Brewer
The Dictionary of
Phrase
& Fable

Brewer

The Dictionary of

Phrase

& Fable

WORDSWORTH REFERENCE

Preface
To the New and Enlarged Edition
of
'Phrase and Fable' 1894.

It is now about a quarter of a century since the first
Edition of 'Phrase and Fable' was published, and the continuous
sale of the book is a proof that it supplies a want very largely
felt. —

In the interval much new information has been unearthed
on the subjects treated of in the Dictionary, many errors of
philology have been exposed, and an exactitude has been reached
which was almost impossible when the book was first undertaken
more than 50 years ago. During this length of period time the
book or its manuscript has been always at the author's elbow,
that new matter might be laid in store, errors corrected, and
suggestions utilized, to render the work more generally useful,
and more thoroughly to be depended on. —

It has been thought by those concerned, that, as the author
is now in the 85th year of his age, it would be desirable
for him finally to overhaul the entire book, — a revision not
compatible with such clipping and verbal changes as can be
made in stereotyped plates; this 'New and Enlarged Edition'
has, accordingly, been thoroughly recast, and every item has been
printed in a fresh type. This has enabled the author to make
additions and corrections, and to substitute new articles for less
useful ones ad libitum; so that this 'New and Enlarged Edition'
is virtually a new work on the old lines. —

The last ten years of this Nineteenth Century have been
preeminently distinguished for researches in English philology. More dictionaries on our gigantic and magnificent language
have been published in this decade than in any preceding one,
and thousands of ripe scholars in Great Britain and America
have contributed to improve their character; so that now no dictionary

of any other language can touch even the fringe of our best English exponents of a tongue spoken by more than a hundred-million of the earth's inhabitants. The research, the accuracy, the precision now demanded are quite unprecedented, and the great public interest taken in the matter might justify our calling the period "The Era of English Philology."—

In this present "New and Enlarged Edition" of this "Dictionary of Phrase and Fable" advantage has been taken of this great literary movement from every available source. More than one-third of the book consists of entire new matter. Some 350 extra pages have been added, and all that has been retained of previous editions has been subjected to the severest scrutiny.—

Thanks are most deservedly due, and are here most gratefully tendered to the many hundreds of correspondents who have written to the author on the subjects contained in his book. Some have been specialists; some have suggested new articles; some have sent apt quotations; and others have gone diligently through the edition in their possession from beginning to end, and have sent their observations to the author, with permission to use them according to his judgment.—

Of these last, especial mention should be made of the Rev. Arthur M. Rendell, M.S. of Goston Rectory, Melton Mowbray,—of Dr Huxley of Bath, Mr J. Edward Cooper, Stapleford (a most judicious and pains-taking critic), of George Martin Esq.", Principal of Wirral Academy, Birkenhead, F Tolhausen Esq.", a well-known author, and of a Barrister-at-Law whose name I have not obtained permission to publish.—

To set down the names of others whose correspondence fills a box of no inconsiderable size, would serve no useful purpose, and would not interest the general reader; but it may, without vanity, be hoped, with all this help, and all the pains of the author for more than half a century, that this Treasury of Literary bric-à-brac will become a standard book of reference, and a guide to be relied on.—

E Cobham Brewer.—

Edwinstowe Newark
Autumn 1894—

THE

DICTIONARY

OF

PHRASE AND FABLE.

—◆—

A. This letter is modified from the Hebrew א (*aleph* = an ox), which was meant to indicate the outline of an ox's head.

A among the Egyptians is denoted by the hieroglyphic which represents the ibis. Among the Greeks it was the symbol of a bad augury in the sacrifices.

A in logic is the symbol of a universal affirmative. *A* asserts, *E* denies. Thus, syllogisms in b*A*rb*A*r*A* contain three universal affirmative propositions.

A1 means first-rate—the very best. In Lloyd's Register of British and Foreign Shipping, the character of the ship's hull is designated by *letters*, and that of the anchors, cables, and stores by figures. A1 means hull first-rate, and also anchors, cables, and stores ; A2, hull first-rate, but furniture second-rate. Vessels of an inferior character are classified under the letters Æ, E, and I.

"She is a prime girl, she is ; she is A1."—*Sam Slick.*

A.B. (*See* ABLE.)

A.B.C. = Aerated Bread Company.

A B C Book. A primer, a book in which articles are set in alphabetical order, as the *A B C Railway Guide.* The old Primers contained the Catechism, as is evident from the lines :—

"That is question now ;
And then comes answer like an Absey book."
Shakespeare: King John, i. 1.

A.B.C. Process (*The*) of making artificial manure. An acrostic of Alum, Blood, Clay, the three chief ingredients.

A. E. I. O. U. The device adopted by Frederick V., Archduke of Austria

(the Emperor Frederick III. — 1440-1493).

Austria Est Imperare Orbi Universo.
Alles Erdreich Ist Oesterreich Unterthan.
Austria's Empire Is Overall Universal.

To which wags added after the war of 1866,

Austria's Emperor Is Ousted Utterly.

Frederick II. of Prussia is said to have translated the motto thus :—

"Austria Erit In Orbe Ultima" (*Austria will one day be lowest in the world*).

A.U.C. *Anno urbis condĭtæ* (Latin), "from the foundation of the city"—*i.e.*, Rome.

Aaron. *An Aaron's serpent.* Something so powerful as to swallow up minor powers.—Exodus vii. 10-12.

Ab. *Ab ovo.* From the very beginning. Stasīnos, in the epic poem called the *Little Iliad*, does not rush *in medias res*, but begins with the eggs of Leda, from one of which Helen was born. If Leda had not laid this egg, Helen would never have been born. If Helen had not been born, Paris could not have eloped with her. If Paris had not eloped with Helen, there would have been no Trojan War, etc.

Ab ovo usque ad mala. From the first dish to the last. A Roman *cœna* (dinner) consisted of three parts. The first course was the appetiser, and consisted chiefly of eggs, with stimulants ; the second was the "dinner proper ;" and the third the dessert, at which *māla* (*i.e.*, all sorts of apples, pears, quinces, pomegranates, and so on) formed the most conspicuous part. —*Hor. Sat.* I. iii. 5.

Aback'. *I was taken aback*—I was greatly astonished—taken by surprise—startled. It is a sea term. A ship is "taken aback" when the sails are suddenly carried by the wind back against the mast, instantly staying the ship's progress—very dangerous in a strong gale.

Ab'acus. A small frame with wires stretched across it. Each wire contains ten movable balls, which can be shifted backwards or forwards, so as to vary *ad libitum* the number in two or more blocks. It is used to teach children addition and subtraction. The ancient Greeks and Romans employed it for calculations, and so do the Chinese. The word is derived from the Phœn. *abak* (dust); the Orientals used tables covered with dust for ciphering and diagrams. In Turkish schools this method is still used for teaching writing. The multiplication table invented by Pythagoras is called *Ab'acus Pythagor'icus.* (Latin, *abacus;* Greek, ἄβαξ.)

Abaddon. The angel of the bottomless pit (Rev. ix. 11). The Hebrew *abad* means "he perished."

"The angell of the bottomlesse pytt, whose name in the hebrew tonge is Abadon."—*Tindale.*

Abam'bou. The evil spirit of the Camma tribes in Africa. A fire is kept always burning in his house. He is supposed to have the power of causing sickness and death.

Abandon means put at anyone's orders; hence, to give up. (Latin, *ad,* to; *bann-um,* late Latin for "a decree.")

Abandon fait larron. As opportunity makes the thief, the person who neglects to take proper care of his goods, leads into temptation, hence the proverb, "Neglect leads to theft."

Ab'aris. *The dart of Abaris.* Abaris, the Scythian, was a priest of Apollo; and the god gave him a golden arrow on which to ride through the air. This dart rendered him invisible; it also cured diseases, and gave oracles. Abaris gave it to Pythag'oras.

"The dart of Abaris carried the philosopher wheresoever he desired it."—*Willmott.*

Abate (2 syl.) means properly to knock down. (French, *abattre,* whence a *battue, i.e.,* wholesale destruction of game; O.E. *a-beátan.*)

Abate, in horsemanship, is to perform well the downward motion. A horse is said to abate when, working upon curvets, he puts or *beats down* both his hind legs to the ground at once, and keeps exact time.

Abatement, in heraldry, is a mark of dishonour annexed to coat armour, whereby the honour of it is abated.

Ab'aton. (Greek *a,* not; βαίνω, I go.) *As inaccessible as Abãton.* Artemisia, to commemorate her conquest of Rhodes, erected two statues in the island, one representing herself, and the other emblematical of Rhodes. When the Rhodians recovered their liberty they looked upon this monument as a kind of palladium, and to prevent its destruction surrounded it with a fortified enclosure which they called Abaton, or the inaccessible place. (Lucan speaks of an island difficult of access in the fens of Memphis, called Abãton.)

Abb'assides (3 syl.). A dynasty of caliphs who reigned from 750-1258. The name is derived from Abbas, uncle of Mahomet. The most celebrated of them was Haroun-al-Raschid (born 765, reigned 786-808).

Abbey Laird (*An*). An insolvent debtor sheltered by the precincts of Holyrood Abbey.

"As diligence cannot be proceeded with on Sunday, the Abbey Lairds (as they were jocularly called) were enabled to come forth on that day to mingle in our society."—*R. Chambers.*

Abbey-lubber (*An*). An idle, well-fed dependent or loafer.

"It came into a common proverbe to call him an *Abbay-lubber,* that was idle, wel fed, a long, lewd, lither loiterer, that might worke and would not."—*The Burnynge of Paules Church, 1563.*

It is used also of religions in contempt; see Dryden's *Spanish Friar.*

Abbot of Misrule, or *Lord of Misrule.* A person who used to superintend the Christmas diversions. In France the "Abbot of Misrule" was called *L'abbé de Liesse* (jollity). In Scotland the master of revels was called the "Master of Unreason."

Abbotsford. A name given by Sir Walter Scott to Clarty Hole, on the south bank of the Tweed, after it became his residence. Sir Walter devised the name from a fancy he loved to indulge in, that the *abbots* of Melrose Abbey, in ancient times, passed over the *fords* of the Tweed.

Abd in Arabic = slave or servant, as Abd-Allah (*servant of God*), Abd-el-Kader (*servant of the Mighty One*), Abd-ul-Latif (*servant of the Gracious One*), etc.

Abdael (2 syl.). George Monk, third Duke of Albemarle.

"Brave Abdael o'er the prophets' school was placed;
Abdael, with all his father's virtues graced. . .
Without one Hebrew's blood, restored the crown."
Dryden and Tait: Absalom and Achitophel, Part ii.

⁂ Tate's blunder for Abdiel (*q.v.*).

Abdall'ah, the father of Mahomet, was so beautiful, that when he married Ami'na, 200 virgins broke their hearts from disappointed love.—*Washington Irving: Life of Mahomet.*

Abdall'ah. Brother and predecessor of Giaffir, pacha of Aby'dos. He was murdered by Giaffir (2 syl.).—*Byron: Bride of Abydos.*

Ab'dals. Persian fanatics, who think it a merit to kill anyone of a different religion; and if slain in the attempt, are accounted martyrs.

Abde'ra. A maritime town of Thrace, said in fable to have been founded by Abdēra, sister of Diomede. It was so overrun with rats that it was abandoned, and the Abderītans migrated to Macedonia.

Abderi'tan. A native of Abdēra, a maritime city of Thrace. The Abderītans were proverbial for stupidity, hence the phrase, "You have no more mind than an Abderite." Yet the city gave birth to some of the wisest men of Greece : as Democrītos (the laughing philosopher), Protagŏras (the great sophist), Anaxarchos (the philosopher and friend of Alexander), Hecatæos (the historian), etc.

Abderitan Laughter. Scoffing laughter, incessant laughter. So called from Abdēra, the birthplace of Democrītos, the laughing philosopher.

Ab'derite (3 syl.). A scoffer, so called from Democ'ritos.

Abde'rus. One of Herakles's friends, devoured by the horses of Diomede. Diomede gave him his horses to hold, and they devoured him.

Ab'diel. The faithful seraph who withstood Satan when he urged the angels to revolt. (See *Paradise Lost*, Bk. v., lines 896, etc.)

"[He] adheres, with the faith of Abdiel, to the ancient form of adoration."—*Sir W. Scott.*

Abeceda'rian. One who teaches or is learning his A B C.

Abecedarian hymns. Hymns which began with the letter A, and each verse or clause following took up the letters of the alphabet in regular succession. (*See* ACROSTIC POETRY.)

Abel and Cain. The Mahometan tradition of the death of Abel is this : Cain was born with a twin sister who was named Aclima, and Abel with a twin sister named Jumella. Adam wished Cain to marry Abel's twin sister, and Abel to marry Cain's. Cain would not consent to this arrangement, and Adam proposed to refer the question to God by means of a sacrifice. God rejected Cain's sacrifice to signify his disapproval of his marriage with Aclima, his twin sister, and Cain slew his brother in a fit of jealousy.

Abel Keene. A village schoolmaster, afterwards a merchant's clerk. He was led astray, lost his place, and hanged himself. – *Crabbe : Borough, Letter* xxi.

A'belites (3 syl.), *Abel'ians*, or *Abelo'nians*. A Christian sect of the fourth century, chiefly found in Hippo (N. Africa). They married, but lived in continence, as they affirm Abel did. The sect was maintained by adopting the children of others. No children of Abel being mentioned in Scripture, the Abelites assume that he had none.

Abes'sa. The impersonation of Abbeys and Convents, represented by Spenser as a damsel. When Una asked if she had seen the Red Cross Knight, Abessa, frightened at the lion, ran to the cottage of blind Superstition, and shut the door. Una arrived, and the lion burst the door open. The meaning is, that at the Reformation, when Truth came, the abbeys and convents got alarmed, and would not let Truth enter, but England (the lion) broke down the door.—*Faërie Queen*, i. 3.

Abesta. A book said to have been written by Abraham as a commentary on the Zend and the Pazend. It is furthermore said that Abraham read these three books in the midst of the furnace into which he was cast by Nimrod.—*Persian Mythology.*

Abey'ance really means something gaped after (French, *bayer*, to gape). The allusion is to men standing with their mouths open, in expectation of some sight about to appear.

Abhigit. The propitiatory sacrifice made by an Indian rajah who has slain a priest without premeditation.

Abhor' (Latin, *ab*, away from, and *horreo*, to shrink; originally, to shudder, have the hair on end). To abhor is to have a natural antipathy, and to show it by shuddering with disgust.

Abiala. Wife of Makambi; African deities. She holds a pistol in her hand, and is greatly feared. Her aid is implored in sickness.

Abida. A god of the Kalmucks, who receives the souls of the dead at the moment of decease, and gives them permission to enter a new body, either human or not, and have another spell of life on earth. If the spirit is spotless it may, if it likes, rise and live in the air.

Abidhar'ma. The book of metaphysics in the Tripit'aka (*q.v.*).

Ab'igail. A lady's maid, or lady-maid. Abigail, wife of Nabal, who introduced herself to David and afterwards married him, is a well-known Scripture heroine (1 Sam. xxv. 3). Abigail was a popular middle class Christian name in the seventeenth century. Beaumont and Fletcher, in *The Scornful Lady*, call the "waiting' gentlewoman" Abigail, a name employed by Swift, Fielding, and others, in their novels. Probably "Abigail Hill," the original name of Mrs. Masham, waiting-woman to Queen Anne, popularised the name.

Abim'elech is no proper name, but a regal title of the Philistines, meaning *Father-king*.

Able. *An able seaman* is a skilled seaman. Such a man is termed an A.B. (Able-Bodied); *unskilled* seamen are called " boys " without regard to age.

Able-bodied Seaman. A sailor of the first class. A crew is divided into three classes :— (1) able seamen, or skilled sailors, termed A.B. ; (2) ordinary seamen ; and (3) boys, which include green - hands, or inexperienced men, without regard to age or size.

Aboard. *He fell aboard of me*—met me ; abused me. A ship is said to fall aboard another when, being in motion, it runs against the other.

To go aboard is to embark, to go on the board or deck.

Aboard main tack is to draw one of the lower corners of the main-sail down to the chess-tree. Figuratively, it means " to keep to the point."

Aboll'a. An ancient military garment worn by the Greeks and Romans, opposed to the *toga* or robe of peace. The abolla being worn by the lower orders, was

affected by philosophers in the vanity of humility.

Abom'inate (*abominor*, I pray that the omen may be averted ; used on mentioning anything unlucky). As ill-omened things are disliked, so, by a simple figure of speech, what we dislike we consider ill-omened.

Abomina'tion of Desolation (*The*). The Roman standard is so called (Matt. xxiv. 15). As it was set up in the holy temple, it was an abomination ; and, as it brought destruction, it was the "abomination of desolation."

Abon Hassan. A rich merchant, transferred during sleep to the bed and palace of the Caliph Haroun-al-Raschid. Next morning he was treated as the caliph, and every effort was made to make him forget his identity. *Arabian Nights* ("The Sleeper Awakened"). The same trick was played on Christopher Sly, in the Induction of Shakespeare's comedy of *Taming of the Shrew ;* and, according to Burton (*Anatomy of Melancholy*, ii. 2, 4), by Philippe the Good, Duke of Burgundy, on his marriage with Eleono'ra.

"Were I caliph for a day, as honest Abon Hassan, I would scourge me these jugglers out of the Commonwealth."—*Sir Walter Scott.*

Abonde (*Dame*). The French Santa Claus, the good fairy who comes at night to bring toys to children while they sleep, especially on New Year's Day.

Abortive Flowers are those which have stamens but no pistils.

Abou ebn Sina, commonly called *Avicenna.* A great Persian physician, born at Shiraz, whose canons of medicine were those adopted by Hippoc'ratës and Aristotle. Died 1037.

Abou-Bekr, called *Father of the Virgin, i.e.,* Mahomet's favourite wife. He was the first caliph, and was founder of the sect called the Sunnites. (571-634.)

Abou Jahi'a. The angel of death in Mohammedan mythology. Called Azrael by the Arabs, and Mordad by the Persians.

Aboulomri (*in Mohammedan mythology*). A fabulous bird of the vulture sort which lives 1,000 years. Called by the Persians Kerkës, and by the Turks Ak-Baba.—*Herbelot.*

Above properly applies only to matter on the same page, but has been extended to any previous part of the book, as *See above*, p. *.

Above-board. In a straightforward manner. Conjurers place their hands *under* the table when they are preparing their tricks, but *above* when they show them. "Let all be above-board" means "let there be no *under*-hand work, but let us see everything."

Above par. A commercial term meaning that the article referred to is more than its nominal value. Thus, if you must give more than £100 for a £100 share in a bank company, a railway share, or other stock, we say the stock is "above par."

If, on the other hand, a nominal £100 worth can be bought for less than £100, we say the stock is "below par."

Figuratively, a person in low spirits or ill health says he is "below par."

Above your hook—*i.e.*, beyond your comprehension; beyond your mark. The allusion is to hat-pegs placed in rows; the higher rows are above the reach of small statures.

Abracada'bra. A charm. It is said that Abracadabra was the supreme deity of the Assyrians. Q. Sevērus Sammon'icus recommended the use of the word as a powerful antidote against ague, flux, and toothache. The word was to be written on parchment, and suspended round the neck by a linen thread, in the form given below :—

```
A B R A C A D A B R A
  A B R A C A D A B R
    A B R A C A D A B
      A B R A C A D A
        A B R A C A D
          A B R A C A
            A B R A C
              A B R A
                A B R
                  A B
                    A
```

Abrac'ax, also written *Abrax'as* or *Abras'ax*, in Persian mythology denotes the Supreme Being. In Greek notation it stands for 365. In Persian mythology Abracax presides over 365 impersonated virtues, one of which is supposed to prevail on each day of the year. In the second century the word was employed by the Basilid'ians for the deity; it was also the principle of the Gnostic hierarchy, and that from which sprang their numerous Æons. (*See* ABRAXAS STONES.)

Abraham.

His parents. According to Mohammedan mythology, the parents of Abraham were Prince Azar and his wife, Adna.

His infancy. As King Nimrod had been told that one shortly to be born would dethrone him, he commanded the death of all such ; so Adna retired to a cave where Abraham was born. He was nourished by sucking two of her fingers, one of which supplied milk and the other honey.

His boyhood. At the age of fifteen months he was equal in size to a lad of fifteen, and very wise; so his father introduced him to the court of King Nimrod.—*Herbelot: Bibliothèque Orientale.*

His offering. According to Mohammedan tradition, the mountain on which Abraham offered up his son was Arfaday; but is more generally thought to have been Morīah.

His death. The Ghebers say that Abraham was thrown into the fire by Nimrod's order, but the flame turned into a bed of roses, on which the child Abraham went to sleep.—*Tavernier.*

"Sweet and welcome as the bed
For their own infant prophet spread,
When pitying Heaven to roses turned
The death-flames that beneath him burned."
          T. *Moore : Fire Worshippers.*

To Sham Abraham. To pretend illness or distress, in order to get off work. (*See* ABRAM-MAN.)

"I have heard people say *Sham Abram* you may,
But must not sham Abraham Newland."
          T. *Dibdin* or *Upton.*

Abraham Newland was cashier of the Bank of England, and signed the notes.

Abraham's Bosom. The repose of the happy in death (Luke xvi. 22). The figure is taken from the ancient custom of allowing a dear friend to recline at dinner on your bosom. Thus the beloved John reclined on the bosom of Jesus.

There is no leaping from Deli'lah's lap into Abraham's bosom—*i.e.*, those who live and die in notorious sin must not expect to go to heaven at death.—*Boston: Crook in the Lot.*

Abraham Newland (*An*). A banknote. So called because, in the early part of the nineteenth century, none were genuine but those signed by this name.

Abraham'ic Covenant. The covenant made by God with Abraham, that Messiah should spring from his seed. This promise was given to Abraham, because he left his country and father's house to live in a strange land, as God told him.

Abrahamites (4 syl.). Certain Bohemian deists, so called because they professed to believe what Abraham believed before he was circumcised. The sect was forbidden by the Emperor Joseph II. in 1783.

Abram - colour. Probably a corruption of Abron, meaning auburn. Halliwell quotes the following from *Coriolanus*, ii. 3 : " Our heads are some brown, some black, some Abram, some bald." And again, " Where is the eldest son of Priam, the Abram-coloured Trojan ? " " A goodly, long, thick Abram-coloured beard."—*Blurt, Master Constable.*

Hall, in his *Satires*, iii. 5, uses *abron* for auburn. " A lusty courtier . . . with abron locks was fairly furnished."

Abram-Man, or *Abraham Cove*. A Tom o' Bedlam ; a naked vagabond ; a begging impostor.

The Abraham Ward, in Bedlam, had for its inmates begging lunatics, who used to array themselves " with partycoloured ribbons, tape in their hats, a fox-tail hanging down, a long stick with streamers," and beg alms ; but " for all their seeming madness, they had wit enough to steal as they went along." —*Canting Academy.*

See *King Lear*, ii. 3.

In Beaumont and Fletcher we have several synonyms :—

"And these, what name or title e'er they bear, *Jackman* or *Pat'rico, Cranke* or *Clapper-dudgeon, Fraier* or *Abram-man*, I speak to all." *Beggar's Bush*, ii. 1.

Abrax'as Stones. Stones with the word *Abraxas* engraved on them, and used as talismans. They were cut into symbolic forms combining a fowl's head, a serpent's body, and human limbs. (*See* ABRACAX.)

Abreast. Side by side, the breasts being all in a line.

The ships were all abreast—i.e., their heads were all equally advanced, as soldiers marching abreast.

Abridge is not formed from the word *bridge ;* but comes from the Latin *abbreviāre*, to shorten, from *brevis* (short), through the French *abréger* (to shorten).

Abroach. *To set mischief abroach* is to set it afoot. The figure is from a cask of liquor, which is broached that the liquor may be drawn from it. (Fr., *brocher*, to prick, *abrocher*.)

Abroad. *You are all abroad.* Wide of the mark ; not at home with the subject. Abroad ; in all directions.

" An elm displays her dusky arms abroad." *Dryden.*

Ab'rogate. When the Roman senate wanted a law to be passed, they asked the people to give their votes in its favour. The Latin for this is *rogāre legem* (to solicit or propose a law). If they wanted a law repealed, they asked the people to vote against it ; this was *abrogāre legem* (to solicit against the law).

Ab'salom. James, Duke of Monmouth, the handsome but rebellious son of Charles II. in Dryden's *Absalom and Achitophel* (1649-1685).

Absalom and Achitophel. A political satire by Dryden (1649-1685). David is meant for Charles II.; Absalom for his natural son James, Duke of Monmouth, handsome like Absalom, and, like him, rebellious. Achitophel is meant for Lord Shaftesbury, Zimri for the Duke of Buckingham, and Abdael for Monk. The selections are so skilfully made that the history of David seems repeated. Of Absalom, Dryden says (Part i.) :—

" Whate'er he did was done with so much ease, In him alone 'twas natural to please ; His motions all accompanied with grace, And paradise was opened in his face."

Abscond' means properly to *hide ;* but we generally use the word in the sense of stealing off secretly from an employer. (Latin, *abscondo.*)

Ab'sent. " Out of mind as soon as out of sight." Generally misquoted " Out of sight, out of mind."—*Lord Brooke.*

The absent are always wrong. The translation of the French proverb, *Les absents ont toujours tort.*

Absent Mar. (*The*). The character of Bruyère's *Absent Man*, translated in the *Spectator* and exhibited on the stage, is a caricature of Comte de Brancas.

Ab'solute. *A Captain Absolute*, a bold, despotic man, determined to have his own way. The character is in Sheridan's play called *The Rivals.*

Sir Anthony Absolute, a warm-hearted, testy, overbearing country squire, in the same play. William Dowton (1764-1851) was nick-named " Sir Anthony Absolute."

Absquat'ulate. To run away or abscond. A comic American word, from *ab* and *squat* (to go away from your squatting). A squatting is a tenement taken in some unclaimed part, without purchase or permission. The persons who take up their squatting are termed *squatters.*

Abste'mious, according to Fabius and Aulus Gellius, is compounded of *abs* and *teme'tum*. "Teme'tum" was a strong, intoxicating drink, allied to the Greek *methu* (strong drink).

"Vinum prisca lingua *temetum* appellabant."—*Aulus Gellius*, x. 23.

Abstract Numbers are numbers considered abstractly—1, 2, 3 ; but if we say 1 year, 2 feet, 3 men, etc., the numbers are no longer abstract, but *concrete*.

Taken in the abstract. Things are said to be taken in the abstract when they are considered absolutely, that is, without reference to other matters or persons. Thus, in the abstract, one man is as good as another, but not so socially and politically.

Abstraction. *An empty Abstraction*, a mere ideality, of no practical use. Every noun is an abstraction, but the narrower genera may be raised to higher ones, till the common thread is so fine that hardly anything is left. These high abstractions, from which everything but one common cord is taken, are called *empty* abstractions.

For example, *man* is a genus, but may be raised to the genus *animal*, thence to *organised being*, thence to *created being*, thence to *matter* in the abstract, and so on, till everything but one is emptied out.

Absurd means strictly, quite deaf. (Latin, *ab*, intensive, and *surdus*, deaf.)

Reductio ad absurdum. Proving a proposition to be right by showing that every supposable deviation from it would involve an absurdity.

Abu'dah. A merchant of Bagdad, haunted every night by an old hag ; he finds at last that the way to rid himself of this torment is to "fear God, and keep his commandments."—*Tales of the Genii.*

"Like Abudah, he is always looking out for the Fury, and knows that the night will come with the inevitable hag with it."—*Thackeray.*

Abundant Number (*An*). A number such that the sum of all its divisors (except itself) is greater than the number itself. Thus 12 is an abundant number, because its divisors, 1, 2, 3, 4, 6 = 16, which is greater than 12.

A *Deficient* number is one of which the sum of all its divisors is less than itself, as 10, the divisors of which are 1, 2, 5 = 8, which is less than 10.

A *Perfect* number is one of which the sum of all its divisors exactly measures itself, as 6, the divisors of which are 1, 2, 3 = 6.

Abus, the river Humber.

"For by the river that whylome was hight
The ancien Abus . . . [was from] . . .
Their chieftain, Humber, named aright."

And Drayton, in his *Polyolbion*, 28, says :—

"For my princely name,
From Humber, king of Huns, as anciently it came."

See Geoffrey's *Chronicles*, Bk. ii. 2.

Ab'yla. A mountain in Africa, opposite Gibraltar. This, with Calpē in Spain, 16 m. distant, forms the *pillars of Hercules.*

"Heaves up huge Abyla on Afric's sand,
Crowns with high Calpē Europe's salient strand."
Darwin: Economy of Vegetation.

Abyssin'ians. A sect of Christians in Abyssinia, who admit only one nature in Jesus Christ, and reject the Council of Chalce'don.

Acace'tus. One who does nothing badly. It was a name given to Mercury or Hermēs for his eloquence. (Greek, *a*, not; *kakos*, bad.)

Academ'ics The followers of Plato were so called, because they attended his lectures in the Acad'emy, a garden planted by Acade'mos.

"See there the olive grove of Acadēmus, Plato's retreat." *Milton : Paradise Lost*, Book iv.

Acad'emy. Divided into—*Old*, the philosophic teaching of Plato and his immediate followers; *Middle*, a modification of the Platonic system, taught by Arcesila'os ; *New*, the half-sceptical school of Car'neadēs.

Plato taught that matter is eternal and infinite, but without form or order : and that there is an intelligent cause, the author of everything. He maintained that we could grasp truth only so far as we had elevated our mind by thought to its divine essence.

Arcesila'os was the great antagonist of the Stoics, and wholly denied man's capacity for grasping truth.

Car'neadēs maintained that neither our senses nor our understanding could supply us with a sure criterion of truth.

The talent of the Academy, so Plato called Aristotle (B.C. 384-322).

Academy Figures. Drawings in black and white chalk, on tinted paper, from living models, used by artists. So called from the Royal Academy of Artists.

Aca'dia—*i.e.,* Nova Scotia, so called by the French from the river *Shubenacadie.* The name was changed in 1621.

In 1755 the old French inhabitants were driven into exile by order of George II.

"Thus dwelt together in love those simple Acadian farmers." *Longfellow : Evangeline.*

Acadine. A fountain of Sicily which revealed if writings were authentic and genuine or not. The writings to be tested were thrown into the fountain, and if spurious they sank to the bottom. Oaths and promises were tried in the same way, after being written down.— *Diodorus Siculus.*

Acan'thus. The leafy ornament used in the capitals of Corinthian and composite columns. It is said that Callim'-achos lost his daughter, and set a basket of flowers on her grave, with a tile to keep the wind from blowing it away. The next time he went to visit the grave an acanthus had sprung up around the basket, which so struck the fancy of the architect that he introduced the design in his buildings.

Accep'tance. A bill or note accepted. This is done by the drawee writing on it "accepted," and signing his name. The person who accepts it is called the "acceptor."

Ac'cessory. *Accessory before the fact* is one who is aware that another intends to commit an offence, but is himself absent when the offence is perpetrated.

Accessory after the fact is one who screens a felon, aids him in eluding justice, or helps him in any way to profit by his crime. Thus, the receiver of stolen goods, knowing or even suspecting them to be stolen, is an accessory *ex post facto.*

Ac'cident. *A logical accident* is some property or quality which a thing possesses, but which does not essentially belong to it, as the tint of our skin, the height of our body, the redness of a brick, or the whiteness of paper. If any of these were changed, the substance would remain intact.

Accidental or Subjective Colours. Those which depend on the state of our eye, and not those which the object really possesses. Thus, after looking at the bright sun, all objects appear dark; that dark colour is the accidental colour of the bright sun. When, again, we come from a dark room, all objects at first have a yellow tinge. This is especially the case if we wear blue glasses, for a minute or two after we have taken them off.

The accidental colour of *red* is bluish green, of *orange* dark blue, of *violet* yellow, of *black* white ; and the converse.

Acciden'tals in music are those sharps and flats, etc., which do not properly belong to the key in which the music is set, but which the composer arbitrarily introduces.

Accidente ! (4 syl.) An Italian curse or oath : "Ce qui veut dire en bon français, 'Puisses-tu mourir d'accident, sans confession,' damné."—*E. About : Tolla.*

Ac'cidents, in theology. After consecration, say the Catholics, the *substance* of the bread and wine is changed into that of the body and blood of Christ, but their *accidents* (flavour, appearance, and so on) remain the same as before.

Ac'cius Na'vius. A Roman augur in the reign of Tarquin the Elder. When he forbade the king to increase the number of the tribes without consulting the augurs, Tarquin asked him if he thought then in his mind was feasible. "Undoubtedly," said Accius. "Then cut through this whetstone with the razor in your hand." The priest gave a bold cut, and the block fell in two. This story (from Livy, Bk. i., chap. 36) is humorously retold in Bon Gaultier's Ballads.

Accolade (3 syl.). The touch of a sword on the shoulder in the ceremony of conferring knighthood ; originally an embrace or touch by the hand on the neck. (Latin, *ad collum*, on the neck.)

Accommoda'tion. A loan of money, which accommodates us, or fits a want. *Accommodation Note* or *Bill.* An acceptance given on a Bill of Exchange for which value has not been received by the acceptor from the drawer, and which, not representing a commercial transaction, is so far fictitious.

Accommodation Ladder. The light ladder hung over the side of a ship at the gangway.

Accord' means "heart to heart." (Latin, *ad corda*.) If two persons like and dislike the same things, they are heart to heart with each other.

Similarly, "con-cord" means heart with heart ; "dis-cord," heart divided from heart ; "re-cord" properly means to recollect—*i.e., re-cordāre*, to bring again to the mind or heart ; then to set down in writing for the purpose of recollecting.

Accost' means to "come to the side" of a person for the purpose of speaking to him. (Latin, *ad costam*, to the side.)

Account. *To open an account*, to enter a customer's name on your ledger for the first time. (Latin, *accomputāre*, to reckon with.)

To keep open account is when merchants agree to honour each other's bills of exchange.

A current account or "account current, *a/c*. A commercial term, meaning that the customer is entered by name in the creditor's ledger for goods purchased but not paid for at the time. The account runs on for a month or more, according to agreement.

To cast accounts. To give the results of the debits and credits entered, balancing the two, and carrying over the surplus.

A sale for the account in the Stock Exchange means : the sale of stock not for immediate payment, but for the fortnightly settlement. Generally this is speculative, and the broker or customer pays the difference of price between the time of purchase and time of settlement.

We will give a good account of them— *i.e.* we will give them a thorough good drubbing.

Ac'curate means well and carefully done. (Latin, *ad-curāre, accurātus*.)

Accu'sative (*The*). Calvin was so called by his college companions. We speak of an "accusative age," meaning *searching*, one eliminating error by *accusing* it.

"This hath been a very accusative age."—*Sir E. Dering.*

Ace (1 syl.). The unit of cards or dice, from *as*, the Latin unit of weight. (Italian, *asso;* French and Spanish, *as*.)

Within an ace. Within a shave. An ace is the lowest numeral, and he who wins within an ace, wins within a single mark. (*See* AMBES-AS.)

To bate an ace is to make an abatement, or to give a competitor some start or other advantage, in order to render the combatants more equal. It is said that the expression originated in the reign of Henry VIII., when one of the courtiers named Bolton, in order to flatter the king, used to say at cards, "Your Majesty must bate me an ace, or I shall have no chance at all." Taylor, the water poet (1580-1654), speaking of certain women, says—

"Though bad they be, they will not bate an ace
To be cald Prudence, Temp'rance, Faith, and Grace."

Acel'dama. A battle-field, a place where much blood has been shed. To

the south of Jerusalem there was a field so called ; it was purchased by the priests with the blood-money thrown down by Judas, and appropriated as a cemetery for strangers (Matt. xxvii. 8; Acts i. 19). (Aramaic, *ōkēl-damā*.)

Aceph'alites (4 syl.) properly means men without a head. (1) A faction among the Eutych'ians in the fifth century after the submission of Mongus their chief, by which they were "deprived of their head." (2) Certain bishops exempt from the jurisdiction and discipline of their patriarch. (3) A sect of levellers in the reign of Henry I., who acknowledged no leader. (4) The fabulous Blemmyes of Africa, who are described as having no head, their eyes and mouth being placed elsewhere. (Greek, *a-keph'ale*, without a head.)

Aces'tes (3 syl.). *The Arrow of Acestes*. In a trial of skill Acestes, the Sicilian, discharged his arrow with such force that it took fire. (*Æn.* 5, line 525.)

" Like Acestes' shaft of old,
The swift thought kindles as it flies."
Longfellow.

Achæ'an League. A confederacy of the twelve towns of Achæa. It was broken up by Alexander the Great, but was again reorganised B.C. 280, and dissolved by the Romans in 147 B.C.

Achar in Indian philosophy means the All-in-All. The world is spun out of Achar as a web from a spider, and will ultimately return to him, as a spider sometimes takes back into itself its own thread. Phenomena are not independent realities, but merely partial and individual manifestations of the All-in-All.

Acha'tes (3 syl.). A *fidus Achatēs*. A faithful companion, a bosom friend. Achates in Virgil's *Æneid* is the chosen companion of the hero in adventures of all kinds.

"He has chosen this fellow for his *fidus Achates*."—*Sir Walter Scott.*

Ache'mon, or Achmon, and his brother Basālas were two Cercōpes for ever quarrelling. One day they saw Hercules asleep under a tree and insulted him, but Hercules tied them by their feet to his club and walked off with them, heads downwards, like a brace of hares. Everyone laughed at the sight, and it became a proverbial cry among the Greeks, when two men were seen quarrelling—"Look out for Melampy'gos ! " (*i.e.* Hercules).

"Ne insidas in Melampygum."

✢ According to Greek fable, monkeys

are degraded men. The Cercōpĕs were changed into monkeys for attempting to deceive Zeus.

Ac'heron. The "River of Sorrows" (Greek, *achos roös*); one of the five rivers of the infernal regions.

"Sad Acheron of sorrow, black and deep."
Milton: Paradise Lost, ii. 578.

Pabulum Acherontis. Food for the churchyard; said of a dead body.

Acheron'tian Books. The most celebrated books of augury in the world. They are the books which the Etruscans received from Tagĕs, grandson of Jupiter.

Acheru'sia. A cavern on the borders of Pontus, said to lead down to the infernal regions. It was through this cavern that Hercules dragged Cer'berus to earth.

Achillea. The Yarrow, called by the French the *herbe aux charpentiers*— *i.e.*, carpenter's wort, because it was supposed to heal wounds made by carpenters' tools. Called Achillēa from Achillĕs, who was taught the uses and virtues of plants by Chiron the centaur. The tale is, that when the Greeks invaded Troy, Telĕphus, a son-in-law of King Priam, attempted to stop their landing; but Bacchus caused him to stumble over a vine, and, when he had fallen, Achillĕs wounded him with his spear. The young Trojan was told by an oracle that "Achillĕs (meaning milfoil or yarrow) would cure the wound;" but, instead of seeking the plant, he applied to the Grecian chief, and promised to conduct the host to Troy if he would cure the wound. Achillĕs consented to do so, scraped some rust from his spear, and from the filings rose the plant milfoil, which, being applied to the wound, had the desired effect.

Achilles (3 syl.). King of the Myr'-midons (in Thessaly), the hero of Homer's epic poem called the *Iliad*. He is represented as brave and relentless. The poem begins with a quarrel between him and Agamemnon, the commander-in-chief of the allied Greeks; in consequence of which Achilles refused to go to battle. The Trojans prevail, and Achilles sends forth his friend Patroc'los to oppose them. Patroc'los fell; and Achilles, in anger, rushing into the battle, killed Hector, the commander of the Trojans. He himself, according to later poems, fell in battle a few days afterwards, before Troy was taken.

Achilles.

Army : The Myrmidons followed him to Troy.
Death of : It was Paris who wounded Achilles in the heel with an arrow (a post-Homeric story).
Father : Peleus (2 syl.), King of Thessaly.
Friend : Patroclos.
Horses : Balios (= swift-footed) and Xanthos (= chestnut-coloured), endowed with human speech.
Mistress in Troy : Hippodamia, surnamed Briseis (2 syl.).
Mother : Thetis, a sea goddess.
Son : Pyrrhos, surnamed Neoptolĕmos (= the new warrior).
Tomb : In Sigœum, over which no bird ever flies. —*Pliny*, x. 29.
Tutors : First, Phœnix, who taught him the elements ; then Chiron the centaur.
Wife : Deidamia. (5 syl.) De-i-da-my'-ah.

Achilles (pronounce A-kil'-leez). The *English*, John Talbot, first Earl of Shrewsbury (1373-1453).

Achilles *of England*, the Duke of Wellington (1769-1852).

Of Germany, Albert, Elector of Brandenburg (1414-1486).

Of Lombardy, brother of Sforza and Palamēdēs. All the three brothers were in the allied army of Godfrey (*Jerusalem Delivered*). Achilles of Lombardy was slain by Corinna. This was not a complimentary title, but a proper name.

Of Rome, Lucius Sicin'ius Dentātus, the Roman tribune; also called the *Second Achilles*. Put to death B.C. 450.

Achilles of the West. Roland the Paladin; also called "The Christian Theseus " (2 syl.).

Achilles' Spear. (*See* ACHILLEA.)

Achilles' Tendon. A strong sinew running along the heel to the calf of the leg. The tale is that Thetis took her son Achilles by the heel, and dipped him in the river Styx to make him invulnerable. The water washed every part, except the heel covered with his mother's hand. It was on this vulnerable point the hero was slain ; and the sinew of the heel is called, in consequence, *tendo Achillis*. A post-Homeric story.

The Heel of Achilles. The vulnerable or weak point in a man's character or of a nation. (*See above.*)

Aching Void (*An*). That desolation of heart which arises from the recollection of some cherished endearment no longer possessed.

" What peaceful hours I once enjoyed !
How sweet their memory still !
But they have left an aching void
The world can never fill."
Cowper : Walking with God.

Achit'ophel. (*See* ABSALOM AND ACHITOPHEL.) Achitophel was David's traitorous counsellor, who deserted to

Absalom ; but his advice being disregarded, he hanged himself (2 Sam. xv.). The Achitophel of Dryden's satire was the Earl of Shaftesbury :—

"Of these (*the rebels*) the false Achitophel was first ;
A name to all succeeding ages curst ;
For close designs and crooked counsels fit ;
Sagacious, bold, and turbulent of wit ;
Restless, unfixed in principles and place ;
In power unpleased, impatient in disgrace."
Part i. 150-5.

A'chor. God of flies, worshipped by the Cyre'neans, that they might not be annoyed with these tiny tormentors. (*See* FLIES, *God of.*)

A'cis. The son of Faunus, in love with Galate'a. Polyphe'mos, his rival, crushed him under a huge rock.

Ac'me. The crisis of a disease. Old medical writers used to divide the progress of a disease into four periods : the *ar-che*, or beginning ; the *anab'asis*, or increase ; the *ac'me*, or term of its utmost violence ; and the *pa-rac'-me*, or decline. Figuratively, the highest point of anything.

Acmon'ian Wood (*The*). The trysting-place of unlawful love. It was here that Mars had his assignation with Harmoni̇a, who became the mother of the Amazons.

"C'est là que . . . Mars eut les faveurs de la nymphe Harmonie, commerce dont naquirent les Amazones."—*Etienne : Géographie.*

Acoime'tæ. An order of monks in the fifth century who watched day and night. (Greek, *watchers.*)

Ac'olyte (3 syl.). A subordinate officer in the Catholic Church, whose duty is to light the lamps, prepare the sacred elements, attend the officiating priests, etc. (Greek, *a follower.*)

Aconite. The herb Monkshood or Wolfsbane. Classic fabulists ascribe its poisonous qualities to the foam which dropped from the mouths of the three-headed Cerbĕrus, when Hercules, at the command of Eurystheus, dragged the monster from the infernal regions. (Greek, ἀκόνιτον ; Latin, *aconītum.*)

"Lurida terribiles miscent Aconita novercæ."
Ovid : Metamorphoses, i. 147.

Acra'sia (*Self-indulgence*). An enchantress who lived in the "Bower of Bliss," situate in "Wandering Island." She transformed her lovers into monstrous shapes, and kept them captives. Sir Guyon having crept up softly, threw a net over her, and bound her in chains of adamant ; then broke down her bower and burnt it to ashes.—*Spenser : Faëry Queen*, ii. 12.

Acra'tes (3 syl.), *i.e.*, *incontinence ;* called by Spenser the father of Cymoch'-lēs and Pyroch'lēs.—*Faëry Queen*, ii. 4.

Acre. "God's acre," a cemetery or churchyard. The word "acre," Old English, *æcer*, is akin to the Latin *ager* and German *acker* (a field).

A'cre-fight. A duel in the open field. The combats of the Scotch and English Borderers were so called.

Acre-shot. A land tax. "Acre" is Old English, *æcer* (land), and "shot" is *scot* or *sceat* (a tax).

A'cres. *A Bob Acres—i . .*, a coward. From Sheridan's comedy called *The Rivals.* His courage always "oozed out at his fingers' ends."

Acroamat'ics. Esoter'ical lectures ; the lectures of Aristotle, which none but his chosen disciples were allowed to attend. Those given to the pubic generally were called *exoter'ic.* (Acroamatic is a Greek word, meaning *delivered to an audience ;* ακροάομαι, to attend lectures.)

Acroat'ic. Same as *esoter'ic.* (*See* ACROAMATICS.)

Ac'robat means one who *goes on his extremities*, or uses only the tips of his fingers and toes in moving about. (It is from the two Greek words, *akros baino*, to go on the extremities of one's limbs.)

Acrop'olis. The citadel of ancient Athens.

Of course, the word is compounded of *akros* and *polis* = the city on the height, *i.e.*, the high rock.

Acros'tic (Greek, *akros stichos*). The term was first applied to the verses of the Erythræan sibyl, written on leaves. These prophecies were excessively obscure ; but were so contrived that when the leaves were sorted and laid in order, their initial letters always made a word. —*Dionys.*, iv. 62.

Acrostic poetry among the Hebrews consisted of twenty-two lines or stanzas beginning with the letters of the alphabet in succession, as Psalm cxix., etc.

Acrostics. Puzzles, generally in verse, consisting of two words of equal length. The initial letters of the several lines constitute one of the secret words, and the final letters constitute the other word.

Also words re-arranged so as to make other words of similar significance, as "Horatio Nelson" re-arranged into

Honor est a Nilo. Another form of acrostic is to find a sentence which reads the same backwards and forwards, as E.T.L.N.L.T.E., the initial letters of "Eat To Live, Never Live To Eat;" which in Latin would be, E.U.V.N.V.U.E. (*Ede Ut Viras, Ne Viras Ut Edas*).

Act and **Opponency.** An "Act," in our University language, consists of a thesis and "disputation" thereon, covering continuous parts of three hours. The person "disputing" with the "keeper of the Act" is called the "opponent," and his function is called an "opponency." In some degrees the student is required to keep his Act, and then to be the opponent of another disputant. Much alteration in these matters has been introduced of late, with other college reforms.

Act of Faith (*auto da fé*), in Spain, is a day set apart by the Inquisition for the punishment of heretics, and the absolution of those who renounce their heretical doctrines. The sentence of the Inquisition is also so called ; and so is the ceremony of burning, or otherwise torturing the condemned.

Act of God (*An*). "Damnum fatāle," such as loss by lightning, shipwreck, fire, etc. ; loss arising from fatality, and not from one's own fault, theft, and so on. A Devonshire jury once found a verdict—"That deceased died by the act of God, brought about by the flooded condition of the river."

Actæ'on. A hunter. In Grecian mythology Actæon was a huntsman, who surprised Diana bathing, was changed by her into a stag, and torn to pieces by his own hounds. Hence, a man whose wife is unfaithful. (*See* HORNS.)

"Go thou, like Sir Actæon, with Ringwood at thy heel." *Shakespeare: Merry Wives*, ii. 1.
"Divulge Page himself for a secure and wilful Actæon." *Ibid.* iii. 2.

Ac'tian Years. Years in which the Actian games were celebrated. Augustus instituted games at Actium to celebrate his naval victory over Antony. They were held every five years.

Action Sermon. A sacramental sermon (in the Scots Presbyterian Church).

"I returned home about seven, and addressed myself towards my Action Sermon, Mrs. Olivant."—*E. Irving.*

Ac'tive. *Active verbs,* verbs which act on the noun governed.

Active capital. Property in actual employment in a given concern.

Active commerce. Exports and imports carried to and fro in our own ships. *Passive commerce* is when they are carried in foreign vessels. The commerce of England is *active,* of China *passive.*

Activity. *The sphere of activity,* the whole field through which the influence of an object or person extends.

Acton. A taffeta, or leather-quilted dress, worn under the habergeon to keep the body from being chafed or bruised. (French, *hocqueton.*)

Actresses. Female characters used to be played by boys. Coryat, in his *Crudities* (1611), says, "When I went to a theatre (in Venice) I observed certain things that I never saw before ; for I saw women acte. . . . I have heard that it hath sometimes been used in London" (Vol. ii.).

"Whereas, women's parts in plays have hitherto been acted by men in the habits of women . . . we do permit and give leave for the time to come that all women's parts be acted by women, 1662."—*Charles II.*
The first female actress on the English stage was Mrs. Coleman (1656), who played Ianthe in the *Siege of Rhodes.*
The last male actor that took the part of a woman on the English stage, in serious drama, was Edward Kynaston, noted for his beauty (1619-1687).

Acu tetigisti. You have hit the nail on the head. (Lit., you have touched it with a needle.) Plautus (*Rudens,* v. 2, 19) says, "Rem acu tetigisti ; " and Cicero (*Pro Milōne,* 24) has "Vulnus acu punctum," evidently referring to a surgeon's probe.

Acutia'tor. A person in the Middle Ages who attended armies and knights to sharpen their instruments of war. (Latin, *acuo,* to sharpen.)

Ad Græcas Calendas. (Deferred) to the Greek Calends—*i.e.,* for ever. (It shall be done) on the Greek Calends —*i.e.,* never. There were no Calends in the Greek notation of the months. (*See* NEVER.)

Ad inquirendum. A judicial writ commanding an inquiry to be made into some complaint.

Ad lib'itum. Without restraint.

Ad rem (Latin). To the point in hand ; to the purpose. (*Acu rem tetigisti.*) (*See above,* ACU.)

Ad unum omnes. All to a man (Latin).

Ad valo'rem. According to the price charged. Some custom-duties vary according to the different values of the goods imported. Thus, at one time teas paid duty *ad valorem*, the high-priced tea paying more duty than that of a lower price.

Ad vitam aut culpam. A Latin phrase, used in Scotch law, to indicate the legal permanency of an appointment, unless forfeited by misconduct.

Adam. The Talmudists say that Adam lived in Paradise only twelve hours, and account for the time thus :—
The first hour, God collected the dust and animated it.
The second hour, Adam stood on his feet.
The fourth hour, he named the animals.
The sixth hour, he slept and Eve was created.
The seventh hour, he married the woman.
The tenth hour, he fell.
The twelfth hour, he was thrust out of Paradise.
The Mohammedans tell us he fell on Mount Serendib, in Ceylon, where there is a curious impression in the granite resembling a human foot, above 5 feet long and 2½ feet broad. They tell us it was made by Adam, who stood there on one foot for 200 years to expiate his crime ; when Gabriel took him to Mount Arafath, where he found Eve. (*See* ADAM'S PEAK.)
Adam was buried, according to Arabian tradition, on Aboucais, a mountain of Arabia.

Adam. *The old Adam ; beat the offending Adam out of thee ; the first Adam.* Adam, as the head of unredeemed man, stands for "original sin," or "man without regenerating grace."
The second Adam ; the new Adam, etc.; I will give you the new Adam. Jesus Christ, as the covenant head, is so called ; also the "new birth unto righteousness."
When Adam delved and Eve span. "Au temps passé, Berthe filait." This Bertha was the wife of King Pepin.

"When Adam delved and Eve span,
Who was then the gentleman?"

Adam. A sergeant, bailiff, or any one clad in buff, or a skin-coat, like Adam.

"Not that Adam that kept Paradise, but that Adam that keeps the prison." — *Shakespeare: Comedy of Errors,* iv. 3.

A faithful Adam. A faithful old servant. The character is taken from Shakespeare's comedy of *As You Like It,* where a retainer of that name, who had served the family sixty-three years, offers to accompany Orlando in his flight,

and to share with him his thrifty savings of 500 crowns.

Adam Bell. A northern outlaw, whose name has become a synonym for a good archer. (*See* CLYM OF THE CLOUGH.)

Adam Cupid—*i.e.*, Archer Cupid, perhaps with allusion to Adam Bell, the celebrated archer. (See *Percy's Reliques,* vol. i., p. 7.)

Adam's Ale. Water as a beverage ; from the supposition that Adam had nothing but water to drink. In Scotland water for a beverage is called *Adam's Wine.*

Adam's Apple. The protuberance in the fore-part of a man's throat ; so called from the superstition that a piece of the forbidden fruit which Adam ate stuck in his throat, and occasioned the swelling.

Adam's Needle. The yucca, so called because it is sharp-pointed like a needle.

Adam's Peak, in Ceylon, is where the Arabs say Adam bewailed his expulsion from Paradise, and stood on one foot till God forgave him. It was the Portuguese who first called it " Pico de Adam." (*See* KAABA.)

In the granite is the mark of a human foot, above 5 feet long by 2½ broad, said to have been made by Adam, who, we are told, stood there on one foot for 200 years, to expiate his crime. After his penance he was restored to Eve. The Hindûs assert that the footprint is that made by Buddha, when he ascended to heaven.

Adam's Profession. Gardening, agriculture. Adam was appointed by God to dress the garden of Eden, and to keep it (Gen. ii. 15) ; and after the fall he was sent out of the garden " to till the ground " (Gen. iii. 23).

"There is no ancient gentlemen, but gardeners, ditchers, and grave-makers ; they hold up Adam's profession."—*The Clown in " Hamlet,"* v. 1.

Adams. *Parson Adams,* the ideal of a benevolent, simple-minded, eccentric country clergyman ; ignorant of the world, bold as a lion for the truth, and modest as a girl. The character is in Fielding's novel of *Joseph Andrews.*

Adamant is really the mineral corundum ; but the word is indifferently used for rock crystal, diamond, or any hard substance, and also for the magnet or loadstone. It is often used by poets for no specific substance, but as hardness or firmness in the abstract. Thus, Virgil, in his *Æneid* vi. 552, speaks of "adamantine pillars " merely to express solid and strong ones ; and Milton frequently uses the word in the same way.

Thus, in *Paradise Lost*, ii. 436, he says the gates of hell were made of burning adamant:

> "This huge convex of fire
> Outrageous to devour, immures us round
> Ninefold, and gates of burning adamant
> Barred over us prohibit all egress."

Satan, he tells us, wore adamantine armour (Book vi. 110):

> "Satan, with vast and haughty strides advanced,
> Came towering, armed in adamant and gold."

And a little further on he tells us his shield was made of adamant (vi. 255):

> "He [Satan] hasted, and opposed the rocky orb
> Of ten-fold adamant, his ample shield
> A vast circumference."

Tasso (canto vii. 82) speaks of *scudo di lucidissimo diamante* (a shield of clearest diamond).

Other poets make adamant to mean the *magnet*. Thus, in *Troilus and Cressida*, iii. 2:

> "As true as steel, as plantage to the moon,
> As sun to day, as turtle to her mate,
> As iron to adamant."

("Plantage to the moon," from the notion that plants grew best with the increasing moon.)

And Green says:

> "As true to thee as steel to adamant."

So, in the *Arabian Nights*, the "Third Calendar," we read:

> "To-morrow about noon we shall be near the black mountain, or mine of adamant, which at this very minute draws all your fleet towards it, by virtue of the iron in your ships."

Adamant is *a* (negative) and *damao* (to conquer). Pliny tells us there are six unbreakable stones (xxxvii. 15), but the classical *adamas* (gen. *adamant-is*) is generally supposed to mean the diamond. *Diamond* and *adamant* are originally the same word.

Adamas'tor. The spirit of the stormy Cape (Good Hope), described by Camoëns in the *Lusiad* as a hideous phantom. According to Barre'to, he was one of the giants who invaded heaven.

Adam'ic Covenant. The covenant made with God to Adam, that "the seed of the woman should bruise the serpent's head" (Gen. iii. 15).

Ad'amites (3 syl.). A sect of fanatics who spread themselves over Bohemia and Moravia in the fifteenth and sixteenth centuries. One Picard, of Bohemia, was the founder in 1400, and styled himself "Adam, son of God." He professed to recall his followers to the state of primitive innocence. No clothes were worn, wives were in common, and there was no such thing as good and evil, but all actions were indifferent.

Ad'aran', according to the Parsee superstition, is a sacred fire less holy than that called Behram (*q.v.*).

Adays. *Nowadays*, at the present time (or day). So in Latin, *Nunc diērum* and *Nunc tempŏris.* The prefix "a" = *at*, *of*, or *on*. Simularly, *anights*, *of late*, *on Sundays.* All used adverbially.

Ad'dison of the North—*i.e.*, Henry Mackenzie, the author of the *Man of Feeling* (1745-1831).

Addix'it, or *Addixe'runt* (Latin). All right. The word uttered by the augurs when the "birds" were favourable.

Ad'dle is the Old English *adela* (filth), hence rotten, putrid, worthless.

Addled egg, better "addle-egg," a worthless egg. An egg which has not the vital principle.

Addle - headed, *addle - pate*, emptyheaded. As an addle-egg produces no living bird, so an addle-pate lacks brains.

Addle Parliament (*The*)—5th April to 7th June, 1614. So called because it did not pass one single measure. (*See* PARLIAMENT.)

Adelantado. A big-wig, the great boss of the place. It is a Spanish word for "his excellency" (*adelantar*, to excel), and is given to the governor of a province.

> "Open no door. If the adelantado of Spain were here he should not enter."—*Ben Jonson: Every Man out of his Humour*, v. 4.

Ad'emar, or *Adema'ro* (in *Jerusalem Delivered*). Archbishop of Pog'gio, an ecclesiastical warrior, who with William, Archbishop of Orange, besought Pope Urban on his knees that he might be sent on the crusade. He took 400 armed men from Poggio, but they sneaked off during a drought, and left the crusade (Book xiii.). Ademar was not alive at the time, he had been slain at the attack on Antioch by Clorinda (Book xi.); but in the final attack on Jerusalem, his spirit came with three squadrons of angels to aid the besiegers (Book xviii.).

Adept' properly means one who has attained (from the Latin, *adeptus*, participle of *adipiscor*). The alchemists applied the term *vere adep'tus* to those persons who professed to have "attained to the knowledge of" the elixir of life or of the philosopher's stone.

Alchemists tell us there are always 11 adepts, neither more nor less. Like the sacred chickens of Compostella, of which there are only 2 and always 2—a cock and a hen.

> "In Rosicrucian lore as learn'd
> As he that *vere adeptus* earn'd."
> *S.'Butler : Hudibras.*

Ades'sena'rians. A term applied to those who hold the real presence of Christ's body in the eucharist, but do not maintain that the bread and wine lose any of their original properties. (The word is from the Latin *adesse*, to be present.)

Ades'te Fide'lës. Composed by John Reading, who wrote "Dulce Domum." It is called the "Portuguese Hymn," from being heard at the Portuguese Chapel by the Duke of Leeds, who supposed it to be a part of the usual Portuguese service.

Adfil'iate, Adfilia'tion. The ancient Goths adopted the children of a former marriage, and put them on the same footing as those of the new family. (Latin, *ad-filius*, equal to a real son.)

Adha, *al* (*the slit-eared*). The swiftest of Mahomet's camels.

Ad'hab-al-Cabr. The first purgatory of the Mahometans.

Adiaph'orists. Followers of Melanchthon ; moderate Lutherans, who hold that some of the dogmas of Luther are matters of indifference. (Greek, *adiaph'oros*, indifferent.)
Macaulay : Essay, Burleigh.

Adieu, good-b'ye. *A Dieu,* an elliptical form for *I commend you to God.* Good-b'ye is *God be with ye.*

Adis'sechen. The serpent with a thousand heads which sustains the universe. (*Indian mythology.*)

Adjective Colours are those which require a mordant before they can be used as dyes.

Adjourn'. Once written *ajorn.* French, *à-journer*, to put off to another day.
"He ajorned tham to relie in the North of Carlele."—*Longtoft : Chronicle,* p. 309.

Adjournment of the House. (*See* MOVING THE ADJOURNMENT.)

Admirable (*The*). Aben-Ezra, a Spanish rabbi, born at Toledo (1119-1174).

Ad'mirable Crichton (*The*). James Crichton (*kry-ton*). (1551-1573.)

Admirable Doctor (*Doctor admirābilis*). Roger Bacon (1214-1292).

Admiral, corruption of *Amir-al.* Milton, speaking of Satan, says :—

> "His spear (to equal which the tallest pine
> Hewn on Norwegian hills, to be the mast
> Of some tall amiral, were but a wand)
> He walked with."—*Paradise Lost,* i. 292.

The word was introduced by the Turks or Genoese in the twelfth century, and is the Arabic *Amir* with the article *al* (lord or commander) ; as *Amir-al-ma* (commander of the water), *Amir-al-Omra* (commander of the forces), *Amir-al-Mūminim* (commander of the faithful).

English admirals used to be of three classes, according to the colour of their flag—

Admiral of the Red, used to hold the centre in an engagement.

Admiral of the White, used to hold the van.

Admiral of the Blue, used to hold the rear.

The distinction was abolished in 1864 ; now all admirals carry the white flag.

Admirals are called *Flag Officers.*

Admiral of the Blue. A butcher who dresses in blue to conceal blood-stains. A tapster also is so called, from his blue apron. A play on the rear-admiral of the British navy, called "Admiral of the Blue (Flag)."

> "As soon as customers begin to stir
> The Admiral of the Blue cries, 'Coming, Sir.'"
> *Poor Robin, 1731.*

Admiral of the Red. A punning term applied to a wine-bibber whose face and nose are very red.

Admittance. Licence. Shakespeare says. "Sir John, you are a gentleman of excellent breeding, of great admittance " —*i.e.,* to whom great freedom is allowed (*Merry Wives*, ii. 2). The allusion is to an obsolete custom called *admission*, by which a prince avowed another prince to be under his protection. Maximilian, Emperor of Mexico, was the "admittant" of the Emperor Napoleon III.

Admonitionists, or **Admonitioners.** Certain Puritans who in 1571 sent an *admonition* to the Parliament condemning everything in the Church of England which was not in accordance with the doctrines and practices of Gene'va.

Adobe [EDOBE.]

Adolpha. Daughter of General Kleiner, governor of Prague and wife of Idenstein. Her only fault was "excess of too sweet nature, which ever made another's grief her own."— *Knowles : Maid of Mariendorpt* (1838).

Ado'nai. Son of the star-beam, and god of light among the Rosicru'cians.

One of the names given by the Jews to Jehovah, for fear of breaking the command, "Thou shalt not take the name of the Lord [Jehovah] thy God in vain."

Adona'is (4 syl.). The song about Ado'nis; Shelley's elegy on Keats is so called. *See* Bion's *Lament for Adonis.*

Ado'nies. Feasts of Adonis, celebrated in Assyria, Alexandria, Egypt, Judea, Persia, Cyprus, and all Greece, for eight days. Lucian gives a long description of them. In these feasts wheat, flowers, herbs, fruits, and branches of trees were carried in procession, and thrown into the sea or some fountain.

Ado'nis. A beautiful boy. The allusion is to Ado'nis, who was beloved by Venus, and was killed by a boar while hunting.

> "Rose-cheeked Adonis hied him to the chase;
> Hunting he loved; but love he laughed to scorn.
> Sick-thoughted Venus makes amain unto him,
> And, like a bold-faced suitor,'gins to woo him."
> *Shakespeare: Venus and Adonis.*

Adonis of 50. Leigh Hunt was sent to prison for applying this term to George IV. when Regent.

Adonis Flower (*The*), according to Bion, is the rose; Pliny (i. 23) says it is the anemone; others say it is the field poppy, certainly the prince of weeds; but what we now generally mean by the Adōnis flower is pheasant's eye, called in French *goute-de-sang*, because in fable it sprang from the blood of the gored hunter.

> "Αιμα ροδον τικτει, τα δε δακρυα ταν ανεμωναν."
> (Blood brings forth roses, tears anemone.)—*Bion: Elegy on Adonis.* See also *Ovid: Metamorphoses*, Bk. x., Fable 15.)

Adonis Garden, or *A garden of Adonis* (Greek). A worthless toy; a very perishable good. The allusion is to the fennel and lettuce jars of the ancient Greeks, called "Adonis gardens," because these herbs were planted in them for the annual festival of the young huntsman, and thrown away the next morning. (1 *Henry VI.*, i. 6.)

Adonis River. A river in Phœnicia, which always runs red at the season of the year when the feast of Adonis is held. The legend ascribes this redness to sympathy with the young hunter; others ascribe it to a sort of minium, or red earth, which mixes with the water.

> "Thammuz came next behind,
> Whose annual wound in Lebanon allured
> The Syrian damsels to lament his fate
> In amorous ditties all a summer's day,
> While smooth Adonis from his native rock
> Ran purple to the sea, supposed with blood
> Of Thammuz yearly wounded."
> *Milton: Paradise Lost*, Book 1, line 445, etc.

Ado'nists. Those Jews who maintain that the proper vowels of the word Jehovah are unknown, and that the word is never to be pronounced *Ado'nai.* (Hebrew, *adon*, lord.)

Adop'tion. *Adoption by arms.* An ancient custom of giving arms to a person of merit, which laid him under the obligation of being your champion and defender.

Adoption by baptism. Being godfather or godmother to a child. The child by baptism is your god-child.

Adoption by hair. Cutting off your hair, and giving it to a person in proof that you receive him as your adopted father. Thus Bo'son, King of Arles, cut off his hair and gave it to Pope John VIII., who adopted him.

Adoption Controversy. Elipand, Archbishop of Tole'do, and Felix, Bishop of Urgel, maintained that Jesus Christ in his *human* nature was the son of God by adoption only (Rom. viii. 29), though in his pre-existing state he was the "begotten Son of God" in the ordinary catholic acceptation. Duns Scotus, Durandus, Calixtus, and others supported this view.

Adop'tionist. A disciple of Elipand, Archbishop of Tole'do, and Felix, Bishop of Urgel (in Spain), is so called.

Adore (2 syl.) means to "carry to one's mouth" "to kiss" (*ad-os, adorāre*). The Romans performed adoration by placing their right hand on their mouth and bowing. The Greeks paid adoration to kings by putting the royal robe to their lips. The Jews kissed in homage: thus God said to Elijah he had 7,000 in Israel who had not bowed unto Baal, "every mouth which hath not kissed him" (1 Kings xix. 18; *see also* Hos. xiii. 2). "Kiss the Son lest He be angry" (Psalm ii. 12), means worship, reverence the Son. Even in England we do homage by kissing the hand of the sovereign.

Adram'melech. God of the people of Sepharva'im, to whom infants were burnt in sacrifice (Kings xvii. 31). Probably the sun.

Adrastus. An Indian prince from the banks of the Ganges, who aided the King of Egypt against the crusaders. He wore a serpent's skin, and rode on an elephant. Adrastus was slain by Rinaldo.—*Tasso: Jerusalem Delivered*, Book xx.

Adrian (*St.*), represented, in Christian art, with an anvil, and a sword or axe close by it. He had his limbs cut off on a smith's anvil, and was afterwards beheaded. St. Adrian is the patron saint of the Flemish brewers.

Adriel, in Dryden's *Absalom and Achitophel*, is meant for the Earl of Mulgrave.

> "Sharp-judging Adriel, the muses' friend,
> Himself a muse : in Sanhedrim's debate
> True to his prince, but not a slave of state ;
> Whom David's love with honours did adorn,
> That from his disobedient son were torn."
> *Part I.*

Adrift. *I am all adrift. He is quite adrift. To turn one adrift.* Sea phrases. A ship is said to be adrift when it has broken from its moorings, and is driven at random by the winds. To be adrift is to be wide of the mark, or not in the right course. To turn one adrift is to turn him from house and home to go his own way.

Adroit' properly means "to the right" (French, *à droite*). The French call a person who is not adroit *gauche* (left-handed), meaning awkward, boorish.

Adsidel'ta. The table at which the flamens sat during sacrifice.

Adullamites (4 syl.). The adherents of Lowe and Horsman, seceders in 1866 from the Reform Party. John Bright said of these members that they retired to the cave of Adullam, and tried to gather round them all the discontented. The allusion is to David in his flight from Saul, who "escaped to the cave Adullam ; and every one that was in distress, and every one that was in debt, and every one that was discontented, gathered themselves unto him" (1 Sam. xxii. 1, 2).

Advauncer. The second branches of a stag's horn.

> "In a hart the main horne itself they call the *beame.* The lowest antlier is called the *brow-antlier;* the next, *roial ;* the next that, *surroial ;* and then the top.
> "In a buck, they say *bur, beame, braunch, ad-vauncers, palme,* and *speilers."—Marwood : Forest Lawes.*

Advent. Four weeks to commemorate the first and second coming of Christ ; the first to redeem, and the second to judge the world. The season begins on St. Andrew's Day, or the Sunday nearest to it. (Latin, *ad-ventus, the* coming to.)

Ad'versary (*The*). Satan. (1 Pet. v. 8.)

Advocate (*An*) means one called to assist clients in a court of law. (Latin, *advocāre.*)

The Devil's Advocate. One who brings forward malicious accusations. When any name is proposed for canonisation in the Roman Catholic Church, two advocates are appointed, one to oppose the motion and one to defend it. The former, called *Advoca'tus Diab'oli* (the Devil's Advocate), advances all he can against the person in question ; the latter, called *Advoca'tus Dei* (God's Advocate), says all he can in support of the proposal.

Advocates' Library, in Edinburgh, founded 1682, is one of the five libraries to which copyright books are sent. (*See* COPYRIGHT.)

Advow'son means the right of appointing the incumbent of a church or ecclesiastical benefice. In mediæval times the "advocacy" or patronage of bishoprics and abbeys was frequently in the hands of powerful nobles, who often claimed the right to appoint in the event of a vacancy ; hence the word (from Latin, *advocatio,* the office of a patron).

A presentative advowson is when the patron presents to the bishop a person to whom he is willing to give the place of preferment.

A collative advowson is when the bishop himself is patron, and collates his client without any intermediate person.

A don'ative advowson is where the Crown gives a living to a clergyman without presentation, institution, or induction. This is done when a church or chapel has been founded by the Crown, and is not subject to the ordinary.

Advowson in gross is an advowson separated from the manor, and belonging wholly to the owner. While attached to the manor it is an advowson *appendant.* "Gross" (French) means absolute, entire ; thus gross weight is the entire weight without deductions. A *villain in gross* was a villain the entire property of his master, and not attached to the land. A *common in gross* is one which is entirely your own, and which belongs to the manor.

Sale of Advowsons. When lords of manors built churches upon their own demesnes, and endowed them, they became private property, which the lord might give away or even sell, under certain limitations. These livings are called *Advowsons appen'dant,* being appended to the manor. After a time they became regular "commercial property," and we still see the sale of some of them in the public journals.

Ad'ytum. The Holy of Holies in the Greek and Roman temples, into which the general public were not admitted. (Greek, *a-duton* = not to be entered; *duo*, to go.)

Æ'diles (2 syl.). Those who, in ancient Rome, had charge of the public buildings (*ædes*), such as the temples, theatres, baths, aqueducts, sewers, including roads and streets also.

Ægeus (2 syl.). A fabulous king of Athens who gave name to the Ægēan Sea. His son, Theseus, went to Crete to deliver Athens from the tribute exacted by Minos. Theseus said, if he succeeded he would hoist a white sail on his home-voyage, as a signal of his safety. This he neglected to do ; and Ægeus, who watched the ship from a rock, thinking his son had perished, threw himself into the sea.

This incident has been copied in the tale of Sir Tristram and Ysolde. Sir Tristram being severely wounded in Brittany, sent for Ysolde to come and see him before he died. He told his messenger, if Ysolde consented to come to hoist a white flag. Sir Tristram's wife told him the ship was in sight with a black flag at the helm, whereupon Sir Tristram bowed his head and died. [TRISTRAM.]

Ægine'tan Sculptures. Sculptures excavated by a company of Germans, Danes, and English (1811), in the little island of Ægi'na. They were purchased by Ludwig, Crown Prince of Bavaria, and are now the most remarkable ornaments of the Glyptothek, at Münich.

Ægir'. God of the ocean, whose wife is Rana. They had nine daughters, who wore white robes and veils (*Scandinavian mythology*). These daughters are the billows, etc. The word means " to flow."

Æ'gis. The shield of Jupiter made by Vulcan was so called, and symbolised "Divine protection." The shield of Minerva was called an *ægis* also. The shield of Jupiter was covered with the skin of the goat Amalthæa, and the Greek for goat is, in the genitive case, *aigos*. The ægis made by Vulcan was of brass.

I throw my ægis over you, I give you my protection.

Ægro'tat. *To sport an ægrōtat.* In university parlance, an ægrōtat is a

medical certificate of indisposition to exempt the bearer from attending chapel and college lectures.

A E I (*A—i*), a common motto on jewellery, means " for ever and for aye." (Greek.)

Ælu'rus. The cat. An Egyptian deity held in the greatest veneration. Herodŏtus (ii. 66) tells us that Diana, to avoid being molested by the giants, changed herself into a cat. The deity used to be represented with a cat's head on a human body. (Greek, *ailouros*, a cat.)

Æmilian Law. Made by Æmilius Mamercus the prætor. It enjoined that the oldest priest should drive a nail every year into the capitol on the ides of September (September 5).

Æmonia Æmo'nian (HÆMONIA HÆMONIAN).

Æne'as. The hero of Virgil's epic. He carried his father Anchi'sēs on his shoulders from the flames of Troy. After roaming about for many years, he came to Italy, where he founded a colony which the Romans claim as their origin. The epithet applied to him is *pius* = pious, dutiful.

Æne'id. The epic poem of Virgil, (in twelve books). So called from *Æne'as* and the suffix *-is*, plur. *idēs* (belonging to).

"The story of Sinon," says Macrŏbius, "and the taking of Troy is bor'owed from Pisander.
"The loves of Did and Ænēus are taken from those of Medēa an Jason, in Apollōnius of Rhodes.
"The story of the Wooden Horse and burning of Troy is from Arctinus of Milētus."

Æol'ic Digamma. An ancient Greek letter (Ϝ), sounded like our *w*. Thus *oinos* with the digamma was sounded *woinos ;* whence the Latin *vinum*, our *wine*. Gamma, or *g*, was shaped thus Γ, hence digamma = double *g*.

Æolic Mode, in music, noted for its simplicity, fit for ballads and songs. The Phrygian Mode was for religious music, as hymns and anthems.

Æ'olus, in Roman mythology, was " god of the winds."

Æolian harp. The wind-harp. A box on which strings are stretched. Being placed where a draught gets to the strings, they utter musical sounds.

Æon (Greek, *aion*), eternity, an immeasurable length of time ; any being that is eternal. Basilidēs reckons there have been 365 such æons, or gods ; but

Valentinius restricts the number to 30. Sometimes written "ēon."

In geology each series of rocks covers an æon, or an indefinite and immeasurable period of time.

Æra. [ERA.]

Aërated Bread. Bread made light by means of carbonic acid gas instead of leaven.

Aërated Water. Water impregnated with carbonic acid gas, called *fixed air*.

Ae'rians. Followers of Ae'rius, who maintained that there is no difference between bishops and priests.

Æs'chylus (Greek, Αισχυλος), the most sublime of the Greek tragic poets. He wrote 90 plays, only 7 of which are now extant. Æschylus was killed by a tortoise thrown by an eagle (to break the shell) against his bald head, which it mistook for a stone (B.C. 535-456). *See* Horace, *Ars Poetica*, 278.

Pronounce *Ees'-ke-lus*.

Æs'chylus of France. Prosper Jolyot de Crébillon. (1674-1762.)

Æscula'pius. The Latin form of the Greek word Asklēpios, the god of medicine and of healing. Now used for "a medical practitioner."

Æsir, plural of As or Asa, the celestial gods of Scandinavia, who lived in Asgard (god's ward), situate on the heavenly hills between earth and the rainbow. The chief was Odin. We are told that there were twelve, but it would be hard to determine who the twelve are, for, like Arthur's knights, the number seems variable. The following may be mentioned:—(1) Odin ; (2) Thor (his eldest son, the god of thunder) ; (3) Tyr (another son, the god of wisdom) ; (4) Baldur (another son, the Scandinavian Apollo) ; (5) Bragi (the god of eloquence) ; (6) Vidar (god of silence) ; (7) Hödur the blind (Baldur's twin brother) ; (8) Hermod (Odin's son and messenger) ; (9) Hœnir (divine intelligence) ; (10) Odur (husband of Freyja, the Scandinavian Venus) ; (11) Loki (the god of mischief, though not an asa, lived in Asgard) ; (12) Vali (Odin's youngest son) ; another of Odin's sons was Kvasir the keen-sighted. Then there were the Vanir, or gods of air, ocean, and water ; the gods of fire ; the gods of the Lower World ; and the Mysterious Three, who sat on three thrones above the rainbow. Their names were Har (the perfect), the Like-perfect, and the Third person.

Wives of the Æsir : Odin's wife was Frigga ; Thor's wife was Sif (beauty) ;

Baldur's wife was Nanna (daring); Bragi's wife was Iduna ; Odur's wife was Freyja (the Scandinavian Venus) ; Loki's wife was Sigūna.

The Æsir built Asgard themselves, but each god had his own private mansion. That of Odin was Gladsheim ; but his wife Frigga had also her private abode, named Fensalir ; the mansion of Thor was Bilskirnir ; that of Baldur was Broadblink ; that of Odur's wife was Folkbang ; of Vidar was Landvidi (wide land) ; the private abode of the goddesses generally was Vingolf.

The refectory or banquet hall of the Æsir was called Valhalla. •

Niörd, the water-god, was not one of the Æsir, but chief of the Vanir ; his son was Frey ; his daughter, Freyja (the Scandinavian Venus) ; his wife was Skadi ; and his home, Noatun.

Æson's Bath. Sir Thomas Browne (*Religio Medici*, p. 67) rationalises this into "hair-dye." The reference is to Medea renovating Æson, father of Jason, with the juices of a concoction made of sundry articles. After Æson had imbibed these juices, Ovid says :—

"Barba comæque,
Canitie posita, nigrum rapuēre, colorem."
Metamorphoses, vii. 288.

Æsonian Hero (*The*). Jason, who was the son of Æson.

Æ'sop's Fables were compiled by Ba'brios, a Greek, who lived in the Alexandrian age.

Æsop, a Phrygian slave, very deformed, and the writer of fables. He was contemporary with Pythagŏras, about B.C. 570.

Almost all Greek and Latin fables are ascribed to Æsop, as all our Psalms are ascribed to David. The Latin fables of Phædrus are supposed to be translations of Æsopian fables.

Æsop of Arabia. Lokman (?). Nasser, who lived in the fifth century, is generally called the "Arabian Æsop."

Æsop of England. John Gay. (1688-1732.)

Æsop of France. Jean de la Fontaine. (1621-1695.)

Æsop of Germany, Gotthold Ephraim Lessing. (1729-1781.)

Æsop of India. Bidpay or Pilpay. (About three centuries before the Christian era.)

A'etites (3 syl.). Eagle - stones. (Greek, *aĕtos*, an eagle.) Hollow stones composed of several crusts, one within another. Supposed at one time to form part of an eagle's nest. Pliny mentions them. Kirwan applies the name to clay-ironstones having a globular crust of oxide investing an ochreous kernel. Mythically, they are supposed to have the property of detecting theft.

Ætolian Hero (*The*). Diomede, who was king of Ætolia. *Ovid.*

Affable means "one easy to be spoken to." (Latin, *ad fari*, to speak to.)

Affect'. To love, to desire. (Latin, *affecto*.)

"Some affect the light, and some the shade."
      Blair: Grave.

l'Affection aveugle raison (French). Cassius says to Brutus, "A friendly eye could never see such faults." "L'esprit est presque toujours la dupe du cœur." (La Rochefoucauld: *Maximes*.)

Again, "a mother thinks all her geese are swans."

Italian : A ogni grolla paion belli i suoi grollatini. Ad ogni uccello, suo nido è bello.

French : A chaque oiseau son nid parait beau.

Latin : Asinus asino, sus sui, pulcher. Sua cuique res est carissima.

Affront' properly means to stand front to front. In savage nations opposing armies draw up front to front before they begin hostilities, and by grimaces, sounds, words, and all conceivable means, try to provoke and terrify their *vis-à-vis*. When this "affronting" is over, the adversaries rush against each other, and the fight begins in earnest.

Affront. A salute; a coming in front of another to salute.

"Only, sir, this I must caution you of, in your affront, or salute, never to move your hat."—
Green: Tu Quoque, vii. 95.

Afraid. *He who trembles to hear a leaf fall should keep out of the wood.* This is a French proverb: "Qui a peur de feuilles, ne doit aller au bois." Our corresponding English proverb is, "He who fears scars shouldn't go the wars." The timid should not voluntarily expose themselves to danger.

"Little boats should keep near shore,
   Larger ones may venture more."

Africa. *Teneo te, Africa* (I take possession of thee, O Africa). When Cæsar landed at Adrumētum, in Africa, he tripped and fell—a bad omen; but, with wonderful presence of mind, he pretended that he had done so intentionally, and kissing the soil, exclaimed, "Thus do I take possession of thee, O Africa." Told also of Scipio. (*See Don Quixote*, Pt. II. Bk. vi. ch. 6.)

Africa semper aliquid novi affert. "Africa is always producing some novelty." A Greek proverb quoted

(in Latin) by Pliny, in allusion to the ancient belief that Africa abounded in strange monsters.

African Sisters (*The*). The Hesperīdes (4 syl.) who lived in Africa. They were the daughters of Atlas.

Afriet, or "Afrit." The beau ideal of what is terrible and monstrous in Arabian superstition. A sort of ghoul or demon. Solomon, we are told, once tamed an Afrit, and made it submissive to his will.

Aft. The hinder part of a ship.
Fore and Aft. The entire length (of a ship), from stem to stern.

After-cast. A throw of dice after the game is ended ; anything done too late.

"Ever he playeth an after-cast
   Of all that he shall say or do."—*Gower.*

After-clap. *Beware of after-claps.* An after-clap is a catastrophe or threat after an affair is supposed to be over. It is very common in thunderstorms to hear a "clap" after the rain subsides, and the clouds break.

"What plaguy mischief and mishaps
   Do dog him still with after-claps."
      Butler: Hudibras, Pt. i. 3.

After Meat, Mustard. In Latin, "Post bellum, auxilium." We have also, "After death, the doctor," which is the German, "Wann der kranke ist todt, so kommt der arztnei" (when the patient's dead, comes the physic). To the same effect is "When the steed is stolen, lock the stable door." Meaning, doing a thing, or offering service when it is too late, or when there is no longer need thereof.

After us, the Deluge. "I care not what happens when I am dead and gone." So said Mdme. de Pompadour, the mistress of Louis XV. (1722-1764). Metternich, the Austrian statesman (1773-1859), is credited with the same ; but probably he simply quoted the words of the French marchioness.

Aft-meal. An extra meal; a meal taken after and in addition to the ordinary meals.

"At aft-meals who shall pay for the wine ?"
      Thynne: Debate.

A'gag, in Dryden's satire of *Absalom and Achit'ophel*, is meant for Sir Edmondbury Godfrey, the magistrate before whom Titus Oates made his declaration, and was afterwards found barbarously murdered in a ditch near

Primrose Hill. Agag was hewed to pieces by Samuel (1 Sam. xv.).

"And Corah (*Titus Oates*) might for Agag's murder call
In terms as coarse as Samuel used to Saul."
1. 675-6.

Agamarshana. A passage of the Veda, the repetition of which will purify the soul like absolution after confession.

Agamem'non. King of Argos, in Greece, and commander-in-chief of the allied Greeks who went to the siege of Troy. The fleet being delayed by adverse winds at Aulis, Agamemnon sacrificed his daughter Iph'igeni'a to Diana, and the winds became at once favourable. —*Homer's Iliad.*

"Till Agamemnon's daughter's blood
Appeased the gods that them withstood."
Earl of Surrey.

His *brother* was Menelãos.
His *daughters* were Iphigenia, Electra, Iphianassa, and Chrysothemis (*Sophocles*).
He was *grandson* of Pelops.
He was *killed* in a bath by his wife Clytemnestra, after his return from Troy.
His *son* was Orestës, who slew his mother for murdering his father, and was called Agamemnonidês.
His *wife* was Clytemnestra, who lived in adultery with Egistheus. At Troy he fell in love with Cassandra, a daughter of King Priam.

Virēre fortes antĕ Agamemnona ("there are hills beyond Pentland, and fields beyond Forth"), *i.e.*, we are not to suppose that our own age or locality monopolises all that is good.—*Hor. Od.* iv. 9, 25. We might add, *et post Agamemnŏna vivent.*

"Great men there lived ere Agamemnon came,
And after him will others rise to fame."—*E. C. B.*

Aganice (4 syl.), or Aglaonicē, the Thessalian, being able to calculate eclipses, she pretended to have the moon under her command, and to be able when she chose to draw it from heaven. Her secret being found out, her vaunting became a laughing-stock, and gave birth to the Greek proverb cast at braggarts, "Yes, as the Moon obeys Aganicē."

Aganippe (4 syl.). A fountain of Bœotia at the foot of Mount Helicon, dedicated to the Muses, because it had the virtue of imparting poetic inspiration. From this fountain the Muses are called Aganippedēs (5 syl.) or Aganippidēs (5 syl.).

Ag'ape (3 syl.). A love-feast. The early Christians held a love-feast before or after communion, when contributions were made for the poor. These feasts became a scandal, and were condemned at the Council of Carthage, 397. (Greek, *agapē*, love.)

Agapem'one (5 syl.). A somewhat disreputable association of men and women living promiscuously on a common fund, which existed for a time at Charlynch, near Bridgewater, in Somersetshire. (Greek, *agapē*, love.)

Agape tæ. Women under vows of virginity, who undertook to attend the monks. (The word is Greek, and means *beloved.*)

Ag'ate (2 syl.). So called, says Pliny (xxxvii. 10), from Acha'tēs or Gaga'tēs, a river in Sicily, near which it is found in abundance.

"These, these are they, if we consider well,
That saphirs and the diamonds doe excell,
The pearle, the emerauld, and the turkesse bleu,
The sanguine corrall, amber's golden hiew,
The christall, jacinth, *achate*, ruby red."
Taylor: The Waterspout (1630).

Agate is supposed to render a person invisible, and to turn the sword of foes against themselves.

Ag'ate. A very diminutive person. Shakespeare speaks of Queen Mab as no bigger than an agate-stone on the forefinger of an alderman.

"I was never manned with an agate till now."
Shakespeare: 2 Hen. IV. i. 2.

Ag'atha. Daughter of Cuno, the ranger, in love with Max, to whom she is to be married, provided he carries off the prize in the annual trial-shot. She is in danger of being shot by Max unwittingly, but is rescued by a hermit, and becomes the bride of the young huntsman.—*Weber's Opera of Der Freischütz.*

Agatha (*St.*). Represented in Christian art with a pair of shears, and holding in her hand a salver, on which her breasts are placed. The reference is to her martyrdom, when her breasts were cut off by a pair of shears.

Agave (3 syl.) or "American aloe," from the Greek, *agauos*, admirable. The Mexicans plant fences of Agavē round their wigwams, as a defence against wild beasts. The Mahometans of Egypt regard it as a charm and religious symbol; and pilgrims to Mecca indicate their exploit by hanging over the door of their dwelling a leaf of Agavē, which has the further charm of warding off evil spirits. The Jews in Cairo attribute a similar virtue to the plant, every part of which is utilised.

Agdistes (*self-indulgence*). The god who kept the porch of the "Bower of Bliss." He united in his own person the two sexes, and sprang from the stone Agdus, parts of which were taken by Deucalion and Pyrrha to cast over their shoulders, after the flood, for re-peopling the world. (*Spenser : Faërie Queene*, book ii. 12.) Ag-dis'-tes in 3 syl.

Age as accords (*To*). To do what is fit and right (Scotch law term). Here " Age " is from the Latin *agĕre*, to do.

"To set about the matter in a regular manner, or, as he termed it . . . to 'age as accords.'"—
Sir W. Scott: Redgauntlet, chap. 2.

Age of Animals. An old Celtic rhyme, put into modern English, says :—

" Thrice the age of a dog is that of a horse ;
Thrice the age of a horse is that of a man ;
Thrice the age of a man is that of a deer ;
Thrice the age of a deer is that of an eagle."

Age of Women (*The*). Though many women are mentioned in the Bible, the age of only one (Sarah, Abraham's wife) is recorded, and that to show at her advanced age she would become the mother of Isaac.

"Elizabeth, the mother of the Baptist," we a e told by St. Luke, " was well-stricken in age."

Age of the Bishops (*The*). The ninth century. (*Hallam : Middle Ages.*)

Age of the Popes (*The*). The twelfth century. (*Hallam : Middle Ages.*)

Agĕ hoc. " Attend to this." In sacrifice the Roman crier perpetually repeated these words to arouse attention. In the " Common Prayer Book " the attention of the congregation is frequently aroused by the exhortation, " Let us pray," though nearly the whole service is that of prayer.

Ages. Varro (*Fragments*, p. 219, Scaliger's edition, 1623) recognises three ages :—

(1) From the beginning of mankind to the Deluge, a time wholly unknown.

(2) From the Deluge to the First Olympiad, called the mythical period.

(3) From the first Olympiad to the present time, called the historic period.

Titian symbolised the three ages of man thus :—

(1) An infant in a cradle.
(2) A shepherd playing a flute.
(3) An old man meditating on two skulls.

According to Lucre'tius also, there are three ages, distinguished by the materials employed in implements (v. 1282), viz. :

(1) *The age of stone*, when celts or implements of stone were employed.

(2) *The age of bronze*, when implements were made of copper or brass.

(3) *The age of iron*, when implements were made of iron, as at present.

Hesiod names five ages, viz. :—

The Golden or patriarchal, under the care of Saturn.
The Silver or voluptuous, under the care of Jupiter.
The Brazen or warlike, under the care. of Neptune.
The Heroic or renaissant, under the care of Mars.
The Iron or present, under the care of Pluto.

** The present is sometimes called the wire age, from its telegraphs, by means of which well-nigh the whole earth is in intercommunication.

Fichte names five ages also : the antediluvian, post-diluvian, Christian, satanic, and millennian.

Ag'elas'ta. The stone on which Ce'rēs rested when worn down by fatigue in searching for her daughter. (Greek, *joyless.*)

Agenor'ides (5 syl.). Cadmos, who was the son of Agĕnor.

Agent. *Is man a free agent ?* This is a question of theology, which has long been mooted. The point is this : If God fore-ordains all our actions, they must take place as he fore-ordains them, and man acts as a watch or clock ; but if, on the other hand, man is responsible for his actions, he must be free to act as his inclination leads him. Those who hold the former view are called *necessitarians ;* those who hold the latter, *libertarians.*

Agglu'tinate Languages. The Tura'nian family of languages are so called because every syllable is a word, and these are *glued* together to form other words, and may be unglued so as to leave the roots distinct, as "inkstand."

Aghast'. Frightened, as by a ghost; from Anglo-Saxon *gást*, a ghost.

Agi'o. The percentage of charge made for the exchange of paper money into cash. (Italian).

"The profit is called by the Italians aggio."—
Scarlett.

Agis. King of Sparta, who tried to deliver Greece from the Macedonian yoke, and was slain in the attempt.

"To save a rotten state, Agis, who saw
E'en Sparta's self to servile avarice sink."
Thomson : Winter, 488-9.

Agist'. To take the cattle of another to graze at a certain sum. The feeding of these beasts is called *agistment.* The words are from the Norman *agiser* (to be levant and couchant, rise up and lie down), because, says Coke, beasts are levant and couchant whilst they are on the land.

Ag'la. A cabalistic name of God, formed from the initial letters of **A**ttâh, **G**ibbor, **L**eholâm, **A**donâi (*Thou art strong for ever, O Lord!*). (*See* NOT-ARICA.)

Aglaos. The poorest man in Arcadia, pronounced by Apollo to be far happier than Gygēs, because he was "contented with his lot."

> "Poor and content is rich and rich enough;
> But riches endless are as poor as winter
> To him who ever fears he shall be poor."
> *Shakespeare: Othello* iii. 3.

Agnes. *She is an Agnes* (*elle fait l'Agnès*)—*i.e.*, she is a sort of female "Verdant Green," who is so unsophistic-ated that she does not even know what love means. It is a character in Mo-lière's *L'École des Femmes*.

Agnes (*St.*) is represented by Dom-enichino as kneeling on a pile of fagots, the fire extinguished, and the executioner about to slay her with the sword. The introduction of a lamb (*agnus*) is a modern innovation, and play on the name. St. Agnes is the patron of young virgins.

"St. Agnes was first tied to a stake, but the fire of the stakes went out; whereupon Aspasius, set to watch the martyrdom, drew his sword, and cut off her head."

Agnes' Day (*St.*), 21st January. Upon St. Agnes' night, you take a row of pins, and pull out every one, one after another. Saying a pater-noster, stick a pin in your sleeve, and you will dream of him or her you shall marry.—*Aubrey: Mis-cellany*, p. 136.

Ag'noites (3 syl.). *Ag'-no-i'tes*, or **Ag-no'-i-tæ** (4 syl.).
(1) Certain heretics in the fourth century who said "God did *not know* everything."
(2) Another sect, in the sixth century, who maintained that Christ "did *not know* the time of the day of judgment." (Greek, *a*, not; γιγνώσκω, to know.)

Agnostic (*An*). A term invented by Prof. Huxley in 1885 to indicate the mental attitude of those who withhold their assent to whatever is incapable of proof, such as the absolute. In regard to miracles and revelation, agnostics neither dogmatically accept nor reject such matters, but simply say *Agnosco*—I do not know—they are not capable of proof.

Agnus-castus. A shrub of the Vitex tribe, called *agnos* (chaste) by the Greeks, because the Athenian ladies, at the feast of Cerēs, used to strew their couches with vitex leaves, as a palladium of chástity. The monks, mistaking *agnos* (chaste) for *agnus* (a lamb), but knowing the use made of the plant, added *castus* to explain its character, making it chaste-lamb. (For another similar blunder, *see* I.H.S.)

Agnus Dei. A cake of wax or dough stamped with the figure of a lamb supporting the banner of the Cross, and distributed by the Pope on the Sunday after Easter as an amulet. Our Lord is called *Agnus Dei* (the Lamb of God). There is also a prayer so called, because it begins with the words, *Agnus Dei, qui tollis pecca'ta mundi* (O Lamb of God, that takest away the sins of the world).

Agog'. *He is all agog*, in nervous anxiety; on the *qui vive*, like a horse in clover. (French, *à gogo*, or *vivre à gogo*, to live in clover.)

Agonis'tes (4 syl.). *Samson Agonistes* (the title of Milton's drama) means Samson wrestling with adversity—Sam-son combating with trouble. (Greek, *agoni'zomai*, to combat, to struggle.)

Agonis'tics. A branch of the Dona-tists of Africa who roamed from town to town affirming they were ministers of justice. The Greek *agōn* (an assembly) = the Latin *nundinæ*, days when the law-courts were opened, that country people might go and get their law-suits settled.

Ag'ony properly means contention in the athletic games; and to *agonise* is the act of contending. (Greek, *agōn*, a game of contest, as well as a "place of assembly").
Agony, meaning "great pain," is the wrestle with pain or struggle with suffer-ing.

Agony Column of a newspaper. A column containing advertisements of missing relatives and friends; indicating great distress of mind in the advertiser.

Agra'rian Law, from the Latin *ager* (land), is a law for making land the common property of a nation, and not the particular property of individuals. In a modified form, it means a re-distribution of land, giving to each citizen a portion.

Agrimony. The older spelling was Argemony, and Pliny calls it *argemonia*, from the Greek *argemos*, a white speck on the eye, which this plant was supposed to cure.

Ague (*A cure for*). (*See* HOMER.)

Ague-cheek. *Sir Andrew Ague-cheek*, a straight-haired country squire, stupid even to silliness, self-conceited, living to eat, and wholly unacquainted with the world of fashion. The character is in Shakespeare's *Twelfth Night*.

A'gur's Wish (Prov. xxx. 8). "Give me neither riches nor poverty."

Ahasue'rus, or Ahashverosh. A title common to several Persian kings. The three mentioned in the Bible are supposed to be Cyaxares (Dan. xi. 1); Xerxes (Esther); and Cambyses (Ezra iv. 6).

An alabaster vase found at Halicarnassus gives four renderings of the name Xerxes, viz., Persian, *Khshâyarsha*; Assyrian, *Khsiharsha*; Egyptian, *Khshyarsha*; and the Greek, *Xerxes*; the Sanskrit root *Kshi* means "to rule," *Kshathra* (Zend *Ksathra*), a king.

Ahead. *The wind's ahead—i.e.*, blows in the direction towards which the ship's head points; in front. If the wind blows in the opposite direction (*i.e.*, towards the stern) it is said to be astern. When one ship is ahead of another, it is *before* it, or further advanced. "Ahead of his class," means at the head. Ahead in a race, means before the rest of the runners.

To go ahead is to go on without hesitation, as a ship runs ahead of another.

Ahith'ophel, or *Achit'ophel*. A treacherous friend and adviser. Ahithophel was David's counsellor, but joined Absalom in revolt, and advised him "like the oracle of God" (2 Sam. xvi. 20-23). In Dryden's political satire, Achitophel stands for the Earl of Shaftesbury. (*See* ACHITOPHEL.)

Ah'med (Prince). Noted for the tent given him by the fairy Pari-ban'ou, which would cover a whole army, but might be carried in one's pocket; and for the apple of Sa narcand', which would cure all diseases. — *Arabian Nights, Prince Ahmed, etc.*

This tent coincides in a marvellous manner with the Norse ship called Skidbladnir (*q.v.*). (*See* SOLOMON'S CARPET.)

Aholibah (Ezek. xxiii. 4, 11, etc.). The personification of prostitution. Used by the prophet to signify religious adultery or harlotry. (*See* HARLOT.)

"The great difficulty in exposing the immoralities of this Aholibah is that her [acts] are so revolting."—*Papers on the Social Evil*, 1885.

Aholiba'mah. A granddaughter of Cain, loved by the seraph Samia'sa. She is a proud, ambitious, queen-like beauty, a female type of Cain. When the flood came, her angel-lover carried her under his wings to some other planet.—*Byron: Heaven and Earth.*

Ah'riman, or *Ahrim'anēs*. The principle or angel of darkness and evil in the Magian system. (*See* ORMUSD.)

"I recognise the evil spirit, sir, and do honour to Ahrimanes in this young man."—*Thackeray.*

Aide toi et le Ciel t'aidera (*God will help those who help themselves*). The party-motto of a political society of France, established in 1824. The object of the society was, by agitation and the press, to induce the middle classes to resist the Government. Guizot was at one time its president, and *Le Globe* and *Le National* its organs. This society, which doubtless aided in bringing about the Revolution of 1830, was dissolved in 1832.

Ai'grette (2 syl.). A lady's headdress, consisting of feathers or flowers. The French call the down of thistles and dandelions, as well as the tuft of birds, *aigrette*.

Aim. *To give aim*, to stand aloof. A term in archery, meaning to stand within a convenient distance from the butts, to *give* the archers information how near their arrows fall to the mark *aimed at*.

"But, gentle people, give me aim awhile,
For nature puts me to a heavy task;
Stand all aloof."
Shakespeare: Titus Andronicus, v. 3.

To cry aim. To applaud, encourage. In archery it was customary to appoint certain persons to cry *aim*, for the sake of encouraging those who were about to shoot.

"All my neighbours shall cry aim."
Shakespeare: Merry Wives of Windsor, iii. 2.

Aim-crier. An abettor, one who encourages. In archery, the person employed to "cry aim." (*See above.*)

"Thou smiling aim-crier at princes' fall."
English Arcadia.

Air, *an element*. Anaxag'oras held air to be the primary form of matter.

Aristotle gives Fire, Air, Earth, and Water as the four elements.

Air, *a manner*, as "the air of the court," the "air of gentility;" "a good air" (manner, deportment) means the pervading habit.

Air, *in music*, is that melody which predominates and gives its character to the piece.

Air one's opinions (*To*). To state opinions without having firmly based them on proper data. To let them fly loose, like a caged bird.

To *ventilate* an opinion means to suggest for the purpose of having it duly tested. A conceited man *airs* his opinions, a discreet one *ventilates* them, as corn when it is winnowed, and the chaff is blown off.

Air-brained. Giddy, heedless. This word is now generally spelt "hare-brained;" but, by ancient authors, *hair-brained*. In C. Thomson's *Autobiography* it is spelt "Air-brained," which seems plausible.

Air-line signifies (in the United States) the most direct and shortest possible route between two given places, as the Eastern and Western Air-line Railway.

Air-ship (*An*). A balloon.

"Presently a north-easterly current of wind struck the air-ship, and it began to move with great velocity upon a horizontal line."—*Max Adeler : The Captain's MS.*

Air-throne. Odin's throne in Gladsheim. His palace was in Asgard.

Airs. *To give oneself mighty airs :* to assume, in manner, appearance, and tone, a superiority to which you have no claim. The same as *Air*, manner (*q.v.*).

The plural is essential in this case to take it out of the category of mere eccentricity, or to distinguish it from "air" in the sense of deportment, as "he had a fine, manly air," "his air was that of a gentleman." Air, in the singular, being generally complimentary, but "airs" in the plural always conveying censure. In Italian, we find the phrase, *Si da dell' arie.*

Airap'adam. The white elephant, one of the eight which, according to Indian mythology, sustain the earth.

Aisle (pronounce *ile*). The north and south wings of a church. Latin, *ala* (axilla, ascella), through the French, *aile*, a wing. In German the nave of a church is *schiff*, and the aisle *flügel* (a wing). In some church documents the aisles are called *alleys* (walks), and hence the nave is still sometimes called the "middle aisle " or alley. The choir of Lincoln Cathedral used to be called the "Chanters' alley ; " and Olden tells us that when he came to be church-warden, in 1638, he made the Puritans "come up the middle alley on their knees to the raile."

Aitch-bone of beef. Corruption of "Naitch-bone," *i.e.* the haunch-bone (Latin, *nates*, a haunch or buttock).

Similarly, "an apron" is a corruption of *a napperon ;* "an adder" is a corruption of *a nadder* (Old Eng., *nœddre*). In other words, we have reversed the order ; thus "a newt" is *an ewt ;* "a nag" is *an ög* (Danish). Latin, *eq[uus]*, a horse.

Ajax, *the Greater.* King of Sal'amis, a man of giant stature, daring, and self-confident. Generally called Tel'amon

Ajax, because he was the son of Tel'amon. When the armour of Hector was awarded to Ulysses instead of to himself, he turned mad from vexation and stabbed himself.—*Homer's Iliad,* and later poets.

Ajax, *the Less.* Son of Oïleus (3 syl.), King of Locris, in Greece. The night Troy was taken, he offered violence to Cassandra, the prophetic daughter of Priam ; in consequence of which his ship was driven on a rock, and he perished at sea. —*Homer's Iliad,* and later poets.

" Ipsa (Juno), Jovis rapidum jaculata e nubibus ignem,
Disjecitque rates, evertitque æquora ventis ;
Illum (Ajax) expirantem transfixo pectore flammas
Turbine corripuit, scopuloque infixit acuto."
Virgil : Æneid, i. 42, etc.

Akbar. An Arabic word, meaning "Very Great." Akbar-Khan, the "very great Khan," is applied especially to the Khan of Hindûstan who reigned 1556-1605.

Ak'uan, the giant whom Rustan slew. (*Persian mythology.*)

Ak'uman. The most malevolent of all the Persian gods.

Alabama, U. S. America. The name of an Indian tribe of the Mississippi Valley, meaning " here we rest."

Alabaster. A stone of great purity and whiteness, used for ornaments. So called from " Alabastron," in Upper Egypt, where it abounds.

Alad'din, in the *Arabian Nights' Tales,* obtains a magic lamp, and has a splendid palace built by the genius of the lamp. He marries the daughter of the sultan of China, loses his lamp, and his palace is transported to Africa. Sir Walter Scott says, somewhat incorrectly :—

"Vanished into air like the palace of Aladdin."

❖ The palace did not vanish into air, but was transported to another place.

Aladdin's Lamp. The source of wealth and good fortune. After Aladdin came to his wealth and was married, he suffered his lamp to hang up and get rusty.

"It was impossible that a family, holding a document which gave them access to the most powerful noblemen in Scotland, should have suffered it to remain unemployed, like Aladdin's rusty lamp."—*Senior.*

Aladdin's Ring, given him by the African magician, was a " preservative against every evil."—*Arabian Nights : Aladdin and the Wonderful Lamp.*

Aladdin's Window. *To finish Aladdin's Window—i.e.* to attempt to complete something begun by a great genius, but left imperfect. The genius of the lamp built a palace with twenty-four windows, all but one being set in frames of precious stones; the last was left for the sultan to finish; but after exhausting his treasures, the sultan was obliged to abandon the task as hopeless.

Tait's second part of Dryden's *Absalom and Achitophel* is an *Aladdin's Window.*

Al'adine (3 syl.). The sagacious but cruel old king of Jerusalem in Tasso's *Jerusalem Delivered*, book xx. This is a fictitious character, inasmuch as the Holy Land was at the time under the dominion of the caliph of Egypt. Aladine was slain by Raymond.

Al'ako. Son of Baro-De'vel, the great god of the gipsies. The gipsies say that he will ultimately restore them to Assas in Assyria, their native country. The image of Alako has a pen in his left hand and a sword in his right.

Alans. Large dogs, of various species, used for hunting deer.

"Skins of animals slain in the chase were stretched on the ground . . . and upon a heap of these lay 3 *alans*, as they were called, *i.e.*, wolf greyhounds of the largest size."—*Sir W. Scott: The Talisman*, chap. vi.

Alar'con. King of Barca, who joined the armament of Egypt against the Crusaders. His men were only half armed.—*Jerusalem Delivered.*

Alarm. An outcry made to give notice of danger. (Italian, *all' arme,* "to arms;" French, *alarme.*)

Alar'um Bell. In feudal times a 'larum bell was rung in the castle in times of danger to summon the retainers to arms. A variant of alarm (*q.v.*).

"Awake! awake! Ring the alarum bell! Murder and treason!"
Shakespeare: Macbeth, ii. 3.

Alas'nam. *Alasnam's lady.* In the *Arabian Nights' Tales* Alasnam has eight diamond statues, but had to go in quest of a ninth more precious still, to fill the vacant pedestal. The prize was found in the lady who became his wife, at once the most beautiful and the most perfect of her race.

"There is wanting one pure and perfect model, and that one, wherever it is to be found, is like Alasnam's lady, worth them all."—*Sir Walter Scott.*

Alasnam's Mirror. The "touchstone of virtue," given to Alasnam by one of the Genii. If he looked in this mirror it informed him whether a damsel would remain to him faithful or not. If the mirror remained unsullied so would the maiden; if it clouded, the maiden

would prove faithless.—*Arabian Nights: Prince Zeyn Alasnam.*

Alas'tor. The evil genius of a house; a Nemesis. Cicero says: "Who meditated killing himself that he might become the *Alastor* of Augustus, whom he hated." Shelley has a poem entitled "Alastor, or The Spirit of Solitude." The word is Greek (*alastōr*, the avenging god, a title applied to Zeus); the Romans had their Jupiter Vindex; and we read in the Bible, "Vengeance is mine. I will repay, saith the Lord" (*Rom.* xii. 19).

Alauda. A Roman legion raised by Julius Cæsar in Gaul, and so called because they carried a *lark's tuft* on the top of their helmets.

Alawy. The Nile is so called by the Abyssinians. The word means "the giant."

Alb. The long white tunic (Latin, *albus*, white) bound round the waist with a girdle. The dress is emblematical of purity and continence, and worn by priests when saying Mass.

Albadara. A bone which the Arabs say defies destruction, and which, at the resurrection, will be the germ of the new body. The Jews called it Luz (*q.v.*); and the "Os sacrum" (*q.v.*) refers probably to the same superstition.

Alban (*St.*), like St. Denis, is represented as carrying his head between his hands. His attributes are a sword and a crown.

St. Aphrodisius, St. Aventine, St. Desiderius, St. Chrysolius, St. Hilarian, St. Leo, St. Lucanus, St. Lucian, St. Proba, St. Solangia, and several other martyrs, are represented as carrying their heads in their hands. An artist's bungling way of identifying a headless trunk.

Albania, Turkey, or rather the region about the Caucasus. The word means the "mountainous region."

Albanian Hat (*An*). "Un chapeau à l'Albanaise." A sugar-loaf hat, such as was worn by the Albanians in the sixteenth century.

Alba'no Stone or Peperi'no, used by the Romans in building; a volcanic tufa quarried at Alba'no.

Albany. Scotland. (*See* ALBIN.)

Alba'ti. The white brethren. Certain Christian fanatics of the fourteenth century, so called because they dressed in white. Also the recently baptised. (Latin.)

Al'batross. The largest of webfooted birds, called by sailors the *Cape Sheep*, from its frequenting the Cape of

Good Hope. It gorges itself, and then sits motionless upon the waves. It is said to sleep in the air, because its flight is a gliding without any apparent motion of its long wings. Sailors say it is fatal to shoot an albatross. Coleridge's *Ancient Mariner* is founded on this superstition.

Albert (*An*). A chain from the waistcoat pocket to a button in front of the waistcoat. So called from Prince Albert, the consort of Queen Victoria. When he went to Birmingham, in 1849, he was presented by the jewellers of the town with such a chain, and the fashion took the public fancy.

Albertaz'zo (in *Orlando Furioso*) married Alda, daughter of Otho, Duke of Saxony. His sons were Hugh or Ugo, and Fulke or Fulco. From this family springs the Royal Family of England.

Albia'zar (in *Jerusalem Delivered*). One of the leaders of the Arab host which joined the Egyptian armament against the Crusaders. "A chief in rapine, not in knighthood bred." (Book xvii.)

Albigen'ses (4 syl.). A common name for *heretics* prior to the Reformation ; so called from the Albigeois, inhabitants of the district which now is the department of the Tarn, the capital of which was Albi. It was here the persecution of the Reformers began, under the direction of Pope Innocent III., in 1209. The Waldenses rose after them, but are not unfrequently confounded with them.

Albin. A name at one time applied to the northern part of Scotland, called by the Romans "Caledonia." This was the part inhabited by the Picts. The Scots migrated from Scotia in the North of Ireland, and acquired mastery under Kenneth M'Alpin in 843. In poetry Scotland is called Albin.

Gaelic, *ailp*; Keltic, *alp*, our *Alps*. Alpin is either *Ailp-ben* son of the hills, *i.e.*, the hill-country, or *Alp-inn* (hilly island). Albania means the "hilly country."
"Woe to his kindred, and woe to his cause,
When Albin her claymore indignantly draws."
Campbell : Lochiel's Warning.

Albi'no. A term originally applied by the Portuguese to those negroes who were mottled with white spots ; but now applied to those who are born with red eyes and white hair. Albinos are found among *white* people as well as among negroes. The term is also applied to beasts and plants. (Latin, *albus*, white.)

Albino-poets, Oliver Wendell Holmes, in the *Autocrat of the Breakfast Table* (chap. viii.), speaks of Kirke

White as one of the "sweet Albino poets," whose "plaintive song" he admires. It implies some deficiency of virility, as albinism suggests weakness, and possibly is meant as a play upon the name in this particular instance.

Al'bion. England, so named from the ancient inhabitants called Albio'nēs. The usual etymology of *albus* (white), said to have been given by Julius Cæsar in allusion to the "white cliffs," is quite untenable, as an old Greek treatise, the *De Mundo*, formerly ascribed to Aristotle, mentions the islands of Albion and Iērnē three hundred years before the invasion of Cæsar. Probably "Albion" or Albany was the Celtic name of all Great Britain, subsequently restricted to Scotland, and then to the Highlands of Scotland. Certainly the inhabitants of the whole island are implied in the word *Albionēs* in Festus Avienus's account of the voyage of Hamilcar in the fifth century B.C. (*See* ALBIN.)

"Beyond the Pillars of Herculēs is the ocean which flows round the earth, and in it are 2 very large islands called Britannia, viz., Albion and Iērnē."—*De Mundo*, Sec. iii.

Al'bion. Son of the king of this island when Oberon held his court in what we call Kensington Gardens. He was stolen by the elfin Milkah, and brought up in fairyland. When nineteen years of age, he fell in love with Kenna, daughter of King O'beron, but was driven from the empire by the indignant monarch. Albion invaded the territory, but was slain in the battle. When Kenna knew this, she poured the juice of moly over the dead body, and it changed into a snow-drop.—*T. Tickell.*

Albion the Giant. Fourth son of Neptune, sixth son of Osiris, and brother of Herculēs, his mother being Amphitrīta. Albion the Giant was put by his father in possession of the isle of Britain, where he speedily subdued the Samotheans, the first inhabitants. His brother Bergion ruled over Ireland and the Orkneys. Another of his brothers was Lestrigo, who subjected Italy. (*See* W. Harrison's *Introduction to Holinshed's Chronicle.*)

Albrac'ca's Damsel (in *Orlando Furioso*) is Angelica. Albracca is the capital of Cathay (*q.v.*).

Album. A blank book for scraps. The Romans applied the word to certain tables overlaid with gypsum, on which were inscribed the annals of the chief priests, the edicts of the prætors, and rules relating to civil matters. In the Middle Ages, "album" was the general name of a register or list; so called from being kept either on a white (*albus*) board with black letters, or on a black board with white letters. For the same reason the boards in churches for notices, and the boards in universities containing the names of the college men, are called albums.

Alca'de (3 syl.). A magistrate is so called in Spain and Portugal. The word is the Arabic *al cadi* (the judge).

Alca'ic Verse or *Alcaïcs*. A Greek and Latin metre, so called from *Alcæos*, a lyric poet, who invented it. Each line is divided into two parts, thus:

∪ — | ∪ — | — ‖ — ∪ ∪ — | ∪ — |

The first two lines of each stanza of the ninth ode of Horace are in Alcaics. The first two lines of the ode run thus, and in the same metre:

"See how Soracté groans with its wintry snow,
And weary woodlands bend with the toilsome
weight."

Alcan'tara (*Order of*). A military and religious order instituted in 1214 by Alfonso IX., King of Castile, to commemorate the taking of Alcantara from the Moors. The sovereign of Spain is, *ex-officio*, head of the Order. A resuscitation of the order of *St. Julian of the Pear-tree*, instituted by Fernando Gomez in 1176, better known by the French title *St. Julien du Poirier*. The badge of the order was a pear-tree.

Alcastus (in *Jerusalem Delivered*). The Cap'aneus of the Crusaders, leader of 6,000 foot soldiers from Helvetia.

Al'ce (2 syl.). One of the dogs of Actæ'on. The word means "strength."

Alces'te (2 syl.). The hero of Molière's *Misanthrope*. Not unlike Shakespeare's character of Timon.

Alchemilla or Lady's Mantle. The alchemist's plant; so called because alchemists collected the dew of its leaves for their operations. Lady means the Virgin Mary, to whom the plant was dedicated.

Alchemy (Al'-ki-mĕ) is the Arabic *al kimia* (the secret art); so called not only because it was carried on in secret, but because its main objects were the three great secrets of science—the transmutation of baser metals into gold, the universal solvent, and the elixir of life.

Alcim'edon. A generic name for a first-rate carver in wood.

" Pocula ponam
Fagina, cœlätum divini opus Alcimedontis."
Virgil: Eclogue, iii. 36.

Alci'na. The personification of carnal pleasure in *Orlando Furioso;* the *Circê* of classic fable, and *Latê* of the Arabians. She enjoyed her lovers for a time, and then changed them into trees, stones, fountains, or beasts, as her fancy dictated.

Alcinoo poma dare (to give apples to Alcinŏus). To carry coals to Newcastle ; sending cider to Herefordshire. The orchards of Alcinŏus, King of Corcyra (Corfu), were famous for their fruits.

Alcofribas. The pseudonym of Rabelais in his *Gargantua and Pantagruel*. Alcofribas Nasier is an anagram of "François Rabelais." The introduction runs thus: "The inestimable life of the great Gargantua, father of Pantagruel, heretofore composed by M. Alcofribas, abstractor of the quintessence, a book full of pantagruelism."

Alcuith, mentioned by the Venerable Bede, is Dumbarton.

Aldabella or *Aldabelle* (in *Orlando Furioso*). Sister of Olivie'ro and Brandimarte, daughter of Monodantēs, and wife of Orlando.

Aldabella. A marchioness of Florence, who gave entertainment to the magnates of the city. She was very handsome, heartless, and arrogant. When Fazio became rich with Bartoldo's money, Aldabella inveigled him from his wife, and his wife, out of jealousy, accused her husband of being privy to Bartoldo's death. Fazio being condemned for murder and robbery, his wife Bianca accused Aldabella of inveigling him, and the marchioness was condemned by the Duke of Florence to spend the rest of her life in a nunnery. —*Dean Milman : Fazio.*

Aldeb'aran. The sun in Arabian mythology. In astronomy, the star called the *Bull's eye* in the constellation Taurus. (Arabic *al* the, *debaran*.)

Alderman. One of the seniors or elders. Now applied to a class of magistrates in corporate towns. In London an alderman is the chief magistrate in a ward appointed by election. There are also aldermen of the County Council.

A *turkey* is called an alderman, both from its presence in aldermanic feasts, and also because of its red and purple colours about the head and neck, which make it a sort of poultry alderman.

An alderman in chains, by a similar effort of wit, is a turkey hung with sausages.

Alderman (*An*). A burglar's tool; a crowbar for forcing safes. So called from the high rank it holds with burglars.

Alderman (*An*). A cant term for half-a-crown. An alderman as chief magistrate is half a king in his own ward; and half a crown is half a king.

Aldgate Pump. *A draught on Aldgate Pump.* A cheque with no effects. A worthless bill. The pun is on the word draught, which means either an order on a bank for money or a sup of liquor.

Al'dibo-ron'te-phos'co-phor'nio. A courtier in Henry Carey's farce called *Chro'non-ho'ton-thol'ogos.*

Aldiger (in *Orlando Furioso*). Buo'vo's son, of the house of Clarmont, who lived in Ag'rismont Castle. He was brother of Malagi'gi and Vivian; all Christians.

Aldine (2 syl.). Leader of the second squadron of Arabs who joined the Egyptian armament against the Crusaders. — *Tasso : Jerusalem Delivered.* (*See* SYPHAX.)

Aldine Editions. Editions of the Greek and Latin classics, published and printed under the superintendence of Aldo Manuz'io, his father-in-law Andrea of Asolo, and his son Paolo (1490-1597); most of them in small octavo, and all noted for their accuracy. The father invented the type called *italics*, once called *Aldine*, and first used in printing *Virgil*, 1501.

Al'dingar (*Sir*). Steward of Queen Eleanor, wife of Henry II. He impeached her fidelity, and submitted to a combat to substantiate his charge; but an angel, in the shape of a child, established the queen's innocence. — *Percy's Reliques.*

Ale is the Scandinavian *öl*, called *ealo* in our island. Beer, written *bere*, even in the reign of James I., is the Anglo-Saxon *beor*, from *bere* (barley). A beverage made from barley is mentioned by Tacitus and even Herodotus. Hops were introduced from Holland and used for brewing in 1524, but their use was prohibited by Act of Parliament in 1528—a

prohibition which soon fell into disuse. Ale is made from pale malt, whence its light colour; porter and stout from malt more highly dried. Beer is the general word, and in many parts of England includes ale, porter, and stout. The word *ale* was introduced by the Danes, and the word *beer* by the Teutons. Among London brewers *beer* means the dark form, called also stout or porter.

" Called ale among men ; but by the gods called beer."—*The Alvismál.*

Aleberry, a corruption of ale-bree. A drink made of hot ale, spice, sugar, and toast. Burns speaks of the barley-bree (Anglo-Saxon *brin*, broth).

" Cause an aleberry to be made for her, and put into it powder of camphor."—*The Pathway to Health.*

Ale-dagger (*An*). A dagger used in self-defence in ale-house brawls.

" He that drinkes with cutlers must not be without his ale-dagger." (1589). (*See* N. E. D.)
Pierce Pennilesse says :—" All that will not . . . weare ale-house daggers at your backes [should abstain from taverns]."—*See Shakespeare Society,* p. 55.

Ale-draper, a tapster. *Ale-drapery,* the selling of ale, etc.

" No other occupation have I but to be an ale-draper."—*H. Chettle : Kind-harts' Dreame,* 1592.

Ale Knight (*An*). A knight of the ale-tub, a tippler, a sot.

Ale-silver. A yearly tribute paid to the corporation of London, as a licence for selling ale.

Ale-stake. The pole set up before ale-houses by way of " sign." A bush was very often fixed to its top. A tavern.

" A garland had he set upon his head
As great as it werein for an ale-stake."
Chaucer.
" I know many an ale-stake."
Hawkins : English Drama, i. 100.

Ale-wife. The landlady of an ale-house or ale-stand.

Alec'to. One of the Furies, whose head was covered with snakes.

" Then like Alecto, terrible to view,
Or like Medusa, the Circassian grew."
Hoole : Jerusalem Delivered, b. vi.

Alectorian Stone (*An*). A stone, said to be of talismanic power, found in the stomach of cocks. Those who possess it are strong, brave, and wealthy. Milo of Crotōna owed his strength to this talisman. As a philtre it has the power of preventing thirst or of assuaging it. (Greek, *alectōr,* a cock.)

Alectromancy. Divination by a cock. Draw a circle, and write in succession round it the letters of the alphabet, on each of which lay a grain of corn. Then put a cock in the centre of the circle, and watch what grains he eats. The letters will prognosticate the answer. Libanius and Jamblicus thus discovered who was to succeed the emperor Valens. The cock ate the grains over the letters t, h, e, o, d = Theod [orus]. Greek *alector*, cock; *manteia*, divination.

Ale'ria (in *Orlando Furioso*). One of the Amazons, and the best beloved of the ten wives of Guido the Savage.

Alert. To be on the watch. From the Latin *erectus*, part. of *erigĕre*, to set upright; Italian, *erto;* French, *erte,* a watch-tower. Hence the Italian *starè all' erta*, the Spanish *estar alerta*, and the French *être à l'erte*, to be on the watch.

Alessio. The lover of Liza, in Bellini's opera of *La Sonnambula* (Scribe's libretto).

Ale'thes (3 syl.). An ambassador from Egypt to King Al'adine. He is represented as a man of low birth raised to the highest rank, subtle, false, deceitful, and wily.—*Tasso : Jerusalem Delivered.*

Alexander and the Robber. The robber's name was Diomedēs.—*Gesta Romanorum,* cxlvi.

You are thinking of Parmenio, and I of Alexander—i.e., you are thinking what you ought to receive, and I what I ought to give; you are thinking of those castigated, rewarded, or gifted; but I of my own position, and what punishment, reward, or gift is consistent with my rank. The allusion is to the tale about Parmen'io and Alexander, when the king said, "I consider not what Parmenio should receive, but what Alexander should give."

Only two Alexanders. Alexander said, "There are but two Alexanders—the invincible son of Philip, and the inimitable painting of the hero by Apellès."

The continence of Alexander. Having gained the battle of Issus (B.C. 333) the family of King Darīus fell into his hand; but he treated the ladies as queens, and observed the greatest decorum towards them. A eunuch, having escaped, told Darius of this noble continence, and Darius could not but admire such nobility in a rival.—*Arrian Anabasis of Alexander,* iv. 20. (*See* CONTINENCE.)

Alexander, so Paris, son of Priam,

was called by the shepherds who brought him up.

Alexander of the North. Charles XII. of Sweden, so called from his military achievements. He was conquered at Pultowa, in Russia (1709), by Czar Peter the Great (1682-1718).

" Repressing here
The frantic Alexander of the North."
Thomson: Winter.

The Persian Alexander. Sandjar (1117-1158).

Alexander the Corrector. Alexander Cruden, author of the "Concordance to the Bible," who petitioned Parliament to constitute him "Corrector of the People," and went about constantly with a sponge to wipe out the licentious, coarse, and profane chalk scrawls which met his eye. (1701-1770.)

Alexander's Beard. A smooth chin, no beard at all. An Amazōnian chin.

" Disgracéd yet with Alexander's bearde."
Gascoigne: The Steele Glas.

Alexandra (in *Orlando Furioso*). Oronthea's daughter ; the Amazon queen.

Alexandra, so Cassandra, daughter of Priam, is called. The two names are mere variants of each other.

Alexan'drian. Anything from the East was so called by the old chroniclers and romancers, because Alexandria was the depôt from which Eastern stores reached Europe.

"Reclined on Alexandrian carpets (*i.e., Persian*).
Rose: Orlando Furioso, x. 37.

Alexandrian Codex. A manuscript of the Scriptures in Greek, which belonged to the library of the patriarchs of Alexandria, in Africa, A.D. 1098. In 1628 it was sent as a present to Charles I., and (in 1753) was placed in the British Museum. It is on parchment, in uncial letters, and contains the Septuagint version (except the Psalms), a part of the New Testament, and the Epistles of Clemens Romānus.

Alexandrian Library. Founded by Ptolemy So'ter, in Alexandria, in Egypt. The tale is that it was burnt and partly consumed in 391 ; but when the city fell into the hands of the calif Omar, in 642, the Arabs found books sufficient to "heat the baths of the city for six months." It is said that it contained 700,000 volumes.

Alexandrian School. An academy of literature by Ptolemy, son of La'gos, especially famous for its grammarians and mathematicians. Of its *grammarians* the most noted are Aristarchos, Harpocra'tion, and Eratos'thenēs; and of its mathematicians, Ptolemy and Euclid, the former an astronomer, and the latter the geometer whose *Elements* are still very generally used.

Alexandrine Age. From A.D. 323 to 640, when Alexandria, in Egypt, was the centre of science and literature.

Alexandrine Philosophy. The system of the Gnostics, or Platonised form of Christianity.

Alexan'drines (4 syl.). Iambic verses of 12 or 13 syllables, divided into two parts between the sixth and seventh syllable; so called because they were first employed in a metrical romance of *Alexander the Great*, commenced by Lambert-li-Cors, and continued by Alexandre de Bernay, also called Alexandre de Paris. The final line of the Spenserian stanza is an Alexandrine.

" A needless Alexandrine ends the song,
Which, like a wounded snake, | drags its slow
　　length along."
Pope: Essay on Criticism, Part ii., lines 356-7.

Alexandrito (4 syl.). A variety of chrysobery found in the mica-slate of the Urals. So named from Czar Alexander II. (1818, 1855-1881), because it shows the Russian colours, green and red.

Alexis (*St.*). Patron saint of hermits and beggars. The story goes that he lived on his father's estate as a hermit till death, but was never recognised.

He is represented, in Christian art, with a pilgrim's habit and staff. Sometimes he is drawn as if extended on a mat, with a letter in his hand, dying.

Alfa'der (*father of all*). The most ancient and chief of the Scandina'vian gods. Odin, father of the Æsir, or gods.

Alfa'na. (*See* HORSE.)

Alfar'. The good and bad genii of the Scandina'vians.

Alf'heim (*home of the good genii*). A celestial city inhabited by the elves and fairies. (*Scandinavian mythology*.)

Alfonsin. An instrument for extracting balls. So called from Alfonse Ferri, a surgeon of Naples, who invented it. (1552.)

Alfonsine Tables. Astronomical tables constructed in 1252, by Isaac Hazan, a Jewish rabbi, who named

them in honour of his patron, Alfonso X., King of Castile, surnamed "The Wise."

Alfonso, to whom Tasso dedicated his *Jerusalem Delivered*, was Alfonso d'Este, Duke of Ferrara.

Alfonso XI., *of Castile*, whose "favourite" was Leonora de Guzman. Being threatened with excommunication unless he put her away (as Leonora was in love with Ferdinando, a brave officer), the king created Ferdinando Marquis of Montreal, and gave him the hand of his mistress in marriage. As soon as Ferdinando discovered who Leonora was, he restored her to the king, and retired to a monastery. — *Donizetti's Opera, La Favorita.*

Alfred's Scholars. Werfrith, Bishop of Worcester; Ethelstan and Werwulf, two Mercian priests; Plegmund (a Mercian), afterwards Archbishop of Canterbury; Asser a Welshman; Grimbald, a great French scholar, etc., invited over to England by King Alfred.

Al'garsife (3 syl.). Son of Cambuscan, and brother of Cam'balo, who "won Theod'ora to wife." It was in the "Squire's Tale," by Chaucer, but was never finished. (*See* CANACE.)

" Call him up that left half told
The story of Cambuscan bold,
Of Camball, and of Algarsife,
And who had Canace to wife."
Milton: Il Penseroso.

Al'gebra is the Arabic *al gebr* (the equalisation), "the supplementing and equalising (process);" so called because the problems are solved by equations, and the equations are made by supplementary terms. Fancifully identified with the Arabian chemist Gebir.

Algrind, of Spenser, is meant for Grindal, Bishop of London in the beginning of Elizabeth's reign. He was a Marian exile, and not a very cordial co-operator with Bishop Parker.

"The hills where dwellēd holy saints
　I reverence and adore;
Not for themselves, but for the saints,
　Which had been dead of yore.
And now they been to heaven for went,
　Their good is with them go;
Their sample to us only lent,
　That als we mought do so.
" Shepherds they weren of the best,
　And lived in lowly leas,
And sith their souls be now at rest,
　Why done we them disease?
Such one he was (as I have heard)
　Old Algrind often saine,
That whilome was the first shepherd,
　And lived with little gain."
Eclogue vii.

Alham'bra. The palace of the ancient Moors in Grana'da. The word is the Arabic *al-hamra*, or at full length *kal'-at al hamra* (the red castle).

Ali. Cousin and son-in-law of Mahomet, the beauty of whose eyes is with the Persians proverbial; insomuch that the highest term they employ to express beauty is *Ayn Hali* (eyes of Ali).— *Chardin.*

Alias. "You have as many aliases as Robin of Bagshot," one of Macheath's gang: he was Robin of Bagshot, *alias* Gordon, *alias* Bluff Bob, *alias* Carbuncle, *alias* Bob Booty.— *Gay: The Beggar's Opera.*

Alibi (elsewhere). A plea of having been at another place at the time that an offence is alleged to have been committed.

"Never mind the character, and stick to the alley bi. Nothing like an alley bi, Sammy, nothing."—*Dickens: Pickwick Papers.*

Alibi Clock (*An*), 1887. A clock which strikes one hour, while the hands point to a different time, the real time being neither one nor the other.

Aliboron. *Maitre Aliboron.* Mr. Jackass. Aliboron is the name of a jackass in La Fontaine's *Fables.* (*See* GONIN.)

Alice. The foster-sister of Robert le Diable, and bride of Rambaldo, the Norman troubadour. She came to Palermo to place in the duke's hand her mother's will, which he was enjoined not to read till he was a virtuous man. When Bertram, his fiend-father, tempted his son to evil, Alice proved his good genius; and when, at last, Bertram claimed his soul as the price of his ill deeds, Alice read the "will," and won him from the evil one. — *Meyerbeer's Opera, Roberto il Diavolo.*

Alice Brand. Wife of Lord Richard, cursed with the "sleepless eye." Alice signed Urgan the dwarf thrice with the sign of the cross, and he became "the fairest knight in all Scotland;" when Alice recognised in him her own brother. —*Sir Walter Scott : The Lady of the Lake*, iv. 12.

Alichi'no (*wing-drooped*). A devil, in *The Inferno* of Dante.

Alick and **Sandie.** Contractions of Alexander; the one being Alex' and the other 'xander.

Al'icon. The seventh heaven, to which Azrael conveys the spirits of the just. (*Mahometan mythology.*)

Alien Priory (*An*). A priory which owes allegiance to another priory. A

sub-priory, like Rufford Abbey, Notts, which was under the prior of Rievaulx in Yorkshire.

Alifan'faron, the giant. Don Quixote attacked a flock of sheep, which he declared to be the army of the giant Alifanfaron. Similarly Ajax, in a fit of madness, fell upon a flock of sheep, which he mistook for Grecian princes.

Al'ilat. The name by which the Arabs adore nature, which they represent by a crescent moon.

Aliprando (in *Jerusalem Delivered*). One of the Christian knights. Having discovered the armour of Rinaldo cast on one side, he took it to Godfrey, who very naturally inferred that Rinaldo had been slain. (*See* Gen. xxxvii. 31-35.)

Al'iris. Sultan of Lower Bucharia. Under the disguised name of Fer'amorz, he accompanied Lalla Rookh, his betrothed, from Delhi, and won her heart by his ways, and the tales he told on ·the journey. The lady fell in love with the poet, and was delighted to find, on the morning of the wedding, that Feramorz was, in fact, the sultan, her intended husband.—*T. Moore : Lalla Rookh.*

Al Kader (*the Divine decree*). A particular night in the month Ramadhan, when the Arabs say that angels descend to earth, and Gabriel reveals to man the decrees of God.—*Al Koran*, ch. xcviii.

Alkahest. The hypothetical universal solvent. The word was invented by Paracelsus.

Al Rakim (pronounce Rah-keem'). The dog in the legend of the Seven Sleepers of Ephesus.

Al-Sirat (Arabian, *the path*). The bridge over hell, no wider than the edge of a sword, across which every one who enters heaven must pass. (*Mahometan theology.*)

All. Everything. "Our all," everything we possess.

"Our all is at stake."
            Addison : State of War.

All and Some. "One and all."· (Old English, *ealle æt somme*, all at once, altogether.)

"Now stop your noses, readers, all and some."
        Dryden : Absalom and Achitophel.

All and Sundry. All without exception.

"He invited all and sundry to partake freely of the oaten cake and ale."—*Hall Caine.*

All cannot do all. Horace says, "Non omnia possumus omnes." German proverb, "Ein jeder kann nicht alles." All are not equally clever. Or rather, "Be not surprised that I cannot do what you can do, for we are not all exactly alike."

All Fools' Day (April 1st). (*See* APRIL FOOL.)

All Fours. A game of cards; so called from the four points that are at stake, viz. High, Low, Jack, and Game.

To go on all fours is to crawl about on knees and hands like a little child.

It does not go on all fours means it does not suit in every minute particular; it does not fully satisfy the demand. It limps as a quadruped which does not go on all its four legs. *Omnis comparatio claudicat* (all similes limp).

" No simile can go on all-fours."
Macaulay.

All-hallown Summer. The second summer, or the summerly time which sets in about All-Hallows-tide. Called by the French, *L'été de St. Martin* (from October 9th to November 11th). Also called St. Luke's Summer (St. Luke's Day is October 18th). The Indian summer. Shakespeare uses the term—

" Farewell, thou latter spring ; farewell, All-
hallown Summer !"
1 *Henry IV.* i. 2.

All Hallow's Day (November 1st). The French call it *Toussaint*, which we have translated All Saints' Day. Hallowmas is All-Saints' festival. (Anglo-Saxon, *hálig*, but *Hálig-mónáth* was September, and *Hálig-dæg* was simply a Holy-day.)

All Hallows' Eve. The Scotch tradition is, that those born on All Hallows' Eve have the gift of double sight, and commanding powers over spirits. Mary Avenel, on this supposition, is made to see the White Lady, invisible to less gifted visions.

" Being born on All-hallows' Eve, she (Mary
Avenel) was supposed to be invested with power
over the invisible world." (*See* Sir Walter Scott :
The Monastery, chap. xiv.)

All in all. *He is all in all to me*, that is, the dearest object of my affection. *God shall be all in all* means all creation shall be absorbed or gathered into God. The phrase is also used adverbially, meaning altogether, as :—

" Take him for all in all,
I shall not look upon his like again."
Shakespeare : Hamlet, ii. 2.

All in the Wrong. A drama, by Murphy, borrowed from Destouches, the French dramatist.

2

All is lost that is put in a riven dish. In Latin, "Pertūsum quicquid infundĭtur in dolium, perit." (It is no use helping the insolvent.)

All is not gold that glitters or **glisters.** Trust not to appearances. In Latin, "Nulla fides fronti."

" Not all that tempts your wandering eyes
And heedless hearts is lawful prize,
Nor all that glisters gold."
Gray : The Cat and the Gold-Fish.

All my Eye (and) **Betty Martin.** All nonsense. Joe Miller says that a Jack Tar went into a foreign church, where he heard some one uttering these words—*Ah ! mihi, bea'te Martine* (Ah ! [grant] me, Blessed Martin). On giving an account of his adventure, Jack said he could not make much out of it, but it seemed to him very like "All my eye and Betty Martin." Grose has "Mihi beatæ Martinis " [*sic*]. The shortened phrase, " All my eye," is very common.

All one. The same in effect. Answers the same purpose.

All-overish. A familiar expression meaning *all over ill at ease.* " I feel all-overish," not exactly ill, but uncomfortable all over. The precursor of a fever, influenza, ague, etc.

All Saints or *All Hallows.* In 610 the Pope of Rome ordered that the heathen Pantheon should be converted into a Christian church, and dedicated to the honour of all martyrs. The festival of All Saints was first held on May 1st, but in the year 834 it was changed to November 1st. " Hallows " is from the Anglo-Saxon *hálig* (holy).

All Serene, derived from the Spanish word *serena.* In Cuba the word is used as a countersign by sentinels, and is about equivalent to our "All right," or " All's well."

All Souls' Day. The 2nd of November, so called because the Roman Catholics on that day seek by prayer and almsgiving to alleviate the sufferings of souls in purgatory. It was first instituted in the monastery of Clugny, in 993. According to tradition, a pilgrim, returning from the Holy Land, was compelled by a storm to land on a rocky island, where he found a hermit, who told him that among the cliffs of the island was an opening into the infernal regions through which huge flames ascended, and where the groans of the tormented were distinctly audible. The pilgrim told Odilo, abbot of Clugny, of this ; and the abbot appointed the day following, which was November 2nd, to be set apart for the benefit of souls in purgatory.

All the go. All the fashion. Drapers will tell you that certain goods "go off well." They are in great demand, all the mode, quite in vogue.

> "Her *carte* is hung in the West-end shops,
> With her name in full on the white below ;
> And all day long there's a big crowd stops
> To look at the lady who's "all the go."
> *Sims : Ballads of Babylon* (" Beauty and the Beast ").

All there. Said of a sharp-witted person. *Not all there*, said of one of weak intellect. The one has all his wits about him, the other has not.

All this for a Song ! The exclamation of Burleigh, when Queen Elizabeth ordered him to give £100 to Spenser for a royal gratuity.

All to break (Judges ix. 53). " A certain woman cast a piece of millstone upon Abimelech's head, and all to brake his skull " does not mean for the sake of breaking his skull, but that she wholly smashed his skull. A spurious form, owing its existence to a typographical mistake. The *to* really belongs to the verb ; and in the last passage quoted it should be read " all to-brake." The *to* is a Teutonic particle, meaning *asunder, in pieces*. It is very common in Old English, where we have " To-bite," *i.e.* bite in pieces, to-cleave, to-rend, to-tear. *All* is the adverb = entirely, wholly. So " all to bebattered "=wholly battered to pieces. All-to-frozen. Here to-frozen is intensive. So in Latin dis-crucior = valde crucior. Plautus (in his *Menæchmi*, ii. line 24) uses the phrase " dis-caveas malo," *i.e.* be fully on your guard, etc., be very much beware of.

> Gothic, *dis ;* O. N., *tor ;* Old High German, *zar ;* Latin, *dis ;* Greek, *de.*
> " Mercutio's icy hand had all-to-frozen mine"
> (*i.e.* wholly frozen up mine).—*Romeo and Juliet* (1562).
> "Her wings . . . were al-to-ruffled and sometimes impaired."—*Milton : Comus.*

All waters (*I am for*). I am a Jack of all trades, can turn my hand to anything, a good all-round man. Like a fish which can live in salt or fresh water.

> "I am for all waters."
> *Shakespeare : Twelfth Night,* iv. 2.

All-work. *A maid of all work.* A general servant who does all the work of a house ; at once nurse-maid, house-maid, and cook.

Alla or *Allah* (that is, *al-iláh*). " The adorable." The Arabic name of the Supreme Being.

> "The city won for Allah from the Giaour."
> *Byron : Childe Harold,* ii. 77.

Alla Akbar'. *Allah is most mighty.* The cry of the Arabs.—*Ockley.*

Allan-a-Dale. The minstrel of Robin Hood's yeomen. He was assisted by Robin Hood in carrying off his bride, when on the point of being married against her will to a rich old knight.

Allemand. "Une querelle d' Allemand," a quarrel about nothing. We call pot valour " Dutch courage."

Allen. (*See* ALLWORTHY.)

Allestree. Richard Allestree, of Derby, was a noted almanac maker in Ben Jonson's time.

> " A little more
> Would fetch all his astronomy from Allestree."
> *Ben Jonson: Magnetic Lady,* iv. 2 (1632).

Alley (*The*). The Stock Exchange Alley.

> "John Rive, after many active years in the Alley, retired to the Continent, and died at the age of 118."—*Old and New London,* p. 476.

Alliensis (*Dies*) (June 16th, B.C. 390), when the Romans were cut to pieces by the Gauls near the banks of the river Allía ; and ever after held to be a *dies nefastus*, or unlucky day.

Alligator. When the Spaniards first saw this reptile in the New World, they called it *el lagarto* (the lizard). Sir Walter Raleigh called these creatures *lagartos*, and Ben Jonson *alligartas.*

> "To the present day the Europeans in Ceylon apply the term alligator to what are in reality crocodiles."—*J. E. Tennent: Ceylon* (vol. I. part 2, chap. iii. p. 186).

Alligator Pears (the fruit of *Persea gratissima*) is a curious corruption. The aboriginal Carib word for the tree is " aouacate," which the Spanish discoverers pronounced " avocado," and English sailors called " alligator," as the nearest approach which occurred to them.

Alliteration.

DR. BETHEL OF ETON.

> "Didactic, dry, declamatory, dull,
> Big, burly Bethel bellows like a bull."
> *Eton College.*

CARDINAL WOLSEY.

> " Begot by butchers, but by bishops bred,
> How high his Honour holds his haughty head."

¶ Hucbald composed an alliterative poem on Charles the Bald, every word of which begins with *c*.

Henry Harder composed a poem of 100 lines, in Latin hexameters, on cats, every word of which begins with *c*. The title is *Canum cum Catis certamen carmine compositum currente calamo C Catulli Caninii.* The first line is—

> "Cattorum canimus certamina clara canimque."

Hamonicus wrote the *Certamen catho-licum cum Calvinistis*, every word of which begins with *c*.

⁂ It is a curious coincidence that the names of these three men all begin with H.

¶ In the *Materia more Magistralis* every word begins with *m*.

¶ Placentius, the Dominican, who died 1548, wrote a poem of 258 Latin hexa-meters, called *Pugna Porcorum*, every word of which begins with *p*. It begins thus :—

" Plaudite, Porcelli, porcorum pigra propago."

Which may be translated—

" Praise, Paul, prize pig's prolific progeny."

¶ Tusser, who died 1580, has a rhym-ing poem of twelve lines, every word of which begins with *t*.

¶ The Rev. B. Poulter, prebendary of Winchester, composed in 1828 the famous alliterative alphabetic poem in rhymes. Each word of each line begins with the letter of the alphabet which it represents. It begins thus :—

" An Austrian army awfully arrayed,
Boldly by battery besieged Belgrade ;
Cossack commanders, cannonading come,
Dealing destruction's devastating doom ; . . ."

⁂ Some ascribe this alliterative poem to Alaric A. Watts (1820). (*See* H. SOUTHGATE, *Many Thoughts on Many Things*.)

Another attempt of the same kind begins thus :—

" About an age ago, as all agree,
Beauteous Belinda, brewing best Bohea
Carelessly chattered, controverting clean,
Dublin's derisive, disputatious dean . . ."

Allo'dials. Lands which are held by an absolute right, without even the bur-den of homage or fidelity; opposed to feudal. The word is Teutonic—*all-ōd* (all property).

Allop'athy is in opposition to *Ho-mœop'athy*. The latter word is from the Greek, *homœon pathos*, similar disease ; and the former is *allo pathos*, a different disease. In one case, " like is to cure like " ; and in the latter, the disease is cured by its " antidote."

Alls. *The five Alls.* A public-house sign. It has five human figures, with a motto to each :—

(1) A king in his regalia .. motto *I govern all.*
(2) A bishop, in his pontificals „ *I pray for all.*
(3) A lawyer, in his gown .. „ *I plead for all.*
(4) A soldier in regimentals „ *I fight for all.*
(5) A labourer, with his tools „ *I pay for all.*

Several of these signs still exist.

Alls. Tap-droppings. The refuse of all sorts of spirits drained from the

glasses, or spilt in drawing. The mixture is sold in gin-houses at a cheap rate.

Allworth. In *A New Way to Pay Old Debts*, by Massinger.

Allworthy, in Fielding's *Tom Jones*, is designed for the author's friend, Ralph Allen, of Bristol.

" Let humble Allen, with an awkward shame,
Do good by stealth, and blush to find it fame."
Pope : Epilogue to Sat. i. 135, 136.

Al'ma (*the human soul*), queen of " **Body Castle**," beset by enemies for seven years (*the Seven Ages of Man*). The besiegers are a rabble rout of evil desires, foul imaginations, and silly conceits. Alma conducted Arthur and Sir Guyon over her castle. " The *divine* part of a man," says Spenser, " is *circular*, a circle being the emblem of eternity ; but the mortal part *tri-angular*, as it consists of three things—blood, flesh, and bones."—*Prior's Poem*.

Alma Ma'ter. A collegian so calls the university of which he is a member. The words are Latin for " fostering mother."

" Expulsion from his Alma Mater."—*The Col-legian and the Porter.*

Almack's. A suite of assembly rooms in King Street, St. James's (London), built in 1765 by a Scotchman named Macall, who inverted his name to obviate all prejudice and hide his origin. Balls, presided over by a committee of ladies of the highest rank, used to be given at these rooms ; and to be admitted to them was as great a distinction as to be presented at Court. The rooms were afterwards known as Willis's, from the name of the next proprietor, and used chiefly for large dinners. They were closed in 1890.

Almagest. The *Syntaxis-megistē* of Ptolemy, translated by the Arabians in 800, by order of the calif Al Maimon, and then called *Al-maghesti*, *i.e.* " the megistē." It contains numerous obser-vations and problems of geometry and astronomy. It is very rare, and more precious than gold.

Alman, a German. The French *Allemand*, a German, which, of course, is the classic *Alamani* or *Alamanni*. Similarly, Almany = Germany, French, *Allemagne*.

" Chonodomarius and Vestralpus, Aleman kings,
. . . sat them downe neere unto Argentoratum."
Holland : Ammianus Marcellius.

" Now Fulko comes . . . And dwelt in Amany."—*Harrington : Orlando Furioso*, iii. 30.

Al'manac is the Arabic *al manac* (the diary). Verstegen says it is the Saxon *al-mon-aght* (all moon heed), and that it refers to the tallies of the full and new moons kept by our Saxon ancestors. One of these tallies may still be seen at St. John's College, Cambridge.

Before printing, or before it was common:

By Solomon Jarchi	..	..in and after	1150
„ Peter de Dacia	..	..	about 1300
„ Walter de Elvendene	..	..	1327
„ John Some's, Oxford	..	..	1380 !!
„ Nicholas de Lynna	..	..	1386
„ Purbach	..	..	1150-1461
First printed by Gutenberg, at **Mentz**			1457
By Regiomontanus, at Nuremberg		..1472-3
„ Zainer, at Ulm	..	..	1478
„ Richard Pynson (*Sheapeheard's*			
Kalendar)	..	..	1497 !!
„ Stöffler, in Venice	..	..	1499
„ Poor Robin's Almanack	..	..	1652
„ Francis Moore's Almanack be-			
tween..	..	..	1698 and 1713

Stamp duty imposed 1710, repealed 1834.

The Man i' the Almanac stuck with pins (Nat. Lee), is a man marked with points referring to signs of the zodiac, and intended to indicate the favourable and unfavourable times of letting blood.

I shan't consult your almanac (French), I shall not come to you to know what weather to expect. The reference is to the prognostications of weather in almanacs.

Almesbury. It was in a sanctuary at Almesbury that Queen Guenever took refuge, after her adulterous passion for Lancelot was revealed to the king (Arthur). Here she died ; but her body was buried at Glastonbury.

Almighty Dollar. Washington Irving first made use of this expression, in his sketch of a "Creole Village" (1837).

"The almighty dollar, that great object of universal devotion throughout our land. . . ."—*W. Irving: Wolfert's Roost, Creole Village*, p. 40.

⁂ Ben Jonson speaks of "almighty gold."

Almond Tree. Grey hairs. The Preacher thus describes old age :—

"In the day when the keepers of the house (*the hands*) shall tremble, and the strong men (*the legs*) bow themselves, and the grinders (*the teeth*) cease because they are few, and those that look out of the windows (*the eyes*) be darkened . . . and the almond-tree shall flourish (*grey hairs* on a bald pate), and the grasshopper be a burden, and desire shall fail . . . when the silver cord (*the spinal marrow*) shall be loosed, the golden bowl (*intellect*) broken, and the pitcher broken at the cistern (*the pulse of the heart stopped*)."—*Eccles.* xii. 3-6.

Almonry. The place where the almoner resides, or where alms are distributed. An almoner is a person whose duty it is to distribute alms,

which, in ancient times, consisted of one-tenth of the entire income of a monastery. (*See* AMBRY.)

Alms. Gifts to the poor.

Dr. Johnson says the word has no *singular*; whereas Todd says it has no plural. Like *riches*, it is wholly singular in construction, but is used both as a noun singular and noun plural. Of course it is Almos-ine, almos-ie, Almose, almesse, almes, alms, the *s* is not the plural suffix. Riches is the French *richesse*. Both words are singular, but, as nouns of multitude, prefer the plural construction. (Latin *alimosina*, Greek *eleemosyně*, from the verb *eleeō*, I pity.)

Alms Basket. *To live on the alms basket.* To live on charity.

Alms-drink. Another's leavings ; for alms consists of broken bread and the residue of drink. It is also applied to the liquor which a drinker finds too much, and therefore hands to another.

Alms-fee. Peter's pence, or Rome scot. Abolished in England by Henry VIII.

Alms-house. A house where paupers are supported at the public expense ; a poor-house. Also a house set apart for the aged poor free of rent.

"Only, alas ! the poor who had neither friends nor attendants,
Crept away to die in the alms-house, home of the homeless."
Longfellow: Evangeline, part ii. 5, 2.

Alms-man. One who lives on alms.

Alnaschar Dream (*An*). Counting your chickens before they are hatched. Alnaschar, the barber's fifth brother, invested all his money in a basket of glass-ware, on which he was to make a certain profit. The profit, being invested, was to make more, and this was to go on till he grew rich enough to marry the vizier's daughter. Being angry with his imaginary wife he gave a kick, overturned his basket, and broke all his wares.

"To indulge in Alnaschar-like dreams of compound interest *ad infinitum*."—*The Times.*

Alnaschar of Modern Literature. Coleridge has been so called because he "dreamt" his *Kubla Khan*, and wrote it out next morning. (1772-1834.)

⁂ Probably he had been reading Purchas's *Pilgrimage*, for none can doubt the resemblance of the two pieces.

Aloe. A Hebrew word, Greek *aloē*. A very bitter plant ; hence the proverb, *Plus aloes quam mellis habet*, " (Life) has more bitters than sweets." The French say, "La côte d'Adam contient plus d'aloès que de miel," where *côte d' Adam*, of course, means woman or one's wife.

Socotrine Aloes came originally from the island called Socotra, in the Indian Ocean.

Along-shore Men or Longshoremen, that is stevedores (2 syl.), or men employed to load and unload vessels.

Alonzo of A'guilar'. When Fernando, King of Ar'agon, was laying siege to Grana'da, after chasing Za'gal from the gates, he asked who would undertake to plant his banner on the heights. Alonzo, "the lowmost of the dons," undertook the task, but was cut down by the Moors. His body was exposed in the wood of Oxije'ra, and the Moorish damsels, struck with its beauty, buried it near the brook of Alpuxarra.

Aloof. *Stand aloof*, away. A sea term, meaning originally to bear to windward, or *luff*. (Norwegian, German, etc., *luft*, wind, breeze.)

Alorus, so the Chaldeans called their first king, who, they say, came from Babylon.

A l'outrance. To the uttermost. (Anglo-French for *à outrance*.)

"A champion has started up to maintain *à l'outrance* her innocence of the great offence." —*Standard.*

Alp. The Adrian renegade, a Venetian by extraction, who forswore the Christian faith to become a commander in the Turkish army. He led the host to the siege of Corinth, while that country was under the dominion of the Doge. He loved Francesca, daughter of Minotti, governor of Corinth, but she died of a broken heart because he deserted his country and was an apostate. The renegade was shot in the siege.— *Byron : Siege of Corinth.*

Alph. A mythical "sacred river in Xanadu," which ran "through caverns measureless to man."—*Coleridge : Kubla Khan.*

Al'pha. "*I am Alpha and Omega, the first and the last*" (Rev. i. 8). "Alpha" is the first, and "O-meg'a" the last letter of the Greek alphabet. A Ω.

Alphabet. This is the only word compounded of letters only. The Greek *alpha* (a) *beta* (b) ; our A B C (book), etc.

⁂ The number of letters in an alphabet varies in different languages. Thus there are

21	letters in the Italian alphabet.	
22	„	Hebrew & Syriac alphabet
23	„	Latin „
24	„	Greek „
25	„	French „
26	„	English, German, Dutch „
27	„	Spanish „
28	„	Arabic „
32	„	Coptic „
33	„	Russian „
38	„	Armenian „
39	„	Georgian „
40	„	Slavonic „
45	„	Persian (Zend) „
49	„	Sanskrit „

⁂ The Chinese have no alphabet, but about 20,000 syllabic characters.

Ezra vii. 21 contains all the letters of the English language, presuming *I* and *J* to be identical. Even the Italian alphabet is capable of more than seventeen trillion combinations ; that is, 17 followed by eighteen other figures, as—

17,000,000,000,000,000,000 ;

while the English alphabet will combine into more than twenty-nine thousand quatrillion combinations ; that is, 29 followed by twenty-seven other figures, as—

29,000,000,000,000,000,000,000,000,000.

Yet we have no means of marking the several sounds of our different vowels ; nor can we show how to pronounce such simple words as *foot*, (pull and dull), *sugar* (father and rather), (*gin* and be-gin), *calm*, *Bourges*, *Bœuf* in "Bœuf-gras," *œufs*, and thousands of other words.

⁂ We want the restoration of *th* to distinguish between *this* and *thin ;* a Greek *ch* to distinguish between *Church* and *Christ*, two *g*'s (one soft and one hard), two *c*'s, two *o*'s, half a dozen *a*'s, and so on.

⁂ Take *a*, we have *fate, fat, Thames* (e), *war* (o), *salt* (au), etc. So with *e*, we have *prey* (a), *met* (e), England (i), *sew* (o), *herb* (u), etc. The other vowels are equally indefinite.

Alphe'os and Arethu'sa. The Greek fable says that Alphe'os, the river-god, fell in love with the nymph Arethu'sa, who fled from him in affright. The god pursued under the sea, but the nymph was changed into a spring, which comes up in the harbour of Syracuse.

"We have seen a moustachioed Alpheos, at Ramsgate, pursue an affrighted Arethusa." — *London Review.*

Alphe'us (in *Orlando Furioso*). A magician and prophet in the army of Charlemagne, slain in sleep by Clorida'no.

Alphesibe'a or "Arsinöe," wife of Alcmēon. She gave her spouse the fatal collar, the source of numberless evils.

So was the necklace of Harmonia, and so were the collar and veil of Eriphylē, wife of Amphiaräos.

Alphonso, etc. (*See* ALFONSO, etc.)

Alpleich or "Elfenreigen" (the weird spirit-song), that music which some hear before death. Faber refers to it in his *Pilgrims of the Night.*

"Hark, hark, my soul ! Angelic songs are
    swelling."

Pope also says, in the *Dying Christian*—

"Hark! they whisper; angels say,
    Sister spirit, come away."

Alpue, Alpieu (*Alpu*), in the game of Basset, doubling the stake on a winning card.

"What pity 'tis those conquering eyes
    Which all the world subdue,
Should, while the lover gazing dies,
    Be only on alpue."   *Etherege: Basset.*

Alquife (*al-kē-fy*). A famous enchanter, introduced into the romances of ancient times, especially those relating to Am'adis of Gaul.

Alrinach. The demon who presides over floods and earthquakes, rain and hail. It is this demon who causes shipwrecks. When visible, it is in a female form. (*Eastern mythology.*)

Alruna-wife (*An*). The Alrunes were the larēs or penatēs of the ancient Germans. An Alruna-wife was the household goddess of a German family. An Alruna-maiden is a household maiden goddess.

"She (Hypatia) looked as fair as the sun, and talked like an Alruna-wife."—*Kingsley: Hypatia,* chap. xii.

Alsa'tia. The Whitefriars sanctuary for debtors and law-breakers. Cunningham thinks the name is borrowed from Alsace, in France, which being a frontier of the Rhine, was everlastingly the seat of war and the refuge of the disaffected. Sir Walter Scott, in his *Fortunes of Nigel,* has described the life and state of this rookery. He has borrowed largely from Shadwell's comedy, *The Squire of Alsatia.* (*See* PETAND.)

Alsvidur. (*See* HORSE.)

Altamo'rus (in *Jerusalem Delivered*). King of Samarcand', who joined the Egyptian armament against the Crusaders. "He was supreme in courage as in might." (Book xvii.) He surrendered himself to Godfrey. (Book xx.)

Altan Kol or *Gold River* (Thibet). So called from the gold which abounds in its sands.

Altar (*An*), in Christian art. St. Stephen (the Pope), and Thomas Becket are represented as immolated before an altar. St. Canute is represented as lying before an altar. St. Charles Borromeo is represented as kneeling before an altar. St. Gregory (the Pope) is represented as *offering sacrifice* before an altar. And the attribute of Victor is an altar overthrown, in allusion to his throwing down a Roman altar in the presence of the Emperor Maximian.

Led to the altar, i.e. married. Said of a lady. The altar is the communion-table railed off from the body of the church, where marriages are solemnised. The bride is led up the aisle to the rail.

Alter eg'o. My double or counterpart. In *The Corsican Brothers,* the same actor performs the two brothers, the one being the *alter ego* of the other. (Latin, "a second I"). One who has full powers to act for another.

Althæa's Brand, a fatal contingency. Althæa's son was to live so long as a log of wood, then on the fire, remained unconsumed. She contrived to keep the log unconsumed for many years, but being angry one day with Meleāger, she pushed it into the midst of the fire, and it was consumed in a few minutes. Meleager died at the same time.—*Ovid: Metamorphoses,* viii. 4.

"The fatal brand Althæa burned."
    Shakespeare: 2 *Henry VI.,* Act i. 1.

Althe'a (*Divine*). The divine Althe'a of Richard Lovelace was Lucy Sacheverell, called by the poet, "Lucretia."

"When love with unconfinēd wings
    Hovers within my gates,
And my divine Althea brings
    To whisper at my grates."

The "grates" referred to were the prison grates. Lovelace was thrown into prison by the Long Parliament for his petition from Kent in favour of the king.

Altisido'ra (in the "Curious Impertinent"), an episode in *Don Quixote.*

Altis. The plot of ground on which the Greeks held their public games.

Alto relie'vo. Italian for "high relief." A term used in sculpture for figures in wood, stone, marble, etc., so cut as to project at least one-half from the tablet. It should be *rilievo* (3 syl.)

Alumbra'do, a perfectionist; so called from a Spanish sect which arose in 1575, and claimed special illumination. (Spanish, meaning "illuminated," "enlightened").

Alvina Weeps, or "Hark! Alvina weeps," *i.e.* the wind howls loudly, a Flemish saying. Alvina was the daughter of a king, who was cursed by her parents because she married unsuitably. From that day she roamed about the air invisible to the eye of man, but her moans are audible.

Alyface (*Annot*), servant of Dame Christian Custance, the gay widow, in Udall's comedy *Ralph Roister Doister*.

Alzir'do (in *Orlando Furioso*). King of Trem'izen, in Africa. He was overthrown by Orlando on his way to join the allied army of Ag'ramant.

A.M. or **M.A.** When the Latin form is intended the A comes first, as *Artium Magister;* but where the English form is meant the M precedes, as *Master of Arts.*

Am'adis of Gaul. The hero of a romance in prose of the same title, originally written in Portuguese in four books. These four were translated into Spanish by Montalvo, who added a fifth. Subsequent romancers added the exploits and adventures of other knights, so as to swell the romance to fourteen books. The French version is much larger still, one containing twenty-four books, and another running through seven volumes. The original author was Vasco de Lobeira, of Oporto, who died 1403.

The *hero*, called the "Lion-knight," from the device on his shield, and "Beltenebros" (*darkly beautiful*), from his personal appearance, was a love-child of Per'ion, King of Gaul, and Eliz'ena, Princess of Brittany. He is represented as a poet and musician, a linguist and a gallant, a knight-errant and a king, the very model of chivalry.

Other names by which Am'adis was called were the *Lovely Obscure*, the *Knight of the Burning Sword*, the *Knight of the Dwarf*, etc. Bernardo, in 1560, wrote "Amadigi di Gaula."

Am'adis of Greece. A supplemental part of the romance called *Am'adis of Gaul*, added by Felicia'no de Silva.

Amai'mon (3 syl.). One of the chief devils whose dominion is on the north side of the infernal gulf. He might be bound or restrained from doing hurt from the third hour till noon, and from the ninth hour till evening.

"Amaimon sounds well ; Lucifer well."
Shakespeare: Merry Wives of Windsor, ii. 2.

Amal'fitan Code. A compilation of maritime laws, compiled in the eleventh century at Amalfi, then an important trading town.

Amaliv'aca. An American spirit, who had seven daughters. He broke their legs to prevent their running away, and left them to people the forests.

Amalthæa. (*See* SIBYLLINE BOOKS.)

Amalthe'a's Horn. The cornucopia or horn of plenty. The infant Zeus was fed with goats' milk by Amalthēa, one of the daughters of Melisseus, King of Crete. Zeus, in gratitude, broke off one of the goat's horns, and gave it to Amalthēa, promising that the possessor should always have in abundance everything desired. (*See* ÆGIS.)

Aman'da, the impersonation of love in Thomson's *Spring*, is Miss Young, afterwards married to Admiral Campbell.

Am'arant. A cruel giant slain by Guy of Warwick.—*Guy and Amarant, Percy's Reliques.*

Am'aranth. Clement of Alexandria says—*Amarantus flos, sym'bolum est immortalita'tis.* The word is from the Greek *amaran'tos* (everlasting). So called because its flowers never fade like other flowers, but retain to the last much of their deep blood-red colour.

"Immortal amarant—a flower which once
In Paradise, fast by the tree of life,
Began to bloom ; but soon, for man's offence,
To heaven removed, where first it grew, there grows
And flowers aloft, shading the fount of life. . . .
With these, that never fade, the spirits elect
Bind their resplendent locks."
Milton: Paradise Lost iii. 353-61.

⁂ In 1653 Christina, Queen of Sweden, instituted the Order of the "Knights of the Amaranth," but it ceased to exist at the death of the Queen. Among the ancients it was the symbol of immortality.

The best known species are "Love lies bleeding" (*amarantus caudātus*), and "Prince's feather" (*amarantus hypochondriacus*). "Cock's comb" is now ranked under the genus *Celosia.*

Amaryl'lis. A pastoral sweetheart. The name is borrowed from the pastorals of Theoc'ritos and Virgil.

"To sport with Amaryllis in the shade."
Milton: Lycidas, 68.

Amasis (*Ring of*), same as Polycrătēs' Ring. Polycrătēs, tyrant of Samos, was so fortunate in everything that Amasis, King of Egypt, advised him to part with something which he highly prized. Polycrătēs accordingly threw into the sea an engraved ring of extraordinary value. A few days afterwards, a fish was presented to the tyrant, in which the ring was found. Amasis now renounced all friendship with Polycrătēs, as a man doomed by the gods; and not long afterwards, a satrap, having entrapped the too fortunate despot, put him to death by crucifixion.—*Herodotus*, iii. 40.

Ama'ti. A first-rate violin; properly, one made by Ama'ti of Cremona (*c.* 1600). (*See* CREMONA.)

Amaurot (Greek, the shadowy or unknown place), the chief city in *Utopia* (no-place), a political novel by Sir Thomas More. Rabelais, in his *Pantagruel*, had previously introduced the word, and tells us that the Amaurots conquered the Dipsodes (or Duplicians).

Amaurote, a bridge in Utopia. Sir Thomas More says he could not recollect whether Raphael Hyghloday told him it was 500 paces or 300 paces long; and he requested his friend Peter Giles, of Antwerp, to put the question to the adventurer.

" I cannot recollect whether the reception room of the Spaniard's Castle in the Air is 200 or 300 feet long. I will get the next aeronaut who journeys to the moon to take the exact dimensions for me, and will memorialise the learned society of Laputa."—*Dean Swift: Gulliver's Travels.*

Amazement. *Not afraid with any amazement* (1 Peter iii. 6), introduced at the close of the marriage service in the Book of Common Prayer. The meaning is, you will be God's children so long as you do his bidding, and are not drawn aside by any distraction (πτόησις). No doubt St. Peter meant " by any terror of persecution." Cranmer, being so afraid, was drawn aside from the path of duty.

Amazia, meant for Charles II., in Pordage's poem of *Azaria and Hushai.* We are told by the poet, " his father's murtherers he destroyed ; " and then he preposterously adds—

" Beloved of all, for merciful was he,
Like God, in the superlative degree."

To say that such a selfish, promise-breaking, impious libertine was " like God, in the superlative degree," is an outrage against even poetical licence and court flattery.

Am'azon. A horsewoman, a fighting or masculine woman. The word means *without breast*, or rather, " deprived of a pap." According to Grecian story, there was a nation of women in Africa of a very warlike character. There were no men in the nation ; and if a boy was born, it was either killed or sent to his father, who lived in some neighbouring state. The girls had their right breasts burnt off, that they might the better draw the bow.

" These dreadful Amazons, gallant viragoes who . . . carried victorious arms . . . into Syria and Asia Minor."—*J. E. Chambliss : David Livingstone* (Introduction, p. 24).

Amazo'nia. In South America, originally called Mar'anon'. The Spaniards first called it Orella'na ; but after the women joined their husbands in attacking the invaders, the Spaniards called the people Am'azons and the country Amazo'nia.

Amazonian Chin (*An*). A beardless chin, like that of a woman warrior.

" When with his Amazonian chin he drove
The bristled lips before him."
Shakespeare : Coriolanus, ii. 2.

Ambassador, a practical joke played on greenhorns aboard ship. A tub full of water is placed between two stools, and the whole being covered with a green cloth, a sailor sits on each stool, to keep the cloth tight. The two sailors represent Neptune and Amphitritē, and the greenhorn, as ambassador, is introduced to their majesties. He is given the seat of honour between them ; but no sooner does he take his seat than the two sailors rise, and the greenhorn falls into the tub, amidst the laughter of the whole crew.

Am'ber. This fossilised vegetable resin is, according to legend, a concretion of birds' tears. The birds were the sisters of Meleāger, who never ceased weeping for the death of their brother.—*Ovid : Metamorphoses*, viii. line 270, etc.

" Around thee shall glisten the loveliest amber
That ever the sorrowing sea-bird hath wept."
T. Moore : Fire Worshippers.

Amber, a repository. So called because insects and small leaves are preserved in amber.

" You may be disposed to preserve it in your amber."—*Notes and Queries.—W. Dowe.*
" Pretty ! in amber, to observe the forms
Of hairs, or straws, or dirt, or grubs, or worms,
The things, we know, are neither rich nor rare,
But wonder how the devil they got there."
Pope : Ep. to Arbuthnot, 169-72.

Amberabad'. Amber-city, one of the towns of Jinnistan, or Fairy Land.

Ambes'-as or *Ambes-ace.* Two aces, the lowest throw in dice ; figuratively, bad luck. (Latin, *ambo-asses*, both or two aces.)

" I had rather be in this choice than throw ames-ace for my life."—*All's Well*, etc., ii. 3.

Ambi-dexter properly means both hands right hands ; a double dealer ; a juror who takes money from both parties for his verdict ; one who can use his left hand as deftly as his right.

Ambition, strictly speaking, means "the going from house to house" (Latin, *ambitio*, going about canvassing). In Rome it was customary, some time before an election came on, for the candidates to go round to the different dwellings to solicit votes, and those who did so were ambitious of office.

Ambree (*Mary*). An English heroine, who has immortalised her name by her valour at the siege of Ghent, in 1584. Her name is a proverbial one for a woman of heroic spirit.

"My daughter will be valiant,
And prove a very Mary Ambry i' the business."
Ben Jonson: Tale of a Tub, i. 4.

Ambrose (*St.*), represented in Christian art in the costume of a bishop. His attributes are (1) a *bee-hive,* in allusion to the legend that a swarm of bees settled on his mouth when lying in his cradle; (2) a *scourge,* by which he expelled the Arians from Italy.

The penance he inflicted on the Emperor Theodosius has been represented by Rubens, a copy of which, by Vandyck, is in the National Gallery.

Ambro′sia. The food of the gods (Greek, *a* privative, *brotos,* mortal); so called because it made them not mortal, *i.e.* it made them immortal. Anything delicious to the taste or fragrant in perfume is so called from the notion that whatever is used by the celestials must be excellent.

"A table where the heaped ambrosia lay."
Homer, by Bryant: Odyssey, v. line 141.
"Husband and wife must drink from the cup of conjugal life; but they must both taste the same ambrosia, or the same gall."—*R. C. Houghton: Women of the Orient,* part iii.

Ambro′sian Chant. The choral music introduced from the Eastern to the Western Church by St. Ambrose, the Bishop of Mil′an, in the fourth century. It was used till Gregory *the Great* changed it for the Gregorian.

Ambro′sian Library. A library in Mil′an, so called in compliment of St. Ambrose, the patron saint.

Ambrosio, the hero of Lewis's romance, called *The Monk.* Abbot of the Capuchins at Madrid. The temptations of Matilda overcome his virtue, and he proceeds from crime to crime, till at last he sells his soul to the devil. Ambrosio, being condemned to death by the Inquisition, is released by Lucifer; but no sooner is he out of prison than he is dashed to pieces on a rock.

Am′bry, a cupboard, locker, or recess. In church, for keeping vestments, books, or other articles. Used by a confusion for *almonry,* or niche in the wall where alms, etc., were deposited. Now used for holding the sacramental plate, consecrated oil, and so on. The secret drawers of an escritoire are called ambries. (Archaic English *almary,* Latin *armarium,* French *armoire.*)

"Ther avarice hath almaries,
And yren-bounden cofres."
Piers Ploughman, p. 288.

Almonry is from the Latin *eleemosynarium,* a place for alms.

"The place wherein this Chapel or Almshouse stands was called the 'Elemosinary' or Almonry, now corrupted into Ambrey, for that the alms of the Abbey are there distributed to the poor."—*Stow: Survey.*

Ambusca′de (3 syl.) is the Italian *imbosca′ta* (concealed in a wood).

Ame damnée (French), a scape-goat.

"He is the *ame damnée* of everyone about the court—the scapegoat, who is to carry away all their iniquities."—*Sir Walter Scott: Peveril of the Peak,* chap. 48.

Amedieu (3 syl.). "Friends of God;" a religious body in the Church of Rome, founded in 1400. They wore no breeches, but a grey cloak girded with a cord, and were shod with wooden shoes.

Amo′lia. A model of conjugal affection, in Fielding's novel so called. It is said that the character is intended for his own wife.

Amelon. A Chaldean hero, who reigned thirteen sares. A sare = 3,600 years.—*Banier: Mythology,* vol. i.

Amenon is another hero of Chaldea, who reigned 12 sares. Amphis reigned 6 sares.

Amen Corner, London, the end of Paternoster Row, where the monks finished their *Pater Noster,* on Corpus Christi Day, as they went in procession to St. Paul's Cathedral. They began in Paternoster Row with the Lord's prayer in Latin, which was continued to the end of the street; then said *Amen,* at the corner or bottom of the Row; then turning down Ave-Maria Lane, commenced chanting the "Hail, Mary!" then crossing Ludgate, they chanted the *Credo.* Amen Lane no longer exists.

Amende honorable, in France, was a degrading punishment inflicted on traitors, parricides, and sacrilegious persons, who were brought into court with a rope round their neck, and made to beg pardon of God, the king, and the court.

Now the public acknowledgment of the offence is all that is required.

Amen′thes (3 syl.). The Egyptian Ha′dēs. The word means *hiding-place.*

2*

American Flag. The American Congress resolved (June 14, 1777), that the flag of the United States should have thirteen stripes, alternately red and white, to represent the thirteen States of the Union, together with thirteen white stars, on a blue ground. General Washington's escutcheon contained two stripes, each alternated with red and white, and, like the American stars, those of the General had only five points instead of six. A new star is now added for each new State, but the stripes remain the same.

However, before the separation the flag contained thirteen stripes of alternate red and white to indicate the thirteen colonies; and the East India Company flag, as far back as 1704, had thirteen stripes. The Company flag was cantoned with St. George's Cross, the British American flag with the Union Jack.

American Peculiarities:—

Natives of New England .. .. say *Guess.*
  ,, N. York & Middle States ,, *Expect.*
  ,, Southern States .. .. ,, *Reckon.*
  ,, Western States .. .. ,, *Calculate.*

American States. The Americans are rich in nicknames. Every state has, or has had, its sobriquet. The people of

Alabama	..	are lizards.
Arkansas	..	,, toothpicks
California	..	,, gold-hunters.
Colorado	..	,, rovers.
Connecticut	..	,, wooden nutmegs.
Delaware	..	,, musk rats.
Florida	..	,, fly-up-the-creeks.
Georgia ..	..	,, buzzards.
Illinois ..	..	,, suckers.
Indiana..	..	,, hoosiers.
Iowa ..	..	,, hawk-eyes.
Kansas ..	..	,, jay-hawkers.
Kentucky	..	,, corn-crackers.
Louisiana	..	,, creoles.
Maine ..	..	,, foxes.
Maryland	..	,, craw-thumpers.
Michigan	..	,, wolverines.
Minnesota	..	,, gophers.
Mississippi	..	,, tadpoles.
Missouri	..	,, pukes.
Nebraska	..	,, bug-eaters.
Nevada ..	..	,, sage-hens.
New Hampshire	..	,, granite-boys.
New Jersey	..	,, Blues *or* clam-catchers.
New York	..	,, knickerbockers.
North Carolina	..	,, tar-boilers *or* Tuckoes.
Ohio ..	..	,, buck-eyes.
Oregon ..	..	,, web-feet *or* hard cases.
Pennsylvania..	..	,, Pennamites *or* Leather-heads.
Rhode Island ..	..	,, gun-flints.
South Carolina	..	,, weasels.
Tennessee	..	,, whelps.
Texas ..	..	,, beef-heads.
Vermont	..	,, green-mountain boys.
Virginia	..	,, beadies.
Wisconsin	..	,, badgers.

American States. The eight states which retain the Indian names of the chief rivers, as: Alabama, Arkansas, Illinois, Kentucky, Mississippi, Missouri, Ohio, and Wisconsin.

Ameth'ea. (*See* HORSE.)

Am'ethyst. A species of rock-crystal supposed to prevent intoxication (Greek, *a-methusta*, the antidote of intoxication). Drinking-cups made of amethyst were supposed to be a charm against inebriety.

∴ It was the most cherished of all precious stones by Roman matrons, from the superstition that it would preserve inviolate the affection of their husbands.

Amiable Numbers. (*See* AMICABLE, etc.)

Amicable Numbers. Numbers which are mutually equal to the sum of all their aliquot parts: as 220, 284. The aliquot parts of 220 are 1, 2, 4, 5, 10, 11, 20, 22, 44, 55, 110, the sum of which is 284. Again, the aliquot parts of 284 are 1, 2, 4, 71, 142, the sum of which is 220.

Ami'cus cu'riæ (Latin, *a friend to the court*). One in the court who informs the judge of some error he has detected, or makes some suggestion to assist the court.

Ami'cus Plato, sed magis ami'ca Ver'itas (Plato I love, but I love Truth more). A noble dictum attributed to Aristotle, but certainly a very free translation of a phrase in the *Nicomache'an Ethics* ("Where both are friends, it is right to prefer Truth").

Am'iel (3 syl.). A form of the name Eliam (*friend of God*). In Dryden's satire of *Absalom and Achitophel* it is meant for Sir Edward Seymour, Speaker of the House of Commons. (2 Sam. xxii. 34.)

" Who can Amiel's praise refuse?
Of ancient race by birth, but nobler yet
In his own worth, and without title great.
The Sanhedrim long time as chief he ruled,
Their reason guided and their passion cooled."
Dryden; Absalom and Achitophel, i. 899-903.

Am'iens (3 syl.). *The Peace of Amiens,* March 27, 1802, a treaty signed by Joseph Bonaparte, the Marquis of Cornwallis, Azara, and Schimmelpenninck, to settle the disputed points between France, England, Spain, and Holland. It was dissolved in 1803.

Ami'na. An orphan adopted by a miller, and beloved by Elvi'no, a rich farmer. The night before her espousals she is found in the bed of Count Rodolpho, and is renounced by her betrothed husband. The count explains to the young farmer and his friends that Ami'na is innocent, and has wandered in her sleep. While he is still talking, the orphan is seen getting out of the window of the mill, and walking in her sleep along the edge of the roof under which the mill-wheel is rapidly revolving. She crosses a crazy bridge, and comes among the spectators. In a few minutes she awakes, flies to Elvi'no, and is claimed by him as his beloved and innocent bride.—*Belli'ni's best opera, La Sonnambula.*

Amin'adab. A Quaker. The Scripture name has a double *m*, but in old comedies, where the character represents a Quaker, the name has generally only one. *Obadiah* is used, also, to signify a Quaker, and *Rachel* a Quakeress.

Am'ine (3 syl.). Wife of Sidi Nouman, who ate her rice with a bodkin, and was in fact a ghoul. "She was so hard-hearted that she led about her three sisters like a leash of greyhounds." —*Arabian Nights.*

Aminte (2 syl.). The name assumed by Cathos as more aristocratic than her own. She is courted by a gentleman, but discards him because his manners are too simple and easy for "bon ton;" he then sends his valet, who pretends to be a marquis, and Aminte is charmed with his "distinguished style of manners and talk." When the game has gone far enough, the trick is exposed, and Aminte is saved from a mésalliance.— *Molière: Les Précieuses Ridicules.*

It was a prevailing fashion in the Middle Ages to change names ; Voltaire's proper name was *Arouet* (1694-1778) ; Melancthon's was *Schwarzerde* (1497-1560). The real names of Desiderius Erasmus were *Gheraerd Gheraerd* (1467-1536) ; Anacharsis Clootz was *Jean Baptiste* Clootz, etc.

Am'iral or *Ammiral.* An early form of the word "admiral." (French, *amiral ;* Italian, *ammiraglio.*) (*See* ADMIRAL.)

Am'let (*Richard*). The gamester in Vanbrugh's drama called *The Confederacy.*

Am'mon. The Libyan Jupiter; so called from the Greek *ammos* (sand), because his temple was in the desert. Herodotus calls it an Egyptian word (ii. 42).

Son of Jupiter Ammon. Alexander the Great. His father, Philip, claimed to be a descendant of Hercules, and therefore of Jupiter ; and the son was saluted by the priests of the Libyan temple as son of Ammon. Hence was he called the son or descendant both of Jupiter and of Ammon.

Ammonian Horn (*The*), the cornucopia. It was in reality a tract of very fertile land, in the shape of a ram's horn, given by Ammon, King of Libya, to his mistress, Amalthea (q.v.) (the mother of Bacchus).

Am'monites (3 syl.). *Fossil molluscs* allied to the nautilus and cuttlefish. So called because they resemble the horn upon the ancient statues of Jupiter Ammon. (*See above.*)

A'mon's Son (in *Orlando Furioso*) is Rinaldo. He was the eldest son of Amon or Aymon, Marquis d'Este, and nephew of Charlemagne.

Am'oret, brought up by Venus in the courts of love. She is the type of female loveliness—young, handsome, gay, witty, and good ; soft as a rose, sweet as a violet, chaste as a lily, gentle as a dove, loving everybody and by all beloved. She is no Diana to make "gods and men fear her stern frown"; no Minerva to "freeze her foes into congealed stone with rigid looks of chaste austerity"; but a living, breathing virgin, with a warm heart, and beaming eye, and passions strong, and all that man can wish and woman want. She becomes the loving, tender wife of Sir Scu'damore. Tim'ias finds her in the arms of Corflambo (*sensual passion*) ; combats the monster unsuccessfully, but wounds the lady.—*Spenser: Faëry Queen,* book iii.

Amoret, a love-song, love-knot, love-affair, love personified. A pretty word, which might be reintroduced.

"He will be in his amorets, and his canzonets, his pastorals, and his madrigals."—*Heywood : Love's Mistress.*

"For not icladde in silke was he,
But all in flouris and flourettes,
I-paintid all with amorettes."
Romance of the Rose, 892.

Amorous (*The*). Philippe I. of France; so called because he divorced his wife Berthe to espouse Bertrade, who was already married to Foulques, count of Anjou. (1061-1108.)

Amour propre. One's self-love, vanity, or opinion of what is due to self. *To make an appeal to one's amour propre,* is to put a person on his metal. *To wound one's amour propre,* is to gall his good opinion of himself—to wound his vanity. (French.)

Ampa'ro de Pobres. A book exposing the begging impostors of Madrid, written by Herrera, physician to Felipe III.

Ampersand, the character made thus, "&" = and. In the old Horn-books, after giving the twenty-six letters, the character & was added, and was called "Ampersand," a corruption of

"and per-se &" (and by itself, and).
A B C D . . . . X Y Z &.

" Any odd shape folks understand
To mean my Protean amperzand."
Punch (17 April, 1869, p. 153, col. 2).

The martyr Bradford, says Lord Russell, was "A per se A" with them, "to their comfort," etc.—*i.e.* stood alone in their defence.

Amphi'alus, son of Cecropia, in love with Philoclea ; but he ultimately married Queen Helen of Corinth.—*Sir Philip Sidney : The Countess of Pembroke's Arcadia.*

Amphictyon'ic Council. A council of confederate Greeks from twelve of their tribes, each of which had two deputies. The council met twice a year —in the spring at Delphi, and in the autumn at Thermop'ylæ. According to fable, it was so called from Amphic'tyon, son of Deuca'lion, its supposed founder. (Greek, *amphictionēs,* dwellers round about.)

Amphig'ons. Words strung together without any real connection. The two pleaders in *Pantagruel* by Rabelais (book ii. c. 11-13) give an excellent example.

Amphigouri, nonsense verse, rigmarole.

" A kind of overgrown amphigouri, a heterogeneous combination."—*Quarterly Review,* i. 50, 1809.

⁑ Porson's "Three Children sliding on the Ice" is a good specimen of amphigouri.

Amphi'on is said to have built Thebes by the music of his lute, which was so melodious that the stones danced into walls and houses of their own accord. Tennyson has a rhyming *jeu d'esprit.*

Amphitri'te (either 3 or 4 syl.). The sea. In classic mythology, the wife of Neptune (Greek, *amphi-trio* for *tribo,* rubbing or wearing away [the shore] on all sides).

" His weary chariot sought the bowers
Of Amphitritè and her tending nymphs."
Thomson: Summer. (1625-6).

Amphit'ryon. *Le véritable Amphitryon est l' Amphitryon où l'on dine* (Molière). That is, the person who *provides the feast* (whether master of the house or not) is the real host. The tale is that Jupiter assumed the likeness of Amphit'ryon, and gave a banquet ; but Amphitryon himself came home, and claimed the honour of being the master of the house. As far as the servants and guests were concerned, the dispute was soon decided—" he who gave the feast was to them the host."

Amphrys'ian Prophetess (*Amphrysia Vatēs*). The Cumæan sibyl ; so called from Amphrÿsos, a river of Thessaly, on the banks of which Apollo fed the herds of Adme'tos ; consequently Amphrys'ian means Apollo'nian.

Ampoulle (*Sainte*). The jug or bottle containing oil used in anointing the kings of France, and said to have been brought from heaven by a dove for the coronation service of St. Louis. It was preserved at Rheims till the first Revolution, when it was destroyed.

Amram's Son. Moses. (Exodus vi. 20.)

" As when the potent rod
Of Amram's son, in Egypt's evil day,
Waved round the coast."
Milton: Paradise Lost, i. 338-40.

Amri, in the satire of *Absalom and Achitophel,* by Dryden and Tate, is designed for Heneage Finch, Earl of Nottingham and Lord Chancellor.

" Our list of nobles next let Amri grace,
Whose merits claimed the Abethdin's (*Lord Chancellor's*) high place—
To whom the double blessing does belong,
With Moses' inspiration, Aaron's tongue."
Part ii.

Amri'ta. The elixir of immortality, made by churning the milk-sea (*Hindu mythology*). Sir William Jones speaks of an apple so called, because it bestows immortality on those who partake of it. The word means *immortal.* (*See* AMBROSIA.)

Amsanc'tus. A lake in Italy, in the territory of Hirpi'num, said to lead down to the infernal regions. The word means *sacred water.*

Amuck'. *To run amuck.* To talk or write on a subject of which you are wholly ignorant ; to run foul of. The Malays, under the influence of opium, become so excited that they sometimes rush forth with daggers, yelling "*Amoq ! amoq !*" (Kill ! kill !), and fall foul of any one they chance to meet.

" Satire's my weapon, but I'm too discreet
To run amuck and tilt at all I meet."
Pope: Satires, i. 69-70.

Am'ulet. Something worn, generally round the neck, as a charm. (Arabic, *hamulet,* that which is suspended.)
The early Christians used to wear amulets called *Ichthus,* fish ; the word is composed of the initial letters of Ie'sos CHristos THeou Uios Sotēr (Jesus Christ, Son of God, our Saviour). (*See* NOTARICA.)

Amun'deville. *Lady Adeline Amundeville,* a lady who " had a twilight tinge of blue," could make epigrams, give delightful soirées, and was fond of making matches.—*Byron: Don Juan*, **xv.**, xvi.

Amyclæan Brothers (*The*). Castor and Pollux, who were born at Amyclæ.

Amyclæ'an Silence. *More silent than Amyclæ.* The inhabitants of Amyclæ were so often alarmed by false rumours of the approach of the Spartans, that they made a decree no one should ever again mention the subject. When the Spartans actually came against the town, no one durst mention it, and the town was taken.

Amyris plays the fool, *i.e.* a person assumes a false character with an ulterior object, like Junius Brutus. Amyris was a Sybarite (3 syl.) sent to Delphi to consult the Oracle, who informed him of the approaching destruction of his nation. Amyris fled to Peloponnesus and his countrymen called him a fool; but, like the madness of David, his "folly" was true wisdom, for thereby he saved his life.

A'mys and **Amyl'ion.** The Pyl'adēs and Ores'tēs of mediæval story. — *Ellis's Specimens.*

Anabaptists. A nickname of the Baptist Dissenters; so called because, in the first instances, they had been baptised in infancy, and were again baptised on a confession of faith in adult age. The word means the *twice baptised*.

Anabaptists. A sect which arose in Germany in 1521.

Anachar'sis. *Anacharsis among the Scythians.* A wise man amongst fools; "Good out of Nazareth"; "A Sir Sidney Smith on Salisbury Plain." The opposite proverb is "Saul amongst the Prophets," *i.e.* a fool amongst wise men. Anacharsis was a Scythian by birth, and the Scythians were proverbial for their uncultivated state and great ignorance.

Anacharsis Clootz. Baron Jean Baptiste Clootz, a Prussian by birth, but brought up in Paris, where he adopted the revolutionary principles, and called himself *The Orator of the Human Race.* (1755-1794.)

Anacleth'ra. The stone on which Cerēs rested after searching in vain for her daughter. It was kept as a sacred deposit in the Prytane'um of Athens.

Anac'reon. A Greek poet, who wrote chiefly in praise of love and wine. (B.C. 563-478.)

Anacreon of the Twelfth Century.

Walter Mapes, also called "The Jovial Toper." (1150-1196). His best-known piece is the famous drinking-song, "Meum est propos'itum in taber'na mori," translated by Leigh Hunt.

Anacreon Moore. Thomas Moore, who not only translated Anacreon into English, but also wrote original poems in the same style. (1779-1852.)

Anacreon of the Guillotine. Bertrand Barère de Vieuzac, president of the National Convention; so called from the flowery language and convivial jests used by him towards his miserable victims. (1755-1841.)

Anacreon of the Temple. Guillaume Amfrye, abbé de Chalieu; the "Tom Moore" of France. (1639-1720.)

The French Anacreon. Pontus de Tyard, one of the Pleiad poets (1521-1605). P. Laujon. (1727-1811.)

The Persian Anacreon. Mohammed Hafiz. (Fourteenth century.)

The Scotch Anacreon. Alexander Scot, who flourished about 1550.

The Sicilian Anacreon. Giovanni Meli. (1740-1815.)

Anacreon of Painters. Francesco Alba'no, a famous painter of lovely females. (1578-1660.)

Anacreon'tic. In imitation of Anac'-reon (*q.v.*).

Anach'ronism. An event placed at a wrong date; as when Shakespeare, in *Troilus and Cressida*, makes Nestor quote Aristotle. (Greek, *ana chronos*, out of time.)

Anag'nostes (Greek). A domestic servant employed by the wealthy Romans to read to them at meals. Charlemagne had his reader; and monks and nuns were read to at meals. (Greek, *anaginosko*, to read.)

Anagrams.

Dame Eleanor Davies (prophetess in the reign of Charles I.) = *Never so mad a lady.*

Gustavus = *Augustus.*

Horatio Nelson= *Honor est a Nilo* (made by Dr. Burney).

Queen Victoria's Jubilee Year = *I require love in a subject.*

Quid est Veritas (John xviii. 38) ?= *Vir est qui adest.*

Marie Touchet (mistress of Charles IX. of France = *Je charme tout* (made by Henri IV.).

Voltaire is an anagram of *Arouet l(e)j(eune).*

These are interchangeable words :—

Alcuinus and Calvinus ; Amor and Roma; Eros and Rose ; Evil and Live ; and many more.

Anah, a tender-hearted, pious, meek, and loving creature, granddaughter of Cain, and sister of Aholiba'mah. Japhet loved her, but she had set her heart on the seraph Aza'ziel, who carried her off to some other planet when the flood came.—*Byron : Heaven and Earth*.

Ana′na. The pine-apple (the Brazilian *ananas*).

"Witness thou, best Anana ! thou the pride
Of vegetable life." *Thomson : Summer*, 685,686.

Anastasia (*St.*). Her attributes are a stake and faggots, with a palm branch in her hand. The allusion is, of course, to her martyrdom at the stake.

Anathe′ma. A denunciation or curse. The word is Greek, and means to *place*, or *set up*, in allusion to the mythological custom of hanging in the temple of a patron god something devoted to him. Thus Gordius hung up his yoke and beam ; the shipwrecked hung up their wet clothes ; workmen retired from business hung up their tools, etc. Hence *anything set apart for destruction ;* and so, set apart from the Church as under a curse.

"Me tabula sacer
Votiva paries indicat uvida
Suspendisse potenti
Vestimenta maris deo."
Horace : Odes (v. 13—16).

꙰ Horace, having escaped the love-snares of Pyrrha, hangs up his votive tablet, as one who has escaped the dangers of the sea.

Anat′omy. *He was like an anatomy—i.e.* a mere skeleton, very thin, like one whose flesh had been anatomised or cut off. Shakespeare uses atomy as a synonym. Thus the hostess *Quickly* says to the *Beadle :* " Thou atomy, thou ! " and *Doll Tearsheet* caps the phrase with, " Come, you thin thing ; come, you rascal."—*2 Henry IV.*, v. 4.

Anaxarete (5 syl.) of Salamis was changed into stone for despising the love of Iphis, who hung himself.—*Ovid : Metamorphoses*, xiv. 750.

Anaxar′te (4 syl.). A knight whose adventures and exploits form a supplemental part of the Spanish romance called *Am′adis of Gaul*. This part was added by Feliciano de Silva.

Ancæ′os. Helmsman of the ship *Argo*, after the death of Ti′phys. He was told by a slave that he would never live to taste the wine of his vineyards. When a bottle made from his own grapes was set before him, he sent for the slave to laugh at his prognostications ; but the slave made answer, " There's many a slip 'twixt the cup and the lip." At this instant a messenger came in, and told Ancæos that

a wild boar was laying his vineyard waste, whereupon he set down his cup, went out against the boar, and was killed in the encounter.

Ancal′ites (4 syl.) Inhabitants of parts of Berkshire and Wiltshire, referred to by Cæsar in his *Commentaries*.

An′chor. *That was my sheet anchor —i.e.* my best hope, my last refuge. The sheet anchor is the largest anchor of a ship, which, in stress of weather, is the sailor's chief dependence. The word *sheet* is a corruption of the word *shote* (thrown out), meaning the anchor " thrown out " in foul weather. The Greeks and Romans said, " my *sacred* anchor," because the sheet anchor was always dedicated to some god.

Anchor (*The*), in Christian art, is given to Clement of Rome and Nicolas of Bari. Pope Clement, in A.D. 80, was bound to an anchor and cast into the sea. Nicolas of Bari is the patron saint of sailors.

The anchor is apeak—that is, the cable of the anchor is so tight that the ship is drawn completely over it. (*See* BOWER ANCHOR, SHEET ANCHOR.)

The anchor comes home, the anchor has been dragged from its hold. Figuratively, the enterprise has failed, notwithstanding the precautions employed.

To weigh anchor, to haul in the anchor, that the ship may sail away from its mooring. Figuratively, to begin an enterprise which has hung on hand.

Anchor Watch (*An*). A watch of one or two men, while the vessel rides at anchor, in port.

Ancien Régime. An antiquated system of government. This phrase, in the French Revolution, meant the monarchical form of government, or the system of government, with all its evils, which existed prior to that great change.

Ancient. A corruption of *ensign*—a flag and the officer who bore it. Pistol was Falstaff's " ancient."

"Ten times more dishonourably ragged than an old-faced ancient."—*Shakespeare:* 1 *Henry IV.*, iv. 21.
" My whole charge consists of ancients, corporals, lieutenants, gentlemen of companies . . . ."—*Shakespeare:* 1 *Henry IV.*, iv. 2.

Ancient Mariner. Having shot an albatross, he and his companions were subjected to fearful penalties. On repentance he was forgiven, and on reaching land told his story to a hermit.

At times, however, distress of mind drove him from land to land, and wherever he abode he told his tale of woe, to warn from cruelty and persuade men to love God's creatures.—*Coleridge.*

Ancient of Days (Daniel iii. 9). Jehovah.

Ancile (3 syl.). The Palladium of Rome. It was the sacred buckler which Numa said fell from heaven. To prevent its being stolen, he caused eleven others to be made precisely like it, and confided them to twelve priests called Salii, who bore them in procession through the city every year at the beginning of March.

" Idque ancile vocat, quod ab omni parte recisum est,
Quemque notes oculis, angulus omnis abest."
Ovid: Fasti, iii. 377.

And. The character " & " is a monogram of *et* (and), made in Italian type, &°.

Andirons or **Hand-irons,** a corruption of *anderia, andēra, andēla,* or *andēna.* Ducange says, " Andena est ferrum, quo appodiantur ligna in foco, ut melius luceant, et melius comburantur." Farther on he gives anderia, anderius, andellus, etc., as variants. Called "dogs" because they were often made in the resemblance of dogs. The derivation of *anderons* is not clear ; Ducange says, "dicitur andena, quasi *ante vaporem, i.e.* calorem," but this probably will satisfy no one. The modern French word is *landier,* old French *andier,* Low Latin *andæus.*

And'rea Ferra'ra. A sword. So called from a famous sword-maker of the name. (Sixteenth century.)

"We'll put in bail, my boy ; old Andrea Ferrara shall lodge his security."—*Scott: Waverley,* ch. 50.

Andrew, a name commonly used in old plays for a valet or man-servant. Probably a Merry Andrew is simply the mirth-making Andrew or domestic jester. (*See* MERRY ANDREW.)

Similarly, Abigail is used in old plays for a waiting gentlewoman. (*See* ABIGAIL.)

Andrew (*An*). A merchant vessel, probably so called from Andrew Doria, the famous Genoese admiral.

"I should think of shallows and of flats,
And see my wealthy Andrew docked in sand."
Shakespeare: Merchant of Venice, i. 1.

Andrew (*St.*), depicted in Christian art as an old man with long white hair and beard, holding the Gospel in his right hand, and leaning on a cross like the letter X, termed St. Andrew's cross. The great pictures of St. Andrew are his *Flagellation* by Domenichino, and the *Adoration of the Cross* by Guido, which

has also been depicted by Andrea Sacchi, in the Vatican at Rome. Both the *Flagellation* and the *Adoration* form the subjects of frescoes in the chapel of St. Andrea, in the church of San Gregorio, at Rome. His day is November 30th. It is said that he suffered martyrdom in Patræ (A.D. 70). (*See* ST. RULE.)

The "adoration of the cross" means his fervent address to the cross on which he was about to suffer. "Hail, precious cross, consecrated by the body of Christ ! I come to thee exulting and full of joy. Receive me into thy dear arms." The "flagellation" means the scourging which always preceded capital punishments, according to Roman custom.

St. Andrew's Cross is represented in the form of an X (white on a blue field). The cross, however, on which the apostle suffered was of the ordinary shape, if we may believe the relic in the convent of St. Victor, near Marseilles. The error rose from the way in which that cross is exhibited, resting on the end of the cross-beam and point of the foot.

According to J. Leslie (*History of Scotland*), this sort of cross appeared in the heavens to Achaius, King of the Scots, and Hungus, King of the Picts, the night before their engagement with Athelstane. As they were the victors, they went barefoot to the kirk of St. Andrew, and vowed to adopt his cross as their national emblem. (*See* CONSTANTINE'S CROSS.)

Andrew Macs (*The*). The crew of H.M.S. *Androm'achē.* Similarly, the *Beller'ophon* was called by English sailors " Billy ruffian," and the *Achilles* the " Ash heels." (*See* BEEFEATER, etc.)

Androcles and the Lion. Androcles was a runaway slave who took refuge in a cavern. A lion entered, and instead of tearing him to pieces, lifted up his fore paw that Androcles might extract from it a thorn. The slave being subsequently captured, was doomed to fight with a lion in the Roman arena. It so happened that the same lion was let out against him, and, recognising his benefactor, showed towards him every demonstration of love and gratitude.

In the *Gesta Romanorum* (Tale civ.) the same story is told, and there is a similar one in Æsop's *Fables.* The original tale, however, is from Aulus Gellius, on the authority of Plistonices, who asserts that he was himself an eye-witness of the encounter.

Android. An automaton figure of a

human being (Greek, *andros-eidos*, a man's likeness). One of the most famous of these machines is that by M. Vaucanson, called the flute-player. The chess-player by Kempelen is also celebrated. (*See* AUTOMATON.)

Androm'eda. Daughter of Cepheus (2 syl.) and Cassiopeia. Her mother boasted that the beauty of Androměda surpassed that of the Nereids; so the Nereids induced Neptune to send a sea-monster on the country, and an oracle declared that Andromeda must be given up to it. She was accordingly chained to a rock, but was delivered by Perseus (2 syl.). After death she was placed among the stars. (*See* ANGELICA.)

Ovid: Metamorphoses, v. 1, etc.

Androni'ca (in *Orlando Furioso*). One of Logistilla's handmaids, famous for her beauty. She was sent with Sophros'ynē to conduct Astolpho from India to Arabia.

Anent. Over against; concerning. (Old English, *on-emn;* later forms, *on-efen, on-efent, an-'ent.*)

Ange de Grève (French), a hang-man or executioner. The "Place de Grève" was at one time the Tyburn of Paris.

Angel. Half a sovereign in gold; so called because, at one time, it bore the figure of the archangel Michael slaying the dragon.

✢ When the Rev. Mr. Patten, vicar of Whitstable, was dying, the Arch-bishop of Canterbury sent him £10. The wit said, " Tell his Grace that now I am sure he is a man of God, for I have seen his angels."

Angel (*a public-house sign*), in compli-ment to Richard II., who placed an angel above his shield, holding it up in his hands.

To write like an angel (French). The angel referred to was Angelo Vergece [Vergezio], a Cretan of the sixteenth century. He was employed both by Henri II. and by François I., and was noted for his caligraphy. (*Didot: Nouvelle Biographie Universelle* [1852-66]).

Angel of the Schools. St. Thomas Aquīnas. (*See* ANGELIC DOCTOR.)

Angels, say the Arabs, were created from pure, bright gems; the genii, of *fire;* and man, of *clay.*

Angels, according to Dionysius the

Areop'agite, were divided into nine or-ders :—

(i) Seraphim, Cherubim, and Thrones, in the first circle.
(ii) Dominions, Virtues, and Powers, in the second circle.
(iii) Principalities, Archangels, and Angels, in the third circle.

St. Gregory the Great: Homily 34.

" In heaven above,
The effulgent bands in triple circles move."
Tasso: Jerusalem Delivered, xi. 13.

Angels. The seven holy angels are— Abdiel, Gabriel, Michael, Raguel, Raphael, Simiel, and Uriel. Michael and Gabriel are mentioned in the Bible, Raphael in the Apocrypha.

✢ Milton (*Paradise Lost*, book i., from 392) gives a list of the fallen angels.

Angel-beast. A favourite round game of cards, which enabled gentlemen to let the ladies win small stakes. Five cards are dealt to each player, and three heaps formed—one for the king, one for play, and the third for Tri'olet. The name of the game was *la bête* (beast). Angel was the stake. Thus we say, Shilling-whist.

"This gentleman offers to play at Angel-beast, though he scarce knows the cards."—*Mulberry Garden.*

Angel Visits. Delightful intercourse of short duration and rare occurrence.

" (Visits) Like those of angels, short and far between." *Blair: Grave,* pt. ii. 586.
" Like angel-visits, few and far between."
Campbell: Pleasures of Hope, line 375.

Angel-water, a Spanish cosmetic, made of roses, trefoil, and lavender. Short for Angel'ica-water, because ori-ginally it was chiefly made of the plant Angelica.

"Angel-water was the worst scent about her."
—*Sedley: Bellam.*

Angelic Doctor. Thomas Aqui'nas was so called, because he discussed the knotty points in connection with the being and nature of angels. An ex-ample is, " *Utrum An'gelus moveatur de loco ad locum transeundo per me'dium ?* " The Doctor says that it depends upon circumstances.

∴ It is said, by way of a quiz, that one of his questions was: " How many angels can dance on the point of a pin ? "

Angelic Hymn. The hymn begin-ning with *Glory be to God on high,* etc. (Luke ii. 14); so called because the former part of it was sung by the angel host that appeared to the shepherds of Beth-lehem.

Angelica. Daughter of Gal'aphron, king of Cathay, the capital of which was Albrac'ca. She was sent to sow discord among the Christians. Charlemagne sent her to the Duke of Bavaria, but she made her escape from the duke's castle. Being captured in her flight, she was bound to a rock, and exposed to sea-monsters. Rogéro delivered her, but she escaped out of his hands by a magic ring. Orlando greatly loved her, but she married Medo ro, a young Moor, and returned to India, where Medo'ro succeeded to the crown in right of his wife. (*Orlando Furioso.*) (*See* ANDROMEDA).

Angelica's Draught, something which completely changes affection. The tale is that Angelica was passionately in love with Rinaldo, who hated her, whereas Orlando, whom she hated, actually adored her shadow. Angelica and Rinaldo drink from a certain fountain, when a complete change takes place; Rinaldo is drunk with love, and Angelica's passion changes to abhorrence. Angelica ultimately married Medo'ro, and Orlando went mad. (*Ariosto : Orlando Furioso.*)

Angel'ical Stone. The speculum of Dr. Dee. He asserted that it was given him by the angels Raphael and Gabriel. It passed into the possession of the Earl of Peterborough, thence to Lady Betty Germaine, by whom it was given to the Duke of Argyll, whose son presented it to Horace Walpole. It was sold in 1842, at the dispersion of the curiosities of Strawberry Hill.

Angel'ici. Certain heretics of the second century, who advocated the worship of angels.

An'gelites (3 syl.). A branch of the Sabellian heretics; so called from Angel'ius, in Alexandria, where they used to meet. (*Dr. Hook: Church Dictionary.*)

An'gelo. (*See* MICHAEL ANGELO.)

Angelo and Raffaelle. Michael Angelo criticised Raffaelle very severely.

" Such was the language of this false Italian
       [Angelo]:
  One time he christened Raphael a Pyg-
       malion,
  Swore that his maidens were composed
       of stone ;
  Swore his expressions were like owls, so
       tame,
  His drawings, like the lamest cripple, lame ;
  And as for composition, he had none."
              Peter Pindar: Lyric Odes, viii.
(*See* MICHAEL ANGELO.)

Angelus (*The*). A Roman Catholic devotion in honour of the Incarnation, instituted by Urban II. It consists of three texts, each said as versicle and response, and followed by the salutation of Gabriel. The name is derived from the first words, Angelus Domini (The angel of the Lord, etc.).

The prayer is recited three times a day, generally about 6 a.m., at noon, and about 6 p.m., at the sound of a bell called the *Angelus.*

The Angelus bell (often wrongly called the Curfew) is still rung at 8 p.m. in some country churches.

" Sweetly over the village the bell of the An-
       gelus sounded."
              Longfellow : Evangeline.

Anger. Athenodo'rus, the Stoic, told Augustus the best way to restrain unruly anger was to repeat the alphabet before giving way to it. (*See* DANDER.)

" The sacred line he did but once repeat,
  And laid the storm, and cooled the raging
       heat."   *Tickell : The Horn Book.*

Angevin, adjective of Anjou.

John was not the last of the Angevin kings of England, though he was the last king of England who reigned over Anjou.

Angioli'na (4 syl.). The young wife of Mari'no Falie'ro, the doge. She was the daughter of Loreda'no. (*Byron : Marino Faliero.*)

Anglant'e's Lord. Orlando, who was lord of Anglant and knight of Brava.

An'gle. *A dead angle.* A term in fortification applied to the plot of earth before an angle in a wall which can neither be seen nor defended from the parapet.

Angle with a Silver Hook (*To*). To buy fish at market.

An'gling. *The father of angling,* Izaak Walton (1593-1683). Angling is called " the gentle craft "; shoe-making was also so called. Probably there is a pun concealed in the first of these ; a common bait of anglers being a " gentle." In the second case, St. Crispin was a Roman gentleman of high birth, and his craftsmen took from him their title of " gentle " (*generōsi*).

Angoulaffre of the Broken Teeth, a giant " 12 cubits in height." His face measured 3 feet across; his nose was 9 inches long; his arms and legs were each 6 feet; his fingers 6 inches and 2 lines; his enormous mouth was armed with sharp-pointed yellow tusks. He was descended from Goliath, and assumed the title of " Governor of Jerusalem." Angoulaffre had the strength of 30 men, and his mace was the trunk of an oak-tree 300 years old. Some say the Tower of Pisa lost its perpendicularity by the weight of this giant, who one day leaned against it to rest himself. He was slain by Roland, the paladin, in single combat at the Fronsac. (*Croquemitaine.*)

Angry (*The*). Christian II., of Denmark, Norway, and Sweden, was so called on account of his ungovernable temper. (1513-1559.)

An'gular. Cross-grained ; of a patchy temper ; one full of angles, whose temper is not smooth.

Angurva'del. Frithiof's sword, inscribed with Runic letters, which blazed in time of war, but gleamed with a dim light in time of peace. (*See* SWORD.)

An'ima Mundi [*the soul of the world*], with the oldest of the ancient philosophers, meant "the source of life" ; with Plato, it meant "the animating principle of matter," inferior to pure spirit ; with the Stoics, it meant "the whole vital force of the universe."

Stahl (1710) taught that the phenomena of animal life are due to an immortal *anima*, or vital principle distinct from matter.

Animal. *To go the entire animal*, a facetious euphuism for "To go the whole hog." (*See* HOG.)

Animal Spirits. Liveliness and animation arising from physical vigour.

Animals admitted into Heaven (*The*). They are ten : (1) Jonah's *whale* ; (2) Solomon's *ant* ; (3) the *ram* caught by Abraham and sacrificed instead of Isaac ; (4) the *cuckoo* of Belkis ; (5) the *camel* of the prophet Saleh ; (6) Balaam's *ass* ; (7) the *ox* of Moses ; (8) the *dog* Kratim of the Seven Sleepers ; (9) Mahomet's ass, called Al Borak ; and (10) Noah's *dove.*

Animals in Christian Art. The *ant* symbolises prudence ; the *ape*, malice, lust, and cunning ; the *ass*, sobriety, or the Jewish nation ; the *asp*, Christ, or Christian faith ; the *bee*, industry ; the *camel*, submission ; the *cock*, vigilance ; the *dog*, fidelity ; the *fox*, fraud and cunning ; the *hog*, impurity ; the *lamb*, innocence ; the *leopard*, sin ; the *ox*, pride ; the *wolf*, cruelty.

Some animals are appropriated to certain saints : as the calf or ox to *Luke* ; the cock to *Peter* ; the eagle to *John the Divine* ; the lion to *Mark* ; the raven to *Benedict*, etc.

The lamb, the pelican, and the unicorn, are symbols of Christ.

The dragon, serpent, and swine, symbolise Satan and his crew.

Animals sacred to special Deities. To Apollo, the *wolf*, the *griffon*, and the *crow* ; to Bacchus, the *dragon* and the *panther* ; to Diana, the *stag* ; to Æsculapius, the *serpent* ; to Hercules, the *deer* ; to Isis, the *heifer* ; to Jupiter, the *eagle* ; to Juno, the *peacock* and the *lamb* ; to the Larēs, the *dog* ; to Mars, the *horse* and the *vulture* ; to Mercury, the *cock* ; to Minerva, the *owl* ; to Neptune, the *bull* ; to Tethys, the *halycon* ; to Venus, the *dove*, the *swan*, and the *sparrow* ; to Vulcan, the *lion*, etc.

Animals (*Symbolical*). The ant, *frugality and prevision* ; ape, *uncleanness* ; ass, *stupidity* ; bantam cock, *pluckiness*, *priggishness* ; bat, *blindness* ; bear, *ill-temper*, *uncouthness* ; bee, *industry* ; beetle, *blindness* ; bull, *strength*, *straightforwardness* ; bull-dog, *pertinacity* ; butterfly, *sportiveness*, *living in pleasure* ; cat, *deceit* ; calf, *lumpishness*, *cowardice* ; cicada, *poetry* ; cock, *vigilance*, *overbearing insolence* ; crow, *longevity* ; crocodile, *hypocrisy* ; cuckoo, *cuckoldom* ; dog, *fidelity*, *dirty habits* ; dove, *innocence*, *harmlessness* ; duck, *deceit* (French, *canard*, a hoax) ; eagle, *majesty*, *inspiration* ; elephant, *sagacity*, *ponderosity* ; fly, *feebleness*, *insignificance* ; fox, *cunning*, *artifice* ; frog and toad, *inspiration* ; goat, *lasciviousness* ; goose, *conceit*, *folly* ; gull, *gullibility* ; grasshopper, *old age* ; hare, *timidity* ; hawk, *rapacity*, *penetration* ; hen, *maternal care* ; horse, *speed*, *grace* ; jackdaw, *vain assumption*, *empty conceit* ; jay, *senseless chatter* ; kitten, *playfulness* ; lamb, *innocence*, *sacrifice* ; lark, *cheerfulness* ; lion, *noble courage* ; lynx, *suspicious vigilance* ; magpie, *garrulity* ; mole, *blindness*, *obtuseness* ; monkey, *tricks* ; mule, *obstinacy* ; nightingale, *forlornness* ; ostrich, *stupidity* ; ox, *patience*, *strength* ; owl, *wisdom* ; parrot, *mocking verbosity* ; peacock, *pride* ; pigeon, *cowardice* (pigeon-livered) ; pig, *obstinacy*, *dirtiness* ; puppy, *empty-headed conceit* ; rabbit, *fecundity* ; raven, *ill luck* ; robin red-breast, *confiding trust* ; serpent, *wisdom* ; sheep, *silliness*, *timidity* ; sparrow, *lasciviousness* ; spider, *wiliness* ; stag, *cuckoldom* ; swallow, *a sunshine friend* ; swan, *grace* ; swine, *filthiness*, *greed* ; tiger, *ferocity* ; tortoise, *chastity* ; turkey-cock, *official insolence* ; turtle-dove, *conjugal fidelity* ; vulture, *rapine* ; wolf, *cruelty*, *savage ferocity*, and *rapine* ; worm, *cringing* ; etc.

Animals (*The cries of*). Apes *gibber* ; asses *bray* ; bees *hum* ; beetles *drone* ; bears *growl* ; bitterns *boom* ; blackbirds *whistle* ; blackcaps — we speak of the

" chick-chick" of the blackcap; bulls *bellow;* canaries *sing* or *quaver;* cats *mew, purr, swear,* and *caterwaul;* calves *bleat* and *blear;* chaffinches *chirp* or *pink;* chickens *pip;* cicadæ *sing;* cocks *crow;* cows *moo* or *low;* crows *caw;* cuckoos cry *cuckoo;* deer *bell;* dogs *bark, bay, howl,* and *yelp;* doves *coo;* ducks *quack;* eagles *scream;* falcons *chant;* flies *buzz;* foxes *bark* and *yelp;* frogs *croak;* geese *cackle* and *hiss;* goldfinch—we speak of the "merry twinkle" of the female; grasshoppers *chirp* and *pitter;* grouse— we speak of the "drumming" of the grouse; guineafowls cry "*come back*"; guineapigs *squeak;* hares *squeak;* hawks *scream;* hens *cackle* and *cluck;* horses *neigh* and *whinny;* hyenas *laugh;* jays *chatter;* kittens *mew;* lambs *baa* and *bleat;* larks *sing;* linnets *chuckle* in their call; lions *roar;* magpies *chatter;* mice *squeak* and *squeal;* monkeys *chatter* and *gibber;* nightingales *pipe* and *warble*—we also speak of its "jug-jug"; owls *hoot* and *screech;* oxen *low* and *bellow;* parrots *talk;* peacocks *scream;* peewits cry *pee-wit;* pigeons *coo;* pigs *grunt, squeak,* and *squeal;* ravens *croak;* redstarts *whistle;* rooks *caw;* screech-owls *screech* or *shriek;* sheep *baa* or *bleat;* snakes *hiss;* sparrows *chirp* or *yelp;* stags *bellow* and *call;* swallows *twitter;* swans *cry*—we also speak of the "bombilation" of the swan; thrushes *whistle;* tigers *growl;* tits—we speak of the "twit-twit" of the bottle-tit; turkey-cocks *gobble;* vultures *scream;* whitethroats *chirr;* wolves *howl.*

Animosity means animation, spirit, as the fire of a horse, called in Latin *equi animos'itas.* Its present exclusive use in a bad sense is an instance of the tendency which words originally neutral have to assume a bad meaning. (Compare *churl, villain.*)

Animula.

" Animula, vagula, blandula,
   Hospes, comesque, corporis ;
   Quæ nunc abibis in loca,
   Pallidula, rigida, nudula ? "
        The Emperor Hadrian to his Soul.

Sorry-lived, blithe-little, fluttering Sprite,
  Comrade and guest in this body of clay,
Whither, ah ! whither, departing in flight,
Rigid, half-naked, pale minion, away ?
                                    E. C. B.

Anna (*Donna*). A lady beloved by Don Otta'vio, but seduced by Don Gio-vanni, who also killed her father, the "Commandant of the City," in a duel. (*Mozart's opera of Don Giovanni.*)

An'nabel, in Dryden's satire of

Absalom and Achitophel is designed for the Duchess of Monmouth. Her maiden name and title were Anne Scott, Countess of Buccleuch, the richest heiress in Europe. The duke was faithless to her, and after his death, the widow, still handsome, married again.

"To all his [Monmouth's] wishes, nothing he
    [David] denied ;
  And made the charming Annabel his bride."
                            Part i. lines 33, 34.

Anna Matilda (*An*), an ultra-senti-mental girl. Mrs. Hannah Cowley used this pen-name in her responses in the *World* to Della Crusca (R. Merry). (*See the Baviad* by Gifford.)

An'nates (2 syl.). One entire year's income claimed by the Pope on the appointment of a bishop or other eccle-siastic in the Catholic Church. This is called the *first fruits* (Latin, *annus,* a year). By the Statute of Recusants (25 Hen. VIII. c. 20, and the Confirm-ing Act), the right to English Annates and Tenths was transferred to the Crown; but, in the reign of Queen Anne, annates were given up to form a fund for the augmentation of poor livings. (*See* BOUNTY, QUEEN ANNE'S.)

Anne. *Sister Anne.* Sister of Fat'ima, the seventh and last of Bluebeard's wives.

Anne's Fan (*Queen*). Your thumb to your nose and your fingers spread.

Anne's Great Captain. The Duke of Marlborough (1650-1722).

Annie Laurie was eldest of the three daughters of Sir Robert Laurie, of Maxwellton, born December 16, 1682. William Douglas, of Fingland (Kirk-cudbright), wrote the popular song, but Annie married, in 1709, James Fer-gusson, of Craigdarroch, and was the mother of Alexander Fergusson, the hero of Burns's song called *The Whistle.*

William Douglas was the hero of the song
" Willie was a wanton wag."

Annulo Dei figuram ne gestato (*In*). Wear not God's image in a ring (or *inscribe* . . . .), the 24th symbol of the *Protreptics.* Jamblicus tells us that Pythagoras wished to teach by this prohibition that God had an "incor-poreal subsistence." In fact, that it meant "thou shalt not liken God to any of His works."

Probably the ring, symbolising eternity, bore upon the special prohibition.

Annuncia'tion. *Day of the Annun-ciation.* The 25th of March, also called *Lady Day,* on which the angel announced to the Virgin Mary that she would be the mother of the Messiah.

Annus Luctus, the period during which a widow is morally supposed to remain chaste. If she marries within about nine months from the death of her late husband and a child is born, a doubt might arise as to the paternity of the child. Such a marriage is not illegal, but it is inexpedient.

Annus Mirab'ilis. The year of wonders, 1666, memorable for the great fire of London and the successes of our arms over the Dutch. Dryden has written a poem with this title, in which he describes both these events.

Anodyne Necklace (*An*), a halter. An anodyne is a medicine to relieve pain. Probably a pun on *nodus*, a knot, is intended also. George Primrose says: "May I die by an anodyne necklace, but I had rather be an under-turnkey than an usher in a boarding-school."

Anomœ'ans or *Unlikists*. A sect in the fourth century which maintained that the essence of the Son is wholly unlike that of the Father. (Greek, *an'omoios*, unlike.)

Anon, immediately, at once. The Old English *an-on* or *an-ane* = at once. Variants, *on one, anone*.

"They knewye hym in brekyng of brede, and onone he vanyste awaye fro hem."—*MS. Lincoln,*
A 1, 17.

"Spek the lion . . . .
To the fox anone his wille."
Wright's Political Songs.

∵ "For the nonce" is a corrupt form of "For the-n once," where *the-n* is the accusative case, meaning "For the once" or "For this once."

Anon-rightes. Right quickly.

"He had in town five hundred knightes,
He hem [*them*] of [*off*] sent anon-rightes."
Arthur and Merlin, p. 88.

Ansa'rian. The Moslems of Medi'na were called Ansarians (*auxiliaries*) by Mahomet, because they received him and took his part when he was driven from house and home by the Koreishites (*Kore-ish'-ites*).

Answer is the Old English *and-swaru*, verb *and swar-ian* or *swerian*, where *And* is the preposition = the Latin *re* in *re-spond-eo*. (*See* SWEAR.)

To answer like a Norman, that is, evasively.

"We say, in France, 'Answering like a Norman,' which means to give an evasive answer, neither yes nor no."—*Max O'Rell: Friend M'Donald,*
ch. v.

To answer its purpose, to carry out

what was expected or what was intended. Celsus says, "Medicīna sæpius respondet, interdum tamen fallit."

To answer the bell is to go and see what it was rung for.

To answer the door is to go and open it when a knock or ring has been given.

In both the last two instances the word is "answering to a summons." To *swear* means literally "to affirm something," and to *an-swear* is to "say something" by way of rejoinder; but figuratively both the "swer" and the "answer" may be made without words.

". . . . My story being done, . . .
She [*Desdemona*] swore [*affirmed*] 'twas strange, ...
'Twas pitiful, 'twas wondrous pitiful."
Shakespeare: Othello, i. 3.

Answer more Scotico (*To*). To divert the direct question by starting another question or subject.

"'Hark you, sirrah,' said the doctor, 'I trust you remember you are owing to the laird 4 stone of barleymeal and a bow of oats. . . . .'
"'I was thinking,' replied the man *more Scotico,* that is, returning no direct answer on the subject on which he was addressed, 'I was thinking my best way would be to come down to your honour, and take your advice, in case my trouble should come back.'"—*Sir Walter Scott: The Abbot,* ch. xxvi.

Antæ'os, in Greek mythology, was a gigantic wrestler, whose strength was invincible so long as he touched the earth; and every time he was lifted from it, was renewed by touching it again. (*See* MALE'GAR.)

"As once Antæos, on the Libyan strand,
More fierce recovered when he reached the sand."
Hoole's Ariosto, book iv.

It was Hercules who succeeded in killing this charmed giant. He

"Lifts proud Antæos from his mother's plains,
And with strong grasp the struggling giant strains;
Back falls his panting head and clammy hair,
Writhe his weak limbs and flits his life in air."
Darwin: Economy of Vegetation.

Antece'dents. *I know nothing of his antecedents*—his previous life, character, or conduct. (Latin, *antecedens*, fore-going.)

Antedilu'vian. Before the Deluge, meaning the Scripture Deluge.

Anthi'a. The lady-love of Abroc'-omas in Xenophon's romance, called *Ephesi'aca.* Shakespeare has borrowed from this Greek novel the leading incidents of his *Romeo and Juliet,* especially that of the potion and mock entombment. N.B. This is not the historian, but a Xenophon who lived in the fourth Christian century.

Anthony.

Anthony (St.). Patron saint of swine-herds, because he always lived in woods and forests.

St. Anthony's Cross. The taucross, T, called a lace.

St. Anthony's Fire. Erysip'elas is so called from the tradition that those who sought the intercession of St. Anthony recovered from the pestilential erysipelas called the *sacred fire*, which proved extremely fatal in 1089.

St. Anthony's Pig. A pet pig, the smallest of the whole litter. St. Anthony was originally a swineherd, and, therefore, the patron saint of pigs.

Anthropos'ophus. The nickname of Dr. Vaughan, rector of St. Bride's, in Bedfordshire. So called from his *Anthroposoph'ia Teomagica*, to show the condition of man after death.

Anti-Christ, or the *Man of Sin,* expected by some to precede the second coming of Christ. St. John so calls every one who denies the incarnation of the eternal Son of God.

Antig'one. *The Modern Antigone.* Marie Thérèse Charlotte, Duchesse d'Angoulême, daughter of Louis XVI.; so called for her attachment to Louis XVIII., whose companion she was. (1778-1851.)

An'timony. Said to be derived from the Greek *antimon'achos* (bad for monks). The tale is that Valentine once gave some of this mineral to his convent pigs, who thrived upon it, and became very fat. He next tried it on the monks, who died from its effects; so Valentine said, "tho' good for pigs, it was bad for monks." This fable is given by Furetière.

Another derivation is *anti-monos* (averse to being alone), because it is found in combination with sulphur, silver, or some other substance.

Littré suggests *isthimmit*, and connects it with *stibium.*

Antino'mian. [Greek, *anti-nomos*, exempt from the law.] One who believes that Christians are not bound to observe the "law of God," but "may continue in sin that grace may abound." The term was first applied to John Agricola by Martin Luther.

Antin'ous (4 syl.). A model of manly beauty. He was the page of Hadrian, the Roman Emperor.

"The polished grace of Antinöus." — *Daily Telegraph.*

Antipathy (of human beings) To *Animals :* Henri III. and the Duke of Schoenberg felt faint at the sight of a cat; Vanghelm felt the same at the sight of a pig, and abhorred pork; Marshal Brézé sickened at the sight of a rabbit; the Duc d'Epernon always swooned at the sight of a leveret, though he was not affected at the sight of a hare.

To *Fish :* Erasmus felt grievous nausea at the smell of fresh fish.

To *Flowers* and *Fruits :* Queen Anne, Grétry the composer, Faverite the Italian poet, and Vincent the painter, all abhorred the smell of roses; Scaliger had the same aversion to watercresses; and King Vladislas sickened at the smell of apples.

To *Music :* Le Mothe de Nayer felt faint at the sound of any musical instrument; Nicano had a strong aversion to the sound of a flute.

To *Thunder :* Augustus trembled at the noise of thunder, and retired to a vault when a thunderstorm was apprehended.

Witches have an antipathy to running water.

"Some men there are love not a gaping pig,
Some that are mad if they behold a cat."
Shakespeare: Merchant of Venice, iv. 1.

Antip'athy (of animals). According to tradition, wolves have a mortal antipathy to scillaroots; geese to the soil of Whitby; snakes to soil of Ireland; cats to dogs; all animals dislike the castoroil plant; camphor keeps off insects; Russian leather is disliked by bookworms; paraffin by flies; cedar-wood is used for wardrobes, because its odour is disliked by moths. Ants dislike green sage.

Anti-pope is a pope elected by a *king* in opposition to the pope elected by the cardinals; or one who usurps the popedom in opposition to the rightful pope. Geddes gives a list of twenty-four anti-popes, three of whom were deposed by the council of Constance.

Antis'thenes. Founder of the Cynic School in Athens. He wore a ragged cloak, and carried a wallet and staff like a beggar. Soc'ratēs wittily said he could "see rank pride peering through the holes of Antis'thenes' rags."

Antoni'nus. *The Wall of Antonine* A turf entrenchment raised by the Romans from Dunglass Castle, on the Clyde, to Caer Ridden Kirk, near the Firth of Forth, under the direction of Lollius Urb'icus, legate of Antoni'nus Pius, A.D. 140.

An'tony. (*See* ANTHONY.)

Antrus'tions. The chief followers of the Frankish kings, who were specially trusty to them. (Old German, *tröst*, trust, fidelity.)

"None but the king could have antrustions."
—*Stubbs: Constitutional History.*

Ants. "*Go to the ant, thou sluggard, ... which provideth her meat in the summer*" (Proverbs vi. 6-8; and xxx. 25). The notion that ants in general gather food in harvest for a winter's store is quite an error; in the first place, they do not live on grain, but chiefly on animal food; and in the next place they are torpid in winter, and do not require food. Colonel Sykes, however, says there is in Poonah a grain-feeding species, which stores up millet-seed; and according to Lubbock and Moggridge, ants in the south of Europe and in Texas make stores.

⁂ What are called "ant eggs" are not eggs, but the pupæ of ants.

Anu'bis. In Egyptian mythology, similar to the Hermēs of Greece, whose office it was to take the souls of the dead before the judge of the infernal regions. Anu'bis is represented with a human body and jackal's head.

Anvil. *It is on the anvil,* under deliberation; the project is in hand. Of course, the reference is to a smithy.

"She had another arrangement on the anvil."
—*Le Fanu: The House in the Churchyard.*

Any-how, *i.e.* in an irregular manner. "He did it any-how," in a careless, slovenly manner. "He went on any-how," in a wild, reckless manner. *Any-how, you must manage it for me;* by hook or crook; at all events. (Old English, *ænig-hú.*)

Aōn'ian. Poetical, pertaining to the Muses. The Muses, according to Grecian mythology, dwelt in Aōn'ia, that part of Bœo'tia which contains Mount Hel'icon and the Muses' Fountain. Thomson calls the fraternity of poets

"The Aonian hive
Who praisèd are, and starve right merrily."
Castle of Indolence, ii. 2.

A outrance. (French.) To the farthest point. The correct form of the phrase. (*See* A L'OUTRANCE.)

Ape. *The buffoon ape,* in Dryden's poem called *The Hind and the Panther,* means the Free-thinkers.

"Next her [*the bear*] the buffoon ape, as atheists use,
Mimicked all sects, and had his own to choose."
Part i. 39, 40.

He keeps them, like an ape, in the corner of his jaw; first mouthed, to be last swallowed (*Hamlet* iv. 2). Most of the Old World monkeys have cheek pouches, used as receptacles for food.

To lead apes or *To lead apes in hell.* It is said of old maids. Hence, to die an old maid.

"I will even take sixpence in earnest of the bear-ward, and lead his apes into hell."—*Shakespeare: Much Ado about Nothing,* ii. 1.

Fadladin'da says to Tatlanthe (3 syl.):

"Pity that you who've served so long and well
Should die a virgin, and lead apes in hell."
H. Carey: Chrononhotonthologos.

"Women, dying maids, lead apes in hell."—*The London Prodigal,* i. 2.

To play the ape, to play practical jokes; to play silly tricks; to make facial imitations, like an ape.

To put an ape into your hood (or) *cap—i.e.* to make a fool of you. Apes were formerly carried on the shoulders of fools and simpletons.

To say an ape's paternoster, is to chatter with fright or cold, like an ape.

Apel'lēs. A famous Grecian painter, contemporary with Alexander the Great.

"There comelier forms embroidered rose to view
Than e'er Apelles' wondrous pencil drew."
Ariosto: Orlando Furioso, book xxiv.

Ap'eman'tus. A churlish philosopher, in Shakespeare's *Timon of Athens.*

"The cynicism of Apemantus contrasted with the misanthropy of Timon."—*Sir Walter Scott.*

A-per-se. An A 1; a person or thing of unusual merit. "A" all alone, with no one who can follow, *nemo proximus aut secundus.*

Chaucer calls Cresseide "the floure and A-per-se of Troi and Greek."

"London, thou art of townēs *A-per-se.*"—*Lansdowne MSS.*

Apex, the topmost height, really means the pointed olive-wood spike on the top of the cap of a Roman priest. The cap fitted close to the head and was fastened under the chin by a fillet. It was applied also to the crest or spike of a helmet. The word now means the summit or tiptop.

Aph'rodite (4 syl.). The Greek Venus; so called because she sprang from the foam of the sea. (Greek, *aphros,* foam.)

Aph'rodite's Girdle. Whoever wore Aphrodite's magic girdle, immediately became the object of love. (*Greek mythology.*)

Apic'ius. A gourmand. Apicius was a Roman gourmand, whose income being reduced by his luxurious living to £80,000, put an end to his life, to avoid the misery of being obliged to live on plain diet.

A-pigga-back. (*See* PIG-BACK.)

A'pis, in Egyptian mythology, is the bull symbolical of the god Apis. It was not suffered to live more than twenty-five years, when it was sacrificed and buried in great pomp. The madness of Cambysês is said to have been in retribution for his killing a sacred bull.

Aplomb means true to the plumbline, but is generally used to express that self-possession which arises from perfect self-confidence. We also talk of a dancer's aplomb, meaning that he is a perfect master of his art. (French, *à plomb*.)

"Here exists the best stock in the world . . . men of aplomb and reserve, of great range and many moods, of strong instincts, yet apt for culture."—*Emerson: English Traits*, p. 130.

Apocalyp'tic Number. The mystic number 666. (Rev. xiii. 18.) (*See* NUMBER OF THE BEAST.)

Apo'crypha. Those books included in the Septuagint and Vulgate versions of the Old Testament, but not considered to be parts of the original canon. They are accepted as canonical by Catholics, but not by Protestants, and are not printed in Protestant Bibles in ordinary circulation. The word means hidden (Greek, *apokrupto*), "because they were wont to be read not openly. . . . but, as it were, in secret and apart" (*Bible*, 1539, *Preface to the Apocrypha*). As the reason why these books are not received as canonical is because either their genuineness or their authenticity is doubtful, therefore the word "apocryphal" means not genuine or not authentic.

Apollina'rians. An ancient sect founded in the middle of the fourth century by Apollina'ris, bishop of Laodice'a. They denied that Christ had a human soul, and asserted that the *Logos* supplied its place. The Athanasian creed condemns this heresy.

Apollo. The sun, the god of music. (*Roman mythology*.)

"Apollo's angry, and the heavens themselves Do strike at my injustice." *Shakespeare: Winter's Tale*, iii. 2.

A perfect Apollo. A model of manly beauty, referring to the Apollo Belvidere (*q.v.*).

The Apollo of Portugal. Luis Camoëns, author of the *Lusiad;* so called, not for his beauty, but for his poetry. He was god of poetry in Portugal, but was allowed to die in the streets of Lisbon like a dog, literally of starvation. Our own Otway suffered a similar fate. (1527-1579.)

Apollo Belvidere [*Bel'-ve-dear*]. A marble statue, supposed to be from the chisel of the Greek sculptor Cal'amis,

who flourished in the fifth ante-Christian era. It represents the god holding a bow in his left hand, and is called Belvidere from the Belvidere Gallery of the Vat'ican, in Rome, where it stands. It was discovered in 1503, amidst the ruins of An'tium, and was purchased by Pope Julius II.

Apollodo'ros. Plato says: "Who would not rather be a man of sorrows than Apollodoros, envied by all for his enormous wealth, yet nourishing in his heart the scorpions of a guilty conscience?" (*The Republic*). This Apollodoros was the tyrant of Cassan'drea (formerly *Potide'a*). He obtained the supreme power B.C. 379, exercised it with the utmost cruelty, and was put to death by Antig'onos Gon'atas.

Apollo'nius. Master of the Rosicrucians. He is said to have had the power of raising the dead, of making himself invisible, and of being in two places at the same time.

Apoll'yon. King of the bottomless pit. (Rev. ix. 11.) His contest with Christian, in Bunyan's allegory, has made his name familiar. (Greek, *the destroyer*.)

Apos'tate (*The*). Julian, the Roman emperor. So called because he forsook the Christian faith and returned to Paganism again. (331, 361-363.)

A poster'io'ri [Latin, *from the latter*]. An *a posteriori* argument is proving the cause from the effect. Thus, if we see a watch, we conclude there was a watchmaker. Robinson Crusoe inferred there was another human being on the desert island, because he saw a human footprint in the wet sand. It is thus the existence and character of Deity is inferred from his works. (*See* A PRIORI.)

Apos'tles. The badges or symbols of the fourteen apostles.

Andrew, *a cross*, because he was crucified on a cross shaped like the letter X.

Bartholomew, *a knife*, because he was flayed with a knife.

James the Greater, *a scallop-shell, a pilgrim's staff*, or *a gourd bottle*, because he is the patron saint of pilgrims. (*See* SCALLOP-SHELL.)

James the Less, *a fuller's pole*, because he was killed by a blow on the head with a pole, dealt him by Simeon the fuller.

John, *a cup with a winged serpent flying out of it*, in allusion to the tradition about Aristode'mos, priest of Diana, who challenged John to drink a cup of poison. John made the sign of a cross on the cup, Satan like a dragon flew from it, and John then drank the cup, which was quite innocuous.

Judas Iscariot, *a bag*, because he had the bag and "bare what was put therein" (John xii. 6).

Jude, *a club*, because he was martyred with a club.

Matthew, *a hatchet* or *halbert*, because he was slain at Nad'abar with a halbert.

Matthias, *a battle-axe*, because he was first stoned, and then beheaded with a battle-axe.

Paul, *a sword*, because his head was cut off with a sword. The convent of La Lisla, in Spain, boasts of possessing the very instrument.

Peter, *a bunch of keys*, because Christ gave him the "keys of the kingdom of heaven." *A cock*, because he went out and wept bitterly when he heard the cock crow. (Matt. xxvi. 75.)

Philip, *a long staff surmounted with a cross*, because he suffered death by being suspended by the neck to a tall pillar.

Simon, *a saw*, because he was sawn to death, according to tradition.

Thomas, *a lance*, because he was pierced through the body, at Mel'iapour, with a lance.

(*See* EVANGELISTS.)

Apostles, where buried. According to Catholic legend, seven of the Apostles are buried at Rome. These seven are distinguished by a star (*).

ANDREW lies buried at Amalfi (Naples).
BARTHOLOMEW,* at Rome, in the church of Bartholomew Island, on the Tiber.
JAMES THE GREATER was buried at St. Jago de Compostella, in Spain.
JAMES THE LESS,* at Rome, in the church of the Holy Apostles.
JOHN, at Ephesus.
JUDE,* at Rome.
MATTHEW, at Salerno (Naples).
MATTHIAS,* at Rome, under the altar of the Basilica.
PAUL, somewhere in Italy.
PETER,* at Rome, in the church of St. Peter.
PHILIP,* at Rome.
SIMON or SIMEON,* at Rome.
THOMAS, at Ortōna (Naples). (? Madras.)
¶ MARK THE EVANGELIST is said to have been buried at Venice.
LUKE THE EVANGELIST is said to have been buried at Padua.
N.B.—Italy claims thirteen of these apostles or evangelists—Rome seven, Naples three, Paul somewhere in Italy, Mark at Venice, Luke at Padua.

Apostles of

Abyssinians, St. Frumentius. (Fourth century.)
Alps, Felix Neff. (1798-1829.)
Ardennes, St. Hubert. (656-730.)
Armenians, Gregory of Armenia. (256-331.)
English, St. Augustine. (Died 607.) St. George.
Ethiopia. (*See* ABYSSINIANS.)
Free Trade, Richard Cobden. (1804-1865.)
French, St. Denis. (Third century.)
Frisians, St. Wilbrod. (657-738.)
Gauls, St. Irenæus (130-200); St. Martin. (316-397.)
Gentiles, St. Paul.
Germany, St. Boniface. (680-755.)
Highlanders, St. Columb. (521-597.)
Hungary, St. Anastatius. (954-1044.)
Indians (American), Bartolomé de Las Casas (1474-1500); Rev. John Eliot. (1603-1690.)
Indies (East), St. Francis Xavier. (1506-1552.)
Infidelity, Voltaire. (1694-1778.)
Ireland, St. Patrick. (372-493.)
Netherlands, St. Armand, Bishop of Maestricht. (589-679.)
North, St. Ansgar or Anscarius (801- 864); Bernard Gilpin. (1517-1583.)
Picts, St. Ninian.
Scottish Reformers, John Knox. (1505-1572.)
Slavs, St. Cyril. (Died 868.)
Spain, St. James the Greater. (Died 44.)
Temperance, Father Mathew. (1790-1856.)
Yorkshire, Pauli'nus, bishop of York and Rochester. (597-644.)
Wales, St. David. (480-544.)

¶ *The Twelve Apostles*. The last twelve names on the poll ŏr list of ordinary degrees were so called, when the list was arranged in order of merit, and not alphabetically, as now; they were also called the *Chosen Twelve*. The last of the twelve was designated *St. Paul* from a play on the verse 1 Cor. xv. 9. The same term is now applied to the last twelve in the Mathematical Tripos.

Apostle of the Sword. So Mahomet was called, because he enforced his creed at the point of the sword. (570-632.)

Prince of the Apostles. St. Peter. (Matt. xvi. 18, 19.)

Apostle Spoons. Spoons formerly given at christenings; so called because one of the apostles figured at the top of the handle. Sometimes twelve spoons, representing the twelve apostles; sometimes four, representing the four evangelists; and sometimes only one, was presented. Sometimes, but very rarely, a set occurs containing in addition the "Master Spoon" and the "Lady Spoon." We still give at christenings a silver spoon, though the apostolic handle is no longer retained.

Apostles' Creed (*The*). A church creed supposed to be an epitome of Scripture doctrines, or doctrines taught by the apostles. It was received into the Latin Church, in its present form, in the eleventh century; but a formula somewhat like it existed in the second century. Items v̄ere added in the fourth and fifth centuries, and verbal alterations much later.

∴ It is said that Tullo, Bishop of Antioch, introduced the Cr̄.ed as part of the daily service in 471.

Apostolic Fathers. Christian authors born in the first century, when the apostles lived. John is supposed to have died about A.D. 99, and Polycarp, the last of the Apostolic Fathers, born about 80, was his disciple. These three are tolerably certain: Clement of Rome (30-100), Ignatius (died 115), and Polycarp (80-169). Three others are Barnabas, Hermas, and Papias. Barnabas was the companion of Paul, Hermas is a very doubtful name, and Papias (Bp. of Hierapolis) is mentioned by Eusebius.

∵ Polycarp could hardly have been a disciple of John, although he might have received Christian instruction from the old "beloved one."

Apostolic Majesty. A title borne by the Emperor of Austria, as King of Hungary. It was conferred by Pope Sylvester II. on the King of Hungary in 1000.

Apparel. Dress. The ornamental parts of the alb, at the lower edge and at the wrists. Catechu'mens used to talk of putting on their apparels, or fine

white surplices, for the feast of Pentecost.

Pugin says: "The albe should be made with
apparels worked in silk or gold, embroidered with
ornaments."
Rock tells us—" That apparels were stitched on
the upper part of the amice, like a collar to it."

Appeal to the Country (*An*).
Asking electors by their choice of representatives to express their opinion of
some moot question. In order to obtain
the public opinion Parliament is dissolved,
and a new election must be made.

Ap'piades (4 syl.). Five divinities
whose temple stood near the fountains
of Ap'pius, in Rome. Their names are
Venus, Pallas, Concord, Peace, and
Vesta. They were represented on horseback, like Amazons.

Ap'pian Way. The oldest and best
of all the Roman roads, leading from the
Porta Cape'na of Rome to Cap'ua. This
"queen of roads" was commenced by
Appius Claudius, the decemvir, B.C.
313.

Apple (*Newton and the*). Voltaire
tells us that Mrs. Conduit, Newton's
niece, told him that Newton was at
Woolsthorpe, when, seeing an apple fall,
he was led into a train of thought
which resulted in his discovery of gravitation (1666).

His mother had married a Rev. B. Smith, and
in 1656 had returned to Woolsthorpe. Her granddaughter was the wife of Mr. Conduit, who succeeded Newton in the Mint. Newton was on a
visit to his mother.

The apple of discord. A cause of
dispute; something to contend about.
At the marriage of Thetis and Pe'leus,
where all the gods and goddesses met
together, Discord threw on the table a
golden apple " for the most beautiful."
Juno, Minerva, and Venus put in their
separate claims; and not being able to
settle the point, referred the question
to Paris, who gave judgment in favour
of Venus. This brought upon him the
vengeance of Juno and Minerva, to
whose spite the fall of Troy is attributed.

* The " apple " plays a large part in
Greek story. Besides the " Apple of
Discord," related above, we have the
three apples thrown down by Hippo-
mĕnēs when he raced with Atalanta.
The story says that Atalanta stopped to
pick up the apples, whereby Hippo-
mĕnēs won the race, and according to
the terms obtained her for wife.

Then there are the golden apples of
the Hesperĭdēs, guarded by a sleepless
dragon with a hundred heads; but
Herculēs slew the dragon and carried

some of the apples to Eurystheus.
This was the twelfth and last of his
" labours."

Of course, the Bible story of Eve and
the Apple will be familiar to every
reader of this dictionary.

Apples of Istakhar are " all sweetness
on one side, and all bitterness on the
other."

Apples of Paradise, according to tradition, had a bite on one side, to commemorate the bite given by Eve.

Apples of Pyban, says Sir John Mandeville, fed the pigmies with their odour
only.

Apples of Sodom. Thevenot says—
" There are apple-trees on the sides of
the Dead Sea which bear lovely fruit,
but within are full of ashes." Josephus
speaks of these apples. Witman says
the same is asserted of the oranges there.
(See *Tacitus, Hist.,* v. 7.)

" Like to the apples on the Dead Sea's shore,
All ashes to the taste."
Byron: Childe Harold, iii. 34.

The apple of perpetual youth. This is
the apple of Idun, daughter of the
dwarf Svald, and wife of Bragi. It is
by tasting this apple that the gods preserve their perpetual youth. (*Scandinavian mythology.*)

The singing apple had the power of
persuading any one to anything. (*Chery
and Fairstar : Countess D'Anois.*)

Prince Ahmed's apple — a cure for
every disorder. This apple the prince
purchased at Samarcand'. (*Arabian
Nights, Prince Ahmed,* etc.)

The apple of the eye. The pupil, of
which perhaps it is a corruption. If
not, it is from an erroneous notion that
the little black spot of the eye is a little
round solid ball like an apple. Anything extremely dear or extremely sensitive.

" He kept him as the apple of his eye."—Deut.
xxxii. 3.

Apple-john (*An*). An apple so
called from its being at maturity about
St. John's Day (May 6th). We are told
that apple-johns will keep for two
years, and are best when shrivelled.

" I am withered like an old apple-john."
Shakespeare : 1 Henry IV. iii. 3.
∴ Sometimes called the Apples of King John,
which, if correct, would militate against the
notion about "St. John's Day."
" There were some things, for instance, the
Apples of King John, . . . I should be tempted
to buy."—*Bigelow : Life of B. Franklin.*
∴ In the United States there is a drink called
" Apple-Jack," which is apple or cider brandy.

Apple-pie Bed. A bed in which the
sheets are so folded that a person cannot

get his legs down; from the *apple turnover;* or, more probably, a corruption of "a *nap-pe-pli* bed." (French, *nappe pliée,* a folded sheet.)

Apple-pie Order. Prim and precise order.

The origin of this phrase is still doubtful. Some suggest *cap-à-pie,* like a knight in complete armour. Some tell us that apples made into a pie are quartered and methodically arranged when the cores have been taken out. Perhaps the suggestion made above of *nap-pe-pli* (French, *nappes pliées,* folded linen, neat as folded linen, Latin, *plico,* to fold) is nearer the mark.

It has also been suggested that "Apple-pie order" may be a corruption of *alpha, beta,* meaning as orderly as the letters of the alphabet.

"Everything being in apple-pie order, . . . Dr. Johnson . . . proposed that we should accompany him . . . to M'Tassa's kraal."—*Adventures in Mashonaland,* p. 294 (1893).

April. The opening month, when the trees unfold, and the womb of nature opens with young life. (Latin, *aperi're,* to open.)

April Fool. Called in France *un poisson d'Avril* (*q.v.*), and in Scotland a *gowk* (cuckoo). In Hindustan similar tricks are played at the Huli Festival (March 31st). So that it cannot refer to the uncertainty of the weather, nor yet to the mockery trial of our Redeemer, the two most popular explanations. A better solution is this: As March 25th used to be New Year's Day, April 1st was its octave, when its festivities culminated and ended.

For the same reason that the "Mockery of Jesus" is rejected as a solution of this custom, the tradition that it arose from Noah sending out the dove on the first of the month may be set aside.

Perhaps it may be a relic of the Roman "Cerealia," held at the beginning of April. The tale is that Proserpina was sporting in the Elysian meadows, and had just filled her lap with daffodils, when Pluto carried her off to the lower world. Her mother, Cerês, heard the echo of her screams, and went in search of "the voice;" but her search was a fool's errand, it was hunting the gowk, or looking for the "echo of a scream." ∴ Of course this fable is an allegory of seed-time.

My April morn—*i.e.* my wedding day; the day when I was made a fool of. The allusion is to the custom of making fools of each other on the 1st of April.

April Gentleman (*An*). A man newly married, who has made himself thus "an April fool."

April Squire (*An*). A *novus homo.* A man who has accumulated money, and has retired into the country, where his money may give him the position of a squire.

A prio'ri [Latin, *from an antecedent*]. An *a priori* argument is when we deduce a fact from something antecedent, as when we infer certain effects from given causes. All mathematical proofs are of the *a priori* kind, whereas judgments in the law courts are of the *a posteriori* evidence; we infer the *animus* from the act. (*See* A POSTERIORI.)

Apron. This is a strange blunder. *A napperon,* converted into *An apperon.* "Napperon" is French for a napkin, from *nappe* (cloth in general). Halliwell, in his *Archaic Dictionary,* p. 571, gives Nappern (an apron) *North.*

Other examples of *n* attached to the following noun, or detached from it, are an *odder* for a nadder (Old English, *nœddre*); a *newt* for an ewt; a *nag* (Danish, *ög*); *nuncle* (Shakespeare), mine uncle; For the *nonce* (this once), where *n* is transferred from the preceding pronoun *tha-n* or *the-n. i.e.* this-n (accusative case after "for").

Apron-string Tenure (*An*). A tenure held in virtue of one's wife.

Tied to his mother's apron-string, completely under his mother's thumb. Applied to a big boy or young man who is still under mother rule.

A propos de bottes (French). Turning to quite another subject; *à propos de rien.*

Aqua Re'gia [*royal water*]. So called because it dissolves gold, *the king of metals.* It consists of one part of nitric acid, with from two to four of hydrochloric acid.

Aqua Tofa'na or *Acqua Tofan'ica.* A poisonous liquid much used in Italy in the seventeenth century by young wives who wanted to get rid of their husbands. It was invented by a woman named Tofâna, who called it the *Manna of St. Nicholas of Bari,* from the widespread notion that an oil of miraculous efficacy flowed from the tomb of that saint. In Italian called also *Aquella di Napoli.*

Aqua Vitæ [*water of life*]. Certain ardent spirits used by the alchemists. Ben Jonson terms a seller of ardent spirits an "aqua-vitæ man" (*Alchemist,* i. 1). The "elixir of life" was made from distilled spirits, which were thought to have the power of prolonging life. (*See* EAU-DE-VIE.)

Aqua'rians. A sect in the early Christian Church which insisted on the use of water instead of wine in the Lord's Supper.

Aqua'rius [*the water-bearer*]. One of the signs of the zodiac (January 20th to February 18th). So called because it appears when the Nile begins to overflow.

A'queous Rocks. Rocks produced by the agency of water, such as bedded limestones, sandstones, and clays ; in short, all the geological rocks which are arranged in layers or strata.

Aq'uilant (in *Orlando Furioso*). A knight in Charlemagne's army, son of Olive'ro and Sigismunda. He was called *black* from his armour, and his brother Gryphon *white*. While Aquilant was searching for his brother he met Marta'no in Gryphon's armour, and took him bound to Damascus, where his brother was.

Aq'uiline (3 syl.). Raymond's matchless steed, bred on the banks of the Tagus. (*Georgics*, iii. 271-277 ; and *Tasso, Jerusalem Delivered*, book vii.) (*See* HORSE.)

Aquin'ian Sage (*The*). Ju'venal is so called because he was born at Aqui'num, a town of the Volscians.

Arabesque [*Arrabesk'*]. The gorgeous Moorish patterns, like those in the Alhambra, especially employed in architectural decoration. During the Spanish wars, in the reign of Louis XIV., arabesque decorations were profusely introduced into France. (French, "Arab-like.")

Arabian Bird (*The*). The phœnix ; a marvellous man, quite *sui generis*.

"O Antony ! O thou Arabian bird !"
Shakespeare : Antony and Cleopatra, iii. 2.

Arabian Nights (*The*). First made known in Europe by Antoine Galland, a French Oriental scholar, who translated them and called them *The Thousand and One Nights* (from the number of nights occupied in their recital). They are of Indian, Persian, Egyptian, and Arabian origin.
Common English translations—
4 vols. 12mo, 1792, by R. Heron, published in Edinburgh and London.
3 vols. 12mo, 1794, by Mr. Beloe, London.
  „   „   1798, by Richard Gough, enlarged. Paris edition.
5 vols. 8vo, 1802, by Rev. Edward Foster.
  „   „   1830, by Edw. Wm. Lane.
The Tales of the Genii, by Sir Charles Morell (*i.e.* Rev. James Ridley), are excellent imitations.

Arabians. A class of Arabian heretics of the third century, who maintained that the soul dies with the body.

Ar'abic Figures. The figures 1, 2, 3, 4, etc. So called because they were introduced into Europe (Spain) by the Moors or Arabs, who learnt them from the Hindus. Far more important than the characters, is the decimalism of these figures : 1 figure = units, 2 figures = tens, 3 figures = hundreds, and so on *ad infinitum*.

The figures i, ii, iii, iv, v, vi, vii, viii, ix, x, etc., are called Roman figures.
The Greeks arranged their figures under three columns of nine figures, units, tens, and hundreds, and employed the letters of the alphabet. As there are but twenty-four letters, a sansculotte letter had to be introduced into each column. In the units column it represented 6, and was called *episëmon*. In the tens column it represented 90, and was called *koppos*. And; in the third column it represented 900, and was called *sanpi*. Thousands were represented by a dash under some letter of the first three columns :
As, $\beta = 2$, but $\underset{|}{\beta} = 2,000$;

$$\epsilon = 5, \text{ but } \underset{|}{\epsilon} = 5,000 ;$$

$$\sigma = 200, \text{ but } \underset{|}{\sigma} = 200,000 ;$$

and so on.

Ar'abs. *Street Arabs.* The houseless poor ; street children. So called because, like the Arabs, they are nomads or wanderers with no settled home.

Arach'nē's Labours. Spinning and weaving. Arachne was so skilful a needlewoman that she challenged Minerva to a trial of skill, and hanged herself because the goddess beat her. Minerva then changed her into a spider.

"Arachnē's labours ne'er her hours divide,
Her noble hands nor looms nor spindles guide."
Hoole's Jerusalem Delivered, book ii.

A'raf, Al [*the partition*]. A region, according to the Koran, between Paradise and Jehennam, for those who are neither morally good nor bad, such as infants, lunatics, and idiots. The inmates of Al Araf will be allowed to converse with the blessed and the cursed ; to the former this region will appear a hell, to the latter a heaven. (*See* LIMBO.)

Aras'pes (in *Jerusalem Delivered*), King of Alexandria, more famed for devices than courage. He joined the Egyptian armament against the Crusaders.

Ara'tos of Achæa, in Greece, murdered Nic'oclēs, the tyrant, in order to restore his country to liberty, and would not allow even a picture of a king to exist. He was poisoned by Philip of Macedon.

"Aratus, who awhile relumed the soul
Of fondly-lingering liberty in Greece."
Thomson : Winter, 491, 492.

Arba'ces (3 syl.). A Mede and Assyrian satrap, who conspired against

Sardanapa'lus, and founded the empire of Me'dia on the ruins of the Assyrian kingdom. (*Byron: Sardanapalus.*)

Arbor Day. A day set apart in Canada and the United States for planting trees. (See *Historic Note Book,* p. 42.)

Arbor Judæ. Said to be so called because Judas Iscariot hanged himself thereon. This is one of those word-resemblances so delusive to etymologists. Judæ is the Spanish jud'ia (a French bean), and Arbor Judæ is a corruption of *Arbol Judia* (the bean-tree), so called from its bean-like pods.

Arcades Ambo [*Arcădes* 3 syl.], both sweet innocents or simpletons, both Verdant Greens. From Virgil's *Eclogue,* vii. v. 4. (*See below,* ARCADIAN YOUTH.) Byron's translation was " blackguards both."

Arca'dian. A shepherd, a fancy farmer; so called because the Arcadians were a pastoral people, and hence pastoral poetry is called *Arca'dic.*
An Arcadian youth. A dunce or blockhead; so called because the Arcadians were the least intellectual of all the Greeks. Juvenal (vii. 160) uses the phrase *Arcadĭcus juvĕnis* for a stupid fool.

Arcadian Nightingales. Asses.
" April is the month of love ; and the country of Chastellerauld abounds with Arcadian nightingales."—*Rabelais: Pantagruel.* v. 7 (note).

Archangels. According to the Koran, there are four archangels. *Ga'briel,* the angel of revelations, who writes down the divine decrees ; *Mi'chael,* the champion, who fights the battles of faith ; *Az'rael,* the angel of death ; and *Az'rafil,* who is commissioned to sound the trumpet of the resurrection.

Arch-monarch of the World. Napoleon III. of France. (1808, 1852-1870, *died* 1873.)

Archers. The best archers in British history and story are Robin Hood and his two comrades Little John and Will Scarlet.
The famous archers of Henry II. were Tepus his bowman of the Guards, Gilbert of the white hind, Hubert of Suffolk, and Clifton of Hampshire.
Nearly equal to these were Egbert of Kent and William of Southampton.
Domitian, the Roman emperor, we are told, could shoot four arrows between the spread fingers of a man's hand.
Tell, who shot an apple set on the head of his son, is a replica of t''e Scandinavian tale of Egil,

who, at the command of King Nidung, performed a precisely similar feat.
Robin Hood, we are told, could shoot an arrow a mile or more.

Arches (*The Court of*). The most ancient consistory court of England, the dean of which anciently held his court under the arches of Bow church. Of course we refer to the old church, the steeple of which was supported on arches. The present structure was the work of Sir Christopher Wren.

Arche'us (3 syl.), according to the Paracelsians, is that immaterial principle which energises all living substances. There were supposed to be numerous archēi, but the chief one was said to reside in the stomach.

Archiloch'ian Bitterness. Ill-natured satire, so named from Archil'ochos, the Grecian satirist (B.C. 714-676).

Ar'chimage (3 syl.). The name given by Thomson to the " demon Indolence." Archima'gus is the title borne by the High Priest of the Persian Magi.
" ' I will,' he cried, ' so help me God ! destroy
That villain Archimage.' "
Thomson: Castle of Indolence, c. ii.

Archima'go [*Hypocrisy*]. In Spenser's *Faërie Queene* (ii. 1). He assumes the guise of the Red Cross Knight, and deceives Una ; but Sansloy sets upon him, and reveals his true character. When the Red Cross Knight is about to be married to Una, he presents himself before the King of Eden, and tells him that the Knight is betrothed to Duessa. The falsehood being exposed, Archimago is cast into a vile dungeon (book i.). In book ii. the arch-hypocrite is loosed again for a season, and employs Braggadocchio to attack the Red Cross Knight. These allegories are pretty obvious: thus the first incident means that Truth (*Una*), when Piety (the *Red Cross Knight*) is absent, is in danger of being led astray by Hypocrisy ; but any Infidel (*Sansloy*) can lay bare religious hypocrisy.
" Such whenas Archimago them did view
He weenèd well to worke some uncouth wyle."
Spenser: Faërie Queene, ii. 1, st. 8.
⁂ Sometimes Spenser employs the shortened form " Archimage."

Archime'des Principle. The quantity of water removed by any body immersed therein will equal in bulk the bulk of the body immersed. This scientific fact was noted by the philosopher Archime'dēs. (*See* EUREKA.)

Archime'des Screw. An endless screw, used for raising water, propelling ships, etc., invented by Archime'dēs of Syracuse.

Ar'chitect of his own Fortune. Appius says, "*Fabrum suæ esse quemque fortunæ.*" Longfellow says, "All are architects of Fate." (*The Builders.*)

Archon'tics. Heretics of the second century, who held a number of idle stories about creation, which they attributed to a number of agents called "archons." (Greek, *archon*, a prince or ruler.)

Ar'cite (2 syl.). A young Theban knight, made captive by Duke Theseus, and shut up with Pal'amon in a prison at Athens. Here both the captives fell in love with Emily, the duke's sister-in-law. After a time both captives gained their liberty, and Emily was promised by the duke to the victor in a tournament. Arcite was the victor, but, as he was riding to receive the prize of his prowess, he was thrown from his horse, and died. So Emily became the bride of Pal'amon. (*Chaucer : The Knight's Tale.*)

The story is perhaps better known through Dryden's version, *Palamon and Arcite.*

Ar'cos Barbs. War steeds of Arcos, in Andalu'sia, very famous in Spanish ballads. (*See* BARBED STEEDS.)

Arctic Region means the region of *Arctu'ros* (the Bear stars). *Ark* in Sanskrit means "to be bright," applied to stars or anything bright. The Greeks translated *ark* into *arkt(os)*, "a bear"; hence Arctu'rus (*the Bear stars*), and Arctic region, the region where the north star is found.

Arden (*Enoch*). Mr. G. R. Emerson, in a letter to the *Athenæum* (August 18th, 1866), points out the resemblance of this tale by Tennyson to one entitled *Homeward Bound,* by Adelaide Anne Procter, in a volume of *Legends and Lyrics,* 1858. Mr. Emerson concludes his letter thus : "At this point (*i.e.* when the hero sees his wife 'seated by the fire, whispering baby words and smiling on the father of her child ') Tennyson departs from the story. Enoch goes away broken-hearted to die, without revealing his secret; but Miss Procter makes the three recognise each other, and the hero having blessed his wife, leaves her, to roam 'over the restless ocean.'"

Mrs. Gaskell's *Manchester Marriage* is a similar tale. In this tale "Frank" is made to drown himself; and his wife (then Mrs. Openshaw) never knows of his return.

Area-sneak. A boy or girl who sneaks about areas to commit petty thefts.

Areop'agus or *Mars' Hill.* The seat of a famous tribunal in Athens; so called because the first cause tried there was that of Mars or Arēs, accused by Neptune of the death of his son Halirrhoth'ius.

"Then Paul stood in the midst of Mars' Hill." —Acts xvii. 22.

Ar'etine (3 syl.), or rather Pietro Aretino, patronised by François I. of France. A poet noted for his disreputable life and licentious verses. (1492-1557.)

"[Shakespeare] tried his hand with Aretine on a licentious subject."—*Steevens.*

Aretin'ian Syllables. *Ut, re, mi, fa, sol, la,* used by Guido d'Arezzo in the eleventh century for his system of hexachords. Hexachord means a scale of six notes. They are the first syllables of some words in the opening stanza of a hymn for St. John's Day. "*Ut* queant laxis *re*-sonare fibris," etc. *Si,* the seventh note, was not introduced till the seventeenth century. Originally the scale consisted of six notes only. (*See* Do.)

"Auparavant on ne se servait que de six notes ; et on remplaçait le *si* au moyen de combinaisons appelées *nuances.*"—*Bou.llet : Dictionnaire des Sciences,* p. 1523, col. 2.)

Argan, a miserly hypochondriac. He reduced himself to this dilemma : if his apothecary would not charge less, he could not afford to be sick; but if he swallowed fewer drugs, he would suffer in health. (*Molière's Le Malade Imaginaire.*)

Argand' Lamp. A lamp with a circular wick, through which a current of air flows, to supply oxygen to the flame, and increase its brilliancy. Invented by Aimé Argand, 1789.

Argan'te (3 syl.). A giantess of unbridled licentiousness, in Spenser's *Faërie Queene,* iii. 7.

"That geauntesse Argantè is behight,
A daughter of the Titans . . . .
Her sire Typhœus was. . . . ."
Book iii. 7, st. 47,

Argan'tes (3 syl.). A Circassian of high rank and matchless courage, but fierce to brutality, and an ultra-despiser of the sect of the Nazarenes. He was sent as an ambassador from Egypt to King Al'adine. He and Solyman were by far the most doughty of the Pagan knights. The former was slain by Rinaldo, and the other by Tancred. (*Tasso : Jerusalem Delivered.*)

"Bonaparte stood before the deputies like the Argantès of Italy's heroic poet. and gave them the choice of peace and war, with the air of a superior being, capable at once of dictating their fate."—*Sir Walter Scott.*

Ar'genis. A political allegory by John Barclay, containing allusions to the state of Europe, and more especially to France, during the time of the league. (1582-1621.) (*See* UTOPIA.)

Ar'gentile and Cur'an. Argentile was the daughter of King Ad'elbright, who, on his deathbed, committed her in charge to King Edel. Edel kept her a close prisoner, under hope of getting into his possession her lands and dominion. Curan, the son of a Danske king, in order to woo her, became a kitchen drudge in Edel's household, and Edel resolved to marry Argentile to this drudge, but she fled away. Curan now turned shepherd, and fell in love with a neatherd's maid, who turned out to be Argentile. The two were married, and Curan claiming his wife's dominions, became King of Northumberland, and put Edel to death. (*Percy's Reliques.*)

Argent'ine Republic. The Republic of the Argentine, or Silver River; in other words, the Confederation of the Rio de la Plata.

Arge'o (in *Orlando Furioso*). Baron of Servia, and husband of Gabri'na. He is a sort of Potiphar. His wife tried to seduce Philander, a young Dutch knight, and failing in her effort, she accused him to her husband of adultery; whereupon Arge'o threw the "faithless guest" into durance. In the course of time Gabri'na implored the young captive to defend her against a wicked knight who had assailed her virtue. He consented to be her champion, and was placed in concealment. Presently a knight drew near, and Philander, rushing on him, dispatched him; but the supposed "adulterer" was, in reality, Arge'o himself; and Gabri'na, being now a widow, was free to marry her Dutch "Joseph."

Ar'gillan (in *Jerusalem Delivered*). A haughty, turbulent knight, born on the banks of the Trent. Accusing Godfrey and his brother of having murdered Rinaldo, he induced the Latians to revolt. The revolt spread to the Swiss and English, but Godfrey succeeded in restoring order. Argillan was arrested, but made his escape, and was slain in battle by Solyman. (Books viii. ix.)

Ar'go. A ship sailing on an adventure. The galley of Jason that went in search of the Golden Fleece was so called, from the Greek *argos* (swift).

Ar'gonauts. The sailors of the ship *Argo.* Apollo'nios of Rhodes wrote an epic poem on the subject. (Greek, *argo naus.*)

Argosy. A merchant ship. A corruption of "ragusea." Ships of the largest size were built at Ragusa in Dalmatia and Venice.

" He hath an argosy bound to Tripolis, another to the Indies . . . . a third to Mexico, a fourth to England."—*Shakespeare: Merchant of Venice,* i. 3.

Argot [*Ar'go*]. Slang or flash language (French).

" Sans le (*le mot d'argot*) faire venir du grec *argos*, *e.g.* comme l'on a prétendu avant nous, nous y verrions logiquement undiminute du vieux mot *argu* qui signifiait *injure, reproche,* et aussi *ruse, finesse, subtilité."—Larchey: Dictionnaire d'Argot.* Francisque-Michel, however, in his *Philologie Comparée,* says, " L'ancienne langue Française avait le mot *argu,* mais dans un sens bien différent, que l'on peut établir par les passages suivant . . ." He then gives five examples.

Ar'gus-eyed. Jealously watchful. According to Grecian fable, Argos had 100 eyes, and Juno set him to watch Io, of whom she was jealous.

Argyle (2 syl.)—of whom Thomson says, in his *Autumn* (928-30)—

" On thee, Argyle,
Her hope, her stay, her darling, and her boast,
Thy fond, imploring country turns her eye—"

was John, the *great duke,* who lived only two years after he succeeded to the dukedom. Pope (*Ep. Sat.* ii. 86, 87) says—

" Argyle the state's whole thunder born to wield,
And shake alike the senate and the field."

Arians. The followers of Arius, a presbyter of the church of Alexandria, in the fourth century. He maintained (1) that the Father and Son are distinct beings; (2) that the Son, though divine, is not equal to the Father; (3) that the Son had a state of existence previous to His appearance on earth, but not from eternity; and (4) that the Messiah was not real man, but a divine being in a case of flesh.

Arideus [*A-ree'-de-us*] in *Jerusalem Delivered,* herald in the Christian army. The other herald is Pindo'rus.

Ariel. A spirit of the air and guardian of innocence. He was enslaved to the witch Syc'orax, who overtasked him; and in punishment for not doing what was beyond his power, shut him up in a pine-rift for twelve years. On the death of Sycorax, Ariel became the slave of Cal'iban, who tortured him most cruelly. Pros'pero liberated him from the pine-rift, and the grateful fairy served him for sixteen years, when he was set free. (*Shakespeare : Tempest.*)

A'riel. The sylph that watched over Belinda. (*Pope : Rape of the Lock,* i.)

A'riel. One of the angels cast out of heaven. The word means *lion of God.* (*Milton : Paradise Lost*, book vi. 371.)

A'ries. The Ram. The sign of the Zodiac in which the sun is from March 21st to April 20th.

" At last from Aries rolls the bounteous sun."
Thomson : Spring, 20.

Ariman'es (4 syl.). "The prince of earth and air," and the fountain-head of evil. It is a personage in Persian mythology, introduced into Grecian fable under the name of Ariman'nis. Byron introduces him in his drama called *Manfred.*

Arimas'pians. A one-eyed people of Scythia, who adorned their hair with gold. They were constantly at war with the gryphons who guarded the gold mines.

" As when a gryphon, through the wilderness ...
Pursues the Arimaspian, who by stealth
Had from his wakeful custody purloined
The guarded gold."
Milton : Paradise Lost, ii. 943-6.

Ar'ioch. One of the fallen angels cast out of heaven. The word means *a fierce lion.* (*Milton : Paradise Lost*, vi. 371.)

Ari'on. A Greek musician, cast into the sea by mariners, but carried to Tænaros on the back of a dolphin.

Ari'on. The wonderful horse which Herculēs gave to Adras'tos. It sprang from Cerēs and Neptune, had the power of speech, and its feet on the right side were the feet of a man. (*See* HORSE.)

Arios'to was privately married to Alessandra Benucci, widow of Tito Strozzi; she is generally called his mistress.

Ariosto of the North. So Lord Byron calls Sir Walter Scott. (*Childe Harold*, iv. 40.)

Ariste'as. The wandering Jew of Grecian fable. (*See* JEW.)

Aristi'des (4 syl.). Surnamed *The Just.* An Athenian statesman.

" Then Aristides lifts his honest front,
Spotless of heart ; to whom the unflattering voice
Of Freedom gave the noblest name of 'Just.' "
Thomson : Winter, 459-61.

The British Aristides. Andrew Marvell (1620-1678).

The French Aristides. Mons. Grévy, born 1813, president of the Third Republic 1879-1887, died 1891. He was a barrister by profession.

Aristippos. (*See* HEDONISM.)

Aristoc'racy. *The cold shade of the aristocracy — i.e.* the unsympathising

patronage of the great. The expression first occurs in Sir W. F. P. Napier's *History of the Peninsular War.*

The word "aristocracy" is the Greek *aristo-cratia* (rule of the best-born).

Aristoph'anes. *The English* or *modern Aristophanes.* Samuel Foote (1722-1777).

The French Aristophanes. J. Baptiste Poquelin de Molière (1622-1673).

Aristotle.

Aristotle of China. Tehuhe, who died A.D. 1200, called the "Prince of Science."

Aristotle of the nineteenth century. Baron Cuvier, the great naturalist (1769-1832).

Aristote'lian Philosophy. Aristotle maintained that four separate causes are necessary before anything exists : the material cause, the formal, the final, and the moving cause. The first is the antecedents from which the thing comes into existence ; the second, that which gives it its individuality ; the moving or efficient cause is that which causes matter to assume its individual forms ; and the final cause is that for which the thing exists. According to Aristotle, matter is eternal.

Aristote'lian Unities. Aristotle, the Greek philosopher, laid it down as a rule that every tragedy, properly constructed, should contain but one catastrophe ; should be limited to one denoument ; and be circumscribed to the action of one single day. These are called the *Aristotel'ic* or *Dramatic unities.* To these the French have added a fourth, the unity of *uniformity, i.e.* in tragedy all the " dramatis personæ " should be *tragic* in style, in comedy *comic,* and in farce *farcical.*

Ark. *You must have come out of the ark,* or *you were born in the ark ;* because you are so old-fashioned, and ignorant of current events.

Arma'da. *The Spanish Armada.* The fleet assembled by Philip II. of Spain, in 1588, for the conquest of England. Used for any fleet.

Arme'nians. A religious sect so called from Arme'nia, where Christianity was introduced in the second century. They attribute only one nature to Christ and hold that the Spirit proceeds from the Father only. They enjoin the adoration of saints, have some peculiar ways of administering baptism and the Lord's Supper, but do not maintain the doctrine of purgatory.

Armi'da. One of the prominent female characters in Tasso's *Jerusalem Delivered*. She was a beautiful sorceress, with whom Rinaldo fell in love, and wasted his time in voluptuous pleasure. Two messengers were sent from the Christian army with a talisman to disenchant him. After his escape, Armida followed him in distraction, but not being able to allure him back, set fire to her palace, rushed into the midst of a combat, and was slain.

In 1806, Frederick William of Prussia declared war against Napoleon, and his young queen rode about in military costume to arouse the enthusiasm of the people. When Napoleon was told of it, he wittily said of her : " She is Armi'da, in her distraction setting fire to her own palace."

Armin'ians (Anti - Calvinists), so called from James Harmensen, of Holland, whose name, Latinised, is Jaco'bus Armin'ius. He asserted that God bestows forgiveness and eternal life on all who repent and believe ; that He wills all men to be saved ; and that His predestination is founded on His foreknowledge.

Ar'mory. Heraldry is so called, because it first found its special use in direct connection with military equipments, knightly exercises, and the *mêlée* of actual battle.

"Some great man's badge of war or armory."
　　　　　Morris : Earthly Paradise, ii. 167.

Armoury. The place where armour is kept.　"But the sword
　　Of Michael from the armoury of God
　　Was given him."
Milton : Paradise Lost, vi. 320. *See also* vii. 200.

Arms. In the Bayeux tapestry, the Saxons fight on foot with javelin and battle-axe, and bear shields with the British characteristic of a boss in the centre. The men were moustached.

The Normans are on horseback, with long shields and pennoned lances. The men are not only shaven, but most of them have a complete tonsure on the back of the head, whence the spies said to Harold, " There are more priests in the Norman army than men in Harold's."

Arms of England (*The Royal*). The three lions leopardised were the cognisance of William the Conqueror ; the lion rampant in the second quarter is from the arms of Scotland ; and the harp in the fourth quarter represents Ireland. The lion supporter is in honour of England, and the unicorn in honour of Scotland. These two supporters were introduced by James I.

William I. had only two lions *passant gardant ;* the third was introduced by Henry II. The lion rampant first appeared on Scotch seals in the reign of Alexander II. (1214-1249). The harp was assigned to Ireland in the time of Henry VII. ; before that time the arms of Ireland were *three crowns*. The unicorn was not a supporter of the royal arms of Scotland before the reign of Mary Stuart.

Which arm of the service. Military or naval ?

The secular arm. Civil, in contradistinction to ecclesiastical jurisdiction.

"The relapsed arm delivered to the secular arm."—*Priestley : Corruptions of Christianity.*

To arm a magnet. To put an armature on a loadstone.

A coat of arms. An heraldic device.

A passage of arms. A literary controversy ; a battle of words.

An assault at arms (or *of arms*). An attack by fencers ; a hand-to-hand military exercise.

At arm's length. At a distance. To keep one at arm's length is to repel familiarity.

In arms. A child in arms is an infant carried about in one's arms.

A city in arms is one in which the people are armed for war.

King of arms. A chief herald in the College of Heralds. Here arms means heraldic devices.

Small arms. Those which do not, like artillery, require carriages.

To appeal to arms. To determine to decide a litigation by war.

To arms ! Make ready for battle.

"To arms ! cried Mortimer,
And couched his quivering lance."
　　　　　　Gray : The Bard.

Come to my arms. Come, and let me embrace you.

To lay down their arms. To cease from armed hostility ; to surrender.

Under arms. Prepared for battle ; in battle array.

Up in arms. In open rebellion ; roused to anger, as the clergy were up in arms against Colenso for publishing his *Lectures on the Pentateuch.* The latter is a figure of speech.

With open arms. Cordially ; as persons receive a dear friend when they open their arms for an embrace.

Arnauts [*brave men*] Albanian mountaineers.

"Stained with the best of Arnaut's blood."
　　　　　Byron : The Giaour.

Arn-monat. Anglo - Saxon, *arn-monath*, barn month. The Anglo-Saxon name for August, because it was the month for garnering the corn.

Arnold, of Melch'thal, patriarch of the forest cantons of Switzerland. He was in love with Matilda, a sister of Gessler, the Austrian governor of the district. When the tyranny of Gessler drove the people into rebellion, Arnold gave up Matilda and joined the insurgents; but when Gessler was shot by William Tell, he became united to her in marriage. (*Rossini's opera of Guglielmo Tell.*)

Arnol'dists. The partisans of Arnold of Brescia, who raised his voice against the abuses and vices of the papacy in the twelfth century. He was burnt alive by Pope Adrian IV.

Arod, in the satire of *Absalom and Achitophel*, by Dryden and Tate, is designed for Sir William Waller.

> " But in the sacred annals of our plot
> Industrious Arod never be forgot,
> The labours of this midnight magistrate
> May vie with Corah [Titus Oates] to preserve
> the state." *Part ii.*

Aroint thee. Get ye gone, be off. In Cheshire they say, *rynt ye, witch;* and milk-maids say to their cows when they have done milking them, *rynt ye,* (or *'roint*) *my beauties;* but it is doubtful whether this is connected with the word in question.

Aron'teus (4 syl.), in *Jerusalem Delivered.* An Asiatic king, who joined the Egyptian armament against the Crusaders, " not by virtue fired, but vain of his titles and ambitious of fame."

Ar'oundight. The sword of Sir Launcelot of the Lake. (*See* SWORD.)

> " It is the sword of a good knight,
> Though homespun was his mail,
> What matter if it be not bright,
> Joyeuse, Cola'da, Durindale,
> Excalibar, or Aroundight ? " *Longfellow.*

Arras, tapestry. So called from Arras, in Artois, famed for its manufacture. When rooms were hung with tapestry it was a common thing for persons to hide behind it, especially the arras curtain before the door. Hubert concealed the two villains who were to put out Arthur's eyes behind the arras. Polo'nius was slain by Hamlet while concealed behind the arras. Falstaff proposed to hide behind the arras at Windsor, etc.

Arria, a Roman lady, the wife of Cæcina Pætus. Pætus being accused of conspiring against the Emperor Claudius

was condemned to death and sent by sea to Rome. Arria accompanied him, and stabbed herself in the boat, then presenting the dagger to her husband, she said: " Pætus, it gives no pain" (*non dolet*). (*Pliny,* vii.)

✻ Her daughter Arria, wife of Thraseas, when her husband was condemned to death by Nero, opened her veins; but Thraseas entreated her to live, for the sake of her children.

Arrière Pensée (plural *arrières pensées*), a hidden or reserved motive, not apparent on the surface.

Arrot, the weasel, in the tale of *Reynard the Fox.*

Arrow. *The broad arrow,* thus ⋏. A mark used by the British Board of Ordnance, and placed on their stores. (*See* BROAD ARROW.)

Arrowroot is *araruta,* the Indian word *ara* is the name of the plant. There is no evidence of its being used to absorb the poison of poisoned arrows in fleshy wounds.

Arse'tēs (in *Jerusalem Delivered*). The aged eunuch who brought up Clorin'da, and attended her steps.

Artaxerx'es, called by the Persians Kai-Ardeshir, and surnamed *diraz-dest* (long-handed), because his right hand was longer than his left. The Romans translated *diraz-dest* into *longi-manus;* the Greek *Arta* into *Arde* (" noble ").

Art'egal (*Sir*) (in Spenser's *Faërie Queene*), is the hero of the fifth book, and impersonates Justice, the foster-child of Astræa. In the previous books he occasionally appears, and is called Sir Arthegal. It is said that Arthur, Lord Grey of Wilton, was the prototype of this character. He was sent to Ireland as Lord Lieutenant in 1580, and the poet was his secretary. In book iv., canto 6, Sir Art'egal is married to Brit'omart, and proceeds to succour Ire'na (Ireland), whose heritage had been withheld by the tyrant Grantorto. (*See* ARTHEGAL.)

Ar'temus Ward. A showman, very cute, and very American. The hypothetical writer of the essays or papers so called, the real author being Charles F. Browne.

Being asked if his name was Artĕmus or Artēmus, he wrote on his address card :—

> " Don't bother me with your etas and short e's,
> Nor ask me for more than you have on my
> card ;
> Oh ! spare me from etymological sorties,
> And simply accept me as Artemus Ward."

✝ Which, however, leaves the pronunciation of "Ward" doubtful.

Arte'sian Wells. So called from *Arte'sium* (the Latin for Artois), in France, where they were first bored.

Artful Dodger. A young thief, a most perfect adept in villainy, up to every sort of wicked dodge. (*Dickens: Oliver Twist.*)

Ar'thegal. Uterine brother of Prince Arthur. Spenser, in his *Faërie Queene* (book iii.), makes Brit'omart see his person and name in the magic glass. She falls in love with the looking-glass hero, and is told by Merlin that she will marry him, and become the mother of a line of kings that would supersede both the Saxons and Normans. He referred, of course, to the Tudors, who were descendants of Cadwallader. (*See* ARTEGAL.)

Arthur, King of the Sil'urēs, a tribe of ancient Britons, was mortally wounded in the battle of Camlan, in Cornwall, raised by the revolt of his nephew, Modred. He was taken to Glastonbury, where he died.

His wife was Guinever, who committed adultery with Sir Launcelot of the Lake, one of the Knights of the Round Table.

He was the natural *son* of Uther and Igerna (wife of Gorlois, duke of Cornwall), and was brought up by Sir Ector.

He *was born* at Tintad'gel or Tintagel, a castle in Cornwall.

His habitual *residence* was Caerleon, in Wales; and he was buried at Av'alon.

His *sword* was called *Excal'ibar* or *Excal'ibor ;* his *spear, Rone* (1 syl.), and his *shield, Pridwin.* His *dog* was named Cavall. (*See* ROUND TABLE KNIGHTS.)

Arthurian Romances. These may be divided into six parts :

(1) The romance of the *San Graal.* By Robert Borron.

(2) *The Merlin,* which celebrates the birth and exploits of King Arthur. By Walter Mapes.

(3) *The Launcelot.* Perhaps by Ulrich.

(4) The search or *Quest of the San Graal.* It is found by Sir Gal'ahad, a knight of pure heart and great courage ; but no sooner does he find it than he is taken up to heaven. By (?) Walter Mapes.

(5) The *Mort d'Arthur,* or *Death of* Arthur. By (?) Walter Mapes.

(6) *Sundry Tales,* but especially the adventures of Sir Tristan. By Luke Gast, of Salisbury.

Arthur's Seat, a hill near Edinburgh, is *A'rd Seir* (hill of arrows), where people shot at a mark.

Articles of Roup (Scotch). Conditions of sale at an auction announced by a crier. (Roup is the Teutonic *re-open,* to cry out.)

Artists, The Prince of, Albert Dürer ; so called by his countrymen. (1471-1528.)

Ar'toty'rites (4 syl.). Certain heretics from among the Montanists ; so called because they used bread and cheese in the Eucharist. They admitted women to the priesthood. (Greek, *artos,* barley-bread, and *turos,* cheese.)

Arts. *Degrees in Arts.* In the mediæval ages the full course consisted of the three subjects which constituted the *Triv'ium,* and the four subjects which constituted the *Quadriv'ium :*—

The *Triv'ium* was grammar, logic, and rhetoric.

The *Quadriv'ium* was music, arithmetic, geometry, and astronomy.

The Master of Arts was the person qualified to teach or be the master of students in arts ; as the Doctor was the person qualified to teach theology, law, or medicine.

Ar'undel. The heraldic device of the family is six swallows (*hirondelles*), a pun upon the name.

Arundel. (*See* HORSE.)

Arunde'lian Marbles. A collection of ancient sculptures collected at great expense by Thomas Howard, Earl of Arundel, and presented to the University of Oxford in 1667 by his grandson, Henry Howard, afterwards Duke of Norfolk. They contain tables of ancient chronology, especially that of Athens, from B.C. 1582 to 264, engraved in old Greek capitals. Date of the tables, B.C. 263.

Arvakur'. (*See* HORSE.)

A'ryans. The parent stock of what is called the Indo-European family of nations. They lived probably in Bactria, *i.e.* between the river Oxus and the Hindu-koosh mountains. The Aryan family of languages include the Persian and Hindû, with all the European except Basque, Turkish, Hungarian, and Finnic. Sometimes called the Indo-European, sometimes the Indo-Germanic, and sometimes the Japetic.

Sanskrit, Zend, Latin, Greek, and Celtic are, of course, included.

Arzi'na. A river that flows into the North Sea, near Wardhus, where Sir Willoughby's three ships were frozen, and the whole crew perished of starvation.

> 'In these fell regions, in Arzina caught,
> And to the stony deep his idle ship
> Immediate sealed, he with his hapless crew . . .
> Froze into statues."
> *Thomson : Winter*, 934.

As you were, in military drilling, means, Return to the position in which you were before the last exercise. As you were before.

Asa was a term of address to all the gods of Gladsheim ; as Asa Odin, Asa Thor, Asa Loki, Asa Tyr, etc.

> "'That's all very well, Asa Odin,' answered Frey ; 'but who, let me ask, is to undertake the feeding of the human animal ?'"—*Keary : Heroes of Asgard*, p. 73.

Asa Loki. Descended from the giants and received among the celestials. He is represented as a treacherous malignant power, fond of assuming disguises, and plotting evil. One of his progeny is Hela (*q.v.*). (*Scandinavian mythology.*) (*See* ÆSIR.)

Asa Thor. Eldest son of Asa Odin, and the first-born of mortals. (*Scandinavian mythology.*)

A'saph. A famous musician in David's time (1 Chron. xxv. 1, 2). Mr. Tate, who wrote the second part of *Absalom and Achitophel*, lauds Dryden under this name.

> "While Judah's throne and Sion's rock stand fast,
> The song of Asaph and the fame shall last."
> *Absalom and Achitophel*, part ii. 1063-4.

As'bolos. One of Actæon's dogs. The word means *soot-coloured*. (*See* AMARYNTHOS.)

Ascal'aphos. Turned by Proserpine, for mischief-making, into an owl. (*Greek fable.*)

As'capart. A giant conquered by Sir Bevis of Southampton. He was thirty feet high, and the space between his eyes was twelve inches. This mighty giant, whose effigy figures on the city gates of Southampton, could carry under his arm without feeling distressed Sir Bevis with his wife and horse. (*See* GIANTS.)

> "As Bevis of Southampton fell upon Ascapart."
> *Shakespeare : 2 Henry VI.*, act ii. 3.

Ascendant. In casting a horoscope the easternmost star, representing the house of life, is called the ascendant, because it is in the act of ascending. This is a man's strongest star, and so long as it is above the horizon his fortune is said to be in the ascendant. When a man's circumstances begin to improve, and things look brighter, we say *his star is in the ascendant.* (*See* HOUSES, STARS.)

House of the Ascendant includes five degrees of the zodiac above the point just rising, and twenty-five below it. Usually, the point of birth is referred to.

The lord of the Ascendant is any planet within the "house of the Ascendant." The house and lord of the Ascendant at birth were said by astrologers to exercise great influence on the future life of the child. Perhaps Deborah referred to the influence of the stars when she said "the stars in their courses fought against Sisera." (Judges v. 20.)

Ascension Day or *Holy Thursday*. The day set apart by the Catholic and Anglican Church to commemorate the ascent of our Lord from earth to heaven.

> Formerly it was customary to *beat the bounds* of each respective parish on this day, and many practical jokes were played even during the first quarter of the nineteenth century ; to make the boys remember the delimitations : such as " bumping them ;" pouring water clandestinely on them from house windows, beating them with thin rods, etc. Beating the bounds was called in Scotland *Riding the marches* (bounds).

Asclepi'adics or *Asclepiadic Metre*. A Greek and Latin verse, so called from Asclepi'ades, the inventor. Each line is divided into two parts, thus :—

$$- - \mid - \smile \smile - \parallel - \smile \smile - \mid \smile -$$

The first ode of Horace is Asclepi'adic. The first and last two lines run thus, and in the same metre :—

> Dear friend, patron of song, sprung from the race of kings ;
> Thy name ever a grace and a protection brings.

> . . . .
> My name, if to the lyre haply you chance to wed,
> Pride would high as the stars lift my exalted head.   E. C. B.

Ascod'rogites (4 syl.). Certain heretics who said "they were vessels full of new wine." (Greek, *askos*). By new wine they meant the Gospel. (Matt. ix. 17.)

Ascot Races. A very fashionable "meet," run on Ascot Heath, Berkshire (6 miles from Windsor). The best horses of all England compete, and at a somewhat more advanced age than at the "great classic races" (*q.v.*).

Ascræ'an Poet or *Sage*. Hesiod, the Greek didactic poet, born at Ascra, in Bœotia. Virgil calls him the "Old Ascræon." (*Eclogues*, vii. 70.)

As'gard. The fortress of the *Æsir* or the Northern gods, the Olympos of

Scandina'vian mythology. It is said to be situated in the centre of the universe, and accessible only by the rainbow-bridge (*Bifrost*). The word *As* means a "god," and *gard* an "enclosure," our "yard." Odin was priest of Asgard before he migrated to the Lake Logur or Mœlar Sea.

Ash Tree, or "Tree of the Universe." (*See* YGGDRASIL.)

Ash Wednesday. The first Wednesday in Lent, so called from an ancient Roman Catholic custom of sprinkling ashes on the heads of those condemned to do penance on this day.

The ashes were those of the palms burnt on Palm Sunday. The *pessimi* were sprinkled with ashes, the less offending were signed on the forehead with the sign of the cross, the officiating minister saying, "*Memento, homo, quia pulvis es, et in pulverem reverteris.*" The custom, it is said, was introduced by Gregory the Great.

Ashmo'lean Museum. Presented to the University of Oxford in 1682 by Elias Ashmole. Sometimes called the Trades'cant, because it belonged to the Tradescant family.

Ash'taroth. The goddess-moon in Syrian mythology, called by Jeremiah (vii. 18, xliv. 17, 25) "the queen of heaven." Goddess of the Zidonians.

" Moonèd Ashtaroth,
Heaven's queen and mother both."
Milton: The Hymn.

Ashur. The highest god of the Assyrians. It had the head of an eagle and four wings, but the body of a man.

"Out of that land went forth Asshur, and builded Nineveh."—Gen. x. 11.

As'inus. *As'inus as'inum fricat* (Latin, " one ass rubs another "), that is, we fraternise with persons like ourselves ; or, in other words, "Birds of a feather flock together." The allusion needs no explanation.

A'sir. [*See* ÆSIR.]

Ask. The vulgar *Ax* is the more correct (Saxon, *axian*, to ask). In assenting to Bills, the king used to reply, " Be it as it is axed." Chaucer says in the *Doctor of Medicine's Tale*, " For my werke nothing will I axe." Launfal, 1027, has, " Ho that wyll there axsy justus." Other quotations could easily be added.

Ask and **Embla.** The Adam and Eve made by Odin, one from ash-wood and the other from elm.

Aslo. (*See* HORSE.)

Asmode'us [*the destroyer*]. The demon of vanity and dress, called in the Talmud " the king of devils."

The Asmode'us of domestic peace (in the Book of Tobit). Asmode'us falls in love with Sara, daughter of Rag'uel, and causes the death of seven husbands in succession, each on his bridal night. After her marriage to Tobit, he was driven into Egypt by a charm, made by Tobias of the heart and liver of a fish burnt on perfumed ashes, and being pursued was taken prisoner and bound.

" Better pleased
Than Asmode'us with the fishy fume
That drove him, though enamoured, from the spouse
Of Tobit's son, and with a vengeance sent
From Media post to Egypt, there fast bound."
Milton : Paradise Lost, iv. 167-71.

Asmode'us. The companion of Don Cle'ofas in *The Devil on Two Sticks.* (Chap. iii.)

Asmode'us flight. Don Cle'ofas, catching hold of his companion's cloak, is perched on the steeple of St. Salva'dor. Here the foul fiend stretches out his hand, and the roofs of all the houses open in a moment, to show the Don what is going on privately in each respective dwelling.

"Could the reader take an Asmodeus-flight, and, waving open all roofs and privacies, look down from the roof of Notre Dame, what a Paris were it !"—*Carlyle : French Revolution II.,* vi. chap. vi.

As'oka of Magad'ha. In the third century the " nursing father" of Buddhism, as Constantine was of Christianity. He is called " the king beloved of the gods."

Aso'ors. Evil genii of the Indians.

Aspa'sia, a courtesan. She was the most celebrated of the Greek Hetæræ, to whom Per'iclēs attached himself. On the death of Pericles she lived with Lys'iclēs, a cattle-dealer.

⁕ The Hetæræ of Athens were, many of them, distinguished for talents and accomplishments. Those of Corinth were connected with the worship of Aphrodītē (Venus).

Aspa'tia, in the *Maid's Tragedy*, of Beaumont and Fletcher, is noted for her deep sorrows, her great resignation, and the pathos of her speeches. Amyn'tor deserts her, women point at her with scorn, she is the jest and bye-word of every one, but she bears it all with patience.

Aspen. The aspen leaf is said to tremble, from shame and horror, because our Lord's cross was made of this wood. The fact is this : the leaf is broad, and placed on a long leaf-stalk so flexible as scarcely to be able to support it in an upright position. The upper part of the stalk, on which the play mainly depends, is flattened; and, being at right angles with the leaf, is peculiarly liable to be acted on by the least breath of air.

Aspen leaf. Metaphorically, a chattering tongue, never quiet.

"Those aspen leaves of theirs never leave wagging."—*Sir T. More.*

Asper'sions properly means "sprinklings" or "scatterings." Its present meaning is base insinuations or slanders.

"No sweet aspersion [*rain*] shall the heavens let fall
To make this contract grow."
Shakespeare: The Tempest, iv. 1.

Casting aspersions on one, i.e. sprinkling with calumnies, slandering or insinuating misconduct.

"I defy all the world to cast a just aspersion on my character."—*Fielding: Tom Jones.*

Asphal'tic Lake. The Dead Sea, where asphalt abounds both on the surface of the water and on the banks. Asphalt is a bitumen. (From the Greek *asphaltos.*)

As'rael. (*See* AZRAEL.)

Ass. (*See* GOLDEN ASS.)

Ass. The ass on which Mahomet went to heaven to learn the will of God was called *Al Borak* (the lightning).

Ass. There is a dark stripe running down the back of an ass, crossed by another at the shoulders. The tradition is that this cross was communicated to the creature when our Lord rode on the back of an ass in His triumphant entry into Jerusalem. (*See* CHRISTIAN TRADITIONS.)

Ass, deaf to music. This tradition arose from the hideous noise made by "Sir Balaam" in braying. Because Midas had no power to appreciate music, Apollo gave him the ears of an ass. (*See* ASS-EARED.)

"Avarice is as deaf to the voice of virtue, as the ass to the voice of Apollo."—*Orlando Furioso,* xvii.

An ass in a lion's skin. A coward who hectors, a fool that apes the wise man. The allusion is to the fable of an ass that put on a lion's hide, but was betrayed when he began to bray.

An ass with two panniers. A man walking the streets with a lady on each arm. This occupies the whole pavement, and is therefore bad manners well meriting the reproach. In Italy they call such a simpleton a *pitcher with two handles,* his two arms akimbo forming

the two handles. In London we call it walking *bodkin,* because the man is sheathed like a bodkin and powerless. Our expression is probably a corruption of the French *Faire le panier à deux anses* ("put your arms akimbo" or "make yourself a basket with two handles").

The ass waggeth his ears. This proverb is applied to those who lack learning, and yet talk as if they were very wise; men wise in their own conceit. The ass, proverbial for having no "taste for music," will nevertheless wag its ears at a "concord of sweet sounds," just as if it could well appreciate it.

Till the ass ascends the ladder—i.e. never. A rabbinical expression. The Romans had a similar one, *Cum as'inus in teg'ulis ascen'derit* (when the ass climbs to the tiles). And Buxtorf has *Si ascen'derit as'inus per scalas.*

Sell your ass. Get rid of your foolish ways.

That which thou knowest not perchance thine ass can tell thee. An allusion to Balaam's ass.

To make an ass of oneself. To do something very foolish. To expose oneself to ridicule.

To mount the ass (French). To become bankrupt. The allusion is to a custom very common in the sixteenth century of mounting a bankrupt on an ass, with his face to its tail. Thus mounted, the defaulter was made to ride through the principal thoroughfares of the town.

Asses have ears as well as pitchers. Children, and even the densest minds, hear and understand many a word and hint which the speaker supposed would pass unheeded.

Asses that carry the mysteries (*as'inus portat myste'ria*). A classical knock at the Roman clergy. The allusion is to the custom of employing asses to carry the *cista* which contained the sacred symbols, when processions were made through the streets. (*Warburton: Divine Legation,* ii. 4.)

Well, well! honey is not for the ass's mouth. Persuasion will not persuade fools. The gentlest words will not divert the anger of the unreasonable.

Wrangle for an ass's shadow. To contend about trifles. The tale told by Demosthĕnēs is, that a man hired an ass to take him to Megăra; and at noon, the sun being very hot, the traveller dismounted, and sat himself down in the shadow of the ass. Just then the owner came up and claimed the right of sitting in this shady spot, saying that he let out the ass for hire, but there was no bargain made about the ass's shade. The two men then fell to blows to settle the point in dispute. A passer-by told the traveller to move on, and leave the owner of the beast to walk in the ass's shadow as long as he thought proper.

Ass's Bridge (*The*). Prop. 5, book i. of Euclid. This is the first difficult proposition in geometry, and stupid boys rarely get over it the first time without tripping.

It is the ass's *pitfall*, not his bridge.

If this be rightly called the "Bridge of Asses," He's not the fool who sticks, but he that passes. E. C. B.

Asses (*Feast of*). (*See* FOOLS.)

Ass-eared. Midas had the ears of an ass. The tale says Apollo and Pan had a contest, and chose Midas to decide which was the better musician. Midas gave sentence in favour of Pan; and Apollo, in disgust, changed his ears into those of an ass.

Assas'sins. A band of Carmathians, collected by Hassan, subah of Nish'-apour, called the *Old Man of the Mountains*, because he made Mount Leb'anon his stronghold. This band was the terror of the world for two centuries, when it was put down by Sultan Bib'aris. The assassins indulged in *haschisch* (bang), an intoxicating drink, and from this liquor received their name. (A.D. 1090.)

"The Assassins . . . . before they attacked the enemy, would intoxicate themselves with a powder made of hemp-leaves . . . . called *hashish*."—*J. Wolff.*

Assay' or **Essay'**. To take the *assay* is to taste wine to prove it is not poisoned. Hence, to *try*, to *taste*; a *savour*, *trial*, or *sample*. Holinshed says, "Wolsey made dukes and earls serve him of wine with a *say* taken" (p. 847).

Edmund, in *King Lear* (v. 5), says to Edgar, "Thy tongue, some *say* of breeding breathes;" *i.e.* thy speech gives indication of good breeding—it savours of it. Hence the expression, *I make my first assay* (trial).

"[He] makes vow before his uncle never more To give the assay of arms against your majesty." *Shakespeare: Hamlet,* ii. 2.

A cup of assay. A cup for the assay of wine.

To put it in assay. To put it to the test.

Assaye Regiment. The 74th Foot, so called because they first distinguished themselves in the battle of Assaye, where 2,000 British and 2,500 Sepoy troops under Wellington defeated 50,000 Mahrattas, commanded by French officers, in 1803. This regiment is now called "the 2nd Battalion of the Highland Light Infantry." The first battalion was the old No. 71.

Assien'to Treaties. [Spanish, *agreement treaties*.] Contracts entered into by Spain with Portugal, France, and England, to supply her South American colonies with negro slaves. England joined in 1713, after the peace of Utrecht.

Ass'ine'go. A young ass, a simpleton (a Portuguese word).

"Thou hast no more brain than I have in mine elbows; an assinego may tutor thee."—*Shakespeare: Troilus and Cressida,* ii. 1.

Assumption (*Feast of the*). The 15th of August, so called in honour of the Virgin Mary, who (according to the Roman and Greek Churches) was taken to heaven that day (A.D. 45), in her corporeal form, being at the time seventy-five years of age.

This seems very improbable, if Christ was crucified A.D. 33. It would make Mary survive her son twelve years, and to have been thirty years old at his birth instead of about fifteen.

Assurance. Audacity, brazen self-confidence. "His assurance is quite unbearable."

To make assurance double sure. To make security doubly secure.

"But yet I'll make assurance double sure, And take a bond of fate." *Shakespeare: Macbeth,* iv. 1.

Astag'oras (in *Jerusalem Delivered*). A female fiend, who had the power of raising storms, and whose partners were the three Furies: Tisiph'onē, Meg'ara, and Alec'to.

Astar'te (3 syl.). Goddess of the Moon, in Phœnician mythology.

"With these in troop Came Astoreth, whom the Phœnicians called Astartē, queen of heaven, with crescent horns." *Milton: Paradise Lost,* i. 437-9.

Astarte (3 syl.). The lady beloved by Manfred. In order to see and speak to her, the magician entered the hall of Arima'nēs, and the spirits called up the phantom of the young lady, which told the count that "to-morrow would end his earthly ills." When Manfred asked her if she loved him, she sighed "Manfred," and vanished. (*Byron: Manfred.*)

"Astarte, my belovèd, speak to me." *Manfred,* ii. 4.

As'tolat. By some identified with Guildford, in Surrey.

Astol'pho (in *Orlando Furioso*). An English duke (son of Otho), who joined Charlemagne against the Saracens. He was carried on the back of a whale to Alci'na's isle; but when Alcina tired of him, she turned him into a myrtle. He was disenchanted by Melissa. Astolpho descended into the infernal regions, and his flight to the moon (book xviii.) is one of the best parts of the whole poem. (*See* INFERNO.)

It came upon them like a blast from Astolpho's horn — *i.e.* it produced a panic. Logistilla gave Astolpho a magic horn, and whatever man or beast heard its blast was seized with panic, and became an easy captive. (*Orlando Furioso*, book viii.)

Like Astolpho's book, it told you everything. The same fairy gave Astolpho a book, which would not only direct him aright in his journeys, but would tell him anything he desired to know. (*Ariosto : Orlando Furioso*, book viii.)

As'toreth. (*See* ASHTAROTH.)

Astræ'a. Equity, innocence. During the Golden Age this goddess dwelt on earth, but when sin began to prevail, she reluctantly left it, and was metamorphosed into the constellation *Virgo*.

" When hard-hearted interest first began
To poison earth, Astræa left the plain."
Thomson: Castle of Indolence, canto 1.

Astral Body (*The*). The noumenon of a phenomenal body. This "spirit body" survives after the death of the material body, and is the "ghost" or "double." Macbeth's dagger was an astral body; so, in theosophy, is the "kama-rupa" or mind body; and in transubstantiation the veritable "blood and flesh" of Christ is the astral body of the accidents "bread and wine."

Man is supposed to consist of body, soul, and spirit. The last is the astral body of man.

Astral Spirits. The spirits of the stars. According to the mythology of the Persians, Greeks, Jews, etc., each star has its special spirit. Paracelsus maintained that every man had his attendant star, which received him at death, and took charge of him till the great resurrection.

Astre'a. A poetical name of Mrs. Aphra Behn, born of good family in the reign of Charles I. Her works are very numerous and very indecent, including seventeen dramatic pieces. She died 1689, and was buried in Westminster Abbey.

"The stage how loosely does Astrea tread."
Pope : Satires, v. 290.

Astrology. (*See* DIAPASON, MICROCOSM.)

Astronomer of Dublin (*The*). The head of the chief rebel of Dublin, set on a tall white-painted stake on the highest point of Dublin Castle, where it remains till it falls to decay or is replaced by the head of a greater rebel. The Irish say: "God send to Dublin many more astronomers."

" His head is poled high
Upon the castle here,
Beholding stars as though he were
A great astronomer." *Derrick.*

Astronomers Royal: (1) Flamsteed, 1675 ; (2) Halley, 1719 ; (3) Bradley, 1742 ; (4) Bliss, 1762 ; (5) Maskelyne, who originated the Nautical Almanack, 1765 ; (6) Pond, 1811 ; (7) Airy, 1835 ; (8) Christie, 1881.

As'trophel. Sir Philip Sidney. "Phil. Sid." being a contraction of Philos Sidus, and the Latin *sidus* being changed to the Greek *astron*, we get *astron-philos* (star-lover). The "star" that he loved was Penelope Devereux, whom he called *Stella* (star), and to whom he was betrothed. Edmund Spenser wrote a pastoral called *Astrophel*, to the memory of his friend and patron, who fell at the battle of Zutphen. (1554-1586.)

Asy'lum means, literally, a place where pillage is forbidden (Greek, *a* (negative), *sulon*, right of pillage). The ancients set apart certain places of refuge, where the vilest criminals were protected, both from private and public assaults.

Asyniur. The goddesses of Asgard. The gods were called the Æsir, the singular of which is *Asa*.

At. *Strain at a gnat* (Matt. xxiii. 24). Greek, *di-aulizo*, to strain off. Here "at" is an error, probably in the first instance typographical, for "out." "Out" is given in the Bible of 1603, and has been restored by the Revisers.

Ate (2 syl.). Goddess of vengeance and mischief. This goddess was driven out of heaven, and took refuge among the sons of men.

"With Atě by his side come hot from hell, . . .
Cry ' Havoc,' and let slip the dogs of war."
Shakespeare: Julius Cæsar, iii. 1.

Atella'næ or *Atell'an Fables.* Interludes in the Roman theatres, introduced from Atella, in Campa'nia. The characters of Macchus and Bucco are the foundations of our Punch and Clown. (*See* PUNCH.)

Ater'gata. A deity with the upper part like a woman and the lower part like a fish. She had a temple at As'calon. (*See* DAGON.)

Athana'sian Creed, so called because it embodies the opinions of Athana'sius respecting the Trinity. It was compiled in the fifth century by Hilary, Bishop of Arles.
⁎⁎ In the Episcopal Prayer Book of America this creed is omitted.

Athel'stane (3 syl.), surnamed "The Unready" (*i.e.* impolitic, unwise), thane of Coningsburgh. (*Sir Walter Scott: Ivanhoe.*)

Athenæum (the review so called) was founded by James Silk Buckingham in 1829. It was named after the institution founded by Hadrian, where works of art and learning were dedicated to Athēnē.

Athe'nian Bee. Plato, a native of Athens, was so called because his words flowed with the sweetness of honey.

Athens. *The Modern Athens, i.e.* Edinburgh. Willis says that its singular resemblance to Athens, approached from the Piræus, is very striking.

"An imitation Acrop'olis is commenced on the Calton Hill, and has the effect of the Parthenon. Hymettus is rather more lofty than t.e Pentland hills, and Pentel'icus is farther off and grander than Arthur's Seat ; but the old Castle of Edinburgh is a noble feature, superbly magnificent."—*Pencillings.*

Athens of Ireland. Belfast.

Athens of the New World. Boston, noted for its literary merit and institutions.

Athens of the West. Cor'dova, in Spain, was so called in the Middle Ages.

Athole Brose (Scotch). A compound of oatmeal, honey, and whisky.

At Home (*An*). A notification sent to friends that the lady who sends it will be at home on the day and at the hour specified, and will be glad to see the persons mentioned in the card of invitation. These "At homes" are generally held in an afternoon before dinner. Light refreshments are provided, and generally some popular games are introduced, occasionally music and dancing.

Not at Home. Not disengaged, or prepared for the reception of visitors ; not in the house.

Atin. *Strife.* The squire of Pyrochlēs, and stirrer up of contention. (*Spenser : Faërie Queene,* book ii.)

Atkins. (*See* TOMMY ATKINS.)

Atlante'an Shoulders. Shoulders able to bear a great weight, like those of Atlas, which, according to heathen mythology, supported the whole world.

"Sage he stood,
With Atlantean shoulders fit to bear
The weight of mightiest monarchies."
Milton : Paradise Lost, book ii. 305-7.

Atlan'tes. Figures of men, used in architecture instead of pillars. So called from Atlas, who in Greek mythology supported the world on his shoulders. Female figures are called Caryat'idēs (*q.v.*). (*See* TELAMONES.)

Atlan'tes (3 syl.) (in *Orlando Furioso*). A sage and a magician who lived in an enchanted palace, and brought up Roge'ro to all manly virtues.

Atlan'tic Ocean. An ocean, so called from the Atlas mountains.

Atlant'is. A mythic island which contained the Elysian Fields.
The New Atlantis. An island imagined by Lord Bacon, where was established a philosophical commonwealth bent on the cultivation of the natural sciences. (*See* UTOPIA, CITY OF THE SUN.)

Atlas. King of Maurita'nia in Africa, fabled to have supported the world upon his shoulders. Of course, the tale is merely a poetical way of saying that the Atlas mountains prop up the heavens, because they are so lofty. We call a book of maps an "Atlas," because it contains or holds the world. The word was first employed in this sense by Merca'tor, and the title-page of his collection of maps had the figure of Atlas with the world on his back.

"Bid Atlas, propping heaven, as poets feign,
His subterranean wonders spread !"
Thomson : Autumn, 797-8.

Atman, in Buddhist philosophy, is the noumenon of one's own self. Not the Ego, but the ego divested of all that is objective ; the "spark of heavenly flame."

"The unseen and unperceivable, which was formerly called the soul, was now called the self, Atman. Nothing could be predicated of it except that it was, that it perceived and thought, and that it must be blessed." — *Max Müller: Nineteenth Century,* May, 1893, p. 777.

Atom'ic Philosophy. The hypothesis of Leucippus, Democri̇tus, and Epicūrus, that the world is composed of a congeries of atoms, or particles of matter so minute as to be incapable of further diminution.

Of course it is quite impossible even to think of a portion of matter which has not an upper and under side, with some breadth and thickness.

"According to Democritus, the expounder of the Atomic Theory of matter, images composed of the finest atoms floated from the object to the mind."—*McCosh: Psychological Cognitive Powers*, p. 23.

Atom'ic Theory. That all elemental bodies consist of aggregations of atoms, not united fortuitously, but according to fixed proportions. The four laws of Dalton are—constant proportion, reciprocal proportion, multiple proportion, and compound proportion.

∵ This has nothing to do with the atomic theory of Leucippus. It merely means that gases and other elements always combine in certain known ratios or units.

Atom'ic Volume. The space occupied by a quantity, compared with, or in proportion to, atomic weight.

Atom'ic Weight. The weight of an atom of an element, compared with an atom of hydrogen, the standard of unity.

Atos'sa. Sarah, Duchess of Marlborough, so called by Pope, because she was the friend of Lady Mary Wortley Montague, whom he calls *Sappho*. Herod'otus says that Atossa, the mother of Xerxes, was a follower of Sappho.

Atrip. The anchor is *atrip* when it has just been drawn from the ground in a perpendicular direction. A sail is *atrip* when it has been hoisted from the cap, and is ready for trimming. The word is from the Norwegian and Danish *trip*, a short step.

Attaint. A term in chivalry, meaning to strike the helmet and shield of an antagonist so firmly with the lance, held in a direct line, as either to break the lance or overthrow the person struck. Hence to "attaint of treason," etc.

"Attaint was a term of tilting, used to express the champion's having attained his mark, or, in other words, struck his lance straight and fair against the helmet or breast of his adversary."—*Sir Walter Scott: The Monastery* (note).

At'tercop. An ill-tempered person, who mars all sociability. Strictly speaking, the attercop is the poison-spider. (Anglo-Saxon, *atter*, poison; *cop*, spider. Our cob-web should be cop-web, *i.e.* spider-web.)

Attic Bee (*The*). Soph'oclēs, the tragic poet, a native of Athens; so called from the great sweetness of his compositions. (B.C. 495-405.)

Attic Bird (*The*). The nightingale;

3*

so called because Philomel was the daughter of the King of Athens.

" Where the Attic bird
Trills her thick-warbled notes the summer long."
Milton: Paradise Regained, iv. 245-6.

Attic Boy (*The*). Cephălos, beloved by Aurora or Morn; passionately fond of hunting.

" Till civil-suited Morn appear,
Not tricked and frounced, as she was wont
With the Attic boy to hunt,
But kerchiefed in a comely cloud."
Milton: Il Penseroso.

Attic Faith. Inviolable faith, the very opposite of "Punic Faith."

Attic Muse (*The*). Xenophon, the historian, a native of Athens; so called because the style of his composition is a model of elegance. (B.C. 444-359.)

Attic Order, in architecture, a square column of any of the five orders. (*See* ORDERS.)

Attic Salt. Elegant and delicate wit. Salt, both in Latin and Greek, was a common term for *wit*, or sparkling thought well expressed: thus Cicero says, " *Scipio omnes sale supera'bat* " (Scipio surpassed all in wit). The Athenians were noted for their wit and elegant turns of thought, and hence Attic salt means wit as pointed and delicately expressed as by the Athenians. "Attic point," wit.

Attic Science. A knowledge of Attic Greek.

Attics, Attic Storey. Attics are the rooms in the attic storey, and the attic storey generally is an extra storey made in the roof. In the Roman and Renaissance styles of architecture the low storey above the cornice or entablature is called the "Attic." Professor Goldstücker derives the word from the Sanskrit *attaka* (a room on the top of a house). (*See* The Transactions of the Philological Society, 1854.)

Attic storey. The head; the body being compared to a house, the head is the highest, or attic storey.

" Here a gentleman present, who had in his attic
More pepper than brains, shrieked: 'The man's a fanatic.'"
Lowell: Fable for Critics (stanza 50).

Ill furnished in the attic storey. Not clever, dull.

Queer in the attic storey. Fuddled, partially intoxicated.

At'ticus. The most elegant and finished scholar of the Romans. His admirable taste and sound judgment were so highly thought of that even Cicero submitted to him several of his treatises.

The English Atticus. Joseph Addison; so called by Pope, on account of his refined taste and philosophical mind. (1672-1719.)

The Christian Atticus. Reginald Heber, Bishop of Calcutta. (1783-1826.)

The Irish Atticus. George Faulkner; so called by Lord Chesterfield. (1700-1775.)

Attin'gians. Heretics of the eighth century, who solemnised baptism with the words, "I am the living water." (Attin, a name of Neptune.)

Attock. The forbidden river, beyond which no pure Hindoo can pass.

Attorney, Solicitor (French, *atourner*, to attorn, or turn over to another). One legally qualified to manage matters in law for others, and to prosecute or defend others, as the case may be. A *solicitor* is one who solicits or petitions in Courts of Equity on behalf of his clients. At one time solicitors belonged to Courts of Equity, and attorneys to the other courts.

From and after Act 36, 37 Vict. lxvi. 87, "all persons admitted as solicitors, attorneys, or proctors . . . . empowered to practise in any court, the jurisdiction of which is hereby transferred to the High Court of Justice, or the Court of Appeal, shall be called Solicitors of the Supreme Court." (1873.)

Power of Attorney. Legal authority given to another to collect rents, pay wages, invest money, or to act in matters stated in the instrument on your behalf, according to his own judgment. In such cases *quod aliquis facit per aliquem, facit per se.*

Warrant of Attorney. The legal instrument which confers on another the "Power of Attorney."

A'tys. Metamorphosed into a fir-tree by Cyb'elē. *See* the poem by Catullus, translated by Leigh Hunt.

Au Courant (French), "acquainted with " (lit. = in the current [of events]). *To keep one au courant of everything that passes,* is to keep one familiar with, or informed of, passing events.

Au Fait (French). Skilful, thorough master of; as, *He is quite au fait in those matters, i.e.* quite master of them or conversant with them.

Au Grand Sérieux (French). In sober earnest.

"We are not asked to take these narratives *au grand sérieux.* They are rather sketches of the past, illustrating what could have been done, and may be done again by women . . . ."—*Notes and Queries (Notes on Books,* June 10, 1893, p. 459).

Au Pied de la Lettre (French). *Literatim et verbatim;* according to the strict letter of the text.

"In reading *au pied de la lettre* the story of his [Buddha's] fatal illness supervened on a meal of 'dried boar's flesh,' served to him by a certain Kunda."—*Nineteenth Century* (June, 1893, p. 1020).

Au Revoir (French). "Good bye for the present." Literally, *till seeing you again.*

Aubry's Dog. (*See* Dog.)

Au'deanism. The doctrine of Au'deus of Mesopotamia, who lived in the fourth century. He maintained that the Old Testament justifies the belief that God has a sensible form (Gen. i. 26).

Audhum'la [*the nourishing power*], in Scandinavian mythology, is the cow created by Surt to nourish Ymir. She supplied him with four rivers of milk, and was herself nourished by licking the rocks. (*See* Ymir.)

⁛ Bör, the first man, was made by Audhumla licking salt from the snow. Odin was the son of Bör.

The breath of Audhumla was very sweet, but her milk was bitter.

Audley. *We will John Audley it, i.e.* abridge it. A theatrical phrase. In the eighteenth century one Shuter had a travelling company which visited different fairs. It was his custom to lengthen out his performance till a goodly number of newcomers had collected on the open stage of his theatre, when a boy called out *John Audley,* and the play which was going on inside was brought to an end as soon as possible. (1759.)

Aud'rey. A country wench, who jilted William for Touchstone. (*Shakespeare: As You Like It.*)

Auge'an Stables. The stables of Augēas, King of Elis, in Greece. In these stables he had kept 3,000 oxen, and the stalls had not been cleansed for thirty years. When Herculēs was appointed to cleanse these stables, he caused two rivers to run through them.

To cleanse the Augean stables. To clear away an accumulated mass of corruption, moral, religious, physical, or legal. To reform wrongs almost past the power of man to tackle.

Augsburg Confession. The chief standard of faith in the Lutheran church. So called because, while the Diet of the German Empire was sitting at Augsburg, in 1530, the confession of faith drawn up by Melancthon and Luther was presented to Charles V.

Au'gury means properly the function of an augur (perhaps from *avium garritus*). St. Pierre says: "The first navigators, when out of sight of land, watched the flight of birds, as indications of the shore, and with no other guidance discovered many new islands." From this custom (he says) arose the practice of consulting birds before entering on any important enterprise. (*Studies.*)

August. The sixth month (beginning from March) was once called *sextilis*, but was changed to Augustus in compliment to Augustus Cæsar of Rome, whose "lucky month" it was, in which occurred many of his most fortunate events.

The preceding month (July), originally called *Quintilis*, had already been changed to Julius in honour of Julius Cæsar.

Augusta. London; so called by the Romans.

> "Oft let me wander o'er the dewy fields,
> . . . . or ascend
> Some eminence, Augusta, in thy plains,
> And see the country far diffused around."
> *Thomson: Spring*, 102, 107-9.

Augustan Age. The best literary period of a nation; so called from Augustus, the Emperor of Rome, the most palmy time of Latin literature. Horace, Ovid, Propertius, Tibullus, Virgil, etc., flourished in this reign.

Augustan Age of English Literature. Beginning in the reign of Elizabeth and ending in that of James I. For list of authors, see *Historic Note-book*, p. 59.

Augustan Age of China, France, Germany, Hindustan, Portugal, etc., see ditto.

Augustan History. A series of histories of the Roman Empire from 157 to 285, ascribed to the six following authors: Delius Spartianus, Julius Capitolinus, Ælius Lampridius, Vulcatius Gallicanus, Trebellius Pollio, and Flavius Vopiscus.

Augustine (*The Second*). Thomas Aquinas, also called the *Angelic Doctor*. (1224-1275.)

Augustinians. Friars or nuns of the Augustine Order, established in the eleventh century in commemoration of St. Augustine, and in imitation of the ancient order founded by him in the fourth century.

Those who believe, on the authority of St. Augustine, in absolute predestination and effectual grace. That is, that predestination is quite independent of man, and that grace has no reference to

preceding piety and moral conduct, but is vouchsafed by God's own absolute will. Whom He would He did predestinate, and "whom He did predestinate, them He also called" (Romans viii. 30).

Augustus. No proper name, but a mere title given to Octavian, because he was head of the priesthood. In the reign of Diocle'tian the two emperors were each styled *Augustus* (sacred majesty), and the two viceroys *Cæsar*. Prior to that time Ha'drian limited the title of *Cæsar* to the heir presumptive.

Augustus. Philippe II. of France; so called because he was born in the month of August. (1165, 1180-1223.)

Sigismund II. of Poland. (1520, 1548-1572.)

Aulay, in Indian mythology, is the horse with a huge trunk, on which Baly the giant rode.

> "Through these wide portals oft had Baly rode
> Triumphant from his proud abode,
> When, in his greatness, he bestrode
> The Aulay, hugest of four-footed kind.
> The Aulay-horse, that in his force
> With elephantine trunk, could bind
> And lift the elephant, and on the wind
> Whirl him away, with sway and swing,
> E'en like a pebble from the practised sling."
> *Southey: Curse of Kehama*, xvi. 2.

Auld Brig and **New Brig**, of Robert Burns, refers to the bridges over the river Ayr, in Scotland.

Auld Hornie. After the establishment of Christianity, the heathen deities were degraded by the Church into fallen angels; and Pan, with his horns, crooked nose, goat's beard, pointed ears, and goats' feet, was transformed to his Satanic majesty, and called Old Horny.

> "O thou, whatever title suit thee,
> Auld Hornie, Satan, Nick, or Clootie."
> *Burns.*

Auld Reekie. Edinburgh old town; so called because it generally appears to be capped by a cloud of "reek" or smoke.

Aulic Council. The council of the Kaiser in the old German Empire, from which there was no appeal (1495-1806) (Latin, *aula*, a court). The name is now given in Austria to a council of Vienna which manages the war department of the Austrian Empire.

Aunt Sally. A game in which a wooden head is mounted on a pole. The fun of the game is to knock the nose of the figure, or break the pipe stuck in its mouth. This is to be done by throwing at it, from a stated distance, a short club. The word *aunt* was anciently applied to any old woman: thus, in Shakespeare, Puck speaks of

> "The wisest aunt telling the saddest tale."
> *Midsummer Night's Dream*, ii. 1.

Aure'ola. A circle of light, emblematical of glory, placed by the old painters round the heads of martyrs and saints. The notion was derived from Exod. xxv. 25. *Facies coro'nam aure'olam* ("Thou shalt by thine own merits make for thyself a crown, besides that of gold which God has promised to the faithful") (*Donne: Sermons*). Strictly speaking, the glory confined to the head alone is a *nimbus*, and only when it envelops the entire body, is it called an aureola.

Du Cange informs us that the aureola of nuns is *white*, of martyrs *red*, and of doctors *green*.

∴ The nimbus of a Christ should contain a cross; of the Virgin Mary, a circlet of stars; of God the Father, a triangle with rays; of a living saint, a square without rays.

> "They say, who know the life divine,
> And upward gaze with eagle eyne,
> That by each golden crown on high,
> Rich with celestial jewelry,
> Which for our Lord's redeemed is set,
> There hangs a radiant coronet,
> All gemmed with pure and living light
> Too dazzling for a sinner's sight,
> Prepared for virgin souls, and them
> Who seek the martyr's diadem."
> *Keble: Christian Year.*

Au'ri. *Auri sacra famēs* (the cursed hunger for wealth), applied to that restless craving for money which is almost a monomania.

Auro'ra. Early morning. According to Grecian mythology, the goddess Aurora, called by Homer "rosy-fingered," sets out before the sun, and is the pioneer of his rising.

> "You cannot shut the windows of the sky,
> Through which Aurora shows her brightening face."
> *Thomson: Castle of Indolence*, canto ii. 3.

Aurora's tears. The morning dew.

Auro'ra Austra'lis. The Southern lights, a similar phenomenon to the "Aurora Borealis."

Auro'ra Borea'lis (Latin). The electrical lights occasionally seen in the northern part of the sky; also called "Northern Lights," and "Merry Dancers." (*See* DERWENTWATER.)

Aurora Raby. A rich, noble English orphan; left to the care of guardians; a Catholic in religion; and in person

> "A rose with all its sweetest leaves yet folded."
> *Byron: Don Juan*, xv. 43.

Auro'ra Septentriona'lis. Same as Aurora Austrālis (*q.v.*).

Auso'nia. An ancient name of Italy; so called from Auson, son of Ulysses, and father of the Auso'nēs.

> "All the green delights Ausonia pours."
> *Thomson: Summer*, 956.

Aus'pices. *Under your good auspices*, *i.e.* through your influence, or the influence of your good name. In Rome only the Commander-in-Chief was allowed to take the auspices of war. If a legate gained a victory, he was said to win it under the good auspices of his superior in command.

"Auspex" is from *avispex* (*avis* and *spicio*), one who observes the flight, etc., of birds.

Aus'ter. A wind pernicious to flowers and health. In Italy one of the *South* winds was so called; its modern name is the *Sirocco.* (Greek, *auste'ros*, hot, dry). In England it is a damp wind, generally bringing wet weather.

> "Nought but putrid streams and noisome fogs,
> For ever hung on drizzly Auster's beard."
> *Thomson: Castle of Indolence*, ii. 78.

Austin Friars. Friars of the Order of St. Augustine. (*See* BEGGING.)

Austrian Lip. The thick under-lip, characteristic of the house of Haps'burg. Derived from Cymburgis, daughter of Ziemovitz, Duke of Maso'via, and niece of the then King of Poland. Cymburgis was noted for her beauty and unusual strength.

Aut Cæsar aut nullus [Latin, *Either Cæsar or no one*], everything or nothing; all or not at all. Cæsar used to say, "he would sooner be first in a village than second at Rome." Milton makes Satan say,

> "Better to reign in Hell, than serve in Heaven."
> *Milton: Par. Lost*, i. 263.

(*See* SIX.)

Authen'tic Doctor. Gregory of Rim'ini. (Fourteenth century.)

Auto da Fe. [*An act of faith.*] A day set apart by the Inquisition for the examination of "heretics." Those not acquitted were burnt. The reason why inquisitors *burnt* their victims was, because they are forbidden to "shed blood"; an axiom of the Roman Catholic Church being, "*Ecclesia non novit san'guinem*" (the church is untainted with blood).

Autol'ycus. The craftiest of thieves. He stole the flocks of his neighbours, and changed their marks. Si'syphos outwitted him by marking his sheep under their feet, a device which so tickled the rogue that he instantly "cottoned" to him. Shakespeare introduces him in *The Winter's Tale* as a pedlar, and says he was called the son of Mercury, because he was born under that "thieving planet."

"Autolycus is no lapidary, though he drives a roaring trade in flash jewellery." — *Pall Mall Gazette.*

Autom'aton—plural, *automatons* or *automata.* Machines which imitate the actions, etc., of living creatures. The most famous are the following :—(1) The *pigeon* that could fly, made, B.C. 400, by Archy'tas, of Tarentum ; (2) the wooden *eagle* of Regiomonta'nus, the German, which flew from the city of Kœnigsberg to meet the emperor, saluted him, and returned, 1436-1476 ; (3) the *duck* of Vaucanson of Grenoble, which could eat and drink, and, even in a way digest food; its wings, viscera, bones, etc., minutely resembled those of a living animal. Vaucanson also made an image of Pan, which, at the beck of Syrinx, rose from his seat, played on his pipe, bowed when applauded, and sat down again. He also made an asp which, on being touched by an actress, in the character of Cleopatra, flew at her breast with a malignant hiss. Louis XV. set him to make a human figure, but he died before he had completed it. (Greek, *autos-mao,* I self-move.) (*See* ANDROID.)

.* Pierre Droz and his son Louis were noted for their automatons ; so was Frederick of Knause (Vienna). The chess-player of Wolfgang, baron of Kempelen, in 1784, created quite a furor in Paris. Napoleon on one occasion played chess with this automaton. (*See* BRAZEN HEADS.)

Autom'edon. A coachman. He was the charioteer of Achilles.

Autumn. *He is come to his autumn, i.e.* to be hanged, to his "fall." A pun on the plan of "turning a man off" by dropping the plank on which he stands. The drop is the "leaf," and autumn is called the "fall," or "fall of the leaf."

A'va, in Burmah, has marble quarries of which idols are made, and only priests are allowed to trade there. (*Symes,* vol. ii. p. 376.)

"As on Ava's shore,
Where none but priests are privileged to trade
In that best marble of which gods are made."
T. Moore: Lalla Rookh, part 1.

Av'alanche (3 syl.) means properly something which goes downwards (French, *à val*). The word is applied to a mass of snow mixed with earth, ice, and stones, which slips down a mountain side to the lower ground. Metaphorically, we speak of an "avalanche of applause," an "avalanche of bouquets" showered on the stage, etc.

Av'alon. An ocean island, where King Arthur resided and was buried. The word means "Apple island" (*aval,* apple ; *yn',* island) ; and it is generally thought to mean Glastonbury, a name derived from the Saxon *glastn* (green like glass).

Avant Courier. (French, *avant courier.*) A "messenger sent before" to get things ready for a party of travellers, or to announce their approach. Anything said or done to prepare the way for something more important to follow ; a feeler, a harbinger.

Avant Garde. (French.) The van or advanced guard of an army.

Av'atar'. The advent to earth of a deity in a visible form. The ten avâta'ras of Vishnu, in Hindû mythology, are by far the most celebrated. 1st advent, in the form of a fish ; 2nd, in that of a tortoise ; 3rd, of a hog ; 4th, of a monster, half man and half lion, to destroy the giant Iranian ; 5th, in the form of a dwarf (this Avâtar is called Varumna) ; 6th, in human form, under the name of Râma ; 7th, under the same figure and name, to slay the thousand-armed giant Cartasuciriargunan; 8th, as a child named Krishna, who performed numerous miracles (this is the most memorable of all the advents) ; 9th, under the form of Buddha. These are all past. The 10th advent will be in the form of a white horse (Kalki) with wings, to destroy the earth.

"In Vishnu land what avatar?
Or who in Moscow, towards the czar?"
Browning.

Ave Mari'a [*Hail, Mary !*] (*Ave,* 2 syl.). The first two words of the angel's salutation to the Virgin Mary. (Luke i. 28.) In the Roman Catholic Church the phrase is applied to an invocation to the Virgin beginning with those words ; and also to the smaller beads of a rosary, the larger ones being termed *pater-nosters.*

Aven'el (2 syl.). *White Lady of Avenel.* A tutelary spirit in Scott's *Monastery.*

Avenger of Blood (*The*). The man who, in the Jewish polity, had the right of taking vengeance on him who had slain one of his kinsmen. The Avenger in Hebrew is called *goël.*

Cities of refuge were appointed for the protection of homicides, and of those who had caused another's death by accident. The Koran sanctions the Jewish custom. Family feuds have been a common hunting ground of poets and novelists.

Aver'nus (Greek, *a-ornis,* "without a bird "). A lake in Campa'nia, so called from the belief that its sulphurous and mephitic vapours killed any bird that happened to inhale them. Poets call it the entrance to the infernal regions; hence the proverb, *The descent to Avernus is easy, but coming back again is quite another matter,* meaning that all bad habits are easily acquired, but very hard to be abandoned.

Av'ertin (*St.*). The patron saint of lunatics; so called from the French *avertineux* (lunatics).

Aves'ta. The sacred Scriptures of the Magians, composed by Zoroaster. Better known as the Zend-Avesta or "living word in the Zend language."

Aveu'gle. Son of Erebus and Nox. (*Spenser : Faërie Queene.*)

Avie'nus. A writer of fables in the decline of the Roman empire. In the Middle Ages, a collection of fables used to be called Av'ynet, or E'sopet.

A vinculo matrimonii (Latin). Divorced from marriage ties. A total divorce. A divorce *a mensa et thoro* is a partial divorce. The divorce *a vinculo matrimonii* is because the marriage was never legal, as in the case of bigamy, or marriage within the prohibited degrees; but a divorce *a mensa et thoro* is because the parties cannot live together from incompatibility of temper, in which case they may, if they choose, come together again.

Aviz. An order of knighthood in Portugal, founded by Sancho I., and having for its object the subjugation of the Moors.

Avoid Etxremes. The wise saw of Pit'tacos of Mityle'nē. (B.C. 652-569.)

Avoir. *Avoir Martel en tête* (French). To be distracted. Martel is a hammer, hence distraction, torment, torture.

Avoirdupois. French, *avoir, aver* or *avier,* goods in general, and *poise=poids* (weight). Not the verb, but the noun *avoir.* Properly *avoir de poids* (goods having weight), goods sold by weight. We have the word *aver,* meaning goods in general, hence also cattle; whence such compounds as aver-corn, aver-penny, aver-silver, aver-land, and so on. We have also the noun "having, havings" =possessions.

There is a common French phrase *avoir du poids* (to be weight), with which our word *avoirdupois* has been muddled up.
"Pared my present havings [property] to bestow
My bounties upon you."
Shakespeare: Henry VIII., iii. 2.

"One of your having, and yet cark and care."
Muses' Looking Glass.
Even medicines, as wholesale goods, are bought and sold by avoirdupois weight.

A-weather. The reverse of *a-lee.* "A-weather" is towards the weather, or the side on which the wind strikes. "A-lee" is in the lee or shelter, and therefore opposite to the wind side; as helm a-weather.

Awkward. French, *gauche,* not dexterous. Awk means the left hand. Hence in Holland's *Plutarch* we have "The *awke* or left hand"; and again, "They receive her *awkly* when she presenteth . . . the right hand." (*See* SINISTER.)

Awkward Squad. In military language means recruits not yet fitted to take their place in the regimental line.

∴ A squad is a troop or company of soldiers under a sergeant. It is a contraction of squadron. A squadron of cavalry is the unit of a regiment. Three or four squadrons make a regiment, and a certain number of regiments constitute an army. In naval affairs a squadron is a section of a fleet.

Awl. "*I'll pack up my awls and be gone,*" *i.e.* all my goods. The play is on awl and all.

Axe. "*To hang up one's axe.*" To retire from business, to give over a useless project. The allusion is to the ancient battle-axe, hung up to the gods when the fight was done. All classical scholars will call to mind the allusion of Horace to a similar Roman custom. Being snubbed by Pyrrha, he says, "He will hang up his axe upon her wall," or more literally, his "drenched garments on the temple-walls of Neptune." (1 *Odes,* V. 14-17.) (*See* ASK.)

To put the axe on the helve. To solve a difficulty. To hit the right nail on the head.

To send the axe after the helve. To spend good money after bad, or under the hope of recovering bad debts.

He has an axe to grind. Some selfish motive in the background; some personal interest to answer. Franklin tells of a man who wanted to grind his axe, but had no one to turn the grindstone. Going to the yard where he saw young Franklin, he asked the boy to show him how the machine worked, and kept praising him till his axe was ground, and then laughed at him for his pains.

Ax'inoman'cy. Divination by an axe; much practised by the ancient Greeks with a view of discovering crime. An agate was placed on a red-hot axe, and indicated the guilty person by its motion. (Greek, *ax'inē manteia*.)

A'yah (Anglo-Indian). A native Hindû nurse or lady's maid.

"The ayahs, or nurses, are said to be the best in the world."—*B. Taylor: Visit to India*, chap. ii. p. 37.

Aye'shah (3 syl.). Mahomet's second and favourite wife. He married her when she was only nine years old, and died in her arms.

Ayr'shire Poet. Robert Burns, born near the town of Ayr. (1759-1796.)

Azaz'el. The scape-goat; so called by the Jews, because the high priest cast lots on two goats; one lot was *for the Lord*, and the other lot *for Azaz'el* or Satan, and the goat on which the latter lot fell was the scape-goat.

Azaz'iel. A seraph who fell in love with An'ah, a granddaughter of Cain. When the flood came, he carried her under his wing to some other planet. (*Byron: Heaven and Earth.*)

Azaz'il. In Milton's *Paradise Lost*, Azazil is the standard-bearer of the infernal host. According to the Koran, when God commanded the angels to worship Adam, Azazil replied, "Why should the son of fire fall down before a son of clay?" and God cast him out of heaven. His name was then changed to *Eblis*, which means "despair."

"Then straight commands that at the warlike sound
Of trumpets loud, and clarions, be upreared
His mighty standard ; that proud honour claimed
Azazil, as his right, a cherub tall."
Milton: Paradise Lost, book i. 531-4.

Azim. The young convert who joined "the creed and standard" of the veiled prophet of Khorassan, in Moore's *Lalla Rookh*. When he was witness of the prophet's infamy, he joined the caliph's army, and was mainly instrumental in defeating that of the veiled prophet.

Az'o, Marquis of Estē, married Pari-si'na, who fell in love with Hugo, a natural son of Azo. The marquis ordered Hugo to be beheaded; but no one knows what the fate of Parisi'na was. Azo, at any rate, married again, and had a family. This Azo was in reality Niccolo of Ferra'ra. (*Byron: Parisina.*)

A'zor's Mirror. Zemi'ra is the name of the lady, and Azor that of the bear, in Marmontel's tale of *Beauty and the Beast*. Zemi'ra entreats the kind

monster to let her see her father, if only for a few moments ; so drawing aside a curtain, he shows him to her in a magic mirror. This mirror was a sort of tele-scope, which rendered objects otherwise too far off distinctly visible.

Az'oth. The panace'a of Paracelsus, regarded by his followers as "the tincture of life."

Az'rael (3 syl.). The angel that watches over the dying, and takes the soul from the body. The angel of death. He will be the last to die, but will do so at the second trump of the archangel.

"The Mohammedan doctors say that Azrael was commissioned to inflict the penalty of death on all mankind."—*H. Christmas.*

The wings of Azrael. The approach of death ; the signs of death coming on the dying.

"Those who listen in the . . . watches of the night for the wings of Azrael."—*Besant.*

Az'rafil. The archangel commissioned to blow the trumpet of the resurrection. (*The Koran*)

Aztecs. An indigenous people of Mexico who, in 1325, founded Tenoch-titlan. They were in the zenith of their power in the fourteenth and fif-teenth centuries. When the Spaniards arrived, their king was Montezuma ; their supreme god was Taoti ; and Huitzilopochtli was the divine protector of their nation, to whom they offered human victims.

Azuce'na. An old gipsy who stole Man'rico, infant son of Garzia, the Conte di Luna's brother. (*Verdi: Il Trovatore.*)

Azure. Sky blue. Represented in royal arms by the planet Jupiter, in noblemen's by the sapphire. The ground of the old shield of France was azure. Emblem of fidelity and truth. Represented in heraldic devices by hori-zontal lines.

Azu'riel. The fairy who owned what we call Holland Park. King O'beron gave him his daughter Kenna in mar-riage when he drove Albion from his empire. Albion invaded Kensington, the territory of King Oberon, but was slain in battle by Azuriel. (*Tickell.*)

Az'ymites (3 syl.). The Roman Cath-olics are so called by the Greek Church, because the holy wafers used by them in the eucharist are made of unleavened bread. (Greek, *azūmos*, unleavened.)

B

B. This letter is the outline of a house. It is called in Hebrew *beth* (a house). In Egyptian hierology this letter is a sheep.

B stands for 300. *Scit B. trecentum sibi cognātum retinēre.* And, again, *Et B. trecentum per se retinere videtur.* But with a *line above*, it denotes 3,000.

For *Becarre* and *Bemol* (French for B sharp and B flat), see BECARRE.

Marked with a B (French), *i.e.* a poor thing. In the French language almost all personal defects begin with the letter B; *e.g. bigle* (squint-eyed), *borgne* (one-eyed), *bossu* (humpty), *boiteux* (lame), etc.

Not to know B from a battledoor. To be quite illiterate, not to know even his letters. Miege tells us that *hornbooks* used to be called battledoors. The phrase might therefore originally mean not to know the B of, from, or out of, your hornbook. But its more general meaning is "not able to distinguish one letter from another."

"He knoweth not a B from a battledoore."—*Howell: English Proverbs.*

"Distinguish a B from a battledore."—*Dekker: Guls Hornebook.*

I know B from a Bull's foot. Similar to the proverb, "I know a hawk from a hernshaw." (*See* HAWK.) The bull's parted hoof somewhat resembles a B.

"There were members who scarcely knew B from a bull's foot." — *Brackenbridge: Modern Chivalry.*

B. C. *Marked with B.C.* (bad character). When a soldier disgraced himself by insubordination he was formerly marked with "B. C." before he was drummed out of the regiment.

B. and S. Brandy and soda-water.

B. K. S. The name of "residence" given to officers in mufti, who do not wish to give up their address. The word stands for *BarracKS.*

B Flats. Bugs. The pun is "B" (the initial letter), and "flat," from the flatness of the obnoxious insect. Also called *Norfolk Howards*, from Mr. Bugg, who advertised in the *Times* that he should in future change his name into "Norfolk Howard." (*See* F SHARP.)

B.'s. *Four B.'s essential for social success.* Blood, brains, brass, brads (money). (American.)
Beware of the B.'s, i.e. the British. A Carlow caution.

B. of B. K. Some mysterious initials applied to himself in his diary by

Arthur Orton, "the Tichborne Claimant." Supposed to denote "Baronet of British Kingdom."

Baal-Peor or *Bel'phegor.* The *Priapus* of the Mo'abites and Midianites.

Baal Samin. The god of celestial places.

Baal Shemesh. The Sun-god.

Baal Zeboub [Beelzebub], god of corruption or of flies. (*See* FLIES.)

Ba'ba. Same as *papa* (Turkish). Ali-baba is "father Ali."

Babau. The bogie with which nurses in Languedoc terrify unruly children.

Babes in the Wood. (1) Simple trustful folks, never suspicious, and easily gulled.
(2) Insurrectionary hordes that infested the mountains of Wicklow and the woods of Enniscorthy towards the close of the eighteenth century. (*See* CHILDREN.)
(3) Men in the stocks or in the pillory.

Babes (*Deities of*), in Rome. VATICAN, or, more correctly, VAGITAN-US (*q.v.*), the god who caused infants to utter their first *cry.* FABULIN-US (*q.v.*), the god to whom Roman parents made an offering when an infant uttered its first *word.* CUBA (*q.v.*), the goddess who kept infants quiet in their cots. DOMIDU'CA, the goddess who brought young children safe home, and kept guard over them when out of their parents' sight.

Babies in the Eyes. That is, love in the expression of the eyes. Love is the little babe Cupid, and hence the conceit, originating from the reflection of the onlooker in the pupil of another's eyes.

"In each of her two crystal eyes
Smileth a naked boy [Cupid]."
Lord Surrey.

She clung about his neck, gave him ten kisses,
Toyed with his locks, looked babies in his eyes."
Heywood: Love's Mistress.

Babel. *A perfect Babel.* A thorough confusion. "A Babel of sounds." A confused uproar, in which nothing can be heard but hubbub. The allusion is to the confusion of tongues at Babel. (Genesis xi.)

"God . . . comes down to see their city,
. . . . . . and in derision sets
Upon their tongues a various spirit, to raze
Quite out their native language, and instead
To sow a jangling noise of words unknown.
Forthwith a hideous gabble rises loud
Among the builders; each to other calls
Not understood. . . . Thus was the building left
Ridiculous, and the work Confusion named."
Milton: Paradise Lost, xii. 48-62.

Babouc. (*See* BACBUC.)

Babouin. *Taisez-vous, petite babouin; laissez parlez votre mère, qui est plus sage que vous.* The tale or fable is this: A girl one day went to make an offering to Venus, and prayed the goddess to give her for husband a young man on whom she had fixed her affections. A young fellow happened at the time to be behind the image of Cupid, and hearing the petition, replied, "So fine a gentleman is not for such as you." The voice seemed to proceed from the image, and the girl replied, "Hold your tongue, you little monkey; let your mother speak, for she is wiser than you."

Baby Charles. So James I. used to call his son Charles, afterwards Charles I.

Babylon. *The modern Babylon.* So London is sometimes called, on account of its wealth, luxury, and dissipation.

Babylonian Numbers. *Ne Babylonios tentāris numeros.* Do not pry into futurity by astrological calculations and horoscopes. Do not consult fortune-tellers. The Chaldæans were the most noted of astrologers. (*Horace : Odes,* book i. xi. 2.)

Babylonish Captivity. The seventy years that the Jews were captives in Babylon. They were made captives by Nebuchadnezzar, and released by Cyrus (B.C. 538).

Babylonish Garment (*A*). *Babylonica vestis,* a garment woven with divers colours. (*Pliny,* viii. 74.)

"I saw among the spoils a goodly Babylonish garment."—Joshua vii. 21.

Baca. *The Valley of Baca,* also called the Valley of Tears, translated in the New Version "the Valley of Weeping," apparently a dry sterile valley, the type of this earth spoilt by sorrow and sin. "Blessed is the man . . . in whose heart are the ways of them. Who passing through the valley of Baca make it a well . . ." (Psalm lxxxiv. 6). That man is blessed whose trust in God converts adverse circumstances into proofs of divine love. "Whom He loveth He chasteneth." They "go from strength to strength."

In the mountains of Lebanon is a valley called Baca, but it is described as fertile and very delicious. The Valley of Lebanon (Joshua xi. 17) is encompassed by mountains, one of which is very barren, and abounds in thorns, rocks, and flints. but another is called

a terrestrial paradise. Baca means "mulberry trees," but Bekah means a "plain." Perowne says Bacah is from a Hebrew root which means "weeping."

"Our sources of common pleasure dry up as we journey on through the vale of Ba'cha."—*Sir Walter Scott : The Antiquary.*

Bacbuc. The Holy Bottle, and also the priestess of the Holy Bottle, the oracle of Lantern-land consulted by Panurge on the momentous question whether or not he ought to marry. The Holy Bottle answered with a click like the noise made by a glass snapping. Bacbuc told Panurge the noise meant *trinc* (drink), and that was the response, the most direct and positive ever given by the oracle. Panurge might interpret it as he liked, the obscurity would always save the oracle.

So Pic or Glück (say I) or neither,
Or both, for aught I care, or either ;
More undecided than Bacbuc,
Here's heads for Pic, and tails for Glück.
E. C. B.

Bacchanalia. Festivals in honour of Bacchus, distinguished for their licentiousness and debauchery. Plato says he has seen the whole population of Athens drunk at these festivals.

Bacchanalian. Drunken, rollicksome, devoted or pertaining to Bacchus (*q.v.*).

Bacchant. A person given to habits of drinking ; so called from the "bacchants," or men admitted to the feasts of Bacchus. Bacchants wore fillets of ivy.

Bacchante (2 syl.). A female wine-bibber ; so called from the "bacchantes," or female priestesses of Bacchus. They wore fillets of ivy.

Bacchis. A sacred bull which changed its colour every hour of the day. (*Egyptian mythology.*)

Bacchus [*wine*]. In Roman mythology the god of wine. He is represented as a beautiful youth with black eyes, golden locks, flowing with curls about his shoulders and filleted with ivy. In peace his robe was purple, in war he was covered with a panther's skin. His chariot was drawn by panthers.

The famous statue of Bacchus in the palace of Borghese (3 syl.) is represented with a bunch of grapes in his hand and a panther at his feet. Pliny tells us that, after his conquest of India, Bacchus entered Thebes in a chariot drawn by elephants.

⁂ The Etruscan Bacchus was called *Esar* or *Nesar ;* the Umbrian *Desar ;* the

Assyrian *Issus;* the Greek *Dion-ysus;*
the Galatian *Nyssus;* the Hebrew *Nizziz;*
a Greek form was *Iacchus* (from *Iachē*,
a shout); the Latin *Bacchus;* other
forms of the word are the Norse *Eis;*
the Indian *Ies;* the Persian *Yez.;* the
Gaulish *Hes;* the German *Hist;* and
the Chinese *Jos.*

"As jolly Bacchus, god of pleasure,
Cha'med the wide world with drink and dances,
And all his thousand airy fancies,
Alas ! he quite forgot the while
His favourite vines in Lesbos' isle." *Parnell.*

Bacchus, in the *Lusiad,* is the evil
demon or antagonist of Jupiter, the lord
of destiny. As Mars is the guardian
power of Christianity, Bacchus is the
guardian power of Mohammedanism.

Bacchus sprang from the thigh of Zeus.
The tale is that Sem'elē asked Zeus to
appear before her in all his glory, but
the foolish request proved her death.
Zeus saved the child which was prema-
turely born by sewing it up in his thigh
till it came to maturity. The Arabian
tradition is that the infant Bacchus was
nourished during infancy in a cave of
Mount Meros. As "Meros" is Greek
for a *thigh,* the Greek fable is readily
explained.

What has that to do with Bacchus?
i.e. what has that to do with the matter
in hand? When Thespis introduced
recitations in the vintage songs, the
innovation was suffered to pass, so long
as the subject of recitation bore on the
exploits of Bacchus ; but when, for
variety sake, he wandered to other
subjects, the Greeks pulled him up with
the exclamation, "What has that to do
with Bacchus?" (*See* HECUBA, MOU-
TONS.)

*Bacchus a noyé plus d'hommes que
Neptune.* The ale-house wrecks more
men than the ocean.

A priest of Bacchus. A toper.
"The jolly old priests of Bacchus in the parlour
make their libations of claret."—*J. S. Le Fanu:
The House in the Churchyard,* p. 113.

A son of Bacchus. A toper.

Baccoch. The travelling cripple of
Ireland. Generally, a talkative, facetious fellow, prompt at repartee, and
not unlike the ancient jester.

Bachelor. A man who has not
been married. Probably from *baccalaris,*
"a man employed on a grazing-farm"
(Low Latin, *bacca,* for *vacca,* a cow).
French, *bachelier, bachelette* (a damsel).

A Bachelor of Arts. The student who
has passed his examination, but is not
yet of standing to be a master. Formerly the bachelor was the candidate
for examination. The word used to

be spelt *bachiller;* thus in the *Proceedings of the Privy Council,* vol. i.
p. 72, we read:—"The king ordered
that the bachillers should have reasonable pay for their trouble."

Froissart styles Richard II. *le jeune
damoisel Richart.* The Italian is *don-
zella.*

Bachelor of Salamanca (*The*). Don
Cherubim. He is placed in different
situations of life, and is made to associate with all classes of society. (*Le
Sage : The Bachelor of Salamanca* (a
novel).)

Bachelor's Buttons. Several flowers
are so called. Red Bachelor's Buttons,
the double red campion; yellow Bachelor's Buttons, the "upright crowfoot";
white Bachelor's Buttons, the white
ranunculus and white campion.

"The similitude these flowers have to the
jagged cloath buttons anciently worne . . . gave
occasion . . . to call them Bachelour's Buttons."—
Gerard: Herbal.

Or else from a custom still sometimes
observèd by rustics of carrying the
flower in their pockets to know how
they stand with their sweethearts. If
the flower dies, it is a bad omen ; but if
it does not fade, they may hope for the
best.

To wear bachelor's buttons. To remain
a bachelor. (*See above.*)

Bachelor's Fare. Bread and cheese
and kisses.

Bachelor's Porch. The north door
used to be so called. The menservants
and other poor men used to sit on
benches down the north aisle, and the
maidservants, with other poor women,
on the south side. Even when married
the custom was not discontinued. After
service the men formed one line and the
women another, down which the clergy
and gentry passed amidst salutations,
and the two lines filed off. In some
country churches these arrangements
are still observed.

Bachelor's Wife (*A*). A hypothetical
wife. A bachelor has only an imaginary
wife.

"Bachelors' wives and old maids' children be
well taught."—*Heywood: Proverbs.*

Back (*To*). To support with money,
influence, or encouragement: as to
"back a friend." A commercial term
meaning to *endorse.* When a merchant
backs or endorses a bill, he guarantees
its value.

Falstaff says to the Prince :—

"You care not who sees your back. Call you

that backing of your friends? A plague upon such backing!"—*Shakespeare*: 1 *Henry IV.*, ii. 4.
"Englishmen will fight now as well as ever they did; and there is ample power to back them."—*W. Robertson: John Bright*, chap. xxxi. p. 298.

Back and Edge. Entirely, heartily, tooth and nail, with might and main. The reference is to a wedge driven home to split wood.

"They were working back and edge for me."—*Boldrewood: Robbery under Arms*, ch. ii.

To back and fill. A mode of tacking, when the tide is with the vessel and the wind against it. Metaphorically, to be irresolute.

To back out. To draw back from an engagement, bargain, etc., because it does not seem so plausible as you once thought it. Many horses are unwilling to go out of a stable head foremost, and are backed out.

"Octavius backs out; his caution and reserve come to her rescue."—*C. Clarke: Shakespeare.*

To back the field. To bet on all the horses bar one. A sporting term used in betting.

To back the sails. So to arrange them that the ship's way may be checked.

To back up. To uphold, to support. As one who stands at your back to support you.

At the back of. Behind, following close after. Figure from following a leader.

"With half the city at his back."
         Byron: Don Juan.

To see his back; to see the back of anything. To get rid of a person or thing; to see it leave.

Back the oars or *back water* is to row backwards, that the boat may move the reverse of its ordinary direction.

On the back of. Immediately after. Figure from soldiers on the march.

To the back, that is, to the backbone, entirely.

To break the back of a thing. To surmount the hardest part.

His back is up. He is angry, he shows that he is annoyed. The allusion is to a cat, which sets its back up when attacked by a dog or other animal.

To get one's back up. To be irritated (*See above*).

To have his back at the wall. To act on the defensive against odds. One beset with foes tries to get his back against a wall that he may not be attacked by foes behind.

"He planted his back against a wall, in a skilful attitude of fence, ready with his bright glancing rapier to do battle with all the heavy fierce unarmed men, some six or seven in number."—*Mrs. Gaskell: The Poor Clare*, iii.

To set one's back up. (*See above.*)
"That word set my back up."
         Dame Huddle's Letter (1710).

To turn one's back on another. To leave, forsake, or neglect him. To leave one by going away.

"At length we . . . turn our backs on the outskirts of civilisation."—*Tristram: Moab*, ii. 19.

Behind my back. When I was not present. When my back was turned.

Laid on one's back. Laid up with chronic ill-health; helpless. Figure from persons extremely ill.

Thrown on his back. Completely worsted. A figure taken from wrestlers.

Backbite (*To*). To slander behind one's back.

"The only thing in which all parties agreed was to backbite the manager."—*W. Irving: Traveller, Buckthorn*, p. 183.

Backbone (*The*). The main stay.

"Sober . . . . practical men . . . . constitute the moral backbone of the country."—*W. Booth: In Darkest England* (Part i. 2, p. 17).

To the backbone. Thoroughly, as true to the backbone.

"A union man, and a nationalist to the backbone."—*T. Roosevelt: T. H. Benton*, chap. v. p. 113.

Backgammon is the Anglo-Saxon *bac oamen* (back game); so called because the pieces (in certain circumstances) are taken up and obliged to go back to enter at the table again.

Background. *Placed in the background*, *i.e.* made of no consequence. Pictures have three distances, called grounds: the foreground, where the artist is supposed to be; the middle ground, where the most salient part of the picture is placed; and the background or distance, beyond which the eye cannot penetrate.

Back-hander. A blow on the face with the back of the hand. Also one who takes *back* the decanter in order to *hand* himself another glass before the decanter is passed on.

"I'll take a back-hander, as Clive don't seem to drink."—*Thackeray: The Newcomes.*

Back-speer (*To*). To cross-examine. (Scotch.)

"He has the wit to lay the scene in such a remote . . . country that nobody should be able to back-speer him."—*Sir W. Scott: The Betrothed* (Introduction).

Back-stair Influence. Private or unrecognised influence. It was customary to build royal palaces with a staircase for state visitors, and another for those who sought the sovereign upon private matters. If any one wanted a private interview with royalty, it was highly desirable to conciliate those appointed to guard the back stairs, as they could admit or exclude a visitor.

"Once, we confess, beneath the patriot's cloak,
From the cracked bag the dropping guineas broke,
And, jingling down the back stairs, told the crew
'Old Cato is as great a rogue as you.'"
Pope: Epistle to Lord Bathurst, 35-8.

Backwardation (*Stockbrokers' term*). The sum paid by a speculator on a "bear account" (*i.e.* a speculation on a *fall* in the price of certain stock), in order to postpone the completion of the transaction till the next settling day. (*See* CONTANGO.)

Backward Blessing (*Muttering a*). Muttering a curse. To say the Lord's Prayer backwards was to invoke the devil.

Backwater. (1) Water at the lower end of a millrace to check the speed of the wheel. (2) A current of water from the *inland*, which clears off the deposit of sand and silt left by the action of the sea; as the Backwater of Weymouth.

Bacon. *The Bacon of Theology.* Bishop Butler, author of the *Analogy.* (1692-1752.)

Bacon's brazen head. (*See* BRAZEN.)

To baste your bacon. To strike or scourge one. The Saxons were called "hogs" by their Norman lords. Henry VIII. spoke of the common people as the "swinish multitude"; and Falstaff says to the travellers at Gadshill, "On, bacons, on!" (1 *Henry IV.*, ii. 2). Bacon is the outside portion of the sides of pork, and may be considered generally as the part which would receive a blow.

To save one's bacon. To save oneself from injury.

"But as he rose to save his bacon,
By hat and wig he was forsaken."
Coombe: Dr. Syntax, canto vi. line 240.

There seems to be another sense in which the term is used—viz. to escape loss; and in this sense the allusion is to the care taken by our forefathers to save from the numerous dogs that frequented their houses the bacon which was laid up for winter store, the loss of which would have been a very serious calamity.

A chaw-bacon. A rustic. Till comparatively modern times the only meat which rustics had to eat was bacon. I myself know several farm labourers who never taste any meat but bacon, except on club and feast days.

He may fetch a flitch of bacon from Dunmow, i.e. he is so amiable and good-tempered he will never quarrel with his wife. The allusion is to a custom founded by Juga, a noble lady, in 1111, and restored by Robert de Fitzwalter in 1244; which was, that "any person from any part of England going to Dunmow, in Essex, and humbly kneeling on two stones at the church door, may claim a gammon of bacon, if he can swear that for twelve months and a day he has never had a household brawl or wished himself unmarried."

Baco'nian Philosophy. A system of philosophy based on principles laid down by Francis Bacon, Lord Ver'ulam, in the 2nd book of his *Novum Organum.* It is also called inductive philosophy.

Baconian Theory. The theory that Lord Bacon wrote the plays attributed to Shakespeare.

Bac'trian Sage. Zoroaster, a native of Bactria (Balkh), about 500 years before the birth of Christ.

Bad. *Charles le mauvais.* Charles II. of Navarre (1332-1387).

He is gone to the bad. Has become a ruined man, or a depraved character. He has gone amongst bad people, in bad ways, or to bad circumstances.

To the bad. On the wrong side of the account; in arrears.

Bad Blood. Vindictiveness, ill-feeling.

"If there is any bad blood in the fellow he will be sure to show it."— *Brother Jonathan.*

To make bad blood, to stir up bad blood. To create or renew ill-feeling and a vindictive spirit.

Bad Books. *You are in my bad books.* Under disgrace. Also *In my black books.* (*See under* BLACK BOOKS.)

Bad Debts. Debts not likely to be paid.

Bad Form, not *comme il faut.* Not in good taste.

Bad Lot (*A*). A person of bad moral character, or one commercially unsound. Also a commercial project or stock of worthless value. The allusion is to auctioneering slang, meaning a lot which no one will bid for. So an inefficient soldier is called one of the Queen's *bad bargains.*

Bad Shot (*A*). A wrong guess. A sporting phrase; a bad shot is one which does not bring down the bird shot at, one that misses the mark.

Badaud. A booby. *C'est un franc badaud* he is a regular booby. Le badaud de Paris, a French cockney. From the Italian, *badare*, to gaze in the air, to stare about one.

Badge of Poverty. In former times those who received parish relief had to wear a badge. It was the letter P, with the initial of the parish to which they belonged, in red or blue cloth, on the shoulder of the right sleeve. (*See* DYVOUR.)

Badge-men. Alms-house men; so called because they wear some special dress, or other badge, to indicate that they belong to a particular foundation.

"He quits the gay and rich, the young and free,
Among the badge-men with a badge to be."
Crabbe: Borough.

Badger (*A*). A licensed huckster, who was obliged to wear a badge. By 5 Eliz., c. 12, it was enacted that "Badgers were to be licensed annually, under a penalty of £5."

"Under Dec. 17, 1565, we read of 'Certain persons upon Humber side who . . . by great quantities of corn, two of whom were authorised badgers.'"—*State Papers (Domestic Series).*

Badger (*To*). To tease or annoy by superior numbers. In allusion to the ancient custom of badger-baiting. A badger was kennelled in a tub, where dogs were set upon him to worry him out. When dragged from his tub the poor beast was allowed to retire to it till he recovered from the attack. This process was repeated several times.

Badger. It is a vulgar error that the legs of a badger are shorter on one side than on the other.

"I think that Titus Oates was as uneven as a badger."—*Lord Macaulay.*

Drawing a badger is drawing him out of his tub by means of dogs.

Badinage. Playful raillery, banter (French), from the verb *badiner*, to joke or jest. The noun *badine* means a switch, and in France they catch wild ducks by covering a boat with switches, in which the ducks seek protection. A person quizzed is like these wild ducks.

Badinguet. A nickname given to Napoleon III. It was the name of the workman whose clothes he wore when he contrived to escape from the fort of Ham, in 1846.

"If Badinguet and Bismarck have a row together let them settle it between them with their fists, instead of troubling hundreds of thousands of men who . . . have no wish to fight."—*Zola: The Downfall*, chap. ii. (1892).

Badingueux. The party of the Emperor Napoleon III. The party of the Empress were called "Montijoyeux" and "Montijocrisses," from Montijo in

Spain. She was the second daughter of the Count of Montijo.

Bad'minton is properly a "copus cup," made of claret spiced and sweetened, a favourite with the Duke of Beaufort of Badminton. As the duke used to be a great patron of the prize ring, Badminton was used as equivalent to claret as the synonym of blood.

Also a game similar to lawn tennis, only played with shuttlecocks instead of balls.

Baffle. To erase the cognisance of a recreant knight. To degrade a knight from his rank. To be knocked about by the winds.

"I am disgraced, impeached, and baffled here."
Shakespeare: Richard II., act i. 1.

Bag. *Bag and Baggage*, as "Get away with you, bag and baggage," *i.e.* get away, and carry with you all your belongings. The bag or sack is the pouch in which a soldier packs his few articles when he moves from place to place. Baggage is a contemptuous term for a woman, either because soldiers send their wives in the baggage wagons, or from the Italian *bagascia* (a harlot), French *bagasse*, Spanish *bagazo*, Persian, *baga.*

Bag and baggage policy. In 1876 Mr. Gladstone, speaking on the Eastern question, said, "Let the Turks now carry away their abuses in the only possible manner, namely, by carrying away themselves. . . . One and all, *bag and baggage*, shall, I hope, clear out from the province they have desolated and profaned." This was termed by the Conservatives the bag and baggage policy.

A bag of bones. Very emaciated; generally "A mere bag of bones."

A bag of game. A large battue. From the custom of carrying game home in "bags."

A bag of tricks or *A whole bag of tricks.* Numerous expedients. In allusion to the fable of the *Fox and the Cat.* The fox was commiserating the cat because she had only one shift in the case of danger, while he had a thousand tricks to evade it. Being set upon by a pack of hounds, the fox was soon caught, while puss ran up a tree and was quite secure.

A good bag. A large catch of game, fish, or other animals sought after by sportsmen.

Got the bag. Got his dismissal. (*See* SACK.)

The bottom of the bag. The last

expedient, having emptied every other one out of his bag.

To empty the bag. To tell the whole matter and conceal nothing. (French, *vider le sac*, to expose all to view.)

To let the cat out of the bag. (*See* under CAT.)

Bag (*To*). To steal, or slip into one's bag, as a poacher or pilferer who slyly slips into his bag what he has contrived to purloin.

Bags. A slang word for trousers, which are the bags of the body. When the pattern was very staring and "loud," they once were called *howling-bags*.

Bag-man (*A*). A commercial traveller, who carries a bag with specimens to show to those whose custom he solicits. In former times commercial travellers used to ride a horse with saddle-bags sometimes so large as almost to conceal the rider.

Bag o' Nails. Some hundreds of years ago there stood in the Tyburn Road, Oxford Street, a public-house called *The Bacchanals:* the sign was Pan and the Satyrs. The jolly god, with his cloven hoof and his horns, was called "The devil;" and the word Bacchanals soon got corrupted into "Bag o' Nails." The *Devil and the Bag o' Nails* is a sign not uncommon even now in the midland counties.

Baga de Secrētis. Records in the Record Office of trials for high treason and other State offences from the reign of Edward IV. to the close of the reign of George III. These records contain the proceedings in the trials of Anne Boleyn, Sir Walter Raleigh, Guy Fawkes, the regicides, and of the risings of 1715 and 1745. (Baga = Bag.)

Bagatelle (*A*). A trifle; a thing of no consideration. "Oh! nothing. A mere bagatelle." In French, "*Il dépense tout son argent en bagatelles*" means, he squanders his money on trash. "*Il ne s'amuse qu'à des bagatelles*," he finds no pleasure except in frivolities. Bagatelle! as an exclamation, means Nonsense! as "*Vous dites qu'il me fera un procès. Bagatelle!*" (fiddlesticks!)

"He considered his wife a bagatelle, to be shut up at pleasure" [*i.e.* a toy to be put away at pleasure].—*The Depraved Husband.*

Baguette d'Armide (*La*). The sorcerer's wand. Armida is a sorceress in Tasso's *Jerusalem Delivered*. Baguette is a rod or wand.

Bahagnia, Bohemia; **Bahaignons,** Bohemians. (1300.)

Bahr Geist (*A*). A banshee or grey-spectre.

"Know then (said Eveline) it [the Bahr Geist] is a spectre, usually the image of the departed person, who, either for wrong suffered, sustained during life, or through treasure hidden, . . . haunts the spot from time to time, becomes familiar to those who dwell there, and takes an interest in their fate."—*Sir W. Scott: The Betrothed*, chap. 15.

Bail (French, *bailler*). To deliver up. *Common bail* or *bail below.* A bail given to the sheriff, after arresting a person, to guarantee that the defendant will appear in court at any day and time the court demands.

Special bail or *bail above*, consists of persons who undertake to satisfy all claims made on the defendant, and to guarantee his rendering himself up to justice when required.

Bail. (*See* LEG-BAIL.)

To bail up. To disarm before robbing, to force to throw up the arms. (Australian.)

Bailey. The space enclosed within the external walls of a castle, not including the "Keep." The entrance was over a drawbridge, and through the embattled gate (Middle-age Latin *balium* or *ballium*, a corruption of *vallum*, a rampart).

When there were two courts to a castle, they were distinguished as the outer and inner bailey (rampart). Subsequently the word included the court and all its buildings; and when the court was abolished, the term was attached to the castle, as the Old Bailey (London) and the Bailey (Oxford).

Bailiff. At Constantinople, the person who had charge of the imperial children used to be called the *bajulus*, from *baios*, a child. The word was subsequently attached to the Venetian consul at Constantinople, and the Venetian ambassador was called the *balio*, a word afterwards extended to any superintendent or magistrate. In France the *bailli* was a superintendent of the royal domains and commander of the troops. In time, any superintendent of even a private estate was so called, whence our *farmer's bailiff*. The sheriff is the king's bailiff—a title now applied almost exclusively to his deputies or officers. (*See* BUMBAILIFF.)

Bailleur. *Un bon bâilleur en fait bâiller deux* (French). Yawning is catching.

Baillif (*Herry*). Mine host in Chaucer's *Canterbury Tales*. When the poet began the second "Fit" of the

Rime of Sir Thopas, Herry Baillif interrupts him with unmitigated contempt:—

"'No mor of this, for Goddes dignitie !'
Quod our host, 'for thou makest me
So wery . . . that
Mine eerës aken for thy nasty speeche.'"
Verse 15327.

Bain Marie. A saucepan containing hot water into which a smaller saucepan is plunged, either to keep it hot, or that it may boil without burning. A glue pot is a good example. Mons. Bouillet says, "*Ainsi appelé du nom de l'inventeur*" (Balneum Mariæ). But derivations from proper names require authentication.

Bairam (3 syl.). The name given to two movable Moslem feasts. The first, which begins on the first day of the moon which follows that of Ramadan, and lasts three days, is a kind of Paschal feast. The second, seventy days later, lasts four days, and is not unlike the Jewish Feast of Tabernacles.

⁂ As the Mohammedan year is a lunar one, in 33 years these feasts will have occurred at all the four seasons.

Baisser. *Il semble qu'il n'y a qu'à se baisser et en prendre* (French). One would think he has only to pick and choose. Said of a person who fancies that fortune will fall into his lap, without his stirring. Literally, "to stoop down and pick up what he wants."

Bait. Food to entice or allure, as *bait for fish*. Bait for travellers is a "feed" by way of refreshment taken *en passant*. (Anglo-Saxon, *bætan*, to bait or feed.)

Bajaderes. Indian dancing girls. A corruption of the Portuguese *bailadeira*, whence *bai'adera*, *bajadere*.

Bajulus. A pedagogue. A Grand Bajulus, a "big" pedagogue. In the Greek court, the preceptor of the Emperor was called the Grand Bajulus. Originally "porter." (*Cf.* BAILIFF.)

Bajura. Mahomet's standard.

Baked. *Half-baked.* Imbecile, of weak mind. The metaphor from half-baked food.

Baked Meat means meat-pie. "The funeral baked meats did coldly furnish forth the marriage table" (*Hamlet*); *i.e.* the hot meat-pies (venison pasties) served at the funeral and not eaten, were served cold at the marriage banquet.

Baker (*The*). Louis XVI. was called "the Baker," the queen was called

"the baker's wife" (or *La Boulangère*), and the dauphin the "shop boy;" because a heavy trade in corn was carried on at Versailles, and consequently very little was brought to Paris.

"The return of the baker, his wife, and the shop-boy to Paris [after the king was brought from Versailles] had not had the expected effect. Flour and bread were still scarce."—*A. Dumas: The Countess de Charny*, chap. ix.

Baker's Dozen. Thirteen for twelve. When a heavy penalty was inflicted for short weight, bakers used to give a surplus number of loaves, called the *inbread*, to avoid all risk of incurring the fine. The 13th was the "vantage loaf."

Mr. Riley (*Liber Albus*) tells us that the 13th loaf was "the extent of the profit allowed to retail dealers," and therefore the *vantage* loaf means, the loaf allowed for profit.

To give one a baker's dozen, in slang phraseology, is to give him a sound drubbing—*i.e.* all he deserves and one stroke more.

Baker's Knee (*A*). A knop-knee, or knee bent inwards, from carrying the heavy bread-basket on the right arm.

Bakshish. A Persian word for a gratuity. These gifts are insolently demanded by all sorts of officials in Turkey, Egypt, and Asia Minor, more as a claim than a gratuity.

Bal. *Donner le bal à quelqu'un* (French). To make one dance for it; to abuse one. In several games played with a ball, the person who catches the ball or to whom the ball is given, is put to an immense amount of labour. Thus, in Hurling, the person who holds the ball has one of the labours of Hercules to pass through. His opponent tries to lay hold of him, and the hurler makes his way over hills, dales, hedges, and ditches, through bushes, briars, mire, plashes, and even rivers. Sometimes twenty or thirty persons lie tugging together in the water, scrambling and scratching for the ball. (*See* Strutt, *Sports and Pastimes*, section xii.) (*See* BALL.)

Balaam. The Earl of Huntingdon, one of the rebels in Monmouth's army.

"And, therefore, in the name of dulness, be
The well-hung Balaam."
Dryden: Absalom and Achitophel, 1573-4.

Balaam. A "citizen of sober fame," who lived hard by the Monument of London; "he was a plain, good man; religious, punctual, and frugal," his week-day meal being only "one solid dish." He grew rich; got knighted;

seldom went to church ; became a courtier ; "took a bribe from France ; " was hanged for treason, and all his goods were confiscated to the State. (*See* Diamond Pitt.) It was Thomas Pitt, grandfather of the Earl of Chatham, who suggested to Pope this sketch. (*Pope: Moral Essays*, Ep. iii.)

Balaam. Matter kept in type for filling up odd spaces in periodicals. These are generally refuse bits—the words of an oaf, who talks like "Balaam's ass." (Numb. xxii. 30.) (American.)

Balaam Basket or **Box** (*A*). An ass's pannier. In printer's slang of America, it is the place where rejected articles are deposited. (*See* BALAAM.)

Balafré, Le [*the gashed*]. Henri, son of François, second Duke of Guise. In the Battle of Dormans he received a sword-cut which left a frightful scar on his face (1550-1588). So Ludovic Lesly, an old archer of the Scottish Guards, is called, in Sir Walter Scott's *Quentin Durward*.

Balai. *Donner trois tours de balai par la cheminée* (French). To be a witch. Literally, to run your brush three times up the chimney. According to an ancient superstition, all witches had to pass their brooms on which they rode three times up the chimney between one Sabbath and the following.

Balak, in the second part of *Absalom and Achitophel*, a satire by Dryden and Tate, is meant for Dr. Burnet, author of *Burnet's Own Time*.

Balâm the ox, and the fish Nun, are the food of Mahomet's paradise ; the mere lobes of the livers of these animals will suffice for 70,000 saints. (*Al Koran*.)

Balan. Bravest and strongest of the giant race. Vasco de Lobeira, in *Amadis of Gaul.* Also, Emir of the Saracens, and father of Ferumbras or Fierabras (*q.v.*).

Balance (*The*). "Libra," the 7th sign of the zodiac, which contains the autumnal equinox. According to fable it is Astræa, who, in the iron age, returned from earth to heaven. Virgil, to praise the equity of Augustus, promises him a future residence in this sign.

❧ According to Persian mythology, at the last day there will be a huge balance big as the vault of heaven. The two scale pans will be called that of light and that of darkness. In the former all good will be placed, in the latter all evil. And each individual will receive an award according to the judgment of the balance.

Balance. *He has a good balance at his bankers.* His credit side shows a large balance in his favour.

Balance of power. The States of Europe being so balanced that no one nation shall have such a preponderance as to endanger the independence of another.

Balance of trade. The money-value difference between the exports and imports of a nation.

To balance an account. To add up the debit and credit sides, and subtract the less of the two from the greater. The remainder is called the balance.

To strike a balance. To calculate the exact difference, if any, between the debit and credit side of an account.

Balayer. *Chacun doit balayer devant sa porte* (French), "Let everyone correct his own faults." The allusion is to a custom, nearly obsolete in large towns, but common still in London and in villages, for each housewife to sweep and keep clean the pavement before her own dwelling.

Balclutha (*The tower of*), in Ossian, is Dun-dee, where Dun means a tower. Those circular buildings so common in the Orkney and Shetland Islands, the Hebrides, and all the north of Scotland, are *duns*. Dee is a corruption of *Tay*, the river on which the city is built ; in Latin, *Tao-dunum*.

Bald. *Charles le Chauve.* Charles I., son of Louis *le Débonnaire* (823, 840-877).

Baldachin. The daïs or canopy under which, in Roman Catholic processions, the Holy Sacrament is carried (Italian, baldacchino, so-called from Baldacco (Italian for Bagdad), where the cloth was made). Also the canopy above an altar.

Baldassare. Chief of the monastery of St. Jacopo di Compostella. (*Donizetti's opera La Favorita.*)

Balder, the god of peace, second son of Odin and Frigga. He was killed by the blind war-god Höder, at the instigation of Loki, but restored to life at the general request of the gods. (*Scandinavian mythology.*)

N.B.—Sydney Dobell (*born* 1824) has a poem entitled *Balder*, published in 1854.

Balder is the sun or daylight which is killed by the blind-god at the instigation of Loki or darkness, but is restored to life the next day.

Balder's abode was Broadblink (*vast splendour*).

Balderdash. Ribaldry, jargon. (Danish *balder*, tattle, clatter.)

Baldwin. The youngest and comeliest of Charlemagne's paladins ; and the nephew of Sir Roland.

Baldwin (in *Jerusalem Delivered*). The restless and ambitious Duke of Bologna, leader of 1,200 horse in the allied Christian army. He was Godfrey's brother ; not so tall, but very like him.

Baldwin, the Ass (in the tale of *Reynard the Fox*). In the third part of the Beast-epic he is called " Dr. Baldwin." (Old German, *bold friend*.)

Bale. *When bale is highest, boot is nighest.* When things have come to the worst they must needs mend.

Balearica Tormenta. Here *tormenta* means instruments for throwing stones. Cæsar (*Gallic War*, iv. 25) says : " *Fundis, tormentis, sagittis hostes propellere.*" The inhabitants of the Balearic Islands were noted slingers, and indeed owe their name to this skill. (Greek, *ballo*, to cast or hurl.) Pronounce *Bale-ari-ca.*

Balfour of Burley. Leader of the Covenanters in Scott's *Old Mortality*, a novel (1816).

Balios. (*See* HORSE.)

Balisar'da or *Balisardo*. Roge'ro's sword, made by a sorceress, and capable of cutting through enchanted substances.

" With Balisarda's slightest blow
Nor helm, nor shield, nor cuirass could avail,
Nor strongly-tempered plate, nor twisted mail."
Ariosto. Orlando Furioso, book xxiii.

Balistra'ria. Narrow apertures in the form of a cross in the walls of ancient castles, through which cross-bowmen discharged their arrows.

Baliverso (in *Orlando Furioso*). The basest knight in the Saracen army.

Balk means the high ridge between furrows (Anglo-Saxon *balca*, a beam, a ridge) ; hence a rising ground.

A balk of timber is a beam running across the ceiling, etc., like a ridge. As the balk is the part not cut by the plough, therefore " to balk " means to leave untouched, or to disappoint.

To make a balk. To miss a part of the field in ploughing. Hence to disappoint, to withhold deceitfully.

To make a balk of good ground. To throw away a good chance.

Balker. One who from an eminence balks or directs fishermen where shoals of herrings have gathered together. (Anglo-Saxon, *bœlc-an*, to shout.)

Balkis. The Queen of Sheba or Saba, who visited Solomon. (*Al Koran*, c. ii.)

Ball. *To strike the ball under the line.* To fail in one's object. The allusion is to the game of tennis, in which a line is stretched in the middle of the court, and the players standing on each side have, with their rackets, to knock it alternately over the line.

" Thou hast stricken the ball under the line."—
John Heywoode's Works (London, 1566).

To take the ball before the bound. To anticipate an opportunity ; to be over-hasty. A metaphor from cricket, as when a batsman runs up to meet the ball at full pitch, before it bounds. (*See* BALLE.)

Ball of Fortune (*A*). One tossed, like a ball, from pillar to post ; one who has experienced many vicissitudes of fortune.

" Brown had been from infancy a ball for fortune to spurn at."—*Sir Walter Scott : Guy Mannering*, chap. xxi.

The ball is with you. It is your turn now.

To have the ball at your feet. To have a thing in one's power. A metaphor from foot-ball.

" We have the ball at our feet ; and, if the government will allow it . . . we can now crush out the rebellion."—*Lord Auckland.*

To keep the ball a-rolling. To continue without intermission. To keep the fun alive ; to keep the matter going. A metaphor from the game of bandy, or *la jeu de la cross*.

" It is Russia that keeps the ball rolling [the Servian and Bulgarian War, 1885, fomented and encouraged by Russian agents]." — *Newspaper paragraph*, 1885.

To keep the ball up. Not to let conversation or fun flag ; to keep the thing going. A metaphor taken from several games played with balls.

" I put in a word now and then to keep the ball up."—*Bentham.*

To open the ball. To lead off the first dance at a ball. (Italian, *ballaro*, to dance.)

Balls. *The three golden balls.* The emblem of St. Nicholas, who is said to have given three purses of gold to three virgin sisters to enable them to marry.

As the cognisance of the Medici family, they probably represent three golden pills —a punning device on the name. Be this, however, as it may, it is from the

Lombard family (the first great money-lenders in England) that the sign has been appropriated by pawnbrokers. (*See* MUGELLO for another account.)

Ballad means, strictly, a song to dance-music, or a song sung while dancing. (Italian, *ballare*, to dance, *ballata*, our *ballad*, *ballet* [*q.v.*]).

Ballads. " *Let me make the ballads, and who will may make the laws.*" Andrew Fletcher of Saltoun, in Scotland, wrote to the Marquis of Montrose, "I knew a very wise man of Sir Christopher Musgrave's sentiment. He believed, if a man were permitted to make all the ballads, he need not care who should make the laws " (1703).

Ballambangjan (*The Straits of*). A sailor's joke for a place where he may lay any wonderful adventure. These straits, he will tell us, are so narrow that a ship cannot pass through without jamming the tails of the monkeys which haunt the trees on each side of the strait; or any other rigmarole which his fancy may conjure up at the moment.

Ballast. *A man of no ballast.* Not steady; not to be depended on. Unsteady as a ship without ballast. A similar phrase is, "The man wants ballast."

Balle. *Prendre la balle au bond* (French). Strike while the iron is hot; make hay while the sun shines. The allusion is to certain games at ball, which must be struck at the moment of the rebound.

Renvoyer la balle à quelqu'un (French). To pay one off in his own coin. Literally, to strike back the ball to the sender.

Ballendino (*Don Antonio*). Intended for Anthony Munday, the dramatist. (Ben Jonson, *The Case Altered*, a comedy.)

Ballet (pronounce *bal-lay*). A theatrical representation of some adventure or intrigue by pantomime and dancing. Baltazari'ni, director of music to Catherine de' Medici, was the inventor of modern ballets.

Balliol College, Oxford, founded in 1263, by John de Baliol, Knight (father of Baliol, King of Scotland).

Balloon (*A pilot*). Metaphorically, a feeler, sent to ascertain public opinion.

"The pilot balloon sent from . . . ., has shown [the sender] the direction of the wind, and he now trims his sails accordingly." — *Newspaper paragraph*, January, 1886.

Balloon Post. During the siege of Paris, in 1871, fifty-four balloon posts were dispatched, carrying two-and-a-half million letters, weighing ten tons.

Balm (French, *baume*). Contraction of balsam (*q.r.*). The Balm of Gilead = the balsam of Gilead.

Is there no balm in Gilead ? Is there no remedy, no consolation, not even in religion ?

Balmawhapple. A stupid, obstinate Scottish laird in Scott's *Waverley*, a novel (1805).

Balmérino (*Lord*) was beheaded, but the executioner at the first stroke cut only half through the neck, and (we are told) his lordship turned round and grinned at the bungler.

Balmung or *Gram*. The sword of Siegfried, forged by Wieland, the Vulcan of the Scandinavians. Wieland, in a trial of merit, clove Amil'ias, a brother smith, through steel helmet and armour, down to the waist; but the cut was so fine that Amilias was not even aware that he was wounded till he attempted to move, when he fell into two pieces. (*Scandinavian mythology.*)

Balmy. " *I am going to the balmy* " —*i.e.* to " Balmy sleep; " one of Dick Swiveller's pet phrases. (*Dickens: Old Curiosity Shop.*)

Balmy-stick (*To put on the*). In prison slang means to feign insanity; and the " Balmy Ward " is the prison ward in which the insane, real or feigned, are confined.

Balnibar'bi. A land occupied by projectors. (*Swift: Gulliver's Travels.*)

Baltha'zar. One of the kings of Cologne—*i.e.* the three Magi, who came from the East to pay reverence to the infant Jesus. The two other magi were Melchior and Gasper.

Baltic. The Mediterranean of the north (Swedish, *balt*; Danish, *bælté*; Latin, *baltēus*; English, *belt*), the sea of the " Belts."

Balwhidder (*The Rev. Micah*). A Scotch Presbyterian minister, full of fossilised national prejudices, but both kind-hearted and sincere. (*Galt: Annals of the Parish*, a novel (1821).)

Bambi'no. A picture or image of the infant Jesus, swaddled (Italian, *bambi'no*, a little boy). The most celebrated is that in the church of Sta. Maria, in the Ara Cœli of Rome.

Bamboc'ciades (4 syl.). Pictures of grotesque scenes in low life, such as country wakes, penny weddings, and so on. They are so called from the Italian word *bamboccio* (a cripple), a nickname given to Pieter van Laer, the first Dutch painter of such scenes, distinguished in Rome.

Bamboc'cio or *Bamboche.* (*See* MICHAEL-ANGELO DES BAMBOCHES.)

Bamboo'zle. To cheat by cunning, or daze with tricks.

"The third refinement observable in the letter I send you, consists of the choice of certain words invented by some pretty fellows, such as *banter, bamboozle* . . . and *kidney* . . . some of which are now struggling for the vogue, and others are in possession of it."—*Swift: The Tatler* (Sept. 28, 1710).

To bamboozle into (doing something). To induce by trickery.

To bamboozle one out of something. To get something by trickery.

Bampton Lectures. Founded by the Rev. John Bampton, canon of Salisbury. He left an estate to the university of Oxford, to pay for eight divinity lectures on given subjects, to be preached at Great St. Mary's, and printed afterwards.

Ban. A proclamation of outlawry; a denunciation by the church (Anglo-Saxon, *ge-ban*, a proclamation; verb, *ge-bannan*).

Marriage bans. (*See* BANNS.)

To ban is to make a proclamation of outlawry. To *banish* is to proclaim a man an exile. (*See* BANDIT.)

Lever le ban et l'arrière ban (French). To levy the *ban* was to call the king's vassals to active service; to levy the *arrière ban* was to levy the vassals of a suzerain or under-lord.

"Le mot *ban*, qui signifie bannière, se disait de l'appel fait par le seigneur à ses vassaux pour les convoquer sous son étendard. On distinguait le *ban* composé des vassaux immédiats, qui etaient convoqués par le *roi* luimême, et l'*arrière ban*, composé des vassux convoqués par leurs suzerains."—*Bouillet: Dictionnaire d'Histoire, etc.*

Banagher. (*See under* BEATS.)

Ban'at. A territory under a *ban* (lord), from the Illyrican word *bojan*, a lord. The Turks gave this title to the lords of frontier provinces—*e.g.* the Banat of Croatia, which now forms part of the kingdom of Hungary.

Banbury. *A Banbury-man—i.e.* a Puritan (*Ben Jonson*); a bigot. From the reign of Elizabeth to that of Charles II. Banbury was noted for its number of Puritans and its religious "zeal."

As thin as Banbury cheese. In *Jack Drum's Entertainment* we read, "You are like a Banbury cheese, nothing but paring;" and Bardolph compares Slender to Banbury cheese (*Merry Wives*, i. 1). The Banbury cheese is a rich milk cheese about an inch in thickness.

Banco. *Sittings in Banco.* Sittings of the Superior Court of Common Law in its own bench or court, and not in circuit, as a judge of *Nisi Prius* (*q.v.*). (*Banc* is Italian for "bench" or "seat of justice.")

So much banco—i.e. so much bank money, as distinguished from current coin. At Hamburg, etc., currency is inferior to "bank money." (Not money in the bank, but the fictitious value set on cash by bankers.)

Bancus Regius. The king's or queen's bench. *Bancus Communis*, the bench of common pleas.

Bandan'a or **Bandanna.** A pocket-handkerchief. It is an Indian word, properly applied to silk goods, but now restricted to cotton handkerchiefs having a dark ground of Turkey red or blue, with little white or yellow spots. (Hindû, *bandhnū*, a mode of dyeing.)

Bandbox. *He comes out of a bandbox—i.e.* he is so neat and precise, so carefully got up in his dress and person, that he looks like some company dress, carefully kept in a bandbox.

Neat as a bandbox. Neat as clothes folded and put by in a bandbox.

Bandbox Plot (*The*). Rapin (*History of England*, iv. 297) tells us that a bandbox was sent to the lord-treasurer, in Queen Anne's reign, with three pistols charged and cocked, the triggers being tied to a pack-thread fastened to the lid. When the lid was lifted, the pistols would go off, and shoot the person who opened the lid. He adds that [dean] Swift happened to be by at the time, and seeing the pack-thread, cut it, thereby saving the life of the lord-treasurer.

"Two ink-horn tops your Whigs did fill
    With gunpowder and lead;
 Which with two serpents made of quill,
    You in a bandbox laid;
 A tinder-box there was beside,
    Which had a trigger to it,
 To which the very string was ty'd
    That was designed to do it."
            Plot upon Plot (about 1713).

Bande Noire. Properly, a *black band;* metaphorically, the *Vandal Society.* Those capitalists that bought up the Church property confiscated in the great French revolution were so called, because they recklessly pulled down ancient buildings and destroyed relics of great antiquity.

Bandit, plural *banditti* or *bandits,* properly means outlaw (Italian, *bandito,* banished), men pronounced "banned"). As these outlaws very often became robbers, the term soon came to signify banded highwaymen.

Bands. *Clerical bands* are a relic of the ancient *amice,* a square linen tippet tied about the neck of priests during the administration of mass. (Discontinued by the parochial clergy the latter part of the 19th century, but still used by clerics on the Continent.)

Legal bands are a relic of the wide collars which formed a part of the ordinary dress in the reign of Henry VIII., and which were especially conspicuous in the reign of the Stuarts. In the showy days of Charles II. the plain bands were changed for lace ends.

" The eighth Henry, as I understand,
Was the first prince that ever wore a band."
John Taylor, the Water Poet (1580-1654).

Bandy. *I am not going to bandy words with you—i.e.* to dispute about words. The reference is to a game called Bandy. The players have each a stick with a crook at the end to strike a wooden or other hard ball. The ball is bandied from side to side, each party trying to beat it home to the opposite goal. (Anglo-Saxon, *bendan,* to bend.)

" The bat was called a bandy from its being bent."—*Brand: Popular Antiquities* (article "Golf," p. 538).

Bane really means ruin, death, or destruction (Anglo-Saxon, *bana,* a murderer) ; and " I will be his bane," means I will ruin or murder him. Bane is, therefore, a mortal injury.

" My bane and antidote are both before it.
This [sword] in a moment brings me to an end.
But this [Plato] assures me I shall never die."
Addison: Cato.

Bango'rian Controversy. A theological paper-war stirred up by a sermon preached March 31st, 1717, before George I., by Dr. Hoadly, Bishop of Bangor, on the text, " My kingdom is not of this world." The best reply is by Law, in a series of *Letters to Hoadly.*

Bang-up, or *Slap-bang.* First-rate, thumping, as a " thumping legacy." It is a slang punning synonym of thumping or striking. Slap-bang is double bang, or doubly striking.

Banian or **Banyan** (*A*). A loose coat (Anglo-Indian).

" His coat was brownish black perhaps of yore,
In summer time a banyan loose he wore."
Lowell: FitzAdam's Story (stanza 15).

Banian Days [*Ban-yan*]. Days when no meat is served to a ship's crew. The

term is derived from the Banians, a class of Hindu merchants, who carried on a most extensive trade with the interior of Asia, but being a caste of the Vaisya, abstained from the use of meat. (Sanskrit, *banij,* a merchant.)

Bank. A money-changer's bench or table. (Italian *banco* or *banca.*)

Bank of a River. Stand with your back to the source, and face to the sea or outlet : the *left* bank is on your left, and *right* bank on your right hand.

Sisters of the Bank, i.e. of the bankside, " the brothel quarter " of London. Now removed to a different quarter, and divided into "North" and "South."

" On this side of the Banke was sometimes the bordello or stewes."—*Stow : Survey.*

Bankrupt. Money-lenders in Italy used to display the money they had to lend out on a *banco* or bench. When one of these money-lenders was unable to continue business, his bench or counter was broken up, and he himself was spoken of as a *bancorotto—i.e.* a bankrupt.

Bankside. Part of the borough of Southwark, noted in the time of Shakespeare for its theatres and retreats of the *demi - monde,* called " Sisters of the Bank."

" Come, I will send for a whole coach or two of Bankside ladies, and we will be jovial."—*Randolph : The Muses' Looking Glass.*

Banks's Horse. A learned horse, called Marocco, belonging to one Banks, in the reign of Queen Elizabeth. It is said that his shoes were of silver. One of his exploits was " the ascent of St. Paul's steeple."

Ban'natyne Club. A literary club which takes its name from George Bannatyne, to whose industry we owe the preservation of very much of the early Scotch poetry. It was instituted in 1823 by Sir Walter Scott, and had for its object the publication of rare works illustrative of Scotch history, poetry, and general literature. The club was dissolved in 1859.

Banner means a piece of cloth. (Anglo-Saxon, *fana;* Latin, *pannus;* Welsh, *baner;* Italian, *bandie'ra;* French, *banniere.*)

" An emperor's banner should be sixe foote longe, and the same in breadth ; a king's banner five foote ; a prince's and a duke's banner, four foote ; a marquys's, an erle's, a viscount's, a baron's, and a banneret's banner shall be but three foote square."—*Park.*

The banner of the Prophet is called

Sanjek-sherif, and is kept in the Eyab mosque of Constantinople.

The two black banners borne before the Califs of the house of Abbas were called *Night* and *Shadow*.

The sacred banner of France is the *Oriflamme* (*q.v.*).

Banners in churches. These are suspended as thank-offerings to God. Those in St. George's Chapel, Windsor, Henry VII.'s Chapel, Westminster, etc., are to indicate that the knight whose banner is hung up, avows himself devoted to God's service.

Ban'neret. One who leads his vassals to battle under his own banner. A knight made in the field was called a banneret, because the chief ceremony was cutting or tearing off the pointed ends of his banner.

Bannière. *Cent ans bannière, cent ans civière.* The ups and downs of life. A grand seigneur who has had his banner carried before him for a century, may come to drive his hand-barrow through the streets as a costermonger.

Bannière. *Il faut la croix et la bannière pour l'avoir.* If you want to have him, you must make a great fuss over him—you must go to meet him with cross and banner, "*aller au devant de lui avec un croix et la bannière.*"

Banns of Marriage. The publication in the parish church for three successive Sundays of an intended marriage. It is made after the Second Lesson of the Morning Service. To announce the intention is called "Publishing the banns," from the words "I publish the banns of marriage between . . . ." (Anglo-Saxon, *ge-bannan*, to proclaim, to announce).

To forbid the banns. To object to the proposed marriage.

"And a better fate did poor Maria deserve than to have a banns forbidden by the curate of the parish who published them."—*Sterne: Sentimental Journey.*

Banquet used at one time to mean the dessert. Thus, Taylor, in the *Pennyless Pilgrim*, says: "Our first and second course being threescore dishes at one boord, and after that, always a banquet." (French, *banquet; banc*, a bench or table. We use "table" also for a meal or feast, as "the funeral baked meats did coldly furnish forth the marriage table," *i.e.* feast.)

"After supper . . . . a delicate banquet, with abundance of wine."—*Cogan* (1583).

A banquet of brine. A flood of tears.

"My heart was charged to overflowing, and forced into my eyes a banquet of brine."—*C. Thomson: Autobiography*, p. 263.

Ban'quo. A Scotch general of royal extraction, who obtained several victories over the Highlanders and Danes in the reign of Donald VII. He was murdered by the order of Macbeth, and his ghost haunted the guilty usurper. (*Shakespeare: Macbeth.*)

Banshee. The supposed domestic spirit of certain Irish or Highland Scottish families, supposed to take an interest in its welfare, and to wail at the death of one of the family. The Welsh "Cyhyraeth" is a sort of Banshee.

⁘ The distinction of a Banshee is allowed only to families of pure Milesian stock. (Gaelic, *ban-sith*, a woman-fairy.)

Bantam. *A little bantam cock.* A little plucky fellow that will not be bullied by a person bigger than himself. The bantam cock will encounter a dunghill cock five times his own weight, and is therefore said to "have a great soul in a little body." The bantam originally came from Bantam, in Java.

Banting. *Doing Banting.* Reducing superfluous fat by living on meat diet, and abstaining from beer, farinaceous food, and vegetables, according to the method adopted by William Banting, a London cabinet-maker, once a very fat man (*born* 1796, *died* 1878). The word was introduced about 1864.

Bantling. A child. Mahn suggests the German, *bänkling*, a bastard. (Query, *bandling*, a little one in swaddling-clothes.)

Banyan. A Hindû shopkeeper. In Bengal it denotes a native who manages the money concerns of a European, and also serves as an interpreter. In Madras such an agent is called Dubash (*i.e.* one who can speak two languages). (*See* BANIAN DAYS.)

Bap or *Bap'homet.* An imaginary idol or symbol, which the Templars were said to employ in their mysterious rites. The word is a corruption of Mahomet. (French, *Baphomet ;* Old Spanish, *Matomat.*)

Bap'tes (2 syl.). Priests of the goddess Cotyt'to, whose midnight orgies were so obscene that they disgusted even Cotytto, the goddess of obscenity. They received their name from the Greek verb *bapto*, to wash, because they bathed themselves in the most effeminate manner. (*Juvenal*, ii. 91.)

Baptist. *John the Baptist.* His symbol is a sword, the instrument by which he was beheaded.

Bar. The whole body of barristers; as *bench* means the whole body of bishops.

" A dinner was given to the English Bar."—*The Times.*

Bar, excepting. In racing phrase a man will bet "Two to one, bar one," that is, two to one against any horse in the field with one exception. The word means " barring out " one, shutting out, or debarring one.

Bar. *At the bar.* As the prisoner at the bar, the prisoner in the dock before the judge.

Trial at bar, i.e. by the full court of judges. The bar means the place set apart for the business of the court.

To be called to the bar. To be admitted a barrister. The bar is the partition separating the seats of the benchers from the rest of the hall. Students having attained a certain status used to be called from the body of the hall within the bar, to take part in the proceedings of the court. To disbar is *to discard from the bar.* Now, "to be called within the bar " means to be appointed king's (or queen's) counsel; and to disbar means to expel a barrister from his profession.

Bar, in heraldry. An honourable ordinary, consisting of two parallel lines drawn across the shield and containing a fifth part of the field.

"A barre . . . is drawne overthwart the escochon . . . it containeth the fifth part of the Field."—*Gwillim: Heraldry.*

A Bar sinister in an heraldic shield means one drawn the reverse way; that is, not from left to right, but from right to left. Popularly but erroneously supposed to indicate bastardy.

Bar (*Trial at*). The examination of a difficult cause before the four judges in the superior courts.

Barabas. The hero of Marlow's tragedy, *The Jew of Malta.*

"A mere monster, brought in with a large painted nose. . . . He kills in sport, poisons whole nunneries, invents infernal machines. . . ."—*C. Lamb.*

Barata'ria. Sancho Panza's island-city, over which he was appointed governor. The table was presided over by Doctor Pedro Rezio de Ague'ro, who caused every dish set upon the board to be removed without being tasted—some because they heated the blood, and others because they chilled it; some for one ill effect, and some for another; so that Sancho was allowed to eat nothing. The word is from *barato* (cheap).

"The meat was put on the table, and whisked away, like Sancho's inauguration feast at Barataria."—*Thackeray.*

Barathron. A deep ditch behind the Acropolis of Athens into which malefactors were thrown: somewhat in the same way as criminals at Rome were cast from the "Tarpeian Rock."

Barb. An arrow. The feathers under the beak of a hawk were called *barb feathers* (beard feathers). The point of an arrow has two iron "feathers," which stick out so as to hinder the extraction of the arrow. (Latin, *barba,* a beard.)

N.B.—The *barb* is not the feather on the upper part of the *shaft,* but the hooked iron point or head.

Barb. A Barbary steed, noted for docility, speed, endurance, and spirit. (*See* BARBED STEEDS.)

Bar'bari. *Quod non fece'runt Barbari, fece'runt Barberi'ni* (What the barbarians left standing, Barberini contrived to destroy). Pope Barberini robbed the roof of the Pantheon to build the Baldacchi'no, or canopy of St. Peter's. It is made entirely of bronze, and weighs ninety tons.

Barbarians is certainly not derived from the Latin *barba* (a beard), as many suppose, because it is a Greek word, and has many analogous ones. The Greeks and Romans called all foreigners *barbarians* (babblers; men who spoke a language not understood by them); the Jews called them *Gentiles* (other nations); the Russians *Ostiaks* (foreigners). The reproachful meaning crept in from the natural egotism of man. It is not very long ago that an Englishman looked with disdainful pity on a foreigner, and the French still retain much of the same national exclusiveness. (*See* WUNDERBERG.)

"If then I know not the meaning of the voice [*words*], I shall be to him that speaketh a barbarian [*a foreigner*], and he that speaketh will be a barbarian unto me."—1 Cor. xiv. 11.

Barbarossa [*Red-beard,* similar to *Rufus*]. The surname of Frederick I. of Germany (1121-1190). Also Khaireddin Barbarossa, a famous corsair of the sixteenth century.

Barbary. *St. Barbary,* the patron saint of arsenals and powder magazines. Her father delivered her up to Martian, governor of Nicome'dia, for being a Christian. After she had been subjected to the most cruel tortures, her unnatural father was about to strike off her head, when a lightning flash laid him dead at her feet. Hence, those who invoke saints select St. Barbary in thunderstorms. (*See* BARBE.)

Roan Barbary. The favourite horse of Richard II. (*See* HORSE.)

"O, how it yearned my heart when I beheld
In London streets that coronation day,
When Bolingbroke rode on roan Barbary !
That horse that thou [Rich. II.] so often last bestrid,
That horse that I so carefully have dressed."
Shakespeare: Richard II., v. 5.

Bar'bason. A fiend mentioned by Shakespeare in the *Merry Wives of Windsor,* ii. 2, and in *Henry V.,* ii. 1.

" Amaimon sounds well, Lucifer well, Barbason well ; yet they are . . . the names of fiends."— *Merry Wives.*

Barbazure (or *Blue-Beard*). *See* "*Punch's* Prize Novelists," by Thackeray.

Barbe (*Ste.*). The powder-room in a French ship ; so called from St. Barbara, the patron saint of artillery. (*See* BARBARY.)

A barbe de fou apprend-on à raire (French). An apprentice is taught to shave on the chin of a fool.

Tel a fait sa barbe, qui n'est pas beau fils (French). You may waste half the day on making your toilet, and yet not come forth an Adonis. You cannot make a silk purse of a sow's ear. Not every block will make a Mercury.

" Heap lying curls a million on your head,
On socks, a cubit high, plant your proud tread,
You're just what you are—that's all about it."
Goethe: Faust (Dr. Anster), p. 163.

Bar'becue (3 syl.). A West Indian dish, consisting of a hog roasted whole, stuffed with spice, and basted with Madeira wine. Any animal roasted whole is so called.

" Oldfield. with more than harpy throat subdued,
Cries, 'Send me, ye gods, a whole hog barbecued !' " *Pope : Satires,* ii. 25, 26.

Barbed Steed (a corruption of *barded*). A horse in armour. (French, *bardé,* caparisoned.)

" And now, instead of mounting barbèd steeds
To fright the souls of fearful adversaries,
He capers nimbly in a lady's chamber,
To the lascivious pleasing of a lute."
Shakespeare : Richard III., act i. 1.

Barbel. Latin, *barbellus* (the barbed fish) ; so called from the barbules, or fleshy appendages round the mouth.

Barbeliots. A sect of Gnostics. Their first immortal son they called Barbeloth, omniscient, eternal, and incorruptible. He engendered light by the instrumentality of Christ, author of Wisdom. From Wisdom sprang Autogenês, and from Autogenês, Adam (male and female),

and from Adam, matter. The first angel created was the Holy Ghost, from whom sprang the first prince, named Protarchontês, who married Arrogance, whose offspring was Sin.

Barber. *Every barber knows that*

" Omnibus notum tonsoribus."
Horace : 1 *Satires,* VII. 3.

In Rome the *tonstri'næ* or barbers' shops were the fashionable resort of loungers and idlers. Here every scandal was known, and all the talk of the town was repeated.

Barber Poet. Jacques Jasmin, last of the Troubadours, who was a barber of Gascony. (1798-1864.)

Barber's Pole. The gilt knob at the end represents a brass basin, which is sometimes actually suspended on the pole. The basin has a notch cut in it to fit the throat, and was used for lathering customers who came to be shaved. The pole represents the staff held by persons in venesection ; and the two spiral ribbons painted round it represent the two bandages, one for twisting round the arm previous to blood-letting, and the other for binding. Barbers used to be the surgeons, but have fallen from "their high estate" since science has made its voice " to be heard on high."

N.B. — The Barbers' Hall stood in Monkwell Street, Cripplegate. The last barber-surgeon in London was Middleditch, of Great Suffolk Street, in the Borough. He died 1821.

"To this year" (1541), says Wornum . . . "belongs the Barber-Surgeons' picture of Henry (VIII.) granting a charter to the Corporation. The barbers and surgeons of London, originally constituting one company, had been separated, but were again, in the 32 Henry VIII., combined into a single society, and it was the ceremony of presenting them with a new charter which is commemorated by Holbein's picture, now in their hall in Monkwell Street."

Barbican (*The*) or *Barbacan.* The outwork intended to defend the drawbridge in a fortified town or castle (French, *barbacane*). Also an opening or loophole in the wall of a fortress, through which guns may be fired.

Barbier. *Un barbier rase l'autre* (French). Caw me and I'll caw thee. One good turn deserves another. One barber shaves another.

Barcarole (3 syl.). A song sung by Venetian *barcaroli,* as they row their gondolas. (Italian, *barcarolo,* a boatman.)

Barcelona (*A*). A fichu, piece of velvet for the neck, or small neck-tie, made at Barcelona, and common in

England in the first quarter of the nineteenth century. Also a neckcloth of some bright colour, as red with yellow spots.

"And on this handkerchief so starch and white
She pinned a Barcelona black and tight."
    Peter Pindar: Portfolio (Dinah).
"A double Barcelona protected his neck."—
Scott: Peveril of the Peak (Prefatory Letter.)

Bar'clayans. (*See* BERE'ANS.)

Barco'chebah or **Barchōchebas** (Shimeon). A fanatical leader of the Jews who headed a revolt of the Jews against the Romans A.D. 132, took Jerusalem in 132, and was slain by Julius Sevērus in an assault of Bethel, A.D. 135. (*Didot: Nouvelle Biographie Universelle.*)

"Shared the fall of the Antichrist Barcochebah."—*Professor Seeley : Ecce Homo.*

Bardesanists. Followers of Bardesanes, of Edessa, founder of a Gnostic sect in the second century. They believed that the human body was ethereal till it became imbruted with sin. Milton, in his *Comus*, refers to this :—

"When Lust
By unchaste looks, loose gestures, and foul talk,
But most by lewd and lavish acts of sin,
Lets in defilement to the inward parts,
The soul grows clotted by contagion,
Imbodies and imbrutes."

Bardit. The ancient German chant, which incited to war.

Bardo de' Bardi. A wealthy Florentine scholar, father of Romola, in George Eliot's *Romola*, a novel (1863).

Bardolph. One of Falstaff's inferior officers. Falstaff calls him "the knight of the burning lamp," because his nose was so red, and his face so "full of meteors." He is a low-bred, drunken swaggerer, without principle, and poor as a church mouse. (*Merry Wives ; Henry IV.,* i., ii.)

"We must have better assurance for Sir John than Bardolf's. We like not the security."—*Lord Macaulay.*

Bards. The oldest bardic compositions that have been preserved are of the fifth century ; the oldest existing manuscript is the *Psalter of Cashel,* a collection of bardic legends, compiled in the ninth century by Cormac Mac Culinan, bishop of Cashel and king of Munster.

Bard of Avon. Shakespeare, who was born and buried at Stratford-upon-Avon. Also called "The bard of all times." (1564-1616.)

Bard of Ayrshire. Robert Burns, a native of Ayrshire. (1759-1796.)

Bard of Hope. Thomas Campbell, author of *The Pleasures of Hope.* (1777-1844.)

Bard of the Imagination. Mark Akenside, author of *Pleasures of the Imagination.* (1721-1770.)

Bard of Memory. Rogers, author of *The Pleasures of Memory.* (1762-1855.)

Bard of Olney. Cowper, who resided at Olney, in Bucks, for many years. (1731-1800.)

The Bard of Prose.
    "He of the hundred tales of love."
        Childe Harold, iv. 56.
i.e. Boccaccio.

The Bard of Rydal Mount. William Wordsworth ; so called because Rydal Mount was his mountain home. Also called the "Poet of the Excursion," from his principal poem. (1770-1850.)

Bard of Twickenham. Alexander Pope, who resided at Twickenham. (1688-1744.)

Barebone Parliament (*The*). The Parliament convened by Cromwell in 1653 ; so called from Praise-God Barebone, a fanatical leader, who was a prominent member.

Barefaced. Audacious, shameless, impudent. This seems to imply that social and good manners require concealment, or, at any rate, to veil the face with "white lies." In Latin — *retecta facie ;* in French—*à visage découvert.* Cassius says to his friend Brutus, "If I have veiled my looks . . .," that is, concealed my thoughts from you.

Barefooted. Certain monks and nuns, who use sandals instead of shoes. The Jews and Romans used to put off their shoes in mourning and public calamities, by way of humiliation. The practice is defended by the command of our Lord to His disciples: "Carry neither purse, nor scrip, nor shoes" (Luke x. 4).

Bare Poles (*Under*) implies that the weather is rough and the wind so high that the ship displays no sails on the masts. Figuratively applied to a man reduced to the last extremity. Figuratively, a disingenuous person sails under bare poles.

"We were scudding before a heavy gale, under bare poles."—*Capt. Marryat.*

Bargain. *Into the bargain.* In addition thereto ; besides what was bargained for.

To make the best of a bad bargain. To bear bad luck, or a bad bargain, with equanimity.

Bark. Dogs in their wild state never bark ; they howl, whine, and growl, but do not bark. Barking is an acquired habit ; and as only domesticated dogs bark, this effort of a dog to speak is no indication of a savage temper.

Barking dogs seldom bite. Huffing, bouncing, hectoring fellows rarely possess cool courage. Similar proverbs are found in Latin, French, Italian, and German.

To bark at the moon. To rail at those in high places, as a dog thinks to frighten the moon by baying at it. There is a superstition that it portends death or ill-luck.

" I'd rather be a dog, and bay the moon,
  Than such a Roman."
            Shakespeare: Julius Cæsar, iv. 3.

His bark is worse than his bite. He scolds and abuses roundly, but does not bear malice, or do mischief. The proverb says, "Barking dogs never bite."

Barker. A pistol, which barks or makes a loud report.

Barkis is willin'. The message sent by Barkis to Peggotty by David Copperfield, expressing his desire to marry. It has passed into a proverbial expression indicating willingness or consent. (*Dickens: David Copperfield.*)

Barktan. The famous black stone in the eastern corner of the Kaaba; it is 4½ feet in length, and is surrounded with a circle of gold. The legend is that when Abraham wished to build the Kaaba, the stones came to him of their own accord, and the patriarch commanded all the faithful to kiss the Barktan.

Bar'laham. A hermit who converted Jos'aphat, an Indian prince. This German romance, entitled *Barlaham and Josaphat,* was immensely popular in the Middle Ages. It was written by Rudolf of Ems (13th century).

Barley. *To cry barley.* To ask for truce (in children's games). Query, a corruption of parley.

" A proper lad o' his quarters, that will not cry barley in a brulzie."—*Sir W. Scott: Waverley,* xiii.

Barley-bree. Barley-broth; that is, malt liquor brewed from barley (*Scotch*).

" The cock may craw, the day may daw,
  And aye we'll taste the barley-bree."
            Burns: Willie Brew'd a Peck o' Maut.

Barley Cap. *To wear the barley cap.* To be top-heavy or tipsy with barley-bree. The liquor got into the head.

Barleycorn. *John* or *Sir John Barleycorn.* A personification of malt liquor. The term has been made popular by Robert Burns.

" Inspiring bold John Barleycorn,
  What dangers thou canst make us scorn ! "
            Burns: Tam o' Shanter, 105, 106.

Barley-mow. A heap of barley housed, or where it is housed. (Anglo-Saxon, *mowe,* a heap; Italian, *mucchio;* Spanish, *mucho.*)

Barley Sugar. Sugar boiled in a decoction of barley. It is not now made so, but with saffron, sugar, and water, flavoured with oil of citron, orange, or lemon.

" Barley sugar was prepared by boiling down ordinary sugar in a decoction of pearl-barley."—*Knowledge* (July 6th, 1883).

Bar'mecide (3 syl.). The word is used to express the uncertainty of things on which we set our heart. As the beggar looked forward to a feast, but found only empty dishes; so many a joy is found to be mere illusion when we come to partake of it.

" To-morrow ! the mysterious unknown guest
  Who cries aloud, ' Remember Barmecide !
  And tremble to be happy with the rest.' "
            Longfellow.

Bar'mecide's Feast. A feast where there is nothing to eat; any illusion. Barmecide asked Schac'abac, a poor, starving wretch, to dinner, and set before him an empty plate. "How do you like your soup ?" asked the merchant. "Excellently well," replied Schac'abac. "Did you ever see whiter bread ?" "Never, honourable sir," was the civil answer. Wine was then brought in, and Schac'abac was pressed to drink, but excused himself by saying he was always quarrelsome in his cups. Being over-persuaded, he fell foul of his host, and was provided with food to his heart's content. (*Arabian Nights: Barber's Sixth Brother.*)

Bar'nabas. *St. Barnabas' Day,* June 11. St. Barnabas was a fellow-labourer of St. Paul. His symbol is a rake, because the 11th of June is the time of hay-harvest.

Bar'nabites (3 syl.). An Order of monks, so called because the church of St. Barnabas, in Milan, was given to them to preach in. They are also called "Canons of St. Paul," because the original society made a point of reading St. Paul's Epistles.

Barnaby Lecturers. Four lecturers in the University of Cambridge, elected annually on St. Barnabas' Day (June 11), to lecture on mathematics, philosophy, rhetoric, and logic.

Barnaby Rudge. A half-witted lad whose companion is a raven. (*Dickens: Barnaby Rudge.*)

Bar'nacle. The Solan goose. The strange tales of this creature have arisen

4

from a tissue of blunders. The Latin *pernac'ula* is a "small limpet," and *bernacula* (Portuguese, *bernaca;* French, *barnache*) is the Scotch *bren-clake* or "Solan goose." Both words being corrupted into "barnacle," it was natural to look for an identity of nature in the two creatures, so it was given out that the goose was the offspring of the limpet. Gerard, in 1636, speaks of "broken pieces of old ships on which is found certain spume or froth, which in time breedeth into shells, and the fish which is hatched therefrom is in shape and habit like a bird."

Barnacles. Placemen who stick to their offices but do little work, like the barnacles which live on the ship but impede its progress.

"The redundants would be ' Barnacles' with a vengeance . . . and the work be all the worse done for these hangers-on."—*Nineteenth Century* (August, 1888, p. 280).

Bar'nacles. Spectacles, or rather reading-glasses ; so called because in shape they resemble the twitchers used by farriers to keep under restraint unruly horses during the process of bleeding, dressing, or shoeing. This instrument, formerly called a barnacle, consisting of two branches joined at one end by a hinge, was fixed on the horse's nose. Dr. Latham considers the word a corruption of *binocles* (double-eyes), Latin, *binus oculus.* Another suggestion is "binnacle," the case on board ship in which the steering compass is placed, illuminated when it is dark by a lamp.

Barnardine. A reckless, dissolute fellow, "fearless of what's past, present, and to come." (*Shakespeare : Measure for Measure.*)

Barn-burners. Destructives, who, like the Dutchman of story, would burn down their barns to rid themselves of the rats.

Barnet. An epicure who falls in love with, and marries, a lady on account of her skill in dressing a dish of stewed carp. (*Edward*, a novel by Dr. John Moore, 1796.)

Barnwell (*George*). The chief character in a prose tragedy, so called, by George Lillo. He was a London apprentice, who fell in with a wanton in Shoreditch, named Sarah Millwood, whom he visited, and to whom he gave £200 of his master's money, and ran away. He next robbed his uncle, a rich grazier at Ludlow, and beat out his brains. Having spent the money, Sarah turned him out of doors, and each informed against the other. Sarah Millwood and George Barnwell were both hanged. (*Lillo*, 1693-1739.)

Baro-Devel. The great god of the gipsies. His son is named Alako.

Baron properly means a man (Old High German, *baro*). It was a term applied to a serving-soldier, then to a military chief, and ultimately to a lord. The reverse of this is seen in our word *slave* (a servile menial), which is the Slavonic word *slav* (noble). (*See* IDIOT.)

Baron Bung. Mine host, master of the beer bung.

Baron Munchausen (pron. *Moohnkow'-zn*). Said to be a satire on Bruce, the Abyssinian traveller, to whom the work was dedicated. The author was Raspé, a German fugitive from the officers of justice, living in Cornwall (1785). The chief incidents were compiled from various sources.

Baron of Beef. Two sirloins left uncut at the backbone. The *baron* is the backpart of the ox, called in Danish, the *rug*. Jocosely, but wrongly, said to be a pun upon *baron* and *sir* loin.

Barons' War (*The*). An historical poem by Michael Drayton (1603),

"The pictures of Mortimer and the queen, and of Edward's entrance into the castle, are splendid and spir.ted.—*Campbell*.

Barrack Hack (*The*). A lady who hangs on the sleeve of a military officer, attends all barrack fêtes of every description, and is always ready to get up a dance, dinner, or picnic, to please the officers on whom she dances attendance.

Barracks means huts made of the branches of trees (Gaelic, *barr*, the top of anything ; *barrach*, the top-branches of trees ; *barrachad*, a hut made of branches). Our word is plural, indicative of the whole collection ; but the French *baraque* is singular. (*See* B. K. S.)

Barrack (*To*). To jeer at, to receive with derisive applause. The substantive *barracking* = derisive cheers and shouts, is also in use. These terms were introduced during the visit of the Australian cricketers in 1899.

Barratry or *Barretry*. *Qui fait barat, barat lui vient* (French). With what measure ye mete, it shall be measured to you again. Barratry is false faith to one's employers. It is a sea term, and means the commission of a fraud on the owners or insurers of a ship by the captain or the crew. The fraud may consist of many phases, such as deserting the ship, sinking her, falsifying her cargo, etc. The French have other proverbs to the same effect: as, *La tricherie revient presque toujours à son maitre.* "He made a pit and . . . is fallen into the ditch which he made. His mischief shall return upon his own head." (Psalm vii. 14, 15, 16.)

Barrel Fever. Intoxication or illness from intemperance in drink.

Barrell's Blues. The 4th Foot; so called from the colour of their facings, and William Barrell, colonel of the regiment (1734-1739). Now called "The King's Own (Royal Lancaster Regiment)." They were called "Lions" from their badge, *The Lion of England.*

Barrette. *Parler à la barrette* (French). To give one a thump o' the head. The word *barrette* means the cap worn by the lower orders.

"Et moi, je pourrais bien parler à ta barrette."
Molière: L'Avare.

It is also used to signify the ordinary *birretta* of ecclesiastics and (probably) of French lawyers. *Il à reçu le chapeau* or *la barrette.* He has been made a cardinal.

"Le pape lui envoyait la barrette, mais elle ne servit qu' à le faire mourir cardinal."—*Voltaire: Siècle de Louis XIV.,* chap. xxxix.

Barrica'de (3 syl.). To block up. The term rose in France in 1588, when Henri de Guise returned to Paris in defiance of the king's order. The king sent for his Swiss Guards, and the Parisians tore up the pavement, threw chains across the streets, and piled up barrels filled with earth and stones, behind which they shot down the Swiss as they passed through the streets. The French for barrel is *barrique,* and to barricade is to stop up the streets with these barrels.

The day of the Barricades:
(1) May 12th, 1588, when the people forced Henri III. to flee from Paris.
(2) August 5th, 1648, the beginning of the Fronde War.
(3) July 27th, 1830, the first day of *le grand semain* which drove Charles X. from the throne.
(4) February 24th, 1848, which drove Louis Philippe to abdicate and flee to England.
(5) June 23rd, 1848, when Affre, Archbishop of Paris, was shot in his attempt to quell the insurrection.
(6) December 2nd, 1851, the day of the *coup d'état,* when Louis Napoleon

made his appeal to the people for re-election to the Presidency for ten years.

Barrier Treaty, November 5th, 1715, by which the Dutch reserved the right of holding garrisons in certain fortresses of the Spanish Netherlands.

Bar'rikin. Jargon, words not understood. (Old French, *baracan,* from the Breton, *bara gwyn,* "white bread," taken as a type of barbarous words; modern French, *baragouin,* gibberish.)

Barring-out. A practice of barring the master out of the schoolroom in order to dictate terms to him. It was once common, but is now numbered with past customs. Miss Edgeworth has a tale so called.

Barrister. One admitted to plead at the bar; one who has been "called to the bar." The bar is the rail which divides the counsel from the audience, or the place thus enclosed. Tantamount to the rood-screen of a church, which separates the chancel from the rest of the building. Both these are relics of the ancient notion that the laity are an inferior order to the privileged class.

᛭ A *silk* gown or bencher pleads *within* the bar, a *stuff* gown or outer barrister pleads without the bar.

An Outer or Utter Barrister. This phrase alludes to an ancient custom observed in courts of law, when certain barristers were allowed to plead; but not being benchers (king's counsel or sergeants-at-law) they took their seats "at the end of the forms called the bar." The Utter Barrister comes next to a bencher, and all barristers inferior to the Utter Barristers are termed "Inner Barristers."

᛭ The whole society is divided into three ranks: Benchers, Utter Barristers, and Inner Barristers.

An Inner Barrister. A barrister inferior in grade to a Bencher or Utter Barrister.

A Revising Barrister. One appointed to revise the lists of electors.

A Vacation Barrister. One newly called to the bar, who for three years has to attend in "long vacation."

Barristers' Bags. In the Common Law bar, barristers' bags are either red or dark blue. Red bags are reserved for King's Counsel and sergeants; but a stuff gownsman may carry one "if presented with it by a silk." Only red bags may be taken into Common Law Courts; blue bags must be carried no farther than the robing room. In the Chancery Courts the etiquette is not so strict.

Barristers' Gowns. "Utter barristers wear a stuff or bombazine gown, and the puckered material between the shoulders of the gown is all that is now left of the purse into which, in early days, the successful litigant . . . dropped his . . . pecuniary tribute . . . for services rendered" (*Notes and Queries*, 11 March, 1893, p. 124). The fact is that the counsel was supposed to appear merely as a friend of the litigant. Even now he cannot recover his fees.

Barry Cornwall, poet. A *nom de plume* of Bryan Waller Procter. It is an anagram of his name. (1788-1874.)

Barsa'nians. Heretics who arose in the sixth century. They made their sacrifices consist in taking wheat flour on the tip of their first finger, and carrying it to their mouth.

Bar-sur-Aube (*Prévot*). *Je ne voudrais pas être roi, si j'étais prévot de Bar-sur-Aube* (French). I should not care to be king, if I were Provost of Bar-sur-Aube [the most lucrative and honourable of all the provostships of France]. Almost the same idea is expressed in the words

" And often to our comfort we shall find,
The sharded beetle in a safer hold
Than is the full-winged eagle."

Almost to the same effect Pope says :

" And more true joy Marcellus exiled feels,
Than Cæsar with a senate at his heels."

⁂ See CASTLE OF BUNGAY.

Bartholo. A doctor in the comedies of *Le Mariage de Figaro*, and *Le Barbier de Séville*, by Beaumarchais.

Barthol'omew (*St.*). The symbol of this saint is a knife, in allusion to the knife with which he was flayed alive.
St. Bartholomew's Day, August 24th. Probably Bartholomew is the apostle called "Nathanael" by St. John the Evangelist (i. 45-51).
Massacre of St. Bartholomew. The slaughter of the French Protestants in the reign of Charles IX., begun on St. Bartholomew's Day, *i.e.* between the 24th and 25th August, 1572. It is said that 30,000 persons fell in this dreadful persecution.

Bartholomew Fair. Held in West Smithfield (1133-1855) on St. Bartholomew's Day.
A Bartholomew doll. A tawdry, overdressed woman ; like a flashy, bespangled doll offered for sale at Bartholomew Fair.

A Bartholomew pig. A very fat person. At Bartholomew Fair one of the chief attractions used to be a pig, roasted whole, and sold piping hot. Falstaff calls himself,

" A little tidy Bartholomew boar-pig."—2 *Henry IV.* ii. 4.

Barthram's Dirge (in Sir Walter Scott's *Border Minstrelsy*). Sir Noel Paton, in a private letter, says : "The subject of this dirge was communicated to Sir Walter as a genuine fragment of the ancient *Border Muse* by his friend Mr. Surtees, who is in reality its author. The ballad has no foundation in history ; and the fair lady, her lover, and the nine brothers, are but the creation of the poet's fancy." Sir Noel adds : "I never painted a picture of this subject, though I have often thought of doing so. The engraving which appeared in the *Art Journal* was executed without my concurrence from the oil sketch, still, I presume, in the collection of Mr. Pender, the late M.P., by whom it was brought to the Exhibition of the Royal Scottish Academy here" (at Edinburgh) November 19th, 1866.

Bartol'do. A rich old miser, who died of fear and penurious self-denial. Fazio rifled his treasures, and, being accused by his own wife Bianca, was put to death. (*Dean Milman : Fazio.*)

Bartôle (2 syl.). *He knows his "Bartole" as well as a cordelier his "Dormi"* (French). Bartole was an Italian lawyer, born in Umbria (1313-1356), whose authority amongst French barristers is equal to that of Blackstone with us. The cordeliers or Franciscans were not great at preaching, and perhaps for this reason used a collection called *Dormi*, containing the best specimens of the fourteenth and fifteenth centuries. This compilation was called *Dormi* from the first word in the book. The compilation is anonymous.

Bartolist. One skilled in law. (*See above.*)

Barzil'lai (3 syl.). The Duke of Ormond, a friend and staunch adherent of Charles II. The allusion is to Barzillai, who assisted David when he was expelled by Absalom from his kingdom (2 Sam. xvii. 27-29).

" Barzillai crowned with honours and with years . . . .
In exile with his godlike prince he mourned,
For him he suffered, and with him returned."
Dryden: Absalom and Achitophel, l. 817-24.

Bas Bleu. (*See* BLUE STOCKING.)

Base. The basis, or that on which an animal walks (Greek, *baino*, to go, and *basis*, a footstep). The foot is the foundation—hence, base of a pillar, etc. It is also the lowest part, and hence the notion of worthless. Bass in music (Italian, *basso*) is the lowest part, or the part for the lowest compass of voice.

Base Tenure. Holding by copy of court-roll, in opposition to freeholders.

Base of Operation, in war. That is, a fortified or otherwise secure spot, where the magazines of all sorts can be formed, whence the army can derive stores, and upon which (in case of reverse) it can fall back. If a fleet, it is called a *movable* base; if a fortified or other immovable spot, it is called a *fixed* base. The line from such a base to the object aimed at is called "the Line of Operation."

Bashaw'. An arrogant, domineering man; so called from the Turkish vice-roys and provincial governors, each of whom bears the title of *bascha* (pacha).

A three-tailed bashaw. A beglerbeg or prince of princes among the Turks, having a standard of three horse-tails borne before him. The next in rank is the bashaw with two tails, and then the bey, who has only one horse-tail.

Basil'ian Monks. Monks of the Order of St. Basil, who lived in the fourth century. This Order has produced 14 popes, 1,805 bishops, 3,010 abbots, and 11,085 martyrs.

Basil'ica. Originally the court of the Athenian archon, called the *basileus*, who used to give judgment in the *stoa basil'ikē*. At Rome these courts of justice had their nave, aisles, porticoes, and tribunals; so that when used for Christian worship very little alteration was needed. The church of St. John Lat'eran at Rome was an ancient basilica.

Basilics or *Basil'ica*. A digest of laws begun by the Byzantine emperor Basilius in 867, and completed by his son Leo, the philosopher, in 880.

Basilid'ians. A sect of Gnostic heretics, followers of Basilīdēs, an Alexandrian Gnostic, who taught that from the unborn Father "Mind" was begotten; from Mind proceeded "The Word"; from the Word or *Logos* proceeded "Understanding"; from Understanding "Wisdom" and "Power"; from Wisdom and Power "Excellencies," "Princes," and "Angels,"

the agents which created heaven. Next to these high mightinesses come 365 celestial beings, the chief of whom is Abraxas (*q.v.*), and each of whom has his special honour. What we call Christ is what the Basilidians term *The first-begotten "Mind."*

Basilisco. A braggart; a character in an old play entitled *Solyman and Perseda.* Shakespeare makes the Bastard say to his mother, who asks him why he boasted of his ill-birth, "Knight, knight, good mother, Basilisco-like"—*i.e.* my boasting has made me a knight. (*King John*, i. 1.)

Basilisk. The king of serpents (Greek, *basileus*, a king), supposed to have the power of "looking any one dead on whom it fixed its eyes." Hence Dryden makes Clytus say to Alexander, "Nay, frown not so; you cannot look me dead." This creature is called a king from having on its head a mitre-shaped crest. Also called a *cockatrice,* and fabulously alleged to be hatched by a serpent from a cock's egg.

> "Like a boar
> Plunging his tusk in mastiff's gore;
> Or basilisk, when roused, whose breath,
> Teeth, sting, and eyeballs all are death."
> *King: Art of Love.*

Basket. *To be left in the basket.* Neglected or uncared for. Left in the waste-basket.

To give a basket. To refuse to marry. In Germany a basket [*korb*] is fixed on the roof of one who has been jilted, or one who, after long courtship, cannot persuade the lady courted to become his wife.

Baso'chians. Clerks of the basilica or palace. When the Kings of France inhabited the "Palace of Justice," the judges, advocates, proctors, and lawyers went by the common name of the *clercs de la basoche;* subsequently (in 1303) divided into "Clerks of the Palace," and "Clerks of the Châtelet." The chief of the basochians was called *Le roi de la basoche,* and had his court, coin, and grand officers. He reviewed his "subjects" every year, and administered justice twice a week. Henri III. suppressed the title of the chief, and transferred all his functions and privileges to the Chancellor.

Bass. Matting made of bast, that is the lime or linden tree. Dutch, *bast,* bark; Swedish, *basta,* to bind; so called because used for binding. "Ribbons from the linden tree give a wreath no charms to me." The shepherds of

Carniola make a cloth of the outer bark. The inner bark is made into Russian matting, and is serviceable to gardeners for packing, tying up plants, protecting trees, etc. Other materials are now used for the same purposes, and for *hassocks*, etc., but the generic word *bass* designates both bast-bark and all its imitations.

Bastard. Any sweetened wine, but more correctly applied to a sweet Spanish wine (white or brown) made of the bastard muscadine grape.

"I will pledge you willingly in a cup of bastard."—*Sir Walter Scott: Kenilworth*, chap. iii.

Ba'ste (1 syl.). *I'll baste your jacket for you, i.e.* cane you. *I'll give you a thorough basting, i.e.* beating. (Spanish, *baston*, a stick; Italian, *bastone*; French, *bâton*.)

Ba'stille means simply a building (French, *bastir*, now *bâtir*, to build). Charles V. built it as a royal château; Philippe-Auguste enclosed it with a high wall; St. Louis administered justice in the park, under the oak-trees; Philippe de Valois demolished the old château and commenced a new one; Louis XI. first used it as a state prison; and it was demolished by the rabble in the French Revolution, July 14th, 1789.

Bastina'do. A beating (Italian, *bastone*; French, *baston*, now *bâton*, a stick). The Chinese, Turks, and Persians punish offenders by beating them on the soles of the feet. The Turks call the punishment *zarb*.

Bastion (*A*), in fortification, is a work having two faces and two flanks, all the angles of which are *salient*, that is, pointing outwards towards the country. The line of rampart which joins together the flanks of two bastions is technically called a curtain.

Bastions in fortifications were invented in 1480 by Achmet Pasha; but San Michaeli of Verona, in 1527, is said by Maffei and Vasari to have been the real inventor.

Bat. Harlequin's lath wand (French, *batte*, a wooden sword).

To carry out one's bat (in cricket). Not to be "out" when the time for drawing the stumps has arrived.

Off his own bat. By his own exertions; on his own account. A cricketer's phrase, meaning runs won by a single player.

Bat-horses and *Bat-men*.- Bat-horses are those which carry officers' baggage during a campaign (French, *bât*, a pack-saddle). Bat-men are those who look after the pack-horses.

Batavia. The Netherlands; so called from the Bata'vi, a Celtic tribe who dwelt there.

"Flat Batavia's willowy groves."
Wordsworth.

Bate me an Ace. (*See* BOLTON.)

Bath. *Knights of the Bath.* This name is derived from the ceremony of bathing, which used to be practised at the inauguration of a knight, as a symbol of purity. The last knights created in this ancient form were at the coronation of Charles II. in 1661. G.C.B. stands for *Grand Cross of the Bath* (the first-class); K.C.B. *Knight Commander of the Bath* (the second class); C.B. *Companion of the Bath* (the third class).

King of Bath. Richard Nash, generally called Beau Nash, a celebrated master of the ceremonies at Bath for fifty-six years. (1674-1761.)

There, go to Bath with you! Don't talk nonsense. Insane persons used to be sent to Bath for the benefit of its mineral waters. The implied reproof is, what you say is so silly, you ought to go to Bath and get your head shaved.

Bath Brick. Alluvial matter made in the form of a brick, and used for cleaning knives and polishing metals. It is not made at Bath, but at Bridgwater, being dredged from the river Parrett, which runs through Bridgwater.

Bath Chair (*A*). A chair mounted on wheels and used for invalids. Much used at Bath, frequented by invalids for its hot springs.

Bath Metal. The same as Pinchbeck (*q.v.*). An alloy consisting of sixteen parts copper and five of zinc.

Bath Post. A letter paper with a highly-glazed surface, used by the highly-fashionable visitors of Bath when that watering-place was at its prime. (*See* POST.) Since the introduction of the penny post and envelope system, this paper has gone out of general use.

Bath Shillings. Silver tokens coined at Bath in 1811-1812, and issued for 4s., for 2s., and for 1s., by C. Culverhouse, J. Orchard, and J. Phipps.

Bath Stone. A species of limestone, used for building, and found in the Lower Oolite, in Wiltshire and Somersetshire. It is easily wrought in the quarry, but hardens on exposure to the air. Called "Bath" stone because several of the quarries are near Bath, in Somersetshire.

Bath (*Major*). A poor, high-minded officer, who tries to conceal his poverty by bold speech and ostentatious bearing. Colman's *Poor Gentleman* (Lieutenant Worthington) is a similar character. (*Fielding : Amelia* (a novel) 1751.)

Bath-kol (*daughter of the voice*). A sort of divination common among the ancient Jews after the gift of prophecy had ceased. When an appeal was made to Bath-kol, the first words uttered after the appeal were considered oracular.

Bathos [Greek, *bathos*, depth]. A ludicrous descent from grandiloquence to commonplace. A literary mermaid.

> "Humano capiti cervicem pictor equinam
> Jungere si velit . . . ut turpiter atrum
> Desinat in piscem mulier formosa superne."
> "Parturiunt montes, nascetur ridiculus mus."
>   *Horace : De Arte Poetica*, line 139.

A good example is the well-known couplet :

> "And thou, Dalhousie, the great god of war,
> Lieutenant-general to the earl of Mar."

Bath'sheba. The Duchess of Portsmouth, a favourite court lady of Charles II. The allusion is to the wife of Uri'ah the Hittite, criminally beloved by David (2 Sam. xi.). The Duke of Monmouth says :

> "My father, whom with reverence yet I name,
> Charmed into ease, is careless of his fame;
> And, bribed with petty sums of foreign gold,
> Is grown in Bathsheba's embraces old."
>   *Dryden : Absalom and Achitophel*, i. 707-10.

Bathyllus. A beautiful boy of Samos, greatly beloved by Polycrătēs the tyrant, and by the poet Anacreon. (*See Horace : Epistle* xiv. 9.)

> "To them [*i.e.* the æsthetic school] the boyhood of Bathyllus is of more moment than the manhood of Napoleon."—*Mallock : The New Republic*, book iv. chap. i.

Batiste. The fabric is so called from Baptiste of Cambrai, who first manufactured it.

Ba'trachomy'omach'ia (pronounce *Ba-trak'o-my'o-mak'ia*). A storm in a puddle ; much ado about nothing. The word is the name of a mock heroic poem in Greek, supposed to be by Pi'grēs of Caria, and means *The Battle of the Frogs and Mice.*

Batta or *Batty* (Hindustanee). Perquisites ; wages. Properly, an allowance to East Indian troops in the field. In garrison they are put on half-batta.

> "He would rather live on half-pay in a garrison that could boast of a fives-court, than vegetate on full batta where there was none."—*G. R. Gleig: Thomas Munro*, vol. i. chap. iv. p. 227.

Battar, *Al* [*the Trenchant*]. One of Mahomet's swords, confiscated from the Jews when they were exiled from Medi'na.

Battels. Rations or "commons" allowed to students at the University of Oxford. (To *batten*, to feast.)

Battel Bills. Buttery bills at the universities. (*See above.*)

Battersea. *You must go to Battersea to get your simples cut.* A reproof to a simpleton, or one who makes a very foolish observation. The market gardeners of Battersea used to grow simples (medicinal herbs), and the London apothecaries went there to select or cut such as they wanted. (*See* NAVIGA.)

Battle. Professor Creasy says there are fifteen *decisive* battles, which led to some great political change : B.C. 490, Mar'athon ; 413, Syracuse ; 331, Arbe'la : 207, Metau'rus ; the defeat of the Romans under Varus by Arminius, 9 ; Chalons, A.D. 451 ; Tours, 732 ; Hastings, 1066 ; Joan of Arc's victory at Orléans, 1429 ; the Arma'da, 1588 ; Blenheim, 1704 ; Pultow'a, 1709 ; Sarato'ga, 1777 ; Valmy, 1792 ; and Waterloo, 1815.

Battle royal. A certain number of cocks, say sixteen, are pitted together ; the eight victors are then pitted, then the four, and last of all the two ; and the winner is victor of the battle royal. Metaphorically, the term is applied to chess, etc.

Battle scenes. Le Clerc could arrange on a small piece of paper not larger than one's hand an army of 20,000 men.

The Battle-painter or *Delle Battaglie.* (*See* MICHAEL ANGELO.)

Battle of the Books. A satire, by Dean Swift, on the contention among literary men whether ancient or modern authors were the better. In the battle the ancient books fight against the modern books in St. James's Library.

Battle of the Giants ; i.e. the battle of Marignan (*Ma-rin-yan'*) in 1515, when François I. won a complete victory over 12,000 Swiss, allies of the Milanese.

Battle of the Herrings, in 1429. A sortie made by the men of Orléans, during the siege of their city, to intercept a supply of salt herrings sent to the besiegers.

Battle of the Moat. A skirmish or battle between Mahomet and Abu Sofian (chief of the Koreishites) before Medi'na ; so called because the "prophet" had a moat dug before the city to keep off the invaders ; and in the moat much of the fighting took place.

Battle of the Standard, in 1138, when

the English overthrew the Scotch, at Northallerton, in Yorkshire. The standard was a high crucifix borne by the English on a wagon.

Battle of the Spurs (1302), in which the allied citizens of Ghent and Bruges won a famous victory over the chivalry of France under the walls of Courtray. After the battle more than 700 gilt spurs (worn by French nobles) were gathered from the field.

In English history the Battle of Guinegate (1513) is so called, " because the French *spurred* their horses to flight, almost as soon as they came in sight of the English troops."

A close battle. A naval fight at " close quarters," in which opposing ships engage each other side by side.

A line of battle. The position of troops drawn up in battle array. At sea, the arrangement formed by ships in a naval engagement. A *line-of-battle ship* is a ship fit to take part in a main attack. *Frigates* do not join in a general engagement.

A pitched battle. A battle which has been planned, and the ground pitched on or chosen beforehand, by both sides.

Half the battle. Half determines the battle. Thus, " The first stroke is half the battle," that is, the way in which the battle is begun half determines what the end will be.

Trial by battle. The submission of a legal suit to a combat between the litigants, under the notion that God would defend the right. It was legal in England till the nineteenth century.

Wager of Battle. One of the forms of ordeal or appeal to the judgment of God, in the old Norman courts of the kingdom. It consisted of a personal combat between the plaintiff and the defendant, in the presence of the court itself. Abolished by 59 Geo. III. c. 46.

Battle of the Frogs and Mice (*The*). [*See* BATRACHOMYOMACHIA.]

Battle of the Kegs (*The*). A mockheroic by Francis Hopkinson (1738-1791). In the War of Independence certain machines, in the form of kegs, charged with gunpowder, were sent down the river to annoy the British at Philadelphia. When the British found out the nature of these machines, they waged relentless war with everything they saw floating about the river.

Battle of the Poets (*The*). A satirical poem by John [Sheffield], Duke of Buckingham, in which all the

versifiers of the time are brought into the field (1725).

Battle of the Whips. The Scythian slaves once rose in rebellion against their masters, and many a bloody encounter followed. At length, one of the Scythian masters said to his followers : Let us throw away our spears and swords, and fight in future with whips. We get killed by the former weapons and weakened. So in the next encounter they armed themselves with whips, and immediately the slaves saw the whips, remembering former scourgings, they turned tail and were no more trouble.

Battle (*Sarah*), who considered whist the business of life and literature one of the relaxations. When a young gentleman, of a literary turn, said to her he had no objection to unbend his mind for a little time by taking a hand with her, Sarah was indignant, and declared it worse than sacrilege to speak thus of her noble occupation. Whist " was her life business ; her duty ; the thing she came into the world to do, and she did it. She unbent her mind afterwards over a book." (*C. Lamb : Elia.*)

Bat'tledore (3 syl.) means, properly, a baton for washing linen by striking on it to knock out the dirt. The plan is still common in France. The word is the French *battoir*, a beater used by washerwomen ; Portuguese, *Batidor*, Spanish, *batidero*, a wash-board.

Battu. *Autant pleure mal battu que bien battu* (French). It little matters whether stripes are given maliciously or not, as they smart the same. Whether misfortunes come from God or Satan, they are misfortunes still. A slight variant is " *Autant vaut bien battu que mal battu,*" which means, it is of no consequence whether badly beaten or not, enough that I am beaten ; " over shoes, over boots."

Battu de fol Oiseau (*Etre*), or " *être battu de l'oiseau,*" to be utterly dismayed ; to be dazed. The allusion is to bird-catching at night, when a candle or lantern is held up before the birds aroused from their sleep ; the birds, being dazed, are beaten down easily with sticks.

Battus paieront (*Les*). Væ victis ! Those who lose must pay the piper. " *C'est le loi du pays de Béarn que le battu paie l'amende.*" Again, " *C'est la coutume de Lorris. les battus paient* *l'amende.*" This is certainly the general custom in law and war.

Baubee. (*See* BAWBEE.)

Bauble. *A fool should never hold a bauble in his hand.* "'Tis a foolish bird that fouls its own nest." The bauble was a short stick, ornamented with ass's ears, carried by licensed fools. (French, *babiole*, a plaything; Old French, *baubel*, a child's toy.)

If every fool held a bauble, fuel would be dear. The proverb indicates that the world contains so many fools that if each had a separate bauble there would be but little wood left for lighting fires.

To deserve the bauble. To be so foolish as to be qualified to carry a fool's emblem of office.

Baucis. (*See* PHILEMON.)

Ba'viad (*The*). A merciless satire by Gifford on the Della Cruscan poetry, published 1794. The word is from Virgil's *Eclogue*, iii. 9.

He may with foxes plough, and milk he-goats,'
Who praises Bavius or on Mævius dotes."
E. C. B.

Bavie'ca. The Cid's horse.

Ba'vius. Any bad poet. (*See* BA-VIAD.)

" May some choice patron bless each grey goose
quill,
May every Bavius have his Bufo still."
Pope: Prologue to the Satires, 249-50.

Bawbee.

" Wha'll hire, wha'll hire, wha'll hire me?
Three plumps and a wallop for ae bawbee."

The tale is that the people of Kirkmahoe were so poor, they could not afford to put any meat into their broth. A 'cute cobbler invested all his money in buying four sheep-shanks, and when a neighbour wanted to make mutton broth, for the payment of one halfpenny the cobbler would " plump " one of the sheep-shanks into the boiling water, and give it a " wallop " or whisk round. He then wrapped it in a cabbage-leaf and took it home. This was called a *gustin bone,* and was supposed to give a rich " gust " to the broth. The cobbler found his *gustin bone* very profitable.

Jenny's bawbee. Her marriage portion. The word means, properly, a debased copper coin, equal in value to a halfpenny, issued in the reign of James V. of Scotland. (French, *bas billon,* debased copper money.)

☞ The word " bawbee " is derived from the laird of Sillebawby, a mintmaster. That there was such a laird is quite certain from the Treasurer's account, September 7th, 1541, "*In argento*

receptis a Jacobo Atzinsone, et Alexandro Orok de Sillebawby respective."

Bawley Boat (*A*). A small fishing-smack used on the coasts of Kent and Essex, about the mouth of the Thames and Medway. Bawleys are generally about 40 feet long, 13 feet beam, 5 feet draught, and from 15 to 20 tons measurement. They differ in rig from a cutter in having no booms to the mainsail, which is, consequently, easily brailed up when working the trawl nets. They are half-decked, with a wet well to keep fish alive.

Bawtry. *Like the saddler of Bawtry, who was hanged for leaving his liquor* (Yorkshire proverb). It was customary for criminals on their way to execution to stop at a certain tavern in York for a "parting draught." The saddler of Bawtry refused to accept the liquor and was hanged. If he had stopped a few minutes at the tavern, his reprieve, which was on the road, would have arrived in time to save his life.

Baxte'rians. Those who entertain the same religious views as Richard Baxter. The chief points are—(1) That Christ died in a spiritual sense for the elect, and in a general sense for all; (2) that there is no such thing as reprobation; (3) that even saints may fall from grace. Dr. Isaac Watts and Dr. Doddridge held these views.

Bay.
Supposed to be an antidote against lightning, because it was the tree of Apollo. Hence Tibe'rius and some other of the Roman emperors wore a wreath of bay as an amulet, especially in thunder-storms. (*Pliny.*)

" Reach the bays—
I'll tie a garland here about his head ;
'Twill keep my boy from lightning."
The White Devil.

The withering of a bay-tree was supposed to be the omen of a death.

" 'Tis thought the king is dead. We'll not stay—
The bay-trees in our country are withered."
Shakespeare: Richard II., ii. 4.

Crowned with bays, in sign of victory. The general who obtained a victory among the Romans was crowned with a wreath of bay leaves.

Bay. The reason why Apollo and all those under his protection are crowned with bay is a pretty fable. Daphnê, daughter of the river-god Penēos, in Thessaly, was very beautiful and resolved to pass her life in perpetual virginity. Apollo fell in love with her,

4*

but she rejected his suit. On one occasion the god was so importunate that Daphnē fled from him and sought the protection of her father, who changed her into the bay-tree. The gallant god declared henceforth he would wear bay leaves on his brow and lyre instead of the oak, and that all who sought his favour should follow his example.

The Queen's Bays. The 2nd Dragoon Guards; so called because they are mounted on bay horses. Now called *The Queen's.*

Bay. The colour of a horse is Varro's *equus badius*, given by Ainsworth as, "brown, bay, sorrel, chestnut colour." Coles gives the same. Our bayard; bright bay, light bay, blood bay, etc.

Bay the Moon (*To*). To bark at the moon. (French, *aboyer*, to bark at.) (*See* BARK.)

Bay Salt is salt of a bay colour. It is the salt of sea-water hardened by the heat of the sun.

Bayadere (*bah-ya-dare*). A dancing girl dressed in Eastern costume ; so called from the *bajaderes* of India, whose duty is to dance before the images of the gods; but the grandees employ similar dancers for their private amusements. The word is a corruption of the Portuguese *bailadeira*.

Bayard (*Chevalier*), Pierre du Terrail, a celebrated French knight (1476-1524). *Le chevalier sans peur et sans reproche.*

The British Bayard. Sir Philip Sidney. (1554-1584.)

The Polish Bayard. Prince Joseph Poniatowski. (1763-1814.)

Bayard of the East (*The*) or *Of the Indian Army.* Sir James Outram (1803-1863).

Ba'yard. A horse of incredible swiftness, belonging to the four sons of Ay'mon. If only one of the sons mounted, the horse was of the ordinary size ; but if all four mounted, his body became elongated to the requisite length. The name is used for any valuable or wonderful horse, and means a "high-bay" (*bay - ard*). (*Villeneuve : Les Quatre-Filz Aymon.*) (*See* HORSE.)

Keep Bayard in the stable, i.e. keep what is of value under lock and key. (*See above.*)

Bold as Blind Bayard. Foolhardy. If a blind horse leaps, the chance is he will fall into a ditch. Grose mentions the following expression, *To ride bayard of ten toes*—"Going by the marrow-bone stage"—*i.e.* walking.

Bayar'do. The famous steed of Rinaldo, which once belonged to Am'adis of Gaul. (*See* HORSE.)

Bayardo's Leap. Three stones, about thirty yards apart, near Sleaford. It is said that Rinaldo was riding on his favourite steed Bayardo, when the demon of the place sprang behind him ; but the animal in terror took three tremendous leaps and unhorsed the fiend.

Bayes, in the *Rehearsal*, by the Duke of Buckingham, was designed to satirise John Dryden, the poet laureate.

Bayes's Troops. *Dead men may rise again, like Bayes's troops, or the savages in the Fantoci'ni (Something New).* In the *Rehearsal*, by George Villiers, Duke of Buckingham, a battle is fought between foot-soldiers and great hobby-horses. At last Drawcan'sir kills all on both sides. Smith then asks how they are to go off, to which Bayes replies, "As they came on—upon their legs " ; upon which they all jump up alive again.

Bayeux Tapestry. Supposed to be the work of Matilda, wife of William the Conqueror. It represents the mission of Harold to the duke, and all the incidents of his history from that event till his death at Hastings in 1066. It is called Bayeux from the place where it is preserved. A drawing, on a reduced scale, of this curious antique is preserved in the Guildhall Library.

Bayle (2 syl.). Dances of the common people were so called in Spain, in opposition to the stately court dances, called *danza.* The Baylē were of Moorish invention, the most celebrated being *La Sarabanda, La Chacona, Las Gambelas,* and *El Hermano Bartolo.*

Bay'onet. So called from La Bayonette, a lower ridge of the Montagne d'Arrhune. A Basque regiment, early in the seventeenth century, running short of powder, stuck their knives into their muskets, and charged the Spaniards with success. Some derive this word from Bayonne.

Bayonets. A synonym of "rank and file," that is, privates and corporals of infantry. As, "the number of bayonets was 25,000."

"It is on the bayonets that a Quartermaster-General relies for his working and fatigue parties." —*Howitt: Hist. of Eng.* (year 1854, p. 260). .

Bead (Anglo-Saxon, *béd*, a prayer). When little balls with a hole through them were used for keeping account of the number of prayers repeated, the term was applied to the prayers also. (*See* BEADSMAN.)

To count one's beads. To say one's prayers. In the Catholic Church beads are threaded on a string, some large and some small, to assist in keeping count how often a person repeats a certain form of words.

To pray without one's beads. To be out of one's reckoning. (*See above.*)

Baily's Beads. When the disc of the moon has (in an eclipse) reduced that of the sun to a thin crescent, the crescent assumes the appearance of a string of beads. This was first observed by Francis Baily, whence the name of the phenomenon.

St. Cuthbert's Beads. Single joints of the articulated stems of encrinites. They are perforated in the centre, and bear a fanciful resemblance to a cross; hence, they were once used for *rosaries* (beads). St. Cuthbert was a Scotch monk of the sixth century, and may be called the St. Patrick of the north of England and south of Scotland.

St. Martin's beads. Flash jewellery. St. Martins-le-Grand was at one time a noted place for sham jewellery.

Bead-house. An almshouse for beadsmen.

Bead-roll. A list of persons to be prayed for; hence, also, any list.

Beadle. A person whose duty it is to *bid* or cite persons to appear to a summons; also a church servant, whose duty it is to *bid* the parishioners to attend the vestry, or to give notice of vestry meetings. (Anglo-Saxon, *bædel*, from *beodan*, to bid or summon.)

Beadsman or *Bedesman*. An inhabitant of an almshouse; so called because in Catholic times most charities of this class were instituted that the inmates might "pray for the soul of the founder." (*See* BEAD.)

"Seated with some grey beadsman."
Crabbe: Borough.

Beak. A magistrate. (Anglo-Saxon *beag*, a gold collar worn by civic magistrates.)

⁂ W. H. Black says, "The term is derived from a Mr. Beke, who was formerly a resident magistrate at the Tower Hamlets.

Beaker. A drinking-glass; a rummer. (Greek, *bikos*, a wine jar.)

"Here, Gerard, reach your beaker."
Browning: Blot in the 'Scutcheon, i. 1.

Beam. *Thrown on my beam-ends.* Driven to my last shift. A ship is said to be on her beam-ends when she is laid by a heavy gale completely on her beams or sides. Not unfrequently the only means of righting her in such a case is to cut away her masts.

On the starboard beam. A distant point out at sea on the right-hand side, and at right angles to the keel.

On the port beam. A similar point on the left-hand side.

On the weather beam. On that side of a ship which faces the wind.

Beam (*of a stag*). That part of the head from which the horns spring. (Anglo-Saxon *béam*, a tree; the horns are called branches.)

Bean. *Every bean has its black.* *Nemo sine vitiis nas'citur*, "everyone has his faults." The bean has a black eye. (*Ogni grano ha la sua semola.*)

He has found the bean in the cake, he has got a prize in the lottery, has come to some unexpected good fortune. The allusion is to twelfth cakes in which a bean is buried. When the cake is cut up and distributed, he who gets the bean is the twelfth-night king.

Beans, slang for property, money, is the French *biens*, goods. "A bean" = a guinea, is in Grose.

"Like a beane [alms-money] in a monkeshood."
—*Cotgrave*

(*See* BARRISTERS' GOWNS.)

Beans. Pythag'oras forbade the use of beans to his disciples—not the use of beans as a food, but the use of beans for political elections. Magistrates and other public officers were elected by beans cast by the voters into a helmet, and what Pythag'oras advised was that his disciples should not interfere with politics or "love beans"—*i.e.* office.

Aristotle says the word *bean* means ven'ery, and that the prohibition to "abstain from beans" was equivalent to "keeping the body chaste."

⁂ The French have the proverb, "If he gives me peas I will give him beans," *S'il me donne des pois, je lui donnerai des fèves, i.e.* I will give him tit for tat, a Rowland for an Oliver.

Beans are in flower, les fèvres fleurissent, and this will account for your being so silly. Our forefathers imagined that the perfume of the flowering bean was bad for the head, and made men silly or light-headed.

He knows how many beans go to make

up five. He is "up to snuff;" he is no
fool; he is not to be imposed upon. The
reference is to the ancient custom of
moving beans in counting.

"I was a fool, I was, and didn't know how many
beans make five [that is, how many beans must
be moved to make up five]."—*Parjeon.*
"Few men better knew how many blue beans
it takes to make five."—*Galt.*

❧ Blue Beans: "Three blue beans in
a blue bladder." A rattle for children.

"*F.* Hark! does it rattle?
S. Yes, like three blue beans in a blue bladder."
Old *Fortunatus* (*Ancient Dramas*), iii. p. 128.

❧ "Blue beans" are bullets or shot.
Three small bullets or large shot in a
bladder would make a very good rattle
for a child. (*See* BLUE BEANS.)
Full of beans. Said of a fresh and
spirited horse.
To get beans. To incur reproof.
I'll give him beans. A licking; a
jolly good hiding. A very common
phrase. Probably from the French referred to above, meaning as good as I
got; "beans for his peas."

Bean Feast. Much the same as
wayz-goose (*q.v.*). A feast given by an
employer to those he employs.

Bean Goose (*The*). A migratory
bird which appears in England in the
autumn of the year, and is so named
from a mark on its bill like a horse-
bean. It is next in size to the Grey
Lag-goose. The term comes from the
northern counties where the bean (*goose*)
is common.

"Espèce d'oie dont les mandibules sont taillées
en forme de féveroles."—*Royal Dictionnaire.*

Bean-king (*The*). *Rey de Habas,*
the child appointed to play the part of
king on twelfth-night. In France it
was at one time customary to hide a
bean in a large cake, and he to whom
the bean fell, when the cake was distributed, was for the nonce the bean
king, to whom all the other guests
showed playful reverence. The Greeks
used beans for voting by ballot.
Bean-King's festival. Twelfth-night.
(*See above.*)

Bear (*A*). (Stock Exchange), a fall,
or a speculator for a fall. *To operate for a bear. To realise a profitable
bear.*
Bearing the market is using every
effort to depress the price of stocks in
order to buy it.
The arena of bears and bulls, i.e. the
Stock Exchange.
❧ Dr. Warton says the term bear came
from the proverb of "Selling the skin

before you have caught the bear," and
referred to those who entered into
contracts in the South Sea Scheme to
transfer stock at a stated price. (*See*
BULL.)

"So was the huntsman by the bear oppressed,
Whose hide he sold before he caught the beast."
Waller: Battle of the Summer Islands, c. ii.

A Bear account. A speculation in
stocks on the chance of a *fall* in the
price of the stock sold, with a view of
buying it back at a lower price or receiving the difference. (*See* BULLS.)

Bear (*The*). Albert, margrave of
Brandenburg. He was also called "The
Fair" (1106-1170).
The bloody Bear, in Dryden's poem
called *The Hind and Panther,* means
the Independents.

"The bloody bear, an independent beast,
Unlicked to form, in groans her hate expressed."
Pt. i. 35, 36.

The Great Bear and *Little Bear.* The
constellations so called are specimens of
a large class of blunders founded on
approximate sounds. The Sanskrit *rakh*
means "to be bright;" the Greeks corrupted the word into *arktos,* which
means a bear; so that the "bear"
should in reality be the "bright ones."
The fable is that Calisto, a nymph of
Diana, had two sons by Jupiter, which
Juno changed into bears, and Jupiter
converted into constellations.

"The wind-shaked surge, with high and mon-
strous mane,
Seems to cast water on the burning bear,
And quench the guards of th' ever-fixèd pole."
Shakespeare: Othello, ii. 1.

"'Twas here we saw Calisto's star retire
Beneath the waves, unawed by Juno's ire."
Camoens: Lusiad, book v.

The Bear or *Northern Bear.* Russia.

"France turns from her abandoned friends afresh,
And soothes the bear that growls for patriot
flesh."   *Campbell: Poland,* stanza 5.

A Bridled Bear. A young nobleman
under the control of a travelling tutor.
(*See* BEAR-LEADER.)
The Bear and Ragged Staff. A public-
house sign in compliment to Warwick,
the king-maker, whose cognisance it
was. The first earl was Arth or Arth-
gal, of the Round Table, whose cognisance was a *bear,* because *arth* means
a bear (Latin, *urs'*). Morvid, the second
earl, overcame, in single combat, a
mighty giant, who came against him
with a club, which was a tree pulled
up by the roots, but stripped of its
branches. In remembrance of his victory
over the giant he added "the ragged
staff."
The Bear and the Tea-kettle (Kamschatka). Said of a person who injures

himself by foolish rage. One day a bear entered a hut in Kamschatka, where a kettle was on the fire. Master Bruin went to the kettle, and smelling at it burnt his nose; being greatly irritated, he seized the kettle with his paws, and squeezed it against his breast. This, of course, made matters worse, for the boiling water scalded him terribly, and he growled in agony till some neighbours put an end to his life with their guns.

A bear sucking his paws. It is said that when a bear is deprived of food, it sustains life by sucking its paws. The same is said of the English badger. Applied to industrious idleness.

As savage as a bear with a sore (or *scalt*) *head.* Unreasonably ill-tempered.

As a bear has no tail, for a lion he'll fail. The same as *Ne sutor supra crep'-idam,* "let not the cobbler aspire above his last." Robert Dudley, Earl of Leicester, being a descendant of the Warwick family, changed his own crest, which was "a green lion with two tails," for the Warwick crest, a "bear and ragged staff." When made governor of the Low Countries, he was suspected of aiming at absolute supremacy, or the desire of being the monarch of his fellows, as the lion is monarch among beasts. Some wit wrote under his crest the Latin verse, "*Ursa caret cauda non queat esse leo.*"

"Your bear for lion needs must fail,
Because your true bears have no tail."

To take the bear by the tooth. To put your head into the lion's mouth; needlessly to run into danger.

You dare as soon take a bear by his tooth. You would no more attempt such a thing, than attempt to take a bear by its tooth.

Bear (*To*). *Come, bear a hand!* Come and render help! In French, "*Donner un coup à quelqu'un.*" Bring a hand, or bring your hand to bear on the work going on.

To bear arms. To do military service.

To bear away (Nautical). To keep away from the wind.

To bear one company. To be one's companion.

"His faithful dog shall bear him company."
Pope: Essay on Man, epistle i. 112.

To bear down. To overpower; to force down.

"Fully prepared to bear down all resistance."—
Cooper: The Pilot, chap. xviii.

To bear down upon (Nautical). To approach from the weather side.

To bear in mind. Remember; do not forget. Carry in your recollection.

"To learn by heart," means to learn *memoriter.* Mind and heart stand for memory in both phrases.

To bear out. To corroborate, to confirm.

To bear up. To support; to keep the spirits up.

To bear with. To show forbearance; to endure with complacency.

"How long shall I bear with this evil congregation?"—Numbers xiv. 27.

To bear the bell. (*See* BELL.)

Bear of Bradwardine (*The*) was a wine goblet, holding about an English pint, and, according to Scott, was made by command of St. Duthac, Abbot of Aberbrothoc, to be presented to the Baron of Bradwardine for services rendered in defence of the monastery. Inscribed upon the goblet was the motto; "Beware the bear."

Bear Account (*A*). (*See* BEAR.)

Bear Garden. *This place is a perfect bear-garden*—that is, full of confusion, noise, tumult, and quarrels. Bear-gardens were places where bears used to be kept and baited for public amusement.

Bear-leader. One who undertakes the charge of a young man of rank on his travels. It was once customary to lead muzzled bears about the streets, and to make them show off in order to attract notice and gain money.

"Bear! [said *Dr. Pangloss* to his pupil]. Under favour, young gentleman, I am the bear-leader, being appointed your tutor."—*G. Colman: Heir-at-Law.*

Bears are caught by Honey. In French, "*Il faut avoir mauvaise bête par douceur,*" for, as La Fontaine says, "*Plus fait douceur que violence.*" Bears are very fond of honey. Bribes win even bears.

∴ There is another phrase: *Divide honey with a bear,* i.e. It is better to divide your honey with a bear than to provoke its anger.

Beard. *Cutting the beard.* The Turks think it a dire disgrace to have the beard cut. Slaves who serve in the seraglio have clean chins, as a sign of their servitude.

Kissing the beard. In Turkey wives kiss their husband, and children their father on the beard.

To make one's beard (Chaucer). This is the French "*Faire la barbe à quelqu'un,*" and refers to a barber's taking hold of a man's beard to dress it, or to his shaving the chin of a customer. To make one's beard is to have him wholly at your mercy.

I told him to his beard. I told him to his face, regardless of consequences; to speak openly and fearlessly.

Beard (*To*). To beard one is to defy him, to contradict him flatly, to insult by plucking the beard. Among the Jews, no greater insult could be offered to a man than to pluck or even touch his beard.

To beard the lion in his den. To contradict one either in his own growlery, or on some subject he has made his hobby. To defy personally or face to face.

> "Dar'st thou, then,
> To beard the lion in his den,
> The Douglas in his hall?"
> *Sir W. Scott: Marmion,* canto vi. stanza 14.

Maugre his beard. In spite of him.
To laugh at one's beard. To attempt to make a fool of a person—to deceive by ridiculous exaggeration.

> "'By the prophet! but he laughs at our beards,'
> exclaimed the Pacha angrily. 'These are foolish
> lies.'"—*Marryat: Pacha of Many Tales.*

To laugh in one's beard ["*Rire dans sa barbe*"] To laugh in one's sleeve.
To run in one's beard. To offer opposition to a person; to do something obnoxious to a person before his face. The French say, "*à la barbe de quel-qu'un,*" under one's very nose.
With the beard on the shoulder (Spanish). In the attitude of listening to overhear something; with circumspection, looking in all directions for surprises and ambuscades.

> "They rode, as the Spanish proverb expresses
> it, 'with the beard on the shoulder,' looking
> round from time to time, and using every pre-
> caution . . . against pursuit."—*Sir W. Scott:
> Peveril of the Peak,* chap. vii.

Tax upon beards. Peter the Great imposed a tax upon beards. Every one above the lowest class had to pay 100 roubles, and the lowest class had to pay a copec, for enjoying this "luxury." Clerks were stationed at the gates of every town to collect the beard-tax.

Bearded. *Bearded Master* (*Magister barba'tus*). So Persius styled Socratēs, under the notion that the beard is the symbol of wisdom. (B.C. 468-399.)
Pogona'tus (Bearded). Constantine IV., Emperor of Rome (648, 668-685).
The Bearded. Geoffrey the Crusader, and Bouchard of the house of Montmorency.
Handsome-beard. Baldwin IV., Earl of Flanders. (1160-1186.)
John the Bearded. Johann Mayo, the German painter, whose beard touched the ground when he stood upright.

Bearded Women:
Bartel Grætjë, of Stuttgard, born 1562.
The Duke of Saxony had the portrait taken of a poor Swiss woman, remarkable for her large bushy beard.
In 1726 a female dancer appeared at Venice, with a large bushy beard.
Charles XII. had in his army a woman whose beard was a yard and a half long. She was taken prisoner at the battle of Pultowa, and presented to the Czar, 1724.
Mlle. Bois de Chêne, born at Geneva in 1834, was exhibited in London in 1852-3; she had a profuse head of hair, a strong black beard, large whiskers, and thick hair on her arms and back.
Julia Pastra'na was exhibited in London in 1857; died, 1862, at Moscow; was embalmed by Professor Suckaloff; and the embalmed body was exhibited at 191, Piccadilly. She was found among the Digger Indians of Mexico.
Margaret of Holland had a long, stiff beard.

Bearings. *I'll bring him to his bearings.* I'll bring him to his senses. A sea term. The bearings of a ship at anchor is that part of her hull which is on the water-line when she is in good trim. To bring a ship to her bearings is to get her into this trim. (*Dana: The Seaman's Manual,* 84.)
To lose one's bearings. To become bewildered; to get perplexed as to which is the right road.
To take the bearings. To ascertain the relative position of some object.

Bearnais (*Le*). Henri IV. of France; so called from *Le Be'arn,* his native province (1553-1610).

Beasts (*Heraldic*):
Couchant, lying down.
Counter-passant, moving in opposite directions.
Dormant, sleeping.
Gardant, full-faced.
Issuant, rising from the top or bottom of an ordinary.
Nascent, rising out of the middle of an ordinary.
Passant, walking.
Passant gardant, walking, and with full face.
Passant regardant, walking and looking behind.
Rampant, rearing.
Regardant, looking back.
Sejant, seated.
Salient, springing.
Statant, standing still.

Beastly Drunk. It was an ancient notion that men in their cups exhibited the vicious qualities of beasts. Nash describes seven kinds of drunkards:—
(1) The *Ape-drunk*, who leaps and sings;
(2) The *Lion-drunk*, who is quarrelsome;
(3) The *Swine-drunk*, who is sleepy and puking; (4) The *Sheep-drunk*, wise in his own conceit, but unable to speak;
(5) The *Martin-drunk*, who drinks himself sober again; (6) The *Goat-drunk*, who is lascivious; and (7) The *Fox-drunk*, who is crafty, like a Dutchman in his cups. [*See* MAUDLIN.]

Beat. A track, line, or appointed range. A walk often trodden or beaten by the feet, as a *policeman's beat*. The word means a beaten path.
Not in my beat. Not in my line; not in the range of my talents or inclination.
Off his beat. Not on duty; not in his appointed walk; not his speciality or line.

"Off his own beat his opinions were of no value."—*Emerson: English Traits*, chap. i.

On his beat. In his appointed walk; on duty.
Out of his beat. In his wrong walk; out of his proper sphere.
To beat up one's quarters. To hunt out where one lives; to visit without ceremony. A military term, signifying to make an unexpected attack on an enemy in camp.

"To beat up the quarters of some of our less-known relations."—*Lamb: Essays of Elia.*

Beat (*To*). To strike. (Anglo-Saxon, *beatan*.)
To beat an alarm. To give notice of danger by beat of drum.
To beat or *drum a thing into one.* To repeat as a drummer repeats his strokes on a drum.
To beat a retreat (French, *battre en retraite*); *to beat to arms; to beat a charge.* Military terms similar to the above.
To beat the air. To strike out at nothing, merely to bring one's muscles into play, as pugilists do before they begin to fight; to toil without profit; to work to no purpose.

"So fight I, not as one that beateth the air."—1 Cor. ix. 26.

To beat the bush. One beat the bush and another caught the hare. "*Il a battu les buissons, et autre a pris les oiseaux.*" "*Il bat le buisson sans prendre les oisillons*" is a slightly different idea, meaning he has toiled in vain. "Other men laboured, and ye are entered into their labours" (John iv. 48). The allusion is to beaters, whose business it is to beat the bushes and start the game for a shooting party.
To beat the Devil's Tattoo. (*See* TATTOO.)
To beat the Dutch. To draw a very long bow; to say something very incredible.

"Well! if that don't beat the Dutch!"

To beat time. To mark time in music by beating or moving the hands, feet, or a wand.
To beat up supporters. To hunt them up or call them together, as soldiers are by beat of drum.

Beat (*To*). To overcome or get the better of. This does not mean to strike, which is the Anglo-Saxon *beátan*, but to better, to be better, from the Anglo-Saxon verb *bétan*.
Dead beat. So completely beaten or worsted as to have no leg to stand on. Like a dead man with no fight left in him; quite tired out.

"I'm dead beat, but I thought I'd like to come in and see you all once more."—*Roe: Without a Home*, p. 32.

Dead beat escapement (of a watch). One in which there is no reverse motion of the escape-wheel.
That beats Banagher. Wonderfully inconsistent and absurd — exceedingly ridiculous. Banagher is a town in Ireland, on the Shannon, in King's County. It formerly sent two members to Parliament, and was, of course, a famous pocket borough. When a member spoke of a family borough where every voter was a man employed by the lord, it was not unusual to reply, "Well, that beats Banagher."

"'Well,' says he, 'to gratify them I will. So just a morsel. But, Jack, this beats Bannagher' (*sic*)."—*W. B. Yeats: Fairy Tales of the Irish Peasantry*, p. 196.

That beats Termagant. Your ranting, raging pomposity, or exaggeration, surpasses that of Termagant (*q.v.*).
To beat hollow is to beat wholly, to be wholly the superior.
To beat up against the wind. To tack against an adverse wind; to get the better of the wind.

Beat. (French, *abattre*, to abate.)
To beat down. To make a seller "abate" his price.

Beaten to a Mummy. Beaten so that one can distinguish neither form nor feature.

Beaten with his own Staff. Confuted by one's own words. An *argumentum ad hominem.*

"Can High Church bigotry go farther than this? And how well have I since been beaten with mine own staff."—*J. Wesley.* (He refers to his excluding Bolzius from "the Lord's table," because he had not been canonically baptized.)

Beating about the Bush. Not coming directly to the matter in hand, but feeling your way timidly by indirection, as persons beat bushes to ascertain if game is lurking under them.

Beating the Bounds. On Holy Thursday, or Ascension Day, it used to be customary for the parish school children, accompanied by the clergymen and parish officers, to walk through their parish from end to end. The boys were struck with willow wands all along the lines of boundary. Before maps were common, the boys were thus taught to know the bounds of their own parish. The custom still prevails in some parishes.

Beati Possidentes. Blessed are those who have [for they shall receive]. "Possession is nine points of the law."

Beatific Vision. The sight of the Deity, or of the blessed in the realms of heaven. (*See* Isaiah vi. 1-4, and Acts vii. 55, 56.)

Beatrice, beloved from girlhood by Dante, a native of Florence, was of the Portinari family. She died under twenty-four years of age (1266-1290). Beatrice married Simone de' Bardi, and Dante married Gemma Donati.

Beau.
Beau Brummel. George Bryan. (1778-1840.)
Le Beau D'Orsay. Father of Count D'Orsay, and called by Byron *Jeune Cupidon.*
Beau Fielding, called "Handsome Fielding" by Charles II., whose name was Hendrome Fielding. He died in Scotland Yard, London.
Beau Hewitt. The "Sir Fopling Flutter" of Etheredge. (*The Man of Mode ; or, Sir Fopling Flutter.*)
Beau Nash. Son of a Welsh gentleman, a notorious diner-out. He undertook the management of the bath-rooms at Bath, and conducted the public balls with a splendour and decorum never before witnessed. In old age he sank into poverty. (1674-1761.)
Beau Tibbs, noted for his finery, vanity, and poverty. (*Goldsmith : Citizen of the World.*)

Beau Id'eal. The model of beauty or excellency formed by fancy.

Beau Jour beau Retour (*A*). My turn will come next. (Never used in a good sense, but always to signify the resentment of an injury.)

Beau Lion (*Un*). A fine dashing fellow ; an aristocrat every inch ; the "lion" of society. The lion is the king of beasts.

Beau Monde. The fashionable world; people who make up the coterie of fashion.

Beau Trap. A loose pavement under which water lodges, and which squirts up filth when trodden on, to the annoyance of the smartly dressed.

Beauclerc [*good scholar*]. Applied to Henry I., who had clerk-like accomplishments, very rare in the times in which he lived (1068, 1100-1135).

Beaumontague [pronounce *bo-mon-taig*]. Bad work, especially ill-fitting carpenter's work ; literary padding; paste and scissors literature ; so called from putty used by carpenters, etc., for filling up cracks and bad joinery. German, *teig*, dough ; and Emile Beaumont, the geologist (1798-1851), who also gives his name to "Beaumontite."

Beautiful. *Beautiful* or *fair as an angel.* Throughout the Middle Ages it was common to associate beauty with virtue, and ugliness with sin ; hence the expressions given above, and the following also—"Seraphic beauty," "Cherubic loveliness," "Ugly as sin," etc.

Beautiful Parricide. Beatrice Cenci, the daughter of a Roman nobleman, who plotted the death of her father because he violently defiled her. (Died 1599.)

"Francesco Cenci (xvi. siècle) . . . avait quatre fils et une fille (Béatrix). Il les maltraitait cruellement, ou les faisait servir à ses plaisirs brutaux. . . . Révoltée de tant d'horreurs, Béatrix, sa fille, de concert avec deux de ses frerès, et Lucrece leur mère, fit assassiner Francesco Cenci. Accusés de parricide, ils périrent tous quatre sur l'échafaud par la sentence de Clément VIII. (1605)."—*Bouillet.*
∴ This is Muratori's version of the affair, but it is much disputed. It is a favourite theme for tragedy.

Beauty. *Tout est beau sans chandelles.* "*La nuit tous les chats sont gris.*" *Beauty is but skin deep.*

"O formose puer, nimium ne crede colori."
        Virgil, Bucolics, ii.

Beauty and the Beast. The hero and heroine of Madame Villeneuve's fairy tale. Beauty saved the life of her father by consenting to live with the Beast ; and the Beast, being disenchanted by Beauty's love, became a handsome prince, and married her. (*Contes Marines,* 1740.)

∵ A handsome woman with an uncouth or uncomely male companion.

Beauty of Buttermere. Mary Robinson, married to John Hatfield, a heartless impostor, executed for forgery at Carlisle in 1803.

Beauty Sleep. Sleep taken before midnight. Those who habitually go to bed, especially during youth, after midnight, are usually pale and more or less haggard.

"Would I please to remember that I had roused him up at night . . . . [in] his beauty sleep."—*Blackmore: Lorna Doone*, chap. 64.

Beaux Esprits (French). Men of wit or genius (singular number, *Un bel esprit*, a wit, a genius).

Beaux Yeux (French). Beautiful eyes or attractive looks. "I will do it for your *beaux yeux*" (because you are so pretty, or because your eyes are so attractive).

Beaver. A hat; so called from its being made of beaver-skins.

Beaver. That part of the helmet which lifted up to enable the wearer to drink. Similarly *bever*, the afternoon draught in the harvest-field, called *fours's*. (Italian, *bevere*, to drink; Spanish, *beber;* Latin, *bibo;* French, *buveur*, a drinker; Armoric, *beuvrauh*, beverage, etc.)

"*Hamlet:* Then you saw not his face?
"*Horatio:* O, yes, my lord; he wore his beaver up." *Shakespeare: Hamlet*, i. 2.

Becarre, Bemol. *Sauter de bécarre en bémol* (French), to jump from one subject to another without regard to pertinence; "*Sauter du coq à l'ane*," from Genesis to Revelation. Literally, to jump from sharps to flats. Becarre is the Latin *B quadratum* or *B quarré*. In old musical notation B sharp was expressed by a square B, and B flat by a round B.

∵ Bémol is B *mollis*, soft (flat).

Becasse. You goose; you simpleton; you booby. Bécasse is a woodcock. "*C'est une bécasse*," he or she is a fool.

Becket's Assassins. William de Tracy, Hugh de Morville, Richard Brito (or le Bret), and Fitz-Urse.

Bed. *The great bed of Ware.* A bed twelve feet square, and capable of holding twelve persons; assigned by tradition to the Earl of Warwick, the king-maker. It is now in Rye House.

"Although the sheet were big enough for the bed of Ware in England."—*Shakespeare: Twelfth Night*, iii. 2.

To make the bed. To arrange it and make it fit for use. In America this sense of "make" is much more common than it is with us. "Your room is made," arranged in due order. To make it all right.

As you make your bed you must lie on it. Everyone must bear the consequences of his own acts. "As you sow, so must you reap." "As you brew, so must you bake."

To bed out. To plant what are called "bedding-out plants" in a flower-bed.

∵ Bedding-out plants are reared in pots, generally in a hot-house, and are transferred into garden-beds early in the summer. Such plants as geraniums, marguerites, fuchsias, penstemons, petunias, verbenas, lobelias, calceolarias, etc., are meant.

You got out of bed the wrong way, or *with the left leg foremost.* Said of a person who is patchy and ill-tempered. It was an ancient superstition that it was unlucky to set the left foot on the ground first on getting out of bed. The same superstition applies to putting on the left shoe first, a "fancy" not yet wholly exploded.

∵ Augustus Cæsar was very superstitious in this respect.

Bed of Justice. (*See* LIT.)

Bed of Roses (*A*). A situation of ease and pleasure.

Bed of Thorns (*A*). A situation of great anxiety and apprehension.

Bed-post. *In the twinkling of a bed-post.* As quickly as possible. In the ancient bed-frames movable staves were laid as we now lay iron laths; there were also staves in the two sides of the bedstead for keeping the bed-clothes from rolling off; and in some cases a staff was used to beat the bed and clean it. In the reign of Edward I., Sir John Chichester had a mock skirmish with his servant (Sir John with his rapier and the servant with the bed-staff), in which the servant was accidentally killed. Wright, in his *Domestic Manners*, shows us a chambermaid of the seventeenth century using a bed-staff to beat up the bedding. "Twinkling" means a rapid twist or turn. (Old French, *guincher:* Welsh, *gwing*, *gwingaw*, our *wriggle*.)

"I'll do it instantly, in the twinkling of a bed-staff."—*Shadwell: Virtuoso*, 1676.
"He would have cut him down in the twinkling of a bed-post."—"*Rabelais*," *done into English.*

Bobadil, in *Every Man in his Humour*,

and Lord Duberley, in the *Heir-at-Law*, use the same expression.

Bede (*Adam*). A novel by George Eliot (Marian Evans), 1859. One of the chief characters is Mrs. Poyser, a woman of shrewd observation, and as full of wise saws as Sancho Panza.

Bedell. *The Vice-chancellor's bedell* (not *beadle*). The officer who carries the mace before the Vice-Chancellor, etc., in the universities is not a beadle but a bedell (the same word in an older form).

Be'der. A valley famous for the victory gained by Mahomet, in which "he was assisted by 3,000 angels, led by Gabriel, mounted on his horse Haïzum." (*Al Koran.*)

Beder. King of Persia, who married Giauha're, daughter of the most powerful of the under-sea emperors. Queen Labê tried to change him into a horse, but he changed her into a mare instead. (*Arabian Nights*, "*Beder and Giauharê.*")

Bedford. Saxon, *Bedean-forda* (fortress ford)—that is, the ford at the fortress of the river Ouse.

Bedford Level. Land drained by the Earl of Bedford in 1649. This large tract of fenny land lay in the counties of Norfolk, Suffolk, Cambridge, Huntingdonshire, Northamptonshire, and Lincolnshire.

Bedfordshire. *I am off to Bedfordshire.* To the land of Nod, to bed. The language abounds with these puns, *e.g.* "the marrowbone stage," "A Dunse scholar," "Knight of the beer-barrel," "Admiral of the blue," "Master of the Mint" (*q.v.*), "Master of the Rolls" (*q.v.*), etc. And the French even more than the English.

Bed'iver. A knight of the Round Table, and the butler of King Arthur.

Bedlam. A lunatic asylum or madhouse; a contraction for *Bethlehem*, the name of a religious house in London, converted into a hospital for lunatics. *Tom o' Bedlam.* (*See* TOM.)

∴ St. Mary of Bethlehem, London, was founded as a *priory* in 1247, and in 1547 it was given to the mayor and corporation of London, and incorporated as a royal foundation for lunatics.

Bed'lamite (3 syl.). A madman, a fool, an inhabitant of a Bedlam.

Bedouins [*Bed-wins*]. The homeless street poor are so called. Thus the *Times* calls the ragged, houseless boys "the Bedouins of London." The Bedouins are the nomadic tribes of Arabia (Arabic, *bedawin*, a dweller in a desert; *badw*, a desert). (*See* STREET ARABS.)

"These Bedouins of the prairie invariably carry their lodges with them."—*A. D. Richardson: Beyond the Mississippi*, chap. V.

Bed'reddin' Hassan, in the story of *Nour'eddin' and his Son*, in the *Arabian Nights*.

"Comparing herself to Bedreddin Hassan, whom the vizier ... discovered by his superlative skill in composing cream-tarts without pepper in them."—*Scott: Heart of Midlothian.*

Bed-rock. American slang for one's last shilling. A miner's term, called in England the "stone-head," and in America, the "Bed-rock," the hard basis rock. When miners get to this bed the mine is exhausted. "I'm come down to the bed-rock," *i.e.* my last dollar.

"'No, no!' continued Tennessee's partner, hastily, 'I'll play this yer hand alone. I've come down to the bed-rock; it's just this: Tennessee, thar, has played it pretty rough and expensive, like, on a stranger. ... Now what's the fair thing? Some would say more, and some would say less. Here's seventeen hundred dollars in coarse gold and a watch—it's about all my pile—and call it square.'"—*Bret Harte: Tennessee's Partner.*

Bedver. King Arthur's butler; Caius or Kaye was his sewer. (*Geoffrey: British History*, ix. 13.)

Bee. *The Athenian Bee.* Plato. (*See* ATHENIAN BEE, page 72, col. 1.)

It is said that when Plato was in his cradle, a swarm of bees alighted on his mouth. The story is good enough for poets and orators. The same tale is told of St. Ambrose. (*See* AMBROSE, page 41, col. 1.)

The Bee of Athens. Soph'oclēs. (*See* ATTIC BEE, page 73, col. 1.)

Xenophon (B.C. 444-359) is also called "the Bee of Athens," or "the Athenian Bee."

❊ *See* also ANIMALS (SYMBOLICAL), page 50, col. 2.

To have your head full of bees. Full of devices, crotchets, fancies, inventions, and dreamy theories. The connection between bees and the soul was once generally maintained: hence Mahomet admits bees to Paradise. Porphyry says of fountains, "they are adapted to the nymphs, or those souls which the ancients called bees." The moon was called a *bee* by the priestesses of Cerēs, and the word lunatic or moon-struck still means one with "bees in his head."

"Il a des rats dans la tête."—*French Proverb.*

(*See* MAGGOT.)

To have a bee in your bonnet. To be cranky; to have an idiosyncrasy; also, to carry a jewel or ornament in your cap. (*See* BIGHES.)

> " For pity, sir, find out that bee
> That bore my love away—
> ' I'll seek him in your bonnet brave.' . . ."
> *Herrick: The Mad Maid's Song.*

Bee. A social gathering for some useful work. The object generally precedes the word, as a spelling - bee (a gathering to compete in spelling). There are apple-bees, husking-bees, and half a dozen other sorts of bees or gatherings. It is an old Devonshire custom, which was carried across the Atlantic in Elizabethan times.

Bee-line. The line that a bee takes in making for the hive; the shortest distance between two given points.

" Our footmarks, seen afterwards, showed that we had steered a bee-line to the brig."—*Kane: Arctic Explorations*, vol. i. chap. xvii. p. 198.

Bees.
Jupiter was nourished by bees in infancy. (*See* ATHENIAN BEE, p. 72, col. 1.)
Pindar is said to have been nourished by bees with honey instead of milk.
The coins of Ephesus had a bee on the reverse.
The Greeks consecrated bees to the moon.
With the Romans a flight of bees was considered a bad omen. Appian (*Civil War*, book ii.) says a swarm of bees lighted on the altar and prognosticated the fatal issue of the battle of Pharsalia.
The priestesses of Cerēs were called bees.
In Christian Art St. Ambrose is represented with a beehive, from the tradition that a swarm of bees settled on his mouth in his infancy.

Beef, Ox. The former is Norman, and the latter Saxon. The Normans had the cooked meat, and when set before them used the word they were accustomed to. The Saxon was the herdsman, and while the beast was under his charge called it by its Saxon name.

" Old Alderman Ox continues to hold his Saxon title while he is under the charge of serfs and bondsmen ; but becomes *Beef*, a fiery French gallant, when he arrives before the worshipful jaws that are destined to consume him."—*Ivanhoe*.

Weaver's beef of Colchester, *i.e.* sprats, caught abundantly in the neighbourhood. (*Fuller: Worthies*.)

Beefeaters. Yeomen of the Guard in the royal household, appointed, in 1485, by Henry VII., to form part of the royal train in banquets and other grand occasions. The old theory was that the word means " an attendant on the royal buffets," Anglicised into

buffeters or *buffeteers*, and corrupted into *Beefeaters*; but Professor Skeat says no such word as *buffeter* has yet been found in any book; nor does *buffetier* exist in French.

A plausible reply to this objection is that the word may have got corrupted almost *ab initio* in those unlettered days; and the earliest quotation of " Beefeater," already adduced, is above 150 years from the institution of the force, and even then the allusions are either satirical or humorous : as " Begone, yee greedy beefe-eaters, y' are best " (*Histrio-mastix*, iii. 1 ; A.D. 1610); " Bows, or Beefeaters, as the French were pleased to terme us " (1628); " You beef-eater, you saucy cur " (1671). Not one of the quotations fixes the word on the Yeomen of the Guard, and that the English have been called Beefeaters none will deny. Even if the allusion given above could be certainly affixed to Yeomen of the Guard it would only prove that 150 or 160 years after their establishment in the palace they were so called (corruptly, humorously or otherwise).

Arguments in favour of the old derivation :—

(1) Certainly Henry VII. himself did not call these yeomen " beef-eaters." He was as much French as Welsh, and must have been familiar with the buffet (*bu-fey*) ; he had no spark of humour in his constitution, and it is extremely doubtful whether beef was a standing dish at the time, certainly it was not so in Wales. We have a good number of *menus* extant of the period, but beef does not appear in any of them.

(2) We have a host of similar corruptions in our language, as *Andrew Macs* (*q.v.*), *Billy-ruffians* (*see* BELLEROPHON), *Bull and Mouth* (*q.v.*), *Charles's Wain* (*q.v.*), *Bag-o'-Nails*, *Goat and Compasses*, *Sparrow-grass* (asparagus), *ancient* (ensign), *lutestring* (lustring, from lustre), *Dog-cheap* (god-kepe, *i.e.* a good bargain), and many more of the same sort.

(3) There can be no doubt that the " beefeaters " waited at the royal table, for in 1602 we read that " the dishes were brought in by the halberdiers [beefeaters], who are fine, big fellows " (quoted in *Notes and Queries*, February 4th, 1893, p. 86).

(4) If beef was a general food in the sixteenth century, which is extremely doubtful, it would be supremely ridiculous to call a few yeomen " eaters of beef," unless beef was restricted to them. In the present Argentine Republic, beef dried, called " jerked beef,"

is the common diet, and it would be foolish indeed to restrict the phrase " eaters of jerked beef " to some half-score waiters at the President's table.

(5) That the word *buffeteer* or *buffetier* is not to be found (in the English sense) in any French author, does not prove that it was never used in Anglo-French. We have scores of perverted French words, with English meanings, unrecognised by the French ; for example : *encore*, *double entendre*, *surtout* (a frock coat), *epergne*, and so on.

(6) Historic etymology has its value, but, like all other general rules, it requires to be narrowly watched, or it may not unfrequently over-ride the truth. Historically, *Rome* comes from Romulus, *Scotland* from Scota or Scotia, *Britain* from Brutus. All sorts of rubbishy etymology belong to the historic craze.

Beefeaters. Yeomen Extraordinary of the Guard appointed as warders of the Tower by Edward VI. They wear the same costume as the Yeomen of the Guard mentioned above. (*See* BUPHA-GOS.)

Beef-steak Club owed its origin to an accidental dinner taken by Lord Peterborough in the scene-room of Rich, over Covent Garden Theatre. The original gridiron on which Rich broiled the peer's steak is still preserved in the palladium of the club, and the members have it engraved on their buttons. (*History of the Clubs of London.*)

Beefington or *Milor Beefington*, a character in Canning's mock tragedy, *The Rovers*, a burlesque, in the *Anti-Jacobin*, on the sentimental German dramas of the period. Casimere is a Polish emigrant, and Beefington an English nobleman, exiled by the tyranny of King John.

Beelzebub. God of flies, supposed to ward off flies from his votaries. One of the gods of the Philistines. (*See* ACHOR.) The Greeks had a similar deity, *Zeus Apomy'ios.* The Jews, by way of reproach, changed Beelzebub into Baal Zeboub (q.v.), and placed him among the dæmons. Milton says he was next in rank to Satan, and stood

" With Atlante'an shoulders, fit to bear
The weight of mightiest monarchies."
(Book ii.)
" One next himself in power, and next in crime,
Long after known in Palestine, and named
Beëlzebub."   *Paradise Lost,* i. 79-81.

Beer. Cerēs, when wandering over the earth in quest of her daughter, taught men the art of making beer, because "*ils me ne purent apprendre l'art*

de faire le vin." (*Mem. de l'Academie des Inscriptiones,* xvii.) (*See* ALE.)
He does not think small beer of himself. [*See* SMALL BEER.]

Beer and Skittles. *Life is not all beer and skittles, i.e.* not all eating, drinking, and play ; not all pleasure ; not all harmony and love.

" Sport like life, and life like sport,
Isn't all skittles and beer."

Beer aux Mouches, or *Béer aux corneilles.* To stand gaping in the air (at the flies or the rooks). *Béer,* Old French for *bayer,* to gape.

Beeswing. The film which forms on the sides of a bottle of good old port. This film, broken up into small pieces, looks like the wings of bees. A port drinker is very particular not to " break the beeswing " by shaking the bottle, or turning it the wrong way up.

∴ Beeswinged port is old port which has formed its second crust or beeswing.

Beetle (*To*). To overhang, to threaten, to jut over (Anglo-Saxon, *beot-ian,* to menace). Hence beetle or beetled brow.

" Or to the dreadful summit of the cliff,
That beetles o'er his base into the sea."
Shakespeare: Hamlet, i. 4.

Beetle-crusher. A large, flat foot. The expression was first used in *Punch,* in one of Leech's caricatures. Those who know London know how it is over-run with cockroaches, wrongly called black-beetles.

Befa'na. The good fairy of Italian children, who is supposed to fill their stockings with toys when they go to bed on Twelfth Night. Some one enters the children's bedroom for the purpose, and the wakeful youngsters cry out, "*Ecco la Befa'na."* 'According to legend, Befana was too busy with house affairs to look after the Magi when they went to offer their gifts, and said she would wait to see them on their return ; but they went another way, and Befana, every Twelfth Night, watches to see them. The name is a corruption of *Epiphania.*

Before the Lights, in theatrical parlance, means on the stage, before the foot-lights.

Before the Mast. *To serve before the mast.* To be one of the common sailors, whose quarters are in the forward part of the ship. The half-deck is the sanctum of the second mate, and, in Greenland fishers, of the spikeneer, harpooners, carpenters, coopers, boatswains, and all secondary officers; of low birth.

"*I myself come from before the mast.*—*Sir W. Scott: The Antiquary,* chap. xx.

Beg the Question (*To*). (*See* BEGGING.)

Beggar. *A beggar may sing before a pickpocket.* (In Latin, "*Cantabit vacuus coram latrone viator.*") A beggar may sing before a highwayman because he has nothing in his pocket to lose.

Set a beggar on horseback, and he'll ride to the de'il. There is no one so proud and arrogant as a beggar who has suddenly grown rich.

"Such is the sad effect of wealth—rank pride— Mount but a beggar, how the rogue will ride!" *Peter Pindar: Epistle to Lord Lonsdale.*

Latin: "Asperius nihil est humili cum surgit in altum."

French: "Il n'est orgueil que de pauvre enrichi."

Italian: "Il vilan nobilitado non connosce il parentado" (A beggar ennobled does not know his own kinsmen).

Spanish: "Quando el villano está en el mulo, non conoze a dios, ni al mundo" (when a beggar is mounted on a mule, he knows neither gods nor men).

Beggars. *King of the Beggars.* Bampfylde Moore Carew (1693-1770).

Beggars should not be choosers. Beggars should take what is given them, and not dictate to the giver what they like best. They must accept and be thankful.

Beggars' Barm. The thick foam which collects on the surface of ponds, brooks, and other pieces of water where the current meets stoppage. It looks like barm or yeast, but, being unfit for use, is only beggarly barm at best.

Beggars' Bullets. Stones.

Beggar's Bush. *To go by beggar's bush,* or *Go home by beggar's bush*—*i.e.* to go to ruin. Beggar's bush is the name of a tree which once stood on the left hand of the London road from Huntingdon to Caxton; so called because it was a noted rendezvous for beggars. These punning phrases and proverbs are very common.

Beggar's Daughter. *Bessee, the beggar's daughter of Bednall Green.* Bessee was very beautiful, and was courted by four suitors at once—a knight, a gentleman of fortune, a London merchant, and the son of the innkeeper at Romford. She told them that they must obtain the consent of her father, the poor blind beggar of Bethnal Green. When they heard that, they all slunk off except the knight, who went to ask the beggar's leave to wed the "pretty Bessee." The beggar gave her £3,000 for her dower, and £100 to buy her wedding gown. At the wedding feast he explained to the guests that he was Henry, son and heir of Sir Simon de Montfort. At the battle of Evesham the barons were routed, Montfort slain, and himself left on the field for dead. A baron's daughter discovered him, nursed him with care, and married him; the fruit of this marriage was "pretty Bessee." Henry de Montfort assumed the garb and semblance of a beggar to escape the vigilance of King Henry's spies. (*Percy: Reliques.*)

Begging Hermits were of the Augustine order; they renounced all property, and lived on the voluntary alms of "the faithful."

¿ *Begging Friars* were restricted to four orders: Franciscans (*Grey Friars*), Augustines (*Black Friars*), Carmelites (*White Friars*), and Dominicans (*Preaching Friars*).

Begging the Question. Assuming a proposition which, in reality, involves the conclusion. Thus, to say that parallel lines will never meet because they are parallel, is simply to assume as a fact the very thing you profess to prove. The phrase is a translation of the Latin term, *petitio princip'ii,* and was first used by Aristotle.

Beghards. A brotherhood which rose in the Low Countries in the twelfth century, and was so called from Lambert Bègue. The male society were *Beghards,* the female, *Beguins.* They took no vows, and were free to leave the society when they liked. In the seventeenth century, those who survived the persecutions of the popes and inquisition joined the Tertiarii of the Franciscans. (*See* BEGUINS.)

Begtash'i. A religious order in the Ottoman Empire, which had its origin in the fourteenth century. The word is derived from Hadji Begtash, a dervish, its founder.

Begue d'entendement. This is a really happy phrase for one whose wits are gone wool-gathering; he is a man of "stammering understanding."

Béguins. A sisterhood instituted in the twelfth century, founded by Lambert Bègue or Lambert le Bègue. The members of the male society were called Beghards (*q.v.*). The Béguins were at liberty to quit the cloister, if they chose, and marry. The cap called a *beguin* was named from this sisterhood.

"Secta quædam pestifera illorum qui Beguini vulgariter appellantur, qui se Fratres Pauperes de tertia ordine S. Francisci communiter nomina- bant, ex quibus plures fuerunt tanquam hæretici condemnati et combusti."—*Bernard Guido: Life of John*, xxii.

Begum. A lady, princess, or woman of high rank in India; the wife of a ruler. (*Bey* or *Beg*, governor of a Turkish province, a title of honour.)

Behe'moth (Hebrew). The hippo- pot'amus; once thought to be the rhino- ceros. (*See* Job xl. 15.)

"Behold ! in plaited mail, Behe'moth rears his head." *Thomson: Summer*, 709, 710.

⁇ The word is generally, but incor- rectly, pronounced Be'hemoth; but Mil- ton, like Thomson, places the accent on the second syllable.

"Scarce from his mold Behemoth, biggest born of earth, upheaved His vastness." *Milton: Paradise Lost*, vii. 471.

Beh'menists. A sect of visionary religionists, so called from Jacob Beh- men (Böhme), their founder. (1575- 1625.)

Behram. The most holy kind of fire, according to Parseeism. (*See* ADA- RAN.)

Be'jan. A freshman or greenhorn. This term is employed in the French and Scotch universities, and is evidently a corruption of *bec jaune* (yellow beak), a French expression to designate a nestling or unfledged bird. In the university of Vienna the freshman is termed *beanus*, and in France footing- money is *bejaunia*.

"His grandmother yielded, and Robert was straightway a bejan or yellow-beak."—*Macdonald: R. Falconer.*

Bel-à-faire-peur. A handsome, dare- devil of a fellow.

Bel Esprit (French). A vivacious wit; a man or woman of quick and lively parts, ready at repartee. (Plural, *beaux esprits.*)

Belch. *Sir Toby Belch.* A reckless, roistering, jolly knight of the Eliza- bethan period. (*Shakespeare: Twelfth Night.*)

Belcher. A pocket-handkerchief— properly, a blue ground with white spots; so called from Jim Belcher, the pugilist, who adopted it.

Beldam. An old woman; literally, a grandmother. The French also use *bel age* for old age.

"Old men and beldames in the streets Do prophesy upon it dangerously." *Shakespeare: King John*, iv. 2.

Bele'ses (3 syl.). A Chaldean sooth- sayer and Assyrian satrap, who told Arba'cēs, governor of Me'dia, that he would one day sit on the throne of Sar- danapa'lus, King of Nineveh and As- syria. His prophecy was verified, and he was rewarded by Arba'cēs with the government of Babylon. (*Byron: Sar- danapalus.*)

Belfast Regiment (*The*). The 35th Foot, which was raised in Belfast in 1701. There is no such regiment now in the British Army. What used to be called No. 35 is now called the 1st bat- talion of the Royal Sussex, the 2nd battalion being the old No. 107.

Bel-fires. *Between Bel's two fires.* Scylla on one side and Charybdis on the other. In Irish, *Itter dha teine Bheil*, in a dilemma. The reference is to the two fires kindled on May Eve in every village, between which all men and beasts devoted to sacrifice were com- pelled to pass.

Bel'ford. A friend of Lovelace in Richardson's *Clarissa Harlowe*. These "friends" made a covenant to pardon every sort of liberty which they took with each other.

Belfry. A military tower, pushed by besiegers against the wall of a be- sieged city, that missiles may be thrown more easily against the defenders. Pro- bably a church steeple is called a belfry from its resemblance to these towers, and not because bells are hung in it. (French, *beffroi*, a watch-tower, Old French, *berfreit, belefreit*, from German, *berg-frit, bergen*, to protect, *frit [vride]*, a place fenced in for security.)

"Alone, and warming his five wits, The white owl in the belfry sits." *Tennyson: The Owl*, stanza 1.

Be'lial (Hebrew). The worthless or lawless one, *i.e.* the devil. Milton, in his pandemonium, makes him a very high and distinguished prince of dark- ness. (*Paradise Lost.*)

"What concord hath Christ with Belial?"—2 Cor. vi. 15.

"Belial came last—than whom a spirit more lewd Fell not from heaven, or more gross to love Vice for itself." *Milton: Paradise Lost*, book i. 490-2.

Sons of Belial. Lawless, worthless, rebellious people. (*See above.*)

"Now the sons of Eli were sons of Belial."— 1 Sam. ii. 12.

Belin'da. The heroine of Pope's serio-comical poem, entitled the *Rape of the Lock.* The poem is based on a real incident:—Lord Petre cut off a lock of Miss Fermor's hair, and this liberty gave rise to a bitter feud between the two noble families. The poet says that Belinda wore on her neck two curls, one of which the baron cut off with a pair of scissors borrowed of Clarissa. Belinda, in anger, demanded back the ringlet; but it had flown to the skies and become a meteor, which "shot through liquid air, and drew behind a radiant trail of hair." (*See* BERENICE.)

Belinun'cia. A herb sacred to Belis, with the juice of which the Gauls used to poison their arrows.

Belisa'rius. *Belisarius begging for an ob'olus.* Belisa'rius, the greatest of Justinian's generals, being accused of conspiring against the life of the emperor, was deprived of all his property; and his eyes being put out, he lived a beggar in Constantinople. The tale is that he fastened a bag to his road-side hut, and had inscribed over it, "Give an obolus to poor old Belisarius." This tradition is of no historic value.

Bell. *Acton, Currer,* and *Ellis.* Assumed names of Anne, Charlotte, and Emily Brontë.

Bell. *As the bell clinks, so the fool thinks,* or, *As the fool thinks, so the bell clinks.* The tale says when Whittington ran away from his master, and had got as far as Hounslow Heath, he was hungry, tired, and wished to return. Bow Bells began to ring, and Whittington fancied they said, "Turn again, Whittington, Lord Mayor of London." The bells clinked in response to the boy's thoughts. "*Les gens de peu de jugement sont comme les cloches, à qui l'on fait dire tout ce que l'on veut.*" Dickens has the same idea in his *Christmas Chimes.*

The Passing Bell is the hallowed bell which used to be rung when persons were *in extremis,* to scare away evil spirits which were supposed to lurk about the dying, to pounce on the soul while "passing from the body to its resting-place." A secondary object was to announce to the neighbourhood the fact that all good Christians might offer up a prayer for the safe passage of the dying person into Paradise. We now call the bell rung at a person's decease the "passing bell."

The Athenians used to beat on brazen kettles at the moment of a decease to scare away the Furies.

Ringing the hallowed bell. Bells were believed to disperse storms and pestilence, drive away devils, and extinguish fire. In France it is still by no means unusual to ring church bells to ward off the effects of lightning. Nor is this peculiar to France, for even in 1852 the Bishop of Malta ordered the church bells to be rung for an hour to "lay a gale of wind." Of course, the supposed efficacy of a bell resides in its having been consecrated.

"Fu'nera plango, ful'gura frango, sab'bata pango,
Ex'cito lentos, dis'sipo ventos, paco cruentos."

(Death's tale I tell, the winds dispel, ill-feeling quell,
The slothful shake, the storm-clouds break, the Sabbath wake.   E. C. B.)

(*See* RINGING THE BELLS BACKWARDS.)

Sound as a bell. (*See* SIMILES.)

Tolling the bell (for church). A relic of the Avē Bell, which, before the Reformation, was tolled before service to invite worshippers to a preparatory prayer to the Virgin.

To bear the bell. To be first fiddle; to carry off the palm; to be the best. Before cups were presented to winners of horse-races, etc., a little gold or silver bell used to be given for the prize.

"Jockey and his horse were by their masters sent
To put in for the bell. . . .
They are to run and cannot miss the bell."
            North: Forest of Varieties.

∴ It does not refer to bell-wethers, or the leading horse of a team, but "bear" means bear or carry off.

Who is to bell the cat? Who will risk his own life to save his neighbours? Any one who encounters great personal hazard for the sake of others undertakes to "bell the cat." The allusion is to the fable of the cunning old mouse, who suggested that they should hang a bell on the cat's neck to give notice to all mice of her approach. "Excellent," said a wise young mouse, "but who is to undertake the job?" (*See* BELL-THE-CAT.)

"Is there a man in all Spain able and willing to bell the cat [*i.e.* persuade the queen to abdicate]?"
—*The Times.*

Bells. The Koran says that bells hang on the trees of Paradise, and are set in motion by wind from the throne of God, as often as the blessed wish for music. (*Sale.*)

"Bells as musical
As those that, on the golden-shafted trees
Of Eden, shook by the eternal breeze."
            T. Moore: Lalla Rookh, part i.

At three bells, at five bells, etc. A term on board ship pretty nearly tantamount to our expression *o'clock.* Five out of the seven watches last four hours, and each half-hour is marked by a bell, which gives a number of strokes corresponding to the number of half-hours passed. Thus, "three bells" denotes the third half-hour of the watch, "five bells" the fifth half-hour of the watch, and so on. The two short watches, which last only two hours each, are from four to six and six to eight in the afternoon. At eight bells a new watch begins. (*See* WATCH.)

"Do you there hear? Clean shirt and a shave for muster at five bells."—*Basil Hall.*

I'll not hang all my bells on one horse. I'll not leave all my property to one son. The allusion is manifest.

Give her the bells and let her fly. Don't throw good money after bad; make the best of the matter, but do not attempt to bolster it up. When a hawk was worthless, the bells were taken off, and the bird was suffered to escape, but the advice given above is to "leave the bells" and let the hawk go.

Ringing the bells backwards, is ringing a muffled peal. *Backwards* is often used to denote "in a contrary direction" (*tout le contraire*), as, "I hear you are grown rich—" "Yes, backwards." To *ring* a muffled peal, is to ring a peal of sorrow, not of joy.

⁂ In olden times bells were rung backwards as a tocsin, or notice of danger.

"Beacons were lighted upon crags and eminences ; the bells were rung backwards in the churches ; and the general summons to arm announced an extremity of danger."—*Sir W. Scott: The Betrothed,* chap. iii.

Like sweet bells jangled, out of tune and harsh (Hamlet, iii. 1). A most exquisite metaphor for a deranged mind, such as that of Don Quixote.

Warwick shakes his bells. Beware of danger, for Warwick is in the field. Trojans beware, Achilles has donned his armour. The bells mean the bells of a hawk, the hawk shakes his bells.

"Neither the king, nor he that loves him best,
Dares stir a wing, if Warwick shakes his bells."
Shakespeare: 3 *Henry VI.,* i. 1.

Bell, Book, and Candle. A ceremony in the greater excommunication introduced into the Catholic Church in the eighth century. After reading the sentence a bell is rung, a book closed, and a candle extinguished. From that moment the excommunicated person is excluded from the sacraments and even divine worship.

"Bell, book, and candle shall not drive me back."—*Shakespeare: King John,* iii. 3.

In spite of bell, book, and candle, i.e. in spite of all the opposition which the Christian hierarchy can offer. (*See* CURSING.)

Bell of Patrick's Will (*clog an eadhachta Phatraic*) is six inches high, five broad, and four deep. It certainly was in existence in the sixth century. In the eleventh century a shrine was made for it of gold and silver filigree, adorned with jewels.

Bell Savage, or La Belle Sauvage = Pocahontas. According to one derivation it is a contraction of Isabelle Savage, who originally kept the inn. It is somewhat remarkable that the sign of the inn was a pun on the Christian name, a "bell on the Hope" (hoop), as may be seen in the Close Roll of 1453. The hoop seems to have formed a garter or frame to most signs. The site of the inn is now occupied by the premises of Messrs. Cassell & Co.

"They now returned to their inn, the famous Bell Savage."—*Scott: Kenilworth,* xiii.

Bell-the-Cat. Archibald Douglas, Earl of Angus, was so called. James III. made favourites of architects and masons. One mason, named Cochrane, he created Earl of Mar. The Scotch nobles held a council in the church of Lauder for the purpose of putting down these upstarts, when Lord Gray asked, "Who will bell the cat?" "That will I," said Douglas, and he fearlessly put to death, in the king's presence, the obnoxious minions. (*See* BELL.)

Bell-wavering. Vacillating, swaying from side to side like a bell. A man whose mind jangles out of tune from delirium, drunkenness, or temporary insanity, is said to have his wits gone bell-wavering.

"I doubt me his wits have gone bell-wavering by the road."—*Sir W. Scott: The Monastery,* chap. vii.

Belladonna (Italian, *beautiful lady*). This name was given to the Deadly Nightshade, from a practice once common among ladies of touching their eyes with it to make the pupils large and lustrous.

Bell'armine (*A*). A large Flemish gotch, *i.e.* a corpulent beer-jug of some strong ware, originally made in Flanders in ridicule of Cardinal Bellarmine, the great persecutor of the reformed party there. These jugs had at the neck a rude likeness of the cardinal with his large, square, ecclesiastical beard.

> " . . . like a larger jug, that some men call
> A bellarmine . . .
> Whereon the lewder hand of pagan workmen,
> Over the proud ambitious head, hath carved
> An idol large, with beard episcopal,
> Making the vessel look like tyrant Eglon."
> *Cartright : The Ordinary.*

"One of the Fellows of Exeter [College], when Dr. Prideaux was rector, sent his servitor, after nine o'clock at night, with a large bottle to fetch some ale from the alehouse. When he was coming home with it under his gown the proctor met him, and asked him what he did out so late, and what he had under his gown ? The man answered that his master had sent him to the stationers to borrow *Bellarmine*, which book he had under his arm ; and so he went home, Whence a bottle with a big belly is called a Bellarmine to this day, 1667."—*Oxoniana*, vol. i. p. 232.

Bell'aston (*Lady*). A profligate, whose conduct and conversation are a life-like photograph of the court "beauties" of Louis XV. (*Fielding : Tom Jones.*)

Belle. A beauty. *The Belle of the room.* The most beautiful lady in the room (French).
La belle France. A common French phrase applied to France, as "Merry England" is to our own country.

Belles Lettres. Polite literature (French) ; similarly, *Beaux arts*, the fine arts.

Bellefontaine (*Benedict*). The most wealthy farmer of Grand Pré (*Nova Scotia*), and father of Evangeline. When the inhabitants of his village were exiled, and he was about to embark, he died of a broken heart, and was buried on the sea-shore. (*Longfellow : Evangeline.*)

Beller'ophon. One of the ships which took part in the Battle of the Nile, and was called by the English sailors "the Bully-ruffran," or "Belly-ruffron."

"Why, she and the Belly-ruffron seem to have pretty well shared and shared alike."—*Captain Marryat : Poor Jack*, chap. xiii.

Beller'ophon. The Joseph of Greek mythology ; Antæa, the wife of Prœtos, being the "Potiphar's wife" who tempted him, and afterwards falsely accused him. Being successful in various enterprises, he attempted to fly to heaven on the winged horse Peg'asos, but Zeus sent a gad-fly to sting the horse, and the rider was overthrown.
Letters of Bellerophon. Letters or other documents either dangerous or prejudicial to the bearer. Prœtos sent Bellerophon with a letter to the King of Lycia, his wife's father, recounting the charge, and praying that the bearer might be put to death.
Pausa'nias, the Spartan, sent messengers from time to time to King Xerxes, with similar letters ; the discovery by one of the bearers proved the ruin of the traitor.
David's letter sent by Uriah (2 Sam. xi. 14) was of a similar treacherous character ; hence the phrase, "Letters of Uriah."

Belle'rus. Belle'rium is the Land's End, Cornwall, the fabled land of the giant Belle'rus.

> "Sleep'st by the fable of Bellerus old."
> *Milton : Lycidas*, 160.

Bellicent. Daughter of Gorloise and Igerna. According to Tennyson, she was the wife of Lot, King of Orkney ; but in *La Morte d'Arthur* Margause is called Lot's wife.

Bellin. The ram, in the tale of *Reynard the Fox.*

Bellisant. Sister to King Pepin of France, wife of Alexander, Emperor of Constantinople. Being accused of infidelity, the emperor banished her, and she became the mother of Valentine and Orson. (*Valentine and Orson.*)

Bellman. Before the new police force was established, watchmen or bellmen used to parade the streets at night, and at Easter a copy of verses was left at the chief houses in the hope of obtaining an offering. These verses were the relics of the old incantations sung or said by the bellman to keep off elves and hobgoblins. The town crier.

Bello'na. Goddess of war and wife of Mars. (*Roman mythology.*)

"Her features, late so exquisitely lovely, inflamed with the fury of frenzy, resembled those of a Bellona."—*Sir Walter Scott.*

Bellows. The pit of the stomach. To knock a man on the "bellows" takes his "wind (breath) away."
Sing old rose and burn the bellows. (*See* SING.)

Bellwether of the Flock. A jocose and rather depreciating term applied to the leader of a party. Of course the allusion is to the wether or sheep which leads the flock with a bell fastened to its neck.

Belly. *The belly and its members.* The fable of Menenius Agrippa to the Roman people when they seceded to the *Sacred Mount :* "Once on a time the members refused to work for the lazy belly ; but, as the supply of food was thus stopped, they found there was a necessary and mutual dependence between them." Shakespeare introduces the fable in his *Coriolanus*, i. 1.

The belly has no ears. A hungry man will not listen to advice or arguments. The Romans had the same proverb, *Venter non habet aures;* and in French, *Ventre affamé n'a point d'oreilles.*

Belly-timber. Food.

"And now, Dame Peveril, to dinner, to dinner. The old fox must have his belly-timber, though the hounds have been after him the whole day."
—*Sir W. Scott: Peveril of the Peak*, chap. 48.

Belomancy (Greek). Divination by arrows. Labels being attached to a given number of arrows, the archers let them fly, and the advice on the label of the arrow which flies farthest is accepted and acted on. This practice is common with the Arabs.

Beloved Disciple. St. John. (John xiii. 23, etc.)

Beloved Physician. St. Luke. (Col. iv. 14.)

Below the Belt. (*See* BELT.)

Bel'phegor. A nasty, licentious, obscene fellow. Bel-Phegor was a Moabitish deity, whose rites were celebrated on Mount Phegor, and were noted for their obscenity. The *Standard*, speaking of certain museums in London, says, "When will men cease to be deluded by these unscrupulous Bel'phegors?" (meaning "quacks").

✝ Phegor, Phogor, or Peor, a famous mountain beyond the Jordan. Nebo and Pisgah were neighbouring mountains. Beth-Peor is referred to in Deut. iii. 29.

Belphœbe, meant for Queen Elizabeth. She was sister of Am'oret. Equally chaste, but of the Diana and Minerva type. Cold as an icicle, passionless, immovable. She is a white flower without perfume, and her only tender passion is that of chivalry. Like a moonbeam, she is light without warmth. You admire her as you admire a marble statue. (*Spenser: Faërie Queene*, book iii.)

Belt. *To hit below the belt.* To strike unfairly. It is prohibited in prize-fighting to hit below the waist-belt.

To call men knaves and fools, to charge a man with nepotism, to make a slanderous report which is not actionable, indeed to take away a man's character in any way where self-defence is impossible, is "hitting him below the belt."
"Lord Salisbury hits hard, but never hits below the belt."—*Daily Telegraph*, November, 1885.

To hold the belt. To be the champion. In pugilism, etc., a belt is passed on to the champion.

Bel'tane (2 syl.). A festival observed in Ireland on June 21st, and in some parts of Scotland on May Day. A fire is kindled on the hills, and the young people dance round it, and feast on cakes made of milk and eggs. It is supposed to be a relic of the worship of Baal. The word is Gaelic, and means *Bel's fire;* and the cakes are called *beltane-cakes.*

Belted Knight. The right of wearing belt and spurs. Even to the present day knights of the shire are "girt with a belt and sword," when the declaration of their election is officially made.

Belted Will. Lord William Howard, warden of the western marches (1563-1640).

"His Bilboa blade, by marchmen felt,
Hung in a broad and studded belt;
Hence, in rude phrase, the borderers still
Called noble Howard *Betted Will.*" *Scott.*

Belten'ebros. Am'adis of Gaul so calls himself after he retires to the Poor Rock. His lady-love is Oria'na. (*Amadis of Gaul*, ii. 6.)

Belvawney (*Miss*), of the Portsmouth theatre. She always took the part of a page, and wore tights and silk stockings. (*Dickens: Nicholas Nickleby*, 1838.)

Belvedere [*bel-ve-dear*]. A sort of pleasure-house or look-out on the top of a house. The word is Italian, and means a *fine prospect.*

Belvide'ra (in Otway's *Venice Preserved*). Sir Walter Scott says, "More tears have been shed for the sorrows of Belvide'ra and Monim'ia than for those of Juliet and Desdemona."

"And Belvidera pours her soul in love."
Thomson: Winter.

Bemuse (2 syl.). To get into a dreamy, half-intoxicated state.

"Bemusing himself with beer."—*Sala: Gaslight and Daylight.*

Ben. The Neptune of the Saxons.

Ben (a theatrical word). Benefit. "A big ben," a good or bumping benefit.

Big Ben of Westminster. A name given to the large bell, which weighs 13 tons 10 cwt., and is named after Sir Benjamin Hall, the Chief Commissioner of Works when the bell was cast. (1856.)

Ben Joc'hanan', in the satire of *Absalom and Achitophel*, by Dryden and Tate, is meant for the Rev. Samuel Johnson, who suffered much persecution for his defence of the right of private judgment.

"A Jew [*Englishman*] of humble parentage was he ;
By trade a Levite [*clergyman*], though of low degree."   Part ii. 354, 355.

Ben trovato (Italian). Well found ; a happy discovery or invention.

Benai'ah (3 syl.), in the satire of *Absalom and Achitophel*, by Dryden and Tate, is meant for George Edward Sackville, called General Sackville, a gentleman of family, and a zealous partisan of the Duke of York. Benaiah was captain in David's army, and was made by Solomon generalissimo. (1 Kings ii. 35.)

"Nor can Benaiah's worth forgotten lie,
Of steady soul when public storms were high ;
Whose conduct, while the Moors fierce onsets made,
Secured at once our honour and our trade."
          Part ii. 819-20.

Bena'res (3 syl.). One of the "most holy" cities of the Hindus, reverenced by them as much as Mecca is by the Mohammedans.

Benbow (*Admiral*), in an engagement with the French near St. Martha, on the Spanish coast, in 1701, had his legs and thighs shivered into splinters by a chain-shot, but, supported in a wooden frame, he remained on the quarter-deck till morning, when Du Casse bore away. Almey'da, the Portuguese governor of India, in his engagement with the united fleet of Cambay'a and Egypt, had his legs and thighs shattered in a similar manner ; but, instead of retreating, had himself bound to the ship's mast, where he "waved his sword to cheer on the combatants," till he died from loss of blood. (*See* CYNÆGEROS, JAAFER, etc.)

"Whirled by the cannon's rage, in shivers torn,
His thighs far shattered o'er the waves are borne ;
Bound to the mast the god-like hero stands,
Waves his proud sword and cheers his woeful bands ;
Though winds and seas their wonted aid deny,
To yield he knows not, but he knows to die."
          Camoens : Lusiad, book x.

Benbow. A sot, generous, free, idle, and always hanging about the ale-house. He inherited a good estate, spent it all, and ended life in the workhouse. The tale is in Crabbe's *Borough*.

"Benbow, a boon companion, long approved
By jovial sets, and (as he thought) beloved,
Was judged as one to joy and friendship prone,
And deemed injurious to himself alone."
          Letter xvi.

Bench. The seat of a judge in the law courts ; the office of judge.

To be raised to the bench. To be made a judge.

The King's [queen's] bench. The Supreme Court of Common Law ; so called because at one time the sovereign presided in this court, and the court followed the sovereign when he moved from one place to another. Now a division of the High Court of Judicature.

Bench. *Bench of bishops.* The whole body of English prelates, who sit together on a bench in the House of Lords.
To be raised to the Episcopal bench. To be made a bishop.

Bench and Bar. Judges and pleaders. The bench is the seat on which a judge sits. The bar of a court was formerly a wooden barrier, to separate the counsel from the audience. Now, silk gowns (*q.v.*) sit nearer the judge, and their juniors behind them. (*See* BARRISTERS.)

Benchers. Senior members of the Inns of Court ; so called from the bench on which they used to sit. They exercise the function of calling students to the bar, and have the right of expelling the obnoxious. (*See* BAR, page 94, col. 1.)

"He was made successively Barrister, Utter Barrister, Bencher, and Reader."—*Wood*.

Bend, meaning power, as *Beyond my bend*, *i.e.* my means or power. The allusion is to a bow or spring ; if strained beyond its bending power, it breaks. (*See* BENT.)

Bend Sinister. *He has a bend sinister.* He was not born in lawful wedlock. In heraldry, a band running from the upper right-hand corner to the lower left-hand corner (as the shield appears before you on paper) is called a bend-sinister, and is popularly, but erroneously, supposed to indicate bastardy.

Ben'demeer'. A river that flows near the ruins of Chil'minar' or Istachar', in the province of Chusistan' in Persia.

"There's a bower of roses by Bendemeer's stream,
And the nightingale sings round it all the day long."   *T. Moore : Lalla Rookh*, Part I.

Bender. Sixpence.

Ben'digo. A rough fur cap, named from a noted pugilist, William Thompson, nicknamed Abednego, which was contracted to Bendigo.

Bendy (*Old*). The devil, who is willing to bend to anyone's inclination. The way of sin is so broad that every shade of error can be admitted without obstruction.

Benedicite (5 syl.). "Bless you:" a benediction used in the Roman Catholic Church; also the canticle.

Benedick. A sworn bachelor caught in the wiles of matrimony, like Benedick in Shakespeare's comedy of *Much Ado about Nothing.*

"Let our worthy Cantab be bachelor or Benedick, what concern is it of ours."—*Mrs. Edwards: A Girton Girl,* chap. xv.

⁎ Benedick and Benedict are used indiscriminately, but the distinction should be observed.

Benedict. A bachelor, not necessarily one pledged to celibacy, but simply a man of marriageable age, not married. St. Benedict was a most uncompromising stickler for celibacy.

"Is it not a pun? There is an old saying, 'Needles and pins; when a man marries his trouble begins.' If so, the unmarried man is *benedictus.*"—*Life in the West.*

Benedictines (4 syl.). Monks who follow the rule of St. Benedict, viz. implicit obedience, celibacy, abstaining from laughter, spare diet, poverty, the exercise of hospitality, and unremitting industry.

Ben'efice (3 syl.). Under the Romans certain grants of lands made to veteran soldiers were called *beneficia,* and in the Middle Ages an estate held *ex mero beneficio* of the donor was called "a benefice." When the popes assumed the power of the feudal lords with reference to ecclesiastical patronage, a "living" was termed by them a benefice held under the pope as superior lord. This assumption roused the jealousy of France and England, and was stoutly resisted.

Benefit of Clergy. Exemption of the clerical order from civil punishment, based on the text, "Touch not mine anointed, and do my prophets no harm" (1 Chron. xvi. 22). In time it comprehended not only the ordained clergy, but all who, being able to write and read, were capable of entering into holy orders. This law was abolished in the reign of George IV. (1827).

Ben'en-ge'li. (*See* HAMET.)

Benet (French). A simpleton, so called because they were supposed to be, in a special way, the objects of God's care. (French, *béni,* Old French, *beneit,* from Latin, *benedictus.*) We call an idiot an "Innocent" (*q.v.*).

Benevolence. A "forced" gratuity, under the excuse of a loan, exacted by some of the Plantagenet kings. First enforced in 1473, it was declared illegal by the Bill of Rights in 1689.

"Royal benevolences were encroaching more and more on the right of parliamentary taxation."—*Green: History of the English People,* vol. ii. book vi. chap. i. p. 197.

Benev'olus, in Cowper's *Task,* is John Courtney Throckmorton of Weston Underwood.

Bengal Tigers. The old 17th Foot, whose badge, a royal tiger, was granted them for their services in India (1802-23). Now the Leicester Regiment.

Bengalese (3 syl.) for Ben'galis or Bengalees. Natives of Bengal. (Singular, Ben'gali or Bengalee.)

Bengo'di. A wonderful country where "they tie the vines with sausages, where you may buy a fat goose for a penny and have the giblets given into the bargain. In this place there is a mountain of Parmesan cheese, and people's employment is making cheesecakes and macaroons. There is also a river which runs Malmsey wine of the very best quality. (*Boccaccio: Eighth Day, Novel* iii.)

Benicia Boy. John C. Heenan, the American pugilist, who challenged and fought Tom Sayers for "the belt" in 1860; so called from Benicia in California, his birthplace.

Benjamin. The pet, the youngest. Queensland is the Benjamin of our colonial possessions. The allusion is to Benjamin, the youngest son of Jacob (Gen. xxxv. 18).

Ben'jamin. A smart overcoat; so called from a tailor of the name, and rendered popular by its association with Joseph's "coat of many colours."

Benjamin's Mess. The largest share. The allusion is to the banquet given by Joseph, viceroy of Egypt, to his brethren. "Benjamin's mess was five times so much as any of theirs" (Gen. xliii. 34).

Bennaskar. A wealthy merchant and magician of Delhi, in Ridley's *Tales of the Genii.*

"Like the jeweller of Delhi, in the house of the magician Bennaskar, I at length reached a vaulted room dedicated to secrecy and silence."—*Sir W. Scott.*

Benshie, Benshee (*see* BANSHEE). The Scotch *Bodach Glay,* or Grey Spectre, is a similar superstition; and the *Pari-Banou* (Nymph of the Air) of the *Arabian Nights* is also a sort of Benshee.

"How oft has the Benshee cried !" [How busy death has been of late with our notables.]—*T. Moore: Irish Melodies*, No. ii.

Bent. Inclination ; talent for something. *Out of my bent*, not in my way, not in the range of my talent. *Bent on it*, inclined to it. As a thing bent is inclined, so a bent is an inclination or bias. Genius or talent is a bent or bias,

"Whatever is done best, is done from the natural bent and disposition of the mind."—*Hazlitt: Table Talk.*

They fool me to the top of my bent, i.e. as far as the bow can be bent without snapping. (*Hamlet*, iii. 2.) (*See* BEND.)

Benvo'lio. Nephew to Montague, a testy, litigious gentleman, who would "quarrel with a man that had a hair more or a hair less in his beard than he had." Mercutio says to him, "Thou hast quarrelled with a man for coughing in the street, because he hath wakened thy dog that hath lain asleep in the sun." (*Shakespeare : Romeo and Juliet*, iii. 1.)

Beppo. The contraction of Giuseppe, and therefore equal to our Joe. Husband of Laura, a Venetian lady. He was taken captive in Troy, turned Turk, joined a band of pirates, grew rich, and, after several years' absence, returned to his native land, where he discovered his wife at a carnival ball with her *cavaliero servente*. He made himself known to her, and they lived together again as man and wife. (*Byron : Beppo*.)

Berch'ta [*the white lady*]. This fairy, in Southern Germany, answers to Hulda (*the gracious lady*) of Northern Germany; but after the introduction of Christianity, when pagan deities were represented as demons, Berchta lost her former character, and became a bogie to frighten children.

Bere'ans (3 syl.). The followers of the Rev. John Barclay, of Kincardineshire (1773). They believe that all we know of God is from revelation ; that all the Psalms refer to Christ; that assurance is the proof of faith; and that unbelief is the unpardonable sin. They took their name from the Bereans, mentioned in the Book of the Acts (xvii. 11), who "received the Word with all readiness of mind, and searched the Scriptures daily."

Berecyn'thian Hero. Midas, the Phrygian king ; so called from Mount Berecyntus, in Phrygia.

Berenga'rians. Followers of Berenger, archdeacon of Angers, the learned opponent of Lanfranc (eleventh century). He said that the bread by consecration did not become the very body of Christ "generated on earth so many years before, but becomes to the faithful, nevertheless, the blessed body of Christ."

Bereni'ce (4 syl.). The sister-wife of Ptolemy III., who vowed to sacrifice her hair to the gods, if her husband returned home the vanquisher of Asia. She suspended her hair in the temple of the war-god, but it was stolen the first night, and Conon of Samos told the king that the winds had wafted it to heaven, where it still forms the seven stars near the tail of Leo, called *Coma Berenīcēs*.

✢ Pope, in his *Rape of the Lock*, converts the purloined ringlet into a star or meteor, "which drew behind a radiant trail of hair." (Canto v.)

Berg Folk. Pagan spirits doomed to live on the Scandinavian hills till the day of redemption. (*Scandinavian mythology*.)

Bergæan (*A*). A great liar ; so called from Antiphanes Berga.

Bergelmir. A frost-giant, father of the Jötuns, or second dynasty of giants. (*Scandinavian mythology*.)

Berger. *L'heure du Berger* (French). The shepherd's hour, *i.e.* the swain's or lover's hour ; the happy hour of tryst ; the critical moment.

Bergomask. A clown or merry-andrew ; a native of Bergamo. Compare, a gasconader ; a Bœotian.

Berkley (*Mr.*). An Englishman of fortune, good-humoured, and humane. He is a bachelor and somewhat eccentric, but sound common sense is a silver thread which is never lost. (*Longfellow: Hyperion* (a romance), 1839.)

Berkshire (Saxon, *Bearoc - scire*, forest-shire), a name peculiarly appropriate to this county, which contains the forest districts of Windsor and Bagshot.

Berlin Decree. A decree issued at Berlin by Napoleon I., forbidding any of the nations of Europe to trade with Great Britain (1806). This mad fancy was the first step to the great man's fall.

Berlin Time. The new Berlin Observatory is 44′ 14″ east of Paris, and 53′ 35″ east of Greenwich. The Berlin day begins at noon, but our civil day begins the midnight preceding.

Berliners. The people of Berlin, in Prussia.

Berme'ja. Insula de la Torre, from which Amadis of Gaul starts when he goes in quest of the Enchantress-Damsel, daughter of Fin'etor the necromancer.

Bermoothes. An hypothetical island feigned by Shakespeare to be enchanted, and inhabited by witches and devils. Supposed by some to be Bermudas; but a correspondent in *Notes and Queries* (January 23rd, 1886, p. 72) utterly denies this, and favours the suggestion that the island meant was Lampedusa.

"From the still-vexed Bermoothes, there she's hid."   *Shakespeare: The Tempest*, i. 2.

Bermudas. *To live in the Bermudas, i.e.* in some out-of-the-way place for cheapness. The shabby genteel hire a knocker in some West-end square, where letters may be left for them, but live in the Bermudas, or narrow passages north of the Strand, near Covent Garden.

Bernard (*St.*). Abbot of the monastery of Clairvaux in the twelfth century. His fame for wisdom was very great, and few church matters were undertaken without his being consulted.

Petit Bernard. Solomon Bernard, engraver of Lyons. (Sixteenth century.)

Poor Bernard. Claude Bernard, of Dijon, philanthropist (1588-1641).

Lucullus. Samuel Bernard, capitalist (1651-1739).

Le gentil Bernard. Pierre Joseph Bernard, the French poet (1710-1775).

Bernard. *Bonus Bernardus non videt omnia* (*see above*). We are all apt to forget sometimes; events do not always turn out as they are planned beforehand.

"Poor Peter was to win honours at Shrewsbury school, and carry them thick to Cambridge: and after that a living awaited him, the gift of his godfather, Sir Peter Arley: but *Bonus Bernardus non videt omnia*, and Poor Peter's lot in life was very different to what his friends had planned." —*Mrs. Gaskell: Cranford*, chap. vi.

Bernard Soup (*St.*). (*See* STONE SOUP.)

Bernardo, in Dibdin's *Bibliomania* (a romance), is meant for Joseph Hazlewood, antiquary and critic (1811).

Bernar'do del Car'pio. One of the most favourite subjects of the Spanish minstrels; the other two being the Cid and Lara's seven infants.

Bernard's Inn. Formerly called Mackworth Inn, from Dean Mackworth, who died 1454.

'This house was, in the thirty-first year of the reign of Henry VI., a messuage belonging to Dr. John Mackworth, dean of the cathedral church of Lincoln, and at that time in the holding of one Lionel Bernard . . . , and it hath ever since retained the name of Bernard's Inn."—*Harleian MSS.* No. 1104.

Berners or **Barnes** (*Juliana*). Prioress of Sopewell nunnery, near St. Albans, reputed authoress of the *Bokys of Hawking and Hunting* (1486). Generally called "Dame Berners." Another book ascribed to her is the *Boke of the Blazing of Arms* (1485).

Bernese (2 syl.). A native of Berne, in Switzerland.

Bernesque Poetry. Serio-comic poetry; so called from Francesco Berni, of Tuscany, who greatly excelled in it. (1490-1536.)

Bernouilli's Numbers or the properties of numbers first discovered by James Bernouilli, professor of mathematics at Basle (1654-1705).

Berser'ker. Grandson of the eight-handed Starka'der and the beautiful Alfhilde, called *bær-serce* (bare of mail) because he went into battle unharnessed. Hence, any man with the fighting fever on him.

"You say that I am berserker. And . . . baresark I go to-morrow to the war."—*Rev. C. Kingsley: Hereward the Wake.*

Berth. *He has tumbled into a nice berth.* A nice situation or fortune. The place in which a ship is anchored is called its berth, and the sailors call it a *good* or *bad* berth as they think it favourable or otherwise. The space also allotted to a seaman for his hammock is called his berth. (Norman, *berth*, a cradle.)

To give a wide berth. Not to come near a person; to keep a person at a distance. The place where a ship lies in harbour is called her berth: hence, to give a "wide berth" is to give a ship plenty of room to swing at anchor.

Bertha. The betrothed of John of Leyden, but, being a vassal of Count Oberthal, she was unable to marry without her lord's consent. When she went with her mother to ask permission of marriage, the count, struck with her beauty, determined to make her his mistress. She afterwards makes her escape from the castle, and, fancying that the "prophet" had caused the death of her lover, goes to Munster fully resolved to compass his death by setting fire to the palace. She is apprehended, and, being brought before the prophet-king, recognises her lover in him, saying, " I loved thee once, but now my love is turned to hate," and stabs herself. (*Meyerbeer's opera, Le Prophète.*)

Bertha. The blind daughter of Caleb Plummer in Dickens's *Cricket on the Hearth* (a Christmas story), 1845.

Bertha (*Frau*). A German impersonation of the Epiphany, corresponding to the Italian Befana. Represented as a white lady, who steals softly into nurseries and rocks infants asleep in the absence of negligent nurses; she is, however, the terror of all naughty children. Her feet are very large, and she has an iron nose. (*See* BEFANA.)

Berthas [*Stock Exchange term*]. The London, Brighton, & South Coast Railway Deferred Stock.

Berthe au Grand Pied. Mother of Charlemagne, and great granddaughter of Charles Martel ; so called because she had a club-foot.

Bertolde [*Bar-told*]. *Imperturbable as Bertolde*, i.e. not to be taken by surprise, thrown off your guard, or disconcerted at anything. Bertolde is the hero of a little *jeu d'esprit* in Italian prose, J. Cesare Croce. He is a comedian by profession, whom nothing astonishes, and is as much at his ease with kings and queens as with persons of his own rank and vocation.

Bertram. One of the conspirators against the Republic of Venice "in whom there was a hesitating softness fatal to a great enterprise." He betrayed the conspiracy to the senate. (*Byron: Marino Faliero.*)

Bertram (*Henry*), in Sir W. Scott's novel of *Guy Mannering*, was suggested by James Annesley, Esq., rightful heir of the earldom of Anglesey, of which he was dispossessed by his uncle Richard. He died in 1743.

Bertram, Count of Rousillon, beloved by Helěna, the hero of Shakespeare's comedy, *All's Well that Ends Well.*

" I cannot reconcile,my heart to Bertram,a man noble without generosity, and young without truth ; who marries Helena as a coward, and leaves her as a profligate."—*Dr. Johnson.*

Bertram Risingham. The vassal of Philip of Mortham. Oswald Wycliffe induced him to shoot his lord at Marston Moor, and for this vile deed the vassal demanded of him all the gold and movables of his late master. Oswald, being a villain, tried to outwit Bertram,

and even murder him ; but in the end it turns out that Mortham was not killed, neither was Oswald his heir, for Redmond O'Neale, the page of Rokeby, is found to be Mortham's son. (*Scott : Rokeby.*)

Bertra´mo. The fiend-father of Robert le Diable. After alluring his son to gamble away all his possessions, he meets him near the rocks St. Ire´ne, and Hel´ena seduces him in the " Dance of Love." When Bertra´mo at last comes to claim his victim, he is resisted by Alice, the foster-sister of the duke, who reads to him his mother's will, and angels come to celebrate the triumph of good over evil. (*Meyerbeer's opera of Roberto il Diavolo.*)

Berwicks [*Stock Exchange term*], meaning the North-Eastern Railway shares. The line runs to Berwick.

Beryl Molozane (3 syl.). The lady beloved by George Geith ; a laughing, loving beauty, all sunshine and artlessness ; tender, frank, full of innocent chatter ; helping everyone and loving everyone. Her lot is painfully unhappy, and she dies. (*F. G. Trafford* [*J. H. Riddell*] : *George Geith.*)

Berzak [*the interval*]. The space between death and the resurrection. (*The Koran.*)

Besaile. A great grandfather (French, *bisaieul*). This word should be restored.

Besants or **Bezants.** Circular pieces of bullion without any impression, supposed to represent the old coinage of Byzantium, and to have been brought to Europe by the Crusaders.

Beside the Cushion. Beside the question ; not to the point ; not pertinent to the matter in hand. French, *hors de propos ;* Latin, *nihil ad rhombum.* It was Judge Jeffreys who used the phrase, " Besides [*sic*] the cushion."

Besom. *To hang out the besom.* To have a fling when your wife is gone on a visit. To be a quasi bachelor once more. Taking this in connection with the following phrase, it evidently means, holding the marriage service in abeyance.

"This is French argot. *Rotir le balai* (to burn the besom) means to live the life of a libertine, whence *balochard,* Paris slang for a libertine. Probably our phrase, " burn the bellows," is pretty much the same as *rotir le balai.*

Jumping the besom. Omitting the marriage service after the publication of banns, and living together as man and wife. In Southern Scotch, a street-walker is called a *besom*, and in French *balai* (a besom) means the life of a liber-tine, as *Rôtir le balai ; Il ont bien rôti le balai ensemble,* where *balai* means a de-bauch or something worse. No further explanation can be needed or could be given.

Bess. *Good Queen Bess.* Queen Eliza-beth (1533, 1558-1603).

Bess o' Bedlam. A female lunatic vagrant. Bedlam is a common name for a madhouse, and Bess is a national name for a woman, especially of the lower order. The male lunatic is a *Tom o' Bedlam.*

Bess of Hardwicke. Elizabeth, Countess of Shrewsbury, to whose charge, in 1572, Mary Queen of Scots was committed. The countess treated the captive queen with great harshness, being jealous of the earl her husband. Bess of Hardwicke married four times : Alexander Barley (when she was only fourteen years of age); William Caven-dish ; Sir William St. Loe, Captain of Queen Elizabeth's Guard ; and lastly, George, Earl of Shrewsbury. She built Hardwicke Hall, and founded the wealth and dignity of the Cavendish family.

Bessemer Iron. Pig-iron refined, and converted into steel or malleable iron by passing currents of air through the molten metal, according to a process discovered by Sir H. Bessemer, and patented in 1856.

Bessie Bell and Mary Gray. A ballad. The tale is that these two young ladies, natives of Perth, to avoid the plague of 1666, retired to a rural retreat called the Burnbraes, about a mile from Lynedock, the residence of Mary Gray. A young man, in love with both, carried them provisions. Both ladies died of the plague, and were buried at Dornock Hough.

Bessus. A cowardly, bragging cap-tain, a sort of Bob'adil (*q.v.*). (*Beaumont and Fletcher : A King and no King.*)

Best. *At best* or *At the very best.* Looking at the matter in the most favourable light. Making every allow-ance.

"Life at best is but a mingled yarn."

At one's best. At the highest or best point attainable by the person referred to.

For the best. With the best of motives; with the view of obtaining the best results.

I must make the best of my way home,

It is getting late and I must use my utmost diligence to get home as soon as possible.

To have the best of it, or, *To have the best of the bargain.* To have the advan-tage or best of a transaction.

To make the best of the matter. To submit to ill-luck with the best grace in your power.

Best Man (at a wedding). The bride-groom's chosen friend who waits on him, as the bride's maids wait on the bride.

Best Things (*The Eight*), according to Scandinavian mythology :—

(1) The ash Yggdrasil is the best of trees ;
(2) Skidbladnir, of ships ;
(3) Odin, of the Æsir ;
(4) Sleipnir, of steeds ;
(5) Bifrost, of bridges ;
(6) Bragi, of bards ;
(7) Habrok, of hawks
(8) Garm, of hounds.

Bestiaries or **Bestials.** Books very popular in the eleventh, twelfth, and thirteenth centuries, containing the pic-tures of animals and their symbolisms.

"The unicorn has but one horn in the middle of its forehead. It is the only animal that ven-tures to attack the elephant ; and so sharp is the nail of its foot, that with one blow it can rip the belly of that beast. Hunters can catch the unicorn only by placing a young virgin in its haunts. No sooner does he see the damsel, than he runs towards her, and lies down at her feet, and so suffers himself to be captured by the hunters. The unicorn represents Jesus Christ, who took on Him our nature in the virgin's womb, was be-trayed to the Jews, and delivered into the hands of Pontius Pilate. Its one horn signifies the Gospel of Truth. . . ."—*Le Bestiaire Divin de Guillaume, Clerc de Normandie* (13th century).

Bête. *Morte la bête, mort le venin.* Dead men tell no tales ; dead dogs don't bite. When one is dead his power of mischief is over. Literally, if the beast is dead, its poison is dead also.

Quand Jean-Bête est mort, il à laissé bien des héritiers. Casimir Delavigne says to the same effect, *Les sots depuis Adam sont en majorité.* Jean-Bête means a fool or dolt.

Bête Noire. The thorn in the side, the bitter in the cup, the spoke in the wheel, the black sheep, the object of aversion. A black sheep has always been considered an eyesore in a flock, and its wool is really less valuable. In times of superstition it was looked on as bearing the devil's mark.

"The Dutch sale of tin is the *bête noire* of the Cornish miners."—*The Times.*

Beth Gelert, or "the Grave of the Greyhound." A ballad by the Hon. William Robert Spencer. The tale is that one day Llewellyn returned from hunting, when his favourite hound, covered with gore, ran to meet him. The chieftain ran to see if anything had happened to his infant son, found the cradle overturned, and all around was sprinkled with gore and blood. Thinking the hound had eaten the child, he stabbed it to the heart. Afterwards he found the babe quite safe, and a huge wolf under the bed, quite dead. Gêlert had killed the wolf and saved the child.

Beth'lemenites (4 syl.). Followers of John Huss, so called because he used to preach in the church called Bethlehem of Prague.

Betrothed (*The*). One of the *Tales of the Crusaders*, by Sir Walter Scott, 1832. Lady Eveline Berenger is the betrothed of Sir Damian de Lacy, whom she marries.

Better. *My better half.* A jocose way of saying my wife. As the twain are one, each is half. Horace calls his friend *ánimæ dimidium meæ.* (1 *Odes* iii. 8.)

To be better than his word. To do more than he promised.

To think better of the matter. To give it further consideration; to form a more correct opinion respecting it.

Better kind Friend, etc. *Better kind friend than friend kind.* Friend is a corruption of *fremd*, meaning a stranger. Better [a] kind stranger than a kinsman who makes himself a stranger, or an estranged kinsman.

Better off. In more easy circumstances.

Bettina. A mascotte who always brought good luck wherever she went. Though a mere peasant, she is taken to the Prince of Piombino's palace of Laurent, to avert his ill-luck; but by marrying Pippo (a shepherd) she loses her gift. However, the prince is reminded that the children of a mascotte are hereditary mascottes, and makes Bettina promise that her first child shall be adopted by the prince. (*See* MASCOTTE.)

Bettina. The name under which Elizabeth Brentano translated into English Goethe's *Letters to a Child* in 1835. She was the wife of Ludwig Achim von Arnim, and it was her correspondence with Goethe which were the *Letters to a Child* referred to. Elizabeth Brentano was born 1785.

Betty. A name of contempt given to a man who interferes with the duties of female servants, or occupies himself in female pursuits; also called a "Molly."

Betty. A skeleton key; the servant of a picklock. Burglars call their short crowbars for forcing locks *Jennies* and *Jemmies*. "Jenny" is a "small engine," *i.e.'ginie*, and Jemmy is merely a variant.

Betu'bium. Dumsby, or the Cape of St. Andrew, in Scotland.

" The north-inflated tempest foams
O'er Orka's and Betubium's highest peak."
Thomson: Autumn, 891, 2.

Between. *Between hay and grass.* Neither one thing nor yet another; a hobbledehoy, neither a man nor yet a boy.

Between cup and lip. (*See* SLIP.)

Between Scylla and Charybdis. Between two equal dangers; on the horns of a dilemma. (*See* CHARYBDIS.)

Between two fires. Between two dangers. In war, an army fired upon from opposite sides is in imminent danger.

Between two stools you come to the ground. "Like a man on double business bound, I stand in pause where I shall first begin, and both neglect." He who hunts two hares leaves one and loses the other." *Simul sorbēre ac flare non possum.* The allusion is to a children's game called "The Ambassador," also a practical joke at one time played at sea when the ship crossed the line. Two stools are set side by side, but somewhat apart, and a cloth is covered over them. A person sits on each stool to keep the cloth taut, and the ambassador is invited to sit in the middle; but, as soon as he is seated, the two rise and the ambassador comes to the ground.

Between you and me (French, *entre nous*). In confidence be it spoken. Sometimes, *Between you and me and the gate-post.* These phrases, for the most part, indicate that some ill-natured remark or slander is about to be made of a third person, but occasionally they refer to some offer or private affair. "Between ourselves" is another form of the same phrase.

Betwixt and Between. Neither one nor the other, but somewhere between the two. Thus, grey is neither white nor black, but betwixt and between the two.

Beurre. *Avoir beurre sur la tête.* To be covered with crimes. Taken from a Jewish saying, "If you have butter on your head (*i.e.* have stolen butter and put it in your cap), don't go into the sun." (*Vidocq: Voleurs*, vol. i. p. 16.)

J'y suis pour mon beurre. Here *beurre* means *argent.* I paid for it through the nose. *Beurre* or butter has the same relation to food as wealth has to civil life ; it does not take the place of it, and does not make it, but it makes it go down more pleasantly, and adds somewhat to its wholesomeness. As Shakespeare says, " Where virtue is, it makes more virtuous."

Promettre plus de beurre que de pain. To promise much, but perform little. To promise more than one can, or chooses to, perform. The butter of a promise is of no use without substantial bread. " Be thou fed" will not fill an empty stomach. A little help is worth a deal of pity.

Beuves (1 syl.), or *Buo'vo of Ayyre'-mont.* The father of Malagigi, and uncle of Rinaldo. (*Ariosto : Orlando Furioso.*)

Bev'er. A "drink" between meals (Italian, *bevere,* to drink—our *beverage ;* Latin, *bibere*—our *im-bibe*). At Eton they used to have " Bever days," when extra beer and bread were served during the afternoon in the College Hall to scholars, and any friends whom they might bring in.

" He . . . will devour three breakfasts . . . without prejudice to his bevers."—*Beaumont and Fletcher : Woman Hater,* i. 3.

Bev'il. A model gentleman in Steele's *Conscious Lovers.*

" Whate'er can deck mankind,
Or charm the heart, in generous Bevil showed."
Thomson : Winter, 654-5.

Be'vis. The horse of Lord Marmion. (*Sir Walter Scott.*) (*See* HORSE.)

Bevis of Southampton. A knight of romance, whose exploits are recounted in Drayton's *Polyolbion.* The French call him *Beuves de Hantone.*

Bevoriskius, whose *Commentary on the Generations of Adam* is referred to by Sterne in the *Sentimental Journey,* was Johannes Bevoricius, physician and senator, author of a large number of books. The *Commentary* will be found at fol. 1 (1652).

Bev'y. *A bevy of ladies.* A throng or company ; properly applied to roe-bucks, quails, and pheasants. Timid gregarious animals, in self-defence, go down to a river to drink in bevies or small companies. Ladies, from their timidity, are placed in the same category (Italian, *bevere,* to drink).

" And upon her deck what a bevy of human flowers—young women, how lovely !—young men, how noble !"—*De Quincey : Dream-fugue.*

Beza'liel, in the satire of *Absalom*

and Achitophel, by Dryden and Tate, is meant for the Marquis of Worcester, afterwards Duke of Beaufort.

" Bezaliel with each grace and virtue fraught,
Serene his looks, serene his life and thought ;
On whom so largely Nature heaped her store,
There scarce remained for arts to give him more." Part ii. 947-56.

Bezo'nian. A new recruit ; applied originally in derision, to young soldiers sent from Spain to Italy, who landed both ill-accoutred and in want of everything (Ital. *besogni,* from *bisogno,* need ; French *besoin*).

" Base and pilfering besognios and marauders.'
—*Sir W. Scott : Monastery,* xvi.

" Great men oft die by vile bezonians."
Shakespeare : 2 Henry VI., act iv. 1.

" Under which king, Bezonian? Speak or die" (*2 Hen. IV.,* act v. 3). Choose your leader or take the consequences —Cæsar or Pompey ? " Speak or die."

Bheem or *Bhima.* One of the five Pandoos, or brotherhoods of Indian demi-gods, famous for his strength. He slew the giant Kinchick, and dragged his body from the hills, thereby making the Kinchick ravine.

Bixum, in rhetoric, means convertir; the proof into a disproof. As thus : That you were the murderer is proved by your being on the spot at the time. *Reply :* Just the contrary, if I had been the guilty person most certainly I should have run away. (Greek, *biaion.*)

Bian'ca. Wife of Fazio. When Fazio became rich, and got entangled with the Marchioness Aldabella, she accused him to the Duke of Florence of being privy to the death of Bartoldo, an old miser. Fazio was arrested and condemned to death. Bianca now repented of her jealous rashness, and tried to save her husband, but failing in her endeavours, went mad, and died of a broken heart. (*Dean Milman : Fazio.*)

N. B. — The name is employed by Shakespeare both in his *Taming of the Shrew* and also in *Othello.*

Bianchi. (*See* NERI.)

Bias. The weight in bowls which makes them deviate from the straight line ; hence any favourite idea or pur-suit, or whatever predisposes the mind in a particular direction.

Bowls are not now loaded, but the bias depends on the shape of the bowls. They are flattened on one side, and therefore roll obliquely.

" Your stomach makes your fabric roll,
Just as the bias rules the bowl."
Prior ; Alma, iii, line 1261,

Biberius Caldius Mero. The punning nickname of Tiberius Claudius Nero. Biberius [Tiberius], drink-loving, Caldius Mero [Claudius Nero], by metathesis for *calidus mero*, hot with wine.

Bible means simply a book, but is now exclusively confined to the "Book of Books." (Greek, *biblos*, a book.)

The headings of the chapters were prefixed by Miles Smith, Bishop of Gloucester, one of the translators.

(i) BIBLES NAMED FROM ERRORS OF TYPE, or from archaic words:—

The Breeches Bible. So called because Genesis iii. 7 was rendered, "The eyes of them bothe were opened . . . . and they sowed figge-tree leaves together, and made themselves breeches." By Whittingham, Gilby, and Sampson, 1579.

The Idle Bible, 1809. In which the "idole shepherd" (Zech. xi. 17) is printed "the idle shepherd."

The Bug Bible, 1551. So called because Psalm xci. 5 is translated, "Thou shalt not be afraid of bugges [bogies] by nighte."

The Great Bible. The same as Matthew Parker's Bible (*q.v.*).

The Place-maker's Bible. So called from a printer's error in Matt. v. 9, "Blessed are the placemakers [peacemakers], for they shall be called the children of God."

The Printers' Bible makes David pathetically complain that "the printers [princes] have persecuted me without a cause" (Ps. cxix. 161).

The Treacle Bible, 1549 (Beck's Bible), in which the word "balm" is rendered "treacle." The Bishops' Bible has *tryacle* in Jer. iii. 28 ; xlvi. 11 ; and in Ezek. xxvii. 17.

The Unrighteous Bible, 1652 (Cambridge Press). So called from the printer's error, "Know ye not that the unrighteous shall inherit the Kingdom of God?" (1 Cor. vi. 9).

The Vinegar Bible. So called because the heading to Luke xx. is given as "The parable of the Vinegar" (instead of Vineyard). Printed at the Clarendon Press in 1717.

The Wicked Bible. So called because the word *not* is omitted in the seventh commandment, making it, "Thou shalt commit adultery." Printed by Barker and Lucas, 1632.

To these may be added : the Discharge Bible, the Ears to Ear Bible, Rebecca's Camels Bible, the Rosin Bible, the Standing Fishes Bible, and some others.

(ii) BIBLES NAMED FROM PROPER NAMES, or dignities.

Bishop's Bible. The revised edition of Archbishop Parker's version. Published 1568.

Coverdale's Bible, 1535. Translated by Miles Coverdale, afterwards Bishop of Exeter. This was the first Bible sanctioned by royal authority.

Cranmer's Bible, 1539. This is Coverdale's Bible corrected by Archbishop Cranmer. It was printed in 1540, and in 1549 every parish church was enjoined to have a copy under a penalty of 40s. a month.

The Douay Bible, 1581. A translation made by the professors of the Douay College for the use of English boys designed for the Catholic priesthood.

The Geneva Bible. The Bible translated by the English exiles at Geneva. The same as the "Breeches Bible" (*q.v.*).

King James's Bible. The Authorised Version ; so called because it was undertaken by command of James I. Published 1611.

Matthew Parker's Bible, or "The Great Bible," published in the reign of Henry VIII. under the care of Archbishop Parker and his staff (1539-1541). In 1572 several prolegomena were added.

Matthews' Bible is Tindal's version. It was so called by John Rogers, superintendent of the English churches in Germany, and was published with notes under the fictitious name of Thomas Matthews, 1537.

The Mazarine Bible. The earliest book printed in movable metal type. It contains no date. Copies have been recently sold from £3,900 to £5,000. Called the Mazarine Bible from the *Bibliothèque Mazarine*, founded in Paris by Cardinal Mazarine in 1648.

Sacy's Bible. So called from Isaac Louis Sacy (*Le-maistre*), director of the Port Royal Monastery. He was imprisoned for three years in the Bastille for his Jansenist opinions, and translated the Bible during his captivity (1666-1670).

Tyndale's Bible. William Tyndale, or Tindal, having embraced the Reformed religion, retired to Antwerp, where he printed an English translation of the Scriptures. All the copies were bought up, whereupon Tyndale printed a revised edition. The book excited the rancour of the Catholics, who strangled the "heretic" and burnt his body near Antwerp in 1536.

Wyclif's Bible, 1380, but first printed in 1850.

(iii) VERSIONS.

The Authorised Version, 1611. (*See* KING JAMES'S BIBLE.)

The Revised Version. Published in May, 1885. The work was begun in June, 1870, by twenty-five scholars, ten of whom died before the version was completed, the eighty-five sessions extending over fourteen years. The Apocrypha was issued in 1895.

Bible-backed. Round-shouldered, like one who is always poring over a book.

Bible-carrier (*A*). A pogram; creak-shoes; or saint, in a scornful sense.

"Of all bookes, they least respect the Bible. Many will have statute bookes, cronicles, yea play-bookes, and such-like toyish pamphlets, but not a bible in their house or hands. . . . Some vse to carry other bookes with them to church . . . to draw away their mindes from hearing God's word when it is read and preached to them. Some goe yet further, and will not suffer their wives, children, or other of their household to reade the Word. And some scoffe at such as carry the scriptures with them to church, terming them in reproach *Bible-carriers.*"—*Gouge: Whole Armour of God,* p. 318 (1616).

Bible Christians. A Protestant sect founded in 1815 by William O'Bryan, a Wesleyan, of Cornwall; also called Bryanites (3 syl.).

Bible-Clerk. A sizar of the Oxford university; a student who gets certain pecuniary advantages for reading the Bible aloud at chapel. The office is almost a sinecure now, but the emolument is given, in some colleges, to the sons of poor gentlemen, either as a free gift, or as the reward of merit tested by examination.

Bible Statistics.

The Number of Authors is 50.

About 30 books are mentioned in the Bible, but not included in the canon.

	In the Old Testament.	In the New Testament.	Total.
Books	39	27	66
Chapters	929	260	1,189
Verses	23,214	7,959	31,173
Words	592,439	181,253	773,692
Letters	2,728,800	838,380	3,567,180

Apocrypha. Books, 14; chapters, 183; verses, 6,081; words, 252,185; letters, 1,063,876.

Middle book .. .. Proverbs
Middle chapter .. Job xxix.   2 Thess.
Middle verse .. 2 Chron. xx.   Rom. xiii. & xiv.   Acts xvii. 17.
(between verses 17 and 18)
Least verse .. .. 1 Chron. i. 25, John xi. 35.
Smallest chapter   Psalm cxvii.
Longest chapter   Psalm cxix.

Ezra vii. 21 contains all the letters of the alphabet, except j.

2 Kings xix. and Isaiah xxxvi. are exactly alike.

The last two verses of 2 Chron. and the opening verses of Ezra are alike.

Ezra ii. and Nehemiah vii. are alike.

The word *and* occurs in the Old Testament 35,543 times.

The word *and* occurs in the New Testament 10,684 times.

The word *Jehovah* occurs 6,855 times.

The letter *Mem* in the Hebrew text occurs 77,778 times.

The letter *Vau* in the Hebrew text occurs 76,922 times. (These are the most frequent.)

The letter *Teth* occurs 11,052 times.

The letter *Samech* occurs 13,580 times. (These are the least frequent.)

The Bible was divided into *chapters* by Cardinal Hugo de Sancto-Caro, about 1236.

The Old Testament was divided into *verses* by Rabbi Mordecai Nathan; and the New Testament, in 1544, by R. Stephens, a French printer, it is said, while on horseback.

Of the 3,000 languages and dialects on the earth, the Bible has been translated into 180.

The Septuagint, a translation into Greek, was made in Egypt 285 B.C.

The first complete English translation was by Wicklif, A.D. 1380; the first French translation, in 1160; the first German, in 1460; the first American edition was printed at Boston in 1752.

The oldest MS. of the Bible in the British Museum is the "Codex Alexandrinus." Parts of the New Testament are omitted. The "Codex Vaticānus" is the oldest in the Vatican Library at Rome.

Bib'lia Pau'perum [*the poor man's Bible*]. Some forty or fifty pictures of Bible subjects used in the Middle Ages, when few could read, to teach the leading events of Scripture history. (*See* MIRROR OF HUMAN SALVATION.)

Biblical. *Father of Biblical criticism and exegesis.* Origen (185-254).

Bibliomancy. Forecasting future events by the Bible. The plan was to open the sacred volume at random, and lay your finger on a passage without looking at it. The text thus pointed out was supposed to be applicable to the person who pointed it out. (Greek, *biblia,* Bible; *manteia,* prophecy.) (*See* SORTES.)

✢ Another process was to weigh a person suspected of magic against a Bible. If the Bible bore down the other scale, the accused was acquitted.

Bib'ulus. Colleague of Julius Cæsar, a mere cipher in office, whence his name has become proverbial for one in office who is a mere *fainéant.*

Biceps. Muscular strength of the arm; properly, the prominent muscles of the upper arm; so called because they have two heads. (Latin, *biceps,* two heads.)

Biceps Parnassus (*Pers. Prol.* 2), *i.e.* Parnassus with two heads or tops (*bis caput*).

"Nec fonte labra prolui caballino,
Nec in bicipiti somniasse Parnasso
Memini, ut repente sic poeta prodirem"
Persius : Satires (prologue).

Bick'erstaff (*Isaac*). A name assumed by Dean Swift in a satirical pamphlet against Partridge, the almanack-maker. This produced a paper war so diverting that Steele issued the *Tatler* under the editorial name of "Isaac Bickerstaff, Esq., Astrologer" (1709).

Bicorn. An hypothetical beast supposed to devour all men under petticoat government. It is described as very fat and well liking. There was another beast called Chichevache, which fed on obedient wives, but the famished beast was thinner than the most rascal of Pharaoh's lean kine, for its food always fell short. Of course, *bi-corn* (two-horns) contains an allusion familiar to all readers of our early literature.

Bid. *To bid fair.* To seem likely: as "He bids fair to do well;" "It bids fair to be a fine day." (Anglo-Saxon, *bédan* or *beódan*, to promise, to offer.)

To bid for [votes]. To promise to support in Parliament certain measures, in order to obtain votes.

To bid against one. To offer or promise a higher price for an article at auction.

I bid him defiance. I offer him defiance; I defy him.

Bid. *I bid you good night.* I wish you good night, or I pray that you may have a good night. This is the Anglo-Saxon *biddan*, to ask, pray, or intreat. Whence "beads-men" (*q.v.*), "bidding prayer" (*q.v.*). "Bid him welcome."

"Neither bid him God-speed."—2 John 10, 11.

To bid the [*marriage*] *banns.* To ask if anyone objects to the marriage of the persons named. " *Si quis* " (*q.v.*).

To bid to the wedding. In the New Testament is to ask to the wedding feast.

Bid-ale. An invitation of friends to assemble at the house of a poor man to drink ale, and thus to raise alms for his relief.

"The ordinary amusements in country parishes (in 1632) were church-ales, clerk-ales, and bid-ales, . . . consisting of drinking and sports, particularly dancing."—*T. V. Short, D.D.: History of the Church of England*, p. 392.

"Denham, in 1634, issued an order in the western circuit to put an end to the disorders attending church-ales, bid-ales, clerk-ales, and the like."—*Howitt: History of England* (Charles I., chap. iii. p. 159).

Bidding Beads. Telling off prayers by beads (Anglo-Saxon, *biddan*, to ask, to pray).

Bidding-Prayer. The prayer for *the souls of benefactors* said before the sermon; a relic of this remains in the prayer used in cathedrals, university churches, etc. Bidding is from *bead* or *bede*. (Anglo-Saxon, *biddan*, to pray for the souls of benefactors.) (*See* BEADSMAN.)

Biddy (*i.e.* Bridget). A generic name for an Irish servant-maid, as Mike is for an Irish labourer. These generic names are very common: for example, Tom Tug, a waterman; Jack Pudding, a buffoon; Cousin Jonathan, an American of the United States; Cousin Michel, a German; John Bull, an Englishman; Moll and Betty, English female servants of the lower order.; John Chinaman, a Chinese; Colin Tompon, a Swiss; Nic Frog, a Dutchman; Mossoo, a Frenchman; and many others.

⁂ In Arbuthnot's *John Bull* Nic Frog is certainly a Dutchman; and Frogs are called "Dutch Nightingales." The French sometimes serve Liège frogs at table as a great delicacy, and this has caused the word to be transferred to the French; but, properly, Nic Frog is a Dutchman.

Bideford Postman. Edward Capern, the poet (born 1819), so called because at one time he was a letter-carrier at Bideford. He died in 1894.

Bidpai. [*See* PILPAI.]

Biforked Letter of the Greeks. The capital U, made thus Y, which resembles a bird flying.

"[The birds] flying, write upon the sky
The biforked letter of the Greeks."
Longfellow : The Wayside Inn, prelude.

Bif'rost, in Scandinavian mythology, is the name of the bridge between heaven and earth; the rainbow may be considered to be this bridge, and its various colours are the reflections of its precious stones. (Icelandic, *bifa*, tremble, and *rost*, path.)

⁂ The keeper of the bridge is Heimdall. It leads to Doomstead, the palace of the Norns or Fates.

Big. *To look big.* To assume a consequential air.

To talk big. To boast or brag.

"The archdeacon waxed wroth, talked big, and looked bigger."—*Trollope: The Warden*, chap. 20.

Big Bird. *To get the big bird* (*i.e.* the goose). To be hissed on the stage. A theatrical expression.

Big-en'dians. A religious party in the empire of Lilliput, who made it a matter of conscience to break their eggs at the *big end;* they were looked on as heretics by the orthodox party, who broke theirs at the small end. The Big-endians are the Catholics, and the Little-endians the Protestants.

Big Gooseberry Season (*The*). The time when Parliament is not assembled.

It is at such times that newspapers are glad of any subject to fill their columns and amuse their readers; monster gooseberries will do for such a purpose for the nonce, or the sea-serpent.

Big-wig (*A*). A person in authority, a "nob." Of course, the term arises from the custom of judges, bishops, and so on, wearing large wigs. Bishops no longer wear them.

Bigaroon. Incorrectly spelt *Bica-roon*. A white-heart cherry. (French, *bigarreau*; Latin, *bigarella*; *i.e. bis var-ellus*, double-varied, red and white mixed. The French word, *bigarrure*, means party-colour, *bigarrer*).

Bighes (pron. *bees*). Jewels, female ornaments. (Also written *bie*.)
She is all in her bighes to-day—i.e. in full fig, in excellent spirits, in good humour.

Bight. *To hook the bight—i.e.* to get entangled. The bight is the bend or doubled part of a rope, and when the rope of one anchor gets into the "bight" of another, it gets "hooked."

Bigorne (2 syl.). A corruption of "Bicorn" (*q.v.*).

Big'ot means simply a worshipper (Anglo-Saxon, *bigan*, to worship; German, *bigott*). Various explanations have been given from time to time, but none are well supported.

Bigot and his Castle of Bungay. (*See* CASTLE, etc.)

Bil'bo. A rapier or sword. So called from Bilba'o, in Spain, once famous for its finely-tempered blades. Falstaff says to Ford :

"I suffered the pangs of three several deaths; first, an intolerable fright, to be detected . . . next, to be compassed, like a good bilbo . . . hilt to point, heel to head; and then . . ."—*Merry Wiv-s*, iii. 5.

Bilboes. A bar of iron with fetters annexed to it, by which mutinous sailors are linked together. The word is de-rived from Bilba'o, in Spain, where they were first made. Some of the bilboes taken from the Spanish Arma'da are still kept in the Tower of London.

Bile. *It rouses my bile.* It makes me angry or indignant. In Latin, *biliosus* (a bilious man) meant a choleric one. According to the ancient theory, bile is one of the humours of the body, and

when excited abnormally it produces choler or rage.
"It raised my bile to see him so reflect their grief aside."—*Hood: Plea of Midsummer Fairies*, stanza 54.

✝ Black bile is melancholy.

Bilge Water. Filthy drainings. The bilge is the lowest part of a ship, and, as the rain or sea-water which trickles down to this part is hard to get at, it is apt to become foul and very offensive.

Bilk. To cheat, to obtain goods and decamp without paying for them.
"The landlord explained it by saying that 'a bilk' is a man who never misses a meal and never pays a cent."—*A. K. McClure: Rocky Mountains*, letter xxii. p. 211.

✝ To "bilk" in cribbage is to spoil your adversaries' score; to *balk* him. Perhaps the two words are mere variants.

Bilker (*A*). A person who gives a cabman less than his fare, and, when remonstrated with, gives a false name and address. Sometimes a "bilker" gets out and says, "Cabby, I shall be back in a minute," turns the corner and is no more seen.
"The time for taking out a summons expires in seven days, and it often takes longer than that to hunt a 'bilker' down."—*Nineteenth Century* (March, 1893, p. 177).
Also a cabman who does not pay the owner for the cab.

Bill (*The*). The nose, also called the beak. Hence, "Billy" is slang for a pocket-handkerchief.
" Lastly came Winter, clothèd all in frize,
   Chattering his teeth for cold that did him
      chill ;
   Whilst on his hoary beard his breath did freeze ;
   And the dull drops that from his purple bill
      [nose],
   As from a limbeck, did adown distill."
            Spenser : Faërie Queene, canto vii.

Bill (*A*). The draft of an Act of Parliament.
A public bill is the draft of an Act of Parliament affecting the general public.
A private bill is the draft of an Act of Parliament for the granting of some-thing to a company, corporation, or certain individuals.
A true bill. I confess what you say is true. The case against the accused is first submitted to the grand jury. If they think the charge has a fair colour, they write on the declaration "A true bill," and the case is submitted to the petty jury. Otherwise, they write "No true bill," or "Not found," and the case is at once dismissed or "ignored."
To ignore a bill is to write on it *igno-ramus*.
"'Ignoramus' is the word properly used by the Grand Enquest . . . and written upon the bill."—*Cowell*.

Bills payable. Bills of exchange, promissory notes, or other documents promising to pay a sum of money.

Bills receivable. Promissory notes, bills of exchange, or other acceptances held by a person to whom the money stated is payable.

Bill of Fare (*A*). A list of the *menu* provided, or which may be ordered, at a restaurant.

Bill of Health. *A clean bill of health.* A document, duly signed by the proper authorities, to certify that when the ship set sail no infectious disorder existed in the place.

A foul bill of health is a document to show that the place was suffering from some infection when the ship set sail. If a captain cannot show a *clean bill*, he is supposed to have a foul one.

Bill of Lading. A document signed by the master of a ship in acknowledgment of goods laden in his vessel. In this document he binds himself to deliver the articles in good condition to the persons named in the bill, certain exceptions being duly provided for. These bills are generally in triplicate—one for the sender, one for the receiver, and one for the master of the vessel.

Bill of Pains and Penalties (*A*). A legislative act imposing punishment (less than capital) upon a person charged with treason or other high crimes.

Bill of Quantities. An abstract of the probable cost of a building.

Bill of Rights. The declaration delivered to the Prince of Orange on his election to the British throne, confirming the rights and privileges of the people. (Feb. 13th, 1689.)

Bill of Sale. When a person borrows money and delivers goods as security, he gives him a bill of sale, that is, permission to sell the goods if the money is not returned on a stated day.

Bills of Mortality took their rise in 1592, when a great pestilence broke out, which continued till 1595. The term is now used for those abstracts from parish registers which show the births, deaths, and baptisms of the district.

Within the Bills of Mortality = within the district.

Bills of Parcels. An itemised statement of articles purchased. These bills are itemised by the seller.

Billee' (*Little*). The youngest of "Three sailors of Bristol city," who "took a boat and went to sea."

" There was gorging Jack, and guzzling Jimmy,
    And the youngest—he was little Billee.
Now, when they got as far as the equator,
    They had nothing left but one split pea.
To gorging Jack says guzzling Jimmy,
    ' We've nothing left, we must eat we.' "
                                        Thackeray.

[They decide to eat Little Billee, but he contrives to escape.]

Billet-doux [pronounce *billy doo*]. French, a love-letter, a sweet or affectionate letter.

Billiards. A corrupt form of the French *billard.* "*Autrefois, le bâton avec lequel on poussait les billes*" ; then "*la table verte sur laquelle on joue*"; and, lastly, the "game itself."

Similar plural forms are the games called bowls, cards, dominoes, draughts, marbles, quoits, skittles, tops, etc.

Billings (*Josh*). The *nom de plume* of H. W. Shaw, an American humorist, who died 1885. His *Book of Sayings* was published in 1866.

Billingsgate (London). *Gate* = quay, and *bellan* is to bawl or bellow. This quay is so called from the shouting of the fishermen in trying to attract attention and vend their fish.

That's Billingsgate. Vulgar and coarse, like the manners and language of Billingsgate fish-fags.

" Parnassus spoke the cant of Billingsgate."
            Dryden : Art of Poetry, c. l.

To talk Billingsgate, i.e. to slang, to scold in a vulgar, coarse style.

You are no better than a Billingsgate fish-fag, i.e. you are as rude and ill-mannered as the women of Billingsgate fish-market. The French say "Maubert" instead of Billingsgate, as *Your compliments are like those of the Place Maubert, i.e.* no compliments at all, but vulgar dirt-flinging. The " Place Maubert " has long been noted for its market.

Billingsgate Pheasant (*A*). A red herring.

Billy. A policeman's staff, which is a little bill or billet.

A pocket-handkerchief. "A blue billy" is a handkerchief with blue ground and white spots.

Billy Barlow. A street droll, a merry Andrew ; so called from a half-idiot of the name, who fancied himself "some great personage." He was well known in the East of London, and died in Whitechapel workhouse. Some of his sayings were really witty, and some of his attitudes really droll.

Billycock Hats. First used by Billy Coke (Mr. William Coke) at the great shooting parties at Holkham. The old-established hatters in the West End still call them "Coke hats."

Bi-metallism. The employment of two metals, silver and gold, of fixed relative value. Now gold is the only standard metal in England and some other countries. Silver coins are mere tokens, like copper coins; and if given in payment of large sums are estimated at the market value, so much an ounce; but a gold sovereign is always of one fixed legal value.

Binary Arithmetic. Arithmetic in which the base of the notation is 2 instead of 10. The unit followed by a *cipher* signifies two, by another *unit* it signifies three, by *two ciphers* it signifies four, and so on. Thus, 10 signifies two, 100 signifies four; while 11 signifies 3, etc.

Bi'nary Theory. A theory which supposes that all definite chemical salts are combinations of two radicles or elements, one of which is electro-positive (basic), and the other electro-negative (acid).

Bingham's Dandies. The 17th Lancers; so called from their colonel, the Earl of Lucan, formerly Lord Bingham. The uniform is noted for its admirable fit and smartness. Now called "The Duke of Cambridge's Own Lancers."

Bin'nacle. The case of the mariner's compass, which used to be written *bittacle*, a corruption of the Portuguese *bitacola*, French, *habitacle*, properly an abode.

Birchin Lane. *I must send you to Birchin Lane, i.e.* whip you. The play is on *birch* (a rod).
A suit in Birchin Lane. Birchin Lane was once famous for all sorts of apparel; references to second-hand clothes in Birchin Lane are common enough in Elizabethan books.

"Passing through Birchin Lane amidst a camp-royal of hose and doublets, I took ... occasion to slip into a captain's suit—a valiant buff doublet stuffed with points and a pair of velvet slops scored thick with lace."—*Middleton : Black Book* (1604).

Bird. An endearing name for girl.

"And by my word, your bonnie bird
In danger shall not tarry;
So, though the waves are raging white,
I'll row you o'er the ferry."
Campbell : Lord Ullin's Daughter.

Bird is the Anglo-Saxon *brid*, the young of any animal, hence *bride*, verb, *beran*, to bring forth.

A bird of ill-omen. A person who is regarded as unlucky; one who is in the habit of bringing ill-news. The ancients thought that some birds indicated good luck, and others evil. Even to the present day many look upon owls, crows, and ravens as unlucky birds; swallows and storks as lucky ones.

Ravens, by their acute sense of smell, discern the savour of dying bodies, and, under the hope of preying on them, light on chimney-tops or flutter about sick rooms; hence the raven indicates death. Owls screech when bad weather is at hand, and as foul weather often precedes sickness, so the owl is looked on as a funeral bird.

A bird of passage. A person who shifts from place to place; a temporary visitant, like a cuckoo, the swallows, starlings, etc.

A jail-bird. (*See* JAIL.)
The bird of Juno. The peacock.
⁎⁎ Minerva's bird is either the cock or the owl; that of Venus is the dove.

The bird of Washington. The American or baldheaded eagle.

"The well-known bald-headed eagle, sometimes called the Bird of Washington."—*Wood.*

The Arabian bird. The phœnix.
The green bird tells everything a person wishes to know. (*Cherry and Fairstar.*)
The talking bird spoke with a human voice, and could bid all other birds join in concert. (*Arabian Nights.*)
Old birds are not to be caught with chaff. Experience teaches wisdom.
One beats the bush, and another takes the bird. The workman does the work, the master makes the money.
'Tis the early bird that catches the worm.

"Early to bed and early to rise,
Makes a man healthy, wealthy, and wise."

A little bird told me so. From Eccles. x. 20: "Curse not the king, no not in thy thought, ... for a bird of the air shall carry the voice, and that which hath wings shall tell the matter."

Bird in the hand. *A bird in the hand is worth two in the bush.* Possession is better than expectation.

Italian: "E meglio aver oggi un novo, che dimani una gallina."
French: "Il vaut mieux avoir l'œuf aujourd'hui, que la poule demain" (*Turkish*).
"Un tien vaut mieux que deux tu l'auras."
"Un sou, quand il est assuré, vaut mieux que cinq en espérance."
German: "Ein vogel in der hand ist besser als zehen über land."

"Besser ein spatz in der hand, als ein storch auf dem dache."
Latin : " Ego spem pretio non emam."
English : "A pound in the purse is worth two in the book."
On the other side we have : " Qui ne s'aventure, n'a ni cheval ni mule." "Nothing venture, nothing have." "Give a sprat to catch a mackerel." "Chi non s'arrischia, non guadagna."

Bird in thy Bosom. *Thou hast kept well the bird in thy bosom.* Thou hast remained faithful to thy allegiance or faith. The expression was used by Sir Ralph Percy (slain in the battle of Hedgly Moor in 1464) to express his having preserved unstained his fidelity to the House of Lancaster.

Bird of Estë. The white eagle, the cognisance of the house.

" His dazzling way
The bird of Estö soars beyond the solar ray."
Tasso : Jerusalem Delivered, x.

Birds. *Birds of a feather flock together.* Persons associate with those of a similar taste and station as themselves. *Qui se ressemble s'assemble.* Cicero says, " *Similes similibus gaudent, pares cum paribus facillime congregantur.*" " *Ne nous associons qu'avec nos égaux* " (*La Fontaine*).
To kill two birds with one stone. To effect two objects with one outlay of trouble.

Birds (protected by superstitions).
Choughs are protected in Cornwall, because the soul of King Arthur migrated into a chough.
The Hawk is held sacred by the Egyptians, because it is the form assumed by Ra or Horus.
The Ibis is sacred in Egypt, and to kill one was at one time a capital offence. It is said that the god Thoth escaped (as an Ibis) from the pursuit of Typhon.
Mother Carey's Chickens, or Storm Petrels are protected by sailors, from a superstition that they are the living forms of the souls of deceased sailors.
The Robin is protected, both from Christian tradition and nursery legend. (*See* ROBIN REDBREAST.)
The Stork is a sacred bird in Sweden, from the legend that it flew round the cross, crying *Styrka, Styrka,* when Jesus was crucified. (*See* STORK.)
Swans are superstitiously protected in Ireland from the legend of the Fionnuala (daughter of Lir), who was metamorphosed into a swan and condemned to wander in lakes and rivers till Christianity was introduced. (See *Irish Melodies, Silent O' Moyle.*)
∴ The *bat* (a winged animal) was regarded by the Caribs as a good angel, which protected their

dwellings at night ; and it was accounted sacrilegious to kill one.

Bird's-eye View. A mode of perspective drawing in which the artist is supposed to be *over* the objects delineated, in which case he beholds them as a *bird* in the air would see them. A general, view.

Birdcage Walk (St. James's Park, London) ; so called from an aviary.

Birmingham Poet. John Freeth, who died at the age of seventy-eight in 1808. He was wit, poet, and publican, who not only wrote the words and tunes of songs, but sang them also, and sang them well.

Birthday Suit. *He was in his birthday suit.* Quite nude, as when first born.

Bis. *Bis dat, qui cito dat* (he gives twice who gives promptly)—*i.e.* prompt relief will do as much good as twice the sum at a future period (*Publius Syrus Proverbs.*)
Purple and bis, i.e. purple and fine linen (Latin, *byssus,* fine flax). The spelling is sometimes *biss, bys,* etc.

Biscuit (French-Latin, *bis,* twice ; *cuit,* baked). So called because it was originally twice ovened. The Romans had a bread of this kind.
In pottery, earthenware or porcelain, after it has been hardened in the fire, but has not yet been glazed, is so called.

Bise. A wind that acts notably on the nervous system. It is prevalent in those valleys of Savoy that open to the north.

" The Bise blew cold."
Rogers : Italy, part 1, div. ii. stanza 4.

Bishop (*Evêque*), the same word, *episcopus ;* whence *episc, evesc, evesque, evêque ;* also *'piscop, bishop.*

Bishop, Cardinal, Pope (as beverages) :
Bishop is made by pouring *red* wine (such as claret or burgundy), either hot or cold, on ripe bitter oranges. The liquor is then sugared and spiced to taste. In Germany, " bishop " is a mixture of wine, sugar, nutmeg, and orange or lemon. It is sometimes called " Purple Wine," and has received its name of *bishop* from its colour.
Cardinal is made by using *white* wine instead of red.
Pope is made by using *tokay.*
" When I was at college, *Cup* was spiced audit ale ; *Bishop* was " cup" with wine (properly claret or burgundy) added ; *Cardinal* was " cup" with brandy added. All were served with a hedge-hog [*i.e.* a whole lemon or orange bristling

5*

with cloves] floating in the midst. Each guest had his own glass or cup filled by a ladle from the common bowl (a large silver one)."

The bishop hath put his foot in it. Said of milk or porridge that is burnt, or of meat over-roasted. Tyndale says, "If the podech be burned-to, or the meate ouer rosted, we saye the byshope hath put his fote in the potte," and explains it thus, "because the bishopes burn who they lust." Such food is also said to be *bishopped*.

Bishop Barnaby. The May-bug, lady-bird, etc.

Bishop in Partibus. (*See* IN PARTIBUS.)

Bishop of Hippo. St. Augustine (354-430) is often so referred to. He held the See for many years.

Bishop's Apron represents the short cassock which, by the 74th canon, all clergymen were enjoined to wear.

Bishop's Bible (*The*). (*See* under BIBLE, page 131, col. 2.)

Bishop's Mitre. Dean Stanley tells us that the cleft of a bishop's mitre represents the mark of the crease of the mitre, when folded and carried under the arm, like an opera hat. (*Christian Institutions*, p. 154.)

Bissextile. Leap-year. We add a day to February in leap-year, but the Romans counted the 24th of February twice. Now, the 24th of February was called by them "*dies bissextus*" (*sexto calendas Martias*), the sextile or sixth day before March 1st; and this day being reckoned twice (*bis*) in leap-year, was called "*annus bissextus*."

Bisson or *Bisen* [blind] is the Anglo-Saxon *bisen*. Shakespeare (*Hamlet*, ii. 2) speaks of *bisson rheum* (blinding tears), and in *Coriolanus*, ii. 1, "What harm can your bisson conspectuities glean out of this character?"

Biston'ians. The Thracians; so called from Biston, son of Mars, who built Biston'ia on the Lake Bis'tonis.

"So the Bistonian race, a maddening train, Exult and revel on the Thracian plain; With milk their bloody banquets they allay. Or from the lion rend his panting prey; On some abandoned savage fiercely fly, Seize, tear, devour, and think it luxury." *Pitt: Statius*, Book ii.

Bit. A piece.
A bit of my mind, as "I'll tell him a bit of my mind," I'll reprove him. Same word as *bite*, meaning a piece bitten off, hence a piece generally. (Anglo-Saxon, *bitan*, to bite.)
Bit by bit. A little at a time; piecemeal.

Not a bit, or *Not the least bit*. Not at all; not the least likely. This may be not a morsel, or not a doit, rap, or sou. "Bit" used to be a small Jamaica coin. We still talk of a threepenny-bit. *Bit*, of course, is the substantive of *bite*, as *morsel* (French *morçeau*) of *mordre*.

Bit (*of a horse*). *To take the bit in* (or *between*) *his teeth*. To be obstinately self-willed; to make up one's mind not to yield. When a horse has a mind to run away, he catches the bit "between his teeth," and the driver has no longer control over him.

"Mr. X. will not yield. He has taken the bit between his teeth, and is resolved to carry out his original measure."—*Newspaper paragraph*, April, 1886.

Bit. Money. The word is used in the West Indies for a half pistareen (fivepence). In Jamaica, a bit is worth sixpence, English; in America, $12\frac{1}{2}$ cents; in Ireland, tenpence.
The word is still thieves' slang for money generally, and coiners are called *bit-makers*.

⁂ In English we use the word for a coin which is a fraction of a unit. Thus, a shilling being a unit, we have a sixpenny bit and threepenny bit (or not in *bits* but in divers pieces). So, taking a sovereign for a unit, we had seven-shilling bits, etc.

Bite. A cheat; one who *bites* us. "The biter bit" explains the origin. We say "a man was bitten" when he "burns his fingers" meddling with something which promised well but turned out a failure.
To bite the dust, as "Their enemies shall bite the dust," *i.e.* be slain in battle.

Bite. *To bite one's thumb at another*. To insult; to provoke to a quarrel.

"*Gregory.* I will frown as I pass by: and let them take it as they list.
"*Sampson.* Nay, as they dare. I will bite my thumb at them; which is a disgrace to them, if they bear it."—*Shakespeare: Romeo and Juliet*, i. 1.

To bite the lip, indicative of suppressed chagrin, passion, or annoyance.
"She had to bite her lips till the blood came in order to keep down the angry words that would rise in her heart."—*Mrs. Gaskell: Mary Barton*, chap. xi.

To bite upon the bridle. To champ the bit, like an impatient or restless horse.

Bit'elas. Sister of Fairlimb, and daughter of Rukenaw, the ape, in the story of *Reynard the Fox*. (*Alkmar*.)

Bites and Bams. Hoaxes and quizzes; humbugery.
"[His] humble efforts at jocularity were chiefly confined to ... bites and bams."—*Sir W. Scott: Guy Mannering*, chap. 3.

Biting Remark (*A*). *A remark more biting than Zeno's.* Near'chos ordered Ze'no the philosopher to be pounded to death in a mortar. When he had been pounded some time, he told Nearchos he had an important secret to communicate to him; but, when the tyrant bent over the mortar to hear what Zeno had to say, the dying man bit off his ear.

"That would have been a biting jest."
Shakespeare: *Richard III.*, act ii. 4.

Bitt. *To bitt the cable* is to fasten it round the "bitt" or frame made for the purpose, and placed in the fore part of the vessel.

Bitten. Imposed upon, let in, made to suffer loss. "I was terribly bitten in that affair." I suffered great loss. To bite is to cheat or suffer retaliation. Thus, Pope says, "The rogue was bit," he intended to cheat, but was himself taken in. "The biter bit" is the moral of Æsop's fable called *The Viper and the File;* and Goldsmith's mad dog, which, "for some private ends, went mad and bit a man," but the biter was bit, for "The man recovered of the bite, the dog it was that died."

Bitter End (*The*). *A outrance;* with relentless hostility; also applied to affliction, as, "she bore it to the bitter end," meaning to the last stroke of adverse fortune. "All Thy waves have gone over me, but I have borne up under them to the bitter end." Here "bitter end" means the end of the rope. The "bitterend" is a sea term meaning "that part of the cable which is "abaft the bitts." When there is no windlass the cables are fastened to bitts, that is, pieces of timber so called; and when a rope is payed out to the bitter-end, or to these pieces of timber, all of it is let out, and no more remains. However, we read in Prov. v. 4, "Her end is bitter as wormwood," which, after all, may be the origin of the phrase.

Bitter as Gall, as soot, as wormwood. Absinthe is made of wormwood. (*See* SIMILES.)

Bittock. A little bit; -ock as a diminutive is preserved in bull-ock, hill-ock, butt-ock, etc." "A mile and a bittock" is a mile and a little bit. (*Sir Walter Scott: Guy Mannering,* i.)

Biz, in theatrical slang. means "business." *Good biz* means full houses; but an actor's "biz" is quite another thing, meaning by-play. Thus, Hamlet trifling with Ophelia's fan, Lord Dundreary's

hop, and so on, are the special "business" of the actor of the part. As a rule, the "business" is invented by the actor who creates the part, and is handed down by tradition.

Black for mourning was a Roman custom (*Juvenal*, x. 245) borrowed from the Egyptians.
Black, in blazonry, means constancy, wisdom, and prudence.
Black, in several of the Oriental nations, is a badge of servitude, slavery, and low birth. Our word *blackguard* seems to point to this meaning. The Latin *niger* meant *bad, unpropitious.* (*See* BLACKGUARD.)

Black. (*See* under COLOURS for its symbolisms, etc.).

Black as a Crow (or as a *raven*); "as a raven's wing;" as ink; as hell, *i.e.* hades (2 syl.), meaning death or the grave; as your hat, etc. (*See* SIMILES.)

Black as a Newgate Knocker. A Newgate knocker is the fringe or lock of hair which costermongers and thieves twist back towards the ear.

Black in the Face. Extremely angry. The face discoloured with passion or distress.

"Mr. Winkle pulled . . . till he was black in the face."—*Dickens: Pickwick Papers.*
"He swore himself black in the face."—*Peter Pindar (Wolcott).*

Black is White. (*See* SWEAR.)
Beaten black and blue. So that the skin is black and blue with the marks of the beating.
I must have it in black and white, i.e. in plain writing; the paper being white and the ink black.
To say black's his eye, i.e. to vituperate; to blame. The expression, *Black's the white of his eye,* is a modern corruption. To say the eye is black or evil, is to accuse a person of an evil heart or great ignorance. The Latin *niger* also meant evil. (*See* BLACK PRINCE.)

"A fool may do all things, and no man say black's his eye."—*The Tell Tale.*

Black Act. 9 Geo. I. c. 22 is so called, because it was directed against the Waltham deer-stealers, who blackened their faces for disguise, and, under the name of *Blacks,* appeared in Epping Forest. This Act was repealed in 1827.

Black Acts. Acts of the Scottish Parliament between the accession of James I. and the year 1587; so called because they were printed in black characters.

Black Art. The art practised by conjurors, wizards, and others, who professed to have dealings with the devil. Black here means diabolical or wicked. Some derive it from *nigromancy*, a corruption of necromancy.

Black Assize. July 6th, 1577, when a putrid pestilence broke out at Oxford during the time of assize.

Black-balled. Not admitted to a club; the candidate proposed is not accepted as a member. In voting by ballot, those who accept the person proposed drop a white or red ball into the box, but those who would exclude the candidate drop into it a black one. It is now more usually done by two compartments, for "yes" and "no" respectively.

Black Book. A book exposing abuses in Church and State, which furnished much material for political reform in the early part of the present century. (*See* BLACK BOOKS.)

❞ Amherst speaks of the Proctor's black book, and tells us that no one can proceed to a degree whose name is found there. (1726.) It also appears that each regiment keeps a black book or record of ill-behaviour.

Black Book of the Admiralty. An old navy code, said to have been compiled in the reign of Edward III.

Black Books. *To be in my black books.* In bad odour; in disgrace; out of favour. The black books were those compiled in the reign of Henry VIII. to set forth the scandalous proceedings of the English monasteries, and were so called from the colour of their binding. We have similarly the Blue Book, the Red Book, and so on.

Black Books of the Exchequer. An official account of the royal revenues, payments, perquisites, etc., in the reign of Henry II. Its cover was black leather. There are two of them preserved in the Public Record Office.

Black Brunswickers. A corps of 700 volunteer hussars under the command of Frederick William, Duke of Brunswick, who had been forbidden by Napoleon to succeed to his father's dukedom. They were called "Black" because they wore mourning for the deceased Duke. Frederick William fell at Quatre-Bras, 1815. One of Millais's best pictures is called "The Black Brunswicker."

Black Cap, or the *Judgment Cap,* worn by a judge when he passes sentence of death on a prisoner. This cap is part of the judge's full dress. The judges wear their black caps on November 9th, when the Lord Mayor is presented in the Court of Exchequer. Covering the head was a sign of mourning among the Israelites, Greeks, Romans, and Anglo-Saxons. (2 Sam. xv. 30.)

Black Cattle. Oxen for slaughter; so called because black is their prevailing colour, at least in the north.

Black Cattle. Negro slaves.

"She was chartered for the West Coast of Africa to trade with the natives, but not in black cattle, for slavery was never our line of business."
—*J. Grant: Dick Rodney,* chap. xi.

Black Death. A putrid typhus, in which the body turned black with rapid putrefaction. It occurred in 1348, and carried off twenty-five millions in Europe alone, while in Asia and Africa the mortality was even greater.

Black Diamonds. Coals; also clever fellows of the lower orders. Coals and diamonds are both carbon.

Black Dog. A fiend still dreaded in many country places. (*See* DOG.)
Black Dog. Base silver coin in the reign of Anne. Made of pewter double washed.

Black Doll (*A*). The sign of a marine store shop. The doll was a dummy dressed to indicate that cast-off garments were bought.

Black Douglas. William Douglas, Lord of Nithsdale. Died 1390.

Black Flag (*A*) denotes a pirate, and is called the "Jolly Roger."

Black Flags. Moslem soldiers. The banner of the Abbasides (3 syl.) is *black;* that of the Fatimites (3 syl.) *green;* and that of the Ommiades (3 syl.) *white.* Hence the banner of the Kalif of Bagdad is black, but that of the Sultan of Damascus is green. (*Gibbon,* chap. iii.)
Black Flags. Pirates of the Chinese Sea who opposed the French in Tonquin, etc.

Black-foot. There is a powerful and numerous tribe of North American Indians called Black-feet. A black-foot is an intermediary in love affairs; but if perfidious to the wooer he was called a white-foot.

Blackfoot (*The*). One of the many Irish factions which disturbed the peace in the first half of the nineteenth century.

"And the Blackfoot, who courted each foeman's approach,
Faith! 'tis hot-foot [*speedily*] he'd fly from the stout Father Roach." *Lover.*

Black Friars. The Dominicans were formerly so called in England.

Black Friday. December 6th, 1745, the day on which the news arrived in London that the Pretender had reached Derby.

Black Game. Heath-fowl; in contradistinction to red game, as grouse. The male bird is called a blackcock.

Black Genevan (*A*). A black preaching gown; once used in some Anglican churches, and still used by some Dissenters in the pulpit. So called from Geneva, where Calvin preached in such a robe.

"The Nonconformist divine leaves his vestry in his black Genevan, toadied by his deacons and elders."—*Newspaper paragraph*, July 18th, 1885 (on Sunday bands).

Black-guards. Those horse-boys and unmilitary folk, such as cooks with their pots, pans, and other kitchen utensils, which travel with an army, and greatly impede its march.

Gifford, in his edition of Ben Jonson, says: "In all great houses there were a number of dirty dependents, whose office it was to attend the wool-yards, sculleries, etc. Of these the most forlorn were selected to carry coals to the kitchen. They rode with the pots and pans, and were in derision called the black-guards."

In the Lord Steward's office a proclamation (May 7th, 1683) begins thus: "Whereas . . . a sort of vicious, idle, and masterless boyes and rogues, commonly called the Black-guard, with divers other lewd and loose fellows . . . do usually haunt and follow the court. . . . Wee do hereby strictly charge . . . all those so called, . . . with all other loose, idle . . . men . . . who have intruded themselves into his Majesty's court and stables . . . to depart upon pain of imprisonment."

Black Hole of Calcutta. A dark cell in a prison into which Suraja Dowlah thrust 146 British prisoners. Next morning only twenty-three were found alive (1756).

∵ The punishment cell or lock-up in barracks.

Black Horse. The 7th Dragoon Guards, or "the Princess Royal's D. G." Their "facings" are black. Also called "Strawboots," "The Blacks."

Black Jack. *Black Jack rides a good horse* (Cornish). The miners call blende or sulphide of zinc "Black Jack," the occurrence of which is considered by them a favourable indication. The blende rides upon a lode of good ore.

Black Jack (*A*). A large leather *gotch* for beer and ale, so called from the outside being tarred.

Black Joke. An old tune, now called *The Sprig of Shillelagh.* Tom Moore has adapted words to the tune, beginning, "Sublime was the warning which Liberty spoke."

Black Leg. A swindler, especially in cards and races. Also, one who works for less than trade-union wages; a non-union workman.

"Pledging the strikers not to return to work so long as a single Black-leg was retained in the service."—*Nineteenth Century*, February, 1891, p. 243.

Black Letter. The Gothic or German type. So called because of its black appearance. The initial items of this book are now called "black letter," sometimes called "Clarendon type."

Black Letter Day. An unlucky day; one to be recalled with regret. The Romans marked their unlucky days with a piece of black charcoal, and their lucky ones with white chalk.

Black-letter dogs. Literary antiquaries who poke and pry into every hole and corner to find out black-letter copies of books.

"By fell black-letter dogs . . .
That from Gothic kennels eager strut."
Matthias: Pursuits of Literature.

Black Lists. Lists of insolvency and bankruptcy, for the private guidance of the mercantile community. (*See* BLACK BOOKS.)

Black Looks. Looks of displeasure. *To look black.* To look displeased. The figure is from black clouds indicative of foul weather.

Black Mail. Money given to freebooters by way of exempting property from depredation. (Anglo-Saxon, *mal*, "rent-tax;" French, *maille*, an old coin worth ·083 farthing). *Grass mail* was rent paid for pasturage. *Mails* and *duties* (Scotch) are rents of an estate in money or otherwise. "Black" in this phrase does not mean wicked or wrongful, but is the Gaelic, to cherish or protect. Black mail was a rent paid to Free Companies for protecting the property paid for, from the depredations of freebooters, etc.

To levy black mail now means to exact exorbitant charges; thus the cabs and omnibuses during the Great Exhibition years " levied black mail " on the public.

Black Man (*The*). The Evil One.

Black Maria. The black van which conveys prisoners from the police courts to jail. The French call a mud-barge a " Marie-salope." The tradition is that the van referred to was so called from Maria Lee, a **n**egress, who kept a sailors' boarding house in Boston. She was a woman of such great size and strength that the unruly stood in dread of her, and when constables required help, it was a common thing to send for Black Maria, who soon collared the refractory and led them to the lock-up. So a prison-van was called a " Black Maria."

Black Monday. Easter Monday, April 14th, 1360, was so called. Edward III. was with his army lying before Paris, and the day was so dark, with mist and hail, so bitterly cold and so windy, that many of his horses and men died. Monday after Easter holidays is called " Black Monday," in allusion to this fatal day. Launcelot says:

" It was not for nothing that my nose fell a-bleeding on Black Monday last, at six o'clock i' the morning."—*Shakespeare: Merchant of Venice*, ii. 5.

February 27th, 1865, was so called in Melbourne from a terrible sirocco from the N.N.W., which produced dreadful havoc between Sandhurst and Castlemaine.

Black Monday. In schoolboy phraseology is the first Monday after the holidays are over, when lessons begin again.

Black Money. Base coin brought to England by foreigners, and prohibited by Edward III.

Black Ox. *The black ox has trod on his foot*—*i.e.* misfortune has come to him. Black oxen were sacrificed to Pluto and other infernal deities.

Black Parliament. The Parliament held by Henry VIII. in Bridewell.

Black Prince. Edward, Prince of Wales, son of Edward III. Froissart says he was "styled black by terror of his arms " (c. 169). Strutt confirms this saying: "for his martial deeds surnamed Black the Prince " (*Antiquities*). Meyrick says there is not the slightest proof that Edward, Prince of Wales,

ever wore black armour (vol. ii.); indeed, we have much indirect proof against the supposition. Thus Shaw (vol. i. plate 31) gives a facsimile from a picture on the wall of St. Stephen's Chapel, Westminster, in which the prince is clad in *gilt* armour. Stothard says " the effigy is of copper gilt." In the British Museum is an 'llumination of Edward III. granting to his son the duchy of Aquitaine, in which both figures are represented in silver armour with gilt joints. The first mention of the term " Black Prince " occurs in a parliamentary paper of the second year of Richard II.; so that Shakespeare has good reason for the use of the word in his tragedy of that king :—

" Brave Gaunt, thy father and myself
Rescued the Black Prince, that young Mars of men,
From forth the ranks of many thousand French."
Richard II., ii. 3.
" That black name, Edward, black Prince of Wales."—*Henry V.* ii. 4.

Black Republicans. The Republicans were so called by the pro-slavery party of the States, because they resisted the introduction of slavery into any State where it was not already recognised.

Black Rod, *i.e.* " Gentleman Usher of the Black Rod," so called from his staff of office—a black wand surmounted by a lion.

Black Rood of Scotland. The "piece of the true cross " or *rood*, set in an *ebony* crucifix, which Margaret, the wife of King Malcolm, left at death to the Scottish nation. It passed into various hands, but was lost at the Reformation.

Black Russia. Central and Southern Russia is so called from its black soil.

" The winter crops in the whole of European Russia are very good, especially in the black-earth regions. In the government of Northern Russia the condition is less favourable."—*Newspaper paragraph*, December, 1893.

Black Saturday. August 4th, 1621; so called in Scotland, because a violent storm occurred at the very moment the Parliament was sitting to enforce episcopacy on the people.

Black Sea. So called from the abounding black rock in the extensive coal-fields between the Bos'phorus and Heracle'a.

Black Sheep [*Kârâ-Koin-loo*]. A tribe of Turkomans, so called from their standards. This tribe was extirpated by the *White Sheep* (*q.v.*).

A Black Sheep. A disgrace to the

family; a *mauvais sujet;* a workman who will not join in a strike. Black sheep are looked on with dislike by shepherds, and are not so valuable as white ones.

Black Standard. The dress, turbans, and standards of the Abbasside caliphs were all black. (*D'Herbelot.*)

Black Strap. Bad port wine. A sailor's name for any bad liquor. In North America, "Black-strap" is a mixture of rum and molasses, sometimes vinegar is added.

"The seething blackstrap was pronounced ready for use."—*Pinkerton: Molly Maguires,* chap. xvii. p. 174.

Black Swan. (*See* RARA AVIS.)

Black-thorn Winter (*The*). The cold weather which frequently occurs when the black-thorn is in blossom. (*See* BORROWED DAYS.)

Black Thursday. February 6th, 1851; so called in the colony of Victoria, from a terrible bush-fire which then occurred.

Black Tom. The Earl of Ormonde, Lord Deputy of Ireland in the reign of Elizabeth; so called from his ungracious ways and "black looks."

"He being very stately in apparel, and erect in port, despite his great age, yet with a dark, dour, and menacing look upon his face, so that all who met his gaze seemed to quake before the same."—*Hon. Emily Lawless: With Essex in Ireland,* p. 105.

Black Watch. Companies employed to watch the Islands of Scotland. They dressed in a "black" or dark tartan (1725). Subsequently they were enrolled into the 42nd regiment, under the Earl of Crawford, in 1737. Their tartan is still called "The Black Watch Tartan." The regiment is now called "The Royal Highlanders."

Black...White. *To swear black is white.* To persist in an obvious untruth. The French locution, *Si vous lui dites blanc, il répondra noir,* means, He will contradict what you say point blank.

Blacks. Mutes at funerals, who wore a black cloak; sometimes called the Black Guards.

"I do pray ye
To give me leave to live a little longer.
You stand about me like my Blacks."
Beaumont and Fletcher: Mons. Thomas, iii. 1.

Blacks (*The*), or "The 7th Dragoon Guards," or "The Princess Royal's D. G." Called *blacks* from their facings. Nicknames: "The Virgin Mary's Guard," "Straw boots," "Lingoniers," etc.

Blackacre (*Widow*). The best of Wycherley's comic characters; she is a masculine, litigious, pettifogging, headstrong woman. (*The Plain Dealer.*)

Blackamoor. *Washing the blackamoor white—i.e.* engaged upon a hopeless and useless task. The allusion is to one of Æsop's fables so entitled.

Blackness. *All faces shall gather blackness* (Joel ii. 6)—*i.e.* be downcast in consequence of trouble.

Blacksmith. *The learned blacksmith.* Elihu Burritt, U.S. (1811-1879.)

Blad'amour. The friend of Par'idel in Spenser's *Faërie Queene.* The poet had his eye upon the Earl of Northumberland, one of the leaders in the northern insurrection of 1569. (*See* PAR'IDEL.)

Blade. *A knowing blade,* a sharp fellow; *a regular blade,* a buck or fop. (Anglo-Saxon, *blad* or *blœd,* a branch or sprig.)

⁂ *Blœd* = "branch," whence "fruit, prosperity, glory," etc. The compound, *Blœd-dœg* = a prosperous day; *blœd-gifa,* a glory-giver, *i.e.* a king, a "regular blade."

Bladud. A mythical king of England, and father of King Lear. He built the city of Bath, and dedicated the medicinal springs to Minerva. Bladud studied magic, and, attempting to fly, fell into the temple of Apollo and was dashed to pieces. (*Geoffrey of Monmouth.*)

"Inexhaustible as Bladud's well."—*Thackeray.*

Blanche fleur. The heroine of Boccaccio's prose romance called *Il Filocopo.* Her lover, Florès, is Boccaccio himself, and Blanchefleur was a young lady passionately beloved by him, the natural daughter of King Robert. The story of Blanchefleur and Florès is substantially the same as that of Dor'igen and Aurelius by Chaucer, and that of Diano'ra and Ansaldo in the *Decameron.* (*See* DIANORA and DORIGEN.)

Blan'diman. The faithful manservant of fair Bellisant (*q.v.*), who attended her when she was divorced. (*Valentine and Orson.*)

Blaney. A wealthy heir, ruined by dissipation, in Crabbe's *Borough.*

"Misery and mirt') are blended in his face,
Much innate vileness and some outward grace:...
The serpent's cunning and the sinner's fall,"
Letter xiv.

Blank Cartridge. Cartridge with powder only, that is, without shot, bullet, or ball. Used in drill and in saluting. Figuratively, empty threats.

Blank Cheque. A cheque duly signed, but without specifying any sum of money; the amount to be filled in by the payee.

Blank Practice. Shooting for practice with blank cartridges.

Blank Verse. English verse without rhyme.

Blanket. *The wrong side of the blanket.* A love-child is said to come of the wrong side of the blanket.

"He grew up to be a fine *vaule* fallow, like mony ane that comes o' the wrang side o' the blanket."—*Sir W. Scott: The Antiquary*, chap. xxiv.

A wet blanket. A discouragement, a marplot. A person is a wet blanket who discourages a proposed scheme. "Treated with a wet blanket," discouraged. "A wet blanket influence," etc. A wet blanket is used to smother fire, or to prevent one escaping from a fire from being burnt.

Blanketeers. The Coxeyites were so called in 1894. "General" Coxey of the United States induced 50,000 persons to undertake a 700 miles' march to Washington, with blankets on their backs, to terrorise Congress into finding work for the unemployed.

Previous to this, the word had been applied to some 5,000 Radical operatives who assembled on St. Peter's Field, near Manchester, March 10, 1817. They provided themselves with blankets and rugs, intending to march to London, to lay before the Prince Regent a petition of grievances. Only six got as far as Ashbourne Bridge, when the expedition collapsed.

"The Americans have no royal dukes, no bench of bishops, no House of Lords, no effete monarchy; but they have Home Rule, one man one vote, and Coxey with his blanketeers."—*Liberty Review*, May 5th, 1894, p. 354.

Blare. To cry with a great noise, like a child in a tricky temper; to bellow. (Latin, *ploro*, to weep with noise.)

Blarney. *None of your blarney.* Soft, wheeling speeches to gain some end; sugar-words. Cormack Macarthy held the castle of Blarney in 1602, and concluded an armistice with Carew, the Lord President, on condition of surrendering the fort to the English garrison. Day after day his lordship looked for the fulfilment of the terms, but received nothing except protocols and soft speeches, till he became the laughing-stock of Elizabeth's ministers, and the dupe of the Lord of Blarney.

To kiss the Blarney Stone. Whoever does this shall be able to persuade to anything. The Blarney Stone is triangular, lowered from the north angle of the castle, about twenty feet from the top, and containing this inscription: "Cormac Mac Carthy *fortis me fieri fecit*, A.D. 1446." Blarney is near Cork.

Blasé (pronounce *blah-zay*). Surfeited with pleasure. A man *blasé* is one who has had full swing to all the pleasures of life, and has no longer any appetite for any of them. A worn out *debauchée* (French, *blaser*, to exhaust with enjoyment).

Blasphemous Balfour. Sir James Balfour, the Scottish judge, was so called because of his apostasy. He died 1583.

Blast. *In full blast.* In the extreme. In America will be heard such a sentence as this: "When she came to the meeting in her yellow hat and feathers, wasn't she in full blast?" A metaphor from the blast furnace in full operation.

Blast. To strike by lightning; to make to wither. The "blasted oak." This is the sense in which the word is used as an exclamation.

"If it 'the [ghost] assume my noble father's person,
I'll cross it, though it blast me."
Shakespeare: Hamlet, i. 1.

Blatant Beast (*The*). "A dreadful fiend of gods and men, ydrad;" type of "Common Rumour" or "Slander." He has 100 tongues and a sting; with his tongues he speaks things "most shameful, most unrighteous, most untrue;" and with his sting "steeps them in poison." Sir Calidore muzzled the monster, and drew him with a chain to Faërie Land. After a time the beast broke his chain and regained his liberty. (Saxon, *blœtan*, to bellow.) (*Spenser: Faërie Queene*, books v. vi.)

Blayney's Bloodhounds. The old 89th Foot; so called because of their unerring certainty, and untiring perseverance in hunting down the Irish rebels in 1798, when the corps was commanded by Lord Blaney.

This regiment is now called "the Second Battalion of the Princess Victoria's Irish Fusiliers." The *first* battalion is the old 87th Foot.

Blaze. A white mark in the forehead of a horse. (Icelandic, *blesi*, a white star on the forehead of a horse; German, *blasz*, pale.)

❦ A star is a sort of white diamond in the forehead. A blaze is an elongated star or dash of white.

To blaze a path. To notch trees as a clue. Trees so notched are called in America " blazed trees," and the white wood shown by the notch is called " a blaze." (*See above.*)

"Guided by the blazed trees . . . they came to the spot."—*Goulding : The Young Marooners,* 118.

"They buried him where he lay, a blazed tree marking his last resting-place."—*Adventures in Mashonaland,* p. 158.

Blaze (*To*). *To blaze abroad.* To noise abroad is the German verb *blasen,* to blow or sound. Shakespeare uses the noun *blazon :*

" But this eternal blazon must not be
      To ears of flesh and blood."
                              Hamlet, i. 5.

Blazer (*A*). A boatman's jacket. Properly and originally applied to the Johnian crew (Camb.), whose boat jackets are the brightest possible scarlet.

" A blazer is the red flannel boating jacket worn by the Lady Margaret, St. John's College, Cambridge, Boat Club."—*Daily News,* August 22nd, 1889.

Blazon [*Blazonry*]. To blazon is to announce with a trumpet, hence the Ghost in *Hamlet* says, " But this eternal blazon must not be to ears of flesh and blood," *i.e.* this babbling about eternal things, or things of the other world, must not be made to persons still in the flesh. Knights were wont to be announced by the blast of a trumpet on their entrance into the lists ; the flourish was answered by the heralds, who described aloud the arms and devices borne by the knight ; hence, to blazon came to signify to " describe the charges borne " ; and blazonry is " the science of describing or deciphering arms." (German, *blasen,* to blow.)

Blé. *Manger son blé en herbe* (French), to eat the calf before it is cast ; to spend your fortune before it comes to you ; to spend your income in advance. Literally, to feed off your green wheat.

Blear-eyed (*The*). Aurelius Brandoli'ni, the Italian poet, called *Il Lippo* (1440-1497).

Bleed. *To make a man bleed* is to make him pay dearly for something ; to victimise him. Money is the life-blood of commerce.

It makes my heart bleed. It makes me very sorrowful.

" She found them indeed,
      But it made her heart bleed."
                              Little Bo-Peep.

Bleeding of a Dead Body (*The*). It was at one time believed that, at the approach of a murderer, the blood of the murdered body gushed out. If in a dead body the slightest change was observable in the eyes, mouth, feet, or hands, the murderer was supposed to be present. The notion still survives in some places.

Blefus'cu. An island severed from Lilliput by a channel 800 yards wide, inhabited by pigmies. Swift meant it for France. (*Gulliver's Travels.*)

Bleidablik [*vast splendour*]. The abode of Baldur, the Scandinavian Apollo.

Blemmye' (of Africa). Men said to have no head, their eyes and mouth being placed in the breast. (*See* ACEPHALITES ; CAORA.)

Blenheim Dog. A small spaniel ; so called from Blenheim Palace in Oxfordshire, where the breed has been preserved ever since the palace was built.

Blenheim House (Oxfordshire). The house given by the nation to the Duke of Marlborough, for his victory over the French at Blenheim, in Bavaria, in the reign of Queen Anne (1704).

" When Europe freed confessed the saving power
      Of Marlborough's hand, Britain. who sent him forth,
Chief of confederate hosts, to fight the cause
      Of liberty and justice, grateful raised
This palace, sacred to the leader's fame."
                              Littleton : Blenheim.

Blenheim Steps. Once noted for an anatomical school, over which Sir Astley Cooper presided. Here "resurrectionists" were sure to find a ready mart for their gruesome wares, for which they received sums of money varying from £3 to £10, and sometimes more. Such phrases as "going to Blenheim Steps," meant going to be dissected, or unearthed from one's grave.

" The body-snatchers, they have come,
      And made a snatch at me;
'Tis very hard them kind of men
      Won't let a body be.
The cock it crows—I must be gone—
      My William, we must part;
But I'll be yours in death although
      Sir Astley has my heart."
                              Hood : Mary's Ghost.

Bless. *He has not a* [*sixpence*] *to bless himself with, i.e.* in his possession ; wherewith to make himself happy. This expression may probably be traced to the time when coins were marked with a deeply-indented cross. *Cf.* To keep the devil out of one's pocket.

Blessing with *three fingers* is symbolical of the Trinity, in the name of the Father, and of the Son, and of the Holy Ghost.

Blest. *I'll be blest if I do it.* I am resolved not to do it. A euphemism for *curst.*

Blikian'dabol [*splendid misery*]. The canopy of the goddess Hel or Hela (*q.v.*).

Blimber (*Miss*). A blue-stocking, who knows the dead languages, and wears learned spectacles. She is the daughter of Dr. Blimber, a fossil schoolmaster of the high and dry grammar type. (*Dickens: Dombey and Son.*)

Blind. *That's a mere blind.* A pretence; something ostensible to conceal a covert design. The metaphor is from window-blinds, which prevent outsiders from seeing into a room.

Blind as a bat. A bat is not blind, but when it enters a room well lighted, it cannot see, and blunders about. It sees best, like a cat, in the dusk. (*See* SIMILES.)

Blind as a beetle. Beetles are not blind, but the dor-beetle or hedge-chafer, in its rapid flight, will occasionally bump against one as if it could not see.

Blind as a mole. Moles are not blind, but as they work underground, their eyes are very small. There is a mole found in the south of Europe, the eyes of which are covered by membranes, and probably this is the animal to which Aristotle refers when he says, "the mole is blind." (*See* SIMILES.)

Blind as an owl. Owls are not blind, but being night birds, they see better in partial darkness than in the full light of day. (*See* SIMILES.)

You came on his blind side. His soft or tender-hearted side. Said of persons who wheedle some favour out of another. He yielded because he was not wide awake to his own interest.

"Lincoln wrote to the same friend that the nomination took the democrats on the blind side."—*Nicolay and Hay: Abraham Lincoln,* vol. i. chap. xv. p. 275.

Blind leaders of the blind. The allusion is to a sect of the Pharisees, who were wont to shut their eyes when they walked abroad. and often ran their heads against a wall or fell into a ditch. (Matt. xv. 14.)

The Blind :—
Francesco Bello, called *Il Cieco*.
Lui'gi Grotto, called *Il Cieco*, the Italian poet. (1541-1585.)
Lieutenant James Holman, *The Blind Traveller.* (1787-1857.)
Ludwig III., Emperor of Germany, *L'Aveugle.* (880, 890-934.)

Blind Alley (*A*). A "cul de sac," an alley with no outlet. It is blind because it has no "eye" or passage through it.

Blind Beggar of Bethnal Green (*The*). A public-house sign in the Whitechapel Road. (*Hotten: History of Sign-Boards.*) (*See* BEGGAR.)

Blind Department (*The*). In Post Office parlance, means that department where letters with incoherent, insufficient, or illegible addresses are examined, and, if possible, put upon the proper track for delivery. The clerk so employed is called "The Blind Man."

"One of these addresses was "Santlings, Hilewite" (St. Helen's, Isle of Wight). I, myself, had one from France addressed, 'A Mons. E. Cobham, brasseur, Angleterre,' and it reached me. Another address was 'Haselfeach in no famtshere' (Hazelbeach, Northamptonshire)."

Blind Ditch (*A*). One which cannot be seen. Here blind means obscure, as *a blind village.*

Blind Harper (*The*). John Parry, who died 1739.

Blind Harry. A Scotch minstrel of the fifteenth century. His epic of *Sir William Wallace* runs to 11,861 lines.

Blind Hedge (*A*). A hawhaw hedge, not easily seen. Milton uses the word *blind* for concealed, as "In the blind mazes of this tangled wood." (*Comus,* line 181.)

Blind old Man of Scio's rocky Isle. Homer is so called by Byron in his *Bride of Abydos.*

Blind Magistrate (*The*). Sir John Fielding, knighted in 1761, was born blind. He was in the commission of the Peace for Middlesex, Surrey, Essex, and the liberties of Westminster.

Blindman's Holiday. The hour of dusk, when it is too dark to work, and too soon to light candles.

Blindman's Lantern (*The*), or "Eyes to the Blind." A walking stick with which a blind man guides his way. In French argot *bougie* means a walking stick.

Blindmen's Dinner (*The*). A dinner unpaid for. A dinner in which the landlord is made the victim. Eulenspiegel being asked for alms by twelve blind men, said, "Go to the inn; eat, drink, and be merry, my men; and here are twenty florins to pay the fare." The blind men thanked him; each supposing one of the others had received the money. Reaching the inn, they told the landlord of their luck, and were at once provided with food and drink to the amount of twenty florins. On asking for payment, they all said, "Let him who received the money pay for the dinner;" but none had received a penny.

Blinkers. Spectacles; the allusion is to a horse's blinkers.

Block. *To block a Bill.* In parliamentary language means to postpone or prevent the passage of a Bill by giving notice of opposition, and thus preventing its being taken after half-past twelve at night.

"By blocking the Bill [he] denied to two million persons the right of having votes."—*Contemporary Review*, August, 1884, p. 171.

Blockhead. A stupid person; one without brains. The allusion is to a wig-maker's dummy or *tête à perruque*, on which he fits his wigs.

"Your wit will not so soon out as another man's will ; 'tis strongly wedged up in a block-head."— *Shakespeare: Coriolanus*, ii. 3.

Blood. A buck, an aristocratic rowdy. A term taken from blood horses.

"A blood or dandy about town."—*Thackeray: Vanity Fair*, chap. x. p. 49.

Blood. Family descent.

"And hath made of one blood all nations of men."—Acts xvii. 26.

Blood thicker than water. Relationship has a claim which is generally acknowledged. It is better to seek kindness from a kinsman than from a stranger. Water soon evaporates and leaves no mark behind; not so blood. So the interest we take in a stranger is thinner and more evanescent than that which we take in a blood relation.

"Weel! blude's thicker than water. She's welcome to the cheeses and the hams just the same."—*Sir W. Scott: Guy Mannering.*

A Prince of the Blood. One of the Royal Family.

Bad blood. Anger, quarrels; as, *It stirs up bad blood.* It provokes to ill-feeling and contention.

Blue blood. (*See under* BLUE.)

Young blood. Fresh members; as, "To bring young blood into the concern."

In cold blood. Deliberately; not in the excitement of passion or of battle.

It makes one's blood boil. It provokes indignation and anger.

It runs in the blood. It is inherited or exists in the family race.

"It runs in the blood of our family."—*Sheridan: The Rivals*, iv. 2.

My own flesh and blood. My own children, brothers, sisters, or other near kindred.

Laws written in blood. Dema'dēs said that the laws of Draco were written in blood, because every offence was punished by death.

The field of blood. Acel'dama (Acts i. 19), the piece of ground purchased with the blood-money of our Saviour, and set apart for the burial of strangers.

The field of the battle of Cannæ, where Hannibal defeated the Romans, B.C. 216.

Blood of our Saviour. An order of knighthood in Mantua; so called because their special office was to guard "the drops of the Saviour's blood" preserved in St. Andrew's church, Mantua.

Blood and iron policy—i.e. war policy. No explanation needed.

Blood-guiltiness. The guilt of murder.

Blood-horse (*A*). A thorough-bred.

Bloodhound. Figuratively, one who follows up an enemy with pertinacity. Bloodhounds used to be employed for tracking wounded game by the blood spilt; subsequently they were employed for tracking criminals and slaves who had made their escape, and were hunters of blood, not hunters *by* blood. The most noted breeds are the African, Cuban, and English.

Blood Money. Money paid to a person for giving such evidence as shall lead to the conviction of another; money paid to the next of kin to induce him to forego his "right" of seeking blood for blood; money paid to a person for betraying another, as Judas was paid blood-money for showing the band the place where Jesus might be found.

Blood Relation (*A*). One in direct descent from the same father or mother; one of the same family stock.

Blood-thirsty. Eager for shedding blood.

Blood of the Grograms (*The*). Taffety gentility; make-believe aristocratic blood. Grogram is a coarse silk taffety stiffened with gum (French, *grosgrain*).

"Our first tragedian was always boasting of his being 'an old actor,' and was full of the 'blood of the Grograms.'"—*C. Thomson: Autobiography*, p. 200.

Bloody, used as an expletive in such phrases as "A bloody fool," "Bloody drunk," etc., arose from associating folly and drunkenness, etc., with what are called "Bloods," or aristocratic rowdies. Similar to "Drunk as a lord."

"It was bloody hot walking to-day."—Swift: Journal to Stella, letter xxii.

Bloody (*The*). Otho II., Emperor of Germany. (955, 973-983.)

The Bloody Eleventh. The old 11th Foot was so called from their having been several times nearly annihilated, as at Almanza, Fontenoy, Roucoux, Ostend, and Salamanca (1812), in capturing a French standard. Now called "The Devonshire Regiment."

Bloody Assizes. The infamous assizes held by Judge Jeffreys in 1685. Three hundred were executed, more whipped or imprisoned, and a thousand sent to the plantations for taking part in Monmouth's rebellion.

Bloody Bill. The 31 Henry VIII., c. 14, which denounced death, by hanging or burning, on all who denied the doctrine of transubstantiation.

Bloody-bones. A hobgoblin ; generally "Raw-head and Bloody-Bones."

Bloody Butcher. (*See* BUTCHER.)

Bloody Hand. A man whose hand was bloody, and was therefore presumed to be the person guilty of killing the deer shot or otherwise slain. (*Cf.* RED HAND.) Also the badge of a baronet.

Bloody Wedding. St. Bartholomew's slaughter in 1572 is so called because it took place during the marriage feast of Henri (afterwards Henri IV.) and Marguerite (daughter of Catherine de Medici).

Bloody Week (*The*). The week ending on Sunday, May 28th, 1871, when Paris was burning, being set on fire by the Communists in hundreds of places. The destruction was frightful, but Nôtre Dame, the Hôtel Dieu, and the magnificent collection of pictures in the Louvre, happily escaped demolition.

Bloom. *From bloom to bloom.* A floral rent. The Lord of the Manor received a red rose or gillyflower, on the Feast of John the Baptist, yearly (July 5th, O. S.). (See *Notes and Queries*, Feb. 13th, 1886, p. 135.)

Bloom'erism. A female costume ; so called from Mrs. Amelia Bloomer, of New York, who tried in 1849 to introduce the fashion. The dress consisted of a short skirt and loose trousers gathered closely round the ankles— becoming enough to young ladies in

their teens, but ridiculous for "the fat and forty."

Blount (*Charles*). Author of some deistical writings in the time of Charles II. (1654-1693.)

"He heard of Blount, etc." Crabbe: Borough.

Blouse. A short smock-frock of a blue colour worn commonly by French workmen. *Bleu* is French argot for *manteau.*

"A garment called bliant or bliaus, which appears to have been another name for a surcoat.... In this bliaus we may discover the modern French blouse, a . . . smock-frock."—Planché: British Costume.

1. **Blow** (*To*). As the wind blows ; or to blow with the breath. (Anglo-Saxon, *blawan,* to blow or breathe.)

It will soon blow over. It will soon be no longer talked about ; it will soon come to an end, as a gale or storm blows over or ceases.

✦ *To blow off* is another form of the same phrase.

To blow great guns. The wind blows so violently that its noise resembles the roar of artillery.

To blow hot and cold, (or) *To blow hot and cold with the same breath.* To be inconsistent. The allusion is to the fable of a traveller who was entertained by a satyr. Being cold, the traveller blew his fingers to warm them, and afterwards blew his hot broth to cool it. The satyr, in great indignation, turned him out of doors, because he blew both hot and cold with the same breath.

To blow off the steam. To get rid of superfluous energy. The allusion is to the forcible escape of superfluous steam no longer required.

2. **Blow** (*To*). To sound a trumpet.

"But when the blast of war blows in our ears, Let us be tigers in our fierce deportment." Shakespeare: Henry V., iii. 1.

To blow. To inform against a companion ; to "peach." The reference is to the announcing of knights by blast of trumpet.

3. **Blow** (*To*). To blast as with gunpowder.

I will blow him up sky high. Give him a good scolding. *A regular blowing up* is a thorough jobation. The metaphor is from blasting by gunpowder.

✦ But to *blow up a bladder,* etc., means to inflate it.

4. **Blow.** A stroke. (German, *bläuen,* to beat or strike.)

At one blow. By one stroke.

The first blow is half the battle. Well begun is half done. Pythagoras used to

say, " The beginning is half the whole."
"*Incipe : Dimidium facti est cœpisse*"
(*Ausonius*). "*Dimidium facti, qui cœpit,
habet*" (*Horace*). "*Ce n'est que le
premier pas qui coûte.*"

Without striking a blow. Without
coming to a contest.

Blow a Cloud. To smoke a cigar or
pipe. This term was in use in Queen
Elizabeth's reign.

Blow Me (an oath). *You be blowed*
(an oath), a play on the word *Dash me*,
which is a euphemism for a more offensive oath.

"' Well, if you won't stand a pint,' quoth the tall
man, ' I will, that's all, and blow temperance.' "—
Kingsley : Alton Locke, chap. ii.

Blow Out (*A*). A " tuck in," or feast
which swells out the paunch.

Blow-point. A game similar to our
pea-puffing, only instead of peas small
wooden skewers or bits of pointed wood
were puffed through the tube. The
game is alluded to by Florio, Strutt,
and several other authors.

Blown, in the phrase " fly-blown,"
has nothing to do with the verb *to blow*
(as the wind blows). It means that flies
have deposited their eggs and tainted
the article. In French, *déposer des œufs
de mouches sur* . . . and a fly-blow is
un œuf de mouche. The word seems to be
connected with *blot*, the egg of a moth
or other insect.

Blown Herrings are bloated herrings. The French *bouffi* (blown) is
analogous to both expressions. Blown
herrings are herrings bloated, swollen,
or cured by smoking.

Blown upon. Made the subject of a
scandal. His reputation has been blown
upon, means has been the subject of
talk wherein something derogatory was
hinted at or even asserted. Blown upon
by the breath of slander.

" Blown," meaning stale, tainted, is probably
the same as the above ; but blown *upon* cannot be.

Blowzelin'da. A country maiden in
Gay's pastoral called *The Shepherd's
Week.*

" Sweet is my toil when Blowzelind is near ;
Of her bereft, 'tis winter all the year. . . .
Come, Blowzelinda, ease thy swain's desire,
My summer's shadow and my winter's fire."
Pastoral i.

Blowzy. Coarse, red-faced, bloated ;
applied to women. The word is allied
to blush, blaze, etc. (Dutch, *bloozen*
and *blaazen ;* Danish, *blusser*, to blaze.)

Blubber. To cry like a child, with

noise and slavering. Connected with
slobber, slaver.

" I play the boy, and blubber in thy bosom."
Otway : Venice Preserved, i. 1.

Blubber Cheeks. Fat, flabby cheeks,
like whale's blubber. " The blubber
cheeks of my friend the baronet."

Bluchers. Half boots ; so called after
Field-Marshal von Blucher (1742—1819).

Blue or *Azure* is the symbol of Divine
eternity and human immortality. Consequently, it is a mortuary colour—
hence its use in covering the coffins of
young persons. When used for the garment of an angel, it signifies faith and
fidelity. As the dress of the Virgin, it
indicates modesty. In *blazonry*, it signifies chastity, loyalty, fidelity, and a
spotless reputation.

The *Covenanters* wore blue as their
badge, in opposition to the scarlet of
royalty. They based their choice on
Numb. xv. 38, " Speak unto the children
of Israel, and bid them that they make
them fringes in the borders of their
garments . . . and that they put upon
the fringe . . . a *ribband of blue.*"

(*See* COLOURS for its symbolisms.)

Blue (*A*), or a " staunch blue," descriptive of political opinions, for the
most part means a Tory, for in most
counties the Conservative colour is blue.
(*See* TRUE BLUE.)

" This was a blue demonstration, a gathering of
the Conservative clans."—*Holme Lee.*

A blue. (*See* BLUE STOCKING.)

A dark blue. An Oxford man or
Harrow boy.

A light blue. A Cambridge man or
Eton boy.

An old blue. One who has pulled in
a University boat-race, or taken part in
any of their athletic contests.

" There were five old blues playing."—*Standard,*
May 8th, 1883.

True blue. This is a Spanish phrase,
and refers to the notion that the veins
shown in the skin of aristocratic families
are more blue than that of inferior persons. (*See* SANG.)

True blue will never stain. A really
noble heart will never disgrace itself.
The reference is to blue aprons and
blouses worn by butchers, which do not
show blood-stains.

True as Coventry blue. The reference
is to a blue cloth and blue thread made
at Coventry, noted for its permanent
dye.

'*Twas Presbyterian true blue* (*Hudibras,*
i. 1). The allusion is to the blue apron

which some of the Presbyterian preachers used to throw over their preaching-tub before they began to address the people. In one of the Rump songs we read of a person going to hear a lecture, and the song says—

"Where I a tub did view,
Hung with an apron blue;
'Twas the preacher's, I conjecture."

To look blue. To be disconcerted. *He was blue in the face.* Aghast with wonder. The effect of fear and wonder is to drive the colour from the cheeks, and give them a pale-bluish tinge.

Blue-apron Statesman (*A*). A lay politician, a tradesman who interferes with the affairs of the nation. The reference is to the blue apron once worn by almost all tradesmen, but now restricted to butchers, poulterers, fishmongers, and so on.

Blue Beans. Bullets. Lead is blue.

"Many a valiant Gaul had no breakfast that morning but what the Germans call 'blue beans,' *i.e.* bullets.—*W. Maccall: My School Days*, 1885.

Three blue beans in a blue bottle or *bladder.* (*See under* BEANS.)

Bluebeard. A bogey, a merciless tyrant, in Charles Perrault's *Contes du Temps*. The tale of Bluebeard (Chevalier Raoul) is known to every child, but many have speculated on the original of this despot. Some say it was a satire on Henry VIII., of wife-killing notoriety. Dr. C. Taylor thinks it is a type of the castle lords in the days of knighterrantry. Holinshed calls Giles de Retz, Marquis de Laval, the original Bluebeard. This Giles or Gilles who lived at Machecoul, in Brittany, was accused of murdering six of his seven wives, and was ultimately strangled and burnt in 1440.

"The Bluebeard chamber of his mind, into which no eye but his own must look."—*Carlyle.*

∵ Campbell has a Bluebeard story in his *Tales of the Western Highlands*, called *The Widow and her Daughters*. A similar one is No. 39 of Visentini's collection of Italian stories. So is No. 3 of Bernoni's collection.

Bluebeard's Key. When the blood stain of this key was rubbed out on one side, it appeared on the opposite side ; so prodigality being overcome will appear in the form of meanness ; and friends, over-fond, will often become enemies.

Blue Billy (*A*). A blue neckcloth with white spots, worn by William Mace. More likely the allusion is to the bill or nose. (*See* BILLY.)

Blue Blood. (*See* page 149, *True Blue.*)

Blue Boar. A public-house sign ; the cognisance of Richard III. In Leicester is a lane in the parish of St. Nicholas, called the *Blue Boar Lane*, because Richard slept there the night before the battle of Bosworth Field.

"The bristly boar, in infant gore,
Wallows beneath the thorny shade."
Gray: The Bard.

Blue Bonnets (*The*). The Scotch Highlanders ; the Scotch generally. So called from the blue woollen cap at one time in very general use in Scotland, and still far from uncommon.

"England shall many a day
Tell of the bloody fray,
When the blue bonnets came over the border."
Sir W. Scott.

Blue Books. In England, parliamentary reports and official publications presented by the Crown to both Houses of Parliament. Each volume is in folio, and is covered with a blue wrapper.

∵ Short Acts of Parliament, etc., even without a wrapper, come under the same designation.

In America, the "Blue Books" (like our "Red Books") contain lists of those persons who hold government appointments. The official colour of Spain is *red*, of Italy *green*, of France *yellow*, of Germany and Portugal *white*.

Blue Bottle. A beadsman, a policeman ; so called from the colour of his dress. Shakespeare makes Doll Tearsheet denounce the beadle as a "bluebottle rogue."

"You proud varlets, you need not be ashamed to wear blue, when your master is one of your fellows."—*Dekker: The Honest Whore* (1602).

"I'll have you soundly swinged for this, you blue-bottle rogue." — *Shakespeare: 2 Hen. IV.*, act v. 4.

Blue Caps or *Blue Bonnets.* The Scotch.

"He is there, too, . . . and a thousand blue caps more."—*Shakespeare: 1 Henry IV.*, ii. 4.

Blue-coat School. Christ's Hospital is so called because the boys there wear a long *blue coat* girded at the loins with a leather belt. Some who attend the mathematical school are termed *King's boys*, and those who constitute the highest class are *Grecians*.

Founded by Edward VI. in the year of his death. There are several other blue-coat schools in England besides Christ's Hospital.

Blue Devils, or *A fit of the blues*. A fit of spleen, low spirits. Roach and Esquirol affirm, from observation, that indigo dyers are especially subject to melancholy ; and that those who dye scarlet are choleric. Paracelsus also asserts that blue is injurious to the health and spirits. There may, therefore, be more science in calling melancholy *blue* than is generally allowed. The German *blei* (lead) which gives rise to our slang word *blue* or *bluey* (lead) seems to bear upon the " leaden downcast eyes " of melancholy.

Blue-eyed Maid (*The*). Minerva, the goddess of wisdom, is so called by Homer.

" Now Prudence gently pulled the poet's ear,
And thus the daughter of the Blue-eyed Maid,
In flattery's soothing sounds, divinely said,
'O Peter, eldest-born of Phœbus, hear.'"
    Peter Pindar : A Falling Minister.

Blue Fish (*The*). The shark, technically called *Carcharias glaucus*, the upper parts of which are blue.

Blue Flag. *He has hoisted the blue flag*. He has turned publican or fishmonger, in allusion to the blue apron at one time worn by publicans, and still worn by fishmongers.

Blue Gown (*A*). A harlot. Nares tells us that " a blue gown was a dress of ignominy for a harlot in the House of Correction. (*See below.*)

Blue-gowns. The bedesmen, to whom the kings of Scotland distributed certain alms. Their dress was a cloak or gown of coarse blue cloth, with a pewter badge. The number of these bedesmen was equal to that of the king's years, so that an extra one was added every returning birthday. These paupers were privileged to ask alms through the whole realm of Scotland. No new member has been added since 1833. (*See* GABERLUNZIE.)

Blue Guards (*The*). So the Oxford Blues, now called the Royal Horse Guards, were called during the campaign in Flanders (1742-1745).

Blue Hen. Captain Caldwell used to say that no cock could be truly game whose mother was not a blue hen. As Caldwell commanded the 1st Delaware regiment in the war, the State of Delaware was nicknamed *Blue Hen*.

Your mother was a blue hen, no doubt. A reproof given to a braggart. (*See above.*)

Blue-jackets. Sailors ; so called because the colour of their jackets is blue.

Blue John (*A*). A petrefaction of blue fluor-spar, found in the Blue John mine of Tre Cliff, Derbyshire ; and so

called to distinguish it from the Black Jack, an ore of zinc. Called John from John Kirk, a miner, who first noticed it.

Blue Laws (*The*). These were puritanical laws enacted in 1732, at New Haven, Connecticut, in the United States of America. Their object was to stamp out " heresy," and enforce a strict observance of the Sunday. Many persons insist that they are apocryphal ; but in October, 1891, the German American Lincoln Club protested against their enforcement by a democratic judge, and resolved—

"To call upon all right-thinking citizens to assist in an effort to have the laws repealed, by supporting and voting only for such candidates for the legislature as would pledge themselves to vote for their repeal."

Blue-light Federalists. A name given to those Americans who were believed to have made friendly (" bluelight ") signals to British ships in the war. (1812.)

Blue-mantle. The English pursuivant at arms is so called from his official robe.

Blue Monday. The Monday before Lent, spent in dissipation. (German, *der blaue Montag*.) It is said that dissipation gives everything a blue tinge. Hence " blue " means tipsy. (*See* BLUE DEVILS.)

" Drink till all is blue.
Cracking bottles till all is blue."
    Fraser's Magazine, xvii. (1838).

Blue Moon. *Once in a blue moon.* Very rarely indeed.

⁂ On December 10th, 1883, we had a " blue moon." The winter was unusually mild.

Blue Mould. Applied to cheese which has become the bed of a fungus, technically called *Aspergillus glaucus*.

The blue mould of bread, paste, jams, etc., is the fungus called *Mucor Mucedo*.

Blue Murder. *To shout blue murder.* Indicative more of terror or alarm than of real danger. It appears to be a play on the French exclamation *morbleu ;* there may also be a distinct allusion to the common phrase " blue ruin."

Blue-noses. The Nova Scotians.

" 'Pray, sir,' said one of my fellow-passengers, ' can you tell me the reason why the Nova Scotians are called " Blue-noses " ? '
" ' It is the name of a potato,' said I, ' which they produce in the greatest perfection, and boast to be the best in the world. The Americans have, in consequence, given them the nickname of *Blue Noses*.' "—*Haliburton : Sam Slick.*

Blue Peter. A flag with a blue ground and white square in the centre, hoisted as a signal that the ship is about to sail. Peter is a corruption of the

French *partir* (leave or notice of departure). The flag is hoisted to give notice to the town that any person having a money-claim may make it before the ship starts, and that all about to sail are to come on board.

According to Falconer, it is a corruption of the "blue repeater."

In whist, it is a "call for trumps"; that is, laying on your partner's card a higher one than is required.

To hoist the blue Peter. To leave.

"'When are you going to sail?'
"'I cannot justly say. Our ship's bound for America next voyage . . . but I've got to go to the Isle of Man first . . . And I may have to hoist the blue Peter any day.'"—*Mrs. Gaskell: Mary Barton*, chap. xiii.

Blue-pigeon Flyer. A man who steals the lead off of a house or church. "Bluey" is slang for lead, so called from its colour. To "pigeon" is to gull, cheat, or fub. Hence, blue-pigeon, one who cheats another of his lead, or fubs his lead. "Flyer," of course, is one who flies off with the stolen lead.

Blue Ribbon (*The*). "To be adorned with the blue ribbon," to be made knight of the garter, or adorned with a blue ribbon at the knee. Blue ribbon is also a temperance badge. (*See* CORDON BLEU.)

"Lord Lansdown is to be made Knight of the Garter . . . . though there is no vacancy. Lord Derby received the Blue Ribbon in 1859, although there was no vacancy."—*Truth :* March, 1894.

The Blue Ribbon of the Turf. The Derby. Lord George Bentinck sold his stud, and found to his vexation that one of the horses sold won the Derby a few months afterwards. Bewailing his ill-luck, he said to Disraeli, "Ah! you don't know what the Derby is." "Yes, I do," replied Disraeli; "it is the blue ribbon of the turf," alluding to the term *cordon bleu* (*q.v.*); or else to the blue garter, the highest of all orders.

⁂ "The blue ribbon of the profession" is the highest point of honour attainable therein. The blue ribbon of the Church is the Archbishopric of Canterbury, that in law is the office of Lord Chancellor.

Blue Ribbon (*A*). A wale from a blow. A bruise turns the skin blue.

"'Do you want a blue ribbon round those white sides of yours, you monkey?' answered Orestes; 'because, if you do, the hippopotamus hide hangs ready outside.'"—*Kingsley: Hypatia*, chap. iv.

Blue Ruin. Gin. Called *blue* from its tint, and *ruin* from its effects.

Blue Squadron (*The*). One of the three divisions of the British Fleet in the seventeenth century. (*See* ADMIRAL OF THE BLUE.)

Blue Stocking A female pedant. In 1400 a society of ladies and gentlemen was formed at Venice, distinguished by the colour of their stockings, and called *della calza*. It lasted till 1590, when it appeared in Paris and was the rage among the lady *savantes*. From France it came to England in 1780, when Mrs. Montague displayed the badge of the Bas-bleu club at her evening assemblies. Mr. Benjamin Stillingfleet was a constant attendant of the *soirées*. The last of the clique was Miss Monckton, afterwards Countess of Cork, who died 1840.

"'You used to be fond enough of books . . . . a regular blue-stocking Mr. Bland called you.'"—*E. S. Phelps: The Gates Ajar*, chap. iv.

Blue Talk. Indecent conversation, from the French, *Bibliothèque Bleu*. (Harlots are called "Blues" from the blue gown they were once compelled to wear in the House of Correction.)

Blue Wonder (*A*). The German *Blaues Wunder*, which means "a queer story," as *Du sollst dein blaues wunder sehen*, You will be filled with amazement (at the queer story I have to relate). A "blue wonder" is a cock and bull story, an improbable tale, something to make one stare. The French, *contes bleus*.

Blue and **Red**, in public-house signs, are heraldic colours, as the Blue Pig, the Blue Cow, the Red Lion, the Red Hart, etc.

Blue and Yellow (*The*). The *Edinburgh Review;* so called from its yellow and blue cover. The back is yellow, the rest of the cover is blue.

Blues (*The*), applied to troops. *The Oxford Blues.* The Royal Horse Guards were so called in 1690, from the Earl of Oxford their commander and the blue facings. Wellington, in one of his despatches, writes:—"I have been appointed colonel of the Blues."

"It was also known as the 'Blue Guards' during the campaign in Flanders (1742-1745)."—*Trimen: Regiments of the British Army.*

Bluff (*To*), in the game called *Poker*, is to stake on a bad hand. This is a dodge resorted to by players to lead an adversary to throw up his cards and forfeit his stake rather than risk them against the "bluffer."

"The game proceeded. George, although he affected no ignorance of the ordinary principles of poker, played like a novice—that is to say, he bluffed extravagantly on absurdly low hands."—*Truth: Queer Stories*, Sept. 3rd, 1885.

Bluff Harry or Hal. Henry VIII., so called from his bluff and burly manners (1491, 1509-1547.)

Blunderbore. A giant, brother of Cormoran, who put Jack the Giant Killer to bed and intended to kill him; but Jack thrust a billet of wood into the bed, and crept under the bedstead. Blunderbore came with his club and broke the billet to pieces, but was much amazed at seeing Jack next morning at breakfast-time. When his astonishment was abated he asked Jack how he had slept. "Pretty well," said the Cornish hero, "but once or twice I fancied a mouse tickled me with its tail." This increased the giant's surprise. Hasty pudding being provided for breakfast, Jack stowed away such huge stores in a bag concealed within his dress that the giant could not keep pace with him. Jack cut the bag open to relieve "the gorge," and the giant, to effect the same relief, cut his throat and thus killed himself. (*See* GIANTS.)

Blunderbuss. A short gun with a large bore. (Dutch, *donderbus*, a thunder-tube.)

Blunt. Ready money.

Blunt (*Major - General*). An old cavalry officer, rough in speech, but very brave and honest, of good understanding, and a true patriot. (*Shadwell: The Volunteers.*)

Blurt out (*To*). To tell something from impulse which should not have been told. To speak incautiously, or without due reflection. Florio makes the distinction, to "flurt with one's fingers, and blurt with one's mouth."

Blush. *At the first blush.* At the first glance; speaking off-hand without having given the subject mature deliberation. The allusion is to blushing at some sudden or unexpected allusion; the first time the thought has flashed into your mind.

To put to the blush. To make one blush with shame, annoyance, or confusion.

"England might blush in 1620, when Englishmen trembled at a fool's frown [*i.e.* James I.], but not in 1649, when an enraged people cut off his son's [Charles I.] head."—*Wendell Phillips: Orations,* p. 419.

Bo or *Boh*, in old Runic, was a fierce Gothic captain, son of Odin. His name was used by his soldiers when they would take the enemy by surprise. (*Sir William Temple.*)

From this name comes our *bogie*, a hobgoblin or little Bo. Gifford Castle is called Bo Hall, being said to have been constructed by bogies or magic. Compare Greek, *boi*, bah! verb, *boaō*, to shout out; Latin, *bōo*, to bellow like a bull (*bos*). (*See* BOGIE.)

You cannot say Bo! to a goose—i.e. you are a coward who dare not say bo! even to a fool. When Ben Jonson was introduced to a nobleman, the peer was so struck with his homely appearance that he exclaimed, "What! are you Ben Jonson? Why, you look as if you could not say Bo! to a goose." "Bo!" exclaimed the witty dramatist, turning to the peer and making his bow. (Latin, *bo-are;* Greek, *boa-ein*, to cry aloud.)

Bo-tree. A corruption of *bodhi* or *bodhiru'ma* (the tree of wisdom), under which Sakyamuni used to sit when he concocted the system called Buddhism.

Boa. Pliny says the word is from *bos* (a cow), and arose from the supposition that the boa sucked the milk of cows.

Boanergēs (sons of thunder). A name given to James and John, the sons of Zeb'edee, because they wanted to call down "fire from heaven" to consume the Samaritans for not "receiving" the Lord Jesus. (Luke ix. 54; *see* Mark iii. 17.)

Boar. *The Boar.* Richard III.; so called from his cognisance.

"The wretched, bloody, and usurping boar
That spoiled your summer fields and fruitful vines;
. . . This foul swine . . . lies now . . .
Near to the town of Leicester, as we learn."
Shakespeare: Richard III., v. 3.

The bristled Baptist boar. So Dryden denominates the Anabaptists in his *Hind and Panther.*

"The bristled Baptist boar, impure as he [the ape],
But whitened with the foam of sanctity,
With fat pollutions filled the sacred place,
And mountains levelled in his furious race."
Part i. 43-6.

The wild boar of Ardennes [*Le sanglier des Ardennes*]. Guillaume, Comte de la Marck, so called because he was fierce as the wild boar, which he delighted to hunt. Introduced by Sir Walter Scott as William, Count of la Marck, in *Quentin Durward.*

Boar (*The*), eaten every evening in Valhalla by the Æsir, was named SÆHRIMNIR. It was eaten every evening and next morning was restored whole again.

Boar's Flesh. *Buddha died from a meal of dried boar's flesh.* Mr. Sinnett tells us that the "boar" referred to was the boar avatar of Vishnu, and that "dried boar's flesh" means esoteric knowledge prepared for popular use. None but Buddha himself must take the responsibility of giving out occult secrets, and he died while so occupied, *i.e.* in preparing for the general esoteric knowledge. The protreptics of Jamblicus are examples of similar interpretations. (See *Nineteenth Century*, June, 1893, p. 1021.)

Boar's Head. [The Christmas dish.] Freyr, the Scandinavian god of peace and plenty, used to ride on the boar Gullinbursti; his festival was held at Yuletide (*winter solstice*), when a boar was sacrificed to his honour.

The Boar's Head. This tavern, made immortal by Shakespeare, used to stand in Eastcheap, on the site of the present statue of William IV. It was the cognisance of the Gordons, the progenitor of which clan slew, in the forest of Huntley, a wild boar, the terror of all the Merse (1093).

Board. A council which sits at a board or table; as " Board of Directors," " Board of Guardians," " School Board," " Board of Trade," etc. (Anglo-Saxon, *bord*, a board, table, etc.)

To sweep the board. To win and carry off all the stakes in a game of cards.

2. *Board*, in sea phrases, is all that space of the sea which a ship passes over in tacking.

On board. In the ship. " To go on board," to enter the ship or other sea vessel.

Overboard. Fallen out of the ship into the sea.

To board a ship is to get on board an enemy's vessel.

To make a good board. To make a good or long tack in beating to windward.

To make a short board. To make a short tack. " To make short boards," to tack frequently.

To make a stern board. To sail stern foremost.

To run aboard of. To run foul of [another ship].

3. *To board.* To feed and lodge together, is taken from the custom of the university members, etc., dining together at a common table or board.

Board. To accost. (French, *aborder*, to accost.)

" I'll board her, though she chide as loud
    As thunder."
          Shakespeare : Taming of the Shrew, i. 2.
(See also *Hamlet,* ii. 2.)

Board of Green Cloth. So called because the lord steward and his board sat at a table covered with green cloth. It existed certainly in the reign of Henry I., and probably earlier, and was abolished in 1849.

"Board of Green Cloth, June 12th, 1681. Order was this day given that the Maides of Honour should have cherry-tarts instead of gooseberry-tarts, it being observed that cherrys are three-pence a pound."

Board School (*A*). An undenominational elementary school managed by a School Board, and supported by a parliamentary grant collected by a rate.

Boarding School. *I am going to boarding school.* Going to prison to be taught good behaviour.

Boards. *He is on the boards, i.e.* an actor by profession.

Boast (*The*). The vainglory, the ostentation, that which a person boasts of, or is proud of.

" The boast of heraldry, the pomp of power,
  Awaits [*sic*] alike the inevitable hour."
          Gray : The Elegy, stanza 9.

Boast of England (*The*). Tom Thumb or Tom-a-lin. Richard Johnson, in 1599, published a "history of this ever-renowned soldier, the Red Rose Knight, surnamed The Boast of England, showing his honorable victories in foreign countries, with his strange fortunes in Faëry Land, and how he married the fair Angliterra, daughter of Prester John. . . ."

Boat. *Both in the same boat.* Both treated alike; both placed in the same conditions. The reference is to the boat launched when a ship is wrecked.

To be represented in a boat is the ordinary symbol of apotheo'sis. Many sovereigns are so represented on coins.

Boatswain. The officer who has charge of the boats, sails, rigging, anchors, cordage, cables, and colours. Swain is the Saxon *swein* (a boy, servant), Swedish *sven*. Hence, a shepherd is a swain, and a sweetheart is a woman's servant or swain.

Boatswain. The name of Byron's favourite dog, buried in Newstead Abbey garden.

Boaz and **Jachin.** The names of the two brazen pillars set up by Solomon at the entrance of his temple—Boaz (*strength*) on the left hand, and Jachin (*stability*) on the right. (1 Kings vii. 21.)

" Two pillars raising by their skill profound,
  Boaz and Jachin, thro' the East renowned."
          Crabbe : Borough.

Bob. A shilling. A "bender" is a sixpence. (Compare BAWBEE.)

Bob. A set of changes rung on [church] bells: as a "bob major," a "bob-minor," a "triple bob."

To give the bob to any one. To deceive, to balk. This word is a corruption of *pop.* The bob of a pendulum or mason's plumb-line is the weight that pops backwards and forwards. The bob of a fishing-line pops up and down when fish nibble at the bait. To bob for apples or cherries is to try and catch them while they swing backwards and for-wards. As this is very deceptive, it is easy to see how the word signifies to balk, etc.

To *bob* means also to thump, and a *bob* is a blow.

"He that a fool doth very wisely hit,
  Doth very foolishly, although he smart,
  Not to seem senseless of the bob."
          Shakespeare : As You Like It, ii. 7.

Bear a bob. Be brisk. The allusion is to bobbing for apples, in which it requires great agility and quickness to catch the apple.

A bob wig. A wig in which the bottom locks are turned up into bobs or short curls.

Bob'adil. A military braggart of the first water. Captain Bobadil is a character in Ben Jonson's comedy of *Every Man in his Humour.* This name was probably suggested by Bobadilla, first governor of Cuba, who sent Columbus home in chains. (*See* VINCENT.)

"Bobadil is the author's best invention, and is worthy to march in the same regiment with Bessus and Pistol, Parolles, and the Copper Captain" (*q.v.*).—*B. W. Procter.*

✱ See all these names in their proper places.

Bobbery, as "Kicking up a bobbery," making a squabble or tumult, kicking up a shindy. It is much used in India, and Colonel Yule says it is of Indian origin.

Bobbish. *Pretty bobbish.* Pretty well (in spirits and health), from *bob,* brisk. (*See above.*) A very ancient expression.

Bobbit. *If it isn't weel bobbit we'll bob it again.* If it is not done well enough, we will try again. To bob is to dance, and literally the proverb means, "If it is not well danced, we will dance over again."

Bobby. A policeman; so called because Sir *Robert* Peel introduced the

force, at least into Ireland. (*See* PEELER.)

"But oh ! for the grip of the bobby's hand
  Upon his neck that day."
          Punch : July 26, 1884.

Boccus (*King*). A kind of Solomon, who not only drank strong poison "in the name of the Trinite" without hurt ; but also answered questions of wisdom, morality, and natural-science. (*The History of King Boccus and Sydrack,* from the French.)

Bockland or *Bookland.* Land severed from the *folcland,* and converted into a private estate of perpetual inheritance by a short and simple deed or bock.

Bod. The divinity invoked by Indian women who desire fecundity. Children born after an invocation to Bod must be redeemed, or else serve in the temple of the goddess. (*Indian mythology.*)

Boden-See. The Lake of Constance ; so called because it lies in the Boden, or low country at the foot of the Alps. (Latin, *Sinus Bodamicus.*)

Bodies. *Compound bodies,* in chemical phraseology, mean those which have two or more simple bodies or elements in their composition, as water.

Simple bodies, in chemical phraseology, mean the elements.

The heavenly bodies. The sun, moon, stars, and so on.

The seven bodies (of alchemists). The seven metals supposed to correspond with the seven "planets."

Planets.	Metals.
1. Apollo, or the Sun	Gold.
2. Diana, or the Moon	Silver.
3. Mercury	Quicksilver.
4. Venus	Copper.
5. Mars	Iron.
6. Jupiter	Tin.
7. Saturn	Lead.

Bodkin. A dagger. (Welsh, *bodogyn,* a small dagger.)

Bodkin. *When he himself might his quietus make with a bare bodkin* (*Hamlet,* iii. 1). A stiletto worn by ladies in the hair, not a dagger. In the *Seven Champions,* Castria took her silver bodkin from her hair, and stabbed to death first her sister and then herself. Praxida stabbed herself in a similar manner. Shakespeare could not mean that a man might kill himself with a naked dagger, but that even a hair-pin would suffice to give a man his quietus.

Bodkin. *To ride bodkin.* To ride in a carriage between two others, the accommodation being only for two.

✱ Dr. Payne says that bodkin in this sense is a contraction of bodykin, a little body, which may be squeezed into a small space.

"If you can bodkin the sweet creature into the coach."—*Gibbon.*

"There is hardly room between Jos and Miss Sharp, who are on the front seat, Mr. Osborne sitting bodkin opposite, between Captain Dobbin and Amelia."—*Thackeray: Vanity Fair.*

Bodle. A Scotch coin, worth the sixth of a penny; so called from Both-well, a mint-master.

"Fair play, he car'd na deils a boddle."
   Burns: Tam o' Shanter, line 110.

To care not a bodle = our English phrase, "Not to care a farthing."

Bodle'ian Library (Oxford). So called because it was restored by Sir Thomas Bodley in 1597.

Body. (Anglo-Saxon, *bodig.*)

A regular body, in geometry, means one of the five regular solids, called "Platonic" because first suggested by Plato. (*See* PLATONIC BODIES.)

To body forth. To give mental shape to an ideal form.

"Imagination bodies forth
The forms of things unknown."
Shakespeare : Midsummer Night's Dream, v. 1.

Body and Soul. *To keep body and soul together.* To sustain life; from the notion that the soul gives life. The Latin *anima,* and the Greek *psyche,* mean both soul and life; and, according to Homeric mythology, the departed soul retains the shape and semblance of the body, hence the notion of ghosts. Indeed, if the soul is the "principle of life," it must of necessity be the fac-simile of every living atom of the body. (*See* ASTRAL BODY.)

Body-colour (*A*). Is a paint con-taining a body or consistency. In water-colours it is mixed with white lead and laid on thickly.

Body Corporate (*A*). An aggregate of individuals legally united into a cor-poration.

Body Politic (*A*). A whole nation considered as a political corporation; the state. In Latin, *totum corpus reipublicæ.*

Body-snatcher (*A*). One who snatches or purloins bodies, newly buried, to sell them to surgeons for dissection. By a play on the words, a bum-bailiff was so called, because his duty was to snatch or capture the body of a delinquent.

⁂ The first instance of body-snatching on record was in 1777. It was the body of Mrs. Jane Sainsbury from the burial ground near Gray's Inn Lane. The men, being convicted, were imprisoned for six months.

Bœmond. The Christian King of Antioch, who tried to teach his subjects arts, laws, and religion. Pyrrhus de-livered to him a fort, by which Antioch was taken by the Christians after an eight months' siege. Bœmond and Roge'ro were two brothers, the sons of Roberto Guiscardo, of the Norman race. (*Tasso : Jerusalem Delivered.*)

Bœo'tia. According to fable it is so-called because Cadmus was conducted by an ox (Greek *bous*) to the spot where he built Thebes; but, according to fact, it was so called because it abounded in cattle. (Greek, *Boiōtia.*)

Bœo'tian. A rude, unlettered person, a dull blockhead. The ancient Bœotians loved agricultural and pastoral pursuits, so the Athenians used to say they were dull and thick as their own atmosphere; yet Hesiod, Pindar, Corinna, Plutarch, Pelop'idas, and Epaminondas, were all Bœotians.

Bœo'tian Ears. Ears unable to ap-preciate music or rhetoric.

"Well, friend, I assure thee thou hast not got Bœotian ears [*because you can appreciate the beauties of my sermons*]."— *Le Sage: Gil Blas,* vii. 3.

Boë'thius. Last of the Latin authors, properly so called (470–524). Alfred the Great translated his *De Consolatio'ne Philosophiæ* into Anglo-Saxon.

Bogie. A scarecrow, a goblin. (Bul-garian, *bog,* a god; Slavonic, *bogu;* Welsh, *bwg,* a goblin, our *bugbear.*)

The Assyrian mothers used to scare their children with the name of Narsēs (*Gibbon*); the Syrians with that of Richard Cœur de Lion; the Dutch with Boh, the Gothic general (*Warton*); the Jews with Lilith; the Turks with Mathias Corvi'nus, the Hungarian king; and the English with the name of Luns-fort (*q.v.*). (*See* BO.)

Bo'gio (in *Orlando Furioso*). One of the allies of Charlemagne. He promised his wife to return within six moons, but was slain by Dardinello.

Bogle Swindle. A gigantic swindle concocted in Paris by fourteen persons, who expected to net at least a million sterling. It was exposed in the *Times.*

Bogomi'li. A religious sect of the twelfth century, whose chief seat was Thrace. So called from their constant repetition of the words, "Lord, have mercy upon us," which, in Bulgarian, is *bog* (Lord), *milui* (have mercy).

Bogtrotters. Irish tramps; so called from their skill in crossing the Irish bogs, from tussock to tussock, either as guides or to escape pursuit.

Bogus. *Bogus currency.* Forged or sham bills. *Bogus transactions.* Fraudulent transactions. The word is by some connected with bogie.

Lowell (*Biglow Papers*) says, "I more than suspect the word to be a corruption of the French *bagasse.*"

In French argot is another word (*bogue*), the rind of a green chestnut, or case of a watch; a bogus chestnut or watch.

Bohême (*La*). A Bohemian, that is, one living on his wits, such as a penny-a-liner, journalist, politician, artist, dancer, or in fact any chevalier of unsettled habits and no settled home. From the French, *Bohémien*, a gipsy.

Une maison de Bohême means a house where no regularity is observed, but all things are at sixes and sevens.

Bohe'mia. *The Queen of Bohemia.* A public-house sign in honour of Lady Elizabeth Stuart, daughter of James I., who was married to Frederick, elector palatine, for whom Bohemia was raised into a separate kingdom. It is through this lady that the Brunswick family succeeded to the throne of Great Britain.

Bohe'mian. A gipsy, an impostor. The first gipsies that entered France came from Bohemia, and appeared before Paris in 1427. They were not allowed to enter the city, but were lodged at La Chapelle St. Denis.

A slang term applied to literary men and artists of loose and irregular habits, living by what they can pick up by their brains.

"Never was there an editor with less about him of the literary Bohemian. A strong contrast to his unhappy contemporary, Chatterton."—*Fortnightly Review: Paston Letter.*

Bohe'mian Brethren. A religious sect formed out of the remnants of the Hussites. They arose at Prague in the fifteenth century, and were nicknamed *Cave-dwellers*, because they lurked in caves to avoid persecution.

Bohemian Life (*A*). An irregular, restless way of living, like that of a gipsy.

Bohort (*Sir*). A knight of Arthur's Round Table, brother of Sir Lionel, and nephew of Lancelot of the Lake. Also called Sir Bors.

Boi'es (2 syl.). Priests of the savages of Florida. Each priest has his special idol, which must be invoked by the fumes of tobacco. (*American Indian mythology.*)

Boiling-point. *He was at boiling-point.* Very angry indeed. Properly the point of heat at which water, under

ordinary conditions, boils. (212° Fahrenheit, 100° Centigrade, 80° Réaumur.)

Boiley or *Boily.* Bread soaked in water. A word used in baby-farming establishments (French, *bouillie*). (*Pall Mall Budget*, Aug. 22, 1889.)

Boissere'an Collection. A collection at Stuttgart of the early specimens of German art, made by the three brothers Boisserée.

Bo'lay or *Boley.* The giant which the Indians say conquered heaven, earth, and the inferno. (*Indian mythology.*)

Bold. *Bold as Beauchamp* (Beech-um). It is said that Thomas Beauchamp, Earl of Warwick, with one squire and six archers, overthrew 100 armed men at Hogges, in Normandy, in 1346.

This exploit is not more incredible than that attributed to Captal-de-Buch, who, with forty followers, cleared Meaux of the insurgents called "La Jacquerie," 7,000 of whom were slain by this little band, or trampled to death in the narrow streets as they fled panic-struck (1358).

Bold as brass. Downright impudent; without modesty. Similarly, we say "brazen-faced."

I make bold to say. I take the liberty of saying; I venture to say.

Bole'rium Promontory. The Land's End.

Bole'ro. A Spanish dance; so called from the name of the inventor.

Bolingbroke. Henry IV. of England; so called from Bolingbroke, in Lincolnshire, where he was born. (1366, 1399-1413.)

Bollandists. Editors of the *Acta Sanctorum* begun by John Bolland (1596-1665); the sixty-first folio volume was published in 1875.

Bollen. Swollen. (Anglo-Saxon, *bolla*, a bowl.) Hence "joints bolne-big" (*Golding*), and "bolne in pride" (*Phaer*). The seed capsule or pod of flax is called a "boll."

"The barley was in the ear, and the flax was bolled."—Exod. ix. 31.

Bolo'gna Stone. A variety of barite, found in masses near Bologna. After being heated, powdered, and exposed to the light it becomes phosphorescent in the dark.

Bolognese School. There were three periods to the Bolognese School in painting—the Early, the Roman, and the Eclectic. The first was founded by

Marco Zoppo, in the fifteenth century, and its best exponent was Francia. The second was founded in the sixteenth century by Bagnacavallo, and its chief exponents were Primaticio, Tibaldi, and Nicolo dell' Aba'te. The third was founded by the Carracci, at the close of the sixteenth century, and its best masters have been Domenichi'no, Lanfranco, Guido, Schido'ne, Guerci'no, and Alba'ni.

Bolt. An arrow, a shaft (Anglo-Saxon, *bolta*; Danish, *bolt*; Greek, *ballo*, to cast; Latin, *pello*, to drive). A *door bolt* is a shaft of wood or iron, which may be shot or driven forward to secure a door. A *thunderbolt* is an hypothetical shaft cast from the clouds ; an aerolite. *Cupid's bolt* is Cupid's arrow.

The fool's bolt is soon spent. A foolish archer shoots all his arrows so heedlessly that he leaves himself no resources in case of need.

I must bolt. Be off like an arrow.

To bolt food. To swallow it quickly without waiting to chew it.

To bolt out the truth. To blurt it out ; also *To bolt out*, to exclude or shut out by bolting the door.

To bolt. To sift, as flour is bolted. This has a different derivation to the above (Low Latin, *bult-ella*, a boulter, from an Old French word for coarse cloth).

" I cannot bolt this matter to the bran,
As Bradwarden and holy Austin can."
Dryden's version of the Cock and Fox.

Bolt from the Blue (*A*). *There fell a bolt from the blue.* A sudden and wholly unexpected catastrophe or event occurred, like a "thunderbolt" from the blue sky, or flash of lightning without warning and wholly unexpected.

" Namque Diespiter
Igni corusco nubila dividens,
Plerumque, per purum tonantes
Egit equos volucremque currum. . . ."
Horace: 1 Ode xxxiv. 5, etc.

" On Monday, Dec. 22nd [1890], there fell a bolt from the blue. The morning papers announced that the men were out [on strike]."—*Nineteenth Century,* February, 1891, p. 240.

☞ In this phrase the word " bolt " is used in the popular sense for lightning, the Latin *fulmen*, the French *foudre* and *tonnerre*, in English sometimes for an aerolite. Of course, in strict scientific language, a flash of lightning is not a thunderbolt. Metaphorically, it means a sudden and wholly unexpected catastrophe, like a thunderbolt [flash of lightning] from a blue or serene sky.

German: Wie ein Blitzstrahl aus blauem Aether.
Italian: Comme un fulmine a ciel sereno.
Latin: Audiit et cœli genitor de parte serena
Intonuit lævum. (*Virgil: Æneid,* ix. 630.)

Bolt in Tun, a public-house sign, is heraldic. In heraldry it is applied to a bird-bolt, in pale, piercing through a tun. The punning crest of Serjeant Bolton, who died 1787, was " on a wreath a tun erect proper, transpierced by an arrow fesseways or." Another family of the same name has for crest " a tun with a bird-bolt through it proper." A third, harping on the same string, has " a bolt gules in a tun or." The public-house sign distinguished by this device or name adopted it in honour of some family claiming one of the devices mentioned above.

Bolt Upright. Straight as an arrow. A bolt is an arrow with a round knob at the end, used for shooting at rooks, etc.

Bolted. *Bolted out.* Either ran off suddenly, or being barred out of the house.

The horse bolted. The horse shot off like a bolt or arrow.

Bolted Arrow. A blunt arrow for shooting young rooks with a cross-bow ; called " bolting rooks." A gun would not do, and an arrow would mangle the little things too much.

Bolton. *The Bolton Ass.* This creature is said to have chewed tobacco and taken snuff. (*Dr. Doran.*)

Bate me an ace, quoth Bolton. Give me some advantage. What you say must be qualified, as it is too strong. Ray says that a collection of proverbs were once presented to the Virgin Queen, with the assurance that it contained all the proverbs in the language ; but the Queen rebuked the boaster with the proverb, " Bate me an ace, quoth Bolton," a proverb omitted in the compilation. John Bolton was one of the courtiers who used to play cards and dice with Henry VIII., and flattered the king by asking him to allow him an *ace* or some advantage in the game.

Bolus. An apothecary. Apothecaries are so called because they administer *boluses.* Similarly Mrs. Suds is a washerwoman ; Boots is the shoeblack of an inn, etc.

George Colman adopts the name for his apothecary, who wrote his labels in rhyme, one of which was—

" When taken,
To be well shaken " ;

but the patient being shaken, instead of the mixture, died.

Bomb. A shell filled with gunpowder. (Greek, *bombos*; Latin, *bombus*, any deep noise. Thus *Festus* says : "*Bombus, sonus non apium tantum, aut poculi bilbientis, sed etiam tonitrûs.*" And Catullus applies it to the blast of a trumpet, "*efflabant cornua bombis,*" lxiv. 263.)

Bomba. *King Bomba.* A nickname given to Ferdinand II., King of Naples, in consequence of his cruel bombardment of Messi'na in 1848, in which the slaughter and destruction of property was most wanton.

Bomba II. was the nickname given to his son Francis II. for bombarding Palermo in 1860. He was also called *Bombali'no* (Little Bomba).

Another meaning equally applicable is *Vox et præter'ea nihil,* Bomba being the explosion made by puffing out the cheeks, and causing them suddenly to collapse. Liar, break-promise, worthless.

Bombast literally means the produce of the bombyx (Middle Latin *bombax,* Greek *bombux*), and applied to cotton-wool used for padding. The head of the cotton plant was called "bombast" or "bombace" in the sixteenth century. Bombast was much used in the reign of Henry VIII. for padding, and hence inflated language was so called.

"We have received your letters full of love, . . .
And in our maiden council rated them . . .
As bombast and as lining to the time."
Shakespeare: Love's Labour's Lost, v. 2.

Bombastes Furio'so. One who talks big and uses long sesquipedalian words; the ideal of bombast. He is the hero of a burlesque opera so called, by William Barnes Rhodes. (1790.)

Bombas'tus. The family name of Aureolus Paracelsus (1493-1541). He is said to have kept a small devil prisoner in the pommel of his sword.

"Bombastus kept a devil's bird
Shut in the pommel of his sword,
That taught him all the cunning pranks
Of past and future mountebanks."
S. Butler: Hudibras, part ii. 3.

Bon Gaultier Ballads. Parodies of modern poetry by W. E. Aytoun and Theodore Martin (Sir).

Bon gré mal gré. Willing or unwilling, willy nilly, *nolens volens.*

Bon Mot (French). A good or witty saying ; a pun ; a clever repartee.

Bon Ton (French). Good manners, or manners accredited by good society.

Bon Vivant (French). A free liver; one who indulges in the "good things of the table."

Bona Fide. Without subterfuge or deception ; really and truly. Literally, *in good faith* (Latin).

Bona-ro'ba. A courtesan (Italian); so called from the smartness of their robes or dresses.

"We knew where the bona-robas were."
Shakespeare: 2 *Henry IV.,* iii. 2.

Bonduca = Boadicea. (*Fletcher's Tragedy,* 1647.)

Bone. *Bred in the bone.* A part of one's nature. "What's bred in the bone will come out in the flesh." A natural propensity cannot be repressed. *Naturam furcâ expellas, autem usque redibit.*

Bone in my Throat. *I have a bone in my throat.* I cannot talk; I cannot answer your question.

I have a bone in my leg. An excuse given to children for not moving from one's seat. Similarly, "I have a bone in my arm," and must be excused using it for the present.

Bone of Contention. A disputed point ; a point not yet settled. The metaphor is taken from the proverb about "Two dogs fighting for a bone," etc.

Bones. Deuca'lion, after the Deluge, was ordered to cast behind him the *bones of his mother, i.e.* the stones of mother earth. Those thrown by Deuca'lion became men, and those thrown by his wife, Pyrrha, became women.

Pindar suggests that *laas,* a stone, is a pun on *laos,* the people. Both words, in the genitive case singular, are alike *laou. (Olynthics,* ix. 66.)

Bone to pick (*A*). A sop to Cerbĕrus. A lucrative appointment given to a troublesome opponent in order to silence him. Thus Chisholm Anstey was sent to Hong-Kong as a judge to keep him away from the House of Commons. Of course the allusion is to throwing a bone to a dog barking at you.

"In those days the usual plan to get rid of an oratorical patriot in the House was to give him 'a bone to pick.'"—*Anthony Collins.*

I have a bone to pick with you. An unpleasant matter to settle with you. At the marriage banquets of the Sicilian poor, the bride's father, after the meal, used to hand the bridegroom a bone, saying, "Pick this bone, for you have taken in hand a much harder task."

Bone. (*See* ALBADARA ; LUZ ; OS SACRUM.)

Bone (*To*). To filch, as, *I boned it.* Shakespeare (2 *Henry VI.,* act i. 3) says, "By these ten bones, my lord . . ." meaning his ten fingers ; and (*Hamlet,* iii. 2) calls the fingers "pickers and stealers." Putting the two together, there can be no doubt that "to bone" means to finger, that is, "to pick and steal."

> "You thought that I was buried deep
> Quite decent-like and chary,
> But from her grave in Mary-bone,
> They've come and boned your Mary!"
>   *Hood: Mary's Ghost.*

Bone-grubber (*A*). A person who grubs about dust-bins, gutters, etc., for refuse bones, which he sells to bone-grinders, and other dealers in such stores.

Bone-lace. Lace woven on bobbins made of trotter-bones.

Bone-shaker (*A*). A four-wheel cab; also an old bicycle.

> "A good swift hansom is worth twice as much as a 'bone-shaker' any day."—*Nineteenth Century*, March, 1893, p. 473.

Boned. *I boned him.* Caught or seized him. (*See above*, To BONE.)

Bones. The man who rattles or plays the bones in nigger troupes.

To make no bones about the matter, i.e. no difficulty, no scruple. Dice are called "bones," and the French, *flatter le dé* (to mince the matter), is the opposite of our expression. To make no bones of a thing is not to flatter, or "make much of," or humour the dice in order to show favour.

Napier's bones. (*See under* NAPIER.)

Without more bones. Without further scruple or objection. (*See above, "Make no bones,"* etc.)

Bonese (2 syl.). The inhabitants of Bo'ni, one of the Celebēs.

Bonfire. *Ignis ossium.* The *Athenæum* shows that the word means a fire made of *bones;* one quotation runs thus, "In the worship of St. John, the people . . . made three manner of fires: one was of clean bones and no wood, and that is called a bonefire; another of clean wood and no bones, and that is called a wood-fire . . . and the third is made of wood and bones, and is called 'St. John's fire'" (*Quatuor Sermones*, 1499). Certainly *bone* (Scotch, *bane*) is the more ancient way of spelling the first syllable of the word; but some suggest that "bon-fire" is really "boon-fire."

> "In some parts of Lincolnshire . . . they make fires in the public streets . . . with bones of oxen, sheep, etc. . . . heaped together . . . hence came the origin of bonfires."—*Leland*, 1552.

⁂ Whatever the origin of the word, it has long been used to signify either a *beacon* fire, or a *boon* fire, *i.e.* a fire expressive of joy. We often find the word spelt "bane-fire," where *bane* may mean "bone" or beacon. Welsh *ban*, lofty; allied to the Norwegian *baun*, a beacon or cresset.

Bon'homie'. Kindness, good nature; free and easy manners; cordial benevolence. (French.)

> "I never knew a more prepossessing man. His *bonhomie* was infectious."—*C. D. Warner: Little Journey*, chap. vi.

Bonhomme (*Un*). A goody man; according to Dr. Young's line, "What is mere good nature, but a fool?" The word, divided into two, is used in a good sense, as *Etre un bon homme. Jacques Bonhomme* means a peasant.

Jacques Bonhomme (French). A peasant who ventures to interfere in politics. Hence, the peasants' rebellion in 1358 was called *La Jacquerie.* The term means "James Goodfellow"; we also often address the poor as "My good fellow."

Bon'iface. A sleek, good-tempered, jolly landlord. From Farquhar's comedy of *The Beaux' Stratagem.*

> "A regular British Boniface."—*The John Bull.*

St. Boniface. The apostle of Germany, an Anglo-Saxon whose original name was *Winifrid* or *Winfrith.* (680-750.)

St. Boniface's cup. An extra cup of wine (to the health of the Pope). Pope Boniface, we are told in the *Ebrietatis Encomium,* instituted an indulgence to those who drank his good health after grace, or the health of the Pope of the time being. An excuse for an extra glass.

Bonne (French). A nursemaid, a nursery governess.

Bonne Bouche (*A*). A delicious morsel; a tit-bit (tid-bit).

> "Now I'll give you a real *bonne-bouche*. This is a bottle of the famous comet port of 1811."—*The Epicure.*

Bonnet. A pretended player at a gaming-table, or bidder at an auction, to lure others to play; so called because he blinds the eyes of his dupes, just as if he had struck their bonnet over their eyes.

> "A man who sits at a gaming table, and appears to be playing against the table; when a stranger appears the Bonnet generally wins."—*The Times.*

Bonnet.

Braid Bonnet. The old Scotch cap, made of milled woollen, without seam or lining.

Glengarry Bonnet. The Highland bonnet, which rises to a point in front.

He has a green bonnet. Has failed in trade. In France it used to be customary, even in the seventeenth century, for bankrupts to wear a green bonnet (cloth cap).

He has a bee in his bonnet. (*See* BEE.)

Bonnet Lairds. Local magnates of Scotland, who wore the Braid Bonnet.

Bonnet-piece. A gold coin of James V. of Scotland, the king's head on which wears a bonnet.

Bonnet Rouge. The red cap of Liberty worn by the leaders of the French revolution. It is the emblem of Red Republicanism.

Bonnie Dundee. John Graham, of Claverhouse, Viscount Dundee (1650-1689).

Bonnyclabber. A drink made of beer and buttermilk. (Irish, *bainne*, milk ; *claba*, thick or thickened.)

> " With beer and buttermilk, mingled together, . .
> To drink such . . . bonny-clapper."
> *Ben Jonson : The New Inn*, i. 3.

Bono Johnny. John Bull is so called in the East Indies.

Bontemps. *Roger Bontemps* (French). The personification of " Never say die." The phrase is from Béranger.

> " Vous pauvres, pleins d'envie :
>   Vous riches, désireux ;
> Vous, dont le char devie
>   Après un cours heureux ;
> Vous, qui perdrez peut-être
>   Des titres éclatants,
> Eh ! gai ! prenez pour maître
>   Le gros Roger Bontemps." *Béranger.*

> Ye poor, with envy goaded ;
> Ye rich, for more who long ;
> Ye who by fortune loaded
>   Find all things going wrong
> Ye who by some disaster
>   See all your cables break
> From henceforth for your master
>   Bluff Roger Bontemps take.
>   *E. C. B.*

Bonus. A bounty over and above the interest of a share in any company. (Latin, *bonus quæstus*, a good profit or bounty. The interest or fruit of money put out in an investment was by the Romans called the *quæstus*.)

Bonus Homērus. (*See* HOMER.)

Bonzes (sing. *Bon'ze*). Indian priests. In China they are the priests of the Fohists ; their number is 50,000, and they are represented as idle and dissolute. In Japan they are men of rank and family. In Tonquin every pagoda has at least two bonzes, and some as many as fifty.

Booby. A spiritless fool, who suffers himself to be imposed upon. In England the Solan goose is called a booby or noddy. (Spanish, *bobo ;* German, *bube*.)

A booby will never make a hawk. The bird called the booby, that allows itself to be fleeced by other birds, will never become a bird of prey itself.

Booby (*Lady*). A caricature on Richardson's *Pam'ela*. A vulgar upstart, who tries to seduce Joseph Andrews. (*Fielding : Joseph Andrews.*)

Booby-trap (*A*). A pitcher of water, book, or something else, balanced gingerly on the top of a door set ajar, so that when the booby or victim is entice . to pass through the door, the pitcher or book falls on him.

Book (Ang.-Saxon, *boc;* Danish, *beuke;* German, *buche*, a beech-tree). Beech-bark was employed for carving names on before the invention of printing.

> " Here on my trunk's surviving frame,
> Carved many a long-forgotten name. . .
> As love's own altar, honour me :
> Spare, woodman, spare the beechen tree."
>   *Campbell: Beech Tree's Petition.*

Book. *The dearest ever sold.* A Mazarin Bible at the Thorold sale, in 1884, bought by Mr. Quaritch, bookseller, Piccadilly, London, for £3,900. In 1873 Lord Ashburnham gave £3,400 for a copy.

Book. *The oldest in the world.* That by Ptah-Hotep, the Egyptian, compiled in the reign of Assa, about B.C. 3366. This MS. is preserved in the Bibliothèque Nationale in Paris. It is written on papyrus in hieratic characters, and is a compilation of moral, political, and religious aphorisms. It strongly insists on reverence to women, politeness, and monotheism. Ptah-Hotep was a prince of the blood, and lived to the age of 110 years.

Book. Logistilla gave Astolpho, at parting, a book which would tell him anything he wanted to know, and save him from the power of enchantment. (*Ariosto : Orlando Furioso*, book viii)

Beware of a man of one book. Never attempt to controvert the statement of any one in his own special subject. A shepherd who cannot read will know more about sheep than the wisest bookworm. This caution is given by St. Thomas Aqui'nas.

That does not suit my book. Does not accord with my arrangements. The reference is to betting-books, in which the bets are formally entered.

To bring him to book. To make him prove his words ; to call him to account. Make him show that what he says accords with what is written down in the indentures, the written agreement, or the book which treats of the subject.

To book it. To take down an order ; to make a memorandum ; to enter in a book.

To speak by the book. With minute

6

exactness. To speak *literatim*, according to what is in the book.

To speak like a book. To speak with great precision and accuracy; to be full of information.

To speak without book. Without authority; from memory only, without consulting or referring to the book.

Bell, book, and candle. (*See under* BELL.)

Book of Books (*The*). The Bible.

Book of Life (*The*). In Bible language, is a register of the names of those who are to inherit eternal life. (Phil. iv. 3; Rev. xx. 12.)

Books.

He is in my books, or *in my good books.* The former is the older form; both mean to be in favour. The word book was at one time used more widely, a single sheet, or even a list being called a book. To be in my books is to be on my list of friends.

"I was so much in his books, that at his decease he left me his lamp."—*Addison.*

"If you want to keep in her good books, don't call her 'the old lady.'"—*Dickens.*

He is in my black (or *bad*) *books.* In disfavour. (*See* BLACK BOOKS.)

On the books. On the list of a club, on the list of candidates, on the list of voters, etc. At Cambridge university they say "on the boards."

Out of my books. Not in favour; no longer in my list of friends.

The battle of the books. The Boyle controversy (*q.v.*). (*See* BATTLE.)

To take one's name off the books. To withdraw from a club. In the passive voice it means to be excluded, or no longer admissible to enjoy the benefits of the institution. The Cambridge university phrase is "to take my name off the boards," etc.

Book-keeper. One who borrows books, but does not return them.

Book-keeping. The system of keeping the debtor and creditor accounts of merchants in books provided for the purpose, either by single or by double entry.

Waste-book. A book in which items are not posted under heads, but are left at random, as each transaction occurred.

Day-book. A book in which are set down the debits and credits which occur day by day. These are ultimately sorted into the ledger.

Ledger (Dutch, *leggen*, to lay). The book which is laid up in counting-houses. In the ledger the different items are regularly sorted according to the system in use. (LEDGER-LINES.)

By single entry. Book-keeping in which each debit or credit is entered only once into the ledger, either as a debit or credit item, under the customer's or salesman's name.

By double entry. By which each item is entered twice into the ledger, once on the debit and once on the credit side.

Bookworm. One always poring over his books; so called in allusion to the insect that eats holes in books, and lives both in and on its leaves.

Boom. A sudden and great demand of a thing, with a corresponding rise in its price. The rush of a ship under press of sail. The word arises from the sound of booming or rushing water.

"The boom was something wonderful. Everybody bought, everybody sold."—*Mark Twain: Life on the Mississippi,* chap. 57.

Boom-Passenger (*A*). A convict on board ship, who was chained to the boom when made to take his daily exercise.

Boon Companion (*A*). A convivial companion. A *bon vivant* is one fond of good living. "Who leads a good life is sure to live well." (French, *bon,* good.)

Boot. *I will give you that to boot, i.e.* in addition. The Anglo-Saxon *boot* or *bôt* means "compensation." (Gothic, *bóta,* profit.)

"As anyone shall be more powerful . . . . or higher in degree, shall he the more deeply make boot for sin, and pay for every misdeed."—*Laws of King Ethelred.*

Boot-jack. (*See under* JACK.)

Boots. *Seven-leagued boots.* The boots worn by the giant in the fairy tale, called *The Seven-leagued Boots.* These boots would stride over seven leagues at a pace.

I measure five feet ten inches without my boots The allusion is to the chopine or high-heeled boot, worn at one time to increase the stature. Hamlet says of the lady actress, "You are nearer heaven than when I saw you last, by the altitude of a chopine." (ii. 2.)

Boots (an instrument of torture). They were made of four pieces of narrow board nailed together, of a competent length to fit the leg. The leg being placed therein, wedges were inserted till the sufferer confessed or fainted.

"All your empirics could never do the like cure upon the gout as the rack in England or your Scotch boots."—*Marston: The Malcontent.*

Boots. The youngest bishop of the House of Lords, whose duty it is to read prayers; so called because he walks into the house in a dead man's shoes or boots, *i.e.* he was not in the house till some bishop there died, and left a vacancy.

Boots. *To go to bed in his boots.* To be very tipsy.

Boots at an Inn. A servant whose duty it is to clean the boots. *The Boots of the Holly-tree Inn*, a Christmas tale by Charles Dickens (1855).

Bootless Errand. An unprofitable or futile message. The Saxon *bot* means "reparation"—"overplus to profit": as "I will give you that to boot"; "what boots it me?" (what does it profit me?).

> "I sent him
> Bootless home and weather-beaten back."
> *Shakespeare:* 1 *Henry IV.*, iii. 1.

Boötes (*Bo-o'-tees*), or the ox-driver, a constellation. According to ancient mythology, Boötes invented the plough, to which he yoked two oxen, and at death, being taken to heaven with his plough and oxen, was made a constellation. Homer calls it "the wagoner."

> "Wide o'er the spacious regions of the north,
> That see Boötes urge his tardy wain."
> *Thomson: Winter*, 834-5.

Booth. Husband of Amelia. (*Fielding: Amelia.*)

Boozy. Partly intoxicated. (Russian, *busá*, millet-beer; Latin, *buza*, from *buo*, to fill; Welsh, *bozi*; Old Dutch, *buyzen*, to tipple; Coptic, *bouza*, intoxicating drink.)

> "In Egypt there is a beer called 'Boozer,' which is intoxicating."—*Morning Chronicle, Aug. 27th*, 1852.

Bor (in Norfolk) is a familiar term of address to a lad or young man; as, "Well, bor, I saw the mother you spoke of"—*i.e.* "Well, sir, I saw the lass. . . ." "Bor" is the Dutch *boer*, a farmer; and "mor" the Dutch *moer*, a female.

Borach'io. A drunkard. From the Spanish *borach'oe* or *borrach'o*, a bottle made of pig's skin, with the hair inside, dressed with resin and pitch to keep the wine sweet. (*Minsheu.*)

Borachio. A follower of Don John, in *Much Ado About Nothing*, who thus plays upon his own name:—

> "I will, like a true drunkard [*borachio*], utter all to thee."—*Act* iii. 5.

Bor'ak or *Al Borak* (the lightning). The animal brought by Gabriel to carry Mahomet to the seventh heaven. It had the face of a man, but the cheeks of a horse; its eyes were like jacinths, but brilliant as the stars; it had the wings of an eagle, spoke with the voice of a man, and glittered all over with radiant light. This creature was received into Paradise. (*See* ANIMALS, CAMEL.)

Bord Halfpenny. A toll paid by the Saxons to the lord for the privilege of having a bord or bench at some fair for the sale of articles.

Borda'rii or *Bordmen.* A class of agriculturists superior to the Villa'ni, who paid their rent by supplying the lord's board with eggs and poultry. (*Domesday Book.*)

Border (*The*). The frontier of England and Scotland, which, from the eleventh to the fifteenth century, was the field of constant forays, and a most fertile source of ill blood between North and South Britain.

> "March, march, Ettrick and Teviotdale;
> Why the deil dinna ye march forward in order?
> March, march, Eskdale and Liddesdale—
> All the Blue Bonnets are bound for the border."
> *Sir Walter Scott: The Monastery.*

Border Minstrel. Sir Walter Scott, because he sang of the border. (1771-1832.)

Border States (*The*). The five "slave" states (Delaware, Maryland, Virginia, Kentucky, and Missouri) which lay next to the "free states" were so called in the Civil War, 1861-1865.

Bordlands. Lands kept by lords in Saxon times for the supply of their own board or table. (Anglo-Saxon, *bord*, a table.)

Bordlode. Service paid for the land.

Bore (*A*). A person who bestows his tediousness on you; one who wearies you with his prate, his company, or his solicitations. Verb *bear, bore, borne*, to endure. A bore is someone we bore with or endured.

> "At this instant
> He bores me with some trick."
> *Shakespeare: Henry VIII.*, i. 1.

Bore. A tidal wave.

The most *celebrated* bores are those of the Brahmaputra, Ganges, Hooghly, Indus, and Tsintang (in China). Bores occur *regularly* in the Bristol Channel and Solway Frith; *occasionally* (in high tides), in the Clyde, Dee (Cheshire), Dornoch Frith, Lune, Severn, Trent (*eygre*), and Wye. The bore of the Bay of Fundy is caused by the *collision of the tides.* (Icelandic *bára*, a wave or billow.)

Bore (in pugilistic language) is one who *bears* or presses on a man so as to force him to the ropes of the ring by his physical weight; figuratively, one who bears or presses on you by his pertinacity.

" All beggars are liable to rebuffs, with the cer-
,ainty besides of being considered bores."—*Prince
Albert*, 1859.

Bor'eal. Northern.

" In radiant streams,
Bright over Europe, bursts the Boreal morn."
         Thomson : Autumn, 98.

Bor'eas. The north wind. According to mythology, he was the son of Astræus, a Titan, and Eos, the morning, and lived in a cave of Mount Hæmus, in Thrace. (Greek, *boros,* voracious ; *Bŏreas,* the north wind ; Russian, *boria,* storm.)

" Cease, rude Boreas ! blustering railer."
         Geo. Alex. Stevens.
" Omnia pontus haurit saxa vorax." *Lucan.*

Borghese (*Bor-ga'-zy*). *The Princess Borghese* pulled down a church contiguous to her palace, because the incense turned her sick and the organ made her head uneasy.

Bor'gia. (*See* LUCREZIA.)

Born. *Not born yesterday.* Not to be taken in ; worldly wise.

Born Days. *In all my born days.* Ever since I was born.

Born in the Purple (a translation of *porphyrogenitus*). The infant of royal parents in opposition to *born in the gutter,* or child of beggars. This has nothing to do with the purple robes of royalty. It refers to the chamber lined with porphyry by one of the Byzantine empresses for her accouchement. (See *Nineteenth Century,* March, 1894, p. 510.)

" Zoe, the fourth wife of Leo VI., gave birth to
the future Emperor Constantine Porphyrogenitus
in the purple chamber of the imperial palace."—
*Finlay: History of the Byzantine and Greek Em-
pires*, vol. i.

Born with a Silver Spoon, or *Born with a silver spoon in one's mouth. Born* to good luck ; born with hereditary wealth. The reference is to the usual gift of a silver spoon by the godfather or godmother of a child. The lucky child does not need to wait for the gift, for it is born with it in its mouth or inherits it from infancy.

Borough English is where the youngest son inherits instead of the eldest. It is of *Saxon* origin, and is so called to distinguish it from the Norman custom.

-" The custom of Borough English abounds in
Kent, Sussex, Surrey, the neighbourhood of
London, and Somerset. In the Midlands it is
rare, and north of the Humber . . . it does not
seem to occur."—*F. Pollock: Macmillan's Magazine*, xlvi. (1882).

Borowe. *St. George to borowe, i.e.* St. George being surety. (Danish, *borgen,* bail ; Swedish, *borgan,* a giving of bail.)

Borr. Son of Ymer, and father of Odin, Ville, Ve, and Hertha or Earth. The Celtic priests claimed descent from this deity. (*Celtic mythology.*)

Borrow. A pledge. *To borrow* is to take something which we pledge ourselves to return. (Anglo-Saxon, *borg,* a loan or pledge ; verb *borg-ian.*)

" Ye may retain as borrows my two priests."—
Scott: Ivanhoe, chap. xxxiii.

Borrowed days of February (*The*). 12th, 13th and 14th of February, said to be borrowed from January. If these days prove stormy, the year will be favoured with good weather ; but if fine, the year will be foul and unfavourable. These three days are called by the Scotch *Faoilteach,* and hence the word *faoilteach* means execrable weather.

Borrowed days of March. The last three days of March are said to be " borrowed from April."

' March said to Aperill,
  I see 3 hoggs [hoggets, sheep] upon a hill ;
  And if you'll lend me dayes 3
  I'll find a way to make them dee [die].
  The first o' them wus wind and weet,
  The second o' them wus snaw and sleet,
  The third o' them wus sic a freeze
  It froze the birds' nebs to the trees.
  When the 3 days were past and gane
  The 3 silly hoggs came hirpling [limping] hame."

Bortell. The bull, in the tale of *Reynard the Fox.* (*Heinrich von Alk-man.*)

Bos[ei] **in lingua.** He is bribed to silence ; he has a coin (marked with a bull's head) on his tongue. Adalardus, in *Statutis Abbatiæ Corbeiensis* (bk. i. c. 8), seems to refer to the *bos* as a coin. " *Boves et reliquam pecuniam habeat . . . unde et ipse et omnis familia ejus vivere possit*" (*i.e.* plenty of gold and silver...). Plautus, however, distinctly says (*Persa,* ii. 5, 16), " *Boves bini hic sunt in cru-mēna*" (Two bulls in a purse.) The Greeks had the phrase, βους επι γλωττης. Servius tells us that even the Romans had a coin with a bull stamped on it. (See *Pliny,* 18, 3.) Presuming that there was no such coin, there cannot be a doubt that the word *Bos* was used as the equivalent of the price of an ox.

Bosh. A Persian word meaning *non-sense*. It was popularised in 1824 by James Morier in his *Adventures of Hajji Baba of Ispahan*, a Persian romance. (Turkish, *bosh lakerdi*, silly talk.)

"I always like to read old Darwin's *Loves of the Plants ;* bosh as it is in a scientific point of view."
—*Kingsley : Two Years Ago* (chap. x.).

Bosky. On the verge of drunkenness. University slang, from *boskō*, to pasture, to feed. Everyone will remember how Sir John Falstaff made sack his meat and drink.

Bosom Friend (*A*). A very dear friend. Nathan says, "It lay in his bosom, and was unto him as a daughter." (2 Sam. xii. 3.) Bosom friend, *amie du cœur*. St. John is represented in the New Testament as the "bosom friend" of Jesus.

Bosom Sermons. Written sermons, not extemporary ones or from notes. Does it not mean committed to memory or learnt by heart ?

"The preaching from 'bosom sermons,' or from writing, being considered a lifeless practice before the Reformation."—*Blunt : Reformation in England*, p. 179.

Bosphorus=Ox ford. The Thracian Bosphorus, or Bosporus, unites the Sea of Marmŏra with the Euxine (2 syl.) or Black Sea. According to Greek fable, Zeus (Jupiter) greatly loved Io, and changed her into a white cow or heifer from fear of Hera or Juno ; to flee from whom she swam across the strait, which was thence called *bos poros*, the passage of the cow. Hera discovered the trick, and sent a gadfly to torment Io, who was made to wander, in a state of phrenzy, from land to land. The wanderings of Io were a favourite subject of story with the ancients. Ultimately, the persecuted Argive princess found rest on the banks of the Nile.

Dionysius of Halicarnassus and *Valerius Flaccus* give this account, but Accarion says it was a ship, with the prow of an ox, sent by some Thracians through the straits, that gave name to this passage.

Boss, a master, is the Dutch *baas*, head of the household. Hence the great man, chief, a masher, a swell.

"Mr. Stead calls Mr. O'Connor the 'Boss of the House.'"

Bossum. One of the two chief deities of the negroes on the Gold Coast, the other being Demonio. Bossum, the principle of good, is said to be *white ;* and Demonio, the principle of evil, black. (*African mythology*.)

Bostal or *Borstall*. A narrow road-way up the steep ascent of hills or downs. (Anglo-Saxon *biorh*, a hill ; *stigelĕ*, a rising path ; our *stile*.)

Bot'anomancy. Divination by leaves. Words were written on leaves which were exposed to the wind. The leaves left contained the response. (*See* BOTANY.)

Bot'any means a treatise on fodder (Greek, *bot'ănē*, fodder, from *boskein*, to feed). The science of plants would be "phytol'ogy," from *phyton-logos* (plant-treatise).

Botch. A patch. *Botch* and *patch* are the same word ; the older form was *bodge*, whence *boggle*. (Italian *pezzo*, pronounced *patzo*.)

Bother, *i.e. pother* (Hibernian). Halliwell gives us *blother*, which he says means to chatter idly.

"'Sir,' cries the umpire, 'cease your pother,
The creature's neither one nor t'other.'"
    Lloyd : The Chameleon.

⁂ The Irish *bódhar* (*buaidhirt*, trouble), or its cognate verb, to deafen, seems to be the original word.

Bothie System. The Scotch system of building, like a barrack, all the out-houses of a farmstead, as the byres, stables, barns, etc. The farm men-servants live here. (Gaelic, *bothag*, a cot or hut, our *booth*.)

"The bothie system prevails, more or less, in the eastern and north-eastern districts."—*J. Begg, D.D.*

Botley Assizes. The joke is to ask a Botley man, "When the assizes are coming on ?" and an innuendo is supposed to be implied in the tradition that the men of Botley once hanged a man because he could not drink so deep as his neighbours.

Bottes. *A propos de bottes.* By the by, thus : *Mais, Mons., à propos de bottes, comment se porte madame votre mère ?*

"That venerable personage [the Chaldæan Charon] not only gives Izdubar instructions how to regain his health, but tells him, somewhat *a propos des bottes* . . . the long story of his perfidious adventure."—*Nineteenth Century*, June, 1891, p. 911.

Bottle. *Looking for a needle in a bottle of hay.* Looking for a very small article amidst a mass of other things. Bottle is a diminutive of the French -*botte*, a bundle; as *botte de foin*, a bundle of hay.

Hang me in a bottle. (*See* CAT.)

Bottle-chart. A chart of ocean surface currents to show the track of sealed bottles thrown from ships into the sea.

Bottle-holder. One who gives moral but not material support. The allusion is to boxing or prize-fighting, where each combatant has a bottle-holder to wipe off blood, refresh with water, and do other services to encourage his man to persevere and win.

"Lord Palmerston considered himself the bottle-holder of oppressed States. . . . He was the steadfast partisan of constitutional liberty in every part of the world."—*The Times.*

Bottle-imps. The Hebrew word for familiar spirits is *oboth*, leather bottles, to indicate that the magicians were wont to imprison in bottles those spirits which their spells had subdued.

Bottle-washer (*Head*). Chief agent; the principal man employed by another; a factotum. Head waiter or butler (*botteller*).

Bottled Beer is said to have been discovered by Dean Nowell as a most excellent beverage. The Dean was very fond of fishing, and took a bottle of beer with him in his excursions. One day, being disturbed, he buried his bottle under the grass, and when he disinterred it some ten days afterwards, found it so greatly improved that he ever after drank bottled beer.

Bottled Moonshine. Social and benevolent schemes, such as Utopia, Coleridge's Pantisocracy, the dreams of Owen, Fourier, St. Simon, the New Republic, and so on.

"Godwin! Hazlitt! Coleridge! Where now are their 'novel philosophies and systems'? Bottled moonshine, which does not improve by keeping."—*Birrell: Obiter Dicta,* p. 109 (1885).

Bottom.
A ship's bottom is that part which is used for freight or stowage.

Goods imported in British bottoms are those which come in our own vessels.

Goods imported in foreign bottoms are those which come in foreign ships.

A full bottom is where the lower half of the hull is so disposed as to allow large stowage.

A sharp bottom is when a ship is capable of speed.

At bottom. Radically, fundamentally: as, the young prodigal lived a riotous life, but was good at bottom, or below the surface.

At the bottom. At the base or root.

"Pride is at the bottom of all great mistakes." —*Ruskin: True and Beautiful,* p. 426.

From the bottom of my heart. Without reservation. (*Imo corde.*)

"If one of the parties . . . be content to forgive from the bottom of his heart all that the other hath trespassed against him."—*Common Prayer Book.*

He was at the bottom of it. He really instigated it, or prompted it.

Never venture all in one bottom—i.e. one ship. "Do not put all your eggs into one basket."

"My ventures are not in one bottom trusted."— *Shakespeare: Merchant of Venice,* i. 1.

To have no bottom. To be unfathomable.

To get to the bottom of the matter. To ascertain the entire truth; to bolt a matter to its bran.

To stand on one's own bottom. To be independent. "Every tub must stand on its own bottom."

To touch bottom. To reach the lowest depth.

A horse of good bottom means of good stamina, good foundation.

Bottom (*Nick*), *the weaver.* A man who fancies he can do everything, and do it better than anyone else. Shakespeare has drawn him as profoundly ignorant, brawny, mock heroic, and with an overflow of self-conceit. He is in one part of *Midsummer Night's Dream* represented with an ass's head, and Titania, queen of the fairies, under a spell, caresses him as an Ado'nis.

⁂ The name is very appropriate, as the word *bottom* means a ball of thread used in weaving, etc. Thus in Clark's *Heraldry* we read, "The coat of Badland is *argent*, three bottoms in fess *gules*, the thread *or*."

"When Goldsmith, jealous of the attention which a dancing monkey attracted, said, 'I can do that,' he was but playing Bottom."—*R. G. White.*

Bottomless. *The bottomless pit.* An allusion to William Pitt, who was remarkably thin.

Botty. Conceited. The frog that tried to look as big as an ox was a "botty" frog (*Norfolk*). A similar word is "swell," though not identical in meaning. "Bumpkin" and "bumptious" are of similar construction. (Welsh, *bot*, a round body, our *bottle; both*, the boss of a shield; *bothel*, a rotundity.)

Boucan. *Donner un boucan.* To give a dance. Boucan or Bocan was a musician and dancing master in the middle of the seventeenth century. He was alive in 1645.

"Thibaut se dit estre Mercure,
Et l'orgueilleux Colin nous jure
Qu'il est aussi bien Apollon
Que Boccan est bon violon."
Sieur de St. Amant (1661).

"Les musiciens qui jouent au ballet du roi sont appelés 'disciples de Bocan.'"—*Histoire Comique de Francion* (1655).

Bouders or *Boudons*. A tribe of giants and evil genii, the guard of Shiva. (*Indian mythology*.)

Boudoir, properly speaking, is the room to which a lady retires when she is in the sulks. (French, *bouder*, to pout or sulk.)

The first boudoirs were those of the mistresses of Louis XV. (*See* BOWER.)

Boues de St. Amand (*Les*). The mud baths of St. Amand (that is, St. Amand-les-Eaux, near Valenciennes, famous for its mineral waters). These mud-baths are a "*sorte de limon qui se trouve près des eaux minérales.*" By a figure of speech, one says, by way of reproof, to an insolent, foul-mouthed fellow, "I see you have been to the mud-baths of St. Amand."

Bought and Sold, or *Bought, sold, and done for.* Ruined, done for, outwitted.

"Jocky of Norfolk, be not too bold,
For Diccon, thy master, is bought and sold."
　　　　Shakespeare: Richard III., act v. 3.

"It would make a man mad as a buck to be so bought and sold."—*Comedy of Errors*, iii. 1.

Bougie. A wax candle; so called from Bougiah, in Algeria, whence the wax was imported. A medical instrument used for dilating strictures or removing obstructions.

Boule or *Boule-work* (not Buhl). A kind of marquetry; so called from André Charles Boule, a cabinetmaker, to whom Louis XIV. gave apartments in the Louvre. (1642-1732.)

Boul'janus. An idol worshipped at Nantes, in ancient Gaul. An inscription was found to this god in 1592. (*Celtic mythology*.)

Bouncer. *That's a bouncer.* A gross exaggeration, a braggart's lie. (Dutch, *bonz*, verb *bonzen*, to bounce or thump. A *bouncing* lie is a *thumping* lie, and a *bouncer* is a *thumper*.)

"He speaks plain cannon, fire, and smoke, and bounce."—*Shakespeare: King John*, ii. 2.

Bounty. *Queen Anne's Bounty.* The produce of the first-fruits and tenths due to the Crown, made over by Queen Anne to a corporation established in the year 1704, for the purpose of augmenting church livings under £50 a year.

Bouquet. French for nosegay.

"Mr. Disraeli was able to make a financial statement burst into a bouquet of flowers."—*McCarthy: Our Own Times*, vol. iii. chap. xxx. p. 11.

The bouquet of wine, also called its nosegay, is its aro'ma.

Bourbon. So named from the castle and seigniory of Bourbon, in the old

provin e of Bourbonnais. The *Bourbon family* is a branch of the Cap'et stock, throug 1 the brother of Philippe le Bel.

Bourgeois (French), our burgess. The class between the "gentleman" and the peasantry. It includes all merchants, shopkeepers, and what we call the "middle class."

Bourgeoisie (French). The merchants, manufacturers, and master-tradesmen considered as a class. *Citoyen* is a freeman, a citizen of the State; *bourgeois*, an individual of the Bourgeoisie class. Molière has a comedy entitled *Le Bourgeois Gentilhomme.*

"The commons of England, the Tiers-Etat of France, the bourgeoisie of the Continent generally, are the descendants of this class [artisans] generally."—*Mill: Political Economy* (Prelim. p. 12).

Bouse. (*See* BOOZY.)

Boustrap'a. Napoleon III. The word is compounded of the first syllables *Bou*-logne, *Stra*-sbourg, *Pa*-ris, and alludes to his escapades in 1836 and 1840.

Boustroph'edon. A method of writing or printing, alternately from right to left and left to right, like the path of oxen in ploughing. (Greek, *bous-strepho*, ox-turning.)

Bouts-rimés [*rhymed-endings*]. A person writes a line and gives the last word to another person, who writes a second to rhyme with it, and so on. Dean Swift employs the term for a poem, each stanza of which terminates with the same word. He has given a poem of nine verses, each of which ends with Domitilla, to which, of course, he finds nine rhymes. (French.)

Bovey Coal. A lignite found at Bovey Tracy, in Devonshire.

Bow (to rhyme with *flow*). (Anglo-Saxon, *boga;* verb, *bogan* or *bugan*, to arch.)

Draw not your bow till your arrow is fixed. Have everything ready before you begin.

He has a famous bow up at the castle. Said of a braggart or pretender.

He has two strings to his bow. Two means of accomplishing his object; if one fails, he can try the other. The allusion is to the custom of the British bowmen carrying a reserve string in case of accident.

To draw a bow at a venture. To attack with a random remark; to make a random remark which may hit the truth.

"A certain man drew a bow at a venture and smote the King of Israel."—1 Kings xxii. 34.

To draw the long bow. To exaggerate. The long-bow was the famous English weapon till gunpowder was introduced, and it is said that a good archer could hit between the fingers of a man's hand at a considerable distance, and could propel his arrow a mile. The tales told about long-bow adventures are so wonderful that they fully justify the phrase given above.

To unstring the bow will not heal the wound (Italian). René of Anjou, king of Sicily, on the death of his wife, Isabeau of Lorraine, adopted the emblem of a bow with the string broken, and with the words given above for the motto, by which he meant, " Lamentation for the loss of his wife was but poor satisfaction."

Bow (to rhyme with *now*). The fore-end of a boat or ship. (Danish and Norwegian, *boug* or *bov*, a shoulder; Icelandic, *bogr*.)

On the bow. Within a range of 45° on one side or the other of the prow.

Bow Bells. *Born within sound of Bow bells.* A true cockney. St. Mary-le-Bow has long had one of the most celebrated bell-peals in London. John Dun, mercer, gave in 1472 two tenements to maintain the ringing of Bow bell every night at nine o'clock, to direct travellers on the road to town ; and in 1520 William Copland gave a bigger bell for the purpose of " sounding a retreat from work." Bow church is nearly the centre of the City. (This *bow* rhymes with *flow*.)

Bow-catcher (*A*). A corruption of " Beau Catcher," a love-curl, termed by the French an *accroche cœur*. A love-curl worn by a man is a Bell-rope, *i.e.* a rope to pull the *belles* with.

Bow-hand. The left hand ; the hand which holds the bow. (This *bow* rhymes with *flow*.)

To be too much of the bow-hand. To fail in a design ; not be sufficiently dexterous.

Bow-street Runners. Detectives who scoured the country to find criminals, before the introduction of the police force. Bow Street, near Covent Garden, London, is where the principal police-court stands. (This *bow* rhymes with *flow*.)

Bow-window in Front (*A*) A big corporation.

" He was a very large man, . . . with what is termed a considerable bow-window in front."— *Capt. Marryat: Poor Jack,* i.

Bow-wow Word. A word in imitation of the sound made, as hiss, cackle, murmur, cuckoo, whip-poor-will, etc. (Max Müller.)

Bowden. *Not every man can be vicar of Bowden.* Not everyone can occupy the first place. Bowden is one of the best livings in Cheshire. (*Cheshire proverb.*)

Bowdlerise (*To*). To expurgate a book in editing it. Thomas Bowdler, in 1818, gave to the world an expurgated edition of Shakespeare's works. We have also Bowdlerite, Bowdlerist, Bowdleriser, Bowdlerism, Bowdlerisation, etc. (*See* GRANGERISE.)

Bowels of Mercy. Compassion, sympathy. The affections were at one time supposed to be the outcome of certain secretions or organs, as the bile, the kidneys, the heart, the head, the liver, the bowels, the spleen, and so on. Hence such words and phrases as *melancholy* (black bile) ; the Psalmist says that his *reins*, or kidneys, instructed him (Psa. x. 7), meaning his inward conviction ; the *head* is the seat of understanding ; the *heart* of affection and memory (hence "learning by heart"), the *bowels* of mercy, the *spleen* of passion or anger, etc.

His bowels yearned over him (*upon* or *towards him*). He felt a secret affection for him.

" Joseph made haste, for his bowels did yearn upon his brother."—Gen. xliii. 30 ; see also 1 Kings iii. 26.

Bower. A lady's private room. (Anglo-Saxon *bur*, a chamber.) (To rhyme with *flower*.) (*See* BOUDOIR.)

" By a back staircase she slipped to her own bower."—*Bret Harte : Thankful Blossoms,* part ii.

Bower Anchor. An anchor carried at the bow of a ship. There are two : one called the *best bower*, and the other the *small bower*. (To rhyme with *flower*.)

" Starboard being the best bower, and port the small bower."—*Smyth : Sailor's Word-book.*

Bower-woman (*A*). A lady's maid and companion. The attendants were admitted to considerable freedom of speech, and were treated with familiarity and kindness. (" Bower " to rhyme with *flower*.)

" ' This maiden,' replied Eveline, ' is my bower-woman, and acquainted with my most inward thoughts. I beseech you to permit her presence at our conference.' "—*Sir W. Scott : The Betrothed,* chap. xi.

Bower of Bliss, in Wandering Island, the enchanted residence of Acra-sia, destroyed by Sir Guyon. (*Spenser : Faërie Queene,* book ii.) (" Bower " to rhyme with *flower*.)

Bowie Knife. A long, stout knife, carried by hunters in the Western States of America. So called from Colonel James Bowie, one of the most daring characters of the States. Born in Logan, co. Kentucky. A bowie knife has a horn handle, and the curved blade is 15 in. long, and 1¼ wide at the hilt. ("Bowie" to rhyme with *showy*.)

Bowing. We uncover the head when we wish to salute anyone with respect; but the Jews, Turks, Siamese, etc., uncover their feet. The reason is this: With us the chief act of investiture is crowning or placing a cap on the head; but in the East it is putting on the slippers. To take off our symbol of honour is to confess we are but "the humble servant" of the person whom we thus salute. ("Bowing" to rhyme with *ploughing* or *plowing*.)

Bowled. *He was bowled out.* A term in cricket. (Pronounce *bold*.)

Bowling. *Tom Bowling.* The type of a model sailor in Smollett's *Roderick Random.* (To rhyme with *rolling*.)
⁂ The Tom Bowling referred to in Dibdin's famous sea-song was Captain Thomas Dibdin, brother of Charles Dibdin, who wrote the song, and father of Dr. Dibdin, the bibliomaniac.

"Here a sheer hulk lies poor Tom Bowling,
The darling of the crew."   *Dibdin.*

Bowls. *They who play bowls must expect to meet with rubbers.* Those who touch pitch must expect to defile their fingers. Those who enter upon affairs of chance, adventure, or dangerous hazard must make up their minds to encounter crosses, losses, or difficulties. Those who play with edged instruments must expect to get cut. Soldiers in battle must look out for wounds, gamblers for losses, libertines for diseases.
⁂ "Bowls" to rhyme with *rolls.*

Bowse. (*See* BROWSE.)

Bowyer God. The same as the "archer god," meaning Cupid. ("Bower" to rhyme with *grower*.)

Box. *I've got into the wrong box.* I am out of my element. Lord Lyttelton used to say he ought to have been brought up to some business; that whenever he went to Vauxhall and heard the mirth of his neighbours, he used to fancy pleasure was in every box but his own. Wherever he went for happiness, he somehow always got into the wrong box. (*See* CHRISTMAS BOX.)

6*

Box and Cox. The two chief characters in John M. Morton's farce, usually called *Box and Cox.*

Box the Compass. Repeat in order the 32 points. (Spanish, *boxar*, to sail round.)

Box Days. Two days in spring and autumn, and one at Christmas, during vacation, in which pleadings may be filed. This custom was established in 1690, for the purpose of expediting business. Each judge has a private box with a slit, into which informations may be placed on box days, and the judge, who alone has the key, examines the papers in private.

Box Harry (*To*), among commercial travellers, is to shirk the *table d'hôte* and take something substantial for tea, in order to save expense. Halliwell says, "to take care after having been extravagant." To box a tree is to cut the bark to procure the sap, and these travellers drain the landlord by having a cheap tea instead of an expensive dinner. To "box the fox" is to rob an orchard.

Boxing-Day. (*See* CHRISTMAS BOX.)

Boy in sailor language has no reference to age, but only to experience in seamanship. A boy may be fifty or any other age. A crew is divided into able seamen, ordinary seamen, and boys or greenhorns. A "boy" is not required to know anything about the practical working of the vessel, but an "able seaman" must know all his duties and be able to perform them.
"A boy does not ship to know anything."

Boy Bachelor. William Wotton, D.D., was admitted at St. Catherine's Hall before he was ten, and took his B.A. when he was twelve and a half. (1666-1726.)

Boy Bishop. St. Nicholas. From his cradle he is said to have manifested marvellous indications of piety, and was therefore selected for the patron saint of boys. (Fourth century.)
Boy Bishop. The custom of choosing a boy from the cathedral choir, etc., on St. Nicholas Day (December 6th), as a mock bishop, is very ancient. The boy possessed episcopal honour for three weeks, and the rest of the choir were his prebendaries. If he died during the time of his prelacy, he was buried *in pontifica'libus*. Probably the reference is to Jesus Christ sitting in the Temple among the doctors while He was a boy. The

custom was abolished in the reign of Henry VIII.

Boy in buttons (*A*). (*See* BUTTONS.)

Boycott (*To*). *To boycott a person* is to refuse to deal with him, to take any notice of him, or even to sell to him. The term arose in 1881, when Captain Boycott, an Irish landlord, was thus ostracised by the Irish agrarian insurgents. The custom of ostracising is of very old standing. St. Paul exhorts Christians to "boycott" idolaters (2 Cor. vi. 17); and the Jews "boycotted" the Samaritans. The French phrases, *Damner une boutique* and *Damner une ville*, convey the same idea; and the Catholic Church anathematises and interdicts freely.

"One word as to the way in which a man should be boycotted. When any man has taken a farm from which a tenant has been evicted, or is a grabber, let everyone in the parish turn his back on him; have no communication with him; have no dealings with him. You need never say an unkind word to him; but never say anything at all to him. If you must meet him in fair, walk away from him silently. Do him no violence, but have no dealings with him. Let every man's door be closed against him; and make him feel himself a stranger and a castaway in his own neighbourhood."—*J. Dillon, M.P.* (*Speech to the Land League*, Feb. 26, 1881).

Boyle Controversy. A book-battle between the Hon. Charles Boyle, third Earl of Orrery, and the famous Bentley, respecting the *Epistles of Phal'aris*. Charles Boyle edited the *Epistles of Phalaris* in 1695. Two years later Bentley published his celebrated *Dissertation*, to prove that the epistles were not written till the second century after Christ instead of six centuries before that epoch. In 1699 he published another rejoinder, and utterly annihilated the Boyleists.

Boyle's Law. "The volume of a gas is inversely as the pressure." If we double the pressure on a gas, its volume is reduced to one-half; if we quadruple the pressure, it will be reduced to one-fourth; and so on; so called from the Hon. Robert Boyle. (1627-1691.)

Boyle Lectures. Eight sermons a year in defence of Christianity, founded by the Hon. Robert Boyle.

Boz. Charles Dickens (1812-1870).

"Boz, my signature in the *Morning Chronicle*," he tells us, "was the nickname of a pet child, a younger brother, whom I had dubbed Moses, in honour of the *Vicar of Wakefield*, which, being pronounced *Bozes*, got shortened into *Boz*."

"Who the dickens ' Boz' could be
Puzzled many a learned elf;
But time revealed the mystery,
For ' Boz' appeared as Dickens' self."
Epigram in the Carthusian.

Bozzy. James Boswell, the biographer of Dr. Johnson (1740-1795).

Brabançonne. A Belgian patriotic song, composed in the revolution of 1830, and so named from Brabant, of which Brussels is the chief city.

Brabançons. Troops of adventurers and bandits, who made war a trade and lent themselves for money to anyone who would pay them; so called from Brabant, their great nest. (Twelfth century.)

Brace. *The Brace Tavern*, southeast corner of King's Bench; originally kept by two brothers named Partridge, *i.e.* a brace of birds.

Brace of Shakes. *In a brace of shakes.* Very soon. (*See* SHAKES.) Similar phrases are: "In the twinkling of an eye." (*See* EYE.) "In the twinkling of a bed-post." (*See* BED-POST.)

Brad amant or *Bradaman'te*. Sister of Rinaldo, in Ariosto's *Orlando Furioso.* She is represented as a most wonderful Christian Am'azon, possessed of an irresistible spear, which unhorsed every knight that it touched. The same character appears in the *Orlando Innamora'to* of Bojardo.

Bradshaw's Guide was started in 1839 by George Bradshaw, printer, in Manchester. The *Monthly Guide* was first issued in December, 1841, and consisted of thirty-two pages, giving tables of forty-three lines of English railway.

Brad'wardine (*Rose*). The daughter of Baron Bradwardine, and the heroine of Scott's *Waverley*. She is in love with young Waverley, and ultimately marries him.

Brag. A game at cards: so called because the players brag of their cards to induce the company to make bets. The principal sport of the game is occasioned by any player *bragging* that he holds a better hand than the rest of the party, which is declared by saying "I brag," and staking a sum of money on the issue. (*Hoyle.*)

Brag is a good dog, but Holdfast is a better. Talking is all very well, but doing is far better.

Jack Brag. A vulgar, pretentious braggart, who gets into aristocratic society, where his vulgarity stands out in strong relief. The character is in Theodore Hook's novel of the same name.

"He was a sort of literary Jack Brag."—*T. H. Burton.*

Braggado'chio. A braggart. One who is very valiant with his tongue, but a great coward at heart. A barking dog that bites not. The character is from Spenser's *Faërie Queene*, and a type of the "Intemperance of the Tongue." After a time, like the jackdaw in borrowed plumes, Braggadochio is stripped of all his "glories": his shield is claimed by Sir Mar'inel; his lady is proved by the golden girdle to be the false Florimel; his horse is claimed by Sir Guyon; Talus shaves off his beard and scourges his squire; and the pretender sneaks off amidst the jeers of everyone. It is thought that the poet had Felipe of Spain in his eye when he drew this character. (*Faërie Queene*, iii. 8, 10; v. 3.)

Bra'gi. Son of Odin and Frigga. According to Scandinavian mythology, he was the inventor of poetry; but, unlike Apollo, he is always represented as an old man with a long white beard. His wife was Iduna.

Bragi's Apples. An instant cure of weariness, decay of power, ill temper, and failing health. These apples were inexhaustible, for immediately one was eaten its place was supplied by another.

Bragi's Story. Always enchanting, but never coming to an end.

"But I have made my story long enough; if I say more, you may fancy that it is Bragi who has come among you, and that he has entered on his endless story."—*Keary: Heroes of Asgard*, p. 224.

Bragmar'do. When Gargantua took the bells of Notre Dame de Paris to hang about the neck of his horse, the citizens sent Bragmardo to him with a remonstrance. (*Rabelais: Gargantua and Pantag'ruel.*)

Brah'ma (*Indian*). The self-existing and invisible Creator of the universe; represented with four heads looking to the four corners of the world. The divine triad is Brahma, Vishnu, and Siva.

Brahma. One of the three beings created by God to assist in the creation of the world. The Brahmins claim him as the founder of their religious system.

"Whate'er in India holds the sacred name
Of piety or lore, the Brahmins claim;
In wildest rituals, vain and painful, lost,
Brahma, their founder, as a god they boast."
　　　　　Camoens: Lusiad, book vii.

Brah'mi. One of the three goddess-daughters of Vishnu, representing "creative energy."

Brahmin. A worshipper of Brahma, the highest caste in the system of Hinduism, and of the priestly order.

Bramble (*Matthew*). A testy, gouty, benevolent, country squire, in Smollett's novel of *Humphrey Clinker*. Colman has introduced the same character as Sir Robert Bramble in his *Poor Gentleman*. Sheridan's "Sir Anthony Absolute" is of the same type.

"A'n't I a baronet? Sir Robert Bramble at Blackberry Hall, in the county of Kent? 'Tis time you should know it, for you have been my clumsy, two-fisted valet-de-chambre these thirty years."—*The Poor Gentleman*, iii. 1.

Bran. *If not Bran, it is Bran's brother.* If not the real "Simon Pure," it is just as good. A complimentary expression. Bran was Fingal's dog, a mighty favourite.

Bran-new or **Brand-new.** (Anglo-Saxon, *brand*, a torch.) Fire new. Shakespeare, in *Love's Labour Lost*, i. 1, says, "A man of fire-new words." And again in *Twelfth Night*, iii. 2, "Fire-new from the mint"; and again in *King Lear*, v. 3, "Fire-new fortune"; and again in *Richard III.*, act i. 3, "Your fire-new stamp of honour is scarce current." Originally applied to metals and things manufactured in metal which shine. Subsequently applied generally to things quite new.

Brand. *The Clicquot brand*, etc., *the best brand*, etc. That is the merchant's or excise mark branded on the article itself, the vessel which contains the article, the wrapper which covers it, the cork of the bottle, etc., to guarantee its being genuine, etc. Madame Clicquot, of champagne notoriety, died in 1866.

He has the brand of villain in his looks. It was once customary to brand the cheeks of felons with an **F**. The custom was abolished by law in 1822.

Brandenburg. *Confession of Brandenburg.* A formulary or confession of faith drawn up in the city of Brandenburg, by order of the elector, with the view of reconciling the tenets of Luther with those of Calvin, and to put an end to the disputes occasioned by the confession of Augsburg.

Bran'dimart, in *Orlando Furioso*, is Orlando's brother-in-law.

Brandon, the juggler, lived in the reign of Henry VIII.

Brandons. Lighted torches. *Dominica de brandonibus* (St. Valentine's Day), when boys used to carry about brandons (Cupid's torches).

Brandy is Latin for Goose. Here is a pun between *anser*, a goose, and *answer*, to reply. What is the Latin for

goose? Answer [*anser*] brandy. (*See*
TACE THE LATIN FOR CANDLE.)

Brandy Nan. Queen Anne, who
was very fond of brandy (1664, 1702-
1714). On the statue of Queen Anne
in St. Paul's Churchyard a wit wrote—

"Brandy Nan, Brandy Nan, left in the lurch,
 Her face to the gin-shop, her back to the
 church."

A "gin palace" used to stand at the
south corner of St. Paul's Churchyard.

Branghtons (*The*). Vulgar, malicious,
jealous women. The characters are taken
from Miss Burney's novel called *Evelina*.
One of the brothers is a Cockney snob.

Brank. A gag for scolds. (Dutch,
prang, a fetter; German, *pranger*, Gaelic,
brancas, a kind of pillory.)

Brasenose (Oxford). Over the gate
is a brass nose, the arms of the college;
but the word is a corruption of *brasen-
huis*, a brasserie or brewhouse. (Latin,
brasin'ium.)

Brass. Impudence. A lawyer said
to a troublesome witness, "Why, man,
you have brass enough in your head to
make a teakettle." "And you, sir,"
replied the witness, "have water enough
in yours to fill it."

Sampson Brass. A knavish attorney;
servile, affecting sympathy, but making
his clients his lawful prey. (*Dickens:
Old Curiosity Shop.*)

Brat. A child; so called from the
Welsh, *brat*, a child's pinafore; and *brat*
is a contraction of *brattach*, a cloth, also
a standard.

"Every man must repair to the brattach of his
 tribe."—*Scott.*
"O Israel! O household of the Lord!
 O Abraham's brats! O brood of blessed seed!"
          Gascoigne: De Profundis.

Brave. *The Brave.*
Alfonso IV. of Portugal (1290, 1324-
1357).
John Andr. van der Mersch, patriot,
The brave Fleming (1734-1792).

Bravery. Finery is the French *brave-
rie.* The French for courage is *bravoure.*

"What woman in the city do I name
 When that I say the city woman bears
 The cost of princes on unworthy shoulders?
 Who can come in and say that I mean her? . . .
 Or what is he of basest function
 That says his bravery is not of my cost?"
          Shakespeare: As You Like It, ii. 7.

Bravest of the Brave. Marshal
Ney. So called by the troops of Friedland (1807), on account of his fearless
bravery. Napoleon said of him, "That
man is a lion." (1769-1815.)

Brawn. *The test of the brawn's head.*
A little boy one day came to the court of
King Arthur, and, drawing his wand
over a boar's head, declared, "There's
never a cuckold's knife can carve this
head of brawn." No knight in the
court except Sir Cradock was able to
accomplish the feat. (*Percy's Reliques.*)

Bray. (*See* VICAR.)

Brazen Age. The age of war and
violence. It followed the silver age.

"To this next came in course the brazen age,
 A warlike offspring, prompt to bloody rage,
 Not impious yet. Hard steel succeeded then,
 And stubborn as the metal were the men."
          Dryden: Metamorphoses, i.

Brazen-faced. Bold (in a bad sense),
without shame.

"What a brazen-faced varlet art thou!"
          Shakespeare: King Lear, ii. 2.

Brazen Head. The following are
noted:—One by Albertus Magnus, which
cost him thirty years' labour, and was
broken into a thousand pieces by Thomas
Aqui'nas, his disciple. One by Friar
Bacon.

"Bacon trembled for his brazen head."
          Pope: Dunciad, iii. 104.
"Quoth he, 'My head's not made of brass,
 As Friar Bacon's noddle was.'"
          S. Butler: Hudibras, ii. 2.

The brazen head of the Marquis de
Ville'na, of Spain.
Another by a Polander, a disciple of
Escotillo, an Italian.

.'. It was said if Bacon heard his head
speak he would succeed; if not, he would
fail. Miles was set to watch, and while
Bacon slept the Head spoke thrice:
"Time is"; half an hour later it said,
"Time was." In another half-hour it
said, "Time's past," fell down, and was
broken to atoms. Byron refers to this
legend.

"Like Friar Bacon's brazen head, I've spoken,
 'Time is,' 'Time was,' 'Time's past.'"
          Don Juan, i. 217.

Brazen Head. A gigantic head kept
in the castle of the giant Fer'ragus, of
Portugal. It was omniscient, and told
those who consulted it whatever they
required to know, past, present, or to
come. (*Valentine and Orson.*)

Brazen out (*To*). To stick to an
assertion knowing it to be wrong; to
outface in a shameless manner; to disregard public opinion.

Breaches, meaning *creeks* or *small
bays*, is to be found in Judges v. 17.
Deborah, complaining of the tribes who
refused to assist her in her war with
Sisera, says Reuben continued in his
sheepfolds, Gilead remained beyond

Jordan, Dan in ships, and Asher in his breaches, that is, creeks on the sea-shore.

Bread. *To break bread.* To partake of food. Common in Scripture language. *Breaking of bread.* The Eucharist.

"They continued . . . in breaking of bread, and in prayers."—Acts ii. 42 ; and again verse 46.

Bread. *He took bread and salt, i.e.* he took his oath. Bread and salt were formerly eaten when an oath was taken.

Cast thy bread upon the waters: for thou shalt find it after many days (Eccles. xi. 1). When the Nile overflows its banks the weeds perish and the soil is disintegrated. The rice-seed being cast into the water takes root, and is found in due time growing in healthful vigour.

Don't quarrel with your bread and butter. Don't foolishly give up the pursuit by which you earn your living.

To know which side one's bread is buttered. To be mindful of one's own interest.

To take the bread out of one's mouth. To forestall another ; to say something which another was on the point of saying ; to take away another's livelihood. (*See under* BUTTER.)

Bread-basket (*One's*). The stomach.

Bread and Cheese. The barest necessities of life.

Break (*To*). To become a bankrupt. (*See* BANKRUPT.)

To break a bond. To dishonour it.

To break a journey. To stop before the journey is accomplished.

To break a matter to a person. To be the first to impart it, and to do so cautiously and by piecemeal.

To break bread. To partake of the Lord's Supper.

"Upon the first day of the week, when the disciples came together to break bread, Paul preached to them."—Acts xx. 7.

To break one's fast. To take food after long abstinence ; to eat one's breakfast after the night's fast.

To break one's neck. To dislocate the bones of one's neck.

To break on the wheel. To torture one on a "wheel" by breaking the long bones with an iron bar. (*Cf.* COUP DE GRÂCE.)

To break a butterfly on a wheel. To employ superabundant effort in the accomplishment of a small matter.

"Satire or sense, alas ! can Sporus feel,
Who breaks a butterfly upon a wheel."
Pope : Epistle to Dr. Arbuthnot, 307-8.

To break out of bounds. To go beyond the prescribed limits.

Break Cover (*To*). To start forth from a hiding-place.

Break Down (*To*). To lose all control of one's feelings.

Break Faith (*To*). To violate one's word or pledge.

Break Ground (*To*). To commence a new project. As a settler does.

Break In (*To*). To interpose a remark. To train a horse to the saddle or to harness.

Break of Day. Day-break.

"'At break of day I will come to thee again."
Wordsworth : Pet Lamb, stanza 15.

Break the Ice (*To*). To prepare the way ; to cause the stiffness and reserve of intercourse with a stranger to relax ; to impart to another bit by bit distressing news or a delicate subject.

Break your Back (*To*). Make you bankrupt. The metaphor is from carrying burdens on the back.

Break up Housekeeping (*To*). To discontinue keeping a separate house.

Break with One (*To*). To cease from intercourse.

"What cause have I given him to break with me ?"—*Florence Marryat.*

Breakers Ahead. Hidden danger at hand. Breakers in the open sea always announce sunken rocks, sand-banks, etc.

Breaking a Stick. Part of the marriage ceremony of the American Indians, as breaking a wine-glass is part of the marriage ceremony of the Jews. (*Lady Augusta Hamilton : Marriage Rites,* etc., 292, 298.)

In one of Raphael's pictures we see an unsuccessful suitor of the Virgin Mary breaking his stick. This alludes to the legend that the several suitors were each to bring an almond stick, which was to be laid up in the sanctuary over-night, and the owner of the stick which budded was to be accounted the suitor which God approved of. It was thus that Joseph became the husband of Mary. (*Pseudo-Matthew's Gospel,* 40, 41.)

In Florence is a picture in which the rejected suitors break their sticks on Joseph's back.

Breast. *To make a clean breast of it.* To make a full confession ; concealing nothing.

Breath. *All in a breath.* Without taking breath. (Latin, *continenti spiritu.*)

It takes away one's breath. The news is so astounding it causes one to hold his breath with surprise.

Out of breath. Panting from exertion; temporarily short of breath.

Save your breath to cool your porridge. Don't talk to me, it is only wasting your breath.

" You might have saved your breath to cool your porridge."—*Mrs. Gaskell: Libbie Marsh* (Era 111).

To catch one's breath. To check suddenly the free act of breathing.

"'I see her,' replied I, catching my breath with joy."—*Capt. Marryat: Peter Simple.*

To hold one's breath. Voluntarily to cease breathing for a time.

To take breath. To cease for a little time from some exertion in order to recover from exhaustion of breath.

Under one's breath. In a whisper or undertone of voice.

Breathe. *To breathe one's last.* To die.

Brèche de Roland. A deep defile in the crest of the Pyrenees, some three hundred feet in width, between two precipitous rocks. The legend is that Roland, the paladin, cleft the rock in two with his sword Durandal, when he was set upon by the Gascons at Roncesvalles.

" Then would I seek the Pyrenean breach
    Which Roland clove with huge two-handed
    sway."   *Wordsworth.*

Breeches. *To wear the breeches.* Said of a woman who usurps the prerogative of her husband. Similar to *The grey mare is the better horse.* (*See* GREY.)

The phrase is common to the French, Dutch, Germans, etc., as *Elle porte les braies. Die vrouw die hosen anhaben. Sie hat die Hösen.*

Breeches Bible. (*See* BIBLE.)

Breeze. House-sweepings, as fluff, dust, ashes, and so on, thrown as refuse into the dust-bin. We generally limit the meaning now to small ashes and cinders used for coals in burning bricks. The word is a corruption of the French, *débris* (rubbish, or rather the part broken or rubbed off by wear, tear, and stress of weather). The French, *braise,* older form *brese,* means small coke or charcoal.

The Breeze-fly. The gad-fly; so called from its sting. (Anglo-Saxon, *briôse;* Gothic, *bry,* a sting.)

Breeze. A gentle wind or gale. (French, *brise,* a breeze.) Figuratively, a slight quarrel.

Breidablik [*wide - shining*]. The palace of Baldur, which stood in the Milky Way. (*Scandinavian mythology.*)

Brennus. A Latin form of the Kymric word *Brenhin* (a war-chief). In times of danger the Druids appointed a *brenn* to lead the confederate tribes to battle.

Brent. Without a wrinkle. Burns says of John Anderson, in his prime of life, his "locks were like the raven," and his "bonnie brow was brent" (without a wrinkle).

Brent-goose (*A*). Properly a *brant-goose,* the *branta bernicla,* a brownish-grey goose of the genus *branta.*

" For the people of the village
    Saw the flock of brant with wonder."
    Longfellow: Hiawatha, part xvi. stanza 32.

Brent-hill means the eyebrows.

Looking or *gazing from under brent-hill.* In Devonshire means "frowning at one;" and in West Cornwall *to brend* means to wrinkle the brows. It is very remarkable that the word should have such opposite meanings.

Brentford. *Like the two kings of Brentford smelling at one nosegay.* Said of persons who were once rivals, but have become reconciled. The allusion is to an old farce called *The Rehearsal,* by the Duke of Buckingham. "The two kings of Brentford enter hand in hand," and the actors, to heighten the absurdity, used to make them enter "smelling at one nosegay" (act ii. s. 2).

Bressommer, or *Brest-summer.* (French, *sommier,* a lintel or bressummer.) A beam supporting the whole weight of the building above it; as, the beam over a shop-front, the beam extending over an opening through a wall when a communication between two contiguous rooms is required. Sometimes these beams support a large superstructure. (The word *bress, brest,* or *breast,* in carpentry, means a rafter, and the German *brett* = a plank.)

Bretwalda (*ruler of Britain*). The chief of the kings of the heptarchy who exercised a certain undefined power over the other rulers; something like that of Hugues Cap'et over his peers.

"The office of Bretwalda, a kind of elective chieftainship, of all Britain, was held by several Northumbrian kings, in succession."—*Earle: English Tongue,* p. 26.

Brevet Rank is rank one degree higher than your pay. Thus, a brevet-major has the title of major, but the pay of captain. (French, *brevet*, a patent, a concession.)

Breviary. An epitome of the old office of matins and lauds for daily service in the Roman Catholic Church. The Breviary contains the daily "Divine Office," which those in orders in the Catholic Church are bound to recite. The office consists of psalms, collects, readings from Scripture, and the life of some saint or saints.

Brew. *Brew me a glass of grog, i.e.* mix one for me. *Brew me a cup of tea, i.e.* make one for me. *The tea is set to brew, i.e.* to draw. The general meaning of the word is to boil or mix ; the restricted meaning is to make malt liquor.

Brewer. *The Brewer of Ghent.* James van Artevelde. (Fourteenth century.)

It may here be remarked that it is a great error to derive proper names of any antiquity from modern words of a similar sound or spelling. As a rule, very few ancient names are the names of trades ; and to suppose that such words as Bacon, Hogg, and Pigg refer to swineherds, or Gaiter, Miller, Tanner, Ringer, and Bottles to handicrafts, is a great mistake. A few examples of a more scientific derivation will suffice for a hint :—

BREWER. This name, which exists in France as Bruhière and Brugière, is not derived from the Saxon *briwan* (to brew), but the French *bruyère* (heath), and is about tantamount to the German "Plantagenet" (*broom-plant*). (*See* Rymer's *Fœdera*, William I.)

BACON is from the High German verb *bagan* (to fight), and means "the fighter."

PIGG and BIGG are from the old High German *pichan* (to slash).

HOGG is the Anglo-Saxon *hyge* (scholar), from the verb *hogan* (to study). In some cases it may be from the German *hoch* (high).

BOTTLE is the Anglo-Saxon *Bod'-el* (little envoy). Norse, *bodi ;* Danish, *bud.*

GAITER is the Saxon *Gaid er* (the darter). Celtic, *gais,* our *goad.*

MILLER is the old Norse, *melia,* our *mill* and *maul,* and means a "mauler" or "fighter."

RINGER is the Anglo-Saxon *hring gar* (the mailed warrior).

SMITH is the man who smites.

TANNER (German *Thanger,* old German *Danegaud*) is the Dane-Goth.

This list might easily be extended.

Briar'eos or *Æge'on.* A giant with fifty heads and a hundred hands. Homer says the gods called him Briar'eos, but men called him Ægeon. (*Iliad,* i. 403.)

" Not he who brandished in his hundred hands
His fifty swords and fifty shields in fight,
Could have surpassed the fierce Argantes'
might."
Tasso: Jerusalem Delivered, book vii.

The Briareus of languages. Cardinal Mezzofanti, who knew fifty-eight different tongues. Byron called him "a walking polyglot ; a monster of languages ; a Briareus of parts of speech." (1774 - 1849.) Generally pronounced *Bri-a-ruce.*

Bold Briareus. Handel (1685-1756).

Briar-root Pipe. A pipe made from the root-wood of the large heath(*bruyère*), which grows in the south of France.

Bribo'ci. Inhabitants of part of Berkshire and the adjacent counties referred to by Cæsar in his *Commentaries.*

Bric-à-brac. Odds and ends of curiosities. In French, a *marchand de bric-à-brac* is a seller of rubbish, as old nails, old screws, old hinges, and other odds and ends of small value ; but we employ the phrase for odds and ends of vertu. (*Bricoler* in archaic French means *Faire toute espèce de metier,* to be Jack of all trades. *Brac* is the ricochet of *bric,* as fiddle faddle and scores of other double words in English.)

" A man with a passion for bric-a-brac is always stumbling over antique bronzes, intaglios, mosaics, and daggers of the time of Benvenuto Cellini."—*Aldrich : Miss Mehetable's Son,* chap. ii.

Brick. *A regular brick.* A jolly good fellow. (Compare τετράγωνος ἀνήρ ; "square" ; and " four-square to all the winds that blow.")

" A fellow like nobody else, and, in fine, a brick."—*George Eliot: Daniel Deronda,* book ii. chap. 16.

Brick-and-mortar Franchise. A Chartist phrase for the £10 household system, now abolished.

Brickdusts. The 53rd Foot ; so called from the brickdust-red colour of their facings. Also called *Five-and-thre'pennies,* a play on the number and daily pay of the ensigns.

Now called the 1st battalion of the " King's Shropshire Light Infantry." The 2nd battalion is the old 85th.

Brick-tea. The inferior leaves of the tea-plant mixed with sheep's blood and pressed into cubes; the ordinary drink of the common people south of Moscow.

"The Tartars swill a horrible gruel, thick and slab, of brick-tea, suet, salt, pepper, and sugar, boiled in a chaldron (sic)."—*The Daily Telegraph*, Friday, October 16th, 1891.

Bride. *The bridal wreath* is a relic of the *coro'na nuptia'lis* used by the Greeks and Romans to indicate triumph.

Bride Cake. A relic of the Roman Confarrea'tio, a mode of marriage practised by the highest class in Rome. It was performed before ten witnesses by the Pon'tifex Max'imus, and the contracting parties mutually partook of a cake made of salt, water, and flour (*far*). Only those born in such wedlock were eligible for the high sacred offices.

Bride or Wedding Favours represent the *true lover's knot*, and symbolise union.

Bride of Aby'dos. Zuleika, daughter of Giaffir, Pacha of Aby'dos. As she was never wed, she should be called the affianced or betrothed. (*Byron*.)

Bride of Lammermoor. Lucy Ashton. (*Scott : Bride of Lammermoor*.)

Bride of the Sea. Venice; so called from the ancient ceremony of the Doge, who threw a ring into the Adriatic, saying, "We wed thee, O sea, in token of perpetual domination."

Bridegroom is the old Dutch *gom* (a young man). Thus, *Groom of the Stole* is the young man over the wardrobe. Groom, an ostler, is quite another word, being the Persian *garma* (a keeper of horses), unless, indeed, it is a contracted form of stable-groom (stable-boy). The Anglo-Saxon *Bryd-guma* (guma = man) confused with *groom*, a lad.

Bridegroom's Men. In the Roman marriage by *confarreatio*, the bride was led to the Pon'tifex Max'imus by bachelors, but was conducted home by married men. Polydore Virgil says that a married man preceded the bride on her return, bearing a vessel of gold and silver. (*See* BRIDE CAKE.)

Bridewell. The city Bridewell, Bridge Street, Blackfriars, was built over a holy well of medical water, called St. Bride's Well, where was founded a hospital for the poor. After the Reformation, Edward VI. chartered this hospital to the city. Christ Church was given to the education of the young; St. Thomas's Hospital to the cure of the sick; and Bridewell was made a penitentiary for unruly apprentices and vagrants.

Bridge of Gold. According to a German tradition, Charlemagne's spirit crosses the Rhine on a golden bridge at Bingen, in seasons of plenty, to bless the vineyards and cornfields.

" Thou standest, like imperial Charlemagne, Upon thy bridge of gold."
Longfellow : Autumn.

Made a bridge of gold for him ; i.e. enabling a man to retreat from a false position without loss of dignity.

Bridge of Jehennam. (*See* SERAT.)

Bridge of Sighs, which connects the palace of the Doge with the state prisons of Venice. Over this bridge the state prisoners were conveyed from the judgment-hall to the place of execution.

" I stood in Venice, on the Bridge of Sighs, A palace and a prison on each hand."
Byron : Childe Harold's Pilgrimage, iv. 1.

∵ Waterloo Bridge, in London, used, some years ago, when suicides were frequent there, to be called *The Bridge of Sighs*.

Bridgewater Treatises. Instituted by the Rev. Francis Henry Egerton, Earl of Bridgewater, in 1825. He left the interest of £8,000 to be given to the author of the best treatise on "The power, wisdom, and goodness of God, as manifested in creation." Eight are published by the following gentlemen :— (1) The Rev. Dr. Chalmers, (2) Dr. John Kidd, (3) the Rev. Dr. Whewell, (4) Sir Charles Bell, (5) Dr. Peter M. Roget, (6) the Rev. Dr. Buckland, (7) the Rev. W. Kirby, and (8) Dr. William Prout.

Bridle. *To bite on the bridle* is to suffer great hardships. The bridle was an instrument for punishing a scold ; to bite on the bridle is to suffer this punishment.

Bridle Road or **Way.** A way for a riding-horse, but not for a horse and cart.

Bridle up (*To*). In French, *se rengorger*, to draw in the chin and toss the head back in scorn or pride. The metaphor is to a horse pulled up suddenly and sharply.

Bridlegoose (*Judge*), or Bridoie, who decided the causes brought to him by the throw of dice. (*Rabelais : Gargantua and Pantag'ruel*, iii. 39.)

Bridport. *Stabbed with a Bridport dagger, i.e.* hanged. Bridport, in Dorsetshire, was once famous for its hempen goods, and monopolised the manufacture of ropes, cables, and tackling for the British navy. The hangman's rope being made at Bridport gave birth to the proverb. (*Fuller : Worthies.*)

Brig'adore (3 syl.). (*See* HORSE.)

Brigand properly means a seditious fellow. The *Brigands* were light-armed, irregular troops, like the Bashi-Bazouks, and like them were addicted to marauding. The *Free Companies* of France were Brigands. (Italian, *brigante*, seditious; *briga*, variance.)

Brigandine. The armour of a brigand, consisting of small plates of iron on quilted linen, and covered with leather, hemp, or something of the kind.

Brigantine (3 syl.) or *Hermaphrodite Brig.* A two-masted vessel with a brig's foremast and a schooner's mainmast. (*Dana's Seaman's Manual.*) A pirate vessel.

Bright's Disease. A degeneration of the tissues of the kidneys into fat, first investigated by Dr. Bright. The patient under this disease has a flabby, bloodless appearance, is always drowsy, and easily fatigued.

Brigians. The Castilians; so called from one of their ancient kings, named Brix or Brigus, said by monkish fabulists to be the grandson of Noah.

" Edward and Pedro, emulous of fame . . .
Thro' the fierce Brigians hewed their bloody
    way,
Till in a cold embrace the striplings lay."
            Camoens: Lusiad, v.

Brigliado'ro. (*See* HORSE.)

Brilliant Madman (*The*). Charles XII. of Sweden. (1682-1697-1718.)

"Macedonia's madman or the Swede."
        Johnson: Vanity of Human Wishes.

Briney or **Briny.** *I'm on the briny.* The sea, which is salt like brine.

Bring About (*To*). To cause a thing to be done.

Bring Down the House (*To*). To cause rapturous applause in a theatre.

Bring into Play (*To*). To cause to act, to set in motion.

Bring Round (*To*). To restore to consciousness or health; to cause one to recover [from a fit, etc.].

Bring To (*To*). To restore to consciousness; to resuscitate. Many other meanings.

"'I'll bring her to,' said the driver, with a brutal grin; ' I'll give her something better than camphor.'"—*Mrs. Stowe: Uncle Tom's Cabin.*

Bring to Bear (*To*). To cause to happen successfully.

Bring to Book (*To*). To detect one in a mistake.

Bring to Pass (*To*). To cause to happen.

Bring to the Hammer (*To*). To offer or sell by public auction.

Bring Under (*To*). To bring into subjection.

Bring Up (*To*). To rear from birth or an early age. Also numerous other meanings.

Brioche (2 syl.). A sort of bun or cake common in France, and now pretty generally sold in England. When Marie Antoinette was talking about the bread riots of Paris during the 5th and 6th October, 1789, the Duchesse de Polignac naïvely exclaimed, " How is it that these silly people are so clamorous for *bread*, when they can buy such nice brioches for a few sous?" This was in spirit not unlike the remark of our own Princess Charlotte, who avowed "that she would for her part *rather eat beef than starve*," and wondered that the people should be so obstinate as to insist upon having bread when it was so scarce.

Bris. Il conte di San Bris, governor of the Louvre, was father of Valentina, and leader of the St. Bartholomew massacre. (*Meyerbeer's Opera: Gli Ugonotti.*)

Brisëis (3 syl.). The patronymic name of Hippodamia, daughter of Briseus (2 syl.). A concubine of Achilles, to whom he was greatly attached. When Agamemnon was compelled to give up his own concubine, who was the daughter of a priest of Apollo, he took Brisëis away from Achilles. This so annoyed the hero that he refused any longer to go to battle, and the Greeks lost ground daily. Ultimately, Achilles sent his friend Patroclos to supply his place. Patroclos was slain, and Achilles, towering with rage, rushed to battle, slew Hector, and Troy fell.

Brisingamen. Freyja's necklace made by the fairies. Freyja left her husband Odin in order to obtain this necklace; and Odin deserted her because her love was changed into vanity. It is not possible to love Brisingamen and Odin too, for no one can serve two masters.

As a moral tale this is excellent. If Freyja personifies "the beauty of the year," then the *necklace* means the rich autumn tints and flowers, which (soon as Freyja puts on) her husband leaves her—that is, the fertility of the genial year is gone away, and winter is at hand.

Brisk as a Bee. (*See* SIMILES.)

Brissotins. A nickname given to the advocates of reform in the French Revolution, because they were "led by the nose" by Jean Pierre Brissot. The party was subsequently called the Girondists.

Bristol Board. A stiff drawing-paper, originally manufactured at Bristol.

Bristol Boy (*The*). Thomas Chatterton the poet (1752-1770).

"The marvellous boy,
The sleepless soul that perished in his pride."
Wordsworth: Resolution and Independence.

Bristol Diamonds. Brilliant crystals of colourless quartz found in St. Vincent's Rock, Clifton, near Bristol.

Bristol Fashion (*In*). Methodical and orderly. More generally "Shipshape and Bristol fashion."

"In the great mass meeting, October 18th, 1884, a route of above three miles was observed in one unbroken line. No cheering disturbed the stately solemnity; no one ran to give any direction; no noise of any kind was heard; but on, in one unbroken line, steady and stately, marched the throng in 'Bristol fashion.'"—*Daily News*, October 20th, 1884.

Bristol Milk. Sherry sack, at one time given by the Bristol people to their friends.

"This metaphorical milk, whereby Xeres or Sherry-sack is intended."—*Fuller: Worthies.*

Bristol Waters. Mineral waters of Clifton, near Bristol, with a temperature not exceeding 74°; formerly celebrated in cases of pulmonary consumption. They are very rarely used now.

Britain. By far the most probable derivation of this word is that given by Bochart, from the Phœnician *Baratanic* (country of tin), contracted into B'ratan'. The Greek *Cassiterides* (tin islands) is a translation of Baratanic, once applied to the whole known group, but now restricted to the Scilly Isles. Aristotle, who lived some 350 years before the Christian era, calls the island *Britannic*, which is so close to *B'ratanic* that the suggestion of Bochart can scarcely admit of a doubt. (*De Mundo*, sec. 3.)

Pliny says, "Opposite to Celtiberia are a number of islands which the Greeks called 'Cassiterides'" (evidently he means the British group). Strabo says the Cassiterides are situated about the same latitude as Britain.

Great Britain consists of "Britannia prima" (England), "Britannia secunda" (Wales), and "North Britain" (Scotland), united under one sway.

Greater Britain. The whole British empire.

Britannia. The first known representation of Britannia as a female figure sitting on a globe, leaning with one arm on a shield, and grasping a spear in the other hand, is on a Roman coin of Antoninus Pius, who died A.D. 161. The figure reappeared on our copper coin in the reign of Charles II., 1665, and the model was Miss Stewart, afterwards created Duchess of Richmond. The engraver was Philip Roetier, 1665. In 1825 W. Wyon made a new design.

"The King's new medall, where, in little, there is Mrs. Stewart's face, . . . and a pretty thing it is, that he should choose her face to represent Britannia by."—*Pepys' Diary* (25 Feb.).

British Lion (*The*). The pugnacity of the British nation, as opposed to the *John Bull*, which symbolises the substantiality, solidity, and obstinacy of the people, with all their prejudices and national peculiarities.

To rouse the British Lion is to flourish a red flag in the face of John Bull; to provoke him to resistance even to the point of war.

"To twist the lion's tail" is a favourite phrase and favourite policy with some rival unfriendly powers.

Brit'omart [*sweet maid*] (*see below*). Daughter of King Ryence of Wales, whose desire was to be a heroine. She is the impersonation of saintly chastity and purity of mind. She encounters the "savage, fierce bandit and mountaineer" without injury; is assailed by "hag and unlaid-ghost, goblin, and swart fairy of the mine," but "dashes their brute violence into sudden adoration and blank awe." Britomart is not the impersonation of celibacy, as she is in love with an unknown hero, but of "virgin purity." (*Spenser: Faërie Queene*, book iii. Her marriage, book v. 6.)

"She charmed at once and tamed the heart, Incomparable Britomart." *Scott.*

Brit'omartis. A Cretan nymph, very fond of the chase. King Minos fell in love with her, and persisted in his advances for nine months, when she threw herself into the sea. (Cretan, *britus-martis*, sweet maiden.)

Briton (*Like a*). Vigorously, perseveringly. "To fight like a Briton" is to fight with indomitable courage. "To work like a Briton" is to work hard and perseveringly. Certainly, without the slightest flattery, dogged courage and perseverance are the strong characteristics of John Bull. A similar phrase is "To fight like a Trojan."

Brit'tany. *The damsel of Brittany.* Eleanora, daughter of Geoffrey, second son of Henry II., King of England and Duke of Brittany. At the death of

Prince Arthur she was the real heir to the crown, but John confined her in the castle of Bristol till death (1241).

Broach. *To broach a new subject.* To start one in conversation. The allusion is to beer tubs. If one is flat, another must be tapped. A broach is a peg or pin, and to broach a cask is to bore a hole in the top for the vent-peg.

"I did broach this business to your highness."
Shakespeare: Henry VIII., ii. 4.

Broad as Long. *'Tis about as broad as it is long.* One way or the other would bring about the same result.

Broad Arrow on Government stores. It was the cognisance of Henry, Viscount Sydney, Earl of Romney, master-general of the ordnance. (1693-1702.)

※ It seems like a symbol of the Trinity, and Wharton says, "It was used by the Kelts to signify holiness and royalty."

Broad Bottom Ministry (1744). Formed by a coalition of parties: Pelham retained the lead; Pitt supported the Government; Bubb Doddington was treasurer of the navy.

Broadcloth. The best cloth for men's clothes. So called from its great breadth. It required two weavers, side by side, to fling the shuttle across it. Originally two yards wide, now about fifty-four inches; but the word is now used to signify the best quality of (black) cloth.

Broadside. Printed matter spread over an entire sheet of paper. The whole must be in one type and one measure, *i.e.* must not be divided into columns. A folio is when the sheet is folded, in which case a page occupies only *half* the sheet.

"Pamphlets and broadsides were scattered right and left."—Fiske: American History, chap. vii. p. 341.

In naval language, a *broadside* means the whole side of a ship; and to "open a broadside on the enemy" is to discharge all the guns on one side at the same moment.

Brobdingnag. The country of gigantic giants, to whom Gulliver was a pigmy "not half so big as a round little worm plucked from the lazy finger of a maid."

"You high church steeple, you gawky stag,
   Your husband must come from Brobdingnag."
Kane O'Hara: Midas.

Brobdingnag'ian. Colossal; tall as a church steeple. (*See above.*)

"Limbs of Brobdingnagian proportions."—The Star.

Brocken. *The spectre of the Brocken.* This is the shadow of men and other objects greatly magnified and reflected in the mist and cloud of the mountain opposite. The Brocken is the highest summit of the Harz range.

Brocklehurst (*The Rev. Robert*). A Calvinistic clergyman, the son of Naomi Brocklehurst. of Brocklehurst Hall, part founder of Lowood Institution, where young ladies were boarded, clothed, and taught for £15 a year, subsidised by private subscriptions. The Rev. Robert Brocklehurst was treasurer, and half starved the inmates in order to augment his own income, and scared the children by talking to them of hell-fire, and making capital out of their young faults or supposed shortcomings. He and his family fared sumptuously every day, but made the inmates of his institution deny themselves and carry the cross of vexation and want. (*C. Brontë: Jane Eyre.*)

Brogue (1 syl.) properly means the Irish *brog*, or shoe of rough hide. The application of *brog* to the dialect or manner of speaking is similar to that of buskin to tragedy and sock to comedy.

"And put my clouted brogues from off my feet."
Shakespeare: Cymbeline, iv. 2.

Brogues (1 syl.). Trousers. From the Irish *brog*, resembling those still worn by some of the French cavalry, in which trousers and boots are all one garment.

Broken Feather (*A*). *A broken feather in his wing.* A scandal connected with one's character.

"If an angel were to walk about, Mrs. Sam Hurst would never rest till she had found out where he came from; and perhaps whether he had a broken feather in his wing."—Mrs. Oliphant: Phœbe.

Broken Music. A "consort" consisted of six viols, usually kept in one case. When the six were played together it was called a "whole consort," when less than the six were played it was called "a broken consort." Sometimes applied to open chords or arpeggios.

"Here is good broken music."
Shakespeare: Troilus and Cressida, iii. 1.

※ Lord Bacon in his *Sylva Sylvarum* gives a different explanation: he says certain instruments agree together and produce concordant music, but others (as the virginal and lute, the Welsh and Irish harps) do not accord.

Broken on the Wheel. (*See* BREAK.)

Broker. Properly speaking, is one who sells refuse. In German, called *mäklers*, that is, "sellers of damaged stores." (Teutonic, *brak* or *wrak*, refuse, allied with German *brauchen*.)

✝ Generally some special word is prefixed: as bill-broker, cotton-broker, ship-broker, stock-broker, etc.

Brontes (2 syl.). A blacksmith personified; one of the Cyclops. The name signifies *Thunder.*

"Not with such weight, to frame the forky
    brand,
The ponderous hammer falls from Brontes'
    hand."
        Hoole: Jerusalem Delivered, book xx.

Bronzomar'te. (*See* HORSE.)

Brook (*Master*). The name assumed by Ford when he visits Sir John Falstaff. The amorous knight tells Master Brook all about his amour with Mrs. Ford, and how he duped her husband by being stowed into a basket of dirty linen.

"[Ford. I'll give you a pottle of burnt sack to give me recourse to him, and tell him my name is Brook, only for a jest.
" *Host.* My hand, bully. Thou shalt have egress and regress, . . . and thy name shall be Brook."—*Shakespeare: Merry Wives of Windsor,* ii. 1.

Brooks of Sheffield. An imaginary individual mentioned in *David Copperfield.* (*See* HARRIS, MRS.)

Broom. A broom is hung at the mast-head of ships about to be sold, to indicate that they are to be swept away. The idea is popularly taken from Admiral Tromp; but probably this allusion is more witty than true. The custom of hanging up something to attract notice seems very common. Thus an old piece of carpet from a window indicates household furniture for sale; a wisp of straw indicates oysters for sale; a bush means wine for sale; an old broom, ships to sell, etc. etc. (*See* PENNANT.)

A new broom. One fresh in office.

New brooms sweep clean. Those newly appointed to an office find fault and want to sweep away old customs.

Brosier. Eating one out of house and home. At Eton, when a dame keeps an unusually bad table, the boys agree together on a day to eat, pocket, or waste everything eatable in the house. The censure is well understood, and the hint is generally effective. (Greek, *broso,* to eat.)

Brother or *Frère.* A friar not in orders. (*See* FATHER.)

Brother (So-and-so). A fellow-barrister.

Brother Benedict. A married man. (*See* BENEDICT.)

Brother Birch. A fellow-schoolmaster.

Brother Blade. A fellow-soldier,

properly; but now anyone of the same calling as yourself.

Brother Brush. A fellow-painter.

Brother Bung. A fellow-tapster.

Brother Buskin. A fellow-comedian or actor.

A Brother Chip. A fellow-carpenter.

A Brother Clergyman. A fellow-clergyman.

A Brother Crispin. A fellow-shoemaker.

A Brother Mason. A fellow-Freemason.

A Brother Quill. A fellow-author.

A Brother Salt. A fellow-seaman or sailor.

A Brother Shuttle. A fellow-weaver.

A Brother Stitch. A fellow-tailor.

A Brother String. A fellow-violinist.

A Brother Whip. A fellow-coachman.

Brother German. A real brother. (Latin, *germānus,* of the same stock; *germen,* a bud or sprout.)

"Te in germani fratris dilexi loco."—*Terence: Andria,* l. 5, 58.

A uterine brother is a brother by the mother's side only. (Latin, *uterīnus,* born of the same mother, as "frater uterīnus," utĕrus.)

Brother Jonathan. When Washington was in want of ammunition, he called a council of officers, but no practical suggestion could be offered. "We must consult brother Jonathan," said the general, meaning his excellency, Jonathan Trumbull, the elder governor of the State of Connecticut. This was done, and the difficulty was remedied. To consult brother Jonathan then became a set phrase, and brother Jonathan grew to be the John Bull of the United States. (*J. R. Bartlett: Dictionary of Americanisms.*)

Brother Sam. The brother of Lord Dundreary (*q.v.*), the hero of a comedy based on a German drama, by John Oxenford, with additions and alterations by E. A. Sothern and T. B. Buckstone. (*Supplied by T. B. Buckstone, Esq.*)

Browbeat. To beat or put a man down by knitting the brows.

Brown. A copper coin, a penny; so called from its colour. Similarly a sovereign is a "yellow boy." (*See* BLUNT.)

To be done brown. To be roasted, deceived, taken in.

Brown as a Berry. (*See* SIMILES.)

Brown, Jones, and Robinson. Three Englishmen who travel together. Their adventures were published in

Punch, and were the production of Richard Doyle. They typify the middle-class English abroad; and hold up to ridicule their gaucherie and contracted notions, their vulgarity and extravagance, their conceit and snobbism.

Brown Bess means brown barrel. The barrels were browned to keep them from rusting. (Dutch, *bus*, a gun-barrel; Low German, *büsse;* Swedish, *byssa.* Our *arquebus, blunderbuss.*) In 1808 a process of browning was introduced, but this has, of course, nothing to do with the distinctive epithet. Probably *Bess* is a companion word to *Bill.* (*See below.*)

Brown Bill. A kind of halbert used by English foot-soldiers before muskets were employed. We find in the mediæval ballads the expressions, "brown brand," "brown sword," "brown blade," etc. Sometimes the word *rusty* is substituted for brown, as in Chaucer: "And in his side he had a rousty blade"; which, being the god Mars, cannot mean a bad one. Keeping the weapons *bright* is a modern fashion; our forefathers preferred the honour of blood stains. Some say the weapons were varnished with a brown varnish to prevent rust, and some affirm that one Brown was a famous maker of these instruments, and that Brown Bill is a phrase similar to Armstrong gun and Colt's revolver. (*See above.*)

"So, with a band of bowmen and of pikes,
Brown bills and targetiers."
    Marlowe: Edward II. (1622.)

‽ Brown also means shining (Dutch, *brun*), hence, "My bonnie brown sword," "brown as glass," etc., so that a "brown bill" might refer to the shining steel, and "brown Bess" to the bright barrel.

Brown Study. Absence of mind; apparent thought, but real vacuity. The corresponding French expression explains it—*sombre rêverie. Sombre* and *brun* both mean sad, melancholy, gloomy, dull.

"Invention flags, his brain grows muddy,
And black despair succeeds brown study."
    Congreve: An Impossible Thing.

Browns. *To astonish the Browns.* To do or say something regardless of the annoyance it may cause or the shock it may give to Mrs. Grundy.

Anne Boleyn had a whole host of Browns, or "country cousins," who were welcomed at Court in the reign of Elizabeth. The queen, however, was quick to see what was *gauche*, and did not scruple to reprove the Browns if she noticed anything in their conduct not *comme il faut.* Her bluntness of speech often "astonished the Browns."

Brownie. The house spirit in Scottish superstition. He is called in England *Robin Goodfellow.* At night he is supposed to busy himself in doing little jobs for the family over which he presides. Farms are his favourite abode. Brownies are brown or tawny spirits, in opposition to fairies, which are fair or elegant ones. (*See* FAIRIES.)

"It is not long since every family of considerable substance was haunted by a spirit they called Browny, which did several sorts of work; and this was the reason why they gave him offerings . . . on what they called 'Browny's stone.'"—*Martin: Scotland.*

Brownists. Followers of Robert Brown, of Rutlandshire, a violent opponent of the Established Church in the time of Queen Elizabeth. The present "Independents" hold pretty well the same religious tenets as the Brownists. Sir Andrew Aguecheek says:

"I'd as lief be a Brownist as a politician."—*Shakespeare: Twelfth Night*, iii. 2.

Browse his Jib (*To*). A sailor's phrase, meaning to drink till the face is flushed and swollen. The *jib* means the face, and to *browse* here means "to fatten."

‽ The only correct form of the phrase, however, is "to bowse his jib." To bowse the jib means to haul the sail taut; and as a metaphor signifies that a man is "tight."

Bruel. The goose, in the tale of *Reynard the Fox.* The word means *little-roarer.*

Bruin. One of the leaders arrayed against Hudibras. He was Talgol, a Newgate butcher, who obtained a captain's commission for valour at Naseby. He marched next Orsin (Joshua Gosling, landlord of the bear-gardens at Southwark).

Sir Bruin. The name of the bear in the famous German beast-epic, called *Reynard the Fox.* (Dutch for *brown.*)

Brumaire. The celebrated 18th Brumaire (Nov. 9th, 1799) was the day on which the Directory was overthrown and Napoleon established his supremacy.

Brum'magem. Worthless or very inferior metallic articles made in imitation of better ones. Birmingham is the great mart and manufactory of gilt toys, cheap jewellery, imitation gems, mosaic gold, and such-like. Birmingham was called by the Romans "Bremenium."

Brums. In Stock Exchange phraseology this means the "London and

North-Western Railway shares." The Brum, *i.e.* the Birmingham line.

Brunehild (3 syl.) or *Brunehil'da.* Daughter of the King of Issland, beloved by Günther, one of the two gr-at chieftains of the Nibelungenlied or Teutonic *Iliad.* She was to be carried off by force, and Günther asked his friend Siegfried to help him. Siegfried contrived the matter by snatching from her the talisman which was her protector, but she never forgave him for his treachery. (Old German, *bruni,* coat of mail ; *hilt,* battle.)

Brunello (in *Orlando Furioso*). A deformed dwarf of Biserta, to whom King Ag'ramant gave a ring which had the virtue to withstand the power of magic (book ii.). He was leader of the Tingita'nians in the Saracen army. He also figures in Bojardo's *Orlando Innamorato.*

Brunswicker. A native of Brunswick. (*See* BLACK BRUNSWICKER.)

Brunt. *To bear the brunt.* To bear the stress, the heat, and collision. The same word as " burn." (Icelandic, *bruni,* burning heat, *bren ;* Anglo-Saxon, *brenning,* burning.) The " brunt of a battle " is the hottest part of the fight. (Compare " fire-brand.")

Brush. The tail of a fox or squirrel, which is *brushy.*
Brush away. Get along.
Brush off. Move on.
He brushed by me. He just touched me as he went quickly past. Hence also *brush,* a slight skirmish.
All these are metaphors from brushing with a brush.
Give it another brush. A little more attention ; bestow a little more labour on it ; return it to the file for a little more polish.

Brush up (*To*). To renovate or revive ; to bring again into use what has been neglected, as, " I must brush up my French." When a fire is slack we brush up the hearth and then sweep clean the lower bars of the stove and stir the sleepy coals into activity.

Brut. A rhyming chronicle, as the *Brut d'Angleterre* and *Le Roman de Brut,* by Wace (twelfth century). Brut is the Romance word *bruit* (a rumour, hence a tradition, or a chronicle based on tradition). It is by mere accident that the word resembles " Brute " or " Brutus," the traditional king. (*See* next column.)

Brut d'Angleterre. A chronicle of the achievements of King Arthur and his Knights of the Round Table. Arthur is described as the natural son of Uther, pendragon (or chief) of the ancient Britons. He succeeded his father, in 516, by the aid of Merlin, who gave him a magic sword, with which he conquered the Saxons, Picts, Scots, and Irish. Besides the *Brut* referred to, several other romances record the exploits of this heroic king. (*See* ARTHUR.)

Brute, in Cambridge University slang, is a man who has not yet matriculated. The play is evident. A "man," in college phrase, is a collegian ; and, as matriculation is the sign and seal of acceptance, a scholar before that ceremony is not a "man," and therefore only a " biped brute."

Brute (*Sir John*). A coarse, potvaliant knight, ignobly noted for his absurdities. (*Vanbrugh : The Provoked Wife.*)

Brute or **Brutus,** in the mythological history of England, the first king of the Britons, was son of Sylvius (grandson of Ascanius and great grandson of Æne'as). Having inadvertently killed his father, he first took refuge in Greece and then in Britain. In remembrance of Troy, he called the capital of his kingdom Troy-novant (New Troy), now London.
⁂ The pedigree was as follows:—
(1) Æne'as, (2) Ascanius, (3) Silvius, (4) Brutus. (*See* TROY NOVANT.)

Brutum Fulmen (Latin). A noisy but harmless threatening ; an innocuous thunderbolt.
" His [the Pope's] denunciations are but a *brutum fulmen.*"—*The Standard.*

Brutus (*Junius*), the first consul of Rome. He condemned to death his own two sons for joining a conspiracy to restore to the throne the banished Tarquin.
" The public father [Brutus], who the private quelled,
And on the dread tribunal sternly sat."
　　　　　　　Thomson : Winter.

The Spanish Brutus. Alphonso Perez de Guzman (1258-1320). While he was governor, Castile was besieged by Don Juan, who had revolted from his brother, Sancho IV. Juan, who held in captivity one of the sons of Guzman, threatened to cut his throat unless Guzman surrendered the city. Guzman replied, "Sooner than be a traitor, I would myself lend you a sword to slay him," and he threw a sword over the city wall. The son, we are told, was slain by the father's sword before his eyes.

Brutus (*Marcus*). Cæsar's friend, joined the conspirators to murder him, because he made himself a king.

"And thou, unhappy Brutus, kind of heart,
Whose steady arm, by awful virtue urged,
Lifted the Roman steel against thy friend."
Thomson: Winter, 524-6.

Et tu, Brute. What! does my own familiar friend lift up his heel against me? The reference is to that Marcus Brutus whose "bastard hand stabbed Julius Cæsar." (*Suetonius.*)

Bruxellois. The inhabitants of Brussels or Bruxelles.

Brydport Dagger. (*See* BRIDPORT.)

Bub. Drink. (Connected with *bubble* —Latin, *bibo*, to drink; our *imbibe*.) (*See* GRUB.)

"Drunk with Helicon's waters and double-brewed bub."—*Prior: To a Person who wrote ill.*

Bubas'tis. The Diana of Egyptian mythology; the daughter of Isis and sister of Horus.

Bubble (*A*). A scheme of no sterling worth and of very ephemeral duration —as worthless and frail as a bubble.

"The whole scheme [the Fenian raid on British America] was a collapsed bubble."—*The Times.*

The Bubble Act, 6 George I., cap. 18; published 1719, and repealed July 5th, 1825. Its object was to punish the promoters of bubble schemes.

A bubble company. A company whose object is to enrich themselves at the expense of subscribers to their scheme.

A bubble scheme. A project for getting money from subscribers to a scheme of no value.

Bubble and Squeak. Cold boiled meat and greens fried. They first bubbled in water when boiled, and afterwards hissed or squeaked in the frying-pan.

Something pretentious, but of no real value, such as "rank and title," or a bit of ribbon in one's button hole.

Bucca. A goblin of the wind, supposed by the ancient inhabitants of Cornwall to foretell shipwrecks.

Buc'caneer' means sellers of smoke-dried meat, from the Caribbean word *boucan*, smoke-dried meat. The term was first given to the French settlers in Hayti, whose business it was to hunt animals for their skins. The flesh they smoke-dried and sold, chiefly to the Dutch.

When the Spaniards laid claim to all America, many English and French adventurers lived by buccaneering, and hunted Spaniards as lawful prey. After the peace of Ryswick this was no longer tolerated, and the term was then applied to any desperate, lawless, piratical adventurer.

Bucen'taur. A monster, half-man and half-ox. The Venetian state-galley employed by the Doge when he went on Ascension Day to wed the Adriatic was so called. (Greek, *bous*, ox; *centauros*, centaur.)

Buceph'alos [*bull-headed*]. A horse. Strictly speaking, the charger of Alexander the Great, bought of a Thessalian for thirteen talents (£3,500).

"True, true; I forgot your Bucephalus."—*Sir W. Scott: The Antiquary.*

Buc'hanites (3 syl.). A sect of fanatics who appeared in the west of Scotland in 1783. They were named after Mrs. or Lucky Buchan, their founder, who called herself "Friend Mother in the Lord," claiming to be the woman mentioned in Rev. xii., and maintaining that the Rev. Hugh White, a convert, was the "man-child."

"I never heard of alewife that turned preacher, except Luckie Buchan in the West."—*Scott: St. Roman's Well, c. 11.*

Buck. A dandy. (*See below.*)

"A most tremendous buck he was, as he sat there serene, in state, driving his greys."—*Thackeray: Vanity Fair,* chap. vi.

Buck-basket. A linen-basket. To buck is to wash clothes in lye; and a buck is one whose clothes are buck, or nicely got up. When Cade says his mother was "descended from the Lacies," two men overhear him, and say, "She was a pedlar's daughter, but not being able to travel with her furred pack, she washes bucks here at home." (*2 Henry VI.,* iv. 2.) (German, *beuchen,* to steep clothes in lye; *beuche,* clothes so steeped. However, compare "bucket," a diminutive of the Anglo-Saxon *buc.*)

Buck-bean. A corruption of *bog-bean,* a native of wet bog-lands.

Buck-rider (*A*). A dummy fare who enables a cabman to pass police-constables who prevent empty cabs loitering at places where cabs will be likely to be required, as at theatres, music-halls, and large hotels. A cabman who wants to get at such a place under hope of picking up a fare gives a "buck" a shilling to get into his cab that he may seem to have a fare, and so pass the police.

"Constables are stationed at certain points to spot the professional 'buck-riders.'"—*Nineteenth Century* (March, 1893, p. 576).

Buck-tooth. A large projecting front-tooth. (*See* BUTTER TOOTH.)

Buckwheat. A corruption of *boc.* German, *buche,* beech-wheat; it is so called because it is triangular, like beech-mast. The botanical name is *Fago-pyrum* (beech-wheat).

" The buckwheat
Whitened broad acres, sweetening with its flowers
The August wind."
        Bryant : The Fountain, stanza 7.

Buckhorse. A severe blow or slap on the face. So called from a boxer of that name.

Buckingham. (Saxon, *boccen-ham,* beech - tree village.) Fuller, in his *Worthies,* speaks of the beech-trees as the most characteristic feature of this county.

Bucklaw, or rather *Frank Hayston, lord of Bucklaw,* a wealthy nobleman, who marries Lucia di Lammermoor (*Lucy Ashton*), who had pledged her troth to Edgar, master of Ravenswood. On the wedding-night Lucy murders him, goes mad, and dies. (*Donizetti's opera of Lucia di Lammermoor. Sir Walter Scott's Bride of Lammermoor.*)

Buckle. *I can't buckle to.* I can't give my mind to work. The allusion is to buckling on one's armour or belt.

To cut the buckle. To caper about, to heel and toe it in dancing. In jigs the two feet buckle or twist into each other with great rapidity.

" Throth, it wouldn't lave a laugh in you to see the parson dancin' down the road on his way home, and the ministher and methodist praicher cuttin' the buckle as they went along."—*W. B. Yeats: Fairy Tales of the Irish Peasantry,* p. 98 (*see also* p. 196).

To put into buckle. To put into pawn at the rate of 40 per cent. interest.

To talk buckle. To talk about marriage.

" I took a girl to dinner who talked buckle to me."—*Vera,* 154.

Buckler. (*See* SHIELD.)

Bucklersbury (London) was at one time the noted street for druggists and herbalists ; hence Falstaff says—

" I cannot cog, and say thou art this and that, like a many of these lisping hawthorn buds, that come like women in men's apparel, and smell like Bucklersbury in simple time." — *Shakespeare : Merry Wives of Windsor,* iii. 3.

Buckmaster's Light Infantry. The 3rd West India Regiment was so called from Buckmaster, the tailor, who used to issue "Light Infantry uniforms" to the officers of the corps without any authority from the Commander-in-Chief.

Buckra. Superior, excellent. *That's buckra. A buckra coat* is a smart coat; *a buckra man,* a man of consequence.

This word among the West Indians does the service of *burra* among the Anglo-Indians : as *burra saïb* (great master, *i.e.* white man), *burra khana* (a magnificent spread or dinner).

Buckshish or *Baksheesh.* A gratuity, *pour boire.* A term common to India, Persia, and indeed all the East.

Buddha means the *Wise One.* From the Indian word *budh,* to know. The title was given to Prince Siddhar'tha, generally called Saky'a-muni, the founder of Buddhism. His wife's name was Gopa.

Buddhism. A system of religion established in India in the third century. The general outline of the system is that the world is a transient reflex of deity ; that the soul is a "vital spark" of deity ; and that after death it will be bound to matter again till its "wearer" has, by divine contemplation, so purged and purified it that it is fit to be absorbed into the divine essence.

Buddhist. One whose system of religion is Buddhism.

Bude or **Gurney Light.** The latter is the name of the inventor, and the former the place of his abode. (Goldsworthy Gurney, of Bude, Cornwall.)

Budge is lambskin with the wool dressed outwards, worn on the edge of capes, bachelors' hoods, and so on. Budge Row, Cannon Street, is so-called because it was chiefly occupied by budge-makers.

" O foolishness of men! that lend their ears
   To those budge-doctors of the stoic fur."
       Milton : Comus, 706, 707.

Budge (*To*) is the French *bouger,* to stir.

Budge Bachelors. A company of men clothed in long gowns lined with budge or lambs' wool, who used to accompany the Lord Mayor of London at his inauguration.

Budget. The statement which the Chancellor of the Exchequer lays before the House of Commons every session, respecting the national income and expenditure, taxes and salaries. The word is the old French *bougette,* a bag, and the present use arose from the custom of bringing to the House the papers pertaining to these matters in a leather bag, and laying them on the table. Hence, *to open the budget* or bag, *i.e.* to take the papers from the bag and submit them to the House.

A budget of news is a bagful of news, a large stock of news.

Cry Budget. A watchword or shibboleth. Thus Slender says to Shallow—

" We have a nay-word how to know one another.
I come to her in white and cry *mum;* she cries
budget; and by that we know one another.'
Shakespeare: Merry Wives of Windsor, v. 2.

Buff. Buff is a contraction of *buffle* or *buffalo;* and buff skin is the skin of the buffalo prepared. "To stand in buff" is to stand without clothing in one's bare skin. "To strip to the buff" is to strip to the skin. The French for "buff" is *buffle,* which also means a buffalo.

To stand buff, also written *bluff,* meaning firm, without flinching. Sheridan, in his *School for Scandal,* ii. 3, says, "That he should have stood bluff to old bachelor so long, and sink into a husband at last." It is a nautical term; a "bluff shore" is one with a bold and almost perpendicular front. The word *buff,* a blow or buffet, may have got confounded with bluff, but without doubt numerous instances of "buff" can be adduced.

" And for the good old cause stood buff,
'Gainst many a bitter kick and cuff."
Butler: Hudibras's Epitaph.
"I must even stand buff and outface him."—
Fielding.

BUFF in "Blind-man's buff," the well-known game, is an allusion to the three buffs or pats which the "blindman" gets when he has caught a player. (Norman-French, *buffe,* a blow; Welsh, *paff,* verb, *paffio,* to thump; our *buffet* is a little slap.)

Buffalo Bill. Colonel Cody.

Buffalo Robe (*A*). The skin of a bison dressed without removing the hair, and used as a travelling rug. The word "robe" is often omitted.

"The large and roomy sleigh was decked with buffalo robes, red-bound, and furnished with sham eyes and ears."—*The Upper Ten Thousand,* p. 4.
"Leaving all hands under their buffaloes."—
Kane: Arctic Expedition.

Buffer of a railway carriage is an apparatus to *rebuff* or deaden the force of collision.

Buffer (*A*). A chap. The French *bouffer* (older form, *bauffer*) meant to eat, as *il bauffera tout seul.* If this is the basis of the word, a buffer is one who eats with us, called a Commoner in our universities.

"I always said the old buffer would."—*Miss Braddon: Lady Audley's Secret.*

Buffoon means one who puffs out his cheeks, and makes a ridiculous explosion by causing them suddenly to collapse. This being a standing trick with clowns, caused the name to be applied to low jesters. The Italian *buffare* is "to puff out the cheeks for the purpose of making an explosion;" our *puff.* (Italian *buffone,* a buffoon; French *bouffon.*)

Buffoons. Names synonymous with *Buffoon :*—

Bobêche. A clown in a small theatre in the Boulevart du Temple, Paris. (1815-1825.)
Galimafré. A contemporary and rival of the former.
Tabarin. | (Of the seventeenth
Bruscambille. | century.)
Grimaldi. (1779-1837.) (*See* SCARA-MOUCH.)

Buffs. The old 3rd regiment of foot soldiers. The men's coats were lined and faced with buff; they also wore buff waistcoats, buff breeches, and buff stockings. These are the "Old Buffs," raised in 1689.

At one time called the Buff Howards, from Howard their colonel (1737-1749).
The "Young Buffs" are the old 31st Foot raised in 1702; now called the "Huntingdonshire Regiment," whose present uniform is scarlet with buff facings.

The Rothshire Buffs. The old 78th, now the second battalion of the Seaforth Highlanders.

Bugaboo. A monster, or goblin, introduced into the tales of the old Italian romancers. (*See below.*)

Bugbear. A scarecrow. Bug is the Welsh *bwg,* a hobgoblin, called in Russia *buka.* Spenser says, "A ghastly bug doth greatly them affear" (book ii. canto 3); and *Hamlet* has "bugs and goblins" (v. 2).

" Warwick was a bug that feared us all."
Shakespeare: 3 Henry IV., v. 3.
" To the world no bugbear is so great
As want of figure and a small estate."
Pope: Satires, iii. 67-68.

⁂ The latter half of this word is somewhat doubtful. The Welsh *bâr*=ire, fury, wrath, whence *barog,* spiteful, seems probable.

Buggy. A light vehicle without a hood, drawn by one horse. (Hindustani, *bâghi.*)

Buhl-work. Cabinet - work, inlaid with brass; so called from Signor Boule, the inventor, who settled in Paris during the reign of Louis XIV. (The word should be spelt BOULE-WORK.)

Build, for make, as, *A man of strong build,* a man of robust make. The metaphor is evident.

Build. Applied to dress. *Not so bad a build after all,* not badly made.

Builder's Square. Emblematic of St. Thomas, patron of architects.

Bulbul. The nightingale. A Persian word, familiarised by Tom Moore.

> "'Twas like the notes, half-ecstasy, half-pain,
>   The bulbul utters."
> Moore : *Lalla Rookh* (Veiled Prophet, part 1, stanza 14).

Bulis, metamorphosed into a drake ; and his son, Egypios, into a vulture.

Bull. One of the twelve signs of the Zodiac (April 20 to May 21). The time for ploughing, which in Egypt was performed by oxen or bulls.

> "At last from Aries rolls the bounteous sun,
>   And the bright Bull receives him."
> *Thomson : Spring*, 26, 27.

Bull. A blunder, or inadvertent contradiction of terms, for which the Irish are proverbial. *The British Apollo*, 1740, says the term is derived from one Obadiah Bull, an Irish lawyer of London, in the reign of Henry VII., whose blundering in this way was notorious.

Bull is a five-shilling piece. "Half a bull" is half-a-crown. From *bulla,* a great leaden seal. Hood, in one of his comic sketches, speaks of a crier who, being apprehended, "swallowed three hogs (shillings) and a bull."

The pope's bull. So called from the *bulla* or capsule of the seal appended to the document. Subsequently the seal was called the *bulla,* and then the document itself.

The edict of the Emperor Charles IV. (1356) had a golden *bulla,* and was therefore called the golden bull. (*See* GOLDEN BULL.)

Bull. A public-house sign, the cognisance of the house of Clare. The bull and the boar were signs used by the partisans of Clare, and Richard, Duke of Gloucester (Richard III.).

Bull.

A bull in a china shop. A maladroit hand interfering with a delicate business ; one who produces reckless destruction.

A brazen bull. An instrument of torture. (*See* PHALARIS.)

He may bear a bull that hath borne a calf (*Erasmus : Proverbs*)—"He that accustometh hym-selfe to lytle thynges, by lytle and lytle shalbe able to go a waye with greater thynges (*Taverner*).

To take the bull by the horns. To attack or encounter a threatened danger fearlessly ; to go forth boldly to meet a difficulty. The figure is taken from bullfights, in which a strong and skilful

matadore will grasp the horns of a bull about to toss him and hold it prisoner.

John Bull. An Englishman. Applied to a native of England in Arbuthnot's ludicrous *History of Europe.* This history is sometimes erroneously ascribed to Dean Swift. In this satire the French are called *Lewis Baboon,* and the Dutch *Nicholas Frog.*

> "One would think, in personifying itself, a nation would . . . picture something grand, heroic, and imposing, but it is characteristic of the peculiar humour of the English, and of their love for what is blunt, comic, and familiar, that they have embodied their national oddities in the figure of a sturdy, corpulent old fellow . . . with red waistcoat, leather breeches, and a stout oaken cudgel . . . [whom they call] John Bull."—*Washington Irving.*

Bull and Gate. Bull and Mouth. Public-house signs. A corruption of Boulogne Gate or Mouth, adopted out of compliment to Henry VIII., who took Boulogne in 1544.

Bull-dog (*A*). A man of relentless, savage disposition is sometimes so called. A "bull-dog courage" is one that flinches from no danger. The "bulldog" was the dog formerly used in bullbaiting.

Bull-dogs, in University slang, are the two myrmidons of the proctor, who attend his heels like dogs, and are ready to spring on any offending undergraduate like bull-dogs. (*See* MYRMIDONS.)

Bull-necked. *The Bull-necked Forger.* Cagliostro, the huge impostor, was so called. (1743-1795.)

Bull-ring. (*See* MAYOR OF THE BULL-RING.)

Bull's Eye. A small cloud suddenly appearing, seemingly in violent motion, and growing out of itself. It soon covers the entire vault of heaven, producing a tumult of wind and rain. (1 Kings xviii. 44.)

Bull's Eye. The inner disc of a target.

> "A little way from the centre there is a spot where the shots are thickly gathered ; some few have hit the bull's-eye."—*Fiske : Excursions*, etc., chap. vi. p. 178.

To make a bull's eye. To gain some signal advantage ; a successful *coup.* To fire or shoot an arrow right into the centre disc of the target.

Bulls, in Stock Exchange phraseology, means those dealers who "bull," or try to raise the price of stock, with the view of effecting sales. A bull-account is a speculation made under the hope that the stock purchased will rise before the day of settlement. (*See* BEAR.)

Bullet. *Every bullet has its billet.* Nothing happens by chance, and no act is altogether without some effect. "There is a divinity that shapes our ends, rough hew them as we will." Another meaning is this: an arrow or bullet is not discharged at random, but at some mark or for some deliberate purpose.

"Let the arrow fly that has a mark."—*Cæsar Borgia*, chap. xx.

Bulletin. French for a certificate. An official report of an officer to his superior, or of medical attendants respecting the health of persons of notoriety; so called because they were authenticated by an official *bulla* or seal. (Spanish, *boletin*, a warrant; Italian, *bullettino*, a roll.)

Bulling the Barrel is pouring water into a rum cask, when it is nearly empty, to prevent its leaking. The water, which gets impregnated with the spirit and is very intoxicating, is called *bull*.

Seamen talk of *bulling the teapot* (making a second brew), *bulling the coffee*, etc.

Bullion properly means the mint where *bolla*, little round coins, are made. Subsequently the metal in the mint.

Bully. To overbear with words. *A bully* is a blustering menacer. (Anglo-Saxon, *bulgian*, to bellow like a bull.) It is often used, without any mixture of reproof, as a term of endearment, as:—

"O sweet bully Bottom."—*Midsummer Night's Dream*, iv. 4.
"Bless thee, bully doctor." — *Merry Wives of Windsor*, ii. 3.

Bully-boy (*A*). A jolly companion, a "brick." (German, *buhle*, a lover; *buhler*, a gallant.)

"We be three poor mariners
Newly come from the seas,
We spend our lives in jeopardy,
While others live at ease;
Shall we go dance the round, the round,
Shall we go dance the round?
And he that is a bully boy
Come pledge me on this ground."
Deuteromelia. (1609.)

Bully-rook. A blustering cheat. Like *bully*, it is sometimes used without any offensive meaning. Thus the Host, in *The Merry Wives of Windsor*, addresses Sir John Falstaff, Ford, and Page, etc., as *bully-rook*—"How now, my bully-rook?" equal to "my fine fellow."

∵ A *bully rake* is "one who fights for fighting's sake." To *bully-rag* is to intimidate; *bully-ragging* is abusive intimidation. According to Halliwell, a *rag* is a scold, and hence a "ragging" means a scolding. Connected with *rage*.

Bum-bailiff.
The French *pousse-cul* seems to favour

the notion that *bum*-bailiff is no corruption. These officers are frequently referred to as *bums*.

"Scout me for him at the corner of the orchard, like a bum-bailiff."
Shakespeare: Twelfth Night, iii. 4.

Bum-boat. A small wide boat to carry provisions to vessels lying off shore. Also called "dirt-boats," being used for removing filth from ships lying in the Thames. (Dutch, *bumboot*, a wide fishing boat. In Canada a punt is called a *bun*. A *bun* is a receptacle for keeping fish alive.)

Bumble. A beadle. So called from the officious, overbearing beadle in Dickens's *Oliver Twist*.

Bumbledom. The dominion of an overbearing parish officer, the arrogance of parish authorities, the conceit of parish dignity. (*See above.*)

Bummarees. A class of middlemen or fish-jobbers in Billingsgate Market, who get a living by *bummareeing, i.e.* buying parcels of fish from the salesmen, and then retailing them. A corruption of *bonne marée*, good fresh fish, or the seller thereof. According to the *Dictionnaire de l'Académie*, *marée* means *toute sorte de poisson de mer que n'est pas salé*. *Bonne marée, marée fraiche*.

Bumper. A full glass, generally connected with a "toast." Dr. Arn says a bumper is when the surface of the wine bumps up in the middle. (French, *bomber*, to render convex, to bulge or swell out.)

"A fancied connection with bump, a swelling, has not only influenced the form of the word, but [has] added the notion of fulness."—*Skea: Etymological Dictionary*.

Bumpkin. A loutish person. (Dutch, *boomken*, a sprout, a fool.) This word very closely resembles the word "chit." (*See* CHITTY.)

Bumptious. Arrogant, full of mighty airs and graces; apt to take offence at presumed slights. A corruption of presumptuous, first into "sumptious," then to bumptious.

Bun. A small cake. (Irish, *boinneog*, Scotch, *bannock*.)

∵ In regard to "hot cross buns" on Good Friday, it may be stated that the Greeks offered to Apollo, Diana, Hecate, and the Moon, cakes with "horns." Such a cake was called a *bous*, and (it is said) never grew mouldy. The "cross" symbolised the four quarters of the moon.

"Good Friday comes this month: the old woman runs
With one a penny, two a penny, 'hot cross buns.'"

Whose virtue is, if you believe what's said,
They'll not grow mouldy like the common
bread."

         Poor Robin: Almanack, 1733.

Bunch of Fives. A slang term for
the hand or fist.

Buncle (*John*). "A prodigious hand
at matrimony, divinity, a song, and a
peck." He marries seven wives, loses all
in the flower of their age, is inconsolable
for two or three days, then resigns himself to the decrees of Providence, and
marries again. (*The Life and Opinions of
John Buncle, Esq., by Thomas Amory.*)

"John is a kind of innocent Henry VIII. of
private life."—*Leigh Hunt.*

Bundle. *Bundle off.* Get away. *To
bundle a person off,* is to send him away
unceremoniously. Similar to *pack off.*
The allusion is obvious.

Bundle of Sticks. Æsop, in one of
his fables, shows that sticks one by one
may be readily broken; not so when
several are bound together in a bundle.
The lesson taught is, that "Union gives
strength."

"They now lay to heart the lesson of the bundle of sticks."—*The Times.*

Bundschuh [*highlows*]. An insurrection of the peasants of Germany in
the sixteenth century. So called from
the highlows or clouted shoon of the
insurgents.

Bung. A cant term for a toper.
"Away, . . . you filthy bung," says
Doll to Pistol. (2 *Henry IV.,* ii. 4.)

    Brother Bung. A cant term for a
publican.

    Bung up. Close up, as a bung closes
a cask.

Bun'galow (Indian). The house of
a European in India, generally a ground
floor with a verandah all round it, and
the roof thatched to keep off the hot
rays of the sun. There are English
bungalows at Birchington and on the
Norfolk coast near Cromer. A *dâk-
bungalow* is a caravansary or house
built by the Government for the use of
travellers. (Hindustani, *banglā.*)

Bungay. *Go to Bungay with you!*—
i.e. get away and don't bother me, or
don't talk such stuff. Bungay, in
Suffolk, used to be famous for the manufacture of leather breeches, once very
fashionable. Persons who required new
ones, or to have their old ones new-
seated, went or sent to Bungay for that
purpose. Hence rose the cant saying,
"Go to Bungay, and get your breeches
mended," shortened into "Go to Bungay
with you!"

Bungay. *My castle of Bungay.* (*See
under* CASTLE.)

Bunkum. Claptrap. A representative at Washington being asked why he
made such a flowery and angry speech,
so wholly uncalled for, made answer, "I
was not speaking to the House, but to
Buncombe," which he represented (North
Carolina).

"America, too, will find that caucuses, stump-
oratory, and speeches to Buncombe will not carry
men to the immortal gods."—*Carlyle: Latter-day
Pamphlets* (Parliaments, p. 93).

Bunny. A rabbit. So called from
the provincial word *bun,* a tail. The
Scotch say of the hare, "she cocks her
bun." Bunny, a diminutive of bun,
applied to a rabbit, means the animal
with the "little tail."

"Bunny, lying in the grass,
Saw the shiny column pass."
    Bret Harte: Battle Bunny, stanza 1.

Bunsby (*Jack*). Captain Cuttle's
friend; a Sir Oracle of his neighbours;
profoundly mysterious, and keeping his
eye always fixed upon invisible dreamland somewhere beyond the limits of
infinite space. (*Dickens: Dombey and
Son.*)

Bunting. In Somersetshire bunting
means sifting flour. Sieves were at one
time made of a strong gauzy woollen
cloth, which being tough and capable of
resisting wear, was found suitable for
flags, and now has changed its reference
from sieves to flags. A "bunt-mill" is
a machine for sifting corn.

"Not unlike . . . a baker's bunt, when he separates the flour from the bran."—*Stedman.*

Buphagos. Pausanias (viii. 24) tells
us that the son of Japhet was called Buphagos (glutton), as Hercules was called
Adephagus, because on one occasion he
ate a whole ox (*Athenæos* x.). The
French call the English "Beefeaters,"
because they are eaters of large joints of
meat, and not of delicate, well-dressed
viands. Neither of these has any relation to our Yeomen of the Guards.
(*See* BEEFEATERS, page 115.)

Burbon. A knight assailed by a
rabble rout, who batter his shield to
pieces, and compel him to cast it aside.
Talus renders him assistance, and is informed by the rescued knight that Fourde'lis, his own true love, had been enticed
away from him by Grantorto. When
the rabble is dispersed, and Fourde'lis
recovered, Burbon places her on his
steed, and rides off as fast as possible.
Burbon is *Henri IV.* of France; Fourde'-
lis, the *kingdom of France;* the rabble
rout, the *Roman Catholic party* that tried

to set him aside ; the shield he is compelled to abandon is *Protestantism ;* his carrying off Fourde'lis is his obtaining the kingdom by a *coup* after his renunciation of the Protestant cause. (*Spenser : Faërie Queene,* v. 11.)

Burchardise. To speak *ex cathedra ;* to speak with authority. Burchard (who died 1026) compiled a volume of canons of such undisputed authority, that any sentence it gave was beyond appeal.

Burchell (*Mr.*). A baronet who passes himself off as a poor man, his real name and title being Sir William Thornhill. His favourite cant word is "Fudge." (*Goldsmith : Vicar of Wakefield.*)

Burd (*Helen*). The Scotch female impersonation of the French *preux* or *prud'homme,* with this difference, that she is discreet, rather than brave and wise.

Burden of a Song. The words repeated in each verse, the chorus or refrain. It is the French *bourdon,* the big drone of a bagpipe, or double-diapason of an organ, used in forté parts and choruses.

Burden of Isaiah. Tho "measure" of a prophecy announcing a calamity, or a denunciation of hardships on those against whom the burden is uttered. (Isa. xiii. 1, etc.)

The burden of proof. The obligation to prove something.

"Tho burden of proof is on the party holding the affirmative" [because no one can prove a negative, except by *reductio ad absurdum*].— *Greenleaf: On Evidence* (vol. i. part 2, chap. iii. p. 105).

Bure (2 syl.). The first woman, and sister of Borr, the father of Odin. (*Scandinavian mythology.*)

Bureauc'racy. A system of government in which the business is carried on in bureaux or departments. The French *bureau* means not only the office of a public functionary, but also the whole staff of officers attached to the department. As a word of reproach, bureaucracy has nearly the same meaning as Dickens's word, *red-tapeism* (*q.v.*).

Burglar [*burg-larron*]. The robber of a burgh, castle, or house. Burglary is called, in ancient law-books, *hamesecken* or *hám-secn,* house-violation.

Burgun'dian. *A Burgundian blow,* *i.e.* decapitation. The Duc de Biron, who was put to death for treason by Henri IV., was told in his youth, by a fortune-teller, "to beware of a Burgundian blow." When going to execution,

he asked who was to be his executioner, and was told he was a man from Burgundy.

Burial of an Ass. No burial at all.
"He shall be buried with the burial of an ass, drawn and cast forth beyond the gates of Jerusalem."—Jer. xxii. 19.

Bu'ridan's Ass. A man of indecision ; like one "on double business bound, who stands in pause where he should first begin, and both neglects." Bu'ridan the scholastic said : "If a hungry ass were placed exactly between two hay-stacks in every respect equal, it would starve to death, because there would be no motive why it should go to one rather than to the other."

Burke. To murder by placing something over the mouth of the person attacked to prevent his giving alarm. So called from Burke, an Irishman, who used to suffocate his victims and murder them for the sole purpose of selling the dead bodies to surgeons for dissection. Hanged at Edinburgh, 1829.

To burke a question. To strangle it in its birth. *The publication was burked :* suppressed before it was circulated.

Burkers. Body-snatchers; those who kill by burking.

Burl, Burler. In Cumberland, a *burler* is the master of the revels at a bidden-wedding, who is to see that the guests are well furnished with drink. To *burl* is to carouse or pour out liquor. (Anglo-Saxon, *byrlian.*)

"Mr. H. called for a quart of beer. . . . He told me to burl out the beer, as he was in a hurry, and I burled out the glass and gave it to him."—*The Times : Law Reports.*

Burlaw or **Byrlaw.** A sort of Lynch-law in the rural districts of Scotland. The inhabitants of a district used to make certain laws for their own observance, and appoint one of their neighbours, called the *Burlaw-man,* to carry out the pains and penalties. The word is a corrupt form of *byr-law,* byr=a burgh, common in such names as *Derby,* the burgh on the Derwent; *Grimsby* (*q.v.*), Grims-town.

Burlesque. *Father of burlesque poetry.* Hippo'nax of Ephesus. (Sixth century B.C.)

Burlond. A giant whose legs Sir Try'amour cut off. (*Romance of Sir Tryamour.*)

Burn. *His money burns a hole in his pocket.* He cannot keep it in his pocket, or forbear spending it.

To burn one's boats. To cut oneself off from all means or hope of retreat. The allusion is to Julius Cæsar and other generals, who burned their boats or ships when they invaded a foreign country, in order that their soldiers might feel that they must either conquer the country or die, as retreat would be impossible.

To burn one's fingers. To suffer loss by speculation or interference. The allusion is to taking chestnuts from the fire.

"He has been bolstering up these rotten ironworks. I told him he would burn his fingers."—*Mrs. Lynn Linton.*

You cannot burn the candle at both ends. You cannot do two opposite things at one and the same time; you cannot exhaust your energies in one direction, and yet reserve them unimpaired for something else. If you go to bed late you cannot get up early. You cannot eat your cake and have it too. You cannot serve God and Mammon. You cannot serve two masters. *Poursuis deux lièvres, et les manques.* (*La Fontaine.*) *Simul sorbēre ac flare non possum.*

We burn daylight. We waste time in talk instead of action. (*Shakespeare: Merry Wives of Windsor,* ii. 1.)

Burn, a stream. A variant of bourn (Anglo-Saxon, *burne,* a brook, as in Winterbourne, Burnham, Swinburn, etc.).

Burning Crown (*A*). A crown of red-hot iron set on the head of regicides.

"He was adjudged
To have his head seared with a burning crown."
Tragedy of Hoffmann. (1631.)

Burnt. *The burnt child dreads the fire.* Once caught, twice shy. "What! wouldst thou have a serpent sting thee twice?"

Burnt Candlemas Day. Feb. 2, 1355-6, when Edward III. marched through the Lothians with fire and sword. He burnt to the ground Edinburgh and Haddington, and then retreated from want of provisions. The Scots call the period "Burnt Candlemas." (*See* "Epochs of History," *England under the Plantagenets;* and Macmillan's series, *Little History of Scotland,* edited by Prof. Freeman.)

Bursa (a bull's hide). So the citadel of Carthage was called. The tale is that when Dido came to Africa she bought of the natives "as much land as could be encompassed by a bull's hide." The agreement was made, and Dido cut the hide into thongs, so as to enclose a space sufficient for a citadel.

The following is a similar story: The Yakutsks granted to the Russian explorers as much land as they could encompass with a cow's hide; but the Russians, cutting the hide into strips, obtained land enough for the port and town of Yakutsk.

The Indians have a somewhat similar tradition. The fifth incarnation of Vishnu was in the form of a dwarf called Vamen. Vamen, presenting himself before the giant Baly, asked as a reward for services as much land as he could measure in three paces to build a hut on. Baly laughed at the request, and freely granted it. Whereupon the dwarf grew so prodigiously large that, with three paces, he strode over the whole world. (*Sonnerat: Voyages,* vol. i. p. 24.)

Burst. To inform against an accomplice. Slang variety of "split" (turn king's evidence, impeach). The person who does this *splits* or breaks up the whole concern.

Bury the Hatchet. Let by-gones be by-gones. The "Great Spirit" commanded the North American Indians, when they smoked the cal'umet or peace-pipe, to bury their hatchet, scalping-knives, and war-clubs in the ground, that all thought of hostility might be buried out of sight.

"It is much to be regretted that the American government, having brought the great war to a conclusion, did not bury the hatchet altogether."
—*The Times.*

"Buried was the bloody hatchet;
Buried was the dreadful war-club;
Buried were all warlike weapons,
And the war-cry was forgotten;
Then was peace among the nations."
Longfellow: Hiawatha, xiii.

Burying, *Cremation.* The Parsees neither bury or burn their dead, because they will not defile the elements (fire and earth). So they carry their dead to the Tower of Silence, and leave the body there to be devoured by vultures. (*See Nineteenth Century,* October, 1893, p. 611.)

Burying at Cross Roads. (*See* CROSS-ROADS.)

Bus. A contraction of *Omnibus.* Of course, Omnibi, as a plural, though sometimes used, is quite absurd.

Busby (*A*). A frizzled wig. Doctor Busby, master of Westminster school, did not wear a frizzled wig, but a close cap, somewhat like a Welsh wig. (*See* WIGS.)

Busby. The tall cap of a hussar, artillery-man, etc., which hangs from the top over the right shoulder.

Bush. *One beats the bush, but another has the hare, i.e.* one does the work, but another reaps the profit. The Latins said, *Sic vos non vobis.* The allusion is to beating the bush to start game. (*See* BEATING.)

Good wine needs no bush. A good article will make itself known without being puffed. The booths in fairs used to be dressed with ivy, to indicate that wine was sold there, ivy being sacred to Bacchus. An ivy-bush was once the common sign of taverns, and especially of private houses where beer or wine could be obtained by travellers. In France, a peasant who sells his vineyard has to put a green bush over his door.

The proverb is Latin, and shows that the Romans introduced the custom into Britain. "*Vino vendibili hedera non opus est*" (*Columella*). It was also common to France. "*Au vin qui se vend bien, il ne faut point de lierre.*"

"If it be true that good wine needs no bush, 'tis
true that a good play needs no prologue."
Shakespeare: As You Like It (Epilogue).

To take to the bush. To become bushrangers, like runaway convicts who live by plunder. The bush in this case means what the Dutch call *bosch*, the uncleared land as opposed to towns and clearings.

"Everything being much cheaper in Toronto
than away in the bush."—*Geikie: Life in the
Woods.*

Bushel. *To measure other people's corn by one's own bushel.* To make oneself the standard of right and wrong; to appraise everything as it accords or disagrees with one's own habits of thought and preconceived opinions; to be extremely bigoted and self-opiniated.

Under a bushel. Secretly; in order to hide it.

"Do men light a candle and put it under a
bushel?"—Matt. v. 15.

Bushman (Dutch, *Boschjesman*). Natives of South Africa who live in the "bush"; the aborigines of the Cape; dwellers in the Australian "bush;" a bush farmer.

"Bushmen .... are the only nomades in the
country. They never cultivate the soil, nor rear
any domestic animal save wretched dogs."—
Livingstone: Travels, chap. ii. p. 55.

Bushrangers. Escaped convicts who have taken refuge in the Australian "bush," and subsist by plunder.

"The bushrangers at first were absentees [*i.e.*
escaped convicts] who were soon allured or
driven to theft and violence. So early as 1808
they had, by systematic robbery, excited feelings
of alarm."—*West: Tasmania.*

Business, Busy. Saxon, *bysgian,* the verb, *bysig* (busy); Dutch, *bezigen;* German, *besorgniss* (care, management);

sorge (care); Saxon, *seogan* (to see). From the German *sorgen* we get the French *soigner* (to look after something), *soigne,* and *be-sogne* (business, or that which is our care and concern), with *be-soin* (something looked after but not found, hence "want"); the Italian *besognio* (a beggar).

Business To-morrow. When the Spartans seized upon Thebes, they placed Arch'ias over the garrison. Pelop'idas, with eleven others, banded together to put Archias to the sword. A letter containing full details of the plot was given to the Spartan polemarch at the banquet table; but Archias thrust the letter under his cushion, saying, "Business tomorrow." But long ere that sun arose he was numbered with the dead.

Bu'sirane (3 syl.). An enchanter bound by Brit'omart. (*Spenser: Faërie Queene,* book iii. 11, 12.)

Busi'ris. A king of Egypt, who used to immolate to the gods all strangers who set foot on his shores. Hercules was seized by him; and would have fallen a victim, but he broke his chain, and slew the inhospitable king.

Busi'ris, according to Milton, is the Pharaoh who was drowned in the Red Sea.

"Vex'd the Red-Sea coast, whose waves o'er-
threw
Busiris and his Memphian chivalry."
Paradise Lost, book i. 306, 307.

Buskin. Tragedy. The Greek tragic actors used to wear a sandal some two or three inches thick, to elevate their stature. To this sole was attached a very elegant buskin, and the whole was called *cothur'nus.* (*See* SOCK.)

"Or what (though rare) of later age
Ennobled hath the buskined stage."
Milton: Il Penseroso, 79, 80.

Buss. To kiss. (Welsh, *bus,* the human lip; Gaelic, *bus,* the mouth; French, *baiser,* a kiss.)

"Yon towers, whose wanton tops do buss the
clouds,
Must kiss their own feet."
Shakespeare: Troilus and Cressida, iv. 5.

Busterich. A German god. His idol may still be seen at Sondershusa, the castle of Schwartzenburg.

Busy as a Bee. The equivalent Latin phrase is "*Satãgis tamquam mus in matella.*" (*See* SIMILES.)

Butcher. *The Butcher.* Achmed Pasha was called *djezzar* (the butcher), and is said to have whipped off the heads of his seven wives. He is famous for his defence of Acre against Napoleon I.

The Butcher. John, ninth lord Clifford, also called *The Black,* died 1461.

The Bloody Butcher. The Duke of Cumberland, second son of George II. So called from his barbarities in suppressing the rebellion of the young Pretender.

The Royalist Butcher. Blaise de Montluc, distinguished for his cruelties to the Protestants in the reign of Charles IX. of France (1502-1572).

Butcher Boots. The black boots worn *en petite tenue* in the hunting field.

Butter. Soft soap, soft solder (pron. *saw-der*), "wiping down" with winning words. *Punch* expressively calls it "the milk of human kindness churned into butter." (Anglo-Saxon, *butere* or *butyre*, Latin, *butyrum*, Greek, *boutyron*, *i.e. bou-turos*, cow-cheese, as distinguished from goat- or ewe-butter.)

Soft words butter no parsnips. Saying "'Be thou fed,' will not feed a hungry man." Mere words will not find salt to our porridge, or butter to our parsnips.

"Fine words, says our homely old proverb, butter no parsnips."—*Lowell.*

He looks as if butter would not melt in his mouth. He looks like a dolt. He looks quite harmless and expressly made to be played upon. Yet beware, and "touch not a cat but a glove."

"She smiles and languishes, you'd think that butter would not melt in her mouth."—*Thackeray: Pendennis,* lx.

He knows on which side his bread is buttered. He knows his own interest. *Scit uti foro.*

He that has good store of butter may lay it thick on his bread. Cui multum est piperis, etiam oleribus immiscet.

To butter one's bread on both sides. To be wastefully extravagant and luxurious.

Butter-fingers. Said of a person who lets things fall out of his hand. His fingers are slippery, and things slip from them as if they were greased with butter. Often heard on the cricket field.

"I never was a butter-fingers, though a bad batter."—*H. Kingsley.*

Butter-tooth (*A*). A wide front tooth. (*See* BUCK-TOOTH.)

Buttered Ale. A beverage made of ale or beer (without hops) mixed with butter, sugar, and cinnamon.

Buttercups. So called because they were once supposed to increase the butter of milk. No doubt those cows give the best milk that pasture in fields where buttercups abound, not because these flowers produce butter, but because they grow only on sound, dry, old pastures, which afford the best food. Miller, in his *Gardener's Dictionary,* says they were so called "under the notion that the

yellow colour of butter is owing to these plants."

Butterflies, in the cab trade, are those drivers who take to the occupation only in summer-time, and at the best of the season. At other times they follow some other occupation.

"The feeling of the regular drivers against these 'butterflies' is very strong."—*Nineteenth Century* (March 1893, p. 177).

Butterfly Kiss (*A*). A kiss with one's eyelashes, that is, stroking the cheek with one's eyelashes.

Button. A decoy in an auction-room; so called because he buttons or ties the unwary to bargains offered for sale. The button fastens or fixes what else would slip away.

The button of the cap. The tip-top. Thus, in *Hamlet,* Guildenstern says: "On fortune's cap we are not the very button" (act ii. sc. 2), *i.e.* the most highly favoured. The button on the cap was a mark of honour. Thus, in China to the present hour, the first grade of literary honour is the privilege of adding a gold button to the cap, a custom adopted in several collegiate schools of England. This gives the expression quoted a further force. Also, the several grades of mandarins are distinguished by a different coloured button on the top of their cap.

Button (of a foil). The piece of cork fixed to the end of a foil to protect the point and prevent injury in fencing.

Buttons. The two buttons on the back of a coat, in the fall of the back, are a survival of the buttons on the back of riding-coats and military frocks of the eighteenth century, occasionally used to button back the coat-tails.

A boy in buttons. A page, whose jacket in front is remarkable for a display of small round buttons, as close as they can be inserted, from chin to waist.

"The titter [tingle] of an electric bell brought a large fat buttons, with a stage effect of being dressed to look small."—*Howell: Hazard of New Fortunes,* (vol. i. part i. chap. vii. p. 58).

He has not all his buttons. He is half-silly; "not all there"; he is "a button short."

Dash my buttons. Here, "buttons" means lot or destiny, and "dash" is a euphemistic form of a more offensive word.

The buttons come off the foils. Figuratively, the courtesies of controversy are neglected.

"Familiarity with controversy ... will have accustomed him to the misadventures which arise when, as sometimes will happen in the heat of fence, the buttons come off the foils."—*Nineteenth Century* (June, 1891, p. 925).

'Tis in his buttons. He is destined to obtain the prize; he is the accepted lover. It is still common to hear boys count their buttons to know what trade they are to follow, whether they are to do a thing or not, and whether some favourite favours them. (*See* BACHELOR.)

"'Tis in his buttons: he will carry't."—*Shakespeare: Merry Wives of Windsor,* iii. 2.

'Tis not in his buttons. 'Tis not in his power, 'tis not in his lot.

To have a soul above buttons. To be worthy of better things; to have abilities too good for one's present employment. This is explained by George Colman in *Sylvester Daggerwood:* "My father was an eminent button-maker ... but I had a soul above buttons ... and panted for a liberal profession."

To put into buttons. To dress a boy as a "page," with a jacket full in the front with little buttons, generally metallic and very conspicuous.

To take by the button. To detain one in conversation; to apprehend, as, "to take fortune by the button." The allusion is to a custom, now discontinued, of holding a person by the button or button-hole in conversation.

Button-hole. *To button-hole a person.* To bore one with conversation. The French have the same locution: *Serrer le bouton* [à quel qu'un].

"He went about button-holing and boring everyone."—*H. Kingsley: Mathilde.*

To take one down a button-hole. To take one down a peg; to lower one's conceit.

"Better mind yerselves, or I'll take ye down a button-hole lower."—*Mrs. B. Stowe: Uncle Tom's Cabin,* iv.

Button-hole (*A*). A flower inserted in the button-hole of a coat.

"In fine weather he [the driver of a hansom] will sport a button-hole—generally a dahlia, or some flower of that ilk."—*Nineteenth Century* (March, 1893, p. 473).

Buy in (*To*). To collect stock by purchase; to withhold the sale of something offered at auction, because the bidding has not reached the "reserve price."

Buy Off (*To*). To give a person money to drop a claim or put an end to contention, or to throw up a partnership.

Buy Out (*To*). To redeem or ransom.

"Not being able to buy out his life . . . .
Dies ere the weary sun set."
Shakespeare: Comedy of Errors, i. 2.

Buy Over (*To*). To induce one by a bribe to renounce his claim; to gain over by bribery.

To buy over a person's head. To outbid another.

Buy Up (*To*). To purchase stock to such an amount as to obtain a virtual monopoly, and thus command the market; to make a corner, as "to buy up corn," etc.

Buying a Pig in a Poke. (*See* PIG, etc.)

Buzfuz (*Serjeant*). A driving, chaffing, masculine bar orator, who twists "Chops and Tomato Sauce" into a declaration of love. (*Dickens: Pickwick Papers.*)

Buzz. Empty the bottle. A corruption of *bouse* (to drink).

"In bousing a bout 'twas his gift to excel,
And of all jolly topers he bore off the bell."

(*See* BOOZY.)

Buzz (*A*). A rumour, a whispered report.

"Yes, that, on every dream,
Each buzz, each fancy . . .
He may enguard his dotage."
Shakespeare: King Lear, i. 4.

Buzzard (*The*) is meant for Dr. Burnett, whose figure was lusty.

"The noble Buzzard ever pleased me best."
Dryden: Hind and Panther, part iii. 1121.

Buzzard called hawk by courtesy. It is a euphemism—a brevet rank—a complimentary title.

"Of small renown, 'tis true; for, not to lie,
We call [your buzzard] "hawk" by courtesy."
Dryden: Hind and Panther, iii. 1122-3.

Between hawk and buzzard. Not quite a lady or gentleman, nor quite a servant. Applied to tutors in private houses, bear-leaders, and other grown-up persons who are allowed to come down to dessert, but not to be guests at the dinner-table.

By. Meaning *against.* "I know nothing by myself, yet am I not thereby justified." (1 Cor. iv. 4.)

By-and-by now means a little time hence, but when the Bible was translated it meant instantly. "When persecution ariseth . . . by-and-by he is offended" (Matt. xiii. 21); rendered in Mark iv. 17 by the word "immediately." Our *presently* means in a little time hence, but in French *présentement* means now, directly. Thus in France we see, *These apartments are to be let presently,* meaning *now*—a phrase which would in English signify by-and-by.

Bygones. *Let bygones be bygones.* Let old grievances be forgotten and never brought to mind.

7

By-laws. Local laws. From *by*, a borough. Properly, laws by a Town Council, and bearing only on the borough or company over which it has jurisdiction.

By-road (*A*). Not a main road; a local road.

By-the-by. *En passant*, laterally connected with the main subject. "By-play" is side or secondary play; "By-lanes and streets" are those which branch out of the main thoroughfare. The first "by" means *passing from one to another*, as in the phrase "Day by day." Thus "By-the-by" is passing from the main subject to a *by* or secondary one.

By-the-way is an incidental remark thrown in, and tending the same way as the discourse itself.

Byron. *The Polish Byron.* Adam Mickiewicz (1798-1855).
The Russian Byron. Alexander Sergeivitch Puschkin (1799-1837).

Byrsa. ·(*See* page 191, col. 1, BURSA.)

Byzantine Art. That symbolical system which was developed by the early Greek or Byzantine artists out of the Christian symbolism. Its chief features are the circle, dome, and round arch; and its chief symbols the lily, cross, vesica, and nimbus. St. Sophia, at Constantinople, and St. Mark, at Venice, are excellent examples.

Byzantine Empire (*The*). The Eastern or Greek Empire from 395 to 1453.

Byzantine Historians. Certain Greek historians who lived under the Eastern empire between the sixth and fifteenth centuries. They may be divided into three groups:—(1) Those whose works form a continuous history of the Byzantine empire, from the fourth century to the conquest of Constantinople by the Turks; (2) general chroniclers who wrote histories of the world from the oldest period; and (3) writers on Roman antiquities, statistics, and customs.

Byzan'tines (3 syl.). Coins of the Byzantine empire, generally called *Besants.*

C

C. This letter is the outline of the hollow of the hand, and is called in Hebrew *caph* (the hollow of the hand).
C. The French *c*, when it is to be sounded like *s*, has a mark under it (*ç*):

this mark is called a *cedilla*. (A diminutive of *z*; called *zeta* in Greek, *ceda* in Spanish.)

C. There is more than one poem written of which every word begins with C. For example:
(1) One composed by HUEBALD in honour of Charles le Chauve. It is in Latin hexameters and runs to somewhat more than a hundred lines, the last two of which are
"Conveniet claras claustris componere cannas
Completur clarus carmen cantabile CALVIS."
(2) One by HAMCONIUS, called "*Certamen catholicum cum Calvinistis.*"
(3) One by HENRY HARDER, of 100 lines in Latin, on "Cats," entitled: "*Canum cum Catis certamen carmine compositum currente calamo C. Catulli Caninii.*" The first line is—
"Cattorum canimus certamina clara canumque."
Cats' canine caterwauling contests chant.
See M and P for other examples.

Ça Ira (*it will go*). Called emphatically *Le Carillon National* of the French Revolution (1790). It went to the tune of the *Carillon National*, which Marie Antoinette was for ever strumming on her harpsichord.
"*Ça Ira*" was the rallying cry borrowed by the Federalists from Dr. Franklin of America, who used to say, in reference to the American revolution, "*Ah! ah! ça ira, ça ira!*" ('twill be sure to do). The refrain of the *carillon* is—
Ha! ha! It will speed, it will speed, it will speed!
Resistance is vain, we are sure to succeed.

Caa'ba (3 syl.). The shrine of Mecca, said by the Arabs to be built on the exact spot of the tabernacle let down from heaven at the prayer of repentant Adam. Adam had been a wanderer for 200 years, and here received pardon. The shrine was built, according to Arab tradition, by Ishmael, assisted by his father Abraham, who inserted in the walls a black stone "presented to him by the angel Gabriel."

Cab. A contraction of cabriolet (*a little caperer*), a small carriage that scampers along like a kid.

Cabal'. A junto or council of intriguers. One of the Ministries of Charles II. was called a cabal (1670), because the initial letters of its members formed this acrostic: **C**lifford, **A**shley, **B**uckingham, **A**rlington, and **L**auderdale. This accident may have popularised the word, but, without doubt, we borrowed it from the French *cabale*, "an intriguing faction," and Hebrew *cab'ala*, "secret knowledge." A *junto* is merely an assembly ; Spanish, *junta*, a council. (*See* NOTARICA ; TAMMANY RING.)

> " In dark cabals and mighty juntos met."
> *Thomson.*

> " These ministers were emphatically called the Cabal, and they soon made the appellation so infamous that it has never since . . . . been used except as a term of reproach." — *Macaulay : England*, vol. i. chap. ii. p. 165.

Cab'ala. The oral law of the Jews delivered down from father to son by word of mouth. Some of the rabbins say that the angel Raziel instructed Adam in it, the angel Japhiel instructed Shem, and the angel Zedekiel instructed Abraham ; but the more usual belief is that God instructed Moses, and Moses his brother Aaron, and so on from age to age.

N.B.—The promises held out by the cabala are : the abolition of sin and sickness, abundant provision of all things needful for our well-being during life, familiar intercourse with deity and angels, the gift of languages and prophecy, the power of transmuting metals, and also of working miracles.

Cab'alist. A Jewish doctor who professed the study of the Cab'ala, a mysterious science said to have been delivered to the Jews by revelation, and transmitted by oral tradition. This science consisted mainly in understanding the combination of certain letters, words, and numbers, said to be significant.

Cabalis'tic. Mystic word-juggling. (*See* CABALIST.)

Caballe'ro. A Spanish dance, grave and stately ; so called from the ballad-music to which it was danced. The ballad begins—

> " Esta noche le mataron al caballero."

Cabbage. It is said that no sort of food causes so much thirst as cabbage, especially that called colewort. Pausanias tells us it first sprang from the sweat of Jupiter, some drops of which fell on the earth. Cœlius, Rhodiginus, Ovid, Suidas, and others repeat the same fable.

> " Some drops of sweat happening to light on the earth produced what mortals call cabbage."
> —*Rabelais : Pantagruel*, book iv. (Prologue).

Cabbage (*To*). To filch. Sometimes a tailor is called " cabbage," from his pilfering cloth given him to make up. Thus in Motteux's *Rabelais*, iv. 52, we read of " Poor Cabbage's hair." (Old French, *cabas*, theft, verb *cabasser ;*

Dutch, *kabassen ;* Swedish, *grabba ;* Danish, *griber*, our *grab*.)

> " Your tailor, instead of shreds, cabbages whole yards of cloth."—*Arbuthnot's John Bull.*

Cabbage is also a common schoolboy term for a literary crib, or other petty theft.

Cabinet Ministers. The chief officers of state in whom the administrative government is vested. It contains the First Lord of the Treasury (*the Premier*), the Lord High Chancellor, Lord President of the Council, Lord Privy Seal, Chancellor of the Exchequer, six Secretaries of State, the First Lord of the Admiralty, Lord Lieutenant and Lord Chancellor of Ireland, President of the Board of Trade, Chancellor of the Duchy of Lancaster, the President of the Board of Agriculture. The five Secretaries of State are those of the Home Department, Foreign Affairs, Colonies, War, India, and Chief-Secretary to the Lord-Lieutenant of Ireland. Sometimes other members of the Government are included, and sometimes one or two of the above left out of the Cabinet. These Ministers are privileged to consult the Sovereign in the private cabinet of the palace.

Cabi'ri. Mystic divinities worshipped in ancient Egypt, Phœnicia, Asia Minor, and Greece. They were inferior to the supreme gods. (Phœnician, *kabir*, powerful.)

Cable's Length. 100 fathoms.

⁂ Some think to avoid a difficulty by rendering Matthew xix. 24 " It is easier for a cable to go through the eye of a needle . . . .", but the word is κάμηλον, and the whole force of the passage rests on the " impossibility " of the thing, as it is distinctly stated in Mark x. 24, " How hard is it for them that *trust* in [their] riches, ἐπὶ τοῖς χρήμασιν. . ." It is impossible by the virtue of *money* or by bribes to enter the kingdom of heaven. (*See* page 205, col. 1, CAMEL.)

Cabochon (*En*). Uncut, but only polished ; applied to emeralds, rubies, and other precious stones. (French, *cabochon*.)

Cachecope Bell. A bell rung at funerals, when the pall was thrown over the coffin. (French, *cache corps*, cover over the body.)

Ca'chet (pron. *cah'shay*). *Lettres de cachet* (letters sealed). Under the old French régime, carte-blanche warrants, sealed with the king's seal, might be obtained for a consideration, and the person who held them might fill in any name. Sometimes the warrant was to set a prisoner at large, but it was more frequently for detention in the Bastille. During the administration of Cardinal Fleury 80,000 of these cachets were issued, the larger number being against the Jan'senists. In the reigns of Louis XV. and XVI. fifty-nine were obtained against the one family of Mirabeau. This scandal was abolished January 15th, 1790.

Cac'odæ'mon. An evil spirit. Astrologers give this name to the Twelfth House of Heaven, from which only evil prognostics proceed. (Greek, *kakos daimon.*)

"Hie thee to hell for shame, and leave the world,
 Thou cacodemon."
    Shakespeare: Richard III., i. 3.

Cacoe'thes (Greek). A "bad habit."
Cacoethes loquendi. A passion for making speeches or for talking.
Cacoethes scribendi. The love of rushing into print; a mania for authorship.

Ca'cus. A famous robber, represented as three-headed, and vomiting flames. He lived in Italy, and was strangled by Hercules. Sancho Panza says of the Lord Rinaldo and his friends, "They are greater thieves than Cacus." (*Don Quixote.*)

Cad. A low, vulgar fellow; an omnibus conductor. Either from cadet, or a contraction of *cadger* (a packman). The etymology of cad, *a cadendo*, is only a pun. N.B.—The Scotch *cadie* or *cawdie* (a little servant, or errand-boy, or carrier of a sedan-chair), without the diminutive, offers a plausible suggestion.

"All Edinburgh men and boys know that when sedan-chairs were discontinued, the old cadies sank into ruinous poverty, and became synonymous with roughs. The word was brought to London by James Hannay, who frequently used it."—*M. Pringle.*

Caddice or *Caddis.* Worsted galloon, crewel. (Welsh, *cadas*, brocade; *cadach* is a kerchief; Irish, *cadan.*)

"He hath ribands of all the colours i' the rainbow; . . . caddisses, cambrics, lawns."—*Shakespeare: Winter's Tale*, iv. 3.

Caddice-garter. A servant', a man of mean rank. When garters were worn in sight, the gentry used very expensive ones, but the baser sort wore worsted galloon ones. Prince Henry calls Poins a "caddice-garter." (1 *Henry IV.*, ii. 4.)

"Dost hear,
My honest caddis-garter?"
 Glapthorne: Wit in a Constable, 1639.

Caddy. A ghost, a bugbear. A caddis is a grub, a bait for anglers.

"Poor Mister Leviathan Addy !
 Lo ! his grandeur so lately a sun,
Is sinking (sad fall !) to a caddy."
Peter Pindar: Great Cry and Little Wool, epistle 1.

Cade. *Jack Cade legislation.* Pressure from without. The allusion is to the insurrection of Jack Cade, an Irishman, who headed about 20,000 armed men, chiefly of Kent, "to procure redress of grievances " (1450).

"You that love the commons, follow me ;
 Now show yourselves men ; 'tis for liberty.
We will not leave one lord, one gentleman ;
Spare none but such as go in clouted shoon."
   Shakespeare: 2 *Henry VI.*, iv. 2.

Cader Idris or *Arthur's Seat.* If any man passes the night sitting on this "chair," he will be either a poet or a madman.

Cades'sia (*Battle of*) gave the Arabs the monarchy of Persia. (A.D. 636.)

Cadet. Younger branches of noble families are called cadets, because their armorial shields are marked with a difference called a cadency.
Cadet is a student at the Royal Military Academy at Woolwich, the Royal Military College at Sandhurst, or in one of her Majesty's training ships, the *Excellent* and the *Britannia.* From these places they are sent (after passing certain examinations) into the army as ensigns or second lieutenants, and into the navy as midshipmen. (French, *cadet*, junior member of a family.)

Cadger. One who *carries* butter, eggs, and poultry to market ; a packman or huckster. From *cadge* (to carry). Hence the frame on which hawks were carried was called "a cadge," and the man who carried it, a "cadger." A man of low degree.

"Every cadger thinks himself as good as an earl."—*McDonald: Malcolm*, part ix. chap. xlv. p. 183.

Ca'di, among the Turks, Arabs, etc., is a town magistrate or inferior judge. "Cadi Lesker" is a superior cadi. The Spanish Alcaydë is the Moorish *al cadi.* (Arabic, *the judge.*)

Cadme'an Letters (*The*). The simple Greek letters introduced by Cadmus from Phœnicia. (*Greek myth.*)

Cadme'an Victory (Greek, *Kadmeia nikê* ; Latin, *Cadmea Victoria*). A victory purchased with great loss. The allusion is to the armed men who sprang out of the ground from the teeth of the dragon sown by Cadmus. These men fell foul of each other, and only five of them escaped death.

Cadme'ans. The people of Carthage are called the *Gens Cadmēa*, and so are the Thebans.

Cadmus having slain the dragon which guarded the fountain of Dircë, in Bœotia, sowed the teeth of the monster, when a number of armed men sprang up and surrounded Cadmus with intent to kill him. By the counsel of Minerva, he threw a precious stone among the armed men, who, striving for it, killed one another. The foundation of the fable is this : Cadmus having slain a famous free-booter that infested Bœotia, his banditti set upon him to revenge their captain's death ; but Cadmus sent a bribe, for which they quarrelled and slew each other.

Cadog'an (Ca-dug'-an). A club of hair worn by young French ladies ; so called from the portrait of the first Earl of Cadog'an, a print at one time very popular in France. The fashion was introduced at the court of Montbéliard by the Duchesse de Bourbon.

Cadu'ceus (4 syl.). A white wand carried by Roman officers when they went to treat for peace. The Egyptians adorned the rod with a male and female serpent twisted about it, and kissing each other. From this use of the rod, it became the symbol of eloquence and also of office. In mythology, a caduceus with wings is placed in the hands of Mercury, the herald of the gods ; and the poets feign that he could therewith give sleep to whomsoever he chose ; wherefore Milton styles it " his opiate rod " in *Paradise Lost*, xi. 133.

"So with his dread caduceus Hermes led
From the dark regions of the imprisoned dead ;
Or drove in silent shoals the lingering train
To Night's dull shore and Pluto's dreary reign."
Darwin : Loves of the Plants, ii. 291.

Cadur'ci. The people of Aquita'nia. Cahors is the modern capital.

Cædmon. Cowherd of Whitby, the greatest poet of the Anglo-Saxons. In his wonderful romance we find the bold prototype of Milton's *Paradise Lost*. The portions relating to the fall of the angels are most striking. The hero encounters, defeats, and finally slays Grendel, an evil being of supernatural powers.

Cærite Franchise (*The*). The franchise of a Roman subject in a præfecture. These subjects had the right of self-government, and were registered by the Roman censor as tax-payers ; but they enjoyed none of the privileges of a Roman citizen. Cærē was the first community placed in this dependent position, whence the term *Cærite* franchise.

Ca'erle'on, on the Usk, in Wales. The habitual residence of King Arthur, where he lived in splendid state, surrounded by hundreds of knights, twelve of whom he selected as Knights of the Round Table.

Cæsar was made by Hadrian a title, conferred on the heir presumptive to the throne (A.D. 136). Diocle'tian conferred the title on the two viceroys, calling the two emperors *Augustus* (sacred majesty). The German Emperor still assumes the title of kaiser (*q.v.*).

"Thou art an emperor, Cæsar, keisar, and Phee-zar."—*Shakespeare : Merry Wives of Windsor*, i. 3.
" No bending knees shall call thee Cæsar now."
Shakespeare : 3 *Henry VI.*, iii. 1.

Cæsar, as a title, was pretty nearly equivalent to our *Prince of Wales* and the French *dauphin*.

Cæsar's wife must be above suspicion. The name of Pompe'ia having been mixed up with an accusation against P. Clodius, Cæsar divorced her ; not because he believed her guilty, but because the wife of Cæsar must not even be suspected of crime. (*Suetonius : Julius Cæsar*, 74.)

Cæsar. (*See* page 76, 2, AUT CÆSAR.)
Julius Cæsar's sword. Crocea Mors (*yellow death*). (*See* page 76, 2, SWORD.)
Julius Cæsar won 320 triumphs.

Cæsa'rian Operation or *Cesa'rean Operation.* The extraction of a child from the womb by cutting the abdomen (Latin, *cæso*, cut from the womb). Julius Cæsar is said to have been thus brought into the world.

Cæ'sarism. The absolute rule of man over man, with the recognition of no law divine or human beyond that of the ruler's will. (*See* CHAUVINISM.)

Cæteris paribus (Latin). Other things being equal ; presuming all other conditions to be equal.

Caf (*Mount*). In Mohammedan mythology is that huge mountain in the middle of which the earth is sunk, as a night light is placed in a cup. Its foundation is the emerald Sakhrat, the reflection of which gives the azure hue to the sky.

Caf'tan. A garment worn in Turkey and other Eastern countries. It is a sort of under-tunic or vest tied by a girdle at the waist.

"Picturesque merchants and their customers, no longer in the big trousers of Egypt, but [in] the long caftans and abas of Syria."—*B. Taylor : Lands of the Saracen*, chap. ix. p. 122.

Cag Mag. Offal, bad meat; also a tough old goose; food which none can relish. (Gaelic and Welsh, *cag magu*.)

Cage. *To whistle* or *sing in the cage.* The cage is a jail, and to whistle in a cage is to turn Queen's evidence, or peach against a comrade.

Caglios'tro. *Conte de Cagliostro*, or Giuseppe Balsamo of Palermo, a charlatan who offered everlasting youth to all who would pay him for his secret (1743-1795).

Cagots. A sort of gipsy race in Gas'cony and Bearne, supposed to be descendants of the Visigoths, and shunned as something loathsome. (*See* CAQUEUX, COLLIBERTS.)

"Cagoti non fuerunt monachi, anachoritæ, aut leprosi; . . . sed genus quoddam hominum cæteris odiosum. Vasconibus *Cagots*, nonnullis *Capoti*, Burdegalentibus *Gaheti*, Vascis et Navarris *Agoti*, dicuntur."—*Ducange: Glossarium Manuale*, vol. ii., pp. 23, 24.

Cahors. *Usuriers de Cahors.* In the thirteenth century there was a colony of Jewish money-lenders settled at Cahors, which was to France what Lombard Street was to London.

Cai'aphas. The country-house of Caiaphas, in which Judas concluded his bargain to betray his Master, stood on "The Hill of Evil Counsel."

Cain - coloured Beard. Yellow, symbolic of treason. In the ancient tapestries Cain and Judas are represented with yellow beards. (*See* YELLOW.)

"He hath but a little wee face, with a little yellow beard, a Cain-coloured beard."—*Shakespeare: Merry Wives of Windsor*, i. 4.

Cain'ites (2 syl.). Disciples of Cain, a pseudo-Gnostic sect of the second century. They renounced the New Testament, and received instead *The Gospel of Judas*, which justified the false disciple and the crucifixion of Jesus. This sect maintained that heaven and earth were created by the evil principle, and that Cain with his descendants were the persecuted party.

Cairds or *Jockeys.* Gipsy tribes. Halliwell tells us "Caird" in Northumberland = tinker, and gipsies are great menders of pots and pans. (Irish, *ceard*, a tinker; Welsh, *cerdd*, art or craft.)

"Donald Caird's come again." *Popular Song.*

Caius (*Dr.*). A French physician in Shakespeare's *Merry Wives of Windsor.*

"The clipped English of Dr. Caius."—*Macaulay.*

Caius College (Cambridge). Elevated by Dr. John Key (*Caius*), of Norwich,

into a college, being previously only a hall called Gonville. Called Keys. (1557.)

Cake. A fool, a poor thing. (*Cf.* HALF-BAKED.)

Cake. *To take the cake.* To carry off the prize. The reference is to the prize-cake to the person who succeeded best in a given competition. In *Notes and Queries* (Feb. 27th, 1892, p. 176) a correspondent of New York tells us of a "cake walk" by the Southern negroes. It consists of walking round the prize cake in pairs, and umpires decide which pair walk the most gracefully. In ancient Greece a cake was the award of the toper who held out the longest.

In Ireland the best dancer in a dancing competition was rewarded, at one time, by a cake.

"A churn-dish stuck into the earth supported on its flat end a cake, which was to become the prize of the best dancer. . . . At length the competitors yielded their claims to a young man . . . who, taking the cake, placed it gallantly in the lap of a pretty girl to whom . . . he was about to be married."—*Bartlett and Coyne: Scenery and Antiquities of Ireland*, vol. ii. p. 64.

You cannot eat your cake and have it too. You cannot spend your money and yet keep it. You cannot serve God and Mammon.

Your cake [or *my cake*] *is dough.* All my swans are turned to geese. *Occisa est res tua* [or *mea*]. *Mon affaire est manquée;* my project has failed.

Cake...Dough. *I wish my cake were dough again.* I wish I had never married. Bellenden Ker says the proverb is a corruption of *Ei w'hissche my keke was d'how en geen*, which he says is tantamount to "Something whispers within me—repentance; would that my marriage were set aside."

Cakes. *Land of Cakes.* Scotland, famous for its oatmeal cakes.

"Land o' cakes and brither Scots." *Burns.*

Cal'abash. A drinking cup or water-holder; so called from the calabash nut of which it is made.

Calamanco Cat (*A*). A tortoise-shell cat. Calamanco is a glossy woollen fabric, sometimes striped or variegated. It is the Spanish word *Calamáco.*

Calam'ity. The beating down of standing corn by wind or storm. The word is derived from the Latin *calamus* (a stalk of corn). Hence, Cicero calls a storm *Calamito'sa tempestas* (a corn-levelling tempest).

"Another ill accident is drought, and the spoiling of the corn; inasmuch as the word 'calamity' was first derived from *calamus* (stalk), when the corn could not get out of the ear."—*Bacon.*

Calandri'no. A typical simpleton frequently introduced in Boccaccio's *Decameron;* expressly made to be befooled and played upon.

Calatra'va (*Red Cross Knights of*). Instituted at Calatra'va, in Spain, by Sancho III. of Castile in 1158; their badge is a red cross cut out in the form of lilies, on the left breast of a white mantle.

Calauri'a. *Pro Delo Calauria* (*Ovid: Metamorphoses*, vii. 384). Calauria was an island in the Sinus Saronĭcus which Latōna gave to Neptune in exchange for Delos. A *quid pro quo.*

Calceola'ria. Little-shoe flowers; so called from their resemblance to fairy slippers. (Latin, *cal'ceolus.*)

Calceos mutavit. He has changed his shoes, that is, has become a senator. Roman senators were distinguished by their shoes, which were sandalled across the instep and up the ankles.

Calculate is from the Latin *calculi* (pebbles), used by the Romans for counters. In the ab'acus, the round balls were called cal'culi, and it was by this instrument the Roman boys were taught to count and calculate. The Greeks voted by pebbles dropped into an urn—a method adopted both in ancient Egypt and Syria; counting these pebbles was "calculating" the number of voters. (*See* page 2, col. 1, ABACUS.)

I calculate. A peculiarity of expression common in the western states of North America. In the southern states the phrase is " I reckon," in the middle states " I expect," and in New England " I guess." All were imported from the mother country by early settlers.

" Your aunt sets two tables, I calculate ; don't she?"—*Susan Warner: Queechy* (vol. i. chap. xix.)

Calculators (*The*). Alfragan, the Arabian astronomer. Died 820.
Jedediah Buxton, of Elmeton, in Derbyshire. (1705-1775.)
George Bidder and Zerah Colburn (an American), who exhibited publicly.
Inaudi exhibited " his astounding powers of calculatin'" at Paris in 1880, his additions and subtractions were from left to right.

" Buxton, being asked 'How many cubical eighths-of-an-inch there are in a body whose three sides are 23,145,786 yards, 5,642,732 yards, and 54,965 yards?' replied correctly without setting down a figure."
"Colburn, being asked the square root of 106,929 and the cube root 268,336,125, replied before the audience had set the figures down."—*Price: Parallel History*, vol. ii. p. 570.

Cale. [*See* KALE.]

Caleb. The enchantress who carried off St. George in infancy.
Caleb, in Dryden's satire of *Absalom and Achitophel*, is meant for Lord Grey of Wark (Northumberland), one of the adherents of the Duke of Monmouth.

" And, therefore, in the name of dulness, be
The well-hung Balaam [Earl of Huntingdon]
and old Caleb free."   *Lines* 512-13.

Ca'leb Quo'tem. A parish clerk or jack-of-all-trades, in Colman's play called *The Review, or Wags of Windsor,* which first appeared in 1808. Colman borrowed the character from a farce by Henry Lee (1798) entitled *Throw Physic to the Dogs.*

" I resolved, like Caleb Quotem, to have a place at the review."—*Washington Irving.*

Caledon. Scotland. (*See next article.*)

" Not thus, in ancient days of Caledon,
Was thy voice mute amid the festal crowd."
Sir W. Scott.

Caledo'nia. Scotland. A corruption of *Celyddon*, a Celtic word meaning " a dweller in woods and forests." The word Celt is itself a contraction of the same word (*Celyd*), and means the same thing.

" Sees Caledonia in romantic view."
Thomson.

" O Caledonia, stern and wild,
Meet nurse for a poetic child."
Sir W. Scott: Lay of the Last Minstrel.

Calembour (French). A pun, a jest. From the "Jester of Kahlenberg," whose name was Wigand von Theben; a character introduced in *Tyll Eulenspiegel*, a German tale. Eulenspiegel (a fool or jester) means Owl's looking-glass, and may probably have suggested the title of the periodical called the *Owl*, the witty but satirical "looking-glass" of the passing follies of the day. The jester of Calembourg visited Paris in the reign of Louis XV., and soon became noted for his blunders and puns.

Calendar.
The Julian Calendar, introduced B.C. 46. It fixed the ordinary year to 365 days, with an extra day every fourth year (leap year). This is called " The Old Style."
The Gregorian Year. A modification of the Julian Calendar, introduced in 1582 by Pope Gregory XIII., and adopted in Great Britain in 1752. This is called " the New Style."
The Mohammedan Calendar, used in Mohammedan countries, dates from July 16th, 622, the day of the Hegira. It consists of 12 lunar months (29 days, 12 hours, 44 minutes). A cycle is 30 years.
The Revolutionary Calendar was the

work of Fabre d'Eglantine and Mons. Romme.

Calendar. *A Newgate Calendar* or "Malefactors' Bloody Register," containing the biography, confessions, dying speeches, etc., of notorious criminals. Began in 1700.

Calendars (*The Three*) were three royal princes, disguised as begging dervishes, the subjects of three tales in the *Arabian Nights*.

Cal'ends. The first of every month was so called by the Romans. Varro says the term originated in the practice of *calling together* or assembling the people on the first day of the month, when the pontifex informed them of the time of the new moon, the day of the nones, with the festivals and sacred days to be observed. The custom continued till A.U.C. 450, when the fasti or calendar was posted in public places. (*See* GREEK CALENDS.)

Cal'epin (*A*). A dictionary. (Italian, *calepino*.) Ambrosio Calepino, of Calepio, in Italy, was the author of a dictionary, so that "my Calepin," like my Euclid, my Johnson, according to Cocker, etc., have become common nouns from proper names. Generally called Cal'epin, but the subjoined quotation throws the accent on the *le*.

"Whom do you prefer
For the best linguist? And I seelily
Said that I thought Calepine's Dictionary."
        Dr. Donne: Fourth Satire.

Caleys (A Stock Exchange term). Caledonian Railway Ordinary Stock. A contraction of Calĕ-donians. (*See* STOCK EXCHANGE SLANG.)

Calf-love. Youthful fancy as opposed to lasting attachment.

"I thought it was a childish besotment you had for the man—a sort of calf-love. . . ."—*Rhoda Broughton.*

Calf-skin. Fools and jesters used to wear a calf-skin coat buttoned down the back. In allusion to this custom, Faulconbridge says insolently to the Archduke of Austria, who had acted most basely to Richard Cœur-de-Lion—

"Thou wear a lion's hide! Doff it, for shame,
And hang a calf-skin on those recreant limbs."
        Shakespeare: King John, iii. 1.

Cal'iban. Rude, uncouth, unknown; as a Caliban style, a Caliban language. The allusion is to Shakespeare's Caliban (*The Tempest*), in which character Lord Falkland, etc., said that Shakespeare had not only invented a *new creation*, but also a *new language*.

"Satan had not the privilege, as Caliban, to use new phrases, and diction unknown."—*Dr. Bentley.*

Coleridge says, "In him [Caliban], as in some brute animals, this advance to the intellectual faculties, without the moral sense, is marked by the appearance of vice."
(Caliban is the "missing link" between brute animals and man.)

Calibre [*kal'i-ber*]. *A mind of no calibre :* of no capacity. *A mind of great calibre :* of large capacity. Calibre is the *bore* of a gun, and, figuratively, the bore or compass of one's intelligence.

"The enemy had generally new arms . . . of uniform caliber."—*Grant: Memoirs*, vol. i. chap. xxxix. p. 572.

"We measure men's calibre by the broadest circle of achievements."—*Chapin: Lessons of Faith*, p. 16.

Caliburn. Same as *Excalibur*, King Arthur's well-known sword. (*See* SWORD.)

"Onward Arthur paced, with hand
On Caliburn's resistless brand."
        Scott: Bridal of Triermain.

Cal'ico. So called from Cali'cut, in Malabar, once the chief port and emporium of Hindustan.

Cal'idore (3 syl.). Sir Cal'idore is the type of *courtesy*, and hero of the sixth book of Spenser's *Faërie Queene*. He is described as the most courteous of all knights, and is entitled the "all-beloved." The model of the poet was Sir Philip Sidney. His adventure is against the Blatant Beast, whom he muzzles, chains, and drags to Faërie Land.

"Sir Gawain was the Calidore of the Round Table."—*Southey.*

Calig'orant. An Egyptian giant and cannibal who used to entrap strangers with a hidden net. This net was made by Vulcan to catch Mars and Venus; Mercury stole it for the purpose of catching Chloris, and left it in the temple of Anu'bis; Calig'orant stole it thence. At length Astolpho blew his magic horn, and the giant ran affrighted into his own net, which dragged him to the ground. Whereupon Astolpho made the giant his captive, and despoiled him of his net. This is an allegory. Caligorant was a great sophist and heretic in the days of Ariosto, who used to entangle people with his talk; but being converted by Astolpho to the true faith, was, as it were, caught in his own net, and both his sophistry and heresy were taken from him. (*Ariosto: Orlando Furioso.*)

Calig'ula. A Roman emperor; so called because he wore a military sandal called a caliga, which had no upper leather, and was used only by the common soldiers. (12, 37-41.)

"The word *caligæ*, however,' continued the Baron . . . 'means, in its primitive sense, sandals ; and Caius Cæsar . . . received the cognomen of Caligula, *a caligis, sive cal'igis levioribus, quibus adolescentior non fuerat in exercitu German'ici patris sui.* And the *caligæ* were also proper to the monastic bodies ; for we read in the ancient Glossarium, upon the rule of St. Benedict . . . that *caligæ* were tied with latchets."—*Scott : Waverley,* xlviii.

Caligula's Horse. Incita'tus. It was made a priest and consul, had a manger of ivory, and drank wine from a golden goblet. (*See* HORSE.)

Ca'liph or *Calif.* A title given to the successors of Mahomet. Among the Saracens a caliph is one vested with supreme dignity. The caliphat of Bagdad reached its highest splendour under Haroun al Raschid, in the ninth century. For the last 200 years the appellation has been swallowed up in the titles of *Shah, Sultan, Emir,* and so on. (Arabic, *Khalifah,* a successor ; *khalafa,* to succeed.)

Calis'ta. The heroine of Rowe's *Fair Penitent.*

Calis'to and Arcas. Calisto was an Arcadian nymph metamorphosed into a she-bear by Jupiter. Her son Arcas having met her in the chase, would have killed her, but Jupiter converted him into a he-bear, and placed them both in the heavens, where they are recognised as the Great and Little Bear.

Calix'tines (3 syl.). A religious sect of Bohemians in the fifteenth century ; so called from *Calix* (the chalice), which they insisted should be given to the laity in the sacrament of the Lord's Supper, as well as the bread or wafer.

Call (*A*). A "divine" summons or invitation, as "a call to the ministry."
A call before the curtain. An applause inviting a favourite actor to appear before the curtain, and make his bow to the audience.
A Gospel call. The invitation of the Gospel to men to believe in Jesus to the saving of their souls.
A morning call. A short morning visit.
A call on shareholders. A demand to pay up a part of the money due for shares allotted in a company.
Payable at call. To be paid on demand.

Call Bird (*A*). A bird trained as a decoy.

Call-boy (*The*). A boy employed in theatres to "call" or summon actors, when it is time for them to make their appearance on the stage.

7*

Call of Abraham. The invitation or command of God to Abraham, to leave his idolatrous country, under the promise of being made a great nation.

Call of God. An invitation, exhortation, or warning, by the dispensations of Providence (Isa. xxii. 12) ; divine influence on the mind to do or avoid something (Heb. iii. 1).

Call of the House. An imperative summons sent to every Member of Parliament to attend. This is done when the sense of the whole House is required. At the muster the names of the members are *called over,* and defaulters reported.

Call to Arms (*To*). To summon to prepare for battle. "*Ad arma vocare.*"

Call to the Bar. The admission of a law student to the privileges of a barrister. The names of those qualified are *called over.* (*See* page 94, col. 1, BAR.)

Call to the Pastorate. An invitation to a minister by the members of a Presbyterian or Nonconformist church to preside over a certain congregation.

Call to the Unconverted. An invitation accompanied with promises and threats, to induce the unconverted to receive the gospel. Richard Baxter wrote a book so entitled.

Call (*To*). *I call God to witness.* I solemnly declare that what I state is true.
To call. To invite : as, the trumpet calls.

"If honour calls, where'er she points the way,
The sons of honour follow and obey."
Churchill : The Farewell, stanza 7.

To call [a man] *out.* To challenge him ; to appeal to a man's honour to come forth and fight a duel.
To call in question. To doubt the truth of a statement ; to challenge the truth of a statement. "*In dubium vocare.*"
To call over the coals. (*See* COALS.)
To call to account. To demand an explanation ; to reprove.

Called. *He is called to his account.* He is removed by death. Called to the judgment seat of God to give an account of his deeds, whether they be good, or whether they be evil. (*See* page 202, col. 1, CALLING.)

Calla'bre or *Calaber.* A Cala'brian fur. Ducange says, "At Chichester the 'priest vicars' and at St. Paul's the 'minor canons' wore a calabre amyce ; " and Bale, in his *Image of Both Churches,* alludes to the "fair rochets of Raines (*Rennes*), and costly grey amices of calaber and cats' tails."

"The Lord Mayor and those aldermen above the chair ought to have their coats furred with grey amis, and also with changeable taffeta; and those below the chair with calabre and with green taffeta."—*Hutton: New View of London.*

Caller Herrings. Fresh herrings. Hence "caller air." (Anglo-Saxon, *calian*, to cool.)

Calligraphy (*The art of*). Writing very minutely and yet clearly. Peter Bale, in the sixteenth century, wrote in the compass of a silver penny the Lord's Prayer, the Creed, the Ten Commandments, two Latin prayers, his own name, the day of the month and date of the year since the accession of Queen Elizabeth, and a motto. With a glass this writing could be read. By photography a sheet of the *Times* newspaper has been reduced to a smaller compass. (Greek, *calos-grapho*, I write beautifully.)

Callim'achos. *The Italian Callimachos.* Filippo Buonaccorsi (1437-1496).

Calling. A vocation, trade, or profession. The allusion is to the calling of the apostles by Jesus Christ to follow Him. In the legal profession persons must still be called to the bar before they can practise.
Effectual calling. An invitation to believe in Jesus, rendered effectual by the immediate operation of the Holy Ghost.

Calliope [*Kal-lĭ-o-pe*, 4 syl., Greek, καλὸς, ὂψ, *beautiful voice*]. The muse of epic or heroic poetry. Her emblems are a stylus and wax tablets. The painting of this Muse by Ercolana Ercolanetti (1615-1687) and her statue by Clementi (who died in 1580) are very celebrated.
‡ The Greek word is Καλλιόπη, in which the *i* is short. Erroneously called "Caliope."

Callip'olis. A character in the *Battle of Alcazar* (1594) by George Peele. It is referred to by Pistol in 2 *Henry IV.*, act ii. 4 ; and Sir W. Scott uses the word over and over again as the synonym of lady-love, sweetheart, charmer. Sir Walter always spells the word Callipŏlis, but Peele calls it Calipŏlis. The drunken Mike Lambourne says to Amy Robsart—

"Hark ye, most fair Callipolis, or most lovely countess of clouts, and divine duchess of dark corners."—*Kenilworth,* chap. xxxiii.

And the modest Roland Græme calls the beautiful Catherine his "most fair Callipŏlis." (*The Abbot,* chap. xi.)

Callippic Period. The correction of the Meton'ic cycle by Callippos. In four cycles, or seventy-six years, the Metonic calculation was seven and a-half in excess. Callippos proposed to quadruple the period of Meton, and deduct a day at the end of it : at the expiration of which period Callippos imagined that the new and full moons returned to the same day of the solar year.

Callir'rhoe (4 syl.). The lady-love of Chæ'reas, in Chariton's Greek romance, entitled the *Loves of Chæ'reas and Callirrhoë,* written in the eighth century.

Cal'omel. Hooper says—
"This name, which means 'beautiful black,' was originally given to the Æthiop's mineral, or black sulphuret of mercury. It was afterwards applied in joke by Sir Theodore Mayerne to the chloride of mercury, in honour of a favourite negro servant whom he employed to prepare it. As calomel is a *white* powder, the name is merely a jocular misnomer."—*Medical Dictionary.*

Greek, καλός, beautiful, μέλας, black.

Calo'yers. Monks in the Greek Church, who follow the rule of St. Basil. They are divided into *cen'obites,* who recite the offices from midnight to sunrise ; *an'chorites,* who live in hermitages ; and *recluses,* who shut themselves up in caverns and live on alms. (Greek, καλὸς and γέρων, beautiful old man.)

Calpe (2 syl.). *Calpë and Ab'yla.* The two pillars of Hercules. According to one account, these two were originally only one mountain, which Hercules tore asunder ; but some say he piled up each mountain separately, and poured the sea between them.
"Heaves up huge Abyla on Afric's sand,
Crowns with high Calpë Europe's salient strand,
Crests with opposing towers the splendid scene,
And pours from urns immense the sea between."
Darwin: Economy of Vegetation.

Cal'umet [*the peace-pipe*]. When the North American Indians make peace or form an alliance, the high contracting parties smoke together to ratify the arrangement.
The peace-pipe is about two and a-half feet long, the bowl is made of highly-polished red marble, and the stem of a reed, which is decorated with eagles' quills, women's hair, and so on.
"The Great Spirit at an ancient period called the Indian nations together, and standing on the precipice of the red pipe-stone rock, broke off a piece which he moulded into the bowl of a pipe, and fitting on it a long reed, filled the pipe with the bark of red willow, and smoked over them, turning to the four winds. He told them the *red* colour of the pipe represented their flesh, and when they

smoked it they must bury their war-clubs and scalping-knives. At the last whiff the Great Spirit disappeared."

To present the calumet to a stranger is a mark of hospitality and good-will; to refuse the offer is an act of hostile defiance.

"Wash the war-paint from your faces,
Wash the war-stains from your fingers,
Bury your war-clubs and your weapons; . . .
Smoke the calumet together,
And as brothers live henceforward."
Longfellow: Hiawatha, i.

Cal'vary [*bare skull*], **Gol'gotha** [*skull*]. The place of our Lord's crucifixion; so called from some fanciful resemblance which it bore to a human skull. The present church of "the Holy Sepulchre" has no claim to be considered the site thereof; it is far more likely that the "mosque of Omar," or *the dome of the rock,* occupies the real site.

A Calvary. A representation of 'the successive scenes of the Passion of Christ in a series of pictures, etc., in a church. The shrine containing the representations.

Calvary Clover said to have sprung up in the track made by Pilate when he went to the cross to see his "title affixed" [Jesus of Nazareth, king of the Jews]. It is a common trefoil, probably a native of India or Turkey. Each of the three round leaves has a little carmine spot in the centre. In the day-time the three leaves of the trefoil form a sort of cross; and in the flowering season the plant bears a little yellow flower, like a "crown of thorns." Julian tells us that each of the three leaves had in his time a white cross in the centre, and that the centre cross lasts visible longer than the crosses of the other two leaves. (*See* CHRISTIAN TRADITIONS.)

Calvary Cross (*A*). A Latin cross mounted on three steps (or grises).

Calvert's Entire. The 14th Foot. Called *Calvert* from their colonel, Sir Harry Calvert (1806-1826), and *entire,* because three entire battalions were kept up for the good of Sir Harry, when adjutant-general. The term is, of course, a play on Calvert's malt liquor. The regiment is now called The Prince of Wales's Own (West Yorks. Regiment).

Calves. The inhabitants of the *Isle of Wight* are so called from a legendary joke which states that a calf once got its head firmly wedged in a wooden pale, and, instead of breaking up the pale, the farm-man cut off the calf's head.

Calves gone to Grass (*His*). Said of a spindle-legged man. And another

mocking taunt is, "Veal will be dear, because there are no calves."

Calves' Head. *There are many ways of dressing a calf's head.* Many ways of saying or doing a foolish thing; a simpleton has many ways of showing his folly; or, generally, if one way won't do we must try another. The allusion is to the great Calves' Head Club banquet, when the board was laden with calves' heads cooked in sundry ways and divers fashions.

Calves' Head Club. Instituted in ridicule of Charles I. The great annual banquet was held on the 30th January, and consisted of a cod's head, to represent the person of Charles Stuart, independent of his kingly office; a pike with little ones in its mouth, an emblem of tyranny; a boar's head with an apple in its mouth to represent the king preying on his subjects; and calves' heads dressed in sundry ways to represent Charles in his regal capacity. After the banquet, the king's book (*Icon Basil'ikë*) was burnt, and the parting cup was, "To those worthy patriots who killed the tyrant."

Calvinism. The five chief points of Calvinism are:

(1) Predestination, or particular election.

(2) Irresistible grace.

(3) Original sin, or the total depravity of the natural man, which renders it morally impossible to believe and turn to God of his own free will.

(4) Particular redemption.

(5) Final perseverance of the saints.

Cal'ydon. A forest supposed, in the romances relating to King Arthur, to occupy the northern portion of England.

Calyp'so, in Fénelon's *Télémaque,* is meant to represent Madame de Montespan. In fairy mythology, she was queen of the island Ogyg'ia on which Ulysses was wrecked, and where he was detained for seven years.

Calypso's Isle. Gozo, near Malta. Called in classic mythology Ogyg'ia.

Cam and Isis. The universities of Cambridge and Oxford; so called from the rivers on which they stand.

"May you, my Cam and Isis, preach it long,
'The right divine of kings to govern wrong.'"
Pope: Dunciad, iv. 187.

Cama. The God of love and marriage in Indian mythology.

Cama'cho, "richest of men," makes grand preparations for his wedding with

Quite'ria, "fairest of women"; but, as the bridal party were on their way, Basil'ius cheats him of his bride by pretending to kill himself. As he is supposed to be dying, Quiteria is given to him in marriage as a mere matter of form; but, as soon as this is done, up jumps Basilius, and shows that his wounds were a mere pretence. (*Cervantes: Don Quixote*, pt. ii. bk. 2, ch. 3, 4.)

Camal'dolites (4 syl.). A religious order of great rigidity of life, founded in the vale of Camal'doli, in the Tuscan Apennines, by St. Romuald, a Benedictine. (Eleventh century.)

Camaral'zaman (*Prince*) fell in love with Badou'ra, Princess of China, the moment he saw her. (*Arabian Nights: Prince Camaralzaman.*)

Camarilla (Spanish). A clique; the confidants or private advisers of the sovereign. It literally means a small private chamber, and is in Spain applied to the room in which boys are flogged.

"Encircled with a dangerous camarilla."—*The Times.*

Camari'na. *Ne moveas Camarinam* (Don't meddle with Camarina). Camarīna was a lake in Sicily, which, in time of drought, yielded a pestilential stench. The inhabitants consulted an oracle about draining it, and Apollo replied, "Don't meddle with it." Nevertheless, they drained it, and ere long an enemy marched an army over the bed of the lake and plundered the city. The proverb is applied to those who remove one evil, but thus give place to a greater. The Channel may be an evil to those who suffer sea-sickness, but it is a million times better to endure this evil than to make it a high road to invaders. The application is very extensive, as: Don't kill the small birds, or you will be devoured by insects. One pest is a safeguard against a greater one.

∵ A similar Latin phrase is *Anagyrin movēre.*

"When the laird of Ellangowan drove the gipsies from the neighbourhood, though they had been allowed to remain there undisturbed hitherto, Dominie Sampson warned him of the danger by quoting the proverb 'Ne moveas Camarinam.'"—*Sir W. Scott: Guy Mannering*, chap. vii.

Cam'balo's Ring. Given him by his sister Can'acë. It had the virtue of healing wounds. (*See* CAMBEL.) (*Spenser: Faërie Queene*, bk. iv.)

"Well mote ye wonder how that noble knight,
After he had so often wounded been,
Could stand on foot now to renew the fight ...
All was through virtue of the ring he wore;
The which, not only did not from him let
One drop of blood to fall, but did restore
His weakened powers, and dulled spirits
whet." *Spenser: Faërie Queene*, iv. 3.

Cambel. Called by Chaucer, Cam'-balo; brother of Can'acë, a female paragon. He challenged every suitor to his sister's hand, and overthrew all except Tri'amond, who married the lady. (*Spenser: Faërie Queene*, book iv.) (*See* CANACE.)

Camber. Second son of King Brute, to whom Wales was left, whence its name of Cambria. (*British fable.*)

Cam'bria. The ancient name of Wales, the land of the Cimbri or Cymry.

"Cambria's fatal day."
Gray: Bard.

Cam'brian. Pertaining to Wales; Welsh. (*See above.*)

"The Cambrian mountains, like far clouds,
That skirt the blue horizon, dusky rise."
Thomson: Spring, 961—62.

Cam'brian Series (in geology). The earliest fossiliferous rocks in North Wales. So named by Professor Sedgwick.

Cambric. A kind of very fine white linen cloth, so named from Cambray or Cameryk, in Flanders, where it is still the chief manufacture.

"He hath ribbons of all the colours of the rainbow; inkles, caddisses, cambricks, and lawns."—*Shakespeare: Winter's Tale,* iv. 3.

Cam'buscan'. King of Sarra, in the land of Tartary; the model of all royal virtues. His wife was El'feta; his two sons, Algarsife and Cam'balo; and his daughter, Can'acë. On her birthday (October 15th) the King of Arabia and India sent Cambuscan a "steed of brass, which, between sunrise and sunset, would carry its rider to any spot on the earth." All that was required was to whisper the name of the place in the horse's ear, mount upon his back, and turn a pin set in his ear. When the rider had arrived at the place required, he had to turn another pin, and the horse instantly descended, and, with another screw of the pin, vanished till it was again required. This story is told by Chaucer in the *Squire's Tale*, but was never finished. Milton (*Il Penseroso*) accents the word Cambus'-can.

"Him that left half-told
The story of Cambuscan bold."
(*See* CANACE.)

Camby'ses (3 syl.). A pompous, ranting character in Preston's lamentable tragedy of that name.

"Give me a cup of sack, to make mine eyes look red; for I must speak in passion, and I will do it in King Cambyses' vein."—*Shakespeare:* 1 *Henry IV.,* ii. 4.

Camden Society, for the publication of early historic and literary remains, is named in honour of William Camden, the historian.

Camel. The name of Mahomet's favourite camel was Al Kaswa. The mosque at Koba covers the spot where it knelt when Mahomet fled from Mecca. Mahomet considered the kneeling of the camel as a sign sent by God, and remained at Koba in safety for four days. The swiftest of his camels was *Al Aḋha.*

Camel. The prophet Mahomet's camel performed the whole journey from Jerusalem to Mecca in four bounds, for which service he had a place in heaven with Al-borak (the prophet's "horse"), Balaam's ass, Tobit's dog, and Ketmir (the dog of the seven sleepers). (*Curzon.*)

Camel. "It is easier for a camel to go through the eye of a needle, than for a rich man to enter into the kingdom of God" (Matt. xix. 24). In the Koran we find a similar expression: "The impious shall find the gates of heaven shut; nor shall he enter till a camel shall pass through the eye of a needle." In the Rabbinical writings we have a slight variety which goes to prove that the word "camel" should not be changed into "cable," as Theophylact suggests : "Perhaps thou art one of the Pampe-dith'ians, who can make an elephant pass through the eye of a needle." (*See* CABLE.)

"It is as hard to come, as for a camel
To thread the postern of a needle's eye."
Shakespeare: Richard II., v. 5.

Camellia. The technical name of a genus, and the popular name of the species of evergreen shrubs ; so named in honour of G. J. Kamel (Latin *Camellius*), a Spanish Jesuit. Introduced into England in 1739.

Camelot (Somersetshire), where King Arthur held his court. (*See* WINCHESTER.)

Camelote (2 syl.). Fustian, rubbish, trash. The cloth so called ought to be made of goats' hair, but is a mixture of wool and silk, wool and hair, or wool, silk, and hair, etc. (French, *camelot ;* Arabic, *camlat.*) (*See* page 206, CAMLET.)

Cameo. An anaglyph on a precious stone. The *anaglyph* is when the figure is raised in relief ; an *intaglio* is when the figure is hollowed out. The word cameo means an onyx, and the most famous cameo in the world is the onyx containing the *apotheosis of Augustus.* These precious stones have two layers

of different colours, one serving for the figure, and the other for the ground.

Cameron Highlanders. The 79th Regiment of Infantry, raised by Allan Cameron, of Errock, in 1793. Now called "The Queen's Own Cameron Highlanders."

Cameronian Regiment. The 26th Infantry, which had its origin in a body of Cameronians (*q.v.*), in the Revolution of 1688. Now the 1st Battalion of the Scottish Rifles ; the 2nd Battalion is the old No. 90.

Cameronians. The strictest sect of Scotch Presbyterians, organised in 1680, by Richard Cam'eron, who was slain in battle at Aird's Moss in 1680. He objected to the alliance of Church and State. In 1876 most of the Cameronians were merged in the Free Church. In history the Cameronians are generally called the Covenanters.

Camilla. Virgin queen of the Volscians. Virgil (*Æneid*, vii. 809) says she was so swift that she could run over a field of corn without bending a single blade, or make her way over the sea without even wetting her feet.

" Not so when swift Camilla scours the plain,
Flies o'er the unbending corn and skims along the main."
Pope: Essay on Criticism, 372-3.

Camillus, five times Dictator of Rome, was falsely accused of embezzlement, and went into voluntary exile ; but when the Gauls besieged Rome, he returned and delivered his country.

"Camillus, only vengeful to his foes."
Thomson: Winter.

Camisard. In French history, the Camisards are the Protestant insurgents of the Cevennes, who resisted the violence of the dragonnades, after the revocation of the edict of Nantes. Their leader was Cavalier, afterwards Governor of Jersey.

Camisarde or *Camisa'do.* A night attack ; so called because the attacking party wore a *camise* or peasant's smock over their armour, both to conceal it, and that they might the better recognise each other in the dark.

Camisole (3 syl.). A loose jacket worn by women when dressed in *negligée* (French).

Camisole de Force. A strait-waistcoat. Frequently mentioned in accounts of capital punishments in France.

Camlan (*Battle of,* Cornwall), which put an end to the Knights of the Round

Table. Here Arthur received his death wound from the hand of his nephew Modred. (A.D. 542.)

Cam'let is not connected with the word camel ; it is a fine cloth made of *goats'* hair, called Turkish yarn, and is from the Arabic word *camlat,* which Littré says is so called from *seil el camel* (the Angora goat).

Cam'mock. *As crooked as a cammock.* The cammock is a piece of timber bent for the knee of a ship ; a hockey-stick ; a shinny-club. (*Anglo-Saxon.*)

"Though the cammock, the more it is bowed the better it is ; yet the bow, the more it is bent the weaker it waxeth."—*Lily.*

Camorra. A secret society of Italy organised early in the nineteenth century. It claimed the right of settling disputes, etc.

Camorrist. One of the desperadoes belonging to the Camorra. "Camorrism," the gospel of the league.

Camp Candlestick (*A*). A bottle, or a soldier's bayonet.

Camp-followers. Non-combatants (such as servants, carriers, hostlers, suttlers, laundresses, and so on), who follow an army. We are told that in 1859 as many as 85,000 camp-followers were in attendance on 15,000 combatants in a Bengal army.

Campaign Wig (*A*), imported from France. It was made very full, was curled, and was eighteen inches in length in the front, with drop locks. In some cases the back part of the wig was put in a black silk bag. Of course the campaign referred to the victories of Marlborough. (*Social Life in the Reign of Queen Anne,* chap. xii.)

☙ There were also campaign coats, campaign lace, campaign shoes, campaign shirts, campaign gowns, campaign waistcoats, etc.

Campa'nia. Properly the *Terra di Lavo'ro* of Italy, *i.e.* the plain country about Cap'ua.

"Disdainful of Campania's gentle plains."
Thomson : Summer.

Campaspe (3 syl.). A beautiful harlot, whom Alexander the Great handed over to Apellês. Apelles drew her in the nude.

"When Cupid and Campaspe played
At cards for kisses, Cupid paid." *Lily.*

Campbells are Coming (*The*). This soul-stirring song was composed in 1715, when the Earl of Mar raised the standard for the Stuarts against George I.

John Campbell was Commander-in-Chief of his Majesty's forces, and the rebellion was quashed. The main interest now attached to the famous song is connected with the siege of Lucknow in the Indian rebellion, 1857. Nana Sahib had massacred women and children most foully, and while the survivors were expecting instant death, a Scotch woman lying ill on the ground heard the pibroch, and exclaimed, "Dinna ye hear it ? Dinna ye hear it ? The pipes o' Havelock sound." And soon afterwards the rescue was accomplished.

The first verse runs thus :—

"The Campbells are coming, O-ho ! O-ho !
The Campbells are coming, O-ho !
The Campbells are coming to bonnie Loch Leven,
The Campbells are coming, O-ho !

Campbellite (3 syl.). A follower of John McLeod Campbell, who taught the universality of the atonement, for which, in 1831, he was deposed.

Campceiling. A ceiling sloping on one side from the vertical wall towards a plane surface in the middle. A corruption of *cam* (twisted or bent) ceiling. (Halliwell gives *cam,* " awry.")

Campeador (*cam-pa'-dor*). The Cid (*q.v.*).

Can'ace (3 syl.). A paragon of women, the daughter of King Cambuscan', to whom the King of Arabia and India sent as a present a mirror and a ring. The mirror would tell the lady if any man on whom she set her heart would prove true or false, and the ring (which was to be worn on her thumb) would enable her to understand the language of birds and to converse with them. It would also give the wearer perfect knowledge of the medicinal properties of all roots. Chaucer never finished the tale, but probably he meant to marry Can'acë to some knight who would be able to overthrow her two brothers, Cam'balo and Al'garsife, in the tournament. (*Squire's Tale.*) (*See below.*)

Can'acë was courted by a crowd of suitors, but her brother, Cam'balo or Cambel, gave out that anyone who pretended to her hand must encounter *him* in single combat and overthrow him. She ultimately married Tri'amond, son of the fairy Ag'apë. (*Spenser : Faërie Queene,* bk. iv. 3.) (*See* CAMBEL.)

Can'ache (3 syl.). One of Actæon's dogs. (Greek, "the clang of metal falling.")

Can'ada Balsam. Made from the *Pinus balsamea,* a native of Canada,

Canaille (French, *can-nay'e*). The mob; the rabble (Italian, *canaglia*, a pack of dogs, from Latin *canis*, a dog).

Canard. A hoax. Cornelissen, to try the gullibility of the public, reported in the papers that he had twenty ducks, one of which he cut up and threw to the nineteen, who devoured it greedily. He then cut up another, then a third, and so on till nineteen were cut up; and as the nineteenth was gobbled up by the surviving duck, it followed that this one duck actually ate nineteen ducks—a wonderful proof of duck voracity. This tale had the run of all the papers, and gave a new word to the language. (French, *cane*, a duck.) (*Quetelet.*)

Canary (*A*). Slang for "a guinea" or "sovereign." Gold coin is so called because, like a canary, it is yellow.

Canary-bird (*A*). A jail-bird. At one time certain desperate convicts were dressed in yellow; and jail was the *cage* of these "canaries."

Cancan. *To dance the cancan.* A free-and-easy way of dancing quadrilles invented by Rigolboche, and adopted in the public gardens, the opera comique, and the casinos of Paris. (*Cancan* familiarity, tittle-tattle.)

"They were going through a quadrille with all those supplementary gestures introduced by the great Rigolboche, a notorious *danseuse*, to whom the notorious cancan owes its origin."—*A. Egmont Hake: Paris Originals (the Chiffonier).*

Cancel, to blot out, is merely "to make lattice-work." This is done by making a cross over the part to be omitted. (Latin, *cancello*, to make trellis.) (*See* CROSS IT OUT.)

Cancer (the Crab) appears when the sun has reached his highest northern limit, and begins to go backward towards the south; but, like a crab, the return is sideways (June 21st to July 23rd).

⁂ According to fable, Cancer was the animal which Juno sent against Hercules, when he combated the Hydra of Lernê. Cancer bit the hero's foot, but Hercules killed the creature, and Juno took it up to heaven, and made it one of the twelve signs of the zodiac.

Candaules (3 syl.). King of Lydia, who exposed the charms of his wife to Gyges; whereupon the queen compelled Gyges to assassinate her husband, after which she married the murderer, who became king, and reigned twenty-eight years. (716–678.)

Candidate (3 syl.) means "clothed in white." Those who solicited the office of consul, quæstor, prætor, etc.,

among the Romans, arrayed themselves in a loose white robe. It was loose that they might show the people their scars, and white in sign of fidelity and humility. (Latin, *candidus*, whence *candidāti*, clothed in white, etc.)

Candide (2 syl.). The hero of Voltaire's novel so called. All sorts of misfortunes are heaped upon him, and he bears them all with cynical indifference.

Candle.
Bell, Book, and Candle. (*See* page 120, col. 1, BELL, etc.)

Fine (or *Gay*) *as the king's candle.* "*Bariolé comme la chandelle des rois*," in allusion to an ancient custom of presenting, on January 6th, a candle of various colours to the three kings of Cologne. It is generally applied to a woman overdressed, especially with gay ribbons and flowers. "Fine as fivepence."

The game is not worth the candle (Le jeu ne vaut pas la chandelle). Not worth even the cost of the candle that lights the players.

To burn the candle at both ends. In French, "*Brûler la chandelle par les deux bouts*." To indulge in two or more expensive luxuries or dissipated habits at the same time; to haste to rise up early and late take rest, eating the bread of carefulness.

To hold a candle to the devil. To aid or countenance that which is wrong. The allusion is to the practice of Roman Catholics, who burn candles before the image of a favourite saint, carry them in funeral processions, and place them on their altars.

⁂ When Jessica (in the *Merchant of Venice*, ii. 6) says to Lorenzo: "What, must I hold a candle to my shame?" she means, Must I direct attention to this disguise, and blazon my folly abroad? Why, "Cupid himself would blush to see me thus transformed to a boy." She does not mean, Must I glory in my shame?

To sell by the candle. A species of sale by auction. A pin is thrust through a candle about an inch from the top, and bidding goes on till the candle is burnt down to the pin, when the pin drops into the candlestick, and the last bidder is declared the purchaser. This sort of auction was employed in 1893, according to the *Reading Mercury* (Dec. 16), at Aldermaston, near Reading.

"The Council thinks it meet to propose the way of selling by 'inch [of candle,' as being the most probable means to procure the true value of the goods."—*Milton: Letters*, etc.

To smell of the lamp (or *candle*). To betray laborious art, but the best literary work is the art of concealing art ; to manifest great pains and long study by night.

To vow a candle to the devil. To propitiate the devil by a bribe, as some seek to propitiate the saints in glory by a votive candle.

What is the Latin for candle?—*Tacë.* Here is a play of words : *ta'ce* means hold your tongue, don't bother me. (*See* GOOSE.)

Candles used by Roman Catholics at funerals are the relic of an ancient Roman custom.

Candle-holder. An abettor. The reference is to the practice of holding a candle in the Catholic Church for the reader, and in ordinary life to light a workman when he requires more light.

"I'll be candle-holder and look on."—*Shakespeare: Romeo and Juliet,* i. 4.

Candles of the Night. The stars are so called by Shakespeare, in the *Merchant of Venice,* v. 1. Milton has improved upon the idea :—

" Else, O thievish Night,
Why shouldst thou, but for some felonious end,
In thy dark lantern thus close up the stars
That Nature hung in heaven, and filled their lamps
With everlasting oil, to give due light
To the misled and lonely traveller ? "
Comus, 200-206.

Candlemas Day. The feast of the purification of the Virgin Mary, when Christ was presented by her in the Temple. February 2nd, when, in the Roman Catholic Church, there is a candle procession, to consecrate all the candles which will be needed in the church during the year. The candles symbolise Jesus Christ, called " the light of the world," and " a light to lighten the Gentiles." It was the old Roman custom of burning candles to the goddess Feb'rua, mother of Mars, to scare away evil spirits.

" On Candlemas Day
Candles and candlesticks throw all away."

Candour (*Mrs.*). A type of female backbiters. In Sheridan's comedy of *The School for Scandal.*

"The name of ' Mrs. Candour' has become one of those formidable by-words, which have had more power in putting folly and ill-nature out of countenance than whole volumes of remonstrance."—*T. Moore.*

Canens. A nymph, wife of Picus, King of the Laurentës. When Circë had changed Picus into a bird, Canens lamented him so greatly that she pined away, till she became a *vox et præterea nihil.* (*Ovid: Metamorphoses,* 14 fab. 9.)

Caneph'oræ (in architecture). Figures of young persons of either sex bearing a basket on their head. (Latin, *canephoræ,* plural ; singular, Greek, κανηφόρος.) The English singular is " canephor " (3 syl.).

Canicular Days. The dog-days, corresponding with the overflow of the Nile. From the middle of July to the beginning of the second week in September. (Latin, *canicŭla,* diminutive of *canic,* a dog.)

Canicular Period. A cycle of 1461 years or 1460 Julian years, called a " Sothic period." When it was supposed that any given day had passed through all the seasons of the year.

Canicular Year. The ancient Egyptian year, computed from one heliacal rising of the Dog-star (*Sirius*) to the next.

Canid'ia. A sorceress, who could bring the moon from heaven. Alluded to by Horace. (*Epodes,* v.)

" Your ancient conjurors were wont
To make her [the moon] from her sphere dismount,
And to their incantations stoop."
Butler: Hudibras, part ii. 3.

Canister. The head (pugilistic term). " To mill his canister " is to break his head. A " canister cap " is a covering for the head, whether hat or cap. A " canister " is a small coffer or box, and the head is the " canister " or coffer of man's brains.

Canker. The briar or dog-rose.

" Put down Richard, that sweet lovely rose,
And plant this thorn, this canker, Bolingbroke."
Shakespeare: 1 *Henry IV.,* i. 3.

Cannæ. The place where Han'nibal defeated the Romans under L. Æmil'ius Paulus. Any fatal battle that is the turning point of a great general's prosperity is called his Cannæ. Thus, we say, " Moscow was the Cannæ of Napoleon Bonaparte."

Cannel Coal. A corruption of *candle coal,* so called from the bright flame, unmixed with smoke, which it yields in combustion.

Cannibal. A word applied to those who eat human flesh. The usual derivation is *Caribbee,* corrupted into Canibbee, supposed to be man-eaters. Some of the tribes of these islands have no *r*.

" The natives live in great fear of the canibals (*i.e.* Caribals, or people of Cariba)."—*Columbus.*

Cannon (in billiards). A corruption of *carrom,* which is short for *carambole.* A cannon is when the player's ball strikes the adversary's ball in such a way as to glance off and strike a second ball.

Canoe' (2 syl.). A boat. (Spanish, *canóa*, a canoe; Dutch, *cano;* German, *kahn*, a boat; Old French, *cane*, a ship, and *canot*, a boat; Latin, *canna*, a hollow stem or reed; our *cane*, *can* = a jug; *cannon, canal*, etc.)

Canon. The canons used to be those persons who resided in the buildings contiguous to the cathedral, employed either in the daily service, or in the education of the choristers. The word is Greek, and means a measuring rod, the beam of a balance; then, a roll or register containing the names of the clergy who are licensed to officiate in a cathedral church.

Canon. A divine or ecclesiastical law.

"Or that the Everlasting had not fixed
His canon 'gainst self-slaughter."
    Shakespeare: Hamlet, i. 2.

Can'on Law. A collection of ecclesiastical laws which serve as the rule of church government. (*See below.*)

Canon'ical. Canon is a Greek word, and means the index of a balance, hence a rule or law. (*See above.*)

The sacred canon means the accepted books of Holy Scripture, which contain the inspired laws of salvation and morality; also called *The Canonical Books.*

Canonical Dress. The costume worn by the clergy according to the direction of the canon. Archdeacons, deans, and bishops wear canonical hats.

Canonical Epistles. The seven catholic epistles, *i.e.* one of James, two of Peter, three of John, and one of Jude. The epistles of Paul were addressed to specific churches or to individuals.

"The second and third epistles of John are certainly not catholic. One is to a specific lady and her children; and the other is to Gaius. If the word "canonical" in this phrase means appointed to be read in church, then the epistles of Paul are canonical. In fact there are only five canonical epistles.

Canon'ical Hours. The times within which the sacred offices may be performed. In the Roman Catholic Church they are seven—viz. matins, prime, tierce, sext, nones, vespers, and compline. Prime, tierce, sext, and nones are the first, third, sixth, and ninth hours of the day, counting from six in the morning. Compline is a corruption of *completo'rium* (that which completes the services of the day). The reason why there are seven canonical hours is that David says, "Seven times a day do I praise thee" (Psalm cxix. 164).

⁑ In England the phrase means the time of the day within which persons can be legally married, *i.e.* from eight in the morning to three p.m.

Canonical Obedience. The obedience due by the inferior clergy to the superior clergy set over them. Even bishops owe canonical obedience to the archbishop of the same province.

Canon'ical Punishments are those punishments which the Church is authorised to inflict.

Canonicals.
The *pouch* on the gown of an M.D., designed for carrying drugs.

The *coif* of a serjeant-at-law, designed for concealing the tonsure.

The *lamb-skin* on a B.A. hood, in imitation of the *toga can'dida* of the Romans.

The *strings* of an Oxford undergraduate, to show the wearer is still in leading strings. At Cambridge, however, the strings are the mark of a graduate who has won his ribbons.

The *tippet* on a barrister's gown, meant for a wallet to carry briefs in.

The proctors' and pro-proctors' *tippet,* for papers—a sort of sabretache.

Cano'pic Vases. Used by the Egyptian priests for the viscera of bodies embalmed, four vases being provided for each body. So called from Cano'pus, in Egypt, where they were first used.

Cano'pus. The Egyptian god of water. The Chaldeans worshipped fire, and sent all the other gods a challenge, which was accepted by a priest of Cano'pus. The Chaldeans lighted a vast fire round the god Canopus, when the Egyptian deity spouted out torrents of water and quenched the fire, thereby obtaining the triumph of water over fire.

Can'opy properly means a *gnat curtain*. Herod'otus tells us (ii. 95) that the fishermen of the Nile used to lift their nets on a pole, and form thereby a rude sort of tent under which they slept securely, as gnats will not pass through the meshes of a net. Subsequently the tester of a bed was so called, and lastly the canopy borne over kings. (Greek, κώνωψ, a gnat; κωιωπεῖον, a gnat-curtain; Latin, *conōpēum*, a gnat-curtain.)

Canossa. Canossa, in the duchy of Modēna, is where (in the winter of 1076-7) Kaiser Heinrich IV. went to humble himself before Pope Gregory VII. (Hildebrand).

Has the Czar gone to Canossa ? Is he about to eat humble pie?

When, in November, 1887, the Czar went to Berlin to visit the Emperor of Germany, the *Standard* asked in a leader, " Has the Czar gone to Canossa ? "

Cant. A whining manner of speech ; class phraseology, especially of a religious nature (Latin, *canto,* to sing, whence chant). It is often derived from a proper name. We are told that Alexander and Andrew Cant maintained that all those who refused the " Covenant " ought to be excommunicated, and that those were cursed who made use of the prayer-book. These same Cants, in their grace before meat, used to " pray for all those who suffered persecution for their religious opinions." (*Mercurius Publicus,* No. ix., 1661.)

⁂ The proper name cannot have given us the noun and verb, as they were in familiar use certainly in the time of Ben Jonson, signifying " professional slang," and " to use professional slang."

" The doctor here,
When he discourses of dissection,
Of *vena cava* and of *vena porta* . . . .
What does he do but cant ? Or if he run
To his judicial astrology,
And trowl out the *trine,* the *quartile,* and the *sextile.*
Does he not cant ? "
Ben Jonson (1574—1637) ; *Andrew Cant* died 1664.

Cantabrian Surge. The Bay of Biscay. So called from the Cantábri who dwelt about the Biscayan shore. Suetonius tells us that a thunderbolt fell in the Cantabrian Lake (Spain) " in which twelve axes were found." (*Galba,* viii.)

" She her thundering army leads
To Calpē [Gibraltar] . . . . or the rough
Cantabrian Surge."
Akenside: Hymn to the Naiades.

Cantāte Sunday. Fourth Sunday after Easter. So called from the first word of the introït of the mass : " Sing to the Lord." Similarly " Lætāre Sunday " (the fourth after Lent) is so called from the first word of the mass.

Canteen' means properly a wine-cellar. Then a refreshment-house in a barrack for the use of the soldiers. Then a vessel, holding about three pints, for the use of soldiers on the march. (Italian, *cantina,* a cellar.)

Canterbury. *Canterbury is the higher rack, but Winchester the better manger.* Canterbury is the higher see in rank, but Winchester the one which produces the most money, This was the reply of William Edington, Bishop of Winchester, when offered the archbishopric of Canterbury (1366). Now Canterbury is £15,000 a year, and Winchester £6,500.

Canterbury Tales. Chaucer supposed that he was in company with a party of pilgrims going to Canterbury to pay their devotions at the shrine of Thomas à Becket. The party assembled at an inn in Southwark, called the *Tabard,* and there agreed to tell one tale each, both in going and returning. He who told the best tale was to be treated with a supper on the homeward journey. The work is incomplete, and we have none of the tales told on the way home.

A Canterbury Tale. A cock-and-bull story ; a romance. So called from Chaucer's *Canterbury Tales.*

Canting Crew (*The*). Beggars, gipsies, and thieves, who use what is called the canting lingo.

Canucks. The Canadians. So called in the United States of America.

Canvas means cloth made of hemp. *To canvas a subject* is to strain it through a hemp strainer, to sift it ; and *to canvass a borough* is to sift the votes. (Latin, *can'nabis,* hemp.)

Canvas City (*A*). A military encampment.

" The Grand Master assented, and they proceeded accordingly, ... avoiding the most inhabited parts of the canvas city."—*Sir W. Scott: The Talisman,* chap. x.

" In 1851, during the gold rush, a town of tents, known as Canvas Town, rose into being on the St. Kilda Road, Melbourne. Several thousand inhabitants lived in this temporary settlement, which was laid out in streets and lasted for several months."—*Cities of the World ; Melbourne.*

Ca'ora. A river, on the banks of which are a people whose heads grow beneath their shoulders. Their eyes are in their shoulders, and their mouths in the middle of their breasts. (*Hakluyt : Voyages,* 1598.) Raleigh, in his *Description of Guiana,* gives a similar account of a race of men. (*See* BLEMMYES.)

" The Anthropophagi and men whose heads
Do grow beneath their shoulders."
Shakespeare: Othello, i. 3.

Cap.

Black cap. (*See* page 140, BLACK CAP.)

Cater cap. A square cap or mortarboard. (French, *quartier.*)

College cap. A trencher like the caps worn at the English Universities by students and bachelors of art, doctors of divinity, etc.

Fool's cap. A cylindrical cap with feather and bells, such as licensed Fools used to wear.

Forked cap. A bishop's mitre. For the paper so called, *see* FOOLSCAP.

John Knox cap (*A*). A cap made of black silk velvet.

"A cap of black silk velvet, after the John Knox fashion."—*Edinburgh University Calendar.*

Monmouth cap (*A*). (*See* MONMOUTH.)

Phrygian cap (*A*). Cap of liberty (*q.v.*).

Scotch cap. A cloth cap worn commonly in Scotland.

Cap and bells. The insignia of a professional fool or jester.

A feather in one's cap. An achievement to be proud of; something creditable.

Square cap. A trencher or "mortarboard," like the University cap.

Statute cap. A woollen cap ordered by statute to be worn on holidays by all citizens for the benefit of the woollen trade. To a similar end, persons were obliged to be buried at death in flannel.

"Well, better wits have worn plain statute caps."—*Shakespeare: Love's Labour Lost,* v. 2.

Trencher cap, or mortar-board. A cap with a square board, generally covered with black cloth.

I must put on my considering cap. I must think about the matter before I give a final answer. The allusion is to a conjurer's cap.

If the cap fits, wear it. If the remark applies to you, apply it to yourself. Hats and caps differ very slightly in size and appearance, but everyone knows his own when he puts it on.

Setting her cap at him. Trying to catch him for a sweetheart or a husband. The lady puts on the most becoming of her caps, to attract the attention and admiration of the favoured gentleman.

To gain the cap. To obtain a bow from another out of respect.

"Such gains the cap of him that makes them fine, But keeps his book uncrossed."
     Shakespeare: Cymbeline, iii. 3.

To pull caps. To quarrel like two women, who pull each other's caps.

Your cap is all on one side. The French have the phrase *Mettre son bonnet de travers,* meaning "to be in an ill-humour." M. Hilaire le Gai explains it thus: "*La plupart des tapageurs de profession portent ordinairement le chapeau sur l'oreille.*" It is quite certain that workmen, when they are bothered, push their cap on one side of the head, generally over the right ear, because the right hand is occupied.

Cap (the verb).

I cap to that, i.e. assent to it. The allusion is to a custom observed in France amongst the judges in deliberation. Those who assent to the opinion stated by any of the bench signify it by lifting their toque from their heads.

To cap. To excel.

"Well, that caps the globe."—*C. Brontë: Jane Eyre.*

Cap Verses (*To*). Having the metre fixed and the last letter of the previous line given, to add a verse beginning with the given letter (of the same metre or not, according to prearrangement) thus:

English.
The way was long, the wind was cold (D).
Dogs with their tongues their wounds do heal (L).
Like words congealed in northern air (R).
Regions Cæsar never knew (W).
With all a poet's ecstasy (Y).
You may deride my awkward pace, etc. etc.

Latin.
Nil pictis timidus navita puppibus (S).
Sunt quos curriculo pulverem Olympicum (M).
Myrtoum pavidus nauta secet mare (E).
Est qui nec veteris pocula Massici (I).
Illum, si proprio condidit horreo (O).
O, et presidium .... (*as long as you please*).

⁂ It would make a Christmas game to cap proper names: as Plato, Otway, Young, Goldsmith, etc., or to cap proverbs, as: "Rome was not built in a day"; "Ye are the salt of the earth"; "Hunger is the best sauce"; "Example is better than precept"; "Time and tide wait for no man"; etc.

Cap and Bells. *Wearing the cap and bells.* Said of a person who is the butt of the company, or one who excites laughter at his own expense. The reference is to licensed jesters formerly attached to noblemen's establishments. Their headgear was a cap with bells.

"One is bound to speak the truth .... whether he mounts the cap and bells or a shovel hat [like a bishop]."—*Thackeray.*

Cap and Feather Days. The time of childhood.

"Here I was got into the scenes of my cap-and-feather days."—*Cobbett.*

Cap and Gown. The full academical costume of a university student, tutor, or master, worn at lectures, examinations, and after "hall" (dinner).

"Is it a cap and gown affair?"—*C. Bede: Verdant Green.*

Cap in Hand. Submissively. To wait on a man cap in hand is to wait on him like a servant, ready to do his bidding.

Cap of Fools (*The*). The chief or foremost fool; one that exceeds all others in folly.

"Thou art the cap of all the fools alive."
     Shakespeare: Timon of Athens, iv. 3.

Cap of Liberty. When a slave was manumitted by the Romans, a small red cloth cap, called *pil'ēus,* was placed on his head. As soon as this was done, he was termed *liberti'nus* (a freedman), and his name was registered in the city tribes. When Saturni'nus, in 263, possessed himself of the capitol, he hoisted a cap on the top of his spear, to indicate that all slaves who joined his standard should be free. When Ma'rius incited the slaves to take up arms against Sylla, he employed the same symbol; and when Cæsar was murdered, the conspirators marched forth in a body, with a cap elevated on a spear, in token of liberty. (*See* LIBERTY.)

Cap of Maintenance. A cap of dignity anciently belonging to the rank of duke ; the fur cap of the Lord Mayor of London, worn on days of state ; a cap carried before the British sovereigns at their coronation. Maintenance here means defence.

Cap of Time. *They wear themselves in the cap of time.* Use more ceremony, says Parolles, for these lords do "wear themselves in the cap of time," *i.e.* these lords are the favours and jewels worn in the cap of the time being, and have the greatest influence. In the cap of time being, they are the very jewels, and most honoured. (*Shakespeare : All's Well, etc.*, ii. 1.)

Cap-acquaintance (*A*), now called a bowing acquaintance. One just sufficiently known to bow to.

Cap-money. Money collected in a cap or hat ; hence an improvised collection.

Cap-a-pie. The general etymology is the French *cap à pied*, but the French phrase is *de pied en cap.*

"Armed at all points exactly cap-a-pie."
    Shakespeare : Hamlet, i. 2.
" I am courtier, cap-a-pe."
    Shakespeare : Winter's Tale, iv. 3.

✢ We are told that *cap à pie* is Old French, but it would be desirable to give a quotation from some old French author to verify this assertion. I have hunted in vain for the purpose. Again, is *pie* Old French for *pied ?* This is not a usual change. The usual change would be *pied* into *pie.* The Latin might be *De capite ad pedem.*

Capfull of Wind. Olaus Magnus tells us that Eric, King of Sweden, was so familiar with evil spirits that what way soever he turned his cap the wind would blow, and for this he was called *Windy Cap.* The Laplanders drove a profitable trade in selling winds ; but, even so late as 1814, Bessie Millie, of Pomo'na (Orkney Islands), helped out her living by selling favourable winds to mariners for the small sum of sixpence. (*See* MONT ST. MICHEL.)

Cape. *Spirit of the Cape.* (*See* page 14, col. 1, ADAMASTOR.)

Cape of Storms. (*See* STORMS.)

Capel Court. A speculation in stocks of such magnitude as to affect the money market. Capel Court is the name of the place in London where transactions in stocks are carried on.

Caper. *The weather is so foul not even a caper would venture out.* A Manx proverb. A caper is a fisherman of Cape Clear in Ireland, who will venture out in almost any weather.

Caper Merchant. A dancing-master who cuts "capers." (*See* CUT CAPERS.)

Capet (*Cap-pay*). Hugues, the founder of the French monarchy, was surnamed *Cap'etus* (clothed with a capot or monk's hood), because he always wore a clerical costume as abbot of St. Martin de Tours. This was considered the family name of the kings of France ; hence, Louis XVI. was arraigned before the National Convention under the name of Louis Capet.

Capital. Money or money's worth available for production.

" His capital is continually going from him [the merchant] in some shape, and returning to him in another."—*Adam Smith : Wealth of Nations,* vol. i. book ii. chap. i. p. 276.

Active capital. Ready money or property readily convertible into it.

Circulating capital. Wages, or raw material. This sort of capital is not available a second time for the same purpose.

Fixed capital. Land, buildings, and machinery, which are only gradually consumed.

Political capital is something employed to serve a political purpose. Thus, the Whigs make political capital out of the errors of the Tories, and *vice versâ.*

" He tried to make capital out of his rival's discomfiture."—*The Times.*

Capital Fellow (*A*). A stockjobber ; in French called *Un Capitaine, par allusion aux capitaux sur lesquels on agiote habituellement.* A good-tempered, jovial, and generous person.

Capitals. *To speak in capitals.* To emphasise certain words with great stress. Certain nouns spelt with a capital letter are meant to be emphatic and distinctive.

Cap'ite Censi. The lowest rank of Roman citizens ; so called because they were counted simply by *the poll*, as they had no taxable property.

Capit'ulars. The laws of the first two dynasties of France were so called, because they were divided into chapters. (French, *capitulaire*.)

Capon. Called *a fish out of the coop* by those friars who wished to evade the Friday fast by eating chickens instead of fish. (*See* YARMOUTH.)

Capon (*A*). A castrated cock.
A Crail's capon. A dried haddock.
A Severn capon. A sole.
A Yarmouth capon. A red herring.
❧ We also sometimes hear of a Glasgow capon, a salt herring.

Capon (*A*). A love-letter. In French, *poulet* means not only a chicken but also a love-letter, or a sheet of note-paper. Thus Henri IV., consulting with Sully about his marriage, says: "My niece of Guise would please me best, though report says maliciously that she loves poulets in paper better than in a fricasee."

"Boyet . . break up this capon [*i.e.* open this love-letter]."—*Shakespeare: Love's Labour's Lost*, iv. 1.

Cap'ricorn. Called by Thomson, in his *Winter*, "the centaur archer." Anciently, the winter solstice occurred on the entry of the sun into Capricorn; but the stars, having advanced a whole sign to the east, the winter solstice now falls at the sun's entrance into Sagittarius (the centaur archer), so that the poet is strictly right, though we vulgarly retain the ancient classical manner of speaking. Capricornus is the tenth, or, strictly speaking, the eleventh sign of the zodiac. (Dec. 21-Jan. 20.)
❧ According to classic mythology, Capricorn was Pan, who, from fear of the great Typhon, changed himself into a goat, and was made by Jupiter one of the signs of the zodiac.

Captain. *Capitano del Popolo, i.e.* Garibaldi (1807-1882).
The Great Captain (*el gran capita'no*). Gonzalvo di Cor'dova (1453-1515.)
Manuel Comne'nus of Treb'izond (1120, 1143-1180).

Captain Cauf's Tail. The commander-in-chief of the mummers of Plough Monday.

Captain Copperthorne's Crew. All masters and no men.

Captain Podd. A showman. So called from "Captain" Podd, a famous puppet-showman in the time of Ben Jonson.

Captain Stiff. *To come Captain Stiff over one.* To treat one with cold formality.
"I shouldn't quite come Captain Stiff over him."—*S. Warren: Ten Thousand a Year.*

Cap'tious. Fallacious, deceitful; now it means ill-tempered, carping. (Latin, *captio'sus*.)
"I know I love in vain, strive against hope;
  Yet in this captious and intenible sieve
  I still pour in the waters of my love."
Shakespeare: All's Well that Ends Well, i. 3.

Cap'ua. *Capua corrupted Hannibal.* Luxury and self-indulgence will ruin anyone. Hannibal was everywhere victorious over the Romans till he took up his winter quarters at Capua, the most luxurious city of Italy. When he left Capua his star began to wane, and, ere long, Carthage was in ruins and himself an exile.
Capua was the Cannæ of Hannibal. As the battle of Cannæ was most disastrous to the Roman army, so was the luxury of Capua to Hannibal's army. We have a modern adaptation to this proverb: "Moscow was the Austerlitz of Napoleon."

Cap'uchin. A friar of the order of St. Francis, of the new rule of 1528; so called from their "cap'uce" or pointed cowl.

Cap'ulet. A noble house in Vero'na, the rival of that of Mon'tague (3 syl.); Juliet is of the former, and Romeo of the latter. Lady Capulet is the beau-ideal of a proud Italian matron of the fifteenth century. The expression so familiar, "the tomb of all the Capulets," is from Burke. (*Shakespeare: Romeo and Juliet*.)

Cap'ut Mor'tuum. Latin for *head of the dead*, used by the old chemists to designate the residuum of chemicals, when all their volatile matters had escaped. Anything from which all that rendered it valuable has been taken away. Thus, a learned scholar paralysed is a mere *caput mortuum* of his former self. The French Directory, towards its close, was a mere *caput mortuum* of a governing body.

Caqueux. A sort of gipsy race in Brittany, similar to the Cagots of Gascony, and Colliberts of Poitou.

Car'abas. *He is a Marquis of Carabas.* A fossil nobleman, of unbounded pretensions and vanity, who would fain restore the slavish foolery of the reign of Louis XIV.; one with Fortunatus's purse, which was never empty. The character is taken from Perrault's tale of *Puss in Boots*.

> " Prêtres que nous vengeons
> Levez la dîme et partageons ;
> Et toi, peuple animal,
> Porte encor le bât féodal. . . .
> Chapeau bas ! Chapeau bas !
> Gloire au marquis de Carabas ! "
> *Béranger*, 1816.

Caracal'la [*long-mantle*]. Aure'lius Antoni'nus was so called because he adopted the Gaulish caracalla in preference to the Roman toga. It was a large, close-fitting, hooded mantle, reaching to the heels, and slit up before and behind to the waist. Aure'lius was himself born in Gaul, called Caracal in Ossian. (*See* CURTMANTLE.)

Carac'ci (pron. *Kar - rah' - che*). Founder of the eclectic school in Italy. Luis and his two cousins Augustin and Annibale founded the school called *In-cammina'ti* (progressive), which had for its chief principle the strict observance of nature. Luis (1554-1619), Augustin (1558-1601), Annibale (1560-1609).

The Caracci of France. Jean Jouvenet, who was paralysed on the right side, and painted with his left hand. (1647-1707.)

The Annibale Caracci of the Eclectic School. Bernardi'no Campi, the Italian, is so called by Lanzi (1522-1590).

Carack or *Carrack*. A ship of great bulk, constructed to carry heavy freights. (Spanish, *caraca*.)

> " The rich-laden carack bound to distant shores."
> *Pollok: Course of Time*, book vii. line 60.

Carad'oc. A Knight of the Round Table, noted for being the husband of the only lady in the queen's train who could wear "the mantle of matrimonial fidelity." Also in history, the British chief whom the Romans called Caractacus.

Caraites. A religious sect among the Jews, who rigidly adhered to the words and letters of Scripture, regardless of metaphor, etc. Of course, they rejected the rabbinical interpretations and the Cab'ala. The word is derived from *Caraïm*, equivalent to *scripturarii* (textualists). Pronounce *Carry-ites*.

Caran D'Ache. The pseudonym of M. Emanuel Poirié, the French caricaturist.

Carat of Gold. So called from the carat bean, or seed of the locust tree, formerly employed in weighing gold and silver. Hence the expressions "22 carats fine," "18 carats fine," etc.,

meaning that out of 24 parts, 22 or 18 are gold, and the rest alloy.

> " Here's the note
> How much your chain weighs to the utmost carat."
> *Shakespeare: Comedy of Errors*, iv. 1.

Caraway. Latin, *carum*, from Caria in Asia Minor, whence the seeds were imported.

> "Nay, you shall see my orchard, where in an arbour we will eat a last year's pippin of my own grafting, with a dish of caraways."—*Shakespeare: 2 Henry IV.*, v. 3 (Justice Shallow to Falstaff).

Carbineer' or *Carabineer*. Properly a skirmisher or light horseman, from the Arabic *carabine*. A carbine is the light musket used by cavalry soldiers.

> "He . . . left the Rhinegrave, with his company of mounted carbineers, to guard the passage."—*Motley: Dutch Republic* (vol. i. part i. chap. ii. p. 179).

Carbona'do. A chop; mince meat. Strictly speaking, a carbonado is a piece of meat cut crosswise for the gridiron. (Latin, *carbo*, a coal.)

> "If he do come in my way, so ; if he do not—if I come in his willingly, let him make a carbonado of me."—*Shakespeare: 1 Henry IV.*, v. 3.

Carbona'ri means *charcoal-burners*, a name assumed by a secret political society in Italy (organised 1808-1814). Their place of muster they called a "hut;" its inside, "the place for selling charcoal;" and the outside, the "forest." Their political opponents they called "wolves." Their object was to convert the kingdom of Naples into a republic. In the singular number, *Carbonaro*. (*See* CHARBONNERIE.)

Carbuncle of Ward Hill (*The*). A mysterious carbuncle visible enough to those who stand at the foot of the hill in May, June or July; but never beheld by anyone who has succeeded in reaching the hill top.

> "I have distinguished, among the dark rocks, that wonderful carbuncle, which gleams ruddy as a furnace to them who view it from beneath, but has ever become invisible to him whose daring foot has scaled the precipice from which it darts its splendour."—*Sir W. Scott: The Pirate*, chap. xix.

⁂ Dr. Wallace thinks it is water trickling from a rock, and reddened by the sun.

Car'canet. A small chain of jewels for the neck. (French, *carcan*, an iron collar.)

> "Like captain jewels in a carcanet."
> *Shakespeare: Sonnets*.

Car'cass. The shell of a house before the floors are laid and walls plastered; the skeleton of a ship, a wreck, etc. The body of a dead animal, so called from the Latin *caro-cassa* (lifeless flesh). (French, *carcasse*.)

> "The Goodwins, I think they call the place ; a

very dangerous flat and fatal, where the carcases of many a tall ship lie buried."—*Shakespeare: Merchant of Venice*, iii. 1.

Car'casses. Shells with three fuze-holes. They are projected from mortars (*q.v.*), howitzers (*q.v.*), and guns. They will burn furiously for eight 'or ten minutes, do not burst like shells, but the flames, rushing from the three holes, set on fire everything within their influence.

"Charlestown, . . . having been fired by a car-cass from Copp's Hill, sent up dense columns of smoke."—*Lessing: United States.*

Card.

That's the card. The right thing; the ticket. The reference is to tickets of admission, cards of the races, and pro-grammes.

"10s. is about the card."—*Mayhew: London Labour, etc.*

A queer card. An eccentric person, "indifferent honest." A difficult lead in cards to play to.

A knowing card. A sharp fellow, next door to a sharper. The allusion is to card-sharpers and their tricks.

"Whose great aim it was to be considered a knowing card."—*Dickens: Sketches, etc.*

A great card. A big wig; the boss of the season; a person of note. A big card.

A leading card. A star actor. A person leads from his strongest suit.

A loose card. A worthless fellow who lives on the loose.

"A loose card is a card of no value, and, con-sequently, the properest to throw away."—*Hoyle: Games, etc.*

A sure card. A person one can fully depend on; a person sure to command success. A project to be certainly de-pended on. As a winning card in one's hand.

He is the card of our house. The man of mark, the most *distingué.* Osric tells Hamlet that Laer'tës is "the card and calendar of gentry" (v. 2). The card is a card of a compass, containing all its points. Laertës is the card of gentry, in whom may be seen all its points. We also say "a queer card," meaning an odd fish.

That was my best trump card. My best chance. The allusion is to loo, whist, and other games played with cards.

To play one's best card. To do that which one hopes is most likely to secure success.

To speak by the card. To speak by the book, be as precise as a map or book. A merchant's expression. The card is the document in writing containing the agreements made between a merchant and the captain of a vessel. Sometimes the owner binds himself, ship, tackle, and furniture for due performance, and the captain is bound to deliver the cargo committed to him in good condition. To speak by the card is to speak according to the indentures or written instructions. In some cases the reference is to the card of a mariner's compass.

"Law . . . is the card to guide the world by."—*Hooker: Ecc. Pol.*, part ii. sec. 5.
"We must speak by the card, or equivocation will undo us."—*Shakespeare: Hamlet*, v. 1.

Cards.

It is said that there never was a good hand of cards containing four clubs. Such a hand is called "The Devil's Four-poster."

Lieuben, a German lunatic, bet that he would succeed in turning up a pack of cards in a certain order stated in a written agreement. He turned and turned the cards ten hours a day for twenty years; and repeated the opera-tion 4,246,028 times, when at last he succeeded.

In Spain, spades used to be *columbines ;* clubs, *rabbits ;* diamonds, *pinks ;* and hearts, *roses.* The present name for spades is *espados* (swords); of clubs, *bastos* (cudgels); of diamonds, *dineros* (square pieces of money used for paying wages); of hearts, *copas* (chalices).

The French for spades is *pique* (pike-men or soldiers); for clubs, *trèfle* (clover, or husbandmen); of diamonds, *carreaux* (building tiles, or artisans) ; of hearts, *chœur* (choir-men, or ecclesiastics).

The English spades is the French form of a pike, and the Spanish name ; the clubs is the French trefoil, and the Spanish name ; the hearts is a corruption of *chœur* into *cœur.* (*See* VIERGE.)

Court cards. So called because of their heraldic devices. The king of clubs originally represented the arms of the Pope ; of spades, the King of France ; of diamonds, the King of Spain ; and of hearts, the King of England. The French kings in cards are called David (spades), Alexander (clubs), Cæsar (dia-monds), and Charles (hearts)—repre-senting the Jewish, Greek, Roman, and Frankish empires. The queens or dames are Argine—*i.e.* Juno (hearts), Judith (clubs), Rachel (diamonds), and Pallas (spades) — representing royalty, forti-tude, piety, and wisdom. They were likenesses of Marie d'Anjou, the queen of Charles VII. ; Isabeau, the queen-mother ; Agnes Sorel, the king's mis-tress ; and Joan d'Arc, the dame of spades, or war.

He felt that he held the cards in his own hands. That he had the whip-end of the stick; that he had the upper hand, and could do as he liked. The allusion is to games played with cards, such as whist.

He played his cards well. He acted judiciously and skilfully, like a whist-player who plays his hand with judgment. To play one's cards *badly* is to manage a project unskilfully.

The cards are in my hands. I hold the disposal of events which will secure success. The allusion is obvious.

"The Vitelli busied at Arezzo; the Orsini irritating the French; the war of Naples imminent; —the cards are in my hands."—*Cæsar Borgia*, xxix.

On the cards. Likely to happen, projected, and talked about as likely to occur. On the programme or card of the races; on the "agenda.'"

To count on one's cards. To anticipate success under the circumstances. The allusion is to holding in one's hand cards likely to win.

To go in with good cards. To have good patronage; to have excellent grounds for expecting success.

To throw up the cards. To give up as a bad job; to acknowledge you have no hope of success. In some games of cards, as loo, a player has the liberty of saying whether he will play or not, and if one's hand is hopelessly bad he throws up his cards and sits out till the next deal.

Cardinal Humours. Blood, phlegm, yellow bile, and black bile.

Cardinal Numbers. Such numbers as 1, 2, 3, etc. 1st, 2nd, 3rd, etc., are *ordinal* numbers.

Cardinal Points of the Compass. Due north, west, east, and south. So called because they are the points on which the intermediate ones, such as N.E., N.W., N.N.E., etc., hinge or hang. (Latin, *cardo*, a hinge.)

Cardinal Signs [of the Zodiac]. The two equinoctial and the two solsticial signs, Aries and Libra, Cancer and Capricornus.

Cardinal Virtues. Justice, prudence, temperance, and fortitude, on which all other virtues hang or depend.

Cardinal Winds. Those that blow due East, West, North, and South.

Cardinals. Hinges. (Latin, *cardo*.) The election of the Pope "hinges" on the voice of the sacred college, and on the Pope the doctrines of the Church depend; so that the cardinals are in fact the hinges on which the Christian Church turns. There may be six cardinal bishops, fifty cardinal priests, and fourteen cardinal deacons, who constitute the Pope's council, and who elect the Pope when a vacancy occurs.

Cardinal's Red Hat. Some assert that Innocent IV. made the cardinals wear a red hat "in token of their being ready to lay down their life for the gospel."

Car'duel or *Kartel.* Carlisle. The place where Merlin prepared the Round Table.

Care-cloth (*The*). The fine linen cloth laid over the newly-married in the Catholic Church. (Anglo-Saxon, *cear*, large, as *cear wind* (a big wound), *cear sorh* (a great sorrow), etc.)

Care killed the Cat. It is said that "a cat has nine lives," yet care would wear them all out.

Care Sunday (the fifth Sunday in Lent). Professor Skeat tells us (*Notes and Queries*, Oct. 28th, 1893), that "care" means trouble, suffering; and that Care-Sunday means Passion-Sunday. In Old High German we have *Kar-woche* and *Kar-fritag.*

The Latin *cura* sometimes meant "sorrow, grief, trouble," as "Curam et angŏrem animi levāre."—*Cicero: Att.* i. 15.

Carême (2 syl.). Lent; a corruption of *quadragesima.*

Car-goose (*A*) or **Gargoose.** The crested diver, belonging to the genus Colymbus. (Anglo-Saxon, *gar* and *gos.*)

Caricatures mean "sketches over-drawn." (Italian, *caricatu'ra*, from *carica're*, to load or burden.)

Car'illons, in France, are chimes or tunes played on bells; but in England the suites of bells that play the tunes. Our word *carol* approaches the French meaning nearer than our own. The best chimes in the world are those in *Les Halles*, at Bruges.

Cari'næ. Women hired by the Romans to weep at funerals; so called from Caria, whence most of them came.

Carle or *Carling* **Sunday** [*Pea Sunday*]. The octave preceding Palm Sunday; so called because the special food of the day was *carling*—*i.e.* peas fried in butter. The custom is a continuation of the pagan bean-feast. The fifth Sunday in Lent.

Carlovin'gian Dyn'asty. So called from Car'olus or Charles Martel.

Carludovi'ca. A Pan'ama hat, made of the *Carludovica pal'mata ;* so called in compliment to Carlos IV. of Spain, whose second name was Ludovic.

Car'magnole (3 syl.). A red Republican song and dance in the first French revolution; so called from Carmag'nola, in Piedmont, the great nest of the Savoyards, noted for street music and dancing. The refrain of "Madame Veto," the Carmagnole song, is " *Dansons la Carmagnole — vive le son du canon !* " The word was subsequently applied to other revolutionary songs, such as *Ça ira,* the *Marseillaise,* the *Chant 'du Depart.* Besides the songs, the word is applied to the dress worn by the Jacobins, consisting of a blouse, red cap, and tri-coloured girdle ; to the wearer of this dress or any violent revolutionist ; to the speeches in favour of the execution of Louis XVI., called by M. Barrière *des Carmagnoles ;* and, lastly, to the dance performed by the mob round the guillotine, or down the streets of Paris.

Car'melites (3 syl.). An order of mendicant friars of Mount Carmel, the monastery of which is named Eli'as, from Elijah the prophet, who on Mount Carmel told Ahab that rain was at hand. Also called White Friars, from their white cloaks.

Car'milhan. The phantom ship on which the Kobold of the Baltic sits when he appears to doomed vessels.

Carmin'ative. A charm medicine. Magic and charms were at one time the chief "medicines," and the fact is perpetuated by the word carminative, among others. Carminatives are given to relieve flatulence. (Latin, *carmen,* a charm.)

Carmi'ne (2 syl). The dye made from the carmës or kermës insect, whence also *crimson,* through the Italian *cremisino.*

Carnation. "Flesh-colour." (Latin, *caro ;* genitive, *carnis,* flesh.)

Car'ney. To wheedle, to keep caressing.

Carnival. The season immediately preceding Lent ; shrove-tide. Ducange gives the word *carne-levale.* (Modern Italian, *carnovále ;* Spanish and French, *carnaval.*)

Italis, *carnevale, carnovale, carnaval.* Quidam scriptores Itali "carne-vale" dictum putant, quasi *carne vale* (good-bye meat) ; sed id etymon non probat Octav. Ferrarius. Cangius . . . . appellasse Gallos existimat, *carn-a-val,* quod sonat caro abscêdit . . . [We are referred to a

charter, dated 1195, in which occurs the word *carne-levamen,* and a quotation is given in which occurs the phrase *in carnis levamen].—Ducange,* vol. ii. p. 222.

Carot'id Artery. An artery on each side of the neck, supposed by the ancients to be the seat of drowsiness, brought on by an increased flow of blood through it to the head. (Greek, *carōticos,* inducing sleep.)

Carouse (2 syl.). Mr. Gifford says the Danes called their large drinking cup a *rouse,* and to rouse is to drink from a rouse ; ca-rouse is gar-rouse, to drink all up, or to drink all—*i.e.* in company.

"The king doth wake to-night, and takes his rouse." *Shakespeare : Hamlet,* i. 4.

Carouse the hunter's hoop. Drinking cups were anciently marked with hoops, by which every drinker knew his stint. Shakespeare makes Jack Cade promise his friends that " seven halfpenny loaves shall be sold for a penny ; and the three-hooped pot have ten hoops." Pegs or pins (*q.v.*) are other means of limiting the draught of individuals who drank out of the same tankard.

Carpathian Wizard. Proteus (2 syl.), who lived in the island of Car'-pathos, between Rhodes and Crete. He was a wizard and prophet, who could transform himself into any shape he pleased. He is represented as carrying a sort of crook in his hand. Carpathos, now called Scarpanto.

"By the Carpathian wizard's hook." *Milton : Comus,* 893.

Carpe Diem. Enjoy yourself while you have the opportunity. Seize the present day. (*Horace :* 1 *Odes,* xi. 8.) "*Dum vivimus, vivāmus.*"

Carpenter is from the Low Latin *carpentarius,* a maker of *carpenta* (two-wheeled carts and carriages). The *carpentum* was used for ladies ; the *carpentum funebre* or *carpentum pompaticum* was a hearse. There was also a *carpentum* (cart) for agricultural purposes. There is no Latin word for our "carpenter"; the phrase *faber lignarius* is used by Cicero. Our forefathers called a carpenter a "smith" or a "wood-smith." (French, *charpentier.*)

Carpet.

The magic carpet of Tangu. A carpet to all appearances worthless, but if anyone sat thereon, it would transport him instantaneously to the place he wished to go. So called because it came from Tangu, in Persia. It is sometimes termed *Prince Housain's carpet,* because it came into his hands, and he made use of it. (*Arabian Nights : Prince Ahmed.*) (*See below.*)

Solomon's carpet. The Eastern writers say that Solomon had a green silk carpet, on which his throne was placed when he travelled. This carpet was large enough for all his forces to stand upon ; the men and women stood on his right hand, and the spirits on his left. When all were arranged in order, Solomon told the wind where he wished to go, and the carpet, with all its contents, rose in the air and alighted at the place indicated. In order to screen the party from the sun, the birds of the air with outspread wings formed a canopy over the whole party. (*Sale : Koran.*) (*See above.*)

Such and such a question is on the carpet. The French *sur le tapis* (on the table-cloth) — *i.e.* before the house, under consideration. The question has been laid on the table-cloth of the house, and is now under debate.

Carpet-bag Adventurer (*A*). A passing adventurer, who happens to be on the road with his travelling or carpet-bag.

Carpet-bag Government. The government of mere adventurers. In America, a state in the South reorganised by "carpet-baggers," *i.e.* Northern political adventurers, who sought a career in the Southern States after the Civil War of 1865. [It may be noted that in America members of Congress and the State legislatures almost invariably reside in the district which they represent.]

Carpet Knight. One dubbed at Court by favour, not having won his spurs by military service in the field. Mayors, lawyers, and other civilians knighted as they kneel *on a carpet* before their sovereign. "Knights of the Carpet," "Knights of the Green Cloth," "Knights of Carpetry."

"The subordinate commands fell to young patricians, carpet-knights, who went on campaigns with their families and slaves."—*Froude: Cæsar*, chap. iv. p. 91.

Carpocra′tians. Gnostics ; so called from Carpo′cratēs, who flourished in the middle of the second century. They maintained that the world was made by angels,—that only the soul of Christ ascended into heaven, — and that the body will have no resurrection.

Carriage Company. Persons who keep their private carriage.

"Seeing a great deal of carriage company."—*Thackeray.*

Carriages. Things carried, luggage.

"And after those days we took up our carriages, and went up to Jerusalem."—Acts xxi. 15.

Car′ronades (3 syl.). Short, light iron guns. As they have no trunnions they differ in this respect from guns and howitzers (*q.v.*). They were invented in 1779 by Mr. Gascoigne, director of the Carron foundry, in Scotland, whence the name. Carronades are fastened to their carriages by a loop underneath, and are chiefly used in the arming of ships, to enable them to throw heavy shot at close quarters, without over-loading the decks with heavy guns. On shore they are used as howitzers.

Carry Arms ! Hold your gun in the right hand, the barrel nearly perpendicular, and resting against the hollow of the shoulder, the thumb and fore-finger embracing the guard. (A military command.) (*See* CARRY SWORDS.)

Carry Coals. (*See* COALS.)

Carry Everything before One (*To*). To be beyond competition ; to carry off all the prizes. A military phrase. Similarly, a high wind carries everything before it.

Carry Fire in one Hand and Water in the other (*To*). To say one thing and mean another ; to flatter, to deceive ; to lull suspicion in order the better to work mischief.

" Altera manu fert aquam, altera ignem.
Altera manu fert lapidem, altera panem ostentat."   *Plautus.*

Carry One's Point (*To*). To succeed in one's aim. Candidates in Rome were balloted for, and the votes were marked on a tablet by points. Hence, *omne punctum ferre* meant "to be carried *nem. con.*," or to gain every vote ; and "to carry one's point" is to carry off the points at which one aimed.

Carry Out (*To*) or *Carry through.* To continue a project to its completion.

Carry out one's Bat (*To*). A cricketer is said to carry out his bat when he is not "out" at the close of the game.

Carry Swords ! Hold the drawn sword vertically, the blade against the shoulder. (A military command.) (*See above,* CARRY ARMS.)

Carry the Day (*To*). To win the contest ; to carry off the honours of the day. In Latin, *victoriam reportare.*

Carry Weight (*To*), in races, etc., means to equalise the weight of two or more riders by adding weights to the lighter ones, till both (or all) the riders are made of one uniform weight.

" He carries weight ! he rides a race !
'Tis for a thousand pounds."
                    Cowper : John Gilpin.

To carry weight. To have influence.

Cart before the Horse. *To put the cart before the horse* is to reverse the right order or allocation of things.

French : " Mettre la charrette avant les bœufs."
Latin : " Currus bovem trahit
            Præpostere."
Greek : " Hysteron proteron." |
German : " Die pferde hinter den wagen spannen."
Italian : " Metter il carro inanzi ai buoi."

Carte Blanche (French). A blank cheque signed by the giver, but left to be filled in by the receiver, with a sum of money drawn on the bank-account of the giver. Power to act at discretion in an affair placed under your charge.

Carte de Visite (French). A visiting card ; a photographic likeness on a card for the albums of friends, etc. This custom originated, in 1857, with the Duke of Parma.

Carte'sian Philosophy. The philosophical system of René Descartes (Latin, *Carte'sius*), of La Haye, in Touraine. The basis of his system is *cog'ito ergo sum*. Thought must proceed from soul, and therefore man is not wholly material ; that soul must be from some Being not material, and that Being is God. As for physical phenomena, they must be the result of motion excited by God, and these motions he termed *vortices*. (1596-1650.)

⁕ Of course, he begs the whole question in his first assertion. (*See* COGITO.)

Carthage of the North. Lubeck was so called, when it was the head of the Hanseatic League.

Carthage'na. Capital of New Grana'da, in South America, unsuccessfully attacked in 1747 by Admiral Vernon.

" Wasteful, forth
Walks the dire power of pestilent disease . . .
Such as, of late, at Carthagena quenched
The British fire. You, gallant Vernon, saw
The miserable scene ; you, pitying, saw
To infant-weakness sunk the warrior's arm."
                    Thomson : Summer, 1034-43.

Carthag'inem esse Delendam (*censeo*) were the words with which Cato the Elder concluded every speech in the Roman senate. More usually quoted " *Delenda est Carthago.*" They are now proverbial, and mean, " That which stands in the way of our greatness must be removed at all hazards."

Carthagin'ian Faith. Treachery. (*See* PUNICA FIDES.)

Carthu'sians. Founded, in 1086, by St. Bruno, of Cologne, who, with six companions, retired to the solitude of La Chartreuse, near Greno'ble, in Vienne.

Cartoons. Designs drawn on *cartone* (pasteboard), like those of Raffaelle, formerly at Hampton Court, but now at Kensington Museum. They were bought by Charles I.. and are seven in number : " The Miraculous Draught of Fishes," " Feed my Lambs," " The Beautiful Gate of the Temple," " Death of Ani'as," " El'ymas the Sorcerer," " Paul at Lystra," and " Paul on the Mars Hill."

" They were designs for tapestries to be worked in Flanders."—*Julia B. De Forest : Short History of Art*, p. 246.

Cart'ridge Paper was originally manufactured for soldiers' cartridges. The word is a corruption of *cartouche*, from *carta* (paper).

Carya'tes or **Caryat'ids.** Figures of women in Greek costume, used in architecture to support entablatures. Ca'ryæ, in Arca'dia, sided with the Persians in the battle of Thermop'ylæ ; in consequence of which the victorious Greeks destroyed the city, slew the men, and made the women slaves. Praxit'elês, to perpetuate the disgrace, employed figures of these women, instead of columns. (*See* page 72, col. 2, ATLANTES ; page 208, col. 2, CANEPHORÆ.)

Caryat'ic Order or **Caryatid'ic Order.** Architecture in which Caryat'ids are introduced to support the entablature.

Casabian'ca was the name of the captain of the French man-of-war, *L'Orient*. At the battle of Aboukir, having first secured the safety of his crew, he blew up his ship, to prevent it falling into the hands of the English. His little son, refusing to leave him, perished with his father. Mrs. Hemans has made a ballad, *Casabianca*, on this subject, modifying the incident. The French poets Lebrun and Chénier have also celebrated the occurrence.

Cas'ca. A blunt-witted Roman, one of the conspirators against Julius Cæsar. (*Shakespeare : Julius Cæsar*.)

Case (*To*). To skin an animal. In the *Cookery* by Mrs. Glasse is the direction, " Take your hare when it is cased, . . . and make a pudding . . ." The witticism, " First catch your hare," may possibly have been suggested by this direction, but it is not in the *Art of Cookery made Plain and Easy.*

Case-hardened. Impenetrable to all sense of honour or shame. The allusion is to iron toughened by carbonising the surface in contact with charcoal in a case or closed box. It is done by heat.

Cashier' (2 syl.). To dismiss an officer from the army, to discard from society. (French, *casser;* to break; Italian, *cassa'rë,* to blot out; Ger. *kassiren.*)

"The ruling rogue, who dreads to be cashiered,
Contrives, as he is hated, to be feared."
Swift: Epistle to Mr. Gay, line 137.

Casi'no. Originally, a little *casa* or room near a theatre, where persons might retire, after the play was over, for dancing or music.

Casket Homer. Alexander the Great's edition, with Aristotle's corrections. After the battle of Arbe'la a golden casket, studded with jewels, was found in the tent of Dari'us. Alexander, being asked to what purpose it should be applied, made answer, "There is but one production in the world worthy of so costly a depository," and placed therein his edition of Homer, which received from this circumstance the term of Casket Homer.

Caspar. A huntsman who sold himself to Za'miel, the Black Huntsman. The night before the expiration of his lease of life he bargained for three years' respite on condition of bringing Max into the power of the evil one. Zamiel replied, "To-morrow either he or you." On the day appointed for the trial-shot, Caspar places himself in a tree. Max is told by the prince to aim at a dove. The dove flies to the tree where Caspar is concealed. Max shoots at the dove, but kills Caspar, and Zamiel comes to carry off his victim. (*Weber's Opera of Der Freischütz.*)

Cassan'dra. Daughter of Priam, gifted with the power of prophecy; but Apollo, whom she had offended, brought it to pass that no one believed her predictions. (*Shakespeare: Troilus and Cressida.*)

"Those who foresee and predict the downfall, meet with the fate of Cassandra."—*The Times.*

Cassa'tion. *The court of cassation,* in France, is the court which can *casser* (or quash) the judgment of other courts.

Cassi. Inhabitants of what is now Cassio hundred, Hertfordshire, referred to by Cæsar in his *Commentaries.*

Cassib'elan. Great-uncle to Cymbeline. He granted Cæsar a yearly tribute of £3,000. (*Shakespeare: Cymbeline.*)

Cassio (in Shakespeare's *Othello*). Michael Cassio was a Florentine, and Othello's lieutenant. Iago made him drunk, and then set on Roderi'go to quarrel with him. Cassio wounded Roderigo, and a brawl ensued, which offended Othello. Othello suspended Cassio, but Iago induced Desdemo'na to plead for his restoration. This interest in Cassio, being regarded by the Moor as a confirmation of Desdemona's illicit love, hinted at broadly by Iago, provoked the jealousy of Othello. After the death of the Moor, Cassio was appointed governor of Cyprus.

Cassiope'ia [*the lady in the chair*]. The chief stars of this constellation form the outline of a chair. The lady referred to is the wife of Ce'pheus (2 syl.), King of Ethiopia. She boasted that the beauty of her daughter Andromĕda surpassed that of the sea-nymphs. The sea-nymphs complained to the sea god of this affront, and Andromeda, to appease their wrath, was chained to a rock to be devoured by sea-monsters. Perseus (2 syl.) delivered her, and made her his wife. The vain mother was taken to heaven out of the way, and placed among the stars.

"That starred Ethiop queen that strove
To set her beauty's praise above
The sea-nymphs and their powers offended."
Milton: Il Penseroso.

N.B.—" Her beauty's praise " means that of her beautiful daughter. Andromĕda was her mother's " beauty."

Cassiter'ides (5 syl.).The tin islands, generally supposed to be the Scilly Islands and Cornwall, but probably the isles in Vigo Bay are meant. It is said that the Veneti procured tin from Cornwall, and carried it to the Isles of Vigo Bay, but kept as a profound secret the place from which they obtained it. The Phœnicians were the chief customers of the Veneti.

Cast About (*To*). To deliberate, to consider, as, "I am casting about me how I am to meet the expenses." A sporting phrase. Dogs, when they have lost scent, "cast for it," *i.e.* spread out and search in different directions to recover it.

Cast Accounts (*To*). To balance or keep accounts. *To cast up a line of figures* is to add them together and set down the sum they produce. To cast or throw the value of one figure into another till the whole number is totalled.

Cast Anchor (*To*). To throw out the anchor in order to bring the vessel to a standstill. (Latin, *anchoram jacĕre*.)

Cast Aside (*To*). To reject as worthless.

Cast Down. Dejected. (Latin, *dejectus*.)

Cast a Sheep's Eye at One (*To*). To look askance or sideways at one; to look wantonly at one.

Cast beyond the Moon. To form wild conjectures. One of Heywood's proverbs. At one time the moon was supposed to influence the weather, to affect the ingathering of fruits, to rule the time of sowing, reaping, and slaying cattle, etc.

"I talke of things impossible, and cast beyond
     the moon."   *Heywood.*

Cast in One's Lot (*To*). To share the good or bad fortune of another.

Cast into One's Teeth (*To*). To throw a reproof at one. The allusion is to knocking one's teeth out by stones.

"All my faults observed, set in a note book,
Learned and conned by rote, to cast into my
     teeth."   *Shakespeare: Julius Cæsar.*

Cast of the Eye (*A*). A squint. One meaning of the word cast is to twist or warp. Thus, a fabric is said to "cast" when it warps; and seamen speak of "casting," or turning the head of a ship on the tack it is to sail. We also speak of a "casting" or turning vote.

"My goode bowe clene cast [twisted] on one
side."—*Ascham : Toxophilus.*

Cast Pearls before Swine (*To*). If pearls are cast to swine, the swine would only trample them under foot.

Casting Vote. The vote of the presiding officer when the votes of the assembly are equal. This final vote casts, turns, or determines the question.

Castagnette (*Captain*). A hero noted for having his stomach replaced by Desgenettes by a leather one. His career is ended by a bomb, which blows him into fragments. An extravaganza from the French of Manuel.

Cas'taly. A fountain of Parnassus sacred to the Muses. Its waters had the power of inspiring with the gift of poetry those who drank of them.

"The drooping Muses [Sir Industry]
         Brought to another Castalie,
Where Isis many a famous nursling breeds,
Or, where old Cam soft paces o'er the lea
In pensive mood."
         Thomson: Castle of Indolence, ii. 21.

"Isis" means the University of Oxford,

and "Cam" the University of Cambridge, so called from the respective rivers on which they stand.

Caste (1 syl.), race. The Portuguese *casta*. In Sanskrit the word used for the same purpose is *varna* (colour). The four Hindu castes are *Brahmins* (the sacred order), *Shatri'ya* (soldiers and rulers), *Vaisy'a* (husbandmen and merchants), *Sudra* (agricultural labourers and mechanics). The first issued from the mouth of Brahma, the second from his arms, the third from his thighs, and the fourth from his feet. Below these come thirty-six inferior classes, to whom the Vedas are sealed, and who are held cursed in this world and without hope in the next. The Jews seem to have entertained the same notion respecting the common people, and hence the Sanhedrim say to the officers, "This people, who know not the law, are cursed." (John vii. 49.)

To lose caste. To lose position in society. To get degraded from one caste to an inferior one.

Castle Builder (*A*). One who entertains sanguine hopes. One who builds air-castles which have no existence except in a dreamy imagination. (*See below.*)

Castle in the Air. A splendid edifice, but one which has no existence. In fairy tales we often have these castles built at a word, and vanishing as soon, like that built for Aladdin by the Genius of the Lamp. These air-castles are called by the French *Châteaux d'Espagne*, because Spain has no châteaux. We also find the expression *Châteaux en Asie* for a similar reason. (*See* CHATEAUX.)

Castle of Bungay (*My*).

"Were I in my Castle of Bungay
 Vpon the riuer of Waueney,
 I would ne care for the King of Cockney."

Attributed to Lord Bigod of Bungay. The lines are in Camden's *Britannia* (edit. 1607). The events referred to in the ballad belong to the reign of Stephen or Henry II. (*See* BAR-SUR-AUBE, page 100, col. 1.)

Castle of Indolence. In the land of Drowsiness, where every sense is steeped in enervating delights. The owner of the castle was an enchanter, who deprived all who entered his domains of their energy and free-will. (*Thomson: Castle of Indolence.*)

Castle Terabil (or "Terrible") in Arthurian legends stood in Launceston. It had a steep keep environed with a triple wall. Sometimes called Dun-heved Castle. It was within ten miles of Tintagel.

Castor. A hat. Castor is the Latin for a beaver, and beaver means a hat made of the beaver's skin.

"Tom Trot
Took his new castor from his head."
Randall: Diary.

Castor and Pollux. What we call *comazants*. Electric flames sometimes seen in stormy weather playing about the masts of ships. If only one flame showed itself, the Romans called it *Helen*, and said that it portended that the worst of the storm was yet to come; but two or more luminous flames they called *Castor and Pollux*, and said that they boded the termination of the storm.

But when the sons of Leda shed
Their star-lamps on our vessel's head,
The storm-winds cease, the troubled spray
Falls from the rocks, clouds flee away,
And on the bosom of the deep
In peace the angry billows sleep. E. C. B.
Horace: 3 Odes xii., 27-32.

Castor's Horse. Cyll'aros. Virgil ascribes him to Pollux. (*Geor.*, iii.) (*See* HORSE.)

Cas'uist (3 syl.). One who resolves *casus conscientiæ* (cases of conscience). M. le Fevre calls casuistry "the art of quibbling with God."

Casus Belli (Latin). A ground for war; an occurrence warranting international hostilities.

Cat. Called a "familiar," from the mediæval superstition that Satan's favourite form was a black cat. Hence "witches" were said to have a cat as their familiar.

Cat. A symbol of liberty. The Roman goddess of Liberty was represented as holding a cup in one hand, a broken sceptre in the other, and with a cat lying at her feet. No animal is so great an enemy to all constraint as a cat.

Cat. Held in veneration by the Egyptians under the name of Ælu'rus. This deity is represented with a human body and a cat's head. Diodo'rus tells us that whoever killed a cat, even by accident, was by the Egyptians punished by death. According to Egyptian tradition, Diana assumed the form of a cat, and thus excited the fury of the giants.

The *London Review* says the Egyptians worshipped the cat as a symbol of the moon, not only because it is more active after sunset, but from the dilation and contraction of its pupil, symbolical of the waxing and waning of the night-goddess. (*See* PUSS.)

Hang me in a bottle like a cat. (*Much*

Ado about Nothing, i. 1.) In olden times a cat was for sport enclosed in a bag or leather bottle, and hung to the branch of a tree, as a mark for bowmen to shoot at. Steevens tells us of another sport: "A cat was placed in a soot bag, and hung on a line; the players had to beat out the bottom of the bag without getting besmudged, and he who succeeded in so doing was allowed to hunt the cat afterwards.

Some . . . are mad if they behold a cat. (*Merchant of Venice*, iv. 1.) Henri III. of France swooned if he caught sight of a cat, and Napoleon I. showed a morbid horror of the same; so did one of the Ferdinands, Emperor of Germany. (*See* ANTIPATHY, page 53; PIG.)

Cat-call. A kind of whistle used at theatres by the audience to express displeasure or impatience. A hideous noise like the *call* or *waul* of a *cat*.

"I was very much surprised with the great consort of cat-calls . . . . to see so many persons of quality of both sexes assembled together at a kind of caterwauling."—*Addison, Spectator*, No. 361.

Cat-eyed. Able to see in the dark. *Cat's eye* is an opalescent mineral gem.

Cat Jumps (*The*). *See how the cat jumps*, "which way the wind blows"; which of two alternatives is likely to be the successful one before you give any opinion of its merit or adhesion to it, either moral or otherwise. The allusion is to the game called tip-cat. Before you strike, you must observe which way the "cat" has jumped up.

⁂ We are told that our forefathers had a cruel sport, which consisted in placing a cat in a tree as a mark to shoot at. A wily sportsman would, of course, wait to see which way it jumped before he shot at her. This sort of sport was very like that of hanging two cats by their tails over a rope. (*See* page 224, KILKENNY CAT.)

"He soon saw which way the cat did jump,
And his company he offered plump."
The Dog's-meat Man (See *Universal Songster*, 1825.)

Cat Stane. Battle stone. A monolith in Scotland (sometimes wrongly called a Druidical stone). The Norwegian term, *bauta stein*, means the same thing. (Celtic, *cath*, battle.)

Cat and Dog. *To live a cat and dog life.* To be always snarling and quarrelling, as a cat and dog, whose aversion to each other is intense.

"There will be jealousies, and a cat-and-dog life over yonder worse than ever."—*Carlyle: Frederick the Great* (vol. ii. book ix. p. 346.).

It is raining cats and dogs. Very heavily. We sometimes say, "It is raining pitchforks," which is the French locution, "*Il tombe des hallebardes.*"

Cat and Fiddle, a public-house sign, is a corruption of Caton le fidèle, meaning Caton, Governor of Calais.

Cat and Kittens. A public-house sign, alluding to the pewter-pots so called. Stealing these pots is termed "Cat and kitten sneaking." We still call a large kettle a *kitchen,* and speak of a soldier's *kit.* (Saxon, *cytel,* a pot, pan, or vessel generally.)

Cat and Tortoise, or *Boar and Sow.* Names given to the testu'do.

Cat has nine Lives (*A*). (*See under* NINE.)

Cat i' the Adage (*The*). The adage referred to is, the cat loves fish, but does not like to wet her paws.

"Letting 'I dare not' wait upon 'I would,'
Like the poor cat i' the adage."
Shakespeare: Macbeth, i. 7.

Cat may look at a King (*A*). An insolent remark of insubordination, meaning, "I am as good as you"; or "Are you too mighty to be spoken to or looked at?" "You may wear stars and ribbons, and I may be dressed in hodden grey, but a man's a man for a' that."

Cat-o'-nine-tails. A whip, first with three, then with six, and lastly with nine lashes, used for punishing offenders, and briefly called *a cat.* Lilburn was scourged, in 1637, with a whip having only three lashes, but there were twenty knots in each tail, and, as he received a lash every three paces between the Fleet and Old Palace Yard, Cook says that 60,000 stripes were inflicted. Titus Oates was scourged, in the reign of James II., with a cat having six lashes, and, between Newgate and Tyburn, received as many as 17,000 lashes. The cat-o'-nine-tails once used in the British army and navy is no longer employed there, but garotters and some other offenders are still scourged. Probably the punishment was first used on board ship, where ropes would be handy, and several ropes are called *cats,* as "cat-harpings," for bracing the shrouds ; "cat-falls," which pass over the *cat-head* and communicate with the *cat-block,* etc. The French *martinet* (*q.v.*) had twelve leather thongs.

Cat Proverbs.
A cat has nine lives. A cat is more tenacious of life than other animals, because it generally lights upon its feet without injury, the foot and toes being

padded so as to break the fall. (*See* NINE.)

"*Tyb.* What wouldst thou have with me ?
Mer. Good king of cats, nothing but one of your nine lives."
Shakespeare : Romeo and Juliet, iii. 1.

All cats love fish. (*See previous column,* CAT I' THE ADAGE.)

Before the cat can lick her ear—i.e. before the Greek kalends. Never. No cat can lick her ear. (*See* NEVER.)

Care killed the cat. (*See* page 216, 2, CARE.)

In the dark all cats are gray. All persons are undistinguished till they have made a name.

Not room to swing a cat. Swinging cats as a mark for sportsmen was at one time a favourite amusement. There were several varieties of this diversion. Sometimes two cats were swung by their tails over a rope. Sometimes a cat was swung to the bough of a tree in a bag or sack. Sometimes it was enclosed in a leather bottle.

Sick as a cat. Cats are very subject to vomiting. Hence the vomit of a drunkard is called "a cat," and the act of discarding it is called "shooting the cat."

Let the cat out of the bag. To disclose a secret. It was formerly a trick among country folk to substitute a cat for a sucking-pig, and bring it in a bag to market. If any greenhorn chose to buy a "pig in a poke" without examination, all very well ; but if he opened the sack, "he let the cat out of the bag," and the trick was disclosed.

"She let the cat out of her bag of verse . . . she almost proposed to her hero in rhyme."—
George Meredith : The Egotist, iii.

To bell the cat. (*See* page 119, BELL.)
To turn cat-in-pan. To turn traitor, to be a turncoat. The phrase seems to be the French *tourner côte en peine* (to turn sides in trouble). I do not think it refers to turning pancakes.

"When George in pudding-time came o'er
And moderate men looked big, sir.
I turned a cat-in-pan once more,
And so became a Whig, sir."
Vicar of Bray.

∴ Bacon says, "There is a cunning which we in England call the turning of the *cat in the pan;* which is, when that which a man says to another, he says it as if another had said it to him."

Touch not a cat but a glove. Here "but" is used in its original meaning of "beout," *i.e.* without. (For another example of "but" meaning *without,* see Amos iii. 7.) The words are the motto of Mackintosh, whose crest is "cat-a-mountain salient guardant proper"; *supporters,* two cats proper. The whole is a pun on the word Catti, the Teutonic settlers of Caithness, *i.e.* Catti-ness, and mean, "Touch not the clan Cattan or Mountain Cat without a glaive." The same words are the adopted motto of Grant of Ballindalloch, and are explained by the second motto, *ensë et an'imo.*

In French: On ne prend pas tel chat sans moufles.

What can you have of a cat but her skin? The thing is useless for any purpose but one. In former times the cat's fur was used for trimming cloaks and coats, but the flesh is utterly useless.

Who ate the cat? A gentleman who had his larder frequently assailed by bargees, had a cat cooked and placed there as a decoy. It was taken like the other foods, and became a standing jest against these larder pilferers.

A Cheshire cat. He grins like a Cheshire cat. Cheese was formerly sold in Cheshire moulded like a cat. The allusion is to the grinning cheese-cat, but is applied to persons who show their teeth and gums when they laugh. (See *Alice in Wonderland.*)

A Kilkenny cat. The story is that, during the rebellion of Ireland, Kilkenny was garrisoned by a troop of Hessian soldiers, who amused themselves in barracks by tying two cats together by their tails and throwing them across a clothes-line to fight. The officers, hearing of this, resolved to put a stop to the practice. The look-out man, enjoying the sport, did not observe the officer on duty approaching the barracks; but one of the troopers, more quick-sighted, seizing a sword, cut the two tails, and the cats made their escape. When the officer inquired the meaning of the two bleeding tails, he was coolly told that two cats had been fighting and had devoured each other all but the tails.

∵ Whatever the true story, it is certain that the municipalities of Kilkenny and Irishtown contended so stoutly about their respective boundaries and rights to the end of the seventeenth century, that they mutually impoverished each other, leaving little else than "two tails" behind.

Whittington's cat. A cat is a ship formed on the Norwegian model, having a narrow stern, projecting quarters, and deep waist. It is strongly built, and used in the coal trade. Harrison speaks of it as a " cat " or " catch." According to tradition, Sir Richard Whittington made his money by trading in coals,

which he conveyed in his "cat" from Newcastle to London. The black faces of his coal-heavers gave rise to the tale about the Moors. In confirmation of this suggestion, it may be added that Whittington was Lord Mayor in 1397, and coal was first made an article of trade from Newcastle to London in 1381.

Cat's Cradle. A child's play, with a piece of twine. Corrupt for cratch-cradle or manger cradle, in which the infant Saviour was laid. Cratch is the French *crèche* (a rack or manger), and to the present hour the racks which stand in fields for cattle to eat from are called *cratches.*

Cat's Foot. *To live under the cat's foot.* To be under petticoat government; to be henpecked. A mouse under the paw of a cat lives but by sufferance and at the cat's pleasure.

Cat's Melody (*The*). Squalling.

"The children were playing the cat's melody to keep their mother in countenance."— *W. B. Yeats: Fairy Tales of the Irish Peasantry,* p. 238.

Cat's Paw. *To be made a cat's paw of, i.e.* the tool of another, the medium of doing another's dirty work. The allusion is to the fable of the monkey who wanted to get from the fire some roasted chestnuts, and took the paw of the cat to get them from the hot ashes.

"I had no intention of becoming a cat's paw to draw European chestnuts out of the fire."—*Com. Rodgers.*

At sea, light air during a calm causing a ripple on the water, and indicating a storm, is called by sailors a *cat's paw,* and seamen affirm that the frolics of a cat indicate a gale. These are relics of a superstition that cats are witches or demons in disguise.

Cat's Sleep. A sham sleep, like that of a cat watching a mouse.

Cats.
Mistress Tofts, the singer, left legacies at death to twenty cats.

"Not Niobē mourned more for fourteen brats, Nor Mistress Tofts, to leave her twenty cats."
Peter Pindar : Old Simon.

Catacomb. A subterranean place for the burial of the dead. The Persians have a city they call *Comb* or *Coom,* full of mausoleums and the sepulchres of the Persian saints. (Greek, *kata-kumbē,* a hollow place underground.) (*See* KOOM.)

"The most awful idea connected with the catacombs is their interminable extent, and the possibility of going astray in the labyrinth of darkness."—*Hawthorne: Marble Faun,* iii.

Catai'an (3 syl.). A native of Cathay or China; outlandish, a foreigner generally, a liar.

"I will not believe such a Cataian, though the priest of the town commended him for a true man."—*Shakespeare: Merry Wives*, ii. 1.

Catalogue Raisonné (French). A catalogue of books arranged under subjects.

Catamaran. A scraggy old woman, a vixen; so called by a play on the first syllable. It properly means a raft consisting of three sticks, lashed together with ropes; used on the coasts of Coromandel and Madras.

"No, you old catamaran, though you pretend you never read novels. . . . ."—*Thackeray: Lovel the Widower*, chap. i.

Cataphryg'ians. Christian heretics, who arose in the second century; so called because the first lived in *Phrygia*. They followed the errors of Monta'nus.

Catarrh. A cold in the head. The word means a down-running; from the Greek *katarrheo* (to flow down).

Catas'trophe (4 syl.). A turning upside down. The termination of a drama is always a "turning upside down" of the beginning of the plot. (Greek, *kata-strepho*.)

Catch.
To lie upon the catch. To lie in wait. "*Quid me captas?*"

"They sent certain of the Pharisees . . . . to catch Him in His words."—*Mark* xii. Here the Greek word is ἀγρεύω, to take by hunting. They were to lie upon the catch till they found occasion against Him.

You'll catch it. You'll get severely punished. Here "it" stands for the indefinite punishment, such as a whipping, a scolding, or other unpleasant consequence.

Catch a Crab (*To*). In rowing, is to be struck with the handle of one's oar; to fall backwards. This occurs when the rower leaves his oar too long in the water before repeating the stroke. In Italian *granchio* is a crab, and *pigliar il granchio* is to "catch a crab," or a Tartar.

Catch a Tartar. The biter bit. Grose says an Irish soldier in the Imperial service, in a battle against the Turks, shouted to his comrade that he had caught a Tartar. "Bring him along, then," said his mate. "But he won't come," cried Paddy. "Then come along yourself," said his comrade. "Arrah!"

replied Paddy, "I wish I could, but he won't let me."

"We are like the man who boasted of having caught a Tartar, when the fact was that the Tartar had caught him."—*Cautions for the Times.*

Catch as Catch can. Get by hook or crook all you can.

"All must catch that catch can."—*Johnson: Rambler*, No. 197.

Catch Me at It! Most certainly I shall never do what you say.

"'Catch me going to London!' exclaimed Vixen."—*Miss Braddon: Vixen.*

Catch the Speaker's Eye (*To*). To find the eye of the Speaker fixed on you; to be observed by the Speaker. In the House of Commons the member on whom the eye of the Speaker is fixed has the privilege of addressing the House.

"He succeeded in catching the Speaker's eye."—*A. Trollope.*

Catch Out (*To*). In cricket, is to catch the ball of a batsman, whereby the striker is ruled out, that is, must relinquish his bat.

Catch your Hare (*First*). It is generally believed that "Mrs. Glasse," in her *Cookery Book*, gave this direction; but the exact words are, "Take your hare when it is cased, and make a pudding, . . . etc." To "case" means to take off the skin. Thus, in *All's Well that Ends Well*, iii. 6, we have these words, "We'll make you some sport with the fox ere we case him." Scatch also means to skin, and this word gave rise to the misquoted *catch*. Though scatch and case both mean to skin, yet the word used in the book referred to is *case*, not scatch. Mrs. Glasse was the penname of Dr. John Hill (1716-1775), author of *The Cookery Book*. (*See* CASE.)

Bracton, however (book iv. tit. i. chap. xxi. sec. 4), has these words: "*Vulgariter dicitur, quod primo oportet cervum capere, et postea (cum captus fuerit) illum excoriare.*"

☞ The Welsh word *cach* = ordure, dung, and to cach (*cachu*) would be to clean and gut the hare.

Catch-Club. *A member of the Catch-club.* A bum-bailiff, a tipstaff, a constable. The pun is obvious.

Catchpenny. A worthless article puffed off to catch the pennies of those who are foolish enough to buy them.

Catchpole. A constable; a law officer whose business it was to apprehend criminals. Pole or poll means head, person; and the word means one

8

who catches persons by the poll or neck. This was done by means of an instrument something like a shepherd's crook.

"Cacchepoles, from *catch* and *pole*, because these officers lay hold of a man's neck."—*Wiclif : New Testament* (Acts xvi., *Glossary*).

Catch Weights, in racing, means without restrictions as to weight.

Catch-word. A popular cry, a word or a phrase adopted by any party for political or other purposes. "Three acres and a cow," "A living wage," are examples.

Catch-word. The first word on any page of a book or manuscript which is printed or written at the foot of the preceding page. In the early days of printing the catch-word was generally used, but for the last two hundred years the practice has been gradually dying out. Its purpose was, among other things, to enable the reader to avoid an awkward pause when turning over a leaf. The first book so printed was a *Tacitus*, by John de Spira, 1469.

Catch-word. In theatrical parlance, is the last word or so of the previous speaker, which is the cue of the person who follows.

Catechu'men [*kat'y-ku'men*]. One taught by word of mouth (Greek, *kate-chou'menos*). Those about to be baptised in the early Church were first taught by word of mouth, and then catechised on their religious faith and duties.

Cater-cousin. An intimate friend; a remote kinsman. (French, *quatre-cousin*, a fourth cousin).

"His master and he, saving your worship's reverence, are scarce cater-cousins."—*Shakespeare : Merchant of Venice*, ii. 2.

Caterpillars. Soldiers. In 1745 a soldier, quartered at Derby, was desired by the landlord to call on him whenever he passed that way, for, added Boniface, "I consider soldiers the pillars of the state." When the rebellion was put down, it so happened that the same regiment was quartered in Derby, and the soldier called on his old host, but was very coldly and somewhat uncivilly received. The soldier reminded Boniface of what he said at parting—"I consider soldiers the pillars of the state." "Did I say so?" said mine host, "Well, I meant cater-pillars."

Caterwauling. The wawl or wrawl of cats; the *er* being either a plural,

similar to "childer" (*children*), or a corrupted genitive.

"What a caterwauling do you keep here!"— *Shakespeare : Twelfth Night*, ii. 3.

Catgut. A contracted form of cattle-gut, especially a sheep. Another form is *catling*-gut, *i.e.* cattle-ing gut. In Gen. xxx. 40 we read that Jacob did separate "his own flocks by themselves, and put them not unto Laban's cattle [*i.e.* sheep]." Again, in xxxi. 9, Jacob said, "God hath taken away the cattle [sheep and lambs] of your father, and given them to me;" and verse 43 he says, "These cattle [sheep and lambs] are my cattle."

‡ Musical strings never were made from the gut of a cat.

Catgut Scraper (*A*). A fiddler.

Cath'ari. Novatian heretics. The Waldenses were subsequently so called. (*Ducange :* vol. ii. p. 288, col. 2.)

Cath'arine. *To braid St. Catharine's tresses.* To live a virgin.

"Thou art too fair to be left to braid St. Catharine's tresses."   *Longfellow : Evangeline.*

Catharine (*Knights of St.*), 1714. A Russian military order founded by Peter the Great after his naval victory of Aland, and so named in compliment to his wife Catharine.

Catharine of Russia. A sutler. When Czar Peter wished to marry her, it was needful to make her of noble birth ; so a private person was first converted into her brother, and then into a great lord *by birth*. Hence Catharine, being the sister of a "great lord," was made fit to be the wife of the Czar. (*De Cusine : Russia*, chap. iv.)

Catharine Theot (1725-1795). A visionary born at Avranches, who gave herself out to be (like Joanna Southcott) the mother of God, and changed her name Theot into Theos (God). She preached in Paris in 1794, at the very time that the worship of the Supreme Being was instituted, and declared that Robespierre was the forerunner of the WORD. The Comité de la Sûreté Génerale had her arrested, and she was guillotined. Catharine Theot was called by Dom Gerle " *la mère de dieu*," and Catharine called Robespierre "her well-beloved son and chief prophet."

Catharine Wheel (*A*). A sort of firework. (*See below.*)

Catharine Wheels. *To turn Catharine Wheels.* To turn head over heels

on the hands. Boys in the streets, etc.,
often do so to catch a penny or so from
trippers and others.

A Catharine-wheel window. A wheel-
window, sometimes called a rose-win-
dow, with radiating divisions. St.
Catharine was a virgin of royal descent
in Alexandria, who publicly confessed
the Christian faith at a sacrificial feast
appointed by the Emperor Maximi'nus,
for which confession she was put to
death by torture by means of a wheel
like that of a chaff-cutter.

Catharine-wheel Politicians.
Lovers of political changes.

Catharine-wheel Republics. "Republics," says Mr. Lowell, "always in
revolution while the powder lasts."

Cath'arists. A sect of the Manicheans; so called from their professed
purity of faith. (Greek, *kath'aros*, pure.)
They maintained that matter is the
source of all evil; that Christ had not a
real body; that the human body is incapable of newness of life; and that the
sacraments do not convey grace. (*See
Ducange:* vol. ii. p. 289, col. 1.)

Cathay'. China, or rather Tartary,
the capital of which was Albrac'ca, according to *Orlando Furioso.* It was
called Khita'i by the Tartars, and China
was first entered by Europeans in the
Middle Ages from the side of Tartary.

"Better fifty years of Europe than a cycle of
Cathay."   *Tennyson: Lockgley Hall.*

Cathedræ Molles (Latin). Luxurious women. Properly, *soft chairs.*
The cathedra was a chair for women,
like our ottoman; and Juvenal applies
the soft chair used by women of dainty
habits to the women who use them.

**Cathedrals of the Old Founda-
tion.** Those which have never been
monastic, but which have *ab initio* been
governed by a dean and chapter, with
the statutable dignities of precentor,
chancellor, and treasurer.

Catherans or *Caterans.* Highland
freebooters or marauders. (Lowland
Scotch, *catherein*, peasantry.)

Catherine. (*See* CATHARINE.)

Cath'olic (*The*). "Cathol'icus," a
title inherited by the King of Spain; as
the monarch of England is entitled
"Fidei Defensor," and the King of
France was styled "Christianissimus."
(*See* page 228, CATHOLIC MAJESTY.)

Catholic Association (*The*), 1756.
The first Catholic Association was formed

for the purpose of obtaining relief from
disabilities. In 1760 the association was
re-established on a more representative
basis, but it became moribund in 1763.
Another association was organised in
1773, which fell under the control of
Lord Kenmare; this society was broken
up 1783. In 1793 a new society was
formed on a still wider basis, and Wolfe
Tone was elected secretary. In 1793 the
Catholic Relief Bill received the Royal
Assent.

In Ireland, 1823; suppressed 1825 (6
Geo. iv. c. 4); dissolved itself February,
1829. The association was first suggested
by Daniel O'Connell at a dinner-party
given by Mr. O'Mara at Glancullen, and
on Monday, May 12th, the first meeting
of the association was held in Dempsey's
Rooms, Sackville Street. It became one of
the most powerful popular movements
ever organised. The objects were: (1) to
forward petitions to Parliament; (2) to
afford relief to Catholics assailed by
Orange lodges; (3) to support a Liberal
press both in Dublin and London; (4)
to circulate cheap publications; (5) to
aid the Irish Catholics of America; and
(6) to aid English Catholics. Indirectly
it undertook the repeal of the Union,
and the redress of Irish grievances
generally. Everyone who paid 1d. a
month was a member. (*See* CATHOLIC
EMANCIPATION.)

Catholic Church (*The*). The Church
considered as a whole, as distinguished
from parish churches. When the Western Church broke off from the Eastern,
the Eastern Church called itself the
Orthodox Church, and the Western
Church adopted the term Catholic. At
the Reformation the Western Church
was called by the Reformers the Roman
Catholic Church, and the British Established Church was called the "Protestant Church," the "Reformed National
Church," or the "Anglo-Catholic
Church." It is foolish and misleading
to call the Anglican Church the Catholic
Church, as at most it is only a branch
thereof. No Protestant would think of
calling himself a Catholic.

Catholic Emancipation Act (*The*).
10 Geo. IV. c. 7, April 13th, 1829,
whereby Catholics were admitted to all
corporate offices, and to an equal enjoyment of all municipal rights. The army
and navy had been already opened to
them. They were, however, excluded
from the following offices: (1) Regent;
(2) Chancellor of England or Ireland;
(3) Viceroy of Ireland; (4) all offices

connected with the Church, universities, and public schools ; and (5) the disposal of Church patronage.

Catholic Epistles (*The*) of the New Testament are those Epistles not addressed to any particular church or individual. Conventionally they are seven—viz. 1 James, 2 Peter, 1 Jude, and 3 John ; but 2 John is addressed to a "lady," and 3 John to Gaius, and, of course, are not Catholic Epistles either in matter or otherwise.

Catholic King (*The*) or *His Catholic Majesty.* A title given by the Pope to Ferdinand, King of Aragon (1452, 1474-1516), for expelling the Moors from Spain. This was about as unwise as the revocation of the Edict of Nantes by Louis XIV.

Catholic League (*The*), 1614. A confederacy of Catholics to counter-balance the Evangelic League (*q.v.*) of Bohemia. The two Leagues kept Germany in perpetual disturbance, and ultimately led to the Thirty Years' War (1618-1648).

Catholic Majesty, 759. A title given by Gregory III. to Alfonso I., King of Asturias.

Catholic Relief. (*See* CATHOLIC ASSOCIATION.)

Catholic Rent (*The*), 1823. The subscription of 1d. per month towards the expenses of the Catholic Association (*q.v.*).

Catholic Roll (*The*). A document which each Roman Catholic was obliged to swear to on taking his seat as a Member of Parliament. It was abolished, and a single oath prescribed to all members by the 29, 30 Victoria, c. 19 (1866).

Catholi'con. A panace'a. (Greek, *katholicon iāma,* a universal remedy.)

"Meanwhile, permit me to recommend,
As the matter admits of no delay,
My wonderful catholicon."
            Longfellow : The Golden Legend, i.

Catholicos. The head of the Assyrian Nestorians. Now called the Patriarch of Armenia.

Catiline's Conspiracy. Lucius Sergius Catilina, B.C. 64, conspired with a large number of dissolute young nobles to plunder the Roman treasury, extirpate the senate, and fire the capitol. Cicero, who was consul, got full information of the plot, and delivered his *first* Oration against Catiline November

8th, 63, whereupon Catiline quitted Rome. Next day Cicero delivered his *second* Oration, and several of the conspirators were arrested. On December 4th Cicero made his *third* Oration, respecting what punishment should be accorded to the conspirators. And on December 5th, after his *fourth* Oration, sentence of death was passed. Catiline tried to escape into Gaul, but, being intercepted, he was slain fighting, B.C. 64.

Catilines and **Cethe'gi** (*The*). Synonyms for conspirators who hope to mend their fortunes by rebellion.

"The intrigues of a few impoverished Catilines and Cethegi."—*Motley : Dutch Republic.*

Catius. In Pope's *Moral Essays* (Epist. i.), intended for Charles Dartineuf, a kind of Lucullus, who preferred "A rogue with venison to a rogue without."

Catkins. The inflorescence of hazel, birch, willow, and some other trees ; so called from their resemblance to a cat's tail.

"See the yellow catkins cover
All the slender willows over."
Mary Howitt : Voice of Spring, stanza 2.

Cat-lap. Milk or weak tea, only fit for the cat to lap.

"A more accomplished old woman never drank cat-lap."—*Sir W. Scott : Redgauntlet,* chap. xii.

Cato. *He is a Cato.* A man of simple life, severe morals, self-denying habits, strict justice, brusque manners, blunt of speech, and of undoubted patriotism, like the Roman censor of that name.

Cato-Street Conspiracy. A scheme entertained by Arthur Thistlewood and his fellow-conspirators to overthrow the Government by assassinating the Cabinet Ministers. So called from Cato Street, where their meetings were held. (1820.)

✲ The other names of these conspirators are Brunt, Davidson, Harrison, Ings, Monument, Tidd, and Wilson. All eight were sent to the Tower, March 3rd, 1820, by warrant of the Secretary of State.

Catsup or *Ketchup.* The Eastern *kitjap* (soy sauce).

Catted. The anchor hung on the cathead, a piece of timber outside the ship to which the anchor is hung to keep it clear of the ship.

"The decks were all life and commotion ; the sailors on the forecastle singing, 'Ho ! cheerly, men !' as they catted the anchor."—*H. Melville: Omoo,* xxxvi. p. 191.

Cat'ual. Chief minister of the Zam'-orin or ancient sovereign of India.

"Begirt with high-plumed nobles, by the flood
The first great minister of India stood,
His name 'the Catual' in India's tongue."
Camoens: Lusiad, book vii.

Catum (*Al*) [*the strong*]. A bow which fell into the hands of Mahomet when the property of the Jews of Medi'na was confiscated. In the first battle the prophet drew it with such force that it snapped in two.

Catwater. The estuary of the Plym (Plymouth). A corruption of *château* (chat-eau) ; as the castle at the mouth of the Plym used to be called.

Caucas'ians, according to Blumen-bach's ethnological system, represent the European or highest type of the human race ; so called from Cau'casus, the mountainous range. Whilst the professor was studying ethnology, he was supplied with a skull from these regions, which he considered the stand-ard of the human type.

Caucus. A meeting of citizens in America to agree upon what members they intend to support, and to concert measures for carrying out their political wishes. The word arose from the caulkers of Boston, who had a dispute with the British soldiers a little before the Revolution. Several citizens were killed, and meetings were held at the caulkers' house or *calk-house*, to concert measures for redress of grievances.

"The whole Fenian affair is merely a caucus in disguise."—*The Times.*

"This day the caucus club meets . . . in the garret of Tom Dawes, the adjutant of the Boston regiment."—*John Adams: Diary*, vol. ii. p. 164, February, 1763.

Caudine Forks. A narrow pass in the mountains near Capua, now called the Valley of Arpaia. It was here that the Roman army, under the consuls T. Veturius Calvi'nus and Sp. Postu'mius fell into the hands of the Samnites, and were made to pass under the yoke.

"Hard as it was to abandon an enterprise so very dear to him . . . . he did not hesitate to take the more prudent course of passing under (*sic*) the Caudine Forks of the Monroe doctrine, and leave Maximilian and the French bondholders to their fate."—*Standard*, Nov. 17th, 1866.

Caudle is any sloppy mess, especially that sweet mixture given by nurses to gossips who call to see the baby during the first month. The word simply means something warm. (Latin, *calidus ;* French, *chaudeau ;* Italian, *caldo.*)

Caudle (*Mrs.*). A curtain lecturer. The term is derived from a series of papers by Douglas Jerrold, which were published in *Punch*. These papers re-present Job Caudle as a patient sufferer of the curtain lectures of his nagging wife.

Caught Napping (*To be*). To suffer some disadvantage while off one's guard. Pheasants, hares, and other animals are sometimes surprised "napping." I have myself caught a cock-pheasant napping.

Caul. The membrane on the heads of some new-born infants, supposed to be a charm against death by drowning.

To be born with a caul was with the Romans tantamount to our phrase, " To be born with a silver spoon in one's mouth," meaning " born to good luck." M. Francisque-Michel, in his *Philologie-Comparée*, p. 83, 4, says : "*Calle, espèce de coiffure, est synonyme de coiffé,*" and quotes the proverb, " *Ste. Migoree ! nous sommes nées coiffées.*" (*La Comédie des Proverbes*, act ii. 4.)

Cauld-lad (*The*) of Hilton Hall. A house-spirit, who moved about the fur-niture during the night. Being resolved to banish him, the inmates left for him a green cloak and hood, before the kitchen-fire, which so delighted him that he never troubled the house any more ; but sometimes he might be heard singing—

" Here's a cloak, and here's a hood,
The cauld-lad of Hilton will do no more good."

Cauline (*Sir*) (2 syl.). A knight who lived in the palace of the King of Ire-land, and " used to serve the wine." He fell in love with Christabelle, the king's daughter, who plighted her troth to him secretly, for fear of the king. The king discovered the lovers in a bower, and banished Sir Cauline. After a time an eldridge came, and demanded the lady in marriage. Sir Cauline slew the "Soldain," but died of the wounds received in the combat ; and the fair Christabelle died of grief, having "burst her gentle hearte in twayne." (*Percy's Reliques*, iv.)

Cau'rus or **Co'rus.** The west-north-west wind, which blew from Caurus (Argestēs).

" The ground by piercing Caurus seared."
Thomson: Castle of Indolence, ii. 78.

Causa Causans. The initiating cause ; the primary cause.

Causa Causata. The cause which owes its existence to the " causa causans " ; the secondary cause.

∵ The *vera causa* is (*a*) the immediate predecessor of an effect; (*b*) a cause verifiable by independent evidence. (*Mill.*)

In theology God is the *causa causans*, and creation the *causa causāta*. The presence of the sun above the horizon is the *vera causa* of daylight, and his withdrawal below the horizon is the *vera causa* of night.

Cause (*The*). A mission; the object or project.

To make common cause. To abet the same object. Here "cause" is the legal term, meaning *pro* or *con*, as it may be, the cause or side of the question advocated.

Cause Celèbre. Any famous law case.

Causes. *Aristotelian causes* are these four:

(1) The *Efficient Cause.* That which immediately produces the effect.

(2) The *Material Cause.* The matter on which (1) works.

(3) The *Formal Cause.* The Essence or "Form" (= group of attributes) introduced into the matter by the efficient cause.

(4) The *Final* or *Ultimate Cause.* The purpose or end for which the thing exists or the causal change takes place. But God is called the ultimate Final Cause, since, according to Aristotle, all things tend, so far as they can, to realise some Divine attribute.

∵ God is also called *The First Cause*, or the Cause Causeless, beyond which even imagination cannot go.

Cau'telous. Cautious, cunning, treacherous. (Latin, *cautēla*; French, *cauteleux*; Spanish, *cauteloso.*)

"Caught with cautelous baits."
Shakespeare: Coriolanus, iv. 1.

"Swear priests and cowards and men cautelous."
Shakespeare: Julius Cæsar, ii. 1.

Cau'ther (*Al*). The lake of Paradise, the waters of which are sweet as honey, cold as snow, and clear as crystal. He who once tastes thereof will never thirst again. (*The Koran.*)

Caution Money. A sum deposited before entering college, by way of security.

Caut'ser. (*See* CAUTHER.)

Cava. *Cava's traitor sire.* Cava or Florinda was the daughter of St. Julian. It was the violation of Cava by Roderick that brought about the war between the Goths and the Moors. St. Julian, to avenge his daughter, turned traitor to Roderick, and induced the Moors to invade Spain. King Roderick was slain at Xerës on the third day. (A.D. 711.)

Cavalerie à Pied. The Zouaves (pronounce *zwav*) and Zephyrs of the French army are so called because of their fleetness and swiftness of foot.

Cavalie'r (3 syl.). A horseman; whence a knight, a gentleman. (Latin, *caballus*, a horse.)

The Cavalier.

Eon de Beaumont, the French soldier; *Chevalier d'Eon.* (1728-1810.)

Charles Breydel, the Flemish landscape painter. (1677-1744.)

Francesco Cairo (*Cavaliere del Cairo*), historian. (1598-1674.)

Jean le Clerc, *le chevalier.* (1587-1633.)

J. Battista Marini, Italian poet; *Il cavalier* (1569-1656).

Andrew Michael Ramsay (1686-1743).

Cavalier' or *Cheval'ier de St. George.* James Francis Edward Stuart, called "the Pretender," or "the Old Pretender" (1688-1765).

The Young Cavalier or *the Bonnie Chevalier.* Edward, the "Young Pretender" (1720-1785).

Cavalier Servant, in Italian *cicisbe'o*, and in Spanish *corte'jo.* A gentleman that chaperones married ladies.

"Coach, servants, gondola, he goes to call,
And carries fan and tippet, gloves and shawl."
Byron: Beppo, st. xl.

Cavalie'rs. Adherents of Charles I. Those of the opposing Parliament party were called Roundheads (*q.v.*).

Cavall'. "King Arthur's hound of deepest mouth." (*Idylls of the King; Enid.*)

Cave-dwellers. (*See* page 157, col. 1, BOHEMIAN BRETHREN.)

Cave In. Shut up! have done! *I'll cave in his head* (break it). *His fortune has caved in* (has failed). *The bank has caved in* (come to a smash). *The affair caved in* (fell through). Common American expressions.

In the lead diggings, after a shaft has been sunk, the earth round the sides falls or *caves* in, unless properly boarded; and if the mine does not answer, no care is taken to prevent a caving in.

Cavê ne literas Bellerophontis adferras. Take care that the letter you carry is not a warrant for your death. (*See* page 121, col. 1, BELLEROPHON.)

Cave of Achadh Aldai. A cairn in Ireland, so called from Aldai, the ancestor of the Tuatha de Danaan kings.

Cave of Adullam (*The*). (*See* page 17, col. 1, ADULLAMITES.)

Cave of Mammon. The abode of the god of wealth in Spenser's *Faërie Queene*, ii. 7.

Cav'eat (3 syl.). *To enter a caveat.* To give legal notice that the opponent is not to proceed with the suit in hand until the party giving the notice has been heard; to give a warning or admonition.

Cav'eat Emptor. The buyer must be responsible for his own free act. Let the buyer keep his eyes open, for the bargain he agrees to is binding. In English law, Chief Justice Tindal modified this rule. He said if the buyer gives notice that he relies on the vendor's judgment, and the vendor warrants the article, then the vendor is bound to furnish an article "reasonable and fit for the purpose required."

Cavell or *Cavel.* A parcel or allotment of land measured by a cord or cable. (German, *kabel*, whence *kaveln*, to assign by lot.)

Cavendish Tobacco. An American brand of chewing or smoking tobacco, prepared for use by softening, sweetening with molasses, and pressing into plugs. Called "Cavendish" from the original manufacturer.

Cav'iare (3 syl.). *Caviare to the general.* Above the taste or comprehension of ordinary people. Caviare is a kind of pickle made from the roe of sturgeons, much esteemed in Muscovy. It is a dish for the great, but beyond the reach of the general public. (*Hamlet*, ii. 2.)

"All popular talk about lacustrine villages and flint implements . . , is *caviare* to the multitude."
—*Pall Mall Gazette.*

Cavo-rilie've. "Relief," cut below the original surface, the highest parts of the figure being on a level with the surface. Also called Intaglio-rilievato (pronounce *cah'-vo-rel-ye'-vo*).

Caxon. A worn-out wig; also a big cauliflower wig, worn out or not. It has been suggested that the word is from the proper name, but nothing whatever is known about such a person.

"People scarce could decide on its phiz,
  Which looked wisest—the caxon or jowl.
      Peter Pindar : The Portfolio.

C. D. *i.e. Cætera desunt* (Latin). The rest [of the MS.] is wanting.

Ce'an. *The Cean poet.* Simon'ides, of Ce'os.

"The Cean and the Teian muse."
      Byron: Don Juan (The Poet's Song).

Ceca to Mecca (*From*). From one end of the world to the other; from pillar to post. It is a Spanish phrase meaning to roam about purposelessly. Ceca and Mecca are two places visited by Mohammedan pilgrims. (Compare: *From Dan to Beersheba;* and *From Land's End to John o' Groat's.*)

"'Let us return home,' said Sancho, 'no longer ramble about from Ceca to Mecca.'"—*Cervantes: Don Quixote,* I. iii. 4.

Cecil'ia (*St.*). A Roman lady who underwent martyrdom in the third century. She is the patron saint of the blind, being herself blind; she is also patroness of musicians, and "inventor of the organ."

"At length dívine Cecilia came,
  Inventress of the vocal frame."
      Dryden: Alexander's Feast.

According to tradition, an angel fell in love with her for her musical skill, and used nightly to visit her. Her husband saw the heavenly visitant, who gave to both a crown of martyrdom which he brought from Paradise. Dryden and Pope have written odes in her honour, and both speak of her charming an angel by her musical powers:

"He [Timotheus] raised a mortal to the skies,"
  She [Cecilia] brought an angel down."
      Dryden: Alexander's Feast.

Cecil's Fast. A dinner off fish. W. Cecil (Lord Burleigh) introduced a Bill to enjoin the eating of fish on certain days in order to restore the fish trade.

Ced, *Kêd,* or *Ceridwen.* The Arkite goddess or Ceres of the Britons.

"I was first modelled into the form of a pure man in the hall of Ceridwen, who subjected me to penance."—*Taliesin (Davies's Translation'.*

Cedar. Curzon says that Solomon cut down a cedar, and buried it on the spot where the pool of Bethes'da used to stand. A few days before the crucifixion, this cedar floated to the surface of the pool, and was employed as the upright of the Saviour's cross. (*Monasteries of the Levant.*) (*See* CROSS.)

Cedilla. The mark (ِ) under a French sibilant c. This mark is the letter z, and the word is from the Italian *zediglia* ("zeticula," a little z. (Greek, *zēta;* Spanish, *ceda,* with a diminutive.)

Cee'lict (*St.*) or *St. Calixtus,* whose *day* is the 14th of October, the day of the Battle of Hastings.

Brown Willis tells us there was a tablet once in Battle parish church with these words:

"This place of war is Battle called, because in battle here

Quite 'conquered and o'erthrown the English nation were.
This slaughter happenëd to them upon St. Ceelict's day," etc.

Ceinture de la Reine. The octroi levied at Paris, which at one time was the queen's pin-money or private purse.

Celadon. The lover of Amelia, a "matchless beauty." Being overtaken by a storm, Amelia became alarmed, but Celadon, folding her in his arms, exclaimed, "'Tis safety to be near thee, sure, and thus to clasp perfection." As he spoke, a flash of lightning struck Amelia dead. (*Thomson: The Seasons; Summer.*)

Celandine, a shepherdess in love with Marina. Finding his suit too easily granted, he waxed cold, and discarded the "matchless beauty." (*W. Browne: Britannia's Pastorals;* 1613.)

Celestial City (*The*). Heaven is so called by John Bunyan in his *Pilgrim's Progress.*

Celestial Empire (*The*). China; so called because the first emperors were all celestial deities.

Celes'tians. Followers of Celes'tius, disciple of Pela'gius. St. Jerome calls him "a blockhead swollen with Scotch pottage"—Scotch being, in this case, what we now call Irish.

Ce'lia [*heavenliness*]. Mother of Faith, Hope, and Charity. She lived in the hospice called Holiness. (*Spenser: Faërie Queene,* bk. i. 10.)
Celia or *Cælia.* A common poetical name for a lady or lady-love. Thus, Swift had an ode in which Strephon describes Cælia's dressing-room.

" Five hours, and who can do it less in,
By haughty Cælia spent in dressing."

Celt. A piece of stone, ground artificially into a wedge-like shape, with a cutting edge. Used, before the employment of bronze and iron, for knives, hatchets, and chisels.

Celts (*The*), or *The Kelts.* This family of nations includes the Irish, Erse, Manx, Welsh, Cornish, and Low Bretons. According to historic fable, Celtina was the daughter of Britannus. She had a son by Hercules, named Celtus, the progenitor of the Celts.

Cem'etery properly means a sleeping-place. The Jews used to speak of death as *sleep.* The Persians call their cemeteries "The Cities of the Silent." The Greeks thought it unlucky to pronounce the name of Death. (Greek, *koimētērion.*)

Cen'obites (3 syl.). Monks. So called because they live in common. Hermits and anchorites are not cenobites, as they live alone. (Greek, *koinŏbiŏtes.*)

Cenoman'ni. The inhabitants of Norfolk, Suffolk, and Cambridge, referred to by Cæsar in his *Commentaries.*

Cenotaphs. The most noted in ancient times—

ÆNEAS to Deiphŏbus (*Æneid,* i. 6 ; v. 505).
ANDROMACHE (4 syl.) to Hector (*Æneid,* i. 3 ; v. 302)
ARGENTIER to Kallaischros (*Anthologia,* bk. iii. 22).
ARISTOTLE to Hermias and Eulŭlos (*Diogenēs Laertius*).
The ATHENIANS to the poet Euripĭdes.
CALLIMACHOS to Sopolis, son of Dioclĭdēs (*Epigram of Callimachos,* 22).
CATULLUS to his brother (*Epigram of Catullus,* 103).
DIDO to Sichæus (*Justin,* xviii. 6).
EUPOLIS and Aristodŏcē to their son Theotimos.
GERMAIN DE BRIE to Hervé, the Breton, in 1512.
ONESTOS to Tîmŏclēs (*Anthologia,* iii. p. 366).
The ROMANS to Drusus in Germany, and to Alexander Sevĕrus, the emp., in Gaul (*Suetonius: Life of Claudius;* and the *Anthologia*).
STATIUS to his father (*The Sylvæ of Statius,* v. — Epicēdium, 3).
TIMARES to his son Teleutagŏras.
XENOCRATES to Lysidicēs (*Anthologia*).
∴ A cenotaph (Greek, κενός τάφος, an empty tomb) is a monument or tablet to the memory of a person whose body is buried elsewhere. A mausoleum is an imposing monument enshrining the dead body itself.

Censorius et Sapiens. Cato Major was so called. (B.C. 234-149.)

Cent Nouvelles Nouvelles. French imitations of Granuc'ci, Malespi'ni, and Campeg'gi, Italian tale-writers of the seventeenth century.

Cen'taur (2 syl.). A huntsman. The Thessalian centaurs were half-horses, half-men. They were invited to a marriage feast, and, being intoxicated, behaved with great rudeness to the women. The Lap'ithæ took the women's part, fell on the centaurs, and drove them out of the country.

" Feasts that Thessalian centaurs never knew."
Thomson: Autumn.

Cent-cyne. One of the upper ten; a person of high birth, a descendant of the race of kings. (Anglo-Saxon *cyne,* royal; *cyne-dom,* a kingdom; also noble, renowned, chief.)

" His wife, by birth a Cent-cyne, went out as a day-servant."— *Gaboriau: Promise of Marriage,* chap. v.

Cento. Poetry made up of lines borrowed from established authors. Auso'nius has a nuptial idyll composed from verses selected from Virgil. (Latin, *cento,* patchwork.)

∵ The best known are the *Homĕro-centones* (3 syl.), the *Cento Virgilianus* by Proba Falconia (4th century), and the *Cento Nuptiālis* of Ausonius. Metellus made hymns out of the Odes of Horace by this sort of patchwork. Of modern centos, the *Comédie des Comédies*, made up of extracts from Balzac, is pretty well known.

Central Sun. That body or point about which our whole system revolves. Mädler believed that point to be *eta* in Taurus.

Cen'tre. In the Legislative Assembly *The Centre* were the friends of order. In the Fenian rebellion, 1866, the chief movers were called Head Centres, and their subordinates Centres.

Centre of Gravity. That point on which a body acted on by gravity is balanced in all positions.

Centum'viri. A court under whose jurisdiction the Romans placed all matters pertaining to testaments and inheritances.

Centu'rion. A Roman officer who had the command of 100 men. His badge was a vine-rod. (Latin, *centum*, a hundred.)

Century White. John White, the Nonconformist lawyer. So called from his chief publication, *The First Century of Scandalous, Malignant Priests, made and admitted into Benefices by the Prelates*, etc. (1590-1645).

Ceph'alus and Procris. Made familiar to us by an allusion to them in the play of *Pyramus and Thisbê*, where they are miscalled Shafalus and Procrus. Cephalus was the husband of Procris, who, out of jealousy, deserted him. Cephalus went in search of her, and rested awhile under a tree. Procris, knowing of his whereabouts, crept through some bushes to ascertain if a rival was with him. Cephalus heard the noise, and thinking it to be made by some wild beast, hurled his javelin into the bushes and slew Procris. When the unhappy man discovered what he had done, he slew himself in anguish of spirit with the same javelin.

"*Pyramus:* Not Shafalus to Procrus was so true.
Thisbe: As Shafalus to Procrus, I to you."
   Shakespeare: Midsummer Night's Dream, v. 1.

Ce'pheus (2 syl.). One of the northern constellations, which takes its name from Cepheus, King of Ethiopia, husband of Cassiope'ia and father of Androm'eda.

Ce'pola. *Devices of Cépola.* Quips of law are so called from Bartholomew Cépola whose law-quirks for prolonging lawsuits have been frequently reprinted.

8*

Ce'quiel (3 syl.). A spirit who transported Torral'ba from Valladolid' to Rome and back again in an hour and a half. (*Pellicer.*)

Cerau'nium. The opal. So called by the ancients from a notion that it was a thunder-stone. (Latin, *ceraunium*; Grèek, *kerau'nios*.)

Cer'berus. A grim, watchful keeper, house-porter, guardian, etc. Cerberus, according to Roman mythology, is the three-headed dog that keeps the entrance of the infernal regions. Herculës dragged the monster to earth, and then let him go again. (*See* SOP.)

❖ Orpheus (2 syl.) lulled Cerberus to sleep with his lyre; and the Sibyl who conducted Ænëas through the Inferno, also threw the dog into a profound sleep with a cake seasoned with poppies and honey.

The origin of the fable of Cerberus is from the custom of the ancient Egyptians of guarding graves with dogs.

❖ The exquisite cameo by Dioscorìdês, in the possession of the King of Prussia, and the painting of Hercules and Cerberus, in the Farnésé Gallery of Rome, are of world-wide renown.

Cerdo'nians. A sect of heretics, established by Cerdon of Syria, who lived in the time of Pope Hygi'nus, and maintained most of the errors of the Manichees.

Ceremonious (*The*). Peter IV. of Aragon. (1319, 1336-1387.)

Cer'emony. When the Romans fled before Brennus, one Albi'nus, who was carrying his wife and children in a cart to a place of safety, overtook at Janic'ulum the Vestal virgins bending under their load, took them up and conveyed them to Cæ̈rë, in Etru'ria. Here they remained, and continued to perform their sacred rites, which were consequently called "Cæ̈re-monia." (*Livy*, v.)

❖ Scaliger says the word comes from *cerus=sanctus*. *Cerus manus=*Creator; and *Cereo* (according to Varro) is by metathesis for *creo*. *Ceres*, according to Scaliger, is also from *creo*. By this etymology, "Ceremony" means sacred rites, or solemn acts in honour of the Creator. The great objection to this etymology is that Cicero, Tacitus, and other classic authors spell the word *Cære-monia* and not *Cere-monia*.

Master of the Ceremonies. An officer, first appointed by James I., to superintend the reception of ambassadors and strangers of rank, and to prescribe the formalities to be observed in levees and other grand public functions.

Ce'res (2 syl.). Corn. Ceres was the Roman name of *Mother-Earth*, the protectress of agriculture and of all the fruits of the earth.

" Dark frowning heaths grow bright with Ceres' store." *Thomson : Castle of Indolence,* ii. 27.

Cerin'thians. Disciples of Cerin'-thus, a heresiarch of the first century. They denied the divinity of Christ, but held that a certain virtue descended into Him at baptism, which filled Him with the Holy Ghost.

Cerulean Brother of Jove (*The*). Neptune. Here cerulean means green.

Cess. Measure, as ex-cess, excess-ive. *Out of all cess* means excessively, *i.e. ex* (out of all) cess.

" Poor jade, is wrung in the withers out of all cess."—*Shakespeare :* 1 *Henry IV.,* ii. 1.

Cess. A tax, contracted from assessment (" sess ") ; as a " church-cess." In Ireland the word is used sometimes as a contraction of success, meaning luck, as " bad cess to you ! "

Cestui que Vie is the person for whose life any lands or hereditaments may be held.
Cestui que use, the person entitled to a use. *Cestui que trust,* the person for whose benefit a trust may be created.

Ces'tus, in Homer, is the girdle of Venus, of magical power to move to ardent love. In *Jerusalem Delivered,* Ar'mida wore a similar cestus.

Cf. Latin, *confer* = compare.

Chabouk. (*See* CHIBOUQUE, p. 245.)

Chabouk or *Chabuk.* A long whip, or the application of whips and rods ; a Persian and Chinese punishment. (*Dubois.*)

" Drag forward that fakir, and cut his robe into tatters on his back with your chabouks."—*Scott : The Surgeon's Daughter,* c. xiv.

The criticism of the chabuk. The application of whips or rods (Persian). (*Dubois.*)

" If that monarch did not give the chabuk to Feramorz, there would be an end to all legitimate government in Bucharia." — *T. Moore : Lalla Rookh.*

Chacun a son Goût. " Everyone has (*a*) his taste " ; or, " Everyone to (*à*) his taste." The former is French, the latter is English-French. The phrase is much more common with us than it is in France, where we meet with the phrases —*Chacun a sa chacunerie* (everyone has

his idiosyncrasy), and *chacun a sa marotte* (everyone has his hobby). In Latin *sua cuique voluptas,* " as the good-man said when he kissed his cow."

Chad-pennies. Whitsuntide offerings at St. Chad's cathedral, Lichfield, for keeping it in repair.

Chaff. *An old bird is not to be caught with chaff.* An experienced man, or one with his wits about him, is not to be deluded by humbug. The reference is to throwing chaff instead of bird-seed to allure birds. Hence—
You are chaffing me. Making fun of me. A singular custom used to exist in Notts and Leicestershire some half a century ago. When a husband ill-treated his wife, the villagers emptied a sack of chaff at his door, to intimate that " thrashing was done within," which some think to be the origin of the word.
⁂ " *To chaff,*" meaning to banter, is a variant of *chafe,* to irritate.

Chair (*The*). The office of chief magistrate in a corporate town.
Below the chair. An alderman who has not yet served the mayoralty.
Passed the chair. One who has served the chief office of the corporation.
⁂ The word is also applied to the office of a professor, etc., as " The chair of poetry, in Oxford, is now vacant." The word is furthermore applied to the president of a committee or public meeting. Hence—
To take the chair. To become the chairman or president of a public meeting. The chairman is placed in a chair at the head of the table, or in some conspicuous place like the Speaker of the House of Commons, and his decision is absolutely final in all points of doubt. Usually the persons present nominate and elect their own chairman ; but in some cases there is an *ex officio* chairman.

Chair. When members of the House of Commons and other debaters call out " Chair," they mean that the chairman is not properly supported, and his words not obeyed as they ought to be. Another form of the same expression is, " Pray support the chair."
Groaning chair. The chair in which a woman is confined or sits afterwards to receive congratulations. Similarly " groaning cake " and " groaning cheese " are the cake and cheese which used to be provided in " Goose month."

" For a nurse, the child to dandle,
Sugar, soap, spiced pots, and candle,
A groaning chair, and eke a cradle."
Poor Robin's Almanack, 1676.

Chair-days. Old age.

"I had long supposed that chair-days, the beautiful name for those days of old age . . . was of Shakespeare's own invention . . . but this is a mistake . . . the word is current in Lancashire still."—*Trench: English Past and Present,* v.

"In thy reverence and thy chair-days, thus
    To die in ruffian battle."
        Shakespeare: 2 *Henry VI.,* act v. 2.

Chair of St. Peter (*The*). The office of the Pope of Rome, said to be founded by St. Peter, the apostle; but *St. Peter's Chair* means the Catholic festival held in commemoration of the two episcopates founded by the apostle, one at Rome, and the other at Antioch (January 18th and February 22nd).

Chalced'ony [*kalced'ony*]. A precious stone, consisting of half - transparent quartz; so called from Chalce'don, in Asia Minor, where it was first found. Its chief varieties are agate, carnelian, cat's-eye, chrysoprase, flint, hornstone, onyx, plasma, and sard.

❖ Albertus Magnus (book i. chap. 2) says: "It dispels illusions and all vain imaginations. If hung about the neck as a charm, it is a defence against enemies, and keeps the body healthful and vigorous.

Chaldee's (*Kal-dees*). *The Land of the Chaldees.* Babylo'nia.

Chalk.

I'll chalk out your path for you—i.e. lay it down or plan it out as a carpenter or ship-builder plans out his work with a piece of chalk.

I can walk a chalk as well as you. I am no more drunk than you are. The allusion is to the ordeal on board ship of trying men suspected of drunkenness. They were required to walk along a line chalked on the deck, without deviating to the right or left.

The tapster is undone by chalk, i.e. credit. The allusion is to scoring up credit on a tally with chalk. This was common enough early in the nineteenth century, when milk scores, bread scores, as well as beer scores were general.

Chalk it up. Put it to his credit.

❖ As good-humoured sarcasm, *Chalk it up!* is tantamount to saying, "What you have done so astonishes me that I must make some more or less permanent record of it."

Chalk and Cheese. *I know the difference between chalk and cheese.* Between what is worthless and what is valuable, between a counterfeit and a real article. Of course, the resemblance of chalk to cheese has something to do with the saying, and the alliteration helps to popularise it.

"This Scotch scarecrow was no more to be compared to him than chalk was to cheese."—*Sir W. Scott: Woodstock,* xxiv.

I cannot make chalk of one and cheese of the other. I must treat both alike; I must show no favouritism.

They are no more like than chalk is like cheese. There may be a slight apparent resemblance, but there is no real likeness.

Chalks.

I beat him by long chalks. Thoroughly. In allusion to the ancient custom of making merit marks with chalk, before lead pencils were so common.

Walk your chalks. Get you gone. Lodgings wanted for the royal retinue used to be taken arbitrarily by the marshal and sergeant-chamberlain, the inhabitants were sent to the right about, and the houses selected were notified by a chalk mark. When Mary de Medicis, in 1638, came to England, Sieur de Labat was employed to mark "all sorts of houses commodious for her retinue in Colchester." The same custom is referred to in the *Life and Acts of Sir William Wallace,* in Edinburgh. The phrase is "Walk, you're chalked," corrupted into *Walk your chalks.*

❖ In Scotland, at one time, the landlord gave the tenant notice to quit by chalking the door.

"The prisoner has cut his stick, and walked his chalk, and is off to London."—*C. Kingsley.*

Challenge to the Array (*A*). An objection to the whole panel or body of jurymen, based on some default of the sheriff, or his officer who arrayed the panel.

Challenge to the Polls (*A*). An objection or protest to certain persons selected for a jury. If a man is not qualified to serve, or if he is supposed to be biassed, he may be challenged. In capital cases a prisoner may challenge persons without assigning any reason, and in cases of treason as many as thirty-five. (22 *Henry VIII.,* c. 14; 7, 8 *George IV.,* c. 28, s. 3.)

Challenging a Jury. This may be to object to all the jurors from some informality in the way they have been "arrayed" or empanelled, or to one or more of the jurors, from some real or supposed disqualification or bias of judgment. The word "challenge" is Norman, and is exactly equivalent to "call out;'" hence we say Captain A challenged or called out Captain B.

Cham (*kam*). The sovereign prince of Tartary, now written "khan."

"Fetch you a hair off the great Cham's beard."
—*Shakespeare: Much Ado About Nothing,* ii. 1.

The great Cham of Literature. Dr. Samuel Johnson (1709-1784).

Chambre Ardente (French), "A lighted chamber" (A darkened court). Before the Revolution, certain offences in France were tried in a court from which daylight was excluded, and the only light admitted was by torches. These inquisitorial courts were devised by Cardinal Lorraine. The first was held in the reign of François I., for trying heretics. Brinvilliers and his associates were tried in a darkened court in 1680. Another was held in 1716, during the regency. When judges were ashamed to be seen, prisoners could not expect much leniency.

Chameleon. *You are a chameleon, i.e.* very changeable—shifting according to the opinions of others, as the chameleon changes its hue to that of contiguous objects.

" As the chameleon, who is known
To have no colours of its own,
But borrows from his neighbour's hue,
His white or black, his green or blue."
Prior.

⁎ Pliny tells us that Democritus wrote a book on superstitions connected with the chameleon.

C'est un cameleon. One who shifts his opinions according to circumstances; a vicar of Bray.

To chameleonise is to change one's opinions as a chameleon changes its colour.

Champ de Manœuvre (*Le*). The soldiers' exercise ground.

Champs de Mai. The same as the Champs de Mars (*q.v.*), transferred after 755 to the month of May. Napoleon I. revived these meetings during the "Hundred Days" (June 1st, 1815).

Champs de Mars. The March meetings held by Clovis and his immediate followers, sometimes as mere pageants for the amusement of the freedmen who came to offer homage to their lord, and pay their annual gifts; sometimes for business purposes, especially when the king wished to consult his warriors about some expedition.

Champak. An Indian tree (*Michelia Champaca*). The wood is sacred to Buddha, and the strongly-scented golden flowers are worn in the black hair of Indian women.

" The Champak odours fail."
Shelley : Lines to Indian Air.

Champerty (Latin, *campi partitio*, division of the land) is a bargain with some person who undertakes at his own cost to recover property on condition of receiving a share thereof if he succeeds.

"Champerty is treated as a worse offence ; for by this a stranger supplies money to carry on a suit, on condition of sharing in the land or other property."—*Parsons : Contracts* (vol. ii. part ii. chap. 3, page 264.)

Champion and Severall. A "champion" is a common, or land in allotments without enclosures. A "severall" is a private farm, or land enclosed for individual use. A champion also means one who holds a champion.

" The *champion* differs from *severall* much
For want of partition, closier, and such."
Tusser : Five Hundred Points, etc. (Intro.).

Champion of England. A person whose office it is to ride up Westminster Hall on a Coronation Day, and challenge any one who disputes the right of succession. The office was established by William the Conqueror, and was given to Marmion and his male descendants, with the manor of " broad Scrivelsby." De Ludlow received the office and manor through the female line ; and in the reign of Richard II. Sir John Dymoke succeeded through the female line also. Since then the office has continued in the Dymoke family.

" These Lincoln lands the Conqueror gave,
That England's glove they might convey
To knight renowned amongest the brave—
The baron bold of Fonteney."
An Anglo-Norman Ballad modernised.

Chance. (*See* MAIN CHANCE.)

Chancel means a lattice-screen. In the Roman law courts the lawyers were cut off from the public by such a screen. (Latin, *cancellus.*)
Chancel of a church. That part of a church which contains the altar, and the seats set apart for the choir. It is generally raised a step or more above the floor of the nave.

Chancellor. A petty officer in the Roman law courts stationed at the chancel (*q.v.*) as usher of the court. In the Eastern Empire he was a secretary or notary, subsequently invested with judicial functions. The office was introduced into England by Edward the Confessor, and under the Norman kings the chancellor was made official secretary of all important legal documents. In France, the chancellor was the royal notary, president of the councils, and keeper of the Great Seal.

Chancellor of England (*The*). The *Lord Chancellor,* or the *Lord High Chancellor.* The highest judicial functionary of the nation, who ranks above all peers. except princes of the blood and the Archbishop of Canterbury. He is " Keeper of the Great Seal," is called " Keeper of His (or Her) Majesty's Conscience," and presides on the Woolsack in the House of Lords.

Chancellor of the Exchequer (*The*). The minister of finance in the Privy Council.

Chan'cery. The part of the Court occupied by the lawyers.

To get a man's head into chancery is to get it under your arm, where you can pummel it as long as you like, and he cannot get it free without great difficulty. The allusion is to the long and exhausting nature of a Chancery suit. If a man once gets his head there, the lawyers punish him to their heart's content.

" When I can perform my mile in eight minutes, or a little less, I feel as if I had old Time's head in chancery."—*Holmes : Autocrat,* chap. vii. p. 191.

Chaneph. The island of religious hypocrites, inhabited by sham saints, tellers of beads, mumblers of *ave marias,* and friars who lived by begging. (The word meant hypocrite in Hebrew.) (*See Rabelais : Pantagruel,* iv. 63, 64.)

Change. *Ringing the changes.* Repeating the same thing in different ways. The allusion is to bell-ringing.

❧ To know how many changes can be rung on a peal of bells, multiply the known preceding number by the next subsequent one, thus : 1 bell no change ; 2 bells, 1 × 2 = 2 changes ; 3 bells, 2 × 3 = 6 changes ; 4 bells, 6 × 4 = 24 changes ; 5 bells, 24 × 5 = 120 changes ; 6 bells, 720 changes, etc.

Take your change out of that. Said to a person who insults you when you give him a *quid pro quo,* and tell him to take out the change. It is an allusion to shopping transactions, where you *settle* the price of the article, and put the surplus or change in your pocket.

Changeling (2 syl.). A peevish, sickly child. The notion used to be that the fairies took a healthy child, and left in its place one of their starveling elves which never did kindly.

" Oh, that it could be proved
That some night-tripping fairy had exchanged
In cradle-clothes our children as they lay,
And called mine Percy, his Plantagenet !
Then would I have his Harry, and he mine."
Shakespeare: 1 *Henry IV.,* i. 1.

Chant du Depart. After the *Marseillaise,* the most celebrated song of the first French Revolution. It was written by M. J. Chénier for a public festival, held June 11th, 1794, to commemorate the taking of the Bastille. The music is by Méhul. A mother, an old man, a child, a wife, a girl, and three warriors sing a verse in turn, and the sentiment of each is, " We give up our claims on the men of France for the good of the Republic." (*See* page 217, col. 1, CARMAGNOLE.)

" La republique nous appelle,
Sachons vaincre ou sachons perir ;
Un Français doit vivre pour elle,
Pour elle un Français doit mourir."
M. J. Chenier.

The Republic invites,
Let us conquer or fall ;
For her Frenchmen live,
And die at her call. *E. C. B.*

Chantage. A subsidy paid to a journal. Certain journals will pronounce a company to be a " bubble one " unless the company advertises in its columns ; and at gaming resorts will publish all the scandals and mischances connected with the place unless the proprietors subsidise them, or throw a sop to Cerberus. This subsidy is technically known as Chantage in France and Italy.

Chan'ticleer. The cock, in the tale of *Reynard the Fox,* and in Chaucer's *Nonne Prestes Tale.* The word means "shrill-singer." (French *chanter-clair,* to sing *clairment, i.e.* distinctly.)

" My lungs began to crow like chanticleer."
Shakespeare : As You Like It, ii. 7.

Chaonian Bird (*The*). The dove. So called because it delivered the oracles of Chaonia (*Dodōna*).

" But the mild swallow none with toils infest,
And none the soft Chaonian bird molest."
Ovid : Art of Love, ii.

Chaon'ian Food. Acorns. So called from the oak trees of Chaonia or Dodona. Some think *beech-mast* is meant, and tell us that the bells of the oracle were hung on beech-trees, not on oaks.

❧ The Greek word is φηγὸς ; Latin, *fagus.* Hence Strabo, Δωδώνην, φηγόυ τε Πελασγῶν ἑδρανον ἥκεν. (He to Dodona came, and the hallowed oak or beech [*fagus*], the seat of the Pelasgi.) Now, "fagus" means the *food-tree,* and both acorns and mast are food, so nothing determinate can be derived from going to the root of the word, and, as it is extremely doubtful where Dodona was, we get no light by referring to the locality. Our text says Chaonia (in Epirus), others place it in Thessaly.

Cha'os (*ka'os*). Confusion ; that confused mass of elemental substances supposed to have existed before God reduced creation into order. The poet Hesiod is the first extant writer that speaks of it.

" Light, uncollected, through the chaos urged
Its infant way ; nor order yet had drawn
His lovely train from out the dubious gloom."
Thomson : Autumn, 733-4.

Chap. A man, properly a merchant. A chap-man is a merchantman or tradesman. "If you want to buy, I'm your chap." A good chap-man or chap became in time a good fellow. Hence, *A good sort of chap*, *A clever chap*, etc. (Anglo-Saxon, *ceáp-mann*.)

✝ An awkward *customer* is an analogous phrase.

Chap-book (*A*). A cheap little book containing tales, ballads, lives, etc., sold by chapmen.

Chapeau or **Chapel de Roses.** C'est un petit mariage, car quand on demande ce qu'un père donne à une fille, et qu'on veut répondre qu'il donne peu, on dit qu'il lui donne un chapeau de roses. Les roses sont consacrés à Venus, aux Grâces, et à l'Amour. (*Les Origines de quelques Coutumes Anciennes*, 1672.)

N.B.—"Chapel" we now call a chaplet.

Chapeau-bras. A soft hat which can be folded and carried under the arm (*bras*, French for arm). Strictly speaking, it should be a three-cornered hat.

Chapel is the chest containing relics, or the shrine thereof (Latin, *capella;* French, *chape*, a cope). The kings of France in war carried St. Martin's cope into the field, and kept it in a tent as a talisman. The place in which the cope was kept was called the *chapelle*, and the keeper thereof the *chapelain*.

Chapel (*A*). Either a place subsidiary to the parish church, or a place of worship not connected with the State, as a Methodist Chapel, a Baptist Chapel, etc.

Chapel, in printers' parlance, meant his workshop. In the early days of printing, presses were set up in the chapels attached to abbeys, as those of Caxton in Westminster Abbey. (*See* MONK, FRIAR, etc.)

Chapel. The "caucus" of journeymen printers assembled to decide any point of common interest. The chairman is called the "father of the chapel."

To hold a chapel. To hold a printers' caucus.

Chapel-of-Ease. A place of worship for the use of parishioners residing at a distance from the parish church.

Chap'eron. A lady's attendant and protector in public. So called from the Spanish hood worn by duennas. (English-French.) (*See* TAPISSERIE.)

To chaperone. To accompany a young unmarried lady *in loco parentis*, when she appears in public or in society.

Chapter. *To the end of the chapter.* From the beginning to the end of a proceeding. The allusion is to the custom of reading an entire chapter in the first and second lesson of the Church service. This is no longer a general rule in the Church of England.

Chapter and Verse. *To give chapter and verse* is to give the exact authority of a statement, as the name of the author, the title of the book, the date thereof, the chapter referred to, and any other, particular which might render the reference easily discoverable.

Chapter of Accidents (*A*). Unforeseen events. ·To trust to the chapter of accidents is to trust that something unforeseen may turn up in your favour. The Roman laws were divided into books, and each book into chapters. The chapter of accidents is that under the head of accidents, and metaphorically, the sequence of unforeseen events.

Chapter of Possibilities (*The*). A may-be in the course of events.

Character. *In character.* In harmony with a person's actions, etc.

Out of character. Not in harmony with a person's actions, writings, profession, age, or status in society.

Character (*A*). An oddity. One who has a distinctive peculiarity of manner: Sam Weller is a character, so is Pickwick. And Sam Weller's conduct in the law-court was "in character," but had he betrayed his master it would have been "out of character."

Charbon'nerie Democrat'ique. A new Carbona'ri society, founded in Paris on the principles of Babeuf. The object of these Republicans was to make Paris the centre of all political movements. (*See* page 214, col. 2, CARBONARI.)

Charge.

Curate in charge. A curate placed by a bishop in charge of a parish where there is no incumbent, or where the incumbent is suspended.

To charge oneself with. To take upon oneself the onus of a given task.

To give charge over. To set one in authority over.

"I gave my brother Hanani . . . . charge over Jerusalem."—Nehemiah vii. 2.

To give in charge. To hand over a person to the charge of a policeman.

To have in charge. To have the care of something.

To take in charge. To "take up" a person given in charge; to take upon oneself the responsibility of something.

Charge (*To*). To make an attack or onset in battle. "To charge with bayonets" is to rush on the enemy with levelled bayonets.

To return to the charge. To renew the attack.

Chargé d'Affaires. The proxy of an ambassador, or the diplomatic agent where none higher has been appointed.

Charicle'ia. The lady-love of The-ag'enës in the exquisite erotic Greek romance called *The Loves of Theagenēs and Charicle'ia*, by Heliodo'ros, Bishop of Trikka, in the fourth century.

Charing Cross. Not from *chère reine*, in honour of Eleanor, the dear wife of Edward I., but *la chère reine* (the Blessed Virgin). Hence, in the Close Roll, Richard II., part 1 (1382), we read that the custody of the falcons at Charryng, near Westminster, was granted to Simon Burley, who was to receive 12d. a day from the Wardrobe.

※ A correspondent in *Notes and Queries*, Dec. 28th, 1889, p. 507, suggests the Anglo-Saxon *cérran* (to turn), alluding to the bend of the Thames.

"Queen Eleanor died at Harby, Nottinghamshire, and was buried at Westminster. In every town where the corpse rested the king caused a cross 'of cunning workmanship' to be erected in remembrance of her. There were fourteen, some say fifteen, altogether. The three, which remain are in capitals: Lincoln, Newark, Grantham, Leicester, Stamford, GEDDINGTON, NORTHAMPTON, Stony-Stratford, Woburn, Dunstable, St. Albans, WALTHAM, West-Cheap (Cheapside), Charing, and (15th Herdly?)."

∴ In front of the South Eastern Railway station (Strand) is a model, in the original dimensions, of the old cross, which was made of Caen stone, and was demolished in 1643.

Char'iot. According to Greek mythology, the chariot was invented by Erichtho'nius to conceal his feet, which were those of a dragon.

"Seated in car, by him constructed first
To hide his hideous feet."
Rose : Orlando Furioso, xxxvii. 27.

Chariot of the Gods. So the Greeks called Sierra Leo'ne, in Africa, a ridge of mountains of great height. A sierra means a saw, and is applied to a ridge of peaked mountains.

"Her palmy forests, mingling with the skies,
Leona's rugged steep behind us flies."
Camoens : Lusiad, book 5.

Chariots or **Cars.** That of

ADME'TOS was drawn by lions and wild boars.
BACCHUS by panthers.
CERES (2 syl.) by winged dragons.
CYB'ELE (3 syl.) by lions.
DIANA by stags.
JUNO by peacocks.
NEPTUNE by sea-horses.
PLUTO by black horses.
The SUN by seven horses (the seven days of the week).
VENUS by doves.

Charioteers (in Rome) were classed under four factions, distinguished by their liveries:— white, red, sky-blue, and green. Dómitian added two more, viz. the golden and the purple.

Charities. Masks.

"Our ladies laugh at bare-faced trulls when they have those mufflers on, which they call masks, and which were formerly much more properly called charity, because they cover a multitude of sins."— *Rabelais : Pantagruel,* v. 27.

Charity. *Charity begins at home.* "Let them learn first to show piety at home" (1 Tim. v. 4 and 8).

Cold as charity. Than which what's colder to him who gives and him who takes?

Chariva'ri. The clatter made with pots and pans, whistling, bawling, hissing, and so on. Our concert of "marrow-bones and cleavers"; the German *Katzenmusik*, got up to salute with ridicule unequal marriages. *Punch* is our national Charivari, and clatters weekly against political and social wrong-sidedness.

Charlatan. The following etymology is suitable to a book of Phrase and Fable. It is said that one Latan, a famous quack, used to go about Paris in a gorgeous car, in which he had a travelling dispensary. A man with a horn announced the approach of this magnate, and the delighted sightseers used to cry out, "*Voila! le char de Latan.*" When I lived in Paris I often saw this gorgeous car; the horn-man had a drum also, and M. Latan, dressed in a long showy robe, wore sometimes a hat with feathers, sometimes a brass helmet, and sometimes a showy cap. He was a tooth-extracter as well as dispenser.

Probably "Latan" was an assumed name, for charlatan is undoubtedly the Italian *ciarlatano*, a babbler or quack.

Charlemagne. His nine wives were Hamiltrude, a poor Frankish woman, who bore him several children; Desiderata, who was divorced; Hildegarde, Fastrade (daughter of Count Rodolph the Saxon), and Luitgarde the German, all three of whom died before him; Maltegarde; Gersuinde the Saxon; Regi'na; and Adalinda.

Charlemagne's peers. (*See* PALADINS.)
Charlemagne's sword. La Joyeuse.

Faire Charlemagne. To carry off one's winnings without giving the adversaries "their revenge."

"Faire Charlemagne c'est se retirer du jeu avec tout son gain, ne point donner de revanche. Charlemagne garda jusqu' à la fin toutes ses conquêtes et quitta le jeu de la vie sans avoir rien rendu du fruit de ses victoires. Le joueur qui se retire les mains pleins, fait comme Charlemagne."
—*Génin : Récréations,* i. 186.

Charles. An ill-omened name for kings:

England : Charles I. was beheaded by his subjects.

Charles II. lived long in exile.

Charles Edward, the Young Pretender, died in poverty and disgrace in France.

France : Charles I:, the Bald, marching to repel the invading Saracens, was forsaken by his followers, and died of poison at Brios.

Charles II., the Fat, reigned wretchedly, and died a beggarly dependent on the stinting bounty of the Archbishop of Metz.

Charles III., the Simple, died in the dungeon of Château Thierry.

Charles IV., the Fair, reigned six years, married thrice, but buried all his children except one daughter, who was forbidden by the Salic law to succeed to the crown.

Charles VI. lived and died an idiot or madman.

Charles VII. starved himself to death.

Charles VIII. smashed his head against the lintel of a doorway in the Château Amboise, and died in agony.

Charles IX. died at the age of twenty-four, harrowed in conscience for the part he had taken in the " Massacre of St. Bartholomew."

Charles X. spent a quarter of a century in exile, and when he succeeded to the throne, fled for his life and died in exile.

Charles le Téméraire, of Burgundy, lost his life at Nancy, where he was utterly defeated by the Swiss.

Naples : Charles I. saw the French massacred in the " Sicilian Vespers," and experienced only disasters.

Charles II., the Lame, was in captivity at his father's death.

Charles III., his grandson, was assassinated. (*See* JANE.)

Charles I. When Bernini's bust of Charles I. was brought home, the King was sitting in the garden of Chelsea Palace. He ordered the bust to be uncovered, and at the moment a hawk with a bird in its beak flew by, and a drop of the blood fell on the throat of the bust. The bust was ultimately destroyed when the palace was burnt down.

Charles and the Oak. When Charles II. fled from the Parliamentary army, he took refuge in Boscobel House; but when he deemed it no longer safe to remain there, he concealed himself in an oak. Dr. Stukeley says that this tree " stood just by a horse-track passing through the wood, and the king, with Colonel Carlos, climbed into it by means of the hen-roost ladder. The family reached them victuals with a nut-hook." (*Itinerarium Curio'sum,* iii. p. 57, 1724.)

Charles's Wain. The constellation called the Great Bear, which forms the outline of a wheelbarrow or rustic wagon. " Charles " is a corruption of the word *churles,* the farmer's wagon. (Anglo-Saxon, *ceorles wæn.*)

⁂ Sometimes still further corrupted into " King Charles's wain."

Charleys, or *Charlies.* The old night watch, before the police force was organised in 1829. So called from Charles I., in whose reign the system was re-organised. (1640.)

Charlotte Elizabeth. Mrs. Tonna (1792-1846).

Charm means a song. Incantation is singing on or against some one. Enchant is the same. (Latin, *carmen.*)

Charon's Toll [*care'-un*]. A coin, about equal to a penny, placed in the mouth or hand of the dead to pay Charon for ferrying the spirit across the river Styx to the Elysian fields.

Charter. (*See* PEOPLE'S CHARTER.)

Chartism. The political system of the Chartists, who, in 1838, demanded the *People's Charter;* consisting of five principles : universal suffrage, annual parliaments, stipendiary members, vote by ballot, and electoral districts.

Charyb'dis [*ch* = *k*]. A whirlpool on the coast of Sicily. Scylla and Charybdis are employed to signify two equal dangers. Thus Horace says an author trying to avoid Scylla, drifts into Charybdis, *i.e.* seeking to avoid one fault, falls into another. The tale is that Charybdis stole the oxen of Hercules, was killed by lightning, and changed into the gulf.

"Thus when I shun Scylla, your father, I fall into Charybdis, your mother." — *Shakespeare* : *Merchant of Venice,* iii. 5.

Chase (*A*). A small deer-forest held, for the most part, by a private individual, and protected only by common law. Forests are *royal* prerogatives, protected by the " Forest Laws."

Chase (*A*). An iron frame used by printers for holding sufficient type for one side of a sheet. The type is first set up letter by letter in the "composing stick," and is then transferred to the "galley," where it appears in columns. It is next divided into pages, and then transferred to the chase, where it is held tight by quoins, or small wedges of wood. The word is French, *chasse* (a frame); our *case-ment*. (*See* STICK.)

Chas′idim and **Zad′ikim.** After the Babylonish captivity the Jews were divided into two groups—those who accepted and those who rejected the Persian innovation. The former were called *pietists* (chasidim), and the latter *uprights* (zadikim).

Chasseurs de Vincennes (French). The Duke of Orleans' rifle corps; so called because they were garrisoned at Vincennes. (1835.)

Chat. *Nid d'une souris dans l'oreille d'un chat.* A mare's nest. This French phrase is the translation of a line in Wynkyn de Worde's *Amusing Questions*, printed in English in 1511. "*Demand:* What is that that never was and never will be? *Response:* A mouse's nest in a cat's ear." (*See* MARE'S NEST.)

Chat de Beaugency (*Le*). Keeping the word of promise to the ear, but breaking it to the sense. The legend is this: An architect was employed to construct a bridge over the Loire, opposite Beaugency, but not being able to accomplish it, made a league with the devil to give his sable majesty the first living being which crossed the bridge. The devil supposed it would be the architect himself, but when the bridge was finished the man threw a cat forwards, and it ran over the bridge like a wild thing. The devil was furious, but a bargain's a bargain, and the "cat of Beaugency" became a proverb.

Châteaux en Espagne. [*Castles in Spain.*] A castle in the air; something that exists only in the imagination. In Spain there are no châteaux. (*See* CASTLE.)

Château. Many wines are named after the manor on which the grapes are grown: as *Château Lafitte, Château La Tour, Château Margaux, Château Rose* (and Bordeaux), *Château Yquem* (a white Bordeaux), etc.

Chat′telin's. A fashionable coffee-house in the reign of Charles II.

"Met their servant coming to bring me to Chatelin's, the French house, in Covent Garden, and there with music and good company . . . mighty merry till ten at night. The Duke of Monmouth and a great many blades were at Chatelin's, and I left them there."—*Pepys: Diary, April 22nd,* 1668.

Chatterbox. A talkative person. The Germans have *Plaudertasche* (chatterbag). Shakespeare speaks of the clack-dish. "His use was to put a ducat in her clack-dish" (*Measure for Measure,* iii. 2)—*i.e.* the box or dish used by beggars for collecting alms, which the holder clatters to attract attention. We find also chatter-basket in old writers, referring to the child's rattle.

Chatterhouse. *To go through the chatterhouse.* Between the legs of one or more boys, set apart like an inverted Λ, who strike, with their hands or caps, the victim as he creeps through. Halliwell (*Archaic Dict.*) gives *chat*, a small twig, and *chatter*, to bruise; also *chattocks*, refuse wood left in making faggots. Probably, the boys used little twigs or sticks instead of caps or hands. And to go through chatterhouse means to get a trouncing or tunding. The pun between chatterhouse and charterhouse is obvious.

Chatterpie. Same as chatterbox. The pie means the magpie. (*Mag*, to chatter.) (*See Halliwell.*)

Chaucer of Painting (*The*). Albert Dürer of Nurnberg (1471-1528). "The prince of artists."

Chauvin. A blind idolator of Napoleon the Great. The name is taken from *Les Aidès de Camp*, by Bayard and Dumanoir, but was popularised in Charet's *Conscrit Chauvin.*

Chauvinism. A blind idolatry of Napoleon the Great. Now it means a blind and pugnacious patriotism: a warlike spirit.

"Chauvin, patriote ardent, jusqu'à l'exagération. Allusion au nom d'un type de caricature populaire, comme le prouve cet exemple: 1820, époque où un liberalism plus large commença à se moquer de ces éloges donnés aux conscrit Chauvin, fit justice de ces niaiseries de l'opinion."—*Lorédan Larchey: Dictionnaire de l'Argot Parisien,* 1872.

Chawbacon (*A*). An uncouth rustic, supposed to eat no meat but bacon.

I myself knew a most respectable day-labourer, who had saved up enough money to keep himself in old age, who told me he never saw or touched any meat in his cottage but bacon, except once a year, and that was on club-day (1879). He never ate rabbit, game, chicken, or duck.

Chawed up. Done for, utterly discomfited, demolished. (*American.*)

Che sa′ra, sa′ra. What shall be will be. The motto of the Russells (Bedford).

"What doctrine call ye this, *Che sara, sara?*"—*Faust* (*Anster's* translation), i. 1.

Cheap as a Sardinian. A Roman phrase referring to the great crowds of

Sardinian prisoners brought to Rome by Tiberius Gracchus, and offered for sale at almost any price.

Cheap Jack. Jack, the chap-man. Not cheap, meaning low-priced, but cheap meaning merchant, as in "chapman," "Cheap-side," etc. Jack is a term applied to inferior persons, etc. (Saxon, *cepa*, a merchant; *ceapian*, to buy; *ceapmann*, a tradesman.) (*See* JACK.)

Cheapside Bargain (*A*). A very weak pun, meaning that the article was bought cheap or under its market value.

Cheater (2 syl.) originally meant an *Escheator* or officer of the king's exchequer appointed to receive dues and taxes. The present use, of the word shows how these officers were wont to fleece the people. (*See* CATCHPOLE).

✶ Compare with escheator the New Testament word "Publicans," or collectors of the Roman tax in Judæa, etc.

Chech. Called also stone-chest, kistvaen (a sepulchral monument or cromlech).

"We find a rude chech or flat stone of an oval form, about three yards in length, five feet over where broadest, and ten or twelve inches thick."—*Camden.*

Checkmate, in the game of chess, means placing your adversary's king in such a position that he can neither cover nor move out of check. Figuratively, "to checkmate" means to foil or outwit another; *checkmated*, outmanœuvred. "Mate" (Arabic, *māt*, dead; Spanish, *matar*, to kill). The German *schach* means both chess and check, and the Italian *scacco* means the squares of the chess-board; but *schach-matt* and *scacco-matto* = check-mate. The French *échec* is a "stoppage," whence *donner* or *faire échec et mat*, to make a stoppage (check) and dead; the Spanish, *xaque de mate* means the check of death (or final check).

✶ If we go to Arabic for "mate," why not go there for "check" also? And "sheik mat" = the king dead, would be consistent and exact. (*See* CHESS.)

Cheek. *None of your cheek.* None of your insolence. "None of your jaw" means none of your nagging or word irritation.

✶ We say a man is very *cheeky*, meaning that he is saucy and presumptuous.

To give cheek. To be insolent. "Give me none of your cheek."

To have the cheek. To have the face or assurance. "He hadn't the cheek to ask for more."

"On account of his having so much cheek"—*Dickens: Bleak House.*

Cheek (*To*). To be saucy. "You must cheek him well," *i.e.* confront him with fearless impudence; face him out.

Cheek by Jowl. In intimate confabulation; *tête-à-tête.* Cheek is the Anglo-Saxon *ceca*, *céac-bán*, cheek-bone; and jowl is the Anglo-Saxon *ceole* (the jaw); Irish, *gial*.

"I'll go with thee, cheek by jowl."—*Shakespeare: Midsummer Night's Dream*, iii. 2.

Cheese.
Tusser says that a cheese, to be perfect, should not be like (1) Gehazi, *i.e.* dead white, like a leper; (2) not like Lot's wife, all salt; (3) not like Argus, full of eyes; (4) not like Tom Piper, "hoven and puffed," like the cheeks of a piper; (5) not like Crispin, leathery; (6) not like Lazarus, poor; (7) not like Esau, hairy; (8) not like Mary Magdalene, full of whey or maudlin; (9) not like the Gentiles, full of maggots or gentils; and (10) not like a bishop, made of burnt milk. (*Five Hundred Points of Good Husbandry.*)

✶ A cheese which has no resemblance to these ten defects is "quite the cheese."

Bread and cheese. Food generally, but of a frugal nature. "Come and take your bread and cheese with me this evening."

A green cheese. An unripe cheese.

The moon made of green cheese. A slight resemblance, but not in the least likely. "You will persuade him to believe that the moon is made of green cheese." (*See above.*)

'Tis an old rat that won't eat cheese. It must be a wondrously toothless man that is inaccessible to flattery; he must be very old indeed who can abandon his favourite indulgence; only a very cunning rat knows that cheese is a mere bait.

Cheese. Something choice (Anglo-Saxon, *ceos-an*, to choose; German, *kiesen*; French, *choisir*). Chaucer says, "To cheese whether she wold him marry or no."

"Now thou might cheese
How thou couetist [covetest] to calme, now thou
Knowist all mi names."
P. Ploughman's Vision.

It is not the cheese. Not the right thing; not what I should choose.

He is quite the cheese or *just the cheese* —*i.e.* quite the thing. By a double refinement we get the slang varieties, *That's prime Stilton,* or *double Glo'ster*— *i.e.* slap bang up.

Cheeseparer (*A*). A skinflint; a man of small savings; economy carried to excess—like one who pares or shaves off very thinly the rind of his cheese instead of cutting it off. The tale is well known of the man who chose his wife out of three sisters by the way they ate their cheese. One pared it—she (he said) was mean ; one cut it off extravagantly thick—she was wasteful ; the third sliced it off in a medium way, and there his choice fell.

Cheeseparing Economy. A useless economy. The French say, " *Une économie de bouts de chandelles.*" The allusion is to the well-known tale of a man who chose one of three sisters for wife by the way they pared their cheese. (*See above.*)

Cheese-Toaster (*A*). A sword; also called a "toasting-fork." " Come ! out with your toaster." In Latin *veru* means a dart, a spit used in roasting, or a toasting-fork. Thùs we have "*pugnant mucrone veruque Sabello*" (*Æn.* vii. 663), and in *Æn.* i. 210, etc., we read that the men prepared their supper, after slaying the beasts, "*pars in frustra secant, verubusque trementia figunt.*" In the former example *veru* is used for an instrument of war, and in the latter for a toasting-fork or spit.

Cheesewring (Lynton, Devon). A mass of eight stones, towering to the height of thirty-two feet ; so called because it looks like a gigantic cheesepress. This is probably a natural work, the effect of some convulsion. The Kilmarth Rocks, and part of Hugh Lloyd's Pulpit, present somewhat similar piles of stone.

Chef d'Œuvre. A masterpiece. (French.) (Pronounce *sha deuvr*.)

Chem'istry [*kem'istry*] is from the Arabic *kimia*, whence *al-kimia* (the occult art), from *kamai* (to conceal).
Inorganic chemistry is that branch of chemistry which is limited to metallic and non-metallic substances, which are not organised bodies.
Organic chemistry is devoted to organised bodies and their elements.

Che'mos or *Che'mosh* [*Kee'mosh*]. War-god of the Moabites ; god of lust.

" Next, Chemos, the obscene dread of Moab's sons,
From Ar'oer to Nebo, and the wild
Of southmost Ab'arim."
    Milton : Paradise Lost, book i, 406-8.

Chennap'pa. *The city of Chennappa.* So Madras is called by the natives.

Chenu (French). Hoary, grey-headed. This word is much used in Paris to signify *good, delicate, exquisite in flavour, delicious, de bon goût.* It was originally applied to wine which is improved by age. Thus we hear commonly in Paris the expression, " *Voilà du vin qui est bien chenu* " (mellow with age). Sometimes *gris* (grey, with age) is substituted, as, " *Nous en boirons tant de ce bon vin gris* " (*Le Tresor des Chansons Nouvelles*, p. 78). The word, however, is by no means limited to wine, but is applied to well-nigh everything worthy of commendation. We even hear *Chenu Reluit*, good morning ; and *Chenu sorgue*, good night. " Reluit," of course, means " sunshine," and " sorgue " is an old French word for evening or brown. " Chenument " = *à merveille*.

Chequers. A public-house sign. In England without doubt the arms of Fitzwarren, the head of which house, in the days of the Henrys, was invested with the power of licensing vintners and publicans, may have helped to popularise this sign, which indicated that the house was duly licensed ; but the sign has been found on houses in exhumed Pompeii, and probably referred to some game, like our draughts, which might be indulged in on the premises. Possibly in some cases certain public-houses were at one time used for the payment of doles, etc., and a chequer-board was provided for the purpose. In such cases the sign indicated the house where the parish authorities met for that and other purposes.

Cherone'an [ch=k]. *The Cheronean Sage.* Plutarch, who was born at Chærone'a, in Bœotia (46-120).

" This phrase, O Cheronean sage, is thine."
    Beattie : Minstrel.

Cherry. *The whole tree or not a cherry on it.* " *Aut Cæsar aut nullus.*" All in all or none at all.

" This Hospitaller seems to be one of those pragmatical knaves who must have the whole tree, or they'll not have a cherry on it."

To make two bites of a cherry. To divide something too small to be worth dividing.

Cherry Fairs. Now called teagardens. Nothing to do with cherries ; it is cheery fairs—*i.e.* gay or recreation fairs. A " cheering " is a merrymaking. Halliwell tells us that " Cherry (or rather *chery*) fairs are still held in Worcestershire." Gower says of this world, "Alle is but a cherye-fayre," a phrase frequently met with.

"This life, my son, is but a chery-fayre."—*MS. Bodl.* 221 (quoted by *Halliwell*).

Cherry Trees and the Cuckoo. The cherry tree is strangely mixed up with the cuckoo in many cuckoo stories, because of the tradition that the cuckoo must eat three good meals of cherries before he is allowed to cease singing.

"Cuckoo, cuckoo, cherry-tree,
Good bird, prithee, tell to me
How many years I am to see."

The answer is made by the cuckoo repeating its cry the prophetic number of times.

Cher'ubims. The 11th Hussars are so called, by a bad pun, because their trousers are of a *cherry* colour.

Chery and Fair-Star. Chery was the son of a king's brother and Brunetta ; Fair-star was the daughter of the king and Blond'ina, the two fathers being brothers, and the two mothers sisters. They were cast on the sea adrift, but were found and brought up by a corsair and his wife. Ultimately they are told of their birth by a green bird, and marry each other. This tale is imitated from *The Sisters who Envied their Younger Sister*, in *Arabian Nights*.

N.B.—The name is from the French *cher* (dear), and is about equal to "deary" or "dear one." It is quite wrong to spell it with a double *r*. (*Comtesse d'Aulnoy : Fairy Tales.*)

Cheshire is the Latin *castra'-shire*, called by the Romans *Deva'na castra* (the camp town of Deva, or Deemouth).

Chess. Called by the Hindus *cheturanga* (the four angas)—*i.e.* the four members of the army—viz. elephants, horses, chariots, and foot-soldiers; called by the ancient Persians *chetrang*. The Arabs, who have neither *c* nor *g*, called it *shetranj*, which modern Persians corrupted into *sacchi*, whence the Italian *scacchi*, German *schach*, French *échec*, our *chess*. (*See* page 242, CHECKMATE.)

Ches'terfield, lauded by Thomson in his *Winter* is the fourth earl, author of *Chesterfield's Letters to His Son* (1694-1773).

Chesterfield House (London) was built by Isaac Ware for Philip, fourth earl of Chesterfield. (*See above.*)

Chestnut. A stale joke. In *The Broken Sword*, an old melodrama by William Dillon, Captain Xavier is for ever

telling the same jokes with variations. He was telling about one of his exploits connected with a cork-tree, when Pablo corrects him, " A chestnut-tree you mean, captain." " Bah ! (replied the captain) I say a cork-tree." " A chestnut-tree," insists Pablo. " I must know better than you (said the captain) ; it was a cork-tree, I say." " A chestnut (persisted Pablo). I have heard you tell the joke twenty-seven times, and I am sure it was a chestnut."

"Is not this an illustration of the enduring vitality of the 'chestnut'? [joke]."—*Notes and Queries.*

Chestnut Sunday. Rogation Sunday, or the Sunday before Ascension Day.

Cheval (French, *à cheval*). Troops are arranged *à cheval* when they command two roads, as Wellington's army at Waterloo, which, being at the apex of two roads, commanded that between Charleroi and Brussels, as well as that to Mons.

"The Western Powers will assuredly never permit Russia to place herself again *à cheval* between the Ottoman empire and Persia."—*The Times.*

Cheval de Bataille (*His*). His strong argument. (See *Notes and Queries*, May 22nd, 1886, p. 410.)

Chevalier d'Industrie. A man who lives by his wits and calls himself a gentleman.

"Denicheur de fauvettes, chevalier de l'ordre de l'industrie, qui va chercher quelque bon nid, quelque femme qui lui fasse sa fortune."—*Gongam, ou l'Homme Prodigieux* (1713).

Chevalier du Brouillard (*Le*). The French Jack Sheppard. A drama.

Chevaux de Frise (French). Horses of Friesland. A beam filled with spikes to keep off horses; so called from its use in the siege of Gron'ingen, Friesland, in 1594. A somewhat similar engine had been used before, but was not called by the same name. In German it is "a Spanish horseman" (*ein Spanischer Reiter*).

Cheveril. *He has a cheveril conscience.* One that will easily stretch like cheveril or kid leather.

"Oh, here's a wit of cheveril, that stretches from an inch narrow to an ell broad !"—*Shakespeare : Romeo and Juliet,* ii. 4.

"Your soft cheveril conscience would receive,
If you might please to stretch it."
Shakespeare : Henry VIII., ii. 3.

Chevy Chase. There had long been a rivalry between the families of Percy and Douglas, which showed itself by incessant raids into each other's territory. Percy of Northumberland one day vowed he would hunt for three days in the Scottish border, without condescending to ask leave of Earl Douglas. The Scotch warden said in his anger, "Tell this vaunter he shall find one day more than sufficient." The ballad called *Chevy Chase* mixes up this hunt with the battle of Otterburn, which, Dr. Percy justly observes, was "a very different event." (Chaucer, *chevachie*, a military expedition on horseback.)

"To louder strains he raised his voice, to tell
  What woful wars in 'Chevy Chase' befell,
When Percy drove the deer with hound and horn,
Wars to be wept by children yet unborn."
                Gay: Pastoral VI.

Chiabreres'co (Italian). Poetry formed on the Greek model; so called from Gabriel Chiabre'ra, surnamed the "Pindar of Italy" (1552-1637).

Chiar-oscuro [pronounce *ke-ar-rosku'-ro*]. A style of painting now called "black and white."

"Chiar-oscuro . . . . is the art of representing light in shadow and shadow in light, so that the parts represented in shadow shall have the clearness and warmth of those in light; and those in light, the depth and softness of those in shadow."—*Chambers: Encyclopædia*, iii. p. 171.

Chib'ia'bos. The musician; the harmony of nature personified. He teaches the birds to sing and the brooks to warble as they flow. "All the many sounds of nature borrow sweetness from his singing."

"Very dear to Hiawatha
  Was the gentle Chibiabos.
For his gentleness he loved him,
  And the magic of his singing."
             Longfellow: Hiawatha, vi.

Chibouque (*A*). A smoking-pipe with a long tube, used in the East (Turkish).

Chic. Fashionable; *comme il faut;* the mode. This is an archaic French word in vogue in the seventeenth century. It really is the Spanish *chico*, little, also a little boy, and *chica*, a little girl or darling. Similarly, *wee* in Scotch is a loving term of admiration and pride. (Chic is an abbreviation of the German *geschickt*, apt, clever.)

"J'use de mots de l'art, je met en marge *hic;*
J'espere avec le tems que j'entendrai le chic."
    Les Satyres de Du Lorens, xii. p. 97.

Avoir le chic. To have the knack of doing the thing smartly.

Chicard and *chicandard* = elegant, *de grand style*, are very common expressions with artists.

Chich'ivache (3 syl.). French for the "sorry cow," a monster that lived only on good women—all skin and bone,

because its food was so extremely scarce. The old English romancers invented another monster, which they called Bicorn, as fat as the other was lean; but, luckily, he had for food "good and enduring husbands," of which there is no lack. (*See* BICORN.)

"O noble wyvës, ful of heigh pruden'ce,
  Let noon humilitie your tongës nayle:
Ne lat no clerk have cause or diligen'ce
  To write of you a story of such mervayle
As of Griseldes, pacient and kynde,
Lest Chichi-vache you swolwe in hir entraile."
    Chaucer: L'Envoye de Chaucer, v. 9064.

The French *chiche-face* means "thin-face." Lydgate wrote a poem entitled *Bycorne and Chichevache*.

Chick-a-biddy (*A*). A child's name for a young chicken, and a mother's word of endearment to her young child. "Biddy" is merely the call of a child, bid-bid-bid-bid to a chicken.

"Do you, sweet Rob? Do you truly, cnickabiddy?"—*Dickens: Dombey and Son.*

Chicken (plural *chickens*). It is quite a mistake to suppose "chickens" to be a double plural. The Anglo-Saxon is *cicen*, plural *cicen-u*. We have a few plural forms in -en, as ox-en, brack-en, children, brethren, hosen, and eyen; but of these *children* and *brethren* are not the most ancient forms. "Chick" is a mere contraction of *chicken*.

The old plural forms of "child" are *child-r-e*, dialectic *child-er; children* is a later form. The old plural forms of "brother" are *brothru, brothre, brethre;* later forms are *brethren* and *brothres* (now *brothers*).

Children and chicken must always be pickin'. Are always hungry and ready to eat food.

To count your chickens ere they are hatched (Hudibras). To anticipate profits before they come. One of Æsop's fables describes a market woman saying she would get so much for her eggs, with the money she would buy a goose; the goose in time would bring her so much, with which she would buy a cow, and so on; but in her excitement she kicked over her basket, and all her eggs were broken. The Latins said, "Don't sing your song of triumph before you have won the victory" (*ante victo'rium can'ere triumphum*). "Don't crow till you are out of the wood" has a similar meaning. (*See* page 36, col. 2, ALNASCHAR'S DREAM.)

Curses like chickens come home to roost. (*See* under CURSES.)

Mother Carey's chickens. (*See* MOTHER CAREY.)

She's no chicken. Not young. The young child as well as the young fowl is called a chicken or chick.

Chicken of St. Nicholas (*The*). So the Piedmontese call the ladybird, or little red beetle with spots of black, called by the Russians "God's little cow," and by the Germans, "God's little horse" sent as a messenger of love.

Chicken-hearted. Cowardly. Young fowls are remarkably timid, and run to the wing of the hen upon the slightest cause of alarm.

Chien. *Entre chien et loup.* Dusk, between daylight and lamp-light; owl-light.

"The best time to talk of difficult things is *entre chien et loup*, as the Guernsey folk say."—*Mrs. Edwardes: A Girton Girl*, chap. xlvi.

Chien de Jean de Nivelle (*Le*), which never came when it was called. Jean de Nivelle was the eldest son of Jean II. de Montmorency, born about 1423. He espoused the cause of the Duke of Burgundy against the orders of Louis XI. and the wish of his father, who disinherited him. Bouillet says: Jean de Nivelle était devenu en France à cause du refus qu'il fit de répondre à l'appel de son roi un objet de haine et de mépris; et le peuple lui donna le surnom injurieux de *chien*, de là le proverbe.

" C'est le chien de Jean de Nivelle
Qui s'en fuit toujours quand on l'appelle

The Italians call this Arlotto's dog.

Child, at one time, meant a female infant, and was the correlative of boy.

"Mercy on 's ! A barne, a very pretty babe. A boy or a child, I wonder ?"—*Shakespeare: Winter's Tale*, iii. 3.

Child of God (*A*), in the Anglican and Catholic Church, means one who has been baptised; others consider the phrase to mean one converted by special grace and adopted into the holy family of God's Church.

" In my baptism, wherein I was made a member of Christ, the child of God, and an inheritor of the Kingdom of Heaven."—*Church Catechism.*

Child of the Cord. So the defendant was called by the judges of the vehmgericht in Westphalia, because everyone condemned by the tribunal was hanged to the branch of a tree.

Childe, as *Childe Harold, Childe of Ellechilde Waters, Childe Roland, Childe Tristram, Childe Arthur*, etc. In all these cases the word "Childe" is a title of honour, like the infante and infanta of Spain. In the times of chivalry, the noble youths who were candidates for knighthood were, during their time of probation, called *infans, valets, damoysels*, and *bacheliers*. Childe

or infant was the term given only to the most noble. (In Anglo-Saxon, the same word [*eniht*] means both a child and a knight.)

Childe Harold. A man sated of the world, who roams from place to place to flee from himself. The "childe" is, in fact, Lord Byron himself, who was only twenty-one when he began, and twenty-eight when he finished the poem. In canto i. (1809), he visited Portugal and Spain; in canto ii. (1810), Turkey in Europe; in canto iii. (1816), Belgium and Switzerland; and in canto iv. (1817), Venice, Rome, and Florence.

Children. *The children in the wood.* The master of Wayland Hall, Norfolk, on his deathbed left a little son, three years old, and a still younger daughter, named Jane, to the care of his wife's brother. The boy was to have £300 a year when he came of age, and the girl £500 as a wedding portion; but, if the children died previously, the uncle was to inherit. After twelve months had elapsed, the uncle hired two ruffians to murder the two babes. As they went along one of the ruffians relented, and killed his fellow; then, putting down the children in a wood, left them. The poor babes gathered blackberries to allay their hunger, but died during the night, and " Robin Redbreast" covered them over with strawberry leaves. All things went ill with the cruel uncle; his sons died, his barns were fired, his cattle died, and he himself perished in gaol. After the lapse of seven years, the ruffian was taken up for highway robbery, and confessed the whole affair. (*Percy: Reliques*, iii. ii. 18.)

" Then sad he sung 'The Children in the Wood.'
(Ah! barbarous uncle, stained with infant
  blood!)
How blackberries they plucked in deserts wild,
And fearless at the glittering falchion smiled ;
Their little corpse the robin-redbreast found,
And strewed with pious bill the leaves around."
                              Gay : Pastoral VI.

Children. Three hundred and sixty-five at a birth. It is said that the Countess of Henneberg accused a beggar of adultery because she carried twins, whereupon the beggar prayed that the countess might carry as many children as there are days in the year. According to the legend, this happened on Good Friday, 1276. All the males were named John, and all the females Elizabeth. The countess was forty-two at the time.

Children as plural of "child." (*See* under **Chicken**, page 245, col. 2.)

Chile'nos. People of Chili.

Chil'ian. A native of Chili, pertaining to Chili, etc.

Chil'iasts [*kil'iasts*]. Another word for *Millen'arians;* those who believe that Christ will return to this earth and reign a thousand years in the midst of His saints. (Greek, *chilias*, a thousand.)

Chillingham Cattle. A breed of cattle (*bos taurus*) in the park of the Earl of Tankerville, supposed to be the last remnant of the wild oxen of Britain.

Chillon'. *Prisoner of Chillon.* François de Bonnivard, of Lunes. Lord Byron makes him one of six brothers, all of whom suffered as martyrs. The father and two sons died on the battle-field; one was burnt at the stake; three were incarcerated in the dungeon of Chillon, near the lake of Gene'va—of these, two died, and François was set at liberty by "the Bearnais." Byron says that Bonnivard has left traces of his footsteps in the pavement of the dungeon. He was put in prison for "republican principles" by the Duke-Bishop of Savoy. (1496-1570.)

Chilminar' and **Balbec.** Two cities built by the Genii, acting under the orders of Jan ben Jan, who governed the world long before the time of Adam. Chilminar, or the "Forty Pillars," is Persep'olis. These two cities were built as lurking places for the Genii to hide in.

Chiltern Hundreds (*The*). There are three, viz. Stoke, Desborough, and Bonenham (or Burnham). At one time the Chiltern Hills, between Bedford and Hertford, etc., were covered with beech trees which formed shelter for robbers; so a steward was appointed by the Crown to put down these marauders and protect the inhabitants of the neighbourhood from depredations. The necessity of such watch and ward has long since ceased, but the office remains; and, since 1750, when a Member of Parliament wishes to vacate his seat, one way of doing so is by applying for the stewardship of the three Chiltern Hundreds. The application being granted, the Member is advanced to an *office under the Crown*, and his seat in the House is *ex officio* vacated. Immediately the Member has effected his object, he resigns his office again. The gift is in the hands of the Chancellor of the Exchequer. It was refused to a Member for Reading in 1842.

⁕ The Stewardships used for a similar purpose were Old Sarum (in Sussex),

East Hendred (in Berks), the Manor of Poynings (in Sussex), Hempholwic (in Yorkshire), all of which have dropped out of use. The Stewardship of the Manor of Northstead (in Yorks) survives (1894), but the Escheatorships of Munster and Ulster were abolished in 1838.

The *London Gazette* of August 4, 1893, announced that the "Chancellor of the Exchequer has appointed William Henry Grenfell to be steward and bailiff of the Chiltern Hundreds in the room of John Morrogh, resigned."

Chimæra [*kime'ra*]. An illusory fancy, a wild, incongruous scheme, a castle in the air. Homer describes the chimæra as a monster with a goat's body, a lion's head, and a dragon's tail. It was born in Lycia, and was slain by Bellerophon. (Greek, *chimaira*, a she-goat.)

Chime in with (*To*). To be in harmony with, to accord with, to fall in with. The allusion is to chiming bells.

"This chimed in with Mr. Dombey's own hope and belief."—*Dickens: Dombey and Son.*

Chimney Money or *Hearth money.* A Crown duty for every fire-place in a house (14 Car. ii. c. 2). Repealed by 1 Will. & Mary, i. c. 2.

Chimneypot Hat (*A*). The ordinary cylindrical black-silk hat, generally worn as more dressy than the soft felt hats or stiff billycocks. Called by the French *cheminée.*

Chinese Gordon. General Gordon (afterwards killed at Khartoum), who succeeded in putting down the Taëping rebellion, which broke out in 1851 and lasted fifteen years. The rebels had ravaged sixteen of the eighteen provinces, and had destroyed six hundred cities. In 1861 Ward raised an army called the "Ever Victorious," which was placed under General Gordon, and in 1864 the rebellion was stamped out.

Chingachgook. The Indian chief in Fenimore Cooper's *Last of the Mohicans, Pathfinder, Deerslayer*, and *Pioneer.* Called in French *Le Gros Serpent.*

Chink or *Jink.* Money; so called because it chinks or jingles in the purse. Thus, if a person is asked if he has money, he rattles that which he has in his purse or pocket.

"Have chinks in thy purse." *Tusser.*

Chintz means spotted. The cotton goods originally manufactured in the East. (Persian, *chinz*, spotted, stained; Hindu, *chint*, plur. *chints;* Sanscrit. *chitra*, variegated.)

Chios (*Ki'os*). *The man of Chios.*
Homer, who lived at Chios, near the
Æge'an Sea. Seven cities claim to be
his place of birth—

> "Smyrna, Rhodos, Colŏphon, Salamis, Chios,
> Argos, Athe'næ."—*Varro.*

Chip or **Chips.**
A carpenter is known by his chips. A
man is known to be a carpenter by the
chips in his workshop, so the profession
or taste of other men may be known by
their manners or mode of speech. There
is a broadcloth slang as well as a corduroy slang; a military, naval, school, and
university slang.
Such carpenters, such chips. As the
workman, so his work will be.
Brother Chip. Properly a brother
carpenter, but in its extended meaning
applied to anyone of the same vocation
as ourselves. (*Es nostræ fasciæ;* Petronius.)

∴ The ship's carpenter is, at sea, commonly
addressed as "chips."

Saratoga chips. Potatoes sliced thin
while raw, and fried crisp. Sometimes
called chipped potatoes.

Chip of the Old Block (*A*). A son
or child of the same stuff as his father.
The chip is the same wood as the block.
Burke applied the words to W. Pitt.

Chi'ron [*Ki'ron*]. The centaur who
taught Achilles music, medicine, and
hunting. Jupiter placed him in heaven
among the stars, where he is called
Sagitta'rius (*the Archer*).
Chi'ron, according to Dantë, has watch
over the lake of boiling blood, in the
seventh circle of hell.

Chirping Cup or **Glass.** A merry-
making glass or cup of liquor. Wine
that maketh glad the heart of man, or
makes him sing for joy.

> "A chirping cup is my matin song,
> And my vesper bell is my bowl; Ding dong!"
>   *A Friar of Orders Grey.*

Chisel. *I chiselled him* means, I
cheated him, or cut him out of something.

Chitty-faced. Baby-faced, lean. A
chit is a child or sprout. Both *chit* and
chitty-faced are terms of contempt.
(Anglo-Saxon, *cith,* a twig, etc.)

Chivalry.
The paladins of Charlemagne were all
scattered by the battle of Roncesvallës.
The champions of Did'erick were all
assassinated at the instigation of Chriem-
hil'da, the bride of Ezzel, King of the
Huns.
The Knights of the Round Table were

all extirpated by the fatal battle of
Camlan.
Chivalry. The six following clauses
may be considered almost as axioms of
the Arthu'rian romances:—
(1) There was no braver or more noble
king than Arthur.
(2) No fairer or more faithless wife
than Guin'iver.
(3) No truer pair of lovers than Tristan
and Iseult (or Tristram and Ysolde).
(4) No knight more faithful than Sir
Kaye.
(5) None so brave and amorous as Sir
Laun'celot.
(6) None so virtuous as Sir Gal'ahad.
The flower of Chivalry. William
Douglas, Lord of Liddesdale. (Fourteenth century.)

Chiv'y. A chase in the school game
of "Prisoners' Base" or "Prison Bars."
Probably a gipsy word. One boy sets a
chivy, by leaving his bar, when one
of the opposite side chases him, and if
he succeeds in touching him before he
reaches "home," the boy touched, becomes a prisoner.

Chivy or **Chivvy.** Slang for the face.
Much slang is due to rhyme, and when
the rhyme is a compound word the
rhyming part is sometimes dropped and
the other part remains. Thus Chivy
[Chevy]-chase rhymes with "face," by
dropping "chase" *chivy* remains, and
becomes the accepted slang word. Similarly, daisies = boots, thus: daisy-roots
will rhyme with "boots," and by dropping "roots," the rhyme, *daisy* remains.
By the same process *sky* is the slang for
pocket, the compound word which gave
birth to it being "sky-rocket." "Christmas" the slang for a railway guard, as
"Ask the Christmas," is, of course, from
the rhyme "Christmas-card"; and
"raspberry" the slang for heart, is
from the rhyme "raspberry-tart."

> "Then came a knock at the Rory o' More [door],
> Which made my raspberry beat."

Other examples given under their
proper heads.

Chlo'e (*Klo'ee*). The shepherdess beloved by Daphnis in the pastoral romance
of Longus, entitled *Daphnis and Chloe.*
St. Pierre's tale of *Paul and Virginia* is
founded on the exquisite romance of
Longus.

∵ Prior calls Mrs. Centlivre "Cloe."

Chloe, in Pope's *Moral Essays* (epist.
ii.), Lady Suffolk, mistress of George II.
"Content to dwell in decencies for
ever."

Chœ'reas [*Ke'reas*]. The lover of Callir'rhoë, in Cha'riton's Greek romance, called the *Loves of Chœreas and Callir'rhoë.* (Eighth century.)

Choice Spirit (*A*) or "Choice Spirit of the Age," a gallant of the day, being one who delights to exaggerate the whims of fashion.

Hobson's Choice. (*See* HOBSON.)

Choke. *May this piece of bread . . oke me, if what I say is not true.* In ancient times a person accused of robbery had a piece of barley bread, on which the mass had been said, given him to swallow. He put it in his mouth uttering the words given above, and if he could swallow it without being choked, he was pronounced innocent. Tradition ascribes the death of the Earl Godwin to choking with a piece of bread, after this solemn appeal. (*See* CORSNED.)

Choke-pear. An argument to which there is no answer. Robbers in Holland at one time made use of a piece of iron in the shape of a pear, which they forced into the mouth of their victim. On turning a key, a number of springs thrust forth points of iron in all directions, so that the instrument of torture could never be taken out except by means of the key.

Choker (*A*). A neckcloth. A *white choker* is a white neckcloth or necktie, worn in full dress, and generally by waiters and clergymen. Of course, the verb *to choke* has supplied the word.

Chop and **Chops.**
Chop and change (*To*). To barter by the rule of thumb. Boys "chop" one article for another (Anglo Saxon, *oip an*, or *ceáp-ian*, to sell or barter).
A mutton chop is from the French *coup-er*, to cut off. A piece chopped off.
The wind chops about. Shifts from point to point suddenly. This is *cip-an*, to barter or change hands. (*See above* To CHOP AND CHANGE.)

"How the House of Lords and House of Commons chopped round."—*Thackeray: The Four Georges* (George I.).

Chop-fallen. Crest-fallen; down in the mouth. (*See next column,* CHOPS.)

Chop-House (*A*). An eating-house where chops and steaks are served.

"John Bull . . . would set up a chop-house at the very gates of paradise."—*Washington Irving*: vol. i. chap. vi. p. 61.

⁂ A Chinese custom-house is called a Chop-house (Hindu, *chap*, a stamp).

Chop Logic (*To*). To bandy words; to altercate. Lord Bacon says, "Let not the council chop with the judge." (*See* CHOP AND CHANGE.)

"How now, how now, chop logic! What is this? 'Proud,' and 'I thank you,' and 'I thank you not,'
And yet 'not proud.'"
Shakespeare: Romeo and Juliet, iii. 5.

Chops. The face, is allied to the Latin *caput*, the head; Greek κέφαλ-ος, Anglo-Saxon *ceafel*, the snout; in the plural, the cheeks. We talk of a "pig's chap."

⁂ The Latin *cap-ut* gives us the word *chap*, a fellow or man; and its alliance with *chop* gives us the term "chapped" hands, etc. Everyone knows the answer given to the girl who complained of *chapped lips*: "My dear, you should not let the chaps come near your lips."
Down in the chops—i.e. down in the mouth; in a melancholy state; with the mouth drawn down. (Anglo-Saxon, *cealf*, the snout or jaw; Icelandic, *kiaptr*.)

Chops of the Channel. The short broken motion of the waves, experienced in crossing the English Channel; also the place where such motion occurs.

Chop'ine (2 syl.), or *Chopin*. A high-heeled shoe. The Venetian ladies used to wear "high-heeled shoes like stilts." Hamlet says of the actress, "Your ladyship is nearer to heaven, than when I saw you last, by the altitude of a chopine" (act ii. s. 2). (Spanish, *chapin*, a high cork shoe.)

Choreu'tæ [*Koru'tee*]. A sect of heretics, who, among other errors, persisted in keeping the Sunday a fast.

Choriambic Metre. Horace gives us a great variety, but the main feature in all is the prevalence of the choriambus (− ᴗ ᴗ −). Specimen translations of two of these metres are subjoined ·
(1) Horace, 1 *Odes*, viii.

−ᴗ| | −−| −ᴗᴗ−| −ᴗᴗ | ᴗ−−

Lydia, why on Stanley,
By the great gods, tell me, I pray, ruinous love
you centre?
Once he was strong and manly,
Never seen now, patient of toil, Mars' sunny camp to enter. E. C. B.

(2) The other specimen is 1 *Odes*, xii.

−−|−ᴗᴗ−|ᴗ−−
−−|−ᴗᴗ−|ᴗ−−|ᴗ−−

When you, with an approving smile,
Praise those delicate arms, Lydy, of Telephus,
Ah me! how you stir up my bile!
Heart-sick that for a boy you should forsake me
thus. E. C. B.

Chouans (2 syl.). French insurgents of the Royalist party during the Revolution. Jean Cotterean was their leader, nicknamed *chouan* (owl), because he was accustomed to warn his companions of danger by imitating the screech of an owl. Cottereau was followed by George Cadoudal.

⁎⁎ It is an error to suppose Chouan to be a proper name.

Choughs Protected. (*See* page 137, col. 1, BIRDS, etc.)

Chouse (1 syl.). To cheat out of something. Gifford says the interpreter of the Turkish embassy in England is called *chiaus*, and in 1609 this chiaus contrived to defraud his government of £4,000, an enormous sum at that period. From the notoriety of the swindle the word *chiaus* or *to chouse* was adopted.

" He is no chiaus."
Ben Jonson: Alchemist, i. 1 (1610).

Chriem-hil'da or **Chriem-hild.** A woman of unrivalled beauty, sister of Gunther, and beloved by Siegfried, the two chief heroes of the Nibelungenlied. Siegfried gives her a talisman taken from Gunther's lady-love, and Gunther, in a fit of jealousy, induces Hagen to murder his brother-in-law. Chriemhild in revenge marries Ezzel, King of the Huns; invites the Nibelungs to the wedding feast; and there they are all put to the sword, except Hagen and Gunther, who are taken prisoners, and put to death by the bride. (*See* KRIEM-HILD.)

Chriss-cross Row (*row* to rhyme with *low*). The alphabet in a horn-book, which had a cross at the beginning and end.

" Philosophy is all the go,
And science quite the fashion;
Our grandams learnt the Chriss-cross Row,
L—d, how their daughters dash on."
Anon. in the Eaglet.

Chrisom or **Chrism** signifies properly "the white cloth set by the minister at baptism on the head of the newly anointed with chrism"—*i.e.* a composition of oil and balm. In the Form of Private Baptism is this direction: " Then the minister shall put the white vesture, commonly called the chrisome, upon the child." The child thus baptised is called a chrisom or chrisom child. If it dies within the month, it is shrouded in the vesture; and hence, in the bills of mortality, even to the year 1726, infants that died within the month were termed chrisoms. (The cloth is so called because it was anointed. Greek, *chrisma*, verb *chrio*, to anoint.)

" A' made a finer end and went away an it had been any chrisom child."—*Shakespeare: Henry V.*, ii. 3.

Christabel [*Kris'tabel*]. The heroine of Coleridge's fragmentary poem of that name.

Christabelle [*Kris'tabel*]. Daughter of a "bonnie king" in Ireland. She fell in love with Sir Cauline (*q.v.*).

Christendom [*Kris-en-dum*] generally means all Christian countries; but Shakespeare uses it for *baptism*, or "Christian citizenship." Thus, in *King John*, the young prince says:—

" By my christendom !
So I were out of prison and kept sheep,
I should be merry as the day is long."
Act iv. sc. 1.

Christian [ch = k]. The hero of John Bunyan's allegory called *The Pilgrim's Progress.* He flees from the "City of Destruction," and journeys to the "Celestial City." He starts with a heavy burden on his back, but it falls off when he stands at the foot of the cross.

Christian. A follower of Christ. So called first at Antioch (Acts xi. 26).

Most Christian Doctor. John Charlier de Gerson (1363-1429).

Most Christian King. The style of the King of France. (1469.)

Pepin le Bref was so styled by Pope Stephen III. (714-768).

Charles le Chauve was so styled by the council of Savonnières (823, 840-877).

Louis XI. was so styled by Pope Paul II. (1423, 1461-1483).

Since which time (1469) it was universally adopted in the French monarchy.

" And thou, O Gaul, with gaudy trophies plumed,
' Most Christian king.' Alas ! in vain assumed."
Camoens: Lusiad, book vii.

Founder of Christian Eloquence. Louis Bordaloue, the French preacher (1632-1704).

Christian Traditions, connected with natural objects.

1. *Birds, Beasts, and Fishes.*
The *Ass:* Cross on the back. (*See* ASS.)

Bunting. (*See* YELLOW-HAMMER.)

⁎⁎ The *Crossbill* has nothing to do with the Christian cross; the bird is so called, because its mandibles cross each other.

Haddock: The finger-marks on the Haddock and John Dory. (*See* HADDOCK, etc.)

Ichthus, a fish. (*See* ICHTHUS.)

Pike's Head (*q.v.*).

Pigeons or *Doves:* The Russians are averse to pigeons as a food, because the Holy Ghost assumed the form of a dove at the baptism of Jesus. (*Sporting Magazine*, January, 1825, p. 307.)

Robin Redbreast : The red breast. (*See* ROBIN.)

Stork : The cry of the Stork. (*See* STORK.)

Swallow : The cry of the Swallow. (*See* SWALLOW.)

Swine : The holes in the forefeet of Swine. (*See* PIGS.)

2. *The Vegetable World.*

The Arum, Aspen, Calvary-clover, Cedar (*see also* CROSS), Dwarf-elder, Judas-tree, Passion-flower, Purple Orchis, Red Anemone, Rood Selken, Spotted Persicaria, Thistle.

(*See these articles,* and FLOWERS WITH TRADITIONS OF CHRIST.)

3. The Number Thirteen. (*See* THIR-TEEN.)

Christian′a [ch = k]. The wife of Christian, who started with her children and Mercy from the "City of Destruction" long after her husband. She was placed under the guidance of Mr. Great-Heart, and went, therefore, in "silver slippers" along the thorny road (*Bunyan : The Pilgrim's Progress,* part ii.).

Christmas (*Krist′mas*). "Christmas comes but once a year." (*Thomas Tusser.*)

Christmas. Slang for a railway-guard. Explained under CHIVY (*q.v.*).

Christmas Box. A small gratuity given to servants, etc., on Boxing Day (the day after Christmas Day). In the early days of Christianity boxes were placed in churches for promiscuous charities, and opened on Christmas Day. The contents were distributed next day by the priests, and called the "dole of the Christmas box," or the "box money." It was customary for heads of houses to give small sums of money to their subordinates "to put into the box" before mass on Christmas Day.

Somewhat later, apprentices carried a box round to their master's customers for small gratuities. The custom since 1836 has been gradually dying out.

" Gladly the boy, with Christmas-box in hand,
Throughout the town his devious route pursues,
And of his master's customers implores
The yearly mite."
                                                Christmas.

Christmas Carols are in commemoration of the song of the angels to the shepherds at the nativity. Durand tells us that the bishops with the clergy used to sing carols and play games on Christmas Day. (Welsh, *carol,* a love-song ; Italian, *carola,* etc.)

Christmas Day. Transferred from the 6th of January to the 25th of December by Julius I. (337-352).

Old Christmas Day. January 6th. When Gregory XIII. reformed the Calendar in 1582, he omitted *ten* days ; but when the New Style was adopted in England in 1752, it was necessary to cut off *eleven* days, which drove back January 6th to December 25th of the previous year. So what we now call January 6th in the Old Style would be Christmas Day, or December 25th.

Christmas Decorations. The great feast of Saturn was held in December, when the people decorated the temples with such green things as they could find. The Christian custom is the same transferred to Him who was born in Bethlehem on Christmas Day. The holly or holy-tree is called Christ's-thorn in Germany and Scandinavia, from its use in church decorations and its putting forth its berries about Christmas time. The early Christians gave an emblematic turn to the custom, referring to the "righteous branch," and justifying the custom from Isaiah lx. 13— "The glory of Lebanon shall come unto thee ; the fir-tree, the pine-tree, and the box together, to beautify the place of my sanctuary."

Christmas Trees and **Maypoles** are remnants of the Scandinavian Ash, called Yggdräsil′, the Tree of Time, whose roots penetrate to heaven, Niff-heim and Ginnungagap (the gap of gaps). In Ginnungagap the frost giants dwell, in Niffheim is the great serpent Nidhögg ; and under this root is Helheim, the home of the dead.

⁂ We are told that the ancient Egyptians, at the Winter Solstice, used a palm branch containing twelve leaves or shoots to symbolise the "completion of the year." The modern custom comes from Germany.

Chris′tolytes [*Kris′-to-lites*]. A sect of Christians that appeared in the sixth century. They maintained that when Christ descended into hell, He left His soul and body there, and rose only with His heavenly nature.

Christopher (*St.*). The giant carried a child over a brook, and said, "Chylde, thou hast put me in grete peryll. I might bere no greater burden." To which the child answered, "Marvel thou nothing, for thou hast borne all the world upon thee, and its sins likewise." This is an allegory : Christopher means

Christ-bearer; the *child* was Christ, and the *river* was the river of death.

Chronicle Small Beer (*To*). To note down events of no importance whatsoever.

"He was a wight, if ever such wight were . . .
To suckle fools and chronicle small beer."
Shakespeare: Othello, ii. 1.

Chron'icon ex Chron'icis is by Florence, a monk of Worcester, the earliest of our English chroniclers. It begins from Creation, and goes down to 1119, in which year the author died; but it was continued by another hand to 1141. Printed in 4to at London, 1592. Its chief value consists in its serving as a key to the Saxon chronicle.

Chronon-hoton-thol'ogos [ch = k]. A burlesque pomposo in Henry Carey's farce, so called. Anyone who delivers an inflated address.

" Aldiborontephoscophornio, where left you Chrononhotonthologos?"—*H. Carey.*

Chrys'alis [ch = k]. The form which caterpillars assume before they are converted into butterflies or moths. The chrysalis is also called an aure'lia, from the Latin *aurum,* gold. The external covering of some species has a metallic, golden hue, but others are green, red, black, etc. (Greek, *chrusos,* gold.)
∵ The plural is either *chrysalises* or *chrys'alides* (4 syl.).

Chrysa'or [ch = k]. Sir Artegal's sword, "that all other swords excelled." (*Spenser: Faërie Queene.*) (*See* SWORD.)

Chrysippus. *Nisi Chrysippus fuisset, Porticus non esset.* Chrysippus of Soli was a disciple of Zeno the Stoic, and Cleanthes his successor. He did for the Stoics what St. Paul did for Christianity —that is, he explained the system, showed by plausible reasoning its truth, and how it was based on a solid foundation. Stoicism was founded by Zeno, it is true; but if Chrysippus had not advocated it, the system would never have taken root.

Chubb (*Thomas*). A deistical writer who wrote upon miracles in the first half of the eighteenth century.

"He heard of Blount, of Mandeville, and Chubb."
Crabbe: Borough.

Chuck Full. Probably a corruption of *chock full* or *choke full*—*i.e.* full enough to choke one.

"Ayr was holding some grand market; streets and inn had been chokefull during the sunny hours."—*Carlyle, in Froude's Jane W. Carlyle,* vol. i. letter lxxxvii. p. 275.

Chukwa. The tortoise at the South Pole on which the earth is said to rest.

Chum. A crony, a familiar companion, properly a bedfellow; a corruption either of *chamber-mate* or *comrade.*

"To have a good chum is one of the pleasantest parts of a voyage."—*Nordhoff: Merchant Vessels,* chap. xii. p. 164.

Chum in with (*To*). To be on friendly terms with. (*See above.*)

Church. The etymology of this word is generally assumed to be from the Greek, *Kuriou oikos* (house of God); but this is most improbable, as the word existed in all the Celtic dialects long before the introduction of Greek. No doubt the word means "a circle." The places of worship among the German and Celtic nations were always circular. (Welsh, *cyrch;* French, *cirque;* Scotch, *kirk;* Greek, *kirk-os,* etc.) Compare Anglo-Saxon *circe,* a church, with *circol,* a circle.

High, Low, and *Broad Church.* Dr. South says, "The High Church are those who think highly of the Church and lowly of themselves; the Low Church, those who think lowly of the Church and highly of themselves" (this may be epigrammatic, but the latter half is not true). Broad Church are those who think the Church is broad enough for all religious parties, and their own views of religion are chiefly of a moral nature, their doctrinal views being so rounded and elastic that they can come into collision with no one.

∵ By the "High Church" now are meant those who follow the "Oxford Movement"; the "Low Church" party call themselves the "Evangelical" Church party.

The Church of Latter-day Saints. The Mormons.

The Anglican Church. That branch of the Protestant Church which, at the Reformation, was adopted in England. It disavowed the authority of the Pope, and rejected certain dogmas and rules of the Roman Church.

∵ Since 1532 generally called the "Established Church," because established by Act of Parliament.

The Catholic Church. The Western Church called itself so when it separated from the Eastern Church. It is also called the Roman Catholic Church, to distinguish it from the Anglican Church or Anglican Catholic Church, a branch of the Western Church.

The Established Church. The State Church, which, in England, is Episcopalian and in Scotland Presbyterian.

Before the Reformation it was, in both countries, "Catholic;" before the introduction of Christianity it was Pagan, and before that Druidism. In Turkey it is Mohammedanism; in Russia the Greek Church; in China, India, etc., other systems of religion.

To go into the Church. To take holy orders, or become an "ordained" clergyman.

Church-goer (*A*). One who regularly attends the parish church.

Church Invisible (*The*). Those who are known to God alone as His sons and daughters by adoption and grace. (*See* CHURCH VISIBLE.)

"Oh, may I join the choir invisible."
G. Eliot.

Church Militant. The Church on earth means the whole body of believers, who are said to be "waging the war of faith" against "the world, the flesh, and the devil." It is therefore militant, or in warfare. (*See* CHURCH TRIUMPHANT.)

Church Porch (*The*) was used in ancient times for settling money transactions, paying dowries, rents, and purchases of estates. Consequently, it was furnished with benches on both sides. Hence, Lord Stourton sent to invite the Hartgills to meet him in the porch of Kilmington church to receive the £2,000 awarded them by the Star Chamber. (*Lord de Ros : Tower of London.*)

Church Triumphant (*The*). Those who are dead and gone to their rest. Having fought the fight and triumphed, they belong to the Church triumphant in heaven. (*See* CHURCH MILITANT.)

Church Visible (*The*). All ostensible Christians; all who profess to be Christians; all who have been baptised and admitted into Church Communion. (*See* CHURCH INVISIBLE.)

Churched. Baptized.

To church a woman is to read the appointed service when a woman comes to church to return thanks to God for her "safe deliverance" and restored health.

Churchwarden (*A*). A long clay pipe, such as churchwardens used to smoke some half a century ago when they met together in the parish tavern, after they had made up their accounts in the vestry, or been elected to office at the Easter meeting.

"Thirty years have enabled these 'briar-root pipes] to destroy short clays, ruin meerschaums, and even do much mischief to the venerable 'churchwarden.'"—*Notes and Queries,* April 25th, 1885, p. 323.

Churchyard Cough (*A*). A consumptive cough indicating the near approach of death.

Chuz'zlewit (*Martin*). The hero of Dickens's novel so called. Jonas Chuzzlewit is a type of mean tyranny and sordid greed.

Chyndo'nax. A chief Druid, whose tomb, with a Greek inscription, was discovered near Dijon in 1598.

Ci-devant (French). Former, of times gone by. As *Ci-devant governor*— *i.e.* once a governor, but no longer so. *Ci-devant philosophers* means philosophers of former days.

" The appellation of mistress put her in mind of her ci-devant abigailship."—*Jane Porter : Thaddeus of Warsaw,* chap. xxi.

Cic'ero. So called from the Latin, *cicer* (a wart or vetch). Plutarch says "a flat excrescence on the tip of his nose gave him this name." His real name was (Tullius) Tully.

La Bouche de Ciceron. Philippe Pot, prime minister of Louis XI. (1428-1494.)

The Cicero of France. Jean Baptiste Massillon (1663-1742.)

The Cicero of Germany. Johann III., elector of Brandenburg. (1455-1499.)

The Cicero of the British Senate. George Canning (1770-1827.)

The British Cicero. William Pitt, Earl of Chatham (1708-1778.)

The Christian Cicero. Lucius Cœlius Lactantius, a Christian father, who died 330.

The German Cicero. Johann Sturm, printer and scholar. (1507-1589.)

Cicero'ne (4 syl.). A guide to point out objects of interest to strangers. So called in the same way as Paul was called by the men of Lystra "Mercu'rius, because he was the chief speaker" (Acts xiv. 12). Cicero was the speaker of speakers at Rome; and certainly, in a party of sight-seers, the guide is "the chief speaker." It is no compliment to the great orator to call the glib patterer of a show-place a Cicero; but we must not throw stones at our Italian neighbours, as we have conferred similar honour on our great epic poet in changing "Grub Street" into "Milton Street."

⁎ Pronounce *chich-e-ro'ny.*

" Every glib and loquacious hireling who shows strangers about their pleasure-galleries, palaces, and ruins is called [in Italy] a *cicerone* or a Cicero."—*Trench : On the Study of Words,* lecture iii. p. 88.

⁎ In England, generally called "a guide."

Cicisbe'o [*che-chĭz-bee'-o*]. A dangler about women; the professed gallant of a married woman. Also the knot of silk or ribbon which is attached to fans, walking-sticks, umbrellas, etc. *Cicisbeism*, the practice of dangling about women.

Cicle'nius or *Cylle'nius.* Mercury. So called from mount Cylle'në, in Peloponne'sus, where he was born.

Cicuta. In Latin *cicūta* means the length of a reed up to the knot, such as the internodes made into a Pan-pipe. Hence Virgil (*Ecl.* ii. 36) describes a Pan-pipe as "*septem compacta cicūtis fistula.*" It is called Cow-bane, because cows not unfrequently eat it, but are killed by it. It is one of the most poisonous of plants, and some think it made the fatal draught given to Socratês.

"Sicut cicuta homini venenum est, sic cicutæ vinum."—*Pliny*, xiv. 7.
"Quæ poterunt unquam satis expurgāre cicutæ."
Horace: 2 Epist. ii. 53.

Cid. Arabic for *lord.* Don Roderi'go Laynez, Ruy Diaz (son of Diaz), Count of Bivar'. He was called "*mio cid el campëador*," my lord the champion (1025-1099). Corruption of Saïd.
The Cid's horse. Babie'ca. (3 or 4 syl.). (*See* HORSE.)
The Cid's sword. Cola'da. The sword taken by the Cid Roderi'go from King Bucar was called Tizo'na. (*See* SWORD.)
The Portuguese Cid. Nunez Alva'rez Perei'ra, general diplomatist. (1360-1431.)

Cid Hamet Benengeli. The supposititious author of *Don Quixote's Adventures.*

Cigogne (French). A stork. *Conte de la cigogne.* An old wife's tale; silly tittle-tattle. "*On conte des choses merveilleuses de la cigogne*" (wonderful stories are told of the stork). This, no doubt, refers to the numerous Swedish legends of the stork, one of which is that its very name is derived from a stork flying round the cross of Christ, crying, *Styrka! Styrka!* (strengthen, strengthen, or bear up), and as the stork has no voice at all, the legend certainly is a "*Conte de la cigogne*," or old wife's fable.

"J'apprehende qu'on ne croye que tout ce que j'ai rapporté jusqu'a present ne passe pour des contes de la cigogne, ou de ma mère l'oie."—*Le Roman Bourgeois*, 1713.

Cil'laros. (*See* HORSE.)

Cimmer'ian Bos'phorus. The strait of Kaffa.

Cimmer'ian Darkness. Homer (possibly from some story as to the Arctic night) supposes the Cimmerians to dwell in a land "beyond the ocean-stream," where the sun never shone. (*Odys.*, xi. 14.)

"In dark Cimmerian desert ever dwell."
Milton: L'Allegro.

Cincho'na or *Quinine.* So named from the wife of the Contë del Chinchon, viceroy of Peru, whence the bark was first sent to Europe in 1640. Linnæus erroneously named it Cinchona for Chinchona. (*See* PERUVIAN BARK.)

Cincinna'tus, the Roman, was ploughing his field, when he was saluted as Dictator. After he had conquered the Volsci and delivered his country from danger, he laid down his office and returned to his plough.

"And Cincinnatus, awful from the plough."
Thomson: Winter, 512.
The Cincinnatus of the Americans. George Washington (1732-1799).

Cinderel'la [*little cinder girl*]. Heroine of a fairy tale. She is the drudge of the house, dirty with housework, while her elder sisters go to fine balls. At length a fairy enables her to go to the prince's ball; the prince falls in love with her, and she is discovered by means of a glass slipper which she drops, and which will fit no foot but her own.
The *glass* slipper is a mistranslation of *pantoufle en vair* (a fur slipper), not *en verre.* (*R. C. Perrault : Contes de Fées.*)

Cinque Cento. An epithet applied to art between 1500-1600; called in France *Renaissance*, and in England *Elizabethan.* It was the revival of the classical or antique, but is generally understood as a derogatory term, implying debased or inferior art. The great schools of art closed with 1500. The "immortal five" great painters were all born in the previous century: viz. Leonardo da Vinci, born 1452; Michel Angëlo, 1474; Titian, 1477; Raphael, 1480; and Correggio, 1494. *Cinque Cento* is the Italian for 500, omitting the *thousand = mil cinque cento.*

Cinque Ports (*The*). Originally the five seaports: Hastings, Sandwich, Dover, Romney, and Hythe. Subsequently Winchelsea and Rye were added.

Cinter (*A*). The framing erected between piers to hold up the stones of an arch during the making thereof.

"Certain crude beliefs may be needful in the infancy of a nation, but when the arch is made, when the intelligence is fully developed, the cinter is thrown down and truth stands unsupported."—*E. D. Fawcett.*

Cipher. Dr. Whewell's riddle is—

" A headless man had a letter (o) to write,
He who read it (*naught*) had lost his sight;
The dumb repeated it (*naught*) word for word,
And deaf was the man who listened and heard
(*naught*).

Cir'ce (2 syl.). A sorceress. She lived in the island of Ææa. When Ulysses landed there, Circë turned his companions into swine, but Ulysses resisted this metamorphose by virtue of a herb called *moly*, given him by Mercury.

" Who knows not Circe,
The daughter of the Sun, whose charmëd cup
Whoever tasted lost his upright shape,
And downward fell into a grovelling swine ? "
Milton: Comus, 50—53.

Circle of Ul'loa. A white rainbow or luminous ring sometimes seen in Alpine regions opposite the sun in foggy weather.

Circuit. The journey made through the counties of Great Britain by the judges twice a year. There are six circuits in England, two in Wales, and three in Scotland. Those in England are called the Home, Norfolk, Midland, Oxford, Western, and Northern ; those of Wales, the North and South circuits ; and those of Scotland, the Southern, Western, and Northern.

Circumbendibus (*A*). *He took a circumbendibus, i.e.* he went round about and round about before coming to the point.

" Partaking of what scholars call the periphrastic and ambagitory, and the vulgar the circumbendibus."—*Sir W. Scott: Waverley*, chap. xxiv.

Circumcell'ians. A sect of the African Don'atists in the fourth century ; so called because they rambled from town to town to redress grievances, forgive debts, manumit slaves, and set themselves up as the oracles of right and wrong. (Latin, *circum-cello*, to beat about.)

Circumcised Brethren (in *Hudibras*). They were Prynne, Bertie or Burton, and Bastwick, who lost their ears and had their noses slit for lampooning Henrietta Maria and the bishops.

Circumlocu'tion Office. A term applied in ridicule to our public offices, because each person tries to shuffle off every act to some one else ; and before anything is done it has to pass through so many departments, that every fly is crushed on a wheel. The term was invented by Charles Dickens, and appears in *Little Dorrit*.

Ciric-Sceat or **Church Scot.** An ecclesiastical due, paid chiefly in corn, in the reign of Canute, etc., on St. Martin's Day.

Cist (Greek *kistê*, Latin *cista*). A chest or box. Generally used as a coffer for the remains of the dead. The Greek and Roman cist was a deep cylindrical basket made of wickerwork, like a lady's work-basket. The basket into which voters cast their tablets was called a "cist; " but the mystic cist used in the rites of Cerës was latterly made of bronze.

Cist Urn (*A*). An urn for the ashes of those buried in cists.

Cister'cians. A religious order, so called from the monastery of Cister'cium, near Dijon, in France. The abbey of Cistercium or Citeaux was founded by Robert, abbot of Molême, in Burgundy, at the close of the eleventh century.

Citadel (*A*), in fortification, a small strong fort, constructed either within the place fortified, or on the most' inaccessible spot of its general outline ; to give refuge for the garrison, that it may prolong the defence after the place has fallen, or to hold out for the best terms of capitulation. Citadels generally command the interior of the place, and are useful, therefore, for overawing a population which might otherwise strive to shorten a siege. (French, *citadelle ;* Italian, *citadella*, a little city.)

Cities.
Cities of Refuge. Moses, at the command of God, set apart three cities on the east of Jordan, and Joshua added three others on the west, whither any person might flee for refuge who had killed a human creature inadvertently. The three on the east of Jordan were Bezer, Ramoth, and Golan ; the three on the west were Hebron, Shechem, and Kedesh. (Deut. iv. 43 ; Josh. xx. 1-8.)
The Cities of the Plain. Sodom and Gomorrah.

" Abram dwelled in the land of Canaan, and Lot dwelled in the cities of the plain, and pitched his tent toward Sodom."—Gen. xiii. 12.

The Seven Cities. Egypt, Jerusalem, Babylon, Athens, Rome, Constantinople, and either London for commerce, or Paris for beauty. (*See* PENTAPOLIS.)

Citizen King (*The*). Louis Philippe of France. So called because he was elected king by the citizens of Paris. (Born 1773, reigned 1830-1848, died 1850.)

City (*A*), strictly speaking is a *large* town with a corporation and cathedral;

but any large town is so called in ordinary speech. In the Bible it means a town having walls and gates.

"The eldest son of the first man [Cain] builded a city (Gen. iv. 17)—not, of course, a Nineveh or a Babylon, but still a city."—*Rawlinson: Origin of Nations*, part i. chap. i. p. 10.

City College (*The*). Newgate. The wit is now a thing of the past.

City of Bells (*The*). Strasburg.

"He was a Strasburgher, and in that city of bells had been a medical practitioner."—*Mayne Reid: The Scalp Hunters*, chap. xxv.

City of David (*The*). Jerusalem. So called in compliment to King David. (2 Sam. v. 7, 9.)

City of Destruction (*The*). This world, or rather, the world of the unconverted. Bunyan makes Christian flee from the "City of Destruction" and journey to the "Celestial City," by which he allegorises the "walk of a Christian" from conversion to death.

City of God (*The*). The church or whole body of believers; the kingdom of Jesus Christ, in contradistinction to the city of the World, called by John Bunyan the City of Destruction. The phrase is that of St. Augustine; one of his chief works bearing that title, or rather *De Civitate Dei*.

City of Lanterns (*The*). A supposititious city in Lucian's *Veræ Historiæ*, situate somewhere beyond the zodiac. (*See* LANTERN-LAND.)

City of Palaces (*The*). Agrippa, in the reign of Augustus, converted Rome from "a city of brick huts to one of marble palaces." (*Cf. Suetonius*.) Calcutta is called the "City of Palaces." Modern Paris well deserves the compliment of being so called.

City of Refuge (*The*). Medina, in Arabia, where Mahomet took refuge when driven by conspirators from Mecca. He entered the city, not as a fugitive, but in triumph, A.D. 622. (*See under* CITIES OF REFUGE, page 255.)

City of St. Michael (*The*). Dumfries, of which city St. Michael is the patron saint.

City of Saints. Montreal, in Canada, is so named because all the streets are named after saints.

"Mr. Geo. Martin . . . said he came from [Montreal] a city of saints, where all the streets were named after saints."—*Secular Thought*, September 10th, 1891.

City of the Great King (*The*)—*i.e.* Jerusalem. (Psa. xlviii. 2 ; Matt. v. 35.)

City of the Seven Hills (*The*). Rome, built on seven hills (*Urbs septacollis*). The hills are the Aventine, Cælian, Capitöline, Esquiline, Palätine, Quirïnal, and Viminal.

The AVENTINE HILL was given to the people. It was deemed unlucky, because here Remus was slain. It was also called "Collis Dianæ," from the Temple of Diana which stood there.

The CÆLIAN HILL was given to Cælius Vibenna, the Tuscan, who came to the help of the Romans in the Sabine war.

The CAPITOLINE HILL or "Mons Tarpeius," also called "Mons Saturni," on which stood the great castle or capitol of Rome. It contained the Temple of Jupiter Capitolïnus.

The ESQUILINE HILL was given by Augustus to Mæcenas, who built thereon a magnificent mansion.

The PALATINE HILL was the largest of the seven. Here Romulus held his court, whence the word "palace" (*palatium*).

The QUIRINAL HILL was where the Quirës or Curës settled. It was also called "Cabalïnus," from two marble statues of a horse, one of which was the work of Phidias, the other of Praxitëlës.

The VIMINAL HILL was so called from the number of osiers (*vimines*) which grew there. It contained the Temple of Jupiter Viminälis.

City of the Sun (*The*). A romance by Campanella, similar to the *Republic* of Plato, *Utopia* of Sir Thomas More, and *Atlantis* of Lord Bacon (1568-1639).

City of the Violet Crown. Athens is so called by Aristophanës (ἰοστέφᾰνος —*see Equites*, 1323 and 1329; and *Acharnians*, 637). Macaulay refers to Athens as the "violet-crowned city." Ion (a violet) was a representative king of Athens, whose four sons gave names to the four Athenian classes; and Greece, in Asia Minor, was called Ionïa. Athens was the city of "Ion crowned its king" or "of the Violet crowned." Similarly Paris is the "city of lilies"—*i.e.* fleurs-de-luce or Louis-flowers.

※ I do not think that Athens was called ἰοστέφᾰνος from "the purple hue which Hymettus assumed in the evening sky."

Civic Crown. (*See under* CROWN.)

Civil List. Now applied to expenses voted annually by Parliament to pay the personal expenses of the Sovereign, the household expenses, and the pensions awarded by Royal bounty; but before the reign of William III. it embraced all the heads of public expenditure, except those of the army and navy.

Civil Magistrate (*A*). A civic or municipal magistrate, as distinguished from ecclesiastical authority.

Civil Service Estimates (*The*), C.S.E. The annual Parliamentary grant to cover the expenses of the diplomatic services, the post-office and telegraphs, the grant for national education, the collection of the revenue, and other expenses neither pertaining to the Sovereign, the army, nor the navy.

Civil War. War between citizens (*civilés*). In English history the term is applied to the war between Charles I. and his Parliament; but the War of the Red and White Roses was a civil war. In America the War of Secession (1861-1865) was a civil war.

Civis Romanus Sum. This single plea sufficed to arrest arbitrary condemnation, bonds, and scourging. Hence, when the centurion commanded Paul "to be examined by scourging," he virtually pleaded " Civis Romānus sum "; and asked, " Is it lawful for you to *scourge* a Roman citizen, and *uncondemned ?* " (1) No Roman citizen could be condemned unheard; (2) by the Valerian Law he could not be bound; (3) by the Sempronian Law it was forbidden to *scourge* him, or to beat him with rods. (*See also* Acts xvi. 37, etc.)

Civitas Solis. A political and philosophical romance by Thomas Campanella (1568-1639), born at Stillo, or Stilo, in Italy. This romance is a kind of Utopia, formed on the model of Plato's *Republic.* His society is a sort of convent-life established on the principles of a theocratic communism.

Clabber Napper's Hole. Near Gravesend; said to be named after a free-booter; but more likely the Celtic *Caer-ber l'arber* (water-town lower camp).

Clack Dish. A dish or basin with a movable lid. Some two or three centuries ago beggars used to proclaim their want by clacking the lid of a wooden dish.

"Can you think I get my living by a bell and clack-dish ?
" .... How's that ?
" Why, begging, sir." *Family of Love* (1608).

Claft. An Egyptian head-dress with long lappets pendent on the shoulders, as in the statue of Amenophis III.

Clak-ho-har'yah. At Fort Vancouver the medium of intercourse is a mixture of Canadian-French, English, Indian, and Chinese. An Englishman goes by the name of *Kint-shosh,* a corruption of King George; an American is called *Boston ;* and the ordinary salutation is *clak-ho-haryah.* This is explained by the fact that the Indians, frequently hearing a trader named Clark addressed by his companions, "Clark, how are you? " imagined this

to be the correct English form of salutation. (*Taylor : Words and Places.*)

Clam. (*See* CLOSE AS A CLAM.)

Clan-na-Gael (*The*). An Irish Fenian organisation founded in Philadelphia in 1870, and known in secret as the "United Brotherhood "; its avowed object being to secure "the complete and absolute independence of Ireland from Great Britain, and the complete severance of all political connection between the two countries, to be effected by unceasing preparation for armed insurrection in Ireland." (*See* DYNAMITE SATURDAY.)

∴ In 1883 Alexander Sullivan was elected one of the three heads of this club, to which is due the dynamite outrages in London (January, 1885), and the design to murder the Queen's ministers.

Clap-trap. Something introduced to win applause; something really worthless, but sure to take with the groundlings. A *trap* to catch applause.

Clapper. A plank bridge over a stream ; a ferry-gate. A roofing-board is called a clap-board.

" A little low and lonesome shed,
With a roof of clap-boards overhead."
Alice Cary : Settlers' Christmas Eve.

Probably a corruption of clath-board, a covering board, from Anglo-Saxon, *clath,* a covering, whence our clothes.

✢ Boards for making casks are also called " clap-boards."

Clapperclaw. To jangle and claw each other about. (Dutch and German, *klappen,* to strike, clatter.)

"Now they are clapper-clawing one another ;
I'll go look on."—*Shakespeare : Troilus and Cressida,* v. 4.

✢ A clapper-claw is a back-scratcher.

Clapper - dudgeons. Abram-men (*q.v.*). The *clapper* is the tongue of a bell, and in cant language the human "tongue." Dudgeon is a slang word for a beggar.

Clapping the Prayer Books, or stamping the feet, in the Roman Catholic Church, on Good Friday, is designed to signify the abandonment of our Saviour by His disciples. This is done when twelve of the thirteen burning candles are put out. The noise comes from within the choir.

Claque ; Claqueurs. Applause by clapping the hands ; persons paid for doing so. M. Sauton, in 1820, established in Paris an office to ensure the success of dramatic pièces. He was the first to organise the Parisian *claque.* The manager sends an order to his office for any number of claqueurs, sometimes for

9

500, or even more. The class is divided into *commissaires*, those who commit the pieces to memory and are noisy in pointing out its merits; *rieurs*, who laugh at the puns and jokes; *pleureurs*, chiefly women, who are to hold their pocket-handkerchiefs to their eyes at the moving parts; *chatouilleurs*, who are to keep the audience in good humour; and *bisseurs*, who are to cry (*bis*) encore. The Romans had their Laudicœni (*q.v.*).

Claras (Stock Exchange term). The Chatham, London, and Dover Railway Ordinary Stock (C.L.R.S.).

Clare (*St.*). A religious order of women, the second that St. Francis instituted. It was founded in 1213, and took its name from its first abbess.

Clarenceux King-of-Arms. One of the two provincial heralds, with jurisdiction over the southern provinces. The name was taken in honour of the Duke of Clarence, third son of Edward III. The herald of the northern provinces is called Norroy King-of-Arms.

✗ Garter-King-of-Arms, also "Principal King-of-Arms," has to attend on Knights of the Garter, and arrange whatever is required in connection with these knights. There is a Bath King-of-Arms, not a member of the college, to attend on Knights of the Bath.

Clarendon. *The Constitutions of Clarendon.* Laws made by a general council of nobles and prelates, held at Clarendon, in Wiltshire, in 1164, to check the power of the Church, and restrain the prerogative of ecclesiastics. These famous ordinances, sixteen in number, define the limits of the patronage and jurisdiction of the Pope in these realms.

Clarendon Type. The black letters which head these articles are so called.

Claret. The wine so called does not receive its name from its colour, but the colour so called receives its name from the wine. The word means clarified wine (*vinum clare'tum*). What we call hippocras was called *clare'tum*, made of wine and honey clarified.

Claret. Blood. *To broach one's claret.* To give one a bloody nose; so called from the claret colour.

Claret Cup. A drink made of claret, brandy, lemon, borage, sugar, ice, and carbonated water.

Claret Jug (*One's*). One's nose. (*See above*, CLARET.)
To tap one's claret jug. To give one a

bloody nose. "Tap" is meant for a pun—to broach and to knock.

Classic Races (*The*). The five chief horse-races in England, viz. the 2,000 and 1,000 guinea races for two-year-olds, run at Newmarket, the Derby for fillies and colts, the Oaks for fillies only, and the St. Leger.

Classics. The best authors. The Romans were divided by Ser'vius into six classes. Any citizen who belonged to the highest class was called *class'icus*, all the rest were said to be *infra classem*. From this the best authors were termed *class'ici aucto'res* (classic authors), *i.e.* authors of the best or first class. The high esteem in which Greek and Latin were held at the revival of letters obtained for these authors the name of classic, emphatically; and when other first-rate works are intended some distinctive name is added, as the English, French, Spanish, etc., classics.

Claude Lorraine (*i.e.* of Lorraine). This incorrect form is generally used in English for the name of Claude le Lorrain, or Claude Gelée, the French landscape painter, born at the Château-de-Chamage, in Lorraine. (1600-1682.)
The Scotch Claude. Thomas of Duddingston (near Edinburgh).

Claus (*Santa*). (*See* SANTA CLAUS.)

Clause. *Letter-clause*, a close letter, sealed with the royal signet or privy-seal; in opposition to *letters-patent*, which are left open, the seal being attached simply as a legal form. ("Clause," Latin *clausus*, shut, closed. "Patent," Latin *patens*, open.)

Clause Rolls (*Rotuli clausi*). Close Rolls. (*See* CLOSE ROLLS.)
"Clause Rolls contain all such matters of record as were committed to close writs. These Rolls are preserved in the Tower."—*Jacob: Law Dictionary.*

Clavie. *Burning of the Clavie* on New-year's eve (old style) in the village of Burghead, on the southern shore of the Moray Frith. The clavie is a sort of bonfire made of casks split up. One of the casks is split into two parts of different sizes, and an important item of the ceremony is to join these parts together with a huge nail made for the purpose. Whence the name *clavus* (Latin), a nail. Chambers, who in his *Book of Days* (vol. ii. p. 789) minutely describes the ceremony, suggests that it is a relic of Druid worship, but it seems to me to be connected with the Roman ceremony observed on the 13th September, and called the *clavus annalis*. The two divisions of the cask, I think, symbolise the old and the new year, which are joined together by a nail. The two parts are unequal, because the part of the new year joined on to the old is very small in comparison.

Clavile'no. The wooden horse on which Don Quixote got astride, in order to disenchant the Infanta Antonoma'sia and her husband, who were shut up in the tomb of Queen Magun'cia, of Canday'a. It was the very horse on which Peter of Provence carried off the fair Magalo'na; it was constructed by Merlin, and was governed by a wooden pin in the forehead. (The word means *Wooden Peg.*) (*Don Quixote*, part ii. book 3, chaps. 4, 5.) (*See* CAMBUSCAN.)

Claw means the foot of an animal armed with claws; a hand. *To claw* is to lay one's hands upon things. It also means to tickle with the hand; hence to please or flatter, puff or praise. (Anglo-Saxon, *clawu*, a claw, with the verb *clawian*, to claw.)

Claw me and I will claw thee, means, "praise me, and I will praise you," or, scratch my back, and I will do the same for you.

- "Laugh when I am merry, and claw no man in his humour."—*Shakespeare: Much Ado, etc.*, i. 3.

Claw-backs. Flatterers. Bishop Jewel speaks of "the Pope's claw-backs." (*See above*, and CLAPPERCLAWS.)

Clay'more or *Glay'more* (2 syl.) is the Celtic *glaif* (a bent sword), Gaelic *claidheamh* (a sword), and *mór* (great). (*See* MORGLAY.)

    "I've told thee how the Southrons fell
    Beneath the broad claymore."
      Aytoun: Execution of Montrose, stanza 2.

Clean. Free from blame or fault.

"Ye are clean, but not all."—*John* xiii. 10.

BILL. *To show a clean bill of health.* (*See* page 135, col. 1, BILL OF HEALTH.)

BREAST. *To make a clean breast* or *Make a clean breast of it.* To make a full and unreserved confession.

HANDS. *To have clean hands.* To be quite clear of some stated evil. Hence "clean-handed."

To keep the hands clean. Not to be involved in wrong-doing.

HEART. *To have a clean heart.* A righteous spirit.

"Create in me a clean heart, and renew a right spirit within me."—*Psalm* li. 10.

HEELS. *To show a clean pair of heels.* To make one's escape, to run away. Here "clean" means free from obstruction.

"The Maroons were runaway slaves who had . . . . shown their tyrants a clean pair of heels" —*Sala.*

LIFE. *To live a clean life.* Blameless and undefiled.

TONGUE. *A clean tongue.* Not abusive, not profane, not foul.

Clean (*To*).
Clean away! Scrub on, go on cleaning, etc.
To clean down. To sweep down, to swill down.
To clean out. To purify, to make tidy. Also, to win another's money till his pocket is quite empty.
To clean up. To wash up, to put in order.
∵ Clean, used adverbially, means entirely, wholly; as, "you have grown clean out of knowledge," *i.e.* wholly beyond recognition.

Clean and Unclean Animals. Pythagoras taught the doctrine of the transmigration of the soul, but that it never entered into those animals which it is lawful to eat. Hence those animals which were lawful food for man were those into which the human soul never entered; but those into which the human soul entered were unclean or not fit for human food. This notion existed long before the time of Pythagoras, who learnt it in Egypt.

∵ In the Old Testament, those animals which chew the cud and part the hoof were clean, and might be eaten. Hares and rabbits could not be eaten because (although they chew the cud) they do not part the hoof. Pigs and camels were unclean, because (although they part the hoof) they do not chew the cud. Birds of prey were accounted unclean. Fish with fins and scales were accounted fit food for man. (Lev. xi.)

Cleaned Out. Impoverished of everything. De Quincey says that Richard Bentley, after his lawsuit with Dr. Colbatch, "must have been pretty well cleaned out."

Clear (verb).
Clear away. Remove.
Clear off! Away with you! Take away.
Clear out. Empty out, make tidy. (*See below*, CLEAR OUT FOR GUAM.)
Clear up. Become fine after rain or cloudiness; to make manifest; to elucidate what was obscure.
To clear an examination paper. To floor it, or answer every question set.
To clear the air. To remove the clouds, mists, and impurities.
To clear the dishes. To empty them of their contents.

To clear the room. To remove from it every thing or person not required.

To clear the table. To remove what has been placed on it.

Clear the Court. Remove all strangers, or persons not officially concerned in the suit.

Clear the Decks. Prepare for action by removing everything not required.

❧ Clear used adverbially means wholly, entirely ; as, "He is gone clear away," "Clear out of sight."

Clear (the adjective).
A clear head.—A mind that can understand clearly anything which it grasps.
A clear statement. A straightforward and intelligible statement.
A clear style [of writing]. A lucid method of expressing one's thoughts.

Clear as Crystal. Clear as Mud. (*See* SIMILES.)

Clear-coat. A mixture of size, alum, and whitening, for sizing walls. To cover over whatever might show through the coat of colour or paper to be put on it, also to make them stick or adhere more firmly.

Clear Day (*A*). A bright day, an entire day, as, "The bonds must be left three clear days for examination," to examine them before the interest is paid.

Clear Grit (*The*). The real thing, as "champagne is . . . if it be but the clear grit" (Anglo-Saxon, *gryt*, bolted flour).

❧ A man of grit, or clear grit, is one of decision, from whom all doubt or vacillation has been bolted out, as husks from fine flour.

Clear out for Guam (*To*). The ship is bound for no specific place. In the height of the gold fever, ships were chartered to carry passengers to Australia without having return cargoes secured for them. They were, therefore, obliged to leave Melbourne in ballast, and to sail in search of homeward freights. The Custom House regulations required, however, that, on clearing outwards, some port should be named ; and it became the habit of captains to name "Guam" (a small island of the Ladrone group) as the hypothetical destination. Hence, "to clear out for Guam" came to mean, clear out for just anywhere—we are bound for whatever coast we may choose to venture upon. (See *Notes and Queries*, April 18th, 1885, p. 314.)

Clear Voice (*A*). A voice of pure intonation, neither husky, mouthy, nor throaty.

Cleared out. *I am quite cleared out.* I have spent all my money ; I have not a farthing left. In French, *Je suis Anglé.* (*See* FRENCH LEAVE.) Cleared out means, my purse or pocket is cleared out of money.

Clearing House. A building in Lombard Street, set apart, since 1775, for interchanging bankers' cheques and bills. Each bank sends to it daily all the bills and cheques not drawn on its own firm ; these are sorted and distributed to their respective houses, and the balance is settled by transfer tickets. The origin of this establishment was a post at the corner of Birchin Lane and Lombard Street, where banking clerks met and exchanged memoranda.

Railway lines have also their "Clearing Houses" for settling the "tickets" of the different lines.

A "clearing banker" is a banker who has the *entrée* of the clearing house.

"London has become the clearing-house of the whole world, the place where international debts are exchanged against each other. And something like 5,000 million pounds'-worth of checks and bills pass that clearing yearly."—*A. C. Perry: Elements of Political Economy,* p. 363.

Cleave. Either to *stick to* or to *part from.* A man "shall cleave to his wife" (Matt. xix. 5). As one that "cleaveth wood" (Psalm cxli. 7). The former is the Anglo-Saxon *clif-an,* to stick to, and the latter is *cleof-an,* to split.

Cle'lia. A vain, frivolous female butterfly, with a smattering of everything. In youth she coquetted ; and, when youth was passed, tried sundry ways of earning a living, but always without success. It is a character in Crabbe's *Borough.*

Cle'lie. A character in Madam Scudéri's romance so called. This novel is a type of the buckram formality of Louis XIV. It is full of high-flown compliments, theatrical poses, and cut-and-dry sentiments.

Clement (*St.*). Patron saint of tanners, being himself a tanner. His symbol is a pot, because November the 23rd, St. Clement's Day, is the day on which the early Danes used to go about begging for ale.

Clementina (*The Lady*). In love with Sir Charles Grandison, who marries Harriet Biron. (*Richardson : Sir Charles Grandison.*)

Clench and **Clinch.** To clench is to grasp firmly, as, "He clenched my arm firmly," "He clenched his nerves bravely to endure the pain." (Anglo-Saxon, *be-clencan*, to hold fast.)

To *clinch* is to make fast, to turn the point of a nail in order to make it fast. Hence, to clinch an argument. (Dutch, *klinken*, to rivet. Whence "clinker-built," said of a ship whose planks overlap each other, and are riveted together.)

I gave him a clencher (should be "*clincher*"). I nailed him fast.

Cleom'brotos (4 syl.). A philosopher who so admired Plato's *Phædon* that he jumped into the sea in order to exchange this life for a better. He was called *Ambracio'ta* (*of Ambra'cia*), from the place of his birth in Epirus.

> "He who to enjoy
> Plato's elysium, leaped into the sea,
> Cleombrotus."
> *Milton: Paradise Lost*, iii. 471-3.

Cleon. The personification of glory in Spenser's *Faërie Queene*.

Cleopatra was introduced to Julius Cæsar by Apollodōrus in a bale of rich Syrian rugs. When the bale was unbound, there was discovered the fairest and wittiest girl of all the earth, and Cæsar became her captive slave.

Cleopa'tra and her Pearl. It is said that Cleopatra made a banquet for Antony, the costliness of which excited his astonishment; and, when Antony expressed his surprise, Cleopatra took a pearl ear-drop, which she dissolved in a strong acid, and drank to the health of the Roman triumvir, saying, "My draught to Antony shall far exceed it." There are two difficulties in this anecdote—the first is, that vinegar would not dissolve a pearl; and the next is, that any stronger acid would be wholly unfit to drink. Probably the solution is this: the pearl was sold to some merchant, whose name was synonymous with a strong acid, and the money given to Antony as a present by the fond queen. The pearl melted, and Cleopatra drank to the health of Antony as she handed him the money. (*See* "Gresham" in *Reader's Handbook*.)

Clergy. The men of God's lot or inheritance. In St. Peter's first epistle (ch. v. 3) the Church is called "God's heritage" or lot. In the Old Testament the tribe of Levi is called the "lot or heritage of the Lord." (Greek, κλῆρος; Latin, *clerus* and *clericus*, whence Norman *clerex* and *clerkus*; French, *clergé*.)

Benefit of clergy. (*See* BENEFIT.)

Cler'gymen. The dislike of sailors to clergymen on board ship arises from an association with the history of Jonah. Sailors call them a *kittle cargo*, or kittlish cargo, meaning dangerous. Probably the disastrous voyage of St. Paul confirmed the prejudice.

Cler'ical Titles.

(1) CLERK. As in ancient times the clergyman was about the only person who could write and read, the word *clerical*, as used in "clerical error," came to signify an orthographical error. As the respondent in church was able to read, he received the name of *clerk*, and the assistants in writing, etc., are so termed in business. (Latin, *cler'icus*, a clergyman.)

(2) CURATE. One who has the cure of souls. As the cure of the parish used to be virtually entrusted to the clerical stipendiary, the word *curate* was appropriated to this assistant.

(3) RECTOR. One who has the parsonage and great tithes. The man who rules or guides the parish. (Latin, "a ruler.")

(4) VICAR. One who does the "duty" of a parish for the person who receives the tithes. (Latin, *vicarius*, a deputy.)

(5) INCUMBENT and PERPETUAL CURATE are now termed Vicars. (*See* PARSONS.)

∴ The French *curé* equals our vicar, and their *vicaire* our curate.

Cler'ical Vestments.

(1) *White.* Emblem of purity, worn on all feasts, saints' days, and sacramental occasions.

(2) *Red.* The colour of blood and of fire, worn on the days of martyrs, and on Whit-Sunday, when the Holy Ghost came down like tongues of fire.

(3) *Green.* Worn only on days which are neither feasts nor fasts.

(4) *Purple.* The colour of mourning, worn on Advent Sundays, in Lent, and on Ember days.

(5) *Black.* Worn on Good Friday, and when masses are said for the dead.

Cler'imond. Niece of the Green Knight (*q.v.*), bride of Valentine the brave, and sister of Fer'ragus the giant. (*Valentine and Orson.*)

Clerk. A scholar. Hence, *beau-clerc*. (*See above*, CLERICAL TITLES.)

> "All the clerks,
> I mean the learned ones, in Christian kingdoms,
> Have their free voices."
> *Shakespeare: Henry VIII.*, ii. 2.

St. Nicholas's Clerks. Thieves. An equivoque on the word Nick.

"I think there came prancing down the hill a couple of St. Nicholas's clerks."—*Rowley: Match at Midnight*, 1633.

Clerk-ale and **Church-ale.** Mr. Douce says the word "ale" is used in such composite words as bride-ale, clerk-ale, church-ale, lamb-ale, Midsummer-ale, Scot-ale, Whitsun-ale, etc., for revel or feast, ale being the chief liquor given.

"The multitude call Church-ale Sunday their revelyng day, which day is spent in bulbeatings, bearbeating, ... dicying, ... and drunkenness."—*W. Kethe* (1570).

Clerkenwell (London) means the Clerks'-well, where the parish clerks of London used to assemble yearly to play some sacred piece.

Clerkly. Cleverly; like a scholar.

"I thank you, gentle servant: 'tis very clerkly done."
Shakespeare: Two Gentlemen of Verona, iii. 1.

Client. In Roman history meant a plebeian under the patronage of a patron. The client performed certain services, and the patron protected the life and interests of the client. The word is now a legal one, meaning a person who employs the services of a legal adviser to protect his interests.

Clifford (*Paul*). A highwayman, reformed by the power of love, in Sir L. Bulwer Lytton's novel so called.

Climacteric. It was once believed that 7 and 9, with their multiples, were critical points in life; and 63, which is produced by multiplying 7 and 9 together, was termed the *Grand Climacteric*, which few persons succeeded in outliving.

"There are two years, the seventh and the ninth, that commonly bring great changes in a man's life, and great dangers; wherefore 63, that contains both these numbers multiplied together, comes not without heaps of dangers."—*Levinus Lemnius*.

Climacteric Years are seventh and ninth, with their multiples by the odd numbers 3, 5, 7, 9—viz. 7, 9, 21, 27, 35, 45, 49, 63, and 81, over which astrologers supposed Saturn, the malevolent planet, presided. Hippocrates recognises these periods. (*See* NINE.)

Climax means a *stair* (Greek), applied to the last of a gradation of arguments, each of which is stronger than the preceding. The last of a gradation of words of a similar character is also called a climax. The point of highest development.

"In the very climax of his career ... he was stricken down."—*Chittenden: Recollections of Lincoln*, chap. xiv, p. 454.

Climb. *On the climb.* Under the hope of promotion. Thomas Becket, after he became Cardinal-archbishop of Canterbury, was at the top of the tree, and no further promotion was in the power of the king to bestow. Being no longer on the climb, he could set the king at defiance, and did do so.

Clinch. To bend the point of a nail after it is driven home. The word is sometimes written *clench*, from the French *clenche*, the lift of a latch. (German, *klinke*; Dutch, *klinken*, to rivet.) (*See* page 261, col. 1, CLENCH.)

That was a clincher. That argument was not to be gainsaid; that remark drove the matter home, and fixed it "as a nail in a sure place."

A lie is called a *clincher* from the tale about two swaggerers, one of whom said, "I drove a nail right through the moon." "Yes," said the other, "I remember it well, for I went the other side and clinched it." The French say, *Je lui ai bien rivé son clou* (I have clinched his nail for him).

Clinker (*Humphrey*). Hero of Smollett's novel so called. The general scheme of *Oliver Twist* resembles it. Humphrey is a workhouse boy, put out apprentice; but being afterwards reduced to great want, he attracts the notice of Mr. Bramble, who takes him into his service. He turns out to be Bramble's natural son, and falls in love with Winifred Jenkins, Miss Bramble's maid.

Clio was one of the nine Muses, the inventress of historical and heroic poetry.

Clio. Addison is so called because his papers in the *Spectator* are signed by one of the four letters in this word, probably the initial letters of Chelsea, London, Islington, Office. (*See* NOTARICA.)

❖ *See* Professor Morley's "Introduction to the *Spectator*," on the subject.

Clipper. A fast-sailing ship.

"We shall have to catch the *Aurora*, and she has a name for being a clipper."—*A. C. Doyle: The Sign of Four*, chap. x.

She's a clipper. Said of a stylish or beautiful woman. A first-class craft.

Clipping Pace (*A*). Very fast. A clipper is a fast-sailing vessel.

"Leaving Bolus Head, we scudded on at a clipping pace, and the skiff yielded so much to the breeze that Bury said we must reef the mainsail."—*W. S. Trench: Realities of Irish Life*, chap. x.

Cliquot (of *Punch* celebrity). A nickname of Frederick William **IV.** of

Prussia; so called from his fondness for champagne (1795, 1840-1861).

Cloaci′na. Goddess of sewers. (Latin, *cloa′ca,* a sewer.)

" Then Cloacina, goddess of the tide,
Whose sable streams beneath the city glide,
Indulged the modish flame ; the town she roved,
A mortal scavenger she saw, she loved."
                 Gay : Trivia, ii.

Cloak and Sword Plays. Modern comedy, played in the ordinary costume of modern life. The phrase was adopted by Canderon, who lived in Spain while gentlemen were accustomed to wear cloaks and swords. For tragedy the men actors wore either heraldic or dramatico-historic dresses. In England actors in tragedy and old comedy wore the costume of Charles II.'s period, till quite recently.

Clock. So church bells were once called. (German, *glocke ;* French, *cloche ;* Mediæval Latin, *cloca.*)

" Wel sikerer [surer] was his crowyng in his logge
Than is a clok [bell] or abbay orologge."
     Chaucer : The Nonne Prestes Tale (1639-40).

Clock. The tale about St. Paul's clock striking thirteen is given in Walcott's *Memorials of Westminster,* and refers to John Hatfield, who died 1770, aged 102. He was a soldier in the reign of William III., and was brought before a courtmartial for falling asleep on duty upon Windsor Terrace. In proof of his innocence he asserted that he heard St. Paul's clock strike thirteen, which statement was confirmed by several witnesses.

Clodhopper. A farmer, who hops or walks amongst the clods. The cavalry call the infantry clodhoppers, because they have to walk instead of riding horseback.

Clog Almanac. A primitive almanac or calendar, originally made of a " clog," or log of wood, with four faces or parallelograms ; the sharp edge of each face or side was divided by notches into three months, every week being marked by a big notch. The face left of the notched edge contained the saints' days, the festivals, the phases of the moon, and so on in Runic characters, whence the " clog " was also called a Runic staff. These curiosities are not uncommon, and specimens may be seen in the British Museum, the Bodleian (Oxford), the Ashmolean Museum, St. John's (Cambridge), the Cheetham Library (Manchester), and other places both at home and abroad.

Cloister. *He retired into a cloister,* a monastery. Almost all monasteries have a cloister or covered walk, which generally occupied three sides of a quadrangle.

Clootie. *Auld Clootie.* Old Nick. The Scotch call a cloven hoof a cloot, so that Auld Clootie is Old Cloven-foot.

Clorida′no (in *Orlando Furioso*). A humble Moorish youth, who joins Medo′ro in seeking the body of King Dardinello to bury it. Medo′ro being wounded, Cloridano rushed madly into the ranks of the enemy and was slain.

Clorin′da (in *Jerusalem Delivered*). A female knight who came from Persia to oppose the Crusaders, and was appointed by Al′adine leader of all the Pagan forces. Tancred fell in love with her ; but not knowing her in a night attack, slew her after a most dreadful combat. Before she died she received Christian baptism at the hands of Tancred, who mourned her death with great sorrow of heart. (Book xii.)

Sena′pus of Ethiopia (a Christian) was her father ; but her being born white alarmed her mother, who changed her babe for a black child. Arse′tës, the eunuch, was entrusted with the infant Clorinda, and as he was going through a forest he saw a tiger, dropped the child, and sought safety in a tree. The tiger took the babe and suckled it, after which Arsetës left Ethiopia with the child for Egypt.

Close as a Clam. A clam is a bivalve mollusca, which burrows in sand or mud. It is about the size of a florin, and may be eaten raw or fried like an oyster. Clams are gathered only when the tide is out. When the tide is in they are safe from molestation, hence the saying "Happy as a clam at high tide." (Anglo-Saxon, *clam,* mud ; verb *clæm-ian,* to glue ; German, *klamm,* close.)

Close Rolls are mandates, letters, and writs of a private nature, addressed, in the Sovereign's name, to individuals, and folded or *closed* and sealed on the outside with the Great Seal.

✱ *Patent* Rolls are left *open,* with the seal hanging from the bottom.

Close-time for Game. (*See* SPORTING SEASONS.)

Closh (*Mynherr*). A Dutch Jacktar. Closh is corrupt form of Claus, a contraction of Nicholas, a name as common with the Dutch as Jack is with the English people.

Clo'ten. A vindictive lout who wore his dagger in his mouth. He fell in love with Im'ogen, but his love was not reciprocated. (*Shakespeare: Cymbeline.*)

Cloth (*The*). The clergy; the clerical office; thus we say "having respect for the cloth." Formerly the clergy used to wear a distinguishing costume, made of grey or black cloth.

Clotha'rius or *Clothaire* (in *Jerusalem Delivered*). At the death of Hugo he takes the lead of the Franks, but is shot by Clorinda (*q.v.*) with an arrow (book xi.). After his death, his troops sneak away and leave the Christian army (book xiii.).

Clotho, in Classic mythology. One of the Three Fates. She presided over birth, and drew from her distaff the thread of life; Atropos presided over death and cut the thread of life; and Lachesis spun the fate of life between birth and death. (Greek, *klótho*, to draw thread from a distaff.)

"A France slashed asunder with Clotho-scissors and civil war."—*Carlyle.* (This is an erroneous allusion. It was Atropos who cut the thread.)

Cloud, Clouds.
He is in the clouds. In dreamland; entertaining visionary notions; having no distinct idea about the matter in question.
He is under a cloud. Under suspicion, in disrepute.
To blow a cloud is to smoke a cigar or pipe.

Cloud. A dark spot on the forehead of a horse between the eyes. A white spot is called a star, and an elongated star is a blaze. (*See* BLAZE.)

"*Agrippa.* He [Antony] has a cloud on his face.
Enobarbus. He were the worse for that were he a horse."
    Shakespeare: Antony and Cleopatra, iii. 2.

Cloud (*St.*). Patron saint of nailsmiths, by a play upon the French word *clou,* a nail.

Clouded Cane (*A*). A malacca cane clouded or mottled from age and use. These canes were very fashionable in the first quarter of the present century.

Cloven Foot. *To show the cloven foot, i.e.* to show a knavish intention; a base motive. The allusion is to Satan, represented with the legs and feet of a goat; and, however he might disguise himself, he could never conceal his cloven feet. (*See* BAG O' NAILS, GOAT.)

"Real grief little influenced its composition

. . . and the cloven foot peeps out in some letters written by him at the period."—*St. James's Magazine.*

Clover. *He's in clover.* In luck, in prosperous circumstances, in a good situation. The allusion is to cattle feeding in clover fields.

Clowns. The three most celebrated are Joseph Grimaldi (1779-1837), the French Carlin (1713-1783), and Richard Tarlton, in the days of Queen Elizabeth, who acted at the galleried inn called the *Belle Sauvage.*

"To sit with Tarlton on an alehouse signe."
    Bishop Hall: Satires.

Club. A society of persons who club together, or form themselves into a knot or lump.
The word was originally applied to persons bound together by a vow. (German, *gelübde.*) (*See* CARDS, 4 clubs.)

"[1190] was the era of chivalry, ... for bodies of men uniting themselves by a sacred vow, *gelubde,* which word and thing have passed over to us in a singularly dwindled condition, ' club' we call it ; and the vow . . . . does not rank very high."—*Carlyle: Frederick the Great,* vol. i. p. 111.

Club-bearer (*The*). Periphe'tēs, the robber of Ar'golis, is so called because he murdered his victims with an iron club.

Club-land. That part of the West End of London where the principal clubs are situated; the members of such clubs.

Club-law. The law of might or compulsion through fear of chastisement. Do it or get a hiding.

Clue. *I have not yet got the clue : to give a clue, i.e.* a hint. A clue is a ball of thread (Ang.-Saxon, *cleowen*). The only mode of finding the way out of the Cretan labyrinth was by a skein of thread, which, being laid along the proper route, indicated the right path.

Clumsy (Norwegian, *klump,* a lump; Swedish, *klummsen,* benumbed ; Icelandic, *klumsa*). Piers Plowman has " thou klompsist for cold," and Wiclif has " Our hondis ben aclumpsid." Halliwell gives us *clumpish* = awkward, and *clump* = lazy.

Clu'ricaune (3 syl.). An elf of evil disposition who usually appears as a wrinkled old man, and has knowledge of hid treasures. (*Irish mythology.*)

Clydesdale Horses. Scotch draughthorses, not equal to Shire-horses in size, but of great endurance. (*See* SHIRE-HORSES.)

Clym of the Clough, with Adam Bell and William of Cloudesly, were noted outlaws, whose skill in archery rendered them as famous in the north of England as Robin Hood and Little John in the midland counties. Their place of resort was in Englewood Forest, near Carlisle. N.B. — Englewood means firewood. Clym of the Clough means Clement of the Cliff.

Clyt'ie (3 syl.). A water-nymph, in love with Apollo. Meeting with no return, she was changed into a sunflower, which, traditionally, still turns to the sun, following him through his daily course.

Cneph. The name under which the Egyptians adore the Creator of the world.

Cnidian Venus (*The*). The exquisite statue of Venus or Aphroditê by Praxitĕlês, placed in the temple of Venus, at Cnidus.

Co. A contraction of *company*; as Smith and Co.

Coach (*A*). A private tutor. The term is a pun on *getting on fast*. To get on fast you take a coach; you cannot get on fast without a private tutor— *ergo*, a private tutor is the coach you take in order that you may get on quickly. (*University slang.*)

"The books . . . . are expensive, and often a further expense is entailed by the necessity of securing 'a coach.'"—*Stedman: Oxford*, chap. x. p. 188.

To dine in the coach. In the captain's private room. The coach or couch of a ship is a small apartment near the stern, the floor being formed of the aftmost part of the quarter-deck, and the roof by the poop.

A slow coach. A dull, unprogressive person, somewhat fossilised.

"What a dull, old-fashioned chap thou be'st . . . but thou wert always a slow-coach." — *Mrs. Gaskell: Cibbie Marsh* (Era 2).

Coach-and-four (or *Coach-and-six*). It is said one may drive a coach-and-four through an Act of Parliament, *i.e.* lawyers can always find for their clients some loophole of escape.

"It is easy to drive a coach-and-four through wills, and settlements, and legal things."—*H. R. Haggard.*
"[Rice] was often heard to say . . . . that he would drive a coach and six horses through the Act of Settlement."—*Wellwood.*

Coach-and-pair (*A*). A coach drawn by a pair of horses. Coach-and-four, coach-and-six, etc.

Coach Away. Get on a little faster. Your coach drags; drive on faster.

Coached Up. Taught by a private tutor for examination. "Well coached up," well crammed or taught.

9*

Coal. *Hot as a coal.* The expression has an obvious allusion.

To post the coal or *cole*. To pay or put down the cash. Coal = money has been in use in the sporting world for very many years. Buxton, in 1863, used the phrase "post the coal," and since then it has been in frequent use. Probably rhyming slang: "Coal," an imperfect rhyme of *gool* = gold. (*See* page 248, CHIVY, and page 266, COALING.)

"It would not suit me to write . . . . even if they offered, . . . to post the cole."—*Hood.*

Coal Brandy. Burnt brandy. The ancient way to set brandy on fire was to drop in it a live or red-hot coal.

Coals.
To blow the coals. To fan dissensions, to excite smouldering animosity into open hostility, as dull coals are blown into a blaze by a pair of bellows.

To carry coals. To be put upon. "Gregory, o' my word, we'll not carry coals"—*i.e.* submit to be "put upon" (*Romeo and Juliet*, i. 1). So in *Every Man out of his Humour*, "Here comes one that will carry coals, *ergo*, will hold my dog." The allusion is to the dirty, laborious occupation of coal-carriers. Gifford, in his edition of Bon Jonson, says, "Of these (*i.e.* scullions, etc.), the most forlorn wretches were selected to carry coals to the kitchen, halls, etc." (*See* page 141, col. 1, BLACKGUARD.)

To carry coals to Newcastle. To do what is superfluous. As Newcastle is the great coal-field, it would be quite superfluous to carry coals thither. The French say, "*Porter de l'eau à la rivière*" (to carry water to the river). There are numerous Latin equivalents: as, "To carry wood to the forests;" "*Poma Alcinoo dare*" (*See* ALCINOO); "*Noctuas Athenas ferre*" (*See* NOCTUAS); "*Crocum in Ciliciam ferre*" (*See* CROCUM).

To haul over the coals. To bring to task for shortcomings; to scold. At one time the Jews were "bled" whenever the kings or barons wanted money; and one very common torture, if they resisted, was to haul them over the coals of a slow fire, to give them a "roasting." (See *Ivanhoe*, where Front-de-Bœuf threatens to haul Isaac over the coals.)

Coals of Fire. *To heap coals of fire on the head of a foe.* To melt down his animosity by deeds of kindness.

"If thine enemy be hungry, give him bread to eat; and if he be thirsty, give him water to drink; for thou shalt heap coals of fire upon his head."—*Prov.* xxv. 21, 22.

Coaling, in theatrical slang, means telling phrases and speeches, as, "My part is full of ' coaling lines.'" Coal being money, means profit, whence *coaling.* (*See* p. 265, To POST THE COAL . . .)

Coalition Government. A Government formed by various parties by a mutual surrender of principles. The administration of Lord North and Charles Fox, 1783, was a coalition, but it fell to pieces in a few months. That of Lord Salisbury with the old Whig party headed by Lord Hartington was a coalition (1886-1892).

Coast Clear. *Is the coast clear? The coast is clear.* There is no likelihood of interference. None of the coastguards are about.

Coast Men of Attica. The merchant class who lived along the coastlands (*Par'ali*).

Coasting Lead (*A*). A sounding lead used in shallow water.

Coasting Trade. Trade between ports of the same country carried on by coasting vessels.

Coasting Waiter. An officer of Customs in the Port of London, whose duty it was to visit and make a return of coasting vessels trading from one part of the kingdom to another, and which (from the nature of their cargo) were not required to report or make entry at the Custom House. These vessels were liable to the payment of certain small dues, which it was the duty of the Coasting Waiter to exact. He was also expected to search the cargo, that no contraband goods were illicitly on board. Like Tide Waiters, these Coasting Waiters were abolished in the latter half of the nineteenth century, and their duties have since been performed by the Examining Officer. Their salary was about £40 a year.

Coat.
Cut your coat according to your cloth. Curtail your expenses to the amount of your income ; live within your means. *Si non possis quod velis, velis id quod possis.*
Near is my coat, but nearer is my skin. "*Tunica pallio propior est.*" "*Ego proximus mihi.*"
To baste one's coat. To dust his jacket ; to beat him.
To wear the king's coat. To be a soldier.
Turning one's coat for luck. It was an ancient superstition that this was a charm against evil spirits. (*See* TURN-COAT.)

"William found
A means for our deliverance : 'Turn your cloaks,'
Quoth hee,' for Pucke is busy in these oakes.'"
Bishop Corbett : Iter Boreale.

Coat of Arms. A surcoat worn by knights over their armour, decorated with devices by which heralds described the wearer. Hence the heraldic device of a family. Coat-armour was invented in the Crusading expeditions, to distinguish the various noble warriors when wrapped in complete steel, and it was introduced into England by Richard Lion-heart.

Coat of many Colours (Gen. xxxvii. 3). Harmer, in his *Observations* (vol. ii. p. 386), informs us that "many colours" in this connection does not mean striped, flowered, embroidered, or "printed" with several colours, but having "divers pieces of different colours sewed together" in patchwork. The Hebrew word is *passeem.* In 2 Sam. xiii. 18 we are told that king's daughters wore a garment of many colours or divers *pieces.* Dr. Adam Clarke says that similar garments "are worn by persons of distinction in Persia, India, and some parts of China to the present day." The great offence was this : Jacob was a sheik, and by giving Joseph a "prince's robe" he virtually announced him his heir. (*See* DIVERS COLOURS.)

Coats, Hosen, and Hats (Dan. iii. 21). These were not articles of dress, but badges of office. It will be recollected that Shadrach and his two companions had recently been set over provinces of Babylon ; and Nebuchadnezzar degraded them by insisting on their wearing their insignia of office. The word *cap* would be better than "hat," their caps of office ; and *sandals* would be better than "hosen." Coats or cloaks have always designated office. "Hosen" means what the Romans called *calceus patricius,* which were sandalled up to the calf of the leg. Every Latin scholar knows that *calceos mutare* means to "become a senator."

Cob (*A*). Between a pony and a horse in size, from thirteen to nearly fifteen hands high. The word means big, stout. The original meaning is a tuft or head, hence eminent, large, powerful. The "cob of the county" is the great boss thereof. A rich cob is a plutocrat. Hence also a male, as a cob-swan.
⁂ Riding horses run between fifteen and sixteen hands in height, and carriage

horses, between sixteen and seventeen hands.

Cobalt. From the German *Kobold* (a gnome). The demon of mines. This metal was so called by miners, because it was long thought to be useless and troublesome. It was consequently attributed to the ill offices of the mine demon.

Cobbler. A drink made of wine (sherry), sugar, lemon, and ice. It is sipped up through a straw. (*See* COBBLER'S PUNCH.)

"This wonderful invention, sir, . . . is called cobbler,—Sherry cobbler, when you name it long; cobbler when you name it short."—*Dickens: Martin Chuzzlewit*, xvii.

Cobbler. *Let not the cobbler overstep his last* (*Ne su'tor ultra crep'idam*). Let no one presume to interfere in matters of which he is ignorant. The tale goes that a cobbler detected a fault in the shoe-latchet of one of Apelles' paintings, and the artist rectified the fault. The cobbler, thinking himself very wise, next ventured to criticise the legs; but Apelles answered, "Keep to your trade"—you understand about shoes, but not about anatomy.

Cobbler Poet (*The*). Hans Sachs of Nuremberg, prince of the mastersingers of Germany (1494-1574).

Cobbler's Punch. Gin and water, with a little treacle and vinegar.

Cobbler's Toast. School-boys' bread and butter, toasted on the dry side and eaten hot.

Cob'ham, referred to by Thomson in his *Autumn*, was Sir Richard Temple, created Lord Cobham in 1714.

Cob-nut. A nut with a tuft. (Welsh, *cob* or *cop*, a tuft; German, *kopf*, the head.)

Coburgs. A corded or ribbed cotton cloth made in Coburg (Saxony), or in imitation thereof. Chiefly used for ladies' dresses.

Cob'web. *Cob*, Teutonic for "spider." Dutch, *spinnekop*; Saxon, *attercop* (poisonous spider); Chaldee, *kopi* (spider's web).

Cock. Mahomet found in the first heaven a cock of such enormous size that its crest touched the second heaven. The crowing of this celestial bird arouses every living creature from sleep except man. The Moslem doctors say that Allah lends a willing ear to him who reads the Koran, to him who prays for

pardon, and to the cock whose chant is divine melody. When this cock ceases to crow, the day of judgment will be at hand.

Cock. Dedicated to Apollo, the sun-god, because it gives notice of the rising of the sun. It was dedicated to Mercury, because it summons men to business by its crowing. And to Æsculapius, because "early to bed and early to rise, makes a man healthy."

A cock on church spires is to remind men not to deny their Lord as Peter did, but when the cock crew he "went out and wept bitterly." Peter Le Neve affirms that a cock was the warlike ensign of the Goths, and therefore used in Gothic churches for ornament.

Every cock crows on its own dunghill, or *Ilka cock crows on his own midden*. It is easy to brag of your deeds in your own castle when safe from danger and not likely to be put to the proof.

Latin : Gallus in suo sterquilinio plurimum potest.

French : Chien sur son fumier est hardi.

Spanish : Cada Galla canta en su muladar.

Nourish a cock, but offer it not in sacrifice. This is the eighteenth Symbolic Saying in the Protreptics of Iamblichus. The cock was sacred to Minerva, and also to the Sun and Moon, and it would be impious to offer a sacrilegious offering to the gods. What is already consecrated to God cannot be employed in sacrifice.

That cock won't fight. That dodge wouldn't answer; that tale won't wash. Of course, the allusion is to fighting cocks. A bet is made on a favourite cock, but when pitted he refuses to fight.

To cry cock. To claim the victory; to assert oneself to be the superior. As a cock of the walk is the chief or ruler of the whole walk, so to cry cock is to claim this cockship.

Cock and Bottle. A public-house sign, probably meaning that draught and bottled ale may be had on the premises. If so, the word "cock" would mean the tap.

Cock and Bull Story. A corruption of a *concocted and bully story*. The catch-pennies hawked about the streets are still called *cocks*— *i.e.* concocted things. Bully is the Danish *bullen* (exaggerated), our *bull-rush* (an exaggerated rush), *bull-frog*, etc.

Another etymology may be suggested:

The idol Nergal was the most common idol of the ancient Phœnicians, Indians, and Persians, and Nergal means a *dunghill cock*. The Egyptian *bull* is equally notorious under the name of Osi'ris. A cock-and-bull story may therefore mean a *myth*, in reference to the mythological fables of Nergal and Osiris.

The French equivalents are *faire un coq à l'âne* and *un conte de ma mère l'oie* (a mother goose tale).

Cock and Pie (*By*). We meet with *cock's bones*, *cock's wounds*, *cock's mother*, *cock's body*, *cock's passion*, etc., where we can have no doubt that the word is a minced oath, and stands for the sacred name which should never be taken in vain. The *Pie* is the table or rule in the old Roman offices, showing how to find out the service for each day, called by the Greeks *pi'nax* (an index). The latter part of the oath is equivalent to "the Mass book."

"By cock and pie, sir, you shall not away to-night."—*Shakespeare: 2 Henry IV.*, act v. 1.

Cock and Pie (as a public-house sign) is probably "The Cock and Magpie."

Cock of Hay (*A*) or *a haycock*. A small heap of hay thrown up temporarily. (German, *kocke*, a heap of hay; Norwegian, *kok*, a heap.)

Cock of the North. The Duke of Gordon. So called on a monument erected to his honour at Fochabers, in Aberdeenshire. (Died 1836.)

Cock of the Walk. The dominant bully or master spirit. The place where barn-door fowls are fed is called *the walk*, and if there is more than one cock they will fight for the supremacy of this domain.

Cock-a-hoop or *Cock-a-houp*. *To sit cock-a-houp*. Boastful, defiant, like a game-cock with his houpe or crest erect; eagerly expectant. (French, *coq à huppe*.)

"And having routed a whole troop,
With victory was cock-a-hoop."
Butler: Hudibras, i. 3.

Cock apace. Set off as fast as you can run. A cock is a tap through which liquor runs. "To cock" is to walk lightly or nimbly.

"If storms be nigh then cock apace," says Tusser (1174).

Cockboat or *Cockle Boat*. A small boat made of a wicker frame, and covered with leather or oil-cloth. The Welsh fishers used to carry them on their backs. (Welsh, *cwch*, a boat;

French, *coche*, a passage boat; Irish, *coca*; Italian, *cocca*; Norwegian, *kog*, ι cockboat.)

Cock-crow. The Hebrews divided the night into four watches : 1, The "beginning of the watches" or "even" (Lam. ii. 19) ; 2, "The middle watch" or "midnight" (Judg. vii. 19) ; 3, "The cock - crowing ; " 4, "The morning watch" or "dawning" (Exod. xiv. 24).

"Ye know not when the master of the house cometh, at even, or at midnight, or at the cock-crowing, or in the morning."—*Mark* xiii. 35.

⁎⁎ The Romans divided the night into sixteen parts, each one hour and a-half, beginning at midnight. The third of these divisions (3 a.m.) they called *gallicinium*, the time when cocks begin to crow ; the next was *conticinium*, when they ceased to crow ; and fifth was *diluculum*, dawn.

Probably the Romans sounded the hour on a trumpet (bugle) three times, and if so it would explain the diversity of the Gospels : "Before the cock crow" (John xiii. 38, Luke xxii. 34, and Matt. xxvi. 34) ; but "Before the cock crow *twice*" (Mark xiv. 30)—that is, before the "bugle" has finished sounding.

Apparitions vanish at cock crow. This is a Christian superstition, the cock being the watch-bird placed on church spires, and therefore sacred.

"The morning cock crew loud,
And at the sound it [the Ghost] shrunk in haste away,
And vanished from our sight."
Shakespeare: Hamlet, i. 2.

Cock-eye. A squint. Cock-eyed, having a squint ; cross-eyed. (Irish and Gaelic, *caog*, a squint ; "caogshuil," squint-eyed.)

Cock-fighting was introduced into Britain by the Romans. It was a favourite sport both with the Greeks and with the Romans.

That beats cock-fighting. That is most improbable and extraordinary. The allusion is to the extravagant tales told of fighting-cocks.

"He can only relieve his feelings by the ... frequent repetition, ' Well, that beats cock-fighting ! ' "—*Whyte-Melville*.

To live like fighting-cocks. To live in luxury. Before game-cocks are pitted they are fed plentifully on the very best food.

Cock-horse. *To ride-a-cock-horse*. To sit astride a person's foot or knee while he dances or tosses it up and down.

Cock Lane Ghost. A tale of terror without truth ; an imaginary tale of horrors. In Cock Lane, Stockwell (1762), certain knockings were heard, which Mr. Parsons, the owner, declared proceeded from the ghost of Fanny Kent, who died suddenly, and Parsons wished people to suppose that she had been murdered by her husband. All London was agog with this story; but it was found out that the knockings were produced by Parsons' daughter (a girl twelve years of age) rapping on a board which she took into her bed. Parsons was condemned to stand in the pillory. (*See* STOCKWELL GHOST.)

Cock-pit. The judicial committee of the privy council is so called, because the council-room is built on the old cock-pit of Whitehall palace.

"Great consultations at the cockpit about battles, duels, victories, and what not."—*Poor Robin's Almanack*, 1730.

Cock Sure is *cocky sure*—pertly confident. We call a self-confident, overbearing prig a cocky fellow, from the barnyard despot; but Shakespeare employs the phrase in the sense of "sure as the cock of a firelock."

"We steal as in a castle, cock-sure."—*Shakespeare:* 1 *Henry IV.*, ii. 1.

✻ The French phrase is *à coup sûr*, as: "*Nous réussirons à coup sûr*," we are certain of success, "*Cela est ainsi à coup sûr*," etc., and the phrase "Sure as a gun," seem to favour the latter derivation.

Cock the Ears (*To*). To prick up the ears, or turn them as a horse does when he listens to a strange sound. Here "cock" means to turn, and seems to be connected with the Greek κύκλος, a circle, and the verb κυκλόω.

Cock the Nose or *Cock up the nose.* To turn up the nose in contempt. (*See* COCK YOUR EYE.)

Cock up your Head [foot, etc.]. Lift up, turn up your head or foot. The allusion is to cocking hay, *i.e.* lifting it into small heaps or into the hay-cart. (*See* COCK OF HAY.)

Cock your Eye (*To*) is to shut one eye and look with the other; to glance at. A "cock-eye" is a squinting eye, and "cock-eyed" is having squinting eyes. In many phrases, *cock* means to turn. (*See above.*)

Cock your Hat (*To*). To set your hat more on one side of the head than on the other; to look knowing and pert. Soldiers cock their caps over the left side to "look smart." (*See* COCKED HAT.)

Cockade. The men-servants of the military wear a small black cockade on their hat, the Hanoverian badge. The Stuart cockade was white. At the battle of Sherra-Muir, in the reign of George I., the English soldiers wore a black rosette in their hats. In the song of Sherra-Muir the English soldiers are called "the red-coat lads wi' black cockades." (French, *cocarde;* German, *kokarde*.)

In the British Army and Navy the cockade, since the·Hanoverian accession, has been *black.*

AUSTRIAN cockade is black and yellow. All sentry boxes and boundary posts are so painted. *Ein schwarz-gelber* was the nickname of an Austrian Imperialist in 1848.

BAVARIA, light blue and white are the royal colours.

BELGIUM, black, yellow, and red.

FRANCE (*regal*), the royal colour was white.

HANOVER, the cockade was black. Black enters into all the German cockades.

PRUSSIA, black and white are the royal colours.

RUSSIA, green and white are the royal colours.

To mount the cockade. To become a soldier. From time immemorial the partisans of different leaders have adopted some emblem to show their party; in 1767 an authoritative regulation determined that every French soldier should wear a white cockade, and in 1782 the badge was restricted to the military. The phrase given above is common both to England and France.

Cockaigne (*Land of*). An imaginary land of idleness and luxury. The subject of a burlesque, probably "the earliest specimen of English poetry which we possess." London is generally so called, but Boileau applies the phrase to Paris. (*See* page 270, col. 2, COCKNEY.)

Allied to the German, *kuchen*, a cake. Scotland is called the "land of cakes"; there is the old French word *cocaigne*, abundance. Compare Latin *coquo*, to cook, *coquinaria, coquina*, etc.

✻ Ellis, in his *Specimens of Early English Poets* (i. 83-95), has printed at length an old French poem called "The Land of Cockaign" (thirteenth century), where "the houses were made of barley sugar and cakes, the streets were paved with pastry, and the shops supplied goods for nothing."

Cock·atrice (3 syl.). A monster with the wings of a fowl, tail of a dragon,

and head of a cock. So called because
it was said to be produced from a cock's
egg hatched by a serpent. According to
legend, the very look of this monster
would cause instant death. In consequence of the *crest* with which the head
is crowned, the creature is called a
basilisk, from the Greek, *basiliskos* (a
little king). Isaiah says, "The weaned
child shall put his hand on the cockatrice den" (xi. 8), to signify that the
most noxious animal should not hurt the
most feeble of God's creatures.

Figuratively, it means an insidious,
treacherous person bent on mischief.

"They will kill one another by the look, like
cockatrices."—*Shakespeare: Twelfth Night,* iii. 4.

Cocked Hat (*A*). A hat with the
brim turned, like that of a bishop, dean,
etc. It is also applied to the *chapeau
bras*, and the military full-dress hat,
pointed before and behind, and rising
to a point at the crown, the *chapeau à
cornes*. "Cock" in this phrase means to
turn; *cocked*, turned up.

Knocked into a cocked hat. In the
game of nine-pins, three pins were set
up in the form of a triangle, and when
all the pins except these three were
knocked down, the set was technically
said to be "knocked into a cocked hat."
Hence, utterly out of all shape or
plumb. A somewhat similar phrase is
"Knocked into the middle of next
week."

Cocked-hat Club (*The*). A club of
the Society of Antiquaries. A cocked
hat was always placed before the president when the club met.

There was another club so called in
which the members, during club sittings,
wore cocked hats.

Cocker. *According to Cocker. All
right, according to Cocker.* According
to established rules, according to what is
correct. Edward Cocker (1631-1677) published an arithmetic which ran through
sixty editions. The phrase, "According
to Cocker," was popularised by Murphy
in his farce called *The Apprentice*.

Cockie or **Cocky**. Bumptious, overbearing, conceited, and dogmatical; like
a little bantam cock.

Cockle Hat. A pilgrim's hat. Warburton says, as the chief places of devotion were beyond sea, or on the coasts,
pilgrims used to put cockle-shells upon
their hats, to indicate that they were
pilgrims. Cockles are symbols of St.

James, patron saint of Spain. Cockle=
scallop, as in heraldry.

" And how shall I your true love know
    From many another one ?
Oh, by his cockle hat and staff,
    And by his sandal shoon."
Beaumont and Fletcher: The Friar of Orders Grey.

Cockle Shells. Favourite tokens
worn by pilgrims in their hats. The
polished side of the shell was scratched
with some rude drawing of the "blessed
Virgin," the Crucifixion, or some other
subject connected with the pilgrimage.
Being blessed by the priest, they were
considered amulets against spiritual
foes, and might be used as drinking
vessels.

Cockles. *To cry cockles.* To be
hanged; from the gurgling noise made
in strangulation.

Cockles of the Heart. " *To warm
the cockles of one's heart*," said of good
wine. (Latin, *cochleæ cordis*, the ven-
tricles of the heart.)

" Fibræ quidem rectis hisce exterioribus in
dextro ventriculo proxime subjectæ oblique dex-
trorsum ascendentes in basim cordis terminantur,
et spirali suo ambitu helicem sive *cochleam* satis
apte referunt."—*Lower: Tractatus de Corde,* p. 25.
(1669.)

Cockledemoy (*A*). An amusing
rogue, a sort of Tyll Eulenspiegel. A
character in Marston's comedy of *The
Dutch Courtesan*. He cheats Mrs. Mulli-
grub, a vintner's wife, of a goblet and
salmon.

Cockney. One born within sound of
Bow-bells, London ; one possessing
London peculiarities of speech, etc.;
one wholly ignorant of country sports,
country life, farm animals, plants, and
so on.

Camden says the Thames was once
called " the Cockney."

The word has been spelt *Cockeney,
Cockaneys, Cocknell,* etc. " Cocknell "
would be a little cock. " *Puer in deliciis
matris nutritus*," Anglice, a *kokenay*, a
pampered child. " Niais " means a
nestling, as *faucon niais*, and if this is the
last syllable of " Cockney," it confirms
the idea that the word means an *enfant
gâté*.

Wedgwood suggests *cocker* (to fondle),
and says a cockerney or cockney is one
pampered by city indulgence, in contradistinction to rustics hardened by outdoor work. (Dutch, *kokkeler*, to pamper;
French, *coqueliner*, to dangle.)

Chambers in his *Journal* derives
the word from a French poem of the
thirteenth century, called *The Land of
Cocagne*, where the houses were made
of barley-sugar and cakes, the streets

paved with pastry, and the shops supplied goods without requiring money in payment. The French, at a very early period, called the English *cocagne men*, *i.e. bons vivants* (beef and pudding men).

"Cry to it, nuncle, as the cockney did to the eels, when she put them into the paste alive."— *Shakespeare: Lear*, ii. 4.

The king of cockneys. A master of the revels chosen by students of Lincoln's Inn on Childermas Day (Dec. 28th).

Cockney School. Leigh Hunt, Hazlitt, Shelley, and Keats ; so called by Lockhart. (1817.)

"If I may be permitted to have the honour of christening it, it may be henceforth referred to by the designation of the ' Cockney School.' " —*Z., Blackwood's Magazine*, Oct., 1817.

Cockpit of Europe. Belgium is so called because it has been the site of more European battles than any other country ; for example, Oudenarde, Ramillies, Fontenoy, Fleurus, Jemmapes, Ligny, Quatre Bras, Waterloo.

Cockshy (*A*). A free fling or "shy" at something. The allusion is to the once popular Shrove-Tuesday sport of shying or casting stones or sticks at cocks. This sport is now superseded by pigeon-shooting, which is thought to be more aristocratic ! but can hardly be deemed more humane.

Cockswain, or COXSWAIN [*cox'n*]. The swain or servant of the cock or boat, together with its crew. (Anglo-Saxon, *swan* or *swein*, a youth or servant, and *cock*, a boat.) (*See* COCKBOAT.)

Cocktail. The *New York World*, 1891, tells us that this is an Aztec word, and that "the liquor was discovered by a Toltec noble, who sent it to the king by the hand of his daughter Xochitl. The king fell in love with the maiden, drank the liquor, and called them xoc-tl, a name perpetuated by the word cocktail.

∴ Cocktail is an iced drink made of spirits mixed with bitters, sugar, and some aromatic flavouring. Champagne cocktail is champagne flavoured with Angostura bitters ; soda cocktail is soda-water, sugar, and bitters.

"Did ye iver try a brandy cocktail, Cornel ?"— *Thackeray : The Newcomes*, xiii.

Cocqcigrues. *At the coming of the Cocqcigrues.* That good time coming, when every mystery shall be cleared up.

"'That is one of the seven things,' said the fairy Bedonebyasyoudid, 'I am forbidden to tell till the coming of the Cocqcigrues.'."—*C. Kingsley : The Water Babies*, chap. vi.

Cocy'tus [*Ko-ky'tus*]. One of the five rivers of hell. The word means the "river of lamentation." The unburied were doomed to wander about its banks for 100 years. (Greek, *kōku'o*, to weep.)

"Cocytus, named of lamentation loud
Heard on the rueful stream."
Milton : Paradise Lost, ii. 579.

Codds. Codgers. Thackeray says, "The Cistercian lads call the poor brethren of the Charterhouse *codds*," adding, "but I know not wherefore." (Turkish, *kodjah*, an old man or woman.) We say "Well, old boy," without referring to age.

"I say, do you know any of the old codds . . . ? Colonel Newcome is going to be a codd."—*Nineteenth Century*, October, 1893, p. 589.

Codille (2 syl.). Triumph. A term in the game of Ombre. When one of the two opponents of Ombre has more tricks than Ombre, he is said to have won Codille, and takes all the stake that Ombre played for. Thus Belinda is said, in the *Rape of the Lock*, to have been "between the jaws of ruin and Codille." She wins with the "king of hearts," and *she wins codille*.

Codlin's your Friend, not Short. (*Dickens : Old Curiosity Shop*, chap. xix.). Codlin had a shrewd suspicion that little Nell and her grandfather had absconded, and that a reward would be offered for their discovery. So he tried to bespeak the goodwill of the little girl in the hope of making something of it.

"None of the speakers has much to say in actual hostility to Lord Salisbury's speech, but they all harp upon the theory that Codlin is the friend, not Short."—*Newspaper paragraph*, Oct. 13th, 1885.

Coehorns (2 syl.). Small howitzers of about 4⅗ inches calibre ; so called from Baron van Coe'horn, of Holland.

Coe'nobites or *Cenobites* (3 syl.). Monks who live in common, in contradistinction to the hermits or anchorites. (Greek, *koinosbios*.)

Cœur de Lion.

Richard I. of England ; so called from the prodigies of personal valour performed by him in the Holy Land. (1157, 1189-1199.)

Louis VIII. of France, more frequently called *Le Lion*. (1187, 1223-1226.)

Boleslas I. of Poland, also called "The Intrepid." (960, 992-1025.)

Coffee. The Turkish word is Kauhi, *Kauveh* or *Kauvey*.

Coffee. In Ardennes ten cups of coffee are taken after dinner, and each cup has its special name. (1) Café, (2) Gloria, (3) Pousse Café, (4) Goutte, (5) Regoutte, (6) Sur-goutte, (7) Rincette, (8) Re-rincette, (9) Sur-rincette, and (10) Coup de l'étrier.

Gloria is coffee with a small glass of brandy in lieu of milk; all the following have more and more l'eau de vie; and the last is the "stirrup-cup."

Coffin. A raised crust, like the lid of a basket. Hence Shakespeare speaks of a "custard coffin" (*Taming of the Shrew*, iv. 3). (Greek, *koph'inos*, a basket.) (*See* MAHOMET'S COFFIN.)

"Of the paste a coffin will I rear.'
Shakespeare: Titus Andronicus, v. 2.

Cog'geshall. *A Coggeshall job.* The saying is, that the Coggeshall folk wanted to divert the current of a stream, and fixed hurdles in the bed of it for the purpose. Another tale is that a mad dog bit a wheelbarrow, and the people, fearing it would go mad, chained it up in a shed. (*See* GOTHAM.)

Cogito, ergo sum. Descartes' axiom. This is a *petitio principii.* "I think" can only prove this: that "I think." And he might just as well infer from it the existence of *thought* as the existence of *I.* He is asked to prove the latter, and immediately assumes that it exists and does something, and then infers that it exists *because* it does something. Suppose I were asked to prove the existence of ice, and were to say, ice is cold, therefore there is such a thing as ice. Manifestly I first assume there is such a thing as ice, then ascribe to it an attribute, and then argue back that this attribute is the outcome of ice. This is not proof, but simply arguing in a circle.

Cohens (Stock Exchange term). The Turkish '69 loan, floated by the firm of that name.

Coif (1 syl.). The coif of the old serjeant-at-law was a relic of his ecclesiastical character. The original *serjeants-at-law* were clerical lawyers, and the coif is the representation of the tonsure.
Serjeants of the Coif. Serjeants-at-law (now abolished). (*See above.*)

Coiffé. *Il est né coiffé.* He is born with a silver spoon in his mouth; born to fortune. (*See* page 229, col. 2, CAUL.)

"Quelques enfans viennent au monde avec une pellicule . . . que l'on appelle du nom de coëffe; et que l'on croit estre une marque de bonheur. Ce qui a donné lieu au proverbe françois. . . . *Il est né coëffé.*"—*Traité des Superstition*, 1679.

Coiffer to Sainte Catherine. To remain an old maid. "St. Catherine est la patronne des filles à marier et des vieilles filles. Ce sont ces dernières qui restent ordinairement pour soigner les chapelles consacrées à la sainte, et qui sont chargées de sa toilette." (*Hetaire*

le Gai: Encyclopédie des Proverbes Français.)

"Il crois peut-être que je le regrette, que, de désespoir je vais coiffer St. Catherine. Ah! ah! mais non! moi aussi je veux me marier."—*La Mascotte* (an opera).

Coin. *Paid in his own coin.* Tit for tat. "*Par pari referre.*"

Coin Money (*To*). To make money with rapidity and ease.

"For the last four years . . . I literally coined money."—*F. Kemble: Residence in Georgia.*

Coins.

BRITISH. Iron rings were used for money by the ancient Britons, and Segonax, a petty king under Cassivelän, is the first whose head was impressed on the coin. Gold, silver, and copper coins were struck by Cunobelin.

The ROMANS introduced their own coins into the island.

The oldest ANGLO-SAXON coin was the *sceatta* (pl. *sceattæ*), sixth century. In the reign of Ethelbert, King of Kent, money accounts were kept in *pounds, mancuses, shillings,* and *pence.* One of the last being equal to about 3 pence of our money. 5 pence = one scilling, 30 scillings one *manca* or *mancus,* and 40 one pound. Mancuses were in gold and silver also.

The NORMANS introduced pence with a cross so deeply impressed that the coin could be broken either into two or four parts, hence the terms half-pence and fourthings.

The *Angel,* a gold coin (7s. 6d.), was introduced by Edward IV., and had a figure of Michael slaying the dragon.

The *Bawbee* first came into use in the reign of James VI. of Scotland. (French, *bas-billon,* base copper coin.)

The *Carolus* (20s.) was a gold coin of the reign of Charles I.

The *Crown* (5s.) was first issued in 1553. Crowns and half-crowns are still in common circulation.

English *Dollars* (4s. 6d.) were introduced in 1798.

Florins, a gold coin (6s.), were issued by Edward III.; but the silver florin (2s.) in 1849.

The *Guinea* (a gold coin = 21s.) was first issued in 1717; but a gold coin so-called, of the value of 30s., was issued in 1673, reduced in 1696 to 22s.

Our *Sovereign* was first issued in 1816, but there were coins so called in the reigns of Henry I. (worth 22s.), Edward VI. (from 24s. to 30s.).

Shillings of the present value date from 1503; pence made of bronze in

1862, but copper pence were coined in 1620, half-pence and farthings in 1665.

Coke. *To cry coke.* To cry pecca'vi; to ask for mercy. Ruddiman says "coke" is the sound which cocks utter when they are beaten.

Coke upon Littleton. Tent and brandy.

"Another ... sipping Coke upon Littleton, *i.e.* tent and brandy."—*Nichols: Illustrations of Literature* (1743).

Col'bronde or *Colbrand.* The Danish giant slain by Sir Guy of Warwick. By the death of this giant the land was delivered from Danish tribute.

" I am not Samson, nor Sir Guy, nor Colbrand,
    To mow 'em down before me."
        Shakespeare: Henry VIII., v. 4.

Colcannon. Potatoes and cabbage pounded together and then fried in butter (Irish). "Col" is cole or cale, *i.e.* cabbage.

"About 1774 Isaac Sparks, the Irish comedian, founded in Long Acre a Colcannon Club."—*The Athenæum*, January 20th, 1875.

Cold as Charity. (*See* CHARITY.)

Cold-Bath Fields. So called from the cold baths established there by Mr. Bains, in 1697, for the cure of rheumatism, convulsions, and other nervous disorders.

Cold Blood. *Done in cold blood.* (French, *sang froid.*) Not in the heat of temper; deliberately, and with premeditation. The allusion is to the ancient notion that the blood grew hot and cold, and this difference of temperature ruled the temper.

Cold-blooded Animals. As a rule, all invertebrate animals, and all fishes and reptiles, are called cold-blooded, because the temperature of their blood is about equal to the medium in which they live.

Cold-blooded Persons. Those not easily excited; those whose passions are not easily roused; those whose circulation is sluggish.

Cold-chisel (*A*). A chisel of tempered steel for cutting cold metal.

Cold Drawn Oil. Castor oil, obtained by pressure in the cold.

Cold Pigeon (*A*). A message sent in place of a love-letter. The love-letter would have been a poulet (*q.v.*). A pigeon pie is called a dove-tart, and dove is symbolical of love. Pyramus says of Thisbe, "What dead, my dove?" A verbal message is "cold comfort" to a lover looking out for a letter.

Cold Pudding settles Love by giving the pains of indigestion, colic, etc.

Cold Shoulder. *To show* or *give one the cold shoulder* is to assume a distant manner towards a person, to indicate that you wish to cut his acquaintance. The reference is to a cold shoulder of mutton served to a stranger at dinner; there is not much of it, and even what is left is but moderate fare.

Cold Steel. *The persuasion of cold steel* is persuasion enforced at the point of the sword or bayonet.

Cold Water Ordeal. An ancient method of testing the guilt or innocence of the common sort of people. The accused, being tied under the arms, was thrown into a river. If he sank to the bottom, he was held to be guiltless, and drawn up by the cord; but if he floated, the water rejected him, because of his guilt.

Cold Without. An elliptical expression, meaning spirits mixed with *cold* water *without* sugar.

Coldbrand. (*See* COLBRONDE.)

Coldstream Guards. One of the three regiments of Foot Guards. It was originally under the command of Colonel Monk (1650-1660), and in January, 1660, marched under him from Coldstream in Berwickshire with the object of bringing back Charles II. to the throne.

Cole = money. (*See* COAL.)

Cole (*King*). A legendary British king, described as "a merry old soul" fond of his pipe, fond of his glass, and fond of his "fiddlers three." (*Ky. Coïl*, i.)

Colemi'ra (3 syl.). A poetical name for a cook; being, of course, compounded of *coal* and *mire*.

"' Could I,' he cried, ' express how bright a grace
    Adorns thy morning hands and well-washed face,
Thou wouldst, Colemira, grant what I implore,
And yield me love, or wash thy face no more.'"
        Shenstone: Colemira, an Eclogue.

Colin Clout. A name which Spenser assumes in *The Shepherd's Calendar*, and in the pastoral entitled *Colin Clout's Come Home Again*, which represents his return from a visit to Sir Walter Raleigh, "the Shepherd of the Ocean."

Colin Tampon. The nickname of a Swiss, as John Bull is of an Englishman, Brother Jonathan of a North American, and Monsieur Crapaud of a Frenchman.

Collapse. *The scheme collapsed.* Came to nothing. An inflated balloon is said to collapse when the gas has escaped and the sides fall together, or pucker into wrinkles. As a collapsed balloon will not mount, a collapsed scheme will not go off. (Latin, *collapsus, collabor,* to fall or sink together.)

Collar.
Against the collar. Somewhat fatiguing. When a horse travels up-hill the collar distresses his neck, so foot-travellers often find the last mile or so "against the collar," or distressing. Authors of long books often find the last few pages wearisome and against the grain.

In collar. In harness. The allusion is to a horse's collar, which is put on when about to go to work.

Out of collar. Out of work, out of place. (*See above.*)

To slip the collar. To escape from restraint; to draw back from a task begun.

To work up to the collar. To work tooth and nail; not to shirk the work in hand. A horse that lets his collar lie loose on his neck without bearing on it does not draw the vehicle at all, but leaves another to do the real work.

"As regarded himself, the path lay plain. He must work up to the collar, hot and hard, leaving himself no time to feel the parts that were galled and wrung."—*Mrs. Edwardes: A Girton Girl,* chap. iv.

Collar (verb). *To collar one.* To seize by the collar; to prig; to appropriate without leave.

To collar the cole or *coal.* To prig the money. (*See* COAL.)

Collar-day (*A*). In royal levees, means that attendants are to wear all their insignia and decorations, such as medals, stars, ribbons, and orders. This is done on grand occasions by order of the Crown. The Queen's Collar-day is when she wears the Order of the Garter.

Collar of Arsinoë (4 syl.) or *Collar of Alphesibēa,* given by her to her husband Alcmēon, was a fatal gift; so was the collar and veil of Eriph'ylē, wife of Amphiarāos. (*See* FATAL GIFTS.)

Collar of SS. A decoration restricted to the Lord Chief Justices of the Queen's Bench, the Lord Chief Baron of the Exchequer, the Lord Mayor of London, the Kings-of-Arms, the Heralds, the Sergeant-at-Arms, and the Sergeant Trumpeter. (*Coussan's Heraldry.*) (*See* SS.)

Collectivists. Collectivism is the opposite of Individualism. In the latter system, everyone is to be his own master, and everything is to be free and in common. In the former system, government is to be the sole employer, the sole landlord, and the sole paymaster. Private property is to be abolished, competition to be stamped out; everyone must work for his living, and the State must find the work. Bellamy's novel of *Looking Backward* will give a pretty fair notion of what is meant by Collectivism. (*See* INDIVIDUALISTS.)

College (*New*). Newgate prison. "To take one's final degree at New College" is to be hanged. "King's College" is King's Bench Prison, now called Queen's College. Prisoners are "collegiates." College is the Latin *collegium,* and has a very wide range, as, College of the Apostles, College of Physicians, College of Surgeons, Heralds' College, College of Justice, etc.; and on the Continent we have College of Foreign Affairs, College of War, College of Cardinals, etc.

College Colours.

CAMBRIDGE BOAT CREWS, light blue.

Caius, light blue and black.
Catherine's, blue and white.
Christ's, common blue.
Clare, black and golden yellow.
Corpus, cherry-colour and white.
Downing, chocolate.
Emmanuel, cherry-colour and dark blue
Jesus, red and black.
John's, bright red and white.
King's, violet.
Magdalen, indigo and lavender.
Pembroke, claret and French grey.
Peterhouse, dark blue and white.
Queen's, green and white.
Sydney, red and blue.
Trinity, dark blue.
Trinity Hall, black and white.

OXFORD BOAT CREWS, dark blue.

St. Alban's, blue with arrow-head.
Balliol, pink, white, blue, white, pink. ¶
Brazenose, black, and gold edges.
Christ Church, blue with red cardinal's hat
Corpus, red with blue stripe.
St. Edmond's, red, and yellow edges
Exeter, black, and red edges.
Jesus, green, and white edges
John's, yellow, black, red.
Lincoln, blue with mitre.
Magdalen, black and white.
St. Mary's, white, black, white.
Merton, blue, with white edges and red cross.
New College, three pink and two white stripes.
Oriel, blue and white.
Pembroke, pink, white, pink.
Queen's, red, white, blue, white, blue, white. red.
Trinity, blue, with double dragon's head, yellow and green, or blue, with white edges.
University, blue, and yellow edges.
Wadham, light blue.
Worcester, blue, white, pink, white, blue.

College Colours (America) in football matches, boating, etc.

Adelbert, Bismarck brown and purple.
Alleghany, cadet blue and old gold.

Amherst, white and purple.
Bates, garnet.
Boston University, scarlet and white.
Bowdoin, white.
Brown, brown and white.
Buchtel, orange and blue.
California, blue and gold.
C.C.N.Y., lavender.
Colby, silver grey.
Columbia, blue and white.
Cornell, cornelian and white.
Dartmouth, dark green.
Dickinson, red and white.
Hamilton, rose pink.
Harvard, crimson.
Hobart, orange and purple.
Kenyon, mauve.
Lafayette, white and maroon.
Madison, orange and maroon.
Michigan, blue and maize.
New York University, violet.
Ohio University, blue.
Princeton, orange and black.
Rensselaer Polytechnic, cherry.
Rochester, blue and grey.
Rutgers, scarlet.
Swarthmore, garnet.
Syracuse, blue and pink.
Trinity, white and green.
Tufts, blue and brown.
Union, garnet.
University of North Carolina, white and blue.
   of South Carolina, red and blue.
   of Pennsylvania, blue and red.
   of the South, red and blue.
   of Vermont, old gold and green.
   of Virginia, cardinal and grey.
Vassar, pink and grey.
Wesleyan, cardinal and black.
Williams, royal purple.
Wooster, old gold.
Yale, blue.

College Port. The worst species of red wine that can be manufactured and palmed off upon young men at college. (*See* WIDOWS' PORT.)

"We all know what college port is like."—*The Times.*

Col'liberts. A sort of gipsy race in Poitou, Maine, and Anjou, similar to the *Cagots* of Gascony and the *Caqueux* of Brittany. In feudal times a collibert was a serf partly free, but bound to certain services. (Latin, *col-libertus*, a fellow freedman.)

Collu'thians. A religious sect which rose in the fourth century; so called from Collu'thos of Alexandria, their founder.

Colly my Cow. A corruption of *Calainos*, the most ancient of Spanish ballads. Calainos the Moor asked a damsel to wife, who said the price of winning her should be the heads of the three paladins of Charlemagne, named Rinaldo, Roland, and Olivier. Calainos went to Paris and challenged the paladins. First Sir Baldwin, the youngest knight, accepted the challenge and was overthrown; then his uncle Roland went against the Moor and smote him.

Collyrid'ians. A sect of Arabian Christians, chiefly women, which first appeared in 373. They worshipped the Virgin Mary, and made offerings to her in a twisted cake, called a *collyris*. (Greek, *kollura*, a little cake.)

Collywobbles. The gripes, usually accompanied with sundry noises in the stomach. These noises are called the "borbarigmus." (The wobbling caused by a slight colic.)

Cologne. *The three kings of Cologne.* The three magi, called Gaspar, Melchior, and Baltha'zar. They are called by other names, but those given are the most generally accepted.

Co'lon. One of the rabble leaders in *Hudibras* was Noel Perryan, or Ned Perry, an ostler, who loved bear-baiting, but was a very straight-laced Puritan of low morals.

Col'ophon. The end of a book. Col'ophon was a city of Io'nia, the inhabitants of which were such excellent horsemen that they would turn the scale of battle to the side on which they fought; hence, the Greek phrase, *To add a colopho'nian*, means "to put a finishing stroke to any matter." (*Strabo.*) In the early times of printing, the statement containing the date, place, printer, and edition was given at the end of the book, and was called the colophon.

❧ Now called the "imprint."

"The volume was uninjured . . . from title-page to colophon."—*Scott : The Antiquary.*

Coloquin'tida or **Colocynth.** Bitter-apple or colocynth. (Greek, *kolokunthis.*)

"The food that to him now is luscious as locusts, shall be to him shortly as bitter as coloquintida."—*Shakespeare : Othello,* i. 3.

Coloquin'tida (*St.*). Charles I. was so called. He was bitter as gall to the Levellers.

"The Levellers styled him [Charles I.] an Ahab, and a Coloquintida, a man of blood, and the ever-lasting obstacle to peace and liberty."—*Howitt : History of England* (" Charles I.," chap. vi. p. 284).

Colorado (U.S. America). A Spanish word meaning *red*, referring to the red hue of the water of the river.

Colossal. Gigantic. As a colossal scheme. (*See below.*)

Colossus or **Colossos** (Latin, *colossus*). A giant. The Rhodian Colossos was a gigantic statue of brass, 126 feet high, executed by Charēs. It is said that ships could pass full sail under the legs of this statue, but the notion of a striding statue rose in the sixteenth century, and is due to Blaise de Vigenère, who was the first to give the *chef d'œuvre* of Charēs this impossible position. The Comte de Caylus has demonstrated that the Apollo of Rhodes was never planted at the mouth of the Rhodian port, that it was not a striding statue, and that ships never passed under it. Neither Strabo nor Pliny makes mention of any of these things, though both describe the gigantic statue minutely. Philo (the architect of Byzantium, third century) has a treatise on the seven wonders of the world, and says that the Colossos *stood on a block of white marble*; and Lucius Ampellius, in a similar treatise, says it *stood in a car.* Tickell out-herods Herod in the following lines :

" So, near proud Rhodes, across the raging flood,
Stupendous form ! the vast Colossus stood,
While at one foot the thronging galleys ride,
A whole hour's sail scarce reached the farther
      side ;
Betwixt his brazen thighs, in loose array,
Ten thousand streamers on the billows play."
                      On the Prospect of Peace.
",He doth bestride the narrow world
Like a Colossus." *Shakespeare : Julius Cæsar,* i. 2.

❖ The twin Colossi of Amenophis III., on the banks of the Nile, near Thebes, are seated. The statue of Liberty, New York, is colossal.

Colour. (*See* RANK.)

Colour, Colours. *A man of colour.* A negro, or, more strictly speaking, one with negro blood. (*See* COLOURS.)

"There are three great classes: (1) the pure whites ; (2) the people of colour ; (3) negroes and mulattoes."—*Edwards : St. Domingo,* i.

Colours.

(1) Black :

In blazonry, sable, signifying prudence, wisdom, and constancy.
In art, signifying evil, falsehood, and error.
As a mortuary colour, signifying grief, despair, death. In the Catholic Church violet may be substituted for black).
In metals it is represented by lead.
In precious stones it is represented by the diamond.
In planets it stands for Saturn.
In heraldry it is engraved by perpendicular and horizontal lines crossing each other at right angles.

(2) Blue :

In blazonry, azure, signifying chastity, loyalty, fidelity.
In art (as an angel's robe) it signifies fidelity and faith.
In art (as the robe of the Virgin Mary) it signifies modesty.
In art (in the Catholic Church) it signifies humility and expiation.
As a mortuary colour it signifies eternity (applied to Deity), immortality (applied to man).
In metals it is represented by tin
In precious stones it is represented by sapphire.
In planets it stands for Jupiter.
In heraldry it is engraved by norizontal lines.

(3) Green :

In blazonry, vert, signifying love, joy, abundance.
In art, signifying hope, joy, youth, spring (among the Greeks and Moors it signified victory).
In church ornaments, signifying God's bounty, mirth, gladness, the resurrection.
In metals it is represented by copper.
In precious stones it is represented by the emerald.
In planets it stands for Venus.
As a railway signal it means caution, go slowly.
In heraldry it is engraved from left to right.

(4) Purple :

In blazonry, purpure, signifying temperance.
In art, signifying royalty.
In metals it is represented by quicksilver.
In precious stones it is represented by amethyst.
In planets it stands for Mercury.
In heraldry it is engraved by lines slanting from right to left.

(5) Red :

In blazonry, gules ; blood-red is called sanguine. The former signifies magnanimity, and the latter, fortitude.
In metals it is represented by iron (the metal of war).
In precious stones it is represented by the ruby.
In planets it stands for Mars.
In heraldry it is engraved by perpendicular lines.

(6) White :

In blazonry, argent ; signifying purity, truth, innocence.
In art, priests, Magi, and Druids are arrayed in white. Jesus after the resurrection should be draped in white.
As a mortuary colour it indicates hope.
In metals it is represented by silver.
In precious stones it is represented by the pearl.
In planets it stands for Diana or the Moon.
In heraldry it is engraved by shields left white.

(7) Yellow :

In blazonry or signifying faith, constancy, wisdom, glory.
In modern art or signifying jealousy, inconstancy, incontinence. In France the doors of traitors used to be daubed with yellow, and in some countries Jews were obliged to dress in yellow. In Spain the executioner is dressed in red and yellow.
In Christian art Judas is arrayed in yellow ; but St. Peter is also arrayed in golden yellow.
In metals it is represented by gold.
In precious stones it is represented by the topaz.
In planets it stands for Apollo or the Sun.
In heraldry it is engraved by dots.

Colours for Church Decoration.

White, for festivals of our Lord, for Easter, and for all saints except martyrs.
Red, for martyrs, for Ash Wednesday, the last three days of Holy Week, and Whit Sunday.
Blue, for all week-days after Trinity Sunday.
Blue or *Green,* indifferently, for ordinary Sundays.
Violet, Brown, or *Grey,* for Advent and Lent.
Black, for Good Friday.

Colours of the University Boats, etc. (*See* COLLEGE COLOURS.)

Colours.
Accidental colours. Those colours seen on a white ground after looking for some time at a bright-coloured object, like the sun.
Complementary colours. Colours which, in combination, produce white light.

"The colour transmitted is always complementary to the one reflected."—*Brewster : Optics,* xii.

Fundamental colours. The seven colours of the spectrum : violet, indigo, blue, green, yellow, orange, and red. Or red, yellow, blue, also called *primary* or *simple* colours.

Secondary colours. Those which result from the mixture of two or more primary or simple colours.

Colours. *He was with the colours.* In active military service.

"The period . . . was raised from seven to nine years, *five* years being passed with the colours, and *four* in the reserve."—*Edinburgh Review* (1886).

His coward lips did from their colours fly. He was unable to speak. As cowards run away from their regimental colours, so [Cæsar's] lips, when he was ill, ran away from their colour and turned pale.

To come out in his true colours. To reveal one's proper character, divested of all that is meretricious.

To describe [*a matter*] *in very black colours.* To see them with a jaundiced eye, and describe them accordingly ; to describe [the matter] under the bias of strong prejudice.

To desert one's colours. To become a turncoat ; to turn tail. The allusion is to the military flag.

To give colour or *To give some plausible colour to the matter.* To render the matter more plausible ; to give it a more specious appearance.

To paint in bright colours. To see or describe things in *couleur de rose.* Also "to paint in lively colours."

To put a false colour on a matter. · To misinterpret it, or put a false construction on it.

To see things in their true colours. To see them as they really are.

Under colour of. . . . Under pretence of . . . ; under the alleged authority of . . . .

Wearing his colours. Taking his part ; being strongly attached to one. The idea is from livery.

"Jim could always count on every man, woman, and child, wherever he lived, wearing his colours, and backing him . . . through thick and thin."—*Boldrewood : Robbery Under Arms*, chap. xiv.

Without colour. "*In nudâ veritate,*" without disguise.

Colours. *National colours—*

Great Britain	Red and blue.
America, U.S. ..	Stars on blue, white with red stripes.
Austria	Red, white, and red.
Bavaria	Red
Denmark	Red, with white cross.
France	Blue, white, and red.
Netherlands ..	Red, white, and blue.
Portugal	Blue and white.
Prussia	White.
Russia	White, with blue cross.
Spain	Red, yellow, and red.
Sweden	Blue, with yellow cross.
Switzerland ..	Red, with white cross.

Colours Nailed to the Mast (*With our*), *à outrance.* If the colours are nailed to the mast, they cannot be lowered to express submission.

"If they catch you at disadvantage, the mines for your life is the word ; and so we fight them with our colours nailed to the mast."—*Sir W. Scott : The Pirate*, chap. xxi.

Colour-blindness. Incapacity of discerning one colour from another. The term was introduced by Sir David Brewster. It is of three sorts : (1) inability to discern any colours, so that everything is either black or white, shade or light ; (2) inability to distinguish between primary colours, as red, blue, and yellow ; or secondary colours, as green, purple, and orange ; and (3) inability to distinguish between such composite colours as browns, greys, and neutral tints. Except in this one respect, the colour-blind may have excellent vision.

Colour Sergeant. A sergeant who carries or has charge of the regimental colours.

Colour (verb). *To colour up*, to turn red in the face ; to blush.

Coloured Frontispiece by Phiz (*A*). A blush.

Colporteur'. A hawker or pedlar ; so called because he carries his basket or pack round his neck. The term is more especially applied to hawkers of religious books. (Latin, *collum*, the neck ; *porto*, to carry.)

Colt (*A*). A piece of knotted rope eighteen inches long for the special benefit of ship boys ; a cat-o'-nine-tails.

"Look alive there, lads, or as sure as my name is Sam Weston I'll give the colt to the last man off the deck."—*J. Grant : Dick Rodney*, chap. vii.

Colt (*A*). A barrister who attends a sergeant-at-law at his induction.

"I accompanied the newly-made Chief Baron as his colt."—*Pollock.*

"Then Mr. Bailey, his colt, delivered his ring to the Lord Chancellor."—*Wynne.*

Colt (*To*). To befool, to gull. (Italian, *colto*, cheated, befooled.)

Colt-pixy (*A*). A pixy, puck, or fairy. To colt-pixy is to take what belongs to the pixies, and is specially applied to the gleaning of apples after the crop has been gathered in ; these apples were the privilege of the pixies, and to colt-pixy is to deprive the pixies of their perquisites.

Colt's Revolver. A fire-arm which, by means of revolving barrels, can be fired several times without intermission. This instrument was patented by Colonel Samuel Colt, U.S., in 1835.

Colt's-tooth. The love of youthful pleasure. Chaucer uses the word "coltish" for skittish. Horses have at three years old the colt's-tooth. The allusion is to the colt's teeth of animals, a period of their life when their passions are strongest.

> " Her merry dancing-days are done ;
> She has a colt's-tooth still, I warrant."
> *King : Orpheus and Eurydice.*
> " Well said, Lord Sands ;
> Your colt's-tooth is not cast yet."
> *Shakespeare : Henry VIII.*, i. 3.

Col'umbine (3 syl.). The sweetheart of Harlequin, and, like him, supposed to be invisible to mortal eyes. *Columbina* in Italian is a pet-name for a lady-love, and means a little dove, a young coquette.

Columbus. His signature was—

S.	*i.e.*	Servidor
S. A. S.		Sus Altezas Sacras
X. M. Y.		Jesus Maria Isabel
Xto. FERENS		Christo-pher
El Almirante		El Almirante.

In English, "Servant—of their Sacred Highnesses—Jesus Mary and Isabella —Christopher—the Admiral."

The second Columbus. Cyrus West Field was so called by John Bright when he completed the Atlantic Cable. Born at Stockbridge, Massachusetts, 1819.

Columbus of the Skies (*The*). Sir F. William Herschel, discoverer of Georgium Sidus (Urănus), 1738-1822.

Column.

The Alexandrine Column. Made of granite ; in memory of the Emperor Alexander.

The Column of Antonīnus. At Rome ; made of marble, 176 feet high ; in memory of the Emperor Marcus Aurelius Antonīnus. Like that of Trajan, this column is covered externally with spiral bas-reliefs representing the wars carried on by the emperor.

Sixtus V. caused the original statue of this column to be supplanted by a figure of St. Paul. (See *Trajan's Column.*)

The Column of Arcadius. At Constantinople ; made of marble.

Column at Boulogne. To commemorate the camp of Boulogne. This formidable army was intended for the invasion of England. England also girded herself for battle, and here the matter ended. The Column perpetuates the memory of this threat.

The Duke of York's Column, in London, at the top of the steps leading into St. James's Park. Erected in 1830-1833 in memory of Frederick, Duke of York, second son of George III., who died in 1827. It is of the Tuscan order, was designed by R. Wyatt, and is made of Aberdeenshire granite. On the summit is a statue of the duke by Sir R. Westmacott.

The Column of July. 1832, **Paris** ; made of bronze, and erected on the spot where the Bastille stood, to commemorate the revolution of July, 1830, when Charles X. abdicated. It is surmounted with a statue of Liberty standing on one foot.

London's Column. (*See* MONUMENT.)

Nelson's Column. In Trafalgar Square, London ; was erected in 1843. The four lions, by Landseer, were added in 1867. The order of the Column is Corinthian, and the material Devonshire granite. The reliefs are (*north side*) the battle of the Nile, where Nelson was wounded ; (*south side*) Nelson's death at the battle of Trafalgar ; (*east side*) the bombardment of Copenhagen ; and (*west side*) the battle of St. Vincent. The column is surmounted by a statue of Nelson by E. H. Baily.

Column of the Place Vendôme. Paris, 1806-1810 ; made of bronze, and erected in honour of Napoleon I. The spiral outside represents in bas-relief the battles of Napoleon I., ending with Austerlitz in 1805. It is a facsimile of Trajan's Column.

In 1871 the statue of Napoleon, which surmounted this column, was hurled to the ground by the Communists, but in 1874 a statue of Liberty was substituted for the original one.

Pompey's Column. In Egypt ; made of marble.

Trajan's Column. At Rome ; made of marble, A.D. 114, by Apollodorus. It is 132 feet in height, and has inside a spiral staircase of 185 steps, and 40 windows to let in light. It was surmounted by a statue of the Emperor Trajan, but Sixtus V. supplanted the original statue by that of St. Peter. The spiral outside represents in bas-reliefs the battles of the emperor.

Columns of Herculēs. Two large pyramidal columns set up by the Phœnicians as lighthouses and landmarks, dedicated, one to Herculēs (the sun), and the other to Astartē (the moon).

By the Greeks and Romans the two pyramidal mountains at the Straits of Gibraltar (Calpē and Abўla), the former in Europe and the latter in Africa, were termed the *Pillars of Herculēs.*

Co'ma Bereni'ces (4 syl.). (*See* BERENICE.)

Com'azants. Called St. Elmo fires by the French, Castor and Pollux by the Romans. A celestial light seen occasionally to play round mast-heads, etc.

(Latin, *co'ma*, hair.) Virgil makes good use of this phenomenon while Æneas is hesitating whether to leave burning Troy or not :

" Ecce levis summo de vertice visus Iuli
 Fundere lumen apex, tractuque innoxia mo...
 Lambere flamma comas, et circum tempora pasci
 Nos, pavidi trepidare metu, crinemque flagran-
 tem
 Excutere, et sanctos restinguere fontibus
 ignes."

When old Anchises interferes, and a falling star is interpreted to mean that Jupiter will lead them forth securely. (*Æneid*, ii. 682, etc.)

Comb.

A crabtree comb. A cudgel applied to the head. To smooth your hair with a crabtree comb, is to give the head a knock with a stick.

Reynard's wonderful comb. This comb existed only in the brain of Master Fox. He said it was made of the Pan'thera's bone, the perfume of which was so fragrant that no one could resist following it ; and the wearer of the comb was always cheerful and merry. (*Reynard the Fox*, chap. ii.)

To comb one's head. To humiliate a person, or to give him a " set down."

" I'll carry you with me to my country box, and keep you out of harm's way, till I find you a wife who will comb your head for you."—*Bulwer-Lytton : What will he do with it?* iv. 16.

To comb your noddle with a three-legged stool (*Taming of the Shrew*, i. 1) is to beat you about the head with a stool. Many stools, such as those used by milk-maids, are still made with three legs ; and these handy weapons seem to have been used at one time pretty freely, especially by angry women.

To cut one's comb. To take down a person's conceit. In allusion to the prac-tice of cutting the combs of capons.

To set up one's comb is to be cockish and vainglorious.

Comb the Cat (*To*). To run your fingers through the lashes of a cat-o'-nine-tails to disentangle them.

Come and take Them. The reply of Leon'idas, King of Sparta, to the messengers sent by Xerxes to Thermop'-ylæ. Xerxes said, " Go, and tell those madmen to deliver up their arms." Leonidas replied, " Go, and tell Xerxes to come and take them."

Come Ather (pron. *ah-ther*) means, when addressed to horses, "come hither" —*i.e.* to the *left*, the side on which the teamsman walks. (*See* WOO'ISH.)

Come Down a Peg. Humiliated ; lowered in dignity, tone, demands, etc.

" Well, he has come down a peg or two, and he don't like it."—*Haggard.*

A come down. Loss of prestige or position.

" ' Now I'm your worship's washerwoman.' The dignitary coloured, and said that ' this was rather a come down.' "—*Reade.*

Come Down upon One (*To*). To reproach, to punish severely, to make a peremptory demand.

Come Home. Return to your house ; to touch one's feelings or interest.

" No poetry was ever more human than Chau-cer's ; none ever came more generally . . . home to its readers."—*Green : Short History of the Eng-lish People*, chap. v.

Come it. *Has he come it?* Has he lent the money? Has he hearkened to your request? Has he come over to your side? Also, " Out with it ! "

Come it Strong. Lay it on thick ; to exaggerate or overdo. (*See* DRAW IT MILD.)

Come Lightly. *Lightly come, lightly go.* There is a somewhat similar Latin proverb, *male parta, male dilabuntur.*

Come Of. *What's to come of it? What's to come of him?* A contracted form of *become.* To come of [a good stock] is to be descended from [a good family].

Come Off (*To*). To occur, to take place. (Anglo-Saxon, *of-cuman* = Latin, *pro-cedo*, to proceed.)

To come off with honours is to proceed to the end successfully.

Come On ! A challenge to fight with fists.

Come Out. Said of a young lady after she has been introduced at Court, or has entered into society as a " grown-up " person. She " comes out into society."

Come Over One (*To*). To wheedle one to do or give something. (Anglo-Saxon, *ofer-cuman*, to overcome.) To come over one is in reality to conquer or get your own way.

Come Round. (*See* COMING, etc.).

Come Short (*To*). Not to be suffi-cient. " To come short of " means to miss or fail of attaining.

Come That, as, *Can you come that? I can't come that.* Here, " come " means to arrive at, to accomplish.

Come the Religious Dodge (*To*) means to ask or seek some favour under pretence of a religious motive. Here " come " means to come and introduce. (*See* DODGE.)

Come to. Amount to, to obtain possession. "It will not come to much."

Come to Grief (*To*). To fail, to prove a failure, as, "the undertaking (or company) came to grief," *i.e.* to a grievous end.

Come to Hand (*It has*). Been received. "Come into my hand." In Latin, *ad manus* (*alicujus*) *pervenire*.

"Your letter came to hand yesterday."—*A. Trollope.*

Come to Pass (*To*). To happen, to befall, to come about.

"What thou hast spoken is come to pass."—Jer. xxxii. 24.

"It came to pass [ἐγένετο] in those days that there went out a decree."—Luke ii. 1.

Come to an End. To terminate. The allusion is to travelling, when the traveller has come to the end of his journey.

Come to the Hammer. To be sold by auction.

Come to the Heath. To tip. A pun taken from the place called Tip-tree Heath, in Essex. Our forefathers, and the French too, delighted in these sort of puns. A great source of slang. (*See* CHIVY.)

Come to the Point. Speak out plainly what you want; do not beat about the bush, but state at once what you wish to say. The point is the gist or grit of a thing. Circumlocution is wandering round the point with words; to come to the point is to omit all needless speech, and bring all the straggling rays to a focus or point.

Come to the Scratch. (*See* SCRATCH.)

Come to the Worst. *If the worst come to the worst ;* even if the very worst occurs.

Come Under (*To*). To fall under; to be classed under.

Come Up. *Marry, come up !* (*See* MARRY.) "To come up to" means to equal, to obtain the same number of marks, to amount to the same quantity.

Come Upon the Parish (*To*). To live in the workhouse; to be supported by the parish.

Come Yorkshire over One (*To*). To bamboozle one, to overreach one. Yorkshire has always been proverbial for shrewdness and sharp practice. "I's Yorkshire too" means, I am 'cute as you are, and am not to be taken in.

Comedy means a village-song (Greek, *komē-ōdē*), referring to the village merrymakings, in which comic songs still take a conspicuous place. The Greeks had certain festal processions of great licentiousness, held in honour of Diony'sos, in the suburbs of their cities, and termed *ko'moi* or village-revels. On these occasions an ode was generally sung, and this ode was the foundation of Greek comedy. (*See* TRAGEDY.)

The Father of comedy. Aristoph'anês, the Athenian (B.C. 444-380).

Comes (2 syl.). A Latin military title, now called count on the continent of Europe, but earl in England from the Saxon *earldorman* (alderman), Danish *eorle.* The wife of an earl is called countess.

Comet Wine. A term of praise to signify wine of superior quality. A notion prevails that the grapes in comet years are better in flavour than in other years, either because the weather is warmer and ripens them better, or because the comets themselves exercise some chemical influence on them. Thus, wine of the years 1811, 1826, 1839, 1845, 1852, 1858, 1861, etc., have a repute.

"The old gentleman yet nurses some few bottles of the famous comet year (*i.e.* 1811), emphatically called comet wine."—*The Times.*

Coming Round. *He is coming round.* Recovering from sickness ; recovering from a fit of the sulks ; returning to friendship. Death is the end of life, and therefore recovering from "sickness nigh unto death" is coming back to health, or coming round the corner.

Command Night. In theatrical parlance, a night on which a certain play is performed by command of some person of authority or influence.

Commandment. *The eleventh commandment.* Thou shalt not be found out.

"After all, that Eleventh Commandment is the only one that is vitally important to keep in these days."—*B. H. Buxton : Jennie of the Prince's,* iii. 314.

The · ten commandments. The ten fingers or nails. (*Shakespeare : 2 Henry VI.,* i. 3.)

Comme il Faut (French, pronounce *cum cel fo*), as it should be ; quite proper ; quite according to etiquette or rule.

Commen'dam. *A living in commendam* is a living held by a bishop till an incumbent is appointed. When a clergyman accepts a bishopric he loses all his previous preferment ; but in order that these livings may not be uncared for, they are *commended* by the Crown to the care of the new bishop till they can be properly transferred. Abolished in 1836.

Commendation Ninepence. A bent silver ninepence, supposed to be lucky, and commonly used in the seventeenth century as a love-token, the giver or sender using these words, "From my love, to my love." Sometimes the coin was broken, and each kept a part.

> "Like commendation ninepence, crooked,
> With 'To and from my love,' it looked."
> *Butler: Hudibras,* i. 1.
> "*Filbert:* As this divides, thus are we torn in twain.
> *Kitty:* And as this meets, thus may we meet again."
> *Gay: What d'ye Call It?*

Commis-voyageur (*A*). A commercial traveller.

Committee. *A committee of the whole house,* in Parliamentary language, is when the Speaker leaves the chair and all the members form a committee, where anyone may speak once or more than once. In such cases the chair is occupied by the chairman of committees, elected with each new Parliament.

A standing committee, in Parliamentary language, is a committee which continues to the end of the current session. To this committee are referred all questions which fall within the scope of their appointment.

Committing Falsehood. Swindling.

The Earl of Rosebery pointed out that the expression "committing falsehood" in Scotch law was synonymous with what in England was called swindling (April 25th, 1885).

Commodity of Brown Paper (*A*). Rubbish served as make-weight; worthless stock; goods palmed off on the inexperienced. In most auctions the buyer of a lot has a fair share of the commodity of brown paper. Rubbish given to supplement a loan.

> "Here's young Master Rash! he's in for a commodity of brown paper and old ginger, nine-score and seventeen pounds [*i.e.* £197, a part of the advance being old ginger and brown paper]."—*Shakespeare: Measure for Measure,* iv. 3.

Commodore. A corruption of "commander" (French, *commandeur;* Spanish, *comendador*). A naval officer in temporary command of a squadron or division of a fleet. He has the pay of a rear-admiral.

Common Pleas. Civil actions at law brought by one subject against another—not by the Crown against a

subject. The *Court of Common Pleas* is for the trial of civil [not capital] offences. In 1875 this court was abolished, and in 1880 it was represented by the Common Pleas Division and merged in the King's [or Queen's] Bench Division.

Common Prayer. *The Book of Common Prayer.* The book used by the Established Church of England in "divine service." Common, in this case, means *united.*

Common Sense does not mean that good sense which is common, or commonly needed in the ordinary affairs of life, but the sense which is common to all the five, or the point where the five senses meet, supposed to be the seat of the soul, where it judges what is presented by the senses, and decides the mode of action. (*See* SEVEN SENSES.)

Commoner. *The Great Commoner.*
1. Sir John Barnard, who, in 1737, proposed to reduce the interest of the national debt from 4 per cent. to 3 per cent., any creditor being at liberty to receive his principal in full if he preferred it. Mr. Goschen (1889-90) reduced the 3 per cents. to 2½.
2. William Pitt, the statesman (1759-1806).

Commons. *To put one on short commons.* To stint him, to give him scanty meals. In the University of Cambridge the food provided for each student at breakfast is called his *commons;* hence food in general or meals.

To come into commons. To enter a society in which the members have a common or general dinner table.

Commons in Gross — that is, at large. These are commons granted to individuals and their heirs by deed, or claimed by prescription as by a parson or corporation.

Commonwealths (*Ideal*). "Utopia" by Sir Thomas More, "The New Atlantis" by Lord Bacon, "The City of the Sun" by Campanella, etc.

Companion Ladder. The ladder leading from the poop to the main deck. The "companion way" is the staircase to the cabin. (*Dana: Seaman's Manual.*)
✵ The staircase from the deck to the cabin.

Companions of Jehu. The *Chouans* were so called, from a fanciful analogy between their self-imposed task and that appointed to Jehu, on being set over the kingdom of Israel. Jehu was to cut off

Ahab and Jez'ebel, with all their house, and all the priests of Baal. The Chouans were to cut off all who assassinated Louis XVI., and see that his brother (*Jehu*) was placed on the throne.

Comparisons are Odorous. So says Dogberry. (*Much Ado About Nothing*, iii. 5.)

> "We own your verses are melodious,
> But then comparisons are odious."
> *Swift: Answer to Sheridan's "Simile."*

Complementary Colours. (*See* COLOURS.)

Complexion literally means "what embraces or contains," and the idea implies that the colour of the skin corresponds to the habit of body, and the habit of body answers to the element which predominates. If fire predominates, the person is *bilious* or full of bile; if air, he is *sanguine* or full of blood; if earth, the body is *melancholic* or full of black bile; if water, it is *phleg'matic* or full of phlegm. The first is hot and dry, the second hot and moist, the third cold and dry, and the last moist and cold like water.

> "'Tis ill, tho' different your complexions are [*i.e.* dispositions]."   *Dryden.*
> "Cretans through mere complexion lie."
>   *Pitt: Hymn of Callimachus.*

Com'pline (2 syl.). The last service of the day in the Roman Catholic Church. First appointed by the abbot Benedict in the sixth century. The word is a corruption of *completo'rium.* In ecclesiastical Latin *vesperinus*, from *vesper*, means evening service, and *completinus* is formed on the same model.

Compostella. A corruption of *Giacomo-postolo* (James the Apostle). So called after his relics were transferred thither from Iria Flavia (El Padron) on the borders of Galicia, in the ninth century. Leo III. transferred the See of Iria Flavia to Compostella. (Somewhere between 810 and 816.)

Compte rendu. The account already sent; the account of particulars delivered; a report of proceedings.

Com'rade (2 syl.). The name of Fortu'nio's fairy horse. It ate but once a week; knew the past, present, and future; and spake with the voice of a man. (*Grimm's Goblins: Fortunio.*) (*See* HORSE.)

Com'rades (2 syl.). Those who sleep in the same bed-chamber. It is a Spanish military term derived from the custom of dividing soldiers into chambers. The proper spelling is *camerades*, men of the same *cam'era* (chamber).

Co'mus. God of revelry. Milton represents him as a male Circē. (Greek, *komos*, carousal.)

> "This nymph [Circe], that gazed upon his [Bacchus's] clustering locks, ...
> Had by him, ere he parted thence, a son,
> Much like his father, but his mother more,
> Whom therefore she brought up, and Comus named."   *Milton: Comus*, 54-58.

Comus. The elder brother in this domestic drama is meant for Lord Viscount Brackley, eldest son of John, Earl of Bridgewater, president of Wales. The younger brother is Mr. Thomas Egerton. The lady is Lady Alice Egerton. (*Milton.*)

Comus's Court. A social gathering formerly held at the Half-Moon Tavern in Cheapside, London.

Con Amo're (Italian). With heart and soul; as, "He did it *con amo're*"— *i.e.* lovingly, with delight, and therefore in good earnest.

Con Commodo (Italian). At a convenient rate. A musical term.

Con Spirito (Italian). With quickness and vivacity. A musical term.

Co'nan. The Thersi'tēs of "Fingal;" brave even to rashness.

Blow for blow or *claw for claw, as Conan said.* Conan made a vow never to take a blow without returning it; when he descended into the infernal regions, the arch-fiend gave him a cuff, which Conan instantly returned, saying "Claw for claw."

> "'Blow for blow,' as Conan said to the devil."— *Scott: Waverley*, chap. xxii.

Concert Pitch. The degree of sharpness or flatness adopted by a number of musicians acting in concert, that all the instruments may be in accord. Generally, a particular note is selected for the standard, as A or C; this note is put into the proper pitch, and all other notes are regulated by it.

Concerto (Italian). A composition intended to display the powers of some particular instrument, with orchestral accompaniments.

Con'cierge (3 syl.). French. The door-porter of a public or private "hotel," or house divided into flats, or of a prison.

Conciergerie. (French.) The office or room of a concierge or porter's lodge; a state prison. During the Revolution it was the prison where the chief victims were confined prior to execution.

Conclave (2 syl.). A set of rooms, all of which are entered by one common key (Latin, *con cla′vis*). The word is applied to the little deal cells erected in some large apartment for the cardinals who meet to choose a new Pope, because the long gallery of the Vatican between the cells and the windows of the palace is common ground to all the conclavists. The assembly itself is, by a figure of speech, also called a conclave.

Conclama′tio, amongst the ancient Romans, was similar to the Irish howl over the dead; and, as in Ireland, women led the funeral cortège, weeping ostentatiously and gesticulating. "One not howled over" (*corpus nondum conclama′tum*) meant one at the point of death; and "one howled for" was one given up for dead or really deceased. Virgil tells us that the ululation was a Phœnician custom; and therefore he makes the palace ring with howls when Dido burnt herself to death.

"Lamentis, gemituque, et fœmineo ululato,
  Texta fremunt."   *Æneid*, iv. 667.

Conclamatum est. He is dead past all hope. The sense of hearing is generally the last to fail in the hour of death, hence the Romans were accustomed to call on the deceased three times by name, and if no indication of hearing was shown death was considered certain. *Conclamatum est*, he has been called and shows no sign.

Concord is Strength. The wise saw of Periander, "tyrant" of Corinth (B.C. 665-585).

Concor′dat. An agreement made between a ruler and the Pope relative to the collation of benefices. As the Concordat of 1801 between Napoleon Bonaparte and Pope Pius VII.; the Concordat of 1516 between François I. and Pope Leo X. to abolish the "pragmatic sanction;" and the Germanic Concordat of 1448 between Frederick III. and Pope Nicholas V.

Condign′. Latin, *condignus* (well worthy); as condign punishment—*i.e.* punishment well deserved.

"In thy con′dign praise."
  Shakespeare: Love's Labour's Lost, i. 2.

Condottie′ri. Leaders of military adventurers in the fifteenth century. The most noted of these brigand leaders in Italy were Guarnie′ri, Lando, Frances′co of Carmag′nola, and Francesco Sforza. Giac′omo Sforza, the son of Francesco, married the daughter of the Duke of Milan, and succeeded his father-in-law. The singular is Condottiere (5 syl.).

Confed′erate States. The eleven States which revolted from the Union in the late American Civil War (1861-1866) —viz. Georgia, North and South Caroli′na, Virgin′ia, Tennessee′, Alaba′ma, Louisia′na, Arkan′sas, Mississip′pi, and Flor′ida and Texas.

Confedera′tion of the Rhine. Sixteen German provinces in 1806 dissolved their connection with Germany, and allied themselves with France. At the downfall of Napoleon in 1814 this confederation melted away of itself.

Confession. John of Nep′omuc, canon of Prague, suffered death rather than violate the seal of confession. The Emperor Wenceslas ordered him to be thrown off a bridge into the Moldau, because he refused to reveal the confession of the empress. He was canonised as St. John Nepomu′cen.

Confis′cate (3 syl.). To forfeit to the public treasury. (Latin, *con fiscus*, with the tribute money.)

"If thou doet shed one drop of Christian blood,
Thy lands and goods are, by the laws of Venice,
Confiscate to the State of Venice."
   Shakespeare; Merchant of Venice, iv. 1.

Confusion Worse Confounded. Disorder made worse than before.

"With ruin upon ruin, rout on rout,
Confusion worse confounded."
   Milton: Paradise Lost, ii. line 996.

Congé. "To give a person his congé" is to dismiss him from your service. "To take one's congé" is to give notice to friends of your departure. This is done by leaving a card at the friend's house with the letters P.P.C. (*pour prendre congé*) inscribed on the left-hand corner. (French, *donner congé* and *donner à son congé*.)

Congé d'Elire (Norman - French, *leave to elect*). A royal warrant given to the dean and chapter of a diocese to elect the person nominated by the Crown to their vacant see.

Congle′ton Bears. The men of Congleton. It is said that the Congleton parish clerk sold the church Bible to buy a bear.

Congrega′tionalists. Those Protestant Dissenters who maintain that each congregation is an independent community, and has a right to make its own laws and choose its own minister. They rose in the time of Queen Elizabeth.

Con'greve Rockets. (1808.) So called from Sir William Congreve, eldest son of Lieut.-Colonel Sir William Congreve (1772-1828).

Congreves. A predecessor of Lucifer matches. The splints were first dipped in sulphur, and then tipped with the chlorate of potash paste, in which gum was substituted for sugar, and there was added a small quantity of sulphide of antimony. The match was ignited by being drawn through a fold of sandpaper with pressure. These matches, being dangerous, were prohibited in France and Germany. (*See* PROME-THEANS; LUCIFERS.)

Con'jugal. What pertains to *conjugēs* (yoke-fellows). In ancient times a yoke (*jugum*) was put on a man and woman by way of marriage ceremony, and the two were said to be yoked together by marriage.

Con'juring Cap. *I must put on my conjuring cap—i.e.* your question requires deliberate thought, and I must reflect on it. Eric XIV., King of Sweden, was a great admirer of magic, and had an "enchanted cap" made, either to keep his head warm or for mystification. He pretended to have power over the elements; and when a storm arose, his subjects used to say "The king has got on his conjuring cap."

Connecticut, U.S. America, is the Indian *Quin - neh - tuk - qut,* meaning "land of the long tidal river."

Connubialis de Mulcibre fecit Apellem. Love turned a blacksmith into a great artist. Said of Quentin Matsys, the blacksmith of Antwerp, who was in love with an artist's daughter. The father scorned the alliance, and said he should not be accepted unless he made himself a worthy artist. This did Matsys and won his bride. The sentence may be seen still on the monument of Quentin Matsys outside Antwerp cathedral.

Conqueror. *The Conqueror.*
Alexander the Great. *The conqueror of the world.* (B.C. 356, 336-323.)
Alfonso of Portugal. (1094, 1137-1185.)
Aurungzebe the Great. *Alemgir.* The most powerful of the great Moguls. (1618, 1659-1707.)
James I. of Aragon. (1206, 1213-1276.)
Othman or Osman I. Founder of the Turkish power. (1259, 1299-1326.)
Francisco Pizarro. *Conquistador.* So

called because he conquered Peru. (1475-1541.)
William, Duke of Normandy. So called because he obtained England by conquest. (1027, 1066-1087.)

Conqueror's Nose (*A*). A prominent straight nose, rising at the bridge. Charlemagne had such a nose, so had Henry the Fowler (Heinrich I. of Germany); Rudolf I. of Germany; Friedrich I. of Hohenzollern, famous for reducing to order his unruly barons by blowing up their castles (1382-1440); our own "Iron Duke;" Bismarck, the iron Chancellor of Prussia; etc.

Conquest (*The*). The accession of William I. to the crown of England. So called because his right depended on his conquest of Harold, the reigning king. (1066.)

Con'rad (*Lord*). Afterwards called Lara, the corsair. A proud, ascetic, but successful captain. Hearing that the Sultan Seyd was about to attack the pirates, Conrad assumed the disguise of a dervish and entered the palace, while his crew set fire to the sultan's fleet. The trick being discovered, Conrad was taken prisoner, but was released by Gulnare, the sultan's favourite concubine, whom he had rescued from the flaming palace. Gulnare escaped with the corsair to the Pirates' Isle, and when Conrad found Medo'ra dead, he left the island, and no one knew whither he went. The rest of his adventures are recorded under his new name of Lara. (*Byron: The Corsair.*)

Conscience.
Have you the conscience to [demand such a price]. Can your conscience allow you to [demand such a price]. Conscience is the secret monitor within man which accuses or excuses him, as he does what he thinks to be wrong or right.
In all conscience. As, "And enough too, in all conscience." Meaning that the demand made is as much as conscience would tolerate without accusing the person of actual dishonesty; to the verge of that fine line which separates honesty from dishonesty.
My conscience! An oath. I swear by my conscience.
Court of Conscience. Established for the recovery of small debts in London and other trading places. These courts have been superseded by county courts.

" Why should not Conscience have vacation,
As well as other courts o' the nation ? "
         Butler: Hudibras, ii. 2.

Nonconformist Conscience. (*See* NON-
CONFORMIST.)

Conscience Clause (*A*). A clause
in an Act of Parliament to relieve persons with conscientious scruples from
certain requirements in it.

Conscience Money. Money paid
anonymously to Government by persons
who have defrauded the revenue. Their
conscience being uneasy, they send the
deficit to the Treasury, and the sum is
advertised in the *Gazette.*

Conscious Water. *The conscious
water saw its God, and blushed* (*Nympha
pudica Deum vidit, et erubuit*). Crashaw's
epigram on the miracle of Cana in
Galilee. "The *modest* water" would
be a closer rendering.

Conscript Fathers. In Latin, *Patres
Conscripti.* The Roman senate. Romulus instituted a senate consisting of a
hundred elders, called *Patres* (Fathers).
After the Sabines joined the State,
another hundred were added. Tarquinius Priscus, the fifth king, added a
third hundred, called *Patres Minorum
Gentium.*. When Tarquinius Superbus,
the seventh and last king of Rome, was
banished, several of the senate followed
him, and the vacancies were filled up by
Junius Brutus, the first consul. The
new members were enrolled in the sena-
torial register, and called *Conscripti;* the
entire body was then addressed as *Patres
[et] Conscripti* or *Patres, Conscripti.*

Consen'tes Dii. The twelve chief
Roman deities—
Jupiter, Apollo, Mars, Neptune, Mer-
cury, and Vulcan.
Juno, Vesta, Minerva, Ceres, Diana,
and Venus.
Ennius puts them into two hexameter
verses—
"Juno, Vesta, Minerva, Ceres, Diana, Venus,
Mars,
Mercurius, Jovi', Neptunus, Vulcanus, Apollo."
✻ Called "*consentes,*" says Varro,
"Quia in consilium Jovis adhibebantur."—*De
Lingua Latina,* vii. 28.

Consenting Stars. Stars forming
configurations for good or evil. In
Judges v. 20 we read that "the stars in
their courses fought against Sisera," *i.e.*
formed unlucky or malignant configurations.
".... Scourge the bad revolting stars
That have consented unto Henry's death."
Shakespeare: 1 *Henry VI.,* i. 1.

Conser'vative (4 syl.). A medium
Tory—one who wishes to preserve the
union of Church and State, and not
radically to alter the constitution. The
word was first used in this sense in 1830,
in the January number of the *Quarterly
Review*—"We have always been con-
scientiously attached to what is called
the *Tory,* and which might with more
propriety be called the *Conservative*
party" (p. 276).
✻ Canning, ten years previously, had
used the word in a speech delivered at
Liverpool in March, 1820. In Lord
Salisbury's Ministry those Whigs and
Radicals who joined the Conservatives
were called "Liberal Unionists" because
they objected to give Ireland a separate
parliament (1885).

Consistory (*A*). An ecclesiastical
court. In Rome it consists of the cardinals, presided over by the Pope. In
England it is a diocesan court, presided
over by the chancellor of the diocese.

Consolidated Fund (*The*). In 1757
an Act was passed for consolidating the
nine loans bearing different interests,
into one common loan bearing an interest
of three per cent. In 1890 this interest
was reduced to two and three-quarter
per cent.; and in 1903 will be still further
reduced to two and a-half per cent.
This fund is pledged for the payment of
the interest of the national debt, the
civil list, the salaries of the judges, ambassadors, and other high officials, etc.

Consols. A contraction of Consolidated Fund. (*See above.*)

Con'sort is, properly, one whose *lot*
is cast in *with* another. As the Queen
does not lose by marriage her separate
existence, like other women, her husband
is called a consort, because he consorts
with the Queen, but does not share her
sovereignty.
"Wilt thou be our consort?"
Shakespeare: Two Gentlemen of Verona, iv. 1.

Conspirators. Members of a commercial ring or corner. (*See* CORNER,
TRUSTS.) These merchants "conspire"
to fix the price of articles, and make the
public bleed *ad libitum.* In criminal
law it means persons who league together to do something unlawful.

Con'stable (Latin, *comes-stab'uli*)
means "Master of the Horse." The
constable of England and France was at
one time a military officer of state, next
in rank to the crown.
To overrun or *outrun the constable.* To
get into debt; spend more than one's
income; to talk about what you do not
understand. (*See below.*)
"Quoth Hudibras, Friend Ralph, thou hast
Outrun the constable at last;

For thou hast fallen on a new
Dispute, as senseless as untrue."
Butler: Hudibras, i. 3.

Who's to pay the constable ? Who is
to pay the score?

The constable arrests debtors, and, of
course, represents the creditor ; wherefore, to overrun the constable is to
overrun your credit account. To pay
the constable is to give him the money
due, to prevent an arrest.

Constable de Bourbon. Charles,
Duc de Bourbon, a powerful enemy of
François I. He was killed while heading
the assault on Rome. (1527.)

Constantine Tolman (Cornwall).
A vast egg-like stone, thirty-three feet
in length, eighteen in width, and fourteen in thickness, placed on the points
of two natural rocks, so that a man may
creep under it. The stone upheld weighs
750 tons.

Constantine's Cross. In Latin,
vincēs in hoc ; in English, *By this conquer.* It is said that Constantine, on his
march to Rome, saw a luminous
cross in the sky, in the shape and
with the motto here given. In
the night before the battle of
Saxa Rubra a vision appeared
to him in his sleep, commanding
him to inscribe the cross and the motto
on the shields of his soldiers. He obeyed
the voice of the vision, and prevailed.
The monogram is ΧΡιστος (Christ). (*See
Gibbon : Decline and Fall,* chap. xix. n.)

This may be called a standing miracle
in legendary history ; for, besides Andrew's cross, and the Dannebrog or red
cross of Denmark (*q.v.*), we have the
cross which appeared to Don Alonzo
before the battle of Ourique in 1139,
when the Moors were totally routed with
incredible slaughter. As Alonzo was
drawing up his men, the figure of a cross
appeared in the eastern sky, and Christ,
suspended on the cross, promised the
Christian king a complete victory. This
legend is commemorated by the device
assumed by Alonzo, in a field argent five
escutcheons azure, in the form of a cross,
each escutcheon being charged with five
bezants, in memory of the five wounds
of Christ. (*See* LABARUM.)

Constit'uent Assembly. The first
of the national assemblies of the French
Revolution ; so called because it took
an oath never to separate till it had
given to France a constitution. (1788-
1791.)

Constit'uents. Those who constitute
or elect members of Parliament. (Latin,
constit'uo, to place or elect, etc.)

Constitution. The fundamental laws
of a state. It may be either despotic,
aristocratic, democratic, or mixed.

To give a nation a constitution is to
give it fixed laws even to the limitation
of the sovereign's rights, so that the
people are not under the arbitrary
caprice of a ruler, but under a known
code of laws. A despotism or autocracy
is solely under the unrestricted will of
the despot or autocrat.

Constitu'tions of Clar'endon. (*See*
CLARENDON.)

Apostolic Constitutions. A "Catholic"
code of both doctrine and discipline
collected by Clemens Romānus. The
word " Apostolic," as in the " Apostles'
Creed," does not mean made by the
Apostles, but what the " Church " considered to be in accordance with apostolic teaching.

Con'strue. To translate. To translate into English means to set an English
word in the place of a foreign word,
and to put the whole sentence in good
grammatical order. (Latin, *construo,* to
construct.)

Consuelo (4 syl.). The impersonation of moral purity in the midst of
temptations. The heroine of George
Sand's (*Mad. Dudevant's*) novel of the
same name.

Contango. The sum paid by a
speculator on a " bull account " (*i.e.* a
speculation on the *rise* in the price of
certain stock), to defer completing the
bargain till the next settling day. (*See*
BACKWARDATION.)

Con'template (3 syl.). To inspect or
watch the temple. The augur among the
Romans, having taken his stand on the
Capit'oline Hill, marked out with his
wand the space in the heavens he intended to consult. This space he called
the *templum.* Having divided his
templum into two parts from top to
bottom, he watched to see what would
occur ; the watching of the templum was
called *contemplating.*

Contempt' of Court. Refusing to
conform to the rules of the law courts.
Consequential contempt is that which
tends to obstruct the business or lower
the dignity of the court by indirection.
Direct contempt is an open insult or
resistance to the judge or others officially
employed in the court.

Contenement. A word used in
Magna Charta, meaning the lands and
chattels connected with a tenement ;

also whatever befits the social position of a person, as the arms of a gentleman, the merchandise of a trader, the ploughs and wagons of a peasant, etc.

"In every case the contenement (a word expressive of chattels necessary to each man's station) was exempted from seizure."—*Hallam: Middle Ages*, part ii. chap. viii. p. 342.

Contentment is true Riches. The wise saw of Democritos, the laughing philosopher. (B.C. 509-400.)

"Content is wealth, the riches of the mind ;
And happy he who can such riches find."
Dryden: Wife of Bath's Tale.

Contests of Wartburg (*The*), sometimes called *The Battles of the Minstrels*. An annual contest held in Wartburg, in Saxe Weimar, for a prize given by Hermann, Margrave of Thuringia, for the best poem. About 150 specimens of these poems are still extant, by far the best being those of Walter of Vogelweide, in Thuringia (1168-1230).

.˙. The poem called *The Contest of Wartburg* is by Wolfram, a minnesinger. It records the contest of the two great German schools of poetry in the thirteenth century—the Thuringian and the Suabian. Henry of Vogel-weide and Henry of Ofterdingen represent the two schools.

Continence of a Scip'io. It is said that a beautiful princess fell into the hands of Scipio Africa'nus, and he refused to see her, "lest he should be tempted to forget his principles." The same is said of Cyrus (*see* PANTHEA), of Anson (*see* THERESA), and of Alexander.

Continental System. A name given to Napoleon's plan for shutting out Great Britain from all commerce with the continent of Europe. He forbade under pain of war any nation of Europe to receive British exports, or to send imports to any of the British dominions. It began Nov. 21st, 1806.

Contin'gent (*A*). The quota of troops furnished by each of several contracting powers, according to agreement. The word properly means the number which falls to the lot of each ; hence we call a fortuitous event a contingency.

Contra bonos Mores (Latin). Not in accordance with good manners; not *comme il faut* (*q.v.*).

Contretemps (French). A mischance, something inopportune. Literally, "out of time."

Conven'ticle means a "little convent," and was originally applied to a cabal of monks against the election of

a proposed abbot. It now means a religious meeting of dissenters. (Latin, *conventus*, an assembly, with a diminutive.) (*See* CHAPEL.)

Conversation Sharp. Richard Sharp, F.R.S., the critic. (1759-1835.)

Convey. A polite term for *steal*. Thieves are, by a similar euphemism, called *conveyers*. (Latin, *con-veho*, to carry away.)

"Convey, the wise it call. Steal! foh ! a fico for the phrase."—*Shakespeare: Merry Wives of Windsor*, i. 3.

Conveyers. Thieves. (*See above*.)

"*Bolingbroke*. 'Go, some of you, convey him to the Tower.'
Rich. II. 'O, good ! "Convey." Conveyers are ye all,
That rise thus nimbly by a true king's fall.'"
Shakespeare: Richard II., iv. 4.

Conway Cabal (*The*), 1777. A faction organised to place General Gates at the head of the American army. He conquered Burgoyne, October, 1777, at Saratoga, and hoped to supplant Washington The Conway referred to is the town in New Brunswick, North America, where the cabal was formed.

General Gates was conquered in 1780 by Lord Cornwallis.

Con'yger or **Con'igry.** A warren for conies, a cony-burrow.

Cooing and Billing, like Philip and Mary on a shilling. The reference is to coins struck in the year 1555, in which Mary and her consort are placed face to face, and not cheek by jowl, the usual way.

"Still amorous, and fond, and billing,
Like Philip and Mary on a shilling."
Hudibras, part iii. 1.

Cook your Goose. (*See* GOOSE.)

Cooked. *The books have been cooked.* The ledger and other trade books have been tampered with, in order to show a balance in favour of the bankrupt. The term was first used in reference to George Hudson, the railway king, under whose chairmanship the Eastern Counties Railway accounts were falsified. The allusion is to preparing meat for table.

Cooking.
Terms belonging to cuisine applied to man under different circumstances:
Sometimes he is well *basted ;* he *boils* with rage, is *baked* with heat, and *burns* with love or jealousy. Sometimes he is *buttered* and well buttered ; he is often *cut up, devoured* with a flame, and *done brown.* We *dress his jacket* for him ; sometimes he is *eaten up* with care ; sometimes he

is *fried*. We cook his *goose* for him, and sometimes he makes a goose of himself. We make a *hash* of him, and at times he makes a hash of something else. He gets into *hot water*, and sometimes into a *mess*. Is made into *mincemeat*, makes mincemeat of his money, and is often in a *pickle*. We are often asked to *toast* him, sometimes he gets well *roasted*, is sometimes *set on fire*, put into a *stew*, or is in a *stew* no one knows why. A "*soft*" is *half-baked*, one severely handled is well *peppered*, to falsify accounts is to *salt* them, wit is *Attic salt*, and an exaggerated statement must be taken *cum grano salis*. A pert young person is a *sauce box*, a shy lover is a *spoon*, a rich father has to *fork out*, and is sometimes *dished* of his money.

ii. *Connected with foods and drinks.*

A conceited man does not think small *beer* (or small potatoes) of himself, and our mouth is called a potato-*trap*. A simpleton is a *cake*, a gudgeon, and a pigeon. Some are *cool as a cucumber*, others hot as a quail. A chubby child is a little *dumpling*. A man or woman may be a *cheese* or *duck*. A courtesan is called a *mutton*, and a large coarse hand is a mutton fist. A greedy person is a *pig*, a fat one is a *sausage*, and a shy one, if not a sheep, is certainly *sheepish ;* while a Lubin casts *sheep's eyes* at his lady-love. A coward is *chicken*-hearted, a fat person is *crummy*, and a cross one is *crusty*, while an aristocrat belongs to the *upper crust* of society. A yeoman of the guards is a *beef-eater*, a soldier a *red herring*, a policeman a *lobster*, and a stingy, ill-tempered old man is a *crab*. A walking advertiser between two boards is a *sandwich*. An alderman in his chair is a *turkey hung with sausages*. Two persons resembling each other are like as *two peas*. A chit is a mere *sprat*, a delicate maiden a *tit-bit*, and a colourless countenance is called a *whey-face*. "How now ? . . . Where got ye that whey-face ?"

Cooks. Athenæus affirms that cooks were the first kings of the earth.

In the luxurious ages of ancient Greece Sicilian cooks were most esteemed, and received very high wages. Among them Trimal'cio was very celebrated. It is said that he could cook the most common fish, and give it the flavour and look of the most highly esteemed. ·

In the palmy days of Rome a chief cook had £800 a year. Antony gave the cook who arranged his banquet for Cleopatra the present of a city.

Modern Cooks.

CAREME. Called the "Regenerator of Cookery" (1784-1833).

FRANCATELLI (*Charles Elmé*), who succeeded Ude at Crockford's. Afterwards he was appointed to the Royal household, and lastly to the Reform Club (1805-1876).

SOYER (*Alexis*), who died 1858. His epitaph is *Soyer tranquille.* ·

UDE. The most learned of modern cooks, author of *Science de Gueule.* It was Ude who said, "A cook must be born a cook, he cannot be made." Another of his sayings is this : "Music, dancing, fencing, painting, and mechanics possess professors under the age of twenty years, but pre-eminence in cookery can never be attained under thirty years of age." Ude was *chef* to Louis XIV., then to Lord Sefton, then to the Duke of York, then to Crockford's Club. He left Lord Sefton's because on one occasion one of the guests added pepper to his soup.

VATEL. At a fête given by the great Condé to Louis XIV. at Cantilly the *roti* at the twenty-fifth table was wanting. Vatel being told of it exclaimed that he could not survive such a disgrace. Another messenger then announced that the lobsters for the turbot-sauce had not arrived, whereupon Vatel retired to his room and, leaning his sword against the wall, thrust himself through, and at the third attempt succeeded in killing himself (1671).

WELTJE. Cook to George while Prince Regent.

Cool Card. *You are a cool card* (or *pretty cool card*). A person who coolly asks for something preposterous or outrageous. Card = character, hence a queer card, a rum card, etc. And "cool" in this connection means coolly impudent.

⁂ Gifford says the phrase means a "cooling-card, or *bolus*"; but this is not likely, as a cool-card acts generally as an irritant. A person's card of address is given at the door, and represents the person himself, and this without doubt is the card referred to.

"You're a shaky old card ; and you can't be in love with this Lizzie."—*Dickens: Our Mutual Friend*, book iii. chap. i. p. 192.

Cool as a Cucumber. Perfectly composed ; neither angry nor agitated in the least.

Cool Hundred (*A*) or *Cool Thousand* (or any other sum) means entire, or the whole of £100. Cool, in this case, means not influenced by hot-headed enthusiasm or exaggeration.

"I lost a cool hundred myself."—*Mackenzie.*

Cool Tankard (*A*) or *Cool Cup.* A drink made of wine and water, with lemon, sugar, and borage; sometimes also slices of cucumber.

Coon (*A*) means a racoon, a small American animal valued for its fur. It is about the size of a fox, and lodges in hollow trees.

A gone coon. A person in a terrible fix; one on the verge of ruin. The coon being hunted for its fur is a "gone coon" when it has no escape from its pursuers. It is said that Colonel Crockett was one day out racoon-shooting in North America, when he levelled his gun at a tree where an "old coon" was concealed. Knowing the colonel's prowess, it cried out, in the voice of a man, "Hallo, there! air you Colonel Crockett? for if you air, I'll jist come down, or I know I am a gone 'coon."

⁂ Martin Scott, lieutenant-general of the United States, is said to have had a prior claim to this saying.

Cooper. Half stout and half porter. The term arises from the practice at breweries of allowing the coopers a daily portion of stout and porter. As they do not like to drink porter after stout, they mix the two together.

Cooper. A coop for wine bottles. The bottles lie in a slanting position in the coop, and may be transported in it from place to place. We find allusions to "six-bottle coopers" not unfrequently, *i.e.* coops or cases containing six bottles. Compare "hen-coops," "cooped up," etc. (Latin, *cupa*, a cask; our "cup.")

"(Enter waiter with a cooper of wine.)
Waiter: Six bottles of wine for Corporal Foddy."   *O'Keeffe: Rogues All*, iii. 4.

Cooper. *Do you want a cooper?* This question is asked of those who have an order to visit the wine cellars of the London Docks. The "cooper" bores the casks and gives the visitor different wines to taste.

Cooper's Hill. Near Runnymede and Egham. Both Denham and Pope have written in praise of this hill.

"If I can be to thee
A poet, thou Parnassus art to me."
Denham.

Coot. *A silly old coot. Stupid as a coot.* The coot is a small water-fowl.

Bald as a coot. The coot has a strong, straight, and somewhat conical bill, the base of which tends to push up the forehead, and there dilates, so as to form a remarkable naked patch.

Cop (*A*). A policeman.

Cop (*A*). A copperhead (*q.v.*).

Cop. To throw, as *cop it here.* The word properly means to beat or strike, as to cop a shuttlecock or ball with a bat. (Greek, *copto*, to beat); but in Norfolk it means to "hull" or throw.

Cop (*To*). To catch [a fever, etc.]. To "get copped" is to get caught by the police. (Latin, *capere*, to take, etc.) A similar change of *a* into *o* is in *cotched* (caught).

"They thought I was sleepin', ye know,
And they sed as I'd copped it o' Jim;
Well, it come like a bit of a blow,
For I watched by the deathbed of him."
Sims: Dagonet Ballads (The Last Letter).

"'I shall cut this to-morrow, ...' said the younger man. 'You'll be copped, then,' replied the other."—*T. Terrell: Lady Delmar.*

Copenhagen. The Duke of Wellington's horse, on which he rode in the Battle of Waterloo, "from four in the morning till twelve at night." It was a rich chestnut, 15 hands high. It was afterwards a pensioner in the paddocks of Strathfieldsaye. It died quite blind, in 1835, at the age of twenty-seven, and was buried with military honours. (*See* HORSE.)

Copernicanism. The doctrine that the earth moves round the sun, in opposition to the doctrine that the sun moves round the earth; so called after Nicolas Copernicus, the Prussian astronomer. (1473-1543.)

"Even Bellarmine does not by any means hold the consensus to be decisive against Copernicanism; for, in his letter to F. Foscarini, he says that though he does not believe that any proof of the earth's motion can be adduced, yet, should such proof occur, he is quite prepared to change his views as to the meaning of the Scripture text."—*Nineteenth Century*, May, 1886 (*The Case of Galileo*).

"Whereas it has come to the knowledge of the Holy Congregation that that false Pythagorean doctrine altogether opposed to Holy Scripture, on the mobility of the earth and the immobility of the sun, taught by Nicholas Copernicus. . . . . This congregation has decreed that the said book of Copernicus be suspended until it be corrected."—*Decree of the H. Congregation of the Index*, A.D. 1616. (Quoted in the *Nineteenth Century*, as above.)

Copes'mate (2 syl.). A companion. "Copesmate of ugly night" (*Rape of Lucrece*), a mate who copes with you.

Cophet'ua. An imaginary king of Africa, of great wealth, who "disdained all womankind." One day he saw a beggar-girl from his window, and fell in love with her. He asked her name; it was Penel'ophon, called by Shakespeare Xenel'ophon (*Love's Labour's Lost*, iv. 1).

10

They lived together long and happily, and at death were universally lamented. (*Percy's Reliques,* book ii. 6.)

"King Cophetua loved the beggar-maid."
Shakespeare: Romeo and Juliet. ii. 1.

Copper (*A*). A policeman. Said to be so called from the copper badge which Fernando Wood, of New York, appointed them to wear ; but more likely a variant of " cop " (*q.v.*).

" There were cries of ' Coppers, Coppers !' in the yard, and then a violent struggle. . . . . Whoever it was that was wanted had been evidently secured and dragged off to gaol."—*T. Terrell: Lady Delmar,* 1.

Copper was by the ancient alchemists called Venus ; gold, symbol of Apollo (the sun) ; silver, of Diana (the moon) ; iron, of Mars ; quicksilver, of Mercury ; tin, of Jupiter ; and lead, of Saturn.

Copper. *Give us a copper, i.e.* a piece of copper money. *I have no coppers—* no ha'pence.

Copper Captain (*A*). A Brummagem captain ; a " General von Poffenburgh." Michael Perez is so called in *Rule a Wife and have a Wife,* by Beaumont and Fletcher.

" To this copper-captain was confided the command of the troops."—*W. Irving.*

Copper Nose. Oliver Cromwell ; also called " Ruby Nose," " Nosey," and " Nose Almighty," no doubt from some scorbutic tendency which showed itself in a big red nose.

Copper-nosed Harry. Henry VIII. When Henry VIII. had spent all the money left him by his miserly father, he minted an inferior silver coin, in which the copper alloy soon showed itself on the more prominent parts, especially the nose of the face ; and hence the people soon called the king " Old Copper-nose."

Copperheads. Secret foes. Copperheads are poisonous serpents of America that give no warning, like rattlesnakes, of their attack. In the great Civil War of the United States the term was applied by the Federals to the peace party, supposed to be the covert friends of the Confederates.

Cop'ple. The hen killed by Reynard, in the tale of *Reynard the Fox.*

Copronymus. So Constantine V. was surnamed (718, 741-775). " Kopros " is the Greek for dung, and Constantine V. was called Copronymus: " *Parce qu'il salit les fonts baptismaux lorsqu'on le baptisait.*"

Copts. The Jacobite Christians of Egypt, who have for eleven centuries been in possession of the patriarchal chair of Alexandria. The word is probably derived from Coptos, the metropolis of the Theba'id. These Christians conduct their worship in a dead language called " Coptic " (language of the Copts).

" The Copts [of Egypt] circumcise, confess to their priests, and abstain from swine's flesh. They are Jacobites in their creed."—*S. Olin ; Travels in Egypt* (vol. i. chap. viii. p. 102).

Co'pus. A drink made of beer, wine, and spice heated together, and served in a " loving-cup." Dog-Latin for *cupellon Hippoc'ratis* (a cup of hippocras).

Copy. *That's a mere copy of your countenance.* Not your real wish or meaning, but merely one you choose to present to me.

Copy is a printer's term both for original MS. and printed matter that is to be set up in type.

Cop'yhold Estate. Land which a tenant holds [or rather, *held*] without any deed of transfer in his own possession. His only document is a copy of the roll made by the steward of the manor from the court-roll kept in the manor-house.

" The villein took an'oath of fealty to his lord for the cottage and land which he enjoyed from his bounty. . . . These tenements were suffered to descend to their children . . . and thus the tenure of copyhold was established."—*Lingard: England* (vol. ii. chap. i. p. 27, note).

Copyright. The law of copyright was made in 1814 (54 Geo. III. c. 156). It enacted that an author should possess a right in his work for life, or for twenty-eight years. If he died before the expiration of twenty-eight years, the residue of the right passed to the heirs.

By Talfourd's or Lord Mahon's Act (1842) the time was extended to forty-two years, and at least seven years after decease : for example, if the time unexpired exceeds seven years, the heirs enjoy the residue ; if less, the heirs claim seven years.

∴ In the first case eleven copies of the work had to be given for public use ; by Lord Mahon's Act the number was reduced to five: *i.e.* one to each of the following institutions, viz. the British Museum, the Bodleian (Oxford), the University library (Cambridge), the Advocates' library (Edinburgh), and the library of Trinity College (Dublin).

The six omitted are Sion College, the Scotch Universities of Glasgow, Aberdeen, and St. Andrews, and King's Inn (Dublin).

Coq-à-l'âne. A cock-and-bull story ; idle nonsense, as " *Il fait toujours des coq-à-l'âne* "—he is always doing silly things, or talking rubbish.

Il m'a répondu par un coq-à-l'âne—
His reply was nothing to the purpose.

Co'rah, in Dryden's satire of *Absalom and Achitophel*, is meant for Dr. Titus Oates (Numbers xvi.). North describes him as a short man, extremely ugly : if his mouth is taken for the centre, his chin, forehead, and cheek-bones would fall in the circumference.

"Sunk were his eyes, his voice was harsh and
    loud ;
Sure signs he neither choleric was, nor proud ;
His long chin proved his wit ; his saint-like
    grace
A church vermilion, and a Mosca' face.
His memory, miraculously great,
Could plots, exceeding man's belief, repeat."
    Dryden : Absalom and Achitophel, i. 646-51.

Coral Beads. The Romans used to hang beads of red coral on the cradles and round the neck of infants, to "preserve and fasten their teeth," and save them from "the falling sickness." It was considered by soothsayers as a charm against lightning, whirlwind, shipwreck, and fire. Paracelsus says it should be worn round the neck of children as a preservative "against fits, sorcery, charms, and poison." The coral *bells* are a Roman Catholic addition, the object being to frighten away evil spirits by their jingle.

"Coral is good to be hanged about the neck of
children ... to preserve them from the falling
sickness. It has also some special sympathy with
nature, for the best coral ... will turn pale and
wan if the party that wears it be sick, and it
comes to its former colour again as they recover."
—*Plat: Jewel-House of Art and Nature.*

Cor'al Master. A juggler. So called by the Spaniards. In ancient times the juggler, when he threw off his mantle, appeared in a tight scarlet or coral dress.

Coram Judice (Latin). Under consideration ; still before the judge.

Cor'anach, or CORONACH. Lamentation for the dead, as anciently practised in Ireland and Celtic Scotland. (Gaelic, *comh ranaich*, crying together.) Pennant says it was called by the Irish *hululoo*.

Cor'bant. The rook, in the tale of *Reynard the Fox*. (Latin, *corvus;* French, *corbeau*.) Heinrich von Alkmar.

Corbeaux. Bearers, *i.e.* persons who carry the dead to the grave ; mutes, etc. So called from the corbillards, or *coches d'eau*, which went from Paris to Corbeil with the dead bodies of those who died in the 16th century of a fatal epidemic.

"J'ai lu quelque part que ce coche [the Corbil-
lard] servit, sous Henri IV., à transporter des
morts, victimes d'une épidémie de Paris à Corbeil.
Le nom de Corbillard resta depuis aux voitures
funèbres."—*Alf. Bonnardot.*

Corcēca [*Blind-heart*]. Superstition is so named in Spenser's *Faërie Queene*. Abessa tried to make her understand that danger was at hand, but, being blind, she was dull of comprehension. At length she was induced to shut her door, and when Una knocked would give no answer. Then the lion broke down the door, and both entered. The meaning is that England, the lion, broke down the door of Superstition at the Reformation. Corcēca means Romanism in England. (Book i. 3.)

Corcyre'an Sedition (*The*), B.C. 479. Corcyra was a colony of Corinth, but in the year of the famous Battle of Platæa revolted from the mother country and formed an alliance with the Athenians. The Corinthians made war on the colony and took 1,000 prisoners; of these 250 were men of position, who promised as the price of liberty to bring back the Corcyrēans to the mother country. This was the cause of the sedition. The 250 returned captives represented the oligarchical party ; their opponents represented the democratic element. The latter prevailed, but it would be difficult to parallel the treachery and brutality of the whole affair. (*Thucydidēs*, book iv. 46, 48.)

Corde'lia. The youngest of Lear's three daughters, and the only one that loved him. (*Shakespeare : King Lear.*)

Cordelia's Gift. A "voice ever soft, gentle, and low ; an excellent thing in woman." (*Shakespeare: King Lear*, v. 3.)

"It is her voice that he hears prevailing over
the those [*sic*] of the rest of the company, ...
for she has not Cordelia's gift."—*Miss Broughton:
Dr. Cupid.*

Corde'liers, *i.e.* "cord-wearers," 1215. A religious order of the Minor Brothers of St. Francis Assisi. They wore a large grey cloth vestment, girt about the loins with a rope or cord. It was one of the mendicant orders, not allowed to possess any property at all ; even their daily food was a gift of charity. The Cordeliers distinguished themselves in philosophy and theology. Duns Scotus was one of their most distinguished members.

The tale is that in the reign of St. Louis these Minorites repulsed an army of infidels, and the king asked who those *gens de cordelies* (corded people) were. From this they received their appellation.

Cordeliers (*The*), 1790. A French political club in the Great Revolution. It held its meetings in the "Convent des Cordeliers," which was in the "Place de l'École de Médecine." The Cordeliers were the rivals of the Jacobins, and numbered among its members Paré (the president), Danton, Marat, Camille Desmoulins, Hébert, Chaumette, Dufournoy de Villiers, Fabre d'Eglantine (a journalist), and others. The Club of the Cordeliers was far in advance of the Jacobins, being the first to demand the abolition of the monarchy and the establishment of a commonwealth instead. Its leaders were put to death between March 24th and April 5th, 1794.

This club was nicknamed "The Pandemonium," and Danton was called the "Archfiend." When Bailly, the mayor, locked them out of their hall in 1791, they met in the Tennis Court (Paris), and changed their name into the "Society of the Rights of Man"; but they are best known by their original appellation.

Cordon (*The*), in fortification, is the flat stone covering of the revetment (*q.v.*), to protect the masonry from the rain.

Cordon (*Un grand*). A member of the *Legion d'Honneur*. The cross is attached to a *grand* (broad) ribbon.

Cordon Bleu (*Un*) (French). A knight of the ancient order of the *St. Esprit* (Holy Ghost); so called because the decoration is suspended on a blue ribbon. It was at one time the highest order in the kingdom.

Un repas de cordon bleu. A well-cooked and well-appointed dinner. The commandeur de Souvé, Comte d'Olonne, and some others, who were cordons bleus (*i.e.* knights of St. Esprit), met together as a sort of club, and were noted for their excellent dinners. Hence, when anyone had dined well he said, "*Bien, c'est un vrai repas de cordon bleu.*"

Une Cordon Bleu. A facetious compliment to a good female cook. The play is between *cordon bleu*, and the blue ribbons or strings of some favourite cook.

Cordon Noir (*Un*). A knight of the Order of St. Michael, distinguished by a black ribbon.

Cordon Rouge (*Un*) (French). A chevalier of the Order of *St. Louis*, the decoration being suspended on a red ribbon.

Cord'uroy. A corded fabric, originally made of silk, and worn by the kings of France in the chase. (French, *cord du roy*.)

Corduroy Road. A term applied to roads in the backwoods and swampy districts of the United States of America, formed of the halves of trees sawn in two longitudinally, and laid transversely across the track. A road thus made presents a ribbed appearance, like the cloth called corduroy.

"Look well to your seat, 'tis like taking an airing
On a corduroy road, and that out of repairing."
Lowell: Fable for Critics, stanza 2.

Cord'wainer. Not a twister of cord, but a worker in leather. Our word is the French *cordouannier* (a maker or worker of *cordouan*); the former a corruption of *Cordovanier* (a worker in Cordovan leather).

Corea (*The*). The dancing mania, which in 1800 appeared in Tennessee, Kentucky, and Virginia. The usual manifestations were laughing, shouting, dancing, and convulsions. (Latin *chorĕa*, a dance where many dance simultaneously.)

Corflam'bo. The impersonation of sensual passion in Spenser's *Faërie Queene.* (Book iv. 8.)

Cori'neus (3 syl.). A mythical hero in the suite of Brute, who conquered the giant Goëm'agot, for which achievement the whole western horn of England was allotted him. He called it Corin'ea, and the people Corin'eans, from his own name.

"In meed of these great conquests by them got,
Corineus had that province utmost west
To him assyned for his worthy lot,
Which of his name and memorable gest,
He called Cornwall."
Spenser: Faërie Queene, ii. 10.

Corinnus. A Greek poet before the time of Homer. He wrote in heroic verse the *Siege of Troy,* and it is said that Homer is considerably indebted to him. (*Suidas.*)

Corinth. *Non cuivis homini contingit adire Corinthum* (It falls not to every man's lot to go to Corinth). Gellius, in his *Noctes Atticæ,* i. 8, says that Horace refers to Laïs, a courtesan of Corinth, who sold her favours at so high a price that not everyone could afford to purchase them; but this most certainly is not the meaning that Horace intended. He says, "To please princes is no little praise, for it falls not to every man's lot to go to Corinth." That is, it is as hard to please princes as it is to enter Corinth, situated between two seas, and hence called Bimăris Corinthus. (1 *Odes,* vii. line 2.)

☞ Still, without doubt, the proverb was applied as Aulus Gellius says: "The courtesans of Corinth are not every man's money." Demosthenes tells us that Laïs sold her favours for 10,000 [Attic] drachmæ (about £300), and adds *tanti non emo pœnitere*. (*Horace*: 1 *Epistles*, xvii. line 36.)

Corinth. *There is but one road that leads to Corinth.* There is only one right way of doing anything. The Bible tells us that the way of evil is broad, because of its many tracks ; but the way of life is narrow, because it has only one single footpath.

" All other ways are wrong, all other guides are false. Hence my difficulty!—the number and variety of the ways. For you know, 'There is but one road that leads to Corinth.'"—*Pater : Marius the Epicurean*, chap. 24.

Corinth's Pedagogue. Dionys'ios the younger, on being banished a second time from Syracuse, went to Corinth and became schoolmaster. He is called Dionysios the *tyrant*. Hence Lord Byron says of Napoleon—

" Corinth's pedagogue hath now Transferred his by-word to thy brow." *Ode to Napoleon*, stanza xiv.

Corin'thian (*A*). A licentious libertine. The immorality of Corinth was proverbial both in Greece and Rome. To *Corin'thianise* is to indulge in licentious conduct. A gentleman sportsman who rides his own horses on the turf, or sails his own yacht.

A Corinthian. A member of the pugilistic club, Bond Street, London.

Corinthian Brass. A mixed metal made by a variety of metals melted at the conflagration of Corinth in B.C. 116, when the city was burnt to the ground by the consul Mummius. Vases and other ornaments were made by the Romans of this metal, of greater value than if they had been made of silver or gold.

The Hong-hee vases (1426) of China were made of a similar mixed metal when the Imperial palace was burnt to the ground. These vessels are of priceless value.

" I think it may be of Corinthian brass, Which was a mixture of all metals, but The brazen uppermost." *Byron : Don Juan*, vi. 56.

Corin'thian Order. The most richly decorated of the five orders of Greek architecture. The shaft is fluted, and the capital adorned with acanthus leaves. (*See* ACANTHUS.)

Corinthian Tom. The sporting rake in Pierce Egan's *Life in London*. A " Corinthian " was the " fast man " of Shakespeare's period.

" I am no proud Jack, like Falstaff ; but a Corinthian, a lad of mettle, a good boy."—*Shakespeare*: 1 *Henry IV.*, ii. 4.

Corinthian War (*The*), B.C. 395-387. A suicidal contention between the Corinthians and the Lacedemonians. The

allies of Corinth were Athens, Thebes, and Argos. The only battle of note was that of Coronea won by the Lacedemonians. Both the contending parties, utterly exhausted, agreed to the arbitration of Artaxerxes, and signed what is called The Peace of Antalkidas.

Not long after this destructive contest Epaminondas and Pelopidas (Theban generals) won the battle of Leuctra (B.C. 371), from which defeat the Lacedemonians never recovered.

Corked. *This wine is corked—i.e.* tastes of the cork.

Corker or **Calker.** The nail in a horse's shoe to prevent slipping in frosty weather. (Latin, *calx*.)

Corking-pins. Pins at one time used by ladies to keep curls on the forehead fixed and in trim.

Cor'moran'. The Cornish giant who fell into a pit twenty feet deep, dug by Jack the Giant-killer, and filmed over with grass and gravel. The name means cormorant or great eater. For this doughty achievement Jack received a belt from King Arthur, with this inscription—

" This is the valiant Cornish man That slew the giant Cormoran." *Jack the Giant-killer.*

Corn ... Horn. *Up corn, down horn.* When corn is high or dear, beef is down or cheap, because persons have less money to spend on meat.

Corn in Egypt (*There's*). There is abundance ; there is a plentiful supply. Of course, the reference is to the Bible story of Joseph in Egypt.

Corn - Law Rhymer. Ebenezer Elliot, who wrote philippics against the corn laws (1781-1849).

" Is not the corn-law rhymer already a king?" —*Carlyle*.

Cornstalks. In Australia and the United States, youths of colonial birth are so called from being generally both taller and more slender than their parents.

Corns. *To tread on one's corns.* To irritate one's prejudices ; to annoy another by disregard to his pet opinions or habits.

Cor'nage (2 syl.), horn-service. A kind of tenure in grand serjeanty. The service required was to blow a horn when any invasion of the Scots was perceived. " Cornagium " was money paid instead of the old service.

Corneille du Boulevard. Guilbert de Pixérécourt (1773-1844).

Corneille d'Esope (*La*). Motley work. " *C'est la corneille d'Esope.*"

The allusion is to the fable of the Jackdaw which decked itself with the plumage of the peacocks. The jackdaw not only lost its borrowed plumes, but got picked well-nigh to death by the angry peacocks.

Corner (*A*). The condition of the market with respect to ·a commodity which has been largely bought up, in order to create a virtual monopoly and enhance its market price; as a salt-corner, a corner in pork, etc. The idea is that the goods are piled and hidden in a corner out of sight.

"The price of bread rose like a rocket, and speculators wished to corner what little wheat there was."—*New York Weekly Times* (June 13, 1894).

Corner. *Driven into a corner.* Placed where there is no escape; driven from all subterfuges and excuses.

Corner (*The*). Tattersall's horse-stores and betting-rooms, Knightsbridge Green. They were once at *the corner* of Hyde Park.

To make ·a corner. To combine in order to control the price of a given article, and thus secure enormous profits. (*See* CORNER.)

What have I done to deserve a corner? To deserve punishment. The allusion is to setting naughty children in a corner by way of punishment.

"There's nothing I have done yet, o' my conscience,
Deserves a corner."
    Shakespeare: Henry VIII., iii. 1.

Corner-stone (*The*). *The chief corner-stone.* A large stone laid at the base of a building to strengthen the two walls forming a right angle. These stones in some ancient buildings were as much as twenty feet long and eight feet thick. Christ is called (in Eph. ii. 20) the chief corner-stone because He united the Jews and Gentiles into one family. Daughters are called corner-stones (Psalm cliv. 12) because, as wives and mothers, they unite together two families. In argument, the minor premise is the chief corner-stone.

Cornet. *The terrible cornet of horse.* William Pitt, first Earl of Chatham (1708-1778). His son William was "the pilot that weathered the storm" (meaning the French Revolution and Napoleon).

Cornette. *Porter la cornette.* To be domineered over by the woman of the house; to be a Jerry Sneak. The cornette is the mob-cap anciently worn by the women of France. *Porter les culottes* (to wear the breeches) is the same idea;

only it shows who has the mastery, and not who is mastered. In the latter case it means the woman wears the dress of the man, and assumes his position in the house. Probably our expression about "wearing the horns" may be referred to the "cornette" rather than to the stag or deer.

Corn'grate (2 syl.). A term given in Wiltshire to the soil in the north-western border, consisting of an irregular mass of loose gravel, sand, and limestone.

Cornish Hug. A hug to overthrow you. The Cornish men were famous wrestlers, and tried to throttle their antagonist with a particular grip or embrace called the Cornish hug.

Cornish Language was virtually extinct 150 years ago. Doll Pentreath, the last person who could speak it, died, at the age of ninety-one, in 1777. (*Notes and Queries.*)

Cornish Names.
  "By Tre, Pol, and Pen,
   You shall know the Cornishmen."

Thus, *Tre* [a town] gives Trefry, Tregengon, Tregony, Tregothnan, Trelawy, Tremayne, Trevannion, Treveddoe, Trewithen, etc.

Pol [a head] gives Polkerris Point, Polperro, Polwheel, etc.

Pen [a top] gives Penkevil, Penrice, Penrose, Pentire, etc.

Cornish Wonder (*The*). John Opie, of Cornwall, the painter. (1761-1807.)

Cornubian Shore (*The*). Cornwall, famous for its tin mines.

". . . from the bleak Cornubian shore
Dispense the mineral treasure, which of old
Sidonian pilots sought."
    Akenside: Hymn to the Naiads.

Cornu-co'pia. (*See* AMALTHÆA'S HORN.)

Cornwall. (*See* BARRY, CORINEUS.)

Cor'onach. (*See* CORANACH.)

Coronation Chair consists of a stone so enclosed as to form a chair.

It was probably the stone on which the kings of Ireland were inaugurated on the hill of Tara. It was removed by Fergus, son of Eric, to Argyleshire, and thence by King Kenneth (in the ninth century) to Scone, where it was enclosed in a wooden chair. Edward I. transferred it to Westminster.

The monkish legend says that it was the very stone which formed "Jacob's pillow."

The tradition is, "Wherever this stone

is found, there will reign some of the Scotch race of kings." (*See* Scone.)

Cor'oner means properly the crown-officer. In Saxon times it was his duty to collect the Crown revenues; next, to take charge of Crown pleas; but at present to uphold the paternal solicitude of the Crown by searching into all cases of sudden or suspicious death. (Vulgo, *crowner*; Latin, *coro'na*, the crown.)

" But is this law ?
Ay, marry, is't: crowner's quest law."
Shakespeare: Hamlet, v. 1.

Cor'onet. A crown inferior to the royal crown. A duke's coronet is adorned with strawberry leaves above the band; that of a *marquis* with strawberry leaves alternating with pearls; that of an *earl* has pearls elevated on stalks, alternating with leaves above the band; that of a *viscount* has a string of pearls above the band, but no leaves; that of a *baron* has only six pearls.

Coro'nis. Daughter of a King of Pho'cis, changed by Athe'na into a crow. There was another Coro'nis, loved by Apollo, and killed by him for infidelity.

Corporal Violet. (*See* Violet.)

Corporation. A large paunch.
A municipal corporation is a body of men elected for the local government of a city or town.

Corps de Garde (French). The company of men appointed to watch in a guard-room; the guard-room.

Corps Diplomatique (French). A diplomatic body [of men].

Corps Legislatif (French). The lower house of the French legislature. The first assembly so called was when Napoleon I. substituted a *corps legislatif* and a tribunal for the two councils of the Directory, Dec. 24, 1799. The next was the *corps legislatif* and *conseil d'état* of 1807. The third was the *corps legislatif* of 750 deputies of 1849. The legislative power under Napoleon III. was vested in the Emperor, the *senate*, and the *corps legislatif*. (1852.)

Corpse Candle. The *ignis fatuus* is so called by the Welsh because it was supposed to forbode death, and to show the road that the corpse would take. Also a large candle used at lich wakes—*i.e.* watching a corpse before interment. (German *leiche*, a corpse.)

Corpus Christi [*body of Christ*]. A festival of the Church, kept on the first Thursday after Trinity Sunday, in honour of the eucharist. There are colleges both at Cambridge and Oxford so named.

Corpus Delicti (Latin). The fundamental fact that a crime has really been committed; thus finding a murdered body is " corpus delicti " that a murder has been committed by someone.

Corpuscular Philosophy, promulgated by Robert Boyle. It accounts for all natural phenomena by the position and motion of corpuscles. (*See* Atomic Philosophy.)

Corrector. (*See* Alexander the Corrector.)

Corre'ggio. *The Corre'ggio of sculptors.* Jean Goujon, who was slain in the massacre of St. Bartholomew. (1510-1572.)

Corrob'oree. An Australian war-dance.
" He roared, stamped, and danced corroboree, like any black fellow."—*Kingsley: Water-Babies*, chap. viii. p. 300.

Corrouge. The sword of Sir Ot'uel in mediæval romance. (*See* Sword.)

Corrugated Iron. Sheet iron coated with zinc. It is called corrugated or wrinkled because the sheet is made wavy by the rollers between which it is made to pass.

Corruptic'olæ. A sect of heretics of the sixth century, who maintained that Jesus Christ was *corruptible.*

Corruption of Blood. Loss of title and entailed estates in consequence of treason, by which a man's *blood* is *attainted* and his issue suffers.

Corsair' means properly " one who gives chase." Applied to the pirates of the northern coast of Africa. (Italian *corso*, a chase; French *corsaire;* Latin *cursus*.)

Cors'ned means the " cursed mouthful." It was a piece of bread " consecrated for exorcism," and given to a person to swallow as a test of his guilt. The words of " consecration " were, " May this morsel cause convulsions and find no passage if the accused is guilty, but turn to wholesome nourishment if he is innocent." (Saxon, *corse,* curse; *snæd*, mouthful.) (*See* Choke.)

Cor'tes (2 syl.). The Spanish or Portuguese parliament. The word means " court officers."

Corti'na. The skin of the serpent Pytho, which covered the tripod of the Pythoness when she delivered her oracles. " Tripodas cortina tegit " (*Prudentius : Apophthegmata*, 506) ; also the tripod itself, or the place where the oracle was delivered. (*Virgil : Æneid*, vi. 345.) " Neque te Phœbi cortina fefellit."

Corvi'nus [*a raven*]. Ja'nos Hun'yady, Governor of Hungary, is so called from the raven on his shield.

There were two Romans so called—viz. Vale'rius Max'imus Corvi'nus Messa'la, and Vale'rius Messa'la Corvi'nus.

Marcus Vale'rius was so called because, in a single combat'with a gigantic Gaul during the Gallic war, a raven flew into the Gaul's face and so harassed him that he could neither defend himself nor attack his adversary.

Corybantic Religion. An expression applied by Prof. Huxley to the Salvation Army and its methods. The rowdy processions of the Salvation Army (especially at Eastbourne, 1891), resembling the wild ravings of the ancient Corybantēs, or devotees of Bacchus, more than sober, religious functions, have given colour to the new word.

Corycian Cave (*The*), on Mount Parnassus ; so called from the nymph Corycia. The Muses are sometimes called Corycĭdes (4 syl.).

" The immortal Muse
To your calm habitations, to the cave
Corycian . . . will guide his footsteps."
Akenside : Hymn to the Naiads.

Corycian Nymphs (*The*). The Muses. (*See above.*)

Cor'ydon. A swain ; a brainless, love-sick spooney. It is one of the shepherds in Virgil's eclogues.

Coryphæ'us (*The*) or " Coryphēus." The leader and speaker of the chorus in Greek dramas. In modern English it is used to designate the chief speaker and most active member of a board, company, or expedition.

Coryphæus of German Literature (*The*). Goethe, "prince of German poets " (1749-1812).

"The Polish poet called upon . . . . the great Coryphæus of German literature."—See *Notes and Queries*, 27th April, 1878.

Coryphæus of Grammarians. Aristarchos of Sam'othrace. A coryphæus was the leader of the Greek chorus ; hence the chief of a department in any of the sciences or fine arts. Aristarchos, in the second century B.C., was the chief or prince of grammarians. (Greek, *koruphaios*, leader.)

Coryphée. A ballet-dancer. (*See preceding column.*)

Cosa (plu. Cosas). A theoretic speculation ; a literary fancy ; a whim of the brain (*Indian*).

Cos'miel (3 syl.). The genius of the world. He gave Theodidac'tus a boat of asbestos, in which he sailed to the sun and planets. (*Kircher : Ecstatic Journey to Heaven.*)

Cosmop'olite (4 syl.). A citizen of the world. One who has no partiality to any one country as his abidingplace ; one who looks on the whole world with " an equal eye." (Greek, *cosmospoli'tēs.*)

Cos'set. A house pet. Applied to a pet lamb brought up in the house ; any pet. (Anglo-Saxon, *cot-seat*, cottagedweller ; German, *kossat*.)

Cos'tard. A clown in *Love's Labour's Lost* (Shakespeare), who apes the court wit of Queen Elizabeth's time, but misapplies and miscalls like Mrs. Malaprop or Master Dogberry.

Costard. A large apple, and, metaphorically, a man's head. (*See* COSTERMONGER.)

"Take him over the costard with the hilts of thy sword."—*Shakespeare : Richard III.*, i. 4.

Cos'termonger. A seller of eatables about the streets, properly an appleseller (from *costard*, a sort of apple, and *monger*, "a trader ;" Saxon, *mangian*, "to trade "), a word still retained in ironmonger, cheese-monger, fish-monger, news-monger, fell-monger, etc.

"Her father was an Irish costarmonger."
B. Jonson : The Alchemist, iv. 1.

Cote-hardi. A tight-fitting tunic buttoned down the front.

"He was clothed in a cote-hardi upon the gyse of Almayne [Germany]."—*Geoffroi de la Tour : Landry.*

Cotereaux (French). Cut-throats. The King of England, irritated at the rising in Brittany in the twelfth century, sent the Brabançons (*q.v.*) to ravage the lands of Raoul de Fourgères. These cut-throats carried knives (*couteaux*) with them, whence their name.

Co'terie' (3 syl.). A French word, originally tantamount to our " guild," a society where each paid his *quota*—*i.e.* his quote-part or gild (*share*). The French word has departed from its original meaning, and is now applied to an exclusive set, more especially of ladies.

"All coteries . . . it seems to me, have a tendency to change truth into affectation."—*E. C. Gaskell : Charlotte Brontë* (vol. ii. chap. xi. p. 47).

Cotillon (*co-til'-yon*) means properly the "under-petticoat." The word was applied to a brisk dance by eight persons, in which the ladies held up their gowns and showed their under-petticoats. The dance of the present day is an elaborate one, with many added figures.

Cotset. The lowest of bondsmen. So called from *cot-seat* (a cottage-dweller). These slaves were bound to work for their feudal lord. The word occurs frequently in *Domesday Book*.

Cotswold Barley. *You are as long a-coming as Cotswold barley.* Cotswold, in Gloucestershire, is a very cold, bleak place on the wolds, exposed to the winds, and very backward in vegetation, but yet it yields a good late supply of barley.

Cotswold Lion. A sheep for which Cotswold hills are famous. *Fierce as a Cotswold lion* (ironical).

Cotta, in Pope's *Moral Essays* (Epistle 2). John Holles, fourth Earl of Clare, who married Margaret, daughter of Henry Cavendish, Duke of Newcastle, and was created Duke of Newcastle in 1694 and died 1711.

Cottage Countess (*The*). Sarah Higgins, of Shropshire, daughter of a small farmer, in 1790 married Henry Cecil, Marquis of Exeter and Lord of Burleigh. The bridegroom was at the time living under the name of John Jones, separated from his wife, whose maiden name was Emma Vernon. She eloped with a clergyman, and subsequently to the second marriage "John Jones," the lord of Burleigh, obtained a divorce and an Act of Parliament to legitimatise the children of his second wife. Sarah Higgins was seventeen at the time of her marriage, and "John Jones" was thirty. They were married by licence in the parish church of Bolas. Tennyson has a poem on the subject called *The Lord of Burleigh*, but historically it is not to be trusted.

Cottage Orné (*A*) (French). A cottage residence belonging to persons in good circumstances.

Cottys. One of the three Hundred-handed giants, son of Heaven and Earth. His two brothers were Briareus [*Bri-a-ruce*] and Gygēs or Gyēs. (*See* HUNDRED-HANDED, GIANTS.)

Cotton. *To cotton to a person.* To cling to one or take a fancy to a person. To stick to a person as cotton sticks to our clothes.

10*

Cotton Lord. *A great cotton lord.* A rich Manchester cotton manufacturer, a real lord in wealth, style of living, equipage, and tenantry.

Cotto'nian Library. In the British Museum. Collected by Sir R. Cotton, and added to by his son and grandson, after which it was invested in trustees for the use of the public.

Cottonopolis. Manchester, the great centre of cotton manufactures.

"His friends thought he would have preferred the busy life of Cottonopolis to the out-of-way county of Cornwall." — *Newspaper paragraph*, January, 1886.

Cotyt'to. The Thracian goddess of immodesty, worshipped at Athens with nocturnal rites.

"Hail! goddess of nocturnal sport,
Dark-veiled Cotytto."
Milton: Comus, 129, 130.

Coucy. Enguerrand III., Sire de Coucy, has won fame by his arrogant motto:

"Roi je ne suis,
Ni Prince, ni comte, aussi,
Je suis Le Sire de Coucy."

Couleur de Rose (French). Highly coloured; too favourably considered, overdrawn with romantic embellishments, like objects viewed through glass tinted with rose pink.

Coulin. A British giant, pursued by Debon (one of the companions of Brute) till he came to a chasm 132 feet across, which he leaped; but slipping on the opposite side, he fell back into the chasm and was killed. (*Spenser: Faërie Queene.*) (*See* GIANTS.)

Councils. *Œcumenical Councils.* There are twenty-one recognised, nine Eastern and twelve Western.

THE NINE EASTERN: (1) Jerusalem; (2 and 8) Nice, 325, 787; (3, 6, 7, 9) Constantinople, 381, 553, 680, 869; (4) Ephesus, 431; (5) Chalcēdon, 451.

THE TWELVE WESTERN: (10, 11, 12, 13, 19) Lat'eran, 1123, 1139, 1179, 1215, 1517; (14, 15) Synod of Lyon, 1245, 1274; (16) Synod of Vienne, in Dauphiné, 1311; (17) Constance, 1414; (18) Basil, 1431-1443; (20) Trent, 1545-1563; (21) Vatican, 1869.

⁑ Of these, the Church of England recognises only the first six, viz.:

325 of *Nice*, against the Arians.
381 of *Constantinople*, against "heretics."
431 of *Ephesus*, against the Nestorians and Pelagians.
451 of *Chalcē'don*, when Athanasius was restored.
553 of *Constantinople*, against Origen.
680 of *Constantinople*, against the Monothelites (4 syl.).

Counsel. *Keep your own counsel.* Don't talk about what you intend to do. Keep your plans to yourself.

"Now, mind what I tell you, and keep your own counsel." — *Boldrewood : Robbery Under Arms*, chap. vi.

Count Kin with One. (*To*), is a Scotch expression meaning to compare one's pedigree with that of another.

Count not your Chickens . . . (*See* CHICKENS.)

Count out the House (*To*). To declare the House of Commons adjourned because there are not forty members present. The Speaker has his attention called to the fact, and must himself count the number present. If he finds there are not forty members present, he declares the sitting over.

Count Upon (*To*). To rely with confidence on some one or some thing; to reckon on.

Countenance (*To*). To sanction; to support. Approval or disapproval is shown by the countenance. The Scripture speaks of "the light of God's countenance," *i.e.* the smile of approbation; and to "hide His face" (or countenance) is to manifest displeasure.

"General Grant, neither at this time nor at any other, gave the least countenance to the efforts . . ."—*Nicolay and Hay: Abraham Lincoln* (vol. ix. chap. ii. p. 51).

To keep in countenance. To encourage, or prevent one losing his countenance or feeling dismayed.
To keep one's countenance. To refrain from smiling or expressing one's thoughts by the face.
Out of countenance. Ashamed, confounded. With the countenance fallen or cast down.
To put one out of countenance is to make one ashamed or disconcerted. To "discountenance" is to set your face against something done or propounded.

Counter-caster. One who keeps accounts, or casts up accounts by counters. Thus, in *The Winter's Tale*, the Clown says, "Fifteen hundred shorn; what comes the wool to? I cannot do 't without counters." (Act iv. s. 3.)

"And what was he?
Forsooth, a great arithmetician, . . .
And I . . . must be belee'd and calmed
By debitor and creditor, this counter-caster."
Shakespeare: Othello, i. 1.

Countercheck Quarrelsome (*The*). Sir, how dare you utter such a falsehood? Sir, you know that it is not true. This is the third remove from the lie direct;

or rather, the lie direct in the third degree.

The Reproof Valiant, the Countercheck Quarrelsome, the Lie Circumstantial, and the Lie Direct, are not clearly defined by Touchstone. *That* is not true; how *dare* you utter such a falsehood; *if* you say so, you are a liar; you lie, or are a liar, seem to fit the four degrees.

Counterforts, in permanent fortification. The sides of ditches strengthened interiorly by buttresses some fifteen or eighteen feet apart. (*See* REVETMENTS.)

Counter-jumper. A draper's assistant, who jumps over the counter to go from one part of the shop to another.

Counterpane. A corruption of *counterpoint*, from the Latin *cul cita* (a wadded wrapper, a quilt). When the stitches were arranged in patterns it was called *cul'cita puncta*, which in French became *courte-pointe*, corrupted into *contre-pointe, counter-point*, where point is pronounced "poyn," corrupted into "pane."

Counterscarp, in fortification, the side of a ditch next to the open country. The side next to the place fortified is the *escarp.*

Countess di Civillari (*The*). A bog, sewer, cesspool, into which falls the filth of a city. Two wags promised Simon da Villa an introduction to the Countess di Civillari, and tossed him, in his scarlet gown, into a ditch where farmers "emptied the Countess of Civillari for manuring their lands." Here the doctor floundered about half the night, and, having spoilt his robes, made the best of his way home, to be rated soundly by his wife. (*Boccaccio: Decameron*, Eighth day, ix.)

Country.
To appeal to the country. To dissolve Parliament in order to ascertain the wish of the country by a new election of representatives.
Father of his country. (*See* FATHER.)

Country-dance. A corruption of the French *contre danse* (a dance where the partners face each other).

Coup [*coo*]. *He made a good coup.* A good hit or haul. (French.)

Coup d'Etat (French) means a state stroke, and the term is applied to one of those bold measures taken by Government to prevent a supposed or actual danger; as when a large body of men are arrested suddenly for fear they should overturn the Government.

The famous *coup d'état*, by which Louis Napoleon became possessed of absolute power, took place on December 2nd, 1851.

Coup de Grâce. The finishing stroke. When criminals were tortured by the wheel or otherwise, the executioner gave him a *coup de grâce*, or blow on the head or breast, to put him out of his misery.

"The Turks dealt the *coup de grâce* to the Eastern empire."—*Times.*

❊ The following is taken from a note (chap. **xxx.**) of Sir W. Scott's novel *The Betrothed.*

"This punishment [being broken on the wheel] consists in the executioner, with a bar of iron, breaking the shoulder-bones, arms, thigh-bones, and legs—taking alternate sides. The punishment is concluded by a blow across the breast, called the *coup de grâce*, or blow of mercy, because it removes the sufferer from his agony. Mandrin, the celebrated smuggler, while in the act of being thus tortured, tells us that the sensibility of pain never continues after the nervous system has been shattered by the first blow."

Coup de Main (French). A sudden stroke ; a stratagem whereby something is effected suddenly. Sometimes called a *coup* only, as "The *coup* [the scheme] did not answer."

"London is not to be taken by a *coup de main.*"—*Public Opinion.*

Coup d'Œil (French). A view ; glance ; prospect ; effect of things in the mass.

These principles are presented at a single *coup d'œil.*

The *coup d'œil* was grand in the extreme.

Coup de Pied de l'Ane (kick from the ass's foot). A blow given to a vanquished or fallen man ; a cowardly blow ; an insult offered to one who has not the power of returning or avenging it. The allusion is to the fable of the sick lion kicked by the ass. (French.)

Coup de Soleil (French). A sunstroke, any malady produced by exposure to the sun.

Coup de Théâtre. An unforeseen or unexpected turn in a drama to produce a sensational effect. In ordinary life, something planned for effect. Burke and his dagger was meant for a *coup de théâtre*, but it was turned into farce by a little ready wit. (*See* DAGGER-SCENE.)

Coup Manqué (*A*). A false stroke.

"Shoot dead, or don't aim at all ; but never make a *coup manqué.*"—*Ouida: Under Two Flags,* chap. xx.

Coupon. A certificate of interest which is to be cut off [French, *couper*] from a bond and presented for payment. It bears on its face the date and amount of interest to be paid. If the coupons

are exhausted before the principal is paid off, new ones are gratuitously supplied to the holder of the bond.

Most foreign state-bonds expire in a stated term of years, generally a portion being paid off annually at par. Suppose there are 1,000 bonds, and 10 are paid off annually, then in 100 years all are paid off and the obligation is cancelled.

Courage of One's Opinion. To have the courage of one's opinion means to utter, maintain, and act according to one's opinion, be the consequences what they may. The French use the same locution. Martyrs may be said to have had the courage of their opinions.

Courland Weather. Very boisterous, uncongenial weather, with high winds, driving snow and rain, like the weather of Courland, in Russia.

Course. *Another course would have done it.* A little more would have effected our purpose. It is said that the peasants of a Yorkshire village tried to wall in a cuckoo in order to enjoy an eternal spring. They built a wall round the bird, and the cuckoo just skimmed over it. "Ah!" said one of the peasants, "another carse would a' done it."

"There is a school of moralists who, connecting sundry short-comings . . . . with changes in manners, endeavour to persuade us that only 'another carse' is wanted to wall in the cuckoo." —*Nineteenth Century,* December, 1892, p. 920.

Course. *To keep on the course.* To go straight ; to do one's duty in that course [path] of life in which we are placed. The allusion is to racing horses.

"We are not the only horses that can't be kept on the courses—with a good turn of speed, too." —*Boldrewood : Robbery under Arms,* chap. xv.

Court originally meant a coop or sheepfold. It was on the Latium hills that the ancient Latins raised their *cors* or *cohors*, small enclosures with hurdles for sheep, etc. Subsequently, as many men as could be cooped or folded together were called a *corps* or *cohort.* The "cors" or cattle-yard being the nucleus of the farm, became the centre of a lot of farm cottages, then of a hamlet, town, fortified place, and lastly of a royal residence.

Court. A short cut, alley, or paved way between two main streets. (French, *court,* "short," as *prendre un chemin court,* "to take a short cut.")

Out of court. Not worth consideration ; wholly to be discarded, as such and such an hypothesis is wholly out of court, and has been proved to be untenable. "No true bill."

Court Circular. Brief paragraphs supplied to certain daily papers by an officer (the Court Newsman) specially appointed for the purpose. He announces the movements of the sovereign, the Prince of Wales, and the court generally; gives reports of the levees, drawing-rooms, state balls, royal concerts, meetings of the Cabinet ministers, deputations to ministers, and so on. George III., in 1803, introduced the custom to prevent misstatements on these subjects.

Court-cupboard. The buffet to hold flagons, cans, cups, and beakers. There are two in Stationers' Hall.

" Away with the joint-stools, remove the court-cupboard, look to the plate." — *Shakespeare: Romeo and Juliet*, i. 5.

Court Fools. (*See* FOOLS.)

Court Holy Water. Fair speeches, which look like promises of favour, but end in nothing.

Court Plaster. The plaster of which the court ladies made their patches. These patches, worn on the face, were cut into the shape of crescents, stars, circles, diamonds, hearts, crosses; and some even went so far as to patch their face with a coach-and-four, a ship in full sail, a château, etc. This ridiculous fashion was in vogue in the reign of Charles I.; and in the reign of Anne was employed as the badge of political partisanship. (*See* PATCHES.)

" Your black patches you wear variously,
Some cut like stars, some in half-moons, some lozenges."
Beaumont and Fletcher: Elder Brother, iii. 2.

Court of Love. A judicial court for deciding affairs of the heart, established in Provence during the palmy days of the Troubadours. The following is a case submitted to their judgment: A lady listened to one admirer, squeezed the hand of another, and touched with her toe the foot of a third. Query, Which of these three was the favoured suitor?

Court of Pie-powder. (*See* PIE-POUDRE.)

Court of the Gentiles (*The*). *They are but in the Court of the Gentiles.* They are not wholly God's people; they are not the elect, but have only a smattering of the truth. The "Court of the Israelites" in the Jewish temple was for Jewish men; the "Court of the Women" was for Jewish women; the "Court of the Gentiles" was for those who were not Jews.

" Oh, Cuddie, they are but in the Court of the Gentiles, and will ne'er win farther ben, I doubt."
—*Sir W. Scott: Old Mortality*, chap. viii.

Courtesy. Civility, politeness. It was at the courts of princes and great feudatories that minstrels and pages practised the refinements of the age in which they lived. The word originally meant the manners of the court.

Courtesy Titles. Titles assumed or granted by social custom, but not of any legal value. The courtesy title of the eldest son of a duke is *marquis;* of a marquis is *earl;* of the eldest son of an earl is *viscount.* Younger sons of peers are by courtesy called lord or honourable, and the daughters are lady or honourable. These titles do not give the holders official rank to sit in the House of Lords. Even the Marquis of Lorne, the Queen's son-in-law, is only a commoner (1894).

Cousin. Blackstone says that Henry IV., being related or allied to every earl in the kingdom, artfully and constantly acknowledged the connection in all public acts. The usage has descended to his successors, though the reason has long ago failed. (*Commentaries*, i. 398.)

Cousin. All peers above the rank of baron are officially addressed by the Crown as *cousin.*
A *viscount* or *earl* is "Our right trusty and well-beloved cousin."
A *marquis* is "Our right trusty and entirely-beloved cousin."
A *duke* is "Our right trusty and right-entirely-beloved cousin."

Cousin Betsy. A half-witted person, a "Bess of Bedlam" (*q.v.*).

" [None] can say Foster's wronged him of a penny, or gave short measure to a child or a cousin Betsy."—*Mrs. Gaskell.*

Cousin-german. The children of brothers and sisters, first cousins; kinsfolk. (Latin, *germa′nus*, a brother, one of the same stock.)

" There is three cozen-germans that has cozened all the hosts of Reading, of Maidenhead, of Colebrook, of horses and money."—*Shakespeare: Merry Wives of Windsor*, iv. 5.

Cousin Jack. So Cornishmen are called in the western counties.

Cousin Michael (or *Michel*). The Germans are so called. *Michel*, in Old German, means "gross," cousin Michel is meant to indicate a slow, heavy, simple, unrefined, coarse-feeding people.

Coûte que Coûte (French). Cost what it may, at any price, be the consequences what they may.

" His object is to serve his party *coûte que coûte*."—*Standard.*

Couvade (2 syl.). A man who takes the place of his wife when she is in child-bed. (See *Reader's Handbook*, p. 217, col. 2.)

Cove (1 syl.). An individual; as a *flash cove* (a swell), a *rum cove* (a man whose position and character is not quite palpable), a *gentry cove* (a gentleman), a *downy cove* (a very knowing individual), etc. (Gipsy, *cova*, a thing; *covo*, that man; *covi*, that woman.)

Cov'enanters. A term applied, during the civil wars, to the Scotch Presbyterians, who united by "solemn league and covenant" to resist the encroachments of Charles I. on religious liberty.

Covent Garden. A corruption of Convent Garden; the garden and burial ground attached to the convent of Westminster, and turned into a fruit and flower market in the reign of Charles II. It now belongs to the Duke of Bedford.

Cov'entry. *To send one to Coventry.* To take no notice of him; to let him live and move and have his being with you, but pay no more heed to him than to the idle winds which you regard not. According to Messrs. Chambers (*Cyclopædia*), the citizens of Coventry had at one time so great a dislike to soldiers that a woman seen speaking to one was instantly tabooed. No intercourse was ever allowed between the garrison and the town; hence, when a soldier was sent to Coventry, he was cut off from all social intercourse.

Hutton, in his *History of Birmingham*, gives a different version. He says that Coventry was a stronghold of the parliamentary party in the civil wars, and that all troublesome and refractory royalists were sent there for safe custody. The former explanation meets the general scope of the phrase the better. (*See* BOYCOTT.)

Coventry Mysteries. Miracle plays acted at Coventry till 1591. They were published in 1841 for the Shakespeare Society.

Parliaments held at Coventry. Two parliaments have been held in this city, one in 1404, styled *Parliamentum Indoctorum;* and the other in 1459, called *Parliamentum Diabolicum.*

Cover. *To break cover.* To start from the covert or temporary lair. The usual earth-holes of a fox being covered up the night before a hunt, the creature makes some gorse-bush or other cover its temporary resting-place, and as soon as it quits it the hunt begins.

Covers were laid for . . . Dinner was provided for. . . . A cover (*couvert*) in French means knife, fork, spoon, and napkin. Hence, *mettre le couvert*, to lay the cloth; and *lever* (or *ôter*) *le couvert*, to clear it away.

Covered Way, in fortification. (*See* GLACIS.)

Covering the Face. No malefactor was allowed, in ancient Persia, to look upon a king. So, in Esther vii. 5, when Haman fell into disgrace, being seen on the queen's divan, "they instantly cover Haman's face," that he might not look on the face of Ahasuerus.

⁂ In India a low caste man covers his mouth when speaking to one of high caste.

Cov'erley. *Sir Roger de Coverley.* A member of an hypothetical club in the *Spectator*, "who lived in Soho Square when he was in town." Sir Roger is the type of an English squire in the reign of Queen Anne. He figures in thirty papers of the *Spectator*.

"Who can be insensible to his unpretending virtues and amiable weaknesses; his modesty, generosity, hospitality, and eccentric whims; the respect for his neighbours, and the affection of his domestics?"—*Hazlitt.*

Covotous Man. A Tantalus (*q.v.*).

" In the full flood stands Tan'talus, his skin
  Washed o'er in vain, for ever dry within.
  He catches at the stream with greedy lips—
  From his parched mouth the wanton torrent
      slips...
  Change but the name, this fable is thy story:
  Thou in a flood of useless wealth dost glory,
  Which thou canst only touch, but never taste."
      Cowley: Horace, satire i.

Cow. The cow that nourished Ymir with four streams of milk was called Audhumla. (*Scandinavian mythology.*) (*See* AUDHUMLA.)

Curst cows. (*See under* CURST.)

The whiter the cow, the surer is it to go to the altar. The richer the prey, the more likely is it to be seized.

"The system of impropriations grew so rapidly that, in the course of three centuries, more than a third part of all the benefices in England became such, and those the richest, for the whiter the cow, the surer was it to go to the altar."—*Blunt: Reformation in England,* p. 63.

Cow's Tail. "Always behind, like a cow's tail." "Tanquam coda vituli." (*Petronius.*)

The cow knows not the worth of her tail till she loses it, and is troubled with flies, which her tail brushed off.

" What we have we prize not to the worth
  Whiles we enjoy it; but being lack'd and lost,
  Why, then we rack the value."
      Shakespeare: Much Ado about Nothing, iv. 1.

Cow-lick. A tuft of hair on the human forehead, sometimes called a feather; it cannot be made to lie in the same direction as the rest of the hair by brushing, or even by pomatum. When cows lick their hides they make the hair stand on end.

"This term must have been adopted from a comparison with that part of a . . . cow's hide where the hairs, having different directions, meet and form a projecting ridge, supposed to be occasioned by the animals licking themselves."— *Brochett: Glossary of North-Country Words.*

Coward (anciently written *culvard*) is either from the French, *couard*, originally written *culvert*, from *culver* (a pigeon), pigeon-livered being still a common expression for a coward; or else from the Latin, *culum ver'tere*, to turn tail (Spanish, *cobarde*; Portuguese, *covarde*; Italian, *codardo*, "a coward;" Latin, *cauda*, "a tail"). A beast *cowarded*, in heraldry, is one drawn with its coue or tail between its legs. The allusion is to the practice of beasts, who sneak off in this manner when they are cowed.

Cowper. Called "Author of *The Task*," from his principal poem. (1731-1800.)

Cowper Law, a corruption of *Cupar*, etc., is trying a man *after* execution. Similar expressions are Jedwood, Jeddart, and Jedburgh justice. Cowper justice had its rise from a baron-baile in Coupar-Angus, before heritable jurisdictions were abolished. (*See* LYDFORD LAW.)

"Cowper Law, as we say in Scotland—hang a man first, and then judge him."—*Lord de Ros: Tower of London.*

Coxcomb. An empty-headed, vain person. The ancient licensed jesters were so called because they wore a cock's comb in their caps.

" Coxcombs, an ever empty race, Are trumpets of their own disgrace." *Gay: Fables*, xix.

" Let me hire him too ; here's my coxcomb." *Shakespeare: King Lear*, i. 4.

The Prince of Coxcombs. Charles Joseph, Prince de Ligne. (1535-1614.) Richard II. of England is sometimes called the Coxcomb. (1366, 1377-1400.) Henri III. of France was called *le Mignon*, which means pretty well the same thing. (1551, 1574-1589.)

Coxeyites (3 syl.). Followers of Mr. ["General"] Coxey, of the United States, who induced 50,000 labourers from sundry states "to march" to Washington to overawe the Government into giving employment to the unemployed. The word is now employed to express labour processions and masses organised to force concessions to workmen.

Coxswain. *Kog* is Norwegian for a cockboat; Welsh, *cwch*; Italian, *cocca*, etc.; and *swain*, Anglo-Saxon for a servant, superintendent, or bailiff. (*See* COCKBOAT.)

Coyne and Livery. Food and entertainment for soldiers, and forage for their horses, exacted by an army from the people whose lands they passed through, or from towns where they rested on their march.

Coys'tril, *Coystrel*, or *Kestrel.* A degenerate hawk; hence, a paltry fellow. Holinshed says, "costerels or bearers of the arms of barons or knights " (vol. i. p. 162); and again, " women, lackeys, and costerels are considered as the unwarlike attendants on an army" (vol. iii. 272). Each of the life-guards of Henry VIII. had an attendant, called a coystrel or coystril. Some think the word is a corruption of *costerel*, which they derive from the Latin *coterellus* (a peasant); but if not a corruption of *kestrel*, I should derive it from *costrel* (a small wooden bottle used by labourers in harvest time). "*Vasa quædam quæ costrelli vocantur.*" (*Matthew Paris.*)

" He's a coward and a coystril that will not drink to my niece."—*Shakespeare: Twelfth Night*, i. 3.

Cozen. To cheat. (Armoric, *couçzyein*; Russian, *kosnodei*; Arabic, *gausa*; Ethiopic, *chasawa*; our *chouse*.)

" I think it no sin To cozen him that would unjustly win." *Shakespeare: All's Well that Ends Well*, iv. 2.

Crab (*A*). An ill-tempered fellow; sour as a crab-apple.

To catch a crab, in rowing. (*See* CATCH A CRAB.)

Crab-cart. The carapace of a crab. So called because it is used very commonly by children for a toy-cart.

Crack, as a *crack man*, a first-rate fellow; a *crack hand* at cards, a first-rate player; a *crack article*, an excellent one, *i.e.* an article *cracked up* or boasted about. This is the Latin *crepo*, to crack or boast about. Hence Lucretius ii. 1168, " crepas antiquum genus."

" Indeed, ha ! 'tis a noble child; a crack, madam." *Shakespeare: Coriolanus*, i. 3.

A gude crack. A good talker.

"To be a gude crack . . . was essential to the trade of a 'puir body' of the more esteemed class."—*Sir W. Scott: The Antiquary* (Introduction).

In a crack. Instantly. In a snap of the fingers, *crep'itu digito'rum* (in a crack of the fingers). (French, *craquer*.)

" Une allusion au bruit de l'ongle contre la dent que les Orientaux du moyen âge touchaient du

doight quand ils voulaient affirmer solennclle-
ment une chose." Hence—

" Sire, bien vous croi seur les Dieux;
Mais assès vous querroie mieux
Sé vous l'ongle hurties au dent."
Théatre Francois de Moyen Age, p. 167.

Crack-brained. Eccentric ; slightly
mad. Another form is " A crack-skull."

Crack a Bottle — *i.e.* drink one.
The allusion is to the mischievous pranks
of the drunken frolics of times gone
by, when the bottles and glasses were
broken during the bout. Miss Oldbuck
says, in reference to the same custom,
" We never were glass-breakers in this
house, Mr. Lovel " (*Antiquary*); meaning they were not bottle-crackers, or
given to drunken orgies. (*See* CRUSH.)

" Dear Tom, this brown jug that now foams with
mild ale,
From which I now drink to sweet Nan of the
Vale,
Was once Toby Filpot's, a thirsty old soul
As e'er cracked a bottle, or fathomed a bowl."
O'Keefe : Poor Soldier.

Crack a Crib (*To*). To break into a
house as a thief. (*See* CRIB.)

Crack Up a Person (*To*). To praise
him highly. (*See* CRACK.)

Cracked. Made a bankrupt. A play
on " rupt," which is from the Latin
rumpo, to break.

Cracked Pipkins. *Cracked pipkins
are discovered by their sound.* Ignorance
is betrayed by speech.

" They bid you talk—my honest song
Bids you for ever hold your tongue;
Silence with some is wisdom most profound—
Cracked pipkins are discovered by the sound."
Peter Pindar : Lord B. and his Motions.

Cracker. So called from the noise it
makes when it goes off.

Cracknells (from the French *craque-
lin*). A hard, brittle cake.

Cradle-land. The same as " borough
English," under which lands descend to
the youngest son. By *Gavelkind*, land
passes to all sons in equal proportions.
If the father has no son, then (in
cradle-land tenures) the youngest daughter is sole heiress. If neither wife, son,
nor daughter, the youngest brother
inherits ; if no brother, the youngest
sister is heir ; if neither brother nor yet
sister, then the youngest next of kin.

Craft (*A*). A trade (Anglo-Saxon,
cræft). A *craftsman* is a mechanic. A
handicraft is manual skill, *i.e.* mechanical
skill. And *leechcraft* is skill in medicine.
(Anglo-Saxon *læce-cræft* ; *læce*, a doctor.)

Craft (*A*). A general term for a
vessel employed in loading and unloading
ships.

Small craft. Such vessels as schooners,
sloops, cutters, and so on. A ship-
builder was at one time the prince of
craftsmen, and his vessels were work of
craft emphatically.

Craft. Cunning, or skill in a bad
sense. Hence *Witchcraft*, the art or
cunning of a witch.

Craigmillar Castle. So called from
Henry de Craigmillar, who built the
castle in the twelfth century.

Cra′kys of War. Cannons were so
called in the reign of Edward III.

Cram. To tell what is not true. A
crammer, an untruth. The allusion is to
stuffing a person with useless rubbish.

Crambe bis Cocta [" cabbage boiled
twice "]. A subject hacked out. Juvenal says, " *Occidit miseros crambe repe-
tita magistros* " (vii. 155), alluding to the
Greek proverb " *Dis krambē thanatos.* "

" There was a disadvantage in treading this
Border district, for it had been already ransacked
by the author himself, as well as by others; and,
unless presented under a new light, was likely to
afford ground to the objection of *Crambe bis
cocta*.''—*Sir W. Scott: The Monastery* (Introduction).

Crambo. Repetition. So called from
a game which consists in some one
setting a line which another is to
rhyme to, but no one word of the first
line must occur in the second.

Dumb crambo. Pantomime of a word
in rhyme to a given word. Thus if
" oat " is the given word, the pantomimists would act Bat, Fat, Hat, Mat,
Pat, Rat, Sat, etc., till the word acted is
guessed.

Crampart (*King*). The king who
made a wooden horse which would
travel 100 miles an hour. (*Alkmaar .
Reynard the Fox*, 1498.)

Swifter than Crampart's horse. Quick
as lightning ; quick as thought. (*See
above.*)

Cramp-ring. *To scour the cramp-
ring.* To be put into fetters ; to be
imprisoned. The allusion is obvious.

" There's no muckle hazard o' scouring the
cramp-ring."—*Sir W. Scott: Guy Mannering*, chap.
xxiii.

Crane means long-shanks. (Welsh,
gar, " the shanks," whence our *gaiter*
and *garter*.) Garan is the long-shanked
bird, contracted into *g'ran*, crane ; *heron*
is another form of the same word.

Crank. An Abram man (*q.v.*). So
called from the German *krank* (sickly),
whence *cranky*, " idiotic, foolish, full of
whims," and *cranks* (simulated sickness). These beggars were called *cranks*

because they pretended madness and sickness to excite compassion.

Cran'nock. An Irish measure which, in the days of Edward II., contained either eight or sixteen pecks.

"Crannocus continebit xvj pecks. Crannoco continente octo pecks."—*Exchequer of Ireland* (*Rec.*).

Cra'paud or *Johnny Crapaud.* A Frenchman; so called from the device of the ancient kings of France, "three toads erect, saltant." (Guillim's *Display of Heraldrie*, 1611.) Nostrada'mus, in the sixteenth century, called the French "crapauds."

Les anciens crapauds prenderont Sara (Nostrada'mus). Sara is the word *Aras* reversed, and when the French under Louis XIV. took Aras from the Spaniards, this verse was quoted as a prophecy.

Crape . . . . Lawn. *A saint in crape is twice a saint in lawn.* (*Pope: Ep. to Cobham*, 136.) Crape (a sort of bombazine, or alpaca) is the stuff of which cheap clerical gowns used to be made, and here means one of the lower clergy; "lawn" refers to the lawn sleeves of a bishop, and here means a prelate. A good curate is all very well, but the same goodness in a bishop is exalted as something noteworthy.

Cravat'. A corruption of Crabat or Croät. It was introduced into France by some French officers on their return from Germany in 1636. The Croäts, who guarded the Turkish frontiers of Austria, and acted as scouts on the flanks of the army, wore linen round their necks, tied in front, and the officers wore muslin or silk. When France organised a regiment on the model of the Croäts, these linen neckcloths were imitated, and the regiment was called "The Royal Cravat."

The Bonny Cravat. A public-house sign at Woodchurch, Kent; a corruption of *La bonne corvette.* Woodchurch was noted for its smuggling proclivities, and the "Bonnie Cravat" was a smuggler's hostelry.

To wear a hempen cravat. To be hanged.

Cra'ven means "your mercy is craved." It was usual in former times to decide controversies by an appeal to battle. The combatants fought with bâtons, and if the accused could either kill his adversary or maintain the fight till sundown, he was acquitted. If he wished to call off, he cried out"Craven!" and was held infamous, while the defendant was advanced to honour. (*Blackstone.*)

Crawley. *Crooked as Crawley* (or) *Crawley brook,* a river in Bedfordshire. That part called the brook, which runs into the Ouse, is so crooked that a boat would have to go eighty miles in order to make a progress direct of eighteen. (*Fuller: Worthies.*)

Cray'on (*Geoffrey*). The *nom de plume* under which Washington Irving published *The Sketch-Book*. (1820.)

Creaking Doors hang the Longest. "*Un pot fêlé dure plus qu'un neuf.*" "*Tout se qui branle ne chet pas*" (tumbles not). Delicate persons often outlive the more robust. Those who have some personal affliction, like the gout, often live longer than those who have no such vent.

Create. Make.

God created the heavens and the earth (Gen. i. 1.)
   (Hebrew, *carah*; Greek, κτίζω.)
God made the firmament .. .. (Gen. i. 7.)
   (Greek, ποιέω).
God made the sun and moon .. .. .. (Gen. i. 16.)
God created the great fishes .. .. .. (Gen. i. 21.)
God made the terrestrial animals .. (Gen. i. 25.)
God created man and *made* him "God-
   like" .. .. (Gen. i. 27.)
   God said " Let us *make* man in our own image"
(verse 26), and so God *created* man in His image
(verse 27).
Chap. ii. 3. He rested from all the works which
He had *created and made.*
Chap. ii. 4. He *made* the earth and the heavens;
He also created them.
Chap. ii. 22. He *made* woman, but *created* man.
Most certainly *create* does not of necessity mean
to make out of nothing, as fishes were "created"
from water, and man was created from "earth."

Creature (*The*). Whisky or other spirits. A contracted form of " Creature-comfort."

" When he chanced to have taken an overdose of the creature."—*Sir W. Scott: Guy Mannering,* chap. xliv.

A drop of the creature. A little whisky. The Irish call it " a drop of the crater."

Creature - comforts. Food and other things necessary for the comfort of the body. Man being supposed to consist of body and soul, the body is the creature, but the soul is the " vital spark of heavenly flame."

" Mr. Squeers had been seeking in creature-comforts [brandy and water] temporary forgetfulness of his unpleasant situation."—*Dickens: Nicholas Nickleby.*

Credat Judæus or **Credat Judæus Apella.** Tell that to the Marines. That may do for Apella, but I don't believe a word of it. Who this Apella was, nobody knows. (*Horace: 1 Satires,* v. line 100.)

⁂ Cicero mentions a person of this name in *Ad Atticum* (12, *ep.* 19); but *see* DUCANGE.

Cre′dence Table. The table near the altar on which the bread and wine are deposited before they are consecrated. In former times food was placed on a credence-table to be tasted previously to its being set before the guests. This was done to assure the guests that the meat was not poisoned. The Italian *credenza′re* means to taste meats placed on the *creden′za*. (Italian, *la credenza*, a shelf or buffet; Greek, *kreas*, food.)

Crédit Foncier (French). A company licensed to borrow money for city and other improvements connected with estates. A board of guardians may form such a company, and their security would be the parish rates. The money borrowed is repaid by instalments with interest. The word *foncier* means "landed," as *impôt foncier* (land-tax), *bien foncier* (landed property), and so on.

Crédit Mobilier (French). A company licensed to take in hand all sorts of trading enterprises, such as railways, and to carry on the business of stockjobbers. The word *mobilier* means personal property, general stock, as *bien mobilier* (personal chattels), *mobilier vif et mort* (live and dead stock).

Cre′kenpit. A fictitious river near Husterloe, according to the invention of Master Reynard, who calls on the Hare to attest the fact. (*Reynard the Fox.*)

Cremo′na. An organ stop, a corruption of the Italian *cormorne*, which is the German *krummhorn*, an organ stop of eight feet pitch; so called from a wind-instrument made of wood, and bent outwards in a circular arc (*krummhorn*, crooked horn).

Cremo′nas. Violins of the greatest excellence; so called from Cremo′na, where for many years lived some makers of them who have gained a world-wide notoriety, such as An′drea Ama′ti and Antonio his son, Anto′nius Stradiva′rius his pupil, and Giuseppe Guarne′rius the pupil of Stradiva′rius. Cremona has long since lost its reputation for this manufacture.

"In silvis viva silui ; cano′ra jam mor′tua cano."
A motto on a Cremona.

Speechless, alive, I heard the feathered throng ;
Now, being dead, I emulate their song. *E. C. B.*

Cre′ole (2 syl.). A descendant of white people born in Mexico, South America, and the West Indies. (Spanish *criado*, a servant; diminutive *criadillo*, contracted into *creollo*, *creole*.) (*See* MULATTO.)

Creole dialects. The various jargons spoken by the West India slaves.

Crep′idam. *Supra crep′idam.* Talking about subjects above one's *metier*, meddling and muddling matters of which you know little or nothing. (*See* COBBLER.)

Cres′cent. Tradition says that "Philip, the father of Alexander, meeting with great difficulties in the siege of Byzan′tium, set the workmen to undermine the walls, but a crescent moon discovered the design, which miscarried ; consequently the Byzantines erected a statue to Diana, and the crescent became the symbol of the state."

Another legend is that Othman, the Sultan, saw in a vision a crescent moon, which kept increasing till its horns extended from east to west, and he adopted the crescent of his dream for his standard, adding the motto, "*Donec rep′leat orbem.*"

Crescent City (*The*). New Orleans, in Louisiana, U.S.

Cres′cit. *Crescit sub pon′dere Virtus* (Virtue thrives best in adversity). The allusion is to the palm-tree, which grows better when pressed by an incumbent weight.

Many plants grow the better for being pressed, as grass, which is wonderfully improved by being rolled frequently with a heavy roller, and by being trodden down by sheep.

Cressell′e (2 syl.). A wooden rattle used formerly in the Romish Church during Passion week, instead of bells, to give notice of Divine worship. Supposed to represent the rattling in the throat of Christ while hanging on the cross.

Cres′set. A beacon-light ; properly "a little cross." So called because originally it was surmounted by a little cross. (French, *croisette*.)

Cress′ida, daughter of Calchas the Grecian priest, was beloved by Troïlus, one of the sons of Priam. They vowed eternal fidelity to each other, and as pledges of their vow Troïlus gave the maiden a sleeve, and Cressid gave the Trojan prince a glove. Scarce had the vow been made when an exchange of prisoners was agreed to. Diomed gave up three Trojan princes, and was to receive Cressid in lieu thereof. Cressid vowed to remain constant, and Troïlus swore to rescue her. She was led off to the Grecian's tent, and soon gave all her affections to Diomed—nay, even bade him wear the sleeve that Troïlus had given her in token of his love.

"As false
As air, as water, wind, or sandy earth,
As fox to lamb, as wolf to heifer's calf,
Pard to the hind, or step-dame to her son ;
'Yea,' let them say, to stick the heart of false-hood,
'As false as Cressid.'"
Shakespeare: Troilus and Cressida, iii. 2.

Cresswell (*Madame*). A woman of infamous character who bequeathed £10 for a funeral sermon, in which nothing ill should be said of her. The Duke of Buckingham wrote the sermon, which was as follows : "All I shall say of her is this—she was born *well*, she married *well*, lived *well*, and died *well;* for she was born at Shad-well, married to Cress-well, lived at Clerken-well, and died in Bride-well."

Cressy (*Battle of*). Won by Edward III. and the Black Prince over Philippe VI. of France, August 26, 1346.

"Cressy was lost by kickshaws and soup meagre."
Fenton: Prol. to Southern's Spartan Dame.

Crestfallen. Dispirited. The allusion is to fighting cocks, whose crest falls in defeat and rises rigid and of a deep red colour in victory.

"Shall I seem crest-fallen in my father's sight ?"
Shakespeare: Richard II., i. 1.

Crete. *Hound of Crete.* A bloodhound.

"*Coupe le gorge.* that's the word. I thee defy again,
O hound of Crete."
Shakespeare: Henry V., ii. 1.

The Infamy of Crete. The Minotaur.

"There lay stretched
The infamy of Crete, detested brood
Of the feigned heifer."
Dante: Hell, xii. (Cary's translation).

Cre'ticus. Metellus, the Roman general, was so called because he conquered Crete (Candia).

Cre'tinism. Mental imbecility accompanied by goître. So called from the Crétins of the Alps. The word is a corruption of Christian (*Chrétien*), because, being baptised, and only idiots, they were "washed from original sin," and incapable of actual sin. Similarly, idiots are called *innocents*. (French *crétin*, *crétinisme*.)

Crex. White buliace. (Dutch, *kriecke*, cherry ; Latin, *cer'asum*.)

Crib (*A*). Slang for a house or dwelling, as a "Stocking Crib" (*i.e.* a hosiery), a "Thimble Crib" (*i.e.* a silversmith's). Crib is an ox - stall. (Anglo-Saxon, *crib*, a stall, a bed, etc.)

"Where no oxen are, the crib is clean."—*Prov.* xiv. 4.

A child's crib is a child's bed. (*See* preceding column.)

Crib (*A*). A petty theft ; a literal translation of some foreign work, stealthily employed to save trouble.

"We are glad to turn from the choruses of Æschylus, or the odes of Horace, confected in English verse by some petty scholar, to the original text, and the homely help of a school-boy's crib."—*Balzac's Shorter Stories: Prefatory Notice*, p. 16.

Crib. To steal small articles. (Saxon, *crybb* ; Irish, *grib* ; our *grab*, *grapple*, *grip*, *gripe*, etc.)

Cricket.
The diminutive of the Anglo-Saxon *cric*, a staff or crutch. In the Bodleian library is a MS. (1344) picture of a monk bowling a ball to another monk, who is about to strike it with a cric. In the field are other monks. There are no wickets, but the batsman stands before a hole, and the art of the game was either to get the ball into the hole, or to catch it.

Perhaps the earliest mention of the word "crickett" is 1593. John Derrick, gent., tells us when he attended the "free school of Guldeforde, he and his fellowes did runne and play there at crickett and other plaies." It was a Wykehamist game in the days of Elizabeth.

A single stump was placed in the seventeenth century at each hole to point out the place to bowlers and fielders. In 1700 two stumps were used 24 inches apart and 12 inches high, with long bails atop.

A middle stump was added by the Hambledon Club in 1775; and the height of the stumps was raised to 22 inches.

In 1814 they were made 26 inches, and in 1817 they were reduced to 22 inches. the present height. The length of run is 22 yards.

The first cricket club was Hambledon, which practically broke up in 1791, but existed in name till 1825.

Cri'key. A profane oath ; a perverted form of the word *Christ*.

Cril'lon. *Where wert thou, Crillon ?* Crillon, surnamed *the Brave*, in his old age went to church, and listened intently to the story of the Crucifixion. In the middle of the narrative he grew excited, and, unable to contain himself, cried out, "*Où étais - tu, Crillon ?*" (What were you about, Crillon, to allow of such things as these ?).

N.B. Louis de Berton des Balbes de Crillon was one of the greatest captains of the sixteenth century. Born in Provence 1541, died 1615.

Henri IV., after the battle of Argives (1589), wrote to Crillon the following letter: "*Prend-toi, brave Crillon, nous avons vaincu à Arques, et tu n'y étais pas.*" The first and last part of this letter have become proverbial.

Crimen læsæ Majestatis (Latin). High treason.

Crimp. A decoy; a man or woman that is on the look-out to decoy the unwary. It is more properly applied to an agent for supplying ships with sailors, but these agents are generally in league with public-houses and private lodging-houses of low character, into which they decoy the sailors and relieve them of their money under one pretence or another. (Welsh, *crimpiaw*, to squeeze or pinch; Norwegian, *krympe*, a sponge.)

Crimp of Death (*A*). A thief-catcher. A crimp is a decoy, especially of soldiers and sailors. (*See above.*)

"Here lie three crimps of death, knocked down
    by Fate,
Of justice the staunch blood-hounds, too, so
    keen."
            *Peter Pindar: Epitaph on Townsend,
                    Macmanus, and Jealous.*

Cringle (*Tom*). An excellent sailor character in the naval story by Michael Scott, called *Tom Cringle's Log*, first published in *Blackwood's Magazine*.

Crip'ple. A battered or bent sixpence; so called because it is hard to make it go.

Crip'plegate. St. Giles is the patron saint of cripples and beggars, and was himself a cripple. Churches dedicated to this saint are, therefore, in the suburbs of large towns, as St. Giles of London, Norwich, Cambridge, Salisbury, etc. Cripplegate, London, was so called before the Conquest from the number of cripples who resorted thither to beg. (*Stowe*.)

Criss-cross Row (*Christ-cross row*). The A B C horn-book, containing the alphabet and nine digits. The most ancient of these infant-school books had the letters arranged in the form of a Latin cross, with A at the top and Z at the bottom; but afterwards the letters were arranged in lines, and a + was placed at the beginning to remind the learner that "The fear of the Lord is the beginning of wisdom."

"Mortals ne'er shall know
More than contained of old the Chris'-cross row."
            Tickell: The Horn-Book.

Crish'na. An incarnate deity of perfect beauty. King Canza, being informed that a child of the family of Devaci would overturn his throne, gave orders to destroy all the male infants that were born. When Crishna was born, his brother conveyed him secretly to the house of a shepherd king; but Canza discovered his retreat, and sent the monster Kâkshas to poison him. The tale says the infant child sucked the monster to death, and so escaped. As he grew up, his beauty was so divine that all the princesses of Hindustan fell in love with him, and even to the present hour he is the Apollo of India and the "idol of women." His images are always painted a deep azure colour. (*Sir W. Jones.*) (*See* RAMA.)

Cri'sis properly means the "ability to judge." Hippoc'ratēs said that all diseases had their periods, when the humours of the body ebbed and flowed like the tide of the sea. These tidal days he called *critical days*, and the tide itself a *crisis*, because it was on these days the physi'cian could determine whether the disorder was taking a good or a bad turn. The seventh and all its multiples were critical days of a favourable character. (Greek, *krino*, to judge or determine.)

Crispin. A shoemaker. St. Crispin was a shoemaker, and was therefore chosen for the patron saint of the craft. It is said that two brothers, Crispin and Crispian, born in Rome, went to Soissons, in France (A.D. 303), to propagate the Christian religion, and maintained themselves wholly by making and mending shoes. Probably the tale is fabulous, for *crepis* is Greek for a shoe, Latin *crepid-a*, and St. Crepis or Crepid became Crepin and Crespin.

St. Crispin's Day. October 25th, the day of the battle of Agincourt. Shakespeare makes Crispin Crispian one person, and not two brothers. Hence Henry V. says to his soldiers—

"And Crispin Crispian shall ne'er go by ...
But we in it shall be remembered."
            Shakespeare: Henry V., iv. 3.

St. Crispin's holiday. Every Monday, with those who begin the working week on Tuesday; a no-work day with shoemakers. (*See* CRISPIN.)

St. Crispin's lance. A shoemaker's awl. In French, "*Lance de St. Crépin.*" Crispin is the patron saint of shoemakers.

The French argot for a leather purse is *une crépine.*

Crite'rion. A standard to judge by. (Greek, *krino*, to judge.)

Crit'ic. A judge; an arbiter. (Greek, *krino*, to judge.)

Critic. A captious, malignant critic is called a Zoïlus (*q.v.*)

"'And what of this new book the whole world makes such a rout about?' 'Oh, it is out of all plumb, my lord; quite an irregular thing! not one of the angles at the four corners is a right angle. I had my rule and compasses in my pocket.' 'Excellent critic!'

"'And for the epic poem your lordship bade me look at, upon taking the length, breadth, height, and depth of it, and trying them at home upon an exact scale of Bossu's [Bossut's], 'tis out, my lord, in every one of its dimensions.' 'Admirable connoisseur!'"—*Sterne: Tristram Shandy,* vol. iii. chap. xii.

⁂ The abbé Charles Bossut (1730-1814) was a noted mathematician and geometer.

Prince of critics. Aristarchos, of Byzantium, who compiled the rhapsodies of Homer. (Second century B.C.)

Stop-watch critics.

"'And how did Garrick speak the soliloquy last night?' 'Oh, against all rule, my lord, most ungrammatically. Betwixt the substantive and the adjective, which should agree together in number, case, and gender, he made a breach, thus—stopping as if the point wanted settling; and betwixt the nominative case, which, your lordship knows, should govern the verb, he suspended his voice in the epilogue a dozen times, three seconds and three-fifths by a stop-watch, my lord, each time.' 'Admirable grammarian!' 'But in suspending his voice was the sense suspended likewise? Did no expression of attitude or countenance fill up the chasm? Was the eye silent? Did you narrowly look?' 'I looked only at the stop-watch, my lord.' 'Excellent observer!'"—*Sterne: Tristram Shandy,* vol. iii. chap. xii.

Croak'er (2 syl.). A raven, so called from its croak; one who takes a desponding view of things. Goldsmith, in his *Good-natured Man,* has a character so named.

Croakumshire. Northumberland is so called from the peculiar croaking of the natives in speaking. This is especially observable in Newcastle and Morpeth, where the people are said to be born with a burr in their throats, which prevents their giving effect to the letter *r.*

Croc mitaine (*A*). A fire-eater; one always ready to quarrel and fight. (*See* CROQUEMITAINE.)

Croc'odile (3 syl.). A symbol of deity among the Egyptians, because it is the only aquatic animal, says Plutarch, which has its eyes covered with a thin transparent membrane, by reason of which it sees and is not seen; so God sees all, Himself not being seen. To this he subsequently adds another reason, saying, "The Egyptians worship God symbolically in the crocodile, that being the only animal without a tongue, like the Divine Logos, which standeth not in need of speech." (*De Iside et Osiride,* vol. ii. p. 381.)

⁂ Achilles Tatius says, "The number of its teeth equals the number of days in a year." Another tradition is, that during the seven days held sacred to Apis, the crocodile will harm no one.

Crocodile (*King*). A king who devours his people, or at least their substance. Browne, in his *Travels,* tells us that there is a king crocodile, as there is a queen bee. The king crocodile has no tail.

Crocodile's Eye. Hieroglyphic for the morning.

Croc'odile's Tears. Hypocritical tears. The tale is, that crocodiles moan and sigh like a person in deep distress, to allure travellers to the spot, and even shed tears over their prey while in the act of devouring it.

" As the mournful crocodile
With sorrow snares relenting passengers."
Shakespeare: 2 Henry VI., iii. 1.

Crocum in Ciliciam ferre. To carry coals to Newcastle. As Cilicia abounds with saffron, to send it there would be needless and extravagant excess. For similar phrases, *see* ALCINOO POMA DARE, NOCTUAS ATHENAS, COALS.

Crœsus. *Rich as Crœsus.* Crœsus, King of Lydia, was so rich and powerful that all the wise men of Greece were drawn to his court, and his name became proverbial for wealth. (B.C. 560-546.) (*See* GYGES.)

Crom'eruach'. Chief idol of the Irish before the preaching of St. Patrick. It was a gold or silver image surrounded by twelve little brazen ones.

Cromlech. A large stone resting on two or more others, like a table. (Welsh, *crom,* bent; *llech,* a flat stone.)

Weyland Smith's cave (Berkshire), Trevethy stone (Cornwall), Kit's Coty House (Kent). Irby and Mangles saw twenty-seven structures just like these on the banks of the Jordan; at Plas Newydd (Anglesey) are two cromlechs; in Cornwall they are numerous; so are they in Wales; some few are found in Ireland, as the "killing-stone" in Louth. In Brittany, Denmark, Germany, and some other parts of Europe, cromlechs are to be found.

Cromwell in the part of "Tactus." (*See* TACTUS.)

Crone, properly speaking, means a ewe whose teeth are worn out; but metaphorically it means any toothless old beldam. (Irish, *criona,* old; allied to the Greek *gerōn,* an old man.)

"Take up the bastard; take 't up, I say; give 't to thy crone."—*Shakespeare: Winter's Tale,* ii. 3.

Cro'nian Sea. The north polar sea. Pliny says, " *A Thule unius diei naviga- tio'nĕ marĕ* concretum, *a nonnullis* cronium *appella'tur.*" (*Natural History,* iv. 16.)

> "As when two polar winds blowing adverse
> Upon the Cronian sea."
> *Milton: Paradise Lost,* x. 290.

Cro'ny. A familiar friend. *An old crony* is an intimate of times gone by. Probably *crone* with the diminutive *ie* for endearment, and equivalent to " dear old fellow," "dear old boy." (*See* CRONE.)

Crook in the Lot. *There is a crook in the lot of everyone.* There is vexa- tion bound up in every person's lot of life, a skeleton in the cupboard of every house. A crook in a stick is a bend, a part where the stick does not run straight, hence a "shepherd's crook." When lots were drawn by bits of stick, it was desirable to get sticks which were smooth and straight ; but it is very hard to find one without a crook, knot, or some other defect. Boston has a book entitled *The Crook in the Lot.*

Crooked as Crawley. (*See* CRAW- LEY.)

Crooked Sixpence (*A*). Said to bring luck. (*See* MONEY.)

Crooked Stick (*A*). A self-willed fellow who will neither lead nor drive, neither be led nor driven. (*See* CROOK.)

Crop Up (or) **Out.** To rise out of, to appear at the surface. A mining term. Strata which rise to the surface are said to *crop out.* We also say, such and such a subject *crops up* from time to time—*i.e.* rises to the surface ; such and such a thing *crops out* of what you were saying—*i.e.* is *apropos* thereof.

Cropper. *He came a cropper.* He fell head over heels. *To get a cropper.* To get a bad fall. "Neck and crop" means altogether, and to "come a cropper" is to come to the ground neck and crop.

Croquemitaine [*croak-mit-tain*], the bogie raised by fear. The romance so called, in three parts. The first relates the bloody tournament at Fransac, be- tween the champions of the Moorish King Marsillus and the paladins of Charlemagne. The second is the Siege of Saragossa by Charlemagne. The third is the allegory of Fear-Fortress. The epilogue is the disaster at Ronces- vallës. The author is M. l'Epine. There is an English version by Tom Hood,

illustrated by Gustave Doré (1867). (*See* FEAR-FORTRESS, MITAINE, etc.)

Croquet. A game played with a sort of bandy stick. The crook was superseded by a kind of mallet. Du Cange gives " *Croque, croquebois, croquet, bâton armé d'un croc, ou qui est recourbé*" (vol. vii. p. 115). The art of the game is to strike your balls through very small hoops arranged in a given order.

Crore (*A*), in the East Indies, means a hundred lacs of rupees, equal nomi- nally, in round numbers, to a million sterling. (Pronounce *cror,* Hindustanee *karor.*)

Cross. The cross is said to have been made of four sorts of wood (palm, cedar, olive, and cypress), to signify the four quarters of the globe.

> " Ligna crucis palma, cedrus, cupressus, oli'va."

We are accustomed to consider the sign of the cross as wholly a Christian symbol, originating with the crucifixion of our Redeemer. This is quite errone- ous. In ancient Carthage it was used for ornamental purposes. Runic crosses were set up by the Scandinavians as boundary marks, and were erected over the graves of kings and heroes. Cicero tells us (*De Divinatione,* ii. 27, and 80, 81) that the augur's staff with which they marked out the heaven was a cross. The ancient Egyptians employed the same as a sacred symbol, and we see on Greek sculptures, etc., a cake with a cross ; two such buns were discovered at Hercula'neum.

It was a sacred symbol among the Aztecs long before the landing of Cortes. (*Malinche.*) In Cozumel it was an ob- ject of worship ; in Tabasco it symbolised the god of rain ; in Palinque (the Pal- myra of America) it is sculptured on the walls with a child held up adoring it.

> "The cross is not only a Christian symbol, it was also a Mexican symbol. It was one of the em- blems of Quetzalcoatl, as lord of the four cardinal points, and the four winds that blow therefrom." —*Fiske: Discovery of America,* vol. ii. chap. viii. p. 250.)

Cross (*in heraldry*). There are twelve crosses in heraldry, called (1) the ordi- nary cross ; (2) the cross humetté, or couped ; (3) the cross urdé, or pointed ; (4) the cross potent ; (5) the cross cross- let ; (6) the cross botonné, or treflé ; (7) the cross moline ; (8) the cross potence ; (9) the cross fleury ; (10) the cross paté ; (11) the Maltese cross (or eight-pointed cross) ; (12) the cross cleché and fitché. Some heraldic writers enumerate 285 different kinds of crosses.

Cross (*a mystic emblem*) may be reduced to these four :

The Greek cross (✚), found on Assyrian tablets, Egyptian and Persian monuments, and on Etruscan pottery.

The crux decussāta (✕), generally called St. Andrew's cross. Quite common in ancient sculpture.

The Latin cross (✝), or "crux immissa." This symbol is also found on coins, monuments, and medals, long before the Christian era.

The tau cross (T), or "crux commissa." Very ancient indeed, and supposed to be a phallic emblem.

❧ The tau cross with a handle (✝) is common to several Egyptian deities, as Isis, Osiris, etc. ; and is the emblem of immortality and life generally.

Everyone must bear his own cross. His own burden or troubles. The allusion is to the law that the person condemned to be crucified was to carry his cross to the place of execution.

Get on the cross. Get into bad ways ; not go straight.

"It's hard lines to think a fellow must grow up and get on the cross in spite of himself, and come to the gallow's foot at last, whether he likes it or not."—*Boldrewood: Robbery Under Arms,* chap. viii.

The judgment of the cross. An ordeal instituted in the reign of Charlemagne. The plaintiff and defendant were required to cross their arms upon their breast, and he who could hold out the longest gained the suit.

On the cross. Not "on the square," not straightforward. To get anything "on the cross" is to get it unfairly or surreptitiously.

See ROSICRUCIANS.

Cross (*To*).
Cross it off or out. Cancel it by running your pen across it. To cancel (*q.v.*) means to mark it with lattice lines.

Cross, ill-tempered, is the Anglo-Saxon *crous.*

"Azeyn [against] hem was he kene and crous."
Cursor Mundi.

Cross Buns. (*See* BUNS.)

Cross-grained. Patchy, ill-tempered, self-willed. Wood must be worked with the grain ; when the grain crosses we get a knot or curling, which is hard to work uniform.

Cross-legged Knights indicate that the person so represented died in the Christian faith. As crusaders were supposed so to do, they were generally represented on their tombs with crossed legs.

"Sometimes the figure on the tomb of a knight has his legs crossed at the ankles, this meant that the knight went *one* crusade. If the legs are crossed at the knees, he went *twice;* if at the thighs he went *three times.*"—*Ditchfield: Our Villages,* 1889.

Cross Man (*A*). Not straightforward ; ungain ; not honest.

"The storekeepers know who are their best customers, the square people or the cross ones." —*Boldrewood: Robbery Under Arms,* chap. xvii.

Cross-patch. A disagreeable, ill-tempered person, male or female. Patch means a fool or gossip ; so called from his parti-coloured or patched dress. A cross-patch is an ill-tempered fool or gossip. Patch, meaning "fellow," is common enough ; half a dozen examples occur in Shakespeare, as a "scurvy patch," a "soldier's patch," "What patch is made our porter ? " "a crew of patches," etc.

" Cross-patch, draw the latch,
Sit by the fire and spin ;
Take a cup, and drink it up,
Then call your neighbours in.
Old Nursery Rhyme.

Cross-roads. All (except suicides) who were excluded from holy rites were piously buried at the foot of the cross erected on the public road, as the place next in sanctity to consecrated ground. Suicides were ignominiously buried on the highway, with a stake driven through their body.

Cross and Ball, so universally marked on Egyptian figures, is a circle and the letter T. The circle signifies the eternal preserver of the world, and the T is the monogram of Thoth, the Egyptian Mercury, meaning wisdom.

The coronation orb is a sphere or ball surmounted by a cross, an emblem of empire introduced in representations of our Saviour. In this case the cross stands *above* the ball, to signify that the spiritual power is above the temporal.

Cross and Pile. Money ; pitch and toss. Hilaire le Gai tells us that some of the ancient French coins had a cross, and others a column, on the reverse ; the column was called a pile, from which comes our word "pillar," and the phrase "pile-driving." Scaliger says that some of the old French coins had a *ship* on the reverse, the arms of Paris, and that *pile* means "a ship," whence our word "pilot."

"A man may now justifiably throw up cross and pile for his opinions."—*Locke: Human Understanding.*

Cross or pile. Heads or tails. The French say *pile ou face.* The "face" or

cross was the *obverse* of the coin, the
"pile" was the reverse; but at a later
period the cross was transferred to the
reverse, as in our florins, and the
obverse bore a "head" or "poll."

"Marriage is worse than cross I win, pile you
    lose."   *Shadwell: Epsom Wells.*

*Cross nor pile. I have neither cross
nor pile.* Not a penny in the world.
The French phrase is, "*N'avoir ni croix
ni pile*" (to have neither one sort of
coin nor another).

"Whacum had neither cross nor pile."
    Butler: Hudibras, part ii. 3.

Cross as a Bear, or *Cross as a bear
with a sore head.*

Cross as the Tongs. The reference is to tongs which open like a pair
of scissors.

Cross as Two Sticks. The reference is to the cross (X).

Crossing the Hand. Fortune-tellers of the gipsy race always bid their
dupe to "cross their hand with a bit of
silver." This, they say, is for luck.
Of course, the sign of the cross warded
off witches and all other evil spirits, and,
as fortune-telling belongs to the black
arts, the palm is signed with a cross to
keep off the wiles of the devil. "You
need fear no evil, though I am a fortune-
teller, if by the sign of the cross you
exorcise the evil spirit."

Crossing the Line—*i.e.* the equator.

Crot'alum. A sort of castanet, rattled
in dancing. Aristopha'nēs calls a great
talker *krot'alon* (a clack).

Crot'chet. A whim; a fancy; a
twist of the mind, like the crotch or
crome of a stick. (*See* CROOK.)

"The duke hath crotchets in him."
    Shakespeare: Measure for Measure, iii. 2.

Croto'na's Sage. Pytha'goras. So
called because at Crotona he established
his first and chief school of philosophy.
Such success followed his teaching that
the whole aspect of the town became
more moral and decorous in a marvellously short time. About B.C. 540.

Crouchback. (*See* RED ROSE.)

Crouchmas, from the Invention of
the Cross to St. Helen's Day (May 3rd
to August 18th). Not Christ-mas, but
Cross-mas. Rogation Sunday is called
Crouchmas Sunday, and Rogation week
is called Crouchmas.

" From bull-cow fast,
    Till Crouchmas be past " [*i.e.* August 18th].
                    Tusser: May Remembrances.

Crow. *As the crow flies.* **The**
shortest route between two given places.
The crow flies straight to its point of
destination. Called the bee - line in
America.

Crow. (*See* RAVEN.)

*I must pluck a crow with you ; I have a
crow to pick with you.* I am displeased
with you, and must call you to account.
I have a small complaint to make against
you. In Howell's proverbs (1659) we
find the following, "I have a *goose* to
pluck with you," used in the same sense ;
and Chaucer has the phrase "Pull a
finch," but means thereby to cheat or
filch. Children of distinction among the
Greeks and Romans had birds for their
amusement, and in their boyish quarrels used to pluck or pull the feathers
out of each other's pets. Tyn'darus,
in his *Captives,* alludes to this, but
instances it with a *lapwing.* In hieroglyphics a crow symbolises contention,
discord, strife.

"If a crow help us in, sirrah, we'll pluck a crow
together."—*Shakespeare: Comedy of Errors,* iii. 1.

" If not, resolve before we go,
    That you and I must pull a crow."
                Butler: Hudibras, part ii. 2.

Crow over Ono (*To*), is to exult over
a vanquished or abased person. The allusion is to cocks, who always crow when
they have vanquished an adversary.

Crowbar. An iron with a crook,
used for leverage. (Anglo-Saxon, *cruc.*)

"Science is as far removed from brute force as
this sword from a crowbar."—*Bulwer-Lytton:
Leila,* book ii. chap. i. p. 33.

Crowd or **Crouth.** A species of fiddle
with six or more strings. The last noted
player on this instrument was John
Morgan, who died 1720. (Welsh, *crwth.*)

" O sweet consent, between a crowd and a Jew's
harp ! "   *Lyly.*

Crowde'ro. One of the rabble leaders
encountered by Hudibras at a bear-
baiting. The original of this character
was one Jackson or Jephson, a milliner,
who lived in the New Exchange, Strand.
He lost a leg in the service of the Roundheads, and was reduced to the necessity
of fiddling from alehouse to alehouse for
his daily bread. The word means fiddler.
(*See above,* CROWD.)

Crown. In heraldry nine crowns are
recognised : The oriental, the triumphal
or imperial, the diadem, the obsidional
crown, the civic, the crown vallery, the
mural crown, the naval, and the crown
celestial.

The blockade crown (*coro'na obsidio-
na'lis*), presented by the Romans to the
general who liberated a beleaguered

army. This was made of grass and wild flowers gathered from the spot.

A camp crown was given by the Romans to him who first forced his way into the enemy's camp. It was made of gold, and decorated with palisades.

A civic crown was presented to him who preserved the life of a *civis* or Roman citizen in battle. This crown was made of oak leaves, and bore the inscription, H.O.C.S.—*i.e. hostem occidit, ci'vem serva'vit (a foe he slew, a citizen saved).*

A mural crown was given by the Romans to that man who first scaled the wall of a besieged town. It was made of gold and decorated with battlements.

A naval crown was by the Romans given to him who won a naval victory. It was made of gold, and decorated with the beaks of ships.

An olive crown was by the Romans given to those who distinguished themselves in battle in some way not specially mentioned in other clauses.

An ova'tion crown (cord'na ova'lis) was by the Romans given to the general who vanquished pirates or any despised enemy. It was made of myrtle.

A triumphal crown was by the Romans given to the general who obtained a triumph. It was made of laurel or bay leaves. Sometimes a massive gold crown was given to a victorious general. (*See* LAUREL.)

⁕ *The iron crown of Lombardy* is the crown of the ancient Longobardic kings. It is now at Monza, in Italy. Henry of Luxembourg and succeeding kings were crowned with it. Napoleon I. put it on his head with his own hands. It is a thin fillet of iron, said to be hammered from a nail of the true cross, covered with a gold circle, enamelled with jewels, etc.

Crown Glass is window glass blown into a crown or hollow globe. It is flattened before it is fit for use.

Crown Office (*The*). A department belonging to the Court of Queen's Bench. There are three Crown officers appointed by the Lord Chief Justice—viz. (1) Queen's Coroner and Attorney ; (2) the Master ; and (3) the Assistant Master. The offices are held during good behaviour.

Crown of the East—*i.e.* Antioch, capital of Syria, which consisted of four walled cities, encompassed by a common rampart, that "enrounded them like a

coronet." It was also surnamed "the beautiful."

Crowns (worn by heathen deities) :

APOLLO wore a crown of laurels.
BACCHUS, of grapes or ivy.
CERES, of blades of wheat.
COMUS, of roses.
CYBĔLĒ, of pine leaves.
FLORA, of flowers.
FORTUNE, of fir-slips.
The GRACES, of olive-leaves.
HERCULES, of poplar-leaves.
HYMEN, of roses.
JUNO, of quince-leaves.
JUPITER, of oak-leaves.
The LARĔS, of rosemary.
MERCURY, of ivy, olive-leaves, or mulberries.
MINERVA, of olive-leaves.
The MUSES, of flowers.
PAN, of pine-leaves.
PLUTO, of cypress.
POMŎNA, of fruits.
SATURN, of vine-leaves.
VENUS, of myrtle or roses.

Crowner. Coroner—*i.e.* an officer of the Crown.

"The crowner hath sat on her, and finds it Christian burial."—*Shakespeare: Hamlet,* v. 1.

Crow's-Nest (*The*), in a Greenlander's galley, is a small room constructed of staves, something like an empty cask. It is fitted up with seats and other conveniences, and here the person on watch continues for two hours looking out for whales. The whale generally announces his approach by a "blowing," which may in favourable circumstances be heard several miles off.

Crowquill (*Alfred*). Alfred Henry Forrester (1805-1872).

Croysa'do. *The Great Croysado.* General Lord Fairfax. (*Hudibras.*)

Cro'zier or *Cro'sier*. An archbishop's staff terminates in a floriated cross, while a bishop's crook has a curved, bracken-like head. A bishop turns his crook *outwards*, to denote his wider authority ; an abbot (whose crook is the same as a bishop's) carries it turned *inwards*, to show that his jurisdiction is limited to his own inmates. When walking with a bishop an abbot covers his crook with a veil hanging from the knob, to show that his authority is veiled in the presence of his superior.

Cru'cial. *A crucial test.* A very severe and undeniable one. The allusion is to a fancy of Lord Bacon's, who said that two different diseases or sciences might run parallel for a time, but would ultimately cross each other : thus, the plague might for a time resemble other diseases, but when the *bubo* or boil appeared, the plague would assume its specific character. Hence the phrases *instan'tia crucis* (a crucial or unmistakable symptom), a crucial experiment, a crucial example, a crucial question, etc.

Crude Forms in grammar. The roots or essential letters of words. The words are crude or unfinished. Thus *am-* is the crude form of the verb *amo;* *bon-* of the adjective *bonus;* and *domin-* of the noun *dominus.*

Cruel (*The*). Pedro, King of Castile (1334, 1350-1369).

Pedro I. of Portugal; also called *le Justicier* (1320, 1357-1367).

Cruel (now **Crewel**) **Garters.** Garters made of worsted or yarn.

> "Ha ! ha ! look, he wears cruel garters."
> *Shakespeare: King Lear,* ii. 4.
> "Wearing of silk, why art thou so cruel ?"
> *Woman's a Weathercock* (1612).

Crummy. *That's crummy,* that's jolly good. *She's a crummy woman,* a fine handsome woman. Crummy means fat or fleshy. The crummy part of bread is the fleshy or main part. The opposite of " crusty " = ill-tempered.

Crump. "*Don't you wish you may get it, Mrs. Crump ?* " Grose says Mrs. Crump, a farmer's wife, was invited to dine with Lady Coventry, who was very deaf. Mrs. Crump wanted some beer, but, awed by the purple and plush, said, in a half-whisper, " I wish I had some beer, now." Mr. Flunkey, conscious that his mistress could not hear, replied in the same *aside,* " Don't you wish you may get it ? " At this the farmer's wife rose from table and helped herself. Lady Coventry, of course, demanded the reason, and the anecdote soon became a standing joke.

Crusades (2 syl.). Holy wars in which the warriors wore a cross, and fought, nominally at least, for the honour of the cross. Each nation had its special colour, which, says Matthew Paris (i. 446), was *red* for France ; *white* for England ; *green* for Flanders ; for Italy it was blue or *azure ;* for Spain, *gules ;* for Scotland, a St. Andrew's cross ; for the Knights Templars, red on white.

The seven Crusades.
(1) 1096-1100. Preached up by Peter the Hermit. Led by Godfrey of Bouillon, who took Jerusalem. As a result of this crusade, Geoffrey of Bouillon became the virtual king of Jerusalem.

(2) 1147-1149. At the instigation of St. Bernard. Led by Louis VII. and the Emperor Conrad. To secure the union of Europe.

(3) 1189-1193. Led by Richard *Lionheart.* For knightly distinction. This was against Saladin or Salah-Eddin.

(4) 1202-1204. Led by Baldwin of Flanders and the doge. To glorify the Venetians.

(5) 1217. Led by John of Brienne, titular King of Jerusalem. To suit his own purpose.

(6) 1228-1229. Led by Frederick II. As a result, Palestine was ceded to Frederick (Kaiser of Germany), who was crowned king of Jerusalem.

(7) 1248-1254 and (8) 1268-1270. To satisfy the religious scruples of Louis IX.

Crush. *To crush a bottle—i.e.* drink one. *Cf.* Milton's *crush the sweet poison.* The idea is that of crushing the grapes. Shakespeare has also *burst* a bottle in the same sense (Induction of *Taming the Shrew*). (*See* CRACK.)

> " Come and crush a cup of wine."
> *Shakespeare: Romeo and Juliet,* i. 2.

To crush a fly on a wheel. To crack a nut with a steam-hammer ; to employ power far too valuable for the purpose to be accomplished. The wheel referred to is the rack. (*See* BREAK A BUTTERFLY.)

Crush-room (*The*) of an opera or theatre. A room provided for ladies where they can wait till their carriages are called. Called *crush* because the room is not only crowded, but all crush towards the door, hoping each call will be that of their own carriage. " Mrs. X.'s carriage stops the way," " Lord X.'s carriage," etc.

Cru'soe (*A*). A solitary man ; the only inhabitant of a place. The tale of Defoe is well known, which describes Robinson Crusoe as cast on a desert island, where he employs the most admirable ingenuity in providing for his daily wants.

> " Whence creeping forth, to Duty's call he yields
> And strolls the Crusoe of the lonely fields."
> *Bloomfield: Farmer's Boy.*

Crust. *The upper crust* (of society). The aristocracy; the upper ten-thousand.

Crus'ted Port. When port is first bottled its fermentation is not complete ; in time it precipitates argol on the sides of the bottle, where it forms a crust. Crusted port, therefore, is port which has completed its fermentation.

⁖ The " crust " is composed of argol, tartrate of lime, and colouring matter, thus making the wine more ethereal in quality and lighter in colour.

Crus'ty. Ill-tempered, apt to take offence. This is formed from the old word *crous*, cross, peevish.

> " Azeyn [against] hem was he kene ane crous,
> And said, ' Goth out my Fader hous.' "
> *Cursor Mundi.*

Crutched Friars is the Latin *crucia'ti* (crossed)—*i.e.* having a cross embroidered on their dress. They were of the Trinitarian order.

Crux (*A*). A knotty point, a difficulty. *Instantia crucis* means a crucial test, or the point where two similar diseases *crossed* and showed a special feature. It does not refer to the cross, an instrument of punishment; but to the crossing of two lines, called also a *node* or knot ; hence a trouble or difficulty. *Quæ te mala crux agitat ?* (Plautus) ; What' evil cross distresses you?—*i.e.* what difficulty, what trouble are you under ?

Crux Ansa'ta. The tau cross with a loop or handle at the top. (*See* CROSS.)

Crux Decussata. A St. Andrew's cross

> "Crux decussāta est in qua duo ligna directa et æqualibilia inter se obliquantur, cujus formam refert litera **X** quæ, ut ait Isidorus (Orig. 1, iii.) 'in figura crucem et in numero decem demonstrat.' Hæc vulgo Andreana vocatur, quod vetus traditio sit in hac S. Antream fuisse necatum."— *Gretser : De Cruce*, book i. p. 2.

Crux Pectora'lis. The cross which bishops of the Church of Rome suspend over their breast.

> "Crucem cum pretioso ligno vel cum reliquis Sanctorum ante pectus portare suspensum ad collum, hoc est quod vocant encolpium [*or* crux Pectorālis]."—See *Ducange*, vol. iii. p. 302, col. 2, article ENCOLPIUM.

Cry.
Great cry and little wool. This is derived from the ancient mystery of *David and Abigail*, in which Nabal is represented as shearing his sheep, and the Devil, who is made to attend the churl, imitates the act by "shearing a hog." Originally, the proverb ran thus, "Great cry and little wool, as the Devil said when he sheared the hogs." N.B. —Butler alters the proverb into "All cry and no wool."

Cry of Animals (*The*). (*See* ANIMALS.)

Cry (*To*).
To cry over spilt milk. To fret about some loss which can never be repaired.

Cry Cavē (*To*). To ask mercy ; to throw up the sponge ; to confess oneself beaten. (Latin, *caveo.*) (*See* CAVE IN.)

Cry Havock! No quarter. In a tract entitled *The Office of the Constable and Mareschall in the Tyme of Werre*

(contained in the Black Book of the Admiralty), one of the chapters is, "The peyne of hym that crieth havock, and of them that followeth him "—"*Item si quis inventus fuerit qui clamorem inceperit qui vocatur havok.*"

> " Cry Havock, and let slip the dogs of war."
> *Shakespeare : Julius Cæsar*, iii. 1

Cry Quits. (*See* QUITS.)

Cry Vinegar (*To*). In French, *Crier Vinaigre.* The shout of sportsmen when a hare is caught. He cries "Vinegar !" he has caught the hare ; metaphorically it means, he has won success. "*C'étoit, dit le Duchat, la coutume en Languedoc, entre les chasseurs, de s'écrier l'un à l'autre 'Vinaigre,' dès qu'ils avaient tiré un lièvre, parceque la vraie sauce de cet animal est le vinaigre.*"

Crier au Vinaigre has quite another meaning. It is the reproof to a landlord who serves his customers with bad wine. In a figurative sense it means *Crier au Voleur.*

Cry Wolf. (*See* WOLF.)

Crystal Hills. On the coast of the Caspian, near Badku, is a mountain which sparkles like diamonds, from the sea-glass and crystals with which it abounds.

Crystal'line (3 syl.). *The Crystalline sphere.* According to Ptolemy, between the "primum mobile" and the firmament or sphere of the fixed stars comes the crystal'line sphere, which oscillates or has a shimmering motion that interferes with the regular motion of the stars.

> " They pass the planets seven, and pass the 'fixed'
> And that crystal'line sphere, whose balance weighs
> The trepidation talked (of)."
> *Milton : Paradise Lost*, iii.

Cub. An ill-mannered lout. The cub of a bear is said to have no shape until its dam has licked it into form.

> " A bear's a savage beast, of all
> Most ugly and unnatural ;
> Whelped without form until the dam
> Has licked it into shape and frame."
> *Butler : Hudibras*, i. 3.

Cuba. The Roman deity who kept guard over infants in their cribs and sent them to sleep. Verb *cubo*, to lie down in bed.

Cube. *A faultless cube.* A truly good man ; a regular brick. (*See* BRICK.)

> Ὁ γ' ὡς ἀληθῶς ἀγαθὸς καὶ τετράγωνος ἄνευ ψόγου.—*Aristotle : Nicomachean Ethics*, i. 11, sec. 11.

Cucking-stool (*The*) or *Choking-stool*, for ducking scolds, is not connected with *choke* (to stifle), but the French *choquer ;* hence the archaic verb *cuck* (to throw), and one still in use, *chuck*

(chuck-farthing). The cucking-stool is the stool which is chucked or thrown into the water.

"Now, if one cucking-stool was for each scold,
Some towns, I fear, would not their numbers
hold." *Poor Robin* (1746).

Cuckold. (*See* ACTÆON.)

Cuckold King (*The*). Mark of Cornwall, whose wife Yseult intrigued with Sir Tristram, one of the Knights of the Round Table.

Cuckold's Point. A spot on the riverside near Deptford. So called from a tradition that King John made there successful love to a labourer's wife.

Cuckoo. A cuckold. The cuckoo occupies the nest and eats the eggs of other birds ; and Dr. Johnson says " it was usual to alarm a husband at the approach of an adulterer by calling out ' Cuckoo,' which by mistake was applied in time to the person warned." Green calls the cuckoo " the cuckold's quirister " (*Quip for an Upstart Courtier*, 1620). This is an instance of how words get in time perverted from their original meaning. The Romans used to call an adulterer a " cuckoo," as " *Te cuculum uxor ex lustris rapit*" (*Plautus : Asinaria*, v. 3), and the allusion was simple and correct ; but Dr. Johnson's explanation will hardly satisfy anyone for the modern perversion of the word.

"The cuckoo, then, on every tree,
Mocks married men ; for thus sings he,
Cuckoo !
Cuckoo ! cuckoo ! O word of fear,
Unpleasing to a married ear ! "
Shakespeare : Love's Labour's Lost, v. 2.

Cuckoo (*A*). A watch or clock. The French have the same slang word *coucou* for a watch or clock. Of course, the word is derived from the German cuckoo-clocks, which, instead of striking the hour, cry cuckoo.

Cuckoo Oats and Woodcock Hay. *Cuckoo oats and woodcock hay make a farmer run away.* If the spring is so backward that oats cannot be sown till the cuckoo is heard (*i.e.* April), or if the autumn is so wet that the aftermath of hay cannot be got in till woodcock shooting (middle of November), the farmer must be a great sufferer.

Cuckoo - Spit, " Frog - Spit," or " Froth-Spit." The spume which forms the nidus of an insect called the *Cicada Spumaria*, or, more strictly speaking, the *Cercopis Spumaria* (one of the three divisions of the Cicadariæ). This spume is found on lavender-bushes, rosemary, fly-catch, and some other plants. Like the cochineal, the cicada spumaria exudes a foam for its own warmth, and for protection during its transition state. The word "cuckoo" in this case means spring or cuckoo-time.

Cu'cumber Time. The dull season in the tailoring trade. The Germans call it *Die saure Gurken Zeit* (pickled gherkin time). Hence the expression *Tailors are vegetarians*, because they live on " cucumber " when without work, and on " cabbage " when in full employ. (*Notes and Queries.*) (*See* GHERKIN.)

Cuddy. An ass ; a dolt. A gipsy term, from the Persian *gudda* and the Hindustanee *ghudda* (an ass).

"Hast got thy breakfast, brother cuddy?"
D. Wingate.

Cudgel One's Brains (*To*). To make a painful effort to remember or understand something. The idea is from taking a stick to beat a dull boy under the notion that dulness is the result of temper or inattention.

"Cudgel thy brains no more about it ; for your
dull ass will not mend his pace with beating."—
Shakespeare ; Hamlet, v. 1.

Cudgels. *To take up the cudgels.* To maintain an argument or position. To fight, as with a cudgel, for one's own way.

"For some reason he did not feel as hot to take
up the cudgels for Almira with his mother."—*M.
E. Wilkins : A Modern Dragon.*

Cue (1 syl.). The tail of a sentence (French, *queue*), the catch-word which indicates when another actor is to speak ; a hint ; the state of a person's temper, as " So-and-so is in a good cue (or) bad cue."

"When my cue comes, call me, and I will
answer." — *Shakespeare : Midsummer Night's
Dream*, iv. 1.

To give the cue. To give the hint. (*See above.*)

Cuffy. A negro ; both a generic word and proper name.

"Sambo and Cuffey expand under every sky."—
Mrs. Beecher Stowe : Uncle Tom's Cabin.

Cui bono ? Who is benefited thereby ? To whom is it a gain ? The more usual meaning attached to the words is, What good will it do? For what good purpose ? It was the question of Judge Cassius. (See *Cicero : Pro Milone*, 12, sec. 32.)

"Cato, that great and grave philosopher, did
commonly demand, when any new project was
propounded unto him, *cui bono*, what good will
ensue in case the same is effected?"—*Fuller :
Worthies* (The Design, i.).

Cuirass. Sir Arthur's cuirass was " carved of one emerald, centred in a sun of silver rays, that lightened as he breathed." (*Tennyson : Élaine.*)

Cuish'es or *Cuisses* (2 syl.). Armour for the thighs. (French, *cuisse*, the thigh.)

"Soon o'er his thighs he placed the cuishes bright." *Jerusalem Delivered*, book xi.
" His cuisses on his thighs, gallantly armed."
    Shakespeare : 1 *Henry IV., iv.* 1.

Cul de Sac (French). A blind alley, or alley blocked up at one end like a sack. Figuratively, an argument, etc., that leads to nothing.

Culdees. A religious order of Ireland and Scotland, said to have been founded in the sixth century by St. Columba. So called from the Gaelic *cylle-dee* (a house of cells) or *ceilede* (servants of God, *ceile*, a servant). Giraldus Cambrensis, going to the Latin for its etymology, according to a custom unhappily not yet extinct, derives it from *colo-deus* (to worship God).

Cullis. A very fine and strong broth, well strained, and much used for invalids. (French, *coulis*, from *couler*, to strain.)

Cully. A fop, a fool, a dupe. A contracted form of cullion, a despicable creature (Italian, *coglione*). Shakespeare uses the word two or three times, as "Away, base cullions!" (2 *Henry VI.*, i. 3), and again in *Taming of the Shrew*, iv. 2 —"And makes a god of such a cullion." (Compare GULL.)

    "You base cullion, you."
Ben Jonson : Every Man in his Humour, iii. 2.

Cul'minate (3 syl.). Come to a crisis. The passage of a celestial body over the meridian at the upper transit is called its culmination. (Latin, *culmen*, the top.)

Culross Girdles. The thin plate of iron used in Scotland for the manufacture of oaten cakes is called a "girdle," for which Culross was long celebrated.

" Locks and bars, plough-graith and harrow-teeth ! and why not grates and fireprongs, and Culross girdles ?"—*Scott : Fair Maid of Perth*, chap. ii.

Cul'ver. Pigeon. (Old English, *col-ver ;* Latin, *columba ;* hence culver-house, a dove-cote.)

    " On liquid wing,"
    The sounding culver shoots."
        Thomson : Spring 452.

Cul'verin properly means a serpent (Latin, *colubri'nus*, the col'uber), but is applied to a long, slender piece of artillery employed in the sixteenth century to carry balls to a great distance. Queen Elizabeth's "Pocket Pistol" in Dover Castle is a culverin.

Cul'verkeys. The keys or flowers of the culver or columba, *i.e.* columbine. (Anglo-Saxon *culfre*, a dove.)

Cum Grano Salis. With its grain of salt ; there is a grain of wheat in the bushel of chaff, and we must make the proper abatement.

Cum Hoc, Propter Hoc. Because two or more events occur consecutively or simultaneously, one is not necessarily the outcome of the other. Sequence of events is not always the result of cause and effect. The swallows come to England in the spring, but do not bring the spring.

" [Free trade and revival of trade] says Lord Penzance, came simultaneously, but, he adds, 'There is no more dangerous form of reasoning than the *cum hoc, propter hoc*.' "—*Nineteenth Century*, April, 1886.,

Cumberland Poet (*The*). William Wordsworth, born at Cockermouth. (1770-1850.)

Cummer. A gammer, gudewife, old woman. A variety of gammer which is *grande-mère* (our grandmother), as gaffer is *grand-père* or grandfather. It occurs scores of times in Scott's novels.

Cuncta'tor [*the delayer*]. Quintus Fa'bius Max'imus, the Roman general who baffled Hannibal by avoiding direct engagements, and wearing him out by marches, countermarches, and skirmishes from a distance. This was the policy by which Duguesclin forced the English to abandon their possessions in France in the reign of Charles V. (*le Sage*). (*See* FABIAN.)

Cu'neiform Letters. Letters like wedges (Latin, *cu'neus*, a wedge). These sort of letters occur in old Persian and Babylonian inscriptions. They are sometimes called *Arrow-headed characters*, and those found at Babylon are called *nail-headed*. This species of writing is the most ancient of which we have any knowledge ; and was first really deciphered by Grotefend in 1802.

Cunning Man or **Woman.** A fortune-teller, one who professes to discover stolen goods. (Anglo-Saxon, *cunnan*, to know.)

Cu'no. The ranger, father of Agatha, in Weber's opera of *Der Freischütz*.

Cu'nobelin's Gold Mines. Caverns in the chalk beds of Little Thurrock, Essex ; so called from the tradition that King Cu'nobelin hid in them his gold. They are sometimes called Dane-holes, because they were used as lurking-places by the Norsemen.

Cunstance. A model of Resignation, daughter of the Emperor of Rome. The Sultan of Syria, in order to have her for his wife, renounced his religion and turned Christian; but the Sultan's mother murdered him, and turned Cunstance adrift on a raft. After a time the raft stranded on a rock near Northumberland, and the constable rescued Cunstance, and took her home, where she converted his wife, Hermegild. A young lord fell in love with her; but, his suit being rejected, he murdered Hermegild, and laid the charge of murder against Cunstance. King Ella adjudged the cause, and Cunstance being proved innocent, he married her. While Ella was in Scotland, Cunstance was confined with a boy, named Maurice; and Ella's mother, angry with Cunstance for the introduction of the Christian religion, put her on a raft adrift with her baby boy. They were accidentally found by a senator, and taken to Rome. Ella, having discovered that his mother had turned his wife and child adrift, put her to death, and went to Rome in pilgrimage to atone for his crime. Here he fell in with his wife and son. Maurice succeeded his grandfather as Emperor of Rome, and at the death of Ella, Cunstance returned to her native land. (*Chaucer: The Man of Lawes Tale.*)

Cuntur. A bird worshipped by the ancient Peruvians. It is generally called the "condor," and by the Arabians the "roc."

Cup.

A deadly cup. Referring to the ancient practice of putting persons to death by poison, as Socratēs was put to death by the Athenians.

"In the hand of the Lord there is a cup [a deadly cup], the dregs thereof all the wicked of the earth shall wring them out and drink them."—Psalm lxxv. 8.

Let this cup pass from me. Let this trouble or affliction be taken away, that I may not be compelled to undergo it. The allusion is to the Jewish practice of assigning to guests a certain portion of wine—as, indeed, was the custom in England at the close of the eighteenth century and the first quarter of the nineteenth. This cup is "full of the wine of God's fury," let me not be compelled to drink it.

Many a slip 'twixt the cup and the lip. (*See* ANCÆUS.)

My [or *his*] *cup runs over.* My blessings overflow. Here cup signifies portion or blessing.

"My cup runneth over . . . goodness and mercy follow me all the days of my life."—Psalm xxiii. 5, 6.

We must drink the cup. We must bear the burden awarded to us, the sorrow which falls to our lot. The allusion is to the words of our Lord in the garden of Gethsem'anë (Matt. xxvi. 39; also xx. 22). One way of putting criminals to death in ancient times was by poison; Socratēs had hemlock to drink. In allusion to this it is said that Jesus Christ *tasted* death for every man (Heb. ii. 9).

Cup, in the university of Cambridge, means a mixture of strong ale with spice and a lemon, served up hot in a silver cup. Sometimes a roasted orange takes the place of a lemon. If wine is added, the cup is called *bishop;* if brandy is added, the beverage is called *cardinal.* (*See* BISHOP.)

Cup Tosser. A juggler (French, *joueur de gobelet*). The old symbol for a juggler was a goblet. The phrase and symbol are derived from the practice of jugglers who toss in the air, twist on a stick, and play all sorts of tricks with goblets or cups.

Cup of Vows (*The*). It used to be customary at feasts to drink from cups of mead, and vow to perform some great deed worthy of the song of a skald. There were four cups: one to Odin, for victory; one to Frey, for a good year, one to Niörd, for peace; and one to Bragi, for celebration of the dead in poetry.

Cups. *He was in his cups.* Intoxicated. (Latin, *inter pocula, inter vina.*) (*Horace: 3 Odes,* vi. 20.)

Cu'par. *He that will to Cupar maun to Cupar.* He that will have his own way, must have it even to his injury. The reference is to the Cistercian monastery, founded here by Malcolm IV.

Cupar Justice. Same as "Jedburgh Justice," hang first and try afterwards. Abingdon Law is another phrase. It is said that Major-General Brown, of Abingdon, in the Commonwealth, first hanged his prisoners and then tried them.

Cupboard Love. Love from interested motives. The allusion is to the love of children to some indulgent person who gives them something nice from her cupboard.

"Cupboard love is seldom true."—*Poor Robin.*

Cupid. The god of love, and son of Venus. According to fable he wets with blood the grindstone on which he sharpens his arrows.

> "Ferus et Cupido,
> Semper ardentes acuens sagittas."
> *Horace: 2 Odes,* viii. 14,15.

✸ The best statues of this little god are "Cupid Sleeping," in Albano (Rome) ; "Cupid playing with a Swan," in the Capitol; "Cupid mounted on a Tiger," (Negroni) ; and "Cupid stringing his Bow," in the Louvre (Paris). Raphael's painting of Cupid is in the Farnesina (Rome).

Cupid and Psyche. An exquisite episode in the *Golden Ass* of Apule'ius. It is an allegory representing the progress of the soul to perfection. Mrs. Tighe has a poem on the same subject ; and Molière a drama entitled *Psyche.* (*See* Morris, *Earthly Paradise* [May].)

Cupid's Golden Arrow. Virtuous love. "Cupid's leaden arrow," sensual passion.

> " Deque sagittifera promsit duo tela pharetra
>   Diversorum operum ; fugat hoc, facit illud
>   amorem.
> Quod facit auratum est, et cuspide fulget acuta,—
>   Quod fugat obtusum est, et habet sub arundine
>   plumbum."
> *Ovid: Tale of Apollo and Daphnë.*
> " I swear to thee by Cupid's strongest bow ;
> By his best arrow with the golden head . . . .
> By that which knitteth souls and prospers love."
> *Shakespeare: Midsummer Night's Dream.*

Cupidon (*Le jeune*). Count d'Orsay was so called by Lord Byron (1798-1852). The Count's father was styled *Le beau d'Orsay.*

Cur. A fawning, mean-spirited fellow ; a crop-tailed dog (Latin, *curtus,* crop-tailed ; French, *court ;* our *curt*). According to forest laws, a man who had no right to the privilege of the chase was obliged to cut off the tail of his dog. Hence, a degenerate dog or man is called a cur.

> " What would you have, you curs,
>   That like nor peace nor war ? "
> *Shakespeare: Coriolanus,* i. 1.

Curate. (*See* CLERICAL TITLES.)

Curé de Meudon—*i.e.* Rabelais, who was first a monk, then a leech, then prebend of St. Maur, and lastly curé of Meudon. (1483-1553.)

Cure'tes (3 syl.). A mythical people of Crete, to whom the infant Zeus or Jupiter was entrusted by his mother Rhea. By clashing their shields they drowned the cries of the infant, to prevent its father (Cronos) from finding the place where the babe was hid,

Curfew Bell. The bell rung in the reigns of William I. and II. at sunset, to give notice to their subjects that they were to put out their fires and candles (French, *couvre feu,* cover-fire). The Klokans in Abo, even to the present day, traverse the towns crying the "go-to-bed time." Those abroad are told to "make haste home," and those at home to "put out their fires." Abolished, as a police regulation, by Henry I.

> "The curfew tolls the knell of parting day."
> *Gray: Elegy.*

Curmud'geon (3 syl.). A grasping, miserly churl. Dr. Johnson gives the derivation of this word thus, "*cœur mechant,* unknown correspondent." Dr. Ash, in his dictionary, says, "*cœur,* unknown ; *mechant,* correspondent," a blunder only paralleled by the schoolboy translation of the Greek, *me genoito,* by μὴ (God) γένοιτο (forbid) (Luke xx. 6).

Currant. A corruption of *Corinth,* hence called by Ju'venal *Corinthi'aca uvæ.*

Current. *The drift of the current* is the rate per hour at which the current runs.
The setting of the current is that point of the compass towards which the waters of the current run.

Currente Cal'amo (Latin). Offhand ; without premeditation ; written off at once, without making a rough copy first.

Currer Bell. The *nom de plume* of Charlotte Brontë.

Curry Favour. The French *courir,* to hunt after, to seek, as *courir une charge, courir un bénéfice,* to sue for a living ; *courir les tables,* to go a spunging. Similarly, *courir les faveurs,* to sue for, court, or seek favours.

Curse or **Cuss.** *Not worth a curse. I don't care a curse* (or *cuss*). Here "curse" is a corruption of *cerse* or *kerse.* Similarly, the Latin *nihil* [*nihilum*] is *ne hilum,* not [worth] the black eye of a bean. Other phrases are "not a straw," "not a pin," "not a rap," "not a dam," "not a bit," "not a jot," "not a pin's point," "not a button." (Anglo-Saxon, *cerse,* cress ; German, *kirsche,* a cherry.)

> " Wisdom and witt nowe is not worthe a kerse."
> *Robert Langeland: Piers Ploughman.*

Curse of Scotland. The nine of diamonds. The two most plausible suggestions are these : (1) The nine of diamonds in the game of *Pope Joan* is called the Pope, the Antichrist of the

Scotch reformers. (2) In the game of *comette*, introduced by Queen Mary, it is the great winning card, and the game was the curse of Scotland because it was the ruin of so many families.

Other suggestions are these. (3) The word "curse" is a corruption of *cross*, and the nine of diamonds is so arranged as to form a St. Andrew's Cross ; but as the nine of hearts would do as well, this explanation must be abandoned. (4) Some say it was the card on which the "Butcher Duke" wrote his cruel order after the Battle of Cullod'en ; but the term must have been in vogue at the period, as the ladies nicknamed Justice-Clerk Ormistone "The Nine of Diamonds" (1715). (5) Similarly, we must reject the suggestion that it refers to the arms of Dalrymple, Earl of Stair— viz. or, on a saltire azure, nine lozenges of the first. The earl was justly held in abhorrence for the massacre of Glencoe ; so also was Colonel Packer, who attended Charles I. on the scaffold, and had for his arms "gules a cross lozengy or."

Grose says of the nine of diamonds : " Diamonds . . . imply royalty . . . . and every ninth King of Scotland has been observed for many ages to be a tyrant and a curse to the country."—*Tour Thro' Scotland*, 1789.
.*. It is a pity that Grose does not give the names of these kings. Malcolm III. was assassinated in 1046 by Macbeth, William was taken prisoner by Henry II. (died 1214), James I. was assassinated in 1437.

Curses. *Curses, like chickens, come home to roost.* Curses fall on the head of the curser, as chickens which stray during the day return to their roost at night.

Cursing by Bell, Book, and Candle, is reading the anathema in the church, then closing the Bible, tolling the bell, and extinguishing all the candles, saying "*Fiat, fiat ! Do-to* (close) the Book, quench the candles, ring the bell. Amen, amen."

Cursitor (Latin, *clericus de cursu*). Formerly a clerk of the course ; a chancery clerk, who made out original writs for the beat, course, or part of the county allotted him. A Newgate solicitor was called a cursitor in depreciation of his office.

Curst. *Curst cows have curt horns.* Angry men cannot do all the mischief they wish. Curst means "angry" or "fierce," and curt is "short," as curtmantle, curt-hose. The Latin proverb is, "*Dat Deus immi'ti cor'nua curta bovi.*"

" You are called plain Kate,
And bonny Kate, and sometimes Kate the curst."
Shakespeare : Taming of the Shrew, ii. 1.

Curtail. To cut short. (French, *court tailler*, to short cut, whence the old French *courtault*.)

Curtain (*The*). In fortification, the line of rampart which joins together the flanks of two "bastions" (*q.v.*).

Curtain. *To ring down the curtain.* To bring a matter to an end. A theatrical term. When the act or play is over, the bell rings and the green curtain comes down.

" A few more matters of routine will be accomplished, and then the curtain will be rung down on the Session of 1891."—*Newspaper Paragraph*, July 27th, 1891.

Curtain Lecture. The nagging of a wife after her husband is in bed. The lectures of Mrs. Caudle in *Punch* are first-rate caricatures of these "small cattle."

" Besides what endless brawls by wives are bred,
The curtain lecture makes a mournful bed."
Dryden.

Curtal Friar. A friar who served as an attendant at the gate of a monastery court. As a curtal dog was not privileged to hunt or course, so a curtal friar virtually meant a worldly-minded one.

" Some do call me the curtal Friar of Fountain Dale ; others again call me in jest the Abbot of Fountain Abbey ; others still again call me simply Friar Tuck."—*Howard Pyle : The Merry Adventures of Robin Hood*, ii. p. 141.

Curta'na. The sword of Edward the Confessor, which, having no point, was the emblem of mercy. The royal sword of England was so called to the reign of Henry III.

" But when Curtana will not do the deed,
You lay the pointless clergy-weapon by,
And to the laws, your sword of justice, fly."
Dryden : Hind and Panther, part ii. 419-21.

Curthose (2 syl.). Robert II., Duc de Normandie (1087-1134).

Curtis'e (2 syl.). The little hound in the tale of *Reynard the Fox*, by Heinrich von Alkman (1498). (High German, *kurz* ; French, *courte*, short or small.)

Curtmantle. The surname of Henry II. He introduced the Anjou mantle, which was shorter than the robe worn by his predecessors. (1133, 1154-1189.) (*See* CARACALLA.)

Curule Chair. Properly a chariot chair, an ornamental camp-stool made of ivory placed by the Romans in a chariot for the chief magistrate when he went to attend the council. As dictators, consuls, prætors, censors, and the chief ediles occupied such a chair, they were termed *curule* magistrates or *curu′lēs.* Horace calls the chair *curule ebur* (1 *Epist.*, vi. 53).

Curzon Street (London). Named after the ground landlord, George August Curzon, third Viscount Howe.

Cussedness. Ungainliness; perversity; an evil temper; malice prepense. Halliwell gives *cuss* = surly.

"The turkey-cock is just as likely as not to trample on the young turkeys and smash them, or to split their skulls by a savage dig of his powerful beak. Whether this is 'cussedness' pure and simple . . . . has not been satisfactorily determined."—*Daily News*, December 22nd, 1885.

Cus′tard. A slap on the hand with a ferula. The word should be *custid*, unless a play is meant. (Latin, *custis*, a club or stick.)

Custard Coffin. (*See* COFFIN.)

Cus′tomer. A man or acquaintance. *A rum customer* is one better left alone, as he is likely to show fight if interfered with. A shop term. (*See* CARD.)

"Here be many of her old customers."
    Shakespeare: Measure for Measure, iv. 3.

Custos Rotulo′rum (*keeper of the rolls*). The chief civil officer of a county, to whose custody are committed the records or rolls of the sessions.

Cut. To renounce acquaintance. There are four sorts of cut—

(1) The *cut direct* is to stare an acquaintance in the face and pretend not to know him.

(2) The *cut indirect*, to look another way, and pretend not to see him.

(3) The *cut sublime*, to admire the top of some tall edifice or the clouds of heaven till the person cut has passed by.

(4) The *cut infernal*, to stoop and adjust your boots till the party has gone past.

There is a very remarkable Scripture illustration of the word *cut*, meaning to renounce: "Jehovah took a staff and cut it asunder, in token that He would break His covenant with His people; and He cut another staff asunder, in token that He would break the brotherhood between Judah and Israel" (Zech. xi. 7-14).

Cut.

Cut and come again. Take a cut from the joint, and come for another if you like.

To cut the ground from under one (or *from under his feet*). To leave an adversary no ground to stand on, by disproving all his arguments.

He has cut his eye-teeth. He is wide awake, he is a knowing one. The eye-teeth are the canine teeth, just under the eyes, and the phrase means he can bite as well as bark. Of course, the play is on the word "eye," and those who have cut their eye-teeth are wide awake.

Cut your wisdom teeth. Wisdom teeth are those at the extreme end of the jaws, which do not make their appearance till persons have come to years of discretion. When persons say or do silly things, the remark is made to them that "they have not yet cut their wisdom teeth," or reached the years of discretion.

Cut the knot. Break through an obstacle. The reference is to the Gordian knot (*q.v.*) shown to Alexander, with the assurance that whoever loosed it would be made ruler of all Asia; whereupon the Macedonian cut it in two with his sword, and claimed to have fulfilled the prophecy.

I must cut my stick—i.e. leave. The Irish usually cut a shillelah before they start on an expedition. *Punch* gives the following witty derivation:—"Pilgrims on leaving the Holy Land used to cut a palm-stick, to prove that they had really been to the Holy Sepulchre. So brother Francis would say to brother Paul, 'Where is brother Benedict?' 'Oh (says Paul), he has cut his stick!' —*i.e.* he is on his way home."

I′ll cut your comb for you. Take your conceit down. The allusion is to the practice of cutting the combs of capons.

He′ll cut up well. He is rich, and his property will cut into good slices.

Cut Blocks with a Razor (*To*). To do something astounding by insignificant means; to do something more eccentric than inexpedient. According to Dean Swift, to "make pincushions of sunbeams." The tale is that Accius, or Attus Navius, a Roman augur, opposed the king Tarquin the Elder, who wished to double the number of senators. Tarquin, to throw ridicule on the augur, sneered at his pretensions of augury, and asked him if he could do what was then in his thoughts. "Undoubtedly," replied Navius; and Tarquin with a laugh, said, "Why, I was thinking whether I could cut through this whetstone with a razor." "Cut boldly," cried Navius, and the whetstone was cleft in two. This story forms the subject of one of Bon Gaultier's ballads, and Goldsmith refers to it in his *Retaliation:*

"In short, 'twas his [Burke's] fate, unemployed or in place, sir,
To eat mutton cold, and cut blocks with a razor."

Cut neither Nails nor Hair at Sea.
Petronius says, "*Non licere cuiquam
mortalium in nave neque ungues neque
capillos deponere, nisi cum pelago ventus
irascitur.*" The cuttings of the nails
and hair were votive offerings to Proserpine, and it would excite the jealousy
of Neptune to make offerings to another
in his own special kingdom.

Cut Off with a Shilling. Disinherited. Blackstone tells us that the
Romans set aside those testaments which
passed by the natural heirs unnoticed;
but if any legacy was left, no matter
how small, it proved the testator's intention. English law has no such
provision, but the notion at one time
prevailed that the name of the heir
should appear in the will; and if he was
bequeathed "a shilling," that the testator had not forgotten him, but disinherited him intentionally.

Cut out. Left in the lurch; superseded. In cards, when there are too
many for a game (say whist), it is customary for the players to cut out after
a [rubber], in order that another player
may have a turn. This is done by the
players cutting the cards on the table,
and the lowest turn-up gives place to
the new hand, who "supersedes" him,
or takes his place.
✢ It does not refer to cutting out a
ship from an enemy's port.
He is cut out for a sailor. His natural propensities are suited for the
vocation. The allusion is to cutting out
cloth, etc., for specific purposes.

**Cut your Coat according to your
Cloth.** Stretch your arm no farther
than your sleeve will reach.

"Little barks must keep near shore,
Larger ones may venture more."

French : "Selon ta bourse nourris ta
bouche." "Selon le pain il faut le
couteau." "Fou est, qui plus dépense
que sa rente ne vaut."
Italian : "Noi facciamo la spese se-
condo l'entrata."
Latin : "Ex quovis ligno non fit
Mercurius." "Parvum parva decent"
(*Horace*). "Messe tenus propria vive"
(*Persius*). "Cui multum est piperis,
etiam oleribus immiscet." "Sumptus
censum ne superat" (*Plautus*). "Si
non possis quod velis, velis id quod
possis." "Ne te quæsiveris extra"
(*Horace*).

Cut a Dash. Make a show. Cut is
the French *couper*, better seen in the

noun *coup*, as a *grand coup*, a *coup de
maître* (a masterly stroke), so "to cut"
means to make a masterly coup, to do
something to be looked at and talked
about. Dashing means *striking—i.e.*
showy, as a "dashing fellow," a "dashing equipage." To cut a dash is to
get one's self looked at and talked about
for a showy or striking appearance.

Cut and Dry. Already prepared.
"He had a speech all cut and dry."
The allusion is to timber cut, dry, and
fit for use.

"Sets of phrases, cut and dry,
Evermore thy tongue supply." *Swift.*

Cut and Run. Be off as quickly as
possible. A sea phrase, meaning cut
your cable and run before the wind.

Cut Away. Be off at once. This is
a French phrase, *couper* (cut away)—*i.e.*
to break through the enemy's ranks by
cutting them down with your swords.

Cut Capers (*To*). To act in an unusual manner.

"The quietest fellows are forced to fight for
their *status quo*, and sometimes to cut capers like
the rest."—*Le Fanu: The House in the Churchyard,* p. 143.

To cut capers (in dancing) is to spring
upwards, and rapidly interlace one foot
with the other.
Cut your capers! Be off with you !
I'll make him cut his capers, i.e. rue
his conduct.

Cut it Short. (*See* AUDLEY.)

Cut of his Jib. The contour or expression of his face. This is a sailor's
phrase. The cut of a jib or foresail of
a ship indicates her character. Thus, a
sailor says of a suspicious vessel, he
"does not like the cut of her jib."

Cut Short is to shorten. "Cut short
all intermission" (*Macbeth*, iv. 3). *To
cut it short* means to bring to an end
what you are doing or saying.
His life was cut short. He died pre-
maturely. The allusion is to Atropos,
one of the three Parcæ, cutting the
thread of life spun by her sister Clo'tho.

Cut up Rough (*To*). To be disagreeable or quarrelsome about anything.

Cuthbert. *St. Cuthbert's beads.* Joints
of the articulated stems of encrinites,
used for rosaries. St. Cuthbert was a
Scotch monk of the sixth century, and
may be termed the St. Patrick of Great
Britain. He is said to sit at night on a
rock in Holy Island, and to use the opposite rock as his anvil while he forges

the en'trochites (*en'-tro-kites*). (*See* BEAD.)

> "On a rock of Lindisfarn
> St. Cuthbert sits, and toils to frame
> The sea-born beads that bear his name."
> *Scott: Marmion.*

St. Cuthbert's Stone. A granite rock in Cumberland.

St. Cuthbert's Well. A spring of water close by St. Cuthbert's Stone.

Cuthbert Bede. A *nom de plume* of the Rev. Edward Bradley, author of *Verdant Green*. (1827-1889.)

Cutler's Poetry. Mere jingles or rhymes. Knives had, at one time, a distich inscribed on the blade by means of aqua fortis.

> "Whose posy was
> For all the world like cutler's poetry
> Upon a knife."
> *Shakespeare: Merchant of Venice, v. 1.*

Cutpurse. Now called "pickpocket." The two words are of historical value. When purses were worn suspended from a girdle, thieves cut the string by which the purse was attached; but when pockets were adopted, and purses were no longer hung on the girdle, the thief was no longer a cutpurse, but became a pickpocket.

> "To have an open ear, a quick eye, and a nimble hand, is necessary for a cutpurse."—*Shakespeare: Winter's Tale, iv. 3.*

Cutter's Law. Not to see a fellow want while we have cash in our purse. Cutter's law means the law of purse-cutters, robbers, brigands, and highwaymen.

> "I must put you in cash with some of your old uncle's broad-pieces. This is cutter's law; we must not see a pretty fellow want, if we have cash ourselves."—*Sir W. Scott: Old Mortality,* chap. ix.

Cuttle. *Captain Cuttle.* An eccentric, kind-hearted sailor, simple as a child, credulous of every tale, and generous as the sun. He is immortalised by the motto selected by *Notes and Queries,* "When found make a note of." (*Dickens: Dombey and Son.*)

> "Unfortunately, I neglected Captain Cuttle's advice, and am now unable to find it."—*W. H. Husk: Notes and Queries.*

Cutty. Scotch for short, as a cutty pipe, cutty sark. (A diminutive of *curt.*)

Cutty Pipe. A short clay pipe. Scotch, *cutty* (short), as cutty spoons, cutty sark, a cutty (little girl), etc., a cutty gun (a pop-gun).

Cutty Stool. A small stool on which offenders were placed in the Scotch church when they were about to receive a public rebuke.

Cwt. is C wt.—*i.e.* C. *centum,* wt. *weight,* meaning hundred-weight. (*See* DWT.)

Cyan'ean Rocks (*The*). The Symple'gadēs at the entrance of the Euxine Sea. Said to close together when a vessel attempted to sail between them, and thus crush it to pieces. Cyanĕan means *dark,* and Symplegădēs means *dashers together.*

> "Here are those hard rocks of trap, of a greenish-blue, coloured with copper, and hence called the Cyanean."—*Olivier.*

Cy'cle. A period or series of events or numbers which recur everlastingly in precisely the same order.

Cycle of the moon, called "Meton's Cycle," from Meton, who discovered it, is a period of nineteen years, at the expiration of which time the phases of the moon repeat themselves on the same days as they did nineteen years previously. (*See* CALLIPIC PERIOD.)

Cycle of the sun. A period of twenty-eight years, at the expiration of which time the Sunday letters recur and proceed in the same order as they did twenty-eight years previously. In other words, the days of the month fall again on the same days of the week.

The Platonic cycle or *great year* is that space of time which elapses before all the stars and constellations return to any given state. Tycho Brahë calculated this period at 25,816 years, and Riccio'li at 25,920.

Cyc'lic Poets. Inferior epic poets. On the death of Homer a host of minstrels caught the contagion of his poems, and wrote continuations, illustrations, or additions thereto. These poets were called *cyclic* because they confined themselves to the cycle of the Trojan war. The chief were Ag'ias, Arcti'nos, Eu'gamon, Les'chēs, and Strasīnos.

> "Besides the Homeric poems, the Greeks of this age possessed those of the poets named *Cyclic,* as they sang a traditional cycle of events . . . ."—*Keightley: Greece,* part i. chap. xiv. p. 150.

Cyclopæ'dia. *The living cyclopædia.* Longi'nus, so called for his extensive information. (213-273.)

Cyclo'pean. Huge, massive, like the Cyclops of classic mythology.

Cyclo'pean Masonry. The old Pelasgic ruins of Greece, Asia Minor, and Italy, such as the Gallery of Ti'ryns, the Gate of Lyons, the Treasury of Athens, and the Tombs of Phoro'neus (3 syl.) and Dan'aos. They are said to have been the work of the Cyclops. They are huge blocks fitted together without mortar, with marvellous nicety.

Cyclops. One of a group of giants with only one eye, and that in the centre of their forehead, whose business it was to forge iron for Vulcan. They were probably Pelasgians, who worked in quarries, and attached a lantern to their forehead to give them light underground. The lantern was their *one eye as big as the full moon*. (Greek, "circular-eye.") (*See* ARIMASPIANS.)

" Roused with the sound, the mighty family
Of one-eyed brothers hasten to the shore,
And gather round the bellowing Polypheme."
Addison : Milton Imitated.

Cyll'aros, according to Virgil, was the celebrated horse of Pollux (*Geor.*, iii. 90), but, according to Ovid, it was Castor's steed (*Met.*, xii. 408).

" He, O Castor, was a courser worthy thee . . .
Coal-black his colour, but like jet it shone ;
His legs and flowing tail were white alone."
Dryden : Ovid's Metamorphose, xii.

Cymbeline. (*See* IMOGEN, ZINEURA.)

Cymoch'les. A man of prodigious might, brother of Pyroch'lēs, son of Malice (Acra'tēs) and Despite, and husband of Acra'sia, the enchantress. He sets out to encounter Sir Guyon, but is ferried over the idle lake by Wantonness (Phæ'dria), and forgets himself ; he is slain by King Arthur (canto viii.). The word means, "one who seeks glory in troubles." (*Spenser : Faërie Queene*, ii. 5.)

Cymod'oce (4 syl.). A sea nymph and companion of Venus. (*Virgil : Georgic*, iv. 338 ; and again, *Æneid*, v. 826.) The word means "wave-receiving."

The Garden of Cymod'oce. Sark, one of the Channel islands. It is the title of a poem by Swinburne, 1880.

Cynægi'ros. It is said that when the Persians were pushing off from shore after the battle of Mar'athon, Cynægīros, the brother of Æschylos, the poet, seized one of their ships with his right hand, which was instantly lopped off ; he then grasped it with his left, which was cut off also ; lastly, he seized hold of it with his teeth and lost his head. (*See* BENBOW.)

Cynic. A snarling, churlish person, like a cynic. The Cynics were so called because Antis'thenēs held his school in the gymnasium called Cynosar'gēs, set apart for those who were not of pure Athenian blood. Cynosargēs means *white dog*, and was so called because a white dog once carried away part of a

victim which Diome'os was offering to Herculēs. The sect was often called the Dog-sect ; and the effigy over Diogĕnēs' pillar was a dog, with this inscription :

" Say, dog, I pray, what guard you in that tomb ? "
" A dog."—" His name ? "—" Diogĕnēs."—" From far ? "
" Sino'pē."—" What ! who made a tub his home ? "
" The same ; now dead, amongst the stars a star."
                                   E. C. B.

Cynic Tub (*The*). The tub from which Diogenēs lectured. Similarly we speak of the "Porch," that is, the Porch Pœcilē, meaning Stoic philosophy ; the "Garden," meaning Epicurēan philosophy ; the "Academy," meaning Platonic philosophy ; the "Colonnade," meaning Aristotelian philosophy.

" [They] fetch their doctrines from the Cynic tub."
                     Milton : Comus, line 708.

Cynics. The chief were Antis'thenēs of Athens (the founder), Diogĕnēs, Onesic'ritos, Mon'imos, Cra'tēs and his wife Hippar'chia, Metroc'lēs, Menip'pos, and Menede'mos the madman.

Cy'nosure (3 syl.). The polar star ; the observed of all observers. Greek for *dog's tail*, and applied to the constellation called *Ursa Minor*. As seamen guide their ships by the north star, and observe it well, the word "cynosure" is used for whatever attracts attention, as "The cynosure of neighbouring eyes" (*Milton*), especially for guidance in some doubtful matter, as—

" Richmond was the cynosure on which all
Northern eyes were fixed [in the American war]."
—*The Times.*

Cyn'thia. The moon ; a surname of Ar'temis or Diana. The Roman Diana, who represented the moon, was called Cynthia from Mount Cynthus, where she was born.

" And from embattled clouds emerging slow,
Cynthia came riding on her silver car."
                   Beattie : Minstrel.

Cynthia. Pope, speaking of the inconstant character of woman, "matter too soft a lasting mark to bear," says—

" Come, then, the colours and the ground prepare !
Dip in the rainbow, trick her off in air ;
Choose a firm cloud, before it fall, and in it
Catch, ere she change, the Cynthia of the minute."
                  Epistle ii. 17-20.

Cypress (*The*) is a funeral tree, and was dedicated by the Romans to Pluto, because when once cut it never grows again.

" Cypresse garlands are of great account at funerals amongst the gentiler sort, but rosemary and bayes are used by the commons both at funerals and weddings. They are plants which fade not a good while after they are gathered . . . . and intimate that the remembrance of the present solemnity might not dye presently."—*Coles : Introduction to the Knowledge of Plants.*

The magic cypress branch. In the opera of *Roberto il Diav'olo,* after the "dance of love," in which Hel'ena seduces the duke, he removes the cypress branch, which has the power of imparting to him whatever he wishes. With this he enters the palace of Isabella, princess of Sicily, and transfixes the princess and her attendants in a magic sleep, but afterwards relenting, he breaks the branch, and is dragged away by the guards.

Cyprian Brass, or "æs Cyprium," copper. Pliny (book xxxiv. c. ii.) says, "*in Cypro enim prima æris inventio fuit.*"

Cypriote. A native of Cyprus; the dialect spoken on the island; pertaining or special to Cyprus.

D

D. This letter is the outline of a rude archway or door. It is called in Hebrew *daleth* (a door). In Egyptian hiero-glyphics it is a man's hand.

D or **d,** indicating a penny or pence, is the initial letter of the Latin *dena'rius,* a silver coin equal to 8¾d. during the commonwealth of Rome, but in the Middle Ages about equivalent to our penny. The word was used by the Romans for money in general.

D stands for 500, which is half ⌀, a form of ∞ or M, which stands for *mille.*

D̄ stands for 5,000.

D.O.M. *Deo Op'timo Max'imo. Datur om'nibus mori* (It is allotted to all to die).

D.T. A contraction of *delirium tremens.*

"They get a look, after a touch of D.T., which nothing else that I know of can give them."— *Indian Tale.*

Da Capo or **D.C.** From the beginning—that is, finish with a repetition of the first strain. A term in music. (*Italian.*)

Dab. Clever, skilled; as "a dab-hand at it"; a corrupt contraction of the Latin *adeptus* (an adept). "Dabster" is another form. *Apt* is a related word.

"An Eton stripling, training for the law,
A dunce at learning, but a dab at taw [marbles]."
    Anon.: Logic; or, The Biter Bit.

Dab, Din, etc.

"Hab Dab and David Din
Ding the deil o'er Dabson's Linn."

"Hab Dab" means Halbert Dobson; "David Din" means David Dun; and "Dabson's Linn," or Dob's Linn, is a waterfall near the head of Moffat Water.

Dobson and Dun were two Cameronians who lived for security in a cave in the ravine. Here, as they said, they saw the devil in the form of a pack of dried hides, and after fighting the "foul fiend" for some time, they dinged him into the waterfall.

Daba'ira. An idol of the savages of Pan'ama', to whose honour slaves are burnt to death. (*American mythology.*)

Dab'bat [*the Beast*]. The Beast of the Apocalypse, which the Mahometans say will appear with Antichrist, called by them *dag'gial.* (Rev. xix. 19; xx. 10.)

Dabble. *To dabble in the funds; to dabble in politics—i.e.* to do something in them in a small way. (Dutch, *dabbelen,* our *dip* and *tap.*)

Dab'chick. The lesser grebe. Dab is a corruption of *dap,* the old participle of dip, and chick (any young or small fowl), literally the dipping or diving chick.

Dactyl (*Will*). The "smallest of pedants." (*Steele : The Tatler.*)

Dactyls (*The*). Mythic beings to whom is ascribed the discovery of iron. Their number was originally three—the Smelter, the Hammer, and the Anvil; but was afterwards increased to five males and five females, whence their name Dactyls or Fingers.

Dad or **Daddy.** Father. The person who acts as father at a wedding; a stage-manager. The superintendent of a casual ward is termed by the inmates "Old Daddy." (*A Night in a Work-house, by an Amateur Casual* [*J. Green-wood*].)

In the *Fortunes of Nigel,* by Sir W. Scott, Steenie, Duke of Buckingham, calls King James "My dear dad and gossip." (Welsh, *tad;* Irish, *daid,* father; Sanskrit, *tada;* Hindu, *dada.*)

Daddy Long-legs. A crane-fly; sometimes applied to the long-legged spiders called "harvestmen."

Dæ'dalos. A Greek who formed the Cretan labyrinth, and made for himself wings, by means of which he flew from Crete across the Archipel'ago. He is said to have invented the saw, the axe, the gimlet, etc.

Daffodil (*The*), or "Lent Lily," was once white; but Persephŏnē, daughter of Demetēr (Cerēs), delighted to wander about the flowery meadows of Sicily. One spring-tide she tripped over the meadows, wreathed her head with wild lilies, and, throwing herself on the grass, fell asleep. The god of the Infernal Regions, called by the Romans Pluto, fell in love with the beautiful maid, and carried her off for his bride. His touch turned the white flowers to a golden yellow, as some of them fell in Acheron, where they grew luxuriantly; and ever since the flower has been planted on graves. Theophilus and Pliny tell us that the ghosts delight in the flower, called by them the Asphodel. It was once called the Affodil. (French, *aspho-dèle*; Latin, *asphodilus*; Greek, *aspho-dilos*.)

"Flour of daffodil is a cure for madness."—*Med. MS. Lincoln Cathedral,* f. 282.

Dag (*day*). Son of Natt or night. (*Scandinavian mythology.*)

Dagger or *Long Cross* (†), used for reference to a note after the asterisk (*), is a Roman Catholic character, originally employed in church books, prayers of exorcism, at benedictions, and so on, to remind the priest where to make the sign of the cross. This sign is sometimes called an obelisk—that is, "a spit." (Greek, *ob'elos*, a spit.)

Dagger, in the City arms of London, commemorates Sir William Walworth's dagger, with which he slew Wat Tyler in 1381. Before this time the cognisance of the City was the sword of St. Paul.

" Brave Walworth, knight, lord mayor, that slew
Rebellious Tyler in his alarmes;
The king, therefore, did give him in lieu
The dagger to the city armes."
Fourth year of Richard II. (1381),
Fishmongers' Hall.

Dagger Ale is the ale of the *Dagger*, a celebrated ordinary in Holborn.

" My lawyer's clerk I lighted on last night
In Holborn, at the *Dagger*."
Ben Jonson: The Alchemist, i. 1.

Dagger-scene in the House of Commons. Edmund Burke, during the French Revolution, tried a bit of bunkum by throwing down a dagger on the floor of the House, exclaiming as he did so, "There's French fraternity for you! Such is the weapon which French Jacobins would plunge into the heart of our beloved king." Sheridan spoilt the dramatic effect, and set the House in a roar by his remark, "The gentleman, I see, has brought his knife with him, but where is his fork?" (*See* COUP DE THEATRE.)

Daggers. *To speak daggers, To look daggers.* To speak or look so as to wound the sensibilities.

" I will speak daggers to her; but will use none."—*Shakespeare: Hamlet,* iii. 2.

Daggers Drawn (*At*). At great enmity, as if with daggers drawn and ready to rush on each other.

, Daggle-tail or **Draggle-tail.** A slovenly woman, the bottom of whose dress trails in the dirt. *Dag* (Saxon) means loose ends, mire or dirt; whence *dag-locks*, the soiled locks of a sheep's fleece, and *dag-wool*, refuse wool. (Compare TAG.)

Dagobert. *King Dagobert and St. Eloi.* There is a French song very popular with this title. St. Eloi tells the king his coat has a hole in it, and the king replies, " *C'est vrai, le tien est bon ; prête-le moi.*" Next the saint complains of the king's stockings, and Dagobert makes the same answer. Then of his wig and cloak, to which the same answer is returned. After seventeen complaints St. Eloi said, " My king, death is at hand, and it is time to confess," when the king replied, " Why can't you confess, and die instead of me?"

Da'gon (Hebrew, *dag On*, the fish On). The idol of the Philistines; half woman and half fish. (*See* ATERGATA.)

" Dagon his name; sea-monster, upward man
And downward fish; yet had his temple high
Rear'd in Azo'tus, dreaded through the coast
Of Palestine, in Gath and As'calon,
And Accaron and Gaza's frontier bounds."
Milton: Paradise Lost, book i. 462.

Dag'onet (*Sir*). In the romance *La Mort d'Arthure* he is called the *fool* of King Arthur, and was knighted by the king himself.

" I remember at Mile-End Green, when I lay at Clement's Inn, I was then Sir Dagonet in Arthur's show."—*2 Henry IV.,* iii. 2. (Justice Shallow).

⁂ "Dagonet" is the pen-name of Mr. G. R. Sims.

Daguer'reotype (4 syl.). A photographic process. So named from M. Daguerre, who greatly improved it in 1839. (*See* TALBOTYPE.)

Da'gun. A god worshipped in Pegu. When Kiak'iak destroyed the world, Dagun reconstructed it. (*Indian mythology.*)

Dahak. The Satan of Persia. According to Persian mythology, the ages of the world are divided into periods of 1,000 years. When the cycle of " chiliasms" (1,000-year periods) is complete, the reign of Ormuzd will begin, and men will be all good and all happy; but this event will be preceded by the loosing of Dahak, who will break his chain and fall upon the world, and bring on man the most dreadful calamities. Two prophets will appear to cheer the oppressed, and announce the advent of Ormuzd.

Dahlia. A flower. So called from Andrew Dahl, the Swedish botanist.

Dahomey is not derived from Daho, the founder of the palace so called, but is a corruption of Danh-homen, "Danh's Belly." The story is as follows: Ardrah divided his kingdom at death between his three sons, and Daho, one of the sons, received the northern portion. Being an enterprising and ambitious man, he coveted the country of his neighbour Danh, King of Gedavin, and first applied to him for a plot of land to build a house on. This being granted, Daho made other requests in quick succession, and Danh's patience being exhausted, he exclaimed, "Must I open my belly for you to build on?" On hearing this, Daho declared himself insulted, made war on Danh, and slew him. He then built his palace where Danh fell, and called it Danh-homen. (*Nineteenth Century*, October, 1890, pp. 605-6.)

Daïboth (3 syl.). A Japanese idol of colossal size. Each of her hands is full of hands. (*Japanese mythology.*)

Daïkoku (4 syl.). The god invoked specially by the artisans of Japan. He sits on a ball of rice, holding a hammer in his hand, with which he beats a sack; and every time he does so the sack becomes full of silver, rice, cloth, and other useful articles. (*Japanese mythology.*)

Daïri (3 syl.). The royal residence in Japan; the court of the mikado, used by metonomy for the sovereign or chief pontiff himself.

Dairy. A corrupt form of "dey-ery," Middle English *deierie* and *deyyerye*, from *deye*, a dairymaid.

"The dey or farm-woman entered with her pitchers, to deliver the milk for the family."—*Scott: Fair Maid of Perth*, chap. xxxii.

Daïs. The raised floor at the head of a dining-room, designed for guests of distinction (French, *daïs*, a canopy). So called because it used to be decorated with a canopy. The proverb "*Sous le dais*" means "in the midst of grandeur."

Daisies. Slang for boots. Explained *under* CHIVY.

Daïsy. Ophelia gives the queen a daisy to signify "that her light and fickle love ought not to expect constancy in her husband." So the daisy is explained by Greene to mean a *Quip for an upstart courtier*. (Anglo-Saxon *dæges eáge*, day's eye.)

The word is *Day's eye*, and the flower is so called because it closes its pinky lashes and goes to sleep when the sun sets, but in the morning it expands its petals to the light. (*See* VIOLET.)

" That well by reason men calle it maie,
The daisie, or else the eie of the daie."
Chaucer.

Daisy (*Solomon*). Parish clerk of Chigwell. He had little, round, black, shiny eyes like beads; wore rusty black breeches, a rusty black coat, and a long-flapped waistcoat with queer little buttons. Solomon Daisy, with Phil Parkes, the ranger of Epping Forest, Tom Cobb, the chandler and post-office keeper, and John Willet, mine host, formed a quadrilateral or village club, which used to meet night after night at the *Maypole*, on the borders of the forest. Daisy's famous tale was the murder of Mr. Reuben Haredale, and the conviction that the murderer would be found out on the 19th of March, the anniversary of the murder. (*Dickens: Barnaby Rudge*, chap. i., etc.)

Daisy-cutter (*A*). In cricket, a ball that is bowled all along the ground.

Daisy-roots, like dwarf-elder berries, are said to stunt the growth; hence the fairy Milkah fed her royal foster-child on this food, that his standard might not exceed that of a pigmy. This superstition arose from the notion that everything had the property of bestowing its own speciality on others. (*See* FERN SEED.)

" She robbed dwarf-elders of their fragrant fruit,
And fed him early with the daisy root,
Whence through his veins the powerful juices ran,
And formed the beauteous *miniature* of man."
Tickell: Kensington Gardens.

Dalaï-Lama [*grand lama*]. Chief of the two Tartar priests—a sort of incarnate deity. The other lama is called the "Tesho-lama."

Dal'dah. Mahomet's favourite white mule.

Dalgar'no (*Lord*). A heartless profligate in Scott's *Fortunes of Nigel.*

Dalget'ty (*Dugald*). Jeffrey calls him "a compound of Captain Fluellen and Bob'adil," but this is scarcely just. Without doubt, he has all the pedantry and conceit of the former, and all the vulgar assurance of the latter; but, unlike Bobadil, he is a man of real courage, and wholly trustworthy to those who pay him for the service of his sword, which, like a thrifty mercenary, he lets out to the highest bidder. (*Scott: Legend of Montrose.*)

"Neither Schiller, Strada, Thuanus, Monroe, nor Dugald Dalgetty makes any mention of it."—*Carlyle.*

Dalkey (*King of*). A kind of "Mayor of Garrat" (*q.v.*) at Kingstown, in Ireland. A full description is given of this mock mayor, etc., in a book entitled *Ireland Ninety Years Ago.*

Dalle (French), écu de six francs (5s.). Money generally.

"Quiconque parleroit de paix . . . . payeroit à la bourse de l'Union certaine quantité de dales, pour l'entretenement des docteurs." — *Satyre Menippee,* 1824, p. 163.

Dalmat'ica or *Dalmat'ic.* A robe, open in front, reaching to the knees; worn at one time by deacons over the *alb* or *stole,* when the Eucharist was administered. It is in imitation of the regal vest of Dalma'tia, and was imported into Rome by the Emperor Com'modus. A similar robe was worn by kings, in the Middle Ages, at coronations and other great solemnities, to remind them of their duty of bountifulness to the poor. The right sleeve was plain and full, but the left was fringed and tasselled. Deacons had broader sleeves than sub-deacons, to indicate their duty to larger generosity; for a similar reason the sleeves of a bishop are larger than those of a priest. The two stripes before and behind were to show that the wearer should exercise his charity to all.

Dam. An ancient Indian copper coin, of which 1,600 went to a rupee. Hence some compare the expression "Not worth a damn," though wrongly, with "not worth a farthing," "not worth a sou." [TWOPENNY DAMN.]

Dam'age. *What's the damage?* What have I to pay? how much is the bill? The allusion is to the law assessing damages in remuneration to the plaintiff.

Dam'ask Linen. So called from Damascus, where it was originally manufactured.

Damaskeen'ing. Producing upon steel a blue tinge and ornamental figures, sometimes inlaid with gold and silver, as in Damascus blades; so called from

Damascus, which was celebrated in the Middle Ages for this class of ornamental art.

Dambe'a or *Dembe'a.* A lake in Gojam, Abyssinia, the source of the *Blue* Nile. Captain Speke traced the *White* Nile to Lake Victoria N'yanza, which, no doubt, is fed by the Mountains of the Moon.

" He [the Nile] thro' the lucid lake
Of fair Dambea rolls his infant stream."
Thomson: Summer, 807-8.

Dame du Lac. A fay, named Vivienne, who plunged with the infant Lancelot into a lake. This lake was a kind of mirage, concealing the demesnes of the lady "*en la marche de la petite Bretaigne.*" (*See* VIVIENNE.)

" En ce lieu . . . . avoit la dame moult de belles maisons et moult riches; et au plain dessoubs elle avoit une gente petite rivière."

Damiens' Bed of Steel. R. F. Damiens, in 1757, attempted the life of Louis XV. He was taken to the Conciergerie; an iron bed, which likewise served as a chair, was prepared for him, and to this he was fastened with chains. He was then tortured, and ultimately torn to pieces by wild horses. (*Smollet: History of England,* v. 12, p. 39.)

" The uplifted axe, the agonising wheel,
Luke's iron crown, and Damiens' bed of steel."
Goldsmith: The Traveller (1768).

Damn with Faint Praise. To praise with such a voice and in such measured terms as to show plainly secret disapproval.

" Damn with faint praise, assent with civil leer,
And, without sneering, teach the rest to sneer."
Pope: Epistle to Arbuthnot.

Dam'ocles' Sword. Evil foreboded or dreaded. Dam'ocles, the sycophant of Dionysius the elder, of Syracuse, was invited by the tyrant to try the felicity he so much envied. Accordingly he was set down to a sumptuous banquet, but overhead was a sword suspended by a hair. Damocles was afraid to stir, and the banquet was a tantalising torment to him. (*Cicero.*)

" These fears hang like Damocles' sword over every feast, and make enjoyment impossible." —*Chambers's Cyclopædia.*

Da'mon and Musido'ra. Two lovers in Thomson's *Summer.* One day Damon caught Musidora bathing, and his delicacy so won upon her that she promised to be his bride.

Da'mon and Pyth'ias. Inseparable friends. They were two Syracu'sian youths. Damon, being condemned to death by Dionysius the tyrant, obtained leave to go home to arrange his affairs if Pythias became his security. Damon being delayed, Pythias was led to execution, but his friend arrived in time to save him. Dionysius was so struck with this honourable friendship that he pardoned both of them.

Damper (*A*). A snap before dinner, which damps or takes off the edge of appetite. "That's a damper" also means a wet-blanket influence, a rebuff which damps or cools one's courage.

Also a large thin cake of flour and water baked in hot ashes. The mute of a stringed instrument to deaden the sound is also called a "damper."

Dam'sel. (*See* DOMISELLUS.)

Dam'son. A corruption of Damascène, a fruit from Damascus.

Dam'yan (3 syl.). A "silke squyer," whose illicit love was accepted by May, the youthful bride of January, a Lombard knight, sixty years old. (*Chaucer: The Marchaundes Tale*.)

Dan. A title of honour, common with the old poets, as Dan Phœbus, Dan Cupid, Dan Neptune, Dan Chaucer, etc. (Spanish, *don*.)

"Dan Chaucer, well of English undefiled,
On Fame's eternal beadroll worthy to be filed."
   Spenser : Faërie Queene, book iv. canto ii. 32.

From Dan to Beer'sheba. From one end of the kingdom to the other; all over the world; everywhere. The phrase is Scriptural, Dan being the most northern and Beersheba the most southern city of the Holy Land. We have a similar expression, "From John o' Groats to the Land's End."

Dan Tucker. *Out o' de way*, old *Dan Tucker*. The first Governor of Bermu'da was Mr. Moore, who was succeeded by Captain Daniel Tucker. These islands were colonised from Virginia.

Dan'ace (3 syl.). A coin placed by the Greeks in the mouth of the dead to pay their passage across the ferry of the Lower World.

Dan'aë. An Argive princess whom Zeus (Jupiter) seduced under the form of a shower of gold, while she was confined in an inaccessible tower. She thus became the mother of Perseus (2 syl.).

Dana'ïdes (4 syl.). Daughters of Dan'aos (King of Argos). They were fifty in number, and married the fifty sons of Ægyptos. They all but one murdered their husbands on their wedding-night, and were punished in the infernal regions by having to draw water everlastingly in sieves from a deep well.

This is an allegory. The followers of Dan'aos taught the Argives to dig wells, and irrigate their fields in the Egyptian manner. As the soil of Argos was very dry and porous, it was like a sieve.

The names of the fifty Danaïdes and their respective husbands are as follows :

Actæa ..	.. wife of	Per'iphas.
Adianta ..	.. ,,	Daïph'ron.
Adyta ..	.. ,,	Menal'cēs.
Aga'yē ..	.. ,,	Lycos.
Amymon'ē	.. ,,	Encel'ados.
Anaxib'ia	.. ,,	Archela'os.
Antod'icɛ	.. ,,	Clytos.
Aster'ia ..	.. ,,	Chœtos.
Autho'lea	.. ,,	Cisseus.
Autom'ata	.. ,,	Archite'los.
Auton'oē	.. ,,	Euryl'ochos.
Bry'cea ..	.. ,,	Chthon'ios.
Callid'icē	.. ,,	Pandi'on.
Cele'no ..	.. ,,	Hyxo'bios.
Chrysip'pē	.. ,,	Chrysip'pos.
Chrysoth'emis	,,	As'teris.
Cleodo'ra	.. ,,	Lixos.
Cleopat'ra	.. ,,	Age'nor.
Cli'o ..	.. ,,	Aster'ias.
Critome'dia	.. ,,	Antipaph'os.
Damo'nē	.. ,,	Amyn'tor.
Dioxip'pē	.. ,,	Ægyptos.
Electra ..	.. ,,	Peris'thenēs.
Er'ato ..	.. ,,	Bro'mios.
Euphe'no	.. ,,	Hyper'bios.
Euryd'icē	.. ,,	Dryas.
Evip'pē ..	.. ,,	Imbros.
Glauca ..	.. ,,	Alcis.
Glaucip'pa	.. ,,	Pot'amon.
Gorga ..	.. ,,	Hyppoth'oöa.
Gorg'ophon	.. ,,	Pro'teus.
Hel'cita ..	.. ,,	Cassos.
Hippodami'a	.. ,,	Ister.
Hippod'ica	.. ,,	Idras.
Hippomedu'sē *,*	.. ,,	Alcme'non.
Hyperip'pa	.. ,,	Hippocoris'tēs.
Hypermnes'tra	.. ,,	Lynceus.*
Iphimedu'sa	.. ,,	Euche'nor.
Mnestia ..	.. ,,	Egi'os.
Ocyp'etē	.. ,,	Lampos.
O'nē ..	.. ,,	Arbe'los.
Phartē ..	.. ,,	Euryd'amas.
Pilar'ʒa ..	.. ,,	Idmon.
Pire'nē ..	.. ,,	Agaptole'mos.
Podar'ca	.. ,,	Œ'neus.
Rhoda ..	.. ,,	Hippol'ytos.
Rho'dia ..	.. ,,	Chalce'don.
Stben'ela	.. ,,	Sthen'elos.
Stygna ..	.. ,,	Polyc'tor.
Thea'no ..	.. ,,	Phanthēs.

⁑ Lynceus (2 syl.), the one saved by his wife, is marked with an asterisk (*).

Dan'aos. According to the *Roman de Rose*, Denmark means the country of Dan'aos, who settled here with a colony after the siege of Troy, as Brutus is said by the same sort of name-legend to have settled in Britain. Saxo-German'icus, with equal absurdity, makes Dan, the son of Humble, the first king, to account for the name of the country.

Danaw. The Danube (German).

"To pass
Rhone or the Danaw."
   Milton : Paradise Lost, book i. 353.

Dance. The Spanish *danza* was a grave and stately court dance. Those of the seventeenth century were called the *Turdion, Paba'na, Madama Orleans, Piedelgiba'o, El Rey Don Alonzo,* and *El Caballe'ro.* Most of the names are taken from the ballad-music to which they were danced.

The light dances were called *Baylë* (*q.v.*).

Dance (*Pyrrhic*). (*See* PYRRHIC).
St. Vitus's Dance. (*See* VITUS).

Dance of Death. A series of wood-cuts, said to be by Hans Holbein (1538), representing Death dancing after all sorts of persons, beginning with Adam and Eve. He is beside the judge on his bench, the priest in the pulpit, the nun in her cell, the doctor in his study, the bride and the beggar, the king and the infant; but is "swallowed up at last."

This is often called the *Dance Maca'bre,* from a German who wrote verses on the subject.

On the north side of Old St. Paul's was a cloister, on the walls of which was painted, at the cost of John Carpenter, town clerk of London (15th century), a "Dance of Death," or "Death leading all the estate, with speeches of Death, and answers, by John Lydgate" (*Stow*). The Death-Dance in the Dominican Convent of Basle was retouched by Holbein.

¶ PHRASES.

I'll lead you a pretty dance, i.e. I'll bother or put you to trouble. The French say, *Donner le bal à quelqu'un.* The reference is to the complicated dances of former times, when all followed the leader.

To dance attendance. To wait obsequiously, to be at the beck and call of another. The allusion is to the ancient custom of weddings, where the bride on the wedding-night had to dance with every guest, and play the amiable, though greatly annoyed.

" Then must the poore bryde kepe foote with a
dauncer, and refuse none, how scabbed, foule,
droncken, rude, and shameless soever be be."—
Christen: State of Matrimony, 1543.

      " I had thought
They'had parted so much honesty among them
(At least, good manners) as not thus to suffer
A man of his place, and so near our favour,
To dance attendance on their lordships' plea-
   sures."   *Shakespeare: Henry VIII.,* v. 2.

To dance upon nothing. To be hanged.

Dances (*National Dances*) :

Bohemian : the *redo'wa.*
English : the *hornpipe* and *lancers.*
French : the *contredanse* (country dance), *cotillon,*
   and *quadrille.*
German : the *gallopade* and *waltz.*
Irish : the *jig.*
Neapolitan : the *taran'tella.*
Polish : the *mazurka* and *krakovieck.*

11*

Russian : the *cossac.*
Scotch : the *reel.*
Spanish : the *bole'ro* and *fandango.*

⁂ When Handel was asked to point out the peculiar taste of the different nations of Europe in dancing, he ascribed the *minuet* to the French, the *sar'aband* to the Spaniard, the *arietta* to the Italian, and the *hornpipe* and the *morris-dance* to the English.

Dances (*Religious Dances*) :

Astronomical dances, invented by the Egyptians, designed (like our orreries) to represent the movements of the heavenly bodies.
The Bacchic dances were of three sorts : grave (like our minuet), gay (like our gavotte), and mixed (like our minuet and gavotte combined).
The dance Champêtre, invented by Pan, quick and lively. The dancers (in the open air) wore wreaths of oak and garlands of flowers.
Children's dances, in Lacedemonia, in honour of Diana. The children were nude; and their movements were grave, modest, and graceful.
Corybantic dances, in honour of Bacchus, accompanied with timbrels, fifes, flutes, and a tumultuous noise produced by the clashing of swords and spears against brazen bucklers.
Funereal dances, in Athens, slow, solemn dances in which the priests took part. The performers wore long white robes, and carried cypress slips in their hands.
Hymeneal dances were lively and joyous. The dancers being crowned with flowers.
Of the Lapithæ, invented by Pirithöus. These were exhibited after some famous victory, and were designed to imitate the combats of the Centaurs and Lapithæ. These dances were both difficult and dangerous.
May-day dances at Rome. At daybreak lads and lasses went out to gather "May" and other flowers for themselves and their elders ; and the day was spent in dances and festivities.
Military dances. The oldest of all dances, executed with swords, javelins, and bucklers. Said to be invented by Minerva to celebrate the victory of the gods over the Titans.
Nuptial dances. A Roman pantomimic performance resembling the dances of our harlequin and columbine.
Sacred dances (among the Jews). David danced in certain religious processions (2 Sam. vi. 14). The people sang and danced before the golden calf (Exod. xxxii. 19). And in the book of Psalms (cl. 4) we read, "Let [the people] praise [the Lord] with timbrel and dance. Miriam, the sister of Moses, after the passage of the Red Sea, was followed by all the women with timbrels and dances (Exod. xv. 20).
Salic dances, instituted by Numa Pompilius in honour of Mars. They were executed by twelve priests selected from the highest of the nobility, and the dances were performed in the temple while sacrifices were being made and hymns sung to the god.

⁂ The Dancing Dervishes celebrate their religious rites with dances, which consist chiefly of spinning round and round a little allotted space, not in couples, but each one alone.

In ancient times the Gauls, the Germans, the Spaniards, and the English too had their sacred dances. In fact, in all religious ceremonies the dance was an essential part of divine worship. In India dancing is a part of religious worship in which the priests join.

See DANSE.

Dancing-water (*The*), which beautifies ladies, makes them young again, and enriches them. It fell in a cascade in the Burning Forest, and could only be reached by an underground passage. Prince Chery fetched a bottle of this water for his beloved Fair-star, but was aided by a dove. (*Fairy Tales*, by the Comtesse d'Aulnoy.) (*See* YELLOW WATER.)

Dandeli'on. A flower. The word is a corruption of the French *dent de lion* (lion's tooth). Also called *Leon'todon* (lion-tooth, Greek), from a supposed resemblance between its leaves and the teeth of lions.

Dander. *Is your dander up* or *riz?* Is your angry passion up? This is generally considered to be an Americanism; but Halliwell gives, in his *Archaic Dictionary*, both *dander* (anger) and *dandy* (distracted), the former common to several counties, and the latter peculiar to Somersetshire.

Dandie Dinmont. A jovial, true-hearted store-farmer, in Sir Walter Scott's *Guy Mannering.* Also a hardy hairy short-legged terrier.

"From this dog descended Davidson of Hyndlee's breed, the original Dandie-Dinmont."—*T. Brown: Our Dogs*, p. 104.

Dandin (French). A ninny, a snob. From Molière's comedy of *George Dandin.* (*See* GANDIN.)

Dandin (*George*). A French cit, who marries a sprig of nobility, and lives with his wife's parents. Madame appeals on all occasions to her father and mother, who, of course, take her part against her husband. Poor George is in a sad plight, and is for ever lamenting his fate with the expression, *Vous l'avez voulu, George Dandin* ('Tis your own fault, George Dandin). George Dandin stands for anyone who marries above his sphere, and is pecked by his wife and mother-in-law. The word means "a ninny." (*Molière's comedy so called.*)

Perrin Dandin. A sort of Lynch judge in Rabelais, who seated himself on the trunk of the first tree he came to, and there decided the causes submitted to him.

Dan'diprat or *Dandëprat*, according to Camden, is a small coin issued in the reign of Henry VII. Applied to a little fellow, it is about equal to our modern expression, a little "twopenny-ha'penny" fellow.

Dando (*A*). One who frequents hotels, eating-houses, and other such places, satisfies his appetite, and decamps without payment.

Dandy. A coxcomb; a fop. The feminine of "dandy" is either *dandilly* or dandizett. Egan says the word was first used in 1813, but examples of the word occur at least one hundred years before that date. (French, *dandin*, a ninny, a vain, conceited fellow.)

Dandy-horse. (*See* VELOCIPEDE.)

Dandyism. The manners, etc., of a dandy; like a dandy.

Dane's Skin (*A*). A freckled skin. Red hair and a freckled skin are the traditional characteristics of Danish blood.

Dangle. A theatrical amateur in Sheridan's *Critic.* It was designed for Thomas Vaughan, a playwright.

Daniel Lambert weighed 739 lbs. In 1841 eleven young men stood within his waistcoat buttoned. (1770-1809.)

Danism. Lending money on usury. (Greek, *daneisma*, a loan.)

Dan'nebrog or **Danebrog.** The old flag of Denmark. The tradition is that Waldemar II. of Denmark saw in the heavens a fiery cross which betokened his victory over the Estho'nians (1219). This story is very similar to that of Constantine (*q.v.*), and of St. Andrew's Cross. (*See* ANDREW, *St.*)

The order of Danebrog. The second of the Danish orders. Brog means "cloth" or banner.

Dan'nocks. Hedging - gloves. A corruption of Tournay, where they were originally manufactured.

Danse. *La danse commence là-bas,* fighting has broken out yonder.

"Mon Caporal, there is great news: *La danse commence là-bas.*"—*Ouida: Under Two Flags*, chap. XXV.

A la danse. On the march.

"The regiment was ordered out *à la danse.* There was fresh war in the interior."—*Ouida: Under Two Flags*, chap. XXV. (*See* DANCE.)

Dans'ker. A Dane. Denmark used to be called Danskë. Hence Polo'nius says to Reynaldo, "Inquire me first what Danskers are in Paris." (*Hamlet*, ii. 1.)

Dante and Be'atri'ce—*i.e.* Beatrice Portina'ri, who was only eight years old when the poet first saw her. His abiding love for her was chaste as snow and pure as it was tender. Beatrice married a nobleman named Simo'ne de Bardi, and died young, in 1290. Dante married Gemma, of the powerful house of Do-na'ti. In the *Divi'na Comme'dia* the poet is conducted first by Virgil (who represents human reason) through hell and purgatory; then by the spirit of Be'atri'ce (who represents the wisdom of faith); and finally by St. Bernard (who represents the wisdom from on high).

Dantes'que (2 syl.). Dante-like— that is, a minute life-like representation of the infernal horrors, whether by words, as in the poet, or in visible form, as in Doré's illustrations of the *Inferno*.

Daphna'ida. An elegy on Douglas Howard, daughter and heiress of Lord Howard. (*Spenser*, 1591.)

Daphne. Daughter of a river-god, loved by Apollo. She fled from the amorous god, and escaped by being changed into a laurel, thenceforth the favourite tree of the sun-god.

"Nay, lady, sit. If I but wave this wand,
Your nerves are all chain'd up in alabaster,
And you a statue, or, as Daphne was,
Root-bound, that fled Apollo."
Milton: Comus, 678-681.

Daph'nis. A Sicilian shepherd who invented pastoral poetry.

Daph'nis. The lover of Chloe in the exquisite Greek pastoral romance of Longos, in the fourth century. Daphnis was the model of Allan Ramsay's *Gentle Shepherd*, and the tale is the basis of St. Pierre's *Paul and Virginia*.

Dapper. A little, nimble, spruce young clerk in Ben Jonson's *Alchemist*.

Dap'ple. The name of Sancho Panza's donkey in Cervantes' romance of *Don Quixote*. Bailey derives dapple from the Teutonic *dapper* (streaked or spotted like a pippin). A *dapple-grey* horse is one of a light grey shaded with a deeper hue; a *dapple-bay* is a light bay spotted with bay of a deeper colour. (Icelandic, *depill*, a spot.)

Dar'bies (2 syl.). Handcuffs. This is derived from "Darby and Joan," because originally two prisoners were linked together as Darby and Joan.

"Hark ye! Jem Clink will fetch you the darbies."—*Sir W. Scott: Peveril of the Peak*.

✢ Johnny Darbies, policemen, is a perversion of the French *gensdarmes*, in conjunction with the above.

Darby and Joan. A loving, old-fashioned, virtuous couple. The names belong to a ballad written by Henry Woodfall, and the characters are those of John Darby, of Bartholomew Close, who died 1730, and his wife, "As chaste as a picture cut in alabaster. You might sooner move a Scythian rock than shoot fire into her bosom." Woodfall served his apprenticeship to John Darby.

"Perhaps some day or other we may be Darby and Joan."—*Lord Lytton*.

✢ The French equivalent is *C'est St. Roch et son chien*.

Dar'byites (3 syl.). The Plymouth Brethren are so called on the Continent from Mr. Darby, a barrister, who abandoned himself to the work, and was for years the "organ" of the sect.

Darics (or) *State'res Dari'ci*. Celebrated Persian coins. So called from Dari'us. They bear on one side the head of the king, and on the other a chariot drawn by mules. Their value is about twenty-five shillings.

Dariolet, Dariolette (French). An intriguant, a confidant, a go-between, a pander. Originally a *dariole* meant a little sweetmeat or cake rayed with little bands of paste.

"Dariolette, employé comme un des nombreux synonymes de *soubrette*, a eu d'abord la mission particulière de designer les suivantes de roman."—*Roland de Villarceaux*.
"Mdlle. Vitry, confidente de Mdlle. de Guise, était la dariolette."—*Tallemant*, vol. i. p. 125.

Dari'us. A classic way of spelling *Durawesh* (king), a Persian title of royalty. Gushtasp or Kishtasp assumed the title of darawesh on ascending the throne, and is the person generally called Darius the Great.

Darius. Seven princes of Persia agreed that he should be king whose horse neighed first; as the horse of Darius was the first to neigh, Darius was proclaimed king.

Dari'us, conquered by Alexander, was Dara, surnamed *kuchek* (the younger). When Alexander succeeded to the throne, Dara sent to him for the tribute of golden eggs, but the Macedonian returned for answer, "The bird which laid them is flown to the other world, where Dara must seek them." The Persian king then sent him a bat and ball, in ridicule of his youth; but Alexander told the messengers, with the bat he would beat the ball of power from their master's hand. Lastly, Dara sent him a bitter melon, as emblem of the grief in store for him; but the Macedonian declared that he would make the Shah eat his own fruit.

Dark. *To keep dark.* To lie perdu ; to lurk in concealment. (Ang.-Sax. *deorc.*)

"We'd get away to some of the far-out stations .... where we could keep in the dark."—*Boldrewood: Robbery Under Arms*, xvi.

Keep it in the dark. Keep it a dead secret ; don't enlighten anyone about the matter.

Dark Ages. The era between the death of Charlemagne and the close of the Carlovingian dynasty.

Dark Continent (*The*). Africa, the land of the dark race or darkies.

Dark Horse (*A*). A racing term for a horse of good pretensions, but of which nothing is positively known by the general public. Its merits are kept dark from betters and book-makers.

"At last a Liberal candidate has entered the field at Croydon. The Conservatives have kept their candidate back, as a dark horse."—*Newspaper paragraph*, January, 1886.

Darkest Hour is that before the Dawn (*The*). When Fortune's wheel is lowest, it must turn up again. When things have come to their worst, they must mend. In Latin, *Post nubila, Phœbus.*

Darky. A negro.

Darley Arabians. A breed of English racers, from an Arab stallion introduced by Mr. Darley. This stallion was the sire of the *Flying Childers*, and great-grandsire of *Eclipse.*

Daron, Daronne (French). The sobriquet given, at the present day, by workmen to shopkeepers and cobblers.

"Il étoit maitre de tout, jusqu'à manier l'argent de la daronne."—*Histoire de Guillaume, cocher.*

Daronne. The confidant of Elisenne, mother of Amadis, and wife of Perion des Gaules. (*Amadis de Gaule.*)

Dart. (*See* ABARIS.)

Darwin'ian Theory. Charles Darwin, grandson of the poet, published in 1859 a work entitled *Origin of Species*, to prove that the numerous species now existing on the earth sprang originally from one or at most a few primal forms ; and that the present diversity is due to special development and natural selection. Those plants and creatures which are best suited to the conditions of their existence survive and become fruitful ; certain organs called into play by peculiar conditions of life grow with their growth, and strengthen with their strength, till they become so much a part and parcel of their frames as to be transmitted to their offspring. The conditions of life being very diverse, cause a great diversity of organic development, and, of course, every such diversity which has become radical is the parent of a new species. (*See* EVOLUTION.)

Dash, in printer's copy. *One* dash under a word in MS. means that the part so dashed must be printed in italics; *two* dashes means small capitals; *three* dashes, large capitals.

Cut a dash. (*See* CUT.)

Dash my Wig. Dash my Buttons. Dash is a euphemism for a common oath ; and wig, buttons, etc., are relics of a common fashion at one time adopted in comedies and by "mashers" of swearing without using profane language.

Date. *Not quite up to date.* Said of books somewhat in arrears of the most recent information.

Daughter. Greek, *thugater*, contracted into *thug'ter ;* Dutch, *dogter ;* German, *tochter ;* Persian, *dochtar ;* Sanskrit, *duhiter ;* Saxon, *dohter ;* etc.

Daughter of Pene'us (*The*). The bay-tree is so called because it grows in greatest perfection on the banks of the river Penēus (3 syl.).

Daughter of the Horseleech. One very exigeant ; one for ever sponging on another. (Prov. xxx. 15.)

"Such and many such like were the morning attendants of the Duke of Buckingham—all genuine descendants of the daughter of the horseleech, whose cry is 'Give, give.'"—*Sir W. Scott : Peveril of the Peak*, chap. xxviii.

Dau'phin. The heir of the French crown under the Valois and Bourbon dynasties. Guy VIII., Count of Vienne, was the first so styled, because he wore *a dolphin* as his cognisance. The title descended in the family till 1349, when Humbert II., *de la tour de Pisa*, sold his seigneurie, called the Dauphiné, to King Philippe VI. (de Valois), on condition that the heir of France assumed the title of *le dauphin*. The first French prince so called was Jean, who succeeded Philippe ; and the last was the Duc d'Angoulême, son of Charles IX., who renounced the title in 1830.

Grand Dauphin. Louis, Duc de Bourgogne, eldest son of Louis XIV., for whose use was published the Latin classics entitled *Ad Usum Delphi'ni.* (1661-1711.)

Second or *Little Dauphin.* Louis, son of the Grand Dauphin. (1682-1712.)

Davenport. A kind of small writing-desk with drawers each side, named after the maker.

Dav'enport (*The Brothers*), from America. Two impostors, who professed that spirits would untie them when bound with cords, and even that spirits played all sorts of instruments in a dark cabinet. The imposition was exposed in 1865.

David, in Dryden's satire called *Absalom and Achitophel,* represents Charles II.; Absalom, his beautiful but rebellious son, represents the Duke of Monmouth; Achitophel, the traitorous counsellor, is the Earl of Shaftesbury; Barzillaï, the faithful old man who provided the king sustenance, was the Duke of Ormond; Hushaï, who defeated the counsel of Achitophel, was Hyde, Duke of Rochester; Zadok the priest was Sancroft, Archbishop of Canterbury; Shimeï, who cursed the king in his flight, was Bethel, the lord mayor; etc. etc. (2 Sam. xvii.-xix.)

"Once more the godlike David was restored,
And willing nations knew their lawful lord."
  Dryden: Absalom and Achitophel, part i.

David (*St.*) or *Dewid,* was son of Xantus, Prince of Cereticu, now called Cardiganshire; he was brought up a priest, became an ascetic in the Isle of Wight, preached to the Britons, confuted Pela'gius, and was preferred to the see of Caerleon, since called St. David's. He died 544. (*See* TAFFY.)

St. David's (Wales) was originally called Mene'via (*i.e. main aw,* narrow water or frith). Here St. David received his early education, and when Dyvrig, Archbishop of Caerleon, resigned to him his see, St. David removed the archiepiscopal residence to Mene'via, which was henceforth called by his name.

David and Jonathan. Inseparable friends. Similar examples of friendship were Pyladēs and Orestēs (*q.v.*); Damon and Pythias (*q.v.*); etc.

"I am distressed for thee, my brother Jonathan. Very pleasant hast thou been to me. Thy love to me was wonderful, passing the love of women."
—2 Sam. i. 26.

Davide'is. An epic poem in four books, describing the troubles of King David. (*Abraham Cowley* [1618-1667].)

There is another sacred poem so called, by Thomas Elwood (1712).

Da'vus. *Davus sum, non Œdipus* (I am a plain, simple fellow, and no solver of riddles, like Œdipus). The words are from Terence's *An'dria,* i. 2, 23.

Non te credas Davum ludere. Don't imagine you are deluding Davus. "Do you see any white in my eye?" I am not such a fool as you think me to be.

Davy. *I'll take my davy of it.* I'll take my "affidavit" it is true.

Davy (*Snuffy*). David Wilson. (*See* Sir Walter Scott, *The Antiquary,* chap. iii. and note.)

Davy Jones's Locker. *He's gone to Davy Jones's locker, i.e.* he is dead. Jones is a corruption of Jonah, the prophet, who was thrown into the sea. *Locker,* in seaman's phrase, means any receptacle for private stores; and *duffy* is a ghost or spirit among the West Indian negroes. So the whole phrase is, "He is gone to the place of safe keeping, where duffy Jonah was sent to."

"This same Davy Jones, according to the mythology of sailors, is the fiend that presides over all the evil spirits of the deep, and is seen in various shapes . . . . warning the devoted wretch of death and woe."—*Smollett: Peregrine Pickle,* xiii.

Da'vy's Sow. *Drunk as Davy's sow.* Grose says: One David Lloyd, a Welshman, who kept an ale-house at Hereford, had a sow with six legs, which was an object of great curiosity. One day David's wife, having indulged too freely, lay down in the sty to sleep, and a company coming to see the sow, David led them to the sty, saying, as usual, "There is a sow for you! Did you ever see the like?" One of the visitors replied, "Well, it is the drunkenest sow I ever beheld." Whence the woman was ever after called "Davy's sow." (*Classical Dictionary of the Vulgar Tongue.*)

Dawson (*Bully*). A noted London sharper, who swaggered and led a most abandoned life about Blackfriars, in the reign of Charles II. (*See* JEMMY DAWSON.)

"Bully Dawson kicked by half the town, and half the town kicked by Bully Dawson."—*Charles Lamb.*

Day. When it begins. (1) With *sun-set:* The Jews in their "sacred year," and the Church—hence the eve of feast-days; the ancient Britons "*non die'rum nu'merum, ut nos, sed noc'tium com'putant,*" says Tacitus—hence "se'n-night" and "fort'night;" the Athenians, Chinese, Mahometans, etc., Italians, Austrians, and Bohemians. (2) With *sun-rise:* The Babylonians, Syrians, Persians, and modern Greeks. (3) With *noon:* The ancient Egyptians and modern astronomers. (4) With *midnight:* The English, French, Dutch, Germans, Spanish, Portuguese, Americans, etc.

A day after the fair. Too late; the fair you came to see is over.

Day in, day out. All day long.

"Sewing as she did, day in, day out."—*W. E. Wilkins: The Honest Soul.*

Every dog has its day. (*See under* DOG.)

I have had my day. My prime of life is over ; I have been a *man of light and leading, but am now " out of the swim."*

"Old Joe, sir . . . was a bit of a favourite . . . once; but he has had his day."—*Dickens.*

I have lost a day (*Per'didi diem*) was the exclamation of Titus, the Roman emperor, when on one occasion he could call to mind nothing done during the past day for the benefit of his subjects.

To-day a man, to-morrow a mouse. In French, "*Aujourd' hui roi, demain rien.*" Fortune is so fickle that one day we may be at the top of the wheel, and the next day at the bottom.

Day of the Barricades. (*See* BARRICADES.)

Day of the Dupes, in French history, was November 11th, 1630, when Marie de Me'dicis and Gaston Duc d'Orléans extorted from Louis XIII. a promise that he would dismiss his Minister, the Cardinal Richelieu. The cardinal went in all speed to Versailles, the king repented, and Richelieu became more powerful than ever. Marie de Me'dicis and Gaston were the dupes who had to pay dearly for their short triumph.

Day-dream. A dream of the imagination when the eyes are awake.

Daylight, in drinking bumpers, means that the wine-glass is not full to the brim ; between the wine and the rim of the wine-glass light may be seen. Toastmasters used to cry out, "Gentlemen, no daylights nor heeltaps"—the heeltap being a little wine left at the bottom of the glass. The glass must be filled to the brim, and every drop of it must be drunk.

Daylights. The eyes, which let daylight into the sensorium.

To darken one's daylights. To give one such a blow on the eyes with the fist as to prevent seeing. (Pugilistic slang.)

Days set apart as Sabbaths. *Sunday* by Christians ; *Monday* by the Greeks ; *Tuesday* by the Persians ; *Wednesday* by the Assyrians ; *Thursday* by the Egyptians ; *Friday* by the Turks ; *Saturday* by the Jews.

Christians worship God on *Sunday,*
Grecian zealots hallow *Monday,*
Tuesday Persians spend in prayer,
Assyrians *Wednesday* revere,
Egyptians *Thursday, Friday* Turks,
On *Saturday* no Hebrew works. *E. C. B.*

Daysman. An umpire, judge, or intercessor. The word is *dais-man* (a-man who sits on the daïs) ; a sort of *lit de justice.* Hence Piers Ploughman—

"And at the day of doom
At the height Deys sit."

Dayspring. The dawn : the commencement of the Messiah's reign.

"The dayspring from on high hath visited us." —Luke i. 78.

Daystar (*The*). The morning star. Hence the emblem of hope or better prospects.

"Again o'er the vine-covered regions of France,
See the day-star of Liberty rise."
   Wilson: Noctes (Jan., 1831, vol. iv. p. 231).

De Bonne Grâce (French). Willingly ; with good grace.

De Die in Diem. From day to day continuously, till the business is completed.

"The Ministry have elected to go on *de die in diem.*"—*Newspaper paragraph*, December, 1885.

De Facto. Actually, in reality ; in opposition to *de jure,* lawfully or rightfully. Thus John was *de facto* king, but Arthur was so *de jure.*

De Haut en Bas. Superciliously.

"She used to treat him a little *de haut en bas.*" —*C. Reade.*

⁂ But *Du haut en bas.* From top to bottom.

De Jure (Latin). By right, rightfully, lawfully, according to the law of the land. Thus a legal axiom says : "*De jure Judices, de facto Juratores, respondent*" (Judges look to the law, juries to the facts).

De Lunatico Inquirendo (Latin). A writ issued to inquire into the state of a person's mind, whether it is sound or not. If not of sound mind, the person is called *non compos,* and is committed to proper guardians.

De Mortuis Nil Nisi Bonum. Of the dead speak kindly or not at all.

De Nihilo Nihil Fit (Latin). You cannot make anything out of nothing.

De Novo (Latin). Afresh ; over again from the beginning.

De Profundis [Out of the depths]. The 130th Psalm is so called from the first two words in the Latin version. It is sung by Roman Catholics when the dead are committed to the grave.

De Rigueur. Strictly speaking, quite *comme il faut,* in the height of fashion.

De Trop (French). Supererogatory, more than enough. *Rien de trop*, let nothing be in excess. Preserve in all things the golden mean. Also "one too many," in the way; when a person's presence is not wished for, that person is *de trop*.

Dead. *Dead as a door-nail.* The door-nail is the plate or knob on which the knocker or hammer strikes. As this nail is knocked on the head several times a day, it cannot be supposed to have much life left in it.

> "Come thou and thy five men, and if I do not leave you all as dead as a door-nail, I pray God I may never eat grass more."—*Shakespeare*: *2 Henry VI.*, iv. 10. (Jack Cade.)

> "*Falstaff.* What! is the old king dead?
> *Pistol.* As nail in door."
> *Shakespeare*: *2 Henry IV.*, v. 3.

Dead as a herring. (*See* HERRING.)

Dead. *He is dead.* "Gone to the world of light." "Joined the majority." *The wind is dead against us.* Directly opposed to our direction. Instead of making the ship more lively, its tendency is quite the contrary. It makes a "dead set" at our progress.

Dead. *Let the dead bury the dead.* Let bygones be bygones. Don't rake up old and dead grievances.

> "Let me entreat you to let the dead bury the dead, to cast behind you every recollection of bygone evils, and to cherish, to love, to sustain one another through all the vicissitudes of human affairs in the times that are to come."—*Gladstone: Home Rule Bill* (February 13th, 1893).

Dead Drunk. So intoxicated as to be wholly powerless.

> "Pythagoras has finely observed that a man is not to be considered dead drunk till he lies on the floor and stretches out his arms and legs to prevent his going lower."—*S. Warren.*

Dead-eye, in nautical phrase, is a block of wood with three holes through it, for the lanyards of rigging to reeve through, without sheaves, and with a groove round it for an iron strap. (*Dana: Seaman's Manual*, p. 92.)

⁘ The holes are eyes, but they are dead eyes.

Dead-flat (*A*), in ship architecture, one of the bends amidship. (*Dana.*)

Dead Freight. That part of a cargo which does not belong to the freight. Dead freight is not counted in the freight, and when the cargo is delivered is not to be reckoned.

Dead Hand (*A*). A first-rate. One that would dead-beat. (*See* MORTMAIN.)

> "First-rate work it was too; he was always a dead hand at splitting."—*Boldrewood: Robbery Under Arms*, xv.

Dead-heads, in theatrical language, means those admitted by orders without payment. They count for nothing. In the United States, persons who receive something of value for which the tax-payer has to pay.

⁘ In *nautical* language, a log floating so low in the water that only a small part of it is visible.

Dead Heat. A race to be run again between two horses that have "tied." A *heat* is that part of a race run without stopping. One, two, or more heats make a race. A dead heat is a heat which goes for nothing.

Dead Horse. *Flogging a dead horse.* Attempting to revive a question already settled. John Bright used the phrase in the House of Commons.

Working for a dead horse. Working for wages already paid.

Dead Languages. Languages no longer spoken.

Dead Letter. A written document of no value; a law no longer acted upon. Also a letter which lies buried in the post-office because the address is incorrect, or the person addressed cannot be found.

Dead-letter Office (*The*). A department in the post-office where unclaimed letters are kept. (*See above.*)

Dead Lift. *I am at a dead lift.* In a strait or difficulty where I greatly need help; a hopeless exigency. A dead lift is the lifting of a dead or inactive body, which must be done by sheer force.

Dead Lights. Strong wooden shutters to close the cabin windows of a ship; they deaden or kill the daylight.

To ship the dead lights. To draw the shutter over the cabin window; to keep out the sea when a gale is expected.

Dead Lock. A lock which has no spring catch. Metaphorically, a state of things so entangled that there seems to be no practical solution.

> "Things are at a dead-lock."—*The Times.*

Dead Men. Empty bottles. *Down among the dead men let me lie.* Let me get so intoxicated as to slip from my chair, and lie under the table with the empty bottles. The expression is a witticism on the word *spirit*. Spirit means life, and also alcohol (the spirit of full bottles); when the spirit is out the man is dead, and when the bottle is empty its spirit is departed. Also, a loaf of bread smuggled into the basket for the private use of the person who carries the bread out is called a "dead man."

Dead Men's Shoes. *Waiting for dead men's shoes.* Looking out for legacies; looking to stand in the place of some moneyed man when he is dead and buried.

Dead Pan (*The*). A poem founded on the tradition that at the crucifixion a cry swept across the ocean in the hearing of many, "Great Pan is Dead," and that at the same time the responses of the oracles ceased for ever. Elizabeth Barrett Browning has a poem so called (1844).

Dead Reckoning. A calculation of the ship's place without any observation of the heavenly bodies. A guess made by consulting the log, the time, the direction, the wind, and so on. Such a calculation may suffice for many practical purposes, but must not be fully relied on.

Dead Ropes. Those which are fixed or do not run on blocks; so called because they have no activity or life in them.

Dead Sea. So the Romans called the "Salt Sea." Jose'phus says that the vale of Siddim was changed into the Dead Sea at the destruction of Sodom (*Antiq.* i. 8, 3, etc.). The water is of a dull green colour. Few fish are found therein, but it is not true that birds which venture near its vapours fall down dead. The shores are almost barren, but hyenas and other wild beasts lurk there. Called the "Salt Sea" because of its saltness. The percentage of salt in the ocean generally is about three or four, but of the Salt Sea it is twenty-six or more.

Dead-Sea Fruit. Fair to the eye, but nauseous to the taste; full of promise, but without reality. (*See* APPLES OF SODOM.)

Dead Set. *He made a dead set at her.* A pointed or decided determination to bring matters to a crisis. The allusion is to a setter dog that has discovered game, and makes a dead set at it.

To be at a dead set is to be set fast, so as not to be able to move. The allusion is to machinery.

To make a dead set upon someone is to attack him resolutely, to set upon him; the allusion being to dogs, bulls, etc., set on each other to fight.

Dead Shares. In theatrical sharing companies three or more supernumerary shares are so called. The manager has one or more of these shares for his expenses; a star will have another; and sometimes a share, or part of a share, is given to an actor who has brought down the house, or made a hit.

Dead Water. The eddy-water closing in with the ship's stern, as she passes through the water. It shifts its place, but is like taking money from one pocket and putting it into another.

Dead Weight. The weight of something without life; a burden that does nothing towards easing its own weight; a person who encumbers us and renders no assistance. (*See* DEAD LIFT.)

Dead Wind (*A*). A wind directly opposed to a ship's course; a wind dead ahead.

Dead Wood, in shipbuilding. Blocks of timber laid on the ship's keel. This is no part of the ship, but it serves to make the keel more rigid.

Dead Works, in theology. Such works as do not earn salvation, or even assist in obtaining it. For such a purpose their value is nil. (Heb. ix. 14.)

Deaf.
Deaf as an adder. (*See below,* DEAF ADDER.)

Deaf as a post. Quite deaf; or so inattentive as not to hear what is said. One might as well speak to a gate-post or log of wood.

Deaf as a white cat. It is said that white cats are deaf and stupid.

None so deaf as those who won't hear. The French have the same locution: "Il n'y a de pire sourd que celui qui ne veut pas entendre."

Deaf Adder. "The deaf adder stoppeth her ears, and will not hearken to the voice of the charmer, charm he never so wisely" (Psalm lviii. 4, 5). Captain Bruce says, "If a viper enters the house, the charmer is sent for, who entices the serpent, and puts it into a bag. I have seen poisonous vipers twist round the bodies of these psylli in all directions, without having their fangs extracted." According to tradition, the asp stops its ears when the charmer utters his incantation, by applying one ear to the ground and twisting its tail into the other. In the United States the copperhead is so called.

Deal. A portion. "A tenth deal of flour." (Exodus xxix. 40.) (German, *theil;* Anglo-Saxon, *dæl,* verb, *dælan,* to share ; Irish, *dail;* English, *dole.*)

To deal the cards is to give each his dole or portion.

Deal-fish. So called because of some fancied resemblance to a deal-board, from its length and thinness.

Dean (the Latin *Deca'nus*). The chief over ten prebends or canons.

The Dean (Il Piova'no). Arlotto, the Italian humorist. (1395-1483.)

Jonathan Swift, Dean of St. Patrick. (1667-1745.)

Deans (*Effie*), in Scott's *Heart of Midlothian,* is Helen Walker. She is abandoned by her lover, Geordie Robertson [Staunton], and condemned for child-murder.

Jeanie Deans. Half-sister of Effie Deans, who walks all the way to London to plead for her sister. She is a model of good sense, strong affection, and disinterested heroism. (*See* WALKER.)

"We follow Pilgrim through his progress with an interest not inferior to that with which we follow Elizabeth from Siberia to Moscow, and Jeanie Deans from Edinburgh to London."—*Lord Macaulay.*

Dear. *Oh, dear me !* Regarded, but without evidence, as a corruption of the Italian *O Dio mio !*

Dear Bought and Far Brought or *Dear bought and far felt.* A gentle reproof for some extravagant purchase of luxury.

Dearest. Most hateful, as *dearest foe.* The word dear, meaning " beloved," is the Saxon *deor* (dear, rare) ; but dear, "hateful," is the Anglo-Saxon *derian* (to hurt), Scotch *dere* (to annoy).

"Would I had met my dearest foe in heaven,
Or ever I had seen that day, Horatio."
Shakespeare : Hamlet, i. 2.

Death, according to Milton, is twin-keeper with Sin, of Hell-gate.

"The other shape
(If shape it might be called that shape had none
Distinguishable in member, joint, or limb :
Or substance might be called that shadow seemed ;) . . . .
The likeness of a kingly crown had on."
Milton : Paradise Lost, ii. 666—673.

Death. (*See* BLACK DEATH.)

Death stands, like Mercuries, in every way. (*See* MERCURY.)

Till death us do part. (*See* DEPART.)

Angel of Death. (*See* ABOU-JAHIA, AZRAEL.)

At death's door. On the point of death ; very dangerously ill.

In at the death. Present when the fox was caught and killed.

Death and Doctor Hornbook. Doctor Hornbook was John Wilson the apothecary, whom the poet met at the Torbolton Masonic Lodge. (*Burns.*)

Death from Strange Causes.

Æs'chylus was killed by the fall of a tortoise on his bald head from the claws of an eagle in the air. (*Valerius Maximus,* ix. 12, and *Pliny : History,* vii. 7.)

Agath'ocles (4 syl.), tyrant of Sicily, was killed by a toothpick at the age of ninety-five.

Anac'reon was choked by a grapestone. (*Pliny : History,* vii. 7.)

Bassus (Quintus Lucānus) died from the prick of a needle in his left thumb.

Chalchas, the soothsayer, died of laughter at the thought of having outlived the predicted hour of his death.

Charles VIII., of France, conducting his queen into a tennis-court, struck his head against the lintel, and it caused his death.

Fab'ius, the Roman prætor, was choked by a single goat-hair in the milk which he was drinking. (*Pliny: History,* vii. 7.)

Frederick Lewis, Prince of Wales, died from the blow of a cricket-ball.

Gallus (Cornelius), the prætor, and Titus Haterĭus, a knight, each died while kissing the hand of his wife.

Gabrielle (La belle), the mistress of Henri IV., died from eating an orange.

Itadach died of thirst in the harvest-field because (in observance of the rule of St. Patrick) he refused to drink a drop of anything.

Lep'idus (Quintus Æm'ilius), going out of his house, struck his great toe against the threshold and expired.

Louis VI. met with his death from a pig running under his horse and causing it to stumble.

Margutte died of laughter on seeing a monkey trying to pull on a pair of boots.

Otway, the poet, in a starving condition, had a guinea given him, on which he bought a loaf of bread, and died while swallowing the first mouthful.

Pamphilius (Cnew' Babius), a man of prætorian rank, died while asking a boy what o'clock it was.

Philom'enes (4 syl.) died of laughter at seeing an ass eating the figs provided for his own dessert. (*Valerius Maximus.*)

Placut (Phillipot) dropped down dead while in the act of paying a bill. (*Bacaberry the Elder.*)

Quenelault, a Norman physician, of Montpellier, died from a slight wound made in his hand in extracting a splinter.

Saufeius (*Appius*) was choked to death supping up the white of an under-boiled egg. (*Pliny : History*, vii. 33.)

Torqua'tus (*Aulus Manlius*), a gentleman of consular rank, died in the act of taking a cheesecake at dinner.

Valla (*Lucius Tuscius*), the physician, died in the act of taking a draught of medicine.

William III. died from his horse stumbling over a mole-hill.

Zeuxis, the great painter, died of laughter at sight of a hag which he had just depicted.

⁜ It will be observed that four of the list died of laughter. No doubt the reader will be able to add other examples.

Death in the Pot. During a dearth in Gilgal, there was made for the sons of the prophets a pottage of wild herbs, some of which were poisonous. When the sons of the prophets tasted the pottage, they cried out, "There is death in the pot." Then Elisha put into it some meal, and its poisonous qualities were counteracted. (2 Kings iv. 40.)

Death under Shield. Death in battle.

"Her imagination had been familiarised with wild and bloody events . . . and had been trained up to consider an honourable 'death under shield' (as that in a field of battle was termed) a desirable termination to the life of a warrior."—*Sir W. Scott : The Betrothed*, chap. 6.

Death-bell. A tinkling in the ears, supposed by the Scotch peasantry to announce the death of a friend.

"O lady, 'tis dark, an' I heard the death-bell,
An' I darena gae yonder for gowd nor fee."
James Hogg : Mountain Bard.

Death-meal (*A*). A funeral banquet.

"Death-meals, as they were termed, were spread in honour of the deceased."—*Sir W. Scott : The Betrothed*, chap. 7.

Death-watch. Any species of Anobium, a genus of wood-boring beetles that make a clicking sound, once supposed to presage death.

Death's Head. Bawds and procuresses used to wear a ring bearing the impression of a death's head in the time of Queen Elizabeth. Allusions not uncommon in plays of the period.

"Sell some of my cloaths to buy thee a death's-head, and put [it] upon thy middle finger. Your least considering bawds do so much."—*Messenger : Old Laws*, iv. 1.

Death's Head on a Mopstick. A thin, sickly person, a mere anatomy, is so called. When practical jokes were more common it was by no means unusual to mount on a mopstick a turnip with holes for eyes, and a cand'e inside, to scare travellers at night time.

Deaths-man. An executioner ; a person who kills another brutally but lawfully.

"Great Hector's deaths-man."
Heywood : Iron Age.

Debateable Land. A tract of land between the Esk and Sark, claimed by both England and Scotland, and for a long time the subject of dispute. This tract of land was the hotbed of thieves and vagabonds.

De'bon. One of the heroes who accompanied Brute to Britain. According to British fable, Devonshire is the county or share of Debon. (*See* DEVONSHIRE.)

Debonair' [*Le Débonnaire*]. Louis I. of France, sometimes called in English *The Meek*, son and successor of Charlemagne ; a man of courteous manners, cheerful temper, but effeminate and deficient in moral energy. (778, 814-840.)

Débris. *The débris of an army.* The remnants of a routed army. Débris means the fragments of a worn-down rock. It is a geological term (*débriser*, to break down).

Debt of Nature. *To pay the debt of Nature.* To die. Life is a loan, not a gift, and the debt is paid off by death.

"The slender debt to Nature's quickly paid."
Quarles : Emblems.

Decam'eron. A volume of tales related in *ten days* (Greek, *deka, hem'era*), as the *Decameron of Boccac'cio*, which contains one hundred tales related in ten days.

Decamp'. *He decamped in the middle of the night.* Left without paying his debts. A military term from the Latin *de-campus* (from the field) ; French, *décamper*, to march away.

Decaniller. To be off, to decamp, to escape. A curious instance of argot. Canille is old French for *chenille*, a pupa, imago, or chrysalis. These afterwards become winged insects and take their flight. So a visitor says in France, "*Il faut me sauver*," or "*Il faut decaniller*." I must be off.

December. (Latin, *the tenth month*.) So it was when the year began in March with the vernal equinox ; but since January and February have been inserted before it, the term is quite incorrect.

Deception.

"Doubtless the pleasure is as great
Of being cheated as to cheat ;
As lookers-on feel most delight
That least perceive a juggler's sleight,
And still the less they understand,
The more they admire his sleight of hand."
     Butler : Hudibras, part ii. 3.

Deci′de (2 syl.) means "to knock out." Several things being set before a person, he eliminates all but one, which he selects as his choice. A *decided man* is one who quickly eliminates every idea but the one he intends to adhere to.

Decimo. *A man in decimo—i.e.* a hobby-de-hoy. Jonson uses the phrase *in decimo-sexto.*

Deck. A pack of cards, or that part of the pack which is left after the hands have been dealt.

"But whilst he thought to steal the single ' ten,'
The ' king ' was slyly fingered from the deck."
     Shakespeare: 3 Henry VI., v. 1.

To sweep the deck. To clear off all the stakes. (*See above.*)

To deck is to decorate or adorn. (Anglo-Saxon, *decan ;* Dutch, *dekken,* to cover.)

"I thought thy bride-bed to have decked, sweet maid,
And not have strewed thy grave."
     Shakespeare: Hamlet, v. 1.

Clear the decks—i.e. get out of the way ; your room is better than your company ; I am going to be busy. A sea term. Decks are cleared before action.

Decking Churches. Isaiah (lx. 13) says : "The glory of Lebanon shall come unto thee; the fir-tree, the pine-tree, and the box together, to beautify the place of my sanctuary." The "glory of Lebanon" is the cedar-tree. These are not the evergreens mainly used in church decorations. At Christmas the holly is chiefly used, though those mentioned by Isaiah abound.

Décolleté [*da-coal-ta*]. *Nothing even décolleté should be uttered before ladies— i.e.* bearing the least semblance to a *double entendre.* Décolleté is the French for a " dress cut low about the bosom."

Decoration Day. May 30th ; set apart in the United States for decorating the graves of those who fell in the " War of the Union " (1861-5).

Decoy Duck. A bait or lure ; a duck taught to allure others into a net, and employed for this purpose.

Decrep′it. Unable to make a noise. It refers rather to the mute voice and silent footstep of old age than to its broken strength. (Latin, *de-crepo.*)

Dec′uman Gate. The gate where the 10th cohorts of the legions were posted. It was opposite the Prætorian gate, and farthest from the enemy. (Latin, *decem,* ten.)

Deda′lian. Intricate ; variegated. So called from *Dæ′dalos,* who made the Cretan labyrinth.

Dedlock (*Sir Leicester*). An honourable and truthful gentleman, but of such fossilised ideas that no " tongue of man " could shake his prejudices. (*Charles Dickens : Bleak House.*)

Dee—*i.e.* D for a detective. *Look sharp ! the dees are about.*

Dee (*Dr. John*). A man of vast knowledge, whose library, museum, and mathematical instruments were valued at £2,000. On one occasion the populace broke into his house and destroyed the greater part of his valuable collection, under the notion that Dee held intercourse with the devil. He ultimately died a pauper, at the advanced age of eighty-one, and was buried at Mortlake. He professed to be able to raise the dead, and had a magic mirror, afterwards in Horace Walpole's collection at Strawberry Hill (1527-1608).

Dee's speculum or *mirror,* in which persons were told they could see their friends in distant lands and how they were occupied. It is a piece of solid pink-tinted glass about the size of an orange. It is now in the British Museum.

Dee Mills. *If you had the rent of Dee Mills, you would spend it all.* Dee Mills, in Cheshire, used to yield a very large annual rent. (*Cheshire proverb.*)

"There was a jolly miller
Lived on the river Dee ;
He worked and sung from morn to night—
No lark so blithe as he ;
And this the burden of his song
For ever used to be—
I care for nobody, no, not I,
If nobody cares for me.'"
     Bickerstaff : Love in a Village (1762).

Deer. Supposed by poets to shed tears. The drops, however, which fall from their eyes are not tears, but an oily secretion from the so-called tear-pits.

"A poor sequestered stag . . . .
Did come to languish . . . . and the big round tears
Coursed one another down his innocent nose
In piteous chase."
     Shakespeare: As You Like It, ii. 2.

Small deer. Any small animal; and used metaphorically for any collection of trifles or trifling matters.

"But mice and rats, and such small deer,
Have been Tom's food for seven long year."
     Shakespeare: Lear, iii. 4.

Deerslayer. The hero of a novel so called, by F. Cooper. He is the beau-ideal of a man without cultivation—honourable in sentiment, truthful, and brave as a lion ; pure of heart, and without reproach in conduct. The character appears, under different names, in five novels—*The Deerslayer*, *The Pathfinder*, *The Last of the Mo'hicans*, *The Pioneers*, and *The Prairie*. (*See* NATTY BUMPO.)

Dees (*The*). (*See above* DEE.)

Deev-Binder. Tamnuras, King of Persia, who defeated the Deev king and the fierce Demrush, but was slain by Houndkonz, another powerful Deev.

Default. *Judgment by default* is when the defendant does not appear in court on the day appointed. The judge gives sentence in favour of the plaintiff, not because the plaintiff is right, but from the default of the defendant.

Defeat. "What though the field be lost? all is not lost." (*Milton: Paradise Lost*, i. line 105-6.)

"All is lost but honour" (*Tout est perdu, madame, fors l'honneur*) is what François I. is said to have written to his mother, after the Battle of Pavia in 1525.

Defeat. There is a somewhat strange connection between *de-feat* and *de-feature*. Defeat is the French *de-fait*, un-made or un-done; Latin, *de-factus* (*defectus*, our "defect"); and *feature* is the Norman *faiture*, Latin *factu'ra*, the make-up, frame, or form. Hence old writers have used the word "defeat" to mean disfigure or spoil the form.

"Defeat thy favour [face] with an usurped beard."—*Shakespeare: Othello*, i. 3.

Defen'der of the Faith. A title given by Pope Leo X. to Henry VIII. of England, in 1521, for a Latin treatise *On the Seven Sacraments*. Many previous kings, and even subjects, had been termed "defenders of the Catholic faith," "defenders of the Church," and so on, but no one had borne it as a title. The sovereign of Spain is entitled *Catholic*, and of France *Most Christian*.

"God bless the king! I mean the 'faith's defender!'
God bless—no harm in blessing the Pretender.
But who Pretender is, or who is king—
God bless us all! that's quite another thing."
John Byron: Shorthand Writer.

∵ Richard II., in a writ to the sheriffs, uses these words: "*Ecclesia cujus nos defensor sumus*," and Henry VII., in the Black Book, is called "Defender of the Faith;" but the pope gave the title to Henry VIII., and from that time to this it has been perpetuated. (*See* GRACELESS FLORIN.)

De'ficit (*Madame*). Marie Antoinette. So called because she was always demanding money of her ministers, and never had any. According to the Revolutionary song:

"La Boulangère a des ecus,
Qui ne lui content guère."

(*See* BAKER.)

Degen'erate (4 syl.) is to be worse than the parent stock. (Latin, *de genus*.)

Dei Gratia. By God's grace. Introduced into English charters in 1106; as much as to say, "*dei non hominum gratia*," by divine right and not man's appointment. The archbishops of Canterbury from 676 to 1170 assumed the same style.

∵ From the time of Offa, King of Mercia (A.D. 780), we find occasionally the same or some similar assumption as, *Dei dono*, *Christo donante*, etc. The Archbishop of Canterbury is now *divina providentia*.

Dei Gratia omitted on a florin. (*See* GRACELESS FLORIN.)

Dei Judicium (Latin). The judgment of God; so the judgment by ordeals was called, because it was supposed that God would deal rightly with the appellants.

De'iani'ra. Wife of Herculēs, and the inadvertent cause of his death. Nessos told her that anyone to whom she gave a shirt steeped in his blood, would love her with undying love; she gave it to her husband, and it caused him such agony that he burnt himself to death on a funeral pile. Deianira killed herself for grief.

Deiph'obus (4 syl.). One of the sons of Priam, and, next to Hector, the bravest and boldest of all the Trojans. On the death of his brother Paris, he married Helen; but Helen betrayed him to her first husband, Menela'os, who slew him. (*Homer's Iliad* and *Virgil's Æneid*.)

Deities.

Air: Ariel, Elves (singular, Elf).
Caves or *Caverns:* Hill-people (Hög-folk, hög = height).
Corn: Ceres (2 syl.) (Greek, Demēter).
Domestic Life: Vesta.
Eloquence: Mercury (Greek, Hermēs).
Evening: Vesper.
Fates (The): Three in number (Greek, Parcæ, Moiræ, 2 syl., Kēres).
Fire: Vulcan (Greek, Hephaistŏs, 3 syl.), Vesta, Mulciber.
Fairies: (*q.v.*).
Furies: Three in number (Greek, Eumenides, 4 syl., Erinn'yes).

Gardens: Priāpus, Vertumnus with his wife Pomōna.

Graces (The): Three in number (Greek, Chartes).

Hills: Trolls. There are also Wood Trolls and Water,Trolls. (*See below* Mountains.)

Home Spirits (q.v.): Penātes (3 syl.), Lares (2 syl.).

Hunting: Diana (Greek, Artĕmis).

Infernal Regions: Pluto, with his wife Proserpine, 3 syl. (Greek, A'idēs and Persephŏnē).

Justice: Them'is, Astræa, Nemesis.

Love: Cupid (Greek, Eros).

Marriage: Hymen.

Medicine: Æsculāpius.

Mines: Trolls.

Morning: Aurora (Greek, Eŏs).

Mountains: Orĕads or Orēades (4 syl.), from the Greek, όρος, a mountain; Trolls.

Ocean (The): Ocean'ides.

Poetry and *Music:* Apollo, the nine Muses.

Rainbow (The): Iris.

Riches: Plutus. Shakespeare speaks of "Plutus' mine," (*Julius Cæsar,* iv. 3).

Rivers and *Streams:* Fluviāles, 4 syl. (Greek, Potamēides, 5 syl.).

Sea (The): Neptune (Greek, Poseidon, 3 syl.), his son Triton, Necks, Mermaids, Nereids (3 syl.). (*See* Sea.)

Shepherds and their *Flocks:* Pan, the Satyrs.

Springs, Lakes, Rivers, etc.: Nēreides or Naiads (2 syl.).

Time: Saturn (Greek, Chrŏnos).

War: Mars (Greek, Arēs), Bellōna, Thor.

Water-nymphs: Naiads (2 syl.), Undine (2 syl.).

Winds (The): Æōlus.

Wine: Bacchus (Greek, Diony'sŏs).

Wisdom: Minerva (Greek, Pallas, Athēnē, or Pallas-Athēnē).

Woods: Dryads (A Hama-Dryad presides over some particular tree), Wood-Trolls.

Youth: Hēbē.

☞ Of course this is not meant for a complete list of heathen and pagan deities. Such a list would require a volume.

Déjeuner à la Fourchette (French). Breakfast with forks; a cold collation; a breakfast in the middle of the day, with meat and wine; a lunch.

Delaware, U.S. America, was granted by charter in 1701 to Lord De la Ware, who first explored the bay into which the river empties itself.

Delec'table Mountains (*The*), in Bunyan's *Pilgrim's Progress,* are a range of mountains from which the "Celestial City" may be seen. They are in Immanuel's land, and are covered with sheep, for which Immanuel had died.

Delf, or more correctly *Delft.* A common sort of pottery made at Delft in Holland, about 1310.

De'lia, of Pope's line, "Slander or poison dread from Delia's rage," was Lady Deloraine, who married W. Windam of Carsham, and died 1744. The person said to have been poisoned was Miss Mackenzie. (*Satires and Epistles,* i. 81.)

Delia is not better known to our yard-dog—i.e. the person is so intimate and well known that the yard-dog will not bark at his approach. It is from Virgil, who makes his shepherd Menalcas boast "That his sweetheart is as well known to his dog as Delia the shepherdess." (*Eclogues,* iii. 67.)

Delias. The sacred vessel made by Theseus (2 syl.) and sent annually from Athens to Delos. This annual festival lasted 30 days, during which no Athenian could be put to death, and as Socrates was condemned during this period his death was deferred till the return of the sacred vessel. The ship had been so often repaired that not a stick of the original vessel remained at the time, yet was it the identical ship. So the body changes from infancy to old age, and though no single particle remains constant, yet the man 6 feet high is identical with his infant body a span long. (Sometimes called *Theoris.*)

Delight is "to make light." Hence Shakespeare speaks of the disembodied soul as "the delighted spirit". . . . blown with restless violence round about the pendant world" (*Measure for Measure,* iii. 1). So again he says of gifts, "the more delayed, delighted" (*Cymbeline,* v. 5), meaning the longer they are delayed the "lighter" or less valuable they are esteemed. Delighted, in the sense of "pleased," means light-hearted, with buoyant spirits.

The delight of mankind. So Titus, the Roman emperor, was entitled (40, 79-81).

Delir'ium. From the Latin *lira* (the ridge left by the plough), hence the verb *de-lira're,* to make an irregular ridge or balk in ploughing. *Deli'rus* is one whose mind is not properly tilled or cultivated, a person of irregular intellect; and *delirium* is the state of a person whose mental faculties are like a field full of balks or irregularities. (*See* PREVARICATION.)

Della Crus'cans or *Della Crus'can School.* So called from Crusca, the Florentine academy. The name is applied to a school of poetry started by some young Englishmen at Florence in the latter part of the eighteenth century. These silly, sentimental affectations, which appeared in the *World* and the *Oracle,* created for a time quite a *furore.* The whole affair was mercilessly gibbeted in the *Baviad* and *Mæviad* of Gifford. (Academia della Crusca literally means, the Academy of Chaff, and its object was to sift the chaff from the Italian language, or to purify it.)

Delmon'ico. The great American cuisinier, of New York.

"The table service is of heavy silver, French cut glasses, and handsome china; and the meals are worthy of Delmonico."—*The Oracle,* August 2nd, 1884, p. 495.

De'los. A floating island ultimately made fast to the bottom of the sea by Posei'don (Neptune). Apollo having become possessor of it by exchange, made it his favourite retreat. It is one of the Cyclades.

Delphi or *Delphos.* A town of Pho'cis, famous for a temple of Apollo and for an oracle celebrated in every age and country. So called from its twin peaks, which the Greeks called brothers (*adelphoi*).

Delphin Classics. A set of Latin classics edited in France by thirty-nine scholars, under the superintendence of Montausier, Bossuet, and Huet, for the use of the son of Louis XIV., called the *Grand Dauphin.* Their chief value consists in their verbal indexes or concordances.

Del'ta. The island formed at the mouth of a river, which usually assumes a triangular form, like the Greek letter (Δ) called *delta;* as the delta of the Nile, the delta of the Danube, Rhine, Ganges, Indus, Niger, Mississippi, Po, and so on.

Del'uge. *After me the Deluge* ["*Après moi le Déluge*"]. When I am dead the deluge may come for aught I care. Generally ascribed to Prince Metternich, but the Prince borrowed it from Mme. Pompadour, who laughed off all the remonstrances of ministers at her extravagance by saying, "*Après nous le déluge*" (Ruin, if you like, when we are dead and gone).

Del'uges (3 syl.). The chief, besides that recorded in the Bible, are the following:—The deluge of *Fohi,* the Chinese; the *Satyavra'ta,* of the Indians; the *Xisuth'rus,* of the Assyrians; the Mexican deluge; and the Greek deluges of *Deuca'lion* and *Og'ygès.*

✱ The most celebrated painting of Noah's Flood is by Poussin, in Paris; and that by Raphael is in the Vatican (Rome).

Demerit has reversed its original meaning (Latin, *demereo,* to merit, to deserve). Hence Plautus, *Demeritas dare laudas* (to accord due praise); Ovid, *Numina culta demeruisse;* Livy, *demerēri beneficio civitatem.* The *de-* is intensive, as in "de-mand," "describe," "de-claim," etc.; not the privative *deorsum,* as in the word "defame."

"My demerits [deserts] May speak unbonneted."
Shakespeare : Othello, i. 2.

Demijohn (*A*). A glass vessel with a large body and small neck, enclosed in wickerwork like a Florence flask, and containing more than a bottle. (French, *dame-jeanne,* "Madam Jane," a corruption of *Damaghan,* a town in Persia famous for its glass works.)

Demi-monde. Lorettes, courtezans. *Le beau monde* means "fashionable society," and *demi-monde* the society only half acknowledged.

"Demi-monde implies not only recognition and a *status,* but a certain social standing."—*Saturday Review.*

Demi-rep. A woman whose character has been blown upon. Contraction of *demi-reputation.*

Dem'iurge (3 syl.), in the language of Platonists, means that mysterious agent which made the world and all that it contains. The Logos or Word spoken of by St. John, in the first chapter of his gospel, is the Demiurgus of Platonising Christians. In the Gnostic systems, Jehovah (as an eon or emanation of the Supreme Being) is the Demiurge.

"The power is not that of an absolute cause, but only a world-maker, a demiurge; and this does not answer to the human idea of deity."—*Winchell: Science and Religion,* chap. x. p. 295.

Demobilisa'tion of troops. The disorganisation of them, the disarming of them. This is a French military term. To "mobilise" troops is to render them liable to be moved on service out of their quarters; to "demobilise" them is to send them home, so that they cannot be moved from their quarters against any one. To change from a war to a peace footing.

Democ'racy. A Republican form of government, a commonwealth. (Greek, *demos-kratia,* the rule of the people.)

Democ'ritos. The laughing philosopher of Abde'ra. He should rather be termed the *deriding* philosopher, because he derided or laughed at people's folly or vanity. It is said that he put out his eyes that he might think more deeply.

"Democritus, dear droll, revisit earth, And with our follies glut thy heightened mirth." *Prior.*

Democ'ritus Junior. Robert Burton, author of *The Anatomy of Melancholy* (1576-1640).

Demod'ocos. A minstrel who, according to Homer, sang the amours of Mars and Venus in the court of Alcin'oös while Ulysses was a guest there.

Demogorgon. A terrible deity, whose very name was capable of producing the most horrible effects. Hence Milton speaks of "the dreaded name of Demogorgon" (*Paradise Lost*, ii. 965). This tyrant king of the elves and fays lived on the Himalayas, and once in five years summoned all his subjects before him to give an account of their stewardship. Spenser (book iv. 2) says, "He dwells in the deep abyss where the three fatal sisters dwell." (Greek *daimon*, demon ; *gorgos*, terrible.)

> "Must I call your master to my aid,
> At whose dread name the trembling furies quake,
> Hell stands abashed, and earth's foundations
> shake?"   *Rowe: Lucan's Pharsalia*, vi.
>
> "When the morn arises none are found,
> For cruel Demogorgon walks his round,
> And if he finds a fairy lag in light,
> He drives the wretch before, and lashes into
> night."
>   *Dryden: The Flower and the Leaf*, 492-5.

Demon of Matrimonial Unhappiness. Asmode'us, who slew the seven husbands of Sara. (*Tobit*.) (*See* ASMODÆUS.)

Prince of Demons. Asmode'us. (*Talmud*.)

Demos (*King*). The electorate ; the proletariat. Not the mob, but those who choose and elect our senators, and are therefore the virtual rulers of the nation.

Demos'thenes' Lantern. A chora'gic monument erected by Lysic'ratēs in Athens, originally surmounted by the tripod won by Lysicratēs. A "tripod" was awarded to everyone in Athens who produced the best drama or choral piece of his tribe. The street in which Demosthenēs' Lantern stood was full of these tripods.

Demurrage. An allowance made to the master or owners of a ship by the freighters for detaining her in port longer than the time agreed upon. (Latin, *demorari*, to delay.)

> "The extra days beyond the lay days . . . . are called days of demurrage."—*Kent: Commentaries*, vol. iii. part v. lecture xlvii. p. 159.

Demy'. A size of paper between royal and crown. Its size is 22½ in. × 17½ in. It is from the French word *demi* (half), and means demi-royal (a small royal), royal being 25 in. × 20 in. The old watermark is a *fleur-de-lis*.

A Demy' of Magdalene College, Oxford, is a "superior" sort of scholar, half a Fellow.

Den. Evening. *God ye good den !*— *i.e.* God (give) ye good evening. This is the final *d* of good joined to the "en," a contraction of evening.

Dena'rius. A Roman silver coin, equal in value to ten ases (*deni-ases*). The word was used in France and England for the inferior coins, whether silver or copper, and for ready money generally. Now d (*denarius*) stands for money less than a shilling, as £ s. d.

> "The denarius . . . . shown to our Lord . . . . was the tribute-money payable by the Jews to the Roman emperor, and must not be confounded with the tribute paid to the Temple."—*F. H. Madden : Jewish Coinage*, chap. xi. p. 247.

Denarius Dei [God's penny]. An earnest of a bargain, which was given to the church or poor.

Denarii St. Petri [Peter's pence]. One penny from each family, given to the Pope.

Denarius tertius comita'tus. One-third of the pence of the county, which was paid to the earl. The other two-thirds belonged to the Crown. (*See* D.)

Den'izen. A made citizen—*i.e.* an alien who has been naturalised by letters patent. (Old French *deinzein ;* Latin *de-intus*, from within.)

> "A denizen is a kind of middle state, between an alien and a natural-born subject, and partakes of both."—*Blackstone : Commentaries*, book i. chap. x. p. 374.

Dennis (*John*), called the "best abused man in England." Swift and Pope both satirised him. He is called Zoïlus.

Dénouement (3 syl.). The untying of a plot ; the winding-up of a novel or play. (French *dénouer*, to untie.)

Denys (*St.*), according to tradition, carried his head, after martyrdom, for six miles; and then deliberately laid it down on the spot where stands the present cathedral bearing his name. This absurd tale took its rise from an ancient *painting*, in which the artist, to represent the martyrdom of the bishop, drew a headless body ; but, in order that the trunk might be recognised, placed the head in front, between the martyr's hands.

Sir Denys Brand, in Crabbe's *Borough*, is a country magnate who apes humility. He rides on a sorry brown pony "not worth £5," but mounts his lackey on a racehorse, "twice victor for a plate." Sir Denys Brand is the type of a character by no means uncommon.

Deo Gratias (Latin). Thanks to God.

Deo Juvante (Latin). With God's help.

Deo, non Fortunâ (Latin). From God, not from mere luck ; [I attribute it] to God and not to blind chance.

Deo Volente, contracted into D. V. (Latin). God being willing ; by God's will.

De'odand means something "given to God" (*deo-dandum*). This was the case when a man met with his death through injuries inflicted by some chattel, as by the fall of a ladder, the toss of a bull, or the kick of a horse. In such cases the cause of death was sold, and the proceeds given to the Church. The custom was based on the doctrine of purgatory. As the person was sent to his account without the sacrament of extreme unction, the money thus raised served to pay for masses for his repose. Deodands were abolished September 1st, 1846.

Depart. To part thoroughly ; to separate effectually. The marriage service in the ancient prayer-books had "till death us depart," or "till alimony or death us departs," a sentence which has been corrupted into "till death us do part."

"Before they settle hands and hearts, ·
  Till alimony or death departs."
        Butler : Hudibras, iii. 3.

Depart'ment. France is divided into departments, as Great Britain and Ireland are divided into counties or shires. From 1768 it was divided into *governments*, of which thirty-two were *grand* and eight *petit*. In 1790, by a decree of the Constituent Assembly, it was mapped out *de novo* into eighty-three departments. In 1804 the number of departments was increased to 107, and in 1812 to 130. In 1815 the territory was reduced to eighty-six departments, and continued so till 1860, when Savoy and Nice were added. The present number is eighty-seven.

Dependence. An existing quarrel. (A term used among swordsmen.)

"Let us pause . . . until I give you my opinion on this dependence . . . for if we coolly examine the state of our dependence, we may the better apprehend whether the sisters three have doomed one of us to expiate the same with our blood."— *Sir W. Scott : The Monastery*, chap. xxi.

De'pinges (2 syl.) or *Deep'ings*. A breadth of netting to be sewed on a *hoddy* (net) to make it sufficiently large. Sometimes the breadth is called a *depth*, and the act of sewing one depth on another is called *deepening* the net. In 1574 the Dutch settlers at Yarmouth

were required "to provide themselves with twine and depinges in foreign places."

Deputa'tions. *The year of deputations.* The eighth of the Hedj'rah, after Mahomet's victory over the Arabs near Taïf, when deputations from all parts flocked to do him homage.

Depu'te (2 syl.). To depute means to prune or cut off a part ; deputation is the part cut off. A deputation is a slip cut off to represent the whole. (Latin, *depu'to*.)

Derbend [*iron*]. A town on the Caspian, commanding the coast road. D'Herbelot says : "Les Turcs appellent cette ville ' Demir Capi ' (porte de fer) ; ce sont les *Caspiæ Portæ* des anciens."

"Beyond the Caspian's iron gates."
        Moore : Fire Worshippers.

Derby Stakes. Started by Edward Smith Stanley, the twelfth Earl of Derby, in 1780, the year after his establishment of the Oaks stakes (*q.v.*).

The Derby Day is the day when the Derby stakes are run for ; it is the second Wednesday of the great Epsom Spring Meeting, in May.

The Derby Day.

✷ The Derby, the Oaks, and the St. Leger are called "The Classic Races." The Oaks is the classic race for fillies only, three years' old (£1,000) ; the Derby (Darby) for colts and fillies three years' old ; the St. Leger for colts and fillies, those which have run in the Oaks or Derby being eligible.

Deri've (2 syl.) means "back to its channel or source" (Latin, *de rivo*). The Latin *rivus* (a river) does not mean the stream or current, but the source whence it flows, or the channel through which it runs. As Ulpian says, "*Fons sive locus per longitu'dinem depressus, quo aqua decurrat.*"

Dernier Ressort (French). A last resource.

Der'rick. A hangman ; a temporary crane to remove goods from the hold of a vessel. So called from Derrick, the Tyburn hangman early in the seventeenth century, who for more than a hundred years gave his name to gibbets. (*See* HANGMAN.)

"He rides circuit with the devil, and Derrick must be his host, and Tyborne the inn at which he will light."—*Bellman of London*, 1616.

Der'wentwa'ter. Lord *Derwentwater's lights.* The Auro'ra borea'lis ; so called from James, Earl of Derwentwater, beheaded for rebellion February

24th, 1716. It is said that the northern lights were unusually brilliant on that night.

Desdemo'na (in Shakespeare's *Othello*). Daughter of Brabantio. She fell in love with Othello, and eloped with him. Iago, acting on the jealous temper of the Moor, made him believe that his wife had an intrigue with Cassio, and in confirmation of this statement told the Moor that she had given Cassio a pocket-handkerchief, the fact being that Iago's wife, to gratify her husband, had purloined it. Othello asked his bride for it, but she was unable to find it; whereupon the Moor murdered her and then stabbed himself.

"She ... was ready to listen and weep, like Desdemona, at the stories of his dangers and campaigns."—*Thackeray.*

Desmas. (*See* DYSMAS.)

Despair. *The Giant Despair*, in Bunyan's *Pilgrim's Progress*, lived in "Doubting Castle."

Dessert' means simply the cloth removed (French, *desservir*, to clear the cloth); and dessert is that which comes after the cloth is removed.

Destruction. *Prince of Destruction.* Tamerlane or Timour the Tartar (1335, 1360-1405.)

Destructives (*The*), as a political term, arose in 1832.

"The *Times* newspaper, hitherto the most effective advocate of the [Reform] bill, has been obliged to designate those whom it formerly glorified as *Radicals*, by the more appropriate and emphatic title of the *Destructives*."—*Quarterly Review* (Dec., 1832, p. 545.)

Des'ultory. Those who rode two or more horses in the circus of Rome, and used to leap from one to the other, were called *desulto'res;* hence *desultor* came in Latin to mean one inconstant, or who went from one thing to another; and desultory means after the manner of a desultor.

Detest' is simply to witness against. (Latin, *de-testor*.)

Deuca'lion, after the Deluge, was ordered to cast behind him the *bones of his mother* (*i.e.* the stones of mother earth). Those thrown by Deucalion became men, and those thrown by his wife, Pyrrha, became women. For the interchange between λαός (people), and λᾶας (a stone), see *Pindar: Olympic Games,* ix. 66.

Deucalion's flood. According to Greek mythology, Deucalion was a king of Thessaly, in whose reign the whole world was covered with a deluge in consequence of the great impiety of man. (*See* DELUGES.)

Deuce. The Kelts called wood-demons *dus.* (Compare the Latin *deus*.)

"In the popular mythology both of the Kelts and Teutons there were certain hairy wood-demons, called by the former *dus*, and by the latter *scrat* (? scratz). Our common names of 'Deuce' and 'Old Scratch' are plainly derived from these."—*Lowell: Among my Books* (Witchcraft), p. 109.

It played the deuce with me. It made me very ill; it disagreed with me; it almost ruined me.

The deuce is in you. You are a very demon.

Deuce take you. Get away! you annoy me.

What the deuce is the matter? What in the world is amiss?

Deuce-ace. A throw of two dice, one showing *one* spot and the other showing *two* spots.

Deuce of Cards (*The*). The two (French, *deux*). The three is called "Tray" (French, *trois;* Latin, *tres*).

"A gentleman being punched by a butcher's tray, exclaimed, 'Deuce take the tray.' 'Well,' said the boy, 'I don't know how the deuce is to take the tray.'"—*Jest Book.*

Deus (2 syl.). *Deus ex ma'china.* The intervention of a god, or some unlikely event, in order to extricate from difficulties in which a clumsy author has involved himself; any forced incident, such as the arrival of a rich uncle from the Indies to help a young couple in their pecuniary embarrassments. Literally, it means "a god (let down upon the stage or flying in the air) by machinery."

De'va's Vale. The valley of the river Dee or Deva, in Cheshire, celebrated for its pastures and dairy produce.

"He chose a farm in Deva's vale, Where his long alleys peeped upon the main." *Thomson: Castle of Indolence,* canto ii.

Development. (*See* EVOLUTION.)

Devil. Represented with a cloven foot, because by the Rabbinical writers he is called *seirissim* (a goat). As the goat is a type of uncleanness, the prince of unclean spirits is aptly represented under this emblem.

Devil among the Tailors (*The*). On Dowton's benefit at the Haymarket, some 7,000 journeymen tailors congregated in and around the theatre to prevent a burlesque called *The Tailors: a Tragedy for Warm Weather,* which they considered insulting to the trade. Fair-burn's edition of this play is headed *The Devil among the Tailors*, and contains an account of this fracas. (See also *Biographia Dramatica*, article TAILORS.) There is a Scotch reel so called.

Devil and Bag o' Nails (*The*). The public-house by Buckingham Gate was so called, but the sign was *The Blackamoor's Head and the Woolpack*. (*Remarkable Trials*, ii. p. 14; 1765.)

Devil and Dr. Faustus (*The*). Faust was the first printer of Bibles, and issued a large number in imitation of those sold as manuscripts. These he passed off in Paris as genuine, and sold for sixty crowns apiece, the usual price being five hundred crowns. The uniformity of the books, their rapid supply, and their unusual cheapness excited astonishment. Information was laid against him for magic, and, in searching his lodgings, the brilliant red ink with which his copies were adorned was declared to be his blood. He was charged with dealings with the Devil, and condemned to be burnt alive. To save himself, he revealed his secret to the Paris Parlement, and his invention became the admiration of the world. N.B.—This tradition is not to be accepted as history.

Devil and his Dam (*The*). Either the Devil and his *mother*, or the Devil and his *wife*. Numerous quotations may be adduced in support of either of these interpretations. Shakespeare uses the phrase six times, and in *King John* (ii. 1) dam evidently means mother; thus Constance says that her son Arthur is as like his *father* as the Devil is like his dam (*mother*); and in *Titus Andronicus* Tamora is called the "dam" of a black child. We also read of the Devil's daughter and the Devil's son.

In many mythologies the Devil is supposed to be an animal: Thus in Cazotte's *Diable Amoureux* he is a *camel;* the Irish and others call him a *black cat;* the Jews speak of him as a *dragon* (which idea is carried out in our George and the Dragon); the Santons of Japan call him a species of *fox;* others say he is a *goat;* and Dante associates him with *dragons, swine,* and *dogs.* In all which cases dam for mother is not inappropriate.

On the other hand, dam for leman or wife has good support. We are told that Lilith was the wife of Adam, but was such a vixen that Adam could not live with her, and she became the Devil's dam. We also read that Belphegor "came to earth to seek him out a dam."

⁂ As women when they go wrong are for the most part worse than the other sex, the phrase at the head of this article means the Devil and something worse.

Devil and the Deep Sea (*Between the*). Between Scylla and Charybdis; between two evils, each equally hazardous. The allusion seems to be to the herd of swine and the devils called Legion.

"In the matter of passing from one part of the vessel to another when she was rolling, we were indeed between the devil and the deep sea."—*Nineteenth Century*, April, 1891, p. 664.

Devil and Tom Walker (*The*). An American proverb, used as a caution to usurers. Tom Walker was a poor, miserly man, born at Massachusetts in 1727, and it is said that he sold himself to the Devil for wealth. Be this as it may, Tom suddenly became very rich, and opened a counting-house at Boston during the money panic which prevailed in the time of Governor Belcher. By usury he grew richer and richer; but one day, as he was foreclosing a mortgage with a poor land-jobber, a black man on a black horse knocked at the office door. Tom went to open it, and was never seen again. Of course the good people of Boston searched his office, but all his coffers were found empty; and during the night his house caught fire and was burnt to the ground. (*Washington Irving: Tales of a Traveller.*)

Devil catch the Hindmost (*The*). In Scotland (? Salamanca) it is said when a class of students have made a certain progress in their mystic studies, they are obliged to run through a subterranean hall, and the last man is seized by the devil, and becomes his imp.

Devil in Dublin City (*The*). The Scandinavian form of Dublin was *Divelin[a]*, and the Latin *Dublinia*. (See *Notes and Queries*, April 9th, 1881, p. 296, for another explanation.)

"Is just as true's the deil's in hell
Or Dublin city."
Burns: Death and Dr. Hornbook.

Devil looking Over Lincoln (*The*). Sir W. Scott in his *Kenilworth* has, "Like the Devil looking over Lincoln." A correspondent of *Notes and Queries*, September 10th, 1892, says—

"The famous devil that used to overlook Lincoln College, in Oxford, was taken down (Wednesday, September 15th, 1731), having about two years since [previously] lost his head in a storm."—*Gentleman's Magazine*, 1831, p. 402.

⁂ We have other similar phrases, as "The devil looking over Durham."

Devil loves Holy Water (*As the*). That is, not at all. The Roman Catholics teach that holy water drives away the Devil. The Latin proverb is, " *Sicut sus amaricinum amat* " (as swine love marjoram). Lucretius, vi. 974, says " *amaricinum fugitat sus.*"

Devil-may-care (*A*). A reckless fellow.

Devil must be Striking (*The*) (German). Said · when it thunders. The old Norse *Donar* means Thor, equal to Jupiter, the god of thunder, and *donner* is the German for thunder or Devil, as may be seen in the expression, "The runaway goose is gone to the Devil" (*donner*).

Devil on the Neck (*A*). An instrument of torture used by persecuting papists. It was an iron winch which forced a man's neck and legs together.

Devil rides on a Fiddlestick (*The*). Much ado about nothing. Beaumont and Fletcher, Shakespeare, and others, use the phrase. "Fiddlesticks!" as an exclamation, means rubbish! nonsense! When the prince and his merry companions are at the *Boar's Head*, first Bardolph rushes in to warn them that the sheriff's officers are at hand, and anon enters the hostess to put her guests on their guard. But the prince says, "Here's a devil of a row to make about a trifle " (or "The devil rides on a fiddlestick") (1 *Henry IV.*, ii. 2), and hiding some of his companions, he stoutly faces the sheriff's officers and browbeats them.

Devil Sick would be a Monk (*The*).

" *Dæmon languebat, monachus bonus esse volebat; Sed cum convaluit, manet ut ante fuit.*"

" When the Devil was sick, the devil a monk would be ;
When the Devil got well, the devil a monk was he."

Said of those persons who in times of sickness or danger make pious resolutions, but forget them when danger is past and health recovered.

Devil to Pay and no Pitch Hot (*The*). The "devil" is a seam between the garboard-strake and the keel, and to "pay" is to cover with pitch. In former times, when vessels were often careened for repairs, it was difficult to calk and pay this seam before the tide turned. Hence the locution, the ship is careened, the devil is exposed, but there is no pitch hot ready, and the tide will turn before the work can be done. (French, *payer*, from *paix*, *po'ix*, pitch.)

⁂ *The Devil to Pay* is the name of a farce by Jobson and Nelly.

Here's the very devil to pay. Is used in quite another sense, meaning : Here's a pretty kettle of fish. I'm in a pretty mess ; this is confusion worse confounded.

PROVERBIAL PHRASES.

Cheating the devil. Mincing an oath ; doing evil for gain, and giving part of the profits to the Church, etc. It is by no means unusual in monkish traditions. Thus the "Devil's Bridge" is a single arch over a cataract. It is said that his Satanic Majesty had knocked down several bridges, but promised the abbot, Giraldus of Einsiedel, to let this one stand, provided the abbot would consign to him the first living thing that crossed it. When the bridge was finished, the abbot threw across it a loaf of bread, which a hungry dog ran after, and "the rocks re-echoed with peals of laughter to see the Devil thus defeated." (*Longfellow : Golden Legend*, v.)

⁂ The bridge referred to by Longfellow is that over the Fall of the Reuss, in the canton of the Uri, Switzerland.

Rabelais says that a farmer once bargained with the Devil for each to have on alternate years what grew under and over the soil. The canny farmer sowed carrots and turnips when it was his turn to have the under-soil share, and wheat and barley the year following. (*Pantagruel*, book iv. chap. xlvi.)

Give the devil his due. Give even a bad man or one hated like the devil the credit he deserves.

Gone to the devil. To ruin. The *Devil and St. Dunstan* was the sign of a public house, No. 2, Fleet Street, at one time much frequented by lawyers.

"Into the Devil Tavern three booted troopers strode."

Pull devil, pull baker. Lie, cheat, and wrangle away, for one is as bad as the other. (In this proverb baker is not a proper name, but the trade.)

" Like Punch and the Deevil rugging about the Baker at the fair."—*Sir W. Scott : Old Mortality*, chap. xxxviii.

Talk of the devil and he's sure to come. Said of a person who has been the subject of conversation, and who unexpectedly makes his appearance. An older proverb still is, "Talk of the Dule and he'll put out his horns ;" but the modern euphemism is, "Talk of an angel and you'll see its wings." If "from the fulness of the heart the mouth speaketh," their hearts must be full of the evil one who talk about him, and if the heart is full of the devil he cannot be far off.

"Forthwith the devil did appear,
For name him, and he's always near."
Prior: Hans Carvel.

To hold a candle to the devil is to abet an evildoer out of fawning fear. The allusion is to the story of an old woman who set one wax taper before the image of St. Michael, and another before the Devil whom he was trampling under foot. Being reproved for paying such honour to Satan, she naïvely replied: "Ye see, your honour, it is quite uncertain which place I shall go to at last, and sure you will not blame a poor woman for securing a friend in each."

To kindle a fire for the devil is to offer sacrifice, to do what is really sinful, under the delusion that you are doing God service.

To play the very devil with [the matter]. To so muddle and mar it as to spoil it utterly.

When the devil is blind. Never. Referring to the utter absence of all disloyalty and evil.

"Ay, Tib, that will be [*i.e.* all will be true and loyal] when the de'il is blind ; and his e'en's no sair yet."—*Sir W. Scott: Guy Mannering* (Dandie Dinmont to Tib Mumps), chap. xxii.

Devil (*A*), in legal parlance, is a leader's fag who gets up the facts of a brief, with the laws bearing on it, and arranges everything for the pleader in methodical order.

These juniors have surplus briefs handed to them by their seniors. A good fag is a good devil and is sure to get on.

The Attorney-General's devils are the Counsel of the Treasury, who not unfrequently get promoted to the bench.

A printer's devil. Formerly, the boy who took the printed sheets from the tympan of the press. Old Moxon says: "They do commonly so black and bedaub themselves that the workmen do jocosely call them devils." The errand-boy is now so called. The black slave employed by Aldo Manuzio, Venetian printer, was thought to be an imp. Hence the following proclamation:

"I, Aldo Manuzio, printer to the Doge, have this day made public exposure of the printer's devil. All who think he is not flesh and blood may come and pinch him.'—*Proclamation of Aldo Manuzio,* 1490.

Robert the Devil, of Normandy. (*See* ROBERT LE DIABLE.)

The French Devil. Jean Bart, an intrepid French sailor, born at Dunkirk. (1650-1702.)

Son of the Devil. Ezzeli'no, chief of the Gibelins, and Governor of Vicenza, was

so called for his infamous cruelties. (1215-1259.)

"Fierce Ezelin, that most inhuman lord,
Who shall be deemed by men the child of hell."
Rose: Orlando Furioso, iii. 32.

The White Devil of Walla'chia. George Castrio'ta was so called by the Turks. (1404-1467.)

Devil's Advocate (*The*). In the Catholic Church when a name is suggested for canonisation, some person is appointed to oppose the proposition, and is expected to give reasons why it should not take place. This person is technically called *Advocātus Diaboli.* Having said his say, the conclave decides the question.

Devil's Apple. The mandrake.

Devil's Arrows (Yorkshire). Three remarkable "Druid" stones near Boroughbridge, like *Harold's Stones,* and probably marking some boundary.

Devil's Bird (*The*). The yellow bunting ; is so called from its note, *deil.*

Devil's Bones. Dice, which are made of bones and lead to ruin.

Devil's Books. Playing cards. A Presbyterian phrase, used in reproof of the term King's Books, applied to a pack of cards, from the French *livre des quatre rois* (the book of the four kings). Also called the Devil's Bible.

Devil's Cabinet (*The*). Belphego, the Devil's ambassador in France ; Hutgin, in Italy ; Belial, in Turkey ; Tharung, in Spain ; and Martinet, in Switzerland. His grand almoner is Dagon ; chief of the eunuchs is Succor Benoth ; banker is Asmodēus ; theatrical manager is Kobal ; master of ceremonies, Verdelet ; court fool is Nybbas. (*Victor Hugo : Toilers of the Sea.*)

Devil's Candle. So the Arabs call the mandrake, from its shining appearance at night. (*Richardson.*)

"Those hellish fires that light
The mandrake's charnel leaves at night."
T. Moore : Fire Worshippers.

Devil's Current (*The*). Part of the current of the Bosphorus is so called, from its great rapidity.

Devil's Daughter's Portion (*The*). The saying is—

"Deal, Dover, and Harwich,
The devil gave with his daughter in marriage,"

because of the scandalous impositions practised in these seaports on sailors and occasional visitors. (*Grose : Classical Dictionary,* etc.)

Devil's Den. A cromlech in a valley, near Marlborough. It now consists of two large uprights and an impost. The third upright has fallen. Some of the farm labourers, a few years ago, fastened a team of horses to the impost, and tried, but without effect, to drag it down.

Devil's Dust. Old rags torn up by a machine called the "devil," and made into shoddy by gum and pressure. Mr. Ferrand brought the subject before Parliament, March 4th, 1842. It is so called from the dishonesty and falsehood which it covers. (*Latimer's Sermons.*)

Devil's Dyke (*The*). A ravine in the South Downs, Brighton. The legend is, that St. Cuthman, walking on the downs, plumed himself on having Christianised the surrounding country, and having built a nunnery where the dyke-house now stands. Presently the Devil appears and tells him all his labour is vain, for he would swamp the whole country before morning. St. Cuthman went to the nunnery and told the abbess to keep the sisters in prayer till after midnight, and then illuminate the windows. The Devil came at sunset with mattock and spade, and began cutting a dyke into the sea, but was seized with rheumatic pains all over the body. He flung down his mattock and spade, and the cocks, mistaking the illuminated windows for sunrise, began to crow ; whereupon the Devil fled in alarm, leaving his work not half done.

Devil's Four-Poster (*The*). A hand at whist with four clubs. It is said that such a hand is never a winning one.

Devil's Frying-pan (*The*). A Cornish tin-mine worked by the Romans.

Devil's Livery (*The*). Black and yellow. Black for death, yellow for quarantine.

Devil's Luck (*The*). Astounding good luck. Persons always lucky were thought at one time to have compounded with the Devil.

"You won't have to pay his annuity very long ; you have the Devil's luck in bargains, always."—*Dickens.*

Devil's Mass (*The*). Swearing at everybody and everything.

"Whin a bad egg is shut av the army, he says the devil's mass .... an' manes svearin' at ivry-ching, from the commandher-in-chief down to the room-corp'ril."—*Soldiers Three*, p. 95.

Devil's Nostrils (*The*). Two vast caverns separated by a huge pillar of natural rock in the mainland of the Zetland Islands. (See *The Pirate*, chap. xxii.)

Devil's Own. (CONNAUGHT BOYS.) The 88th Foot. So called by General Picton from their bravery in the Peninsular War, 1809-1814.

Applied also to the Inns of Court Volunteers, the members of which are lawyers.

Devil's Paternoster (*To say the*). To grumble ; to rail at providence.

Devil's Snuff-box (*The*). A puff-ball ; a fungus full of dust; one of the genus Lycoperdon.

Devil's Tattoo (*The*). Tapping on the table with one's finger a wearisome number of times ; tapping on the floor with one's foot in a similar manner; repeating any sound with wearisome pertinacity, giving those who hear the "blue devils" or the "fidgets."

Devil's Throat (*The*). Cromer Bay. So called from its danger to navigation.

Devils (in Dante's *Divine Comedy*) :

Alichino. (The allurer.)
Barbariccia. (The malicious.)
Calcobrina. (The grace-scorner.)
Cagnazzo. (The snarler.)
Ciriato Sannuto. (The tusked boar.)
Draghignazzo. (The fell dragon.)
Farfarello. (The scandalmonger.)
Graffiacane. (The doggish.)
Libicocco. (The ill-tempered.)
Rubicante. (The red with rage.)
Scarmiglione. (The baneful.)
The blue Devils. The fidgets or megrims.

Devonshire, according to English mythology, is a corruption of Debon's-share. This Debon was one of the heroes who came with Brute from Troy. One of the giants that he slew in the south coasts of England was Coulin, whom he chased to a vast pit eight leagues across. The monster trying to leap this pit, fell backwards, and lost his life in the chasm. When Brutus allotted out the island, this portion became Debon's-share.

" And eke that ample pit, yet far renowned
For the large leap which Debon did compell
Coulin to make, being eight lugs of grownd,
Into the which retourning back he fell . . .
In mede of these great conquests by them got
Cori'neus had that province utmost west . . .
And Debon's share was that is Devonshire."
Spenser : Faërie Queene, book ii. canto x. 11, 12.

Devonshire Poet. O. Jones, a journeyman wool-comber, who lived at the close of the 18th century. Edward Capern, called "The rural Postman of Bideford" (born 1819), and John Gay, author of the *Beggar's Opera,* etc. (1688-1732), of Barnstaple (Devonshire).

Dew-beaters. The feet ; shoes to resist the wet.

"Hold out your dew-beaters till I take off the darbies [iron shoes or fetters]."—*Peveril of the Peak.*

Dew-bit (*A*). A snack before breakfast.

Dew-drink. A draught before breakfast. In harvest the men are allowed, in some counties, a drink of beer before they begin work.

Dexterity means *right-handed* skill (Latin, *dexter*, the right hand). "Awkward" (*q.v.*) means *left-handed; gauche* is the French, and *sinister* the Latin for the left hand. Certainly the German left-handed marriages are sinister ones.

Dgellabæ'an. The Persian era. Dgella Eddin, son of Togrul Beg, appointed eight astronomers to reform the calendar. The era began A.D. 1075, and is followed to this day.

Dhul'dul. (*See* HORSE.)

Diable (*Le*). Olivier Ledain, the tool of Louis XI., and once the king's barber. So called because he was as much feared as his Satanic Majesty, and even more disliked. (Hanged 1484.)

Robert le Diable. Meyerbeer's grand opera. (*See* ROBERT.)

Di'adem meant, originally, a fillet wound round the head. The diadem of Bacchus was a broad band, which might be unfolded so as to make a veil. Hieronymus, king of Syracuse (B.C. 216-215), wore a diadem. Constantine the Great (306-337) was the first of the Roman emperors who wore a diadem. After his time it was set with rows of pearls and precious stones. (Greek, *dia-deo*, to bind entirely.)

Dialec'tics. Metaphysics; the art of disputation; that strictly logical discussion which leads to reliable results. The product or result is ideas, which, being classified, produce knowledge; but all knowledge being of the divine types, must conduce more or less to practical results and good morals. (Greek, *dialego*, to speak thoroughly.)

∵ Kant used the word to signify the theory of fallacies, and Hegel for that concept which of necessity develops its opposite.

The following questions from John of Salisbury are fair specimens of the Middle-age subjects of discussion:—

(1) When a person buys a whole cloak, does the cowl belong to his purchase?

(2) When a hog is driven to market with a rope round its neck, does the man or the rope take him?

Di'amond. A corruption of *adamant.* So called because the diamond, which cuts other substances, can be cut or polished with no substance but itself. (Greek, *a damao*, what cannot be subdued. Latin, *adamas*, gen. *adamant-is;* French, *diamant.*)

Di'amond (3 syl.). Son of Ag'apë, a fairy. He was very strong, and fought either on foot or horse with a battle-axe. He was slain in single combat by Cam'-balo. (*See* TRIAMOND.) (*Spenser: Faërie Queene*, book iv.)

A diamond of the first water. A man of the highest merit. The colour or lustre of a pearl or diamond is called its "water." One of the "first water" is one of the best colour and most brilliant lustre. We say also, "A man of the first water."

A rough diamond. An uncultivated genius; a person of excellent parts, but without society manners.

"As for Warrington, that rough diamond had not had the polish of a dancing-master, and he did not know how to waltz."—*Thackeray.*

Diamond cut diamond. Cunning outwitting cunning; a hard bargain overreached. A diamond is so hard that it can only be ground by diamond dust, or by rubbing one against another.

Diamond (Newton's favourite little dog). One winter's morning, while attending early service in Trinity College, Newton inadvertently left Diamond shut up in his room. On returning from chapel he found that the little fellow had upset a candle on his desk, by which several papers containing minutes of many years' experiments, were destroyed. On perceiving this irreparable loss, he exclaimed, "Oh, Diamond, Diamond, thou little knowest the mischief thou hast done!" (*Diffusion of Useful Knowledge: Life of Newton*, p. 25, col. 2.)

∵ Huygens, 1694, referring to this accident says: "Newtonum incidisse in phrenitin abhinc anno ac sex mensibus. An ex nimia studii assiduitate, an dolore infortunii, quod in incendio laboratorium chemicum et scripta quædam amiserat."

Diamond Hammer (*A*). A hammer or pick for "whetting" millstones. The diamond hammer is provided with several sharp-pointed teeth to give a uniform roughness to the surface of the stone. Also to a steel pick with diamond-shaped point at each extremity to recut grooves in stone.

Diamond Jousts (*The*). Jousts instituted by King Arthur, "who by that name had named them, since a diamond was the prize." Ere he was king, he came by accident to a glen in Lyonnesse, where two brothers had met in combat. Each was slain; but one had worn a crown of diamonds, which Arthur picked up, and when he became king offered the nine diamonds as the prize of nine several jousts, "one every year, a joust for one." Lancelot had won eight, and intended to present them all to the queen "when all were won." When the knight laid them before the queen, Guinevere, in a fit of jealousy, flung them out of the palace window into the river which ran below. (*Idylls of the King ; Elaine.*)

Diamond Necklace (*The*) (1785). A necklace presented, through Mme. de Lamotte, by Cardinal de Rohan (as he supposed) to Marie Antoinette. The cardinal, a profligate churchman, entertained a sort of love passion for the queen; and the Countess de Lamotte induced him to purchase for the queen, for £85,000, a diamond necklace, made for Mme. Dubarry. The cardinal handed the necklace to the countess, who sold it to an English jeweller and kept the money. When the time of payment arrived Boehmer, the jeweller, sent his bill in to the queen, who denied all knowledge of the matter. A trial ensued, which lasted nine months, and created immense scandal.

Diamond Sculls (*The*), or "The Diamond Challenge Sculls" of the Henley Royal Regatta, are a pair of crossed silver sculls not quite a foot in length, surmounted by an imitation wreath of laurel, and having a pendant of diamonds. They lie in a box lined with velvet, which contains also the names of all the winners. The prize is rowed for every year, and the sculls pass from winner to winner; but each winner receives a silver cup, which becomes his own absolute property. Established 1844 by the Royal Regatta Committee.

Diamonds. (*See* BLACK DIAMONDS.)

Dian'a (3 syl.). The temple of Diana at Eph'esus, built by Dinochărēs, was set on fire by Heros'tratos, for the sake of perpetuating his name. The Ionians decreed that any one who mentioned his name should be put to death, but this very decree gave it immortality. The temple was discovered in 1872 by Mr. Wood.

Diana of Ephesus. This statue, we are told, fell from heaven. If so, it was an aerolite ; but Minucius says he *saw* it, and that it was a wooden statue (second century, A.D.). Pliny, a contemporary of Minucius, tells us it was made of ebony. Probably the real

"image" was a meteorite, and in the course of time a wooden or ebony image was substituted.

∵ The palladium of Troy, the sacred shield of the Romans, the shrine of our Lady of Loretto, and other similar religious objects of veneration, were said to have been sent from heaven. The statue of Cybĕle (3 syl.) "fell from heaven" ; and Elagabălas, of Syro-Phœnicia, was a great conical stone which fell from heaven.

Great is Diana of the Ephesians. Nothing like leather ; self-interest blinds the eyes. Deme'trios was a silversmith of Eph'esus, who made gold and silver shrines for the temple of Diana. When Christianity was preached in the city, and there was danger of substituting the simplicity of the Gospel for the grandeur of idolatry, the silversmiths, headed by Demetrios, stirred the people to a riot, and they cried out with one voice for the space of two hours, "Great is Diana of the Ephesians!" (Acts xix. 24-28.)

Dian's Worshippers. Midnight revellers. So called because they return home by moonlight. Dian means the moon.

Diano'ra was the wife of Gilberto of Friu'li, but was passionately beloved by Ansaldo. In order to get rid of his importunity, she told him she would never grant his suit and prove untrue till he made her garden at midwinter as full of flowers and odours as if it were midsummer. By the aid of a magician, Ansaldo accomplished this, and claimed his reward. Diano'ra went to meet him, and told him she had obeyed the command of her husband in so doing. Ansaldo, not to be outdone in courtesy, released her ; and Gilberto became the firm friend of Ansaldo from that day to the end of his life. (*Boccaccio : Decameron,* day x. 5.) (*See* DORIGEN.)

Diapa'son. Dryden says—

" From harmony, from heavenly harmony
        The universal frame began ;
 From harmony to harmony
        Thro' all the compass of the notes it ran,
        The diapason closing full in man."
                        Song for St. Cecilia's Day.

According to the Pythagore'an system, the world is a piece of harmony, and man the full chord.

Diaper. A sort of cloth said to be corrupted from Ypres (where it is manufactured), on analogy with calico from Calicut, nankeen from Nankin, worsted from Worsted, in Norfolk, and other similar words. But the French *diapré,* variegated (connected with Lat.

iaspis = a jasper), is the source of this word. Diaper is cloth variegated with flowers, etc., like damask.

Diav'olo (*Fra*). Michele Pozza, an insurgent of Cala'bria (1760 - 1806). Scribe wrote a libretto on this hero for Auber.

Dibs or *Dibbs*. Money. (Compare *tips*, gifts to schoolboys; and *diobolus*. Compare also *dot* with *tot*, *jot*, and *yod*.)

The huckle-bones of sheep used for gambling purposes are called dibbs; and Locke speaks of stones used for the same game, which he calls *dibstones*.

Dicers' Oaths. *False as dicers' oaths.* Worthless or untrustworthy, as when a gambler swears never to touch dice again. (*Shakespeare: Hamlet*, iii. 4.)

Dicil'la (in *Orlando Furioso*). One of Logistilla's handmaids, famous for her chastity.

Dick. *That happened in the reign of Queen Dick*—*i.e.* never; there never was a Queen Richard.

Dick's Hatband. (Richard Cromwell, 1626-1712.)

(1) *Dick's hatband, which was made of sand.* His regal honours were "a rope of sand."

(2) *As fine as Dick's hatband.* The crown of England would be a very fine thing for anyone to get.

(3) *As queer as Dick's hatband.* Few things have been more ridiculous than the exaltation and abdication of the Protector's son.

(4) *As tight as Dick's hatband.* The hatband of Richard Cromwell was the crown, which was too tight for him to wear with safety.

Dick = Richard. The diminutive "Dicky" is also common.

" Jockey of Norfolk [Lord Howard], be not too
    bold,
For Dicky [or Dickon], thy master, is bought
    and sold."
        Shakespeare : Richard III., v. 3.
    (Dicky or Dickon is Richard III.)

Dickens. (*See* BOZ.)

Dickens is a perverted oath corrupted from "Nick." Mrs. Page says—

" I cannot tell what the dickens his name is."—
Shakespeare : Merry Wives of Windsor, iii. 2.

❖ The three poets who express a conflagration are "Dickens! How-itt, Burns ! "

Dickey or *Dicky*. A donkey; anciently called a Dick-ass, now termed Jack-ass. It is a term of endearment, as we call a pet bird a *dicky-bird*. The ass is called Dick-y (little Richard),

Cuddy (little Cuthbert), Neddy (little Edward), Jack-ass, Moke or Mil'e, etc.

Dickey. The rumble behind a carriage; also a leather apron, a child's bib, and a false shirt or front. All these are from the same root. (Dutch, *dekken ;* German, *decken ;* Anglo-Saxon, *thecan ;* Latin, *tego*, to cover.)

Dicky (*A*), in George III.'s time, meant a flannel petticoat. It was afterwards applied to what were called false shirts—*i.e.* a shirt front worn over a dirty shirt, or in lieu of a shirt. These half-shirts were first called Tommies.

" A hundred instances I soon could pick ye—
    Without a cap we view the fair,
    The bosom heaving alto bare,
The hips ashamed, forsooth, to wear a dicky."
    Peter Pindar : Lord Auckland's Triumph.

So again :—

" And sister Peg, and sister Joan,
    With scarce a flannel dicky on . . . ."
            Middlesex Election, letter iv.
(Hair, whalebone, or metal vestments, called dress-improvers, are hung on women's backs, as a " dicky " is hung on a coach behind.)

Dicky Sam. A native-born inhabitant of Liverpool, as Tim Bobbin is a native of Lancashire.

Dicta'tor of Letters. François Marie Arouet de Voltaire, called the *Great Pan.* (1694-1778.)

Didactic Poetry is poetry that teaches some moral lesson, as Pope's *Essay on Man.* (Greek, *didasko*, I teach.)

Diddle (*To*). To cheat in a small way, as " I diddled him out of . . . ." Edgar Allan Poe has an article on the art of " Diddling." Rhyming slang is very common. (*See* CHIVY.) Fiddle and diddle rhyme. " Fiddle " is slang for a sharper, and "diddle " is the act of a sharper. The suggestive rhyme was

" Hi diddle diddle !
    The cat and the fiddle."

" A certain portion of the human race
Has certainly a taste for being diddled."
        Hood : A Black Job, stanza 1.

Diddler (*Jeremy*). An artful swindler ; a clever, seedy vagabond, borrowing money or obtaining credit by his wit and wits. From Kenny's farce called *Raising the Wind.*

Did'erick. (*See* DIETRICH.)

Di'do. It was Porson who said he could rhyme on any subject ; and being asked to rhyme upon the three Latin gerunds, gave this couplet—

" When Dido found Æneas would not come,
She mourned in silence, and was Di-do dum(b)."

❖ In the old Eton Latin grammar the three gerunds are called -*di*, -*do*,

-dum. In modern school primers they are *-dum, -di, -do.*

> When Dido saw Æneas needs must go,
> She wept in silence, and was dum(b) Di-do.
>   *E. C. B.*

⁂ Dido was queen of Carthage, who fell in love with Æneas, driven by a storm to her shores. After abiding a-while at Carthage, he was compelled by Mercury to leave the hospitable queen. Dido, in grief, burnt herself to death on a funeral pile. (*Virgil:* from *Æneid,* i. 494 to iii. 650.)

Die. *The die is cast.* The step is taken, and I cannot draw back. So said Julius Cæsar when he crossed the Rubicon.

> "I have set my life upon the cast,
> And I will stand the hazard of the die."
>   *Shakespeare: Richard III.,* v. 4.

Die.
Whom the gods love die young. This is from Menander's *fragments* (*Hon hoi theoi philousin apothnēskei neos*). Demosthenes has a similar apophthegm. Plautus has the line, "*Quem Di diligunt adolescens moritur.*" (See *Byron : Don Juan,* canto iv. 12.) Those who die young are "taken out of the miseries of this sinful life" into a happy immortality.

Die-hards. The 57th Foot. Their colonel (Inglis) in the battle of Albuera (1811), addressing his men, said, "Die hard, my lads; die hard!" And they did die hard, for their banner was pierced with thirty bullets. Only one officer out of twenty-four survived, and only 168 men out of 584. This fine regiment is now called the West Middlesex; the East Middlesex (the Duke of Cambridge's own) is the old 77th.

Diego (*San*). A corruption of Santiago (St. James), champion of the red cross, and patron saint of Spain.

Diēs Alliensis. (*See* ALLIENSIS.)

Diēs Iræ. A famous mediæval hymn on the last judgment, probably the composition of Thomas of Cela'no, a native of Abruzzi, who died in 1255. Sir Walter Scott has introduced the former part of it into his *Lay of the Last Minstrel.*

> "Dies iræ, dies illa,
> Solvet sæclum in favilla,
> Testē David cum Sibylla."
> On that day, that wrathful day,
> David and the Sibyl say,
> Heaven and earth shall melt away.
>   *E. C. B.*

Diēs Non. A non-business day. A law phrase, meaning a day when the courts do not sit, as on Sundays; the Purification, in Hilary term ; the Ascension, in Easter term ; St. John the Baptist, in Trinity term ; and All Saints, with All Souls, in Michaelmas term. A contracted form of "Dies non juridicus," a non-judicial day.

Diēs San'guinis. The 24th March, called Bello'na's Day, when the Roman votaries of the war-goddess cut themselves and drank the sacrificial blood to propitiate the deity.

Dietrich (2 syl.), of Berne or Vero'na, a name given by the German minnesängers (*minstrels*) to Theod'oric the Great, king of the Ostrogoths. One of the liegemen of King Etzel. In the terrible broil stirred up by Queen Kriemhild in the banquet-hall of the Hunnish king, after the slaughter of Sir Rudiger, his friend Dietrich interfered, and succeeded in taking prisoners the only two surviving Burgundians, kings Gunther and Hagan, whom he handed over to Kriemhild, praying that she would set them free, but the angry queen cut off both their heads with her own hands. (*The Nibelungen-Lied.*)

Dicu. *Dieu et mon droit* (God and my right). The parole of Richard I. at the battle of Gisors (1198), meaning that he was no vassal of France, but owed his royalty to God alone. As the French were signally beaten, the battle-word was adopted as the royal motto of England.

Difference. Ophe'lia says to the queen, "You may wear your rue with a difference." In heraldry *differences* or *marks of cadency* indicate the various branches of a family.

(1) The eldest son, during the lifetime of his father, bears a *label* (or *lambel*), *i.e.* a piece of silk, stuff, or linen, with three pendants, broader at the bottom than at the top.

(2) The second son bears a *crescent.*

(3) The third, a *mullet* (or star with five points).

(4) The fourth, a *martlet.*

(5) The fifth, an *annulet.*

(6) The sixth, a *fleur-de-lis.*

(7) The seventh, a *rose.*

(8) The eighth, a *cross-moline.*

(9) The ninth, a *double quatre foil.*

Ophelia says both she and the Queen are to wear rue : the one as the affianced of Hamlet, eldest son of the late king ; the other as the wife of Claudius his brother, and the cadet branch. The latter was to have a "difference," to signify it was a cadet branch. "I [says Ophelia] shall wear the rue, but you [the Queen] must now wear it with a 'difference.'"

Digest (*The*). The collection of all the laws of Rome compiled by Tribonian and sixteen assistants, by order of Justinian. It amounted to 2,000 volumes, and was finished in three years (A.D. 533). (*See* PANDECTS.)

Diggings. *Come to my diggings.* To my rooms, residence, office, sanctum. A word imported from California and its gold diggings.

"My friend here wants to take diggings; and as you were complaining that you would get some-one to go halves with you, I thought I had better bring you together."—*A. O. Doyle : A Study in Scarlet*, chap. i.

Dig'gory. A barn labourer, taken on grand occasions for butler and foot-man to Mr. and Mrs. Hardcastle. He laughs and talks while serving, and is as *gauche* as possible. (*Goldsmith : She Stoops to Conquer.*)

Digit. The first nine numerals ; so called from the habit of counting as far as ten on the fingers. (Latin, *digitus*, a finger.)

Dignitary (*A*). A clergyman who holds preferment to which jurisdiction is annexed, as bishops, deans, archdeacons, canons, etc.

Dignus Vin'dice No'dus (Latin). A knot or difficulty worthy of such hands to untie. Literally, a knotty point worthy to be made a civil action. The person who brought a civil action was called in Roman law a *vindex*, and the action was called a *vindicātio*. If the rightful possessor was a matter of dispute, the question became a *lis vindi-ciārum*, and was referred to the prætor to determine. A knotty point referred to the prætor was a "*dignus vindice nodus.*"

Dii Penatēs (Latin). Household gods ; now used for such articles of furniture or decoration as the lady of the house especially prizes.

Dilem'ma. *The horns of a dilemma.* "Lemma" means a thing taken for granted (Greek, *lam'bano*, to take). "Dilemma" is a double lemma, a two-edged sword which strikes both ways, or a bull which will toss you whichever horn you lay hold of. A young rhetori-cian said to an old sophist, "Teach me to plead, and I will pay you when I gain a cause." The master sued for payment, and the scholar pleaded, "If

I gain the cause I shall not pay you, because the judge will say I am not to pay ; and if I lose my cause I shall not be required to pay, according to the terms of our agreement." To this the master replied, "Not so ; if you gain your cause you must pay me according to the terms of our agreement ; and if you lose your cause the judge will condemn you to pay me."

Dilettan'të (Italian). An amateur of the fine arts, in opposition to a pro-fessor. Plural, *dilettanti*.

"These gentlemen are to be judged, not as dilettanti, but as professors."—*Athenæum*.

Diligence is that energy and in-dustry which we show when we do what we like (Latin, *dil'igo*, I like) ; but indolence is that listless manner with which we do what thoroughly vexes us. (Latin, *in*, intensive ; *doleo*, to grieve.)

Diligence. A four-wheeled stage-coach, drawn by four or more horses. Common in France before the intro-duction of railroads. The pun is well known.

Si vis placēre magistro, utĕre diligentia (*i.e.* his diligence).

Dilly (plural, **Dillies**). Stage-coaches. They first began to run in 1779. An abbreviation of the French word *dili-gence* (*q.v.*). "Derby dilly."

Dim and Distant Future (*The*). In November, 1885, Mr. W. E. Glad-stone said that the disestablishment and disendowment of the Anglican Church were questions in "the dim and distant future."

Diman'che (*Monsieur*). A dun. The term is from Molière's *Don Juan*, and would be, in English, *Mr. Sunday*. The word *dimanche* is a corruption and con-traction of *dies Domin'ica* (the Lord's day).

Dimetæ. The ancient Latin name for the inhabitants of Carmarthenshire, Pembrokeshire, and Cardiganshire.

Dim'issory. *A letter dimissory* is a letter from the bishop of one diocese to some other bishop, giving leave for the bearer to be ordained by him. (Latin, *di-mitto*, to send away.)

Dim'ity. A cloth said to be so called from Damietta, in Egypt, but really from the Greek *di-mitos* (double-thread). (*See* SAMITE.)

Di'nah (*Aunt*), in Sterne's *Tristram Shandy*. She leaves Mr. Walter Shandy

£1,000, which he fancies will enable him to carry out all the wild schemes that enter into his head.

Dinde (1 syl.). The French for a turkey is *poulet d'Inde* (an Indian fowl). This is an error, as the bird comes from America ; unless, indeed, the whole Western continent, with all its contiguous islands, be called by the name of West Indies. Our word "turkey" is no better, if indeed it means a native of Turkey.

Dine (*To*).

Qui dort dîne. The seven sleepers and others required no food till they woke from their long sleep. The same may be said of all hibernating animals.

To dine with Democritos. To be cheated out of one's dinner. Democritos was the derider, or philosopher who laughed at men's folly.

To dine with Sir Thomas Gresham. To go without one's dinner; to be dinnerless. Sir Thomas Gresham founded the Royal Exchange, which was a favourite lounge for those who could not afford to provide themselves with a dinner.

To dine with Duke Humphrey. (*See* HUMPHREY.)

To dine with Mahomet. To die, and dine in paradise.

To dine with the cross-legged knights. (*See next column*, DINNERLESS.)

Dine Out (*To*). To be dinnerless; to go without a dinner.

Ding (*A*). A blow. *To ding it in one's ears.* To repeat a subject over and over again ; to teach by repetition.

To ding. To strike. (Anglo-Saxon, *dency* [*un*], to knock, strike, beat.) Hence "ding-dong," as "They were at it ding-dong."

" The butcher's axe, like great Achilles' bat,
   Dings deadly downe ten-thousand-thousand
   flat."   *Taylor: Works* (1630).

Ding-dong. *They went at it ding-dong.* Fighting in good earnest. To ding is to beat or bruise (Saxon, *dencgan*); dong is a responsive word. One gives a ding and the other a dong.

" Din is the Anglo-Saxon *dyn-ian*, to make a din; *dinung*, a dinning noise.

Dingley Dell. The home of Mr. Wardle and his family, and the scene of Tupman's love adventure with Miss Rachel. (*Dickens: Pickwick Papers*.)

Dinner (*Waiting for*). The "mauvais quart d'heure."

Dinnerless. *Their hosts are the cross-legged knights.* That is, the stone effigies of the Round Church. In this church at one time lawyers met their clients, and here a host of vagabonds used to loiter about all day, under the hope of being hired as witnesses. Dining with the cross-legged knights meant much the same thing as dining with duke Humphrey (*q.v.*).

Di'nos. (*See* HORSE.)

Dint. *By dint of war ; by dint of argument ; by dint of hard work.* Dint means a blow or striking (Anglo-Saxon, *dynt*) ; whence perseverance, power exerted, force ; it also means the indentation made by a blow.

Diocle'tian. The Roman Emperor, noted for his fierce persecution of the Christians, 303. The Emperor Constantine, on the other hand, was the "nursing father" of the Church.

" To make the Church's glory shine,
   Should Diocletian reign, not Constantine."
                      Crabbe: Borough.

Diocle'tian was the king, and Erastus the prince, his son, in the Italian version of the *Seven Wise Masters* (*q.v.*).

Diog'enes (4 syl., *g=j*). The cynic philosopher is said to have lived in a tub.

" The whole world was not half so wide
   To Alexander, when he cried
   Because he had but one to sub'due,
   As was a paltry narrow tub to
   Diogenes."   *Butler: Hudibras*, i. 3.

Diog'enes. Romanus IV., emperor of the East (1067-1071).

Di'omed's Horses. Dinos (*dreadful*) and Lampon (*bright-eyed*). (*See* HORSE.)

Diom'ede'an Swop. An exchange in which all the benefit is on one side. This proverbial expression is founded on an incident related by Homer in the *Iliad*. Glaucus recognises Diomed on the battle-field, and the friends change armour.

" For Diomed's brass arms, of mean device,
   For which nine oxen paid (a vulgar price),
   He [Glaucus] gave his own, of gold divinely
   wrought,
   An hundred beeves the shining purchase
   bought."   *Pope: Iliad*, vi.

Diome'dēs or **Diomēd.** King of Æto'lia, in Greece, brave and obedient to authority. He survived the siege of Troy ; but on his return home found his wife living in adultery, and saved his life by living an exile in Italy. (*Homer: Iliad*.)

Dio'ne (3 syl.). Venus, who sprang from the froth of the sea, after the mutilated body of U'ranus (*the sky*) had been thrown there by Saturn.

" So young Dionē, nursed beneath the waves,
 And rocked by Nereids in their coral caves ....
 Lisped her sweet tones, and tried her tender
 smiles." *Darwin: Economy of Vegetation,* ii.

Dionys'ius (*the younger*), being banished a second time from Syracuse, retired to Corinth, where he turned schoolmaster for a living. Posterity called him a *tyrant*. Byron, in his *Ode to Napoleon*, alludes to these facts in the following lines :—

" Corinth's pedagogue hath now
 Transferred his byword to thy brow."

That is, Napoleon is now called *tyrant*, like Dionysius.

Diony'sos. The Greek name of Bacchus (*q.v.*).

Father: Zeus (Jupiter).
Feasts of Bacchus in Rome, Bromalia or Brumalia, in March and September.
Mother: Semēlē, daughter of Cadmus
Nurse: Brisa.
Owls were his aversion.
Panthers drew his chariot.
Rams were the most general sacrifices offered to him.
Wife: Ariad'nē.

The most famous statue of this god was by Praxitĕlēs.

Attalus gave above £18,000 sterling for a painting of the god by Aristídēs.

Diophan'tine Anal'ysis. Finding commensurate values of squares, cubes, triangles, etc. ; or the sum of a given number of squares which is itself a square ; or a certain number of squares, etc., which are in arithmetical progression. The following examples will give some idea of the theory :

1. To find two whole numbers, the *sum* of whose squares is a square ;

2. To find three square numbers which are in arithmetical progression ;

3. To find a number from which two given squares being severally subtracted, each of the remainders is a square.

⁕ Diophantus was an Alexandrian Greek (5th cent. A.D.)

Dioscu'ri. Castor and Pollux. (Greek, *Dios kouros,* young men of Zeus ; *dios* is gen. of Zeus.)

The horses of the Dioscuri. Cyl'laros and Har'pagos. (*See* HORSE.)

Diotrephes. One who loves to have the pre-eminence among others. (3 John 9.)

'Neither a desperate Judas, like the prelate Sharpe [archbishop of St. Andrew's, who was murdered], that's gone to his place ; nor a sanctuary-breaking Holofernēs, like the bloody-minded Claverhouse ; nor an ambitious Diotrephēs, like the lad [Lord] Evandale .... shall resist the arrows that are whetted and the bow that is bent against you."—*Sir W. Scott: Old Mortality,* chap. x. v.

Dip (*A*). A tallow-chandler, one who makes or sells candles or "dips." These candles are made by dipping into melted tallow the cotton which forms the wick. (Anglo-Saxon *dippan,* to dip.)

Diph'thera. The skin of the goat Amalthe'a, on which Jove wrote the destiny of man. Diphtheria is an infectious disease of the throat ; so called from its tendency to form a false membrane.

Diplo'ma literally means something folded (Greek). Diplomas used to be written on parchment, folded, and sealed. The word is applied to licences given to graduates to assume a degree, to clergymen, to physicians, agents, and so on.

Diplom'acy. The tact, negotiations, privileges, etc., of a diplomatist, or one who carries a diploma to a foreign court to authorise him to represent the Government which sends him out.

Diplomatic Cold (*A*). An excuse to get over a disagreeable engagement. Mr. Healy, M.P. (1885), said that Lord Hartifigton and Mr. Gladstone had "diplomatic colds," when they pleaded indisposition as an excuse for not giving addresses at public meetings in which they were advertised to speak. The day after the meetings both gentlemen were "much better."

Diplomatics. The science of palæography—that is, deciphering old charters, diplomas, titles ; investigating their authenticity and genuineness, and so on. Papebröch, the Bollandist, originated the study in 1675 ; but Mabillon, another Bollandist, reduced it to a science in his work entitled *De re Diplomatĭca,* 1681. Toustain and Tassin further developed it in their treatise entitled *Nouveau Traité de Diplomatique,* 1750-1760.

Diptych [*dip'tik*]. A register folded into two leaves, opening like our books, and not like the ancient scrolls. The Romans kept in a book of this sort the names of their magistrates, and the Roman Catholics employed the word for the registers in which were written the names of those bishops, saints, and martyrs who were to be specially commemorated when oblations were made for the dead. (Greek, *diptuchos,* folded in two.)

" The Greeks executed small works of great elegance, as may be seen in the diptychs, or ivory covers to consular records, or sacred volumes used in the church service."—*T. Flaxman: Lectures on Sculpture,* iii. p. 98.

Dircæ′an Swan. Pindar; so called from Dircē, a fountain in the neighbourhood of Thebes, the poet's birthplace (B.C. 518-442).

Direct Tax is one collected *directly* from the owner of property subject to the tax, as when the tax-gatherer goes direct to the owner of a house and demands five, ten, or twenty pounds, as it may be, for Government uses. *Indirect taxes* are taxes upon marketable commodities, such as tea and sugar, the tax on which is added to the article taxed, and is paid by the purchasers indirectly.

Direc′tory. The French constitution of 1795, when the executive was vested in five persons called directors, one of whom retired every year. After a sickly existence of four years, it was quashed by Napoleon Bonaparte. An alphabetical list of the inhabitants, etc., of a given locality, as a "London Directory."

Dirleton. *Doubting with Dirleton, and resolving those doubts with Stewart.* Doubting and answering those doubts, but doubting still. It applies to law, science, religion, morals, etc. Sir John Nisbett of Dirleton's *Doubts* on points of law, and Sir James Stewart's *Doubts Resolved*, are works of established reputation in Scotland, but the *Doubts* hold a higher place than the *Solutions*.

Dir′los (*Count*). A Paladin, the beau-ideal of valour, generosity, and truth. The story says he was sent by Charlemagne into the East, where he conquered Aliar′dē, a great Moorish prince. On his return he found his young wife, who thought he was dead, betrothed to Celi′nos, another of Charlemagne's peers. The matter being set right, the king gave a grand banquet. Dirlos is D′Yrlos.

Dirt is matter in the wrong place. (*Lord Palmerston.*) This is not true: a diamond or sovereign lost on a road is matter in a wrong place, but certainly is not dirt.

Throw plenty of dirt and some will be sure to stick. Scandal always leaves a trail behind.

Dirt cheap. Very low-priced. Dirt is so cheap that persons pay others to take it away.

To eat dirt is to put up with insults and mortification. An Eastern method of punishment.

"If dirt were trumps what a capital hand you would hold!"—*Charles Lamb to Martin Burney.*

Dirty Half-Hundred. The 50th Foot, so called from the men wiping their faces with their black cuffs. Now called "The Queen's Own."

Dirty Lane. Now called Abingdon Street, Westminster.

Dirty Shirts (*The*). The 101st Foot, which fought at Delhi in their shirt-sleeves (1857). Now called "The Royal Bengal Fusileers."

Dis. Pluto.

"Proser′pine gathering flowers,
Herself a fairer flower, by gloomy Dis
Was gathered."
Milton: Paradise Lost, iv. 270.

Disas′ter is being under an evil star (Greek, *dus-aster*, evil star). An astrological word.

"The stars in their courses fought against Sisera."—*Judges* v. 20.

Disas′trous Peace (*La Paix Malheureuse*). It followed the battle of Gravelines (2 syl.), and was signed at Cateau - Cambre′sis. By this treaty Henri II. renounced all claim to Gen′oa, Naples, Mil′an, and Cor′sica (1559).

Disbar (*To*). To deprive a barrister of his right to plead. The bar is the part barred off in courts of law and equity for barristers or pleaders.

Discard. To throw out of one's hands such cards as are useless.

Discharge Bible (*The*), 1806. "I discharge [charge] thee before God." (1 Tim. v. 21.)

Discipline (*A*). A scourge used by Roman Catholics for penitential purposes.

"Before the cross and altar a lamp was still burning, . . . and on the floor lay a small discipline or penitential scourge of small cord and wire, the lashes of which were stained with recent blood."—*Sir W. Scott: The Talisman,* chap. iv.

Dis′cord means severance of hearts (Latin, *discorda*). It is the opposite of *concord*, the coming together of hearts. In music it means disagreement of sounds, as when a note is followed by another which is disagreeable to a musical ear. (*See* APPLE.)

Discount. *At a discount.* Not in demand; little valued; less esteemed than formerly; less than their nominal value. (Latin *dis-computo*, to depreciate.)

Discuss. *To discuss a bottle.* To drink one with a friend. Same as "*crush*" or "*crack* a bottle." (Discuss is the Latin *dis-quatio;* French, *casser.* The Latin *quassa′rĕ vasa* is to break a drinking-vessel.)

"We all . . . . drew round the table, an austere silence prevailing, while we discussed our meal."—*E. Brontë: Wuthering Heights,* chap. ii.

Disease, meaning discomfort, want of ease, *mal aise,* as

"In the world ye shall have disease."— *Wyclif:* John xvi. 33.

Dished (1 syl.). *I was dished out of it.* Cheated out of it ; or rather, some one else contrived to obtain it. A contraction of *disherit.* The heir is dish't out of his inheritance when his father marries again and leaves his property to the widow and widow's family.

"Where's Brummel? Dished!"
      Byron: Don Juan.

Dish-washer (*A*). A scullery-maid.

Dismal. Daniel Finch, second earl of Nottingham.

"No sooner was Dismal among the Whigs . . . but Lady Char[lot]te is taken knitting in St. James's Chapel [*i.e.* Lady Charlotte Finch, his daughter]."—*Examiner,* April 20-24th, 1713, No. 44.

Dismas (*St.*). The penitent thief. [DYSMAS.]

Disney Professor. The Professor of Archæology in the University of Cambridge. This chair was founded in 1851 by John Disney, Esq., of the Hyde, Ingatestone.

Disor'der, says Franklin, "breakfasts with Plenty, dines with Poverty, sups with Misery, and sleeps with Death."

Dispensa'tion. The system which God chooses to *dispense* or establish between Himself and man. The dispensation of *Adam* was that between Adam and God ; the dispensation of *Abraham,* and that of *Moses,* were those imparted to these holy men ; the *Gospel* dispensation is that explained in the Gospels. (Latin, *dis-penso,* to spread forth, unroll, explain, reveal.)

A dispensation from the Pope. Permission to *dispense* with something enjoined ; a licence to do what is forbidden, or to omit what is commanded by the law of the Church, as distinct from the moral law.

"A dispensation was obtained to enable Dr. Barrow to marry."—*Ward.*

Dispu'te (2 syl.) means, literally, to "lop down" (Latin, *dis-puto*) ; debate means to "knock down" (French, *débattre*) ; discuss means to "shake down" (Latin, *dis-quatio*) ; object' is to "cast against" (Latin, *ob-jacio*) ; contend is to "pull against" (Latin, *contendo*) ; quarrel is to throw darts at each other (Welsh, *cwarel,* a dart) ; and wrangle is to strain by twisting (Swedish, *vränga ;* Anglo-Saxon, *wringan*).

Dis'solute is one that runs loose, not restrained by laws or any other bonds. (Latin, *dissolvo,* like horses unharnessed.)

Dis'taff. A woman. Properly the staff from which the flax was drawn in spinning. The allusion is to the ancient custom of women, who spun from morning to night. (*See* SPINSTER.)

"The crown of France never falls to the distaff."
     —*Kersey.*

To have tow on the distaff. To have work in hand. Froissart says, "*Il aura en bref temps autres estoupes en sa quenouille.*"

"He haddë more tow on his distaf
Than Gerveys knew."
   Chaucer : Canterbury Tales, 3,772.

St. Distaff's Day. The 7th of January. So called because the Christmas festival terminated on Twelfth Day, and on the day following the women returned to their distaffs or daily occupations. It is also called *Rock Day,* a distaff being called a rock. "In old times they used to spin with rocks." (*Aubrey : Wilts.*)

"Give St. Distaff all the right,
Then give Christmas sport good night,
And next morrow every one
To his own vocation."   (1657.)
"What! shall a woman with a rock drive thee away?
Fye on thee, traitor!"
    Digby : Mysteries, p. 11.

Distaffi'na. To whom Bombastës Furio'so makes love. (*Thomas Barnes Rhodes : Bombastes Furioso.*)

Distem'per means an undue mixture. In medicine a distemper arises from the redundancy of certain secretions or morbid humours. The distemper in dogs is an undue quantity of secretions manifested by a running from the eyes and nose. (Latin, *dis-temp'ero,* to mix amiss.)

Applied to painting, the word is from another source, the French *détremper* (to soak in water), because the paints, instead of being mixed with oil, are mixed with a vehicle (as yolk of eggs or glue) soluble in water.

Distinguished Member of the Humane Society. The name of this dog was Paul Pry. Landseer says, "Mr. Newman Smith was rather disappointed when his dog appeared in character rather than 'the property of Newman Smith, Esq., of Croydon Lodge.'" (*Notes and Queries,* March 21st, 1885, p. 225.)

Distraction. An excellent example of how greatly the meaning of words may change. To "distract" means now, to harass, to perplex; and "distraction" confusion of mind from a great multiplicity of duties; but in French to "distract" means to divert the mind, and "distraction" means recreation or amusement (Latin, *dis - traho*). (*See* SLAVE.)

Distrait (French). Absent-minded.

Dithyram'bic. *The father of dithyrambic poetry.* Ari'on of Lesbos.

Dit'tany. When Godfrey was wounded with an arrow, an "odoriferous pan'acy" distilled from dittany was applied to the wound; whereupon the arrow-head fell out, and the wound healed immediately. (*Tasso: Jerusalem Delivered*, book xi.)

Ditto. (*See* Do.)

Dittoes (*A suit of*). Coat, waistcoat, and trousers all alike, or all ditto (the same).

Divan' (Arabic and Persian, *diwan*) means a register kept on a white table exactly similar to our *board*. Among the Orientals the word is applied to a council-chamber or court of justice; but in England we mean a coffee-house where smoking is the chief attraction.

Divers Colours [*in garments*]. We are told, in 2 Sam. xiii. 18, that kings' daughters were arrayed in a garment of divers colours, and Dr. Shaw informs us that only virgins wore drawers of needle-work; so that when the mother of Sisera (Judges v. 30) says, "Have they not sped? Have they not divided the spoil? To Sisera a prey of divers colours, of divers colours of needle-work?" she means—is not the king's daughter allotted to Sisera as a portion of his spoil? (*See* COAT OF MANY COLOURS.)

Divert. To turn aside. Business is the regular walk or current of our life, but pleasure is a diversion or turning aside for a time from the straight line. What we call diversion is called in French *distraction*, drawing aside. (Latin, *di-verto*, to turn aside; *dis-traho*, to draw aside.)

Dives (1 syl.), *Divs* or *Deevs*. Demons of Persian mythology. According to the Koran, they are ferocious and gigantic spirits under the sovereignty of Eblis.

"At Lahore, in the Mogul's palace, are pictures of Dews and Dives with long horns, staring eyes, shaggy hair, great fangs, ugly paws, long tails, and such horrible deformity, that I wonder the poor women are not frightened."—*William Finch: Purchas' Pilgrims*, vol. i.

Dives (2 syl.). The name popularly given to the rich man in our Lord's parable of the Rich Man and Lazarus

(Luke xvi.). The Latin would be *Dives et Lazarus*.

Divi'de (2 syl.). When the members in the House of Commons interrupt a speaker by crying out *divide*, they mean, bring the debate to an end and put the motion to the vote—*i.e.* let the ayes divide from the noes, one going into one room or lobby, and the others into another.

Divide and Govern. Divide a nation into parties, or set your enemies at loggerheads, and you can have your own way. A maxim of Machiavelli, a noted political writer of Florence (1469-1527).

"Every city or house divided against itself shall not stand."—Matthew xii. 25.

Divination. There are numerous species of divination referred to in the Bible. The Hebrew word is added in italics.

JUDICIAL ASTROLOGY (*Meonen*).
AUGURY (*Menachesch*).
WITCHCRAFT (*Mecascheph*).
ENCHANTMENT (*Ithoboron*).
CASTING LOTS (*Indeoni*).
By INTERROGATING SPIRITS.
By NECROMANCY (1 Sam. xxviii. 12).
By RHABDOMANCY (Hosea iv. 12).
By TERAPHIM or household idols.
By HEPATOSCOPY or inspecting the liver of animals.
By DREAMS and their interpretations.
Divination by fire, air, and water; thunder, lightning, and meteors; etc.
The *Urim and Thummim* was a prophetic breastplate worn by the High Priest.
(Consult: Gen. xxxvii. 5—11; xl. xli.; 1 Sam. xxviii. 12; 2 Chron. xxxiii. 6; Prov. xvi. 33; Ezek. xxi. 21; Hosea iii. 4, 5, etc.)

Divine. *The divine right of kings.* The notion that kings reign by divine right, quite independent of the people's will. This notion arose from the Old Testament Scriptures, where kings are called "God's anointed," because they were God's vicars on earth, when the Jews changed their theocracy for a monarchy.

"The right divine of kings to govern wrong."
Pope.

Divine (*The*). Ferdinand de Herre'ra, a Spanish poet (1516-1595).
Raphael, the painter, *il Divi'no* (1483-1520).
Luis Mora'lēs, Spanish painter, *el Divi'no* (1509-1586).

Divine Doctor. Jean de Ruysbroek, the mystic (1294-1381).

Divine Pagan (*The*). Hypa'tia, who presided over the Neoplaton'ic School at Alexandria. She was infamously torn to pieces (A.D. 415) by a Christian mob, not without the concurrence of the Archbishop Cyril.

Divine Plant (*The*). Vervain, called by the Romans Herba Sacra (*q.v.*).

Divine Speaker (*The*). So Aristotle called Tyr'tamos, who therefore adopted the name of Theophrastos (B.C. 370-287).

Divi'ning Rod. A forked branch of hazel, suspended by the two prongs between the balls of the thumbs. The inclination of the rod indicates the presence of water-springs, precious metal, and anything else that simpletons will pay for. (*See* DOUSTERSWIVEL.)

Divinity in Odd Numbers. Falstaff tells us (in the *Merry Wives of Windsor*, v. 1) that this divinity affects "nativity, chance, and death." A Trinity is by no means confined to the Christian creed. The Brahmins represent their god with three heads; the Greeks and Romans had three Graces, three Fates, three Furies, and a threefold Hecate. Jupiter had his three thunderbolts, Neptune his trident, and Pluto his three-headed dog. The Muses were three times three. Pythagoras says God is threefold—"the beginning, middle, and end of all things." Then, again, there are five features, five parts to the body, five vowels, five lines in music, five acts to a play, etc.; seven strings to a harp, seven planets (anciently, at any rate), seven musical notes, etc.

Chance. There's luck in odd numbers "*Numero Deus impăre gaudet*" (*Virgil: Eclogue* viii. 75). The seventh son of a seventh son was always held notable. Baalam would have seven altars, and sacrificed on them seven bullocks and seven rams. Naaman was commanded to dip seven times in Jordan, and Elijah sent his servant seven times to look out for rain. Climacteric years are seven and nine with their multiples by odd numbers.

Death. The great climacteric year of life is 63 (*i.e.* 7×9), and Saturn presides over all climacteric years.

Divi'no Lodovi'co. Ariosto, author of *Orlando Furioso*, an epic poem in twenty-four books. (1474-1533.)

Division. The sign $\div$ for division was invented by John Pell of Cambridge in 1668.

Divorcement. *A writing,* or *bill of divorcement.* "Whosoever shall put away his wife, let him give her a writing of divorcement" (Matt. v. 31).

Adalet tells in the *Nineteenth Century* (July, 1892, p. 137):

"A woman [in Turkey] divorced from her husband is not treated with contumely . . . and often marries again. . . . A man simply states to his wife that he has divorced her, on which she will go away; and the man, having repeated the same to the cadi, will receive an act of divorce written, which he will send to her. If it is the first or second time that this has occurred, he may take her back again without any formality ensuing, but, after a third divorce, she will be lost to him for ever. Seeing the ease with which this may be done, it is not surprising if men abuse the licence, and sometimes divorce their wives for [a very small] fault . . . as a badly-cooked dinner, or a button unsewed, knowing very well that if he repents of it he can have her back before evening. I know a lady who has been divorced from five husbands, and is now living with a sixth."

Divus in Latin, attached to a proper name, does not mean *divine*, but simply deceased or canonised; excellently translated in *Notes and Queries* (May 21st, 1892, p. 421), "of blessed memory." Thus, *Divus Augustus* means Augustus of blessed memory, not divine Augustus. Of course, the *noun* "divus" opposite to a proper noun = a god, as in Horace, 3 *Odes* v. 2, "*Præsens divus habebitur Augustus.*" While living, Augustus will be accounted a god. Virgil (*Ecl.* i. 6) says, "*Deus nobis hæc otia fecit;*" the "deus" was Augustus.

Dix'ie Land. Nigger land. Mason and Dixon drew a line which was to be the northern limit of slavery. In the third quarter of the 19th century the southern part of this line was called Dixie or nigger land.

Dizzy. A nickname of Benjamin Disraeli (Lord Beaconsfield) (1805-1881).

Djin'nestan'. The realm of the djinns or genii of Oriental mythology.

Do. A contraction of *ditto*, which is the Italian *détto* (said), Latin *dictus.*

How do you do? i.e. How do you fare? It should be, *How do you du?* (Anglo-Saxon, *dug-an* = *valëre*); in Latin, *Quomodo vales.*

Well to do. This, again, is not the transitive verb (*facĕre*) but the intransitive verb (*valëre*), and means "well to fare." (Anglo-Saxon, *dug-an* = *valëre.*)

To do him, i.e. cheat or trick a person out of something.

I have done the Jew, i.e. over-reached him. The same as *outdo* = excel.

Do (to rhyme with *go*). The first or tonic note of the solfeggio system of music.

Do, re, mi, fa, sol, la, Italian; *ut, re, mi, fa, sol, la,* French. The latter are borrowed from a hymn by Paulus Piaconus, addressed to St. John, which Guido, in the eleventh century, used in teaching singing :

> " *Ut* queant laxis, *Re*-sonare fibris,
> *Mi*-ra gestorum *Fa*-muli tuorum,
> *Sol*-ve pollutis *La*-biis reatum."
> *Sanctè Joannès.*
>
> *Ut*-tered be thy wondrous story,
> *Re*-prehensive though I be,
> *Me* make mindful of thy glory,
> *Fa*-mous son of Zacharee ;
> *Sol*-ace to my spirit bring,
> *La*-bouring thy praise to sing.
> *E. C. B.*

(*See* WEIZIUS in *Heortologio*, p. 263.) Le Maire added *si* (seventeenth century). (*See* ARETINIAN SYLLABLES.)

Do for. *I'll do for him.* Ruin him ; literally, provide for him in a bad sense. "Taken in and done for," is taken in and provided for ; but, jocosely, it means "cheated and fleeced."

Do up (*To*). To set in order ; to make tidy. "Dup the door." (*See* DUP.)

Doab (Indian). A tract of land between two rivers. (Pronounce *du'-ab*.)

Dobbin. A steady old horse, a child's horse. *Dobby*, a silly old man. *Dobbies*, house-elves similar to brownies. All these are one and the same word. The dobbies lived in the house, were very thin and shaggy, very kind to servants and children, and did many a little service when people had their hands full.

> "Sober Dobbin lifts his clumsy heel."
> *Bloomfield : Farmer's Boy.* (Winter, stanza 9.)

Dobbins (*Humphrey*). The valet-de-chambre and factotum of Sir Robert Bramble, of Blackbury Hall, in the county of Kent. A blunt, rough-spoken old retainer, full of the milk of human kindness, and most devoted to his master. (*G. Colman : The Poor Gentleman.*)

Dobby's Walk. The goblin's haunt or beat. Dobby is an archaic word for a goblin or brownie. (*See* Washington Irving's *Bracebridge Hall*, ii. 183-6.) Dobby also means an imbecile old man.

> "The Dobby's walk was within the inhabited domains of the Hall."—*Sir W. Scott : Peveril of the Peak*, chap. x.

Doce'tes (3 syl.). An early heretical sect, which maintained that Jesus Christ was only God, and that His visible form was merely a phantom ; that the crucifixion and resurrection were illusions. (The word is Greek, and means *phantomists*.)

Dock-Alfar. The dark Alfs whose abode is underground. They are in appearance blacker than pitch. (*Scandinavian mythology*.)

Dock-side Lumper (*A*). One engaged in delivering and loading ships' cargoes.

> "Judging of my histrionic powers by my outward man, he probably thought me more fit for a dock-side lumper than an actor."—*C. Thomson : Autobiography*, p. 191.

Dock Warrant (*A*). An order authorising the removal of goods warehoused in the dock.

Doctor. A seventh son used to be so dubbed from the notion of his being intuitively skilled in the cure of agues, the king's evil, and other diseases.

> " Plusieurs croyent qu'en France les septiennes garçons, nez de legitimes mariages (sans que la suitte des sept ait, esté interrompue par la naissance d'aucune fille) peuvent aussi guerir des fievres tierces, des fievres quartes, et mesme des ecrouelles, après avoir jeûne trois ou neuf jours avant que de toucher les malades."—*Jean Baptiste Thiers : Traité des Superstitions, etc.*, i. p. 436.

Doctor (*The*). The cook on board ship, who "doctors" the food. Any adulterated or doctored beverage ; hence the mixture of milk, water, nutmeg, and a little rum, is called Doctor ; the two former ingredients being "doctored" by the two latter.

Doctor (*The*). Brown sherry, so called because it is concocted from a harsh, thin wine, by the addition of old boiled mosto stock. Mosto is made by heating unfermented juice in earthen vessels, till it becomes as thick and sweet as treacle. This syrup being added to fresh "must" ferments, and the luscious produce is used for doctoring very inferior qualities of wine. (*Shaw : On Wine.*)

To doctor the wine. To drug it, or strengthen it with brandy. The fermentation of cheap wines is increased by fermentable sugar. As such wines fail in aroma, connoisseurs smell at their wine. To doctor wine is to make weak wine stronger, and "sick" wine more palatable.

Doctored Dice. Loaded dice.

To doctor the accounts. To falsify them. They are *ill* (so far as you are concerned) and you falsify them to make them look *better*. The allusion is to drugging wine, beer, etc., and to adulteration generally.

Dr. Diafoirus in Molière's *Malade Imaginaire*. A man of fossilised ideas, who, like the monk, refused to change his time - honoured *mumpsimus* (*q.v.*), for the new-fangled *sumpsimus*. Dr. Diafoirus used to say, what was good enough for his forefathers was good enough for their posterity, and he had no patience with the modern fads about the rotundity of the earth, its motion round the sun, the circulation of the blood, and all such stuff.

Dr. Dove. The hero of Southey's *Doctor.*

Dr. Fell. *I do not like thee, Dr. Fell.* A correspondent of *Notes and Queries* says the author was Tom Brown, who wrote *Dialogues of the Dead,* and the person referred to was Dr. Fell, Dean of Christchurch (1625-1686), who expelled him, but said he would remit the sentence if he translated the thirty-third Epigram of Martial:

" Non amo te, Zabidi, nec possum dicere quare;
   Hoc tantum possum dicere ,non amo te."
   " I do not like thee, Dr. Fell,
   The reason why I cannot tell;
   But this I know, I know full well,
   I do not like thee, Dr. Fell."   *T. Brown.*

Doctor Mirabilis. Roger Bacon (1214-1292).

Doctor My-Book. Dr. John Aberne'thy, so called because he used to say to his patients, " Read *my book* "—on *Surgical Observations.* (1765-1830.)

Dr. Rez'io or *Pedro Rezio of Ague'ro.* The doctor of Barata'ria, who forbade Sancho Panza to taste any of the meats set before him. Roasted partridge was forbidden by Hippoc'ratēs; podri'da was the most pernicious food in the world; rabbits are a sharp-haired diet; veal is prejudicial to health; but the governor might eat a " few wafers, and a thin slice or two of quince." (*Don Quixote,* part ii. book iii. chap. 10.)

Dr. Sangra'do, of Vall'adolid', a tall, meagre, pale man, of very solemn appearance, who weighed every word he uttered, and gave an emphasis to his sage dicta. " His reasoning was geometrical, and his opinions angular." He said to the licentiate Sedillo, who was sick, " If you had drunk nothing else but pure water all your life, and eaten only such simple food as boiled apples, you would not now be tormented with gout." He then took from him six porringers of blood to begin with; in three hours he repeated the operation; and again the next day, saying: " It is a gross error to suppose that blood is necessary for life." With this depletion, the patient was to drink two or three pints of hot water every two hours. The result of this treatment was death " from obstinacy." (*Gil Blas,* chap. ii.)

Doctor Slop. An enthusiast, who thinks the world hinges on getting Uncle

Toby to understand the action of a new medical instrument. (*Sterne: Tristram Shandy.*)

A nickname given by William Hone to Sir John Stoddart, editor of the *New Times.* (1773-1856.)

Doctor Squintum. George Whitefield, so called by Foote in his farce entitled *The Minor.* (1714-1770.)

Theodore Hook applied the same sobriquet to the Rev. Edward Irving, who had an obliquity of the eyes. (1792-1834.)

Doctor Syntax. A simple-minded, pious henpecked clergyman, very simple-minded, but of excellent taste and scholarship, who left home in search of the picturesque. His adventures are told in eight-syllable verse in *The Tour of Dr. Syntax,* by William Combe. (*See* DUKE COMBE.)

Dr. Syntax's horse. Grizzle, all skin and bone. (*See* HORSE.)

Doctors. False dice, which are doctored, or made to turn up winning numbers.

" 'The whole antechamber is full, my lord—knights and squires, doctors and dicers.'
" 'The dicers with their doctors in their pockets, I presume.' "—*Scott: Peveril of the Peak,* chap. xxviii.
" Or chaired at White's, amidst the doctors sit."
   .*Dunciad,* book i. 203.

Doctors. *The three best doctors are Dr. Quiet, Dr. Diet,* and *Dr. Merryman.*

" Si tibi deficiant medici, medici tibi fiant
   Hæc tria: Mens-læta, Requies, Moderata-Diæta."

Doctors' Commons. A locality near St. Paul's, where the ecclesiastical courts were formerly held, and wills preserved. To " common " means to dine together; a term still used at our universities. Doctors' Commons was so called because the doctors of civil law had to dine together four days in each term. This was called *eating their terms.*

Doctors Disagree. *Who shall decide when doctors disagree.* When authorities differ, the question *sub judice* must be left undecided. (*Pope: Moral Essays,* epistle iii. line 1.)

Doctor's Stuff. Medicine; stuff sent from the doctor.

Doctored Wine. (*See* TO DOCTOR.)

Doctour of Phisikes Tale, in Chaucer, is the Roman story of Virginius, given by Livy. There is a version of this tale in the *Roman de la Rose,* vol. ii. p. 74; and another, by Gower, in his *Confessio Amantis,* book vii.

Doctrinists or *Doctrinaires.* A political party which has existed in France since 1815. They maintain that true liberty is compatible with a monarchical Government ; and are so called because they advocate what is only a *doctrine* or dream. M. Guizot was one of this party.

Dodge (1 syl.). An artful device to evade, deceive, or bilk some one. (Anglo-Saxon, *deogian,* to conceal or colour.)
The religious dodge. Seeking alms by trading on religion.
The tidy dodge. To dress up a family clean and tidy so as to excite sympathy, and make passers-by suppose you have by misfortune fallen from a respectable state in society.

Dodge About (*To*), in school phrase, is to skip about and not go straight on through a lesson. A boy learns a verb, and the master does not hear him conjugate it straight through, but dodges him about. Also in class not to call each in order, but to pick a boy here and there.

Dodger. A "knowing fellow." One who knows all the tricks and ways of London life, and profits by such knowledge.

Dodger. *The Artful Dodger.* John Dawkins, a young thief, up to every artifice, and a perfect adept in villainy. A sobriquet given by Dickens to such a rascal, in his *Oliver Twist,* chap. viii.

Dodington, whom Thomson invokes in his *Summer,* was George Bubb Dodington, Lord Melcomb-Regis, a British statesman, who associated much with the wits of the time. Churchill and Pope ridiculed him, while Hogarth introduced him in his wig into his picture called the *Orders of Periwigs.*

Dod'ipoll. *As wise as Dr. Dodipoll* (or) *Doddipole*—*i.e.* not wise at all ; a dunce. (*Doddy* in dodi-poll and doddy-pate is probably a variant of *totty,* small, puny. Doddy-poll, one of puny intellect.)

Dodman or *Doddiman.* A snail. A word still common in Norfolk ; but Fairfax, in his *Bulk and Selvedge* (1674), speaks of "a snayl or dodman."

 "Doddiman, doddiman, put out your horn,
 Here comes a thief to steal your corn."
 Norfolk rhyme.

Dodo'na. A famous oracle in Epi'ros, and the most ancient of Greece. It was dedicated to Zeus (*Jupiter*), and situate in the village of Dodōna.

⁂ The tale is, that Jupiter presented his daughter Thebē with two black pigeons which had the gift of human speech. Lemprière tells us that the Greek word *peleiai* (pigeons) means, in the dialect of the Epīrots, *old women ;* so that the two black doves with human voice were two black or African women. One went to Libya, in Africa, and founded the oracle of Jupiter Ammon ; the other went to Epīrus and founded the oracle of Dodōna. We are also told that plates of brass were suspended on the oak trees of Dodona, which being struck by thongs when the wind blew, gave various sounds from which the responses were concocted. It appears that this suggested to the Greeks the phrase *Kalkos Dodōnēs* (brass of Dodona), meaning a babbler, or one who talks an infinite deal of nothing.

Dods (*Meg*). The old landlady in Scott's novel called *St. Ronan's Well.* An excellent character, made up of consistent inconsistencies ; a mosaic of oddities, all fitting together, and forming an admirable whole. She was so good a housewife that a cookery book of great repute bears her name.

Dodson and Fogg. The lawyers employed by the plaintiff in the famous case of "Bardell *v.* Pickwick," in the *Pickwick Papers,* by Charles Dickens.

Doe (1 syl.). *John Doe and Richard Roe.* Any plaintiff and defendant in an action of ejectment. They were sham names used at one time to save certain "niceties of law ; " but the clumsy device was abolished in 1852. Any mere imaginary persons, or men of straw. John Doe, Richard Roe, John o' Noakes, and Tom Styles are the four sons of "Mrs. Harris," all bound apprentices to the legal profession.

Doeg (2 syl.), in the satire of *Absalom and Achitophel,* by Dryden and Tate, is meant for Elka'nah Settle, a poet who wrote satires upon Dryden, but was no match for his great rival. Doeg was Saul's herdsman, who had charge of his mules and asses. He told Saul that the priests of Nob had provided David with food ; whereupon Saul sent him to put them to death, and eighty-five were ruthlessly massacred. (1 Sam. xxi. 7 · xxii. 18.)

 "Doëg, though without knowing how or why,
 Made still a blundering kind of melody ....
 Let him rail on ; let his invective Muse
 Have four-and-twenty letters to abuse,
 Which if he jumbles to one line of sense,
 Indict him of a capital offence."
 Absalom and Achitophel, part ii.

Doff is do-off, as "Doff your hat."
So *Don* is do-on, as "Don your clothes."
Dup is do-up, as "Dup the door" (*q.v.*).

"Doff thy harness, youth . . .
And tempt not yet the brushes of the war."
Shakespeare: Troilus and Cressida, v. 3.

Dog. This long article is subdivided into eleven parts:

1 Dogs of note.
2. Dogs of noted persons.
3. Dogs models of their species.
4. Dogs in phrases.
5. Dogs used metaphorically, etc.
6. Dogs in Scripture language.
7. Dogs in art.
8. Dogs in proverbs and fables
9. Dogs in superstitions.
10. Dogs the male of animals.
11. Dogs inferior plants.

(1) Dogs *of Note:*

Barry. The famous mastiff of Great St. Bernard's, in the early part of the present century instrumental in saving forty human beings. His most memorable achievement was rescuing a little boy whose mother had been destroyed by an avalanche. The dog carried the boy on his back to the hospice. The stuffed skin of this noble animal is kept in the museum of Berne.

Gelert (*q.v.*).

Tonton. The dog which was enclosed in an acorn.

Tray—i.e. Trag = runner, or else from the Spanish *traér*, to fetch.

(2) Dogs *of noted persons:*

Actæon's fifty dogs. Alcē (*strength*), Amaryn'thos (*from Amary'thia, in Eubœa*), As'bolos (*soot-colour*), Ban'os, Bor'eas, Can'achē (*ringwood*), Chediæ'-tros, Cisse'ta, Co'ran (*cropped, crop-eared*), Cyllo (*halt*), Cyllop'otēs (*zig-zag runner*), Cyp'rios (*the Cyprian*), Draco (*the dragon*), Drom'as (*the courser*), Dro'mios (*seize-'em*), Ech'nobas, Eu'dromos (*good-runner*), Har'palē (*voracious*), Harpie'a (*tear-'em*), Ichnob'atē (*track-follower*), La'bros (*furious*), Lacæna (*lioness*), Lach'nē (*glossy-coated*), Lacon (*Spartan*), La'don (*from Ladon, in Arca'dia*), Læ-laps (*hurricane*), Lampos (*shining-one*), Leu'cos (*grey*), Lycis'ca, Lynce'a, Mach'imos (*boxer*), Melampē (*black*), Melan-che'tē (*black-coat*), Melan'ea (*black*), Menele'a, Molossos (*from Molossos*), Na'pa (*begotten by a wolf*), Nebroph'onos (*fawn-killer*), Oc'ydroma (*swift-runner*), Or'esit'rophos (*mountain-bred*), Ori'basos (*mountain-ranger*), Pachy'tos (*thick-skinned*), Pam'phagos (*ravenous*), Poe'-menis (*leader*), Pter'elas (*winged*), Stricta (*spot*), Therid'amas (*beast-tamer* or *sub-duer*), The'ron (*savage-faced*), Thoös (*swift*), U'ranis (*heavenly-one*).

✳ Several modern names of dogs are

of Spanish origin, as *Ponto* (pointer), *Tray* (fetch), etc.

King Arthur's favourite hound. Cavall.

Aubry's dog. Aubry of Montdid'ier was murdered, in 1371, in the forest of Bondy. His dog, Dragon, showed a most unusual hatred to a man named Richard of Macaire, always snarling and ready to fly at his throat whenever he appeared. Suspicion was excited, and Richard of Macaire was condemned to a judicial combat with the dog. He was killed, and in his dying moments confessed the crime.

Belgrade, the camp-sutler's dog: Clumsy.

Browning's (Mrs.) little dog Flush, on which she wrote a poem.

Lord Byron's favourite dog. Boat-swain, buried in the garden of Newstead Abbey.

Catherine de Medici's favourite lap-dog was named Phœbé.

Cathullin's hound was named Luath (*q.v.*).

Douglas's hound was named Luffra or Lufra (*q.v.*).

Elizabeth of Bohemia's dog was named Apollon.

Fingal's dog was named Bran.

"'Mar e Bran, is e a brathair' (If it be not Bran, it is Bran's brother) was the proverbial reply of Maccombich."—*Waverley*, chap. xlv.

Frederick of Wales had a dog given him by Alexander Pope, and on the collar were these words—

" I am his Highness' dog at Kew ;
Pray tell me, sir, whose dog are you ? "

Ge'ryon's dogs. Gargittios and Orthos. The latter was the brother of Cer'beros, but had one head less. Herculēs killed both these monsters.

Icarios's dog. Mæra (*the glistener*). Icarios was slain by some drunken peasants, who buried the body under a tree. His daughter Erig'onē, searching for her father, was directed to the spot by the howling of Mæra, and when she discovered the body she hung herself for grief. Icarios became the constellation *Boötēs,* Erig'one the constellation *Virgo,* and Mæra the star *Pro'cyon,* which rises in July, a little before the Dog-star. (Greek, *pro-kuon.*)

Kenneth's (*Sir*) famous hound was called Roswal. (*Sir W. Scott: The Talisman.*)

Lamb's (*Charles*) dog was named Dash.

Landor's (*Savage*) dog was named Giallo.

Landseer's greyhound was named Brutus. "The Invader of the Larder."

Llewellyn's greyhound was named Gelert' (*q.v.*).

Ludlam's dog. (*See* LAZY.)

Lurgan's (*Lord*) greyhound was named Master M'Grath, from an orphan boy who reared it. It won three Waterloo Cups, and was presented at Court by the express desire of Queen Victoria, the very year it died (1866-1871).

Neville's dog. It ran away whenever it was called. In the corresponding Italian proverb the dog is called that of the Vicar Arlotto. (*See* CHIEN.)

Mauthe dog. (*See* MAUTHE.)

Sir Isaac Newton's, Diamond (*q.v.*).

Dog of Montargis. The same as Aubry's dog. A picture of the combat was for many years preserved in the castle of Montargis. (*See* AUBRY'S DOG.)

Ori'on's dogs were Arctoph'onos (*bearkiller*), and Ptooph'agos (Ptoon-glutton.) (Ptoon is in Bœotia.)

Pope's dog was named Bounce.

Punch's dog is Toby.

Richard II.'s greyhound was named Mathe. It deserted the king and attached itself to Bolingbroke.

Roderick the Goth's dog was named Theron.

Rupert's (*Prince*) dog, killed at Marston Moor, was named Boy.

Scott's (*Sir Walter*) dogs: his favourite deerhound was named Maida; his jetblack greyhound was called Hamlet. He also had two Dandy Dinmont terriers.

Seven Sleepers (*Dog of the*). This famous dog, admitted by Mahomet to heaven, was named Katmir. The seven noble youths that fell asleep for 309 years had a dog, which accompanied them to the cavern in which they were walled up. It remained standing for the whole time, and neither moved from the spot, ate, drank, nor slept. (*Sale's Koran*, xviii., *notes*.)

Tristran's dog was named Leon or Lion.

Ulysses' dog, Argos, recognised him after his return from Troy, and died of joy.

(3) DOGS, *models of their species :*

Argoss (a Russian terrier); *Baroness Cardiff* (a Newfoundland); *Black Prince* (a mastiff); *Bow-wow* (a schipperke); *Corney* (a bull-terrier); *Countess of Warwick* (a great Dane); *Dan O'Connor* (an Irish water-spaniel); *Dude* (a pug); *Fascination* (a black cockerspaniel); *Fritz* (a French poodle); *Judith* (a bloodhound); *Kilcree* (a Scotch terrier); *King Lud* (a bulldog); *King of the Heather* (a dandie-dinmont); *Mikado*

(a Japanese spaniel); *Olga* (a deerhound); *Romeo* (a King Charles spaniel); *Royal Krueger* (a beagle); *Scottish Leader* (a smooth-coated St. Bernard); *Sensation* (a pointer); *Sir Bedivere* (a rough - coated St. Bernard); *Spinaway* (a greyhound); *Toledo Blade* (an English setter); *Woodmansterne Trefoil* (a collie).

(4) DOG *in phrases :*

A dog in a doublet. A bold, resolute fellow. In Germany and Flanders the boldest dogs were employed for hunting the wild boar, and these dogs were dressed in a kind of buff doublet buttoned to their bodies. Rubens and Sneyders have represented several in their pictures. A false friend is called a dog in one's doublet.

Between dog and wolf. The hour of dusk. "*Entre chien et loup.*"

St. Roch and his dog. Two inseparables. "Toby and his dog." One is never seen without the other.

They lead a cat and dog life. Always quarrelling.

To lead the life of a dog. To live a wretched life, or a life of debauchery.

(5) DOG, *used metaphorically or symbolically :*

The dog. Diogĕnēs, the Cynic (B.C. 412-323). When Alexander went to see him, the young King of Macedonia introduced himself with these words: "I am Alexander, surnamed the Great," to which the philosopher replied : "And I am Diogĕnēs, surnamed the Dog." The Athenians raised to his memory a pillar of Parian marble, surmounted by a dog. (*See* CYNIC.)

Dog of God. So the Laplanders call the bear. The Norwegians say it "has the strength of ten men and the wit of twelve." They never presume to speak of it by its proper appellation, *quouztija*, lest it should revenge the insult on their flocks and herds, but they call it *Möddaaigja* (the old man with a fur cloak).

A dead dog. Something utterly worthless. A phrase used two or three times in the Bible. (*See* (6).)

A dirty dog. In the East the dog is still held in abhorrence, as the scavenger of the streets. "Him that dieth in the city shall the dogs eat" (1 Kings xiv. 11). The French say, *Crotté comme un barbet* (muddy or dirty as a poodle), whose hair, being very long, becomes filthy with mud and dirt. Generally speaking, "a dirty dog" is one morally filthy, and is applied to those who talk and act nastily. Mere skin dirt is quite another matter, and those who are so defiled we call dirty *pigs*.

A surly dog. A human being of a surly temper, like a surly dog.

Is thy servant a dog, that he should do this thing? (2 Kings viii. 12, 13). Hazael means, "Am I such a brute as to set on fire the strongholds of Israel, slay the young men with the sword, and dash their children to the ground, as thou, Elijah, sayest I shall do when I am king?"

Sydney Smith being asked if it was true that he was about to sit to Landseer, the animal painter, for his portrait, replied, in the words of Hazael, "What! is thy servant a dog, that he should do this thing?"

The Thracian dog. Zoïlus.

" Like curs, our critics haunt the poet's feast,
And feed on scraps refused by every guest ;
From the old Thracian dog they learned the
    way
To snarl in want, and grumble o'er their prey."
    Pitt : To Mr. Spence.

Dogs of war. The horrors of war, especially famine, sword, and fire.

" And Cæsar's spirit, ranging for revenge,
With Até by his side, come hot from hell,
Shall in these confines, with a monarch's voice,
Cry ' Havoc,' and let slip the dogs of war."
    Shakespeare : Julius Cæsar, iii. 1.

(6) Dog (*in Scripture language*), whether dead or living, is a most degrading expression: "After whom is the King of Israel come out? After a dead dog?" (1 Sam. xxiv. 14.) "Beware of dogs" (Phil. iii. 2), *i.e.* sordid, noisy professors. Again, "Without are dogs" (Rev. xxii. 15), *i.e.* false teachers and sinners, who sin and return to their sins (2 Peter ii. 21).

There is no expression in the Bible of the fidelity, love, and watchful care of the dog, so highly honoured by ourselves.

(7) Dog *in art*.

Dog, in mediæval art, symbolises fidelity.

A dog is represented as lying at the feet of St. Bernard, St. Benignus, and St. Wendelin ; as licking the wounds of St. Roch ; as carrying a lighted torch in representations of St. Dominic.

Dogs in monuments. The *dog* is placed at the feet of women in monuments to symbolise affection and fidelity, as a *lion* is placed at the feet of men to signify courage and magnanimity. Many of the Crusaders are represented with their feet on a dog, to show that they followed the standard of the Lord as faithfully as a dog follows the footsteps of his master.

(8) Dog *in proverbs, fables, and proverbial phrases :*

Barking dogs seldom bite. (*See* Barking.)

Dog don't eat dog. Ecclesia ecclesiam non decimat; government letters are not taxed; church lands pay no tithes to the church.

A black dog has walked over him. Said of a sullen person. Horace tells us that the sight of a black dog with its pups was an unlucky omen. (*See* Black Dog.)

A dog in the manger. A churlish fellow, who will not use what is wanted by another, nor yet let the other have it to use. The allusion is to the well-known fable of a dog that fixed his place in a manger, and would not allow an ox to come near the hay.

Every dog has his day. In Latin, " *Hodie mihi, cras tibi*." " *Nunc mihi, nunc tibi, benigna*" [*fortuna*]. In German, " *Heute mir, morgen dir*." You may crow over me to-day, but my turn will come by-and-by. The Latin proverb, " *Hodie mihi*," etc., means, " I died to-day, your turn will come in time." The other Latin proverb means, fortune visits every man once. She favours me now, but she will favour you in your turn.

" Thus every dog at last will have his day—
He who this morning smiled, at night may
    sorrow ;
The grub to-day's a butterfly to-morrow."
    Peter Pindar : Odes of Condolence.

Give a dog a bad name and hang him. If you want to do anyone a wrong, throw dirt on him or rail against him.

Gone to the dogs. Gone to utter ruin ; impoverished.

He has not a dog to lick a dish. He has quite cleared out. He has taken away everything.

He who has a mind to beat his dog will easily find a stick. In Latin, " *Qui vult cædere canem facile invenit fustem*." If you want to abuse a person, you will easily find something to blame. Dean Swift says, " If you want to throw a stone, every lane will furnish one."

" To him who wills, ways will not be wanting." " Where there's a will there's a way."

Hungry dogs will eat dirty pudding. Those really hungry are not particular about what they eat, and are by no means dainty. When Darius in his flight from Greece drank from a ditch defiled with dead carcases, he declared he had never drunk so pleasantly before.

It was the story of the dog and the shadow—i.e. of one who throws good money after bad; of one who gives *certa pro incertis.* The allusion is to the well-known fable.

"Illudit species, ac den'tibus aëra mordit."
(Down sank the meat in the stream for the fishes to hoard it.)

Love me love my dog. "*Qui m'aime aime mon chien,*" or "*Qui aime Bertrand aime son chien.*"

Old dogs will not learn new tricks. People in old age do not readily conform to new ways.

To call off the dogs. To break up a disagreeable conversation. In the chase, if the dogs are on the wrong track, the huntsman calls them off. (French, *rompre les chiens.*)

Throw it to the dogs. Throw it away, it is useless and worthless.

What! keep a dog and bark myself! Must I keep servants and myself do their work?

You are like Neville's dog, which runs away when it is called. (*See* CHIEN.)

(9) DOG, DOGS, *in Superstitions:*
Dogs howl at death. A wide-spread superstition.

" In the rabbinical book it saith
The dogs howl when, with icy breath,
Great Sammaël, the angel of death,
Takes thro' the town his flight."
Longfellow: Golden Legend, iii.

The hair of the dog that bit you. When a man has had a debauch, he is advised to take next morning "a hair of the same dog," in allusion to an ancient notion that the burnt hair of a dog is an antidote to its bite.

(10) DOG, *to express the male of animals,* as dog-ape, dog-fox, dog-otter.

(11) DOG, *applied to inferior plants:* dog-brier, dog-berry, dog-cabbage, dog-daisy, dog-fennel, dog-leek, dog-lichen, dog-mercury, dog-parsley, dog-violets (which have no perfume), dog-wheat. (*See below,* DOG-GRASS, DOG-ROSE.

Dog and Duck. A public-house sign, to announce that ducks were hunted by dogs within. The sport was to see the duck dive, and the dog after it. At Lambeth there was a famous pleasure-resort so called, on the spot where Bethlehem Hospital now stands.

Dog-cheap. A perversion of the old English *god-chepe* (a good bargain). French, *bon marché* (good-cheap or bargain).

" The sack . . . . would have bought me lights as *good-cheap* at the dearest chandler's in Europe." —*Shakespeare:* 1 *Henry IV.,* iii. 3.

Dog-days. Days of great heat. The Romans called the six or eight hottest weeks of the summer *canicula'rēs diēs.*

According to their theory, the dog-star or Sirius, rising with the sun, added to its heat, and the dog-days bore the combined heat of the dog-star and the sun. (July 3rd to August 11th.)

Dog-fall (in wrestling), when both wrestlers fall together.

Dog-grass (*triticum repens*). Grass eaten by dogs when they have lost their appetite; it acts as an emetic and purgative.

Dog-head (in machinery). That which bites or holds the gun-flint.

Dog-headed Tribes *of India.* Mentioned in the Italian romance of *Gueri'no Meschi'no.*

Dog-Latin. Pretended or mongrel Latin. An excellent example is Stevens' definition of a kitchen:

As the law classically expresses it, a kitchen is " camera necessaria pro usus cookare ; cum saucepannis, stewpannis, scullero, dressero, coalhoio, stovis, smoak-jacko ; pro roastandum, boilandum, fryandum, et plum-pudding-mixandum. . . ."—*A Law Report* (Daniel *v.* Dishclout).

Dog-leech (*A*). A dog-doctor. Formerly applied to a medical practitioner ; it expresses great contempt.

Dog-rose. Botanical name, *Cynorrhodos*—*i.e.* Greek *kuno-rodon,* dog-rose ; so called because it was supposed to cure the bite of a mad dog (*Rosa Canina,* wild brier).

"A morsu vero [*i.e.* of a mad dog] unicum remedium oraculo quodam nuper repertum, radix sylvestris rosæ, quæ cynorrhodos appellatur."— *Pliny: Natural History,* viii. 63 ; xxv. 6.

Dog-sick. Sick as a dog. We also say "Sick as a cat." The Bible speaks of dogs "returning to their vomit again" (Prov. xxvi. 11 ; 2 Pet. ii. 22).

Dog-sleep (*A*). A pretended sleep. Dogs seem to sleep with "one eye open."

Dog-star. The brightest star in the firmament. (*See* DOG-DAYS.)

Dog-vane (*A*). A cockade.

" Dog-vane is a term familiarly applied to a cockade."—*Smyth: Sailors' Word-book.*

Dog-watch. A corruption of dodge-watch : two short watches, one from four to six, and the other from six to eight in the evening, introduced to *dodge* the routine, or prevent the same men always keeping watch at the same time. (*See* WATCH.)

Dog-whipper (*A*). A beadle who whips all dogs from the precincts of a church. At one time there was a church officer so called. Even so recently as 1856 Mr. John Pickard was appointed "dog-whipper" in Exeter Cathedral, "in the room of Mr. Charles Reynolds, deceased." (*Exeter Gazette*.)

Dog-whipping Day. October 18th (St. Luke's Day). It is said that a dog once swallowed the consecrated wafer in York Minster on this day.

Dogs (a military term). The 17th Lancers or Duke of Cambridge's Own Lancers. The crest of this famous cavalry regiment is a Death's Head and Cross-bones, OR GLORY, whence the acrostic **D**eath **O**r **G**lory (D.O.G.).

The Spartan injunction, when the young soldier was presented with his shield, was, " With this, or On this," which meant the same thing.

Dogs, in Stock-Exchange phraseology, means Newfoundland Telegraph shares —that is, Newfoundland dogs. (*See* STOCK-EXCHANGE SLANG.)

Dogs. *Isle of Dogs.* When Greenwich was a place of royal residence, the kennel for the monarch's hounds was on the opposite side of the river, hence called the "Isle of Dogs."

Dogs (*Green*). Extinct like the Dodo. Brederode said to Count Louis, "I would the whole race of bishops and cardinals were extinct, like that of green dogs." (*Motley : Dutch Republic,* part ii. 5.)

Dogs'-ears. The corners of leaves crumpled and folded down.
Dogs'-eared. Leaves so crumpled and turned up. The ears of many dogs turn down and seem quite limp.

Dogs'-meat. Food unfit for consumption by human beings.
Dogs'-meat and cats'-meat. Food cheap and nasty.

Dog's-nose. Gin and beer.
"' Dog's-nose, which is, I believe, a mixture of gin and beer.'
"' So it is,' said an old lady."—*Pickwick Papers.*

Dogged. He *dogged* me, *i.e.* followed me about like a dog; shadowed me.

Dogged (2 syl.). Sullen, snappish, like a dog.

Do'gares'sa ($g = j$). The wife of a doge.

Dogberry. An ignorant, self-satisfied, overbearing, but good-natured night-constable in Shakespeare's *Much Ado about Nothing*.

Doge (1 syl., $g = j$). The chief magistrate in Venice while it was a Republic. The first duke or doge was Anafesto Paoluc'cio, created 697. The chief magistrate of Gen'oa was called a doge

down to 1797, when the Republican form of Government was abolished by the French. (Latin, *dux,* a "duke" or "leader."

"For six hundred years . . . . her [Venice's] government was an elective monarchy, her . . . . doge possessing, in early times at least, as much independent authority as any other European sovereign."—*Ruskin: Stones of Venice,* vol. i. chap. i. p. 3.,

Doge. The ceremony of wedding the Adriatic was instituted in 1174 by Pope Alexander III., who gave the doge a gold ring from off his own finger in token of the victory achieved by the Venetian fleet at Istria over Frederick Barbarossa, in defence of the Pope's quarrel. When his Holiness gave the ring he desired the doge to throw a similar one into the sea every year on Ascension Day, in commemoration of the event. (*See* BUCENTAUR.)

Dirty dog. (*See under* DOG, No. 5.)
This alludes more to the animal called a dog, but implies the idea of *badness*.

Dogget. *Dogget's coat and badge.* The first prize in the Thames rowing-match, given on the 1st of August every year. So called from Thomas Dogget, an actor of Drury Lane, who signalised the accession of George I. to the throne by giving a waterman's coat and badge to the winner of the race. The Fishmongers' Company add a guinea to the prize. The race is from the "Swan" at London Bridge to the "Swan" at Chelsea.

Doggerel. Inferior sort of verse in rhymes.

Dogma (Greek). A religious doctrine formally stated. It now means a statement resting on the *ipse dixit* of the speaker. Dogmatic teaching used to mean the teaching of religious doctrines, but now dogmatic means overbearing and dictatorial. (Greek *dogma,* gen. *dogmatos,* a matter of opinion; verb *dokeo,* to think, whence *dogmatizo.*)

Dogmatic Facts.
(1) The supreme authority of the Pope of Rome over all churches.
(2) His right to decide arbitrarily all controversies.
(3) His right to convoke councils at will.
(4) His right to revise, repeal, or confirm decrees.
(5) His right to issue decrees bearing on discipline, morals and doctrine.
(6) The Pope is the centre of communion, and separation from him is excommunication.

(7) He has ultimate authority to appoint all bishops.

(8) He has power to depose any ecclesiastic.

(9) He has power to judge every question of doctrine, and pronounce infallibly what the Church shall or shall not accept.

Dogmatic School of Medicine-Founded by Hippoc'ratēs, and so called because it set out certain dogmas or theoretical principles which it made the basis of practice.

Dogmatic Theology is that which treats of the *dog'mata* (doctrines) of religion.

Doiley. (*See* DOYLEY.)

Doit (1 syl.). *Not a doit.* The doit was a Scotch silver coin = one-third of a farthing. In England the doit was a base coin of small value prohibited by 3 Henry V. c. 1.

"When they will not give a doit to relieve a lame beggar, they will lay out ten to see a dead Indian."—*Shakespeare : The Tempest*, ii. 2.

Dola'bra. A Roman axe.
Dolābra fossōria. The pickaxe' used by miners and excavators.
Dolābra pontificālis. The priest's hatchet for slaughtering animals.

Dolce far Niente (Italian). Delightful idleness. Pliny has "*Jucundum tamen nihil agere*" (Ep. viii. 9).

Doldrums (*The*). The name given to that region of the ocean near the equator noted for calms, squalls, and baffling winds, between the N.E. and S.E. trade-winds.

"But from the bluff-head, where I watched to-day, I saw her in the doldrums."
Byron: The Island, canto ii. stanza 21.

In the doldrums. In the dumps.

Dole, lamentation, from the Latin *doleo*, to grieve.

"He [the dwarf] found the dead bodies, wherefore he made great dole."—*S. Lanier : King Arthur*, book i. chap. xiv.

Dole, a portion allotted, is the Anglo-Saxon *dál*, a portion.

"Heaven has in store a precious dole."
Keble: Christian Year (4th Sunday after Trinity).

Happy man be his dole. May his share or lot be that of a happy or fortunate man.

"Wherein, happy man be his dole, I trust that I Shall not speed worst, and that very quickly."
Damon and Pythias, i. 177.

Dole-fish. The share of fish allotted to each one of a company of fishermen in a catch. Dole = the part *dealt* to anyone. (Anglo-Saxon, *dál* or *dæl*, from the verb *dæl-an*, to divide into parts.)

Doll Money. A lady of Duxford left a sum of money to be given away annually in the parish, and to be called *Doll Money*. Doll is a corruption of *dole*, Saxon *dál* (a share distributed).

Dollar. Marked thus $, either *scutum* or 8, a dollar being a "piece of eight" [reals]. The two lines indicate a contraction, as in ℔.

The word is a variant of *thaler* (Low German, *dahler ;* Danish, *daler*), and means "a valley," our *dale.* The counts of Schlick, at the close of the fifteenth century, extracted from the mines at *Joachim's thal* (Joachim's valley) silver which they coined into ounce-pieces. These pieces, called *Joachim's-thalers,* gained such high repute that they became a standard coin. Other coins being made like them were called *thalers* only. The American dollar equals 100 cents, in English money a little more than four shillings.

Dolly Murrey. A character in Crabbe's *Borough,* who died playing cards.

"'A vole! a vole !' she cried, ''tis fairly won.'...
This said she, gently, with a single sigh,
Died as one taught and practised how to die."
Crabbe: Borough.

Dolly Shop. A shop where rags and refuse are bought and sold. So called from the black doll suspended over it as a sign. Dolly shops are, in reality, no better than unlicensed pawnshops. A black doll used to be the sign hung out to denote the sale of silks and muslins which were fabricated by Indians.

Dolmen. A name given in France to what we term "cromlechs." These ancient remains are often called by the rural population devils' tables, fairies' tables, and so on. (Celtic, *stone tables.*) It consists of a slab resting on unhewn upright stones. Plural *dolmens* (*dol,* a table ; *men,* a stone).

"The Indian dolmens ... may be said to be identical with those of Western Europe."—*J. Lubbock: Prehistoric Times*, chap. v. p. 129.

Dolopa'tos. A French metrical version of San'dabar's *Parables,* written by Hebers or Herbers or Prince Philippe, afterwards called Philippe *le Hardi.* Dolopa'tos is the Sicilian king, and Virgil the tutor of his son Lucinien. (*See* SEVEN WISE MASTERS.)

Dolorous Dettie (*The*). John Skelton wrote an elegy on Henry Percy, fourth Earl of Northumberland, who fell a victim to the avarice of Henry VII. (1489). This elegy he entitled thus: "Upon the Dolorous Dettie and

Much Lamentable Chaunce of the Most Honorable Earl of Northumberland."

Dolphin. Called a sea-goose (*oie de mer*) from the form of its snout, termed in French *bec d'oie* (a goose's beak). The dolphin is noted for its changes of colour when taken out of the water.

" Parting day
Dies like the dolphin, whom each pang imbues
With a new colour as it gasps away,
The last still loveliest."
Byron: Childe Harold, canto iv. stanza 29.

Dolphin (*The*), in mediæval art, symbolises social love.

Dom. A title applied in the Middle Ages to the Pope, and at a somewhat later period to other Church dignitaries. It is now restricted to priests and choir monks among the Benedictines, and some few other monastic orders, as Dom Mabillon, Dom Calmet. The Spanish *don*, Portuguese *dom*, German *von*, and French *de*, are pretty well equivalent to it. (Latin, *dom'inus*.)

Dombey (*Florence*). A motherless child, hungering and thirsting to be loved, but regarded with frigid indifference by her father, who thinks that sons alone are worthy of his regard. (*Dickens: Dombey and Son.*)

Mr. Dombey. A self-sufficient, purseproud, frigid merchant, who feels satisfied there is but one Dombey in the world, and that is himself. (*Dickens: Dombey and Son.*)

Dom-Daniel. The abode of evil spirits, gnomes, and enchanters, somewhere " under the roots of the ocean," but not far from Babylon. (*Continuation of the Arabian Tales.*)

" In tɔe Domdaniel caverns
Under the roots of the ocean." *Southey.*

Domesday Book consists of two volumes, one a large folio, and the other a quarto, the material of each being vellum. It was formerly kept in the Exchequer, under three different locks and keys, but is now kept in the Record Office. The date of the survey is 1086. Northumberland, Cumberland, Westmoreland, and Durham are not included in the survey, though parts of Westmoreland and Cumberland are taken.

The value of all estates is given, firstly, as in the time of the Confessor; secondly, when bestowed by the Conqueror; and, thirdly, at the time of the survey. It is also called *The King's Book*, and *The Winchester Roll* because it was kept there. Printed in facsimile in 1783 and 1816.

Stow says the book was so called because it was deposited in a part of Winchester Cathedral called *Domus-dei*, and that the word is a contraction of Domus-dei book ; more likely it is connected with the previous surveys made by the Saxon kings, and called *dom-bocs* (libri judicia'les), because every case of dispute was decided by an appeal to these registers.

" Then seyde Gamelyn to the Justice . .
Thou hast given domes that bin evil dight,
I will sitten in thy sete, and dressen him aright."
Chaucer: Canterbury Tales (The Cookes Tale).

Domestic. *England's domestic poet.* William Cowper, author of *The Task*. (1731-1800.)

Domestic Poultry, in Dryden's *Hind and Panther*, means the Roman Catholic clergy. So called from an establishment of priests in the private chapel at Whitehall. The nuns are termed " sister partlet with her hooded head."

Domiciliary Visit (*A*). An official visit to search the house.

Dominic (*St.*). (1170-1221.) A Spanish priest who founded the Inquisition, and the order called the Dominicans or Preaching Friars. He was called by the Pope " Inquisitor - General," and was canonised by Gregory IX.

⁂ Some say the Inquisition existed in 1184, when Dominic was under fourteen years of age.

He is represented with a sparrow at his side, and a dog carrying in its mouth a burning torch. The devil, it is said, appeared to the saint in the form of a sparrow, and the dog refers to a dream which his mother had during pregnancy. She dreamt that she had given birth to a dog, spotted with black and white spots, which lighted the world with a burning torch.

He is also represented sometimes with a city in his hand and a star either on his forehead or on his breast ; sometimes also with a sword in his hand and a pile of books burning beside him, to denote his severity with heretics.

Domin'ical Letters. The letters which denote the Sundays or *diēs domin'ica*. The first seven letters of the alphabet are employed ; so that if A stands for the first Sunday in the year, the other six letters will stand for the other days of the week, and the octave Sunday will come round to A again. In this case A will be the Sunday or Dominical Letter for the whole year.

Domin'icans. Preaching friars founded by Dominic de Guzman, at Toulouse, in 1215. Formerly called in

England *Black Friars*, from their black dress, and in France *Jac'obins*, because their mother-establishment in Paris was in the Rue St. Jacques.

Dom'inie Sampson. A village schoolmaster and scholar, poor as a church mouse, and modest as a girl. He cites Latin like a *porcus litera'rum*, and exclaims "Prodigious!" (*Scott: Guy Mannering.*) (*See* STILLING.)

Dominions. One of the orders of angels, symbolised in Christian art by an ensign.

Domino (*A*). A hood worn by canons; a mask.

"Ce nom, qu'on donnait autrefois, par allusion à quelque passage de la liturgie, au *camail* dont les prêtres se couvrent la tête et les épaules pendant l'hiver, ne désigne aujourd'hui qu'un habit de déguisement pour les bals masqués."—*Bouillet: Dictionnaire des Sciences*, etc.

Dom'inoes (3 syl.). The teeth; also called ivories. Dominoes are made of ivory.

Domisel'lus. The son of a king, prince, knight, or lord before he has entered on the order of knighthood. Also an attendant on some abbot or nobleman. The person domiciled in your house. Hence the king's body-guards were called his *damoiseaux* or *damsels*.

Froissart styles Richard II. *le jeune damoisel Richart.* Similarly Louis VII. (*Le Jeune*) was called the *royal damsel*.

"Damoisel ou Damoiseau désignait autrefois les fils de chevaliers, de barons, et toutes les jeunes gentilshommes qui n'étaient pas encore chevaliers. On le donnait aussi aux fils des rois qui n'étaient pas encore en état de porter les armes."—*Bouillet: Dict. Universel.*

Domisellus and domisella are diminutives of *dominus*, a lord. In old French we find *damoiseau* and *damoiselle*. The word Ma-demoiselle is ma domisella or damoiselle.

Don is do-on, as "Don your bonnet." (*See* DOFF, DUP.)

"Then up he rose, and donned his clothes,
And dupp'd the chamber door."
Shakespeare: Hamlet, iv. 5.

Don. A man of mark, an aristocrat. At the universities the masters, fellows, and noblemen are termed *dons*. (Spanish.)

Don Giovan'ni. Mozart's best opera. (*See* DON JUAN.)

Don Ju'an. A native of Sev'ille, son of Don José and Donna Inez, a blue-stocking. When Juan was sixteen years old he got into trouble with Donna Julia, and was sent by his mother, then a widow, on his travels. His adventures form the story of the poem, which is incomplete. (*Byron: Don Juan.*)

A Don Juan. A libertine of the aristocratic class. The original of this character was Don Juan Teno'rio of Seville, who lived in the fourteenth century. The traditions concerning him have been dramatised by Tirso de Mo'lina; thence passed into Italy and France. Glück has a musical ballet of *Don Juan*, and Mozart has immortalised the character in his opera of *Don Giovanni* (1787).

Don Quixote (2 syl.). A gaunt country gentleman of La Mancha, gentle and dignified, affectionate and simple-minded, but so crazed by reading books of knight-errantry that he believes himself called upon to redress the wrongs of the whole world, and actually goes forth to avenge the oppressed and run a tilt with their oppressors. The word Quixote means *The cuish-armed*. (*See* QUIXOTIC.)

A Don Quixote. A dreamy, unpractical man, with a "bee in his bonnet."

Donation of Pepin (*The*). When Pepin conquered Ataulf the ex-archate of Ravenna fell into his hands. Pepin gave both the ex-archate and the Republic of Rome to the Pope, and this munificent gift is the famous "Donation" on which rested the whole fabric of the temporal power of the Popes of Rome (A.D. 755).

Victor Emmanuel, King of Italy, dispossessed the Pope of his temporal dominions, and added the Papal States to the united kingdom of Italy (1870).

Don'atists. Followers of Dona'tus, a Numidian bishop who opposed Cecilia'nus. Their chief dogma is that the outward church is nothing, "for the letter killeth, it is the spirit that giveth life." (Founded 314.)

Doncaster. Sigebert, monk of Gemblours, in 1100, derived this word from Thong-ceaster, the "Castle of the thong," and says that Hengist and Horsa purchased of the British king as much land as he could encompass with a leather thong. The thong was cut into strips, and encompassed the land occupied by the city of Doncaster.

This is the old tale of Dido and the hide, and so is the Russian Yakutsks. (*See* BURSA.)

⁂ Of course it means the "City on the river Don." (Celtic, *Don*, that which spreads.)

Dondasch'. An Oriental giant contemporary with Seth, to whose service he was attached. He needed no weapons, as he could destroy anything by the mere force of his arms.

Done Brown. *He was done brown.* Completely bamboozled or made a fool of. This is a variety of the many expressions of a similar meaning connected with cooking, such as "I gave him a roasting," "I cooked his goose," "I cut him into mince-meat," "I put him into a pretty stew," "I settled his hash," "He was dished up," "He was well dressed" [drubbed], "He was served out," etc. (*See* COOKING.)

Done For or *Regularly done for.* Utterly ruined. This "for" is the adverb = thoroughly, very common as a prefix.

Done Up. Thoroughly tired and wearied out. Up means ended, completed, as the "game is up" (over, finished), and adverbially it means "completely," hence to be "done up" is to be exhausted completely.

Don'egild (3 syl.). The wicked mother of Alla, King of Northumberland. Hating Cunstance because she was a Christian, she put her on a raft with her infant son, and turned her adrift. When Alla returned from Scotland and discovered this cruelty of his mother, he put her to death. (*Chaucer: Man of Lawes Tale.*)

⁎⁎ The tradition of St. Mungo resembles the *Man of Lawes Tale* in many respects.

Donkey. An ass. It was made to rhyme with "monkey," but is never now so pronounced. The word means a little tawny or dun-coloured animal.

Donkey. The cross of the donkey's back is popularly attributed to the honour conferred on the beast by our Lord, who rode on an ass in "His triumphant entry" into Jerusalem on Palm Sunday. (*See* CHRISTIAN TRADITIONS.)

The donkey means one thing and the driver another. Different people see from different standpoints, their own interest in every case directing their judgment. The allusion is to a fable in Phædrus, where a donkey-driver exhorts his donkey to flee, as the enemy is at hand. The donkey asks if the enemy will load him with double pack-saddles. "No," says the man. "Then," replies the donkey, "what care I whether you are my master or someone else?"

To ride the black donkey. To be pig-headed, obstinate like a donkey. Black is added, not so much to designate the colour, as to express what is bad.

Two more, and up goes the donkey—*i.e.* two pennies more, and the donkey shall be balanced on the top of the pole or ladder. It is said to a braggart, and means—what you have said is wonderful, but if we admit it without gainsaying we shall soon be treated with something still more astounding.

Who ate the donkey? When the French were in their flight from Spain, after the battle of Vittoria, some stragglers entered a village and demanded rations. The villagers killed a donkey, and served it to their hated foes. Next day they continued their flight, and were waylaid by the villagers, who assaulted them most murderously, jeering them as they did so with the shout, "Who ate the donkey?"

Who stole the donkey? This was for many years a jeer against policemen. When the force was first established a donkey was stolen, but the police failed to discover the thief, and this failure gave rise to the laugh against them.

Who stole the donkey? Answer: "The man with the white hat." It was said, in the middle of the nineteenth century, that white hats were made of the skins of donkeys, and that many donkeys were stolen and sold to hatters.

Donkey Engine (*A*). A small engine of from two to four horse-power.

Do'ny. Florimel's dwarf. (*Spenser: Faërie Queene*, book iii. canto 5.)

Don'zel (Italian). A squire or young man of good birth.

"He is esquire to a knight-errant, donzel to the damsels."—*Butler: Characters.*

Doo'lin of Mayence. The hero of a French romance of chivalry, and the father of Ogier the Dane.

Doolin's Sword. Merveilleuse (wonderful). (*See* SWORD.)

Doom. *The crack of doom.* The signal for the final judgment.

Doom Book (*dom-boc*) is the book of dooms or judgments compiled by King Alfred. (*See* DOOMSDAY BOOK.)

Doom-rings, or *Circles of Judgment.* An Icelandic term for circles of stones resembling Stonehenge and Avebury.

Dooms'day Sedgwick. William Sedgwick, a fanatical prophet and preacher during the Commonwealth. He pretended to have had it revealed to him in a vision that doomsday was at hand; and, going to the house of Sir Francis Russell, in Cambridgeshire, he called upon a party of gentlemen playing at bowls to leave off and prepare for the approaching dissolution.

Doomstead. The horse of the Scandinavian Nornes or Fates. (*See* HORSE.)

Door. (Greek, *thura;* Anglo-Saxon, *dora.*)

The door must be either shut or open. It must be one way or the other. This is from a French comedy called *Le Grondeur,* where the master scolds his servant for leaving the door open. The servant says that he was scolded the last time for shutting it, and adds: "Do you wish it shut?"—"No."—"Do you wish it open?"—"No."—"Why," says the man, "it must be either shut or open."

He laid the charge at my door. He accused me of doing it.

Next door to it. As, if not so, it was next door to it, *i.e.* very like it, next-door neighbour to it.

Sin lieth at the door (Gen. iv. 7). The blame of sin lies at the door of the wrong-doer, and he must take the consequences.

Door Nail. (*See* DEAD.) Scrooge's partner is "dead as a door-nail." (*Dickens: Christmas Carol,* chap. i.)

Door-opener (*The*). So Cratēs, the Theban, was called, because every morning he used to go round Athens and rebuke the people for their late rising.

Door-tree (*A*). The wooden bar of a door to secure it at night from intruders. Also a door-post.

Doors [*house*]. As, come indoors, go indoors. So Virgil: "*Tum foribus divæ* . . [*Dido*] . . *resedit.*" (Then Dido seated herself in the house or temple of the goddess.) (*Æneid,* i. 505.)

Out of doors. Outside the house; in the open air.

Doorm. An earl called "the Bull," who tried to make Enid his handmaid; but, when she would neither eat, drink, nor array herself in bravery at his bidding, "he smote her on the cheek;" whereupon her lord and husband, Count Geraint, starting up, slew the "russet-bearded earl" in his own hall. (*Tennyson: Idylls of the King; Enid.*)

Dora. The first wife of David Copperfield; she was a child-wife, but no help-meet. She could do nothing of practical use, but looked on her husband with idolatrous love. Tennyson has a poem entitled *Dora.*

Dorado (*El*). (*See* EL DORADO.)

Dorax. A Portuguese renegade, in Dryden's *Don Sebastian*—by far the best of all his characters.

Dor'cas Society. A society for supplying the poor with clothing. So called from Dorcas, mentioned in Acts ix. 39.

Dor'chester. *As big as a Dorchester butt.* Very corpulent, like the butts of Dorchester. Of Toby Filpot it is said:

" His breath-doors of life on a sudden were shut,
And he died full as big as a Dorchester butt."
O'Keefe: Poor Soldier.

Do'ric. The oldest, strongest, and simplest of the Grecian orders of architecture. So called from Doris, in Greece, or the Dorians who employed it. The Greek Doric is simpler than the Roman imitation. The former stands on the pavement without fillet or other ornament, and the flutes are not scalloped. The Roman column is placed on a plinth, has fillets, and the flutings, both top and bottom, are scalloped.

Doric Dialect. The dialect spoken by the natives of Doris, in Greece. It was broad and hard. Hence, any broad dialect.

Doric Land. Greece, Doris being a part of Greece.

"Through all the bounds
Of Doric land."
Milton: Paradise Lost, book i. 519.

Do'ric Reed. Pastoral poetry. Everything Doric was very plain, but cheerful, chaste, and solid. The Dorians were the pastoral people of Greece, and their dialect was that of the country rustics. Our own Bloomfield and Robert Burns are examples of British Doric.

" The Doric reed once more
Well pleased, I tune."
Thomson: Autumn, 3-4.

Dor'icourt. A sort of Tremaine of the eighteenth century, who, having over-refined his taste by the "grand tour," considers English beauties insipid. He falls in love with Letitia Hardy at a masquerade, after feeling aversion to her in her assumed character of a hoyden. (*Mrs. Cowley: The Belle's Stratagem.*)

Dor'igen. A lady of high family, who married Arvir'agus out of pity for his love and meekness. She was greatly beloved by Aurelius, to whom she had been long known. Aurelius, during the absence of Arviragus, tried to win the heart of the young wife; but Dorigen made answer that she would never listen to him till the rocks that beset the coast of Britain are removed "and there n'is no stone yseen." Aurelius, by the aid of a young magician of Orleans, caused all the rocks to disappear, and claimed his reward. Dorigen was very sad, but her husband insisted that she should keep her word, and she went to meet Aurelius. When Aurelius saw how sad she was, and heard what Arviragus had counselled, he said he would rather die than injure so true a wife and noble a gentleman. So she returned to her husband happy and untainted. (*See* DIANORA.) (*Chaucer : Franklines Tale.*)

Dor'imant. Drawn from the Earl of Rochester ; a witty, aristocratic libertine, in Etherege's *Man of Mode.*

Dorinda, in the verses of the Earl of Dorset, is Catherine Sedley, Countess of Dorchester, mistress of James II.

Dormer Window. The window of an attic standing out from the slope of the roof. (O. French, *dormeor*=a sleeping room formerly fitted with windows of this kind.)

"Thatched were the roofs, with dormer windows."
Longfellow : Evangeline, part i. stanza 1.

Dornock. Stout figured linen for tablecloths ; so called from a town in Scotland, where it was originally made.

Dorothea (*St.*), represented with a rose-branch in her hand, a wreath of roses on her head, and roses with fruit by her side ; sometimes with an angel carrying a basket with three apples and three roses. The legend is that Theophilus, the judge's secretary, scoffingly said to her, as she was going to execution, "Send me some fruit and roses, Dorothea, when you get to Paradise." Immediately after her execution, while Theophilus was at dinner with a party of companions, a young angel brought to him a basket of apples and roses, saying, "From Dorothea, in Paradise," and vanished. Theophilus, of course, was a convert from that moment.

Dorset. Once the seat of a British tribe, calling themselves *Dwr-trigs* (waterdwellers). The Romans colonised the settlement, and Latinised *Dwr-trigs* into *Duro-triges.* Lastly came the Saxons, and translated the original words into their own tongue, *dor-sætta* (waterdwellers).

Dorse'tian Downs. The Downs of Dorsetshire.

"Spread the pure Dorsetian downs
In boundless prospect."
Thomson : Autumn.

Dosith'eans. A religious sect which sprang up in the first century ; so called because they believed that Dosith'eus had a divine mission superior to that of prophets and apostles.

Do'son. A promise-maker and a promise-breaker. Antig'onos, grandson of Demetrios *the besieger*, was so called.

Doss. A hassock stuffed with straw; a bed—properly, a straw bed ; whence the cant word for a lodging-house is a dossingken. *Dossel* is an old word for a bundle of hay or straw, and *dosser* for a straw basket. These words were common in Elizabeth's reign. The French *dossier* means a "bundle."

Doss-house (*A*). A cheap lodginghouse where the poorer classes sleep on bundles of straw. (*See above.*)

In the *New Review* (Aug., 1894) there is an article entitled "In a Woman's Doss-house," which throws much light on the condition of the poor in London.

Dosser. One who sleeps in a low or cheap hired dormitory. The verb *doss* =to sleep.

Do-the-Boys' Hall. A school where boys were taken in and done for by a Mr. Squeers, a puffing, ignorant, overbearing brute, who starved them and taught them nothing. (*Dickens : Nicholas Nickleby.*)

.: It is said that Mr. Squeers is a caricature of Mr. Shaw, a Yorkshire schoolmaster ; but Mr. Shaw was a kindhearted man, and his boys were well fed, happy, and not ill-taught. Like Squeers he had only one eye, and like Squeers he had a daughter. It is said that his school was ruined by Dickens's caricature.

Dot and go One (*A*). An infant just beginning to toddle ; one who limps in walking ; a person who has one leg longer than the other.

Dot'terel or *Dottrel.* A doting old fool ; an old man easily cajoled. The bird thus called, a species of plover, is said to be so fond of imitation that any one who excites its curiosity by strange antics may catch it.

To dor the dotterel. Dor is an archaic word meaning to trick or cheat. Whence the phrase to "dor the dotterel" means to cheat the simpleton.

Dou'ay Bible. The English translation of the Bible sanctioned by the Roman Catholic Church. The Old Testament was published by the English college at Douay, in France, in 1609 ; but the New Testament was published at Rheims in 1582. The English college at Douay was founded by William Allen (afterwards cardinal) in 1568. The Douay Bible translates such words as *repentance* by the word *penance*, etc., and the whole contains notes by Roman Catholic divines.

Double (*To*). To pass or sail round, as "to double the cape." The cape (or point) is twice between the ship and the land. (French, *doubler;* Latin, *duo-plico.*)

"What capes he doubled, and what continent,
The gulfs and straits that strangely he had past."
Dryden: Ideas, stanza 1.

Double Dealing. Professing one thing and doing another inconsistent with that promise.

"[She] was quite above all double-dealing. She had no mental reservation."—*Maria Edgeworth.*

Double Dutch. Gibberish, jargon, or a foreign tongue not understood by the hearer. Dutch is a synonym for foreign; and double is simply excessive, in a twofold degree.

Double-edged Sword. Literally, a sword which cuts either way; metaphorically, an argument which makes both for and against the person employing it, or which has a double meaning.

"'Your Delphic sword,' the panther then replied,
'Is double-edged, and cuts on either side.'"
Dryden: Hind and Panther, part iii. 191—2.

Double Entendre (English-French for *Un mot à double entente,* or *à deux ententes*). Words which secretly express a rude or coarse covert meaning, generally of a licentious character. "Entendre" is the infinitive mood of a verb, and is never used as a noun.

Double First (*A*). In the first class both of the classical and mathematical final examination in the Oxford University; or of the classical and mathematical triposes of the University of Cambridge.

Double-headed Eagle (*The*). The German eagle has its head turned to our left hand, and the Roman eagle to our right hand. When Charlemagne was made "Kaiser of the Holy Roman Empire," he joined the two heads together, one looking east and the other west.

Double-tongued. One who makes contrary declarations on the same subject at different times; deceitful.

"Be grave, not double-tongued."—1 Tim. iii. 8.

Double up (*To*). To fold together. "To double up the fist" is to fold the fingers together so as to make the hand into a fist.

I doubled him up. I struck him in the wind, so as to make him double up with pain, or so as to leave him "all of a heap."

Double X. (*See* XX.)

Double or Quits. The winner stakes his stake, and the loser promises to pay twice the stake if he loses again; but if he wins the second throw he pays nothing, and neither player loses or wins anything. This is often done when the stake is 3d., and the parties have no copper : if the loser loses again, he pays 6d. ; if not, the winner does not claim his 3d.

Doubles or **Double-walkers.** Those aerial duplicates of men or women who represent them so minutely as to deceive those who know them. We apply the word to such persons as the Dromio brothers, the Corsican brothers, and the brothers Antiph'olus. The "head centre Stephens" is said to have had a double, who was perpetually leading astray those set to hunt him down.

Doubting Castle. The castle of the giant Despair, in which Christian and Hopeful were incarcerated, but from which they escaped by means of the key called "Promise." (*Bunyan : Pilgrim's Progress.*)

Douceur'. (French.) A gratuity for service rendered or promised.

Doug'las. The tutelary saint of the house of Douglas is St. Bridget. According to tradition, a Scottish king in 770, whose ranks had been broken by the fierce onset of the Lord of the Isles, saw the tide of battle turned in his favour by an unknown chief. After the battle the king asked who was the "Du-glass" chieftain, his deliverer, and received for answer *Sholto Du-glass* (Behold the dark-grey man you inquired for). The king then rewarded him with the Clydesdale valley for his services.

"'Let him not cross or thwart me,' said the page; 'for I will not yield him an inch of way, had he in his body the soul of every Douglas that has lived since the time of the Dark Gray Man.'"—*Scott : The Abbot,* chap. xxviii.

Black Douglas, introduced by Sir Walter Scott in *Castle Dangerous,* is James, eighth Lord Douglas, who twice took Douglas Castle from the English by stratagem. The first time he partly burnt it, and the second time he utterly razed it to the ground. The castle, says Godscroft, was nicknamed the hazardous or dangerous, because every one who attempted to keep it from the "gud schyr James" was in constant jeopardy by his wiles.

"The Good Sir James, the dreadful blacke Douglas',
That in his dayes so wise and worthie was,
Wha here and on the infidels of Spain,
Such honour, praise, and triumphs did obtain."
Gordon.

❊ The person generally called "Black Douglas" is William Douglas, lord of Nithsdale, who died in 1390. It was of this Douglas that Sir W. Scott said—

"The name of this indefatigable chief has become so formidable, that women used, in the northern counties, to still their froward children by threatening them with the Black Douglas."—*History of Scotland*, chap. xi.

Douglas Tragedy (*The*). A ballad in Scott's *Border Minstrelsy*. Lord William steals away Lady Margaret Douglas, but is pursued by her father and two brothers. Being overtaken, a fight ensues, in which the father and his two sons are sore wounded. Lord William, wounded, creeps to his mother's house, and there dies; the lady before sunrise next morning dies also.

Douse the Glim. Put out the light; also knock out a man's eye. To douse is to lower in haste, as "Douse the top-sail" Glim, gleam, glimmer, are variants of the same word.

"'And so you would turn honest, Captain Goffe, agrazing, would ye,' said an old weather-beaten pirate who had but one eye; 'what though he . . . . made my eye dowse the glim . . .'. . he is an honest man' . . . ."—*The Pirate*, chap. xxxiii.

Dousterswivel. A German swindler, who obtains money under the promise of finding buried wealth by a divining-rod. (*Scott: Antiquary*.)

Dout. A contraction of *do-out*, as don is of *do-on*, doff of *do-off*, and dup of *do-up*.

In Devonshire and other southern counties they still say *Dout the candle* and *Dout the fire*. In some counties extinguishers are called *douters*.

"The dram of base
Doth all the noble substance dout."
Shakespeare: Hamlet, i. 4.

Dove—*i.e.* the diver-bird; perhaps so called from its habit of ducking the head. So also *columba* (the Latin for dove) is the Greek *kolumbis* (a diver).

Dove (*The*). The dove, in Christian art, symbolises the Holy Ghost. In church windows the seven rays proceeding from the dove signify the seven gifts of the Holy Ghost. It also symbolises the human soul, and as such is represented coming out of the mouth of saints at death.

A dove with six wings is emblematic of the Church of Christ.

The seven gifts of the Holy Ghost are: (1) counsel, (2) the fear of the Lord, (3) fortitude, (4) piety, (5) understanding, (6) wisdom, and (7) knowledge.

Doves or *pigeons* not eaten as food in Russia. (*See* CHRISTIAN TRADITIONS.)

Doves or *pigeons*. The clergy of the Church of England are allegorised under this term in Dryden's *Hind and Panther*, part iii. 947, 998-1002.

"A sort of doves were noused too near the hall . . . [*i.e.* the private chapel at Whitehall] Our pampered pigeons, with malignant eyes, Beheld these inmates [the Roman Catholic clergy]. Tho' hard their fare, at evening and at morn, A cruse of water and an ear of corn, Yet still they grudged that modicum."

Soiled doves. Women of the demimonde.

Doves' Dung. In 2 Kings vi. 25, during the siege of Samaria, "there was a great famine . . . . and . . . . an ass's head was sold for fourscore pieces of silver, and the fourth part of a cab of dove's dung [*hariyonim*] for five pieces of silver." This "hariyonim" was a plant called chickpea, a common article of food still sold to pilgrims on their way to Mecca.

"In Damascus there are many tradesmen whose sole occupation is preparing [hariyonim] for sale. They have always been esteemed as provision meet for a lengthy journey, and are a necessary part of the outfit of all who travel in the remote parts of Syria and Asia Minor."—*Bible Flowers*, p. 71.

Dover (*A*). A réchauffé or cooked food done over again. In the professional slang of English cooks a *resurrection dish* is still called a *dover* (do over again).

Dover. *When Dover and Calais meet* —*i.e.* never.
A jack of Dover. A "jack" is a small drinking vessel made of waxed leather, and a "*jack*" of Dover" is a bottle of wine made up of fragments of opened bottles. It is customary to pour the refuse into a bottle, cork it up, and sell it as a fresh bottle. This is called dovering, a corruption of *do-over*, because the cork is done over with wax or resin.

"Many a jack of Dover hast thou sold."
Chaucer: Coke's Prologue.

Dovers (Stock Exchange term). The South-Eastern railway shares. The line runs to Dover. (*See* CLARAS; STOCK EXCHANGE SLANG.)

Dovercot or *Dovercourt*. A confused gabble; a Babel. According to legend, Dover Court church, in Essex, once possessed a cross that spoke; and Foxe says the crowd to the church was so great "that no man could shut the door." The confusion of this daily throng gave rise to the term.

"And now the rood of Dovercot did speak, Confirming his opinions to be true."
Collier of Croydon.

Dovetail. Metaphorically, to fit on or fit in nicely; to correspond. It is a word in carpentry, and means the fitting one board into another by a tenon in the shape of a dove's tail, or wedge reversed.

Dowgate Ward (London). Some derive it from *Dour* (water), it being next to the Thames, at the foot of the hill; others say it is "Down-gate," the gate of the down, dune, or hill, as Brighton Downs (hills), South-downs, etc.

Dowlas (*Mr.*). A generic name for a linendraper, who sells dowlas, a coarse linen cloth, so called from Doulens in Picardy, where it is manufactured.

Dowling (*Captain*). A character in Crabbe's *Borough;* a great drunkard, who died in his cups.

"'Come, fill my glass.' He took it and he went "
(*i.e.* died).   *Letter* xvi.

Down. *He is quite down in the mouth.* Out of spirits; disheartened. When persons are very sad and low-spirited, the corners of the mouth are drawn down. "Down in the jib" is a nautical phrase of the same meaning.

Down in the Dumps. Low-spirited.

Down on Him (*To be*). *I was down on him in a minute.* I pounced on him directly; I detected his trick immediately. Also to treat harshly. The allusion is to birds of prey.

Down on his Luck. In ill-luck.

"'I guess, stranger, you'll find me an ex-president down on his luck.'"—*A. Egmont Hake: Paris Originals* (Professors of Languages).

Down to the Ground. *That suits me down to the ground.* Entirely.

Down - hearted. Without spirit; the heart prostrated.

Down Town. *I am going down town,* *i.e.* to the business part of the town.

Down the country properly means down the slope of the land, or as the rivers run.

⁂ We say "I am going up to town" when we mean out of the country into the chief city.

Down-trod. Despised, as one trodden under foot.

"I will lift
The down-trod Mortimer as high i' the air
As this ungrateful king."
Shakespeare: 1 *Henry IV.*, i. 3.

Downfall (*A*). A heavy shower of rain; a loss of social position.

Downing Professor. The Professor of the Laws of England in the University of Cambridge. This chair was founded in 1800 by Sir George Downing, Bart.

Downing Street (London). Named after Sir George Downing, who died 1684. He was elected M.P. for Morpeth in 1661.

Downpour (*A*). A very heavy shower of rain. "A regular downpour."

Downright. Thoroughly, as "downright honest," "downright mad"; outspoken; utter, as a "downright shame." The word means from top to bottom, throughout.

Downright Dunstable. Very blunt, plain speaking. The present town of Dunstable is at the foot of the Chiltern Hills, in Bedfordshire. There was somewhere about the same site a Roman station called Magionium or Magintum, utterly destroyed by the Danes, and afterwards overgrown by trees. Henry I. founded the present town, and built there a palace and priory.

"If this is not plain speaking, there is no such place as downright Dunstable."—*Sir W. Scott: Redgauntlet*, chap. xvii.

Downstairs. Stairs leading from a higher to a lower floor; on the lowest floor, as "I am downstairs."

Downy (*The*). Bed. *Gone to the downy,* gone to bed. Bed being stuffed with down.

Downy Cove (*A*). A knowing fellow, *up* to every dodge. On the "*lucus a non lucendo*" principle, contraries are often substituted in slang and facetious phrases. (*See* LUCUS A NON LUCENDO.)

Dow'sabell. Daughter of Cassamen, a knight of Arden, who fell in love with a shepherd. The two make love with Arcadian simplicity, and vow eternal fidelity.

"With that she bent her snow-white knee,
Down by the shepherd kneelèd she,
    And him she sweetly kist.
With that the shepherd whooped for joy.
Quoth he, 'There's never shepherd boy
    That ever was so blist.'"
Drayton: Dowsabel.' (a ballad).

Dowse on the Chops (*A*). A ding or blow on the face. "A dowse on the blubber-chops of my friend the baronet" means a setting down, a snubbing.

Doxy. A baby; a plaything; a paramour. In the West of England babies are called *doxies.*

Doyleys. Now means a small cloth used to cover dessert plates; but originally it had a much wider meaning. Thus Dryden speaks of "doyley petticoats;"

and Steele, in No. 102 of the *Tatler*, speaks of his "doiley suit." The Doyleys were linen-drapers, No. 346, east corner of Upper Wellington Street, Strand, from the time of Queen Anne to the year 1850.

Dozen. (*See* BAKER'S DOZEN.)

D. P. or **Dom. Proc.** The House of Lords. (Latin, *Domus Procĕrum.*)

Drac. A sort of fairy in human form, whose abode is the caverns of rivers. Sometimes these dracs will float like golden cups along a stream to entice women and children bathing, and when they attempt to catch the prize drag them under water. (*South of France mythology.*)

Fare le drac, same as "Faire le diable." Irish, "Play the Puck;" English, "Play the deuce."

"Belomen qu' yeu faré le Drac
Se jamay trebi dins un sac
Cinc ô siés milante pistolos
Espessos como de redolos."
Goudelin: Castle en l'Ayre.

Dra'chenfels (Dragon-rocks). So called from the legendary dragon killed there by Siegfried, the hero of the Nibelungen-Lied.

"The castled crag of Drachenfels
Frowns o'er the wide and winding Rhine,
Whose breast of waters broadly swells
Between the banks which bear the vine."
Byron: Childe Harold, iii. 55.

Draco'nian Code. One very severe. Draco was an Athenian law-maker. As every violation of a law was made in this code a capital offence, Dema'dēs the orator said "that Draco's code was written in human blood."

Draft. The Druids borrowed money on promises of repayment after death (*Patricius*). Purchas tells us of some priests of Pekin, who barter with the people in bills of exchange, to be paid in heaven a hundredfold.

Draft on Aldgate (*A*), or *A draft on Aldgate pump.* A worthless note of hand; a fraudulent draft or money order. The pun is between draft or draught of drink, and draft a money order on a bank.

Drag in, Neck and Crop, or *To drag in, head and shoulders.* To introduce a subject or remark abruptly. (*See* A PROPOS DE BOTTES.)

Draggle-tail. A slut; a woman who allows her petticoats to trail in the dirt. The word should be "daggletail" (*q.v.*), from the Scotch *dag* (dew on the grass), *daggle* (wet with the grass-dew), like the Latin *collu'tulo irro'ro.*

Drag'oman (plural, *Dragomans*). A cicerone; a guide or interpreter to foreigners. (Arabic *targuman*, an interpreter; whence *targum.*)

"My dragoman had me completely in his power, and I resolved to become independent of all interpreters."—*Baker: Albert Nyanza*, chap. i. p. 3.

Dragon. The Greek word *drakŏn* comes from a verb meaning "to see," to "look at," and more remotely "to watch" and "to flash."

The animal called a dragon is a winged crocodile with a serpent's tail; whence the words serpent and dragon are sometimes interchangeable.

From the meaning *a watcher* we get the notion of one that watches; and from the meaning "to flash," we connect the word with *meteors.*

"Swift, swift, ye dragons of the night !—that dawning
May bare the raven's eye."
Shakespeare: Cymbeline, ii. 2.

Dragon. This word is used by ecclesiastics of the Middle Ages as the symbol of sin in general and paganism in particular. The metaphor is derived from Rev. xii. 9, where Satan is termed "the great dragon." In Ps. xci. 13 it is said that the saints "shall trample the dragon under their feet." In the story of the Fall, Satan appeared to Eve in the semblance of a serpent, and the promise was made that in the fulness of time the seed of the woman should bruise the serpent's head.

Another source of dragon legends is the Celtic use of the word for "a chief." Hence *pen-dragon* (summus rex), a sort of dictator, created in times of danger. Those knights who slew a chief in battle slew a dragon, and the military title soon got confounded with the fabulous monster. Dragon, meaning "quick-sighted," is a very suitable word for a general.

Some great *inundations* have also been termed serpents or dragons. Hence Apollo (the sun) is said to have destroyed the serpent Python (*i.e.* dried up the overflow). Similarly, St. Roma'nus delivered the city of Rouen from a dragon, named *Gargouille* (waterspout), which lived in the river Seine.

From the-idea of *watching*, we have a dragon placed in the garden of the Hesper'īdēs; and a duenna is poetically called a dragon :

"In England the garden of beauty is kept
By a dragon of prudery placed within call ;
But so oft the unamiable dragon hath slept,
That the garden's but carelessly watched after all."
T. Moore: Irish Melodies, No. 2 (" We may roam through this world," etc.).

" A spiteful, violent, tyrannical woman is called a dragoness.

The blind dragon, the third party who plays propriety in flirtations.

"This state of affairs was hailed with undisguised thankfulness by the rector, whose feeling for harmony had been rudely jarred by the necessity of his acting the blind dragon."—*J. O. Hobbes: Some Emotions and a Moral*, chap. iv.

Dragon in Christian art symbolises Satan or sin. In the pictures of St. Michael and St. Margaret it typifies their conquest over sin. Similarly, when represented at the feet of Christ and the Virgin Mary. The conquest of St. George and St. Silvester over a dragon means their triumph over paganism. In the pictures of St. Martha it means the inundation of the Rhone, spreading pestilence and death; similarly, St. Romanus delivered Rouen from the inundation of the Seine, and Apollo's conquest of the python means the same thing. St. John the Evangelist is sometimes represented holding a chalice, from which a winged dragon is issuing.

Ladies guarded by dragons. The walls of feudal castles ran winding round the building, and the ladies were kept in the securest part. As adventurers had to scale the walls to gain access to the ladies, the authors of romance said they overcame the serpent-like defence, or the dragon that guarded them. Sometimes there were two walls, and then the bold invader overcame two dragons in his attempt to liberate the captive damsel. (*See* ENCHANTED CASTLES.)

A flying dragon. A meteor.

The Chinese dragon. In China, the drawing of a five-clawed dragon is not only introduced into pictures, but is also embroidered on state dresses and royal robes. This representation is regarded as an amulet.

The Green Dragon. A public-house sign in compliment to St. George.

The Red Dragon. A public-house sign in compliment to Henry VII., who adopted this device for his standard at Bosworth Field. It was the ensign of Cadwallader, the last of the British kings, from whom the Tudors descended.

Dragon Slayers.

(1) St. Philip the Apostle is said to have destroyed a huge dragon at Hierapolis, in Phrygia.

(2) St. Martha killed the terrible dragon called Tarasque at Aix (la Chapelle).

(3) St. Florent killed a dragon which haunted the Loire.

(4) St. Cado, St. Maudet, and St. Paul did similar feats in Brittany.

(5) St. Keyne of Cornwall slew a dragon.

(6) St. Michael, St. George, St. Margaret, Pope Sylvester, St. Samson (Archbishop of Dol), Don'atus (fourth century), St. Clement of Metz, and many others, killed dragons.

(7) St. Romain of Rouen destroyed the huge dragon called La Gargouille, which ravaged the Seine.

Dragon of Wantley (*i.e.* Warncliff, in Yorkshire). A monster slain by More, of More Hall, who procured a suit of armour studded with spikes; and, proceeding to the well where the dragon had his lair, kicked it in the mouth, where alone it was vulnerable. Dr. Percy says this dragon was an overgrown, rascally attorney, who cheated some children of their estate, but was made to disgorge by a gentleman named More, who went against him, "armed with the spikes of the law," after which the dragon attorney died of vexation. (*Reliques.*)

Dragon's Hill (Berkshire) is where the legend says St. George killed the dragon. A bare place is shown on the hill, where nothing will grow, and there the blood of the dragon ran out.

In Saxon annals we are told that Cedric, founder of the West Saxon kingdom, slew there Naud, the pendragon, with 5,000 men. This Naud is called Natan-leod, a corruption of *Naudan ludh* (Naud, the people's refuge).

Dragon's Teeth. Subjects of civil strife; whatever rouses citizens to rise in arms. The allusion is to the dragon that guarded the well of A'res. Cadmus slew it, and sowed some of the teeth, from which sprang up the men called Spartans, who all killed each other except five, who were the ancestors of the Thebans. Those teeth which Cadmus did not sow came to the possession of Æe'tēs, King of Colchis; and one of the tasks he enjoined Jason was to sow these teeth and slay the armed warriors that rose therefrom.

"Citizens rising from the soil, richly sown with dragon's teeth, for the rights of their several states."—*The Times.*

To sow dragons' teeth. To foment contentions; to stir up strife or war. The reference is to the classical story of Jason or that of Cadmus, both of whom sowed the teeth of a dragon which he had slain, and from these teeth sprang up armies of fighting men, who attacked each other in fierce fight. Of course, the figure means that quarrels often arise out of a contention supposed to have been allayed (or slain). The Philistines sowed dragons' teeth when they took Samson, bound him, and put out his eyes. The ancient Britons sowed dragons' teeth when they massacred the Danes on St. Bryce's Day.

Drag'onades (3 syl.). A series of religious persecutions by Louis XIV., which drove many thousand Protestants out of France. Their object was to root out "heresy ; " and a bishop, with certain ecclesiastics, was sent to see if the heretics would recant; if not, they were left to the tender mercies of the dragoons who followed these "ministers of peace and goodwill to man."

" France was drifting toward the fatal atrocities of the dragonade.'—F. . arkman : The Old Régime, chap. ix, p. 16?

Dragoons. So called because they used to be armed with dragons, *i.e.* short muskets, which spouted out fire like the fabulous beast so named. The head of a dragon was wrought on the muzzle of these muskets.

Drake means the " duck-king." The old English word *end* means a duck, and *end-ric* becomes 'dric, drake. Similarly the German *tauber-rich* is a male dove, and *ganse-rich*, a male goose, or gander.

Drama. *Father of the French drama.* Etienne Jodelle (1532-1573).
Father of the Greek drama. Thespis (sixth century B.C.).
Father of the Spanish drama. Lopë de Ve'ga (1562-1635).

Drama of Exile (*A*). A poem by Elizabeth Barrett Browning (1844). The exile is Eve, driven out of Paradise into the wilderness. Luci"er, Gabriel, and Christ are introduced into the poem, as well as Adam and Eve.

Dramatic Unities (*The three*). One catastrophe, one locality, one day. These are Aristotle's rules for tragedy, and the French plays strictly follow them.

The French have added a fourth, one style. Hence comedy must not be mixed with tragedy. Addison's *Cato* is a good example. Unity of style is called the Unity of Uniformity. Shakespeare disregards all these canons.

Dram'atis Perso'næ. The characters of a drama, novel, or actual transaction.

" The dramatis personæ were nobles, country gentlemen, justices of the quorum, and custo'des rotulo'rum [keepers of the rolls]."—*The Times.*

Drap. One of Queen Mab's maids of honour. (*Drayton.*)

Dra'pier's Letters. A series of letters written by Dean Swift to the people of Ireland, advising them not to take the copper money coined by William Wood, by patent granted by George I. These letters crushed the infamous job, and the patent was cancelled.

Dean Swift signed himself M. B. Dra-' pier in these letters.

Drat 'em! A variant of *Od rot 'em !* The first word is a minced form of the word God, as in " Od's blood ! " " Od zounds ! "= God's wounds, " Od's bodikins," etc. (*See* OD'S.) A correspondent in *Notes and Queries* suggests "[May] God out-root them ! " but we have the words *drattle* and *throttle* (to choke) which would better account for the *a* and the *o*, and which are also imprecations.

Draught of Thor (*The*). The ebb of the sea. When Asa Thor visited Jötunheim he was set to drain a bowl of liquor. He took three draughts, but only succeeded in slightly reducing the quantity. On leaving Jötunheim, the king, Giant Skrymir, told him he need not be ashamed of himself, and showed him the sea at low ebb, saying that he had drunk all the rest in his three draughts. We are told it was a quarter of a mile of sea-water that he drank.

Draupnir. Odin's magic ring, from which every ninth night dropped eight rings equal in size and beauty to itself.

Draw.
To draw amiss. To follow scent in the wrong direction. Fox-hunting term, where *to draw* means to follow scent.
To draw a furrow. To plough or draw a plough through a field so as to make a furrow.
To draw a person out. To entice a person to speak on any subject, often with the intention of ridiculing his utterances.

Draw it Mild (*To*). We talk of remarks being highly flavoured, of strong language, of piquant remarks, of spicy words ; so that to " draw it mild " refers to *liquor;* let it be mild, not too highly-flavoured, not too spicy and strong.

Draw the Long Bow (*To*). To exaggerate. Some wonderful tales are told of Robin Hood and other foresters practised in the long bow. (*See* BOW.)

Drawback. Something to set against the profits or advantages of a concern. In commerce, it is duty charged on goods paid back again when the goods are exported.

"It is only on goods into which dutiable commodities have entered in large proportion and obvious ways that drawbacks are allowed."—*H. George: Protection or Free Trade?* chap ix. p. 92.

Draw'cansir. A burlesque tyrant in *The Rehearsal*, by G. Villiers, Duke of Buckingham (1672). He kills every one, "sparing neither friend nor foe." The name stands for a blustering braggart, and the farce is said to have been a satire on Dryden's inflated tragedies. (*See* BAYES, BOBADIL.)

"[He] frights his mistress, snubs up kings, bafftes armies, and does what he will, without regard to numbers, good sense, or justice."—*Bayes: The Rehearsal.*

Drawing-room. A room to which ladies *withdraw* or retire after dinner. Also a levée where ladies are presented to the sovereign.

Drawing the Cork. Giving one a bloody nose. (*See* CLARET.)

Drawing the King's (or Queen's) **Picture.** Coining false money.

Drawing the Nail, *i.e.* absolving oneself of a vow. In Cheshire, two or more persons would agree to do something, or to abstain from something, say drinking beer ; and they would go into a wood, and register their vow by driving a nail into a tree, swearing to keep their vow as long as that nail remained in the tree. If they repented of their vow, some or all of the party went and drew out the nail, whereupon the vow was cancelled.

Drawlatches. Thieves, robbers, wasters, and roberdsmen (5 Edward III. c. 14). About equal to door-openers and shop-lifters.

Drawn. *Hanged, drawn, and quartered,* or *Drawn, hanged, and quartered.* The question turns on the meaning of drawn. The evidence seems to be that traitors were drawn to the place of execution, then hanged, then "drawn" or disembowelled, and then quartered. Thus the sentence on Sir William Wallace was that he should be drawn (*detrahatur*) from the Palace of Westminster to the Tower, etc., then hanged (*suspendatur*), then disembowelled or drawn (*devaletur*), then beheaded and quartered (*decolletur et decapitetur*). (See *Notes and Queries*, August 15th, 1891.)

⁂ If by "drawn" is meant conveyed to the place of execution, the phrase should be "Drawn, hanged, and quartered ; " but if the word is used as a synonym of disembowelled, the phrase

should be "Hanged, drawn, and quartered."

"Lord Ellenborough used to say to those condemned, 'You are drawn on hurdles to the place of execution, where you are to be hanged, but *not* till you are dead ; for, while still living, your body is to be taken down, your bowels torn out and burnt before your face; your head is then cut off, and your body divided into four quarters.'" —*Gentleman's Magazine*, 1803, part i. pp. 177, 275.

Drawn Battle. A battle in which the troops on both sides are *drawn off*, neither combatants claiming the victory.

Dreadnought. The Seaman's Hospital Society ; a floating hospital.

Dream Authorship. It is said that Coleridge wrote his *Kubla Khan*, a poem, in a dream.

Coleridge may have dreamt these lines, but without doubt Purchas's *Pilgrimage* haunted his dreams, for the resemblance is indubitable.

Dream'er. *The Immortal Dreamer.* John Bunyan (1628-1688).

Dreng. A servant boy, similar to the French *garçon* and Latin *puer*. A Danish word, which occurs in Domesday Book.

Dress your Jacket (or hide). *I'll dress your jacket for you.* I'll give you a beating. *I'll give you a dressing*, or *a good dressing*. To dress a horse is to curry it, rub it, and comb it. To dress ore is to break it up, crush it, and powder it in the stamping mill. The original idea of dressing is preserved, but the method employed in dressing horses, ore, etc., is the prevailing idea in the phrases referred to.

Dreyfusard', Drey'fusite. An advocate of the innocence of Capt. Dreyfus, a Jewish officer of the French artillery, condemned in 1895 for betraying military secrets, degraded and sent to Devil's Island. In 1899 the first trial was annulled. He was brought back to France, retried, and again condemned, but shortly afterwards pardoned. It was believed that he was sacrificed to save the General Staff.

Drink Deep. Drink a deep draught. The allusion is to the peg tankards. Those who drank deep, drank to the lower pegs. (*Hamlet*, i. 2.) (*See* PEG.)

Drinke and Welcome. One of the numerous publications of John Taylor, the Water Poet (1637). The subject is thus set forth : "The famous Historie of the most parts of Drinks in use now in the Kingdomes of G. Britaine and Ireland ; with an especiall declaration of the potency, vertue, and operation of our English Ale. With a description of all sorts of Waters, from the Ocean-sea to the Teares of a Woman. As also the causes of all sorts of weather, faire or foule, sleet, raine, haile, frost, snow, fogges, mists, vapours, clouds, stormes, windes, thunder, and lightning. Compiled first in High Dutch Tongue by the painefull and industrious Huldricke van Speagle, a grammatical brewer of Lubeck; and now most learnedly enlarged, amplified, and translated into English verse and prose, by John Taylor, the Water Poet."

Drink like a Fish (*To*). To drink abundantly. Many fish swim with their mouths open.

Drinking Healths was a Roman custom. Thus, in Plautus, we read of a man drinking to his mistress with these words: "*Bene vos, bene nos, bene te, bene me, bene nostrum etiam Stepha'nium*" (Here's to you, here's to us *all*, here's to thee, here's to me, here's to our dear ——). (*Stich.* v. 4.) Persius (v. 1, 20) has a similar verse: "*Bene mihi, bene vobis, bene ami'cæ nostræ*" (Here's to myself, here's to you, and here's to I shan't say who). Martial, Ovid, Horace, etc., refer to the same custom.

The ancient Greeks drank healths. Thus, when Theramēnēs was condemned by the Thirty Tyrants to drink hemlock, he said: "*Hoc pulcro Critiæ*"—the man who condemned him to death.

The ancient Saxons followed the same habit, and Geoffrey of Monmouth says that Hengist invited King Vortigern to a banquet to see his new levies. After the meats were removed, Rowe'na, the beautiful daughter of Hengist, entered with a golden cup full of wine, and, making obeisance, said, "*Lauerd kining, wacht heil*" (Lord King, your health). The king then drank and replied, "*Drinc heil*" (Here's to you). (*Geoffrey of Monmouth*, book vi. 12.) Robert de Brunne refers to this custom:

"This is ther custom and hev gest
When they are at the ale or fest:
Ilk man that levis gware him drink
Salle say 'Wosseille' to him drink;
He that biddis sall say 'Wassaile,'
The tother salle say again 'Drinkaille.
That says 'Woisseille' drinks of the cup,
Kiss and his felaw he gives it up."
                    Robert de Brunne.

⁂ In drinking healths we hold our hands up towards the person toasted and say, "Your health ...." The Greeks handed the cup to the person toasted and said, "This to thee," "*Græci in epūlis pocūlum alicui tradituri, eum*

nominare solent." Our holding out the wine-glass is a relic of this Greek custom.

Drinking Song. The oldest in the language is in the second act of *Gammer Gurton's Needle*, by John Still, called *The Jolly Bishop.* It begins:

"I cannot eat but little meat,
My stomach is not good."

Drinking at Freeman's Quay, that is, drinking gratis. At one time, all porters and carmen calling at Freeman's Quay, near London Bridge, had a pot of beer given them gratis.

Drive. (Anglo-Saxon *drif-an*.)
To drive a good bargain. To exact more than is quite equable.
"Heaven would no bargain for its blessings drive."　　*Dryden: Astræa Redux,* i 137.

To drive a roaring trade. To be doing a brisk business. The allusion is to a coachman who drives so fast that his horses pant and *roar* for breath.
To drive the swine through the hanks of yarn. To spoil what has been painfully done; to squander thrift. In Scotland, the yarn wrought in the winter (called the gude-wife's thrift) is laid down by the burn-side to bleach, and is peculiarly exposed to damage from passing animals. Sometimes a herd of pigs driven along the road will run over the hanks, and sometimes they will stray over them from some neighbouring farmyard and do a vast amount of harm.

Drive at (*To*). *What are you driving at?* What do you want to prove? What do you want me to infer? We say the "wind drove against the sails," *i.e.* rushed or moved violently against them. Falstaff tells us of "four rogues in buckram [who] let drive at him," where *at* means against or towards. "What are you driving at?" is, against or towards what object are you driving or moving?

Drive Off. To defer, to procrastinate. The idea is, running away or drawing off from something that ought to be done, with the promise of coming to it at a future time.

Driv'eller. An idiot, an imbecile, whose saliva drivels out of his mouth.
"And Swift expires a driveller and a show."

Drivelling Dotage. In weak old age saliva drops unconsciously from the mouth.
"This exhibition of drivelling dotage was attended with many other incoherent expressions."—*J. P. Kennedy: The Swallow Barn,* chap. xlvii. p. 463.

Driver of Europe (*Le Cocher de l'Europe*). So the Empress of Russia used to call the Duc de Choiseul, minister of Louis XV., because he had spies all over Europe, and thus ruled its political cabals.

Drivers, in the Irish uprising about 1843, were persons engaged by landlords to drive all the live stock of defaulting tenants and lodge them in a pound [like that at Carrickmacross]. They were resisted by the Molly Maguires.

Drives fat Oxen (*Who*). Brook, in his *Gustavus Vasa*, says: "Who rules o'er freemen should himself be free," which Dr. Johnson parodied thus: "Who drives fat oxen should himself be fat." (*Boswell's Life*, year 1784.)

Driving for Rent, in Ireland, was a summary way of recovering rent by driving cattle to a pound, and keeping them till the rent was paid, or selling them by auction.

"It was determined that I and the bailiffs should go out in a body and 'drive for rent.'"—*Trench: Realities of Irish Life*, chap. v.

Driving Pigs. *He is driving pigs,* or *driving pigs to market—i.e.* snoring like pigs, whose grunt resembles the snore of a sleeper.

Droit d'Aubaine. In France the king was entitled, at the death of foreign residents (except Swiss and Scots), to all their movable estates; the law was only abolished in 1819. *Aubain* means "alien," and *droit d'aubaine* the "right over an alien's property."

"Had I died that night of an indigestion, the whole world could not have suspended the effects of the *droits d'aubaine* : my shirts and black pair of breeches, portmanteau and all, must have gone to the king of France."—*Sterne : Sentimental Journey* (Introduction).

Drôle. "*C'est un drôle,*" or "*C'est un drôle d'homme*" (he is a rum customer). "*Un joyeux drôle*" means a boon companion. "*Une drôle de chose*" means a queer thing; something one can make neither head nor tail of.

Dro'mio. *The brothers Dromio.* Two brothers exactly alike, who serve two brothers exactly alike, and the mistakes of masters and men form the fun of Shakespeare's *Comedy of Errors*, based on the *Menæch'mi* of Plautus.

Drone (1 syl.). The largest tube of a bagpipe; so called because it sounds only one continuous note. (German, *drohne*, verb, *drohnen*, to groan or drone.) *A drone.* An idle person who lives on the means of another, as drones on the honey collected by bees; a sluggard. (Anglo-Saxon *dræn*, a male bee.)

Drop. *To take a drop.* A euphemism for taking what the drinker chooses to call by that term. It may be anything from a sip to a Dutchman's draught. *A drop of the cratur.* In Ireland means a drink of whisky, or "creature-comfort." *To take a drop too much.* To be intoxicated. If it is the "last feather which breaks the camel's back," it is the drop too much which produces intoxication. *To take one's drops.* To drink spirits in private.

Drop (*To*). *To drop an acquaintance* is quietly to cease visiting and inviting an acquaintance. The opposite of picking up or taking up an acquaintance.

Drop in (*To*). To make a casual call, not invited; to pay an informal visit. The allusion is to fruit and other things falling down suddenly, unexpectedly, or accidentally. It is the *intransitive* verb, not the transitive, which means to "let fall."

Drop off (*To*). "Friends drop off," fall away gradually. "To drop off to sleep," to fall asleep (especially in weariness or sickness).

Drop Serene (*gutta sere'na*). An old name for amauro'sis. It was at one time thought that a transparent, watery humour, distilling on the optic nerve, would produce blindness without changing the appearance of the eye.

"So thick a 'drop serene' hath quenched these orbs." *Milton : Paradise Lost*, iii. 25.

Drown the 'Miller (*To*). To put too much water into grog or tea. The idea is that the supply of water is so great that even the miller, who uses a water wheel, is drowned with it.

Drowned Rat. *As wet as a drowned rat—i.e.* soaking wet. Drowned rats certainly look deplorably wet, but so also do drowned mice, drowned cats, and drowned dogs, etc.

Drowned in a Butt of Malmsey. George, Duke of Clarence, being allowed to choose by what death he would die, chose drowning in malmsey wine (1477). *See* the continuation of *Monstrelet*, 196 : *Fulgosus*, ix. 12 : Martin du Bellais's *Memoirs* (year 1514).

Admitting this legend to be an historic fact, it is not unique : Michael Harslob, of Berlin, wished to meet death in a similar way in 1571, if we may credit the inscription on his tomb :—

" In cyatho vini pleno cum musca periret,
Sic, ait Oeneus, sponte perire velim."

" When in a cup of wine a fly was drowned,
So, said Vinarius, may my days be crowned."

Drowning Men. *Drowning men catch at straws.* Persons in desperate circumstances cling in hope to trifles wholly inadequate to rescue or even help them.

Drows or *Trows.* A sort of fairy race, residing in hills and caverns. They are curious artificers in iron and precious metals. (*Zetland superstition*)

" I hung about thy neck that gifted chain,
which all in our isles know was wrought by no
earthly artist, but by the Drows in the secret
recesses of their caverns."—*Scott: The Pirate*,
chap. x.

Drub, Drubbing. To flog, a flogging. Compare Greek *tribo*, to rub, bruise ; Anglo-Saxon, *drepan*, to beat.

Drug. *It is a mere drug in the market.* Something not called for, which no one will buy. French *drogue* = rubbish, as *Ce n'est que de la drogue ;* hence *droguet* (drugget), inferior carpet-cloth made of rubbish or inferior wool, etc.

Druid. A chief priest (Celtic, *der*, superior ; *wydd*, priest or instructor). In Taliesin we read, *Bûm gwŷdd yngwarth an* (at length I became a priest or *wydd*). It was after this period that the *wydds* were divided into two classes, the Der-wydds and the Go-wydds (D'ruids and Ovidds). Every chief had his druid, and every chief druid was allowed a guard of 'hirty men (*Strabo*). The order was very wealthy. (Not derived from the Greek *drus*, an oak.)

✝ Patricius tells us that the Druids were wont to borrow money to be repaid in the life to come. His words are, "Druidæ pecuniam mutuo accipiebant in posteriore vita redditure."

' Like money by the Druids borrowed,
In t'other world to be restored."
Butler : Hudibras, part iii. canto ...

Drum. A crowded evening party, a contraction of "drawing - room" (dr'-'oom). Cominges, the French ambassador, writing to Louis XIV., calls these assemblies *drerums* and *driwcromes.* (*See* ROUT, HURRICANE.)

" The Comte de Broglie . . . goes sometimes to
the drerums, and sometimes to the driwrome of
the Princess of Wales."—*Nineteenth Century :
Comte de Cominges ;* Sept., 1891, p. 461.

" It is impossible to live in a drum."—*Lady M.
W. Montagu.*

John Drum's entertainment. Turning an unwelcome guest out of doors. The allusion is to drumming a soldier out of a regiment.

Drum Ecclesiastic. The pulpit cushion, often vigorously thumped by what are termed " rousing preachers."

" When Gospel trumpeter, surrounded
With long-eared rout, to battle sounded ;
And pulpit, drum ecclesiastic,
Was beat with fist instead of a stick."
Butler : Hudibras, part i. canto 1.

Drum-head Court-martial. One held in haste ; like a court-martial summoned on the field round the big drum to deal summarily with an offender.

Drummers. So commercial travellers are called in America, because their vocation is to drum up recruits or customers.

Drum'mond Light. The limelight. So named from Captain Thomas Drummond, R.E.

" Wisdom thinks, and makes a solar *Drummond
Light* of a point of dull lime."—*Geikie: Entering
on Life* (Reading, p. 211).

Drumsticks. Legs. The leg of a cooked fowl is called a *drumstick.*

Drunk. (Anglo-Saxon *drinc-an.*) *Drunk as a fiddler.* The reference is to the fiddler at wakes, fairs, and on board ship, who used to be paid in liquor for playing to rustic dancers.

Drunk as a lord. Before the great temperance movement set in, in the latter half of the nineteenth century, those who could afford to drink thought it quite *comme il faut* to drink two, three, or even more bottles of port wine for dinner, and few dinners ended without placing the guests under the table in a hopeless state of intoxication. The temperate habits of the last quarter of the nineteenth century renders this phrase now almost unintelligible.

Drunk as blazes. " Blazes " of course means the devil.

Drunk as Chloe. Chloe, or rather Cloe (2 syl.), is the cobbler's wife of Linden Grove, to whom Prior, the poet, was attached. She was notorious for her drinking habits.

Drunk as David's sow. (*See* DAVY'S Sow.)

Drunkard's Cloak (*A*). A tub with holes for the arms to pass through. At one time used for drunkards and scolds by way of punishment.

Drunken Deddington. One dead drunk. The proper name is a play on the word *dead.*

Drunkenness. *The seven degrees :* (1) Ape drunk; (2) Lion drunk; (3)

Swine drunk; (4) Sheep drunk; (5) Martin drunk; (6) Goat drunk; (7) Fox drunk. (*Nash*.)

Drunkenness. It is said that if children eat owl's eggs they will never be addicted to strong drinks.

"Tous les oiseaux lui [*i.e.* to Bacchus] étaient agréable, excepté la chouette dont les œufs avaient la vertu de rendre les enfans qui les mangeaient ennemis du vin."—*Noel : Dictionnaire de la Fable*, vol. i. p. 206.

Drupner [*the dripper*]. A gold ring given to Odin; every ninth night other rings dropped from it of equal value to itself. (*The Edda.*)

Drury Lane (London) takes its name from the habitation of the great Drury family. Sir William Drury, K.G., was a most able commander in the Irish wars. Drury House stood on the site of the present Olympic theatre.

Dru'ses (2 syl.). A people of Syria governed by emirs. Their faith is a mixture of the Pentateuch, the Gospel, the Koran, and Sufism. They offer up their devotions both in mosques and churches, worship the images of saints, and yet observe the fast of Ram'adan. Their language is pure Arabic. (Hakem, the incarnate spirit, was assisted by Darási in propounding his religion to these Syrians; and the word *Druse* is said to be derived from Darasi, shortened into D'rasi.)

Dry. Thirsty. Hence to drink is to " wet your whistle " (*i.e.* throat) ; and malt liquor is called " heavy wet." (Anglo-Saxon *dryg*, dry.)

Dry Blow (*A*). A blow which does not bring blood.

Dry Goods (in merchandise), such as cloths, stuffs, silks, laces, and drapery in general, as opposed to groceries.

Dry Lodgings. Sleeping accommodation without board. Gentlemen who take their meals at clubs live in dry lodgings.

" Dry Lodging of seven weeks. £0 4s. 1d."—*Sir W. Scott: Old Mortality* (Intr. Rob. Patterson *deb.* to Margaret Chrystale).

Dry-nurse. When a superior officer does not know his duty, and is instructed in it by an inferior officer, he is said to be dry-nursed. The inferior nurses the superior, as a dry-nurse rears an infant.

Dry Rot. The spontaneous rot of timber or wall-paper, not unfrequently produced by certain fungi attaching themselves thereto. It is called dry rot because the wood is not purposely exposed to wet, although, without doubt, damp from defective ventilation is largely present, and the greenness of wood employed contributes greatly to the decay.

Dry Sea (*A*). A sandy desert. The camel is the ship of the desert. We read of the Persian sea of sand.

" The see that men slepen the gravely see, that is alle gravelle and sond with outen ony drope of watre."—*Mandeville : Travels.*

Dry Shave (*A*). A shave without soaping the face ; to scrape the face with a piece of iron hoop ; to scratch the face ; to box it and bruise it. Sometimes it means to beat and bruise generally ; ill usage.

" The fellow will get a dry shave."
Peter Pindar : Great Cry and Little Wool, Ep. 1.
" I'll shave her, like a punished soldier, dry."
Peter Pindar : The Lousiad, canto ii.

Dry Style (of writing). Without pathos, without light and shade ; dull level, and unamusing.

Dry Wine. Opposed to sweet or fruity wine. In sweet wine some of the sugar is not yet decomposed ; in *dry* wine all the sugar has been converted into alcohol. The doctoring of wine to improve its quality is called dosage.

" Upon the nature and amount of the dosage, the character of the wine (whether it be dry or sweet, light or strong) very much depends."— *Vizetelly : Facts about Champagne*, chap. v. p. 59.

Dry'ads. Nymphs of the trees. (Greek, *drus*, any forest tree.) They were supposed to live in the trees and die when the trees died. Eurydĭcē, the wife of Orpheus (2 syl.) the poet, was a dryad.

Dry'asdust (*Rev. Dr.*). A heavy, plodding author, very prosy, very dull, and very learned ; an antiquary. Sir Walter Scott employs the name to bring out the prefatory matter of some of his novels.

"The Prussian Dryasdust . . . excels all other 'Dryasdusts' yet known."—*Carlyle.*

Du'alism. A system of philosophy which refers all things that exist to two ultimate principles. It is eminently a Persian doctrine. The Orphic poets made the ultimate principles of all things to be Water and Night, or Time and Necessity. In theology the Mani-che'an doctrine is dualistic. In modern philosophy it is opposed to monism (*q.v.*), and insists that the creator and creation, mind and body, are distinct entities. That creation is not deity, and that mind is not an offspring of matter. (*See* MONISM.)

13

Dub. To make a knight by giving him *a blow.* Dr. Tusler says, "The ancient method of knighting was by a box on the ear, implying that it would be the last he would receive, as he would henceforth be free to maintain his own honour." The present ceremony is to tap the shoulder with a sword. (Anglo-Saxon, *dubban*, to strike with a blow.)

Dub Up! Pay down the money. A dub is an Anglo-Indian coin, hence "down with your dubs," money down. A "doubloon" is a double pistole.

Dublin (the Irish *dubh-linn*, the "black pool"). The chief part of the city stands on land reclaimed from the river Liffey or the sea.
True as the De'il is in Dublin city. (*Burns: Death and Dr. Hornbook.*) Probably Burns refers to the Scandinavian name *Divelin*, which suggested first *Divel* and then *Devil or Deil.*

Dubs in "marbles" is a contraction of double or doublets. Thus, if a player knocks two marbles out of the ring, he cries *dubs*, before the adversary cries "no dubs," and claims them both.

Duc'at. A piece of money; so called from the legend on the early Sicilian pieces: *Sit tibi, Christe, datus, quem tu regis, istë ducātus* (May this duchy [*ducat-us*] which you rule be devoted to you, O Christ).

Duchesne (2 syl.). *Le père Duchésne.* Jacques Réné Hébert, chief of the Cordelier Club in the French Revolution, the members of which were called Hébertists. He was called "Father Duchésne," from the name of his vile journal. (1755-1794.)

Duchess. The wife or widow of a duke; but an old woman is often jocosely termed *an old duchess* or a *regular old duchess.* The longevity of the peers and peeresses is certainly very striking.

Duck. *A lame duck.* A stock-jobber who will not, or cannot, pay his losses. He has to "waddle out of the alley like a lame duck."
Like a dying duck in a thunderstorm. Quite chop-fallen.
To get a duck. A contraction of duck's egg or 0, in cricket. A player who gets no run off his bat is marked down 0.

Duck Lane. A row for old and second-hand books which stood formerly near Smithfield, but has given way to city improvements. It might be called

the Holywell Street of Queen Anne's reign.
"Scotists and Thomists now in peace remain
Amidst their kindred cobwebs in Duck Lane."
Pope: Essay on Criticism.

Duck's Egg. *Broke his duck's egg.* Took his first school prize. In cricket a "duck's egg" or 0 in a score is broken by a run.
"What a proud and happy day it was to Lucy when little Herbert, in public-school parlance, 'broke his duck's egg'—otherwise, took his first prize."—*A Fellow of Trinity*, chap. i.

Duck's-foot Lane [City.] A corruption of Duke's Foot Lane ; so called from the Dukes of Suffolk, whose manor-house was there.

Ducks and Drakes. The ricocheting or rebounding of a stone thrown from the hand to skim along the surface of a pond or river.
To make ducks and drakes of one's money. To throw it away as stones with which "ducks and drakes" are made on water. The allusion is to the sport of throwing stones to skim over water for the sake of seeing them ricocheting or rebounding.
"What figured slates are best to make
On watery surface duck and drake."
Butler : Hudibras, ii. 3.
"Mr. Locke Harper found out, a month after his marriage, that somebody had made ducks and drakes of his wife's money."—*Dinah M. Craik: Agatha's Husband*, chap. xxiii.

Duckie. Diminutive of "duck," a term of endearment = darling or beloved one. (Norwegian and Danish, *dukke*, a doll, a baby.)

Ducking (*A*). A drenching. (German, *ducken*, to dive under water.)

Duckweed. A weed which floats on the surface of stagnant water and forms a harbour for insects which ducks feed on. Its Latin name is "Lemna;" Greek, *limnē* (a stagnant pool).

Dude. A masher. One who renders himself conspicuous by affectation of dress, manners, and speech. The word was first familiarised in London in 1881, and is a revival of the old word *dudes* (clothes). We have several derivations, as *dudder*, one who sells dress-pieces; *duddery*, a rag-shop; *duddle*, to wrap up warmly (*Halliwell*), etc. It is not of American origin.
"I should just as soon expect to see Mercutio smoke a cigarette, as to find him ambling about the stage with the mincing manners of a dude."—*Jefferson: Century Magazine*, January, 1890, p. 383.

Dudeism (3 syl.). The tomfoolery of a dude (2 syl.).

Dudgeon (*The*). The handle of a dagger, at one time made of box-wood root, called "dudgeon-wood;" a dagger with such a handle. Shakespeare does not say, "and on the blade o' the dudgeon gouts of blood," but "on the blade *and* dudgeon . . ," both blade and handle.

Dud'man and Ramhead. *When Dudman and Ramhead meet.* Never. Dudman and Ramhead (now spelt Ramehead) are two forelands on the Cornish coast, about twenty miles asunder. (*See* NEVER.)

"Make yourself scarce! depart! vanish! or we'll have you summoned before the mayor of Hal'gaver, and that before Dudman and Ramhead meet."—*Scott: Kenilworth,* iv.

Duds. Old clothes, tattered garments (Gaelic, *dud,* a rag; Dutch, *tod;* Italian, *tozzi*). A dudder or dudsman is a scarecrow, or man of straw dressed in cast off garments to fray birds; also a pedlar who sells duds or gown-pieces. (Compare the Greek *duo,* to put on [clothes]; Latin, *in-duo,* to clothe.)

Dudu. A pensive maiden of seventeen, "who never thought about herself at all." (*Byron: Don Juan,* vi. vii.)

Duen'de (3 syl.). A Spanish goblin or house-spirit. Cal'deron has a comedy called *La Dama Duenda.* (*See* FAIRY.)

Duen'na [*Lady*]. The female of don. The Spanish *don* is derived from the Latin *dominus* = a lord, a master. A duenna is the chief lady-in-waiting on the Queen of Spain; but in common parlance it means a lady who is half companion and half governess, in charge of the younger female members of a nobleman's or gentleman's family in Portugal or Spain.

"There is no duenna so rigidly prudent and inexorably decorous as a superannuated coquette." —*W. Irving : Sketch-Book (Spectre Bridegroom).*

Duer'gar (2 syl.). Dwarfs who dwell in rocks and hills; noted for their strength, subtilty, magical powers, and skill in metallurgy. They are the personification of the subterranean powers of nature. According to the Gotho-German myth, the duergar were first maggots in Ymir's flesh, but afterwards assumed the likeness of men. The first duergar was Modsogn'er, the next Dyrin. N.B.—The Giant Ymir is Chaos. (*See* HELDENBUCH.)

Dues'sa (*Double-mind* or *False-faith*). Daughter of Falsehood and Shame, who assumes divers disguises to beguile the Red Cross Knight. At one time she takes the name of Fidessa, and entices the knight into the Palace of Pride (*Lucife'ra*). The knight having left the palace, is overtaken by Duessa, and

drinks of an enchanted fountain, which paralyses him, in which state he is taken captive by the giant Orgoglio. Prince Arthur slays the giant and rescues the knight; Duessa, being stripped of her gorgeous disguise, is found to be a hideous hag, and flees into the wilderness for concealment. She appears again in book ii. (*Spenser: Faërie Queene,* book i. 2-7; v. 9.)

Dufarge. Jacques and Madame Dufarge are the presiding genii of the Faubourg St. Antoine, and chief instigators of many of the crimes committed by the Red Republicans in Dickens's *Tale of Two Cities.*

Duffer (*A*) now means a person easily bamboozled, one of slow wit; but originally it meant one who cheated or bamboozled. To *duff* = to cheat. Persons who sell inferior goods as "great bargains," under the pretence of their being smuggled, are duffers; so are hawkers generally. At the close of the eighteenth century passers of bad money were so called. Now the word is applied to persons taken in, and by artists to inferior pictures.

"Robinson a thorough duffer is."
Alexander Smith: Summer Idyll.

Duglas, the scene of four Arthurian battles. It is a river which falls into the Ribble. Mr. Whittaker says, "six cwt. of horse-shoes were taken up from a space of ground near the spot during the formation of a canal."

Duke. *The Great Duke.* The Duke of Wellington, called "the Iron Duke." (1769-1852.)

Duke Coombe. William Coombe, author of *Dr. Syntax, The Devil upon Two Sticks,* etc., who in the days of his prosperity was noted for the splendour of his dress, the profusion of his table, and the magnificence of his deportment. Having spent all his money he turned author, but passed the last fifteen years of his life in the King's Bench. (1743-1823.)

Duke Ernest. (*See* ERNEST.)

Duke Humphrey. (*See* HUMPHREY.)

Duke Street (Strand), so named from George Villiers, Duke of Buckingham.

Duke and Duchess in *Don Quixote,* who play so many tricks on the Knight of the Woeful Countenance, were Don Carlos de Borja, Count of Ficallo, who married Donna Maria of Ar'agon, Duchess of Villaher'mora. in whose right the count had extensive estates on the banks of the Ebro ; among others he had a country seat called Buena'via, which was the place Cervantes referred to.

Duke of Exeter's Daughter (*The*). A rack in the Tower of London, so called from a minister of Henry VI., who sought to introduce it into England.

Duke or Darling. Heads or tails ; pitch and toss. When the scandals about the Duke of York and Mrs. Clarke were the common talk of the town, the street boys, instead of crying *Heads or tails*, used to say *Duke or Darling*. (*Lord Colchester : Diary*, 1861.)

Duke's. A fashionable theatre in the reign of Charles II. It was situate in Portugal Street, Lincoln's Inn Fields. It was named from its great patron, James, Duke of York, afterwards James II. The modern Duke's theatre.

Duke's Walk. *To meet one in the Duke's Walk.* An invitation to fight a duel. In the vicinity of Holyrood House is a place called the Duke's Walk, from being the favourite promenade of the Duke of York, afterwards James II., during his residence in Scotland. This walk was the common rendezvous for settling affairs of honour, as the site of the British Museum was in England.

" If a gentleman shall ask me the same question, I shall regard the incivility as equivalent to an invitation to meet him in the Duke's Walk."— *Scott : Bride of Lammermoor*, chap. xxxiv.

Dukeries. A district in Nottinghamshire, so called from the number of ducal residences in the vicinity, including Welbeck Abbey, Thoresby, Clumber, Worksop, Kiveton Hall, etc.

Dulcar'non. The horns of a dilemma. (or *Syllogismum cornu'tum*) ; at my wits' end ; a puzzling question. Dulcar'nein is the Arabic *dhu'lkarnein* (double-horned, having two horns). Hence the 47th proposition of the First Book of Euclid is called the Dulcarnon, as the 5th is the *pons asinorum*. Alexander the Great is called Iscander Dulcarnein, and the Macedonian æra the *æra of Dulcarnein*. Chaucer uses the word in *Troylus and Cryseyde*, book iii. 126, 127.

∵ The *horns* of the 47th proposition are the two squares which contain the right angle.

To be in Dulcarnon. To be in a quandary, or on the horns of a dilemma.

To send one to Dulcarnon. To daze with puzzles.

Dulce Domum. The holiday song of Winchester school. Mr. Brandon

says it was composed by a boy of St. Mary's College, Winchester, who was confined for misconduct during the Whitsun holidays, " as report says, tied to a pillar." On the evening preceding the Whitsun holidays, " the master, scholars, and choristers of the above college walk in procession round the ' pillar,' chanting the six stanzas of the song." In the March number of the *Gentleman's Magazine*, 1796, a translation, signed " J. R.," was given of the song ; and Dr. Milner thinks the original is not more than a century old. ⸗ It is rather remarkable that the author has made " domum " a neuter noun. (*See* ADESTE FIDELES.)

CHORUS:

" Domum, domum, dulce domum !
Domum, domum, dulce domum ;
Dulce, dulce. dulce domum !
Dulce domum resone'mus."

Home, home, joyous home !
Home, home, joyous home !
Joyous, joyous, joyous home !
Hurrah for joyous home !   *E. C. B.*

Dulce est Desipere in Loco. It is delightful to play the fool occasionally ; it is nice to throw aside one's dignity and relax at the proper time. (*Horace : 4 Odes*, xii. 28.)

Dulce et Decorum est pro Patria Mori (Latin). It is sweet and becoming to die on our country's behalf, or to die for one's country.

Dul'cimer (Italian *docimello*), according to Bishop (*Musical Dictionary*, p. 45), is " a triangular chest strung with wires, which are struck with a little rod held in each hand ; " but the word " symphonia," translated dulcimer in Daniel iii. 5, was a species of bagpipe. Fürst deduces it from the Hebrew *smpn* (a pipe).

" The sound of cornet, flute, harp, sackbut, psaltery, [symphony] or dulcimer, and all kinds of music."— Dan. iii. 5.

Dulcin'ea. A lady - love. Taken from Don Quixote's *amie du cœur*. Her real name was Aldonza Lorenzo, but the knight dubbed her Dulcin'ea del Tobo'so.

" I must ever have some Dulcinea in my head— it harmonises the soul."— *Sterne.*

Dul'cinists. Heretics who followed the teaching of Dulcin, who lived in the fourteenth century. He said that God reigned from the beginning to the coming of Messiah ; and that Christ reigned from His ascension to the fourteenth century, when He gave up His dominion to the Holy Ghost. Dulcin was burnt by order of Pope Clement IV.

Duli'a. An inferior degree of worship or veneration, such as that paid by

Roman Catholics to saints and angels; Hyper-duli'a is a superior sort of veneration reserved for the Virgin; but that worship which is paid to God alone is called latri'a. "Dulia" means that sort of veneration which slaves pay to their lords (Greek, *doulos*, a slave); "Latria" means that sort of veneration which mortals pay to the gods (Greek, *latreu'o*, to worship the gods).

Dull as a Fro. A frow or fro is a kind of wedge for splitting wood. It is not a sharp-edged instrument like a chisel, but a blunt or dull one.

Dull as Ditch-water. Uninteresting; ditch-water is stagnant and has no go in it.

Dulness. *King of dulness.* Colley Cibber, poet laureate after Eusden.

"'God save king Cibber!' mounts in every
note . . . .
So when Jove's block descended from on
high . . . .
Loud thunder to the bottom shook the bog,
And the hoarse nation croaked, 'God save king
Log!'"
Pope: Dunciad, book i.

Dum Sola (Latin). While single or unmarried.

Dum Spiro, Spero. While I live, I hope; or, While there's life, there's hope.

Hope while you live, for who would care to
cope
With life's three foes, unpanoplied with hope?
Hope against hope, while fed with vital breath,
Hope be your anchor in the hour of death.
E. C. B.

Dum Vivimus, Vivamus (Latin). While we live, let us enjoy life. The motto of Dr. Doddridge's coat of arms, which he converted into the subjoined epigram—

"'Live, while you live,' the epicure would say,
'And seize the pleasures of the present day.'
'Live, while you live,' the sacred preacher cries,
'And give to God each moment as it flies.'
Lord, in *my* views let each united be;
I live in pleasure, when I live to thee."

Du'machus. The impenitent thief, called Dysmas in the apocryphal Gospel of Nicodemus. In Longfellow's *Golden Legend* Dumachus and Titus were two of a band of robbers who attacked Joseph in his flight into Egypt. Titus said, "Let these good people go in peace," but Dumachus replied, "First let them pay for their release." Upon this Titus gave his fellow-robber forty groats, and the infant Jesus said—

"When thirty years shall have gone by,
I at Jerusalem shall die . . . .
On the accursèd tree.
Then on my right and my left side,
These thieves shall both be crucified;
And Titus thenceforth shall abide
In Paradise with me."
The Miracle Play, iii.

Dumb-barge (*A*). A barge without sails, used for a pier, and not for conveying merchandise up and down a river.

Dumb-bell Nebula (*The*). A still condensing mass; so called from being of the shape of a dumb-bell.

Dumb-bells. A corruption of Dumpels or Dumples, the same word as Dumplings, and meaning heavy (weights). (German and Danish, *dumm*, heavy, dull, insipid; *dumpling*, a heavy, insipid pudding; *dumps*, heavy, stupid moroseness.) (*See* DUMP.)

Dumb-bells. In New College, Oxford, there still is an apparatus for developing the muscles similar to that which sets church-bells in motion. It consists of a fly-wheel with a weight attached, and the gymnast is carried by it up and down to bring his muscles into play. The present apparatus was substituted for it, and answers a similar purpose, though the name is greatly obscured.

Dumb-bidding. A sale by auction effected thus: The owner fixes an upset-price on an article, writes it on a slip of paper, and covers the slip up. The article is then offered to the bidders, and withdrawn unless some, bid reaches the upset price.

Dumb-cow (*To*). To brow-beat; to cow. (Anglo-Indian.)

Dumb Crambo. (*See* CRAMBO.)

Dumb Dog (*A*). One who remains silent when he ought to speak.

Dumb Ox of Cologne (*The*). Thomas Aquinas (1224-1274), known afterwards as "the Angelic Doctor" or "Angel of the Schools." Albertus Magnus, the tutor of the "dumb ox," said of him: "The dumb ox will one day fill the world with his lowing." He was born at Naples, but was a student in the monastery of Cologne.

Dumb-waiter. A piece of dining-room furniture, fitted with shelves, to hold glasses, dishes, and plate. So called because it answers all the purposes of a waiter, and is not possessed of an insolent tongue; a lift for carrying food from a kitchen to the dining-room, etc.

Dum'my. In three-handed whist the exposed hand is called dummy.

Dum'mies (2 syl.). Empty bottles or drawers in a druggist's shop; wooden heads in a hairdresser's shop; lay figures in a tailor's shop ; persons on the stage who appear before the lights, but have nothing to say. These all are dumb, actually or figuratively.

Dump. A Brazilian copper coin, worth about 2½d. ; also a round flat lump of lead used on board ship for playing quoits and chuck-penny. Hence *dumpy* or *dumpty* (squat or small). An egg is called a *humpty-dumpty* in the nursery verses beginning with "Humpty Dumpty sat on a wall," etc.

" Death saw two players playing cards,
- But the game was not worth a dump."
Hood : Death's Ramble, stanza 14.

Dumps. *To be in the dumps.* Out of spirits ; in the " sullens." According to etymological fable, it is derived from Dumops, King of Egypt, who built a pyramid and died of melancholy. Gay's Third Pastoral is *Wednesday, or the Dumps.* (German, *dumm*, stupid, dull.)

"Why, how now, daughter Katharine ? in your dumps ?"—*Shakespeare : Taming of the Shrew*, ii. 1.

Dun. One who importunes for payment of a bill (Anglo-Saxon, *dunan*, to din or clamour). The tradition is that it refers to Joe Dun, a famous bailiff of Lincoln in the reign of Henry VII. The *British Apollo* says he was so active and dexterous in collecting bad debts that when anyone became " slow to pay " the neighbours used to say to the creditors, " Dun him " (send Dun after him).

"An Universitie dunne .... is an inferior creditor of some ten shillings or downewards, contracted for horse-hire, or perchance drinke, too weake to be put in suite."—*Bishop Earle : Microcosmographia* (1601-1695).

Squire Dun. The hangman between Richard Brandin and Jack Ketch.

" And presently a halter got,
Made of the best strong hempen teer ;
And, ere a cat could lick his ear,
Had tied him up with as much art
As Dun himself could do for 's heart."
Cotton : Virgil Travestied, book iv.

Dun Cow. The dun cow of Dunsmore heath was a savage beast slain by Sir Guy, Earl of Warwick. A huge tusk, probably that of an elephant, is still shown at Harwich Castle as one of the horns of the dun-cow. (*See* GUY.)

The fable is that this cow belonged to a giant, and was kept on Mitchell Fold (middle fold), Shropshire. Its milk was inexhaustible ; but one day an old woman who had filled her pail, wanted to fill her sieve also. This so enraged the cow, that she broke loose from the fold and wandered to Dunsmore heath, where she was slain by Guy of Warwick.

᠄ Isaac Taylor, in his *Words and Places* (p. 269), says the dun cow is a corruption of the *Dena Gau* or Danish settlement in the neighbourhood of Warwick. Gau, in German, means region, country. If this explanation is correct, the great achievement of Guy was a victory over the Danes, and taking from them their settlement near Warwick.

Dun in the Mire. *To draw Dun out of the mire.* To lend a helping hand to one in distress. The allusion is to an English game, explained by Mr. Gifford in his edition of *Ben Jonson*, vii. 283. A log of wood is brought into a room. The log, called Dun, is supposed to have fallen into the mire, and the players are to pull him out. Every player does all he can to obstruct the others, and as often as possible the log is made to fall on someone's toes. Constant allusion is made to this game.

" Sires, what ? Dun is in the mire."—*Chaucer : Prologue to Maunciples Tale.*
" If thou art dun, we'll draw thee from the mire."
Shakespeare : Romeo and Juliet, i. 4.
" Well done, my masters, lend 's your hands ;
Draw Dun out of the ditch.
Draw, pull, helpe all. So, so ; well done."
Duchesse of Suffolke (1631).

Dunce. A dolt ; a stupid person. The word is taken from Duns Scotus, the learned schoolman and great supporter of the immaculate conception. His followers were called Dunsers. Tyndal says, when they saw that their hairsplitting divinity was giving way to modern theology, " the old barking curs raged in every pulpit " against the classics and new notions, so that the name indicated an opponent to progress, to learning, and hence a dunce.

" He knew what's what, and that's as high
As metaphysic wit can fly ....
A second Thomas, or at once
To name them all, another Dunse."
Butler : Hudibras, i. 1.

Dunce. (*See* ABDERITAN, ARCADIAN, BŒOTIAN.)

Dun'ciad. The dunce-epic, a satire by Alexander Pope. Eusden, the poet laureate, being dead, the goddess of Dulness elects Colley Cibber to be his successor. The installation is celebrated by games, the most important being the proposal to read, without sleeping, two voluminous works—one in verse and the other in prose ; as everyone falls asleep, the games come to an end. King Cibber is now taken to the temple of Dulness, and is lulled to sleep on the lap of the goddess ; and, during his slumber, sees in a vision the past, present, and future triumphs of the empire. Finally, the goddess, having destroyed order and science, establishes her kingdom on a firm basis; and, having given directions to her several agents to prevent thought and keep people to foolish and trifling pursuits, Night and Chaos are restored, and the poem ends. (*See* DENNIS.)

Dun'derhead. A blockhead, or, rather, a muddle-headed person. Dunder is the lees or dregs of wine, etc.; more correctly, the overflow of fermented liquors (yeast). (Spanish, *redundar*, to overflow or froth over.)

"The use of Dunder in the making of rum answers the purpose of yeast in the fermentation of flour."—*Edwards: West Indies.*

Dundrea'ry (*Lord*) (3 syl.). The impersonation of a good-natured, indoient, blundering, empty-headed swell. The chief character in Tom Taylor's dramatic piece called *Our American Cousin.* Mr. Sothern created the character of Lord Dundreary by the power of his conception and the genius of his acting. (*See* BROTHER SAM.)

Dungaree. A coarse blue cloth worn by sailors; coarse and vulgar. Dungaree is the Wapping of Bombay.

Dunghill! Coward! Villain! This is a cockpit phrase; all cocks, except gamecocks, being called dunghills.

"Out, dunghill! dar'st thou brave a nobleman?"
    Shakespeare: King John, iv. 3.

That is, Dare you, a dunghill cock, brave a thoroughbred gamecock?

Dunghill. *Thou hast it, ad dunghill, at thy fingers' ends.* To this Holofernes replies: "Oh, I smell false Latin; 'dunghill' for '*unguem.*'" (*Shakespeare: Love's Labour's Lost,* v. 1.)

Dunkers. (*See* TUNKERS.)

Dunmow. *To eat Dunmow bacon.* To live in conjugal amity, without even wishing the marriage knot to be less firmly tied. The allusion is to the institution of Robert Fitzwalter. Between 1244 and 1772 eight claimants have been admitted to eat the flitch. Their names merit immortality:

1445. Richard Wright, labourer, Bauburgh, near Norwich.

1467. Steven Samuel, of Little Ayston, Essex.

1510. Thomas Ley, fuller, Coggeshall, Essex.

1701. William and Jane Parsley, butcher, Much-Easton, Essex. Same year, John and Ann Reynolds, Hatfield Regis.

1751. Thomas Shakeshaft, woolcomber, Weathersfield, Essex.

1763. *Names unknown!!*

1772. John and Susan Gilder, Tarling, Essex.

The attempt to revive this "premium for humbug" is a mere "get-up" for the benefit of the town.

"Ah, madam! cease to be mistaken;
Few married fowl peck Dunmow bacon."
    Prior: Turtle and Sparrow, 233.

Dunmow Flitch. The oath administered was in the doggerel subjoined:

"You shall swear, by the custom of our confession,
That you never made any nuptial transgression
Since you were married man and wife,
By household brawls or contentious strife;
Or, since the parish clerk said '*Amen,*'
Wished yourselves unmarried again;
Or, in a twelvemonth and a day,
Repented not in thought any way.
If to these terms, without all fear,
Of your own accord you will freely swear,
A gammon of bacon you shall receive,
And bear it hence with our good leave.
For this is our custom at Dunmow well known—
The sport is ours, but the bacon your own."

Duns Scotus. A schoolman, called Duns from Dunce in Berwickshire. (1265–1308.) Not John Scotus, Erigĕna, the schoolman, who died A.D. 875.

Dun'stable. Bailey, as if he actually believed it, gives the etymology of this word *Duns' stable;* adding Duns or "Dunus was a robber in the reign of Henry I., who made it dangerous for travellers to pass that way." (*Dunes* or *duns tavell,* our table—*i.e.* the table-land or flat of the hills.)

Downright Dunstable. (*See* DOWNRIGHT.)

Plain as the road to Dunstable; or, as Shakespeare says, "Plain as way to parish church." The road leading to Dunstable is the confluence of many leading to London, but the play is on the word *dunce.*

Dun'stan (*St.*). Patron saint of goldsmiths, being himself a noted worker in gold. He is represented generally in pontifical robes, but carrying a pair of pincers in his right hand. The pontificals refer to his office as Archbishop of Canterbury, and the pincers to the legend of his holding the Devil by the nose till he promised never to tempt him again.

St. Dunstan and the devil. Dunstan was a painter, jeweller, and blacksmith. Being expelled from court, he built a cell near Glastonbury church, and there he worked at his handicrafts. It was in this cell that tradition says the Devil had a gossip with the saint through the lattice window. Dunstan went on talking till his tongs were red hot, when he turned round suddenly and caught his Satanic Majesty by the nose. One can trace in this legend the notion that all knowledge belonged to the Black Art; that the "saints" are always more than conquerors over the spirits of evil; and the singular cunning which our forefathers so delighted to honour.

Duodec'imo. A book whose sheets are folded into twelve leaves each. This word, which differs from both the Italian and French, is from the Latin *duodecim* (twelve). It is now called twelvemo, from the contraction 12mo. The term is still applied to books that are the same size as the old duodecimo, irrespective of the number of leaves into which the sheet is folded.

A man in duodec'imo is a dwarf. (*See* Decimo.)

Duomo (*The*). The cathedral.

"The supreme executive of Florence suspended Savonarola from preaching in the 'Duomo."—*Symonds: Renaissance in Italy.*

Dup is *do up.* Thus Ophelia says, in one of her snatches, he "dupt the chamber door," *i.e.* did up or pushed up the latch, in order to open the door, that he might "let in the maid" (*Hamlet,* iv. 1). A portcullis and some other doors were lifted up or dupped.

"Iche weene the porters are drunk. Will they not dup the gate to-day."—*Edwards: Damon and Pithias* (1571).

Dupes. (*See* Day of the Dupes.)

Duranda'na or *Durin'dana.* Orlando's sword, given him by his cousin Malagi'gi. It once belonged to Hector, and was made by the fairies. It could cleave the Pyrenees at a blow. N.B.—In French romance Orlando is called *Roland,* Malagigi *Maugis,* and the sword *durandal* or *durin'dal.* (*See* Sword.)

"Nor plaited shield, nor tempered casque defends, Where Durindana's trenchant edge descends." *Hoole: Orlando Furioso,* book v.

Du'randar'të. A knight who fell at Roncesvalles, cousin to Montesi'nos. The tale says he loved Belerma, whom he served seven years, at the expiration of which time he was slain. In his last breath he told Montesi'nos to take his heart and give it to Belerma. He is described by Lewis as

"Sweet in manners, fair in favour, Mild in temper, fierce in fight."

Durante.
Durante bene placito (Latin). During pleasure.
Durante minore ætate (Latin). During minority.
Durante viduitate (Latin). During widowhood.
Durante vita (Latin). For life.

Durbar (Indian word). A levée.

"Durbars which might rival in splendour of colour and jewelled bravery the glories of the court of Byzantium."—*McCarthy: England under Gladstone,* chap. iv. p. 60.

Dur'den (*Dame*). A notable housewife. Dame Durden, of the famous English song, kept five serving girls to carry the milking pails, and also kept five serving men to use the spade and flail. The five men loved the five maids.

"'Twas Moll and Bet, and Doll and Kate, and Dorothy Draggletail; And John and Dick, and Joe and Jack, and Humphrey with his flail." *Anon.*

Dürer (*Albert*), of Nürnberg, called by his countrymen "the prince of artists," and by many the "Chaucer of painting." (1471-1528.)

⁎ Dürer's portraits of Charlemagne and other emperors are unrivalled; but Lucas Kranach's (1472-1553) portraits of Luther and other reformers are said to run them very close in merit.

Duresley. *You are a man of Duresley, i.e.* a great liar and cheat. Duresley is a market-town in Gloucestershire, famous for its broadcloth manufactory. Now called Dursley. (*See Fuller: Worthies.*) The word "cabbage," connected with tailors, seems to confirm the notion that our forefathers had no very high opinion of their honesty.

Dur'ham Book. By Eadfrid, Bishop of Lindisfarne, who died in 721, one of the most splendid examples of illumination in the world.

Durham Mustard. So called from the residence of Mrs. Clements, who first conceived the idea of grinding mustard in a mill, instead of pounding it in a mortar. George I. stamped it with his approval, hence the pots labelled "Durham mustard" bear the royal initials in a medallion.

Dus or *Deuce.* The chief god of the Brigan'tës, one of whose altars, bearing an inscription, was discovered at Gretland. (*Camden: Britannia.*)

Du'siens. The name given by the Gauls to those demons that produce nightmares.

"Dæmones quos 'duscios' Galli nuncupant."—*St. Augustine: De Civitate Dei,* chap. xxiii.

Dust. Money; so called because it is made of gold-dust. It is said that Dean Swift took for the text of a charity sermon, "He who giveth to the poor, lendeth to the Lord." Having thrice repeated his text, he added, "Now, brethren, if you like the security, down with your dust." That ended his sermon.

Dust. The wild Irish peasantry believe that dust is raised on roads by fairies on a journey, and raise their hats to it, saying, "God speed you, gentlemen." The Arabs think the whirlwind and waterspout are caused by evil jinns.

I'll dust your jacket for you. Give you a good beating. The allusion is to dusting carpets, etc., by beating them with a stick.

To raise a dust, To kick up a dust. To make a commotion or disturbance.

To throw dust in one's eyes, To mislead. The allusion is to a Mahometan practice of casting dust into the air for the sake of "confounding" the enemies of the faith. This was done by Mahomet on two or three occasions, as in the battle of Honein; and the Koran refers to it when it says, "Neither didst thou, O Mahomet, cast dust into their eyes; but it was God who confounded them." But the following incident will suffice: One day the Koreishites surrounded the house of Mahomet, resolved to murder him. They peeped through the crevice of his chamber-door, and saw him lying asleep. Just at this moment his son-in-law Ali opened the door silently and threw into the air a handful of dust. Immediately the conspirators were confounded. They mistook Ali for Mahomet, and Mahomet for Ali; allowed the prophet to walk through their midst uninjured, and laid hands on Ali. No sooner was Mahomet safe, than their eyes were opened, and they saw their mistake.

"When the English king pursued the Imaum who had stolen the daughter of Allah, Allah threw dust in his eyes to check his pursuit."—*Legend at Gori* (respecting the beauty of the Georgians).

Dustman has arrived (*The*), or "The sandman is about." It is bed-time, for the children rub their eyes, as if dust or sand was in them.

Dusty. *Well, it is none so dusty,* or *Not so dusty.* I don't call it bad; rather smart. Here *dusty* is the opposite of *neat,* and neat = spruce. "None so dusty" or "Not so dusty" means therefore, *Not so unspruce,* or *rather smart.*

Dusty-foot. (*See* PIE POUDRE.)

Dutch. *The Dutch have taken Holland.* A quiz when anyone tells what is well known as a piece of wonderful news. Similar to *Queen Bess* (or *Queen Anne*) *is dead; the Ark rested on Mount Ararat;* etc.

Dutch Auction. An "*auction*" in which the bidders *decrease* their bids till they come to the minimum price. Dutch gold is no gold at all; Dutch courage is no real courage; Dutch concert is no music at all, but mere hubbub; and Dutch auction is no *auction,* or increase of bids, but quite the contrary.

Dutch Clocks, *i.e.* German clocks, chiefly made in the Black Forest. As many as 180,000 are exported annually from Friburg. (German, *Deutsch,* German.)

" A woman, that is like a German clock,
Still a-repairing, ever out of frame,
And never going aright."
Shakespeare: Love's Labour's Lost, iii. 1.

Dutch Comfort. 'Tis a comfort it was no worse. The comfort derivable from the consideration that how bad soever the evil which has befallen you, a worse evil is at least conceivable.

Dutch Concert. A great noise and uproar, like that made by a party of Dutchmen in sundry stages of intoxication, some singing, others quarrelling, speechifying, wrangling, and so on.

Dutch Courage. The courage excited by drink; pot valour.

" In the Dutch wars (in the time of Charles II.), ... the captain of the *Hollander* man-of-war, when about to engage with our ships, usually set .... a hogshead of brandy abroach before the mast, and bid the men drink .... and our men felt the force of the brandy to their cost."—*Notes and Queries* (Oct. 15, 1892, p. 304).

Dutch Gleek. Tippling. Gleek is a game, and the phrase means the game loved by Dutchmen is drinking.

"Nor could be partaker of any of the good cheer except it were the liquid part of it, which they call 'Dutch Gleek.'"—*Gayton.*

Dutch Gold. Deutsche or German gold. An alloy of copper and zinc, invented by Prince Rupert of Bavaria.

Dutch Nightingales. Frogs. Similarly, Cambridgeshire nightingales; Liège nightingales, etc.

Dutch School of painting is a sort of "pre-Raphaelite" exactness of detail without selection. It is, in fact, photographing exactly what appears before the artist, as faithfully as his art will allow. The subjects are generally the lower classes of social life, as pothouse scenes, drunken orgies, street groups, Dutch boors, etc., with landscapes and still-life. The greatest of the Dutch masters are: for *portraits,* Rembrandt, Bol, Flinck, Hals, and Vanderhelst; for *conversation pieces,* Gerhard Douw, Terburg, Metzu, Mieris, and Netscher; for *low life,* Ostade, Brower, and Jan Steen; for *landscapes,* Ruysdael, Hobbema, Cuyp, Vanderneer, Berchem, and A. Both; for *battle scenes,* Wouvermans

13*

and Huchtenburg; for *marine pieces*, Vandevelde and Bakhuizen; for *still-life and flowers*, Kalf, A. Van Utrecht, Van Huysum, and De Heem.

Dutch Toys, chiefly made in Meiningen, part of the duchy of Coburg-Gotha. (Dutch, *i.e. Deutsch*, German.)

Dutch Uncle. *I will talk to you like a Dutch uncle.* Will reprove you smartly. Uncle is the Latin notion of *pat'ruus*, " an uncle," " severe guardian," or " stern castigator." Hence Horace, 3 *Od.* xii. 3, " *Metuentes patruæ verbera linguæ*" (dreading the castigations of an uncle's tongue) ; and 2 *Sat.* iii. 88, " *Ne sis patruus mihi* " (Don't come the uncle over me).

Dutchman. *I'm a Dutchman if I do.* A strong refusal. During the rivalry between England and Holland, the word Dutch was synonymous with all that was false and hateful, and when a man said, " I would rather be a Dutchman than do what you ask me," he used the strongest term of refusal that words could express.

If not, I'm a Dutchman, means, I will do it or I will call myself a Dutchman.

Well, I'm a Dutchman! An exclamation of strong incredulity.

Duty means what is due or owing, a debt which should be paid. Thus obedience is the debt of citizens to rulers for protection, and service is the debt of persons employed for wages received.

" Strictly considered, all duty is owed originally to God only ; but . . . duties to God may be distributed . . . into duties towards self, towards manhood, and towards God."—*Gregory : Christian Ethics*, part ii. division i. p. 172.

Duum'virs (3 syl.) or *Duumviri.* Certain Roman officers who were appointed in pairs, like our London sheriffs. The chief were the two officers who had charge of the Sibylline books, the two who had the supervision of the municipal cities, and the two who were charged with naval matters.

Dwarf (*The*). Richard Gibson, painter (1615–1690), a page of the backstairs in the court of Charles I. He married Anne Shepherd, a dwarf also, and the King honoured the wedding with his presence. Each measured three feet ten inches.

" Design or chance makes others wive,
But Nature did this match contrive."
Waller.

The Black Dwarf. A fairy of the most malignant character ; a genuine northern Duergar, and once held by the dalesmen of the border as the author of all the mischief that befell their flocks and herds. Sir Walter Scott has a novel so called, in which the " black dwarf " is introduced under the *aliases* of Sir Edward Mauley ; Elshander, the recluse ; Cannie Elshie ; and the Wise Wight of Mucklestane Moor.

Dwarf Alberich (in the *Nibelungen Lied*) is the guardian of the famous " hoard " won by Siegfried from the Nibelungs. The dwarf is twice vanquished by the hero, who gets possession of his *Tarn-kappë* (cloak of invisibility). (*See* ELBERICH.)

Dwarf Peter (*das Peter Manchen*). An allegorical romance by Ludwig Tieck. The dwarf is a castle spectre that advises and aids the family ; but all his advice turns out evil, and all his aid productive of trouble. The dwarf represents that corrupt part of human nature called by St. Paul the " law in our members which wars against the law of our minds, and brings us into captivity to the law of sin."

Dwarfs (under three feet in height).

ANDROM'EDA, 2 ft. 4 in. One of Julia's free maids. (*See below*, CONOPAS.)

ARIS'TRATOS, the poet, was so small that Athenæos says, "no one could see him."

BEBE, or Nicholas Ferry, 2 ft. 9 in. A native of France (1714–1737). He had a brother and sister, both dwarfs.

BORUWLASKI (*Count Joseph*), 2 ft. 4 in. at the age of twenty. (1739–1837).

BUCKINGER (*Matthew*), a German, born 1674. He was born without hands, legs, or feet. Facsimiles of his writing are amongst the Harleian MSS.

CHE-MAH (a Chinese), 2 ft. 1 in., weight 52 lbs. Exhibited in London in 1880.

COLO'BRI (*Prince*) of Sleswig, 2 ft. 1 in., weight 25 lbs. at the age of 25 (1851).

CONOPAS, 2 ft. 4 in. One of the dwarfs of Julia, niece of Augustus. (*See above*, ANDROMEDA.)

COPPERNIN, the dwarf of the Princess of Wales, mother of George III. The last court dwarf in England.

CRACH'AMI' (*Caroline*). Born at Palermo; 1 ft. 8 in. at death. (1814–24.) Exhibited in Bond Street, London, 1824.

DECKER or DUCKER (*John*), 2 ft. 6 in. An Englishman (1610).

FAIRY QUEEN (*The*), 1 ft. 4 in., weight 4 lbs. Exhibited in Regent Street, London, 1850. Her feet were less than two inches.

GIBSON (*Richard*), a good portrait painter. His wife's maiden name was Anne Shepherd. Each measured 3 ft. 10 in. Waller sang their praises. (In the reign of Charles I.)

HUDSON (*Sir Jeffrey*). Born at Oakham, Rutlandshire ; 1 ft. 6 in. at the age of thirty (1619–78).

JARVIS (*John*), 2 ft. Page of honour to Queen Mary (1508–56).

LOLKES (*Wybrand*), 2 ft. 3 in., weight 57 lbs. Exhibited at Astley's in 1790.

LU'CIUS, 2 ft., weight 17 lbs. The dwarf of the Emperor Augustus.

MARINE (*Lizzie*), 2 ft. 9 in., weight 45 lbs.

MIDGETS, THE. Lucia Zarate, the eldest sister, 1 ft. 8 in., weight 4½ lbs. at the age of eighteen. Her sister was a little taller. Exhibited in London, 1881.

MILLER (*Miss*), of Virginia, 2 ft. 2 in.

MITE (*General*), 1 ft. 9 in. (weight 9 lbs.) at the age of seventeen. Exhibited in London, 1881.

PAAP (*Simon*). A Dutch dwarf, 2 ft. 4 in., weight 27 lbs.

PHILE'TAS, a poet, contemporary with Hippocratês. So thin "that he wore leaden shoes lest the wind should blow him away." (Died B.C. 280.)

SAWYER (A. L.), 2 ft. 6½ in., weight 39 lbs. Editor in 1883, etc., of the *Democrat*, a paper of considerable repute in Florida.

STOBERIN (C. H.), of Nuremberg, 2 ft. 11 in. at the age of twenty.

STOCKER (*Nannette*), 2 ft. 9 in. Exhibited in London in 1815.

STRASSE DAVIT Family. Man, 1 ft. 8 in.; woman, 1 tt. 6 in.; child, at age of seventeen, only 6 in. Embalmed in the chemical library of Rastadt.

TERESIA (*Madame*). A Corsican, 2 ft. 10 in., weight 27 lbs. Exhibited in London 1773.

TOM THUMB (*General*), whose name was Charles S. Stratton, born at Bridgeport in Connecticut, U.S., 2 ft. 1 in., weight 25 lbs. at the age of twenty-five. (1838-83.) Exhibited first in London in 1844. In 1863 he married Betsy Bump (Lavina Warren).

TOM THUMB, a Dutch dwarf, 2 ft. 4 in. at the age of eighteen.

WANMER (*Lucy*), 2 ft. 6 in., weight 45 lbs. Exhibited in London, 1801, at the age of forty-five.

WARREN (*Lavina*), married to General Tom Thumb in 1863, was also a dwarf, and in 1885 she married another dwarf, Count Primo Magri, who was 2 ft. 8 in.

WORMBERG (*John*), 2 ft. 7 in. at the age of thirty-eight (Hanoverian period).

XIT was the dwarf of Edward VI.

ZARATE (*Lucia*), 1 ft. 3 in.. An excellent linguist of Shigaken Osara (b. 1851).

∴ Nicephorus Galistus tells us of an Egyptian dwarf not bigger than a partridge.

The names of several infants are known whose heads have not exceeded in size an ordinary billiard ball. The son of D. O. Miller, of Candelaria, born October 27th, 1882, weighed only 8¾ oz. A silver dollar would entirely hide its face, and its mouth was too small to admit an ordinary lead pencil.

The head of the son of Mrs. Charles Tracy, of Kingsbridge, N.Y., was not bigger than a horse-chestnut, and the mouth would hardly grasp a goose-quill. The mother's wedding ring would slip easily up its legs and thighs.

The head of Mr. Marion Poe's child was not so big as a billiard ball and the mother's ring would slip up the arm as high as the shoulder. Mr. Poe stands over six feet in height.

I have a list of several other babies of similar dimensions.

Dwile, or Dwyel. A house-flannel for cleaning floors, common in Norfolk, and called in the piece " dweyeling." (Dutch, *dweil*, a clout or swab.)

Dwt. is D-wt., *i.e. denarius-weight* (penny-weight). (*See* CWT.)

Dyed Beards. The dyeing of beards is mentioned by Strabo, and Bottom the Weaver satirises the custom when he undertakes to play Pyramus, and asks, " what beard were I best to play it in ? "

" I will discharge it in either your straw-colour beard, your orange-tawny beard, your purple-in-grain beard, or your French-crown-colour beard (your perfect yellow)."—*Shakespeare: Midsummer Night's Dream*, i. 2.

∴ The French couronne = twenty-five francs, was a gold piece, and therefore the French-crown colour was a golden yellow; but the word French-crown also means baldness brought on by licentiousness. Hence the retort, " some of your ' French-crowns' have no hair at all."

Dyeing Scarlet. Drinking deep. Drinking dyes the face scarlet.

" They call drinking deep, dyeing scarlet."— *Shakespeare: 1 Henry IV.* ii. 4.

Dying Sayings (real or traditional):

ADAMS (*President*) : "Independence for ever."

ADAMS (*John Q.*) : " It is the last of earth. I am content."

ADDISON : "See how a Christian dies," *or* "See in what peace a Christian can die." (*See* BERRY.)

ALBERT (*Prince Consort*) : " I have such sweet thoughts."

ALEXANDER I. (of Russia) : "Que vous devez être fatiguée " (to his wife Elizabeth).

ALEXANDER II. (of Russia) : " I am sweeping through the gates, washed in the blood of the Lamb."

ALEXANDER III. (of Russia) : "This box was presented to me by the Emperor [sic] of Prussia."

ALFIERI : "Clasp my hand, dear friend, I am dying."

ANAXAG'ORAS (the philosopher, who maintained himself by keeping a school, being asked if he wished for anything, replied) : "Give the boys a holiday."

ANGELO (*Michael*) : "My soul I resign to God, my body to the earth, my worldly goods to my next akin."

ANNE BOLEYN (on the scaffold) : " It [my neck] is very small, very small."

ANTOINETTE. (*See below*, MARIE.)

ANTONY (of Padua) : " I see my God. He calls me to Him."

ARCHIMEDES (being ordered by a Roman soldier to follow him, replied) : " Wait till I have finished my problem." (*See* LAVOISIER.)

ARRIA : "My Pætus, it is not painful."

AUGUSTUS (having asked how he had played his part, and being, of course, commended, said) : " Vos plaudite."

BACON (*Francis*) : " My name and memory I leave to men's charitable speeches, to foreign nations and to the next age."

BAILLEY : "Yes ! it is very cold." (This he said on his way to the guillotine, when one said to him, "Why, how you shake.")

BEAUFORT (*Cardinal Henry*) : " I pray you all pray for me."

BEAUMONT (*Cardinal*) : "What! is there no escaping death ?"

BECKET (*Thomas à*) : " I confide my soul and the cause of the Church to God, to the Virgin Mary, to the patron saints of the Church, and to St. Dennis." (This was said as he went to the altar in Canterbury Cathedral, where he was assassinated.)

BEDE (*The Venerable*) : "Glory be to the Father, and to the Son, and to the Holy Ghost."

BEETHOVEN (who was deaf) : " I shall hear in heaven."

BERRY (*Madame de*) : "Is not this dying with courage and true greatness ?" (*See* ADDISON.)

BOILEAU : " It is a great consolation to a poet on the point of death that he has never written a line injurious to good morals."

BRONTE (father of the authoresses) : " While there is life there is will." (Like Louis XVIII., Vespasian, Siward, and others, he died standing.)

BROUGHTON (*Bishop*) : " Let the earth be filled with His glory."

BURNS : " Don't let the awkward squad fire over my grave."

BYRON : " I must sleep now."

CÆSAR (*Julius*) : " Et tu, Brute ?" (This he said to Brutus, his most intimate friend, when he stabbed him.)

CAMERON (*Colonel James*) : "Scots, follow me !" (He was killed at Bull-Run, 21st July, 1861.)

CASTLEREAGH : "Bankhead, let me fall into your arms. It is all over." (Said to Dr. Bankhead.)

CATESBY (one of the conspirators in the Gunpowder Plot) : "Stand by me, Tom, and we will die together."

CHARLEMAGNE : "Lord, into Thy hand I commend my spirit." (*See* COLUMBUS and TASSO.)

CHARLES I. (of England, just before he laid his head on the block, said to Juxon, Archbishop of Canterbury) : " Remember."

CHARLES II. (of England) : "Don't forget poor Nell," *or* " Don't let poor Nell starve" (meaning Nell Gwynne).

CHARLES V. : "Ah ! Jesus."

CHARLES VIII. (of France): "I hope never again to commit a mortal sin, nor even a venial one, if I can help it." (With these words in his mouth, says Cominges, he gave up the ghost.)

CHARLES IX. (of France, in whose reign occurred the Bartholomew slaughter): "Nurse, nurse, what murder! what blood! Oh! I have done wrong: God pardon me."

CHARLOTTE (The Princess): "You make me drunk. Pray leave me quiet. I feel it affects my head."

CHESTERFIELD (Lord): "Give Dayrolles a chair."

CHRIST (Jesus): "It is finished!" (John xix. 30.)

CHRYSOSTOM: "Glory to God for all things. Amen."

CICERO (to his assassins): "Strike!"

COLIGNY: "Honour these grey hairs, young man." (Said to the German who assassinated him.)

COLUMBUS: "Lord, into Thy hands I commend my spirit." (See CHARLEMAGNE and TASSO.)

CONDE (Duc d'Enghien): "I die for my king and for France." (Shot by order of Napoleon I. in 1804.)

COPER'NICUS: "Now, O Lord, set thy servant free." (See Luke ii. 29.)

CORDAY (Charlotte): "One man have I slain to save a hundred thousand."

CRANMER (Archbishop of Canterbury): "That unworthy hand! That unworthy hand!" (This he said, according to a popular tradition, as he held in the flames his right hand which had signed his apostasy.)

CROMBE (John): "O Hobbema, Hobbema, how I do love thee!"

CROMWELL: "My design is to make what haste I can to be gone."

CUVIER (to the nurse who was applying leeches): "Nurse, it was I who discovered that leeches have red blood."

DANTON (to the executioner): "Be sure you show the mob my head. It will be a long time ere they see its like."

DEMO'NAX (the philosopher): "You may go home, the show is over" (Lucian). (See RABELAIS.)

DERBY (Earl of): "Douglas, I would give all my lands to save thee."

DICKENS (said in reply to his sister-in-law, who urged him to lie down): "Yes, on the ground."

DIDEROT: "The first step towards philosophy is incredulity."

DIOGENES (requested that his body should be buried, and when his friends said that his body would be torn to pieces he replied): "Quid mihi nocebunt ferarum dentes nihil sentienti."

DOUGLAS (Earl): "Fight on, my merry men."

EDWARDS (Jonathan): "Trust in God, and you need not fear."

ELDON (Lord): "It matters not where I am going whether the weather be cold or hot."

ELIZABETH (Queen): "All my possessions for a moment of time."

ELIZABETH (sister of Louis XVI., on her way to the guillotine, when her kerchief fell from her neck): "I pray you, gentlemen, in the name of modesty, suffer me to cover my bosom."

ELPHEGE (Archbishop of Canterbury): "You urge me in vain. I am not the man to provide Christian flesh for Pagan teeth, by robbing my flock to enrich their enemy."

EPAMINONDAS (wounded; on being told that the Thebans were victorious): "Then I die happy." (See WOLFE.)

ETTY: "Wonderful! Wonderful this death!"

EULER: "I am dying."

FARR (M.D.): "Lord, receive my spirit."

FELTON (John): "I am the man" (i.e. who shot the Duke of Buckingham).

FONTENELLE: "I suffer nothing, but I feel a sort of difficulty of living longer."

FRANKLIN: "A dying man can do nothing easily."

FREDERICK V. (of Denmark): "There is not a drop of blood on my hands." (See PERICLES.)

GAINSBOROUGH: "We are all going to heaven, and Vandyke is of the company." (See CROME.)

GARRICK: "Oh, dear!"

GASTON DE FOIX (called "Phœbus" for his beauty): "I am a dead man! Lord, have mercy upon me!"

GEORGE IV.: "Watty, what is this? It is death, my boy. They have deceived me." (Said to his page, Sir Wathen Waller.)

GIBBON: "Mon Dieu! Mon Dieu!"

GŒTHE: "More light."

GOLDSMITH: "No, it is not." (Said in reply to Dr. Turton, who asked him if his mind was at ease.)

GRANT (General): "I want nobody distressed on my account."

GREGORY VII.: "I have loved justice and hated iniquity, therefore I die in exile." (He had embroiled himself with Heinrich IV., the Kaiser, and had retired to Salerno.)

GREY (Lady Jane): "Lord, into Thy hands I commend my spirit." (See CHARLEMAGNE.)

GROTIUS: "Be serious."

GUSTAVUS ADOLPHUS: "My God!"

HALLER: "My friend, the pulse has ceased to beat." (This was said to his medical attendant.)

HANNIBAL: "Let us now relieve the Romans of their fears by the death of a feeble old man."

HARRISON (W. H.): "I wish you to understand the true principles of government. I wish them carried out, and ask nothing more."

HAYDN died singing "God preserve the emperor!"

HAZLITT: "I have led a happy life."

HENRY II. (of England): "Now let the world go as it will; I care for nothing more." (This he said when he was told that his favourite son John was one of those who were conspiring against him. (Shakespeare makes Macbeth say:
"I 'gin to be aweary of the sun,
And wish th' estate o' the world were now undone.")

HENRY III.: "I am Harry of Winchester." (These can hardly be called his dying words, but only the last recorded. They were spoken on the field of battle when a man was about to slay him. The battle of Evesham was fought August 4th, 1265, but Henry III. died November 16th, 1272.)

HENRY VII.: "We heartily desire our executors to consider how behoofful it is to be prayed for."

HENRY VIII.: "All is lost! Monks, monks, monks!"

HENRY (Prince): "Tie a rope round my body, pull me out of bed, and lay me in ashes, that I may die with repentant prayers to an offended God."

HERBERT (George): "Now, Lord, receive my soul."

HOBBES: "Now I am about to take my last voyage—a great leap in the dark."

HOFER (Andreas): "I will not kneel. Fire!" (Spoken to the soldiers commissioned to shoot him.)

HOOD: "Dying, dying."

HOOPER: "Lord, receive my spirit."

HUMBOLDT: "How grand these rays! They seem to beckon earth to heaven."

HUNTER (Dr. William): "If I had strength to hold a pen, I would write down how easy and pleasant a thing it is to die."

IRVING (Edward): "If I die, I die unto the Lord. Amen."

JACKSON (surnamed "Stonewall"): "Send Hill to the front."

JAMES V. (of Scotland): "It [the crown of Scotland] came with a lass and will go with a lass." (This he said when told that the queen had given birth to a daughter—the future Mary Queen of Scots.)

JEFFERSON (of America): "I resign my spirit to God, my daughter to my country."

JEROME (of Prague): "Thou knowest, Lord, that I have loved the truth."

JESUS (See CHRIST).

JOAN of ARC: "Jesus! Jesus! Jesus! Blessed be God."

JOHNSON (Dr.): "God bless you, my dear" (to Miss Morris).

JOSEPHINE (the divorced wife of Napoleon I.): "L'ile d'Elbe! Napoleon!"

JULIAN (called the "Apostate"): "Vicisti, O Galilee."

KEATS: "I feel the flowers growing over me."

KEN (Bishop): "God's will be done."

KNOX: "Now it is come."

LAMB (Charles): "My bed-fellows are cramp and cough—we three all in one bed."

LAMBERT (the Martyr): "None but Christ! None but Christ!" (This he said as he was pitched into the flames.)

LAVOISIER, being condemned to die, asked for a respite of two weeks that he might complete some experiments in which he was engaged. He was told that the Republic was in no need of experiments. (*See above,* ARCHIME'DES.)

LAWRENCE (*St.*). Said to have been broiled alive on a gridiron, A.D. 258.
" This side enough is toasted, so turn me, tyrant, eat,
: And see whether raw or roasted I make the better meat." *Foxe : Book of Martyrs.*

LAWRENCE (*Com. James*): "Don't give up the ship." (Mortally wounded on the *Chesapeake*.)

LEICESTER (*Earl of*) : " By the arm of St. James, it is time to die."

LEOPOLD I. (*the Kaiser*) : "Let me die to the sound of sweet music." (*See* MIRABEAU.)

LISLE (*Sir George*) : "Ay! but I have been nearer to you, my friends, many a time, and you have missed me."

LOCKE (*John*) : "Oh! the depth of the riches of the goodness and knowledge of God. Cease now." (This was said to Lady Masham, who was reading to him some of the Psalms.)

LOUIS I. : "Huz! huz!" (Bouquet says, "He turned his face to the wall, twice cried *huz! huz!* [out ; out !] and then died.)

LOUIS IX. : "I will enter now into the house of the Lord."

LOUIS XI. : "Notre dame d'Embrun, ma bonne maitresse, aidez moi."

LOUIS XIV. : "Why weep you? Did you think I should live for ever? I thought dying had been harder."

LOUIS XVI. (on the scaffold): "Frenchmen, I die guiltless of the crimes imputed to me. Pray God my blood fall not on France!"

LOUIS XVIII. : "A king should die standing." (*See* VESPASIAN and SIWARD.)

MADISON (*James*): "I always talk better lying down."

MAHOMET or MOHAMMED: "O Allah! be it so! Henceforth among the glorious host of Paradise."

MALESHERBES (to the priest): "Hold your tongue! your wretched chatter disgusts me."

MARAT (stabbed in his bath by Charlotte Corday): "Help! help me, my dear !" (To his housekeeper.)

MARGARET (of Scotland, wife of Louis XI. of France): "Fi de la vie! qu'on ne m'en parle plus."

MARIE ANTOINETTE: "Farewell, my children, for ever. I am going to your father."

MARTIN (*St.*) : "What dost thou here, thou cruel beast?" (Said to the devil). (*St. Sulpicius: Epistle to Bassula*.)

MARTINUZZI (*Cardinal*), the Wolsey of Hungary. He was assassinated uttering the words, "Jesu, Maria !"

MARY (*Queen of England*) : "You will find the word *Calais* written on my heart."

MASANIELLO: "Ungrateful traitors !" (To his assassins.)

MATHEWS (*Charles*): " I am ready."

MAXIMILIAN (*Emperor of Mexico*): "Poor Carlotta !" (Referring to his wife.)

MELANCTHON (in reply to the question, "Do you want anything ?") : "Nothing but heaven."

MIRABEAU: "Let me fall asleep to the sound of delicious music." (*See* LEOPOLD.)

MONICA (*St.*): "In peace I will sleep with Him and take my rest." (*St. Augustin: Confessions.*)

MOODY (the actor):
" Reason thus with life:
If I do lose thee, I do lose a thing
That none but fools would keep."
(The same is said of Paterson, an actor in the Norwich Company.)

MOORE (*Hannah*): "Patty, Joy."

MOORE (*Sir John*) : "I hope my country will do me justice."

MORE (*Sir Thomas*): "For my coming down, let me shift for myself."

MOZART: "You spoke of a refreshment, Emilie ; take my last notes, and let me hear once more my solace and delight."

MURAT (*King of Naples*): "Soldiers, save my face ; aim at my heart. Farewell." (Said to the men appointed to shoot him.)

NAPOLEON I.: " Mon Dieu ! La nation Française. Tête d'armée !"

NAPOLEON III. : " Were you at Sedan ?" (To Dr. Conneau.)

NELSON: "I thank God I have done my duty. Kiss me, Hardy."

NERO: "Qualis artifex perio."

PALMER (the actor): " There is another and a better world." (This he said on the stage. It is a line in the part he was performing—*The Stranger.*)

PASCAL : "My God, forsake me not."

PER'ICLES (of Athens) : " I have never caused any citizen to put on mourning on my account." (*See* FREDERICK V.)

PITT (*William*) : " Alas, my country !"

PIZARRO : "Jesu!"

POMPADOUR (*Mdme. de*) : "Stay a little longer, M. le Curé, and we will go together."

PONIATOWSKI (after the bridge over the Pliesse was blown up) : "Gentlemen, it behoves us now to die with honour."

POPE : "Friendship itself is but a part of virtue."

RABELAIS : "Let down the curtain, the farce is over." (*See* DEMO'NAX.)

RALEIGH : "It matters little how the head lies." (Said on the scaffold where he was beheaded.)

RENAN : " We perish, we disappear, but the march of time goes on for ever."

RICHARD I. (of England) : "Youth, I forgive thee !" (This was said to Bertrand de Gourdon, who shot him with an arrow at Chalus.) Then to his attendants he added, " Take off his chains, give him 100 shillings, and let him go."

RICHARD III. (of England) : "Treason ! treason !" (At Bosworth, where his best men deserted him and joined the army of Richmond, afterwards Henry VII.)

ROBESPIERRE (taunted with the death of Danton) : "Cowards ! Why did you not defend him?" (This must have been before his jaw was broken by the shot of the gendarme the day before he was guillotined.)

ROCHEJAQUELAIN (the Vendean hero) : "We go to meet the foe. If I advance, follow me ; if I retreat, slay me ; if I fall, avenge me."

ROLAND (*Madame*): "O liberty ! What crimes are committed in thy name !"

SALADIN : " When I am buried, carry my winding-sheet on the point of a spear, and say these words: Behold the spoils which Saladin carries with him ! Of all his victories, realms, and riches, nothing remains to him but this." (*See* SEVERUS.)

SAND (*George*): " Laissez la verdure." (That is, leave the plot green, and do not cover the grave with bricks or stone.)

SCARRON : " Ah, my children, you cannot cry for me so much as I have made you laugh."

SCHILLER : "Many things are growing plain and clear to my understanding."

SCOTT (*Sir Walter*): "God bless you all. I feel myself again." (To his family.)

SERVE'TUS (at the stake): "Christ, Son of the eternal God, have mercy upon me." (Calvin insisted on his saying, "the eternal Son of God," but he would not, and was burnt to death.)

SEVE'RUS : "I have been everything, and everything is nothing. A little urn will contain all that remains of one for whom the whole world was too little." (*See* SALADIN.)

SEYMOUR (*Jane*): "No, my head never committed any treason ; but, if you want it, you can take it." (As Jane Seymour died within a fortnight of the birth of her son Edward—the cause of unbounded delight to the king—I cannot believe that this traditionary speech is correct.)

SHARPE (*Archbishop*) : "I shall be happy."

SHERIDAN : "I am absolutely undone."

SIDNEY (*Algernon*) : "I know that my Redeemer liveth. I die for the good old cause." (He was condemned to death by Judge Jeffries as an accomplice in the Rye House plot.)

SIDNEY (*Sir Philip*) : "I would not change my joy for the empire of the world."

SIWARD (the Dane) : "Lift me up that I may die standing, not lying down like a cow." (*See* LOUIS XVIII. and VESPASIAN.)

SOCRATES : "Crito, we owe a cock to Æsculapios."

STAEL (*Madame de*) : "I have loved God, my father, and liberty."

STEPHEN (the first Christian martyr) : "Lord, into thy hands I commend my spirit."

SWEDENBORG : "What o'clock is it ?" (After being told, he added) "Thank you, and God bless you."

TALMA: "The worst is, I cannot see." (But his last word was) "Voltaire."

TASSO: "Lord, into Thy hands I commend my spirit." (*See* CHARLEMAGNE, and COLUMBUS.)

TAYLOR (*General Zachary*): "I have tried to do my duty, and am not afraid to die. I am ready."

TENTERDEN (*Lord Chief Justice*): "Gentlemen of the jury, you may retire."

THERAMENES (the Athenian, condemned by Critias to drink hemlock, said as he drank the poison): "This to the fair Critias."

THIEF (*The Penitent*): "Lord, remember me when Thou comest into Thy Kingdom."

THURLOW (*Lord*): "I'll be shot if I don't believe I'm dying."

TYLER (*Wat*): "Because they are all under my command, they are sworn to do what I bid them."

VANE (*Sir Harry*): "It is a bad cause which cannot bear the words of a dying man."

VESPASIAN: "A king should die standing" (*See* LOUIS XVIII. and SIWARD); but his last words were, "Ut puto, deus fio" (referring to the fact that he was the first of the Roman emperors who died a natural death, if, indeed, Augustus was poisoned, as many suppose).

VICARS (*Hedley*): "Cover my face."

VOLTAIRE: "Do let me die in peace."

WASHINGTON: "It is well. I die hard, but am not afraid to go."

WESLEY: "The best of all is, God is with us."

WILBERFORCE (His father said to him, "So He giveth His beloved sleep"; to which Wilberforce replied): "Yes, and sweet indeed is the rest which Christ giveth." (Saying this, he never spoke again.)

WILLIAM I.: "To my Lady, the Holy Mary, I commend myself; that she, by her prayers, may reconcile her beloved Son to me."

WILLIAM II.: "Shoot, Walter, in the devil's name!" (Walter Tyrrell did shoot, but killed the king.)

WILLIAM III.: "Can this last long?" (To his physician. He suffered from a broken collarbone.)

WILLIAM (of Nassau): "O God, have mercy upon me, and upon this poor nation." (This was just before he was shot by Balthasar Gerard.)

WILSON (the ornithologist): "Bury me where the birds will sing over my grave."

WOLFE (*General*): "What! do they run already? Then I die happy." (*See* EPAMINONDAS.)

WOLSEY (*Cardinal*): "Had I but served my God with half the zeal that I have served my king, He would not have left me in my grey hairs."

WORDSWORTH: "God bless you! Is that you, Dora?"

WYATT (*Thomas*): "What I then said [about the treason of Princess Elizabeth] I unsay now; and what I now say is the truth." (This was said to the priest who waited on him on the scaffold.)

ZISKA (*John*): "Make my skin into drum-heads for the Bohemian cause."

Many of these sayings, like all other history, belong to the region of Phrase and Fable, but the collection is interesting and fairly exhaustive.

Dymph'na. The tutelar saint of those stricken in spirit. She was a native of Britain, and a woman of high rank. It is said that she was murdered, at Geel, in Belgium, by her own father, because she resisted his incestuous passion. Geel, or Gheel, has long been a famous colony for the insane, who are sent thither from all parts of Europe, and are boarded with the peasantry.

Dy'namite (3 syl.) An explosive compound consisting of some absorbent (as infusorial earth) saturated with nitroglycerine. (Greek, *dunamis*, power.)

Dynamite Saturday. January 24th, 1885, when great damage was done to the Houses of Parliament and the Tower of London by explosions of dynamite. The Law-Courts and some other public buildings were to have been attacked by the dynamiters, but happily were well guarded. (*See* CLAN-NA-GAEL.)

Dyot Street, Bloomsbury Square, London; now called George Street, St. Giles. Made familiar by a well-known song in *Bombastes Furioso:*

"My lodging is in heather lane,
A parlour that's next to the sky . . ."
Rhodes.

Dyser. The deities who conduct the souls of the deceased to the palace of Odin. (*Scandinavian mythology*.)

Dy'vour. The debtor's badge in Scotland (French, *devoir*, to own). Bankrupts were compelled to wear an upper garment, half yellow and half brown, with a parti-coloured cap. This law was abolished in the reign of William IV.

Dyz'emas Day. Tithe day. (Portuguese, *diz'imas*, tithes; Law Latin, *dec'imæ*.)

E.

E. This letter represents a window; in Hebrew it is called *he* (a window).

E.G. or *e.g.* (Latin for *exempli gra'tia*). By way of example; for instance.

E Pluribus Unum (Latin). One unity composed of many parts. The motto of the United States of America.

Eager or *eagre.* Sharp, keen, acid; the French *aigre.* (Latin, crude form, *acr-* "acer," sharp.)

"It doth posset
And curd, like eager droppings into milk."
Shakespeare: Hamlet, i. 5.

"Vex him with eager words."
Shakespeare: Henry VI., ii. 4.

Eagle (in royal banners). It was the ensign of the ancient kings of Babylon and Persia, of the Ptolemies and Seleu'cidēs. The Romans adopted it in conjunction with other devices, but Ma'rius made it the ensign of the legion, and confined the other devices to the cohorts. The French under the Empire assumed the same device.

Eagle (in Christian art) is emblematic of St. John the Evangelist, because, like the eagle, he looked on "the sun of glory"; the eagle was one of the four figures which made up the cherub (Ezek. i. 10).

Eagle (in funerals). The Romans used to let an eagle fly from the funeral pile of a deceased emperor. Dryden alludes to this custom in his stanzas on Oliver Cromwell after his funeral, when he says, "Officious haste did let too soon the sacred eagle fly."

Eagle (in heraldry) signifies fortitude.

Eagle (for lecterns in churches). The eagle is the natural enemy of the serpent. The two Testaments are the two outspread wings of the eagle.

⁙ Pliny in his *Natural History* (book x. chap. 3) enumerates six kinds of eagles: (1) Melænactos, (2) Pygargus, (3) Morphnos, which Homer (*Iliad*, xxiv. 316) calls perknos, (4) Percnopterus, (5) Gnesios, the royal eagle, and (6) Haliæetos, the osprey.

Eagle (in phrases).
Thy youth is renewed like the eagle's (Ps. ciii. 5). This refers to the superstition feigned by poets that every ten years the eagle soars into the "fiery region," and plunges thence into the sea, where, moulting its feathers, it acquires new life.

" She saw where he upstarted brave
  Out of the well. . . .
  As eagle fresh out of the ocean wave,
  Where he hath lefte his plumes all hory gray,
  And decks himself with fethers youthly gay."
      Spenser : Faërie Queene, i. 11, 34.

Eagle, a public-house sign, is in honour of Queen Mary, whose badge it was. She put it on the dexter side of the shield, and the sun on the sinister—a conjugal compliment which gave great offence to her subjects.
The Golden Eagle and the *Spread Eagle* are commemorative of the crusades; they were the devices of the emperors of the East.

Eagle. *The spread eagle.* A device of the old Roman or Eastern Empire, brought over by the crusaders.
Eagle of the doctors of France. Pierre d'Ailly, a French cardinal and great astrologer, who calculated the horoscope of our Lord, and maintained that the stars foretold the great deluge. (1350-1425.)
Eagle of Brittany. Bertrand Duguesclin, Constable of France. (1320-1380.)
Eagle of Meaux [*mo*]. Jacques Bénigne Bossuet, Bishop of Meaux, the grandest and most sublime of the pulpit orators of France. (1627-1704.)

Eagle. *The two-headed eagle.* Austria, Prussia (representing Germany), and Russia have two-headed eagles, one

facing to the right and the other to the left. The one facing to the west indicates direct succession from Charlemagne, crowned the sixty-ninth emperor of the Romans from Augustus. In Russia it was Ivan Basilovitz who first assumed the two-headed eagle, when, in 1472, he married Sophia, daughter of Thomas Palæologus, and niece of Constantine XIV., the last Emperor of Byzantium. The two heads symbolise the Eastern or Byzantine Empire and the Western or Roman Empire.

Eagle-stones or *Aetītes* (ἀετίτης). Yellow clay ironstones supposed to have sanative and magical virtues. They are so called because they are found in eagles' nests. Epiphanius says, "In the interior of Scythia there is a valley inaccessible to man, down which slaughtered lambs are thrown. The small stones at the bottom of the valley adhere to these pieces of flesh, and eagles, when they carry away the flesh to their nests, carry the stones with it." The story of Sindbad in the Valley of Diamonds will occur to the readers of this article (*Epiphanius : De duodecim gemmis*, etc., p. 30 ; 1743).
It is said that without these stones eagles cannot hatch their eggs.

Ear. (Anglo-Saxon, *eáre.*)
A deaf ear. One that refuses to listen ; as if it heard not.
Bow down Thine ear. Condescend to hear or listen. (Ps. xxxi. 2.)
By ear. To sing or play by ear means to sing or play without knowledge of musical notes, depending on the ear only.
Give ear to . . . Listen to ; give attention to.
I am all ear. All attention.

      "I was all ear,
And took in strains that might create a soul
Under the ribs of death."
        Milton: Comus, 574.

I'll send you off with a flea in your ear. With a cuff or box of the ear. The allusion is to domestic animals, who are sometimes greatly annoyed with these "tiny torments." There seems also to be a pun implied—*flea* and *flee*.
⁙ The French equivalent is "*Mettre la puce à l'oreille,*" to give one a good jobation.
In at one ear, and out at the other. Forgotten as soon as heard.
No ear. A bad ear for musical intonations ; "ear-blind " or "sound-blind."
Dionysius's Ear. A bell-shaped chamber connected by an underground passage with the king's palace. Its object was

that the tyrant of Syracuse might overhear whatever was passing in the prison.

Ear-finger. The little finger, which is thrust into the ear if anything tickles it.

Ear-marked. Marked so as to be recognised. The allusion is to marking cattle and sheep on the ear, by which they may be readily recognised.

"The increase [of these wild cattle] were duly branded and ear-marked each year."—*Nineteenth Century* (May, 1893), p. 789.
"The late president [Balmaceda] took on board a large quantity of silver, which had been ear-marked for a particular purpose."—*Newspaper paragraph*, Sept. 4, 1891.

Ear-shot. *Within ear-shot.* Within hearing. The allusion is palpable.

Ears.
About one's ears. Causing trouble. The allusion is to a house falling on one, or a hornet's nest buzzing about one's head.

Bring the house about your ears. Set the whole family against you.

¶ If your ears burn, people say some one is *talking of you*. This is very old, for Pliny says, "When our ears do glow and tingle, some do talk of us in our absence." Shakespeare, in *Much Ado About Nothing* (iii. 1), makes Beatrice say, when Ur'sula and Hero had been talking of her, "What fire is in mine ears?" Sir Thomas Browne ascribes this conceit to the superstition of guardian angels, who touch the right ear if the talk is favourable, and the left if otherwise. This is done to cheer or warn.

"One ear tingles ; some there be
  That are snarling now at me."
          Herrick: Hesperides.

Little pitchers have large ears. (*See* PITCHERS.)

Mine ears hast thou bored. Thou hast accepted me as thy bond-slave for life. If a Hebrew servant declined to go free after six years' service, the master was to bring him to the doorpost, and bore his ear through with an awl, in token of his voluntary servitude. (Exod. xxi. 6.)

Over head and ears (in love, in debt, etc.). Wholly, desperately.

"He is over head and ears in love with the maid. He loves her better than his own life."—*Terence in English.*

To give's one's ears [to obtain an object]. To make a considerable sacrifice for the purpose. The allusion is to the ancient practice of cutting off the ears of those who loved their own offensive opinions better than their ears.

To have itching ears. Loving to hear news or current gossip. (2 Tim. iv. 3.)

To prick up one's ears. To listen attentively to something not expected, as horses prick up their ears at a sudden sound.

"At which, like unbacked colts, they pricked their ears."
          Shakespeare: The Tempest, iv. 1.

To set people together by the ears. To create ill-will among them ; to set them quarrelling and pulling each other's ears.

"When civil dudgeon first grew high,
  And men fell out, they knew not why ;
  When hard words, jealousies, and fears,
  Set folks together by the ears."
          Butler: Hudibras (The opening).

To tickle the ears. To gratify the ear either by pleasing sounds or flattering words.

Walls have ears. Things uttered in secret get rumoured abroad. Chaucer says, "That field hath eyen, and the wood hath ears." (*Canterbury Tales*, v. 1,524.)

Ears to ear Bible (*The*). (1810.) "Who hath ears to ear, let him hear." (Matt. xiii. 43.) (*See* BIBLE.)

Earing. Ploughing. (Anglo-Saxon, *erian*, to plough ; Latin, *aro*.)

"And yet there are five years, in the which there shall neither be earing nor harvest."—Genesis xlv. 6.
"In earing time and in harvest thou shalt rest."—Exodus xxxiv. 21.

Earl (Anglo-Saxon, *eorl*, a man of position, in opposition to *ceorl*, a churl, or freeman of the lowest rank ; Danish, *jarl*). William the Conqueror tried to introduce the word Count, but did not succeed, although the wife of an earl is still called a *countess*.

"The sheriff is called in Latin vice-comès, as being the deputy of the earl or comès, to whom the custody of the shire is said to have been committed."—*Blackstone: Commentaries*, book i. chap. ix. p. 339.

Earl of Mar's Grey Breeks. The 21st Foot are so called because they wore *grey breeches* when the Earl of Mar was their colonel. (1678-1686.)
The 21st Foot is now called the "Royal Scots Fusiliers."

Early to Bed. "Early to bed and early to rise, makes a man healthy, wealthy, and wise."

"Lever à cinq, dîner à neuf,
  Souper à cinq, coucher à neuf,
  Font vivre d'ans nonante neuf."
        (The older of the two.)
"Lever à six, dîner à dix,
  Super à six, coucher à dix,
  Fait vivre l'homme dix fois dix."

Earth. *To gather strength from the earth.* The reference is to Antæos, son of Posei'don and Ge, a giant and wrestler of Lib'ya (Africa). So long as he touched the earth his strength was irresistible. Hercules, knowing this, lifted him into the air and crushed him to death. Near the town of Tingis, in Maurita'nia, is a hill in the shape of a man, and called *The hill of Antæos.* Tradition says it is the wrestler's tomb. (*See* MALEGEA.)

Earthmen (*The*). Gnomes and fairies of the mines: a solemn race, who nevertheless can laugh most heartily and dance most merrily.

"We [earthmen] work at the mines for men; we put the ore in readiness for the miners."— *Besant and Rice: Titania's Farewell.*

Earthquakes. According to Indian mythology, the world rests on the head of a great elephant, and when, for the sake of rest, the huge monster refreshes itself by moving its head, an earthquake is produced. The elephant is called "Muha-pudma."

"Having penetrated to the south, they saw the great elephant 'Muha-pudma,' equal to a huge mountain, sustaining the earth with its head."— *The Ramayuna* (section xxxiii.).

✵ The Lamas say that the earth is placed on the back of a gigantic frog, and when the frog stretches its limbs or moves its head, it shakes the earth. Other Eastern mythologists place the earth on the back of a tortoise.

Greek and Roman mythologists ascribe earthquakes to the restlessness of the giants which Jupiter buried under high mountains. Thus Virgil (*Æneid*, iii. 578) ascribes the eruption of Etna to the giant Encelädus.

Earwig. A corruption of the Saxon *ear-wiega* (ear-insect); so called because the hind wings resemble in shape the human ear. The word has engendered the notion that these insects are apt to get into our cars.

An earwig, metaphorically, is one who whispers into our ears all the news and scandal going, in order to curry favour; a flatterer.

"Court earwigs banish from your ears."
Political Ballads.

Ease. (Anglo-Saxon, *eath;* Latin, *oti-um.*)

At ease. Without pain or anxiety.

Ill at ease. Uneasy, not comfortable, anxious.

Stand at ease! A command given to soldiers to rest for a time. The "gentlemen stood at ease" means in an informal manner.

To ease one of his money or *purse.* To steal it. (*See* LITTLE EASE.)

Ease (*Chapel of*). (*See* CHAPEL.)

Ease Her! A command given on a steamer to reduce speed. The next

order is generally "Stop her!"—*i.e.* **the** steamboat.

East. The custom of *turning to the east* when the creed is repeated is to express the belief that Christ is the Dayspring and Sun of Righteousness. The altar is placed at the east end of the church to remind us of Christ, the "Dayspring" and "Resurrection"; and persons are buried with their feet to the east to signify that they died in the hope of the Resurrection.

The ancient Greeks always buried their dead with the face *upwards*, looking towards heaven; and the feet turned to the east or the rising sun, to indicate that the deceased was on his way to Elysium, and not to the region of night or the inferno. (*Diogenês Laertius: Life of Solon*, in Greek.)

East Indies.

(1) *He came safe from the East Indies, and was drowned in the Thames.* He encountered many dangers of great magnitude, but was at last killed where he thought himself secure.

(2) *To send to the East Indies for Kentish pippins.* To go round about to accomplish a very simple thing. To crush a fly on a wheel. To send to the Chancellor of the Exchequer for a penny postage-stamp.

Easter. April was called Ostermonath—the month of the Ost-end wind (wind from the east). Easter is therefore the April feast, which lasted eight days. Our Easter Sunday must be between March 21st and April 25th. It is regulated by the paschal moon, or first full moon between the vernal equinox and fourteen days afterwards. (Teutonic, *ostara;* Anglo-Saxon, *eastre.*)

Easter. The Saxon goddess of the east, whose festival was held in the spring.

Easter-day Sun. It was formerly a common belief that the sun danced on Easter Day. Sir Thomas Browne combats the notion in his *Vulgar Errors.*

"But oh, she dances such a way,
No sun upon an Easter day
Is half so fine a sight."
Sir John Suckling.

Easter Eggs, or *Pasch eggs*, are symbolical of creation, or the re-creation of spring. The practice of presenting eggs to our friends at Easter is Magian or Persian, and bears allusion to the mundane egg, for which Ormuzd and Ahriman were to contend till the consummation of all things. It prevailed not only with the Persians, but also among the Jews, Egyptians, and Hindus. Christians adopted the custom to symbolise the resurrection, and they colour the eggs red in allusion to the blood of their redemption. There is a tradition, also, that the world was "hatched" or created at Easter-tide.

"Bless, Lord, we beseech thee, this Thy creature of eggs, that it may become a wholesome sustenance to Thy faithful servants, eating it in thankfulness to Thee, on account of the resurrection of our Lord."—*Pope Paul V.: Ritual.*

Eat. *To eat humble pie.* (*See* HUMBLE PIE.)

To eat one out of house and home. To eat so much that one will have to part with house and home in order to pay for it.

To eat one's words. To retract in a humiliating manner; to unsay what you have said; to eat your own lick.

To eat the mad cow. A French phrase, implying that a person is reduced to the very last extremity, and is willing to eat even a cow that has died of madness; glad to eat cat's meat.

"Il mangea de cette chose inexprimable qu'on appelle de la vache enragée."—*Victor Hugo: Les Misérables.*

To eat the leek. (*See* LEEK.)

To eat well. To have a good appetite. But "It eats well" means that what is eaten is agreeable or flavorous. To "eat badly" is to eat without appetite or too little; not pleasant to the taste.

Eat not the Brain. This is the 31st Symbol in the Protreptics of Iamblichus; and the prohibition is very similar to that of Moses forbidding the Jews to eat the blood, because the blood is the life. The brain is the seat of reason and the ruler of the body. It was also esteemed the Divine part—at least, of man.

Eat not the Heart. This is the 30th Symbol in the Protreptics of Iamblichus. Pythagoras forbade judges and priests to eat animal food at all, because it was taking away life. Other persons he did not wholly forbid this food, but he restricted them from eating the *brain* (the seat of wisdom) and the *heart* (the seat of life).

Eat One's Heart Out (*To*). To fret or worry unreasonably; to allow one grief or one vexation to predominate over the mind, tincture all one's ideas, and absorb all other emotions.

Eats his Head Off (*The horse*). Eats more than he is worth, or the work done does not pay for the cost of keeping.

A horse which stands in the stable unemployed eats his head off.

Eating One's Terms. To be studying for the bar. Students are required to dine in the Hall of the Inns of Court at least three times in each of the twelve terms before they are "called" [to the bar]. (*See* DOCTORS' COMMONS.)

Eating Together. To eat together in the East was at one time a sure pledge of protection. A Persian nobleman was once sitting in his garden, when a man prostrated himself before him, and implored protection from the rabble. The nobleman gave him the remainder of a peach which he was eating, and when the incensed multitude arrived, and declared that the man had slain the only son of the nobleman, the heart-broken father replied, "We have eaten together; go in peace," and would not allow the murderer to be punished.

Eau de Cologne. A perfumed spirit, prepared at Cologne. The most famous maker was Jean Maria Fari'na.

Eau de Vie. Brandy. A French translation of the Latin *aqua vitæ* (water of life). This is a curious perversion of the Spanish *acqua di vite* (water or juice of the vine), rendered by the monks into *aqua vitæ* instead of *aqua vitis*, and confounding the juice of the grape with the alchemists' elixir of life. The same error is perpetuated in the Italian *acqua vite;* the Scotch *whisky,* which is the Celtic *uisc-lyf;* and the Irish *usquebaugh,* which is the Gaelic and Irish *uisgæ-beatha.* (*See* AQUA VITÆ.)

Eaves-dropper. One who listens stealthily to conversation. The derivation of the term is not usually understood. The owners of private estates in Saxon times were not allowed to cultivate to the extremity of their possessions, but were obliged to leave a space for eaves. This space was called the *yfesdrype* (eaves-drip). An eaves-dropper is one who places himself in the eaves-drip to overhear what is said in the adjacent house or field.

"Under our tents I'll play the eaves-dropper,
To hear if any mean to shrink from me."
    Shakespeare: Richard III., v. 3.

Eb'ionism. The doctrine that the poor only shall be saved. *Ebion,* plural *ebionim* (poor).

"At the end of the second century the Ebionites were treated as heretics, and a pretended leader (Ebion) was invented by Tertullian to explain the name."—*Renan: Life of Jesus,* chap. xi.

Eb'ionites (4 syl.). A religious sect of the first and second centuries, who maintained that Jesus Christ was merely an inspired messenger, the greatest of all prophets, but yet a man and a man only, without any existence before His birth in Bethlehem. (*See above.*)

Eb'lis or *Ibleis*. A jinn, and the ruler of the evil genii, or fallen angels. Before his fall he was called Azaz'el or Hha'ris. When Adam was created, God commanded all the angels to worship him; but Eblis replied, "Me thou hast created of smokeless fire, and shall I reverence a creature made of dust?" God was very angry at this insolent answer, and turned the disobedient fay into a Sheytân (devil), and he became the father of devils.

"His majesty was a hundred feet in height; his skin, striped with red, was covered with small scales, which made it glisten like armour; his hair was so long and curly a snake might have lost its way in it; his flat nose was pierced with a ring of admirable workmanship; his small eyes assumed all the prismatic colours; his ears, which resembled those of an elephant, flapped on his shoulders; and his tail, sixty feet long, terminated in a hooked claw."—*Croquemitaine*, ii. 10.

"When he said unto the angels, 'Worship Adam,' all worshipped him except Eblis."—*Al Koran*, ii.

Eb'ony. *God's image done in ebony.* Negroes. Thomas Fuller gave birth to this expression.

Ebu'dæ. The Heb'rides. (*Ariosto: Orlando Furioso.*)

Ecce Homo. A painting by Correg'gio of our Lord crowned with thorns and bound with ropes, as He was shown to the people by Pilate, who said to them, "*Ecce homo!*" (Behold the man!) (John xix. 5.)

Other conceptions of this subject, either painted or engraved, are by Albert Durer (1471-1528), Titian (1477-1576), Cigoli (1559-1613), Guido (1574-1642), Albani (1578-1660), Vandyck (1599-1641), Rembrandt (1608-1669), Poussin (1613-1675), and some others.

Ecce Signum. See it, in proof; Behold the proof!

"I am eight times thrust through the doublet, four through the hose; my buckler cut through and through; my sword hacked like a handsaw—ecce signum!"—*Shakespeare:* 1 *Henry IV.*, ii. 4.

Eccen'tric means deviating from the centre; hence irregular, not according to rule. Originally applied to those planets which wander round the earth, like comets, the earth not being in the centre of their orbit. (Latin, *ex centrum*.)

Eccentric Sensation. The sensations of the brain transferred to objects without. For example: we see a tree; this tree is a reflection of the tree on the

retina transferred to the brain; but the tree seen is the tree without, not the tree in the brain. This transferred perception is called an "Eccentric Sensation."

Eccentric Theory (*The*) in astronomy. A theory which uses an eccentric instead of an epicycle in accounting for the sun's motion.

Ecclesias'tes (5 syl.). One of the books in the Old Testament, arranged next to Proverbs, generally ascribed to Solomon, because it says (verse 1), "The words of the Preacher, the son of David, king in Jerusalem." This seems, so far, to confirm the authorship to Solomon; but verse 12 says, "I, the Preacher, *was king over Israel*, in Jerusalem," which seems to intimate that he was *once* a king, but was so no longer. If so, it could not be Solomon, who died king of the twelve tribes. "Son of David" often means a descendant of David, Christ himself being so called.

Ecclesias'tical. *The father of ecclesiastical history.* Euse'bius of Cæsare'a (264-340).

Ecclesias'ticus is so called, not because the writer was a priest, but because the book (in the opinion of the fathers) was the chief of the apocryphal books, designated by them *Ecclesias'tici Libri* (books to be read in churches), to distinguish them from the canonical Scriptures.

Echidna (*E-kid'-na*). Half-woman, half-serpent. She was mother of the Chimæra, the many-headed dog Orthos, the hundred-headed dragon of the Hesperides, the Col'chian dragon, the Sphinx, Cer'beros, Scylla, the Gorgons, the Lernæan hydra, the vulture that gnawed away the liver of Prome'theus, and the Nem'ean lion. (*Hesiod.*)

"[She] seemed a woman to the waist, and fair
But ended foul in many a scaly fold,
Voluminous and vast."
Milton: Paradise Lost, book ii. 650-2.

Echo. The Romans say that Echo was a nymph in love with Narcissus, but her love not being returned, she pined away till only her voice remained. We use the word to imply similarity of sentiment: as *You echo my ideas; That is an echo to my opinion.*

"Sweet Echo, sweetest nymph, that liv'st unseen
Within thy airy shell,
By slow Meänder's margent green. . . .
Canst thou not tell me of a gentle pair
That likest thy Narcissus are?"
Milton: Comus, 230, etc.

Echo. (Gr. *ēko*; verb, *ēkeo*, to sound.) *To applaud to the echo.* To applaud so loudly as to produce an echo,

Eck'hardt. *A faithful Eckhardt, who warneth everyone* (German). Eckhardt, in German legends, appears on the evening of Maundy Thursday to warn all persons to go home, that they may not be injured by the headless bodies and two-legged horses which traverse the streets on that night.

Eclec'tics. Ancient philosophers, who selected what they thought best in all other systems, and made a patchwork therefrom. There is the eclectic school of painters, of which Paul Delaroche was the founder and best exponent; the eclectic school of modern philosophy, founded by Victor Cousin; the eclectic school of architecture; and so on. (Greek, *ek-lego*, to pick out.)

Eclectics or *Modern Platonists.* A Christian sect which arose in the second century. They professed to make *truth* their sole object of inquiry, and adopted from existing systems whatever, in their opinion, was true. They were called Platonists because they adopted Plato's notions about God and the human soul.

Eclipses were considered by the ancient Greeks and Romans as bad omens. Nicias, the Athenian general, was so terrified by an eclipse of the moon, that he durst not defend himself from the Syracusans; in consequence of which his whole army was cut to pieces, and he himself was put to death.

The Romans would never hold a public assembly during an eclipse. Some of their poets feign that an eclipse of the moon is because she is gone on a visit to Endymion.

A very general notion was and still is among barbarians that the sun or moon has been devoured by some monster, and hence the custom of beating drums and brass kettles to scare away the monster.

The Chinese, Laps, Persians, and some others call the evil beast a dragon. The East Indians say it is a black griffin.

The notion of the ancient Mexicans was that eclipses were caused by sun and moon quarrels, in which one of the litigants is beaten black and blue.

Eclip'tic. The path apparently described by the sun in his annual course through the heavens. Eclipses happen only when the moon is in or near the same plane.

Ec'logue (2 syl.). Pastoral poetry not expressed in rustic speech, but in the most refined and elegant of which the language is capable. (Greek, meaning "elegant extracts," "select poetry.")

Ecne'phia. A sort of hurricane, similar to the Typhon.

"The circling Typhon, whirled from point to
point. . . .
And dire Ecnephia reign."
Thomson: Summer.

École des Femmes. Molière borrowed the plot of this comedy from the novelletti of *Ser Giovanni*, composed in the fourteenth century.

Econ'omy means the rules or plans adopted in managing one's own house. As we generally prevent extravagant waste, and make the most of our means in our own homes, so the careful expenditure of money in general is termed house-management. The word is applied to time and several other things, as well as money. (Greek, *oikos nomos*, house-law.)

Animal economy. The system, laws, and management whereby the greatest amount of good accrues to the animal kingdom.

"Animal . . . economy, according to which animal affairs are regulated and disposed."—*Shaftesbury: Characteristics.*

Political economy. The principles whereby the revenues and resources of a nation are made the most of. Thus: Is Free Trade good or bad economy? Articles are cheaper, and therefore the buying value of money is increased; but, on the other hand, competition is increased, and therefore wages are lowered.

Vegetable economy. The system, laws, and management, whereby the greatest amount of good is to be derived by the vegetable kingdom.

The Christian Economy. The religious system based on the New Testament. That is, what is the best economy of man, taking into account the life that now is, and that which is to come? The answer is thus summed up by Christ: "What is a man profited though he gain the whole world and lose his own soul? For what should a man give in exchange for his soul?"

The Mosaic economy. The religious system taught by God: that is, the system whereby man obtains the greatest amount of value for his conduct, whether by serving God or living for this life only. Also called "The Jewish Economy."

Economy is a great income. "No alchemy like frugality." "Ever save, ever have." The following also are to a similar effect: "A pin a day is a groat a year." "Take care of the pence, and the pounds will take care of themselves." "Many a little makes a mickle." "Frae saving, comes having." "A penny saved is a penny gained." "Little and often fills the purse."

Latin : "Non intelligunt homines quam magnum vectīgal sit parsimonia" (*Cicero*). "Sera in fundo est parsimonia" (*Seneca*).

French : "Plusieurs Peu font un Beaucoup." "Denier sur denier bâtit la maison."

German : "Die sparsamkeit ist ein grosser zyll" (Parsimony is a great income).

Economy of Nature (*The*). The laws of nature, whereby the greatest amount of good is obtained ; or the laws by which the affairs of nature are regulated and disposed.

Écorcheurs. Freebooters of the twelfth century, in France; so called because they stripped their victims of everything, even their clothes. (French, *écorcher*, to flay.)

Ec'stasy (Greek ἔκ-στασις, from ἐξ-ίστημι, to stand out of [the body or mind]). To stand out of one's mind is to lose one's wits, to be beside oneself. To stand out of one's body is to be disembodied. St. Paul refers to this when he says he was caught up to the third heaven and heard unutterable words, "whether in the body, or out of the body, I cannot tell" (2 Cor. xii. 2-4). St. John also says he was "in the spirit"—*i.e.* in an ecstasy—when he saw the apocalyptic vision (i. 10). The belief that the soul left the body at times was very general in former ages, and is still the belief of many. (*See* ECSTATICI.)

Ecstat'ic Doctor (*The*). Jean de Ruysbroek, the mystic (1294-1381).

Ecstat'ici (*The*). A class of diviners among the ancient Greeks, who used to lie in trances, and when they came to themselves gave strange accounts of what they had seen while they were "out of the body." (Greek, *ex-iste'mi.*)

Ector (*Sir*). The foster-father of King Arthur.

Edda. There are two religious codes, so called, containing the ancient Scandinavian mythology. One is in verse, composed in Iceland in the eleventh century by Sæmund Sigfusson, *the Sage ;* and the other in prose, compiled a century later by Snorri Sturleson, who wrote a commentary on the first edda. The poetical edda contains an account of creation, the history of *Odin, Thor, Freyr, Balder,* etc., etc. The prose one

contains the exploits of such conquerors as *Vœlsung, Sigurd, Attle,* etc., and is divided into several parts. The first part contains historical and mythological traditions ; the second a long poetical vocabulary ; and the third Scandinavian prosody, or the modes of composition adopted by the ancient *Skalds.* The poetical compilation is generally called *Sæmund's Edda,* and the prose one *Snorri's Edda.*

Eden. Paradise, the country and garden in which Adam and Eve were placed by God (Gen. ii. 15). The word means *delight, pleasure.*

Eden Hall. *The luck of Eden Hall.* An old painted drinking-glass, supposed to be sacred. The tale is that the butler once went to draw water from St. Cuthbert's Well, in Eden Hall garden, Cumberland, when the fairies left their drinking-glass on the well to enjoy a little fun. The butler seized the glass, and ran off with it. The goblet is preserved in the family of Sir Christopher Musgrave. Longfellow wrote a poem on the subject. The superstition is—

" If that glass either break or fall,
Farewell the luck of Eden Hall."

✷ Readers of the *Golden Butterfly,* by Besant and Rice, will remember how the luck of Gilead P. Beck was associated with a golden butterfly.

Edenburgh, *i.e.* Edwin's burgh. The fort built by Edwin, king of Northumbria (616-633). Dun Eden or Dunedin, is a Saxon form ; Edina a poetical one.

Edgar or **Edgar'do.** Master of Ravenswood, in love with Lucy Ashton (*Lucia di Lammermoor*). While absent in France on an important embassy, the lady is led to believe that her lover has proved faithless to her, and in the torrent of her indignation consents to marry the laird of Bucklaw, but stabs him on the wedding-night, goes mad, and dies. In the opera Edgardo stabs himself also ; but in the novel he is lost in the quicksands at Kelpies-Flow, in accordance with an ancient prophecy. (*Donizetti's opera of " Lucia di Lammermoor " ; Sir Walter Scott's " Bride of Lammermoor."*)

Edge. (Anglo-Saxon, *ecg.*)
Not to put too fine an edge upon it. Not to mince the matter ; to speak plainly.
" He is, not to put too fine an edge upon it, a thorough scoundrel."—*Lowell.*

. To be on edge. To be very eager or impatient.
To set one's teeth on edge. To give one

the horrors; to induce a tingling or grating sensation in one's teeth, as from acids or harsh noises.

> " I had rather hear a brazen canstick turned,
> Or a dry wheel grate on the axle-tree;
> And that would set my teeth nothing on edge,
> Nothing so much as mincing poetry."
> *Shakespeare* : 1 *Henry IV.,* iii. 1.

Edge Away (*To*). To move away very gradually, as a ship moves from the edge of the shore. Often called *egg*. (Anglo-Saxon, *ecg*, an edge; *ecg-clif*, is a sea cliff.)

Edge-bone. (*See* AITCH-BONE.)

Edge on. (*See* EGG ON.)

Edge of the Sword.
To fall by the edge of the sword. By a cut from the sword; in battle.

Edgewise. *One cannot get in a word edgewise.* The [conversation is so engrossed by others] that there is no getting in a word.

Edged Tools. *It is dangerous to play with edged tools.* It is dangerous to tamper with mischief or anything that may bring you into trouble.

Edhilin'gi. The aristocratic class among the Anglo-Saxons; the second rank were termed the *Frilingi;* and the third the *Lazzi.* (Anglo-Saxon, *ædele* or *edele,* noble; *free-ling,* free-born. Ricardo says of the third class, they were the " unwilling to work, the dull " —quos hodie *lazie* di'cimus.)

Edict of Mil'an. Proclaimed by Constantine, after the conquest of Italy (313), to secure to Christians the restitution of their civil and religious rights.

Edict of Nantes. An edict published by Henri IV. of France, granting toleration to his Protestant subjects. It was published from Nantes in 1598, but repealed in 1685 by Louis XIV.

Edie Ochiltree. In Scott's *Antiquary.*

> "Charles II. would be as sceptical as Edie Ochiltree about the existence of circles and avenues, altar-stones and cromlechs."—*Knight: Old England.*

Ed'ify is to build a house (Latin, *ædes-facio*); morally, to build instruction in the mind methodically, like an architect. The Scripture word *edification* means the building-up of " believers " in grace and holiness. St. Paul says, " Ye are God's building," and elsewhere he carries out the figure more fully, saying—

> " All the building [or body of Christians], fitly framed together, groweth unto a holy temple in the Lord."—Eph. ii. 21.

E'diles (2 syl.). Roman officers who had charge of the streets, bridges, aqueducts, temples, and city buildings generally. We call our surveyors *city ediles* sometimes. (Latin, *ædes,* a house.)

E'dith, called the *Maid of Lorn* (Argyleshire), was about to be married to Lord Ronald, when Robert, Edward, and Isabel Bruce, tempest-tossed, sought shelter at the castle. Edith's brother recognised the Bruce, and being in the English interest, a quarrel ensued, in the course of which the abbot arrived, but refused to marry the bridal pair amidst such discord. Edith fled, and, assuming the character of a page, passed through divers adventures. At length Robert Bruce won the battle of Bannockburn, and when peace was restored Ronald married the " Maid of Lorn." (*Scott : Lord of the Isles.*)

Ednam, in Roxburghshire, near the Tweed, where Thomson, the author of *The Seasons,* was born.

> " The Tweed, pure *parent-stream,*
> Whose pastoral banks first heard my Doric reed."
> *Autumn* (888-9).

Edo'be (2 syl.). *Edobe cottages* are those made of sun-dried bricks, like the buildings of ancient Egypt. (*W. Hepworth Dixon : New America,* i. 16.) ⁂ The present and proper form of this word is Adobe (Spanish, *adobar,* plaster).

> "They make adobes, or sun-dried bricks, by mixing ashes and earth with water, which is then moulded into large blocks and dried in the sun."—*Bancroft: Native Races,* vol. i. p. 535.

Edward. *Edward the Confessor's sword.* Curta'na (*the cutter*), a blunt sword of state, emblematical of mercy.

The Chevalier Prince Charles Edward. The Young Pretender. Introduced by Sir Walter Scott in *Redgauntlet,* first as "Father Buonaventura," and afterwards as Pretender to the Crown. Again in *Waverley.*

Ed'widge. Wife of William Tell. (*Rossini's opera of Guglielmo Tell.*)

Edwin. The hero of Beattie's *Minstrel.*

> " And yet poor Edwin was no vulgar boy;
> Deep thought oft seemed to fix his infant eye,
> Dainties he heeded not, nor gaud, nor toy,
> Save one short pipe of rudest minstrelsy;
> Silent when glad; affectionate, though shy.
> And now his look was most demurely sad;
> And now he laughed aloud, yet none knew why.
> The neighbours stared and sighed, yet blessed the lad;
> Some deemed him wondrous wise, and some believed him mad." Canto i. 16.

Ed'yrn. Son of Nudd; called the " Sparrowhawk." He ousted the Earl

of Yn'iol from his earldom, and tried to
win E'nid, the earl's daughter, but failing in this, became the evil genius of
the gentle earl. Being overthrown in
a tournament by Prince Geraint', he
was sent to the court of King Arthur,
where his whole nature was completely
changed, and "subdued to that gentleness which, when it weds with manhood,
makes a man." (*Idylls of the King;
Enid.*)

Eel. A nickname for a New Englander.

"The eels of New England and the corncrackers of Virginia."—*Haliburton: Clockmaker.*

Eel. *A salt eel.* A rope's end, used
for scourging. At one time celskins
were used for whips.

"With my salt eele, went down in the parler,
and there got my boy and did beat him."—*Pepys'
Diary* (April 24th).

Eel. (Anglo-Saxon, *œl.*)
Holding the eel of science by the tail.
That is, to have an ephemeral smattering
of a subject, which slips from the memory
as an eel would wriggle out of one's
fingers if held by the tail.

"Cauda tenes anguillam, in eos apte dicetur,
quibus res est cum hominibus lubrica fide, per-
fidisque, aut qui rem fugitivam atque incertam
aliquam habent, quam tueri diu non possint."—
Erasmus: Adagia, p. 324. (1629.)

To get used to it, as a skinned eel, i.e.
as an eel is used to being skinned. It
may be unpleasant at first, but habit
will get the better of such annoyance.

"It ain't always pleasant to turn out for morning chapel, is it, Gig-lamps? But it's just like the
eels with their skinning: it goes against the
grain at first, but you soon get used to it."—
Cuthbert Bede [Bradley]: Verdant Green, chap. vii.

To skin an eel by the tail is to do things
the wrong way.

Eelkhance Tables. The celebrated
calculation of Nazir' u Dien, the Persian
astronomer, grandson of Zenghis Khan,
brought out in the middle of the thirteenth century.

Effen'di. A Turkish title, about equal
to our "squire," given to emirs, men of
learning, and the high priests of mosques.
The title is added after the name, as Ali
effendi (Ali *Esquire*).

Ef'figy. *To burn* or *hang one in effigy.*
To burn or hang the representation of a
person, instead of the person himself,
in order to show popular hatred, dislike,
or contempt. The custom comes from
France, where the public executioner
used to hang the effigy of the criminal
when the criminal himself could not be
found.

Ef'frontery. Out-facing, rude per-
sistence, and overbearing impudence.
(Latin, *ef-frons,* i.e. *ex-frons,* out-face.)

Egalité. Philippe, Duc d'Orléans,
father of Louis-Philippe, King of the
French, was so called because he sided
with the revolutionary party, whose
motto was "Liberty, fraternity, and
equality." Philippe *Egalité* was guillotined in 1793.

Ege'ria. The nymph who instructed
Numa in his wise legislation. Numa
used to meet her in a grove near Aric'ia.

Egg. Eggs. (Anglo-Saxon, *œg.*)
A bad egg. A bad speculation; a man
who promises, but whose promises are
pie-crust.

A duck's egg, in cricket. (*See* DUCK.)
Golden eggs. Great profits. (*See*
GOOSE.)

"I doubt the bird is flown that laid the golden
eggs."—*Scott: The Antiquary.*

The mundane egg. The Phœnicians,
and from them the Egyptians, Hindus,
Japanese, and many other ancient
nations, maintained that the world was
hatched from an egg made by the
Creator. Orpheus speaks of this egg.

Eggs of Nuremberg. (*See* NUREMBERG.)
Pasch eggs. (*See* EASTER EGGS.)
The serpent's egg of the Druids. This
wonderful egg was hatched by the joint
labour of several serpents, and was
buoyed into the air by their hissing.
The person who caught it had to ride off
at full speed, to avoid being stung to
death; but the possessor was sure to
prevail in every contest or combat, and
to be courted by those in power. Pliny
says he had seen one of these eggs, and
that it was about as large as a moderate
sized apple.

PHRASES AND PROVERBS:
Don't put all your eggs in one basket.
Don't venture all you have in one speculation; don't put all your property in
one bank. The allusion is obvious.
From the egg to the apples. (Latin,
"*ab ovo usque ad mala.*") From first to
last. The Romans began their "dinner"
with eggs, and ended with fruits called
"mala."
I have eggs on the spit. I am very
busy, and cannot attend to anything
else. The reference is to roasting eggs
on a spit. They were first boiled, then
the yolk was taken out, braided up with
spices, and put back again; the eggs
were then drawn on a "spit," and
roasted. As this required both despatch
and constant attention, the person in

charge could not leave them. It must be remembered that the word "spit" had at one time a much wider meaning than it has now. Thus toasting-forks and the hooks of a Dutch oven were termed spits.

"I forgot to tell you, I write short journals now ; I have eggs on the spit."—*Swift.*

I got eggs for my money means I gave valuable money, and received instead such worthless things as eggs. When Wolsey accused the Earl of Kildare for not taking Desmond prisoner, the Earl replied, "He is no more to blame than his brother Ossory, who (notwithstanding his high promises) is glad to take eggs for his money," *i.e.* is willing to be imposed on. (*Campion : History of Ireland*, 1633.)

Like as two eggs. Exactly alike.

"They say we are almost as like as eggs."— *Shakespeare : Winter's Tale*, i. 2.

Sure as eggs is eggs. Professor de Morgan suggests that this is a corruption of the logician's formula, "*x is x*." (*Notes and Queries.*)

Teach your grandmother to suck eggs. Attempting to teach your elders and superiors. The French say, "The goslings want to drive the geese to pasture" (*Les oisons veulent mener les ois paître*).

There is reason in roasting eggs. Even the most trivial thing has a reason for being done in one way rather than in some other. When wood fires were usual, it was more common to roast eggs than to boil them, and some care was required to prevent their being "ill-roasted, all on one side," as Touchstone says (*As You Like It*, iii. 2).

" One likes the pheasant's wing, and one the leg ; The vulgar boil, the learnèd roast an egg."
Pope : Epistles, ii.

To tread upon eggs. To walk gingerly, as if walking over eggs, which are easily broken.

Will you take eggs for your money ? "Will you allow yourself to be imposed upon ? Will you take kicks for halfpence ?" This saying was in vogue when eggs were plentiful as blackberries.

"My honest friend, will you take eggs for money ?"—*Shakespeare : Winter's Tale*, i. 2.

Egg Feast. In Oxford the Saturday preceding Shrove Tuesday is so called ; it is also called Egg-Saturday, because pasch eggs are provided for the students on that day.

Egg-flip, Egg-hot, Egg-nog. Drinks composed of warm spiced ale, with sugar, spirit and eggs ; or eggs beaten up with wine, sweetened and flavoured, etc.

Egg-on or **Edge-on.** A corruption of the Saxon *eggian* (to incite). The Anglo-Saxon *ecg*, and Scandinavian *eg*, means a " sharp point "—hence *edge-hog* (hedgehog), a hog with sharp points, called in Danish *pin-swin* (thorny swine), and in French *porc-épic*, where *épic* is the Latin *spic'ula* (spikes).

Egg Saturday (*See above*, EGG-FEAST.)

Egg-trot. A cautious, jog-trot pace, like that of a good housewife riding to market with eggs in her panniers.

Egil. Brother of Weland, the Vulcan of Northern mythology. Egil was a great archer, and a tale is told of him the exact counterpart of the famous story about William Tell : One day King Nidung commanded Egil to shoot an apple off the head of his son. Egil took two well-selected arrows from his quiver, and when asked by the king why he took two, replied (as the Swiss peasant to Gessler), "To shoot thee, O tyrant, with the second, if I fail."

Egis. (*See* ÆGIS.)

Eg'lantine (3 syl.). Daughter of King Pepin, and bride of her cousin Valentine, the brother of Orson. She soon died. (*Valentine and Orson.*)

Madame Eglantine. The prioress in Chaucer's *Canterbury Tales.* Goodnatured, wholly ignorant of the world, vain of her courtly manners, and noted for her partiality to lap-dogs, her delicate oath, "by seint Eloy," her entuning the service swetely in her nose," and her speaking French " after the scole of Stratford atte Bowe."

Ego and **Non-Ego.** "Ego" means I myself ; " Non-ego" means the objective world. They are terms used by Fichté (1762-1814) to explain his Idealism. According to this philosopher, the Ego posits or embraces the Non-ego. Take an example : A tree is an object out of my personality, and therefore a part of the Non-ego. I see a tree ; the tree of my brain is a subjective tree, the tree itself is an objective tree. Before I can see it, the objective tree and the subjective tree must be like the two clocks of a telegraphic apparatus   the sender and reader must be in connection, the reader must " posit," or take in the message sent. The message, or non-ego, must be engrafted into the ego. Applying this rule generally, all objects known, seen, heard, etc., by me become part of me, or the ego posits the non-ego by subjective objectivity.

Egoism. The theory in Ethics which places man's *summum bonum* in self. The correlative of altruism, or the theory which places our own greatest happiness in making others happy. Egoism is selfishness pure, altruism is selfish benevolence. " Egoist," a disciple of egoism.

" To say that each individual shall reap the benefits brought to him by his own powers . . . . is to enunciate egoism as an ultimate principle of conduct."—*Spencer: Data of Ethics*, p. 189.

Eg'otism. The too frequent use of the word I ; the habit of talking about oneself, or of paia ling one's own doings. " Egotist," one addicted to egotism.

E'gypt, in Dryden's satire of *Absalom and Achitophel*, means France.

" Egypt and Tyrus [Holland] intercept your trade, And Jebusites [Papists] your sacred rites invade." Part i. 705-6.

Egyptian Crown (*The*). That of Upper Egypt was a high conical *white* cap, terminating in a knob. That of Lower Egypt was *red*. If a king governed both countries he wore both crowns (that of Lower Egypt outside the other). This double crown was called a pschent.

Egyptian Days. The last Monday in April, the second Monday of August, and the third Monday of December. So called because Egyptian astrologers marked them out.

" Three days there are in the year which we call Egyptian Days."—*Saxon MS.* (British Museum).

Egyptian Festivals (*The*). The six great festivals of the ancient Egyptians were—

1. That of Bubastis (= Diana, or the moon);
2. That of Busīris, in honour of Isis ;
3. That of Saïs (= Minerva, Hermēs, or Wisdom) ;
4. That of Heliopôlis, in honour of the sun ;
5. That of Butis, or Buto, the goddess of night ; and
6. That of Papremis (= Mars or Arēs, the god of War).

Eider - down. The down of the eider duck. This duck is common in Greenlana, Iceland, and the Islands north and west of Scotland. It is about the size of a goose, and receives its distinctive name from the river Eider, in Denmark.

Eikon Basil'ikē [*Portraiture of the King*]. A book attributed to Charles I., but claimed by John Gauden, Bishop of Exeter. " The Εἰκων is wholly and only my invention." (*Gauden : Letter to the Lord Chancellor.*)

Eisell. Wormwood wine. Hamlet says to Laertes, *Woul't drink up eisell—* *i.e.* drink wormwood wine to show your love to the dead Ophelia ? In the *Troy Book* of Ludgate we have the line " Of *bitter* eysell and of eager [sour] wine." And in Shakespeare's sonnets :

" I will drink
Potions of eysell, 'gainst my strong infection ;
No *bitterness* that I will bitter think,
Nor double penance to correct correction."
Sonnet cxi.

Eisteddfod. The meetings of the Welsh bards and others, now held annually, for the encouragement of Welsh literature and music. (Welsh, " a sessions," from *eistedd*, to sit.)

Either. (Greek, *hekater'* ; Irish, *ceach-tar* ; Saxon, *ægther*. *Ceach'*, our " each," and *ægther*, our " either.")

Ejus'dem Fari'næ (Latin). Of the same kidney ; of the same sort.

" Lord Hartington, Lord Derby, Mr. Childers, and others *ejusdem farinæ*."—*Newspaper paragraph*, November, 1885.

El Dora'do. Golden illusion ; a land or means of unbounded wealth. Orella'na, lieutenant of Pizarro, pretended he had discovered a land of gold (*el dorado*) between the rivers Orino co and Am'azon, in South America. Sir Walter Raleigh twice visited Guia'na as the spot indicated, and published a highly-coloured account of its enormous wealth. Figuratively, a source of wit, wealth, or abundance of any kind.

The real " land of gold " is California, and not Guiana. (*See* BALNIBARBI.)

"The whole comedy is a sort of El Dorado of wit."—*T. Moore.*

⁕ *El Dorado* (masculine), "the gilt one," can hardly refer to a country ; it seems more likely to refer to some prince ; and we are told of a prince in South America who was every day powdered with gold-dust blown through a reed. If this is admitted, no wonder those who sought a golden country were disappointed.

El Infante de Anteque'ra is the Regent Fernando, who took the city of Anteque'ra from the Moors in 1419.

El Islam. The religion of the Moslems. The words mean " the resigning one's-self to God."

El Khi'dr. One of the good angels, according to the Koran.

Elagab'alus. A Syro-Phœnician sun-god, represented under the form of a huge conical stone. The Roman emperor, Marcus Aurelius Antonīnus, was so called because in childhood he was priest of the

Sun-god. Of all the Roman emperors none exceeded him in debauchery and sin. He reigned about four years (B.C. 218-222), and died at the age of eighteen.

This madman invited the principal men of Rome to a banquet, and smothered them in a shower of roses.

Ela'ine (2 syl.). The "lily maid of As'tolat" (*Guildford, in Surrey*), who loved Sir Lancelot "with that love which was her doom." Sir Lancelot, being sworn to celibacy, could not have married her, even if he had been willing; and, unhappily, what little love he had was bestowed on the queen. Elaine felt that her love was a vain thing, and died. According to her last request, the bed on which she died was placed on a barge, and on it was laid her dead body, arrayed in white, a lily in her right hand, and a letter avowing her love in the left. An old dumb servitor steered and rowed the barge up the river, and when it stopped at the palace staith, King Arthur ordered the body to be brought in. The letter being read, Arthur directed that the maiden should be buried like a queen, with her sad story blazoned on her tomb. The tale is taken from Sir T. Malory's *History of Prince Arthur*, part iii. Tennyson turned it into blank verse. (*Idylls of the King ; Elaine.*)

Elas'mothe'rium (Greek, *the metal-plate beast*). An extinct animal, between the horse and the rhinoceros.

El'berich. The most famous dwarf of German romance. He aided the Emperor Otnit (who ruled over Lombardy) to gain for wife the Soldan's daughter. (*The Heldenbuch.*)

Elbow. (Anglo-Saxon, *el-boga ; el=* an ell, *boga=* a bow.)
A knight of the elbow. A gambler.
At one's elbow. Close at hand.
To elbow one's way in. To push one's way through a crowd ; to get a place by hook or crook.
To elbow out ; to be elbowed out. To supersede ; to be ousted by a rival.
Up to one's elbow [in work]. Very busy, or full of work. Work piled up to one's elbows.

Elbow Grease. Perspiration excited by hard manual labour. They say *"Elbow grease* is the best furniture oil."

Elbow Room. Sufficient space for the work in hand.

Elbows. *Out at elbows.* Shabbily dressed (applied to men only) ; metaphorically, short of money ; hackneyed ;

stale ; thus, we say of a play which has been acted too often that it is worn out at elbows. It is like a coat which is no longer presentable, being out at the elbows.

Elden Hole. *Elden Hole needs filling.* A reproof given to great braggarts. Elden Hole is a deep pit in Derbyshire Peak, said to be fathomless. (See *Sir W. Scott : Peveril of the Peak*, ch. iii.)

Elder Brethren. (*See* TRINITY HOUSE.)

Elder-tree. Sir John Maundeville, speaking of the Pool of Sil'oe, says, "Fast by is the elder-tree on which Judas hanged himself . . . . when he sold and betrayed our Lord." Shakespeare, in *Love's Labour's Lost*, v. 2, says, "Judas was hanged on an elder." (*See* FIG-TREE.)

> " Judas he japed
> With Jewish siller,
> And sithen on an elder tree
> Hanged himsel."
> *Piers Plowman : Vision.*

Eleanor Crosses. (*See* CHARING CROSS.)

Eleat'ic Philosophy. Founded by Xenoph'anes of El'ea about B.C. 530. The Ionic school believed there was but one element ; the Eleatics said there were four or six, as heat and cold, moisture and dryness, odd and even, from the antagonisms of which visible objects sprang : Thus, *Fire* is heat acting on dryness ; *Air* is heat acting on moisture ; *Water* is cold acting on moisture ; and *Earth* is cold acting on dryness. (*See below.*)

The New Eleatic School was founded by Leucippos of El'ea, a disciple of Zeno. He wholly discarded the phantasmagoric theory, and confined his attention to the physical properties of the visible world. He was the father of the *Atomic System*, in which the agency of *chance* was again revived.

Elecampane and Amrida. Sweetmeats which confer immortality (Latin, *helenium campāna* or *inula campāna*). Pliny tells us the plant so called sprang from Helen's tears. The sweetmeat so called is a coarse sugar-candy. There was also an electuary so called, said to cure wounds given in fight.

> "Here, take this essence of elecampane ;
> Rise up, Sir George, and fight again."
> *Miracle Play of St. George.*

Elector. A prince who had a vote in the election of the Emperor of Germany. Napoleon broke up the old German empire, and the college of electors fell asunder.

The Great Elector. Frederick William of Brandenburg (1620-1688).

Electricity (from the Greek *elektron*, amber). Thalēs (B.C. 600) observed that amber when rubbed attracted light substances, and this observation followed out has led to the present science of electricity.

" Bright amber shines on his electric throne."
    Darwin : Economy of Nature, i. 2.

Negative and positive electricity. Two opposite conditions of the electric state of bodies. At one time electricity was considered a fluid, as heat was thought to be caloric. Everybody was thought to have a certain quantity. If a body contained more than its normal quantity it was said to be *positive ;* if less, it was said to be *negative* in this respect. Another theory was that there were two different electric fluids, which neutralised each other when they came in contact. Electricity is now supposed to be a mere condition, like heat and motion ; but its energy is set in action by some molecular disturbance, such as friction, rupture, and chemical action. The old terms are still retained.

Electro-Biology. The science of electricity as it is connected with the phenomena of living beings. Also the effect of " animal magnetism " on living creatures, said to produce sleep, stupor, anesthesia, etc.

Electro-Chemistry. That branch of chemistry which treats of electricity as an energy affecting chemical changes.

Elec'tuary. Something to be licked up ; a medicine made " thick and slab," which cannot be imbibed like a liquid nor bolted like a pill, but which must be licked up like honey. (Greek, *ek-leicho.*)

Eleemos'ynam. *Eleemos'ynam sepulcri patris tui* (Alms on your father's grave). (*See* MEAT.)

Elegant Extracts. The 85th Foot, remodelled in 1813, after the numerous court-martials which then occurred. The officers of the regiment were removed, and officers drafted from other regiments were substituted in their places. The 85th is now called the " Second Battalion of the Shropshire Light Infantry." The first battalion is the old 23rd.

¶ At the University of Cambridge, in the good old times, some few men were too good to be plucked and not good enough for the poll : a line was drawn below the poll-list, and these lucky unfortunates, allowed to pass, were nicknamed the *Elegant Extracts.* There was a similar limbo in the honour-list, called the Gulf, in allusion to a Scripture passage well known and thus parodied, " Between them [*in the poll*] and us [*in the honour-lists*] there is a great gulf fixed," etc.

Elegiacs. (*See* HEXAMETERS and PENTAMETERS.)

El'ements, according to Aristotle. Aristotle maintained that there are four elements—fire, air, water, and earth ; and this assertion has been the subject of very unwise ridicule. Modern chemists maintain the same fact, but have selected four new words for the four old ones, and instead of the term " element," use " material forms." We say that matter exists under four forms : the imponderable (caloric), the gaseous (air), the liquid (water), and the solid (earth), and this is all the ancient philosophers meant by their four elements or elemental forms. It was Empedʹoclēs of Sicily who first maintained that fire, air, earth, and water are the four elements ; but he called them Zeus, Hera, Gœa, and Poseiʹdon. (Latin, *eleo* for *oleo.* Vossius says : *ab* ant. *eleo* pro *oleo, i.e.* cresco, quod omnia crescant ac nascantur." Latin, *elementum.* to grow out of.)

" Let us the great philosopher [Aristotle] attend . . .
    His elements,‘ Earth, Water, Air, and Fire ’; . . .
    Tell why these simple elements are four ;
    Why just so many ; why not less or more ? "
        Blackmore: Creation, v.

∵ The first of these forms — viz. "Caloric," or the imponderable matter of heat, is now attributed to a mere condition of matter, like motion.

Elephant. The elephant which supports the world is called " Muha-pudma," and the tortoise which supports the elephant is called " Chukwa." In some of the Eastern mythologies we are told that the world stands on the backs of eight elephants, called " Achtequedjams."

Elephant (*The*). Symbol of temperance, eternity, and sovereignty. (*See* WHITE ELEPHANT.)

" L'eternité est désignée sur une médaille de l'empereur Philippe, par un eléphant sur lequel est monté un petit garçon armé de flèches."—*Noel : Dictionnaire de la Fable,* vol. i. p. 506.

Elephant. (*See* WHITE ELEPHANT.)
Only an elephant can bear an elephant's load. An Indian proverb: Only a great man can do the work of a great man ; also, the burden is more than I can bear ; it is a load fit for an elephant.

Elephant Paper. A large - sized drawing-paper, measuring 20 inches by 23. There is also a "double elephant paper," measuring 40 inches by 26¾.

Elephant and Castle. A public-house sign at Newington, said to derive its name from the skeleton of an elephant dug up near Battle Bridge in 1714. A flint-headed spear lay by the remains, whence it is conjectured that the creature was killed by the British in a fight with the Romans. (*The Times.*)

There is another public-house with the same sign in St. Pancras, probably intended to represent an elephant with a howdah.

Elephan'ta, in Bombay, is so called from a stone elephant, which carried a tiger on its back, and formerly stood near the landing-place on the south side of the island. It has now nearly disappeared. The natives call it Gahrapooree (cave town), from its cave, 130 feet long. (*Chow-chow.*)

Elephan'tine (4 syl.). Heavy and ungainly, like an elephant. In Rome, the registers of the senate, magistrates, generals, and emperors were called elephantine books, because they were made of ivory. In geology, the elephantine period was that noted for its numerous large thick-skinned animals. The *disease* called elephanti'asis is when the limbs swell and look like those of an elephant more than those of a human being.

Eleusin'ian Mysteries. The religious rites in honour of Deme'ter or Ceres, performed at Eleu'sis, in At'tica.

Elevation of the Host (*The*). The celebrant lifting up the "consecrated wafers" above his head, that the people may see the paten and adore "the Host" while his back is turned to the congregation.

Eleven (Anglo - Saxon, *œndlefene,* œnd = *ain*, lefene = *lef*, left). One left or one more after counting ten (the fingers of the two hands). Twelve is Twa lef (two left); all the other teens up to 20 represent 3, 4, 5, etc. + ten. It would seem that at one time persons did not count higher than twelve, but in a more advanced state they required higher numbers, and introduced the "teen" series, omitting eleven and twelve, which would be *enteen* and *twateen.*

Eleven Thousand Virgins. Ur'sula being asked in marriage by a pagan prince, fled towards Rome with her eleven thousand virgins. At Cologne they were all massacred by a party of Huns, and even to the present hour "their bones" are exhibited to visitors through windows in the wall. Maury says that Ursula's handmaid was named *Undecimella,* and that the legend of her eleven thousand virgins rose out of this name. (*Légendes Pieuses.*)

Eleventh Hour (*At the*). Just in time (Matt. xx. 1).

Elf (*plural,* Elves, Anglo-Saxon, *œlf*). Properly, a mountain fay, but more loosely applied to those airy creatures that dance on the grass or sit in the leaves of trees and delight in the full moon. They have fair golden hair, sweet musical voices, and magic harps. They have a king and queen, marry and are given in marriage. They impersonate the shimmering of the air, the felt but indefinable melody of Nature, and all the little prettinesses which a lover of the country sees, or thinks he sees, in hill and dale, copse and meadow, grass and tree, river and moonlight. Spenser says that Prome'theus called the man he made "Elfe," who found a maid in the garden of Ado'nis, whom he called "Fay," of "whom all Fayres spring."

" Of these a mighty people shortly grew,
   And puissant kings, which all the world warrayd,
And to themselves all nations did subdue."
     Faërie Queene, ii. 9, stanza 70. etc.

Elf and Goblin, as derived from Guelf and Ghibelline, is mentioned in Johnson (article GOBLIN), though the words existed long before those factions arose. Heylin (in his *Cosmography,* p. 130) tells us that some supported that opinion in 1370. Skinner gives the same etymology.

Red Elf. In Iceland, a person gaily dressed is called a red elf (*raud álfr*), in allusion to a superstition that dwarfs wear scarlet or red clothes. (*Nial's Sagas.*) Black elves are evil spirits; white elves, good ones.

Elf-arrows. Arrow-heads of the neolithic period. The shafts of these arrows were reeds, and the heads were pieces of flint, carefully sharpened, and so adjusted as to detach themselves from the shaft and remain in the wounded body. At one time they were supposed to be shot by elves at people and cattle out of malice or revenge.

" There every herd by sad experience knows
   How, winged with fate, their elf-shot arrows fly,
When the sick ewe her summer food forgoes,
Or stretched on earth the heart-smit heifers lie."   *Collins : Popular Superstitions.*

Elf-fire. The ignis-fatuus. The name of this elf is Will o' the Wisp, Jack o' lanthorn, Peg-a-lantern, or Kit o' the canstick (candlestick).

Elf-land. The realm ruled over by Oberon, King of Faëry. King James says: "I think it is liker Vir'gilis *Campi Elysii* nor anything that ought to be believed by Christians."(*Dæmonology*,iii.5.)

Elf-locks. Tangled hair. It is said that one of the favourite amusements of Queen Mab is to tie people's hair in knots. When Edgar impersonates a madman, "he elfs all his hair in knots." (*Lear*, ii. 3.)

> "This is that very Mab
> That plats the manes of horses in the night,
> And bakes [? cakes] the elf-locks in foul sluttish
> hairs."
> *Shakespeare: Romeo and Juliet,* i. 4.

Elf-marked. Those born with a natural defect, according to the ancient Scottish superstition, are marked by the elves for mischief. Queen Margaret called Richard III.—

> "Thou elfish-marked, abortive, rooting hog!"—
> *Shakespeare: Richard III.,* i. 3.

Elf-shot. Afflicted with some unknown disease, and supposed to have been wounded by an elfin arrow. The rinderpest would, in the Middle Ages, have been ascribed to elf-shots. (*See* ELF-ARROWS.)

Elfin. The first fairy king. He ruled over India and America. (*Middle Age Romance.*)

El'gin Marbles. A collection of ancient bas-reliefs and statues made by Lord Elgin, and sent to England in 1812. They are chiefly fragments of the Par'-thenon at Athens, and were purchased by the British Government for £35,000, to be placed in the British Museum (1816). (Elgin pronounced 'gin,' as in *begin*.)

Elia. A *nom de plume* adopted by Charles Lamb. (*Essays of Elia.*)

"The adoption of this signature was purely accidental. Lamb's first contribution to the *London Magazine* was a description of the old South-Sea House, where he had passed a few months' novitiate as a clerk, . . . and remembering the name of a gay light-hearted foreigner, who fluttered there at the time, substituted his nan e for his own."—*Talfourd.*

Eli'ab, in the satire of *Absalom and Achitophel,* by Dryden and Tate, is meant for Henry Bennet, Earl of Arlington. Eliab was one of the chiefs of the Gadites who joined David at Ziklag. (1 Chron. xii. 9.)

> "Hard the task to do Eliab right;
> Long with the royal wanderer [Charles II.] he
> roved,
> And firm in all the turns of fortune proved."
> *Absalom and Achitophel,* part ii. 986-8.

Eli'akim. Jehoiakim, King of Judah. (B.C. 635, 610-598.)

El'idure (3 syl.). A legendary king of Britain, advanced to the throne in place of his elder brother, Arthgallo, supposed by him to be dead. Arthgallo, after a long exile, returned to his country, and Elidure resigned to him the throne. Wordsworth has a poem on the subject.

Eligibles and **Detrimentals.** Sons which are socially good and bad *parties,* to be introduced to daughters with a view of matrimony.

"The *County Families of the United Kingdom* is useful to all who are concerned with questions of precedence, and especially useful to mothers who desire to distinguish between 'eligibles' and 'detrimentals.'"—*Notes and Queries,* February 1st, 1886, p. 119.

Elijah's Melons. Certain stones on Mount Carmel are so called. (*See* Stanley, *Sinai and Palestine.*)

⁂ Similar formations are those called "The Virgin Mary's Peas" (*q.v.*). Compare also the Bible story of Lot's wife.

The story is that the owner of the land refused to supply the wants of the prophet, and consequently his melons were transformed into stones.

Elim'inate (4 syl.). To turn out of doors; to turn out of an equation everything not essential to its conditions. (Latin, *e limine,* out of doors.)

Eliot (*George*). A *nom de plume* of Marian Evans (Mrs. Cross), author of *Adam Bede,* etc. (1820-1880).

Eliott's Tailors. The 15th Hussars, now the 15th [King's] Hussars, previously called the 15th, or king's own royal light dragoon guards. In 1759 Lieutenant-Colonel Eliott enlisted a large number of tailors on strike into a cavalry regiment modelled after the Prussian hussars. This regiment so highly distinguished themselves, that George III. granted them the honour of being called "the king's royal."

Elissa. Dido, Queen of Carthage. A Phœnician name signifying heroic, brave.

> "Nec me meminisse pigebit Elissæ."
> *Virgil: Æneid,* iv. 335.

⁂ Dido was the niece of the Bible Jezebel. Ithobal I., king of Tyre (1 Kings xvi. 13), had for children Belus, Margĕnus, and Jezebel. Of these Belus was the father of Pygmalion and Dido. Hence Jezebel was Dido's aunt.

Elis'sa (*deficiency* or parsimony; Greek, *ellipsis*). Step-sister of Medi'na and Peris'sa, but they could never agree upon any subject. (*Spenser: Faërie Queene,* book ii.)

Elivâ′ger (4 syl.). A cold venomous stream which issued from Niflheim, and in the abyss called the Ginnunga Gap, hardening into layer upon layer of ice. (*Scandinavian mythology*.)

Elixir of Life. A ruby, supposed by the alchemists to prolong life indefinitely. The tincture for transmuting metals was also called an elixir. (Arabic, *el* or *al iksir*, the iksir (? coction).) (*See* AM-RITA.)

" He that has once the Flower of the Sun,
The perfect ruby which we call Elixir. . . .
Can confer honour, love, respect, long life,
Give safety, valour, yea, and victory,
To whom he will. In eight-and-twenty days
I'll make an old man of fourscore a child.
Ben Jonson: The Alchemist, ii. 1.

Elizabeth had pet names for all her favourite courtiers ; *q.e.* :
The mother of Sir John Norris she called " My own Crow."
Burghley was her " Spirit."
Mountjoy she termed her " Kitchen-maid in Ireland."

Elizabeth has given more variants than any other Christian name : Eliza, Isa, Isabel, Lizzy, Elizabeth, Elisabetta, Betty, Bettina, Bess, Bessy, etc.

Elizabeth of Hungary (*St.*). Patron saint of queens, being herself a queen. (1207-1231.)

Elizabe′than. After the style of things in the reign of Queen Elizabeth. Elizabethan architecture is a mixture of Gothic and Italian, prevalent in the reigns of Elizabeth and James I.

Ell (Anglo-Saxon *eln*, an ell). It is said that the English ell was the length of Henry I.'s arm, but the ordinary length of a man's arm is about a yard.
Give him an inch, and he'll take an ell.
Give him a little licence, and he will take great liberties, or make great encroachments. The ell was no definite length. The English ell was 45 inches, the Scotch ell only 37 inches, while the Flemish ell was three-quarters of a yard and a French ell a yard and a half. This indefinite measure expresses the uncertainty of the length to which persons will go to whom you give the inch of liberty. Some will go the French ell ; while others of more modesty or more limited desires will be satisfied with the shorter measures.

Ell-wand (*The King's*). The group of stars called " Orīon's Belt."
" The King's Ellwand, now foolishly termed the ' Belt of Orion.' "—*Hogg: Tales*, etc.

Ella, or **Alla.** King of Northumberland, who married Cunstance. (*Chaucer : Man of Lawes Tale.*) (*See* CUNSTANCE.)

Elliot. In the *Black Dwarf*, by Sir Walter Scott, are seven of that name, viz. Halbert or Hobbie Elliot, of the Heugh-foot (a farmer) ; Mrs. Elliot, his grandmother ; John and Harry, his brothers ; and Lilias, Jean, and Arnot, his sisters.

Ellyl′lon. The souls of the ancient Druids, which, being too good for hell, and not good enough for heaven, are permitted to wander upon earth till the judgment day, when they will be admitted to a higher state of being. (*Welsh mythology*.)

Elmo's Fire (*St.*). *Comazants*, or electric lights occasionally seen on the masts of ships before and after a storm ; so called by the Spaniards because St. Elmo is with them the patron saint of sailors. (*See* CASTOR AND POLLUX.)
" Sudden, breaking on their raptured sight,
Appeared the splendour of St. Elmo's light."
Hoole : Orlando Furioso, book ix.

Elohim. The genus of which ghosts, Chemosh, Dagon, Baal, Jahveh, etc., were species. The ghost or spectre which appeared to Saul (1 Sam. xxviii. 14-20) is called Elohim. " I see Elohim coming up out of the earth," said the witch ; and Saul asked, " What is HE like ? " (*Huxley : Nineteenth Century*, March, 1886.)
"The word Elôhim is often applied in the Bible to the gods of the Gentiles."—*Lenormant : Beginnings of History*, chap. vii.

¶ In theology, Elŏhim (the plural of Elŏah) means the " Lord of Hosts," or Lord of all power and might. Jehŏvah signifies rather the God of mercy and forgiveness. Hence, Elohim is used to express the God of creation, but Jehŏvah the God of the covenant of mercy.
"Elohim designates the fulness of Divine power."—*Religious Encyclopædia*.

Elohis′tic *and* **Jehovis′tic Scriptures.** The Pentateuch is supposed by Bishop Colenso and many others to have been written at two widely different periods, because God is invariably called Elo′him in some paragraphs, while in others He is no less invariably called Jehovah. The Elohistic paragraphs, being more simple, more primitive, more narrative, and more pastoral, are said to be the older ; while the Jehovistic paragraphs indicate a knowledge of geography and history, seem to exalt the priestly office, and are altogether of a more elaborate character. Those who maintain this theory think that some late transcriber has compiled the two Scriptures and combined them into one, much the same as if the four Gospels were collated and welded together into a single one. To give one or two examples :— Gen. i. 27, it is said, "So God (*Elohim*) created man in His own image, (both) male and female"; whereas, in the next chapter (21-24), it is said that God (*Jehovah*) caused a deep sleep to fall on Adam, and that He then took from the sleeping man a rib and made it a woman; and therefore (says the writer) a man shall cleave unto his wife, and the two be considered one flesh. Again (Gen. vi. 19) Elohim tells Noah, "Two of every sort shalt thou bring into the ark, a male and a female"; and (vii. 9) "There went in two and two unto Noah into the ark, the male and the female, as God (*Elohim*) commanded Noah." In Gen. vii. 2 Jehovah tells Noah he is to make a distinction between clean and unclean beasts, and that he is to admit the former by sevens and the latter by twos. In the first example, the priestly character is indicated by the moral, and in the latter by the distinction made between clean and unclean animals. We pass no opinion on this theory, but state it as fairly as we can in a few lines.

Eloi (*St.*). Patron saint of artists and smiths. He was a famous worker in gold and silver, and was made Bishop of Noyon in the reign of Dag'obert. Probably the St. Eloi of Chaucer's Prioress was St. Louis (St. 'Loy).

" Ther was also a nonne, a prioresse,
That of hire smylyng was ful symple and coy !
Hire grettest ooth was but by Seynt Loy."
Chaucer : Canterbury Tales, Prol. 18-20.

⁂ We find reference to "Seynt Loy" again in verse 7143.

Eloquent. *The old man eloquent.* Isoc'ratēs, the Greek orator. When he heard that Grecian liberty was extinguished by the battle of Chæronē'a, he died of grief.

" That dishonest victory
At Chæronea, fatal to liberty,
Killed with report that old man eloquent."
Milton : Sonnets (To Lady Margaret Ley).

The eloquent doctor. Peter Aure'olus, Archbishop of Aix, a schoolman.

Elshender or *Cannie Elshie.* The Black Dwarf, *alias* Sir Edward Mauley, *alias* the Recluse, *alias* the Wise Wight of Mucklestane Moor. (*Sir Walter Scott: The Black Dwarf.*)

Elsie. The daughter of Gottlieb, a farm tenant of Prince Henry of Hoheneck. The prince was suffering severely from some malady, and was told that he would be cured if any maiden would give her life as a substitute. Elsie vowed to do so, and accompanied the prince from Germany to Salerno. Here Elsie surrendered herself to Lucifer, but was rescued by the prince, who married her. His health was perfectly re-established by the pilgrimage. (*Longfellow : The Golden Legend.*)

Elves. (*See under* ELF.)

Elvidna. The hall of the goddess Hel (*q.v.*).

Elvi'no. A rich farmer, in love with Ami'na, the somnambulist. The fact of Ami'na being found in the bed of Count Rodolpho the day before the wedding, induces Elvino to reject her hand and promise marriage to Liza; but he is soon undeceived—Ami'na is found to be innocent, and Liza to have been the paramour of another; so Ami'na and Elvi'no are wedded under the happiest auspices. (*Belli'ni's opera, La Sonnambula.*) (*See* LIZA.)

Elvi'ra (*Donna*). A lady deceived by Don Giovanni, who deluded her into a liaison with his valet, Leporello. (*Mozart's opera, Don Giovanni.*)

Elvira. A lady who loved Erna'ni, the robber-captain, and head of a league against Don Carlos, afterwards Charles V. of Spain. She was betrothed to Don Ruy Gomez de Silva, an old Spanish grandee, whom she detested, and Ernani resolved to rescue her; but it so happened that the king himself fell in love with her, and tried to win her. When Silva learned this, he joined the league; but the king, overhearing the plot in concealment, arrested the conspirators. Elvira interceded for them, and the king granted them a free pardon. When Ernani was on the point of wedding Elvira, Ernani, being summoned to death by Silva, stabbed himself. (*Verdi's opera of Ernani.*)

El'vish or **Elfish.** Irritable, peevish, spiteful; full of little mischievous ways, like the elves. Our superstitious forefathers thought such persons were actually "possessed" by elves; and elvishmarked is marked by elves or fairies.

" Thou elvish-marked, abortive, rooting hog."
Shakespeare: Richard III., i. 3.

Ely'sium. *Elysian Fields.* The Paradise or Happy Land of the Greek poets. *Elysian* (the adjective) means happy, delightful.

" O'er which were shadowy cast Elysian gleams."
Thomson: Castle of Indolence, i. 44.

" Would take the prisoned soul,
And lap it in Elysium."
Milton: Comus 261-2.

El'zevir. An edition of a classic author, published and printed by the family of Elzevir, and said to be immaculate. Virgil, one of the masterpieces, is certainly incorrect in some places. (1592-1626.)

Em. The unit of measure in printing. The standard is a pica M ; and the width of a line is measured by the number of such M's that would stand side by side in the "stick." This dictionary is in double columns ; each column equals 11 pica M's in width, and one M is allowed for the space between. Some work is made up to $10\frac{1}{2}$, $20\frac{1}{2}$, etc., ems ; and for the half-em printers employ the letter N, which is in width half a letter M. As no letter is wider than the M, and all narrower letters are fractions of it, this letter forms a very convenient standard for printing purposes.

Embargo. *To lay an embargo on him* or *it* is to impose certain conditions before you give your consent. It is a Portuguese and Spanish word, meaning an order issued by authority to prevent ships leaving port for a fixed period.

Embarras de Richesse. More matter than can be used ; overcrowded with facts or material. A publisher or editor who is overwhelmed with MSS., or contributions ; an author who has more incidents or illustrations in support of his theory than he can produce, etc., have an *embarras de richesse*.

Ember Days are the Wednesday, Friday, and Saturday of Ember Weeks (*q.v.*).

Ember Weeks. A corruption of *quat'uor tem'pora*, through the Dutch *quatemper* and German *quatember*. The four times are after Quadragesima Sunday, Whit Sunday, Holyrood Day (*September*), and St. Lucia's Day (*December*). The supposition that persons sat in embers (or ashes) on these days is without foundation.

Emblem is a picture with a hidden meaning ; the meaning is "cast into" or "inserted in" the visible device. Thus, a *balance* is an emblem of justice, *white* of purity, a *sceptre* of sovereignty. (Greek, *en-ballo*, which gives the Greek *emblēma*.) (*See* APOSTLES, PATRON SAINTS.)

Some of the most common and simple emblems of the Christian Church are—

A chalice. The eucharist.

The circle inscribed in an equilateral triangle. To denote the co-equality and co-eternity of the Trinity.

A cross. The Christian's life and conflict ; the death of Christ for man's redemption.

A crown. The reward of the perseverance of the saints.

A dove. The Holy Ghost.

A hand from the clouds. To denote God the Father.

A lamb, fish, pelican, etc., etc. The Lord Jesus Christ.

A phœnix. The resurrection.

Emblems of the Jewish Temple. (*See* Exod. xxv. 30-32 ; Rev. i. 12-20.)

Golden candlestick. The Church. Its seven lights, the seven spirits of God. (Rev. iv. 6.)

The *shewbread.* The twelve loaves the twelve tribes of Israel. Represented in the Gospel by the twelve apostles.

The *incense* of sweet spices. Prayer, which rises to heaven as incense. (Rev. viii. 3, 4.)

The *Holy of Holies.* The nation of the Jews as God's peculiar people. When the veil which separated it from the temple was "rent in twain," it signified that thenceforth Jews and Gentiles all formed one people of God.

Em'bryo means that which swells inside something (Greek, *en-bru'o*, which gives the Greek *embruon*) ; hence the child in the womb ; the rudiment in a plant before it shows itself in a bud ; an idea not developed, etc.

Em'elye. The sister-in-law of "Duke Theseus," beloved by the two knights, Pal'amon and Ar'cyte, the former of whom had her to wife. It is of this lady the poet says, "Up roos the sun, and up roos Emelye" (v. 2275).

" This passeth yeer by yeer, and day and day,
Till it fel oon̄es in a morne of May,
That Emelie, that fairer was to scene
Than is the lilie on hire stalkēs grene,
And fresscher than the May with flourēs newe . . . .
Er it was day, as sche was wont to do,
Sche was arisen."
Chaucer : Canterbury Tales (The Knighte's Tale).

Em'erald Isle. Ireland. This term was first used by Dr. Drennan (1754-1820), in the poem called *Erin.* Of course, it refers to the bright green verdure of the island.

" An emerald set in the ring of the sea."
Cushlamachree.
" Nor one feeling of vengeance presume to defile
The cause or the men of the Emerald Isle."
E. J. Drennan : Erin.

Em'eralds. According to tradition, if a serpent fixes its eyes upon an emerald it becomes blind. (*Ahmed ben Abdalaziz : Treatise on Jewels.*)

Emer'gency. *A sudden emergency* is something which starts suddenly into view, or which rises suddenly out of the current of events. (Latin, *e-mergo,* to rise out of "the water.")

Emergency Man (*An*). One engaged for some special service, as in Irish evictions.

Emeute (French). A seditious rising or small riot. Literally, a moving-out. (Latin, *e-mov'eo*.)

Emile (2 syl.). The French form of Emil'ius. The hero of Jean Jacques Rousseau's novel of the same name, and his ideal of a perfectly educated young man.

Emil'ia (in Shakespeare's *Othello*). Wife of Iago. She is induced by her husband to purloin Desdemona's handkerchief, which Iago conveys to Cassio's chamber, and tells the Moor that Desdemo'na had given it to the lieutenant as a love-token. At the death of Desdemona, Emilia (who, till then, never suspected the real state of the case) reveals the fact, and Iago kills her.

Emil'ia. The sweetheart of Peregrine Pickle, in Smollett's novel.

Emilie (*The divine*), to whom Voltaire wrote verses, was Madame Châtelet, with whom he lived at Circy for ten years.

Emmet contracted into *Ant : thus, Em't, ent, ant* (Anglo-Saxon, *œmete*).

"A bracelet made of emmets' eyes."
Drayton : Court of Fairies.

Emne. *Your emne Christen* (*Bosworth*), *i.e.* your even or fellow Christian. Shakespeare (*Hamlet*, v. 1) has "your even Christian." (Anglo-Saxon, *Emnecristen*, fellow-Christian.)

Emol'ument. Literally, that which comes out of the mill. (Latin, *e-mola*.) It originally meant toll on what was ground. (*See* GRIST.)

Emo'tion. Literally, the movement of the mind brought out by something which affects it. The idea is this: The mind, like electricity, is passive till something occurs to affect it, when it becomes roused ; the active state thus produced is its emotion, and the result thereof is passion or affection. (Latin, *e-moveo*.)

Empan'el or *Impanel* is to write the names of a jury on a *panel*, or piece of parchment. (French, *panneau*, *i.e.* pan de peau, piece of skin.)

Empannel, To put the pack-saddle on a beast of burden.

"Saddle Rozinante, and empannel thine ass."—
Don Quixote, ii. 326.

Emped'oclēs (4 syl.) *of Sicily.* A disciple of Pythag'oras According to Lu'cian, he threw himself into the crater of Etna, that persons might suppose he was returned to the gods; but Etna threw out his sandal, and destroyed the illusion. (*Horace : Ars Poetica*, 404.) (*See* CLEOMBROTOS.)

" He who, to be deemed
A god, leaped fondly into Ætna flames,
Empedoclēs."
Milton : Paradise Lost, iii. 471.

Emperor. *Emperor, not for myself, but for my people.* The maxim of Ha'-drian, the Roman emperor (117-138).

Emperor of Believers. Omar I., father-in-law of Mahomet, and second caliph of the Mussulmans (581-644).

Emperor of the Mountains, *king of the woods, and lord of the highways from Florence to Naples.* A title assumed by Peter the Calabrian, a famous bandit-chief (1812).

Empire City (*The*). New York, the great commercial city of the United States.

Empire of Reason ; the Empire of Truth, etc., *i.e.* reason or truth as the governing principle. Empire is the Latin *imper'ium*, a jurisdiction, and an *emperor* is one who holds command.

Em'pirics. Quacks. A school of medicine founded by Serap'ion of Alexandria, who contended that it is not necessary to obtain a knowledge of the nature and functions of the body in order to treat diseases, but that experience is the surest and best guide. They were opposed to the Dogmatics (*q.v.*). (Greek, *peirao*, to try, which gives the Greek *empeiria*, experience.)

" We must not
So stain our judgment, or corrupt our hope,
To prostitute our past-cure malady
To empirics."
Shakespeare : All's Well That Ends Well, ii. 1.

Employé. (French). One in our employ : such as clerks, shopmen, servants, etc. Employée, a female employed by a master. Employee, either sex.

" In Italy, all railroad employées are subjected to rigorous examination."—*Harlan : Eyesight*, v. 64.

" All these employées should be women of character."—*Macmillan's Magazine* (July, 1862, p. 257).

Empson. The favourite flageolet-player of Charles II., introduced into Scott's *Peveril of the Peak*.

" Julian could only bow obedience, and follow Empson, who was the same person that played so rarely on the flageolet."—Chap. xxx.

Empty as Air. (Ang.-Sax., *œmtig.*)

" Dead men's cries to fill the empty air."
Shakespeare : 2 Henry VI., v. 2.

Empty Champagne Bottles. Fellow-commoners at Cambridge used to be so called, their academical dress being a gaudy purple and silver gown, resembling the silver foil round the neck

14

of a champagne bottle. Very few of these wealthy magnates took honours.

The nobleman's gown was silk.

Empty Chance. A chance not worth calculating on. The ace of dice was, by the Greeks and Romans, left *empty*, because the number of dice was equal to the number of aces thrown. As ace is the lowest chance, the empty chance was the least likely to win.

Empyre'an. According to Ptolemy, there are five heavens, the last of which is pure elemental fire and the seat of deity ; this fifth heaven is called the empyrean (from the Greek *en-pur*, in fire). (*See* HEAVEN.)

" Now had the Almighty Father from above,
From the pure empyrean where He sits
High throned above all height, bent down his
  eye." *Milton : Paradise Lost*, iii. 56-58.

And again, book vi. 833 :

" The steadfast empyrēan shook without."

En Evidence (French). To the fore.

" Mr. ——— has been much *en evidence* of late in the lobby ; but ;as he has no seat, his chance of being in the ministry is very problematical."—*Newspaper paragraph*, February, 1886.

En Garçon. As a bachelor. " To take me en garçon," without ceremony, as a bachelor fares in ordinary life.

En Masse. The whole lot just as it stands ; the whole.

En Rapport. In harmony with; in sympathetic lines with.

En Route. On the way ; on the road or journey

Enal'io-saurians(Greek, *sea-lizards*). A group of fossil saurians, including the Ich'thyosaur, Ple'siosaur, Sauropter'ygy, etc., etc.

Encel'ados. The most powerful of the giants that conspired against Zeus (Jupiter). The king of gods and men cast him down, and threw Mount Etna over him. The poets say that the flames of this volcano arise from the breath of this giant. The battle-field of his contest was Phleg'ra, in Macedonia.

" So fierce Enceladus in Phlegra stood."
          Hoole: Jerusalem Delivered.
" I tell you, younglings, not Encelados,
  With all his threat'ning band of Typhon's
  brood . . .
Shall seize this prey out of his father's hands."
  Shakespeare : Titus Andronicus, iv. 2.

Enchanted Castles. De Saint Foix says that women and girls were subject to violence whenever they passed by an abbey quite as much as when they approached a feudal castle. When these victims were sought for and demanded

back, the monks would sustain a siege rather than relinquish them ; and, if close pressed, would bring to the walls some sacred relic, which so awed the assailants that they would desist rather than incur the risk of violating such holy articles. This, he says, is the origin of enchanters, enchantments, and enchanted castles. (*Historical Essays.*)

Enchanter is one who sings incantations. (Latin, *in-canto*, to sing over or against some one.)

Encomium. The Greek *kōmos* is a revel in honour of [Bacchus], in which the procession marches from *kōmē* to *kōmē*: *i.e.* village to village. *En-kōmion* is the hymn sung in these processions in honour of Bacchus; hence, praise, eulogy.

Encore (French). Our use of this word is unknown to the French, who use the word *bis* (twice) if they wish a thing to be repeated. The French, however, say *encore un tasse* (another cup), *encore une fois* (still once more). It is strange how we have perverted almost every French word that we have naturalised. (*See* ENGLISH FRENCH.)

Encrat'ites (4 syl.). A sect of the second century, who condemned marriage, forbade eating flesh or drinking wine, and rejected all the luxuries and comforts of life as " things sinful." The sect was founded by Ta'tian, a heretic of the third century, who compiled from four other books what he called a *Diatessaron*—an heretical gospel. (See *Eusebius*, book iv. chap. xxix.) (Greek, *egcrates*, self-mastery.)

❧ This heretic must not be confounded with Tatian the philosopher, a disciple of Justin Martyr, who lived in the second century.

Encroach means literally to put on a hook, or to hook on. Those who hook on a little here and a little there. (French, *en croc*, on a hook.)

End. (Ang.-Sax. *ende*, verb *endian*.) *At my wits' end.* At a standstill· how to proceed farther ; at a non-plus.

He is no end of a fellow. A capital chap ; a most agreeable companion ; an A1 [A one] (*q.v.*). He is an " all round " man, and therefore has no end.

To be [one's] *end.* The cause or agent of [his] death.

" This apoplexie will be his end."
          Shakespeare : 2 Henry IV., iv. 4.

To begin at the wrong end. To attempt to do something unmethodically. **This** is often done in education, where children are taught grammar before they are taught words. No one on earth would teach his child to talk in such a manner. First talk anyhow, and when words are familiar, teach the grammar of sentences. The allusion may be to thread wound on a card or bobbin; if anyone attempts to unwind it at the wrong end, he will entangle the thread and be unable to unwind it.

To come to the end of one's tether. To do all that one has ability or liberty to do. The allusion is to an animal tied to a rope; he can graze only so far as his tether can be carried out.

To have it at my finger's end. To be perfectly *au fait;* to remember perfectly, and with ease; *tanquam unguis scire.* The allusion is to work done with the fingers (such as knitting), which needs no thought after it has become familiar.

To have it on [or *at*] *the tip of my tongue.* (*See* TIP OF MY TONGUE.)

A rope's end. A short length of rope bound at the end with thread, and used for punishing the refractory.

A shoemaker's end. A length of thread pointed with a bristle, and used by shoemakers.

My latter end. At the close of life. "At the latter end," towards the close.

"At the latter end of a dinner."
Shakespeare: All's Well, etc., ii. 5.

On end. Erect.

To put an end to. To terminate or cause to terminate.

West end, East end, etc. The quarter or part of a town east or west of the central or middle part.

End-irons. Two movable iron cheeks or plates, still used in cooking-stoves to enlarge or contract the grate at pleasure. The term explains itself, but must not be mistaken for *andirons* or "dogs."

End Paper. The blank fly-leaves of a book.

End of the World (*The*). According to rabbinical mythology, the world is to last six thousand years. The reasons assigned are (1) because the name Jehova contains six letters; (2) because the Hebrew letter *m* occurs six times in the book of Genesis; (3) because the patriarch Enoch, who was taken to heaven without dying, was the sixth generation from Adam (Seth, Enos, Cainan, Mahalaleel, Jared, Enoch); (4) because God created the world in six days; (5) because six contains three binaries—the first 2000 years were for the law of nature, the next 2000 years the written law, and the last 2000 the law of grace.

Seven would suit this fancy quite as well: there are seven days in a week; Jehovah contains seven letters; and Enoch was the seventh generation of the race of man; and the first two binaries were not equal periods.

Ends.

To burn the candle at both ends. To be like a man on double business bound, who both neglects. Of course, no candle could burn at both ends, unless held horizontally, as the lower end would be extinguished by the melted wax or tallow.

To make two or *both ends meet.* To make one's income cover expenses; to keep out of debt. The allusion is to a belt somewhat too tight. The French say *joindre les deux bouts.*

Endemic. Pertaining to a locality. An endemic disease is one common to a particular district, from which it shows no tendency to spread. Thus intermittent fevers are endemic in marshy places.

Endorse. *I endorse that statement.* I accept it; I fully accord with it. The allusion is to the commercial practice of writing your name on the back of a bill of exchange or promissory note if you choose to make yourself responsible for it. (Latin, *in-dorsum,* on the back.)

Endym'ion, in Greek mythology, is the setting sun with which the moon is in love. Endym'ion was condemned to endless sleep and everlasting youth, and Sele'ne kisses him every night on the Latmian hills.

"The moon sleeps with Endymion,
And would not be awaked."
Shakespeare: Merchant of Venice, v. 1.

Enemy. *How goes the enemy?* or *What says the enemy?* What o'clock is it? Time is the enemy of man, especially of those who are behind time.

Enfant Terrible (*An*) [lit., a terrible child]. A moral or social nuisance.

Enfield Rifle. So called from the factory at Enfield where it is made.

Enfilade (French) means literally to spin out; to put thread in [a needle], as *enfiler une aiguille;* to string beads by putting them on a thread, as *enfiler des perles.* Soldiers being compared to thread, we get the following metaphors: to go through a place as thread through a needle—to string artillery by placing it in a line and directing it against an enemy; hence, to scour or rake with shot.

England. Verstegan quaintly says that Egbert was "chiefly moved" to call his kingdom England "in respect of

Pope Gregory's changing the name of *Engelisce* into *Angellyke*." And this "may have moved our kings upon their best gold coins to set the image of an angel." (*Restitution of Decayed Intelligence int Antiquities concerning . . . the English Nation*, p. 147.)

☙ The Angles migrated from the east of the Elbe to Schleswig (between the Jutes and the Saxons). They passed over in great numbers to Britain during the 5th century, and in time established the kingdoms of the heptarchy.

England Expects that Every Man will do his Duty. The parole signalled by Horatio Nelson to his fleet before the battle of Trafalgar.

England's Darling. Hereward the Wake, in the time of William the Conqueror. The "Camp of Refuge" was established in the Isle of Ely, and the Earl of Morcar joined it in 1071. It was blockaded for three months by William, and Hereward (3 syl.) with some of his followers escaped.

Englentyne (3 syl.). The Nonne or Prioress of Chaucer's pilgrims. An admirable character sketch. (*Canterbury Tales ; Prologue*, 118-164.) (*See* ELOI.)

English French. A kind of perversity seems to pervade many of the words which we have borrowed from the French. Thus curate (French *vicaire*) ; Vicar (French *curé*).
Encore (French *bis*).
Epergne (French *surtout*) ; Surtout (French *pardessus*).
Screw (French *vis*), whereas the French *écrou* we call a nut ; and our vice is *étau* in French.
Some still say à l'outrance (French *à outrance*).
We say double entendre, the French *à deux ententes*.

☙ The reader will easily call to mind other examples.

Englishman. The national nickname of an Englishman is "a John Bull." The nation, taken in the aggregate, is nicknamed "John Bull." The French nickname for an Englishman is "Godam'." (*See* BULL.)

Englishman's Castle. His house is so called, because so long as a man shuts himself up in his own house, no bailiff can break through the door to arrest him or seize his goods. It is not so in Scotland.

E'nid. The daughter and only child of Yn'iol, and wife of Prince Geraint',

one of the Knights of the Round Table. Ladies called her "Enid the Fair," but the people named her "Enid the Good." (*Idylls of the King ; Geraint and Enid*.)

Enlightened Doctor (*The*). Raymond Lully, of Palma, one of the most distinguished men of the thirteenth century. (1234-1315.)

Enniskillens. The 6th Dragoons ; instituted 1689, on account of their brave defence of the town of Enniskillen, in favour of William III.

☙ This cavalry regiment must not be confounded with the Inniskillings or Old 27th Foot, now called the "1st battalion of the Royal Inniskilling Fusiliers," which is a foot regiment.

En'nius. The Chaucer or father of Roman poets. (B.C. 239-169.)
The English Ennius. Layamon, who wrote a translation in Saxon of Wace's *Brute.*
The French Ennius. Guillaume di Lorris (1235-65), author of the *Romance of the Rose*, called the *Iliad* of France. Sometimes Jehan de Meung (1260-1320), who wrote the continuation of the same romance, is so called.
The Spanish Ennius. Juan de Mena, born at Cor'dova. (1412-56.)

Enough. (Anglo-Saxon, *genoh* or *genog*.) Enough ! Stop now, you have said all that is needful.
Enough is as good as a feast.
Latin : "Illud satius est, quod satis est."
French : "On est assez riche, quand on a le nécessaire."
☙ At one time Enow was used for numbers reckoned by tale, as : There are chairs enow, nails enow, men enow, etc. ; but now *enough* does duty for both words, and *enow* is archaic.

Ensconce (2 syl.). To hide ; to put under cover. Literally, to cover with a *sconce*, or fort. (German, *schanze*, a fort ; Danish, *schans ;* Swedish, *skans ;* Latin, *abscondo*, to hide.)

Ensemble. *The tout ensemble.* The general effect ; the effect when the whole is regarded. (French.)

Ensign. (French, *enseigner*.)
Of ancient Athens. An owl.
America. The Stars and Stripes.
The British Navy. The Union Jack (*q.v.*). The *white* ensign (Royal Navy) is the banner of St. George with the Jack cantoned in the first quarter. The *red* ensign is that of the merchant service.

The *blue* ensign is that of the navy reserve.

China. A dragon.

Ancient Corinth. A flying horse—*i.e.* Peg'asos.

Ancient Danes. A raven.

Ancient Egypt. A bull, a crocodile, a vulture.

England (in the Tudor era). St. George's cross.

Ancient France. The cape of St. Martin; then the oriflamme.

The Franks (Ripua'rian). A sword with the point upwards.

The Franks (Salian). A bull's head.

The Gauls. A wolf, bear, bull, cock.

The ancient Lacedemonians. The Greek capital letter L (*lambda* Λ).

The ancient Messe'nians. The Greek letter mu (M).

The ancient Persians. A golden eagle with outstretched wings on a white field ; a dove ; the sun.

The Paisdad'ian dynasty of Persia. A blacksmith's apron. (*See* STANDARD.)

The ancient Romans. An eagle for the legion ; a wolf, a horse, a boar, etc.

Rom'ulus. A handful of hay or fern (manip'ulus).

The ancient Saxons. A trotting horse.

The ancient Thebans. A sphinx.

The Turks. Horses' tails.

The ancient Welsh. A dragon.

Ensilage. A method of preserving green fodder by storing it in mass under pressure in deep trenches cut in a dry soil.

Entail'. An entail is an estate cut from the power of a testator. The testator cannot bequeath it ; it must go to the legal heirs. (French, *en-tailler*.)

Entangle. The Anglo-Saxon *tan* means a twig, and twigs smeared with birdlime were used for catching small birds, who were "en-tangled" or twigged.

Ente'le'chy. The kingdom of Queen Quintessence in the famous satirical romance of Rabelais called the *History of Gargan'tua and Pantagruel'.* Pantagruel and his companions went thither in search of the Holy Bottle. It may be called the city of speculative science.

❋ The word is used to express the realisation of a *beau ideal.* Lovers have preconceived notions of human perfections, and imagine that they see the realities in the person beloved, who is the entelechy of their *beau ideal.*

" O lumiere ! enrichie
D'un feu divin, qui m'ard si vivement,
Pour me donner l'etre et le movement,
Etes-vous pas ma seul entelechie."
       Ronsard : sonnet 68 (1524-85).

Enter a House right Foot foremost (*Petronius*). It was thought unlucky to enter a house or to leave one's chamber left foot foremost. Augustus was very superstitious on this point. Pythagoras taught that it is necessary to put the shoe on the right foot first. "When stretching forth your feet to have your sandals put on, first extend your right foot " (*Protreptics of Iamblichus,* symbol xii.). Iamblichus tells us this symbolised that man's first duty is reverence to the gods.

Entering Short. When bills are paid into a banker's hands to receive the amount when due, it is called "entering them short." In this case, if the banker fails, the assignees must give them up. Bills in the hands of factors may be so entered.

Enthu'siast is one who believes that he himself is *in God,* or that *God is in him* (Greek, *en theos*). Our word *inspired* is very similar, being the Latin *in spiritu* (in the spirit).

Entire. Ale, in contradistinction to "cooper," which is half ale and half porter. As Calvert's entire, etc.

Entre Nous (French). Between you and me ; in confidence.

N.B.—One of the most common vulgarisms of the better class is "Between you and I."

Entrée (*To have the*). To be eligible for invitations to State balls and concerts.

Entremets [*arn-tre-may*]. Sweet foods or kickshaws served at table between the main dishes, courses, or removes ; literally, *entre-mets* (French), things put between. We now use two words, *entrées* and *entremets,* the former being subordinate animal foods handed round between the main dishes, and the latter being sweet made dishes.

Eo'lian. *An Eolian harp.* A box fitted with strings, like a fiddle. The strings, however, are not sounded by a bow, but by a current of air or wind passing over them.

" Awake, Eolian harp, awake,
And give to rapture all thy trembling strings."
      Gray: Progress of Poetry, lines 1, 2.

Eolus. God of the winds. (*Roman mythology.*)

Epact. The excess of the solar over the lunar year, the former consisting of 365 days, and the latter of 354, or eleven days fewer. The epact of any year is the number of days from the last new moon of the old year to the 1st of the following January. (Greek, *epactos*, feminine *epactē*, adscititious.)

Eper'gne (2 syl.). A large ornamental stand placed in the middle of a dining-table. It is generally said to be a French word, but the French call such an ornamental stand a *surtout*, strangely adopted by us to signify a frock-coat, which the French call a *pardessus*. The nearest French word is *épargne*, saving, as *caisse d'épargne*, a savings bank; verb *épargner*, to spare or save. (*See* ENGLISH FRENCH.)

Ephe'bi. Youths between the age of eighteen and twenty were so called at Athens. (Greek, *arrived at puberty*.)

Ephe'sian. A jovial companion; a thief; a roysterer. A pun on the verb to pheese—A-pheeze-ian. Pheeze is to flatter.

" It is thine host, thine Ephesian, calls."
Shakespeare: Merry Wives of Windsor, iv. 5.

Ephesian Letters. Magic characters The Ephesians were greatly addicted to magic. Magic characters were marked on the crown, cincture, and feet of Diana; and, at the preaching of Paul, many which used curious [magical] books burnt them. (Acts xix. 19.)

The Ephesian poet. Hippo'nax, born at Ephesus in the sixth century B.C.

Eph'ial'tes (4 syl.). A giant who was deprived of his left eye by Apollo, and of his right eye by Herculēs.

Ephialtes (4 syl.). The nightmare. (Greek, *ephialtēs*, an incubus; from *epihallomai*, to leap upon.)

" Feverish symptoms all, with which those who are haunted by the night-hag, whom the learned call Ephialtes, are but too well acquainted."—
Sir W. Scott: The Antiquary, chap. x.

Eph'ori or *Ephors.* Spartan magistrates, five in number, annually elected from the ruling caste. They exercised control even over the kings and senate.

Epic. *Father of epic poetry.* Homer (about 950 B.C.), author of the *Iliad* and *Odyssey.*

∴ Celebrated epics are the *Iliad, Odyssey, Æneid, Paradise Lost.*

The great Puritan epic. Milton's *Paradise Lost.*

" Speaking of M. Doré's performances as an illustrator of the great Puritan epic."—*The Times.*

Ep'icure (3 syl.). A sensualist; one addicted to good eating and drinking. So called from Epicu'ros (*q.v.*).

Sir Epicure. A worldly sensualist in *The Alchemist*, by Ben Jonson. His surname is "Mammon."

Epicure'an. Carnal; sensual; pertaining to good eating and drinking. (*See* EPICUROS.)

T. Moore has a prose romance entitled *The Epicurean.*

" Epicurean cooks
Sharpen with cloyless sauce his appetite."
Shakespeare: Antony and Cleopatra, ii. 1.

Epicu'ros. (Latin form, *Epicurus.*) The Greek philosopher who founded the Epicure'an school. His axiom was that "happiness or enjoyment is the *summum bonum* of life." His disciples corrupted his doctrine into "Good living is the object we should all seek," or, according to the drinking song, "Who leads a good life is sure to live well."

" Blest be the day I 'scaped the wrangling crew,
From Pyrrho's [*q v.*] maze and Epicurus' sty."
Beattie: Minstrel.

The Epicurus of China. Tao-tse, who commenced the search for the "elixir of life." Several of the Chinese emperors lost their lives by drinking his "potion of immortality" (B.C. 540).

Epi-dem'ic is from the two Greek words *epi-de'mos* (upon the people), a disease that attacks a number of people at once, either from bad air, bad drainage, or other similar cause.

Epigram. A short pointed or antithetical poem; or any short composition happily or antithetically expressed.

Ep'ilepsy was called by the Romans the *Comitial* or *Congress sickness* (morbus comitia'lis), because the polling for the comitia centuria'ta was null and void if any voter was seized with epilepsy while the votes were being taken.

Epimen'ides (5 syl.). A philosopher of Crete, who fell asleep in a cave when a boy, and did not wake again for fifty-seven years, when he found himself endowed with miraculous wisdom. (*Pliny: Natural History.*) (*See* RIP VAN WINKLE.)

" Like Epimenides, I have been sleeping in a cave; and, waking, see those whom I left children are bearded men.—*Bulwer Lytton (Lord Lytton).*

Epiph'any. The time of appearance, meaning the period when the star appeared to the wise men of the East. The 6th January is the Feast of the Epiphany.

⁂ The word is not special to Christianity. One of the names of Zeus was *Epiphanes* (the manifest one), and festivals in his honour were called "Epiphanies." (Greek, *epi-phaino*, to shine upon, to be manifest [in creation].)

Epise'mon, in Greek numerals, is a sign standing for a numeral. Thus, ἐπισημον βαῦ, generally called *Fau.*

Episēmon, stands for 6, and *iota-episemon* for 16. There are two other symbols—viz. *koppa* for 90, and *sampi* [san-pi] for 900. The reason is this: The Greek letters were used for numerals, and were ranged in three columns of nine figures each: but 24 letters will not divide by 9, so the 3 symbols, episēmon, koppa, and sampi were added to make up 3 × 9. Col. 1, from 1 to 20; col. 2, from 20 to 100; col. 3, from 100 to 1,000.

Bau and Fau are identical, the B or F being the dijamma. Thus οἶνος (wine) was pronounced *Foinos*, called in Latin *Vinum*, and ὠόν (an egg) was pronounced *Qfon*, in Latin *Ovum*.

A dash *under* a letter multiplied it a hundredfold. Thus, $a = 1$, but $\underline{a} = 1000$. For intermediate figures between full tens a mark was made *above* the unit. Thus ι (*iota*) = 10; but ί = 10 + 1 = 11, ίβ = 10 + 2 = 12; ίγ = 10 + 3 = 13, and so on.

Ep'isode (3 syl.) is the Greek *epi-eis-odos* (coming in besides—*i.e.* adventitious), meaning an adventitious tale introduced into the main story.

In music, an intermediate passage in a fugue, whereby the subject is for a time suspended.

"In ordinary fugues . . . it is usual to allow a certain number of bars to intervene from time to time, after which the subject is resumed. The intervening bars . . . are called Episodes."—*Ouseley: Counterpoint,* xxii. 169.

Epis'tle is something sent to another. A letter sent by messenger or post. (Greek, *epi-stello.*)

Epi-zoot'ic is *epi-zoon* (upon the herds and flocks). Zoology is used to signify a treatise on animals, but we generally except man; so epi-zootic is used, *demos* (man) not being included.

E'poch means that which bounds in or holds in hand. The starting-point of a sequence of events harnessed together like a team of horses; also the whole period of time from one epoch to another. Our present epoch is the Birth of Christ; previous to this epoch it was the Creation of the World. In this latter sense the word is synonymous with era. (Greek, *epi-echo.*)

"The incarnation of Christ is the greatest moral epoch in the universe of God."—*Stevens: Parables Unfolded* ("The Lost Sheep," p. 104).

Epode (2 syl.). In the Greek epode the chorus returned to their places and remained stationary. It followed the strophe (2 syl.).

Father of choral epode. Stesichoros of Sicily (B.C. 632-552).

Ep'som Races. Horse races held in May, and lasting four days. They are held on Epsom Downs, and were instituted by Charles I. The second day (Wednesday) is the great Derby day, so called from Lord Derby, who instituted the stakes in 1780. The fourth day (Friday) is called the Oaks, so called from "Lambert's Oaks." The "Oaks Estate" passed into the Derby family, and the twelfth Earl of Derby established the stakes.

❧ The Derby, the Oaks, and the St. Leger (held at Doncaster) are called the Three Classic Races. N.B.—There are other races held at Epsom besides the great four-day races mentioned above—for instance, the City Suburban and the Great Metropolitan (both handicap races).

Epsom Salts. A salt formerly obtained by boiling down the mineral water in the vicinity of Epsom, but now chemically prepared. It is the sulphate of magnesia.

Equal-to, in mathematics. The symbol (=), two little parallel lines, was invented by Robert Recorde, who died 1558.

"As he said, nothing is more equal than parallel lines."

Equation of Time. The difference between mean and apparent time—*i.e.* the difference between the time as shown by a good clock and that indicated by a sundial. The greatest difference is in November, at the beginning of which month the sun is somewhat more than sixteen minutes too slow. There are days in December, April, June, and September when the sun and the clocks agree.

Eques Aura'tus. A knight bachelor, called *aura'tus* because he was allowed to gild his armour—a privilege confined to knights.

Eq'uipage (3 syl.). *Tea equipage.* A complete tea-service. To equip means to arm or furnish, and equipage is the furniture of a military man or body of troops. Hence *camp equipage* (all things necessary for an encampment); *field equipage* (all things necessary for the field of battle); a prince's equipage, and so on.

Equity. (*See* ASTRÆA.)

Era. A series of years beginning from some epoch or starting-point, as:

	B.C.
The Era of the Greek Olympiads	776
,, the Foundation of Rome	753
,, Nabonassar	747
,, Alexander the Great	324
,, the Seleucidæ	312
,, Julian Era	45

¶ THE MUNDANE ERA, or the number of years between the Creation and the Nativity:

According to the modern Greek Calendar 7,388
,,   Josephus 7,282
,,   Scaliger 5,829
,,   the ancient Greek Church 5,508
,,   Professor Hales 5,411
,,   L'art de Vérifier les Dates 4,968
,,   Archbishop Ussher 4,004
,,   Calmet 4,000
,,   the Jews 3,700

¶ OTHER ERAS:

The Era of Abraham starts from Oct. 1, B.C. 2016.
,,   Actium starts from Jan. 1, B.C. 30.
,,   Alexander, or of the Lagidæ, starts from Nov. 12, B.C. 324.
,,   American Independence, July 4, A.D. 1776.
,,   Augustus, B.C. 27.
,,   Diocletian, Aug. 29, A.D. 284.
,,   Tyre, Oct. 19, B.C. 125.
,,   the Chinese, B.C. 2697.
,,   the French Republic, Sept. 22, A.D. 1792.
,,   the Heg'ira, July 16, A.D. 622. (The flight of Mahomet from Mecca.)
,,   the Maccabees, B.C. 166.
,,   the Martyrs, Feb. 23, A.D. 313.

¶ The Christian Era begins from the birth of Christ.

Erac′lius, the emperor, condemned a knight to death because the companion who went out with him returned not. "Thou hast slain thy fellow," said the emperor, "and must die. Go," continued he, to another knight, "and lead him to death." On their way they met the knight supposed to be dead, and returned to Eraclius, who, instead of revoking his sentence, ordered all three to be put to death—the first because he had already condemned him to death; the second because he had disobeyed his orders; and the third because he was the real cause of the death of the other two. Chaucer tells this anecdote in his *Sompnoures Tale.* It is told of Cornelius Piso by Sene′ca in his *De Ira,* lib. i. 16; but in the *Gesta Romano′rum* it is ascribed to Eraclius.

Eras′tians. The followers of Thomas Lieber, Latinised into Erastus, a German "heretic" of the sixteenth century. (1524-1583.)

Eras′tianism. State supremacy or interference in ecclesiastical affairs. Thus the Church of England is sometimes called "Erastian," because the two Houses of Parliament can interfere in its ritual and temporalities, and the sovereign, as the "head" of it, appoints bishops and other dignitaries thereof.

E′rebus. Darkness. The gloomy cavern underground through which the Shades had to walk in their passage to Hadës. "A valley of the shadow of death."

   "Not Erebus itself were dim enough
   To hide thee from prevention."
      Shakespeare: Julius Cæsar, ii. 1.

Eret′rian. *The Eretrian bull.* Mene-de′mos of Eret′ria, in Eubœa; a Greek philosopher of the fourth century B.C., and founder of the Eretrian school, which was a branch of the Socrat′ic. He was called a "bull" from the bull-like gravity of his face.

Eri′gena. John Scotus, called "Scotus the Wise," who died 886. He must not be confounded with Duns Scottus the schoolman, who lived some four centuries after him (1265-1308).

Erin. Ireland (*q.v.*).

Erin′nys or *Erin′ys.* The goddess of vengeance, one of the Furies. (*Greek mythology.*)

Eriph′ila. The personification of avarice, who guards the path that leads to pleasure, in *Orlando Furioso,* vi. 61.

Erix, son of Goliah (*sic*) and grandson of Atlas. He invented legerdemain. (*Duchat: Œuvres de Rabelais;* 1711.)

Erl-king. King of the elves, who prepares mischief for children, and even deceives men with his seductions. He is said to haunt the Black Forest.

Er′meline (*Dame*). Reynard's wife, in the tale of *Reynard the Fox.*

Ermie′nes (4 syl.). A renegade Christian, whose name was Clement. He was entrusted with the command of the caliph's "regal host," and was slain by Godfrey. (*Tasso: Jerusalem Delivered.*)

Er′mine or **Hermine.** Littré derives the word from Armenia, and says it is the "Pontic rat" mentioned by Pliny; if so, the better spelling would be "Armine." Prof. Skeat derives the word from the French *hermine,* through *harmo,* the ermine, stoat, or weazel. The ermine is technically called the *Mustela erminea.*

Er′mine Street. One of the four great public ways made in England by the Romans. The other three are *Watling Street, Ikenild Street,* and the *Fosse.* German′icus derives Ermin from *Hermës,* whence *Irminsull* (a column of Mercury), because Mercury presided over public roads. This is not correct; Irminsul, or rather Ermensul, is the Scandinavian Odin, not a "Column of Mercury" at all; and Erming Street really means Odin's Street.

" Fair weyes many on ther ben in Englond,
But four most of all ben zunderstond , . .
Fram the south into the north takit *Erming-
strete;*
Fram the east into the west goeth *Ikeneld-strete;*
Fram south-est [east] to North-west (that is
sum del grete)
Fram Dorer [Dover] into Chestre go'th *Watling-
strete;*
The forth is most of all that tills from Totē-
neys—
Fram the one end of Cornwall anon to Catenays
[Caithness]—
Fram the south to North-est into Englondes end
Fosse men callith thisk voix."
Robert of Gloucester.

Ermin'ia. The heroine of *Jerusalem Delivered*. When her father, the King of Antioch, was slain at the siege of Antioch, and Erminia fell captive into the crusader's hands, Tancred gave her her liberty, and restored to her all her father's treasures. This generous conduct quite captivated her heart, and she fell in love with the Christian prince. Al'adine, King of Jerusalem, took charge of her. When the Christian army besieged Jerusalem, she dressed herself in Clorinda's armour to go to Tancred, but, being discovered, fled, and lived awhile with some shepherds on the banks of the Jordan. Meeting with Vafri'no, sent as a secret spy by the crusaders, she revealed to him the design against the life of Godfrey, and, returning with him to the Christian camp, found Tancred wounded. She cured his wounds, so that he was able to take part in the last great day of the siege. We are not told the ultimate fate of this fair Syrian.

Erna'ni. The bandit-captain, Duke of Segor'bia and Cardo'na, Lord of Ar'agon, and Count of Ernani, in love with Elvi'ra, who is betrothed to Don Ruy Gomez de Silva, an old Spanish grandee, whom she detests. Charles V. of Spain also loves her, and tries to win her. Silva, finding that the king has been tampering with his betrothed, joins the league of Ernani against the king. The king in concealment overhears the plotters, and, at a given signal, they are arrested by his guards, but, at the intercession of Elvira, are pardoned and set free. Erna'ni is on the point of marrying Elvira, when a horn is heard. This horn Ernani had given to Silva when he joined the league, saying, " Sound but this horn, and at that moment Ernani will cease to live." Silva insists on the fulfilment of the compact, and Ernani stabs himself. (*Verdi's opera of Ernani.*)

Ernest (*Duke*). A poetical romance by Henry of Veldig (Waldeck), contemporary with Frederick Barbarossa.

14*

Duke Ernest is son-in-law of Kaiser Konrad II. Having murdered his feudal lord, he went on a pilgrimage to the Holy Land to expiate his crime, and the poem describes his adventures on the way. It is a mixture of Homeric and Oriental myths, and the tales of crusaders. Duke Ernest fulfilled his pilgrimage, returned to Germany, and received absolution.

Eros, the Greek equivalent to Cupid.

Eros'tratus. The man who set fire to the temple of Diana in Ephesus, on the day Alexander the Great was born. This he did to make his name immortal. In order to defeat his vainglory, the Ephesians forbade his name to be mentioned, but such a prohibition would be sure to defeat its object.

Erra-Pater. An almanack. William Lilly, the almanack-maker and astrologer, is so called by Butler. It is said to have been the "name" of an eminent Jewish astrologer. (*Halliwell: Archaic Dictionary.*)

" In mathematics he was greater
Than Tycho Brahe or Erra Pater."
Butler: Hudibras, i. 1.

Erse (1 syl.). The native language of the West Highlanders of Scotland, who are of Irish origin. It is a variant of Irish. Applied by the Scotch Lowlanders to the Highland dialect of Gaelic. In the eighteenth century Scotch was often called Erse, without distinction of Highland and Lowland; and Irish was spoken of as Irish Gaelic. The practice now is to limit the word *Erse* to Irish, and *Gaelic* to Scotch Highlanders.

Er'udite. *Most erudite of the Romans.* Marcus Terentius Varro, a man of vast and varied erudition in almost every department of literature. (B.C. 116-27.)

Erythre'os. (*See* HORSE.)

Erythynus. *Have no doings with the Erythynus.* This is the thirty-third Symbol of the Protreptics of Iamblichus. The Erythynus is a fish called by Pliny (ix. 77) *erythrinus,* a red fish with a white belly. Pythagoras used this fish as a symbol of a braggadocio, which has a lily liver. Have no doings with those who are tongue-doughty, but have white stomachs (where stomach means true courage).

Escapa'de (3 syl.). French. Means literally an escape [from restraint]; hence a spree, lark, or prank. (Spanish, *escapar,* escape.)

" His second escapade was made for the purpose of visiting the field of Rullion Green."—*Scott; Guy Mannering,* xxxvi.

Esclandre. An event which gives rise to scandal. "By the famous Boulogne *esclandre*."

"Since the last 'esclandre' he had held little or no communication with her." — *Lady Herbert: Edith*, 18.

Escu'age (3 syl.) means "shield service," and is applied to that obligation which bound a vassal to follow his lord to war at his own private charge. (French, *escu, écu*, a shield.)

Escula'pios (Latin, *Esculapius*). *A disciple of Esculapius* means a medical student. *Escula'pian*, medical. Escula'pios, in Homer, is a "blameless physician," whose sons were the medical attendants of the Greek army. Subsequently, he was held to be the "god of the medical art."

Escu'rial. The palace of the Spanish sovereigns, about fifteen miles northwest of Madrid. It is one of the most superb structures in Europe, but is built among rocks, as the name signifies.

Escutcheon of Pretence (*An*). That of a wife, either heiress or coheiress, placed in the centre of her husband's shield.

Esin'gæ. A title given to the kings of Kent, from Esē, their first king, sometimes called Ochta.

Esmond (*Henry*). A chivalrous cavalier in the reign of Queen Anne. The hero of Thackeray's novel entitled *Esmond*.

Esoter'ic (Greek, *those within*). Exoter'ic, those without. The term originated with Pythag'oras, who stood behind a curtain when he gave his lectures. Those who were allowed to attend the lectures, but not to see his face, he called his *exoteric disciples;* but those who were allowed to enter the veil, his *esoteric*.
Aristotle adopted the same terms, though he did not lecture behind a curtain. He called those who attended his evening lectures, which were of a popular character, his *exoterics;* and those who attended his more abstruse morning lectures, his *esoterics*.

Espiet (*Es-pe-a*). Nephew of Oriande la Fée. A dwarf, not more than three feet high, with yellow hair as fine as gold, and though above a hundred years old, a seeming child of seven. He was one of the falsest knaves in the world, and knew every kind of enchantment. (*Romance of Maugis d'Aygremont et de Viviason frère*.)

Esplan'dian. Son of Am'adis and Oria'na. He is the hero of Montalvo's continuation of *Amadis*, called *The Fifth Book*.

Esprit de Corps. Fellow-feeling for the society with which you are associated. A military term—every soldier will stand up for his own corps.

Esprit Follet. A bogle which delights in misleading and tormenting mortals.

Esquire. One who carried the *escu* or shield of a knight. (Latin, *scut'iger*, a shield-bearer.)
Copy of a letter from C. H. ATHILL, ESQ., "*Richmond Herald*":—

"Herald's College, E.C., January 26th, 1893.
"The following persons are legally 'Esquires':—
"The sons of peers, the sons of baronets, the sons of knights, the eldest sons of the younger sons of peers, and their eldest sons in perpetuity, the eldest son of the eldest son of a knight, and his eldest son in perpetuity, the kings of arms, the heralds of arms, officers of the Army or Navy of the rank of captain and upwards, sheriffs of counties for life, J.P.'s of counties whilst in commission, serjeants-at-law, Queen's counsel, serjeants-at-arms, Companions of the Orders of Knighthood, certain principal officers in the Queen's household, deputy lieutenants, commissioners of the Court of Bankruptcy, masters of the Supreme Court, those whom the Queen, in any commission or warrant, styles esquire, and any person who, in virtue of his office, takes precedence of esquires."

⁂ Add to these, graduates of the universities not in holy orders.

Es'says. Lord Bacon's essays were the first in English that bore the name.

"To write just treatises requireth leisure in the writer and leisure in the reader . . . which is the cause which hath made me choose to write certain brief notes . . . which I have called essays."— *Dedication to Prince Henry*.

Esse'nes (2 syl.). A sect among the Jews in the time of our Saviour. They were communists who abjured every sort of fleshly indulgence. They ate no animal food, and drank only water. Their sacrifices to God were only fruits of the earth. They kept the Sabbath so strictly that they would not even wash a plate or rinse a cup on that day. They always dressed in white, took no part in public matters, but devoted themselves to contemplative studies. They held the Jewish Scriptures in great reverence, but interpreted them allegorically.

Essex. *East seaxë* (the territory of the East Saxons).

Essex Lions. Calves, for which the county is famous,
Valiant as an Essex iion (ironical).

Essex Stile. A ditch. As Essex is very marshy, it abounds in ditches, and has very few stiles.

Est-il-possible. A nickname of Prince George of Denmark, given him by James II. The story goes that James, speaking of those who had deserted his standard, concluded the catalogue with these words, "And who do you think besides? Why, little Est-il-possible, my worthy son-in-law." James applied this cognomen to the prince because, when George was told of his father-in-law's abdication, all he did was to exclaim, "Est-il-possible?" and when told, further, of the several noblemen who had fallen away from him, "Est-il-possible?" exhausted his indignation.

Estafette (French; Spanish, *estafe'ta*). Military couriers sent express. Their duty is to deliver the dispatches consigned to them to the postillions appointed to receive them.

Estates. *Estates of the realm.* The powers that have the administration of affairs in their hands. The three estates of our own realm are the Lords Spiritual, the Lords Temporal, and the Commons; popularly speaking, the public press is termed the fourth estate. It is a great mistake to call the three estates of England the Sovereign, the Lords, and the Commons, as many do. The word means that on which the realm stands. (Latin, *sto*, to stand.) (*See* FOURTH ESTATE.)

"Herod ... made a supper to his ... chief estates."—Mark vi. 21.

"The king and the three estates of the realm assembled in parliament."—*Collect for Nov. 5.*

Este. The house of Este had for their armorial bearing a white eagle on an azure shield. Rinaldo, in *Jerusalem Delivered*, adopted this device; and Ariosto, in his *Orlando Furioso*, gives it both to Mandricardo and Roge'ro, adding that it was borne by Trojan Hector. As the Dukes of Brunswick are a branch of the house of Este, our Queen is a descendant of the same noble family.

D'Este was the surname adopted by the children of the Duke of Sussex and Lady Augusta Murray.

Estot'iland. An imaginary tract of land near the Arctic Circle in North America, said to have been discovered by John Scalvë, a Pole.

"The snow
From cold Estotiland."
Milton: Paradise Lost, x. 685.

Estramaçon (French). A blow or cut with a sword, hence also "estramaçonner," to play at backsword. Sir Walter Scott uses the word in the sense of a feint or pretended cut. Hence Sir Jeffrey Hudson, the dwarf, says:—

"I tripped a hasty morris ... upon the dining-table, now offering my sword [to the Duke of Buckingham], and now recovering it, I made ... a sort of estramaçon at his nose, the dexterity of which consists in coming mightily near to the object without touching it."—*Peveril of the Peak*, chap. xxxiv.

Estrich Wool is the soft down of the estrich, called in French, *duvet d' autriche*. It lies immediately under the feathers of the ostrich.

Estrildis or *Estrild*. Daughter of a German king, and handmaid to the mythical King Humber. When Humber was drowned in the river that bears his name, King Locrin fell in love with Estrildis, and would have married her, had he not been betrothed already to Guendolœ'na; however, he kept Estrildis for seven years in a palace underground, and had by her a daughter named Sabri'na. After the death of Locrin, Guendolœ'na threw both Estrildis and Sabri'na into the Severn. (*Geoffrey: British History*, ii. ch. ii.-v.)

Es'tuary. Literally, the boiling place; the mouth of a river is so called because the water there seems to seethe and boil. (Latin, *œstuo*, to boil.)

Eter'nal City (*The*). Rome. Virgil makes Jupiter tell Venus he would give to the Romans *impe'rium sine fine* (an eternal empire). (*Æneid*, i. 79.)

Eternal Fitness of Things. The congruity between an action and the agent.

"Can any man have a higher notion of the rule of right, and the eternal fitness of things?"—*Fielding: Tom Jones*, book iv. chap. iv.

Eternal Tables. A white pearl, extending from east to west, and from heaven to earth, on which, according to Mahomet, God has recorded every event, past, present, and to come.

Etesian Wind (*An*). "*Etesia flabra Aquilorium*," says Lucretius (v. 741). A wind which rises annually about the dog-days, and blows forty days together in the same direction. It is a gentle and mild wind. (Greek, ἐτήσιος, annual.)

"Deem not, good Porteus, that in this my song
I mean to harrow up thy humble mind,
And stay that voice in London known so long;
For balm and softness, an Etesian wind."
Peter Pindar: Nil Admiraro.

Eth'nic Plot. The Popish plot. In Dryden's satire of *Absalom and Achitophel*, Charles II. is called David, the royalists are called the Jews, and the Papists Gentiles or Ethnoi, whence

"Ethnic plot" means the Gentile or Popish plot.

"Saw with disdain an Ethnic plot begun . . .
'Gainst form and order they their power employ,
Nothing to build, and all things to destroy."
Part i. 518, 532-3.

Ethnoph'ronēs (4 syl.). A sect of heretics of the seventeenth century, who practised the observances of the ancient Pagans. (Greek, *ethnos-phrēn*, heathen-minded.)

E'thon. The eagle or vulture that gnawed the liver of Prome'theus.

Et'iquette (3 syl.). The usages of polite society. The word means a ticket or card, and refers to the ancient custom of delivering a card of directions and regulations to be observed by all those who attended court. The original use was a soldier's billet. (French, *etiquette;* Spanish, *etiqueta*, a book of court ceremonies.)

"Etiquette . . . had its original application to those ceremonial and formal observances practised at Court. . . . The term came afterwards . . . to signify certain formal methods used in the transactions between Sovereign States."—*Burke: Works*, vol. viii. p. 329.

Et'na. Virgil ascribes its eruption to the restlessness of Encelădus, a hundred-headed giant, who lies buried under the mountain. (*Æn.* iii. 578, etc.) In Etna the Greek and Latin poets place the forges of Vulcan and the smithy of the Cyclops.

Etrenn'es (2 syl.). New-year's gifts are so called in France. Stren'ia, the Roman goddess, had the superintendence of new-year's gifts, which the Romans called *strenæ*. Ta'tius entered Rome on New-year's Day, and received from some augurs palms cut from the sacred grove, dedicated to the goddess Strenia. Having succeeded, he ordained that the 1st of January should be celebrated by gifts to be called *strenæ*, consisting of figs, dates, and honey; and that no word of ill omen should be uttered on that day.

Ettrick Shepherd. James Hogg, the Scotch poet, who was born in the forest of Ettrick, Selkirkshire. (1772-1835.)

"The Ettrick Shepherd was my guide."
Wordsworth.

Etzel—*i.e. Attila.* King of the Huns, a monarch ruling over three kingdoms and more than thirty principalities; being a widower, he married Kriemhild, the widow of Siegfried. In the Nibelungen-Lied, where he is introduced (part ii.), he is made very insignificant, and sees his liegemen, and even his son and heir, struck down without any effort to save them, or avenge their destruction. He is as unlike the Attila of history as possible.

Eu'charis, in Fénelon's *Télémaque,* is meant to represent Mdlle. de Fontanges.

Eu'charist literally means a thank-offering. Our Lord said, "Do this in remembrance of me"—*i.e.* out of gratitude to me. The elements of bread and wine in the Lord's supper. (Greek, *eu-charistia.*)

Eu'clio. A penurious old hunks in one of the comedies of Plautus (*Aulula'ria*).

Eu'cratēs (3 syl.). *More shifts than Eu'cratēs.* Eucratēs, the miller, was one of the archons of Athens, noted for his shifts and excuses for neglecting the duties of the office.

Eudox'ians. Heretics, whose founder was Eudox'ius, patriarch of Antioch in the fourth century. They maintained that the Son had a will independent of the Father, and that sometimes their wills were at variance.

Euge'nius. This was John Hall Stephenson, author of *Crazy Tales,* a relative of Sterne. In Sterne's *Tristram Shandy,* Eugēnius is made the friend and wise counsellor of Yorick.

Eu'gubine Tables. Seven bronze tables found near Eugu'bium (*Gubbio*) in Italy, in 1444. Of the inscriptions, five are Umbrian and Etruscan, and two are Latin.

"The Umbrian, the tongue of north-eastern Italy, is yet more fully represented to us by the Eugubine tablets . . . supposed to be as old as the third and fourth centuries before our era."—*W. D. Whitney: Study of Languages*, lecture vi. p. 220.

Eu'lalie (*St.*). Eu'lalon is one of the names of Apollo; but in the calendar there is a virgin martyr called Eu'lalie, born at Mer'ida, in Estramadu'ra. When she was only twelve years old, the great persecution of Diocle'tian was set on foot, whereupon the young girl left her maternal home, and, in the presence of the Roman judge, cast down the idols he had set up. She was martyred by torture, February 12th, 308.

Longfellow calls Evangeline the "Sunshine of St. Eulălie."

Eulen-spie'gel (*Thyl*) or *Tyll Owlglass.* The hero of a German tale, which relates the pranks and drolleries, the ups and downs, the freaks and fun of a wandering cottager of Brunswick. The author is said to have been Dr. Thomas Murner (1475-1530).

Eumæ'os or *Eumæus*. A swineherd. So called from the slave and swineherd of Ulysses.

"This second Eumæus strode hastily down the forest glade, driving before him . . . the whole herd of his inharmonious charge."—*Sir Walter Scott*.

Eumen'ides [*the good-tempered goddesses*]. A name given by the Greeks to the Furies, as it would have been ominous and bad policy to call them by their right name, *Erin'nyēs*.

Eumnes'tes [*Memory*], who, being very old, keeps a little boy named Anamnestēs [*Research*] to fetch books from the shelves. (*Spenser : Faërie Queene*, book ii. 9.)

Euno'mians. Heretics, the disciples of Euno'mius, Bishop of Cyz'icum in the fourth century. They maintained that the Father was of a different nature to the Son, and that the Son did not in reality unite Himself to human nature.

Eupat'ridæ. The oligarchy of Attica. These lords of creation were subsequently set aside, and a democratic form of government established.

Eu'phemisms. Words or phrases substituted, to soften down offensive expressions.

Place never mentioned to ears polite.
In the reign of Charles II., a worthy divine of Whitehall thus concluded his sermon : "If you don't live up to the precepts of the Gospel . . . you must expect to receive your reward in a certain place which 'tis not good manners to mention here " (*Laconics*). Pope tells us this worthy divine was a dean :—

" To rest the cushion and soft dean invite,
Who never mentioned hell to ears polite."
Moral Essays, epist. iv. 49, 50.

"His Satanic majesty ; " "light-fingered gentry ; " "a gentleman on his travels" (*one transported*) ; "she has met with an accident" (*has had a child before marriage*) ; "help" or "employé " (*a servant*); "not quite correct " (*a falsehood*) ; "an obliquity of vision " (*a squint*) ; "an innocent " (*a fool*), "beldam " (*an ugly woman*), and hundreds of others.

Eure'ka, or rather *Heure'ka* (I have found it out). The exclamation of Archime'dēs, the Syracusan philosopher, when he discovered how to test the purity of Hi'ero's crown. The tale is, that Hiero delivered a certain weight of gold to a workman, to be made into a

votive crown, but suspecting that the workman had alloyed the gold with an inferior metal, asked Archimedes to test the crown. The philosopher went to bathe, and, in stepping into the bath, which was quite full, observed that some of the water ran over. It immediately struck him that a body must remove its own bulk of water when it is immersed, and putting his idea to the test, found his surmise to be correct. Now then, for the crown. Silver is lighter than gold, therefore a pound-weight of silver will be more bulky than a pound-weight of gold, and being of greater bulk will remove more water. Vitru'vius says: "When the idea flashed across his mind, the philosopher jumped out of the bath exclaiming, 'Heure'ka ! heure'ka !' and, without waiting to dress himself, ran home to try the experiment." Dryden has mistaken the quantity in the lines—

" The deïst thinks he stands on firmer ground,
Cries ' Eu'reka !' the mighty secret's found."
Religio Laïci, 42, 43.

But Byron has preserved the right quantity—

" Now we clap
Our hands and cry 'Eureka !' "
Childe Harold, iv. st. 81.

⁑ The omission of the initial *H* finds a parallel in our word *udometer* for "hudometer," *emerods* for "hemorrhoids," *erpetology* for "herpetology" ; on the other hand, we write *humble-pie* for "umble-pie."

Eu'rus (2 syl.). The east wind. So called, says Buttmann, from *eös*, the east. Probably it is *eos eru'o*, drawn from the east. Ovid confirms this etymology : " *Vires capit Eurus ab ortu.*" Breman says it is a corruption of ἕωρος.

" While southern gales or western oceans roll,
And Eurus steals his ice-winds from the pole."
Darwin : Economy of Vegetation, canto vi.

Euryd'icē (4 syl.). Wife of Orpheus, killed by a serpent on her wedding night. Orpheus went down to the infernal regions to seek her, and was promised she should return on condition that he looked not back till she had reached the upper world. When the poet got to the confines of his journey, he turned his head to see if Eurydice were following, and she was instantly caught back again into Hadēs.

" Restore, restore Eurydicē to life ;
Oh, take the husband or return the wife."
Pope : Ode on St. Cecilia's Day.

Eusta'thians. A denomination so called from Eusta'thius, a monk of the fourth century, excommunicated by the council of Gangra.

Eutych'ians. Heretics of the fifth century, violently opposed to the Nesto'rians. They maintained that Jesus Christ was entirely God previous to the incarnation, and entirely man during His sojourn on earth. The founder was Eu'tychēs, an abbot of Constantinople, excommunicated in 448.

Euxine Sea (*The*)—*i.e.* the hospitable sea. It was formerly called *Axine* (inhospitable). So the "Cape of Good Hope" was called the *Cape of Despair*. "Beneventum" was originally called *Maleventum*, and "Dyrrachium" was called *Epidamnus*, which the Romans thought was too much like *damnum* to be lucky.

Evangelic Doctor (*The*). John Wycliffe, "the morning star of the Reformation." (1324-1384.)

Evan'geline. (4 syl.). The heroine of Longfellow's poem so called. The subject of the tale is the expulsion of the inhabitants of Aca'dia (*Nova Scotia*) from their homes by order of George II.

Evan'gelist, in Bunyan's *Pilgrim's Progress*, represents the effectual preacher of the Gospel, who opens the gate of life to Christian. (*See* WYOMING.)

Evangelists. Symbols of the four:—
Matthew. A man with a pen in his hand, and a scroll before him, looking over his left shoulder at an angel. This Gospel was the first, and the angel represents the Being who dictated it. Matthew a *man*, because he begins his gospel with the descent of Jesus from the man David.
Mark. A man seated writing, and by his side a couchant winged lion. Mark begins his gospel with the sojourn of Jesus in the wilderness, amidst wild beasts, and the temptation of Satan, "the roaring lion." (*See* LION).
Luke. A man with a pen, looking in deep thought over a scroll, and near him a cow or ox chewing the cud. The latter part refers to the eclectic character of St. Luke's Gospel.
John. A young man of great delicacy, with an eagle in the background to denote sublimity.
The more ancient symbols were—for Matthew, *a man's face;* for Mark, *a lion;* for Luke, *an ox;* and for John, *a flying eagle;* in allusion to the four living creatures before the throne of God, described in the Book of Revelation: "The first . . . . was like a lion, and the second . . . . like a calf, and

the third . . . . had a face as a man, and the fourth . . . . was like a flying eagle" (iv. 7). Irenæ'us says: "The lion signifies the royalty of Christ; the calf His sacerdotal office; the man's face His incarnation; and the eagle the grace of the Holy Ghost."

Evans (*Sir Hugh*). A pedantic Welsh parson and schoolmaster of wondrous simplicity and shrewdness. (*Shakespeare: Merry Wives of Windsor.*)

Evans (*William*). The giant porter of Charles I., who carried about in his pocket Sir Geoffrey Hudson, the king's dwarf. He was nearly eight feet high. (Died 1632.) Fuller speaks of him in his *Worthies*, and Sir Walter Scott introduces him in *Peveril of the Peak*.

"As tall a man as is in London, always excepting the king's porter, Master Evans, that carried you about in his pocket, Sir Geoffrey, as all the world has heard tell."—Chap. xxxiii.

Evap'orate (4 syl.). Be off; vanish into thin air.

"Bob and Jonathan, with similar meekness, took their leave and evaporated."—*Dickens: Our Mutual Friend,* part i. 6.

Events. *At all events.* In any case; be the issue what it may; "*utcumque ceciderit.*"
In the event, as "In the event of his being elected," means *in case,* or provided he is elected; if the result is that he is elected.

Ever and Anon. From time to time. (*See* ANON.)

Ever-sworded (*The*). The 29th Regiment of Foot, now called the "Worcestershire Regiment." In 1746 a part of this regiment, then at St. John's Island, was surprised by the French and massacred, when a command was issued that henceforth every officer, even at meals, should wear his sword. In 1842-1859 the regiment was in the East Indies, and the order was relaxed, requiring only the captain and subaltern of the day to dine with their swords on.

Ever - Victorious Army (*The*). Ward's army, raised in 1861, and placed under the charge of General Gordon. By 1864 it had stamped out the Taëping rebellion, which broke out in 1851. (*See* CHINESE GORDON.)

Everlasting Staircase (*The*). The treadmill.

Every Man Jack of Them. Everyone. The older form of everyone was *everichon,* often divided into *every chone,* corrupted first into every-john, then into every Jack, then perverted into every man Jack of 'em.

"I shall them soon vanquish every chone."
Shepherd's Kalender.

"To have hadde theym .... slayne everye chone."—*More: On the Passion Weeks.*

Evidence (*In*). Before the eyes of the people; to the front; actually present (Latin). Evidence, meaning testimony in proof of something, has a large number of varieties, as—

Circumstantial evidence. That based on corroborative incidents.

Demonstrative evidence. That which can be proved without leaving a doubt.

Direct evidence. That of an eye-witness.

External evidence. That derived from history or tradition.

Internal evidence. That derived from conformity with what is known.

Material evidence. That which is essential in order to carry proof.

Moral evidence. That which accords with general experience.

Presumptive evidence. That which is highly probable.

Prima facie evidence. That which seems likely, unless it can be explained away.

Queen's or *King's evidence.* That of an accessory against his accomplices, under the promise of pardon.

Secondary evidence. Such as is produced when primary evidence is not to be obtained.

Self evidence. That derived from the senses; manifest and indubitable.

Evil Communications, etc. He who touches pitch must expect to be defiled. A rotten apple will injure its companions. One scabby sheep will infect a whole flock.

French : Il ne faut qu'une brébis galeuse pour gâter tout un troupeau.

Latin : Mala vicini pecoris contagia lædent (*Virgil*). Tunc tua res agitur, paries cum proximus ardet. Mala consortio bonos mores inquinat. Malorum commercio reddimur deteriores. Hic niger est, hunc tu, Romane, caveto (*Horace*). Uva conspecta livorem ducit ab uva.

To the same effect is the locution, " C'est une brébis galeuse," and the idea implied is, he must be separated from the flock, or else he will contaminate others.

Evil Eye. It was anciently believed that the eyes of some persons darted noxious rays on objects which they glared upon. The first morning glance of such eyes was certain destruction to man or beast, but the destruction was not unfrequently the result of emaciation. Virgil speaks of an evil eye making cattle lean. (*See* MASCOTTE, JETTATOR.)

"Nes'cio quis ten'eros oc'ulus n.ihi fas'cinat agnos."   *Ecl.* iii. 103.

Evil May Day (1517). So called because of the riots made on that day by the London apprentices, who fell on the French residents. The ringleaders, with fifteen others, were hanged ; and

four hundred more of the rioters were carried to Westminster with halters round their necks, but were pardoned by "Bluff Harry the King." The Constable of the Tower discharged his cannon on the mob assembled in tumult in Cheapside Way.

Evil Principle. (*See* AHRIMAN, ARIMANES, ASALOR.)

Evils. "Of two evils, I have chosen the least" (*Prior*).

Evolution (*Darwinian*). Darwin's theory is that different forms of animal and vegetable life are due to small variations, and that natural *selection* is a main agent in bringing them about. If favourable, these variations are perpetuated, if not they die off.

Spencer's theory is that the present multitude of objects have all sprung from separate atoms originally homogeneous.

"Evolution is the integration of matter and concomitant dissipation of motion, during which the matter passes from an indefinite, incoherent homogeneity to a definite coherent heterogeneity ; and during which the retained motion undergoes a parallel transformation."—*Spencer: First Principles,* part ii. chap. xvii. p. 396.

Evolution, its process, according to biologists.

Part i.

Assuming the existence of some element, call it protyle (2 syl.), in time we get *matter,* and *motion.*

From matter and motion proceed *cohesion* and *repulsion,* and from cohesion and repulsion we get *crystals.*

Next comes *chemical action* into play, from which springs *primordial pratoplasm,* or the *protoplasmic clot* of purely chemical origin.

By further development the *chlorophyll cell* is formed, with its power to assimilate, and this will account for air, water, and minerals.

By parasitism next comes the proto-bacillus or fungus, living on the green cells.

And then will follow the *protozoön,* the first example of animal life.

Part ii.

(1) The *Amœba* is the lowest of known animals, a mollusc, with the sole power of locomotion.

(2) The *Syn-amœba* is multicellular, with an organism adapted for sensation, digestion, and the power of reproduction.

(3) Then will come the *Gastrula,* an organised being, with an external mouth.

(4) Next the *Hydra* or *Polyp,* which has localised sense-organs and instincts.

(5) Then the *Medusa,* with nerves, muscles, and nerve functions.

(6) Next come worms, which have special sense-organs ; and

(7) Then the *Himatega,* or *Sack-worm,* which has a rudimentary spinal cord.

Part iii.   *From the Sack-worm to Man.*

(1) The larvæ of Ascidians.

(2) Lowly-organised fish, like the *Lancelet.*

(3) The *Lepidosiren,* and other fish.

(4) The *Amphibians.*

(5) *Birds* and *Reptiles.*

(6) *Monotremata,* which connect reptiles with mammals.

(7) *Marsupials.*

(8) *Placental Mammals.*

(9) The *Lemuridæ.*

(10) The *Simiadæ.*

(11) The *Monkey* tribe, consisting of the New

World monkey (called *Platyrhines*), and the Old World monkeys (called *Catarhines*, 3 syl.).

(12) The Missing Link between the catarhine monkey and man. The Alali is thought by some to supply this link. It is one of the monkey tribe which approaches nearer to the human species than any other yet discovered.

⁂ This is no place to criticise the theory of evolution, but merely to state it as briefly and plainly as possible.

Ewe-lamb (*A*). A single possession greatly prized. (2 Sam. xii. 1-14.)

Ex Cathe'dra (Latin). With authority. The Pope, speaking *ex cathedra*, is said to speak with an infallible voice —to speak as the successor and representative of St. Peter, and in his pontifical character. The words are Latin, and mean "from the chair"—*i.e.* the throne of the pontiff. The phrase is applied to all dicta uttered by authority, and ironically to self-sufficient, dogmatical assertions.

Ex Hypoth'esi, according to what is supposed or assumed.

"The justification of the charge [*i.e.* the tax for betterment] lies *ex hypothesi* in an enhanced value of the property in the Betterment area."—*The Property Protection objection against section 37 of the Betterment clause of the Tower Bridge Southern Approach Bill* (1894).

Ex Luce Lucellum. To make a gain out of light; to make a cheese-paring from lucifer-matches. When Robert Lowe proposed to tax lucifer-matches, he suggested that the boxes should be labelled *Ex luce lucellum.* (*Parliamentary Reports*, 1871.)

"Lucifer aggrediens ex luce haurire lucellum Incidit in tenebras ; lex nova fumus erat."

Ex Officio (Latin, *by virtue of his office*). As, the Lord Mayor for the time being shall be *ex officio* one of the trustees.

Ex Parte (Latin, *proceeding only from one of the parties*). An ex-parte statement is a one-sided statement, a partial statement, a statement made by one of the litigants without being modified by the counter-statement.

Ex Ped'e Her'culem. From this sample you can judge of the whole. Plutarch says that Pythag'oras ingeniously calculated the height of Hercules by comparing the length of various stadia in Greece. A stadium was 600 feet in length, but Hercules' stadium at Olympia was much longer. Now, says the philosopher, as the stadium of Olympia is longer than an ordinary stadium, so the foot of Hercules was longer than an ordinary foot; and as the foot bears a certain ratio to the height, so the height of Hercules can be easily ascertained. (*Varia Scripta.*)

Ex Post Facto (Latin). *An ex post facto law.* A law made to meet and punish a crime after the offence has been committed.

Ex Professo (Latin). Avowedly; expressly.

"I have never written *ex professo* on the subject."—*Gladstone: Nineteenth Century*, Nov., 1885.

Ex Uno Omnes means from the one instance deduced you may infer the nature of the rest. A general inference from a particular example. If one oak-tree bears acorns, all other oak-trees will grow similar fruit.

Exalta'tion. In old astrology, a planet was said to be in its "exaltation" when it was in that sign of the zodiac in which it was supposed to exercise its strongest influence. Thus the exaltation of Venus is in Pisces, and her "dejection" in Virgo.

"And thus, God wot, Merc'ry' is desolate' In Pisces, wher Venus' is exaltate'." *Chaucer: Canterbury Tales*, 6,285.

In chemistry, the refining or subtilising of bodies, or of their qualities, virtues, or strength.

Exaltation of the Cross. A feast held in the Roman Catholic Church, on September 14th, to commemorate the restoration of the cross to Calvary in 628. It had been carried away by Khosroes the Persian.

Examination. Examen is Latin for the needle indicator of a balance. To examine is to watch the indicator, so as to adjust the balance.

Examiners (*Public*). The examiners at the universities, and at the examinations for the military, naval, and civil services, etc.

Excal'ibur (*Ex cal* [*ce*] *liber* [*atus*]). Liberated from the stone. The sword which Arthur drew out of the stone, whereby he proved himself to be the king. (*See* SWORD.)

"No sword on earth, were it the Excalibur of King Arthur, can cut that which opposes no steady resistance to the blow."—*Sir Walter Scott.*

Ex'cellency (*His*). A title given to colonial and provincial governors, ambassadors, and the Lord-Lieutenant of Ireland. (Compare Luke i. 3.)

Excel'sior. Aim at higher things still. It is the motto of the United States, and has been made popular by Longfellow's poem so named. Used also as the synonym of super-excellent.

Exception. *To take exception.* To feel offended; to find fault with.

"Her manner was so . . . respectful, that I could not take exception to this reproof."—*Farjeon.*

Excep'tions prove the Rule. They prove there is a rule, or there could be no exceptions; the very fact of exceptions proves there must be a rule.

"Exceptio probat regulam."—*Columella.*

Excheq'uer. *Court of Exchequer.* In the subdivision of the court in the reign of Edward I., the Exchequer acquired a separate and independent position. Its special duty was to order the revenues of the Crown and recover the king's debts. It was denominated *Scacca'rium,* from *scaccum* (a chess-board), and was so called because a chequered cloth was laid on the table of the court. (*Madox: History of the Exchequer.*)

⁂ Foss, in his *Lives of the Judges,* gives a slightly different explanation. He says: "All round the table was a standing ledge four fingers broad, covered with a cloth bought in the Easter Term, and this cloth was 'black rowed with strekes about a span, like a chess-board. On the spaces of this cloth counters were arranged, marked for checking computations.'"

Exci'se (2 syl.) means literally, a *coupon,* or piece cut off (Latin, *exci'do*). It is a toll or duty levied on articles of home consumption—a slice cut off from these things for the national purse.

"Taxes on commodities are either on production within the country, or on importation into it, or on conveyance or sale within it ; and are classed respectively as excise, customs, or tolls."—*Mill : Political Economy,* book v. chap. iii. p. 562.

Exclu'sion. *Bill of Exclusion.* A bill to exclude the Duke of York from the throne, on account of his being a Papist. Passed by the Commons, but rejected by the Lords, in 1679; revived in 1681.

Excommunica'tion. (1) The *greater* is exclusion of an individual from the seven sacraments, from every legitimate act, and from all intercourse with the faithful. (2) The *lesser* excommunication is sequestration from the services of the Church only. The first Napoleon was excommunicated by Pope Pius VII.; and the kings of Italy were placed under an anathema by Pius IX. for adding the Papal dominions to the United Kingdom of Italy.

"The person excommunicated : *Os, orāre, vale, communio, mensā, negatur* (The person excommunicated is to be boycotted by the faithful in *os* (conversation), *orāre* (prayer), *communio* (communion), *mensā* (board)."—*Professor T. T. Gury : Romish Moral Theology* (3rd ed., 1862).

Excommunication by Bell, Book, and Candle. (*See* CURSING, etc.)

Excommunication by the ancient Jews. This was of three sorts—(1) *Nid'ui* (separation), called in the New Testament "casting out of the synagogue" (John ix. 22); (2) *Cherem,* called by St. Paul "delivering over to Satan" (1 Cor. v. 5); (3) *Anathema Marana'tha* (1 Cor. xvi. 22), delivered over to the Lord, *who is at hand,* to take vengeance. The Sadducees had an interdict called *Tetragram'meton,* which was cursing the offender by Jeho'vah, by the Decalogue, by the inferior courts, and with all the curses of the superior courts.

Excru'ciate (4 syl.). To give one as much pain as crucifying him would do. (Latin, *ex crux,* where *ex* is intensitive.)

Excuse. "*Qui s'excuse, s'accuse,*" or "*Tel s'excuse qui s'accuse.*"

Ex'eat (Latin, *he may go out*). Permission granted by a bishop to a priest to leave his diocese. In the universities, it is permission to a student to leave college before end of term. Sometimes permission is granted to leave college after the gates are closed.

Ex'ecrate (3 syl.). To many Roman laws this tag was appended, "If any one breaks this law, *sacer esto,*" *i.e.* let his body, his family, and his goods be consecrated to the gods. When a man was declared *sacer,* anyone might kill him with impunity. Anyone who hurt a tribune was held a *sacer* to the goddess Cerës. *Ex* in this word is intensitive.

"If anyone hurt a tribune in word or deed, he was held accursed [*sacer*], and his goods were confiscated."—*Livy,* iii. 55 ; see also *Dionysius,* vi. 89, and viii. 17.

Exequatur. An official recognition of a person in the character of consul or commercial agent, authorising him to exercise his power. The word is Latin, and means, "he may exercise" [the function to which he has been appointed].

"The Northern Patriotic League (Oporto) has decided to petition the Government to withdraw the Exequatur from the British Consul here."—*Reuter's Telegram,* Tuesday, Feb. 11th, 1890.

Ex'ercises. Week-day sermons were so called by the Puritans. Hence the title of *Morning Exercises,* week-day sermons preached in the morning.

Ex'eter. *The Duke of Exeter's daughter* was a sort of rack invented by the

Duke of Exeter during the reign of Henry VI. (*Blackstone.*)

> " I was the lad that would not confess one word .... though they threatened to make me hug the Duke of Exeter's daughter."—*Scott : Fortunes of Nigel,* xxv.

Ex'eter Controversy. A controversy raised upon a tract entitled *Plain Truth,* by the Rev. John Agate, of Exeter, an Episcopalian ; replied to by several dissenting ministers, as Withers, Trosse, Pierce, etc. (1707-1715.)

Ex'eter Domesday. A record containing a description of Wilts, Dorset, Somerset, Devon, and Cornwall ; published by Sir Henry Ellis (in 1816) as a Supplement to the Great Domesday-Book (*q.v.*). Called " Exon," either because it was at one time kept among the muniments of the Dean and Chapter of Exeter, or because the Bishop of Exeter was commissioned to make the survey.

Exhibition. *My son has got an exhibition at Oxford.* An allowance of meat and drink ; a benefaction for maintenance. (Latin, *exhibitio,* an allowance of food and other necessaries, " *alimentis exhibēre aliquem.*")

> "They have founded six exhibitions of £15 each per annum, to continue for two years and a half."—*Taylor : History of the University of Dublin,* chap. v. p. 198.

> " I crave fit disposition for my wife, Due reference of place, and exhibition."
> *Shakespeare : Othello,* i. 3.

Exhibition (*The Great*) was held in Hyde Park, London, and lasted from May 1 to October 15, 1851.

Exies or *Axes.* Hysterics ; ague fits ; any paroxysm.

> " Jenny Ritherout has taen the exies, and done naething but laugh and greet . . . for twa days successively."—*Sir W. Scott : The Antiquary,* chap. xxxv.

Exile. *The Neapolitan Exile.* Baron Poe'rio. One of the kings of Naples promised the people a constitution, but broke his word ; whereupon a revolution broke out, and the baron, with many others, was imprisoned for many years in a dreadful dungeon near Naples. He was at length liberated and exiled to America, but compelled the captain to steer for Ireland, and landed at Cork, where he was well received.

Exit (Latin, *he goes out*). A theatrical term placed at the point when an actor is to leave the stage. We also say of an actor, *Exit So-and-so*—that is, So-and-so leaves the stage at this point of the drama.

He made his exit. He left, or died : as, " He made his exit of this life in peace with all the world." Except in the drama, we say, " made or makes his exit." (*See above.*)

> " All the world's a stage,
> And all the men and women merely players ;
> They have their exits and their entrances."
> *Shakespeare : As You Like It,* ii. 7.

Ex'odus. *The Exodus of Israel.* The departure of the Israelites from Egypt under the guidance of Moses. We now speak of the *Exodus of Ireland*—*i.e.* the departure of the Irish in large numbers for America ; the *Exodus of the Aca'dians*—*i.e.* the expulsion of these colonists from Nova Scotia in the reign of George II. ; etc. (Greek, *ex odos,* a journey out.)

Ex'on, *Exon of the Guards.* Any one of the three certain officers of the day in command of the yeomen of the royal guard ; the acting officer who resides at the court ; an exempt. *Capitaines exempts des gardes du corps.* (French, *exoine, ex soin,* exempt from duty or care.)

Exor'bitant means literally out of the rut (Latin, *ex or'bita,* out of the wheel-rut) ; out of the track ; extravagant (*extra-vagant*).

Exoter'ic. (*See* Esoteric.)

Expectation Week. Between the Ascension and Whit Sunday, when the apostles continued praying " in earnest expectation of the Comforter."

Experimental Philosophy. Science founded on experiments or data, in contradistinction to moral and mathematical sciences. Experimental philosophy is also called *natural philosophy,* and by the French *physics.*

Experimen'tum Cru'cis (Latin). A decisive experiment. (*See* Crucial.)

Experto Crede. Believe one who has had experience in the matter.

Explo'sion means literally, driven out by clapping the hands (Latin, *explo'do*—*i.e.* *ex-plaudo*) ; hence the noise made by clapping the hands, a report made by ignited gunpowder, etc.

Expo'nent. One who explains or sets forth the views of another. Thus, a clergyman should be the exponent of the Bible and Thirty-nine Articles. (Latin, *ex pono,* to expose or set forth.)

Exposé (French). An exposing of something which should have been kept out of sight. Thus we say a man *made* *a dreadful exposé—i.e.* told or did something which should have been kept concealed.

Express Train. A fast train between two large towns, with few or no stoppages at intermediate stations.

Expressed Oils are those which are obtained by pressure. Unlike animal and essential oils, they are pressed out of the bodies which contain them.

Expression. *A geographical expression.* A term applied to a tract of country with no recognised nationality.

"This territory is to a very great extent occupied by one race . . . and yet to the present day Germany is little more than a geographical expression."—*Daily Telegraph* (before 1871).

Ex'quisite (3 syl.). One sought out; a coxcomb, a dandy, one who thinks himself superlatively well dressed, and of most unexceptionable deportment.

"Exquisites are out of place in the pulpit; they should be set up in a tailor's window."—*Spurgeon: Lectures to my Students.* (Lecture viii.)

Exten'sive (3 syl.). *Rather extensive, that.* Rather fast. A slang synonym for a *swell.*

Exter. *That's Exter, as the old woman said when she saw Kerton.* This is a Devonshire saying, meaning, I thought my work was done, but I find much still remains before it is completed. "Exter" is the popular pronunciation of Exeter, and "Kerton" is Crediton. The tradition is that the woman in question was going for the first time to Exeter, and seeing the grand old church of Kerton (Crediton), supposed it to be Exeter Cathedral. "That's Exter," she said, "and my journey is over;" but alas! she had still eight miles to walk before she reached her destination.

Extinct Species [since the time of man]. The dodo, great auk, quagga, sea-cow, and white rhinoceros.

Getting very rare: the bison, the Carolina paraket, the giraffe, and the passenger pigeon once common enough.

Extravagantēs Constitutio'nēs, or *Extrav'agants.* The papal constitutions of John XXII., and some few of his successors, supplemental to the "Corpus Juris Canon'ici." So called because they were not ranged in order with the other papal constitutions, but were left "out-wanderers" from the general code.

Extreme Unction. One of the seven sacraments of the Catholic Church, founded on St. James v. 14, "Is any sick among you? let him call for the elders of the Church: and let them pray over him, anointing him with oil in the name of the Lord."

Extremes Meet. In French: *"Les extrêmes se touchent."*

Extricate. Latin, *ex,* out of, and *tricæ,* fetters. "Tricæ" are the hairs, etc., tied round the feet of birds to prevent their wandering. To extricate is to "get out of these *tricæ* or meshes."

Exult' (Latin). To leap out. Thus we say, "I am ready to *leap out* of my skin;" to jump for joy.

Eye. Latin, *oc'ulus;* Italian, *occhio;* Spanish, *ojo:* Russian, *oko;* Dutch, *oog;* Saxon, *eáge* (where *g* is pronounced like *y*); French, *œil.*

In my mind's eye. In my perceptive thought. The eye sees in two ways: (1) from without; and (2) from within. When we look at anything without, the object is reflected on the retina as on a mirror; but in deep contemplation the inward thought "informs the eye." It was thus Macbeth saw the dagger; and Hamlet tells Horatio that he saw his deceased father "in his mind's eye."

In the wind's eye. Directly opposed to the wind.

In the twinkling of an eye. Immediately, very soon. *"Au moindre clin d'œil."* Similar phrases are: "In a brace of shakes," "In the twinkling of a bed-post." (*See* BED-POST.)

My eye! or *Oh, my eye!* an exclamation of astonishment. (*See* ALL MY EYE.)

One might see that with half an eye. Easily; at a mere glance.

The king's eyes. His chief officers. An Eastern expression.

"One of the seven
Who in God's presence, nearest to the throne
Stand ready at command, and are his eyes
That run thro' all the heavens, or down to earth
Bear his swift errands."

Milton: Paradise Lost, iii. 652.

To have an eye on. To keep strict watch on the person or thing referred to.

To have an eye to the main chance. To keep constantly in view the profit to arise; to act from motives of policy. (*See* MAIN CHANCE.)

To see eye to eye. To be of precisely the same opinion; to think both alike.

Eye - service. Superficial service. *"Service qu'on rend sous les yeux du maître."*

"Servants, be obedient to them that are your masters . . . ; not with eye-service, as men pleasers; but as the servants of Christ."—Eph. vi. 5, 6.

Eye-sore. Something that is offensive to the sight. Sore is the Anglo-Saxon *sar* (painful) or *swær* (grievous). It is painful or grievous to the eye.

"Mordecai was an eye-sore to Haman."—*D'Estrange.*

Eye-teeth. The canine teeth are so called because their fangs extend upwards nearly to the orbits of the eyes.

To draw one's eye-teeth. To take the conceit out of a person; to fleece one without mercy; to make one suffer loss without *seeing* the manœuvre by which it was effected.

"I guess these Yanks will get their eye-teeth drawn if they don't look sharp."—*W. Hepworth Dixon: New America,* vol. i.

Eye of a Needle. Lady Duff Gordon, writing from Cairo, says: "Yesterday I saw a camel go through the eye of a needle—*i.e.* a low arched door of an enclosure. He must kneel and bow his head to go through, and thus the rich man must humble himself" (*Wood: Bible Animals,* p. 243). Lord Nugent, in his *Travels,* informs us that when at Hebron he was directed to go out by the Needle's Eye, or small gate of the city.

Eye of Greece (*The*). Athens.

"Athens, the eye of Greece, mother of arts."
        Milton: Paradise Regained, book iv. 240.

Eye of the Baltic (*The*). Gottland, in the Baltic.

Eye of the Storm. An opening between the storm clouds. (*See* BULL'S EYE.)

Eyes.
The Almond Eyes. The Chinese.

"He will not receive a very warm welcome from the Almond Eyes."—*F. Millar: On the Central Saints' Rest* (1891).

Eyes to the blind. A staff. So called in allusion to the staff given to Tire'sias by Athe'na, to serve him for the eyes of which she had deprived him. (*See* TIRESIAS.)

To cast sheep's eyes at one. To look askant with shyness or diffidence.

To make eyes at one. To look wantonly at a person; to look lovingly at another.

To rent the eyes with paint (Jer. iv. 30). The ladies of the East tinge the edge of their eyelids with the powder of lead-ore. They dip into the powder a small wooden bodkin, which they draw "*through*" the eyelids over the ball of the eye." Jezebel is said "to have adjusted her eyes with kohol" (a powder of lead-ore), 2 Kings ix. 30. N.B.—The word "face" in our translation should in both these cases be rendered "eyes." (*Shaw: Travels.*)

Your eyes are bigger than your stomach. You fancied you could eat more, but found your appetite satisfied with less than you expected. "Oculi plus devorā-bant quam capit venter."

Eyed.
One-eyed people. (*See* ARIMASPIANS, CYCLOPS.)

Eyre. *Justices in Eyre.* A corruption of "Justices in itin'ere." At first they made the circuit of the kingdom every seven years, but Magna Charta provided that it should be done annually.

Eyre (*Jane*). The heroine of Charlotte Brontë's novel so called. Jane Eyre is a governess, who stoutly copes with adverse circumstances, and ultimately wins the love of a man of fortune. ('Eyre' pronounce *air.*)

Ezour Ve'da or Yajûr Veda. The second of the sacred books of the Hindûs. The four are :—

(1) The *Rig Veda* (prayers and hymns in verse);

(2) The *Ezour Veda* (prayers in prose);

(3) The *Sama* (prayers to be chanted); and

(4) The *Atharvan Veda* (formulas of consecration, imprecation, expiation, etc.).

Ezzelin (3 syl.). Sir Ezzelin recognised count Lara at the table of Lord Otho, and charged him with being Conrad the corsair. A duel was arranged, and Ezzelin was never heard of more. A serf used to tell how one evening he saw a horseman cast a dead body into the river which divided the lands of Otho and Lara, and that there was a star of knighthood on the breast of the dead body. (*Byron: Lara.*) (*See* CONRAD.)

F

F. *F is written on his face.* "Rogue" is written on his face. The letter F used to be branded near the nose, on the left cheek of felons, on their being admitted to "benefit of clergy." The same was used for brawling in church. The custom was not abolished by law till 1822.

F Sharp. A flea. The pun is F, the initial letter, and sharp because the bite is acute. (*See* B FLATS.)

ff. A corrupt way of making a capital *F* in Old English, and used as low down

as 1750 ; as ffrance for France, ffarring-
ton for Farrington, etc.

F. E. R. T. The letters of the Sardinian motto.

Either *Fortitu'do Ejus Rhodum Ten'uit,*
in allusion to the succour rendered to
Rhodes by the house of Savoy, 1310 ;
Or, *Fœdĕre et Religiōne Tenēmur,* on
the gold doubloon of Victor Amadeus I. ;
Or, *Fortitu'do Ejus Rempublicam Tenet.*

F. O. B. Free on board ; meaning
that the shipper, from the time of ship-
ment, is free from all risk.

F's. *The three f's.* **F**ixed tenure, **F**air
rent, **F**ree sale. The platform of the
Irish League in 1880.

Fa' (Scotch). To get ; to get a share
of ; to lay a claim to.

" Where is the laird or belted knight
That best deserves to fa' that ? "
Burns : Whom Will Ye Send, stanza i.

Fabian Society. An association of
socialists.

"The Fabian Society aims at the reorganisation
of society by the emancipation of land and in-
dustrial capital from individual and class owner-
ship ; and the vesting of them in the community
for the general benefit."—*H. G. Wilshire : Fabian
Essays on Socialism,* June, 1891, p. 91.

✢ The name of the society is derived
from Quintus Fabius, the Roman general,
who won his way against Hannibal by
wariness, not by violence, by caution,
not by defiance.

"Fabian tactics lie in stealing inches, not in
grasping leagues." — *Liberty Review,* May 19th,
1894, p. 395, col. 1.

Fabian Soldiers. A complimentary
phrase for Roman soldiers, the bravest
of the brave.

"Quem [band of trained soldiers] quidem sic
omni disciplina militari [Iphicrātēs] erudivit, ut
quemadmodum quondam ' Fabiāui milĭtes' Romani appellati sunt, sic ' Iphicratenses' apud
Græcos in summa laude fuĕrint."—*Nepos : Iphi-
crates,* ii.

Fa'bian Tactics or *Policy—i.e.* delay. " Win like Fabius, by delay."
The Roman general Fabius wearied out
Hannibal by marches, counter-marches,
ambuscades, and skirmishes, without ever
coming to an open engagement. Fabius
died B.C. 203.

"Met by the Fabian tactics, which proved fatal
to its predecessor."—*The Times.*

Fabianism. The system called Collectivism. (*See* COLLECTIVISTS.)

"It must be evident that the Fabian Society
has a really gigantic task before it, the difficulties
of which will not be lightened when the working
classes come to understand that *small* owmersh p
. . . . and small savings . . . . are just as strongly
condemned by Collectivists as large estates and
colossal fortunes."—*Nineteenth Century* (November, 1892, p. 686).

Fab'ila's sad Fate. The king Don
Fab'ila was a man of very obstinate

purpose and fond of the chase. One day
he encountered a boar, and commanded
those who rode with him to remain quiet
and not interfere ; but the boar overthrew
him and killed him. (*Chronica Antiqua
de España,* p. 121.)

Fa'bius. *The American Fabius.*
Washington (1732-1799), whose military
policy was similar to that of Fabius.
He wearied out the English troops by
harassing them, without coming to a
pitched battle. Duguesclin pursued the
same policy in France, by the advice of
Charles V., whereby all the conquests of
Edward and the Black Prince were re-
trieved.

Fa'bius of the French. Anne, Duc de
Montmorency, grand constable of France ;
so called from his success in almost an-
nihilating the imperial army which had
invaded Provence, by laying the country
waste and prolonging the campaign.
(1493-1567.)

Fables. The most famous writers of
fables are—
Pilpay, among the *Hindus.*
Lokman, among the *Arabs.*
Æsop and Babrios, among the *Greeks.*
Phædrus and Aria'nus, among the
Romans.
Faerne, Abste'mius, and Casti, among
the *Italians.* The last wrote *The Talk-
ing Animals.*
La Fontaine and Florian, among the
French.
John Gay and Edward Moore, among
our own countrymen. The former is
sometimes called "The English Æsop."
Lessing and Pfeffel, among the *Ger-
mans.*
Krilof, among the *Russians.*
(*See* ÆSOP.)

Fab'liaux. The metrical fables of
the Trouvères, or early poets north of
the Loire, in the twelfth and thirteenth
centuries. The word *fable,* in this case,
is used very widely, for it includes not
only such tales as *Reynard the Fox,* but
all sorts of familiar incidents of knavery
and intrigue, all sorts of legends and
family traditions. The fabliau of *Au-
cassin and Nicolette* is full of interesting
incidents, and contains much true pathos
and beautiful poetry.

Fabricius. A Roman hero, representative of inflexible purity and
honesty. The ancient writers love to
tell of the frugal way in which he lived
on his hereditary farm ; how he refused
the rich presents offered him by the
Samnite ambassadors ; and how at death

he left no portion for his daughters, whom the senate provided for.

' "Fabricius, scorner of all-conquering gold."
       Thomson: Seasons (Winter).

Fabuli'nus. The god who taught Roman children to utter their first word. It was the god Vagitan-us (*q.v.*) who taught them to utter their first cry. From *fari*, to speak (Varro).

Fabulous Isles. (*See under* ISLANDS.)

Face. (Latin, *facies*.)
A brazen face. A bold, defiant look. *A brazen-faced person* means one with an impudent, audacious look, especially in a bad cause. Brass metaphorically is generally used in a bad or deprecatory sense, as "You have plenty of brass" [impudence], "I admire your brass."
A rebec face (French, *visage de rebec*). An ugly, grotesque face, like that which used to be cut on the upper part of a rebec or three-stringed fiddle.

"Dead is the noble Badebec,
Who had a face like a rebec."
       Rabelais: Pantagruel, book ii. 4.

⁂ Badebec was the mother of Gargantua, and died in childbirth.
A wry face. The features drawn awry, expressive of distaste.
To draw a long face. To look dissatisfied or sorrowful, in which case the mouth is drawn down at the corners, the eyes are dejected, and the face elongated.

"Of course, it is all right ; if you had not drawn such a long face I should never have doubted."—*Dr. Cupid.*

To fly in the face of . . . . To oppose violently and unreasonably : to set at defiance rashly.
To put a good face on the matter. To make the best of a bad matter : to bear up under something disagreeable ; "*vultu malum dissimulare ;*" "*in adversis vultum secundæ fortunæ gerere.*"
To set one's face against [something]. To oppose it ; to resist its being done. The expression of the face shows the state of the inclination of a person's mind.

Face to Face. In the immediate presence of each other ; two or more persons facing each other. To accuse another "face to face" means not "behind his back" or in his absence, but while present.

Faces.
To keep two faces under one hood. To be double-faced ; to pretend to be very religious, and yet live an evil life.

"We never troubled the Church . . . We knew we were doing what we ought not to do, and scorned to look pious, and keep two faces under one hood."—*Boldrewood : Robbery Under Arms,* chap. ii.

To make faces. To make grimaces with the face.

Face. *To face it out.* To persist in an assertion which is not true. To maintain without changing colour or hanging down the head.
To face down. To withstand with boldness and effrontery.

Faced. With a facing, lining of the cuffs, etc. ; also the preterite of the verb "to face."

Faced.
Bare-faced. Impudence unconcealed. A "bare-faced lie" is a lie told shamelessly and without prevarication.
Shame-faced. Having shame expressed in the face.
Faced with [*silk*, etc.]. An inferior article bearing the surface of a superior one, as when cotton-velvet has a silk surface ; the "facings" (as the lining of coat-cuffs, etc.) made of silk, etc.

Face-card or *Faced-card.* A court card, a card with a face on it.

Facilē Princeps. By far the best ; admittedly first.

"But the *facilē princeps* of all gypsologists is Professor Pott, of Halle."—*Chambers's Cyclopædia.*

Facings. *To put one through his facings.* To examine ; to ascertain if what appears on the surface is superficial only.

"The Greek books were again had out, and Grace . . . . was put through her facings."—*A. Trollope.*

Façon de Parler. Idiomatic or usual form of speech, not meant to be offensive. I once told a waiter in Norway that the meat he brought me for breakfast was not sufficiently cooked, and he bluntly told me *it was not true* (*det er ikke sandt*), but he did not intend to be rude. It was the Norwegian "*façon de parler.*"

Fac'tion. The Romans divided the combatants in the circus into classes, called factions, each class being distinguished by its special colour, like the crews of a boat-race. The four original factions were the leek-green (*pras'ina*), the sea-blue (*ven'eta*), the white (*alba*), and the rose-red (*ros'ea*). Two other factions were added by Domitian, the colours being golden-yellow (*aura'ta*) and purple. As these combatants strove against each other, and entertained a strong *esprit de corps*, the word was easily applied to political partisans.

⁂ In the faction riots of Constantinople, A.D. 532, above 30,000 persons were killed. (Latin, *factio*.)

Fac'tor. An agent; a substitute in mercantile affairs; a commission merchant. (Latin, *facio*, to do, whence the French *facteur*, one who does something for an employer.)

> "Asleep and naked as an Indian lay,
> An honest factor stole a gem away."
> *Pope: Moral Essays*, Ep. iii. 361.

Thomas Pitt, ancestor of the Earl of Chatham, was appointed by Queen Anne Governor of Fort St. George, in the East Indies, and in 1702 purchased there, for £20,400, a diamond weighing 127 carats, which he sold to the King of France. This gem is still called the Pitt diamond. Pope insinuates that Pitt stole the diamond. This is not exactly true. He obtained it for a price much below its value, and threatened the thief with exposure if he made a fuss about the matter.

Facto'tum. One who does for his employer all sorts of services. Sometimes called a *Johan'nes Facto'tum*. Our "Jack-of-all-trades" does not mean a factotum, but one who does odd jobs for anyone who will pay him. (Latin, *facere totum*, to do everything required.)

Fad (*A*). A hobby, a temporary fancy, a whim. A contraction of faddle in "fiddle-faddle."

> "Among the fads that Charley had taken up for a time . . . was that of collecting old prints."—*Eggleston: Faith Doctor*, chap. iii.

Fada. A fée or kobold of the south of France, sometimes called "Hada." These house-spirits, of which, strictly speaking, there are but three, bring good luck in their right hand and ill luck in their left.

Fadda. Mahomet's white mule.

Fadge (1 syl.). To suit or fit together, as, *It won't fadge; we cannot fadge together; he does not fadge with me.* (Anglo-Saxon, *fœgen*, to fit together; Welsh, *ffag*, what tends to unite.)

> "How will this fadge?"
> *Shakespeare: Twelfth Night*, ii. 2.

Fadge. A farthing. A corrupt contraction of fardingal, *i.e.* farthingale. (*See* CHIVY.)

Fa'dha (*Al*). Mahomet's silver cuirass, confiscated from the Jews on their expulsion from Medi'na.

Fad'ladeen'. The great Nazir', or chamberlain of Aurungze'bë's harem,

in *Lalla Rookh.* The criticism of this self-conceited courtier upon the several tales which make up the romance are very racy and full of humour; and his crest-fallen conceit when he finds out that the poet was the Prince in disguise is well conceived.

> "He was a judge of everything—from the pencilling of a Circassian's eyelids to the deepest questions of science and literature; from the mixture of a conserve of rose-leaves to the composition of an epic poem . . . all the cooks and poets of Delhi stood in awe of him."—*T. Moore.*

Faërie or **Feerie.** The land of the fays or faëries. The chief fay realms are Av'alon, an island somewhere in the ocean; O'beron's dominions, situate "in wilderness among the holtis hairy;" and a realm somewhere in the middle of the earth, where was Pari Banou's palace.

> "For learnëd Colin [Spenser] lays his pipes to gage,
> And is to Faëry gone a pilgrimage."
> *Drayton: Eclogue*, iii.

Faërie Queene. A metrical romance in six books, by Edmund Spenser (incomplete). It details the adventures of various knights, who impersonate different virtues, and belong to the court of Gloria'na, Queen of faërie land.

The first book contains the legend of the Red Cross Knight (*the spirit of Christianity*), and is by far the best. The chief subject is the victory of Holiness over Error. It contains twelve cantos.

The second book is the legend of Sir Guyon (*the golden mean*), in twelve cantos.

The third book is the legend of Britomartis (*love without lust*), in twelve cantos. Britomartis is Diana, or Queen Elizabeth the Britoness.

The fourth book is the legend of Cambel and Tri'amond (*fidelity*), in twelve cantos.

The fifth book is the legend of Ar'tegal (*justice*), in twelve cantos.

The sixth book is the legend of Sir Cal'idore (*courtesy*), in twelve cantos.

There are parts of a seventh book—viz. cantos 6 and 7, and two stanzas of canto three. The subject is *Mutability.*

The plan of the *Faërie Queene* is borrowed from the *Orlando Furioso*, but the creative power of Spenser is more original, and his imagery more striking, than Ariosto's. Thomson says of him—

> "[He] like a copious river, poured his song
> O'er all the mazes of enchanted ground."
> *The Seasons* (*Summer*), 1574-5.

Fag. One who does, and perseveres in doing. In public schools, it means a little boy who waits upon a bigger one. Probably a contracted form of *factor*, *factotum* ; Latin, *fac-ĕre*, to do.

Fag. Servant of Captain Absolute, who **apes** his master in all things. (*Sheridan : The Rivals*.)

"Even the mendacious Mr. Fag assures us, though he never scruples to tell a lie at his master's command, yet it hurts his conscience to be found out."—*Sir Walter Scott*.

Fag-end (*A*). The selvedge or coarse end of a piece of cloth. This also is from *facio, factum*, meaning the part added after the piece is finished. The fag-end of a session means the last few days before dissolution.

Fagged Out. Wearied with hard work. Fatigued contracted into *fa'g'ed*.

Fa'gin. An infamous Jew, who teaches boys and girls to rob with dexterity. (*Dickens : Oliver Twist*.)

Fagot. A badge worn in mediæval times by those who had recanted their "heretical" opinions. It was designed to show what they merited, but had narrowly escaped. (*See* FAGOTS.)

Il y a fagots et fagots. There are divers sorts of fagots ; every alike is not the same. The expression is in Molière's *Le Médecin malgré lui*, where Sganarelle wants to show that his fagots are better than those of other persons ; "Ay, but those fagots are not so good as my fagots." (Welsh, *ffag*, that which unites ; Anglo-Saxon, *fægan*, to unite.)

Sentire les fagots. To be heretical ; to smack of the fagots. In allusion to the custom of burning heretics by surrounding them with blazing fagots.

Fagot Votes. Votes obtained by the nominal transfer of property to a person whose income was not otherwise sufficient to qualify him for being a voter. The "fagot" was a bundle of property divided into small lots for the purpose stated above. Abolished.

"The object was to prevent the creation of fagot votes."—*The Times*.

Fagots. Cakes made of the "insides" of pigs, with thyme, scraps of pork, sage, onions, and other herbs, fried together in grease, and eaten with potatoes. (Greek, *phago*, to eat.)

Fah'fah. One of the rivers of Paradise in Mahometan mythology.

Fa'ids. The second class of Druids.

Fai'ence (2 syl.). Majolica. So called from Faen'za, where, in 1299, it was first manufactured. It is termed majolica because the first specimens the Italians

saw came from Majorca. In France it now means a fine ware not equal to porcelain.

Fain'eant. *Les Rois Fainéants* (the cipher or puppet kings). Clovis II. and his ten successors were the puppet kings of the Palace Mayors. Louis V. (last of the Carlovingian dynasty) received the same designation.

"'My signet you shall command with all my heart, madam,' said Earl Philip. . . . 'I am, you know, a complete *Roy Fainéant*, and never once interfered wth my *Maire du Palais* in her proceedings.'"—*Sir Walter Scott: Peveril of the Peak*, chap. XV.

Faint. *Faint heart ne'er won fair lady.*
"The bold a way will find or make."
    King : Orpheus and Eurydice.
"Faint harts faire ladies neuer win." (1569.)
Philobiblion Society's Publications (1827, p. 22).

Faint Hearted. Easily discouraged ; afraid to venture.

Fair (*The*).
Charles IV., King of France, *le Bel* (1294, 1322-1328).
Philippe IV. of France, *le Bel* (1268, 1285-1314).

Fair as Lady Done. A great Cheshire family that has long occupied a mansion at Utkinton. (*Cheshire expression*.)

Fair Geraldine. (*See* GERALDINE.)

Fair Rosamond. (*See* ROSAMOND.)

To bid fair, as "he bids fair to be a good . . . " To give good promise of being . . . ; to indicate future success or excellence ; one *de quo bene sperāre licet*.

Fair as a lily. (*See* SIMILES.)

Fair. (Latin *feriæ*, holidays.)
A day after the fair. Too late for the fun. "*Sero sapiunt Phryges*." The Phrygians were noted for their obstinacy ; hence, *Phryx verberatus melior*. They were thrice conquered : by Hercules, the Greeks, and the Latins, and were wise "after the events."

Fair (*Sloe*). (*See* SLOE-FAIR.)

Fair (*Statute*). (*See* MOP.)

Fair City. Perth ; so called from the beauty of its situation.

Fair Game. A worthy subject of banter ; one who exposes himself to ridicule.

"Bourrienne is fair game ; but the whole of his statements are not worthless."—*The Spectator*, Feb. 18th, 1888.

Fair Maid (*The*).
Fair Maid of Anjou. Lady Edith Plantagenet, who married David, Prince Royal of Scotland.

Fair Maid of February. The snow-drop, which blossoms in February.

Fair Maid of Kent. Joan, Countess of Salisbury, wife of the Black Prince, and only daughter of Edmond Plantagenet, Earl of Kent. She had been twice married ere she gave her hand to the prince.

Fair Maid of Norway. Margaret, daughter of Eric II. of Norway, and granddaughter of Alexander III. of Scotland. Being recognised by the states of Scotland as successor to the throne, she set out for her new kingdom, but died on her passage from sea-sickness. (1290.)

Fair Maid of Perth. Katie Glover, the most beautiful young woman of Perth. Heroine of Scott's novel of the same name.

Fair-star. *The Princess Fair-star,* in love with Prince Chery, whom she sets to obtain for her "the dancing water," "the singing apple," and "the green bird" (*q.v.*). This tale is borrowed from the fairy tales of Straparo'la the Milanese. (1550.) *Chery and Fair-star, by the Countess d' Aulnoy.*

Fair Trade. Smuggling.

"Neither Dirk Hatteraick nor any of his sailors, all well known men in the fair trade, were again seen upon that coast."—*Sir Walter Scott: Guy Mannering,* chap. x.

∴ Latterly the phrase has been introduced into politics to signify reciprocity of protection or free-trade. That is, free-trade to those nations that grant free-trade to us, and *vice versa.*

Fair Way. *In a fair way.* On the right tack. The "fair way" is the proper track through a channel.

Fair and Square. Honestly, justly, with straightforwardness.

Fair fall you. Good befall you.

Fair Play is a Jewel. As a jewel is an ornament of beauty and value, so fair play is an honourable thing and a "jewel in the crown" of the player.

Fairies, good and bad.

AFREET or EFREET, one of the Jinn tribe, of which there are five. (See *Story of the Second Calendar.*)

APPARITION. A ghost.

ARIEL. (See ARIEL.)

BANSHEE or BENSHEE, an Irish fairy attached to a house. (See BANSHEE.)

BOGGART. (Scotch.) A local hobgoblin or spirit.

BOGIE or BOGLE, a bugbear (Scotch form of *bug*). (See BOGIE.)

BROWNIE, a Scotch domestic fairy; the servants' friend if well treated. (See BROWNIE.)

BUG or BUGBEAR, any imaginary thing that frightens a person. (Welsh, *bug.*) (See BUG.)

CAULD LAD (*The*), the Brownie of Hilton Hall. (See CAULD LAD.)

DJINN, JIN, or GINN (Arabian). (See JINN.)

DUENDE (3 syl.), a Spanish house-spirit. (See DUENDE.)

DWARF, a diminutive being, human or super-human. (Anglo-Saxon, *dweorg.*)

DWERGER, DWERGUGH, or DUERGAR, Gotho-German dwarfs, dwelling in rocks and hills. (Anglo-Saxon, *dweorgh.*)

ELF (plu. ELVES), fairies of diminutive size, supposed to be fond of practical jokes. (Anglo-Saxon, *œlf.*) (See ELF.)

ELLE-MAID or ELLE-WOMAN, ELLE-FOLK, of Scandinavia.

ESPRIT FOLLET, the house-spirit of France.

FAIRY or FAERIE (plu. FAIRIES), a supernatural being, fond of pranks, but generally pleasing. (German and French, *fee.*)

FAMILIAR (*A*), an evil spirit attendant on witches, etc. (See FAMILIAR.)

FATA, an Italian fay, or white lady.

FATES, the three spirits (Clotho, Lachĕsis, and Atrŏpos) which preside over the destiny of every individual. (Latin, *fata.*)

FAY (plu. FAYS), same as Fairy (*q.v.*).

FEAR DEARG (*The*), *i.e.* Red Man. A house-spirit of Munster.

GENII (plu.). The sing. *genie* and *genius.* Eastern spirits, whether good or bad, who preside over a man or nation. "He is my evil [or good] genius." (Latin, *genius.*) (See GENIUS.)

GHOST, the immaterial body or noumenon of a human being. Supposed to be free to visit the earth at night-time, but obliged to return to its Hades at the first dawn.

GHOUL, a demon that feeds on the dead. (Persian.)

GNOME (1 syl.), the guardian of mines, quarries, etc. (Greek, γνώμη, a Cabalistic being.) (See GNOMES.)

GOBLIN or HOBGOBLIN, a phantom spirit. (French, *gobelin*; German, *kobold.*)

GOOD FOLK (*The*). The Brownies or house-spirits.

GUARDIAN-ANGEL, an angelic spirit which presides over the destiny of each individual.

HABUNDIA, queen of the White Ladies.

HAG (*A*), a female fury. Milton (*Comus* 445) speaks of "blue meagre hags."

HAMADRYAD, a wood-nymph. Each tree has its own wood-nymph, who dies when the tree dies.

HOBGOBLIN. (See *above,* GOBLIN.) Hob is Robin, as Hodge is Roger.

HORNS or HORNIE, the Devil. (See HORNIE.)

IMP, a puny demon or spirit of mischief. (Welsh, *imp.*)

JACK-A-LANTERN, a bog or marsh spirit who delights to mislead.

JINN or GINN. (See JINN.) These Arabian spirits were formed of "smokeless fire."

KELPIE (2 syl.). In Scotland, an imaginary spirit of the waters in the form of a horse. (See KELPIE.)

KOBOLD, a German household goblin, also frequenting mines. (German, *kobold.*) (See KOBOLD.)

LAM'IA (plu. LAM'LÆ), a hag or demon. Keats's Lamia is a serpent which had assumed the form of a beautiful woman, beloved by a young man, and gets a soul. (Latin, *Lamia.*) (See LAMIES.)

LAMIES, African spectres, having the head of a woman and tail of a serpent. (See LAMIA.)

LAR (plu. LARES) (2 syl.), Latin household deities. (See LARES.)

LEPRECHAUN, a fairy shoemaker.

MAB, the faries' midwife. Sometimes incorrectly called queen of the fairies. (Welsh, *mab.*) (See MAB.)

MANDRAKE. (See MANDRAKE.)

MERMAID, a sea-spirit, the upper part a woman and the lower half a fish.

MERROWS, both male and female, are spirits of the sea, of human shape from the waist upwards, but from the waist downwards are like a fish. The females are attractive, but the males have green teeth, green hair, pig's eyes, and red noses. Fishermen dread to meet them.

MONACIELLO or LITTLE MONK, a house-spirit of Naples.

NAIAD (plu. NAIADES [3 syl.] or NAIADS [2 syl.]), water-nymphs. (Latin.) (See NAIADS.)

NIS or NISSE (2 syl.), a Kobold or Brownie. A Scandinavian fairy friendly to farmhouses. (Contraction of *Nicolaus.*)

NIX (female, NIXIE), a water-spirit. The *nix* has green teeth, and wears a green hat; the *nixie* is very beautiful.

OBERON, king of the fairies.

OGRE [pronounce *og'r*], an inhabitant of fairy-land said to feed on infant children. (French.)

ORENDS, mountain nymphs. (Greek, *oros*.)

OUPHE (2 syl.), a fairy or goblin.

PERI, a Persian fairy. Evil peris are called "Deevs."

PIGWIDGEON, a fairy of very diminutive size.

PIXY or PIXIE (also *pisgy, pisgie*), a Devon-shire fairy, same as Puck.

POUKE (1 syl.), same as Puck. (*See* POUKE.)

PUCK, a merry little fairy spirit, full of fun and harmless mischief. (Icelandic and Swedish, *puke*.) (*See* PUCK.)

ROBIN-GOODFELLOW, another name for PUCK. (*See* ROBIN . . . .)

SALAMANDER, a spirit which lives in fire. (Latin and Greek, *salamandra*.) (*See* SALA-MANDRA.)

SHADES, ghosts.

SPECTRE, a ghost.

SPOOK (in Theosophy), an elemental.

SPRITE, a spirit.

STROMKARL, a Norwegian musical spirit, like Neck. (*See* STROMKARL.)

SYLPH, a spirit of the air; so named by the Rosicrucians and Cabalists. (Greek, *silphe*; French, *sylphide*.) (*See* SYLPHS.)

TRITON, a sea deity, who dwells with Father Neptune in a golden palace at the bottom of the sea. The chief employment of tritons is to blow a conch to smooth the sea when it is ruffled.

TROLL, a hill-spirit. Hence Trolls are called Hill-people or Hill-folk, supposed to be immensely rich, and especially dislike noise. (*See* TROLLS.)

UN'DINE (2 syl.), a water-nymph. (Latin, *unda*.) (*See* UNDINE.)

URCHIN properly means a hedgehog, and is applied to mischievous children and small folk generally. (*See* URCHIN.)

VAMPIRE (2 syl.), the spirit of a dead man that haunts a house and sucks the blood of the living. A Hungarian superstition. (*See* VAMPIRE.)

WERE-WOLF (Anglo-Saxon, *wer-wulf*, man-wolf), a human being, sometimes in one form and sometimes in another. (*See* WERE-WOLF.)

WHITE LADIES OF NORMANDY. (*See* WHITE LADIES.)

WHITE LADY (*The*) of the royal family of Prussia. A "spirit" said to appear before the death of one of the family. (*See* WHITE LADY.)

WHITE LADY OF AVENEL (2 syl.), a tutelary spirit.

WHITE LADY OF IRELAND (*The*), the banshee or domestic spirit of a family.

WHITE MERLE (*The*), of the old Basques. A white fairy bird, which, by its singing, restored sight to the blind.

WIGHT, any human creature, as a "Highland wight" Dwarfs and all other fairy creatures.

WILL-O'-THE-WISP, a spirit of the bogs, whose delight is to mislead belated travellers.

WRAITH (Scotch), the ghost of a person shortly about to die or just dead, which appears to sur-vivors, sometimes at a great distance off. (*See* WRAITH, HOUSEHOLD SPIRITS.)

Fairies are the dispossessed spirits which once inhabited human bodies, but are not yet meet to dwell with the "saints in light."

" All those airy shapes you now behold
Were human bodies once, and clothed with
earthly mould ;
Our souls, not yet prepared for upper light,
Till doomsday wander in the shades of night."
Dryden : The Flower and the Leaf.

Fairing (*A*). A present from a fair. The *ing* is a patronymic = a descendant of, come from, belonging to.

" Fairings come thus plentifully in."
Shakespeare : Love's Labour's Lost, v. 2.

Fair'limb. The sister of Bitelas and daughter of Rukenaw, the ape ; in the tale of *Reynard the Fox.*

Fairservice (*Andrew*). A shrewd Scotch gardener at Osbaldis'tone Hall. (*Sir Walter Scott : Rob Roy.*)

Fairy of nursery mythology is the personification of Providence. The good ones are called fairies, elves, elle-folks, and fays ; the evil ones are urchins, ouphes, ell-maids, and ell-women.

" Fairies, black, grey, green, and white,
You moonshine revellers, and shades of night,
You ouphen-heirs of fixéd destiny,
Attend your office."
Shakespeare : Merry Wives of Windsor, v. 5.

The dress of the fairies. They wear a red conical cap ; a mantle of green cloth, inlaid with wild flowers ; green pantaloons, buttoned with bobs of silk ; and silver shoon. They carry quivers of adder-slough, and bows made of the ribs of a man buried where "three lairds' lands meet ;" their arrows are made of bog-reed, tipped with white flints, and dipped in the dew of hemlock ; they ride on steeds whose hoofs would not "dash the dew from the cup of a harebell." (*Cromek.*)

" Fairies small, two foot tall,
With caps red on their head."
Dodsley's Old Plays : Fuimus Troes, i. 5.

Fairy Darts. Flint arrow-heads, supposed at one time to have been thrown by fairies in their pranks.

Fairy Hillocks. Little knolls of grass, like mole-hills, said in the "good old times" to be the homes of fairies.

Fairy Ladies or *Mage*, such as Urganda, the guardian of Amadi'gi ; the fair Oria'na ; Silva'na, the guardian of Alido'ro ; Luci'na, the protectress of Alido'ro and his lady-love, the maiden-warrior, Mirinda ; Eufros'ina, the sister of Luci'na ; Argea, the protectress of Floridante ; and Filide'a, sister of Ardea ; all in Tasso's *Amadi'gi.*

Fairy Land. The land where fairies are supposed to dwell ; dreamland ; a place of great delight and happiness.

"The fairest of fairy lands—the land of home."
Jean Ingelow : The Letter, part i. stanza 31.

Fairy Loaves or **Fairy Stones.** Fossil sea-urchins (*echi'ni*), said to be made by the fairies.

Fairy Money. Found money. Said to be placed by some good fairy at the spot where it was picked up. "Fairy money" is apt to be transformed into leaves.

Fairy Rings. Circles of rank or withered grass, often seen in lawns, meadows, and grass-plots. Said to be produced by the fairies dancing on the spot. In sober truth, these rings are simply an ag'aric or fungus below the surface, which has seeded in a circular range, as many plants do. Where the ring is *brown* and almost *bare*, the "spawn" is of a greyish-white colour. The grass dies because the spawn envelops the roots so as to prevent their absorbing moisture; but where the grass is rank the "spawn" is dead, and serves as manure to the young grass.

> "You demi-puppets, that
> By moonshine do the green-sour ringlets make.
> Whereof the ewe not bites."
> *Shakespeare: Tempest, v. 1.*

Fairy Sparks. The phosphoric light from decaying wood, fish, and other substances. Thought at one time to be lights prepared for the fairies at their revels.

Fairy of the Mine. A malevolent being supposed to live in mines, busying itself with cutting ore, turning the windlass, etc., and yet effecting nothing. (*See* GNOME.)

> "No goblin, or swart fairy of the mine,
> Hath hurtful power o'er true virginity."
> *Milton: Comus, 447-8.*

Fait Accompli (French). A scheme which has been already carried out with success.

> "The subjection of the South is as much a *fait accompli* as the declaration of independence itself."—*The Times.*

Faith. *Defender of the Faith.* (*See* DEFENDER.)
In good faith. "*Bonâ fide*;" "*de bonne foi*;" with no ulterior motive.

Faithful, in Bunyan's *Pilgrim's Progress*, is seized at Vanity Fair, burnt to death, and taken to heaven in a chariot of fire. A Puritan used to be called *Brother Faithful.* The abiding disciples of any cult are called *the faithful.*
Jacob Faithful. The hero of Captain Marryat's novel so called.
Father of the faithful. Abraham (Rom. iv.; Gal. iii. 6-9).

Fakâr (*Dhu'l*). The scimitar of Mahomet, which fell to his share when the spoil was divided after the battle of Bekr. This term means "The Trenchant."

Fake (1 syl.). *Fake away.* Cut away, make off (Latin, *fac*, do, make). It also means *to do*—i.e. to cheat or swindle.
Fake. A single fold of a coiled cable. (Scotch, *faik*, a fold; Swedish, *vika*, to involve; Saxon, *fœgan*, to unite.)

Fakenham Ghost. A ballad by Robert Bloomfield, author of *The Farmer's Boy.* The ghost was a donkey.

Fakir' (*Indian*). A poor man, a mendicant, a religious beggar. The Fakirs are the lowest in the priesthood of Yesidis. They wear coarse black or brown dresses, and a black turban over which a red handkerchief is tied. Fakirs perform all menial offices connected with burials. They clean the sacred building, trim and light the lamps, and so on.

Falcon and **Falconet.** Pieces of light artillery, the names of which are borrowed from hawks. (*See* SAKER.)

Falcon Gentle (*A*). A goshawk.

Falcon Peregrine or **Pel'erin.** *La seconde lignie est faucons que hom apele "pelerins," par ce que nus ne trouve son ni; ains est pris autresi come en pelerinage, et est mult legiers a norrir, et mult cortis, et vaillans, et de bone maniere.* (*Tresor de Brunst Latin: Des Faucons.*)

> "A faukoun peregryn than semëd sche
> Of fremdë [foreign] land."
> *Chaucer: Canterbury Tales (10,742).*

Fald-stool. A small desk at which the Litany is sung or said. The place at the south side of the altar at which sovereigns kneel at their coronation. (Barbarous Latin, *falda*, a thing which folds or shuts up.)

Faldistory. The episcopal seat in a chancel, which used to fold or lift up.

Falernian, the second best wine in Italy, was so called by the ancient Romans because it was made of grapes from Falernus. There were three sorts —the rough, the sweet, and the dry.

Falkland. In Godwin's novel called *Caleb Williams.* He commits murder, and keeps a narrative of the transaction in an iron chest. Williams, a lad in his employ, opens the chest, and is caught in the act by Falkland. The lad runs away, but is hunted down. This tale, dramatised by Colman, is entitled *The Iron Chest.*

Fal-lals. Nick-nacks; ornaments of small value. (Greek, *phalara*, metal ornaments for horses, etc.)

> "Our god-child passed in review all her gowns, fichus, tags, bobbins, laces, silk stockings, and fallals."—*Thackeray: Vanity Fair,* chap. vi. p. 38.

Fall. *In the fall.* In the autumn, at the fall of the leaf. (*An American revival.*)

> "What crowds of patients the town doctor kills,
> Or how, last fall, he raised the weekly bills."
> *Dryden: Juvenal,*

To try a fall. To wrestle, when each tries to "fall" or throw the other.

> "I am given, sir, ... to understand that your younger brother, Orlando, hath a disposition to come in disguised against me to try a fall."—*As You Like It,* i. 1.

Fall Away (*To*). To lose flesh; to degenerate; to quit a party, as "his adherents fell away gradually [one by one], or rapidly."

Fall Flat (*To*). To lie prostrate or procumbent; to fail to interest, as "the last act fell flat."

Fall Foul. *To fall foul of one* is to make an assault on someone. A sea term. A rope is said to be *foul* when it is entangled; and one ship *falls foul* of another when it runs against her and prevents her free progress. Hence to run up against, to assault.

Fall From (*To*). To violate, as "to fall from his word;" to tumble or slip off, as "to fall from a horse;" to abandon or go away from, as "to fall from grace."

Fall In (*To*). To take one's place with others; to concur with, as "he fell in with my views"—that is, his views or ideas fell into the lot of my views or ideas. (*See* FALL OUT.)

Fall Off (*To*). To detach themselves; to be thrown off [a horse]; to leave. The Latin *decĭdo*.

Fall Out (*To*). To quarrel; to happen. (Latin, *accĭdo*.) (*See* FALL IN.)

    "Three children sliding on the ice
      Upon a summer's day;
      As it fell out they all fell in,
      The rest they ran away."
           Porson: Mother Goose.
"See ye fall not out by the way."—Genesis xlv. 24.

Fall Sick (*To*). To be unwell. A Latin phrase, "*In morbum incidĕre.*"

Fall Through (*To*). To tumble through [an insecure place]; to fail of being carried out or accomplished.

Fall to (*To*). To begin [eating, fighting, etc.].

    "They sat down . . . . and without waiting . . . . fell to like commoners after supper."—*Kane: Arctic Explorations*, vol. i. chap. xxx. p. 419.]

Fall Under (*To*). To incur, as, "to be under the reproach of carelessness;" to be submitted to, as, "to fall under consideration," a Latinism, "*In deliberationem cadĕre.*"

Fall Upon (*To*). To attack, as "to fall upon the rear," a Latin phrase, "*ultimis incidĕre;*" to throw oneself on, as, "he fell on his sword," "*manu sua cadĕre;*" to happen on, as, "On what day will the games fall?"

Fall in With (*To*). To meet accidentally; to come across. This is a Latin phrase, *in aliquam casu incidĕre.*"

Fall into a Snare (*To*), or "To fall into an ambuscade." To stumble accidentally into a snare. This is a Latin phrase, "*insidias incidĕre.*" Similarly, to fall into disgrace is the Latin "*ni offensionem cadĕre.*"

Fall of Man (*The*). The degeneracy of the human race in consequence of the "fall" [or disobedience] of Adam, man's federal head. Adam fell, or ceased to stand his ground, under temptation.

Fall of the Drop (*The*), in theatrical parlance, means the fall of the drop-curtain at the end of the act or play.

Fall Out of (*To*). To tumble or slip from, as, "The weapons fell out of my hands." This is a Latin phrase, "*De manibus meis arma cecidērunt.*"

Fall Short of (*To*). To be deficient of a supply. This is the Latin *excĭdo*, to fail. To fall short of the mark is a figure taken from archery, quoits, etc., where the missile falls to the ground before reaching the mark.

Fall Together by the Ears (*To*). To fight and scratch each other; to contend in strife. "To *fall* together by the ears" is "*inter se certāre;*" but "to *set* together by the ears" is "*discordium concitare.*"

Fall Upon One's Feet (*To*). To escape a threatened injury; to light upon one's feet.

Falling Bands. Neck-bands which fall on the chest, common in the seventeenth century.

Falling Sickness. Epilepsy, in which the patient falls suddenly to the ground.

    " *Brutus.*—He [*i.e.* Cæsar] hath the falling-sickness.
    Cassius.—No, Cæsar hath it not: but you, and I, And honest Casca, we have the *falling-sickness.*"
        Shakespeare: Julius Cæsar, i. 2.

Falling Stars are said by Mahometans to be firebrands flung by good angels against evil spirits when they approach too near the gates of heaven.

Fallow Land. Land ploughed, but not sown; so called from its brown or tawny colour. (German, *fahl*, tawny; Anglo-Saxon, *falu* or *fealo*, pale-red; hence, *fallow deer*, red deer.)

    "Break up the fallow land."—Jer. iv. 3.

False (*The Rule of*). A method of solving certain mathematical questions generally done by equations. Suppose the question is this: "What number is that whose half exceeds its third by 12?"

Assume any number you like as the supposed answer—say 96. Then, by the question, $96 \div 2 = 96 \div 3 + 12$, or $48 = 32 + 12$, i.e. 54, but 48 does not equal 54, the latter is 16 too much.

Well, now state by rule of proportion thus, $16 : 12 :: 96$ to the answer, which is 72, the number required.

False Ceiling. The space between the garret-ceiling and the roof.

Fal'staff. A fat, sensual, boastful, and mendacious knight; full of wit and humour; he was the boon companion of Henry, Prince of Wales. (1 and 2 *Henry IV.*, and *Merry Wives of Windsor*.)

Falutin (*High*). Oratorical bombast; affected pomposity; "*Ercles* vein." (*See* HIFALUTEN.)
None of your high falutin airs with me. None of your swell ways with me. (Dutch, *verlooten*.)

Famil'iar. A cat, dog, raven, or other dumb creature, petted by a "witch," and supposed to be her demon in disguise. (*See below.*)

Famil'iar Spirits. Spirit slaves. From the Latin, *fam'ulus* (an attendant).

"Away with him! he has a familiar under his tongue."—*Shakespeare : 2 Henry VI., iv. 7.*

Familiarity. *Too much familiarity breeds contempt.*
Latin : Nimia familiaritas contemptum parit.
French : La familiarité engendre le mépris.
Italian : La famigliarità fà dispregiamento.

"E tribus optimis rebus tres pessimæ oriuntur : e veritate odium ; e familiaritate contemptus ; e felicitate invidia."—*Plutarch (translated).*

Fam'ilists. Members of the "Family of Love," a fanatical sect founded by David George, of Delft, in 1556. They maintained that all men are of one family, and should love each other as brothers and sisters. Their system is called *Familism.*

Family. *A person of family.* One of aristocratic birth. The Latin *gens.*

"Family will take a person anywhere."—*Warner : Little Journey in the World, chap. iv.*

Fan. *I could brain him with his lady's fan* (1 *Henry IV.*, ii. 3)—i.e. knock his brains out with a fan handle. The ancient fans had long handles, so that ladies used their fans for walking-sticks, and it was by no means unusual for very testy dames to chastise unruly

children by beating them with their fan-sticks.

"Wer't not better
Your head were broken with the handle of a fan ?"
Beaumont and Fletcher : Wit at Several Weapons, v.

Fan-light (*A*), placed over a door, is a semicircular window with radiating bars, like the ribs of an open fan.

Fanat'ic. Those transported with religious or temple madness. Among the Romans there were certain persons who attended the temples and fell into strange fits, in which they pretended to see spectres, and uttered what were termed predictions. (Latin, *fa'num*, a temple.)

"That wild energy which leads
The enthusiast to fanatic deeds."
Hemans : Tale of the Secret Tribunal.

Fancy. Love—i.e. the passion of the *fantasy* or imagination. A *fancy-man* is a man (not your husband) whom you fancy or select for chaperon.

"Tell me where is fancy bred,
Or in the heart or in the head."
Shakespeare : Merchant of Venice, iii. 2.

The fancy. Pugilists. So called because boxing is the chief of sports, and fancy means sports, pets, or fancies. Hence "dog-fanciers," "pigeon-fanciers," etc.

Fancy-free. Not in love.

"In maiden meditation fancy-free."
Shakespeare : Midsummer Night's Dream, ii. 2.

Fancy Man (*A*). A cavalier servant or cicisbeo ; one selected by a married lady to escort her to theatres, etc., to ride about with her, and to amuse her. The man she "fancies" or likes.

Fancy-sick. Love-sick.

"All fancy-sick she is, and pale of cheer."
Shakespeare : Midsummer Night's Dream, iii. 2.

Fane'sii. A Scandinavian tribe far north, whose ears were so long that they would cover their whole body. (*Pliny.*)

Fanfar'on. A swaggering bully ; a cowardly boaster who blows his own trumpet. Sir Walter Scott uses the word for finery, especially for the gold chains worn by military men, common in Spain amongst the conquerors of the New World. (Spanish, *fanfarr'on*, a bully ; French, *fanfare*, a flourish of trumpets, or short piece of military music performed by brass instruments and kettledrums.)

"'Marry, hang thee, with thy fanfarona about thy neck !' said the falconer."—*Scott : The Abbot,* cxvii.

Fanfar'onade (4 syl.). Swaggering ; vain boasting ; ostentatious display. (*See above.*)

"The bishop copied this proceeding from the fanfaronade of M. Boufflers."—*Swift.*

Fang. A sheriff's officer in Shakespeare's 2 *Henry IV.*

Fangs. *I fell into his fangs.* Into his power, his clutches. (Anglo-Saxon, *fang*, a grasp.)

> " To seize,
> Traitors, that vice-like fang the hand ye lick."
>   *Bailey : Festus (A Village Feast)*, sec. 9.

Fangled. *A new-fangled notion* is one just started or entertained. (Saxon, *fengan*, to begin.)

Fanny Fern. A *nom de plume* of Mrs. Sarah Payson Parton, sister of Mr. N. P. Willis, the American poet. (Born 1811, died 1872.)

Fanti'gue (2 syl.). A function; a fussy anxiety; that restless, nervous commotion which persons have who are phantom-struck.

Fantocci'ni [*fanto-chĕ'ny*]. A dramatic performance by puppets. (Italian, *fantoccio*, a puppet.)

Fantom-corn. The mere ghost of corn, having been bewitched. (French, *fantôme*, a ghost.)

Fantom-fellow. A person who is light-headed, and under the ban of some hobgoblin. (*See above.*)

Fantom-flesh. Flesh that hangs loose and flabby—supposed to be under the evil influence of some spectre. (*See above.*)

Far and Away. "*Nullus proximus aut secundus;*" as, "far and away the best;" some person or thing beyond all comparison or rivalry.

Far Cry from. *It is a far cry from . . . to . . . ;* as, it is a far cry from Moses to Moses Montefiore, and from David to Disraeli, but they all were Jews, and had certain features in common. Sir Walter Scott several times uses the phrase " It's a far cry to Lochow [Lochawe]." It is a far cry from O'Connell to Kossuth.

Far fetched. Not closely connected; a remote conceit; as, "a far-fetched simile," a "far-fetched allusion." Also, obtained from a foreign or distant country, "*quod rarum est, carum est.*"

> " The passion for long, involved sentences . . . and far-fetched conceits . . . passed away, and a clearer and less ornate style became popular."—*Lecky : English in the Eighteenth Century*, vol. i. chap. i. p. 91.

Far Gone. Deeply affected : as, " far gone in love."

Far Niente (3 syl.). Italian phrase. The Latin *otium*. *Dolce far niente* is the sweet enjoyment of having nothing to do, *i.e.* of a holiday. (*See* DOLCE.)

Farce (1 syl.). Stuffing. Dramatic pieces of no solid worth, but stuffed full of ludicrous incidents and expressions. They bear the same analogy to the regular drama as force-meat does to a solid joint. (French, *farce;* Latin, *farcio*, to stuff.)

Farceur (*The*). One who writes or acts farces.

Farcy or **Farcin** (Latin, *farcimen*, a sausage, any stuffed meat). A disease in horses, which consists of a swelling of the ganglions and lymphatic vessels. It shows itself in little knots ; glanders.

Fare, meaning the expense of a journey or passage across water, is the Anglo-Saxon *fare* or *fær*, a journey ; verb, *faran*, to travel. (Archaic, *feriage*, the fare for crossing a ferry.)

Fare Well (*To*). *You cannot fare well but you must cry out roast meat.* Don't blazon your good fortune on the house-top. " *Sorex suo perit indicio.*" Terence has the same idea: " *Egomet meo indicio miser, quasi sorex, hodie perii.*" (*Eunuchus*, v. 7, 23.)

Fari'na. *Ejusdem farinæ.* Other rubbish of the same sort. Literally, " Other loaves of the same batch." Our more usual expressions are, " Others of the same kidney," "others of the same feather," "others tarred with the same brush."

Fari'na'ta or *Farinata Degli Uberti.* A nobleman of Florence, chief of the Ghibelline faction, placed by Dante, in his *Inferno*, in a red-hot coffin, the lid of which is suspended over him till the day of judgment. He is represented as faithless and an epicure. (Thirteenth century.)

Farleu or **Farley.** A duty of 6d. paid to the lord of the manor of West Slapton, in Devonshire. (*Bailey.*) Money given by a tenant instead of his best beast (heriot).

Farm means food ; so called because anciently the tenant was required to provide the landlord with food by way of rent. (Anglo-Saxon, *fearme*, food.)

To farm taxes is the French *affermer* (to let or lease), from *ferme*, a letting for the supply of food.

Farmer George. George III. ; so called from his farmer-like manners, taste, dress, and amusements. (1738, 1760-1820.)

> " A better farmer ne'er brushed dew from lawn."
>   *Byron: Vision of Judgment.*

Farmers. A farmer ought to make four rents in order to live : one for rent, one for labour, one for stock, and one for himself.

Farnese Bull [*Far-na'-ze*]. A name given to a colossal group attributed to Apollo'nius and Tauriscus of Trallës, in Asia Minor. They belonged to the Rhodian school, and lived about B.C. 300. The group represents Dirce bound to the horns of a bull by Zethus and Amphi'on, for ill-using their mother. It was restored by Bian'chi in 1546, and placed in the Farnese palace, in Italy.

Farnese Hercules [*Far-na'-ze Hercu-lees*]. A name given to Glykon's copy of the famous statue of Lysippos, the Greek sculptor in the time of Alexander the Great. It represents the hero leaning on his club, with one hand on his back, as if he had just got possession of the apple of the Hesperidës. Farne'se is the name of a celebrated family in Italy, which became extinct in 1731.

"It struck me that an ironclad is to a wooden vessel what the Farnese Hercules is to the Apollo Belvidere. The Hercules is not without a beauty of its own."—*The Times* (Paris correspondent).

Faroese (3 syl.). Belonging to the Faroe Islands ; a native of the islands.

Farra'go. *A farrago of nonsense.* A confused heap of nonsense. Farrago is properly a mixture of *far* (meal) with other ingredients for the use of cattle.

"Anquetil was derided . . , for having suffered a farrago of nonsense to be palmed off upon him by his Parsi teache.s as the works of the sage Zoroaster."—*Whitney : Oriental Studies* (Avesta), chap. vi. p. 184.

Farringdon Ward (London). The aldermanry, etc., granted by John le Feure to William Farendon, citizen and goldsmith of London, in consideration of twenty marks given beforehand as a gersum to the said John le Feure. (1279.)

Far'thing. A fourth part. Penny pieces used to be divided into four parts, thus, ⊕ . One of these quarters was a *feor-   thing* or farthing, and two a halfpenny. (Anglo-Saxon, *feor-thung*.)

I don't care for it a brass farthing. James II. debased all the coinage, and issued, amongst other worthless coins, brass pence, halfpence, and farthings.

∵ The *feorthung* was the fourth part of other coins. Thus, we read in the *Grayfriar's Chronicle* :—

"This yere the kynge made a newe quyne, as the nobylle, half-nobylle, and ferdyng-nobylle."

Far'thingale (3 syl.). A sort of crinoline petticoat. The word means a

"guard for modesty." (French, *vertugarde*, corrupted into verdingade, and then into farthingale.)

Faryndon Inn. Serjeants' Inn, Chancery Lane, used to be so called.

Fascina'tion means "slain or overcome by the eyes." The allusion is to the ancient notion of bewitching by the power of the eye. (Greek, *baskaino*, i.e. *phaësi kaino*, to kill with the eyes. See *Valpy : Etymology of Greek Words*, p. 23, col. 1 ; Latin, *fas'cino*.) (*See* EVIL EYE.)

"None of the affections have been noted to fascinate and bewitch, but love and envy."—*Bacon.*

Fashion [*fash'-un.*] *In a fashion* or *after a fashion.* "In a sort of a way ; " as, "he spoke French in a fashion" (*i.e.* very badly). ("French of Stratford atte Bowe.")

Fashion of Speech (*A*). "*Façon de parler*" (q.v.) ; "*Ratio loquendi !*"

Fast Girl or **Young Lady** (*A*) is one who talks slang, assumes the airs of a knowing one, and has no respect for female delicacy and retirement. She is the ape of the fast young man.

Fast Man (*A*) is one who lives a continual round of "pleasure" so fast that he wears himself out.

Fast and Loose (*To play*). To run with the hare and hold with the hounds ; to blow both hot and cold ; to say one thing and do another. The allusion is to a cheating game practised at fairs. A belt is folded, and the player is asked to prick it with a skewer, so as to pin it *fast* to the table ; having so done, the adversary takes the two ends, and *looses* it or draws it away, showing that it has not been pierced at all.

"He forced his neck into a noose,
To show his play at fast and loose ;
And when he chanced t'escape, mistook,
For art and subtlety, his luck."
        Butler : Hudibras, iii. 2.

Fasti. Working days ; when, in Rome, the law-courts were open. Holy days (*dies non*), when the law-courts were not open, were, by the Romans, called *ne-fasti*.

Fasting. The most ingenious method of fasting I know of is that recorded in the *Mappemonde Papistique*, p. 82. A Venetian saint had certain boxes made like mass-books, and these book-boxes were filled, some with Malmsey wine, and some with the fleshiest parts of capons and partridges. These were supposed to be books of devotion, and the saint lived long and grew fat on them.

Fastra'de (2 syl.). Daughter of the Saxon count Rodolph and Luitgarde the German. One of the nine wives of Charlemagne.

" Those same soft bells at eventide
    Rang in the ears of Charlemagne,
As, seated by Fastra'da's side
At Ingelheim, in all his pride,
He heard their sound with secret pain.
        Longfellow : Golden Legend, vi.

Fat. *All the fat is in the fire.* The allusion is to the process of frying. If the grease is spilt into the fire, the coals smoke and blaze so as to spoil the food. The proverb signifies that something has been let out inadvertently which will cause a "regular flare up."

The Fat :—
Alfonzo II. of Portugal. (1212-1223.)
Charles II. of France, *le Gros.* (832, 881-888.)
Louis VI. of France, *le Gros.* (1078, 1108-1137.)

Fat Men.
Edward Bright, of Essex, weighed 44 stone, or 616 pounds, at death. He was 5 feet 9 inches high, 5 feet round the chest, and 6 feet 11 inches round the paunch. He died 1750, aged thirty.

Daniel Lambert, born at St. Margaret's Leicester, weighed 739 pounds. He was 3 yards 4 inches round the waist, 1 yard 1 inch round the leg. (1770-1809.)

Fat as a Porpoise. The skin of the porpoise is nearly an inch thick, and under it is a layer of fat somewhat thicker, and yielding oil of the finest quality.

Fata. Women introduced in mediæval romance not unlike witches, and under the sway of Demogorgon. In *Orlando Innamora'to* we meet with the "Fata Morga'na;" in *Bojardo,* with the "Fata Silvanella." The Fates Nera and Bianca, the protectresses of Guido'ne and Aquilante ; the "Fata della Fonti," from whom Manricardo obtains the arms of Hector; and "Alci'na," sister of Morga'na, who carries off Astolfo. In Tasso we have the three daughters of Morga'na, whose names are Morganetta, Nivetta, and Carvilia ; we have also Dragonti'na, Monta'na, Argea (called the queen of the Fates), protectress of Floridante), Filidea (sister of Argea), and several others. In the *Ado'ne* of Mari'ni we have the Fata named "Falsire'na."

Fa'ta Morga'na. A sort of mirage occasionally seen in the Straits of Messi'na. *Fata* is Italian for a "fairy," and the fairy Morga'na was the sister of Arthur and pupil of Merlin. She lived

at the bottom of a lake, and dispensed her treasures to whom she liked. She is first introduced in the *Orlando Innamora'to* as "Lady Fortune," but subsequently assumes her witch-like attributes. In Tasso her three daughters are introduced.

Fatal Gifts. Collar of Arsinoe, collar and veil of Eriph'ylē, gold of the Nibelungen, gold of Tolosa, necklace of Cadmos, Harmonia's necklace and robe, opal of Alphonso XII., the Trojan horse, the shirt of Nessus, etc. (*See these subjects.*)

Fate = something destined or suitable, is not the Latin *fatum,* but the French *fait* = share, one's own, that which suits one ; as "*voila mon fait,*" that is the man for me.

" Pour moi, ma sieur, a dit la cadette, j'aime le solide, je veux un homme riche, et le gros don Blanco sera mon fait."—*Le Sage : Diable Boiteux.*

Fa'tes (1 syl.). *The cruel fates.* The Greeks and Romans supposed there were three Parcæ or Fates, who arbitrarily controlled the birth, events, and death of every man. They are called cruel because they pay no regard to the wishes and requirements of anyone.

✢ The three Fates were Clotho (who held the distaff), Lachĕsis (who spun the thread of life), and Atrŏpos (who cut it off when life was ended).

Fa'ther. A friar in holy orders. (*See* BROTHER.)

A father suckled by his daughter. Euphra'sia, the Grecian daughter, so preserved the life of Evan'der, her aged father.

Xantip'pe so preserved the life of her father Cimo'nos in prison. The guard, marvelling the old man held out so long, set a watch and discovered the fact. Byron alludes to these stories in his *Childe Harold.*

" There is a dungeon, in whose dim, drear light
    What do I gaze on ? . . .
An old man, and a female young and fair,
    Fresh as a nursing mother, in whose vein
The blood is nectar. . . .
Here youth offers to old age the food,
    The milk of his own gift :—it is her sire
To whom she renders back the debt of blood....
Drink, drink and live, old man ! heaven's realm
    holds no such tide."
        Byron : Childe Harold, iv. st. 148, 150.

Without father, without mother, without descent, having neither beginning of days nor end of life—i.e. Melchisedec (Heb. vii. 3). He was not the *son* of a priest, either on his father's or mother's side ; his pedigree could not be traced in the priestly line, like that of the ordinary high priests, which can be traced to Aaron ; nor did he serve in courses like the Levites, who begin and end their official duties at stated times.

⁘ Jesus was a "priest after the order of Melchisedec." Neither His reputed father, Joseph, nor His mother, Mary, was of the priestly line. As priest, therefore, He was "without father, without mother," without genealogy. And, like Melchisedec, He is a "priest for ever."

He fathers it on me. He imputes it to me; he says it is my bantling.

Father Mathew. (*See* MATHEW.)

Father Neptune. The ocean.

Father Norbert. Pierre Parisot, the French missionary (1697-1769).

Father Paul. Pie'tro Sarpi, father of the order of Servites in Venice, who changed his Christian name when he assumed the religious habit. (1552-1623.)

Father Prout. Francis Mahoney, a humorous writer in *Fraser's Magazine* and the *Globe* newspaper. (1805-1866.)

Father Thames, or *Old Father Thames.* The Thames, so far as it belongs to London.

> "Say, Father Thames, for thou hast seen
> Full many a sprightly race
> Disporting on thy margent green,
> The paths of pleasure trace."
> *Gray: Distant Prospect of Eton College.*

The epithet is not uncommonly applied to other great rivers, especially those on which cities are built. The river is the father of the city, or the reason why the site was selected by the first settlers there.

> "O Tiber, Father Tiber,
> To whom the Romans pray."
> *Macaulay: Lay of Horatius.*

Father Thoughtful. Nicholas Cat'-inat, a marshal of France; so called by his soldiers for his cautious and thoughtful policy. (1637-1712.)

Father of Waters. The Irawaddy, in Burmah, and the Mississippi, in North America. The Nile is so called by Dr. Johnson in his *Rasselas.* (*See* FATHER THAMES.)

Father of his Country.
Cicero was so entitled by the Roman senate. They offered the same title to Ma'rius, but he refused to accept it.

Several of the Cæsars were so called—Julius, after quelling the insurrection of Spain; Augustus, etc.

Cosmo de' Med'ici (1389-1464).

G. Washington, the defender and paternal counsellor of the American States. (1732-1799.)

15

Andrea Do'rea (1468-1560). Inscribed on the base of his statue by his countrymen of Gen'oa.

Androni'cus Palæol'ogus II. assumed the title (1260-1332).

(*See also* 1 Chron. iv. 14.)

Father of the People.
Louis XII. of France (1462, 1498-1515). Henri IV. was also termed "the father and friend of the people" (1553, 1589-1610).

Christian III. of Denmark (1502, 1534-1559).

Gabriel du Pineau, the French lawyer (1573-1644).

Fathers of the Church. The early advocates of Christianity, who may be thus classified:—

(1) Five *apostolic fathers,* who were contemporary with the apostles—viz. Clement of Rome, Bar'nabas, Hermas, Igna'tius, and Pol'ycarp.

(2) The *primitive fathers.* Those advocates of Christianity who lived in the first three centuries. They consisted of the five apostolic fathers (*q.v.*), together with the nine following:—Justin, Theoph'ilus of Antioch, Irenæ'us, Clement of Alexandria, Cyp'rian of Carthage, Or'igen, Gregory Thaumatur'gus, Dionysius of Alexandria, and Tertullian.

(3) The *fathers,* or those of the fourth and fifth century, who were of two groups, those of the Greek and those of the Latin Church. (*See below.*)

Fathers of the Greek Church. Euse'bius, Athana'sius, Basil the Great, Gregory Nazianze'nus, Gregory of Nyssa, Cyr'il of Jerusalem, Chrys'ostom, Epipha'nius, Cyril of Alexandria, and Ephraim, deacon of Edessa.

Fathers of the Latin Church. Lactantius, Hil'ary, Ambrose of Mil'an, Jer'ome, Augustin of Hippo, and St. Bernard.

The last of the fathers. St. Bernard (1091-1153). The schoolmen who followed treated their subjects systematically.

Founder of the fathers of Christian doctrine. Cæsar de Bus (1544-1607).

Fath'om (*Count*). A villain in Smollet's novel so called. After robbing his benefactors, and fleecing all who trusted him, he is at last forgiven.

Fat'ima. The last of Bluebeard's wives, who was saved from death by the timely arrival of her brother with a party of friends. Mahomet's favourite daughter was called Fatima.

Fatted Calf. *To kill the fatted calf.* To welcome with the best of everything. The phrase is taken from the parable in the third gospel of the prodigal son. (Luke xv. 30.)

Fat'ua Mu'lier. A law term for a courtesan. Fatuus with jurisconsults means one not in a right mind, incorrigibly foolish.

Fault. *At fault.* Not on the right track; doubtful whether right or wrong. Hounds are at fault when the scent is broken because the fox has jumped upon a wall, crossed a river, cut through a flock of sheep, or doubled like a hare.

⁂ In *Geology*, the break or displacement of a stratum of rock is called a fault.

Fault. (French, *faute*, Latin, *fallo*, to fail.)
For fault of a better (*Shakespeare*: *Merry Wives*, i. 4). Having no better.
" I am the youngest of that name, for fault of a worse."—*Shakespeare: Romeo and Juliet*, ii. 4.
In fault. To blame.
" Is Antony or we in fault for this ?"
Shakespeare: Antony and Cleopatra, iii. 13.
To a fault. In excess; as, kind to a fault. Excess of every good is more or less evil.
To find fault. To blame; to express disapprobation.

Faults.
No one is without his faults, i.e. is faultless. " *Vitiis nemo sine nascitur.*"

Fau'na (2 syl.). The animals of a country at any given geological period; so called from the mythological fauns, who were the patrons of wild animals.
" Nor less the place of curious plant he knows—
He both his Flora and his Fauna shows."
Crabbe: Borough.

Faust (1 syl.). The grandest of all Gœthe's dramas. Faust makes a compact with Mephistoph'elēs, who on one occasion provides him with a cloak, by means of which he is wafted through the air whithersoever he chooses. " All that is weird, mysterious, and magical groups round this story." An English dramatic version has been made by Bayle Bernard.
Dr. Faustus, a tragedy by Marlow; *Faust and Marguerite*, by Boucicault; *Faust e Margherito*, an opera by Gounod, etc.

Faux-jour (French). A false or contrary light; meaning that a picture is hung so that the light falls on it in the opposite direction to what it ought. The artist has made his light fall in one direction, but it is so hung that the light falls the other way.

Faux Pas. A " false step " ; a breach of manners or moral conduct. (French.)

Favo'nius. The zephyr or west wind. It means the wind *favourable* to vegetation.

Fa'vours. Ribbons made into a bow; so called from being the *favours* bestowed by ladies on the successful champions of tournaments. (*See* TRUE-LOVE KNOT; CURRY FAVOUR.)
" Here, Fluellen ; wear thou this favour for n e and stick it in thy cap."—*Shakespeare: Henry V* , iv. 7.

Favourite. One to whom a lady gives a "favour" or token. The horse which betting men suppose is most likely to come off the winner of a particular race.

Favourites. False curls on the temples; a curl of hair on the temples plastered with some cosmetic; whiskers made to meet the mouth.
" Yet tell me, sire, don't you as nice appear
With your false calves, bardash, and fav'rites here ?"   *Mrs. Centlivre.*

Fay. (*See* FAIRY.)

Faye (1 syl.). *The way to Faye* (French, " *Faie-la-vineuse*"). A winding or zigzag manner, like "Crooked Lane at Eastcheap." A person who tries to do something indirectly goes by the pathway to Faye. Faye is a little village in France, built on an eminence so steep that there is no getting to it except by a very zigzag path.
"They go in to Paradise . . . as the way is to Faye."— *Rabelais: Gargantua and Pantagruel*, book i. 27. .

Faz'io. A native of Florence, who first tried to make his fortune by alchemy; but being present when Bartoldo, an old miser, died, he buried the body secretly, and stole his money - bags. Being now rich, he became acquainted with the Marchioness Aldabella, with whom he passed his time in licentious pleasure. His wife Bianca, out of jealousy, accused him to the duke of being privy to the death of Bartoldo; and Fazio was condemned to death for murder. Bianca now tried to undo the mischief she had done, but it was too late; she went mad with grief, and died of a broken heart. (*Dean Milman : Fazio.*)

Fear Fortress. An hypothetical castle in a forest near Saragossa. It represents that terrible obstacle which fear conjures up, but which vanishes into thin air as it is approached by a stout heart and clear conscience. The allegory forms the third part of the legend of *Croquemitaine*.

"If a child disappeared, or any cattle were carried off, the trembling peasants said, 'The lord of Fear-fortress has taken them.' If a fire broke out anywhere, it was the lord of Fear-fortress who must have lit it. The origin of all accidents, mishaps, and disasters was traced to the mysterious owner of this invisible castle."—*Croquemitaine*, iii. 1.

> " It sunk before my earnest face,
> It vanished quite away,
> And left no shadow on the place,
> Between me and the day.
> Such castles rise to strike us dumb ;
> But, weak in every part,
> They melt before the strong man's eyes
> And fly the true of heart."
> *C. Mackay : The Giant (slightly altered).*

Fearless [*Sans peur*]. Jean, Duke of Burgundy (1371-1419). (*See* BAYARD.)

Feast of Reason.

> "There St. John [Sin-jn] mingles with the friendly bowl
> The feast of reason and the flow of soul."
> *Pope : Imitations of Horace*, ii. 1.

Feasts. Anniversary days of joy. They are either immovable or movable. *The chief immovable feasts* are the four rent-days — viz. the Annunciation or Lady-Day (March 25th), the Nativity of John the Baptist (June 24th), Michaelmas Day (September 29th), and Christmas Day (December 25th). The Circumcision (New Year's Day, January 1st), Epiphany (January 6th), All Saints' (November 1st), All Souls' (November 2nd), and the several Apostles' days.
The chief movable feasts depend upon Easter Sunday. They are—

Palm Sunday. The Sunday next before Easter Sunday.

Good Friday. The Friday next before Easter Sunday.

Ash Wednesday. The first day of Lent.

Sexagesima Sunday. Sixty days before Easter Sunday.

Ascension Day or Holy Thursday. Fortieth day after Easter Sunday.

Pentecost or Whit - Sunday. The seventh Sunday after Easter Sunday.

Trinity Sunday. The Sunday next after Pentecost, etc. etc.

Feather. Meaning species or kind. From the proverb, " Birds of a feather " —*i.e.* of the same plumage, and therefore of the same sort.

> " I am not of that feather to shake off
> My friend, when he must need me."
> *Shakespeare : Timon of Athens*, i. 1.

Feather. A light, volatile person.

> " A wit's a feather, and a chief a rod ;
> An honest man's the noblest work of God."
> *Pope : Essay on Man*, 247-8.

A broken feather. (*See* BROKEN . .)

An oiled feather. Kindness of manner and speech. An oiled feather will do more to ease a stubborn lock than great force. (*See* Power's Tract called *The Oiled Feather*.)

Birds of a feather flock together. ✪

Latin : Similes similibus gaudent. Pares cum paribus facile congregantur. Cicero says, "Deos novimus ornatu et vestitu."

French : Qui se ressemble, s'assemble.

In full feather. Flush of money. In allusion to birds not on the moult.

In grand feather. Dressed to the nines.

In high feather. In exuberant spirits, joyous. When birds are moulting they mope about, but as soon as they regain their feathers their spirits revive.

Tickled with a feather. Easily moved to laughter. "Pleased with a feather, tickled with a straw," is more usual ; *Rire de la moindre bagatelle.*

Also annoyed by trifles, worried by little annoyances.

> " From day to day some silly things
> Upset you altogether ;
> There's nought so soon convulsion brings
> As tickling with a feather.
> 'Gainst minor evils let him pray
> Who Fortune's favour curries ;
> For one that big misfortunes slay,
> Ten die of little worries."
> *Sims : Ballads of Babylon* (Little Worries).

Cut a feather. A ship going fast is said to cut a feather, in allusion to the ripple which she throws off from her bows. Metaphorically, " to cut a dash."

> " Jack could never cut a feather."—*Sir W. Scott : The Pirate*, xxxiv.

To show a white feather. (*See* WHITE . . . .)

Feather in Your Cap. *That's a feather in your cap.* An honour to you. The allusion is to the very general custom in Asia and among the American Indians of adding a new feather to their head-gear for every enemy slain. The Caufirs of Cabul stick a feather in their turban for every Mussulman slain by them. The Incas and Caciques, the Meunitarris and Mandans (of America), the Abyssinians and Tur'comans, etc., etc., follow the same custom. So did the ancient Lycians, and many others. In Scotland and Wales it is still customary for the sportsman who kills the first woodcock to pluck out a feather and stick it in his cap. In fact, the custom, in one form or another, seems to be almost universal.

∴ When " Chinese " Gordon quelled the Taïping rebellion he was honoured by the Chinese Government with the " yellow jacket and peacock's feather."

In Hungary, at one time, none might wear a feather but he who had slain a Turk. (*Lansdowne MS.* 775, folio 149.)

Feather One's Nest.
He has feathered his nest well. He has made lots of money; has married a rich woman. The allusion is to birds, which line their nests with feathers to make them soft and warm.

Feather One's Oar (*To*).
To feather an oar is to turn the blade parallel with the surface of the water as the hands are moved forward for a fresh stroke. (The Greek *pteron* means both "an oar" and "a feather;" and the verb *pteroō*, to "furnish with oars" or "with feathers.") The oar throws off the water in a feathery spray.

"He feathered his oars with such skill and dexterity."   *Jolly Young Waterman.*

Feather Stone. A federal stone or stone table at which the ancient courts baron were held in the open air, and at which covenants were made. (Latin, *fœdus*, a treaty.)

Feathers (*The*). A public-house sign in compliment to Henry VI., whose cognizance it was.
Fine feathers make fine birds. (Latin, " *Vestis virum facit,*" dress makes the man). The French proverb is "La belle plume fait le bel oiseau."
The Prince of Wales' feathers. The tradition is, that the Black Prince, having slain John of Luxemburg, King of Bohemia, in the Battle of Cressy, assumed his crest and motto. The crest consisted of three ostrich feathers, and the motto was "*Ich dien*" (I serve). John of Arden discovered a contemporary MS., in which it is expressly said that this was the case; but much controversy has arisen on the question. Dr. Bell affirms that the crest is a rebus of Queen Philippa's hereditary title—viz. Countess of *Ostre-vant* (ostrich-feather). Randall Holmes claims an old British origin; and the Rev. H. Longueville asserts that the arms of Roderick Mawe, prior to the division of Wales into principalities, was thus blazoned:—"Argent, three lions passant regardant, with their tails passing between their legs and curling over their backs in a *feathery* form."

Feature means the "make." Spenser speaks of God's "secret understanding of our feature"—*i.e.* make or structure. It now means that part which is most conspicuous or important. Thus we speak of the chief feature of a painting,

a garden, a book, etc., etc. (Norman, *faiture;* Latin, *factura.*)

February. The month of purification amongst the ancient Romans. (Latin, *feb'ruo*, to purify by sacrifice.)
The 2nd of Feb'ruary (Candlemas Day). It is said, if the weather is fine and frosty at the close of January and beginning of February, we may look for more winter to come than we have seen up to that time.
" Si sol splendescat Mari'a Purificantë,
Major erit glaciës post festum quam fuit ante."
            Sir T. Browne: Vulgar Errors.
" If Candlemas Day be dry and fair,
The half o' winter's come and mair ;
If Candlemas Day be wet and foul,
The half o' winter was gane at Youl."
            Scotch Proverb.
"The badger peeps out of his hole on Candlemas Day, and, if he finds snow, walks abroad ; but if he sees the sun shining he draws back into his hole."—*German Proverb.*

Fe'cit (Latin, *he did it*). A word inscribed after the name of an artist, sculptor, etc., as David *fecit*, Goujon *fecit ; i.e.* David painted it, Goujon sculptured it, etc.

Fec'ula means sediment. Starch is a fec'ula, being the sediment of flour steeped in water. (Latin, *fæces*, dregs.)

Fed'eral States. In the late American war the Unionists were so called—*i.e.* those northern states which combined to resist the eleven southern or Confederate states (*q.v.*).

Fee. Anglo-Saxon *feoh*, cattle, goods, money. So in Latin, *pecunia*, from *pecus*, cattle. Capital is *capita*, heads [of cattle], and chattels is a mere variant.

Fee-farm-rent is where an estate is granted, subject to a rent in fee of at least one-fourth its value. It is rent paid on lands let to *farm*, and not let in recompense of service at a greatly reduced value.

Fee-penny. A fine for money overdue. Sir Thomas Gresham often wrote for money "in order to save the fee-penny."

Fee Simple. An estate free from condition or limitation. If restricted by conditions, the inheritance is called a 'Conditional Fee.'

Fee-tail (*A*). An estate limited to a person and his lawful heirs.

Feeble. *Most forcible Feeble.* A writer whose language is very "loud," but whose ideas are very jejune. Feeble is a "woman's tailor," brought to Sir John Falstaff as a recruit. He tells Sir John "he will do his good will," and the knight replies, "Well said, courageous Feeble! Thou wilt be as valiant as the wrathful dove, or most magnanimous mouse . . . most forcible Feeble." (*Shakespeare :* 2 *Henry IV.*, iii. 2.)

Feed of Corn. A quartern of oats, the quantity given a horse on a journey when the ostler is told to give him a feed.

Feet. *How are your poor feet ?* This was the popular street *mot* in the year of the Great Exhibition of London in 1862. The immense labour of walking over the exhibition broke down all but the strongest athletes.

Fehm-gericht or *Vehmgericht* (3 syl.). The secret tribunals of Westpha'lia, for the preservation of public peace, suppression of crime, and maintenance of the "Catholic" religion. The judges were enveloped in profound mystery; they had their secret spies through all Germany; their judgments were certain, but no one could discover the executioner. These tribunals rose in the twelfth century, and disappeared in the sixteenth. Sir Walter Scott, in *Anne of Gierstein*, has given an account of the Westphalian Fehmgericht. (Old German, *fehmen*, to condemn; *Gericht*, a tribunal.)

"This Vigilance Committee [of Denver city] is a modern reproduction of the famous Vehmgericht."—*The Times.*

Felician (*Father*). The priest and schoolmaster of Grand Pré, who accompanied Evangeline in her wanderings to find Gabriel, her affianced husband. (*Longfellow : Evangeline.*)

Felix, a monk who listens to the singing of a milk-white bird for a thousand years, which seemed to him "but a single hour," so enchanted was he by the song. (*Longfellow : The Golden Legend.*)

Fe'lixmar'te (4 syl.). The hero of a Spanish romance of chivalry by Melchior de Or'teza, *Caballe'ro de Ubĕda* (1566). The curate in *Don Quixote* condemned this work to the flames.

Fell (*Dr.*). (*See* DOCTOR FELL.)

Fellow Commoner. A wealthy or married undergraduate of Cambridge, who pays extra to " common " (*i.e.* dine) at the fellows' table. In Oxford, these demi-dons are termed *Gentlemen Commoners.*

Fellow commoner or *gentleman commoner.* An empty bottle; so called because these sort of students are, as a class, *empty-headed.*

Felo de Se. The act of a suicide when he commits self-murder. Murder is felony, and a man who murders himself commits this felony—*felo de se.*

"A *felo-de-se*, therefore, is he that deliberately puts an end to his own existence."—*Blackstone : Commentaries,* book iv. chap. xiv. p. 189.

Feme-covert. A married woman. This does not mean a woman *coverte* by her husband, but a woman whose head is covered, not usual with maidens or unmarried women. In Rome unmarried women wore on their heads only a *corolla* (*i.e.* a wreath of flowers). In Greece they wore an *anade̅ma*, or fillet. The Hungarian spinster is called *hajadon* (bareheaded). Married women, as a general rule, have always covered their head with a cap, turban, or something of the same sort, the head being covered as a badge of subjection. Hence Rebekah (Gen. xxiv. 65), being told that the man she saw was her espoused husband, took a veil and covered her head. Servants wear caps, and private soldiers in the presence of their officers cover their heads for the same reason. (*See* Eph. v. 22, 23.)

⁂ Women do not, like men, uncover their heads even in saluting, but bend their knee, in token of subjection. (*See* SALUTATIONS.)

Feme-sole. A single woman. *Feme-sole merchant.* A woman who carries on a trade on her own account.

Femme de Chambre. (French.) A chambermaid.

Fem'ynye (3 syl.). A mediæval name for the kingdom of the Am'azons. Gower terms Penthesile'a "queen of Feminee." "He [Thessus] conquered al the regne of Femynye." *Chaucer : Canterbury Tales,* 868.

Fon Nightingale. A frog, which sings at night in the fens, as nightingales sing in the groves. (*See* ARCADIAN NIGHTINGALE.)

Fence Month. The close time of deer, from fifteen days before Midsummer to fifteen days after it. This being fawning time, deer-hunting is forbidden.

Fenchurch Street (London). The church in the fens or marshy ground by the "Langbourne" side.

Fencible Regiments. A kind of militia raised in 1759, again in 1778-9, and again in 1794, when a force of 15,000 was raised. The force was disbanded in 1802.

Fenel'la. A pretended deaf and dumb sylph-like attendant on the Countess of Derby, in Scott's *Peveril of the Peak.*

Fe′nians. An anti-British association of disaffected Irishmen, called the Fenian Brotherhood, after the ancient Fenians of Ireland; formed in New York, in 1857, to overthrow the domination of England in Ireland, and make Ireland a republic. The word means a *hunter*—Gaelic, *fianna*, from *feadhach* (pronounced *fee-agh*), a hunt. Before the Germanic invasion, a Celtic race so called occupied not only parts of Ireland and Scotland, but also the north of Germany and the Scandinavian shores. Oisin (Ossian) refers to them, and one passage is thus rendered in *The Antiquary*: "Do you compare your psalms to the tales of the barearmed Fenians?" Oisin was the grandson of Fionn, the "fair-haired righ (*chief*) of the Fenians," and all the high officers of this volunteer association were men of rank. It appears that the Fenians of Ireland (*Eirin*), Scotland (*Alba*), England (*Socring*), and Scandinavia, had a great civil battle at Gabhra, in Ireland, and extirpated each other. Oisin alone escaped, and he had slain "twice fifty men with his own hand." In the great Fenian outbreak of Ireland in 1865, etc., the leaders were termed "head centres," and their subordinates "centres." (*See* CLAN-NA-GAEL.)

Fennel. Said to restore lost vision and to give courage.

> "Above the lowly plants it towers,
> The fennel with its yellow flowers,
> And in an earlier age than ours,
> Was gifted with the wondrous powers
> Lost vision to restore;
> It gave new strength and fearless mood,
> And gladiators fierce and rude
> Mingled it in their daily food;
> And he who battled and subdued
> The wreath of fennel wore."
> *Longfellow: The Goblet of Life*, stanza 6.

Fenrir or **Fenris.** The wolf of sin [*i.e.* of Loki], meaning the goading of a guilty conscience. The "wolf" was the brother of Hel (*q.v.*). When he gapes, one jaw touches earth and the other heaven. In the *Ragnarok* he swallows the sun and conquers Odin; but being conquered by Vidar, he was cast into Niflheim, where Loki was confined.

Fenton. One who seeks to mend his fortune by marriage. He is the suitor of Anne Page. Her father objects to him, he says, because

> "I am too great of birth;
> And that, my state being gall'd with my expense,
> I seek to heal it only by his wealth."
> *Shakespeare: Merry Wives of Windsor*, iii. 4.

Feræ Naturæ. Applied in law to animals living in a wild state, as distinguished from animals which are domesticated.

Fer′amorz. The young Cashmerian poet, who relates poetical tales to Lalla Rookh, in her journey from Delhi to Lesser Buchar′ia. Lalla Rookh is going to be married to the young sultan, but falls in love with the poet. On the wedding morn she is led to her future husband, and finds that the poet is the sultan himself, who had gallantly taken this course to win the heart of his bride and beguile her journey. (*T. Moore.*)

Fer′dinand. Son of the King of Naples, and suitor of Miranda, daughter of Pros′pero, the banished Duke of Milan. (*Shakespeare: Tempest.*) In *Love′s Labour′s Lost*, the same name is given to the King of Navarre.

Ferdinan′do. A brave soldier who obtained a complete victory over the King of Morocco and Grena′da, near Tari′fa, in 1340. Being in love with Leono′ra de Guzman, Alfonso XI., whose life he had saved in the battle, created him Count of Zamo′ra and Marquis of Montreal, and gave him the hand of Leonora in marriage. No sooner was this done, than Ferdinando discovered that Leonora was the king's mistress; so he restored his ranks and honours to the king, repudiated his bride, and retired to the monastery of St. James of Compostella. Leonora entered the same monastery as a novice, obtained the forgiveness of Ferdinando, and died. (*Donizetti's opera of La Favori′ta.*)

Ferdo′si. A Persian poet, fámous for the copious flow of his diction. He wrote in verse the *Shah-Námeh*, or history of the Persian kings, which took thirty years, and contains 120,000 verses.

Ferguson. *It's all very fine, Ferguson; but you don't lodge here.* Capt. Ferguson was the companion of the Marquis of Waterford, when that young nobleman made himself notorious for his practical jokes in the middle of the nineteenth century. In one of their sprees the two companions got separated, and the marquis found his way home to the house of his uncle, the Archbishop of Armagh, Charles Street, St. James's Square. The marquis had gone to bed, when a thundering knock came at the door. The marquis, suspecting who it was that knocked, threw up the window and said, "It is all very fine, Ferguson, but you don't lodge here;" and for many years the saying was popular. (See *Notes and Queries*, Jan. 16, 1886, p. 46.)

Fern. (*See* FANNY FERN.)

Fern Seed. *We have the receipt of fern seed, we walk invisible* (1 *Henry IV.*, act iv. 4). The seed of certain species of fern is so small as to be invisible to the naked eye, and hence the plant was believed to confer invisibility on those who carried it about their person. It was at one time believed that plants have the power of imparting their own speciality to their wearer. Thus, the herb-dragon was said to cure the poison of serpents ; the yellow celandine the jaundice ; wood-sorrel, which has a heart-shaped leaf, to cheer the heart ; liverwort to be good for the liver, and so on.

" Why did you think that you had Gyges' ring,
    Or the herb that gives invisibility ? "
Beaumont and Fletcher : Fair Maid of the Inn, i. 1.

" The seeds of fern, which, by prolific heat
Cheered and unfolded, form a plant so great,
Are less a thousand times than what the eye
Can unassisted by the tube descry."
                    Blackmore : Creation.

Fernando Florestan. A state prisoner of Seville, married to Leonora, who, in man's disguise, and under the name of Fide'lio, became the servant of Rocco, the jailor. Pizarro, governor of the prison, conceived a hatred to Fernando, and resolved to murder him. Rocco and Leonora were sent to dig his grave, and when Pizarro entered the dungeon, Leonora intercepted his purpose. At this juncture the minister of State arrived, and ordered the prisoner's release. (*Beethoven : Fidelio.*)

Ferney. *The patriarch of Ferney.* Voltaire ; so called because he retired to Ferney, a small sequestered village near Gene'va, from which obscure retreat he poured forth his invectives against the French Government, the Church, nobles, nuns, priests, and indeed all classes.

" There are in Paris five or six statues of the patriarch of Ferney."—*The Times.*

Fero'hers. The guardian angels of Persian mythology. They are countless in number, and their chief tasks are for the well-being of man.

Fer'racute [*sharp iron*]. A giant in Turpin's *Chronicle of Charlemagne.* He had the strength of forty men, and was thirty-six feet high. Though no lance could pierce his hide, Orlando slew him by Divine interposition. (*See* FERRAU.)

Fer'ragus. The giant of Portugal, who took Bellisant under his care after she had been divorced by Alexander, Emperor of Constantinople. (*Valentine and Orson.*)

The great " Brazen Head," that told those who consulted it whatever they required to know, was kept in the castle of this giant. (*Valentine and Orson.*) (*See* FERRAU.)

Ferra'ra. *An Andrew Ferrara.* A broadsword or claymore of the best quality, bearing the name of Andrea Ferra'ra, one of the Italian family whose swords were famous in the sixteenth and seventeenth centuries. Genuine " Andrea Ferraras " have a crown marked on the blade.

✷ My father had an Andrea Ferrara, which had been in the family about a century. It had a basket-hilt, and the name was distinctly stamped on the blade.

" We'll put in bail, boy ; old Andrew Ferrara shall lodge his security."—*Scott : Waverley*, chap. 1.

Ferrau (in *Orlando Furioso*). Ferraute, Fer'racute, or Fer'ragus, a Saracen, son of Lanfu'sa. He dropped his helmet in the river, and vowed he would never wear another till he had won that worn by Orlando. Orlando slew him with a wound in the navel, his only vulnerable part.

Ferrex and Porrex. Two sons of Gorboduc, a mythical British king. Porrex drove his brother from Britain, and when Ferrex returned with an army he was slain, but Porrex was shortly after put to death by his mother. One of the first, if not the very first, historical play in the English language was *Ferrex and Porrex*, by Thomas Norton and Thomas Sackville.

Ferumbras. (*See* FIERABRAS.)

Fes'cennine Verses. Lampoons ; so called from Fescennia in Tuscany, where performers at merry-makings used to extemporise scurrilous jests of a personal nature to amuse the audience.

Fess (Latin, *fascia*, a band or covering for the thighs). In heraldry, the fess is a band drawn horizontally across the shield, of which it occupies one - third. It represents the band which was worn by knights low down across the hips.

Fest. A pledge. *Festing-man*, a surety to another. *Festing-penny*, a penny given in earnest to secure a bargain. (Anglo-Saxon, *festing*, an act of confidence, an entrusting.)

Fetch. A wraith—the disembodied ghost of a living person. (*See* FETICHE.)

" Fetches . . . most commonly appear to distant friends and relations, at the very instant preceding the death of those they represent."—*Brand : Popular Antiquities* (Death Omens).

Fetches. Excuses, tricks, artifices. (Saxon.)

"Deny to speak with me? They are sick? they
 are weary?
They have travelled all the night? Mere fetches."
Shakespeare: King Lear, ii. 4.

Fet'iche or **Fet'ish.** The African idol, the same as the American Man'itou. The worship of this idol is called Fet'ichism or Fet'ishism. (Portuguese, *fetisso*, magician, fairy, oracle.)

.·. Almost anything will serve for a fetiche: a fly, a bird, a lion, a fish, a serpent, a stone, a tree struck by lightning, a bit of metal, a shell; but the most potent of all fetiches is the rock Tabra.

The fetiche or fetish of the bottle. The imp drunkenness, or drunkenness itself.

Fetter Lane is probably *feuterer-lane.* A feuterer is a keeper of dogs, and the lane has always been famous for dogfanciers. Howel, with less probability, says it is *Fewtor Lane, i.e.* the lane of *fewtors* or worthless fellows who were for ever loitering about the lane on their way to the gardens. Faitour is an archaic word for a worthless fellow, a lazy vagabond, from the Norman-French.

Fettle, as a verb, means *to repair;* to *smoothe;* as an adjective, it means well-knit, all right and tight. It is connected with our word *feat,* the French *faire,* the Latin *facere.*

Fettled ale, in Lancashire, means ale warmed and spiced.

Feu de Joie (French). A running fire of guns on an occasion of rejoicing.

Feud, meaning "hatred," is the Saxon *fæhth* (hatred); but feud, a "fief," is the Teutonic *fee-odh* (trust-land). (*See below.*)

Feudal or *Feodal* (2 syl.). In Gothic *odh* means "property," hence *odh-all* (entire property); Flemish, *udal.* By transposition we get *all-ohd,* whence our *allodium* (absolute property claimed by the holders of fiefs); and by combining the words *fee* and *odh* we get *fee-odh, feodh,* or *feod* (property given by way of fee for services conferred). (*Pontoppidan.*)

Feudal System (*The*). A system founded on the tenure of feuds or fiefs, given in compensation for military service to the lord of the tenants.

Feuillants. A reformed Cistercian order instituted by Jean de la Barrière in 1586. So called from the convent of Feuillans, in Languedoc, where they were established in 1577.

The club of the Feuillants, in the French Revolution, composed of moderate Jacobins. So called because the convent of the Feuillants, near the Tuileries, was their original club-room (1791-2).

Feuilleton [*feu-yĕ-ton*]. A fly-sheet. Applied to the bottom part of French newspapers, generally devoted to a tale or some other light literature.

"The daily [French] newspapers all had feuilletons with continued stories in them."—*Hale: Ten-times One*, chap. viii. p. 125.

Fever-lurdan or **Fever-lurgan.** A fit of idleness. Lurden means a blockhead. (French, *lourd,* heavy, dull, thickheaded; *lourdand,* a blockhead.)

Fever-lurk. A corruption of *Feverlurg,* as "Fever-lurgan" is of *Feverlurdan.* The disease of laziness.

"Fever-lurk,
Neither play nor work."

Fey. Predestined to early death. When a person suddenly changes his wonted manner of life, as when a miser becomes liberal, or a churl good-humoured, he is said in Scotch to be *fey,* and near the point of death.

"She must be fey (said Triptolemus), and in that case has not long to live."—*Sir W. Scott: The Pirate*, chap. v.

Fe'zon. Daughter of Savary, Duke of Aquitaine, demanded in marriage by a pagan, called the *Green Knight;* but Orson, having overthrown the pagan, was accepted by the lady instead. (*Valentine and Orson.*)

Fi or **Fie!** An exclamation indicating that what is reproved is dirty or indecent. The dung of many animals, as the boar, wolf, fox, marten, and badger, is called *fiants,* and the "orificium ana'le" is called a *fi,* a word still used in Lincolnshire. (Anglo-Norman, *fay,* to clean out; Saxon, *afylan,* to foul; our *defile* or *file,* to make foul; *filth,* etc.)

The old words, *fie-corn* (dross corn), *fi-lands* (unenclosed lands), *fi-mashings* (the dung of any wild beast), etc., are compounds of the same word.

"I had another process against the dungfarmer, Master Fifi."—*Rabelais: Pantagruel*, book ii. 17.

Fi. Fa. A contraction of the two Latin words, *fi'eri facias* (cause it to be done). A judicial writ for one who has recovered damages in the Queen's courts, being a command to the sheriff to see the judgment of the court duly carried out.

Fiacre. A French cab or hackney coach. So called from the Hotel de St. Fiacre, Paris, where the first station of these coaches was established by M. Sauvage, about 1650.

⁂ According to Alban Butler, Fiacre was the son of an Irish king, born in 600, to whose tomb pilgrimages were made in the month of August. His day is August 30th. (*Lives of the Saints*, vol. ii. p. 379.)

Fian (*John*), a schoolmaster at Salt-pans, near Edinburgh, tortured to death and then burnt at the stake on the Castle Hill of Edinburgh, Saturday, January, 1591, because he refused to acknowledge that he had raised a storm at sea, to wreck James I. on his voyage to Denmark to visit his future queen. First, his head was crushed in upon his brain by means of a rope twisted tighter and tighter; then his two legs were jammed to a jelly in the wooden boots; then his nails were pulled out and pins inserted in the raw finger tips; as he still remained silent, he was strangled, and his dead body burnt to ashes.

Fiars. *Striking the fiars.* Taking the average price of corn. Fiars is a Gothic word, still current in Ireland. (Scotch law.)

Fias'co. A failure, a mull. In Italy they cry *Olà, olà, fiasco!* to an unpopular singer. This word, common in France and Germany, is employed as the opposite of *furore*.

⁂ The history of the word is as follows :—In making Venetian glass, if the slightest flaw is detected, the glass-blower turns the article into a *fiasco*—that is, a common flask.

A gentleman from North America (G. Fox, "the Modern Bathylus") furnishes me with the following anecdote : "There was once a clever harlequin of Florence named Dominico Biancolelli, noted for his comic harangues. He was wont to improvise upon whatever article he held in his hand. One night he appeared holding a flask (*fiasco*); but failing to extract any humour whatsoever from his subject, he said, 'It is thy fault, fiasco,' and dashed the flask on the ground. After that a failure was commonly called in Florence a 'fiasco.'" To me it appears incredible that a clever improvisator could draw no matter from an empty bottle, apparently a subject rife with matter.

Fiat. *I give my fiat to that proposal.* I consent to it. A fiat in law is an order of the court directing that something stated be done. (Latin, *fiat*, let it be done.)

Fib. An attendant on Queen Mab in Drayton's *Nymphidia*. Fib, meaning a falsehood, is the Latin *fabula*, a fable.

Fi'co. (*See* FIG.)
"Fico for the phrase."
Shakespeare: Merry Wives of Windsor, i. 3.
"I see contempt marching forth, giving me the fico with his thombe in his mouth."—*Wit's Miserie* (1596).

15*

Fiddle (Latin, *fidis* or *fides*). *He was first fiddle.* Chief man, the most distinguished of the company.

To play second fiddle. To take a subordinate part. The allusion is to the leader of concerts, who leads with a fiddle.

The Scotch fiddle or Caledonian Cremōna. The itch. As fiddlers scratch with a bow the strings of a fiddle, so persons suffering from skin-irritation keep scratching the part irritated.

Fiddle About (*To*). To fiddle about a thing means to "play" business. To fiddle with one's fingers is to move them about as a fiddler moves his fingers up and down the fiddle-strings.

"Mere trifling, or unprofitable fiddling about nothing."—*Barrow: Sermons*, vol. i. sermon 7.

Fiddle - de - dee! An exclamation signifying what you say is nonsense or moonshine. Fiddle-de-dee is meant to express the sound of a fiddle-string vocalised. Hence "sound signifying nothing."

Fiddle-faddle. *It is all fiddle-faddle.* Rubbishy nonsense ; talk not worth attention. A ricochet word, of which we have a vast number, as "flim-flam," "helter-skelter," "wishy-washy," etc. To fiddle is to waste time in playing on the fiddle, and hence fiddle means a trifle, and fiddle-faddle is silly trifle or silly nonsense.

"Pitiful fool that I was to stand fiddle-faddling in that way."
Clough : Amours de Voyage, canto iv. stanza 3.

Fiddleback. The name of Oliver Goldsmith's poor unfortunate pony, on which he made his country excursions.

Fiddler. *Drunk as a fiddler.* Fiddlers at wakes and fairs were allowed meat and drink to their heart's content, and seldom left a merry-making sober.

Oliver's Fiddler. Sir Roger L'Estrange (1616-1704). So called because he, at one time, was playing a fiddle or viole with others in the house of John Hingston when Cromwell was one of the guests.

⁂ *Fiddler* is a slang word for sixpence.

Fiddler's Fare or **Fiddler's Pay.** Meat, drink, and money.

Fiddler's Green. The land of the leal or "Dixie Land" of sailors ; where there is perpetual mirth, a fiddle that never ceases to untiring dancers, plenty of grog, and unlimited tobacco.

Fiddler's Money. A silver penny. The fee given to a fiddler at a wake by each dancer.

Fiddler's News. Stale news carried about by wandering fiddlers.

Fiddlestick. In the Great German epic called *The Nibelungen-Lied*, this word is used six or eight times for a broadsword.

" His fiddlestick he grasped, 'twas massy, broad, and long,
As sharp as any razor."   Stanza 1,841.
" My fiddlestick's no feather ; on whom I let it fall,
If he has friends that love him, 'twill set them weeping all."   Stanza 1,880.
" His fiddlestick, sharp-cutting, can hardest steel divide,
And at a stroke can shiver the morion's beamy pride."   Stanza 2,078.

Fiddlesticks! An exclamation signifying what you say is not worth attention. To fiddle about is to waste time, fiddling. A fiddlestick is the instrument used in fiddling, hence the fiddlestick is even less than the fiddle.

Fide'le (3 syl.). The name assumed by Imogen in Shakespeare's *Cymbeline*. Collins has a beautiful elegy on Fidele.

Fide'lio. Beethoven's only opera. (*See* LEONORA.)

Fides. The goddess of Faith, etc.

Fides (2 syl.). Mother of John of Leyden. Not knowing that her son was the " prophet " and ruler of Westphalia, but thinking that the prophet had caused his death, she went to Munster to curse the new-crowned monarch. The moment she saw him she recognised him, but the " prophet-king," surrounded by his courtiers, pretended not to know her. Fides, to save her son annoyance, declared she had made a mistake, and was confined in the dungeon of the palace at Munster, where John visited her and was forgiven. When her son set fire to his palace, Fides rushed into the flames and perished with him. (*Meyerbeer's opera of Le Prophète.*)

Fides Carbona'rii. Blind faith, faith of a child. A carbona'ro being asked what he believed, replied, "What the Church believes ; " and, being asked again what the Church believes, made answer, "What I believe." (*See* CARBONARI.) (*Roux: Dictionnaire Comique.*)

Field. (Anglo-Saxon, *feld.*)
In *agricultural* parlance, a field is a portion of land belonging to a farm.
In *huntsman's* language, it means all the riders.
In *heraldry*, it means the entire surface of the shield.
In *military* language, it means a battle ; the place where a battle is fought, or is about to be fought ; a campaign.
In *sportsmen's* language it means all the horses of any one race.
Against the field. In horse-racing, to bet against the field means to back a particular horse against all the rest entered for the race.
In the field. A competitor for a prize. A term in horse-races, as, so-and-so was in the field. Also in war, as, the French were in the field already.
Master of the field. In military parlance, means the conqueror in a battle.
To keep back the field, is to keep back the riders.
To take the field. To move the army preparatory to battle.
To win the field. To win the battle.

Field-day. Day of business. Thus, a clergyman jocosely calls a " kept festival " his field-day. A military term, meaning a day when a regiment is taken to the fields for practice.

Field Marshal. A general officer of the highest rank, who commands an army, or, at any rate, more than one corps.

Field Officer. Any officer between captain and a general officer. A major or a lieutenant-colonel may be a field officer, being qualified to command whole battalions, or a " field."

Field Pieces. Small cannon carried into the field with an army.

Field Works. Works thrown up by an army in besieging or defending a fortress, or in strengthening its position.
" Earth-forts, and especially field works, will hereafter play an important part in wars."—*W. T. Sherman: Memoirs,* vol. ii. chap. xxiv. p. 398.

Field of Blood. Acel'dama, the piece of land bought by the chief priests with the money which Judas threw down in the temple ; so called because it was bought with blood-money. (Matt. xxvii. 5 ; Acts i. 19.)
∵ The battle-field of Cannæ (B.C. 216) is so called because it was especially sanguinary.

Field of Ice. A large body of floating ice.

Field of Vision or **Field of View.** The space in a telescope, microscope, stereoscope, etc., within which the object is visible. If the object is not distinctly visible, it must be *brought into the field* by adjustment.

Field of the Cloth of Gold. The plain, near Guisnes, where Henry VIII.

had his interview with François I. in 1520 ; so called from the splendour and magnificence displayed there on the occasion.

Field of the Forty Footsteps. At the back of the British Museum, once called Southampton Fields. The tradition is that two brothers, in the Duke of Monmouth's rebellion, took different sides and engaged each other in fight. Both were killed, and forty impressions of their feet remained on the field for many years, where no grass would grow. The encounter took place at the extreme north-east of Upper Montague Street. The Misses Porter wrote a novel on the subject, and the Messrs. Mayhew a melodrama.

Fielding. *The Fielding of the drama.* George Farquhar, author of the *Beaux' Stratagem*, etc. (1678-1707.)

Fierabras (*Sir*), of Alexandria, son of Balan, King of Spain. The greatest giant that ever walked the earth. For height of stature, breadth of shoulder, and hardness of muscle he never had an equal. He possessed all Babylon, even to the Red Sea ; was seigneur of Russia, Lord of Cologne, master of Jerusalem, and even of the Holy Sepulchre. He carried away the crown of thorns, and the balsam which embalmed the body of Our Lord, one drop of which would cure any sickness, or heal any wound in a moment. One of his chief exploits was to slay the "fearful huge giant that guarded the bridge Mantible," famous for its thirty arches of black marble. His pride was laid low by Olivier, one of Charlemagne's paladins. The giant then became a child of God, and ended his days in the odour of sanctity, "meek as a lamb and humble as a chidden slave." Sir Fierabras, or Ferumbras, figures in several mediæval romances, and is an allegory of Sin overcome by the Cross. (*See* BALAN.)

Fifteen decisive Battles (*The*), according to Sir E. S. Creasy, were :

1. The battle of MARATHON (Sept., 490 B.C.), when Miltīadēs, with 10,000 Greeks, defeated 100,000 Persians under Datis and Artaphernēs.

2. The naval battle at SYRACUSE (Sep., 413 B.C.), when the Athenians under Niclas and Demosthenēs were defeated with a loss of 40,000 killed and wounded, and their entire fleet.

3. The battle of ARBE'LA (Oct., 331 B.C.), when Alexander the Great

overthrew Darīus Codomanus for the third time.

4. The battle of METAURUS (207 B.C.), when the consuls Livius and Nero cut to pieces Hasdrubal's army, sent to reinforce Hannibal.

5. In A.D. 9 Arminius and the Gauls utterly overthrew the Romans under Varus, and thus established the independence of Gaul.

6. The battle of CHALONS (A.D. 451), when Aetius and Theodoric utterly defeated Attīla, and saved Europe from devastation.

7. The battle of TOURS (Oct., 732 A.D.), when Charles Martel overthrew the Saracens under Abderahmen, and thus broke the Moslem yoke from Europe.

8. The battle of HASTINGS (Oct., 1066), when William of Normandy slew Harold II., and obtained the crown of England.

9. The battle of ORLEANS in 1429, when Joan of Arc secured the independence of France.

10. The defeat of the Spanish ARMADA in 1588, which destroyed the hopes of the Pope respecting England.

11. The battle of BLENHEIM (13 Aug., 1704), when Marlborough and Prince Eugene defeated Tallard, and thus prevented Louis XIV. from carrying out his schemes.

12. The battle of PULTOWA (July, 1709), when Czar Peter utterly defeated Charles XII. of Sweden, and thus established the Muscovite power.

13. The battle of SARATOGA (Oct., 1777), when General Gates defeated the British under General Burgoyne, and thus secured for the United States the alliance of France.

14. The battle of VALMY (Sep., 1792), when the French Marshal Kellerman defeated the Duke of Brunswick, and thus established for a time the French republic.

15. The battle of WATERLOO (18 June, 1815), when Napoleon the Great was defeated by the Duke of Wellington, and Europe was restored to its normal condition.

The battle of GETTYSBURG, in Pennsylvania (3 July, 1863), when the Confederates, under the command of General Lee, were defeated by the Northern army, was certainly one of the most important, if not the most important, of the American Civil War.

The battle of SEDAN (Sep., 1870), when Napoleon gave up his sword to William, King of Prussia, which put an end to the empire of France.

Fifth-Monarchy Men. A sect of English fanatics in the days of the Puritans, who maintained that Jesus Christ was about to come a second time to the earth, and establish the fifth universal monarchy. The four preceding

Fig 460 Fighting Prelate

monarchies were the Assyrian, the Persian, the Macedonian, and the Roman. In politics, the Fifth-Monarchy Men were arrant Radicals and levellers.

Fig. *Full fig.* Full dress. A corruption of the Italian *in fioc'chi* (in gala costume). It was derived from the tassels with which horses were ornamented in state processions. Thus we read in Miss Knight's *Autobiography*, "The Pope's throne was set out for mass, and the whole building was in perfect fiocchi" (in full fig). Another etymology has been suggested by a correspondent in *Notes and Queries*, that it is taken from the word full fig. (figure) in fashion books.

"The Speaker sits at one end all in full fig, with a clerk at the table below."—*Trollope: West Indies*, chap. ix. p. 101.

Fig or *Figo. I don't care a fig for you ; not worth a fig.* Anything at all. Here fig is *fico*—a fillip or snap of the fingers. Thus we say, "I don't care that for you," snapping the fingers at the same time. (Italian, *far le fiche*, to snap the fingers ; French, *faire la figue* ; German, *diefeigen weisen ;* Dutch, *de vyghe setten*, etc.) (*See* FICO.)

"A fig for Peter."
            Shakespeare : 2 Henry VI., ii. 9.
"The figo for thy friendship."
            Shakespeare : Henry V., iii. 6.

Fig Sunday. Palm Sunday is so called from the custom of eating figs on that day. The practice arose from the Bible story of Zaccheus, who climbed up into a fig-tree to see Jesus.

⁜ Many other festivals have their special foods ; as, Michaelmas goose, Christmas, plum-pudding, Shrove Tuesday, pancake day ; Ash Wednesday, salt cod ; Good Friday, hot cross-buns ; pasch-eggs, roast-chestnuts, etc., have their special days.

Fig-tree. It is said that Judas hanged himself on a fig-tree. (*See* ELDER-TREE.)

"Quæret aliquis quâ ex ar'bore Judas se suspen'derit ? Arbor ficus fuisse di'citur."—*Barradius.*

Figs. *I shan't buy my Attic figs in future, but grow them.* Don't count your chickens before they are hatched. It was Xerxes who boasted that he did not intend any longer to buy his figs, because he meant to conquer Att'ica and add it to his own empire ; but Xerxes met a signal defeat at Sal'amis, and "never loosed his sandal till he reached Abde'ra."

"*In the name of the Prophet, Figs !*" A burlesque of the solemn language employed in eastern countries in the

common business of life. The line occurs in the imitation of Dr. Johnson's pompous style, in *Rejected Addresses*, by James and Horace Smith.

Figged out. (*See* FIG, *Full Fig.*)

Fig'aro. A type of cunning dexterity, and intrigue. The character is in the *Barbier de Séville* and *Mariage de Figaro*, by Beaumarchais. In the former he is a barber, and in the latter a valet ; but in both he outwits every one. There are several operas founded on these dramas, as Mozart's *Nozze di Figaro*, Paisiello's *Il Barbiere di Siviglia*, and Rossini's *Il Barbiere di Siviglia*.

Fight. (See *Hudibras*, Pt. iii. c. 3.)

" He that fights and runs away
    May live to fight another day ;
    But he that is in battle slain
    Can never rise to fight again."
Sir John Mennes : Musarum Delictæ. (1656.)

Demos'thenēs, being reproached for running away from Philip of Macedon, at Chæro'a, replied, " A man that runs away may fight again (Ἀνὴρ ὁ φεύγων καὶ πάλιν μαχήσεται)." (See *Aulus Gellius*, xvii. 21.)

Fight Shy (*To*). To avoid. A shy person is unwilling to come forward, and to fight is to resist, to struggle in a contest. To "fight shy," therefore, is to resist being brought into contest or conflict.

Fighting-cocks. *To live like fighting-cocks.* To have a profusion of the best food. Fighting-cocks used to be high fed in order to aggravate their pugnacity and increase their powers of endurance.

Fighting Fifth (*The*). The 5th Foot. This sobriquet was given to the regiment during the Peninsular War.

The "Old and Bold Fifth," the Duke of Wellington's Body-guard, is now called the "Northumberland Fusiliers." What a terrible vexation must the abolition of the time-honoured names of our old regiments have been to our army !

Fighting Kings [*Chen-kuo*]. Certain feudatories of China incessantly contending for mastery over each other. (B.C. 770–320.)

Fighting Prelate. Henry Spencer, Bishop of Norwich, who greatly distinguished himself in the rebellion of Wat Tyler. He met the rebels in the field, with the temporal sword, then absolved them, and sent them to the gibbet.

"The Bishop of Norwich, the famous 'fighting prelate,' had led an army into Flanders."—*Lord Campbell.*

Fighting the Tiger. Gaming is so called in the United States of America.

"After seeing 'fighting the tiger,' as gaming is styled in the United States, I have arrived at the conclusion that gaming is more fairly carried on in the Monte Carlo casino than in any American gaming-house." — *The Nineteenth Century*, Feb., 1890, p. 249.

Fighting with Gloves on. Sparring without showing animosity; fighting with weapons or words with coloured friendliness. Fighting, like boxers, with boxing gloves. Tories and Whigs in the two Houses of Parliament fight with gloves on, so long as they preserve all the outward amenities of debate, and conceal their hostility to each other by seeming friendliness.

Figure. *To cut a figure.* This phrase seems applicable more especially to dress and outward bearing. To make a figure is rather to make a name or reputation, but the distinction is not sharply observed.

To make a figure. To be a notability. *Faire quelque figure dans le monde.* "He makes no figure at court;" *Il ne fait aucune figure à la cour.*

Figure. *What's the figure?* The price; what am I to pay? what "figure" or sum does my debt amount to?

Figure-head. A figure on the head or projecting cutwater of a ship.

Figure of Fun (*A*). A droll appearance, whether from untidiness, quaintness, or other peculiarity. 'A precious figure of fun,' is a rather stronger expression. These are chiefly applied to young children.

Figures. A corruption of *fingers*, that is, "digits" (Latin, *digiti*, fingers). So called from the primitive method of marking the monades by the fingers. Thus the first four were simply i, ii, iii, iiii; five was the outline of the hand simplified into a v; the next four figures were the two combined, thus, vi, vii, viii, viiii; and ten was a double v, thus, x. At a later period iiii and viiii were expressed by one less than five (i-v) and one less than ten (i-x). Nineteen was ten-plus-nine (x + ix), etc.—a most clumsy and unphilosophical device.

Filch. To steal or purloin. A filch is a staff with a hook at the end, for plucking clothes from hedges and abstracting articles from shop windows. Probably it is a corruption of pilfer. (Welsh, *yspeilio* and *yspeiliwr;* Spanish,

pellizcar: French, *piller* and *peler.* Filch and *pilfer* are variants of the same word.
" With cunning hast thou filched my daughter's heart."
  Shakespeare : Midsummer Night's Dream, i. 2.

File. To cheat. The allusion is to filing money for the sake of the dust which can be used or sold. A *file* is a cheat. Hence "a jolly file," etc.
" Sorful becom that fals file."
   Cursor Mundi MS.

In single file. Single row; one behind another. (French, *file*, a row.)

Rank and file. Common soldiers. Thus we say, "Ten officers and three hundred rank and file fell in the action." *Rank* refers to men standing abreast, *file* to men standing behind each other.
" It was only on the faith of some grand expedition that the credulous rank and file of the Brotherhood subscribed their dollars." — *The Times.*

Fi'lia Doloro'sa. The Duchesse d'Angoulême, daughter of Louis XVI., also called the modern Antig'one. (1778-1851.)

Filibuster. A piratical adventurer. The most notorious was William Walker, who was shot in 1855. (French, *flibustier*, a corruption of our "freebooter;" German, *freibeuter;* Spanish, *filibustero;* Dutch, *vrijbueter.*) (*See* BUCCANEER.)

Filioque Controversy (*The*) long disturbed the Eastern and Western Churches. The point was this: Did the Holy Ghost proceed from the Father *and* the Son (*Filio-que*), or from the Father only? The Western Church maintained the former, and the Eastern Church the latter dogma. The *filio-que* was added in the Council of Toledo 589. Amongst others, Pope Leo III. was averse to the change. (*Nicene Creed.*)

The gist of the argument is this : If the Son is one with the Father, whatever proceeds from the Father must proceed from the Son also. This is technically called "The Procession of the Holy Ghost."

Fill-dyke. The month of February, when the rain and melted snow fills the ditches to overflowing.

Fillet. A narrow band round the head for binding the hair, or simply for ornament. Aure'lian was the first Roman emperor that wore a royal fillet or diadem in public. In the time of Constantine the fillet was adorned with precious stones.

Filome'na. Longfellow calls Florence Nightingale *St. Filomena*, not only because Filomena resembles the Latin word for a nightingale, but also because this saint, in Sabatelli's picture, is represented as hovering over a group of sick and maimed, healed by her intercession. (*See* THAUMATURGUS.)

Filter. To run through felt, as jelly is strained through flannel. The Romans strained the juice of their grapes through felt into the wine-vat, after which it was put into the casks. (Latin, *feltrum*, felt, *filtrum*, a strainer.)

Fin. The hand. *A contraction of finger.* Thus we say, "Give us your fin"—*i.e.* shake hands. The derivation from a fish's fin is good only for a joke.

Final'ity John. Earl Russell, who maintained that the Reform Bill of 1832 was a *finality*, yet in 1854, 1860, and 1866 brought forth other Reform Bills. ;

Finance (French). Revenue derived from fines or subsidies. In feudal times finance was money paid to a lord for a privilege. In the plural we use the word to signify available money resources. Thus we say, "My finances are exhausted," meaning I have no more funds or available money.

Finch Lane (London). So called from a family of consideration by the name of Finch or Finke. There was once a church in the lane called St. Benet Finke. There is an Irish saint named Finc, in Latin *Fincana*, whose day is October 13th.

Find. *You know what you leave behind, but not what you will find.* And this it is that "makes us rather bear the ills we have, than fly to others that we know not of."

Fin'don Haddocks. Haddocks smoked with green wood. (See *Sir W. Scott : The Antiquary*, xxvi.) Findon or Finnon is a village some six miles south of Aberdeen, where haddocks are cured.

Findy. Plump, full. (Saxon, *findig*.)

"A cold May and a windy
Make barns fat and findy."
Old Proverb.

Fine Arts. Those arts which chiefly depend on a delicate or fine imagination, as music, painting, poetry, and sculpture.

Fine as Fivepence. The ancient Saxon shilling was a coin worth 5d. "To dress fine as fivepence" is to dress very smartly. The Saxon shilling was a far better coin than those made of tin, lead, and other inferior metals.

Fine-ear. One of Fortu'nio's servants, who could hear the grass grow

and the mole work underground. (*Grimm's Goblins : Fortunio.*)

Fin'etor. A necromancer, father of the Enchantress-Damsel, in *Am'adis of Gaul.*

Fingal—*i.e.* Fin-mac-Coul. (See *Sir W. Scott : The Antiquary*, chap. xxii.)

Fingal's Cave. The basaltic cavern of Staffa. So called from *Fion na Gael* (Fingal), the great Gaelic hero, whose achievements have been made familiar by the *Fingal* of Macpherson.

Finger. (Anglo-Saxon, *finger*).
The ear finger, digitus auriculāris—*i.e.* the little finger. The four fingers are the index finger, the middle finger, the ring finger, and the ear finger. In French, *le doigt auriculaire.* The little finger is so called because it can, from its diminutive size, be most easily introduced into the conduit of the ear.

"*Le doigt auriculaire* est le petit doight, ainsi nommé parce qu'a cause de sa petitesse, il peut facilement être introduit dans le conduit auditif externe."—*Dict. des Sciences, etc.*

The index finger. The first finger ; so called because it is used as a pointer.

The medical finger. The ring finger (*q.v.*).

"At last he put on her medical finger a pretty, handsome gold ring, whereinto was enchased a precious toadstone of Beausse."—*Rabelais : Pantagruel*, iii. 17.

The ring finger. The finger between the long and little finger was used by the Romans as a ring-finger, from the belief that a nerve ran through it to the heart. Hence the Greeks and Romans used to call it the *medical* finger, and used it for stirring mixtures, under the notion that nothing noxious could touch it without its giving instant warning to the heart. It is still a very general notion in England that it is bad to rub on salve or scratch the skin with any but the ring finger. The fact that there was no such intimacy between the finger and the heart was not discovered till after the notion was deeply rooted. Pliny calls this *digitus annulāris*.

With a wet finger. Easily. (*See* WET FINGER.)

My little finger told me that. The same as "A little bird told me that," meaning, I know it, though you did not expect it. The former expression is from Molière's *Malade Imaginaire.* (*See* BIRD.)

"By the pricking of my thumbs,
Something wicked this way comes."
Shakespeare : Macbeth, iv. 1.

Cry, baby, cry ; put your finger in your eye, etc. This nursery rhyme seems to be referred to by Shakespeare in his *Comedy of Errors*, ii. 2 :—

> "No longer will I be fool,
> To put the finger in the eye and weep."

To hold up a finger (in an auction room) by way of a bid, was a Roman custom, "digĭtum tollĕre" (*Cicero : In Verrem, Actio* i. 54). Horace confirms this.

To turn up the little finger. (*See* TURN.)

Finger and Glove. *To be finger and glove with another* means to be most intimate.

Finger in the Pie. *To have a finger in the pie.* To assist or mix oneself officiously in any matter. *Esse rei particeps.* In French, *Mettre la main à la pâte.*

Finger Benediction. In the Greek and Roman Church the thumb and first two fingers represent the Trinity. The thumb, being strong, represents the *Father ;* the long or second finger, *Jesus Christ ;* and the first finger, the *Holy Ghost,* which proceedeth from the Father and the Son. (*See* BLESSING.)

Some bishops of the Anglican Church use this gesture while pronouncing the benediction.

Finger-stall. A *hutkin,* a cover for a sore finger. The Germans call a thimble a finger-hut, where hut is evidently the word hut or huth (a tending, keeping, or guarding), from the verb *huten* (to keep watch over). Our *hutkin* is simply a little cap for guarding a sore finger. Stall is the Saxon *stæl* (a place), whence our stall, a place for horses.

Fingers. The old names for the fingers are :—

Thumb (Anglo-Saxon *thuma*).

Towcher (the finger that touches), foreman, or pointer. This was called by the Anglo-Saxons the *scite-finger*, i.e. the shooting finger.

Long-man or long finger.

Lech-man or ring-finger. The former means "medical finger," and the latter is a Roman expression, "*digitus annula'ris.*" Called by the Anglo-Saxons the *gold-finger*.

Little-man or little finger. Called by the Anglo-Saxons the *eár-finger*.

Fingers. Ben Jonson says—

> "The thumb, in chiromancy, we give to Venus ;
> The fore-finger to Jove ; the midst to Saturn ;
> The ring to Sol ; the least to Mercury."
> *Alchemist,* i. 2.

His fingers are all thumbs. Said of a person awkward in the use of his hands. *Ce sont les deux doigts de la main.*

Fingers before Forks.

> "This Vulcan was a smith, they tell us,
> That first invented tongs and bellows ;
> For breath and fingers did their works
> (We'd fingers long before we'd forks)."
> *King : Art of Love.*

Fingers' Ends. *I have it at my fingers' ends.* I am quite familiar with it and can do it readily. It is a Latin proverb (*Scire tanquam un'gues dig'itosq.*), where the allusion is to the statuary, who knows every item of his subject by the touch. (*See* UNGUEM.)

> "*Costard:* Go to ; thou hast it ad dunghill, at the fingers' ends, as they say.
> *Holofernes:* O, I smell false Latin : dunghill for unguem."—*Shakespeare : Love's Labour's Lost,* v. 1.

Fingered.

The light-fingered gentry. Priggers, *qui ungues hamatos et uncos habent.*

Fingle-fangle (*A*). A ricochet word meaning a fanciful trifle. A "new fangle" is a novel contrivance. "New fangled," etc.

Finished to the Finger-nail, or "*ad unguem,*" in allusion to statuaries running their finger-tips over a statue to detect if any roughness or imperfection of surface remains.

Finny Tribe. Fish ; so called because they are furnished with fins.

Finsbury (London). A corruption of Fens-bury, the town in the fens.

Fion, son of Comnal, an enormous giant, who could place his feet on two mountains, and then stoop and drink from a stream in the valley between. (*Gaelic legend.*)

Fir-cone on the Thyrsus. The juice of the fir-tree (*turpentine*) used to be mixed by the Greeks with new wine to make it keep ; hence it was adopted as one of the symbols of Bacchus.

Fir-tree (*The*). Atys was metamorphosed into a fir-tree by Cybelē, as he was about to lay violent hands on himself. (*Ovid : Metamorphoses,* x. fable 2.)

Fire. (Anglo-Saxon, *fyr* ; Greek, *pur.*)
St. Antony's fire. Erysipelas. "*Le feu St. Antoine.*" (*See* ANTHONY.)
St. Helen's fire. "*Ignis sanctæ Helēnæ.*"
"*Feu St. Helme.*" (*See* CASTOR and POLLUX ; and ELMO.)
Hermes's fire. Same as St. Helen's fire (*q.v.*).

I have myself passed through the fire ; I have smelt the smell of fire. I have had experience in trouble. The allusion is to Shadrach, Meshach, and Abednego, who were cast into the fiery furnace by Nebuchadnezzar (Dan. iii.).

If you will enjoy the fire you must put up with the smoke. (Latin, " *Commŏd'-itas quæris sua fert incommŏda secum.*") Every convenience has its inconvenience.

More fire in the bed-straw. More mischief brewing. Alluding to the times when straw was used for carpets and beds.

No fire without smoke. (French, " *Nul feu sans fumée.*") No good without its mixture of evil.

No smoke without fire. To every scandal there is some foundation.

Where there is smoke there is fire. Every effect is the result of some cause.

Fire. *The Great Fire of London* (1666) broke out at Master Farryner's, the king's baker, in Pudding Lane, and after three nights and three days was arrested at Pie Corner. St. Paul's Cathedral, eighty-nine other churches, and 13,200 houses were burnt down.

Fire Away! Say on; say what you have to say. The allusion to firing a gun; as, You are primed up to the muzzle with something you want to say; fire away and discharge your thoughts.

"'Foster, I have something I want you and Miss Caryll to understand.' 'Fire away!' exclaimed Foster."—*Watson: The Web of a Spider*, chap. xv.

Fire away, Flan'agan. A taunt to a boaster. A man threatening you, says he will do this, that, and the other; you reply, " Fire away, Flanagan." Cromwell marched against a castle defended by Flanagan, who threatened to open his cannon on the Parliamentarians unless they withdrew. Cromwell wrote on the corner of the missive sent to him, " Fire away, Flanagan," and the doughty champion took to his heels immediately.

Fire First. *Non, Monsieur, nous ne tirons jamais les premiers.* According to tradition, this was said by the Count D'Auteroches to Lord Charles Hay at the battle of Fontenoy, 30th April, 1745 (old style).

"On c'était de tradition dans l'armée : on laissait toujours par courtoisie, l'avantage du premier feu à l'ennemi." (See *Notes and Queries*, 29th October, 1892, p. 345.)

Fire-balloon. A balloon whose ascensional power is derived from hot air rising from a fire beneath its open mouth. Montgolfier used such a balloon.

Fire-brand. An incendiary ; one who incites to rebellion ; like a blazing brand which sets on fire all it touches.

" Our fire-brand brother, Paris, burns us all."
Shakespeare : Troilus and Cressida, ii. 2.

Fire-drake or **Fire-dragon.** A fiery serpent, an ignis-fatuus of large proportions, superstitiously believed to be a flying dragon keeping guard over hid treasures.

" There is a fellow somewhat near the door, he should be a brazier by his face, for, o' my conscience, twenty of the dog-days now reign in 's nose. . . . That fire-drake did I hit three times on the head."—*Shakespeare: Henry VIII.*, v. 3.

Fire-eaters. Persons ready to quarrel for anything. The allusion is to the jugglers who " eat " flaming tow, pour melted lead down their throats, and hold red-hot metal between their teeth. Richardson, in the seventeenth century —Signora Josephine Girardelli (the original Salamander), in the early part of the nineteenth century—and Chaubert, a Frenchman, of the present century, were the most noted of these exhibitors.

" The great fire-eater lay unconscious upon the floor of the house."—*Nashville Banner*.

Fire-new. Spick and span new (*q.v.*).

" You should have accosted her ; and with some excellent jests fire-new from the mint."—*Shakespeare: Twelfth Night*, iii. 2.

Fire-ship. A ship filled with combustibles to be sent against adverse vessels in order to set them on fire.

Fire Up (*To*). To become indignantly angry. The Latin, " *irâ exardescĕre*," " *Inflammer de colère.*"

Fire Worship was introduced into Persia by Phœ'dima, widow of Smerdis, and wife of Gushtasp *darawesh*, usually called Hystaspes (B.C. 521-485). It is not the sun that is worshipped, but God, who is supposed to reside in it ; at the same time they reverence the sun, not as a deity but as the throne of deity. (*See* PARSEES.)

Fire and Sword. *Letters of fire and sword.* If a criminal resisted the law and refused to answer his citation, it was accounted treason in the Scottish courts ; and " letters of fire and sword " were sent to the sheriff, authorising him to use either or both these instruments to apprehend the contumacious party.

Fire and Water. *I will go through fire and water to serve you.* The reference is the ordeals of fire and water which might be transferred to substitutes. Paul seems to refer to substitutional death in Rom. v. 7: " Scarcely for a righteous man will one die ; yet for a good man some would even dare to die."

Firm as a Rock. (*See* SIMILES.)

First-class Hard Labour. Under this sentence, the prisoner sleeps on a plank bed without a mattress, and spends six or eight hours a day turning a hard crank, or treading a wheel. (*See* SECOND-CLASS HARD LABOUR.)

First-fruits. The first profitable results of labour. In husbandry, the first corn that is cut at harvest. We also use the word in an evil sense; as, the first-fruits of sin, the first-fruits of repentance.

First Water. *A diamond of the first water.* (*See* DIAMOND.)

First Gentleman of Europe. A nickname given to George IV., who certainly was first in rank, but it would be sad indeed to think he was ever the most gentlemanly man in feeling, manners, and deportment. Louis d'Artois was so called also.

First Grenadier of France. A title given by Napoleon to Latour d'Auvergne (1743-1800).

First Stroke is Half the Battle. "Well begun is half done." "A good lather is half the shave."

Latin : " Incipe: dimidium facti est cœpisse."
(*Ausonius.*)
" Dimidium facti, qui cœpit, habet."
(*Horace.*)
French : " Barbe bien savonnée est à moitié faite.
Heureux commencement est la moitié de l'œuvre.
C' n'est que le premier pas qui coûte."

Fish. The French have a remarkable locution respecting fish as a food :

" Après poisson, lait est poison ;
Après poisson, le vin est bon ;
Après poisson, noix est contre-poison."

Fish. The reason why fish are employed as card-counters is from a misapprehension of the French word *fiche* (a five-sou piece). The two points allowed for the "rub" are called in French *la fiche de consolation.* The Spanish word *pez* has also a double meaning—a "winning," or a "fish ; " *pez* is the Welsh *pysg*, Latin *pisc'*, English fish.

A loose fish. One of loose or dissolute habits. *Fish* implying a human being is derogatory, but *bird* is a loving term, as my "bonny bird," etc. *Beast* is most reproachful, as "You are a beast."

A pretty kettle of fish. (*See* KITTLE.)

A queer fish. An eccentric person. (*See above,* LOOSE FISH.)

All is fish that comes to my net. "*Auri bonus est odor ex re qualibet.*" I am willing to deal in anything out of which I can make a profit. I turn everything to some use.

" Al is fishe that cometh to the net.'—*G. Gascoigne : The Steele Glas* (died 1577).

He eats no fish ; he is not a papist ; he is an honest man, and one to be trusted. In the reign of Elizabeth papists were opposed to the Government, and Protestants, to show their loyalty, refused to eat fish on Fridays to show they were not papists.

" I do profess . . . . to serve him truly . . . .
and to eat no fish."—*Shakespeare : King Lear*, i. 4.

I have other fish to fry ; "*J'ai bien d'autres affaires en tête ;*" "*Aliud mihi est agendum ;*" I am busy and cannot attend to [that] now ; I have other matters to attend to.

Mute as a fish. Fish have no language like birds, beasts, and insects. Their utmost power of sound is a feeble cry of pain, the result of intestinal respiration. The French also say "mute comme un poisson."

The best fish smell when they are three days old ; "*l'hôte et le poisson puent passé trois jours.*" "Withdraw thy foot from thy neighbour's house, lest he get weary of thee, and so hate thee" (Prov. xxv. 17). "Don't outstay your welcome."

The best fish swim near the bottom. "*Le meilleur poisson nage près du fond.*" What is most commercially valuable is not to be found on the surface of the earth, nor is anything else really valuable to be obtained without trouble. "*Il faut casser le noyau pour en avoir l'amande,*" for "*Nil sine magno vita labore dedit mortalibus.*"

Fish. *It is neither fish, flesh, nor fowl ;* or *Neither fish, flesh, nor good red herring.* Not fish (food for the monk), not flesh (food for the people generally), nor yet red herring (food for paupers). Suitable to no class of people ; fit for neither one thing nor another.

⁂ Fish comes first because in the Middle Ages the clergy took precedence of the laity.

" She would be a betwixt-and-between : . . . neither fish nor fowl."—*Mrs. Lynn Linton.*

Fish-day (*A*) [*jour maigre*]. A day in the Roman Catholic Church when persons, without ecclesiastical permission, are forbidden to eat meat.

Fish-wife (*A*). A woman who hawks fish about the streets.

Fish and Flesh. *You must not make fish of one and flesh of the other.* You must treat both alike. Fish is an inferior sort of animal food to flesh. The alliteration has much to do with the phrase.

Fish in Troubled Water (*To*). In French, "*Pêcher en eau troublé.*" To scramble for personal advantage in times of rebellion, revolution, or national calamity.

Fish it Out (*To*). This is the Latin *expiscor*.

Fish out of Water. Out of place ; without one's usual occupation ; restless from lack of employment.

Fisher of Souls (*The great*). The devil.

"I trust, young man, that neither idleness nor licentious pleasure . . . . the chief baits with which the great Fisher of souls conceals his hooks, are the causes of your declining the career to which I would incite you."—*Sir W. Scott: The Monastery*, chap. xi.

Fisherman. *The fisherman who was father of three kings.* Abu Shujah al Bouyah was a Persian fisherman in the province of Delēm', whose three sons, Imad, Ruken, and Moez, all rose to sovereign power.

Fishing. *Fishing for compliments.* Laying a bait for praise.

Fisk (in *Hudibras*) was Nicholas Fisk, a physician and astrologer, who used to say that a physician never deserved his bread till he had no teeth to eat it. In his old age he was almost a beggar.

Fitz (Norman). Son of ; as Fitz-Herbert, Fitz-William, Fitz-Peter, etc. It is sometimes applied to illegitimate children, as Fitz-Clarence, Fitz-roy, etc.

Fitz-Fulke (*Hebē*). "A gracious, graceful, graceless grace ; " "fat, fair, and forty." (*Byron : Don Juan*, canto xvi.)

Fitzwilliam Museum (Cambridge University). So called from Earl Fitzwilliam, who left £100,000, with books, paintings, etc., to form the nucleus of a museum for the benefit of the university.

Five, or the pentad, the great mystic number, being the sum of 2 + 3, the first *even* and first *odd* compound. Unity is God alone, *i.e.* without creation. Two is diversity, and three (being 1 + 2) is the compound of unity and diversity, or the two principles in operation since creation, and representing all the powers of nature.

Five-minute Clause. A provision sometimes inserted in deeds of separation, whereby it is stipulated that the deed is null and void if the husband and wife remain together five minutes after the separation is enjoined.

Five Nations (*The*). The five confederated Indian tribes, viz. the Mohawks, Oneidas, Onondagas, Cayugas, and Senecas. Known as the *Iroquois Confederacy*.

Five Points (*The*). (*See* CALVINISM.)

Five Wits. (1) Common sense, (2) imagination, (3) fantasy, (4) estimation, and (5) memory. Common sense is the outcome of the five senses ; imagination is the "wit" of the mind ; fantasy is imagination united with judgment ; estimation estimates the absolute, such as time, space, locality, and so on ; and memory is the "wit" of recalling past events. (*See* SEVEN WITS.)

"Four of his five wits went halting off." *Shakespeare : Much Ado, etc.*, i. 1.
"These are the five witts removyng inwardly : First, 'Common witte,' and then 'Ymagination,' 'Fantasy,' and 'Estimation' truely, And 'Memory.'" *Stephen Hawes : The Passe-tyme of Plesure* (1515).
∴ Notwithstanding this quotation, probably the Five Wits mean the wits of the five senses.

Fiver (*A*). A five-pound note. A "tenner" is a ten-pound note.

Fives. A game similar to court-tennis ; the hand, however, is used instead of a racket. Said to be so called because the game is three fives (15).

"He forgot that cricket and fives are capital training for tennis."—*T. Hughes : Tom Brown at Oxford*, chap. ii.

A bunch of fives. The fist, in which the five fingers are bound in a bunch.

Fix. *I'm in a fix.* A predicament. The allusion is to machinery which will not move. The *Northumberland* was in a terrible fix at the launch, when it refused to leave the dock. (1866.)

Fixed Air. Carbonic dioxide gas. Dr. Black gave it this name, because carbonate of magnesia evolved by heat carbonic acid, that is, MgO, CO_2 evolved CO_2, thereby proving that CO_2 (carbonic acid) is a "fixed air."

Fixed Oils. Oils obtained by simple pressure. These oils do not readily dry or volatilise, but remain fixed in their oily character.

Fixed Stars. Stars whose relative position to other stars is fixed or always the same. Planets are always shifting their relative positions.

Fixt (*The*). That is, the Firmament. According to the Ptolemaic System, the earth is surrounded by nine spheres. These spheres are surrounded by the *Primum Mobīle* (or First Moved) ; and the

Premium Mobíle is enveloped by the empyrēan, or abode of deity.

"They pass the planets seven, and pass the fixt,
And that crystalline sphere whose balance weighs
The trepidation talked, and that first moved."
Milton: Paradise Lost, iii. 481—3.

Flaccus. Horace, the Roman poet, whose full name was Quintus Hora'tius Flaccus.

Flag. (Danish, *flag*.)
A black flag is the emblem of piracy or of no quarter. (*See* BLACK FLAGS.)
To unfurl the black flag. To declare war. The curtain which used to hang before the door of Ayeshah, Mahomet's favourite wife, was taken for a national flag, and is regarded by Mussulmans as the most precious of relics. It is black, and is never unfolded except as a declaration of war.
A red flag. To display a red flag is to defy or dare to battle. Red is the emblem of blood. The Roman signal for battle.
A yellow flag signals contagious disease on board ship.
To get one's flag. To become an admiral. Formerly the captain of a flagship was called a "flag-officer."

"I do not believe that the bullet is cast that is to deprive you of life, Jack; you'll get your flag, as I hope to get mine."—*Kingston: The Three Admirals*, xiii.

To hang the flag half-mast high is in token of mourning or distress.
To hang out the white flag. To sue for quarter; to give in.
To lower one's flag; to eat humble pie: to eat the leek; to confess oneself in the wrong; to eat one's own words.

"The . . . Association . . . after systematically opposing the views of the . . . National Congress, had to lower the flag and pass a resolution in favour of simultaneous examinations."—*Nineteenth Century* (April, 1894, page 670).

To strike the flag. To lower it or pull it down upon the cap, in token of respect or submission. In naval warfare it means to surrender.

Flag, Flags.
Banners of Saints. Flags smaller than standards, and not slit at the extremity.
Royal Banners contain the royal arms.
Standards, much larger and longer than banners, and slit at the extremity. A standard has no armorial bearings.
Burgee. A small flag with the loose end cleft like a **<**.
Pennant. A small triangular flag.
Pennons, much smaller than standards; rounded at the extremity, and charged with arms.
Bannerols, banners of great width, representing alliances and descents.
Pensils, small flags shaped like the vanes on pinnacles.

Flag Lieutenant (*A*). An admiral's aide-de-camp.

Flag-officer. Either an admiral, vice-admiral, rear-admiral, or commodore. These officers alone are privileged to carry a flag denoting rank. Admirals carry their flag at the main, vice-admirals at the fore, and rear-admirals at the mizen. (*See* ADMIRAL.)

Flag-ship. A ship carrying a flag officer. (*See* ADMIRAL.)

Flag Signals (on railroads).
"White is all right; Red is all wrong:
Green is go cautiously bowling along."

Flag's Down (*The*). Indicative of distress. When the face is pale the "flag is down." Alluding to the ancient custom of taking down the flag of theatres during Lent, when the theatres were closed.

"'Tis Lent in your cheeks, the flag's down."—*Dodsley's Old Plays* (vol. v. p. 314, article, "Mad World.")

Flag of Distress. A card at one's window announcing "lodgings" or "board and lodgings." The allusion is evident. A flag reversed, hoisted with the union downwards.

Flagel'lants. A sect of enthusiasts in the middle of the thirteenth century, who went in procession about the streets inflicting on themselves daily flagellations, in order to merit thereby the favour of God. They were put down soon after their appearance, but revived in the fourteenth century. Also called "Brothers of the Cross."

Flam. Flattery for an object; blarney; humbug. (Irish, *flim*, Anglo-Saxon, *flæm*, flight.)

"They told me what a fine thing it was to be an Englishman, and about liberty and property . . . I find it was a flam."—*Godwin: Caleb Williams*, vol. ii. chap. v. p. 57.

Flamberge or **Floberge.** The sword which Maugis took from Anthénor, the Saracen admiral, when he came to attack the castle of Oriande la Feé. It was made by Weyland, the Vulcan of the Northern Olympus. (*Romance of Maugis d'Aygremont et de Vivian son Frère*.)

"Mais si une fois je luy fais essayer ceste-cy plus tranchante que 'Joyeuse, Durandel, Hauteclaire, ou Flamberge,' je le fendray jusques à l'estomach."—*Pierre de l'Arivey: Le Jaloux*, v. 6.

Flamboyant Architecture. A florid style which prevailed in France in the 15th and 16th centuries. So called from its flame-like tracery.

"The great tower [of Antwerp cathedral] . . . most florid and flamboyant . . . is one of the few rivals of the peerless steeple of Strasbourg."—*James: Sketches* (Belgium), p. 394.

Flame. A sweetheart. "An old flame," a quondam sweetheart. In Latin, *flamma* is used for *love*, and so is *feu* in French. *Ardeo*, to burn like fire, is also applied to the passion of love; hence, Virgil (*Ecl.* ii. 4), "*Corydon* *ardebat Alexin ;* " and Horace (Epoch xiii. 9), *"Arsit Anacreon Bathyllo."*

Flaming. Superb, captivating, attractive. The French *flambant.* This word was originally applied to those persons who dressed themselves in rich dresses " flaming " with gold and silver thread. We now speak of a " flaming advertisement," etc.

> " Le velour, trop commun en France,
>   Sous toy reprend son vieil honneur,
> Tellement que ta remontrance
> Nous a fait voir la différence
>   Du valet et de son Seigneur,
> Et du muguet chargé de soye
> Qui à tes princes s'esgaloit,
> Et riche en draps de soye, alloit
> Faisant flamber toute la voye."
>   *Ronsard : Au Roy Henri II.* (1546.)

Flaming Swords. Swords with a wavy or *flamboyant* edge, generally used for state purposes. The Dukes of Burgundy carried swords of this sort, and they were worn in our country till the accession of William III.

Flamin'ian Way. The great northern road of ancient Italy, constructed by C. Flamin'ius, and beginning at the Flaminian gate of Rome, and leading to Ariminium (Rimini).

Flanders (*Moll*). The chief character of De Foe's novel of the same name. She runs through the whole career of female profligacy, then turns religious.

Flanders' Babies. The wooden jointed dolls common in the early part of the nineteenth century, and now almost entirely superseded by " wax dolls."

Flanders' Mare (*The*). So Henry VIII. called Anne of Cleves. She died at Chelsea in 1557.

Flaneur (French). A lounger, gossiper. From *flaner*, to saunter about.

Flap-dragons. Small combustible bodies blazing at one end and floating in a glass of liquor. The liquor was stirred about with a candle-end to promote combustion. A skilful toper would swallow them blazing, as we swallow the blazing raisins of snap-dragons.

> " He drinks off candles' ends for flap-dragons."
> —*Shakespeare : 2 Henry IV.*, ii. 4.

Flare-up. A sudden outburst of anger ; a gas-jet or other ignitible body flares up when lighted with a sudden blaze.

Flare-up (*A*). A rumpus or row. Also a banquet or jovial treat. The first meaning is simply the substantive of the verb. The second meaning refers to dazzle and " splendour " displayed.

Flash. *A mere flash in the pan.* All sound and fury, signifying nothing ; like the attempt to discharge a gun that ends with a flash in the lock-pan, the gun itself " hanging fire."

Flash Men and **Flash Notes.** Between Buxton, Leek, and Macclesfield is a wild country called the *Flash*, from a chapel of that name. Here used to live a set of pedlars, who hawked about buttons, ribbons, and other articles made at Leek, together with handkerchiefs and small wares from Manchester. They were known on the road as Flash-men, and frequented fairs and farmhouses. They paid, at first, ready-money ; but when they had established a credit, paid in promissory notes, which were rarely honoured. They were ultimately put down by the magistracy.

Flat. One who is not sharp ; a suite of rooms on one floor.

> " Oh, Messrs. . . . what flats you are !"—*The Times.*
> " He said he was going to have a flat to let on the top floor." —*Howells : Hazards of New Fortunes.* vol. i. part i. p. 123.

Flat as a flounder. I knocked him down flat as a flounder. A flounder is one of the flat-fish.

Flat as a pancake. Quite flat. A pancake is a thin flat cake, fried in a pan.

Flat-fish. *He is a regular flat-fish.* A dull, stupid fellow, not up to anything. The play is upon *flat* (stupid), and such fish as plaice, dabs, and soles.

Flat Milk. Skimmed milk, that is, milk " fletted " (Anglo - Saxon, *flet*, cream ; Latin, *flos lactis.*)

Flat Race (*A*). A race on the flat or level ground without obstacles.

Flat Simplicity. " *The flat simplicity of that reply was admirable.*" (*Colley Cibber : The Crooked Husband,* i. 1.)

Flatterer. Vitellius, the Roman synonym of flatterer. (*Tacitus, Ann.* vi. 32.)

Flatterers. *When flatterers meet, the devil goes to dinner.* Flattery is so pernicious, so fills the heart with pride and conceit, so perverts the judgment and disturbs the balance of the mind, that Satan himself could do no greater mischief. He may go to dinner and leave the leaven of wickedness to operate its own mischief.

> " Portens, there is a proverb thou shouldst read :
> ' When flatterers meet, the devil goes to dinner.'"
>   *Peter Pindar : Nil Admirari.*

Flay a Fox (*To*). To vomit.

> " At the time of the paroxysm he used to flay a fox by way of antidote."—*Rabelais : Pantagruel,* iv. 44.

Flea. When the Princess Badoura was placed on Prince Camaral'zaman's bed, in order to compare their claims to beauty, the fairy Maimounë changed herself into a flea, and bit the prince on the neck in order to awake him. Next, the genius Danhasch changed himself into a flea and bit the princess on the lip, that she might open her eyes and see the prince. (*Arabian Nights ; Camaralzaman and Badoura.*)

Flea *as a parasite.*

" Hobbes clearly proves that every creature
Lives in a state of war by nature ;
So naturalists observe a flea
Has smaller fleas that on him prey,
And these have smaller still to bite 'em,
And so proceed *ad infinitum.*"
Swift : Poetry ; a Rhapsody.

Sent off with a flea in his ear. Peremptorily. A dog which has a flea in the ear is very restless, and runs off in terror and distress. In French : *Mettre à quelqu'un puce à l'oreille.* Probably our change of word implies a pun.

Flea-bite. *It is a mere flea-bite.* A thing of no moment. Thus, a merchant who has suffered loss by speculation or failure might say that the loss is a mere flea-bite to him. A soldier might call a wound a mere flea-bite. A passing inconvenience which annoys but leaves no permanent injury. Mr. Disraeli spoke of the national debt as a mere flea-bite.

Flea's Jump. Aristoph'anēs, in the *Clouds*, says that Socratēs and Chæ'-rephon tried to measure how many times its own length a flea jumped. They took in wax the size of a flea's foot ; then, on the principle of *ex pede Herculem*, calculated the length of its body. Having found this, and measured the distance of the flea's jump from the hand of Socrates to Chærephon, the knotty problem was resolved by simple multiplication.

Fle'ance (2 syl.). Son of Banquo. (*Shakespeare : Macbeth.*)

Flèche. *Faire flèche de tout bois.* To turn every event into a cause of censure. To make whatever wood falls in your path an arrow to discharge at your adversary.

Flecknoe (*Richard*). An Irish priest, who printed a host of poems, letters, and travels. As a poet, his name, like the names of *Mævius* and *Bavius* among the Romans, is proverbial for vileness. Dryden says he—

" Reigned without dispute
Through all the realms of nonsense absolute."
Dryden : MacFlecknoe.

Fledgeby (2 syl.). An over-reaching, cowardly sneak, who conceals his dirty bill-broking under the trade name of Pubsey & Co. He is soundly thrashed by Alfred Lammle, and quietly pockets the affront. (*Dickens : Mutual Friend.*)

Flee the Falcon (*To*). To let fly the small cannon.

" ' I'll flee the falcon' (so the small cannon was called) ' I'll flee the falcon . . . my certie, she'll ruffle their feathers for them'" [*i.e.* the insurgents].—*Sir W. Scott : Old Mortality, chap. xxv.*

Fleeced (1 syl.). Cheated of one's money ; sheared like a sheep.

Fleet Book Evidence. No evidence at all. The books of the Old Fleet prison are not admissible as evidence to prove a marriage. (*Wharton : Law Dictionary.*)

Fleet Marriages. Clandestine marriages, at one time performed without banns or licence by needy chaplains, in Fleet Prison, London. As many as thirty marriages a day were sometimes celebrated in this disgraceful manner ; and Malcolm tells us that 2,954 were registered in the four months ending with February 12th, 1705. Suppressed by the Marriage Act in 1754. (See *Chaplain of the Fleet,* by Besant and Rice.)

Fleet Street (London). For 200 years after the Conquest London was watered on the west by " the river of Wells," afterwards called " Fleet dyke, because (Stowe says) it runneth past the Fleete." In the middle of the city and falling into the Thames was Wellbrooke ; on the east side, Langbourne ; and in the western suburbs, Oldbourne. Along the Fleete and Oldbourne " ships " used to ply with merchandise. These four, together with the Roding, the Lea, the Ravensbourne, and the Wandle, now serve as sewers to the great metropolis.

Fleet of the Desert. A caravan.

Flemish Account. A sum less than that expected. In Antwerp accounts were kept in *livres, sols,* and *pence ;* but the *livre* or pound was only 12s. In *Notes and Queries* we have an example of a Flemish account, where £373 Flemish becomes £213 2s. 10d. English.

Flemish School. A school of painting established by the brothers Van Eyck, in the fifteenth century. The chief *early* masters were Memling, Weyden, Matsys, Mabus, and Moro. Of the *second* period, Rubens and Vandyck, Snyders, Jordaens, Gaspar de Crayer, and the younger Teniers.

Flesh and Blood. Human nature; as "Flesh and blood cannot stand it."

Flesh-pots. *Sighing for the flesh-pots of Egypt.* Hankering for good things no longer at your command. The children of Israel said they wished they had died "when they sat by the flesh-pots of Egypt" (Exodus xvi. 3)—*i.e.* when they sat watching the boilers which contained the meat they were to have for dinner. The expression also means abundance of appetising food.

Fleshed. *He fleshed his sword.* Used it for the first time. *Men fleshed in cruelty—i.e.* initiated or used to it. A sportsman's expression. When a sportsman wishes to encourage a young dog or hawk, he will allow it to have the first game it catches for its own eating. This "flesh" is the first it has tasted, and fleshing its tooth thus gives the creature a craving for similar food. Hence, also, to eat with avidity.

> "The wild dog
> Shall flesh his tooth on every innocent."
> *Shakespeare:* 2 *Henry IV.,* iv. 5.

Fleshly School (*The*). A class of "realistic" British poets, such as Swinburne, Rossetti, Morris, etc. So called by Thomas Maitland [*R. Buchanan*] in the *Contemporary Review.*

Fle'ta. An excellent treatise on the common law of England, written in the fourteenth century by an unknown writer while a prisoner in the Fleet.

Fleur-de-Luce. A corruption of Fleur-de-Lis. (*See* FLAG.) In Italian the white iris is called *fiordilisa.* Made thus.

> "They may give the dozen white luces in their coat."—*Shakespeare: Merry Wives,* i. 1.

Fleurs-de-Lys. In the reign of Louis VII. (1137-1180) the national standard was thickly charged with flowers. In 1365 the number was reduced by Charles VI. to *three* (the mystical church number). Guillim, in his *Display of Heraldrie,* 1611, says the device is "Three toads erect, saltant;" in allusion to which Nostrada'mus, in the sixteenth century, calls Frenchmen *crapauds* (toads). Recently it has been thought that the device is really a "bee flying," because certain ornaments resembling bees were found in the tomb of Childeric, father of Clovis, when it was opened in 1653. These bees are now generally believed to be the fleurons of horse-trappings, and quite independent of the emblem.

The fleur-de-lys or lily-flower was chosen by Flavio Gio'ja to mark the north point of the compass, out of compliment to the King of Naples, who was of French descent (1302).

Flibbertigibbet. One of the five fiends that possessed "poor Tom." Shakespeare got it from Bishop Harsnet's account of the Spanish invasion, where we are told of forty fiends which the Jesuits cast out, and among the number was Fliberdigibet. Shakespeare says he "is the fiend of mopping and mowing, who possesses chambermaids and waiting women" (*King Lear,* iv. 2). And, again, that he "begins at curfew and walks till the first cock," giving men pins and needles, squint eyes, hare-lips, and so on. (*Shakespeare: Lear,* iii. 4.)

Flic (French). A policeman or *sergeant de ville.* "*Une allusion à l'épée des sergents de ville, ou plutôt aux flèches des archers primitifs*" (Raille). Hence "flic-flacs," thumps and thwacks.

Flick. To strike with a quick jerk. To "flick a whip in one's face" is to strike the face with the lash and draw the whip suddenly back again. (Anglo-Saxon, *fliccerian;* Scotch, *flicker;* Danish, *flikkeren,* to twinkle, etc.)

Flies. (*See* FLY.)

Fling.
I must have a fling at . . . Throw a stone at something. To attack with words, especially sarcastically. To make a haphazard venture. Allusion is to hurling stones from slings.

To have his fling. To live on the loose for a time. To fling about his time and money like "ducks and drakes."

> "If he is young, he desires to have . . . . his 'fling' before he is compelled to settle down."—*Nineteenth Century* (February, 1892, p. 208).

Fling Herself at my Head (*To*). To make desperate love to a man; to angle obviously to catch a certain individual for a husband.

> "'Coxcomb?' said Lance; 'why, 'twas but last night the whole family saw her . . . . fling herself at my head."—*Sir W. Scott: Peveril of the Peak,* chap. vii.

Flins [*a stone*]. An idol of the ancient Vandals settled in Lusace. It was a huge stone, draped, wearing a lion's skin over its shoulders, and designed to represent death. Mr. Lower says that the town of Flint in North Wales is named in honour of this stone deity, and gives Alwin Flint in Suffolk as another example. (*Pat. Brit.*)

The Welsh call Flint *Flint Teg-cingi* (Flin's beautiful band or girdle).

Flint. *To skin a flint.* To act meanly, and exact the uttermost farthing.

Flint Im'plements. Arrow-heads, axe-heads, lance-heads, and knives, made of granite, jade, serpentine, jasper, basalt, and other hard stones. The first were discovered on the banks of the Somme, near Amiens and Abbeville, but others have been discovered in Belgium, Germany, Italy, etc. They were the rude instruments of men before the use of metal was known.

Flint Jack. Edward Simpson, an occasional servant of Dr. Young, of Whitby. So called because he used to tramp the kingdom vending spurious fossils, flint arrow-heads, stone celts, and other imitation antiquities. Professor Tennant charged him with forging these wares, and in 1867 he was sent to prison for theft.

Flipper. *Tip us your flipper.* Give me your hand. A flipper is the paddle of a turtle.

Flirt. A coquette. The word is from the verb flirt, as, "to flirt a fan." The fan being used for coquetting, those who coquetted were called fan-flirts. Lady Frances Shirley, the favourite of Lord Chesterfield, introduced the word. Flirt is allied to *flutter, flit, jerk*, etc.

Flittermouse. A bat. South calls the bat a *flinder-mouse.* (German, *fledermaus.*)

Flo (Old French). A crowd. (Latin, *fluctus.*)

> "Puis lor tramist par buiz ouverz
> Grand flo d'Anglois de fer couverz."
> *Guillaume Guiart,* verse 1692.

Floated (Stock Exchange term). Brought out (said of a loan or company), as the Turkish '69 Loan was floated by the Cohens. The French 6 per cent. was floated by the Morgans.

Floaters (Stock Exchange term). Exchequer bills and other unfunded stock. (*See* STOCK EXCHANGE SLANG.)

Floating Academy (*The*). The hulks.

Flogging the Dead Horse. Trying to revive an interest in a subject out of date. Bright said that Earl Russell's "Reform Bill" was a "dead horse," and every attempt to create any enthusiasm in its favour was like "flogging the dead horse."

Flogged by Deputy. When Henri IV. of France abjured Protestantism and was received into the Catholic Church, in 1595, two ambassadors were sent to Rome who knelt in the portico of St. Peter, and sang the *Miserere.* At each verse a blow with a switch was given on their shoulders.

∴ Strange as this may seem, yet numerous examples occur in the Scriptures ; thus, for David's sin thousands of his subjects were "flogged to death by deputy ;" and what else is meant by the words "by his stripes we are healed" ?

Flood. The almost universal tradition of the East respecting this catastrophe is that the waters were boiling hot. (*See* the *Talmud,* the *Targums,* the *Koran,* etc.)

Floor. *I floored him.* Knocked him down on the floor ; hence, to overcome, beat or surpass. Thus, we say at the university, "I floored that paper," *i.e.* answered every question on it. "I floored that problem"—did it perfectly, or made myself master of it.

Floorer. *That was a floorer.* That blow knocked the man down on the floor. In the university we say, "That paper or question was a floorer ;" meaning it was too hard to be mastered. (*See above.*)

Flora. Flowers ; all the vegetable productions of a country or of a geological period, as the flora of England, the flora of the coal period. Flora was the Roman goddess of flowers.

> "Another Flora there, of bolder hues,
> And richer sweets beyond our garden's pride."
> *Thomson: Summer.*

The animals of a period or country are called the Fauna ; hence, the phrase the Flora and the Fauna of . . . . signifies all its vegetable and animal productions.

Metropolis of Flora. Aranjuez, in Spain, is so called, from its many beautiful gardens.

Flora's Dial. A dial formed by flowers which open or close at stated hours.

I. Dial of flowers which open—

(*a*) The first twelve hours.

A.M. OPENS.
1. (*Scandinavian Sowthistle closes.*)
2. Yellow Goat's-beard.
3. Common Ox-tongue.
4. Hawkweed ; Late-flowering Dandelion ; and Wild Succory.
5. White Water-lily ; Naked-stalked Poppy ; and Smooth Sowthistle.
6. Shrubby Hawkweed and Spotted Cat's-ears.
7. White Water-lily ; Garden Lettuce ; and African Marigold.
8. Scarlet Pimpernel ; Mouse-ear Hawkweed ; and Proliferous Pink.
9. Field Marigold.
10. Red Sandwort.
11. Star of Bethlehem.
Noon. Ice Plant.

(*b*) **The second twelve hours.**

P.M. OPENS.
1. Common Purslane.
2. (*Purple Sandwort closes.*)
3. (*Dandelion closes.*)
4. (*White Spiderwort closes.*)
5. Julap.
6. Dark Crane's-bill.
7. (*Naked-stalked Poppy closes.*)
8. (*Orange Day-lily closes.*)
9. Cactus Opuntia.
10. Purple Bindweed.
11. Night-blooming Catch-fly.
Midnight. (*Late-flowering Dandelion closes.*)

II. Dial of closing flowers—

(*a*) **The first twelve hours.**

A.M. CLOSES.
1. Scandinavian Sowthistle.
2. (*Yellow Goat's-beard opens.*)
3. (*Common Oxtongue opens*).
4. (*Wild Succory opens.*)
5. (*Several Sowthistles open.*)
6. (*Spotted Cat's-ear opens.*)
7. Night-flowering Catch-fly.
8. Evening Primrose.
9. Purple Bindweed.
10. Yellow Goat's-beard.
11. Bethlehem Star (*la dame d'onze heures*).
Noon. Field Sowthistle.

(*b*) **The second twelve hours.**

P.M. CLOSES.
1. Red or Proliferous Pink.
2. Purple Sandwort.
3. Dandelion or Field Marigold.
4. White Spadewort and Field Bindwort.
5. Common Cat's-ears.
6. White Water-lily.
7. Naked-stalked Poppy.
8. Orange Day-lily and Wild Succory.
9. Convolvulus Linnæus and Chickweed.
10. Common Nipple-wort.
11. Smooth Sowthistle.
Midnight. Creeping Mallow and Late Dandelion.

Florence (*The German*). Dresden.

Florentine Diamond (*The*). The fourth in size of cut diamonds. It weighs 139½ carats, belonged to Charles, Duke of Burgundy; was picked up by a peasant and sold for half-a-crown.

Floren'tius. A knight who bound himself to marry a "foul and ugly witch," if she would teach him the solution of a riddle on which his life depended. (*Gower: Confessio Amantis.*)

Flor'ian (*St.*). Patron saint of mercers,. being himself of the same craft.

Floria'ni. A sect of heretics of the second century who maintained that God is the author of evil, and taught the Gnostic doctrine of two principles. Floria'nus was their founder.

Florid Architecture. The latter division of the perpendicular style, often called the Tudor, remarkable for its florid character or profusion of ornament.

Florida (U. S. America). In 1712 Ponce de Leon sailed from France to the West in search of "the Fountain of Youth." He first saw land on Easter Day, and on account of the richness and quantity of flowers, called the new possession "Florida."

Flor'imel [*honey-flower*]. A damsel of great beauty, but so timid that she feared the "smallest monstrous mouse that creeps on floor," and was abused by everyone. Her form was simulated by a witch out of wax, but the wax image melted, leaving nothing behind except the girdle that was round the waist. (*Spenser: Faërie Queene*, book iii. 4, 8; iv. 11, 12.)

"Florimel loved Mar'inel, but Proteus cast her into a dungeon, from which, being released by the order of Neptune, she married the man of her choice."—*Spenser: Faërie Queene*, book iv.

"St. Amand had long since in bitterness repented of a transient infatuation, had long since distinguished the true Florimel from the false."
—*Sir E. B. Lytton: Pilgrims of the Rhine*, iii.

Florimel's Girdle gave to those who could wear it "the virtue of chaste love and wifehood true;" but if any woman not chaste and faithful put it on, it "loosed or tore asunder." It was once the cestus of Venus, made by her husband Vulcan; but when she wantoned with Mars it fell off, and was left on the "Acida'lian mount." (*Spenser: Faërie Queene*, book iv. 11, 12.)

Florin. An English coin representing 2s., or the tenth of a sovereign, issued in 1849. Camden informs us that Edward III. issued gold florins worth 6s., in 1337. The word is generally supposed to be derived from Florence; but as it had a lily on one side, probably it is connected with the Latin *flos*, a flower. (*See* GRACELESS FLORIN.)

Florisan'do. One of the knights in the Spanish version of *Am'adis of Gaul*, whose exploits and adventures are recounted in the 6th and following books. This part of the romance was added by Paez de Ribe'ra.

Flor'isel of Nice'a. A knight whose exploits and adventures form a supplemental part of the Spanish version of *Am'adis of Gaul*. This part was added by Felicia'no de Silva.

Flor'ismart. One of Charlemagne's paladins, and the bosom friend of Roland.

Flor'izel. Prince of Bohemia, in love with Per'dita. (*Shakespeare: Winter's Tale.*)

Florizel. George the Fourth, when prince, corresponded under this name with Mrs. Robinson, actress and poet, generally known as Perdita, that being the character in which she first attracted the prince's attention.

Prince Florizel, in Lord Beaconsfield's novel of *Endymion* (1880), is meant for Napoleon III.

Flotsam and Jetson. Waifs found in the sea or on the shore. "Flotsam," goods found *floating* on the sea after a a wreck. "Jetson," or Jetsam, things thrown out of a ship to lighten it. (Anglo-Saxon, *flotan*, to float ; French, *jeter*, to throw out.) (*See* LIGAN.)

Flower Games. Fêtes held at Toulouse, Barcelōna, Treviso, and other places, where the prizes given consisted of flowers.

Flower Sermon. A sermon preached on Whit-Monday in St. Catherine Cree, when all the congregation wear flowers.

Flower sermons are now (1894) preached very generally once a year, especially in country churches. Every person is supposed to bring a bunch of flowers to the altar, and the flowers next day are sent to some hospital.

Flower of Chivalry. A name given to several *cavaliers : e.g.*

William Douglas, Lord of Liddesdale, in the fourteenth century.

Sir Philip Sidney (1554-1586).

Chevalier de Bayard (*le chevalier sans peur et sans reproche*) (1476-1524).

Flower of Kings. Arthur is so called by John of Exeter. (Sixth century.)

Flower of Paradiso. The Ipomœa or Camala'ta, called by Sir W. Jones "Love's creeper." It symbolises that mythological plant which fulfils all desire.

Flower of the Lev'ant. Zante, noted for its beauty and fertility. "Zanté ! Zanté, flos di Levanti."

Flowers and Trees.

(1) Dedicated to heathen gods :

The Cornel cherry-tree to Apollo	
„ Cypress	„ Pluto.
„ Dittany	„ The Moon.
„ Laurel	„ Apollo.
„ Lily	„ Juno.
„ Maiden's-hair	„ Pluto.
„ Myrtle	„ Venus.
„ Narcissus	„ Cerés.
„ Oak	„ Jupiter.
„ Olive	„ Minerva.
„ Poppy	„ Cerés.
„ Vine	„ Bacchus

(2) Dedicated to saints ;

Canterbury Bells	to St. Augustine of England.
Crocus	„ St. Valentine.
Crown Imperial	„ Edward the Confessor.
Daisy	„ St. Margaret.
Herb Christophe	„ St. Christopher.
Lady's-smock	„ The Virgin Mary.
Rose	„ Mary Magdalene.
St. John's-wort	„ St. John.
St. Barnaby's Thistle	„ St. Barnabas.

(3) National emblems :

Leek	emblem of Wales.
Lily (*Fleur-de-lys*)	„ France.
„ (*Giglio blanco*)	„ Florence.
„ white	„ the Ghibelline badge.
„ red	„ badge of the Guelphs.
Linden	„ Prussia.
Mignonette	„ Saxony.
Pomegranate	„ Spain.
Rose	„ England.
„ red, Lancastrians ; white, Yorkists.	
Shamrock	emblem of Ireland.
Thistle	„ Scotland.
Violet	„ Athens and Napoleon
Sugar Maple	„ Canada.

(4) Symbols :

Box	is a symbol of the resurrection.
Cedars	„ the faithful.
Corn-ears	„ the Holy Communion.
Dates	„ the faithful.
Grapes	„ this is my blood.
Holly	„ the resurrection.
Ivy	„ the resurrection.
Lily	„ purity
Olive	„ peace.
Orange-blossom	„ virginity.
Palm	„ victory.
Rose	„ incorruption.
Vine	„ Christ our Life.
Yew	„ death.

N.B.—The laurel, oak, olive, myrtle, rosemary, cypress, and amaranth are all funereal plants.

Flowers and Trees with Christian Traditions.

The *Aspen* leaf is said to tremble because the cross was made of Aspenwood.

Ah ! tremble, tremble, Aspen-tree,
We need not ask thee why thou shakest,
For if, as holy legend saith,
On thee the Saviour bled to death,
No wonder, Aspen, that thou quakest ;
And, till in judgment all assemble,
Thy leaves accursed shall wail and tremble.
                                        E. C. B.

The *dwarf elder* is called in Wales "the plant of the Blood of Man."

The *wallflower* is known in Palestine as the "Blood-drops of Christ."

The following are also said to owe their stained blossoms to the blood which trickled from the cross :—

The *red anemone ;* the *arum ;* the *purple orchis ;* the crimson-spotted leaves of the *roodselken* (a French tradition) ; the spotted *persicaria*, snakeweed. (*See* CHRISTIAN TRADITIONS.)

Flowers at Funerals. The Greeks crowned the dead body with flowers, and placed flowers on the tomb also. The Romans decked the funeral couch with leaves and flowers, and spread flowers, wreaths, and fillets on the tomb of friends. When Sulla was buried as many as 2,000 wreaths were sent in his honour. Most of our funeral customs are derived from the Romans ; as dressing in black, walking in procession, carrying insignia on the bier, raising a mound over the grave, called *tumulus*, whence our tomb.

Flowered Robes. In ancient Greece to say "a woman wore flowered robes" was to imply that she was a *fille publique*. Solon made it a law that virtuous women should appear in simple and modest apparel, but that harlots should always dress in flashy or flowered robes.

"As fugitive slaves are known by their stigmata, so flowered garments indicate one of the demi-monde [μοιχάλιδα]."—*Clemens of Alexandria.*

Flowing Philosophers. The followers of Heraclítos, referred to by Plato as τοὺς ῥέοντας (*Theœtetus*, 181 A). Heraclitos denied the permanency of everything in nature except change. Tennyson has a poem entitled "Οι ῥέοντες.

Fluellen. A Welsh captain and great pedant, who, amongst other learned quiddities, attempted to draw a parallel between Henry V. and Alexander the Great; but when he had said that one was born at Monmouth and the other at Macedon, both beginning with the same letter, and that there was a river in both cities, he had exhausted his best parallelisms. (*Henry V.*, iv. 7.)

"His parallel is, in all essential circumstances, as incorrect as that which Fluellen drew between Macedon and Monmouth."—*Lord Macaulay.*

Fluke. Hap-hazard. In billiards it means playing for one thing and getting another. Hence an advantage gained by luck more than by skill or judgment. (German, *glück*, chance, our *luck*.)

"We seem to have discovered, as it were by a fluke, a most excellent rule for all future Cabinet arrangements."—*The Times.*

Flummery. Flattering nonsense, palaver. In Wales it is a food made of oatmeal steeped in water and kept till it has become sour. In Cheshire and Lancashire it is the prepared skin of oatmeal mixed with honey, ale, or milk; pap; blanc-mange. (Welsh, *llymry*, wash-brew, from *llym*, sour or sharp.)

"You came ... with your red coats and flashing buttons ... and her head got turned with your flummery."—*Simms: The Partizans*, chap. xxix.

Flummux (*To*). To bamboozle; to deceive; to be in a quandary. "I am regularly flummuxed"—*i.e.* perplexed. The first syllable is probably a variant of *flam*, humbug, deception, and the word seems to be compounded on the model of the word "perplex."

"For the privates, the sergeants, and 'spectors, She flummuxed them all to a coon."
Sims: *Dagonet Ballads* (Moll Jarvis).

Flummuxed. The mark ☉ set on a street, gatepost, house, etc., as a warning to fellow-vagabonds not to go near, for fear of being given in charge.

Flunkey. A livery servant. (Old French, *flanquier*, a henchman.)

Flur. The bride of Cas'sivelaun, "for whose love the Roman Cæsar first invaded Britain." (*Tennyson: Enid.*)

Flush (*A*), in cards, means a whole hand of one suit, as a "flush of clubs," a "flush of hearts," etc. (*See below.*)

Flush of Money. Full of money. Similarly *A flush of water* means a sudden and full flow of water. (Latin, *flux-us.*)

"Strut was not very flush in [the] ready."—*Dr Arbuthnot.*

Flute. *The Magic Flute*, an opera by Mozart (*Die Zauberflöte*). The "flute" was bestowed by the powers of darkness, and had the power of inspiring love. Unless purified the love was only lust, but, being purified by the Powers of Light, it subserved the holiest purposes. Tamino and Pamina are guided by it through all worldly dangers to the knowledge of Divine Truth.

Flutter. A very weak specimen of a fop, in the *Belle's Stratagem*, by Mrs. Cowley.

Flutter the Dovecotes (*To*). To disturb the equanimity of a society. The phrase occurs in *Coriolanus*.

"The important movement in favour of a general school of law fluttered the dovecotes of the Inns of Court."—*Nineteenth Century* (Nov., 1892, p. 779).

Fly (plural *flys*). A hackney coach, a cab. A contraction of *Fly-by-night*, as sedan chairs on wheels used to be called in the regency. These "Fly-by-nights," patronised greatly by George, Prince of Wales, and his boon companions, during their wild night pranks at Brighton, were invented 1809 by John Butcher, a carpenter of Jew Street.

"In the morning we took a fly, an English term for an exceedingly sluggish vehicle, and drove up to the Minister's."—*Hawthorne: Our Old House* (Pilgrimage to Old Boston, p. 171).

Fly (plural *flies*). An insect. All flies shall perish except one, and that is the bee-fly. (*Koran.*)

A Fly has three eyes and two compound eyes, each of which has 4,000 facets.

The god of flies. In the temple of Actium the Greeks used to sacrifice annually an ox to the god of flies. Pliny tells us that at Rome sacrifice was offered to flies in the temple of Hercules Victor. The Syrians undoubtedly offered sacrifice to the same tiny tormentors. It is said that no fly was ever seen in Solomon's temple.

ACHOR, god of the Cyrenians, to whom, according to Pliny, they offered sacrifice.

APOMYIOS, a surname given by the Cyrenians to Zeus, for delivering Herakles [Hercules] from flies during sacrifice. Sacrifices were yearly offered to Zeus Apomyios (Greek, *apo-myia*, from flies.)

BELZEBUB, or BEELZEBUTH (Prince of Flies), was one of the principal Syrian gods, to whom sacrifice was offered on all *ferialia*.

BUCLOPUS, in Roman mythology. (*Rhod.* xxii. 3.)

MYAGROS (the fly-chaser), one of the deities of the Arcadians and Eleans. (*Pliny*, x. 28.) (Greek, *myia*, a fly ; *agra*, taken in hunting or chasing.)

Flies in amber. (*See under* AMBER.)

To crush a fly on a wheel. Making a mountain of a mole-hill. Taking a wheel used for torturing criminals and heretics for killing a fly, which one might destroy with a flapper.

Fly on the coach-wheel (*A*). One who fancies himself of mighty importance, but who is in reality of none at all. The allusion is to the fable of a fly sitting on a chariot-wheel and saying, "See what a dust we make ! "

Not a fly with him. Domitian, the Roman emperor, was fond of catching flies, and one of his slaves, being asked if the emperor was alone, wittily replied, "Not a fly with him."

To rise to the fly. To be taken in by a hoax, as a fish rises to a false fly and is caught.

"He [the professor] rose to the fly with a charming simplicity."—*Grant Allen : The Mysterious Occurrence in Piccadilly*, part ii.

Fly-boy. The boy in a printing-office who lifts the printed sheets off the press. He is called the fly-boy because he catches the sheets as they fly from the tympan (*q.v.*) immediately the frisket (*q.v.*) is opened. This is now generally performed by the pressmen.

Fly a Kite (*To*). To send a begging letter to persons of a charitable reputation, or in easy circumstances, to solicit pecuniary aid, urging poverty, losses, or sickness as an excuse. (*See* KITE-FLYING.)

Fly-by-night (*A*). One who defrauds his creditors by decamping at night-time. (*See* FLY.)

Fly in One's Face (*To*). To get into a passion with a person ; to insult ; as a hawk, when irritated, flies in the face of its master.

Fly in the Face of Danger (*To*). To run in a foolhardy manner into danger, as a hen flies in the face of a dog or cat.

Fly in the Face of Providence (*To*). To act rashly, and throw away good opportunities ; to court danger.

Fly Open (*To*). To open suddenly, as, "the doors flew open," "*les portes

s'ouvrirent," as they do sometimes by the force of the wind.

Fly Out at (*To*). To burst or break into a passion. The Latin, *involo in . . .*

"Poor choleric Sir Brian would fly out at his coachman, his butler, or his gamekeeper, and use language . . . which . . . from any other master, would have brought about a prompt resignation."—*Good Words*, 1887.

Flying Colours (*To come off with*). In triumph ; with the flags unfurled and flying.

Flying Dutchman. A spectral ship, seen in stormy weather off the Cape of Good Hope, and considered ominous of ill-luck. Sir Walter Scott says she was originally a vessel laden with precious metal, but a horrible murder having been committed on board, the plague broke out among the crew, and no port would allow the vessel to enter. The ill-fated ship still wanders about like a ghost, doomed to be sea-tossed, but never more to enjoy rest. Captain Marryat has a novel called *The Phantom Ship*.

Flying without Wings (*No*). Nothing can be done without the proper means.

"Sine pennis vola're haud facile est."—*Plautus*.

Flyman's Plot (*The*). In theatrical language, means a list of all the articles required by the flyman in the play produced. The flyman is the scene-shifter, or the "man in the flies."

Fog-eater. A white bow in the clouds during foggy weather is so called. Such a bow was seen in England during January, 1888. A week preceding, the weather had been clear, sunshiny, and genial, then followed several days of thick fog, during which the white bow appeared. The bow was followed by several days of brilliant mild weather.

Fogie or **Fogey.** *An old fogey.* Properly an old military pensioner. This term is derived from the old pensioners of Edinburgh Castle, whose chief occupation was to fire the guns, or assist in quelling street riots. (Allied to *fogat*, *phogot*, *voget*, *foged*, *fogde*, etc.)

"What has the world come to [said Thackeray] . . when two broken-nosed old fogies like you and me sit talking about love to each other."—*Trollope : W. M. Thackeray*, chap. i. p. 61.

Fo-hi or **Foë.** One of the chief deities of the Chinese. His mother, Moyë, was walking one day along a river bank, when she became suddenly encircled by a rainbow, and at the end of twelve years was the mother of a son. During gestation she dreamed that she was pregnant with a white elephant, and hence the honours paid to this beast. (*Asiatic Researches.*)

Foil. That which sets off something to advantage. The allusion is to the metallic leaf used by jewellers to set off precious stones. (French, *feuille;* Latin, *folium;* Greek, *phullon*, a leaf.)

"Hector, as a foil to set him off."   *Broome.*
" I'll be your foil, Laertes. In mine ignorance
Your skill shall, like a star i' the darkest night,
Stick fiery off indeed."
          Shakespeare: Hamlet, v. 2.

He foiled me. He outwitted me.

"If I be foiled, there is but one ashamed who never was gracious."—*Shakespeare: As You Like It,* i. 2.

To run a foil. To puzzle ; to lead astray. The track of game is called its *foil;* and an animal hunted will sometimes run back over the same foil in order to mislead its pursuers.

Folio. A book of the largest size, formed by folding the paper only once, so that each sheet makes two leaves. It is from the Italian, *un libro in foglio*, through the French, *in-folio.* Fol. is the contraction for folio.

Folio (so-and-so), in mercantile books, means page so-and-so, and sometimes the two pages which lie exposed at the same time, one containing the credit and the other the debit of one and the same account. So called because ledgers, etc., are made in folio. The paging is called the folio also. Printers call a page of MS. or printed matter a folio regardless of size.

Folio. In conveyances seventy-two words, and in Parliamentary proceedings ninety words, make a folio.

Folk. Latin, *vulg'* (the common people) ; German, *volk;* Dutch, *volch;* Saxon, *folc;* Danish, *folk. Folk* and *vulgar* are variants of the same word.

Folk. *Fairies,* also called " people," "neighbours," "wights." The Germans have their *kleine volk* (little folk), the Swiss their hill people and earth people.

"The little folk,
So happy and so gay, amuse themselves
Sometimes with singing . . .
Sometimes with dancing, when they jump and
   spring
Like the young skipping kids in the Alp-grass."
     Wyss : Idyll of Gertrude and Rosy.
" In the hinder end of harvest, at All-hallow e'en,
   When our good neighbours ride, if I read
   right,
Some buckled on beenwand, and some on a been."
     Montgomery : Flyting against Polwart.
" I crouche thee from the elves, and from wights."
     Chaucer : The Millere's Tale.

Folk-lore. Whatever pertains to a knowledge of the antiquities, superstitions, mythology, legends, customs, traditions, and proverbs of a people. A "folklorist" is one who is more or less acquainted with these matters.

Folk-mote [*a folk meeting*]. A word used in England before the Conquest for what we now call a county or even a parish meeting.

Follets. Goblins of the north of France, who live in the houses of simple rustics, and can be expelled neither by water nor exorcism. They can be heard but are never seen. In the singular number, " esprit follet."

Follow. *Follow your nose,* go straight on. *He followed his nose*—he went on and on without any discretion or thought of consequences.

He who follows truth too closely will have dirt kicked in his face. Be not too strict to pry into abuse, for "*odium veritas parit,*" " *Summum jus suprema est injuria.*"

Follower. A male sweetheart who follows the object of his affections. A word very common among servants. Mistresses say to female servants, " I allow no followers "—*i.e.* I do not allow men to come into my house to see you. Also a disciple, a partisan.

"The pretty neat servant-maids had their choice of desirable followers."—*E. C. Gaskell: Cranford,* chap. iii. p. 53.

Folly. *Father of Folly (Abu Jahl),* an aged chief, who led a hundred horse and seven hundred camels against Mahomet and fell at the battle of Bedr. His own people called him Father of Wisdom (*Abu'Lhoem*).

Folly. A fantastic or foolishly extravagant country seat, built for amusement or vainglory. (French, *folie.*)

"We have in' this country a word (namely Folly) which has a technical appropriation to the case of fantastic buildings."—*De Quincey : Essays on the Poets* (Keats, p. 90).

Fisher's Folly. A large and beautiful house in Bishopsgate, with pleasure-gardens, bowling-green, and hot-houses, built by Jasper Fisher, one of the six clerks of Chancery and a Justice of the Peace. Queen Elizabeth lodged there.

" Kirby's castle, and Fisher's folly,
Spinola's pleasure, and Megse's glory."
         Stowe: Surrey.

Fond. *A foolish, fond parent.* Here fond does not mean affectionate, but silly. Chaucer uses the word *fonne* for a simpleton, and the Scotch *fou* is to play the fool. Shakespeare has " fond desire," " fond love," " fond shekels of gold," "fond wretch," "fond mad-woman," etc. "Fondling" means an idiot, or one fond.

> "See how simple and how fond I am."
> *Shakespeare: Midsummer Night's Dream*, iii. 2.
> "Fonder than ignorance."
> *Shakespeare: Troilus and Cressida*, i. 1.

Fons et Origo (Latin). The primary cause. *Fax et focus*, the instigator, as Juno was the *fax et focus* of the Trojan war.

Font, in printing, sometimes called *Fount*, a complete set of type of any one size, with all the usual points and accents; a font consists of about 100,000 characters. The word is French, *fonte*, from *fondre* (to melt or cast). When a letter of a different type to the rest gets into a page it is called a "wrong font," and is signified in the margin by the two letters *w.f.* (*See* TYPE.)

Taken to the font. Baptised. The font is a vessel employed for baptism.

Fontara′bia. Now called Fuenter-rabia (in Latin, *Fons rap′idus*), near the Gulf of Gas′cony. Here, according to Maria′na and other Spanish historians, Charlemagne and all his chivalry fell by the sword of the Spanish Saracens. Mez′eray and the French writers say that, the rear of the king's army being cut to pieces, Charlemagne returned and revenged their death by a complete victory.

> "When Charlemagne with all his peerage fell
> By Fontarabia."
> *Milton: Paradise Lost*, book i. 587.

Food. Sir Walter Scott remarks that *live* cattle go by Saxon names, and *slain* meat by Norman-French, a standing evidence that the Normans were the lords who ate the meat, and the Saxons the serfs who tended the cattle. Examples:

Sheep Ox Calf Hog Pig (*Saxon*).
Mutton Beef Veal Bacon Pork (*Norman-French*).

Food of the gods. (*See* AMBROSIA, NECTAR.)

Food for Powder. Raw recruits levied in times of war.

Foods and Wines. Gastronomic curiosities.

> *Foods.*
> Sterlets from the Volga.
> Eels from the Tiber.
> Grouse from Scotland.
> Bustards from Sweden.
> Bears' feet from the Black Forest.
> Bison humps from America.
> Fillet of beef *à la Chateaubriand*.
> Ortolans *à la Lucullus*.
> *Wines.*
> Old Madeira with the soup.
> Château-Filhot '58 with the side dishes.
> Johannisberger and Pichon-Longueville with the *relevés*.
> Château-Lafitte '48 with the *entrées*.
> Sparkling Moselle with the roast.

Fool. In chess, the French call the "bishop" *fou*, and used to represent the piece in a fool's dress; hence, Regnier says, "*Les fous sont aux échecs les plus proches des Rois*" (14 *Sat.*). *Fou* is a corruption of the Eastern word *Fol* (an elephant), as Thomas Hyde remarks in his *Ludis Orientalibus* (i. 4), and on old boards the places occupied by our "bishops" were occupied by elephants.

A Tom Fool. A person who makes himself ridiculous. (*See* TOM.)

> "The ancient and noble family of Tom Fool."
> —*Quarterly Review.*

Fool [*a food*], as gooseberry fool, raspberry fool, means gooseberries or raspberries pressed. (French, *fouler*, to press.)

Fool Thinks. *As the fool thinks, so the bell clinks* (Latin, "*Quod valde voï′-ümus facile cre′dimus*"). A foolish person believes what he desires.

Fool in his Sleeve. *Every man hath a fool in his sleeve.* No one is always wise. The allusion is to the tricks of jugglers.

The wisest fool in Christendom. James I. was so called by Henri IV., but he learnt the phrase of Sully.

Fool or Physician at Forty. Plutarch tells us that Tiberius said "Every man is a fool or his own physician at forty." (*Treatise on the Preservation of Health.*)

Fools. (French, *fol*, Latin, *follis*.)

(1) *The most celebrated court fools :*

(*a*) Dag′onet, jester of King Arthur; Rayère, of Henry I.; Scogan, of Edward IV.; Thomas Killigrew, called "King Charles's jester" (1611-1682); Archie Armstrong, jester in the court of James I. (died 1672).

(*b*) Thomas Derrie, jester in the court of James I.

(*c*) James Geddes, jester to Mary Queen of Scots. His predecessor was Jenny Colquhoun.

(*d*) Patch, the court fool of Elizabeth, wife of Henry VII.

(*e*) Will Somers, Henry VIII.'s jester. He died 1560.

(*f*) W. F. Wallet, jester in the court of Queen Elizabeth.

(*g*) Trib′oulet, jester of Louis XII. and François I. (1487-1536); Brusquet, of whom Brantôme says "he never had his equal in repartee" (1512-1563); Chicot, jester of Henri III. and IV. (1553-1591); Longely, of Louis XIII.; and An′geli, of Louis XIV., last of the titled fools of France.

(*h*) **Klaus Narr,** jester of Frederick *the Wise,* elector of Prussia.

(*i*) **Yorick,** in the Court of Denmark, referred to by Shakespeare in *Hamlet,* v. 1.

(2) *Not attached to the court :*

(*a*) **Patrick Bonny,** jester of the regent Morton; **John Heywood,** in the reign of Henry VII., dramatist, died 1505; **Dickie Pearce,** fool of the Earl of Suffolk, whose epitaph Swift wrote.

(*b*) **Kunz von der Rosen,** private jester to the Emperor Maximilian I.

(*c*) **Gonnella** the Italian (*q.v.*).

(*d*) **Le Glorieux,** the jester of Charles le Hardi, of Burgundy.

(*e*) **Patche,** Cardinal Wolsey's jester, whom he transferred to Henry VIII. as a most acceptable gift.

(*f*) **Patison,** licensed jester to Sir Thomas More. Introduced by Hans Holbein in his picture of the chancellor.

(3) *Men worthy of the motley :*

(*a*) **Andrew Borde,** physician to Henry VIII., usually called *Merry Andrew* (1500-1549).

(*b*) **Gen. Kyaw,** a Saxon officer, famous for his blunt jests.

(*c*) **Jacob Paul,** Baron Gundling, who was laden with titles in ridicule by Frederick William I. of Prussia.

(*d*) **Seigni Jean** (Old John), so called to distinguish him from Johan "fol de Madame," of whom Marot speaks in his epitaphs. Seigni Jean lived about a century before Caillette.

(*e*) **Richard Tarlton,** a famous clown in the reign of Queen Elizabeth. He died 1588.

(*f*) **Caillette** "flourished" about 1494. In the frontispiece of the "Ship of Fools," printed 1497, there is a picture both of Seigni Jean and also of Caillette.

Feast of Fools. A kind of Saturnalia, popular in the Middle Ages. Its chief object was to honour the ass on which our Lord made His triumphant entry into Jerusalem. This ridiculous mummery was held on the day of circumcision (January 1). The office of the day was first chanted in travesty; then, a procession being formed, all sorts of absurdities, both of dress, manner, and instrumentation, were indulged in. An ass formed an essential feature, and from time to time the whole procession imitated the braying of this animal, especially in the place of "Amen."

Fool's Bolt. *A fool's bolt is soon shot* (*Henry V.,* iii. 7). Simpletons cannot wait for the fit and proper time, but wast their resources in random

endeavours ; a fool and his money are soon parted. The allusion is to the British bowmen in battle; the good soldier shot with a purpose, but the foolish soldier at random. (*See* Prov. xxix. 11.)

Fool's Paradise. Unlawful pleasure, illicit love, vain hopes. Thus, in *Romeo and Juliet,* the Nurse says to Romeo, "If ye should lead her [Juliet] into a fool's paradise, it were a gross . . . . behaviour." The old schoolmen said there were three places where persons not good enough for paradise were admitted : (1) The *limbus patrum,* for those good men who had died before the death of the Redeemer; (2) The *limbus infantum* or paradise of unbaptised infants ; and (3) The *limbus fatuo'rum* or paradise of idiots and others who were *non compos mentis.* (*See* LIMBO.)

Foolscap. A corruption of the Italian *foglio-capo* (folio-sized sheet). The error must have been very ancient, as the water-mark of this sort of paper from the thirteenth to the seventeenth century was a fool's head, with cap and bells.

Foot. (Greek, *pod'* ; Latin, *ped'* ; French, *pied* ; Dutch, *voet* ; Saxon, *fot.* *Foot* and *pedal* are variants of the same word.)

Best foot foremost. Use all possible dispatch. To "set on foot" is to set agoing. If you have various powers of motion, set your best foremost.

> " Nay, but make haste ; the better foot before.'
>   *Shakespeare : King John,* iv. 2.

I have not yet got my foot in. I am not yet familiar and easy with the work. The allusion is to the preliminary exercises in the great Roman foot-race. While the signal was waited for, the candidates made essays of jumping, running, and posturing, to excite a suitable warmth and make their limbs supple. This was "getting their foot in" for the race. (*See* HAND.)

I have the measure or *length of his foot.* I know the exact calibre of his mind. The allusion is to the Pythagore'an admeasurement of Hercules by the length of his foot. (*See* Ex PEDE.)

To light on one's feet. To escape a threatened danger. It is said that cats thrown from a height always light on their feet.

To put down your foot on [*a matter*]. Peremptorily to forbid it.

To show the cloven foot. To betray an evil intention. The devil is represented with a cloven foot.

Turn away thy foot from the Sabbath (Isa. lviii. 13). Abstain from working and doing your own pleasure on that day. The allusion is to the law which prohibited a Jew from walking on a Sabbath more than a mile. He was to turn away his foot from the road and street.

Withdraw thy foot from thy neighbour's house, lest he get weary of thee, and so hate thee. Never outstay your welcome.

With one foot in the grave. In a dying state.

You have put your foot in it nicely. You have got yourself into a pretty mess. (In French, *vous avez mis le pied dedans.*) When porridge is burnt or meat over-roasted, we say, " The bishop hath put his foot in." (*See* BISHOP.)

Afoot. On the way, in progress. (*See* GAME'S AFOOT, MATTER AFOOT.)

> " Mischief, thou art afoot,
> Take thou what course thou wilt."
>   *Shakespeare: Julius Cæsar,* iii. 2.

Foot-breadth or *Quern-biter.* The sword of Thoralf Skolinson *the Strong,* a companion of Hako I. of Norway. (*See* SWORDS.)

Foot-lights. *To appear before the foot-lights.* On the stage, where a row of lights is placed in front along the floor to lighten it up.

Foot Monsters. In the Italian romance of *Guori'no Moschi'no* Indians are spoken of with feet so large that they carry them over their heads like umbrellas.

Foot-notes. Notes placed at the bottom of a page.

> " A trifling sum of misery
> Now added to the foot of thy account."
>   *Dryden.*

Foot-pound. The unit of result in estimating *work done* by machinery. Thus, if we take 1 lb. as the unit of weight and 1 foot as the unit of distance, a foot-pound would be 1 lb. weight raised 1 foot.

Foot of a Page. The bottom of it, meaning the notes at the bottom of a page.

Footing. *He is on good footing with the world.* He stands well with the world. This is a French phrase, *Être sur un grand pied dans le monde.* "Grand pied " means " large foot," and the allusion is to the time of Henry VIII., when the rank of a man was designated by the size of his shoe—the higher the rank the larger the shoe. The proverb would be more correctly rendered, " He has a large foot in society."

To pay your footing. To give money for drink when you first enter on a trade. Entry money for being allowed to put your foot in the premises occupied by fellow-craftsmen. This word is called *foot-ale* by ancient writers. (*See* GARNISH.)

Footman's Wand (*A*). (*See* RUNNING FOOTMEN.)

Footmen. (*See* RUNNING FOOTMEN.)

Fop's Alley. The passage between the tiers of benches, right and left, in the Opera-house, frequented by mashers and other exquisites.

Foppington (*Lord*). An empty coxcomb in Vanbrugh's *Relapse,* of which Sheridan's *Trip to Scarborough* is a modified version.

" The shoemaker in the *Relapse* tells Lord Foppington that his lordship is mistaken in supposing that his shoe pinches."—*Lord Macaulay.*

Forbears. Ancestors, predecessors— *i.e.* those born before the present generation. (Anglo-Saxon, *för-beran.*)

" My name is Græme, so please you,—Roland Græme, whose forbears were designated of Heathergill, in the Debateable Land."—*Sir W. Scott: The Abbot,* chap. xviii.

Forbës, referred to by Thomson in his *Seasons,* was Duncan Forbes, of Cullo'den, lord president of the Court of Session. For many years he ruled the destinies and greatly contributed to the prosperity of Scotland. He was on friendly terms with Pope, Swift, Arbuthnot, etc. The word is now generally pronounced as a monosyllable.

" Thee, Forbës, too, whom every worth attends....
Thy country feels thro' her reviving arts,
Planned by thy wisdom, by thy soul informed."
                   Thomson: Autumn.

Forbidden Fruit (*The*), Mahometan doctors aver, was the banana or Indian fig, because fig-leaves were employed to cover the disobedient pair when they felt shame as the result of sin. Called " Paradisaica." Metaphorically, unlawful = forbidden indulgence.

Forcible Feeble School. (*See* FEEBLE.)

Ford. Mr. and Mrs. Ford are characters in *The Merry Wives of Windsor.* Mrs. Ford pretends to accept Sir John Falstaff's protestations of love, in order to punish him for his devices.

For'delis (in *Orlando Furioso*). Wife of Bran'dimart, Orlando's intimate friend. When Brandimart was slain, she dwelt for a time in his mausoleum in Sicily, and died broken-hearted. (Book xii.)

Fore. *To the fore.* In the front rank; eminent.

To come to the fore. To stand out prominently; to distinguish oneself; to stand forth.

Fore-and-Aft. Lengthwise, in opposition to "athwart-ships" (or across the line of the keel). (*Dana : Seaman's Manual*, p. 96.)

"A slight spar-deck fore-and-aft."—*Sir W. Raleigh.*

Forecastle. Ancient ships had a castle, as may be seen in the tapestry of the House of Lords, representing the Spanish Arma'da. The term forecastle means before the castle. The Romans called the castled ships *navēs turri'tæ.*

"That part of the upper deck forward of the foremast . . . In merchant ships, the forward part of the vessel, under the deck, where the sailors live."—*Dana : Seaman's Manual*, p. 96.

Foreclose. To put an end to. A legal term, meaning to close before the time specified; *e.g.* suppose I held the mortgage of a man called A, and A fails to fulfil his part of the agreement, I can insist upon the mortgage being cancelled, foreclosing thus our agreement.

"The embargo with Spain foreclosed this trade."—*Carew.*

Fore-shortened. Not viewed laterally, but more or less obliquely. Thus, a man's leg lying on the ground, with the sole of the foot nearer the artist than the rest of the body, would be perspectively shortened.

"He forbids the fore-shortenings, because they make the parts appear little."—*Dryden.*

Forfar. *Do as the cow o' Forfar did, tak' a stannin' drink.* A cow, in passing a door in Forfar, where a tub of ale had been placed to cool, drank the whole of it. The owner of the ale prosecuted the owner of the cow, but a learned baillie, in giving his decision, said, " As the ale was drunk by the cow while standing·at the door, it must be considered *deoch an doruis* (stirrup-cup), to make a charge for which would be to outrage Scotch hospitality." (*Sir W. Scott : Waverley.*)

Forget-me-nots of the Angels. The stars are so called by Longfellow. The similitude between a little light-blue flower and the yellow stars is very remote. Stars are more like buttercups than forget-me-nots.

" Silently, one by one, in the infinite meadows of heaven,
Blossom the lovely stars, the forget-me-nots of the angels."   *Evangeline.*

Forgive, blest Shade. This very celebrated epitaph is in Brading church-yard, Isle of Wight, and is attributed to Mrs. Anne Steele (*Theodosia*), daughter of a Baptist minister of Bristol, but was touched up by the Rev. John Gill, curate of Newchurch. Set to music in three parts by J. W. Callcott (1795).

Forgiveness. (Ang.-Sax., *forgifenes.*)

" Forgiveness to the injured doth belong,
But they ne'er pardon who have done the wrong."
Dryden : Conquest of Granada, part ii. act i. 2.

" Proprium humāni generis, odisse quem lacerīs."—*Tacitus.*

Fork Out. Hand over; pay down; stand treat. Fingers are called *forks,* and this may suffice to explain the phrase; if not, we have the Anglo-Saxon verb *feccan* (to draw out, to take), and " fork out " would be " fec out."

Forks. The gallows. (Latin, *furca.*) Cicero (*de Divinitāte,* i. 26) says, " *Ferens furcam ductus est,*" often quoted in proof that criminals condemned to the cross were obliged to carry their own cross to the place of execution. But the ordinary meaning of *furca* is a kind of yoke to which the hands of criminals were fastened. The punishment was of three degrees of severity : (1) The *furca ignominiosa ;* (2) the *furca pænālis ;* and (3) the *furca capitālis.* The first was for slight offences, and consisted in carrying the *furca* on the shoulders, more or less weighted. The second consisted in carrying the *furca* and being scourged. The third was being scourged to death. The word *furcifer* meant what we call a gallows-bad or vile fellow.

Forked Cap (*A*). A bishop's mitre is so called by John Skelton. It is cleft or forked.

Forlorn Hope. Cromwell says, "Our *forlorn* of horse marched within a mile of the enemy," *i.e.* our horse picket sent forward to reconnoitre approached within a mile of the enemy's camp. (German, *verloren.*)

Forlot or **Firlot.** The fourth part of a boll. From *feower* (four), *hlot* (part).

Forma Pau'peris (Latin, *Under plea of poverty*). *To sue in formâ pauperis.* When a person has just cause of a suit, but is so poor that he cannot raise £5, the judge will assign him lawyers and counsel without the usual fees.

For'titer in Re (Latin). Firmness in doing what is to be done ; an un-flinching resolution to persevere to the end. Coupled with *Suaviter in modo* (*q.v.*).

Fortunate Islands. Now called the Cana'ries.

Fortuna'tus. *You have found Fortunatus's purse.* Are in luck's way. The nursery tale of *Fortuna'tus* records that he had an inexhaustible purse. It is from the Italian fairy tales of Straparo'la, called *Nights*. Translated into French in 1585. (*See* WISHING CUP.)

Fortune. *Fortune favours the brave.* ("*Fortes fortu'na ad'juvat.*") (*Terence : Phor'mio,* i. 4.)

Fortu'nio. The assumed name of a damsel, youngest of three sisters, who dressed herself as a cavalier to save her aged father, who was summoned to the army. Fortunio on the way engaged seven servants : Strong-back, who could carry on his back enough liquor to fill a river ; Lightfoot, who could traverse any distance in no time ; Marksman, who could hit an object at any distance ; Fine-ear, who could hear anything, no matter where uttered ; Boisterer, who could do any amount of cudgelling ; Gourmand, who could eat any amount of food ; and Tippler, who could drink a river dry and thirst again. Fortunio, having rendered invaluable services to King Alfourite, by the aid of her seven servants, at last married him. (*Grimm's Goblins : Fortunio. Countess D'Aulnoy : Fairy Tales.*)

Forty. A superstitious number, arising from the Scripture use. Thus Moses was forty days in the mount ; Elijah was forty days fed by ravens ; the rain of the flood fell forty days, and another forty days expired before Noah opened the window of the ark , forty days was the period of embalming ; Nineveh had forty days to repent ; our Lord fasted forty days ; He was seen forty days after His resurrection ; etc.

St. Swithin betokens forty days' rain or dry weather ; a quarantine extends to forty days ; forty days, in the Old English law, was the limit for the payment of the fine for manslaughter ; the privilege of sanctuary was for forty days ; the widow was allowed to remain in her husband's house for forty days after his decease ; a knight enjoined forty days' service of his tenant ; a stranger, at the expiration of forty days was compelled to be enrolled in some tithing ; members of Parliament were protected from arrest forty days after the prorogation of the House, and forty days before the House was convened ; a new-made burgess had

to forfeit forty pence unless he built a house within forty days ; etc., etc.

The ancient physicians ascribe many strange changes to the period of forty ; the alchemists looked on forty days as the charmed period when the philosopher's stone and elixir of life were to appear.

Fool or physician at forty. (*See under* FOOL.)

Forty Stripes save One. The Jews were forbidden by the Mosaic law to inflict more than forty stripes on an offender, and for fear of breaking the law they stopped short of the number. If the scourge contained three lashes, thirteen strokes would equal "forty save one."

Forty stripes save one. The thirty-nine articles of the Anglican Church.

Forty Thieves. In the tale of *Ali Baba'.* (*Arabian Nights' Entertainments.*)

Forty Winks. A short nap. Forty is an indefinite number, meaning a few. Thus, we say, "A, B, C, and forty more." Coriola'nus says, "I could beat forty of them " (iii. 1). (*See* FORTY.)

"The slave had forty thousand lives."
Shakespeare: Othello, iii. 1.
" I loved Ophelia ; forty thousand brothers
Could not, with all their quantity of love,
Make up my sum."
Shakespeare : Hamlet, v. 1.

Forty-five. No. 45. The celebrated number of Wilkes's *North Britain,* in which the Cabinet Ministers are accused of putting a lie into the king's mouth.

Forwards (*Marshal*). G. L. von Blücher was called Marschall Vorwarts, from his constant exhortation to his hussars in the campaigns preceding the great battle of Waterloo. *Vorwärts !* always *Vorwärts !* (1742-1819.)

Fos'cari (*Francis*). Doge of Venice He occupied the office for thirty-five years, added Brescia, Ber'gamo, Crema, and Ravenna to the Republic, greatly improved the city, and raised Venice to the pinnacle of its glory. Of his four sons only one, named Jac'opo, survived ; he was thrice tortured. Before his final banishment, the old doge, then eighty-four years of age, hobbled on crutches to the gaol where his son was confined, but would not mitigate the sentence of "The Ten." His son, being banished to Candia, died, and Francis was deposed. As he descended the Giant Staircase he heard the bell toll for the election of his successor, and dropped down dead. (*Byron: The Two Foscari.*)

Jacopo Fos'cari. Denounced by the Council of Ten for taking bribes of foreign powers. He was tried before his own father, confessed his guilt, and was banished. During his banishment a Venetian senator was murdered, and Jacopo, being suspected of complicity in the crime, was again tortured and banished. He returned to Venice, was once more brought before the council, subjected to torture, and banished to Candia, where in a few days he died.

" Nothing can sympathise with Foscari—
Not e'en a Foscari."
Byron : The Two Foscari.

Foss (*Corporal*). An attendant on Lieutenant Worthington. A similar character to Trim in Sterne's *Tristram Shandy.* (*G. Colman : The Poor Gentleman.*)

Foss-way. One of the four principal highways made by the Romans in England, leading from Cornwall to Lincoln. It had a foss or ditch on each side of it. (*See* ERMINE STREET.)

Fossa et Furca [*pit and gallows*]. An ancient privilege granted by the Crown to its vassals, to cast female felons into a ditch, and hang male ones on a gallows.

According to Wharton (*Law Dictionary*), this *furca* is not the Latin word, but the Hebrew *farkah,* to divide. Hence also the servile tenure called *Furcam et Flagellum.*

Fossils. Things dug up, animal and vegetable remains dug out of the earth. (Latin, *fodio,* to dig up.)

"Many other bodies, which, because we discover them by digging into the bowels of the earth, are called by one common name—*fossils,* under which are comprehended metals and minerals." [Not now.]—*Locke.*

Foster Brother or *Sister.* One brought up by the same nurse.

A *foster-child* is one brought up by those who are not its real parents. (Saxon, *fostrian,* Danish *fostrer,* to nurse.)

Fou Drunk. "Wilbraham has *foudrunk* "—*i.e.* is despicably drunk, dead drunk. French, *fou,* "mad," as *fouenragé;* or simply *fu',* *i.e.* "full," " intensive," as in *full-oft,* "*full-well* ye reject the commandment of God" (Mark vii. 9).

Foul Proof. A proof is a rough impression of a manuscript set up in type, or of a drawing engraved, for the author's correction. The proof with many faults is a *foul* proof, but the "pull," after the errors are corrected, is termed a *clean* proof. These impressions

are called proofs because they must be *approved of* by author and reader before they are finally printed.

Foul-weather Jack. Commodore Byron, said to be as notorious for foul weather as Queen Victoria is for fine. (1723-1786.)

Admiral Sir John Norris, who died 1746.

Fountain of Death. In *Jerusalem Delivered,* the hermit tells Charles and Ubald of a fountain, the sight of which excites thirst, but those who taste its water die with laughter.

Pompo'nius Me'la speaks of a fountain in the Fortunate Islands, "*Qui potavère risu solvuntur in mortem.*" Petrarch alludes to the same.

These fountains symbolise the pleasures of sin.

Fountain of Youth. A fountain supposed to possess the power of restoring youth. It was thought to be in one of the Baha'ma Islands.

Four Kings. *The History of the Four Kings* (*Livre des Quatre Rois*). A pack of cards. In a French pack the four kings are Charlemagne, David, Alexander, and Cæsar, representatives of the Franco-German, Jewish or Christian, Macedonian, and Roman monarchies.

Four Letters, containing the name of God, and called by Rabbins "tetragrammaton." Thus, in Hebrew, JHVH (JeHoVaH) ; in Greek, Θεος ; in Latin, *Deus*; in French, *Dieu*; in Assyrian, *Adat*; Dutch, *Godt*; German, *Gott*; Danish, *Godh*; Swedish, *Goth*; Persian, *Soru*; Arabic, *Alla*; Cabalistic, *Agla*; Egyptian, Θουθ; Sanskrit, *Deva*; Spanish, *Dios*; Italian, *Idio*; Scandinavian, *Odin*, etc.

‡ This probably is a mere coincidence, but it is worthy of note.

Four Masters. Michael and Cucoirighe O'Clerighe, Maurice and Fearfeafa Conry, authors of the *Annals of Donegal.*

Fou'rierism. A communistic system, so called from Charles Fourier, of Besançon. According to Fourier, all the world was to be cantoned into groups, called phalansteries, consisting each of 400 families or 1,800 individuals, who were to live in a common edifice, furnished with workshops, studios, and all sources of amusement. The several groups were at the same time to be associated together under a unitary government like the Cantons of Switzerland or the States of America. Only one language was to be admitted; all the gains of each phalanstery were to belong to the common purse; and though talent and industry were to be rewarded, no one was to be suffered to remain indigent, or without the enjoyment of certain luxuries and public amusement (1772-1837).

Fou'rierists. French communists, so called from Charles Fourier. (*See above.*)

Fourteen, in its connection with Henri IV. and Louis XIV. The following are curious and strange coincidences:

HENRI IV.

14 letters in the name Henri-de-Bourbon. He was the 14th king of France and Navarre on the extinction of the family of Navarre. He was born on Dec. 14, 1553, the sum of which year amounts to 14; he was assassinated on May 14, 1610; and lived 4 times 14 years, 14 weeks, and 4 times 14 days.
14 May, 1552, was born Marguerite de Valois, his first wife.
14 May, 1588, the Parisians rose in revolt against him, because he was a "heretic."
14 March, 1590, he won the great battle of Ivry.
14 May, 1590, was organised a grand ecclesiastical and military demonstration against him, which drove him from the faubourgs of Paris.
14 Nov., 1590, the Sixteen took an oath to die rather than submit to a "heretic" king.
It was Gregory XIV. who issued a Bull excluding Henri from the throne.
14 Nov., 1592, the Paris parlement registered the papal Bull.
14 Dec., 1599, the Duke of Savoy was reconciled to Henri IV.
14 Sept., 1606, was baptised the dauphin (afterwards Louis XIII.), son of Henri IV.
14 May, 1610, Henry was assassinated by Ravaillac.
For the dates see *Histoire de France*, by Bordier and Churton (1859).

LOUIS XIV.

14th of the name. He mounted the throne 1643, the sum of which figures equals 14. He died 1715, the sum of which figures also equals 14. He reigned 77 years, the sum of which two figures equals 14. He was born 1638, died 1715, which added together equals 3353, the sum of which figures comes to 14. Such a strange combination is probably without parallel.

Fourteen Hundred (A Stock Exchange warning). It is to give notice that a stranger has entered 'Change. The term was in use in Defoe's time.

Fourth Estate of the Realm (*The*). The daily press. The most powerful of all. Burke, referring to the Reporters' Gallery, said, "Yonder sits the Fourth Estate, more important than them all."

Fourth of July (*The*). The great national holiday of the United States of America. The Declaration of Independence was July 4, 1776.

Fowler (*Henry the Fowler*). Heinrich I., King of Germany, was so called, because when the deputies announced to him his election to the throne, they found him fowling with a hawk on his fist (876, 919-936).

⁂ This tradition is not mentioned by any historian before the eleventh century; but since that period numerous writers have repeated the story. He was called in Latin, *Henricus Auceps*.

Fox (*The old*). Marshal Soult was so nicknamed, from his strategic talents and fertility of resources. (1769-1851.) (*See* REYNARD.)

Fox. *Antipathy to foxes.* Speaking of natural antipathies, Shakespeare makes Shylock say:

" Some men there be love not a gaping pig,
Some that are mad if they behold a cat."

Tycho Brahé would faint at sight of a *fox*, Marshal d'Albret at sight of a *pig*, Henri III. at sight of a *cat*. (*See* ANTIPATHY.)

A wise fox will never rob his neighbour's hen-roost, because it would soon be found out. He goes farther from home where he is not known.

Every fox must pay his skin to the furrier. The crafty shall be taken in their own wiliness.

"Tutte le volpi si trovano in pellicaria."—*Italian Proverb.*

To set a fox to keep the geese. (Latin, "*Ovem lupo committere.*") He entrusted his money to sharpers.

Fox (*That*). So our Lord called Herod Antipas, whose crafty policy was thus pointed at, "Go ye, and tell that fox, Behold, I cast out devils" (St. Luke xiii. 32). (B.C. 4—A.D. 39.)

⁂ Herod Agrippa I. (A.D. 41-44.) Herod Agrippa II. (A.D. 52-100.)

Fox. An Old English broadsword.
⁂ A correspondent of *Notes and Queries* (May 2nd, 1891, p. 356) says: "The swords were manufactured by Julian del Rei of Toledo, whose trade-mark was a little dog, mistaken for a fox." The usual derivation is the Latin *falx*, French *fauchon*, our *falchion*.

" O signieur Dew, thou diest on point of fox,
Except, O signieur, thou do give to me
Egregious ransom."
        Shakespeare: Henry V., iv. 4.

"I had a sword, ay, the flower of Smithfield for a sword, a right fox i' faith."—*Two Angry Women of Abington* (1599).

Fox (*To*). To steal or cheat; to fub; also "to shadow" a suspect; to watch without seeming so to do. A dog, a fox, and a weasel sleep, as they say, "with one eye open."

Fox-fire—*i.e. fause* or "false fire," the phosphoric light, without heat, which plays round decaying matter.

Fox-tail. *I gave him a flap with a fox-tail.* I cajoled him ; made a fool of him. The fox-tail was one of the badges of the motley, and to flap with a fox-tail is to treat one like a fool.

Fox's Sleep (*A*). A sleep with one eye on the *qui vive.* Assumed indifference to what is going on. (*See above.*)

Foxed. A book stained with reddish-brown marks is said to be foxed. Of course, the stain is so called because it is of the colour of a fox.

Foxglove, called by the Welsh *Fairy's glove* and by the Irish *Fairy-bells,* is either a corruption of Folk's glove— *i.e.* the glove of the good folks or fairies, or else of the Saxon *fox[es]glofa,* red or fox-coloured glove. (French, *gants de Notre Dame.*)

Foxites (2 syl.). The Quakers. So called from George Fox, who organised the sect (1624-1690).

" His muzzle, formed of opposition stuff,
Firm as a Foxite, would not lose its ruff."
Dr. Wolcott [*Peter Pindar*] : *The Razor Seller.*

Foxy. Strong-smelling, or red-haired ; like a fox.

Fra Diav'olo (Michele Pozza). A celebrated brigand and renegade monk, who evaded pursuit for many years amidst the mountains of Calabria. (1760-1806.) Auber has made him the subject of an opera.

Fracassus. Father of Ferrăgus, the giant, and son of Morgantē.

" Primus erat quidam Fracassus prole gigantis,
Cujus stirps olim Morganto venit ab illo,
Qui bacchioconem campanæ ferre solebat,
Cum quo mille hominum colpos fracasset in uno."
Merlin Cocaius (i.e. *Théophile Folengo*) :
Histoire Macaronique (1606).

Fradu'bio [*Brother Doubt*], says Spenser, wooed and won Duessa (*False-faith*) ; but one day, while she was bathing, discovered her to be a " filthy old hag," and resolved to leave her. False - faith instantly metamorphosed him into a tree, and he will never be relieved till "he can be bathed from the well of living water." (*Faërie Queene,* book i. 2.)

ΘFrame of Mind. Disposition. A *printer's* frame is a stand on which the type is disposed ; a *founder's* frame is a mould into which molten metal is disposed or poured ; a *weaver's* frame is a loom where the silk or thread is disposed or stretched for quilting, etc. ; a *picture* frame is an ornamental edging within which the picture is disposed ; a *mental* frame, therefore, is the boundary within which the feelings of the mind are disposed. (Anglo-Saxon, *fremm-an.*)

France. The heraldic device of the city of Paris is a ship. As Sauval says, " *L'ile de la cité est faite comme un grand navire enfoncé dans la vase, et échoué au fil de l'eau vers le milieu de la Seine.*" This form of a ship struck the heraldic scribes, who in the latter part of the Middle Ages emblazoned a ship on the shield of Paris.

Frances'ca. A Venetian maiden, daughter of Minotti, governor of Corinth. She loved Alp, and tried to restore him to his country and faith ; but, as he refused to recant, gave him up, and died broken-hearted. (*Byron : Siege of Corinth.*)

Frances'ca da Rim'ini. Daughter of Guido da Polenta, Lord of Ravenna. Her story is told in Dante's *Inferno* (canto v.). She was married to Lanciotto Malatesta, Lord of Rimini, but committed adultery with Paolo, her husband's brother. Botn were put to death by him in 1389. Leigh Hunt has a poem, and Silvio Pellico a tragedy, on the subject.

Francis's Distemper (*St.*). Impecuniosity ; being moneyless. Those of the Order of St. Francis were not allowed to carry any money about them.

" I saw another case of gentlemen of St. Francis's distemper."—*Rabelais : Pantagruel,* v. 21.

Francis'cans, or *Min'orites* (3 syl.). Founded in 1208 by St. Francis of Assisi, who called poverty " his bride." Poverty was the ruling principle of the order. Duns Scotus, Roger Bacon, Cardinal Ximenës, Ganganelli, etc., were of this order.

Called *Franciscans,* from the name of their
  founder.
  " *Minorites,* from their professed humility.
  " *Grey Friars,* from the colour of their
    outer garment.
  " *Mendicants,* because they were one of
    the Begging or mendicant order.
  " *Observants,* because they strictly ob-
    served the rule of poverty.

\:* The Franciscan *Sisters* were known as Clares, or Poor Clares, Minoresses, Mendicants, and Urbanites.

Frangipa'ni. A powerful Roman family. So called from their benevolent distribution of bread during a famine.

Frangipani. A delicious perfume, made of spices, orris-root, and musk, in imitation of real Frangipani. Mutio Frangipani, the famous Italian botanist, visited the West Indies in 1493. The sailors perceived a delicious fragrance as they neared Antig'ua, and Mutio told them it proceeded from the *Plumé'ria Alba*. The plant was re-named Frangipani, and the distilled essence received the same name.

Frangipani Pudding is pudding made of broken bread. (*Frangere*, to break ; *panis*, bread.)

Frank. A name given by the Turks, Greeks, and Arabs to any of the inhabitants of the western parts of Europe, as the English, Italians, Germans, Spaniards, French, etc.

Frank Pledge. Neighbours bound for each other's good conduct. Hallam says every ten men in a village were answerable for each other, and if one of them committed an offence the other nine were bound to make reparation. The word means the security given by Franklins or free-men.

Frankeleynes Tale, in Chaucer, resembles one in Boccaccio (*Decameron*, Day x. No. 5), and one in the fifth book of his *Philocope*. (*See* DORIGEN.)

Frank'enstein (3 syl.). A young student, who made a soulless monster out of fragments of men picked up from churchyards and dissecting-rooms, and endued it with life by galvanism. The tale, written by Mrs. Shelley, shows how the creature longed for sympathy, but was shunned by everyone. It was only animal life, a parody on the creature man, powerful for evil, and the instrument of dreadful retribution on the student, who usurped the prerogative of the Creator.

"The Southern Confederacy will be the soulless monster of Frankenstein."—*Charles Sumner.*

⁂ Mrs. Shelley, unfortunately, has given no name to her monster, and therefore he is not unfrequently called "Frankenstein" when alluded to. This, of course, is an error, but Frankenstein's monster is a clumsy substitute.

"I believe it would be impossible to control the Frankenstein we should have ourselves created."—*Sir John Lubbock* (a speech, 1886).

Frankforters. People of Frankfort.

Franklin. *The Polish Franklin.* Thaddeus Czacki (1765-1813).

Frankum's Night. A night in June destructive to apple- and pear-trees. The tale is that one Frankum offered sacrifice in his orchard for an extra fine crop, but a blight ensued, and his trees were unproductive.

Frantic. Brain-struck (Greek, *phrēn,*

the heart as the seat of reason), madness being a disorder of the understanding.

" Cebel's frantic rites have made them mad."
Spenser.

Fraserian. One of the eighty-one celebrated literary characters of the 19th century published in *Fraser's Magazine* (1830-1838). Amongst them are Harrison Ainsworth, the countess of Blessington, Brewster, Brougham, Bulwer, Campbell, Carlyle, Cobbett, Coleridge, Cruikshank, Allan Cunningham, D'Israeli (both Isaac and Benjamin), Faraday, Gleig, Mrs. S. C. Hall, Hobhouse, Hogg (the Ettrick shepherd), Theodore Hook, Leigh Hunt, Washington Irving, Knowles, Charles Lamb, Miss Landon, Dr. Lardner, Lockhart, Harriet Martineau, Dr. Moir, Molesworth, Robert Montgomery, Thomas Moore, Jane Porter, Sir Walter Scott, Sydney Smith, Talfourd, Talleyrand, Alaric Watts, Wordsworth, and others to the number of eighty-one.

Fraserian Group (*The*) consists of twenty-seven persons : Magirn. On his *right hand*, Washington Irving, Mahony, Gleig, Sir E. Brydges, Carlyle, and Count d'Orsay. On his *left hand*, Barry Cornwall, Southey, Perceval Banks, Thackeray, Churchill, Serjeant Murphy, Macnish, and Harrison Ainsworth. *Opposite* are Coleridge, Hogg, Galt, Dunlop, Jerdan, Fraser, Croker, Lockhart, Theodore Hook, Brewster, and Moir.

Frater. An Abram-man (*q.v.*). (Latin, *frater*, a brother, one of the same community or society.)

Frat'eret'to. A fiend mentioned by Edgar in the tragedy of *King Lear.*

"Frateretto calls me, and tells me Nero is an angler in the lake of darkness. Pray, innocent, and beware of the foul fiend."—Act iii. 6.

Frat'ery. The refectory of a monastery, or chief room of a frater-house. A frater is a member of a fraternity or society of monks. (Latin, *frater*, a brother.)

Fraticel'lians [*Little Brethren*]. A sect of the Middle Ages, who claimed to be the only true Church, and threw off all subjection to the Pope, whom they denounced as an apostate. They wholly disappeared in the fifteenth century.

Fre'a. The Anglo-Saxon form of Frigga, wife of Odin. Our Friday is *Frea's daeg.*

Free. *A free and easy.* A social gathering where persons meet together without formality to chat and smoke.

Free Bench (*francus bancus*). The widow's right to a copyhold. It is not a dower or gift, but a free right independent of the will of the husband. Called *bench* because, upon acceding to the estate, she becomes a tenant of the manor, and one of the benchers, *i.e.* persons who sit on the bench occupied by the *parēs curiæ.*

Free Coup (in Scotland) means a piece of waste land where rubbish may be deposited free of charge.

Free Lances. Roving companies of knights, etc., who wandered from place to place, after the Crusades, selling their services to anyone who would pay for them. In Italy they were termed Condottie'ri.

Free Lances of Life (*The*). The Aspasias of fashion. The fair frail demi-monde.

Free Spirit. *Brethren of the Free Spirit.* A fanatical sect, between the thirteenth and fifteenth centuries, diffused through Italy, France, and Germany. They claimed "freedom of spirit," and based their claims on Romans viii. 2-14, "The law of the Spirit hath made me free from the law of sin and death."

Free Trade. *The Apostle of Free Trade.* Richard Cobden (1804-65).

Freebooter means a free rover. (Dutch, *buiten*, to rove, whence *vrijbuiter;* German, *freibeuter*, etc.)

"His forces consisted mostly of base people and freebooters."—*Bacon.*

Freeholds. Estates which owe no duty or service to any lord but the sovereign. (*See* COPYHOLD.)

Freeman (*Mrs.*). A name assumed by the Duchess of Marlborough in her correspondence with Queen Anne. The queen called herself Mrs. Morley.

Freeman of Bucks. A cuckold. The allusion is to the buck's horn. (*See* HORNS.)

Freeman's Quay. *Drinking at Freeman's Quay.* (*See* DRINKING.)

Freemasons. In the Middle Ages a guild of masons specially employed in building churches. Called "free" because exempted by several papal bulls from the laws which bore upon common craftsmen, and exempt from the burdens thrown on the working classes.

⁘ St. Paul's, London, in 604, and St. Peter's, Westminster, in 605, were built by Freemasons. Gundulph (bishop of Rochester), who built the White Tower, was a "Grand Master;" so was Peter

of Colechurch, architect of Old London Bridge. Henry VII.'s chapel, Westminster, was the work of a Master Mason; so were Sir Thomas Gresham (who planned the Royal Exchange), Inigo Jones, and Sir Christopher Wren. Covent Garden theatre was founded in 1808 by the Prince of Wales in his capacity of "Grand Master."

"Before the beginning of the 13th century the corporation of freemasons was not sufficiently organised to have had much influence on art."—*J. Fergusson: Historic Archæology,* vol. i. part ii. chap. viii. p. 527.

The lady Freemason was the Hon. Miss Elizabeth St. Leger, daughter of Lord Doneraile, who (says the tale) hid herself in an empty clock-case when the lodge was held in her father's house, and witnessed the proceedings. She was discovered, and compelled to submit to initiation as a member of the craft.

Freeport (*Sir Andrew*). A London merchant, industrious, generous, and of great good sense. He was one of the members of the hypothetical club under whose auspices the *Spectator* was published.

Freestone is Portland stone, which cuts *freely* in any direction.

Freethinker. One who thinks unbiassed by revelation or ecclesiastical canons, as deists and atheists.

"Atheist is an old-fashioned word. I am a freethinker."—*Addison.*

Freezing-point. We generally mean by this expression that degree of Fahrenheit's thermometer which indicates the temperature of frozen water— viz. 32° above zero. If we mean any other liquid we add the name, as the freezing-point of milk, sulphuric ether, quicksilver, and so on. In Centigrade and Réaumur's instruments zero marks the freezing-point.

Freischütz (pronounce *fry-shoots*), the free-shooter, a legendary German archer in league with the Devil, who gave him seven balls, six of which were to hit infallibly whatever the marksman aimed at, and the seventh was to be directed according to the will of his co-partner. F. Kind made the libretto, and Weber set to music, the opera based on the legend, called *Der Freischütz.*

Freki and Geri. The two wolves of Odin.

French Cream. Brandy. In France it is extremely general to drink after dinner a cup of coffee with a glass of brandy in it instead of cream. This "patent digester" is called *a Gloria.*

French Leave. *To take French leave.* To take without asking leave or giving any equivalent. The allusion is to the French soldiers, who in their invasions take what they require, and never wait to ask permission of the owners or pay any price for what they take.

The French retort this courtesy by calling a creditor an Englishman (*un Anglais*), a term in vogue in the sixteenth century, and used by Clement Marot. Even to the present hour, when a man excuses himself from entering a café or theatre, because he is in debt, he says: "*Non, non! je suis Anglé*" ("I am cleared out").

> "Et aujourd'huy je faictz soliciter
> Tous me angloys."
> *Guillaume Creton* (1520).

French leave. Leaving a party, house, or neighbourhood without bidding good-bye to anyone; to slip away unnoticed.

French of Stratford atte Bowe. English-French.

> "And French, she [the nun] spak ful, faire and fetysly,
> After the scole of Stratford atte Bowe,
> For French of Parys was to hire unknowe."
> *Chaucer: Canterbury Tales (The Prologue).*

Frenchman. *Done like a Frenchman, turn and turn again* (1 *Henry VI.*, iii. 4). The French are usually satirised by mediæval English authors as a fickle, wavering nation. Dr. Johnson says he once read a treatise the object of which was to show that a weathercock is a satire on the word *Gallus* (a Gaul or cock).

Frenchman. The nickname of a Frenchman is "Crapaud" (*q.v.*), "Johnny" or "Jean," "Mossoo," "Robert Macaire" (*q.v.*); but of a Parisian "Grenouille" (Frog). (*See* BRISSOTINS.)

> They stand erect, they dance whene'er they walk;
> Monkeys in action, parroquets in talk."
> *Gay: Epistle III.*

French Canadian, "Jean Baptiste."
French Peasantry, "Jacques Bonhomme."
French Reformers, "Brissotins" (*q.v.*).

Fres'co-painting means fresh-painting, or rather paint applied to walls while the plaster is fresh and damp. Only so much plaster must be spread as the artist can finish painting before he retires for the day. There are three chambers in the Pope's palace at Rome done in fresco by Raphael Urbino and Julio Roma'no; at Fontainebleau there is a famous one, containing the travels of Ulysses in sixty pieces, the work of

several artists, as Bollame'o, Martin Rouse, and others.

> "A fading frescoe here demands a sigh."
> *Pope.*

Freshman, at college, is a man not salted. It was anciently a custom in the different colleges to play practical jokes on the new-comers. One of the most common was to assemble them in a room and make them deliver a speech. Those who acquitted themselves well had a cup of caudle; those who passed muster had a caudle with salt water; the rest had the salt water only. Without scanning so deeply, "fresh-man" may simply mean a fresh or new student. (*See* BEJAN.)

Freston. An enchanter introduced into the romance of *Don Belia'nis of Greece.*

> "Truly I can't tell whether it was Freston or Friston; but sure I am that his name ended in 'ton.'"—*Don Quixote.*

Frey. Son of Niörd, the Van. He was the Scandinavian god of fertility and peace, and the dispenser of rain. Frey was the patron god of Sweden and Iceland, he rode on the boar Gullinbursti, and his sword was self-acting. (*See* GERDA.)

> Niörd was not of the Æsir. He, with his son and daughter, presided over the sea, the clouds, the air, and water generally. They belonged to the Vanir.

Freyja. Daughter of Niörd, goddess of love. She was the wife of Odin, who deserted her because she loved finery better than she loved her husband. Her chariot was drawn by two cats, and not by doves like the car of Venus. (*Scandinavian mythology.*)

Friar. *A curtal Friar.* (*See* CURTAL.)

Friar, in printing. A part of the sheet which has failed to receive the ink, and is therefore left blank. As Caxton set up his printing-press in Westminster Abbey, it is but natural to suppose that monks and friars should give foundation to some of the printers' slang. (*See* MONK.)

Friar Bungay is an historical character overlaid with legends. It is said that he "raised mists and vapours which befriended Edward IV. at the battle of Barnet."

> "[Friar Bungay is] the personification of the charlatan of science in the 15th century."—*Lord Lytton* [Bulwer Lytton]: *The Last of the Barons.*

Friar Dom'inic, in Dryden's *Spanish Friar,* designed to ridicule the vices of the priesthood.

Friar Ger'und. Designed to ridicule the pulpit oratory of Spain in the eighteenth century; full of quips and cranks, tricks and startling monstrosities. (*Joseph Isla : Life of Friar Gerund,* 1714-1783.)

Friar John. A tall, lean, wide-mouthed, long-nosed friar of Seville, who dispatched his matins with wonderful celerity, and ran through his vigils quicker than any of his fraternity. He swore lustily, and was a Trojan to fight. When the army from Lerne pillaged the convent vineyard, Friar John seized the staff of a cross and pummelled the rogues most lustily. He beat out the brains of some, crushed the arms of others, battered their legs, cracked their ribs, gashed their faces, broke their thighs, tore their jaws, dashed in their teeth, dislocated their joints, that never corn was so mauled by the thresher's flail as were these pillagers by the "baton of the cross." (*Rabelais : Gargantua and Pantagruel,* book i. 27.)

"If a joke more than usually profane is to be uttered, Friar John is the spokesman. . . . A mass of lewdness, debauchery, profanity, and valour."
—*Foreign Quarterly Review.*

Friar Laurence, in Shakespeare's *Romeo and Juliet.*

Friar Rush. A house-spirit, sent from the infernal regions in the seventeenth century to keep the monks and friars in the same state of wickedness they were then in. The legends of this roysterer are of German origin. (*Bruder Rausch,* brother Tipple.)

Friar Tuck. Chaplain and steward of Robin Hood. Introduced by Sir Walter Scott in *Ivanhoe.* He is a pudgy, paunchy, humorous, self-indulgent, and combative clerical Falstaff. His costume consisted of a russet habit of the Franciscan order, a red corded girdle with gold tassel, red stockings, and a wallet. A friar was nicknamed *tuck,* because his dress was *tucked* by a girdle at the waist. Thus Chaucer says, "Tucked he was, as is a frere about."

"In this our spacious isle I think there is not one
But he hath heard some talk of Hood and Little John ;
Of Tuck, the merry friar, which many a sermon made
In praise of Robin Hood, his outlaws, and their trade." *Drayton : Polyolbion,* s. 26.

Friar's Heel. The outstanding upright stone at Stonehenge is so called. Geoffrey of Monmouth says the devil bought the stones of an old woman in Ireland; wrapped them up in a wyth, and brought them to Salisbury plain. Just before he got to Mount Ambre the wyth broke, and one of the stones fell into the Avon, the rest were carried to the plain. After the fiend had fixed them in the ground, he cried out, "No man will ever find out how these stones came here." A friar replied, "That's more than thee canst tell," whereupon the foul fiend threw one of the stones at him and struck him on the heel. The stone stuck in the ground, and remains so to the present hour.

Friar's Lanthorn. Sir W. Scott calls Jack o'Lantern Friar Rush. This is an error, as Rush was a domestic spirit, and not a field *esprit follet.* He got admittance into monasteries, and played the monks sad pranks, but is never called "Jack." Sir Walter Scott seems to have considered Friar Rush the same as "Friar with the Rush (light)," and, therefore, Friar with the Lantern or Will o' the Wisp.

" Better we had through mire and bush
Been lanthorn-led by Friar Rush."
Sir Walter Scott : Marmion.

⁂ Milton also (in his *L'Allegro*) calls Will o' the Wisp a friar, probably meaning Friar Rush :

"She was pinched, and pulled. she said ;
And he by Friar's lantern led."

but "Rush" in this. name has nothing to do with the verb *rush* [about] or rush [light]. It is the German *Brüder Rausch,* called by the Scandinavians *Broder Ruus.* (Scandinavian, *ruus,* intoxication, in German *rausch,* which shows us at once that Friar Rush was the spirit of inebriety. (*See* ROBIN GOODFELLOW.)

Friars [*brothers*]. Applied to the four great religious orders — Dominicans, Franciscans, Augustinians, and Carmelites. Later, a fifth order was added—that of the Trinitarians. The first two were called *Black* and *Grey* friars, the Carmelites were called *White* friars, and the Trinitarians *Crutched* friars (*q.v.*).

Friars. (*See* BLACK.)

Friars ·Major (*Fratrēs majo'rēs*) The Domin'icans.

Friars Minor (*Fratrēs mino'rēs*). The Francis'cans.

Friar's Tale. A certain archdeacon had a sumpnour, who acted as his secret spy, to bring before him all offenders. One day as he was riding forth on his business he met the devil disguised as a yeoman, swore eternal friendship, and promised to "go snacks" with him. They first met a carter whose cart stuck in the road, and he cried in his anger, "The devil take it, both horse and cart and hay!" Soon the horse drew it out of the slough, and the man cried, "God bless you, my brave boy!" "There," said the devil, "is my own true brother, the churl spake one thing but he thought another." They next came to an old screw, and the sumpnour declared he would squeeze twelve pence out of her for sin, "though of her he knew no wrong;" so he knocked at her door and summoned her "for cursing" to the archdeacon's court, but said he would overlook the matter for twelve pence, but she pleaded poverty and implored mercy. "The foul fiend fetch me if I excuse thee," said the sumpnour, whereat the devil replied that he would fetch him that very night, and, seizing him round the body, made off with him. (*Chaucer : Canterbury Tales.*)

Fribble. An effeminate coxcomb of weak nerves, in Garrick's farce of *Miss in her Teens.*

Friday is the Mahometan Sabbath. It was the day on which Adam was created and our Lord was crucified. The Sabe'ans consecrate it to Venus or Astartē. (*See* FREA.)

✷ Friday is *Frig-dæg = dies Veníris*, called in French Vendredi, which means the same thing. It was regarded by the Scandinavians as the luckiest day of the week. (*See below,* FRIDAY, *Unlucky.*)

Friday. Fairies and all the tribes of elves of every description, according to mediæval romance, are converted into hideous animals on Friday, and remain so till Monday. (*See* the romance of *Gueri'no Meschi'no,* and others.)

Black Friday. (*See* BLACK.)

Long Friday, Good Friday, long being a synonym of great. Thus Mrs. Quickly says, "'Tis a long loan for a poor lone woman to bear" (2 *Henry II.* ii. 1), and the Scotch proverb, "Between you and the long day"—*i.e.* the *great* or judgment day. Good Friday in Danish is *Langfiedag,* and in Swedish *Långfredag.*

Friday. *A man Friday.* A faithful and submissive attendant, ready to turn his hand to anything.

My man Friday. The young savage found by Robinson Crusoe on a Friday, and kept as his servant and companion on the desert island.

Friday Street (London). The street of fishmongers who served Friday markets. (*Stow.*)

16*

Friday and Columbus.

Friday, August 3rd, 1492, Columbus started on his voyage of discovery.

Friday, October 12th, 1492, he first sighted land.

Friday, January 4th, 1493, he started on his return journey.

Friday, March 12th, 1493, he safely arrived at Palos.

Friday, November 22nd, 1493, he reached Hispaniola in his second expedition.

Friday, June 13th, 1494, he discovered the continent of America.

Friday and the United States.

Friday, June 17th, 1775, was fought the battle of Bunker's Hill.

Friday, July 17th, 1776, the motion was made by John Adams that the United States are and ought to be independent.

Friday, October 17th, 1777, Saratoga surrendered.

Friday, September 22nd, 1780, the treason of Arnold was exposed.

✷ To these Fridays should be added :

Friday, July 13th, 1866, the *Great Eastern* sailed from Valentia, and on Friday, July 27th, 1866, landed safely with the cable at Heart's Ease, Newfoundland.

Friday a Lucky Day. Sir William Churchill says, "Friday is my lucky day. I was born, christened, married, and knighted on that day; and all my best accidents have befallen me on a Friday."

✷ In Scotland Friday is a choice day for weddings. Not so in England.

He who laughs on Friday will weep on Sunday. Sorrow follows in the wake of joy. The line is taken from Racine's comedy of *Les Plaideurs.*

Friday, an Unlucky Day. Because it was the day of our Lord's crucifixion ; it is accordingly a fast-day in the Roman Catholic Church. Soames says, "Adam and Eve ate the forbidden fruit on a Friday, and died on a Friday." (*Anglo-Saxon Church,* p. 255.)

"But once on a Friday ('tis ever they say'),
A day when misfortune is aptest to fall."
                  Saxe: Good Dog of Brettè, stanza 3.

✷ In Spain, Friday is held to be an unlucky day. So is it esteemed by Buddhists and Brahmins. The old Romans called it *nefastus,* from the utter overthrow of their army at Gallia Narbonensis. And in England the proverb is that a Friday moon brings foul weather.

Friend (*A*). The second in a duel, as "Name your friend," "Captain B. acted as his friend."

"Mr. Baillie was to have acted as Disraeli's friend, if there had been a duel between that statesman and Daniel O'Connell."—*Newspaper paragraph* (December, 1885).

Better kinde frend than fremd kinde (motto of the Waterton family) means "better kind friend (*i.e.* neighbour) than a kinsman who dwells in foreign parts." Probably it is Prov. xxvii. 10, "Better is a neighbour that is near, than a brother far off." In which case *fremd* would be = stranger. Better a kind friend than a kinsman who is a stranger.

Friend at Court properly means a friend in a court of law who watches the trial, and tells the judge if he can nose out an error; but the term is more generally applied to a friend in the royal court, who will whisper a good word for you to the sovereign at the proper place and season. (*See* AMICUS CURIÆ.)

Friend in Need (*A*). *A friend in need is a friend indeed.* "*Amicus certus in re incerta cernitur.*"

Friend of Man. Marquis de Mira-beau. So called from one of his works, *L'Ami des Hommes* (5 vols.). This was the father of the great Mirabeau, called by Barnave "the Shakespeare of elo-quence." (1715–1789.)

Friends . . . Enemies. *Our friends the enemy.* When, on April 1, 1814, the allied armies entered Paris, Sir George Jackson tells us he heard a *viva* pass along the streets, and the shout "*nos amis, nos ennemis.*"

Friendly Suit (*A*). A suit brought by a creditor against an executor, to compel all the creditors to accept an equal distribution of the assets.

Friendship (*Examples of*):

Achilles and Patroclos, *Greeks.*
Amys and Amylion (*q.v.*), *Feudal History.*
Baccio (Fra Bartholomew) and Mariotto, *artists.*
Basil and Gregory.
Burke and Dr. Johnson.
Christ and the "Beloved disciple," *New Testa-ment.*
Damon and Pythias, *Syracusans.*
David and Jonathan, *Old Testament.*
Diomēdes and Sthenälos, *Greeks.*
Epaminondas and Pelopīdas, *Greeks.*
Goethe and Schiller. (See *Carlyle: Schiller*, p. 168.)
Hadrian and Antinöus.
Harmodíos and Aristogiton, *Greeks.*
Hercules [Heraklēs] and Iolāos, *Greeks.*
Idoméneus (4 syl.) and Merïon, *Greeks.*
Maurice (*F. D.*), and C. Kingsley.
Montaigne and Etienne de la Boëtie, *French.*
Nisus and Euryälus, *Trojans.*
Pylädes and Orestēs, *Greeks.*
Sacharissa and Amöret, *Syracusans.*
Septimios and Alcander, *Greeks.*
Theseus (2 syl.) and Pyrithöos, *Greeks.*
William of Orange and Bentinck. (See *Macaulay: History*, i. p. 411.)

Friendships Broken (Eng. Hist.):

Elizabeth and the Earl of Essex.
Henry II. and Thomas Becket.
Henry VIII. and Cardinal Wolsey.
Newman (J. H.) and Whately.
Wesley and Whitefield.

⁂ Other examples in other histories might be added; as

Brutus and Cæsar.
Innocent III. and Otho IV. (See *Milman: Latin Christianity*, vol. v. p. 234.)

Frigga, in the genealogy of Æsir, is the supreme goddess, wife of Odin, and daughter of the giant Fiörgwyn. She presides over marriages, and may be called the Juno of Asgard. (*Scandi-navian mythology.*)

Frilingi. The second rank of people among the ancient Saxons. (*See* EDHI-LINGI.)

Fringe. The Jews wore fringes to their garments. These fringes on the garments of the priests were accounted sacred, and were touched by the common people as a charm. Hence the desire of the woman who had the issue of blood to touch the fringe of our Lord's gar-ment. (Matt. ix. 20-22.)

Frippery. Rubbish of a tawdry cha-racter; worthless finery; foolish levity. A *friperer* or *fripperer* is one who deals in frippery, either to sell or clean old clothes. (French, *friperie*, old clothes and cast-off furniture.)

"We know what belongs to a frippery."
    Shakespeare: Tempest iv. 1.

"Old clothes, cast dresses, tattered rags,
  Whose works are e'en the frippery of wit."
    Ben Jonson.

Frippery properly means rags and all sorts of odds and ends. French, *fripe* (a rag), *friperie* (old clothes and furni-ture), *fripier* (a broker of old clothes, etc.). Applied to pastry. Eugène Grandet says, "*En Anjou la 'frippe' exprime l'accompagnement du pain, depuis le beurre plus distinguée des frippes.*"

Frisket. The light frame of the printing-press, which folds down upon the tympan (*q.v.*) over the sheet of paper to be printed. Its object is two-fold— to hold the sheet in its place and to keep the margins clean. It is called frisket because it *frisks* or skips up and down very rapidly—*i.e.* the pressman opens it and shuts it over with great alacrity, the movement being called "flying the frisket."

Frith. *By frith and fell.* By wold and wild, wood and common. Frith is the Welsh *frith* or *friz*, and means a "woody place." Fell is the German *fels* (rock), and means barren or stony places, a common.

Frithiof (pron. *Frit-yoff*) means "peace-maker." In the Icelandic myths he married Ingëborg (*In-ge-boy'-e*), the daughter of a petty king of Norway, and widow of Hring, to whose dominions he succeeded. His adventures are recorded in the Saga which bears his name, and which was written at the close of the thirteenth century.

Frithiof's Sword. Angurva'del (*stream of anguish*). (*See* SWORD.)

Fritz (*Old Fritz*). Frederick II. *the Great*, King of Prussia (1712, 1740-1786).

Frog. A frog and mouse agreed to settle by single combat their claims to a marsh; but, while they fought, a kite carried them both off. (*Æsop: Fables*, clxviii.)

> " Old Æsop's fable, where he told
> What fate unto the mouse and frog befel."
> *Cary: Dante*, cxxiii.

Nic Frog is the Dutchman (no† French-man) in Arbuthnot's *History of John Bull*. Frogs are called " Dutch night-ingales."

Frog's March. Carrying an obstrep-erous prisoner, face downwards, by his four limbs.

Frogs. Frenchmen, properly *Paris-ians*. So called from their ancient heraldic device, which was three frogs or three toads. " *Qu'en disent les grenouilles ?* "—What will the frogs (people of Paris) say?—was in 1791 a common court phrase at Versailles. There was a point in the pleasantry when Paris was a quagmire, called *Lute'tia* (mud-land) because, like frogs or toads, they lived in mud, but now it is quite an anomaly. (*See* CRAPAUD.)

Frogs. The Lycian shepherds were changed into frogs for mocking Lato'na. (*Ovid: Metamorphoses*, vi. 4.)

> " As when those hinds that were transformed to frogs
> Railed at Latona's twin-born progeny."
> *Milton: Sonnet*, vii.

It may be all fun to you, but it is death to the frogs. The allusion is to the fable of a boy stoning frogs for his amusement.

Frollo (*Archdeacon Claude*). A priest who has a great reputation for sanctity, but falls in love with a gipsy girl, and pursues her with relentless persecution because she will not yield to him. (*Victor Hugo: Notre Dame de Paris*.)

Fronde (1 syl.). A political squabble during the ministry of Cardinal Maz'-arin, in the minority of Louis XIV. (1648-1653). The malcontents were called *Frondeurs*, from a witty illustra-tion of a councillor, who said that they were " like schoolboys who sling stones about the streets. When no eye is upon them they are bold as bullies; but the moment a 'policeman' approaches, away they scamper to the ditches for

concealment " (*Montglat*). The French for a sling is *fronde*, and for slingers, *frondeurs*.

> " It was already true that the French govern-ment was a despotism . . . and as speeches and lampoons were launched by persons who tried to hide after they had shot their dart, some one compared them to children with a sling (*fronde*), who let fly a stone and run away."—*C. M. Yonge: History of France*, chap. viii. p. 136.

Frondeur. A backbiter; one who throws stones at another.

> " 'And what about Diebitsch ?' began another *frondeur*."—*Vera*, p. 200.

Fronti'no. (*See* HORSE.)

Frost. *Jack Frost.* The personifica-tion of frost.

> " Jack Frost looked forth one still, clear night,
> And he said, 'Now I shall be out of sight ;
> So over the valley and over the height
> In silence I'll take my way.' "
> *Miss Gould.*

Frost Saints. (*See* ICE SAINTS.)

Froth (*Master*). " A foolish gentle-man " in *Measure for Measure*.

Lord Froth. A pompous coxcomb in *The Double Dealer*, by Congreve.

Froude's Cat. This cat wanted to know what was good for life, and every-one gave her queer answers. The owl said, " Meditate, O cat ; " and so she tried to think which could have come first, the fowl or the egg. (*Short Studies on Great Subjects.*)

> " If I were to ask, like Froude's cat, ' What is my duty ?' you would answer, I suppose, like the sagacious animal in the parable, ' Get your own dinner . . . that is my duty, I suppose.' "—*Edna Lyall: Donovan*, chap. ix.

Frozen Music. Architecture. So called by F. Schlegel.

Frozen Words appears to have been a household joke with the ancient Greeks, for Antiph'anēs applies it to the discourses of Plato : " As the cold of certain cities is so intense that it freezes the very words we utter, which remain congealed till the heat of summer thaws them, so the mind of youth is so thoughtless that the wisdom of Plato lies there frozen, as it were, till it is thawed by the ripened judgment of mature age." (*Plutarch's Morals.*)

> " The moment their backs were turned, little Jacob thawed, and renewed his crying from the point where Quilp had frozen him." — *Dickens: Old Curiosity Shop.*

> " Truth in person doth appear
> Like words congealed in northern air."
> *Butler: Hudibras*, pt. i. l, lines 147-8.

Everyone knows the incident of the "frozen horn" related by *Munchausen*.

❧ Pantagruel and his companions, on the confines of the Frozen Sea, heard the uproar of a battle, which had been frozen the preceding winter, released by a thaw. (*Rabelais: Pantagruel*, book iv. chap. 56.)

Frumen'tius (*St.*). Apostle of Ethiopia and the Abyssinians in the fourth century.

Fry. Children (a word of contempt). *Get away, you young fry.* It means properly a crowd of young fishes, and its application to children should be limited to those that obstruct your path, crowd about you, or stand in your way. (French, *frai*, spawn.)

Nothing to fry with (French). Nothing to eat; nothing to live on. (*See* WIDE-NOSTRILS.)

Frying-pan. *Out of the frying-pan into the fire.* In trying to extricate yourself from one evil, you fell into a greater. The Greeks used to say, "Out of the smoke into the flame;" and the French say, "*Tombre de la poêle dans la braise.*"

Fub. To steal, to prig. (French, *fourbi*, "a Jew who conceals a trap;" *fourber*, "to cheat;" *four*, "a false pocket for concealing stolen goods.")

Fuchs [a *fox*]. A freshman of the first year in the German University. In the second year he is called a *Bursch*.

Fudge. Not true, stuff, make-up. (Gaelic, *ffug*, deception; Welsh, *ffug*, pretence; whence *ffugiwr*, a pretender or deceiver.) A word of contempt bestowed on one who says what is absurd or untrue. A favourite expression of Mr. Burchell in the *Vicar of Wakefield.*

Fudge Family. A series of metrical epistles by Thomas Moore, purporting to be written by a family on a visit to Paris. Sequel, *The Fudge Family in England.*

Fuel. *Adding fuel to fire.* Saying or doing something to increase the anger of a person already angry. The French say, "pouring oil on fire."

Fuga ad Salices (*A*). An affectation or pretence of denial; as, when Cæsar thrice refused the crown in the Lu'percal. A "nolo episcopāri." The allusion is to—

"Malo me Galatēa petit, lascīva puella,
  Et fugit ad salīces, et se cupit ante vidēri."
        Virgil: Eclöga, iii, 64, 65.

"Cranmer was not prepared for so great an sudden an elevation. Under pretence that the king's affairs still required his presence abroad, he tarried six months longer, in the hope that Henry might consign the crosier to some other hand. There was no affectation in this—no *fuga ad salices*. Ambition is made of sterner stuff than the spirit of Cranmer."—*Blunt: Reformation in England*, 123.

Fuggers. German merchants, proverbial for their great wealth. "Rich as a Fugger" is common in Old English dramatists. Charles V. introduced some of the family into Spain, where they superintended the mines.

"I am neither an Indian merchant, nor yet a Fugger, but a poor boy like yourself."—*Gusman d'Alfarache.*

Fugleman means properly wingman, but is applied to a soldier who stands in front of men at drill to show them what to do. Their proper and original post was in front of the right wing. (German, *Flügel*, a wing.)

Fulhams, or **Fullams.** Loaded dice; so called from the suburb where the Bishop of London resides, which, in the reign of Queen Elizabeth, was the most notorious place for blacklegs in all England. Dice made with a cavity were called "gourds." Those made to throw the high numbers (from five to twelve) were called "high fullams" or "gourds," and those made to throw the low numbers (from ace to four) were termed "low fullams" or "gourds."

"For gourd and fullam holds
And 'high' and 'low' beguile the rich and poor."
    Shakespeare: Merry Wives of Windsor, i. 3.

Fulhams. Make-believes; so called from false or loaded dice. (*See above.*)

"Fulhams of poetic fiction."
    Butler: Hudibras, pt. ii. 1.
"Have their fulhams at command,
Brought up to do their feats at hand."
    Butler: Upon Gaming.

Full Cry. When all the hounds have caught the scent, and give tongue in chorus.

Full Dress. The dress worn on occasions of ceremony. If a man has no special costume, his "full dress" is a suit of black, open waistcoat, swallow-tailed coat, white neckcloth, and patent-leather boots or half-boots. Academicals are worn in the Universities and on official occasions; and full military dress is worn when an officer is on duty, at court, and at official fêtes, but otherwise, "evening dress" suffices.

Full Fig (*In*). "*En grande tenue.*" Probably "fig" is the contraction of figure in books and journals of fashion, and full fig. would mean the height of fashion. It is outrageous to refer the phrase to the fig-leaves used by Adam and Eve, by way of aprons. (*See* FIG.)

Full Swing (*In*). Fully at work; very busy; in full operation.

Fulsome. "Ful" is the Anglo-Saxon *fúl* (foulness), not *ful* (full); "some" is the affix meaning *united with*, the *basis* of something; as, gladsome mettlesome, gamesome, lightsome, frolicsome, etc., etc.

"No adulation was too fulsome for her [Elizabeth], no flattery of her beauty too great."—
Green: Short History of England, chap. viii. sec. 3, p. 376.

Fum, or *Fung hwang.* One of the four symbolical animals supposed to preside over the destinies of the Chinese Empire. It originated from the element of fire, was born in the Hill of the Sun's Halo, and has its body inscribed with the five cardinal virtues. It has the forepart of a goose, the hind-quarters of a stag, the neck of a snake, the tail of a fish, the forehead of a fowl, the down of a duck, the marks of a dragon, the back of a tortoise, the face of a swallow, the beak of a cock, is about six cubits high, and perches only on the woo-tung tree. It is this curious creature that is embroidered on the dresses of certain mandarins.

Fum the Fourth. George IV.

"And where is Fum the Fourth, our royal bird."
Byron: Don Juan, xi. 78.

Fu'mage (2 syl.). A tax for having a fire, mentioned in Domesday Book, and abolished by William III. (Latin, *fumus*, smoke.)

Fume. *In a fume.* In ill-temper, especially from impatience. The French say, "*Fumer sans tabac; Fumer sans pipe*" (to put oneself into a rage). Smoking with rage, or rather with the ineffectual vapour of anger.

"A ! Rignot, il est courageulx
Pour un homme avantureulx
Et terrible quant il se fume."
L'Acentureulx (a farce).

Fun. *To make fun of.* To make a butt of; to ridicule; to play pranks on one. (Compare Irish *fonn*, delight.)
Like fun. Thoroughly, energetically, with delight.

"On'y look at the dimmercrats, see what they've done,
Jest simply by stickin' together like fun."
Lowell: Biglow Papers (First series iv. stanza 5).

Fund. *The sinking fund* is money set aside by the Government for paying off a part of the national debt. This money is "sunk," or withdrawn from circulation, for the bonds purchased by it are destroyed.

Funds or *Public Funds.* Money lent at interest to Government on Government security. It means the national stock, which is the *foundation* of its operations.
A fall in the funds is when the quotation is lower than when it was last quoted.

A rise in the funds is when the quotation is higher than it was before.
To be interested in the funds is to have money in the public funds.
To be out of funds, out of money.

Funeral means a torchlight procession (from the Latin, *funis*, a torch), because funerals among the Romans took place at night by torchlight, that magistrates and priests might not be violated by seeing a corpse, and so be prevented from performing their sacred duties.

"Funus [a funeral], from *funes* or *funalia* [torches] .... originally made of ropes."
Adams : Roman Antiquities (Funerals).

Funeral Banquet. The custom of giving a feast at funerals came to us from the Romans, who not only feasted the friends of the deceased, but also distributed meat to the persons employed.

"Thrift, thrift, Horatio ! the funeral baked meats
Did coldly furnish forth the marriage tables."
Shakespeare: Hamlet, i. 2.

Funeral Games. Public games were held both in Greece and Rome in honour of the honoured dead. Examples of this custom are numerous : as at the death of Azan (son of Arcas, father of the Arcadians) ; the games instituted by Hercules at the death of Pelops ; those held at the death of Œdipus ; the games held by Achilles in honour of his friend Patroclos (*Homer : Iliad*, book xxiii.) ; those held by Æneas in honour of his father Anchis'es (*Virgil : Æneid*, book v.) ; the games held in honour of Miltiädes (*Herodotos*) ; those in honour of Brasĭdas (*Thucyd'ĭdēs*) ; and those in honour of Timolĕon mentioned by *Plutarch.* The spectators at these games generally dressed in white.

Fungo'so. A character in *Every Man in His Humour*, by Ben Jonson.

"Unlucky as Fungoso in the play."
Pope: Essay on Criticism (328).

Funk. *To be in a funk* may be the Walloon "*In de fonk zün*," literally to "be in the smoke." Colloquially to be in a state of trepidation from uncertainty or apprehension of evil.

Funny Bone. A pun on the word *hu'merus.* It is the inner condyle of the humerus ; or, to speak untechnically, the knob, or *enlarged end* of the bone terminating where the ulnar nerve is exposed at the elbow ; the crazy bone. A knock on this bone at the elbow produces a painful sensation.

Fur'below. A corruption of *falbala.*

a word in French, Italian, and Spanish to signify a sort of flounce.

"Flounced and furbelowed from head to foot."
—*Addison.*

Furca. (*See* FOSSA and FORKS.)

Furcam et Flagellum (gallows and whip). The meanest of all servile tenures, the bondman being at the lord's mercy, both life and limb. (*See* FORKS.)

Furies (*The Three*). Tisiphŏne (*Goel,* or Avenger of blood), Alecto (Implacable), and Megæra (Disputatious). The best paintings of these divinities are those by Il Giottino (Thomas di Stefano) of Florence (1324-1356), Giulio Romano (1492-1546), Pietro da Cortōna (1596-1669), and Titian (1477-1576).

Furies of the Guillotine (*The*). The tricoteuses—that is, Frenchwomen who attended the Convention knitting, and encouraged the Commune in all their most bloodthirsty excesses. Never in any age or any country did women so disgrace their sex.

Furor. Son of Occasion, an old hag, who was quite bald behind. Sir Guyon bound him " with a hundred iron chains and a hundred knots." (*Spenser: Faërie Queene,* book ii.)

Fusber'ta. Rinaldo's sword is so called in *Orlando Furioso.* (*See* SWORD.)

"This awful sword was as dear to him as Durin'da'na or Fusberta to their respective masters."
—*Sir W. Scott.*

Fusilier's. Foot-soldiers that used to be armed with a fusil or light musket. The word is now a misnomer, as the six British and two Indian regiments so called carry rifles like those of the rest of the infantry.

Fuss. Much ado about nothing. (Anglo-Saxon, *fus,* eager.)

"So full of figure, so full of fuss,
She seemed to be nothing but bustle."
Hood: Miss Kilmansegg, part iii. stanza 12.

Fus'tian. Stuff, bombast, pretentious words. Properly, a sort of cotton velvet. (French, *futaine ;* Spanish, *fustan,* from *Fustat* in Egypt, where the cloth was first made.) (*See* BOMBAST ; CAMELOT.)

"Discourse fustian with one's own shadow."—*Shakespeare : Othello,* ii. 3.
"Some scurvy quaint collection of fustian phrases, and uplandish words."—*Heywood : Faire Maide of the Exchange,* ii. 2.

Fustian Words. Isaac Taylor thinks this phrase means toper's words, and derives fustian from *fuste,* Old French for a cask, whence "fusty" (tasting of the cask). It may be so, but we have numerous phrases derived from

materials of dress applied to speech, as velvet, satin, silken, etc. The mother of Artaxerxes said, "Those who address kings must use silken words." In French, " *faire patte de velour* " means to fatten with velvet words in order to seduce or win over.

Futile (2 syl.) is that which will not hold together ; inconsistent. *A futile scheme* is a design conceived in the mind which will not hold good in practice. (Latin, *futio,* to run off like water, whence *futilis.*) (*See* SCHEME.)

G.

G. This letter is the outline of a camel's head and neck. It is called in Hebrew *gimel* (a camel).

G.C.B. (*See* BATH.)

G.H.V.L. on the coin of William III. of the Netherlands is *Groot Hertog Van Luxemburg* (grand duke of Luxembourg).

G.O.M. The initial letters of Grand Old Man ; so Mr. Gladstone was called during his premiership 1881-1885. Lord Rosebery first used the expression 26th April, 1882, and the Right Hon. Sir William Harcourt repeated it, 18th October, the same year ; since then it has become quite a synonym for the proper name.

Gab (*g* hard). *The gift of the gab.* Fluency of speech ; or, rather, the gift of boasting. (French, *gaber,* to gasconade ; Danish and Scotch, *gab,* the mouth ; Gaelic, *gob ;* Irish, *cab ;* whence our *gap* and *gape, gabble* and *gobble.* The gable of a house is its *beak.*)

"There was a good man named Job
Who lived in the land of Uz,
He had a good gift of the gob,
The same thing happened us."
Book of Job, by Zaoß. Boyd.

"Thou art one of the knights of France, who hold it for glee and pastime to gab, as they term it, of exploits that are beyond human power."—*Sir W. Scott : The Talisman,* chap. ii.

Gab'ardine' (3 syl.). A Jewish coarse cloak. (Spanish, *gavardina,* a long coarse cloak.)

"You call me misbeliever, cut-throat dog,
And spit upon my Jewish gabardine."
Shakespeare : Merchant of Venice, i. 3.

Gabel', Gabelle (*g* hard). A salt-tax. A word applied in French history to the monopoly of salt. All the salt made in France had to be brought to the royal warehouses, and was there sold at a price fixed by the Government. The iniquity was that some provinces had to pay twice as much as others. Edward III. jokingly called this monopoly "King Philippe's *Salic* law." It was abolished in 1789. (German, *gabe*, a tax.)

Gaberlunzie, or *A gaberlunzie man* (*g* hard). A mendicant ; or, more strictly speaking, one of the king's bedesmen, who were licensed beggars. The word *gaban* is French for " a cloak with tight sleeves and a hood." *Lunzie* is a diminutive of *laine* (wool) ; so that *gaberlunzie* means " coarse woollen gown." These bedesmen were also called *blue-gowns* (*q.v.*), from the colour of their cloaks. (*See above,* GABARDINE.)

Ga'briel (*g* hard), in Jewish mythology, is the angel of death to the favoured people of God, the prince of fire and thunder, and the only angel that can speak Syriac and Chaldee. The Mahometans call him the chief of the four favoured angels, and the spirit of truth. In mediæval romance he is the second of the seven spirits that stand before the throne of God, and, as God's messenger, carries to heaven the prayers of men. (*Jerusalem Delivered*, book i.) The word means "power of God." Milton makes him chief of the angelic guards placed over Paradise.

" Betwixt these rocky pillars Gabriel sat,
    Chief of the angelic guards."
            Paradise Lost, iv. 549-550.

Longfellow, in his *Golden Legend*, makes him the angel of the moon, and says he brings to man the gift of hope.

' I am the angel of the moon . . .
 Nearest the earth, it is my ray
 That best illumines the midnight way.
 I bring the gift of hope."
            The Miracle Play, iii.

∵ It was Gabriel who (we are told in the Koran) took Mahomet to heaven on Al-burak (*q.v.*), and revealed to him his "prophetic lore." In the Old Testament Gabriel is said to have explained to Daniel certain visions ; and in the New Testament it was Gabriel who announced to Zacharias the future birth of John the Baptist, and that afterwards appeared to Mary, the mother of Jesus. (Luke i. 26, etc.)

Gabriel's horse. Haïzum.

Gabriel's hounds, called also *Gabble Ratchet.* Wild geese. The noise of the bean-goose (*anser segětum*) in flight is like that of a pack of hounds in full cry. The legend is that they are the souls of unbaptised children wandering through the air till the Day of Judgment.

Gab'riell'e (3 syl. ; *g* hard). *La Belle Gabrielle.* Daughter of Antoine d'Estrées, grand-master of artillery, and

governor of the Ile de France. Henri IV., towards the close of 1590, happened to sojourn for a night at the Château de Cœuvres, and fell in love with Gabrielle, then nineteen years of age. To throw a flimsy veil over his intrigue, he married her to Damerval de Liancourt, created her Duchess de Beaufort, and took her to live with him at court.

" Charmante Gabrielle,
    Percé de mille dards,
Quand la gloire m'appelle
    A la suite de Mars." *Henri IV.*

Gabri'na, in *Orlando Furioso*, is a sort of Potiphar's wife. (*See under* ARGEO.) When Philander had unwittingly killed her husband, Gabrina threatened to deliver him up to the law unless he married her ; an alternative that Philander accepted, but ere long she tired of and poisoned him. The whole affair being brought to light, Gabrina was shut up in prison, but, effecting her escape, wandered about the country as an old hag. Knight after knight had to defend her ; but at last she was committed to the charge of Odorico, who, to get rid of her, hung her on an old elm. (*See* ODORICO.)

Ga'briolet'ta (*g* hard). Governess of Brittany, rescued by Am'adis of Gaul from the hands of Balan, " the bravest and strongest of all the giants." (*Amadis of Gaul*, bk. iv. ch. 129.)

Gad (*g* hard). *Gadding from place to place.* Wandering from pillar to post without any profitable purpose.

"Give water no passage, neither a wicked woman liberty to gad abroad."—*Ecclesiasticus* xxv. 25.

Gad-about (*A*). A person who spends day after day in frivolous visits, gadding from house to house.

Gad-fly is not the *roving* but the *goading* fly. (Anglo-Saxon, *gad*, a goad.)

Gad-steel. Flemish steel. So called because it is wrought in *gads*, or small bars. (Anglo-Saxon, *gad*, a small bar or goad ; Icelandic, *gaddr*, a spike or goad.)

" I will go get a leaf of brass,
And with a gad of steel will write these words."
            Shakespeare : Titus Andronicus, iv. 1.

Gadshill, in Kent, near Rochester. Famous for the attack of Sir John Falstaff and three of his knavish companions on a party of four travellers, whom they robbed of their purses. While the robbers were dividing the spoil, Poins and the Prince of Wales set upon them, and "outfaced them from their prize ; " and as for the "Hercules of flesh," he ran and "roared for mercy, and still ran and roared," says the prince," "as ever I heard a bull-calf." Gadshill is also the name of one of the thievish companions of Sir John. (*Shakespeare*: 1 *Henry IV.*, ii. 4.)

⁂ Charles Dickens lived at Gadshill.

Gaels. A contraction of *Gaid-heals* (hidden rovers). The inhabitants of Scotland who maintained their ground in the Highlands against the Celts.

Gaff (*g* hard). *Crooked as a gaff.* A gaff is an iron hook at the end of a short pole, used for landing salmon, etc. The metal spurs of fighting-cocks. In nautical language, a spar to which the head of a fore-and-aft sail is bent. (*Dana: Seaman's Manual*, p. 97.) (Irish, *gaf*; Spanish and Portuguese, *gafa*.)

Gaffer (*g* hard). A title of address, as "Gaffer Grey," "Good-day, Gaffer." About equal to "mate." (Anglo-Saxon, *gefera*, a comrade.) Many think the word is "grandfather." (*See* GAMMER.)

" If I had but a thousand a year, Gaffer Green,
   If I had but a thousand a year."
             Gaffer Green and Robin Rough.

Gags, in theatrical parlance, are interpolations. When Hamlet directs the players to say no more "than is set down," he cautions them against indulgence in gags. (*Hamlet*, iii. 2.) (Dutch, *gaggelen*, to cackle. Compare Anglo-Saxon, *geagl*, the jaw.)

Gala Day (*g* hard). A festive day; a day when people put on their best attire. (Spanish, *gala*, court dress; Italian, *gala*, finery; French, *gala*, pomp.)

Galactic Circle (*The*) is to sidereal astronomy what the ecliptic is to planetary astronomy. The Galaxy being the sidereal equator, the Galactic circle is inclined to it at an angle of 63°.

Gal'ahad, or *Sir Galaad* (*g* hard). Son of Sir Launcelot and Elaine, one of the Knights of the Round Table, so pure in life that he was successful in his search for the Sangrail. Tennyson has a poem on the subject, called *The Holy Grail.*

" There Galaad sat, with manly grace,
   Yet maiden meekness in his face."
      Sir W. Scott: Bridal of Triermain, ii. 13.

Gal'aor (*Don*). Brother of Am'adis of Gaul, a gay libertine, whose adventures form a strong contrast to those of the more serious hero.

Galate'a. A sea-nymph, beloved by Polyphe'me, but herself in love with Acis. Acis was crushed under a huge rock by the jealous giant, and Galatea threw herself into the sea, where she joined her sister nymphs. Carlo Maratti (1625-1713) depicted Galatea in the sea and Polypheme sitting on a rock. Handel has an opera entitled *Acis and Galatea.*

Gal'athe (3 syl.). Hector's horse.

" There is a thousand Hectors in the field ;
   Now here he fights on Galathe his horse,
   And there lacks work."
      Shakespeare: Troilus and Cressida, v. 5.

Galaxy (*The*). The "Milky Way." A long white luminous track of stars which seems to encompass the heavens like a girdle. According to classic fable, it is the path to the palace of Zeus (1 syl.) or Jupiter. (Greek, *gala*, milk, genitive, *galaktos*.)

A galaxy of beauty. A cluster, assembly, or coterie of handsome women.

Gale's Compound. Powdered glass mixed with gunpowder to render it non-explosive. Dr. Gale is the patentee.

Galen (*g* hard). *Galen says " Nay,"* and Hippoc'ratēs " Yea." The doctors disagree, and who is to decide ? Galen was a physician of Asia Minor in the second Christian century. Hippoc'ratēs —a native of Cos, born B.C. 460—was the most celebrated physician of antiquity.

Galen. A generic name for an apothecary. Galenists prefer drugs (called *Galenical medicines*), Paracelsians use mineral medicines.

Galeot'ti (*Martius*). Louis XI.'s Italian astrologer. Being asked by the king if he knew the day of his own death, he craftily replied that he could not name the exact day, but he knew this much: it would be twenty-four hours before the decease of his majesty. Thrasullus, the soothsayer of Tiberius, Emperor of Rome, made verbally the same answer to the same question.

" 'Can thy pretended skill ascertain the hour of thine own death ?'
   " 'Only by referring to the fate of another,' said Galeotti.
   " 'I understand not thine answer,' said Louis.
   " 'Know then, O king,' said Martius, 'that this only I can tell with certainty concerning mine own death, that it shall take place exactly twenty-four hours before your majesty's.' "
      Sir W. Scott: Quentin Durward, chap. xxix.

Galera'na (*g* hard), according to Ariosto, was wife of Charlemagne. (*Orlando Furioso*, bk. xxi.) (*See* CHARLE-MAGNE.)

Galère (2 syl.). *Que diable allait-il faire dans cette galère ?* (What business had he to be on that galley ?) This is from Molière's comedy of *Les Fourberies* *de Scapin.* Scapin wants to bamboozle Géronte out of his money, and tells him that his master (Géronte's son) is detained prisoner on a Turkish galley, where he went out of curiosity. He adds, that unless the old man will ransom him, he will be taken to Algiers as a slave. Géronte replies to all that Scapin urges, "What business had he to go on board the galley?" The retort is given to those who beg money to help them out of difficulties which they have brought on themselves. "I grant you are in trouble, but what right had you to go on the galley?"

Vogue la Galère. (*See* VOGUE.)

Gale′sus (*g* hard). A river of Pug′lia, not far from Tarentum. The sheep that fed on the meadows of Gale′sus were noted for their fine wool. (*Horace : 2 Carminum Liber*, vi. 10.)

Galian′a (*g* hard). A Moorish princess. Her father, King Gadalfe of Tole′do, built for her a palace on the Tagus so splendid that the phrase "a palace of Galiana" became proverbial in Spain.

Galimau′frey or **Gallimau′frey** (*g* hard). A medley; any confused jumble of things; but strictly speaking, a hotchpotch made up of all the scraps of the larder. (French, *galimafrée;* Spanish, *gallofa,* "broken meat," *gallofero,* a beggar.)

"He woos both high and low, both rich and poor,
Both young and old, one with another, Ford ;
He loves thy gaily-mawfry [all sorts]."
Shakespeare : Merry Wives, ii. 1.

Gall and Wormwood. Extremely disagreeable and annoying.

"It was so much gall and wormwood to the family."—*Mrs. E. Lynn Linton.*

Gall of Bitterness (*The*). The bitterest grief; extreme affliction. The ancients taught that grief and joy were subject to the gall, affection to the heart, knowledge to the kidneys, anger to the bile (one of the four humours of the body), and courage or timidity to the liver. The gall of bitterness, like the heart of hearts, means the bitter centre of bitterness, as the heart of hearts means the innermost recesses of the heart or affections. In the Acts it is used to signify "the sinfulness of sin," which leads to the bitterest grief.

"I perceive thou art in the gall of bitterness, and in the bond of iniquity."—*Acts* viii. 23.

Gall of Pigeons. The story goes that pigeons have no gall, because the dove sent from the ark by Noah burst its gall out of grief, and none of the pigeon family have had a gall ever since.

"For sin' the Flood of Noah
The dow she had nae ga'."
Jamieson : Popular Ballads (*Lord of Rorlin's Daughter*).

Gall's Bell (*St.*). A four-sided bell, which was certainly in existence in the seventh century, and is still shown in the monastery of St. Gall, Switzerland.

Gallant′ (*g* hard). Brave, polite, courteous, etc. (French, *galant.*)

Gallery. *To play with one eye on the gallery.* To work for popularity. As an actor who sacrifices his author for popular applause, or a stump political orator "orates" to catch votes.

"The instant we begin to think 'about 'success and the effect of our work—to play with one eye on the gallery—we lose power, and touch, and everything else."—*Rudyard Kipling : The Light that Failed.*

Galley (*g* hard). A printer's frame into which type from the stick (*q.v.*) is emptied. In the galley the type appears only in columns; it is subsequently divided into pages, and transferred to the "chase" (*q.v.*). (French, *galée.*)

Galley Pence. Genoese coin brought over by merchants ("galleymen"), who used the Galley Wharf, Thames Street. These pence, or rather halfpence, were larger than our own.

Gal′lia (*g* hard). France.

"Impending hangs o'er Gallia's humbled coast."
Thomson : Summer.

Gall′ia Bracca′ta [*trousered Gaul*]. Gallia Narbonen′sis was so called from the "braccæ" or trousers which the natives wore in common with the Scythians and Persians.

Gall′ia Coma′ta. That part of Gaul which belonged to the Roman emperor, and was governed by leg′ates (*lega′ti*), was so called from the long hair (*coma*) worn by the inhabitants flowing over their shoulders.

Gallice′næ. The nine virgin priestesses of the Gallic oracle. By their charms they could raise the wind and waves, turn themselves into any animal form they liked, cure wounds and diseases, and predict future events. (*Gallic mythology.*)

Gall′icism (*g* hard). A phrase or sentence constructed after the French idiom; as, "when you *shall have returned* home you will find a letter on your table." Government documents are especially guilty of this fault. In St. Matt. xv. 32 is a Gallicism: "I have compassion on the multitude, because *they continue* with me now three days, and have nothing to eat." (Compare St. Mark viii. 2.)

Gallicum Merleburgæ. French of "Stratford atte Bowe."

"There is a spring which (so they say), if anyone tastes, he murders his French [Gallice barbarizat] ; so that when anyone speaks that language ill, we say he speaks the French of Marlborough [Gallicum Merleburgæ]."—*Walter Map.*

Galligantus. A giant who lived with Hocus-Pocus in an enchanted castle. By his magic he changed men and women into dumb animals, amongst which was a duke's daughter, changed into a roe. Jack the Giant Killer, arrayed in his cap, which rendered him nvisible, went to the castle and read the inscription : "Whoever can this trumpet blow, will cause the giant's overthrow." He seized the trumpet, blew a loud blast, the castle fell down, Jack slew the giant, and was married soon after to the duke's daughter, whom he had rescued from the giant's castle. (*Jack the Giant Killer.*)

Gallimaufry. (*See* GALIMAUFREY.)

Galli'pot (*g* hard) means a glazed pot, as *galletyles* (3 syl.) means glazed tiles. (Dutch, *gleipot*, glazed pot.) In farce and jest it forms a by-name for an apothecary.

Gallo-Bel'gicus. An annual register in Latin for European circulation, first published in 1598.

"It is believed,
And told for news with as much diligence
As if 'twere writ in Gallo-Belgicus."
Thomas May : The Heir. (1615.)

Galloon. (*See* CADDICE.)

Gall'oway (*g* hard). A horse less than fifteen hands high, of the breed which originally came from Galloway in Scotland.

"Thrust him downstairs ! Know we not Galloway nags ?"—*Shakespeare: 2 Henry IV.,* ii. 4.
"The knights and esquires are well mounted on large bay horses, the common people on little Galloways."—*S. Lanier: Boy's Froissart,* book i. chap. xiv. p. 25.

Gallowglass. An armed servitor (or foot-soldier) of an ancient Irish chief.

Gal'lus Numid'icus (*A*). A turkey cock. Our common turkey comes neither from Turkey nor Numidia, but from North America.

"And bedecked in borrowed plumage, he struts over his pages as solemnly as any old Gallus Numidicus over the farmyard."—*Fra. Ollie* (1885).

Galor'e (2 syl., *g* hard). A sailor's term, meaning "in abundance." (Irish, *go leor*, in abundance.)

For his Poll he had trinkets and gold galore,
Besides of prize-money quite a store."
Jack Robinson.

Gal'vanism (*g* hard). So called from Louis Galva'ni, of Bologna. Signora Galvani in 1790 had frog-soup prescribed for her diet, and one day some-skinned frogs which happened to be placed near an electric machine in motion exhibited signs of vitality. This strange phenomenon excited the curiosity of the experimenter, who subsequently noticed that similar convulsive effects were produced when the copper hooks on which the frogs were strung were suspended on the iron hook of the larder. Experiments being carefully conducted, soon led to the discovery of this important science.

Galway Jury. An enlightened, independent jury. The expression has its birth in certain trials held in Ireland in 1635 upon the right of the king to the counties of Ireland. Leitrim, Roscommon, Sligo and Mayo, gave judgment in favour of the Crown, but Galway opposed it ; whereupon the sheriff was fined £1,000, and each of the jurors £4,000.

Gam. (*See* GANELON.)

Ga'ma (*g* hard). Vasco da Gama, the Portuguese, was the first European navigator who doubled the Cape of Good Hope.

" With such mad seas the daring Gama fought ...
Incessant labouring round the stormy Cape."
Thomson : Summer.

Vasco da Gama. The hero of Camoëns' *Lusiad.* He is represented as sagacious, intrepid, tender-hearted, pious, fond of his country, and holding his temper in full command. He is also the hero of Meyerbeer's posthumous opera, *L'Africaine.*

" Gama, captain of the venturous band,
Of bold emprise, and born for high command,
Whose martial fires, with prudence close allied,
Ensured the smiles of fortune on his side."
Camoëns : Lusiad, bk. i.

Gamaheu, a natural cameo, or intaglio. These stones (chiefly agate) contain natural representations of plants, landscapes, or animals. Pliny tells us that the "Agate of Pyrrhus" contained a representation of the nine Muses, with Apollo in the midst. Paracelsus calls them natural talismans. Albertus Magnus makes mention of them, and Gaffaret, in his *Curiosités inouïes,* attributes to them magical powers. (French, *camaïeu,* from the oriental *gamahuia, camchuia,* or *camebouia.*)

⁂ When magic was ranked as a science, certain conjunctions were called "Gamahæan unions."

Gamaliel. In the Talmud is rather a good story about this pundit. Cæsar asked Gamaliel how it was that God robbed Adam in order to make Eve. Gamaliel's daughter instantly replied, the robbery was substituting a golden vessel for an earthen one.

Gambo'ge (2 syl., first *g* hard, second *g* soft). So called from Cambo'dia or Camboja, whence it was first brought.

Game includes hares, pheasants, partridges, grouse, heath-game, or moor-game, black-game, and bustards. (*Game Act*, 1, 2, Will. IV.) (*See* SPORTING SEASON.)

Game.
Two can play at that game. If you claw me I can claw you; if you throw stones at me I can do the same to you. The Duke of Buckingham led a mob to break the windows of the Scotch Puritans who came over with James I., but the Puritans broke the windows of the duke's house, and when he complained to the king, the British Solomon quoted to him the proverb, "Those who live in glass houses shouldn't throw stones."

You are making game of me. You are chaffing me. (Anglo-Saxon, *gamen*, jest, scoffing.)

Game-leg. A bad or lame leg. (Welsh, *cam*; Irish, *gam*, bad, crooked.)

Game for a Spree. *Are you game for a spree?* Are you inclined to join in a bit of fun? The allusion is to game-cocks, which never show the white feather, but are always ready for a fight.

Game is not worth the Candle (*The*). The effort is not worth making; the result will not pay for the trouble. (*See* CANDLE.)

Game's Afoot (*The*). The hare has started; the enterprise has begun.

" I see you stand like greyhounds in the slips,
Straining upon the start. The game's afoot!
Follow your spirit! And upon this charge
Cry 'God for Harry! England! and St. George.'"
Shakespeare: Henry V., iii. 1.

Gam'elyn (3 syl., *g* hard). The youngest of the three sons of Sir Johan de Boundys. On his death-bed the old knight left "five plowes of land" to each of his two elder sons, and the rest of his property to Gamelyn. The eldest took charge of the boy, but entreated him shamefully; and when Gamelyn, in his manhood, demanded of him his heritage, the elder brother exclaimed, "Stand still, gadelyng, and hold thy peace!" "I am no gadelyng," retorted the proud young spirit; "but the lawful son of a lady and true knight." At this the elder brother sent his servants to chastise the youngling, but Gamelyn drove them off with "a pestel." At a wrestling-match held in the neighbourhood, young Gamelyn threw the champion, and carried off the prize ram; but on reaching home found the door shut against him. He at once kicked down the door, and threw the porter into a well. The elder brother, by a manœuvre, contrived to bind the young scapegrace to a tree, and left him two days without food; but Adam, the spencer, unloosed him, and Gamelyn fell upon a party of ecclesiastics who had come to dine with his brother, "sprinkling holy water on the guests with his stout oaken cudgel." The sheriff now sent to take Gamelyn and Adam into custody; but they fled into the woods and came upon a party of foresters sitting at meat. The captain gave them welcome, and in time Gamelyn rose to be "king of the outlaws." His brother, being now sheriff, would have put him to death, but Gamelyn constituted himself a lynch judge, and hanged his brother. After this the king appointed him chief ranger, and he married. This tale is the foundation of Lodge's novel, called *Euphue's Golden Legacy*, and the novel furnished Shakespeare with the plot of *As You Like It.*

Gammer (*g* hard). A corruption of *grandmother*, with an intermediate form "granmer." (See *Halliwell*, sub voce.)

Gammer Gurton's Needle. The earliest comedy but one in the English language. It was "Made by Mr. S., Master of Arts." The author is said to have been Bishop Still of Bath and Wells (1543-1607).

Gam'mon (*g* hard). A corruption of *gamene*. Stuff to impose upon one's credulity; chaff. (Anglo-Saxon, *gamen*, scoffing; our *game*, as "You are making game of me.")

Gammon (*g* hard) means the leg, not the buttock). (French, *jambon*, the leg, *jambe*; Italian, *gamba*.)

Gam'mut, or Gamut (*g* hard). It is *gamma ut*, "ut" being the first word in the Guido-von-Arrezzo scale of *ut*, *re*, *mi*, *fa*, *sol*, *la*. In the eleventh century the ancient scale was extended a note below the Greek proslamban'omy note (our A), the first space of the bass staff. The new note was termed γ (gamma), and when "ut" was substituted by Arrezzo the "supernumerary" note was called *gamma* or *ut*, or shortly *gamm' ut.*

—*i.e.* "Gut." The gammut, therefore, properly means the diatonic scale beginning in the bass clef with "G."

Gamp (*Mrs.*), or *Sarah Gamp* (*g* hard). A monthly nurse, famous for her bulky umbrella and perpetual reference to Mrs. Harris, a purely imaginary person, whose opinions always confirmed her own. (*Dickens: Martin Chuzzlewit.*)

"Mrs. Harris, I says to her, if I could afford to lay out all my fellow creeturs for nothink, I would gladly do it. Such is the love I bear 'em."

Punch caricatures the *Standard* as "Mrs. Sarah Gamp," a little woman with an enormous bonnet and her characteristic umbrella.

A Sarah Gamp, or *Mrs. Gamp.* A big, pawky umbrella, so called from Sarah Gamp. (*See above.*) In France it is called *un Robinson*, from Robinson Crusoe's umbrella. (*Defoe.*)

Gamps and Harrises. Workhouse nurses, real or supposititious. (*See* Gamp.)

"Mr. Gathorne Hardy is to look after the Gamps and Harrises of Lambeth and the Strand."—*The Daily Telegraph.*

Gan'abim. The island of thieves and plagiarists. So called from the Hebrew *ganab* (a thief). (*Rabelais: Pantagruel,* iv. 66.)

Gander (*g* hard). *What's sauce for the goose is sauce for the gander.* Both must be treated exactly alike. Applesauce is just as good for one as the other. (Anglo-Saxon *gós*, related to *gons* and *gans*. The *d* and *r* of *gan-a* are merely euphonic ; the *a* being the masculine suffix. Thus *han-a* was the masculine of *hen*. Latin, *anser*.)

Gander-cleugh. Folly cliff ; that mysterious land where anyone who makes a "goose of himself" takes up his temporary residence. The hypothetical Jedediah Cleishbotham, who edited the *Tales of My Landlord*, lived there, as Sir Walter Scott assures us.

Gander-month. Those four weeks when the "monthly nurse" rules the house with despotic sway, and the master is made a goose of.

Gan'elon (*g* hard). Count of Mayence, one of Charlemagne's paladins, the "Judas" of knights. His castle was built on the Blocksberg, the loftiest peak of the Hartz mountains. Jealousy of Roland made him a traitor ; and in

order to destroy his rival, he planned with Marsillus, the Moorish king, the attack of Roncesvallës. He was six and a-half feet high, with glaring eyes and fiery hair ; he loved solitude, was very taciturn, disbelieved in the existence of moral good, and never had a friend. His name is a by-word for a traitor of the basest sort.

"Have you not held me at such a distance from your counsels, as if I were the most faithless spy since the days of Ganelon?"—*Sir Walter Scott: The Abbot*, chap. xxiv.

"You would have thought him [Ganelon] one of Attila's Huns, rather than one of the paladins of Charlemagne's court."—*Croquemitaine*, iii.

Ga'nem (*g* hard), having incurred the displeasure of Caliph Haroun-al-Raschid, effected his escape by taking the place of a slave, who was carrying on his head dishes from his own table. (*Arabian Nights' Entertainments.*)

Gan'esa (*g* hard). Son of Siva and Parbutta ; also called Gunputty, the elephant god. The god of wisdom, forethought, and prudence. The Mercury of the Hindus.

"Camdeo bright and Ganesa sublime
Shall bless with joy their own propitious clime."
Campbell: Pleasures of Hope, i.

Gang a-gley (*To*). To go wrong. (Scotch.)

"The best-laid schemes of mice and men
Gang aft agley.",   *Burns.*

Gang-board, or **Gang-way** (*g* hard). The board or way made for the rowers to pass from stem to stern, and where the mast was laid when it was unshipped. Now it means the board with cleats or bars of wood by which passengers walk into or out of a ship or steamboat. A *gang* is an alley or avenue.

"As we were putting off the boat they laid hold of the gangboard and unhooked it off the boat's stern."—*Cook: Second Voyage*, bk. iii. chap. iv.

Gang-day (*g* hard). The day in Rogation week when boys with the clergy and wardens used to *gang* round the parish to beat its bounds.

Gangway (*g* hard). *Below the gangway.* In the House of Commons there is a sort of bar extending across the House, which separates the Ministry and the Opposition from the rest of the members. To sit "below the gangway" is to sit amongst the general members, neither among the Ministers nor with the Opposition.
Clear the gangway. Make room for the passengers from the boat, clear the passage. (*See* Gang-board.)

Ganges (*The*) is so named from *gang*, the earth. Often called Gunga or Ganga.

"Those who, through the curse, have fallen from heaven, having performed ablution in this stream, become free from sin ; cleansed from sin by this water, and restored to happiness, they shall enter heaven and return again to the gods. After having performed ablution in this living water, they become free from all iniquity."—*The Ramayuna* (section xxxv.).

Ganna. A Celtic prophetess, who succeeded Velle′da. She went to Rome, and was received by Domitian with great honours. (*Tacitus: Annals*, 55.)

Ganor (*g* hard), **Gineura** (*g* soft), or **Guinever.** Arthur's wife.

Gan′ymede (3 syl. ; *g* hard). Jove's cup-bearer ; the most beautiful boy ever born. He succeeded Hebē in office.

> " When Ganymede above
> His service ministers to mighty Jove."
> *Hoole's Ariosto.*

Ga′ora. A tract of land inhabited by a people without heads. Their eyes are in their shoulders, and their mouth in their breast. (*Hakluyt's Voyages*.) (*See* BLEMMYES.)

Gape (*g* hard). *Looking for gape-seed.* Gaping about and doing nothing. A corruption of " Looking a-gapesing ; " *gapesing* is staring about with one's mouth open. A-gapesing and a-trapesing are still used in Norfolk.

Seeking a gape's nest. (Devonshire.) A *gape's nest* is a sight which people stare at with wide-open mouth. The word "nest" was used in a much wider sense formerly than it is now. Thus we read of a "nest of shelves," a "nest of thieves," a "cosy nest." A gape's nest is the nest or place where anything stared at is to be found. (*See* MARE'S NEST.)

Gar′agan′tua (*g* hard). The giant that swallowed five pilgrims with their staves and all in a salad. From a book entitled *The History of Garagantua*, 1594. Laneham, however, mentions the book of Garagantua in 1575. The giant in Rabelais is called Gargantua (*q.v.*).

> "You must borrow me Gargantua's mouth first [before I can utter so long a word] ; 'tis a word too great for any mouth of this age's size." —*Shakespeare: As You Like It*, iii. 2.

Garagantuan. Threatening, bullying. (*See preceding*.)

Garble (*g* hard) properly means to sift out the refuse. Thus, by the statute of 1 James I. 19, a penalty is imposed on the sale of drugs not garbled. We now use the word to express a mutilated extract, in which the sense of the author is perverted by what is omitted. (French,

garber, to make clean ; Spanish, *garbil-lar*.)

> "A garbled quotation may be the most effectual perversion of an author's meaning."—*McCosh : Divine Government*, p. 14.

⁂ One of the best garbled quotations. is this : David said (Psalm xiv. 1), "There is no God" (omitting the preceding words, " The fool hath said in his heart.")

Garci′as (*g* hard). *The soul of Pedro Garcias.* Money. It is said that two scholars of Salamanca discovered a tombstone with this inscription :—" Here lies the soul of the licentiate Pedro Garci′as ; " and on searching for this " soul " found a purse with a hundred golden ducats. (*Gil Blas*, *Preface*.)

Gar′darike (4 syl., *g* hard). So Russia is called in the Eddas.

Garden (*g* hard). The garden of Joseph of Arimathea is said to be the spot where the rotunda of the Holy Sepulchre now stands.

The Garden or Garden Sect. The disciples of Epicu′rus, who taught in his own private garden.

> " Epicurus in his garden was languid ; the birds of the air have more enjoyment of their food."—*Ecce Homo.*

Garden of England. Worcestershire and Kent are both so called.

Garden of Europe. Italy.

Garden of France. Amboise, in the department of Indre-et-Loire.

Garden of India. Oude.

Garden of Ireland. Carlow.

Garden of Italy. The island of Sicily.

Garden of South Wales. The southern division of Glamorganshire.

Garden of Spain. Andalusia.

Garden of the Sun. The East Indian (or Malayan) archipelago.

Garden of the West. Illinois ; Kansas. is also so called.

Garden of the World. The region of the Mississippi.

Gardener (*g* hard). *Get on, gardener !* Get on, you slow and clumsy coachman. The allusion is to a man who is both gardener and coachman.

Gardener. Adam is so called by Tennyson.

> " From yon blue sky above us bent,
> The grand old gardener and his wife [Adam and Eve]
> Smile at the claims of long descent."
> *Lady Clara Vere de Vere*

> "Thou, old Adam's likeness,
> Get to dress this garden."
> *Shakespeare: Richard II.*, iii. 4.

Gardening (*g* hard). (*See* ADAM'S PROFESSION.)

Father of landscape gardening. Lenotre (1613-1700).

Gargamelle (3 syl., *g* hard) was the wife of Grangousier, and daughter of the king of the Parpaillons (*butterflies*). On the day that she gave birth to Gargantua she ate sixteen quarters, two bushels, three pecks, and a pipkin of *dirt*, the mere remains left in the tripe which she had for supper; for, as the proverb says—

"Scrape tripe as clean as e'er you can,
    A tithe of filth will still remain."

Gargamelle. Said to be meant for Anne of Brittany. She was the mother of Gargantua, in the satirical romance of *Gargantua and Pantagruel*, by Rabelais. Motteux, who makes "Pantagruel" to be Anthony de Bourbon, and "Gargantua" to be Henri d'Albret, says "Gargamelle" is designed for Catherine de Foix, Queen of Navarre. (*Rabelais*, i. 4.)

Gargan'tua (*g* hard), according to Rabelais, was son of Grangousier and Gargamelle. Immediately he was born he cried out "Drink, drink!" so lustily that the words were heard in Beauce and Bibarois; whereupon his royal father exclaimed, "*Que grand tu as!*" which, being the first words he uttered after the birth of the child, were accepted as its name; so it was called "Gah-gran'-tu-as," corrupted into Garg'an-tu-a. It needed 17,913 cows to supply the babe with milk. When he went to Paris to finish his education he rode on a mare as big as six elephants, and took the bells of Notre Dame to hang on his mare's neck as jingles. At the prayer of the Parisians he restored the bells, and they consented to feed his mare for nothing. On his way home he was fired at from the castle at Vede Ford, and on reaching home combed his hair with a comb 900 feet long, when at every "rake" seven bullet-balls fell from his hair. Being desirous of a salad for dinner, he went to cut some lettuces as big as walnut-trees, and ate up six pilgrims from Sebastian, who had hidden themselves among them out of fear. Picrochole, having committed certain offences, was attacked by Gargantua in the rock Clermond, and utterly defeated; and Gargantua, in remembrance of this victory, founded and endowed the abbey of Theleme [*Te-lame*]. (*Rabelais: Gargantua*, i. 7.)

Gargantua is said to be a satire on François I., but this cannot be correct, as he was born in the kingdom of the butterflies, was sent to Paris to finish his education, and left it again to succour his own country. Motteux, perceiving these difficulties, thinks it is meant for Henri d'Albret, King of Navarre.

Gargantua's mare. Those who make Gargantua to be François I. make his "great mare" to be Mme. d'Estampes. Motteux, who looks upon the romance as a satire on the Reform party, is at a loss how to apply this word, and merely says, "It is some lady." Rabelais says, "She was as big as six elephants, and had her feet cloven into fingers. She was of a burnt-sorrel hue, with a little mixture of dapple-grey; but, above all, she had a terrible tail, for it was every whit as great as the steeple pillar of St. Mark." When the beast got to Orléans, and the wasps assaulted her, she switched about her tail so furiously that she knocked down all the trees that grew in the vicinity, and Gargantua, delighted, exclaimed, "*Je trouve beau ce!*" wherefore the locality has been called "Beauce" ever since. The satire shows the wilfulness and extravagance of court mistresses. (*Rabelais: Gargantua and Pantagruel*, book i. 16.)

Gargantua's shepherds, according to Motteux, mean Lutheran preachers; but those who look upon the romance as a political satire, think the Crown ministers and advisers are intended.

Gargantua's thirst. Motteux says the "great thirst" of Gargantua, and "mighty drought" at Pantagruel's birth, refer to the withholding the cup from the laity, and the clamour raised by the Reform party for the wine as well as the bread in the eucharist.

Gargan'tuan. Enormous, inordinate, great beyond all limits. It needed 900 ells of Châtelleraut linen to make the body of his shirt, and 200 more for the gussets; for his shoes 406 ells of blue and crimson velvet were required, and 1,100 cow-hides for the soles. He could play 207 different games, picked his teeth with an elephant's tusk, and did everything in the same "large way."

"It sounded like a Gargantuan order for a dram."—*The Standard.*

A Gargantuan course of studies. A course including all languages, as well ancient as modern, all the sciences, all the -ologies and -onomies, together with calisthenics and athletic sports. Gargantua wrote to his son Pantagruel, commanding him to learn Greek, Latin, Chaldaic, Arabic; all history, geometry, arithmetic, and music; astronomy and natural philosophy, so that "there be not a river in all the world thou dost not know the name of, and nature of all its fishes ; all the fowls of the air ; all the several kinds of shrubs and herbs ; all the metals hid in the bowels of the earth ; with all gems and precious stones. I would furthermore have thee study the Talmudists and Cabalists, and get a perfect knowledge of man. In brief, I would have thee a bottomless pit of all knowledge." (*Rabelais : Pantagruel*, book ii. 8.)

Gargit′tios. One of the dogs that guarded the herds and flocks of Ger′yon, and which Hercules killed. The other was the two-headed dog, named Orthos, or Orthros.

Gargouille, or **Gargoil** (*g* hard). A water-spout in church architecture. Sometimes also spelt *Gurgoyle.* They are usually carved into some fantastic shape, such as a dragon's head, through which the water flows. Gargouille was the great dragon that lived in the Seine, ravaged Rouen, and was slain by St. Roma′nus, Bishop of Rouen, in the seventh century. (*See* DRAGON.)

Garibaldi's Red Shirt. The red shirt is the habitual upper garment of American sailors. Any Liverpudlian will tell you that some fifteen years ago a British tar might be discerned by his *blue* shirt, and a Yankee "salt" by his *red.* Garibaldi first adopted the American shirt, when he took the command of the merchantman in Baltimore.

Garland (*g* hard).

"A chaplet should be composed of four roses . . . and a garland should be formed of laurel or oak leaves, interspersed with acorns."—*J. E. Cussans: Handbook of Heraldry,* chap. vii. p. 105.

Garland. A collection of ballads in *True Lovers' Garland,* etc.

Nuptial garlands are as old as the hills. The ancient Jews used them, according to Selden (*Uxor Heb.,* iii. 655) ; the Greek and Roman brides did the same (Vaughan, *Golden Grove*) ; so did the Anglo-Saxons and Gauls.

"Thre ornamentys pryncipaly to a wyfe: A rynge on hir fynger, a broch on hir brest, and a garlond on hir hede. The rynge betokenethe true love: the broch clennesse in herte and chastitye: the garlond . . . gladness and the dignity of the sacrement of wedlock." — *Leland: Dives and Pauper* (1493).

Garlick is said to destroy the magnetic power of the loadstone. This notion, though proved to be erroneous, has the sanction of Pliny, Solinus, Ptolemy, Plutarch, Albertus, Mathiolas,

Rueus, Rulandus, Reuodæus, Langius, and others. Sir Thomas Browne places it among *Vulgar Errors* (book ii. chap. 3.)

"Martin Rulandus saith that Onions and Garlick . . . hinder the attractive power [of the magnet] and rob it of its virtue of drawing iron, to which Renodæus agrees ;[but this is all lies."— *W. Salmon: The Complete English Physician, etc.,* chap. xxv. p. 182.

Garnish (*g* hard). Entrance-money, to be spent in drink, demanded by jail-birds of new-comers. In prison slang garnish means fetters, and garnish-money is money given for the "honour" of wearing fetters. The custom became obsolete with the reform of prisons. (French, *garnissage,* trimming, verb *garnir,* to decorate or adorn.) (*See* Fielding's and Smollett's novels.)

Garratt (*g* hard). *The Mayor of Garratt.* Garratt is between Wandsworth and Tooting ; the first mayor of this village was elected towards the close of the eighteenth century ; and his election came about thus : Garratt Common had been often encroached on, and in 1780 the inhabitants associated themselves together to defend their rights. The chairman of this association was entitled *Mayor,* and as it happened to be the time of a general election, the society made it a law that a new "mayor" should be chosen at every general election. The addresses of these mayors, written by Foote, Garrick, Wilkes, and others, are satires on the corruption of electors and political squibs. The first Mayor of Garratt was "Sir" John Harper, a retailer of brickdust in London ; and the last was "Sir" Harry Dimsdale, muffin-seller, in 1796. Foote has a farce entitled *The Mayor of Garratt.*

Garraway's, *i.e.* Garraway's coffee-house, in Exchange Alley. It existed for 216 years, and here tea was sold, in 1657, for 16s. up to 50s. a pound. The house no longer exists.

Garrot′e or **Garotte** (2 syl., *g* hard) is the Spanish *garrote* (a stick). The original way of garrotting in Spain was to place the victim on a chair with a cord round his neck, then to twist the cord with a *stick* till strangulation ensued. In 1851 General Lopez was garrotted by the Spanish authorities for attempting to gain possession of Cuba ; since which time the thieves of London, etc., have adopted the method of strangling their victim by throwing their arms round his throat, while an accomplice rifles his pockets.

Garter (*g* hard). *Knights of the Garter.* The popular legend is that Joan, Countess of Salisbury, accidentally slipped her garter at a court ball. It was picked up by her royal partner, Edward III., who gallantly diverted the attention of the guests from the lady by binding the blue band round his own knee, saying as he did so, "*Honi soit qui mal y pense*" (1348).

Wearing the garters of a pretty maiden either on the hat or knee was a common custom with our forefathers. Brides usually wore on their legs a host of gay ribbons, to be distributed after the marriage ceremony amongst the bridegroom's friends; and the piper at the wedding dance never failed to tie a piece of the bride's garter round his pipe. If there is any truth in the legend given above, the impression on the guests would be wholly different to what such an accident would produce in our days; but perhaps the "Order of the Garter," after all, may be about tantamount to "The Order of the Ladies' Champions," or "The Order of the Ladies' Favourites."

Gar'vies (2 syl., *g* soft). Sprats. So called from Inch Garvie, an isle in the Frith of Forth, near which they are caught.

Gascona'de (3 syl., *g* hard). Talk like that of a Gascon—absurd boasting, vainglorious braggadocio. It is said that a Gascon being asked what he thought of the Louvre in Paris, replied, "Pretty well; it reminds me of the back part of my father's stables." The vainglory of this answer is more palpable when it is borne in mind that the Gascons were proverbially poor. The Dictionary of the French Academy gives us the following specimen: "A Gascon, in proof of his ancient nobility, asserted that they used in his father's house no other fuel than the bâtons of the family marshals."

Gaston (*g* hard). Lord of Claros, one of Charlemagne's paladins.

Gastrol'ators. People whose god is their belly. (*Rabelais: Pantagruel*, iv. 58.)

Gat-tooth (*g* hard). Goat-tooth. (Anglo-Saxon, *gæt*.) Goat-toothed is having a lickerish tooth. Chaucer makes the wife of Bath say, "Gat-toothed I was, and that became me wele."

Gate Money. Money paid at the gate for admission to the grounds where some contest is to be seen.

Gate-posts. The post on which the gate hangs and swings is called the "hanging-post"; that against which it shuts is called the "banging post."

Gate of Italy. That part of the valley of the Adige which is in the vicinity of Trent and Rovere'do. A narrow gorge between two mountain ridges.

Gate of Tears [*Babelmandeb*]. The passage into the Red Sea. So called by the Arabs from the number of shipwrecks that took place there.

> "Like some ill-destined bark that steers
> In silence through the Gate of Tears."
> *T. Moore: Fire Worshippers.*

Gath (*g* hard), in Dryden's satire of *Absalom and Achitophel*, means Brussels, where Charles II. long resided while he was in exile.

> "Had thus old David [Charles II.] . . .
> Not dared, when fortune called him, to be king,
> At Gath an exile he might still remain."

Tell it not in Gath. Don't let your enemies hear it. Gath was famous as being the birthplace of the giant Goliath.

> "Tell it not in Gath, publish it not in the streets of Askelon; lest the daughters of the Philistines rejoice, lest the daughters of the uncircumcised triumph."—2 Sam. i. 20.

Gathered = *dead.* The Bible phrase, "He was gathered to his fathers."

> "He was (for he is gathered) a little man with a coppery complexion."—*Dr. Geist*, p. 25.

Gathers (*g* hard). *Out of gathers.* In distress; in a very impoverished condition. The allusion is to a woman's gown, which certainly looks very seedy when "out of gathers"—*i.e.* when the cotton that kept the "pleats" together has given way. (Anglo-Saxon, *gader-ian*, to gather, or pleat.)

Gauche (French, *the left hand*). Awkward. *Awk*, the left hand. (*See* ADROIT.)

Gauch'erie (3 syl., *g* hard). Things not *comme il faut;* behaviour not according to the received forms of society; awkward and untoward ways. (*See above.*)

Gau'difer (*g* hard). A champion, celebrated in the romance of *Alexander.* Not unlike the Scotch Bruce.

Gaudy-day (*A*). A holiday, a feast-day. (Latin *gaudeo*, to rejoice.)

Gaul (*g* hard). France.

> "Insulting Gaul has roused the world to war."
> *Thomson: Autumn.*

> "Shall haughty Gaul invasion threat?"—*Burns.*

Gaunt (*g* hard). *John of Gaunt.* The third son of Edward III.; so called from Ghent, in Flanders, the place of his birth.

Gauntgrim (*g* hard). The wolf.

"'For my part (said he), I don't wonder at my cousin's refusing Bruin the bear and Gauntgrim the wolf. . . . Bruin is always in the sulks, and Gauntgrim always in a passion.'"—*E. B. Lytton: Pilgrims of the Rhine*, chap. xii.

Gauntlet (*g* hard). *To run the gantlet*. To be hounded on all sides. Corruption of *gantlope*, the passage between two files of soldiers. (German, *ganglaufen* or *gassenlaufen*.) The reference is to a punishment common among sailors. If a companion had disgraced himself, the crew, provided with gauntlets or ropes' ends, were drawn up in two rows facing each other, and the delinquent had to run between them, while every man dealt him, in passing, as severe a chastisement as he could.

✲ The custom exists among the North American Indians. (*See* Fenimore Cooper and Mayne Reid.)

To throw down the gauntlet. To challenge. The custom in the Middle Ages, when one knight challenged another, was for the challenger to throw his gauntlet on the ground, and if the challenge was accepted the person to whom it was thrown picked it up.

"It is not for Spain, reduced as she is to the lowest degree of social inanition, to throw the gauntlet to the right and left."—*The Times*.

Gauta'ma (*g* hard). The chief deity of Burmah, whose favourite offering is a paper umbrella.

The four sublime verities of Gauta'ma are as follows:

(1) Pain exists.

(2) The cause of pain is "birth sin." The Buddhist supposes that man has passed through many previous existences, and all the heaped-up sins accumulated in these previous states constitute man's "birth sin."

(3) Pain is ended only by Nirva'na.

(4) The way that leads to Nirvana is —right faith, right judgment, right language, right purpose, right practice, right obedience, right memory, and right meditation (eight in all).

Gau'tier and **Garguille** (French). All the world and his wife.

Se mocquer de Gautier et de Garguille (to make fun of everyone). Gautier-Garguille was a clown of the seventeenth century, who gave himself unbounded licence, and provoked against himself a storm of angry feeling.

Gau'vaine or **Ga'wain** = Gau-wain (2 syl., *g* hard). *Sir Gauvaine the Courteous*. One of Arthur's knights,

and his nephew. He challenged the Green Knight, and struck off his head; but the headless knight picked up his poll again and walked off, telling Sir Gauvaine to meet him twelve months hence. Sir Gauvaine kept his appointment, and was hospitably entertained; but, taking possession of the girdle belonging to the lady of the house, was chastised by the Green Knight, confessed his fault, and was forgiven.

" The gentle Gawain's courteous lore,
Hector de Mares and Pellinore,
And Lancelot that evermore
Looked stol'nwise on the queen."
Sir W. Scott: Bridal of Triermain, ii. 13.

Gav'elkind (*g* hard). A tenure in Wales, Kent, and Northumberland, whereby land descended from the father to *all* his sons in equal proportions. The youngest had the homestead, and the eldest the horse and arms.

∴ Coke (1 *Institutes*, 140 *a*) says the word is *gif eal cyn* (give all the kin); but Lambarde suggests the Anglo-Saxon *gafol* or *gavel*, rent ; and says it means " land which yields rent " ! *gavel cyn*, rent for the family derived from land. There is a similar Irish word, *gabhailcine*, a family tenure.

Gawain (*g* hard). (*See* GAUVAINE.)

Gawrey (*g* hard). One of the race of flying women who appeared to Peter Wilkins in his solitary cave. (*Robert Pultock : Peter Wilkins*.)

Gay (*g* hard). *Gay as the king's candle*. A French phrase, alluding to an ancient custom observed on the 6th of January, called the " Eve or Vigil of the Kings," when a candle of divers colours was burnt. The expression is used to denote a woman who is more showily dressed than is consistent with good taste.

Gay Deceiver (*A*). A Lothario (*q.v.*) ; a libertine.

" I immediately quitted the precincts of the castle, and posted myself on the high road, where the gay deceiver was sure to be intercepted on his return."—*Le Sage : Adventures of Gil Blas* (Smollett's translation). (1749.)

Gay Girl. A woman of light or extravagant habits. Lady Anne Berkeley, dissatisfied with the conduct of her daughter-in-law (Lady Catherine Howard), exclaimed, " By the blessed sacrament, this gay girl will beggar my son Henry." (*See* above.)

" What eyleth you ? Some gay gurl, God it wot,
Hath brought you thus upon the very trot " (*i.e.* put you on your high horse, or into a passion). *Chaucer : Canterbury Tales*, 3,767.

Gaze (1 syl., *g* hard). *To stand at gaze*. To stand in doubt what to do. A term in forestry. When a stag first hears the hounds it stands dazed, looking all round, and in doubt what to do.

Heralds call a stag which is represented full-faced, a "stag at gaze."

"The American army in the central states remained wholly at gaze."—*Lord Mahon: History.*

"As the poor frighted deer, that stands at gaze,
Wildly determining which way to fly."
Shakespeare: Rape of Lucrece, 1149-50.

Gaze-hound. (*See* LYME-HOUND.)

Gazet'te (2 syl., *g* hard). A newspaper. The first newspapers were issued in Venice by the Government, and came out in manuscript once a month, during the war of 1563 between the Venetians and Turks. The intelligence was read publicly in certain places, and the fee for hearing it read was one *gazetta* (a Venetian coin, somewhat less than a farthing in value).

∴ The first official English newspaper, called *The Oxford Gazette,* was published in 1642, at Oxford, where the Court was held. On the removal of the Court to London, the name was changed to *The London Gazette.* The name was revived in 1665, during the Great Fire. Now the official *Gazette,* published every Tuesday and Friday, contains announcements of pensions, promotions, bankruptcies, dissolutions of partnerships, etc. (*See* NEWS-PAPERS.)

Gazet'ted (*g* hard). Published in the London *Gazette,* an official newspaper.

Gaz'nivides, (3 syl.). A dynasty of Persia, which gave four kings and lasted fifty years (999-1049), founded by Mahmoud Gazni, who reigned from the Ganges to the Caspian Sea.

Gear (*g* hard) properly means "dress." In machinery, the bands and wheels that communicate motion to the working part are called the *gearing.* (Saxon, *gearwa,* clothing.)

In good gear. To be in good working order.

Out of gear. Not in working condition, when the "gearing" does not act properly; out of health.

Gee-up! and **Gee-woo!** addressed to horses both mean "Horse, get on." Gee = horse. In Notts and many other counties nurses say to young children, "Come and see the gee-gees." There is not the least likelihood that Gee-woo is the Italian *gio,* because *gio* will not fit in with any of the other terms, and it is absurd to suppose our peasants would go to Italy for such a word. Woa! or Woo! (*q.v.*), meaning stop, or halt, is quite another word. We subjoin the following quotation, although we differ from it. (*See* COME ATHER, WOO'SH.)

"Et cum sic gloriarētur, et cogitāres cum quanta gloria duceretur ad illum virum super equum, dicendo *Gio! Gio!* cepit pede percutēre terram quasi pungeret equum calcaribus."—*Dia-logus Creaturarum* (1480).

Geese (*g* hard). (*See* GANDER, GOOSE.)

Geese save the capitol. The tradition is that when the Gauls invaded Rome a detachment in single file clambered up the hill of the capitol so silently that the foremost man reached the top without being challenged; but while he was striding over the rampart, some sacred geese, disturbed by the noise, began to cackle, and awoke the garrison. Marcus Man'lius rushed to the wall and hurled the fellow over the precipice. To commemorate this event, the Romans carried a golden goose in procession to the capitol every year (B.C. 390).

"Those consecrated geese in orders,
That to the capitol were warders,
And being then upon patrol,
With noise alone beat off the Gaul."
Butler: Hudibras, ii. 3.

All his swans are geese, or *All his swans are turned to geese.* All his expectations end in nothing; all his boasting ends in smoke. Like a person who fancies he sees a swan on a river, but finds it to be only a goose.

The phrase is sometimes reversed thus, "All his geese are swans." Commonly applied to people who think too much of the beauty and talent of their children.

Every man thinks his own geese swans. Everyone is prejudiced by self-love. Every crow thinks its own nestling the fairest. Every child is beautiful in its mother's eyes. (*See* Æsop's fable, *The Eagle and the Owl.*)

Latin: Suum cuique pulchrum. Sua cuique sponsa, mihi meas. Sua cuique res est carissima. Asinus asino, sus suo pulcher.

German: Eine güte mutter halt ihre kinder vor die schönsten.

French: A chaque oiseau son nid paraît beau.

Italian: A ogni grolla paion' belli i suoi grollatini. Ad ogni uccello, suo nido è bello.

The more geese the more lovers. The French newspaper called *L'Europe,* December, 1865, repeats this proverb, and says:—"It is customary in England for every gentleman admitted into society to send a fat goose at Christmas to the lady of the house he is in the habit of visiting. Beautiful women receive a whole magazine . . . . and are thus enabled to tell the number of their lovers by the number of fat geese sent to them." (*The Times,* December 27th, 1865.) Truly the Frenchman knows much more about us than we ever "dreamt of in our philosophy."

Geese. (*See* GOOSE, CAG MAG.)

Gehen'na (Hebrew, *g* hard). The place of eternal torment. Strictly speaking, it means simply the Valley of Hinnom (*Ge-Hinnom*), where sacrifices to Moloch were offered and where refuse of all sorts was subsequently cast, for the consumption of which fires were kept constantly burning.

> "And made his grove
> The pleasant valley of Hinnom, Tophet thence
> And black Gehenna called, the type of hell."
> *Milton : Paradise Lost*, book i. 403-5.

Gel'ert (*g* hard). The name of Llewellyn's dog. One day a wolf entered the room where the infant son of the Welsh prince was asleep ; Gelert flew at it and killed it ; but when Llewellyn returned home and saw his dog's mouth bloody, he hastily concluded that it had killed his child, and thrust it through with his sword. The howl of the dog awoke the child, and the prince saw too late his fatal rashness. Beth-gelert is the name of the place where the dog was buried. (*See* BETH-GELERT, DOG.)

∴ A similar story is told of Czar Piras of Russia. In the *Gesta Romanorum* the story is told of Folliculus, a knight, but instead of a serpent the dog is said to have killed a wolf. The story occurs again in the *Seven Wise Masters*. In the Sanskrit version the dog is called an ichneumon and the wolf a "black snake." In the *Hitopadesa* (iv. 3) the dog is an otter ; in the Arabic a weasel ; in the Mongolian a pole-cat ; in the Persian a cat, etc.

Gellatley (*Davie*). The idiot servant of the Baron of Bradwardine. (*Sir W. Scott : Waverley.*) Also spelt GELLATLY.

Gema'ra (*g* hard), which means "complement," is applied to the second part of the Talmud, which consists of annotations, discussions, and amplifications of the Jewish *Mishna*. There is the Babylonian *Gema'ra* and the Jerusalem *Gema'ra*. The former, which is the more complete, is by the academies of Babylon ; the latter by those of Palestine.

"Scribes and Pharisees . . . set little value on the study of the Law itself, but much on that of the commentaries of the rabbis, now embodied in the *Mishna* and *Gemara*."—*Geikie : Life of Christ*, vol. ii. ch. xxxvi. p. 64.

Gemmagog. Son of the giant Oromēdon, and inventor of the Poulan shoes—*i.e.* shoes with a spur behind, and turned-up toes fastened to the knees. These shoes were forbidden by Charles V. of France in 1365, but the fashion revived again. (*Duchat : Ouvres de Rabelais.*)

∴ According to the same authority, giants were great inventors : Erix invented legerdemain ; Gabbara, drinking healths ; Gemmagog. Poulan shoes ;

Hapmouche, drying and smoking neats' tongues ; etc. etc.

Gems. (*See* JEWELS.)

Gendarmes. "Men at arms," the armed police of France. The term was first applied to those who marched in the train of knights ; subsequently to the cavalry ; in the time of Louis XIV. to a body of horse charged with the preservation of order ; after the revolution to a military police chosen from old soldiers of good character ; now it is applied to the ordinary police, whose costume is half civil and half military.

Gender-words : Billy, nanny ; boar, sow ; buck, doe ; bull, cow ; cock, hen ; dog, bitch ; ewe, tup ; groom = man ; he, she ; Jack, Jenny ; male, female ; man, maid ; man, woman ; master, mistress ; Tom ; tup, dam ; and several "Christian names ; as in the following examples :—

Ape : Dog ape, bitch ape.
Ass : Jack ass and Jenny ; he ass, she ass.
Bear : He bear, she bear.
Bird : Male bird, female bird ; cock bird, hen bird.
Blackcock (grouse) ; moorcock and hen (red grouse).
Bridegroom, bride.
Calf : Bull calf, cow calf.
Cat : Tom cat, lady cat, he and she cat. Gib cat (*q.v.*).
Charwoman.
Child : Male child, female child ; man child, woman child (child is either male or female, except when sex is referred to).
Devil : He and she devil (if sex is referred to).
Donkey : Male and female donkey. (*See* ASS.)
Elephant : Bull and cow elephant ; male and female elephant.
Fox : Dog and bitch fox ; the bitch is also called a vixen.
Game cock.
Gentleman, gentlewoman or lady.
Goat : Billy and Nanny goat ; he and she goat ; buck goat.
Hare : Buck and doe hare.
Heir : Heir male, heir female.
Kinsman, kinswoman.
Lamb : ewe lamb, tup lamb.
Mankind, womankind.
Merman, mermaid.
Milkman, milkmaid or milk-woman.
Moorcock, moorhen.
Otter : Dog and bitch otter.
Partridge : Cock and hen partridge.
Peacock, penhen.
Pheasant : Cock and hen pheasant.
Pig : Boar and sow pig.
Rabbit : Buck and doe rabbit.
Rat : A Jack rat.
Schoolmaster, schoolmistress.
Seal : Bull and cow. The bull of fur seals under six years of age is called a "Bachelor."
Servant : Male and female servant ; man and maid servant.
Singer, songstress ; man and woman singer.
Sir [John], Lady [Mary].
Sparrow : Cock and hen sparrow.
Swan : A cob or cock swan, pen-swan.
Turkey cock and hen.
Wash or washer-woman.
Whale : Bull or Unicorn, and cow.
Wren : Jenny ; cock Robin ; Tom tit ; etc.
Wolf : Dog wolf, bitch or she-wolf.

∴ Generally the name of the animal stands last ; in the following instances, however, it stands *before* the gender-word:—

Blackcock ; bridegroom ; charwoman ; game-cock ; gentleman and gentlewoman ; heir male and female ; kinsman and woman ; mankind, womankind ; milkman, milkmaid or -woman ; moorcock and hen ; peacock and hen ; servant man and maid ; turkey cock and hen ; wash or washer-woman.

⟩ ∵ In a few instances the gender-word does not express gender, as jackdaw, jack pike, roe-buck, etc.

(2) The following require no gender-word :—

Bachelor, spinster or maid.
Beau, belle.
Boar, sow (pig).
Boy, girl (*both* child).
Brother, sister.
Buck, doe (stag or deer).
Bull, cow (black cattle).
Cock, hen (barndoor fowls).
Cockerel, pullet.
Colt, filly (*both* foal).
Dad, father.
Dog, bitch (*both* dog, if sex is not referred to).
Drake, duck (*both* duck, if sex is not referred to).
Drone, bee.
Earl, countess.
Father, mother (*both* parents).
Friar, nun.
Gaffer, gammer.
Gander, goose (*both* geese, if sex is not referred to).
Gentleman, lady (*both* gentlefolk).
Hart, roe (*both* deer).
Husband, wife.
Kipper, shedder or baggit (spent salmon).
King, queen (*both* monarch or sovereign).
Lad, lass.
Mallard, wild-duck (*both* wild fowl).
Man, maid.
Man, woman.
Master, mistress.
Milter, spawner (fish).
Monk, nun.
Nephew, niece.
Papa, mamma.
Ram, ewe (sheep).
Ruff, reeve.
Sir, ma'am.
Sir [John], Lady [Mary].
Sire, dam.
Sloven, slut.
Son, daughter.
Stag, hind (*both* stag, if sex is not referred to).
Stallion, mare (*both* horse).
Steer, heifer.
Tup, dam (sheep).
Uncle, aunt.
Widow, widower.
Wizard, witch.

∵ The females of other animals are made by adding a suffix to the male (-ess, -ina, -ine, -ix, -a, -ee, etc.) ; as, lion, lioness ; czar, czarina ; hero, heroine ; testator, testatrix, etc.

General Funk. A panic.

"The influence of 'General Funk' was, at one time, far too prevalent among both the colonists and the younger soldiers." — *Montague: Campaigning in South Africa,* chap. vi. (1880).

General Issue is pleading "Not guilty" to a criminal charge ; "Never indebted " to a charge of debt ; the issue formed by a general denial of the plaintiff's charge.

Generalis'simo (*g* soft). Called *Tagus* among the ancient Thessalians, *Brennus* among the ancient Gauls, *Pendragon* among the ancient Welsh or Celts.

Gen'erous (*g* soft). *Generous as Hatim.* An Arabian expression. Hatim was a Bedouin chief famous for his war-like deeds and boundless generosity. His son was contemporary with Mahomet.

Geneu'ra (*g* soft). Daughter of the King of Scotland. Lurca'nio carried her off captive, and confined her in his father's castle. She loved Ariodantes, who being told that she was false, condemned her to die for incontinence, unless she found a champion to defend her. Ariodantes himself became her champion, and, having vindicated her innocence, married her. This is a satire on Arthur, whose wife intrigued with Sir Launcelot. (*Orlando Furioso,* bk. 1.)

Gene'va (*g* soft), contracted into *Gin.* Originally made from malt and juniper-berries. (French, *genièvre,* a juniper berry.)

Gene'va Bible. The English version in use prior to the present one ; so called because it was originally printed at Geneva (in 1560).

Geneva Bible (*The*). The wine cup or beer pot. The pun is on Geneva, which is the synonym of gin. (Latin, *bibo,* I drink [gin].)

"Eh bien, Gudyil, lui dit le vieux major, quelle diable de discipline? Vous avez déjà lu la Bible de Genève ce matin."—*Les Puritains d'Ecosse,* part iii. chap. 2.

Gene'va Bull. Stephen Marshall, a preacher who roared like a bull of Bashan. Called Geneva because he was a disciple of John Calvin.

Geneva Courage. Pot valour; the braggadocio which is the effect of having drunk too much gin. Gin is a corrupt contraction of Geneva, or, rather, of *genièvre.* The juniper-berry at one time used to flavour the extract of malt in the manufacture of gin. It may be used still in some qualities of gin. (*See* DUTCH COURAGE.)

Gene'va Doctrines. Calvinism. Calvin, in 1541, was invited to take up his residence in Geneva as the public teacher of theology. From this period Geneva was for many years the centre of education for the Protestant youths of Europe.

Geneva Print (*Reading*). Drinking gin or whisky.

"'Why, John,' said the veteran, 'what a discipline is this you have been keeping? You have been reading Geneva print this morning already.' 'I have been reading the Litany,' said John, shaking his head, with a look of drunken gravity."—*Sir W. Scott: Old Mortality,* chap. xi.

Geneviève (*St.*). The sainted patroness of the city of Paris. (422-512.)

Genii King. King Solomon is supposed to preside over the whole race of genii. (*D'Herbelot: Notes to the Koran*, c. 2.)

Gen'itive Case means the genus case, the case which shows the genus; thus, a bird *of the air, of the sea, of the marshes*, etc. The part in italics shows to what genus the bird belongs. Ou'*s* is the adjective sign, the same as the Sanskrit *syâ*, as *udaka* (water), *udaka-sya* (of water, or aquatic). So in Greek, *demos* (people), *demo-sios* (belonging to the people), or genitive *demo-sio*, softened into *demo- io*. In Chaucer, etc., the genitive is written in full, as *The Clerkes Tale, The Cokes Tale, The Knightes Tale, The Milleres Tale*, etc.

Ge'nius, Genii (Roman mythology) were attendant spirits. Everyone had two of these tutelaries from his cradle to his grave. But the Roman genii differ in many respects from the Eastern. The Persian and Indian genii had a corporeal form, which they could change at pleasure. They were not guardian or attendant spirits, but fallen angels, dwelling in Ginnistan, under the dominion of Eblis. They were naturally hostile to man, though compelled sometimes to serve them as slaves. The Roman genii were tutelary spirits, very similar to the guardian angels spoken of in Scripture (St. Matt. xviii. 10). (The word is the old Latin *geno*, to be born, from the notion that birth and life were due to these *dii genita'les*.)

Genius (birth-wit) is innate talent; hence propensity, nature, inner man. " *Cras genium mero cura'bis* " (to-morrow you shall indulge your inner man with wine), *Horace, 3 Odes,* xvii. 14. "*Indulg'ere genio*" (to give loose to one's propensity), *Persius,* v. 151. " *Defrauda're genium suum*" (to stint one's appetite, to deny one's self), *Terence: Phormio,* i. 1. (*See above.*)

Genius. Tom Moore says that Common Sense went out one moonlight night with Genius on his rambles; Common Sense went on many wise things saying, but Genius went gazing at the stars, and fell into a river. This is told of Thalēs by Plato, and Chaucer has introduced it into his *Milleres Tale*.

" So ferde another clerk with astronomye:
    He walkèd in the feeldès for to prye
Upon the sterrès, what ther shuld befall,
Till he was in a marlè pit i-fall."
                    Canterbury Tales, 3,457.

My evil genius (my ill-luck). The Romans maintained that two genii attended every man from birth to death— one good and the other evil. Good luck was brought about by the agency of "his good genius," and ill luck by that of his "evil genius."

Genius Loci (Latin). The tutelary deity of a place.

" In the midst of this wreck of ancient books and utensils, with a gravity equal to [that of] Marius among the ruins of Carthage, sat a large black cat, which, to a superstitious eye, might have presented the *genius loci*, the tutelar demon of the apartment."—*Sir W. Scott : The Antiquary,* chap. iii.

Gen'oa, from the Latin, *genu* (the knee); so called from the bend made there by the Adriatic. The whole of Italy is called a man's leg, and this is his knee.

Genove'fa (*g* soft). Wife of Count Palatine Siegfried, of Brabant, in the time of Charles Martel. Being suspected of infidelity, she was driven into the forest of Ardennes, where she gave birth to a son, who was nourished by a white doe. In time, Siegfried discovered his error, and restored his wife and child to their proper home.

Genre Painter (*genre* 1 syl.). A painter of domestic, rural, or village scenes, such as *A Village Wedding, The Young Recruit, Blind Man's Buff, The Village Politician*, etc. It is a French term, and means, " Man : his customs, habits, and ways of life." Wilkie, Ostade, Gerard Dow, etc., belonged to this class. In the *drama*, Victor Hugo introduced the genre system in lieu of the stilted, unnatural style of Louis XIV.'s era.

" We call those ' genre' canvases, whereon are painted idyls of the fireside, the roadside, and the farm ; pictures of real life."—*E. C. Stedman · Poets of America,* chap. iv. p. 98.

Gens Braccata. Trousered people. The Romans wore no trousers like the Gauls, Scythians, and Persians. The Gauls wore "braccæ" and were called *Gens braccāta*.

Gens Togata. The nation which wore the toga. The Greeks wore the " pallium " and were called *Gens palliāta*.

Gentle (*g* soft) means having the manners of genteel persons—*i.e.* persons of family, called *gens* in Latin.

"We must be gentle, now we are gentlemen."— Shakespeare : *Winter's Tale,* v. 2.

The gentle craft. The gentleman's trade, so called from the romance of Prince Crispin, who is said to have made shoes. It is rather remarkable that the "gentle craft" should be closely connected with our *snob* (*q.v.*).

"Here Hans Sachs, the cobbler poet, laureate
of the gentle craft,
Wisest of the Twelve Wise Masters, in huge
folios sang and laughed."
Longfellow : Nuremberg, stanza 19.

The gentle craft. Angling. The pun is on *gentle*, a maggot or grub used for baiting the hook in angling.

Gentle Shepherd (*The*). George Grenville, the statesman, a nickname derived from a line applied to him by Pitt, afterwards Earl of Chatham. Grenville, in the course of one of his speeches, addressed the House interrogatively, "Tell me where? tell me where?" Pitt hummed a line of a song then very popular, "Gentle shepherd, tell me where?" and the House burst into laughter (1712-1720).

Gentleman (*g* soft). A translation of the French *gentilhomme*, one who belongs to the *gens* or stock. According to the Roman law, gens-men, or gentlemen, were those only who had a family name, were born of free parents, had no slave in their ancestral line, and had never been degraded to a lower rank.

A gentleman of the four outs. A vulgar upstart, with-*out* manners, with-*out* wit, with-*out* money, and with-*out* credit.

Gentlemen of Paper and Wax. The first of a new line ennobled with knighthood or other dignity, to whom are given titles and coat-armour. They are made "gentlemen" by patent and a seal.

Geoffrey Crayon. The hypothetical author of the *Sketch Book.* Washington Irving, of New York (1783-1859).

Geology (*g* soft). *The father of geology.* William Smith (1769-1840).

Ge'omancy (*g* soft). Divining by the earth. So termed because these diviners in the sixteenth century drew on the earth their magic circles, figures, and lines. (Greek, *ge*, the earth; *mantei'a*, prophecy.)

Geometry (*g* soft) means land-measuring. The first geometrician was a ploughman pacing out his field. (Greek, *ge*, the earth ; *metron*, a measure.)

George II. was nicknamed "Prince Titi." (*See* TITI.)

George III. was nicknamed "Farmer George," or "The Farmer King." (*See* FARMER.)

George IV. was nicknamed "The First Gentleman of Europe," "Fum the Fourth," "Prince Florizel," "The

Adonis of fifty," and "The Fat Adonis of fifty." (*See each of these nicknames.*)

George, Mark, John (*SS.*). Nostradamus wrote in 1566 :

"Quand Georges Dieu crucifera,
Que Marc le ressucitera,
Et que St. Jean le portera,
La fin du monde arrivera."

In 1886 St. George's day fell on Good Friday, St. Mark's day on Easter Sunday, and St. John's day on Corpus Christi—but "the end of the world" did not then arrive.

George (*St.*) (*g* soft). Gibbon, in his *Decline and Fall*, ii. 323, asserts that the patron saint of England was George of Cappadocia, the turbulent Arian Bishop of Alexandria, torn to pieces by the populace in 360, and revered as a saint by the opponents of Athanasius ; but this assertion has been fully disproved by the Jesuit Papebroch, Milner, and others.

That St. George is a veritable character is beyond all reasonable doubt, and there seems no reason to deny that he was born in Armor'ica, and was beheaded in Diocletian's persecution by order of Datianus, April 23rd, 303. St. Jerome (331-420) mentions him in one of his martyrologies ; in the next century there were many churches to his honour. St. Gregory (540-604) has in his Sacramentary a "Preface for St. George's Day;" and the Venerable Bede (672-735), in his martyrology, says, "At last St. George truly finished his martyrdom by decapitation, although the gests of his passion are numbered among the apocryphal writings."

In regard to his connection with England, Ashmole, in his *History of the Order of the Garter*, says that King Arthur, in the sixth century, placed the picture of St. George on his banners ; and Selden tells us he was patron saint of England in the Saxon times. It is quite certain that the Council of Oxford in 1222 commanded his festival to be observed in England as a holiday of lesser rank ; and on the establishment of the Order of the Garter by Edward III. St. George was adopted as the patron saint.

The dragon slain by St. George is simply a common allegory to express the triumph of the Christian hero over evil, which John "the Divine" beheld under the image of a dragon. Similarly, St. Michael, St. Margaret, St. Silvester, and St. Martha are all depicted as slaying dragons ; the Saviour and the Virgin as treading them under their feet ; and St. John the Evangelist as charming a winged dragon from a poisoned chalice given him to drink. Even John Bunyan avails himself of the same figure, when he makes Christian encounter Apollyon and prevail against him.

George (St.), the Red Cross Knight (in Spenser's *Faërie Queene*, bk. i.), represents "Piety." He starts with Una (Truth) in his adventures, and is driven into Wandering Wood, where he encounters Error, and passes the night with Una in Hypocrisy's cell. Being visited by a false vision, the knight abandons Una, and goes with Duessa (False-faith) to the palace of Pride. He leaves this palace clandestinely, but being overtaken by Duessa is persuaded to drink of an enchanted fountain, when he becomes paralysed, and is taken captive by Orgoglio. Una informs Arthur of the sad event, and the prince goes to the rescue. He slays Orgoglio, and the Red Cross Knight, being set free, is taken by Una to the house of Holiness to be healed. On leaving Holiness, both Una and the knight journey towards Eden. As they draw near, the dragon porter flies at the knight, and St. George has to do battle with it for three whole days before he succeeds in slaying it. The dragon being slain, the two enter Eden, and the Red Cross Knight is united to Una in marriage.

St. George and the Dragon. According to the ballad given in Percy's *Reliques*, St. George was the son of Lord Albert of Coventry. His mother died in giving him birth, and the new-born babe was stolen away by the weird lady of the woods, who brought him up to deeds of arms. His body had three marks; a dragon on the breast, a garter round one of the legs, and a blood-red cross on the arm. When he grew to manhood he first fought against the Saracens, and then went to Syle'nē, a city of Libya, where was a stagnant lake infested by a huge dragon, whose poisonous breath "had many a city slain," and whose hide "no spear nor sword could pierce." Every day a virgin was sacrificed to it, and at length it came to the lot of Sabra, the king's daughter, to become its victim. She was tied to the stake and left to be devoured, when St. George came up, and vowed to take her cause in hand. On came the dragon, and St. George, thrusting his lance into its mouth, killed it on the spot. The king of Morocco and the king of Egypt, unwilling that Sabra should marry a Christian, sent St. George to Persia, and directed the "sophy" to kill him. He was accordingly thrust

into a dungeon, but making good his escape, carried off Sabra to England, where she became his wife, and they lived happily at Coventry together till their death.

⁎ A very similar tale is told of Hesionê, daughter of Laomĕdon. (*See* HESIONE, SEA MONSTERS.)

St. George he was for England, St. Denis was for France. This refers to the war-cries of the two nations—that of England was "St. George!" that of France, "Montjoye St. Denis!"

"Our ancient word of courage, fair 'St. George,' Inspire us with the spleen of fiery dragons."
Shakespeare: Richard III., v. 3.

When St. George goes on horseback St. Yves goes on foot. In times of war lawyers have nothing to do. St. George is the patron of soldiers, and St. Ives of lawyers.

St. George's Arm. The Hellespont is so called by the Catholic Church in honour of St. George, the patron saint of England. (*Papebroch : Actes des Saints.*)

St. George's Channel. An arm of the Atlantic, separating Ireland from Great Britain ; so called in honour of St. George, referred to above.

St. George's Cross. Red on a white field.

St. George's Day (April 23rd). A day of deception and oppression. It was the day when new leases and contracts used to be made.

George a' Green. *As good as George a' Green.* Resolute-minded ; one who will do his duty come what may. George a' Green was the famous pinder or pound-keeper of Wakefield, who resisted Robin Hood, Will Scarlett, and Little John single-handed when they attempted to commit a trespass in Wakefield.

" Were ye bold as George-a-Green,
I shall make bold to turn again."
Samuel Butler : Hudibras.

George Eliot. The literary name of Marian Evans [Lewes], authoress of *Adam Bede, Mill on the Floss, Felix Holt*, etc.

George Geith. The hero of a novel by Mrs. Trafford [Riddell]. He is one who will work as long as he has breath to draw, and would die in harness. He would fight against all opposing circumstances while he had a drop of blood left in his veins, and may be called the model of untiring industry and indomitable moral courage.

George Sand. The pen-name of Mme. Dudevant, born at Paris 1804. Her maiden name was Dupin.

George Street (Strand, London) commences the precinct of an ancient mansion which originally belonged to the bishops of Norwich. After passing successively into the possession of Charles Brandon, Duke of Suffolk, the archbishops of York, and the Crown, it came to George Villiers, Duke of Buckingham. The second Duke of Buckingham pulled down the mansion and built the streets and alley called respectively " George" (street), "Villiers" (street), " Duke " (street), " Of " (alley), and " Buckingham " (street).

Geraint' (*g* hard). Tributary Prince of Devon, and one of the knights of the Round Table. Overhearing part of E'nid's words, he fancied she was faithless to him, and treated her for a time very harshly; but Enid nursed him so carefully when he was wounded that he saw his error, "nor did he doubt her more, but rested in her fealty, till he crowned a happy life with a fair death." (*Tennyson : Idylls of the King ; Enid.*)

Geraldine (3 syl., *g* soft). *The Fair Geraldine.* Lady Elizabeth Fitzgerald is so called in the Earl of Surrey's poems.

Gera'nium (*g* soft). The Turks say this was a common mallow changed by the touch of Mahomet's garment.
The word is from the Greek *gerános* (a crane); and the plant is called " Crane's Bill," from the resemblance of the fruit to the bill of a crane.

Gerda (*g* hard). Wife of Frey, and daughter of the frost giant Gymer. She is so beautiful that the brightness of her naked arms illuminates both air and sea. Frey (the genial spring) married Gerda (the frozen earth), and Gerda became the mother of children. (*Scandinavian mythology.*)

German or **Germaine** (*g* soft). Pertaining to, related to, as *cousins-german* (first cousins), *german to the subject* (bearing on or pertinent to the subject). This word has no connection with German (the nation), but comes from the Latin *germa'nus* (of the same germ or stock). First cousins have a grandfather or grandmother in common.
"Those that are germaine to him, though removed fifty times, shall all come under the hangman."—*Shakespeare: Winter's Tale,* iv. 3.

German. Jehan de Maire says, "Germany is so called from Cæsar's sister Germâna, wife of Salvius Brabon." Geoffrey of Monmouth says that Ebrancus, a mythological descendant of Brute, King of Britain, had twenty sons and thirty daughters. All the sons, except the eldest, settled in Germany, which was therefore called the land of the *Germans* or brothers. (*See above.*)

" [*Ebrank.*] An happy man in his first days he was,
  And happy father of fair progeny ;
For all so many weeks as the year has
  So many children he did multiply !
Of which were twenty sons, which did apply
Their minds to praise and chivalrous desire.
These germans did subdue all Germany,
Of whom it hight. . . ."
          Spenser : Faërie Queene, ii. 10.

∵ Probably the name is Ger-man, meaning " war-man." The Germans call themselves *Deutsch-en,* which is the same as Teut-on, with the initial letter flattened into D, and " Teut " means a multitude. The Romans called the people Germans at least 200 years before the Christian era, for in 1547 a tablet (dated B.C. 222) was discovered, recording the victories of the Consul Marcellus over Veridomar, "General of the Gauls and Germans."

Father of German literature. Gotthold Ephraim Lessing. (1729-1781.)

German Comb. The four fingers and thumb. "*Se pygnoit du pygne d'Almaing*" (*Rabelais*), He combed his hair with his fingers. Oudin, in his *Dictionnaire,* explains *pygne d'Aleman* by "*los dedos et la dita.*" The Germans were the last to adopt periwigs, and while the French were never seen without a comb in one hand, the Germans adjusted their hair by running their fingers through it.
" He apparelled himself according to the season, and afterwards combed his head with an Alman comb."—*Rabelais: Gargantua and Pantagruel,* book i. 21.

German Silver is not silver at all, but white copper, or copper, zinc, and nickel mixed together. It was first made in Europe at Hildberg-hausen, in Germany, but had been used by the Chinese time out of mind.

Gerryman'der (*g* hard). So to divide a county or nation into representative districts as to give one special political party undue advantage over others. The word is derived from Elbridge Gerry, who adopted the scheme in Massachusetts when he was governor. Gilbert Stuart, the artist, looking at the map of the new distribution, with a little invention converted it into a salamander. " No, no ! " said Russell, when shown it, " not a Sala-mander, Stuart ; call it a Gerry-mander."
∵ *To gerrymander* is so to hocus-pocus figures, etc., as to affect the balance.

Gerst-Monat. Barley-month. The Anglo-Saxon name for September; so called because it was the time of barley-beer making.

Ger'trude (2 syl., *g* hard). Hamlet's mother, who married Claudius, the murderer of her late husband. She inadvertently poisoned herself by drinking a potion prepared for her son. (*Shakespeare : Hamlet.*)

Gertrude (*St.*), in Christian art, is sometimes represented as surrounded with rats and mice; and sometimes as spinning, the rats and mice running about her distaff.

Gertrude of Wyo'ming. The name of one of Campbell's poems.

Gervais (*St.*). The French St. Swithin, June 19th. (*See* SWITHIN.)

In 1725, Bulliot, a French banker, made a bet that, as it rained on St. Gervais's Day, it would rain more or less for forty days afterwards. The bet was taken by so many people that the entire property of Bulliot was pledged. The bet was lost, and the banker was utterly ruined.

Ger'yon (*g* hard). A human monster with three bodies and three heads, whose oxen ate human flesh, and were guarded by a two-headed dog. Herculēs slew both Geryon and the dog. This fable means simply that Geryon reigned over three kingdoms, and was defended by an ally, who was at the head of two tribes.

Geryon'eo. A giant with three bodies; that is, Philip II. of Spain, master of three kingdoms. (*Spenser : Faërie Queene*, v. 11.)

Ges'mas (*g* hard). (*See* Desmas.)

Gess'ler (*g* hard). The Austrian governor of the three Forest Cantons of Switzerland. A man of most brutal nature and tyrannical disposition. He attempted to carry off the daughter of Leuthold, a Swiss herdsman; but Leuthold slew the ruffian sent to seize her, and fled. This act of injustice roused the people to rebellion, and Gessler, having put to death Melch'tal, the patriarch of the Forest Cantons, insulted the people by commanding them to bow down to his cap, hoisted on a high pole. Tell refusing so to do, was arrested with his son, and Gessler, in the refinement of cruelty, imposed on him the task of shooting with his bow and arrow an apple from the head of his own son. Tell succeeded in this dangerous skill-trial, but in his agitation dropped an arrow from his robe. The governor insolently demanded what the second arrow was for, and Tell fearlessly replied, "To shoot you with, had I failed in the task imposed upon me." Gessler now ordered him to be carried in chains across the lake, and cast into Kusnacht castle, a prey "to the reptiles that lodged there." He was, however, rescued by the peasantry, and, having shot Gessler, freed his country from the Austrian yoke.

Gesta Romano'rum (*g* soft), compiled by Pierre Bercheur, prior of the Benedictine convent of St. Eloi, Paris, published by the Roxburgh Society. Edited by Sir F. Madden, and afterwards by S. J. Herrtage.

Geste or **Gest** (*g* soft). A story, romance, achievement. From the Latin *gesta* (exploits).

"The scene of these *gestes* being laid in ordinary life."—*Cyclopædia Britan.* (*Romance*).

Get (*To*). To gain; to procure; to obtain.

"Get wealth and place, if possible with grace; if not, by any means get wealth and place."

Horace (*Satires*) says:—" Rem facis, recte si possis; si non, rem facis."

Get, Got. (Anglo-Saxon, *git-an*.)

"I got on horseback within ten minutes after I got your letter. When I got to Canterbury I got a chaise for town; but I got wet through, and have got such a cold that I shall not get rid of in a hurry. I got to the Treasury about noon, but first of all got shaved and dressed. I soon got into the scoret of getting a memorial before the Board, but I could not get an answer then; however, I got intelligence from a messenger that I should get one next morning. As soon as I got back to my inn, I got my supper, and then got to bed. When I got up next morning, I got my breakfast, and, having got dressed, I got out in time to get an answer to my memorial. As soon as I got it, I got into a chaise, and got back to Canterbury by three, and got home for tea. I have got nothing for you, and so adieu."—*Dr. Withers.*

Get by Heart (*To*). To commit to memory. In French, "*Apprendre une chose par cœur.*"

Get One's Back Up (*To*). To show irritation, as cats set up their backs when angry.

Get-up (*A*). A style of dress, as "His get-up was excellent," meaning his style of dress exactly suited the part he professed to enact.

Get up (*To*).
To rise from one's bed.
To learn, as "I must get up my Euclid."
To organise and arrange, as "We will get up a bazaar."

Gethsemane. The *Orchis maculata*, supposed in legendary story to be spotted by the blood of Christ.

Gew'gaw (*g* hard). A showy trifle. (Saxon, *ge-gaf*, a trifle; French, *joujou*, a toy.)

17

Ghe'bers or **Gue'bres.** The original
tives of Iran (Persia), who adhered to
e religion of Zoroaster, and (after the
nquest of their country by the Arabs)
came waifs and outlaws. The term is
w applied to fire-worshippers generally.
anway says that the ancient Ghebers
ore a cushee or belt, which they never
id aside.

Ghibelline (*g* hard), or rather Waib-
igen. The war-cry of Conrad's fol-
wers in the battle of Weinsberg (1140).
mrad, Duke of Suabia, was opposed
Henry the Lion, Duke of Saxony,
hose slogan was Guelph or Welfe, his
mily name.

Ghost. *To give up the ghost.* To
e. The idea is that life is independent
the body, and is due to the habitation
the ghost or spirit in the material
dy. At death the ghost or spirit
aves this tabernacle of clay, and either
turns to God or abides in the region of
irits till the general resurrection.
us in Ecc. xii. 7 it is said, "Then
all the dust return to the earth as it
as: and the spirit shall return unto
od who gave it."

Man dieth, and wasteth away : yea, man giveth
the ghost, and where is he ?"—Job xiv. 10.

The ghost of a chance. The least like-
lood. "He has not the ghost of a
ance of being elected," not the shadow
a probability.

Ghoul. (*See* FAIRY.)

Giaffir (*Djaf-fir*). Pacha of Aby'dos,
d father of Zule'ika. He tells her he
tends to marry her to Kara Osman
rloo, governor of Magne'sia ; but Zu-
ka has betrothed herself to her cousin
lim. The lovers flee, Giaffir shoots
lim, Zuleika dies of grief, and the
cha lives on, a heart-broken old man,
er calling to the winds, "Where is
y daughter ?" and echo answers,
Where ?" (*Byron : Bride of Abydos.*)

Giall. The infernal river of Scandi-
vian mythology.

Giallar Bridge. The bridge of
ath, over which all must pass to get to
elheim. (*Scandinavian mythology.*)

Giallar Horn (*The*). Heimdall's
rn, which went out into all worlds
henever he chose to blow it. (*Scandi-
rian mythology.*)

Gian ben Gian (*g* soft). King of
e Ginns or Genii, and founder of the
yramids. He was overthrown by Aza'-
l or Lucifer. (*Arab superstitions.*)

Giant of Literature (*The*). Dr.
Samuel Johnson (1709 - 1783). Also
called "the great moralist."

Giants (*g* soft).

(1) *Of Greek mythology*, sons of Tar'-
taros and Ge. When they attempted to
storm heaven, they were hurled to earth
by the aid of Hercules, and buried under
Mount Etna.

(2) *Of Scandinavian mythology*, were
evil genii, dwelling in Jötunheim (*giant-
land*), who had the power of reducing or
extending their stature at will.

(3) *Of nursery mythology*, are cannibals of vast stature and immense muscular power, but as stupid as they are
violent and treacherous. The best
known are Blunderbore (*q.v.*), Cormoran' (*q.v.*), Galliantus (*q.v.*), Gombo
(*q.v.*), Megadore and Bellygan.

(4) In the romance of *Gargan'tua and
Pantagruel*, by Rabelais, giants mean
princes.

(5) **Giants of Mythology.**

AC'AMAS. One of the Cyclops. (*Greek fable.*)
ADAMAS'TOR (*q.v.*).
ÆGÆ'ON, the hundred-handed. One of the Titans.
   (*Greek fable.*)
AG'RIOS. One of the Titans. He was killed by
   the Parcæ. (*Greek fable.*)
ALCYONEUS [*Al-si-o-nuce*], or AL'CION. Jupiter
   sent Hercules against him for stealing some of
   the Sun's oxen. But Hercules could not do
   anything, for immediately the giant touched
   the earth he received fresh strength. (*See
   below,* ANTÆOS.) At length Pallas carried
   him beyond the moon. His seven daughters
   were metamorphosed into halcyons. (*Argon-
   autic Expedition,* i. 6.)
AL'GEBAR'. The giant Ori'on is so called by the
   Arabs.
ALIFAN'FARON or ALIPHAR'NON (*q.v.*).
ALO'EOS. Son of Poseidon Canacè. Each of his
   two sons was 27 cubits high. (*Greek fable.*)
AM'ERANT. A cruel giant slain by Guy of War-
   wick. (*Percy : Reliques.*)
ANGOULAFFRE (*q.v.*). (*See below,* 21 feet.)
ANTÆ'OS (*q.v.* ; *see above,* ALCYONEUS). (*See
   below,* 105 feet.)
ARGES (2 syl.). One of the Cyclops. (*Greek fable.*)
AS'CAPART (*q.v.*).
ATLAS (*q.v.*).
BALAN (*q.v.*).
BELLE (1 syl.) (*q.v.*).
BELLE'RUS (*q.v.*).
BLUNDERBORE (3 syl.) (*q.v.*).
BRIAR'EOS or BRI'AREUS (3 syl.) (*q.v.*).
BROBDINGNAG (*q.v.*).
BRONTES (2 syl.) (*q.v.*).
BURLOND (*q.v.*).
CA'COS or CACUS (*q.v.*).
CALIG'ORANT (*q.v.*).
CAR'ACULIAM'BO. The giant that Don Quixote
   intended should kneel at the feet of Dulcin'ea.
   (*Cervantes : Don Quixote.*)
CARUS. In the *Seven Champions.*
CHALBROTH. The stem of all the giant race.
   (*Rabelais : Pantagruel.*)
CHRISTOPH'ERUS. (*See* CHRISTOPHER, *St.*)
CLYT'IOS (*q.v.*).
CŒOS. Son of Heaven and Earth. He married
   Phœbè, and was the father of Latöna. (*Greek
   fable.*)
COLBRAND. (*See* COLBRONDE.)
CORFLAM'BO (*q.v.*).
CORMORAN (*q.v.*).
CORMORANT. A giant discomfited by Sir Brian.
   (*Spenser : Faërie Queene,* vi. 4.)

COTTAS (*q.v.*).

COULIN (*q.v.*).

CYCLOPS (The) (*q.v.*).

DESPAIR (*q.v.*).

DONDASCH (*q.v.*).

ENCEL'ADOS (*q.v.*) (*q.v.*).

EPHIALTES (4 syl.) (*q.v.*).

ERIX (*q.v.*).

EU'RYTOS. One of the giants that made war with the gods. Bacchus killed him with his thyrsus. (*Greek fable.*)

FERREGUS, slain by Orgando, was 28 feet in height.

FER'RACUTE (3 syl.) (*q.v.*).

FER'RAGUS (*q.v.*).

FIERABRAS [*Fe-a-ra-brah*] (*q.v.*).

FION (*q.v.*).

FIOR'GWYN, the father of Frigga (*Scandinavian mythology*).

FRACASSUS (*q.v.*).

GAL'BARA. Father of Goliah of Secondille (3 syl.), and inventor of the custom of drinking healths. (*Duchat: Œuvres de Rabelais.* 1711.)

GALAPAS. The giant slain by King Arthur. (*Sir T. Malory: History of Prince Arthur.*)

GALLIGANTUS (*q.v.*).

GARAGANTUA (*q.v.*).

GARGANTUA (*q.v.*).

GARIAN. In the *Seven Champions.*

GEMMAGOG (*q.v.*).

GERYON'EO (*q.v.*).

GIRALDA (*q.v.*).

GODMER (*q.v.*).

GOEMOT or GOEMAGOT (*q.v.*).

GOG'MAGOG. King of the giant race of Albion ; slain by Cori'neus.

GRANGOUSIER. The giant king of Utopia, father of Gargantua. (*Rabelais: Gargantua,*)

GRANTORTO (*q.v.*).

GRIM (*q.v.*).

GRUMBO (*q.v.*).

GUY OF WARWICK (*q.v.*).

GYGES (2 syl.). One of the Titans. He had fifty heads and a hundred hands. (*Greek fable.*)

HAP'MOUCHE (2 syl.) (*q.v.*).

HIPPOL'YTOS. One of the giants who made war with the gods. He was killed by Hermês. (*Greek fable.*)

HRASVELG (*q.v.*).

HRIMTHURSAR (*q.v.*).

HURTALI (*q.v.*).

INDRACIT'TRAN (*q.v.*).

IRUS (*q.v.*).

JOTUN. The giant of Jötunheim or Giant-land. (*Scandinavian mythology.*)

JULIANCE. A giant of Arthurian romance.

JUNNER (*q.v.*).

KIPRI. The giant of atheism and infidelity.

KOTTOS. One of the Titans. He had a hundred hands. (*See* BRIAREOS.) (*Greek fable.*)

MALAMBRU'KO (*q.v.*).

MARGUTTE (*q.v.*).

MAUGYS (*q.v.*).

MAUL (*q.v.*).

MONT-ROGNON (*q.v.*).

MORGANTE (3 syl.) (*q.v.*).

MUGILLO. A giant famous for his mace with six balls.

OFF'ERUS (*q.v.*).

OGIAS (*q.v.*).

ORGOGLIO (*q.v.*).

ORI'ON (*q.v.*). (*See below,* 80½ feet.)

OTOS (*q.v.*).

PALLAS (*q.v.*).

PANTAG'RUEL (*q.v.*).

PHIDON. In the *Seven Champions.*

POLYBO'TES (4 syl.) (*q.v.*).

POL'YPHE'MUS or POLYPHEME (3 syl.) (*q.v.*).

PORPHYR'ION (*q.v.*).

PYRAC'MON. One of the Cyclops. (*Greek fable.*)

RAPHSARUS. In the *Seven Champions.*

RITHO (*q.v.*).

RITHO. The giant who commanded King Arthur to send him his beard to complete the lining of a robe. In the Arthurian romance.

SKRYMIR. (*See* DRAUGHT OF THOR, p. 380.)

SLAY-GOOD (*q.v.*).

S'TER'OPES (3 syl.). One of the Cyclops. (*Greek fable.*)

TARTARQ. The Cyclops of Basque mythology.

TEUTOBOCH'US (*King*). (*See below,* 30 feet.)

THAON. One of the giants who made war with the gods. He was killed by the Parcæ. (*Greek fable.*)

TITANS (The) (*q.v.*).

TIT'YOS (*q.v.*).

TRE'YEAGLE (*q.v.*).

TYPHŒUS (*q.v.*).

TYPHON (*q.v.*).

WIDENOSTRILS (*q.v.*).

YOHAK. The giant guardian of the caves of Babylon. (*Southey: Thalaba,* book v.)

Of these giants the following are noteworthy :

19 feet in height: A skeleton discovered at Lucerne in 1577. Dr. Plater is our authority for this measurement.

21 feet in height: Angoulaffre of the Broken Teeth, was 12 cubits in height. (A cubit was 21 inches.)

30 feet in height : Teutobochus, whose remains were discovered near the Rhone in 1613. They occupied a tomb 30 feet long. The bones of another gigantic skeleton were exposed by the action of the Rhone in 1456. If this was a human skeleton, the height of the living man must have been 30 feet.

80½ feet in height: Orion, according to Pliny, was 46 cubits in height.

105 feet in height: Antæos is said by Plutarch to have been 60 cubits in height. He furthermore adds that the grave of the giant was opened by Serbonios.

300 feet in height: The "monster Polypheme." It is said that his skeleton was discovered at Trapa'ni, in Sicily, in the fourteenth century. If this skeleton was that of a man, he must have been 300 feet in height.

(6) Giants of Real Life.

ANAK (of Bible history), father of the Anakim. The Hebrew spies said they were mere grasshoppers in comparison with these giants (Joshua xv. 14 ; Judges i. 20 ; and Numbers xiii. 33.)

ANAK. (*See* BRICE.)

ANDRONI'CUS II. was 10 feet in height. He was grandson of Alexius Connēnus. Nicētas asserts that he had seen him.

BAMFORD (*Edward*) was 7 feet 4 inches. He died in 1768, and was buried in St. Dunstan's churchyard.

BATES (*Captain*) was 7 feet 11½ inches. He was a native of Kentucky, and was exhibited in London in 1871. His wife (Anna Swann) was the same height.

BLACKER (*Henry*) was 7 feet 4 inches, and most symmetrical. He was born at Cuckfield, in Sussex, in 1724, and was called "The British Giant."

BRADLEY (*William*) was 7 feet 9 inches in height. He was born in 1787, and died 1820. His birth is duly registered in the parish church of Market Weighton, in Yorkshire, and his right hand is preserved in the museum of the College of Surgeons.

BRICE (M. J.) exhibited under the name of Anak, was 7 feet 8 inches in height at the age of 26. He was born in 1840 at Ramonchamp, in the Vosges, and visited England 1862-5. His arms had a stretch of 95½ inches, and were therefore 3½ inches too long for symmetry.

BRUSTED (*Von*) was 8 feet in height. This Norway giant was exhibited in London in 1880.

BUSBY (*John*) was 7 feet 9 inches in height, and his brother was about the same. They were natives of Darfield, in Yorkshire.

CHANG, the Chinese giant, was 8 feet 2 inches in height. The entire name of this Chinese giant was Chang-Woo-Goo. He was exhibited in London in 1865-1866, and again in 1880. He was a native of Fychou.

CHARLEMAGNE was nearly 8 feet in height, and was so strong he could squeeze together three horseshoes with his hands.

COTTER (*Patrick*) was 8 feet 7½ inches in height. This Irish giant died at Clifton, Bristol, in 1802. A cast of his hand is preserved in the museum of the College of Surgeons.

DANIEL, the porter of Oliver Cromwell, was a man of gigantic stature.

ELEA′ZER was 7 cubits (nearly 14 feet). Vitellius sent this giant to Rome ; and he is mentioned by Josephus. N.B.—The height of Goliath was 6 cubits and a span.

Nothing can be a greater proof that the cubit was not 21 inches, for no recorded height of any giant known has reached 10 feet. The nearest approach to it was Gabara, the Arabian giant (9 feet 9 inches) mentioned by Pliny, and Middleton of Lancashire (9 feet 3 inches) mentioned by Dr. Plott. Probably a cubit was about 18 inches.

ELRIZEGUE (*Joachim*). Was 7 feet 10 inches in height. He was a Spaniard, and exhibited in the Cosmorama, Regent Stre t, London.

EVANS (*William*) was 8 feet at death. He was a porter of Charles I., and died in 1632.

FRANK (*Big*). Was 7 feet 8 inches in height. He was an Irishman whose name was Francis Sheridan, and died in 1870.

FRENZ (*Louis*) was 7 feet 4 inches in height. He was called "the French giant."

FUNNUM (court giant of Eugene II.) was 11 feet 6 inches.

GABARA, the Arabian giant, was 9 feet 9 inches. This Arabian giant is mentioned by Pliny, who says he was the tallest man seen in the days of Claudius.

GILLY was 8 feet. This Swedish giant was exhibited in the early part of the nineteenth century.

GOLI′ATH was 6 cubits and a span (11 feet 9 inches, if the cubit = 21 inches, and the span = 9 inches).
See note to the giant ELEAZER. If the cubit was 18 inches, then Goliath was the same height as the Arabian giant Gabara.

GORDON (*Alice*) was 7 feet in height. She was a native of Essex, and died in 1737, at the age of 19.

HALE (*Robert*) was 7 feet 6 inches in height. He was born at Somerton, in Norfolk, and was called "the Norfolk giant" (1820-1862).

HAR′DRADA (*Harold*) was nearly 8 feet in height ("5 ells of Norway"), and was called "the Norway giant." Snorro Sturleson says he was "about 8 feet in height."

HOLMES (*Benjamin*) was 7 feet 6 inches in height. He was a Northumberland man, and was made sword-bearer of the Corporation of Worcester. He died in 1892.

JOHN FREDERICK, Duke of Brunswick, was 8 feet 6 inches in height.

KINTOLOCHUS REX was 15 feet 6 inches in height (!), 5 feet through the chest to the spine (!), and 10 feet across the shoulders (!). This, of course, is quite incredible.

LA PIERRE was 7 feet 1 inch in height. He was born at Stratgard, in Denmark.

LOUIS was 7 feet 4 inches in height. Called "the French giant." His left hand is preserved in the museum of the College of Surgeons.

LOUISHKIN was 8 feet 5 inches in height. This Russian giant was drum-major of the Imperial Guards.

MCDONALD (*James*) was 7 feet 6 inches in height. He was born in Cork, Ireland, and died in 1760.

MCDONALD (*Samuel*) was 6 feet 10 inches in height. This Scotchman was usually called "Big Sam." He was the Prince of Wales's footman, and died in 1802.

MAGRATH (*Cornelius*) was 7 feet 10 inches in height at the age of 16. He was an orphan reared by Bishop Berkeley, and died at the age of twenty (1740–1760).

MAXIMI′NUS was 8 feet 6 inches in height. The Roman emperor, from 235 to 238.

MELLON (*Edmund*) was 7 feet 6 inches in height at the age of nineteen. He was born at Port Leicester, in Ireland (1740-1760).

MIDDLETON (*John*) was 9 feet 3 inches in height. "His hand was 17 inches long and 8½ broad." He was born at Hale, Lancashire, in the reign of James I. (*See above*, GABARA.) (*Dr. Plott: Natural History of Staffordshire*, p. 295.)

MILLER (*Maximilian Christopher*) was 8 feet in height. His hand measured 12 inches, and his forefinger was 9 inches long. This Saxon giant died in London at the age of sixty (1674-1734).

MURPHY was 8 feet 10 inches in height. This Irish giant was contemporary with O'Brien (*see below*), and died at Marseilles.

O'BRIEN, or CHARLES BYRNE, was 8 feet 4 inches in height. The skeleton of this Irish giant is preserved in the College of Surgeons. He died in Cockspur Street, London, and was contemporary with Murphy (1761-1783).

O'BRIEN (*Patrick*) was 8 feet 7 inches in height. He died August 3, 1804, aged thirty-nine.

OG, King of Bashan. According to tradition, he lived 3,000 years, and walked beside the Ark during the Flood. One of his bones formed a bridge over a river. His bed (Deuteronomy iii. 11) was 9 cubits by 4 cubits.
If the cubit was really 21 inches, this would make the bed 15¾ feet by 10¼. The great bed of Ware, Herts, is 12 feet by 12. (*See above*, ELEAZAR —note.)

OSEN (*Heinrich*) was 7 feet 6 inches in height at the age of 27, and weighed above 37 stone. He was born in Norway. (*See above*, HARDRADA.)

PORUS was "5 cubits in height" (7 feet 6 inches). He was an Indian king who fought against Alexander the Great near the river Hydaspes. (*Quintus Curtius : De rebus gestis Alexandri Magni*.)
Whatever the Jewish cubit was, the Roman cubit was not more than 18 inches.

RIECHART (*J. H.*) was 8 feet 4 inches in height. He was a native of Friedberg, and both his father and mother were of gigantic stature.

SALMERON (*Martin*) was 7 feet 4 inches in height. He was called "The Mexican Giant."

SAM (*Big*). (*See* MACDONALD.)

SHERIDAN. (*See above*, FRANK.)

SWANN (*Anne Hanen*) was 7 feet 11½ inches in height. She was a native of Nova Scotia.

TOLLER (*James*) was 8 feet at the age of 24. He died in February, 1819.
Josephus speaks of a Jew 10 feet 2 inches.
Becanus asserts that he had seen a man nearly 10 feet high, and a woman fully 10 feet.
Gasper Bauhin speaks of a Swiss 8 feet in height.
Del Rio tells us he himself saw a Piedmontese in 1572 more than 9 feet in height.
C. F. S. Warren, M.A. (in *Notes and Queries*, August 14th, 1875), tells us that his father knew a lady 9 feet in height, and adds "her head touched the ceiling of a good-sized room."
Vanderbrook says he saw at Congo a black man 9 feet high.
In the museum of Trinity College, Dublin, is a human skeleton 8 feet 6 inches in height.
Thomas Hall, of Willingham, was 3 feet 9 inches at the age of 3.
A giant was exhibited at Rouen in the early part of the eighteenth century 17 feet 10 inches (!) in height.
Gorapus, the surgeon, tells us of a Swedish giantess, who, at the age of 9, was over 10 feet in height.
Turner, the naturalist, tells us he *saw* in Brazil a giant 12 feet in height.
M. Thevet published, in 1575, an account of a South American giant, the skeleton of which he measured. It was 11 feet 5 inches.

Giant's Causeway, in Ireland. A
basaltic mole, said to be the commencement of a road to be constructed by the giants across the channel, reaching from Ireland to Scotland.

Giants' Dance (*The*). Stonehenge,
which Geoffrey of Monmouth says was removed from Killaraus, a mountain in Ireland, by the magical skill of Merlin.

"If you [Aurelius] are desirous to honour the burying-place of these men [who routed Hengist] with an everlasting monument, send for the Giants' Dance, which is in Killaraus, a mountain in Ireland."—*Geoffrey of Monmouth: British History*, book viii. chap. 10.

Giant's Leap (*The*). Lam-Goemagog.
The legend is that Corineus (3 syl.), in

his encounter with Goemagog, or Gogmagog, slung him on his shoulders, carried him to the top of a neighbouring cliff, and heaved him into the sea. Ever since then the cliff has been called Lam-Goemagog. (*Thomas Borcman : Gigantick History;* 1741.)

Giants' War with Jove (*The*). The War of the Giants and the War of the Titans should be kept distinct. The latter was *after* Jove or Zeus was god of heaven and earth, the former was *before* that time. Kronos, a Titan, had been exalted by his brothers to the supremacy, but Zeus made war on Kronos with the view of dethroning him. After ten years' contest he succeeded, and hurled the Titans into hell. The other war was a revolt by the giants against Zeus, which was readily put down by the help of the other gods and the aid of Hercules.

Giaour (*jow'-er*). An unbeliever, one who disbelieves the Mahometan faith. A corruption of the Arabic *Kiafir*. It has now become so common that it scarcely implies insult, but has about the force of the word "Gentile," meaning "not a Jew." Byron has a poetical tale so called, but he has not given the giaour a name.

"The city won for Allah from the Giaour,
The Giaour from Othman's race again may wrest."
  Byron : Childe Harold, canto ii. stanza 77.

Gib (*g* soft). *The cut of his gib.* (*See* JIB.)
To nang one's gib. To be angry, to pout. The lower lip of a horse is called its gib, and so is the beak of a male salmon.

Gib Cat. A tom-cat. The male cat used to be called Gilbert. Nares says that Tibert or Tybalt is the French form of Gilbert, and hence Chaucer in his *Romance of the Rose*, renders "Thibert le Cas" by "Gibbe, our Cat" (v. 6204). Generally used for a castrated cat. (*See* TYBALT.)

"I am as melancholy as a gib cat or a lugged bear."—*Shakespeare : 1 Henry IV.*, i. 2.

Gib'berish (*g* hard). Geber, the Arabian, was by far the greatest alchemist of the eleventh century, and wrote several treatises on "the art of making gold" in the usual mystical jargon, because the ecclesiastics would have put to death any one who had openly written on the subject. Friar Bacon, in 1282, furnishes a specimen of this gibberish.

He is giving the prescription for making gunpowder, and says—

"Sed tamen salis-petræ
LURU MONE CAP URBE
Et sulphuris."

The second line is merely an anagram of *Carbonum pulvere* (pulverised charcoal).

‡ "Gibberish," compare *jabber*, and *gabble*.

Gib'bet (*g* soft). A foot-pad, who "piqued himself on being the best-behaved man on the road." (*George Farquhar : Beaux' Stratagem.*)
To gibbet the bread (Lincolnshire). When bread turns out ropy and is supposed to be bewitched, the good dame runs a stick through it and hangs it in the cupboard. It is gibbeted *in terrorem* to other batches.

Gib'elins or *Ghib'ellines* (*g* hard). (*See* GUELPHS.)

Gib'eonite (4 syl., *g* hard). A slave's slave, a workman's labourer, a farmer's understrapper, or Jack-of-all-work. The Gibeonites were made "hewers of wood and drawers of water" to the Israelites. (Josh. ix. 27.)

"And Giles must trudge, whoever gives command,
A Gibeonite, that serves them all by turn."
  Bloomfield : Farmer's Boy.

Giblets (*The Duke of*). A very fat man. In Yorkshire a fat man is still nicknamed "giblets."

Gibral'tar (*g* soft). A contraction of *Gibel al Tari* (Gib' al Tar), "mountain of Tari." This Tari ben Zeyad was an Arabian general who, under the orders of Mousa, landed at Calpë in 710, and utterly defeated Roderick, the Gothic King of Spain. Cape Tari'fa is named from the same general.
Gibraltar of Greece. A precipitous rock 700 feet above the sea, in Nauplia (Greece).
Gibraltar of the New World. Cape Diamond, in the province of Quebec.

Gif Gaff. Give and take ; good turn for good turn.

"I have pledged my word for your safety, and you must give me yours to be private in the matter—giff gaff, you know."—*Sir W. Scott: Redgauntlet*, chap. xii.

Gift-horse. *Don't look a gift-horse in the mouth.* When a present is made, do not inquire too minutely into its intrinsic value.
Latin : "Noli equi dentes inspicere donati." "Si quis det mannos ne quære in dentibus annos" (*Monkish*).
Italian : "A cavallao daio non guardar in bocca."

French : "A cheval donné il ne faut pas regarder aux dents."

Spanish : "A cavall dato no le mirem el diénte."

Gig (*g* hard). A whipping top, made like a ∇.

"Thou disputest like an infant. Go, whip thy gig."—*Shakespeare: Love's Labour's Lost,* v. 1.

Gig-lamps. Spectacles. Gig-lamps are the "spectacles" of a gig. (*See* VERDANT GREEN.)

Gig-manity. Respectability. A word invented by Carlyle. A witness in the trial of John Thurtell said, "I always thought him [Thurtell] a respectable man." And being asked by the judge what he meant, replied, "He [Thurtell] kept a gig."

"A princess of the blood, yet whose father had sold his inexpressibles . . . in a word, Gigmanity disgigged."—*Carlyle: The Diamond Necklace,* chap. v.

Giggle (*g* hard). *Have you found a giggle's nest ?* A question asked in Norfolk when anyone laughs immoderately and senselessly. The meaning is, "Have you found a nest of romping girls that you laugh so ?" *Giglet* is still in common use in the West of England for a giddy, romping, Tom-boy girl, and in Salop a flighty person is called a "giggle." (*See* GAPE'S-NEST.)

Gil Blas (*g* soft). The hero of Le Sage's novel of the same name. Timid, but audacious ; well-disposed, but easily led astray ; shrewd, but easily gulled by practising on his vanity ; good-natured, but without moral principle. The tale, according to one account, is based on Matteo Aleman's Spanish romance, called the *Life of Guzman ;* others maintain that the original was the comic romance entitled *Relaciones de la Vida del Escudero Marcos de Obregon.*

Gil'bertines (3 syl., *g* hard). A religious order founded in the twelfth century by St. Gilbert of Lincolnshire.

Gild the Pill (*To*). To do something to make a disagreeable task less offensive, as a pill is gilded to make it less offensive to the sight and taste. Children's powders are hidden in jam, and authors are "damned with faint praise."

Gilded Chamber (*The*). The House of Lords.

"Mr. Rowland Winn is now Lord St. Oswald, and after years spent in the Lower House he has retired to the calm of the gilded chamber."—*Newspaper paragraph,* June 26th, 1885.

Gilderoy' (3 syl., *g* hard). A famous robber, who robbed Cardinal Richelieu and Oliver Cromwell. There was a Scotch robber of the same name in the reign of Queen Mary. Both were noted for their handsome persons, and both were hanged.

Gilderoy's Kite. *Higher than Gilderoy's kite.* To be hung higher than Gilderoy's kite is to be punished more severely than the very worst criminal. The greater the crime, the higher the gallows, was at one time a practical legal axiom. Haman, it will be remembered, was hanged on a very high gallows. The gallows of Montrose was 30 feet high. The ballad says :—

" Of Gilderoy sae fraid they were
They bound him mickle strong,
Till Edenburrow they led him thair
And on a gallows hong ;
They hong him high abone the rest,
He was so trim a boy . . . ."

He was "hong abone the rest" of the criminals because his crimes were deemed to be more heinous. So high he hung he looked like "a kite" in the clouds.

Gildip'pe (in *Jerusalem Delivered*). Wife of Edward, an English baron. She accompanied her husband to the Holy War, and performed prodigies of valour (book ix.). Both she and her husband were slain by Solyman (book xx.).

Giles (1 syl., *g* soft). The "farmer's boy" in Bloomfield's poem so called.

Giles (*St.*). Patron saint of cripples. The tradition is that the king of France, hunting in the desert, accidentally wounded the hermit in the knee ; and the hermit, that he might the better mortify the flesh, refusing to be cured, remained a cripple for life.

The symbol of this saint is a hind, in allusion to the "heaven-directed hind" which went daily to his cave near the mouth of the Rhone to give him milk. He is sometimes represented as an old man with an arrow in his knee and a hind by his side.

St. Giles's parish. Generally situated in the outskirts of a city, and originally without the walls, cripples and beggars not being permitted to pass the gates.

Hopping or *Hobbling Giles.* A lame person ; so called from St. Giles, the tutelar saint of cripples. (*See* CRIPPLEGATE.)

Lame as St. Giles', Cripplegate. (*See above.*)

Giles Overreach (*Sir*). *A New Way to Pay Old Debts,* by Massinger. The "Academy figure" of this character was Sir Giles Mompesson, a notorious usurer, banished the kingdom for his misdeeds.

Giles of Antwerp (*g* soft). Giles Coignet, the painter (1530-1600).

Gill (*g* soft) or *Jill*. A generic name for a lass, a sweetheart. (A contraction of *Gillian = Juliana, Julia.*)

"Jack and Jill went up the hill . . . ."
Nursery Rhymes.
"Every Jack has got his Jill (*i.e.* Ilka laddie has his lassie)."—*Burns.*

Gill (*Harry*). A farmer struck with the curse of ever shivering with cold, because he would not allow old Goody Blake to keep a few stray sticks which she had picked up to warm herself by.

"Oh ! what's the matter ? what's the matter ?
What is't that ails young Harry Gill,
That evermore his teeth they chatter,
Chatter, chatter, chatter, still ? . . . .
No word to any man he utters,
A-bed or up, to young or old ;
But ever to himself he mutters—
'Poor Harry Gill is very cold.'"
Wordsworth: Goody Blake and Harry Gill.

Gills (*g* hard). *Wipe your gills* (your mouth). The gills of fishes, like the mouth of man, are the organs of respiration.

Gillie (*g* hard). A servant or attendant ; the man who leads a pony about when a child is riding. A *gillie-wet-foot* is a barefooted Highland lad.

"These gillie-wet-foots, as they were called, were destined to beat the bushes."—*Sir Walter Scott: Waverley,* chap. xiii.

Gillies' Hill. In the battle of Bannockburn (1314) King Robert Bruce ordered all the servants, drivers of carts, and camp followers to go behind a height. When the battle seemed to favour the Scotch, these servants, or gillies, desirous of sharing in the plunder, rushed from their concealment with such arms as they could lay hands on ; and the English, thinking them to be a new army, fled in panic. The height in honour was ever after called The Gillies' Hill. (*Sir Walter Scott: Tales of a Grandfather,* x.)

Gillyflower (*g* soft) is not the *July-flower,* but the French *giroflée,* from *girofle* (a clove), called by Chaucer "gilofre." The common stock, the wallflower, the rocket, the clove pink, and several other plants are so called. (Greek *karuophullon;* Latin, *caryophyllum,* the clove gillyflower.)

"The fairest flowers o' the season
Are our carnations and streaked gillyflowers."
Shakespeare: Winter's Tale, iv. 2.

Gilpin (*John*), of Cowper's famous ballad, is a caricature of Mr. Beyer, an eminent linendraper at the end of Paternoster Row, where it joins Cheapside. He died 1791, at the age of 98. It was Lady Austin who told the adventure to our domestic poet, to divert him from his melancholy. The marriage adventure of Commodore Trunnion in *Peregrine Pickle* is very similar to the wedding-day adventure of John Gilpin.

"John Gilpin was a citizen
Of credit and renown ;
A trainband captain eke was he
Of famous London town."
Cowper: John Gilpin.

⁂ Some insist that the "trainband captain" was one Jonathan Gilpin, who died at Bath in 1770, leaving his daughter a legacy of £20,000.

Gilt (*g* hard). *To take the gilt off the gingerbread.* To destroy the illusion. The reference is to gingerbread watches, men, and other gilded toys, sold at fairs. These eatables were common even in the reign of Henry IV., but were then made of honey instead of treacle.

Gilt-edge Investments. A phrase introduced in the last quarter of the 19th century (when so many investments proved worthless), for investments in which no risks are incurred, such as debentures, preference shares, first mortgages, and shares in first-rate companies.

Giltspur Street (West Smithfield). The route taken by the gilt-spurs, or knights, on their way to Smithfield, where tournaments were held.

Gimlet Eye (*g* hard). A squint-eye ; strictly speaking, "an eye that wanders obliquely," jocosely called a "piercer." (Welsh, *çwim,* a movement round ; *çwimlaw,* to twist or move in a serpentine direction ; Celtic, *guimble.*)

Gimmer (*g* soft), or *Jimmer,* a jointed hinge. In Somersetshire, *gimmace.* We have also *gemel.* A *gimmal* is a double ring ; hence gimmal-bit. (*Shakespeare: Henry V.,* iv. 2.)

Gin Sling. A drink made of gin and water, sweetened and flavoured. "Sling" = Collins, the inventor, contracted into *c'lins,* and perverted into *slings.*

Gin'evra (*g* soft). The young Italian bride who hid in a trunk with a spring-lock. The lid fell upon her, and she was not discovered till the body had become a skeleton. (*Rogers: Italy.*)

"Be the cause what it might, from his offer she shrunk,
And Ginevra-like, shut herself up in a trunk."
Lowell.

Gingerbread. The best used to be made at Grantham, and Grantham gingerbread was as much a locution as Everton toffy, or tuffy as we used to call it in the first half of the nineteenth century.

To get the gilt off the gingerbread. To appropriate all the fun or profit and leave the *caput mortuum* behind. In the first half of the nineteenth century gingerbread cakes were profusely decorated with gold-leaf or Dutch-leaf, which looked like gold.

Gingerbread (*g* soft). Brummagem wares, showy but worthless. The allusion is to the gilt gingerbread toys sold at fairs.

Gingerbread Husbands. Gingerbread cakes fashioned like men and gilt, commonly sold at fairs up to the middle of the nineteenth century.

Gingerly. Cautiously, with faltering steps. The Scotch phrase, "gang that gate," and the Anglo-Saxon *gangende* (going), applied to an army looking out for ambuscades, would furnish the adverb *gangendelic;* Swedish, *gingla,* to go gently.

"Gingerly, as if treading upon eggs, Cuddie began to ascend the well-known pass."— *Scott: Old Mortality,* chap. xxv.

Gingham. So called from Guingamp, a town in Brittany, where it was originally manufactured (Littré). A common playful equivalent of umbrella.

Ginnunga Gap. The abyss between Niflheim (the region of fog) and Muspelheim (the region of heat). It existed before either land or sea, heaven or earth. (*Scandinavian mythology.*)

Gi′ona (*g* soft). A leader of the Anabaptists, once a servant of Comte d'O′berthal, but discharged from his service for theft. In the rebellion headed by the Anabaptists, Giona took the Count prisoner, but John of Leyden set him free again. Giona, with the rest of the conspirators, betrayed their prophet king as soon as the Emperor arrived with his army. They entered the banquet room to arrest him, but perished in the flaming palace. (*Meyerbeer: Le Prophète, an opera.*)

Giotto. *Round as Giotto's O.* An Italian proverb applied to a dull, stupid fellow. The Pope, wishing to obtain some art decorations, sent a messenger to obtain specimens of the chief artists of Italy. The messenger came to Giotto and delivered his message, whereupon the artist simply drew a circle with red paint. The messenger, in amazement, asked Giotto if that were all. Giotto replied, "Send it, and we shall see if his Holiness understands the hint." A specimen of genius about equal to a brick as a specimen of an edifice.

Giovan′ni (*Don*). A Spanish libertine. (*See* JUAN.) His valet, Leporello, says his master had "in Italy 700 mistresses, in Germany 800, in Turkey and France 91, in Spain 1,003." When "the measure of his iniquity was full," the ghost of the commandant whom he had slain came with a legion of "foul fiends," and carried him off to a "dreadful gulf that opened to devour him." (*Mozart: Don Giovanni, Libretto by Lorenzo da Ponte.*)

Gipsy (*g* soft). Said to be a corruption of *Egyptian,* and so called because in 1418 a band of them appeared in Europe, commanded by a leader named Duke Michael of "Little Egypt." Other appellations are:

(2) *Bohe′mians.* So called by the French, because the first that ever arrived in their country came from Bohemia in 1427, and presented themselves before the gates of Paris. They were not allowed to enter the city, but were lodged at La Chapelle, St. Denis. The French nickname for gipsies is *cagoux* (unsociables).

(3) *Ciga′nos.* So called by the Portuguese, a corruption of Zinga′nè. (*See* TCHINGA′NI.)

(4) *Gita′nos.* So called by the Spaniards, a corruption of Zinga′nè. (*See* TCHINGA′NI.)

(5) *Heidens* (heathens). So called by the Dutch, because they are heathens.

(6) *Pharaoh-nepek* (Pharaoh's people). So called in Hungary, from the notion that they came from Egypt.

(7) *Sinte.* So called by themselves, because they assert that they came from Sind, *i.e.* Ind (Hindustan). (*See* TCHINGA′NI.)

(8) *Tatar.* So called by the Danes and Swedes, from the notion that they came from Tartary.

(9) *Tchinga′ni* or *Tshingani.* So called by the Turks, from a tribe still existing at the mouth of the Indus (*Tshin-calo,* black Indian).

(10) *Wala′chians.* So called by the Italians, from the notion that they came from Walachia.

(11) *Zigeü′ner* (wanderers). So called by the Germans.

(12) *Zinca′li* or *Zinga′ni.* Said to be so called by the Turks, because in 1517 they were led by Zinga′neus to revolt from Sultan Selim; but more likely a mere variety of Tchingani (*q.v.*).

✶ Their language, called "Romǎny,"

contains about 5,000 words, the chief of which are corrupt Sanskrit.

✢ There is a legend that these people are waifs and strays on the earth, because they refused to shelter the Virgin and her child in their flight to Egypt. (*Aventinus, Annāles Boiorum*, chap. viii.)

Gipsy (*The*). Anthony de Sola'rio, the painter and illuminator, *Il Zingaro* (1382-1455).

Giral'da (*g* soft). The giantess; a statue of victory on the top of an old Moorish tower in Seville.

Gird. *To gird with the sword.* To raise to a peerage. It was the Saxon method of investiture to an earldom, continued after the Conquest. Thus, Richard I. " girded with the sword " Hugh de Pudsey, the aged Bishop of Durham, making (as he said) " a young earl of an old prelate."

Gird up the Loins (*To*). To prepare for hard work or a journey. The Jews wore a girdle only when at work or on a journey. Even to the present day, Eastern people, who wear loose dresses, gird them about the loins.

" The loose tunic was an inconvenient walking dress ; therefore, when persons went from home, they tied a girdle round it (2 Kings iv. 2 ; ix. 1 ; Isaiah v. 27 ; Jeremiah i. 17 ; John xxi. 7 ; Acts xii. 8)."—*Jahn: Archeologia Biblica* (section 121).

Girder (*A*). A cooper. Hoops are girders. John Girder = John, the cooper, a character in *The Bride of Lammermoor*, by Sir Walter Scott.

Girdle (*g* hard). *A good name is better than a golden girdle.* A good name is better than money. It used to be customary to carry money in the girdle, and a girdle of gold meant a " purse of gold." The French proverb, " *Bonne renommée vaut mieux que ceinture dorée*," refers rather to the custom of wearing girdles of gold tissue, forbidden, in 1420, to women of bad character.

· *Children under the girdle.* Not yet born.

" All children under the girdle at the time of marriage are held to be legitimate."—*Notes and Queries.*

If he be angry, he knows how to turn his girdle (*Much Ado about Nothing*, v. 1). If he is angry, let him prepare himself to fight, if he likes. Before wrestlers, in ancient times, engaged in combat, they turned the buckle of their girdle behind them. Thus, Sir Ralph Winwood writes to Secretary Cecil :

" I said. ' What I spake was not to make him angry.' He replied, ' If I were angry, I might turn the buckle of my girdle behind me.' "—*Dec.* 17, 1602.

He has a large mouth but small girdle. Great expenses but small means. The girdle is the purse or purse-pocket. (*See above.*)

He has undone her girdle. Taken her for his wedded wife. The Roman bride wore a chaplet of flowers on her head, and a girdle of sheep's wool about her waist. A part of the marriage ceremony was for the bridegroom to loose this girdle. (*Vaughan : Golden Grove.*)

The Persian regulation-girdle. In Persia a new sort of " Procrustēs Bed " is adopted, according to Kemper. One of the officers of the king is styled the " chief holder of the girdle," and his business is to measure the ladies of the harem by a sort of regulation-girdle. If any lady has outgrown the standard, she is reduced, like a jockey, by spare diet ; but, if she falls short thereof, she is fatted up, like a Strasburg goose, to regulation size. (*See* PROCRUSTES.)

To put a girdle round the earth. To travel or go round it. Puck says, " I'll put a girdle round about the earth in forty minutes." (*Midsummer Night's Dream*, ii. 2.)

Girdle (*Florimel's*). The prize of a grand tournament in which Sir Satyrane and several others took part. It was dropped by Florimel, picked up by Sir Satyrane, and employed by him to bind the monster sent in her pursuit ; but it came again into the hands of the knight, who kept it in a golden casket. It was a " gorgeous girdle made by Vulcan for Venus, embossed with pearls and precious stones ; " but its chief virtue was

" It gave the virtue of chaste love,
And wifehood true to all that it did bear ;
But whosoever contrary doth prove
Might not the same about her middle wear,
But it would loose, or else asunder tear."
Spenser : Faërie Queene, book iii. canto vii. 31.

✢ King Arthur's Drinking Horn, and the Court Mantel in *Orlando Furioso*, possessed similar virtues.

Girdle (*St. Colman's*) would meet only round the chaste.

" In Ireland it yet remains to be proved whether St. Colman's girdle has not lost its virtue " [the reference is to Charles S. Parnell].—*Nineteenth Century*, Feb., 1891, p. 206.

Girdle of Venus. (*See* CESTUS.)

Girl. This word has given rise to a host of guesses :—

Bailey suggests *garrula*, a chatterbox.
Minshew ventures the Italian *girella*, a weathercock.
Skinner goes in for the Anglo-Saxon *ceorl*, a churl.
Why not *girdle*, as young women before marriage wore a girdle [*gir'le*] ; and part of a Roman marriage ceremony was for the bridegroom to loose the zone.

As for guessing, the word *gull* may put in a claim (1 *Henry* iv. 1); so may the Greek *kourē*, a girl, with a diminutive suffix *koure-la*, whence *gourla, gourl, gurl*, girl.

(The Latin *gerula* means a maid that attends on a child. Chaucer spells the word *gurl*.)
Probably the word is a variation of *darling*, Anglo-Saxon, *deorling*.

Giron'dists (*g* soft). French, *Giron-dins*, moderate republicans in the first French Revolution. So called from the department of Gironde, which chose for the Legislative Assembly five men who greatly distinguished themselves for their oratory, and formed a political party. They were subsequently joined by Brissot, Condorcet, and the adherents of Roland. The party is called *The Gironde*. (1791-93.)

" The new assembly, called the Legislative Assembly, met October 1, 1791. Its more moderate members formed the party called the Girondists."
—*C. M. Yonge: France*, chap. ix. p. 168.

Gir'ouet'te (3 syl., *g* soft). A turncoat, a weathercock (French). The *Dictionnaire des Girouettes* contains the names of the most noted turncoats, with their political veerings.

Gis (*g* soft) *i.e.* Jesus. A corruption of Jesus or J. H. S. Ophelia says " By Gis and by St. Charity." (*Hamlet*, iv. 5.)

Gita'nos. (*See* GIPSY.)

Give and Take (*policy*). One of mutual forbearance and accommodation.

" [His] wife jogged along with him very comfortably with a give and take policy for many years."—*Hugh Conway*.

Give it Him (*To*). To scold or thrash a person. As "I gave it him right and left." "I'll give it you when I catch you." An elliptical phrase, *dare pœnam*. "Give it him well."

Give the Boys a Holiday. Anaxag'-oras, on his death-bed, being asked what honour should be conferred upon him, replied, " Give the boys a holiday."

Give the Devil his Due. Though bad, I allow, yet not so bad as you make him out. Do not lay more to the charge of a person than he deserves. The French say, "*Il ne faut pas faire le diable plus noir qu'il n'est.*" The Italians have the same proverb, "*Non bisognà fare il diablo piu nero che non è.*"

The devil is not so black as he is painted. Every black has its white, as well as every sweet its sour.

Gizzard. *Don't fret your gizzard.* Don't be so anxious ; don't worry yourself. The Latin *stomachus* means temper, etc., as well as stomach or "gizzard." (French, *gésier*.)

That stuck in his gizzard. Annoyed him, was more than he could digest.

Gjallar. Heimdall's horn, which he blows to give the gods notice when any one is approaching the bridge Bifröst (*q.v.*). (*Scandinavian mythology.*)

Glacis. The sloping mass on the outer edge of the *covered way* in fortification. Immediately without the "ditches" of the place fortified, there is a road of communication all round the fortress (about thirty feet wide), having on its exterior edge a covered mass of earth eight feet high, sloping off gently towards the open country. The road is technically called the *covered way*, and the sloping mass the *glacis*.

Gladsheim [*Home of joy*]. The largest and most magnificent mansion of the Scandinavian Æsir. It contains twelve seats besides the throne of Alfader. The great hall of Gladsheim was called "Valhalla."

Gladstone Bag (*A*). A black leather bag of various sizes, all convenient to be hand-carried. These bags have two handles, and are made so as not to touch the ground, like the older carpet bags. Called Gladstone in compliment to W. E. Gladstone, many years leader of the Liberal party.

Glamorgan. Geoffrey of Monmouth says that Cundah' and Morgan, the sons of Gonorill and Regan, usurped the crown at the death of Cordeilla. The former resolved to reign alone, chased Morgan into Wales, and slew him at the foot of a hill, hence called Gla-Morgan or Glyn-Morgan, valley of Morgan. (See *Spenser: Faërie Queene*, ii. 10.)

Glasgow Arms. An oak tree, a bell hanging on one of the branches, a bird at the top of the tree, and a salmon with a ring in its mouth at the base.

St. Kentigern, in the seventh century, took up his abode on the banks of a little stream which falls into the Clyde, the site of the present city of Glasgow. Upon an oak in the clearing he hung a bell to summon the savages to worship, hence the oak and the bell. Now for the other two emblems : A queen having formed an illicit attachment to a soldier, gave him a precious ring which the king had given her. The king, aware of the fact, stole upon the soldier in sleep abstracted the ring, threw it into the Clyde, and then asked the queen for it. The queen, in alarm, applied to St. Kentigern, who knew the whole affair ;

and the saint went to the Clyde, caught a salmon with the ring in its mouth, handed it to the queen, and was thus the means of restoring peace to the royal couple, and of reforming the repentant queen.

✵ The queen's name was Langoureth, the king's name Rederech, and the Clyde was then called the Clud.

> " The tree that never grew,
> The bird that never flew,
> The fish that never swam,
> The bell that never rang."

✵ A similar legend is told of Dame Rebecca Berry, wife of Thomas Elton, of Stratford Bow, and relict of Sir John Berry (1696). Rebecca Berry is the heroine of the ballad called *The Cruel Knight*, and the story says that a knight passing by a cottage, heard the cries of a woman in labour, and knew by his occult science that the child was doomed to be his wife. He tried hard to elude his fate, and when the child was grown up, took her one day to the seaside, intending to drown her, but relented. At the same time he threw a ring into the sea, and commanded her never again to enter his presence till she brought him that ring. Rebecca, dressing a cod for dinner, found the ring in the fish, presented it to Sir John, and became his wife. The Berry arms show a fish, and on the dexter chief point a ring or annulet.

Glasgow Magistrate (*A*). A salt herring. When George IV. visited Glasgow some wag placed a salt herring on the iron guard of the carriage of a well-known magistrate who formed one of the deputation to receive him. I remember a similar joke played on a magistrate, because he said, during a time of great scarcity, he wondered why the poor did not eat salt herrings, which he himself found very appetising.

Glass is from the Celtic *glas* (bluish-green), the colour produced by the woad employed by the ancient Britons in dyeing their bodies. Pliny calls it *glastrum*, and Cæsar *vitrum*.

Glass Breaker (*A*). A wine-bibber. To crack a bottle is to drink up its contents and throw away the empty bottle. A glass breaker is one who drinks what is in the glass, and flings the glass under the table. In the early part of the nineteenth century it was by no means unusual with topers to break off the stand of their wineglass, so that they might not be able to set it down, but were

compelled to drink it clean off, without heel-taps.

> " Troth, ye're nae glass-breaker; and neither am I, unless it be a screed wi' the neighbours, or when I'm on a ramble."—*Sir W. Scott: Guy Mannering*, chap. 45.

> "We never were glass-breakers in this house, Mr. Lovel."—*Sir W. Scott: The Antiquary*, chap. ix.

Glass-eye. A blind eye, not an eye made of glass, but the Danish *glas-öie* (wall-eye).

Glass Houses. *Those who live in glass houses should not throw stones.* When, on the union of the two crowns, London was inundated with Scotchmen, Buckingham was a chief instigator of the movement against them, and parties used nightly to go about breaking their windows. In retaliation, a party of Scotchmen smashed the windows of the Duke's mansion, which stood in St. Martin's Fields, and had so many windows that it went by the name of the "Glass-house." The court favourite appealed to the king, and the British Solomon replied, "Steenie, Steenie, those wha live in glass housen should be careful' how they fling stanes."

✵ This was not an original remark of the English Solomon, but only the application of an existing proverb: "El que tiene tejados de vidro, no tire piedras al de su vezino." (*Nunez de Guzman: Proverbios.*) (*See also* Chaucer's *Troylus*, ii.)

> "Qui a sa maison de verre,
> Sur le voisin ne jette pierre."
> *Proverbes en Rimes* (1664).

Glass Slipper (of Cinderella). A curious blunder of the translator, who has mistaken *vair* (sable) for *verre* (glass). Sable was worn only by kings and princes, so the fairy gave royal slippers to her favourite. Hamlet says he shall discard his mourning and resume "his suit of sables" (iii. 2).

Glasse (*Mrs. Hannah*), a name immortalised by the reputed saying in a cookery book, "First catch your hare," then cook it according to the directions given. This, like many other smart sayings, evidently grew. The word in the cookery-book is "cast" (*i.e.* flay). "Take your hare, and when it is cast" (or *cased*), do so and so. (*See* CASE, CATCH YOUR HARE.)

> "We'll make you some sport with the fox ere we case him."—*Shakespeare: All's Well, etc.*, iii. 6.

> "Some of them knew me,
> Else had they cased me like a cony."
> *Beaumont and Fletcher: Love's Pilgrimage*, ii. 3.

✵ First *scotch* your hare (though not in Mrs. Glasse) is the East Anglian word *scatch* (flay), and might suggest the play of words. Mrs. Glasse is the pseudonym which Dr. John Hill appended to his *Cook's Oracle*.

Glassite (*A*). A Sandemanian; a follower of John Glass (eighteenth century). Members of this Scotch sect are admitted by a "holy kiss," and abstain from all animal food which has not been well drained of blood. John Glass condemned all national establishments of religion, and maintained the Congregational system. Robert Sandeman was one of his disciples.

Glastonbury, in Arthurian legend, was where king Arthur was buried. Selden, in his *Illustrations of Drayton*, says the tomb was "betwixt two pillars," and he adds, "Henry II. gave command to Henry de Blois, the abbot, to make great search for the body, which was found in a wooden coffin some sixteen foote deepe; and afterwards was found a stone on whose lower side was fixt a leaden cross with the name inscribed." The authority of Selden no doubt is very great, but it is too great a tax on our credulity to credit this statement.

Glaswe′gian. Belonging to Glasgow.

Glauber Salts. So called from Johann Rudolph Glauber, a German alchemist, who discovered it in 1658 in his researches after the philosopher's stone. It is the sulphate of soda.

Glaucus (of Bœotia). A fisherman who instructed Apollo in soothsaying. He jumped into the sea, and became a marine god. Milton alludes to him in his *Comus* (line 895):

"[By] old soothsaying Glaucus' spell."

Glaucus (*Another*). In Latin, *Glaucus alter*. One who ruins himself by horses. The tale is that Glaucus, son of Sisyphus, would not allow his horses to breed, and the goddess of Love so infuriated them that they killed him.

Glaucus' Swop (*A*). A one-sided bargain. Alluding to the exchange of armour between Glaucos and Diome′des. As the armour of the Lycian was of gold, and that of the Greek of brass, it was like bartering precious stones for French paste. Moses, in Goldsmith's *Vicar of Wakefield*, made "a Glaucus' swop" with the spectacle-seller.

Glaymore or *Claymore* (2 syl.). The Scottish great sword. It used to be a large two-handed sword, but was subsequently applied to the broadsword with the basket-hilt. (Gaelic, *claidhamh*, a sword; *more*, great.)

Glazier. *Is your father a glazier?* Does he make windows, for you stand in my light and expect me to see through you?

Gleek. A game at cards, sometimes called cleek. Thus, in *Epsom Wells*, Dorothy says to Mrs. Bisket, "*I'll make one at cleek, that's better than any two-handed game.*" Ben Jonson, in the *Alchemist*, speaks of gleek and prim′ero as "the best games for the gallantest company."

Gleek is played by three persons. Every deuce and trois is thrown out of the pack. Twelve cards are then dealt to each player, and eight are left for stock, which is offered in rotation to the players for purchase. The trumps are called Tiddy, Tumbler, Tib, Tom, and Towser. Gleek is the German *gleich* (like), intimating the point on which the game turns, gleek being three cards all alike, as three aces, three kings, etc.

Gleichen (*The Count de*). A German knight married to a lady of his own country. He joined a crusade, and, being wounded, was attended so diligently by a Saracen princess that he married her also.

Gleipnir. The chain made by the fairies, by which the wolf Fenrir or Fenris was securely chained. It was extremely light, and made of such things as "the roots of stones, the noise made by the footfalls of a cat, the beards of women, the spittle of birds, and such like articles."

Glenco′e (2 syl.). *The massacre of Glencoe.* The Edinburgh authorities exhorted the Jacobites to submit to William and Mary, and offered pardon to all who submitted on or before the 31st of December, 1691. Mac-Ian, chief of the Macdonalds of Glencoe, was unable to do so before the 6th of January, and his excuse was sent to the Council at Edinburgh. The Master of Stair (Sir John Dalrymple) resolved to make an example of Mac-Ian, and obtained the king's permission "to extirpate the set of thieves." Accordingly, on the 1st of February, 120 soldiers, led by a Captain Campbell, marched to Glencoe, told the clan they were come as friends, and lived peaceably among them for twelve days; but on the morning of the 13th, the glenmen, to the number of thirty-eight, were scandalously murdered, their huts set on fire, and their flocks and herds driven off as plunder. Campbell has written a poem, and Talfourd a play on the subject.

Glendoveer′, in Hindu mythology, is a kind of sylph, the most lovely of the good spirits. (*See* Southey's *Curse of Kehama.*)

" I am a blessèd Glendoveer,
'Tis mine to speak and yours to hear."
Rejected Addresses (Imitations of Southey).

Glendower (*Owen*). A Welsh chief, one of the most active and formidable enemies of Henry IV. He was descended from Llewellyn, the last of the Welsh princes. Sir Edmund Mortimer married one of his daughters, and the husband of Mortimer's sister was Earl Percy, generally called "Hotspur," who took Douglas prisoner at Homildon Hill. Glendower, Hotspur, Douglas, and others conspired to dethrone Henry, but the coalition was ruined in the fatal battle of Shrewsbury. Shakespeare makes the Welsh nobleman a wizard of great diversity of talent, but especially conceited of the prodigies that "announced" his birth. (*Shakespeare :* 1 *Henry IV.*)

Glim. (*See* DOUSE THE GLIM.)

Globe of Glass (*Reynard's*). *To consult Reynard's globe of glass.* To seek into futurity by magical or other devices. This globe of glass would reveal what was being done, no matter how far off, and would afford information on any subject that the person consulting it wished to know. The globe was set in a wooden frame which no worm would attack. Reynard said he had sent this invaluable treasure to her majesty the queen as a present; but it never came to hand, inasmuch as it had no existence except in the imagination of the fox. (*H. von Alkmar : Reynard the Fox.*)

Your gift was like the globe of glass of Master Reynard. Vox et præterea nihil. A great promise, but no performance. (*See above.*)

Worthy to be set in the frame of Reynard's globe of glass. Worthy of being imperishable ; worthy of being preserved for ever.

Gloria. A cup of coffee with brandy in it instead of milk. Sweetened to taste.

Gloria in Excelsis. The latter portion of this doxology is ascribed to Telesphorus, A.D. 139. (*See* GLORY.)

Gloria′na. (Queen Elizabeth considered as a sovereign.) Spenser says in his *Faërie Queene* that she kept an annual feast for twelve days, during which time adventurers appeared before her to undertake whatever task she chose to impose upon them. On one occasion twelve knights presented themselves before her, and their exploits form the scheme of Spenser's allegory. The poet intended to give a separate book to each knight, but only six and a half books remain.

Glorious John. John Dryden, the poet (1631-1701).

Glorious First of June. June 1st, 1794, when Lord Howe, who commanded the Channel fleet, gained a decisive victory over the French.

Glorious Uncertainty of the Law (*The*), 1756. The toast of Mr. Wilbraham at a dinner given to the judges and counsel in Serjeant's Hall. This dinner was given soon after Lord Mansfield had overruled several ancient legal decisions and had introduced many innovations in the practice.

Glory. Meaning speech or the tongue, so called by the Psalmist because speech is man's speciality. Other animals see, hear, smell, and feel quite as well and often better than man, but rational speech is man's glory, or that which distinguishes the race from other animals.

" I will sing and give praise even with my glory."—Psalm cviii. 1.

" That my glory may sing praise to Thee, and not be silent."—Psalm xxx. 12.

" Awake up my glory, awake psaltery and harp."—Psalm lvii. 8.

Glory Demon (*The*). War.

" Fresh troops had each year to be sent off to glut the maw of the 'Glory Demon.' "—*C. Thomson : Autobiography, 32.*

Glory Hand. In folk lore, a dead man's hand, supposed to possess certain magical properties.

" De hand of glory is hand cut off from a dead man as have been hanged for murther, and dried very nice in de shmoke of juniper wood."—*Sir W. Scott : The Antiquary (Dousterswivel).*

Glory be to the Father, etc. The first verse of this doxology is said to be by St. Basil. During the Arian controversy it ran thus : " Glory be *to* the Father, *by* the Son, and *in* the Holy Ghost." (*See* GLORIA.)

Glossin (*Lawyer*) purchases Ellangowan estate, and is found by Counsellor Pleydell to be implicated in carrying off Henry Bertrand, the heir of the estate. Both Glossin and Dirk Hatteraick, his accomplice, are sent to prison, and in the night the lawyer contrives to enter the smuggler's cell, when a quarrel ensues, in which Hatteraick strangles him, and then hangs himself." (*Sir W Scott: Guy Mannering.*)

Glouces'ter (2 syl.). The ancient Britons called the town *Caer Glou* (bright city). The Romans Latinised Glou or Glove in *Glev-um*, and added *colonia* (the Roman colony of Glev-um). The Saxons restored the old British word *Glou*, and added *ceaster*, to signify it had been a Roman camp. Hence the word means "Glou, the camp city." Geoffrey of Monmouth says, when Arvir'agus married Genuissa, daughter of Claudius Cæsar, he induced the emperor to build a city on the spot where the nuptials were solemnised; this city was called *Caer-Claw'*, a contraction of Caer-Claud, corrupted into Caer-glou, converted by the Romans into Glou-caster, and by the Saxons into Glou-ceaster or Glou-cester. "Some," continues the same "philologist," "derive the name from the Duke Gloius, a son of Claudius, born in Britain on the very spot."

Glove. In the days of chivalry it was customary for knights to wear a lady's glove in their helmets, and to defend it with their life.

"One ware on his headpiece his ladies sleve, and another bare on hys helme the glove of his dearlynge."—*Hall: Chronicle, Henry IV.*

Glove. A bribe. (*See* GLOVE MONEY.)

Hand and glove. Sworn friends; on most intimate terms; close companions, like glove and hand.

"And prate and preach about what others prove, As if the world and they were hand and glove." *Cowper.*

He bit his glove. He resolved on mortal revenge. On the "Border," to bite the glove was considered a pledge of deadly vengeance.

"Stern Rutherford right little said, But bit his glove and shook his head." *Sir Walter Scott: Lay of the Last Minstrel.*

Here I throw down my glove. I challenge you. In allusion to an ancient custom of a challenger throwing his glove or gauntlet at the feet of the person challenged, and bidding him to pick it up. If he did so the two fought, and the vanquisher was considered to be adjudged by God to be in the right. *To take up the glove* means, therefore, to accept the challenge.

"I will throw my glove to Death itself, that there's no maculation in thy heart."—*Shakespeare: Troilus and Cressida, iv. 4.*

To take up the glove. To accept the challenge made by casting a glove or gauntlet on the ground.

Right as my glove. The phrase, says Sir Walter Scott, comes from the custom of pledging a glove as the signal of irrefragable faith. (*The Antiquary.*)

Glove Money. A bribe, a perquisite; so called from the ancient custom of presenting a pair of gloves to a person who undertook a cause for you. Mrs. Croaker presented Sir Thomas More, the Lord Chancellor, with a pair of gloves lined with forty pounds in "angels," as a "token." Sir Thomas kept the gloves, but returned the lining. (*See above.*)

Gloves are not worn in the presence of royalty, because we are to stand unarmed, with the helmet off the head and gauntlets off the hands, to show we have no hostile intention. (*See* SALUTATIONS.)

Gloves used to be worn by the clergy to indicate that their hands are clean and not open to bribes. They are no longer officially worn by the parochial clergy.

Gloves given to a judge in a maiden assize. In an assize without a criminal, the sheriff presents the judge with a pair of white gloves. Chambers says, anciently judges were not allowed to wear gloves on the bench (*Cyclopædia*). To give a judge a pair of gloves, therefore, symbolised that he need not come to the bench, but might wear gloves.

You owe me a pair of gloves. A small present. The gift of a pair of gloves was at one time a perquisite of those who performed small services, such as pleading your cause, arbitrating your quarrel, or showing you some favour which could not be charged for. As the services became more important, the glove was lined with money, or made to contain some coin called glove money (*q.v.*). Relics of this ancient custom were common till the last quarter of a century in the presentation of gloves to those who attended weddings and funerals. There also existed at one time the claim of a pair of gloves by a lady who chose to salute a gentleman caught napping in her company. In *The Fair Maid of Perth*, by Sir Walter Scott, Catherine steals from her chamber on St. Valentine's morn, and, catching Henry Smith asleep, gives him a kiss. The glover says to him :

"Come into the booth with me, my son, and I will furnish thee with a fitting theme. Thou knowest the maiden who ventures to kiss a sleeping man wins of him a pair of gloves."—Chap. v.

In the next chapter Henry presents the gloves, and Catherine accepts them.

A round with gloves. A friendly contest ; a fight with gloves.

"Will you point out how this is going to be a genteel round with gloves?"—*Watson: The Web of the Spider*, chap. ix.

Glubdub'drib. The land of sorcerers and magicians visited by Gulliver in his *Travels.* (*Swift.*)

Gluckist and Picci'nists. A foolish rivalry excited in Paris (1774-1780) between the admirers of Glück and those of Picci'ni—the former a German musical composer, and the latter an Italian. Marie Antoinette was a Glückist, and consequently Young France favoured the rival claimant. In the streets, coffeehouses, private houses, and even schools, the merits of Glück and Piccinini were canvassed ; and all Paris was ranged on one side or the other. This was, in fact, a contention between the relative merits of the German and Italian school of music. (*See* BACBUC.)

Glum had a sword and cloak given him by his grandfather, which brought good luck to their possessors. After this present everything prospered with him. He gave the spear to Asgrim and cloak to Gizur the White, after which everything went wrong with him. Old and blind, he retained his cunning long after he had lost his luck. (*The Nials Saga.*)

To look glum. To look dull or moody. (Scotch, *gloum*, a frown ; Dutch, *loom*, heavy, dull ; Anglo-Saxon, *glōm*, our *gloom, gloaming*, etc.)

Glumdal'clitch. A girl, nine years old, and only forty feet high, who had charge of · Gulliver in Brobdingnag. (*Swift : Gulliver's Travels.*)

"Soon as Glumdalclitch missed her pleasing care,
She wept, she blubbered, and she tore her hair."
Pope.

Glutton (*The*). Vitelius, the Roman emperor (15-69), reigned from January 4 to December 22, A.D. 69.

Gluttony. (*See* APICIUS, etc.)

Gna'tho. A vain, boastful parasite in the *Eunuch* of Terence (Greek, *gnathon*, jaw, meaning "tongue-doughty").

Gnomes (1 syl.), according to the Rosicru'cian system, are the elemental spirits of earth, and the guardians of mines and quarries. (Greek, *gnoma*, knowledge, meaning the knowing ones, the wise ones.) (*See* FAIRY, SALAMANDERS.)

"The four elements are inhabited by spirits called sylphs, gnomes, nymphs, and salamanders. The gnomes, or demons of the earth, delight in mischief ; but the sylphs, whose habitation is in air, are the best conditioned creatures imaginable."—*Pope : Pref. Letter to the Rape of the Lock.*

Gnostics. The *knowers*, opposed to *believers*, various sects in the first ages of Christianity, who tried to accommodate Scripture to the speculations of Pythag'oras, Plato, and other ancient philosophers. They taught that knowledge, rather than mere faith, is the true key of salvation. In the Gnostic creed Christ is esteemed merely as an eon, or divine attribute personified, like Mind, Truth, Logos, Church, etc., the whole of which eons made up this divine plerōma or fulness. Paul, in several of his epistles, speaks of this "Fulness (pleroma) of God." (Greek, *Gnos'ticos*.) (*See* AGNOSTICS.)

Go. (Anglo-Saxon, *gān, ic gā*, I go.)
Here's a go or *Here's a pretty go.* Here's a mess or awkward state of affairs.
It is no go. It is not workable. "*Ça ira*," in the French Revolution (it will go), is a similar phrase.
(*See* GREAT GO, and LITTLE GO.)

Go (*The*). *All the go.* Quite the fashion ; very popular ; *la vogue.*

Go along with You. In French, *Tirez de long*, said to dogs, meaning scamper off, run away. *Au long et au large, i.e.* entirely, go off the whole length and breadth of the way from me to infinite space.
∵ "To go along with some one," with the lower classes, means to take a walk with someone of the opposite sex, with a view of matrimony if both parties think fit.

Go-between (*A*). An interposer ; one who interposes between two parties.

Go-by. *To give one the go-by.* To pass without notice, to leave in the lurch.

Go it Blind. Don't stop to deliberate. In the game called "Poker," if a player chooses to "go it blind," he doubles the *ante* before looking at his cards. If the other players refuse to see his *blind*, he wins the *ante*.

Go it, Warwick! A street cry during the Peninsular War, meaning, "Go it, ye cripples!" The Warwickshire militia, stationed at Hull, were more than ordinarily licentious and disorderly.

Go it, you Cripples! Fight on, you simpletons ; scold away, you silly or quarrelsome ones. A cripple is slang for a dullard or awkward person.

Go of Gin. A quartern. In the Queen's Head, Covent Garden, spirits used to be served in quarterns, neat—water *ad libitum.* (Compare STIRRUP CUP.)

Go on all Fours. Perfect in all points. We say of a pun or riddle, "It does not go on all fours," it will not hold good in every way. Lord Macaulay says, "It is not easy to make a simile go on all fours." Sir Edward Coke says, "*Nullum sim'ile quat'uor ped'ibus currit.*" The metaphor is taken from a horse, which is lame if only one of its legs is injured. All four must be sound in order that it may go.

Go Out (*To*). To rise in rebellion; the Irish say, "To be up." To go out with the forces of Charles Edward. To be out with Roger More and Sir Phelim O'Neil, in 1641.

"I thocht my best chance for payment was e'en to gae out myself."—*Sir W. Scott: Waverley,* 39.

Go through Fire and Water to serve you. Do anything even at personal cost and inconvenience. The reference is to the ancient ordeals by fire and water. Those condemned to these ordeals might employ a substitute.

Go to! A curtailed oath. "Go to the devil!" or some such phrase.

"*Cassius:* I [am] abler than yourself
To make conditions.
Brutus: Go to! You are not, Cassius."
Shakespeare: Julius Cæsar, iv. 3.

Go TO BANFF, and bottle skate.
Go TO BATH, and get your head shaved.
Go TO BUNGAY, and get your breeches mended.
Go TO COVENTRY. Make yourself scarce.
Go TO HEXHAM. A kind of Alsatia or sanctuary in the reign of Henry VIII.
Go TO JERICHO. Out of the way. (*See* JERICHO.)
And many other similar phrases.

Go to the Wall (*To*). To be pushed on one side, laid on the shelf, passed by. Business men, and those in a hurry, leave the wall-side of a pavement to women, children, and loungers.

Go without Saying (*To*). *Cela va sans dire.* To be a self-evident fact; well understood or indisputable.

Goat. Usually placed under seats in church stalls, etc., as a mark of dishonour and abhorrence, especially to ecclesiastics who are bound by the law of continence.

The seven little goats. So the Pleiades are vulgarly called in Spain.

Goat and Compasses. A public-house sign in the Commonwealth; a corruption of "God en-compasses [us]."

⁕ Some say it is the carpenters' arms —three goats and a chevron. The chevron being mistaken for a pair of compasses.

Goats. (Anglo-Saxon, *gāt.*)

The three goats. A public-house sign at Lincoln, is a corruption of the *Three Gowts,* that is, drains or sluices, which at one time conducted the waters of a large lake into the river Witham. The name of the inn is now the *Black Goats.*

Gobbler (*A*). A turkey-cock is so called from its cry.

Gob'bo (*Launcelot*). A clown in Shakespeare's *Merchant of Venice.*

Gob'elin Tapestry. So called from Giles Gob'elin, a French dyer in the reign of François I., who discovered the Gobelin scarlet. His house in the suburbs of St. Marcel, in Paris, is still called the Gobelins.

Goblin. A familiar demon. According to popular belief goblins dwelt in private houses and chinks of trees. As a specimen of forced etymology, it may be mentioned that Elf and Goblin have been derived from Guelph and Ghibelline. (French, *gobelin,* a lubber-fiend; Armoric *gobylin;* German *kobold,* the demon of mines; Greek, *kobalos;* Russian, *colfy;* Welsh *coblyn,* a "knocker;" whence the woodpecker is called in Welsh "*coblyn y coed.*") (*See* FAIRY.)

Goblin Cave. In Celtic called "*Coir nan Uriskin*" (*cove of the satyrs*), in Benvenue, Scotland.

"After landing on the skirts of Benvenue, we reach the *cave* or cove *of the goblins* by a steep and narrow defile of one hundred yards in length. It is a deep circular amphitheatre of at least six hundred yards' extent in its upper diameter, gradually narrowing towards the base, hemmed in all round by steep and towering rocks, and rendered impenetrable to the rays of the sun by a close covert of luxuriant trees. On the south and west it is bounded by the precipitous shoulder of Benvenue, to the height of at least 500 feet; towards the east the rock appears at some former period to have tumbled down, strewing the white course of its fall with immense fragments, which now serve only to give shelter to foxes, wild cats, and badgers."—*Dr. Graham.*

Goblins. In Cardiganshire the miners attribute those strange noises heard in mines to spirits called "Knockers" (goblins). (*See above.*)

God. Gothic, *goth* (god); German, *gott.* (*See* ALLA, ADONIST, ELOHISTIC, etc.)

It was Hiero, Tyrant of Syracuse, who asked Simonidēs the poet, "What is God?" Simonidēs asked to have a day to consider the question. Being asked the same question the next day, he desired two more days for reflection. Every time he appeared before Hiero he doubled the length of time for the consideration of his answer. Hiero, greatly astonished, asked the philosopher why he did so, and Simonidēs made answer, "The longer I think on the subject, the farther I seem from making it out."

It was Voltaire who said, "*Si Dieu n'existait pas, il faudrait l'inventer*."

God and the saints. "*Il vaut mieux s'adresser à Dieu qu'à ses saints.*" "*Il vaut mieux se tenir au tronc qu'aux branches.*" Better go to the master than to his steward or foreman.

God bless the Duke of Argyle. It is said that the Duke of Argyle erected a row of posts to mark his property, and these posts were used by the cattle to rub against. (*Hotten : Slang Dictionary.*)

God helps those who help themselves. In French, "*Aide-toi, le ciel t'aidera.*" "*A toile ourdie Dieu donne le fil*" (You make the warp and God will make the woof).

God made the country, and man made the town. Cowper in *The Task* (The Sofa). Varro says in his *De Re Rustica*, "*Divina Natūra agros dedit; Ars humana ædificavit urbes.*"

"*God save the king.*" It is said by some that both the words and music of this anthem were composed by Dr. John Bull (1563-1622), organist at Antwerp cathedral, where the original MS. is still preserved. Others attribute them to Henry Carey, author of *Sally in our Alley.* The words, "Send him victorious," etc., look like a Jacobite song, and Sir John Sinclair tells us he saw that verse cut in an old glass tankard, the property of P. Murray Threipland, of Fingask Castle, whose predecessors were staunch Jacobites.

No doubt the words of the anthem have often been altered. The air and words were probably first suggested to John Bull by the *Domine Salvum* of the Catholic Church. In 1605 the lines, "Frustrate their knavish tricks," etc., were added in reference to Gunpowder Plot. In 1715 some Jacobite added the words, "Send him [the Pretender] victorious," etc. And in 1740 Henry Carey reset both words and music for the Mercers' Company on the birthday of George II.

God sides with the strongest. Julius Civiles. Napoleon I. said, "*Le bon Dieu est toujours du côté des gros bataillons.*" God helps those that help themselves. The fable of *Hercules and the Carter.*

God tempers the wind to the shorn lamb. Sterne (Maria, in the *Sentimental Journey*). In French, "*A brebis tondue Dieu lui mesure le vent ;*" "*Dieu mesure le froid à la brebis tondue.*" "*Dieu donne le froid selon la robbe.*" Sheep are shorn when the cold north-east winds have given way to milder weather.

Full of the god—inspired, mænadic. (Latin, *Dei plenus.*)

Gods.

BRITONS. *The gods of the ancient Britons.* Taramis (the father of the gods and master of thunder), Teutatēs (patron of commerce and inventor of letters), Esus (god of war), Belinus (= Apollo), Ardena (goddess of forests), Belisarna (the queen of heaven and the moon).

CARTHAGINIAN GODS. Urania and Moloch. The former was implored when rain was required.

"Ista ipsa virgo [Urania] cœlestis pluviarum pollicitatrix."—*Tertullian.*

‡ Moloch was the Latin Saturn, to whom human sacrifices were offered. Hence Saturn was said to devour his own children.

CHALDEANS. *The seven gods of the Chaldeans.* The gods of the seven planets called in the Latin language Saturn, Jupiter, Mars, Apollo [*i.e.* the Sun], Mercury, Venus, and Diana [*i.e.* the Moon].

EGYPTIAN GODS. The two chief deities were Osīris and Isis (supposed to be sun and moon). Of inferior gods, storks, apes, cats, the hawk, and some 20,000 other things had their temples, or at least received religious honours. Thebes worshipped a ram, Memphis the ox [Apis], Bubastis a cat, Momemphis a cow, the Mondosians a he-goat, the Hermopolitans a fish called "Latus," the Paprimas the hippopotamus, the Lycopolitans the wolf. The ibis was deified because it fed on serpents, the crocodile out of terror, the ichneumon because it fed on crocodiles' eggs.

ETRUSCANS. *Their nine gods.* Juno, Minerva, and Tin'ia (the three chief) ; to which add Vulcan, Mars, Saturn, Hercules, Summa'nus, and Vedius. (*See* AESIR.)

"Lars Porsĕna of Clusium,
  By the nine gods he swore
That the great house of Tarquin
  Should suffer wrong no more.
By the nine gods he swore it,
  And named a trysting day."
        Macaulay : Horatius, stanza 1.

GAUL. *The gods of the Gauls* were Esus and Teutatēs (called in Latin Mars and Mercury). Lucan adds a third named Taranēs (Jupiter). Cæsar says they worshipped Mercury, Apollo, Mars, Jupiter, and Minerva. The last was the inventor of all the arts, and presided over roads and commerce.

GREEK AND ROMAN GODS were divided into *Dii Majōrēs* and *Dii Minōrēs*. The Dii Majores were twelve in number, thus summed by Ennius—

Juno, Vesta, Minerva, Cerēs, Diana, Venus, Mars, Mercurius, Jŏvī, Neptunus, Vulcanus, Apollo.

Their blood was *ichor*, their food was *ambrosia*, their drink *nectar*. They married and had children, lived on Olympus in Thessaly, in brazen houses built by Vulcan, and wore golden shoes which enabled them to tread on air or water.

The twelve great deities, according to Ennius were (six male and six female):

LATIN.	GREEK.
JUPITER (*King*)	ZEUS (1 syl.).
Apollo (*the sun*)	Apollŏn.
Mars (*war*)	Arēs.
Mercury (*messenger*)	Hermēs.
Neptune (*ocean*)	Poseidon (3 syl.).
Vulcan (*smith*)	Hephaistos (3 sy
JUNO (*Queen*)	HERA.
Cerēs (*tillage*)	Demētĕr.
Diana (*moon, hunting*)	Artĕmis.
Minerva (*wisdom*)	Athēna.
Venus (*love and beauty*)	Aphroditē.
Vesta (*home-life*)	Hestia.

∴ Juno was the wife of Jupiter, Hera of Zeus; Venus was the wife of Vulcan, Aphroditē of Hephaistos.

Four other deities are often referred to:

Bacchus (wine)	Dionȳsos.
Cupid (*the lad Love*)	Eros.
Pluto (*of the Inferno*)	Plutōn.
Saturn (*time*)	Kronos.

∴ Of these, Proserpine (Latin) and Persephŏnē (Greek) was the wife of Pluto, Cybĕlē was the wife of Saturn, and Rhea of Kronos.

✢ In Hesiod's time the number of gods was thirty thousand, and that none might be omitted the Greeks observed a feast called θεοξένια, or Feast of the Unknown Gods. We have an All Saints' day.

Τρὶς γὰρ μύριοι εἰσὶν ἐπὶ χθονὶ πουλυβοτείρῃ
Ἀθάνατοι Ζηνὸς, φύλακες μερόπων ἀνθρώπων.
                              Hesiod, i. 250.

" Some thirty thousand gods on earth we find
Subjects of Zeus, and guardians of mankind."

PERSIAN GODS. The chief god was Mithra. Inferior to him were the two gods Oromasdēs and Tremanius. The former was supposed to be the author of all the evils of the earth.

SAXON GODS. Odin or Woden (the father of the gods), to whom Wednesday is consecrated; Frea (the mother of the gods), to whom Fri-day is consecrated; Hertha (the earth); Tuesco, to whom Tues-day is consecrated; Thor, to whom Thurs-day is consecrated.

SCANDINAVIAN GODS. The supreme gods of the Scandinavians were the Mysterious Three, called HAR (the mighty), the LIKE MIGHTY, and the THIRD PERSON, who sat on three thrones above the Rainbow. Then came the Æsir, of

which Odin was the chief, who lived in Asgard, on the heavenly hills, between the Earth and the Rainbow. Next came the Vanir', or genii of water, air, and clouds, of which Niörd was chief.

GODS AND GODDESSES. (*See* DEITIES, FAIRIES.)

Gods.

Among the gods. In the uppermost gallery of a theatre, which is near the ceiling, generally painted to resemble the sky. The French call this celestial region *paradis*.

Dead gods. The sepulchre of Jupiter is in Candia. Esculapius was killed with an arrow. The ashes of Venus are shown in Paphos. Hercules was burnt to death. (*Ignatius*.)

Triple gods. (*See* TRINITY.)

God's Acre. A churchyard or cemetery.

" I like that ancient Saxon phrase, which calls
The burial ground God's Acre."—*Longfellow*.

Gods' Secretaries (*The*). The three Parcæ. One dictates the decrees of the gods; another writes them down; and the third sees that they are carried out. (*Martianus Capella*. 5th century.)

God-child. One for whom a person stands sponsor in baptism, A godson or a goddaughter.

Goddess Mothers (*The*). What the French call " *bonnes dames* " or " *les dames blanches*," the prototype of the fays; generally represented as nursing infants on their laps. Some of these statues made by the Gauls or Gallo-Romans are called " Black Virgins."

Godfather. *To stand godfather.* To pay the reckoning, godfathers being generally chosen for the sake of the present they are expected to make the child at the christening or in their wills.

Godfathers. Jurymen, who are the sponsors of the criminal.

" In christening time thou shalt have two godfathers. Had I been judge, thou shouldst have had ten more to bring thee to the gallows, not to the font."—*Shakespeare : Merchant of Venice*, iv. 1.

God'frey. The Agamemnon of Tasso's *Jerusalem Delivered*, chosen by God as chief of the Crusaders. He is represented as calm, circumspect, and prudent; a despiser of " worldly empire, wealth, and fame."

Godfrey's Cordial. A patent medicine given to children troubled with colic. Gray says it was used by the lower orders to " prevent the crying of children in pain " when in want of proper nourishment. It consists of sassafras, opium in some form, brandy or rectified spirit, caraway seed, and treacle. There are seven or eight different preparations. Named after Thomas Godfrey of Hunsdon, in Hertfordshire, in the first quarter of the eighteenth century.

Godi'va (*Lady*). Patroness of Coventry. In 1040, Leofric, Earl of Mercia and Lord of Coventry, imposed certain exactions on his tenants, which his lady besought him to remove. To escape her importunity, he said he would do so if she would ride naked through the town. Lady Godiva took him at his word, and the Earl faithfully kept his promise.

The legend asserts that every inhabitant of Coventry kept indoors at the time, but a certain tailor peeped through his window to see the lady pass. Some say he was struck blind, others that his eyes were put out by the indignant townsfolk, and some that he was put to death. Be this as it may, he has ever since been called "Peeping Tom of Coventry." Tennyson has a poem on the subject.

⁂ The privilege of cutting wood in the Herduoles, by the parishioners of St. Briavel's Castle, in Gloucestershire, is said to have been granted by the Earl of Hereford (lord of Dean Forest) on precisely the same terms as those accepted by Lady Godiva.

"Peeping Tom" is an interpolation not anterior to the reign of Charles II., if we may place any faith in the figure in Smithfield Street, which represents him in a flowing wig and Stuart cravat.

Godless Florin (*The*). Also called "The Graceless Florin." In 1849 were issued florins in Great Britain, with no legend except "Victoria Regina." Both F.D. (Defender of the Faith) and D.G. (by God's Grace) were omitted for want of room. From the omission of "Fidēi Defensor" they were called *Godless* florins, and from the omission of "Dei Gratia" they were called *Graceless* florins.

⁂ These florins (2s.) were issued by Sheil, Master of the Mint, and as he was a Catholic, so great an outcry was made against them that they were called in the same year.

Godliness. *Cleanliness next to godliness*, "as Matthew Henry says." Whether Matthew Henry used the proverb as well known, or invented it, deponent sayeth not.

Godmer. A British giant, son of Albion, slain by Canu'tus, one of the companions of Brute.

"Those three monstrous stones . . .
Which that huge son of hideous Albion,
Great Godmer, threw in fierce contention
At bold Canutus: but of him was slain."
Spenser : Faërie Queene, ii. 10.

Goël. The avenger of blood, so called by the Jews.

Goe'mot or **Goëm'agot.** The giant who dominated over the western horn of England, slain by Corin'eus, one of the companions of Brute. (*Geoffrey : Chronicles*, i. 16.) (*See* CORINEUS.)

Gog and Magog. The Emperor Diocle'tian had thirty-three infamous daughters, who murdered their husbands; and, being set adrift in a ship, reached Albion, where they fell in with a number of demons. The offspring of this unnatural alliance was a race of giants, afterwards extirpated by Brute and his companions, refugees from Troy. Gog and Magog, the last two of the giant race, were brought in chains to London, then called Troy-novant, and, being chained to the palace of Brute, which stood on the site of our Guildhall, did duty as porters. We cannot pledge ourselves to the truth of old Caxton's narrative; but we are quite certain that Gog and Magog had their effigies at Guildhall in the reign of Henry V. The old giants were destroyed in the Great Fire, and the present ones, fourteen feet high, were carved in 1708 by Richard Saunders.

Children used to be told (as a very mild joke) that when these giants hear St. Paul's clock strike twelve, they descend from their pedestals and go into the Hall for dinner.

Gog'gles. A corruption of *oyles*, eyeshades. (Danish, *oog*, an eye ; Spanish, *ojo ;* or from the Welsh, *gogelu*, to shelter.)

Gogmagog Hill (*The*). The higher of two hills, some three miles south-east of Cambridge. The legend is that Gogmagog was a huge giant who fell in love with the nymph Granta, but the saucy lady would have nothing to say to the big bulk, afterwards metamorphosed into the hill which bears his name. (*Drayton : Polyolbion*, xxi.)

Go'jam. A province of Abyssinia (Africa). Captain Speke traced it to Lake Victoria Nyanza, near the Mountains of the Moon (1861).

"The swelling Nile.
From his two springs in Gojam's sunny realm,
Pure-welling out." *Thomson ; Summer.*

Golcon'da, in Hindustan, famous for its diamond mines.

Gold. By the ancient alchemists, gold represented the sun, and silver the moon. In heraldry, gold is expressed by dots.

All he touches turns to gold. It is said of Midas that whatever he touched turned to gold. (*See* RAINBOW.)

"In manu illius plumbum aurum fiebat."—*Petronius.*

Gold. *All that glitters is not gold.* (*Shakespeare: Merchant of Venice,* ii. 7.)

"All thing which that schineth as the gold
Is nought gold."
Chaucer: Canterbury Tales, 12,890.
"Non teneas aurum totum quod splendet ut aurum
Nec pulchrum pomum quodlibet esse bonum."
Ala'nus de In'sulis: Parab'olæ.

He has got the gold of Tolo'sa. His ill gains will never prosper. Cæpio, the Roman consul, in his march to Gallia Narbonensis, stole from Tolo'sa (Toulouse) the gold and silver consecrated by the Cimbrian Druids to their gods. When he encountered the Cimbrians both he and Mallius, his brother-consul, were defeated, and 112,000 of their men were left upon the field (B.C. 106).

The gold of Nibelungen. Brought ill-luck to every one who possessed it. (*Icelandic Edda.*) (*See* FATAL GIFTS.)

Mannheim gold. A sort of pinchbeck, made of copper and zinc, invented at Mannheim, in Germany.

Mosa'ic gold is "*aurum musi'vum,*" a bi-sulphuret of tin used by the ancients in tesselating. (French, *mosaique.*)

Gold Purse of Spain. Andalusia is so called because it is the city from which Spain derives its chief wealth.

Golden. *The Golden* ("Aura'tus"). So Jean Dorat, one of the Pleiad poets of France, was called by a pun on his name. This pun may perhaps pass muster; not so the preposterous title given to him of "The French Pindar." (1507-1588.)

Golden-tongued (Greek, *Chrysol'ogos*). So St. Peter, Bishop of Ravenna, was called. (433-450.)

The golden section of a line. Its division into two such parts that the rectangle contained by the smaller segment and the whole line equals the square on the larger segment. (*Euclid,* ii. 11.)

Golden Age. The best age; as the golden age of innocence, the golden age of literature. Chronologers divide the time between Creation and the birth of Christ into ages; Hesiod describes five,

and Lord Byron adds a sixth, "The Age of Bronze." (*See* AGE, AUGUSTAN.)

i. *The Golden Age of Ancient Nations:*

(1) NEW ASSYRIAN EMPIRE. From the reign of Esar-haddon or Assur Adon (*Assyria's prince*), third son of Sennach'-erib, to the end of Sarac's reign (B.C. 691-606).

(2) CHALDÆO - BABYLONIAN EMPIRE. From the reign of Nabopolassar or Nebopul-Assur (*Nebo the great Assyrian*) to that of Belshazzar or Bel-shah-Assur (*Bel king-of Assyria*) (B.C. 606-538).

(3) CHINA. The Tâng dynasty (626-684), and especially the reign of Tae-tsong (618-626).

(4) EGYPT. The reigns of Sethos I. and Ram'eses II. (B.C. 1336-1224).

(5) MEDIA. The reign of Cyax'ares or Kai-ax-Arës (*the-king son-of "Mars"*) (B.C. 634-594).

(6) PERSIA. The reigns of Khosru I., and II. (531-628).

ii. *The Golden Age of Modern Nations.*

(1) ENGLAND. The reign of Elizabeth (1558-1603).

(2) FRANCE. Part of the reigns of Louis XIV. and XV. (1640-1740).

(3) GERMANY. The reign of Charles V. (1519-1558).

(4) PORTUGAL. From John I. to the close of Sebastian's reign (1383-1578). In 1580 the crown was seized by Felipe II. of Spain.

(5) PRUSSIA. The reign of Frederick the Great (1740-1786).

(6) RUSSIA. The reign of Czar Peter the Great (1672-1725).

(7) SPAIN. The reign of Ferdinand and Isabella, when the crowns of Castile and Aragon were united (1474-1516).

(8) SWEDEN. From Gustavus Vasa to the close of the reign of Gustavus Adolphus (1523-1632).

Golden Apple. "*What female heart can gold despise?*" (*Gray*). In allusion to the fable of Atalanta, the swiftest of all mortals. She vowed to marry only that man who could outstrip her in a race. Milan'ion threw down three golden apples, and Atalanta, stopping to pick them up, lost the race.

Golden Ass. The romance of Apule'ius, written in the second century, and called the *golden* because of its excellency. It contains the adventures of Lucian, a young man who, being accidentally metamorphosed into an ass while sojourning in Thessaly, fell into the hands of robbers, eunuchs, magistrates, and so on, by whom he was ill-treated; but ultimately he recovered his human form. Boccaccio has borrowed largely from this admirable romance; and the incidents of the robbers' cave in *Gil Blas* are taken from it.

Golden Ball (*The*). Ball Hughes, one of the dandies in the days of the Regency. He paid some fabulous prices for his dressing cases (flourished 1820-1830). Ball married a Spanish dancer.

He shirked a duel, and this probably popularised the pun Golden Ball, Leaden Ball, Hughes Ball.

The three golden balls. (*See* BALLS.)

Golden Bay. The Bay of Kieselarke is so called because the sands shine like gold or fire. (*Hans Struys*, 17th cent.)

Golden Bonds. Aurelian allowed the captive queen Zenobia to have a slave to hold up her golden fetters.

Golden Bowl is Broken (*The*). Death has supervened.

"Or ever the silver cord be loosed, or the golden bowl be broken, or the pitcher be broken at the fountain, or the wheel broken at the cistern. Then shall the dust return to the earth as it was: and the spirit shall return unto God who gave it."—Ecclesiastes xii. 6, 7.

"Remember thy Creator":
before the silver cord of health is loosed by sickness;
before the golden bowl of manly strength has been broken up;
before the pitcher or body, which contains the spirit, has been broken up;
before the wheel of life has run its course,
and the spirit has returned to God, who gave it.

Golden Bull. An edict by the Emperor Charles IV., issued at the Diet of Nuremberg in 1356, for the purpose of fixing how the German emperors were to be elected. (*See* BULL.)

Golden Calf. *We all worship the golden calf, i.e.* money. The reference is to the golden calf made by Aaron when Moses was absent on Mount Sinai. (Exod. xxxii.) According to a common local tradition, Aaron's golden calf is buried in Rook's Hill, Lav'ant, near Chichester.

Golden Cave. Contained a cistern guarded by two giants and two centaurs; the waters of the cistern were good for quenching the fire of the cave; and when this fire was quenched the inhabitants of Scobellum would return to their native forms. (*The Seven Champions*, iii. 10.)

Golden Chain. "*Faith is the golden chain to link the penitent sinner unto God*" (Jeremy Taylor). The allusion is to a passage in Homer's *Iliad* (i. 19-30), where Zeus says, If a golden chain were let down from heaven, and all the gods and goddesses pulled at one end, they would not be able to pull him down to

earth; whereas he could lift with ease all the deities and all created things besides with his single might.

Golden Fleece. Ino persuaded her husband, Ath'amas, that his son Phryxos was the cause of a famine which desolated the land, and the old dotard ordered him to be sacrificed to the angry gods. Phryxos being apprised of this order, made his escape over sea on a *ram which had a golden fleece*. When he arrived at Colchis, he sacrificed the ram to Zeus, and gave the fleece to King Æe'tēs, who hung it on a sacred oak. It was afterwards stolen by Jason in his celebrated Argonautic expedition. (*See* ARGO.)

" This rising Greece with indignation viewed,
And youthful Jason an attempt conceived
Lofty and bold : along Pene'us' banks,
Around Olympus' brows, the Muses' haunts,
He roused the brave to re-demand the fleece."
 Dyer : The Fleece, ii.

Golden fleece of the north. The fur and peltry of Siberia is so called.

⁂ Australia has been called "The Land of the Golden Fleece," because of the quantity of wool produced there.

Golden Fleece. An order of knighthood by this title was instituted by Philip III., Duke of Burgundy, in 1429. The selection of the fleece as a badge is perhaps best explained by the fact that the manufacture of wool had long been the staple industry of the Low Countries, then a part of the Burgundian possessions.

Golden Fountain. The property of a wealthy Jew of Jerusalem. "In twenty-four hours it would convert any metal into refined gold; stony flints into pure silver; and any kind of earth into excellent metal." (*The Seven Champions of Christendom*, ii. 4.)

Golden Girdle. Louis VIII. made an edict that no courtesan should be allowed to wear a golden girdle, under very severe penalty. Hence the proverb, *Bonne renommé vault mieux que ceinture dorée*. (*See* GIRDLE.)

Golden Horn. The inlet of the Bosphorus on which Constantinople is situated. So called from its curved shape and great beauty.

Golden House. This was a palace erected by Nero in Rome. It was roofed with golden tiles, and the inside walls, which were profusely gilt, were embellished with mother-of-pearl and precious stones; the ceilings were inlaid with ivory and gold. The banquet-hall had a rotatory motion, and its vaulted ceiling showered flowers and perfumes on the guests. Popes and princes used the materials for their palaces.

Golden Leg. [KILMANSEGG, MISS.]

Golden Legend. A collection of hagiology (*lives of saints*) made by Jaques de Voragine in the thirteenth century; valuable for the picture it gives of mediæval manners, customs, and thought. Jortin says that the young students of religious houses, for the exercise of their talents, were set to accommodate the narratives of heathen writers to Christian saints. It was a collection of these "lives" that Voragine made, and thought deserving to be called "Legends worth their Weight in Gold." Longfellow has a dramatic poem entitled *The Golden Legend.*

Golden Mean. *Keep the golden mean.* The wise saw of Cleobu'los, King of Rhodes (B.C. 630-559).

" Distant alike from each, to neither lean,
But ever keep the happy Golden Mean."
Rowe: The Golden Verses.

Golden-mouthed. Chrysostom; so called for his great eloquence (A.D. 347-407).

Golden Ointment. Eye salve. In allusion to the ancient practice of rubbing "stynas of the eye" with a gold ring to cure them.

" I have a sty here, Chilax,
I have no gold to cure it."
Beaumont and Fletcher: Mad Lovers.

Golden Opinions. "I have bought golden opinions of all sorts of people." (*Shakespeare: Macbeth,* i. 7.)

Golden Palace. (*See* GOLDEN HOUSE.)

Golden Rose. A cluster of roses and rosebuds growing on one thorny stem, all of the purest gold, chiselled with exquisite workmanship. In its cup, among its petals, the Pope, at every benediction he pronounces upon it, inserts a few particles of amber and musk. It is blessed on the fourth Sunday in Lent, and bestowed during the ecclesiastical year on the royal lady whose zeal for the Church has most shown itself by pious deeds or pious intentions. The prince who has best deserved of the Holy See has the blessed sword and cap (*lo stocco e il beretto*) sent him. If no one merits the gift it is laid up in the Vatican. In the spring of 1868 the Pope gave the golden rose to Isabella of Spain, in reward of "her faith, justice, and charity," and to "foretoken the protection of God to his

well - beloved daughter, whose high virtues make her a shining light amongst women." The Empress Eugénie of France also received it.

Golden Rule.
In morals—Do unto others as you would be done by. Or Matt. vii. 12.
In arithmetic—The Rule of Three.

Golden Shoe (*A*). A pot of money. "The want of a golden shoe" is the want of ready cash. It seems to be a superlative of a "silver slipper," or good luck generally, as he "walks in silver slippers."

Golden Shower or *Shower of gold.* A bribe, money. The allusion is to the classic tale of Jupiter and Dan'aē. Acris'ios, King of Argos, being told that his daughter's son would put him to death, resolved that Dan'aē should never marry, and accordingly locked her up in a brazen tower. Jupiter, who was in love with the princess, foiled the king by changing himself into a shower of gold, under which guise he readily found access to the fair prisoner.

Golden Slipper (*The*), in Negro melodies, like "golden streets," etc., symbolises the joys of the land of the leal; and to wear the golden slipper means to enter into the joys of Paradise. The golden shoes or slippers of Paradise, according to Scandinavian mythology, enable the wearer to walk on air or water.

Golden State. California; so called from its gold "diggins."

Golden Stream. Joannes Damasce'nus, author of *Dogmatic Theology* (died 756).

Golden Thigh. Pythagoras is said to have had a golden thigh, which he showed to Abăris, the Hyperborean priest, and exhibited in the Olympic games. Pelops, we are told, had an ivory shoulder. Nuad had a silver hand (*see* SILVER HAND), but this was artificial.

Golden Tooth. A Silesian child, in 1593, we are told, in his second set of teeth, cut "one great tooth of pure gold;" but Libavius, chemist of Coburg, recommended that the tooth should be seen by a goldsmith; and the goldsmith pronounced it to be "an ordinary tooth cleverly covered with gold leaf."

Golden Town (*The*). So Mainz or Mayence was called in Carlovingian times.

Golden Valley (*The*). The eastern portion of Limerick is so called, from its great natural fertility.

Golden Verses. So called because they are "good as gold." They are by some attributed to Epicar'mos, and by others to Emped'oclēs, but always go under the name of Pythag'oras, and seem quite in accordance with the excellent precepts of that philosopher. They are as follows :—

Ne'er suffer sleep thine eyes to close
Before thy mind hath run
O'er every act, and thought, and word,
From dawn to set of sun ;
For wrong take shame, but grateful feel
If just thy course hath been;
Such effort day by day renewed
Will ward thy soul from sin.   *E. C. B.*

Goldy. The pet name given by Dr. Johnson to Oliver Goldsmith. Garrick said of him, "He wrote like an angel and talked like poor Poll." (Born Nov. 29, 1728 ; died April 4, 1774.)

Gol'gotha signifies a *skull*, and corresponds to the French word *chaumont*. Probably it designated a bare hill or rising ground, having some fanciful resemblance to the form of a bald skull.

"Golgotha seems not entirely unconnected with the hill of Gareb, and the locality of Goath, mentioned in Jeremiah xxxi. 39, on the north-west of the city. I am inclined to fix the place where Jesus was crucified . . . on the mounds which command the valley of Hinnom, above Birket-Mamila."—*Renan : Life of Jesus*, chap. xxv. .

Golgotha, at the University church, Cambridge, was the gallery in which the "heads of the houses" sat; so called because it was the place of skulls or heads. It has been more wittily than truly said that Golgotha was the place of empty skulls.

Goli'ath. The Philistine giant, slain by the stripling David with a small stone hurled from a sling. (1 Sam. xvii. 23-54.) (*See* GIANTS.)

Golosh'. It is said that Henry VI. wore half-boots laced at the side, and about the same time was introduced the shoe or clog called the "galage" or "gologe," meaning simply a covering; to which is attributed the origin of our word golosh. This cannot be correct, as Chaucer, who died twenty years before Henry VI. was born, uses the word. The word comes to us from the Spanish *galocha* (wooden shoes); German, *galosche*.

"Ne were worthy to unbocle his galoche."
        Chaucer : Squire's Tale.

Go'marists. Opponents of Armin'ius. So called after Francis Gomar, their leader (1563-1641).

Gombeen Man (*The*). A tallyman; a village usurer ; a money-lender. The word is of Irish extraction.

"They suppose that the tenants can have no other supply of capital than from the gombeen man."—*Egmont Hake: Free Trade in Capital.* p. 375.

Gombo. Pigeon French, or French as it is spoken by the coloured population of Louisiana, the French West Indies, Bourbon, and Mauritius. (Connected with *jumbo*.)

"Creole is almost pure French, not much more mispronounced than in some parts of France; but Gombo is a mere phonetic burlesque of French, interlarded with African words, and other words which are neither African nor French, but probably belong to the aboriginal language of the various countries to which the slaves were brought from Africa."—*The Nineteenth Century*, October, 1891, p. 576.

Gondola. A Venetian boat.

"Venice, in her purple prime . . . . when the famous law was passed making all gondolas black, that the nobles should not squander fortunes upon them."—*Curtis: Potiphar Papers*, i. p. 31.

Gone 'Coon (*A*). (*See* 'COON.)

Gone to the Devil. (*See under* DEVIL.)

Gone Up. Put out of the way, hanged, or otherwise got rid of. In Denver (America) unruly citizens are summarily hung on a cotton tree, and when any question is asked about them the answer is briefly given, "Gone up" —*i.e.* gone up the cotton tree, or suspended from one of its branches. (See *New America*, by W. Hepworth Dixon, i. 11.)

Gon'eril. One of Lear's three daughters. Having received her moiety of Lear's kingdom, the unnatural daughter first abridged the old man's retinue, then gave him to understand that his company was troublesome. (*Shakespeare : King Lear*.)

Gon'falon or *Gonfanon*. An ensign or standard. A *gonfalonier* is a magistrate that has a gonfalon. (Italian, *gonfalo'ne ;* French, *gonfalon ;* Saxon, *guth-fana*, war-flag.) Chaucer uses the word gonfanon; Milton prefers gonfalon. Thus he says:—

"Ten thousand thousand ensigns high advanced, Standards and gonfalons, 'twixt van and rear Stream in the air, and for distinction serve Of hierarchies [3 syl.], of orders, and degrees."
        Paradise Lost, v. 580.

Gonfanon. The consecrated banner of the Normans. When William invaded England, his gonfanon was presented to him by the Pope. It was made of purple silk, divided at the end like the banner attached to the "Cross of the Resurrection." When Harold was wounded in the eye, he was borne to the foot of this sacred standard, and the English rallied round him; but his death gave victory to the invaders. The high altar of Battle Abbey marked the spot where the gonfanon stood, but the only traces now left are a few stones, recently uncovered, to show the site of this memorable place.

Gonin. *C'est un Maître Gonin.* He is a sly dog. Maître Gonin was a famous clown in the sixteenth century. "*Un tour de Maître Gonin*" means a cunning or scurvy trick. (*See* ALIBORON.)

Gonnella's Horse. Gonnella, the domestic jester of the Duke of Ferra'ra, rode on a horse all skin and bone. The jests of Gonnella are in-print.

"His horse was as lean as Gonnella's, which (as the Duke said) 'Osso atque pellis totus erat' (Plautus)."—*Cervantes : Don Quixote.*

Gonsal'ez [*Gon-zalley*]. Fernan Gonsalez was a Spanish hero of the tenth century, whose life was twice saved by his wife Sancha, daughter of Garcias, King of Navarre. The adventures of Gonsal'ez have given birth to a host of ballads.

Gonville College (Cambridge). The same as *Caius College*, founded in 1348 by Edmond Gonville, son of Sir Nicholas Gonville, rector of Terrington, Norfolk. (*See* CAIUS COLLEGE.)

Good. *The Good.*

Alfonso VIII. (or IX.) of Leon, "The Noble and Good." (1158-1214.)

Douglas (*The good Sir James*), Bruce's friend, died 1330.

Jean II. of France, *le Bon.* (1319, 1350-1364.)

Jean III., Duc de Bourgogne. (1286, 1312-1341.)

Jean of Brittany, "The Good and Wise." (1287, 1389-1442.)

Philippe III., Duc de Bourgogne. (1396, 1419-1467.)

Réné, called *The Good King Réné*, titular King of Na'ples. (1439-1452.)

Richard II., Duc de Normandie. (996-1026.)

Richard de Beauchamp, twelfth Earl of Warwick, Regent of France. (Died 1439.)

Good-bye. A contraction of *God be with you.* Similar to the French adieu, which is *à Dieu* (I commend you to God).

⁂ Some object to the substitution of "God" in this phrase, reminding us of our common phrases *good day, good night, good morning, good evening;*

"Good be with ye" would mean may you fare well, or good abide [with you].

Good-Cheap. The French *bon marché*, a good bargain. "Cheap" here means market or bargain. (Anglo-Saxon, *ceap*.)

Good Duke Humphrey. Humphrey Plantagenet, Duke of Gloucester, youngest son of Henry IV., said to have been murdered by Suffolk and Cardinal Beaufort. (*Shakespeare : 2 Henry VI.*, iii. 2.)

⁂ Called "Good," not for his philanthropy, but from his devotion to the Church. He was an out-and-out Catholic.

Good Folk (Scotch *guid folk*) are like the Shetland land-Trows, who inhabit the interior of green hills. (*See* TROWS.)

Good Form, Bad Form. *Comme il faut, bon ton ; mauvais ton, comme il ne faut pas.* Form means fashion, like the Latin *forma.*

Good Friday. The anniversary of the Crucifixion. "Good" means *holy.* Probably *good* = God, as in the phrase "Good-bye" (*q.v.*).

Born on Good Friday. According to ancient superstition, those born on Christmas Day or Good Friday have the power of seeing and commanding spirits.

Good Graces (*To get into one's*). To be in favour with.

"Having continued to get into the good graces of the buxom widow."—*Dickens: Pickwick*, chap. xiv.

Good Hater (*A*). *I love a good hater.* I like a man to be with me or against me, either to be hot or cold. Dr. Johnson called Bathurst the physician a "good hater," because he hated a fool, and he hated a rogue, and he hated a Whig; "he," said the Doctor, "was a very good hater."

Good Lady (*The*). The mistress of the house. "Your good lady," your wife. (*See* GOODMAN.)

⁂ "My good woman" is a deprecatory address to an inferior; but "Is your good woman at home?" is quite respectful, meaning your wife (of the lower grade of society).

Good Neighbours. So the Scotch call the Norse drows.

Good Regent. James Stewart, Earl of Murray, appointed Regent of Scotland after the imprisonment of Queen Mary.

Good Samaritan. One who succours the distressed. The character is from our Lord's Parable of the man who fell among thieves (St. Luke x. 30-37).

Good Time. *There is a good time coming.* This has been for a long, long time a familiar saying in Scotland, and is introduced by Sir Walter Scott in his *Rob Roy.* Charles Mackay has written a song so called, set to music by Henry Russell.

Good Turn (*To do a*). To do a kindness to any one.

Good and All (*For*). Not tentatively, not in pretence, nor yet temporally, but *bonâ fide*, really, and altogether. (*See* ALL.)

"The good woman never died after this, till she came to die for good and all."—*L'Estrange: Fables.*

Good as Gold. Thoroughly good.

Good for Anything. Ripe for any sort of work.

"After a man has had a year or two at this sort of work, he is good .... for anything."—*Boldrewood: Robbery under Arms*, chap. xi.

Not good for anything. Utterly worthless; used up or worn out.

Good Wine needs no Bush. It was customary to hang out ivy, boughs of trees, flowers, etc., at public houses to notify to travellers that "good cheer" might be had within.

"Some ale-houses upon the road I saw,
 And some with bushes showing they wine did draw."
   Poor Robin's Perambulations (1678).

Goods. *I carry all my goods with me* (*Omnia mea mecum porto*). Said by Bias, one of the seven sages, when Priene was besieged and the inhabitants were preparing for flight.

Goodfellow (*Robin*). Sometimes called Puck, son of Oberon, a domestic spirit, the constant attendant on the English fairy-court; full of tricks and fond of practical jokes.

"That shrewd and knavish sprite
 Called Robin Goodfellow."
Shakespeare : Midsummer Night's Dream, ii. 1.

Goodluck's Close (Norfolk). A corruption of Guthlac's Close, so called from a chapel founded by Allen, son of Godfrey de Swaffham, in the reign of Henry II., and dedicated to St. Guthlac.

Goodman. A husband or master is the Saxon *guma* or *goma* (a man), which in the inflected cases becomes guman or goman. In St. Matt. xxiv. 43, "If the goodman of the house had known in what watch the thief would come, he would have watched." Gomman and

gommer, for the master and mistress of a house, are by no means uncommon. The phrase is also used of the devil.

"There's nae luck about the house
 When our gudeman's awa." *Mickle.*

Goodman, or **St. Gutman.** Patron saint of tailors, being himself of the same craft.

Goodman of Bal'lengeich. The assumed name of James V. of Scotland when he made his disguised visits through the country districts around Edinburgh and Stirling, after the fashion of Haroun-al-Raschid, Louis XI., etc.

Goodman's Croft. A strip of ground or corner of a field formerly left untilled, in Scotland, in the belief that unless some such place were left, the spirit of evil would damage the crop.

"Scotchmen still living remember the corner of a field being left for the goodman's croft."—*Tylor: Primitive Culture*, ii. 370.

Goodman's Fields, Whitechapel. Fields belonging to a farmer named Goodman.

"At the which farm I myself in my youth have fetched many a halfpenny-worth of milk, and never had less than three ale-pints for a halfpenny in summer, nor less than one ale-pint in winter always hot from the kine . . . and strained. One Trolop, and afterwards Goodman, were the farmers there, and had thirty or forty kine to the pail."
—*Stow.*

Goodwin Sands consisted at one time of about 4,000 acres of low land fenced from the sea by a wall, belonging to Earl Goodwin or Godwin. William the Conqueror bestowed them on the abbey of St. Augustine, at Canterbury, and the abbot allowed the sea-wall to fall into a dilapidated state, so that the sea broke through in 1100 and inundated the whole. (*See* TENTERDEN STEEPLE.)

Goodwood Races. So called from the park in which they are held. They begin the last Tuesday of July, and last four days; but the principal one is Thursday, called the "Cup Day." These races, being held in a private park, are very select, and admirably conducted. Goodwood Park, the property of the Duke of Richmond, was purchased by Charles, the first Duke, of the Compton family, then resident in East Lav'ant, a village two miles north of Chichester.

Goody. A depreciative, meaning weakly moral and religious. In French, *bon homme* is used in a similar way.

"No doubt, if a Cæsar or a Napoleon comes before some man of weak will . . . especially if he be a goody man, [he] will quail."—*J. Cook: Conscience*, lecture iv. p. 49.

Goody is good-wife, Chaucer's good-lefe ; as, Goody Dobson. Good-woman means the mistress of the house, contracted sometimes into gommer, as goodman is into gomman. (*See* GOODMAN.)

Goody Blake. A poor old woman who was detected by Harry Gill, the farmer, picking up sticks for a wee-bit fire to warm herself by. The farmer compelled her to leave them on the field, and Goody Blake invoked on him the curse that he might never more be warm. From that moment neither blazing fire nor accumulated clothing ever made Harry Gill warm again. Do what he would, "his teeth went chatter, chatter, still." (*Wordsworth: Goody Blake and Harry Gill.*)

Goody Two-Shoes. This tale first appeared in 1765. It was written for Newbery, as it is said, by Oliver Goldsmith.

Goody-goody. Very religious or moral, but with no strength of mind or independence of spirit.

Goose. A tailor's smoothing-iron ; so called because its handle resembles the neck of a goose.

"Come in, tailor ; here you may roast your goose."—*Shakespeare: Macbeth,* ii. 3.

Ferrara geese. Celebrated for the size of their livers. The French *pâte de foie gras,* for which Strasbourg is so noted, is not a French invention, but a mere imitation of a well-known dish of classic times.

"I wish, gentlemen, it was one of the geese of Ferrara, so much celebrated among the ancients for the magnitude of their livers, one of which is said to have weighed upwards of two pounds. With this food, exquisite as it was, did Heliogab'alus regale his hounds."—*Smollett: Peregrine Pickle.*

Wayz Goose. (*See* WAYZ.)

I'll cook your goose for you. I'll pay you out. Eric, King of Sweden, coming to a certain town with very few soldiers, the enemy, in mockery, hung out a goose for him to shoot at. Finding, however, that the king meant business, and that it would be no laughing matter for them, they sent heralds to ask him what he wanted. "To cook your goose for you," he facetiously replied.

He killed the goose to get the eggs. He grasped at what was more than his due, and lost an excellent customer. The Greek fable says a countryman had a goose that laid golden eggs ; thinking to make himself rich, he killed the goose to get the whole stock of eggs at once, but lost everything.

He steals a goose, and gives the giblets in alms. He amasses wealth by over-reaching, and salves his conscience by giving small sums in charity.

The older the goose the harder to pluck. Old men are unwilling to part with their money. The reference is to the custom of plucking live geese for the sake of their quills. Steel pens have put an end to this barbarous custom.

To get the goose. To get hissed on the stage. (*Theatrical.*)

What a goose you are. In the Egyptian hieroglyphics the emblem of a vain silly fellow is a goose.

Goose and Gridiron. A public-house sign, properly the coat of arms of the Company of Musicians—viz. a *swan* with expanded wings, within a *double tressure* [the gridiron], counter, flory, argent. Perverted into a goose striking the bars of a gridiron with its foot, and called "The Swan and Harp," or "Goose and Gridiron."

This famous lodge of the Freemasons, of which Wren was Master (in London Honse Yard), was doomed in 1894.

Goose at Michaelmas. One legend says that St. Martin was tormented by a goose which he killed and ate. As he died from the repast, good Christians have ever since sacrificed the goose on the day of the saint.

The popular tradition is that Queen Elizabeth, on her way to Tilbury Fort (September 29th, 1588), dined at the ancient seat of Sir Neville Umfreyville, where, among other things, two fine geese were provided for dinner. The queen, having eaten heartily, called for a bumper of Burgundy, and gave as a toast, "Destruction to the Spanish Armada ! " Scarcely had she spoken when a messenger announced the destruction of the fleet by a storm. The queen demanded a second bumper, and said, "Henceforth shall a goose commemorate this great victory." This tale is marred by the awkward circumstance that the thanksgiving sermon for the victory was preached at St. Paul's on the 20th August, and the fleet was dispersed by the winds in July. Gascoigne, who died 1577, refers to the custom of goose-eating at Michaelmas as common.

"At Christmas a capon, at Michaelmas a goose, And somewhat else at New Yere's tide, for feare the lease flies loose."

⁂ At Michaelmas time stubble-geese are in perfection, and tenants formerly presented their landlords with one to keep in their good graces.

Although geese were served at table in Michaelmas time, before the destruction of the Armada, still they commemorate that event. So there were doubtless rainbows before the Flood, yet God made the rainbow the token of His promise not to send another Flood upon the world.

Gooseberry. Fox Talbot says this is St. John's berry, being ripe about St. John's Day. [This must be John the Baptist, at the end of August, not John the Evangelist, at the beginning of May.] Hence, he says, it is called in Holland *Jansbeeren.* Jans'-beeren, he continues, has been corrupted into Gansbeeren, and Gans is the German for goose. This is very ingenious, but *gorse* (furze) offers a simpler derivation. *Gorse-berry* (the prickly berry) would be like the German *stachel-beere* (the "prickly berry"), and *kraus-beere* (the rough gooseberry), from *krauen* (to scratch). Krausbeere, Gorse-berry, Gooseberry. In Scotland it is called *grosser.* (*See* BEAR'S GARLICK.)

To play gooseberry is to go with two lovers for appearance' sake. The person "who plays propriety" is expected to hear, see, and say nothing. (*See* GOOSEBERRY PICKER.)

He played up old gooseberry with me. He took great liberties with my property, and greatly abused it; in fact, he made gooseberry fool of it. (*See below.*)

Gooseberry Fool. A corruption of gooseberry *foulé,* milled, mashed, pressed. The French have *foulé de pommes; foulé de raisins; foulé de groseilles,* our "gooseberry fool."

⁂ Gooseberry fool is a compound made of gooseberries scalded and pounded with cream.

Gooseberry Picker (*A*). One who has all the toil and trouble of picking a troublesome fruit for the delectation of others. (*See* TAPISSERIE.)

Goosebridge. *Go to Goosebridge.* "Rule a wife and have a wife." Boccaccio (ix. 9) tells us that a man who had married a shrew asked Solomon what he should do to make her more submissive; and the wise king answered, "Go to Goosebridge." Returning home, deeply perplexed, he came to a bridge where a muleteer was trying to induce a mule to pass over it. The mule resisted, but the stronger will of the muleteer at length prevailed. The man asked the name of the bridge, and was told it was "Goosebridge." Petruchio

tamed Katharine by the power of a stronger will.

Goose Dubbs, of Glasgow. A sort of Seven Dials, or Scottish Alsa'tia. The Scotch use *dubbs* for a filthy puddle. (Welsh, *dwb,* mortar; Irish, *doib,* plaster.)

"The Guse-dubs o' Glasgow: O sirs, what a huddle o' houses, . . . the green middens o' baith liquid and solid matter, soomin' wi' dead cats and auld shoon."—*Noctes Ambrosianæ.*

Goose Gibbie. A half-witted lad, who first "kept the turkeys, and was afterwards advanced to the more important office of minding the cows." (*Sir Walter Scott: Old Mortality.*)

Gopher-wood (נֹפֶר), of which the ark was made.

It was *acacia,* says the Religious Tract Society.
It was *boxwood,* says the Arabian commentators.
It was *bulrushes,* daubed over with slime, says Dawson.
It was *cedar,* says the Targum of Onkelos.
It was *cypress,* says Fuller, and κυπαρ is not unlike *gopher.*
It was *ebony-wood,* says Bockart.
It was *deal* or *fir-wood,* say some.
It was *juniper-wood,* says Castellus.
It was *pine,* say Asenarius, Munster, Persie, Taylor, etc.
It was *wicker-wood,* says Geddes.

Gordian Knot. A great difficulty. Gordius, a peasant, being chosen king of Phrygia, dedicated his waggon to Jupiter, and fastened the yoke to a beam with a rope of bark so ingeniously that no one could untie it. Alexander was told that "whoever undid the knot would reign over the whole East." "Well then," said the conqueror, "it is thus I perform the task," and, so saying, he cut the knot in twain with his sword.

To cut the knot is to evade a difficulty, or get out of it in a summary manner.

"Such praise the Macedonian got
For having rudely cut the Gordian knot."
Waller: To the King.
"Turn him to any cause of policy,
The Gordian knot of it he will unloose,
Familiar as his garter."
Shakespeare: Henry V. i. 1.

Gordon Riots. Riots in 1780, headed by Lord George Gordon, to compel the House of Commons to repeal the bill passed in 1778 for the relief of Roman Catholics. Gordon was undoubtedly of unsound mind, and he died in 1793, a proselyte to Judaism. Dickens has given a very vivid description of the Gordon riots in *Barnaby Rudge.*

Gor'gibus. An honest, simple-minded burgess, brought into all sorts of troubles by the love of finery and the gingerbread gentility of his niece and his daughter. (*Molière: Les Précieuses Ridicules.*)

Gorgon. Anything unusually hideous. There were three Gorgons, with serpents on their heads instead of hair : Medu'sa was the chief of the three, and the only one that was mortal ; but so hideous was her face that whoever set eyes on it was instantly turned into stone. She was slain by Perseus, and her head placed on the shield of Minerva.

" Lest Gorgon rising from the infernal lakes
  With horrors armed, and curls of hissing snakes,
  Should fix me, stiffened at the monstrous sight,
  A stony image in eternal night."
               Odyssey, xi.

" What was that snaky-headed Gorgon shield
  That wise Minerva wore, unconquered virgin,
  Wherewith she freezed her foes to congealed
    stone?
  But rigid looks of chaste austerity,
  And noble grace, that dashed brute violence
  With sudden adoration and blank awe."
         Milton: Comus, 458—463.

Gor'ham Controversy. This arose out of the refusal of the bishop of Exeter to institute the Rev. Cornelius Gorham to the vicarage of Brampford Speke, "because he held unsound views on the doctrine of baptism." Mr. Gorham maintained that "spiritual regeneration is not conferred on children by baptism." After two years' controversy, the Privy Council decided in favour of Mr. Gorham (1851).

Gorlois, Duke of Cornwall, husband of Igerna, who was the mother of King Arthur by an adulterous connection with Uther, pendragon of the Britons.

Gosling. A term applied to a silly fellow, a simpleton.

" Surprised at all they meet, the gosling pair,
  With awkward gait, stretched neck, and silly
    stare,
  Discover huge cathedrals."
      Cowper: Progress of Error, 379—81.

Goslings. The catkins of nut-trees, pines, etc. Halliwell says they are so called from their yellow colour and fluffy texture.

Gospel. A panacea; a scheme to bring about some promised reform ; a beau ideal. Of course the theological word is the Anglo-Saxon *godspell, i.e.* God and *spel* (a story), a translation of the Greek *evangelion,* the good story.

" Mr. Carnegie's gospel is the very thing for the transition period from social heathendom to social Christianity."—*Nineteenth Century* (March, 1891, p. 380).

Gospel according to . . . The chief teaching of [so-and-so]. "The Gospel according to Mammon" is the making and collecting of money. "The Gospel according to Sir Pertinax Mac Sycophant," is bowing and cringing to those who are in a position to lend you a helping hand.

Gospel of Nicodemus (*The*). Sometimes called "The Acts of Pilate" (*Acta Pilāti*), was the main source of the "Mysteries" and "Miracle Plays" of the Middle Ages ; and although now deemed apocryphal, seems for many ages to have been accepted as genuine.

Gospel of Wealth (*The*). The hypothesis that wealth is the great end and aim of man, the one thing needful.

" The Gospel of Wealth advocates leaving free the operation of laws of accumulation."—*Carnegie: Advantages of Poverty.*

Gospellers. Followers of Wycliffe, called the "Gospel Doctor;" any one who believes that the New Testament has in part, at least, superseded the Old.

Hot Gospellers. A nickname applied to the Puritans after the Restoration.

Gossamer. According to legend, this delicate thread is the ravelling of the Virgin Mary's winding-sheet, which fell to earth on her ascension to heaven. It is said to be *God's seam, i.e.* God's thread. Philologically it is the Latin *gossipin-us,* cotton.

Gossip. A tattler ; a sponsor at baptism, a corruption of *gossib,* which is Godsib, a kinsman in the Lord. (*Sib, gesib,* Anglo-Saxon, kinsman, whence *sibman, he is our sib,* still used.)

" 'Tis not a maid, for she hath had gossips [sponsors for her child]; yet 'tis a maid, for she is her master's servant, and serves for wages."—*Shakespeare: Two Gentlemen of Verona,* iii. 1.

Gossip. A father confessor, of a good, easy, jovial frame.

" Here, Andrew, carry this to my gossip, jolly father Boniface, the monk of St. Martin's."—*Sir Walter Scott: Quentin Durward.*

Gossyp'ia. The cotton-plant personified.

" The nymph Gossypia heads the velvet sod,
  And warms with rosy smiles the watery god."
    Darwin: Loves of the Plants, canto ii.

Got the Mitten. Jilted ; got his dismissal. The word is from the Latin *mitto,* to dismiss.

" There is a young lady I have set my heart on; though whether she is agoin' to give me hern, or give me the mitten, I ain't quite satisfied."—*Sam Slick: Human Nature,* p. 90.

Gotch. A large stone jug with a handle (Norfolk). *Fetch the gotch, mor —i.e.* fetch the great water-jug, lassie.

" A gotch of milk I've been to fill."
    Bloomfield: Richard and Kate.

Goth. Icelandic, *got* (a horseman) ; whence *Woden—i.e.* Gothen.

" The Goths were divided by the Dnieper into East Goths (Ostrogoths), and West Goths (Visigoths), and were the most cultured of the German peoples."—*Baring-Gould: Story of Germany,* p. 37.

Last of the Goths. Roderick, the thirty-fourth of the Visigothic line of kings (414-711). (*See* RODERICK.)

Gotham. *Wise Men of Gotham—* fools. Many tales of folly have been fathered on the Gothamites, one of which is their joining hands round a thorn-bush to shut in a cuckoo. The "bush" is still shown to visitors.

It is said that King John intended to make a progress through this town with the view of purchasing a castle and grounds. The townsmen had no desire to be saddled with this expense, and therefore when the royal messengers appeared, wherever they went they saw the people occupied in some idiotic pursuit. The king being told of it, abandoned his intention, and the "wise men" of the village cunningly remarked, "We ween there are more fools pass through Gotham than remain in it." Andrew Boyde, a native of Gotham, wrote *The Merrie Tales of the Wise Men of Gotham*, founded on a commission signed by Henry VIII. to the magistrates of that town to prevent poaching.

N.B. All nations have fixed upon some locality as their limbus of fools; thus we have Phrygia as the fools' home of Asia Minor, Abde'ra of the Thracians, Bœo'tia of the Greeks, Nazareth of the ancient Jews, Swabia of the modern Germans, and so on. (*See* COGGESHALL.)

Gothamites (3 syl.). American cockneys. New York is called satirically Gotham.

"Such things as would strike . . . a stranger in our beloved Gotham, and places to which our regular Gothamites (American cockneys) are wont to repair."—*Fraser's Magazine: Sketches of American Society.*

Gothic Architecture has nothing to do with the Goths, but is a term of contempt bestowed by the architects of the Renaissance period on mediæval architecture, which they termed Gothic or clumsy, fit for barbarians.

"St. Louis . . . built the Ste. Chapelle of Paris, . . . the most precious piece of Gothic in North-ern Europe."—*Ruskin: Fors Clavigera*, vol. i.

∴ Napoleon III. magnificently restored and laid open this exquisite church.

Gouk or **Gowk.** In the Teutonic the word *gauch* means fool; whence the Anglo-Saxon *geac*, a cuckoo, and the Scotch *goke* or *gouk*.

Hunting the gowk [fool], is making one an April fool. (*See* APRIL.)

A gowk storm is a term applied to a storm consisting of several days of tempestuous weather, believed by the peasantry to take place periodically about the beginning of April, at the time that the gowk or cuckoo visits this country.

"That being done, he hoped that this was but a gowk-storm."—*Sir G. Mackenzie: Memoirs*, p. 70.

Gourd. Used in the Middle Ages for corks (*Orlando Furioso*, x. 106); used also for a cup or bottle. (French, *gourde*; Latin, *cucurbita*.)

Jonah's gourd [*kikiven*], the Palma Christi, called in Egypt *kiki*. Niebuhr speaks of a specimen which he himself saw near a rivulet, which in October "rose eight feet in five months' time." And Volney says, "Wherever plants have water the rapidity of their growth is prodigious. In Cairo," he adds, "there is a species of gourd which in twenty-four hours will send out shoots four inches long." (*Travels*, vol. i. p. 71.)

Gourds. Dice with a secret cavity. Those loaded with lead were called Fulhams (*q.v.*).

"Gourds and fullam holds,
And high and low beguile the rich and poor."
Shakespeare: Merry Wives of Windsor, i. 3.

Gourmand and **Gourmet** (French). The *gourmand* is one whose chief pleasure is eating; but a *gourmet* is a connoisseur of food and wines. In England the difference is this : a *gourmand* regards quantity more than quality, a *gourmet* quality more than quantity. (Welsh, *gor*, excess; *gorm*, a fulness; *gourmod*, too much; *gormant*; etc.) (*See* APICIUS.)

" In former times [in France] *gourmand* meant a judge of eating, and *gourmet* a judge of wine . . . Gourmet is now universally understood to refer to eating, and not to drinking."—*Hamerton: French and English*, part v. chap. iv. p. 249.

Gourmand's Prayer (*The*). "O Philoxenos, Philoxenos, why were you not Prometheus ?" Prometheus was the mythological creator of man, and Philoxenos was a great epicure, whose great and constant wish was to have the neck of a crane, that he might enjoy the taste of his food longer before it was swallowed into his stomach. (*Aristotle: Ethics*, iii. 10.)

Gourre (1 syl.). A debauched wo-man. The citizens of Paris bestowed the name on Isabella of Bavaria.

" We have here . . . a man . . . who to his second wife es; oused La grande Gourre."—*Rabelais: Pantag'ruel*, iii. 21.

Gout, from the French *goutte*, a drop, because it was once thought to proceed from a "drop of acrid matter in the joints."

Goutte de Sang. The Adonis flower or pheasant's eye, said to be stained by the blood of Adonis, who was gored by a boar.

"O fleur, si chère à Cytherée
Ta corolle fut, en naissant,
Du sang d'Adonis colorée."

Goven. *St. Goven's Bell.* (*See* INCH-CAPE.)

Government Men. Convicts.

"[He] had always been a hard-working man . . . good at most things, and, like a lot more of the Government men, as the convicts were called, . . . had saved some money."—*Boldrewood: Robbery under Arms*, chap. i.

Gowan. A daisy; a perennial plant or flower.

The ewe-gowan is the common daisy, apparently denominated from the ewe, as being frequently in pastures fed on by sheep.

"Some bit waefu' love story, enough to mak the pinks an' the ewe-gowans blush to the very lip."—*Brownie of Bodsbeck*, i. 215.

Gower, called by Chaucer "The moral Gower."

"O moral Gower, this book I direct
To thee, and to the philosophical Strood,
To vouchsauf there need is to correct
Of your benignities and zealës good."
Chaucer.

Gowk. (*See* GOUK.)

Gowk-thrapple (*Maister*). A pulpit-drumming "chosen vessel" in Scott's *Waverley.*

Gowlee (*Indian*). A "cow-herd." One of the Hindu castes is so called.

Gown. *Gown and town row.* A scrimmage between the students of different colleges, on one side, and the townsmen, on the other. These feuds go back to the reign of King John, when 3,000 students left Oxford for Reading, owing to a quarrel with the men of the town. What little now remains of this "ancient tenure" is confined, as far as the town is concerned, to the bargees and their "tails."

Gownsman. A student at one of the universities; so called because he wears an academical gown.

Graal. (*See* GRAIL.)

Grab. To clutch or seize. *I grabbed it; he grabbed him, i.e.* the bailiff caught him. (Swedish, *grabba*, to grasp; Danish, *griber*; our *grip, gripe, grope, grapple.*)

A land grabber. A very common expression in Ireland during the last two decades of the nineteenth century, to signify one who takes the farm or land of an evicted tenant.

Grace. *The sister Graces.* The Romans said there were three sister Graces, bosom friends of the Muses. They are represented as embracing each other,

to show that where one is the other is welcome. Their names are Aglœa, Thalïa, and Euphrosÿnē.

Grace's Card or **Grace-card.** The six of hearts is so called in Kilkenny. At the Revolution in 1688, one of the family of Grace, of Courtstown, in Ireland, equipped at his own expense a regiment of foot and troop of horse, in the service of King James. William of Orange promised him high honours if he would join the new party, but the indignant baron wrote on a card, "Tell your master I despise his offer." The card was the six of hearts, and hence the name.

‡ It was a common practice till quite modern times to utilise playing-cards for directions, orders, and addresses.

Grace Cup or *Loving Cup.* The larger tankard passed round the table after grace. It is still seen at the Lord Mayor's feasts, at college, and occasionally in private banquets.

‡ The proper way of drinking the cup observed at the Lord Mayor's banquet or City companies' is to have a silver bowl with two handles and a napkin. Two persons stand up, one to drink and the other to defend the drinker. Having taken his draught, he wipes the cup with the napkin, and passes it to his "defender," when the next person rises to defend the new drinker. And so on to the end.

Grace Darling, daughter of William Darling, lighthouse-keeper on Longstone, one of the Farne Islands. On the morning of the 7th September, 1838, Grace and her father saved nine of the crew of the *Forfarshire* steamer, wrecked among the Farne Isles, opposite Bamborough Castle (1815-1842). Wordsworth has a poem on the subject.

The Grace Darling of America. Ida Lewis (afterwards Mrs. W. H. Wilson, of Black Rock, Connecticut). Her father kept the Limerock lighthouse in Newport harbour. At the age of eighteen she saved four young men whose boat had upset in the harbour. A little later she saved the life of a drunken sailor whose boat had sunk. In 1867 she rescued three men; and in 1868 a small boy who had clung to the mast of a sailboat from midnight till morning. In 1869 she and her brother Hosea rescued two sailors whose boat had capsized in a squall. Soon after this she married, and her career at the lighthouse ended. (Born 1841.)

Grace Days or *Days of Grace*. The three days over and above the time stated in a commercial bill. Thus, if a bill is drawn on the 20th June, and is payable in one month, it ought to be due on the 20th of July, but three days of grace are to be added, bringing the date to the 23rd of July.

Gracechurch (London) is Græs-church, or Grass-church, the church built on the site of the old grass-market. Grass at one time included all sorts of herbs.

Graceless Florin. The first issue of the English florins, so called because the letters D.G. ("by God's grace") were omitted for want of room. It happened that Richard Lalor Sheil, the master of the Mint, was a Catholic, and a scandal was raised that the omission was made on religious grounds. The florins were called in and re-cast. (*See* GODLESS FLORIN.)

.: Mr. Sheil was appointed by the Whig ministry Master of the Mint in 1846; he issued the florin in 1849; was removed in 1850, and died at Florence in 1851, aged nearly 57.

Gracio'sa. A princess beloved by Porciuot, who thwarts the malicious schemes of Grognon, her stepmother. (*A fairy tale.*)

Gracio'so. The interlocutor in the Spanish *drame romantique*. He thrusts himself forward on all occasions, ever and anon directing his gibes to the audience.

Gradas'so. A bully; so called from Gradasso, King of Serica'na, called by Ariosto "the bravest of the Pagan knights." He went against Charlemagne with 100,000 vassals in his train, all "discrowned kings," who never addressed him but on their knees. (*Orlando Furioso* and *Orlando Innamorato*.)

Gradely. A north of England term meaning thoroughly; regularly; as *Behave yourself gradely. A gradely fine day.*

"Sammy 'll fettle him graidely."—*Mrs. H. Burnett: That Lass o'Lowrie's*, chap. ii.

Grad'grind (*Thomas*). A man who measures everything with rule and compass, allows nothing for the weakness of human nature, and deals with men and women as a mathematician with his figures. He shows that *summum jus* is *suprema injuria*. (*Dickens: Hard Times.*)

"The gradgrinds undervalue and disparage it." —*Church Review.*

Græmes (*The*). A class of freebooters, who inhabited the debatable land, and were transported to Ireland at the beginning of the seventeenth century.

Graham. A charlatan who gave indecent and blasphemous addresses in the "Great Apollo Room," Adelphi. He sometimes made mesmerism a medium of pandering to the prurient taste of his audience.

Grahame's Dyke. The Roman wall between the friths of the Clyde and Forth, so called from the first person who leaped over it after the Romans left Britain.

"This wall defended the Britons for a time, but the Scots and Picts assembled themselves in great numbers, and climbed over it .... A man named Grahame is said to have been the first soldier who got over, and the common people still call the remains of the wall 'Grahame's Dike.'"—*Sir Walter Scott: Tales of a Grandfather.*

Grail (*The Holy*). In French, *San Graal*. This must not be confounded with the *san-greal* or *sang-real*, for the two are totally distinct. The "Grail" is either the paten or dish which held the paschal lamb eaten by Christ and His apostles at the last supper, or the cup which He said contained the blood of the New Testament. Joseph of Arimathæa, according to legend, preserved this cup, and received into it some of the blood of Jesus at the crucifixion. He brought it to England, but it disappeared. The quest of the Holy Grail is the fertile source of the adventures of the Knights of the Round Table. In some of the tales it is evidently the cup, in others it is the paten or dish (French, *grasal*, the sacramental cup). Sir Galahad discovered it and died; but each of the 150 knights of King Arthur caught sight of it; but, unless pure of heart and holy in conduct, the grail, though seen, suddenly disappeared. (*See* GREAL and GALAHAD.)

Grain. *A knave in grain.* A knave, though a rich man, or magnate. Grain means scarlet (Latin, *granum*, the coccus, or scarlet dye).

"A military vest of purple flowed
  Livelier than Melibœ'an [Thessalian], or the grain
Of Sarra [Tyre] worn by kings and heroes old
In time of truce."
          Paradise Lost, xi. 241-244.

Rogue in grain. A punning application of the above phrase to millers.

To go against the grain. Against one's inclination. The allusion is to wood, which cannot be easily planed the wrong way of the grain.

With a grain of salt. Latin, "*Cum grano salis,*" with great reservation. The French phrase has another meaning —thus, "*Il le mangerait avec un grain de sel*" means, he could double up such a little whipper-snapper as easily as one could swallow a grain of salt. In the Latin phrase *cum* does not mean "with" or "together with," but it adverbialises the noun, as *cum fide,* faithfully, *cum silentio,* silently, *cum lætitia,* joyfully, *cum grano,* minutely ("*cum grano salis,*" in the minute manner that one takes salt).

Gramercy. Thank you much (the French *grand merci*). Thus Shakespeare, "Be it so, Titus, and gramercy too" (*Titus Andronicus,* i. 2). Again, "Gramercies, Tranio, well dost thou advise" (*Taming of the Shrew,* i. 1). When Gobbo says to Bassanio, "God bless your worship!" he replies, "Gramercy. Wouldst thou aught with me?" (*Merchant of Venice,* ii. 2.)

Grammar. Zenod'otos invented the terms singular, plural, and dual.

The scholars of Alexandria and of the rival academy of Per'gamos were the first to distinguish language into parts of speech, and to give technical terms to the various functions of words.

The first Greek grammar was by Dionysios Thrax, and it is still extant. He was a pupil of Aristarchos.

Julius Cæsar was the inventor of the term *ablative case.*

English grammar is the most philosophical ever devised ; and if the first and third personal pronouns, the relative pronoun, the 3rd person singular of the present indicative of verbs, and the verb "to be" could be reformed, it would be as near perfection as possible.

✠ It was Kaiser Sigismund who stumbled into a wrong gender, and when told of it replied, "*Ego sum Imperator Romanorum, et supra grammaticam*" (1520, 1548-1572).

Grammarians. *Prince of Grammarians.* Apollo'nios of Alexandria, called by Priscian *Grammatico'rum princeps* (second century B.C.).

Grammont. *The Count de Grammont's short memory.* When the Count left England he was followed by the brothers of La Belle Hamilton, who, with drawn swords, asked him if he had not forgotten something. "True, true," said the Count; "I promised to marry your sister," and instantly went back to repair the lapse by making the young lady Countess of Grammont.

Granary of Europe. So Sicily used to be called.

Granby. *The Marquis of Granby.* A public-house sign in honour of John Manners, Marquis of Granby, a popular English general (1721-1770).

The Times says the old marquis owes his sign-board notoriety "partly to his personal bravery and partly to the baldness of his head. He still presides over eighteen public-houses in London alone."

Old Weller, in *Pickwick,* married the hostess of the "Marquis of Granby" at Dorking.

Grand (French).

Le Grand Corneille. Corneille, the French dramatist (1606-1684).

Le Grand Dauph'in. Louis, son of Louis XIV. (1661-1711).

La Grande Mademoiselle. The Duchesse de Montpensier, daughter of Gaston, Duc d'Orléans, and cousin of Louis XIV.

Le Grand Monarque. Louis XIV., also called "The Baboon" (1638, 1643-1715).

Le Grand Pan. Voltaire (1696-1778).

Monsieur le Grand. The Grand Equerry of France in the reign of Louis XIV., etc.

Grandee. In Spain, a nobleman of the highest rank, who has the privilege of remaining covered in the king's presence.

Grand Alliance. Signed May 12th, 1689, between England, Germany, and the States General, subsequently also by Spain and Savoy, to prevent the union of France and Spain.

Grand Lama. The object of worship in Thibet and Mongolia. The word lama in the Tangutanese dialect means "mother of souls." It is the representative of the Shigemooni, the highest god.

Grande Passion (*The*). Love.

"This is scarcely sufficient .... to supply the element .... so indispensable to the existence of a *grande* passion."—*Nineteenth Century* (February, 1892. p. 210).

Grandison (*Sir Charles*). The union of a Christian and a gentleman. Richardson's novel so called. Sir Walter Scott calls Sir Charles "the faultless monster that the world ne'er saw." Robert Nelson, reputed author of the *Whole Duty of Man,* was the prototype.

Grandison Cromwell Lafayette. Grandison Cromwell was the witty nickname given by Mirabeau to Lafayette, meaning thereby that he had all the ambition of a Cromwell in his heart, but wanted to appear before men as a Sir Charles Grandison.

Grandmother. *My grandmother's review*, the *British Review*. Lord Byron said, in a sort of jest, "I bribed *my grandmother's review*." The editor of the *British* called him to account, and this gave the poet a fine opportunity of pointing the battery of his satire against the periodical. (*Don Juan.*)

Granë (1 syl.). To strangle, throttle (Anglo-Saxon, *gryn*).

Grange. Properly the *granum* (granary) or farm of a monastery, where the corn was kept in store. In Lincolnshire and other northern counties any lone farm is so called.
Mariana, of the Moated Grange, is the title of a poem by Tennyson, suggested by the character of Mariana in Shakespeare's *Measure for Measure*.
☞ Houses attached to monasteries where rent was paid in grain were also called granges.

"Till thou return, the Court I will exchange
For some poor cottage, or some country grange."
Drayton: Lady Geraldine to Earl of Surrey.

Grangerise. *Having obtained a copy of the poet's works, he proceeded at once to Grangerise them.* Grangerisation is the addition of all sorts of things directly and indirectly bearing on the book in question, illustrating it, connected with it or its author, or even the author's family and correspondents. It includes autograph letters, caricatures, prints, broadsheets, biographical sketches, anecdotes, scandals, press notices, parallel passages, and any other sort of matter which can be got together as an olla podrida for the matter in hand. The word is from the Rev. J. Granger (1710-1776). Pronounce *Grain-jer-ise*. (*See* Bowdlerise.) There are also Grangerist, Grangerism, Grangerisation, etc.

Grangousier (4 syl.). King of Uto'pia, who married, in "the vigour of his old age," Gargamelle, daughter of the king of the Parpaillons, and became the father of Gargantua, the giant. He is described as a man in his dotage, whose delight was to draw scratches on the hearth with a burnt stick while watching the broiling of his chestnuts. When told of the invasion of Picrochole, King of Lerné, he exclaimed, "Alas! alas! do I dream? Can it be true?" and began calling on all the saints of the calendar. He then sent to expostulate with Picrochole, and, seeing this would not do, tried what bribes by way of reparation would effect. In the meantime he sent to Paris for his son, who soon came to his rescue, utterly defeated Picrochole, and put his army to full rout. Some say he is meant for Louis XII., but this is most improbable, not only because there is very little resemblance between the two, but because he was king of Utopia, some considerable distance from Paris. Motteux thinks the academy figure of this old Priam was John d'Albret, King of Navarre. He certainly was no true Catholic, for he says in chap. xlv. they called him a heretic for declaiming against the saints. (*Rabelais: Gargantua*, i. 3.)

Grani (2 syl.). Siegfried's horse, whose swiftness exceeded that of the winds. (*See* Horse.)

Granite City (*The*). Aberdeen.

Granite Redoubt (*The*). The grenadiers of the Consular Guard were so called at the battle of Marengo in 1800, because when the French had given way they formed into a square, stood like flints against the Austrians, and stopped all further advance.

Granite State (*The*). New Hampshire is so called, because the mountain parts are chiefly granite.

Grantorto. A giant who withheld the inheritance of Ire'na (*Ireland*). He is meant for the genius of the Irish rebellion of 1580, slain by Sir Art'egal. (*Spenser: Faërie Queene*, v.) (*See* Giants.)

Grapes. *The grapes are sour.* You disparage it because it is beyond your reach. The allusion is to the well-known fable of the fox, which tried in vain to get at some grapes, but when he found they were beyond his reach went away saying, "I see they are sour."
Wild grapes. What has been translated "wild grapes" (Isaiah v. 2-4) the Arabs call "wolf-grapes." It is the fruit of the deadly nightshade, which is black and shining. This plant is very common in the vineyards of Palestine.

Grass. *Gone to grass.* Dead. The allusion is to the grass which grows over the dead. Also, "Gone to rusticate," the allusion being to a horse which is sent to grass when unfit for work.
Not to let the grass grow under one's feet. To be very active and energetic.
"Captain Cuttle held on at a great pace, and allowed no grass to grow under his feet."—
Dickens: Dombey and Son.

18

To give grass. To confess yourself vanquished.

To be knocked down in a pugilistic encounter is to "go to grass;" to have the sack is also to go to grass, as a cow which is no longer fit for milking is sent to pasture.

A grass-hand is a compositor who fills a temporary vacancy.

Grass Widow was anciently an unmarried woman who has had a child, but now the word is used for a wife temporarily parted from her husband. The word means a *grace* widow, a widow by courtesy. (In French, *veuve de grace;* in Latin, *viduca de gratia;* a woman divorced or separated from her husband by a dispensation of the Pope, and not by death; hence, a woman temporally separated from her husband.)

"Grace-widow ('grass-widow') is a term for one who becomes a widow by grace or favour, not of necessity, as by death. The term originated in the earlier ages of European civilisation, when divorces were granted [only] by authority of the Catholic Church."—*Indianopolis News* (1876).

✶ The subjoined explanation of the term may be added in a book of "Phrase and Fable."

During the gold mania in California a man would not unfrequently put his wife and children to board with some family while he went to the "diggins." This he called "putting his wife to grass," as we put a horse to grass when not wanted or unfit for work.

Grasshopper, as the sign of a grocer, is the crest of Sir Thomas Gresham, the merchant grocer. The Royal Gresham Exchange used to be profusely decorated with grasshoppers, and the brass one on the eastern part of the present edifice is the one which escaped the fires of 1666 and 1838.

✶ There is a tale that Sir Thomas was a foundling, and that a woman, attracted by the chirping of a grasshopper, discovered the outcast and brought him up. Except as a tale, this solution of the combination is worthless. *Gres* = grass (Anglo-Saxon, *græs*), and no doubt grasshopper is an heraldic rebus on the name. Puns and rebuses were at one time common enough in heraldry, and often very far-fetched.

Grasshopper (*The*). A compound of seven animals. (Anglo-Saxon, *græs-hoppa*.)

"It has the head of a horse, the neck of an ox, the wings of a dragon, the feet of a camel, the tail of a serpent, the horns of a stag, and the body of a scorpion."—*Caylus : Oriental Tales (The Four Talisman*).

Grassmarket. At one time the place of execution in Edinburgh.

"I like nane o' your sermons that end in a psalm at the Grassmarket."—*Sir Walter Scott: Old Mortality*, chap. xxxv.

Grassum or **Gersome.** A fine in money paid by a lessee either on taking possession of his lease or on renewing it. (Anglo-Saxon, *gærsum*, a treasure.)

Gratia′no. Brother of the Venetian senator, Brabantio. (*Shakespeare : Othello*.)

Also a character in *The Merchant of Venice*, who "talks an infinite deal of nothing, more than any man in all Venice." He is one of Bassanio's friends, and when the latter marries Portia, Gratiano marries Nerissa, Portia's maid.

Grave. *To carry away the meal from the grave.* The Greeks and Persians used to make feasts at certain seasons (when the dead were supposed to return to their graves), and leave the fragments of their banquets on the tombs (*Eleemos′ynam sepul′cri pat′ris*).

With one foot in the grave. At the very verge of death. The expression was used by Julian, who said he would "learn something even if he had one foot in the grave." The parallel Greek phrase is, "With one foot in the ferry-boat," meaning Charon's.

Grave. Solemn, sedate, and serious in look and manner. This is the Latin *gravis*, grave; but "grave," a place of interment, is the Anglo-Saxon *græf*, a pit; verb, *graf-an*, to dig.

More grave than wise. "*Tertius e cælo cecidit Cato.*"

Grave-diggers (*Hamlet*). "If the water come to the man . . ." The legal case referred to by Shakespeare occurred in the fifth year of Queen Elizabeth's reign, called Hales *v.* Petit, stated at length in *Notes and Queries*, vol. viii. p. 123 (first series).

Grave Maurice. A public-house sign. The head of the [Graf Moritz], Prince of Orange, and Captain-General of the United Provinces (1567-1625). (*Hotten : Book of Signs.*)

Grave Searchers. Monkir and Nakir, so called by the Mahometans. (*Ockley*, vol. ii.) (*See* MONKIR.)

Grave as a Judge. Sedate and serious in look and manner.

Grave as an Owl. Having an aspect of solemnity and wisdom,

Gravelled. *I'm regularly gravelled.* Non-plussed, like a ship run aground and unable to move.

"When you were gravelled for lack of matter."
—*Shakespeare: As You Like It*, iv. 1.

Gray. The authoress of *Auld Robin Gray* was Lady Anne Lindsay, afterwards Lady Barnard (1750-1825).

Gray Cloak. An alderman above the chair; so called because his proper costume is a cloak furred with gray amis. (*Hutton: New View of London*, intro.)

Gray Man's Path. A singular fissure in the greenstone precipice near Ballycastle, in Ireland.

Gray's Inn (London) was the inn or mansion of the Lords Gray.

Grayham's. (*See* GRAHAME'S DYKE.)

Graysteel. The sword of Kol, fatal to the owner. It passed to several hands, but always brought ill-luck. (*Icelandic Edda*.) (*See* FATAL GIFTS; SWORDS.)

Greal (*San*). Properly divided, it is *sang-real*, the real blood of Christ, or the wine used in the last supper, which Christ said was "His blood of the New Testament, shed for the remission of sin." According to tradition, a part of this wine-blood was preserved by Joseph of Arimathæa, in the cup called the Saint Graal. When Merlin made the Round Table, he left a place for the Holy Graal. (Latin, *Sang*[uis] *Reāl*[is].) (*See* GRAAL.)

Grease One's Fist or **Palm** (*To*). To give a bribe.

"Grease my fist with a tester or two, and ye shall find it in your pennyworths."—*Quarles: The Virgin Widow*, iv. 1, p. 40.

"*S.* You must oyl it first.
C. I understand you—
Greaze him i' the fist."
      Cartwright: Ordinary (1651).

Greasy Sunday. *Dominica carnelevale* —*i.e.* Quinquagesima Sunday. (*See* Du Cange, vol. iii. p. 196, col. 2.)

Great (*The*).

ABBAS I., Shah of Persia. (1557, 1585-1628.)
ALBERTUS MAGNUS, the schoolman. (1193-1280.)
ALFONSO III., King of Asturias and Leon. (848, 866-912.)
ALFRED, of England. (849, 871-901.)
ALEXANDER, of Macedon. (B.C. 356, 340-323.)
ST. BASIL, Bishop of Cæsare'a. (329-379.)
CANUTE, of England and Denmark. (995, 1014-1036.)
CASIMIR III., of Poland. (1309, 1333-1370.)
CHARLES I., Emperor of Germany, called *Charlemagne*. (742, 764-814.)
CHARLES III. (or II.), Duke of Lorraine. (1543-1608.)
CHARLES EMMANUEL I., Duke of Savoy. (1562-1630.)
CONSTANTINE I., Emperor of Rome. (272, 306-337.)
COUPERIN, (*Francis*), the French musical composer. (1668-1733.)

DOUGLAS, (*Archibald, the great Earl of Angus*, also called *Bell-the-Cat* [*q.v.*]). (Died 1514.)
FERDINAND I., of Castile and Leon. (Reigned 1034-1065.)
FREDERICK WILLIAM, Elector of Brandenburg, surnamed *The Great Elector*. (1620, 1640-1688.)
FREDERICK II., of Prussia. (1712, 1740-1786.)
GREGORY I., Pope. (544, 590-604.)
HENRI IV., of France. (1553, 1589-1610.)
HEROD AGRIPPA I., Tetrarch of Abile'nē, who beheaded James (Acts xii.). (Died A.D. 44.)
HIAO-WEN-TEE, the sovereign of the Hân dynasty of China. He forbade the use of gold and silver vessels in the palace, and appropriated the money which they fetched to the aged poor. (B.C. 206, 179-157.)
JOHN II., of Portugal. (1455, 1481-1495.)
JUSTINIAN I. (483, 527-565.)
LEWIS I., of Hungary. (1326, 1342-1381.)
LOUIS II., Prince of Condé, Duc d'Enghien. (1621-1686.)
LOUIS XIV., called *Le Grand Monarque.* (1638, 1643-1714.)
MAHOMET II., Sultan of the Turks. (1430, 1451-1481.)
MAXIMILIAN, Duke of Bavaria, victor of Prague. (1573-1651.)
COSMO DI' MEDICI, first Grand Duke of Tuscany. (1519, 1537-1574.)
GONZALES PEDRO DE MENDOZA, *great Cardinal of Spain*, statesman and scholar. (1503-1575.)
NICHOLAS I., Pope (was Pope from 858-867.)
OTHO I., Emperor of Germany. (912, 936-973.)
PETER I., of Russia. (1672, 1689-1725.)
PIERRE III., of Aragon. (1239, 1276-1285.)
SFORZA (*Giacomo*), the Italian general. (1369-1424.)
SAPOR or SHAH-POUR, the ninth king of the Sassan'idēs (*q.v.*). (240, 307-379.)
SIGISMUND, King of Poland. (1466, 1506-1548.)
THEO'DORIC, King of the Ostrogoths. (454, 475-526.)
THEODO'SIUS I., Emperor. (346, 378-395.)
MATTEO VISCONTI, Lord of Milan. (1250, 1295-1322.)
VLADIMIR, Grand Duke of Russia. (973-1014.)
WALDEMAR I., of Denmark. (1131, 1157-1181.)

Great Bullet-head. George Cadoudal, leader of the *Chouans*, born at Brech, in Mor'bihan. (1769-1804.)

Great Captain. (*See* CAPTAIN.)

Great Cham of Literature. So Smollett calls Dr. Johnson. (1709-1784.)

Great Commoner (*The*). William Pitt (1759-1806).

Great Cry and Little Wool. Much ado about nothing. (*See* CRY.)

Great Dauphin. (*See* GRAND.)

Great Elector (*The*). Frederick William, Elector of Brandenburg (1620, 1640-1688).

Great Go. A familiar term for a university examination for degrees: the "previous examination" being the "Little Go."

"Great Go" is usually shortened into "Greats."

"Since I have been reading . . . for my greats, I have had to go into all sorts of deep books."—*Grant Allen: The Backslider*, part iii.

Great Harry (*The*). A man-of-war built by Henry VII., the first of any size constructed in England. It was burnt in 1553. (*See* HENRY GRACE DE DIEU.)

Great Head. Malcolm III., of Scotland; also called *Canmore*, which means the same thing. (Reigned 1057-1093.)

"Malcolm III., called Canmore or Great Head."
—*Sir W. Scott : Tales of a Grandfather*, i. 4.

Great Men (*Social status of*).

ÆSOP, a manumitted slave.
ARKWRIGHT (*Sir Richard*), a barber.
BEACONSFIELD (*Lord*), a solicitor's clerk.
BLOOMFIELD, a cobbler, son of a tailor.
BUNYAN, a travelling tinker.
BURNS, a gauger, son of a ploughman.
CÆDMON, a cowherd.
CERVANTES, a common soldier.
CLARE, a ploughman, son of a farm labourer.
CLAUDE LORRAINE, a pastrycook.
COLUMBUS, son of a weaver.
COOK (*Captain*), son of a husbandman.
CROMWELL, son of a brewer.
CUNNINGHAM (*Allan*), a stonemason, son of a peasant.
DEFOE, a hosier, son of a butcher.
DEMOSTHENES, son of a cutler.
DICKENS, a, newspaper reporter ; father the same.
ELDON (*Lord*), son of a coal-broker.
FARADAY (*Michael*), a bookbinder.
FERGUSON (*James*), the astronomer, son of a day-labourer.
FRANKLIN, a journeyman printer, son of a tallow-chandler.
HARGREAVES, the machinist, a poor weaver.
HOGG, a shepherd, son of a Scotch peasant.
HOMER, a farmer's son (said to have begged his bread).
HORACE, son of a manumitted slave.
HOWARD (*John*), a grocer's apprentice, son of a tradesman.
KEAN (*Edmund*), son of a stage-carpenter in a minor theatre.
JONSON (*Ben*), a bricklayer.
LATIMER, Bishop of Worcester, son of a small farmer.
LUCIAN, a sculptor, son of a poor tradesman.
MONK (*General*), a volunteer.
OPIE (*John*), son of a poor carpenter in Cornwall.
PAINE (*Thomas*), a stay-maker, son of a Quaker.
PORSON (*Richard*), son of a parish clerk in Norfolk.
RICHARDSON, a bookseller and printer, son of a joiner.
SHAKESPEARE, son of a wool-stapler.
STEPHENSON (*George*), son of a fireman at a colliery.
VIRGIL, son of a porter.
WATT (*James*), improver of the steam engine, son of a block-maker.
WASHINGTON, a farmer.
WOLSEY, son of a butcher.
∴ And hundreds more.

Great Men (*Wives of*). (*See under* WIVES.)

Great Mogul. The title of the chief of the Mogul Empire, which came to an end in 1806.

Great Mother. The earth. When Junius Brutus and the sons of Tarquin asked the Delphic Oracle who was to succeed Superbus on the throne of Rome, they received for answer, "He who shall first kiss his mother." While the two princes hastened home to fulfil what they thought was meant, Brutus fell to the earth, and exclaimed, "Thus kiss I thee, O earth, the great mother of us all."

Great Perhaps (*The*). So Rabelais (1485-1553) described a future state.

Great Scott or **Scot!** A mitigated form of oath. The initial letter of the German *Gott* is changed into *Sc.*

"'Great Scott!... Beg pardon!' ejaculated Silas,' astounded."—*A. C. Gunter : Baron Montez*, book iv. chap. xix.

Great Sea (*The*). So the Mediterranean Sea was called by the ancient Greeks and Romans.

Great Unknown (*The*). Sir Walter Scott, who published the *Waverley Novels* anonymously. (1771-1832.)

Great Unwashed (*The*). The artisan class. Burke first used the compound, but Sir Walter Scott popularised it.

Great Wits Jump. Think alike; tally. Thus Shakespeare says, "It jumps with my humour." (1 *Henry IV.*, iv. 2.)

Great Wits to Madness nearly are Allied. (*Pope.*) Seneca says, "*Nullum magnum ingenium absque mixtura dementiæ est.*"

Greatest. *The greatest happiness of the greatest number.* Jeremy Bentham's political axiom. (*Liberty of the People.*) (1821.)

Greatheart (*Mr.*). The guide of Christiana and her family to the Celestial City. (*Bunyan : Pilgrim's Progress*, ii.)

Greaves (*Sir Launcelot*). A sort of Don Quixote, who, in the reign of George II., wandered over England to redress wrongs, discourage moral evils not recognisable by law, degrade immodesty, punish ingratitude, and reform society. His Sancho Panza was an old sea captain. (*Smollett : Adventures of Sir Launcelot Greaves.*)

Grebenski Cossacks. So called from the word *greben* (a comb). This title was conferred upon them by Czar Ivan I., because, in his campaign against the Tartars of the Caucasus, they scaled a mountain fortified with sharp spurs, sloping down from its summit, and projecting horizontally, like a comb. (*Duncan : Russia.*)

Grecian Bend (*The*). An affectation in walking assumed by English ladies in 1875. The silliness spread to America and other countries which affect passing oddities of fashion.

Grecian Coffee-house, in Devereux Court, the oldest in London, was originally opened by Pasqua, a Greek slave, brought to England in 1652 by Daniel

Edwards, a Turkey merchant. This Greek was the first to teach the method of roasting coffee, to introduce the drink into the island, and to call himself a "coffee-man."

Grecian Stairs. A corruption of *greesing stairs.* Greesings (steps) still survives in the architectural word *grees,* and in the compound word *de-grees.* There is still on the hill at Lincoln a flight of stone steps called "*Grecian stairs.*"

"Paul stood on the greezen [*i.e.* stairs]."— *Wicliffe:* Acts xxi. 40.

Greedy (*Justice*). In *A New Way to Pay Old Debts,* by Massinger.

Greegrees. Charms. (*African superstition.*)
A gree-gree man. One who sells charms.

Greek (*The*). Manuel Alva′rez (*el Griego*), the Spanish sculptor (1727-1797).
All Greek to me. Quite unintelligible; an unknown tongue or language. Casca says, "For mine own part, it was all Greek to me." (*Shakespeare: Julius Cæsar,* i. 2.) "*C'est du Grec pour moi.*"
Last of the Greeks. Philopœ′men, of Megalop′olis, whose great object was to infuse into the Achæans a military spirit, and establish their independence (B.C. 252-183).
To play the Greek (Latin, *græcari*). To indulge in one's cups. The Greeks have always been considered a luxurious race, fond of creature-comforts. Thus Cicero, in his oration against "Verres," says: "*Discum′bitur; fit sermo inter eos et invitu′tio, ut Græco more bibere′tur: hospes horta′tur, poscunt majo′ribus poc′ulis; celebra′tur omnium sermo′ne lætitiaque conviv′ium.*" The law in Greek banquets was *E pithi e apithi* (Quaff, or be off!) (Cut in, or cut off!). In *Troilus and Cressida* Shakespeare makes Pan′darus, bantering Helen for her love to Tro′ilus, say, "I think Helen loves him better than Paris;" to which Cressida, whose wit is to parry and pervert, replies, "Then she's a merry Greek indeed," insinuating that she was a "woman of pleasure." (*Troilus and Cressida,* i. 2.)
Un Grec (French). A cheat. Towards the close of the reign of Louis XIV., a knight of Greek origin, named Apoulos, was caught in the very act of cheating at play, even in the palace of the *grand monarque.* He was sent to the galleys, and the nation which gave him birth

became from that time a byword for swindler and blackleg.
Un potage à la Grecque. Insipid soup; Spartan broth.
When Greek joins Greek, then is the tug of war. When two men or armies of undoubted courage fight, the contest will be very severe. The line is from a verse in the drama of *Alexander the Great,* slightly altered, and the reference is to the obstinate resistance of the Greek cities to Philip and Alexander, the Macedonian kings.

"When Greeks joined Greeks, then was the tug of war." *Nathaniel Lee.*

In French the word "*Grec*" sometimes means *wisdom,* as—
Il est Grec en cela. He has great talent that way.
Il n'est pas grand Grec. He is no great conjurer.

Greek Calends. Never. To defer anything to the Greek Calends is to defer it *sine die.* There were no calends in the Greek months. The Romans used to pay rents, taxes, bills, etc., on the calends, and to defer paying them to the "Greek Calends" was virtually to repudiate them. (*See* NEVER.)

"Will you speak of your paltry prose doings in my presence, whose great historical poem, in twenty books, with notes in proportion, has been postponed 'ad Græcas Kalendas'?"—*Sir W. Scott: The Betrothed* (Introduction).

Greek Church includes the church within the Ottoman Empire subject to the patriarch of Constantinople, the church in the kingdom of Greece, and the Russo-Greek Church. The Roman and Greek Churches formally separated in 1054. The Greek Church dissents from the doctrine that the Holy Ghost proceeds from the Father and the Son (*Filioque*), rejects the Papal claim to supremacy, and administers the eucharist in both kinds to the laity; but the two churches agree in their belief of seven sacraments, transubstantiation, the adoration of the Host, confession, absolution, penance, prayers for the dead, etc.

Greek Commentator. Fernan Nunen de Guzman, the great promoter of Greek literature in Spain. (1470-1553.)

Greek Cross. Same shape as St. George's cross (+). The Latin cross has the upright one-third longer than the cross-beam (†).
St. George's Cross is seen on our banners, where the crosses of St. Andrew and St. Patrick are combined with it. (*See* UNION JACK.)

Greek Fire. A composition of nitre, sulphur, and naphtha. Tow steeped in the mixture was hurled in a blazing state through tubes, or tied to arrows. The invention is ascribed to Callini'cos, of Heliop'olis, A.D. 668.

A very similar projectile was used by the Federals in the great American contest, especially at the seige of Charleston.

Greek Gift (*A*). A treacherous gift. The reference is to the Wooden Horse said to be a gift or offering to the gods for a safe return from Troy, but in reality a ruse for the destruction of the city. (*See* FATAL GIFTS.)

"Timeo Danaos et dona ferentes."
Virgil: Æneid, ii. 49.

Greek Life. A sound mind in a sound body. "*Mens sana in corpore sano.*"

"This healthy life, which was the Greek life, came from keeping the body in good tune."—*Daily Telegraph.*

Greek Trust. No trust at all. "*Græca fides*" was with the Romans no faith at all. A Greek, in English slang, means a cheat or sharper, and Greek bonds are sadly in character with *Græca fides.*

Greeks in the New Testament mean Hellenists, or naturalised Jews in foreign countries; those not naturalised were called Aramæan Jews in Syria, Mesopotamia, and Palestine.

"I will praise God that our family has ever remained Aramæan ; not one among us has ever gone over to the Hellenists."—*Eldad the Pilgrim,* chap. ii.

Green. Young, fresh, as *green cheese, i.e.* cream cheese, which is eaten fresh ; *green goose,* a young or midsummer goose.

"If you would fat green geese, shut them up when they are about a month old."—*Mortimer: Husbandry.*

Immature in age or judgment, inexperienced, young.

"The text is old, the orator too green."
Shakespeare: Venus and Adonis, 806.

Simple, raw, easily imposed upon ; a greenhorn (q.v.).

"'He is so jolly green,' said Charley."—*Dickens: Oliver Twist,* chap. ix.

Green. The imperial green of France was the old Merovin'gian colour restored, and the golden bees are the ornaments found on the tomb of Childeric, the father of Clovis, in 1653. The imperial colour of the Aztecs was green ; the national banner of Ireland is green ; the field of many American flags is green, as their Union Jack, and the flags of the admiral, vice-admiral, rear-admiral, and commodore ; and that of the Chinese militia is green.

Green is held unlucky to particular clans and counties of Scotland. The Caithness men look on it as fatal, because their bands were clad in green at the battle of Flodden. It is disliked by all who bear the name of Ogilvy, and is especially unlucky to the Grahame clan. One day, an aged man of that name was thrown from his horse in a fox chase, and he accounted for the accident from his having a green lash to his riding whip. (*See* KENDAL GREEN.)

⁂ For its symbolism, etc., *see under* COLOURS.

N.B. There are 106 different shades of green. (*See* KENDAL GREEN.)

Green Bag. *What's in the green bag ?* What charge is about to be preferred against me? The allusion is to the "Green Bag Inquiry" (*q.v.*).

Green Bird (*The*) told everything a person wished to know, and talked like an oracle. (*Countess D'Aulnoy : Fair Star and Prince Chery.*)

Green Cloth. *The Board of Green Cloth.* A board connected with the royal household, having power to correct offenders within the verge of the palace and two hundred yards beyond the gates. A warrant from the board must be obtained before a servant of the palace can be arrested for debt. So called "because the committee sit with the steward of the household at a board covered with a green cloth in the counting-house, as recorders and witnesses to the truth." It existed in the reign of Henry I., and probably at a still earlier period.

Green Dogs. Any extinct race, like that of the Dodo. Brederode said to Count Louis: "I would the whole race of bishops and cardinals was extinct, like that of green dogs." (*Motley : Dutch Republic,* part ii. 5.)

Green Dragoons (*The*). The 13th Dragoons (whose regimental facings were green). Now called the 13th Hussars, and the regimental facings have been white since 1861.

Green Glasses. *To look through green glasses.* To feel jealous of one ; to be envious of another's success.

"If we had an average of theatrical talent, we had also our quantum of stage jealousies ; for who looks through his green glasses more peevishly than an actor when his brother Thespian brings down the house with applause."—*C. Thomson: Autobiography,* p. 197.

Green Goose (*A*). A young goose not fully grown.

Green Gown (*A*). A tousel in the new-mown hay. To "give one a green gown" sometimes means to go beyond the bounds of innocent playfulness.

"Had any dared to give her [Narcissa] a green
  gown,
The fair had petrified him with a frown. . . .
Pure as the snow was she, and cold as ice."
  Peter Pindar: Old Simon.

Green Hands (a nautical phrase). Inferior sailors, also called boys. A crew is divided into (1) Able seamen; (2) Ordinary seamen; and (3) Green hands or boys. The term "boys" has no reference to age, but merely skill and knowledge in seamanship. Here "green" means not ripe, not mature.

Green Horse (*The*). The 5th Dragoon Guards; so called because they are a *horse* regiment, and have *green* for their regimental facings. Now called "The Princess Charlotte of Wales's Dragoon Guards."

Tarleton's green horse. That is, the horse of General Tarleton covered with green ribbons and housings, the electioneering colours of the member for Liverpool, which he represented in 1790, 1796, 1802, 1807. His Christian name was Banastre.

Green Howards (*The*). The 19th Foot, named from the Hon. Charles Howard, colonel from 1738 to 1748. Green was the colour of their regimental facings, now white, and the regiment is called "The Princess of Wales's Own."

Green Isle, or *The Emerald Isle*. Ireland; so called from the brilliant green hue of its grass.

Green Knight (*The*). A Pagan, who demanded Fezon in marriage; but, overcome by Orson, resigned his claim. (*Valentine and Orson.*)

Green Labour. The lowest-paid labour in the tailoring trade. Such garments are sold to African gold-diggers and agricultural labourers. Soap and shoddy do more for these garments than cotton or cloth. (*See* GREENER.)

Green Linnets. The 39th Foot, so called from the colour of their facings. Now the Dorsetshire, and the facings are white.

Green Man. This public-house sign represents the gamekeeper, who used at one time to be dressed in green.

"But the 'Green Man' shall I pass by unsung,
  Which mine own James upon his sign-post
  hung?
His sign, his image—for he once was seen
A squire's attendant, clad in keeper's green."
  Crabbe: Borough.

The men who let off fireworks were called *Green-men* in the reign of James I.

"Have you any squibs, any green-man in your shows?"—*The Seven Champions of Christendom.*

Green Room (*The*). The common waiting-room in a theatre for the performers; so called because at one time the walls were coloured green to relieve the eyes affected by the glare of the stage lights.

Green Sea. The Persian Gulf; so called from a remarkable strip of water of a green colour along the Arabian coast.

☞ Between 1690 and 1742 the 2nd Life Guards were facetiously called "The Green Sea" from their sea-green facings, in compliment to Queen Catharine, whose favourite colour it was. The facings of this regiment are now blue.

Green Thursday. Maundy Thursday, the great day of absolution in the Lutheran Church. (German, *Grün-donnerstag*; in Latin, *dies viridium*, Luke xxiii. 31.)

Green Tree. *If they do these things in the green tree, what shall be done in the dry?* (Luke xxiii. 31.) If the righteous can find no justice in man, what must not the unrighteous expect? If innocent men are condemned to death, what hope can the guilty have? If green wood burns so readily, dry wood would burn more freely still.

Green Wax. Estreats delivered to a sheriff out of the Exchequer, under the seal of the court, which is impressed upon green wax, to be levied (7 Henry IV. c. 3). (*Wharton: Law Lexicon.*)

Green as Grass. Applied to those easily gulled, and quite unacquainted with the ways of the world. "Verdant Greens."

Green Bag Inquiry. Certain papers of a seditious character packed in a green bag during the Regency. The contents were laid before Parliament, and the committee advised the suspension of the Habeas Corpus Act (1817).

Green Baize Road (*Gentlemen of the*). Whist players. "Gentlemen of the Green Cloth Road," billiard players. (See *Bleak House*, chap. xxvi. par. 1.) Probably the idea of sharpers is included, as "Gentlemen of the Road" means highwaymen.

Green-Eyed Jealousy or **Green-eyed Monster.** Expressions used by

Shakespeare (*Merchant of Venice*, iii. 2 ; *Othello*, iii. 3). As cats, lions, tigers, and all the green-eyed tribe "mock the meat they feed on," so jealousy mocks its victim by loving and loathing it at the same time.

Green in my Eye. *Do you see any green in the white of my eye* (or *eyes*)? Do I look credulous and easy to be bamboozled? Do I look like a greenhorn? Credulity and wonderment are most pronounced in the eye.

Green Man and Still. This public-house sign refers to the distillation of spirits from green herbs, such as peppermint cordial, and so on. The green man is the herbalist, or the greengrocer of herbs, and the still is the apparatus for distillation.

Green Ribbon Day in Ireland is March 17th, St. Patrick's Day, when the shamrock and green ribbon are worn as the national badge.

Green Sleeves and Pudding Pies. This, like Maggie Lauder, is a scurrilous song, in the time of the Reformation, on the doctrines of the Catholic Church and the Catholic clergy. (*See* "John Anderson, my Jo.")

Greens of Constantinople (*The*). A political party opposed to the *Blues* in the reign of Justinian.

Greenbacks. Bank notes issued by the Government of the United States in 1862, during the Civil War ; so called because the back is printed in green. In March, 1878, the amount of greenbacks for permanent circulation was fixed at 346,681,016 dollars ; in rough numbers, about 70 millions sterling.

Greener. A slang term for a foreigner who begins to learn tailoring or shoemaking on his arrival in England.

Greengage. Introduced into England by the Rev. John Gage from the Chartreuse Monastery, near Paris. Called by the French "Reine Claude," out of compliment to the daughter of Anne de Bretagne and Louis XII., generally called *la bonne reine* (1499-1524).

Greenhorn (*A*). A simpleton, a youngster. French, *Cornichon* (a cornicle or little horn), also a simpleton, a calf.

"Panurge le veau cocquart, cornichon, escorné
... viens ici nous ayder, grand veau plourart," etc."—*Rabelais*, book iv. chap. xxi.

Greenlander. A native of Greenland. Facetiously applied to a greenhorn, that is, one from the verdant country called the land of green ones.

Greenlandman's Galley. The lowest type of profanity and vulgarity.

"In my seafaring days the Greenland sailors were notorious for daring and their disrespect of speech, prefacing or ending every sentence with an oath, or some indecent expression. Even in those days [the first quarter of the nineteenth century] a 'Greenlandman's Galley' was proverbially the lowest in' the scale of vulgarity."—*C. Thomson: Autobiography*, p. 118.

Too low for even a Greenlandman's Galley. One whose ideas of decency were degraded below even that of a Greenland crew.

Greenwich is the Saxon Grenë-wic (green village), formerly called Grenawic, and in old Latin authors "*Grenoviam viridis.*" Some think it is a compound of *grian-wic* (the sun city).

Greenwich Barbers. Retailers of sand ; so called because the inhabitants of Greenwich "shave the pits" in the neighbourhood to supply London with sand.

Greg'arines (3 syl.). In 1867 the women of Europe and America, from the thrones to the maid-servants, adopted the fashion of wearing a pad made of false hair behind their head, utterly destroying its natural proportions. The microscope showed that the hair employed for these "uglies" abounded in a pedic'ulous insect called a greg'arine (or little herding animal), from the Latin *grex* (a herd). The nests on the filaments of hair resemble those of spiders and silkworms, and the "object" used to form one of the exhibits in microscopical *soirées*.

Grego'rian Calendar. One which shows the new and full moon, with the time of Easter and the movable feasts depending thereon. The reformed calendar of the Church of Rome, introduced by Pope Gregory XIII. in 1582, corrected the error of the civil year, according to the Julian calendar.

Grego'rian Chant. So called because it was introduced into the church service by Gregory the Great (600).

Grego'rian Epoch. The epoch or day on which the Gregorian calendar commenced—March, 1582.

Grego'rian Telescope. The first form of the reflecting telescope, invented by James Gregory, professor of mathematics in the university of St. Andrews. (1663.)

Grego'rian Tree. The gallows; so named from three successive hangmen—Gregory, sen., Gregory, jun., and Gregory Brandon. Sir William Segar, Garter Knight of Arms, granted a coat of arms to Gregory Brandon. (*See* HANGMEN.)

", This trembles under the black rod, and he
  Doth fear his fate from the Gregorian tree."
           Mercutius Pragmaticus (1641).

Grego'rian Water or **Gringorian Water.** Holy water; so called because Gregory I. was a most strenuous recommender of it.

"In case they should happen to encounter with devils, by virtue of the Gringoriene water, they might make them disappear."—*Rabelais: Gargantua*, book i. 43.

Grego'rian Year. The civil year, according to the correction introduced by Pope Gregory XIII. in 1582. The equinox which occurred on the 25th of March, in the time of Julius Cæsar, fell on the 11th of March in the year 1582. This was because the Julian calculation of 365¼ days to a year was 11 min. 10 sec. too much. Gregory suppressed ten days, so as to make the equinox fall on the 21st of March, as it did at the Council of Nice, and, by some simple arrangements, prevented the recurrence in future of a similar error.

Greg'ories (3 syl.). Hangmen. (*See* GREGORIAN TREE.)

Gregory (*A*). A school-feast, so called from being held on St. Gregory's Day (March 12th). On this day the pupils at one time brought the master all sorts of eatables, and of course it was a *dies non*, and the master shut his eyes to all sorts of licences. Gregories were not limited to any one country, but were common to all Europe.

Gregory (*St.*). The last Pope who has been canonised. Usually represented with the tiara, pastoral staff, his book of homilies, and a dove. The last is his peculiar attribute.

Gregory Knights or *St. Gregory's Knights.* Harmless blusterers. In Hungary the pupils at their Gregories played at soldiers, marched through the town with flying colours, some on pony back and some on foot; as they went they clattered their toy swords, but of course hurt no one.

Grenade (2 syl.). An explosive shell, weighing from two to six pounds, to be thrown by the hand.

Grenadier' (3 syl.). Originally a soldier employed to throw hand-grenades.

Grenadier Guards. The first regiment of Foot Guards. Noted for their size and height.

Grendel. A superhuman monster slain by Beowulf, in the Anglo-Saxon romance of that title. (See *Turner's abridgement.*)

Gresham College (London). Founded by Sir Thomas Gresham in 1575.

Gresham and the Grasshopper. (*See* GRASSHOPPER.)

Gresham and the Pearl. When Queen Elizabeth visited the Exchange, Sir Thomas Gresham, it is said, pledged her health in a cup of wine containing a precious stone crushed to atoms, and worth £15,000. If this tale is true, it was an exceedingly foolish imitation of Cleopatra (*q.v.*).

" Here fifteen thousand pounds at one clap goes
  Instead of sugar ; Gresham drinks the pearl
  Unto his queen and mistress. Pledge it, lords."
Heywood : If You Know Not Me You Know Nobody.

To dine or *sup with Sir Thomas Gresham.* (*See under* DINE.)

Greta Hall. *The poet of Greta Hall.* Southey, who lived at Greta Hall, in the Vale of Keswick. (1774-1843.)

Gretchen. A pet German diminutive of Margaret.

Greth'el (*Gammer*). The hypothetical narrator of the *Nursery Tales* edited by the brothers Grimm.

Gretna Green Marriages. Runaway matches. In Scotland, all that is required of contracting parties is a mutual declaration before witnesses of their willingness to marry, so that elopers reaching the parish of Graitney, or village of Springfield, could get legally married without either licence, banns, or priest. The declaration was generally made to a blacksmith.

Crabbe has a metrical tale called *Gretna Green*, in which young Belwood elopes with Clara, the daughter of Dr. Sidmere, and gets married; but Belwood was a " screw," and Clara a silly, extravagant hussy, so they soon hated each other and parted. (*Tales of the Hall*, book xv.)

Grève (1 syl.). *Place de Grève.* The Tyburn of ancient Paris. The present Hôtel de Ville occupies part of the site. The word *grève* means the strand of a river or the shore of the sea, and is so

18*

called from *gravier* (gravel or sand).
The Place de Grève was on the bank of
the Seine.

"Who has e'er been to Paris must needs know the
  Grève,
The fatal retreat of th' unfortunate brave,
Where honour and justice most oddly contri-
  bute
To ease Hero's pains by a halter or gibbet."
          Prior: The Thief and the Cordelier.

Grey Friars. Franciscan friars, so
called from their grey habit. Black
friars are Dominicans, and White friars
Carmelites.

Grey Hen (*A*). A stone bottle for
holding liquor. Large and small pewter
pots mixed together are called "hen and
chickens."

"A dirty leather wallet lay near the sleeper,
... also a grey-hen which had contained some
sort of strong liquor."—*Miss Robinson: Whitefriars,* chap. viii.

Grey Mare. *The Grey Mare is the
better horse.* The woman is paramount.
It is said that a man wished to buy a
horse, but his wife took a fancy to a grey
mare, and so pertinaciously insisted that
the grey mare was the better horse, that
the man was obliged to yield the point.

¶ Macaulay says: "I suspect [the
proverb] originated in the preference
generally given to the grey mares of
Flanders over the finest coach-horses of
England."

The French say, when the woman is
paramount, *C'est le mariage d'epervier*
('Tis a hawk's marriage), because the
female hawk is both larger and stronger
than the male bird.

"As long as we have eyes, or hands, or breath,
We'll look, or write, or talk you all to death.
Yield, or she-Pegasus will gain her course,
And the grey mare will prove the better horse."
          Prior: Epilogue to Mrs. Manley's Lucius.

Grey Wethers. These are huge
boulders, either embedded or not, very
common in the "Valley of Stones" near
Avebury, Wilts. When split or broken
up they are called sarsens or sarsdens.

Grey-coat Parson (*A*). An impro-
priator; a tenant who farms the tithes.

Grey from Grief.
Ludovico Sforza became grey in a
single night.
Charles I. grew grey while he was on
his trial.
Marie Antoinette grew grey from grief
during her imprisonment. (*See* GRAY.)

Grey Goose Wing (*The*). "The
grey goose wing was the death of him,"
the arrow which is winged with grey
goose feathers.

Grey Mare's Tail. A cataract that
is made by the stream which issues from

Lochskene, in Scotland, so called from
its appearance.

Grey Washer by the Ford (*The*).
An Irish wraith which seems to be washing clothes in a river, but when the
"doomed man" approaches she holds
up what she seemed to be washing, and
it is the phantom of himself with his
death wounds from which he is about to
suffer. (*Hon. Emily Lawlett: Essex in
Ireland,* p. 245-6.)

Greybeard (*A*). An earthen pot
for holding spirits; a large stone jar.
Also an old man. (cf. BELLARMINE.)

"We will give a cup of distilled waters ...
unto the next pilgrim that comes over; and ye
may keep for the purpose the grunds of the last
greybeard."—*Sir W. Scott: The Monastery,* chap.
ix.

Greycoats. Russian soldiers of the
line, who wear grey coats.

"You might think of him thus calm and collected charging his rifle from one more shot at the
advancing greycoats."— *Besant and Rice: By
Celia's Arbour,* chap. xlv.

Greyhound. "A greyhounde shoulde
be heded like a snake, And neked like a
Drake; Foted like a Kat, Tayled like a
Rat; Syded like a Teme, Chyned like a
Beme." (*Dame Berner.*)

"Syded like a teme," probably means both sides
alike; a plough-team being meant.

Greyhound. A public-house sign,
in honour of Henry VII., whose badge
it was.

Greys. *The Scotch Greys.* The 2nd
(Royal North British) Dragoons, so
called because they are mounted on grey
horses.

Grid'iron. Emblematic of St. Laurence, because in his martyrdom he was
broiled to death on a gridiron. In allusion thereto the church of St. Laurence
Jewry, near Guildhall, has a gilt gridiron for a vane. The gridiron is also an
attribute of St. Faith, who was martyred
like St. Laurence; and St. Vincent, who
was partially roasted on a gridiron
covered with spikes, A.D. 258. (*See*
ESCURIAL.)

It is said that St. Laurence uttered the following doggerel during his martyrdom:
"This side enough is roasted, turn me, tyrant, eat,
And see if raw or roasted I make the better
  meat."

Grief. *To come to grief.* To be
ruined; to fail in business. As lots of
money is the fulness of joy, so the want
of it is the grief of griefs. The Americans call the dollar "almighty."

Grievance-monger. One who is
always raking up or talking about his
own or his party's grievances, public or
private.

Griffen Horse (*The*) belonged to Atlantēs, the magician, but was made use of by Roge'ro, Astolpho, and others. It flew through the air at the bidding of the rider, and landed him where he listed. (*Ariosto: Orlando Furioso.*)

Griffin. A cadet newly arrived in India, half English and half Indian.

Griffins, the residue of a contract feast, taken away by the contractor, half the buyer's and half the seller's.

Griffon, Griffen, or **Griffin.** Offspring of the lion and eagle. Its legs and all from the shoulder to the head are like an eagle, the rest of the body is that of a lion. This creature was sacred to the sun, and kept guard over hidden treasures. Sir Thomas Browne says the Griffon is emblematical of watchfulness, courage, perseverance, and rapidity of execution (*Vulgar Errors*, iii. 2.) (*See* ARIMASPIANS.)

Grig. *Merry as a grig.* A grig is the sand-eel, and a cricket. There was also a class of vagabond dancers and tumblers who visited ale-houses so called. Hence Levi Solomon, *alias* Cockleput, who lived in Sweet Apple Court, being asked in his examination how he obtained his living, replied that "he went a-grigging." Many think the expression should be *merry as a Greek*, and have Shakespeare to back them: "Then she's a merry Greek;" and again, "Cressid 'mongst the merry Greeks" (*Troilus and Cressida,* i. 2; iv. 4). Patrick Gordon also says, "No people in the world are so jovial and merry, so given to singing and dancing, as the Greeks."

Grim (*Giant*), in Bunyan's *Pilgrim's Progress*, part ii. He was one who tried to stop pilgrims on their way to the Celestial City, but was slain by Mr. Greatheart. (*See* GIANTS.)

Grima'ce (2 syl.). Cotgrave says this word is from Grima'cier, who was a celebrated carver of fantastic heads in Gothic architecture. This may be so, but our word comes direct from the French *grimace ; grimacier*, one who makes wry faces.

Grimal'kin or **Graymalkin** (French, *gris malkin*). Shakespeare makes the Witch in *Macbeth* say, "I come, Graymalkin," Malkin being the name of a foul fiend. The cat, supposed to be a witch and the companion of witches, is called by the same name.

Grimes (*Peter*). This son of a steady fisherman was a drunkard and a thief.

He had a boy whom he killed by illusage. Two others he made away with, but was not convicted for want of evidence. As no one would live with him, he dwelt alone, became mad, and was lodged in the parish poor-house, confessed his crime in his delirium, and died. (*Crabbe: Borough*, letter xxii.)

Grimm's Law. A law discovered by Jacob L. Grimm, the German philologist, to show how the mute consonants interchange as corresponding words occur in different branches of the A'ryan family of languages. Thus, what is *p* in Greek, Latin, or Sanskrit becomes *f* in Gothic, and *b* or *f* in the Old High German ; what is *t* in Greek, Latin, or Sanskrit becomes *th* in Gothic, and *d* in Old High German ; etc. Thus changing *p* into *f*, and *t* into *th*, "pater" becomes "father."

Grimsby (Lincolnshire). Grim was a fisherman who rescued from a drifting boat an infant named Habloc, whom he adopted and brought up. This infant turned out to be the son of the king of Denmark, and when the boy was restored to his royal sire Grim was laden with gifts. He now returned to Lincolnshire and built the town which he called after his own name. The ancient seal of the town contains the names of Gryme and Habloc. This is the foundation of the mediæval tales about *Havelock the Dane.*

Grim's Dyke or *Devil's Dyke* (Anglo-Saxon, *grima*, a goblin or demon).

Grimwig. A choleric old gentleman fond of contradiction, generally ending with the words "or I'll eat my head." He is the friend of Brownlow. (*Dickens: Oliver Twist.*)

Grin and Bear It (*You must*), or *You must grin and bide it*, for resistance is hopeless. You may make up a face, if you like, but you cannot help yourself.

Grind. To work up for an examination ; to grind up the subjects set, and to grind into the memory the necessary cram. The allusion is to a mill, and the analogy evident.

To grind one down. To reduce the price asked ; to lower wages. A knife, etc., is gradually reduced by grinding.

To take a grind is to take a constitutional walk ; to cram into the smallest space the greatest amount of physical exercise. This is the physical grind. The literary grind is a turn at hard study.

To take a grinder is to insult another by applying the left thumb to the nose and revolving the right hand round it, as if working a hand-organ or coffee-mill. This insulting retort is given when someone has tried to practise on your credulity, or to impose upon your good faith.

Grinders. The double teeth which grind the food put into the mouth. The Preacher speaks of old age as the time when "the grinders cease because they are few" (Ecc. xii. 3). (*See* ALMOND TREE.)

Grisaille. A style of painting in gray tints, resembling solid bodies in relief, such as ornaments of cornices, etc.

Grise. A step. (*See* GRECIAN STAIRS.)

" Which as a grise or step may help these lovers
Into your favour."
          Shakespeare : Othello, i. 3.

Grisilda or **Griselda.** The model of enduring patience and conjugal obedience. She was the daughter of Janic'-ola, a poor charcoal-burner, but became the wife of Walter, Marquis of Saluzzo. The marquis put her humility and obedience to three severe trials, but she submitted to them all without a murmur : (1) Her infant daughter was taken from her, and secretly conveyed to the Queen of Pa'via to bring up, while Grisilda was made to believe that it had been murdered. (2) Four years later she had a son, who was also taken from her, and sent to be brought up with her sister. When the little girl was twelve years old, the marquis told Grisilda he intended to divorce her and marry another ; so she was stripped of all her fine clothes and sent back to her father's cottage. On the " wedding day" the much-abused Grisilda was sent for to receive " her rival " and prepare her for the ceremony. When her lord saw in her no spark of jealousy, he told her the " bride " was her own daughter. The moral of the tale is this : If Grisilda submitted without a murmur to these trials of her husband, how much more ought we to submit without repining to the trials sent us by God.

This tale is the last of Boccaccio's *De-cam'eron ;* it was rendered by Petrarch into a Latin romance entitled *De Obe-dientia et Fide Uxo'ria Mytholo'gia,* and forms *The Clerkes Tale* in Chaucer's *Canterbury Tales.* Miss Edgeworth has a novel entitled *The Modern Griselda.*

Grist. *All grist that comes to my mill.* All is appropriated that comes to me ; all is made use of that comes in my way. Grist is all that quantity of corn which is to be ground or crushed at one time. The phrase means, all that is brought — good, bad, and indifferent corn, with all refuse and waste—is put into the mill and ground together. (*See* EMOLUMENT.)

To bring grist to the mill. To supply customers or furnish supplies.

Griz'el or **Grissel.** Octavia, wife of Marc Antony and sister of Augustus Cæsar, is called the "patient Grizel" of Roman story. (*See* GRISILDA.)

" For patience she will prove a second Grissel."
     Shakespeare : Taming of the Shrew, ii. 1.

Groaning Cake. A cake prepared for those who called at the house of a woman in confinement " to see the baby."

Groaning Chair. The chair used by women after confinement when they received visitors.

Groaning Malt. A strong ale brewed for the gossips who attend at the birth of a child, and for those who come to offer to a husband congratulations at the auspicious event. A cheese, called the Ken-no, or " groaning cheese," was also made for the occasion. (*See* KEN-NO.)

" Meg Merrilies descended to the kitchen to secure her share of the groaning malt."—*Sir W. Scott : Guy Mannering,* chap. iii.

Groat. *From John o' Groat's house to the Land's End.* From Dan to Beer-sheba, from one end of Great Britain to the other. John o' Groat was a Dutch-man, who settled in the most northerly point of Scotland in the reign of James IV., and immortalised himself by the way he settled a dispute respecting precedency. (*See* JOHN O' GROAT.)

Blood without groats is nothing (north of England), meaning "family without fortune is worthless." The allusion is to black-pudding, which consists chiefly of blood and groats formed into a sausage.

Not worth a groat. Of no value. A groat is a silver fourpence. The Dutch had a coin called a *grote,* a contraction of *grote-schware* (great schware), so called because it was equal in value to five little schware. So the coin of Edward III. was the groat or great silver penny, equal to four penny pieces. The modern groat was first issued in 1335, and were withdrawn from circulation in 1887. (French, *gros,* great.) Groats are no longer in circulation.

" He that spends a groat a day idly, spends idly above six pounds a year."—*Franklin : Neces-sary Hints,* p. 131.

Grog. Rum and water, cold without. Admiral Vernon was called *Old Grog* by his sailors because he was accustomed to walk the deck in rough weather in a *grogram cloak*. As he was the first to serve water in the rum on board ship, the mixture went by the name of grog. *Six-water grog* is one part rum to six parts of water. Grog, in common parlance, is any mixture of spirits and water, either hot or cold.

Grog Blossoms. Blotches on the face that are produced by over-indulgence of grog.

Gro'gram. A coarse kind of taffety, stiffened with gum. A corruption of the French *gros-grain*.

"Gossips in grief and grograms clad."
Praed: The Troubadour, canto i. stanza 5.

Groined Ceiling. One in which the arches are divided or intersected. (Swedish, *grena*, to divide.)

Grommet, Gromet, Grumet, or **Grummet.** A younker on board ship. In Smith's *Sea Grammar* we are told that "younkers are the young men whose duty it is to take in the topsails, or top the yard for furling the sails or slinging the yards. . . ." "*Sailors*," he says, "are the elder men." Gromet is the Flemish *grom* (a boy), with the diminutive. It appears in *bride-groom*, etc. Also a ring of rope made by laying a single strand. (*Dana : Seaman's Manual*, p. 98.) Also a powder-wad.

Grongar Hill, in South Wales, has been rendered famous by Dyer's poem called *Grongar Hill*.

Groom of the Stole. Keeper of the stole or state-robe. His duty, originally, was to invest the king in his state-robe, but he had also to hand him his shirt when he dressed. The office, when a queen reigns, is termed *Mistress of the Robes*, but Queen Anne had her "Groom of the Stole." (Greek, *stolē*, a garment.) (*See* BRIDEGROOM.)

Gross. (*See* ADVOWSON.)

Grosted or *Robert Grosseteste*, Bishop of Lincoln, in the reign of Henry III., the author of some two hundred works. He was accused of some dealings in the black arts, and the Pope ordered a letter to be written to the King of England, enjoining him to disinter the bones of the too-wise bishop and burn them to powder. (Died 1253.)

"None a deeper knowledge boasted,
Since Hodge, Bacon, and Bob Grosted."
Butler : Hudibras ii. 3.

Grotes'que (2 syl.) means in "Grotto style." Classical ornaments so called were found in the 13th century in grottoes, that is, excavations made in the baths of Titus and in other Roman buildings. These ornaments abound in fanciful combinations, and hence anything *outré* is termed grotesque.

Grotta del Cane (Naples). *The Dog's Cave*, so called from the practice of sending dogs into it to show visitors how the carbonic acid gas near the floor of the cave kills them.

Grotto. *Pray remember the grotto.* July 25 *new style*, and August 5 *old style*, is the day dedicated to St. James the Greater ; and the correct thing to do in days of yore was to stick a shell in your hat or coat, and pay a visit on that day to the shrine of St. James of Compostella. Shell grottoes with an image of the saint were erected for the behoof of those who could not afford such pilgrimage, and the keeper of it reminded the passer-by to remember it was St. James's Day, and not to forget their offering to the saint.

Grotto of Ephesus (*The*). The test of chastity. E. Bulwer-Lytton, in his *Tales of Milētus* (iii.), tells us that near the statue of Diana is a grotto, and if, when a woman enters it, she is not chaste, discordant sounds are heard and the woman is never seen more ; if, however, musical sounds are heard, the woman is a pure virgin and comes forth from the grotto unharmed.

Ground. (Anglo-Saxon, *grund*.)
It would suit me down to the ground. Wholly and entirely.
To break ground. To be the first to commence a project, etc. ; to take the first step in an undertaking.
To gain ground. To make progress ; to be improving one's position or prospects of success.
To hold one's ground. To maintain one's authority ; not to budge from one's position ; to retain one's popularity.
To lose ground. To become less popular or less successful ; to be drifting away from the object aimed at.
To stand one's ground. Not to yield or give way ; to stick to one's colours ; to have the courage of one's opinion.

Ground Arms (*To*). To pile or stack military arms, such as guns, on the ground (in drill).

Groundlings. Those who stood in the pit, which was the ground in ancient theatres.

"To split the ears of the groundlings."
Shakespeare: Hamlet, iii. 2.

Grove. The "grove" for which the Jewish women wove hangings, and which the Jews were commanded to cut down and burn, was the wooden Ash'-era, a sort of idol symbolising the generative power of Nature.

Growlers and *Crawlers*. The four-wheel cabs; called "growlers" from the surly and discontented manners of their drivers, and "crawlers" from their slow pace.

"Taken as a whole, the average drivers of hansom cabs ... are smart, intelligent men, sober, honest, and hardworking. ... They have little ... in common with the obtrusive, surly, besotted drivers of the 'growlers' and 'crawlers.'"—*Nineteenth Century*, March, 1893, p. 473.

Grub Street. Since 1830 called Milton Street, near Moorfields, London, once famous for literary hacks and inferior literary productions. The word is the Gothic *graban* (to dig), whence Saxon *grab* (a grave) and *groep* (a ditch). (See *Dunciad*, i. 38, etc.)

Gruel. *To give him his gruel.* To kill him. The allusion is to the very common practice in France, in the sixteenth century, of giving poisoned possets—an art brought to perfection by Catherine de Medicis and her Italian advisers.

Grumbo. A giant in the tale of *Tom Thumb*. A raven picked up Tom, thinking him to be a grain of corn, and dropped him on the flat roof of the giant's castle. Old Grumbo came to walk on the roof terrace, and Tom crept up his sleeve. The giant, annoyed, shook his sleeve, and Tom fell into the sea, where a fish swallowed him; and the fish, having been caught and brought to Arthur's table, was the means of introducing Tom to the British king, by whom he was knighted. (*Nursery Tale: Tom Thumb*.)

Grundy. *What will Mrs. Grundy say?* What will our rivals or neighbours say? The phrase is from Tom Morton's *Speed the Plough*. In the first scene Mrs. Ashfield shows herself very jealous of neighbour Grundy, and farmer Ashfield says to her, "Be quiet, wull ye? Always ding, dinging Dame Grundy into my ears. What will Mrs. Grundy zay? What will Mrs. Grundy think? . . ."

Grunth. The sacred book of the Sikhs.

Gruyère. A town in Switzerland which gives its name to a kind of cheese made there.

Gryll. *Let Gryll be Gryll, and keep his hoggish mind.* Don't attempt to wash a blackamoor white; the leopard will never change his spots. Gryll is from the Greek *gru* (the grunting of a hog). When Sir Guyon disenchanted the forms in the Bower of Bliss some-were exceedingly angry, and one in particular, named Gryll, who had been metamorphosed by Acra'sia into a hog, abused him most roundly. "Come," says the palmer to Sir Guyon,

"Let Gryll be Gryll, and have his hoggish mind,
But let us hence depart while weather serves, and wind."
Spenser: Faërie Queene, book ii. 12.

Gryphon (in *Orlando Furioso*), son of Olive'ro and Sigismunda, brother of Aquilant, in love with Origilla, who plays him false. He was called *White* from his armour, and his brother *Black*. He overthrew the eight champions of Damascus in the tournament given to celebrate the king's wedding-day. While asleep Marta'no steals his armour, and goes to the King Norandi'no to receive the meed of high deeds. In the meantime Gryphon awakes, finds his armour gone, is obliged to put on Marta'no's, and, being mistaken for the coward, is hooted and hustled by the crowd. He lays about him stoutly, and kills many. The king comes up, finds out the mistake, and offers his hand, which Gryphon, like a true knight, receives. He joined the army of Charlemagne.

Gryphons. (*See* GRIFFON.)

Guadia'na. The squire of Durandartë. Mourning the fall of his master at Roncesvallës, he was turned into the river which bears the same name. (*Don Quixote*, ii. 23.)

Guaff. Victor Emmanuel was so called from his nose.

Gua'no is the Peruvian word *hua'no* (dung), and consists of the droppings of sea-fowls.

Guarantee. An engagement on the part of a third person to see an agreement fulfilled.

Guard. *To be off one's guard.* To be careless or heedless.

A guardroom is the place where military offenders are detained; and a guard-ship is a ship stationed in a port or harbour for its defence.

Guards of the Pole. The two stars *β* and *γ* in the Great Bear. Shakespeare, in *Othello*, ii. 1, refers to them where he says, the surge seems "to quench the guards of the ever-fixéd pole."

"How to knowe the houre of the night by the [Polar] Gards, by knowing on what point of the compass they shall be at midnight every fifteenth day throughout the whole year."—*Norman: Safeguard of Sailors* (1587).

Guari'nos (*Admiral*). One of Charlemagne's paladins, taken captive at the battle of Roncesvalles. He fell to the lot of Marlo'tes, a Moslem, who offered him his daughter in marriage if he would become a disciple of Mahomet. Guari'nos refused, and was cast into a dungeon, where he lay captive for seven years. A joust was then held, and Admiral Guari'nos was allowed to try his hand at a target. He knelt before the Moor, stabbed him to the heart, and then vaulted on his grey horse Treb'ozond', and escaped to France.

Gubbings. Anabaptists near Brent, in Devonshire. They had no ecclesiastical order or authority, "but lived in holes, like swine; had all things in common; and multiplied without marriage. Their language was vulgar Devonian. . . They lived by pilfering sheep; were fleet as horses; held together like bees; and revenged every wrong. One of the society was always elected chief, and called *King of the Gubbings.*" (*Fuller*.)

N.B. Their name is from *gubbings*, the offal of fish (Devonshire).

Gudgeon. *Gaping for gudgeons.* Looking out for things extremely improbable. As a gudgeon is a bait to deceive fish, it means a *lie*, a *deception*.

To swallow a gudgeon. To be bamboozled with a most palpable lie, as silly fish are caught by gudgeons. (French, *goujon*, whence the phrase *faire avaler le goujon*, to humbug.)

"Make fools believe in their foreseeing
Of things before they are in being;
To swallow gudgeons ere they're catched,
And count their chickens ere they're hatched."
      Butler: Hudibras, ii. 3.

Gudrun. A model of heroic fortitude and pious resignation. She was a princess betrothed to Herwig, but the King of Norway carried her off captive. As she would not marry him, he put her to all sorts of menial work, such as washing the dirty linen. One day her brother and lover appeared on the scene, and at the end she married Herwig, pardoned the "naughty" king, and all went merry as a marriage bell. (*A North-Saxon poem*.)

Gudule (2 syl.) or **St. Gudu'la**, patron saint of Brussels, was daughter of Count Witger, died 172. She is represented

with a lantern, from a tradition that she was one day going to the church of St. Morgelle with a lantern, which went out, but the holy virgin lighted it again with her prayers.

St. Gudule in Christian art is represented carrying a lantern which a demon tries to put out. The legend is a repetition of that of St. Geneviève, as Brussels is Paris in miniature.

Gue'bres or **Ghebers** [*Fire-Worshippers*]. Followers of the ancient Persian religion, reformed by Zoroaster. Called in Persian *gabr*, in the Talmud *Cheber*, and by Origen *Kabir*, a corruption of the Arabic *Kafir* (a non-Mahometan or infidel), a term bestowed upon them by their Arabian conquerors.

Guelder Rose is the Rose de Gueldre, *i.e.* of the ancient province of Guelder or Guelderland, in Holland.

But Smith, in his *English Flora*, says it is a corruption of Elder Rose, that is, the Rose Elder, the tree being considered a species of Elder, and hence called the "Water Elder."

Guelpho (3 syl.), son of Actius IV., Marquis d'Este and of Cunigunda, a German, King of Carynth'ia. He led an army of 5,000 men from Germany, but two-thirds were slain by the Persians. He was noted for his broad shoulders and ample chest. Guelpho was Rinaldo's uncle, and next in command to Godfrey. (*Tasso: Jerusalem Delivered*, iii.)

Guelphs and **Ghibellines.** Two great parties whose conflicts make up the history of Italy and Germany in the twelfth, thirteenth, and fourteenth centuries. Guelph is the Italian form of *Welfe*, and Ghibelline of *Waiblingen*, and the origin of these two words is this: At the battle of Weinsburg, in Suabia (1140), Conrad, Duke of Franconia, rallied his followers with the war-cry *Hie Waiblingen* (his family estate), while Henry the Lion, Duke of Saxony, used the cry of *Hie Welfe* (the family name). The Ghibellines supported in Italy the side of the German emperors; the Guelphs opposed it, and supported the cause of the Pope.

Guen'dolen (3 syl.). A fairy whose mother was a human being. One day King Arthur wandered into the valley of St. John, when a fairy palace rose to view, and a train of ladies conducted him to their queen. King Arthur and Guen'dolen fell in love with each other, and the fruit of their illicit love was a daughter named Gyneth. After the lapse of three months Arthur left Guen'-dolen, and the deserted fair one offered him a parting cup. As Arthur raised the cup a drop of the contents fell on his horse, and so burnt it that the horse leaped twenty feet high, and then ran in mad career up the hills till it was exhausted. Arthur dashed the cup on the ground, the contents burnt up everything they touched, the fairy palace vanished, and Guen'dolen was never more seen. This tale is told by Sir Walter Scott in *The Bridal of Triermain*. It is called *Lyulph's Tale*, from canto i. 10 to canto ii. 28. (*See* GYNETH.)

" Her mother was of human birth,
   Her sire a Genie of the earth,
   In days of old deemed to preside
   O'er lover's wiles and beauty's pride.
              Bridal of Triermain, ii. 3.

Guendolœ'na, daughter of Corin'eus and wife of Locrin, son of Brute, the legendary king of Britain. She was divorced, and Locrin married Estrildis, by whom he already had a daughter named Sabri'na. Guendolœ'na, greatly indignant, got together a large army, and near the river Stour a battle was fought, in which Locrin was slain. Guendolœ'na now assumed the government, and one of her first acts was to throw both Estrildis and Sabri'na into the river Severn. (*Geoffrey : Brit. Hist.*, ii. chaps. 4, 5.)

Guenever. (*See* GUINEVER.)

Gueril'la, improperly *Guerilla wars*, means a petty war, a partisan conflict; and the parties are called Guerillas or Guerilla chiefs. Spanish, *guer'ra*, war. The word is applied to the armed bands of peasants who carry on irregular war on their own account, especially at such time as their Government is contending with invading armies.

"The town was wholly without defenders, and the guerillas murdered people and destroyed property without hindrance."—*Lessing : United States*, chap. xviii. p. 676.

Gueri'no Meschi'no [*the Wretched*]. An Italian romance, half chivalric and half spiritual, first printed in Padua in 1473. Guerin was the son of Millon, King of Alba'nia. On the day of his birth his father was dethroned, and the child was rescued by a Greek slave, and called Meschino. When he grew up he fell in love with the Princess Elize'na, sister of the Greek Emperor, at Constantinople.

Guess (*I*). A peculiarity of the natives of New England, U.S. America.

Guest. *The Ungrateful Guest* was the brand fixed by Philip of Macedon on a Macedonian soldier who had been kindly entertained by a villager, and, being asked by the king what he could give him, requested the farm and cottage of his entertainer.

Gueux. *Les Gueux*. The ragamuffins. A nickname assumed by the first revolutionists of Holland in 1665. It arose thus : When the Duchess of Parma made inquiry about them of Count Berlaymont, he told her they were "the scum and offscouring of the people" (*les gueux*). This being made public, the party took the name in defiance, and from that moment dressed like beggars, substituted a fox's tail in lieu of a feather, and a wooden platter instead of a brooch. They met at a public-house which had for its sign a *cock* crowing these words, *Vive les Gueux par tout le monde!* (See *Motley : Dutch Republic*, ii. 6.)

✷ The word *gueux* was, of course, not invented by Berlaymont, but only applied by him to the deputation referred to. In Spain, long before, those who opposed the Inquisition were so called.

N.B. The revolters of Guienne assumed the name of *Eaters;* those of Normandy *Barefoot;* those of Beausse and Soulogne *Wooden-pattens;* and in the French Revolution the most violent were termed *Sansculottes*.

Gugner. A spear made by the dwarf Eitri and given to Odin. It never failed to hit and slay in battle. (*The Edda*.)

Gui. *Le Gui* (French). The mistletoe or Druid's plant.

Guide'rius. The elder son of Cymbeline, a legendary king of Britain during the reign of Augustus Cæsar. Both Guiderius and his brother Arvir'-agus were stolen in infancy by Bela'rius, a banished nobleman, out of revenge, and were brought up by him in a cave. When grown to man's estate, the Romans invaded Britain, and the two young men so distinguished themselves that they were introduced to the king, and Belarius related their history. Geoffrey of Monmouth says that Guiderius succeeded his father, and was slain by Hamo. (*Shakespeare : Cymbeline*.)

Guides (pron. *gheed*). Contraction of *guidons*. A corps of French cavalry which carries the *guidon*, a standard borne by light horse-soldiers, broad at one end and nearly pointed at the other. The *corps des Guides* was organised in 1796 by Napoleon as a personal bodyguard ; in 1848 several squadrons were created, but Napoleon III. made the corps a part of the Imperial Guard. Great care must be taken not to confound the Guides with the Gardes, as they are totally distinct terms.

Guido, surnamed *the Savage* (in *Orlando Furioso*), son of Constantia and Amon, therefore younger brother of Rinaldo. He was also Astolpho's kinsman. Being wrecked on the coast of the Amazons, he was doomed to fight their ten male champions. He slew them all, and was then compelled to marry ten of the Amazons. He made his escape with Ale'ria, his favourite wife, and joined the army of Charlemagne.

Guido Francischini. A reduced nobleman, who tried to repair his fortune by marrying Pompilia, the putative child of Pietro and Violante. When the marriage was consummated and the money secure, Guido ill-treated Pietro and Violante; whereupon Violante, at confession, asserted that Pompilia was not her child, but one she had brought up, the offspring of a Roman wanton, and she applied to the law-courts to recover her money. When Guido heard this he was furious, and so ill-treated his wife that she ran away under the protection of a young canon. Guido pursued the fugitives, overtook them, and had them arrested; whereupon the canon was suspended for three years, and Pompilia sent to a convent. Here her health gave way, and as the birth of a child was expected, she was permitted to leave the convent and live with her putative parents. Guido went to the house, murdered all three, and was executed. (*Browning: The Ring and the Book.*)

Guildhall. The hall of the city guilds. Here are the Court of Common Council, the Court of Aldermen, the Chamberlain's Court, the police court presided over by an alderman, etc. The ancient guilds were friendly trade societies, in which each member paid a certain fee, called a guild, from the Saxon *gildan* (to pay). There was a separate guild for each craft of importance.

"Gild [guild] signified among the Saxons a fraternity. Derived from the verb *gyld-an* (to pay), because every man paid his share."—*Blackstone: Commentaries*, book i. chap. xviii. p. 474 (*note*).

Guil'lotine (3 syl.). So named from Joseph Ignace Guillotin, a French physician, who proposed its adoption to prevent unnecessary pain (1738-1814).

⁂ It was facetiously called "Mdlle. Guillotin" or "Guillotin's daughter." It was introduced April 25th, 1792, and is still used in France. A previous instrument invented by Dr. Antoine Louis was called a Louisette (3 syl.).

The Maiden (*q.v.*), introduced into Scotland (1566) by the Regent Morton, when the laird of Pennicuick was to be beheaded, was a similar instrument Discontinued in 1681.

"It was but this very day that the daughter of M. de Guillotin was recognised by her father in the National Assembly, and it should properly be called 'Mademoiselle Guillotin.'"—*Dumas: The Countess de Charny*, chap. xvii.

Guinea. Sir Robert Holmes, in 1666, captured in Schelling Bay 160 Dutch sail, containing bullion and gold-dust from Cape Coast Castle in Guinea. This rich prize was coined into gold pieces, stamped with an elephant, and called Guineas to memorialise the valuable capture. (See *Dryden: Annus Mirabilis.*)

Guinea. The legend is M. B. F. et H. Rex. F. D. B. L. D. S. R. I. A. T. et E. —Magnæ Britanniæ, Franciæ, et Hiberniæ Rex; Fidei Defensor; Brunsvicensis, Lunenburgensis Dux; Sacri Romani Imperii Archi Thesaurarius et Elector.

∵ Guinea-pieces = 21s. were first coined in 1663, and discontinued in 1817. The sovereign coined by Henry VII. in 1489 was displaced by the guinea, but recoined in 1815, soon after which it displaced the guinea. Of course, 20s. is a better decimal coin than 21s.

Guinea-dropper. A cheat. The term is about equal to thimble-rig, and alludes to an ancient cheating dodge of dropping counterfeit guineas.

Guinea Fowl. So called because it was brought to us from the coast of Guinea, where it is very common.

"Notwithstanding their harsh cry . . . I like the Guinea-fowl. They are excellent layers. and enormous devourers of insects."—*D. G. Mitchell: My Farm of Edgewood*, chap. iii. p. 192.

Guinea-hen. A courtesan who is won by money.

"Ere . . . . I would drown myself for the love of a Guinea-hen, I would change my humanity with a baboon."—*Shakespeare: Othello*, i. 3.

Guineapig (Stock Exchange term). A gentleman of sufficient name to form a bait who allows himself to be put on a directors' list for the *guinea and lunch* provided for the board. (*See* Floaters.)

Guineapig (*A*). A midshipman. A guineapig is neither a pig nor a native of Guinea; so a middy is neither a sailor nor an officer.

"He had a letter from the captain of the *Indiaman*, offering you a berth on board as guineapig, or midshipman."—*Captain Marryat: Poor Jack*, chap. xxxi.

⁂ A special juryman who is paid a guinea a case; also a military officer assigned to some special duty, for which he receives a guinea a day, are sometimes so called.

Guineapig (*A*), in the Anglican Church, is a clergyman without cure, who takes occasional duty for a guinea a sermon, besides his travelling expenses (second class) and his board, if required.

Guin'ever, or rather *Guanhuma'ra* (4 syl.). Daughter of Leodograunce of Cam'elyard, the most beautiful of women, and wife of King Arthur. She entertained a guilty passion for Sir Launcelot of the Lake, one of the knights of the Round Table, but during the absence of King Arthur in his expedition against Leo, King of the Romans, she "married" Modred, her husband's nephew, whom he had left in charge of the kingdom. Soon as Arthur heard thereof, he hastened back, Guinever fled from York and took the veil in the nunnery of Julius the Martyr, and Modred set his forces in array at Cam'bula, in Cornwall. Here a desperate battle was fought, in which Modred was slain and Arthur mortally wounded. Guinever is generally called the " grey-eyed; " she was buried at Meigle, in Strathmore, and her name has become the synonym of a wanton or adulteress. (*Geoffrey: Brit. Hist.*, x. 13.)

" That was a woman when Queen Guinever of Britain was a little wench."—*Shakespeare: Love's Labour's Lost,* iv. 1.

Guin'evere (3 syl.). Tennyson's *Idyll* represents her as loving Sir Lancelot; but one day, when they were bidding farewell, Modred tracked them, " and brought his creatures to the basement of the tower for testimony." Sir Lancelot hurled the fellow to the ground and got to horse, and the queen fled to a nunnery at Almesbury. (*See* GUINEVER.)

Guingelot. The boat of Wato or *Wade*, the father of Weland, and son of Vilkinr, in which he crossed over the nine-ell deep, called Grœnasund, with his son upon his shoulders. (*Scandinavian mythology.*)

Guisan'do. *The Bulls of Guisando.* Five monster statues of antiquity, to mark the scene of Cæsar's victory over the younger Pompey.

Guise's Motto: "*A chacun son tour,*" on the standards of the Duc de Guise, who put himself at the head of the Catholic League in the sixteenth century, meant, " My turn will come."

Guitar (Greek, *kithara;* Latin, *cithara;* Italian, *chitarra;* French, *guitare.* The Greek *kithar* is the Hindu *cha-tar* (six-strings).

Guitar. The best players on this instrument have been Guilia'ni, Sor, Zoechi, Stoll, and Horetzsky.

Gules [red]. An heraldic term. The most honourable heraldic colour, signifying valour, justice, and veneration. Hence it was given to kings and princes. The royal livery of England is gules or scarlet. In heraldry expressed by perpendicular parallel lines. (Persian, *ghul,* rose; French, *queules,* the mouth and throat, or the red colour thereof; Latin, *gula,* the throat.)

" With man's blood paint the ground, gules, gules."
          Shakespeare: Timon of Athens, iv. 3.
" And threw warm gules on Madeline's fair breast."   *Keats: Eve of St. Agnes.*

Gules of August (*The*). The 1st of August (from Latin, *gula,* the throat), the entrance into, or first day of that month. (*Wharton: Law Lexicon,* p. 332.)

✻ August 1 is Lammas Day, a quarter-day in Scotland, and half-quarter-day in England.

"'Gula Augusti' initium mensis Augusti. Le Gule d'Angust, in statuo Edw. III., a. 31 c. 14, *averagium œstivale fieri debet inter Hokedai et gulam Augusti.*"—*Ducange: Glossarium Manuale,* vol. iii. p. 866.

(" Hokeday est dies Martis, qui quindenam Paschœ expletam proxime excipit."—Vol. iv. p. 65 col. 1.]

Gulf. A man that goes in for honour at Cambridge—*i.e.* a mathematical degree—is sometimes too bad to be classed with the lowest of the three classes, and yet has shown sufficient merit to pass. When the list is made out a line is drawn after the classes, and one or two names are appended. These names are in the gulf, and those so honoured are gulfed. In the good old times these men were not qualified to stand for the classical tripos.

" The ranks of our curatehood are supplied by youths whom, at the very best, merciful examiners have raised from the very gates of 'pluck' to the comparative paradise of the 'Gulf.'"—*Saturday Review.*

A great gulf fixed. An impassable separation or divergence. From the parable of Dives and Lazarus, in the third Gospel. (Luke xvi. 26.)

Gulf Stream. The stream which issues from the Gulf of Mexico, and extends over a range of 3,000 miles, raising the temperature of the water through which it passes, and of the lands against which it flows. It washes the shores of the British Isles, and runs up the coast of Norway.

"It is found that the amount of heat transferred by the Gulf Stream from equatorial regions into the North Atlantic . . . amounts to no less than one-fifth part of the entire heat possessed by the North Atlantic."— *T. Croll: Climate and Time*, chap. i. p. 15.

Gu'listan [*garden of roses*]. The famous recueil of moral sentences by Saadi, the poet of Shiraz, who died 1291. (Persian, *ghul*, a rose, and *tan*, a region.)

Gull (rhymes with *dull*). A dupe, one easily cheated. (*See* BEJAN.)

" The most notorious geck and gull That e'er invention played on." *Shakespeare: Twelfth Night*, v. 1.

Gulliver (*Lemuel*). The hero of the famous *Travels into Several Remote Nations of the World, by Lemuel Gulliver, first a Surgeon, and then a Captain of several Ships*, i.e. to Lilliput, Brobdingnag, Lapu'ta, and the Houyhnhnms (*Whin-nims*), written by Dr. Swift, Dean of St. Patrick's, Ireland.

Gulna're (2 syl.), afterwards called Kaled, queen of the harem, and fairest of all the slaves of Seyd [*Seed*]. She was rescued from the flaming palace by Lord Conrad, the corsair, and when the corsair was imprisoned released him and murdered the Sultan. The two escaped to the Pirate's Isle; but when Conrad found that Medo'ra, his betrothed, was dead, he and Gulnare left the island secretly, and none of the pirates ever knew where they went to. The rest of the tale of Gulnare is under the new name, Kaled (*q.v.*). (*Byron: The Corsair.*)

Gummed (1 syl.). *He frets like gummed velvet* or *gummed taffety*. Velvet and taffeta were sometimes stiffened with gum to make them "sit better," but, being very stiff, they fretted out quickly.

Gumption. Wit to turn things to account, capacity. In Yorkshire we hear the phrase, "I canna gaum it" (understand it, make it out), and gaumtion is the capacity of understanding, etc. (Irish, *gomsh*, sense, cuteness.)

" Though his eyes were dazzled with the splendour of the place, faith he had *gomsh* enough not to let go his hold."—*Dublin and London Magazine*, 1825 (Loughleagh).

Gumption. A nostrum much in request by painters in search of the supposed ".lost medium" of the old masters, and to which their unapproachable excellence is ascribed. The medium is made of gum mastic and linseed-oil.

Gun. (Welsh *gwn*, a gun.)

CANNONS AND RIFLES.

Armstrong gun. A wrought-iron cannon, usually breech-loading, having an iron-hooped steel inner tube. Designed by Sir William Armstrong in 1854, and officially tested in 1861.

Enfield rifles. Invented by Pritchett at the Enfield factory, adopted in the English army 1852, and converted into Snider breech-loaders in 1866.

Gatling gun. A machine gun with parallel barrels about a central axis, each having its own lock. Capable of being loaded and of discharging 1,000 shots a minute by turning a crank. Named from the inventor, Dr. R. J. Gatling.

Krupp gun. A cannon of ingot steel, made at Krupp's works, at Essen, in Prussia.

Lancaster gun. A cannon having a slightly elliptical twisted bore, and a conoid (2 syl.) projectile. Named from the inventor.

Minié rifle. Invented in 1849, and adopted in the English army in 1851. Named after Claude Minié, a French officer. (1810-1879.)

Snider rifle. Invented by Jacob Snider. A breech-loader adopted by the British Government in 1866.

Whitworth gun. An English rifled firearm of hexagonal bore, and very rapid twist. Constructed in 1857. Its competitive trial with the Armstrong gun in 1864. Named after Sir Joseph Whitworth, the inventor (1803-1887).

Woolwich infant (*The*). A British 35-ton rifled muzzle-loading cannon, having a steel tube hooped with wrought-iron coils. Constructed in 1870. (*See* BROWN BESS, MITRAILLEUSE, etc.)

Gun. *A breech-loading gun.* A gun loaded at the breech, which is then closed by a screw or wedge-block.

Evening or *sunset gun.* A gun fired at sunset, or about 9 o'clock p.m.

Gun Cotton. A highly explosive compound, prepared by saturating cotton with nitric and sulphuric acids.

Gun Money. Money issued in Ireland by James II., made of old brass cannons.

Gun Room. A room in the after-part of a lower gun-deck for the accommodation of junior officers.

GUN PHRASES.

He's a great gun. A man of note.

Son of a gun. A jovial fellow.

Sure as a gun. Quite certain. It is as certain to happen as a gun to go off if the trigger is pulled.

Guns. *To blow great guns.* To be very boisterous and windy. Noisy and boisterous as the reports of great guns.

To run away from their own guns. To eat their own words; desert what is laid down as a principle. The allusion is obvious.

"The Government could not, of course, run away from their guns."—*Nineteenth Century*, Feb., 1893, p. 193.

Gunga [pronounce *Gun-jah*]. The goddess of the Ganges. Bishop Heber calls the river by this name.

Gunner. *Kissing the gunner's daughter.* Being flogged on board ship. At one time boys in the Royal Navy who were to be flogged were first tied to the breech of a cannon.

Gunpowder Plot. The project of a few Roman Catholics to destroy James I. with the Lords and Commons assembled in the Houses of Parliament, on the 5th of November, 1605. It was to be done by means of gunpowder when the king went in person to open Parliament. Robert Catesby originated the plot, and Guy Fawkes undertook to fire the gunpowder. (*See* DYNAMITE SATURDAY.)

Gunter's Chain, for land surveying, is so named from Edmund Gunter, its inventor (1581-1626). It is sixty-six feet long, and divided into one hundred links. As ten square chains make an acre, it follows that an acre contains 100,000 square links.

According to Gunter. According to measurement by Gunter's chain.

Günther. King of Burgundy and brother of Kriem'hild. He resolved to wed Brunhild, the martial queen of Issland, who had made a vow that none should win her who could not surpass her in three trials of skill and strength. The first was hurling a spear, the second throwing a stone, and the third was jumping. The spear could scarcely be lifted by three men. The queen hurled it towards Günther, when Siegfried, in his invisible cloak, reversed it, hurled it back again, and the queen was knocked down. The stone took twelve brawny champions to carry, but Brunhild lifted it on high, flung it twelve fathoms, and jumped beyond it. Again the unseen Siegfried came to his friend's rescue, flung the stone still farther, and, as he leaped, bore Günther with him. The queen, overmastered, exclaimed to her subjects, "I am no more your mistress; you are Günther's liegemen now" (*Lied*, vii.). After the marriage the masculine maid behaved so obstreperously that Günther had again to avail himself of his friend's aid. Siegfried entered the chamber in his cloud-cloak, and wrestled with the bride till all her strength was gone; then he drew a ring from her finger, and took away her girdle. After which he left her, and she became a submissive wife. Günther, with unpardonable ingratitude, was privy to the murder of his friend and brother-in-law, and was himself slain in the dungeon of Etzel's palace by his sister Kriemhild. In history this Burgundian king is called Gün'tacher. (*The Nibelungen-Lied.*)

Gurgoils. (*See* GARGOUILLE.)

Gurme (2 syl.). The Celtic Cer'berus. While the world lasts it is fastened at the mouth of a vast cave; but at the end of the world it will be let loose, when it will attack Tyr, the war-god, and kill him.

Gurney Light. (*See* BUDE.)

Guth'lac (*St.*), of Crowland, Lincolnshire, is represented in Christian art as a hermit punishing demons with a scourge, or consoled by angels while demons torment him.

Guthrum. *Silver of Guthrum,* or *silver of Guthrum's Lane.* Fine silver was at one time so called, because the chief gold and silver smiths of London resided there in the thirteenth and fourteenth centuries. The hall of the Goldsmiths' Company is still in the same locality. (*Riley : Munimenta Gildhallæ.*)

Gutt'apercha. The juice of the percha-tree (*Isonandra percha*) of the family called *Sapotaceæ.* The percha trees grow to a great height, and abound in all the Malacca Islands. The juice is obtained by cutting the bark. Gutta-percha was brought over by Dr. William Montgomerie in 1843, but articles made of this resin were known in Europe some time before. (Latin, *gutta,* a drop.)

Gutter. *Out of the gutter.* Of low birth; of the street-Arab class one of the submerged.

Gutter Children. Street Arabs.

Gutter Lane (London). A corruption of Guthurun Lane, from a Mr. Guthurun, Goderoune, or Guthrum, who, as Stow informs us, "possessed the chief property therein." (*See* GUTHRUM.)

All goes down Gutter Lane. He spends

everything on his stomach. The play is between Gutter Lane, London, and *guttur* (the throat), preserved in our word *guttural* (a throat letter).

Guy. The *Guiser* or *Guisard* was the ancient Scotch mummer, who played before Yule; hence our words *guise*, *disguise*, *guy*, etc.

Guy (*Thomas*). Miser and philanthropist. He amassed an immense fortune in 1720 by speculations in the South Sea Stock, and gave £238,292 to found and endow Guy's Hospital.

Guy Fawkes, or Guido Fawkes, went under the name of John Johnstone, the servant of Mr. Percy.

Guy, Earl of Warwick. An Anglo-Danish hero of wonderful puissance. He was in love with fair Phelis or Felice, who refused to listen to his suit till he had distinguished himself by knightly deeds. First, he rescued the daughter of the Emperor of Germany "from many a valiant knight;" then he went to Greece to fight against the Saracens, and slew the doughty Coldran, Elmaye King of Tyre, and the soldan himself. Then returned he to England and wedded Phelis; but in forty days he returned to the Holy Land, where he redeemed Earl Jonas out of prison, slew the giant Am'arant, and many others. He again returned to England, and slew at Winchester, in single combat, Colbronde or Colbrand, the Danish giant, and thus redeemed England from Danish tribute. At Windsor he slew a boar of "passing might and strength." On Dunsmore Heath he slew the "Duncow of Dunsmore, a monstrous wyld and cruell beast." In Northumberland he slew a dragon "black as any cole," with lion's paws, wings, and a hide which no sword could pierce. Having achieved all this, he became a hermit in Warwick, and hewed himself a cave a mile from the town. Daily he went to his own castle, where he was not known, and begged bread of his own wife Phelis. On his death-bed he sent Phelis a ring, by which she recognised her lord, and went to close his dying eyes. (890-958.) His combat with Colbrand is very elaborately told by Drayton (1563-1631) in his *Polyolbion*.

"I am not Sampson, nor Sir Guy, nor Colbrand,
to mow them down before me."—*Shakespeare: Henry VIII.*, v. 3.

Guy-ropes. Guide, or guiding-ropes, to steady heavy goods while a-hoisting. (Spanish and Portuguese *guia*, from *guiar*, to guide.)

Guyon (*Sir*). The impersonation of Temperance or Self-government. He destroyed the witch Acra'sia, and her bower, called the "Bower of Bliss." His companion was Prudence. (*Spenser: Faërie Queene*, book ii.)

The word Guyon is the Spanish *guiar* (to guide), and the word temperance is the Latin *tem'pero* (to guide).

Gwynn (*Nell*). An actress, and one of the courtesans of Charles II. of England (died 1687). Sir Walter Scott speaks of her twice in *Peveril of the Peak;* in chap. xi. he speaks of "the smart humour of Mrs. Nelly;" and in chap. xl. Lord Chaffinch says of "Mrs. Nelly, wit she has; let her keep herself warm with it in worse company, for the cant of strollers is not language for a prince's chamber."

Gygës' Ring rendered the wearer invisible. Gygës, the Lydian, is the person to whom Candau'lēs showed his wife naked. According to Plato, Gygës descended into a chasm of the earth, where he found a brazen horse; opening the sides of the animal, he found the carcase of a man, from whose finger he drew off a brazen ring which rendered him invisible, and by means of this ring he entered into the king's chamber and murdered him.

"Why, did you think that you had Gygēs ring,
Or the herb that gives invisibility [fern-seed]?"
Beaumont and Fletcher: Fair Maid of the Inn, i. 1.

The wealth of Gygēs. Gygës was a Lydian king, who married Nyssia, the young widow of Candaulēs, and reigned thirty-eight years. He amassed such wealth that his name became proverbial. (Reigned B.C. 716-678.)

Gymnas'tics. Athletic games. The word is from *gymna'sium*, a public place set apart in Greece for athletic sports, the actors in which were naked. (Greek, *gumnos*, naked.)

Gymnos'ophists. A sect of Indian philosophers who went about with naked feet and almost without clothing. They lived in woods, subsisted on roots, and never married. They believed in the transmigration of souls. Strabo divides them into Brahmins and Samans. (Greek, *gumnos*, naked; *sophistēs*, sages.)

Gy'neth. Natural daughter of Guen'dolen and King Arthur. Arthur swore to Guendolen that if she brought forth a boy, he should be his heir, and if a girl, he would give her in marriage to the bravest knight of his kingdom. One

Pentecost a beautiful damsel presented herself to King Arthur, and claimed the promise made to Guendolen. Accordingly, a tournament was proclaimed, and the warder given to Gyneth. The king prayed her to drop the warder before the combat turned to earnest warfare, but Gyneth haughtily refused, and twenty knights of the Round Table fell in the tournament, amongst whom was young Vanoc, son of Merlin. Immediately Vanoc fell, the form of Merlin rose, put a stop to the fight, and caused Gyneth to fall into a trance in the Valley of St. John, from which she was never to awake till some knight came forward for her hand as brave as those which were slain in the tournay. Five hundred years passed away before the spell was broken, and then De Vaux undertook the adventure of breaking it. He overcame four temptations—fear, avarice, pleasure, and ambition—when Gyneth awoke, the enchantment was dissolved, and Gyneth became the bride of the bold warrior. (*Sir Walter Scott: Bridal of Triermain*, chap. ii.)

Gyp. A college servant, whose office is that of a gentleman's valet, waiting on two or more collegians in the University of Cambridge. He differs from a bed-maker, inasmuch as he does not make beds; but he runs on errands, waits at table, wakes men for morning chapel, brushes their clothes, and so on. His perquisites are innumerable, and he is called a gyp (*vulture*, Greek) because he preys upon his employer like a vulture. At Oxford they are called *scouts*.

Gypsy. (*See* GIPSY.)

Gyrfalcon, Gerfalcon, or *Jerfalcon*. A native of Iceland and Norway, highest in the list of hawks for falconry. "Gyr," or "Ger," is, I think, the Dutch *gier*, a vulture. It is called the "vulture-falcon" because, like the vulture, its beak is not toothed. The common etymology from *hieros*, sacred, "because the Egyptians held the hawk to be sacred," is utterly worthless. Besides Ger-falcons, we have Gier-eagles, Lammer-geiers, etc. (*See* HAWK.)

Gyromancy. A kind of divination performed by walking round in a circle or ring.

Gytrash. A north-of-England spirit, which, in the form of horse, mule, or large dog, haunts solitary ways, and sometimes comes upon belated travellers.

"I remembered certain of Bessie's tales, wherein figured a . . . spirit called a Gytrash."—*Charlotte Brontë: Jane Eyre*, xii.

H.

H. This letter represents a style or hedge. It is called in Hebrew *heth* or *cheth* (a hedge).

H.B. (Mr. Doyle, father of Mr. Richard Doyle, connected with *Punch*). This political caricaturist died 1868.

H.M.S. His *or* Her Majesty's service *or* ship, as H.M.S. *Wellington*.

H.U. Hard up.

Habeas Corpus. The "Habeas Corpus Act" was passed in the reign of Charles II., and defined a provision of similar character in Magna Charta, to which also it added certain details. The Act provides (1) That any man taken to prison can insist that the person who charges him with crime shall bring him bodily before a judge, and state the why and wherefore of his detention. As soon as this is done, the judge is to decide whether or not the accused is to be admitted to bail. [No one, therefore, can be imprisoned on mere suspicion, and no one can be left in prison any indefinite time at the caprice of the powers that be. Imprisonment, in fact, must be either for punishment after conviction, or for safe custody till the time of trial.]

(2) It provides that every person accused of crime shall have the question of his guilt decided by a jury of twelve men, and not by a Government agent or nominee.

(3) No prisoner can be tried a second time on the same charge.

(4) Every prisoner may insist on being examined within twenty days of his arrest, and tried by jury the next session.

(5) No defendant is to be sent to prison beyond the seas, either within or without the British dominions.

The exact meaning of the words *Habeas Corpus* is this: "You are to produce the body." That is, You, the accuser, are to bring before the judge the body of the accused, that he may be tried and receive the award of the court, and you (the accused) are to abide by the award of the judge.

Suspension of Habeas Corpus. When the Habeas Corpus Act is suspended, the Crown can imprison persons on *suspicion*, without giving any reason for so doing; the person so arrested cannot insist on being brought before a judge to decide whether or not he can be admitted to bail; it is not needful to try the prisoner at the following assize; and the prisoner may be confined in any prison the Crown chooses to select for the purpose.

Haberdasher, from *hapertas,* a cloth the width of which was settled by Magna Charta. A "hapertas-er" is the seller of hapertas-erie.

" To match this saint there was another,
As busy and perverse a brother,
An haberdasher of small wares
In politics and state affairs."
Butler : Hudibras, iii. 2.

Habit is Second Nature. The wise saw of Diogĕnēs, the cynic. (B.C. 412-323.)

Shakespeare : "Use almost can change the stamp of nature" (*Hamlet,* iii. 4).
French : "L'habitude est une seconde nature."
Latin : "Usus est optĭmus magister" (*Columella*).
Italian : "L'abito è una seconda natura."

Habsburg is a contraction of *Habichts - burg* (Hawk's Tower); so called from the castle on the right bank of the Aar, built in the eleventh century by Werner, Bishop of Strasburg, whose nephew (Werner II.) was the first to assume the title of "Count of Habsburg." His great-grandson, Albrecht II., assumed the title of "Landgraf of Sundgau." His grandson, Albrecht IV., in the thirteenth century, laid the foundation of the greatness of the House of Habsburg, of which the imperial family of Austria are the representatives.

Hackell's Coit. A vast stone near Stantin Drew, in Somersetshire; so called from a tradition that it was a *coit* thrown by Sir John Hautville. In Wiltshire three huge stones near Kennet are called the *Devil's coits.*

Hackney Horses. Not thoroughbred, but nearly so. They make the best roadsters, hunters, and carriage horses; their action is showy, and their pace good. A first-class roadster will trot a mile in 2½ minutes. Some American trotters will even exceed this record. The best hackneys are produced from thorough-bred sires mated with half-bred mares. (French, *haquenée;* the Romance word *haque=* the Latin *equus;* Spanish, *hacanéa.*)

⁑ In ordinary parlance, a hackney, hackney-horse, or hack, means a horse "hacked out" for hire. These horses are sometimes vicious private horses sold for "hacks," or worn-out coach-horses,

and cheap animals with broken wind, broken knees, or some other defect.

"The knights are well horsed, and the common people and others on litell *hakeneys* and geldynges."—*Froissart.*

Hackum (*Captain*). A thick-headed bully of Alsa'tia, impudent but cowardly. He was once a sergeant in Flanders, but ran from his colours, and took refuge in Alsa'tia, where he was dubbed captain. (*Shadwell : Squire of Alsatia.*)

Haco I. His sword was called Quern-Biter [*foot-breadth*]. (*See* SWORD.)

Haddock. According to tradition, it was a haddock in whose mouth St. Peter found the *stater* (or piece of money), and the two marks on the fish's neck are said to be the impressions of the apostle's finger and thumb. It is a pity that the person who invented this pretty story forgot that salt-water haddocks cannot live in the fresh water of the Lake Gennesaret. (*See* JOHN DORY and CHRISTIAN TRADITIONS.)

" O superstitious dainty, Peter's fish,
How com'st thou here to make so goodly dish ? "
Metellus : Dialogues (1693).

Hadēs (2 syl.). The places of the departed spirit till the resurrection. It may be either Paradise or "Tartarus."

⁑ It is a great pity that it has been translated "hell" nine or ten times in the common version of the New Testament, as "hell" in theology means the inferno. The Hebrew *sheol* is about equal to the Greek *haidēs,* that is, *a,* privative, and *idein,* to see.

Ha'dith [*a legend*]. The traditions about the prophet Mahomet's sayings and doings. This compilation forms a supplement to the Koran, as the Talmud to the Jewish Scriptures. Like the Jewish *Gema'ra,* the Ha'dith was not allowed originally to be committed to writing, but the danger of the traditions being perverted or forgotten led to their being placed on record.

Hadj. The pilgrimage to Kaa'ba (temple of Mecca), which every Mahometan feels bound to make once at least before death. Those who neglect to do so "might as well die Jews or Christians." These pilgrimages are made by caravans well supplied with water, and escorted by 1,400 armed men for defence against brigands. (Hebrew, *hag,* the festival of Jewish pilgrimages to Jerusalem.)

"The green turban of the Mussulman distinguishes the devout hadji who has been to Mecca."
—*Stephens: Egypt,* vol. i. chap. xvii. p. 240.

Hadji. A pilgrim, a Mahometan who has made the *Hadj* or pilgrimage to the Prophet's tomb at Mecca. Every Hadji is entitled to wear a green turban.

Hæmony. Milton, in his *Comus*, says hæmony is of "sovereign use 'gainst all enchantments, mildew, blast, or damp." Coleridge says the word is *hæma-oinos* (blood-wine), and refers to the blood of Jesus Christ, which destroys all evil. The leaf, says Milton, "had prickles on it," but "it bore a bright golden flower." The *prickles* are the crown of thorns, the *flower* the fruits of salvation. This interpretation is so in accordance with the spirit of Milton, that it is far preferable to the suggestions that the plant ag'rimony or alyssum was intended, for why should Milton have changed the name? (Greek, *haima*, blood.) (See *Comus*, 648-668.)

Dioscor'ides ascribes similar powers to the herb alyssum, which, as he says, "keepeth man and beast from enchantments and witching."

Hæmos. A range of mountains separating Thrace and Mœ'sia, called by the classic writers *Cold Hæmos*. (Greek, *cheimon*, winter; Latin, *hiems*; Sanskrit, *hima*.)

"O'er high Pier'ia thence her course she bore,
O'er fair Emath'ia's ever-pleasing shore;
O'er Hæmus' hills with snows eternal crown'd,
Nor once her flying foot approached the
    ground" *Pope: Homer's Iliad*, xiv.

Hafed. A Gheber or Fire-worshipper, in love with Hinda, the Arabian emir's daughter, whom he first saw when he entered the palace under the hope of being able to slay her father, the tyrant usurper of Persia. He was the leader of a band sworn to free their country or die, and his name was a terror to the Arab, who looked upon him as superhuman. His rendezvous was betrayed by a traitor comrade, but when the Moslem army came to take him he threw himself into the sacred fire, and was burnt to death. (*Thomas Moore.*)

Hafiz. The great Persian lyrist, called the "Persian Anacreon" (fourteenth century). His odes are called *ghazels*, and are both sweet and graceful. The word *hafiz* (retainer) is a degree given to those who know by heart the Koran and Hadith (traditions).

Hag. A witch or sorceress. (Anglo-Saxon, *hægtesse*, a witch or hag.)

"How now, you secret, black, and midnight
    hags?" *Shakespeare: Macbeth*, iv. 1.

Hagan of Trony or *Haco of Norway*, son of Aldrian, liegeman of Günther,

King of Burgundy. Günther invited Siegfried to a hunt of wild beasts, but while the king of Netherland stooped to drink from a brook, Hagan stabbed him between the shoulders, the only vulnerable point in his whole body. He then deposited the dead body at the door of Kriemhi!d's chamber, that she might stumble on it when she went to matins, and suppose that he had been murdered by assassins. When Kriemhild sent to Worms for the "Nibelung Hoard," Hagan seized it, and buried it secretly somewhere beneath the Rhine, intending himself to enjoy it. Kriemhild, with a view of vengeance, married Etzel, King of the Huns, and after the lapse of seven years, invited the king of Burgundy, with Hagan and many others, to the court of her husband, but the invitation was a mere snare. A terrible broil was stirred up in the banquet hall, which ended in the slaughter of all the Burgundians but two (Günther and Hagan), who were taken prisoners and given to Kriemhild, who cut off both their heads. Hagan lost an eye when he fell upon Walter of Spain. He was dining on the chine of a wild boar when Walter pelted him with the bones, one of which struck him in the eye. Hagan's person is thus described in the great German epic :—

"Well-grown and well-compacted was that re-
    doubted guest;
Long were his legs and sinewy, and deep and
    broad his chest;
His hair, that once was sable, with grey was
    dashed of late;
Most terrible his visage, and lordly was his
    gait."
    The Nibelungen-Lied, stanza 1789.

Hagarenes (3 syl.). The Moors are so called, being the supposed descendants of Hagar, Abraham's bondwoman.

"San Diego .... hath often been seen con-
quering .... the Hagarene squadrons."—*Cervantes: Don Quixote*, part ii. book iv. 6.

Hagga'dah (plur. *hagga'doth*). The free rabbinical interpretation of Scripture. (Hebrew, *hagged*, to relate.) (See *Farrar: Life of Christ*, vol. ii. chap. lviii. p. 333.)

Hagi. (*See* HADJ.)

Hag-knots. Tangles in the manes of wild ponies, supposed to be used by witches for stirrups. The term is common in the New Forest. Seamen use the word *hag's-teeth* to express those parts of a matting, etc., which spoil its general uniformity.

Hagring. The Fata Morgana. (*Scandinavian.*)

Ha-ha (*A*). A ditch serving the purpose of a hedge without breaking the prospect. (Anglo-Saxon, *hœh*, a hole.)

Hahnemann (*Samuel*). A German physician, who set forth in his *Orgănon of Medicine* the system which he called "homœopathy" the principles of which are these: (1) that diseases are cured by those medicines which would produce the disease in healthy bodies; (2) that medicines are to be simple and not compounded; (3) that doses are to be exceedingly minute. (1755-1843.)

Haidee (2 syl.). A beautiful Greek girl, who found Don Juan when he was cast ashore, and restored him to animation. "Her hair was auburn, and her eyes were black as death." Her mother, a Moorish woman from Fez, was dead, and her father, Lambro, a rich Greek pirate, was living on one of the Cyc′- ladês. She and Juan fell in love with each other during the absence of Lambro from the island. On his return Juan was arrested, placed in a galliot, and sent from the island. Haidee went mad and, after a lingering illness, died. (*Byron: Don Juan*, cantos ii. iii. iv.)

Hail. Health, an exclamation of welcome, like the Latin *Salve* (Anglo-Saxon, *hēl*, health; but hail = frozen rain is the Anglo-Saxon *hægl.*)

"All hail, Macbeth! Hail to thee, thane of Gla′mis." *Shakespeare: Macbeth*, i. 3.

Hail. To call to.
To hail a ship or *an omnibus.* To call to those on board.

Hail-fellow-well-met (*A*). One on easy, familiar terms. (*See* JOCKEY.)

"Hail fellow well met, all dirty and wet;
Find out, if you can, who's master, who's man."
Swift: My Lady's Lamentation.

Hair. One single tuft is left on the shaven crown of a Mussulman, for Mahomet to grasp hold of when drawing the deceased to Paradise.

"And each scalp had a single long tuft of hair."
Byron: Siege of Corinth.

The scalp-lock of the North American Indians, left on the otherwise bald head, is for a conquering enemy to seize when he tears off the scalp.

Hair (*Absalom's*) (2 Sam. xiv. 25). Absalom used to cut his hair once a year, and the clippings "weighed 200 shekels after the king's weight," *i.e.* 100 oz. avoirdupois. It would be a fine head of hair which weighed five ounces, but the mere clippings of Absalom's hair weighed 43,800 grains (more than 100 oz.). Paul says (1 Cor. xi. 14), "Doth not even nature itself teach you, that if a man have long hair, it is a shame unto him?"

Mrs. Astley, the actress, could stand upright and cover her feet with her flaxen hair.

Hair, Hairs. (Anglo-Saxon, *hær.*)
The greatest events are often drawn by hairs. Events of great pith and moment are often brought about by causes of apparently no importance.

Sir John Hawkins's *History of Music*, a work of sixteen years' labour, was plunged into long oblivion by a pun.

The magnificent discovery of gravitation by Newton is ascribed to the fall of an apple from a tree under which he was musing.

The dog Diamond, upsetting a lamp, destroyed the papers of Sir Isaac Newton, which had been the toil of his life. (*See* page 350.)

A spark from a candle falling on a cottage floor was the cause of the Great Fire of London.

A ballad chanted by a *fille-de-chambre* undermined the colossal power of Alberoni.

A jest of the French king was the death of William the Conqueror.

The destruction of Athens was brought about by a jest on Sulla. Some witty Athenian, struck with his pimply face, called him a "mulberry pudding."

Rome was saved from capture by the Gauls by the cackling of some sacred geese.

Benson, in his *Sketches of Corsica*, says that Napoleon's love for war was planted in his boyhood by the present of a small brass cannon.

The life of Napoleon was saved from the "Infernal Machine" because General Rapp detained Josephine a minute or two to arrange her shawl after the manner of Egyptian women.

The famous "Rye-house Plot" miscarried from the merest accident. The house in which Charles II. was staying happened to catch fire, and the king was obliged to leave for Newmarket a little sooner than he had intended.

Lafitte, the great banker, was a pauper, and he always ascribed his rise in life to his picking up a pin in the streets of Paris.

A single line of Frederick II., reflecting, not on politics, but on the poetry of a French minister, plunged France into the Seven Years' War.

The invention of glass is ascribed to some Phœnician merchants lighting a fire on the sands of the seashore.

The three hairs. When Reynard wanted to get talked about, he told Miss Magpie, under the promise of secrecy, that "the lion king had given him three hairs from the fifth leg of the a′moronthol′ogos′phorus, . . . a beast that lives on the other side of the river Cylinx; it has five legs, and on the fifth leg there are three hairs, and whoever has these three hairs will be young and beautiful for ever." They had effect only on the fair sex, and could be given only to the lady whom the donor married. (*Sir E. B. Lytton: Pilgrims of the Rhine*, xii.)

To a hair or *To the turn of a hair.* To a nicety. A hairbreadth is the forty-eighth part of an inch.

To comb one's hair the wrong way. To cross or vex one by running counter to one's prejudices, opinions, or habits.

Without turning a hair. Without indicating any sign of fatigue or distress. A horse will run a certain distance at a given rate without turning a hair.

Against the hair. Against the grain, contrary to its nature.

"If you should fight, you go against the hair of your professions."—*Shakespeare: Merry Wives of Windsor,* ii. 3.

Hair-brained. (*See* AIR-BRAINED.)

Hair-breadth 'Scape. A very narrow escape from some evil. In measurement the forty-eighth part of an inch is called a "hair-breadth."

"Wherein I spake of most disastrous chances, Of moving accidents by flood and field, Of hair-breadth 'scapes i' th' imminent deadly breach." *Shakespeare: Othello,* i. 3.

Hair Eels. These filiform worms belong to the species *Gordius aquaticus,* found in stagnant pools. Their resemblance to wriggling hairs has given rise to the not uncommon belief that a hair, if left in water for nine days, will turn into an eel.

Hair-Splitting. Cavilling about very minute differences. (*See* HAIR-BREADTH.)

"Nothing is more fatal to eloquence than attention to fine hair-splitting distinctions."— *Mathews :-Oratory and Orators,* chap. ii. p. 36.

Hair Stane (*Celtic*) means boundary stone ; a monolith sometimes, but erroneously, termed a Druidical stone. (*Scotland.*)

Hair by Hair. *Hair by hair you will pull out the horse's tail.* Plutarch says that Serto'rius, in order to teach his soldiers that perseverance and wit are better than brute force, had two horses brought before them, and set two men to pull out their tails. One of the men was a burly Herculēs, who tugged and tugged, but all to no purpose ; the other was a sharp, weasen-faced tailor, who plucked one hair at a time, amidst roars of laughter, and soon left the tail quite bare.

Hair devoted to Proserpine. Till a lock of hair is devoted to Proserpine, she refuses to release the soul from the dying body. When Dido mounted the funeral pile, she lingered in suffering till Juno sent Iris to cut off a lock of her hair. Thanătos did the same for Alcestis, when she gave her life for her husband. And in all sacrifices a forelock was first cut off from the head of the victim as an offering to the black queen.

"'Hunc ego Diti Sacrum jussa fero, teque isto corpore solvo.' Sic ait, et dextra crinem secat . . . . atque in ventos vita recessit." *Virgil: Æneid,* iv. 702-5.

Hair of a Dissembling Colour. Red hair is so-called, from the notion that Judas had red hair.

"*Rosalind.* His very hair is of the dissembling colour [red]. *Celia.* Somewhat browner than Judas's." — *Shakespeare: As You Like It,* iii. 4.

Hair of the Dog that Bit You (*A*). *Similia similĭbus curantur.* In Scotland it is a popular belief that a few hairs of the dog that bit you applied to the wound will prevent evil consequences. Applied to *drinks,* it means, if overnight you have indulged too freely, take a glass of the same wine next morning to soothe the nerves. "If this dog do you bite, soon as out of your bed, take a hair of the tail in the morning."

"Take the hair, it's well written, Of the dog by which you're bitten; Work off one wine by his brother, And one labour with another. . . . Cook with cook, and strife with strife; Business with business, wife with wife." *Athenæus (ascribed to Aristophanes).* "There was a man, and he was wise, Who fell into a bramble-bush And scratched out both his eyes; And when his eyes were out, he then Jumped into the bramble-bush, And scratched them in again."

Hair stand on End. Indicative of intense mental distress and astonishment. Dr. Andrews, of Beresford chapel, Walworth, who attended Probert under sentence of death, says: "When the executioner put the cords on his wrists, his hair, though long and lanky, of a weak iron-grey, rose gradually and stood perfectly upright, and so remained for some time, and then fell gradually down again."

"Fear came upon me and trembling, . . . [and] the hair of my flesh stood up."—Job iv. 14, 15.

Hake. *We lose in hake, but gain in herring.* Lose one way, but gain in another. Herrings are persecuted by the hakes, which are therefore driven away from a herring fishery.

Hal. A familiar contraction of Harry (for Henry). Similarly, *Dol* is a contraction of Dorothy ; *Mol,* of Mary, etc. ⁂ The substitution of *P* for *M* as the initial letter of proper names is seen in such examples as *Polly* for Molly, *Patty* for Martha, *Peggy* for Margy (*i.e.* Margaret), etc. (*See* ELIZABETH.)

Halacha [*rule*]. The Jewish oral law. (*See* GEMA'RA, MISHNA.)

"The halachah, . . . had even greater authority than the Scriptures of the Old Testament, since it explained and applied them."—*Edersheim: Life of Jesus the Messiah,* vol. i. book i chap. i.

Halberjects or **Haubergets.** A coarse thick cloth used for the habits of monks. Thomson says it is the German *al-bergen* (cover-all) or *Hals-bergen* (neck-cover). (*Essay on Magna Charta.*)

Halcyon Days. A time of happiness and prosperity. Halcyon is the Greek for a kingfisher, compounded of *hals* (the sea) and *kuo* (to brood on). The ancient Sicilians believed that the kingfisher laid its eggs and incubated for fourteen days, before the winter solstice, on the surface of the sea, during which time the waves of the sea were always unruffled.

" Amidst our arms as quiet you shall be
As halcyon brooding on a winter's sea."
Dryden.

" The peaceful kingfishers are met together
About the deck, and prophesie calm weather."
Wild: Iter Boreale.

Half. *Half is more than the whole.* (Πλέον ἥμισυ παντὸς). This is what Hesiod said to his brother Perseus, when he wished him to settle a dispute without going to law. He meant "half of the estate without the expense of law will be better than the whole after the lawyers have had their pickings." The remark, however, has a very wide signification. Thus an *embarras de richesse* is far less profitable than a sufficiency. A large estate to one who cannot manage it is impoverishing. A man of small income will be poorer with a large house and garden to keep up than if he lived in a smaller tenement. Increase of wealth, if expenditure is more in proportion, tendeth to poverty.

" Unhappy they to whom God has not revealed,
By a strong light which must their sense control,
That half a great estate's more than the whole."
Cowley : Essays in Verse and Prose, No. iv.

Half. *My better half.* (*See* BETTER.)

Half-baked. *He is only half-baked.* He is a soft, a noodle. The allusion is to bread, piecrust, etc., only half-cooked.

Half-deck. The sanctum of the second mate, carpenters, coopers, boatswain, and all secondary officers. Quarter-deck, the sanctum of the captain and superior officers. In a gun-decked ship, it is the deck below the spar-deck, extending from the mainmast to the cabin bulkheads.

Half-done. *Half-done, as Elgin was burnt.* In the wars between James II. of Scotland and the Douglases in 1452, the Earl of Huntly burnt one-half of the town of Elgin, being the side which belonged to the Douglases, but left the other side standing because it belonged to his own family. (*Sir Walter Scott : Tales of a Grandfather,* xxi.)

Half-faced Groat (*You*). You worthless fellow. The debased groats issued

in the reign of Henry VIII. had the king's head in profile, but those in the reign of Henry VII. had the king's head with the full face. (See *King John,* i. 1 ; and 2 *Henry IV.,* iii. 1.)

" Thou half-faced groat ! You thick-cheeked chitty-face ! "
Munday : The Downfal of Robert, Earle of Huntingdon (1601).

Half-seas Over. Almost up with one. Now applied to a person almost *dead* drunk. The phrase seems to be a corruption of the Dutch *op-zee zober,* " over-sea beer," a strong, heady beverage introduced into Holland from England (*Gifford*). "Up-zee Freese " is Friezeland beer. The Dutch, *half seeunst's over,* more than *half-sick.* (*C. K. Steerman.*)

" I am half-seas o'er to death."
Dryden.

" I do not like the dulness of your eye,
It hath a heavy cast, 'tis upsee Dutch."
Ben Jonson: Alchemist, iv. 2.

Halfpenny. *I am come back again, like a bad ha'penny.* A facetious way of saying "More free than welcome." As a bad ha'penny is returned to its owner, so have I returned to you, and you cannot get rid of me.

Halgaver. *Summoned before the mayor of Halgaver.* The mayor of Halgaver is an imaginary person, and the threat is given to those who have committed no offence against the laws, but are simply untidy and slovenly. Halgaver is a moor in Cornwall, near Bodmin, famous for an annual carnival held there in the middle of July. Charles II. was so pleased with the diversions when he passed through the place on his way to Scilly that he became a member of the "self-constituted " corporation. The mayor of Garratt (*q.v.*) is a similar "magnate."

Halifax. That is, *halig fax* or holy hair. Its previous name was Horton. The story is that a certain clerk of Horton, being jilted, murdered his quondam sweetheart by cutting off her head, which he hung in a yew-tree. The head was looked on with reverence, and came to be regarded as a holy relic. In time it rotted away, leaving little filaments or veins spreading out between the bark and body of the tree like fine threads. These filaments were regarded as the fax or hair of the murdered maiden. (*See* HULL, THREE H's.)

Halifax (in Nova Scotia). So called by the Hon. Edward Cornwallis, the governor, in compliment to his patron, the Earl of Halifax (1749).

Halifax Law. By this law, whoever commits theft in the liberty of Halifax is to be executed on the Halifax gibbet, a kind of guillotine.

> " At Hallifax the law so sharpe doth deale,
> That whoso more than thirteen pence doth
> steale,
> They have a jyn that wondrous quick and well
> Sends thieves all headless into heaven or hell."
> *Taylor (the Water Poet): Works,* ii. (1630).

Hall Mark. The mark on gold or silver articles after they have been assayed. Every article in gold is compared with a given standard of pure gold. This standard is supposed to be divided into twenty-four parts called carats; gold equal to the standard is said to be twenty-four carats fine. Manufactured articles are never made of pure gold, but the quantity of alloy used is restricted. Thus sovereigns and wedding-rings contain two parts of alloy to every twenty-two of gold, and are said to be twenty-two carats fine. The best gold watch-cases contain six parts of silver or copper to eighteen of gold, and are therefore eighteen carats fine. Other gold watch cases and gold articles may contain nine, twelve, or fifteen parts of alloy, and only fifteen, twelve, or nine of gold. The Mint price of standard gold is £3 17s. 10½d. per ounce, or £46 14s. 6d. per pound.

Standard silver consists of thirty-seven parts of pure silver and three of copper. The Mint price is 5s. 6d. an ounce, but silver to be melted or manufactured into " plate " varies in value according to the silver market. To-day (Oct. 20th, 1894) it is 29½d. per ounce.

Suppose the article to be marked is taken to the assay office for the hall mark. It will receive a *leopard's head* for London; an *anchor* for Birmingham; *three wheat sheaves* or a *dagger* for Chester; a *castle with two wings* for Exeter; *five lions and a cross* for York; a *crown* for Sheffield; *three castles* for Newcastle-on-Tyne; a *thistle* or *castle and lion* for Edinburgh; a *tree and a salmon with a ring in its mouth* for Glasgow; a *harp* or *Hibernia* for Dublin, etc. The specific mark shows at once where the article was assayed.

Besides the hall mark, there is also the standard mark, which for England is a *lion passant;* for Edinburgh a *thistle;* for Glasgow a *lion rampant;* and for Ireland a *crowned harp.* If the article stamped contains less pure metal than the standard coin of the realm, the number of carats is marked on it, as eighteen,fifteen,twelve,or nine carats fine.

Besides the hall mark, the standard mark, and the figure, there is a letter called the date mark. Only twenty letters are used, beginning with A, omitting J, and ending with V; one year they are in Roman characters, another year in Italian, another in Gothic, another in Old English; sometimes they are all capitals, sometimes all small letters; so, by seeing the letter and referring to a table, the exact year of the mark can be discovered.

Lastly, the head of the reigning sovereign completes the marks.

Hall' Sunday. The Sunday preceding Shrove Tuesday; the next day is called Hall' Monday, and Shrove Tuesday eve is called Hall' Night. The Tuesday is also called Pancake Day, and the day preceding Callop Monday, from the special foods popularly prepared for those days. All three were days of merrymaking. Hall' or Halle is a contraction of *Hallow* or *Haloghe,* meaning holy or festival.

Hall of Odin. The rocks, such as Halleberg and Hunneberg, from which the Hyperboreans, when tired of life, used to cast themselves into the sea; so called because they were the vestibule of the Scandinavian Elysium.

Hallam's Greek. Byron, in his *English Bards,* etc., speaks of " classic Hallam, much renowned for Greek," referring to " Hallam's severe critique on Payne Knight's *Taste,* in which were some Greek verses most mercilessly lashed. The verses, however, turned out to be a quotation from Pindar."

It appears that Dr. Allen, not Hallam, was the luckless critic. (See *Crabb Robinson: Diary,* i. 277.)

Hallel. There were two series of psalms so called. Jahn tells us in the Feast of Tabernacles the series consisted of Psalms cxiii. to cxviii. both included (*Archæologica Biblica,* p. 416). Psalm cxxxvi. was called the Great Hallel. And sometimes the songs of degrees sung standing on the fifteen steps of the inner court seem to be so called (*i.e.* cxx. to cxxxvii. both included).

> " Along this [path] Jesus advanced, preceded and followed by multitudes with loud cries of rejoicing, as at the Feast of Tabernacles, when the Great Hallel was daily sung in their processions."—*Geikie: Life of Christ,* vol. ii. chap. 55, p. 397.

In the following quotation the Songs of Degrees are called the Great Hallel.

> ' Eldad would gladly have joined in praying the Great Hallel, as they call the series of Psalms from the cxx. to the cxxxvii., after which it was customary to send round the [paschal] cup a fifth time, but midnight was already too near."—*Eldad the Pilgrim,* chap. ix.

Hallelujah is the Hebrew *halelu-Jah*, "Praise ye Jehovah."

Hallelujah Lass (*A*). A young woman who wanders about with what is called " The Salvation Army."

Hallelujah Victory. A victory gained by some newly-baptised Bretons, led by Germa′nus, Bishop of Auxerre (A.D. 429). The conquerors commenced the battle with loud shouts of "Hallelujah ! "

Halloo when out of the Wood, or *Never halloo till you are out of the wood.* Never think you are safe from the attacks of robbers till you are out of the forest. " Call no man happy till he is dead." " Many a slip 'twixt the cup and the lip."

Hallowe'en (October 31st), according to Scotch superstition, is the time when witches, devils, fairies, and other imps of earth and air hold annual holiday. (See *Hallowe'en*, a poem by Robert Burns.)

Halter. A Bridport dagger (*q.v.*). St. Johnstone's tippet.

Halter, or rather **Halster.** A rope for the neck or halse, as a horse's halter. (Anglo-Saxon, *hals*, the neck ; but there is also the word *hælfter*, a halter.)

"A thievisher knave is not on live, more filching,
  no more false;
Many a truer man than he has banged up by the
  halse [neck]."   *Gammer Gurton.*

Haltios. In Laplandic mythology, the guardian spirits of Mount Nie′mi.

" From this height [Nie′mi, in Lapland] we had opportunity several times to see those vapours rise from the lake, which the people of the country call Haltios, and which they deem to be the guardian spirits of the mountain."—*M. de Mau-pertuis.*

Ham and **Heyd.** Storm demons or weather-sprites. (*Scandinavian mytho-logy.*)

" Though valour never should be scorned,
  Yet now the storm rules wide ;
By now again to live returned
  I'll wager Ham and Heyd."
        Frithiof Saga, lay xi.

Ham′adryads. Nymphs of trees supposed to live in forest-trees, and die when the tree dies. (Greek, *hama*, together with *drus*, a forest-tree.)

⁂ The nymphs of *fruit-trees* were called " Melides " or " Hamamelids."

Hameh. In Arabian mythology, a bird formed from the blood near the brains of a murdered man. This bird cries " *Iskoo'nee !* " (Give me drink!), meaning drink of the murderer's blood ;

and this it cries incessantly till the death is avenged, when it flies away.

Hamet. *The Cid Hamet Benenge'li.* The hypothetical Moorish chronicler from whom Cervantés professes to derive his adventures of Don Quixote.

"Of the two bad cassocks I am worth . . . I would have given the latter of them as freely as even Cid Hamet offered his . . . to have stood by."—*Sterne.*

Hamilton. *The reek of Mr. Patrick Hamilton has infected as many as it did blow upon,* i.e. Patrick Hamilton was burnt to death by Cardinal Beaton, and the horror of the deed contributed not a little to the Reformation. As the blood of the martyrs is the seed of the Church, so the smoke or reek of Hamilton's fire diffused the principles for which he suffered (1504-1528).

⁂ Latimer, at the stake, said : "We shall this day light up such a candle in England as shall never be put out."

Hamilto′nian System. A method of teaching foreign languages by inter-linear translations, suggested by James Hamilton, a merchant (1769-1831).

Hamlet. A daft person (Icelandic, *amlod'*), one who is irresolute, and can do nothing fully. Shakespeare's play is based on the Danish story of Amleth' recorded in Saxo-Grammat′icus.

Hammel (Scotch). A cattle-shed, a hovel. (Hame = home, with a diminu-tive affix. Anglo-Saxon, *hām*, home. Compare *hamlet*.)

Hammer. (Anglo-Saxon, *hamer*.)

(1) Pierre d'Ailly, *Le Marteau des Hérétiques,* president of the council that condemned John Huss. (1350-1425.)

(2) Judas Asmonæus, surnamed *Mac-cabæus,* " the hammer." (B.C. 166-136.)

(3) St. Augustine is called by Hake-well " That renowned pillar of truth and hammer of heresies." (354-430.)

(4) John Faber, surnamed *Malleus Heretico'rum,* from the title of one of his works. (1470-1541.)

(5) St. Hilary, Bishop of Poitiers, *Malleus Ariano'rum.* (350-367.)

(6) Charles Martel. (689-741.)

"On prétend qu'on lui donna le 'surnom de Martel, parcequ'il avait écrasé comme avec un marteau les Sarrasins, qui, sous la conduite d'Ab-dérame, avaient envahi la France."—*Bouillet: Dictionnaire Universel,* etc.

Hammer.

PHRASES AND PROVERBS.

Gone to the hammer. Applied to goods sent to a sale by auction ; the auctioneer giving a rap with a small hammer when a lot is sold, to intimate that there is an end to the bidding.

They live hammer and tongs. Are always quarrelling. They beat each other like hammers, and are as "cross as the tongs."

"Both parties went at it hammer and tongs; and hit one another anywhere and with any-thing."—*James Payn.*

To sell under the hammer. To sell by auction. (*See above.*)

Hammer of the Scotch. Edward I. On his tomb in Westminster Abbey is the inscription "*Edwardus longus Scotorum Malleus hic est*" (Here is long Edward, the hammer of the Scots).

Hammercloth. The cloth that covers the coach-box, in which hammer, nails, bolts, etc., used to be carried in case of accident. Another etymology is from the Icelandic *hamr* (a skin), skin being used for the purpose. A third suggestion is that the word *hammer* is a corruption of "hammock," the seat which the cloth covers being formed of straps or webbing stretched between two crutches like a sailor's hammock. Still another conjecture is that the word is a corruption of "hamper cloth," the hamper being used for sundry articles required, and forming the coachman's box. The word *box* seems to favour this suggestion.

Hampton Court Conference. A conference held at Hampton Court in January, 1604, to settle the disputes between the Church party and the Puritans. It lasted three days, and its result was a few slight alterations in the Book of Common Prayer.

Hamshackle. To hamshackle a horse is to tie his head to one of his fore-legs.

Hamstring. To disable by severing the tendons of the ham.

Han. *Sons of Hân.* The Chinese are so called from Hân the founder of the twenty-sixth dynasty, with which modern history commences. (206-220.)

Hanap. A costly goblet used at one time on state occasions. Sometimes the cup used by our Lord at the Last Supper is so called. (Old High German, *hnapp*, a cup.)

"He had, indeed, four silver hanaps of his own, which had been left him by his grandmother."
—*Sir W. Scott: Quentin Durward*, chap. iv. p. 71.

Han'aper. Exchequer. "Hanaper office," an office where all writs relating to the public were formerly kept in a

hamper (*in hanaper'io*). **Hanaper is** a cover for a hanap.

Hand. A measure of length = four inches. Horses are measured up the fore leg to the shoulder, and are called 14, 15, 16 (as it may be), hands high.

i. **Hand** (*A*). A symbol of fortitude in Egypt, of fidelity in Rome. Two hands symbolise concord; and a hand laid on the head of a person indicates the right of property. Thus if a person laid claim to a slave, he laid his hand upon him in the presence of the prætor. (*Aulus Gellius*, xx. 19.) By a closed hand Zeno represented dialectics, and by an open hand eloquence.

⁂ Previous to the twelfth century the Supreme Being was represented by a hand extended from the clouds; sometimes the hand is open, with rays issuing from the fingers, but generally it is in the act of benediction, *i.e.* with two fingers raised.

ii. **Hand.** (The final word.)

BEAR A HAND. Come and help. Bend to your work immediately.

CAP IN HAND. Suppliantly, humbly; as, "To come cap in hand."

DEAD MAN'S HAND. It is said that carrying a dead man's hand will produce a dead sleep. Another superstition is that a lighted candle placed in the hand of a dead man gives no light to anyone but him who carries the hand. Hence burglars, even to the present day in some parts of Ireland, employ this method of concealment.

EMPTY HAND. *An empty hand is no lure for a hawk.* You must not expect to receive anything without giving a return. The Germans say, *Wer schmiert der fährt.* The Latin proverb is *Da, si vis accipĕre*, or *Pro nihilo, nihil fit.*

HEAVY HAND, as "To rule with a heavy hand," severely, with oppression.

OLD HAND (*An*). One experienced.

POOR HAND (*A*). An unskilful one. "He is but a poor hand at it," *i.e.* he is not skilful at the work.

RED HAND, or *bloody hand*, in coat armour is generally connected with some traditional tale of blood, and the badge was never to be expunged till the bearer had passed, by way of penance, seven years in a cave, without companion, without shaving, and without uttering a single word.

In Aston church, near Birmingham, is a coat-armorial of the Holts, the "bloody hand" of which is thus accounted for :—It is said that Sir Thomas

Holt, some two hundred years ago, murdered his cook in a cellar with a spit, and, when pardoned for the offence, the king enjoined him, by way of penalty, to wear ever after a " bloody hand " in his family coat.

In the church of Stoke d'Abernon, Surrey, there is a red hand upon a monument, the legend of which is, that a gentleman shooting with a friend was so mortified at meeting with no game that he swore he would shoot the first live thing he met. A miller was the victim of this rash vow, and the "bloody hand " was placed in his family coat to keep up a perpetual memorial of the crime.

Similar legends are told of the red hand in Wateringbury church, Kent; of the red hand on a table in the hall of Church-Gresly, in Derbyshire; and of many others.

The open red hand, forming part of the arms of the province of Ulster, commemorates the daring of O'Neile, a bold adventurer, who vowed to be first to touch the shore of Ireland. Finding the boat in which he was rowed outstripped by others, he cut off his hand and flung it to the shore, to touch it before those in advance could land.

The open red hand in the armorial coat of baronets arose thus:—James I. in 1611 created two hundred baronets on the payment of £1,000 each, ostensibly "for the amelioration of Ulster," and from this connection with Ulster they were allowed to place on their coat armour the " open red hand," up to that time borne by the O'Neiles. The O'Neile whose estates were made forfeit by King James was surnamed *Lamb-deriq Eirin* (red-hand of Erin).

RIGHT HAND. *He is my right hand.* In France, *C'est mon bras droit*, my best man.

SECOND-HAND. (*See* SECOND.)

UPPER HAND. *To get the upper hand.* To obtain the mastery.

YOUNG HAND (*A*). A young and inexperienced workman.

iii. **Hand.** (Phrases beginning with " To.")

COME TO HAND. To arrive; to have been delivered.

To come to one's hand. It is easy to do.

GET ONE'S HAND IN. To become familiar with the work in hand.

HAVE A HAND IN THE MATTER. To have a finger in the pie. In French, "*Mettre la main à quelque chose.*"

KISS THE HAND (Job xxxi. 27). To worship false gods. Cicero (*In Verrem*, lib. iv. 43) speaks of a statue of Herculēs, the chin and lips of which were considerably worn by the kisses of his worshippers. Hosea (xiii. 2) says, "Let the men that sacrifice kiss the calves." (*See* ADORE.)

" I have left me seven thousand in Israel . . . which have not bowed unto Baal, and . . . which [have] not kissed [their hand to] him."—i Kings xix. 18.

LEND A HAND. To help. In French, " *Prêtez moi la main*."

LIVE FROM HAND TO MOUTH. To live without any provision for the morrow.

TAKE IN HAND. To undertake to do something; to take the charge of.

iv. **Hand** (preceded by a preposition).

AT HAND. Conveniently near. "Near at hand," quite close by. In French, "*A la main.*"

BEFOREHAND. Sooner, before it happened.

BEHINDHAND. Not in time, not up to date.

BY THE HAND OF GOD. "*Accidit divinitus.*"

FROM HAND TO HAND. From one person to another.

IN HAND. Under control, in possession; under progress, as "*Avoir la main à l'œuvre.*"

" Keep him well in hand."
" I have some in hand, and more in expectation."
" I have a new book or picture in hand."

A bird in the hand. (*See* BIRD.)

OFF HAND. At once; without stopping.

Off one's hands. No longer under one's responsibilities; able to maintain oneself.

OUT OF HAND. At once, over.

" We will proclaim you out of hand."
                    Shakespeare : 3 Henry VI., iv. 7.

"And, were these inward wars once out of hand, We would, dear lords, unto the Holy Land."
                    Shakespeare : 2 Henry IV., iii. 1.

WITH A HIGH HAND. Imperiously, arrogantly. In French, "*Faire quelque chose haut la main.*"

v. **Hand.** (Miscellaneous articles.)

LAYING ON OF HANDS. The laying on of a bishop's hands in confirmation or ordination.

PUTTING THE HAND UNDER THE THIGH. An ancient ceremony used in swearing.

" And Abraham said unto his eldest servant . . . Put, I pray thee, thy hand under my thigh : and I will make thee swear . . . that thou shalt not take a wife unto my son of the daughters of the Cananites."—Genesis xxiv. 2, 3.

Hands. Persons employed in a factory. We say so many *head* of cattle :

horse-dealers count *noses*. Races are won by the nose, and factory work by the hand, but cattle have the place of honour.

Hands.

ALL. *It is believed on all hands.* It is generally (or universally) believed.

CHANGE. *To change hands.* To pass from a possessor to someone else.

CLEAN. *He has clean hands.* In French, "*Il a les mains nettes.*" That is, he is incorruptible, or he has never taken a bribe.

FULL. *My hands are full.* I am fully occupied; I have as much work to do as I can manage. A "handful" has the plural "handfuls," as "two handfuls," same as "two barrow-loads," "two cart-loads," etc.

GOOD. *I have it from very good hands.* I have received my information on good authority.

LAY. *To lay hands on.* To apprehend; to lay hold of. (*See* No. v.)

"Lay hands on the villain."
Shakespeare: Taming of the Shrew, v. 1.

LONG. *Kings have long hands.* In French, "*Les rois ont les mains longues.*" That is, it is hard to escape from the vengeance of a king, for his hands or agents extend over the whole of his kingdom.

SHAKE. *To shake hands.* To salute by giving a hand received into your own a shake.

To strike hands (Prov. xvii. 18). To make a contract, to become surety for another. (*See* also Prov. vii. 1 and xxii. 26.) The English custom of shaking hands in confirmation of a bargain has been common to all nations and all ages. In feudal times the vassal put his hands in the hands of his overlord on taking the oath of fidelity and homage.

SHOP "*Hands,*" etc. Men and women employed in a shop.

TAKE OFF. *To take off one's hands.* To relieve one of something troublesome, as "Will no one take this [task] off my hands?"

WASH. *To wash one's hands of a thing.* In French, "*Se lever les mains d'une chose*" or "*Je m'en lave les mains.*" I will have nothing to do with it; I will abandon it entirely. The allusion is to Pilate's washing his hands at the trial of Jesus.

"When Pilate saw that he could prevail nothing, but that rather a tumult was made, he took water, and washed his hands before the multitude, saying, I am innocent of the blood of this just person: see ye to it."—Matt. xxvii. 24.

Hand - book. Spelman says that King Alfred used to carry in his bosom memorandum leaves, in which he made observations, and took so much pleasure therein that he called it his hand-book, because it was always in his hand.

Hand-gallop. A slow and easy gallop, in which the horse is kept well in hand.

Hand Paper. A particular sort of ☞ * paper well known in the Record Office, and so called from its water-mark, which goes back to the fifteenth century.

Hand-post (*A*). A direction-post to direct travellers the way to different places.

Hand Round (*To*). To pass from one person to another in a regular series.

Hand and Glove (*They are*). Inseparable companions, of like tastes and like affections. They fit each other like hand and glove.

Hand and Seal. When writing was limited to a few clerks, documents were authenticated by the impression of the hand dipped in ink, and then the seal was duly appended. As dipping the hand in ink was dirty, the impression of the thumb was substituted. We are informed that "scores of old English and French deeds still exist in which such 'signatures' appear." Subsequently the name was written, and this writing was called "the hand."

"*Hubert:* Here is your hand and seal for what I did.
King John: Oh, when the last account 'twixt heaven and earth
Is to be made, then shall this hand and seal
Witness against us to damnation."
Shakespeare: King John, iv. 2.

Hand-in-Hand. In a familiar or kindly manner, as when persons go hand-in-hand.

"Now we maun totter down, John,
But hand in hand we'll go."
John Anderson, my Jo.

Hand of Cards. The whole deal of cards given to a single player. The cards which he holds in his hand.

"A saint in heaven would grieve to see such 'hand'
Cut up by one who will not understand."
Crabbe: Borough.

Hand of Justice. The allusion is to the sceptre or bâton anciently used by kings, which had an ivory hand at the top of it.

Hand over Hand. To go or to come up hand over hand, is to travel with great rapidity, as climbing a rope or a ladder, or as one vessel overtakes another. Sailors in hauling a rope put one hand over the other alternately as fast as they can. In French, "*Main sur main.*"

"Commandment fait aux matelots qui halent sur une manœuvre pour qu'ils passent alternativement une main sur l'autre sans interruption, et pour que le travail se fasse plus promptement." —*Royal Dictionnaire.*

Hand the Sail, *i.e.* furl it.

Hand Down to Posterity (*To*). To leave for future generations.

Handfasting. A sort of marriage. A fair was at one time held in Dumfriesshire, at which a young man was allowed to pick out a female companion to live with him. They lived together for twelve months, and if they both liked the arrangement were man and wife. This was called *hand-fasting* or *hand-fastening.*

This sort of contract was common among the Romans and Jews, and is not unusual in the East even now.

"'Knowest thou not that rite, holy man?' said Avenel . . . .; 'then I will tell thee. We bordermen . . . . take our wives for a year and a day; that space gone by, each may choose another mate, or, at their pleasure, [they] may call the priest to marry them for life, and this we call handfasting.'" — *Sir W. Scott: The Monastery,* chap. xxv.

Handicap. A game at cards not unlike loo, but with this difference—the winner of one trick has to put in a double stake, the winner of two tricks a triple stake, and so on. Thus : if six persons are playing, and the general stake is 1s., and A gains three tricks, he gains 6s., and has to "hand i' the cap" or pool 3s. for the next deal. Suppose A gains two tricks and B one, then A gains 4s. and B 2s., and A has to stake 3s. and B 2s. for the next deal.

"To the 'Mitre Tavern' in Wood Street, a house of the greatest note in London. Here some of us fell to handicap, a sport I never knew before, which was very good."—*Pepys: His Diary,* Sept. 18th, 1680.

Handicap, in racing, is the adjudging of various weights to horses differing in age, power, or speed, in order to place them all, as far as possible, on an equality. If two unequal players challenge each other at chess, the superior gives up a piece, and this is his handicap. So called from the ancient game referred to by Pepys. (*See* SWEEPSTAKES, PLATE-RACE, etc.)

The Winner's Handicap. The winning horses of previous races being pitted together in a race royal are first handicapped according to their respective merits : the horse that has won three races has to carry a greater weight than the horse that has won only two, and

this latter more than its competitor who is winner of a single race only.

Handkerchief. "*The committee was at a loss to know whom next to throw the handkerchief to*" (*The Times*). The meaning is that the committee did not know whom they were to ask next to make a speech for them ; and the allusion is to the game called in Norfolk "Stir up the dumplings," and by girls "Kiss in the ring."

Handkerchief and Sword. *With handkerchief in one hand and sword in the other.* Pretending to be sorry at a calamity, but prepared to make capital out of it.

"Abbé George . . . . mentions in [a letter] that 'Maria Theresa stands with the handkerchief in one hand, weeping for the woes of Poland, but with the sword in the other hand, ready to cut Poland in sections, and take her share.'" — *Carlyle: The Diamond Necklace,* chap. iv.

Handle. *He has a handle to his name.* Some title, as "lord," "sir," "doctor." The French say *Monsieur sans queue,* a man without a tail (handle to his name).

To give a handle to . . . . To give grounds for suspicion; as, "He certainly gave a handle to the rumour."

"He gave a handle to his enemies, and threw stumbling-blocks in the way of his friends."— *Hazlitt: Spirit of the Age* (James Macintosh), p. 139.

Handsome = liberal. *To do the thing that is handsome; to act handsomely; to do handsome towards one.*

Handwriting on the Wall (*The*). An announcement of some coming calamity. The allusion is to the handwriting on Belshazzar's palace-wall announcing the loss of his kingdom. (Dan. v. 5-31.)

Handycuffs. Cuffs or blows given by the hand. "Fisticuffs" is now more common.

Hang Back (*To*). To hesitate to proceed.

Hang Fire (*To*). To fail in an expected result. The allusion is to a gun or pistol which fails to go off.

Hang On (*To*). To cling to; to persevere; to be dependent on.

Hang Out. *Where do you hang out?* Where are you living, or lodging? The allusion is to the custom, now restricted to public-houses, but once very general, of hanging before one's shop a sign indicating the nature of the business carried on within. Druggists often still place coloured bottles in their windows, and some tobacconists place near their shop door the statue of a Scotchman. (See *Dickens: Pickwick Papers*, chap. xxx.)

Hangdog Look (*A*). A guilty, shamefaced look.

"Look a little brisker, man, and not so hangdog-like."—*Dickens.*

Hang by a Thread (*To*). To be in a very precarious position. The allusion is to the sword of Damŏclēs. (*See* DAMOCLES' SWORD.)

Hang in the Bell Ropes (*To*). To be asked at church, and then defer the marriage so that the bells hang fire.

Hanged or *Strangled*. Examples from the ancient classic writers :—

(1) AC′HIUS, King of Lydia, endeavoured to raise a new tribute from his subjects, and was hanged by the enraged populace, who threw the dead body into the river Pacto′lus.

(2) AMA′TA, wife of King Lati′nus, promised her daughter Lavin′ia to King Turnus ; when, however, she was given in marriage to Æne′as, Ama′ta hanged herself that she might not see the hated stranger. (*Virgil: Æneid*, vii.)

(3) ARACH′NE, the most skilful of needle-women, hanged herself because she was outdone in a trial of skill by Minerva. (*Ovid: Metamorphoses*, vi. fab. 1.)

(4) AUTOL′YCA, mother of Ulysses, hanged herself in despair on receiving false news of her son's death.

(5) BONO′SUS, a Spaniard by birth, was strangled by the Emperor Probus for assuming the imperial purple in Gaul. (A.D. 280.)

(6) IPHIS, a beautiful youth of Salamis, of mean birth, hanged himself because his addresses were rejected by Anaxar′etë, a girl of Salamis of similar rank in life. (*Ovid: Metamorphoses*, xiv. 708, etc.)

(7) LATI′NUS, wife of. (*See* AMATA, *above.*)

(8) LYCAM′BES, father of Neobu′la, who betrothed her to Archil′ochos, the poet. He broke his promise, and gave her in marriage to a wealthier man. Archil′ochos so scourged them by his satires that both father and daughter hanged themselves.

(9) NEOBU′LA. (*See above.*)

(10) PHYLLIS, Queen of Thrace, the accepted of Demoph′oön, who stopped on her coasts on his return from Troy. Demophoön was called away to Athens, and promised to return ; but, failing so to do, Phyllis hanged herself.

Hanged, Drawn, and Quartered. (*See* DRAWN.)

Hanger (*A*). Properly the fringed loop or strap hung to the girdle by which the dagger was suspended, but applied by a common figure of speech to the sword or dagger itself.

"Men's swords in hangers hang fast by their side."—*J. Taylor* (1630).

Hanging. *Hanging and wiving go by destiny.* "If a man is doomed to be hanged, he will never be drowned." And "marriages are made in heaven," we are told.

"If matrimony and hanging go
By dest′ny, why not whipping too ?
What med′cine else can cure the fits
Of lovers when they lose their wits ?
Love is a boy, by poets styled,
Then spare the rod and spoil the child."
Butler: Hudibras, part ii. canto i. 839-844.

Hanging Gale (*The*). The custom of taking six months' grace in the payment of rent which prevailed in Ireland.

"We went to collect the rents due the 25th March, but which, owing to the custom which prevails in Ireland known as 'the hanging gale,' are never demanded till the 29th September."— *The Times*, November, 1885.

Hanging Gardens of Babylon. Four acres of garden raised on a base supported by pillars, and towering in terraces one above another 300 feet in height. At a distance they looked like a vast pyramid covered with trees. This mound was constructed by Nebuchadnezzar to gratify his wife Am′ytis, who felt weary of the flat plains of Babylon, and longed for something to remind her of her native Me′dian hills. One of the "seven wonders of the world."

Hangman's Acre, Gains, and Gain's Alley (London), in the liberty of St. Catherine. Strype says it is a corruption of "Hammes and Guynes," so called because refugees from those places were allowed to lodge there in the reign of Queen Mary after the loss of Calais. (See also *Stow: History*, vol. ii. ; list of streets.)

Hangman's Wages. 13½d. The fee given to the executioner at Tyburn, with 1½d. for the rope. This was the value of a Scotch merk, and therefore points to the reign of James, who decreed that "the coin of silver called the mark-piece shall be current within the kingdom at the value of 13½d." Noblemen who were to be beheaded were expected to give the executioner from £7 to £10 for cutting off their head.

"For half of thirteen-pence ha'penny wages
I would have cleared all the town cages,
And you should have been rid of all the stages
I and my gallows groan."
The Hangman's Last Will and Testament.
(*Rump Songe.*)

⁂ The present price (1894) is about £40. Calcraft's charge was £33 14s., plus assistant £5 5s., other fees £1 1s., to which he added "expenses for erecting the scaffold."

Hangmen and *Executioners.*

(1) BULL is the earliest hangman whose name survives (about 1593).

(2) JOCK SUTHERLAND.

(3) DERRICK, who cut off the head of Essex in 1601.

(4) GREGORY. Father and son, mentioned by Sir Walter Scott (1647).

(5) GREGORY BRANDON (about 1648).

(6) RICHARD BRANDON, his son, who executed Charles I.

(7) SQUIRE DUN, mentioned by Hudibras (part iii. c. 2).

(8) JACK KETCH (1678) executed Lord Russell and the Duke of Monmouth.

(9) ROSE, the butcher (1686); but Jack Ketch was restored to office the same year.

(10) EDWARD DENNIS (1780), introduced as a character in Dickens's *Barnaby Rudge*.

(11) THOMAS CHESHIRE, nicknamed " Old Cheese."

(12) JOHN CALCRAFT ; MARWOOD ; BERRY ; etc.

(13) Of foreign executioners, the most celebrated are Little John ; Capeluche, headsman of Paris during the terrible days of the Armagnacs and Burgundians ; and the two brothers Sanson, who were executioners during the first French Revolution.

❧ Hudibras, under the name of Dun, "personates " Sir Arthur Hazelrig, " the activest " of the five members impeached by King Charles I. The other four were Monk, Walton, Morley, and Alured.

Hankey Pankey. Jugglery ; fraud.

Hanoverian Shield. This escutcheon used to be added to the arms of England ; it was placed in the *centre* of the shield to show that the House of Hanover came to the crown by election, and not by conquest. Conquerors strike out arms of a conquered country, and place their own in lieu.

Hans von Rippach [*rip-pak*]. Jack of Rippach, a Monsieur Nong-tong-pas —*i.e.* someone asked for who does not exist. A gay German spark calls at a house and asks for Herr Hans von Rippach. Rippach is a village near Leipsic.

Hansards. The printed records of Bills before Parliament, the reports of committees, parliamentary debates, and some of the national accounts. Till the business was made into a company the reports commanded a good respect, but in 1892 the company was wound up. Luke Hansard, the founder of the business came from Norwich, and was born in 1752.

❧ Other parliamentary business was printed by other firms.

Hanse Towns. The maritime cities of Germany, which belonged to the Hanseatic League (*q.v.*).

"The Hanse towns of Lübeck, Bremen, and Hamburg are commonwealths even now (1877)."—*Freeman: General Sketch*, chap. x. p. 174.

Hanseatic League. The first trade union ; it was established in the twelfth century by certain cities of Northern Germany for their mutual prosperity and protection. The diet which used to be held every three years was called the *Hansa*, and the members of it *Hansards*. The league in its prosperity comprised eighty-five towns; it declined rapidly in the Thirty Years' War; in 1669 only six cities were represented ; and the last three members of the league (Hamburg, Lübeck, and Bremen) joined the German Customs Unions' in 1889. (German, *am-see*, on the sea ; and the league was originally called the *Am-see-staaten*, free cities on the sea.)

Hansel. A gift or bribe, the first money received in a day. Hence Hansel Monday, the first Monday of the year. To "hansel our swords " is to use them for the first time. In Norfolk we hear of hanselling a coat—*i.e.* wearing it for the first time. Lemon tells us that superstitious people will spit on the first money taken at market for luck, and Misson says, "*Ils le baisent en le recevant, craschent dessus, et le mettent dans une poche apart.*" (*Travels in England*, p. 192.)

Hansel Monday. The Monday after New-Year's Day, when "hansels," or free gifts, were given in Scotland to servants and children. Our boxing-day is the first weekday after Christmas Day. (Anglo-Saxon, *handselen ; hand* and *sellan*, to give.)

Hansom (*A*). A light two-wheeled cab, in which the driver sits behind the vehicle, and communicates with the passenger through a trap-door in the roof. Invented by Aloysius Hansom of York (1803-1882). Hansom was by trade an architect at Birmingham and at Hinckley in Leicestershire.

Hapmouche (2 syl.). The giant fly-catcher. He invented the art of drying and smoking neats' tongues. (*Duchat : Œuvres de Rabelais.*)

Happy Arabia. A mistranslation of the Latin *Arabia felix*, which means simply *on the right hand—i.e.* to the right hand of *Al-Shan* (Syria). It was Ptolemy who was the author of the threefold division *Arabia Petræa*, miscalled "Stony Arabia," but really so called from its chief city Petra ; *Arabia Felix* (or *Yemen*), the south-west coast; and as for *Arabia deserta* (meaning the interior) probably he referred to *Nedjaz*.

Happy Expression (*A*). A well-turned phrase ; a word or phrase peculiarly apt. The French also say " *Une heureuse expression*," and " *S'exprimer heureusement.*"

Happy-go-lucky (*A*). One indifferent to his interests ; one who looks to good luck to befriend him.

Happy Valley, in Dr. Johnson's tale of *Rasselas*, is placed in the kingdom of Amhara, and was inaccessible except in one spot through a cave in a rock. It was a Garden of Paradise where resided the princes of Abyssinia.

Happy as a Clam at High Tide. The clam is a bivalve mollusc, dug from its bed of sand only at low tide ; at high tide it is quite safe from molestation. (*See* CLOSE AS A CLAM.)

Happy as a King. This idea of happiness is wealth, position, freedom, and luxurious living ; but Richard II. says a king is "Woe's slave" (iii. 2).
∵ On the happiness of kings, *see* Shakespeare : *Henry V.*, iv. 1.

Happy the People whose Annals are Tiresome. (*Montesquieu.*) Of course, wars, rebellions, troubles, make up the most exciting parts of history.

Hapsburg. (*See* HABSBURG.)

Har. The first person of the Scandinavian Trinity, which consists of Har (the Mighty), the Like Mighty, and the Third Person. This Trinity is called "The Mysterious Three," and they sit on three thrones above the Rainbow. The next in order are the Æsir (*q.v.*), of which Odin, the chief, lives in Asgard, on the heavenly hills between Earth and the Rainbow. The third order is the Vanir (*see* VAN)—the gods of the ocean, air, and clouds—of which Van Niörd is the chief. Har has already passed his ninth incarnation ; in his tenth he will take the forms first of a peacock, and then of a horse, when all the followers of Mahomet will be destroyed.

Har, in Indian mythology, is the *second* person of the Trinity.

Ha'ram or **Ha'rem**, means in Arabic *forbidden*, or *not to be violated ;* a name given by Mahometans to those apartments which are appropriated exclusively to the female members of a family.

Har'apha. A descendant of Og and Anak, a giant of Gath, who went to mock Samson in prison, but durst not venture within his reach. The word means *the giant.* (*Milton : Samson Agonistes.*)

Har'binger. One who looks out for lodgings, etc. ; a courier ; hence, a forerunner, a messenger. (Anglo-Saxon, *here*, an army ; *bergan*, to lodge.)

" I'll be myself the harbinger, and make joyful
The hearing of my wife with your approach."
Shakespeare : Macbeth, i. 4.

Harcourt's Round Table. A private conference in the house of Sir William Harcourt, January 14, 1887, with

the view of reuniting, if possible, the Liberal party, broken up by Mr. Gladstone's Irish policy.

The phrase "Round Table" is American, meaning what the French call a *cercle*, or club meetings held at each other's houses.

Hard, meaning difficult, is like the French *dur ;* as, "hard of hearing," "*qui a l'oreille dure ;*" "a hard word," "*un terme dur ;*" "'tis a hard case," "*c'est une chose bien dure ;*" "hard times," "*les temps sont durs ;*" so also "hardly earned," "*qu'on gagne bien durement ;*" "hard-featured," "*dont les traits sont durs ;*" "hard-hearted," "*qui a le cœur dur,*" and many other phrases.

Hard By. Near. Hard means close, pressed close together ; hence firm or solid, in close proximity to.
" Hard by a sheltering wood."
David Mallet : Edwin and Emma.

Hard Lines. Hard terms ; "rather rough treatment ;" exacting. Lines mean lot or allotment (measured out by a line measure), as, "The lines have fallen to me in pleasant places ; yea, I have a goodly heritage," *i.e.* my allotment is excellent. Hard lines = an unfavourable allotment (or task).
" That was hard lines upon me, after I had given up everything."—*G. Eliot.*

Hard Up. Short of money. "*N'avoir pas de quibus.*" "Up" often = out, as, "used up," "worn out," "done up," etc. "Hard up" = nearly out [of cash]. In these, and all similar examples, "Up" is the Old English *ofer*, over ; Latin, *s-uper ;* Greek, ὑπέρ.

Hard as Nails. Stern, hard-hearted, unsympathetic ; able to stand hard blows like nails. Religious bigotry, straitlacedness, rigid puritanical pharisaism, make men and women "hard as nails."
" I know I'm as hard as nails already ; I don't want to get more so."—*Edna Lyall : Donovan,* chap. xxiii.

Hard as a Stone, "hard as iron," "hard as brawn," "hard as ice," "hard as adamant," etc. (*See* SIMILES.)

Hard as the Nether Millstone. Unfeeling, obdurate. The lower or "nether" of the two millstones is firmly fixed and very hard ; the upper stone revolves round it on a shaft, and the corn, running down a tube inserted in the upper stone, is ground by the motion of the upper stone round the lower one. Of course, the upper wheel is made to revolve by some power acting on it, as wind, water, or some other mechanical force.

Hardouin (2 syl.). *E'en Hardouin would not object.* Said in apology of an historical or chronological incident introduced into a treatise against which some captious persons take exception. Jean Hardouin, the learned Jesuit, was librarian to Louis le Grand. He was so fastidious that he doubted the truth of all received history, denied the authenticity of the *Æneid* of Virgil, the *Odes* of Horace, etc.; placed no faith in medals and coins, regarded all councils before that of Trent as chimerical, and looked on Descartes, Malebranche, Pascal, and all Jansenists as infidels. (1646-1729.)

"Even Père Hardouin would not enter his protest against such a collection."—*Dr. A. Clarke: Essay.*

Hardy (*Letitia*). Heroine of the *Belle's Stratagem*, by Mrs. Cowley. She is a young lady of fortune destined to marry Doricourt. She first assumes the air of a raw country hoyden and disgusts the fastidious man of fashion; then she appears at a masquerade and wins him. The marriage is performed at midnight, and Doricourt does not know that the masquerader and hoyden are the same Miss Hardy till after the ceremony is over.

HARDY (*The*), *i.e.* brave or daring, hence the phrase, "*hardi comme un lion.*"

(1) William Douglas, defender of Berwick (died 1302).

(2) Philippe III. of France, *le Hardi* (1245, 1270-1285).

(3) Philippe II., Duc de Bourgogne, *le Hardi* (1342, 1363-1382).

Hare. It is unlucky for a hare to cross your path, because witches were said to transform themselves into hares.

"Nor did we meet, with nimble feet,
  One little fearful lepus ;
That certain sign, as some divine,
  Of fortune bad to keep us."
        Ellison : Trip to Benwell, ix.

⁂ In the *Flamborough Village and Headland*, we are told, "if a fisherman on his way to the boats happens to meet a woman, parson, or hare, he will turn back, being convinced that he will have no luck that day."

Antipathy to hares. Tycho Brahe (2 syl.) would faint at the sight of a hare ; the Duc d'Epernon at the sight of a leveret ; Marshal de Brézé at sight of a rabbit ; and Henri III., the Duke of Schomberg, and the chamberlain of the emperor Ferdinand, at the sight of a cat. (*See* ANTIPATHY.)

First catch your hare. (*See* CATCH.)

Hold with the hare and run with the hounds. To play a double and deceitful game, to be a traitor in the camp. To run with the hounds as if intent to catch the hare, but all the while being the secret friend of poor Wat. In the American war these double-dealers were called Copperheads (*q.v.*).

Mad as a March hare. Hares are unusually shy and wild in March, which is their rutting season.

⁂ Erasmus says "Mad as a marsh hare," and adds, "hares are wilder in marshes from the absence of hedges and cover." (*Aphorisms*, p. 266 ; 1542.)

Melancholy as a hare (*Shakespeare :* 1 *Henry IV.*, i. 2). According to mediæval quackery, the flesh of hare was supposed to generate melancholy ; and all foods imparted their own speciality.

The quaking hare, in Dryden's *Hind and Panther*, means the Quakers.

"Among the timorous kind, the quaking hare
  Professed neutrality, but would not swear."
        Part i. 37, 38.

Hare - brained, or **Hair - brained.** Mad as a March hare, giddy, foolhardy.

"Let's leave this town ; for they [the English]
  are hair-brained slaves,
And hunger will enforce them to be more
  eager."   *Shakespeare :* 1 *Henry VI.*, i. 2.

Harefoot. Swift of foot as a hare. The surname given to Harold I., youngest son of Canute (1035-1040).

To kiss the hare's foot. To be too late for anything, to be a day after the fair. The hare has gone by, and left its footprint for you to salute. A similar phrase is *To kiss the post.*

Hare-lip. A cleft lip ; so called from its resemblance to the upper lip of a hare. It was said to be the mischievous act of an elf or malicious fairy.

"This is the foul fiend Flibbertigibbet. He begins at curfew, and walks till the first cock. He . . . . squints the eye and makes the hare-lip."
—*Shakespeare : King Lear*, iii. 4.

Hare-stone = Hour-stone. Boundary stone in the parish of Sancred (Cornwall), with a heap of stones round it. It is thought that these stones were set up for a similar purpose as the column set up by Laban (Genesis xxxi. 51, 52). "Behold this heap, and behold this pillar," said Laban to Jacob, "which I have cast betwixt me and thee. This heap be witness, and this pillar be witness, that I will not pass over this heap to thee, and that thou shalt not pass over this heap unto me, for harm." (Anglo-Saxon, *hora*, or *horu stan*.) (*See* HAROLD'S STONES.)

Hare and the Tortoise (*The*). Everyone knows the fable of the race between the hare and the tortoise, won by the latter ; and the moral, "Slow and steady wins the race." The French equivalent is "*Pas à pas le bœuf prend le lièvre.*"

Hares shift their Sex. It was once thought that hares are sexless, or that they change their sex every year.

"Lepores omnes utrumque sexum habent."
Munsterus.

"Snakes that cast their coats for new,
Cameleons that alter hue,
Hares that yearly sexes change."
Fletcher: Faithful Shepherd, iii. 1.

Har'icot Mutton. A ragoût made with hashed mutton and turnips. In old French *harigot, harligot,* and *haligote* are found meaning a "morsel," a "piece."

"Et li chevalier tuit monté,
Detaillie et dehaligoté."
Chauvenci: Les Tournois, p. 138.

Harikiri. [*Happy despatch.*] A method of enforcing suicide by disembowelling among Japanese officials when government considered them worthy of death.

Hark Back (*To*). To return to the subject. "*Revenons à nos moutons*" (*q.v.*). A call to the dogs in fox-hunting, when they have overrun the scent, "Hark [dogs] come back"; so "Hark for'ards!" "Hark away!" etc.

Harlequin means a species of drama in two parts, the introduction and the harlequinade, acted in dumb show. The prototype is the Roman *atellānæ,* but our Christmas pantomime or harlequinade is essentially a British entertainment, first introduced by Mr. Weaver, a dancing-master of Shrewsbury, in 1702. (*See below.*)

"What Momus was of old to Jove,
The same a harlequin is now.
The former was buffoon above,
The latter is a Punch below."
Swift: The Puppet Show.

⁂ The Roman mime did not at all correspond with our harlequinade. The Roman mimus is described as having a shorn head, a sooty face, flat unshod feet, and a patched parti-coloured cloak. *Harlequin,* in the British pantomime, is a sprite supposed to be invisible to all eyes but those of his faithful Columbine. His office is to dance through the world and frustrate all the knavish tricks of the Clown, who is supposed to be in love with Columbine. In Armóric, *Harlequin* means "a juggler," and Harlequin metamorphoses everything he touches with his magic wand.

⁂ The prince of Harlequins was John Rich (1681-1761). *Harlequin.* So Charles Quint was called by François I. of France.

Harlot is said to be derived from Harlotta, the mother of William the Conqueror, but it is more likely to be a corruption of *horlet* (a little hireling), "hore" being the past participle of *hyran* (to hire). It was once applied to males as well as females. Hence Chaucer speaks of "a sturdy harlot . . . . that was her hostes man." The word *varlet* is another form of it.

"He was gentil harlot, and a kinde ;
A bettre felaw shulde man no wher finde."
Chaucer: Canterbury Tales, prol. 649.

"The harlot king is quite beyond mine arm."
Shakespeare: Winter's Tale, ii. 3.

⁂ Proverbial names for a harlot are Aholibah and Aholah (Ezek. xxiii. 4), probably symbolic characters ; Petrowna (of Russia), and Messalina (of Rome).

Harlowe (*Clarissa*). The heroine of Richardson's novel of that name. In order to avoid a marriage urged upon her by her parents, she casts herself on the protection of a lover, who grossly abuses the confidence thus reposed in him. He subsequently proposes to marry her, but Clarissa rejects the offer, and retires from the world to cover her shame and die.

Harm. *Harm set, harm get.* Those who lay traps for others get caught themselves. Haman was hanged on his own gallows. Our Lord says, "They that take the sword shall perish with the sword" (Matt. xxvi. 52).

Harmless as a Dove. (Matt. x. 16.)

Harmo'nia's Necklace. An unlucky possession, something that brings evil to all who possess it. Harmonia was the daughter of Mars and Venus. On the day of her marriage with King Cadmos, she received a necklace which proved fatal to all who possessed it.

⁂ The collar given by Alphesibēa (or Arsinoë) to her husband Alcmæon was a like fatal gift. So were the collar and veil of Eriphylē, wife of Amphiaraos, and the Trojan horse. (*See* FATAL GIFTS.)

Harmo'nia's Robe. On the marriage of Harmonia, Vulcan, to avenge the infidelity of her mother, made the bride a present of a robe dyed in all sorts of crimes, which infused wickedness and impiety into all her offspring. Both Harmonia and Cadmos, after having suffered many misfortunes, and seen their children a sorrow to them, were changed into serpents. (*Pausanias,* 9, 10.) (*See* NESSUS.)

⁂ Medēa, in a fit of jealousy, sent Creüsa a wedding robe, which burnt her to death. (*Euripídēs : Medea.*)

Harness. *To die in harness.* To continue in one's work or occupation till death. The allusion is to soldiers in armour or harness.

"At least we'll die with harness on our back."
Shakespeare: Macbeth, v. 5.

Harness Cask. A large cask or tub with a rim cover, containing a supply of salt meat for immediate use. Nautical term.

Harness Prize (University of Cambridge), founded by the Rev. William Harness for the best essay connected with Shakespearian literature. Awarded every third year.

Haro. *To cry out haro to anyone.* To denounce his misdeeds, to follow him with hue and cry. "Ha' rou" was the ancient Norman hue-and-cry, and the exclamation made by those who wanted assistance, their person or property being in danger. It is similar to our cry of "Police!" Probably our halloo is the same word.

⁂ In the Channel Isles, *Ha! ho! à l'aide, mon prince!* is a protest still in vogue when one's property is endangered, or at least was so when I lived in Jersey. It is supposed to be an appeal to Rollo, king of Normandy, to come to the aid of him suffering wrongfully.

Harold the Dauntless. Son of Witikind, the Dane. "He was rocked on a buckler, and fed from a blade." He became a Christian, like his father, and married Eivir, a Danish maid, who had been his page. (*Sir W. Scott: Harold the Dauntless.*)

Harold's Stones at Trelech (Monmouthshire). Three stones, one of which is fourteen feet above the ground, evidently no part of a *circle.* Probably boundary stones. (*See* HARE-STONE.)

Haroot and **Maroot.** Two angels who, in consequence of their want of compassion to man, are susceptible of human passions, and are sent upon earth to be tempted. They were at one time kings of Babel, and are still the teachers of magic and the black arts.

Haroun al Raschid. Calif of the East, of the Abbasside race. (765-809.) His adventures form a part of the *Arabian Nights' Entertainments.*

Harp. The arms of Ireland. According to tradition, one of the early kings of Ireland was named David, and this king took for arms the *harp* of Israel's sweet Psalmist. Probably the harp is altogether a blunder, arising from the *triangle* invented in the reign of John to distinguish his Irish coins from the English. The reason why a

triangle was chosen may have been in allusion to St. Patrick's explanation of the Trinity, or more likely to signify that he was king of England, Ireland, and France. Henry VIII. was the first to assume the *harp* positive as the Irish device, and James I. to place it in the third quarter of the royal achievement of Great Britain.

To harp for ever on the same string. To be for ever teasing one about the same subject. There is a Latin proverb, *Eandem cantilēnam recinĕre.* I once heard a man with a clarionet play the first half of "In my cottage near a wood" for more than an hour, without cessation or change. It was in a crowded market-place, and the annoyance became at last so unbearable that he collected a rich harvest to move on.

"Still harping on my daughter."—*Shakespeare: Hamlet*, ii. 1.

Har'pagon (*A*). A miser. Harpagon is the name of the miser in Molière's comedy called *L'Avare.*

Harpal'ice (4 syl.). A Thracian virago, who liberated her father Harpal'icos when he was taken prisoner by the Getæ.

"With such array Harpalicē bestrode
Her Thracian courser." *Dryden.*

Harpe (2 syl.). The cutlass with which Mercury killed Argus; and with which Perseus subsequently cut off the head of Medu'sa.

Harpies (2 syl.). Vultures with the head and breasts of a woman, very fierce and loathsome, living in an atmosphere of filth and stench, and contaminating everything which they came near. Homer mentions but *one* harpy. He'siod gives *two,* and later writers *three.* The names indicate that these monsters were personifications of whirlwinds and storms. Their names were Ocyp'eta (*rapid*), Cele'no (*blackness*), and Aëll'o (*storm*). (Greek *harpuiai,* verb *harpāzo,* to seize; Latin *harpyia.* See *Virgil: Æneid,* iii. 219, etc.).

He is a regular harpy. One who wants to appropriate everything; one who sponges on another without mercy.

"I will . . . . do you any embassage . . . rather than hold three words conference with this harpy."—*Shakespeare: Much Ado About Nothing,* ii. 1.

Harpoc'rates (4 syl.). The Greek form of the Egyptian god Har-pi-kruti (*Horus the Child*), made by the Greeks and Romans the *god of silence.* This arose from a pure misapprehension. It is an Egyptian god, and was represented with its "finger on its mouth," to indicate *youth*, but the Greeks thought it was a symbol of *silence*.

"I assured my mistress she might make herself perfectly easy on that score [his mentioning a certain matter to anyone], for I was the Harpocrates of trusty valets."—*Gil Blas*, iv. 2 (1715).

Har'ridan. A haggard old beldame. So called from the French *haridelle*, a worn-out jade of a horse.

Har'rier (3 syl.). A dog for hare-hunting, whence the name.

Harrington. A farthing. So called from Lord Harrington, to whom James I. granted a patent for making them of brass. Drunken Barnaby says—

"Thence to Harrington he it spoken,
For name-sake I gave a token
To a beggar that did crave it."
Drunken Barnaby's Journal.

"I will not bate a Harrington of the sum."
Ben Jonson: The Devil is an Ass, ii. 1.

Harris. *Mrs. Harris.* An hypothetical lady, to whom Sarah Gamp referred for the corroboration of all her statements, and the bank on which she might draw to any extent for self-praise. (*Dickens: Martin Chuzzlewit.*) (*See* BROOKS OF SHEFFIELD.)

"Not Mrs. Harris in the immortal narrative was more quoted and more mythical."—*Lord Lytton.*

Harry (*To*) = to harass. Facetiously said to be derived from Harry VIII. of England, who no doubt played up old Harry with church property. Of course, the real derivation is the Anglo-Saxon *herian*, to plunder, from *hære* (2 syl.), an army.

Harry. *Old Harry.* Old Scratch. To harry (Saxon) is to tear in pieces, whence our *harrow*. There is an ancient pamphlet entitled *The Harrowing of Hell*. I do not think it is a corruption of "Old Hairy," although the Hebrew *Seirim* (hairy ones) is translated devils in Lev. xvii. 7, and no doubt alludes to the he-goat, an object of worship with the Egyptians. Moses says the children of Israel are no longer to sacrifice to devils (*seirim*), as they did in Egypt. There is a Scandinavian Hari = Baal or Bel.

Harry Soph. A student at Cambridge who has "declared" for Law or Physic, and wears a full-sleeve gown. The word is a corruption of the Greek *Heri-sophos* (more than a Soph or common second-year student). (*Cambridge Calendar.*)

The tale goes that at the destruction of the monasteries, in the reign of Henry VIII., certain students waited to see how matters would turn out before they committed themselves by taking a clerical degree, and that these men were thence called *Sophistæ Henriciani*, or "Henry Sophisters."

Hart. In Christian art, the emblem of solitude and purity of life. It was the attribute of St. Hubert, St. Julian, and St. Eustace. It was also the type of piety and religious aspiration. (Psalm xlii. 1.) (*See* HIND.)

The White Hart, or hind, with a golden chain, in public-house signs, is the badge of Richard II., which was worn by all his courtiers and adherents. It was adopted from his mother, whose cognisance was a white hind.

Hart Royal. A male red deer, when the crown of the antler has made its appearance, and the creature has been hunted by a king.

Hart of Grease (*A*). A hunter's phrase for a fat venison; a stag full of the pasture, called by Jaques "a fat and greasy citizen." (*As You Like It*, i. 1.) (*See* HEART OF GRACE.)

"It is a hart of grease, too, in full season, with three inches of fat on the brisket."—*Sir W. Scott: The Monastery*, chap. xvii.

Harts. There are four harts in the tree Yggdrasil', an eagle and a squirrel; and a serpent gnaws its root.

Hartnet. The daughter of Rukenaw (the ape's wife) in the tale of *Reynard the Fox*. The word in old German means *hard* or *strong strife*.

Harum Scarum. A hare-brained person who scares quiet folk. Some derive it from the French *clameur de Haro* (hue and cry), as if the madcap was one against whom the hue-and-cry is raised; but probably it is simply a jingle word having allusion to the "madness of a March *hare*," and the "scaring" of honest folks from their proprieties.

"Who's there? I s'pose young harum-scarum."
Cambridge Facetiæ: Collegian and Porter.

Haruspex (pl. *harus'pices*). Persons who interpreted the will of the gods by inspecting the entrails of animals offered in sacrifice (old Latin, *haru'ga*, a victim; *specio*, I inspect). Cato said, "I wonder how one haruspex can keep from laughing when he sees another."

Harvard College, in the United States, endowed by the Rev. John Harvard in 1639. Founded 1636.

Harvest Goose. A corruption of *Arvyst Gos* (a stubble goose). (*See* WAYZ-GOOSE.)

"A young wife and an arvyst gos,
Moche gagil [clatter] with both."
Reliquiæ Antiquæ, ii. 113.

Harvest Moon. The full moon nearest the autumnal equinox. The peculiarity of this moon is that it rises for several days nearly at sunset, and about the same time.

Hash (*A*). A mess, a muddle: as, "a pretty hash he made of it." A hash is a mess, and a mess is a muddle.

I'll soon settle his hash for him. I will soon smash him up; ruin his schemes; "give him his gruel"; "cook his goose"; "put my finger in his pie"; "make mince - meat of him." (*See* COOKING.)

Hassan. Caliph of the Ottoman empire; noted for his hospitality and splendour. His palace was daily thronged with guests, and in his seraglio was a beautiful young slave named Leila (2 syl.), who had formed an unfortunate attachment to a Christian called the Giao'ur. Leila is put to death by an emir, and Hassan is slain by the Giaour near Mount Parnassus. (*Byron : The Giaour.*)

Al Hassan. The Arabian emir' of Persia, father of Hinda, in Moore's *Fire-Worshippers.* He was victorious at the battle of Cadessia, and thus became master of Persia.

Hassan-Ben-Sabah. The Old Man of the Mountain, founder of the sect of the Assassins. In Rymer's *Foedera* are two letters by this sheik.

Hassock. A doss or footstool made of *hêsg* (sedge or rushes).

"Hassocks should be gotten in the fens, and laid at the foot of the said bank . . . . where need required."—*Dugdale: Imbanking,* p. 322.
"The knees and hassocks are well-nigh divorced."
Cowper.

Hat. How Lord Kingsale acquired the right of wearing his hat in the royal presence is this: King John and Philippe II. of France agreed to settle a dispute respecting the duchy of Normandy by single combat. John de Courcy, Earl of Ulster, was the English champion, and no sooner put in his appearance than the French champion put spurs to his horse and fled. The king asked the earl what reward should be given him, and he replied, "Titles and lands I want not, of these I have enough; but in remembrance of this day I beg the boon, for myself and successors, to remain covered in the presence of your highness and all future sovereigns of the realm."

Lord Forester, it is said, possessed the same right, which was confirmed by Henry VIII.

☞ The Somerset Herald wholly denies the right in regard to Lord Kingsale; and probably that of Lord Forester is without foundation. (See *Notes and Queries,* Dec. 19th, 1885, p. 504.)

On the other hand, the privilege seems at one time to have been not unusual, for Motley informs us that "all the Spanish grandees had the privilege of being covered in the presence of the reigning monarch. Hence, when the Duke of Alva presented himself before Margaret, Duchess of Parma, she bade him to be covered." (*Dutch Republic.*)

A cockle hat. A pilgrim's hat. So called from the custom of putting cockle-shells upon their hats, to indicate their intention or performance of a pilgrimage.

" How should I your true love know
From another one ?
By his cockle-hat and staff,
And his sandal shoon."
Shakespeare : Hamlet, iv. 5.

A BROWN HAT. *Never wear a brown hat in Friesland.* When at Rome do as Rome does. If people have a very strong prejudice, do not run counter to it. Friesland is a province of the Netherlands, where the inhabitants cut their hair short, and cover the head first with a knitted cap, then a high silk skull-cap, then a metal turban, and lastly a huge flaunting bonnet. Four or five dresses always constitute the ordinary head gear. A traveller once passed through the province with a common brown chimney-hat or wide-awake, but was hustled by the work-men, jeered at by the women, pelted by the boys, and sneered at by the magnates as a regular guy. If you would pass quietly through this "enlightened" province never wear there a brown hat.

A STEEPLE-CROWNED HAT. *You are only fit to wear a steeple-crowned hat.* To be burnt as a heretic. The victims of the Autos-da-Fé of the "Holy" In-quisition were always decorated with such a head-gear.

A white hat. A white hat used to be emblematical of radical proclivities, be-cause Orator Hunt, the great dema-gogue, used to wear one during the Wellington and Peel administration.

¶ The street arabs of Nottingham-shire used to accost a person wearing a white hat with the question, "Who stole the donkey?" and a companion used to answer, "Him wi' the white hat on."

Pass round the hat. Gather subscrip-tions into a hat.

To eat one's hat. "Hattes are made of eggs, veal, dates, saffron, salt, and so forth." (*Robina Napier: Boke of Cookry.*)

19*

⁂ The Scotch have the word *hattit-kit* or *hatted-kit*, a dish made chiefly of sour cream, new milk, or butter-milk.

To hang up one's hat in a house. To make oneself at home; to become master of a house. Visitors, making a call, carry their hats in their hands.

Hat Money. A small gratuity given to the master of a ship, by passengers, for his care and trouble, originally collected in a hat at the end of a good voyage.

Hats and Caps. Two political factions of Sweden in the eighteenth century, the former favourable to France, and the latter to Russia. Carlyle says the latter were called caps, meaning night-caps, because they were averse to action and war; but the fact is that the French partisans wore a French chapeau as their badge, and the Russian partisans wore a Russian cap.

Hatches. *Put on the hatches.* Figuratively, shut the door. (Anglo-Saxon, *hæc*, a gate. Compare *haca*, a bar or bolt.)
Under hatches. Dead and buried. The hatches of a ship are the coverings over the hatchways (or openings in the deck of a vessel) to allow of cargo, etc., being easily discharged.
" And though his soul has gone aloft,
    His body's under hatches."

Hatchet. [Greek *axinē*, Latin *ascia*, Italian *accetta*, French *hachette*, our *hatchet* and *axe*.)
To bury the hatchet. (*See* BURY.)
To throw the hatchet. To tell falsehoods. In allusion to an ancient game where hatchets were thrown at a mark, like quoits. It means the same as drawing the long-bow (*q.v.*).

Hatchway (*Lieutenant Jack*). A retired naval officer, the companion of Commodore Trunnion, in Smollett's *Peregrine Pickle.*

Hatef [*the deadly*]. One of Mahomet's swords, confiscated from the Jews when they were exiled from Medi'na. (*See* SWORDS.)

Hat'temists. An ecclesiastical sect in Holland; so called from Pontin von Hattem, of Zealand (seventeenth century). They denied the expiatory sacrifice of Christ, and the corruption of human nature.

Hatteraick (*Dirk*). Also called "Jans Janson." A Dutch smuggler imprisoned with lawyer Glossin for kidnapping Henry Bertrand. During the night Glossin contrived to enter the smuggler's cell, when a quarrel ensued. Hatteraick strangled Glossin, and then hanged himself. (*Sir Walter Scott: Guy Mannering.*)

Hatto. Archbishop of Mainz, according to tradition, was devoured by mice. The story says that in 970 there was a great famine in Germany, and Hatto, that there might be better store for the rich, assembled the poor in a barn, and burnt them to death, saying, "They are like mice, only good to devour the corn." By and by an army of mice came against the archbishop, and the abbot, to escape the plague, removed to a tower on the Rhine, but hither came the mouse-army by hundreds and thousands, and ate the bishop up. The tower is still called Mouse-tower. Southey has a ballad on the subject, but makes the invaders an army of rats. (*See* MOUSE TOWER; PIED PIPER.)

" And in at the windows, and in at the door,
    And through the walls by thousands they pour,
    And down through the ceiling, and up through
        the floor,
From the right and the left, from behind and
        before,
From within and without, from above and
        below,
And all at once to the bishop they go.
They have wetted their teeth against the
        stones,
And now they are picking the bishop's bones;
They gnawed the flesh from every limb,
For they were sent to do judgment on him."
                    Southey: Bishop Hatto.

A very similar legend is told of Count Graaf, a wicked and powerful chief, who raised a tower in the midst of the Rhine for the purpose of exacting tolls. If any boat or barge attempted to evade the exaction, the warders of the tower shot the crew with cross-bows. Amongst other ways of making himself rich was buying up corn. One year a sad famine prevailed, and the count made a harvest of the distress; but an army of rats, pressed by hunger, invaded his tower, and falling on the old baron, worried him to death, and then devoured him. (*Legends of the Rhine.*)

Widerolf, bishop of Strasburg (in 997), was devoured by mice in the seventeenth year of his episcopate, because he suppressed the convent of Seltzen, on the Rhine.

Bishop Adolf of Cologne was devoured by mice or rats in 1112.

Frei herr von Güttengen collected the poor in a great barn, and burnt them to death; and being invaded by rats and mice, ran to his castle of Güttingen. The vermin, however, pursued him and ate him clean to the bones, after which his castle sank to the bottom of the lake, "where it may still be seen."

A similar tale is recorded in the chronicles of William of Mulsburg, book ii. p. 313 (Bone's edition).

⁂ Mice or rats. Giraldus Cambrensis says: The larger sort of mice are called *rati*. (*Itinerary*, book xi. 2.) On the other hand, many rats are called mice, as *mustēla Alpīna*, the *mus Indīcus*, the *mus aquaticus*, the *mus Pharaōnis*, etc.

Hatton. *The dancing chancellor*. Sir Christopher Hatton was brought up to the law, but became a courtier, and attracted the attention of Queen Elizabeth by his very graceful dancing at a masque. The queen took him into favour, and soon made him both chancellor and knight of the garter. (He died in 1591.)

" His bushy beard, and shoestrings green,
　His high-crowned hat and satin doublet,
　Moved the stout heart of England's queen,
　Though Pope and Spaniard could not trouble
　it."
　　　　　　　　　　　　　　　　Gray.

Hatton Garden (London). The residence of Sir Christopher Hatton, the dancing chancellor. (*See above.*)

Haul over the Coals. Take to task. Jamieson thinks it refers to the ordeal by fire, a suggestion which is favoured by the French corresponding phrase, *mettre sur la sellette* (to put on the culprit's stool).

Hauss'manniza'tion. The pulling down and building up anew of streets and cities, as Baron Haussmann remodelled Paris. In 1868 he had saddled Paris with a debt of about twenty-eight millions.

Hautboy (pron. *Ho' boy*). A strawberry; so called either from the *haut bois* (high woods) of Bohemia whence it was imported, or from its *haut-bois* (long-stalk). The latter is the more probable, and furnishes the etymology of the musical instrument also, which has a *long mouth-reed*.

Haute Claire. The sword of Oliver the Dane. (*See* SWORD.)

Hautville Coit, at Stanton Drew, in the manor of Keynsham. The tradition is that this coit was thrown there by the champion giant, Sir John Hautville, from Mary's Knolle Hill, about a mile off, the place of his abode. The stone on the top of the hill, once thirty tons' weight, is said to have been the clearing of the giant's spade.

⁂ The same is said of the Gog'magog of Cambridge.

Have a Care ! "*Prenez garde !*" Shakespeare has the expression "Have mind upon your health ! " (*Julius Cæsar*, iv. 3.)

Have a Mind for it (*To*). To desire to possess it ; to wish for it. Mind = desire, intention, is by no means uncommon : "I mind to tell him plainly what I think." (2 *Henry VI.*, act iv. 1.) " I shortly mind to leave you." (2 *Henry VI.*, act iv. 1.)

Have at You. To be about to aim a blow at another ; to attack another.

" Have at thee with a downright blow."
　　　　　　　　　　　　　　Shakespeare.

Have it Out (*To*). To settle the dispute by blows or arguments.

Hav'elok (3 syl.), the orphan son of Birkabegn, King of Denmark, was exposed at sea through the treachery of his guardians, and the raft drifted to the coast of Lincolnshire. Here a fisherman named Grim found the young Prince, and brought him up as his own son. In time it so happened that an English princess stood in the way of certain ambitious nobles, who resolved to degrade her by uniting her to a peasant, and selected the young foundling for the purpose ; but Havelok, having learnt the story of his birth, obtained the aid of the king his father to recover his wife's possessions, and became in due time King of Denmark and part of England. ("*Haveloc the Dane,*" by the *Trouveurs.*)

Haver-Cakes. Oaten cakes (Scandinavian, *hafre ;* German, *hafer ;* Latin, *avēna*, oats).

Haveril (3 syl.). A simpleton, April-fool. (French, *poisson d'Avril ;* Icelandic, *gifr*, foolish talk ; Scotch, *haver*, to talk nonsense.)

Havering (Essex). The legend says that while Edward the Confessor was dwelling in this locality, an old pilgrim asked alms, and the king replied, "I have no money, but I *have a ring*," and, drawing it from his fore-finger, gave it to the beggar. Some time after, certain English pilgrims in Jewry met the same man, who drew the ring from his finger and said, "Give this to your king, and say within six months he shall die." The request was complied with, and the prediction fulfilled. The shrine of Edward the Confessor in Westminster Abbey gives colour to this legend.

Haversack. Strictly speaking is a bag to carry oats in. (*See* HAVER-CAKES.)

It now means a soldier's ration-bag slung from the shoulder; a gunner's leather-case for carrying charges.

Havock. A military cry to general massacre without quarter. This cry was forbidden in the ninth year of Richard II. on pain of death. Probably it was originally used in hunting wild beasts, such as wolves, lions, etc., that fell on sheepfolds, and Shakespeare favours this suggestion in his *Julius Cæsar*, where he says Até shall " cry havock ! and let slip the dogs of war." (Welsh, *hafog*, devastation; Irish, *arvach* ; compare Anglo-Saxon *havoc*, a hawk.)

Havre (France). A contraction of *Le havre de notre dame de grace.*

Hawk.

(1) Different parts of a hawk :

Arms. The legs from the thigh to the foot.
Beak. The upper and crooked part of the bill.
Beams. The long feathers of the wings.
Clap. The nether part of the bill.
Feathers summed. Feathers full grown and complete.
Feathers unsummed. Feathers not yet full grown.
Flags. The next to the longest feathers or principals.
Glut. The slimy substance in the pannel.
Gorge. The crow or crop.
Haglurs. The spots on the feathers.
Mails. The breast feathers.
Nares. The two little holes on the top of the beak.
Pannel. The pipe next to the fundament.
Pendent feathers. Those behind the toes.
Petty singles. The toes.
Pounces. The claws.
Principal feathers. The two longest.
Sails. The wings.
Sear or *sere.* The yellow part under the eyes.
Train. The tail.

(2) Different sorts of hawk :

Gerfalcon. A Tercell of a Gerfalcon is for a king.
Falcon gentle and a *Tercel gentle.* For a prince.
Falcon of the rock. For a duke.
Falcon peregrine. For an earl.
Bastard hawk. For a baron.
Sacre and a *Sacrit.* For a knight.
Lanare and *Lanrell.* For a squire.
Merlyn. For a lady.
Hoby. For a young man.
Goshawk. For a yeoman.
Tercel. For a poor man.
Sparehawk. For a priest.
Murkyte. For a holy-water clerk.
Kesterel. For a knave or servant.
          Dame Juliana Barnes.
The " Sore-hawk " is a hawk of the first year ; so called from the French, *sor* or *saure*, brownish-yellow.
The "Spar" or "Sparrow" hawk is a *small*, ignoble hawk (Saxon, *speara* ; Goth, *sparwa* ; our *spare, spar, spur, spear, spire, sparing, sparse,* etc.; Latin, *sparsus ;* all referring to minuteness).

(3) The dress of a hawk :

Bewits. The leathers with bells, buttoned to a hawk's legs. The bell itself is called a *hawk-bell.*
Creanse. A packthread or thin twine fastened to the leash in disciplining a hawk.
Hood. A cover for the head, to keep the hawk in the dark. A *rufter hood* is a wide one, open behind. *To hood* is to put on the hood. *To unhood* is to take it off. *To unstrike the hood* is to draw the strings so that the hood may be in readiness to be pulled off.

Jesses. The little straps by which the leash is fastened to the legs. There is the singular *jess.*
Leash. The leather thong for holding the hawk.

(4) Terms used in falconry :

Casting. Something given to a hawk to cleanse her gorge.
Cawking. Treading.
Cowering. When young hawks, in obedience to their elders, quiver and shake their wings.
Crabbing. Fighting with each other when they stand too near.
Hack. The place where a hawk's meat is laid.
Imping. Placing a feather in a hawk's wing.
Inke or *Ink.* The breast and neck of a bird that a hawk preys on.
Intermewing. The time of changing the coat.
Lure. A figure of a fowl made of leather and feathers.
Make. An old staunch hawk that sets an example to young ones.
Mantling. Stretching first one wing and then the other over the legs.
Mew. The place where hawks sit when moulting.
Muting. The dung of hawks.
Pelf or *pill.* What a hawk leaves of her prey.
Pelt. The dead body of a fowl killed by a hawk.
Perch. The resting-place of a hawk when off the falconer's wrist.
Plumage. Small feathers given to a hawk to make her cast.
Quarry. The fowl or game that a hawk flies at.
Rangle. Gravel given to a hawk to bring down her stomach.
Sharp set. Hungry.
Tiring. Giving a hawk a leg or wing of a fowl to pull at.

✱✱ The peregrine when full grown is called a *blue-hawk.*

The hawk was the av'atar of Ra or Horus, the sun-god of the Egyptians.

See BIRDS (protected by superstitions.)

Hawk and Handsaw. *I know a hawk from a handsaw.* Handsaw is a corruption of *hernshaw* (a heron). I know a hawk from a heron, the bird of prey from the game flown at. The proverb means, I know one thing from another. (See *Hamlet*, ii. 2.)

Hawk nor Buzzard (*Neither*). Of doubtful social position—too good for the kitchen, and not good enough for the family. Private governesses and pauperised gentlefolk often hold this unhappy position. They are not hawks to be fondled and petted—the " tasselled gentlemen " of the days of falconry—nor yet buzzards—a dull kind of falcon synonymous with dunce or plebeian. In French, " *N'être ni chair ni poisson*," "Neither flesh, fowl, nor good red herring."

Hawker's News or "Piper's News." News known to all the world. " *Le secret de polichinelle.*" (German *höker*, a higgler or hawker.)

Hawkubites (3 syl.). Street bullies in the reign of Queen Anne. It was their delight to molest and ill-treat the old watchmen, women, children, and feeble old men who chanced to be in the streets after sunset. The succession of these London pests after the Restoration was in the following order : The Muns, the Tityré Tūs, the Hectors, the Scourers, the Nickers, then the Hawkubites (1711-1714), and then the Mohocks —most dreaded of all. (Hawkubite is the name of an Indian tribe of savages.)

> " From Mohock and from Hawkubite,
>   Good Lord deliver me,
> Who wander through the streets at nigh
>   Committing cruelty,
> They slash our sons with bloody knives,
>   And on our daughters fall ;
> And, if they murder not our wives,
>   We have good luck withal."

Hawse-hole. *He has crept through the hawse-hole,* or *He has come in at the hawse-hole.* That is, he entered the service in the lowest grade ; he rose from the ranks. A naval phrase. The hawse-hole of a ship is that through which the cable of the anchor runs.

Hawthorn, in florology, means "Good Hope," because it shows the winter is over and spring is at hand. The Athenian girls used to crown themselves with hawthorn flowers at weddings, and the marriage-torch was made of hawthorn. The Romans considered it a charm against sorcery, and placed leaves of it on the cradles of new-born infants.

✢ The hawthorn was chosen by Henry VII. for his device, because the crown of Richard III. was discovered in a hawthorn bush at Bosworth.

Hay, Hagh, or **Haugh.** A royal park in " which no man commons" ; rich pasture-land ; as Bilhagh (*Billa-haugh*), Beskwood- or Bestwood-hay, Lindeby-hay, Welley-hay or Wel-hay. These five hays were "special reserves" of game for royalty alone.

A bottle of hay. (*See* BOTTLE.)

Between hay and grass. Too late for one and too soon for the other.

Neither hay nor grass. That hobbyde-hoy state when a youth is neither boy nor man.

Make hay while the sun shines. Strike while the iron is hot.

'Take time by the forelock. One to-day is worth two to-morrows. (*Franklin.*)

Hayston (*Frank*). The laird of Bucklaw, afterwards laird of Girningston. (*Sir Walter Scott : Bride of Lammermoor.*)

Hayward. A keeper of the cattle or common herd of a village or parish. The word *hay* means " hedge," and this herdsman was so called because he had " ward " of the " hedges " also. (Anglo-Saxon, *hēg*, hay ; *hege,* a hedge.)

Hazazel. The Scape-goat (*q.v.*).

Hazel. (*See* DIVINING ROD.)

Hazel-nut. (Anglo - Saxon, *hæsel-hnut*, from *hæsel,* a hat or cap, the cap-nut or the nut enclosed in a cap.)

Head. (Latin, *caput ;* Saxon, *heáfod ;* Scotch, *hafet ;* contracted into *head.*)

Better be the head of an ass than the tail of a horse. Better be foremost amongst commoners than the lowest of the aristocracy ; better be the head of the yeomanry than the tail of the gentry. The Italians say, "*E meglio esser testa di luccio che coda di sturione.*"

He has a head on his shoulders. He is up to snuff (*q.v.*) ; he is a clever fellow, with brains in his head.

He has quite lost his head. He is in a quandary or quite confused.

I can make neither head nor tail of it. I cannot understand it at all. A gambling phrase.

Men with heads beneath the shoulders. (*See* CAORA.)

Men without heads. (*See* BLEMMYES.)

Off one's head. Deranged ; delirious ; extremely excited. Here " head " means intelligence, understanding, etc. His intelligence or understanding has gone away.

To bundle one out head and heels. " *Sans cérémonie,*" altogether. The allusion is to a custom at one time far too frequent in cottages, for a whole family to sleep together in one bed head to heels or *pednam'enē,* as it was termed in Cornwall ; to bundle the whole lot out of bed was to turn them out head and heels.

To head off. To intercept.

To hit the nail on the head. You have guessed aright ; you have done the right thing. The allusion is obvious. The French say, " *Vous avez frappé au but* " (You have hit the mark) ; the Italians have the phrase, " *Havete dato in brocca* " (You have hit the pitcher), alluding to a game where a pitcher stood in the place of Aunt Sally (*q.v.*). The Latin, " *Rem acu tetigisti* " (You have touched the thing with a needle), refers to the custom of probing sores.

To keep one's head above water. To avoid bankruptcy. The allusion is to a person immersed in water ; so long as his head is above water his life remains, but bad swimmers find it hard to keep their heads above water.

To lose one's head. To be confused and muddle-minded.

To make head. To get on.

Head Shaved (*Get your*). You are a dotard. Go and get your head shaved like other lunatics. (*See* BATH.)

" Thou thinkst that monarchs never can act ill,
  Get thy head shaved, poor fool, or think so
  still."   *Peter Pindar : Ode Upon Ode.*

Head and Ears. *Over head and ears* [in debt, in love, etc.], completely ; entirely. The allusion is to a person immersed in water. The French phrase is " *Avoir des dettes pardessus la tête.*"

Head and Shoulders. A phrase of sundry shades of meaning. Thus " head and shoulders taller" means considerably tall ; to turn one out head and shoulders means to drive one out forcibly and without ceremony.

Head of Cattle. Cattle are counted by the *head ;* manufacturing labourers by *hands,* as " How many hands do you employ ? " horses by the *nose (See* NOSE) ; guests at dinner by the *cover,* as " Covers for ten," etc. (*See* NUMBERS, HAND.)

.'. In contracting for meals the contractor takes the job at so much " a head "—*i.e.* for each person.

Head over Heels (*To turn*). To place the hands upon the ground and throw the legs upwards so as to describe half a circle.

Heads or Tails. Guess whether the coin tossed up will come down with headside uppermost or not. The side not bearing the head has various devices, sometimes Britannia, sometimes George and the Dragon, sometimes a harp, sometimes the royal arms, sometimes an inscription, etc. These devices are all included in the word tail, meaning opposite to the head. The ancient Romans used to play this game, but said, " Heads or ships."

"Cum pueri denarios in sublime jactantes,
'capita aut navia,' lusu teste vetustatis exclamant."—*Macrobius Saturnalia,* i. 7.

Neither head nor tail. Nothing consistent. " I can make neither head nor tail of what you say," *i.e.* I cannot bolt the matter to the bran.

Heads I Win, Tails you Lose. In tossing up a coin, with such an arrangement, the person who *makes* the bargain must of necessity win, and the person who accepts it must inevitably lose.

Heady, wilful ; affecting the head, as " The wine or beer is heady." (German, *heftig,* ardent, strong, self-willed.)

Healing Gold. Gold given to a king for " healing " the king's evil, which was done by a touch.

Health. *Your health.* The story is that Vortigern was invited to dine at the house of Hengist, when Rowe'na, the host's daughter, brought a cup of wine which she presented to their royal guest, saying, " *Was hǽ'l, hlaford cyning* " (Your health, lord king). (*See* WASSAIL.)

William of Malmesbury says the custom took its rise from the death of young King Edward the Martyr, who was traitorously stabbed in the back while drinking a cup of wine presented to him by his mother Elfrida.

Drinking healths. The Romans adopted a curious fashion of drinking the health of their lady-loves, and that was to drink a bumper to each letter of her name. Hudibras satirises this custom, which he calls " spelling names with beer-glasses " (part ii. chap. 1).

" Nævia sex cyathis, septem Justina bibatur,
  Quinque Lycas, Lyde quatuor, Ida tribus."
                                   Martial, i. 72.

Three cups to Amy, four to Kate be given,
To Susan five, six Rachel, Bridget seven.
                                   E. C. B.

Heap. *Struck all of a heap.* To be struck with astonishment. " *Être ahuri.*" The idea is that of confusion, having the wits bundled together in a heap.

Hear. *To hear as a hog in harvest.* In at one ear and out at the other ; hear without paying attention. Giles Firmin says, " If you call hogs out of the harvest stubble, they will just lift up their heads to listen, and fall to their shack again." (*Real Christian,* 1670.)

Hearse (1 syl.) means simply a harrow. Those harrows used in Roman Catholic churches (or frames with spikes) for holding candles are called in France *herses.* These frames at a later period were covered with a canopy, and lastly were mounted on wheels.

Heart. A variety of the word *core.* (Latin, *cord',* the heart ; Greek, *kard' ;* Sanskrit, *herd' ;* Anglo-Saxon, *heorte.*)

Heart (in Christian art), the attribute of St. There'sa.

The flaming heart (in Christian art), the symbol of charity. An attribute of St. Augustine, denoting the fervency of his devotion. The heart of the Saviour is frequently so represented.

Heart.

PHRASES, PROVERBS, ETC.

A bloody heart. Since the time of Good Lord James the Douglases have carried upon their shields a bloody heart with a crown upon it, in memory of the expedition of Lord James to Spain with the heart of King Robert Bruce. King Robert commissioned his friend to carry his heart to the Holy Land, and Lord James had it enclosed in a silver casket, which he wore round his neck. On his way to the Holy Land, he stopped to aid Alphonso of Castile against Osmyn the Moor, and was slain. Sir Simon Lockhard of Lee was commissioned to carry the heart back to Scotland. (*Tales of a Grandfather*, xi.)

After my own heart. Just what I like; in accordance with my liking or wish ; the heart being the supposed seat of the affections.

Be of good heart. Cheer up. In Latin, "*Fac, bono animo sis ;*" the heart being the seat of moral courage.

Out of heart. Despondent ; without sanguine hope. In Latin, "*Animum despondere.*" In French, "*Perdre courage.*"

Set your heart at rest. Be quite easy about the matter. In French, "*Mettez votre cœur à l'aise.*" The heart is the supposed organ of the sensibilities (including the affections, etc.).

To break one's heart. To waste away or die of disappointment. "Broken-hearted," hopelessly distressed. In French, "*Cela me fend le cœur.*" The heart is the organ of life.

To learn by heart. To learn memoriter ; to commit to memory. In French, "*Par cœur*" or "*Apprendre par cœur.*" (*See* LEARN.)

To set one's heart upon. Earnestly to desire it. "*Je l'aime de tout mon cœur ;*" the heart being the supposed seat of the affections.

Take heart. Be of good courage. Moral courage at one time was supposed to reside in the heart, physical courage in the stomach, wisdom in the head, affection in the reins or kidneys, melancholy in the bile, spirit in the blood, etc. In French, "*prendre courage.*"

To take to heart. To feel deeply pained [at something which has occurred]. In Latin, "*Percussit mihi animum ;*" "*iniquo animo ferre.*" In French, "*Prendre une affaire à cœur ;*" the heart being the supposed seat of the affections.

To wear one's heart upon one's sleeve. To expose one's secret intentions to general notice ; the reference being to the custom of tying your lady's favour to your sleeve, and thus exposing the secret of the heart. Iago says, "When my outward action shows my secret heart, I will wear my heart upon my sleeve, as one does a lady's favour, for daws [? dows, pigeons] to peck at."
Dows = fools, or simpletons to laugh at or quiz. (*Othello*, i. 1.)

With all my heart. "*De tout mon cœur ;*" most willing. The heart, as the seat of the affections and sensibilities, is also the seat of the will.

Heart-breaker (*A*). A flirt. Also a particular kind of curl. Called in French *Accroche-cœur*. At one time loose ringlets worn over the shoulders were called heart-breakers. At another time a curl worn over the temples was called an *Accroche-cœur*, *crève cœur*.

Heart-rending. Very pathetic. "*Qui déchire le cœur ;*" the heart as the seat of the affections.

Heart-whole. Not in love ; the affections not given to another.

"I in love? . . . . I give you my word I am heart-whole."—*Sir W. Scott : Redgauntlet* (letter 13).

Heart and Soul. *With my whole heart and soul.* With all the energy and enthusiasm of which I am capable. In French, "*S'y porter de tout son cœur.*" Mark xii. 33 says, "Love [God] with all thy heart [affection], all thy soul [or glow of spiritual life], all thy strength [or physical powers], and all thy understanding [that is, let thy love be also a reasonable service, and not mere enthusiasm]."

Heart in his Boots. *His heart fell into his hose* or *sank into his boots.* In Latin, "*Cor illi in genua decidit.*" In French, "*Avoir la peur au ventre.*" The two last phrases are very expressive : Fear makes the knees shake, and it gives one a stomach-ache ; but the English phrase, if it means anything, must mean that it induces the person to run away.

Heart in his Mouth. *His heart was in his mouth.* That choky feeling in the throat which arises from fear, conscious guilt, shyness, etc.

"The young lover tried to look at his ease, . . . but his heart was in his mouth."—*Miss Thackeray: Mrs. Dymond*, p. 156.

Heart of Grace (*To take*). To pluck up courage ; not to be disheartened or down-hearted. This expression is based on the promise, "My grace is sufficient for thee" (2 Cor. xii. 9) ; by this grace St. Paul says, "When I am weak then am I strong." Take grace into your heart, rely on God's grace for strength, with grace in your heart your feeble knees will be strengthened. (*See* HART OF GREASE.)

Heart of Hearts (*In one's*). In one's inmost conviction. The heart is often referred to as a second self. Shakespeare speaks of the "neck of the heart" (*Merchant of Venice*, ii. 2); "the middle of the heart" (*Cymbeline*, i. 7). The heart of the heart is to the same effect.

Heart of Midlothian. The old jail, the Tolbooth of Edinburgh, taken down in 1817. Sir Walter Scott has a novel so called.

Heart's Ease. The *viola tricolor*. It has a host of fancy names; as, the "Butterfly flower," "Kiss me quick," a "Kiss behind the garden gate," "Love in idleness," "Pansy," "Three faces under one hood," the "Variegated violet," "Herba Trinitatis." The quotation annexed will explain the popular tradition of the flower :—

"Yet marked I where the bolt of Cupid fell :
It fell upon a little western flower,
Before milk-white, now purple with love's
    wound,
And maidens call it love-in-idleness. . . .
The juice of it on sleeping eyelids laid
Will make a man or woman madly doat
Upon the next live creature that it sees."
Shakespeare : Midsummer Night's Dream, ii. 1.

Hearth Money. (*See* CHIMNEY MONEY.)

Heat. One course in a race ; activity, action.

"Feigned Zeal, you saw, set out with speedier
    pace,
But the last heat Plain Dealing won the race."
    Dryden.

Heathen. A dweller on a heath or common. Christian doctrines would not reach these remote people till long after they had been accepted in towns, and even villages. (Anglo-Saxon, *hæthen, hæth.* (*See* PAGAN.)

Heaven. (Anglo-Saxon, *heofon*, from *heofen*, elevated, vaulted.)

THE THREE HEAVENS. (According to the Jewish system.) The word heaven in the Bible denotes (1) the air, thus we read of "the fowls of heaven," "the dew of heaven," and "the clouds of heaven" ; (2) the starry firmament, as, "Let there be lights in the firmament of heaven" (Gen. i. 14) ; (3) the palace of Jehovah ; thus we read that "heaven is My throne" (Isa. lxvi. 1, and Matt. v. 34).

∵ Loosely, the word is used in Scripture sometimes simply to express a great height. "The cities are walled up to heaven" (Deut. i. 28). So the builders on Shinar designed to raise a tower whose top should "reach unto heaven" (Gen. xi. 4).

THE FIVE HEAVENS. (According to the Ptolemaic system.) (1) The planetary heaven ; (2) the sphere of the fixed stars ; (3) the crystalline, which vibrates ; (4) the primum mo'bilë, which communicates motion to the lower spheres ; (5) the empyre'an or seat of deity and angels. (*See above.*)

"Sometimes she deemed that Mars had from
    above
Left his fifth heaven, the powers of men to
    prove."
    Hoole : Orlando Furioso, book xiii.

THE SEVEN HEAVENS. (According to the Mahometan system.)

The first heaven, says Mahomet, is of pure silver, and here the stars are hung out like lamps on golden chains. Each star has an angel for warder. In this heaven "the prophet" found Adam and Eve.

The second heaven, says Mahomet, is of polished steel and dazzling splendour. Here "the prophet" found Noah.

The third heaven, says Mahomet, is studded with precious stones too brilliant for the eye of man. Here Az'rael, the angel of death, is stationed, and is for ever writing in a large book or blotting words out. The former are the names of persons born, the latter those of the newly dead. (See below, *Heaven of heavens*.)

The fourth heaven, he says, is of the finest silver. Here dwells the Angel of Tears, whose height is "500 days' journey," and he sheds ceaseless tears for the sins of man.

The fifth heaven is of purest gold, and here dwells the A'venging Angel, who presides over elemental fire. Here "the prophet" met Aaron. (*See below.*)

The sixth heaven is composed of Has'ala, a sort of carbuncle. Here dwells the Guardian Angel of heaven and earth, half-snow and half-fire. It was here that Mahomet saw Moses, who wept with envy.

The seventh heaven, says the same veritable authority, is formed of divine light beyond the power of tongue to describe. Each inhabitant is bigger than the whole earth, and has 70,000 heads, each head 70,000 mouths, each mouth 70,000 tongues, and each tongue speaks 70,000 languages, all for ever employed in chanting the praises of the Most High. Here he met Abraham. (*See below*).

To be in the seventh heaven. Supremely happy. The Cabbalists maintained that there are seven heavens, each rising in happiness above the other, the seventh being the abode of God and the highest class of angels. (*See above.*)

THE NINE HEAVENS. The term heaven was used anciently to denote the orb or sphere in which a celestial body was supposed to move, hence the number of heavens varied. According to one system, the first heaven was that of the Moon, the second that of Venus, the third that of Mercury, the fourth that of the Sun, the fifth that of Mars, the sixth that of Jupiter, the seventh that of Saturn, the eighth that of the "fixt" or firmament, and the ninth that of the *Crystalline.* (*See* NINE SPHERES.)

HEAVEN (in modern phraseology) means : (1) a great but indefinite height, (2) the sky or the vault of the clouds, (3) the special abode of God, (4) the place of supreme felicity, (5) supposed residence of the celestial gods, etc.

The heaven of heavens. A Hebrewism to express the highest of the heavens, the special residence of Jehovah. Similar superlatives are " the Lord of lords," " the God of gods," " the Song of songs." (*Compare our* Very very much, etc.)

" Behold, the heaven and the heaven of heavens is the Lord's."—Deut. x. 14.

Animals admitted into heaven. (*See under* PARADISE.)

Heavies (*The*), means the heavy cavalry, which consists of men of greater build and height than Lancers and Hussars. (*See* LIGHT TROOPS.)

Heavy Man (*The*), in theatrical parlance, means an actor who plays foil to the hero, such as the king in *Hamlet*, the mere foil to the prince ; Iago is another " heavy man's " part as foil to Othello ; the " tigor " in the *Ticket of Leave Man* is another part for the "heavy man." Such parts preserve a degree of importance, but never rise into passion.

Heavy-armed Artillery (*The*). The garrison artillery. The " light-armed artillery " are Royal Horse Artillery.

He'be (2 syl.). Goddess of youth, and cup-bearer to the celestial gods. She had the power of restoring the aged to youth and beauty. (*Greek mythology.*)

" Wreathèd smiles
Such as hang on Hebe's cheek,
And love to live in dimple sleek."
Milton : L'Allegro.

Hebe vases. Small vases like a cotyliscos. So termed because Hebe is represented as bearing one containing nectar for the gods.

Hebertists (3 syl.). The partisans of the vile demagogue, Jacques Réné

Hébert, chief of the Cordeliers, a revolutionary club which boasted of such names as Anacharsis Clootz, Ronsin, Vincent, and Momoro, in the great French Revolution.

Heb'ron, in the satire of *Absalom and Achitophel*, in the first part stands for Holland, but in the second part for Scotland. Heb'ronite (3 syl.), a native of Holland or Scotland.

Hec'ate (3 syl. in Greek, 2 in Eng.). A triple deity, called Phœbē or the Moon in heaven, Diana on the earth, and Hecate or Proserpine in hell. She is described as having three heads—one of a horse, one of a dog, and one of a lion. Her offerings consisted of dogs, honey, and black lambs. She was sometimes called " Tri'via," because offerings were presented to her at cross-roads. Shakespeare refers to the triple character of this goddess :

' And we fairies that do run
By the triple Hecate's team."
Midsummer Night's Dream, v. 2.

Hecate, daughter of Persēs the Titan, is a very different person to the " Triple Hecate," who, according to Hesiod, was daughter of Zeus and a benevolent goddess. Hecate, daughter of Persēs, was a magician, poisoned her father, raised a temple to Diana in which she immolated strangers, and was mother of Mede'a and Circē. She presided over magic and enchantments, taught sorcery and witchcraft. She is represented with a lighted torch and a sword, and is attended by two black dogs.

⁂ Shakespeare, in his *Macbeth*, alludes to both these Hecates. Thus in act ii. 1 he speaks of "*pale* Hecate," *i.e.* the mother of Medéa and Circē, goddess of magicians, whom they invoked, and to whom they made offerings.

" Now . . . [at night] witchcraft celebrates
Pale Hecate's offerings."

But in act iii. 2 he speaks of "*black* Hecate," meaning night, and says before the night is over and day dawns, there

" Shall be done
A deed of dreadful note;" *i.e.* the murder of Duncan.

N.B. Without doubt, sometimes these two Hecates are confounded.

Hecatomb. It is said that Pythagoras offered up 100 oxen to the gods when he discovered that the square of the hypothenuse of a right-angled-triangle equals both the squares of the other two sides. This is the 47th of book i. of " Euclid," called the dulcarnein (*q.v.*). But Pythagoras never sacrificed animals, and would not suffer his disciples to do so.

"He sacrificed to the gods millet and honeycomb, but not animals. [Again] He forbade his disciples to sacrifice oxen."—*Iamblichus: Life of Pythagoras,* xviii. pp. 108-9. .

Hector. Eldest son of Priam, the noblest and most magnanimous of all the chieftains in Homer's *Iliad* (a Greek epic). After holding out for ten years, he was slain by Achilles, who lashed him to his chariot, and dragged the dead body in triumph thrice round the walls of Troy. The *Iliad* concludes with the funeral obsequies of Hector and Patroc'los.

The Hector of Germany. Joachim II., Elector of Brandenburg (1514-1571).

You wear Hector's cloak. You are paid off for trying to deceive another. You are paid in your own coin. When Thomas Percy, Earl of Northumberland, in 1569, was routed, he hid himself in the House of Hector Armstrong, of Harlaw. This villain betrayed him for the reward offered, but never after did anything go well with him; he went down, down, down, till at last he died a beggar in rags on the roadside.

Hector (*A*). A leader; so called from the son of Priam and generalissimo of the Trojans.

Hector (*To*). To swagger, or play the bully. It is hard to conceive how the brave, modest, noble-minded patriot came to be made the synonym of a braggart and blusterer like Ajax.

Hectors. Street bullies and brawlers who delighted in being as rude as possible, especially to women. Robbery was not their object, but simply to get talked about. (*See* HAWKUBITES.)

Hec'uba. Second wife of Priam, and mother of nineteen children. When Troy was taken by the Greeks she fell to the lot of Ulysses. She was afterwards metamorphosed into a dog, and threw herself into the sea. The place where she perished was afterwards called the *Dog's - grave* (cynos-se'ma). (*Homer : Iliad,* etc.)

On to Hecuba. To the point or main incident. The story of Hecuba has furnished a host of Greek tragedies.

Hedge (1 syl.). *To hedge,* in betting, is to defend oneself from loss by cross-bets. As a hedge is a defence, so cross-betting is hedging. (*E. Hunt : The Town,* ix.)

"He [Godolphin] began to think . . . that he had betted too deep . . . and that it was time to hedge."—*Macaulay : England,* vol. iv. chap. xvii. p. 46.

Hedge Lane (London) includes that whole line of streets (Dorset, Whitcomb, Prince's, and Wardour) stretching from Pall Mall East to Oxford Street.

Hedge Priest. A poor or vagabond parson. The use of hedge for vagabond, or very inferior, is common ; as hedge-mustard, hedge-writer (a Grubb Street author), hedge-marriage (a clandestine one), etc. Shakespeare uses the phrase, "hedge-born swain" as the very opposite of "gentle blood." (1 *Henry VI.,* iv. 1.)

Hedge School (*A*). A school kept in the open air, near a hedge. At one time common in Ireland.

"These irregular or 'hedge schools' are tolerated only in villages where no regular school exists within a convenient distance."—*Barnard : Journal of Education,* December, 1862, p. 574.

Hedonism. The doctrine of Aristippus, that pleasure or happiness is the chief good and chief end of man (Greek, *hedōnē,* pleasure).

Heel, Heels. (Anglo-Saxon *hēl.*)

Achilles' heel. (*See under* ACHILLES.)

I showed him a fair pair of heels. I ran away and outran them.

"Two of them saw me when I went out of doors, and chased me, but I showed them a fair pair of heels."—*Sir W. Scott : Peveril of the Peak,* chap. xxiv.

Out at heels. In a sad plight, in decayed circumstances, like a beggar whose stockings are worn out at the heels.

"A good man's fortune may grow out at heels."
Shakespeare : King Lear, ii. 2.

To show a light pair of heels. To abscond.

To take to one's heels. To run off. "*In pedes nos conjicĕre.*"

Heel-tap. *Bumpers all round, and no heel-taps*—i.e. the bumpers are to be drained to the bottom of the glass. Also, one of the thicknesses of the heel of a shoe.

Heenan. *In Heenan style.* "By apostolic blows and knocks." Heenan, the Benicia boy of North America, disputed for the champion's belt against Sayers, the British champion. His build and muscle were the admiration of the ring.

Heep (*Uri'ah*). An abject toady, malignant as he is base ; always boasting of his '*umble* birth, '*umble* position, '*umble* abode, and '*umble* calling. (*Dickens : David Copperfield.*)

Hegem'ony (*g* hard). *The hegemony of nations.* The leadership. (Greek, *hegemon'ia,* from *ago,* to lead.)

Heg'ira. The epoch of the flight of Mahomet from Mecca, when he was expelled by the magistrates, July 16th, 622. Mahometans date from this event. (Arabic, *hejira*, departure.)

Heimdall (2 syl.). In Scandinavian mythology, son of the nine virgins, all sisters. He is called the *god with the golden tooth* or *with golden teeth*. Heimdall was not an Asa (*q.v.*), but a Van (*q.v.*), who lived in the celestial fort Himinsbiorg under the farther extremity of the bridge Bifrost (*q.v.*), and kept the keys of heaven. He is the watchman or sentinel of Asgard (*q.v.*), sleeps less than a bird, sees even in sleep, can hear the grass grow, and even the wool on a lamb's back. Heimdall, at the end of the world, will wake the gods with his trumpet, when the sons of Muspell will go against them, with Loki, the wolf Fenrir, and the great serpent Jormungand.

Heimdall's Horn. The sound of this horn went through all the world.

Heimdaller. The learned humbugs in the court of King Dinu'be of Hisisburg. (*Grimm's Goblins.*)

Heims-kringla (*The*). A prose legend found in the *Snorra Edda*.

Heir-apparent. The person who will succeed as heir if he survives. At the death of his predecessor the heir-apparent becomes *heir-at-law*.

Heir-presumptive. One who will be heir if no one is born having a prior claim. Thus the Princess Royal was heir-presumptive till the Prince of Wales was born; and if the Prince of Wales had been king before any family had been born to him, his brother, Prince Alfred, would have been heir-presumptive.

Hel or **Hela** (in Scandinavian mythology), queen of the dead, is goddess of the ninth earth or nether world. She dwelt beneath the roots of the sacred ash (*yggdrasil*), and was the daughter of Loki. The All-father sent her into Helheim, where she was given dominion over nine worlds, and to one or other of these nine worlds she sends all who die of sickness or old age. Her dwelling is Elvid'nir (*dark clouds*), her dish Hungr (*hunger*), her knife Sullt (*starvation*), her servants Gangla'ti (*tardy-feet*), her bed Kör (*sickness*), and her bed-curtains Blikian'dabōl (*splendid misery*). Half her body was blue.

" Down the yawning steep he rode
That led 'o Hela's drear abode."
Gray: Descent of Odin

Hel Keplein. A mantle of invisibility belonging to the dwarf-king Laurin. (German, *hehlen*, to conceal.) (*The Heldenbuch.*)

Heldenbuch (Book of Heroes). A German compilation of all the romances pertaining to Diderick and his champions, by Wolfram von Eschenbach.

Helen. The type of female beauty, more especially in those who have reached womanhood. Daughter of Zeus and Leda, and wife of Menela'os, King of Sparta.

" She moves a goddess and she looks a queen."
Pope: Homer's Iliad, iii.

The Helen of Spain. Cava or Florinda, daughter of Count Julian. (*See* CAVA.)

St. Helen's fire (feu d'Hélène) ; also called *Feu St. Helme* (St. Helme's or St. Elmo's fire) ; and by the Italians "the fires of St. Peter and St. Nicholas." Meteoric fires seen occasionally on the masts of ships, etc. If the flame is single, foul weather is said to be at hand ; but if two or more flames appear, the weather will improve. (*See* CASTOR.)

Helen of One's Troy (*The*). The ambition of one's life ; the subject for which we would live and die. The allusion, of course, is to that Helen who eloped with Paris, and thus brought about the siege and destruction of Troy.

" For which men all the life they here enjoy
Still fight, as for the Helens of their Troy."
Lord Brooke : Treatie of Humane Learning.

Hel'ena. The type of a lovely woman, patient and hopeful, strong in feeling, and sustained through trials by her enduring and heroic faith. (*Shakespeare : All's Well that Ends Well.*)

Hel'ena (*St.*). Mother of Constantine the Great. She is represented in royal robes, wearing an imperial crown, because she was empress. Sometimes she carries in her hand a model of the Holy Sepulchre, an edifice raised by her in the East ; sometimes she bears a large cross, typical of her alleged discovery of that upon which the Saviour was crucified ; sometimes she also bears the three nails by which He was affixed to the cross.

Hel'enos. The prophet, the only son of Priam that survived the fall of Troy. He fell to the share of Pyrrhos when the captives were awarded ; and because he saved the life of the young Grecian was allowed to marry Androm'-achē, his brother Hector's widow. (*Virgil : Æneid.*)

Hel'icon. The Muses' Mount. It is part of the Parnassos, a mountain range in Greece.

Helicon's harmonious stream is the stream which flowed from Helicon to the fountains of the Muses, called Aganippe and Hip'pocrene (3 syl.).

Heligh-monat (Holy-month). The name given by the Anglo-Saxons to December, in allusion to Christmas Day.

Heliop'olis, the City of the Sun, a Greek form of (1) Baalbek, in Syria; and (2) of On, in ancientEgypt, noted for its temple of Actis, called Beth Shemesh or Temple of the Sun, in Jer. xliii. 13.

He'lios. The Greek Sun-god, who rode to his palace in Colchis every night in a golden boat furnished with wings.

Heliostat. An instrument by which the rays of the sun can be flashed to great distances. Used in signalling.

Hel'iotrope (4 syl.). Apollo loved Clyt'ie, but forsook her for her sister Leucoth'oe. On discovering this, Clytie pined away; and Apollo changed her at death to a flower, which, always turning towards the sun, is called heliotrope. (Greek, "turn-to-sun.")

⁕ According to the poets, heliotrope renders the bearer invisible. Boccaccio calls it a *stone*, but Solīnus says it is the herb. " *Ut herba ejusdem nominis mixta et præcantationibus legitimis consecrata, eum, a quocunque gestabitur, subtrahat visibus obviorum."* (*Georgic*, xi.)

> "No hope had they of crevice where to hide,
>   Or heliotrope to charm them out of view."
>   *Dante: Inferno*, xxiv.
> "The other stone is heliotrope, which renders those who have it invisible." — *Boccaccio: The Decameron,* Novel iii., Eighth day.

Hell. According to Mohammedan faith, there are seven hells—

(1) Jahannam, for wicked Mohammedans, all of whom will be sooner or later taken to paradise;
(2) The Flamer (*Lathā*), for Christians;
(3) The Smasher (*Hutamah*), for Jews;
(4) The Blazer (*Sair*), for Sabians;
(5) The Scorcher (*Sakar*), for Magians;
(6) The Burner (*Jahīm*), for idolaters; and
(7) The Abyss (*Hawiyah*), for hypocrites.

Hell or *Arka* of the Jewish Cabalists, divided into seven lodges, one under another (*Joseph ben Abraham Gikatilla*)—

In the Buddhist system there are 136 places of punishment after death, where the dead are sent according to their degree of demerit. (*See* EUPHEMISMS.)

Hell. This word occurs eighteen times in the New Testament. In nine instances the Greek word is *Hadēs;* in eight instances it is *Gehenna;* and in one it is Tartarus.

Hades: Matt. xi. 23, xvi. 18; Luke xvi. 23; Acts ii. 31; 1 Cor. xv. 55; Rev. i. 18, vi. 8, xx. 13, 14. (*See* HADES.)

Gehenna: Matt. v. 22, 29, x. 28, xiii. 15, xviii. 9, xxiii. 15, 33; James iii. 6. (*See* GEHENNA.)

Tartarus: 2 Peter ii. 4. (*See* TARTAROS.)

Descended into hell (Creed) means the place of the dead. (Anglo-Saxon, *helan,* to cover or conceal, like the Greek "Ha'dēs," the abode of the dead, from the verb *a-eido,* not to see. In both cases it means "the unseen world" or "the world concealed from sight." The god of this nether world was called "Hadēs," by the Greeks, and "Hel" or "Hela" by the Scandinavians. In some counties of England to cover in with a roof is "to hell the building," and thatchers or tilers are termed "helliers."

Lead apes in hell. (*See* APE.)

Hell (*Rivers of*). Classic authors tell us that the Inferno is encompassed by five rivers: Achĕron, Cocўtus, Styx, Phlegĕthon, and Lethē. Acheron from the Greek *achos-reo,* grief-flowing; Cocytus, from the Greek *kōkuo,* to weep, supposed to be a flood of tears; Styx, from the Greek *stugĕo,* to loathe; Phlegethon, from the Greek *phlĕgo,* to burn; and Lethê, from the Greek *lethē,* oblivion.

> Five hateful rivers round Inferno run,
> Grief comes the first, and then the Flood of tears,
> Next loathsome Styx, then liquid Flame appears,
> Lethè comes last, or blank oblivion. *E.C.B.*

Hell Broth. A magical mixture prepared for evil purposes. The witches in *Macbeth* made it. (*See* act iv. 1.)

Presiding Angel.⁕

(1) Gehennom	The heat 60 times that of fire. (Here it "snows fire")		Absalom and Israelites who break the Law	Kushiel
(2) The Gates of Death	„	60 times hotter than No. 1	Doeg	Lahatiel
(3) The Shadow of Death	„	60 times hotter than No. 2	Korah	Shaftiel
(4) The Pit of Corruption	„	60 times hotter than No. 3	Jeroboam	Maccathiel
(5) The Mire of Clay	„	60 times hotter than No. 4	Ahab	Chutriel
(6) Abaddon	„	60 times hotter than No. 5	Micah	Pasiel
(7) Sheol	„	60 times hotter than No. 6, or 420 times hotter than fire	Elisha, son of Abuya, Sabbath-breakers, idolaters, and uncircumcised	Dalkiel

⁕ All these presidents are under Duma, the Angel of Silence, who keeps the three keys of the three gates of hell.

Hell Gate. A dangerous passage between Great Barn Island and Long Island, North America. The Dutch settlers of New York called it Hoellgat (whirling-gut) corrupted into Hellgate. Flood Rock, its most dangerous reef, has been blown up by U.S. engineers.

Hell Gates, according to Milton, are nine-fold—three of brass, three of iron, and three of adamant; the keepers are Sin and Death. This allegory is one of the most celebrated passages of *Paradise Lost.* (*See* book ii. 643-676.)

Hell Kettles. Cavities three miles long, at Oxen-le-Field, Durham. A, B, C communicate with each other, diameter, about 38 yards. The diameter of D, a separate cave, is about 28 yards.
A is 19 feet 6 inches in depth.
B is 14 feet in depth.
C is 17 feet in depth.
D is 5 feet 6 inches in depth.
(See *Notes and Queries*, August 21, 1875.)

Hell Shoon. In Icelandic mythology, indispensable for the journey to Valhalla as the obolus for crossing the Styx.

Hell or Connaught (*To*). This phrase, usually attributed to Cromwell, and common to the whole of Ireland, rose thus : When the settlers designed for Ireland asked the officers of James I. where they were to go, they were answered "to Hell or Connaught," go where you like or where you may, but don't bother me about the matter.

Hellanod'icæ. Umpires of the public games in Greece. They might chastise with a stick anyone who created a disturbance. Lichas, a Spartan nobleman, was so punished by them.

Helle'nes (3 syl.). "This word had in Palestine three several meanings : Sometimes it designated the pagans ; sometimes the Jews, speaking Greek, and dwelling among the pagans ; and sometimes proselytes of the gate, that is, men of pagan origin converted to Judaism, but not circumcised " (John vii. 35, xii. 20 ; Acts xiv. 1, xvii. 4, xviii. 4, xxi. 28). (*Renan : Life of Jesus,* xiv.)
N.B. The present Greeks call themselves "Helle'nēs," and the king is termed " King of the Helle'nēs." The ancient Greeks called their country " Hellas ; " it was the Romans who misnamed it " Græcia."

"The first and truest Hellas, the mother-land of all Hellenes, was the land which we call Greece, with the islands round about it. There alone the whole land was Greek, and none but Hellenes lived in it."—*Freeman: General Sketch,* chap. ii. p. 21.

Helle'nic. The common dialect of the Greek writers after the age of Alexander. It was based on the Attic.

Hellenis'tic. The dialect of the Greek language used by the Jews. It was full of Oriental idioms and metaphors.

Hell'enists. Those Jews who used the Greek or Helle'nic language. (All these four words are derived from Hellas, in Thessaly, the cradle of the race.)

Hellespont (3 syl.), now called the Dardanelles, means the "sea of Hellē," and was so called because Hellē, the sister of Phryxos, was drowned there. She was fleeing with her brother through the air to Colchis on the golden ram to escape from Ino, her mother-in-law, who most cruelly oppressed her, but turning giddy, she fell into the sea.

Helmet, in heraldry, resting on the chief of the shield, and bearing the crest, indicates rank.

Gold, with six bars, or with the visor raised (in full face) for royalty !
Steel, with gold bars, varying in number (in profile) for a nobleman ;
Steel, without bars, and with visor open (in profile) for a knight or baronet ;
Steel, with visor closed (in profile), for a squire or gentleman.

∴ "The pointed helmet in the bas-reliefs from the earliest palace of Nimroud appears to have been the most ancient. . . . . Several were discovered in the ruins. They were iron, and the rings which ornamented the lower part . . . were inlaid with copper."—*Layard : Nineveh and its Remains,* vol. ii. part ii. chap. iv. p. 262.

Helmets. Those of Saragossa were most in repute in the days of chivalry.
Close helmet. The complete head-piece, having in front two movable parts, which could be lifted up or let down at pleasure.
Visor. One of the movable parts ; it was to look through.
Bever, or drinking-piece. One of the movable parts, which was lifted up when the wearer ate or drank. It comes from the Italian verb *beverē* (to drink).
Mo'rion. A low iron cap, worn only by infantry.
Mahomet's helmet. Mahomet wore a double helmet ; the exterior one was called *al mawashah* (the wreathed garland).
The helmet of Perseus (2 syl.) rendered the wearer invisible. This was the " helmet of Ha'dēs," which, with the winged sandals and magic wallet, he took from certain nymphs who held them in possession ; but after he had slain Medusa he restored them again, and presented the Gorgon's head to Athe'na [Minerva], who placed it in the middle of her ægis.

He'lon, in the satire of *Absaiom and Achitophel*, by Dryden and Tate, is meant for the Earl of Feversham.

Helot. A slave in ancient Sparta. Hence, a slave or serf.

Help. (American.) A hired servant.

Helter-skelter. Higgledy-piggledy; in hurry and confusion. The Latin *hilariter-celeriter* comes tolerably near the meaning of post-haste, as Shakespeare' uses the expression (2 *Henry IV.*, v. 3):—

" Sir John, I am thy Pistol and thy friend,
A'nd helter-skelter have I rode to thee,
And tidings do I bring."

Helve. *To throw the helve after the hatchet.* To be reckless, to throw away what remains because your losses have been so great. The allusion is to the fable of the wood-cutter who lost the head of his axe in a river and threw the handle in after it.

Helve'tia. Switzerland. So called from the Helve'tii, a powerful Celtic people who dwelt thereabouts.

" See from the ashes of Helvetia's pile
The whitened skull of old Serve'tus smile."
Holmes.

Hemp. *To have some hemp in your pocket.* To have luck on your side in the most adverse circumstances. The phrase is French (*Avoir de la corde-dependu dans sa poche*), referring to the popular notion that hemp brings good luck.

Hempe (1 syl.). *When hempe is spun England is done.* Lord Bacon says he heard the prophecy when he was a child, and he interpreted it thus: Hempe is composed of the initial letters of *H*enry, *E*dward, *M*ary, *P*hilip, and *E*lizabeth. At the close of the last reign " England was done," for the sovereign no longer styled himself " King of England," but " King of Great Britain and Ireland." (*See* NOTARICA.)

Hempen Caudle. A hangman's rope.

" Ye shall have a hempen caudle then, and the
help of a hatchet."—*Shakespeare* · 2 *Hen. VI.*, iv. 7.

Hempen Collar (*A*). The hangman's rope. In French: "*La cravate de chanvre.*"

Hempen Fever. Death on the gallows, the rope being made of hemp.

Hempen Widow. The widow of a man who has been hanged. (*See above.*)

" Of a hempen widow the kid forlorn."
Ainsworth: Jack Sheppard.

He'mus or **Hæmus.** A chain of mountains in Thrace. According to mythology, Hæmos, son of Bo'reas, was changed into a mountain for aspiring to divine honours.

Hen-pecked. A man who submits to be snubbed by his wife.

Hen and Chickens (in Christian art), emblematical of God's providence. (*See* St. Matthew xxiii. 37.)

A whistling maid and crowing hen is neither fit for God nor men. A whistling maid means a witch, who whistles like the Lapland witches to call up the winds; they were supposed to be in league with the devil. The crowing of a hen was supposed to forbode a death. The usual interpretation is that masculine qualities in females are undesirable.

Hen with one Chick. *As fussy as a hen with one chick.* Over-anxious about small matters; over-particular and fussy. A hen with one chick is for ever clucking it, and never leaves it in independence a single moment.

Henchman. Henchboy. The Anglo-Saxon *hinc* is a servant or page; or perhaps *henges-man*, a horse-man; *henges* or *hengst*, a horse.

" I do but beg a little changeling boy
To be my henchman."
Shakespeare: Midsummer Night's Dream, ii. 1.

Hengist and **Horsa.** German, *hengst* (a stallion), and Horsa is connected with our Anglo-Saxon word *hors* (horse). If the names of two brothers, probably they were given them from the devices borne on their arms.

According to tradition, they landed in Pegwell Bay, Kent.

Henna. The Persian ladies tinge the tips of their fingers with henna to make them a reddish-yellow.

" The leaf of the henna-plant resembles that of
the myrtle. The blossom has a powerful fragrance ; it grows like a feather about 18 inches
long, forming a cluster of small yellow flowers."
— *Baker: Nile Tribes, Abyssinia,* chap. i. p. 3.

Henneberg (*Countess*). One day a beggar woman asked alms of the Countess, who twitted the beggar for carrying twins. The woman, furious with passion, cursed the Countess with the assurance that she should become the mother of 365 children. The tradition is that the Countess had this number all at one parturition. All the boys were named John and all the girls Elizabeth. The story says they all died on the day of their birth, and were buried at Hague.

Hen'ricans or **Henricians.** A religious sect ; so called from Henri'cus, its founder, an Italian monk, who, in the twelfth century, undertook to reform the vices of the clergy. He rejected infant baptism, festivals, and ceremonies. Henricus was imprisoned by Pope Euge'nius III. in 1148.

Henriette (3 syl.), in the French language, means "a perfect woman." The character is from Molière's *Femmes Savantes*.

Henry (*Poor*), a touching tale in poetry by Hartmann von der Aur [*Our*], one of the minnesingers (12th century). Henry, prince of Hoheneck, in Bavaria, being struck with leprosy, was told that he never would be healed till a spotless maiden volunteered to die on his behalf. Prince Henry, never expecting to meet with such a victim, sold most of his possessions, and went to live in the cottage of a small tenant farmer. Here Elsie, the farmer's daughter, waited on him; and, hearing the condition of his cure, offered herself, and went to Salerno to complete the sacrifice. Prince Henry accompanied her, was cured, and married Elsie, who thus became Lady Alicia, wife of Prince Henry of Hoheneck.

Henry Grace de Dieu. The largest ship built by Henry VIII. It carried 72 guns, 700 men, and was 1,000 tons burthen. (*See* GREAT HARRY.)

Hephæs'tos. The Greek Vulcan.

Heptarchy (Greek for *seven governments*). The *Saxon Heptarchy* is the division of England into seven parts, each of which had a separate ruler: as Kent, Sussex, Wessex, Essex, East Anglia, Mercia, and Northumbria.

He'ra. The Greek Juno, the wife of Zeus. (The word means "chosen one," *haireo*.)

Heraclei'dæ (4 syl.). The descendants of Her'aclēs (Latin, *Herculēs*).

Heralds. (Anglo - Saxon *here* (2 syl.), an army, and *ealdor*, a governor or official.

The *coat of arms* represents the knight himself from whom the bearer is descended.

The *shield* represents his body, and the *helmet* his head.

The *flourish* is his mantle.

The *motto* is the ground or moral pretension on which he stands.

The *supporters* are the pages, designated by the emblems of bears, lions, and so on.

Herald's College consists of three kings-of-arms, six heralds, and four pursuivants. The head of the college is called the Earl Marshal of England.

The three kings-of-arms are Garter (*blue*), Clarencieux and Norroy (*purple*).

The six heralds are styled Somerset Richmond, Lancaster, Windsor, Chester, and York.

The four pursuivants are Rouge Dragon, Blue Mantle, Portcullis, and Rouge Croix.

GARTER KING-OF-ARMS is so called from his special duty to attend at the solemnities of election, investiture, and installation of Knights of the Garter.

CLARENCIEUX KING - OF - ARMS. So called from the Duke of Clarence, brother of Edward IV. His duty is to marshal and dispose the funerals of knights on the south side of the Trent.

NORROY KING-OF-ARMS has similar jurisdiction to Clarencieux, only on the north side of the Trent.

"There is a supplementary herald, called 'Bath King of Arms,' who has no seat in the college. His duty is to attend at the election of a knight of the Bath."

¶ In *Scotland* the heraldic college consists of LYON KING-OF-ARMS, six heralds, and five pursuivants.

¶ In *Ireland* it consists of ULSTER KING-OF-ARMS, two heralds, and two pursuivants.

Heraldic Colours. (*See* JEWELS.)

Herb. Many herbs are used for curative purposes simply because of their form or marks: thus, wood-sorrel, being shaped like a heart, is used as a *cordial*; liver-wort for the *liver*; the celandine, which has yellow juice, for the *jaundice*; herb-dragon, which is speckled like a dragon, to counteract the poison of serpents, etc.

Herb of Grace. Rue is so called because of its use in exorcism, and hence the Roman Catholics sprinkle holy water with a bunch of rue. It was for centuries supposed to prevent contagion. Rue is the German *raute*; Greek, *rutē*; Latin, *ruta*, meaning the "preserver," being a preservative of health (Greek, *ruo*, to preserve). Ophelia calls it the "Herb of Grace o' Sundays."

Herb Trinity. The botanical name is *Viŏla tricŏlor*. The word *tricolor* explains why it is called the Herb Trinity. It also explains the pet name of "Three-faces-under-a-hood;" but the very markings of the pansy resemble the name. (*See* HEART'S EASE and PANSY.)

Herba Sacra. The "divine weed," vervain, said by the old Romans to cure the bites of all rabid animals, to arrest the progress of venom, to cure the plague, to avert sorcery and witchcraft, to reconcile enemies, etc. So highly esteemed was it that feasts called *Verbenalia* were annually held in its honour. Heralds wore a wreath of vervain when they declared war; and the Druids held vervain in similar veneration.

> " Lift your boughs of vervain blue,
> Dipt in cold September dew ;
> And dash the moisture, chaste and clear,
> O'er the ground, and through the air.
> Now the place is purged and pure."
>
> *Mason.*

Hercules (3 syl.), in astronomy, a large northern constellation.

> " Those stars in the neighbourhood of Hercules are mostly found to be approaching the earth, and those which lie in the opposite direction to be receding from it."—*Newcomb: Popular Astronomy*, part iv. chap. i. p. 458.

Her'cules (3 syl.). A Grecian hero, possessed of the utmost amount of physical strength and vigour that the human frame is capable of. He is represented as brawny, muscular, shortnecked, and of huge proportions. The Pythian told him if he would serve Eurys'theus for twelve years he should become immortal; accordingly he bound himself to the Argive king, who imposed upon him twelve tasks of great difficulty and danger :

(1) To slay the Nem'ean lion.
(2) To kill the Ler'nean hydra.
(3) To catch and retain the Arca'dian stag.
(4) To destroy the Eryman'thian boar.
(5) To cleanse the stables of King Au'geas.
(6) To destroy the cannibal birds of the Lake Stympha'lis.
(7) To take captive the Cretan bull.
(8) To catch the horses of the Thracian Diome'des.
(9) To get possession of the girdle of Hippol'yte, Queen of the Am'azons.
(10) To take captive the oxen of the monster Ger'yon.
(11) To get possession of the apples of the Hesper'ides.
(12) To bring up from the infernal regions the three-headed dog Cer'beros.

> The Nem'ean *lion* first he killed, then Lerne's *hydra* slew ;
> Th' Arca'dian *stag* and monster *boar* before Eurys'theus drew ;
> Cleansed Au'geas' *stalls*, and made the *birds* from Lake Stympha'lis flee ;
> The Cretan *bull*, and Thracian *mares*, first seized and then set free ;
> Took prize the Amazo'nian *belt*, brought Ger'yon's *kine* from Gades ;
> Fetched *apples* from the Hesperides and Cer'beros from Hades.   *E. C. B.*

The Attic Hercules. Theseus (2 syl.), who went about like Hercules, his great

contemporary, destroying robbers and achieving wondrous exploits.

The Egyptian Hercules. Sesostris. (Flourished B.C. 1500.)

The Farne'se Hercules. A celebrated work of art, copied by Glykon from an original by Lysippos. It exhibits the hero, exhausted by toil, leaning upon his club ; his left hand rests upon his back, and grasps one of the apples of the Hesperi'des. A copy of this famous statue stands in the gardens of the Tuileries, Paris ; but Glykon's statue is in the Farnese Palace at Rome. A beautiful description of this statue is given by Thomson (*Liberty*, iv.).

The Jewish Hercules. Samson. (Died B.C. 1113.)

Hercules' Choice. Immortality the reward of toil in preference to pleasure. Xenophon tells us when Hercules was a youth he was accosted by two women— —Virtue and Pleasure—and asked to choose between them. Pleasure promised him all carnal delights, but Virtue promised immortality. Hercules gave his hand to the latter, and, after a life of toil, was received amongst the gods.

Hercules' Club. A stick of unusual size and formidable appearance.

Hercules' Horse. Ari'on, given him by Adras'tos. It had the power of speech, and its feet on the right side were those of a man. (*See* Horse.)

Hercules' Labour or *The labour of an Hercules.* Very great toil. Hercules was appointed by Eurystheus (3 syl.) to perform twelve labours requiring enormous strength or dexterity.

> " It was more than the labour of an Hercules could effect to make any tolerable way through your town."—*Cumberland : The West Indian.*

Hercules' Pillars. Calpé and Ab'yla, one at Gibraltar and one at Ceuta, torn asunder by Hercules that the waters of the Atlantic and the Mediterranean Sea might communicate with each other. Macro'bius ascribes these pillars to Sesostris (the Egyptian Hercules), and Lucan follows the same tradition.

I will follow you even to the pillars of Hercules. To the end of the world. The ancients supposed that these rocks marked the utmost limits of the habitable globe. (*See above*, Hercules' Pillars.)

Hercules Secundus. Com'modus, the Roman Emperor, gave himself this title. He was a gigantic idiot, of whom it is said that he killed 100 lions in the amphitheatre, and gave none of them more than one blow. He also overthrew 1,000 gladiators. (161, 180-192.)

Hercules of Music (*The*). Christopher Glück (1714-1787).

Hercu'lean Knot. A snaky complication on the rod or cadu'ceus of Mercury, adopted by the Grecian brides as the fastening of their woollen girdles, which only the bridegroom was allowed to untie when the bride retired for the night. As he did so he invoked Juno to render his marriage as fecund as that of Herculēs, whose numerous wives all had families, amongst them being the fifty daughters of Thestius, each of whom conceived in one night. (*See* KNOT.)

Hereford (3 syl.). (Anglo-Saxon, *herĕ-ford*, army ford.)

Herefordshire Kindness. A good turn rendered for a good turn received. Latin proverbs, "*Fricantem refri'ca ;*" "*Manus manum lavat.*" Fuller says the people of Herefordshire "drink back to him who drinks to them."

Heretic means "one who chooses," and *heresy* means simply "a choice." A heretic is one who chooses his own creed, and does not adopt the creed authorised by the national church. (Greek, *hairēsis*, choice.)

HERETICS OF THE FIRST CENTURY were the *Simo'nians* (so called from Simon Magus), *Cerin'thians* (Cerinthus), *Eb'ionites* (Eb'ion), and *Nicola'itans* (Nicholas, deacon of Antioch).

SECOND CENTURY : The *Basilid'ians* (Basil'ides), *Carpocra'tians* (Carpoc'rates), *Valentin'ians* (Valenti'nus), *Gnostics* (Knowing Ones), *Nazare'nes*, *Millena'rians*, *Cain'ites* (Cain), *Seth'ians* (Seth), *Quartodecimans* (who kept Easter on the fourteenth day of the first month), *Cerdo'nians* (Cerdon), *Mar'cionites* (Mar'cion), *Monta'nists* (Monta'nus), *Ta'tianists* (Ta'tian), *Alogians* (who denied the "Word"), *Artoty'rites* (*q.v.*), and *Angel'ics* (who worshipped angels).

✢ Tatianists belong to the third or fourth century. The Tatian of the second century was a Platonic philosopher who wrote *Discourses* in good Greek ; Tatian the heretic lived in the third or fourth century, and wrote very bad Greek. The two men were widely different in every respect, and the authority of the heretic for "four gospels" is of no worth.

THIRD CENTURY : The *Pat'ri-passians*, *Arab'aci*, *Aqua'rians*, *Nova'tians*, *Or'igenists* (followers of Origen), *Melchisedech'ians* (who believed Melchis'edec was the

Messiah), *Sabellians* (from Sabel'lius), and *Maniche'ans* (followers of Mani).

FOURTH CENTURY : The *A'rians* (from Arius), *Colluth'ians* (Collu'thus), *Macedo'nians*, *Agne'tæ*, *Apollina'rians* (Apollina'ris), *Timo'theans* (Timothy, the apostle), *Collyrid'ians* (who offered *cakes* to the Virgin Mary), *Seleu'cians* (Seleu'cius), *Priscillians* (Priscillian), *Anthropomorphites* (who ascribed to God a human form), *Jovin'ianists* (Jovin'ian), *Messa'lians*, and *Bono'sians* (Bono'sus).

FIFTH CENTURY : The *Pela'gians* (Pela'gius), *Nesto'rians* (Nesto'rius), *Eutych'ians* (Eu'tychus), *Theo-paschites* (who said all the three persons of the Trinity suffered on the cross).

SIXTH CENTURY : The *Predestina'rians*, *Incorrup'tibilists* (who maintained that the body of Christ was incorruptible), the new *Agnoe'tæ* (who maintained that Christ did not know when the day of judgment would take place), and the *Monoth'elites* (who maintained that Christ had but one will). ·

Her'iot. A right of the lord of a manor to the best jewel, beast, or chattel of a deceased copyhold tenant. The word is compounded of the Saxon *here* (army), *geatu* (grant), because originally it was military furniture, such as armour, arms, and horses paid to the lord of the fee. (*Canute*, c. 69.)

Hermæ. Busts of the god Hermēs affixed to a quadrangular stone pillar, diminishing towards the base, and between five and six feet in height. They were set up to mark the boundaries of lands, at the junction of roads, at the corners of streets, and so on. The Romans used them also for garden decorations. In later times the block was more or less chiselled into legs and arms.

Hermaph'rodite (4 syl.). A human body having both sexes ; a vehicle combining the structure of a wagon and cart ; a flower containing both the male and female organs of reproduction. The word is derived from the fable of Hermaph'rodi'tus, son of Hermēs and Aph'-rodite. The nymph Sal'macis became enamoured of him, and prayed that she might be so closely united that "the twain might become one flesh." Her prayer being heard, the nymph and boy became one body. (*Ovid : Metamorphoses*, iv. 347.)

✢ The Romans believed that there were human beings combining in one body both sexes. The Jewish Talmud contains several references to them. An old French law allowed them great latitude. The English law recognises them. The ancient Athenians commanded that they should be put to death. The Hindûs and Chinese enact that every hermaphrodite should choose one sex and keep to it. According to fable, all persons who bathed in the fountain Salmăcis, in Caria, became hermaphrodites.

Some think by comparing Gen. i. 27 with Gen. ii. 20-24 that Adam at first combined in himself both sexes.

Her'megyld or **Hermyngyld.** The wife of the constable of Northumberland, who was converted to Christianity by Cunstance, by whose bidding she restored sight to a blind Briton. (*Chaucer : Man of Lawes Tale.*)

Her'mensul or *Ermensul.* A Saxon deity, worshipped in Westpha'lia. Charlemagne broke the idol, and converted its temple into a Christian church. The statue stood on a column, holding a standard in one hand, and a balance in the other. On its breast was the figure of a bear, and on its shield a lion. Probably it was a war-god.

Her'mes (2 syl.). The Greek Mercury; either the god or the metal.

" So when we see the liquid metal fall
   Which chemists by the name of Hermes call."
                    Hoole: Ariosto, book viii.

Milton (*Paradise Lost,* iii. 603) calls quicksilver "Volatil Hermes."

Hermetic Art. The art or science of alchemy; so called from the Chaldean philosopher, Hermēs Trismegis'tus, its hypothetical founder.

Hermet'ic Books. Egyptian books written under the dictation of Thoth (the Egyptian Hermēs), the scribe of the gods. Iamblichus gives their number as 20,000, but Man'etho raises it to 36,525. These books state that the world was made out of fluid; that the soul is the union of light and life; that nothing is destructible; that the soul transmigrates; and that suffering is the result of motion.

Hermet'ic Philosophy. A system which acknowledges only three chemical principles—viz. salt, sulphur, and mercury—from which it explains every phenomenon of nature (*See* HERMES.)

Hermetic Powder. The sympathetic powder, supposed to possess a healing influence from a distance. The mediæval philosophers were very fond of calling books, drugs, etc., connected with alchemy and astrology by the term hermetic, out of compliment to Hermēs

Trismegis'tus. (*Sir Kenelm Digby : Discourse Concerning the Cure of Wounds by Sympathy.*)

" For by his side a pouch he wore
  Replete with strange hermetic powder,
  That wounds nine miles point-blank would
  solder."   *Butler : Hudibras,* i. 2.

Hermet'ically Sealed. Closed securely. Thus we say, "My lips are hermetically sealed," meaning so as not to utter a word of what has been imparted. The French say close-fitting doors and windows "shut hermetically." When chemists want to preserve anything from the air, they heat the neck of the vessel till it is soft, and then twist it till the aperture is closed up. This is called sealing the vessel hermetically, or like a chemist. (From Hermēs, called Trismegistus, or thrice-great, the supposed inventor of chemistry.)

Her'mia. Daughter of Egēus, who betrothed her to Deme'trius; but she refused to marry him, as she was in love with Lysander. (*Shakespeare : Midsummer Night's Dream.*)

Hermi'one (4 syl.). Wife of Leontēs, King of Silicia. Being suspected of infidelity, she was thrown into jail, swooned, and was reported to be dead. She was kept concealed till her infant Per'dita was of marriageable age, when Leontēs discovered his mistake, and was reconciled to his wife. (*Shakespeare : Winter's Tale.*)

Hermit (*The English*). Roger Crab. He subsisted at the expense of three farthings a week, or 3s. 3d. per annum. His food consisted of bran, herbs, roots, dock-leaves, mallows, and grass. Crab died in 1680.

Hermit. *Peter the Hermit.* Preacher of the first crusade. (1050-1115.)

Hermite (2 syl.). *Tristrem l'Hermite* or *Sir Tristan l'Ermite.* Provost-marshal of Louis XI. He was the main instrument in carrying into effect the nefarious schemes of his wily master, who used to call him his gossip. (1405-1493.) Sir Walter Scott introduces him in *Anne of Gierstein,* and again in *Quentin Durward.*

Hermoth or **Hermod** (2 syl.). The deity, who, with Bragi, receives and welcomes to Valhalla all heroes who fall in battle. (*Scandinavian mythology.*)

He'ro. Daughter of Leona'to, governor of Messi'na. Her attachment to

Beatrice is very beautiful, and she serves as a foil to show off the more brilliant qualities of her cousin. (*Shakespeare: Much Ado about Nothing.*)

He'ro and Lean'der. The tale is that Hero, a priestess of Venus, fell in love with Leander, who swam across the Hellespont every night to visit her. One night he was drowned, and heart-broken Hero drowned herself in the same sea.

Hero Children. Children of whom legend relates, that being deserted by their parents, they were suckled by wild beasts, brought up by herdsmen, and became national heroes.

Heroes scratched off Church-doors. Militia officers were so called by Sheridan. The Militia Act enjoined that a list of all persons between eighteen and forty-five years of age must be affixed to the church door of the parish in which they reside three days before the day of appeal, Sunday being one. Commission officers who had served four years in the militia being exempt, their names " were scratched off."

Hero'ic Age. That age of a nation which comes between the purely mythical period and the historic. This is the age when the sons of the gods take unto themselves the daughters of men, and the offspring partake of the twofold character.

Heroic Medicines. Those which either kill or cure.

Heroic Size in sculpture denotes a stature superior to ordinary life, but not colossal.

Heroic Verse. That verse in which epic poetry is generally written. In Greek and Latin it is *hexameter* verse, in English it is ten-syllable iambic verse, either in rhymes or not; in Italian it is the *ottava rima.* So called because it is employed to celebrate heroic exploits.

Her'od. A child-killer; from Herod the Great, who ordered the massacre of the babes in Bethlehem. (Matt. ii. 16.)

To out-herod Herod. To out-do in wickedness, violence, or rant, the worst of tyrants. Herod, who destroyed the babes of Bethlehem, was made (in the ancient mysteries) a ranting, roaring tyrant ; the extravagance of his rant being the measure of his bloody-mindedness. (*See* PILATE.)

" Oh, it offends me to the soul to hear a robustious, periwig-pated fellow tear a passion to tatters, to very rags, to split the ears of the groundlings . . . . it out-herods Herod."—*Shakespeare: Hamlet,* iii. 2

Herod's Death (Acts xii. 23). The following died of a similar disease [phthiriāsis] : L. Sylla ; Pherecȳdēs the Syrian (the preceptor of Pythagōras) ; the Greek poet Alcmæon, and Philip II. of Spain.

Phthiri'asis is an affection of the skin in which parasites are engendered so numerously as to cover the whole surface of the body. The vermin lay their eggs in the skin and multiply most rapidly.

Herodotus of Old London (*The*). John Stow, author of the *Survey of London* (1525-1605).

Her'on-crests. The Uzbeg Tartars wear a plume of white heron feathers in their turbans.

Heros'tratos or *Erostratos.* An Ephesian who set fire to the temple of Ephesus in order that his name might be perpetuated. The Ephesians made it penal to mention the name, but this law defeated its object (B.C. 356).

Herring. *Dead as a shotten herring.* The shotten herring is one that has shot off or ejected its spawn. This fish dies the very moment it quits the water, from want of air. Indeed, all the herring tribe die very soon after they are taken from their native element. (*See* BATTLE.)

" By gar de herring is no dead so as I vill kill him."—*Shakespeare: Merry Wives of Windsor,* ii. 2.

Neither barrel the better herring. Much of a muchness ; not a pin to choose between you ; six of one and half a dozen of the other. The herrings of both barrels are so much alike that there is no choice whatever. In Spanish : " *Qual mas qual menos, toda la lana es pelos.*"

"Two feloes being like flagicious, and neither barell better herring, accused either other, the kyng Philippus . . . sitting in iudgement vpon them . . . . condemned both the one and the other with banishmente." — *Erasmus: Apophtheymes.*

Herring-bone (in building). Courses of stone laid angularly, thus: . Also applied to strutting placed between thin joists to increase their strength.

Also a peculiar stitch in needlework, chiefly used in working flannel.

Herring-pond (*The*). The British Channel ; the Atlantic, which separates America from the British Isles ; the sea between Australasia and the United Kingdom, are all so called.

" He'll plague you now he's come over the herring-pond." — *Sir W. Scott: Guy Mannering,* chap. xxxiv.

Hertford. (Anglo-Saxon, *heort-ford*, the hart's ford). The arms of the city are " a hart couchant in water."

Hertford, invoked by Thomson in his *Spring*, was Frances Thynne, who married Algernon Seymour, Earl of Hertford, afterwards Duke of Somerset.

Hertha. Mother earth. Worshipped by all the Scandinavian tribes with orgies and mysterious rites, celebrated in the dark. Her veiled statue was transported from district to district by cows which no hand but the priest's was allowed to touch. Tacitus calls this goddess Cyb'ele.

Hesi'one (4 syl.). Daughter of Laom'edon, King of Troy, exposed to a sea-monster, but rescued by Hercules. (*See* ANDROMEDA.)

Hesper'ia. Italy was so called by the Greeks, because it was to them the "Western Land;" and afterwards the Romans, for a similar reason, transferred the name to Spain.

Hesper'ides (4 syl.). Three sisters who guarded the golden apples which He'ra (*Juno*) received as a marriage gift. They were assisted by the dragon La'don. Many English poets call the place where these golden apples grew the "garden of the Hesperides." Shakespeare (*Love's Labour's Lost*, iv. 3) speaks of climbing trees in the Hesperides." (See *Comus*, lines 402-406.)

" Show thee the tree, leafed with refined gold,
Whereon the fearful dragon held his seat.
That watched the garden called Hesperides."
Robert Grene: Friar Bacon and Friar Bungay. (1508.)

Hes'perus. The evening star.

" Ere twice in murk and occidental damp,
Moist Hesperus hath quenched his sleepy lamp."
Shakespeare: All's Well that Ends Well, ii. 1.

He'sychasts (pron. *He'-se-kasts*). The "Quietists" of the East in the fourteenth century. They placed perfection in contemplation. (Greek, *hesu'chia*, quiet.) (*See* Gibbon, *Roman Empire*, lxiii.) Milton well expresses their belief in his *Comus* :—

" Till oft converse with heavenly habitants
Begin to cast a beam on the outward shape,
And turns it by degrees to the soul's essence,
Till all be made immortal." (470-474.)

Hetærism (3 syl.). Prostitution. The Greek *hetaira* (a concubine). According to Plato, " *Meretrix, specioso nomine rem odiosam denotante.*" (*Plut. et Athen.*)

Hetman. The chief of the Cossacks of the Don used to be so called. He was elected by the people, and the mode of choice was thus : The voters threw their fur caps at the candidate they voted for, and he who had the largest number of caps at his feet was the successful candidate. The last Hetman was Count Platoff (1812-1814).

A general or commander-in-chief. (German, *hauptmann*, chief man.)

" After the peace, all Europe hailed their hetman, Platoff, as the hero of the war."—*J. S. Mosby: War Reminiscences*, chap. xi. p. 146.

Heu-monat' or **Heg-monath**. Hay-month, the Anglo-Saxon name for July.

Hewson. *Old Hewson the cobbler*. Colonel John Hewson, who (as Hume says) " rose from the profession of a cobbler to a high rank in Cromwell's army."

Hexameron (*The*). The six days of creation; any six days taken as one continuous period.

"'Every winged fowl' was produced on the fourth day of the Hexameron."—*W. E. Gladstone: Nineteenth Century*, January, 1866.

Hexameter and Pentameter. An alternate metre ; often called elegiac verse. Hexameter as described below. Pentameter verse is divided into two parts, each of which ends with an extra long syllable. The former half consists of two metres, dactyls or spondees; the latter half must be two dactyls. The following is a rhyming specimen in English :

Would you be happy an hour, dine well ; for a day, tend a wedding ;
If for a week, buy a house ; if for a month, wed a spouse ;
Would you be happy six months, buy a horse : if for twelve, start a carriage ;
Happiness long as you live, only contentment can give. *E. C. B.*

This metre might be introduced, and would suit epigrams and short poems.

Hexameter Verse. A line of poetry consisting of six measures, the fifth being a dactyl and the sixth either a spondee or a trochee. The other four may be either dactyls or -spondees. Homer's two epic poems and Virgil's *Æneid* are written in hexameters. The latter begins thus :

Arms and the | man I | sing, who | driven from | Troy by ill- | fortune
First into | Italy | came, as | far as the | shores of La- | vina.
Much was he harassed by land, much tossed on the pitiless ocean,
All by the force of the gods, and relentless anger of Juno. *E. C. B.*

Or rhyming with the Latin,

" Arma virumque cano Trojæ qui primus ab oris.'
Arms and the man I sing who first from the Phrygian shore is.
" Italiam Fato profugus, Lavinaque venit . . ."
Tossed to the land of Lavina, although Jove's queen didn't mean it. *E. C. B.*

⁂ Longfellow's *Evangeline* is in English hexameters.

Hex'apla. A book containing the text of the Bible in Hebrew and Greek, with four translations, viz. the Sep'tuagint, with those of Aquila, Theodo'tion, and Symmachus. The whole is printed in six columns on the page. This was the work of Origen, who also added marginal notes.

Hext. *When bale is hext, boot is next.* When things come to the worst they must soon mend. *Bale* means misery, hurt, misfortune; *hext* is highest, as *next* is nighest; *boot* means help, profit.

Heyday of Youth. The prime of youth. (Anglo-Saxon, *heh-dæg*, highday or mid-day of youth.)

Hiawath'a. Son of Mudjekee'wis (the west wind) and Weno'nah. His mother died in his infancy, and Hiawatha was brought up by his grandmother, Noko'mis, daughter of the Moon. He represents the progress of civilisation among the American Indians. He first wrestled with Monda'min (Indian maize), whom he subdued, and gave to man bread-corn. He then taught man navigation; then he subdued the Mishe-Nahma or sturgeon, and told the people to "bring all their pots and kettles and make oil for winter." His next adventure was against Megissog'won, the magician, "who sent the fiery fever on man; sent the white fog from the fen-lands; sent disease and death among us;" he slew the terrible monster, and taught man the science of medicine. He next married "Laughing Water," setting the people an example to follow. Lastly, he taught the people picture-writing. When the white man landed and taught the Indians the faith of Jesus, Hiawatha exhorted them to receive the words of wisdom, to reverence the missionaries who had come so far to see them, and departed "to the kingdom of Pone'mah, the land of the Hereafter."

Longfellow's song of Hiawath'a may be termed the "Edda" of the North American Indians.

Hiawatha's mittens. "Magic mittens made of deer-skin; when upon his hands he wore them, he could smite the rocks asunder." (*Longfellow: Hiawatha*, iv.)

Hiawatha's moc'casins. Enchanted shoes made of deer-skin. "When he bound them round his ankles, at each stride a mile he measured." (*Longfellow; Hiawatha*, iv.)

Hiber'nia. A variety of Ierne (*Ireland*). Pliny says the Irish mothers feed their babes with swords instead of spoons.

" While in Hibernia's fields the labouring swain,
Shall pass the plough o'er skulls of warriors slain,
And turn up bones and broken spears.
Amazed, he'll show his fellows of the plain
The relics of victorious years,
And tell how swift thy arms that kingdom did regain."
Hughes: House of Nassau.

Hic Ja'cets. Tombstones, so called from the first two words of their inscriptions; "Here lies . . ."

" By the cold *Hic Jacets* of the dead."
Tennyson: Idylls of the King (Vivien).

Hick'athrift (*Tom* or *Jack*). A poor labourer in the time of the Conquest, of such enormous strength that, armed with an axletree and cartwheel only, he killed a giant who dwelt in a marsh at Tilney, Norfolk. He was knighted and made governor of Thanet. He is sometimes called *Hickafric.*

Hick'ory. *Old Hickory.* General Andrew Jackson. Parton says he was first called "Tough," from his pedestrian powers; then "Tough as hickory;" and lastly, "Old Hickory."

Hidal'go. The title in Spain of the lower nobility. (According to Bishop St. Vincent, the word is compounded of *hijo del Goto*, son of a Goth; but more probably it is *hijo* and *dalgo*. *Hija* = child or son, and *dalgo* = respect, as in the phrase, "*Facer mucho dalgo*," to receive with great respect. In Portuguese it is *Fidalgo.*

Hide of Land (*A*). No fixed number of "acres," but such a quantity as was valued at a stated geld or tax. A hide of good arable land was smaller than a hide of inferior quality.

Hiero'clean Legacy. The legacy of jokes. Hiĕroclēs, in the fifth Christian century, was the first person who hunted up and compiled jokes. After a life-long labour he mustered together as many as twenty-eight, which he has left to the world as his legacy.

Higgledy-piggledy. In great confusion; at sixes and sevens. A higgler is a pedlar whose stores are all huddled together. Higgledy means after the fashion of a higgler's basket; and *piggledy* is a ricochet word suggested by litter; as, a pig's litter.

High-born. Of aristocratic birth; "*D'une haute naissance ;*" "*Summo loco natus.*"

High Church. Those who believe the Church [of England] the only true Church; that its baptism is regeneration; and that its priests have the delegated power of absolution (on confession and promise of repentance).

High Days = festivals. *On high days and holidays.* Here "high" = grand or great; as, "*un grand jour.*"

High Falu'tin or **Hifalu'ten.** Tall talk. (Dutch, *verlooten*, high - flown, stilted.)

"The genius of hifaluten, as the Americans call it . . . has received many mortal wounds lately from the hands of satirists. . . . A quizzical Jenkins lately described the dress of a New York belle by stating that 'she wore an exquisite hyphaluten on her head, while her train was composed of transparent fol-de-rol, and her petticoat of crambambuli flounced with Brussels three-ply of A No. 1.'"—*Hingston: Introduction to Josh Billings.*

High Hand. *With a high hand.* Arrogantly. To carry things with a high hand in French would be: "*Faire une chose haut la main.*"

High Heels and **Low Heels.** The High and Low Church party. The names of two factions in Swift's tale of Lilliput. (*Gulliver's Travels.*)

High Horse. *To be on the high horse* or *To ride the high horse.* To be overbearing and arrogant. (For explanation *see* HORSE, "*To get upon your high horse.*")

High Jinks. *He is at high jinks.* The present use of the phrase expresses the idea of uproarious fun and jollity.

"The frolicsome company had begun to practise the ancient and now forgotten pastime of *High Jinks.* The game was played in several different ways. Most frequently the dice were thrown by the company, and those upon whom the lot fell were obliged to assume and maintain for a time a certain fictitious character, or to repeat a certain number of fescennine verses in a particular order. If they departed from the characters assigned . . . they incurred forfeits, which were compounded for by swallowing an additional bumper."—*Sir W. Scott: Guy Mannering,* xxxvi.

High Life. *People of high life.* The upper ten, the "*haut monde.*"

High Places, in Scripture language, means elevated spots where sacrifices were offered. Idolatrous worship was much carried on in high places. Some were evidently artificial mounds, for the faithful were frequently ordered to remove or destroy them. Hezekiah removed the high places (2 Kings xviii. 4), so did Asa (2 Chronicles xiv. 3), Jehoshaphat (2 Chronicles xvii. 6), Josiah, and others. On the other hand, Jehoram and Ahaz made high places for idolatrous worship.

High Ropes. *To be on the high ropes.* To be very grand and mighty in demeanour.

High Seas. All the sea which is not the property of a particular country. The sea three miles out belongs to the adjacent coast, and is called *mare clausum.* High-seas, like high-ways, means for the public use. In both cases the word *high* means "chief," "principal." (Latin, *altum,* "the main sea;" *altus,* "high.")

High Tea (*A*). The meal called tea served with cold meats, vegetables, and pastry, in substitution of dinner.

"A well-understood 'high tea' should have cold roast beef at the top of the table, a cold Yorkshire pie at the bottom, a mighty ham in the middle. The side dishes will comprise soused mackerel, pickled salmon (in due season), sausages and potatoes, etc., etc. Rivers of tea, coffee, and ale, with dry and buttered toast, sally-lunns, scones, muffins, and crumpets, jams and marmalade."—*The Daily Telegraph,* May 9th, 1893.

High Words. Angry words.

Highgate has its name from a gate set up there about 400 years ago, to receive tolls for the bishop of London, when the old miry road from Gray's Inn Lane to Barnet was turned through the bishop's park. The village being in a *high* or elevated situation explains the first part of the name.

Sworn at Highgate. A custom anciently prevailed at the public-houses in Highgate to administer a ludicrous oath to all travellers who stopped there. The party was sworn on a pair of horns fastened to a stick—

(1) Never to kiss the maid when he can kiss the mistress.

(2) Never to eat brown bread when he can get white.

(3) Never to drink small beer when he can get strong—unless he prefers it.

Highland Bail. Fists and cuffs; to escape the constable by knocking him down with the aid of a companion.

"The mute eloquence of the miller and smith, which was vested in their clenched fists, was prepared to give highland bail for the 'r arbiter [Edie Ochiltree]."—*Sir W. Scott: The Antiquary,* chap. xxix.

Highland Mary. A name immortalised by Burns, generally thought to be Mary Campbell, but more probably Mary Morison. In 1792 we have three songs to Mary: "Will ye go to the Indies, my Mary?" "Highland Mary" ("Ye banks and braes of bonnie Doon"), and "To Mary in Heaven" ("Thou lingering star," etc.). These were all written some time after the consummation of his marriage with Jean Armour

(1788), from the recollection of "one of the most interesting passages of his youthful days." Four months after he had sent to Mr. Thomson the song called "Highland Mary" he sent that entitled "Mary Morison," which he calls "one of his juvenile works." Thus all the four songs refer to some youthful passion, and three of them at least were sent in letters addressed to Mr. Thomson, so that little doubt can exist that the Mary of all the four is one and the same person, called by the author Mary Morison.

> "How blythely wad I bide the stoure.
> A weary slave frae sun to sun,
> Could I the rich reward secure—
> The lovely Mary Morison."

Highlands of Scotland (*The*) include all the country on the northern side of a line drawn from the Moray Frith to the river Clyde, or (which is about the same thing) from Nairn to Glasgow.

High'landers of At'tica. The operative class, who had their dwellings on the hills (*Diacrii*).

High'ness. The Khedive of Egypt is styled "Your Highness," or "His Highness;"
The children of kings and queens, "Your Royal Highness," or "His Royal Highness;"
The children of emperors, "Your Imperial Highness," or "His Imperial Highness."
Till the reign of Henry VIII. the kings of England were styled "Your Highness," "Your Grace," "Your Excellent Grace," etc., or "His . . . . " etc.

Highwaymen. The four most celebrated are:—
Claude Duval, who died 1670.
James Whitney, who died 1694, at the age of 34.
Jonathan Wild, of Wolverhampton (1682-1725).
Jack Sheppard, of Spitalfields (1701-1724).

Hil'ary Term, in the Law Courts, begins on Plough Monday (*q.v.*) and ends the Wednesday before Easter. It is so called in honour of St. Hilary, whose day is January 14.

Hil'debrand (*Meister*). The Nestor of German romance. Like Maugis among the heroes of Charlemagne, he was a magician as well as champion.
Hildebrand. Pope Gregory VII. (1013, 1073-1085).
A Hildebrand. One resembling Pope Gregory VII., noted for subjugating the

power of the German emperors; and specially detested by the early reformers for his ultra-pontifical views.

Hil'debrod (*Duke*). President of the Alsa'tian club. (*Sir W. Scott : Fortunes of Nigel.*)

Hildesheim. A monk of Hildesheim doubting how with God a thousand years could be as one day, listened to the singing of a bird in a wood, as he thought for three minutes, but found the time had been three hundred years. Longfellow has borrowed this tale and introduced it in his *Golden Legend*. (*See* FELIX.)

Hill (*Sir John*), M.D., botanist (1716-1775). He wrote some farces, which called forth from Garrick the following couplet:
> "For physic and farces his equal there scarce is,
> His farces are physic, his physic a farce is."

Hill-folk. The Cameronian Scotch Covenanters, who met clandestinely among the hills. Sometimes the Covenanters generally are so called. Sir W. Scott used the words as a synonym of Cameronians.

Hill-people or **Hill-folk.** A class of beings in Scandinavian tradition between the elves and the human race. They are supposed to dwell in caves and small hills, and are bent on receiving the benefits of man's redemption.

Hill Tribes. The barbarous tribes dwelling in remote parts of the Deccan or plateau of Central India.

Hills. Prayers were offered on the tops of high hills, and temples built on "high places," from the notion that the gods could better hear prayers on such places, as they were nearer heaven. As Lucian says, ὅτι τῶν εὐχωλέων ἀγχόθεν ἐπαίουσιν οἱ θεοί. And Tacitus says, "maxime cœlo appropinquare, precesque mortalium a Deo nusquam propius audīre." It will be remembered that Balak (Numbers xxiii. xxiv.) took Balaam to the top of Peor and other high places when Balaam wished to consult God. We often read of "idols on every high hill." (Ezek. vi. 13.)
⁂ The Greek gods dwelt on Mount Olympus.

Himiltrude (3 syl.). Wife of Charlemagne, who surpassed all other women in nobleness of mien.

> "Her neck was tinged with a delicate rose, like that of a Roman matron in former ages. Her locks were bound about her temples with gold and purple bands. Her dress was looped up with ruby clasps. Her coronet and her purple robes gave her an air of surpassing majesty."—*Croquemitaine.* iii.

Hinc illæ Lacrymæ. This was the real offence; this was the true secret of the annoyance; this, *entre nous*, was the real source of the vexation.

" Perchance 'tis Mara's song that gives offence—
 Hinc illæ lacrymæ—I fear
 The song that once could charm the royal sense,
 Delights, alas! no more the royal ear."
        Peter Pindar : Ode upon Ode.

Hind. Emblematic of St. Giles, because "a heaven-directed hind went daily to give him milk in the desert, near the mouth of the Rhone." (*See* HART.)

The hind of Sertorius. Serto'rius was invited by the Lusita'nians to defend them against the Romans. · He had a tame white hind, which he taught to follow him, and from which he pretended to receive the instructions of Dian'a. By this artifice, says Plutarch, he imposed on the superstition of the people.

" He feigned a demon (in a hind concealed)
 To him the counsels of the gods revealed."
        Camoens : Lusiad, i.

The milk-white hind, in Dryden's poem, *The Hind and the Panther,* means the Roman Catholic Church, milk-white because "infallible." The panther, full of the spots of error, is the Church of England.

" Without unspotted, innocent within,
 She feared no danger, for she knew no sin."
        Part i. lines 3, 4.

Hin'da. Daughter of Al Hassan, the Arabian ameer of Persia. Her lover, Hafed, was a Gheber or Fire-worshipper, the sworn enemy of Al Hassan and all his race. Al Hassan sent her away for safety, but she was taken captive by Hafed's party, and when her lover (betrayed to Al Hassan) burnt himself to death in the sacred fire, Hinda cast herself headlong into the sea. (*T. Moore : The Fire-Worshippers.*)

Hin'der is to hold one behind; whereas *pre-vent* is to go before (Anglo-Saxon *hinder,* behind, verb *hindrian*).

Hindustan. The country of the Hindûs. (*Hind* [Persic] and *Sind* [Sanskrit] means "black," and *tan* = territory is very common, as Afghanistan, Beloochistan, Farsistan, Frangistan, Koordistan [the country of the Koords], Kohistan [the high-country], Kafiristan [the infidel country], etc.)

Hindustan Regiment. The 76th; so called because it first distinguished itself in Hindustan. It is also called the *Seven and Sixpennies,* from its number. Now the 2nd battalion of the West Riding, the 1st being the old No. 33.

Hinzelmann. The most famous house-spirit or kobold of German legend. He lived four years in the old castle of Hudemühlen, where he had a room set apart for him. At the end of the fourth year (1588) he went away of his own accord, and never again returned.

Hip (*To*). A hip means a hyp-ochondriac. To hip means to make melancholy; to fret; to make one dismal or gloomy with forebodings. Hipped means melancholy, in low spirits.

" For one short moment let us cease
 To mourn the loss of many ships—
 Forget how tax and rates increase,
 And all that now the nation hips."
     Sims : The Dagonet Ballads (A Set-off).

Hip and Thigh. *To smite hip and thigh.* To slay with great carnage. A Hebrew phrase. (German, *Arm und bein.*)

✢ Perhaps there may be some reference to the superstition about the os sacrum (*q.v.*).

" And he smote them hip and thigh with great slaughter."—Judges xv. 8.

Hip! Hip! Hurrah! Hip is said to be a notarica, composed of the initial letters of *Hierosolyma Est Per'dita.* Henri van Laun says, in *Notes and Queries,* that whenever the German knights headed a Jew-hunt in the Middle Ages, they ran shouting "Hip! Hip!" as much as to say "Jerusalem is destroyed." (*See* NOTARICA.)

Timbs derives Hurrah from the Sclavonic *hu-raj* (to Paradise), so that *Hip! hip! hurrah!* would mean "Jerusalem is lost to the infidel, and we are on the road to Paradise." These etymons may be taken for what they are worth. The word *hurrah!* is a German exclamation also.

" *Now, infidel, I have thee on the hip*" (*Merchant of Venice*); and again, "*I'll have our Michael Cassio on the hip*" (*Othello*), to have the whip hand of one. The term is derived from wrestlers, who seize the adversary by the hip and throw him.

" In fine he doth apply one speciall drift,
 Which was to get the pagan on the hip,
 And having caught him right, he doth him lift
 By nimble sleight, and in such wise doth trip,
 That down he threw him." *Sir J. Harington.*

Hipper - switches. Coarse willow withes. A *hipper* is a coarse osier used in basket-making, and an osier field is a *hipper-holm.*

Hippo. *Bishop of Hippo.* A title by which St. Augustine is sometimes designated. (354-430.)

Hip'pocampus (4 syl.). A seahorse, having the head and fore-quarters of a horse, with the tail and hind-quarters of a fish or dolphin. (Greek, *hippos*, a horse ; *kampos*, a sea monster.)

Hip'pocras. A cordial made of Lisbon and Canary wines, bruised spices, and sugar ; so called from the strainer through which it is passed, called by apothecaries *Hippoc'rates' sleeve*. Hippocratēs in the Middle Ages was called " Yypocras " or " Hippocras." Thus :

> " Well knew he the old Esculapius,
> And Deiscorides, and eek Rufus,
> Old Yypocras, Haly, and Galien."
> *Chaucer : Canterbury Tales (Prologue,* 431).

Hippocrat'ean School. A school of medicine, so called from Hippoc'ratēs. (*See* DOGMATIC.)

Hippoc'rates' Sleeve. A woollen bag of a square piece of flannel, having the opposite corners joined, so as to make it triangular. Used by chemists for straining syrups, decoctions, etc.

Hip'pocrene (3 syl.). The fountain of the Muses, produced by a stroke of the hoof of Peg'asos (Greek, *hippos*, horse ; *krēnē*, fountain).

Hip'pogriff. The winged horse, whose father was a griffin and mother a filly (Greek, *hippos*, a horse, and *gryphos*, a griffin). A symbol of love. (*Ariosto : Orlando Furioso*, iv. 18, 19.)

> " So saying, he caught him up, and without wing
> Of hippogrif, bore through the air sublime,
> Over the wilderness and o'er the plain."
> *Milton : Paradise Regained*, iv. 541-3.

(*See* SIMURGH.)

Hippol'yta. Queen of the Am'azons, and daughter of Mars. Shakespeare has introduced the character in his *Midsummer Night's Dream*, where he betroths her to Theseus, Duke of Athens. In classic fable it is her sister An'tiopē who married Theseus, although some writers justify Shakespeare's account. Hippolyta was famous for a girdle given her by her father, and it was one of the twelve labours of Herculēs to possess himself of this prize.

Hippol'ytos. Son of Theseus (2 syl.), King of Athens. He was dragged to death by wild horses, and restored to life by Escula'pios.

Hippol'ytus, the cardinal to whom Ariosto dedicated his *Orlando Furioso*.

Hippom'enes (4 syl.). A Grecian prince, who ran a race with Atalanta for her hand in marriage. He had three golden apples, which he dropped one by one, and which the lady stopped to pick up. By this delay she lost the race.

20

Hippothadee. The theologian consulted by Panurge (2 syl.) on the all-important question, "*S'il doit se marier ?*" (*Rabelais : Pantagruel*, book iii.)

Hired Grief. Mutes and other undertakers' *employees* at funerals. The Undersheriff Layton, in his will, desired that he might be " buried without hired grief " (1885).

Hiren. A strumpet. From Peele's play, *The Turkish Mahomet and Hyren the Fair Greek*. (*See* 2 *Henry IV.*, ii. 4.)

Hispa'nia. Spain. So called from the Punic word *Span* (a rabbit), on account of the vast number of rabbits which the Carthaginians found in the peninsula. Others derive it from the Basque *Expana* (a border).

Historicus. The *nom de plume* in the *Times* of Sir W. Vernon Harcourt, now (1895) Chancellor of the Exchequer.

History. Our oldest historian is the Venerable Bede, who wrote in Latin an *Ecclesiastical History* of very great merit (672-735). Of secular historians, William of Poitiers, who wrote in Latin *The Gests or Deeds of William, Duke of Normandy and King of the English* (1020-1088). His contemporary was Ingulphus, who wrote a history of Croyland Abbey (1030-1109). The oldest prose work in Early English is Sir John Mandeville's account of his Eastern travels in 1356.
The Father of History. Herod'otos, the Greek historian (B.C. 484-408). So called by Cicero.
The Father of Ecclesiastical History. Eusebius of Cæsarēa (264-340).
Father of French History. André Duchesne (1584-1640).
Father of Historic Painting. Polygno'tos of Thaōs (flourished B.C. 463-435).

History of Croyland Abbey, by Ingulphus, and its continuation to 1118 by Peter of Blois, were proved to be literary impositions by Sir F. Palgrave in the *Quarterly Review*, vol. xxxiv., No. 67.

Histrion'ic is from the Etruscan word *hister* (a dancer), *histrio'nes* (ballet-dancers). Hence, *histrio* in Latin means a stage-player, and our word *histrionic*, pertaining to the drama. History is quite another word, being the Greek *historia, histor*, a judge, allied to *histamai*, to know.

Hit. *A great hit.* A piece of good luck. From the game *hit and miss*, or the game of backgammon, where " two hits equal a gammon."

Hit it Off (*To*). To describe a thing tersely and epigrammatically ; to make a sketch truthfully and quickly. The French say, " *Ce peintre vous saisit la resemblance en un clin d'œil.*"
To hit it off together. To agree together, or suit each other.

Hit the Nail on the Head (*To*). (*See* HEAD.)

Hitch. *There is some hitch.* Some impediment. A horse is said to have a hitch in his gait when he is lame. (Welsh, *hecian*, to halt or limp.)
To hitch. To get on smoothly; to fit in consistently : as, " You and I hitch on well together ; " "These two accounts do not hitch in with each other." A lame horse goes about jumping, and to jump together is to be in accord. So the two meanings apparently contradictory hitch together. Compare *prevent*, meaning to aid and to resist.

Hivites (2 syl.). The students of St. Bee's College, Cumberland. (Bee-hives.)

Hoâng. The ancient title of the Chinese kings, meaning " sovereign lord." (*See* KING.)

Hoare (37, Fleet Street, London). The golden bottle over the fanlight is said to contain the half-crown with which James Hoare started in business.

Hoarstone. A landmark. A stone marking out the boundary of an estate.

Hoax. (*See* CANARD.)

Hob of a grate. From the Anglo-Saxon verb *habban* (to hold). The chimney-corner, where at one time a settle stood on each side, was also called " the hob."

Hob and Nob together. To drink as cronies, to clink glasses, to drink *tête-à-tête*. In the old English houses there was a hob at each corner of the hearth for heating the beer, or holding what one wished to keep hot. This was from the verb *habban* (to hold). The little round table set at the elbow was called a *nob ;* hence to hob-nob was to drink snugly and cosily in the chimney-corner, with the beer hobbed, and a little nob-table set in the snuggery. (*See* HOB NOB.)

Hob'bema.
The English Hobbema. John Crome, the elder (of Norwich), whose last words were, " O Hobbema, Hobbema, how I do love thee ! "

The Scotch Hobbema. P. Nasmyth, a Scotch landscape painter (born 1831).

Hob'bididance (4 syl.). The prince of dumbness, and one of the five fiends that possessed "poor Tom." (*Shakespeare : King Lear*, iv. 1.)

Hob'binol. The shepherd (Gabriel Harvey, the poet, 1545-1630) who relates a song in praise of Eliza, queen of shepherds (Queen Elizabeth). (*Spenser : Shepherd's Calendar.*)

Hob'bism. The principles of Thomas Hobbes, author of *Leviathan* (1588-1670). He taught that religion is a mere engine of state, and that man acts wholly on a consideration of self ; even his benevolent acts spring from the pleasure he experiences in doing acts of kindness. A follower of Hobbes is called a *Hobbist.*

Hobbler or *Clopinel.* Jean de Meung, the poet, who wrote the sequel to the *Romance of the Rose* (1260-1320).
Tyrtæus, the Greek elegiac poet, was called *Hobbler* because he introduced the alternate pentameter verse, which is one foot short of the old heroic metre.

Hobby. A favourite pursuit. The *hobby* is a falcon trained to fly at pigeons and partridges. As hawks were universal pets in the days of falconry, and hawking the favourite pursuit, it is quite evident how the word hobby got its present meaning. Hobby-horse is a corruption of *Hobby-hause* (hawk-tossing), or throwing off the hawk from the wrist. Hobby is applied to a little pet riding-horse by the same natural transposition as a mews for hawks is now a place for horses. (French, *hobereau*, a hawk, a hobby.)

Hobby-horse. A child's plaything, so called from the hobby-horse of the ancient morris-dance ; a light frame of wicker-work, appropriately draped, in which someone was placed, who performed ridiculous gambols.

" The hobby-horse doth hither prance,
Maid Marrian and the Morris dance."
(1221.)

Hob'edy-hoig, sometimes written *Hob'bledehoy* and *hobidy-hoy*, between a man and a boy ; neither hay nor grass. Tusser says the third age of seven years (15 to 21) is to be kept "under Sir Hobbard de Hoy."

Hobgob'lin. Puck or Robin Goodfellow. Keightley thinks it a corruption of Rob-Goblin — *i.e.* the goblin Robin, just as Hodge is the nickname of

Roger, which seems to agree with the subjoined quotation :

"Those that Hobgoblin call you, and sweet Puck,
You do their work, and they shall have good
luck."
Shakespeare: Midsummer Night's Dream, ii. 1.

∴ Hob is certainly sometimes used for a sprite or fairy, as a *hob-lantern*—*i.e.* an *ignis fatuus* or fairy-lantern, but this may mean a "Puck-lantern" or "Robin Goodfellow-lantern."

Hob'inol. (*See* HOBBINOL.)

Hob'lers or **Hovellers.** Men who keep a light nag that they may give instant information of threatened invasion, or ugly customers at sea. (Old French, *hober,* to move up and down ; our *hobby, q.v.*) In mediæval times hoblers were like the German *uhlands.* Their duties were to reconnoitre, to carry intelligence, to harass stragglers, to act as spies, to intercept convoys, and to pursue fugitives. Spelman derives the word from *hobby.*

"Hobblers were another description of cavalry more lightly armed, and taken from the class of men rated at 15 pounds and upwards."—*Lingard : History of England,* vol. iv. chap. ii. p. 116.
"Sentinels who kept watch at beacons in the Isle of Wight, and ran to the governor when they had any intelligence to communicate, were called hoblers."—*MS. Lansd.* (1033).

Hobnail. When the London sheriff is sworn in, the tenants of a manor in Shropshire are directed to come forth and do service, whereupon the senior alderman below the chair steps forward and chops a stick, in token that the tenants of this county supplied their feudal lord with fuel.

The owners of a forge in St. Clements are then called forth to do suit and service, when an officer of the court produces six horse-shoes and sixty-one hobnails, which he used to count before the cursitor baron till that office was abolished in 1857.

Hob Nob. A corruption of *hab nab,* meaning "have or not have," hence hit or miss, at random ; and, secondarily, give or take, whence also an open defiance. A similar construction to willy nilly. (Anglo-Saxon, *habban,* to have ; *nabban,* not to have.)

"The citizens in their rage shot habbe or nabbe [hit or miss] at random."—*Holinshed : History of Ireland.*

"He writes of the weather hab nab [at random], and as the toy [fancy] takes him, chequers the year with foul and fair."—*Quack Astrologer* (1673).
"He is a devil in private brawls . . . . hob nob is his word, give 't or take 't."—*Shakespeare : Twelfth Night,* iii. 4.
"Not of Jack Straw, with his rebellious crew,
That set king, realm, and laws at nab or nab [defiance]." *Sir J. Harington : Epigram,* iv.

Hob's Pound. *To be in Hob's pound* is to be under difficulties, in great embarrassment. Hob is a clownish rustic, and *hoberd* is a fool or ne'er-do-well. To be in Hob's pound is to be in the pound of a hob or hoberd—*i.e.* paying for one's folly.

Hobson's Choice. This or none. Tobi'as Hobson was a carrier and innkeeper at Cambridge, who erected the handsome conduit there, and settled "seven lays" of pasture ground towards its maintenance. "He kept a stable of forty good cattle, always ready and fit for travelling ; but when a man came for a horse he was led into the stable, where there was great choice, but was obliged to take the horse which stood nearest to the stable-door ; so that every customer was alike well served, according to his chance, and every horse ridden with the same justice." (*Spectator,* No. 509.)

Milton wrote two quibbling epitaphs upon this eccentric character.

"Why is the greatest of free communities reduced to Hobson's choice ?"—*The Times.*

Hock. So called from Hockheim, on the Maine, where the best is supposed to be made. It used to be called hockamore (3 syl.).

"As unfit to bottle as old hockamore."—*Mortimer.*

Hock Cart. The high cart, the last cart-load of harvest.

"The harvest swains and wenches bound
For joy, to see the hock-cart crowned."
Herrick : Hesperides, p. 114.

Hock-day or **Hock Tuesday.** The day when the English surprised and slew the Danes, who had annoyed them for 255 years. This Tuesday was long held as a festival in England, and landlords received an annual tribute called *Hock-money,* for allowing their tenants and serfs to commemorate Hock-day, which was the second Tuesday after Easter-day. (See *Kenilworth,* chap. xxxix.)

∴ Hock-tide was the time of paying church dues.
"Hoke Monday was for the men, and Hock Tuesday for the women. On both days the men and women alternately, with great merryment, obstructed the public road with ropes, and pulled passengers to them, from whom they exacted money to be laid out in pious uses."—*Brand : Antiquities* (Hoke day), vol. i. p. 187.

Hock'ey. A game in which each player has a hooked stick or bandy with which to strike the ball. Hockey is simply the diminutive of *hook.* Called Shinty in Scotland.

Hocking. Stopping the highways with ropes, and demanding a gratuity from passengers before they were allowed to pass. (*See* quotation from Brand *under* HOCK-DAY.)

Hockley-i'-the-Hole. Public gardens near Clerkenwell Green, famous for bear- and bull-baiting, dog- and cock-fights, etc. The earliest record of this garden is a little subsequent to the Restoration.

Ho'cus Po'cus. The words uttered by a conjuror when he performs a trick, to cheat or take surreptitiously. The Welsh, *hocea pwca* (a goblin's trick, our *hoax*) is a probable etymology. But generally supposed to be *Hoc est corpus.*

❖ Ochus Bochus was the name of a famous magician of the North invoked by jugglers. He is mentioned in the French *Royal Dictionary.*

Ho'cussed. Hoaxed, cheated, tampered with; as, "This wine is hocussed."

> "Was ever man so hocussed?"
> *Art of Wheedling,* p. 322.

Hod'eken (3 syl.) means *Little-hat,* a German goblin or domestic fairy; so called because he always wore a little felt hat over his face. Our *hudkin.*

Hodge. A generic name for a farm-labourer or peasant. (Said to be an abbreviated form of Roger, as Hob is of Rob or Robin.)

> "Promises held out in order to gain the votes of the agricultural labourers; promises given simply to obtain the vote of 'Hodge,' who will soon find out that his vote was all that was wanted."—*Newspaper paragraph,* Dec., 1885.

Hodge-podge (2 syl.). A medley. A corruption of hotch-pot, *i.e.* various fragments mixed together in the "pot-au-feu." (*See* HOTCH-POT.)

Ho'dur. Balder's twin brother; the God of Darkness; the blind god 'who killed Balder, at the instigation of Loki, with an arrow made of mistletoe. Hödur typifies night, as Balder typifies day. (*Scandinavian mythology.*)

> "And Balder's pile of the glowing sun
> A symbol true blazed forth;
> But soon its splendour sinketh down
> When Höder rules the earth."
> *Frithiof-Saga: Balder's Bale-Fire.*

Hog, meaning a piece of money, is any silver coin—sixpence, shilling, or five-shilling. It is probably derived from the largess given on New Year's Eve called *hog-manay,* pronounced *hog-money.*

❖ In the Bermudas the early coins bore the image of a hog.

Hog seems to refer to age more than to any specific animal. Thus, boars of the second year, sheep between the time of their being weaned and shorn, colts, and bullocks a year old, are all called hogs or hoggets. A boar three years old is a "hog-steer."

❖ Some say a hogget is a sheep after its first shearing, but a "hogget-fleece" is the first shearing.

To go the whole hog. An American expression meaning unmixed democratical principles. It is used in England to signify a "thorough goer" of any kind. In Virginia the dealer asks the retail butcher if "he means to go the whole hog, or to take only certain joints, and he regulates his price accordingly." (*Men and Manners of America.*)

❖ Mahomet forbade his followers to eat *one* part of the pig, but did not particularise what part he intended. Hence, strict Mahometans abstain from pork altogether, but those less scrupulous eat any part they fancy. Cowper refers to this in the lines:

> "With sophistry their sauce they sweeten,
> Till quite from tail to snout 'tis eaten."
> *Love of the World Reproved.*

Another explanation is this: A *hog* in Ireland is slang for "a shilling," and to go the whole hog means to spend the whole shilling. (*See* HOG.)

You have brought your hogs to a fine market. You have made a pretty kettle of fish.

> "You have brought your hogs to a fine market."
> —*Howell* (1659).

Hogs-Norton. A village in Oxfordshire, now called Hook Norton. *I think you were born at Hogs-Norton.* A reproof to an ill-mannered person.

> "I think thou wast born at Hoggs-Norton, where piggs play upon the organs."—*Howell: English Proverbs,* p. 16.

Hog in Armour. A person of awkward manners dressed so fine that he cannot move easily. A corruption of "Hodge in armour."

Hogg. (*See under the word* BREWER.)

Ho'garth (*William*), called the "Juvenal of Painters" (1695-1764). *The Scottish Hogarth,* David Allan (1744-1796).

Ho'gen Mo'gen. Holland or the Netherlands; so called from *Hoogë en Mogendé* (high and mighty), the Dutch style of addressing the States-General.

> "But I have sent him for a token
> To your Low-country Hogen-Mogen."
> *Butler: Hudibras.*

Hogmanay', Hogmena', or Hagmen'a. Holy month.

New Year's Eve is called *hogmanay'-night* or *hogg-night,* and it is still the custom in parts of Scotland for persons to go from door to door on that night asking in rude rhymes for cakes or money. (*See* Hog.)

In Galloway the chief features are "taking the cream off the water," wonderful luck being attached to a draught thereof; and "the first foot," or giving something to drink to the first person who enters the house. A grand bonfire and a procession, in which all persons are masked and in bizarre costume.

King Haco, of Norway, fixed the feast of Yole on Christmas Day, the eve of which used to be called hogg-night, which in the old style is New Year's Eve.

Hogshead, a large cask = ½-pipe or butt, is a curious instance of the misuse of *h.* The word is from the Danish *Oxe-hud* (ox-hide), the larger skins in contradistinction to the smaller *goat* skins. An oxe-hud contained 240 Danish quarts.

Hoi Polloi (*The*). The poll-men in our Universities, that is, those who take their degrees without "honours." The proletariat. (Greek, meaning "the many," "the general.")

Hoist. *Hoist with his own petard.* Beaten with his own weapons, caught in his own trap. The petard was a thick iron engine, filled with gunpowder, and fastened to gates, barricades, and so on, to blow them up. The danger was lest the engineer who fired the petard should be blown up in the explosion.

" Let it work;
For 'tis the sport to have the engineer
Hoist with his own petard ; and it shall go hard
But I will delve one yard below their mines,
And blow them at the moon."
Shakespeare : Hamlet, iii. 4.

Hoity-toity.

(1) Hoity-toity spirits means high spirits, extremely elated and flighty. Selden, in his *Table Talk,* says : " In Queen Elizabeth's time gravity and state were kept up . . . but in King Charles's time there was nothing but Frenchmore [French manners] . . . tolly-polly, and *hoit-comme-toit,*" where *hoit comme toit* means flightiness.

(2) As an exclamation of reproof it means, Your imagination or spirits are running out of all bounds ; hoit-a-toit ! hity-tity ! "Hoity-toity ! What have I to do with dreams?" (*Congreve.*)

We have the verb " to hoit " = to assume ; to be elated in spirits, and perhaps hoity-toity is only one of those words with which our language abounds;

as, harum-scarum, titty-totty, namby-pamby, hugger-mugger, fiddle-faddle, and scores of others.

Hoky or **Hockey Cake.** Harvest cake. The cake given out to the harvesters when the hock cart reached home. (*See* Hock Cart.)

Holborn is not a corruption of Old Bourne, as Stowe asserts, but of Hole-burne, the *burne* or stream in the *hole* or hollow. It is spelt Holeburne in *Domesday Book,* i. 127a ; and in documents connected with the nunnery of St. Mary, Clerkenwell (during the reign of Richard II.), it is eight times spelt in the same way. (*The Times ;* J. G. Waller.)

He rode backwards up Holborn Hill. He went to be hanged. The way to Tyburn from Newgate was up Holborn Hill, and criminals in ancient times sat with their backs to the horse, when drawn to the place of execution.

Hold of a ship is between the lowest deck and the keel. In merchant vessels it *holds* the main part of the cargo. In men of war it holds the provisions, water for drinking, etc., stores, and berths. The *after* hold is *aft* the main-mast ; the *main* hold is before the same ; and the *fore* hold is about the fore hatches.

Hold. (Anglo-Saxon, *heald-an,* to hold.)

He is not fit to hold the candle to him. He is very inferior. The allusion is to link-boys who held candles in theatres and other places of night amusement.

" Others say that Mr. Handel
To Bononcini can't hold a candle." *Swift.*

To cry hold. Stop. The allusion is to the old military tournaments ; when the umpires wished to stop the contest they cried out "Hold ! "

" Lay on Macduff,
And damn'd be him that first cries, ' Hold,
enough !' " *Shakespeare : Macbeth,* v. 8.

Hold Forth (*To*). To speak in public; to harangue ; to declaim. An author holds forth certain opinions or ideas in his book, *i.e.* exhibits them or holds them out to view. A speaker does the same in an oratorical display.

Hold Hard. Keep a firm hold, seat, or footing, as there is danger else of being overthrown. A caution given when a sudden change of *vis inertiæ* is about to occur.

Hold In (*To*). To restrain. The allusion is to horses reined up tightly when running too fast.

Hold Off! Keep at a distance. In French, "*Tenez-vous à distance!*"

Hold On. Cling fast; to persist. The idea is clinging firmly to something to prevent falling or being overset.

Hold Out. Not to succumb to. "*Tenir ferme;*" "*Cette place ne saurait tenir.*"

Hold Water (*To*). To bear close inspection; to endure a trial. A vessel that will hold water is safe and sound.

Hold One Guilty (*To*). To adjudge or regard as guilty. The French *tenir*.

Hold One in Hand (*To*). To amuse in order to get some advantage. The allusion is to horses held in hand or under command of the driver.

Hold One's Own (*To*). To maintain one's own opinion, position, way, etc. Maintain means to hold with the hand. (Latin, *manus teneo*.)

Hold the Fort. Immortalised as a phrase from its use by General Sherman, who signalled it to General Corse from the top of Kenesaw in 1864.

Holdfast. *Brag is a good dog, but Holdfast is a better.* Promises are all very good, but acts are far better.

> "Holdfast is the only dog, my duck."
> *Shakespeare: Henry V.*, ii. 3.

Holdfast. A means by which something is clamped to another; a support.

Hole. *Pick a hole in his coat.* To find out some cause of blame. The allusion is to the Roman custom of dressing criminals in rags (*Livy*, ii. 61). Hence, a holey coat is a synonym for guilt.

> "Hear, Land o' cakes and brither Scots
> Frae Maidenkirk to Johnny Groat's
> If there's a hole in a' your coats
> I rede you tent it;
> A chield's amang you taking notes,
> And, faith, he'll prent it."
> *Burns: On the late Capt. Grose*, stanza 1.

Hole and Corner (business). Underhand and secret.

Holiday Speeches or *Words*. Fine or well-turned speeches or phrases; complimentary speeches. We have also "holiday manners," "holiday clothes," meaning the best we have.

> "Aye, aye, sir. I know your worship loves no holiday speeches."—*Sir W. Scott: Redgauntlet*, chap. iii.

> "With many holiday and lady terms
> He questioned me."
> *Shakespeare:* 1 *Henry IV.*, i. 3 (Hotspur's defence).

Holipher'nes (4 syl.), called English Henry (in *Jerusalem Delivered*). One of the Christian knights in the first crusade, slain by Dragu'tes (book ix.).

Holland. The country of paradoxes. The "houses are built on the sand;" the sea is higher than the shore; the keels of the ships are above the chimney-tops of the houses; and the cow's tail does not "grow downward," but is tied up to a ring in the roof of the stable. Butler calls it:

> "A land that rides at anchor and is moored,
> In which they do not live, but go aboard."
> *Description of Holland.*

(See also *Don Juan*, canto x. 63.)

Holland. A particular kind of cloth; so called because it used to be sent to Holland to be bleached. *Lawn* is cloth bleached on a lawn; and *grass-lawn* is lawn bleached on a grass-plat. Bleaching is now performed by artificial processes.

Hollow. *I beat him hollow.* A corruption of "I beat him wholly."

Holly used to be employed by the early Christians at Rome to decorate churches and dwellings at Christmas; it had been previously used in the great festival of the Saturnālia, which occurred at the same season of the year. The pagan Romans used to send to their friends holly-sprigs, during the Saturnalia, with wishes for their health and well-being.

Hollyhock is the Anglo-Saxon, *holi-hŏc*, the marsh-mallow. It is a mistake to derive it from Holy-oak.

Holman (*Lieutenant James*). The blind traveller (1787-1857).

Holopher'nes (4 syl.). *Master Tubal Holophernes.* The great sophister-doctor, who, in the course of five years and three months, taught Gargantua to say his A B C backward. (*Rabelais: Gargantua*, book i. 14.)

Holofernes, in *Love's Labour's Lost.* Shakespeare satirises in this character the literary affectations of the Lyly school. An anagram of Joh'nes Florio.

Holy Alliance. A league formed by Russia, Austria, and Prussia to regulate the affairs of Europe "by the principles of Christian charity,"—meaning that each of the contracting parties was to keep all that the league assigned them (1816).

Holy City. That city which the religious consider most especially connected with their religious faith, thus:

All'ahabad' is the Holy City of the Indian Mahometans.

Bena'res (3 syl.) of the Hindus.

Cuzco of the ancient Incas.

Fez of the Western Arabs.

Jerusalem of the Jews and Christians.

Kairwan, near Tunis. It contains the Okbar Mosque, in which is the tomb of the prophet's barber.

Kief, the Jerusalem of Russia, the cradle of Christianity in that country.

Mecca and Medina of the Mahometans.

Moscow and Kief of the Russians.

Solovetsk, in the Frozen Sea, is a holy Island much visited by pilgrims.

Holy Coat of Treves, said to be the seamless coat of our Saviour. Deposited at Treves by the Empress Hele'na, who discovered it in the fourth century.

Holy Communion (*The*). The fellowship of Christians manifested by their mutual partaking of the eucharist. The eucharist itself is, by a figure of speech, so called.

Holy Family. The infant Saviour and his attendants, as Joseph, Mary, Elizabeth, Anna, and John the Baptist. All the five figures are not always introduced in pictures of the "Holy Family."

Holy Isle. Lindisfarne, in the German Ocean, about eight miles from Berwick-upon-Tweed. It was once the see of the famous St. Cuthbert, but now the bishopric is that of Durham. The ruins of the old cathedral are still visible.

Ireland used to be called the Holy Island on account of its numerous "saints."

Guernsey was so called in the tenth century in consequence of the great number of monks residing there.

Rugen was so called by the Slavonic Varini.

Scattery, to which St. Senanus retired, and swore that no female should set foot there, is the one referred to by Thomas Moore in his *Irish Melodies*, No. ii. 2.

"Oh! haste and leave this sacred isle
. . . For on thy deck, though dark it be,
A female form I see."

Holy Land (*The*).

(1) Christians call Palestine the Holy Land, because it was the site of Christ's birth, ministry, and death.

(2) Mahometans call Mecca the Holy Land, because Mahomet was born there.

(3) The Chinese Buddhists call India the Holy Land, because it was the native land of Sakya-muni, the Buddha (*q.v.*).

(4) The Greek considered Elis as Holy Land, from the temple of Olympian Zeus

and the sacred festival held there every four years.

(5) In America each of the strange politico-religious sects calls its own settlement pretty much the same thing. (*See* HOLY CITY.)

Holy League (*The*). A combination formed by Pope Julius II. with Louis XII. of France, Maximilian of Germany, Ferdinand III. of Spain, and various Italian princes, against the republic of Venice in 1508.

There was another league so called in the reign of Henri III. of France, in 1576, under the auspices of Henri de Guise, "for the defence of the Holy Catholic Church against the encroachments of the reformers." The Pope gave it his sanction, but its true strength lay in Felipe II. of Spain.

Holy Orders, in the English Church, are those of priest and deacon. In the Roman Church the term includes the sub-diaconate. (*See* MINOR ORDERS.)

Holy Places. Places in which the chief events of our Saviour's life occurred, such as the Sepulchre, Gethsemane, the Supper-room, the Church of the Ascension, the tomb of the Virgin, and so on.

Holy Thursday. The day of our Lord's ascension.

Holy Saturday. The Saturday before Easter Sunday.

Holy Wars are to extirpate "heresy," or to extend what the state supposes to be the one true religion. The Crusades, the Thirty-Years' War, the wars against the Albigenses, etc., were so called.

Holy Water. Water blessed by a priest or bishop for holy uses.

As the devil loves holy water; i.e. not at all. This proverb arose from the employment of holy water in exorcisms in the Holy Church.

"I love him as the devil loves holy water."

Holy Week. The last seven days of Passion Week or the Great Week. It begins on Palm Sunday, and ends with Holy Saturday (*q.v.*). The fourth day is called "Spy Wednesday;" the fifth is "Maundy Thursday;" the sixth is "Good Friday;" and the last "Holy Saturday" or the "Great Sabbath."

Holy Week has been called *Hebdomada Muta* (Silent Week); *Hebdomada Passionis; Hebdomada Incfficiosa* (Vacant Week); *Hebdomada Penitentialis; Hebdomada Indulgentiæ; Hebdomada Luctuosa; Hebdomada Nigra;* and *Hebdomada Ultima.*

Holy Writ. The Bible.

Holy Maid of Kent (*The*). Elizabeth Barton, who incited the Roman Catholics to resist the progress of the Reformation, and pretended to act under direct inspiration. She was hanged at Tyburn in 1534.

Holy of Holies (*The*). The innermost apartment of the Jewish temple, in which the ark of the covenant was kept, and into which only the High Priest was allowed to enter, and that but once a year—the day of atonement.

Holy Water Sprinkler. A military club set with spikes. So called facetiously because it makes the blood to flow as water sprinkled by an aspergillum.

Holywell Street (London). Fitzstephens, in his description of London in the reign of Henry II., speaks of "the excellent springs at a small distance from the city," whose waters are most sweet, salubrious, and clear, and whose runnels murmur over the shining stones. "Among these are Holywell, Clerkenwell, and St. Clement's well."

Holystone. A soft sandstone used for scrubbing the decks of vessels.

Home (1 syl.). (Anglo-Saxon, *hām*.) Our *long home*, the grave.

Who goes home? When the House of Commons breaks up at night the door-keeper asks this question of the members. In bygone days all members going in the direction of the Speaker's residence went in a body to see him safe home. The question is still asked, but is a mere relic of antiquity.

Home, Sweet Home. Words by John Howard Payne (an American), introduced in the melodrama called *The Maid of Milan*.

Homer.
Called Melesigenĕs (*q.v.*); the Man of Chios (*see* CHIOS); the Blind Old Man; Mæon'idĕs (*q.v.*), or Mæonius, either from his father Mæon, or because he was a native of Mæonia (Lydia). He is spoken of as *Mæonius senex*, and his poems as *Mæoniæ chartæ* or *Mæonia carmĭna*.

The Casket Homer. An edition corrected by Aristotle, which Alexander the Great always carried about with him, and laid under his pillow at night with his sword. After the battle of Arbe'la, a golden casket richly studded with gems was found in the tent of Darius; and Alexander being asked to what purpose it should be assigned, replied, "There is but one thing in the world worthy of so costly a depository,"

saying which he placed therein his edition of Homer.

The British Homer. Milton (1608-74).

The Celtic Homer. Ossian, son of Fingal, King of Morven.

The Homer of dramatic poets. Shakespeare is so called by Dryden. (1564-1616.)

"Shakespeare was the Homer of our dramatic poets; Jonson was the Virgil. I admire rare Ben, but I love Shakespeare."—*Dryden.*

Homer of Ferra'ra. Ariosto is so called by Tasso (1474-1533).

Homer of the Franks. Charlemagne called Angilbert his *Homer* (died 814).

The Oriental Homer. Firdusi, the Persian poet, who wrote the *Châh Nâmeh* (or history of the Persian kings). It contains 120,000 verses, and was the work of thirty years (940-1020).

The Homer of philosophers. Plato (B.C. 429-347).

The prose Homer of human nature. Henry Fielding; so called by Byron. (1707-1768.)

The Scottish Homer. William Wilkie, author of *The Epigoniad* (1721-1772).

Homer a Cure for the Ague. It was an old superstition that if the fourth book of the *Iliad* was laid under the head of a patient suffering from quartan ague it would cure him at once. Serēnus Sammonĭcus, preceptor of Gordian and a noted physician, vouches for this remedy.

"Mæoniæ Iliados quartum suppone timenti." —*Præcepta de Medicina,* 50.

⁂ The subject of this book is as follows: While Agamemnon adjudges that Menelãos is the winner, and that the Trojans were bound to yield, according to their compact, Pandãros draws his bow, wounds Menelaos, and the battle becomes general. The reason why this book was selected is because it contains the cure of Menelãos by Machãon, "a son of Æsculapius."

Homer in a Nutshell. Cicero says that he himself saw Homer's *Iliad* enclosed in a nutshell.

Homer Sometimes Nods.
"Quando'que bonus dormi'tat Home'rus."
Horace: Ars Poetica (359)

Homer's Critics.
Dorotheus spent his whole life trying to elucidate one single word of Homer.

Zoilos (3 syl.), the grammarian, was called "Homer's Scourge" (*Homēromastix*), because he assailed the *Iliad* and *Odyssey* with merciless severity.

As some deny that Shakespeare is the author of the plays which are generally ascribed to him, so Wolf, a German critic (1759-1824), in his *Prolegomena ad Homērum*, denies that Homer was the author of the *Iliad* and *Odyssey*.

Homer'ic Verse. Hexameter verse; so called because Homer adopted it in his two great epics. (*See* HEXAMETER VERSE.)

Homœop'athy (5 syl.). The plan of curing a disease by very minute doses of a medicine which would in healthy persons produce the very same disease. The principle of vaccination is a sort of homœopathy, only it is producing in a healthy person a mitigated form of the disease guarded against. You impart a mild form of small-pox to prevent the patient from taking the virulent disease. (Greek, *homoios pathos*, like disease.) (*See* HAHNEMANN.)

"Tut, man! one fire burns out another's burn-
    ing!
One pain is lessened by another's anguish . . . .
Take thou some new infection to the eye,
And the rank poison of the old will die."
    Shakespeare: Romeo and Juliet, i. 2.

Hon'est (*h* silent). *Honest Jack Bannister*. An actor in London for thirty-six years. (1760-1836.)

"After his retirement he was once accosted by Sir George Rose, when Honest Jack, being on the other side of the street, cried out, 'Stop a moment, Sir George, and I will come over to you.' 'No, no,' replied his friend, 'I never yet made you *cross*, and will not begin now."—*Grinsted: Relics of Genius.*

Honest George. General Monk (1608-1670).

Honest Lawyer (*An*). The oldest allusion to this strange expression is the epigram on St. Ives (1251-1303), of whom Dom Lobineau says: "*Il distribuait avec une sainte profusion aux pauvres les revenus de son bénéfice et ceux de son patrimoine, qui étaient de £60 de rente, alors une somme très notable, particulièrement en Basse Bretagne.*" (*Lives of the Saints of Great Britain.*)

" Sanctus Yvo erat Brito,
  Advocatus, et non latro,
  Res miranda populo."

St. Ives was of the land of beef,
An advocate, and not a thief ;
A stretch on popular belief.   *E. C. B.*

The phrase was facetiously applied by some wag to Sir John Strange, Master of the Rolls, who died, at the age of fifty-eight, in 1754.

"Here lies an honest lawyer, that is Strange."

* Of course this line forms no part of the inscription in Leyton churchyard, Essex, where Sir John was buried.

Honey Madness. There is a rhododendron about Trebizond, the flowers of which the bees are fond of, but if anyone eats the honey he becomes mad. (*Tourneford.*)

Honey Soap contains no portion of honey. Some is made from the finest yellow soap; and some is a mixture of palm-oil soap, olive-soap, and curd-soap. It is scented with oil of verbena, rose-geranium, ginger-grass, bergamot, etc.

Honey better than Vinegar. " *On prend plus de mouches avec du miel, qu'avec du vinaigre.*" "*Plus fait douceur que violence.*" "*Il faut avoir mauvaise bête par douceur.*"

It is better to be preserved in vinegar than to rot in honey. It is better to suffer affliction if thereby the heart is brought to God, than to lose body and soul by worldly indulgences.

Honeycomb. The hexagonal shape of the bees' cells is generally ascribed to the instinctive skill of the bee, but is simply the ordinary result of mechanical laws. Solitary bees always make *circular* cells ; and without doubt those of hive bees are made cylindrical, but acquire their hexagonal form by mechanical pressure. Dr. Wollaston says all cylinders made of soft pliable materials become hexagonal under such circumstances. The cells of trees are circular towards the extremity, but hexagonal in the centre of the substance; and the cellular membranes of all vegetables are hexagonal also. (*See* ANT.)

Will Honeycomb. A fine gentleman. One of the members of the imaginary club from which the *Spectator* issued.

Honeydew. A sweet substance found on lime-trees and some other plants. Bees and ants are fond of it. It is a curious misnomer, as it is the excretion of the aphis or vine-fretter. The way it is excreted is this: the ant beats with its antennæ the abdomen of the aphis, which lifts up the part beaten, and excretes a limpid drop of sweet juice called honeydew.

Honeymoon. The month after marriage, or so much of it as is spent away from home ; so called from the practice of the ancient Teutons of drinking honey-wine (*hydromel*) for thirty days after marriage. Attila, the Hun, indulged so freely in hydromel at his wedding-feast that he died.

" It was the custom of the higher order of the Teutons . . . to drink mead or metheglin (a beverage made from honey) for thirty days after every wedding. From this comes the expression 'to spend the honeymoon."—*W. Pulleyn: Etymological Compendium,* § 9, p. 142.

20*

Honeywood. A yea-nay type, illustrative of what Dr. Young says: "What is mere good nature but a fool?" (*Goldsmith : The Good-natured Man.*)

Hong Merchants. Those merchants who were alone permitted by the government of China to trade with China, till the restriction was abolished in 1842. The Chinese applied the word hong to the foreign factories situated at Canton.

Hon'i. *Honi soit qui mal y pense* (Evil be [to him] who thinks evil of this). The tradition is that Edward III. gave a grand court ball, and one of the ladies present was the beautiful Countess of Salisbury, whose garter of blue ribbon accidentally fell off. The king saw a significant smile among the guests, and gallantly came to the rescue. "*Honi soit qui mal y pense*" (Shame to him who thinks shame of this accident), cried the monarch. Then, binding the ribbon round his own knee, he added, "I will bring it about that the proudest noble in the realm shall think it an honour to wear this band." The incident determined him to abandon his plan of forming an order of the *Round Table*, and he formed instead the order of the "Garter." (*Tighe and Davis : Annals of Windsor.*)

Honour (*h* silent). A superior seigniory, on which other lordships or manors depend by the performance of customary services.

An affair of honour. A dispute to be settled by a duel. Duels were generally provoked by offences against the arbitrary rules of etiquette, courtesy, or feeling, called the "laws of honour;" and, as these offences were not recognisable in the law courts, they were settled by private combat.

Debts of honour. Debts contracted by betting, gambling, or verbal promise. As these debts cannot be enforced by law, but depend solely on good faith, they are called debts of honour.

Laws of honour. Certain arbitrary rules which the fashionable world tacitly admits; they wholly regard deportment, and have nothing to do with moral offences. Breaches of this code are punished by duels, expulsion from society, or suspension called "sending to Coventry" (*q.v.*).

Point of honour. An obligation which is binding because its violation would offend some conscientious scruple or notion of self-respect.

Word of honour. A gage which cannot be violated without placing the breaker of it beyond the pale of respectability and good society.

Honour and Glory Griffiths. Capt. Griffiths (in the reign of William IV.) was so called, because all his despatches were addressed "To their Honours and Glories at the Admiralty."

Honour paid to Learning. Dionysius, King of Syracuse, wishing to see Plato, sent the finest galley in his kingdom royally equipped, and stored with every conceivable luxury to fetch him; and, on landing, the philosopher found the royal state carriage waiting to convey him to the palace.

Ben Jonson, in 1619, made a journey from London to Scotland expressly to see William Drummond, the Scotch poet.

Honours (*h* silent). *Crushed by his honours.* The allusion is to the Roman damsel who agreed to open the gates of Rome to King Ta'tius, provided his soldiers would give her the ornaments which they wore on their arms. As they entered they threw their shields on her and crushed her, saying as they did so, "These are the ornaments worn by Sabines on their arms." Roman story says the maid was named Tarpe'ia, and that she was the daughter of Tarpeius, the governor of the citadel.

Draco, the Athenian legislator, was crushed to death in the theatre of Ægi'na, by the number of caps and cloaks showered on him by the audience, as a mark of their high appreciation of his merits.

Elagab'alus, the Roman Emperor, invited the leading men of Rome to a banquet, and, under the pretence of showing them honour, rained roses upon them. But the shower continued till they were all buried and smothered by the flowers.

Two or four by honours. A term in whist. If two "partners" hold three court cards, they score two points; if they hold four court cards, they score four points. These are *honour* points, or points not won by the merit of play, but by courtesy and laws of honour. The phrases mean, "I score or claim two points by right of honours," and "I score or claim four points by right of four court or honour cards."

Honours of War. The privilege allowed to an honoured enemy, on capitulation, of being permitted to retain their offensive arms. This is the highest honour a victor can pay a vanquished foe. Sometimes the soldiers so honoured are required to pile arms ; in other cases they are allowed to march with all their arms, drums beating, and colours flying.

Hood. *'Tis not the hood that makes the monk (Cucul'lus non facit mon'achum).* We must not be deceived by appearances, or take for granted that things and persons are what they seem to be.

"They should be good men ; their affairs are
righteous ;
But all hoods make not monks."
Shakespeare : Henry VIII., iii. 1.

Hood (*Robin*). Introduced by Sir Walter Scott in *Ivanhoe.* (*See* ROBIN.)

Hoods (Anglo-Saxon *hŏd*).
BLACK silk *without* lining :—M.A. Cambridge, non Regius (abolished 1858) ; B.D. Cambridge, Oxford, Dublin.
Black stuff, with broad white *fur* trimming :—B.A. or LL.B. Cambridge.
Black corded silk, with narrow white fur trimming :—B.A. Oxford.
Black silk hood, *with lining* :—With white silk lining, M.A. Cambridge ; with dark red silk lining, M.A. Oxford ; with dark blue silk lining, Dublin ; with russet-brown lining, M.A. London.
BLUE silk hood, with white fur trimming, B.C.L. Oxford.
BROWN (silk or stuff) hood, edged with russet-brown, B.A. London.
SCARLET cloth hood :—Lined with crimson silk, D.C.L. Oxford ; lined with pink silk, D.C.L. Dublin ; lined with pink silk, D.D. Cambridge ; lined with black silk, D.D. Oxford ; lined with light cherry-coloured silk, LL.D. Cambridge.
Scarlet *cashmere* hood :—Lined with silk, D.D. Dublin ;—Lined with white silk, D.C.L. Durham.
VIOLET hoods are St. Andrew's.
✢ The longer the hood the higher the degree ; thus, a bachelor's hood only reaches to the thighs, but a doctor's hood reaches to the heels.

Hoodlum (American slang). A Californian rough.

Hoodman Blind. Now called "Blindman's Buff."

" What devil was't
That thus hath cozened you at hoodman blind ?"
Shakespeare : Hamlet, iii. 4.

Hook, Hooks. *He is off the hooks.* Done for, laid on the shelf, superseded, dead. The bent pieces of iron on which the hinges of a gate rest and turn are called *hooks* ; if a gate is off the hooks it is in a bad way, and cannot readily be opened and shut.

On one's own hook. On one's own responsibility or account. An angler's phrase.

To fish with a golden hook. To give bribes. "*Pêcher avec un hameçon d'or.*" Risk a sprat to catch a mackerel. To buy fish, and pretend to have caught it.

With a hook at the end. My assent is given with a hook at the end means not intended to be kept. In some parts of Germany, even to the present day, when a witness swears falsely, he *crooks* one finger into a sort of hook, and this is supposed sufficient to avert the sin of perjury. It is a crooked oath, or an oath "with a hook at the end." (*See* OVER THE LEFT, *under* LEFT.)

Hook It ! *Take your hook* ; *Sling your hook.* Be off ! Be off about your business !

Hook or Crook (*By*). Either rightfully or wrongfully ; in one way or another. Formerly the poor of a manor were allowed to go into the forests with a hook and crook to get wood. What they could not reach they might pull down with their crook. The French equivalent is "*A droit ou à tort,*" or "*De bric et de broc.*" Either with the thief's hook or the bishop's crook. Mrs. S. C. Hall, in her *Ireland* (vol. ii. p. 149 *n.*), states, as the origin of this phrase, that when the ships of Strongbow were entering Waterford harbour he noticed a tower on one side and a church on the other. Inquiring their names, he was told it was the "Tower of Hook" and the "Church of Crook." Then said he, "We must take the town by Hook and by Crook." There is no such person as St. Crook mentioned by the Bollandists.

" Dynmure Wood was ever open and common to the . . . inhabitants of Bodmin . . . to bear away upon their backs a burden of lop, crop, hook, crook, and bag wood."—*Bodmin Register* (1525).

Hookey Walker. (*See* WALKER.)

Hooligan. A violent young rough. The term originated in the last years of the nineteenth century from the name of one of this class. From it is derived the verb *to hooligan* = to indulge in violent horseplay (often ending in the robbery of the victim), and the substantive, *hooliganism*, to express such conduct.

Hooped Pots. Drinking pots at one time were made with hoops, that when two or more drank from the same tankard no one of them should take more than his share. Jack Cade promises his followers that "seven halfpenny loaves shall be sold for a penny ;

the three-hooped pot shall have ten hoops; and I will make it felony to drink small beer." (*Shakespeare: 2 Henry VI.*, iv. 2,)

Hoopoe (*Upupa Epops*). A small crested bird revered by all the ancient Egyptians, and placed on the sceptre of Horus, to symbolise joy and filial affection. (Latin *upupa*, the hoopoe.)

Hop. The plant, called by Tusser "Robin Hop." (Danish *hop*.) To hop on one leg is the Anglo-Saxon *hopetan* or *hoppian*.

"Get into thy hopyard, for now it is time
To teach Robin Hop on his pole how to climb."
Five Hundred Points of Good Husbandry, xli. 17.

Thick as hops. Very numerous; very compact.

"And thousand other things as thicke as hops."
Taylor the Water Poet (1630).

Hop-o'-my-Thumb. A nix, the same as the German *daumling*, the French *le petit pouce*, and the Scotch *Tom-a-lin* (or Tamlane). Tom Thumb in the well-known nursery tale is quite another character. He was the son of peasants, knighted by King Arthur, and killed by a spider.

❖ Several dwarfs have assumed the name of Tom Thumb. (*See* DWARFS.)

"You Stump-o'-the-Gutter, you Hop-o'-my-Thumb,
Your husband must from Lilliput come."
Kane O'Hara: Midas.

"Plaine friend, Hop-o'-my-Thumb, know you who we are?"—*Taming of the Shrew* (1594).

To hop the twig. To run away from one's creditors, as a bird eludes a fowler, "hopping from spray to spray."

❖ Also to die. The same idea as that above. There are numerous phrases to express the cessation of life; for example, "To kick the bucket" (*q.v.*); "To lay down one's knife and fork;" "Pegging out" (from the game of cribbage); "To be snuffed out" (like a candle); "He has given in;" "To throw up the sponge" (*q.v.*); "To fall asleep;" "To enter Charon's boat" (*See* CHARON); "To join the majority;" "To cave in;" a common Scripture phrase is "To give up the ghost."

Hope. Before Alexander set out for Asia he divided his kingdom among his friends. "My lord," said Perdiccas, "what have you left for yourself?" "Hope," replied Alexander. Whereupon Perdiccas rejoined, "If hope is enough for Alexander, it is enough for Perdiccas," and declined to accept any bounty from the king.

The Bard of Hope. Thomas Campbell (1777-1844), the author of *The*

Pleasures of Hope. The entire profits on this poem were £900.

The Cape of Good Hope. (*See* STORMS.)

Hopeful. The companion of Christian after the death of Faithful. (*Bunyan: Pilgrim's Progress.*)

Hope-on-High Bomby. A puritanical character drawn by Beaumont and Fletcher.

"'Well,' said Wildrake, 'I think I can make a "Hope-on-High Bomby" as well as thou canst.'"
—*Sir Walter Scott: Woodstock*, c. vii.

Hopkins (*Matthew*), of Manningtree, Essex, the witch-finder of the associated counties of Essex, Suffolk, Norfolk, and Huntingdonshire. In one year he hanged sixty reputed witches in Essex alone. Dr. Z. Grey says that between three and four thousand persons suffered death for witchcraft between 1643 and 1661.

Nicholas Hopkins. A Carthusian friar, confessor of the Duke of Buckingham, who prophesied "that neither the king (Henry VIII.) nor his heirs should prosper, but that the Duke of Buckingham should govern England.

"1 *Gent.*   That devil-monk
Hopkins that made this mischief.
2 *Gent.*   That was he
That fed him with his prophecies."
Shakespeare: Henry VIII., ii. 1.

Hopkins'ians. Those who adopt the theological opinions of Dr. Samuel Hopkins, of Connecticut. These sectarians hold most of the Calvinistic doctrines, but entirely reject the doctrines of imputed sin and imputed righteousness. The speciality of the system is that true holiness consists in disinterested benevolence, and that all sin is *selfishness.*

Hopping Giles. A lame person; so called from St. Giles, the tutelar saint of cripples, who was himself lame.

Hopton. *When in doubt, kill Hopton.* Sir Ralph Hopton was a Royalist general. During the Civil Wars we read that Hopton was killed over and over again; thus, in *Diurnal Occurrences*, Dec. 5th, 1642, we read, "It was likewise this day reported that Sir Ralph Hopton is either dead or dangerously sicke." Five months later we read in *Special Passages*, May 6th, 1643, of Hopton's death after a fight on Roborough Down, in Devonshire. And again, May 15th, 1643, we read of his death in *A True Relation of the Proceedings of the Cornish Forces.*

Hor'ace. The Roman lyric poet.

Horaces of England. George, Duke of Buckingham, preposterously declared Cowley to be the Pindar, Horace, and

Virgil of England (1618-1667). Ben Jonson is invariably called Horace by Dekker.

Horaces of France. Jean Macrinus or Salmon (1490-1557) ; Pierre Jean de Beranger, the *French Burns* (1780-1857).

Horaces of Spain. The brothers Argen'sola, whose Christian names were Lupercio and Bartolme.

Horatian Metre (*An*). Book i. Ode iv. In alternate lines, one of seventeen syllables and the other of eleven, thus :

‒◡◡ | ‒◡◡ | ‒‒ | ‒◡◡ | ‒◡◡ | ‒◡ | ‒◡
◡‒ | ◡‒ | ‒ | ‒◡◡ | ‒◡ | ‒◡ | ‒◡

Below is a translation of the first four lines in this Horatian metre (rhyming) :

Now that the winter is past, blithe spring to
  the balmy fields inviteth,
And lo! from the dry sands men their keels
  are hauling ;
Cattle no longer their stalls affect, nor the hind
  his hearth delighteth,
Nor deadly Frost spreads over meads her
  falling.   E. C. B.

⁂ *See* ALCAIC, ASCLEPIADIC, CHORI-AMBIC, SAPPHIC, etc. (*See also* HEXA-METERS, and HEXAMETERS AND PENTA-METERS)

Hora′tio. Hamlet's intimate friend. (*Shakespeare : Hamlet.*)

Horn. Logistilla gave Astolpho at parting a horn that had the virtue to appal and put to flight the boldest knight or most savage beast. (*Ariosto : Orlando Furioso,* book viii.)

Astolpho's horn. (*See above.*)

Cape Horn. So named by Schouten, a Dutch mariner, who first doubled it. He was a native of Hoorn, in north Holland, and named the cape after his native place.

Drinking horn. Drinking cups used to be made of the rhinoceros's horn, from an Oriental belief that "it sweats at the approach of poison." (*Calmet : Biblical Dictionary.*)

King Horn. The hero of a French metrical romance, and the original of our *Horne Childe,* generally called *The Geste of Kyng Horn.* The nominal author of the French romance is Mestre Thomas. Dr. Percy ascribes the English romance of *King Horne* to the twelfth century, but this is probably a century too early. (See *Ritson's Ancient Romances.*)

Horn, Horns.

PHRASES.

My horn hath He exalted (1 Sam. ii. 10 ; Ps. lxxxix. 24, etc.). Mr. Buckingham says of a Tyrian lady, "She wore on her head a hollow silver horn, rearing itself upwards obliquely from the forehead. It was some four inches in diameter at the root, and pointed at its extremity. This peculiarity reminded me forcibly of the expression of the Psalmist, 'Lift not up your horn on high : speak not with a stiff neck. All the horns of the wicked also will I cut off ; but the horns of the righteous shall be exalted' (Ps. lxxv. 5, 10)." Bruce found in Abyssinia the silver horns of warriors and distinguished men. In the reign of Henry V. the "horned head-gear" was introduced into England, and from the effigy of Beatrice, Countess of Arundel, at Arundel church, who is represented with two horns outspread to a great extent, we may infer that the length of the head-horn, like the length of the shoe-point in the reign of Henry VI., etc., marked the degree of rank. "To cut off " such horns would be to degrade; and to exalt or extend such horns would be to add honour and dignity to the wearer.

To draw in one's horns. To retract, or mitigate, a pronounced opinion ; to restrain pride. In French, "*Rentrer les cornes.*" The allusion is to the snail.

To put to the horn. To denounce as a rebel, or pronounce a person an outlaw, for not answering to a summons. In Scotland the messenger-at-arms goes to the Cross of Edinburgh and gives three blasts with a horn before he heralds the judgment of outlawry.

"A king's messenger must give three blasts with his horn, by which the person is understood to be proclaimed rebel to the king for contempt of his authority."—*Erskine : Institutes,* book ii. 5.

To wear the horns. To be a cuckold. In the rutting season, the stags associate with the fawns : one stag selects several females, who constitute his harem, till another stag comes who contests the prize with him. If beaten in the combat, he yields up his harem to the victor, and is without associates till he finds a stag feebler than himself, who is made to submit to similar terms. As stags are horned, and made cuckolds of by their fellows, the application is palpable. (*See* CORNETTE.)

Horn-book. The alphabet-book, which was a thin board of oak about nine inches long and five or six wide, on which was printed the alphabet, the nine digits, and sometimes the Lord's Prayer. It had a handle, and was covered in front with a sheet of thin horn to prevent its being soiled ; the back-board was ornamented with a rude sketch of St. George and the Dragon. The board and its horn cover were held together by a narrow frame or border of brass. (*See* CRISSCROSS ROW.)

" Thee will I sing, in comely wainscoat bound,
And golden verge inclosing thee around ;
The faithful horn before, from age to age
Preserving thy invulnerable page ;
Behind, thy patron saint in armour shines,
With sword and lance to guard the sacred
    lines . . .
Th' instructive handle's at the bottom fixed,
Lest wrangling critics should pervert the text."
    Tickell : The Horn Book.
" Their books of stature small they took in hand
Which with pellucid horn secured are,
To save from finger wet the letters fair."
    Shenstone : Schoolmistress.

Horn-gate. One of the two gates of "Dreams;" the other is of ivory. Visions which issue from the former come true. This whim depends upon two Greek puns; the Greek for horn is *keras*, and the verb *krano* or *karanoo* means "to bring to an issue," "to fulfil; so again *elephas* is ivory, and the verb *elephairo* means "to cheat," "to deceive." The verb *kraino*, however, is derived from *kra*, "the head," and means "to bring to a head ;" and the verb *elephairo* is akin to *elăchus*, "small."

Anchi'ses dismisses Æne'as through the ivory gate, on quitting the infernal regions, to indicate the unreality of his vision.

"Sunt geminæ somni portæ, quarum altera
    fertur
Cornea, qua veris facilis datur exîtus umbris ;
Altera candenti perfecta nitens elephanto ;
Sed falsa ad cœlum mittunt insomnia Manês."
    Virgil : Æneid, vi. 894, etc.

Horn of Fidelity. Morgan la Faye sent a horn to King Arthur, which had the following " virtue " :—No lady could drink out of it who was not " to her husband true ; " all others who attempted to drink were sure to spill what it contained. This horn was carried to King Marke, and " his queene with a hundred ladies more " tried the experiment, but only four managed to " drinke cleane." Ariosto's *enchanted cup* possessed a similar spell. (*See* CHASTITY.)

Horn of Plenty [*Cornu-co'pia*]. Emblem of plenty.

Ce'rēs is drawn with a ram's horn in her left arm, filled with fruits and flowers. Sometimes they are being poured on the earth from " the full horn," and sometimes they are held in it as in a basket. Diodo'rus (iii. 68) says the horn is one from the head of the goat by which Jupiter was suckled. He explains the fable thus : " In Libya," he says, " there is a strip of land shaped like a horn,

bestowed by King Ammon on his bride Amalthæa, who nursed Jupiter with goat's milk.

"When Amalthe'a's horn
O'er hill and dale the rose-crowned Flora pours,
And scatters corn and wine, and fruits and
    flowers."
    Camoens : Lusiad, book ii.

Horn of Power. When Tam'ugin assumed the title of Ghengis Khan, he commanded that a white horn should be thenceforward the standard of his troops. So the great Mogul " lifted up his horn on high," and was exalted to great power.

Horn of the Son of Oil (*The*) (Isa. v. 1). The son of oil means Syria, famous for its olives and its olive oil, and the *horn* of Syria means the strip of land called Syria, which has the sea bounding it on the west and the desert on the east.

Horn with Horn or **Horn under Horn.** The promiscuous feeding of bulls and cows, or, in fact, all horned beasts that are allowed to run together on the same common.

Horns of a Dilemma. A difficulty of such a nature that whatever way you attack it you encounter an equal amount of disagreeables. Macbeth, after the murder of Duncan, was in a strait between two evils. If he allowed Banquo to live, he had reason to believe that Banquo would supplant him ; if, on the other hand, he resolved to keep the crown for which " he had 'filed his hands," he must " step further in blood," and cut Banquo off.

Lemma is something that has been proved, and being so is assumed as an axiom. It is from the Greek word *lam'bano* (I assume or take for granted). *Di-lemma* is a double lemma, or two-edged sword which strikes either way. The *horns* of a dilemma is a figure of speech taken from a bull, which tosses with either of his horns.

" Teach me to plead," said a young rhetorician to a sophist, " and I will pay you when I gain a cause." The master sued for payment at once, and the scholar pleaded, " If I *gain* my cause you must pay me, and if I lose it I am not bound to pay you by the terms of our contract." The master pleaded, " If you *gain* you must pay me by the terms of the agreement, and if you lose the court will compel you to pay me."

Horns of Moses' Face. This is a mere blunder. The Hebrew *karan* means " to shoot out beams of light," but has by mistake been translated in some versions " to wear horns." Thus Moses is conventionally represented with horns. " Moses wist not that the skin of his face shone" (Exod. xxxiv. 29) ; *compare* 2 Cor. iii. 7-13 : " The children of Israel could not stedfastly behold the face of Moses for the glory of his countenance."

Horns of the Altar (*To the*). *Usque ad aras amicus.* Your friend even to the horns of the altar—*i.e.* through thick and thin. In swearing, the ancient Romans held the horns of the altar, and one who did so in testimony of friendship could not break his oath without calling on himself the vengeance of the angry gods.

Horne. *I'll chance it, as old Horne did his neck.* The reference is to Horne, a clergyman of Notts, who committed murder, but contrived to escape to the Continent. After several years of absence, he returned to England, and when told of the risk he ran, he replied, " I'll chance it." He did chance it ; but being apprehended, he was tried, condemned, and executed. (*The Newgate Calendar.*)

Horner. One who blows the hunting-horn ; a huntsman or master of the hounds. Little Jack Horner was master of the Abbot of Glastonbury's hounds.

Hornets (Josh. xxiv. 12). " And I sent the hornet before you, which drave them out from before you, even the two kings of the Amorites." The Egyptian standard was a hornet, and in this passage, " I sent the hornet before you," the word *hornet* must be taken to mean the Egyptian army.

Hornet's Nest. *To poke your head into a hornet's nest. To bring a hornet's nest about your ears.* To get into trouble by meddling and making. The bear is very fond of honey, and often gets stung by poking its snout by mistake into a hornet's nest in search of its favourite dainty.

Hor'nie (2 syl.). *Auld Hornie.* The devil, so called in Scotland. The allusion is to the horns with which Satan is generally represented. (*See* FAIRY.)

Horn'pipe (2 syl.). The dance is so called because it used to be danced in the west of England to the pib-corn or horn-pipe, an instrument consisting of a pipe each end of which was made of horn.

Horology. The art of measuring time; or constructing instruments to indicate time, *i.e.* clocks and watches.

Hor'oscope (3 syl.). The scheme of the twelve houses by which astrologers tell your fortune. The word means the "hour-scrutinised," because it is the hour of birth only which is examined in these star-maps. (*Hora-skopeo*, Greek.)

Horrors (*The*). Delirium tremens.

Hors de Combat (French). *Out of battle.* Incapable of taking any further part in the fight.

¶ **Horse.** Notabilia.

The fifteen points of a good horse :

" A good horse sholde have three propyrtees of a man, three of a woman, three of a foxe, three of a haare, and three of an asse.

" *Of a man.* Bolde, prowde, and hardye.

" *Of a woman.* Fayre-breasted, faire of heere, and easy to move.

" *Of a foxe.* A fair taylle, short eers, with a good trotte.

" *Of a haare.* A grate eye, a dry head, and well rennynge.

" *Of an asse.* A bygge chynn, a flat legge, and a good hoof."—*Wynkyn de Worde* (1496).

Horse. *Creator of the horse.* According to classical mythology, Poseidon [Neptune] created the horse. When the goddess of Wisdom disputed with the Sea-god which of them should give name to Athens, the gods decided that it should be called by the name of that deity which bestowed on man the most useful boon. Athēnē (the goddess of Wisdom) created the olive tree, but Poseidon or Neptune created the horse. The vote was given in favour of the olive-tree, and the city called Athens.

⁂ It was a remarkable judgment, but it must be remembered that an olive branch was the symbol of *peace*, and was also the highest prize of the victor in the Olympic games. The horse, on the other hand, was the symbol of *war*, and peace is certainly to be preferred to war.

Horse (four-in-hand). The first person that drove a four-in-hand was Erichthon'ius, according to Virgil :

" Primus Erichthonius currus et quatuor ausus Jungere equos."   *Georg.* iii. 113.

(Erichthon was the first who dared command A chariot yoked with horses four in hand.)

A horse wins a kingdom. On the death of Smerdis, the several competitors for the throne of Persia agreed that he should be king whose horse neighed first when they met on the day following. The groom of Darius showed his horse a mare on the place appointed, and immediately it arrived at the spot on the following day the horse began to neigh, and won the crown for its master.

¶ *Horse* (in the Catacombs). Emblem of the swiftness of life. Sometimes a palm-wreath is placed above its head to denote that " the race is not to the swift."

Horse (in Christian art). Emblem of courage and generosity. The attribute of St. Martin, St. Maurice, St. George, and St. Victor, all of whom are represented on horseback. St. Léon is represented on horseback, in pontifical robes, blessing the people.

Brazen horse. (*See* CAMBUSCAN; *see also* BARBED STEED, DOBBIN.)

§ *Flesh-eating horses.* The horses of Diomed, Tyrant of Thrace (not Diomede, son of Tydeus); he fed his horses on the strangers who visited his kingdom. Hercules vanquished the tyrant, and gave the carcase to the horses to eat.

> Like to the Thracian tyrant who, they say,
> Unto his horses gave his guests for meat,
> Till he himself was made their greedy prey,
> And torn to pieces by Alcidēs great."
>   *Spenser: Faërie Queene,* book v., canto 8.

Wooden horse. (*See* WOODEN.)

¶ **Horse,** in the British Army:

Elliott's Light Horse. The 15th Hussars of the British Army; so called from Colonel Elliott. They are now called the "King's Hussars."

Paget's Irregular Horse. The 4th Hussars; so called from their loose drill, after their return from India in 1839. Now called "The Queen's Hussars."

The Black Horse. The 7th Dragoon Guards, or Princess Royal's Dragoon Guards; called "black" from its facings.

The Blue Horse. The 4th Dragoon Guards; called "blue" from their facings.

The Green Horse or "The Green Dragoon Guards." The 5th Dragoon Guards; called "green" from their facings. "The Princess Charlotte of Wales's Dragoon Guards."

The Royal Horse Guards (called, in 1690, *Oxford Blues* from their blue facings) are the three heavy cavalry regiments of the Household Brigade, first raised in 1661.

The White Horse. The old 8th Foot; now called "The King's" (Liverpool Regiment); called the "White Horse" from one of the badges—a white horse within the garter.

Horse. The public-house sign.

(1) *The White Horse.* The standard of the Saxons, and therefore impressed on hop pockets and bags as the ensign of Kent. On Uffington Hill, Berks, there is formed in the chalk an enormous white horse, supposed to have been cut there after the battle in which Ethelred and Alfred defeated the Danes (871). This rude ensign is about 374 feet long, and 1,000 feet above the sea-level. It may be seen twelve miles off.

(2) *The galloping white horse* is the device of the house of Hanover.

(3) *The rampant white horse.* The device of the house of Savoy, descended from the Saxons.

HORSES FAMOUS IN HISTORY AND FABLE:

Abakur (Celtic). One of the horses of Sunna. The word means the "hot one." (*Scandinavian mythology.*)

Abas'ter (Greek). One of the horses of Pluto. The word means "away from the stars" or "deprived of the light of day."

Ab'atos (Greek). One of the horses of Pluto. The word means "inaccessible," and refers to the infernal realm.

Abraxas (Greek). One of the horses of Auro'ra. The letters of this word in Greek make up 365, the number of days in the year.

Actæ'on (Greek, "effulgence"). One of the horses of the Sun.

Æthon (Greek, "fiery red"). One of the horses of the Sun.

A'eton. One of the horses of Pluto. Greek, "swift as an eagle."

Agnes. (See below, *Black Agnes.*)

Alborak. (See *Borak.*)

Alfa'na. Gradasso's horse. The word means "a mare." (*Orlando Furioso.*)

Alige'ro Clavile'no. The "wooden-pin wing-horse" which Don Quixote and his squire mounted to achieve the deliverance of Dolori'da and her companions.

Alsvi'dur. One of the horses of Sunna. The word means "all scorching." (*Scandinavian mythology.*)

Amethe'a (Greek). One of the horses of the Sun. The word means "no loiterer."

Aq'uiline (3 syl.). Raymond's steed, bred on the banks of the Tagus. The word means "like an eagle." (*Tasso: Jerusalem Delivered.*)

Ari'on (Greek). Hercules' horse, given to Adras'tos. The horse of Neptune, brought out of the earth by striking it with his trident; its right feet were those of a human creature, it spoke with a human voice, and ran with incredible swiftness. The word means "martial," *i.e.* "war-horse."

Ar'undel. The horse of Bevis of Southampton. The word means "swift as a swallow." (French, *hirondelle*, "a swallow.")

Arva'kur. One of the horses of Sunna. The word means "splendid." (*Scandinavian mythology.*)

Aslo. One of the horses of Sunna. (*Scandinavian mythology.*)

Babiéca (Spanish, "a simpleton"). The Cid's horse. He survived his master two years and a half, during which time no one was allowed to mount him; and when he died he was buried before the gate of the monastery at Valencia, and two elms were planted to mark the site. The horse was so called because, when Rodrigo in his youth was given the choice of a horse, he passed by the most esteemed ones and selected a rough colt; whereupon his godfather called the lad *babiéca* (a dolt), and Rodrigo transferred the appellation to his horse.

Bajar'do. Rinaldo's horse, of a bright bay colour, once the property of Am'adis of Gaul. It was found by Malagi'gi, the wizard, in a cave guarded by a dragon, which the wizard slew. According to tradition, it is still alive, but flees at the approach of man, so that no one can ever hope to catch him. The word means of a "bay colour." (*Orlando Furioso.*)

Bal'ios (Greek, "swift"). One of the horses given by Neptune to Peleus. It afterwards belonged to Achilles. Like Xanthos, its sire was the West-wind, and its dam Swift-foot the harpy.

Bayard. The horse of the four sons of Aymon, which grew larger or smaller as one or more of the four sons mounted it. According to tradition, one of the foot-prints may still be seen in the forest of Soignes, and another on a rock near Dinant. The word means "bright bay colour."

Also the horse of FitzJames.

"Stand, Bayard, stand ! The steed obeyed
With arching neck, and bended head,
And glaring eye, and quivering ear,
As if he loved his lord to hear."
Sir W. Scott: Lady of the Lake, xviii.

Barbary. (See *Roan Barbary.*)

Be'vis. The horse of Lord Mar'mion. The word is Norse, and means "swift." (*Sir W. Scott.*)

Black Agnes. The palfrey of Mary Queen of Scots, given her by her brother Moray, and named after Agnes of Dunbar, a countess in her own right.

Black Bess. The famous mare ridden by the highwayman Dick Turpin, which, tradition says, carried him from London to York.

Black Saladin. Warwick's famous horse, which was coal-black. Its sire was Malech, and, according to tradition, when the race of Malech failed, the race of Warwick would fail also. And it was so.

Borak (Al). The "horse" which conveyed Mahomet from earth to the seventh heaven. It was milk-white, had the wings of an eagle, and a human face,

with horse's cheeks. Every pace she took was equal to the farthest range of human sight. The word is Arabic for "the lightning."

Brig'adore (3 syl.) or *Brigliadore* [Bril-yar-dore]. Sir Guyon's horse, which had a distinguishing black spot in its mouth, like a horse-shoe in shape. (*Spenser : Faërie Queene,* v. 2.)

Brigliado'ro [Bril-ya-do'ro]. Orlando's famous charger, second only to Bayardo in swiftness and wonderful powers. The word means "golden-bridle." (*Orlando Furioso,* etc.)

Bronte (2 syl.). One of the horses of the Sun. The word means "thunder."

Bronzomarte (3 syl.). The horse of Sir Launcelot Greaves. The word means "a mettlesome sorrel."

Brown Hal. A model pacing stallion.

Buceph'alos (Greek). The celebrated charger of Alexander the Great. Alexander was the only person who could mount him, and he always knelt down to take up his master. He was thirty years old at death, and Alexander built a city for his mausoleum, which he called Buceph'ala. The word means "ox-head."

Capilet (Grey). The horse of Sir Andrew Aguecheek. (*Shakespeare : Twelfth Night,* iii. 4.) A capilet or capulet is a small wen on the horse's hock.

Carman. The Chevalier Bayard's horse, given him by the Duke of Lorrain. It was a Persian horse from Kerman or Carmen (Laristan).

Ce'ler. The horse of the Roman Emperor Ve'rus. It was fed on almonds and raisins, covered with royal purple, and stalled in the imperial palace. (Latin for "swift.")

Cerus. The horse of Adrastos, swifter than the wind (*Pausanias*). The word means "fit."

Cesar. A model Percheron stallion.

Clavileño. (See *Aligero.*)

Comrade (2 syl.). Fortunio's fairy horse.

Copenha'gen. Wellington's charger at Waterloo. It died in 1835 at the age of twenty-seven. Napoleon's horse was *Marengo.*

Curtal (Bay). The horse of Lord Lafeu. (*Shakespeare : All's Well that Ends Well,* ii. 3.) The word means "cropped."

Cut. The carrier's horse. (*Shakespeare :* 1 *Henry IV.,* act ii. 1.) A familiar name of a horse. The word may be taken to mean either "castrated" or "cropped."

Cyl'laros (Greek). Named from Cylla, in Troas, a celebrated horse of Castor or of Pollux.

Dapple. Sancho Panza's ass (in the *History of Don Quixote de la Mancha*, by Cervantes). So called from its colour.

Di'nos (Greek). Diomed's horse. The word means "the marvel."

Dhuldul. The famous horse of Ali, son-in-law of Mahomet.

Doomstead. The horse of the Norns or Fates. (*Scandinavian mythology.*)

Eōos (Greek, "dawn"). One of the horses of Aurora.

Eryth'reos (Greek, "red-producer"). One of the horses of the Sun.

Ethon (Greek, "fiery"). One of the horses of Hector.

Fadda. Mahomet's white mule.

Ferrant d'Espagne. The horse of Oliver. The word means "the Spanish traveller."

Fiddle-back. Oliver Goldsmith's unfortunate pony.

Frontaletto. Sacripant's charger. The word means "little head." (*Ariosto: Orlando Furioso.*)

Fronti'no or *Frontin.* Once called "Balisarda." Roge'ro's or Rugie'ro's horse. The word means "little head." (*Ariosto: Orlando Furioso,* etc.)

Gal'athē (3 syl.). One of Hector's horses. The word means "cream-coloured."

Giblas. A model German coach stallion.

Granē (2 syl.). Siegfried's horse, of marvellous swiftness. The word means "grey-coloured."

Grey Capilet. (See *Capilet.*)

Grizzle. Dr. Syntax's horse, all skin and bone. The word means "grey-coloured."

Haïz'um. The horse of the archangel Gabriel. (*Koran.*)

Har'pagos (Greek, "one that carries off rapidly.") One of the horses of Castor and Pollux.

Hip'pocam'pēs (4 syl.). One of Neptune's horses. It had only two legs, the hinder quarter being that of a dragon's tail or fish.

Honest Tom. A model shire stallion, 1105.

Hrimfaxi. The horse of Night, from whose bit fall the "rime-drops" which every night bedew the earth [*i.e.* frost-mane]. (*Scandinavian mythology.*)

Ilderim. A model Arabian stallion.

Incita'tus. The horse of the Roman Emperor Calig'ula, made priest and consul. It had an ivory manger, and drank wine out of a golden pail. The word means "spurred-on."

Jenny Geddes (1 syl.). Robert Burns's mare.

Kan'taka. The white horse of Prince Gautăma of India (Budda).

Kelpy or *Kelpie.* The water-horse of fairy mythology. The word means "of the colour of kelp or sea-weed."

Kervela. A model French coach stallion, 1342.

Lampon (Greek, "the bright one"). One of the horses of Diomed.

Lampos (Greek, "shining like a lamp"). One of the steeds of the Sun at noon.

Lamri. King Arthur's mare. The word means "the curveter."

Leiston. A model Suffolk stallion, 1415.

Leonatus. A model thorough-bred stallion.

Maren'go. The white stallion which Napoleon rode at Waterloo. Its remains are now in the Museum of the United Services, London. It is represented in Vernet's picture of *Napoleon Crossing the Alps.* Wellington's horse was called *Copenhagen.*

Matchless of Londesborough. A model hackney stallion.

Malech. (See *Black Saladin.*)

Marocco. Banks's famous horse. Its shoes were of silver, and one of its exploits was to mount the steeple of St. Paul's.

Molly. Sir Charles Napier's mare. It died at the age of 35.

Nobbs. The steed of Dr. Dove of Doncaster. (*Southey.*)

Nonios. One of the horses of Pluto.

Ore'lia. The charger of Roderick, last of the Goths, noted for its speed and symmetry. (*Southey.*)

Pale Horse (The) on which Death rides. (Rev. vi. 8.)

Palo Alto. A model trotting stallion.

Passe Brewell. Sir Tristram's charger. (*Hist. of Prince Arthur,* ii. 68.)

Peg'asos. The winged horse of Apollo and the Muses. (Greek, "born near the pēge or source of the ocean.") Perseus rode him when he rescued Andromeda.

Pha'eton (Greek, "the shining one"). One of the steeds of Auro'ra.

Phallas. The horse of Herac'lios. The word means "stallion."

Phleg'on (Greek, "the burning or blazing one"). One of the horses of the Noon-day Sun.

Phre'nicos. The horse of Hiero, of Syracuse, that won the Olympic prize for single horses in the seventy-third Olympiad. It means "intelligent,"

Podar'ge (3 syl.). One of the horses of Hector. The word means "swift-foot."

Prince Royal. A model Belgian stallion.

Pu'roeis [pu'-rŏ-ice]. One of the horses of the Noon-day Sun. (Greek, "fiery hot.")

Rabica'no or *Rab'ican.* Argali'a's horse in *Orlando Innamorato*, and Astolpho's horse in *Orlando Furioso.* Its dam was Fire, its sire Wind; it fed on unearthly food. The word means a horse with a "dark tail but with some white hairs."

"Rabicano (adj.), que se applica al caballo que tiene algunas cerdas blancas in la cola."—*Salva: Spanish Dictionary.*

Reksh. Rustem's horse.

Rimfaxi. (See *Hrimfaxi.*)

Roan Barbary. The favourite horse of King Richard II.

" When Bolingbroke rode on Roan Barbary,
That horse that thou so often hast bestrid."
Shakespeare: Richard II., v. 5.

Ronald. Lord Cardigan's thorough-bred chestnut, with white stockings on the near hind and fore feet. It carried him through the Balaclava Charge.

Ros'abelle (3 syl.). The favourite palfrey of Mary Queen of Scots.

Rosinan'te (4 syl.). Don Quixote's horse, all skin and bone. The word means "formerly a hack."

Ros'signol. The palfrey of Madame Châtelet of Cirey, the lady with whom Voltaire resided for ten years.

Royalty. A model Cleveland bay stallion.

Suludin. (See *Black Saladin.*)

Savoy. The favourite black horse of Charles VIII. of France; so called from the Duke of Savoy who gave it him. It had but one eye, and "was mean in stature."

Shib'diz. The Persian Buccph'alos, fleeter than the wind. It was the charger of Chosroes II. of Persia.

Skinfaxi. The steed which draws the car of day. The word means "shining mane." (*Scandinavian mythology.*)

Sleipnir (Slipe'neer). Odin's grey horse, which had eight legs and could traverse either land or sea. The horse typifies the wind which blows over land and water from eight principal points.

Sorrel. The horse of William III., which stumbled by catching his foot in a mole-heap. This accident ultimately caused the king's death. *Sorrel*, like *Savoy*, was blind of one eye, and "mean of stature."

Spumador. King Arthur's horse. The word means "the foaming one."

Strymon. The horse immolated by Xerxes before he invaded Greece.

Named from the river Strymon, in Thrace, from which vicinity it came.

Suleiman. The favourite charger of the Earl of Essex.

Tachebrune (*q.v.*). The horse of Ogier the Dane.

Tre'bizond. The grey horse of Admiral Guari'nos, one of the French knights taken at Roncesvallês.

Veglianti'no [Vail-yan-te'-no]. The famous steed of Orlando, called in French romance *Veillantif*, Orlando being called Roland. The word means "the little vigilant one."

White Surrey. The favourite horse of King Richard III.

" Saddle White Surrey for the field to-morrow."
Shakespeare: Richard III., v. 3.

Wzmakh. A model Orloff stallion.

Wooden Horse. (*See* WOODEN.)

Xanthos. One of the horses of Achilles, who announced to the hero his approaching death when unjustly chidden by him. Its sire was *Zephyros*, and dam *Podargē* (*q.v.*). The word means "chestnut-coloured."

(*See* HUNTERS AND RUNNERS.)

⁂ *O'Donohue's white horse.* Those waves which come on a windy day, crested with foam. The spirit of the hero reappears every May-day, and is seen gliding, to sweet but unearthly music, over the lakes of Killarney, on his favourite white horse. It is preceded by groups of young men and maidens, who fling spring-flowers in his path. (*Derrick's Letters.*)

T. Moore has a poem on the subject in his *Irish Melodies*, No. vi.; it is entitled *O'Donohue's Mistress*, and refers to a tradition that a young and beautiful girl became enamoured of the visionary chieftain, and threw herself into the lake that he might carry her off for his bride.

¶ **Horse.**

IN PHRASE AND PROVERB.

A dark horse. A horse whose merits as a racer are not known to the general public.

Flogging the dead horse. (*See* FLOGGING.)

Riding the wooden horse. A military punishment now discontinued. It was a flogging-stool.

I will win the horse or lose the saddle. Neck or nothing; double or quits. Milton makes Satan say, "Better to reign in hell than serve in heaven."

Latin: " Aut ter sex, aut tres tes-seræ." (*See* TER SEX.)
" Au Cæsar, aut nullus."

French : " Tout ou rien."

" Je veux risquer le tout pour le tout."

They cannot draw (or *set*) *horses together.* They cannot agree together. The French say, " *Nos chiens ne chassent pas ensemble.*"

¶ *'Tis a Trojan horse* (Latin proverb). A deception, a concealed danger. Thus Cicero says, " *Intus, intus, inquam, est equus Troja'nus* " (*Pro Murēna*, 78). It was Epēos who made the Trojan horse.

¶ *'Tis a good horse that never stumbles.* Everyone has his faults. Every black has its white, and every sweet its sour.

Latin : " Quandoque bonus dorm.tat Homerus."
Horace : Ars Poetica, 359.
" Humanum est errare."

French : " Il n'y a bon cheval qui ne bronche." or " Il n'est si bon cheval qui ne bronche."

To get upon one's high horse. To give oneself airs. (*See* HIGH HORSE.)

To set the cart before the horse. (*See* CART.)

When the horse (or *steed*) *is stolen, lock the stable door.* The French say : " *Après la mort, le medicine.*" Somewhat similar is : " After beef, mustard."

Working on the dead horse. (*See* WORKING.)

Horse. Coarse, acrid or pungent, inferior of its kind, rough. " Hoarse " is the Anglo-Saxon *hās.*

Horse-bean. The bean usually given to horses for food.

Horse-chestnut. If a slip is cut off obliquely close to a joint, it will present a perfect miniature of a horse's hock and foot, shoe and nails. I have cut off numerous specimens. Probably this has given the name *horse* to the tree. (*See* HORSE-VETCH.)

Horse-faced. Having a long, coarse face.

Horse Latitudes. A region of calms between 30° and 35° North ; so called because ships laden with horses bound to America or the West Indies were often obliged to lighten their freight by casting the horses overboard when calmbound in these latitudes.

" Nothing could have been more delightful than our run into the horse latitudes. Gales and dead calms, terrible thunderstorms and breezes, fair one hour and foul the next, are the characteristics of these parallels. Numbers of horses were exported from the mother country, and it was reckoned that more of the animals died in these . . . latitudes than in all the rest of the passage."—*Clark Russell : Lady Maud*, vol. i. chap. vii. p. 186.

Horse-laugh. A coarse, vulgar laugh.

" He plays rough pranks . . . and has a big horse-laugh in him when there is a fop to be roasted."—*Carlyle : Frederick the Great*, vol. i. book iv. chap. ii. p. 305.

Horse Marines (*The*). There is no such force. The Royal Marines are either artillery or infantry ; there are no cavalry marines. To belong to the " Horse Marines " is a joke, meaning an awkward lubberly recruit.

Horse-milliner. Properly, one who makes up and supplies decorations for horses.

A horse-soldier more fit for the toilet than the battle-field. The expression was first used by Rowley in his *Ballads of Charitie,* but Sir Walter Scott revived it.

" One comes in foreign trashery
Of tinkling chain and spur,
A walking haberdashery
Of feathers, lace, and fur ;
In Rowley's antiquated phrase,
Horse milliner of modern days."
Bridal of Triermain, ii. 3.

Horse-mint. The pungent mint.

Horse-play. Rough play.

Similarly *hoarse*, having a rough voice from inflammation of the throat ; *gorse*, a rough, prickly plant ; *goose-berry*, a rough berry ; *goose-grass*, the grass whose leaves are rough with hair, etc.

Horse-power. A measure of force. Watt estimated the " force " of a London dray-horse, working eight hours a day, at 33,000 foot-pounds (*q.v.*) per minute. In calculating the horse-power of a steam-engine the following is the formula :—

$$\frac{P \times A \times L \times N}{33,000} \text{ deduct } \tfrac{1}{16} \text{ for friction.}$$

P, pressure (in lbs.) per sq. inch on the piston.
A, area (in inches) of the piston.
L, length (in feet) of the stroke.
N, number of strokes per minute.

Horse Protestant. *As good a Protestant as Oliver Cromwell's horse.* This expression arises in a comparison made by Cromwell respecting some person who had less discernment than his horse in the moot points of the Protestant controversy.

Horse-radish. The pungent root.

Horse-shoes were at one time nailed up over doors as a protection against witches. Aubrey says, " Most houses at the west-end of London have a horseshoe on the threshold." In Monmouth Street there were seventeen in 1813, and seven so late as 1855.

" Straws laid across my path retard ;
The horse-shoes nailed, each threshold's guard." *Gay : Fable* xxiii. part I.

It is lucky to pick up a horse-shoe. This is from the notion that a horse-shoe was a protection against witches. For the same reason our superstitious forefathers loved to nail a horse-shoe on their house-door.· Lord Nelson had one nailed to the mast of the ship *Victory.*

⁂ There is a legend that the devil one day asked St. Dunstan, who was noted for his skill in shoeing horses, to shoe his "single hoof." Dunstan, knowing who his customer was, tied him tightly to the wall and proceeded with his job, but purposely put the devil to so much pain that he roared for mercy. Dunstan at last consented to release his captive on condition that he would never enter a place where he saw a horse-shoe displayed.

Horse-vetch. The vetch which has pods shaped like a horse-shoe; sometimes called the "horse-shoe vetch." (*See* HORSE CHESTNUT.)

Horse and his Rider. One of Æsop's fables, to show that nations crave the assistance of others when they are aggrieved, but become the tools or slaves of those who rendered them assistance. Thus the Celtic Britons asked aid of the Saxons, and the Danish Duchies of the Germans, but in both cases the rider made the horse a mere tool.

Horse-shoes and Nails (for rent). In 1251 Walter le Brun, farrier, in the Strand, London, was to have a piece of land in the parish of St. Clements, to place there a forge, for which he was to pay the parish six horse-shoes, which rent was paid to the Exchequer every year, and is still rendered to the Exchequer by the Lord Mayor and citizens of London, to whom subsequently the piece of ground was granted.

"In the reign of King Edward I. Walter Marescullus paid at the *crucem lapideam* six horse-shoes with nails, for a certain building which he held of the king *in capite* opposite the stone cross."—*Blount: Ancient Tenures.*

Horsemen.

Light horsemen. Those who live by plundering ships.

Heavy horsemen. Those who go aboard to clear ships.

Horsey Man (*A*). One who affects the manners and style of a jockey or horse-dealer.

Hortus Siccus. (Latin, "a dry garden.") A collection of plants dried and arranged in a book.

Ho'rus. The Egyptian day-god, represented in hieroglyphics by a sparrow-hawk, which bird was sacred to him. He was son of Osi'ris and Isis, but his birth being premature he was weak in the lower limbs. As a child he is seen carried in his mother's arms.

wearing the pschent or atf, and seated on a lotus-flower with his finger on his lips. As an adult he is represented hawk-headed. (Egyptian, *har* or *hor*, "the day" or "sun's path.") Strictly speaking, Horus is the rising sun, Ra the noonday sun, and Osiris the setting sun. (Whence Greek and Latin *hora*, and our *hour*.)

Hose. Stockings, or stockings and breeches both in one. French, *chausses.* There were the *haut de chausses* and the *bas de chausses.*

"Their points being broken, down fell their hose."—*Shakespeare:* 1 *Henry IV.,* ii. 4.

Hos'pital. From the Latin *hospes* (a guest), being originally an inn or house of entertainment for pilgrims; hence our words *host* (one who entertains), *hospitality* (the entertainment given), and *hospitaller* (the keeper of the house). In process of time these receptacles were resorted to by the sick and infirm only, and the house of entertainment became an asylum for the sick and wounded. In 1399 Katherine de la Court held a "hospital" at the bottom of the court called Robert de Paris; after the lapse of four years her landlord died, and the tavern or hospital fell to his heirs Jehan de Chevreuse and William Cholet.

Hospital (*The*), in Post-office phraseology, is the department where loose packages are set to rights.

Hos'pitallers. First applied to those whose duty it was to provide *hospitium* (lodging and entertainment) for pilgrims. The most noted institution of the kind was at Jerusalem, which gave its name to an order called the Knights Hospitallers. This order was first called that of the Knights of St. John at Jerusalem, which still exists; afterwards they were styled the Knights of Rhodes, and then Knights of Malta, because Rhodes and Malta were conferred on them by different monarchs.

"The first crusade ... led to the establishment of the Christian kingdom of Jerusalem, in 1099. The chief strength of the kingdom lay in the two orders of military monks—the Templars and the Hospitallers or Knights of St. John."—*Freeman: General Sketch,* chap. xi.

Host. A victim. The consecrated bread of the Eucharist is so called in the Latin Church because it is believed to be a real victim consisting of flesh, blood, and spirit, offered up in sacrifice. (Latin, *hostia.*) At the service known as the Benediction it is set up for adoration, and with it the blessing is given in a transparent vessel called a "monstrance." (Latin, *monstrāre,* to show.)

Host. An army. At the breaking up of the Roman Empire the first duty of every subject was to follow his lord into the field, and the proclamation was *banni're in hostem* (to order out against the foe), which soon came to signify " to order out for military service," and *hostem facere* came to mean "to perform military service." Hostis (military service) next came to mean the *army* that went against the foe, whence our word *host.*

" Like the leaves of the forest, when summer is
green,
That host with their banners at sunset was
seen ;
Like the leaves of the forest, when autumn has
blown,
That host on the morrow lay withered and
strown."
Byron: Destruction of Sennacherib, stanza 2.

To reckon without your host. To reckon from your own standpoint only. Guests who calculate what their expenses at an hotel will come to always leave out certain items which the landlord adds in.

" Found in few minutes, to his cost,
He did but count without his host."
Butler : Hudibras, pt. i. canto iii. lines 22-3.

Hos'tage (2 syl.) is connected with the Latin *obses*, through the Mid. Latin *hostagium*, French *ôtage* or *ostage*, Italian *ostaggio*.

Hos'tler is properly the keeper of an hostelry or inn.

Hot. *I'll make the place too hot to hold him.* (*See* TALUS.)
I'll give it him hot and strong. I'll rate him most soundly and severely. Liquor very hot and strong takes one's breath away, and is apt to choke one.

Hot Cockles. A Christmas game. One blindfolded knelt down, and being struck had to guess who gave the blow.

" Thus poets passing time away,
Like children at hot-cockles play." (1653.)

Hot Cross Buns. Fosbroke says these buns were made of the dough kneaded for the host, and were marked with the cross accordingly. As the Good Friday buns are said to keep for twelve months without turning mouldy, some persons still hang up one or more in their house as a " charm against evil." (*See* CROSS.)
✽ The round bun represents the full moon, and the cross represents the four quarters of the moon. They were made in honour of Diana by the ancient Roman priests, somewhere about the vernal equinox. Phœnicians, Carthaginians, Egyptians, as well as the Greeks and Romans, worshipped the moon.

Hot-foot. With speed ; fast.
" And the Blackfoot who courted each foeman's
approach,
Faith, 'tis hotfoot he'd fly from the stout Father
Roach." *Lover.*
N.B. The Blackfoot was an Irish faction, similar to the Terry Alts in the early part of the nineteenth century.

Hot Water (*In*). In a state of trouble, or of anxiety. The reference is to the ordeal by hot water (*q.v.*).

Hotch-pot. Blackstone says hotch-pot is a pudding made of several things mixed together. Lands given in frank-marriage or descending in fee-simple are to be mixed, like the ingredients of a pudding, and then cut up in equal slices among all the daughters. (Book ii. 12.)
As to *personality : Hotch-pot* may be explained thus : Suppose a father has advanced money to one child, at the decease of the father this child receives a sum in addition enough to make his share equal to the rest of the family. If not content, he must bring into hotch-pot the money that was advanced, and the whole is then divided amongst all the children according to the terms of the will.
French, *hochepot,* from *hocher,* to shake or jumble together ; or from the German *hoch-pot,* the huge pot or family caldron. Wharton says it is *haché en poche.*

Hotch-potch. A confused mixture or jumble ; a thick broth containing meat and vegetables.
" A sort of soup, or broth, or brew,
Or hotchpotch of all sorts of fishes."
Thackeray : Ballad of Bouillabaisse, stanza 2.

Hot'spur. A fiery person who has no control over his temper. Harry Percy was so called. Lord Derby was sometimes called the " *Hotspur of debate.*" Lytton, in *New Timon,* calls him, "frank haughty, bold, the Rupert of debate." (See *Shakespeare : 1 Henry IV.*)

Hottentot. Rude, uncultured, a boor. As "You are a perfect Hottentot."

Hou'goumont is said to be a corruption of *Château Goumont ;* but Victor Hugo says it is *Hugo-mons,* and that the house was built by Hugo, Sire de Sommeril, the same person that endowed the sixth chapelry of the abbey of Villers.

Hound. *To hound a person* is to persecute him, or rather to set on persons to annoy him, as hounds are let from the slips at a hare or stag.
" As he who only lets loose a greyhound out of
the slip is said to hound him at the hare."—
Bramhall.

Hou'qua. A superior quality of tea; so called from Hoque, the celebrated Hong-Kong tea merchant; died 1846.

Hour. (Greek and Latin, *hora*.)

At the eleventh hour. Just in time not to be too late; only just in time to obtain some benefit. The allusion is to the parable of labourers hired for the vineyard (Matt. xx.).

My hour is not yet come. The time of my death is not yet fully come. The allusion is to the belief that the hour of our birth and death is appointed and fixed.

"When Jesus knew that His hour was come..."
—John xiii. 1.

In an evil hour. Acting under an unfortunate impulse. In astrology we have our lucky and unlucky hours.

In the small hours of the morning. One, two, and three, after midnight.

To keep good hours. To return home early every night; to go to bed betimes. " *Se retirer la nuit de bonne heure.*" In Latin, " *Tempestive se domum recipĕre.*"

Hou'ri (pl. *Houris*). The large black-eyed damsels of Paradise, possessed of perpetual youth and beauty, whose virginity is renewable at pleasure. Every believer will have seventy-two of these houris in Paradise, and his intercourse with them will be fruitful or otherwise, according to his wish. If an offspring is desired, it will grow to full estate in an hour. (Persian, *huri*; Arabic, *hūriya*, nymphs of paradise. Compare *ahivar*, black-eyed.) (*The Koran.*)

House (1 syl.). In astrology the whole heaven is divided into twelve portions, called "houses," through which the heavenly bodies pass every twenty-four hours. In casting a man's fortune by the stars, the whole host is divided into two parts (beginning from the east), six above and six below the horizon. The eastern ones are called the *ascendant*, because they are about to rise; the other six are the *descendant*, because they have already passed the zenith. The twelve houses are thus awarded :—

(1) House of life ; (2) House of fortune and riches; (3) House of brethren; (4) House of relatives; (5) House of children ; (6) House of health.

(7) House of marriage ; (8) House of death (the upper portal); (9) House of religion ; (10) House of dignities; (11) House of friends and benefactors; (12) House of enemies.

¶ **House.** A dwelling.

Like a house afire. Very rapidly. "He is getting on like a house afire" means he is getting on excellently.

To bring down the house (in a theatre, etc.) is to receive unusual and rapturous applause.

To keep house. To maintain a separate establishment. "To go into house-keeping " is to start a private establishment.

To keep a good house. To supply a bountiful table.

To keep open house. To give free entertainment to all who choose to come. " *Omnes benigne mensâ occipĕre.*" In French, " *Tenir table ouverte.*"

To throw the house out of the windows. To throw all things into confusion from exuberance of spirit (*à des excès de joie*). " *Cœlum terræ, terram cœlo miscēre ;* " or "*Omnia confundĕre.*" In French, "*Jeter le maison par le fenêtres.*"

¶ **House.** Race or lineage; as, " fhe House of Hanover," "the House of Austria."

House-bote. A sufficient allowance of wood to repair the dwelling and to supply fuel.

House-flag (*A*). The distinguishing flag of a company of shipowners or of a single ship-owner, as, for instance, that of the Cunard Company.

House-leek [*Jove's beard*]. Grown on house-roofs, from the notion that it warded off lightning. Charlemagne made an edict that every one of his subjects should have house-leek on his house roof. The words are, " *Et habet quisque supra domum suum Jovis barbam.*" It was thought to ward off all evil spirits. Fevers as well as lightning were at one time supposed to be due to evil spirits.

" If the herb house-leek or syngreen do grow on the house-top, the same house is never stricken with lightning or thunder."—*Thomas Hill : Natural and Artf. Conclusion.*

House Spirits.

Of DENMARK, Nis or Nisse (2 syl.).
Of ENGLAND, Puck or Robin Goodfellow.
Of FAROE ISLANDS, Niagruisar.
Of FINLAND, Para.
Of FRANCE, Esprit Follet.
Of GERMANY, Kobold.
Of MUNSTER, Fear Dearg or Red Man.
Of NAPLES, Monaciello or Little Monk.
Of NORWAY, same as Denmark.
Of SCOTLAND, Brownie.
Of SPAIN, Duende (3 syl.).
Of SWITZERLAND, Jack of the Bowl.
Of VAUDOIS, Servant.
∴ Others o' particular houses.

House-top. *To cry from the house-top. To proclaim [it] from the house-top.* To announce something in the most public manner possible. Jewish houses had flat roofs, which were paved. Here the ancient Jews used to assemble for gossip; here, too, not unfrequently, they slept; and here some of their festivals were held. From the house-tops the rising of the sun was proclaimed, and other public announcements were made.

" That which ye have spoken [whispered] in the ear . . . shall be proclaimed upon the housetops."
—*Luke* xii. 3.

House and Home. *He hath eaten me out of house and home* (*Shakespeare: 2 Henry IV.*, ii. 1). It is the complaint of hostess Quickly to the Lord Chief Justice when he asks for " what sum " she had arrested Sir John Falstaff. She explains the phrase by " he hath put all my substance into that fat belly of his; " "I am undone by his going."

House of Correction. A gaol governed by a keeper. Originally it was a place where vagrants were made to work, and small offenders were kept in ward for the correction of their offences.

House of God (*The*). Not solely a church, or a temple made with hands, but any place sanctified by God's presence. Thus, Jacob in the wilderness, where he saw the ladder set up leading from earth to heaven, said, " This is none other but the house of God, and this is the gate of heaven (Gen. xxviii. 17).

House that Jack Built (*The*). There are numerous similar glomerations. For example the Hebrew parable of *The Two Zuzim.* The summation runs thus:—

10. This is Yavah who vanquished
9. Death which killed
8. The butcher which slew
7. The ox which drank
6. The water which quenched
5. The fire which burnt
4. The stick which beat
3. The dog which worried
2. The cat which killed
1. The kid which my father bought for two zuzim.

(A zuzim was about = a farthing.)

Household Gods. Domestic pets, and all those things which help to endear home. The Romans had household gods called *pe-na'-tes*, who were supposed to preside over their private dwellings. Of these pe-na'-tes some were called la'res, the special *genii* or *angels* of the family. One was Vest'a, whose office was to preserve domestic unity. Jupiter and Juno were also among the pe-na'-tes. The modern use of the term is a playful adaptation.

" Bearing a nation with all its household gods into exile."   *Longfellow : Evangeline.*

Household Troops. Those troops whose special duty it is to attend the sovereign and guard the metropolis. They consist of the 1st and 2nd Lifeguards, the Royal Horseguards, and the three regiments of Footguards called the Grenadier, Coldstream, and Scots Fusilier Guards.

Housel. To give or receive the Eucharist. (Anglo-Saxon, *huslian*, to give the *hu'sel* or host.)

" Children were christened, and men houseled and assoyled through all the land, except such as were in the bill of excommunication by name expressed."—*Holinshed : Chronicle.*

Houssain (*Prince*). Brother of Prince Ahmed. He possessed a piece of carpet or tapestry of such wonderful power that anyone had only to sit upon it, and it would transport him in a moment to any place to which he desired to go.

" If Prince Houssain's flying tapestry or Astolpho's hippogriff had been shown, he would have judged them by the ordinary rules, and preferred a well-hung chariot."—*Sir Walter Scott.*

Houyhnhnms (*whin' hims*). A race of horses endowed with reason, who bear rule over a race of men. Gulliver, in his *Travels*, tells us what he " saw " among them. (*Swift.*)

" Nay, would kind Jove my organ so dispose
To hymn harmonious Houyhnhnms through the nose,
I'd call thee Houhnhnm, that high-sounding name;
Thy children's noses all should twang the same."
          Pope.

How Do You Do ? (*See* Do.)

How'ard. A philanthropist. John Howard is immortalised by his efforts to improve the condition of prisoners. "He visited all Europe," says Burke, "not to survey the sumptuousness of palaces or the stateliness of temples; not to make accurate measurements of the remains of ancient grandeur, nor to form a scale of the curiosity of modern art; not to collect manuscripts—but to dive into the depths of dungeons; to plunge into the infection of hospitals; to survey the mansions of sorrow and pain; to take the dimensions of misery, depression, and contempt; to remember the forgotten ; to attend to the neglected ; to visit the forsaken, and to compare the distress of all men in all countries. His plan is original, and it is as full of genius as it is of humanity. It was a voyage of discovery ; a circumnavigation of charity." (John Howard, 1726-1790.)

" The radiant path that Howard trod to Heaven."
          Bloomfield : Farmer's Boy.

The female Howard. Mrs. Elizabeth Fry (1780-1844).

All the blood of all the Howards. All the nobility of our best aristocracy. The ducal house of Norfolk stands at the head of the English peerage, and is interwoven in all our history.

" What could ennoble sots, or slaves, or cowards?
Alas ! not all the blood of all the Howards."
Pope: *Essay on Man*, Ep. iv. line 216.

⁜ What will "all the blood of all the Howards" say to Mr. Walter Rye who, in his *History of Norfolk* (1885), tells us that "Howard is from hog-ward," and that the original Howards were so called from their avocation, which was to tend the pigs.

Howard. Mr. Bug, late of Epsom (Surrey), then of Wakefield (Yorkshire), landlord of the Swan Tavern, changed his name (June, 1862) to Norfolk Howard.

Howdah. A canopy, or seat fixed on the back of an elephant.

" Leading the array, three stately elephants marched, bearing the Woons in gilded howdahs under gold umbrellas."—*J. W. Palmer: Up and Down the Irrawaddi*, chap. xx. p. 169.

How'die (2 syl.). A midwife.

Howitzers are guns used to fire buildings, to reach troops behind hills or parapets, to bound their shells along lines and against cavalry, to breach mud walls by exploding their shells in them, etc. They project common shells, common and spherical case-shot, carcasses, and, if necessary, round shot. In a *mortar* the trunnions are at the end ; in *howitzers* they are in the middle.

" The howitzer was taken to pieces, and carried by the men to its destination."—*Grant : Personal Memoirs*, chap. xi. p. 158.

Howleglass (2 syl.). A clever rascal, the hero of an old German romance by Thomas Murner, popular in the eighteenth century.

Hrimfax'i. (*See* HORSE.)

Hub. The nave of a wheel ; a boss ; also a skid. (Welsh, *hob*, a swelling, a protuberance; compare also a *hwb*.) The Americans call Boston, Massachusetts, "The hub [*boss*] of the solar system."

" Boston State-house is the hub of the solar system." — *Holmes : Autocrat of the Breakfast Table*, chap. vi. p. 143.

" Calcutta swaggers as if it were the hub of the universe."—*Daily News*, 1886.

Hu'bal. An Arab idol brought from Bulka, in Syria, by Amir Ibn-Lohei, who asserted that it would procure rain when wanted. It was the statue of a man in red agate ; one hand being lost, a golden one was supplied. He held in his hand seven arrows without wings of feathers, such as the Arabians use in divination. This idol was destroyed in the eighth year of "the flight."

Hub'bard (*Old Mother*). The famous dame of nursery mythology, who went to the cupboard to fetch her poor dog a bone ; but when she got there the cupboard was bare, so the poor dog had none.

Hubert (*h* silent), in Shakespeare's *King John*, is Hubert de Burgh, Justice of England, created Earl of Kent. He died 1243.

St. Hubert. Patron saint of huntsmen. He was son of Bertrand, Duc d'Acquitaine, and cousin of King Pepin. Hubert was so fond of the chase that he neglected his religious duties for his favourite amusement, till one day a stag bearing a crucifix menaced him with eternal perdition unless he reformed. Upon this the merry huntsman entered a cloister, became in time Bishop of Liège, and the apostle of Ardennes and Brabant. Those who were descended of his race were supposed to possess the power of curing the bite of mad dogs.

St. Hubert in Christian art is represented sometimes as a bishop with a miniature stag resting on the book in his hand, and sometimes as a noble huntsman kneeling to the miraculous crucifix borne by the stag.

Hu'dibras. Said to be a caricature of Sir Samuel Luke, a patron of Samuel Butler. The *Grub Street Journal* (1731) maintains it was Colonel Rolle, of Devonshire, with whom the poet lodged for some time, and adds that the name is derived from Hugh de Bras, the patron saint of the county. He represents the Presbyterian party, and his squire the Independents.

" 'Tis sung there is a valiant Mameluke,
In foreign land ycleped [*Sir Samuel Luke*]."
Butler : Hudibras, i. 1.

Sir Hudibras. The cavalier of Elissa of Parsimony. (*Spenser : Faërie Queene*, book. ii.)

Hudibras'tic Verse. A doggerel eight-syllable rhyming verse, after the style of Butler's *Hudibras*.

Hud'son (*Sir Jeffrey*). The famous dwarf, at one time page to Queen Henrietta Maria. Sir Walter Scott has introduced him in his *Peveril of the Peak*, chap. xxxiv. Vandyke has immortalised him by his brush ; and his clothes are said to be preserved in Sir Hans Sloane's museum. (1619-1678.)

❧ The person slain in a duel by this dwarf was the Hon. Mr. Crofts.

"We fought on horseback—breaking ground and advancing by signal ; and, as I never miss aim, I had the misfortune to kill [my adversary] at the first shot."—*Sir W. Scott: Peveril of the Peak,* chap. xxxiv.

Hue and Cry. A phrase used in English law to describe a body of persons joining in pursuit of a felon or suspected thief. (French, *huée*, verb *huer*, to hoot or shout after ; Anglo-Saxon, *hui*, ho !)

Hug the Shore (*To*). In the case of a ship, to keep as close to the shore as is compatible with the vessel's safety, when at sea. "*Serrer la terre.*"

Hug the Wind (*To*). To keep a ship close hauled. "*Serrer le vent.*"

Hugger - mugger. The primary meaning is clandestinely. The secondary meaning is disorderly, in a slovenly manner. To *hugger* is to lie in ambush, from the Danish *hug*, *huger*, *huggring*, to squat on the ground ; mugger is the Danish *smug*, clandestinely, whence our word smuggle.

The king in *Hamlet* says of Polo'-nius : "We have done but greenly in hugger-mugger to inter him"—*i.e.* to smuggle him into the grave clandestinely and without ceremony.

Sir T. North, in his *Plutarch*, says : "Antonius thought that his body should be honourably buried, and not in hugger-mugger" (clandestinely).

Ralph says :—

"While I, in hugger-mugger hid,
Have noted all they said and did."
Butler : Hudibras, iii. 3.

Under the secondary idea we have the following expressions :—*He lives in a hugger-mugger sort of way ; the rooms were all hugger-mugger* (disorderly).

Huggins and Muggins. Mr. and Mrs. Vulgarity, of Pretension Hall.

Hugh Lloyd's Pulpit (Merioneth-shire). A natural production of stone. One pile resembles the Kilmarth Rocks. There is a platform stone with a back in stone. (Hugh *pron.* You.)

Hugh Perry. An English perversion of "Euper'ion," a predecessor of lucifer matches invented by Heurtner, who opened a shop in the Strand, and advertised his invention thus—

"To save your knuckles time and trouble,
Use Heurter's Euper'ion."

(*See* PROMETHEANS, VESUVIANS.)

Hugh of Lincoln. It is said that the Jews in 1255 stole a boy named Hugh, whom they tortured for ten days and then crucified. Eighteen of the richest Jews of Lincoln were hanged for taking part in this affair, and the boy was buried in state. This is the subject of *The Prioress's Tale* of Chaucer, which Wordsworth has modernised. In Rymer's *Fœdera* are several documents relating to this event.

Hugin and Mun'in [*mind* and *memory*]. The two ravens that sit on the shoulders of Odin or Alfader.

"Perhaps the nursery saying, 'A little bird told me that,' is a corruption of Hugo and Munin, and so we have the old Northern superstition lingering among us without our being aware of it."—*Julia Goddard: Joyce Dormer's Story,* ii. 11. (*See* BIRD.)

Hu'go, in *Jerusalem Delivered,* Count of Vermandois, brother of Philippe I. of France, leader of the Franks. He died before Godfrey was appointed leader of the united armies (book i.), but his spirit was seen by Godfrey amongst the angels who came to aid in taking Jerusalem (book xviii.).

Hugo, natural son of Azo, Marquis of Estë, who fell in love with Parisi'na, his father's young wife. Azo discovered the intrigue, and condemned Hugo to be beheaded. (*Byron : Parisina.*)

Hu'gon (*King*). The great hobgoblin of France.

Hu'guenot (*U-gŭe-no*). First applied to the Reformed Church party in the Amboise Plot (1560). From the German *eidgenossen* (confederates).

Huguenot Pope (*La pape des Huguenots*). Philippe de Mornay, the great supporter of the French Protestants. (1549-1623.)

Hul'da [*the Benignant*]. Goddess of marriage and fecundity, who sent bridegrooms to maidens and children to the married. (German.) (*See* BERCHTA.)

Hulda is making her bed. It snows. (*See above.*)

Hulk. An old ship unfit for service. (Anglo-Saxon, *hulc,* from Mid. Latin *hulca,* connected with Greek ὁλκάς = a ship which is towed, a merchant ship.)

Hulking. *A great hulking fellow.* A great overgrown one. A hulk is a big, lubberly fellow, applied to Falstaff by Shakespeare. It means the body of an old ship. (*See above.*)

The monster sausage brought in on Christmas day was called a *haulkin* or *haukin.*

Hull.

"From Hull, Hell, and Halifax
Good Lord, deliver us."

This occurs in Taylor, the water poet. Hull is not the town so called, but a furious river in Kingston, very dangerous. In regard to Halifax, the allusion is to the law that the theft of goods to the value of 13d. shall subject the thief to execution " by a jyn."

Hull Cheese. Strong ale, or rather intoxicating cake, like " tipsy cake," thus described by Taylor, the water-poet : " It is much like a loafe out of a brewer's basket; it is compcsed of two simples—mault and water, . . . and is cousin-germane to the mightiest ale in England. (*See* vol. ii. of *Taylor's Works*.)

Hull'abaloo. Uproar. Irish *pullalue*, a coronach or crying together at funerals. (*See* HURLY-BURLY.)

" All this the poor ould creathure set up such a pullalue, that she brought the seven parishes about her."—*Dublin and London Magazine* (Loughleagh), 1825.

Hul'sean Lectures. Instituted by the Rev. John Hulse, of Cheshire, in 1777. Every year some four or six sermons are preached at Great St. Mary's, Cambridge, by what is now called the Hulsean Lecturer, who, till 1860, was entitled the *Christian Advocate*. Originally twenty sermons a year were preached and afterwards printed under this benefaction.

Hum and Haw (*To*). To hesitate to give a positive plain answer ; to hesitate in making a speech. To introduce *hum* and *haw* between words which ought to follow each other freely.

Hum'a (*The*). A fabulous Oriental bird which never alights, but is always on the wing. It is said that every head which it overshadows will wear a crown (*Richardson*). The splendid little bird suspended over the throne of Tippoo Saib at Seringapatam represented this poetical fancy.

In the first chapter of the *Autocrat of the Breakfast Table* a certain popular lecturer is made to describe himself, in allusion to his many wanderings, to this bird : " Yes, I am like the Huma, the bird that never lights ; being always in the cars, as the Huma is always on the wing."

Hu'man Race (*h* soft). *Father of the human race*. Adam.

Human Sacrifice. A custom still subsisting seems to prove that the Egyptians formerly sacrificed a young virgin to the god of the Nile, for they now make a statue of clay in shape of a girl, which they call the " betrothed bride," and throw it into the river. (*Savary*.)

Humanita'rians. Those who believe that Jesus Christ was only man. The disciples of St. Simon are so called

also, because they maintain the perfectibility of human nature without the aid of grace.

Human'ities or Humanity Studies. Grammar, rhetoric, and poetry, with Greek and Latin (*literæ humaniores*) ; in contradistinction to divinity (*literæ divinæ*).

" The humanities . . . is used to designate those studies which are considered the most specially adapted for training . . . true humanity in every man."—*Trench : On the Study of Words*, Lecture iii. p. 69.

Humber. Chief of the Huns, defeated by Locrin, King of England, and drowned in the river Abus, ever since called the Humber. (*Geoffrey of Monmouth : Chronicles*.)

" Their chieftain Humber naméd was aright
Unto the mighty streame him to betake,
Where he an end of battall and of life did make."
Spenser : Faërie Queene, ii. 10.

Humble Bee. A corruption of the German *hummel bee*, the buzzing bee. Sometimes called the Dumble-dor. Also Bumble-bee, from its booming drone.

Humble Cow (*A*). A cow without horns.

" ' That,' said John with a broad grin, was Grizzel chasing the humble cow out of the close."
—*Sir W. Scott : Guy Mannering*, chap. ix.

Humble Pie. *To eat humble pie*. To come down from a position you have assumed, to be obliged to take " a lower room." " Umbles " are the heart, liver, and entrails of the deer, the huntsman's perquisites. When the lord and his household dined the venison pasty was served on the daïs, but the umbles were made into a pie for the huntsman and his fellows.

N.B. Pie and patty are both diminutives of pasty. Pasty and patty are limited to venison, veal, and some few other meats ; pie is of far wider signification, including fruit, mince, etc.

Hum'bug. A correspondent in *Notes and Queries* (March 5th, 1892) suggests as the *fons et origo* of this word the Italian *Uomo bugiardo*, a lying man.

⁂ To *hum* used to signify " to applaud," " to pretend admiration," hence " to flatter," " to cajole for an end," " to deceive."

" He threatened, but behold ! 'twas all a hum."
Peter Pindar, i. 436.

" ' Gentlemen, this humming [expression of applause] is not at all becoming the gravity of this court."—*State Trials* (1660).

Hume (*David*), the historian, takes the lead among modern philosophical sceptics. His great argument is this : It is more likely that testimony should be false than that miracles should be true. (1711-1776.)

Humming Ale. Strong liquor that froths well, and causes a humming in the head of the drinker.

Hummums (in Covent Garden). So called from the Persian *humoun* (a sweating or Turkish bath).

Hu'mour. As *good humour, ill* or *bad humour*, etc. According to an ancient theory, there are four principal humours in the body: phlegm, blood, choler, and black bile. As any one of these predominates it determines the temper of the mind and body; hence the expressions sanguine, choleric, phlegmatic, and melancholic humours. A just balance made a good compound called "good humour;" a preponderance of any one of the four made a bad compound called an ill or evil humour. (See *Ben Jonson: Every Man Out of His Humour* (Prologue).

Humpback *(The)*.
Gero'nimo Amelunghi, *Il Gobo di Pisa* (sixteenth century).
Andre'a Sola'ri, the Italian painter, *Del Gobbo* (1470-1527).

Humphrey *(Master)*. The imaginary collector of the tales in *Master Humphrey's Clock*, by Charles Dickens.
The good Duke Humphrey. (*See* GOOD DUKE HUMPHREY.)
To dine with Duke Humphrey. To have no dinner to go to. Humphrey, Duke of Gloucester, son of Henry IV., was renowned for his hospitality. At death it was reported that a monument would be erected to him in St. Paul's, but his body was interred at St. Albans. When the promenaders left for dinner, the poor stay-behinds who had no dinner used to say to the gay sparks who asked if they were going, that they would stay a little longer and look for the monument of the "good duke."

To dine with Duke Humphrey in Powl's Walk.

☞ A similar locution is *To sup with Sir Thomas Gresham.* The Exchange built by Sir Thomas being a common lounge.

" Though little coin thy purseless pocket line,
  Yet with great company thou art taken up;
For often with Duke Humphrey thou dost dine,
  And often with Sir Thomas Gresham sup."
    Hayman: Quodlibet (Epigram on a Loafer), 1628.

Humpty Dumpty. An egg, a little deformed dwarf. Dumpty is a corruption of dumpy (short and thick). A *dump* is a piece of lead used in chuck-farthing. Humpty is having a hump or hunch. The two mean short, thick, and round-shouldered.

Hunchback. Styled *My Lord.* Grose says this was done in the reign of Richard III., when many deformed men were made peers; but probably the word is the Greek *lordos* (crooked).

Hundred. *Hero of the hundred fights* or *battles.*
Lord Nelson (1758-1805).
Conn, a celebrated Irish hero, is so called by O'Gnive, the bard of O'Niel:
" Conn, of the hundred fights, sleeps in thy grass-grown tomb."

Hundred. A county division mentioned in Domesday Book, and supposed to embrace ten tithings for military and constabulary purposes. If a crime was committed (such as robbery, maiming cattle, stack-burning, etc.), these sureties were bound to make it good, or bring the offender to justice.
Northumberland, Cumberland, Westmoreland, and Durham are divided into "wards" *(q.v.).*
Yorkshire, Lincolnshire, and Notts, into "wapentakes" *(q.v.).* Yorkshire has also a special division, called "ridings" *(q.v.).*
Kent is divided into five lathes, with subordinate hundreds. (*See* LATHES.)
Sussex is divided into six rapes (1 syl.), with subordinate hundreds. (*See* RAPES.)

Hundred Days. The days between March 20, 1815, when Napoleon reached the Tuileries, after his escape from Elba, and June 28, the date of the second restoration of Louis XVIII. These hundred days were noted for five things:

The additional Act to the constitutions of the empire, April 22;
The Coalition;
The Champ de Mai, June 1;
The battle of Waterloo, June 18;
The second abdication of Napoleon in favour of his son, June 22.

He left Elba February 26; landed at Cannes March 1, and at the Tuileries March 20. He signed his abdication June 22, and abdicated June 28.

The address of the Count de Chambord, the prefect, begins thus: "A hundred days, sire, have elapsed since the fatal moment when your Majesty was forced to quit your capital in the midst of tears." This is the origin of the phrase.

Hundred-eyed *(The).* Argus, in Greek and Latin fable. Juno appointed him guardian of Io [the cow], but Jupiter caused him to be put to death; whereupon Juno transplanted his eyes into the tail of her peacock.

Hundred-handed *(The).* Three of the sons of Uranus were so called, viz. Ægæon or Briareus [*Bri'-a-ruce*], Kottos, and Gygēs or Gyēs. Called in Greek

Hekatogcheiros [*hek'-ka-ton-ki'ros*]. After the war between Zeus and the Titans, when the latter were overcome and hurled into Tartarus, the Hundred-handed ones were set to keep watch and ward over them. (*See* GIANTS.)

❖ Sometimes the three-headed Cerberus is so called, because the necks were covered with snakes instead of hair.

Hundred Miles (*A*). *Not a hundred miles off.* An indirect way of saying in this very neighbourhood, or very spot. The phrase is employed when it would be indiscreet or dangerous to refer more directly to the person or place hinted at ; as, "Not a hundred miles off, there is . . ."

Hundred Years' War (*The*). The struggle between France and England, beginning in the reign of Edward III., 1337, and ending in that of Henry VI., 1453.

"Sous les règnes de Philippe VI. (de Valois), de Jean II., de Charles V., VI., et VII., en France."—*Bouillet: Dictionnaire d'Histoire*, p. 367, col. 2.

Hunga'rian. One half-starved ; intended as a pun on the word *hunger* (a dinnerless fop).

Hun'gary Water. Made of rosemary, sage, and spices ; so called because the receipt was given by a hermit to the Queen of Hungary.

Hunger seasons Food.
English :—
 "Hunger is the best sauce."
 "Hunger is good kitchen meat."
French :—
 "Il n'y a sauce que d'appétit."
 "L'appétit assaisonne tout."
Latin :—
 "Optimum condimentum fames." (*Socrates.*)
 "Optimum tibi condimentum est fames, potionis sitis." (*Cicero.*)
 "Manet hodieque vulgo tritum proverbium : Famem efficere ut crudæ etiam fabæ saccharium sapiant." (*Erasmus.*)
Italian :—
 "La fame e il miglior intingolo."
 "Appetito non vuol salsa."
The contrary : —
 "The full soul loatheth a honeycomb." (Prov. xxvii. 7.)
 "It must be a delicate dish to tempt the o'ergorged appetite."
                              (*Southey.*)
 "He who is not hungry is a fastidious eater." (*Spanish.*)
 "Plenty makes dainty."

Hungr (*hunger*). The dish out of which the goddess Hel (*q.v.*) was wont to feed.

Hungry.
Hungry as a dog. In Latin, "*Rabidus fame, ceu canis.*"
Hungry as a hawk.
Hungry as a hunter.
Hungry as a kite. In Latin, *Milvinam appententiam habēre.*" (*Plautus.*)
Hungry as a wolf. In French, "*Avoir une faim de loup.*" Another French phrase is "*Avoir un faim de diable.*"

Hungry Dogs. *Hungry dogs will eat dirty puddings.*
 "To the hungry soul every bitter thing is sweet." (Prov. xxvii. 7.)
 "When bread is wanting oaten cakes are excellent."
Latin :—
 "Jejunus raro stomachus vulgaria temnit." (*Horace.*)
French :—
 "A la faim il n'y a point de mauvais pain."
 "A ventre affamé tout est bon."
 "Ventre affamé n'a point d'oreilles."
Italian :—
 "L'asino chi a fame mangia d'ogni strame."
German :—
 "Wem kase und brod nicht schmeckt, der ist nicht hungrig."

Hunia'des, Hunniades, or **Hunyady** (4 syl.). One of the greatest captains of the fourteenth century. The Turks so much feared him that they used his name for scaring children. (1400-1456.) (*See* BOGIE.)

"The Turks employed this name to frighten their perverse children. He was corruptly denominated 'Jancus Lain.'"—*Gibbon: Decline and Fall of the Roman Empire*, xii. 166.

Hunks. *An old hunks.* A screw, a hard, selfish, mean fellow. (Icelandic, *hunskur*, sordid.)

Hunt. *Like Hunt's dog, he would neither go to church nor stay at home.* One Hunt, a labouring man in Shropshire, kept a mastiff, which, on being shut up while his master went to church, howled and barked so terribly as to disturb the whole congregation ; whereupon Hunt thought he would take his *Lycisca* with him the next Sunday, but on reaching the churchyard the dog positively refused to enter. The proverb is applied to a tricky, self-willed person, who will neither be led or driven.

Hunter. *Mr. and Mrs. Leo Hunter.* Two lion hunters, or persons who hunt up all the celebrities of London to grace their parties. (*Dickens : Pickwick Papers.*)

The mighty hunter. Nimrod is so called (Gen. x. 9). The meaning seems to be a conqueror. Jeremiah says, "I [the Lord] will send for many hunters [warriors], and they shall hunt [chase] them [the Jews] from every mountain . . . and out of the holes of the rocks" (xvi. 16).

"Proud Nimrod first the bloody chase began—
A mighty hunter, and his prey was man."
Pope: Windsor.

Hunter's Moon (*The*). The month or moon following the "harvest moon" (*q.v.*). Hunting does not begin until after harvest.

Hunters and Runners of classic renown :

ACASTOS, who took part in the famous Calydonian hunt (a wild boar).
ACTÆON, the famous huntsman who was transformed by Diana into a stag, because he chanced to see her bathing.
ADONIS, beloved by Venus, slain by a wild boar while hunting.
ADRASTOS, who was saved at the siege of Thebes by the speed of his horse Arion, given him by Hercules.
ATALANTA, who promised to marry the man who could outstrip her in running.
CAMILLA, the swiftest-footed of all the companions of Diana.
LADAS, the swiftest-footed of all the runners of Alexander the Great.
MELEA'GER, who took part in the great Calydonian boar-hunt.
ORI'ON, the great and famous hunter, changed into the Constellation, so conspicuous in November.
PHEIDIPPIDES, who ran 135 miles in two days.

Hunting of the Hare. A comic romance, published in Weber's collection. A yeoman informs the inhabitants of a village that he has seen a hare, and invites them to join him in hunting it. They attend with their curs and mastiffs, pugs and house-dogs, and the fun turns on the truly unsportsmanlike manner of giving puss the chase.

Hunting the Gowk. (*See* APRIL FOOL.)

Hunting the Snark. A child's tale by "Lewis Carroll," a pseudonym, adopted by C. Lutwidge Dodgson, author of *Alice's Adventures in Wonderland*, with its continuation, *Through the Looking-glass*, etc. (*See* SNARK.)

Hunting two Hares. *He who hunts two hares leaves one and loses the other.* No one can do well or properly two things at once. "No man can serve two masters."

French :—

"Poursuis deux lièvres, et les manques" (*La Fontaine*).

"On ne peut tirer à deux cibles."

Latin :—

"Duos qui sequitur lepores, neutrum capit."

"Simul sorbere ac flare non possum."

"Like a man to double business bound,
I stand in pause where I shall first begin, .
And both neglect."
Shakespeare: Hamlet, iii. 3.

Hunt'ingdon (called by the Saxons *Huntantun,* and in Doomsday *Hunter's dune*) appears to have derived its name from its situation in a tract of country which was anciently an extensive forest abounding with deer, and well suited for the purposes of the chase.

Huntingdon Sturgeon (*A*). An ass's foal. Pepys, in his *Diary,* tells us that during a high flood between the meadows of Huntingdon and Godmanchester something was seen floating on the water, which the Huntingdonians insisted was a sturgeon, but, being rescued, it proved to be a young donkey.

Huon de Bordeaux encounters in Syria an old follower of the family named Gerasmes (2 syl.), whom he asks the way to Babylon. Gerasmes told him the shortest and best way was through a wood sixteen leagues long, and full of fairies ; that few could go that way because King O'beron was sure to encounter them, and whoever spoke to this fay was lost for ever. If a traveller, on the other hand, refused to answer him, he raised a most horrible storm of wind and rain, and made the forest seem one great river. "But," says the vassal, "the river is a mere delusion, through which anyone can wade without wetting the soles of his shoes." Huon for a time followed the advice of Gerasmes, but afterwards addressed Oberon, who told him the history of his birth. They became great friends, and when Oberon went to Paradise he left Huon his successor as lord and king of Mommur. He married Esclairmond, and was crowned "King of all Faerie." (*Huon de Bordeaux, a romance*).

Hurdle Race (*A*). A race in which the runners have to leap over three or more hurdles, fixed in the ground at unequal distances.

Hurdy-gurdy. A stringed instrument of music, like a rude violin ; the notes of which are produced by the friction of a wheel.

Hurlo-Thrumbo. A ridiculous burlesque, which in 1730 had an extraordinary run at the Haymarket theatre. So great was its popularity that a club called "The Hurlo-Thrumbo Society" was formed. The author was Samuel Johnson, a half-mad dancing master, who put this motto on the title-page when the burlesque was printed:—

"Ye sons of fire, read my *Hurlo-Thrumbo*,
Turn it betwixt your finger and your thumbo,
And being quite undone, be quite struck
   dumbo."

Hurly-burly. Uproar, tumult, especially of battle. A reduplication of *hurly*. *Hurlu-berlu* is the French equivalent, evidently connected with *hurler*, to howl or yell. (*See* HULLABALOO.)

✸ In the *Garden of Eloquence* (1577) the word is given as a specimen of onom'atopœ'ia.

   "When the hurly-burly's done,
   When the battle's lost and won."
      The Witches, in *Macbeth* i. 1.

Hurrah', the Hebrew הָרִיעַ. Our "Old Hundredth Psalm" begins with "Shout joyfully [hurrah] to Jehovah!" The word is also of not uncommon occurrence in other psalms. See *Notes and Queries*, October 16th, 1880. (Norwegian and Danish, *hurra!*) (*See* HUZZA.)

✸ The Norman battle-cry was "Ha Rollo!" or "Ha Rou!" (French, *huzzer*, to shout aloud; Russian, *hoera* and *hoezee*.)

   "The Saxon cry of 'Out! Out, Holy Crosse!'
   rose high above the Norman sound 'of 'Ha Rou!
   Ha Rou, Notre Dame!'"—*Lord Lytton: Harold*,
   book xii. chap. 8.

✸ Wace (*Chronicle*) tells us that *Tur aie* (Thor aid) was the battle cry of the Northmen.

Hurricane (3 syl.). A large private party or rout; so called from its hurry, bustle and noise. (*See* DRUM.)

Hurry. The Mahouts 'cheer on their elephants by repeating *ur-ré*, the Arabs their camels by shouting *ar-ré*, the French their hounds by shouts of *hare*, the Germans their horses by the word *hurs*, the herdsmen of Ireland their cattle by shouting *hurrish*. (Welsh, *gyru*, to drive; Armenian, *haura*, to hasten; Latin, *curro*, to run; etc.)

Don't hurry, Hopkins. A satirical reproof to those who are not prompt in their payments. It is said that one Hopkins, of Kentucky, gave his creditor a promissory note on which was this memorandum, "The said Hopkins is not to be hurried in paying the above."

Hurry-skurry. Another ricochet word with which our language abounds. It means a confused haste, or rather, haste without waiting for the due ordering of things; pell-mell,

Hus'band is the house farmer. *Bonde* is Norwegian for a "farmer," hence *bondë-by* (a village where farmers dwell); and *hus* means "house." *Hus-band-man* is the man-of-the-house farmer. The husband, therefore, is the master farmer, and the husband-man the servant or labourer. "Husbandry" is the occupation of a farmer or husband; and a *bondman* or *bondslave* has no connection with *bond* = fetters, or the verb to *bind*. It means simply a cultivator of the soil. (*See* VILLEIN.) Old Tusser was in error when he derived the word from "houseband," as in the following distich:—

   "The name of the husband, what is it to say?
   Of wife and of *house*-hold the *band* and the
      stay."
      Five Hundred Points of Good Husbandry.

Husband's Boat (*The*). The boat which leaves London on Saturday, and takes to Margate those fathers of families who live in that neighbourhood during the summer months.

   "I shall never forget the evening when we
   went down to the jetty to see the Husbands' boat
   come in."—*The Mistletoe Bough.*

Husband's Tea. Very weak tea.

Hush-money. Money given to a person who knows a secret to keep him from mentioning it. A bribe for silence or "hushing" a matter up.

Hush'ai (2 syl.), in Dryden's satire of *Absalom and Achitophel*, is Hyde, Earl of Rochester. Hushai was David's friend, who counteracted the counsels of Achitophel, and caused the plot of Absalom to miscarry; so Rochester defeated the schemes of Shaftesbury, and brought to nought the rebellion of the Duke of Monmouth.

N.B. This was not John Wilmot, Earl of Rochester, the wit.

Hussars. Matthias Corvīnus compelled every twenty families to provide him with one horse-soldier free of all charge. This was in 1458, and in confirmation of this story we are told that *huss* is an Hungarian word meaning "twenty," and that *ar* means "pay."

✸ When Matthias Corvīnus succeeded to the crown of Hungary (1458), Mohammed III. and Frederick III. conspired to dethrone "the boy king"; but Matthias enrolled an army of Hussars, and was able to defy his enemies.

   "Item si contigerit ut aliqui predones aut
   huzarii Hungari aliquam rapinam .... intule-
   rint ...."—*A clause in a truce between the Turks
   and George Brankovich, May 21st*, 1449.

Hus'sites (2 syl.). Followers of John Huss, the Bohemian reformer, in the fourteenth century. (*See* BETHLEM-ENITES.)

Hussy. *A little hussy.* A word of slight contempt, though in some counties it seems to mean simply *girl*, as "Come hither, hussy." Of course, the word is a corruption of *housewife* or *hussif.* In Swedish *hustru* means woman in general. It is rather remarkable that *mother* in Norfolk has given rise to a similar sort of word, *morther*, as "Come hither, morther"—*i.e.* girl. Neither hussy nor morther is applied to married women. In Norfolk they also say *mor* for a female, and *bor* for the other sex. *Moer* is Dutch for woman in general, and *boer* for peasant, whence our *boor*.

Hus'terloe. A wood in Flanders, where Reynard declared his vast treasures were concealed. (*Reynard the Fox.*)

Hus'tings. House - things or city courts. London has still its *court of Hustings* in Guildhall, in which are elected the lord mayor, the aldermen, and city members. The hustings of elections are so called because, like the court of Hustings, they are the places of elective assemblies. (Anglo-Saxon, *husting*, a place of council.)

Hutchinso'nians. Followers of Anne Hutchinson, who retired to Rhode Island. Anne and fifteen of her children were subsequently murdered by the Indians (died 1643).

Hu'tin. *Louis le Hutin.* Louis X. Mazerai says he received the name because he was tongue-doughty. The *hutinet* was a mallet used by coopers which made great noise, but did not give severe blows; as we should say, the *barker* or barking dog. It is my belief that he was so named because he was sent by his father against the "Hutins," a seditious people of Navarre and Lyons. (1289, 1314-1316.)

Hutkin. A cover for a sore finger, made by cutting off the finger of an old glove. The word *hut* in this instance is from the German *huten* (to guard or protect). It is employed in the German noun *finger-hut* (a thimble to protect the finger), and in the word *huth* or *hut.* (*See* HODEKEN.)

Huzza! (Old French, *huzzer*, "to shout aloud;" German, *hussah?* (*See* HURRAH.)

Huzzy. (*See* HUSSY.)

Hvergel'mer. A boiling cauldron in Niflheim, whence issues twelve poisonous springs, which generate ice, snow, wind, and rain. (*Scandinavian mythology.*)

Hy'acinth, according to Grecian fable, was the son of Amyclas, a Spartan king. The lad was beloved by Apollo and Zephyr, and as he preferred the sun-god, Zephyr drove Apollo's quoit at his head, and killed him. The blood became a flower, and the petals are inscribed with the boy's name. (*Virgil : Eclogues,* iii. 106.)

" The hyacinth bewrays the doleful ' A I,'
And culls the tribute of Apollo's sigh.
Still on its bloom the mournful flower retains
The lovely blue that dyed the stripling's veins.'
Camoens : Lusiad, ix.

Hy'ades (3 syl.). Seven nymphs placed among the stars, in the constellation Taurus, which threaten rain when they rise with the sun. The fable is that they wept the death of their brother Hyas so bitterly, that Zeus (1 syl.), out of compassion, took them to heaven, and placed them in the constellation Taurus. (Greek, *huein,* to rain.)

Hybla. A mountain in Sicily, famous for its honey. (*See* HYMETTUS.)

Hy'dra. A monster of the Ler'nean marshes, in Ar'golis. It had nine heads, and Hercules was sent to kill it. As soon as he struck off one of its heads, two shot up in its place.

Hydra-headed. Having as many heads as the hydra (*q.v.*) ; a difficulty which goes on increasing as it is combated.

Hydra-headed multitude. The rabble, which not only is many-headed numerically, but seems to grow more numerous the more it is attacked and resisted.

Hye'nas were worshipped by the ancient Egyptians. Pliny says that a certain stone, called the "hyænia," found in the eye of the creature, being placed under the tongue, imparts the gift of prophecy (xxxvii. 60).

Hygeia (3 syl.). Goddess of health and the daughter of Æsculapios. Her symbol was a serpent drinking from a cup in her hand.

Hyksos. A tribe of Cuthites (2 syl.), driven out of Assyria by Ara'lius and the Shemites. They founded in Egypt a dynasty called Hyksos (shepherd kings), a title assumed by all the Cuthite chiefs. This dynasty, which gave Egypt six or eight kings, lasted 259 years, when the whole horde was driven from Egypt, and retired to Palestine. It is from these refugees that the lords of the Philistines arose. The word is compounded of *hyk* (king) and *sós* (shepherd).

Hyl'as. A boy beloved by Hercules, carried off by the nymphs while drawing water from a fountain in Mys'ia.

Hylech (in Astrology). That planet, or point of the sky, which dominates at man's birth, and influences his whole life.

Hy'men. God of marriage, a sort of overgrown Cupid. His symbols are a bridal-torch and veil in his hand.

Hy'mer. The giant in Celtic mythology who took Thor in his boat when that god went to kill the serpent; for which service he was flung by the ears into the sea. (*See* GIANTS.)

Hymettus. A mountain in Attica, famous for its honey. (*See* HYBLA.)

Hymn Tunes.
"The Heavens are Telling." (From *Haydn's Creation.*)
"Marching to Glory." The tune of *Marching to Georgia.*
"Onward, Christian Soldiers." *One of Haydn's Symphonies.*
"Lo! He comes with clouds descending." The tune of a *hornpipe* danced at Saddler's Wells in the eighteenth century. (*Helmsley.*)
"There is a Happy Land." *An Indian air.*
"The Land of the Leal." *Scots wha hae wi' Wallace bled.*
"Brightest and best of the Sons of the Morning." *Mendelssohn's Lieder No. 9.*
"Sweet the Moments." *The first sixteen bars of Beethoven's Piano Sonata, Op. 26.*

Hymnus Eucharis'ticus. Sung as the clock strikes 5 a.m. by Magdalen choir on the summit of Wolsey's Tower (Oxford) on May morning to greet the rising sun. Some say the custom dates from the reign of Henry VIII.; if this overshoots the mark, no one knows for certainty a more exact period.

"Te Deum Patrem colïmus,
Te laudibus prosequimur ;
Qui corpus ciborificis,
Cœlesti mentem gratia."
Hymnus Eucharisticus.

Hyperbo'reans (5 syl.). The most northern people, who dwell *beyond* Bo'reas (the seat of the north wind), placed by Virgil under the North Pole. They are said to be the oldest of the human race, the most virtuous, and the most happy; to dwell for some thousand years under a cloudless sky, in fields yielding double harvests, and in the enjoyment of perpetual spring. When sated of life they crown their heads with flowers, and plunge headlong from the mountain Hunneberg or Halleberg into the sea, and enter at once the paradise of Odin. (*Scandinavian mythology.*)

The *Hyperbo'reans,* it is said, have not an atmosphere like our own, but one consisting wholly of feathers. Both Herod'otos and Pliny mention this fiction, which they say was suggested by the quantity of snow observed to fall in those regions. (*Herodotos,* iv. 31.)

Hyper'ion. Properly, the father of the Sun and Moon, but by poets made a surname of the Sun. Shakespeare makes it a synonym of Apollo. The proper pronunciation is Hyperi'on. Thus Ovid—

"Placat equo Persis radiis Hyperiŏne cinctum."
Fasti, i. 385.
"So excellent a king, that was to this
Hyper'ion to a satyr."
Shakespeare: Hamlet, i. 9.

Hypermnestra'. Wife of Lynceus (2 syl.), and the only one of the fifty daughters of Danäos who did not murder her husband on their bridal night.

Hypnotism. The art of producing trance-sleep, or hypno'sis; or the state of being hypnotised. (Greek, *hupnos,* sleep.)

"The method, discovered by Mr. Braid, of producing this state . . . appropriately designated . . . hypnotism, consists in the maintenance of a fixed gaze for several minutes . . . on a bright object placed somewhat above [the line of sight], at so short a distance [as to produce pain]."—
Carpenter: Principles of Mental Physiology, book ii. chap. i. p. 65.

Hypochon'dria (Greek, *hypo chondros,* under the cartilage)—*i.e.* the spaces on each side of the epigastric region, supposed to be the seat of melancholy as a disease.

Hypoc'risy. *L'hypoorisio oot un hommage que le vice rend à la vertu.* (*Rochefoucauld.*)

Hyp'ocrite (3 syl.). *Prince of hypocrites.* Tibe'rius Cæsar was so called, because he affected a great regard for decency, but indulged in the most detestable lust and cruelty (B.C. 42, 14 to A.D. 37).

Abdallah Ibn Obba and his partisans were called *The Hypocrites* by Mahomet, because they feigned to be friends, but were in reality disguised foes.

Hyp'ocrites' Isle, called by Rabelais *Chaneph,* which is the Hebrew for "hypocrisy." Rabelais says it is wholly inhabited by sham saints, spiritual comedians, bead-tumblers, mumblers of avemari'as, and such like sorry rogues, who lived on the alms of passengers, like the

21

hermit of Lormont. (*Pantagruel*, iv. 63.)

Hyposta'tic Union. The union of two or more persons into one undivided unity, as, for example, the three persons of the eternal Godhead. The Greek *hypos'tasis* corresponds to the Latin *per-so'na*. The *three persons of the God* and *three hypos'tases of the Godhead* mean one and the same thing.

"We do not find, indeed, that the hypostatic pre-existence of Christ was an article of their creed [*i.e.* of the Nazarenes]."—*Fisher: Supernatural Origin of Christianity*, essay v. p. 319.

Hypped [*hipt*]. Melancholy, low-spirited. Hyp. is a contraction of *hypochondria.*

Hy'son. One of the varieties of green tea. "*Ainsi nommé d'un mot chinois qui veut dire* printemps, *parce que c'est au commencement de cette saison qu'on le cueille.*" (*M. N. Bouillet.*)

Hyssop. David says (Ps. li. 7): "Purge me with hyssop, and I shall be clean." The reference is to the custom of someone who was ceremonially "clean" sprinkling the unclean (when they came to present themselves in the Temple) with a bunch of hyssop dipped in water, in which had been mixed the ashes of a red heifer. This was done as they left the Court of the Gentiles to enter the Court of the women (Numbers xix. 17).

Hys'teron Prot'eron (Greek). The cart before the horse.

I

I. This letter represents a finger, and is called in Hebrew *yod* or *jod* (a hand).

I *per se* [I by itself], *i.e.* without compeer, pre-eminently so.

"If then your I [yes] agreement want,
  I to your I [yes] must answer, 'No.'
Therefore leave off your spelling plea,
  And let your I [yes] be I per se."
i.e. let your yes be yes decidedly.
         Wits Interpreter, p. 116.

❊ Many other letters are similarly used; as, *A per se.* (*See* A-PER-SE.) Thus in *Restituta* Eliza is called "The *E per se* of all that ere hath been." So again, "O," signifies a crier, from "O yes! O yes!" We have "Villanies descovered by . . . the help of a new crier, called O per se [*i.e.* superior to his predecessors]." 1666.

Shakespeare, in *Troilus and Cressida*, i. 2, even uses the phrase "a very man per se"=A 1.

I.H.S.—*i.e.* the Greek IHΣ, meaning IHΣοῦς (Jesus), the long e (H) being mistaken for a capital H, and the dash perverted into a cross. The letters being thus obtained, St. Bernardine of Siena, in 1347, hit upon the Latin anagram, *Jesus Hom'inum Salvator*. In Greek, Iησουε Ἡμετερος Σωτηρ. In German, *Jesus Heiland Seligmacher*. In English, *Jesus Heavenly Saviour*.

I.H.S. A notarica of Japheth, Ham, Seth, the three sons of Noah, by whom the world was peopled after the Flood.

I.H.S. "*In hac salus*"—*i.e.* "*Hac cruce.*"

I.O.U. The memorandum of a debt given by the borrower to the lender. It must not contain a promise to pay. The letters mean, "I owe You."

An I.O.U. requires no stamp, unless it specifies a day of payment, when it becomes a *bill*, and must have a stamp.

I.R.B. Irish Republican Brotherhood, meaning the Fenian conspiracy.

Iach'imo [*Yak-e-mo*]. An Italian libertine in Shakespeare's *Cymbeline*.

Iago [*Ya'go* or *E-a'-go*]. Othello's ensign or ancient. He hated the Moor both because Cassio, a Florentine, was preferred to the lieutenancy instead of himself, and also from a suspicion that the Moor had tampered with his wife; but he concealed his hatred so well that Othello wholly trusted him. Iago persuaded Othello that Desdemo'na intrigued with Cassio, and urged him on till he murdered his bride. His chief argument was that Desdemona had given Cassio a pocket-handkerchief, the fact being that Iago had set on his wife to purloin it. After the death of Desdemona, Emilia (Iago's wife) revealed the fact, and Iago was arrested.

Shakespeare generally makes three syllables of the name, as—

"Let it not gall your patience, good I-a-go. ⎫
Left in the conduct of the bold I-a-go. ⎬ii. 1.
'Tis one I-a-go, ancient to the genera!." ⎭

Iam'bic. *Father of Iambic verse.* Archil'ochos of Paros (B.C. 714-676).

Ian'the (3 syl.), to whom Lord Byron dedicated his *Childe Harolde*, was Lady Charlotte Harley, born 1809, and only eleven years old at the time.

Iap'etos. The father of Atlas and ancestor of the human race, called *genus Iăp'eti*, the progeny of Iapetus (Greek and Latin mythology). By many considered the same as Japheth, one of the sons of Noah.

Ibe'ria. Spain; the country of the Ibe'rus or Ebro. (See *Rowe: On the Late Glorious Successes.*)

Ibe'ria's Pilot. Christopher Columbus. Spain is called "Iberia," and the Spaniards the "Ibēri." The river *Ebro* is a corrupt form of the Latin *Ibērus.*

" Launched with Iberia's pilot from the steep,
To worlds unknown, and isles beyond the deep."
Campbell: The Pleasures of Hope, ii.

Ibid. A contraction of *ibidem* (Lat.), in the same place.

I'bis or *Nile-bird.* The Egyptians call the sacred Ibis *Father John.* It is the avatar' of the god Thoth, who in the guise of an Ibis escaped the pursuit of Typhon. The Egyptians say its white plumage symbolises the light of the sun, and its black neck the shadow of the moon, its body a heart, and its legs a triangle. It was said to drink only the purest of water, and its feathers to scare or even kill the crocodile. It is also said that the bird is so fond of Egypt that it would pine to death if transported elsewhere. It appears at the rise of the Nile, but disappears at its inundation. If, indeed, it devours crocodiles' eggs, scares away the crocodiles themselves, devours serpents and all sorts of noxious reptiles and insects, no wonder it should be held in veneration, and that it is made a crime to kill it. (*See* BIRDS.)

Ibis. The Nile-bird, says Solīnus, "rummages in the mud of the Nile for serpents' eggs, her most favourite food."

Iblis or *Eblis.* The Lucifer of Mozlem theology. Once called Azazel (prince of the apostate angels). (*See* EBLIS.) He has five sons :—

(1) *Tir,* author of fatal accidents ; (2) *Awar,* the demon of lubricity ; (3) *Dásim,* author of discord ; (4) *Sût,* father of lies ; and (5) *Zalambúr,* author of mercantile dishonesty.

Ib'raham. The Abraham of the Koran.

Icar'ian. Soaring, adventurous. (*See* ICAROS.) Also a follower of Cabet, the Communist, a native of Icaria (last half of the nineteenth century).

Ic'aros. Son of Dæ'dalos, who flew with his father from Crete ; but the sun melted the wax with which his wings were fastened on, and he fell into the sea, hence called the Ica'rian. (See *Shakespeare: 3 Henry VI., v. 6.*)

Ice (1 syl.). *To break the ice.* To broach a disagreeable subject ; to open the way. In allusion to breaking ice for bathers. (Latin, *scin'dere glaciem ;*

Italian, *romper il giaccio.*) (Anglo-Saxon, *îs.*)

" [We] An' if you break the ice, and do this feat ....
Will not so graceless be, to be ingrate."
Shakespeare: Taming of the Shrew, i. 2.

Ice-blink (*The*). An indication of pack-ice or of a frozen surface by its reflection on the clouds. If the sky is dark or brown, the navigator may be sure that there is water ; if it is white, rosy, or orange-coloured, he may be certain there is ice, for these tints are reflected from the sun's rays, or of light. The former is called a "water sky," the latter an " ice sky."

Ice-brook. *A sword of ice-brook temper.* Of the very best quality. The Spaniards used to plunge their swords and other weapons, while hot from the forge, into the brook Salo [Xalon], near Bilbilis, in Celtiberia, to harden them. The water of this brook is very cold.

" It is a sword of Spain, the ice-brook temper."
Shakespeare : Othello, v. 2.

" Sævo Bilbilin op'timam metallo
Et ferro Plat'eam suo sonantem
Quam fluctu tenui sed inquie'to
Armo'rum Salo tempera'tor ambit."
Martial.

Ice Saints or *Frost Saints.* Those saints whose days fall in what is called " the black-thorn winter "—that is, the second week in May (between 11 and 14). Some give only three days, but whether 11, 12, 13 or 12, 13, 14 is not agreed. May 11th is the day of St. Mamertus, May 12th of St. Pancratius, May 13th of St. Servatius, and May 14th of St. Boniface.

"Ces saincts passent pour saincts gresleurs, geleurs, et gateurs du bourgeon."—*Rabelais.*

Iceberg. A hill of ice, either floating in the ocean, or aground. The magnitude of some icebergs is very great. One seen off the Cape of Good Hope was two miles in circumference, and a hundred and fifty feet high. For every cubic foot above water there must be at least eight feet below.

Iceland Dogs. Shaggy white dogs, once great favourites with ladies. Shakespeare mentions them (*Henry V.*, ii. 1).

" Use and custome hath intatained . . . Iceland dogges curled and rough all over, which, by reason of the length of their heire make showe neither of face nor of body." — *Fleming: Of English Dogges* (1576).

Ich Dien. According to a Welsh tradition, Edward I. promised to provide Wales with a prince "who could speak no word of English," and when his son Edward of Carnarvon was born he presented him to the assembly, saying in Welsh *Eich dyn* (behold the man).

The more general belief is that it was the motto under the plume of John, King of Bohemia, slain by the Black Prince at Cressy in 1346, and that the Black Prince who slew the Bohemian assumed it out of modesty, to indicate that "he served under the king his father."

Ichneu'mon. An animal resembling a weasel, and well worthy of being defended by priest and prince in Egypt, as it feeds on serpents, mice, and other vermin, and is especially fond of crocodiles' eggs, which it scratches out of the sand. According to legend, it steals into the mouths of crocodiles when they gape, and eats out their bowels. The ichneumon is called "Pharaoh's rat."

Ichor (*I'-kor*). The colourless blood of the heathen deities. (Greek, *ichor*, juice.)

Ichthus for *Ie'sous, CHristos, THeou Uios, Soter*. This notarica is found on many seals, rings, urns, and tombstones, belonging to the early times of Christianity, and was supposed to be a "charm" of mystical efficacy.

Icon Basil'ike (4 syl.). Portraiture of King Charles I.

"The εἰκὼν, or Portraiture of hys Majesty in hys solitudes and sufferings . . . was wholly and only my invention."—*Gauden: Letter to Clarendon.*

Icon'oclasts (Greek, "image breakers"). Reformers who rose in the eighth century, especially averse to the employment of pictures, statues, emblems, and all visible representations of sacred objects. The crusade against these things began in 726 with the Emperor Leo III., and continued for one hundred and twenty years. (Greek, *ikon*, an image; *klao*, I break.)

"The eighth century, the age of the Iconoclasts, had not been favourable to literature."—*Isaac Taylor: The Alphabet*, vol. ii. chap. viii. p. 159.

Idæ'an Mother. Cyb'ele, who had a temple on Mount Ida, in Asia Minor.

Idealism. The doctrines taught by Idealists.

Subjective idealism, taught by Fechte (2 syl.), supposes the object (say a tree) and the image of it on the mind is all one. Or rather, that there is no object outside the mental idea.

Objective idealism, taught by Schelling, supposes that the tree and the image thereof on the mind are distinct from each other.

Absolute idealism, taught by Hegel, supposes there is no such thing as phenomena; that mind, through the senses, creates its own world. In fact, that there is no real, but all is mere ideal.

These are three German philosophers:
Hegel (1770-1831).
Schelling (1770-1854).
Fechte (1762-1814).

Ide'alists. Those who believe in idealism. They may be divided into two distinct sections—

(1) Those who follow Plato, who taught that before creation there existed certain types or ideal models, of which *ideas* created objects are the visible images. Malebranche, Kant, Schelling, Hegel, etc., were of this school.

(2) Those who maintain that all phenomena are only subjective—that is, mental cognisances only within ourselves, and what we see and what we hear are only brain impressions. Of this school were Berkeley, Hume, Fichte, and many others.

I'des (1 syl.). In the Roman calendar the 15th of March, May, July, and October, and the 13th of all the other months. (Latin and Etruscan, *iduâre*, to divide. The middle of the month. Always eight days after the Nones.)

"Remember March ; the ides of March remember."   *Shakespeare: Julius Cæsar*, iv. 3.

Id'iom. A mode of expression peculiar to a language, as a Latin idiom, a French idiom. (Greek, *id'ios*, peculiar to oneself.)

Id'iosyncrasy. A crotchet or peculiar one-sided view of a subject, a monomania. Properly a peculiar effect produced by medicines or foods; as when coffee acts as an aperient; the electrical current as an emetic, as it does upon me. (Greek, *idios sun krasis*, something peculiar to a person's temperament.)

Id'iot meant originally a private person, one not engaged in any public office. Hence Jeremy Taylor says, "Humility is a duty in great ones, as well as in idiots" (private persons). The Greeks have the expressions, "a priest or an idiot" (layman), "a poet or an idiot" (prose-writer). As idiots were not employed in public offices, the term became synonymous with incompetency to fulfil the duties thereof. (Greek, *idio'tēs*.) (*See* BARON.)

I'dle Lake. The lake on which Phædria or Wantonness cruised in her gondola. It led to Wandering Island. (*Spenser : Faërie Queene*, book ii.)

Idle Wheel. The middle of three wheels, which simply conveys the motion of one outside wheel to the other outside wheel.

Suppose A, B, C to be three wheels, B being the idle or gear wheel. B simply conveys the motion of A to C, or of C to A.

I'dle Worms. It was once supposed that little worms were bred in the fingers of idle servants. To this Shakespeare alludes—

> "A round little worm
> Pricked from the lazy finger of a maid."
> *Shakespeare: Romeo and Juliet,* i. 4.

I'dleness. *The Lake of Idleness.* Spenser says whoever drank of this lake grew "instantly faint and weary." The Red Cross Knight drank of it, and was made captive by Orgoglio. (*Spenser: Faërie Queene,* book i.)

Idol Shepherd (*The*), Zech. ii. 17. "Woe to the idol shepherd that leaveth his flock." Idol shepherd means self-seeking, counterfeit, pseudo; the shepherd that sets up himself to be worshipped by his people instead of God.

Idom'eneus (4 syl.). King of Crete, and ally of the Greeks in the siege of Troy. After the city was burnt he made a vow to sacrifice whatever he first encountered, if the gods granted him a safe return to his kingdom. It was his own son that he first met, and when he offered him up to fulfil his vow he was banished from Crete as a murderer. (*Homer: Iliad.*)

Compare the story of Jephthah in Judges xi.

Idun'a or **Idun'.** Daughter of the dwarf Svald, and wife of Bragi. She kept in a box the golden apples which the gods tasted as often as they wished to renew their youth. Loki on one occasion stole the box and hid it in a wood; but the gods compelled him to restore it. (*Scandinavian mythology.*)

❧ Iduna seems to personify the year between March and September, when the sun is north of the equator. Her apples indicate fruits generally. Loki carries her off to Giant-Land, when the Sun descends below the equator, and he steals her apples. In time, Iduna makes her escape, in the form of a sparrow, when the Sun again, in March, rises above the equator; and both gods and men rejoice in her return.

Ifa'kins. A corruption of *In good faith.* I' fa' kin, where *kin* is equivalent to *dear* or *good.*

Ifreet or *Afreet* or *Afrit.* A powerful evil jin or spirit of Arabian mythology. (*See* AFRIET.)

If'urin. The Hadēs of the ancient Gauls. A dark region infested by serpents and savage beasts. Here the wicked are chained in loathsome caverns, plunged into the lairs of dragons, or subjected to a ceaseless distillation of poison. (*Celtic mythology.*)

Iger'na, Igerne, or **Igrayne.** Wife of Gorloïs, Duke of Tintag'el, in Cornwall, and mother of King Arthur. His father was Uther, pendragon of the Britons, who married Igerna thirteen days after her husband was slain.

Igna'ro. Foster-father of Orgoglio. Whatever question Arthur asked, the old dotard answered, "He could not tell." Spenser says this old man walks one way and looks another, because ignorance is always "wrong-headed." (*Spenser: Faërie Queene,* book i.)

❧ (*See* NON MI RECORDO.)

Igna'tius (*St.*) is represented in Christian art accompanied by lions, or chained and exposed to them, in allusion to his martyrdom. The legend is that he was brought before the Emperor Trajan, who condemned him to be made the food of lions and other wild beasts for the delectation of the people. According to tradition, St. Ignatius was the little child whom our Saviour set in the midst of His disciples for their example. (About 29–115.)

Brother Ignatius. The Rev. James Leycester Lyne, for some time head of the English Benedictines at the Norwich Protestant monastery. Now at Llanthony.

Father Ignatius. The Hon. and Rev. Geo. Spencer, formerly a clergyman of the Church of England, who joined the Roman communion, and became Superior of the order of Passionists. (1799–1864.)

Ignatius Loy'ola, founder of the order of Jesuits, is depicted in art sometimes with the sacred monogram I.H.S. on his breast, and sometimes as contemplating it, surrounded by glory in the skies, in allusion to his boast that he had a miraculous knowledge of the mystery of the Trinity vouchsafed to him. He is so represented in Rubens' famous picture in Warwick Castle.

Ig'neous Rocks. Those which have been produced by the agency of fire, as the granitic, the trappean, and the volcanic. (Latin, *ignis,* fire.)

Ignis Fat'uus means strictly a fatuous fire; it is also called "*Jack o'*

Lantern," "*Spunkie,*" "*Walking Fire,*" "*Will o' the Wisp,*" and "*Fair Maid of Ireland.*" Milton calls it *Friar's Lanthern,* and Sir Walter Scott *Friar Rush with a lantern.* Morally speaking, a Uto'pian scheme, no more reducible to practice than the meteor so called can be turned to any useful end. (Plural, *Ignes fatŭi.*) (*See* FRIAR'S LANTHORN.)

"When thou rannest up Gadshill in the night to catch my horse, if I did not think thou hadst been an *ignis fatuus* or a ball of wildfire, there's no purchase in money."—*Shakespeare :* 1 *Henry IV.,* iii. 3.

✢ According to a Russian superstition, these wandering fires are the spirits of still-born children which flit between heaven and the Inferno.

Ignora'mus. One who ignores the knowledge of something ; one really unacquainted with it. It is an ancient law term. The grand jury used to write *Ignoramus* on the back of indictments "not found" or not to be sent into court. Hence *ignore.* The present custom is to write "No true bill."

Ignoramus Jury (*An*). The Grand Jury. (*See above.*)

Ignoran'tines (4 syl.). A religious association founded by the Abbé de la Salle in 1724, for educating gratuitously the children of the poor.

Igrayne. (*See* IGERNA.)

Ihram. The white cotton dress worn by Mohammedan pilgrims to Mecca, For *men,* two scarfs, without seams or ornament of any kind, of any material except silk ; one scarf is folded round the loins, and the other is thrown over the neck and shoulders, leaving the right arm free ; the head is uncovered. For *women,* an ample cloak, enveloping the whole person.

Il Pastor Fi'do [*the Faithful Swain*]. This standard of elegant pastoral composition is by Giovanni Battista Guari'ni, of Ferrara (1537-1612).

Il'iad (3 syl.). The tale of the siege of Troy, an epic poem by Homer, in twenty-four books. Men'ela'os, King of Sparta, received as his guest Paris, a son of Priam (King of Troy), who ran away with Helen, his hostess. Men'ela'os induced the Greeks to lay siege to Troy to avenge the perfidy, and the siege lasted ten years. The poem begins in the tenth year with a quarrel between Agamemnon, commander-in-chief of the allied Greeks, and Achilles, the hero who retired from the army in ill-temper. The Trojans

now prevail, and Achilles sends his friend Patroc'los to oppose them, but Patroclos is slain. Achilles, in a desperate rage, rushes into the battle, and slays Hector, the commander of the Trojan army. The poem ends with the funeral rites of Hector. (Greek, *Ilias,* genitive, *Iliad[os]*, the land of Ilium. It is an adjective, and the word means, "a poem about the land of Ilium.")

✢ Probably "Æneid" is the genitive of Æneas, *Ænēados,* and means a poem about *Ænēas.* (*See* ÆNEID for another derivation.)

Wolf, Herne, and our own Grote, believed the *Iliad* to be the work of several poets. R. W. Browne says :—
"No doubt was ever entertained by the ancients respecting the personality of Homer. Pindar, Plato, Aristotle, and others, all assumed this fact ; nor did they even doubt that the *Iliad* and *Odyssey* were the work of one mind."—*Historical Classical Literature,* book i. chap. iv. p. 59.

The "Iliad" in a nutshell. Pliny (vii. 21) tells us that the *Iliad* was copied in so small a hand that the whole work could lie in a walnut-shell. Pliny's authority is Cicero (*Apud Gellium,* ix. 421). Huet, Bishop of Avranches, demonstrated the possibility of this achievement by writing eighty verses of the *Iliad* on a single line of a page similar to this "Dictionary." This would be 19,000 verses to the page, or 2,000 more than the *Iliad* contains.

✢ In the Harleian MSS. (530) we have an account of Peter Bales, an Englishman, clerk of the Court of Chancery in the reign of Queen Elizabeth, under date of 1590, who wrote out the whole Bible so small that he inclosed it in a walnut shell of English growth. (*See* NUTSHELL.)

"Whilst they (as Homer's *Iliad* in a nut)
A world of wonders in one closet shut."
On the Monumental stone of the Tradescants in Lambeth Churchyard.

The French Iliad. The Romance of the Rose, begun by Guillaume di Lorris in the latter half of the thirteenth century, and continued by Jean de Meung in the early part of the fourteenth. The poem is supposed to be a dream. The poet in his dream is accosted by Dame Idleness, who conducts him to the Palace of Pleasure, where he meets Love, accompanied by Sweet-looks, Riches, Jollity, Courtesy, Liberality, and Youth, who spend their time in dancing, singing, and other amusements. By this retinue the poet is conducted to a bed of roses, where he singles out one and attempts to pluck it, when an arrow from Cupid's bow stretches him fainting on the ground, and he is carried far away from the flower of his choice. As soon as he recovers, he finds himself alone, and resolves to return to his rose. Welcome goes with him; but Danger, Shame-face, Fear, and Slander obstruct him at every turn. Reason advises him to abandon the pursuit, but this he will not do; whereupon Pity and Liberality aid him in reaching the rose of his choice, and Venus permits him to touch it with his lips. Meanwhile, Slander rouses up Jealousy, who seizes Welcome, whom he casts into a strong castle, and gives the key of the castle door to an old hag. Here the poet is left to mourn over his fate, and the original poem ends. Meung added 18,000 lines as a sequel.

The German Iliad. The Nibelungen-lied, put into its present form in 1210 by a wandering minstrel of Austria. It consists of twenty parts. (*See* NIBE-LUNG.)

The Portuguese Iliad. The Lusiad (*q.v.*), by Camoens.

The Scotch Iliad. The Epigo'niad, by William Wilkie, called *The Scottish Homer* (1721-1772). The *Epigo'niad* is the tale of the Epig'oni, or seven Grecian heroes who laid siege to Thebes. When Œ'dipos abdicated, his two sons agreed to reign alternate years; but at the expiration of the first year, the elder son, named Etē'oclēs, refused to give up the throne, whereupon Polynīkēs, the younger brother, induced six chiefs to espouse his cause. The allied army laid siege to Thebes, but without success. Subsequently, seven sons of the chiefs resolved to avenge their fathers' deaths, marched against the city, took it, and placed Terpander, one of their number, on the throne. The Greek tragic poets Æ'schylus and Eurip'idēs have drama-tised this subject.

Il'iad of Ills (*An*). *Il'ias malo'rum* (*Cicero: Ad Atticum,* viii. 11). A number of evils falling simultaneously; there is scarce a calamity in the whole catalogue of human ills that finds not mention in the *Iliad,* hence the Homeric poem was the fountain of classic tragedy.

Ilk. The surname of the person spoken of is the same as the name of his estate. It is quite a mistake to use the phrase "All that ilk" to signify all of that name or sort. *Bethune of that ilk* means "Bethune of Bethune." (Gaelic, *ilk,* clan; Anglo-Saxon, *ilc,* the same.)

Ill-got, Ill-spent. Treasures of wickedness profit nothing. (Prov. x. 2.)

Ill May-day. The 1st of May, 1517, when the London apprentices rose up against the resident foreigners, and did great mischief. More commonly known as *Evil* May-day (*q.v.*).

Ill Omens averted.

Leotych'idēs II., of Sparta, was told by his augurs that his projected expedition would fail, because a viper had got entangled in the handle of the city key. "Not so," he replied. "The key caught the viper."

When Julius Cæsar landed at Adrume'-tum, in Africa, he happened to trip and fall on his face. This would have been considered a fatal omen by his army; but, with admirable presence of mind, he exclaimed, "Thus I take possession of thee, O Africa!" Told of Scipio also.

When William the Conqueror leaped upon the shore at Bulverhythe he fell on his face, and a great cry went forth that it was an ill-omen; but the duke exclaimed, "I have taken seisin of this land with both my hands."

When the Duke was arming for the battle, his squire by accident handed him the *back* piece before the breast-plate, an evil omen, signifying flight. But the Duke, with ready wit, said, "Yes, the last shall be first"—*i.e.* the duke shall be king.

Napoleon III. did a graceful thing to avert an ill omen. Captain Jean Cœur-preux, in a ball given at the Tuileries, tripped and fell; but Napoleon held out his hand to help him up, saying as he did so, "Monsieur le Command-ant, this is the second time I have seen you fall. The first time was by my side in the field of Magenta." Then, turning to the lady, he added, "Henceforth Captain Cœurpreux is commandant of my Guides."

Ill-starred. Unlucky; fated to be unfortunate. Othello says of Desde-mona, "O ill-starred wench!" Of course, the allusion is to the astrological dogma that the stars influence the fortunes of mankind.

"Where'er that ill-starred home may lie."
     Moore: Fire Worshippers.

Ill Wind. *'Tis an ill wind that blows nobody any good.* Someone profits by every loss; someone is benefited by every misfortune.

"Except wind stands as never it stood,
  It is an ill-wind turns none to good."
*Tusser: Five Hundred Points of Good
               Husbandry,* xiii.

Illinois, U.S. America. The Dela-ware Indian word *illini* (real men) with the French termination *-ois.*

Illumina'ted Doctor. Raymond Lully (1235-1315).

John Tauler, the German mystic (1294-1361).

Illumina'ti. The baptised were at one time so called, because a lighted candle was given them to hold as a symbol that they were illuminated by the Holy Ghost.

Four religious societies have been so called, viz. :

(1) The Hesychasts in the fourteenth century.

(2) The Alombra'dos of Spain in the sixteenth century.

(3) The Guerinets of France in the seventeenth century.

(4) The Mystics of Belgium in the eighteenth century.

Add to these the Rosicrucians (*q.v.*).

The Order of the Illuminati. A republican society, founded at Ingoldstadt in Bavaria, 1776; having for its object the establishment of a religion consistent with " sound reason."

Illuminations. Characteristics of Anglo-Saxon illuminations from the eighth to the eleventh century. Extreme intricacy of pattern.

Interlacings of knots in a diagonal or square form, sometimes interwoven with animals and terminating with heads of serpents or birds. (*Sir F. Madden.*)

The *Durham Book*, the work of Eadfrid, Bishop of Lindisfarne, who died 721, is a most splendid specimen of illumination.

The *Benedictional of St. Ethelwold*, an illuminated MS. by Godemann, in the Duke of Devonshire's library, is worthy of Raphael or Michael Angelo. It was executed between 963 and 984, and is full of miniatures and designs in the highest style of art. Beautiful engravings of it may be seen in the *Archæologia.*

Illuminator. Gregory, the apostle of Christianity among the Armenians (257-331).

Illustrious (*The*).

Albert V., Duke and second Emperor of Austria (1398-1439).

Nicome'des II. *Epiph'anĕs* (149-191).

Ptolemy V. *Epiph'anĕs* (210, 205-181 B.C.).

Jam-sheid (Jam *the Illustrious*), nephew of Tah Omurs, fifth king of the Paisdadian dynasty of Persia (B.C. 840-800).

Kien-lông, fourth of the Manchoo dynasty of China (1736-1796).

Image of God. *Wear not the image of God in a ring.* This is the twenty-fourth symbolic saying in the Protreptics of Iamblichus, and is tantamount to the commandment " Thou shalt not take the name of God in vain." Pythagoras meant to teach his disciples by this restriction that God was far too holy a being to be used as a mere ornamental device, and engraved on a ring worn on a man's finger, which might be used for any ordinary purpose.

" In annulo Dei figuram ne gestato."

Images which fell from Heaven. Diana of Ephesus (Acts xix. 35). The same is said of the image of Cybĕle (3 syl.), set up in the temple of Victory, at Rome.

Im'aum (2 syl.) or **Imam.** One of the Ule'ma or priestly body of the Mahometans. He recites the prayers and leads the devotions of the congregation. Im'aums wear a high turban. The sultan as " head of the Moslems " is an Imaum. The word means *teacher* or *guide.*

Ima'us (3 syl.). The Him'alay'a. The word means *snow* hills (*hima,* snow).

" The huge incumbrance of horrific woods
From Asian Taurus, from Imaus stretched
Athwart the roving Tartar's sullen bounds."
Thomson: Autumn.

Im'becile (3 syl.). One mentally weak. Literally, one who leans " on a stick." (Latin, *imbecillis,* from *in-bacillum.*)

Imbroca'do (Spanish). Cloth of gold or silver.

Imbroca'ta, in fencing, is a thrust over the arm. (Italian.)

" If your enemie bee cunning and skilfull, never stand about giving any foine or imbrocata, but this thrust or stoccata alone, neither it also [never attempt] unlesse you be sure to hit him."—*Saviolo : Practise of the Duello* (1595).

Imbro'glio (Italian). A complicated plot; a misunderstanding between nations and persons of a complicated nature.

Immac'ulate Conception. The dogma that the Virgin Mary was conceived without Original sin. This dogma was first broached by St. Bernard, and was stoutly maintained by Duns Scotus and his disciples, but was not received by the Roman Catholic Church as an article of faith till 1854.

Im'molate (3 syl.). To sacrifice; literally, "put meal on one." The reference is to the ancient custom of sprinkling meal and salt on the head of

a victim to be offered in sacrifice. (Latin, *in-molo*.)

"In the picture of the immolation of Isaac, or Abraham sacrificing his son, Isaac is described as a little boy."—*Brown*.

Immor'tal (*The*). Yông - Tching, third of the Manchoo dynasty of China, assumed the title. (1723-1736.)

Immortal Four of Italy (*The*).
Dante (1265-1321).
Petrarch (1301-1374).
Ariosto (1474-1533), and
Tasso (1544-1595).

"The poets read he o'er and o'er,
And most of all the immortal four
Of Italy." *Longfellow: The Wayside Inn*.

Immortal Three (*The*). Homer, Dante, and Milton.

"Three poets, in three distant ages born,
Greece, Italy, and England did adorn;
The first in *loftiness of thought* surpassed,
The next in *majesty*; in both the last:
The force of nature could no farther go,
To make a third, she joined the other two."
Dryden: A Tablet to the Memory of John Milton
(St. Mary-le-Bow, Cheapside).

∴ It was originally in the church of All Hallows, Bread Street.

Immortal Tinker (*The*). John Bunyan, a tinker by trade. (1628-1688.)

Immortals. A regiment of 10,000 choice foot-soldiers, which constituted the body-guard of the Persian kings. There was also an army so named at Constantinople, according to Ducange, first embodied by Major Ducas.

∵ The 76th Foot were called "The Immortals," because so many were wounded, but not killed, in Hindûstan (1788-1806). This regiment, with the old 33rd, now form the two battalions of the West Riding.

Immortality. Poseidon (Neptune) bestowed immortality on Taphian, and confined the gift in a golden lock of hair. His daughter cut off the lock, and the gift was lost. This seems very like the Bible tale of Samson and Delilah. (*See* ELECAMPANE.)

Immu'ring (Latin). Burying in a wall. The Vestal virgins among the Romans, and the nuns among the Roman Catholics, who broke their vows of chastity, were buried in a niche sufficiently large to contain their body with a small pittance of bread and water. The sentence of immuring was *Vade in pace*, or more correctly, *Vade in pacem* (Go *into* peace—*i.e.* eternal rest). Some years ago a skeleton, believed to be the remains of an immured nun, was discovered in the walls of Coldingham Abbey.

21*

The immuring of Constance, a nun who had broken her vows, forms **a** leading incident in Scott's poem of *Marmion*.

Im'ogen. Daughter of Cymbeline, the "most tender and artless of all Shakespeare's characters." (*Cymbeline*.)

Imogine. The lady who broke her vow and was carried off by the ghost of her former lover, in the ballad of *Alonzo the Brave*, by Matthew Gregory Lewis, generally called *Monk* Lewis.

"Alonzo the brave was the name of the knight,
And the maiden's the fair Imogine."

Imp (Anglo-Saxon). A graft; whence also a child; as, "You little imp." In hawking, "to imp a feather" is to engraft or add a new feather for a broken one. The needles employed for the purpose were called "imping needles." Lord Cromwell, writing to Henry VIII., speaks of "that noble imp your son."

"Let us pray for . . . the king's most excellent majesty and for . . . his beloved son Edward, our prince, that most angelic imp."—*Pathway to Prayer*.

Imp of Darkness (*An*). Milton calls the serpent "fittest imp of fraud." (*Paradise Lost*, ix. 89.)

Impana'tion. The dogma of Luther that the body and soul of Christ are infused into the eucharistic elements after consecration; and that the bread and wine are united with the body and soul of Christ in much the same way as the body and soul of man are united. The word means *putting into the bread*.

Impanna'ta. *The Madonna del Impannata*, by Raphael, takes its distinctive name from the *oiled paper* window in the background. (Italian, *impannata*, oiled paper.)

Impar Congressus Achilli. No match for Achillès; the combatants were not equally matched. Said of Troïlus. (*Virgil: Æneid*, i. 475.)

Imperial (*An*). A tuft of hair on the chin, all the rest of the beard and all the whiskers being shaved off. So called from the Emperor Napoleon III., who set the fashion.

Imperium in Imperio. A government independent of the general authorised government.

Imper'tinence (4 syl.). A legal term meaning matter introduced into an affidavit, etc., not pertinent to the case.

Impon'derables (Latin, *things without weight*). Heat, light, electricity.

and magnetism were, it was at one time supposed, the phenomena of imponderable substances; that of heat was called *caloric*. This theory is now exploded, but the hypothetical ether is without appreciable weight.

Imposition. A task given as a punishment. Of course the word is taken from the verb *impose*, as the task is imposed. The term is common in schools, colleges, and universities. In the sense of a *deception* it means to "put a trick on a person," hence, the expressions "to put on one," "to lay it on thick," etc.

Imposition of Hands. The bishop, laying his hand on persons confirmed or ordained. (Acts vi., viii., xix.)

Impossibilities. Latin phrases:

Æthiopem de-albāre.
Arēnas arāre.
Latērem lavāre.
Pumĭce aridius.
In asino lanam.

English phrases:

Gathering grapes from thistles.
Fetching water in a sieve.
Washing a blackamoor white.
Catching wind in cabbage nets.
Flaying eels by the tail.
Making cheese of chalk.
Squaring the circle.
Turning base metal into gold.
The elixir of life.
Making a silk purse of a sow's ear.
(And hundreds more.)

Impropria'tion. Profits of ecclesiastical property in the hands of a layman. *Appropriation* is when the profits of a benefice are in the hands of a college.

Impro'priator. A layman who has church lands or ecclesiastical preferment. (Latin, *in-proprius*, belonging to.)

Improve the Occasion (*To*). To draw a moral lesson from some event which has occurred. In French, "*Profitons de l'occasion.*"

Improvis'ators. Persons who utter verses impromptu. The art was introduced by Petrarch, and is still a favourite amusement of the Italians. The most celebrated are:

ACCOLTI (*Bernardo*), of Arezzo, called the "Unico Areti'no" (1465-1535).
ANTONIANO (*Silvio*). Eighteenth century.
AQUILANO (*Seraff'no*), of Aquila (1466-1500).
BANDETTINI. (*See* IMPROVISATRIX.)
BERONICIUS (*P. J.*), who could convert extempore, into Greek or Latin verse, a Dutch newspaper or anything else (died 1676).
CHRISTOFORO, surnamed *Altissimo*, an Italian (1514).
CORILLA. (*See* IMPROVISATRIX.)
GIANNI (*Francis*). An Italian, made imperial poet by Napoleon, whose victories he celebrated in verse (1759-1824).
JEHAN (*Núr*). (*See* IMPROVISATRIX.)
KARSCHIN (*Anna Louisa*). (*See* IMPROVISATRIX.)
MARONE (*Andreas*). An Italian (1474-1527).

METASTASIO (*P. A. D. B.*), of Assisi, who developed, at the age of ten, a great talent for extemporising in verse (1698-1782).
PERFETTI (*Bernardino*), of Sienna, who received a laurel crown in the capital, an honour conferred only on Petrarch and Tasso (1681-1747).
QUERNO (*Camillo*). An Italian (1470-1528).
ROSSI. Beheaded at Naples in 1799.
SERAFINO. (*See above*, AQUILANO.)
SESTINI (*Bartolomeo*). An Italian (died 1822).
SGRICCI (*Tommaso*), of Tuscany (1788-1832). His *Death of Charles I., Death of Mary Queen of Scots*, and *Fall of Missolonghi*, are very celebrated.
TADDEI (*Rosa*). (*See* IMPROVISATRIX.)
ZUCCO (*Marco Antonio*, of Verona (died 1764).

∴ To these add Ciccioni, Bindocci, the brothers Clerc of Holland, Wolf of Altöna, Langenschwarz of Germany, Eugène de Pradel of France, and our own Thomas Hood (1798-1845).

Improvis'atrix or **Improvisatrice.** The most famous improvisatrices or female improvisators are:

MARIA MAGDALE'NA MORELLI FERNANDEZ, surnamed the Olympic Corilla, crowned at Rome for improvisation (1740-1800).
TERE'SA BANDETTI'NI (1763-*).
ROSA TADDEI (1801-*).
SIGNORA MAZZEI, the most talented of all.
NUR JEHAN, of Bengal (*d.* 1645). She was the inventor of the Otto of Roses.
ANNA LOUISA KARCHIN, a German (1722-1791.)

In Cæna Dom'ini. A papal bull, containing a collection of extracts from different constitutions of the popes, with anathemas against those who violate them; so called from the words with which it commences.

In Commen'dam (Latin). The holding of church preferment for a time, on the recommendation of the Crown, till a suitable person can be provided. Thus a clergyman who has been elevated to the bench retains for a time his "living," *in commendam.*

In Esse (Latin). In actual existence. Thus a child *living* is "in esse," but before birth is only "in posse."

In Exten'so (Latin). At full length, word for word, without abridgment.

In Extremis. At the very point of death. "*In articŭlo mortis.*"

In Fi'eri. In the course of accomplishment; on the way.

In Flagrante Delicto. Red-handed; in the very fact. "*Il a été pris en flagrant délit*," *i.e.* "*Sur le fait.*"

In for a Penny in for a Pound. I may as well "be hung for a sheep as a lamb." If the punishment is the same, then it is worth the risk to commit the offence which brings the greatest profit.

In for It. About "to catch it;" on the point of being in trouble.

"You are in for it, I can tell you. I would not stand in your shoes for something."

In Forma Pau'peris. A person who will swear he is not worth £5 has writs, etc., gratis, and is supplied gratuitously with attorney and counsel (Henry VII., c. 12).

In Gremio Legis. Under the protection of the law.

In Lim'ine (Latin) At the outset, at the threshold.

In Loco Parentis. One who stands in a parent's place.

In Medias Res. In the middle of the subject. In novels and epic poetry, the author generally begins with some catastrophe, which is explained as the tale unfolds. In history, on the other hand, the author begins *ab ovo*.

In Memoriam. In memory of.

In Nubibus. In the clouds; not in actual existence; in contemplation.

In Par'tibus [*Infidelium*]. In a non-Christian country. A "bishop *in partibus*" means a bishop in any country, Christian or otherwise, whose title is from some old see which has fallen away from the Catholic faith. Thus, in England, the Bishop of Cisamus, the Bishop of Emmaus, the Bishop of Amycla, are bishops *in partibus*. Dr. Wiseman was Bishop of Melipotamus before he was Archbishop of Westminster. A bishop *in partibus* does not mean a bishop in a land of infidels; he may be so, but this would not make him a bishop *in partibus*.

In Perpet'uam (Latin). In perpetuity, for ever.

In Petto (Italian). Held in reserve, kept back, something done privately, and not announced to the general public. (*In pec'tore* [Latin], in the breast.)
Cardinals in petto. Cardinals about to be elected, but not yet publicly announced. Their names are *in pectore* (of the Pope).

In Posse (Latin). What may be considered probable, but has not yet any real existence.

In Pro'pria Perso'na (Latin). Personally, and not by deputy or agents.

In Prospect'u (Latin). What is intended or in contemplation to be done at some future time.

In Re (Latin). In the matter of; on the subject of; as *In re* Jones *v.* Robinson. But *in rem*, against the property or thing referred to.

In Si'tu (Latin). In its original place.

In Stat'u Quo or *In stat'u quo ante* (Latin). In the condition things were before the change took place. Thus, two nations arming for war may agree to lay down arms on condition that all things be restored to the same state as they were before they took up arms.

In Terro'rem (Latin). As a warning, to deter others by terrifying them.

In To'to (Latin). Entirely, altogether.

In Vac'uo (Latin). In a vacuum— *i.e.* in a space from which, nominally altogether, and really almost, all the air has been taken away.

In-and-In. A game with four dice, once extremely common, and frequently alluded to. "In" is a throw of doubles, "in-and-in" a throw of double doubles, which sweeps the board.

"I have seen three persons sit down at twelve-penny *in-and-in*, and each draw 40s. a-piece."— *Nicker Nicked.*

Ins and Outs of the Matter (*The*). All the details, both direct and indirect.

"If you want to know the ins and outs of the Yankees . . . I know all their points, shape, make, and breed."—*Haliburton.*

✲ Sometimes the "Ins" means those in office, and the "Outs" those out of office, or in Opposition.

Inau'gurate (4 syl.) means to be led in by augurs. The Roman augurs met at their college doors the high officials about to be invested, and led them up to the altar; hence to install.

Inca. A king or royal prince of the ancient Peruvians. The empire of the Incas was founded by Manco Capac.

"The Inca was a war-chief, elected by the Council to carry out its decision."—*Brinton: The American Race (South American Tribes),* part i. chap. ii. p. 211.

Incanta'tion. A *singing against,* that is, singing a set form of words in order to bring Divine wrath upon persons or nations.

Incarnadine (*To*). To make red. (Latin, *incarnātus color,* carnation).

"No, this my hand will rather
The multitudinous sea incarnadine,
Making the green—one red."
Shakespeare: Macbeth, ii. 2.

Inch of Candle (*Sold by*). A sale by auction. Instead of the hammer of the auctioneer concluding the bids, the purchaser was the last bidder before the candle went out. Another plan is to stick a pin in a candle, and when the pin drops down, the sale of the article is concluded.

"Down were tumbled miracle and martyr,
Put up in lots, and sold by inch of candle."
Peter Pindar : Lyric Odes, xiii.

Inchcape Rock. Twelve miles from land, in the German Sea. It is dangerous for navigators, and therefore the abbot of Aberbrothok fixed a bell on a float, which gave notice to sailors of its whereabouts. Ralph the Rover, a sea pirate, cut the bell from the float, and was wrecked on his return home on the very rock. Southey has a ballad on the subject.

Precisely the same tale is told of St. Goven's bell, in Pembrokeshire. In the chapel was a silver bell, which was stolen one summer evening by pirates, but no sooner had the boat put to sea than all the crew was wrecked. The silver bell was carried by sea-nymphs to the brink of a well, and whenever the stone of that well is struck the bell is heard to moan.

N.B. Inch or Innis means *island*.

Incog.—*i.e.* **Incog'nito** (Italian). Under an assumed name or title. When a royal person travels, and does not wish to be treated with royal ceremony, he assumes some inferior title for the nonce, and travels *incog*.

Incorruptible (*The*). Robespierre (1754–1794). Robert Walpole says that William Shippen was the only man he knew who was proof against a bribe.

"Even the 'Incorruptible' himself fell from his original ideal."—*Nineteenth Century*, August, 1893, p. 272.

In'cubus. A nightmare, anything that weighs heavily on the mind. At one time supposed to consort with women in their sleep. (Latin, *in cubo*, to lie on.)

"Merlin was the son of no mortal father, but of an Incubus ; one of a class of beings not absolutely wicked, but far from good, who inhabit the regions of the air."—*Bulfinch: Age of Chivalry*, part i. chap. iii. p. 50.

Indenture. A written contract; so called because the skin on which it was written in duplicate was divided with an indented edge, to fit into each other.

Indepen'dence. *The Declaration of Independence.* A declaration made July 4th, 1776, by the American States, declaring the colonies free and independent, absolved from all allegiance to Great Britain.

Independence Day (July 4th). So called in the United States of America. (*See above.*)

Indepen'dents. Certain Dissenters are so called, whose fundamental principle is that every congregation is an independent church, and has a right to choose its own minister and make its own laws.

Index (*The*). The "Roman Index" contains both the *Index Librōrum Prohibitōrum* and the *Index Expurgatōrius*. The former contains a list of such books as are absolutely forbidden to be read by faithful Catholics. The latter contains such books as are forbidden till certain parts are omitted or amended. The lists are made out by a board of cardinals called the "Congregation of the Index." Of course, it is wholly impossible to keep pace with the present issue of books; but, besides the Protestant Bibles, and the works of such heretics as Arius and Calvin, we find in the lists the following well-known names :—

Of *English authors :* Addison, Bacon, Gibbon, Goldsmith, Hallam, Locke, J. S. Mill, Milton, Robertson, Archbishop Whately, etc., and even some children's tales.

Of *French authors :* Arnauld, Calvin, Descartes, Fénelon, l'Abbé Fleury, Malebranche, Voltaire, etc.

Of *Italian authors :* Dante, Guicciardini, Sismondi, etc.

Of *German authors :* Kant, Luther, etc.

"Under the auspices of Cardinal Caraffa (part iv.), the Inquisition was introduced into Italy (1542), and exerted the utmost vigilance and severity in crushing out the new faith, and the index of prohibited books was established."—*Fisher : Universal History*, part iii. period ii. chap. iv. p. 414.

India Ink or *Chinese ink*. So called because it was first brought from China. It is now made at home of lampblack and glue.

India Paper. A printing-paper made in China and Japan from vegetable fibre, and used for taking off the finest proofs of engraved plates. Pronounce *Indi' paper*.

India Proof. The proof of an engraving on India paper, before lettering.

Indian Arrowroot. The root which the Indians apply to arrow-wounds to neutralise the venom of the arrow. They mash the meal, and apply it as a poultice. (*Miller.*)

Indian Drug (*The*). Tobacco.

"His breath compounded of strong English beere,
And th' Indian drug, would suffer none come neere."
Taylor, the Water Poet (1630).

Indian File (*In*). One by one. The American Indians, when they go on an expedition, march one by one. The one behind carefully steps in the footprints of the one before, and the last man of the file obliterates the footprints. Thus, neither the track nor the number of invaders can be traced.

"Each man followed his leader in Indian file."
—*Captain Burnaby: On Horseback through Asia Minor.*

Indian Red. Red hæmatite (peroxide of iron), found abundantly in the Forest of Dean, Gloucestershire. It is of a deep, lakey hue, used for flesh tints.

The *Persian Red*, which is of a darker hue with a sparkling lustre, is imported from the island of Ormuz in the Persian Gulf.

The Romans obtained this pigment from the island of Elba. "*Insulam exhaustis chalybum generosa metallis.*" (*Ovid.*)

Indian Summer (*The*). The autumnal summer; generally the finest and mildest part of the whole year, especially in North America.

"The gilding of the Indian summer mellowed the pastures far and wide. The russet woods stood ripe to be stript, but were yet full of leaf. The purple of heath-bloom, faded but not withered, tinged the hills. . . Fieldhead gardens bore the seal of gentle decay ; . . . its time of flowers and even of fruit was over."—*C. Brontë: Shirley*, chap. xxvii.

Indians. *American Indians.* When Columbus landed at Cat Island, he thought that he had landed on one of the Indian islands, and in this belief gave the natives the name of Indians.

India proper is so named from Indus (the river), in Sanskrit *Sindhu,* in Persic *Hind,* whence the Greek *Hindus. Hindustan* is the *tan* or "country" of the river *Hindus.*

Indiarubber. A substance made from the sap of various tropical plants, and used for erasing pencil marks, and many other purposes. Pronounce *Indi'-rubber.*

"He was a man with an indiarubber coat on, indiarubber shoes, an indiarubber cap, and in his pocket an indiarubber purse, and not a cent in it."—*Cyclopædia of American Biography (Charles Goodyear),* vol. ii. p. 684.

Individualists. Individualists hold that as little as possible should be done for its subjects by the State, as much as possible being left to free individual initiative.

Socialism tends to treat the individual as merely a part of the State, holding his possessions (if any) simply by its permission, while Individualism regards the state as a collection of separate units, with rights of life and property independently, which the State does not confer but merely guarantees.

Extreme individualists hold that all government is an evil, though it may be a necessary evil, and the "anarchists" profess the extremest form of the creed.

"Individualism rests on the principle that a man shall be his own master."—*Draper: Conflict between Religion and Science,* chap. xi. p. 295.

Indoors. In the house. Virgil makes Dido sit "*in foribus divæ.*" (*Æneid,* i 505.)

Induc'tion (Latin, *the act of leading in*). When a clergyman is inducted to a living he is led to the church door, and the ring which forms the handle is placed in his hand. The door being opened, he is next led into the church, and the fact is announced to the parish by tolling the bell.

Indul'gence (3 syl.), in the Roman Catholic Church, is the entire or partial remission of punishment due to sin either in this world or in purgatory. It is supposed that the Church is the bank of the infinite merits of Christ, and can give such indulgences like cheques on a bank. (Latin, *indulgentia.*)

Iner'tia. That want of power in matter to change its state either from rest to motion, or from motion to rest. Kepler calls it *Vis inertiæ.* (*Ars* in Latin is the Greek *ar'etē,* power or inherent force ; *In-ars* is the absence of this power.)

Inexorable Logic of Facts (*The*). This was Mazzini's happy expression : "*Nella genesi dei fatti la logica è inesorabile.*"

Infallibility (of the Church of Rome) is the doctrine that the Church of Rome cannot at any time cease to be orthodox in her doctrine, and that what she declares *ex cathedrâ* is substantially true. The doctrine is based on the Divine promise to the disciples, "Howbeit when the Spirit of Truth is come, he will guide you into all truth " (John xvi. 13).

⁂ The dogma of the "Infallibility of the Pope " was decreed by the Vatican Council in 1870.

In'famous means not allowed to speak or give witness in a court of justice. (Latin, *in,* negative *fari,* to speak ; Greek, *phēmi* or *phāmi.*)

Infant. Used as a synonym of "childe," meaning a knight or squire;

as, "Childe Harold." King Arthur is so called. (See also *Spenser : Faërie Queene*, book ii. canto viii. 56.)

Infant of Lubeck. Christian Henry Heinecken (1721-1725). At one year old he knew the chief events of the Pentateuch; at thirteen months he knew the history of the Old Testament; at fourteen months he knew the history of the New Testament; at two and a half years he could answer any ordinary question of history or geography; at three years he knew well both French and Latin. At least, so says Schöneich, his preceptor.

"Another of these pitiable prodigies was John Philipp Baratier, of Schwaback, near Nürnberg, born the same year as the Lubeck prodigy (1721-1740). At the age of five he knew Greek, Latin, and French, besides his native German. At nine he knew Hebrew into French and Chaldee, and could convert German into Latin. At thirteen he could translate Hebrew into French or French into Hebrew. His life was written by Formey, and his name appears in most biographical dictionaries."

Infanta. Any princess of the blood royal, except an heiress of the crown, is so called in Spain and Portugal.

Infan'te (3 syl.). All the sons of the sovereigns of Spain and Portugal bear this title, except the crown prince, who is called in Spain the Prince of Astu'rias. In the Middle Ages the word "childe" was used as a title of honour in England, France, and Germany; hence Childe Harold, Childe-ric, Childe-bert, etc.

Infantry. Foot soldiers. Said to be first applied to a body of men collected by the *Infante* or heir-apparent of Spain for the purpose of rescuing his father from the Moors. The success of the attempt rendered the corps popular. (Spanish, *infanteria ;* Italian, *fanteria ; fante* means a servant.)

Infernal Column. So the corps of Latour d'Auvergne was called, from its terrible charges with the bayonet. (1743-1800.)

Infer'no. We have Dante's notion of the infernal regions in his *Inferno ;* Homer's in the *Odyssey,* book xi. ; Virgil's in the *Æneid,* book vi. ; Spenser's in the *Faërie Queene,* book ii. canto 7; Ariosto's in the *Orlando Furio'so,* book xvii. ; Tasso's in *Jerusalem Delivered,* book iv. ; Milton's in *Paradise Lost ;* Fénelon's in *Télémaque,* book xviii. ; and Beckford's in his romance of *Vathek.*

Infra Dig., *i.e. Dignita'tem.* Not in accordance with one's position and character. (Latin.)

Infralapsa'rians. Those who believe that election and predestination are subsequent to the Fall. The "Supralapsarian " believes that election and predestination were in the eternal counsels of God even before the creation of Adam. (*Infra,* after ; *lapsus,* the fall ; *supra,* before ; *lapsus,* the fall.)

Ingle (*The*). The recess with benches in old-fashioned fireplaces, the fire.

" Sit thee by the ingle when
The scar faggot blazes bright."
Keats : Fancy, stanza 1.

Ingoldsby. The Rev. Richard Harris Barham, author of *Ingoldsby Legends.* (1788-1845.)

Ingrain Colours. Colours dyed in the wool or raw material before manufacture. In French, *tendre en laine.* Such colours are the most durable. We speak of "a rogue ingrain," meaning one hopelessly bad. (In the grain, that is, in the texture.)

" 'Tis ingrain, sir ; 'twill endure wind and weather.—*Shakespeare : Twelfth Night,* i. 5.

Ingulph's "Croyland Chronicle." Proved to be a forgery by H. J. Riley in the *Archæological Journal,* 1862. He dates the forgery between 1393 and 1415, and attributes it to Prior Richard of Croyland and Sergeant William Ludyngton.

Injunc'tion. A writ forbidding a person to encroach on another's privileges ; as, to sell a book which is only a colourable copy of another author's book ; or to violate a patent ; or to perform a play based on a novel without permission of the novelist ; or to publish a book the rights of which are reserved. Injunctions are of two sorts— temporary and perpetual. The first is limited "till the coming on of the defendant's answer " ; the latter is based on the merits of the case, and is of perpetual force.

Ink. Pancirollus says the emperors used a fluid for writing called *encaustum.* (Italian, *inchiostro ;* French, *encre ;* Dutch, *inkt.*)

Inkhorn Terms. This phrase, once common, might be revived to signify pedantic expressions which smell of the lamp.

⁑ Shakespeare uses the phrase, an "Inkhorn mate " (1 *Henry VI.,* iii. 1).

Ink-pot. *Sons and daughters of the ink-pot.* Those who maintain themselves by writing for the press. (*The Silver Domino.*)

Inkle and Yar'ico. The hero and heroine of a drama so called by George Colman. The story is from the *Spectator*, No. 11. Inkle is a young Englishman who is lost in the Spanish main; he falls in love with Yarico, an Indian maiden, whom he lives with as his wife; but no sooner does he find a vessel to take him to Barbadoes than he sells her for a slave.

Inland Navigation. Francis Egerton, Duke of Bridgewater, is called the *Father of British Inland Navigation.* (1729-1803.) A title certainly due to James Brindley (1716-1772).

Inn (Anglo-Saxon). Chamber; originally applied to a mansion, like the French *hôtel.* Hence Clifford's Inn, once the mansion of De Clifford; Lincoln's Inn, the mansion of the Earls of Lincoln; Gray's Inn, that of the Lords Gray, etc.

" Now, whenas Phœbus, with his fiery waine,
  Unto his inne began to draw ajace."
                    Spenser: Faërie Queene, vi. 3.

Inns of Court. The four voluntary societies which have the exclusive right of calling to the bar. They are the Inner Temple, the Middle Temple, Lincoln's Inn, and Gray's Inn. Each is governed by a board of benchers.

Innings, in cricket, is the turn of the team to be bowled to by their opponents. The persons who " bat " are having their " innings given them "; and the innings of an individual is the time he holds the bat.
A good innings. One in which the batsman has made several runs. Figuratively, a run of luck or business.
He has had a long innings. A good long run of luck. A term in cricket for the time that the eleven are *in,* or not out as scouts.

Innis Fodhla [*Island of Destiny*], an old name of Ireland.

" Long before the western districts of *Innis Fodhla* had any settled name . . . a powerful king reigned over this part of the sacred island. [The king referred to was Connedda, who gave his name to the province of Connacht]."—*W. B. Yeats: Fairy Tales and Folk-Lore,* pp. 306, 318.

Innocent (*An*). An idiot or born fool. (*See* BENET.)

" An idiot, or one otherwise deficient in intellect, is called an innocent."—*Trench: On the Study of Words,* lecture iii. p. 97.

Innocents. *Feast of the Holy Innocents.* The 28th December, to commemorate Herod's butchery of the children of Bethlehem under two years old, with the design of cutting off the infant Jesus (Matt. ii. 16.)

Innuen'do. An implied or covert hint of blame. It is a law term, meaning the person nodded to or indirectly referred to (Latin, *in-nuo*).

" Implying or suggesting, instead of stating plainly, often increases the effect of what is intended to give pain or pleasure. This is 'innuendo.' "—*Bain: Composition, etc. (Innuendo),* part i. p. 212.

Inoc'ulate (4 syl.) is to put in an eye (Latin, *in oculus*). The allusion is to a plan adopted by gardeners who insert the " eye " or small bud of a superior plant into the stock of an inferior one, in order to produce flowers or fruits of better quality.

In'ogene or **Ig'noge** (3 syl.). Wife of Brute, the mythological king of Britain.

" Thus Brute this realme unto his rule subdewd,
  And raignëd long in great felicity.
Loved of his friends, and of his foes eschewd,
He left three sons, his famous progeny,
Born of fayre Inogene of Italy."
                    Spenser: Faërie Queene, ii. 10.

Inquisition. A court instituted to inquire into offences against the Roman Catholic religion. Fully established by Pope Gregory IX. in 1235. It was most active in Italy, Spain, and Portugal. Those found guilty were handed over to the secular arm to be dealt with according to the secular laws of the land. Suppressed in France in 1772, and not finally in Spain till 1834. (Latin, *inquisitio,* a searching into.)

Insane Root (*The*). Hemlock. It is said that those who eat hemlock can see subjective things as objects. Thus, when Banquo had encountered the witches, who vanished as mysteriously as they appeared, he said to Macbeth, " Were such things [*really*] here, ... or have we eaten the insane root, that takes the reason prisoner," so that our eyes see things that are not. (*Macbeth,* i. 3.)

⁂ Other plants "take the reason prisoner," as the *Pruna insana,* the " Indian nut," " Hoary nightshade."

Inscription of a Coin. (*See* LEGEND.)

Insolence. (Latin, *in-soleo.*) Unusual conduct, that is, not according to the common courtesies of social life.

Inspired Idiot (*The*). Oliver Goldsmith was so called by Walpole.

Instinct. Something pricked or punctured into one. *Distinguish* is of the same root, and means to prick or puncture separately. *Extinguish* means to prick or puncture out. In all cases the allusion is to marking by a puncture. At college the "markers" at the chapel doors still hold a pin in one hand, and prick with it the name of each "man" who enters. The word is used to express a natural impulse to do something; an inherent habit.

"Although reason may . . . be blended with instinct, the distinction between the two is sufficiently precise. Reason only acts upon a definite and often laboriously acquired knowledge of the relation between means and ends."—*Romanes: Encyclopædia Britannica*, vol. xiii. p. 157 (*ninth edition*).

In'stitutes (3 syl.). Elementary law treatises, as the *Institutes of Gaius* and those of Florentius, Callistrătus, Paulus, Ulpian, and Marcian. The *Institutes of Justinian* were compiled by Antonīnus Pius, and for the most part are mere *rechauffées* of the preceding ones, giving the words and opinions of the respective authors.

Instructions to the Committee. A Parliamentary dodge for empowering a Committee of the House to do what a Committee would not otherwise be empowered to do.

An "Instruction" must be supplementary and auxiliary to the Bill under consideration.

It must fall within the general scope and framework of the Bill in question.

It must not form the substance of a distinct measure.

Insu'bri. The district of Lombardy which contained Milan, Como, Pa'via, Lodi, Nova'ra, and Vercelli.

Insult. To leap on the prostrate body of a foe. To treat with contumely.

Insulter. One who leaps upon you or against you. Thus Terence says, "*Insulta're fores cal'cibus*" (*Eunŭchus*, ii. 2, 54). It will be remembered that the priests of Baal, to show their indignation against their gods, "leaped upon the altar which they had made" (1 Kings xviii. 26). Zephaniah (i. 9) says that God will punish all those that leap on the threshold." (*See* DESULTORY.)

Intag'lio (Italian). A design cut in a gem, like a crest or initials in a stamp. The design does not stand out in relief, as in *cam'eos*, but is hollowed in.

Intellect. The power of reading mentally; hence the power of understanding and quickly grasping what requires intelligence and thought. (Latin, *intus lego*, I read within me.)

Intendance Militaire. *Corps chargé de tout ce qui concerne l'administration et la compatibilité de la guerre.*

The *Intendants Militaire* control the accounts, payments, food, dress, encampments, transport, hospitals, marches, etc., of the army.

Intentions. *Hell is paved with good intentions.* In Spanish: "*El infierno es bleno de buenas intenciones.*" Good intentions without corresponding deeds are self-accusers.

Inter Al'ia (Latin). Among other things or matters.

Inter Cœsa et Porrecta. Out of hand. Many things may occur between the cup and lip. (See *Cicero: Ad Attĭcum*, v. 18.) Literally, between the slaughter (*cæsa*) of the sacrificial victim and its being laid (*porrecta*) on the altar. It was not permitted to speak while the priest struck the animal, nor yet while the sacrifice was being consumed by fire; but between these intervals persons were allowed to talk.

Inter Canem et Lupum. Between two difficulties or dangers equally formidable. Between Scylla and Charyb'dis. Literally, "between dog and wolf."

Inter Nos, or in French *Entre nous.* Confidentially, between ourselves.

Inter Poc'ula. During a drinking bout.

Inter Rex (Latin). A person appointed to hold the office of king during a temporary vacancy.

Intercal'ary (Latin). Inserted between or amongst others. Thus, an intercalary day is a day foisted in between two others, as the 29th February in leap-year. (*See* CALENDS.)

"It was the custom with Greeks to add, or, as it was termed, intercalate, a month every other year."—*Priestley: On History*, xiv.

Interdict and *Excommunicate.* The Pope or some ecclesiastic interdicts a kingdom, province, county, or town, but excommunicates an individual. This sentence excludes the place or individual from partaking in certain sacraments, public worship, and the burial service. The most remarkable instances are:—

586. The Bishop of Bayeux laid an interdict on all the churches of Rouen, in consequence of the murder of the Bishop Prétextat.

1081. Poland was laid under an interdict by Pope Gregory VII., because Boleslas II. had murdered Stanislaus at the altar.

1180. Scotland was put under a similar ban by Pope Alexander III.

1200. France was interdicted by Innocent III., because Philippe Auguste refused to marry Ingelburge, who had been betrothed to him.

1209. England was laid under similar sentence by Innocent III., in the reign of King John, and the interdict lasted for six years.

In France, Robert *the Pious*, Philippe I., Louis VII., Philippe *Auguste*, Philippe IV., and Napoleon I., have all been subjected to the Papal thunder. In England, Henry II. and John. Victor Emmanuel of Italy was excommunicated by Pius IX. for despoiling the Papacy of a large portion of its temporal dominions.

In'terest (Latin). Something that is between the parties concerned. The interest of money is the sum which the borrower agrees to pay the lender for its use. To take an interest in anything is to feel there is something between it and you which may affect your pleasure.

Interest for money. In the Tudor dynasty it was 10 per cent. (37 Henry VIII. chap. 9). In the reign of James it was reduced to 8 per cent.; in Queen Anne's reign to 5 per cent.; in the last quarter of the nineteenth century it was reduced to 2½ per cent.

Interim of Augsburg (*The*). A Concordat drawn up by Charles Quint in 1548 to allay the religious turmoil of Germany. It was a provisional arrangement to be in force till some definite decision could be pronounced by the General Council to be held at Trent. The authors of this instrument were J. Pflug (Bishop of Naumburg), Michael Helding (titular Bishop of Sidon), and John Agricola (a priest of Brandenburg).

Interlard (French). To put lard or fat between layers of meat. Metaphorically, to mix what is the solid part of a discourse with fulsome and irrelevant matter. Thus we say, "To interlard with oaths," to "interlard with compliments," etc.

" They interlard their native drinks with choice
Of strongest brandy." *Philips: Cider*, ii.

Interlo'per. One who runs between traders. One who sets up business, and by so doing interferes with the actual or supposed rights of others. (Dutch, *loopen*, to run, to leap.)

Inter'polate (4 syl.). For two or more persons to polish up something between them. Metaphorically, to insert spurious matter in a book or document; to gag. (Latin, *inter polio*, to polish.)

Inter'preter (*Mr.*). The Holy Spirit personified, in Bunyan's *Pilgrim's Progress*. He is lord of a house a little way beyond the Wicket Gate. Here Christian was kindly entertained and shown many wonderful sights of an allegorical character. Christiana and her party stopped here, and were similarly entertained.

Into'ne (2 syl.). To thunder out; *intonation*, the thundering of the voice. (Latin, *tono*, to thunder.) The Romans said that Cicero and Demosthenes "thundered out their orations." To recite in a musical monotone.

Intoxication. Pliny (xvi. 20) tells us this word is derived from *taxa*, a species of bay-tree used for poisoning arrows. Hence the Greek *toxon* (a bow and arrows), and *toxicon* (rank poison).

Intrigue (2 syl.), comes from the Greek *thrix*, hair, whence the Latin *tricæ*, trifles or hairs, and the verb *intrico*, to entangle; the Germans have the verb *trugen*, to deceive.

Inure (2 syl.) to habituate or harden by use. Ure is an archaic word meaning use. (Latin *opus*, work. French *œuvre;* old French, *eure*.)

Invalide (French). A four-sou piece, so called because it was debased to the value of three sous and a-half.

" Tien, prens cet invalide, à ma santé va boire."
Deux Arlequins (1691).

Invei'gle (3 syl.). To lead blindfold; to entice by misrepresentation. (Norman French, *enveogler;* French, *aveugler;* Italian, *invogliare*.)

Invention of the Cross [*discovery of the cross*]. A festival held on May 3rd, in commemoration of the " discovery of the cross " by the agents of St. Hel'ena, mother of Constantine the Emperor (316). (Latin, *inven'io*, to discover.)

Inventors Punished by their own inventions.

BASTILLE. Hugues Aubriot, Provost of Paris, who built the Bastile, was the first person confined therein. The charge against him was heresy.

BRAZEN BULL. Perillos, who invented the Brazen Bull for Phalăris, Tyrant of Agrigentum, was the first person baked to death in the horrible monster.

CAPTAIN. Cowper Coles, inventor of the turret-ship, perished in the *Captain* off Finisterre September 7th, 1870.

CATHERINE WHEEL. The inventor of St. Catherine's Wheel, a diabolical machine consisting of four wheels turning different ways, and each wheel armed with saws, knives, and teeth, was killed by his own machine; for when St. Catherine was bound on the wheel, she fell off, and the machine flew to pieces. One of the pieces struck the inventor, and other pieces struck several of the men employed to work it, all of whom were killed. (*Metaphrastes*.)

GUILLOTINE. J. B. V. Guillotin, M.D., of Lyons, was guillotined, but it is an error to credit him with the invention of the instrument. The inventor was Dr. Joseph Agnace Guillotin.

HAMAN, son of Hammeda'tha, the Amalekite, of the race of Agag, devised a gallows fifty cubits high on which to hang Mordecai, by way of commencing the extirpation of the Jews; but the favourite of Ahasue'rus was himself hanged on his gigantic gallows. In modern history we have a repetition of this incident in the case of Enguerrand de Marigni, Minister of Finance to Philippe the Fair, who was hung on the gibbet which he had caused to be erected at Montfaucon for the execution of certain felons; and four of his successors in office underwent the same fate.

HOPKINS (*Matthew*), the witch-finder, was himself tried by his own tests, and put to death as a wizard.

IRON CAGE. The Bishop of Verdun, who invented the Iron Cages, too small to allow the person confined in them to stand upright or lie at full length, was the first to be shut up in one; and Cardinal La Balue, who recommended them to Louis XI., was himself confined in one for ten years.

IRON SHROUD. Ludovi'co Sforza, who invented the Iron Shroud, was the first to suffer death by this horrible torture.

MAIDEN. The Regent Morton of Scotland, who invented the Maiden, a sort of guillotine, was the first to be beheaded thereby. This was in the reign of Queen Elizabeth.

OSTRACISM. Clisthênes introduced the custom of Ostracism, and was the first to be banished thereby.

The PERRIERE was an instrument for throwing stones of 3,000 lbs. in weight; and the inventor fell a victim to his own invention by the accidental discharge of a perrière against a wall.

PORTA A FAENZA. Filippo Strozzi counselled the Duke Alessandro de' Medici to construct the Porta a Faenza to intimidate the Florentines, and here he was himself murdered.

SALISBURY (*the Earl of*) was the first to use cannon, and was the first Englishman killed by a cannon ball.

UTROP'IUS induced the Emperor Arcadius to abolish the benefit of sanctuary; but a few days afterwards he committed some offence and fled for safety to the nearest church, St. Chrysostom told him he had fallen into his own net, and he was put to death. (*Life of St. Chrysostom.*)

WINSTANLEY (*Mr.*) erected the first Eddystone lighthouse. It was a wooden polygon, 100 feet high, on a stone base; but it was washed away by a storm in 1703, and the architect himself perished in his own edifice.

Inventors Punished. A curious instance of the *sin* of invention is mentioned in the *Bridge of Allan Reporter*, February, 1803:—

"It is told of Mr. Ferguson's grandfather, that he invented a pair of fanners for cleaning grain, and for this proof of superior ingenuity he was summoned before the Kirk Session, and reproved for trying to place the handiwork of man above the time-honoured practice of cleaning the grain on windy days, when the current was blowing briskly through the open doors of the barn."

Inves'titure. (Latin, *clothing in* or putting on canonicals.) The admission to office is generally made by investiture; thus, a pair of gloves is given to a Freemason in France; a cap is given to a graduate; a crown, etc., to a sovereign, etc. A crosier and ring used to be given to a church dignitary; but are now simply placed in his hands on his induction into office. In the eleventh and twelfth centuries the kings of Europe and the pope were perpetually at variance about the right of investiture; the question was, should the sovereigns or should the pope invest clergymen or appoint them to their livings and dignities? (Latin, *vestis*, a garment; *investio*. (*See* INDUCTION.)

Invin'cible Doctor. William of Occam or Ockham (a village in Surrey), also called *Doctor Singula'ris*. (1270-1347.)

Invisibility, according to fable, may be obtained in a multitude of ways. For example:—

Albric's cloak, called Tarnkappe (3 syl.), which Siegfried got possession of, rendered him invisible. (*Nibelungen Lied.*)

A *chamelon* carried in the breast will render a person invisible.

A *capon stone*, called "Alectoria," will render any person invisible who carries it about his person. (*See* MIRROR OF STONES.)

A *dead hand*. It is believed that a candle placed in a dead man's hand gives no light to any but those who use it. (*See* HAND.)

Fern-seed, mentioned by Shakespeare, and by Beaumont and Fletcher, possesses the same charm.

Gyges' ring, taken from the flanks of a brazen horse, made the wearer invisible, provided he turned the ring inwards.

Hel'iotrope, mentioned by Boccaccio in his *Decamĕron* (Day viii. 3), is a green stone, which renders a person invisible. So does the herb called heliotrope, according to Solīnus, who says, "*Herba etiam ejusdem nominis . . . eum, a quocumque gestabītur, subtrahit visibus obviōrum.*" (*Georgic*, xl.)

The *helmet* of Perseus (2 syl.) and the helmet of Pluto (called *Orci Galĕa*), both rendered the wearer invisible. (*Classic story.*)

The *helmet which Pluto gave to the Cyclops* made them invisible whenever it was worn.

Jack the Giant-killer had a cloak of invisibility as well as a cap of knowledge.

Keplein's mantle. The mantle of Hel Keplein, which belonged to the dwarf-king Laurin, rendered the wearer invisible (*The Heldenbuch ;* thirteenth century.)

The *Moros Musphoron* was a girdle of invisibility. (*Mrs. Centlivre : A Bold Stroke for a Wife.*)

Otnit's ring. The ring of Otnit, King of Lombardy, according to the *Heldenbuch,* possessed a similar charm.

Reynard's wonderful ring had three colours, one of which (the green) caused the wearer to become invisible. (*Reynard the Fox,* 1498.)

Invis'ibles. (1) The Rosicrucians were so called, because they never dared to appear in public.

(2) The disciples of Osiander, Flaccius, Illirĭcus, etc., who denied the perpetual visibility of the Church. (Sixteenth century.)

Invulnerability.

Stones taken from the cassan plant, which grows in Panter, renders the possessor invulnerable. (*Odoricus* in *Hakluyt.*)

A dip in the river Styx rendered Achillēs invulnerable. (*Greek fable.*)

Medēa rendered Jason, with whom she had fallen in love, proof against wounds and fire by anointing him with the Promethe'an unguent. (*Greek fable.*)

Siegfried (2 syl.) was rendered invulnerable by anointing his body with dragon's blood. (*Nibelungen Lied.*)

Iol (pron. *Yol*). The Danish word for Christmas ; the same as *Yule.*

"The savage Dane
At Iol more deep the mead did drain."
Sir W. Scott : Marmion.

Io'nian Mode. A species of church music in the key of C major, in imitation of the ancient Greek mode so called.

Ionic Accomplishments. Gesture and dress.

Ion'ic Architecture. So called from Io'nia, where it took its rise. The capitals are decorated with volutes, and the cornice with dentils. The shaft is fluted ; the entablature either plain or embellished.

"The people of Ionia formed their order of architecture on the model of a young woman dressed in her hair, and of an easy, elegant shape; whereas the Doric had been formed on the model of a robust, strong man."—*Vitruvius.*

Ion'ic School or **Ionic Philosophers.** Thalēs, Anaximander, Anaxime'nēs, Heracli'tos, and Anaxag'oras were all natives of Ionia, and were the earliest of the Greek philosophers. They tried to prove that all created things spring from one principle ; Thalēs said it was water, Anaximenēs thought it was air or gas, Anaxagoras that it was atoms, Heraclitos maintained that it was fire or caloric, while Anaximander insisted that the elements of all things are eternal, for *ex nihilo nihil fit.*

Iormungan'dur. The serpent that encompasses the whole earth, according to Scandinavian mythology.

Io'ta or *Jot.* A very little, the least quantity possible. The iōta [ι] is the smallest letter of the Greek alphabet, called the Lacedemonian letter. (Hebrew, *Yod* [י], the smallest Hebrew letter.)

"This bond doth give thee here no jot of blood.
Shakespeare : Merchant of Venice, iv. 1.

Iphicles' Oxen. *Quid hoc ad Iphicli boves ?* What has that to do with the subject in hand ? So in *L'Avocat* the judge had to pull up the shepherd every minute with the question, "*Mais, mon ami, revenon à nos moutons.*" Iphĭclos or Iphiclēs was the possessor of large herds of oxen, and Neleus (2 syl.) promised to give his daughter in marriage to Bias if he would bring him the oxen of Iphiclēs, which were guarded by a very fierce dog. Melampos contrived to obtain the oxen for his brother, but being caught in the act, he was cast into prison. Melampos afterwards told Astyocha, wife of Iphiclēs, how to become the mother of children, whereupon Iphiclēs gave him the coveted herd, and his brother married the daughter of Neleus. The secret told by Melampos to Astyocha was "to steep the rust of iron in wine for ten days, and drink it." This she did, and became the mother of eight sons. (*Odyssey*, xi. ; *Iliad*, xiii. 23 ; *Apollodoros*, i. 9 ; *Pausanias*, iv. 36.)

❧ When Tressilian wanted Dominie Holiday to tell him of a smith who could shoe his horse, the pedagogue kept starting from the point, and Tressilian says to him :—

"Permit me to ask, in your own learned phrase, *Quid hoc ad Iphycli boves*, what has that to do with my poor nag?"—*Sir W. Scott: Kenilworth*, chap. ix.

❧ Another similar phrase is "*Quid ad Mercurium ?*" Τί πρός τον Ἑρμην:

Another is "*Io Hecuba ?*" What has that to do with Hecuba?

Iphicraten′sians. The best trained and bravest of the Greek soldiers were so called from Iphicrătēs, an Athenian general. (*See* FABIAN SOLDIERS.)

Iphigeni′a. Daughter of Agamemnon and Clytemnestra. Her father having offended Ar′tĕmis (*Diana*) by killing her favourite stag, vowed to sacrifice to the angry goddess the most beautiful thing that came into his possession in the next twelve months ; this was an infant daughter. The father deferred the sacrifice till the fleet of the combined Greeks reached Aulis and Iphigenia had grown to womanhood. Then Calchas told him that the fleet would be wind-bound till he had fulfilled his vow ; accordingly the king prepared to sacrifice his daughter, but Artĕmis at the last moment snatched her from the altar and carried her to heaven, substituting a hind in her place.

The similarity of this legend to the Scripture stories of Jephthah's vow, and Abraham's offering of his son Isaac, is noticeable. (*See* IDOMENEUS.)

Ipse Dixit (Latin). A mere assertion, wholly unsupported. We say it is "your *ipse dixit*," "his *ipse dixit*," "their *ipse dixit*," and so on.

Ipso Facto. Irrespective of all external considerations of right or wrong ; absolutely ; by the very deed itself. It sometimes means the act itself carries the consequences (as excommunication without sentence of excommunication being directly pronounced).

"Whatever the captain does is right *ipso facto* [*i.e.* because it is done by the captain], and any opposition to it is wrong, on board ship."—*R. H. Dana.*

By burning the Pope's bull, Luther *ipso facto* [by the very deed itself] denied the Pope's supremacy. Heresy carries excommunication *ipso facto.*

Ipswich. A corruption of *Gypes-wick*, the town on the river "Gyppen," now called the Orwell.

Iram′. The pilgrim's garb is so called by the Arabs.

Iran. The empire of Persia.

"Avenge the shame
His race hath brought on Iran's name."
Thomas Moore : Fire Worshippers.

Ireland or *Erin* is Celtic ; from *Er*ι or *Iar* (western). Lloyd (*State Worthies*, article "Grandison"), with a gravity which cannot but excite laughter, says the island is called the *land of Ire* because of the broils there, which have extended over four hundred years. Wormius derives the word from the Runic *Yr*, a bow. (*See below.*)

Ireland.
Called by the natives "Erin," *i.e. Eri-innis*, or *Iar-innis* (west island).
By the Welsh "Yver-den" (west valley).
By Apule′ius, "Hiber′nia," which is *Iernia*, a corruption of *Iar-inni-a*.
By Juvenal (ii. 260) "Juverna" or "Juberna," the same as *Ierna* or *Iernia*.
By Claudian "Ouernia," the same.
By moderns "Ireland," which is *Iar-en-land* (land of the west).

¶ *The three great saints of Ireland* are St. Patrick, St. Columba, and St. Bridget.

The fair maid of Ireland. Ignis fatuus (*q.v.*).

"He had read in former times of a Going Fire, called 'Ignis Fatuus,' the fire of destiny ; by some, 'Will with the Wisp,' or 'Jack with the Lantern ;' and likewise, by some simple country people, 'The Fair Maid of Ireland,' which used to lead wandering travellers out of their way."—*The Seven Champions of Christendom*, i. 7.

The three tragic stories of the Irish.
(1) The death of the children of Touran ; (2) the death of the children of Lir ; (3) the death of the children of Usnach. (*O'Flanagan : Transactions of the Gaelic Society of Dublin*, vol. i.)

Dean Ireland's scholarships. Four scholarships of £30 a year in the University of Oxford, founded by Dr. John Ireland, Dean of Westminster, in 1825, for Latin and Greek. They are tenable for four years.

∵ The same person founded an "Exegetical Professorship" of £800 a year.

Ire′na. The impersonation of Ireland

whose inheritance was withheld by the tyrant Grantorto. Sir Artegal (*Justice*) is sent by the Faërie Queene to succour the distressed lady. Grantorto, or the rebellion of 1580, being slain, she is restored to her throne and reigns in peace. (*Spenser: Faërie Queene*, v.)

I'ris. Goddess of the rainbow, or the rainbow itself. In classic mythology she is called the messenger of the gods when they intended *discord*, and the rainbow is the bridge or road let down from heaven for her accommodation. When the gods meant *peace* they sent Mercury. (Greek and Latin, *iris*.)

> "I'll have an Iris that shall find thee out."
> *Shakespeare:* 2 *Henry VI.*, iii. 2.

Irish Agita'tor. Daniel O'Connell (1775-1847).

Irish Apricots. Potatoes.

Irish Stew. A dish of food made by stewing together meat, onions, and potatoes. Called "Irish" from the predominance of potatoes.

Irish Wedding. When a person has a black eye we sometimes say to him, "You have been to an Irish wedding, I see," because the Irish are more famous for giving their guests on these occasions *black eyes* than *white favours*.

Iron. The hieroglyphic for iron is ♂, which denotes "gold at the bottom" (O), only its upper part is too sharp, volatile, and half corrosive (′); this being taken away, iron would become gold. Iron is called Mars.

Strike while the iron is hot. "*Battre le fer pendant qu'il est chaud.*" Make hay while the sun shines.

To have many irons in the fire. To have many affairs in hand.

If you have too many irons in the fire, some will burn. If you have more affairs in hand than you can properly attend to, some of them will be neglected and turn out badly. Both these locutions refer to the "heaters" or irons employed in laundries. If the "heater" is too hot, it will scorch the linen.

To rule with a rod of iron. To rule tyrannically. "*Gouverner avec une verge de fer.*"

Iron. (*See* PIG IRON.)

Iron Age. The era between the death of Charlemagne and the close of the Carlovingian dynasty is so called from its almost ceaseless wars. It is sometimes called the *leaden* age for its worthlessness, and the *dark* age for its barrenness of learned men.

Iron Age. The age of cruelty and hard-heartedness. When Hubert tells Prince Arthur he must burn his eyes out, the young prince replies, "Ah, none but in this iron age would do it." (*Shakespeare: King John*, iv. 1.)

Iron-arm. Francis de Lanoue, the Huguenot soldier, *Bras de Fer* (1531-1591). (*See* FIERABRAS.)

Iron Duke (*The*). The Duke of Wellington was so called from his iron will. (1769-1852.)

Iron-hand or the **Iron-hander.** Goetz von Berlichingen (*Godfrey of Berlichingen*), who lost his right hand at the siege of Landshut, and had one made of iron to supply its place. (1480-1562.) (*See* SILVER-HAND.)

Iron Horse (*The*). The railway locomotive.

> "We can now drive the iron horse from India down the valley of the Irrawaddy, and (*vid* Moulmein) to the very gates of China, without any political impediment."—*Mr. Hallet*, Dec., 1885.

Iron Mask. *The man in the iron mask* (called Lestang) was Count Er'colo Anto'nio Matthio'li, a senator of Mantua, and private agent of Ferdinand Charles, Duke of Mantua. He suffered imprisonment of twenty-four years for having deceived Louis XIV. in a secret treaty for the purchase of the fortress of Casale, the key of Italy. The agents of Spain and Austria bribed him by outbidding the Grande Monarque. The secrecy observed by all parties was inviolate, because "the infamy of the transaction would not bear daylight. (*H. G. A. Ellis: True History of the Iron Mask*.)

⁂ M. Loiseleur utterly denies that Matthioli (sometimes called Giacomo) was the real *homme du masque de fer* (See *Temple Bar*, May, 1872, pp. 182-184); but Marius Topin, in *The Man in the Iron Mask*, maintains it as an indubitable fact. There is an English translation of Topin's book by Vizetelli, published by Smith and Elder.

There are several others "identified" as the veritable Iron Mask, *e.g.*—

(1) Louis, Duc de Vermandois, natural son of Louis XIV. by De la Vallière, who was imprisoned for life because he gave the Dauphin a box on the ears. (*Mémoires Secrets pour servir à l'Histoire de Perse*.) This cannot be, as the duke died in camp, 1683.

(2) A young foreign nobleman, chamberlain of Queen Anne, and real father of Louis XIV. (*A Dutch story*.)

(3) Duc de Beaufort, *King of the*

Markets. (*Legrange-Chancel: L'Année Littéraire*, 1759.) This supposition is worthless, as the duke was slain by the Turks at the siege of Candia (1669).

(4) An elder brother of Louis XIV., some say by the Duke of Buckingham, others by Cardinal Mazarin. (See *Voltaire: DictionnairePhilosophique* [Anna], and *Linguet : Bastile Dévoilée.*)

(5) Abbé Soulavie asserts it was a twin brother of Louis XIV., *Maréchal Richelieu.* This tale forms the basis of Zschokke's German tragedy, and Fournier's drama.

(6) Some maintain that it was Fouquet, the disgraced Minister of Finance to Louis XIV.

(7) Some that it was the Arminian Patriarch, Avedik.

(8) Some that it was the Duke of Monmouth ; but he was executed on Tower Hill in 1685.

(9) In the *Western Morning News* (Plymouth, October 21st, 1893) we are told that Le Commandant Bazeries has deciphered a letter in cipher written by Louvois, Minister of War, to Catinat (Lieutenant-General in command of the army at Piedmont), desiring him to arrest M. de Bulonde for raising the siege of Conti ; and to send him to the citadel of Pignerol.

" He was to be allowed to walk on the ramparts wearing a mask."

Whatever the real name of this mysterious prisoner, he was interred in 1703 under the name of Marchiali, aged about forty-five. And the name is so registered in St. Paul's register, Paris ; witnessed by M. de Rosarge (mayor of the Bastile) and M. Reilh (surgeon).

"The mask was made of black velvet on steel springs."

Iron-tooth [*Dent de Fer*]. Frederick II., Elector of Brandenburg. (1657, 1688-1713.)

Iron Crown of Lombardy is so called from a narrow band of iron within it, said to be beaten out of one of the nails used at the Crucifixion. This band is about three-eighths of an inch broad, and one-tenth of an inch in thickness. According to tradition, the nail was first given to Constantine by his mother, who discovered the cross. The outer circlet of the crown is of beaten gold, and set with precious stones. The crown is preserved with great care at Monza, near Milan ; and Napoleon, like his predecessor Charlemagne, was crowned with it.

After the war between Austria and Italy, the Iron Crown was delivered by the former power to Victor Immanuel.

Iron entered into his Soul (*The*). The anguish or annoyance is felt most keenly. The allusion is to the ancient custom of torturing the flesh with in-struments of iron.

"I saw the iron enter into his soul, and felt what sort of pain it was that ariseth from hope deferred."—*Sterne : Sentimental Journey.*

Iron Maiden of Nuremberg (*The*). An instrument of torture for "heretics," traitors, parricides, etc. It was a box big enough to admit a man, with folding-doors, the whole studded with sharp iron spikes. When the doors were pressed-to these spikes were forced into the body of the victim, who was left there to die in horrible torture. (German, *Eiserne Jungfrau.*)

⁂ One of these diabolical machines was exhibited in 1892 in the Free Trade Hall, Manchester, and in London.

Irons (*In*). In fetters. " *Mettre les fers aux pieds à* [*quelqu'un*]."

Ironclad (*An*). A ship having the hull sheathed wholly or in part with plates of iron, to resist projectiles.

Ironclad Oath (*The*), 1866. An Act passed in North America excluding voters in the States lately in rebellion from the franchise ; practically disfran-chising all Southerners over twenty-five years of age.

Ironside. Edmund II., King of the Anglo-Saxons, was so called, from his iron armour. (989, 1016-1017.)

Nestor Ironside. Sir Richard Steele, who assumed the name in *The Guardian.* (1671-1729.)

Ironsides. The soldiers that served under Cromwell were so called, especially after the battle of Marston Moor, where they displayed an iron resolution.

Irony. A dissembling. (Greek, *eiron*, a dissembler, *eironeia*.)

"So grave a body upon so solemn an occasion should not deal in irony, or explain their meaning by contraries."—*Swift.*

Irony of Fate (*The*). A strange fatality which has brought about some-thing quite the reverse of what might have been expected.

"By the irony of fate the Ten Hours' Bill was carried in the very session when Lord Ashley, having changed his views on the Corn Laws, felt it his duty to resign his seat in Parliament."—*The Leisure Hour,* 1887.

Iroquois (*An*). Anyone of the five (now six) confederate tribes, viz. the Mohawks, Oneidas, Onondagas, Cayugas, Senecas, and sixth the Tuscaroras, added in 1712, now forming "The Six Nations of the Iroquois Confederacy."

Irrefragable Doctor. Alexander Hales, an English friar, founder of the scholastic theology (thirteenth century).

Irrel'evant is not to relieve, not to lighten. Irrelevant matter is that which does not help to bear the burden or make it lighter; something not pertinent or not material to the point in question. (Latin *levis*, light.)

Irresis'tible. Alexander the Great went to consult the Delphic oracle before he started on his expedition against Persia. He chanced, however, to arrive on a day when no responses were made. Nothing daunted, he went in search of the Pythia, and when she refused to attend, took her to the temple by force. "Son," said the priestess, "thou art irresistible." "Enough," cried Alexander; "I accept your words as my response."

Irritable Genus (*The*) or the "*Genus irritabile*" (*Horace: Epistles*, ii. 2, 102). Poets, and authors generally.

"It [publishers'] is a wrathful trade, and the irritable genus comprehends the bookselling as well as the book-writing species."—*Sir W. Scott: The Monastery* (Int.).

Irspilles Felles. Skins having bristly hair like that of goats. (*Hircipilus—i.e.* "goat's hair." (*Festus*.) A *fell* is Anglo-Saxon for "skin," like the Latin *pell-is*, English *peel*. Thus we say still a "wool-fell." Shakespeare speaks of "a fell of hair" (*Macbeth*, v. 5). *Fellmonger*, a dealer in skins.

Irtish Ferry. *To cross the Irtish ferry* is to be laid on the shelf. The ferry of the Irtish is crossed by those who are exiled to Siberia. It is regarded in Russia as the ferry of political death.

Irus. The beggar of gigantic stature, who kept watch over the suitors of Penel'ope. His real name was Ar'neos, but the suitors nicknamed him Iros because he carried their messages for them. Ulysses, on his return, felled him to the ground with a single blow, and flung him out of doors.

Poorer than Irus. A Greek proverb, adopted by the Romans (see *Ovid*), and existing in the French language ("*Plus pauvre qu'Irus*"), alluding to the beggar referred to above.

Ir'vingites (3 syl.). The self-styled *Catholic Apostolic Church*, founded by the Rev. Edward Irving in 1829; they believed in the gift of tongues.

Isaac. A hedge-sparrow, a corruption of Chaucer's word, *heisuagge*.

(Anglo-Saxon, *heag*, hedge ; *sugga*, the sugga bird.)

Isaac of York. The Jew in *Ivanhoe*, and father of Rebecca. (*Sir Walter Scott*.)

Isabel, called *She-wolf of France*. The adulterous queen of Edward II., daughter of Philippe IV. (*le Bel*) of France. According to tradition, she murdered her royal husband by thrusting a hot iron into his bowels.

" Mark the year and mark the night
    When Severn shall re-echo with affright
The shrieks of death through Berkley's roofs that
        ring.
Shrieks of an agonising king.
She-wolf of France, with unrelenting fangs,
That tear'st the bowels of thy mangled mate ! "
        Gray : The Bard.

Is'abel. The Spanish form of Elizabeth. The French form is Isabelle.

Isabella, Princess of Sicily, in love with Robert le Diable, but promised in marriage to the prince of Grana'da, who challenged Robert to mortal combat. Robert was allured from the combat by his fiend-father, but when Alice told him that Isabella "the princess is waiting for him at the altar," a struggle took place between Bertram and Alice, the one trying to drag the duke to the infernal regions, and the other trying to win him to the ways of virtue. Alice prevailed, but the audience is not informed whether Robert married Isabella or not. (*Meyerbeer's opera, Robert il Diavolo.*)

Isabella, daughter of Hercules, Duke of Ferra're, sister of Alfonso and Ippol'ito, and wife of Francisco Gonza'go, lord of Mantua.

Isabella. (*See* POT OF BASIL.)

Isabelle or **Isabella** (in *Orlando Furioso*). Daughter of the king of Galicia, in love with Zerbi'no ; but, being a pagan, Zerbino could not marry her. Zerbino induces her to quit her native land, and gives Odori'co charge of her. She is wrecked, and Odorico escapes with her to Rochelle. Here Odorico assails her virtue, but is alarmed by a vessel which he sees approaching, and flees. She is kept captive by the crew for nine months, but Orlando slays or hangs all the crew, and Isabella being free, accompanies her rescuer. Her lament at the death of Zerbino is one of the best parts of the poem (book xii.). She retires to a chapel to bury Zerbino, and is there slain by Rod'omont.

Isabelle. The *colour* so called is the yellow of soiled calico. A yellow-dun horse

is called in France *un cheval isabelle.* The
tale is attached to Isabel of Austria
and Isabel of Castile. It is said that
Isabel of Austria, daughter of Philip II.,
at the siege of Ostend vowed not to
change her linen till the place was taken.
As the siege lasted three years, we may
well suppose that it was somewhat
soiled by three years' wear.

"His colour was isabel, a name given in allusion to the whimsical vow of Isabella Clara
Eugenia, Governess of the Netherlands, at the
memorable siege of Ostend, which lasted from
1601 till 1604."—*Dillon: Travels in Spain* (1781).

Isabel of Castile, we are told, made a
vow to the Virgin not to change her
linen till Grana'da fell into her hands ;
but this siege lasted longer than ladies
are wont to wear their body-linen.

"Bright-Sun was mounted on a black horse,
that of Felix was a grey, Chery's was white as
milk, and the princess's an isabelle."— *Countess
d'Atnois: Fair-star and Prince Chery.*

Isaf. An Arabian idol in the form of
a man, brought from Syria, and placed
in Es-Safa, near the temple of Mecca.
Some say Isaf was a man converted into
stone for impiety, and that Mahomet
suffered this one "idol" to remain as a
warning to his disciples.

Isenbras or **Sir Isumbras.** A hero
of mediæval romance, first proud and
presumptuous, when he was visited by all
sorts of punishments ; afterwards penitent and humble, when his afflictions
were turned into blessings. It was in
this latter stage that he one day carried
on his horse two children of a poor
woodman across a ford. (*See* YSAM-
BRAS.)

"I warne you first at the begynninge
That I will make no vain carpinge [talk]
Of deeds of armys ne of amours,
As dus mynstrelles and jestours,
That makys carpinge in many a place
Of Octoriane and Isembrase."
William of Nassington.

I'sengrin or **Sir Isgrim,** the wolf,
afterwards created Earl of Pitwood, in
the beast-epic of *Reynard the Fox.*
Isengrin typifies the barons, and Reynard
the church ; and the gist of the tale is to
show how Reynard bamboozles his uncle
Wolf. (German, *Isegrimm,* a wolf, a
surly fellow.)

Iseult. (*See* YSONDE.)

Ishban, in the satire of *Absalom and
Achitophel,* by Dryden and Tate, is Sir
Robert Clayton, who'd "e'en turn loyal
to be made a peer" (part ii.).

Ish'bosheth, in Dryden's satire of
Absalom and Achitophel, is meant for
Richard Cromwell. His father, Oliver,
is called Saul. At the death of Saul,

Ishbosheth was acknowledged king by a
party, and reigned two years, when he
was assassinated. (Part i. 57, 58.)

"They who, when Saul was dead, without a blow,
Made foolish Ishbosheth the crown forego."

Ish'monie'. The petrified city in
Upper Egypt, full of men and women
turned to stone. (*Perry : View of the
Levant.*)
    Marryat has borrowed the idea in his
Pacha of Many Tales.

I'siac Tablet. A spurious Egyptian
monument sold by a soldier to Cardinal
Bembo in 1527, and preserved at Turin.
It is of copper, and on it are represented
most of the Egyptian deities in the
mysteries of Isis. It was said to have
been found at the siege of Rome in 1525.
The word Isiac is an adjective formed
from Isis.

Isido'rian Decre'tals. Also called
Pseudo or *False Decretals.* A spurious
compilation of fifty-nine decretals by
Mentz, who lived in the ninth century,
and fraudulently ascribed them to I'sidore
of Seville, who died in the sixth century.
Prior to the ninth century the only
authentic collection of decretals or letters
of the popes in reply to questions proposed to them by bishops, ecclesiastical
judges, and others, was that of Dionysius
the Little [Exig'uus], a Roman monk,
who lived in the middle of the sixth
century. He commences with Pope
Siricius (fourth century). The Isidorian
decretals contain fifty-nine letters ascribed to persons living between Clement and Siricius, and forty others not
contained in the Dionysian collection.
The object of these forged letters is
either to exalt the Papacy or enforce
some law assuming the existence of such
exaltation. Amongst these spurious
letters are the decretal of St. Anacle'tus,
the decretal of St. Alexander, the letter
of Julius to the Easterns, the synodical
letter of St. Athana'sius, the decretal of
St. Fabian instituting the rite of the
chrism, and so on.

"La réforme pseudo-Isidorienne, adoptée par
S. Nicholas, en 865, par le huitième concile œcu-
menique en 870, confirmé par le concile de Trent
en 1564, elle est depuis neuf siècles le droit com-
mun dans l'église catholique . . . . ce qu'il est
impossible de justifier et même d'excuser, c'est
le moyen employé par le pseudo-Isidore pour
arriver à ses fins."—*Études Religieuses,* No. 47, p.
392.

I'singlass. A corruption of the
Dutch *huyzenblas* (an air-bladder), being
prepared from the bladders and sounds
of sturgeon. (German, *huyen,* a sturgeon.)

I'sis. Sister-wife of Osi'ris. The cow was sacred to her; and she is represented with two long horns from one stem at the top of her head. She is said to have invented spinning and weaving. (*Egyptian mythology*.)

" Inventress of the woof, fair Lina [flax] flings
The flying shuttle thro' the dancing strings. . .
Taught by her labours, from the fertile soil
Immortal Isis clothed the banks of Nile."
Darwin: Loves of the Plants, c. ii.

Milton, in *Paradise Lost*, names Osiris, Isis, and Orus amongst the fallen angels (book i. 478).

Isis, Herodotos thinks, is Deme'ter (Ce'rēs).

Diodo'ros confounds her with the Moon, Demeter, and Juno.

Plutarch confounds her with Athe'na (Minerva), Perseph'onē (Proserpine), the Moon, and Te'thys.

Apule'ius calls her the mother of the gods Minerva, Venus, Diana, Proserpine, Cerēs, Juno, Bello'na, Hecate, and Rhamnu'sia [Nem'esis].

Lockyer says, " Isis represents the idea of rising or becoming visible, Osīris of disappearing." Thus the rising moon, a rising planet, the coming dawn, etc., is Isis; but the setting sun, the waning moon, a setting planet, evening, etc., is Osiris.

" Now the bright moonbeams kissed the water,
. . . and now the mountain and valley, river
and plain, were flooded with white light, for
mother Isis was arisen."—*Rider Haggard: Cleopatra, chap. iii.*

⁂ Isis was the mother of Horus (the rising sun), and is represented as nursing him.

Isis. Some maintain that Isis was at one time the protectress of Paris, and that the word Paris is a contraction of the Greek *Para Isidos* (near the temple of Isis), the temple referred to being the Panthéon or church of St. Geneviève. We are told, moreover, that a statue of Isis was for a long time preserved in the church of St. Germain des Prés, but was broken to pieces by Cardinal Briçonnet because he saw certain women offering candles to it as to the Virgin.

The Young Isis. Cleopatra (69-30 B.C.).

Islam or **Islamism.** The true faith, according to the Mahometan notion. The Moslems say every child is born in Islam, and would continue in the true faith if not led astray into Magism, Judaism, or Christianity. The word means *resignation* or *submission to the will of God*.

Islam consists of five duties:—
(1) Bearing witness that there is but one God.
(2) Reciting daily prayers.
(3) Giving the appointed and legal alms.
(4) Observing the Ramazan (a month's fast).

(5) Making a pilgrimage to Mecca at least once in a lifetime.
⁂ Moslem and Musulman are from the same root.

Is'lamite (3 syl.). A follower of Mahomet or believer in Islam.

Island of Saints. So Ireland was called in the Middle Ages.

Island of St. Brandan. The flying island, the supposed retreat of King Rodri'go. So called from St. Brandan, who went in search of the Islands of Paradise in the sixth century.

Island of the Seven Cities. A kind of Dixie land, where seven bishops, who quitted Spain during the dominion of the Moors, founded seven cities. The legend says that many have visited the island, but no one has ever quitted it.

Islands of the Blessed, called by the Greeks " Happy Islands," and by the Romans " Fortunate Islands." Imaginary islands somewhere in the west, where the favourites of the gods are conveyed at death, and dwell in everlasting joy.

" Their place of birth alone is mute
To sounds that echo farther west
Than your sire's Islands of the Blest."
Byron.

Isle of Dogs. So called from being the receptacle of the greyhounds of Edward III. Some say it is a corruption of the *Isle of Ducks*, and that it is so called in ancient records from the number of wild fowl inhabiting the marshes.

Isle of Lanterns (*The*), or *Lantern-land.* An imaginary country inhabited by pretenders to knowledge. In French, *Lanternois*. (*Rabelais: Pantagruel*, v. 32, 33.)
⁂ Lucian has a similar conceit, called the *City of Lanterns ;* and Dean Swift, in his *Gulliver's Travels*, makes his hero visit Laputa, the empire of quacks, false projectors, and pretenders to science.

Isle of Mist (*The*). The Isle of Skye, whose high hills are almost always shrouded in mist.
" Nor sleep thy hand by thy side, chief of the Isle
of Mist." *Ossian: Fingal,* i.

Islington (*The Marquis of*). One of the skilful companions of Barlow, the famous archer, was so christened by Henry VIII. (*See* SHOREDITCH, *The Duke of*.)

Ismael'ians (4 syl.). A Mahometan sect, which maintained that Isma'el, and not Moussa, ought to be Imaum'. In the tenth century they formed a secret society, from which sprang the Assassins.

Isme'nē (3 syl.) Daughter of Œdipus and Jocasta. Antig'one was buried alive by the order of King Creon, for burying her brother Polyni'cēs, slain in combat by his brother Ete'oclēs. Isme'nē declared that she had aided her sister, and requested to be allowed to share the same punishment.

Isme'nē. The lady-love of Isme'nias, in the erotic romance of Eustathius or Eumathius entitled *Ismene and Ismenias* (twelfth century). Translated by Godfrey of Viterbo. Especially noteworthy from its being reproduced in the *Confessio Amantis* of Gower, and forming the plot of Shakespeare's *Pericles.*

Isme'nias. A Theban musician of whom Ath'eas, King of the Scyth'ians, declared, "I liked the music of Ismenias better than the braying of an ass." (*Plutarch.*)

Isme'no (in *Jerusalem Delivered*). A magician who could "call spirits from the vasty deep." He was once a Christian, but became Mahometan. Ismeno was killed by a stone hurled at him by an engine (book xviii.).

Isobars. Lines on a map connecting places which have the same mean barometric pressure. The closer the isobars are the stronger the wind, the farther the lighter. (Greek, *baros*, weight.)

Isoc'ratēs. *The French Isocrates.* Fléchier, Bishop of Nismes (1632-1710).

Is'olde (2 syl.). Wife of King Mark, of Cornwall, who had an illicit affection for Sir Tristram, Mark's nephew. *Isolde the White,* Sir Tristram's wife.

I'sother'mal Lines. Lines laid down in maps to show the places which have the same mean temperature. (Greek, *isos thermos*, equal heat.)

Is'rael, in Dryden's satire of *Absalom and Achitophel,* stands for England.

Is'rafil'. The angel of music, who possessed the most melodious voice of all God's creatures. This is the angel who is to sound the Resurrection Trump, and will ravish the ears of the saints in paradise. Israfil, Gabriel, and Michael were the three angels that warned Abraham of Sodom's destruction. (*Sale : Koran.*)

"A winged band, commanded by Israfil, the angel of the resurrection, came to meet Roland."
—*Croquemitaine,* ii. 9.

Issa. Jesus.

Is'sachar, in Dryden's satire of *Absalom and Achitophel,* means Thomas Thynne, of Longleate Hall, a friend of the Duke of Monmouth. Thynne was

assassinated in his carriage, in Pall Mall, by ruffians hired by Count Koningsmark. The cause of the murder was jealousy. Both Mr. Thynne and the count were in love with Lady Elizabeth Percy, the widow of the Earl of Ogle. Her friends contracted her to the rich commoner, but before the match was consummated Mr. Thynne was murdered. Within three months the lady married the Duke of Somerset. (*See* MOHUN.)

Issachar's ears. Ass's ears. The allusion is to Gen. xlix. 14 : "Issachar is a strong ass crouching down between two burdens."

" Is't possible that you, whose ears
  Are of the tribe of Issachar's . . .
  Should yet be deaf against a noise
  So roaring as the public voice ? "
        S. Butler : Hudibras to Sidrophel.

Issland. The kingdom of Brunhild is identified by Von der Hagen with Iceland, but Wackernagel says it means Amazonian land, and derives it from the Old German *itis* (a woman). (*The Nibelungen Lied.*)

Issue. The point of law in debate or in question. "At issue," under dispute.

To join issue. To take opposite views of a question, or opposite sides in a suit.

To join issues. To leave a suit to the decision of the court because the parties interested cannot agree.

Isth'mian Games. Epsom races were styled "Our Isthmian Games" by Lord Palmerston, in allusion to the famous games consisting of chariot races, running, wrestling, boxing, etc., held by the Greeks in the Isthmus of Corinth every alternate spring, the first and third of each Olympiad.

Isthmus of Suez. The covered bridge of St. John's College, Cambridge, is so called, because it connects the college with the grounds on the other side of the river. Suez here is a pun on the word *sus* (a hog), the Johnians being nicknamed *hogs* in University slang.

Italian Architecture. The Roman architecture revived in the fifteenth century, and in vogue during that and the two succeeding ones. It is divided into three schools—the Florentine, Roman, and Venetian.

Italian of Asia (*The*). Persian is so called. Noted for its harmony, and its adaptation to verse and the lighter class of music.

Italic School of Philosophy. The Pythagore'an, so called because Pythag'oras taught in Italy.

Italic Version. A version of the Bible from the Septuagint, which preceded the Vulgate, or the version by St. Jerome.

Italics. The type first used by Aldo Manu'zio in printing the Aldine classics. It was called by him " Cursive " letters (a running hand ; from Latin, *curro*, to run). Virgil was the first author printed in this type (1501). Francesco of Bologna cast it.

The words italicised in the Bible have no corresponding words in the original. The translators supplied these words to render the sense of the passage more full and clear.

Italy. The champion of Italy was St. Anthony. (*Seven Champions of Christendom*, part i. 6.)

Itch. *My fingers itch to be at him.* This is a French locution, " *Les poings me démangent de le battre.*"

An itch for gold. A longing desire. (Anglo-Saxon, *giecan*, to itch.)

Itching Ears (*To have*). To have a longing desire to hear news, or some novelty.

" The time will come when they will not endure the sound doctrine ; but, having itching ears, will heap to themselves teachers after their own lusts [or longings]."—2 Timothy iv. 3 (R.V.).

Itching Palm (*An*). A love of money. If the palm of your right hand itches, it betokens that you are going to receive money. So Melton tells us in his *Astrologaster*, p. 23.

" Let me tell you, Cassius, you yourself
Are much condemned to have an itching palm."
Shakespeare · Julius Cæsar, iv. 4.

Itching of the Eye. If the right eye itches it betokens laughter at hand ; if the left eye, it betokens grief ; but Shakespeare does not observe this distinction.

" My right eye itches now, so I shall see
My love." *Theocritus*, i. 37.
" Mine eyes do itch ;
Doth that forebode weeping ? "
Shakespeare : Othello, iv. 3.

Itching of the Lips indicates you are about to receive a kiss, or else kiss somebody.

" If your lips itch, you shall kisse somebody."
—*Melton : Astrologaster*, p. 32.

Itching of the Nose indicates that you are going to see a stranger.

" We shall ha' guests to-day
. . . My nose itcheth so."
Dekker : Honest Whore.

Itching of the Thumb, according to Shakespeare, betokens the approach of evil.

" By the pricking of my thumbs,
Something evil this way comes."
Macbeth, iv. i.

Ithacen'sian Suitors (*The*). The suitors of Penelŏpē (4 syl.), wife of Ulysses, King of Ithăca. While Ulysses was absent, many suitors presented themselves to Penelŏpē, affirming that Ulysses was certainly dead. Penelŏpē put them off, saying she would give a definite answer when she had finished the robe she was weaving for Laertēs ; but at night she unravelled all she had woven during the day. At last Ulysses returned and slew the suitors.

" All the ladies, each and each,
Like the Ithacensian suitors in old time,
Stared with great eyes, and laughed with alien lips." *Tennyson : The Princess*, iv.

Ithu'riel. One of the angels commissioned by Gabriel to search for Satan, who had effected his entrance into Paradise. The other angel who accompanied him was Zephon. (Ithuriel means " the discovery of God.")

" Ithuriel and Zephon, with winged speed
Search through this garden; leave unsearched no nook;
But chiefly where those two fair creatures lodge,
Now laid perhaps asleep, secure of harm."
Milton : Paradise Lost, book iv. 788-791.

Ithu'riel's Spear. The spear of the the angel Ithuriel, the slightest touch of which exposed deceit. Hence, when Satan squatted like a toad " close to the ear of Eve," Ithuriel only touched the creature with his spear, and it resumed the form of Satan.

" Him [*i.e.* Satan], thus intent Ithuriel with his spear
Touched lightly ; for no falsehood can endure
Touch of celestial temper, but returns
Of force to its own likeness."
Milton : Paradise Lost, iv. 810-813.

Itin'erary (*An*). The notification of the route followed by a traveller. The Itinerary of Antoninus marks out all the main roads of the Roman Empire, and the stations of the Roman army. The Itinerary of Peutinger (*Tabula Peutingeriăna*) is also an invaluable document of ancient geography, executed A.D. 393, in the reign of Theodosius the Great, and hence called sometimes the Theodosian Table.

Its did not come into use till the seventeenth century. Dean Trench points out that Chatterton betrayed his forgeries by the line " Life and its goods I scorn," but the word *its* was not in use till several centuries after the death of the monk to whom the words are ascribed. In 1548 *it* was used for *its*.

" The loue and deuotion towardes God also hath it infancie, and hath it commyng forward in growth of age." (1548.)

I'van. The Russian form of John, called *Juan* in Spain, *Giovanni* in Italian.

Ivan the Terrible. Ivan IV. of Russia, infamous for his cruelties, but a man of great energy. He first adopted the title of czar. (1529, 1533-1584.)

I'vanhoe (3 syl.). Sir Wilfred, knight of Ivanhoe, is the disinherited son of Cedric of Rotherwood. He is first introduced as a pilgrim, in which guise he enters his father's hall, where he meets Rowe'na. He next appears as Des̆dichado, the "Disinherited Knight," in the grand tournament where he vanquishes all opponents. At the intercession of King Richard he is reconciled to his father, and ultimately marries Rowena, his father's ward. Rebecca, the Jew's daughter, to whom he had shown many acts of kindness, was in love with him.

Sir Walter Scott took the name from the village of Ivanhoe, or Ivinghoe, in Bucks, a line in a old rhymed proverb —"Tring, King, and Ivanhoe"—having attracted his attention.

Ivanovitch. A lazy, good-natured person, the national impersonation of the Russians as a people, as *John Bull* is of the English, *Brother Jonathan* of the Americans, *Jean Crapaud* of the French, and *Cousin Michael* of the Germans.

Ivories. Teeth ; dice.
To show one's ivories. To display one's teeth.
To wash one's ivories. To rinse the mouth ; to drink.

Ivory Gate of Dreams (*The*). Dreams which delude pass through this gate, those which come true pass through the Gate of Horn. This fancy depends upon two puns : ivory in Greek is *elĕphas*, and the verb *elephairo* means "to cheat with empty hopes ; " the Greek for horn is *keras*, and the verb *karanoō* means "to accomplish."

" Sunt geminæ somni portæ : quarum altera fertur
Cornea, qua veris facilis datur exitus umbris ;
Altera candenti perfecta nitens elephanto ;
Sed falsa ad cœlum mittunt insomnia manes."
Virgil: Æneid, vi. 894-897.

Ivory Palaces are not unfrequently mentioned in the Old Testament. Thus (Psalm xlv. 8), "All thy garments smell of myrrh, aloes, and cassia, out of the ivory palaces ; " in 1 Kings xxii. 39 we read that Ahab built "an ivory house ; " and in Amos iii. 15 we read, "I will smite the winter-house with the summer-house, and the houses of ivory." Lady Mary Wortley Montague, in her *Letters*, speaks of the ivory fittings of the harem of the Kahya's palace at Adrianople. She says, "Its winter apartments are wainscotted with inlaid work of mother-of-pearl and ivory of different colours" (vol. ii. p. 161-162).

"The ceilings of the Eastern houses are of mosaic work, and for the most part of ivory, like those superb Talaar of Persia."—*St. John Chardin.*

Ivory Shoulder. Demēter ate the shoulder of Pelops, served up by Tantălos ; so when the gods restored the body to life, Demēter supplied the lacking shoulder with one of ivory.

"Not Pelops' shoulder whiter than her hands.
W. Browne : Britannia's Pastorals, ii. 3.

Ivy (Old English, *ifig*). Dedicated to Bacchus from the notion that it is a preventive of drunkenness. But whether the Dionysian ivy is the same plant as that which we call *ivy* is doubtful, as it was famous for its golden berries, and was termed *chryso-carpos.*

Ivy (in Christian art). Symbol of everlasting life, from its remaining continually green. An ivy wreath was the prize of the Isth'mian games, till it was superseded by a pine garland. The plant was sacred to Bacchus and Osi'ris.

Ivy Bush. *Like an owl in an ivy-bush.* Having a sapient, vacant look, as some persons have when in their cups ; having a stupid vacant stare. Owls are proverbial for their judge-like solemnity, and ivy is the favourite plant of Bacchus. Gray, in his *Elegy*, refers to the Owl and the Ivy.

"From yonder ivy-mantled tower
The moping owl doth to the moon complain
Of such as, wandering near her secret bower,
Molest her ancient solitary reign."
Stanza 3.

Ivy Lane (London). So called from the houses of the prebendaries of St. Paul, overgrown with ivy, which once stood there.

Ixi'on. A king of the Lapithæ, bound to a revolving wheel of fire in the Infernal regions, for his impious presumption in trying to imitate the thunder of heaven. (*Greek mythology.*)
‡ The treadmill is sometimes called "Ixīon's Wheel."

J

J. (In *Punch*). The signature of Douglas Jerrold, who first contributed to No. 9 of the series.

J. J. (In Hogarth's *Gin Lane*, written on a gibbet), is intended for Sir Joseph Jekyll, obnoxious for his bill for increasing the duty on gin.

Jaafer. At the battle of Muta, Jaafer carried the sacred banner of "the Prophet." One hand being lopped off, he held it with the other; the other being struck off, he embraced it with his two stumps; his head being cleft in twain, he flung himself on the banner staff, and the banner was detained thus till Abdallah seized it and handed it to Khaled. A similar tale is told of Cynægiros (*q.v.*).

Ja′chin. The parish clerk in Crabbe's *Borough.* He appropriated the sacramental money, and died disgraced.

Jachin. (*See* BOAZ.)

Jack.

I. APPLIED TO MEN, but always depreciatingly. (*See* TOM.)

(1) *Jack Adams.* A fool.

(2) *Jack-a-dandy* (*q.v.*).

(3) *Jack-a-dreams.* A man of inaction, a mere dreamer.

(4) *Jack-a-drognes.* A good-natured, lazy fool. (Dutch, *druilen*, to be listless; our *drawl.*)

(5) *Jack-a-Lent.* A half-starved, sheepish booby. Shakespeare says: "You little Jack-a-lent, have you been true to us?" (*Merry Wives of Windsor*, iii. 3.) A kind of Aunt Sally which was thrown at in Lent. (See *Cleveland's Poems* [1660], p. 61.)

(6) *Jack-a-napes* (*q.v.*).

(7) *Jack-at-a-pinch.* One who lends a hand in an emergency; an itinerant clergyman who has no cure, but officiates for a fee in any church where his assistance is required.

(8) *Jack Brag.* (*See* BRAG.)

(9) *Jack Fool.* More generally, Tom Fool (*q.v.*).

(10) *Jack Ketch* (*q.v.*).

(11) *Jack-pudding* (*q.v.*).

(12) *Jack-sauce.* An insolent saucebox, "the worst Jack of the pack." Fluellen says one who challenges another and refuses to fight is a "Jack-sauce." (*Henry V.*, iv. 7.)

(13) *Jack-snip.* A botching tailor.

(14) *Jack-slave.* "Every Jack-slave hath his belly full of fighting." (*Shakespeare: Cymbeline*, ii. 1.)

(15) *Jack-sprat* (*q.v.*).

(16) *Jack-straw.* A peasant rebel.

(17) *Jack-tar* (*q.v.*).

(18) *Jack-in-office.* A conceited official, or upstart, who presumes on his official appointment to give himself airs.

(19) *Jack-in-the-green.* A chimneysweep boy in the midst of boughs, on May Day.

(20) *Jack-in-the-water.* An attendant at the waterman's stairs, etc., willing to wet his feet, if needs be, for a "few coppers."

(21) *Jack-of-all-trades.* One who can turn his hand to anything, but excels in nothing.

(22) *Jack-of-both-sides.* One who tries to favour two antagonistic parties, either from fear or for profit.

(23) *Jack-out-of-office.* "But long I will not be Jack-out-of-office." (*Shakespeare:* 1 *Henry VI.*, i. 1.)

(24) *Cheap Jack.* (*See* CHEAP.)

(25) *Jack will never be a gentleman.* A mere parvenu will never be like a well-bred gentleman.

(26) *Every man-Jack of them.* All without exception, even the most insignificant.

(27) *Remember poor Jack.* Throw a copper to the boys paddling about the jetty or pier, or performing tricks under the hope of getting a small bounty.

II. APPLIED TO BOYS WHO ACT THE PART OF MEN.

(1) *Jack Frost.* Frost personified as a mischievous boy.

(2) *Jack Sprat.* Who bears the same relation to a man as a sprat does to a mackerel or herring.

(3) *Jack and Jill* (nursery rhyme). Jill or Gill is a contraction of Julienne or Gillian, a common Norman name. (*See* JACK, VII.)

(4) *Jack and the Bean-stalk* (*q.v.*).

(5) *Jack and the Fiddler* (*q.v.*).

(6) *Jack of cards.* The Knave or boy of the king and queen of the same suit.

(7) *Jack the Giant-killer* (*q.v.*).

(8) *Glym Jack.* A link boy who carries a glym. (German, *glimmen*.) (*See* GLIM.)

(9) *Little Jack Horner.* (*See* JACK HORNER.)

(10) *The house that Jack built* (nursery tale).

III. APPLIED TO THE MALES OR INFERIOR ANIMALS: as—

Jack-ass, Jack-baker (a kind of owl), *Jack* or dog fox, *Jack-hare, Jack-hern, Jack-rat, Jack-shark, Jack-snipe;* a young pike is called a *Jack,* so also were the male birds used in falconry.

IV. APPLIED TO INSTRUMENTS which supply the place of or represent inferior men or boys:—

(1) *A jack.* Used instead of a turnspit boy, generally called Jack.

(2) *A jack.* Used for lifting heavy weights.

(3) *Jack.* The figure outside old public clocks made to strike the bell.

"Strike like Jack o' the clock-house, never but in season."—*Strode: Floating Island.*

(4) *Jack-roll.* The cylinder round which the rope of a well coils.

(5) *Jack-in-the-basket.* The cap or basket on the top of a pole to indicate the place of a sandbank at sea, etc.

(6) *Jack-in-the-box.* A toy consisting of a box out of which, when the lid is raised, a figure springs.

(7) *Boot-jack.* An instrument for drawing off boots, which used to be done by inferior servants.

(8) *Bottle-jack.* A machine for turning the roast instead of a turnspit.

(9) *Lifting-jack.* A machine for lifting the axle-tree of a carriage when the wheels are cleaned.

(10) *Roasting-jack.* (See *Bottle-jack*, 8.)

(11) *Smoke-jack.* An apparatus in a chimney-flue for turning a spit. It is made to revolve by the upward current of smoke and air.

(12) *Jack-chain.* A small chain for turning the spit of a smoke-jack.

V. APPLIED TO INFERIOR ARTICLES which bear the same relation to the thing imitated as Jack does to a gentleman.

(1) *Jack.* A rough stool or wooden horse for sawing timber on.

(2) *Jack.* A small drinking vessel made of waxed leather.

"Body of me, I am dry still ; give me the jack, boy."—*Beaumont and Fletcher: Bloody Brother*, ii. 2.

(3) *Jack.* Inferior kind of armour. (*See* JACK, No. VIII.)

(4) *A Jack* and *a half-jack.* Counters resembling a sovereign and a half-sovereign. Used at gaming-tables to make up a show of wealth.

(5) *Jack-block.* A block attached to the topgallant-tie of a ship.

(6) *Jack-boots.* Cumbrous boots of tough, thick leather worn by fishermen. Jacks or armour for the legs.

(7) *Jack-pan.* A vessel used by barbers for heating water for their customers.

(8) *Jack-plane.* A menial plane to do the rough work for finer instruments.

(9) *Jack-rafter.* A rafter in a hipped roof, shorter than a full-sized one.

(10) *Jack-rib.* An inferior rib in an arch, being shorter than the rest.

(11) *Jack-screw.* A large screw rotating in a threaded socket, used for lifting heavy weights.

(12) *Jack-timbers.* Timbers in a building shorter than the rest.

(13) *Jack-towel.* A coarse, long towel hung on a roller, for the servants' use.

(14) *Jack of Dover* (*q.v.*).

(15) *Jacket* (*q.v.*).

(16) *Black jack.* A huge drinking vessel. A Frenchman speaking of it says, "The English drink out of their boots." (*Heywood.*)

VI. A TERM OF CONTEMPT.

(1) *Jack-a-lantern* or *Jack-o'-lantern*, the fool fire (*ignis fatuus*).

(2) *Jack-ass.* An unmitigated fool.

(3) *Jack-at-bowls.* The butt of all the players.

(4) *Jack-daw.* A prating nuisance.

(5) *Jack Drum's entertainment* (*q.v.*).

(6) *Jackey.* A monkey.

(7) *Skip-jack.* A toy, an upstart.

(8) *The black jack.* The turnip-fly.

(9) *The yellow jack.* The yellow fever.

VII. USED IN PROVERBIAL PHRASES.

¶ *A good Jack makes a good Jill.* A good husband makes a good wife, a good master makes a good servant. Jack, a generic name for man, husband, or master ; and Gill or Jill, his wife or female servant.

Every Jack shall have his Jill. Every man may find a wife if he likes ; or rather, every country rustic shall find a lass to be his mate.

" Jack shall have his Jill,
    Nought shall go ill ;
The man shall have his mare again, and all shall be well."
Shakespeare : Midsummer Night's Dream, iii. 2.

To play the Jack. To play the rogue or knave ; to deceive or lead astray like Jack-o'-lantern, or *ignis fatuus*.

"——your fairy, which you say is a harmless fairy, has done little better than played the Jack with us."—*Shakespeare : Tempest*, iv. 1.

To be upon their jacks. To have the advantage over one. The reference is to the coat of mail quilted with stout leather, more recently called a jerkin.

VIII. **Jack.** Armour consisting of a leather surcoat worn over the hauberk, from the fourteenth to the seventeenth century, both inclusive. It was formed by overlapping pieces of steel fastened by one edge upon canvas, coated over with cloth or velvet. In short, it was a surcoat padded with metal to make it sword-proof. These jazerines were worn by the peasantry of the English borders when they journeyed from place to place, and in their skirmishes with moss-troopers.

" Jackes quilted and covered over with leather, fustian, or canvas, over thicke plates of iron that are sowed to the same."—*Lily : Euphues.*

¶ *Colonel Jack.* The hero of Defoe's novel so called. He is a thief who goes to Virginia, and becomes the owner of vast plantations and a family of slaves.

Jack-a-Dandy. A term of endearment for a smart, bright little fellow; a Jemmy Jessamy.

"Smart she is, and handy, O !
Sweet as sugar-candy, O ! . . .
And I'm her Jack-a-dandy, O !"

Jack - a - dandy. Slang for brandy. Dandy rhymes with brandy. (*See* CHIVY.)

∴ In Ireland "dandy" means whisky; but whisky = eau de vie; and eau de vie is brandy.

"Dimidium cyathi vero apud Methropolitãnos Herbernicos dicitur Dandy."—*Blackwood's Magazine*, May, 1838 (*Father Tom and the Pope*).

Jack-a-Lantern (*A*). A Will-o'-the-wisp, an *ignis fatuus*.

Jack-a-napes or **Jackanapes** = Jack of apes. An impertinent, vulgar prig. (*See* JEANNOT.)

More likely, it is *Jack* and *ape*, formed on the model of Jack-ass, a stupid fool.

"I will teach a scurvy jackanape priest to meddle or make."—*Shakespeare: Merry Wives of Windsor*, i. 4.

Jack-Amend-All. One of the nicknames given to Jack Cade the rebel, who promised to remedy all abuses.

Jack Brag. (*See* BRAG.)

Jack Drum's Entertainment. A beating. (*See* JOHN DRUM'S, etc.)

Jack Horner. For solution see *Notes and Queries*, xvi. 156; xvii. 83. In Latin alcaics, thus:

"Sedens Johannes parvus in angulo
Hornčrus edit crustula Christmica;
Et dixit, ut pruna extrahebat
Pollice, 'Quam sum ego suavis infans !'"
The Lincoln Herald, Jan. 13, 1832.

Jack Ketch. Although this looks very much like a sobriquet, there seems no sufficient evidence to believe it to be otherwise than a real proper name. We are told that the name Jack was applied to hangmen from Richard Jaquett, to whom the manor of Tyburn once belonged. (*See* HANGMEN.)

Jack Pudding. A buffoon who performs pudding tricks, such as swallowing a certain number of yards of black-pudding. S. Bishop observes that each country names its stage buffoon from its favourite viands: The Dutchman calls him *Pickel-herringë;* the Germans, *Hans Wurst* (John Sausage); the Frenchman, *Jean Potage;* the Italian, *Macaro'ni;* and the English, *Jack Pudding.*

Jack Robinson. *Before you can say Jack Robinson.* Immediately. Grose says that the saying had its birth from a very volatile gentleman of that name, who used to pay flying visits to his neighbours, and was no sooner announced than he was off again; but the following couplet does not confirm this derivation :—

"A warke it ys as easie to be done
As tys to saye *Jacke! robys on.*"
An old Play, cited by Halliwell: Arch. Dict.

Jack Sprat. A dwarf; as if sprats were dwarf mackerels. Children, by a similar metaphor, are called small fry.

Jack Tar. A common sailor, whose hands and clothes are tarred by the ship tackling.

Jack and the Bean Stalk. A nursery tale of German invention. The giant is All-Father, whose three treasures are (1) a harp—*i.e.* the wind; (2) bags full of treasures—*i.e.* the rain; and (3) the red hen which laid golden eggs—that is, the genial sun. Man avails himself of these treasures and becomes rich.

Jack of all Trades is Master of None. In French, "*Tout savoir est ne rien savoir.*"

Jack o' both Sides. A supernumerary who plays on both sides to make up a party; one who for profit or policy is quite colourless.

Jack o' the Clock. The figure which comes out to strike the hours on the bell of a clock. A contraction of Jaquemart (*q.v.*).

"*King Richard.* Well, but what's o'clock ?
Buckingham. Upon the stroke of ten.
K. R. Well, let it strike.
B. Why let it strike ?
K. R. Because that, like a jack, thou keep'st the stroke
Betwixt thy begging and my meditation."
Shakespeare: Richard III., iv. 2.

Jack of Dover. A stockfish, "hake salted and dried." The Latin for a hake is *merlucius*, and lucius is a jack or pike. *Mer*, of course, means the sea, and Dover, the chief Cinque Port, is used as a synonym. Also refuse wine collected into a bottle and sold for fresh wine. "To *do-over* again." (*See* DOVER.)

"Many a Jack of Dover hastow sold
That hath been twyës hot and twyës cold."
Chaucer: Canterbury Tales.

Jack of Newbury. John Winchcomb, the greatest clothier of the world, in the reign of Henry VIII. He kept 100 looms in his own house at Newbury, and equipped at his own expense 100 of his men to aid the king against the Scotch in Flodden Field.

Jack o' the Bowl. The most famous brownie or house-spirit of Switzerland; so called from the custom of placing for him every night on the roof of the cow-house a bowl of fresh sweet cream. The contents of this bowl are sure to disappear before morning.

Jack Out of Office. One no longer in office.

"I am left out ; for me nothing remains.
But long I will not be Jack-out-of-office."
Shakespeare : 1 *Henry VI.,* i. 1.

Jack the Giant-killer owed much of his success to his four marvellous possessions—an invisible coat, a cap of wisdom, shoes of swiftness, and a resistless sword. When he put on his coat no eye could see him; when he had his shoes on no one could overtake him ; his sword would cut through everything ; and when his cap was on he knew everything he required to know. Yonge says the story is based on the Scandinavian tale of Thor and Loki, while Masson maintains it to be a nursery version of the feats of Corin'eus in Geoffrey of Monmouth's marvellous history. I apprehend that neither of these suggestions will find many supporters.

⁂ Military success depends (1) on an *invisible coat*, or secrecy, not letting the foe know your plans ; (2) a *cap of wisdom*, or wise counsel ; (3) *shoes of swiftness*, or attacking the foe before he is prepared ; and (4) a *resistless sword*, or dauntless courage.

Jack the Ripper. An unknown person who so called himself, and committed a series of murders in the East End of London on common prostitutes.

The first was April 2nd, 1888 : the next was August 7th ; the third was August 31st ; the fourth was September 8th ; the fifth was September 30th, when two women were murdered ; the sixth was November 9th ; the seventh was December 20th, in a builder's yard ; the eighth was July 17th, 1889, at Whitechapel ; the ninth was September 17th.

Jack and James. Jewish, *Jacob ;* French, *Jacques,* our "Jack," and *Jacquemes,* our "James." Jacques used to be the commonest name of France, hence the insurrection of the common people was termed the insurrection of the Jacques, or the *Jacquerie ;* and a rustic used to be called a *Jacques bon homme.* The Scotch call Jack *Jock.*

Jackal. A toady. One who does the dirty work of another. It was once thought that the jackals hunted in troops to provide the lion with prey, hence they were called the "lion's providers." No doubt the lion will at times avail himself of the jackal's assistance by appropriating prey started by these "hunters," but it would be folly to suppose that the jackal acted on the principle of *vos non vobis.* (*See* HONEYCOMB.)

Jacket. The French *jaquette,* "little jack," a translation of the German *Hanseline,* a slop cut short.

Jacket. The skin of a potato. Potatoes brought to table unpeeled are said to be "with their jackets on."

To dust one's jacket. (*See* DUST.)

Jackson. (*See* STONEWALL.)

Jackso'nian Professor. The professor of natural and experimental philosophy in the University of Cambridge. This professorship was founded in 1783 by the Rev. Richard Jackson.

Jacob the Scourge of Grammar. Giles Jacob, master of Romsey, in Hampshire, brought up for an attorney. A poetaster in the time of Pope. (See *Dunciad,* iii.)

Jacob's Ladder. A ladder seen by the patriarch Jacob in a vision. It was set on the earth, and reached to heaven, and angels seemed to be ascending and descending on it (Gen. xxviii. 12). Jacob is, on this account, a cant name for a ladder. There is a pretty blue flower so called.

Jacob's Staff. An instrument for taking heights and distances.

"Reach then a soaring quill, that I may write
As with a Jacob's staff to take her height."
Cleveland : The Hecatomb to his Mistress.

The Apostle James is usually represented with a staff.

"As he had travelled many a summer's day
Through boiling sands of Arabie and Ynd ;
And in his hand a Jacob's staff to stay
His weary limbs upon."
Spenser : Faërie Queene, book i. canto vi. 32-35.

Jacob's Stone. The stone inclosed in the coronation chair of Great Britain, brought from Scone by Edward I., and said to be the stone on which the patriarch Jacob laid his head when he dreamt about the ladder referred to above.

This stone was originally used in Ireland as a coronation stone. It was called "Innisfail," or Stone of Destiny. (*See* CORONATION CHAIR.)

Jacobins. The Dominicans were so called in France from the "Rue St. Jacques," Paris, where they first established themselves in 1219.

Jacobins. A political club, originally called the *Club Breton,* formed at Versailles in 1789. On their removal to Paris, they met in the hall of an ex-convent of Jacobins (*see above*), in the Rue St. Honoré.

Jac'obites (3 syl.). The partisans of James II. (when William III. superseded him), his son, and grandson.

Jacobites, nicknamed *Warming-pans.* It is said that Mary d'Este, the wife of James II., never had a living child, but that on one occasion a child, introduced to her bedroom in a warming-pan, was substituted for her dead infant. This "warming-pan child" was the Pretender. Such is the tale, the truth is quite another matter.

Jac'obites. An Oriental sect of Monoph'ysites, so called from Jaco'bus Baradæus (Jacoub Al-Baradei), Bishop of Edessa, in Syria, in the sixth century.

Jaco'bus. A gold coin of the value of 25s., struck in the reign of James I.

Jacquard Loom. So called from Jos. Marie Jacquard, of Lyons, who invented this ingenious device for weaving figures upon silks and muslins. (1752-1834.)

Jacqueline (of Paris). A bell weighing 15,000 lbs., cast in 1400.

Jacquerie (*La*). An insurrection of the peasantry of France in 1358, excited by the oppressions of the privileged classes and Charles the Bad of Navarre, while King Jean was a prisoner in England. When the peasants complained, and asked who was to redress their grievances, they were told in scorn *Jacques Bonhomme* (Johnny Goodman), *i.e.* no one. At length a leader appeared, called himself Jacques Bonhomme, and declared war to the death against every gentleman in France. In six weeks some 12,000 of these insurgents were cut down, and amongst their number was the leader himself. (*See* JACK, JACQUES.)

Jacques. A generic name for the poor artisan class in France. Jaques is a sort of cotton waistcoat without sleeves.

" Jacques, il me faut troubler ton somme ;
 Dans le village, un gros huissier
 Rôde et court, suivi du messier :
 C'est pour l'impôt, las ! mon pauvre homme.
 -Lève-toi, Jacques, lève-toi,
 Voici venir l'huissier du roi."
 Béranger (1831).

Pauvre Jacques. Said to a maiden when she is lackadaisical (French). Marie Antoinette had at the Little Trianon an artificial Swiss village, which she called her "*Petite Suisse,*" and actually sent to Switzerland for a peasant girl to assist in milking the cows. The Swiss maiden was one day overheard sighing for "*Pauvre Jacques,*" and the queen sent for the distant swain, and had the lovers married. To finish this absurd romance, the Marchioness de Travanet wrote an ode on the event, which was for a time wonderfully popular.

" Pauvre Jacques, quand j'etais prés de toi,
 Je ne sentais pas ma misère :
 Mais à présent que tu vis loin de moi,
 Je manque de tout sur la terre."
 Marquise de Travanet.

Jacques Bonhomme. A sort of fairy good-luck, who is to redress all wrongs, and make all the poor wealthy. The French peasants are so called sometimes, and then the phrase is like our term of sneering pity, "my good fellow," or "my fine fellow." (*See* JACQUES.)

Jactitation of Marriage. A false assertion by a person of being married to another. This is actionable.

Jade or *The Divine Stone.* Worn by the Indians as an amulet to preserve them from the bite of venomous animals, and to cure the gravel, epilepsy, etc. (*Hill.*)

" The conversation was interspersed by continual cups of tea drunk out of the most beautiful Chinese-ware, while the Ambar's cup was of a green jade."—*Bonvalot: Across Thibet,* chap. x. p. 252.

Jade. A worthless horse. An old woman (used in contempt). A young woman (not necessarily contemptuous).

Jaf'fier (3 syl.), in *Venice Preserved,* a tragedy by Otway. He joins the conspiracy of Pierre against the Venetian state, but communicates the secret to his wife Belvide'ra. Belvide'ra, being the daughter of a senator, is naturally anxious to save the life of Priu'li, her father, and accordingly induces her husband to disclose the plot, under promise of pardon to all the conspirators. The plot being revealed, the senate condemned the conspirators to death; whereupon Jaffier stabbed Pierre to prevent his being broken on the wheel, and then stabbed himself.

Jagger. A gentleman ; a sportsman. (German, *jager,* a sportsman.)

Jail-bird (*A*). One who has been in jail as a prisoner.

" At this late period of Christianity we are brought up to abhor jail-birds as we do toads."— *Beecher : The Plymouth Pulpit,* August 30th, 1874, vol. ii. 557.

Jamambuxes [*Soldiers of the round valleys*]. Certain fanatics of Japan, who roam about and pretend to hold converse with the Devil. They scourge themselves severely, and sometimes refrain from sleeping for several days, in order to obtain the odour of sanctity. They are employed by the people for the discovery of articles stolen or lost.

Jambon. A gun, so called from its fanciful resemblance to a "betterave" or jambon. The botanical name of the root is *melochia*.

"What would you do to me, brigand? . . . Give me fifty blows of a matraque, as your officer gave you last week for stealing his jambon?"—*Ouida: Under Two Flags*, chap. xvi.

Jambuscha [*Jam-bus-cah*]. Adam's preceptor, according to the pre-Adamites. Sometimes called Boan, and sometime Zagtith.

James. A sovereign; a jacŏbus. A gold coin circulated in the reign of James I. Worth about 25s.

James (*St.*). Patron saint of Spain. At Padron, near Compostella, they used to show a huge stone as the veritable boat in which the apostle sailed from Palestine. His body was discovered in 840 by divine revelation to Bishop Theodomi'rus, and King Alfonso built a church at Compostella for its shrine. According to another legend, it was the *relics* of St. James that were miraculously conveyed to Spain in a ship of marble from Jerusalem, where he was bishop. A knight saw the ship sailing into port, his horse took fright, and plunged with its rider into the sea. The knight saved himself by "boarding the marble vessel," but his clothes were found to be entirely covered with scallop shells.

⁖ In the *Acta Sanctorum* (xi. 37, etc.) we are told, that in Clavigium scarcely a stone is found which does not bear the form of a shell; and if these stones are broken up, the broken bits have also the forms of shells.

In Christian art this saint has sometimes the sword by which he was beheaded, and sometimes he is attired as a pilgrim, with his cloak covered with shells. (*See above*.)

St. James (*the Less*). His attribute is a fuller's club, in allusion to the instrument by which he was put to death, after having been precipitated from the summit of the temple.

St. James's College. So called from James I., who granted a charter to a college founded at Chelsea by Dr. Sutcliffe, Dean of Exeter, to maintain priests to answer all adversaries of religion. Laud nicknamed it "Controversy College." The college was a failure, and Charles II. gave the site to the Royal Society, who sold it for the purpose of erecting the Royal Hospital for Old Soldiers, which now exists.

St. James's Day. July 25th, the day of his martyrdom,

The Court of St. James or *St. James's.* The British court. Queen Victoria holds her drawing-rooms and levées in St. James's Palace, Pall Mall; but Queen Anne, the four Georges, and William IV. resided in this palace.

Jamie or **Jemmie Duffs.** Weepers. So called from a noted Scotchman of the 18th century, who lived at Edinburgh. His great passion, like that of "Old Q.," was to follow funerals in mourning costume, with orthodox weepers. I myself know a gentleman of a similar morbid passion. (*Kay: Original Portraits*, i. 7, and ii. 9, 17, 95.)

Jamshid'. King of the Genii, famous for a golden cup full of the elixir of life. This cup, hidden by the genii, was discovered while digging the foundations of Persep'olis.

" I know too where the genii hid
The jewelled cup of their king Jamshid,
With life's elixir sparkling high."
Thomas Moore: Paradise and the Peri.

Jane. A Genoese halfpenny, a corruption of Januensis or Genoensis.

" Because I could not give her many a jane."
Spenser: Faërie Queene, book iii. canto vii. 58. ⸿

Jane. A most ill-starred name for rulers. To give a few examples: *Lady Jane Grey*, beheaded by Mary for treason; *Jane Seymour; Jane* or *Joan Beaufort*, wife of James I. of Scotland, who was infamously and savagely murdered; *Jane of Burgundy*, wife of Philippe *le Long*, who imprisoned her for adultery in 1314; *Jane of Flanders*, who was in ceaseless war with *Jane of Penthièvre* after the captivity of their husbands. This contest is known in history as "the wars of the two Janes" (fourteenth century). *Jane of France* (de Valois), wife of Louis XII., who repudiated her for being ugly; *Jane d'Albret*, mother of Henri IV. of France. Being invited to Paris to attend the espousals of her son with Margaret de Valo'is, she was poisoned by Catharine de' Medicis (1572); *Jane, Countess of Hainault*, daughter of Baldwin, and wife of Fernand of Portugal, who was made prisoner at the battle of Bouvines in 1214. She refused to ransom him, and is thought to have poisoned her father; *Jane Henriquez*, wife of John II. of Navarre, stirred up war between her husband and his son Carlos by a former marriage, and ultimately made away with the young prince, a proceeding which caused a revolt of the Catalonians (1462); *Jane the Imbecile* of Castle, who lost her reason from grief at the neglect of her husband, Philip the

Handsome, Archduke of Austria; *Jane I. of Naples* married Andrew of Hungary, whom she caused to be murdered, and then married the assassin. Her reign was most disastrous. La Harpe has a tragedy entitled *Jeanne de Naples; Jane II. of Naples*, a woman of most scandalous character, guilty of every sort of wantonness. She married James, Count of March, who put to death her lovers and imprisoned Jane for two years. At her release James fled to France, when Jane had a *liaison* with Caraccioli, whom she murdered. *Joan*, the pope, if indeed such a person ever existed. *Jeanne la Pucelle* [Joan of Arc] cannot be called a ruler, but her lot was not more happy; etc. etc. (*See* JOHN TWO.)

Jane Eyre. The heroine in a novel of the same name, by Currer Bell (*q.v.*).

Jan'issaries or **Jan'izaries**, a celebrated militia of the Ottoman Empire, raised by Orchan in 1326, and called the *Yengi-tscheri* (new corps). It was blessed by Hadji Bektash, a saint, who cut off a sleeve of his fur mantle and gave it to the captain. The captain put the sleeve on his head, and from this circumstance arose the fur cap worn by these footguards. In 1826, having become too formidable to the state, they were abolished.

"There were two classes of Janizaries, one regularly organised . . . and the other composing an irregular militia."—*Chambers: Encyclopædia*, vol. vi. p. 279.

Jan'nes and **Jam'bres.** The two magicians of Pharaoh, who imitated some of the miracles of Moses. The Jannes and Jambres who "withstood Moses," mentioned by St. Paul (2 Tim. iii. 8, 9), are supposed to be the same. The paraphrast Jonathan says they were the sons of Balaam.

Jan'senists. A sect of Christians, who held the doctrines of Cornelius Jansen, Bishop of Ypres, in France. Jansen professed to have formulated the teaching of Augustine, A.D. 1640, which resembled Calvinism in many respects. He taught the doctrines of "irresistible grace," "original sin," and the "utter helplessness of the natural man to turn to God." Louis XIV. took part against them, and they were put down by Pope Clement XI., in 1705, in the famous bull called Unigen'itus (*q.v.*).

Janua'rius (*St.*). A martyr in 305. Two vials of his blood are preserved in the cathedral at Naples, and every year on September 19 (the day of his martyrdom) the blood liquefies.

Order of St. Januarius (patron saint of Naples), instituted in 1738 by Infantë don Carlos.

Jan'uary. The month dedicated by the Romans to Janus (*q.v.*). Janus had two faces, and January could look back to the year past, and forwards to the current year.

Ja'nus. The temple of peace, in Rome. The doors were thrown open in times of war and closed in times of peace. Some think the two faces of this mythical deity allegorise Noah and his sons, who look back on the world before the Flood, and forwards on the world after the deluge had abated. This idea will do very well in poetry.

"Slavery was the hinge on which the gates of the temple of Janus turned" (in the American war).—*The Times*.

Japanese (3 syl.). The language of Japan, a native of Japan, anything pertaining thereto.

Japheth's Stone. According to tradition, Noah gave Japheth a stone which the Turks call *giudëtasch* and *senkjedë*. Whoever possesses this stone has the power of bringing rain from heaven at will. It was for a long time preserved by the Moguls.

Japhet'idie. The supposed posterity of Japheth, son of Noah. The Aryan family is said to belong to this race.

"The Indo-European family of languages as known by various designations. Some style it *Japhetic*, as if it appertained to the descendants of the patriarch Japheth; as the *Semitic* tongues [appertain] to the descendants of Shem."—*Whitney: Languages, etc.*, lecture v. p. 192.

Jaquemart. The automaton of a clock, consisting of a man and woman who strike the hours on a bell. So called from Jean Jaquemart of Di on, a clockmaker, who devised this piece of mechanism.

Jaques (1 syl.). A morose cynical moraliser in Shakespeare's *As You Like It*. It is much disputed whether the word is a monosyllable or not. Charles Lamb makes it a dissyllable—"Where Jaquës fed in solitary vein;" but Sir Walter Scott uses it as a monosyllable— "Whom humorous Jaques with envy viewed."

Jarkman. An Abram-man (*q.v.*). Jark means a *seal*, whence also a safe-conduct. Abram-men were licensed beggars, who had the "seal" or licence of the Bethlehem Hospital to beg.

Jarnac. *Coup de Jarnac.* A peculiar stroke of the sword by which the opponent is ham-strung. The allusion is to the duel between Jarnac and La Châteigneraie, on July 10th, 1547, in the presence of Henri II., when Jarnac dealt his adversary such a blow, from which he died.

Jarndyce v. Jarndyce. An interminable Chancery suit in Dickens's *Bleak House.* The character of Jarndyce is that of a kind-hearted, easy fellow, who is half ashamed that his left hand should know what his right hand gives.

Jarvey. A hackney-coach driver. Said to be a contraction of Geoffrey; and the reason why this name was selected was because coachmen say to their horses *gee-o*, and Ge-o' is a contraction of Geoffrey. Ballantine says, that one Jarvis, a noted hackney-coachman who was hanged, was the original Jarvey.

A Jarvey's benjamin. A coachman's great-coat. (*See* BENJAMIN.)

Jarvie (*Baillie Nicol*). A Glasgow magistrate in Scott's *Rob Roy.* He is petulant, conceited, purse-proud, without tact, and intensely prejudiced, but sincere and kind-hearted.

Jaun'dice (2 syl.) *A jaundiced eye.* A prejudiced eye which sees "faults that are not." It was a popular belief among the Romans that to the eye of a person who had the jaundice everything looked of a yellow tinge. (French, *jaune*, yellow.)

" All seems infected that th' infected spy,
As all seems yellow to the jaundiced eye."
Pope: Essay on Criticism.

Javan [*elay*]. Son of Japheth. In most Eastern languages it is the collective name of the Greeks, and is to be so understood in Isa. lxvi. 19, and Ezek. xxvii. 13.

In the *World Before the Flood*, by James Montgomery, Javan is the hero. On the day of his birth his father died, and Javan remained in the " patriarch's glen " under his mother's care, till she also died. Then he resolved to see the world, and sojourned for ten years with the race of Cain, where he became the disciple of Jubal, noted for his musical talents. At the expiration of that time he returned, penitent, to the patriarch's glen, where Zillah, daughter of Enoch, "won the heart to Heaven denied." The giants invaded the glen, and carried off the little band captives. Enoch reproved him in their fury, but they could not find him, " for he walked with God." As he ascended through the air his mantle fell on Javan, who, " smiting with it as he moved along," brought the captives safely back to the glen again. A tempest broke forth of so fearful a nature that the giant army fled in a panic, and their king was slain by some treacherous blow given by some unknown hand.

Jav'anese (3 syl.). A native of Java, anything pertaining to Java.

Javert. An officer of police, the impersonation of inexorable law in *Les Misérables,* by Victor Hugo.

Jaw. Words of complaint; wrangling, abuse, jabber. "To jaw," to annoy with words, to jabber, wrangle, or abuse. The French *gueule* and *gueuler* are used in the same manner.

Hold your jaw. Hold your tongue or jabber.

What are you jawing about? What are you jabbering or wrangling about?

A break-jaw word. A very long word, or one hard to pronounce.

Jā-wāb. The refusal of an offer of marriage. Thus when one lady says to another that " Mr. A. B. has got his jawab," she means that he made her an offer of marriage, but was refused. (*Calcutta slang.*)

Jawbone (2 syl.). Credit, promises. (*Jaw*, words or talk; *bon*, good.)

Jay (*A*). A wanton.
" This jay of Italy . . . . hath betrayed him."—
Shakespeare : Cymbeline, iii. 4.

Jay. A plunger; one who spends his money recklessly; a simpleton. This is simply the letter J, the initial letter of Juggins, who, in 1887, made a fool of himself by losses on the turf.

Ja'zey. A wig; a corruption of Jersey, and so called because they are made of Jersey flax and fine wool.

Je Maintiendrai (*I will maintain*). The motto of the House of Nassau. When William III. came to England he retained the motto, but added to it, " I will maintain *the liberties of England and the Protestant religion.*"

Je ne Sais Quoi. An indescribable something; as " There was a *je ne sais quoi* about him which made us dislike him at first sight."

Jeames (1 syl.). Any flunkey. Sometimes the *Morning Post* is so called.

Thackeray wrote *Jeames's Diary* (published in *Punch*), of which Jeames de la Pluche was the hero.

Jean Crapaud. A Frenchman. A Frenchman is called both a toad and a frog. (*See* CRAPAUD.)

Jean Farine [*Jack Flour*]. A sort of Scaramouch, generally very tall, and representing a loutish boy dressed all in white, the hair, face, and hands being covered with flour.

"Jean Farine s'en fervient (du manteau d'un gentilhomme Gascon) un bonnet; et à le voir blanchastre, il semble qu'il soit desja enfariné."
—*Les Jeux de l'Inconnu* (1645).

Jean de Lettre (*Mr. Jenkins*). "*Qui pour l'ordinaire, dit Tallemant, est un animal mal idoine à toute autre chose.*" (*Mme. Deshoulières: Histori-ettes,* ix. 209, x. 82.)

Jean de la Suie (French). A Savoyard.

Jean de la Vigne (French). A crucifix. (*See next article.*)

Jean des Vignes (French). So the jonglers call the poupée to which they address themselves. The French Protestants in the sixteenth century called "the host" Jean, and the word is pretty well synonymous with buffoon. Jean des Vignes was a drunken marionette performer of considerable ability; "Jean" was his name, "des Vignes" his sobriquet. Hence when a person does a bad action, the French say, "*Il fait comme Jean des Vignes;*" an illicit marriage is called "*le mariage de Jean des Vignes,*" and a bad fellow is "*un Jean des Vignes.*" Hence Assoucy says, "*Moi, pauvre sot, plus sot que Jean des Vignes !*"

"Jean ! que dire sur Jean ? c'est un terrible nom,
Qui jamais n'accompagne une épithète honnête
Jean des Vignes, Jean ligne. Où vais-je ?
Trouves bon
Qu'en si beau chemin je m'arrête."
Virgile Travesti, vii. (*Juno to Æneas*).

Jeannot (French). One who is minutely great; one who exercises his talents and ingenuity on trifles; one who after great preparation at table to produce some mighty effect, brings forth only a ridiculous mouse.

Jeb'usites (3 syl.), in Dryden's satire of *Absalom and Achitophel,* stands for the Roman Catholics; so called because England was Roman Catholic before the Reformation, and Jerusalem was called Jebus before the time of David.

✱ In this poem, the *Jebusites* are the Catholics, and the *Levites* the dissenting clergy.

"Succeeding times did equal folly call,
Believing nothing, or believing all.
The Egyptian rites the Jebusites embraced,
When gods were recommended by their taste."
[Transubstantiation.]
Dryden: Absalom and Achitophel, Part i. 117-123.

Jedwood Justice. Putting an obnoxious person to death first, and trying him afterwards. This sort of justice was dealt to moss-troopers. Same as *Jedburgh justice, Jeddart justice.* We have also "Cupar justice" and "Abingdon law." Of the last we are told that Major-General Brown, in the Commonwealth, hanged a man first and tried him afterwards.

"Jedwood justice—hang in haste and try at leisure."—*Scott: Fair Maid of Perth,* chap. xxxii.

Jehen'nam. The Gehenna or Inferno of the Arabs. It consists of seven stages, one below the other. The first is allotted to atheists; the second to Manicheans (*q.v.*); the third to the Brahmins of India; the fourth to the Jews; the fifth to Christians; the sixth to the Magians or Ghebers of Persia; and the seventh to hypocrites. (*The Koran.*)

Jehovis'tic. (*See* ELOHISTIC.)

Jehu. A coachman, especially one who drives at a rattling pace.

"The watchman told, saying, ... The driving is like the driving of Jehu the son of Nimshi; for he driveth furiously."—2 Kings ix. 20.

Jejune (2 syl.). *A jejune narrative.* A dry, tedious one. (Latin, *jeju'nus,* dry, spiritless.)

"Till farce itself, most mournfully jejune,
Calls for the kind assistance of a tune."
Sowper: Retirement, 711.

Jekyll. *Dr. Jekyll and Mr. Hyde.* The two phases of one man, "the law of his members warring against the law of his mind." Jekyll is the "would do good," Hyde is "the evil that is present." (*Stevenson: Dr. Jekyll and Mr. Hyde.*)

Jelly Pardons. When Thomas Cromwell was a clerk in the English factory at Antwerp, two of his fellow-countrymen from Boston (Lincolnshire) consulted with him as to the best means of getting the pardons renewed for the repair of Boston harbour. Cromwell, knowing that Pope Julius was very fond of dainties, provided for him some exquisite jelly, and told his Holiness that only royalty ever ate it in England. The Pope was so pleased with the delicacy that he signed the pardons, on condition of having the recipe of the jelly.

Jel'lyby (*Mrs.*). A philanthropist who would spend and be spent to help the poor fan-makers and flower-girls of Borrioboolah Gha, but would bundle into the street a poor beggar dying of starvation on her own doorstep. (*Dickens: Bleak House.*)

Jemmie Duffs. (*See* JAMIE DUFFS.)

Jemmy, a name found in engravings of the eighteenth century, was James Worsdale, the painter and dramatic writer (died 1767).

A housebreaker's crowbar. A variant of Jimmy, Jenny, Jinnie, and a diminutive of en-gine. Similarly a "spinning-jinnie" is a small engine for spinning. These crowbars generally take to pieces that they may be slipped into the pocket.

Jemmy. The head of a slaughtered sheep. There are "boiled jemmies," "baked jemmies," and "sanguinary jemmies" (raw sheep's heads). The tradition is that James IV. of Scotland breakfasted on a sheep's head just before the battle of Flodden Field (Sep. 9, 1513).

"Mr. Sikes made many pleasant witticisms on jemmies, a cant name for sheep's heads, and also for an ingenious implement much used in his profession."—*Dickens: Oliver Twist.*

Jemmy. A great-coat. So called from the Scotch cloth called jemmy.

Jemmy. Spruce, fine. A diminutive of *gim*, spruce or smart (Anglo-Saxon *gemet*). Gimcrack means an ornamental toy, a pretty ornament of no solidity. (*See below,* JEMMY JESSAMY.)

Jemmy Dawson was one of the Manchester rebels, who was hanged, drawn, and quartered on Kennington Common, Surrey, July 30th, 1746. A lady of gentle blood was in love with the gallant young rebel, and died of a broken heart on the day of his execution. (*Percy's Reliques*, series 2, book iii. 26.)

Shenstone has a ballad on it, beginning, "Come, listen to my mournful tale."

Jemmy Jessamy (*A*). A Jack-a-dandy; a lady's fondling, "sweet as sugar-candy." ·

Jenkinson (*Ephraim*). A swindling rascal, who makes a tool of Dr. Primrose. (*Goldsmith: Vicar of Wakefield.*)

Jennet. A small Spanish horse.

Jenny. The spinning jenny means the little spinning engine. The word is a corrupt diminutive, 'ginie. It is an error to derive the word from the inventor's wife or daughter, seeing his wife's name was Elizabeth, and he had no daughter.

Jenny l'Ouvrière. A generic name for a hard-working, poor, but contented needlewoman. The name was devised by Émile Barateau, and rendered popular by his song so called.

"Entendez-vous un oiseau familier?
C'est le chanteur de Jenny l'Ouvrière.
Au cœur content, content de peu
Elle pourrait être riche, et préfère
Ce qui vient de Dieu." (1847.)

Jenny Wren, the sweetheart of Robin Redbreast.

"Robin promised Jenny, if she would be his wife, she should 'feed on cherry-pie and drink currant-wine'; and he says:—
· I'll dress you like a goldfinch,
Or any peacock gay ;
So, dearest Jen, if you'll be mine,
Let us appoint the day.'
Jenny replies:—
'Cherry-pie is very nice,
And so is currant wine ;
But I must wear my plain brown gown,
And never go too fine.'"

Jeofail, *i.e.* **J'ai failli** (*Lapsus sum ;* I have failed), an omission or oversight in a law proceeding. There are several statutes of Jeofail for the remedy of slips or mistakes.

Jeop'ardy (3 syl.). Hazard, danger. Tyrwhitt says it is the French *jeu parti*, and Froissart uses the phrase, "*Si nous les voyons à jeu parti*" (vol. i. c. 234). Jeu parti is a game where the chances are exactly balanced, hence a critical state.

Jereed. A javelin with which the Easterns exercise. (Turkish and Arabic.)

Jeremi'ad (4 syl.). A pitiful tale, a tale of woe to produce compassion ; so called from the "Lamentations" of the prophet Jeremiah.

Jeremiah, derived from "Cucumber." The joke is this: King Jeremiah = *Jere'-king*, contracted in *Jer'-kin'*, or *gher-kin*, and gherkin is a young cucumber.

The British Jeremiah. Gibbon so calls Gildas, author of *Lamentations over the Destruction of Britain* (516-570).

Jeremy Diddler. An adept at raising money on false pretences. From Kenny's farce called *Raising the Wind*.

Jeremy Twitcher. A cunning, treacherous highwayman, in Gay's *Beggar's Opera*. Lord Sandwich, a member of the New Kit Kat Club, was so called in 1765.

Jer'icho. *Gone to Jericho.* No one knows where. The manor of Blackmore, near Chelmsford, was called Jericho, and was one of the houses of pleasure of Henry VIII. When this lascivious prince had a mind to be lost in the embraces of his courtesans, the cant phrase among his courtiers was "He is gone to Jericho." Hence, a place of concealment.

Go to Jericho with you. I wish he had been at Jericho. A euphemistic turn of phrase for "Go and hang yourself," or something more offensive still. This

saying is derived from 2 Sam. x. 5 and
1 Chron. xix. 5.

"And the king said, Tarry at Jericho until your
beards be grown."

I wish you were at Jericho. Anywhere
out of my way. (*See above.*)

Jerked [beef], a corruption of the
Peruvian word *charqui*, meat cut into
strips and dried in the sun to preserve it.
(See *Mayne Reid's novels.*)

Jerkin. A short coat or jacket; a
close waistcoat.

"Mistress line, is not this my jerkin? Now is the
jerkin under the line."—*Shakespeare: The Tempest,*
iv. 1.

Jeroboam of Rum or Claret (*A*).
Eight bottles; but of whisky three pints.
Probably a perversion of "joram."
(*See* TAPPIT-HEN and REHOBOAM.)

"Some 'jeroboams' of very old rum went at
63s. each; several 'tappit-hens, of rum fetched
34s.; and some 'magnums,' 17s. each."—*Truth,*
31st March, 1887.

A magnum = 2 quart bottles; a tap-
pithen = 2 magnums; a jeroboam = 2
tappit-hens; and a rehoboam = 2 jeroboams or 16 quart bottles.

Jerome (*St.*). Generally represented
as an aged man in a cardinal's dress,
writing or studying, with a lion seated
beside him. The best painting of this
saint is *The Communion of St. Jerome,*
by Domenichi'no, in the Vatican. It
is placed opposite Raphael's *Trans-
figuration.*

Jeron'imo. The chief character in
the *Spanish Tragedy* by Thomas Kyd.
On finding his application to the
king ill-timed, he says to himself, "Go
by, Jeronimo," which tickled the fancy
of the audience so that it became for a
time the current street jest.

Jerry-built, unsubstantial. A "jerry-
builder" is a speculative builder who
runs up cheap, unsubstantial houses,
using materials of the commonest kind.
(*See* JURY MAST.)

Jerry-shop, or a **Tom and Jerry
Shop.** A low-class beer-house. Probably
the *Tom and Jerry* was a public-house
sign when Pierce Egan's *Life in London*
was popular.

Jerry Sneak. A henpecked husband, from a celebrated character in
Foote's farce of the *Mayor of Garratt.*

Jerrymander. (*See* GERRYMANDER.)

Jersey is Cæsar's-ey—*i.e.* Cæsar's
island, so called in honour of Julius
Cæsar.

Jeru'salem, in Dryden's satire of
Absalom and Achitophel, means London.
(Part i. verse 86, etc.)

Jerusalem Artichoke. A corruption of *Girasolë articiocco.* Girasole is
the sunflower, which this vegetable resembles both in leaf and stem.

Jerusalem Chamber. The Chapter-house of Westminster Abbey. Henry
IV. died there, March 20, 1413.

"It hath been prophesied to me many years,
I should not die but in Jerusalem."
Shakespeare: 2 Henry IV., iv. 5.

✝ Pope Silvester II. was told the
same thing, and he died as he was saying
mass in a church so called. (*Bacon:
Tusculum.*)

The Lower House of Convocation
now meets in the Jerusalem Chamber.
The Upper House meets at Mr. Hodg-
son's, in Dean's Yard, Westminster.

Jerusalem Delivered. An epic in
twenty books, by Torquato Tasso (1544-
1595).

The crusaders, encamped on the plains
of Torto'sa, chose Godfrey for their
chief, and Alandine, King of Jerusalem,
made preparations of defence. The
overtures of Argantes to Godfrey being
declined, he declared war in the name of
the king of Egypt. The Christian army
having reached Jerusalem, the king of
Damascus sent Armi'da to beguile the
Christians; she told an artful tale by
which she drew off several of the most
puissant. It was found that Jerusalem
could never be taken without the aid of
Rinaldo; but Rinaldo had withdrawn
from the army, because Godfrey had
cited him to answer for the death of
Girnando, slain in a duel. Godfrey,
being informed that the hero was dally-
ing with Armi'da in the enchanted island, sent to invite him back to the
army; he returned, and Jerusalem was
taken in a night attack. As for Armi'da, after setting fire to her palace,
she fled into Egypt, and offered to
marry any knight who slew Rinald;
but when she found the Christian army
was successful she fled from the field.
The love of Rinaldo returned; he pursued her and she relented. The poem
concludes with the triumphant entry of
the Christian army into the Holy City,
and their devotions at the tomb of the
Redeemer. The two chief episodes are
the loves of Olindo (*q.v.*) and Sophro'nia,
and of Tancred (*q.v.*) and Corinda.

Jerusalem Pony. A needy clergyman or minister, who renders temporary
aid to his brother ministers for hire;
so called in humorsome discourtesy.
The Jerusalem pony is a large species of
donkey.

Jess (pl. *Jesses*). A short strap of leather tied about the legs of a hawk to hold it on the fist. Hence a bond of affection, etc.

" If I prove her haggard,
Though that her jesses were my dear heart-
strings,'
I'd whistle her off."
Shakespeare: Othello, iii. 3.

Jessamy Bride is Mary Horneck, with whom Oliver Goldsmith fell in love in 1769.

Jesse Tree. In Christian art, a vine tracing the genealogy of Christ, called a "rod out of the stem of Jesse" (Isa. xi. 1). Jesse is generally represented in a recumbent position, and the vine is made to rise out of his loins.

Jesse Window (*A*). A stained-glass window representing Jesse recumbent, and a tree shooting from him containing the pedigree of Jesus.

Jes'sica. The Jew's daughter in the *Merchant of Venice*, by Shakespeare.

Jesters. (*See* FOOLS.)

Jes'uit (3 syl.). When Ignatius de Loyola was asked what name he would give his order, he replied, "We are a little battalion of Jesus;" so it was called the "Society of Jesus," vulgarised into Jesuits. The society was noted for its learning, political influence, and "pious frauds." The order was driven from France in 1594, from England in 1604, from Venice in 1606, from Spain in 1767, from Naples in 1768; and in 1773 was suppressed by Pope Clement XIV.; but it revived again, and still exists. The word is used by controversialists to express one who "lies like truth," or palters with us in a double sense, that "keeps the word of promise to our ear, and breaks it to our hope."

Jesus Paper. Paper of very large size, chiefly used for engravings. Originally it was stamped with the initials I.H.S. (*q.v.*).

Jet. So called from the River Gages, in Asia Minor, on the banks of which it was collected by the ancients. It was originally called *gagates*, corrupted into *gagat, jet*.

Jet d'Eau (French). A spout or jet of water thrown up into the air, generally from an artificial fountain. The great jet at Versailles rises to a height of 100 feet; that at Chatsworth, the highest in existence, to 267 feet. (French, from the Latin *jactus*, thrown; *jacio*, to throw.)

Jetsam or **Jetson.** Goods cast into the sea to lighten a ship. (French, *jeter*, to cast out.) (*See* FLOTSAM and LIGAN.)

Jettator. One with an evil eye, who always brings ill-luck. The opposite of the Mascotte (*q.v.*), who with a " good eye " always brings good fortune.

The opera called *La Mascotte*. (1893, by Duree and Chivot.)

Jettatura. The evil-eye.

"Their glance, if you meet it, is the jettatura, or evil-eye."—*Mrs. Gaskell: An Accursed Race.*

Jeu d'Esprit (French). A witticism.

Jeu de Mot. A pun; a play on some word or phrase. (French.)

Jeunesse Dorée. The " gilded youth " of a nation; that is, the rich and fashionable young unmarried men.

" There were three of the *jeunesse dorée*, and, as such, were pretty well known to the ladies who promenade the grand circle."—*T. Terrel: Lady Delmar*, ix.

Jew. *The Wandering Jew.*

(1) Said to be KHARTAPH'ILOS, Pilate's porter. When the officers were dragging Jesus out of the hall, Kartaph'ilos struck Him with his fist in the back, saying, " Go quicker, Man; go quicker ! " Whereupon Jesus replied, " I indeed go quickly; but thou shalt tarry till I come again." This man afterwards became a Christian, and was baptised under the name of Joseph. Every 100 years he falls into an ecstasy, out of which he rises again at the age of thirty.

The earliest account of the "Wandering Jew" is in the *Book of the Chronicles of the Abbey of St. Albans*. This tradition was continued by Matthew Paris in 1228. In 1242 Philip Mouskes, afterwards Bishop of Tournay, wrote the *Rhymed Chronicle*.

(2) AHASUE'RUS, a cobbler, who dragged Jesus before Pilate. As the Man of Sorrows was going to Calvary, weighed down with His cross, He stayed to rest on a stone near the man's door, when Ahasuerus pushed Him away, saying, "Away with you; here you shall not rest." The gentle Jesus replied, " I truly go away, and go to rest; but thou shalt walk, and never rest till I come."

This is the legend given by Paul von Eitzen, Bishop of Schleswig (1547). (See *Greve: Memoirs of Paul von Eitzen* (1744).)

(3) In *German* legend, the "Wandering Jew" is associated with JOHN BUTTADÆUS, seen at Antwerp in the thirteenth century; again, in the fifteenth; and again, in the sixteenth century. His last appearance was in 1774, at Brussels.

Leonard Doldius, of Nürnberg, in his *Praxis Alchymiæ* (1604), says that Ahasuerus is sometimes called Buttadæus.

(4) The *French* call "The Wandering Jew" Isaac Lake'dion or Laquedem. (*Mitternacht: Dissertatio in Johannem*, xxi. 19.)

(5) *Dr. Croly*, in his novel, calls the "Wandering Jew" Salathiel ben Sadi, who (he says) appeared towards the close of the sixteenth century at Venice.

⁂ The legend of the Wild Huntsman, called by Shakespeare "Herne, the Hunter," and by Father Mathieu "St. Hubert," is said to be a Jew who would not suffer Jesus to drink from a horse-trough, but pointed out to Him some water in a hoof-print, and bade Him go there and drink. (*Kuhn von Schwarz: Mordd. Sagen*, 499.)

Jew's-eye. *Worth a Jew's-eye.* According to fable, this expression arose from the custom of torturing Jews to extort money from them. The expedient of King John is well known: He demanded 10,000 marks of a rich Jew of Bristol; the Hebrew resisted the atrocious exaction, but the tyrant ordered him to be brought before him, and that one of his teeth should be tugged out every day till the money was forthcoming. This went on for seven days, when the sufferer gave in, and John jestingly observed, "A Jew's eye may be a quick ransom, but Jew's teeth give the richer harvest."

Launcelot, in the *Merchant of Venice*, ii. 5, puns upon this phrase when he says to Jessica :—

"There will come a Christian by
Will be worth a Jewess' eye."

Jew's-harp, called by Bacon *jeutrompe*, by Beaumont and Fletcher, *jew-trump*, by Hakluyt, *jew's-harp*.

The best players on this instrument have been Koch, a Prussian soldier under Frederick the Great; Kunert, Amstein, and some others.

Jew's Myrtle. So called from the popular notion that it formed the crown of thorns placed by the Jews on the Saviour's head.

Jews, in Dryden's satire of *Absalom and Achitophel*, those English who were loyal to Charles II., called David.

"The Jews, a headstrong, moody, murmuring
 race,
God's pampered people, whom, debauched with
 ease,
No king could govern, nor no god could please."
     Part i. verses 45-48.

Jews born with tails. (*See* Raboin.)

Jews' Sabbath. In the *Monasticon de Melsa*, ii. pp. 134, 137, we read that a Jew at Tewkesbury fell into a cesspool.

and Richard, Earl of Gloucester, passing by, offered to pull him out, but the Jew refused, saying—

"Sabbato nostra colo ;
De stercore surgere nolo."

Next day, as the Earl was passing again, the Jew cried to him for help, when Gloucester replied—

"Sabbata nostra quidem,
Solomon, celebrabis ibidem."
    The Rolls Series.

Jewels in heraldry.

The topaz represents " or " (*gold*), or the planet *Sol*.

The pearl or crystal represents "argent " (*silver*), or the planet Luna.

The ruby represents " gules " (*red*), or the planet Mars.

The sapphire represents " azure " (*blue*), or the planet Jupiter.

The diamond represents " sable " (*black*), or the planet Saturn.

The emerald represents " vert " (*green*), or the planet Venus.

The amethyst represents "purpure " (*purple*), or the planet Mercury.

Jewels for the months. Each month is supposed to be under the influence of some precious stone—

January : Garnet. *Constancy.*
February : Amethyst. *Sincerity.*
March : Bloodstone. *Courage.*
April : Diamond. *Innocence.*
May : Emerald. *Success in love.*
June : Agate. *Health and long life.*
July : Cornelian. *Content.*
August : Sardonyx. *Conjugal fidelity.*
September : Chrysolite. *Antidote to madness.*
October : Opal. *Hope.*
November : Topaz. *Fidelity.*
December : Turquoise. *Prosperity.*

Jewels for signs of the zodiac—

Aries : Ruby.
Taurus : Topaz.
Gemini : Carbuncle.
Cancer : Emerald.
Leo : Sapphire.
Virgo : Diamond.
Libra : Jacinth.
Scorpio : Agate.
Sagittarius : Amethyst.
Capricornus : Beryl.
Aquarius : Onyx.
Pisces : Jasper.

Jez'ebel. *A painted Jezebel.* A flaunting woman of bold spirit, but loose morals ; so called from Queen Jezebel, the wife of Ahab.

Jib. A triangular sail borne in front of the foremast. It has the bowsprit for a base in small vessels, and the jib-boom in larger ones, and exerts an important effect, when the wind is abeam, in throwing the ship's head to leeward.

Jib. The under-lip. A sailor's expression ; the under-lip indicating the temper, as the jib indicates the character of a ship.

The cut of his jib. A sailor's phrase, meaning the expression of a person's face. Sailors recognise vessels at sea by the cut of the jibs.

To hang the jib. The jib means the lower lip. To hang the lower lip is to look ill-tempered, or annoyed.

Jib (*To*). To start aside ; a "jibbing horse" is one that is easily startled. It is a sea term, to jib being to shift the boomsail from one side of the mast to the other.

Jib-boom. An extension of the bowsprit by the addition of a spar projecting beyond it. Sometimes the boom is further extended by another spar called the *flying jib-boom.*

Jib-door. A door flush with the outside wall, and intended to be concealed ; forming thus part of the jib or face of the house. (*See above,* line 8.)

Jib-stay (*A*). The stay on which a jib is set.

Jib Topsail (*A*). A light sail flying from the extreme forward end of the flying-jib boom, and set about half-way between the mast and the boom.

Jiffy. *In a jiffy.* In a minute ; in a brace of shakes ; before you can say "Jack Robinson." (French, *vif, vife.*)

Jig, from *gigue.* A short piece of music much in vogue in olden times, of a very lively character, either six-eight or twelve-eight time, and used for dance-tunes. It consists of two parts, each of eight bars. Also a comic song.

"You jig, you amble, and you lisp." — *Shakespeare: Hamlet,* iii. 1.

Jilt (*To*). (*See under* BASKET.) *To give the basket.*

Jim Crow. Brought out at the Adelphi in 1836. The character of Jim Crow played by T. D. Rice, as the original of the "nigger minstrels" since so popular. A renegade or turncoat is called a Jim Crow, from the burden of the song, *Wheel about and turn about.*

Jingo. *By Jingo* or *By the Living Jingo.* Basque "Jainko," the Supreme Being. In corroboration of this derivation it may be stated that Edward I. had Basque mountaineers conveyed to

England to take part in the conquest of Wales, and the Plantagenets held the Basque provinces in possession. The word was certainly used as a juron long before the Crimean War.

" Hey, Jingo ! What the de'il's the matter ?
　Do mermaids swim in Dartford water ?"
　　　Swift : Actæon (or *The Original Horn Fair*)

∵ Dr. Morris, in his *Historic Outlines* (p. 210 *note*), says it is St. Gingulph, and Professor Skeat (*Notes and Queries,* August 25th, 1894, p. 149) is of the same opinion. According to *The Times,* June 25th, 1877, p. 6, col. 1), it is the Persian *jang* = war, and the juron "By St. Jingo" is about equal to " By Mars." But the word had originally no connection with our *jingoism.* It was common enough in the early part of the nineteenth century. Query. A corruption of Jesus, Son of God, thus, *Je-'n-go'.*

Jingoes (*The*). The war party in 1877. They were Russophobists, who felt convinced that the Czar intended to take possession of Constantinople, which would give him command of the Black Sea, and might endanger our Indian possessions. This has nothing to do with the word "jingo" used by Dean Swift ; but was wholly connected with the music-hall song mentioned in the next article.

Jingoism. The British war braggadocio ; called *Chauvinism* in French ; *Spread-eagleism* in the United States of North America. During the Russo-Turkish War in 1877-1878 England was on the point of interfering, and at the music-halls a song became popular containing the following refrain :—

" We don't want to fight ; but, by Jingo, if we do,
　We've got the ships, we've got the men, and got
　　the money too."

Jinn. A sort of fairies in Arabian mythology, the offspring of fire. They propagate their species like human beings, and are governed by a race of kings named Suleyman, one of whom "built the pyramids." Their chief abode is the mountain Kâf, and they appear to men under the forms of serpents, dogs, cats, monsters, or even human beings, and become invisible at pleasure. The evil jinn are hideously ugly, but the good are exquisitely beautiful. According to fable, they were created from fire two thousand years before Adam was made of earth. The singular of jinn is jinnee. (*See* FAIRY.)

Jin'nistan. The country of the Jinn, or Fairy Land, the chief province of which is *The Country of Delight,* and the capital *The City of Jewels.*

Jo'achim (*St.*). The father of the Virgin Mary. Generally represented as an old man carrying in a basket two turtle-doves, in allusion to the offering made for the purification of his daughter. His wife was St. Anne, or St. Anna.

Joan (*Pope*). A supposed female "pope" between Leo IV. and Benedict III. She is said to have been born in England and educated at Cologne, passing under the name of Joannes An'glicus (*John of England*). Blondel, a Calvinist, wrote a book in 1640 to prove that no such person ever occupied the papal chair; but at least a hundred and fifty authors between the thirteenth and seventeenth centuries repeat the tale as an historic fact. The last person who critically examined the question was Döllinger, in 1868. (See *Historic Note Book*, 701-2, for authorities *pro* and *con*.)

Joan Cromwell. *Joan Cromwell's kitchen-stuff tub.* A tub of kitchen perquisites. The filchings of servants sold for "market pennies." The Royalists used to call the Protector's wife, whose name was Elizabeth, *Joan Cromwell*, and declared that she exchanged the kitchen-stuff of the palace for tallow candles.

Joan of Arc or **Jeanne la Pucelle.** M. Octave Delepierre has published a pamphlet, called *Doute Historique*, to deny the tradition that Joan of Arc was burnt at Rouen for sorcery. He cites a document discovered by Father Vignier in the seventeenth century, in the archives of Metz, to prove that she became the wife of Sieur des Armoise, with whom she resided at Metz, and became the mother of a family. Vignier subsequently found in the family muniment-chest the contract of marriage between "Robert des Armoise, knight, and Jeanne D'Arcy, surnamed the Maid of Orleans." In 1740 there were found in the archives of the Maison de Ville (Orléans) records of several payments to certain messengers from Joan to her brother John, bearing the dates 1435, 1436. There is also the entry of a presentation from the council of the city to the Maid, for her services at the siege (dated 1439). M. Delepierre has brought forward a host of other documents to corroborate the same fact, and show that the tale of her martyrdom was invented to throw odium on the English. A sermon is preached annually in France towards the beatification of the Maid, who will eventually become the patron saint of that nation, and Shakespeare will prove a true prophet in the words—

"No longer on St. Denis will we cry,
But Joan la Pucelle shall be France's saint."

Joannes Hagustaldensis is John, Prior of Hexham, author of an old English *Chronicle*, and *Lives of the Bishops of Hexham*, in two books.

Job (*o* long). The personification of poverty and patience. "*Patient as Job*," in allusion to the patriarch whose history is given in the Bible.

Poor as Job. Referring to the patriarch when he was by Satan deprived of all his worldly possessions.

"I am as poor as Job, my lord, but not so patient."—*Shakespeare: 2 Henry IV.*, i. 2.

Job's Comforter. One who pretends to sympathise in your grief, but says that you brought it on yourself; thus in reality adding weight to your sorrow. (*See above.*)

Job's wife. Some call her Rahmat, daughter of Ephraim, son of Joseph; and others call her Makhir, daughter of Manasses. (*Sale: Korán* xxi., note.)

She is also called by some Sitis; and a tradition exists that Job, at the command of God, struck the earth with his foot from the dunghill where he lay, and instantly there welled up a spring of water with which his wife washed his sores, and they were miraculously healed. (*Korán*, xxxvi. 41.)

Job's Pound. Bridewell; prison.

Job (*o* short). A job is a piece of chance work; a public work or office not for the public benefit, but for the profit of the person employed; a sudden blow or "dig" into one.

A bad job. An unsuccessful work; one that brings loss instead of profit; a bad speculation.

To do the job for one. To kill him.

Job (*o* short). *A ministerial job.* Sheridan says:—"Whenever any emolument, profit, salary, or honour is conferred on any person not deserving it—that is a job; if from private friendship, personal attachment, or any view except the interest of the public, anyone is appointed to any public office . . . that is a job."

"No cheek is known to blush, or heart to throb,
Save when they lose a question or a job."
Pope: Essay on Criticism, i. 104.

Job Lot (*A*). A lot of miscellaneous goods to be sold a bargain.

Jobs. A printer's phrase to designate all kinds of work not included in the term "book-work." The French call such work *ouvrage de ville.*

⁂ Allied to the Latin, *op*[*us*]; Spanish, *ob*[*ra*]; French, *ouv*[*rage*]; the *r* occurs in the genitive case, *oper*[*is*].

Job (*To*). To strike. To give one a "job in the eye" is to give one a blow in the eye; and to "job one in the ribs" is to strike one in the ribs, to stab one in the ribs. Job and probe seem to be very nearly allied. Halliwell gives the word "stop," to poke or thrust, which is allied to stab.

Joba'tion. A scolding; so called from the patriarch Job.

"Jobation .... means a long, dreary homily, and has reference to the tedious rebukes inflicted on the patriarch Job by his too obliging friends."
—*G. A. Sala : (Echoes),* Sept. 6, 1884.

Jobber. One who does small jobs; one who buys from merchants to sell to retailers; a middle-man. A "stock-jobber" is one who buys and sells public funds, but is not a sworn stock-broker.

Jobbing Carpenter. One who is ready to do odd jobs (piece-work) in his own line. (*See* JOB.)

Jocelin de Brakelonda, *de Rebus gestis Samsonis,* etc., published by the Camden Society. This record of the acts of Abbot Samson of Edmondsbury contains much contemporary history, and gives a good account of English life and society between 1173 and 1202.

Jockey is a little Jack (boy). So in Scotch, "Ilka Jeanie has her Jockie." (*See* JACK.)
All fellows, Jockey and the laird (man and master). (*Scotch proverb.*)

Jockey (*To*). To deceive in trade; to cheat; to indulge in sharp practice.

Jockey of Norfolk. Sir John Howard, a firm adherent of Richard III. On the night before the battle of Bosworth he found in his tent the warning couplet:
"Jockey of Norfolk, be not too bold,
For Dickon, thy master, is bought and sold."

Joe or a **Joe Miller.** A stale joke; so called from the compilation of jokes under that *nom de plume.* (*See* MILLER.)

Joey. A groat; so called from Joseph Hume, M.P., who strongly recommended the coinage for the sake of paying short cab-fares, etc. (*Hawkins : History of the Silver Coinage of England.*)

Jog. *Jog away ; jog off ; jog on.* Get away; be off; keep moving. Shakespeare uses the word *shog* in the same sense—as, "Will you shog off?" (*Henry V.,* ii. 1); and again in the same play, "Shall we shog?" (ii. 3). Beaumont and Fletcher use the same expression in *The Coxcomb*—"Come, prithee, let us shog off?" and again, in *Pasquill and Katharine*—"Thus it shogges" [goes]. In the *Morte d'Arthur* we have another variety—"He shokkes in sharply"

[rushes in]. The words seem to be connected with the Dutch *schokken,* to jolt, and the Anglo-Saxon *scacan,* to depart, to flee.
"Jog on a little faster, pri'thee,
I'll take a nap and then be wi' thee."
R. Lloyd : The Hare and the Tortoise.

To jog his memory, or *Give his memory a jog.* To remind one of something apparently forgotten. Jog is to shake or stir up. (Welsh, *gogi,* to shake ; French, *choquer ;* our *shock, shake,* etc.)

Jog-trot. A slow but regular pace.

Joggis or **Jogges.** The pillory. Jamieson says, "They punish delinquents, making them stand in 'jogges,' as they call their pillories." (The word is *Yoke :* Latin, *jugum ;* French, *joug ;* Anglo-Saxon, *geoc ;* our *jug,* a jail.)
"Staune ane wholl Sabothe daye in ye joggis."
—*Glen : History of Dumbarton.*

John. A contraction of *Johannes* (Joh'n). The French contract it differently, *Jean—i.e.* Jehan or Jehann ; in Italian, *Giovanni.*

Popes.
JOHN I. died wretchedly in jail.
JOHN II. and III. were nonentities.
JOHN IV. was accused of heresy.
JOHN V., VI., VII., were nonentities.
JOHN VIII. was imprisoned by Lambert, Duke of Spole'to ; at a subsequent period he was dressed in female attire out of mockery, and was at last poisoned.
JOHN IX. had SERGIUS III. for a rival Pope.
JOHN X. was overthrown by Gui, Duke of Tuscany, and died in prison.
JOHN XI. was imprisoned with his mother by Alberic, and died there.
JOHN XII. was deposed for sacrilege, and was at last assassinated.
JOHN XIII. was imprisoned by his nobles and deposed.
JOHN XIV. was deposed, and died imprisoned in the Castle of St. Angelo.
JOHN XV. was a nonentity.
JOHN XVI. was driven from Rome by Crescentius.
JOHN XVII. (antipope) was expelled by Otto III., and barbarously treated by Gregory.
JOHN XVIII. abdicated.
JOHN XIX. was deposed and expelled by Konrad.
JOHN XX. was a nonentity.
JOHN XXI. was crushed to death by the falling in of his palace at Viterbo.
JOHN XXII. was charged with heresy.
JOHN XXIII. fled in disguise, was arrested, and cast into prison for three years.

Certainly a disastrous list of Popes.

John. A proverbially unhappy name with royalty, insomuch that when John Stuart ascended the throne of Scotland he changed his name to Robert; but misfortune never deserted him, and after an evil reign he died overwhelmed with calamities and infirmity. John Baliol was the mere tool of Edward I. ; John of England, a most disastrous reign. *John I. of France* reigned only a few days; John II., having lost the battle of Poitiers, died in captivity in

London; to France his reign was a tissue of evils. *John of Bohemia* was slain at Cressy. *John I. of Aragon* was at ceaseless war with his subjects, by whom he was execrated; John II. was at ceaseless war with his son, Don Carlos. *John I. of Constantinople* was poisoned by Basil, his eunuch; John IV. had his eyes put out; John V. was emperor in name only, and was most unhappy; John VI., harassed with troubles, abdicated, and died in a monastery.

⁂ *John I. of Sweden* was unhappy in his expeditions, and died childless; John II. had his wife driven out of the kingdom by his angry subjects. *Jean sans Peur* of Burgundy engaged in the most horrible massacres and was murdered. *John of Suabia*, called the *Parricide*, because he murdered his father Albert, after which he was a fugitive and a vagabond on the face of the earth, etc., etc.

N.B. John of Portugal was a signal exception.

Ivan IV. of Russia, surnamed the "Terrible" (1529-1584). He murdered with his own hand his eldest son; Ivan V. (1666-1696) was dumb and nearly blind; Ivan VI. (1737-1762) was dethroned, imprisoned, and put to death. (*See* JANE.)

King John and the Abbot of Canterbury. John, being jealous of the state kept by the abbot, declared he should be put to death unless he answered three questions. The first question was, how much the king was worth; the second, how long it would take to ride round the world; and the third, what the king was thinking of. The king gave the abbot three weeks' grace for his answers. A shepherd undertook to answer the three questions, so with crozier, mitre, rochet, and cope, he presented himself before the king. "What am I worth?" asked John. "Well," was the reply, "the Saviour was sold for thirty pence, and your majesty is a penny worse than He." The king laughed, and demanded what he had to say to the next question, and the man replied, "If you rise with the sun and ride with the sun, you will get round the world in a day." Again the king was satisfied, and demanded that the respondent should tell him his thoughts. "You think I am the abbot of Canterbury, but I am only a poor shepherd who am come to ask your majesty's pardon for him and me." The king was so pleased with the jest, that he would have made the shepherd abbot of Canterbury; but the man

pleaded that he could neither write nor read, whereupon the king dismissed him, and gave him a pension of four nobles a week. (*Percy: Reliques*, series 2, bk. iii. 6.)

Mess-John or *Mass-John.* A priest.

Prester John. The supposed Christian king and priest of a mediæval kingdom in the interior of Asia. This Prester John was the Khan Ung who was defeated and slain by Genghis Khan in 1202, said to have been converted by the Nestorian Christians. He figures in Ariosto, and has furnished materials for a host of mediæval legends.

" I will fetch you a tooth-picker now from the farthest inch of Asia ; bring you the length of Prester John's foot : fetch you a hair off the great Cham's beard . . . ."
Shakespeare: Much Ado about Nothing, ii. 1.

The three Johns—an alehouse picture in Little Park Street, Westminster, and in White Lion Street, Pentonville—is John Wilkes between the Rev. John Horne Tooke and Sir John Glynn (serjeant-at-law). (*Hotten: History of Signboards*).

St. John the Evangelist is represented writing his gospel; or bearing a chalice, from which a serpent issues, in allusion to his driving the poison from a cup presented to him to drink. He is sometimes represented in a cauldron of boiling oil, in allusion to the tradition of his being plunged into such a cauldron before his banishment to the isle of Patmos.

St. John. The usual war-cry of the English of the North in their encounters with the Scotch. The person referred to is St. John of Beverley, in Yorkshire, who died 721.

John-a-Dreams. A stupid, dreamy fellow, always in a brown study and half asleep.

" Yet I,
A dull and muddy-mettled rascal, peak,
Like John-a-dreams, unpregnant of my cause,
And can say nothing."
Shakespeare: Hamlet, ii. 2.

John-a-Droynes. A foolish character in Whetstone's *Promos and Cassandra* (1578). Being seized by informers, he stands dazed, and suffers himself to be quietly cheated out of his money.

John-a-Nokes [or **Noakes** (1 syl.)]. A simpleton.

" John-a-Nokes was driving a cart toward Croydon, and by the way fell asleepe therein. Meane time a good fellow came by and stole away his two horses. [John] awakening and missing them, said, 'Either I am John-a-Nokes or I am not John-a-Nokes. If I am John-a-Nokes, then I have lost two horses ; and if I am not John-a-Nokes, then I have found a cart.' "—*Copley: Wits, Fits, and Fancies* (1614).

John Anderson, my Jo. This song, like "Green Sleeves and Pudding Pies," "Maggy Lauder" and some others, were invectives against the Catholic clergy about the time of the Reformation. The first verse refers to their luxurious habits:—

> " John Anderson, my Jo, aim in as ze gae bye,
> And ze sall get a sheip's heid weel baken in a
>   pye ;
> Weel baken in a pye, and the haggis in a pat.
> John Anderson, my Jo, cum in, and ze's get
>   that."

Another verse refers to the seven sacraments or "Seven bairns of Mother Church."

John Audley. *Is John Audley there ?* Get done as soon as possible, for there are persons sufficient for another audience. · John Audley was a noted showman and actor ; when his platform was full, he taught the ticket collector to poke his head behind the green curtain, and cry out : " Is John Audley there ? " This was a signal to the actors to draw their piece to a close, and clear the house as quickly as possible. Audley taught this trick to Richardson.

John Bull. The national nickname for an Englishman, represented as a bluff, kindhearted, bull-headed farmer. The character is from a satire by Dr. Arbuthnot. In this satire the Frenchman is termed *Lewis Baboon*, the Dutchman *Nicholas Frog*, etc.

John Bull. A comedy by George Colman. Job Thornberry is the chief character.

John Chinaman. Either a Chinese or the Chinese as a people.

John Company. Colonel Harold Malet, in *Notes and Queries*, August 6th, 1892. p. 116. says that " John " is a perversion of " Hon.," and John Company is the Hon. Company. No doubt Hon., like Hans, may be equal to John, but probably John Company is allied to the familiar John Bull. The Company was abolished in 1857, in consequence of the Indian Mutiny.

> "In old times ' John Company' employed four
> thousand men in its warehouses."—*Old and New
> London*, ii. 185.

John Doe. At one time used in law pleadings for an hypothetical plaintiff ; the supposititious defendant being "Richard Roe." These fictions are not now used.

John Dory is technically called *Zeus faber*, common in the Mediterranean Sea and round the south-western coasts of England. A corruption of *jaune adorée=* the adorable or sacred yellow fish.

The only interest of this creature in a work like the *Dictionary of Phrase and Fable* is the tradition that it was the fish from which St. Peter took the stater. Hence it is called in French *le poisson de St. Pierre*, and in Gascon, the golden or sacred cock, meaning St. Peter's cock. Like the haddock, it has a remarkable oval black spot on each side, said to be the finger-marks of St. Peter, when he held the fish to extract the coin. As neither the haddock nor dory can live in fresh water, of course this tradition is only an idle tale.

John Dory. A piratical French captain, conquered by Nicholl, a Cornishman.

> " John Dory bought him an ambling nag,
>   To Paris for to ride-a."
>   *Corbett : A Journey to France*, p. 129.

John Long. *To wait for John Long, the carrier.* To wait a long time ; to wait for John, who keeps us a long time.

John Roberts (*A*). An enormous tankard holding enough drink for any ordinary drinker to last through Saturday and Sunday. This measure was introduced into Wales in 1886 to compensate topers for the Sunday closing, and derived its name from John Roberts, M.P., author of the Sunday Closing Act. (*Standard*, March 11th, 1886.)

John Thomas. A generic name for a flunkey ; or footman with large calves and bushy whiskers.

John Drum's Entertainment. Hauling a man by his ears and thrusting him out by the shoulders. The allusion is to "drumming" a man out of the army. There is a comedy so called, published 1601.

> "When your lordship sees the bottom of his
> success in 't . . . if you give him not John Drum's
> entertainment, your inclining cannot be re-
> moved."—*Shakespeare: All's Well that Ends Well*,
> iii. 6.

John in the Wad. A Will-o'-Wisp. A wad is a wisp, and John or Jack is a name for any inferior person unknown. (*See* JACK.)

John of Bruges (1 syl.). John van Eyck, the Flemish painter (1370-1441).

John o' Groat, with his two brothers Malcolm and Gavin, came from Holland in the reign of James IV. of Scotland, and purchased the lands of Warse and Dungisbay. In process of time their families increased, and there came to be eight families of the same name.

They lived together amicably, and met once a year in the original house; but on one occasion a question of precedency arose, who was to go out first, and who was to take the head of the table. John o' Groat promised them the next time they came he would contrive to satisfy them all. Accordingly he built an eight-sided room, with a door and window in each side, and placed a round oak table in the room. This building went ever after with the name of John o' Groat's House. The site of this house is the Berubium of Ptolemy, in the vicinity of Duncansby Head.

> " Hear, land o'cakes and brither Scots,
> Frae Maidenkirk to Johnny Groat's . . .
> A chield's amang you takin' notes,
> And, faith, he'll prent it."
> *Burns : Captain Grose.*

John of Hexham. An English historical writer, twelfth century.

John of Leyden (the prophet), being about to marry Bertha, met with three Anabaptists who observed a strong likeness in him to a picture of David in Munster cathedral. They entered into conversation with him, and finding him apt for their purpose, induced him to join their rebellion. The rebels took the city of Munster, and John was crowned " ruler of Westphalia." His mother met him in the street, and John disclaimed all knowledge of her; but subsequently visited her in prison, and obtained her forgiveness. When the emperor arrived with his army, John's Anabaptist friends deserted him, and " the prophet," setting fire to the banquet-room of his palace, perished with his mother in the flames. (*Meyerbeer : Le Prophète* [*an opera*]).

✴ His real name was John Bockhold.

John the Almoner. Chrysostom was so called, because he bestowed so large a portion of his revenues on hospitals and other charities. (347-407.)

John the Baptist. Patron saint of missionaries. He was sent " to prepare the way of the Lord."

In Christian art he is represented in a coat of sheepskins, in allusion to his life in the desert; either holding a rude wooden cross, with a pennon bearing the words, *Ecce Agnus Dei*, or with a book on which a lamb is seated; or holding in his right hand a lamb surrounded by a halo, and bearing a cross on the right foot.

John Tamson's Man, a henpecked husband; one ordered here, and ordered there, and ordered everywhere. Tameson—*i.e.* spiritless, the slave even of a Tame-son.

> " ' The deil's in the wife ! ' said Cuddie. ' D'ye think I am to be John Tamson's man, and maistered by a woman a' the days o' my life ? "—*Sir W. Scott : Old Mortality,* chap. xxxix.

John with the Leaden Sword. The Duke of Bedford, who acted as regent for Henry VI. in France, was so called by Earl Douglas.

Johnnies. British bourgeois. Byron, February 23rd, 1824, writes to Murray his publisher respecting an earthquake :

> " If you had but seen the *English Johnnies,* who had never been out of a cockney workshop before . . . [running away . . .]."

Johnny Crapaud. A Frenchman, so called by the English sailors in the long Napoleon contest. The ancient Flemings used to call the French " Crapaud Franchos." In allusion to the toads borne originally in the arms of France.

Johnny Raw. A Verdant Green ; a newly-enlisted soldier ; an adult apprentice in the ship-trade.

> " The impulse given to ship-building by the continental war, induced employers to take persons as apprentices who had already passed their majority. This class of men-apprentices, generally from remote towns, were called ' Johnny Raws' by the fraternity."—*C. Thomson : Autobiography,* p. 73.

Johnson (*Dr. Samuel*) lived in Fleet Street—first in Fetter Lane, then in Boswell Court, then in Gough Square, then in the Inner Temple Lane for seven years, then in Johnson's Court (No. 7) for ten years ; and lastly in Bolt Court (No. 8), where he died eight years after. The coffee-house he most frequented was the *Mitre* tavern in Fleet Street, and not that which has assumed the name of " Dr. Johnson's Coffee-house." The church he frequented was St. Clement Danes in the Strand.

Johnstone. The crest of this family is a *winged spur,* or *spur between two wings, leathered,* with the motto. "*Nunquam non parā'tus.*" When King Edward I. was meditating treachery in favour of Balliol, Johnstone sent to Bruce (then in England) a spur with a feather tied to it. Bruce took the hint and fled, and when he became king conferred the crest on the Johnstone family.

Johnstone's Tippet (*St.*). A halter.

Join the Majority. (*See* MAJORITY.)

Joint. *The times are out of joint.* The times are disquiet and unruly. If the body is out of joint it cannot move easily, and so is it with the body corporate.

Jolly. A sailor's nickname for a marine, who, in his opinion, bears the same relation to a "regular" as a jolly-boat or yawl does to a ship. (Danish, *jollë*, a yawl.)

Jolly Dog (*A*). A *bon vivant*. Here "jolly" means jovial.

Jolly God (*The*). Bacchus. The Bible speaks of wine which "maketh glad the heart of man." Here "jolly" means jovial.

Jolly Good Fellow (*A*). A very social and popular person. (French, *joli*.)

"Ali was jolly quiet at Ephesus before St. Paul came thither."—*John Trapp: Commentary* (1656).

"For he's a jolly good fellow [three times].
  And so say all of us,
  With a hip, hip, hip, hoora!"

Jolly Green. Very simple; easily imposed upon, from being without worldly wisdom.

Jolly Roger (*The*). (*See* ROGER.)

Jollyboat. A small boat usually hoisted at the stern of a ship. (Danish, *iollë ;* Dutch, *jol ;* Swedish, *jullë*, a yawl.

Jonah and the Whale. Mr. Colbert, Professor of Astronomy in Chicago, in a chapter on "Star Grouping," tells us that the *whale* referred to is the star-group "Cetus," and that *Jonah* is the "Moon passing through it in three days and nights."

Jo'nas, in Dryden's satire of *Absalom and Achitophel*, is meant for Sir William Jones, Attorney-General, who conducted the prosecution of the Popish Plot (June 25th, 1674); not the great Oriental scholar, who lived 1746–1794. The attorney-general was called in the satire Jonas by a palpable pun.

"Not bull-faced Jonas, who could statutes draw
To mean rebellion and make treason law."
Dryden: Absalom and Achitophel, part i. 520, 521.

Jonathan. *Brother Jonathan.* In the revolutionary war, Washington, being in great want of supplies for the army, and having unbounded confidence in his friend, Jonathan Trumbull, governor of Connecticut, said, "We must consult brother Jonathan." Brother Jonathan was consulted on all occasions by the American liberator, and the phrase becoming popular was accepted as the national name of the Americans as a people.

Jonathan and David. In 1 Sam. xviii. 4 we read that Jonathan (the king's son) "stripped himself of his robe and gave it to David, with his sword, bow, and girdle." This was a mark of honour, as princes and sovereigns nowadays strip themselves of a chain or a ring, which they give to one they delight to honour. In 1519 the Sultan Selim, desirous of showing honour to an imaum of Constantinople, threw his royal robe over him.

Jonathan's. A noted coffee-house in Change Alley, described in the *Tatler* as the general mart of stock-jobbers.

∴ What is now called the Stock Exchange was called Jonathan's.

"Yesterday the brokers and others . . . came to a resolution that [the new building] instead of being called 'New Jonathan's,' should be called 'The Stock Exchange.' . . . . The brokers then collected sixpence each, and christened the house with punch."—Newspaper paragraph (July 15, 1773).

Jonathan's Arrows. They were shot to give warning, and not to hurt. (1 Sam. xx. 36.)

"If the husband would reprove his wife, it should be in such a mood as if he did chide himself ; and his words, like Jonathan's arrows, should be shot, not to hurt, but only to give warning."—*Le Fanu: The House in the Churchyard*, chap. xcix.

Jonc (French). A wedding-ring ; so called because those who were married by compulsion at Ste. Marine wore rings of jonc or straw.

"C'est dans l'église de Ste. Marine que l'on marie ceux que l'on condamne à s'épouser. Anciennement on les mariait avec un anneau de paille : etait-ce pour marquer au mari que la vertu de celle qu'il épousait était bien fragile ?"—*Dulaure.*

Joncs. *Etre sur le joncs* (to be on the straw)—*i.e.* in prison.

"Plantez aux hurmes vos picons
Da paour les bisans si tres-durs
Et aussi d'estre sur les joncz,
Emmanchez en coffre et gros murs."
Villon: *Jargon et Jobelin*, ballade 1.

Jordan Passed. Death over. Jordan is the Styx of Christian mythology, because it was the river which separated the wilderness [of this world] from the promised land.

"If I still hold closely to Him,
  What hath He at last ?
Sorrow vanquished, labour ended,
  Jordan passed."
John Mason Neale, D.D. (*Stephen the Sabaite*).

Jordeloo (3 syl.). Notice given to passengers when dirty water was thrown from chamber windows into the street. Either "*Gare de l'eau,*" or else "*Jorda' lo!*" the mutula being usually called the "Jordan."

"At ten o'clock at night the whole cargo is flung out of a back window that looks into some street or lane, and the maid calls 'Gardy loo'' to the passengers."—*Smollett: Humphrey Clinker.*
"The lass had made the Gardy loo out of the wrong window."—*Sir W. Scott: Heart of Midlothian.*

Jor'mungan'dar or *Midgardsormen* (*i.e.* earth's monster). The great serpent, brother of Hela and Fenrir (*q.v.*), and son of Loki, the spirit of evil. It used to lie at the root of the celestial ash till All-Fader cast it into the ocean; it then grew so large that in time it encompassed the whole world, and was for ever biting its own tail.

Jos'aphat. An Indian prince converted by the hermit Bar'laam, in the Greek religious pastoral entitled *Josaphat and Barlaam*, generally ascribed to St. John of Damascus (eighth century).

Joseph (*A*). One not to be seduced from his continency by the severest temptation. The reference is to Joseph in Potiphar's house. (Gen. xxxix.) (*See* BELLEROPHON.)

A joseph. A great coat, so called after Joseph, who wore a garment or coat of many colours.

"At length, Mrs. Buby herself made her appearance; her venerable person, endued with what was then called a joseph, an ample garment, which had once been green, but now, betwixt stains and patches, had become like the vesture of the patriarch whose name it bore—a garment of divers colours."—*Sir W. Scott: The Pirate,* chap. xi.

Joseph (*St.*). Patron saint of carpenters, because he was of the same craft. This is Joseph, husband of Mary, and the reputed father of Jesus.

In Christian art Joseph is represented as an aged man with a budding staff in his hand.

Joseph Andrews. The hero of a novel written by Fielding to ridicule Richardson's *Pam'ela,* whose brother Joseph is supposed to be.

Joseph of A'rimathe'a brought to Listenise the sanctgraal and also the spear with which Longi'nus wounded the crucified Saviour. When Sir Balin entered this chamber, which was in the palace of King Pellam, he found it "marvellously well dight and richly; the bed was arrayed with cloth of gold, the richest that might be thought, and thereby stood a table of clean gold, with four pillars of silver, and upon the table stood the spear strangely wrought." (*The History of Prince Arthur,* part i. chap. 40.)

Joseph's Coat. (*See under* COAT.)

Joss. The house-god of the Chinese; every family has its joss. A temple is called a joss-house.

Josse. *Vous êtes orfèvre, Monsieur Josse* (You are a jeweller, Mr. Josse). Nothing like leather; great is Diana of the Ephesians; your advice is not disinterested. In Molière's comedy of *L'Amour Médecin,* a silversmith, by the name of Josse, being asked the best way of curing a lady pining from love, recommends a handsome present of jewellery. The father replies, "You advise me like a jeweller, Mr. Josse."

Jot. *Not a jot.* "Jot" is a contraction of *iota,* called the Lacedemonian letter, and the smallest in the alphabet; or the Hebrew *yod.*

Jo'tham, in Dryden's satire of *Absalom and Achitophel,* means Saville, Marquis of Halifax. Jotham was the person who uttered the parable of *The Trees Choosing a King* when the men of Shechem made Abimelech king. (Judges ix.)

Jotunheim (pron. *Utun-hime*). Giant land. The home or region of the Scandinavian giants or joten.

Jour Maigre (French). A day of abstinence, when meat is forbidden to be eaten. (*See* BANIAN DAYS.)

Jourdain (*Monsieur*), in Molière's comedy of *Le Bourgeois Gentilhomme.* He represents a bourgeois placed by wealth in the ranks of gentlemen, and making himself extremely ridiculous by his endeavours to acquire their accomplishments.

Journal. (Latin, *diurnum,* a daily thing; Welsh, *diwrnod;* Italian, *giorno;* French, *journal,* journal, *jour,* a day.) Applied to newspapers, the word strictly means a daily paper; but the extension of the term to weekly papers is sanctioned by custom.

Journey. *A Sabbath-day's journey.* The distance between the farthest tents in the wilderness and the tabernacle of Moses, a radius of about a mile; this would make the entire encampment to cover a circumference of six miles.

Journey-weight. The weight of certain parcels of gold in the mint. A *journey of gold* is fifteen pounds Troy, which is coined into 701 sovereigns, or double that number of half-sovereigns. A *journey of silver* is sixty pounds Troy, which is coined into 3,960 shillings, or double that number of sixpences, half that number of florins, etc. So called because this weight of coin was at one time esteemed a day's mintage. (French, *journée.*)

Jouvence (2 syl.). *You have been to the fountain of Jouvence—i.e.* You have grown young again. This is a French phrase. Jouvence is a town of France in the department of Saône-et-Loire, and has a fountain called *la fontaine de*

Jouvence ; but Jouvence means also *youth,* and *la fontaine de jouvence* may be rendered "the fountain of youth." The play on the word gave rise to the tradition that whoever drank of this fountain would become young again.

Jove (1 syl.). (*See* JUPITER.) The Titans made war against Jove, and tried to dethrone him.

" Not stronger were of old the giant crew,
    Who sought to pull high Jove from regal state."
        Thomson : Castle of Indolence, canto 1.

Milton, in *Paradise Lost,* makes Jove one of the fallen angels (i. 512).

Jo'vial. Merry and sociable, like those born under the planet Jupiter, which astrologers considered the happiest of the natal stars.

"Our jovial star reigned at his birth."
        Shakespeare : Cymbeline, v. 4.

Joy. *The seven joys of the Virgin :* (1) The annunciation ; (2) the visitation ; (3) the nativity ; (4) the adoration of the three kings ; (5) the presentation in the temple ; (6) the discovery of her youthful Son in the temple in the midst of the doctors ; (7) her assumption and coronation. (*See* SORROW.)

Joyeuse (2 syl.). Charlemagne's sword, which bore the inscription *Decem præcepto'rum custos Car'olus ;* the sword of Guillaume au Court-Nez ; anyone's sword. It was buried with Charlemagne. (*See* SWORDS.)

Joyeuse Garde or *Garde-Joyeuse.* The estate given by King Arthur to Sir Launcelot of the Lake for defending the Queen's honour against Sir Mador.

Juan Fernandez. A rocky island in the Pacific Ocean, off the coast of Chili. Here Alexander Selkirk, a buccaneer, resided in solitude for four years, and his history is commonly supposed to be the basis of Defoe's *Robinson Crusoe.*

Sailors commonly believe that this island is the scene of Crusoe's adventures : but Defoe distinctly indicates an island on the *east* coast of South America, somewhere near Dutch Guiana.

Jubal [*a trumpet*]. The son of Lamech and Adah. He is called the inventor of the lyre and flute (Gen. iv. 19-21).

" Then when he [*Javan*] heard the voice of Jubal's
    lyre,
Instinctive genius caught the ethereal fire."
        Montgomery : The World Before the Flood, c. 1.

Ju'bilee (Jewish). *The year of jubilee.* Every fiftieth year, when land that had passed out of the possession of those to whom it originally belonged was restored to them ; all who had been reduced to poverty, and were obliged to let themselves out for hire, were released from bondage ; and all debts were cancelled. The word is from *jobil* (a ram's horn), so called because it was proclaimed with trumpets of rams' horns. (*See* Leviticus xxv. 11-34, 39-54 ; and xxvii. 16-24.)

Jubilee (in the Catholic Church). Every twenty-fifth year, for the purpose of granting indulgences. Boniface VIII. instituted it in 1300, and ordered it to be observed every hundred years. Clement VI. reduced the interval to fifty years, Urban IV. to thirty, and Sixtus IV. to twenty-five.

Protestant Jubilee, celebrated in Germany in 1617, the centenary of the Reformation.

Shakespeare Jubilee, held at Stratford-on-Avon, September 6th, 1769.

Jubilee to commemorate the commencement of the fiftieth year of the reign of George III., October 25th, 1809.

Jubilee to celebrate the close of the Revolutionary War, August 1st, 1814.

1887. The *Jubilee* to commemorate the fiftieth year of the reign of Queen Victoria.

Ju'daise (3 syl.). To convert or conform to the doctrines, rites, or manners of the Jews. A *Judaising spirit* is a desire to convert others to the Jewish religion.

Ju'daism (3 syl.). The religion of the Jews, or anything else which is special to that people.

Ju'das, in the satire of *Absalom and Achitophel,* by Dryden and Tate, was meant for Mr. Furgueson, a Nonconformist. He was ejected in 1662 from his living of Godmersham, in Kent, and afterwards distinguished himself by his political intrigues. He joined the Duke of Monmouth, whom he afterwards betrayed.

Le point de Judas (French). The number thirteen. The Messiah and His twelve disciples made thirteen. And as Judas was the first to die, he was the thirteenth. At the death of the Saviour, the number being reduced to eleven, a twelfth (Matthias) was elected by lot to fill the place of the traitor.

Judas Kiss (*A*). A deceitful act of courtesy. Judas betrayed his Master with a kiss.

"So Judas kissed his Master,
And cried, ' All hail ! ' whenas he meant *all harm.*"
        Shakespeare : 3 Henry VI., v. 7.

Judas Slits or **Judas Holes.** The peep-holes in a prison-door, through which the guard looks into the cell to see if all is right ; when not in use, the holes are covered up.

"It was the faint click made by the cover of the 'Judas' as it falls back into the place over the slit where the eyes have been."—*The Century: Russian Political Prisons*, February, 1888, p. 524.

Judas Tree. A translation of the Latin *arbor Judæ*. The name has given rise to a Greek tradition that it was upon one of these trees that Judas Iscariot hanged himself.

Judas-coloured Hair. Fiery-red. Cain is represented with red hair.

"His very hair is of the dissembling colour, something browner than Judas's."—*Shakespeare: As You Like It*, iii. 4.

Jude (*St.*), in Christian art, is represented with a club or staff, and a carpenter's square, in allusion to his trade.

Judée. *La petite Judée* (French). The prefecture of police ; so called because the bureau is in the Rue de Jérusalem, and those taken there for offences look on the police as their betrayers.

Judge's Black Cap. The judge puts on his black cap (now a three-cornered piece of black silk) when he condemns to death, in sign of mourning. This sign is very ancient. "Haman hasted to his house mourning, having his head covered" (Esther vi. 12). David wept "and had his head covered" (2 Samuel xv. 30). Demosthenes went home with his head covered when insulted by the populace. Darius covered his head on learning the death of his queen. Malcolm says to Macduff in his deep sorrow, "What, man! ne'er pull your hat upon your brows" (*Macbeth*, iv. 3). And the ancient English, says Fosbroke, "drew their hoods forward over their heads at funerals."

Judges' Robes. In the criminal courts, where the judges represent the sovereign, they appear in full court dress, and wear a scarlet robe ; but in Nisi Prius Courts the judge sits merely to balance the law between civilians, and therefore appears in his judicial undress, or violet gown.

Ju'dica (Latin). The fifth Sunday after Lent ; so called from the first word of the service for the day, *Judica me, Dom'ine* (Judge me, O Lord). (Psalm xliii.)

Judicium Crucis was stretching out the arms before a cross, till one of the party could hold out no longer, and lost his cause. The bishop of Paris and abbot of St. Denis appealed to this judgment in a dispute they had about the patronage of a monastery ; each of the disputants selected a man to represent his cause, and the man selected by the bishop gave in, so that the award was given in favour of the abbot.

Judicium Dei (Latin). The trial of guilt by direct appeal to God, under the notion that He would defend the right even by miracle. There were numerous methods of appeal, as by single combat, ordeal by water or fire, eating a crust of bread, standing with arms extended, consulting the Bible, etc., etc.

Ju'dith. The Jewish heroine of Bethu'lia, who perilled her life in the tent of Holofernēs, the general of Nebuchadnezzar, in order to save her native town. The bold adventurer cut off the head of the Assyrian, and her townsmen, rushing on the invaders, defeated them with great slaughter. (*The Book of Judith.*)

Jug (*A*) or a *Stone jug.* A prison. (*See* JOGGIS.)

Juge de Paix (French). A cudgel.

"Albert Mangin, condamné à mort le 7 floreal an. ii. ayant dit que les jacobins étaient tou des scélérats et des coquins, et montrant un gros bâton qu'il tenait à la main : Voilà un 'Juge de paix' qui me servira à leur casser la barre du cou."—*L. P. Prudhomme: Dict. des Individus Condamnés, etc.*

Jugged Hare. The hare being cut up is put into a jug or pipkin, and the pipkin is set in a pan of water. This *bain marie* prevents the contents of the pipkin from being burnt.

Juggernaut or **Jaggernaut.** A Hindu god. The word is a corruption of the Sanscrit *jagannâtha* (lord of the world). The temple of this god is in a town of the same name in Orissa. King Ayeen Akbery sent a learned Brahman to look out a site for a temple. The Brahman wandered about for many days, and then saw a crow dive into the water, and having washed, made obeisance to the element. This was selected as the site of the temple. While the temple was a-building the rajah had a prophetic dream, telling him that the true form of Vishnu should be revealed to him in the morning. When the rajah went to see the temple he beheld a log of wood in the water, and this log he accepted as the realisation of his dream, enshrined it in the temple, and called it Jagannâth.

"The idol Jaggernat is in shape like a serpent, with seven heads ; and on each cheek it hath the form of a wing, and the wings open, and shut, and flap as it is carried in a stately chariot."—*Bruton: Churchill's Collection.*

The car of Juggernaut. An enormous wooden machine adorned with all sorts of figures, and mounted on sixteen wheels. Fifty men drag it annually to the temple, and it is said to contain a bride for the god. Formerly many were crushed to death by the car; some being pushed down by the enormous crowd; some throwing themselves under the wheels, as persons in England under a railway train; some perhaps as devotees. By British police arrangements, such immolation is practically abolished.

Juggler means a player. (Latin, *joculator.*) These jugglers accompanied the minstrels and troubadours, to assist them, and added to their musical talents sleight-of-hand, antics, and feats of prowess, to amuse the company assembled. In time the music was dropped as the least attractive, and tricks became the staple of these wandering performers. (Latin, *joculātor, jocus,* a joke or trick.)

Juggs or **Jougs.** The name given in Scotland to a sort of pillory, consisting of an iron ring or collar fastened by a short chain to a wall, as the "juggs" of Duddingston, Edinburgh. (*See* JOGGIS.)

Ju'lian, the Roman emperor, boasted that he would rebuild Jerusalem, but was mortally wounded by an arrow before the foundation was laid. Much has been made of this by early Christian writers, who dwell on the prohibition and curse pronounced against those who should attempt to rebuild the city, and the fate of Julian is pointed out as an example of Divine wrath against the impious disregarder of the threat.

"Well pleased they look for Sion's coming state,
Nor think of Julian's boast and Julian's fate."
Crabbe: Borough.

St. Julian. Patron saint of travellers and of hospitality. Represented as accompanied by a stag in allusion to his early career as a hunter; and either receiving the poor and afflicted, or ferrying travellers across a river.

"An householdere, and that a gret, was he !
Seynt Julian he was in his countré,
His breed, his ale, was alway after oon [one pattern];
A bettre envyned man was nowhere noon."
Chaucer: The Frankeleyn, Introduction to Canterbury Tales.

St. Julian was he deemed. A great epicure. St. Julian was the epicurean of saints. (*See above.*)

Julian Epoch or **Era.** That of the reformed calendar by Julius Cæsar, which began forty-six years before Christ.

Julian Period is produced by multiplying together the lunar cycle, the solar cycle, and the Roman indiction. The first year of the Christian era corresponded to the year 4713 of the Julian, and therefore to reduce our B.C. dates to the Julian, we must subtract them from 4713, but our A.D. dates we must add to that number. So named from Julius Scaliger, the deviser of it.

Julian period. Multiply 28 by 19 and by 15, which will give 7,980, the time when the solar and lunar periods agree.

Julian Year. The year regulated by Julius Cæsar, which continued to be observed till it was corrected by Pope Gregory XIII. in 1582.

Julienne Soup. Clear meat soup, containing chopped vegetables, especially carrots; so called after Julien, a French cook, of Boston.

Juliet. Daughter of Lady Capulet, and "sweet sweeting" of Romeo, in Shakespeare's tragedy of *Romeo and Juliet.* She has become a household word for a lady-love.

Ju'lium Si'dus. The comet which appeared at the death of Julius Cæsar, and which in court flattery was called the apotheo'sis of the murdered man.

July'. The seventh month, named by Mark Antony, in honour of Julius Cæsar, who was born in it.

Ju'mala. The supreme idol of the ancient Finns and Lapps. The word is sometimes used by the Scandinavian poets for the Almighty.

"On a lonely cliff
An ancient shrine he found, of Jumala the seat,
For many a year gone by closed up and desolate."
Frithiof-Saga: The Reconciliation.

Jump. To jump or to fit or unite with like a graft; as, *both our inventions meet and jump in one.* Hence the adverb exactly, precisely.

"Good advice is easily followed when it jumps with our own ... inclinations."—*Lockhart: Sir Walter Scott,* chap. x. p. 241.

⁂ The Scotch use *jimp,* as, "When she had been married jimp four months." (*The Antiquary.*)

Jump at an Offer (*To*). To accept eagerly.

Jump Over the Broomstick (*To*). To marry in an informal way. A "brom" is the bit of a bridle; to "jump the brom" is to skip over the marriage restraint, and "broomstick" is a mere corruption.

"A Romish wedding is surely better than jumping over a broomstick."—*G. A. Sala.*

Jumper. The longest jumper on record was Phayllos, who is accredited with jumping 55 feet. Half that length would be an enormous jump.

A counter jumper. A draper's apprentice or employé, who is accustomed to jump over the shop counter to save the trouble and time of going round.

June (1 syl.). The sixth month. Ovid says, "*Junius a juvĕnum nomĭne dictus.*" (*Fasti,* v. 78.)

June Marriages Lucky. "Good to the man and happy to the maid." This is an old Roman superstition. The festival of Juno monēta was held on the calends of June, and Juno was the great guardian of the female sex from birth to death.

Ju'nior Op'time. A Cambridge University term, meaning a third-class "honour" man—*i.e.* in the mathematical "honour" examination.

Ju'nior Soph. A man of the second year's standing is so called in the University of Cambridge. (*See* SOPH.)

Ju'nius. *Letters of Junius.* In 1871 was published a book entitled *The Handwriting of Junius Professionally Investigated by Mr. Charles Chabot, expert.* The object of this book is to prove that Sir Philip Francis was the author of these *letters.* On the 22nd May, 1871, appeared an article in the *Times* to show that the case is "not proven" by Mr. Chabot. Mr. Pitt told Lord Aberdeen that he knew who wrote the Junius Letters, and that it was not Francis. Lady Grenville sent a letter to the editor of *Diaries of a Lady of Quality* to the same effect.

Junk, Latin, *juncus,* from *jungo,* to join; used for binding, making baskets, mats. The *juncus maritĭmus* is useful in binding together the loose sands of the sea-shore, and obstructing the incursions of the sea. The *juncus conglomerātus* is used in Holland for giving stability to river-banks and canals. (*See* RUSH.)

Junk. Salt meat supplied to vessels for long voyages; so called because it is hard and tough as old rope-ends so called. Ropes are called junks because they were once made of bulrushes. Junk is often called salt horse. (*See* HARNESS CASK.)

Jun'ket. Curded cream with spice, etc.; any dainty. The word is the Italian *giuncata* (curd or cream-cheese), so called because carried on junk or bulrushes (*giúnco*).

"You know there wants no junkets at the feast."
Shakespeare: Taming of the Shrew, iii. 2.

Junner. A giant in Scandinavian mythology, said in the Edda to represent the "eternal principle." Its skull forms the heavens; its eyes the sun and moon; its shoulders the mountains; its bones the rocks, etc.; hence the poets call heaven "Junner's skull;" the sun, "Junner's right eye;" the moon, "Junner's left eye;" the rivers, "the ichor of old Junner." (*See* GIANTS.)

Ju'no. The "venerable ox-eyed" wife of Jupiter, and queen of heaven. (*Roman mythology.*)

❧ The famous marble statue of the Campana Juno is in the Vatican.

Juno'nian Bird. The peacock, dedicated to the goddess-queen.

Junto. A faction consisting of Russell, Lord-Keeper Somers, Charles Montague, and several other men of mark, who ruled the Whigs in the reign of William III. for nearly twenty years, and exercised a very great influence over the nation. The word is a corruption of the Spanish *junta* (an administrative assembly), but is in English a term of censure.

Ju'piter is the Latin form of Ζευς πατήρ. Verospi's statue of Jupiter is in the Vatican; but one of the seven wonders of the world was the statue of Olympian Jove, by Phidias, destroyed by fire in Constantinople A.D. 475.

This gigantic statue was nearly sixty feet high, though seated on a throne. The statue was made of ivory; the throne of cedar-wood, adorned with ivory, ebony, gold, and precious stones. The god holds in his right hand a golden statue of Victory, and his left hand rested on a long sceptre surmounted with an eagle. The robe of the god was of gold, and so was the footstool supported by golden lions. This wonderful work of art was removed to Constantinople by Theodosius I.

Jupiter. With the ancient alchemists designated tin.

Jupiter Scapin. A nickname of Napoleon Bonaparte, given him by the Abbé de Pradt. Scapin is a valet famous for his knavish tricks, in Molière's comedy of *Les Fourberies de Scapin.*

Jupiter's Beard. House-leek. Supposed to be a charm against evil spirits and lightning. Hence grown at one time very generally on the thatch of houses.

"Et habet quisque supra domum suum Jovis barbam."—*Charlemagne's Edict.*

Jurassic Rocks. Limestone rocks; so called from the Jura; the *Jurassic period* is the geological period when these rocks were formed. Our *oolitic* series pretty nearly corresponds with the Jurassic

Jurisprudence. *The Father of Juris-prudence.* Glanville, who wrote *Tracta'tus de Legibus et Consuetudinibus Angliæ* in 1181 (died 1190).

Jury Leg (*A*). A wooden leg, or leg for the nonce. (*See* JURY MAST.)

"I took the leg off with my saw . . . seared the stump . . . and made a jury leg that he shambles about with as well as ever he did."—*Sir W. Scott: The Pirate*, chap. xxxiv.

Jury Mast. A corruption of *joury mast*—*i.e.* a mast for the day, a temporary mast, being a spar used for the nonce when the mast has been carried away. (French, *jour*, a day.)

Jus Civi'le. Civil law.

Jus Divi'num. Divine law.

Jus Gen'tium (Latin). International law.

Jus Mari'ti (Latin). The right of the husband to the wife's property.

Jus de Réglisse (liquorice). French slang for a negro.

Jus et Norma Loquendi. The right method of speaking and pronouncing established by the custom of each particular nation. The whole phrase is "*Consuetūdo, jus et norma loquendi.*" (*Horace.*)

Just (*The*).

Aristi'dēs, the Athenian (died B.C. 468).

Ba'haram, styled *Shah Endeb* (the Just King), fifth of the Sassan'idæ (*q.v.*) (276-296).

Casimir II., King of Poland (1117, 1177-1194).

Ferdinand I., King of Aragon (1373, 1412-1416).

Haroun al Raschid (*The Just*). The most renowned of the Abbasside califs, and the hero of several of the *Arabian Nights* stories (765, 786-808).

James II., King of Aragon (1261-1327).

Khosru or Chosroes, called by the Arabs *Molk al Adel* (the Just King).

Moran the Just, councillor of Feredach, King of Ireland.

Pedro I. of Portugal (1320, 1357, 1367).

Juste Milieu (French). The golden mean.

Justices in Eyre (pron. *ire*). A contraction and corruption of *Itin'ere*—*i.e.* on circuit.

Justing of Watson and Barbour. A description of a ludicrous tilt between Watson and Barbour, in Scotch verse, by Sir David Lindsay.

Justin'ian. *The English Justinian.* Edward I. (1239, 1272-1307).

Ju'venal (Latin, from *juvenis*). A youth ; common in Shakespeare, thus—

"The juvenal, the prince your master, whos' chin is not yet fledged."—*2 Henry IV.*, i. 2.

Juvenal.

The English Juvenal. John Oldham (1653-1683).

The Juvenal of Painters. William Hogarth (1697-1764).

Juveniles (3 syl.), in theatrical parlance, means those actors who play young men's parts, whether in tragedy, melodrama, or light comedy. Thus a manager scoring a play would write against Hamlet, not the name of the actor, but "the leading Juvenile."

K

K. To be branded with a K (*kalumnia*). So, according to the *Lex Memmia*, false accusers were branded in the forehead.

K. *The three bad K's.* The Greeks so called the Ka'rians, Kre'tans, and Kilik'ians. The Romans retained the same expression, though they spelt the three nations with C instead of K.

K.C.B. Knight Commander of the Bath.

K.G. Knight of the Garter.

K.K. is the German *Kaiserliche Königliche.* The Emperor of Austria is styled K.K. Majestät (His Imperial Royal Majesty).

K.O.B. (*i.e.* the King's Own Borderers). The 25th Foot, so called in 1805.

Ka Me, Ka Thee. One good turn deserves another ; do me a service, and I will give you a helping hand when you require one. (Latin, *Fricantem frica*, or *Muli mutuo scabunt*.)

"Ka me, ka thee, is a proverb all over the world."—*Sir W. Scott: Kenilworth*, chap. v.

Ka'aba (Arabic, *ka'bah*, a square house). A shrine of Mecca, said to have been built by Abraham on the spot where Adam first worshipped after his expulsion from Paradise. In the north-east corner is a stone seven inches long, said to be a ruby sent down from heaven. It is now black, from being kissed so often by sinful man. (*See* ADAM'S PEAK.)

Kab'ibonok'ka (*North - American Indian*). Son of Mudjekee'wis, and the ιndian Boreas, who dwelt in Wabasso (the North). (*See* SHING'EBIS.)

Kaffir (Arabic, *Kâfir*, an infidel). A name given to the Hottentots, who reject the Moslem faith *Kafiristan*, in Central Asia, means "the country of the infidels."

" The affinity of the Kafir tribes . : . including the Kafirs proper and the people of Oungo, is based upon the various idioms spoken by them, the direct representatives of a common, but now extinct, mother tongue. This aggregate of languages is now conveniently known as . . . . the Bantu linguistic system,"—*K. Johnston : Africa*, p. 447.

Kai-Omurs (*the mighty Omurs*), surnamed *Ghil-shah* (earth's king). Son of Du'lavëd, founder of the city Balk, and first of the Kai-Omurs or Paishdad'ian dynasty of Persia (B.C. 940-920). (*See* PAISHDADIAN.)

Kai-an'ians. The sixth Persian dynasty. The semi-historic period (B.C. 660-331). So called because they took for their affix the term *kai* (mighty), called by the Greeks *Ku* (Kuros), and by the Romans *Cy* (Cyrus).

Kail'yal (2 syl.). The heroine of Southey's *Curse of Kehâma*.

Kailyard School, the name given to a school of writers, who take their subjects from Scottish humble life. The name is due to the motto—" There grows a bonnie brier bush in our kailyard"—used by Ian Maclaren for his book, "Beside the Bonnie Brier Bush."

Kain Hens. Hens that a tenant pays to his landlord, as a sort of rent in kind (ill-fed hens). (*Guy Mannering*, v.)

Kaiser. The German Emperor. He receives the title from Dalmatia, Croatia, and the line of the Danube, which, by the arrangement of Diocletian, was governed by a prince entitled Cæsar of the Holy Roman Empire, as successor of the emperor of the old Roman empire. It was Albert II., Duke of Austria, who added the Holy Roman Empire to the imperial throne in 1438 ; and William I., king of Prussia, on being crowned German emperor in 1871, took the title.

Kajak. An Esquimaux boat, used by the men only,

Ka'led is Gulnare (2 syl.) in the disguise of a page in the service of Lara. After Lara was shot, she haunted the spot of his death as a crazy woman, and died of a broken heart. (*Byron : Lara.*)

Kaleda (*Sclavonic mythology*). The god of peace, somewhat similar to the

Latin Janus. His feast was celebrated on the 24th of December.

Kali. A Hindu goddess after whom Calcutta receives its name, Kali-Kutta (*Kali's village*).

Kaliyu'ga. The last of the four Hindu periods contained in the great Yuga, equal to the Iron Age of classic mythology. It consisted of 432,000 solar-sidereal years, and began 3,102 years before the Christian era. The bull, representing truth and right, has but one foot in this period, because all the world delights in wickedness. (*See* KRITA.)

Kalmar'. *The Union of Kalmar.* A treaty made on July 12th, 1397, to settle the succession of Norway, Sweden, and Denmark on Queen Margaret and her heirs for ever. This treaty lasted only till the death of Margaret.

Kalmucks—*i.e. Khalmuiku* (apostates) from Buddhism. A race of western Monguls, extending from western China to the valley of the Volga river.

Kalpa. A day and night of Brahmâ, a period of 4,320,000,000 solar-sidereal years. Some say there are an infinity of Kalpas, others limit the number to thirty. A Great Kalpa is a life of Brahmâ ; the whole duration of time from the creation to the destruction of the world.

Kalpa-Tarou. A tree in Indian mythology from which might be gathered whatever a person desired. This tree is " the tree of the imagination."

Kalyb. The "Lady of the Woods," who stole St. George from his nurse, brought him up as her own child, and endowed him with gifts. St. George enclosed her in a rock, where she was torn to pieces by spirits. (*Seven Champions of Christendom*, part i.)

Kam. Crooked. (Erse *kaam*, squinteyed.) *Clean Kam*, perverted into *Kim Kam*, means wholly awry, clean from the purpose.

"This is clean kam—merely awry."
			Shakespeare : Coriolanus, iii. 1.

Kâma. The Hindu god of love. His wife is Rati (*voluptuousness*), and he is represented as riding on a sparrow, holding in his hand a bow of flowers and five arrows (*i.e.* the five senses).

Ka'mi. The celestial gods of the first mythical dynasty of Japan, the demi-gods of the second dynasty, the spiritual princes, anyone sainted or deified; and now about equal to our lord, a title of respect paid to princes, nobles, ministers, and governors.

Kamsin. A simoom or samiel, a hot, dry, southerly wind, which prevails in Egypt and the deserts of Africa.

Kansas, U.S. America. So named from the Konsos, an Indian tribe of the locality.

Kansas. *Bleeding Kansas.* So called because it was the place where that sanguinary strife commenced which was the prelude of the Civil War of America. According to the Missouri Compromise made in 1820, slavery was never to be introduced into any western region lying beyond 36° 30′ north latitude. In 1851, the slave-holders of Missouri, by a local act, pushed their west frontier to the river-bank, and slave lords, with their slaves, took possession of the Kansas hunting grounds, declaring that they would "lynch, hang, tar and feather any white-livered abolitionist who presumed to pollute the soil." In 1854, thirty New England free-soilers crossed the river in open boats; they were soon joined by others, and dared the slavers to carry out their threats. Many a fierce battle was fought, but in 1861 Bleeding Kansas was admitted into the Union as a free state. (*W. Hepworth Dixon: New America,* vol. i. chap. 2.)

Karaites [*Scripturists*]. A Jewish sect that adhered to the letter of the Scriptures, rejecting all oral traditions. They abhorred the Talmud, and observed the Sabbath with more rigour than even the rabbinists.

Karma. The Buddhist's judgment, which determines at death the future state of the deceased. It is also their fiat on actions, pronouncing them to be meritorious or otherwise.

⁛ In Theosophy, it means the unbroken sequence of cause and effect; each effect being, in its turn, the cause of a subsequent effect. It is a Sanscrit word, meaning "action" or "sequence."

"The laws which determine the physical attribution, condition of life, intellectual capacities, and so forth, of the new body, to which the Ego is drawn by affinities . . . are . . . in Buddhism [called] Karma."—*Nineteenth Century,* June, 1893, p. 1025.

Karma′thians. A Mohammedan sect which rose in Irak in the ninth Christian century. Its founder was Ahmad, a poor labourer who assumed the name of Karmat, and professed to be a prophet.

Karoon or **Korah.** *The riches of Karoon* (Arabic proverb). Korah, according to the commentators of the Koran, was the most wealthy and most beautiful of all the Israelites. It is said that he built a large palace, which he overlaid with gold, and that the doors of his palace were solid gold (*Sale : Koran*). He was the Crœsus of the Mahometans, and guarded his wealth in a labyrinth.

Karrows. A set of gamblers in Ireland, who played away even the clothes on their backs.

"The karrows plaie awaie mantle and all to the bare skin, and then trusse themselves in straw or leaves. They wait for passengers in the highwaie, invite them to game upon the greene and aske no more but companions to make them sport. For default of other stuffe they pawne their glibs, the nailes of their fingers and toes, their dimissaries which they leefe or redeeme at the courtesy of the winner."—*Stanihurst.*

Kaswa (*Al*). Mahomet's favourite camel, which fell on its knees in adoration when "the prophet" delivered the last clause of the Koran to the assembled multitude at Mecca. This is one of the dumb creatures admitted into the Moslem paradise. (*See* PARADISE.)

Katerfelto. A generic name for a quack or charlatan. Katerfelto was a celebrated quack or influenza doctor. He was a tall man, who dressed in a long black gown and square cap. In 1782 he exhibited in London his solar microscope, and created immense excitement by showing the infusoria of [muddy] water. The doctor used to aver that he was the greatest philosopher since the time of Sir Isaac Newton.

" And Katerfelto with his hair on end, At his own wonders wondering for his bread." *Cowper : The Task; The Winter Evening* (1782).

Katharine or **Kathari′na.** Daughter of Baptista, a rich gentleman of Padua. She was very beautiful, but a shrew. Petruchio of Vero′na married her, and so subdued her imperious temper by his indomitable will, that she became the model of a "submissive wife," and gave Bianca, her sister, most excellent advice respecting the duty of submission. (*Shakespeare ;, Taming of the Shrew.*)

The Katherine de' Medici of China. Voochee, widow of King Tae-tsông.

Kathay′. China.

Katmir. (*See* KETMIR.)

Kay or *Sir Key.* Son of Sir Ector, and foster-brother of King Arthur. In Arthurian romance, this seneschal of England is represented as a rude and boastful knight, the first to attempt any achievement, but very rarely successful.

Kayward. The hare, in the tale of *Reynard the Fox.* (The word means "Country-guardian.")

Keber'. A Persian sect (generally rich merchants), distinguished by their beards and dress. When one of them dies, a cock is driven out of the poultry yard ; if a fox seizes it, it is a proof that the soul of the deceased is saved. If this experiment does not answer, they prop the dead body against a wall, and if the birds peck out the right eye first, the Keber is gone to heaven ; if the left eye, the carcase is flung into the ditch, for the Keber was a reprobate.

Kebla. The point of adoration ; *i.e.* the quarter or point of the compass towards which persons turn when they worship. The Persian fire-worshippers turn to the east, the place of the rising sun ; the Jews to Jerusalem, the city of the King of kings; the Mahometans to Mecca ; the early Christians turned to the "east," and the "communion table" even of the "Reformed Church" is placed at the east end of the building, whenever this arrangement is practicable. Any object of passionate desire.

Kebla-Noma. The pocket compass carried by Mussulmans to direct them which way to turn when they pray. (*See above.*)

Kedar's Tents. This world. Kedar was Arabia Deserta, and the phrase Kedar's tents means houses in the wilderness of this world.

> " Ah me ! ah me ! that 1
> In Kedar's tents here stay ;
> No place like that on high ;
> Lord, thither guide my way."
> *Crossman.*

Ke'derli. The St. George of Mahometan mythology. He slew a monstrous dragon to save a damsel exposed to its fury, and, having drunk of the water of life, rode about the world to aid those warriors who invoked him. This tradition is exactly parallel to that of St. George, and explains the reason why the one is the field-word with the Turks, and the latter with the ancient English.

Ked'jeree'. A stew of rice, vegetables, eggs, butter, etc. A corruption of the Indian word *Khichri* (a medley or hotch-potch). The word has been confounded with a place so called, forty miles south-west of Calcutta, on the Hooghly river.

Keel-hauling or **-haling.** A long, troublesome, and vexatious examination or repetition of annoyances from a landlord or government official. In the Dutch and many other navies, delinquents were, at one time, tied to a yard-arm with weights on their feet, and dragged by a rope under the keel of a ship, in at one side and out at the other. The result was often fatal.

Keelman (*A*). A bargeman. (See *Old Mortality* [Introduction], the bill of Margaret Chrystale : "To three chappins of yell with Sandy the keelman, 9d.")

Keelson or **Kelson.** A beam running lengthwise above the keel of a ship, and bolted to the middle of the floor-frames, in order to stiffen the vessel. The word *son* is the Swedish *svin*, and Norwegian *svill*, a sill.)

Keening. A weird lamentation for the dead, common in Galway. The coffin is carried to the burying place, and while it is carried three times round, the mourners go to the graves of their nearest kinsfolk and begin keening, after which they smoke.

Keep Down (*To*). To prevent another from rising to an independent position ; to keep in subjection.

Keep House (*To*). To maintain a separate establishment ; to act as housekeeper.

To keep open house. To admit all comers to hospitable entertainment.

Keep Touch. To keep faith ; the exact performance of an agreement, as, "To keep touch with my promise" (*More*). The idea seems to be embodied in the proverb, "Seeing is believing, but feeling is naked truth."

> " And trust me on my truth,
> If thou keep touch with me,
> My dearest friend, as my own heart,
> Thou shalt right welcome be."
> *Songs of the London 'Prentices,* p. 37.

Keep Up (*To*). To continue, as, "to keep up a discussion;" to maintain, as, "to keep up one's courage ;" to continue *pari passu,* as "Keep up with the rest."

Keep at Arm's Length (*To*). To prevent another from being too familiar.

Keep Body and Soul Together (*To*). To struggle to maintain life ; to continue life. Thus we say, "It is as much as I can do to keep body and soul together ;" and "To keep body and soul together" we did so and so.

Keep Company with (*To*). To associate with someone of another sex with a view of marriage. The phrase is almost confined to household servants and persons of a similar status.

Keep Good Hours (*To*). To retire to bed somewhat early. *To keep bad hours* is to sit up late at night.

Keep it Dark. Keep it as a secret; hide it from public sight or knowledge; do not talk about it.

Keep One's Countenance (*To*). To refrain from laughing; to preserve one's gravity.

Keep One's Own Counsel (*To*). To be reticent of one's own affairs or plans.

Keep your Breath to Cool your Porridge. Look after your own affairs, and do not put your spoke in another person's wheel. Husband your strength to keep your own state safe and well, and do not waste it on matters in which you have really no concern. Don't scold or rail at me, but look at home.

Keep your Powder Dry. Keep prepared for action; keep your courage up.

" Go forth and conquer, Strephon mine,
   This kiss upon your lips retaining ;
A precept that is also thine
   Forbids the teardrop hot and straining.
We're Mars and Venus, you and I,
   And both must ' keep our powder dry.' "
Sims : Dagonet Ballads (In Love and War).

Keepers. A staff of men employed by Irish landlords in 1843, etc., to watch the crops and prevent their being smuggled off during the night. They were resisted by the Molly Maguires.

Keha′ma. A Hindu rajah who obtains and sports with supernatural powers. (*Southey : Curse of Kehama.*)

Kelpie or **Kelpy.** A spirit of the waters in the form of a horse, in Scottish mythology. Not unlike the Irish Phooka. (*See* FAIRY.)

" Every lake has its Kelpie or Water-horse, often seen by the shepherd sitting upon the brow of a rock, dashing along the surface of the deep, or browsing upon the pasture on its verge."—*Graham : Sketches of Perthshire.*

Kelso Convoy (*A*). A step and a half over the door-stone or threshold.

" It's no expected your honour suld leave the land ; it's just a Kelso convoy, a step and a half ower the door stane."—*Sir W. Scott: The Antiquary,* chap. xxx.

Ke′ma. The books containing the secrets of the genii, who, infatuated with love, revealed the marvels of nature to men, and were banished out of heaven. According to some etymologists, the word *chemistry* is derived from this word. (*Zozime Panopolite.*)

Kemp′fer-Hau′sen. The *nom de plume* of Robert Pearce Gillies, one of the speakers in the *Noctēs Ambrosia′næ.* (*Blackwood's Magazine.*)

Kempis. The authorship of the work entitled *De Imitatio′ne Christi,* has afforded as much controversy as the author of *Letters of Junius.* In 1604, a Spanish Jesuit discovered a manuscript copy by the Abbot John Gersen or Gesen; and since then three competitors have had angry and wordy defenders, viz. Thomas à Kempis, J. Charlier de Gerson, Chancellor of the University of Paris, and the Abbot Gersen. M. Malou gives his verdict in favour of the first.

Ken or **Kiun.** An Egyptian goddess similar to the Roman Venus. She is represented as standing on a lion, and holding two serpents in one hand and a flower in the other. (*See* Amos v. 26.)

Kendal Green. Green cloth for foresters ; so called from Kendal, Westmoreland, famous at one time for this manufacture. Kendal green was the livery of Robin Hood and his followers. In Rymer's *Fœdera* (ii. 83) is a letter of protection, dated 1331, and granted by Edward III. to John Kempe of Flanders, who established cloth-weaving in the borough. Lincoln was also famous at one time for dyeing green.

" How couldst thou know these men in Kendal green, when it was so dark thou couldst not see thy hand ? "—*Shakespeare :* 1 *Henry IV.,* ii. 4.

Kenelm (*St.*) was murdered at Clente-in-Cowbage, near Winchelcumb, in Gloucestershire. The murder, says Roger of Wendover, was miraculously notified at Rome by a white dove, which alighted on the altar of St. Peter's, bearing in its beak a scroll with these words :

" In Clent cow pasturé, under a thorn,
   Of head bereft, lies Kenelm king-born."

Kenna. (*See* KENSINGTON.)

Kenna Quhair [*I know not where*]. Scotch for *terra incog′nita.*

Kenne. A stone said to be formed in the eye of a stag, and used as an antidote to poison.

Kennedy. A poker, or to kill with a poker ; so called from a man of that name who was killed by a poker. (*Dictionary of Modern Slang.*)

Kennel. A dog's house; from the Latin *canis* (a dog), Italian *canile ;* but kennel (a gutter), from the Latin *canna* (a cane, whence *canālis*), our *canal, channel,* etc.

Ken'no. This was a large rich cheese, made by the women of the family with a great affectation of secrecy, and was intended for the refreshment of the gossips who were in the house at the "canny minute" of the birth of a child. Called *Ken-no* because no one was supposed to know of its existence—certainly no male being, not excepting the master of the house. After all had eaten their fill on the auspicious occasion, the rest was divided among the gossips and taken home. The Kenno is supposed to be a relic of the secret rites of the *Bona Dea.*

Ken'sington. O'beron, king of the fairies, held his royal seat in these gardens, which were fenced round with spells "interdicted to human touch;" but not unfrequently his thievish elves would rob the human mother of her babe, and leave in its stead a sickly changeling of the elfin race. Once on a time it so fell out that one of the infants fostered in these gardens was Albion, the son of "Albion's royal blood;" it was stolen by a fairy named Milkah. When the boy was nineteen, he fell in love with Kenna, daughter of King Oberon, and Kenna vowed that none but Albion should ever be her chosen husband. Oberon heard her when she made this vow, and instantly drove the prince out of the garden, and married the fairy maid to Azu'riel, a fairy of great beauty and large possessions, to whom Holland Park belonged. In the meantime, Albion prayed to Neptune for revenge, and the sea-god commanded the fairy O'riel, whose dominion lay along the banks of the Thames, to espouse the cause of his lineal offspring. Albion was slain in the battle by Azuriel, and Neptune in revenge crushed the whole empire of Oberon. Being immortal, the fairies could not be destroyed, but they fled from the angry sea-god, some to the hills and some to the dales, some to the caves and others to river-banks. Kenna alone remained, and tried to revive her lover by means of the herb moly. No sooner did the juice of this wondrous herb touch the body than it turned into a snow-drop. When Wise laid out the grounds for the Prince of Orange, Kenna planned it "in a morning dream," and gave her name to the town and garden. (*Tickell: Kensington Gardens.*)

Kent (Latin, *Can'tium*), the territory of the Kantii or Cantii; Old British, *Kant,* a corner or headland). In the reign of Queen Elizabeth Kent was so notorious for highway robbery, that the word signified a "nest of thieves."

"Some bookes are arrogant and impudent :
So are most thieves in Christendome and Kent."
Taylor, the Water Poet (1630).

A man of Kent. One born east of the Medway. These men went out with green boughs to meet the Conqueror, and obtained in consequence a confirmation of their ancient privileges from the new king. They call themselves the *invicti.* The hops of East Kent are liked best.

A Kentish man. A resident of West Kent.

Holy Maid of Kent. Elizabeth Barton, who pretended to the gift of prophecy and power of miracles. Having denounced the doom and speedy death of Henry VIII. for his marriage with Anne Boleyn, she was executed. Sir Walter Scott (*Abbot,* xiii.) calls her "The Nun of Kent." (*See* FAIR [Maid of Kent]).

Kent's Hole. A large cave in the limestone rock near Torquay, Devon.

Kent Street Ejectment. Taking away the street-door : a method devised by the landlords of Kent Street, Southwark, when their tenants were more than a fortnight in arrears.

Kentish Fire. Rapturous applause, or three times three and one more. The expression originated with Lord Winchelsea, who proposed the health of the Earl of Roden, on August 15th, 1834, and added, "Let it be given with the 'Kentish Fire.'" In proposing another toast he asked permission to bring his "Kentish Artillery" again into action. Chambers, in his *Encyclopædia,* says it arose from the protracted cheers given in Kent to the No-Popery orators in 1828-1829.

Kentish Moll. Mary Carlton, nicknamed *The German Princess.* She was transported to Jamaica in 1671 : but, returning without leave, she was hanged at Tyburn, January 22nd, 1673.

Kentishmen's Tails. (*See* TAILS.)

Kentucky (U.S. America), so called in 1782, from its principal river. It was admitted into the union in 1792. The nickname of the inhabitants is *Corncrackers.* Indian Shawnoese *Kentuckee* = "head *or* long river."

Kepler's Fairy. The fairy which guides the planets. Kepler said that each planet was guided in its elliptical orbit by a resident angel.

Kepler's Laws (Johann Kepler, 1571-1630):

(1) That the planets describe ellipses, and that the centre of the sun is in one of the foci.

(2) That every planet so moves that the line drawn from it to the sun describes equal areas in equal times.

(3) That the squares of the times of the planetary revolutions are as the cubes of their mean distances from the sun.

Kerchief of Plesaunce. An embroidered cloth presented by a lady to her knight to wear for her sake. The knight was bound to place it in his helmet.

Kerna. A kind of trumpet used by Tamerlane, the blast of which might be heard for miles.

Kernel (Anglo-Saxon, *cyrnel*, a diminutive of *corn;* seed in general), whence acorn (the *ac* or *oak* corn).

Kersey. A coarse cloth, usually ribbed, and woven from long wool : said to be so named from Kersey, in Suffolk, where it was originally made.

Kerseymere. A corruption of Casimir, a man's name. A twilled woollen cloth made in Abbeville, Amiens, Elbeuf, Louviers, Rheims, Sedan, and the West of England. (French *casimir*, Spanish *casimiro* or *casimiras*.)

Ker'zereh or **Kerz'rah.** A flower which grows in Persia. It is said, if anyone in June or July inhales the hot south wind which has blown over this flower he will die.

Keso'ra. The female idol adored in the temple of Juggernaut. Its head and body are of sandal-wood ; its eyes two diamonds, and a third diamond is suspended round its neck ; its hands are made entirely of small pearls, called *perles à l'once ;* its bracelets are of pearls and rubies, and its robe is cloth of gold.

Kestrel. A hawk of a base breed, hence a worthless fellow. Also used as an adjective.

"No thought of honour ever did assay
    His baser brest ; but in his kestrell kynd
  A pleasant veine of glory he did find . . ."
      Spenser: Faërie Queene, book ii. canto iii. 3.

Ketch. (*See* JACK KETCH.)

Ketch. A kind of two-masted vessel. Bomb-ketches were much used in the last century wars.

Ketchup. A corruption of the Japanese *Kitjap,* a condiment sometimes sold as soy, but not equal to it.

Ketmir or **Katmir.** The dog of the Seven Sleepers. Sometimes called Al Rakim. (*Sale's Koran,* xviii. *n.*)

Kettle (*A*), a watch. A *tin* kittle is a silver watch. A *red* kittle is a gold watch. "Kettle," or rather *kittle,* in slang language is a corrupt rendering of the words *to-tick* read backwards. (Compare Anglo-Saxon *cetel,* a kettle, with *citel-ian,* to tickle.)

Thor's great kettle. The god Thor wanted to brew some beer, but not having a vessel suited for the purpose in Valhalla, stole the kettle of the giant Hymer. (*Scandinavian mythology.*)

Kettle of Fish. A *fête-champêtre* in which salmon is the chief dish provided. In these pic-nics, a large caldron being provided, the party select a place near a salmon river. Having thickened some water with salt to the consistency of brine, the salmon is put therein and boiled ; and when fit for eating, the company partake thereof in gipsy fashion. Some think the discomfort of this sort of pic-nic gave rise to the phrase " A pretty kettle of fish." (*See* KITTLE OF FISH.)

"The whole company go to the waterside to-day to eat a kettle of fish."—*Sir Walter Scott : St. Ronan's Well,* xii.

Kettledrum. A large social party, originally applied to a military party in India, where drum-heads served for tables. On Tweedside it signifies a "social party," met together to take tea from the same tea-kettle. (*See* DRUM, HURRICANE.)

Kettledrum, a drum in the shape of a kiddle or fish-basket.

Kettledrummle (*Gabriel.*) A Covenanter preacher in Sir Walter Scott's *Old Mortality.*

Kev'in (*St.*), like St. Sena'nus (*q.v.*), retired to an island where he vowed no woman should ever land. Kathleen loved the saint, and tracked him to his retirement, but the saint hurled her from a rock. Kathleen died, but her ghost rose smiling from the tide, and never left the place while the saint lived. A bed in the rock at Glendalough (Wicklow) is shown as the bed of St. Kevin. Thomas Moore has a poem on this tradition. (*Irish Melodies,* iv.)

Kex, hemlock. Tennyson says in *The Princess,* "Though the rough kex break the starred mosaic," though weeds break the pavement. Nothing breaks a pavement like the growth of grass or lichen through it. (Welsh, *cecys*, hemlock; French, *ciguë*; Latin, *cicuta*.)

Key. (*See* KAY.)

Key-cold. Deadly cold, lifeless. A key, on account of its coldness, is still sometimes employed to stop bleeding at the nose.

"Poor key-cold figure of a holy king !
Pale ashes of the house of Lancaster !
Thou bloodless remnant of that royal blood !"
    Shakespeare: Richard III., i. 2.

Key-stone. *The Key-stone State.* Pennsylva'nia; so called from its position and importance.

Key and the Bible (*A*). Employed to discover whether plaintiff or defendant is guilty. The Bible is opened either at Ruth, chap. i., or at the 51st Psalm; and a door-key is so placed inside the Bible, that the handle projects beyond the book. The Bible, being tied with a piece of string, is then held by the fourth fingers of the accuser and defendant, who must repeat the words touched by the wards of the key. It is said, as the words are repeated, that the key will turn towards the guilty person, and the Bible fall to the ground.

Key of a Cipher or *of a romance.* That which explains the secret or lays it open ("*La clef d'un chiffre*" or "*La clef d'un romance*").

Key of the Mediterranean. The fortress of Gibraltar; so called because it commands the entrance thereof.

Key of Russia. Smolensk, on the Dnieper.

Key of Spain. Ciudad Rodrigo, taken by the Duke of Wellington, who defeated the French there in 1812.

Keys. (*See* ST. SITHA.)

Keys of stables and cowhouses have not unfrequently, even at the present day, a stone with a hole through it and a piece of horn attached to the handle. This is a relic of an ancient superstition. The *hag, halig,* or holy stone was looked upon as a talisman which kept off the fiendish Mara or night-mare; and the horn was supposed to ensure the protection of the god of cattle, called by the Romans Pan.

Key as an emblem. (Anglo-Saxon, *cœg*.) St. Peter is always represented in Christian art with two keys in his hand; they are consequently the insignia of the Papacy, and are borne saltire-wise, one of gold and the other of silver.

They are the emblems also of St. Serva'tius, St. Hippol'ytus, St. Geneviève,

St. Petronilla, St. Osyth, St. Martha, and St. Germa'nus of Paris.

The Bishop of Winchester bears two keys and sword in saltire.

The bishops of St. Asaph, Gloucester, Exeter, and Peterborough bear two keys in saltire.

The Cross Keys. A public-house sign; the arms of the Archbishop of York.

The key shall be upon his shoulder. He shall have the dominion. The ancient keys were instruments about a yard long, made of wood or metal. On public occasions the steward slung his key over his shoulder, as our mace-bearers carry their mace. Hence, to have the key upon one's shoulder means to be in authority, to have the keeping of something. It is said of Eliakim, that God would lay upon his shoulder the key of the house of David (Isa. xxii. 22); and of our Lord that "the government should be upon His shoulder" (Isa. ix. 6). The chamberlain of the court used to bear a key as his insignia.

The power of the keys—i.e. the supreme authority vested in the pope as successor of St. Peter. The phrase is derived from St. Matt. xvi. 19. (Latin, *Potestas clavium.*)

To throw the keys into the pit. To disclaim a debt; to refuse to pay the debts of a deceased husband. This refers to an ancient French custom. If a deceased husband did not leave his widow enough for her aliment and the payment of his debts, the widow was to throw the bunch of house-keys which she carried at her girdle into the grave, and this answered the purpose of a public renunciation of all further ties. No one after this could come on her for any of her late husband's debts.

Keys (*The House of*). One of the three estates of the Isle of Man. The Crown in council, the governor and his council, and the House of Keys, constitute what is termed "the court of Tynwald." The House of Keys consists of twenty-four representatives selected by their own body, vacancies are filled up by the House presenting to the governor "two of the eldest and worthiest men of the isle," one of which the governor nominates. To them an appeal may be made against the verdicts of juries, and from their decision there is no appeal, except to the Crown in council. (Manx, *kiare-as-feed*, four-and-twenty.)

∴ The governor and his council consists of the governor, the bishop, the attorney-general, two deemsters (or judges), the clerk of the rolls, the water bailiff, the archdeacon, and the vicar-general.

The House of Keys. The board of landed proprietors referred to above, or the house in which they hold their sessions.

Keyne (*St.*). The well of St. Keyne, Cornwall, has a strange superstition attached to it, which is this: "If the bridegroom drinks therefrom before the bride, he will be master of his house; but if the bride gets the first draught, the grey mare will be the better horse." Southey has a ballad on this tradition, and says the man left his wife at the church porch, and ran to the well to get the first draught; but when he returned his wife told him his labour had been in vain, for she had taken with her a "bottle of the water to church."

Khedive d'Egypte. An old regal title revived by the sultan in 1867, who granted it to Ismael I., who succeeded as Pasha of Egypt in 1863. The title is higher than viceroy, but not so high as sultan. (Turkish, *khidiv*; Persian, *khidiw*, king; and *khidēwi*, viceroy.) Pronounce *ke-dive*, in 2 syl.

Khorassan [*Region of the Sun*]. A province of Persia, anciently called Aria'na.

The Veiled Prophet of Khorassan. Mokanna, a prophet chief, who, being terribly deformed, wore a veil under pretence of shading the dazzling light of his countenance.

"Terror seized her lest the love-light which encircled him should fade away, and leave him like the veiled prophet of Khorassan, a sin-stained thing of clay."—*Lady Hardy: A Casual Acquaintance.*

Ki. A Chinese word, signifying age or period, generally applied to the ten periods preceding the first Imperial dynasty, founded B.C. 2205. It extended over some 300,000 years. The first was founded by Puon-ku (highest eternity), and the last by Fo-hi, surnamed *Tien-Tse* (son of heaven).

Kiak-Kiak (*god of gods*). An idol worshipped in Pegu. This god is to sleep 6,000 years, and when he wakes the end of the world will come.

Kick (*A*). Sixpence. "Two-and-a-kick" = two shillings and sixpence. (Anglo-Saxon, *cicel*, a bit. In Jamaica a "bit" = sixpence, and generally it means the smallest silver coin in circulation; thus, in America, a "bit" is fourpence. We speak of a "threepenny bit.")

"*It is hard for thee to kick against the pricks*" (Acts ix. 5; and xxvi. 14.) The proverb occurs in Pindar (2 *Pythian*

Victories, v. 173), in Æschylos (*Agamemnon*, 1,624), in Eurip'idēs (*Bacchæ*, 791), in Terence (*Phormio*, i. ii. 27), in Ovid (*Tristia*, book ii. 15), etc.; but whether the reference is to an ox kicking when goaded, or a horse when pricked with the rowels of a spur, is not certain. The plural *kentra* seems to refer to more than *one*, and *pros kentra* cannot refer to a *repetition* of goad thrusts. Altogether, the rowels of a spur suit the phrase better than the single point of an ox-goad.

N.B. The Greek *pros* with an accusative is not = the Latin *adversus*, such a meaning would require a genitive case; it means in answer to, *i.e.* to kick *when* spurred or goaded.

More kicks than ha'pence. More abuse than profit. Called "monkey's allowance" in allusion to monkeys led about to collect ha'pence by exhibiting "their parts." The poor brutes get the kicks if they do their parts in an unsatisfactory manner, but the master gets the ha'pence collected.

Quite the kick. Quite a dandy. The Italians call a dandy a *chic*. The French *chic* means knack, as *avoir le chic*, to have the knack of doing a thing smartly.

" I cocked my hat and twirled my stick,
And the girls they called me quite the kick."
George Colman the Younger.

Kick Over the Traces (*To*). Not to follow the dicta of a party leader, but to act independently; as a horse refusing to run in harness kicks over the traces.

"If the new member shows any inclination to kick over the traces, he will not be their member long."—Newspaper paragraph, 1893.

Kick the Beam (*To*). To be of light weight; to be of inferior consequence. When one pan of a pair of scales is lighter than the other, it flies upwards and is said to "kick the beam" [of the scales].

"The evil has eclipsed the good, and the scale, which before rested solidly on the ground, now kicks the beam."—*Gladstone.*

Kick the Bucket (*To*). A bucket is a pulley, and in Norfolk a beam. When pigs are killed, they are hung by their hind-legs on a bucket or beam, with their heads downwards, and oxen are hauled up by a pulley. To kick the bucket is to be hung on the balk or bucket by the heels.

Kick Up a Row (*To*). To create a disturbance. "A pretty kick up" is a great disturbance. The phrase "To kick up the dust" explains the other phrases.

Kickshaws. Made dishes, odds and ends, formerly written "kickshose." (French, *quelque chose*.)

Kicksy-wicksy. A horse that kicks and winces in impatience; figuratively, a wife (*grey mare*). Taylor, the water poet, calls it *kicksie-winsie*, but Shakespeare spells it *kicky-wicky*.

" He wears his honour in a box unseen
That hugs his kicky-wicky here at home,
Spending his manly marrow in her arms,
Which should sustain the bound and high
  curvet
Of Mars's fiery steed."
  All's Well that Ends Well, ii. 3 (Globe ed.).

Kid (*A*). A faggot or bundle of firewood. *To kid* is to bind up faggots. In the parish register of Kneelsal church there is the following item : " Leading kids to church, 2s. 6d.," that is, carting faggots to church. (Welsh, *cidys*, faggots.)

Kid (*A*). A young child. A facetious formation from the Anglo-Saxon *ci[l]d*, a child. The *l* is often silent, as in *calm*, *half*, *golf*, etc. At one time fault was pronounced *fau't*.

"'Are these your own kids?' I inquired presently. 'Yes, two of them; I have six, you know.'"—*H. A. Beers: Century Magazine*, June, 1883, p. 282.

Kidderminster Poetry. Coarse doggerel verse, like the coarse woollen manufacture of Kidderminster. The term was first used by Shenstone, who applied it to a Mr. C., of Kidderminster.

" Thy verses, friend, are Kidderminster stuff ;
And I must own you've measured out enough."

Kidnapper (*A*). One who *nabs* or steals " kids " or young children.

"Swarms of kidnappers were busy in every northern town."—*J. B. McMaster: People of the United States*, vol. ii. chap. x. p. 357.

Kidney. *Men of another kidney* or *of the same kidney*. The *reins* or *kidneys* were even by the Jews supposed to be the seat of the affections.

Kilda (*St.*). The farthest of the western isles of Scotland.

Kilda're (2 syl.) is the Irish *Kill dara*, church of the oaks.

Kildare's Holy Fane. Famous for the " Fire of St. Bridget," which was inextinguishable, because the nuns never allowed it to go out. Every twentieth night St. Bridget returned to tend the fire. Part of the chapel of St. Bridget still remains, and is called " The Firehouse."

" Apud Kildariam occurrit ignis Sanctæ Brigidæ quem inextinguebilem vocant."—*Giraldus Cumbrensis: Hibernia*, ii. 34.

Kilken'ny is the Gaelic *Kill Kenny*, church of St. Kenny or Can'ice.

Kilkenny Cats. (*See* CAT.)

Kill (*A*). The slaying of some animal, generally a bullock, tied up by hunters in a jungle, to allure to the spot and attract the attention of some wild beast (such as a lion, tiger, or panther) preparatory to a hunting party being arranged. As a tiger-kill, a panther-kill.

" A shikarie brought us the welcome tidings of a tiger-kill only a mile and a half from the camp. The next day there was no hunt, as the ground round the panther-kill was too unfavourable to permit of any hunting."—*Nineteenth Century*, August, 1886.

Kill Two Birds with One Stone (*To*). To effect some subsidiary work at the same time as the main object is being effected.

Killed by Inches. In allusion to divers ways of prolonging capital punishments in olden times ; *e.g.*: (1) The "iron coffin of Lissa." The prisoner was laid in the coffin, and saw the iron lid creep slowly down with almost imperceptible movement—slowly, silently, but surely ; on, on it came with relentless march, till, after lingering days and nights in suspense, the prisoner was at last as slowly crushed by the iron lid pressing on him. (2) The " baiser de la Vierge " of Baden-Baden. The prisoner, blindfolded and fastened to a chain, was lowered by a windlass down a deep shaft from the top of the castle into the very heart of the rock on which it stands. Here he remained till he was conducted to the torture-chamber, and commanded " to kiss " the brazen statue of the " Virgin " which stood at the end of a passage ; but immediately he raised his lips to give the kiss, down he fell through a trap-door on a wheel with spikes, which was set in motion by the fall. (3) The " iron cages of Louis XI." were so contrived that the victims might linger out for years ; but whether they sat, stood, or lay down, the position was equally uncomfortable. (4) The "chambre à crucer" was a heavy chest, short, shallow, and lined with sharp stones, in which the sufferer was packed and buried alive. (5) The " bernicles " consisted of a mattress on which the victim was fastened by the neck, while his legs were crushed between two logs of wood, on the uppermost of which the torturer took his seat. This process continued for several days, till the sufferer died with the lingering torment. Many other modes of stretching out the torment of death might easily be added. (*See* IRON MAIDEN.)

Killed by Kindness. It is said that Draco, the Athenian legislator, met with his death from his popularity, being smothered in the theatre of Ægi'na by the number of caps and cloaks showered on him by the spectators (B.C. 590).

Killing. Irresistible, overpowering, fascinating, or bewitching; so as to compel admiration and notice.

" Those eyes were made so killing."
Pope: *Rape of the Lock*, v. 64.

A killing pace. Too hot or strong to last; exceptionally great; exhausting.

Killing-stone, in Louth. A stone probably used for human sacrifice.

Killing no Murder. A tract written by Sexby, who was living in Holland at the time of its publication. Probably Sexby was paid for fathering it, and the real author was William Allan.

Kilmansegg (*Miss*). An heiress of great expectations with an artificial leg of solid gold. (*Thomas Hood: A Golden Legend.*)

Kilmarnock Cowls. Nightcaps. The Kilmarnock nightcaps were once celebrated all over Scotland.

Kilmarth Rocks (Scotland). A pile of stones towering 28 feet in height, and overhanging more than 12 feet, like the tower of Pisa (Italy). (*See* CHEESE-WRING.)

Kilwinning, in the county of Ayr, Scotland, the scene of the renowned tournament held in 1839 by the Earl of Eglinton. It was also the cradle of Freemasonry in Scotland.

Kin, Kind.
"*King*. But now, my cousin Hamlet, and my son—
Ham. A little more than kin, and less than kind."
Shakespeare: *Hamlet*, i. 2.

Kin or kinsman is a relative by marriage or blood more distant than father and son.

Kind means of the same sort of genus, as man-kind or man-genus.

Hamlet says he is more than *kin* to Claudius (as he was step-son), but still he is not of the same *kind*, the same class. He is not a bird of the same feather as the king.

Kindhart. A jocular name for a tooth-drawer; so called from a dentist of the name in the reign of Queen Elizabeth. Kindhart, the dentist, is mentioned by Rowland in his *Letting of Humours - Blood in the Head-vaine.* (1600) ; and in Rowley's *New Wonder*.

" Mistake me not, Kindhart . . .
He calls you tooth-drawer."   Act i. 1.

King. The Anglo-Saxon *cyng*, *cyning*, from *cyn* a nation or people, and the termination—*ing*, meaning " of," as " son of," " chief of," etc. In Anglo-Saxon times the king was elected on the Wi'tena-gemòt, and was therefore the *choice of the nation.*

∵ *The factory king.* Richard Oastler, of Bradford, the successful advocate of the " Ten Hours' Bill " (1789-1861).

Rè Galantuomo (the gallant king), Victor Emmanuel of Italy (1820-1878).

King.
A king should die standing. So said Louis XVIII. of France, in imitation of Vespasian, Emperor of Rome. (*See* DYING SAYINGS : *Louis XVIII.*)

Like a king. When Porus, the Indian prince, was taken prisoner, Alexander asked him how he expected to be treated. " Like a king," he replied ; and Alexander made him his friend.

Pray aid of the king. When someone, under the belief that he has a right to the land, claims rent of the king's tenants, they appeal to the sovereign, or " pray aid of the king."

King Ban. Father of Sir Launcelot du Lac. He died of grief when his castle was taken and burnt through the treachery of his seneschal. (*Launcelot du Lac*, 1494.)

King Cash, what the Americans call the " Almighty Dollar."

" Now birth and rank and breeding,
Hardly saved from utter smash,
Have been ousted, rather roughly,
By the onslaught of King Cash."
Truth (*Christmas Number*, 1892, p. 19.)

King Cole. (*See* COLE.)

King Cotton. Cotton, the staple of the Southern States of America, and the chief article of manufacture in England. The expression was first used by James H. Hammond in the Senate of the United States, in 1858. The great cotton manufacturers are called " cotton lords."

King Estmere (2 syl.) of England was induced by his brother Adler to go to King Adland, and request permission to pay suit to his daughter. King Adland replied that Bremor, King of Spain, had already proposed to her and been rejected ; but when the lady was introduced to the English king she accepted him. King Estmere and his brother returned home to prepare for the wedding, but had not proceeded a mile when the king of Spain returned to press his suit, and threatened vengeance if it were not accepted. A page was instantly despatched to inform King Estmere, and request him to return. The two brothers in the guise of harpers rode into the hall of King Adland, when Bremor rebuked them, and bade them leave their steeds in the stable. A quarrel ensued, in which Adler slew "the sowdan," and the two brothers put the retainers to flight. (*Percy's Reliques*, etc., series i. bk. i. 6.)

King Franco′ni. Joachim Murat; so called because he was once a mountebank like Franconi. (1767-1815.)

King Horn or *Childe Horn*. The hero of a metrical romance by *Mestre Thomas*.

King Log. A *roi fainéant*, a king that rules in peace and quietness, but never makes his power felt. The allusion is to the fable of *The Frogs desiring a King*. (*See* LOG.)

King-maker. Richard Neville, Earl of Warwick; so called because, when he sided with Henry VI., Henry was king; but when he sided with Edward IV., Henry was deposed and Edward was king. He was killed at the battle of Barnet. (1420-1471.)

King Mob. The "*ignobile vulgus*."

King Pétaud. *The court of King Pétaud*. A kind of Alsatia, where all are talkers with no hearers, all are kings with no subjects, all are masters and none servants. There was once a society of beggars in France, the chief of whom called himself King Pétaud. (Latin, *peto*, to beg.)

King Ryence, of North Wales, sent a dwarf to King Arthur to say "he had overcome eleven kings, all of which paid him homage in this sort—viz. they gave him their beards to purfell his mantle. He now required King Arthur to do likewise." King Arthur returned answer, "My beard is full young yet for a purfell, but before it is long enough for such a purpose, King Ryence shall do me homage on both his knees." (See *Percy's Reliques*, etc., series iii. book 1.)

Spenser says that Lady Bria′na loved a knight named Crudor, who refused to marry her till she sent him a mantle lined with the beards of knights and locks of ladies. To accomplish this, she appointed Mal′effort, her seneschal, to divest every lady that drew near the castle of her locks, and every knight of his ·beard. (*Faërie Queene*, book vi. canto 1.)

23

King Stork. A tyrant that devours his subjects, and makes them submissive with fear and trembling. The allusion is to the fable of *The Frogs desiring a King*. (*See* LOG.)

King-of-Arms. An officer whose duty it is to direct the heralds, preside at chapters, and have the jurisdiction of armoury. There are three kings-of-arms in England—viz. Garter, Clarencieux, and Norroy; one in Scotland—viz. Lyon; and one in Ireland, called Ulster.

Bath King-of-Arms is no member of the college, but takes precedence next after Garter. The office was created in 1725 for the service of the Order of the Bath. (*See* HERALDS.)

King of Bark. Christopher III. of Scandinavia, who, in a time of great scarcity, had the bark of birchwood mixed with meal for food. (Fifteenth century.)

King of Bath. Richard Nash, generally called Beau Nash, who was leader of fashion and master of the ceremonies at that city for some fifty-six years. He was ultimately ruined by gambling. (1674-1761.)

King of Beasts. The lion.

King of Dalkey. A burlesque officer, like the Mayor of Garratt, the Mayor of the Pig Market, and the Mayor of the Bull-ring (*q.v.*).

⁘ Dalkey is a small island in St. George's Channel, near the coast of Ireland, a little to the south of Dublin Bay.

King of Khorassan. So Anva′ri, the Persian poet of the twelfth century, is called.

King of Metals. Gold, which is not only the most valuable of metals, but also is without its peer in freedom from alloy. It is got without smelting; wherever it exists it is visible to the eye; and it consorts with little else than pure silver. Even with this precious alloy, the pure metal ranges from sixty to ninety-nine per cent.

King of Misrule. Sometimes called LORD, and sometimes ABBOT, etc. At Oxford and Cambridge one of the Masters of Arts superintended both the Christmas and Candlemas sports, for which he was allowed a fee of 40s. These diversions continued till the Reformation. Polydore Vergil says of the feast of Misrule that it was "derived from the Roman Saturnalia," held in

December for five days (17th to 22nd). The Feast of Misrule lasted twelve days.

"If we compare our Bacchanalian Christmases and New Year-tides with these Saturnalia and Feasts of Janus, we shall finde such near affinitye between them both in regard of time . . . and in their manner of solemnising . . . that wee must needs conclude the one to be the very ape or issue of the other."—*Prynne: Histrio-Mastix.*

King of Painters. A title assumed by Parrhas'ios, the painter, a contemporary of Zeuxis. Plutarch says he wore a purple robe and a golden crown. (Flourished 400 B.C.)

King of Preachers. Louis Bourdaloue, a French clergyman (1632-1704).

King of Rome. A *title* conferred by Napoleon I. on his son on the day of his birth. More generally called the Duke of Reichstadt (1811-1832).

King of Shreds and Patches. In the old mysteries Vice used to be dressed as a mimic king in a parti-coloured suit. (*Shakespeare: Hamlet*, iii. 4.) The phrase is metaphorically applied to certain literary operatives who compile books for publishers, but supply no originality of thought or matter.

King of Spain's Trumpeter (*The*). A donkey. A pun on the word *don*, a Spanish magnate.

King of Terrors. Death.

King of Waters. The river Am'azon, in South America.

King of Yvetot (pron. *Ev-to*). A man of mighty pretensions but small merits. Yvetot is near Rouen, and was once a seigneurie, the possessors of which were entitled kings—a title given them in 534 by Clotaire I., and continued far into the fourteenth century.

" Il était un roi d'Yvetot,
 Peu connu dans l'histoire ;
Se levant tard, se couchant tot,
 Dormant fort bien sans gloire ;
Et couronne par Jeanneton
D'un simple bonnet de cotton,
  Dit on ;
Oh ! oh ! oh ! oh ! Ah ! ah ! ah ! ah !
Quel bon petite roi c'était ; la ! la ! la ! "

A king there was, 'roi d'Yvetot' clept,
 But little known in story,
Went soon to bed, till daylight slept,
 And soundly without glory ;
His royal brow in cotton cap
Would Janet, when he took his nap,
  Enwrap.
Oh ! oh ! oh ! oh ! Ah ! ah ! ah ! ah !
A famous king he! La ! la ! la ! *E. C. B.*

King of the Bean (*roi de la fève*). The Twelfth-night king ; so called because he was chosen by distributing slices of Twelfth-cake to the children present, and the child who had the slice with the bean in it was king of the company for the night. This sport was indulged in till the Reformation, even at the two universities.

King of the Beggars or *Gipsies.* Bamfylde Moore Carew, a noted English vagabond (1693-1770).

King of the Forest. The oak, which not only braves the storm, but fosters the growth of tender parasites under its arms.

King of the Herrings (*The*). The *Chimæra*, or sea-ape, a cartilaginous fish which accompanies a shoal of herrings in their migrations.

King of the Jungle (*The*). A tiger.

King of the Peak (*The*). Sir George Vernon.

King of the Sea (*The*). The herring.

"The head of an average-sized whale is from fifteen to sixteen feet [about one-third the length], and the lips open some six or eight feet ; yet to such a mouth there is scarcely any throat, not sufficiently large to allow a herring to pass down it. This little scaly fellow [the herring], some fourteen inches in length, would choke a monster whale, and is hence called 'the king of the sea.'"—*C. Thomson: Autobiography*, p. 132.

King of the Teign. Baldrick of South Devon, son of Eri, who long defended his territory against Algar, a lawless chief.

King of the World (*Shah-Jehan*). The title assumed by Khorrum Shah, third son of Selim Jehan-Ghir, and fifth of the Mogul emperors of Delhi.

King of the World. So the Caledonians, in Ossian's time, called the Roman emperor.

King Chosen by the Neighing of a Horse (*A*). Darius. (*See* HORSE : *A horse wins a kingdom.*)

King Over the Water (*The*). The Young Pretender, or Chevalier Charles Edward.

"My father so far compromised his loyalty as to announce merely 'The king,' as his first toast after dinner, instead of the emphatic 'King George.' . . . Our guest made a motion with his glass, so as to pass it over the water-decanter which stood beside him, and added, 'Over the water.'"—*Sir W. Scott: Redgauntlet*, letter v.

King's [or *Queen's*] **Bench.** This was originally the *Aula Regia*, which followed the king in all his travels, and in which he occupied the *lit de justice*. In the absence of the sovereign the judges were supreme. Of course there is no *lit de justice* or bench for the sovereign in any of our law courts now.

King's Cave. Opposite to Campbelton ; so called because it was here that King Robert Bruce and his retinue lodged when they landed on the mainland from the Isle of Arran. (*Statistical Account of Scotland*, v. p. 167, article "Arran.")

King's Chair. A seat made by two bearers with their hands. On Candlemas Day the children of Scotland used to bring their schoolmaster a present in money, and the boy who brought the largest sum was king for the nonce. When school was dismissed, the "king" was carried on a seat of hands in procession, and the seat was called the "king's chair."

King's Crag. Fife, in Scotland. Called "king" because Alexander III. of Scotland was killed there.

"As he was riding in the dusk of the evening along the sea-coast of Fife, betwixt Burnt-island and King-horn, he approached too near the brink of the precipice, and his horse, starting or stumbling, he was thrown over the rock and killed on the spot. . . The people of the country still point out the very spot where it happened, and which is called 'The King's Crag.' "—*Sir Walter Scott: Tales of a Grandfather*, vi.

King's Cross. Up to the accession of George IV. this locality in London was called "Battle Bridge," and had an infamous notoriety. In 1821 some speculators built there a number of houses, and, at the suggestion of Mr. Bray, changed the name.

King's Evil. Scrofula; so called from a notion which prevailed from the reign of Edward the Confessor to that of Queen Anne that it could be cured by the royal touch. The Jacobites considered that the power did not descend to William III. and Anne because the "divine" hereditary right was not fully possessed by them, but the office remained in our Prayer-Book till 1719. Prince Charles Edward, when he claimed to be Prince of Wales, touched a female child for the disease in 1745; but the last person touched in England was Dr. Johnson, in 1712, when only thirty months old, by Queen Anne. The French kings laid claim to the same divine power even from the time of Anne of Clovis, A.D. 481, and on Easter Sunday, 1686, Louis XIV. touched 1,600 persons, using these words: "*Le roy te touche, Dieu te guerisse.*" The practice was introduced by Henry VII. of presenting the person "touched" with a small gold or silver coin, called a touchpiece. The one presented to Dr. Johnson has St. George and the Dragon on one side and a ship on the other; the legend of the former is *Soli deo gloria*, and of the latter *Anna D:G.M.BR.F:ET.H. REG.* (Anne, by the Grace of God, of

Great Britain, France, and Ireland Queen.)

We are told that Charles II. touched 92,107 persons. The smallest number in one year was 2,983, in 1669; and the largest number was in 1684, when many were trampled to death. (*See* Macaulay's *History of England*, chap. xiv.) John Brown, a royal surgeon, had to superintend the ceremony. (See *Macbeth*, iv. 3.)

King's Keys. The crow-bars, hatchets, and hammers used by sheriffs' officers to force doors and locks. (*Law phrase.*)

"The door, framed to withstand attacks from exciseman, constables, and other personages, considered to use the king's keys . . . set his efforts at defiance."—*Sir W. Scott: Redgauntlet*, chap. xix.

King's Men. The 78th Foot; so called from their motto, "*Cuidich'r Rhi*" (Help the king).

It was raised by Kenneth Mackenzie, Earl of Seaforth, in 1777, and called the Seaforth Highlanders. In 1783 it became the 72nd Foot. From 1830 to 1881 it was called the "Duke of Albany's Highlanders"; and in 1881 it was made the 2nd Battalion of the "Seaforth Highlanders (Ross-shire Buffs), the Duke of Albany's."

King's Mess (*The*). An extra mess of rice boiled with milk—or of almonds, peas, or other pulse—given to the monks of Melrose Abbey by Robert [Bruce], the feast to be held on January 10th, and £100 being set aside for the purpose; but the monks were bound to feed on the same day fifteen poor men, and give to each four ells of broad cloth or six ells of narrow cloth, with a pair of shoes or sandals.

King's Oak (*The*). The oak under which Henry VIII. sat, in Epping Forest, while Anne (Boleyn) was being executed.

King's Picture. Money; so called because coin is stamped with "the image" of the reigning sovereign.

King's Quhair. King's book (James I.). "Cahier" is a copybook.

King's Cheese goes half in Paring. A king's income is half consumed by the numerous calls on his purse.

King's Hanoverian White Horse (*The*). The 8th Foot; called the "King's Hanoverian" for their service against the Pretender in 1715, and called the "White Horse" from their badge; now called the "Liverpool Regiment."

King's Own Scottish Borderers (*The*). Raised by Leven when Claverhouse rode out of Edinburgh.

Kings. Of the 2,550 sovereigns who have hitherto reigned,

300 have been overthrown.
134 have been assassinated.
123 have been taken captive in war.
108 have been executed.

100 have been slain in battle.
64 have been forced to abdicate.
28 have committed suicide.
25 have been tortured to death.
23 have become mad or imbecile.

Kings, etc., of England. Much foolish superstition has of late been circulated respecting certain days supposed to be "fatal" to the crowned heads of Great Britain. The following list may help to discriminate truth from fiction:

[*From* means the regnal year commenced from: *To* is the day of death.]

WILLIAM I., from *Monday*, December 25th, 1066, to *Thursday*, September 9th, 1087; WILLIAM II., from *Sunday*, September 26th, 1087, to *Thursday*, August 2nd, 1100; HENRY I., from *Sunday*, August 5th, 1100, to *Sunday*, December 1st, 1135; STEPHEN, from *Thursday*, December 26th, 1135, to *Monday*, October 25th, 1154.

HENRY II., from *Sunday*, December 19th, 1154, to *Thursday*, July 6th, 1189; RICHARD I., from *Sunday*, September 3rd, 1189, to *Tuesday*, April 6th, 1199; JOHN, from *Thursday*, May 27th, 1199, to *Wednesday*, October 19th, 1216; HENRY III., from *Friday*, October 28th, 1216, to *Wednesday*, November 16th, 1272; EDWARD I., from *Sunday*, November 20th, 1272, to *Friday*, July 7th, 1307; EDWARD II., from *Saturday*, July 8th, 1307, to *Tuesday*, January 20th, 1327; EDWARD III., from *Sunday*, January 25th, 1327 to *Sunday*, June 21st, 1377; RICHARD II., from *Monday*, June 22nd, 1377, to *Monday*, September 29th, 1399; HENRY IV., from *Tuesday*, September 30th, 1399, to *Monday*, March 20th, 1413; HENRY V., from *Tuesday*, March 21st, 1413, to *Monday*, August 31st, 1422; HENRY VI., from *Tuesday*, September 1st, 1422, to *Wednesday*, March 4th, 1461; EDWARD IV., from *Wednesday*, March 4th, 1461, to *Wednesday*, April 9th, 1483; EDWARD V., from *Wednesday*, April 9th, 1483, to *Sunday*, June 22nd, 1483; RICHARD III., from *Thursday*, June 26, 1483, to *Monday*, August 22nd, 1485.

HENRY VII., from *Monday*, August 22nd, 1485, to *Saturday*, April 21st, 1509; HENRY VIII., from *Sunday*, April 22nd, 1509, to *Friday*, January 28th, 1547; EDWARD VI., from *Friday*, January 28th, 1547, to *Thursday*, July 6th, 1553; MARY, from *Thursday*, July 6th, 1553, to *Thursday*, November 17th, 1558; ELIZABETH, from *Thursday*, November 17th, 1558, to *Thursday*, March 24th, 1603.

JAMES I, from *Thursday*, March 24th,

1603, to *Sunday*, March 27, 1625; CHARLES I., from *Sunday*, March 27th, 1625, to *Tuesday*, January 30th, 1649; [Commonwealth—CROMWELL, died *Friday*, September 3-13, 1658;] CHARLES II., restored *Tuesday*, May 29th, 1660, died *Friday*, February 6th, 1685; JAMES II., from *Tuesday*, February 6th, 1685, to *Saturday*, December 11th, 1688; WILLIAM III., from *Wednesday*, February 13th, 1689, to *Sunday*, March 8th, 1702; ANNE, from *Sunday*, March 8th, 1702, to *Sunday*, August 1st, 1714 (Both O.S.)

GEORGE I., from *Sunday*, August 1st, 1714, to *Wednesday*, June 11th, 1727; GEORGE II., from *Wednesday*, June 11th, 1727, to *Saturday*, October 25th, 1760, N.S.; GEORGE III., from *Saturday*, October 25th, 1760, to *Saturday*, January 29th, 1820; GEORGE IV., from *Saturday*, January 29th, 1820, to *Saturday*, June 26th, 1830; WILLIAM IV., from *Saturday*, June 26th, 1830, to *Tuesday*, June 20th, 1837; VICTORIA, from *Tuesday*, June 20th, 1837, to *Tuesday*, January 22nd, 1901; EDWARD VII., from *Tuesday*, January 22nd, 1901, * * (*See* Two.)

Hence six have terminated their reign on Sunday, six on Monday, five on Tuesday, five on Wednesday, six on Thursday, four on Friday, and six on Saturday. Nine have begun and ended their reign on the same day: Henry I., Edward III. and Anne on Sunday; Richard II. on Monday; Victoria on Tuesday; Edward IV. on Wednesday; Mary on Thursday; George III. and George IV. on Saturday.

Kings, etc., of England.

William I. styled himself *King of the English, Normans, and Cinomantians;* Henry I., *King of the English and Duke of the Normans;* Stephen, *King of the English;* Henry II., *King of England, Duke of Normandy and Aquitania, and Count of Anjou;* John, *King of England, Lord of Ireland, Duke of Normandy and Aquitania, and Count of Anjou;* Henry III., in 1259, dropped the titles of "Duke of Normandy" and "Count of Anjou;" Edward I., *King of England, Lord of Ireland, and Duke of Aquitania;* Edward II. made his son "Duke of Aquitania" in the nineteenth year of his reign, and styled himself *King of England and Lord of Ireland;* Edward III., from 1337, adopted the style of *King of France and England, and Lord of Ireland, and Duke of Aquitania;* Richard II., *King of England and France, and Lord of Ireland;* Edward VI., *Of England, France, and Ireland, King, Defender of the Faith*—this last title was given to Henry VIII. in the thirty-fifth year of his reign ; Mary, *Of England, France, and Ireland, Queen, Defender of the Faith, and Supreme Head of the Anglican and Hibernian Church ;* Charles I., *Of Great Britain, France, and Ireland, King, Defender of the Faith,* etc. ; Commonwealth, *The Keepers of the Liberties of England, by the authority of Parliament,* and Cromwell was styled *His Highness ;* Charles II. and James II. as Charles I. ; William and Mary, *Of England, Scotland, France, and Ireland, King and Queen, Defenders of the Faith,* etc. : Anne, *Of Great Britain, France, and Ireland, Queen, Defender of the Faith,* etc. ; George III., in 1801, abandoned the words "King of France," which had been retained for 432 years, and his style was "*George III., by the Grace of God, of the United Kingdom of Great Britain and Ireland, King, Defender of the Faith.*"

Kings have Long Hands. Do not quarrel with a king, as his power and authority reach to the end of his dominions. The Latin proverb is, "*An nescis longas regibus esse manus ;*" and the German, "*Mit grossen herren es ist nicht gut kirschen zu essen*" ("It is not good to eat cherries with great men, as they throw the stones in your eyes ").

"There's such divinity doth hedge a king,
That treason can but peep to what it would."
Shakespeare : King in *Hamlet,* iv. 5.

The books of the four kings. A pack of cards.

"After supper were brought in the books of the four kings."—*Rabelais :* Gargantua and Pantagruel, i. 23.

The three kings of Cologne. The representatives of the three magi who came from the East to offer gifts to the infant Jesus. Tradition makes them three Eastern kings, and at Cologne the names ascribed to them are Kaspar, Melchior, and Balthazar.

Kings may override Grammar. (*See* GRAMMAR.)

Kingly Titles.
Abgarus (The Grand). So the kings of Edessa were styled.

Abim'elech (my father the king). The chief ruler of the ancient Philistines.

Agag (lord). The chief ruler of the Amal'ekites (4 syl.).

Akbar Khan (very-great chieftain). Hindustan.

Anax. The chief ruler of the ancient Greek kingdoms. *Anaxandrōn* was the over-king.

Archon (The). The chief of the nine magistrates of Athens. The next in rank was called *Basileus* (3 syl.) ; and the

third *Polēmarch* (3 syl.), or Field-Marshal.

Asser or *Assyr* (blessed one). The chief ruler of ancient Assyria.

Attabeg (father prince). Persia, 1118.

Augustus. The title of the reigning Emperor of Rome, when the heir presumptive was styled " Cæsar." (*See* AUGUSTUS.)

Autocrat (self-potentate). One whose power is absolute ; Russia.

Beglerbeg. (See *Bey.*)

Ben-Hadad (son of the sun or *Hadad*). The chief ruler of ancient Damascus.

Bey of Tunis. In Turkey, a bey is the governor of a banner, and the chief over the seven banners is the *beglar-bey.*

Brenn or *Brenhin* (war-chief) of the ancient Gauls. A dictator appointed by the Druids in times of danger.

Bretwalda (wielder of Britain). Chief king of the heptarchy.

Cæsar. Proper name adopted by the Roman emperors. (*See* KAISER.)

Calif (successor). Successors of Mahomet ; now the Grand Signior of Turkey, and Sophi of Persia.

Canda'ce. Proper name adopted by the queens of Ethiopia.

Cazique (Ca-zeek'). American Indians ; native princes of the ancient Peruvians, Cubans, Mexicans, etc.

Chagan. The chief of the Avars.

Cham. (See *Khan.*)

Cral. The despot of ancient Servia.

Cyrus (mighty). Ancient Persia. (*See* CYRUS.)

Czar (Cæsar). Russia. Assumed by Ivan III., who married a princess of the Byzantine line, in 1472. He also introduced the double-headed black eagle of Byzantium as the national symbol.

Dari'us, Latin form of *Darawesh* (king). Ancient Persia.

Dey. In Algiers, before it was annexed to France in 1830. (Turkish, *dāi,* uncle.)

Dicta'tor. A military autocrat, appointed by the Romans in times of danger.

Domnu (lord). Roumania.

Emperor. (*See* IMPERATOR.)

Empress. A female emperor, or the wife of an emperor.

Esin'qæ (*q.v.*). Kings of Kent.

Hos'podar. Moldavia and Wallachia ; now borne by the Emperor of Russia.

Impera'tor (ruler or commander). The Latin form of emperor.

Inca. Ancient Peru.

Judge. Ancient Jews (*Shophet*).

Kaiser (same as Cæsar, *q.v.*). The German Emperor.

Khan (chieftain) or *Ghengis-Khan*. Tartary. In Persia, the governor of a province is called a *Khan*.

Khedive (*q.v.*). Modern Egypt.

King or *Queen*. Great Britain, etc. (Anglo-Saxon *cyn*, the people or nation, and *-ing* (a patronymic) = the man of, the choice of, etc.)

Lama or *Dalai Lama* (great mother-of-souls). Thibet.

Melech (king). Ancient Jews.

Mogul' or *Great Mogul'*. Mongolia.

Nejus or *Nejushee* (lord protector). Abyssinia.

Nizam' (ruler). Hyderabad.

Padishah (fatherly king). The Sultan's title.

Pendrag'on (chief of the dragons, or "*summus rex*"). A dictator, created by the ancient Celts in times of danger.

Pha'raoh (light of the world). Ancient Egypt.

President. Republics of America, France, etc.

Ptol'emy (proper name adopted). Egypt after the death of Alexander.

Queen. (Anglo-Saxon, *cwēn*; Greek, *gunē*, a woman.)

Raj'ah or *Maha-rajah* (great king). Hindustan.

Rex (ruler). A Latin word equivalent to our king.

Scherif (lord). Mecca and Medīna.

Shah (protector). Persia.

Sheik (patriarch). Arabia.

Shop'hetim. So the Jewish "judges" were styled.

So'phi (holy). A title of the Shah of Persia.

Stadtholder (city-holder). Formerly chief magistrate of Holland.

Suffetes (dictators). Ancient Carthage.

Sultan or *Soldan* (ruler). Turkey.

Vayvode or *Waywode* (2 syl.) of Transylvania, Moldavia, and Wallachia.

Vladika (ruler). Montenegro.

Also, *Aga, ameer* or *emir, archduke, count, doge, duke, effendi, elector, exarch, herzog* (= duke), *imaum, infanta, land-amman, landgrave, mandarin, margrave,* or *margravine, nabob, pacha* or *bashaw, prince, sachem, satrap, seigneur* or *grand-seigneur, sirdar, subahdar, suzerain, tet-rarch, viceroy, etc.*, in some cases are chief independent rulers, in some cases dependent rulers or governors subject to an over-lord, and in others simply titles of honour without separate dominion.

Kingdom Come. Death, the grave, execution.

"And forty pounds be theirs, a pretty sum,
For sending such a rogue to kingdom come."
Peter Pindar: Subjects for Painters.

Kingsale. Wearing a hat in the presence of Royalty.

Kingsley's Stand, the 20th Foot. Called "Kingsley's" from their colonel (1756-1769); and called "Stand" from their "stand" at Minden in 1759. Now called the "Lancashire Fusiliers."

Kingston Bridge. A card bent, so that when the pack is cut, it is cut at this card. "*Faire le Pont*" is thus described in Fleming and Tibbins's *Grand Dictionnaire*: "*Action de courber quelques-unes des cartes, et de les arranger de telle sorte que celui qui doit couper ne puisse guère couper qu'a l'endroit qu'on vent.*"

Kingston - on - Thames. Named *King's-stone* from a large, square block of stone near the town hall, on which the early Anglo-Saxon monarchs knelt when they were anointed to the kingly office: Edward the Elder, Athelstan, Edmund, Ethelred, Edred, Edwy, and Edward the Martyr received on this stone the royal unction. The stone is now enclosed with railings.

Kingstown (Ireland), formerly called Dunleary. The name was changed in 1821 out of compliment to George IV., who visited Ireland that year, and left Dunleary harbour for his return home on September 5th.

Kingswood Lions. Donkeys; Kingswood being at one time famous for the number of asses kept by the colliers who lived thereabout.

Kinless Loons. The judges whom Cromwell sent into Scotland were so termed. because they condemned and acquitted those brought before them wholly irrespective of party, and solely on the merits of the charge with which they were accused.

Kiosk'. A Turkish summer-house or alcove supported by pillars. (Turkish, *kushk;* Persian, *kushk,* a palace ; French, *kiosque.*) The name is also given to newspaper stands in France and Belgium.

Kirk of Skulls. Gamrie church in Banffshire : so called because the skulls and other bones of the Norsemen who fell in the neighbouring field, called the Bloody Pots, were built into its walls.

Kirke-grim. The nix who looks to order in churches, punishes those who misbehave themselves there, and the persons employed to keep it tidy if they fail in their duty. (*Scandinavian mythology.*)

Kirke's Lambs. The Queen's Royal West Surrey. Called "Kirke" from Piercy Kirke, their colonel, 1682-1691 ; and "Lambs" from their badge, the *Paschal Lamb*, the crest of the house of Braganza, in compliment to Queen Catharine, to whom they were a guard of honour in her progress to London.

Kirkrap′ine (3 syl.). While Una was in the hut of Corcōca, Kirkrapine forced his way in ; but the lion, springing on him, tore him to pieces. The meaning is that Romanism was increased by rapine, but the English lion at the Reformation put an end to the rapacity of monks. (*Spenser : Faërie Queen,* bk. i.)

Kismet. The fulfilment of destiny. (Turkish, *gismet*, a lot.)

"The word *kismet*, which he scarcely comprehended before, seems now to be fraught with ... [meaning]. This is kismet ; this is the fulfilment of destiny ; this is to love."—*Nineteenth Century*, February, 1892, p. 209.

Kiss, as a mode of salutation, comes from its use to express reverence or worship. Thus to adore idols and to kiss idols mean the same thing. Indeed, the word *adore* signifies simply to carry the hand *to the mouth*, that is, to kiss it to the idol. We still kiss the hand in salutation. Various parts of the body are kissed to distinguish the character of the adoration paid. Thus, to kiss the lips is to adore the living breath of the person saluted ; to kiss the feet or ground is to humble oneself in adoration ; to kiss the garments is to express veneration to whatever belongs to or touches the person who wears them. "Kiss the Son, lest He be angry" (Ps. ii. 12), means Worship the Son of God. Pharaoh tells Joseph, "Thou shalt be over my house, and upon thy mouth shall all my people kiss," meaning they shall reverence the commands of Joseph by kissing the roll on which his commands would be written. "Samuel poured oil on Saul, and kissed him," to acknowledge subjection to God's anointed (1 Sam. x. 1). In the Hebrew state, this mode of expressing reverence arose from the form of government established, whether under the patriarchal or matrimonial figure.

A Judas kiss. An act of treachery. The allusion is to the apostle Judas, who betrayed his Master with a kiss.

Kiss Hands (*To*). To kiss the hand of the sovereign either on accepting or retiring from a high government office. (*See* KISS.)

"Kissing the hand to the statue of a god was a Roman form of adoration."—*Spencer : Principles of Sociology,* vol. ii. part iv. chap. 6, p. 123.

Kiss the Book. After taking a legal oath, we are commanded to kiss the book, which in our English courts is the New Testament, except when Jews "are sworn in." This is the kiss of confirmation or promise to act in accordance with the words of the oath (Moravians and Quakers are not required to take legal oaths). The kiss, in this case, is a public acknowledgment that you adore the deity whose book you kiss, as a worshipper.

It is now permitted to affirm, if persons like to do so. Mr. Bradlaugh refused to take an oath, and after some years of contention the law was altered.

Kiss the Dust. To die, or to be slain. In Psalm lxxii. 9 it is said, "his enemies shall lick the dust."

Kiss the Hare's Foot (*To*). To be late or too late for dinner. The hare has run away, and you are only in time to "kiss" the print of his foot. A common proverb.

"You must kiss the hare's foot ; *post festum venisti.*"—*Cole : Dictionary.*

Kiss the Mistress (*To*). To make a good hit, to shoot right into the eye of the target. In bowls, what we now call the *Jack* used to be called the "mistress," and when one ball just touches another it is said "to kiss it." To kiss the Mistress or Jack is to graze another bowl with your own.

"Rub on, and kiss the mistress."—*Shakespeare : Troilus and Cressida,* iii. 2.

Kiss the Rod (*To*). To submit to punishment or misfortune meekly and without murmuring.

Kiss behind the Garden Gate (*A*). A pansy. A practical way of saying "*Pensez de moi,*" the flower-language of the pansy.

Kiss given to a Poet. Margaret, daughter of James I. of Scotland and wife of Louis XI. (when only dauphin), kissed the mouth of Alain Chartier "for uttering so many fine things." Chartier, however, was a decidedly ugly man, and, of course, was asleep at the time.

The tale is sometimes erroneously told of Ronsard the poet.

Kiss the Gunner's Daughter (*To*). To be flogged on board ship, being tied to the breech of a cannon.

"I was made to kiss the wench that never speaks but when she scolds, and that's the gunner's daughter. ... Yes, the minister's son ... has the cat's scratch on his back."—*Sir W. Scott : Redgauntlet,* chap. xiv.

Kiss the Place to make it Well. A relic of a very common custom all over the world of sucking poison from wounds. St. Martin of Tours, when he was at Paris, observed at the city gates a leper full of sores; and, going up to him, he kissed the sores, whereupon the leper was instantly made whole (*Sulpicius Sevērus: Dialogues*). Again, when St. Mayeul had committed some grave offence, he was sent, by way of penance, to kiss a leper who was begging alms at the monastery. St. Mayeul went up to the man, kissed his wounds, and the leprosy left him. Half a score similar examples may be found in the Bollandistes, without much searching.

" Who ran to help me when I fell,
And kissed the place to make it well ? "

Kissing-comfit. The candied root of the Sea-*eryngium maritimum* prepared as a lozenge, to perfume the breath.

Kissing-crust. The crust where the lower lump of bread kisses the upper. In French, *baisure de pain.*

Kissing the Hand. Either kissing the sovereign's hand at a public introduction, or kissing one's own hand to bid farewell to a friend, and kissing the tips of our fingers and then moving the hand in a sort of salutation to imply great satisfaction at some beautiful object, thought, or other charm, are remnants of pagan worship. If the idol was conveniently low enough, the devotee kissed its hand; if not, the devotees kissed their own hands and waved them to the image. God said He had in Israel seven thousand persons who had not bowed unto Baal, " every mouth which hath not kissed him." (*See* KISS.)

" Many . . . whom the fame of this excellent vision had gathered thither, confounded by that matchless beauty, could but kiss the finger-tips of their right hands at sight of her, as in adoration to the goddess Venus herself." — *Pater: Marius the Epicurean,* chap. v.

Kissing the Pope's Toe. Matthew of Westminster says, it was customary formerly to kiss the hand of his Holiness; but that a certain woman, in the eighth century, not only kissed the Pope's hand, but "squeezed it." The Church magnate, seeing the danger to which he was exposed, cut off his hand, and was compelled in future to offer his foot, a custom which has continued to the present hour.

Kissing under the Mistletoe. Balder, the Apollo of Scandinavian mythology, was killed by a mistletoe arrow given to the blind Höder, by Loki, the god of mischief and potentate of our earth. Balder was restored to life, but the mistletoe was placed in future under the care of Friga, and was never again to be an instrument of evil till it touched the earth, the empire of Loki. It is always suspended from ceilings, and when persons of opposite sexes pass under it, they give each other the kiss of peace and love in the full assurance that the epiphyte is no longer an instrument of mischief.

A correspondent in *Notes and Queries* suggests that the Romans dedicated the holly to Saturn, whose festival was in December, and that the early Christians decked their houses with the Saturnian emblems to deceive the Romans and escape persecution.

Kist-vaen (*The*). A rude stone sepulchre or mausoleum, like a chest with a flat stone for a cover.

"At length they reached a grassy mound, on the top of which was placed one of those receptacles for the dead of the ancient British chiefs of distinction, called Kist-vaen, which are composed of upright fragments of granite, so placed as to form a stone coffin. . . ."—*Sir Walter Scott: The Betrothed,* chap. xxix.

Kist of Whistles (*A*). A church-organ (Scotch). *Cist,* a box or chest.

Kist'nerap'pan. The Indian water-god. Persons at the point of death are sometimes carried into the Ganges, and sometimes to its banks, that Kistnerappan may purify them from all defilement before they die. Others have a little water poured into the palms of their hands with the same object.

Kit. (Anglo-Saxon, *kette,* a cist or box [of tools].) Hence that which contains the necessaries, tools, etc., of a workman.

A soldier's kit. His outfit.

The whole kit of them. The whole lot. (*See above.*) Used contemptuously.

Kit. A three-stringed fiddle. (Anglo-Saxon, *cytere ;* Latin, *cithăra.*)

Kit cat Club. A club formed in 1688 by the leading Whigs of the day, and held in Shire Lane (now Lower Serle's Place) in the house of Christopher Cat, a pastry-cook, who supplied the mutton pies, and after whom the club was named. Sir Godfrey Kneller painted forty-two portraits of the club members for Jacob Tonson, the secretary, whose villa was at Barn Elms, and where latterly the club was held. In order to accommodate the paintings to the height of the club-room, he was obliged to make them three-quarter lengths; hence a three-quarter portrait is still called a *kit-cat.*

Strictly speaking, a kit-cat canvas is twenty-eight inches by thirty-six.

"Steele, Addison, Congreve, Garth, Vanbrugh, Manwaring, Stepney, Walpole, and Pulteney were of it ; so was Lord Dorset and the present Duke. Manwaring . . . was the ruling man in all conversat on. . . . Lord Stanhope and the Earl of Essex were also members. . . . Each member gave his [picture]."—*Pope to Spence.*

⁂ Cowley the poet lived at Barn Elms Villas.

Kit Cats. Mutton pies ; so called from Christopher Cat, the pastrycook, who excelled in these pasties. (*See above.*)

Kit's Coty House, on the road between Rochester and Maidstone, a well-known cromlech, is Katigern's or *Kitigern's coty house*—that is, the house or tomb of Kitigern, made of *coits* or huge flat stones. (*See* HACKELL'S COIT and DEVIL'S COIT.)

Katigern was the brother of Vortimer, and leader of the Britons, who was slain in the battle of Aylesford or Epsford, fighting against Hengist and Horsa. Lambarde calls it *Citscotehouse* (1570). The structure consists of two upright side-stones, one standing in the middle as a support or tenon, and a fourth imposed as a roof. Numberless stones lie scattered in the vicinity. Often spelt " Kitt's Cotty House."

Kitchen. Any relish eaten with dry bread, as cheese, bacon, dried fish, etc.

" A hungry heart wad scarce seek better kitchen to a barley scone."—*Sir W. Scott: The Pirate,* chap. xi.

Kitchenmaid (*Mrs.*). So Queen Elizabeth called Lord Mountjoy, her lord-deputy in Ireland. In one of her letters to Lord Mountjoy she writes :—

" With your frying-pan and other kitchen-stuff you have brought to their last home more rebels than those that promised more and did less."

Kite (*A*), in legal phraseology, is a junior counsel who is allotted at an assize court to advocate the cause of a prisoner who is without other defence. For this service he receives a guinea as his honorarium. A kite on Stock Exchange means a worthless bill. An honorarium given to a barrister is in reality a mere kite. (*See below,* KITE-FLYING.)

Kite-flying. *To fly the kite* is to " raise the wind," or obtain money on bills, whether good or bad. It is a Stock Exchange phrase, and means, as a kite flutters in the air by reason of its lightness, and is a mere toy, so these bills fly about, but are light and worthless. (*See* STOCK EXCHANGE SLANG.)

23*

Kitely (2 syl.). A jealous city merchant in Ben Jonson's *Every Man in his Humour.*

Kittle of Fish. *A pretty kittle of fish.* A pretty muddle, a bad job. Corruption of " kiddle of fish." A kiddle is a basket set in the opening of a weir for catching fish. Perhaps the Welsh *hidl* or *hidyl,* a strainer. (*See* KETTLE.)

Klaus (*Peter*). The prototype of Rip Van Winkle, whose sleep lasted twenty years. Pronounce *Klows.* (*See* SANTA KLAUS.)

Klephts (*The*) etymologically means *robbers,* but came to be a title of distinction in modern Greece. Those Greeks who rejected all overtures of their Turkish conquerors, betook themselves to the mountains, where they kept up for several years a desultory warfare, supporting themselves by raids on Turkish settlers. Aristoteles Valaoritis (born 1824) is the great " poet of the Klephts." (See *Nineteenth Century,* July, 1891, p. 130.)

Knack. Skill in handiwork. The derivation of this word is a great puzzle. Minshew suggests that it is a mere variant of *knock.* Cotgrave thinks it a variant of *snap.* Others give the German *knacken* (to sound).

Knave. A lad, a garçon, a servant. (Anglo-Saxon, *cnáfa ;* German, *knabe.*) The knave of clubs, etc., is the son or servant of the king and queen thereof. In an old version of the Bible we read : " Paul, a knave of Jesus Christ, called to be an apostle," etc. (Rom. i. 1).

This version, we are told, is in the Harleian Library, but is generally supposed to be a forgery. But, without doubt, Wycliff (Rev. xii. 5, 13) used the compound " Knave-child," and Chaucer uses the same in the *Man of Lawe's Tale,* line 5130.

Knave of Hearts (*A*). A flirt.

Knave of Sologne (*A*). More knave than fool. The French say " *Un niais de Sologne.*" Sologne is a part of the departments of Loiret et Loire-et-Cher.

Knee. Greek, *gonu ;* Latin, *genu ;* French, *genou ;* Sanskrit, *janu ;* Saxon, *cneow ;* German, *knie ;* English, *knee.*

Knee Tribute. Adoration or reverence, by prostration or bending the knee.

" Coming to receive from us
Knee-tribute yet unpaid, prostration vile."
Milton : Paradise Lost, v. 782.

Kneph. The ram-headed god of ancient Egypt, called also Amen-ra, and by the Greeks, Ammon.

Knickerbocker (*Die'drich*). The imaginary author of a facetious *History of New York*, by Washington Irving.

Knickerbockers. Loose knee-breeches, worn by boys, cyclists, sportsmen, tourists, etc. So named from George Cruikshank's illustrations of Washington Irving's bcok referred to above. In these illustrations the Dutch worthies are drawn with very loose knee-breeches.

Knife is the emblem borne by St. Ag'atha, St. Albert, and St. Christi'na.

The flaying knife is the emblem of St. Bartholomew, because he was flayed.

A sacrificing knife is borne in Christian art by St. Zadkiel, the angel.

The knife of academic knots. Chrysip'-pos, so called because he was the keenest disputant of his age (B.C. 280-207).

War to the knife. Deadly strife.

Knife = sword or dagger.

" Till my keen knife see not the wound it makes."
  Shakespeare : Macbeth, i. 5.

Knife and Fork. *He is a capital knife-and-fork,* a good trencherman.

" He did due honour to the repast ; he ate and drank, and proved a capital knife-and-fork even at the risk of dying the same night of an indigestion."—*Gaboriau: Promise of Marriage,* vi.

Knifeboard. One of the seats for passengers running along the roof of an omnibus. Now almost obsolete.

Knight means simply *a boy.* (Saxon, *cniht.*) As boys (like the Latin *puer* and French *garçon*) were used as servants, so *cniht* came to mean a servant. Those who served the feudal kings bore arms, and persons admitted to this privilege were the king's knights ; as this distinction was limited to men of family, the word became a title of honour next to the nobility. In modern Latin, a knight is termed *aura'tus* (golden), from the gilt spurs which he used to wear.

Last of the knights. Maximilian I. of Germany (1459, 1493-1519).

Knight Rider Street (London). So named from the processions of knights from the Tower to Smithfield, where tournaments were held. Leigh Hunt says the name originated in a sign or some reference to the Heralds' College in the vicinity.

Knight of La Mancha. Don Quixote de la Mancha, the hero of Cervantes' novel, called *Don Quixote.*

Knight of the Bleeding Heart. The Bleeding Heart was one of the many semi-religious orders instituted in the Middle Ages in honour of the Virgin Mary, whose " heart was pierced with many sorrows."

" When he was at Holyrood who would have said that the young, sprightly George Douglas would have been content to play the locksman here in Lochleven, with no gayer amusement than that of turning the key on two or three helpless women ? A strange office for a Knight of the Bleeding Heart."—*Sir W. Scott: The Abbot,* xxiii.

Knight of the Cloak (*The*). Sir Walter Raleigh. So called from his throwing his cloak into a puddle for Queen Elizabeth to step on as she was about to enter her barge. (See *Kenilworth,* chap. xv.)

" Your lordship meaneth that Raleigh, the Devonshire youth,' said Varney, ' the Knight of the Cloak, as they call him at Court."—*Ditto,* chap. xvi.

Elizabeth, in the same novel, addresses him as Sir Squire of the Soiled Cassock.

Knight of the Couching Leopard (*The*). Sir Kenneth, or rather the Earl of Huntingdon, Prince Royal of Scotland, who followed, *incognito,* Richard I. to the Crusade, and is the chief character of the *Talisman,* a novel by Sir Walter Scott.

Knight of the Order of John-William (*A*). In French : " *Chevalier de l'ordre de Jean Guillaume,*" a man hanged. (*See* JOHN-WILLIAM.)

Knight of the Post. A man in the pillory, or that has been tied to a whipping-post, is jestingly so called.

Knight of the Rueful Countenance. Don Quixote.

Knight's Fee. A portion of land held by custom, sufficient to maintain a knight to do service as such for the king. William the Conqueror created 60,000 such fees when he came to England. All who had £20 a year in lands or income were compelled to be knights.

Knight's Ward (*The*). A superior compartment in Newgate for those who paid three pieces by way of " garnish." No longer in existence.

Knights. (*See* CROSS-LEGGED . . .)

Knights Bachelors. Persons who are simply knights, but belong to no order. (French, *bas-chevaliers.*)

Knights Bannerets. Knights created on the field of battle. The king or general cut off the point of their flag, and made it square, so as to resemble a banner. Hence knights bannerets are called *Knights of the Square Flag.*

Knights Baronets. Inferior barons, an order of hereditary rank, created by

James I. in 1611. The title was sold for money, and the funds went nominally towards the plantation of Ulster. These knights bear the arms of Ulster, viz. a field *argent*, a sinister hand couped at the wrist *gules*. (*See* HAND.)

Knights Errant. In France, from 768 to 987, the land was encumbered with fortified castles; in England this was not the case till the reign of Stephen. The lords of these castles used to carry off females and commit rapine, so that a class of men sprang up, at least in the pages of romance, who roamed about in full armour to protect the defenceless and aid the oppressed.

"'Prox'ima quæque metit glad'io' is the perfect account of a knight errant."—*Dryden: Dedication of the Æne'is.*

Knights of Carpetry or *Carpet Knights*, are not military but civil knights, such as mayors, lawyers, and so on; so called because they receive their knighthood kneeling *on a carpet*, and not on the battle-field.

Knights of Industry. Sharpers.

Knights of Labour. Members of a trades union organised in 1834, in the United States of America, to regulate the amount of wages to be demanded by workmen, the degree of skill to be exacted from them, and the length of a day's work. This league enjoins when a strike is to be made, and when workmen of the union may resume work.

Knights of Malta or *Hospitallers of St. John of Jerusalem.* Some time after the first crusade (1042), some Neapolitan merchants built at Jerusalem a hospital for sick pilgrims and a church which they dedicated to St. John; these they committed to the charge of certain knights, called *Hospitallers of St. John.* In 1310 these Hospitallers took Rhode Island, and changed their title into *Knights of Rhodes.* In 1523 they were expelled from Rhodes by the Turks, and took up their residence in the Isle of Malta.

Knights of St. Crispin. Shoemakers. Crispin Crispian was a shoe maker. (See *Henry V.*, iv. 3.)

Knights of St. Patrick. Instituted in 1783, in honour of the patron saint of Ireland.

Knights of the Bag. Bagmen who travel for mercantile orders.

Knights of the Bath. (*See* BATH.)

Knights of the Blade. Bullies who

were for ever appealing to their swords to browbeat the timid.

Knights of the Chamber or *Chamber Knights*, are knights bachelors made in times of peace in the *presence chamber*, and not in the camp. Being military men, they differ from "carpet knights," who are always civilians.

Knights of the Cleaver. Butchers.

Knights of the Garter. (*See* GARTER.)

Knights of the Green Cloth. Same as CARPET KNIGHTS (*q.v.*).

Knights of the Handcuffs. Constables, policemen, etc., who carry handcuffs for refractory or suspicious prisoners taken up by them.

Knights of the Hare. An order of twelve knights created by Edward III. in France, upon the following occasion:— A great shouting was raised by the French army, and Edward thought the shout was the onset of battle; but found afterwards it was occasioned by a hare running between the two armies.

Knights of the Holy Sepulchre. An Order of military knights founded by Godfrey of Bouillon, in 1099, to guard the "Holy Sepulchre."

Knights of the Order of the Golden Fleece. Lawyers.

Knights of the Pencil. The betters in races; so called because they always keep a pencil in hand to mark down their bets.

Knights of the Pestle or **Knights of the Pestle and Mortar.** Apothecaries or druggists, whose chief instrument is the pestle and mortar, used in compounding medicines.

Knights o' the Post. Persons who haunted the purlieus of the courts, ready to be hired for a bribe to swear anything; so called from their being always found waiting at the posts which the sheriffs set up outside their doors for posting proclamations on.

"There are knights of the post and booby cheats enough to swear the truth of the broadest contradictions."—*South.*

"'A knight of the post,' quoth he, 'for so I am termed; a fellow that will sweare you anything for twelve pence.'"—*Nash: Pierce Penilesse* (1592.)

Knights of the Rainbow. Flunkeys; so called from their gorgeous liveries.

"The servants who attended them contradicted the inferences to be drawn from the garb of their masters; and, according to the custom of the knights of the rainbow, gave many hints that they were not people to serve any but men of first-rate consequence."—*Sir W. Scott: Redgauntlet*, chap. 20

Knights of the Road. Footpads. (*See* KNIGHTS OF THE POST.)

Knights of the Round Table. King Arthur's knights, so called from the large circular table round which they sat. The table was circular to prevent any heart-sore about precedency. The number of these knights is variously given. The popular notion is that they were twelve; several authorities say there were forty; but the *History of Prince Arthur* states that the table was made to accommodate 150. King Leodegraunce, who gave Arthur the table on his wedding-day, sent him also 100 knights, Merlin furnished twenty-eight, Arthur himself added two, and twenty "sieges" were left to reward merit (chaps. xlv., xlvi.). These knights went forth into all countries in quest of adventures. The most noted are—

Sir Acolon, Ballamore, Beau'maris, Beleobus, Belvoure, Bersunt, Bors, Ector, Eric, Ewain, Floll, Ga'heris, Gal'ahad, Gal'ohalt, Gareth, Gau'riel, Gawain or Ywain, Grislet, Kay, Lamerock, Launcelot du Lac, Lionell, Marhaus, Palamide, Pa'quinet, Pel'leas, Per'edur or Per'ceval, Sagris, Superab'ilis, Tor, Tristam or Tristan de Le'onnais, Turquine, Wig'alois, Wig'amur, etc., etc.

∴ A list of the knights and a description of their armour is given in the *Theatre of Honour* by Andrew Fairne (1622). According to this list, the number was 151; but in *Lancelot of the Lake* (vol. ii. p. 81), they are said to have amounted to 250.

Knights of the Shears. Tailors. The word *shear* is a play on the word *shire* or county.

Knights of the Shell. The Argonauts of St. Nicholas, a military order, instituted in the 14th century by Carlo III., King of Naples. Their insignia was a "collar of shells."

Knights of the Shire. Now called County Members; that is, members of Parliament elected by counties, in contradistinction to Borough members.

Knights of the Spigot. Landlords of hotels, etc.; mine host is a "knight of the spigot."

"When an old song comes across us merry old knights of the spigot it runs away with our discretion."—*Sir W. Scott: Kenilworth*, chap. viii.

Knights of the Swan. An order of the House of Cleve.

Knights of the Stick. Compositors. The stick is the printer's "composing stick," which he holds in his left hand while with his right hand he fills it with letters from his "case." It holds just enough type not to fatigue the hand of the compositor, and when full, the type is transferred to the "galley."

Knights of the Thistle. Said to have been established in 809 by Achaicus, King of the Scots, and revived in 1540 by James V. of Scotland. Queen Anne placed the order on a permanent footing. These knights are sometimes called *Knights of St. Andrew.*

Knights of the Whip. Coachmen.

Knighten Guild, now called *Portsoken Ward.* King Edgar gave it to thirteen knights on the following conditions:—(1) Each knight was to be victorious in three combats—one aboveground, one underground, and one in the water; and (2) each knight was, on a given day, to run with spears against all comers in East Smithfield. William the Conqueror confirmed the same unto the heirs of these knights. Henry I. gave it to the canons of Holy Trinity, and acquitted it "of all service."

Knipperdollings. A set of German heretics about the time of the Reformation, disciples of a man named Bernard Knipperdolling. (*Blount: Glossographia*, 1681.)

Knock Under (*To*). Johnson says this expression arose from a custom once common of knocking under the table when any guest wished to acknowledge himself beaten in argument. Another derivation is *knuckle under*—*i.e.* to knuckle or bend the knuckle or knee in proof of submission. Bellenden Kerr says it is *Te nŏ'ck ander*, which he interprets "I am forced to yield."

Knocked into a Cocked Hat. Thoroughly beaten; altered beyond recognition; *hors de combat*. A cocked-hat, folded into a *chapeau bras*, is crushed out of all shape.

Knockers. Goblins who dwell in mines, and point out rich veins of lead and silver. In Cardiganshire the miners attribute the strange noises so frequently heard in mines to these spirits, which are sometimes called coblyns (German, *kobolds*).

Knot. (Latin *nodus*, French *nœud*, Danish *knude*, Dutch *knot*, Anglo-Saxon *cnotta*, allied to *knit*.)

He has tied a knot with his tongue he cannot untie with his teeth. He has got married. He has tied the marriage knot by saying, "I take thee for my wedded wife," etc., but the knot is not to be untied so easily.

The Gordian knot. (*See* GORDIAN.)

The marriage knot. (*See* MARRIAGE.)

The ship went six or seven knots an hour. Miles. The log-line is divided into lengths by knots, each length is the same proportion of a nautical mile as half a minute is of an hour. The log-line being cast over, note is taken of the number of knots run out in half a minute, and this number shows the rate per hour.

∴ The length of a knot is 47·33 feet when used with a 28-second glass, but 50·75 feet when the glass runs 30 seconds.

True lovers' knot. Sir Thomas Browne thinks the knot owes its origin to the *nodus Hercula'nus,* a snaky complication in the cadu'ceus or rod of Mercury, in which form the woollen girdle of the Greek brides was fastened.

To seek for a knot in a rush. Seeking for something that does not exist. Not a very wise phrase, seeing there are *jointed* rushes, probably not known when the proverb was first current. The *Juncus acutiflorus,* the *Juncus lampocarpus,* the *Juncus obtusiflorus,* and the *Juncus polycephalus,* are all jointed rushes.

Knot and Bridle (*A*). A mob-cap.

" Upon her head a small mob-cap she placed.
Of lawn so stiff, with large flowered ribbon graced,
Yclept a knot and bridle, in a bow,
Of scarlet flaming, her long chin below."
       Peter Pindar: Portfolio (Dinah).

Knots of May. The children's game. "Here we go gathering nuts of May" is a perversion of "Here we go gathering knots of May," referring to the old custom of gathering knots of flowers on May-day, or, to use the ordinary phrase, "to go a-Maying." Of course, there are no nuts to be gathered in May.

Knotted Stick is Planed (*The*). The house of Orleans is worsted by that of Burgundy. The house of Orleans bore for its badge a *bâton noueux,* the house of Burgundy a *plane;* hence the French saying, "*Le bâton noueux est plané.*"

Knotgrass. Supposed, if taken in an infusion, to stop growth.

" Get you gone, you dwarf ;
You minimus, of hindering knotgrass made."
Shakespeare: Midsummer Night's Dream, iii. 2.

Knout (1 syl.) is a knotted bunch of thongs made of hide. It is a Tartar invention, but was introduced into Russia. (*Knout,* Tartar for knot.)

Know Thyself. The wise saw of Solon, the Athenian lawgiver (B.C. 638-558).

Know the Fitting Moment. The favourite maxim of Pittacos, one of the "seven wise men."

Know Your Own Mind. By Murphy ; borrowed from Destouches, the French dramatist

Know-Nothings. A secret political party of the United States, which arose in 1853, who replied to every question asked about their society, "I know nothing about it." Their object was to accomplish the repeal of the naturalisation laws, and of the law which excluded all but natives from holding office. The party split on the slavery question and died out.

The chief principle of the party was that no one who had not been 21 years in the United States should be permitted to have any part in the government.

Knows which Side his Bread is Buttered (*He*). He is alive to his own interest. In Latin, "*Scit uti foro.*"

Knowledge-box (*Your*). Your head, the brain being the seat of all human knowledge.

Knox's Croft, in Gifford Gate, Haddington ; so called because it was the birthplace of John Knox.

Knuckle-duster. A metal instrument which is fitted to a man's fist, and may be readily used in self-defence by striking a blow. Sometimes these instruments are armed with spikes. It was an American invention, and was used in England in defence against the infamous attacks of Spring-heel Jack. We have the phrase "To dust your jacket for you," meaning to "beat you," as men dust carpets by beating them.

Knuckle Under (*To*). To kneel for pardon. Knuckle here means the knee, and we still say a "knuckle of veal or mutton," meaning the thin end of the leg near the joint. Dr. Ogilvie tells us there was an old custom of striking the under side of a table with the knuckles when defeated in an argument ; and Dr. Johnson, following Bailey, says the same thing.

Kobold. A house-spirit in German superstition ; the same as our Robin Goodfellow, and the Scotch *brownie* (*q.v.*). (*See* FAIRY HINZELMANN.)

Kochla'ni. Arabian horses of royal stock, of which genealogies have been preserved for more than 2,000 years. It is said that they are the offspring of Solomon's stud. (*Niebuhr.*)

Koh-i-Nûr [*Mountain of light*]. A large diamond in the possession of the Queen of England. It was found on the banks of the Godavery (Deccan), 1550, and belonged to Shah Jehan and Aurungzebe the Great (Mogul kings). In 1739 it passed into the hands of Nadir Shah, who called it the Koh-i-nûr. It next went to the monarchs of Afghanistan, and when Shah Sujah was depossessed he gave it to Runjeet Singh, of the Punjaub, as the price of his assistance towards the recovery of the throne of Cabul'. It next went to Dhuleep Singh, but when the Punjaub was annexed to the British crown in 1849, this noble diamond was surrendered to Great Britain. It is valued at £120,664, some say £140,000.

Its present weight is 106 1/16 carats.

Kohol or **Kohl.** Russell says, "The Persian women blacken the inside of their eyelids with a powder made of black Kohol."

" And others mix the Kohol's jetty dye
To give that long, dark languish to the eye."
Thomas Moore : Lalla Rookh, part i.

Koli or the **Kolis.** The 51st Foot, so called in 1821 from the initial letters of the regimental title, King's Own Light Infantry. Subsequently called the " Second Yorkshire (West Riding)," and now called the " 1st Battalion of the South Yorkshire Regiment."

Konx Ompax. The words of dismissal in the Eleusinian Mysteries. A correspondent in *Notes and Queries* says "konx" or "kogx" is the Sanscrit *Canscha* (the object of your desire); "ompax" is *om* (amen), *pacsha* (all is over). If this is correct, the words would mean, *God bless you, Amen, The ceremonies are concluded.* When a judge gave sentence by dropping his pebble into the urn of mercy or death, he said " *Pacsha* " (I have done it). The noise made by the stone in falling was called *pacsha* (fate), and so was the dripping noise of the clepsydra, which limited the pleader's quota of time.

Koppa. A Greek numeral = 90. (*See* EPISEMON.)

Korân, or, with the article, *Al-Korân* [the Reading]. The religious, social, civil, commercial, military, and legal code of Islam. It is rather remarkable that we call our Bible the *writing* (Scripture), but the Arabs call their Bible the *reading* (Korân). We are told to believe that portions of this book were communicated to the prophet at Mecca and Medi'na by the angel Gabriel, with the sound of bells.

Kor'rigans or *Corrigan.* Nine fays of Brittany, of wonderful powers. They can predict future events, assume any shape they like, move quick as thought from place to place, and cure diseases or wounds. They are not more than two feet high, have long flowing hair, which they are fond of combing, dress only with a white veil, are excellent singers, and their favourite haunt is beside some fountain. They flee at the sound of a bell or benediction. Their breath is most deadly. (*Breton mythology.*)

Koumiss or **Kumiss.** Fermented mare's milk used as a beverage by the Tartar tribes of Central Asia. A slightly alcoholic drink of a similar kind is made with great ceremony in Siberia. It consists of slightly sour cow's milk, sugar, and yeast. (Russian, *kumuisu.*)

"Kumiss is still prepared from mare's milk by the Calmucks and Nogais, who, during the process of making it, keep the milk in constant agitation."—*Rawlinson : Herodotus,* vol. iii. book iv. p. 2.

✢ The ceremony of making it is described at full length by Noel, in the *Dictionnaire de la Fable,* vol. i. 833-834.

Kraal. A South African village, being a collection of huts in a circular form. (From *corral.*)

Kraken. A supposed sea-monster of vast size, said to have been seen off the coast of Norway and on the North American coasts. It was first described (1750) by Pontoppidan. Pliny speaks of a sea-monster in the Straits of Gibraltar, which blocked the entrance of ships.

Kratim. The dog of the Seven Sleepers. More correctly called Katmir or Ketmir (*q.v.*).

Kremlin (*The*). A gigantic pile of buildings in Moscow of every style of architecture: Arabesque palaces, Gothic forts, Greek temples, Italian steeples, Chinese pavilions, and Cyclopean walls. It contains palaces and cathedrals, museums and barracks, arcades and shops, the Russian treasury, government offices, the ancient palace of the patriarch, a throne-room, churches, convents, etc. Built by two Italians, Marco and Pietro Antonio, for Ivan III. in 1485. There had been previously a wooden fortress on the spot. (Russian *krem,* a fortress.)

"Towers of every form, round, square, and with pointed roofs, belfries, donjons, turrets, spires, sentry-boxes fixed on minarets, steeples of every height, style, and colour : palaces, domes, watchtowers, walls embattlemented and pierced with loop-holes, ramparts, fortifications of every description, chiosks by the side of cathedrals ; monuments of pride and caprice, voluptuousness, glory, and piety."—*De Custine : Russia,* chap. xxii.

❧ Every city in Russia has its kremlin (citadel); but that of Moscow is the most important.

Krems White takes its name from Krems in Austria, the city where it is manufactured.

Kreuzer (pron. *kroit-zer*). A small copper coin in Southern Germany, once marked with a cross. (German, *kreuz*, a cross; Latin, *crux*.)

Kriem'hild (2 syl.). A beautiful Burgundian lady, daughter of Dancrat and Uta, and sister of Gunther, Gernot, and Gis'elher. She first married Siegfried, King of the Netherlanders, and next Etzel, King of the Huns. Hagan, the Dane, slew her first husband, and seized all her treasures; and to revenge these wrongs she invited her brothers and Hagan to visit her in Hungary. In the first part of the *Nibelungenlied*, Kriemhild brings ruin on herself by a tattling tongue:—(1) She tells Brunehild, Queen of Burgundy, that it is Siegfried who has taken her ring and girdle, which so incenses the queen that she prevails on Hagan to murder the Netherlander; (2) she tells Hagan that the only vulnerable part in Siegfried is between his shoulders, a hint Hagan acts on. In the second part of the great epic she is represented as bent on vengeance, and in executing her purpose, after a most terrible slaughter both of friends and foes, she is killed by Hildebrand. (*See* BRUNEHILD, HAGAN.)

Krish'na (*the black one*). The eighth avâtara or incarnation of Vishnu. Kansa, demon-king of Mathura', having committed great ravages, Brahman complained to Vishnu, and prayed him to relieve the world of its distress; whereupon Vishnu plucked off two hairs, one white and the other black, and promised they should revenge the wrongs of the demon-king. The black hair became Krishna. (*Hindu mythology*.)

Kriss Kringle. A sort of St. Nicholas (*q.v.*). On Christmas Eve Kriss Kringle, arrayed in a fur cap and strange apparel, goes to the bedroom of all good children, where he finds a stocking or sock hung up in expectation of his visit, in which depository he leaves a present for the young wearer. The word means *Christ-child*, and the eve is called "Kriss-Kringle Eve." (*See* SANTA CLAUS.)

Kri'ta. The first of the four Hindu periods contained in the great Yuga, when the genius of Truth and Right, in the form of a bull, stood firm on his four feet, and man gained nothing by iniquity. (*See* KALIYUGA.)

Krupp Gun. (*See* GUN.)

Krupp Steel. Steel from the works of Herr Krupp, of Essen, in Prussia.

Ku-Klux-Klan (*The*). (1864-1876.) A secret society in the Southern States of America against the negro class, to intimidate, flog, mutilate, or murder those who opposed the laws of the society. In Tennessee one murder a day was committed, and if anyone attempted to bring the murderers to justice he was a marked man, and sure to be mutilated or killed. In fact, the Ku-Klux-Klan was formed on the model of the "Molly Maguires" and "Moonlighters" of Ireland. Between November, 1864, and March, 1865, the number of cases of personal violence were 400. (Greek, *kuklos*, a circle.)

Ku'dos. Praise, glory. (*Greek.*)

Ku'fic. Ancient Arabic letters; so called from Kufa, a town in the pashalic of Bagdad, noted for expert copyists of the ancient Arabic MSS.

Kufic Coins. Mahometan coins with Kufic or ancient Arabic characters. The first were struck in the eighteenth year of the Heg'ira (A.D. 638).

Kumara [*youthful*]. The Hindu war-god, the same as Kârttikeya (*q.v.*). One of the most celebrated Hindu poems is the legendary history of this god. R. T. H. Griffith has translated seven cantos of it into English verse.

Kurd. A native of Kurdistan.

Kursaal. Public room at German watering-place for use of visitors.

Kuru. A noted legendary hero of India, the contests of whose descendants form the subject of two Indian epics.

Ky'anise (3 syl.). To apply corrosive sublimate to timber in order to prevent the dry-rot; so called from Dr. Kyan, who invented the process in 1832. (*See* PAYNISING.)

Kyle, *Carrick,* and *Cunningham.* Ayrshire is divided into three parts: Kyle, a strong corn-growing soil; Carrick, a wild hilly portion, only fit for feeding cattle; and Cunningham, a rich dairy land. Hence the saying—

"Kyle for a man, Carrick for a coo [cow],
Cunningham for butter, Galloway for woo°
[wool]."

Kyrie Elei'son [*Ki-ri-e E-li-s'n*]. "Lord, have mercy." The first movement of the Catholic mass. Both the music and the words are so called. In the Anglican Church, after each commandment, the response is, "Lord, have mercy upon us, and incline our hearts to keep this law."

Kyrle Society (*The*). Founded 1878, for decorating the walls of hospitals, school-rooms, mission-rooms, cottages, etc.; for the cultivation of small open spaces, window-gardening, the love of flowers, etc.; and improving the artistic taste of the poorer classes.

L

L. This letter represents an ox-goad, and is called in Hebrew *lamed* (an ox-goad).

L for fifty is half C (*centum*, a hundred).

L, for a pound sterling, is the Latin *libra*, a pound. With a line drawn above the letter, it stands for 50,000.

L. E. L. Letitia Elizabeth Landon (afterwards Mrs. Maclean), a poetess of the "Lara" and "Corsair" school (1802-1839).

LL.D. Doctor of Laws—*i.e.* both civil and canon. The double L is the plural; thus MSS. is the plural of MS. (manuscript); pp., pages.

L. L. Whisky. Lord-Lieutenant whisky. Mr. Kinahan being requested to preserve a certain cask of whisky highly approved of by his Excellency the Duke of Richmond, marked it with the initials L.L., and ever after called this particular quality L.L. whisky. The Duke of Richmond was Lord-Lieutenant from 1807 to 1813.

L.S. *Locus sigilli*, that is, the place for the seal.

L. S. D. Latin, *libra* (a pound); *solidus* (a shilling); and *denarius* (a penny); through the Italian *lire* (2 syl.), *soldi*, *denari*. If farthings are expressed the letter *q* (*quadrans*) is employed. Introduced by the Lombard merchants, from whom also we have *Cr.* (creditor), *Dr.* (debtor), *bankrupt*, *do* or *ditto*, etc.

La-de-da. A yea-nay sort of a fellow, with no backbone. "*Da*," in French, means both *oui* and *nenni*, as *Oui-da* (ay, marry), *Nenni-da* (no forsooth).

> "I wish that French brother of his, the Parisian la-de-da, was more like him, more of an American."—*A. G. Gunter : Baron Montez,* book iii. 8.

La Garde Meurt ne se Rend pas. The words falsely ascribed to General Cambronne, at the battle of Waterloo; inscribed on his monument at Nantes.

La Joyeuse. The sword of Charlemagne. (*See* SWORD.)

La Muette de Portici. Auber's best opera. Also known as *Masaniello*.

La Roche (1 syl.). A Protestant clergyman, whose story is told in *The Mirror*, by Henry Mackenzie.

Lab'adists. A religious sect of the seventeenth century, so called from Jean Labadie, of Bourg in Guyenne. They were Protestant ascetics, who sought reform of morals more than reform of doctrine. They rejected the observance of all holy days, and held certain mystic notions. The sect fell to pieces early in the eighteenth century.

Lab'arum. The standard borne before the Roman emperors. It consisted of a gilded spear, with an eagle on the top, while from a cross-staff hung a splendid purple streamer, with a gold fringe, adorned with precious stones. Constantine substituted a crown for the eagle, and inscribed in the midst the mysterious monogram. (*See* CONSTANTINE'S CROSS.) Rich (*Antiquities*, p. 361) says "probably from the Gaulish *lab*, to raise ; for Constantine was educated in Gaul." The Greek *laba* is a staff. (See *Gibbon : Decline and Fall*, etc. chap. xx.)

La'be (*Queen*). The Circe of the Arabians, who, by her enchantments, transformed men into horses and other brute beasts. She is introduced into the *Arabian Nights' Entertainments*, where Beder, Prince of Persia, marries her, defeats her plots against him, and turns her into a mare. Being restored to her proper shape by her mother, she turns Beder into an owl; but the prince ultimately regains his own proper form.

Labour of Love (*A*). Work undertaken for the love of the thing, without regard to pay.

Labourer is Worthy of his Hire. In Latin: "*Digna canis pabulo.*" "The dog must be bad indeed that is not worth a bone." Hence the Mosaic law, "Thou shalt not muzzle the ox that treadeth out the corn."

Labourers (*The Statute of*). An attempt made in 1349 to fix the rate of wages at which labourers should be compelled to work.

Lab'yrinth. A mass of buildings or garden - walks, so complicated as to puzzle strangers to extricate themselves. Said to be so called from Lab'yris, an Egyptian monarch of the 12th dynasty. The chief labyrinths are :—

(1) The Egyptian, by Petesu'chis or Tithoes, near the Lake Mœris. It had 3,000 apartments, half of which were underground. (B.C. 1800.) *Pliny*, xxxvi. 13 ; and *Pomponius Mela*, i. 9.

(2) The Cretan, by Dæ'dalos, for imprisoning the Mi'notaur. The only means of finding a way out of it was by help of a skein of thread. (See *Virgil: Æneid*, v.)

(3) The Cretan conduit, which had 1,000 branches or turnings.

(4) The Lem'nian, by the architects Zmilus, Rholus, and Theodōrus. It had 150 columns, so nicely adjusted that a child could turn them. Vestiges of this labyrinth were still in existence in the time of Pliny.

(5) The labyrinth of Clu'sium, made by Lars Por'sena, King of Etruria, for his tomb.

(6) The Samian, by Theodo'rus (B.C. 540). Referred to by Pliny ; by Herodotos, ii. 145 ; by Strabo, x. ; and by Diodōrus Sicŭlus, i.

(7) The labyrinth at Woodstock, by Henry II., for the Fair Rosamond.

(8) Of mazes formed by hedges. The best known is that of Hampton Court.

Lac of Rupees. The nominal value of the Indian rupee is 2s., and a lac means 100,000. At this estimate, a lac of rupees=200,000s. or £10,000. Its present value varies according to the market value of silver. In 1894 between 13 and 14 pence.

Lace. *I'll lace your jacket for you*, beat you. (French, *laisse*, a lash ; German, *laschen*, to strike ; our *lash*.)

Laced. *Tea* or *coffee laced with spirits*, a cup of tea or coffee qualified with brandy or whisky.

"Deacon Bearcliff . . . had his pipe, and his teacup . . . laced with a little spirits."—*Sir W. Scott: Guy Mannering*, chap. xi.

"Dandie . . . partook of a cup of tea with Mrs. Allan, just laced with two teaspoonfuls of cogniac."—Ditto, chap. lii.

Lacedæmonian Letter (*The*). The Greek ι (*iota*), the smallest of all letters. Laconic brevity. (*See* LACONIC.)

Lacedæmonians (*The*). The Duke of Cornwall's Light Infantry. So called because in 1777 their colonel made a long harangue, under heavy fire, on the Spartan discipline and military system. (*See* RED FEATHERS.)

Lachesis [*Lak'-ĕ-sis*]. The Fate who spins life's thread, working into the woof the sundry events destined to occur. Clotho held the distaff, and Atropos cut off the thread when life was to be ended. (Greek, *klôtho*, to draw thread from a distaff ; Lachesis from *lagchăno*, to assign by lot ; and *Atropos* = inflexible.)

Lackadaisical. Affected, pensive, sentimental, artificially tender.

Lacon'ic. Very concise and pithy. A Spartan was called a Lacon from Laco'nia, the land in which he dwelt. The Spartans were noted for their brusque and sententious speech. When Philip of Macedon wrote to the Spartan magistrates, " If I enter Laco'nia, I will level Lacedæmon to the ground," the ephors wrote word back the single word, " If." (*See above* LACEDÆMONIAN LETTER.)

⁂ In 1490 O'Neil wrote to O'Donnel : " Send me the tribute, or else——." To which O'Donnel replied : " I owe none, or else——."

Lacus'trine Deposits. Deposits formed at the bottom of fresh-water pools and lakes. (Latin, *lacus*, a lake.)

Lacus'trine Habitations. The remains of human dwellings of great antiquity, constructed on certain lakes in Ireland, Switzerland, etc. They seem to have been villages built on piles in the middle of a lake.

Lad o' Wax. A little boy, a doll of a man. In *Romeo and Juliet* the Nurse calls Paris " a man of wax," meaning a very " proper man." Horace speaks of the " waxen arms of Tel'ephus," meaning well modelled.

La'das. Alexander's messenger, noted for his swiftness of foot, mentioned by Catullus, Martial, and others. Lord Rosebery's horse *Ladas* won the Derby in 1894.

Ladies. (*See after* LADY.)

La'don. One of the dogs of Actæon.

Ladon. The dragon which guarded the apples of the Hesper'ides.

Ladrones. The island of thieves ; so called, in 1519, by Magellan.

Lady. A woman of wealth, of station, or of rank. Verstegan says, " It was anciently written Hleafdian [? hlæfdige], contracted first into Lafdy, and then into Lady. *Laf* or *Hláf* (loaf) means food in general or bread in particular, and *dig-ian* or *dug-an*, to help, serve, or care for; whence lady means the 'bread-server.' The lord (or *loaf-ward*) *sup-plied* the food, and the lady saw that it was properly *served*, for the ladies used to carve and distribute the food to the guests."

Another etymology is *Hláf-weardie* and loaf-wardie, where *ie* stands for a female suffix like -*ina* -*ine*; as Carolus, female *Carol-ina*, or *Carol-ine*; Joseph, *Joseph-ina* or *Joseph-ine*; Czar, *Czar-ina*, etc. etc.

Ladies retire to the drawing-room after dinner, and leave the gentlemen behind. This custom was brought in by the Norsemen. The Vikings always dismissed all women from their drinking parties. (*S. Bunbury*.)

Ladybird, Ladyfly, Ladycow, or *May-bug*. The Bishop Barnaby, called in German, *Unser herrin huhn* (our Lady-fowl), *Marien-huhn* (Mary-fowl), and *Marien Käfer* (Mary's beetle). "Cushcow Lady," as it is called in Yorkshire, is also the German *Marien-kalb* (Lady-calf), in French, *bête à Dieu*. Thus the cockchafer is called the May-bug, where the German *käfer* is rendered bug; and several of the scarabæi are called bugs, as the rose-bug, etc. (*See* BISHOP.)

Lady Bountiful. The benevolent lady of a village. The character of Lady Bountiful is from the *Beaux' Stratagem*, by Farquhar.

Lady Chapel. The small chapel east of the altar, or behind the screen of the high altar; dedicated to the Virgin Mary.

Lady Day. The 25th of March, to commemorate the Annunciation of Our Lady, the Virgin Mary. There is a tradition that Adam was created on this day. Of course, this rests on Jesus being "the Second Adam," or "federal head."

Lady Isabella, the beloved daughter of a noble lord, accompanied her father and mother on a chase one day, when her step-mother requested her to return and tell the master-cook to prepare "the milk-white doe for dinner." Lady Isabella did as she was told, and the master-cook replied, "Thou art the doe that I must dress." The scullion-boy exclaimed, "O save the lady's life, and make thy pies of me;" but the master-cook heeded him not. When the lord

returned he called for his daughter, the fair Isabelle, and the scullion-boy said, "If now you will your daughter see, my lord, cut up that pie." When the fond father comprehended the awful tragedy, he adjudged the cruel step-dame to be burnt alive, and the master-cook "in boiling lead to stand;" but the scullion-boy he made his heir. (*Percy: Reliques*, etc., series iii., bk. 2.)

Lady Magistrate. Lady Berkley was made by Queen Mary a justice of the peace for Gloucestershire and appointed to the quorum of Suffolk. Lady Berkley sat on the bench at assizes and sessions, girt with a sword. Tony Lumpkin says of Mr. Hardcastle—

"He'll persuade you that his mother was an alderman and his aunt a justice of the peace."— *Goldsmith: She Stoops to Conquer.*

Lady Margaret Professor of Divinity, founded in 1502 by the mother of Henry VII. The year following she founded a preachership. Both in the University of Cambridge.

Lady in the Sacque. The apparition of this hag forms the story of the *Tapestried Chamber*, by Sir Walter Scott.

An old woman, whose dress was an old-fashioned gown, which ladies call a sacque; that is, a sort of robe completely loose in the body, but gathered into broad plaits upon the neck and shoulders.

Lady of England. Maud, daughter of Henry I. The title of "*Dom'ina Anglorum*" was conferred upon her by the Council of Winchester, held April 7th, 1141. (*Rymer: Fœdera*, i.)

Lady of Mercy (*Our*). An order of knighthood in Spain, instituted in 1218 by James I. of Aragon, for the deliverance of Christian captives amongst the Moors. Within the first six years, as many as 400 captives were rescued by these knights.

Lady of Shallott'. A maiden who fell in love with Sir Lancelot of the Lake, and died because her love was not returned. Tennyson has a poem on the subject; and the story of Elaine, "the lily maid of As'tolat," in the *Idylls of the King*, is substantially the same. (*See* ELAINE.)

Lady of the Bleeding Heart. Ellen Douglas; so called from the cognisance of the family. (*Sir Walter Scott: Lady of the Lake*, ii. 10.)

Lady of the Broom (*The*). A housemaid.

"Highly disgusted at a farthing candle,
Left by the Lady of the Broom,
Named Susan ..."
Peter Pindar: The Diamond Pin

Lady of the Haystack made her appearance in 1776 at Bourton, near Bristol. She was young and beautiful, graceful, and evidently accustomed to good society. She lived for four years in a haystack; but was ultimately kept by Mrs. Hannah More in an asylum, and died suddenly in December, 1801. Mrs. More called her Louisa ; but she was probably a Mademoiselle La Frülen, natural daughter of Francis Joseph I., Emperor of Austria. (See *World of Wonders*, p. 134.)

Lady of the Lake. Vivien, mistress of Merlin, the enchanter, who lived in the midst of an imaginary lake, surrounded by knights and damsels. Tennyson, in the *Idylls of the King*, tells the story of Vivien and Merlin. (*See* LANCELOT.)

Lady of the Lake. Ellen Douglas, who lived with her father near Loch Katrine. (*Sir Walter Scott: The Lady of the Lake.*)

Lady of the Rock (*Our*). A miraculous image of the Virgin found by the wayside between Salamanca and Ciudad Rodrigo in 1409.

Ladies' Mile (*The*). That part of Hyde Park which is most frequented by ladies on horseback or in carriages.

Ladies' Plate (*The*), in races, is not a race for a prize subscribed for by ladies, but a race run for by women.

" On the Monday succeeding St. Wilfred's Sunday, there were for many years at Roper's Common [a race] called the Lady's Plate, of £15 value, for horses, etc., ridden by women."—*Sporting Magazine*, vol. xx., New Series, p. 287.

Ladies' Smocks. Garden cress, botanically called Cardamine, a diminutive of the Greek *kardamon*, called in Latin *nasturtium*, sometimes called Nose-smart (*Kara-damōn*, head-afflicting) ; so nasturtium is *Nasi-tortium* (nose-twisting), called so in consequence of its pungency.

" When ladies' smocks of silver white
Do paint the meadows with delight."

Called Ladies' smocks because the flowers resemble linen exposed to whiten on the grass—"when maidens bleach their summer smocks." There is, however, a purple tint which mars its perfect whiteness. Another name of the plant is " Cuckoo-flower," because it comes into flower when the cuckoo sings.

Ladies and Gentlemen. Till 1808 public speakers began their addresses with " gentlemen and ladies ; " but since then the order has been reversed.

Læding. The strongest chain that had hitherto been made. It was forged by Asa Thor to bind the wolf Fenrir with ; but the wolf snapped it as if it had been made of tow. Fenrir was then bound with the chain Dromi, much stronger than Læding, but the beast snapped it instantly with equal ease. (*Scandinavian mythology.*)

Lælaps. A very powerful dog given by Diana to Procris ; Procris gave it to Ceph'alos. While pursuing a wild boar it was metamorphosed into a stone. (*See* DOGS, *Actæon's fifty dogs.*)

Laer'tes (3 syl.). Son of Polo'nius and brother of Ophelia. He kills Hamlet with a poisoned rapier, and dies himself from a wound by the same foil. (*Shakespeare: Hamlet.*)

Læta're Sunday. The fourth Sunday in Lent is so called from the first word of the Introit, which is from Isa. lxvi. 10: " *Rejoice* ye with Jerusalem, and be glad with her all ye that love her." It is on this day that the pope blesses the Golden Rose.

Lag'ado. Capital of Balnibarbi, celebrated for its grand academy of projectors, where the scholars spend their time in such useful projects as making pincushions from softened rocks, extracting sunbeams from cucumbers, and converting ice into gunpowder. (*Swift: Gulliver's Travels, Voyage to Lapu'ta.*)

Lager Beer. A light German beer. Lager means a " storehouse," and lager beer means beer stored for ripening before being used.

Laird (Scotch). A landed proprietor.

Lagoon. A shallow lake near river or sea, due to infiltration or overflow of water from the larger body.

Laïs. A courtesan or Greek Hetaira. There were two of the name ; the elder was the most beautiful woman of Corinth, and lived at the time of the Peloponne'sian War. The beauty of the latter excited the jealousy of the Thessalonian women, who pricked her to death with their bodkins. She was contemporary with Phryne (2 syl.), her rival, and sat to Apelles as a model.

Laissez Faire, Laissez Passer. Lord John Russell said : " Colbert, with the intention of fostering the manufactures of France, established regulations limiting the webs woven in looms to a particular size. He also prohibited the introduction of foreign manufactures.

Then the French vine-growers, finding they could no longer get rid of their wine, began to grumble. When Colbert asked a merchant what relief he could give, he received for answer, ' *Laissez faire, laissez passer ;* ' that is to say, Don't interfere with our mode of manufactures, and don't stop the introduction of foreign imports."

The laissez-faire system. The let-alone system.

Lake School (*The*). The school of poetry introduced by the Lake poets Wordsworth, Coleridge, and Southey, who resided in the Lake district of Cumberland and Westmoreland, and sought inspiration in the simplicity of nature. The name was first applied in derision by the *Edinburgh Review* to the class of poets who followed the above-named trio. N.B. Charles Lamb, Lloyd, and Professor William (Christopher North) are sometimes placed among the " Lakers."

Laked'ion or **Laquedem** (*Isaac*). The name given in France, in the fourteenth century, to the Wandering Jew.

La'kin. *By'r Lakin.* An oath, meaning " By our Lady-kin," or Little Lady, where little does not refer to size, but is equivalent to *dear*.

" By'r Lakin, a parlous [perilous] fear."—*Shakespeare : A Midsummer Night's Dream, iii. 1.*

Laks'mi or **Lakshmi.** One of the consorts of Vishnu ; she is goddess of beauty, wealth, and pleasure. (*Hindu mythology.*)

Lalla Rookh [*tulip cheek*] is the supposed daughter of Au-rung-ze'-be, Emperor of Delhi, betrothed to Al'iris, Sultan of Lesser Buchar'ia. On her journey from Delhi to the valley of Cashmere, she is entertained by a young Persian poet named Fer'amorz, who is supposed to relate the four poetical tales of the romance, and with whom she falls in love. (*Thomas Moore : Lalla Rookh.*) (*See* FERAMORZ.)

La'ma, among the Mongols, means the priestly order. Hence the religion of the Mongols and Calmucs is termed Lamaism. The Grand Lamas wear *yellow* caps, the subordinate Lamas *red* caps. (*See* GRAND LAMA.)

La'maïsm [Tibetan, *Blama,* spiritual teacher]. The religion of Tibet and Mongolia, which is Buddhism corrupted by Sivaism and spirit-worship.

Lamb. In Christian art, an emblem of the Redeemer, called the " Lamb of God." It is also the attribute of St.

Agnes, St. Geneviève, St. Catherine, and St. Regi'na. John the Baptist either carries a lamb or is accompanied by one. It is also introduced symbolically to represent any of the " types " of Christ ; as Abraham, Moses, and so on.

Lamb (*The Vegetable*) or *Tartarian lamb ;* technically called Polypodium Barometz. It is a Chinese fern with a decumbent root, covered with a soft, dense yellow wool. Sir Hans Sloane, who calls it the Tartarian lamb, has given a print of it ; and Dr. Hunter has given a print which makes its resemblance to a lamb still more striking. The down is used in India for staunching hæmorrhage.

" Rooted in earth each cloven hoof descends,
And round and round her flexile neck she bends ;
Crops the grey coral moss, and hoary thyme,
Or laps with rosy tongue the melting rime ;
Eyes with mute tenderness her distant dam,
And seems to bleat, a Vegetable Lamb."
    Darwin: Loves of the Plants, 283, etc.

Lamb. *Cold lamb.* A schoolboy's joke. Setting a boy on a cold marble or stone hearth. Horace (*Sat.* i. 5, 22) has " *Dotâre lumbos,*" which may have suggested the pun.

Lamb-pie. A flogging. Lamb is a pun on the Latin verb *lambo* (to lick), and the word " lick " has been perverted to mean flog (*see* LICK) ; or it may be the old Norse *lam* (the hand), meaning hand- or slap-pie. (*See* LAMMING.)

Lamb's Conduit Street (*London*). Stow says, " One William Lamb, citizen and clothworker, born at Sutton Valence, Kent, did found near unto Oldbourne a faire conduit and standard ; from this conduit, water clear as crystal was conveyed in pipes to a conduit on Snow Hill " (26th March, 1577). The conduit was taken down in 1746.

Lamb's Wool. A beverage consisting of the juice of apples roasted over spiced ale. A great day for this drink was the feast of the apple-gathering, called in Irish *la mas ubhal,* pronounced " lammas ool," and corrupted into " lamb's wool."

" The pulpe of the rosted apples, in number foure or five . . . mixed in a wine quart of faire water, laboured together untill it come to be as apples and ale, which we call lambes wool."—*Johnson's Gerard,* p. 1460.

Lambert's Day (*St.*), September 17th. St. Landebert or Lambert, a native of Maestricht, lived in the seventh century.

" Be ready, as your lives shall answer it,
At Coventry, upon St. Lambert's day."
    Shakespeare: Richard II., i. 1.

Lambro was the father of Haidée. Major Lambro, the prototype, was head of the Russian piratical squadron in 1791. He contrived to escape when the rest were seized by the Algerines on the island of Zia. (*Byron : Don Juan*, iii. 26.)

Lame Duck (*A*), in Stock Exchange parlance, means a member of the Stock Exchange who waddles off on settlement day without settling his account. All such defaulters are black-boarded and struck off the list. Sometimes it is used for one who cannot pay his debts, one who trades without money.

> "Pitt . . . gambled and lost :
> But who must answer for the cost ?
> Not he, indeed ! A duck confounded lame
> Not unattended waddling . . ."
>   *Peter Pindar : Proh Impudentiam.*

Lame King. A Grecian oracle had told Sparta to " Beware of a lame king." Agesila'os was lame, and during his reign Sparta lost her supremacy.

Lame Vicegerent (in *Hudibras*). Richard Cromwell.

Lam'erock (*Sir*), of Wales. A knight of the Round Table, son of Sir Pellinore, and brother of Sir Percival. He had an amour with his own aunt, the wife of King Lote. Strange that of all the famous knights of the Round Table, Sir Caradoc and Sir Galahad were the only ones who were continent.

Lam'ia. A female phantom, whose name was used by the Greeks and Romans as a bugbear to children. She was a Lib'yan queen beloved by Jupiter, but robbed of her offspring by the jealous Juno ; and in consequence she vowed vengeance against all children, whom she delighted to entice and murder. (*See* FAIRY.)

> " Keats has a poem so called. His Lamia is a serpent who assumed the form of a beautiful woman, was beloved by a young man and got a soul. The tale was drawn from Philostratus."—*De Vita Apollonii*, book iv., introduced by Burton in his *Anatomy of Melancholy.*

Lammas. *At latter Lammas*—i.e. never. (*See* NEVER.)

Lammas Day (August 1st) means the loaf-mass day. The day of first-fruit offerings, when a loaf was given to the priests in lieu of the first-fruits. (Saxon, *hlam-mæsse*, for *hlaf-mæsse dæg*.)

August 1 Old Style, August 12 New Style.

Lammas-tide. Lammas time, or the season when lammas occurs.

Lammer Beads. Amber beads, once used as charms. (French, *l'ambre ;* Teutonic, *lamertyn-stein*.)

Lammermoor. (*See* EDGAR, LUCIA.)

Lamming (*A*). A beating. (*See* LAMB-PIE.)

Lamminin, Lamkin, Linkin, or *Bold Rakin.* A Scottish ogre, represented in the ballad as a bloodthirsty mason ; the terror of the Scotch nursery.

Lam'ourette's Kiss. On July 7th, 1792, the Abbé Lamourette induced the different factions of the Legislative Assembly of France to lay aside their differences ; so the deputies of the Royalists, Constitutionalists, Girondists, Jacobins, and Orleanists rushed into each other's arms, and the king was sent for to see " how these Christians loved one another ; " but the reconciliation was hollow and unsound. The term is now used for a reconciliation of policy without abatement of rancour.

Lamp. *To smell of the lamp.* To bear the marks of great study, but not enough laboured to conceal the marks of labour. The phrase was first applied to the orations of Demosthenes, written by lamp-light with enormous care.

Lamp of Heaven (*The*). The moon. Milton calls the stars " lamps."

> " Why shouldst thou . . .
> In thy dark lantern thus close up the stars,
> That Nature hung in heaven, and filled their lamps
> With everlasting oil, to give due light
> To the misled and lonely traveller ? "
>   *Comus*, 200—204.

Lamp of Phœbus (*The*). The sun. Phœbus is the mythological personification of the sun.

Lamp of the Law (*The*). Irnerius the German was so called, who first lectured on the Pandects of Justinian after their discovery at Amalphi in 1137.

Lamps. *The seven lamps of sleep.* In the mansion of the Knight of the Black Castle were seven lamps, which could be quenched only with water from an enchanted fountain. So long as these lamps kept burning, everyone within the room fell into a deep sleep, from which nothing could rouse them till the lamps were extinguished. (*See* ROSANA.) (*The Seven Champions of Christendom*, ii. 8.)

Sepulchral lamps. The Romans are said to have preserved lamps in some of their sepulchres for centuries. In the papacy of Paul III. one of these lamps was found in the tomb of Tullia (Cicero's daughter), which had been shut up for 1,550 years. At the dissolution of the monasteries a lamp was found which is said to have been burning 1,200 years. Two are preserved in Leyden museum.

Lampad'ion. The received name of a lively, petulant courtesan, in the later Greek comedy.

Lampoon. Sir Walter Scott says, "These personal and scandalous libels, carried to excess in the reign of Charles II., acquired the name of lampoons from the burden sung to them: 'Lampone, lampone, camerada lampone'—Guzzler, guzzler, my fellow guzzler." (French, *lamper*, to guzzle.) Sir Walter obtained his information from Trevoux.

Lampos and Pha'eton. The two steeds of Auro'ra. One of Actæon's dogs was called Lampos.

Lancashire Lads or " **The Lancashire.**" The 47th Foot. Now called the First Battalion of the North Lancashire Regiment.

Lancaster. The camp-town on the river Lune.

Lancaster Gun. A species of rifled cannon with elliptical bore; so called from Mr. Lancaster, its inventor.

Lancaster'ian (*A*). One who pursues the system of Joseph Lancaster (1778-1838) in schools. By this system the higher classes taught the lower.

Lancastrian (*A*). An adherent of the Lancastrian line of kings, as opposed to the Yorkists. One of the Lancastrian kings (Henry IV., V., VI.).

Lance (1 syl.), in Christian art, is an attribute of St. Matthew and St. Thomas, the apostles; also of St. Longi'nus, St. George, St. Adalbert, St. Oswin, St. Barbara, St. Michael, St. Dome'trius, and several others.

Astolpho had a lance of gold that with enchanted force dismounted everyone it touched. (*Orlando Furioso*, bk. ix.)

A free-lance. One who acts on his own judgment, and not from party motives. The reference is to the Free Companies of the Middle Ages, called in Italy *condottieri*, and in France *Compagnies Grandes*, which were free to act as they liked, and were not servants of the Crown or of any other potentate. It must be confessed, however, that they were willing to sell themselves to any master and any cause, good or bad.

Lance-Corporal and **Lance-Sergeant.** One from the ranks temporarily acting as corporal or sergeant. In the Middle Ages a *lance* meant a soldier.

Lance-Knight. A foot-soldier; a corruption of *lasquenet* or *lancequenet*, a German foot-soldier.

Lance of the Ladies. At the termination of every joust a course was run "*pour les dames*," and called the "Lance of the Ladies."

Lan'celot (*Sir*). "The chief of knights" and "darling of the court." Elaine, the lily of Astolat, fell in love with him, but he returned not her love, and she died. (*See* ELAINE.) (*Tennyson: Idylls of the King; Elaine.*)

Lancelot or **Launcelot Gobbo.** Shylock's servant, famous for his soliloquy whether or not he should run away from his master. (*Shakespeare: Merchant of Venice.*)

Lan'celot du Lac. One of the earliest romances of the "Round Table" (1494). Sir Lancelot was the son of King Ban of Benwicke, but was stolen in infancy by Vivienne, called "*La Dame du Lac*," who dwelt "*en la marche de la petite Bretáigne;*" she plunged with the babe into the lake, and when her *protégé* was grown into man's estate, presented him to King Arthur. The lake referred to was a sort of enchanted delusion to conceal her demesnes. Hence the cognomen of *du Lac* given to the knight. Sir Lancelot goes in search of the Grail or holy cup brought to Britain by Joseph of Arimathe'a, and twice caught sight of it. (*See* GRAAL.) Though always represented in the Arthurian romances as the model of chivalry, Sir Lancelot was the adulterous lover of Guinevere, wife of King Arthur, his friend. At the close of his life the adulterous knight became a hermit, and died in the odour of sanctity.

Sir Lancelot is meant for a model of fidelity, bravery, frailty in love, and repentance; Sir Galahad of chastity; Sir Gawain of courtesy; Sir Kay of a rude, boastful knight; and Sir Modred of treachery.

Sir Lancelot du Lac and Tarquin. Sir Lancelot, seeking some adventure, met a lady who requested him to deliver certain Knights of the Round Table from the power of Tarquin. Coming to a river, he saw a copper basin suspended to a tree, and struck at it so hard that the basin broke. This brought out Tarquin, when a furious encounter took place, in which Tarquin was slain, and Sir Lancelot liberated from durance "threescore knights and four, all of the Table Round." (*Percy: Reliques*, etc., bk. ii. series 1.)

Lancelot of the Laik. A Scottish metrical romance, taken from the French *roman* called *Lancelot du Lac.* Galiot, a neighbouring king, invades Arthur's territory, and captures the castle of Lady Melyhalt among others. Sir Lancelot goes to chastise Galiot, sees Queen Guinevere and falls in love with her. Sir Gawayne is wounded in the war, and Sir Lancelot taken prisoner. In the French romance, Sir Lancelot makes Galiot submit to Arthur, but the Scotch romance terminates with the capture of the knight.

Lancers (*The*). The dance so called was introduced into Paris in 1836. It is in imitation of a military dance in which men used lances.

Land. *See how the land lies.* See what we have to do; see in what state matters are. See in what state the land is that we have to travel or pass over, or in what direction we must go. Joshua sent spies (ii. 1) "to view the land" before he attempted to pass the Jordan.

"Put your blankets down there, boys, and turn in. You'll see how the land lies in the morning."
—*Boldrewood: Robbery under Arms, ch. xi.*

Land-damn. A corruption of *landan* (to rate or reprove severely). According to Dean Milles the word is still used in Gloucestershire.

"You are abused . . . would I knew the villain, I would land-damn him."—*Shakespeare: Winter's Tale,* ii. 1.

Land-loupers. Persons who fly the country for crime or debt. Louper, loper, loafer, and luffer are varieties of the German *läufer,* a vagrant, a runner.

Land-lubber. An awkward or inexpert sailor on board ship. (Lubber, the Welsh *llob,* a dunce.)

Land of Beulah (Isa. lxii. 4). In *Pilgrim's Progress* it is that land of heavenly joy where the pilgrims tarry till they are summoned to enter the Celestial City; the Paradise before the resurrection.

Land of Bondage. Egypt was so called by the Jews, who were bondsmen there to the Pharaohs "who knew not Joseph."

Land of Cakes. Scotland, famous for its oatmeal cakes.

Land of Myrrh. Azab or Saba.

Land of Nod (*The*). To go to the land of Nod is to go to bed. There are many similar puns, and more in French than in English. Of course, the reference is to Gen. iv. 16, "Cain went . . . and dwelt in the land of Nod;" but where the land of Nod is or was nobody knows. In fact, "Nod" means a vagrant or vagabond, and when Cain

was driven out he lived "a vagrant life," with no fixed abode, till he built his "city." (*See* NEEDHAM.)

Land of Promise. Canaan, the land which God promised to give to Abraham for his obedience.

Land of Shadows (*Gone to the*). Fallen asleep. Shadows = dreams, or shadows of realities.

Land of Stars and Stripes (*The*). The United States of America. The reference is to their national flag.

Land o' the Leal (*The*). The Scotch Dixey Land (*q.v.*). An hypothetical land of happiness, loyalty, and virtue. Caroline Oliphant, Baroness Nairne, meant *heaven* in her exquisite song so called, and this is now its accepted meaning. (Leal = faithful, and "Land of the Leal" means the Land of the faithful.)

Landau'. A four-wheeled carriage, the top of which may be thrown back; invented at Landau, in Germany.

Landey'da. (*See* RAVEN.)

Landière (*French,* 3 syl.). A booth in a fair; so called from Le Landit, a famous fair at one time held at St. Denis. *Landit* means a small present such as one receives from a fair.

"Il gambadoit, il faisoit le badin ;
Oncq'on ne vit ung plus parfait landin."
Bourdigné : Légende, c. iii.

"Mercure avec d'avides mains . . .
Met impost et taxes nouvelles . . .
Sur les landis, sur les estrennes."
L. Chamhoury : Le Voyage de Mercure, bk. iii., p. 51 (1633).

Landscape (*A*) is a land picture. (Anglo-Saxon *landscipe,* verb *scap-an,* to shape, to give a form or picture of.) *Father of landscape gardening.* A. Lenotre (1613-1700).

Lane. No evil thing that walks by night, blue meagre hag, or stubborn unlaid ghost, no goblin, or smart fairy of the mine, has power to cross a lane ; once in a lane, the spirit of evil is in a fix. The reason is obvious : a lane is a spur from a main road, and therefore forms with it a sort of T, quite near enough to the shape of a cross to arrest such simple folk of the unseen world as care to trouble the peaceful inmates of the world we live in.

Lane. '*Tis a long lane that has no turning.* Every calamity has an ending. The darkest day, stop till to-morrow, will have passed away.

"Hope peeps from a cloud on our squad,
Whose beams have been long in deep mourning ;
'Tis a lane, let me tell you, my lad,
Very long that has never a turning."
Peter Pindar: Great Cry and Little Wool, epist. 1.

Lane (*The*) and *The Garden.* A short way of saying "Drury Lane" and "Covent Garden," which are two theatres in London.

Lane, of King's Bromley Manor, Staffordshire, bears in a canton "the Arms of England." This honour was granted to Colonel John Lane, for conducting Charles II. to his father's seat after the battle of Worcester. (*See next paragraph.*)

Jane Lane, daughter of Thomas and sister of Colonel John. To save the King after the battle of Worcester, she rode behind him from Bentley, in Staffordshire, the ancient seat of the Lanes, to the house of her cousin, Mrs. Norton, near Bristol. For this act of loyalty the king granted the family to have the following crest : A strawberry-roan horse saliant (couped at the flank), bridled, bitted, and garnished, supporting between its feet a royal crown proper ; motto, *Garde le Roy.*

Lanfu'sa's Son. (*See* FERRAU'.)

Lang Syne (*Scotch*, long since). In the olden time, in days gone by.

"There was muckle fighting about the place lang-syne."—*Scott : Guy Mannering,* chap. xl.

The song called *Auld Lang Syne,* usually attributed to Robert Burns, was not composed by him, for he says expressly in a letter to Thomson, "It is the old song of the olden times, which has never been in print. . . . I took it down from an old man's singing." In another letter he says, "Light be the turf on the heaven-inspired poet who composed this glorious fragment." Nothing whatever is known of the author of the words ; the composer is wholly unknown.

Langbourn Ward (*London*). So called from the long bourn or rivulet of sweet water which formerly broke out of a spring near Magpye Alley. This bourn gives its name to Sharebourne or Southbourne Lane.

Langstaff (*Launcelot*). The name under which *Salmagundi* was published, the real authors being Washington Irving, William Irving, and J. K. Paulding.

Language. *The primeval language.* Psammetichos, an Egyptian king, entrusted two new-born infants to a shepherd, with strict charge that they were never to hear any one utter a word. These children were afterwards brought before the king and uttered the word *bekos* (baked bread). The same experiment was tried by Frederick II. of Sweden, James IV. of Scotland, and one of the Mogul emperors of India.

James IV., in the 15th century, shut up two infant children in the Isle of Inchkeith, with a dumb attendant to wait on them.

The three primitive languages. The Persians say that Arabic, Persian, and Turkish are three primitive languages. The serpent that seduced Eve spoke Arabic, the most suasive language in the world ; Adam and Eve spoke Persian, the most poetic of all languages ; and the angel Gabriel spoke Turkish, the most menacing of all languages. (*Chardin.*)

"*Language given to men to conceal their thoughts,*" is by Montrond, but is generally fathered on Talleyrand.

Characteristics of European languages :
L'Italien se parle aux dames.
Le Français se parle aux hommes.
L'Anglais se parle aux oiseaux.
L'Allemand se parle aux chevaux.
L'Espagnol se parle à Dieux.

⁂ English, according to the French notion, is both singsong and sibilant.

Charles Quint used to say, "I speak German to my horses, Spanish to my God, French to my friends, and Italian to my mistresses."

Langue d'Oc. The Provençal branch of the Gallo-Romaic idiom ; so called from their *oc* (yes).

Langue d'Oïl. Walloon or Germanised Gallo-Romaic ; so called from their pronouncing our yes as *oïl* (o-e). These Gauls lived north of the Loire ; the Provençals dwelt south of that river.

Languish (*Lydia*). A young lady of romantic notions in *The Rivals,* a play by Sheridan.

Lantern. In Christian art, the attribute of St. Gudule and St. Hugh.

The feast of lanterns. Tradition says that the daughter of a famous mandarin, walking alone by a lake one evening, fell in. The father called together his neighbours, and all went with lanterns to look for her, and happily she was rescued. In commemoration thereof an annual festival was held on the spot, and grew in time to the celebrated "feast of lanterns." (*Present State of China.*)

A la lanterne. Hang him with the lantern or lamp ropes. A cry and custom introduced in the French revolution.

Lantern Jaws. Cheeks so thin that one may see daylight through them, as light shows through the horn of a lantern. In French, "*un visage si maigre que si on mettait une bougie allumée dans* *la bouche, la lumière paraitait au travers des joues.*"

Lantern-jawed. Having lantern-jaws.

Lantern-Land. The land of literary charlatans, whose inhabitants are graduates in arts, doctors, professors, prelates, and so on. (*Rabelais: Pantagruel*, v. 33.) (*See* CITY OF LANTERNS.)

Lanterns. Authors, literary men, and other inmates of Lantern-land (*q.v.*). Rabelais so calls the prelates and divines of the Council of Trent, who wasted the time in great displays of learning, to little profit; hence "lanternise" (*q.v.*).

Lanternise. Spending one's time in learned trifles; darkening counsel by words; mystifying the more by attempting to unravel mysteries; putting truths into a lantern through which, at best, we see but darkly. When monks bring their hoods over their faces "to meditate," they are said by the French to lanternise, because they look like the tops of lanterns; but the result of their meditations is that of a "brown study," or "fog of sleepy thought." (*See above.*)

Laocoon [*La-ok'-o-on*]. A son of Priam, famous for the tragic fate of himself and his two sons, who were crushed to death by serpents. The group representing these three in their death agony, now in the Vatican, was discovered in 1506, on the Esquiline Hill (Rome). It is a single block of marble, and was the work of Agesander of Rhodes and two other sculptors. Thomson has described the group in his *Liberty*, pt. iv. (*Virgil: Æneid*, ii. 40 etc., 212 etc.)

"The miserable sire,
Wrapped with his sons in Fate's severest grasp."

Laodami'a. The wife of Protesila'os, who was slain before Troy. She begged to be allowed to converse with her dead husband for only three hours, and her request was granted; when the respite was over, she accompanied the dead hero to the shades of death. Wordsworth has a poem on the subject.

Laodice'an. One indifferent to religion, caring little or nothing about the matter, like the Christians of that church, mentioned in the Book of Revelation (chapter iii. 14-18).

Lapet (*Mons.*). The beau-ideal of poltroonery. He would think the world out of joint if no one gave him a tweak of the nose or lug of the ear. (*Beaumont and Fletcher: Nice Valor, or the Passionate Madman.*)

Mons. Lapet was the author of a book on the punctilios of duelling.

Lap'ithæ. A people of Thessaly, noted for their defeat of the Centaurs. The subject of this contest was represented on the Parthĕnon, the Theseum at Athens, the Temple of Apollo at Basso, and on numberless vases. Raphael painted a picture of the same subject. (*Classic mythology.*)

Lapping Water. When Gideon's army was too numerous, the men were taken to a stream to drink, and 300 of them lapped water with their tongue; all the rest supped it up (Judg. vii. 4-7). All carnivorous animals lap water like dogs, all herbivorous animals suck it up like horses. The presumption is that the lappers of water partook of the carnivorous character, and were more fit for military exploits. No doubt those who fell on their knees to drink exposed themselves to danger far more than those who stood on their feet and lapped water from their hands.

Laprel. The rabbit, in the tale of *Reynard the Fox.* (French, *lapin*, rabbit.)

Lapsus Linguæ (*Latin*). A slip of the tongue, a mistake in uttering a word, an imprudent word inadvertently spoken.

We have also adopted the Latin phrases *lapsus calami* (a slip of the pen), and *lapsus memoriæ* (a slip of the memory).

Laputa. The flying island inhabited by scientific quacks, and visited by Gulliver in his "travels." These dreamy philosophers were so absorbed in their speculations that they employed attendants called "flappers," to flap them on the mouth and ears with a blown bladder when their attention was to be called off from "high things" to vulgar mundane matters. (*Swift.*)

"Realising in a manner the dreams of Laputa, and endeavouring to extract sunbeams from cucumbers."—*De Quincy.*

Lapwing (*The*). Shakespeare refers to two peculiarities of this bird; (1) to allure persons from its nest, it flies away and cries loudest when farthest from its nest; and (2) the young birds run from their shells with part thereof still sticking to their head.

"Far from her nest the lapwing cries away."
Comedy of Errors, iv. 2.
"This lapwing runs away with the shell on his head."—*Hamlet,* v. 2.

Lar Familia'ris (plu. *Lares familiares*). The familiar lar was the spirit of the founder of the house, which never left it, but accompanied his descendants in all their changes. (*See* LARES.)

La'ra. The name assumed by Lord Conrad, the Corsair, after the death of Medo'ra. He returned to his native land, and was one day recognised by Sir Ezzelin at the table of Lord Otho. Ezzelin charged him home, and a duel was arranged for the day following; but Ezzelin was never heard of more. In time Lara headed a rebellion, and was shot by Lord Otho, the leader of the other party. (*Byron: Lara.*) (*See* CONRAD.)

The seven infants of Lara. Gonzales Gustios de Salas de Lara, a Castilian hero of the eleventh century, had seven sons. His brother, Rodri'go Velasquez, married a Moorish lady, and these seven nephews were invited to the feast. A fray took place in which one of the seven slew a Moor, and the bride demanded vengeance. Rodri'go, to please his bride, waylaid his brother Gonzales, and kept him in durance in a dungeon of Cor'dova, and the seven boys were betrayed into a ravine, where they were cruelly murdered. While in the dungeon, Zaida, daughter of the Moorish king, fell in love with Gonzales, and became the mother of Mudarra, who avenged the death of Lara's seven sons by slaying Rodri'go.

Larboard, now called *port* (*q.v.*). (Starboard is from Anglo-Saxon *steorabord*, the steer-board, or right side of a ship.) Larboard is the French *bâbord*, the left-hand side of a ship looking towards the prow; Anglo-Saxon *bœc-bord*.

" She gave a heel, and then a lurch to port,
And going down head foremost—sunk in short."
Byron: Don Juan (The Shipwreck).

❧ "To give a heel" is to sway over on one side. Here it means a heel to the starboard side.

Larceny. Petty theft, means really the peculations and thefts of a mercenary. (Greek *latron*, hire [*latris*, a hireling] ; Latin *latro*, a mercenary, whence *latrocinium* ; French, *larcin*.)

Larder. A place for keeping lard or bacon. This shows that swine were the chief animals salted and preserved in olden times. (Latin, *lardum*, lard.)

The Douglas Larder. The English garrison and all its provisions in Douglas castle massed together by good Lord James Douglas, in 1307.

"He caused all the barrels containing flour, meat, wheat, and malt to be knocked in pieces, and their contents mixed on the floor ; then he staved the great hogsheads of wine and ale, and mixed the liquor with the stores ; and last of all, he killed the prisoners, and flung the dead bodies among this disgusting heap, which his men called, in derision of the English, 'The Douglas Larder.'"
—*Sir Walter Scott: Tales of a Grandfather, ix.*

Wallace's Larder is very similar. It consisted of the dead bodies of the garrison of Ardrossan, in Ayrshire, cast into the dungeon keep. The castle was surprised by Wallace in the reign of Edward I.

Larēs. The Etruscan *lar* (lord or hero). Among the Romans larēs were either domestic or public. *Domestic* lares were the souls of virtuous ancestors exalted to the rank of protectors. *Public* lares were the protectors of roads and streets. Domestic lares were images, like dogs, set behind the "hall" door, or in the lara'rium or shrine. Wicked souls became lem'urēs or ghosts that made night hideous. Pena'tēs were the natural powers personified, and their office was to bring wealth and plenty, rather than to protect and avert danger. (*See* FAIRY.)

Large. *To sail large* is to sail on a large wind—*i.e.* with the wind not straight astern, but what sailors call "abaft the beam."

Set at large, i.e. at liberty. It is a French phrase; *prendre le large* is to stand out at sea, or occupy the main ocean, so as to be free to move. Similarly, to be set at large is to be placed free in the wide world.

Lar'igot. *Boire à tire larigot.* To tope, to bouse. *Larigot* is a corruption of "*l'arigot*" (a limb), and *boire a tire l'arigot* means simply "to drink with all your might," as *jouer de l'arigot* means "to play your best"—*i.e.* "with all your power." It is absurd to derive the word *larigot* from "la Rigaud," according to Noel Taillepied, who says (*Rouen*, xlv.): "Au xiii. siècle, l'archevèque Eudes Rigaud fit présent à la ville de Rouen d'une cloche à laquelle resta son nom. Cette cloche était d'une grandeur et d'une grosseur, telles que ceux qui la mettaient en mouvement ne manquaient pas de boire abondamment pour reprendre des forces. De là l'habitude de comparer ceux qui buvaient beaucoup aux sonneurs chargés *de tirer la Rigaud*," *i.e.* the bell so called.

Lark. A spree ; a corruption of the Anglo-Saxon *lác* (play, fun). (*See* SKYLARK.)

Larks. *When the sky falls we shall catch larks.* A way of stating to a person that his scheme or proposal is absurd or ridiculous.

French: "Si le ciel tombait, il y aurait bien des alouettes."
Latin: "Quid, si redio ad illos, qui aiunt, quid si nunc cœlum ruat?"
Terence: Heautontimoroumenos, iv. 3 ; verse 41.

Larry Dugan's Eye-water. Blacking ; so called from Larry Dugan, a noted shoeblack of Dublin, whose face was always smudged with his blacking.

Lars. The overking of the ancient Etruscans, like the Welsh " pendragon." A satrap, or under-king, was a *lucŭmo.* Thus the king of Prussia is the German *lars*, and the king of Bavaria is a *lucumo.*

> There be thirty chosen prophets,
> The wisest of the land,
> Who always by Lars Por'sena,
> Both morn and evening stand."
> *Macaulay : Lays of Ancient Rome,*
> *(Horatius,* ix.)

Larvæ. Mischievous spectres. The larva or ghost of Caligula was often seen (according to Suetonius) in his palace.

Lascar. A native East Indian sailor in the British service. The natives of the East Indies call camp-followers *lascars.* (Hindu, *lash-kar*, a soldier.)

Last. (Anglo-Saxon *lást*, a footstep, a shoemaker's last.) *The cobbler should stick to his last* (" *Ne sutor ultra crep'-idam*"). Apelles having executed a famous painting, exposed it to public view, when a cobbler found fault because the painter had made too few latchets to the goloshes. Apelles amended the fault, and set out his picture again. Next day the cobbler complained of the legs, when Apelles retorted, " Keep to the shop, friend, but do not attempt to criticise what you do not understand." (*See* WIGS.)

Last Man (*The*). Charles I. was so called by the Parliamentarians, meaning that he would be the last king of Great Britain. His son, Charles II., was called *The Son of the Last Man.*

Last Man. A weirdly grotesque poem by Thomas Hood.

> " So there he hung, and there I stood,
> The last man left alive."

Last Words. (*See* DYING SAYINGS.)

Last of the Fathers. St. Bernard, Abbot of Clairvaux. (1091-1153.)

Last of the Goths. Roderick, who reigned in Spain from 414 to 711. Southey has an historic tale in blank verse on this subject.

Last of the Greeks. Philopœmen of Arcadia. (B.C. 253-183.)

Last of the Knights. (*See* KNIGHTS.)

Last of the Mo'hicans. The Indian chief, Uncas, is so called by Cooper, in his novel of that title.

Last of the Romans.

Marcus Junius Brutus, one of the murderers of Cæsar. (B.C. 85-42.)

Caius Cassius Longi'nus, so called by Brutus. (*Died* B.C. 42.)

Stilicho, the Roman general under Theodosius. (*The Nineteenth Century,* Sepember, 1892.)

Aëtius, a general who defended the Gauls against the Franks and other barbarians, and defeated Attila in the Champs Catalaumques, near Châlons, in 451. So called by Proco'pius.

François Joseph Terasse Desbillons; so called from the elegance and purity of his Latin. (1751-1789.)

Pope calls Congreve *Ultimus Romanorum.* (1670-1729.) (*See* ULTIMUS.)

Last of the Tribunes (*The*). Cola di Rienzi (1314 - 1354). Lord Lytton has a novel so called.

Last of the Troubadours. Jacques Jasmin, of Gascony (1798-1864).

Lat (*El*). A female idol made of stone, and said to be inspired with life; the chief object of adoration by the Arabs before their conversion.

Lăt, at Somanat in India, was a single stone fifty fathoms high, placed in the midst of a temple supported by fifty-six pillars of massive gold. This idol was broken in pieces by Mahmood Ibn-Sabuktigeen, who conquered that part of India. The granite Lat, facing a Jain temple at Mudubidery, near Mangalore, in India, is fifty-two feet high.

> " The granite lăt of Mudubidery, in India, is fifty-two feet high."

Lat'eran. The ancient palace of the Latera'ni, given by the Emperor Constantine to the popes. Lateran, from *lateo*, to hide, and *rana*, a frog. It is said that Nero . . . on one occasion vomited a frog covered with blood, which he believed to be his own progeny, and had it hidden in a vault. The palace which was built on the site of this vault was called the " Lateran," or the palace of the *hidden frog.* (*Buckle: History of Civilisation.*)

> The locality in Rome so called contains the Lateran palace, the Piazza, and the Basilica of St. John Lateran. The Basilica is the Pope's cathedral church. The palace (once a residence of the popes) is now a museum.

Lath or **Lathe.** A division of a county. Sometimes it was an intermediate division between a hundred and a shire, as the *lathes of Kent* and *rapes of Sussex*, each of which contained three or four " hundreds " apiece. In Ireland the arrangement was different. The officer over a lath was called a lathreeve. (Anglo-Saxon *læth*, a canton.)

"If all that tything failed, then all that lath was charged for that tything ; and if the lath failed, then all that hundred was demanded for them [*i.e.* turbulent fellows], and if the hundred, then the shire.—*Spenser : Ireland.*

Lather. *A good lather is half a shave.* This is the French proverb, "*Barbe bien savonné est à moitié faite.*"

Latin. The language spoken by the people of La'tium, in Italy. The Latins are called aborigines of Italy. Alba Longa was head of the Latin League, and, as Rome was a colony of Alba Longa, it is plain to see how the Roman tongue was Latin.

"The earliest extant specimen of the Latin language is a fragment of the hymn of the Fratres Arvāles (3 syl.), a priestly brotherhood, which offered, every 10th of May, a public sacrifice for the fertility of the fields."—*Sellar : Roman Poets of the Republic,* chap. ii. p. 34.

Classical Latin. The Latin of the best authors about the time of Augustus, as Livy, Tacitus, and Cicero (prose), Horace, Virgil, and Ovid (poets).

Late Latin. The period which followed the Augustan age. This period contains the Church Fathers.

Low Latin. Mediæval Latin, mainly bastard German, French, Italian, Spanish, and so on.

Middle Latin. Latin from the sixth to the sixteenth century A.D., both inclusive. In this Latin, prepositions frequently supply the cases of nouns.

New Latin. That which followed the revival of letters in the sixteenth century.

"Latium. The tale is that this word is from *lateo,* to lie hid, and was so called because Saturn lay hid there, when he was driven out of heaven by the gods."

The Latin Church. The Western Church, in contradistinction to the Greek or Eastern Church.

The Latin cross. Formed thus : †

.• The Greek cross has four equal arms, thus : +

Latin Learning, properly so called, terminated with Boe'thius, but continued to be used in literary compositions and in the services of the church.

Lati'nus. King of the Laurentians, a people of Latium. According to Virgil, Latīnus opposed Æneas on his first landing, but subsequently formed an alliance with him, and gave him Lavin'ia in marriage. Turnus, King of the Ru'tuli, declared that Lavinia had been betrothed to him, and prepared to support his claim by arms. It was agreed to decide the rival claims by single combat, and

Æne'as being victor, obtained Lavinia for his wife.

Lati'nus (in *Jerusalem Delivered*), an Italian, went with his five sons to the Holy War. His eldest son was slain by Solyman ; Aramantēs, going to his brother's aid, was also slain ; then Sabi'nus ; and lastly, Picus and Laurentēs, twins. The father now rushed on the soldan, and was slain also. In one hour the father and his five sons were all slain.

Latitudina'rians. A sect of divines in the time of Charles II., opposed both to the High Church party and to the Puritans. The term is now applied to those persons who hold very loose views of Divine inspiration and what are called orthodox doctrines.

Lato'na. Mother of Apollo and Diana. When she knelt by a fountain in Delos (infants in arms) to quench her thirst at a small lake, some Lycian clowns insulted her and were turned into frogs.

"As when those hinds that were transformed to frogs
Railed at Latona's twin-born progeny,
Which after held the sun and moon in fee."
Milton : Sonnets.

Latri'a and Duli'a. Greek words adopted by the Roman Catholics ; the former to express that supreme reverence and adoration which is offered to God alone ; and the latter, that secondary reverence and adoration which is offered to saints. (*Latria* is the reverence of a *latris,* or hired servant, who receives wages ; *dulia* is the reverence of a *doulos* or slave.)

Lattice or *Chequers.* A public-house sign, the arms of Fitzwarren, the head of which house, in the days of the Henrys, was invested with the power of licensing the establishments of vintners and publicans. Houses licensed notified the same by displaying the Fitzwarren arms. (*The Times,* April 29, 1869.)

The Fitzwarren arms were chequy *or* and *gules,* hence public-houses and their signs are still frequently called the "Red Lattices."

"A' calls me e'en now, my lord, through a red lattice."—*Shakespeare :* 2 *Henry IV.,* ii. 2.

Laugh in One's Sleeve (*To*). The French is : "*Rire sous cape,*" or "*Rire sous son bonnet.*" The German is : "*Ins faüstchen lachen.*" The Latin is : "*In stomacho ridēre.*" These expressions indicate secret derision ; laughing *at* one, not *with* one. But such phrases as "*In sinu gaudēre*" mean to feel secret joy, to rejoice in one's heart of hearts.

Laugh on the Other Side of Your Mouth.

To make a person laugh on the other side of his mouth is to make him cry, or to cause him annoyance. To "laugh on the wrong side of one's face" is to be humiliated, or to lament from annoyance.

"Thou laughest there: by-and-by thou wilt laugh on the wrong side of thy face."—*Carlyle: The Diamond Necklace*, chap. iii.

Laughing Philosopher. Democ'ritos of Abde'ra, who viewed with supreme contempt the feeble powers of man. (B.C. 460-357.) (*See* WEEPING PHILOSOPHER.)

Laughing-stock. A butt for jokes.

Laughter. We are told that Jupiter, after his birth, laughed incessantly for seven days.

Calchas, the Homeric soothsayer, died of laughter. The tale is that a fellow in rags told him he would never drink of the grapes growing in his vineyard, and added, if his words did not come true he would be the soothsayer's slave. When the wine was made, Calchas, at a great feast, sent for the fellow, and laughed so incessantly at the non-fulfilment of the prophecy that he died. (*E. Bulwer Lytton: Tales of Miletus*, iv.)

✶ (*See* ANCÆUS and DEATH FROM STRANGE CAUSES.)

Launce. The clownish serving-man of Proteus, famous for his soliloquies to his dog Crab. (*Shakespeare: Two Gentlemen of Verona.*)

Launcelet. (*See* LANCELOT.)

Launched into Eternity. Hanged.

"He ate several oranges on his passage, inquired if his lordship was ready, and then, as old Rowe used to say, 'was launched into eternity'—*Gilly Williams to Lord Harrington.* (This man was his lordship's servant, hanged for robbery.)

Launfal (*Sir*). Steward of King Arthur. He so greatly disliked Queen Gwennere, daughter of Ryon, King of Ireland, that he feigned illness and retired to Carlyoun, where he lived in great poverty. Having obtained the loan of a horse, he rode into a forest, and while he rested himself on the grass two damsels came to him, who invited him to rest in their lady's bower hard by. Sir Launfal accepted the invitation, and fell in love with the lady, whose name was Tryamour. Tryamour gave the knight an unfailing purse, and when he left told him if he ever wished to see her all he had to do was to retire into a private room, and she would instantly be with him. Sir Launfal now returned to court, and excited much attention by

his great wealth; but having told Gwennere, who solicited his love, that she was not worthy to kiss the feet of his lady-love, the queen accused him to Arthur of insulting her person. Thereupon Arthur told him, unless he made good his word by producing this paragon of women, he should be burned alive. On the day appointed, Tryamour arrived; Launfal was set at liberty and accompanied his mistress to the isle of Ole'ron, and no man ever saw him more. (*Thomas Chester: Sir Launfal, a metrical romance of Henry VI.'s time.*)

Laura, the name immortalised by Petrarch, was either the wife of Hugues de Sade, of Avignon, or a fictitious name used by him on which to hang incidents of his life and love. If the former, her maiden name was Laura de Noves.

Laura. Beppo's wife. (*See* BEPPO.)

Lauras. (Greek, *laura.*) An aggregation of separate cells under the control of a superior. In monasteries the monks live under one roof; in lauras they live each in his own cell apart; but on certain occasions they assemble and meet together, sometimes for a meal, and sometimes for a religious service.

Laureate. Poets so called from an ancient custom in our universities of presenting a laurel wreath to graduates in rhetoric and poetry. Young aspirants were wreathed with laurels in berry (*orné de baies de laurier*). Authors are still so "crowned" in France. The poets laureate of the two last centuries have been—

Ben Jonson, 1615, appointed by King James.
Sir William Davenant, 1637.
John Dryden, 1670.
Thomas Shadwell, 1688.
Nahum Tate, 1692.
Nicholas Rowe, 1715.
Laurence Eusden, 1718.
Colley Cibber, 1730.
William Whitehead, 1757
Thomas Warton, 1783.
Henry James Pye, 1790.
Robert Southey, 1813.
William Wordsworth, 1844.
Alfred Tennyson, 1850.
Alfred Austin, 1896.

Six or seven of these are almost unknown, and their productions are seldom read.

Laurel. The Greeks gave a wreath of laurels to the victor in the Pythian games, but the victor in the Olympic games had a wreath of wild olives, the victor in the Neme'an games a wreath of green parsley, and the victor in the Isthmian games a wreath of dry parsley or green pine-leaves. (*See* CROWN.)

Laurel. The ancients believed that laurel communicated the spirit of prophecy and poetry. Hence the custom of crowning the pythoness and poets, and of *putting laurel leaves under one's pillow* to acquire inspiration. Another superstition was that the bay laurel was antagonistic to the stroke of lightning; but Sir Thomas Browne, in his *Vulgar Errors*, tells us that Vicomereatus proves from personal knowledge that this is by no means true.

Laurel, in modern times, is a symbol of victory and peace. St. Gudule, in Christian art, carries a laurel crown.

Laurence (*Friar*). The Franciscan friar who undertakes to marry Romeo and Juliet. To save Juliet from a second marriage he gives her a sleeping draught, and she is carried to the family vault as dead. Romeo finds her there, and believing her sleep to be the sleep of death, kills himself. On waking, Juliet discovers Romeo dead at her side, and kills herself also. (*Shakespeare: Romeo and Juliet*.) (*See* LAWRENCE.)

Lavaine', *Sir* (2 syl.). Brother of Elaine', and son of the lord of As'tolat. He accompanied Sir Lancelot when he went, *incognito*, to tilt for the ninth diamond. Lavaine is described as young, brave, and a true knight. (*Tennyson: Idylls of the King; Elaine*.)

Lavalette (Marquis de), a French statesman who was condemned to death for sending secret despatches to Napoleon, was set at liberty by his wife, who took his place in the prison.

Lord Nithsdale escaped in a similar way from the Tower of London. His wife disguised him as her maid, and with her he passed the sentries and made good his escape.

Lavender. From the Spanish *lavandera* (a laundress), the plant used by laundresses for scenting linen. The botanical name is *Lavandula*, from the Latin *lavo*, to wash. It is a token of affection.

" He from his lass him lavender hath sent,
  Showing his love, and doth requital crave ;
  Him rosemary his sweetheart, whose intent
  Is that he should her in remembrance have."
      Drayton: Eclogue, ix.

Laid up in lavender—i.e. taken great care of, laid away, as women put things away in lavender to keep off moths. Persons who are in hiding are said to be in lavender. The French have the phrase "*Elever dans du coton,*" referring to the custom of wrapping up things precious in cotton wool.

" Je veux que tu sois chez moi, comme dans du coton."—*La Muscotte*, i. 2,

In lavender. In pawn. In Latin, *pignŏri oppŏnĕre.*

"The poor gentleman paies so deare for the lavender it is laid up in, that if it lies long at the broker's house he seems to buy his apparel twice."
—*Greene: Imp. Har. Misc.*, v. 405.

Lavin'ia. Daughter of Lati'nus, betrothed to Turnus, King of the Rutuli. When Æneas landed in Italy, Latinus made an alliance with the Trojan hero, and promised to give him Lavin'ia to wife. This brought on a war between Turnus and Æneas, which was decided by single combat, in which Æneas was victor. (*Virgil: Æneid.*)

Lavinia. The daughter of Titus Andron'icus, bride of Bassia'nus, brother of the Emperor of Rome. Being grossly abused by Chiron and Demetrius, sons of Tam'ora, Queen of the Goths, the savage wantons cut off her hands and pluck out her tongue, that she may not reveal their names. Lavinia, guiding a stick with her stumps, makes her tale known to her father and brothers; whereupon Titus murders the two Moorish princes and serves their heads in a pasty to their mother, whom he afterwards slays, together with the Emperor Saturni'nus her husband. (*Titus Andron'icus, a play published with those of Shakespeare.*)

❡ In the play the word is accented Andron'icus not Androni'cus.

Lavinia. Italy; so called from Lavinia, daughter of Lati'nus and wife of Æneas. Æneas built a town which he called Lavin'ium, capital of La'tium.

" From the rich Lavinian shore
  I your market come to store."
      A well-known Glee.

Lavin'ia and Pale'mon. A free poetical version of Ruth and Boaz, by Thomson in his *Autumn*.

Lavolt or **Lavolta.** (French, *la volte*.) A lively dance, in which was a good deal of jumping or capering, whence its name. Troilus says, "I cannot sing, nor heel the high lavolt" (iv. 4). It is thus described:—

" A lofty jumping or a leaping round,
  Where arm in arm two dancers are entwined,
  And whirl themselves with strict embracements bound,
  And still their feet an anapest do sound."
      Sir John Davies.

Law. *To give one law.* A sporting term, meaning the chance of saving oneself. Thus a hare or a stag is allowed "law"—*i.e.* a certain start before any hound is permitted to attack it; and a tradesman allowed law is one to whom time is given to "find his legs."

Quips of the law, called "devices of Cépola," from Bartholemew Cépola, whose law-quirks, teaching how to elude the most express law, and to perpetuate lawsuits *ad infini'tum*, have been frequently reprinted — once in octavo, in black letter, by John Petit, in 1503.

The Man of Lawes Tale, by Chaucer. This story is found in Gower, who probably took it from the French chronicle of Nicholas Trivet. A similar story forms the plot of *Em'are*, a romance printed in Ritson's collection. The treason of the knight who murders Hermengilde resembles an incident in the French *Roman de la Violette*, the English metrical romance of *Le bone Florence of Rome* (in Ritson), and a tale in the *Gesta Romanorum*, c. 69 (Madden's edition). (*See* CONSTANCE.)

Law Latin. (*See* DOG LATIN.)

Law's Bubble. The famous Mississippi scheme, devised by John Law, for paying off the national debt of France (1716-1720). By this "French South-Sea Bubble" the nation was almost ruined. It was called Mississippi because the company was granted the "exclusive trade of Louisia'na on the banks of the Mississippi."

Laws of the Medes and Persians. Unalterable laws.

"Now, O king, ... sign the writing, that it be not changed, according to the law of the Medes and Persians which altereth not."—*Daniel vi. 8.*

The Laws of Howel Dha, who reigned in South Wales in the tenth century, printed with a Latin translation by Wotton, in his *Leges Wallicæ* (1841).

Lawing. (Scots.) A tavern reckoning.

Lawsuits. Miles d'Illiers, Bishop of Chartres (1459-1493), was so litigious, that when Louis XI. gave him a pension to clear off old scores, and told him in future to live in peace and goodwill with his neighbours, the bishop earnestly entreated the king to leave him some three or four to keep his mind in good exercise. Similarly Panurge entreated Pantag'ruel not to pay off all his debts, but to leave some centimes at least, that he might not feel altogether a stranger to his own self. (*Rabelais: Pantagruel*, iii. 5.) (*See* LILBURN.)

Lawn. Fine, thin cambric bleached on a lawn, instead of the ordinary bleaching grounds. It is used for the sleeves of bishops, and sometimes for ladies' handkerchiefs.

Lawn-market (*The*). *To go up the Lawn-market*, in Scotch parlance, means to go to be hanged.

"Up the Lawn-market, down the West Bow,
Up the lang ladder, down the short low."
Schoolboy Rhyme (Scotland).

"They [the stolen clothes] may serve him to gang up the Lawn-market in, the scoundrel."—*Sir W. Scott: Guy Mannering*, chap. xxxii.

Lawrence (*St.*). Patron saint of curriers, because his skin was broiled on a gridiron. In the pontificate of Sextus I. he was charged with the care of the poor, the orphans, and the widows. In the persecution of Vale'rian, being summoned to deliver up the treasures of the church, he produced the poor, etc., under his charge, and said to the prætor, "These are the church's treasures." In Christian art he is generally represented as holding a gridiron in his hand. He is the subject of one of the principal hymns of Prudentius. (*See* LAURENCE.)

St. Lawrence's tears or *The fiery tears of St. Lawrence*. Meteoric or shooting stars, which generally make a great display on the anniversary of this saint (August 10th).

⁂ The great periods of shooting stars are between the 9th and 14th of August, from the 12th to the 14th of November, and from 6th to 12th December.

Tom Lawrence, alias "Tyburn Tom" or "Tuck." A highwayman. (*Sir Walter Scott: Heart of Mid-Lothian.*)

Lawyer's Bags. Some red, some blue. In the Common Law, *red* bags are reserved for Q.C.'s and Sergeants; but a stuff-gownsman may carry one "if presented with it by a silk." Only *red* bags may be taken into Common Law Courts, *blue* must be carried no farther than the robing-room. In Chancery Courts the etiquette is not so strict.

Lay Brothers. Men not in orders received into the convents and bound by vows. (Greek, *laŏs*, people.)

Lay Figures. Wooden figures with free joints, used by artists chiefly for the study of drapery. This is a metaphorical use of lay. As divines divide the world into two parties, the ecclesiastics and the laity, so artists divide their models into two classes, the living and the lay.

Lay Out (*To*). (*a*) To disburse: *Il dépensa de grandes sommes d'argent.*

(*b*) To display goods: *Mettre des marchandises en montre.* To place in convenient order what is required for wear: *Préparer ses beaux habits.*

(*c*) To prepare a corpse for the coffin,

by placing the limbs in order, and dressing the body in its grave-clothes.

Lay about One (*To*). To strike on all sides.

"He'll lay about him to-day."—*Shakespeare:
Troilus and Cressida,* i. 2.

Lay by the Heels (*To*). To render powerless. The allusion is to the stocks, in which vagrants and other petty offenders were confined by the ankles, locked-in what was called the stocks, common, at one time, to well-nigh every village in the land.

Lay of the Last Minstrel. (For plot *see* MARGARET.)

Lay to One's Charge (*To*). To attribute an offence to a person.

"And he [Stephen] kneeled down, and cried with a loud voice, Lord lay not this sin to their charge."—Acts vii. 60. The phrase occurs again in the Bible, *e.g.* Deut. xxi. 8; Rom. viii. 33, etc.

Lay'amon, who wrote a translation in Saxon of the *Brut* of Wace, in the twelfth century, is called *The English Ennius.* (*See* ENNIUS.)

Layers-over for Meddlers. Nothing that concerns you. A reproof to inquisitive children who want to know what a person is doing or making, when the person so engaged does not think proper to inform them. A "layer-over" is a whip or slap. And a "layer-over for meddlers" is a whip or chastisement for those who meddle with what does not concern them.

Lazar House or **Lazaretto.** A house for poor persons affected with contagious diseases. So called from the beggar Lazarus (*q.v.*).

Laz'arists. A body of missionaries founded by St. Vincent de Paul in 1624, and so termed from the priory of St. Lazáre, at Paris, which was their headquarters from 1632 to 1792.

Lazarillo de Tormës (1553). A comic romance, something in the *Gil Blas* style, the object being to satirise all classes of society. Lazarillo, a light, jovial, audacious man-servant, sees his masters in their undress, and exposes their foibles. This work was written by Diego Hurtado de Mendoza, general and statesman of Spain, author of *War against the Moors.*

Lazaro'ne (3 syl.); Italian *Lazzaro,* plu. *Lazzarŏni.* The mob. Originally applied to all those people of Naples who lived in the streets, not having any habitation of their own. So called from the hospital of St. Lazarus, which

served as a refuge for the destitute of that city. Every year they elected a chief, called the *Capo Lazzaro.* Masaniello, in 1647, with these vagabonds accomplished the revolution of Naples. In 1798 Michele Sforza, at the head of the Lazzaroni, successfully resisted Etienne Championnet, the French general.

Lazarus. Any poor beggar; so called from the Lazarus of the parable, who was laid daily at the rich man's gate (St. Luke xvi.).

La'zy.

Lazy as David Lawrence's dog. Here Lawrence is a corruption of Larrence, an imaginary being supposed by Scottish peasantry to preside over the lazy and indolent. Laziness is called "Larrence." (*See and compare* DAVY JONES.)

Lazy as Joe, the marine, who laid down his musket to sneeze. (*Sailor's proverb.*)

Lazy as Ludlam's dog, which leaned his head against the wall to bark. This Ludlam was the famous sorceress of Surrey, who lived in a cave near Farnham, called "Ludlam's Cave." She kept a dog, noted for its laziness, so that when the rustics came to consult the witch, it would hardly condescend to give notice of their approach, even with the ghost of a bark. (*Ray: Proverbs.*)

Lazy Lawrence of Lubberland. The hero of a popular tale. He served the schoolmaster, the squire's cook, the farmer, and his own wife, which was accounted high treason in Lubberland. One of Miss Edgeworth's tales, in the *Parents' Assistant,* is called *Lazy Lawrence.*

Lazy Lobkin (*A*). A lob (says Halliwell) is "the last person in a race." (*Somersetshire*). (Welsh *llob,* a dolt, our "lubber.")

"A lazy lobkin, like an idle loute."
Breton: Olde Madcappes, etc. (1602).

Lazy Man's Load. One too heavy to be carried; so called because lazy people, to save themselves the trouble of coming a second time, are apt to overload themselves.

Lazyland (*Gone to*). Given up to indolence and idleness.

Lazzaro'ni. (*See* LAZARONE.)

L'État c'est Moi (*I am the State*). The saying and belief of Louis XIV. On this principle he acted with tolerable consistency.

Le Roi le Veut (*French,* The king wills it.) The form of royal assent made by the clerk of parliament to bills submitted to the Crown. The dissent is expressed by *Le roi s'avisera* (the king will give it his consideration).

Le'a. One of the "daughters of men," beloved by one of the "sons of God." The angel who loved her ranked with the least of the spirits of light, whose post around the throne was in the uttermost circle. Sent to earth on a message, he saw Lea bathing and fell in love with her ; but Lea was so heavenly-minded that her only wish was to "dwell in purity, and serve God in singleness of heart." Her angel lover, in the madness of his passion, told Lea the spell-word that gave him admittance into heaven. The moment Lea uttered that word her body became spiritual, rose through the air, and vanished from his sight. On the other hand, the angel lost his ethereal nature, and became altogether earthy, like a child of clay." (*Moore : Loves of the Angels*, story 1.)

Lea'ba na Feine [*Beds of the Feïne*]. The name of several large piles of stones in Ireland. The ancient Irish warriors were called Fe'-i-ne, which some mistake for Phœni (Carthaginians), but which means *hunters*.

Leach, Leachcraft. A leach is one skilled in medicine, and "leach-craft" is the profession of a medical man. (Anglo-Saxon, *læce*, one who relieves pain, *læcecræft*.)

" And straightway sent, with carefull diligence,
To fetch a leach the which had great insight
In that disease."
Spenser : Faërie Queene, book i. canto x. line 23.

Lead (pronounced *led*), the metal, was, by the ancient alchemists, called Saturn. (Anglo-Saxon, *lead*.)

To strike lead. To make a good hit.

"That, after the failure of the king, he should 'strike lead' in his own house seemed . . . an inevitable law."—*Bret Harte : Fool of Five Forks.*

Lead (pronounce *leed*). (Anglo-Saxon *læd-an*.)

To lead apes in hell. (*See* APES.)

To lead by the nose. (*See* under NOSE.)

To lead one a pretty dance. (*See* under DANCE.)

Leaden Hail (*Showers of*). That of artillery in the battlefield.

Leaden Hall (pronounce *led'en*), so named from the ancient manor of Sir Hugh Neville, whose mansion or hall was roofed with lead, a notable thing in his days. "Leadenhall Street" and "Leadenhall Market," London, are on the site of Sir Hugh's manor.

24

Leader (*A*) or *a leading article.* A newspaper article in large type, by the editor or one of the editorial staff. So called because it takes the lead or chief place in the summary of current topics, or because it is meant to lead public opinion.

⁇ The first fiddle of an orchestra and the first cornet-a-piston of a military band is called the *leader.*

Leading Case (*A*). A lawsuit to settle others of a similar kind.

Leading Note in music. The sharp seventh of the diatonic scale, which *leads* to the octave, only half a tone higher.

Leading Question. A question so worded as to suggest an answer. "Was he dressed in a black coat ? " leads to the answer "Yes." In cross-examining a witness, leading questions are permitted, because the chief object of a cross-examination is to obtain contradictions.

Leading Strings. *To be in leading-strings* is to be under the control of another. Leading-strings are those strings used for holding up infants just learning to walk.

Leaf. Before the invention of paper one of the substances employed for writing was the leaves of certain plants. In the British Museum are some writings on leaves from the Malabar coast, and several copies of the Bible written on palm-leaves. The reverse and obverse pages of a book are still called leaves ; and the double page of a ledger is termed a "folio," from *folium* (a leaf).

Leaf. (Anglo-Saxon *leáf.*)

To take a leaf out of [*my*] *book.* To imitate me ; to do as I do. The allusion is to literary plagiarisms.

To turn over a new leaf. To amend one's ways. The French equivalent is : "*Je lui ferai chanter une autre chanson.*" But in English, "To make a person sing another tune," means to make him eat his words, or change his note for one he will not like so well.

League.

The Grey League [*lia grischa*], 15th century. So called from the grey home-spun dress adopted by the leaguers.

The Holy League. Several leagues are so denominated. The three following are the most important : 1511, by Pope Julius II. ; Ferdinand the Catholic, Henry VIII., the Venetians, and the Swiss against Louis XII. ; and that of 1576, founded at Péronne for the maintenance of the Catholic faith and the exclusion of Protestant princes from the throne of France. This league was organised by the Guises to keep Henri IV. from the throne.

Leak Out (*To*). To come clandestinely to public knowledge. As a liquid leaks out of an unsound vessel, so the secret oozes out unawares.

Leal. Loyal, trusty, law-abiding. Norman-French, *leyale*, modern French, *loyale ;* Latin, *legālis*.)

Land of the leal. (*See* LAND . . .)

Lean'der (3 syl.) A young man of Aby'dos, who swam nightly across the Hellespont to visit his lady-love, Hero, a priestess of Sestos. One night he was drowned in his attempt, and Hero leaped into the Hellespont also. This story is told in one of the poems of Musæus, entitled *Hero and Leander*. (*See* Marlowe's poem.) (*See* HERO.)

⁂ Lord Byron and Lieutenant Ekenhead repeated the experiment of Leander and accomplished it in 1 hour 10 minutes. The distance, allowing for drifting, would be about four miles. A young man of St. Croix, in 1817, swam over the Sound from Cronenburgh, in 2 hours 40 minutes, the distance being six miles.

Leaning Tower. The one at Pisa, in Italy, is 178 feet in height, and leans about 14 feet. At Caerphilly, in Glamorganshire, there is a tower which leans eleven feet in eighty.

"The Leaning Tower of Pisa continues to stand because the vertical line drawn through its centre of gravity passes within its base."—*Ganot: Physics.*

Leap Year. Every year divisible by four. Such years occur every fourth year. In ordinary years the day of the month which falls on Monday this year, will fall on Tuesday next year, and Wednesday the year after: but the fourth year will leap over Thursday to Friday. This is because a day is added to February, which, of course, affects every subsequent day of the year. (*See* BISSEXTILE.)

The ladies propose, and, if not accepted, claim a silk gown. St. Patrick, having "driven the frogs out of the bogs," was walking along the shores of Lough Neagh, when he was accosted by St. Bridget in tears, and was told that a mutiny had broken out in the nunnery over which she presided, the ladies claiming the right of "popping the question." St. Patrick said he would concede them the right every seventh year. When St. Bridget threw her arms round his neck,

and exclaimed, "Arrah, Pathrick, jewel, I daurn't go back to the girls wid such a proposal. Make it one year in four." St. Patrick replied, "Bridget, acushla, squeeze me that way agin, an' I'll give ye leap-year, the longest of the lot." St. Bridget, upon this, popped the question to St. Patrick himself, who, of course, could not marry ; so he patched up the difficulty as best he could with a kiss and a silk gown.

⁂ The story told above is of no historic value, for an Act of the Scottish Parliament, passed in the year 1228, has been unearthed which runs thus :—

"Ordonit that during ye reign of her maist blessed maiestie, Margaret, ilka maiden, ladee of baith high and lowe estait, shall hae libertie to speak ye man she likes. Gif he refuses to tak hir to bee his wyf, he shale be mulct in the sum of ane hundridty pundes, or less, as his estait may bee, except and alwais gif he can make it appeare that he is betrothit to anither woman, then he schal be free."

N.B. The year 1228 was, of course, a leap-year.

Leap in the Dark (*A*). Thomas Hobbes is reported to have said on his death-bed, "Now am I about to take my last voyage—a great leap in the dark." Rabelais, in his last moments, said, "I am going to the Great Perhaps." Lord Derby, in 1868, applied the words, "We are about to take a leap in the dark," to the Reform Bill.

Lear (*King*). A legendary king of Britain, who in his old age divided his kingdom between Goneril and Regan, two of his daughters, who professed great love for him. These two daughters drove the old man mad by their unnatural conduct. (*Shakespeare : King Lear.*)

Percy, in his *Reliques of Ancient English Poetry*, has a ballad about *King Leir and his Three Daughters* (series i. book 2).

Camden tells a similar story of Ina, King of the West Saxons (*see Remains*, p. 306, edition 1674). The story of King Lear is given by Geoffrey of Monmouth in his *Chronicles*, whence Holinshed transcribed it. Spenser has introduced the same story into his *Faërie Queene*, book ii. canto 10.

Learn (1 syl.). *Live and learn.*

Cato, the censor, was an old man when he taught himself Greek.

Michael Angelo, at seventy years of age, said, "I am still learning."

John Kemble wrote out Hamlet thirty times, and said, on quitting the stage, "I am now beginning to understand my art."

Mrs. Siddons, after she left the stage, was found studying Lady Macbeth, and said, "I am amazed to discover some new points in the character which I never found out while acting it."

Milton, in his blindness, when past fifty, sat down to complete his *Paradise Lost*.

Scott, at fifty-five, took up his pen to redeem an enormous liability.

Richardson was above fifty when he published his first novel, *Pam'ela*.

Benjamin West was sixty-four when he commenced his series of paintings, one of which is *Christ Healing the Sick*.

Learn by Heart (*To*). The heart is the seat of understanding; thus the Scripture speaks of men "wise in heart;" and "slow of heart" means dull of understanding. To learn by heart is to learn and understand : to learn by *rote* is to learn so as to be able to repeat; to learn by memory is to commit to memory without reference to understanding what is so learnt. However, we employ the phrase commonly as a synonym for committing to memory.

Learned (2 syl.). Coloman, king of Hungary, was called *The Learned* (1095-1114). (*See* BEAUCLERC.)

The Learned Blacksmith. Elihu Burritt, the linguist, who was at one time a blacksmith (1811-1879).

The Learned Painter. Charles Lebrun, so called from the great accuracy of his costumes (1619-1690).

The Learned Tailor. Henry Wild, of Norwich, who mastered, while he worked at his trade, the Greek, Latin, Hebrew, Chaldaic, Syriac, Persian, and Arabic languages (1684-1734).

Least Said the soonest Mended (*The*) or **The Less Said** . . . Explanations and apologies are quite useless, and only make bad worse.

Leather. *Nothing like leather.* My interest is the best nostrum. A town, in danger of a siege, called together a council of the chief inhabitants to know what defence they recommended. A mason suggested a strong wall, a shipbuilder advised "wooden walls," and when others had spoken, a currier arose and said, "There's nothing like leather."

In Botallack, Cornwall, a standing toast is *Tin and Pilchards*, the staples of the town.

.·. Another version is, "Nothing like leather to administer a thrashing."

Leather or Prunella. *It is all leather or prunella.* Nothing of any

moment, all rubbish. **Prunella is a** woollen stuff, used for the uppers of ladies' boots and shoes. (*See* SALT.)

" Worth makes the man, and want of it the fellow;
   The rest is all but leather or prunella."
                              Pope : Essay on Man.

Leathering. *To give one a leathering* is to beat him with a leather belt, such as policemen wear, and boys used to wear. (The Welsh *lathen* is a rod.)

Leatherstocking (*Natty*). The nickname of Natty Bumpo (*q.v.*), in Cooper's novel, called *The Pioneers*. A half-savage and half-Christian hero of American wild life.

Leave in the Lurch (*To*). (*See* LEFT IN THE LURCH.)

Leave out in the Cold (*To*). To slight, to take little or no interest in a person; to pass by unnoticed. The allusion is to a person calling at a house with a friend and the friend not being asked to come in.

Leave some for Manners. In Ecclesiasticus it is written :

" Leave off first for manners' sake ; and be not unsatiable, lest thou offend."—Chap. xxxi. 17.

Leaves without Figs. Show of promise without fulfilment. Words without deeds. Keeping the promise to the ear and breaking it to the sense. Of course, the allusion is to the barren figtree referred to in Luke xiii.

Led Captain (*A*). An obsequious person, who dances attendance on the master and mistress of a house, for which service he has a knife and fork at the dinner table. He is led like a dog, and always graced with the title of captain.

Le'da and the Swan. This has been a favourite subject with artists. In the Orléans gallery is the *chef-d'œuvre* of Paul Veronese. Correggio and Michael Angelo have both left paintings of the same subject.

Ledger (*A*). A book "laid up" in the counting-house, and containing the debits and credits of the merchant or tradesman, arranged under "heads." (Dutch *legen*, to lay ; whence *legger*.)

Ledger-lines, in music, are lines which lie above or below the staff. (Dutch *legger*, to lie.)

Lee. *Under the lee of the land.* Under the shelter of the cliffs which break the force of the winds. (Anglo-Saxon, *hleo*, a shelter.)

Under the lee of a ship. On the side

opposite to the wind, so that the ship shelters or wards it off.

To lay a ship by the lee, or, in modern nautical phraseology, to heave-to, is to arrange the sails of a ship so that they may lie flat against the masts and shrouds, that the wind may strike the vessel broadside so that she will make little or no headway.

Lee Hatch. *Take care of the lee hatch.* Take care, helmsman, that the ship goes not to the leeward of her course—*i.e.* the part towards which the wind blows.

Lee Shore is the shore under the lee of a ship, or that towards which the wind blows. (*See* Lee.)

Lee-side and *Weather-side.* (*See* Leeward.)

Lee Tide, or **Leeward Tide,** is a tide running in the same direction as the wind blows. A tide in the opposite direction is called *a tide under the lee.*

Leeds (a Stock Exchange term). Lancashire and Yorkshire Railway Ordinary Stock. It is the Leeds line.

The Austrian Leeds. Brünn, in Moravia, noted for its woollen cloth. So it was called in the palmy days of Austria.

Leek. *Wearing the leek on St. David's day.* Mr. Brady says St. David caused the Britons under King Cadwallader to distinguish themselves by a leek in their caps. They conquered the Saxons, and recall their victory by adopting that leek on every anniversary (March 1st). (*Clavis Calendaria.*) Wearing the leek is obsolete. (Anglo-Saxon *leác.*)

Shakespeare makes out that the Welsh wore leeks at the battle of Poitiers, for Fluellen says :—

"If your majesties is remembered of it, the Welshmen did good service in a garden where leeks did grow, wearing leeks in their Monmouth caps, which, your majesty know, to this hour is an honourable badge of the service ; and I do believe your majesty takes no scorn to wear the leek upon St. Tavy's Day."—*Henry V.,* iv. 7.

To eat the leek. To be compelled to eat your own words, or retract what you have said. Fluellen (in Shakespeare's *Henry V.*) is taunted by Pistol for wearing a leek in his hat. "Hence," says Pistol, "I am qualmish at the smell of leek." Fluellen replies, "I peseech you . . . at my desire . . . to eat this leek." The ancient answers, "Not for Cadwallader and all his goats." Then the peppery Welshman beats him, nor desists till Pistol has swallowed the entire abhorrence.

Lees. *There are lees to every wine.* The best things have some defect. A French proverb.

"Doubt is the lees of thought."
Boker : Doubt, etc., i. 11.

Settling on the lees. Making the best of a bad job ; settling down on what is left, after having squandered the main part of one's fortune.

Leet (*A*). A manor-court for petty offences ; the day on which such a court was held. (Anglo-Saxon, *lethe,* a law-court superior to the wapentake.)

"Who has a breast so pure,
But some uncleanly apprehensions
Keep leets and law-days and in session sit
With meditations lawful ? "
Shakespeare : Othello, iii. 3.

Leeward and *Windward.* Leeward is toward the lee, or that part towards which the wind blows ; *windward* is in the opposite direction, viz. in the teeth of the wind. "Leeward," pronounced *leu-erd.* · (*See* Lee.)

Lefevre. The poor lieutenant whose story is so touchingly told in Sterne's *Tristram Shandy* book vi. chap. 6).

Left, unlucky ; *Right* lucky. The augur among the Romans having taken his stand on the Capit'oline Hill, and marked out with his wand the space of the heavens to be the field of observation, divided the space into two from top to bottom. If the birds appeared on the left side of the division, the augury was unlucky, but if the birds appeared on the right side the augury was pronounced to be favourable.

"'Hail, gentle bird, turn thy wings and fly on my right hand !' but the bird flew on the left side. Then the cat grew very heavy, for he knew the omen to be unlucky."—*Reynard the Fox,* iii.

The Left, in the Legislative Assembly of France, meant the Girondists ; it was famous for its orators. In the House of Commons the Opposition occupies the left-hand side of the Speaker. In the Austrian Assembly the democratic party is called *The Left.*

Over the left. A way of expressing disbelief, incredulity, or a negative. The allusion is to morganatic marriages (*q.v.*). When a woman so married claimed to be a wedded wife, she was told that such was the case "over the left." (*See below.*)

Sinister (the left hand), meaning not straightforward, dishonest, is far older than morganatic marriages. The ancient Greek augurs considered all signs seen by them over the left shoulder to be unlucky, and foreboding evil to come. Plutarch, following Plato and

Aristotle, gives as the reason, that the west (or left side of the augur) was towards the setting or departing sun.

Left-handed Compliment (*A*). A compliment which insinuates a reproach. (*See below.*)

Left-handed Marriage. A morganat'ic marriage (*q.v.*). In these marriages the husband gives his left hand to the bride, instead of the right, when he says, "I take thee for my wedded wife." George William, Duke of Zell, married Eleanora d'Esmiers in this way, and the lady took the name and title of Lady of Harburg; her daughter was Sophia Dorothe'a, the wife of George I.

Left-handed Oath (*A*). An oath not intended to be binding. (*See above.*)

Left in the Lurch. Left to face a great perplexity. In cribbage a lurch is when a player has scored only thirty holes, while his opponent has made sixty-one, and thus won a double.

Leg (*A*), that is, a blackleg (*q.v.*). *To make a leg*, is to make a bow.

"The pursuivant smiled at their simplicitye,
And making many leggs, tooke their reward."
The King and Miller of Mansfield.

Leg-bail. A runaway. *To give leg-bail*, to cut and run.

Leg-bye (*A*), in cricket, is a run scored from a ball which has glanced off any part of a batsman's person except his hand.

Leg of Mutton School (*The*). So Eckhart called those authors who lauded their patrons in prose or verse, under the hope of gaining a commission, a living, or, at the very least, a dinner for their pains.

Legs. *On his legs.* Mr. So-and-So is on his legs, has risen to make a speech.
On its last legs. Moribund; obsolete; ready to fall out of cognisance.
To set on his legs. So to provide for one that he is able to earn his living without further help.
To stand on one's own legs. To be independent; to be earning one's own living. Of course, the allusion is to being nursed, and standing "alone." (*See* BOTTOM.)

Legal Tender (*A*). The circulating medium of a nation, according to a standard fixed by the government of that nation. It nay be in metal, in paper, or anything else that the government may choose to sanction. In England, at present (1895), the standard is

a gold sovereign, guaranteed of a fixed purity. In some countries it is silver, and in some countries the two precious metals are made to bear a relative value, say twenty silver shillings (or their equivalents) shall equal in commercial value a gold sovereign. In Germany, before 1872, a very base silver was a legal tender, and in Ireland James II. made a farthing the legal tender represented by an English shilling, so that 5d. was really a legal tender for a sovereign. Of course, export and import trade would not be possible under such conditions.

Legem Pone. Money paid down on the nail; ready money. The first of the psalms appointed to be read on the twenty-fifth morning of the month is entitled *Legem pone*, and March 25th is the great pay-day; in this way the phrase "*Legem pone*" became associated with cash down.

"In this there is nothing to be abated; all their speech is *legem pone*." — *Minshall: Essayes in Prison*, p. 26.

"They were all in our service for the *legem pone*."
Ozell: Rabelais.

Legend means simply "something to be read" as part of the divine service. The narratives of the lives of saints and martyrs were so termed from their being read, especially at matins, and after dinner in the refectories. Exaggeration and a love for the wonderful so predominated in these readings, that the word came to signify the untrue, or rather, an event based on tradition.

"A *myth* is a pure and absolute imagination; a *legend* has a basis of fact, but amplifies, abridges, or modifies that basis at pleasure."—*Rawlinson: Historic Evidences*, lecture i. p. 231, note 2.

Legend of a Coin is that which is written round the face of a coin. Thus, on a shilling, the legend is round the head of the reigning sovereign; as, "VICTORIA DEI GRATIA BRITT: REGINA F: D:" (or "BRITANNIAR: REG: F: D:). The words "ONE SHILLING" on the other side of the coin, written across it, we denominate the "inscription."

Legen'da Au'rea, by Jacques de Voragine. A collection of monkish legends in Latin. (1230-1298.)
The Golden Legend, of Longfellow, is a semi-dramatic poem taken from an old German tale by Hartmann von der Aur, called *Poor Henry* (Twelfth century.)

Leger. *St. Leger Stakes* (Doncaster); so called from Colonel Anthony St. Leger, who founded them in 1776. The colonel was governor of St. Lucia, and cousin of the Hon. Elizabeth St. Leger (the lady Freemason).

The St. Leger Stakes are for both colts and mares. Those which have run in the Derby or Oaks are eligible.

Leger-de-Main. Sleight of hand; conjuring which depends chiefly on lightness of hand, or dexterity.

Legion. *"My name is Legion : for we are many "* (St. Mark v. 9). A proverbial expression somewhat similar to hydra-headed. Thus, speaking of the houseless poor we should say, " Their name is Legion ; " so also we should say of the diseases arising from want of cleanliness, the evils of ignorance, and so on.

The Thundering Legion. The Roman legion that discomfited the Marcomanni in 179 is so called, because (as the legend informs us) a thunderstorm was sent in answer to the prayers of certain Christians ; this storm relieved the thirst of the legion. In like manner a hail-storm was sent to the aid of Joshua, at the time when he commanded the sun to stay its course, and assisted the Israelites to their victory. (*Dion Cassius,* lxxi. 8. (*See* Joshua x. 10-12.)

Legion of Honour. An order of merit instituted by the First Consul in 1802, for either military or civil merit. In 1843 there were 49,417 members, but in 1851 one new member was elected for every two extinct ones, so that the honour was no longer a mere farce.

Napoleon III. added a lower order of this Legion, called the Médaille Militaire, the ribbon of which was yellow, not red. The old Legion consisted of Grand Cross, Grand Officers, Commanders, Officers, and Chevaliers, and the ribbon of the order was red.

"The Legion of Honour gives pensions to its military members, and free education to some four hundred of the daughters, sisters, and nieces of its members."

Legislator or **Solon of Parnassus.** Boileau was so called by Voltaire, because of his *Art of Poetry,* a production unequalled ' in the whole range of didactic poetry. (1636-1711.)

Leglin-girth. *To cast a leglin-girth.* To have " a screw loose ; " to have made a *faux pas ;* to have one's reputation blown upon. A leglin-girth is the lowest hoop of a leglin or milk-pail. (See *Sir Walter Scott : Fortunes of Nigel,* chap. xxii.)

Legree. A slave-dealer in *Uncle Tom's Cabin,* by Mrs. Beecher Stowe.

Leibnitz-ism or **Leibnitzian-ism.** The doctrines taught by G. W. von Leibnitz, the German philosopher (1646-1716). The opposite of Spinosa-ism. Spinosa taught that whatever is, is God manifested by phenomena. The light and warmth of the sun, the refreshing breeze, space, and every visible object, is only deity in detail. That God, in fact, is one and all.

Leibnitz, on the other hand, taught that phenomena are separate from deity, as body is from soul ; but although separate, that there is between them a pre-established harmony. The electricity which runs along a telegraph wire is not the message, but it gives birth to the message by pre-established harmony. So all things obey God's will, not because they are identical, but on account of this pre-established harmony.

Leicester (pron. *Les'ter*) is the camp-town on the river Leire, which is now called the Soar.

Leicester Square (London). So called from a family mansion of the Sydneys, Earls of Leicester, which stood on the north-east side.

"The Earl of Leicester, father of Algernon Sidney the patriot . . . built for himself a stately house at the north-east corner of a square plot of ' Lammas Land,' belonging to the parish of St. Martin's, which plot henceforth became known to Londoners as Leicester Fields. A square gradually grew up on the spot, and was completed in 1671."—*Cassell's Magazine, London Legends,* x.

Leigh (*Aurora*) (pron. *Lee*). The heroine of Mrs. Browning's poem so called, designed to show the noble aim of true art.

Leilah [*Li-lah*]. A beautiful young slave, the concubine of Hassan, Caliph of the Ottoman Empire. She falls in love with the Giaour, flees from the seraglio, is overtaken by an emir, and cast into the sea. (*Byron : The Giaour.*)

Lely (*Sir Peter*), the painter, was the son of Vander Vaas or Faes, of Westphalia, whose house had a lily for its sign. Both father and son went by the nickname of Le-lys (the Lily), a sobriquet which Peter afterwards adopted as his cognomen.

Le'man (*Lake*). Geneva ; called in Latin *Lemannus.*

"Lake Leman woos me with its crystal face."
                                    Lord Byron : Childe Harold, iii. 68.

Lemnian Deed (*A*). One of unusual barbarity and cruelty. The phrase arose from two horrible massacres perpetrated by the Lemnians : the first was the murder of all the men and male children on the island by the women; and the other was the murder by the men of all the children born in the island of Athenian parents.

Lem'nian Earth. A species of earth of a yellowish-grey colour, found in the island of Lemnos, said to cure the bites of serpents and other wounds. It was called *terra sigilla'ta*, because it was sealed by the priest before being vended. Philocte'tēs was left at Lemnos when wounded in the foot by Herculēs.

Lemnian Women (*The*). A somewhat similar story is told of these women to that of the Danaidēs (*q.v.*). When they found that their husbands liked the Thracian women better than themselves, they agreed together to murder every man in the island. Hypsiph'ylē saved her father, and was sold to some pirates as a slave.

Lemnos. The island where Vulcan fell when Jupiter flung him out of heaven. Probably it was at one time volcanic, though not so now.

Lemon Soles, which abound on the south coast of England and about Marseilles. Lemon is a corruption of the French *limande*, a dab or flat-fish. The "flounder-sole." There are several varieties. (Latin *lima*, mud.)

Lemster Ore. Fine wool, of which Leominster carpets are made.

"A bank of moss,
Spongy and swelling, and far more
Soft, than the finest Lemster ore."
Herrick: Oberon's Palace.

Lem'ures (3 syl.). The spirits of the dead. Good lem'ures were called Lares, but bad ones Larvæ, spectres who wandered about at night-time to terrify the living. (*Ovid: Fasti,* v.)

"The lars and lemures moan with midnight plaint." *Milton: Ode on the Nativity.*

Lend a Hand. (*See* HAND.)

Length (*A*). Forty-two lines. This is a theatrical term; an actor says he has one. two, or more *lengths* in his part, and, if written out for him, the scribe is paid by the length.

Length-month. (*See* LENT.)

Lens (Latin, a lentil or bean). Glasses used in mathematical instruments are so called because the double convex one, which may be termed the perfect lens, is of a bean shape.

Lenson. *As much akin as Lenson hill to Pilsen pin ; i.e.* not at all. Lenson hill and Pilsen pin are two high hills in

Dorsetshire, called by sailors the Cow and Calf. Out at sea they look like one elevation, though in reality several hills separate them.

Lent (Anglo-Saxon, *lencten*). *Lencwentid* (spring-tide) was the Saxon name for March, because in this month there is a manifest lengthening of the days. As the chief part of the great fast falls in March, this period of fast received the name of the *Lencten-fæsten*, or Lent. It is from Ash Wednesday to Easter.

☙ The Fast of thirty-six days was introduced in the fourth century. Felix III. added four more days in 487, to make it correspond with our Lord's fast in the wilderness.

Galeazzo's Lent. A form of torture devised by Galeazzo Visconti, calculated to prolong the unfortunate victim's life for forty days.

Lent Lily (*The*). The daffodil, which blooms in Lent.

Lenten. Frugal, stinted, as food in Lent. Shakespeare has "lenten entertainment" (*Hamlet,* ii. 2); "a lenten answer" (*Twelfth Night,* i. 5); "a lenten pye" (*Romeo and Juliet,* ii. 4).

"And with a lenten salad cooled her blood."
Dryden: Hind and Panther, iii. 27.

Leod'ogrance, of Camiliard, the father of Guinevere, wife of King Arthur.

Le'on (in *Orlando Furioso*), son of Constantine, the Greek emperor, is promised Bradamant in marriage by her parents, Amon and Beatrice; but Bradamant loves Roge'ro. By-and-by a friendship springs up between Leon and Rogero, and when the prince learns that Bradamant and Roge'ro are betrothed to each other, he nobly withdraws his suit, and Rogero marries Bradamant.

Leonard. A real scholar, forced for daily bread to keep a common school. (*Crabbe : Borough,* letter xxiv.)

St. Leonard is usually represented in a deacon's dress, and holding chains or broken fetters in his hand, in allusion to his untiring zeal in releasing prisoners. Contemporary with Clovis.

Leon'idas of Modern Greece. Marco Bozzaris, who with 1,200 men put to rout 4,000 Turco-Albanians, at Kerpenisi, but was killed in the attack (1823). He was buried at Missolonghi.

Le'onine Contract. A one-sided agreement; so called in allusion to the fable of *The Lion and his Fellow-Hunters.* (*See* GLAUCUS.)

Le'onine Verses, properly speaking, are either hexameter verses, or alternate hexameter verses, or alternate hexameter and pentameter verses, rhyming at the middle and end of each respective line. These fancies were common in the 12th century, and were so called from Leoninus, a canon of the Church of St. Victor, in Paris, the inventor. In English verse, any metre which rhymes middle and end is called a Leonine verse. One of the most noted specimens celebrates the tale of a Jew, who fell into a pit on Saturday and refused to be helped out because it was his Sabbath. His comrade, being a Christian, refused to aid him the day following, because it was Sunday:—

> " Tende manus, *Salomon*, ego te de stercore
> *tollam.*
> Sabbata nostra *colo*, de stercore surgere *nolo*,
> Sabbata nostra *quidem* Salomon celebrabis
> *ibidem.*"

Hexameters and pentameters.

> ' Help for you out of this mire ; here, give me
> your hand, Hezekiah."
> " No ! 'tis the Sabbath, a time labour's accounted
> a crime.
> If on the morrow you've leisure, your aid I'll
> accept with much pleasure."
> " That will be my Sabbath, so, here I will leave
> you and go." E. C. B.

Leonnoys, Leonnesse, or **Lyonnesse.** A mythical country, contiguous to Cornwall.

Leono'ra, wife of Fernando Florestan, a state prisoner in Seville. (*Beethoven: Fidelio, an opera.*) (*See* FERNANDO.)

Leonora. A princess who fell in love with Manri'co, the supposed son of Azucen'a the gipsy. The Conte di Luna was in love with her, and, happening to get Manrico and his reputed mother into his power, condemned them to death. Leonora interceded for Manrico, and promised the count if he would spare his life to " give herself to him." The count consented, and went to the prison to fulfil his promise, when Leonora fell dead from the effect of poison which she had sucked from a ring. Manrico, perceiving this, died also. (*Verdi: Il Trovatore, an opera.*)

Leono'ra de Guzman. The mistress or " favourite " of Alfonso XI. of Castile. Ferdinando, not knowing who she was, fell in love with her; and Alfonso, to save himself from excommunication and reward Ferdinando for services, gave them in marriage to each other. No sooner was this done than the bridegroom, hearing who his bride was, indignantly rejected her, and became a monk. Leonora entered the same monastery as a novice, made herself known to Ferdinando, obtained his forgiveness, and died. (*Donizetti: La Favorita, an opera.*)

Leon'tes (3 syl.), King of Sicilia, invited his friend Polix'enēs, King of Bohemia, to pay him a visit, and being seized with jealousy, ordered Camillo to poison him. Camillo told Polixenes of the king's jealousy, and fled with him to Bohemia. The flight of Polixenes increased the anger of Leontes against Hermi'one, his virtuous queen, whom he sent to prison, where she was confined of a daughter (Per'dita), and it was reported that she had died in giving birth to the child. Per'dita, by order of the jealous king, was put away that she might be no more heard of as his ; but, being abandoned in Bohemia, she was discovered by a shepherd, who brought her up as his own child. In time, Florizel, the son and heir of Polixenes, under the assumed name of Doriclēs, fell in love with Perdita ; but Polixenes, hearing of this attachment, sternly forbade the match. The two lovers, under the charge of Camillo, fled to Sicily, where the mystery was cleared up, Leontes and Hermione re-united, and all " went merry as a marriage bell." (*Shakespeare : Winter's Tale.*)

Leopard, in Christian art, is employed to represent that beast spoken of in the Apocalypse with seven heads and ten horns ; six of the horns bear a nimbus, but the seventh, being " wounded to death " lost its power, and consequently has no nimbus.

Leopard, in heraldry, represents those brave and generous warriors who have performed some bold enterprise with force, courage, promptitude, and activity.

Leopards. So the French designate the English, because their heralds describe our device as 'a *lion leopardé.* Bertrand du Guesclin, the famous Breton, declared that men " *devoyent bien honorer la noble Fleur-de-lis, plus qu'ils ne faisaient le félon Liépard.*"

Lepracaun. The fairy shoemaker. (Irish *leith-bhrogan,* from *leith-brog,* one-shoe maker, so called because he is always seen working at a single shoe.)

> " Do you not catch the tiny clamour,
> Busy click of an elfin hammer.
> Voice of the Lepracaun singing shrill,
> As he merrily plies his trade ?"
> W. B. Yeats: Fairy and Folk Tales, p. 82.

Lerna. *A Lerna of ills (malo'rum Lerna).* A very great evil. Lake Lerna is where Hercules destroyed the hydra which did incalculable evil to Argos.

"Spain was a Lerna of ills to all Europe while it aspired to universal monarchy."—*P. Motteaux: Preface to Rabelais.*

Les Anguilles de Melun. Crying out before you are hurt. When the *Mystery of St. Bartholomew* was performed at Melun, one Languille took the character of the saint, but when the executioner came to "flay him alive," got nervous and began to shriek in earnest. The audience were in hysterics at the fun, and shouted out, *Languille crie avant qu-on l'écorche,*" and "*Les anguilles de Melun*" passed into a French proverb.

Les'bian Poets (*The*). Terpan'der, Alcæ'us, Ari'on, and the poetess Sappho, all of Lesbos.

Lesbian Rule (*The*). A *post facto* law. Making an act the precedent for a rule of conduct, instead of squaring conduct according to law.

Lese Majesty. (*See* LEZE MAJESTY.)

Les'sian Diet. Great abstinence; so called from Lessius, a physician who prescribed very stringent rules for diet. (*See* BANTING.)

Les'trigons. A race of giants who lived in Sicily. Ulysses sent two of his men to request that he and his crew might land, but the king of the place ate one for dinner and the other fled. The Lestrigons assembled on the coast and threw stones against Ulysses and his crew. Ulysses fled with all speed, but lost many of his men. There is considerable resemblance between this tale and that of Polypheme, who ate one of Ulysses' companions, and on the flight of the rest assembled with other giants on the shore, and threw stones at the retreating crew, whereby several were killed.

Let, to permit, is the Anglo-Saxon *læt-an,* to suffer or permit; but *let* (to hinder) is the verb *lett-an.* It is a pity we have dropped the second *t* in the latter word.

"Oftentimes I purposed to come unto you, but was [have been] let hitherto."—*Romans i. 18.*

Let Drive (*To*). To attack; to fall foul of. A Gallicism. "*Se laisser aller à . . .*"—*i.e.* to go without restraint.

"Thou knowest my old ward; here I [Falstaff] lay, and thus I bore my point. Four rogues in buckram let drive at me. . . . These four came all a-front, and mainly thrust at me."—*Shakespeare:* 1 *Henry IV.,* ii. 4.

Let us Eat and Drink; for to-morrow we shall Die (Isaiah xxii. 13).

24*

The Egyptians in their banquets exhibited a skeleton to the guests, to remind them of the brevity of human life, saying as they did so, "Let us eat and drink, for to-morrow we die."

Leth'e (2 syl.), in Greek mythology, is one of the rivers of Hadēs, which the souls of all the dead are obliged to taste, that they may forget everything said and done in the earth on which they lived. (Greek *lētho, lathĕo, lanthăno,* to cause persons not to know.)

Lethe'an Dew. Dreamy forgetfulness; a brown study. Lethē, in mythology, is the river of forgetfulness. Sometimes incorrectly called Le'thean.

" The soul with tender luxury you [Muses] fill,
And o'er the senses Lethean dews distill."
Falconer: The Shipwreck, iii. 4.

Letter-Gae. The precentor is called by Allen Ramsay "The Letter-gae of haly rhyme." " Holy rhyme " means hymns or chants.

"There were no sae mony hairs on the warlock's face as there's on Letter-gae's ain at this moment."
—*Sir W. Scott: Guy Mannering,* chap. xi.

Letter-lock. A lock that cannot be opened unless certain chosen letters are arranged in a certain order.

"A strange lock that opens with A M E N."
Beaumont and Fletcher: Noble Gentleman.

Letter of Credit. A letter written by a merchant or banker to another, requesting him to credit the bearer with certain sums of money. *Circular Notes* are letters of credit carried by gentlemen when they travel.

Letter of Licence (*A*). An instrument in writing made by a creditor, allowing a debtor longer time for the payment of his debt.

Letter of Marque. A commission authorising a privateer to make reprisals on a hostile nation till satisfaction for injury has been duly made. Here "marque " means march, or marca, a border-land (whence our "marquis," the lords appointed to prevent border-incursions). A letter of marque or mart was permission given for reprisals after a border-incursion. Called *jus marchium.*

Letter of Orders (*A*). A certificate that the person named in the letter has been admitted into holy orders.

Letter of Pythag'oras (*The*). The Greek upsilon, ψ

" They placed themselves in the order and figure of ψ, the letter of Pythagoras, as cranes do in their flight."—*Rabelais: Pantagruel,* iv. 33.

Letter of Safe Conduct. A writ under the Great Seal, guaranteeing safety to and fro to the person named in the passport.

Letter of Uriah (2 Sam. xi. 14). A treacherous letter of friendship, but in reality a death-warrant. (*See* BELLEROPHON.)

"However, sir, here is a guarantee. Look at its contents; I do not again carry the letters of Uriah."—*Sir W. Scott: Redgauntlet*, chap. xvi.

Letters. Their proportionate use is as follows :—

E	.. 1,000	H	.. 540	F	.. 236	K ..	88
T	.. 770	R	.. 528	W	.. 190	J ..	55
A	.. 728	D	.. 302	..	184	Q ..	50
I	.. 704	L	.. 360	P	.. 168	X ..	46
S	.. 680	U	.. 295	G	.. 168	Z ..	22
O	.. 672	C	.. 280	B	.. 158		
N	.. 670	M	.. 272	V	.. 120		

Consonants, 5,977. Vowels, 3,400.

As initial letters the order is very different, the proportion being :—

S	.. 1,194	M	.. 439	W	.. 272	Q ..	58
C	.. 937	F	.. 388	G	.. 266	K ..	47
P	.. 804	I	.. 377	U	.. 228	Y ..	23
A	.. 574	E	.. 340	O	.. 206	Z ..	18
T	.. 571	H	.. 308	V	.. 175	X ..	4
D	.. 505	L	.. 298	N	.. 153		
B	.. 463	R	.. 291	J	.. 60		

∴ *E* is the most common letter (except in initials), and *r, s, t, d,* are the most common final letters.

I and *a* are the only single letters which make words. Perhaps *o*, as a sign of the vocative case, should be added. Of two letters, *an, at,* and *on* are the most common, and of three letters *the* and *and.* (*See* LONG WORDS.)

Letters. Philo affirms that letters were invented by Abraham.

Many attribute the invention to Badamanth, the Assyrian.

Blair says they were invented by Memnon, the Egyptian, B.C. 1822.

The same authority says that Menēs invented hieroglyphics, and wrote in them a history of Egypt, B.C. 2122.

Josephus asserts that he had seen inscriptions by Seth, son of Adam.

Lucan says :—

"Phœni'cēs primi, famæ si creditur, ausi
Mansu'r.an ru'dibus vocem signa're figu'ris."
Pharsalia, iii. 220.

Sir Richard Philips says—"Thoth, the Egyptian who invented current writing, lived between B.C. 2806 and 3000."

Many maintain that Jehovah taught men written characters when He inscribed on stone the ten commandments. Of course, all these assertions have a similar value to mythology and fable.

Cadmos, the Phœnician, introduced sixteen of the Greek letters.

Simon'idēs introduced η, ω, ξ; and Epicarmos introduced θ, χ. At least, so says Aristotle. (*See* LACEDEMONIAN LETTER, and LETTER OF PYTHAGORAS.)

Father of Letters (*Père des Lettres*). François I. of France (1494, 1515-1547).

Lorenzo de' Medici, *the Magnificent* (1448-1492).

A man of letters. A man of learning, of erudition.

Letters expletive, and marks on letters.

In French there are two letters expletive—*l* and *t.* The former, called '*l* ephelcystic,' is placed before *on* if the preced ng word ends with a vowel, as *si-l-on.* The latter is called "*t* euphonistic," and is used in interrogative sentences between the third person singular of verbs ending with a vowel, and a pronoun beginning with a vowel, as *gelle-t-il ? a-t-elle ?*

The chief accents are the grave (`), acute (´) and circumflex (^).

Two dots over the latter of two vowels (called *diæresis*), signify that each vowel is to be sounded, as *Aër'ius* (4 syl.).

A *hyphen* between two or more nouns or syllables denotes that they form a compound word, as *mother-in-law.* The hyphen in French is called a "trait d'union," as *irai-je.*

In French, the mark (¸) under the letter *c* is called a *cedilla,* and signifies that the *c* (which would otherwise be = k) is to be pronounced like *s,* as *ça* (*sah*), and *garçon* (*garson*).

A small comma (ˇ) over an *a, o,* or *u,* in Scandinavian languages, is called an *umlau,* and a vowel so marked is called an *umlaute* (3 syl.).

(¨ or ˜) over the vowel *o* in German, is called a *zweipunct* (2 syl.), and gives the vowel the sound of a French *eu,* as in *peu,* etc. ; but over the vowel *u* it gives it the sound of the French *u* in *dût.*

Letters Missive. An order from the Lord Chancellor to a peer to put in an appearance on a bill filed in chancery.

Letters Overt. The same as letters patent (*q.v.*).

Letters Patent. So denominated because they are written upon open sheets of parchment, with the seal of the sovereign or party by whom they were issued pendent at the bottom. Close letters are folded up and sealed on the outside. (*Sir Thomas Duffus Hardy.*)

Letters at the Foot of a Page. Printers affix a letter to the first page of each sheet ; these letters are called *signatures.* They begin with B, and sometimes, but not always, omit J, V, W. A is reserved for the title and preface. After Z, the alphabet is used double—thus, A A or 2 A—and then trebled, quadrupled, etc., as necessity demands. Sometimes figures, 1, 2, 3, etc., are used instead of letters. (*See* SHEET.)

Letters of Administration. The legal instrument granted by the Probate Court to a person appointed administrator to one who has died intestate.

Letters of Beller'ophon. (*See* BELLEROPHON.)

Letters of Horning. (*See under* HORN, HORNS.)

Letters of Junius. (*See* JUNIUS.)

Letters of the Sepulchre. The laws made by Godfrey and the Patriarchs of the court of Jerusalem. There were two codes, one respecting the privileges of the nobles, and the other respecting the rights and duties of the burghers. They were kept in a coffer laid up in the Church of the Holy Sepulchre.

Lettre de Cachet (*French*). An arbitrary warrant of imprisonment; a letter folded and sealed with the king's cachet or little seal. These were secret instructions to the person addressed to proceed against someone named in the letter. The lieutenant-general of police kept an unlimited number of these instruments, and anyone, for a consideration, could obtain one, either to conceal a criminal or to incarcerate someone obnoxious. This power was abolished in the Revolution.

Lettre de Jérusalem. A letter written to extort money. (See *Vidocq: Les Voleurs*, i. 240-253.)

Leuca'dia or **Leucas.** The promontory from which desponding lovers threw themselves into the sea. Sappho threw herself from this rock when she found her love for Phaon was in vain.

" Thence injured lovers, leaping from above,
Their flames extinguish, and forget to love."
Pope: Sappho to Phaon.

Leucippus (Greek, *Leukippos*). Founder of the Atomistic School of Greek philosophy (about B.C. 428).

Leucoth'ea [*White Goddess*]. So Ino was called after she became a seanymph. Her son Palæmon, called by the Romans Portu'nus, or Portumnus, was the protecting genius of harbours.

" By Leucothea's lovely hands,
And her son who rules the strands ! "
Milton: Comus, 896-7.

Leuh. The register of the Recording Angel, in which he enters all the acts of the member of the human race. (According to the Koran.)

Lev'ant and Couchant. Applied to cattle which have strayed into another's field, and have been there long enough to lie down and sleep. The owner of the field can demand compensation for such intrusion. (Latin, " *levantes et cubantes*," rising up and going to bed.)

Lev'ant and Ponent Winds. The east wind is the Lev'ant, and the west wind the Ponent. The former is from *levo*, to rise (sunrise), and the latter from *pono*, to set (sunset).

" Forth rush the Levant and the Ponent winds."
Milton: Paradise Lost, x. 704.

Levant, the region, strictly speaking, means the eastern shore of the Mediterranean ; but is often applied to the whole East.

Levant'. *He has levan'ted*—*i.e.* made off, decamped. A *levan'ter* is one who makes a bet, and runs away without paying his bet if he loses. (Spanish " *levantar el campo, la casa*," to break up the camp or house ; our *leave*.)

In the *Slang Dictionary*, p. 214, we are told that " it was formerly the custom, when a person was in pecuniary difficulties, to give out that he was gone to the Levant." Hence, when one lost a bet and could not or would not pay, he was said to have levanted—*i.e.* gone to the Levant. Of no historic value.

Levée. *Levée en masse* (French). A patriotic rising of a whole nation to defend their country from invasion.

The Queen's Levée. It was customary for the queens of France to receive at the hour of their levée — *i.e.* while making their toilet—the visits of certain noblemen. This custom was afterwards demanded as a right by the court physicians, messengers from the king, the queen's secretary, and some few other gentlemen, so that ten or more persons were often in the dressing-room while the queen was making her toilet and sipping her coffee. The word is now used to express that concourse of gentlemen who wait on the queen on mornings appointed. No ladies except those attached to the court are present on these occasions.

❧ Kings and some nobles have their levées sometimes of an evening.

" When I was very young (said Lord Eldon to Mrs. Forster) Lord Mansfield used to hold levées on Sunday evenings."—*Twiss: Lord Eldon,* vol. i. chap. v. p. 68.

Level Best. *To do one's level best.* To exert oneself to the utmost. *Au gré de nos pouvoirs.* In 1877 Mr. Hale published a book entitled *His Level Best.*

Level Down. To bring society, taxes, wages, etc., to an equality by reducing all to the lowest standard.

Level Up (*To*). To raise the lower strata of society, or standard of wages, etc., to the level of the higher.

Levellers. (April, 1649.) A body of men that first appeared in Surrey, and went about pulling down park palings and levelling hedges, especially those on crown lands. Colonel Lilburne was lodged in prison for favouring the Levellers. (*See* LILBURNE.)

Lev'ellers. Radicals in the time of Charles I. and the Commonwealth, who wanted all men to be placed on a level with respect to their eligibility to office.

Levellers (*in Irish History*), 1740. Agrarian agitators, afterwards called Whiteboys (*q.v.*). Their first offences were levelling the hedges of enclosed commons; but their programme developed into a demand for the general redress of all agrarian grievances.

Lever de Rideau. A light and short dramatic sketch placed on the stage while the manager is preparing to introduce his drama for the night, or "draw up the curtain" on the real business.

"An attempt to pack a romantic tragedy into the space filled by an ordinary *lever de rideau.*"—*Nineteenth Century*, Dec., 1892, p. 964.

Lev'eret. A young hare. The Duke d'Epernon always swooned at the sight of a *leveret*, though he was not affected if he saw a hare. (*See* Fox.)

Levi'athan. The crocodile, or some extinct sea monster, described in the Book of Job (chap. xii.). It sometimes in Scripture designates Pharaoh, King of Egypt, as in Psa. lxxiv. 14, Isa. xxvii. 1, and Ezek. xxix. 3, etc., where the word is translated "dragon."

The Leviathan of Literature. Dr. Johnson (1709-1784).

Lev'ites (2 syl.). In Dryden's *Absalom and Achitophel*, means the Dissenting clergy who were expelled by the Act of Conformity.

Levit'ical. Belonging to the Levites or priestly tribe of Levi; pertaining to the Jewish priesthood, as the *Levitical law*, *Levitical rites*.

Lewd (Anglo-Saxon, *leóde*) simply means folk in general, verb *leod-an*. The present meaning refers to the celibacy of the clergy.

"All that a lewd man hath need to knawe for hele of sowl."—*Caxton Society's Publications.*

Lewis (*Monk*). (*See* Monk.)

Lewis Baboon. Louis XIV. of France is so called in Arbuthnot's *History of John Bull*. Of course, there is a play upon the word Bourbon.

Lewkner's Lane. Now called "Charles Street," Drury Lane, London, always noted for ladies of the pavement.

"The nymphs of chaste Diana's train,
The same with those of Lewkner's Lane."
Butler: Hudibras, part iii. canto 1.

Lex non Scripta. The common law, as distinguished from the statute or written law. Common law does not derive its force from being recorded, and though its several provisions have been compiled and printed, the compilations are not statutes, but simply remembrancers.

Lex Talio'nis (Latin). Tit for tat; the law of retaliation.

Leyden Jar or **Phial.** A glass vessel partly coated, inside and out, with lead-foil, and used in electrical experiments to receive accumulated electricity; invented by Vanleigh, of Leyden.

Leze Majesty. High treason; i.e. "*Crimen læsæ Majestatis.*"

Li-Flambe. The banner of Clovis miraculously displayed to him in the skies. (*See* Toads.)

Lia-fail (of Ireland). The *Fatalé Marmor* or Stone of Destiny. On this stone the ancient Irish kings sat at their coronation, and according to tradition, wherever that stone might be the people there would be dominant. It was removed to Scone; and Edward removed it from Scone Abbey to London. It is kept in Westminster Abbey under the royal throne, on which the English sovereigns sit at their coronation. (*See* Coronation Chair, Scone.)

Liak'ura (3 syl.). Parnassus.

"But where is he that hath beheld
The peak of Liakura unveiled."
Byron: The Giaour.

Liar (*The*). Al Aswad, who set himself up as a prophet against Mahomet. He was called *the Weathercock* because he changed his creed so often, *the Impostor*, and *the Liar*.

Moseïlma, another contemporary, who affirmed that the "belly is the seat of the soul." He wrote to Mahomet, and began his letter: "From Moseïlma, prophet of Allah, to Mahomet, prophet of Allah," and received for answer a letter beginning thus: "From Mahomet the prophet of God, to Moseïlma the Liar." (Anglo-Saxon, *leóg-an*, to tell a falsehood; but to be recumbent is *lieg-an* or *lig-an*.)

Prince of Liars. Ferdinand Mendez Pinto, a Portuguese traveller, whose narrative is so much after Munchausen's style, that Cervantes dubbed him "Prince of Liars." The *Tatler* called him a man "of infinite adventure and unbounded imagination."

Li'bel means a *little book* (Latin, *libellus*). A lampoon, a satire, or any defamatory writings. Originally it meant a plaintiff's statement of his case, which usually "defames" the defendant.

The greater the truth, the greater the libel. The dictum of William Murray, Earl of Mansfield (1704-1793).

"Dost not know that old Mansfield, who writes like the Bible,
Says: 'The more 'tis a truth, sir, the more 'tis a libel'?"
Burns.

Li'ber Albus contains the laws and customs of the city of London, compiled in 1419, by John Carpenter, town clerk.

Li'ber Niger or *The Black Book of the Exchequer*, compiled by Gervase of Tilbury, in the reign of Henry II. It is a roll of the military tenants.

Liberal Arts. Book-learning (Latin, *liber*) ; viz., Grammar, Rhetoric, Philosophy, Arithmetic, Geometry, Astronomy, and Music.

Liberal Unionists or *Tory Democrats.* Those Conservatives or Tories who have a strong bias towards democratic measures.

Liberal Unionists. Those Whigs and Radicals who united, in 1886, with Lord Salisbury and the Conservative party to oppose Home Rule for Ireland. Mr. Gladstone had brought in a Bill to give the Irish Home Rule. Lord Hartington was chief of the Whigs, and Mr. Chamberlain chief of the Radicals, who seceded from Mr. Gladstone's party.

Lib'erals. A political term first employed in 1815, when Lord Byron and his friends set on foot the periodical called *The Liberal*, to represent their views in politics, religion, and literature. The word, however, did not come into general use till about 1831, when the Reform Bill, in Lord Grey's Ministry, gave it prominence.

"Influenced in a great degree by the philosophy and the politics of the Continent, they [the Whigs] endeavoured to substitute cosmopolitan for national principles, and they baptised the new scheme of politics with the plausible name of 'Liberalism.'"—*Disraeli*, June 24, 1872.

Lib'erator (*The*). The Peruvians so call Simon Bolivar, who established the independence of Peru. (1785-1831.) Daniel O'Connell was so called, because he tried to sever Ireland from England. (1775-1847.)

Liberator of the world. So Dr. Franklin has been called. (1706-1790.)

Liberia. An independent republic of western Africa settled by free negroes.

Lib'ertines. A sect of heretics in Holland, led by Quinton a factor, and Copin. They maintained that nothing is sinful but to those who think it sinful, and that perfect innocence is to live without doubt.

⁂ By a "libertine" is now generally meant a profligate, or one who puts no restraint on his personal indulgence.

"A libertine, in earlier use, was a speculative free-thinker in matters of religion and in the theory of morals . . . but [it has come] to signify a profligate."—*Trench: On the Study of Words*, lecture iii. p. 90.

Liberty means "to do what one likes." (Latin, *liber*, free.)

Civil Liberty. The liberty of a subject to conduct his own affairs as he thinks proper, provided he neither infringes on the equal liberty of others, nor offends against the good morals or laws under which he is living.

Moral Liberty. Such freedom as is essential to render a person responsible for what he does, or what he omits to do.

National Liberty. The liberty of a nation to make its own laws, and elect its own executive.

Natural Liberty. Unrestricted freedom to exercise all natural functions in their proper places.

Personal Liberty. Liberty to go out of one's house or nation, and to return again without restraint, except deprived thereof by way of punishment.

Political Liberty. The right to participate in political elections and civil offices ; and to have a voice in the administration of the laws under which you live as a citizen and subject.

Religious Liberty. Freedom in religious opinions, and in both private and public worship, provided such freedom in no wise interferes with the equal liberty of others.

Cap of Liberty. The Goddess of Liberty. in the Aventine Mount, was represented as holding in her hand a cap, the symbol of freedom. In France, the Jacobins wore a *red* cap. In England, a *blue* cap with a white border is the symbol of liberty, and Britannia is sometimes represented as holding such a cap on the point of her spear. (*See* CAP OF LIBERTY.)

Liberty. *The Goddess of Liberty.* On December 10th, 1793, Mlle. Malliard, an actress, was selected to personify the "Goddess of Liberty." Being brought to Notre Dame, Paris, she was seated on the altar, and lighted a large candle to signify that Liberty was the "light of the world." (See *Louis Blanc : History*, ii. 365-367.)

⁂ The statue of Liberty, placed over the entrance of the Palais Royal, was modelled from Mme. Tallien.

The Goddess of Reason. (Aug. 10, 1793.) The Goddess of Reason was enthroned by the French Convention at the suggestion of Chaumette; and the cathedral of Notre Dame de Paris was desecrated for the purpose. The wife of Momoro the printer was the best of these goddesses. The procession was attended by the municipal officers and national guards, while troops of ballet girls carried torches of truth. Incredible as it may seem, Gobet (the Archbishop of Paris), and nearly all the clergy stripped themselves of their canonicals, and, wearing red nightcaps, joined in this blasphemous mockery. So did Julien of Toulouse, a Calvinistic minister.

"Mrs. Momoro, it is admitted, made one of the best goddesses of Reason, though her teeth were a little defective."—*Carlyle : French Revolution*, vol. iii. book v. 4.

Libitina. The goddess who, at Rome, presided over funerals.

"Omnis moriar ; nullaque **pars mei vitabit** Libitinam."

Li'bra [*the balance*]. One of the twelve signs of the Zodiac (September 22 to October 22), when day and night being weighed would be found equal.

Li'brary. One of the most approved materials for writing on, before the invention of paper, was the thin rind between the solid wood and the outside bark of certain trees. This substance is in Latin called *liber*, which came in time to signify also a "book." Hence our *library*, the place for books; *librarian*, the keeper of books; and the French *livre*, a book.

∵ Some interesting facts concerning books and libraries will be found in Disraeli's *Curiosities of Literature.*

A circulating library. A library from which the books may be borrowed and taken by readers to their homes under certain restrictions.

A living or *walking library.* Longi'nus, the philosopher and rhetorician, was so called. (213-273.)

Public Libraries.

¶ *Ancient.* The first public library known was founded at Athens (B.C. 540) by Pisistratos. That of Alexandria, founded (B.C. 47) by the Ptolemies, contained 400,000 books. It was burnt by order of the Calif Omar, A.D. 641.

The first public library of Rome was founded by As'inus Pollio; the second, called the Palatine, by Augustus.

The royal library of the Fatimites of Egypt contained 100,000 manuscripts, splendidly bound. (*Gibbon.*)

The library of the Ommiades of Spain contained 600,000 volumes, 44 of which were catalogues. (*Gibbon.*)

There were seventy public libraries in the kingdom of Andalu'sia. (*Gibbon.*)

When the monastery of Croydon was burnt, in 1091, its library consisted of 900 volumes, 300 of which were very large. (*Ingulphus.*)

¶ *Modern.* The British Museum library contains above 32 miles of book-shelves, 1,250,000 volumes, and 89,000 MSS. Some 40,000 additions are made yearly.

The Bibliothèque Nationale of Paris, founded by Louis XIV., is the largest library in the world. It contains above 1,400,000 volumes, 500,000 pamphlets, 175,000 manuscripts, 300,000 maps and charts, 150,000 coins and medals, 1,400,000 engravings, contained in 10,000 volumes, and 100,000 portraits.

The Impériale, France, contains about 600,000 books, 500,000 pamphlets, and 85,000 manuscripts.

The Munich Library contains about 600,000 books and 10,000 manuscripts.

The Vienna, about 500,000 books and 20,000 manuscripts.

The Vatican, about 200,000 books and 40,000 manuscripts.

The Imperial Library of Russia, about 650,000 books and 21,000 manuscripts.

The Copenhagen Library, about 500,000 books and 15,000 manuscripts.

Lib'ya. Africa, or all the north of Africa between Egypt and the Atlantic Ocean. It was the Greek name for Africa in general. The Romans used the word sometimes as synonymous with Africa, and sometimes for the fringe containing Carthage.

Licen'tiate (4 syl.) One who has a licence to practise some art or faculty, as a *licentiate of medicine.*

Lich. A dead body. (Anglo-Saxon, *lic*; German, *leiche*.)

Lich-field, in Staffordshire. *The field of the dead, i.e.* of the martyred Christians.

Lich-fowls. Birds that feed on carrion, as night-ravens, etc.

Lich-gate. The shed or covered place at the entrance of churchyards, intended to afford shelter to the coffin and mourners, while they wait for the clergyman to conduct the *cortège* into the church.

Lich-owl. The screech-owl, superstitiously supposed to foretell death.

Lich-wake or *Lyke-wake.* The funeral feast or the waking of a corpse, *i.e.* watching it all night.

Lich-way. The path by which a funeral is conveyed to church, which not unfrequently deviates from the ordinary road. It was long supposed that wherever a dead body passed became a public thoroughfare.

Lichten. Belonging to the lich-ground or cemetery. In Chichester, just outside the city walls on the east, are what the common people call the lightnen or liten schools, a corruption of lichten schools, so termed because they stand on a part of the ancient Saxon lich-acre. The spelling usually adopted for these schools is "litten."

Lick, as *I licked him.* I flogged or beat him. (Welsh, *llach*, a slap, verb *llachian;* Anglo-Saxon, *slic*-an, to strike, or slick.)

Lick into Shape (*To*). According to tradition the cubs of bears are cast shapeless, and remain so till the dam has licked them into proper form.

"So watchful Bruin forms, with plastic care,
Each growing lump, and brings it to a bear."
    Pope: Dunciad, i. 101.

Lick the Dust (*To*). To fall in battle.

"His enemies shall lick the dust."—Psalm lxxii. 9.

Licks the Butter. *The very dogs refused to lick the butter from his forehead.* Before the dead body of a Parsee is removed from the house, the forehead is smeared with clarified butter or ghee, and the dogs of the house are admitted. If the dog or dogs lick the butter, it is a good omen ; if not, it signifies perdition.

Lickspittle (*A*). A servile toady.

"His heart too great, though fortune little,
To lick a rascal statesman's spittle." *Swift.*

Lictors. *Binders* (Latin, *ligo*, to bind or tie). These Roman officers were so called because they bound the hands and feet of criminals before they executed the sentence of the law. (*Aulus Gellius*.)

"The lictors at that word, tall yeomen all and strong,
Each with his axe and sheaf of twigs, went down into the throng."
    Macaulay : Virginia.

Lid. Anglo-Saxon, *hlid ;* Dutch and Danish, *lid.* "Close" is the Latin supine *clus-um.*

Lidskial'fa [*the terror of nations*]. The throne of Alfader, whence he can view the whole universe. (*Scandinavian mythology.*)

Lie. (Anglo-Saxon, *lige*, a falsehood.)

Father of lies. Satan (John viii. 44).

The greatest lie. The four P's (a Palmer, a Pardoner, a Poticary, and a Pedlar) disputed as to which could tell the greatest lie. The Palmer said he had never seen a woman out of patience ; whereupon the other three P's threw up the sponge, saying such a falsehood could not possibly be outdone. (*Heywood : The Four P's.*)

White lies. (*See* WHITE.)

Lie Circumstantial (*The*) or *The lie with circumstance.* Sir, if you said so, it was a lie. As Touchstone says, this insult is voidable by this means—"If you said so, I said it was a lie," but the word "if" makes the insult hypothetical. This is the lie direct in the second degree or once removed. (*See* COUNTERCHECK.)

Lie Direct (*The*). Sir, that's a lie. You are a liar. This is an offence no gentleman can take.

"One day as I was walking, with my customary swagger,
Says a fellow to me, 'Pistol, you're a coward, though a bragger.'
Now, this was an indignity no gentleman could take, sir ;
So I told him flat and plump. 'You lie——(under a mistake, sir).'"

Lie Quarrelsome (*The*). To tell one flat and plump "You lie." Touchstone calls this "the countercheck quarrelsome."

"If again [the fifth time] it was not well cut, he would say *I lied :* this is called the countercheck quarrelsome."—*Shakespeare : As You Like It,* v. 4.

Lie hath no Feet (*A*). Because it cannot stand alone. In fact, a lie wants twenty others to support it, and even then is in constant danger of tripping.

Lie. (Anglo-Saxon, *lic̣gan,* to 'bide or rest; but *lie,* to deceive, is the Anglo-Saxon verb *leōg-an.*)

"Lie heavy on him, earth, for he
Laid many a heavy load on thee.

This is part of Dr. Evans's epitaph on Sir John Vanbrugh, the comic poet, herald, and architect. The "heavy loads" referred to were Blenheim, Greenwich Hospital (which he finished), Castle Howard in Yorkshire, and other massive buildings. (1666-1726.)

Lie Low (*To*). To conceal oneself or one's intentions.

"All this while Brer Rabbit lay low."—*Uncle Remus.*

Lie Over (*To*). To be deferred ; as, this question must lie over till next sessions.

Lie-to (*To*). To stop the progress of a vessel at sea by reducing the sails and counterbracing the yards ; to cease from doing something. A nautical phrase.

"We now ran plump into a fog, and were obliged to lie-to."—*Lord Dufferin.*

Lie Up (*To*). To refrain from work ; to rest.

Lie at the Catch (*To*). Thus Talkative says to Faithful, "You lie at the catch, I perceive." To which Faithful replies, "No, not I; I am only for setting things right." "To lie at the catch," or lie on the catch, is to lie in wait or to lay a trap to catch one.

Lie in State (*To*). "*Être couché sur un lit de parade.*" A dead body displayed to the general public.

Lie on Hand (*To*). To remain unsold. "*Rester depuis longtemps en main.*"

Lie to One's Work (*To*). To work energetically.

Lie with One's Fathers (*To*). To be buried in one's native place. "*Reposer avec ses pères.*"

"I will lie with my fathers, and thou shalt carry me out of Egypt."—Genesis xlvii. 30.

Liebenstein and Sternfels. Two ruined castles of the Rhine. According to tradition, Leoline, the orphan, was the sole surviving child of the lord of Liebenstein; and two brothers, named Warbeck and Otho, were the surviving children of the lord of Sternfels. Both the brothers fell in love with Leoline; but, as Leoline gave the preference to Otho, Warbeck joined the Crusades. A Templar in time persuaded Otho to do the same; but, the war being over, Otho stayed at Constantinople, where he fell in love with a Greek, whom he brought home for his bride. Leoline retired to the adjacent convent of Bornhofen. Warbeck defied his brother to single combat for this insult to his betrothed; but Leoline with the nuns interposed to prevent the fight. The Greek wife, in time, eloped with one of the inmates of Sternfels, and Otho died childless. A band of robbers broke into the convent; but Warbeck armed in its defence. He repelled the robbers, but received his death-wound, and died in the lap of Leoline; thus passed away the last lord of Liebenstein. (*Traditions of the Rhine.*)

Liege. The word means one bound, a bondsman (Latin, *ligo*, to bind); hence, vassals were called *liege-men*—*i.e.* men bound to serve their lord. The lord was called the *liege-lord*, being bound to protect the vassals.

"Unarmed and bareheaded, on his knees, and with his hands placed between those of his lord, he [the military tenant] repeated these words: 'Hear, my lord, I have become your liegeman of life and limb, and earthly worship; and faith and truth I will bear to you to live and die."—*Lingard: History of England*, vol. ii. chap. i. p. 27.

Li'en. A bond. (Latin, *liga'men*). Legally, a bond on goods for a debt; a right to retain goods in a creditor's hands till he has satisfied a legal claim for debt.

Liesse (2 syl.). *Abbé de Liesse* or *Abbas Letitiæ*. The French term for the "Boy Bishop," or "Abbot of Unreason." (*See* ABBOT.)

Lieutenant (pronounce *lef-ten'-unt*) is the Latin *locum-tenens*, through the French. A *Lieutenant-Colonel* is the Colonel's deputy. The *Lord-Lieutenant* of Ireland is a viceroy who represents the crown in that country.

Life. (Anglo-Saxon, *lif*.)
Drawn from life. Drawn or described from some existing person or object.
For life. As long as life continues.
For the life of me. True as I am alive. Even if my life depended on it. A strong asseveration.

"Nor could I, for the life of me, see how the creation of the world had anything to do with what I was talking about."—*Goldsmith: Vicar of Wakefield.*

Is life worth living? Schopenhauer decides in the negative. In the "funeral service" we are taught to thank God for delivering the deceased "out of the miseries of this sinful life." On the other hand, we are told that Jesus called Lazarus from the grave, not by way of punishment, but quite the contrary.

"On days like this, one feels that Schopenhauer is wrong after all, and that life is something really worth living for."—*Grant Allen: The Curate of Churnside.*

Large as life. Of the same size as the object represented.
On my life. I will answer for it by my life; as, "*Il le fera j'en répondes sur ma vie.*"
To bear a charmed life. To escape accidents in a marvellous manner.
To know life. In French, "*Savoir vivre*"—that is, "*Savoir ce que c'est que de vivre.*" "Not to know life," is the contrary—"*Ne savoir pas ce que c'est que de vivre.*"
To the life. In exact imitation. "Done to the life." "*Faire le portrait de quelqu'un au naturel*" (or) "*d'après nature.*"

Life-boat (*A*). A boat rendered especially buoyant for the purpose of saving those who are in peril of their life at sea.

Life-buoy (*A*). A float to sustain two or more persons in danger of being drowned at sea.

Life-Guards. Two senior regiments of the mounted body-guard, comprising 878 men, all six feet high; hence, a fine, tall, manly fellow is called "a regular Life-guardsman."

Life Policy (*A*). An assurance to be paid after the death of the person.

Life Preserver (*A*). A buoyant jacket, belt, or other appliance, to support the human body in water; also a loaded staff or knuckle-duster for self-defence.

Lift. *To have one at a lift* is to have one in your power. When a wrestler has his antagonist in his hands and lifts him from the ground, he has him "at a lift," or in his power.

"'Sirra,' says he, 'I have you at a lift.
Now you are come unto your latest shift.'"
Percy: Reliques; Guy and Amarant.

Lift not up your Horn on High. (Psalm lxxv. 5.) Do not behave scornfully, maliciously, or arrogantly. (*See under* HORN.)

Lift up the Heel against Me (*To*). To kick me (physically or morally); to treat with contumely or contempt: to oppose, to become an enemy. As an unruly horse kicks the master who trusts and feeds him.

"Yea, mine own familiar friend, in whom I trusted, which did eat of my bread, hath lifted his heel against me."—Psalm xli. 9.

Lift up the Voice (*To*). To shout or cry aloud; to utter a cry of joy or of sorrow.

"Saul lifted up his voice and wept."—1 Sam. xxiv. 16.

Lifted up. Put to death; to raise on a cross or gibbet.

"When ye have lifted up the Son of Man, then shall ye know that I am He."—John viii. 28.

Lifter. A thief. We still call one who plunders shops a "shop-lifter."

"Is he so young a man, and so old a lifter?"
    Shakespeare: Troilus and Cressida, i. 2.

Lifting (*The*). In Scotland means lifting the coffin on the shoulders of the bearers. Certain ceremonies preceded the funeral.

"When at the funeral of an ordinary husband-man, one o'clock was named as the hour for 'lift-ing,' the party began to assemble two hours previously."—*Saladin: Agnostic Journal*, Jan. 14, 1893, p. 27.

At the first service were offered meat and ale; at the second, shortbread and whisky; at the third, seed-cake and wine; at the fourth, currant-bun and rum; at the last, sugar-biscuits and brandy.

Lifting, or **Lifting the Little Finger.** Tippling. In holding a beaker or glass, most persons stick out or lift up the little finger. "Lifting" is a con-tracted form of the full phrase.

Ligan. Goods thrown overboard, but tied to a cork or buoy in order to be found again. (Latin *ligāre*, to tie or bind.)

***⁎* Flotsam.** The débris of a wreck which floats on the surface of the sea, and is often washed ashore. (Latin *flotare*, to float.)

Jetson or *jetsam.* Goods thrown over-board in a storm to lighten the vessel. (Latin *jacĕre*, to cast forth, through the French *jeter*.)

Light. Life. Othello says, "Put out the light and then put out the light." In May, 1886, Abraham Harper, a mar-ket-gardener, of Oxford, hit his wife in the face, and threatened to "put her light out," for which he was fined 5s. and costs. (*Truth*, May 20th, 1886.)

Light. Graces, holiness. Called "the candle of the Lord," the "lamp of God," as, "The spirit of man is the lamp of the Lord." (Prov. xx. 27.)

"Let your light so shine before men that they may see your good works."—Matt. v. 16.

To stand in one's own light. To act in such a way as to hinder advancement.

"He stands in his own light through nervous fear."—*The Leisure Hour*, 1886.

Light Comedian (*A*), in theatrical parlance, is one who performs in what is called legitimate comedy, but is very different to the "low comedian," who is a farceur. Orlando, in *As You Like It*, might be taken by a "light comedian," but not by a "low comedian." Tony Lumpkin and Paul Pry are parts for a "low comedian," but not for a "light comedian."

Light Horsemen. Those who live by plunder by night. Those who live by plunder in the daytime are Heavy Horsemen. These horsemen take what they can crib aboard ship, such as coffee-beans, which they call *pease;* sugar, which they call *sand;* rum, which they called *vinegar*, and so on. The broker who buys these stolen goods and asks no questions is called a *fence*. (See *Captain Marryat: Poor Jack*, chap. xviii.)

Light Troops, *i.e.* light cavalry, meaning Lancers and Hussars, who are neither such large men as the "Heavies," nor yet so tall. (*See* LIGHT-ARMED ARTILLERY.)

Light-armed Artillery. The Royal Horse Artillery. The heavy artillery are the garrison artillery.

Light as a Feather. (*See* SIMILES.)

Light-fingered Gentry (*The*). Pick-pockets and shop-lifters.

Light Gains make a heavy Purse. Small profits and a quick return, is the best way of gaining wealth. French, "*Le petit gain remplit la bourse;*" Italian, "*I guadagni mediocri empiono la borsa.*"

Light of One's Countenance (*The*). The bright smile of approbation and love.

"Lift up the light of Thy countenance on us."—Psalm iv. 6.

Light of the Age. Maimon'idēs or Rabbi Moses ben Maimon, of Cor'dova (1135-1204).

Light of the Harem. The Sultana Nourmahal', afterwards called *Nour-jehan* (Light of the World). She was the bride of Selim. (*Thomas Moore: Lalla Rookh.*)

Lighthouse. The most celebrated of *antiquity* was the one erected by Ptolemy Soter in the island of Pharos, opposite Alexandria. Josephus says it could be seen at the distance of 42 miles. It was one of the "seven wonders" of the ancient world.

Of *modern* lighthouses the most famous are the Eddystone, 14 miles S.W. of Plymouth Sound; the Tour de Corduan, at the entrance of the Gironde, in France; and the Bell Rock, which is opposite the Frith of Tay.

The largest lighthouses are :—(1) The lighthouse at Hell Gate in New York, 250 feet high, with 9 electric lamps of 6,000 candle-power each. (2) The Bartholdi Statue of Liberty, in New York harbour, 220 feet high. (3) One in Genoa, Italy, 210 feet in height. (4) Cape Hatteras Light, which is 189 feet high. (5) Eddystone Lighthouse is 85 feet high, and lights a radius of 17 miles.

Lightning [*Barca*]. Hamilcar of Carthage was called "Barca," both on account of the rapidity of his march and also for the severity of his attacks. (B.C. 247-228.)

Chain lightning. Two or more flashes of lightning repeated without intermission.
Forked lightning. Zig-zag lightning.
Globular lightning. A meteoric ball [of fire], which sometimes falls on the earth and flies off with an explosion.

Lightning Conductor. A metal rod raised above a building with one end in the earth, to carry off the lightning and prevent its injuring the building.

∴ It must be pointed at the top extremity to ensure a quiet discharge.

Lightning Preservers. The most approved classical preservatives against lightning were the eagle, the sea-calf, and the laurel. Jupiter chose the first, Augustus Cæsar the second, and Tiberius the third. (*Columella*, x.; *Sueton. in Vit. Aug.*, xc. ; ditto *in Vit. Tib.*, lxix.) (*See* HOUSE-LEEK.)

Bodies scathed and persons struck dead by lightning were said to be incorruptible ; and anyone so distinguished was held by the ancients in great honour. (*J. C. Bullenger : De Terræ Motu,* etc., v. 11.)

Lightning Proof. A building protected by lightning conductors (one or more).

Lightning Rod (*A*). (*See* LIGHTNING CONDUCTOR.)

Liguo'rians. A congregation of missionary priests called also Redemptorists, founded in 1732, by St. Alphonsus Liguo'ri. Their object is the religious instruction of the people, and the reform of public morality.

Ligurian Arts. Deception, trickery.

Ligurian Republic (*The*). Venetia, Genoa, and a part of Sardinia, tied up in one bundle by Napoleon I. in 1797, and bound with a constitution similar to that of the French "Directory," so called from Ligu'ria, pretty well commensurate with these districts. It no longer exists.

Ligurian Sage (*The*). Aulus Persius Flaccus, born at Volaterræ, in Etruria, according to ancient authors ; and at Lunæ Portus, in Liguria, according to some modern authorities. (A.D. 34-62.) (See *Satires,* vi. 6.)

Lilburn Shawl. The name of a place in Wensleydale, Yorkshire. Shawl is *shaw*, a hill; *shaw'l* = shaw-hill.

Lilburne. *If no one else were alive, John would quarrel with Lilburne.* John Lilburne was a contentious Leveller in the Commonwealth ; so rancorous against rank that he could never satisfy himself that any two persons were exactly on the same level. (*See* LAWSUITS.)

" Is John departed ? and is Lilburne gone ?
Farewell to both—to Lilburne and to John.
Yet, being gone, take this advice from me :
Let them not both in one grave buried be.
Here lay ye John, lay Lilburne thereabout ;
For if they both should meet, they would fall
out."   *Epigrammatic Epitaph.*

Lil'inau was wooed by a phantom that lived in her father's pines. At nightfall the phantom whispered love, and won the fair Lilinau, who followed his green waving plume through the forest, and was never seen again. (*American-Indian tradition.*)

Li'lis or **Li'lith** (*Rabbinical mythology*). The Talmudists say that Adam had a wife before Eve, whose name was Lilis. Refusing to submit to Adam, she left Paradise for a region of the air. She still haunts the night as a spectre, and is especially hostile to new-born infants. Some superstitious Jews still put in the chamber occupied by their wife four coins, with labels on which the names of Adam and Eve are inscribed, with the words, "Avaunt thee, Lilith !" Gœthe has introduced her in his *Faust.* (*See* LAMIA.)

" It was Lilith, the wife of Adam . . .
Not a drop of her blood was human,
But she was made like a soft sweet woman."
          D. G. Rossetti: Eden Bower.

∵ The fable of Lilis or Lilith was invented to reconcile Gen. i. with Gen. ii. Genesis i. represents the simultaneous creation of man and woman out of the earth; but Genesis ii. represents that Adam was alone, and Eve was made out of a rib, and was given to Adam as a helpmeet for him.

Lilli-Burle'ro or **Lilli-Bulle'ro** and **Bullen-a-lah.** Said to have been the words of distinction used by the Irish Papists in their massacres of the Protestants in 1641. A song with the refrain of "Lilli-burlero, bullen-a-la!" was written by Lord Wharton, which had a more powerful effect than the philippics of either Demosthenês or Cicero, and contributed not a little to the great revolution of 1688. Burnet says, "It made an impression on the [king's] army that cannot be imagined. . . . The whole army, and at last the people, both in city and country, were singing it perpetually . . . never had so slight a thing so great an effect." The song is in Percy's *Reliques of Ancient English Poetry*, series ii. bk. 3. (See *Sterne: Tristram Shandy*, chap. ii.)

" Lilli bullero, lilli bullero bullen a la,
Lero lero, lilli bullero, lero lero bullen a la,
Lero lero, lilli bullero, lero lero bullen a la."

Mr. Chappell attributes the air to Henry Purcell.

Lilliput. The country of pigmies called " Lilliputians," to whom Gulliver was a giant. (*Swift: Gulliver's Travels.*)

Lily (*The*). There is a tradition that the lily sprang from the repentant tears of Eve as she went forth from Paradise.

Lily in Christian art is an emblem of chastity, innocence, and purity. In pictures of the Annunciation, Gabriel is sometimes represented as carrying a lily-branch, while a vase containing a lily stands before the Virgin, who is kneeling in prayer. St. Joseph holds a lily-branch in his hand, to show that his wife Mary was always the virgin.

Lily. (Emblem of France.) Tasso, in his *Jerusalem Delivered*, terms the French *Gigli d'oro* (golden lilies). It is said the people were commonly called *Liliarts*, and the kingdom *Lilium* in the time of Philippe le Bel, Charles VIII., and Louis XII. They were so called from the *fleur-de-lys*, the emblem of France.

" I saw my country's lily torn."
Bloomfield. (A Frenchman is speaking.)
" The burghers of Ghent were bound by solemn oath not to make war upon the lilies."—*Millington: Heraldry*, i.

Lily of France. The device of Clovis was three black toads, but an aged hermit of Joye-en-valle saw a miraculous light stream one night into his cell, and

an angel appeared to him holding a shield of wonderful beauty; its colour was azure, and on it were emblazoned three gold lilies that shone like stars, which the hermit was commanded to give to Queen Clotilde. Scarcely had the angel vanished when Clotilde entered, and, receiving the celestial shield, gave it to her royal husband, whose arms were everywhere victorious. (See *Les Petits Bollandistes*, vol. vi. p. 426.)

" Un hermite apporta à la ditte royne vn drap d'azur à Trois Flevrs de Lis d'or, que l'ange luy auoit donnee et le deliura la ditte royne a son mary le roy Clovis pour le porter comme ses armes en lieu qu'il les portoit d'or à trois crapavz de sable."—*Chifflet.*

** The kings of France were called " Lords of the Silver Lilies."

** Florence is called " The City of Lilies."

Lily of the Valley. The *Convallāria majālis* (the May valley plant); one of the species is Solomon's seal. It is by no means the case that the Convallaria grow only in valleys, although they prefer shady places.

This is not the lily (Matt. vi. 28) which is said to excel " Solomon in all his glory." The Lilium Candidum is the flower alluded to by our Lord; a tall majestic plant, common in Palestine, and known by us as the Garden Lily. It is bell-shaped, with white petals and golden yellow stamens. Jahn (*Archæologia Biblica*, p. 125) tells us that " at festivals the rich and powerful robed themselves in white cotton, which was considered the most splendid dress."

Lily Maid of Astolat. (*See* ELAINE.)

Lim Hay. *Lick it up like Lim hay.* Lim, on the Mersey, is famous for its excellent hay.

Limb. *To tear limb from Warburton.* Lymm cum Warburton forms one rectory in Cheshire. The play is on limb and Lymm.

Limb of the Law (*A*). A lawyer, or a clerk articled to a lawyer. The hands are limbs of the body, and the lawyer's clerks are his *hands* to copy out what the *head* of the office directs.

Limberham. A tame, foolish keeper. The character is in Dryden's comedy of *Limberham, or the Kind Keeper*, and is supposed to satirise the Duke of Lauderdale.

Limbo. A waste-basket; a place where things are stowed, too good to destroy but not good enough to use. In School theology unbaptised infants and good heathens go to Limbo. (Latin, *limbus*, the edge.) They cannot go to heaven, because they are not baptised, and they cannot go to the place of torment, because they have not committed sin at all, or because their good preponderates. (See *Milton : Paradise Lost,* bk. iii.) (*See* ARAF.)

In limbo. Go to limbo — that is, prison.

Limbus, preceded by *in* or *to* becomes *limbo*—as, in limbo, to limbo. Occasionally, *limbo* stands for limbus.

Limbus Fatuo'rum. The Limbus of Fools, or Fool's Paradise. As fools are not responsible for their works, they are not punished in Purgatory, but cannot be received into Heaven ; so they go to a place called the Paradise of Fools.

> " Then might you see
> Cowls, hoods, and habits, with their wearers tossed
> And fluttered into rags ; then relics, beads,
> Indulgences, dispenses, pardons, bulls,
> The sport of winds. All these, upwhirled aloft,
> Into a Limbo large and broad, since called
> The Paradise of Fools."
> *Milton : Paradise Lost,* book iii. 489-95.

Limbus Patrum. The half-way house between earth and heaven, where the patriarchs and prophets, after death, await the coming of Messiah. According to the Roman Catholic notion, this is the "hell," or hadēs, into which Jesus Christ descended after He gave up the ghost on the cross. Limbo, and sometimes limbo patrum, is used for "quod," jail, confinement.

> " I have some of them in limbo patrum, and there they are like to dance these three days."— *Shakespeare : Henry VIII., v. 4.*

Limbus Puero'rum. The Child's Paradise, for children who die before they are responsible for their actions.

Limbus of the Moon. *In the limbo of the moon.* Ariosto (in his *Orlando Furioso,* xxxiv. 70) says, in the moon are treasured up such stores as these : Time misspent in play, all vain efforts, all vows never paid, all intentions which lead to nothing, the vanity of titles, flattery, the promises of princes, deathbed alms, and other like vanities.

Limerick. A nonsense verse or song, in the metre of the example.

> " There was a young lady of Wilts,
> Who walked up to Scotland on stilts ;
> When they said it was shocking ,
> To show so much stocking,
> She answered, 'Then what about kilts ?'"

There is a chorus, " We'll all come up, come up to Limerick," but the connection with the Irish city is not clear.

Lime Street, London. The place where, in former times, lime was sold in public market. It gives its name to one of the wards of London.

Limited Liability. The liability of a shareholder in a company only for a fixed amount, generally the amount of the shares he has subscribed for. The Limited Liability Act was passed 1855.

Limner. A drawer, a painter, an artist. A contraction of *illuminator,* or rather *lumenier* (one who illuminates manuscripts).

> " The limner, or illuminer . . . throws us back on a time when the illumination of MSS. was a leading occupation of the painter."—*Trench : On the Study of Words,* lecture iv. p. 171.

Limp. Formed of the initial letters of Louis (XIV.), James, Mary, Prince (of Wales). A Jacobite toast in the time of William III. (*See* NOTARICA.)

Lina. The Goddess Flax.

> " Inventress of the woof, fair Lina flings
> The flying shuttle through the dancing strings."
> *Darwin : Loves of the Plants,* canto ii.

Lincoln. A contraction of *Lindum-colonia.* Lindum was an old British town, called *Llyn-dune* (the fen-town). If we had not known the Latin name, we should have given the etymology *Llyn-collyne* (the fen-hill, or hill near the pool), as the old city was on a hill.

The devil looks over Lincoln. (*See* DEVIL.)

Lincoln College (Oxford). Founded by Richard Fleming in 1427), and completed by Rotherham, Bishop of Lincoln, in 1479.

Lincoln Green. Lincoln, at one time, was noted for its green, Coventry for its blue, and Yorkshire for its grey. (*See* KENDAL GREEN.)

> " And girls in Lincoln green."
> *Drayton : Polyolbion,* xxv.

Falstaff speaks of Kendal Green (Westmoreland), 1 *Hen. IV.,* ii. 4.)

> " Here be a sort of ragged knaves come in,
> Clothed all in Kendale green."
> *Plays of Robyn Hood.*

Lincoln's Inn. One of the fashionable theatres in the reign of Charles II.

Lincoln's Inn Fields, London. Henry Lacy, Earl of Lincoln, built an inn (mansion) here in the 14th century. The ground belonged to the Black Friars, but was granted by Edward I. to Lacy. Later, one of the bishops of Chichester, in the reign of Henry VII., granted leases here to certain students of law.

Lincolnshire Bagpipes. The croaking of frogs in the Lincolnshire fens. We have Cambridgeshire nightingales, meaning frogs ; fen nightingales, the Liège nightingale. In a somewhat similar way asses are called " Arcadian nightingales."

> " Melancholy as . . . the drone of a Lincolnshire bagpipe."—*Shakespeare :* 1 *Hen. IV., i. 2.*

Lindab'rides. A heroine in *The Mirror of Knighthood*, whose name at one time was a synonym for a kept mistress, in which sense it was used by Scott, *Kenilworth* and *Woodstock*.

Linden Tree (*A*). Baucis was converted into a linden tree. Philēmon and Baucis were poor cottagers of Phrygia, who entertained Jupiter so hospitably that he promised to grant them whatever request they made. They asked that both might die together, and it was so. At death Philēmon became an oak and Baucis a linden tree. Their branches intertwined at the top.

Lindor. A poetic swain of the Cor'ydon type, a lover *en bergère*.

"Do not, for heaven's sake, bring down Corydon and Lindor upon us."—*Sir Walter Scott.*

Line. Trade, business.
What line are you in? What trade or profession are you of? "In the book line"—*i.e.* the book trade. This is a Scripture phrase. "The lines have fallen to me in pleasant places, yea, I have a goodly heritage." The allusion is to drawing a line to mark out the lot of each tribe, hence line became the synonym of lot, and lot means position or destiny; and hence a calling, trade, or profession. Commercial travellers use the word frequently to signify the sort of goods which they have to dispose of; as, one travels "in the hardware line," another "in the drapery line," or "grocery line," etc.

Line (*The*). The equator. (*See* CROSSING THE LINE.)
The deep-sea line. A long line marked at every five fathoms, for sounding the depth of the sea.
The line. All regiments of infantry except the foot-guards, the rifle brigade, the marines, the militia, and the volunteers.

Line a Day (*A*). ("*Nulla dies sine lineā.*") Apelles the artist said he never passed a day without doing at least one line, and to this steady industry he owed his great success.

Line of Battle. The order of troops drawn up so as to present a battle-front. There are three lines—the van, the main body, and the rear. A fleet drawn up in *line of battle* is so arranged that the ships are ahead and astern of each other at stated distances.
All along the line, in every particular. The reference is to line of soldiers.

"The accuracy of the statement is contested all along the line by persons on the spot."—*W. E. Gladstone (Newspaper report*).

To break the enemy's line is to derange their order of battle, and so put them to confusion.

Line of Beauty, according to Hogarth, is a curve thus ‿. Mengs was of the same opinion, but thought it should be more serpentine. Of course, these fancies are not tenable, for the line which may be beautiful for one object would be hideous in another. What would Hogarth have said to a nose or mouth which followed his line of beauty?

Line of Communication, or rather **Lines of Communication,** are trenches made to continue and preserve a safe correspondence between two forts, or two approaches to a besieged city, or between two parts of the same army, in order that they may co-operate with each other.

Line of Demarcation. The line which divides the territories of different proprietors. The space between two opposite doctrines, opinions, rules of conduct, etc.

Line of Direction. The line in which a body moves, a force acts, or motion is communicated. In order that a body may stand without falling, a line let down from the centre of gravity must fall within the base on which the object stands. Thus the leaning tower of Pisa does not fall, because this rule is preserved.

Line of Life (*The*). In French, *La ligne de vie.* So also, line of duty, *La ligne du devoir,* etc. In palmistry, the crease in the left hand beginning above the web of the thumb, and running towards or up to the wrist is so called.

The nearer it approaches the wrist the longer will be the life, according to palm-lorists. If long and deeply marked, it indicates long life with very little trouble; if crossed or cut with other marks, it indicates sickness.

Line of March. The ground from point to point over which an army moves.

Line of Operation (*The*) in war. The line between the base of operation (*q.v.*) and the object aimed at. Thus, if a fleet is the base and the siege of a city is the object aimed at, the line of operation is that drawn from the fleet to the city. If a well-fortified spot is the base and a battle the object, the line of operation is that which lies between the fortified spot and the battle-field.

Line upon Line. Admonition or instruction repeated little by little (a line at a time). Apellēs said "*Nulla dies* *sine lineā.*" A drawing is line upon line, an edifice is brick upon brick or stone upon stone.

"Line upon line, line upon line, here a little and there a little."—Isaiah xxviii. 10.

Lines. *The lines have fallen to me in pleasant places.* The part allotted to me and measured off by a measuring line. (Palms xvi. 6.)

Hard lines. Harsh restrictions. Here lines means an allotment measured out.

To read between the lines. To discern the secret meaning. One method of cryptography is to write in alternate lines; if read line by line, the meaning of the writer is reversed or wholly misunderstood. Thus lines 2, 4, 6 of the following cryptogram would convey the warning to Lord Monteagle of the Gunpowder Plot.

"My lord, having just returned from Paris,
(2) stay away from the house to-night
and give me the pleasure of your company.
(4) for God and man have concurred to punish
those who pay not regard to their health,
and
(6) the wickedness of the time
adds greatly to its wear and tear."

Linen Goods. In 1721 a statute was passed imposing a penalty of £5 upon the *wearer*, and £20 upon the seller of, a piece of calico. Fifteen years later this statute was so far modified that calicoes manufactured in Great Britain were allowed, "provided the warp thereof was entirely of linen yarn." In 1774 a statute was passed allowing printed cotton goods to be used on the payment of threepence a yard duty; in 1806 the duty was raised to threepence halfpenny. This was done to prevent the use of calicoes from interfering with the demand for linen and woollen stuffs. The law for burying in woollen was of a similar character. The following extracts from a London news-letter, dated August 2nd, 1768, are curious. [*Note*—chintz is simply *printed calico.*]

"Yesterday three tradesmen's wives of this city were convicted before the Rt. Hon. the Lord Mayor for wearing chintz gowns on Sunday last, and each of them was fined £5. These make eighty who have been convicted of the above offence within twelve months past .... There were several ladies in St. James's Park on the same day with chintz gowns on, but the persons who gave informas of the above three were not able to discover their names or places of abode. .... Yesterday a waggon loaded with £2,000 worth of chintz was seized at Dartford in Kent by some custom-house officers. Two post-chaises loaded with the same commodity got off with their goods by swiftness of driving."

Lingo. Talk, language. A corruption of *lingua*.

Lingua Franca. A species of corrupt Italian spoken on the coasts of the Mediterranean. The Franks' language mixed with the Italian.

Lining of the Pocket. Money.

"My money is spent : Can I be content
With pockets deprived of their lining?"
The Lady's Decoy, or Man Midwife's Defence, 1738 p. 4.

When the great court tailor wished to obtain the patronage of Beau Brummel, he made him a present of a dress-coat lined with bank-notes. Brummel wrote a letter of thanks, stating that he quite approved of the coat, and he especially admired the lining.

Linnæan System. A system devised by Linnæus of Sweden, who arranged his three kingdoms of animals, vegetables, and minerals into classes, orders, genera, species, and varieties, according to certain characteristics.

Linne (*The Heir of*). The Lord of Linne was a great spendthrift, "who wasted his substance in riotous living." Having spent all, he sold his estates to John o' the Scales, his steward, reserving to himself only a "poor and lonesome lodge in a lonely glen." When he had squandered away the money received for his estates, and found that no one would lend or give him more, he retired to the lodge in the glen, where he found a rope with a running noose dangling over his head. He put the rope round his neck and sprang aloft, when lo! the ceiling burst in twain, and he fell to the ground. When he came to himself he espied two chests of beaten gold, and a third full of white money, and over them was written, "Once more, my son, I set thee clear; amend thy life, or a rope at last must end it." The heir of Linne now returned to his old hall, where he asked his quondam steward for the loan of forty pence; this was refused him. One of the guests proffered the loan, and told John o' the Scales he ought to have lent it, as he had bought the estate cheap enough. "Cheap call you it?" exclaimed John; "why, he shall have it back for 100 marks less." "Done," said the heir of Linne, and counted out the money. He thus recovered his estates, and made the kind guest his forester. (*Percy : Reliques,* series ii. book 2.)

Linsey-woolsy Million (*The*). The great unwashed. The artisan class, supposed to dress in linsey-woolsy. "Broadcloth" being for the gentry.

"Truth needs not, John, the eloquence of oaths ;
Not more than a decent suit of clothes
Requires of broad gold lace th' expensive glare,
That makes the linsey-woolsy million stare."
Peter Pindar : Silvanus Urban.

Linspe (French, 2 syl.) means a *prince* in slang or familiar usage. It comes from the inspector or monitor of the cathedral choir called the *Spé* or the *Inspé* (inspector), because he had to superintend the rest of the boys.

Lion (as an agnomen).

ALP ARSLAN [*the Valiant Lion*], son of Togrul Beg, the Perso-Turkish monarch. (Reigned 1063-1072.)

ALI was called *The Lion of God*.for his religious zeal and great courage. His mother called him at birth Al Haïdara, *the Rugged Lion.* (A.D. 602, 655-661.)

ALI PASHA, called *The Lion of Janina*. overthrown in 1822 by Ibrahim Pasha. (1741, 1788-1822.)

ARIOCH (fifth of the dynasty of Ninu, the Assyrian), called Arioch Ellas'ar— *i.e.* Arioch Melech al Asser, *the Lion King of Assyria.* (B.C. 1927-1897.)

DAMELOWIEZ, Prince of Haliez, who founded Lemberg (*Lion City*) in 1259.

GUSTA'VUS ADOLPHUS, called *The Lion of the North.* (1594, 1611-1632.)

HAMZA, called *The Lion of God and of His Prophet.* So Gabriel told Mahomet his uncle was enregistered in heaven.

HENRY, Duke of Bavaria and Saxony, was called *The Lion* for his daring courage. (1129-1195.)

LOUIS VIII. of France was called *The Lion* because he was born under the sign Leo. (1187, 1223-1226.)

RICHARD I. Cœur de Lion (*Lion's heart*), so called for his bravery. (1157, 1189-1199.)

WILLIAM of Scotland, so called because he chose a red lion *rampant* for his cognisance. (Reigned 1165-1214.)

¶ *The Order of the Lion.* A German Order of civil merit, founded in 1815.

Lion (as an emblem). A lion is emblem of the tribe of Judah ; Christ is called "the lion of the tribe of Judah."

"Judah is a lion's whelp : . . . he couched as a lion, and as an old lion ; who shall rouse him up ?"—Genesis xlix. 9.

A lion emblematic of St. Jerome. The tale is, that while Jerome was lecturing one day, a lion entered the schoolroom, and lifted up one of its paws. All the disciples fled ; but Jerome, seeing that the paw was wounded, drew out of it a thorn and dressed the wound. The lion, out of gratitude, showed a wish to stay with its benefactor. Hence Jerome is typified as a lion, or as accompanied by a lion. (*Kenesman : Lives of the Saints,* p. 784.)

Androclus and the Lion. This is a replica of the tale of ANDROC'LUS. Androclus was a Roman slave, condemned to encounter a lion in the amphitheatre ; but when the beast was let loose it crouched at the feet of the slave and began licking them. The circumstance naturally excited the curiosity of the consul : and the slave, being brought before him, told him the following tale : " I was compelled by cruel treatment to run away from your service while in Africa, and one day I took refuge in a cave from the heat of the sun. While I was in the cave a lion entered, limping, and evidently in great pain. Seeing me, he held up his paw, from which I extracted a large thorn. We lived together in the cave for some time, the lion catering for both of us. At length I left the cave, was apprehended, brought to Rome, and condemned to encounter a lion in the amphitheatre. My enemy was my old friend, and he recognised me instantly." (*A. Gellius: Noctes,* v. 15.)

St. Gerasimus and the Lion. A very similar tale is told of ST. GERAS-IMUS (A.D. 475). One day, being on the banks of the Jordan, he saw a lion coming to him, limping on three feet. When it reached the saint, it held up to him the right paw, from which Gerasimus extracted a large thorn. The grateful beast attached itself to the saint, and followed him about as a dog. (*Vies des Pères des Déserts d'Orient.*)

Sir George Davis and the Lion. Sir George Davis was English consul at Florence at the beginning of the 19th century. One day he went to see the lions of the great Duke of Tuscany. There was one which the keepers could not tame ; but no sooner did Sir George appear than it manifested every symptom of joy. Sir George entered its cage, when the lion leaped on his shoulder, licked his face, wagged its tail, and fawned on him like a dog. Sir George told the great duke that he had brought up the creature ; but as it grew older it became dangerous, and he sold it to a Barbary captive. The duke said that he had bought it of the very same man, and the mystery was solved.

Half a score of such tales are told by the Bollandistes in the *Acta Sanctōrum*.

The lion an emblem of the resurrection. According to tradition, the lion's whelp is born dead, and remains so for three days, when the father breathes on it and it receives life. Another tradition is that the lion is the only animal of the cat tribe born with its eyes open, and it is said that it sleeps with its eyes open. This is not strictly correct, but undoubtedly it sleeps watchfully and lightly.

Mark the *Evangelist* is symbolised by

a *lion*, because he begins his gospel with the scenes of John the Baptist and Jesus in the Wilderness. Matthew is symbolised by a *man*, because he begins his gospel with the humanity of Jesus, as a descendant of David. Luke is symbolised as a *calf*, because he begins his gospel with the priest sacrificing in the temple. John is symbolised by an *eagle*, because he soars high, and begins his gospel with the divinity of the Logos. The four symbols are those of Ezekiel's cherubim.

The American lion. The puma.

A Cotswold lion. A sheep.

Lion (grateful for kindness) :—

ANDROC'LUS. (*See under* LION *as an emblem.*)

SIR IWAIN DE GALLES was attended by a lion, which, in gratitude to the knight, who had delivered it from a serpent with which it had been engaged in deadly combat, ever after became his faithful servant, approaching the knight with tears, and rising on his hind-feet like a dog.

SIR GEOFFREY DE LATOUR was aided by a lion against the Saracens; but the faithful brute was drowned in attempting to follow the vessel in which the knight had embarked on his departure from the Holy Land.

ST. GERASIMUS. (*See under* LION *as an emblem.*)

ST. JEROME. (*See under* LION *as an emblem.*)

Lion, in HERALDRY.

(1) *Couchant.* Lying down; head erect, and tail beneath him. Emblematic of sovereignty.

(2) *Coward* or *Coué.* With tail hanging between his legs.

(3) *Dormant.* Asleep, with head resting on his fore-paws.

(4) *Passant.* Walking, three feet on the ground; in profile. Emblematic of resolution.

(5) *Passant Gardant.* Three feet on the ground; full face. The "Lion of England." Resolution and Prudence.

(6) *Passant Regardant.* Three feet on the ground; side face turned backwards.

(7) *Rampant.* Erect on his hind legs; in profile. Emblematic of magnanimity.

(8) *Rampant Gardant.* Erect on his hind legs; full face. Emblematic of prudence.

(9) *Rampant Regardant.* Erect on his hind legs; side face looking behind. Emblematic of circumspection.

(10) *Regardant.* Looking behind him; emblematic of circumspection.

(11) *Saliant.* In the act of springing forward on its prey. Emblematic of valour.

(12) *Sejant.* Sitting, rising to prepare for action; face in profile, tail erect. Emblematic of counsel.

(13) Sejant *Affronté* (as in the crest of Scotland).

(14) *Statant.* Standing with four legs on the ground.

(15) *Lion of St. Mark.* A winged lion sejant, holding an open book with the inscription "*Pax tibi Marce, Evangelista Meus.*" A sword-point rises above the book on the dexter side, and the whole is encircled by an aureola.

(16) *Lion of Venice.* The same as the lion of St. Mark.

Then there are black, red, and white lions, with many leonine monsters.

A lion at the feet of knights and martyrs, in effigy, signifies that they died for their magnanimity.

The lions in the arms of England. They are three lions passant gardant, *i.e.* walking and showing the full face. The first lion was that of Rollo, Duke of Normandy, and the second represented the country of Maine, which was added to Normandy. These were the two lions borne by William the Conqueror and his descendants. Henry II. added a third lion to represent the Duchy of Aquitaine. which came to him through his wife Eleanor. The French heralds call the lion passant a *leopard*; accordingly Napoleon said to his soldiers, "Let us drive these leopards (the English) into the sea."

⁂ In heraldry any lion not rampant is called a *lion leopardé.*

The lion in the arms of Scotland is derived from the arms of the ancient Earls of Northumberland and Huntingdon, from whom some of the Scotch monarchs were descended. The *tressure* is referred to the reign of King Acha'icus, who made a league with Charlemagne, "who did augment his arms with a double trace formed with Floure-de-lyces, signifying thereby that the lion henceforth should be defended by the ayde of Frenchemen." (*Holinshed: Chronicles.*)

Sir Walter Scott says the lion rampant in the arms of Scotland was first assumed by William of Scotland, and has been continued ever since.

"William, King of Scotland, having chosen for his armorial bearing a Red Lion *rampant*, acquired the name of William the Lion; and this rampant lion still constitutes the arms of Scotland; and the president of the heraldic court . . . is called Lord Lion King-at-Arms."—*Tales of a Grandfather*, iv

A marble lion was set up in honour of Leonidas, who fell at Thermopylæ, and a Belgian lion stands on the field of Waterloo.

¶ *Lions in classic mythology.* CYB'ELE (3 syl.) is represented as riding in a chariot drawn by two tame lions.

PRACRITI, the goddess of nature among the Hindus, is represented in a similar manner.

HIPPOM'ENES and ATALANTA (fond lovers) were metamorphosed into lions by Cybelē.

HERCULES is said to have worn over his shoulders the hide of the Nem'ean lion, which he slew with his club. TER-ROUR is also represented as arrayed in a lion's hide.

The Nem'ean lion, slain by Hercules. The first of his twelve labours. As it could not be wounded by any weapon, Hercules squeezed it to death.

Lion (a public-house sign).

Black lion comes from the Flemings.

> " Au noir lyon la fleur-de-lis
> Prist la terre de ça le Lys."
> *Godefroy de Paris.*

Blue, the badge of the Earl of Mortimer, also of Denmark.

✲ Blue seems frequently to represent silver; thus we have the Blue Boar of Richard III., the Blue Lion of the Earl of Mortimer, the Blue Swan of Henry IV., the Blue Dragon, etc.

Crowned, the badge of Henry VIII.

Golden, the badge of Henry I., and also of Percy, Duke of Northumberland.

Passant gardant (walking and showing a full face), the device of England.

Rampant, the device of Scotland.

Rampant, with the tail between its legs and turned over its back, the badge of Edward IV. as Earl of March.

Red, of Scotland; also the badge of John of Gaunt, Duke of Lancaster, who assumed this badge as a token of his claim to the throne of Castile.

Sleeping, the device of Richard I.

Statant gardant (*i.e.* standing and showing a full face), the device of the Duke of Norfolk.

White, the device of the Dukes of Norfolk; also of the Earl of Surrey, Earl of Mortimer, and the Fitz-Hammonds.

> " For who, in field or foray slack,
> Saw the blanche lion e'er fall back ? [Duke of Norfolk]."
> *Sir Walter Scott : Lay of the Last Minstrel.*

The winged lion. The republic of Venice. Its heraldic device.

White and Red Lions. Prester John, in a letter to Manuel Comnenus, of Constantinople, 1165, says his land is " the home of white and red lions."

Lion-hunter (*A*). One who hunts up a celebrity to adorn or give prestige to a party. Mrs. Leo Hunter, in *Pickwick,* is a good satire on the name and character of a lion-hunter.

Lion-killer (*The*). Jules Gerard (1817-1864).

Lion Sermon (*The*). Preached in St. Katharine Cree church Leadenhall-street, London, in October, to commemorate " the wonderful escape" of Sir John Gayer, about 250 years ago, from a lion which he met with on being shipwrecked on the coast of Africa. Sir John was Lord Mayor in 1647.

Sir John Gayer bequeathed £200 for the relief of the poor on condition that a commemorative sermon was preached annually at St. Katharine Cree. It is said that Sir John was on his knees in prayer when the lion came up, smelt about him, prowled round and round him, and then stalked off.

Lion-sick. Sick of love, like the lion in the fable. (See *Shakespeare : Troilus and Cressida,* ii. 3.)

Lion Tamer (*The*). Ellen Bright, who exhibited at Wombwell's menagerie, was so called. She was killed by a tiger in 1880, at the age of seventeen.

Lion and Unicorn. The animosity which existed between these beasts, referred to by Spenser in his *Faërie Queene,* is allegorical of the animosity which once existed between England and Scotland.

> " Like as a lyon, whose imperiall powre
> A prowd rebellious unicorn defyes."
> Book ii. canto 5.

Lion and Unicorn. Ever since 1603 the royal arms have been supported as now by the English lion and Scottish unicorn; but prior to the accession of James I. the sinister supporter was a family badge. Edward III., with whom supporters began, had a lion and eagle ; Henry IV., an antelope and swan ; Henry V., a lion and antelope ; Edward IV., a lion and bull; Richard III., a lion and boar ; Henry VII., a lion and dragon ; Elizabeth, Mary, and Henry VIII., a lion and greyhound. The lion is dexter—*i.e.* to the right hand of the wearer or person behind the shield.

Lion and the True Prince (*The*). *The lion will not touch the true prince* (1 *Henry IV.,* ii. 4). This is a religious superstition ; the " true prince," strictly speaking, being the Messiah, who is called " the Lion of the tribe of Judah." Loosely it is applied to any prince of blood royal, supposed at one time to be hedged around with a sort of divinity.

> " Fetch the Numidian lion I brought over ;
> If she be sprung from royal blood, the lion
> Will do her reverence, else he'll tear her."
> *Beaumont and Fletcher: The Mad Lover.*

Lion of God. Ali was so called, because of his zeal and his great courage. (602, 655-661.)

Lion of St. Mark. (*See under* LION, *heraldry.*)

Lion of the Reformation (*The*). Spenser says that while Una was seeking St. George, she sat to rest herself, when a lion rushed suddenly out of a thicket, with gaping mouth and lashing tail ; but as he drew near he was awe-struck, and, laying aside his fury, kissed her feet and licked her hands ; for, as the poet adds, "beauty can master strength, and truth subdue vengeance." (The lion is the emblem of England, which waits upon Truth. When true faith was deserted by all the world, England the lion came to its rescue.) The lion then followed Una as a dog, but when Una met Hypocrisy, Sansloy came upon them and killed the lion. That is, during the reigns of Henry VIII. and Edward VI., England the lion followed the footsteps of Truth, but in the reign of Mary, Hypocrisy came and False-faith killed the lion, *i.e.* separated England from Truth by fire and sword.

Lion of the Zodiac. One of the signs of the Zodiac (28th of July to the 23rd of August).

Lion's Claws. Commonly used as ornaments to the legs of furniture, as tables, chairs, etc. ; emblematical of strength and stability. The Greeks and Romans employed, for the same purpose, the hoofs of oxen.

> " Les soutiens des tables et des trépieds [in Greece and Rome] se terminaient souvent en forme de piedes de bœuf, pour exprimer la force et la stabilité."—*Noel : Dictionnaire de la Fable,* vol. i. p. 237, col. 2.

Lion's Head. In fountains the water generally is made to issue from the mouth of a lion. This is a very ancient custom. The Egyptians thus symbolised the inundation of the Nile, which happens when the sun is in Leo. The Greeks and Romans adopted the same device for their fountains.

Lion's Mouth. *To place one's head in the lion's mouth.* To expose oneself needlessly and foolhardily to danger.

Lion's Provider. A jackal ; a foil to another man's wit, a humble friend who plays into your hand to show you to best advantage. The jackal feeds on the lion's leavings, and is supposed to serve the lion in much the same way as a dog serves a sportsman. The dog lifts up its foot to indicate that game is at hand, and the jackals yell to advertise the lion that they have roused up his prey. (*See* JACKAL.)

> ". . . the poor jackals are less foul,
> As being the brave lion's keen providers,
> Than human insects catering for spiders."
> *Byron : Don Juan,* ix. 27.

Lion's Share. The larger part : all or nearly all. In *Æsop's Fables,* several beasts joined the lion in a hunt ; but, when the spoil was divided, the lion claimed one quarter in right of his prerogative, one for his superior courage, one for his dam and cubs, "and as for the fourth, let who will dispute it with me." Awed by his frown, the other beasts yielded and silently withdrew. (*See* MONTGOMERY.)

Lions (*The*). The lions of a place are sights worth seeing, or the celebrities ; so called from the ancient custom of showing strangers, as chief of London sights, the lions at the Tower. The Tower menagerie was abolished in 1834.

Lionise a Person (*To*) is either to show him *the lions,* or chief objects of attraction ; or to make a lion of him, by *fêting* him and making a fuss about him. *To be lionised* is to be so treated.

Liosal'far. The light Alfs who dwell in the city Alf-heim. They are whiter than the sun. (*See* DOCK-ALFAR.) (*Scandinavian mythology.*)

Lip. (Anglo-Saxon, *lippe,* the lip.)

To curl the lip. To express contempt or disgust with the mouth.

To hang the lip. To drop the under lip in sullenness or contempt. Thus' Helen explains why her brother Troilus is not abroad by saying, "He hangs the lip at something." (Act iii. 1.)

> " A foolish hanging of thy nether lip."—*Shakespeare : 1 Henry IV.,* ii. 4.

To shoot out the lip. To show scorn.

> "All they that see me laugh me to scorn. They shoot out the lip ; they shake the head. . ."—Psalm xxii. 7.

Lip Homage. Homage rendered by the lips only, that is, either by a kiss like that of Judas, or by words.

Lip Service. Verbal devotion. Honouring with the lips while the heart takes no part nor lot in the matter. (*See* Matt. xv. 8, Isa. xxix. 13.)

Lips. *The calves of our lips* (Hosea xiv. 2). The sacrifice of praise and thanksgiving.

The fruit of the lips. Thanksgivings.

"Let us offer the sacrifice of praise to God continually, that is, the fruit of our lips giving thanks to His name."—Heb. xiii. 15.

Liquor up. Take another dram.

Lir (*King*). Father of Fionmala. On the death of Fingula, the mother of his daughter, he married the wicked Aoife, who, through spite, transformed the children of Lir into swans, doomed to float on the water till they heard the first mass-bell ring. Thomas Moore has versified this legend.

"Silent, O Moyle, be the roar of thy water,
  Break not, ye breezes, your chain of repose,
While murmuring mournfully, Lir's lovely
    daughter
Tells to the night-stars the tale of her woes."
                    Irish Melodies, No. ii. 9.

Liris. A proud but lovely daughter of the race of man, beloved by Rubi, first of the angel host. Her passion was the love of knowledge, and she was captivated by all her lover told her of heaven and the works of God. At last she requested Rubi to appear before her in all his glory, and as she fell into his embrace was burnt to ashes by the rays which issued from him. (*Moore : Loves of the Angels*, story ii.)

Lisbo'a or **Lis'boa.** Lisbon (*q.v.*)

"What beauties doth Lisbo'a first unfold."
                    Byron : Childe Harold, i. 16.

"And thou, famed Lis'boa, whose embattled wall
Rose by the hand that wrought proud Ilion's
    fall."
                    Mickle : Lusiad.

Lisbon. A corruption of '*Ulyssippo* (Ulysses' polis or city). Said by some to have been founded by Lusus, who visited Portugal with Ulysses, whence "Lusitania" (*q.v.*) ; and by others to have been founded by Ulysses himself This is Camoens' version. (*See above.*)

Lismaha'go (*Captain*), in Smollett's *Humphry Clinker*. Very conceited, fond of disputation, jealous of honour, and brim-full of national pride. This poor but proud Scotch officer marries Miss Tabitha Bramble. The romance of Captain Lismaha'go among the Indians is worthy of Cervantes.

Lisuar'te of Greece. One of the knights whose adventures and exploits are recounted in the latter part of the Spanish version of *Amadis of Gaul*. This part was added by Juan Diaz.

Lit de Justice. Properly the seat occupied by the French king when he attended the deliberations of his *parlement*. The session itself. Any arbitrary edict. As the members of *Parlement* derived their power from the king, when the king himself was present their power

returned to the fountain-head, and the king was arbitrary. What the king then proposed could not be controverted, and, of course, had the force of law. The last *lit de justice* was held by Louis XVI. in 1787.

Little. Thomas Moore published a volume of amatory poems in 1808, under the name of *Thomas Little*.

"When first I came my proper name was Little—
    now I'm Moore."   *Hood : The Wee Man.*

Little. *Little by little.* Gradually ; a little at a time.

Many a little makes a mickle. The real Scotch proverb is : "A wheen o' mickles mak's a muckle," where mickle means *little*, and muckle *much ;* but the Anglo-Saxon *micel* or *mycel* means "much," so that, if the Scotch proverb is accepted, we must give a forced meaning to the word "mickle."

Little Britain or *Brittany*. Same as Armor'ica. Also called Benwic.

Little Corporal (*The*). Napoleon Bonaparte. So called after the battle of Lodi, in 1796, from his low stature, youthful age, and amazing courage. He was barely 5 ft. 2 in. in height.

Little Dauphin (*The*). The eldest son of the Great Dauphin—*i.e.* the Duc de Bourgogne, son of Louis, and grandson of Louis XIV.

Little Ease. The name of a prison cell too small to allow the prisoner to stand upright, or to lie down, or to assume any other position of ease. I have seen such a cell at St. Cyr ; and according to *Curiosity*, or, *The General Library*, p. 69 (1738), cells of this kind were used "at Guildhall for unruly apprentices."

Little-Endians. The two great empires of Lilliput and Blefuscu waged a destructive war against each other, exhausted their treasures, and decimated their subjects on their different views of interpreting this vital direction contained in the 54th chapter of the Blun'decral (*Koran*) : "All true believers break their eggs at the convenient end." The godfather of Calin Deffar Plune, the reigning emperor of Lilliput, happened to cut his finger while breaking his egg at the big end, and very royally published a decree commanding all his liege and faithful subjects, on pains and penalties of great severity, to break their eggs in future at the small end. The orthodox Blefuscu'dians deemed it their duty to resent this innovation, and declared a war of extermination against the heretical Lilliputians. Many hundreds of large treatises were published on both sides, but those of a contrary opinion were put in the *Index expurgato'rius* of the opposite empire. (*Gulliver's Travels Voyage to Lilliput*, iv.)

" The quarrel between the Little-endians and the Big-endians broke out on Thursday, like the after-fire of a more serious conflagration."—*The Times.*

Little Englanders. Those who uphold the doctrine that English people should concern themselves with England only: they are opposed to colonisation and extension of the Empire.

Little-Go. The examination held in the Cambridge University in the second year of residence. Called also "the previous examination," because it precedes by a year the examination for a degree. In Oxford the corresponding examination is called *The Smalls*. (*See* Mods.)

Little Jack Horner. (*See* Jack.)

Little John. A big stalwart fellow, named John Little (or John Nailor), who encountered Robin Hood, and gave him a sound thrashing, after which he was rechristened, and Robin stood godfather. Little John is introduced by Sir Walter Scott in *The Talisman*.

" 'This infant was called John Little,' quoth he ;
   'Which name shall be changed anon.
The words we'll transpose, so wherever he goes,
   His name shall be called Little John."
       Ritson : Robin Hood, xxi.

Little John was executed on Arbor Hill, Dublin.

It will be remembered that Maria in *Twelfth Night*, represented by Shakespeare as a *little* woman, is by a similar pleasantry called by Viola, " Olivia's giant ; " and Sir Toby says to her, " Good night, Penthesile'a "—*i.e.* Amazon.

Little Masters. A name applied to certain designers, who worked for engravers, etc., in the sixteenth and seventeenth centuries. Called *little* because their designs were on a small scale, fit for copper or wood. The most famous are Jost Amman, for the minuteness of his work ; Hans Burgmair, who made drawings in wood illustrative of the triumph of the Emperor Maximilian ; Hans Sebald Beham ; Albert Altdorfer, and Henrich Aldegraver. Albert Dürer and Lucas van Leyden made the art renowned and popular.

Little Nell. A child of beautiful purity of character, living in the midst of selfishness, worldliness, and crime. (*Dickens : Old Curiosity Shop*.)

Little Ones (*The*). The small children, and young children generally.

Little Paris. Brussels, the capital of Belgium, and Milan, in Italy, are so called, from their gaiety and resemblance in miniature to the French capital.

Little Pedlington. The village of quackery and cant, humbug, and egotism, wherever that locality is. A satire by John Poole.

Little Red Ridinghood. This nursery tale is, with slight alterations, common to Sweden, Germany, and France. It comes to us from the French, called *Le Petit Chaperon Rouge*, in Charles Perrault's *Contes des Temps*.

Little Gentleman in Velvet (*The*). The mole. "To the little gentleman in velvet " was a favourite Jacobite toast in the reign of Queen Anne. The reference was to the mole that raised the mole-hill against which the horse of William III. stumbled at Hampton Court. By this accident the king broke his collar-bone, a severe illness ensued, and he died early in 1702.

Little Packs become a Little Pedlar. " Little boats must keep near shore, larger ones may venture more."

" Mainwaring is a clever justice—
In him, my lord, our only trust is—
   Burdett's a rotten meddler ;
Volks slind turn round and see their backs,
And meend [mind] old proverbs : 'Little packs
   Become a little pedlar."
     Peter Pindar : Middlesex Election, letter i.

Liturgy originally meant *public work*, such as arranging the dancing and singing on public festivals, the torch-races, the equipping and manning of ships, etc. In the Church of England it means the religious forms prescribed in the Book of Common Prayer. (Greek, *litourgiā*.)

Live. *He lived like a knave, and died like a fool.* Said by Bishop Warburton of Henry Rich, first Earl of Holland, the turncoat. He went to the scaffold dressed in white satin, trimmed with silver.

Liver-vein (*The*). A love rhapsody. The liver was anciently supposed to be the seat of love. When Longaville reads the verses, Biron says, in an *aside*, "This is the liver-vein, which makes flesh a deity." (*Shakespeare : Love's Labour's Lost*, iv. 3.)

Livered. As, *white-livered, lily-livered.* Cowardly. In the auspices taken by the Greeks and Romans before battle, if the liver of the animals sacrificed was healthy and blood-red, the omen was favourable; but if pale, it augured defeat.

> "Thou lily-livered boy."
> *Shakespeare: Macbeth* v. 3.

Liverpool. Said to be the "liver-pool." The liver is a mythic bird, somewhat like the heron. The arms of the city contain *two livers*.

Liverpud'lian. A native of Liverpool.

Livery. What is delivered. The clothes of a man-servant delivered to him by his master. The stables to which your horse is delivered for keep. During the Merovingian and Carlovingian dynasties, splendid dresses were given to all the members of the royal household; barons and knights gave uniforms to their retainers, and even a duke's son, serving as a page, was clothed in the livery of the prince he served. (French, *livrer*.)

"What livery is we know well enough; it is the allowance of horse-meate to keepe horses at livery; the which word, I guess, is derived of delivering forth their nightly food."—*Spenser on Ireland.*

Livery. The colours of a livery should be those of the field and principal charge of the armorial shield; hence the Queen's livery is gules (scarlet) or scarlet trimmed with gold. The Irish regiments preserve the charge of their own nation. Thus the Royal Irish Dragoon Guards have scarlet uniform with blue facings, and the Royal Irish Lancers have blue uniform with scarlet facings.

Livery-men. The freemen of the ninety-one guilds of London are so called, because they are entitled to wear the livery of their respective companies.

Livy of France (*The*). Juan de Mariana (1537-1624).

Livy of Portugal (*The*). João de Barros, the best of the Portuguese historians. (1496-1570.)

Liza. An innkeeper's daughter in love with Elvi'no, a rich farmer: but Elvi'no loves Ami'na. Suspicious circumstances make the farmer renounce the hand of Amina and promise marriage to her rival; but Liza is shown to be the paramour of another, and Amina, being proved innocent, is married to the man who loves her. (*Bellini: La Sonnambula.*) Or LISA. (*See* ELVINO.)

Lizard (*The*). Supposed, at one time, to be venomous, and hence a "lizard's leg" was an ingredient in the witch's cauldron in *Macbeth*.

Lizard Islands. Fabulous islands where damsels outcast from the rest of the world are received. (*Torquemada: Garden of Flowers.*)

Lizard Point (Cornwall). A corruption of "Lazars' Point," *i.e.* the place of retirement for lazars or lepers.

Lloyd's. An association of underwriters, for marine insurances. So called because the society removed in 1716 from Cornhill to a coffee-house in Lombard Street kept by a man named Lloyd.

Lloyd's Books. Two enormous ledger-like volumes, raised on desks at the entrance (right and left) of Lloyd's Rooms. These books give the principal arrivals, and all losses by wrecks, fire, or other accidents at sea. The entries are written in a fine, bold Roman hand, legible to all readers.

Lloyd's List. A London periodical, in which the shipping news received at Lloyd's Rooms is regularly published.

Lloyd's Register. A register of ships, British and foreign, published yearly.

Lloyd's Rooms. The rooms where Lloyd's Books are kept, and the business of the house is carried on. These rooms were, in 1774, removed from Lombard Street to the Royal Exchange, and are under the management of a committee.

Loaf. *Never turn a loaf in the presence of a Menteith.* Sir John Stewart de Menteith was the person who betrayed Sir William Wallace to King Edward. His signal was, when he turned a loaf set on the table, the guests were to rush upon the patriot, and secure him. (*Sir Walter Scott: Tales of a Grandfather*, vii.)

Loaf held in the Hand (*A*) is the attribute of St. Philip the Apostle, St. Osyth, St. Joanna, Nicholas, St. Godfrey, and of many other saints noted for their charity to the poor.

Loafers. Tramps, thieves, and the ne'er-do-well. Idle fellows who get their living by expedients; *chevaliers d'industrie.* (German, *läufer*, a runner; Dutch, *looper*.)

"Until the differentiation of the labourer from the loafer takes place, the unemployed question can never be properly dealt with."—*Nineteenth Century*, December, 1893, p. 855.

Loathly Lady. A lady so hideous that no one would marry her except Sir Gaw'ain; and immediately after the marriage her ugliness—the effect of enchantment—disappeared, and she became a model of beauty. Love beautifies,

Loaves and Fishes. *With an eye to the loaves and fishes ; for the sake of . . .* With a view to the material benefits to be derived. The crowd followed Jesus Christ, not for the spiritual doctrines which He taught, but for the loaves and fishes which He distributed amongst them.

"Jesus answered them and said, Verily, verily, I say unto you, ye seek Me, not because ye saw the miracles, but because ye did eat of the loaves, and were filled."—John vi. 26.

Lob. A till. Hence *lob-sneak*, one who robs the till ; and *lob-sneaking*, robbing tills. (*See next article.*)

Lob's Pound. A prison, the stocks, or any other place of confinement. (Welsh, *llob*, a dolt). The Irish call it Pook's or Pouk's fold, and Puck is called by Shakespeare "the lob of spirits," and by Milton, "the lubber fiend." Our word *lobby* is where people are confined till admission is granted them into the audience chamber ; it is also applied to that enclosed space near farmyards where cattle are confined.

Lobby. *The Bill will cross the lobbies.* Be sent from the House of Commons to the House of Lords.

Loblolly, among seamen, is spoon-victuals, or pap for lobs or dolts. (*See* LOLLYPOPS.)

Loblolly Boy (*A.*) A surgeon's mate in the navy. Here lob is the Welsh *llob*, a dolt, and loblolly boy is a dolt not yet out of his spoon-meat or baby-pap.

"Loblolly-boy is a person on board a man-of-war who attends the surgeon and his mates, but knows as much about the business of a seaman as the author of this poem."—*The Patent* (1776).

Lobster Sauce. *Died for want of lobster sauce.* Died of mortification at some trifling disappointment. Died from pique, or wounded vanity. At the grand feast given by the great Condé to Louis XIV., at Chantilly, Vatel was told that the lobsters for the turbot sauce had not arrived, whereupon this *chef* of the kitchen retired to his private room, and, leaning on his sword, ran it through his body, unable to survive such a dire disgrace as serving up turbot without lobster sauce.

Lobsters and *Tarpaulings.* Soldiers and sailors. Soldiers are now popularly called lobsters, because they are turned red when enlisted into the service. But the term was originally applied to a troop of horse soldiers in the Great Rebellion, clad in armour which covered them as a shell.

"Sir William Waller received from London (in 1643) a fresh regiment of 500 horse, under the command of Sir Arthur Haslerig, which were so prodigiously armed that they were called by the king's party ' the regiment of lobsters,' because of their bright iron shells with which they were covered, being perfect cuirassiers, and were the first seen so armed on either side."—*Clarendon : History of the Rebellion,* iii. 91.

Lochiel (2 syl.) of Thomas Campbell is Sir Evan Cameron, lord of Lochiel, surnamed *The Black,* and *The Ulysses of the Highlands.* His grandson Donald was called *The Gentle Lochiel.* Lochiel is the title of the head of the clan Cameron.

"And Cameron, in the shock of steel, Die like the offspring of Lochiel." *Sir W. Scott : The Field of Waterloo.*

Lochinvar, being in love with a lady at Netherby Hall, persuaded her to dance one last dance. She was condemned to marry a "laggard in love and a dastard in war," but her young chevalier swung her into his saddle and made off with her, before the " bridegroom " and his servants could recover from their astonishment. (*Sir Walter Scott : Marmion.*)

Lock, Stock, and Barrel. The whole of anything. The lock, stock, and barrel of a gun is the complete instrument.

"The property of the Church of England, lock, stock, and barrel, is claimed by the Liberationists."—*Newspaper paragraph,* 1885.

Lock the Stable Door. *Lock the stable door when the steed is stolen.* To take " precautions " when the mischief is done.

Lockhart. When the good Lord James, on his way to the Holy Land with the heart of King Robert Bruce, was slain in Spain fighting against the Moors, Sir Simon Locard, of Lee, was commissioned to carry back to Scotland the heart, which was interred in Melrose Abbey. In consequence thereof he changed his name to Lock-heart, and adopted the device of *a heart within a fetterlock,* with this motto: " *Corda serrata pando* " (Locked hearts I open). Of course, this is romance. Lockhart is Teutonic, " Strong Beguiler."

"For this reason men changed Sir S'mon's name from Lockhard to Lockheart, and all who are descended from Sir Simon are called Lockhart to this day."—*Sir Walter Scott : Tales of a Grandfather,* xi.

Lockit. The jailer in Gay's *Beggar's Opera.*

Lockitt's. A fashionable coffee-house in the reign of Charles II.

Lockman. An executioner ; so called because one of his dues was a *lock* (or ladleful) of meal from every caskful exposed for sale in the market. In the Isle of Man the under-sheriff is so called.

Locksley. So Robin Hood is sometimes called, from the village in which he was born. (See *Ivanhoe*, ch. xiii.)

Locksley Hall. Tennyson has a poem so called. The lord of Locksley Hall fell in love with his cousin Amy, but Amy married a rich clown. The lord of Locksley Hall, indignant at this, declares he will marry a savage; .but, on reflection, adds: "Better fifty years of Europe than a cycle of Cathay."

Locksmith's Daughter. A key.

Loco Parentis (*Latin*). One acting in the place of a parent, as a guardian or schoolmaster.

Locofo'cos. Lucifer-matches; self-lighting cigars were so called in North America in 1834. (Latin, *loco-foci*, in lieu of fire.)

"In 1835 during an excited meeting of the party in Tammany Hall, New York, when the candles had been blown out to increase the confusion, they were lighted with matches then called "locofocos." — *Gilman : The American People*, chap. xxi.

Locofo'cos. Ultra-Radicals, so called in America because, at a grand meeting in Tammany Hall, New York, in 1835, the chairman left his seat, and the lights were suddenly extinguished, with the hope of breaking up the turbulent assembly; but those who were in favour of extreme measures instantly drew from their pockets their locofocos, and re-lighted the gas. The meeting was continued, and the Radicals had their way. (See *Gilman : The American People*, chap. xxi.)

Locomotive, or **Locomotive Engine.** A steam-engine employed to move carriages from place to place. (Latin, *locus moveo*, to move one's place.)

Locomotive Power. Power applied to the transport of goods, in contradistinction to stationary power.

Locrin or **Locrine** (2 syl.). Father of Sabri'na, and eldest son of the mythical Brutus, King of ancient Britain. On the death of his father he became king of Loe'gria (*q.v.*). (*Geoffrey : Brit. Hist.*, ii. 5.)

"Virgin daughter of Locrine,
Sprung from old Anchises' line."
Milton : Comus, 942-3.

Locum Te'nens (*Latin*). One holding the place of another. A substitute, a deputy; one acting temporarily for another; a lieutenant.

Locus Delicti. The place where a crime was committed.

Locus in quo (*Latin*). The place in question, the spot mentioned.

Locus Pœnitentiæ. (*Latin*.) Place for repentance — that is, the licence of drawing back from a bargain, which can be done before any act has been committed to confirm it. In the interview between Esau and his father Isaac, St. Paul says that the former "found no place for repentance, though he sought it carefully with tears" (Heb. xii. 17)— *i.e.* no means whereby Isaac could break his bargain with Jacob.

Locus pœnitentiæ. Time to withdraw from a bargain (in Scotch law).

Locus Sigilli or **L. S.** The place where the seal is to be set.

Locus Standi (*Latin*). Recognised position, acknowledged right or claim. We say such-and-such a one has no *locus standi* in society.

Locust Bird. A native of Khorassan (Persia), so fond of the water of the Bird Fountain, between Shiraz and Ispahan, that it will follow wherever it is carried.

Locusts. (For food.)

"The bushmen [says Captain Stockenston] consider locusts a great luxury, consuming great quantities fresh, and drying abundance for future emergencies." "They are eaten [says Thomas Bayne] in like manner by the Arabs of the Desert, and by other nomadic tribes in the East."

"Even the wasting locust-swarm,
Which mighty nations dread,
To me no terror brings, nor harm,
I make of them my bread."
African Sketches (1820).

Locus'ta. This woman has become a byword for one who murders those she professes to nurse, or those whom it is her duty to take care of. She lived in the early part of the Roman empire, poisoned Claudius and Britan'nicus, and attempted to destroy Nero; but, being found out, she was put to death.

Lode. The vein that leads or guides to ore. A *dead lode* is one exhausted.

Lode. A ditch that guides or leads water into a river or sewer.

Lodestar. The leading-star by which mariners are guided; the pole-star.

"Your eyes are lodestars."—*Shakespeare : Midsummer Night's Dream*, i. 1.

Lodestone or **Loadstone.** The magnet or stone that guides.

Lodo'na. The Lodden, an affluent of the Thames in Windsor Forest. Pope, in *Windsor Forest*, says it was a nymph, fond of the chase, like Diana. It chanced one day that Pan saw her, and tried to catch her; but Lodona fled from him, imploring Cyn'thia to save her from her persecutor. No sooner had she spoken than she became "a silver stream which ever keeps its virgin coolness."

Loegria or **Lo'gres.** England is so called by Geoffrey of Monmouth, from Logrine, eldest son of the mythical King Brute.

"His [Brute's] three sons divide the land by consent ; Locrine had the middle part, Loëgra . . ."
—*Milton : History of England*, bk. i.

"Thus Cambria to her right, what would herself restore,
And rather than to lose Loegria, looks for more."   *Drayton : Polyolbion*, iv.

"Il est ecrit qu'il est une heure
Ou tout le royaume de Logres,
Qui jaŭis fut la terre es ogres,
Sera detruit par cette lance."
       Chretien de Troyes.

Log. An instrument for measuring the velocity of a ship. It is a flat piece of wood, some six inches in radius, and in the shape of a quadrant. A piece of lead is nailed to the rim to make the log float perpendicularly. To this log a line is fastened, called the log-line (*q.v.*). Other forms are also used.

A king Log. A *roi fainéant*. In allusion to the fable of the frogs asking for a king. Jupiter first threw them down a log of wood, but they grumbled at so spiritless a king. He then sent them a stork, which devoured them eagerly.

Log-board. A couple of boards shutting like a book, in which the "logs" are entered. It may be termed the waste-book, and the *log-book* the journal.

Log-book. The journal in which the "logs" are entered by the chief mate. Besides the logs, this book contains all general transactions pertaining to the ship and its crew, such as the strength and course of the winds, the conduct and misconduct of the men, and, in short, everything worthy of note.

Log-line. The line fastened to the log (*q.v.*), and wound round a reel in the ship's gallery. The whole line (except some five fathoms next the log, called *stray line*) is divided into equal lengths called knots, each of which is marked with a piece of coloured tape or bunting. Suppose the captain wishes to know the rate of his ship; one of the sailors throws the log into the sea, and the reel begins to unwind. The length of line run off in half a minute shows the rate of the ship's motion per hour.

Log-roller (*A*). One engaged in log-rolling, that is (metaphorically) in furthering another's schemes or fads; persons who laud a friend to promote

the sale of his books, etc. The allusion is to neighbours who assist a new settler to roll away the logs of his "clearing."

"The members [of Congress] . . . . make a compact by which each aids the other. This is log-rolling."—*Bryce : Commonwealth*, vol. ii. part iii. chap. lxvii. page 125 (1889).

Log-rolling. The combination of different interests, on the principle of "Claw me, I'll claw you." Applied to mutual admiration criticism. One friend praises the literary work of another with the implied understanding of receiving from him in return as much as he gives. The mutual admirers are called "log-rollers."

⁜ In the last decade of the nineteenth century, it was used politically to signify if A B will help C D to pass their measures through the House, then C D will return the same favour to A B.

Of course, the term is American. If you help me to make my clearance, I will help you to roll away the logs of yours.

Log-rolling Criticism. The criticism of literary men who combine to praise each other's works in press or otherwise.

Logan or **Rocking Stones**, for which Cornwall is famous.

Pliny tells us of a rock near Harpăsa which might be moved with a finger.

Ptolemy says the Gygonian rock might be stirred with a stalk of asphodel.

Half a mile from St. David's is a Logan stone, mounted on divers other stones, which may be shaken with one finger.

At Golcar Hill (Yorkshire) is a rocking stone, which has lost its power from being hacked by workmen who wanted to find out the secret of its rocking mystery.

In Pembrokeshire is a rocking stone, rendered immovable by the soldiers of Cromwell, who held it to be an encouragement to superstition.

The stone called Menamber in Sithney (Cornwall) was also rendered immovable by the soldiers, under the same notion.

There are very many others.

Loggerheads. *Fall to loggerheads ;* to squabbling and fisticuffs.

Logget. A sweetmeat, a toffy cut into small manchets ; a little log of toffy. Common enough in Norfolk.

Logistilla (in *Orlando Furioso*). The good fairy, and sister of Alci'na the sorceress. She teaches Ruggie'ro to manage the hippogriff, and gives Astolpho a magic book and horn. The impersonation of reason.

Logres. (*See* LOEGRIA.)

Lo'gria. England, so called by the old romancers and fabulous historians.

Logris, Locris. Same as Locrin or Locrine (*q.v.*).

Loins. *Gird up the loins*, brace yourself for vigorous action, or energetic endurance. The Jews wore loose garments, which they girded about their loins when they travelled or worked.

"*Gird up the loins of your mind.*"—1 Peter i. 13.

My little finger shall be thicker than my father's loins (1 Kings xii. 10). My lightest tax shall be heavier than the most oppressive tax of my predecessor. The arrogant answer of Rehoboam to the deputation which waited on him to entreat an alleviation of "the yoke" laid on them by Solomon. The reply caused the revolt of all the tribes, except those of Judah and Benjamin.

Loki. The god of strife and spirit of evil. He artfully contrived the death of Balder, when Odin had forbidden everything that springs "from fire, air, earth, and water" to injure him. The mistletoe not being included was made into an arrow, given to the blind Höder, and shot at random; but it struck the beautiful Balder and killed him. This evil being was subsequently chained to a rock with ten chains, and will so continue till the twilight of the gods appears, when he will break his bonds; then will the heavens disappear, the earth be swallowed up by the sea, fire shall consume the elements, and even Odin, with all his kindred deities, shall perish. (*See* BALDER, KISSING.)

Loki's Three Children were Jörmungand (a monstrous serpent), Fenrir (a wolf), and Hela (half corpse and half queen). His wife was Siguna.

⁑ Loki is the personification of sin. Fenrir personifies the gnawings of a guilty conscience. Both Loki and Fenrir were chained by the Æsir, but not with iron chains. (*Scandinavian mythology.*)

Lokmân. A fabulous personage, the supposed author of a collection of Arabic fables. Like Æsop, he is said to have been a slave, noted for his ugliness.

Lollards. The early German reformers and the followers of Wickliffe were so called. An ingenious derivation is given by Bailey, who suggests the Latin word *lolium* (darnel), because these reformers were deemed "tares in God's wheat-field."

⁑ Gregory XI., in one of his bulls against Wickliffe, urges the clergy to extirpate this *lolium*.

"The name of Lollards was first given (in 1300) to a charitable society at Antwerp, who *lulled* the sick by singing to them."—*Dr. Blair : Chronology* (under the date 1300).

German *lollen*, to hum.

Lollop. To lounge or idle about.

Lollypops. Sweets made of treacle, butter. and flour; any sweets which are sucked. A "lolly" is a small lump.

Lombard (*A*). A banker or money-lender, so called because the first bankers were from Lombardy, and set up in Lombard Street (London), in the Middle Ages. The business of lending money on pawns was carried on in England by Italian merchants or bankers as early at least as the reign of Richard I. By the 12 Edward I., a messuage was confirmed to these traders where Lombard Street now stands; but the trade was first recognised in law by James I. The name Lombard (according to Stow) is a contraction of Longobards. Among the richest of these Longobard merchants was the celebrated Medici family, from whose armorial bearings the insignia of three golden balls has been derived. The Lombard bankers exercised a monopoly in pawnbroking till the reign of Queen Elizabeth.

Lombard Fever. Laziness. Pawn-brokers are called Lombard brokers, because they retain the three golden balls of the Lombard money-changers; and lazy folk will pawn anything rather than settle down to steady work.

Lombard Street to a China Orange. Long odds. Lombard Street, London, is the centre of great banking and mercantile transactions. To stake the Bank of England against a common orange is to stake what is of untold value against a mere trifle.

"'It is Lombard Street to a China orange,' quoth Uncle Jack."—*Bulwer Lytton : The Caxtons.*

Lombardic. The debased Roman style of architecture adopted in Lombardy after the fall of Rome.

London, says Francis Crossley, is *Luan-dun* (Celtic), City of the Moon, and tradition says there was once a temple of Diana (the Moon) where St. Paul's now stands. Greenwich he derives from *Grian-wich* (City of the Sun), also Celtic. It would fill a page to give a list of guesses made at the derivation of the word London. The one given above is about the best for fable and mythology. (*See* AUGUSTA, BABYLON, and LUD'S TOWN.)

London Bridge built on Wool-packs. In the reign of Henry II. the new stone bridge over the Thames was paid for by a tax on wool.

⁂ There was a bridge over the Thames in the tenth century. There was a new one of wood in 1014. The stone bridge (1176-1209) was by Peter of Colechurch. New London Bridge, constructed of granite, was begun in 1824, and finished in seven years. It was designed by Sir John Rennie, and cost £1,458,000. In 1894 was opened a new bridge, called the Tower Bridge, to admit of easier traffic.

London Stone. The central millia-rium (*milestone*) of Roman London, simi-lar to that in the Forum of Rome. The British high roads radiated from this stone, and it was from this point they were measured. Near London Stone lived Fitz Alwyne, who was the first mayor of London.

⁂ London Stone was removed for security into the wall of St. Swithin's church, facing Cannon Street station, and secured from damage by an iron railing.

There are two inscriptions, one in Latin and one in English. The latter runs thus :—

"London stone. Commonly believed to be a Roman work, long placed about xxxv feet hence towards the south-west, and afterwards built into the wall of this church, was, for more carefvl pro-tection and transmission to future ages, better secured by the churchwardens in the year of OVR LORD MDCCCLXIX."

Long Chalk (*A*) or **Long Chalks.** *He beat me by a long chalk* or *by long chalks.* By a good deal : by many marks. The allusion is to the game of dominoes, where the notation is made by chalk on a table.

Long Dozen (*A*) is 13. A long hun-dred is 120.

Long-headed. Clever, sharp-witted. Those who believe in the shape and bumps of the head think that a long head indicates shrewdness.

Long Home. *He has gone to his long home.* He is dead. The "long home" means the grave. The French equiva-lent is "*Aller dans une maison où l'on demeurera toujours.*"

Long Lane. (*See* LANE.)

Long Meg of Westminster. A noted virago in the reign of Henry VIII.

Her name has been given to several articles of unusual size. Thus, the large blue-black marble in the south cloister of Westminster Abbey, over the grave of *Gervasius de Blois*, is called "Long Meg of Westminster." Fuller says the term is applied to things "of hop pole height, wanting breadth proportionable there-unto," and refers to a great gun in the Tower so called, taken to Westminster in troublous times.

The large gun in Edinburgh Castle is called *Mons Meg*, and the bomb forged for the siege of Oudenarde, now in the city of Ghent, is called *Mad Meg*.

In the *Edinburgh Antiquarian Maga-zine*, September, 1769, we read of "Peter Branan, aged 104, who was six feet six inches high, and was commonly called *Long Meg of Westminster*. (*See* MEG.)

Long Meg and her daughters. In the neighbourhood of Penrith, Cumberland, is a circle of 67 (Camden says 77) stones, some of them ten feet high, ranged in a circle. Some seventeen paces off, on the south side, is a single stone, fifteen feet high, called *Long Meg*, the shorter ones being called *her daughters*. (Greek. *megas*, great.)

"This, and the Robrick stones in Oxfordshire, are supposed to have been erected at the investi-ture of some Danish kings, like the Kingstoler in Denmark, and the Moresteen in Sweden."—*Cam-den: Britannia.*

Long Odds. The odds laid on a horse which has apparently no chance of win-ning the race. Any similar bet.

Long Parliament. The parliament which assembled November 3rd, 1640, and was dissolved by Cromwell on April 20th, 1653 ; that is, 12½ years.

Long Peter. Peter Aartsen, the Flemish painter ; so called on account of his extraordinary height. (1507-1573.)

Long Run. *In the long run.* Even-tually. Here "long run" is not the correlative of a "short run," but the Latin adverb *demum*, ultimately ; in French, "*A la longue.*"

Long-Sword (*Longue épée*). William, the first Duke of Normandy. (Died 943.)

Long Tail. *Cut and long tail.* One and another, all of every description. The phrase had its origin in the practice of cutting the tails of certain dogs and horses, and leaving others in their natu-ral state, so that cut and long tail horses or dogs included all the species. Master Slender says he will maintain Anne

Page like a gentlewoman. "Ah!" says he—

> "That I will, come cut and long tail under the degree of a squire [*i.e.* as well as any man can who is not a squire]."—*Shakespeare: Merry Wives of Windsor*, iii. 4.

Long-tailed. *How about the long-tailed beggar?* A reproof given to one who is drawing the longbow too freely. The tale is that a boy who had been a short voyage pretended on his return to have forgotten everything belonging to his native home, and asked his mother what she called that "long-tailed beggar," meaning the cat.

Long Tom Coffin. A sailor of noble daring, in *The Pilot*, by Cooper.

Long Words.

Agathokakological. (*Southey : The Doctor*.)

Alcomiroziropoulopilousitounitapignac. The giantess. (*Croquemitaine*, iii. 2.)

Amoronthologosphorus. (*See* HAIR.) (*The Three Hairs*.)

Anantachaturdasivratakatha. (Sanskrit work.) (See *Trübner's Literary Record*.)

Antipericatametanaparbeugedamphicribrationes Toordicantium. One of the books in the library of St. Victor. (*Rabelais : Pantagruel*, ii. 7.)

Batrachomyomachia (battle of the frogs and mice). A Greek mock heroic.

Cluninstaridysarchides. (*Plautus*.)

Deanthropomorphisation.

Don Juan Nepomuceno de Burionagonatotorecagageazcoecha. An *employé* in the finance department of Madrid (1867).

Drimtaidhvrickhillichattan, in the Isle of Mull, Argyleshire.

Honorificabilitudinitatibus, called the longest word in the (?) English language. It frequently occurs in old plays. (See *Bailey's Dictionary*.) The "quadradimensionality" is almost as long.

> "Thou art not so long by the head as honorificabilitudinitatibus."—*Shakespeare: Love's Labour's Lost*, v. 1.

Inanthropomorphisability of deity.

Jungefrauenzimmerdurchschwindsuchttoedtungs-gegenverein (*German*). (See *Notes and Queries*, vol. v. p. 124, first series.)

Kagwadawwacomëgishearg. An Indian chief, who died in Wisconsin in 1866.

Lepadotemachoselachogaleokranioleipsanodrimupotrimmatosilphioparaomelitokatakeclummenokichlepikossuphophattoperisteralektruonoptegkephalokigklopeleiolagoosiraiobaletraganopterugon. It is one of the longest words extant (179

English and 169 Greek letters and consisting of 78 syllables). (*Aristophanes : Ekklesiazousai*, v. 1169.)

Llanfairpwllgwyngyllgogerychwyrndrobwllllandyssiliogogogoch. The name of a Welsh village in Anglesea. In the postal directory the first twenty letters only are given as a sufficient address for practical purposes, but the full name contains 59 letters. The meaning is, "The church of St. Mary in a hollow of white hazel, near to the rapid whirlpool, and to St. Tisilio church, near to a red cave."

> "What, Mr. Manhound, was it not enough thus to have morcrocastebezasteverestegrigeligoscopapondrillated us all in our upper members with your botched mittens, but you must also apply such morcderegrippiatabirofreluchamburdurecaquelurintinmpaniments on our shin-bones with the hard tops and extremities of your cobbled shoes."—*Rabelais*, illustrated by Gustave Dore, p. 438.

They morramborizeverzengirizequoquemorgasacbaquevezinemaffretiding my poor eye. (*Rabelais : Pantagruel*, iv. 15.)

Nitrophenylenediamine. A dye of an intense red colour.

> "Dinitroaniline, chloroxynaphthalic acid, which may be used for colouring wool in intense red; and nitrophenylenediamine of chromatic brilliancy."—*William Crookes: The Times*, October 5th, 1868.

Polyphrasticontinomimegalondulaton.

> "Why not wind up the famous ministerial declaration with 'Konx Ompax' or the mystic 'Om,' or that difficult expression 'Polyphrasticontinomimegalondulaton?'"—*The Star*.

M. N. Rostocostojambedanessé, author of *After Beef, Mustard*. (*Rabelais : Pantagruel*, ii. 7.)

Sankashtachaturthivratodyapana. (Sanskrit work.) (*See* Trübner's *Literary Record*.) Forster gives one of 152 syllables.

Tetramethyldiamidobenzhydrols.

> "The general depth of modern researches in structural chemistry must be explained, even to those who are not interested in the mystery of trypbenylmethans, the tetramethyldiamidobenzhydrols, and other similarly terrific terms used by chemists."—*Nineteenth Century* (Aug., 1893, p. 248).
>
> "Miss Burney has furnished the longest compound in the English tongue: 'the sudden-at-the-moment-though-from-lingering-illness-often-previously-expected death of Mr. Burney's wife."—*De Vere*.

Zürchersalzverbrauchsbuchhaltungsverordnung. (*Ausland*.)

> "Conturbabantur Constantinopolitani, Innumerabilibus sollicitudinibus."
>
> "Constantinopolitan maladministration Superinduces denationalisation."

Longboat. Formerly the largest boat belonging to a ship, built so as to carry a great weight. A long-boat is often from 30 to 40 feet long, having a beam from ·29 to ·25 of its length. It has a heavy flat floor, and is carvel built.

Longbow. *To draw the longbow.* To exaggerate. The force of an arrow in the longbow depends on the strength of the arm that draws it, so the force of a statement depends on the force of the speaker's imagination. The longbow was the favourite weapon of the English from the reign of Edward II. till it was superseded by fire-arms. The "longbow" was the hand-bow, as distinguished from the crossbow or bow fitted on a stock.

Longchamps. On Wednesday, Thursday, and Friday of Passion Week, the Parisians go in procession to Longchamps, near the Bois de Boulogne. This procession is made by private carriages and hired cabs, and is formed by all the smartly-dressed men and women who wish to display the spring fashions. The origin of the custom is this: There was once a famous nunnery at Longchamps, noted for its singing. In Passion Week all who could went to hear these religious women sing the Ténèbres; the custom grew into a fashion, and though the house no longer exists, the procession is as fashionable as ever.

Longcrown. A deep fellow, long-headed.
That caps Longcrown, and he capped the devil. That is a greater falsehood than the "father of lies" would tell.

Longevity. The oldest man of modern times was Thomas Carn, if we may rely on the parish register of St. Leonard's, Shoreditch, where it is recorded that he died in the reign of Queen Elizabeth, aged 207. He was born in 1381, in the reign of Richard II., lived in the reigns of ten sovereigns, and died in 1588. Old Jenkins was only 160 when he died, and remembered going (when he was a boy of twelve) with a load of arrows, to be used in the battle of Flodden Field. Parr died at the age of 152. William Wakley (according to the register of St. Andrew's church, Shifnal, Salop) was at least 124 when he died. He was baptised at Idsal 1590, and buried at Adbaston, November 28, 1714, and he lived in the reigns of eight sovereigns. Mary Yates, of Lizard Common, Shifnal, married her third husband at the age of 92, and died in 1776, at the age of 127.

Longius. The Roman soldier who smote our Lord with his spear. In the romance of King Arthur, this spear was brought by Joseph of Arimathea to Listenise, when he visited King Pellam,

"who was nigh of Joseph's kin." Sir Balim the Savage, being in want of a weapon, seized this spear, with which he wounded King Pellam. "Three whole countries were destoyed" by that one stroke, and Sir Balim saw "the people thereof lying dead on all sides." (*History of Prince Arthur*, vol i. chap. 41.) Generally called LONGINUS.

Longo Intervallo. *Proximus sed longo intervallo.* Next (it is true), but at what a vast distance! Generally quoted "*Longo intervallo.*"

Looby. A simpleton. (Welsh, *lŵb*, a dolt.)
    " The spendthrift and the plodding looby,
     The nice Sir Courtly, and the booby."
                    Hudibras: Redivivus (1707).

Look Alive. Be more active and energetic; look sharp.

Look Black (*To*) and *Black Looks.* (*See* BLACK . . . .)

Look Blue (*To*). To show signs of disappointment, disgust, or displeasure.
" Squire Brown looked rather blue at having to pay £2 10s. for the posting expenses from Oxford."
—*Hughes: Tom Brown at Oxford.*

Look Daggers (*To*). To look very angry, as if to annihilate you. Clytus says to Alexander, "You cannot look me dead."
    "You may look daggers, but use none."

Look as Big as Bull Beef (*To*). To look stout and hearty, as if fed on bull beef. Bull beef was formerly recommended for making men strong and muscular.

Look before You Leap. Consider well before you act. "*Melius est cavēre semper, quam patiri semel.*"
    " And look before you ere you leap,
     For, as you sow, you're like to reap."
    Butler: Hudibras, canto ii. part ii. 502.

Look for a Needle in a Bottle of Hay (*To*). (*See* BOTTLE.)

Look not a Gift Horse in the Mouth. "*Noli dentes equi inspicere donati.*" Do not examine a gift too critically.

Look One Way and Row Another (*To*). "*Olera spectant, lardum tollunt.*" To aim apparently at one thing, but really to be seeking something quite different.

Look through Blue Glasses or **Coloured Spectacles.** To regard actions in a wrong light; to view things distorted by prejudice.

Lookers-on. *The man on the dyke always hurls well.* The man standing on the mound, and looking at those who are playing at hurling, can see the faults and criticise them. Umpires are lookers-on.

Looking Back. Unlucky. This arose from Lot's wife, who looked back towards Sodom and was turned to a pillar of salt (Genesis xix. 26).

Looking-glass. *It is unlucky to break a looking-glass.* The nature of the ill-luck varies ; thus, if a maiden, she will never marry ; if a married woman, it betokens a death, etc. This superstition arose from the use made of mirrors in former times by magicians. If in their operations the mirror used was broken, the magician was obliged to give over his operation, and the unlucky inquirer could receive no answer.

Looking-glass of Lao reflected the mind as well as the outward form. (*Citizen of the World*, xlv.)

Loom means a utensil. (Anglo-Saxon, *loma*). Thus " heir-loom " means a personal chattel or household implement which goes by special custom to the heir. The word was in familiar use in Prior's time (1664-1721), for he says "a thousand maidens ply the purple loom."

Loony or **Luny.** A simpleton ; a natural. Corruption of lunatic.

Loophole. A way of escape, an evasion ; a corruption of "louvre holes." (*See* LOUVRE.)

Loose. *Having a tile loose.* Not quite of sound mind. The head being the roof of the temple called the body.

Out on the loose. Out on the spree ; out of moral bounds.

Loose-coat Field. The battle of Stamford in 1470. So called because the men under Lord Wells, being attacked by the Yorkists, threw off their coats that they might flee the faster.

"Cast off their country's coats to haste their
     speed away ;
Which ' Loose-coat Field ' is called e'en to
     this day."   *Drayton : Polyolbion*, xxii.

Loose Fish (*A*). A dissipated man. We also speak of a "queer fish," and the word "fishy" means of very doubtful character. A loose fish is one that has made its way out of the net ; and applied to man it means one who has thrown off moral restraint.

Loose-girt Boy (*The*). Julius Cæsar was so nicknamed.

Loose-strife. Botanically called *Lysimachia*, a Greek compound meaning the same thing. The author of

Flora Domestica tells us that the Romans put these flowers under the yokes of oxen to keep them from quarrelling with each other ; for (says he) the plant keeps off flies and gnats and thus relieves horses and oxen from a great source of irritation. Similarly in Collins' *Faithful Shepherdess*, we read—

" Yellow Lysimachus, to give sweet rest,
To the faint shepherd, killing, where it comes,
All busy gnats, and every fly that hums."

(Pliny refers the name to one of Alexander's generals, said to have discovered its virtues.)

Lorbrul'grud. The capital of Brobdingnag. The word is humorously said to mean " Pride of the Universe." (*Swift : Gulliver's Travels.*)

Lord. A nobleman.

The word lord is a contraction of *hlaford* (Saxon for "loaf-author " or "bread-earner "). Retainers were called *hlaf-ætas*, or "bread-eaters." Verstegan suggests *hlaf-ford*, "bread-givers." (*See* LADY.)

We have in Anglo-Saxon *hlaf-ord*, *hlaford - gift* (lordship), *hlaford - less* (lordless), *hlafordom* (dominion), and many more similar compounds.

⁛ *Lord*, a hunchback (Greek, *lord-os*, crooked). Generally " My lord."

Lord. *Drunk as a lord.* (*See* DRUNK.)

Lord Burleigh. *As significant as the shake of Lord Burleigh's head.* In *The Critic*, by Sheridan, is introduced a tragedy called the *Spanish Armada*. Lord Burleigh is supposed to be too full of State affairs to utter a word ; he shakes his head, and Puff explains what the shake means.

Lord Fanny. A nickname given to Lord Hervey for his effeminate and foppish manners. He painted his face, and was as pretty in his ways as a boarding-school miss. (In the reign of George II.)

Lord Foppington. A coxcomb who considers dress and fashion the end and aim of nobility. (*Vanbrugh : The Relapse.*)

Lord, Lady. *When our Lord falls in our Lady's lap.* That is, when Good Friday falls on the same date as Lady Day. (March 25th.)

Lord Lovel. The bridegroom who lost his bride on the wedding-day. She was playing at hide-and-seek, and selected an old oak chest for her hiding-place. The chest closed with a spring lock, and many years after her skeleton told the sad story of *The Mistletoe Bough*. Samuel Rogers introduces this story in his *Italy* (part i. 18). He says the bride was Ginevra, only child of Orsini, "an indulgent father." The bridegroom was Francesco Doria, "her playmate from her birth, and her first love." The chest in which she was buried alive in her bridal dress was an heirloom, " richly carved by Antony of Trent, with Scripture stories from the life of Christ." It came from Venice, and had "held the ducal robes of some old ancestor." Francesco, weary of his life, flew to Venice and "flung his life away in battle with the Turk." Orsini went mad, and spent the live-long day " wandering as in quest of something, something he could not find." Fifty years afterwards the chest was removed by strangers and the skeleton discovered.

Lord Mayor's Day, November 9th. So called because the Lord Mayor of London enters into office on that day, and inaugurates his official dignity with a street procession, followed by a grand banquet at the Mansion House.

Lord Peter. The Pope is so called in *The History of John Bull*, by Dr. Arbuthnot.

Lord Strutt. Charles II. of Spain is so called in *The History of John Bull*, by Arbuthnot.

Lord Thomas and the *Fair Annet* or *Elinor*, had a lover's quarrel, when Lord Thomas resolved to forsake Annet for a nut-brown maid who had houses and lands. On the wedding-day Annet, in bridal bravery, went to the church, when Lord Thomas repented of his folly, and gave Annet a rose. Whereupon the nut-brown maid killed her with a " long bodkin from out her gay head-gear." Lord Thomas, seeing Annet fall dead, plunged his dagger into the heart of the murderess, and then stabbed himself. Over the graves of Lord Thomas and fair Annet grew a " bonny briar, and by this ye may ken right well that they were lovers dear." In some ballads the fair Annet is called the fair Elinor. (*Percy : Reliques*, etc., series iii. bk. 3.)

Lord of Creation. Man.

" Replen'sh the earth, and subdue it : and have dominion over the fish of the sea, and o'er the fowl of the air, and over every living thing that moveth upon the earth. . . . Behold, I have given you every herb bearing seed . . . . and every tree . . . ."—Gen. i. 28, 29.

Lord of Misrule, called in Scotland *Abbot of Unreason*, prohibited in 1555. Stow says, " At the feast of Christmas,

in the king's court, there was always appointed, on All-Hallow's eve, a master of mirth and fun," who remained in office till the Feast of Purification. A similar " lord " was appointed by the lord mayor of London, the sheriffs, and the chief nobility. Stubbs tells us that these mock dignitaries had from twenty to sixty officers under them, and were furnished with hobby-horses, dragons, and musicians. They first went to church with such a confused noise that no one could hear his own voice.

Lord of the Isles. Donald of Islay, who in 1346 reduced the Hebrides under his sway. The title had been borne by others for centuries before, and was also borne by his successors. One of Sir Walter Scott's metrical romances is so called. This title is now borne by the Prince of Wales.

Loreda'no (*James*). A Venetian patrician, and one of the " Council of Ten." (*Byron : The Two Foscari*.)

Lorenzo (in Edward Young's *Nights Thoughts*). An atheist, whose remorse ends in despair.

Lorenzo. The suitor of the fair Jessica, daughter of Shylock the Jew. (*Shakespeare : Merchant of Venice*.)

Loretto. *The house of Loretto*. The Santa Casa, the reputed house of the Virgin Mary at Nazareth. It was " miraculously " translated to Fiume in Dalmatia in 1291, thence to Recana'ti in 1294, and finally to Macera'ta in Italy, to a plot of land belonging to the Lady Loretto.

"Our house may have travelled through the air, like the house of Loretto, for aught I care."— *Goldsmith: The Good-natured Man*, iv. 1.

⁂ There are other Lorettos : for instance, the Loretto of Austria, Mariazel (*Mary in the Cell*), in Styria. So called from the miracle-working image of the Virgin. The image, made of ebony, is old and very ugly. Two pilgrimages every year are made to it.

The Loretto of Bavaria (*Altötting*) near the river Inn, where there is a shrine of the Black Virgin.

The Loretto of Switzerland. Einsiedeln, a village containing a shrine of the " Black Lady of Switzerland." The church is of black marble and the image of ebony.

Lorrequer (*Harry*). The hero of a novel so called, by Charles Lever.

Lose. " 'Tis not I who lose the Athenians, but the Athenians who lose me," said Anaxag'oras, when he was driven out of Athens.

Lose Caste (*To*). (*See* CASTE.)

Lose Heart (*To*). To be discouraged or despondent. Heart = courage.

Lose not a Tide. Waste no time; set off at once on the business.

Lose the Day (*To*). To lose the battle; to be defeated. *To win* (or *gain*) *the day* is to be victorious; to win the battle, the prize, or any competition.

Lose the Horse or win the Saddle. Everything or nothing. "*Aut Cæsar, aut nullus.*" A man made the bet of a horse that another could not say the Lord's Prayer without a wandering thought. The bet was accepted, but before half-way through the person who accepted the bet looked up and said, "By-the-bye, do you mean the saddle also?"

Losing a Ship for a Ha'porth o' Tar. Suffering a great loss out of stinginess. By mean savings, or from want of some necessary outlay, to lose the entire article. For example, to save the expense of a nail and lose the horse-shoe as the first result, then to lame the horse, and finally perhaps kill it.

Loss. *To be at a loss.* To be unable to decide. To be puzzled or embarrassed. As: "I am at a loss for the proper word." "*Je m'y perds,*" or "*Je suis bien embarrassée de dire.*"

Lost Island. Cephalo'nia, so called because it was only by chance that even those who had visited it could find it again. It is sometimes called "The Hidden Island."

Lothair. A novel by Benjamin Disraeli (Lord Beaconsfield). The characters are supposed to represent the following persons:—
The Oxford Professor, Goldwin Smith.
Grandison, Cardinal Manning and Wiseman.
Lothair, Marquis of Bute.
Catesby, Monseigneur Capel.
The Duke and Duchess, the Duke and Duchess of Abercorn.
The Bishop, Bishop Wilberforce.
Corisande, one of the Ladies Hamilton.

Lotha'rio. *A gay Lothario.* A gay libertine, a seducer of female modesty, a debauchee. The character is from *The Fair Penitent,* by Rowe, and Rowe's tragedy is from Massinger's *Fatal Dowry.*

Lothian (Scotland). So named from Llew, the second son of Arthur, also

called Lothus. He was the father of Modred, leader of the rebellious army that fought at Camlan, A.D. 537.

Arthur's eldest son was Urien, and his youngest was Arawn.

Lotus. The Egyptians pictured God sitting on a lote-tree, above the watery mud. Jamblichus says the leaves and fruit of the lote-tree being *round* represent "the motion of intellect;" its towering up through mud symbolises the eminency of divine intellect over matter; and the Deity sitting on the lote-tree implies His intellectual sovereignty. (*Myster. Egypt.*, sec. 7, cap. ii. p. 151.)

Lotus. Mahomet says that a lote-tree stands in the seventh heaven, on the right hand of the throne of God.

Dry'opē of Œcha'lia was one day carrying her infant son, when she plucked a lotus flower for his amusement, and was instantaneously transformed into a lotus.

Lotis, daughter of Neptune, fleeing from Pria'pus, was metamorphosed into a lotus.

Lotus-eaters or **Lotoph'agi,** in Homeric legend, are a people who ate of the lotus-tree, the effect of which was to make them forget their friends and homes, and to lose all desire of returning to their native land, their only wish being to live in idleness in Lotus-land. (*Odyssey*, xi.)

A Lotus-eater. One living in ease and luxury. Lord Tennyson has a poem called *The Lotus Eaters.*

✢ The drink is made from the *Zizyphus Lotus,* which grows in Jerbah, an island near Tunis.

Loud Patterns. Flashy, showy ones. The analogy between sound and colour is very striking.

Loud as Tom of Lincoln. The great church bell.

Louis (*St.*) is usually represented as holding the Saviour's crown of thorns and the cross; sometimes, however, he is represented with a pilgrim's staff, and sometimes with the standard of the cross, the allusion in all cases being to his crusades.

Louis Dix-huit was nicknamed *Des Huitres,* because he was a great gourmand, and especially fond of oysters.

Louisiana, U.S. America. So named in compliment to Louis XIV. of France. Originally applied to the French possessions in the Mississippi Valley.

Loup. " *Le loup sait bien ce que mâle bête pense*" [male = méchant]. " *Un fripon reconnaît un fripon au premier coup d'œil.*" We judge others by ourselves. " *Chacun mesure tout à son aune.*" We measure others in our own bushel. The wolf believes that every beast entertains the same wolfish thoughts and desires as it does itself. Plautus expresses the same idea thus: "*Insanire me aiunt ultro cum ipsi insaniunt ;*" and Cicero says, " *Malum conscientia suspiciosum facit.*"

Louvre [*Paris*]. A corruption of *Lupara*, as it is called in old title-deeds.

Dagobert is said to have built here a hunting-seat, the nucleus of the present magnificent pile of buildings.

" He'll make your Paris Louvre shake for it."
  Shakespeare: Henry V., ii. 4.

Louvre. The tower or turret of a building like a belfry, originally designed for a sort of chimney to let out the smoke. (French, *l'ouvert*, the opening.)

Louvre boards in churches. Before chimneys were used, holes were left in the roof, called *loovers* or *leuver holes*. From the French *l'ouvert* (the open boards).

Louvre of St. Petersburg (*The*). The Hermitage, an imperial museum.

Love (*God of*). (Anglo-Saxon *luf*.)
Cam'deo, in Hindu mythology.
Camadé'va, in Persian mythology.
Cupid, in Roman mythology.
Eros, in Greek mythology.
Freya, in Celtic mythology.
Kama or *Cama*, in Indian mythology.
(*See* BOWYER, etc., etc.)

¶ *The family of lore.* Certain fanatics in the sixteenth century, holding tenets not unlike those of the Anabaptists.

There is no love lost. Because the persons referred to have no love for each other. What does not exist cannot be lost.

Love-lock. A small curl gummed to the temples, sometimes called a *beau* or *bow* catcher. When men indulge in a curl in front of their ears, the love-lock is called a *bell-rope—i.e.* a rope to pull the belles after them. At the latter end of the sixteenth century the love-lock was a long lock of hair hanging in front of the shoulders, curled and decorated with bows and ribbons.

Love-powders or **Potions** were drugs to excite lust. Once these love-charms were generally believed in ; thus, Brabantio accuses Othello of having bewitched Desdemona with " drugs to waken motion ; " and Lady Grey was accused of having bewitched Edward IV. " by strange potions and amorous charms." (*Fabian*, p. 495.)

Love and Lordship. *Love and lordship never like fellowship.* French, "*Amour et seigneurie ne veulent point de campagne ;*" German, "*Liebe und herrschaft leiden keine gesellschaft ;*" Italian, "*Amor e signoria non vogliono compagnia.*" (Neither lovers nor princes can brook a rival.)

Love in a Cottage. A marriage for love without sufficient means to maintain one's social status. However, "When poverty comes in at the door, love flies out of the window."

Love-in-Idleness. One of the numerous names of the pansy or heartsease. Originally white, but changed to a purple colour by the fall of Cupid's bolt upon it.

" Yet marked I where the bolt of Cupid fell.
  It fell upon a little Western flower,
  Before, milk-white, now purple with love's wound ;
  The maidens call it Love-in-idleness."
  Shakespeare: Midsummer Night's Dream, ii. 2.

Love me, Love my Dog. St. Bernard quotes this proverb in Latin, "*Qui me amat, amat et canem meam ;*" French, "*Qui aime Bertrand, aime son chien ;*" Spanish, " *Quién bién quiérs a beliram, bien quiére a su can.*" (If you love anyone, you will like all that belongs to him.)

Love's Girdle. (*See* CESTUS.)

Love's Labour's Lost (*Shakespeare*). Ferdinand, King of Navarre, with the three lords, Biron', Longaville, and Dumain, make a vow to spend three years in study, during which time they bind themselves to look upon no woman. Scarce is the vow made when the Princess of France, with Rosaline, Maria, and Catherine are announced, bringing a petition from the King of France. The four gentlemen fall in love with the four ladies, and send them verses ; they also visit them masked as Muscovites. The ladies treat the whole matter as a jest, and when the gentlemen declare their intentions to be honourable impose upon them a delay of twelve months, to be spent in works of charity. If at the expiration of that time they still wish to marry, the ladies promise to lend a favourable ear to their respective suits.

Lovel, the Dog. (*See* RAT, CAT, etc.)

Lovelace The principal male character of Richardson's novel *Clarissa*

Harlowe. He is a selfish voluptuary, a man of fashion, whose sole ambition is to ensnare female modesty and virtue. Crabbe calls him "rich, proud, and crafty; handsome, brave, and gay."

Lover's Leap. The promontory from which Sappho threw herself into the sea; now called Santa Maura. (*See* LEUCADIA.)

Loving or **Grace Cup.** A large cup passed round from guest to guest at state banquets and city feasts. Miss Strickland says that Margaret Atheling, wife of Malcolm Kanmore, in order to induce the Scotch to remain for grace, devised the grace cup, which was filled with the choicest wine, and of which each guest was allowed to drink *ad libitum* after grace had been said. (*Historic Sketches*.)

Loving Cup. On the introduction of Christianity, the custom of wassailing was not abolished, but it assumed a religious aspect. The monks called the wassail bowl the *poc'ulum carita'tis* (loving cup), a term still retained in the London companies, but in the universities the term *Grace Cup* is more general. Immediately after grace the silver cup, filled with sack (spiced wine) is passed round. The master and wardens drink welcome to their guests; the cup is then passed round to all the guests. (*See* GRACE CUP.)

⁂ A loving or grace cup should always have two handles, and some have as many as four.

Loving Cup. This ceremony, of drinking from one cup and passing it round, was observed in the Jewish paschal supper, and our Lord refers to the custom in the words, "Drink ye all of it."

"He [the master of the house] laid hold of the vessel with both hands, lifted it up, and said—'Blessed be Thou, O Lord our God, thou king of the world, who hast given us the fruit of the vine;' and the whole assembly said 'Amen.' Then drinking first himself from the cup, he passed it round to the rest."—*Eldad the Pilgrim*, chap. ix.

Low-bell. Night-fowling, in which birds are first roused from their slumber by the tinkling of a bell, and then dazzled by a light so as to be easily caught. (*Low*, Scotch, *lowe*, a flame, as a "lowe of fyre;" and *bell*.)

"The sound of the low-bell makes the birds lie close, so that they dare not stir whilst you are pitching the net, for the sound thereof is dreadful to them; but the sight of the fire, much more terrible, makes them fly up, so that they become instantly entangled in the net."—*Gent. Recreation*.

Low Church. The *Times* defines a Low Churchman as one "who loves a Jew and hates the Pope." We now call a Calvinistic episcopalian one of the Low Church because he holds "church rituals" and the dogma of "apostolic succession" in lower esteem than personal grace and faith in the "blood of the atonement."

Low Comedian (*The*), in theatrical parlance, is the farceur,—but must not poach on the preserves of the "light comedian." Paul Pry is a part for a "low comedian," Box and Cox are parts for a "light comedian."

Low Mass is a mass without singing. It is called *low* "*quia submissa voce celebrātur*." "Missa alta" is performed musically, and *alta voce*, in a loud voice.

Low Sunday. The Sunday next after Easter; so called because it is at the bottom of the Easter which it closes.

Low to High. *From low St. James's up to high St. Paul's* (*Pope: Satires*). In the Bangorian controversy, Bishop Hoadly, a great favourite at St. James's, was Low Church, but Dr. Hare, Dean of St. Paul's, was High Church.

Lower City (*The*). Acre, north of Zion, was so called.

Lower Empire. The Roman or Western, from removal of the seat of empire to Constantinople to the extinction of that empire by the Turks in 1453.

Lower your Sail. In French, "*Caler la voile*," means to salute; to confess yourself submissive or conquered; to humble oneself.

Lowlanders of Attica were the gentry, so called because they lived on the plains. (*Pedieis*.)

Lownde'an Professor (Cambridge University). A professor of astronomy (and geometry); the chair founded by Thomas Lowndes, Esq., in 1749.

Loy. A long, narrow spade used in cultivating stony lands.

Loyal. Only one regiment of all the British army is so called, and that is the "Loyal North Lancashire," in two battalions, No. 47 and No. 81. It was so called in 1793, and probably had some allusion to the French revolutionists.

Loys [*lo-is*]. So Louis was written in French till the time of Louis XIII.

Luath (2 syl.). Cuthullin's dog in Ossian's *Fingal;* also the name of the poor man's dog representing the peasantry in *The Twa Dogs*, by Robert

Burns. The gentleman's dog is called Cæsar. Also Fingal's dog. (*See* Dog.)

Lubber (*A*). A dolt. Seamen call an awkward sailor a land-lubber. A variant of "looby" (Welsh, *llob*, with a diminutive, "somewhat of a dunce or dolt.")

Lubber's Hole. A lazy cowardly way of doing what is appointed, or of evading duty. A seaman's expression. Sailors call the vacant space between the head of a lower-mast and the edge of the top, the *lubber's hole*, because timid boys get through this space to the top, to avoid the danger and difficulties of the "futtock shrouds."

Lubberkin or **Lubrican.** (Irish, *Lobairein* or *Lep'rechaun*.) A fairy resembling an old man, by profession a maker of brogues, who resorts to out-of-the-way places, where he is discovered by the noise of his hammer. He is rich, and while anyone keeps his eye fixed upon him cannot escape, but the moment the eye is withdrawn he vanishes.

Lubins. A species of goblins in Normandy that take the form of wolves, and frequent churchyards. They are very timorous, and take flight at the slightest noise.
"*Il a peur de lubins*" (Afraid of ghosts). Said of a chicken-hearted person.

Lucasian Professor. A professor of mathematics in the University of Cambridge. This professorship was founded in 1663 by Henry Lucas, Esq., M.P. for the University.

Lucasta, to whom Richard Lovelace sang, was Lucy Sacheverell, called by him *lux casta*, *i.e.* Chaste Lucy.

Luce. *Flower de Luce.* A corruption of *fleur-de-lis* (*q.v.*), more anciently written "*floure delices*," a corruption of *fiordilisa*, the white iris. The French messenger says to the Regent Bedford—

"Cropped are the flower de luces in your arms;
Of England's coat one-half is cut away."
Shakespeare: 1 *Henry VI.*, i. 1.

referring of course to the loss of France.
¶ The luce or lucy is a full-grown pike. Thus Justice Shallow says—"The luce is the fresh fish, the salt fish is an old coat"—*i.e.* Lucy is a new name, the old one was Charlecote. (*Merry Wives of Windsor*, i. 1.) (*See* Fleurs-de-Lys.)

Luce the full-grown pike, is the Latin *luci-us*, from the Greek *lukos* (a wolf), meaning the wolf of fishes.

Lucia di Lammermoor. Called Lucy Ashton by Sir Walter Scott, was the sister of Lord Henry Ashton of Lammermoor, who, to retrieve the fallen fortunes of the family, arranges a marriage between his sister and Lord Arthur Bucklaw (or Frank Hayston, laird of Bucklaw). Unknown to Henry Ashton, Edgardo (or Edgar), master of Ravenswood), whose family has long been in a state of hostility with the Lammermoors, is in love with Lucy, and his attachment is reciprocated. While Edgar is absent in France on an embassy, Lucy is made to believe, by feigned letters, that Edgar is unfaithful to her, and in her frenzy of indignation consents to marry the laird of Bucklaw; but on the wedding night she stabs her husband, goes mad, and dies. (*Donizetti : Lucia di Lammermoor*, *an opera;* and *Sir Walter Scott : Bride of Lammermoor*.)

Lucian. The impersonation of the follies and vices of the age, metamorphosed into an ass. The chief character in the *Golden Ass* of Apuleius.

Lucifer. The morning star. Venus is both an evening and a morning star: When she *follows* the sun, and is an evening star, she is called *Hesperus;* when she *precedes* the sun, and appears before sunrise, she is called *Lucifer* (the light-bringer).
Proud as Lucifer. Very haughty and overbearing. Lucifer is the name given by Isaiah to Nebuchadnezzar, the proud but ruined king of Babylon: "Take up this proverb against the King of Babylon, and say, . . . How art thou fallen, from heaven, O Lucifer, son of the morning!" (Isa. xiv. 4, 12). The poets feign that Satan, before he was driven out of heaven for his pride, was called Lucifer. Milton, in his *Paradise Lost*, gives this name to the demon of "Sinful Pride."

Lucifers (1833). An improvement on the Congreves and Prometheans. Phosphorus was introduced into the paste; but phosphorus made the matches so sensitive that the whole box often ignited, children were killed by sucking the matches, and at Boulogne two soldiers and a woman were poisoned by drinking coffee in which a child had put a "lucifer." The manufacture of these matches was also very deleterious, producing "jaw disease." (*See* Prometheans, Safety Matches.)

Lucifera [*Pride*] lived in a splendid palace, only its foundation was of sand. The door stood always open, and the queen gave welcome to every comer. Her six privy ministers are Idleness, Gluttony, Lechery, Avarice, Envy, and Revenge. These six, with Pride herself, are the seven deadly sins. Her carriage was drawn by six different animals—viz. an ass, swine, goat, camel, wolf, and lion, on each of which rode one of her privy councillors, Satan himself being coachman. While here the Red-Cross Knight was attacked by Sansjoy, who would have been slain if Duessa had not rescued him. (*Spenser : Faërie Queene*, bk. i. 4.)

Lucifer'ians. A sect of the fourth century, who refused to hold any communion with the Arians, who had renounced their "errors" and been readmitted into the Church. So called from Lucifer, Bishop of Cagliari, in Sardinia, their leader.

Lucin'ian. The young prince, son of Dolopatos, the Sicilian monarch, entrusted to the care of Virgil, the philosopher. (*See* SEVEN WISE MASTERS, and DOLOPATOS.)

Lucius. (*See* PUDENS.)

Luck. Accidental good fortune. (Dutch, *luk*; German, *glück*, verb *glücken*, to succeed, to prosper.)
Down on one's luck. Short of cash and credit. "Not in luck's way," not unexpectedly promoted, enriched, or otherwise benefited.
Give a man luck and throw him into the sea. Meaning that his luck will save him even in the greatest extremity. Referring to Jonah and Ari'on, who were cast into the sea, but carried safely to land, the one by a whale and the other by a dolphin.

Luck for Fools. This is a French proverb : "*A fou fortune*." And again, "*Fortune est nourrice de folie.*"

Luck in Odd Numbers. (*See* ODD.)

Luck of Eden Hall (*The*). A drinking cup, said to have been given to Miss Zoe Musgrave on her marriage with Mr. Farquharson, and still in Eden Hall, Cumberland. The tale is, that it was snatched surreptitiously from the fairies, who attached this threat to it :
"If that cup either break or fall,
  Farewell the luck of Eden Hall."
(*See* EDEN HALL.)

Luck or **Lucky Penny.** A trifle returned to a purchaser for good luck. A penny with a hole in it, supposed to ensure good luck.

Lucky. *To cut one's lucky.* To decamp or make off quickly : I must cut my stick. As *luck* means chance, the phrase may signify, "I must give up my chance and be off. (*See* CUT . . .)

Lucky Stone (*A*). A stone with a hole through it. (*See* LUCKY PENNY.)

Lucre'zia di Bor'gia, daughter of Pope Alexander VI., was thrice married, her last husband being Alfonso, Duke of Ferra'ra. Before her marriage with the duke she had a natural son named Genna'ro, who was sent to be brought up by a Neapolitan fisherman. When arrived at man's estate he received a letter informing him that he was nobly born, and offering him a commission in the army. In the battle of Rim'ini he saved the life of Orsi'ni, and they became sworn friends. In Venice he is introduced to the young nobles, who tell him of the ill deeds of Lucrezia Borgia. Each of them has had some relative put to death by her agency. Genna'ro, in his indignation, mutilates the duke's escutcheon with his dagger, knocking off the "B" of his name, and changing Borgia into Orgia (*orgies*). Lucrezia, not knowing who has offered the insult, requests the duke that the perpetrator may be put to death, but when she discovers it to be her own son gives him an antidote to neutralise the poison he has drunk, and releases him from his confinement. Scarcely is he liberated when he and his companions are invited by the Princess Neg'roni to a banquet, where they are all poisoned, Lucrezia tells Gennaro he is her son, and dies herself as soon as her son expires. (*Donizetti's opera.*)

Lucullus sups with Lucullus. Said of a glutton who gormandises alone. Lucullus was a rich Roman soldier, noted for his magnificence and self-indulgence. Sometimes above £1,700 was expended on a single meal, and Horace tells us he had 5,000 rich purple robes in his house. On one occasion a very superb supper was prepared, and when asked who were to be his guests the "rich fool" replied, "Lucullus will sup to-night with Lucullus." (B.C. 110-57.)

Lucus a non Lucendo. An etymological contradiction. The Latin word *lucus* means a "dark grove," but is said to be derived from the verb *luceo*, to shine. Similarly our word *black* (the Anglo-Saxon *blæc*) is derived from the verb *blæc-an*, to bleach or whiten.

Beldam. An ugly hag. From the French *belle dame*.

Bellum [*war*] quia min'ime bellum. (*Priscian.*) *Bellum*, a beautiful thing.

Calid (*hot*) radically the same as the Saxon *cald*, German *kalt* (cold).

Cleave, to *part*, also signifies to *stick together*. (Saxon, *clifan*, to adhere.)

Curta'na (the instrument that *shortens* by cutting off the head ; French *court*, Italian *corto*) is the blunt sword, emblematical of mercy, borne before our sovereigns at their coronation.

Devoted (*attached to*) is the Latin *devotus* (cursed).

Eumenīdēs (the well-disposed) ; the Furies.

Euonyma (good name) ; is poisonous.

Hiren, a sword, a bully. (Gk. *irēnē*, peace.)

Kalo-Johannes, son of Alexius Comnēnēs. Called *Kalos* (handsome) because he was exceedingly ugly and undersized. He was, however, an active and heroic prince, and his son Manual (contemporary with Richard Cœur de Lion) was even more heroic still.

Lambs were ruffians formerly employed at elections to use "physical force" to deter electors from voting for the opposition.

Leucosphere, the inner and brighter portion of the sun's corona. It is neither white nor spherical.

Lily-white, a chimney-sweep.

Religion, bond-service (*re-lĭgo*), is the service of which Christ has made us free.

Speaker of House of Commons. The only member that never makes speeches.

Solomon, George III., so called by Dr. Wolcott, because he was no Solomon.

In their marriage service the Jews *break a wine-glass ;* the symbol being "as this glass can never be rejoined, so may our union be never broken." (*See* MISNOMER.)

Lucy (*St.*). Patron saint for those afflicted in the eyes. It is said that a nobleman wanted to marry her for the beauty of her eyes ; so she tore them out and gave them to him saying, "Now let me live to God." The story says that her eyesight was restored ; but the rejected lover accused her of "faith in Christ," and she was martyred by a sword thrust into her neck. St. Lucy is represented in art carrying a palm branch, and bearing a platter with two eyes on it.

Lucy and Colin. A ballad by Thomas Tickell, translated into Latin by Vincent Bourne. Colin forsook Lucy of Leinster for a bride "thrice as rich." Lucy felt that she was dying, and made request that she might be taken to the church at the time of Colin's wedding. Her request was granted, and when Colin saw Lucy's corpse, "the damps of death bedewed his brow, and he died." Both were buried in one tomb, and to their grave many a constant hind and plighted maid resort to "deck it with garlands and true-love knots."

Lud. A mythical king of Britain. *General Lud.* (*See* LUDDITES.)

Lud's Bulwark. Ludgate prison. (*See above.*)

Lud's Town. London ; so called from Lud, a mythical king of Britain. *Ludgate* is, by a similar tradition, said to be the gate where Lud was buried. (*See* LONDON.)

> "And on the gates of Lud's town set your heads."
>   *Shakespeare: Cymbeline*, iv. 2.

Ludgate. Stow says, "King Lud, repairing the city, called it after his name *Lud's town ;* the strong gate which he built in the west part he likewise named Lud-gate. In the year 1260 the gate was beautified with images of Lud and other kings. Those images, in the reign of Edward VI., had their heads smitten off. . . . . Queen Mary did set new heads upon their old bodies again. The twenty-eighth of Queen Elizabeth the gate was newly and beautifully built, with images of Lud and others, as before." (*Survey of London.*) The more probable etymon of Lud-gate is the Anglo-Saxon *leode* (people), similar to the *Porto del populi* of Rome.

> "[Lud] Built that gate of which his name is hight,
> By which he lies entombèd solemnly."
>   *Spenser: Faërie Queene*, ii. x. 46.

∴ Ludgate was originally built by the barons, who entered London, destroyed the Jews' houses, and erected this gate with their ruins. It was used as a free prison in 1373, but soon lost that privilege. A most romantic story is told of Sir Stephen Forster, who was lord mayor in 1454. He had been a prisoner at Ludgate, and begged at the gate, where he was seen by a rich widow, who bought his liberty, took him into her service, and afterwards married him. To commemorate this strange eventful history, Sir Stephen enlarged the prison accommodation, and added a chapel. The old gate was taken down and rebuilt in 1586. The new-built gate was destroyed in the Great Fire of London, and the next gate (used also as a prison for debtors) was pulled down in 1760, the prisoners having been removed to the London Workhouse, and afterwards to the Giltspur Street Compter.

Luddites (2 syl.). Riotous workmen who went about the manufacturing districts breaking machines, under the notion that machinery threw men out of employ. Miss Martineau says that the term arose from Ned Lud, of Leicestershire, an imbecile who was much hounded by boys. One day he chased a set of tormentors into a house, and broke two stocking-frames, whence the leader of these rioters was called General Lud, his chief abettors Lud's wives, and his followers Luddites. (1811-1816.)

Ludlum. (*See* LAZY.)

Luez. (*See* LUZ.)

Luff. The weather-gauge. The part of a vessel towards the wind. A sailing close to the wind. (Dutch, *loef*, a weather-gauge.)

To luff is to turn the head of a ship towards the wind.

Luff!—i.e. Put the tiller on the leeside. This is done to make the ship sail nearer the wind.

Luff round! Throw the ship's head right into the wind.

Luff a-lee! Same as luff round.

A ship is said to *spring her luff* when she yields to the helm by sailing nearer the wind.

Keep the luff. The wind side.

Lufra. Douglas's dog, "the fleetest hound in all the North." (*Sir Walter Scott: Lady of the Lake*, v. 25.) (*See* DOG.)

Luggie. The warlock who, when storms prevented him from going to sea, used to sit on "Luggie's Knoll," and fish up dressed food.

Luggnagg. An island mentioned in *Gulliver's Travels*, where people live for ever. Swift shows the evil of such a destiny, unless accompanied with eternal youth. (*See* STRULDBRUGS.)

Luke (*St.*). Patron saint of painters and physicians. Tradition says he painted a portrait of the Virgin Mary. From Col. iv. 14 he is supposed to have been a physician.

St. Luke, in Christian art, is usually represented with an ox lying near him, and generally with painting materials. Sometimes he seems engaged painting a picture of the Virgin and infant Saviour, his descriptions of the early life of the Saviour being more minute than that of the other envangelists. Metaphrastus mentions the skill of St. Luke in painting; John of Damascus speaks of his portrait of the Virgin (p. 631: Paris, 1712). Many pictures still extant are attributed to St. Luke; but the artist was probably St. Luke, the Greek hermit; for certainly these meagre Byzantine

productions were not the works of the evangelist. (See *Lanzi: Storia Pittorica dell' Italia*, ii. 10.)

St. Luke's Club or *The Virtuo'sus*. An artists' club, established in England by Sir Antonio Vandyke, and held at the *Rose Tavern* Fleet Street. There was an academy of St. Luke founded by the Paris artists in 1391; one at Rome, founded in 1593, but based on the "Compagnia di San Luca" of Florence, founded in 1345; a similar one was established at Sienna in 1355.

St. Luke's Summer, called by the French *l'été de S. Martin;* hence the phrase "*L'été de la S. Denis à la S. Martin,*" from October 9th to November 11th, meaning generally the latter end of autumn.

". . . . St. Luke's short summer lived these men,
Nearing the goal of threescore years and ten."
Morris: Earthly Paradise (March).

As light as St. Luke's bird (*i.e.* an ox). Not light at all, but quite the contrary. St. Luke is generally represented writing, while behind him is an ox, symbolical of sacrifice. The whole tableau means that Luke begins his gospel with the priest sacrificing in the Temple.

Matthew is symbolised by a *man*, because he begins his gospel with the manhood of Jesus as a descendant of David; Mark, by a *lion*, because he begins his gospel with the baptism in the wilderness; John, by an *eagle*, because he begins his gospel by soaring into heaven, and describing the pre-existing state of the Logos.

Luke's Iron Crown. George and Luke Dosa headed an unsuccessful revolt against the Hungarian nobles in the early part of the sixteenth century. Luke (according to Goldsmith) underwent the torture of the red-hot iron crown, as a punishment for allowing himself to be proclaimed king. History says it was *George*, not Luke. (*The Traveller.*)

Lullian Method. A mechanical aid to the memory, by means of systematic arrangements of ideas and subjects, devised by Raymond Lully, in the thirteenth century.

Lumber (from *Lombard*). A pawnbroker's shop. Thus Lady Murray writes: "They put all the little plate they had in the lumber, which is pawning it, till the ships came home."

Lumine Sicco (*In*). Disinterestedly; as a dry question to be resolved without regard to other matters.

"If physiological considerations have any meaning, it will be always impossible for women to view the subject [of women's suffrage] in *lumine sicco.*"—*The Nineteenth Century* (The Hon. Mrs. Chapman, April, 1886).

Lump. *If you don't like it, you may lump it.* Whether you like to do it or not, no matter; it must be done. Here "lump it" means "to gulp it down," or swallow unwillingly, to put up with it unwillingly but of necessity. Thus we say of medicine, "lump it down," *i.e.* gulp it down. (Danish, *gulpen*, to swallow.)

Lumpkin (*Tony*), in *She Stoops to Conquer*, by Goldsmith. A sheepish, mischievous, idle, cunning lout, "with the vices of a man and the follies of a boy; "fond of low company, but giving himself the airs of the young squire.

Lun. So John Rich called himself when he performed harlequin (1681-1761).

"On the one Folly sits, by some called Fun,
And on the other his arch-patron Lun."
Churchill.

Luna. An ancient seaport of Gen'oa, whence the marble quarried in the neighbourhood is called "marmo lunense." (*Orlando Furioso.*)

Conte di Luna. Garzia, brother of Count Luna, had two sons. One day a gipsy was found in their chamber, and being-seized, was condemned to be burnt alive. The daughter of the gipsy, out of revenge, vowed vengeance, and stole Manri'co, the infant son of Garzia. It so fell out that the count and Manrico both fell in love with the Princess Leonora, who loved Manrico only. Luna and Manrico both fall into the hands of the count, and are condemned to death, when Leonora promises to "give herself" to Luna, provided he liberates Manrico. The count accepts the terms, and goes to the prison to fulfil his promise, when Leonora dies from poison which she has sucked from a ring. Soon as Manrico sees that Leonora is dead, he also dies. (*Verdi: Il Trovatore, an opera.*)

Lunar Month. About four weeks from new moon to new moon.

Lunar Year. Twelve lunar months. There are 13 lunar months in a year, $13 \times 4 = 52$ weeks.

Lunatics. Moon-struck persons. The Romans believed that the mind was affected by the moon, and that "lunatics" were more and more frenzied as the moon increased to its full. (*See* AVERTIN.)

"The various mental derangements ... which have been attributed to the influence of the moon, have given to this day the name *lunatics* to persons suffering from serious mental disorders."—*Crozier: Popular Errors, cha' iv. p. 53.*

Luncheon. (Welsh, *llonc* or *llwnc,* a gulp; *llyncu,* to swallow at a gulp.) The notion of its derivation from the Spanish *once,* eleven, is borrowed from the word nuncheon, *i.e. nón-mete,* a noon repast. Hence *Hudibras:*

"When, laying by their swords and truncheons,
They took their breakfasts, or their nuncheons."
Book i. 1. lines 345, 346.

✢ In *Letter Book* G, folio iv. (27 Edward II.), donations of drink to workmen are called *nonechenche.* (*Riley: Memorials of London.*)

Lungs of London. The parks. In a debate, June 30th, 1808, respecting encroachments upon Hyde Park, Mr. Windham said it was the "lungs of London."

Lunsford. A name used *in terrorem* over children. Sir Thomas Lunsford was governor of the Tower; a man of most vindictive temper, and the dread of everyone.

"Make children with your tones to run for't,
As bad as Bloodybones or Lunsford."
Butler: Hudibras, iii. 2.

Lu'percal (*The*), strictly speaking, meant the place where Romulus and Remus were suckled by the wolf (*lupus*). A yearly festival was held on this spot on Feb. 15, in honour of Lu'percus, the god of fertility. On one of these festivals Antony thrice offered to Julius Cæsar a kingly crown, but seeing the people were only half-hearted, Cæsar put it aside, saying, "Jupiter alone is king of Rome." Shakespeare makes Antony allude to this incident:

"You all did see that on the Lupercal
I thrice presented him a kingly crown,
Which he did thrice refuse."
Julius Cæsar, iii. 2.

✢ Shakespeare calls the Lupercalia "the feast of Lupercal" (act i. 1,), and probably he means the festival in Antony's speech, not the place where the festival was held.

Lupine. *He does not know a libel from a lupine.* In Latin: "*Ignorat quid distent æra lupinis,*" "He does not know good money from a counter, or a hawk from a handsaw." The Romans called counters lupines or beans. A libel was a small silver coin the tenth part of a denarius = the *as.*

Lupus et Agnus. A mere pretence to found a quarrel on. The words are the Latin title of the well-known fable of *The Wolf and the Lamb.*

Lupus in Fabula. (*See above.*)

"' *Lupus in fabula,*' answered the abbot, scornfully. ' The wolf accused the sheep of muddying the stream, when he drank in it above her.'"—*Sir W. Scott: The Monastery, last chapter.*

Lurch. *To leave in the lurch.* To leave a person in a difficulty. In cribbage a person is left in the lurch when his adversary has run out his score of sixty-one holes before he himself has turned the corner (or pegged his thirty-first) hole. In cards it is a slam, that is, when one of the players wins the entire game before his adversary has scored a single point or won a trick.

Lush. Beer and other intoxicating drinks; so called from Lushington the brewer.

Lu'siad or **The Lusiads.** The adventures of the Lusians or Portuguese under Vasquez da Gama in their "discovery of India." The fleet first sailed to Mozambique, in Africa, but Bacchus (the guardian power of the Mahometans) raised a commotion against the Lusians, and a battle ensued in which the Lusians were victorious. The fleet was next conducted by treachery to Quil'oa, a harbour on the east coast of the same continent; but Venus or Divine love, to save her favourites from danger, drove them away by a tempest, and Hermēs.bade Gama steer for Melinda, in Africa. At Melinda the Lusians were hospitably received, and the king of the country not only vowed eternal friendship, but also provided a pilot to conduct the fleet to India. In the Indian Ocean Bacchus tried to destroy the fleet, but "the silver star of Divine love" calmed the sea, and Gama arrived at India in safety. Having accomplished his object, Gama returned to Lisbon.

N.B. Gama sailed three times to India :—(1) with four vessels, in 1497, returning to Lisbon in two years and two months; he was appointed admiral of the Eastern seas. (2) In 1502, with twenty ships, when he was attacked by the Zamorin or king of Calicut, whom he defeated, and returned to Lisbon the year following; and (3) when John III. appointed him viceroy of India. He established his government at Cochin, where he died in 1525. It is the *first* of these voyages which is the subject of the Lusiad by Camoens.

Lusita'nia. Ancient name for Portugal, said to be so called from Lusus. (*See* LUSUS.)

Lusita'nian Prince. Don Henry, third son of John I. "the Great," King of Portugal—

> "Who, heaven-inspired,'
> To love of useful glory roused mankind,
> And in unbounded commerce mixed the world."
> *Thomson : Summer.*

Lustral Water. Water for aspersing worshippers was kept in an aspersorium, that those who entered or left the temple might dip their fingers into the water or be sprinkled by a priest. The same may be said of Indian pagodas, and the custom prevailed in ancient Egypt, and Etruria, with the Hebrews, and almost all the nations of antiquity. In Rome the priest used a small olive or laurel branch for sprinkling the people. Infants were also sprinkled with lustral water.

Lustrum. A space of five years. The word means a purification. These public expiations were made at Rome by one of the censors every fifth year, at the conclusion of the census. (Latin, *lu'ere*, to purify.)

Lus'us. *The sons* or *race of Lusus.* Pliny (iii. 1) tells us that Lusus was the companion of Bacchus in his travels, and settled a colony in Portugal; whence the country was termed *Lusita'nia*, and the inhabitants *Lusians.*

Lusus Natu'ræ. A freak of nature; as a man with six toes, a sheep with two heads, or a stone shaped like some well-known object, etc.

Lutestring. A glossy silk; a corruption of the French word *lustrine* (from *lustre*).

To speak in lutestring. Flash, highly-polished oratory. The expression was first used in *Junius.* Shakespeare has "taffeta phrases and silken terms precise." We call inflated speech "fustian" (*q.v.*) or "bombast" (*q.v.*); say a man talks *stuff;* term a book or speech made up of other men's brains, *shoddy* (*q.v.*); sailors call telling a story "spinning a yarn," etc. etc.

Lute'tia. Mud-hovels; the ancient name of Paris. The Romans call it *Lutetia Parisiōrum*, the mud-town of the Parisii. The former word being dropped, has left the present name Paris.

Luther's Hymn. "Great God, what do I see and hear," and "A safe stronghold," etc.

Lu'therans. Dr. Eck was the first to call the followers of Martin Luther by this name. It was used by way of contempt.

Lu'tin. A sort of goblin in the mythology of Normandy, very similar to the house-spirits of Germany and Scandinavia. Sometimes it assumes the form of a horse ready equipped, and in this shape is called *Le Cheval Bayard*.

To lutin is to twist hair into elf-locks. Sometimes these mischievous urchins so tangle the mane of a horse or head of a child that the hair must be cut off.

Le Prince Lutin, by the Countess D'Aulnoy.

Luxembergers. The people of Luxemberg. Similarly we have Augs-burgers, Carlsburgers, Edinburghers, Fri-burgers, Hamburghers and many more.

Luz or **Luez.** The indestructible bone; the nucleus of the resurrection body.

"'How doth a man revive again in the world to come?' asked Hadrian; and Joshua Ben Hana-ni'ah made answer. 'From luz in the backbone.' He then went on to demonstrate this to him: He took the bone luz, and put it into water, but the water had no action on it; he put it in the fire, but the fire consumed it not; he placed it in a mill, but could not grind it; and laid it on an anvil, but the hammer crushed it not."—*Lightfoot.*

"The learnéd rabbins of the Jews
  Write there's a bone, which they call luez . . ."
        Butler: Hudibras, iii. 2.

Lyb'ius (*Sir*). A very young knight who undertook to rescue the lady of Sinadone. After overcoming various knights, giants, and enchanters, he entered the palace of the lady. Presently the whole edifice fell to pieces about his ears, and a horrible serpent coiled round his neck and kissed him. The spell being broken, the serpent turned into the lady of Sinadone, who married the knight that so gallantly rescued her. (*Libeaux, a romance.*)

Lycaon'ian Tables [*Lycaoniæ mensæ*]. Execrable food. Lyca'on, desirous of testing the divine knowledge of Jove, who had honoured him with a visit, served up human flesh on his table; for which the god changed him into a wolf.

Lyc'idas. The name under which Milton celebrates the untimely death of Edward King, Fellow of Christ College, Cambridge, who was drowned in his passage from Chester to Ireland, August 10th, 1637. He was the son of Sir John King, Secretary for Ireland.

Lycis'ca (*half-wolf, half-dog*). One of the dogs of Actæon. In Latin it is a common term for a shepherd's dog, and is so used by Virgil (*Eclogue* iii. 18). (*See* Dog.)

Lycopo'dium. Wolf's foot, from a fanciful resemblance thereto.

Lydford Law is, punish first and try afterwards. Lydford, in the county of Devon, was a fortified town, in which was an ancient castle, where were held the courts of the Duchy of Cornwall. Offenders against the stannary laws were confined before trial in a dungeon so loathsome and dreary that it gave rise to the proverb referred to. The castle was destroyed by the Danes. (*See* CUPAR JUSTICE, COWPER'S LAW.)

"I oft have heard of Lydford law,
  How in the morn they hang and draw,
  And sit in judgment later."
        A Devonshire Poet.

Lydia, daughter of the King of Lydia, was sought in marriage by Alcestes, a Thracian knight; his suit was refused, and he repaired to the King of Armenia, who gave him an army, with which he laid siege to Lydia. He was persuaded by Lydia to raise the siege. The King of Armenia would not give up the project, and Alcestes slew him. Lydia now set him all sorts of dangerous tasks to "prove the ardour of his love," all of which he surmounted. Lastly, she induced him to kill all his allies, and when she had thus cut off the claws of this love-sick lion she mocked him. Alcestes pined and died, and Lydia was doomed to endless torment in hell, where Astolpho saw her, to whom she told her story. (*Orlando Furioso,* bk. xvii.)

Lydia Languish, in *The Rivals,* by Sheridan.

Lydian Poet (*The*). Alcman of Lydia. (Flourished B.C. 670.)

Lying Traveller (*The*). So Sir John Mandeville has been unjustly called. (1300-1372.)

Lying by the Wall. Dead but not buried. Anglo-Saxon, *wæl* (death). He is lying with the dead.

Lying for the Whetstone. Said of a person who is grossly exaggerating or falsifying a statement. One of the Whitsun amusements of our forefathers was the lie-wage or lie-match; he who could tell the greatest lie was rewarded with a whetstone to sharpen his wit. The nature of these contests may be illustrated by the following well-known extravaganza: one of the combatants declared he could see a fly on the top of a church-steeple; the other replied, "Oh yes, I saw him wink his eye."

When Sir R. Digby declared he had seen the "philosopher's stone," Bacon quizzically replied, "perhaps it was a whetstone."

Lyme-hound and *Gaze-hound.* The stanch lyme-hound tracks the wounded buck over hill and dale. The fleet gaze-hound kills the buck at view.

"Thou art the lyme-hound, I am the gaze-hound. . . . Thou hast deep sagacity and unrelenting purpose, a steady, long-breathed malignity of nature, that surpasses mine. But then, I am the bolder, the more ready, both at action and expedient. . . . I say . . . shall we hunt in couples?"—*Sir W. Scott: Kenilworth*, chap. iv.

Lyn'ceus (2 syl.) was so sharp-sighted he could see through the earth, and distinguish objects nine miles off.

"That Lynceus may be matched with Gautard's sight."   *Hall: Satires*, iv. 1.
"Non possis oculo quantum contendere Lynceus."
          Horace: 1 Epistle, i. 28.

Lynch Law. Mob-law, law administered by private persons. According to Webster, the word lynch refers to a Mr. James Lynch, a farmer, of Piedmont, in Virginia. The tale is that, as Piedmont, on the frontier, was seven miles from any law court, the neighbours, in 1686, selected James Lynch, a man of good judgment and great impartiality, to pass sentence on offenders for the nonce. His judgments were so judicious that he acquired the name of Judge Lynch, and this sort of law went by the name of Lynch law. In confirmation of this story, we are told there was a James Lynch Fitz-Stephen, who was warden of Galway in 1526; and in the capacity of warden he passed sentence of death on his own son for murder. (*See* BURLAW.)

"George was lynched, as he deserved."—*Emerson: English Traits*, chap. ix.

Lynch-pin. (Anglo-Saxon, *lynis*, an axle), whence club. (Qy. lynch-law.)

Lynchno'bians. Booksellers and publishers. Rabelais says they inhabit a little hamlet near Lantern-land, and live by lanterns. (*Pantag'ruel*, v. 33.)

Lynx, proverbial for its piercing eye-sight, is a fabulous beast, half dog and half panther, but not like either in character. The cat-like animal now called a lynx is not remarkable for keen-sightedness.

Lynx-eyed. Having as keen a sight as a lynx. Some think the word lynx is a perversion of Lynceus. (*See above.*)

Lyon King-of-Arms. Chief heraldic officer for Scotland; so called from the *lion rampant* in the Scottish regal escutcheon.

Lyonnesse (3 syl.). "That sweet land of Lyonnesse"—a tract between the Land's End and the Scilly Isles, now submerged full "forty fathoms under water." Arthur came from this mythical country.

Lyre (*The*). That of Terpander and Olympus had only three strings; the Scythian lyre had five; that of Simonídēs had eight; and that of Timotheus (3 syl.) had twelve. It was played either with the fingers or with a plectrum. The lyre is called by poets a "shell," because the cords of the lyre used by Orpheus (2 syl.), Amphíon, and Apollo, were stretched on the shell of a tortoise. Hercules used boxwood instead.

Amphi'on built Thebes with the music of his lyre, for the very stones moved of their own accord into walls and houses.

Ari'on charmed the dolphins by the music of his lyre, and when the bard was thrown overboard one of them carried him safely to Tæ'narus.

Hercules was taught music by Linus. One day, being reproved, the strong man broke the head of his master with his own lyre.

Orpheus charmed savage beasts, and even the infernal gods, with the music of his lyre.

Lysander and Rosicrucius, in the romance called *Bibliomania*, are meant for the author himself, Thomas Frognall Dibdin, D.D., a bibliographer, well known for his *Classics*—i.e. book on the *Rare and Valuable Editions of the Greek and Latin Classics* (1811).

Lyttelton, invoked by Thomson in his *Spring*, was George, Lord Lyttelton, of Hagley, Worcestershire, who procured from the Prince of Wales a pension of £100 a year for the poet. Lucinda was Lucy Fortescue, daughter of Hugh Fortescue, of Devonshire.

M

M. This letter represents the wavy appearance of water, and is called in Hebrew *mem* (water).

M. Every word in the *Materia more Magistralis* begins with the letter m. (*See* C *and* P.)

M (initial of manslaughter). The brand of a person convicted of that offence, and admitted to the benefit of clergy. It was burnt on the brawn of the left thumb.

M in numerals is the initial of *mille*, a thousand.

"Whosoever prayeth for the soul of John Gower he shall, so oft as he so doth, have a M and a D days of pardon."—*Gower's Tablet*.

M, to represent the human face. Add two dots for the eyes, thus, •M•. These dots being equal to O's, we get OMO (*homo*) Latin for man.

> " Who reads the name,
> For *man* upon his forehead, there the M
> Had traced most plainly."
> *Dante : Purgatory*, xxiii.

M. *The five M's :* Mansa, Matsya, Madya, Maithuna, and Mudra (flesh, fish, wine, women, and gesticulation). The five forms of Hindu asceticism.

M', i.e. *Mac.* A Gaelic prefix meaning son. (Gothic, *magus*, a son ; Sanskrit, *mah*, to grow ; Welsh, *magu*, to breed.) The Welsh *ap* is Mac changed to *Map*, and contracted into 'ap or 'p, as Apadam ('*Ap Adam*), Prichard ('*P Richard*).

M or **N** in the Catechism. M is a contraction of NN (names) ; N is for name. The respondent is required to give his *names* if he has more than one, or his *name* if only one.

In the marriage service, M stands for *mas* (the man) or *mari'tus* (the bridegroom), and N for *nupta* (the bride). There are some who think M stands for *Mary*, the patron saint of girls, and N for *Nicholas*, the patron saint of boys.

M. B. Waistcoat. A clerical cassock waistcoat was so called (about 1830) when first introduced by the High Church party. M. B. means " mark of the beast."

" He smiled at the folly which stigmatised an M.B. ' waistcoat.' "—*Mrs. Oliphant : Phœbe Juno*, ii. 3.

M.D. The first woman that obtained this degree was Elizabeth Blackwell, of the United States (1849).

M.P. Member of Parliament, but in slang language Member of the Police.

MS., manuscript ; **MSS.,** manuscripts; generally applied to literary works in penmanship. (Latin *manuscriptum*, that which is written by the hand.)

Mab. The " fairies' midwife "—*i.e.* employed by the fairies as midwife of dreams (to deliver man's brain of dreams). Thus when Romeo says, " I dreamed a dream to-night," Mercutio replies, " Oh, then, I see Queen Mab hath been with you." Sir Walter Scott follows in the same track : " I have a friend who is peculiarly favoured with the visits of Queen Mab," meaning with dreams (*The Antiquary*). When Mab is called "queen," it does not mean sovereign, for Titan'ia was Oberon's wife, but simply female ; both midwives and monthly nurses were anciently called queens or queans. *Quên* or *cwên* in

Saxon means neither more nor less than *woman ;* so " elf-queen," and the Danish *ellequinde,* mean *female elf,* and not "queen of the elves." Excellent descriptions of "Mistress Mab" are given by Shakespeare (*Romeo and Juliet*, i. 4), by Ben Jonson, by Herrick, and by Drayton in *Nymphidea.* (*Mab,* Welsh, a baby.)

MacAlpin. It is said that the founder of this famous family was named Halfpenny, and lived in Dublin in the 18th century. Having prospered in business, he called himself Mr. Halpen. The family, still prospering, dropped the H, and added Mac (son of), making Mac Alpen ; and Kenny MacAlpen called himself Kenneth MacAlpin, the " descendant of a hundred kings." True or not, the metamorphose is ingenious.

MacFarlane's Geese. The proverb is that " MacFarlane's geese like their play better than their meat." The wild geese of Inch-Tavoe (Loch Lomond) used to be called MacFarlane's Geese because the MacFarlanes had a house and garden on the island. It is said that these geese never returned after the extinction of that house. One day James VI. visited the chieftain, and was highly amused by the gambols of the geese, but the one served at table was so tough that the king exclaimed, " MacFarlane's geese like their play better than their meat."

MacFleck'noe in Dryden's famous satire, is Thomas Shadwell, poet-laureate, whose immortality rests on the not very complimentary line, " Shadwell never deviates into sense." (1640-1692.) N.B. Flecknoe was an Irish Roman Catholic priest, doggerel sonneteer, and playwright. Shadwell, according to Dryden, was his double.

" The rest to some slight meaning make pretence,
But Shadwell never deviates into sense."
Dryden : MacFlecknoe, 19, 20.

MacGirdie's Mare, used by degrees to eat less and less, but just as he had reduced her to a straw a day the poor beast died. This is an old Greek joke, which is well known to schoolboys who have been taught the *Analecta Minōra.* (See *Waverley*, p. 54.)

MacGregor. The motto of the MacGregors is, " E'en do and spair nocht," said to have been given them in the twelfth century by the king of Scotland. While the king was hunting he was attacked by a wild boar, when Sir Malcolm requested permission to encounter the creature. " E'en do," said the king, " and spair nocht." Whereupon the strong baronet tore up an oak sapling and despatched the enraged animal. For this defence the king gave Sir Malcolm permission to use the said motto, and, in place of a Scotch fir, to adopt for crest *an oak-tree eradicate, proper*.

✳ Another motto of the MacGregors is—" Sriogal mo dhream."

Rob Roy MacGregor or *Robert Campbell*, the outlaw. A Highland freebooter, the hero of Sir Walter Scott's *Rob Roy*. His wife's name is Helen, and their eldest son Hamish. In the *Two Drovers* MacGregor or MacCombich (Robin Oig) is a Highland drover.

MacIntyre (*Captain Hector*). Brother of Maria MacIntyre, the antiquary's niece, in Sir Walter Scott's *Antiquary*.

MacIvor (*Fergus*). Chief of Glennaquoich, and brother of Flora MacIvor, the heroine of *Waverley*, by Sir W. Scott.

MacPherson. During the reign of David I. of Scotland, a younger brother of the chief of the powerful clan Chattan espoused the clerical life, and in due time became abbot of Kingussie. His elder brother died, childless, and the chieftainship devolved on the abbot. He procured the needful dispensation from the Pope, married the daughter of the thane of Calder, and a swarm of little " Kingussies " was the result. The good people of Inverness-shire called them the *Mac-phersons, i.e.* the sons of the parson.

MacTab. *The Honourable Miss Lucretia MacTab.* A poor Scotch relative of Emily Worthington " on her deceased mother's side, and of the noble blood of the MacTabs." She lived on the Worthingtons, always snubbing them for not appreciating the honour of such a noble hanger-on, and always committing the most ludicrous mistakes from her extravagant vanity and family pride. (*George Colman: The Poor Gentleman.*)

MacTurk (*Captain Mungo* or *Hector*). " The man of peace " at the Spa Hotel, and one of the managing committee. (*Sir Walter Scott: St. Ronan's Well.*)

Maca'ber. *The dance macaber.* The Dance of the dead (*q.v.*) (French, *dance macabre.*) A dance over which Death presides, supposed to be executed by the dead of all ages and conditions. It is an allegory of the mortality of man, and was a favourite subject of artists and poets between the 13th and 15th centuries. It was originally written in German, then in Latin, and then in French. Some think Macaber was the name of the

author, but others think the word is **the** Arabic *makabir*, a cemetery. The best illustrations are those by Minden, Lucerne, Lubeck, Dresden, and Basle. Holbein's painting is very celebrated.

" What are these paintings on the wall around us? The dance macaber."
Longfellow: The Golden Legend.

Macad'amise (4 syl.). Using broken stones for road metal, and making the road convex instead of concave; a method introduced by Sir John L. Macadam (1756-1836).

Macaire (2 syl.). A favourite name in French plays, insomuch that Robert Macaire is sometimes used generically for a Frenchman. It is said that Aubrey de Montdidier was murdered in the forest of Bondy in 1371. His dog conceived such a hatred against Robert Macaire that suspicion was aroused, and it was resolved to pit the man and dog together. The result was fatal to the man, who died confessing his guilt. The story is found in a *chanson de geste* of the 12th century, called *La Reine Sibile*.

Mac'amut. Sultan of Cambaya, who lived upon poison, with which he was so saturated that his breath or touch carried instant death. (*Purchas.*)

Macare (*French*). The impersonation of good temper, in Voltaire's allegory of *Thelème and Macare*.

Macaro'ni. A coxcomb (Italian, *un maccheróne*). The word is derived from the Macaroni Club, instituted by a set of flashy men who had travelled in Italy, and introduced Italian maccheroni at Almack's subscription table. The Macaronies were the most exquisite fops that ever disgraced the name of man; vicious, insolent, fond of gambling, drinking, and duelling, they were (about 1773) the curse of Vauxhall Gardens.

" We are indebted to the Macaronies for only two things: the one is the introduction of that excellent dish . . . macaroni, and the other is the invention of that useful slang word ' bore' (boar), which originally meant any opponent of dandyism."—*Cassell's Magazine: London Legends.*

✳ An American regiment raised in Maryland during the War of Independence, was called The Macaronies from its showy uniform.

Macaron'ic Latin. Dog Latin, or modern words with Latin endings. The law pleadings of G. Steevens, as *Daniel* v. *Dishclout* and *Bullum* v. *Boatum*, are excellent examples. (*See* Dog Latin.)

✳ *Macaron'ic Latin* is a mixture of Latin and some modern language. In Italy *macheroni* is a mixture of coarse meal, eggs, and cheese.

Macaro'nic Verse. Verses in which foreign words are ludicrously distorted and jumbled together, as in Porson's lines on the threatened invasion of England by Napoleon. (*Lingo drawn for the Militia.*) So called by Teof'ilo Folengo, a Mantuan monk of noble family, who published a book entitled *Liber Maca-ronico'rum*, a poetical rhapsody made up of words of different languages, and treating of "pleasant matters" in a comical style (1520). Folengo is generally called Merlinus Coccaius, or Merlino Coccajo. (*See preceding.*) The *Vigonce* of Tossa was published in 1494. The following Latin verse is an hexameter;

"Trumpeter unus erat qui coatum scarlet habebat."

∴ A. Cunningham published in 1801 a *Delectus macaronicorum carminum*, a history of macaronic poetry.

Cane carmen SIXPENCE, pera plena rye,
De multis atris avibus coctis in a pie:
Simul hæc apert'est, cantat omnis grex,
Nonne permirabile, quod vidit ille rex?
Dimidium rex esus, misit ad reginam
Quod reliquit illa, sending back catinum.
Rex fuit in ærario, multo nummo tumens ;
In culina Domina, bread and mel consumens ;
Ancell' in horticulo, hanging out the clothes,
Quum descendens cornix rapuit her nose.
E. C. B.

Macbeth (*Shakespeare*). The story is taken from Holinshed, who copied it from the *History of Scotland*, by Hector Boece or Boyce, in seventeen volumes (1527). The history, written in Latin, was translated by John Bellenden (1531-1535).

∴ "History states that Macbeth slew Duncan at Bothgowan, near Elgin, in 1039, and not, as Shakespeare says, at his castle of Inverness ; the attack was made because Duncan had usurped the throne, to which Macbeth had the better claim. As a king Macbeth proved a very just and equitable prince, but the partisans of Malcolm got head, and succeeded in deposing Macbeth, who was slain in 1056, at Lumphanan. He was thane of Cromarty [Glamis], and afterwards of Moray [Cawdor].—*Lardner : Cabinet Cyclopædia.*

Lady Macbeth. The wife of Macbeth. Ambition is her sin, and to gain the object of her ambition she hesitates at nothing. Her masterful mind sways the weaker Macbeth to "the mood of what she liked or loathed." She is a Mede'a, or Catherine de' Medici, or Cæsar Bor'gia in female form. (*Shakespeare : Macbeth.*)

∴ The real name of Lady Macbeth was Graoch, and instead of being urged to the murder of Duncan through ambition, she was goaded by deadly injuries. She was, in fact, the granddaughter of Kenneth IV., killed in 1003, fighting against Malcolm II.—*Lardner : Cabinet Cyclopædia*, vol. i. 17, etc.

Macbriar (*Ephraim*). An enthusiastic preacher in Sir Walter Scott's *Old Mortality*.
This was the young preacher Maccaul so hideously tortured in the reign of

Charles II. He died "in a rapture." (*See* Cassell's *History of England*, Charles II., vol. iii. p. 422.)

Maccabæ'us. *The Hammerer.* A surname given to Judas Asmonæus; similar to "Martel," the name given to Charles, son of Pepin He'ristel, who beat down the Saracens as with a sledgehammer. Some think the name is a notarica or acrostic: **Mi** **C**amokah **B**aelim **J**ehovah (Who is like to thee among the gods, O Lord?). (Exodus xv. 11.) (*See* NOTARICA.)

Macdonald. *Lord Macdonald's breci.* Parasites. Lord Macdonald (son of the Lord of the Isles) once made a raid on the mainland. He and his followers, with other plunder, fell on the clothes of the enemy, and stripping off their own rags, donned the smartest and best they could lay hands on, with the result of being overrun with parasites.

Macduff. The thane of Fife. A Scotch nobleman whose castle of Kennoway was surprised by Macbeth, and his wife and babes " savagely slaughtered." Macduff vowed vengeance and joined the army of Siward, to dethrone the tyrant. On reaching the royal castle of Dunsinane, they fought, and Macbeth was slain. (*Shakespeare : Macbeth.*)

∴ History states that Macbeth was defeated at Dunsinane, but escaped from the battle and was slain at Lumphanan in 1056.—*Lardner : Cabinet Cyclopædia*, i. p. 17, etc.

Macheath (*Captain*). A highwayman, hero of *The Beggar's Opera*, by Gay. A fine, gay, bold-faced ruffian, game to the very last.

Mac'hiavelli. *The Imperial Machiavelli.* Tiberius, the Roman emperor. (B.C. 42 to A.D. 37.)
His political axiom was—"He who knows not how to dissemble knows not how to reign." It was also the axiom of Louis XI. of France.

Machiavellism. Political cunning and overreaching by diplomacy, according to the pernicious political principles of Niccolo del Machiavelli, of Florence, set forth in his work called *The Prince.* The general scope of this book is to show that rulers may resort to any treachery and artifice to uphold their arbitrary power, and whatever dishonourable acts princes may indulge in are fully set off by the insubordination of their subjects. (1469-1527.)

Mackintosh or **Macintosh.** Cloth waterproofed with caoutchouc, patented by Mr. Macintosh.

Macklin. The real name of this great actor was Charles M'Laughlin, but he changed it on coming to England. (1690-1797.)

Macmill'anites (4 syl.). A religious sect of Scotland, who succeeded the Covenanters; so named from John Macmillan, their leader. They called themselves the " Reformed Presbytery."

Macsyc'ophant (*Sir Pertinax*). In *The Man of the World*, by Charles Macklin, Sir Pertinax " bowed, and bowed, and bowed," and cringed, and fawned, to obtain the object of his ambition.

Mace. Originally a club armed with iron, and used in war. Both sword and mace are ensigns of dignity, suited to the times when men went about in armour, and sovereigns needed champions to vindicate their rights.

Macedon is not Worthy of Thee, is what Philip said to his son Alexander, after his achievement with the horse Buceph'alos, which he subdued to his will, though only eighteen years of age.

Edward III., after the battle of Creçy, in which the Black Prince behaved very valiantly, exclaimed, " My brave boy, go on as you have begun, and you will be worthy of England's crown."

Macedo'nian (*The*). Julius Polyænus, author of *Stratage'mata*, in the second century.

Macedonian Madman (*The*). (*See* MADMAN.)

Macedo'nians. A religious sect, so named from Macedo'nius, Patriarch of Constantinople, in the fourth century. They denied the divinity of the Holy Ghost, and that the essence of the Son is the same in kind with that of the Father.

Macedon'icus. Æmil'ius Paulus, conqueror of Perseus. (230-160 B.C.)

Mackerel Sky (*A*). A sky spotted like a mackerel. (Mackerel from the Latin, *macula*, a spot whence the French *maqu*rean, German *mackrele*, Welsh *macrell*, etc.)

Macon. Mahomet, Mahoun, or Mahound.

"Praised (quoth he) be Macon whom we serve."
Fairfax: Tasso, xii. 10.

Macon. A poetical and romance name of Mecca, the birthplace of Mahomet.

Mac'reons. *The island of the Mac-reons.* Great Britain. The word is Greek, and means long-lived. Rabelais describes the persecutions of the reformers as a terrible storm at sea, in which Pantag'ruel and his fleet were tempest-tossed, but contrived to enter one of the harbours of Great Britain, an island called " Long life," because no one was put to death there for his religious opinions. This island was full of antique ruins, relics of decayed popery and ancient superstitions.

Mac'rocosm (Greek, the *great world*), in opposition to the microcosm (the *little world*). The ancients looked upon the universe as a living creature, and the followers of Paracelsus considered man a miniature representation of the universe. The one was termed the Macrocosm, the other the Microcosm (*q.v.*).

Mad as a March Hare. (*See* HARE.) The French say, " *Il est fou comme un jeune chien.*"

Mad Cavalier (*The*). Prince Rupert, noted for his rash courage and impatience of control. (1619-1682.)

Mad Parliament (*The*). The Parliament which assembled at Oxford in 1258, and broke out into open rebellion against Henry III. The king was declared deposed, and the government was vested in the hands of twenty-four councillors, with Simon de Montfort at their head.

Mad Poet (*The*). Nathaniel Lee, who was confined for four years in Bedlam. (1657-1690.)

Mad as a Hatter. By some said to be a corruption of " Mad as an atter " (*adder*); but evidence is wanting. The word adder is *atter* in Saxon, *nutter* in German.

Madame. So the wife of Philippe, Duc d'Orléans was styled in the reign of Louis XIV.; other ladies were only Madame This or That.

Madame la Duchesse. Wife of Henri-Jules de Bourbon, eldest son of Prince de Condé.

Madame la Princesse. Wife of the Prince de Condé, and natural daughter of Louis XIV. (*See* MONSIEUR.)

Mademoiselle (4 syl.). The daughter of Philippe, Duc de Chartres, grandson of Philippe, Duc d'Orléans, brother of Louis XIV.

La Grande Mademoiselle. The Duchesse de Montpensier, cousin to Louis XIV., and daughter of Gaston, Duc d'Orléans,

Madge. An owl.

Madge Wildfire. The nickname of Margaret Murdochson, a beautiful but giddy girl, whose brain was crazed by seduction and the murder of her infant. (*Sir Walter Scott : Heart of Midlothian.*)

Madman. *Macedonia's madman.* Alexander the Great. (B.C. 356, 336-323.)

The brilliant madman or *Madman of the North.* Charles XII. of Sweden. (1682, 1697-1718.)

"Heroes are much the same, the point's agreed,
From Macedonia's madman to the Swede
   [Charles XII.]." *Pope: Essay on Man,* iv.

Madness. In Perthshire there are several wells and springs dedicated to St. Fillan, which are still places of pilgrimage. These wells are held to be efficacious in cases of madness. Even recently lunatics have been bound to the holy stone at night, under the expectation that St. Fillan would release them before dawn, and send them home in their right minds.

Madoc. The youngest son of Owain Gwyneth, King of North Wales, who died in 1169. According to tradition he sailed away to America, and established a colony on the southern branches of the Missouri. About the same time the Az'tecas forsook Aztlan, under the guidance of Yuhid'thiton, and founded the empire called Mexico, in honour of Mexitli, their tutelary god. Southey has a poem in two parts called *Madoc,* in which these two events are made to harmonise with each other.

Madonna. (Italian, *my lady.*) Specially applied to representations of the Virgin Mary.

Ma'dor (*Sir*). The Scotch knight slain in single combat by Sir Launcelot of the Lake, who volunteered to defend the innocence of Queen Guinever.

Madras System of Education. A system of mutual instruction, introduced by Dr. Andrew Bell into the institution at Madras for the education of the orphan children of the European military. Bell lived 1753-1832.

Mæan'der. To wind like the river Mæander, in Phrygia. The "Greek pattern" of embroidery is so called.

Mæce'nas. A patron of letters; so called from C. Cilnius Mæce'nas, a Roman statesman in the reign of Augustus, who kept open house for all men of letters, and was the special friend and patron of Horace and Virgil. Nicholas Rowe so called the Earl of Halifax on his installation to the Order of the Garter (1714).

The last English Mæcenas. Samuel Rogers, poet and banker. (1763-1855.)

Maelström (Norwegian, *whirling stream*). There are about fifty maelströms off the coast of Norway, but the one Englishmen delight to tremble at is at the foot of the Lofo'ten Islands, between the islands of Moskenës and Mosken, where the water is pushed and jostled a good deal, and when the wind and tide are contrary it is not safe for small boats to venture near.

It was anciently thought that the Maelström was a subterranean abyss, penetrating the globe, and communicating with the Gulf of Bothnia.

Mæon'ides (4 syl.) or **Mæonian Poet.** Homer, either because he was the son of Mæon, or because he was born in Mæon'ia (Asia Minor). (*See* HOMER.)

Mæviad. A merciless satire by Gifford on the Della Cruscan school of poetry. Published 1796. The word is in Virgil's *Eclogue,* iii. 90. (*See* BAVIAD.)

Mag. *What a mag you are !* jabberer, hence to *chatter like a magpie.* Mag is a contraction of magpie. The French have a famous word, "*caquet-bon-bec.*" We call a prating man or woman "a mag." (*See* MAGPIE.)

Not a mag to bless myself with—not a halfpenny.

Mag'a. *Blackwood's Magazine.* A mere contraction of the word maga-zine.

Magalo'na. (*See* MAGUELONE.)

Magazine (3 syl.). A place for stores. (Arabic, *makhzan, gazana,* a place where articles are preserved.)

Mag'dalene (3 syl.). An asylum for the reclaiming of prostitutes; so called from Mary Magdalene or Mary of Mag'-dala, "out of whom Jesus cast seven devils." A great profligate till she met with the Lord and Saviour.

Mag'deburg Centuries. The first great work of Protestant divines on the history of the Christian Church. It was begun at Magdeburg by Matthias Flacius, in 1552 ; and, as each century occupies a volume, the thirteen volumes complete the history to 1300.

Magellan. *Straits of Magellan.* So called after Magellan or Magalhaens, the Portuguese navigator, who discovered them in 1520,

Magen'ta. A brilliant red colour derived from coal-tar, named in commemoration of the battle of Magenta, which was fought in 1859.

Maggot, Maggoty. Whimsical, full of whims and fancies. Fancy tunes used to be called *maggots*, hence we have "Barker's maggots," "Cary's maggots," "Draper's maggots," etc. (*Dancing Master*, 1721.)

When the maggot bites. When the fancy takes us. Swift tells us that it was the opinion of certain virtuosi that the brain is filled with little worms or maggots, and that thought is produced by these worms biting the nerves. "If the bite is hexagonal it produces poetry; if circular, eloquence; if conical, politics, etc. (*Mechanical Operation of the Spirit.*)

Instead of maggots the Scotch say, "His head is full of bees;" the French, "*Il a des rats dans la tête;*" and in Holland, "He has a mouse's nest in his head." (*See* BEE.)

Ma'gi (*The*), according to one tradition, were Mel'chior, Gaspar, and Balthazar, three kings of the East. The first offered *gold*, the emblem of royalty, to the infant Jesus; the second, *frankincense*, in token of divinity; and the third, *myrrh*, in prophetic allusion to the persecution unto death which awaited the "Man of Sorrows."

MELCHIOR means "king of light."
GASPAR, or CASPAR, means "the white one."
BALTHAZAR means "the lord of treasures."
(Klopstock, in his *Messiah*, book v., gives these five names: Hadad, Selima, Zimri, Beled, and Sunith.)

Magi, in Camoens' *Lusiad*, means the Indian "Brahmins." Ammia'nus Marcelli'nus says that the Persian magi derived their knowledge from the Brahmins of India (i. 23); and Aria'nus expressly calls the Brahmins "magi" (i.7.).

Magic Garters. Made of the strips of a young hare's skin saturated with motherwort. Those who wear these garters excel in speed.

"Were it not for my magic garters . . .
I should not continue the business long."
Longfellow: The Golden Legend.

Magic Rings. This superstition arose from the belief that magicians had the power of imprisoning demons in rings. The power was supposed to prevail in Asia, and subsequently in Salamanca, Toledo, and Italy.

☙ Magic *circles* (like magic *squares*) are mathematical puzzles.

Corcud's ring. This magic ring was composed of six metals, and insured the wearer success in any undertaking in which he chose to embark. (*Chinese Tales; Corcud and his Four Sons.*)

Dame Liŏnês's ring, given by her to Sir Gareth during a tournament. It insured the wearer from losing blood when wounded.

"'This ring,' said Dame Lionês, 'increaseth my beauty . . . That which is green it turns red, and that which is red it turns green. That which is blue it turns white, and that which is white it turns blue. Whoever beareth this ring can never lose blood, however wounded.'"—*History of Prince Arthur*, i. 146.

Fairy ring (*A*). Whoever lives in a house built over a fairy ring will wondrously prosper in everything. (*Athenian Oracle*, i. 307.)

Gyges' ring. (*See* GYGES.)

Luned's ring rendered the wearer invisible. Luned or Lynet gave the ring to Owain, one of King Arthur's knights.

"Take this ring, and put it on thy finger, with the stone inside thy hand, and close thy hand upon it. As long as thou concealest the stone, the stone will conceal thee."—*The Mabinogion* (*Lady of the Fountain*).

Reynard's ring. The ring which Reynard pretended he had sent to King Lion. It had three gems: one *red*, which gave light in darkness; one *white*, which cured all blains and sprains; and one *green*, which would guard the wearer from all ills, both in peace and war. (*Henrik von Alkmaar: Reynard the Fox.*)

The steel ring, made by Seidel-Beckit. It enabled the wearer to read the secrets of another's heart. (*Oriental Tales; The Four Talismans.*)

The talking ring given by Tartaro, the Basque Cyclops, to a girl whom he wished to marry. Immediately she put it on, it kept incessantly saying "You there, and I here." In order to get rid of the nuisance, the girl cut off her finger, and threw both finger and ring into a pond. (*Basque legends.*)

☙ This tale appears in Campbell's *Popular Tales of the West Highlands* (i. to iii.), and in Grimm's *Tales* (*The Robber and his Sons*).

Magic Wand.

In *Jerusalem Delivered* the Hermit gives Charles the Dane and Ubaldo a wand which, being shaken, infused terror into all who saw it.

In the *Faërie Queene*, the palmer who accompanies Sir Guyon has a staff of like virtue, made of the same wood as Mercury's caduceus.

Magician. *The Great Magician* or *Wizard of the North.* Professor Wilson calls Sir Walter Scott the Great Magician, from the wonderful fascination of his writings.

Magician of the North. The title assumed by Johann Georg Hamann, of Prussia (1730-1788).

Magliabecchi. The greatest bookworm that ever lived. He never forgot what he had once read, and could even turn at once to the exact page of any reference. He was the librarian of the Great Duke Cosmo III. (1633-1714).

Magna Charta. The *Great Charter* of English liberty extorted from King John, 1215; called by Spelman—

"Augustis'simum Anglica'rum, liberta tum diplo'ma et sacra an'chora."

Magnalia Christi. Cotton Mathers's book, mentioned in Longfellow's *Mayflower.*

Magnanimous (*The*).

Alfonso V. of Aragon (1385, 1416-58). Chosroës or Khosru, twenty-first of the Sassan'idēs, surnamed *Noushir'wan* (the Magnanimous) (531-579).

Magna'no. One of the leaders of the rabble that attacked Hudibras at a bear-baiting. The character is a satire on Simeon Wait, a tinker and Independent preacher. (*Hudibras*, pt. i. 2.) He calls Cromwell the "archangel who did battle with the devil."

Magnet. The loadstone; so called from *Magne'sia*, in Lydia, where the ore was said to abound. The Greeks called it *magnes.* Milton uses the adjective for the substantive in the line "As the magnetic hardest iron draws."

Magnet'ic Mountain. A mountain which drew out all the nails of any ship that approached within its magnetic influence. The ship in which Prince Agib sailed fell to pieces when wind-driven towards it. (*Arabian Nights; The Third Calendar.*)

Magneuse (French). An anonyma or *fille de joie;* so called from the nunnery founded at Rheims in 1654, by Jeanne Canart, daughter of Nicolas Colbert, seigneur de Magneux. The word is sometimes jocosely perverted into Magni-magno.

Magnif'icat. *To sing the Magnificat at matins.* To do things at the wrong time, or out of place. The Magnificat does not belong to the morning service, but to vespers. The Magnificat is Luke i. 46-55 in Latin.

Magnificent (*The*).

Khosru or Chosroës I. of Persia (*, 531-579). The golden period of Persian history was 550-628.

Lorenzo de Medici (1448-1492).

Robert, Duc de Normandie, also called *Le Diable* (*, 1028-1035).

Soliman I., greatest of the Turkish sultans (1493, 1520-1566).

Magnifique . . . Guerre. *" C'est magnifique, mais ce n'est pas la guerre."* Admirable, but not according to rule. The comment of Marshal Canrobert on the charge of the Light Brigade at Balaclava.

" It is because the clergy, as a class, are animated by a high ideal . . . that they, as a class, are incomparably better than they need be . . . *C'est magnifique, mais ce n'est pas la guerre."—Nineteenth Century,* April, 1866.

Magno'lia. A flower so called from Pierre Magnol, professor of medicine at Montpelier. (1638-1715.) ƽ

Magnum Opus. Chief or most important of a person's works. A literary man says of his most renowned book it is his *magnum opus.*

Magnum of Port (*A*), or other wine, a double bottle.

Magnus Apollo (*My*), or *Meus Magnus Apollo.* My leader, authority, and oracle.

Mago the Carthaginian, says Aristotle, crossed the Great Desert twice without having anything to drink.

Magopho'nia. A festival observed by the Persians to commemorate the massacre of the Magi. Smerdis usurped the throne on the death of Camby'ses; but seven Persians, conspiring together, slew Smerdis and his brother; whereupon the people put all the Magi to the sword, and elected Darius, son of Hystaspes, to the throne. (Greek, *magosphonos,* the magi-slaughter.)

Magot (*French*). Money, or rather a mass of secreted money; a corruption of *imago,* the "image and superscription" of coined money.

" Là il vola de même, revint à Paris avec un bon magot."—*La Gazette Noire,* 1784, p. 270.

Magpie. A contraction of magot-pie, or mag'ata-pie. " Mag " is generally thought to be a contraction of Margaret; thus we have Robin red-breast, Tom-tit, Philip—*i.e.* a sparrow, etc.

" Augurs and understood relations have
(By magotpies, and choughs, and rooks) brought forth
The secret'st man of blood."
          Shakespeare: Macbeth, iii. 4.

Magpie. Here is an old Scotch rhyme:

" One's sorrow, two's mirth,
Three's a wedding, four's a birth,
Five's a christening, six a dearth,
Seven's heaven, eight is hell,
And nine's the devil his ane sel'."

Magricio. The champion of Isabella of Portugal, who refused to do homage to France. The brave champion vanquished the French chevalier, and thus vindicated the liberty of his country.

Mag'uelo'ne or **Mag'alo'na** (*the fair*). Heroine of the romance called *The History of the Fair Magalona, Daughter of the King of Naples*, etc. Originally written in French. Cervantēs alludes to it in *Don Quixote*. (*See* PETER OF PROVENCE.)

Magus. (*See* SIMON.)

Mah-abade'an Dynasty (*The*). The first dynasty of Persian mythological history. Mah Abad (*the great Abad*) and his wife were the only persons left on the earth after the great cycle, and from them the world was peopled. Azer Abad, the fourteenth and last of this dynasty, left the earth because "all flesh had corrupted itself," and a period of anarchy ensued.

Mahabharata. One of the two great epic poems of ancient India. Its story is the contests between descendants of Kuru and Pandu. (*See* KURU.)

Ma'hadi or *Hakem*. The Kalif who reigned about 400 years after Mahomet. In one pilgrimage to Mecca he expended six million gold dinars.

Mahâtmas. Initiates who have proved their courage and purity by passing through sundry tests and trials. It is a Hindu word applied to certain Buddhists. They are also called "Masters." According to Theosophists, man has a physical, an intellectual, and a spiritual nature, and a Mahâtma is a person who has reached perfection in each of these three natures. As his knowledge is perfect, he can produce effects which, to the less learned, appear miraculous. Thus, before the telegraph and telephone were invented it would have appeared miraculous to possess such powers; no supernatural power, however, is required, but only a more extensive knowledge.

"Mahâtma is a well-known Sanskrit word applied to men who have retired from the world, who, by means of a long ascetic discipline, have subdued the passions of the flesh, and gained a reputation for sanctity and knowledge. That these men are able to perform most startling feats, and to suffer the most terrible tortures, is perfectly true."—*Max Müller: Nineteenth Century*, May, 1893, p. 775.

Mah'di (*The*). The supreme pontiff of the Shiites (2 syl.) Only twelve of these imaums have really appeared—viz. Ali, Hassan, Hosein, and the nine lineal descendants of Hosein. Mohammed, the last Mahdi, we are told, is not really dead, but sleeps in a cavern near Bagdad, and will return to life in the fulness of time to overthrow Dejal (anti-Christ).

The Mahdi which has of late been disturbing Egypt is hated by the Persians, who are Sunnites (2 syl.); but even the Turks and Persians are looking out for a Mahdi who will stamp out the "infidels."

Mahmoud of Ghizni, the conqueror of India in the 11th century, kept 400 greyhounds and bloodhounds, each of which wore a jewelled collar taken from the necks of captive sultanas.

Mahmut. The name of the famous Turkish spy (*q.v.*).

Mahomet or **Mohammed,** according to Deutsch, means the *Predicted Messiah*. (Hag. ii. 7.) It is the titular name taken by Halabi, founder of Islam. (570-632.)

Angel of. When Mahomet was transported to heaven, he says: "I saw there an angel, the most gigantic of all created beings. It had 70,000 heads, each had 70,000 faces, each face had 70,000 mouths, each mouth had 70,000 tongues, and each tongue spoke 70,000 languages; all were employed in singing God's praises."

∴ This would make more than 31,000 trillion languages, and nearly five billion mouths.

Banner of. Sanjaksherif, kept in the Eyab mosque, at Constantinople.

Bible of. The Koran.

Born at Mecca, A.D. 570.

Bow. Catum (*q.v.*).

Camel (Swiftest). Adha (*q.v.*).

Cave. The cave in which Gabriel appeared to Mahomet was Hoiâ.

Coffin. It is said that Mahomet's coffin, in the Had'gira of Medi'na, is suspended in mid-air without any support. Many explanations have been given of this phenomenon, the one most generally received being that the coffin is of iron, placed midway between two magnets. Burckhardt visited the sacred enclosure, and found the ingenuity of science useless in this case, as the coffin is not suspended at all.

Cuirass. FADHA (*q.v.*).

Daughter (His favourite). Fatĭma.

Died at Medĭna, Monday, June 8th, 632, age of seventy-two. The 10th of the Hedj'rah.

Dove. Mahomet had a dove which he used to feed with wheat out of his ear. When the dove was hungry it used to light on the prophet's shoulder, and thrust its bill into his ear to find its meal. Mahomet thus induced the Arabs to believe that he was inspired by the Holy Ghost in the semblance of

Mahomet (*continued*).

a dove. (*Sir Walter Raleigh: History of the World*, bk. 1. pt. i. chap. vi. (See also *Prideaux: Life of Mahomet.*)

" Was Mahomet inspired with a dove ? "
Shakespeare: 1 *Henry VI.,* i. 2.

Father. Abdall, of the tribe of Koreish. He died a little before or little after the birth of Mahomet.

Father-in-law (father of Ayesha). Abu-Bekr. He succeeded Mahomet and was the first calif.

Flight from Mecca (called the Hedj'-rah), A.D. 622. He retired to Medi'na.

Grandfather (paternal). Abd-el-Mutallib, who adopted the orphan boy, but died in two years.

Hedj'rah. (See above, *Flight.*)

Heir (adopted). Said or Zaid.

Horse. Al Borak [*The Lightning*]. It conveyed the prophet to the seventh heaven. (*See* BORAK.)

" Borak was a fine-limbed, high-standing horse, strong in frame, and with a coat as glossy as marble. His colour was saffron, with one hair of gold for every three of tawny ; his ears were restless and pointed like a reed ; his eyes large and full of fire ; his nostrils wide and steaming ; he had a white star on his forehead, a neck gracefully arched, a mane soft and silky, and a thick tail that swept the ground."—*Croquemitaine,* ii. 9.

Miracles. Chadin mentions several, but some say he performed no miracle. The miracle of the moon is best known.

Moon (The). Habib the Wise told Mahomet to prove his mission by cleaving the moon in two. Mahomet raised his hands towards heaven, and in a loud voice summoned the moon to do Habib's bidding. Accordingly, it descended to the top of the Caaba (*q.v.*), made seven circuits, and, coming to the 'prophet,' entered his right sleeve and came out of the left. It then entered the collar of his robe, and descended to the skirt, clove itself into two plaits, one of which appeared in the east of the skies and the other in the west ; and the two parts ultimately reunited and resumed their usual form.

Mother of. Ami'na, of the tribe of Koreish. She died when Mahomet was six years old.

Mule. Fadda (*q.v.*).

Pond. Just inside the gates of Paradise. It was white as milk, and he who drank thereof would never thirst again. (*Al Koran.*)

Revelation made when he was forty years old by Gabriel, on Mount Hora, in Mecca.

Standard. Baj'ura.

Mahomet (*continued*).

Stepping-stone. The stone upon which the prophet placed his foot when he mounted the beast Al Borak on his ascent to heaven. It rose as the beast rose, but Mahomet, putting his hand upon it, forbade it to follow him, whereupon it remained suspended in mid-air, where the true believer, if he has faith enough, may still behold it.

Swords. Dhu'l Fakar (*the trenchant*), Al Battar (*the beater*), Medham (*the keen*), and Hatef (*the deadly*). (*See* SWORDS.)

Successor. (See above, *Father-in-law.*)

Tribe. On both sides, the Koreish.

Uncle, who took charge of Mahomet at the death of his grandfather, Abu Taleb'.

Wives. Ten in number, viz. (1) Kadidja, a rich widow of the tribe of Koreish, who had been twice married already, and was forty years of age. For twenty-five years she was his only wife, but at her death he married nine others, all of whom survived him.

Mahomet loved Mary, a Coptic girl, and in order to justify the amour, added a new chapter to the Koran, which may be found in Gagnier's *Notes upon Abulfeda,* p. 151.

The nine wives. (1) Ayesha, daughter of Abu Bekr, only nine years old on her wedding-day. This was his youngest and favourite wife.

(2) Sauda, widow of Sokran, and nurse to his daughter Fat'ima.

(3) Hafsa, a widow twenty-eight years old, who also had a son. She was daughter of Omeya.

(4) Zeinab, wife of Zaid, but divorced in order that the prophet might take her to wife.

(5) Barra, wife of a young Arab and daughter of Al Hareth, chief of an Arab tribe. Both father and husband were slain in a battle with Mahomet. She was a captive.

(6) Rehana, daughter of Simeon, and a Jewish captive.

(7) Safi'ya, the espoused wife of Kena'na. Kena'na was put to death. Safiya outlived the prophet forty years.

(8) Omm Habi'ba — *i.e.* mother of Habiba ; the widow of Abu Sof'ian.

(9) Maimu'na, fifty-one years old, and a widow, who survived all his other wives.

Also ten or fifteen concubines, chief of whom was Mari'yeh, mother of Ibrahim, the prophet's son, who died when fifteen months old.

Year of Deputations. A.D. 630, the 8th of the Hedj'rah.

Mahoun' (2 syl.). Name of contempt for Mahomet, a Moslem, a Moor. In Scotland it used to mean *devil*.

"There's the son of the renegade—spawn of Mahoun (son of the Moorish princess)."—*Vengeance of Mudarra.*

Mahound (2 syl.). Mahomet. (*See* MACON.)

"Ofttimes by Termagant and Mahound swore."
    Spenser: Faërie Queene, vii. 47.

Mahu. The fiend-prince that urges to theft.

"Five fiends have been in poor Tom at once: of lust, as Obidicut; Hobbididance, prince of dumbness; Mahu, of stealing; Modo, of murder; Flibbertigibbet, of mopping and mowing."—*Shakespeare: King Lear,* iv. 1.

Maid Ma'rian. A morris dance, or the boy in the morris dance, called *Mad Morion,* from the "morion" which he wore on his head. (*See* MORRIS DANCE.) Maid Marian is a corruption first of the words, and then of the sex. Having got the words Maid Marian, etymologists have puzzled out a suitable character in Matilda, the daughter of Fitz-Walter, baron of Bayard and Dunmow, who eloped with Robert Fitz-Ooth, the outlaw, and lived with him in Sherwood Forest. Some refine upon this tale, and affirm that Matilda was married to the outlaw (commonly called Robin Hood) by Friar Tuck.

"A set of morrice dancers danced a maidmarian with a tabor and pipe."—*Temple.*

    "Next 'tis agreed
That fair Matilda henceforth change her name,
And while [she lives] in Shirewodde . . .
She by maid Marian's name be only called."
    Downfall of Robert, Earl of Huntingdon.

Maid of Athens, immortalised by Byron, was Theresa Macri. Some twenty-four years after this poem was written the maid was in dire poverty, without a single vestige of beauty. She had a large family, and lived in a hovel.

Maid of Norway. Margaret, daughter of Eric II. and Margaret of Norway. On the death of Alexander III. she was acknowledged Queen of Scotland, and was betrothed to Edward, son of Edward I. of England, but she died on her passage to Scotland.

Maid of Orleans. Jeanne d'Arc (1412-1431).

Maid of Perth (*Fair*). Catherine Glover, daughter of Simon Glover, the old glover of Perth. She kisses Smith while asleep on St. Valentine's morning, and ultimately marries him. (*See* SMITH.) (*Scott: Fair Maid of Perth.*)

Maid of Saragossa. Augustina Zaragoza, distinguished for her heroism when Saragossa was besieged in 1808

and 1809. Byron refers to her in his *Childe Harold.*

Maiden. A machine resembling the guillotine for beheading criminals in the sixteenth and seventeenth centuries: brought to Scotland by the Regent Morton from Halifax, in Yorkshire, for the purpose of beheading the laird of Pennycuick. It was also called "the widow."

He who invented the maiden first hanselled it. Referring to Regent Morton, who introduced this sort of guillotine into Scotland, erroneously said to have been the first to suffer by it. Thomas Scott, one of the murderers of Rizzio, was beheaded by it in 1566, fifteen years before Morton's execution.

Maiden Assize (*A*). One in which there is no person to be brought to trial. We have also the expressions *maiden tree,* one never lopped; *maiden fortress,* one never taken; *maiden speech;* etc. In a maiden assize, the sheriff of the county presents the judge with a pair of white gloves. White gloves symbolise innocence. *Maiden* primarily means unspotted, unpolluted, innocent; thus Hubert says to the king—

    "This hand of mine
Is yet a maiden and an innocent hand,
Not painted with the crimson spots of blood."
    Shakespeare: King John, iv. 2.

Maiden King (*The*). Malcolm IV. of Scotland. (1141, 1153-1165.)

"Malcolm . . . son of the brave and generous Prince Henry . . . was so kind and gentle in his disposition, that he was usually called Malcolm the Maiden."—*Scott: Tales of a Grandfather,* iv.

Maiden Lane (London). So called from an image of the Maiden or Virgin Mary, which stood there before the Reformation.

Maiden or **Virgin Queen.** Elizabeth, Queen of England, who never married. (1533, 1558-1603.)

Maiden Town, *i.e.* a town never taken by the enemy. Edinburgh. The tradition is that the maiden daughters of a Pictish king were sent there for protection during an intestine war.

Maiden of the Mist. Anne of Geierstein, in Sir Walter Scott's novel called *Anne of Geierstein.*

Maidenhair (a fern, so-called from its hair-like stalks) never takes wet or moisture.

"His skin is like the herb called true Maiden's hair, which never takes wet or moisture, but still keeps dry, though laid at the bottom of a river as long as you please. For this reason it is called Adiantos."—*Rabelais; Pantagruel,* iv, 24.

Main-brace. *Splice the main-brace,* in sea language, means to take a draught of strong drink to keep the spirits up, and give strength for extra exertion. The main-brace is the rope by which the mainyard of a ship is set in position, and to splice it, in a literal sense, when the rope is broken or injured, is to join the two ends together again.

Main Chance (*The*). Profit or money, probably from the game called hazard.

To have an eye to the main chance, means to keep in view the money to be made out of an enterprise.

✲ In the game of "hazard," the first throw of the dice is called the *main,* which must be between four and nine, the player then throws his *chance,* which determines the main.

Mainote (2 syl.). A pirate that infests the coast of Attica.

"... Like boat
Of island-pirate or Mainote."
Byron : The Giaour.

Maintain is to hold in the hand; hence, to keep; hence, to clothe and feed. (French, *main tenir ;* Latin, *manus teneo.*)

Maitland Club (*The*) of literary antiquities, instituted at Glasgow in 1828. It published a number of works.

Maize (1 syl.). According to American superstition, if a damsel finds a blood-red ear of maize, she will have a suitor before the year is over.

"Even the blood-red ear to Evangeline brought
not her lover." *Longfellow : Evangeline.*

Majesty. Henry VIII. was the first English sovereign who was styled "His Majesty." Henry IV. was "His Grace;" Henry VI., "His Excellent Grace;" Edward IV.,"High and Mighty Prince;" Henry VII., "His Grace," and "His Highness;" Henry VIII., in the earlier part of his reign, was styled "His Highness." "His Sacred Majesty" was a title assumed by subsequent sovereigns, but was afterwards changed to "Most Excellent Majesty."

Majesty, in heraldry. An eagle crowned and holding a sceptre is "an eagle in his majesty."

Majol'ica Ware. A pottery originally made in the island of Majorca or Majolica, and lately revived by Mr. Minton.

Majority. *He has joined the majority.* He is dead. Blair says, in his *Grave,* " 'Tis long since Death had the majority." *"Abiit ad plures ;" " Quin prius me ad plures penetravi"* (*Plautus :*

Trinummus, line 14). " *Beatos eos fore, quando cum pluribus habitarint.*" (See *Polybius,* viii. xxx. 7.)

Make.
What make you here ? What do you want? What are you come here for? A French phrase: *"Que faites-vous ici ?"*
"Now, sir, what make you here?"—*Shake-speare : As You Like It,* i. 1.

Make a hand of or **on** (*To*). To slay, destroy, waste, or spoil.
"So when I came to myself again, I 'cried him mercy ; but he said, ' I know not to show mercy ;' and with that knockt me down again. He had, doubtless, made a hand of me, but that one came by, and bid him forbear."—*Bunyan : Pilgrim's Progress,* p. 93 (first edition).

Make a Hit (*To*). To succeed unexpectedly in an adventure or speculation. (*See* HIT.)

Make a Virtue of Necessity (*To*). See Chaucer's poem of the *Knightes Tale,* line 3,044 ; also *The Two Gentlemen of Verona* and Dryden's poem of *Palămon and Arcite.*

Make away with (*To*). To squander; to put out of the way ; to murder. The French verb *défaire* is used sometimes in a similar way ; as, " *Il tâcha de se défaire secrètement de ses pariers.*"

Make away with Oneself (*To*). To commit suicide.

Make Bricks without Straw (*To*). To attempt to do something without having the necessary material supplied. The allusion is to the Israelites in Egypt, who were commanded by their taskmasters so to do. (Exodus v. 7.)

Make Eyes at (*To*). To flirt with the eyes. " *Ocŭlis venāri.*" (*See* CAST.)

Make Mountains of Molehills (*To*). To make a difficulty of trifles. *"Arcem ex cloācā facĕre.*" The corresponding French proverb is, *"Faire d'un mouche un éléphant.*"

Make one's Bread (*To*). To earn one's living.

Make the Door (*To*). To make it fast by shutting and bolting it. We still say, "Have you made my room ?" —*i.e.* made it tidy. Similarly, to "make the bed" is to arrange it fit for use.
"Why at this time the doors are made against you." *Shakespeare : Comedy of Errors,* iii. 1.
"Make the door upon a woman's wit, and it will out at the casement."—*Shakespeare : As You Like It,* iv. 1.

Make the Ice (*To*). To near the whale-fishing ground. To make *for* the ice is to steer in that direction.
"About the end of April we neared the fishing-ground, or, to be more technical, 'made the ice.'" *C. Thomson : Autobiography,* p. 128.

Make-wage. Wages supplemented by grants or rates. Similarly, a make-weight [loaf] is a small loaf added to make up the proper weight.

Make-weight. A bit [of meat, cheese, bread, or other article] thrown into the scale to make the weight correct.

Makeshift (*A*). A temporary arrangement during an emergency ; a device. (The Anglo-Saxon *seyft* means a division, hence a device.)

Malabar. (*See under* VEUVE.)

Malagi'gi (in *Orlando Furioso*). Son of Buo'vo, and brother of Al'diger and Vivian, of Clarmont's race ; a wizard knight, cousin of Rinaldo. (*See* MAUGIS.)

Malagrowther (*Malachi*). The signature of Sir Walter Scott to a series of letters in 1822 contributed to the *Edinburgh Review* upon the lowest limitation of paper money to £5. They caused immense sensation, not inferior to that produced by *Drapier's Letters* (*q.v.*) in Ireland. No political tract, since Burke's *Reflections on the French Revolution*, ever excited such a stir in Great Britain.

Mal'agrow'ther (*Sir Mungo*). An old courtier soured by misfortune, who tries to make everyone as discontented as himself. (*Scott : Fortunes of Nigel*.)

Mal'akoff (in the Crime'a). In 1831 a sailor and ropemaker, named Alexander Ivanovitch Malakoff, celebrated for his wit and conviviality, lived at Sebastopol. He had many friends and admirers, but, being engaged in a riot, was dismissed the dockyards in which he had been employed. He then opened a liquor-shop on the hill outside the town. His old friends gathered round him, and his shop was called the Malakoff. In time other houses were built around, and the Malakoff became a town, which ultimately was fortified. This was the origin of the famous Malakoff Tower, which caused so much trouble to the allied army in the Crimean War. (*Gazette de France*.)

Malambru'no. The giant, first cousin of Queen Magun'cia, of Canday'a, who enchanted Antonomas'ia and her husband, and shut them up in the tomb of the deceased queen. The infanta he transformed into a monkey of brass, and the knight into a crocodile. Don Quixote achieved their disenchantment by mounting the wooden horse called Clavile'no. (*Cervantes : Don Quixote*, part ii. book iii. chap. xlv.)

Malaprop (*Mrs.*), in *The Rivals*, by Sheridan. (French, *mal à propos*.) Noted for her blunders in the use of words. " As headstrong as an *allegory* on the banks of the Nile " is one of her famous similes. (*See* PARTINGTON.)

Malbec'co. A " cankered, crabbed earl," very wealthy, but miserly and mean. He seems to be the impersonation of self-inflicted torments. He married a young wife named Helenore, who set fire to his house, and eloped with Sir Pari'del. Malbecco cast himself over a high rock, and all his flesh vanished into thin air, leaving behind nothing but his ghost, which was metamorphosed into Jealousy. (*Spenser : Faërie Queene*, book iii.)

Malbrouk or **Marlbrough** (*Marlbro'*), does not date from the battle of Malplaq'uet (1709), but from the time of the Crusades, 600 years before. According to a tradition discovered by M. de Châteaubriand, the air came from the Arabs, and the tale is a legend of Mambron, a crusader. It was brought into fashion during the Revolution by Mme. Poitrine, who used to sing it to her royal foster-child, the son of Louis XVI. M. Ar'ago tells us that when M. Monge, at Cairo, sang this air to an Egyptian audience, they all knew it, and joined in it. Certainly the song has nothing to do with the Duke of Marlborough, as it is all about feudal castles and Eastern wars. We are told also that the band of Captain Cook, in 1770, was playing the air one day on the east coast of Australia, when the natives evidently recognised it, and seemed enchanted. (*Moniteur de l' Armée*.)

> " Malbrouk s'en va-t-en guerre,
> Mironton, mironton, mirontaine ;
> Malbrouk s'en va-t-en guerre,
> Nul sait quand reviendra.
> Il reviendra z'a pâques—
> Mironton, mironton, mirontaine . . .
> Ou à la Trinité."

** The name Malbrouk occurs in the *Chansons de Gestes*, and also in the *Basque Pastorales*.

Malcolm. Eldest son of Duncan, King of Scotland. He was called *Can-More* (Great-head), and succeeded Macbeth (1056). (*Shakespeare : Macbeth*.)

Maldine (French). School. So called because at school " *on dine assez mal*."

Male. (*See* SEX.).

Male Sapphires. Deep indigo-coloured sapphires. The pale blue are the female sapphires. (*Emmanuel: Diamonds and Precious Stones* [1867].)

Male suada Fames. Hunger is a bad counsellor. The French say, "*Vilain affamé, demi enragé.*"

Malebol'ge (4 syl.). The eighth circle of Dante's *Inferno*, which contained in all ten *bolgi* or pits.

" There is a place within the depths of hell
Called Malebolge." *Dante: Inferno*, xviii.

Malecasta. The impersonation of lust. (*Spenser: Faërie Queene*, ii. 1.)

Male'ger [wretchedly thin]. Captain of the rabble rout which attack the castle of Temperance. He was "thin as a rake," and cold as a serpent. Prince Arthur attacks him and flings him to the ground, but Maleger springs up with renewed vigour. Arthur now stabs him through and through, but it is like stabbing a shadow ; he then takes him in his arms and squeezes him as in a vice, but it is like squeezing a piece of sponge ; he then remembers that every time the carl touches the earth his strength is renewed, so he squeezes all his breath out, and tosses the body into a lake. (*See* ANTÆOS.) (*Spenser: Faërie Queene*, book ii. 11.)

Malengin [guile]. On his back he carried a net "to catch fools." Being attacked by Sir Artegal and his iron man, he turned himself first into a fox, then to a bush, then to a bird, then to a hedgehog, then to a snake ; but Talus was a match for all his deceits, and killed him. (*Spenser: Faërie Queene*, v. 9.)

Malepardus. The castle of Master Reynard the Fox, in the tale so called.

Malherbe's Canons of French Poetry.
(1) Poetry is to contain only such words as are in common use by well-educated Parisians.
(2) A word ending with a vowel must in no case be followed by a word beginning with a vowel.
(3) One line in no wise is to run into another.
(4) The cæsura must always be most strictly observed.
(5) Every alternate rhyme must be feminine.

Mal'iom. Mahomet is so called in some of the old romances.

"Send five, send six against me. By Maliom I swear, I'll take them all."—*Fierabras.*

Malkin. The nickname of Mary,

now called Molly. Hence the Maid Marian is so termed.

Malkin. A kitchen wench, now called a Molly, is by Shakespeare termed "the kitchen Malkin. (*Coriolanus*, ii. 1.)

Malkin. A scarecrow or figure dressed like a scullion ; hence, anything made of rags, as a mop.

Malkin. A Moll or female cat, the male being a "Tom." When the cat mews, the witch in *Macbeth* calls out, "I come, Grimalkin" (i. 1).

Mall or *Pall Mall* (London). From the Latin *pellĕre malleo* (to strike with a mallet or bat) ; so called because it was where the ancient game of pell-mall used to be played. Cotgrave says:—

" Pale malle is a game wherein a round box-ball is struck with a mallet through a high arch of iron. He that can do this most frequently wins."

It was a fashionable game in the reign of Charles II., and the walk called the Mall was appropriated to it for the king and his court.

Mall Supper (*A*). A harvest feast (North of England). A *mal* is a feast, our word *meal* (Anglo-Saxon, *mæl*).

Mallows. *Abstain from mallows.* This is the thirty-eighth symbol in the Protreptics. Pythagoras tells us that mallow was the first messenger sent by the gods to earth to indicate to man that they sympathised with them and had pity on them. To make food of mallows would be to dishonour the gods. Mallows are cathartic.

Malmesbury (*William of*). Eleventh century ; author of numerous chronicles. His *Gesta Regum Anglorum* is a *resumé* of English history from the arrival of the English in 440 to the year 1120. His *Historia Novella* gives a retrospect of the reign of Henry I., and terminates abruptly with the year 1143. His third work is called *Gesta Pontificum*. All the three are included in the *Scriptōres post Bedam*.

Malmesbury Monastery. Founded by Maildulf, Meildulf, or Meldun, an Irishman.

Malmsey Wine is the wine of Malva'sia, in Candia.

" Thane spyces unsparyly thay spendyde there-aftyre,
Malvesye and muskadelle, thase mervelyous drynkes." *Morte d'Arthure.*

(*See* DROWNED IN A BUTT OF . . .)

Malt. *The Sermon on Malt* was by John Dod, rector of Fawsley, Northants, called *the decalogist*, from his famous exposition of the Ten Commandments. A Puritan divine. (1547-1645.)

∴ This was not Dr. William Dodd, who was executed for forgery (1729-1777).

Malt . . . Meal. *When the malt gets aboon the meal.* When persons, after dinner, get more or less fuddled.

"When the malt begins to get aboon the meal, they'll begin to speak about government in kirk and state."—*Sir W. Scott: Old Mortality*, chap. iv.

Maltese Cross. Made thus : ✠

Malthu'sian (*A*). A disciple of Malthus, whose political doctrines are laid down in his *Essay on the Principles of Population*.

Malthu'sian Doctrine. That population increases more than the means of increasing subsistence does, so that in time, if no check is put upon the increase of population, many must starve or all be ill-fed. Applied to individual nations, like Britain, it intimated that something must be done to check the increase of population, as all the land would not suffice to feed its inhabitants.

Malum, in Latin, means *an apple*; and "*malus, mala, malum*" means *evil*. Southey, in his *Commonplace Book*, quotes a witty etymon given by Nicolson and Burn, making the noun derived from the adjective, in allusion, I suppose, to the apple eaten by Eve. Of course, *mălum* (an apple) is the Greek *mēlon* or *mălon* (an apple-tree).

Malum in Se (Latin). What is of itself wrong, and would be so even if no law existed against its commission, as lying, murder, theft.

Malum Prohib'itum (Latin). What is wrong merely because it is forbidden, as eating a particular fruit was wrong in Adam and Eve, because they were commanded not to do so. Doing secular work on the Sabbath.

Malvo'lio. Steward to Olivia, in Shakespeare's *Twelfth Night*.

Mamamouchi. A mock honour. Better be a country gentleman in England than a foreign Mamamouchi. The honour is conferred on M. Jourdain. (*Molière : Bourgeois Gentilhomme*.)

Mambri'no's Helmet was of pure gold, and rendered the wearer invulnerable. It was taken possession of by Rinaldo (*Orlando Furioso*). Cervantes tells us of a barber who was caught in a shower, and to protect his hat clapped his brazen basin on his head. Don Quixote insisted that this basin was the enchanted helmet of the Moorish king.

Mam'elon (2 syl., French). A mound in the shape of a woman's breast. These artificial mounds were common in the siege of Sebastopol. (Latin, *mamma*, a breast.)

Mamelukes (2 syl.) or **Mamalukes** (Arabic, *mamluc*, a slave). A name given in Egypt to the slaves of the beys brought from the Caucasus, and formed into a standing army. In 1254 these military "slaves" raised one of their body to the supreme power; and Noureddin Ali, the founder of the Baharites, gave twenty-three sultans; in 1382 the dynasty of the Borjites, also Mamlucs, succeeded, and was followed by twenty-one successors. Selim I., Sultan of Turkey, overthrew the Mamluc kingdom in 1517, but allowed the twenty-four beys to be elected from their body. In 1811, Mohammed Ali by a wholesale massacre annihilated the Mamelukes, and became viceroy of Egypt.

Mamma, Mother. The former is Norman-French, and the latter Anglo-Saxon. (*See* PAPA.)

Mammet. A puppet, a favourite, an idol. A corruption of Mahomet. Mahometanism being the most prominent form of false religion with which Christendom was acquainted before the Reformation, it became a generic word to designate any false faith; even idolatry is called mammetry.

Mammon. The god of this world. The word in Syriac means riches. (*See* Milton : *Paradise Lost*, bk. i. 678.) His speech in the council is book ii. 229, etc.

Mammon. In Spenser's *Faërie Queene*, Mammon says if Sir Guyon will serve him he shall be the richest man in the world; but the knight says money has no charm for him. Mammon then takes him to his smithy, and tells him he may make what orders he likes, but Guyon declines to make any. The god then offers to give him Phil'otine to wife, but Guyon will not accept the honour. Lastly, he takes him to Proserpine's bower, and tells him to pluck the golden fruit, and rest on the silver stool; Sir Guyon again refuses, and after three days' sojourn in the infernal regions is led back to earth. (ii. 7.)

Mammon of Unrighteousness (*The*). Money. A Scripture phrase (Luke xvi. 9). Mammon was the Syrian god of wealth, similar to Plutus of Greek and Roman mythology.

Mammon's Cave. The abode of the Money-god. Sir Guyon visited this cave, and Spenser gives a very full description of it. (*Faërie Queene*, ii. 7.)
Sir Epicure Mammon. A worldly sensualist. (*Ben Jonson : Alchemist.*)

Mammoth Cave (*The*). In Edmonson county, Kentucky, the largest in the world.

Man (*Isle of*), called by the ancient Britons *main-au* (little island), Latinised into *Menav*-ia. Cæsar calls it Mona (*i.e. Mon-ah*), the Scotch pronunciation of Manau. *Mona* and Pliny's *Monabia* are varieties of " Menavia."

Man. Emblematic of St. Matthew, because he begins his gospel by tracing the manhood of Jesus back to David. Mark is symbolised by a *lion*, because he begins his gospel with John the Baptist and Jesus in the wilderness. Luke is symbolised by a *calf*, because he begins his gospel with the Temple sacrifices. And John as a *eagle*, because he looks right into heaven and begins his gospel with Jesus the divine *logos*. The four are indicated in Ezekiel's cherub (i. 10.)
Man. Average weight 150 lbs.: height, 69 inches ; strength, 420 lbs.

Man Friday (*A*). A useful and faithful servant, like the Man Friday in *Robinson Crusoe.*
"Count von Rechberg ... was Prince Bismarck's ' Man Friday.'"—*Athenæum*, 1881.

Man-jack. *Every man-jack of you.* Everyone of you. (*See under* JACK.)

Man . . . Monkey. The Bedouins affirm that the monkeys of Mount Kara were once human beings, thus transformed for disobedience to their prophet. The Arabs have a similar tradition, that the monkey (*Nasnâs*) and the ape (*Wabâr*) were once human beings.

Man-Mountain or *Quinbus Flestrin.* So Gulliver was called Lilliput.

Man Proposes, but *God disposes.* So we read in the *Imitatio Christi ;* Herbert (*Jacula Prudentum*) has nearly the same identical words.

Man Threefold. According to Diog'-enēs Laertius, the body was composed of (1) a mortal part ; (2) a divine and ethereal part, called the *phrēn ;* and (3) an aërial and vaporous part, called the *thumos.*

According to the Romans, man has a threefold soul, which at the dissolution

of the body resolves itself into (1) the *Manes ;* (2) the *An'ima* or Spirit ; (3) the *Umbra.* The Manēs went either to Elysium or Tar'tarus ; the Anima returned to the gods ; but the Umbra hovered about the body as unwilling to quit it.

According to the Jews, man consists of body, soul, and spirit.

Man in Black (*The*). Supposed to be Goldsmith's father. (*Citizen of the World.*) Washington Irving has a tale with the same title.

Man in the Iron Mask (*The*). (*See* IRON MASK.)

Man in the Moon (*The*). Some say it is a man leaning on a fork, on which he is carrying a bundle of sticks picked up on a Sunday. The origin of this fable is from Num. xv. 32-36. Some add a dog also ; thus the prologue in *Midsummer Night's Dream* says, " This man with lantern, dog, and bush of thorns, presenteth moonshine ; " Chaucer says " he stole the bush " (*Test. of Cresseide*). Another tradition says that the man is Cain, with his dog and thorn-bush ; the thorn-bush being emblematical of the thorns and briars of the fall, and the dog being the "foul fiend." Some poets make out the " man " to be Endym'ion, taken to the moon by Diana.
Man in the moon. The nameless person at one time employed in elections to negotiate bribes. Thus the rumour was set flying among the electors that " the Man in the Moon had arrived.'
I know no more about it than the man in the moon. I know nothing at all about the matter.

Man of Be'lial. Any wicked man. Shimei so called David (2 Sam. xvi. 7). The ungodly are called " children of Belial," or " sons of Belial." The word Belial means *worthlessness.*

Man of Blood. David is so called (2 Sam. xvi. 7).
The Puritans applied the term to Charles I., because he made war against his Parliament. Any man of violence.

Man of Blood and Iron (*The*). Otto von Bismarck (Prince Bismarck), called "man of blood" from his great war policy, and " iron " from his indomitable will. Many years Chancellor of Prussia and Germany. (Born September 1st, 1815.)

Man of Brass (*The*). Talos, the work of Hephæstos (Vulcan). He traversed Crete to prevent strangers from setting foot on the island, and threw rocks at the Argonauts to prevent their landing. Talos used to make himself red-hot, and hug intruders to death.

> "That portentous Man of Brass
> Hephæstos made in days of yore,
> Who stalked about the Cretan shore . . .
> And threw stones at the Argonauts."
> *Longfellow: The Wayside Inn.*

Man of December. Napoleon III. He was made President of the French Republic December 11, 1848; made his *coup d'état* December 2, 1851; and was made Emperor December 2, 1852.

Man of Destiny (*The*). Napoleon I. (1761, 1804-1814, died 1821). He looked on himself as an instrument in the hands of destiny.

> "The Man of Destiny . . . had power for a time to bind kings with chains, and nobles with fetters of iron."—*Sir Walter Scott.*

Man of Feeling. The title of a novel by Henry Mackenzie. His "man of feeling" is named Harley—a sensitive, bashful, kind-hearted, sentimental hero.

Man of Letters (*A*). An author.

Man of Remnants (*A*). A tailor.

Man of Ross. John Kyrle, of Ross, in Herefordshire, immortalised by Pope in his epistle *On the Use of Riches.*

Man of Salt. A man like Ænēas, always "melting into salt tears," called "drops of salt."

> "This would make a man a man of salt,
> To use his eyes for garden waterpots."
> *Shakespeare: King Lear,* iv. 6.

Man of Sedan. Napoleon III. was so called, because he surrendered his sword to William, King of Prussia, after the battle of Sedan (September 2, 1870).

Man of Silence (*The*). Napoleon III. (1808, 1852-70, died 1873.)

> "France? You must know better than I your position with the Man of Silence."—*For Sceptre and Crown,* chap. i.

Man of Sin (*The*) (2 Thess. ii. 3). The Roman Catholics say the Man of Sin is Antichrist. The Puritans applied the term to the Pope of Rome; the Fifth-Monarchy men to Cromwell; many modern theologians apply it to that "wicked one" (identical with the "last horn" of Dan. vii.) who is to immediately precede the second advent.

Man of Straw (*A*). A person without capital. It used to be customary for a number of worthless fellows to loiter about our law-courts to become false witness or surety for anyone who would buy their services; their badge was a straw in their shoes.

Man of the Hill (*The*). A tedious "hermit of the vale," which encumbers the story of *Tom Jones,* by Fielding.

Man of the Sea. (*See* OLD, etc.)

Man of the Third Republic (*The*). Napoleon III. (1808, reigned 1852-70, died 1873). (*M. Gambetta;* 1838-1882.)

Man of the World (*A*). One "knowing" in world-craft; no greenhorn. Charles Macklin brought out a comedy (1704), and Henry Mackenzie a novel (1773) with the same title.

Man of Three Letters. (*See* HOMO.)

Man-of-War (*A*). A Government fighting-ship. (Not now often used.)

Man-of-war, or, *Portuguese man-of-war.* A floating hydrozoan (*Physalia pelagica*).

> "Frank went to the captain and told him that Tom had given him leave to have the man-of-war if he could get it."—*Goulding: Adventures of the Young Marooners,* 17.

Man-of-war bird. The frigate-bird.

Man of Wax. A model man; like one fashioned in wax. Horace speaks of the "waxen arms of Telephus," meaning model arms, or of perfect shape and colour; and the nurse says of Romeo, "Why, he's a man of wax" (i. 3), which she explains by saying, "Nay, he's a flower, i' faith a very flower."

Man of Whipcord (*A*). A coachman. The reference is to his whip.

> "He would not have suffered the coachman to proceed while the horses were unfit for service. . . . Yet the man of whipcord escaped some severe . . . reproach."—*Sir W. Scott: The Antiquary,* i.

Manche (French). *Aimer mieux la manche que le bras.* Cupboard love. Manchè is a slang word; a gratuity given to a cicerone, cabman, or porter. It is the Italian *buona mancia.*

Jeter le manche après la cognée. To throw the helve after the hatchet. To abandon what may be useful, out of caprice, because a part of what you expected has not been realised. A horse is stolen, and the man, in ill-temper, throws away saddle and bridle.

Manchester. The first syllable is the Friesic *man* (a common); and the word means the Roman encampment on the common.

Manchester Poet. Charles Swain (1803-1874).

Man'ciple (*A*). A purveyor of food, a clerk of the kitchen. Chaucer has a "manciple" in his *Canterbury Tales,* (Latin *manceps, mancipis.*)

26

Manda'mus (Latin). A writ of King's Bench, commanding the person named to do what the writ directs. The first word is "Mandamus" (We command. . . .).

Manda'na. A stock name in heroic romance, which generally represents the fate of the world turning on the caprice of some beautiful Mandana or Stati'ra.

Mandarin' is not a Chinese word, but one given by the Portuguese colonists at Maca'o to the officials called by the natives *Khiouping* (3 syl.) It is from the verb *mandar* (to command).

The nine ranks of mandarins are distinguished by the button in their cap:— 1, ruby; 2, coral; 3, sapphire; 4, an opaque blue stone; 5, crystal; 6, an opaque white shell; 7, wrought gold; 8, plain gold; and 9, silver.

"The whole body of Chinese mandarins consists of twenty-seven members. They are appointed for (1) imperial birth; (2) long service; (3) illustrious deeds; (4) knowledge; (5) ability; (6) zeal; (7) nobility; and (8) aristocratic birth."—*Gutzlay.*

Mandeville (*Bernard de*). A licentious Deistical writer, author of *The Virgin Unmasked*, and *Free Thoughts on Religion*, in the reign of George II.

Mandou'sians. Very short swords. So called from a certain Spanish nobleman of the house of Mendo'sa, who brought them into use. (*See* SWORDS.)

Man'drabul. *From gold to nothing, like Man'drabul's offering.* Mandrabul, having found a gold-mine in Samos, offered to Juno a golden ram for the discovery; next year he gave a silver one, then a brazen one, and in the fourth year nothing. The proverb "to bring a noble to ninepence, and ninepence to nothing," carries the same meaning.

Mandrake. The root of the mandrag'ora often divides itself in two, and presents a rude appearance of a man. In ancient times human figures were often cut out of the root, and wonderful virtues ascribed to them. It was used to produce fecundity in women (Gen. xxx. 14-16). Some mandrakes cannot be pulled from the earth without producing fatal effects, so a cord used to be fixed to the root, and round a dog's neck, and the dog being chased drew out the mandrake and died. Another superstition is that when the mandrake is uprooted it utters a scream, in explanation of which Thomas Newton, in his *Herball to the Bible*, says, "It is supposed to be a creature having life, engendered under the earth of the seed of some dead person put to death for murder."

"Shrieks like mandrakes' torn out of the earth."
Shakespeare: Romeo and Juliet, iv. 3.

Mandrakes called love-apples. From the old notion that they excited amorous inclinations; hence Venus is called *Mandragori'tis*, and the Emperor Julian, in his epistles, tells Calix'enēs that he drank its juice nightly as a love-potion.

He has eaten mandrake. Said of a very indolent and sleepy man, from the narcotic and stupefying properties of the plant, well known to the ancients.

"Give me to drink mandragora . . .
That I might sleep out this great gap of time
My Antony is away."
Shakespeare: Antony and Cleopatra, i. 5.

Mandrake. Another superstition connected with this plant is that a small dose makes a person vain of his beauty, and conceited; but that a large dose makes him an idiot.

Mandricar'do. King of Tartary, or Scythia, son of Ag'rican. He wore Hector's cuirass, married Dor'alis, and was slain in single combat by Roge'ro. (*Orlando Innamorato*, and *Orlando Furioso.*)

Manduce (2 syl.). The idol Gluttony, venerated by the Gastrol'aters, people whose god was their belly.

"It is a monstrous . . . figure, fit to frighten little children; its eyes are bigger than its belly, and its head larger than all the rest of its body, . . . having a goodly pair of wide jaws, lined with two rows of teeth, which, by the magic of a small twine . . . are made to clash, chatter, and rattle against the other, as the jaws of St. Clement's dragon (called *graulli*) on St. Mark's procession at Metz."—*Rabelais: Pantagruel,* iv. 59.

Manes. *To appease his Mānes.* To do when a person is dead what would have pleased him or was due to him when alive. The spirit or ghost of the dead was by the Romans called his Manes, which never slept quietly in the grave so long as survivors left its wishes unfulfilled. The 19th February was the day when all the living sacrificed to the shades of dead relations and friends.

Manes (2 syl.) from the old word *manis, i.e.* "bonus," "quod eos venerantes manes vocarent, ut Græci *chrēstous.*" (See *Lucretius,* iii. 52.) It cannot come from *māneo,* to remain (because this part of man remains after the body is dead), because the *a* is long.

In the Christian Church there is an All Souls' Day.

Manfred. Count Manfred, son of Count Sig'ismund, sold himself to the Prince of Darkness, and had seven spirits bound to do his bidding, viz. the spirits of "earth, ocean, air, night, mountains, winds," and the star of his own destiny. He was wholly without human sympathies, and lived in splendid solitude among the Alpine mountains. He once loved the Lady As'tarte (2 syl.) who died, but Manfred went to the hall of Arima'nēs to see and speak to her phantom, and was told that he would die the following day. The next day the Spirit of his Destiny came to summon him; the proud count scornfully dismissed it, and died. (*Byron: Manfred.*)

Manger or **Manger le Morceau.** To betray, to impeach, to turn king's evidence. The allusion is to the words of Jesus to the beloved disciple—he will be the traitor " to whom I shall give a sop when I have dipped it," etc. (John xiii. 26.)

Manheim, in Scandinavian mythology, is the abode of man. Vanirheim is the abode of the Vanir. Jötunheim is the abode of the giants. Gladsheim is the abode of Odin. Helheim is the abode of Hela (goddess of death). Muspellheim is the abode of elemental fire. Niflheim is hell. Svartalheim is the abode of the dwarfs.

Ma'ni. The son of Mundilfori; taken to heaven by the gods to drive the mooncar. He is followed by a wolf, which, when time shall be no more, will devour both Mani and his sister Sol.

Mani, Manes, or **Manichæus.** The greatest Persian painter, who lived in the reign of Shah-pour (Sapor' I.). It is said his productions rivalled nature. (226-274.)

Manichæ'ans or **Manichees.** A religious sect founded by Mani or Manichæus, the Persian painter. It was an amalgamation of the Magian and Christian religions, interlarded with a little Buddhism. In order to enforce his religious system, Mani declared himself to be the Paraclete or Comforter promised by Jesus Christ.

Man'itou. The American - Indian *fetish.*

Man'lian Orders. Overstrained severity. Manlius Torqua'tus, the Roman consul, gave orders in the Latin war that no Roman, on pain of death, should engage in single combat; but one of the Latins provoked young Manlius by repeated insults, and Manlius slew him. When the young man took the spoils to his father, Torqua'tus ordered him to be put to death for violating the commands of his superior officer.

Manly, in the *Plain Dealer,* by Wycherly. He is violent and uncouth, but presents an excellent contrast to the hypocritical Olivia (*q.v.*).

Mr. Manly, in *The Provoked Husband,* by Vanbrugh and Cibber.

Manna (Exodus xvi. 15), popularly said to be a corrupt form of *man-hu* (What is this?) The marginal reading gives—" When the children of Israel saw it [the small round thing like hoarfrost on the ground], they said to one another, What is this? for they wist not what it was."

" And the house of Israel called the name thereof manna. It was like coriander seed, white ; and the taste of it was like wafers made with honey." (Verse 31.)

Manna of St. Nicholas of Bari. The name given to a colourless and tasteless poison, sold in phials by a woman of Italy named Tofani, who confessed to having poisoned six hundred persons by this liquid.

Man'nering. *Colonel* or *Guy Mannering; Mrs. Mannering, née* Sophia Wellwood, his wife; *Julia Mannering,* their daughter, who married Captain Bertram ; *Sir Paul Mannering,* the colonel's uncle. In Sir Walter Scott's novel of *Guy Mannering.*

Mannington (*George*). A criminal executed at Cambridge in 1476. It is said that he could cut off a horse's head at a single blow.

" It is in imitation of Mannington's—he that was hanged at Cambridge—that cut off the horse's head at a blow."—*Eastward Ho!*

Manningtree (*Essex*). Noted for its Whitsun fair, where an ox was roasted whole. Shakespeare makes Prince Henry call Falstaff " a roasted Manningtree ox, with the pudding in his belly." (1 *Henry IV.* ii. 4.)

" You shall have a slave eat more at a meale than ten of the guard ; and drink more in two days than all Manningtree does at a Witsun-ale."

Mano'a. The fabulous capital of El Dora'do, the houses of which city were said to be roofed with gold.

Manon Lescaut. A novel by the Abbé Prevost. It is the history of a young man possessed of many brilliant and some estimable qualities, but, being intoxicated by a fatal attachment, he is hurried into the violation of every rule of conduct, and finally prefers the life of a wretched wanderer, with the worthless object of his affection, to all the advantages presented by nature and fortune.

Manor, *Demesne.* " Demesne land " is that near the demesne or dwelling (*domus*) of the lord, and which he kept for his own use. Manor land was all that remained (*maneo*), which was let to tenants for money or service.

In some manors there was *common land* also, *i.e.* land belonging in common to two or more persons, to the whole village, or to certain natives of the village.

Mansard Roof, also called the *curb roof*. A roof in which the rafters, instead of forming a Λ, are broken on each side into an elbow. It was devised by François Mansard, the French architect, to give height to attics. (1598-1666.)

Mansfield. *The Miller of Mansfield.* Henry II. was one day hunting, and lost his way. He met a miller, who took him home to his cottage, and gave him a bed with his son Richard. Next morning the courtiers tracked the king to the cottage, and the miller discovered the rank of his guest. The king, in merry mood, knighted his host, who thus became Sir John Cockle. On St. George's Day, Henry II. invited the miller, his wife and son to a royal banquet, and after being amused with their rustic ways, made Sir John " overseer of Sherwood Forest, with a salary of £300 a year." (*Percy : Reliques.*)

Mansion. The Latin *mansio* was simply a tent pitched for soldiers on the march ; and, hence a " day's journey " (*Pliny*, xii. 14). Subsequently the word was applied to a roadside house for the accommodation of strangers. (*Suetonius : Tit.* 10).

Mantacci'ni. A charlatan who professed to restore the dead to life.

Mantali'ni (*Madame*). A fashionable milliner near Cavendish Square. Her husband, noted for his white teeth, minced oaths, and gorgeous morning gown, is an exquisite man-milliner, who lives on his wife's earnings. (*Dickens : Nicholas Nickleby.*)

Mantel-piece (*A*). A shelf over a fire-place, originally used for drying clothes.

" Around the spacious cupola, over the Italian fire-places, is a ledge to which are affixed pegs, on which postillions hung their wet clothes to dry. We call the shelves over the fire-places 'mantelpieces,' but we no longer hang our mantles on them to dry."—*Memoirs of Col. Macaroni.*

Mantible (*Bridge of*) consisted of thirty arches of black marble, and was guarded by "a fearful huge giant," slain by Sir Fierabras.

Man'tiger. An heraldic monster, having a tiger's body, and the head of an old man with long spiral horns.

Mantle of Fidelity (*The*). A little boy one day presented himself before King Arthur, and showed him a curious mantle, "which would become no wife that was not leal." Queen Guinever tried it, but it changed from green to red, and red to black, and seemed rent into shreds. Sir Kay's lady tried it, but fared no better ; others followed, but only Sir Cradock's wife could wear it. (*Percy : Reliques.*) (*See* CHASTITY.)

Mantra or **Mintra** (Persian mythology). A spell, a talisman, by which a person holds sway over the elements and spirits of all denominations. (*Wilford.*)

Man'tuan Swain, Swan, or **Bard** (*The*). Virgil, a native of Mantua, in Italy. Besides his great Latin epic, he wrote pastorals and Georgics.

Ma'nucodia'ta (*The*). An old name for a bird of paradise. It is a corruption of the Malay *manute-dewata*, the bird of the gods.

" Less pure the footless fowl of heaven, that never
Rests upon earth, but on the wing for ever.
Hovering o'er flowers, their fragrant food inhale.
Drink the descending dew upon the way :
And sleep aloft while floating on the gale."
     Southey : Curse of Kehama, xxi. 6.

Man'umit. To set free ; properly " to send from one's hand " (*e manu mittere*). One of the Roman ways of freeing a slave was to take him before the chief magistrate and say, " I wish this man to be free." The lictor or master then turned the slave round in a circle, struck him with a rod across the cheek, and let him go.

Manure (2 syl.) means hand-work (French, *main-œuvre*), tillage by manual labour. It now means the dressing applied to lands. Milton uses it in its original sense in *Paradise Lost*, iv. 628 :—

" Yon flowery arbours, . . . with branches overgrown
That mock our scant manuring."

⁑ In book xi. 26 he says, the repentant tears of Adam brought forth better fruits than all the trees of Paradise that his hands manured in the days of innocence.

Many. (*See* TOO MANY.)

Many a Mickle makes a Muckle, or *Many a little makes a mickle.* Little and often fills the purse. (*See* LITTLE.)

French : " Les petits ruisseaux font de grandes rivières ; " " Plusieurs peu font un beaucoup."

Greek :

" Εἰ γάρ κεν καὶ σμικρὸν ἐπὶ σμικρῷ καταθεῖο,
Καὶ θαμὰ τοῦτ' ἔρδοις, τάχα κεν μέγα καὶ τὸ
γένοιτο." *Hesiod: Works and Days,* 359, etc.

Many Men, Many Minds.
Latin : "Quot homĭnes tot sententiæ " (*Terence*).

French : "Autant d'hommes, autant
d'avis ; " "Tant de gens, tant de
guises ; " "Autant de testes, autant
d'opinions."

Mao'ri (*The*). The indigenous in-
habitants of New Zealand. It is a New
Zealand word, meaning *natives*. (Plur.,
Mao'ris.)

Ma'ra. A goblin that seized upon
men asleep in their beds, and took from
them all speech and motion.

Mar'abou Feathers. Feathers of
the bird so called, used by ladies for
head-gear. There are two species of
marabou stork, which have white
feathers beneath their wings and tail
especially prized. The word "marabou"
means " devoted to God," and the stork
is a sacred bird. (*See* MARABUTS.)

Mara'bout (in French). A big-
bellied kettle; a very large sail; an
ugly baboon of a man; also a sort of
plume at one time worn by ladies. The
"marabout hat" was a hat adorned
with a marabou feather.

Mara'buts. An Arab tribe which, in
1075, founded a dynasty, put an end to
by the Almohads. They form a priestly
order greatly venerated by the common
people. The Great Marabut ranks next
to the king. (Arabic, *marabath*, devoted
to God.)

Marana'tha (Syriac, *the Lord will
come—i.e.* to execute judgment). A
form of anathematising among the Jews.
The Romans called a curse or improca-
tion a *devotion—i.e.* given up to some
one of the gods.

Maravedi (4 syl.). A very small
Spanish coin, less than a farthing.

Marbles. *The Arundelian Marbles.*
Some thirty-seven statues and 128 busts
with inscriptions, collected by W. Petty,
in the reign of James I., in the island
of Paros, and purchased of him by Lord
Arundel, who gave them to the University of Oxford in 1627.

The Elgin marbles. A collection of
basso-relievos and fragments of statuary
from the Parthenon of Athens (built by
Phid'ias), collected by Thomas, Lord
Elgin, during his mission to the Ottoman
Porte in 1802. They were purchased
from him by the British Government, in
1816, for £35,000. and are now in the

British Museum. (The *gin* of "Elgin"
is like the -*gin* of "begin.")

Money and marbles. Cash and furniture.

Marcassin (*The Prince*). From the
Italian fairy-tales by Straparola, called
Nights, translated into French in 1585.

Marcel'la. A fair shepherdess whose
story forms an episode in *Don Quixote.*

Marcelli'na. The daughter of Rocco,
jailor of the state prison of Seville. She
falls in love with Fide'lio, her father's
servant, who turns out to be Leonora,
the wife of the state prisoner Fernando
Florestan. (*Beethoven : Fidelio.*)

Marcellus (in Dibdin's *Bibliomania,*
a romance,) is meant for Edmund
Malone, the well-known editor of
Shakespeare's works (1811).

March. *He may be a rogue, but he's
no fool on the march.* (French, *sur la
marche* likewise.)

March borrows three days from April.
(*See* BORROWED DAYS.)

March Dust. *A bushel of March
dust is worth a king's ransom.* According to the Anglo-Saxon laws, the fine of
murder was a sliding scale proportioned
to the rank of the person killed. The
lowest was £10, and the highest £60;
the former was the ransom of a churl,
and the latter of a king.

March Hare. *Mad as a March hare.*
Hares in March are very wild; it is
their rutting time. (*See* HARE.)

Marches (boundaries) is the Saxon
mearc ; but marsh, a meadow, is the
Saxon *mersc,* anciently written *marash,*
the French *marais,* and our *moruss.*
The other march is the origin of our
marquis, the lord of the march. The
boundaries between England and Wales,
and between England and Scotland,
were called "marches."

Riding the marches—i.e. beating the
bounds of the parish (Scotch).

Marchaundes Tale (in Chaucer) is
substantially the same as the first Latin
metrical tale of Adolfus, and is not
unlike a Latin prose tale given in the
appendix of T. Wright's edition of
Æsop's Fables. (See *January and May.*)

Marching Watch. A splendid pageant on Midsummer Eve, which
Henry VIII. took Jane Seymour to
Mercers' Hall to see. In 1547 Sir John
Gresham, the Lord Mayor, restored the
pageant, which had been discontinued
on account of the sweating sickness.

Marchington (Staffordshire). Famous for a crumbling short cake. Hence the saying that a man or woman of crusty temper is "as short as Marchington wake-cake."

Marchioness (*The*). The half-starved girl-of-all-work in *The Old Curiosity Shop*, by Charles Dickens.

Marchpane. A confection of pistachio-nuts, almonds, and sugar ; a corruption of the French *masse-pain*. (Italian, *marzapan*.)

Mar'cionites (3 syl.). An ascetic Gnostic sect, founded by Marcion in the second century.

Marck (*William de la*), or "The Wild Boar of Ardennes," A French nobleman, called in French history *Sanglier des Ardennes*, introduced by Sir Walter Scott in *Quentin Durward* (1446-1485).

Marcley Hill (Herefordshire), on February 7th, 1571, at six o'clock in the evening, "roused itself with a roar, and by seven next morning had moved forty paces." It kept on the move for three days, carrying with it sheep in their cotes, hedge-rows, and trees ; overthrew Kinnaston chapel, and diverted two high roads at least 200 yards from their former route. The entire mass thus moved consisted of twenty-six acres of land, and the entire distance moved was 400 yards. (*Speed: Herefordshire.*)

Marcos de Obregon. The model of Gil Blas, in the Spanish romance entitled *Relaciones de la Vida del Escudero Marcos de Obregon.*

Marcos'ians. A branch of the Gnostics ; so called from the Egyptian Marcus. They are noted for their apocryphal books and religious fables.

Mardi Gras. The last day of the Lent carnival in France, when the prize ox is paraded through the principal streets of Paris, crowned with a fillet, and accompanied with mock priests and a band of tin instruments in imitation of a Roman sacrificial procession.

" Tous les ans on vient de la ville
Les marchands dans nos cantons,
Pour les mener aux Tuileries,
Au Mardi-Gras, devant le roi,
Et puit les vendre aux boucheries,
J'aime Jeanne ma femme, eh, ha ! j'aimerais mieux
La voir mourir que voir mourir mes bœufs."
Pierre Dupont : Les Bœufs.

Mardle. To waste time in gossip. (Anglo-Saxon, *mathel-ian*, to talk ; *methel*, a discourse.)

Mardonius (*Captain*), in *A King or No King*, by Beaumont and Fletcher.

Mare. The Cromlech at Gorwell, Dorsetshire, is called the White Mare ; the barrows near Hambleton, the Grey Mare.

Away the mare—i.e. Off with the blue devils, good-bye to care. This mare is the incubus called the nightmare.

To cry the mare (Herefordshire and Shropshire). In harvesting, when the in-gathering is complete, a few blades of corn left for the purpose have their tops tied together. The reapers then place themselves at a certain distance, and fling their sickles at the "mare." He who succeeds in cutting the knot cries out "I have her !" "What have you?" "A mare." "Whose is she ?" The name of some farmer whose field has been reaped is here mentioned. "Where will you send her?" The name of some farmer whose corn is not yet harvested is here given, and then all the reapers give a final shout.

To win the mare or lose the halter—i.e. to play double or quits.

The grey mare is the better horse. (*See* GREY MARE.)

The two-legged mare. The gallows.

Shanks's mare. One's legs or shanks.

Money will make the mare to go.

" ' Will you lend me your mare to go a mile ? '
'No, she is lame leaping over a stile.'
' But if you will her to me spare,
You shall have money for your mare.'
'Oh, ho ! say you so ?
Money will make the mare to go.' "
Old Glees and Catches.

Whose mare's dead? What's the matter? Thus, in 2 *Henry IV.*, when Sir John Falstaff sees Mistress Quickly with the sheriff's officers, evidently in a state of great discomposure, he cries,

"How now ? Whose mare's dead ? What's the matter?"—Act ii. 1.

Mare's Nest. *To find a mare's nest* is to make what you suppose to be a great discovery, but which turns out to be all moonshine.

" Why dost thou laugh ?
What mare's nest hast thou found ? "
Beaumont and Fletcher : Bonduca, v. 2.
" Are we to believe that the governor, executive council, the officers, and merchants have been finding mare's nests only ? "—*The Times.*

N.B. In some parts of Scotland they use instead a *skate's nest.* In Gloucestershire a long-winded tale is called a *Horse-nest.* In Cornwall they say *You have found a wee's nest, and are laughing over the eggs.* In Devon, nonsense is called a *blind mare's nest.* Holinshed calls a gallows a *foul's nest* (iii.). In French the corresponding phrase is

"*Nid de lapin; Nid d'une souris dans l'oreille d'un chat.*" (*See* CHAT.)

Mareotic Luxury. The *Arva Mareotica* mentioned by Ovid (*Metamorphoses*, ix. 73) produced the white grapes, from which was made the favourite beverage of Cleopatra, and mention of which is made both by Horace (*Odes*, i. 37) and Virgil (*Georgics*, ii. 91). The Arva Mareotica were the shores of Lake Mœris, and "Mareotic luxury" is about equal to "Sybaritic luxury."

Marfi'sa. Name of an Indian queen in Bojardo's *Orlando Innamorato*, and in Ariosto's *Orlando Furioso*.

Marfo'rio. A pasquinade (*q.v.*).

Margan Monastery (*Register of*), 1066 to 1232, published in Gale, 1687.

Margaret, Queen of Denmark, Norway, and Sweden, called the "Northern Semiramis" (1353, 1387-1412).

Margaret. A simple, uncultured girl of wonderful witchery, seduced, at the age of fifteen, by Faust. She drowns in a pool the infant of her shame, was sent to prison, where she lost her reason, and was ultimately condemned to death. Faust (whom she calls Henry) visits her in prison, and urges her to make her escape with him; but she refuses, dies, and is taken to heaven; but Mephistopheles carried off Faust to the Inferno. (*Goethe: Faust.*)

Ladye Margaret. "The Flower of Teviot," daughter of the Duchess Margaret and Lord Walter Scott, of Branksome Hall. She was beloved by Baron Henry of Cranstown, whose family had a deadly feud with that of Scott. One day the elfin page of Lord Cranstown inveigled the heir of Branksome Hall, then a lad, into the woods, where he fell into the hands of the Southerners; whereupon 3,000 of the English marched against the castle of the widowed duchess; but, being told by a spy that Douglas with 10,000 men was coming to the rescue, they agreed to decide by single combat whether the boy was to become King Edward's page, or be delivered up to his mother. The champions to decide this question were to be Sir Richard Musgrave on the side of the English, and Sir William Deloraine on the side of the Scotch. In the combat the English champion was slain, and the boy was delivered to the widow; but it then appeared that the antagonist was not William of Deloraine, but Lord Cranstown, who claimed and received the hand of fair Margaret as his reward. (*Scott: Lay of the Last Minstrel.*)

Lady Margaret's preacher. A preacher who has to preach a *Concio ad clerum* before the University, on the day preceding Easter Term. This preachership was founded in 1503 by Lady Margaret, mother of Henry VII.

Lady Margaret professor. A professor of divinity in the University of Cambridge. This professorship was founded in 1502 by Lady Margaret, mother of Henry VII. These lectures are given for the "voluntary theological examination," and treat upon the *Fathers*, the *Liturgy*, and the *priestly duties*. (*See* NORRISIAN.)

Margaret (*St.*). The chosen type of female innocence and meekness.

In Christian art she is represented as a young woman of great beauty, bearing the martyr's palm and crown, or with the dragon as an attribute. Sometimes she is delineated as coming from the dragon's mouth, for the legend says that the monster swallowed her, but on making the sign of the cross he suffered her to quit his maw.

St. Margaret and the dragon. Olyb'ius, Governor of Antioch, captivated by the beauty of St. Margaret, wanted to marry her, and, as she rejected him with scorn, threw her into a dungeon, where the devil came to her in the form of a dragon. Margaret held up the cross, and the dragon fled.

St. Margaret is the patron saint of the ancient borough of Lynn Regis, and on the corporation seal she is represented as standing on a dragon and wounding it with the cross. The inscription of the seal is " SVB · MARGARETA · TERITUR · DRACO · STAT · CRUCE · LÆTA."

Margaret. A magpie.

Margaret or **Marguerite** (*petite*). The daisy; so called from its pearly whiteness, *marguerite* being the French for a pearl. (*See* MARGUERITE.)

" The daise, a flour white and redde,
  In French called 'la belle Marguerite.' "

Margarine Substitute (*A*). A mere imitation. Just as margarine is an imitation and substitute of butter.

" Between a real etching and that margarine substitute a pen-and-ink drawing . . . the difference is this: the margarine substitute is essentially flat . . . but true etching is in sensible relief."—*Nineteenth Century*, May 1891, p. 780.

Margate (Kent), is the sea-gate or opening. (Latin, *mare*; Anglo-Saxon, *mære*, etc.)

Margherit'a di Valois married Henri the Béarnais, afterwards Henri IV. of France. During the wedding solemnities, Catherine de Medicis devised the massacre of the French Protestants, and Margherita was at a ball during the dreadful enactment of this device. (*Meyerbeer: Gli Ugonotti, an opera.*)

Margin. In all our ancient English books, the commentary is printed in the margin. Hence Shakespeare:

" His face's own margent did quote such amazes."
            Love's Labour's Lost, ii. 1.

" I knew you must be edified by the margent."—
Hamlet, v. 2.

" She . . . could pick no meaning . . .
Writ in the glassy margents of such books."
    Shakespeare: Rape of Lucrece, stanza 15.

Margītēs. The first dunce whose name has been transmitted to fame. His rivals are Codrus and Flecknoe.

" Margites was the name . . . whom Antiquity recordeth to have been dunce the first."—*Pope: Dunciad (Martinus Scriblerus).*

Marguerite des Marguerites [*the pearl of pearls*]. So François called his sister (Marguerite de Valois), authoress of the *Heptameron*. She married twice: first, the Duc d'Alençon, and then Henri d'Albret, king of Navarre, and was the mother of Henry IV. of France. Henri [IV.] married a Marguerite, but this Marguerite was the daughter of Henri II. and Catherine de Medicis. The former befriended the Huguenots, the latter was a rigid Catholic, like her mother.

Margutte (3 syl.). A giant ten feet high, who died of laughter on seeing a monkey pulling on his boots. (*Pulci: Morgante Maggiore.*) (*See* DEATH FROM STRANGE CAUSES.)

Mari'a. Heroine of Donizetti's opera *La Figlia del Reggimento*. She first appears as a vivandière or French sutler-girl, for Sulpizio (the sergeant of the 11th regiment of Napoleon's Grand Army) had found her after a battle, and the regiment adopted her as their daughter. Tonio, a Tyrolese, saved her life and fell in love with her, and the regiment agreed to his marriage provided he joined the regiment. Just at this juncture the marchioness of Berkenfield claims Maria as her daughter; the claim is allowed, and the vivandiere is obliged to leave the regiment for the castle of the marchioness. After a time the French regiment takes possession of Berkenfield Castle, and Tonio has risen to the rank of field officer. He claims Maria as his bride, but is told that her mother has promised her hand to the son

of a duchess. Maria promises to obey her mother, the marchioness relents, and Tonio becomes the accepted suitor.

Maria. A fair, quick-witted, amiable maiden, whose banns were forbidden by the curate who published them; in consequence of which she lost her reason, and used to sit by the roadside near Moulines, playing vesper hymns to the Virgin all day long. She led by a ribbon a little dog named Silvio, of which she was very jealous, for she had first made a goat her favourite, but the goat had forsaken her. (*Sterne: Sentimental Journey.*)

Maria There'sa. Wife of Sancho Panza. She is sometimes called Maria, sometimes Teresa Panza. (*Don Quixote.*)

Mariamites (4 syl.). Worshippers of Mary, the mother of Jesus. They said the Trinity consisted of God the Father, God the Son, and Mary the mother of God.

Marian'a. One of the most lovable of Shakespeare's characters. Her pleading for Angelo is unrivalled. (*Measure for Measure.*)

Tennyson has two *Marianas* among his poems.

Mariana. Daughter of the king of Sicily, beloved by Sir Alexander, one of the three sons of St. George, the patron saint of England. Sir Alexander married her, and was crowned king of Thessaly. (*Seven Champions of Christendom*, iii. 3.)

Marigold. So called in honour of the Virgin Mary, and hence the introduction of marigold windows in lady chapels. (*See* MARYGOLD.)

" This riddle, Cuddy, if thou canst, explain . . .
    What flower is that which bears the Virgin's name.
The richest metal added to the same ?"
            Gay: Pastoral.

Marina. Wife of Jacopo Fos'cari, son of the doge. (*Byron: The Two Fos'cari.*)

Marinda or **Maridah.** The fair mistress of Haroun-al-Raschid.

Marine (2 syl.). *The female Marine.* Hannah Snell, of Worcester, who took part in the attack on Pondicherry. She ultimately left the service and opened a public-house in Wapping (London), but retained her male attire (born 1723).

∵ Doubts exist respecting the fact stated above. (See *Notes and Queries*, Dec. 3, 1892.)

Marines (2 syl.). Empty bottles. The marines were at one time looked down upon by the regular seamen, who

considered them useless, like empty bottles. A marine officer was once dining at a mess-table, when the Duke of York said to the man in waiting, "Here, take away these marines." The officer demanded an explanation, when the duke replied, "They have done their duty, and are prepared to do it again."
Tell that to the marines. Tell that to greenhorns, and not to men who know better. Marines are supposed by sailors to be so green that they will swallow the most extravagant story.

"Tell that to the marines, the sailors won't believe it."—*Sir W. Scott: Redgauntlet*, chap. xiii.

Mariner's Compass. The *fleur-de-lis* which ornaments the northern radius of the mariner's compass was adopted out of compliment to Charles d'Anjou, whose device it was. He was the reigning king of Sicily when Flavio Gioja, the Neapolitan, made his improvements in this instrument.

Mari'no Falie'ro. The forty-ninth doge or chief magistrate of the republic of Venice, elected 1354. A patrician named Michel Steno, having behaved indecently to some of the women assembled at the great civic banquet given by the doge, was kicked off the solajo by order of the Duke. In revenge he wrote upon the duke's chair a scurrilous libel against the dogaressa. The insult was referred to the Forty, and the council condemned the young patrician to a month's imprisonment. The doge, furious at this inadequate punishment, joined a conspiracy to overthrow the republic, under the hope and promise of being made a king. He was betrayed by Bertram, one of the conspirators, and was beheaded on the "Giant's Staircase," the place where the doges were wont to take the oath of fidelity to the republic. (*Byron: Marino Falie'ro*.)

Mariotte's Law. At a given temperature, the volume of a gas is inversely as the pressure. So called from Ed. Mariotte, a Frenchman, who died 1684.

Maritor'nes (Spanish, *bad woman*). A vulgar, ugly, stunted servant-wench, whom Don Quixote mistakes for a lord's daughter, and her "hair, rough as a horse's tail," his diseased imagination fancies to be "silken threads of finest gold." (*Cervantes: Don Quixote*.)

Marivaudage (4 syl.). An imitation of the style of Marivaux (1688-1763). He wrote several comedies and novels. "*Il tombe souvent dans une métaphysique alambiquée* [far-fetched, over-strained]

pour laquelle on a créé le nom de marivaudage."

"Ce qui constitue le marivaudage, c'est une recherche affectée dans le style. une grande subtilité dans les sentiments, et une grande complication d'intrigues."—*Bouillet: Dict. Universel*, etc.

Marjoram. *As a pig loves marjoram.* Not at all. Lucretius tells us (vi. 974), "*Amaricinum fugitat sus*," swine shun marjoram. The proverb is applied in somewhat this way: "How did you like so-and-so?" Ans.: "Well, as a pig loves marjoram."

Mark.
God bless the mark! An ejaculation of contempt or scorn. (*See* SAVE THE MARK.)

"To be ruled by my conscience, I should stay with the Jew my master, who, God bless the mark! is a kind of devil."—*Shakespeare: Merchant of Venice*, ii. 2.

To make one's mark. To distinguish oneself. He has written his name (or made his mark) on the page of history.
Up to the mark. Generally used in the negative; as, "Not quite up to the mark," not good enough, not up to the standard fixed by the Assay office for gold and silver articles; not quite well.

Mark (*St.*), in Christian art, is represented as being in the prime of life; sometimes habited as a bishop, and, as the historian of the resurrection, accompanied by a winged lion (*q.v.*). He holds in his right hand a pen, and in his left the Gospel. (*See* LUKE.)

Mark (*Sir*). A mythical king of Cornwall, Sir Tristram's uncle. He lived at Tintag'el Castle, and married Is'olde the Fair, who was passionately enamoured of his nephew, Sir Tristram. The illicit loves of Isolde and Tristram were proverbial in the Middle Ages.

Mark Banco. An hypothetical quantity of fine silver, employed as a money-valuer in the old Bank at Hamburg, and used by the Hanseatic League. Deposits in gold and silver coins were credited in Marco Banco, and all banking accounts were carried on in Marco Banco. The benefit was this: Marco Banco was invariable, but exchange varies every hour. The bank not only credited deposits by this unvarying standard, but paid withdrawals in the same way; so that it was a matter of no moment how exchange varied. I put £1,000 into the bank; the money is not entered to my credit as £1,000, but so much Marco Banco. The same process was adopted on withdrawals also.

Mark Tapley. Ever jolly, who recognises nothing creditable unless it is

26*

overclouded by difficulties. (*Charles Dickens: Martin Chuzzlewit.*)

Mark Time! Move the feet alternately as in marching, but without advancing or retreating from the spot.

Mark of the Beast (*The*). To set the "mark of the beast" on an object or pursuit is to denounce it, to run it down as unorthodox. Thus, many persons set the mark of the beast on theatres, some on dancing, and others on gambling, races, cards, dice, etc. The allusion is to Revelation xvi. 2; xix. 23.

Mark's Eve (*St.*). On St. Mark's Eve all persons fated to be married or to die pass, in procession, the church porch.

> "'Tis now,' replied the village belle,
> 'St. Mark's mysterious eve. . . .
> The ghosts of all whom Death shall doom
> Within the coming year
> In pale procession walk the gloom. . . .'
>   *J. Montgomery.*

Marks in Grammar and Printing.
Printers' marks on the first page of a sheet are called *Signatures*. (*See* LETTERS AT FOOT OF PAGE.)

Serifs are the strokes which finish off Roman letters, top and bottom. A, B, C, are "block" letters, or "sans serifs."

** over the second of two vowels, as aërial, is called "diæresis," and in French, *trema*.

′ An acute accent. In Greek it indicates a rise in the voice. It was not used till Greek became familiar to the Romans.

ˋ A grave accent. In Greek it indicates a fall of the voice. It was not used till Greek became familiar to the Romans.

** over a vowel, as ö, ü, is called in German *zweipunct*.

○ over a vowel, as å, is called in Danish *umlauf*.

~ A circumflex over the letter *n* (as *Oñoro*), in Spanish, is called a *tilde* (2 syl.). A circumflex in French indicates that a letter has been abstracted, as *être* for "*estre*."

t between two hyphens in French, as *parle-t-il?* is called "*t ephelcystic.*" (*See* N.)

& The Tironian sign (*q.v.*). (*See* AND.)

- Hyphen, as horse-guards.
- joining a pronoun to its verb in French, as *irai-je, donnait-on,* is called *le trait d'union.*

, under the letter *c* in French, is called a cedilla, and indicates that

the letter = s. (*See* PRINTERS' MARKS.)

☞ An index-hand, to call attention to a statement.

¶ A blind P, marks a new paragraph indirectly connected with preceding matter.

( ) Called parentheses, and
[ ] Called *brackets*, separate some explanatory or collateral matter from the real sequence.

, is a comma; ; is a semicolon; : is a colon; . is a point or full stop.

— or . . . . in the middle or at the end of a sentence is a *break*, and shows that something is suppressed.

Marks of Gold and Silver.
The date-mark on gold or silver articles is some letter of the alphabet indicating the year when the article was made. Thus, in the Goldsmith's Company of London :— From 1716 to 1755 it was Roman capitals, beginning from A and following in succession year after year; from 1756 to 1775 it was Roman small letters, a to u; from 1776 to 1796, Roman black letters, small, **a** to **u**; from 1796 to 1815, Roman capitals, A to U; from 1816 to 1835, Roman small letters; from 1836 to 1855, Old English capitals; from 1856 to 1875, Old English, small; 1876 to 1895, Roman capitals.

The duty-mark on gold and silver articles is the head of the reigning sovereign, and shows that the duty has been paid. This mark is not now placed on watch-cases, etc.

The Hall-mark, stamped upon gold and silver articles, is a leopard's head crowned for London; three lions and a cross for York; a castle with two wings for Exeter; three wheat sheaves or a dagger for Chester; three castles for Newcastle; an anchor for Birmingham; a crown for Sheffield; a castle and lion for Edinburgh; a tree, salmon, and ring for Glasgow; Hibernia for Dublin. (*See* HALL MARK, SILVER.)

The Standard-mark of gold or silver is a lion passant for England; a thistle for Edinburgh; a lion rampant for Glasgow; and a harp crowned for Ireland.

Market-penny (*A*). Money for refreshments given to those who go to market. Now, however, it means a toll surreptitiously exacted by servants sent out to buy goods for their master.

Markham (*Mrs.*). A *nom de plume* of Elizabeth Cartwright, afterwards Mrs. Penrose.

Marl. Latin, *argill'*; German, *mär-gel*; Spanish and Italian, *marga*; Armoric, *marg*; Irish, *marla*; Welsh, *marl*.

Marlborough. *Statutes of Marlborough.* Certain laws passed in the reign of Henry III., by a parliament held in Marlborough Castle. (*See* MALBROUCK [*S'en va-t'-en guerre*].)

Marlborough Dog. (*See* BLENHEIM DOG.)

Marlow. Both Sir Charles Marlow and his son Young Marlow are characters in *She Stoops to Conquer*, by Goldsmith. Young Marlow is bashful before ladies, but easy enough before women of low degree.

Mar'mion. Ralph de Wilton, being charged with treason, claimed to prove his innocence by the ordeal of battle, and, being overthrown by Lord Marmion, was supposed to be dead, but was picked up by a beadsman, who nursed him carefully; and, being restored to health, he went on a pilgrimage to foreign lands. Now, Lord Marmion was betrothed to Constance de Beverley; and De Wilton to Lady Clare, daughter of the Earl of Gloucester. When De Wilton was supposed to be dead, Lord Marmion proved faithless to Constance, and proposed to Clare, having an eye especially to her rich inheritance. Clare rejected his suit, and took refuge in the convent of St. Hilda, in Whitby; Constance, on the other hand, took the veil in the convent of St. Cuthbert, in Holy Isle. In time, Constance eloped from the convent, but, being overtaken, was buried alive in the walls of a deep cell. In the meantime Lord Marmion was sent by Henry VIII. with a message to James IV. of Scotland, and stopped at the hall of Hugh de Heron for a night. Sir Hugh, at his request, appointed him a guide to conduct him to the king, and the guide wore the dress of a palmer. On his return, Lord Marmion hears that Lady Clare is in Holy Isle, and commands the abbess of Hilda to release her, that she may be placed under the charge of her kinsman, Fitz Clare, of Tantallon Hall. Here she meets De Wilton, the palmer-guide of Lord Marmion. Lord Marmion being killed at the battle of Flodden Field, De Wilton married Lady Clare. (*Sir Walter Scott.*)

Lord Marmion. The hero of Scott's poem so called is a purely fictitious character. There was, however, an historic family so called, descendants of Robert de Marmion, a follower of the Conqueror, who obtained the grant of Tamworth, and the manor of Scrivelby, in Lincolnshire. He was the first royal champion, and his male issue ceased with Philip Marmion in the reign of Edward I. Sir John Dymoke, who married Margery, daughter of Joan, the only surviving child of Philip, claimed the office and manor in the reign of Richard II.; they have remained in his male line ever since.

Marmo Lunense. (*See* LUNA.)

Ma'ro. Virgil, whose name was Publius Virgilius Maro, was born on the banks of the river Mincio, at the village of Andes, near Mantua. (B.C. 70-19.)

" Sweet Maro's muse, sunk in inglorious rest,
  Had silent slept amid the Mincian reeds."
  Thomson: Castle of Indolence.

Maron or **Marron** (*French*). A cat's-paw (*q.v.*). "*Se servir de la patte du chat pour tirer les marrons du feu;*" in Italian, "*Cavare i marroni dal fuoco colla zampa del gatto.*"

" C'est ne se point commettre à faire de l'éclat
  Et tirer les marrons de la patte du chat."
  L'Etourdi, iii. 7.

Mar'onites (3 syl.). A Christian tribe of Syria in the eighth century; so called from the monastery of Maron, on the slopes of Lebanon, their chief seat; so called from John Maron, Patriarch of Antioch, in the sixth century.

Maroon. A runaway slave sent to the Calabonco, or place where such slaves were punished, as the Maroons of Brazil. Those of Jamaica are the offspring of runaways from the old Jamaica plantations or from Cuba, to whom, in 1738, the British Government granted a tract of land, on which they built two towns. The word is from the verb "maroon," to set a person on an inhospitable shore and leave him there (a practice common with pirates and buccaneers). The word is a corruption of *Cimarron*, a word applied by Spaniards to anything unruly, whether man or beast. (See *Scott: Pirate*, xxii.)

Maroon (*To*). To set a man on a desert island and abandon him there. This marooning was often practised by pirates and buccaneers. (*See above.*)

Maro'zia, daughter of Theodora. The infamous offspring of an infamous mother, of the ninth century. Her intrigues have rendered her name proverbial. By one she became the mother of Pope John XI. (*See* MESSALINA.)

Marphi'sa (in *Orlando Furioso*). Sister of Roge'ro, and a female knight of amazing prowess. She was brought up by a magician, but, being stolen at the age of seven, was sold to the king of Persia. The king assailed her virtue when she was eighteen, but she slew him, and seized the crown. She came to Gaul to join the army of Ag'ramant, but hearing that Agramant's father had murdered her mother Galacella, she entered the camp of Charlemagne, and was baptised.

Marplot. A silly, cowardly, inquisitive Paul Pry, in *The Busybody*, by Mrs. Centlivre. H. Woodward's great part.

Marque. (*See* LETTERS OF . . .)

Marriage Knot (*The*). The bond of marriage effected by the legal marriage service. The Latin phrase is *nodus Herculĭus*, and part of the marriage service was for the bridegroom to loosen (*solvĕre*) the bride's girdle, not to *tie* it. In the Hindu marriage ceremony the bridegroom hangs a ribbon on the bride's neck and ties it in a knot. Before the knot is tied the bride's father may refuse consent unless better terms are offered, but immediately the knot is tied the marriage is indissoluble. The Parsees bind the hands of the bridegroom with a sevenfold cord, seven being a sacred number. The ancient. Carthaginians tied the thumbs of the betrothed with leather lace. See *Nineteenth Century*, Oct., 1893, p. 610. (*A. Rogers.*)

" Around her neck they leave
The marriage knot alone."
Southey : Curse of Kehama.

" When first the marriage knot was tied
Between my wife and me,
Her age did mine as much exceed
As three-times-three does three ;
But when ten years and half ten years
We man and wife had been,
Her age came then as near to mine
As eight is to sixteen."
Ans.: 15 and 45 at marriage, 30 and 60 fifteen years afterwards.

❧ The practice of throwing rice is also Indian.

" Hamilcar desired to unite them immediately by an indissoluble betrothal. In Salambo's hands was a lance, which she offered to Narr Havas. Their thumbs were then tied together by a leather lace, and corn was thrown over their heads."— *Flaubert : Salambo*, chap. xi.

Marriage Plates. Sacred plates with a circular well in the centre to hold sweetmeats. They were painted for bridal festivities by Maestro Georgio, Orazio Fontane, and other artists of Urbino and Gubbio, Pesaro and Pavia, Castelli and Savona, Faenza and Ferrara, and all the other art towns of Italy. These plates were hung upon the walls, and looked on with superstitious awe as household gods. They were painted in polychrome, and the chief design was some scriptural subject, like Rebecca and Isaac.

Marriages. *Carrier's republican marriages.* A device of wholesale slaughter, adopted by Carrier, proconsul of Nantes, in the first French Revolution. It consisted in tying men and women together by their hands and feet, and casting them into the Loire. (1794.)

Marriages. *Close times of marriages in the Catholic Church.*

(1) Ab Adventu usque ad Epiphaniam (from Advent to Epiphany).

(2) A Septuagesima usque ad octavus Pasche inclusive (from Septuagesima to the eighth Easter).

(3) A secunda feria in Rogationibus usque ad primam dominicam post Pentacosten (from the second feast in Rogation to the first Sunday after Pentecost exclusive).

(*Liber Sacerdotalis . . . Secundum Ritum Sanctæ Romanæ et Apostolicæ Ecclesiæ ;* 1537.)

Marriages are Made in Heaven. This does not mean that persons in heaven " marry and are given in marriage," but that the partners joined in marriage on earth were foreordained to be so united. As the French proverb more definitely expresses the idea, " *Les mariages se font au ciel et se consomment sur la terre.*" And again, "*Les mariages sont écrits dans le ciel.*" E. Hall (1499-1547) says, " Consider the old proverbe to be true that saieth : Marriage is destinie." Prov. xix. 14 says, " A prudent wife is from the Lord."

Marriages of Men of Genius. (*See* WIVES OF. . . .)

Married Women take their husband's surname. This was a Roman custom. Thus Julia, Octavia, etc., married to Pompey, Cicero, etc., would be called Julia of Pompey, Octavia of Cicero. Our married women are named in the same way, omitting " of."

Marrow (Scotch) a mate, companion, friend. " Not marrow "—that is, not a pair. The Latin word *medulla* (marrow) is used in much the same way as " mihi hæres in medullis " (*Cicero*) ; (very dear, my best friend, etc.).

" Busk ye, busk ye, my bonnie bonnie bride,
Busk ye, busk ye, my winsome marrow."
The Braes of Yarrow.
" One glove [or shoe] is not marrow to the other."
Landsdowne MS.

Marrow-bones. *Down on your marrow-bones*, i.e. knees. That marrow in this phrase is not a corruption of "Mary," meaning the Virgin, is palpable from the analogous phrase, *the marrow-bone stage*—walking. The leg-bone is the marrow-bone of beef and mutton, and the play is on Marylebone (London).

Marrow Controversy (*The*). A memorable struggle in Scotland between Puritanism and Presbyterianism; so called from a book entitled *The Marrow of Modern Divinity*, condemned by the General Assembly in 1720. Abelli, Bishop of Rhodes, wrote the *Medulla Theologica*.

Marrow-men. The twelve ministers who signed the remonstrance to the General Assembly for condemning the evangelical doctrines of the "Marrow." (*See* MARROW CONTROVERSY.)

Marry! An oath, meaning by Mary, the Virgin.

"Yea, marry! you say true."—*Foxe: Book of Martyrs.*

Marry Come Up! An exclamation of disapproval, about equal to "Draw it mild!" May Mary come up to my assistance, or to your discomfort!

"Marry come up, you saucy jade!"—*Nineteenth Century*, November, 1892, p. 797.

Mar's Year. The year 1715, noted for the rebellion of the Earl of Mar.

"Auld uncle John wha wedlock's joys,
Sin Mar's year did desire."
Burns: Halloween, 27.

Mars, with the ancient alchemists, designated iron.

Mars. Under this planet "is borne theves and robbers . . . nyght walkers and quarell pykers, bosters, mockers, and skoffers; and these men of Mars causeth warre, and murther, and batayle. They wyll be gladly smythes or workers of yron . . . lyers, gret swerers. . . . He is red and angry . . . a great walker, and a maker of swordes and knyves, and a sheder of mannes blode . . . and good to be a barboure and a blode letter, and to drawe tethe." (*Compost of Ptholomeus*.)

Mars, in Camoën's *Lusiad*, is "divine fortitude" personified. As Bacchus, the evil demon, is the guardian power of Mahometanism; so Mars or divine fortitude is the guardian power of Christianity.

The Mars of Portugal. Alfonso de Albuquerque, Viceroy of India. (1452-1515.)

Marseillaise (3 syl.). The grand song of the French Revolution. Claude

Joseph Rouget de Lisle, an artillery officer in garrison at Strasbourg, composed both the words and the music for Dietrich, mayor of the town. On July 30th, 1792, the Marseillaise volunteers, invited by Barbaroux at the instance of Madame Roland, marched to Paris singing the favourite song; and the Parisians, enchanted with it, called it the *Hymne des Marseillais.* (Rouget born 1760, died 1835.)

Marseilles' Good Bishop. In 1720 and 1722 the plague made dreadful havoc at Marseilles. The Bishop, H. F. Xavier de Belsunce, was indefatigable in the pastoral office, and spent his whole time visiting the sick. During the plague of London, Sir John Lawrence, the then Lord Mayor, was no less conspicuous in his benevolence. He supported 40,000 dismissed servants so long as his fortune lasted, and, when he had spent his own money, collected and distributed the alms of the nation. Darwin refers to these philanthropists in his *Loves of the Plants*, ii, 433. (*See* BORROMEO.)

Marsh [*Le Marais*]. The pit of the National Convention, between Mountain benches on one side, and those occupied by the ministerial party and the opposition on the other. These middle men or "flats" were "swamped," or *enforcés dans un marais* by those of more decided politics. (*See* PLAIN.)

Marshal means an ostler or groom. His original duty was to feed, groom, shoe, and physic his master's horse. (British, *marc*, a mare; *scalc*, a servant.)

Marshal Forward. Blucher; so called for his dash and readiness in the campaign of 1813.

Marshal of the Army of God, and of Holy Church. The Baron Robert Fitzwalter, appointed by his brother barons to lead their forces in 1215 to obtain from King John redress of grievances. Magna Charta was the result.

Marsham (*Men of*). Those who committed the offence of felling the thorns, etc., in 1646, upon Marsham Heath, Norfolk. The inhabitants of Marshall and tenants of the manor petitioned against the offenders.

Marsiglio or Marsilius. A Saracen king who plotted the attack upon Roland, under "the tree on which Judas hanged himself." With a force of 600,000 men, divided into three armies, he attacked the paladin and overthrew him, but was in turn overthrown by Charlemagne, and hanged on the very tree beneath which he had arranged the attack. (*Turpin : Chronicles.*)

Mar'syas. The Phrygian flute-player who challenged Apollo to a contest of skill, and, being beaten by the god, was flayed alive for his presumption. From his blood arose the river so called. The flute on which Marsyas played was one Athe'na had thrown away, and, being filled with the breath of the goddess, discoursed most excellent music. The interpretation of this fable is as follows : A contest long existed between the lutists and the flautists as to the superiority of their respective instruments. The Dorian mode, employed in the worship of Apollo, was performed on lutes ; and the Phrygian mode, employed in the rites of Cyb'elē, was executed by flutes, the reeds of which grew on the banks of the river Marsyas. As the Dorian mode was preferred by the Greeks, they said that Apollo beat the flute-player.

Martano (in *Orlando Furioso*), who decoyed Origilla from Gryphon. He was a great coward, and fled from the tournament amidst the jeers of the spectators. While Gryphon was asleep he stole his armour, went to King Norandi'no to receive the honours due to Gryphon, and then quitted Damascus with Origilla. A'quilant encountered them, and brought them back to Damascus, when Marta'no was committed to the hangman's mercies (books viii. ; ix.)

Marteau des Heretiques. Pierre d'Ailly, also called *l'Aigle de la France.* (1350-1420.)

Martel. The surname given to Charles, natural son of Pépin d'Héristal, for his victory over the Saracens, who had invaded France under Abd-el-Rahman in 732. It is said that Charles "knocked down the foe, and crushed them beneath his axe, as a martel or hammer crushes what it strikes."

Judas Asmonæus for a similar reason was called *Maccabæus* (the Hammerer).

M. Collin de Plancy says that Charles, the palace mayor, was not called Martel because he *martelé* (hammered) the Saracens, but because his patron saint was *Martellus* (or Martin). (*Bibliothéque des Légendes.*)

Avoir se mettre martel en tête. To have a bee in one's bonnet, to be crotchety. Martel is a corruption of

Martin, an ass, a hobby-horse. **M.** Hilaire le Gai says,• but gives no authority, " *Cette expression nous vient des Italiens, car en Italien martello signifie proprement ' jalousie.' "*

"Ils portent des martels, des capriches."— *Brantome : Des Dames Gallantes.*

"Telle filles ... pourroient bien donner de bons martels à leurs pauvres marys."—*Brantome : Des Dames Gallantes.*

Martello Towers. Round towers about forty feet in height, of great strength, and situated on a beach or river ; so called from the Italian towers built as a protection against pirates. As the warning was given by striking a bell with a martello, or hammer, the towers were called *Torri da Martello.*

Some say that these towers were so called from a tower at the entrance of St. Fiorenzo, in Corsica. Similar towers were common all along the Mediterranean coast as a defence against pirates. They were erected in the low parts of Sussex and Kent in consequence of the powerful defence made (February 8th, 1794) by Le Tellier at the tower of Morteila, with only thirty-eight men, against a simultaneous sea and land attack—the former led by Lord Hood, and the latter by Major-General Dundas.

Martext (*Sir Oliver*). The hedge-priest in *As You Like It* (iii. 3).

Martha (*St.*), patron saint of good housewives, is represented in Christian art as clad in homely costume, bearing at her girdle a bunch of keys, and holding a ladle or pot of water in her hand. Like St. Margaret, she is accompanied by a dragon bound, but has not the palm and crown of martyrdom. The dragon is given to St. Martha from her having destroyed one that ravaged the neighbourhood of Marseilles.

Martial. Pertaining to Mars, the Roman god of war.

Martian Laws. Laws compiled by Martia, wife of Guithelin, great-grandson of Mulmutius, who established in England the Mulmutian Laws. Alfred translated both these codes into Saxon-English.

"Guynteline ... whose queen, ... to show her upright mind,
To wise Malmutius' laws her Martian first did frame." *Drayton : Polyolbion,* viii.

Martin. One of the swallow tribe. Dies derives the word from St. Martin, but St. Martin's bird is the *raven.*

Martin. The ape, in the tale of *Reynard the Fox.*

Martin. A jackass is so called from its obstinacy. "*Il y a plus d'un ane qui s'appelle Martin.*"

"Martinus, qui suam acrius quam par est opinionem tuetur ; (*See* modi fuit Martinus juris consultus celebris sub Friderico I., a quo (inquit Baronius, A.D. 1155) in vulgare proverbium ejus durities in hanc usque diem pertransut, ut Martinum appellent, qui suæ ipsius sententiæ singulari pertinaci studio, in hærescat. Fuit et Martinus Grosia, legum professor in academia Bononiensi."—*Du Cange* (Art. *Martinus*).

Martin. (*See* ALL MY EYE.)

Martin, in Dryden's allegory of the *Hind and Panther,* means the Lutheran party ; so called by a pun on the name of Martin Luther.

Parler d'autre Martin. There are more fools than one in the fair. This phrase is very common. (*See* Bauduin de Seboure : *Romans,* ch. viii. line 855 ; *Godefroid de Bouillon,* p. 537 ; *La branche des royaux lignage,* line 11,419 ; *Le Mystère de S. Crespin et St. Crespinien* [2nd day], p. 43 ; *Reynard the Fox,* vol. ii. p. 17, line 10,096, vol. iii. p. 23, line 20,402, etc.)

✢ Another phrase is "*Parler d'autre Bernart,*" from bernart—a jackass or fool.

"Or vos metron el col la hart
Puis parleron d'autre Bernart."
Le Roman du Renart, iii. p. 75.
"Vous parlerés d'autre Martin."
Ditto, p. 28.

For a hair Martin lost his ass. The French say that Martin made a bet that his ass was black ; the bet was lost because a white hair was found in its coat.

Girt like Martin of Cambray—in a very ridiculous manner. Martin and Martine are the two figures that strike with their marteaux the hours on the clock of Cambray. Martin is represented as a peasant in a blouse girt very tight about the waist.

St. Martin. Patron of drunkards, to save them from falling into danger. This is a mere accident, arising thus : The 11th November (St. Martin's Day) is the Vina'lia or feast of Bacchus. When Bacchus was merged by Christians into St. Martin, St. Martin had to bear the ill-repute of his predecessor.

St. Martin's bird. A cock, whose blood is shed "sacrificially" on the 11th of November, in honour of that saint.

St. Martin's cloak. Martin was a military tribune before conversion, and, while stationed at Amiens in midwinter, divided his military cloak with a naked beggar, who craved alms of him before the city gates of Amiens. At night, the story says, Christ Himself appeared to the soldier, arrayed in this very garment.

St. Martin's goose. The 11th of November, St. Martin's Day, was at one time the great goose feast of France. The legend is that St. Martin was annoyed by a goose, which he ordered to be killed and served up for dinner. As he died from the repast, the goose has been ever since "sacrificed" to him on the anniversary. The goose is sometimes called by the French St. Martin's bird.

St. Martin's jewellery. Counterfeit gems. Upon the site of the old collegiate church of St. Martin's le Grand, which was demolished upon the dissolution of the monasteries, a number of persons established themselves and carried on a considerable trade in artificial stones, beads, and jewellery. These Brummagem ornaments were called St. Martin's beads, St. Martin's lace, or St. Martin's jewellery, as the case might be.

St. Martin's lace. A sort of copper lace for which Blowbladder Street, St. Martin's, was noted. (*Stow.*)

St. Martin's rings. Imitation gold ones. (*See above.*)

St. Martin's tree. St. Martin planted a pilgrim's staff somewhere near Utopia. The staff grew into a large tree, which Gargantua pulled up to serve for a mace or club, with which he dislodged King Picrochole from Clermont Rock. (*Rabelais : Gargantua and Pantag'ruel.*)

Faire la St. Martin or *Martiner.* To feast ; because the people used to begin St. Martin's Day with feasting and drinking.

Martin Drunk. Very intoxicated indeed ; a drunken man "sobered" by drinking more. The feast of St. Martin (November 11) used to be held as a day of great debauch. Hence Baxter uses the word Martin as a synonym of a drunkard :—

"The language of Martin is there [in heaven] a stranger."—*Saint's Rest.*

Martin of Bullions (*St.*). The St. Swithin of Scotland. His day is July 4, and the Scotch say, if it rains then, rain may be expected for forty days.

"'By St. Martin of Bullion—'
'And what hast thou to do with St. Martin ?'
'Nay, little enough, sir, unless when he sends such rainy days that we cannot fly a hawk.'"—*Scott : The Abbott,* xv.

Martin's Running Footman (*St.*). The devil, assigned by legend to St. Martin for a running footman on a certain occasion.

"Who can tell but St. Martin's running footman may still be hatching us some further mischief."—*Rabelais : Pantagruel,* iv. 23.

Martin's Summer (*St.*) (*See under* SUMMER.)

Martine. A sword. (Italian.)

"Quiconque aura affaire à moy, il faut qu'il ait affaire a Martine que me voyla au coste (appellant son espee 'Martine')."—*Brantome : Rodomontade Espagnoles,* vol. ii. p. 16.

Martinet. A strict disciplinarian ; so called from the Marquis of Martinet, a young colonel in the reign of Louis XIV., who remodelled the infantry, and was slain at the siege of Doesbourg, in 1672 (Voltaire, *Louis XIV.,* c. 10). The French still call a cat-o'-nine-tails a "martinet."

The French martinet was a whip with twelve leather thongs.

Martinmas. The feast of St. Martin is November 11. *His Martinmas will come, as it does to every hog*—i.e. all must die.

✝ November was the great slaughter-time of the Anglo-Saxons, when beeves, sheep, and hogs, whose store of food was exhausted, were killed and salted. Martinmas, therefore, was the slaying time, and the proverb intimates that our slaying-time or day of death will come as surely as that of a hog at St. Martin's-tide.

Martyr (*Greek*) simply means a witness, but is applied to one who witnesses a good confession with his blood.

The martyr king. Charles I. of England, beheaded January 30th, 1649. He was buried at Windsor, and was called "The White King."

Martyr to science. Claude Louis, Count Berthollet, who determined to test in his own person the effects of carbolic acid on the human frame, and died under the experiment. (1748-1822.)

Marvedie (*A*). A maravedi (*q.v.*), a small obsolete Spanish copper coin of less value than a farthing.

"What a trifling, foolish girl you are, Edith, to send me by express a letter crammed with nonsense about books and gowns, and to slide the only thing I cared a marvedie about into the postscript."—*Sir W. Scott: Old Mortality,* chap. xi.

Marvellous. *The marvellous boy.* Thomas Chatterton, the poet, author of a volume of poetry entitled *Rowley's Poems,* professedly written by Rowley, a monk. (1752-1770.)

Mary.

As *the Virgin,* she is represented in Christian art with flowing hair, emblematical of her virginity.

As *Mater Dolorosa,* she is represented as somewhat elderly, clad in mourning, head draped, and weeping over the dead body of Christ.

As *Our Lady of Dolours,* she is represented as seated, her breast being pierced with seven swords, emblematic of her seven sorrows.

As *Our Lady of Mercy,* she is represented with arms extended, spreading out her mantle, and gathering sinners beneath it.

As *The glorified Madonna,* she is represented as bearing a crown and sceptre, or a ball and cross, in rich robes and surrounded by angels.

Her seven joys. The Annunciation, Visitation, Nativity, Adoration of the Magi, Presentation in the Temple, Finding Christ amongst the Doctors, and the Assumption.

Her seven sorrows. Simeon's Prophecy, the Flight into Egypt, Christ Missed, the Betrayal, the Crucifixion, the Taking Down from the Cross, and the Ascension, when she was left alone.

Mary, of Lord Byron's poetry, is Miss Chaworth, who was older than his lordship. Both Miss Chaworth and Lord Byron were under the guardianship of Mr. White. Miss Chaworth married John Musters, generally called Jack Musters ; but the marriage was not a happy one, and the parties soon separated. The *Dream* of Lord Byron refers to this love affair of his youth.

Mary, of Robert Burns. (*See* HIGHLAND MARY.)

✝ It may be added to what is said under *Highland Mary* that of Mary Morison the poet wrote :—

" Those smiles and glances let me see,
That make the *miser's treasure* poor."

And in *Highland Mary* we have—

" Still o'er those scenes my mem'ry wakes,
And fondly broods with *miser's care.*"

A statue to her has been recently erected in Edinburgh.

Marys. *The four Marys.* Mary Beaton (or *Bethune*), Mary Livingston (or *Leuson*), Mary Fleming (or *Flemyng*), and Mary Seaton (or *Seyton*) ; called the "Queen's Marys," that is, the ladies of the same age as Mary, afterwards Queen of Scots, and her companions. Mary Carmichael was not one of the four, although introduced in the well-known ballad.

" Yestre'en the queen had four Marys,
This night she'll hae but three :
There was Mary Beaton, and Mary Seaton,
Mary Carmichael, and me."

Mary Anne or **Marianne.** A slang name for the guillotine. (*See below.*)

Mary Anne Associations. Secret republican societies in France. The name comes about thus : Ravaillac was instigated to assassinate Henri IV. by reading the treatise *De Rege et Regio Institutione*, by Mariana, and as Mariana inspired Ravaillac "to deliver France," the republican party was called the Mary-Anne.

"The Mary Annes, which are essentially republicans, are scattered about all the French provinces."—*Disraeli: Lothair.*

Mary Magdalene (*St.*). Patron saint of penitents, being herself the model penitent of Gospel history.

In Christian art she is represented (1) as a *patron saint*, young and beautiful, with a profusion of hair, and holding a box of ointment; (2) as a *penitent*, in a sequestered place, reading before a cross or skull.

Mary Queen of Scots. Shakespeare being under the patronage of Queen Elizabeth, and knowing her jealousy, would not, of course, praise openly her rival queen; but in the *Midsummer Night's Dream*, composed in 1592, that is, five years after the execution of Mary, he wrote these exquisite lines:—

"Thou rememberest
Since once I sat upon a promontory,
And heard a *mermaid* (1) on a *dolphin's* back (2)
Uttering such dulcet and harmonious breath,
That the *rude sea* (3) grew civil at her song ;
And *certain stars* (4) shot *madly from their
spheres* (5),
To hear the sea-maid's music." Act ii. 1,

(1) Mermaid and sea-maid, that is, Mary ; (2) on the dolphin's back, she married the Dolphin or Dauphin of France ; (3) the rude sea grew civil, the Scotch rebels ; (4) certain stars, the Earl of Northumberland, the Earl of Westmoreland, and the Duke of Norfolk ; (5) shot madly from their spheres, that is, revolted from Queen Elizabeth, bewitched by the sea-maid's sweetness.

Marybuds. The flower of the marigold (*q.v.*). Like many other flowers, they open at daybreak and close at sunset.

" And winking marybuds begin
To ope their golden eyes."
Shakespeare: Cymbeline, ii. 3.

Marygold or **Marigold.** A million sterling. A *plum* is £100,000. (*See* MARIGOLD.)

Maryland (U.S. America) was so named in compliment to Queen Henrietta Maria. In the Latin charter it is called *Terra Mariæ.*

Marylebone (London) is not a corruption of *Marie la bonne*, but "Mary on the bourne" or river, as Holborn is "Old Bourne."

Mas (plural, *Masse*). Master, Mr., Messrs. ; as, Mas John King, Masse Fleming and Stebbing.

Ma'saniello. A corruption of TomMASo ANIELLO, a Neapolitan fisherman, who led the revolt of July,

1647. The great grievance was a new tax upon fruit, and the immediate cause of Masaniello's interference was the seizure of his wife (or deaf and dumb sister) for having in her possession some contraband flour. Having surrounded himself with 150,000 men, women, and boys, he was elected chief of Naples, and for nine days ruled with absolute control. The Spanish viceroy flattered him, and this so turned his head that he acted like a maniac. The people betrayed him, he was shot, and his body flung into a ditch, but next day it was interred with a pomp and ceremony never equalled in Naples (1647).

Auber has an opera on this subject called *La Muette de Portici* (1828).

Masche-croute [*gnaw-crust*]. A hideous wooden statue carried about Lyons during Carnival. The nurses of Lyons frighten children by threatening to throw them to Masche-croute.

Mascotte. One who brings good luck, and possesses a "good eye." The contrary of Jettatore, or one with an evil eye, who always brings bad luck.

" Ces envoyés du paradis,
Sont des Mascottes, mes amis,
Heureux celui que le ciel dote d'une Mascotte."
The opera called La Mascotte (1883).

" I tell you, she was a Mascotte of the first water."—*The Ludgate Monthly*, No. 1, vol. ii. ; *Tippitywitchet*, Nov. 1891.

Masdeu (Catalan for *God's field*). The vineyard not far from Perpignan was anciently so called.

Masetto. A rustic engaged to Zerlina ; but Don Giovanni intercepts them in their wedding festivities, and induces the foolish damsel to believe he meant to make her his wife. (*Mozart: Don Giovanni, an opera.*)

Mashack'ering and Misguggling. Mauling and disfiguring.

" I humbly protest against mauling and disfiguring this work ; against what the great Walter Scott would, I think, have called mashackering and misguggling, after the manner of Nicol Musclat (in *The Heart of Midlothian*), when he put an end to his wife Arlie at the spot afterwards called by his name."—*W. E. Gladstone : Nineteenth Century*, November, 1885.

Masher. A dude (*q.v.*) : an exquisite ; a lardy-dardy swell who dresses æsthetically, behaves killingly, and thinks himself a Romeo. This sort of thing used to be called "crushing" or killing, and, as mashing is crushing, the synonym was substituted about 1880. A ladykiller, a crusher, a masher, all mean the same thing.

"The prattle of the masher between the acts."
Daily Telegraph, Oct. 10, 1883,

Mask a Fleet (*To*). To lock up an enemy's fleet that it cannot put to sea.

Mason and Dixon's Line. The southern boundary-line which separated the free states of Pennsylvania from what were at one time the slave states of Maryland and Virginia. It lies in 39° 43′ 26″ north latitude, and was run by Charles Mason and Jeremiah Dixon, two English mathematicians and surveyors (between November 15th, 1763, and December 26th, 1767).

Mass.

High Mass or "Grand Mass" is sung by choristers, and celebrated with the assistance of a deacon and sub-deacon.

Low Mass is simply read without singing; there is one between these two called the "chanted mass," in which the service is chanted by the priest.

Besides these there are a number of special masses, as the *mass of the Beatæ, mass of the Holy Ghost, mass of the dead, mass of a saint, mass of scarcity, dry mass, votive mass, holiday mass, Ambrosian mass, Gallic mass, mass of the presanctified* for Good Friday, *missa Mosara'bum*, etc. etc.

Mass (*The*).

"Pope Celestinus ordained the *introit* and the *gloria in excelsis.*
"Pope Gregory the Great ordered the *kyrie eleison* to be repeated nine times, and introduced the prayer.
"Pope Gelasius ordained the Epistle and Gospel.
"Pope Damasus introduced the *Credo.*
"Pope Alexander put into the canon the following clause : '*Qui pridie quam pateretur.*'
"Pope Sextus introduced the *Sanctus.*
"Pope Innocent the *pax.*
"Pope Leo the *Oráte Fratres,* and the words in the canon ; '*Sanctum Sacrificium et immacul tam Hostiam.*"

E. Kinesman ; Lives of the Saints, p. 187 (1623).

Massachusetts was so named from the bay *massa* [great], *wadehuash* [mountain], *et* [near]. The bay-near-the-great-mountain.

Massacre of the Innocents. The slaughter of the babes of Bethlehem "from two years old and under," when Jesus was born. This was done at the command of Herod the Great in order to cut off "the babe" who was destined to become "King of the Jews."

Micah v. 2 speaks of Bethlehem as a little place, a small village, probably containing about five hundred inhabitants. It will be easy to calculate the probable number of infants under two years of age in such a village. It would be about ten.

Massacre of the Innocents (*The*), in parliamentary phraseology, means the withdrawal at the close of a session of the bills which time has not rendered it possible to consider and pass. The phrase was so used in *The Times,* 1859.

"If the secretarial M.P. is to be condemned for . . . voting against the Miner's Eight Hours Bill, he is equally censurable if he . . . does not support the numerous . . . reforms which get the sanction of the Congress during the Massacre of the Innocents at the close of the sitting."—*Nineteenth Century* October, 189:, p. 619.

Mass'amore (3 syl.) or **Massy More.** The principal dungeon of a feudal castle. A Moorish word.

"Proximus est carcer subterra'neus, sine ut Mauri appellant ' Mazmorra.'"—*Old Latin Itinerary.*

Mast. (*See* BEFORE THE MAST.)

Master Humphrey. Narrator of the story called *The Old Curiosity Shop,* by Charles Dickens.

Master Leonard. Grand-master of the nocturnal orgies of the demons. He is represented as a three-horned goat, with black human face. He marked his novitiates with one of his horns. (*Middle Age demonology.*)

Master Magrath. The dog which won the Waterloo Cup for three successive years, and was introduced to the Queen. "Waterloo" is on the banks of the Mersey, about three miles north of Liverpool.

Master of Sentences. Pierre Lombard, author of a work called *Sentences,* a compilation from the fathers of the leading arguments, *pro* and *con.,* bearing on the hair-splitting theological questions of the Middle Ages. (1100-1164.)

Master of the Mint. A punning term for a gardener.

Master of the Rolls. A punning term for a baker.

Mastic. A tonic which promotes appetite, and therefore only increases the misery of a hungry man.

"Like the starved wretch that hungry mastic chews,
But cheats himself and fosters his disease."
West : Triumphs of the Gout (Lucian).

Matadore (3 syl.). In the game of Ombre, *Spadille* (the ace of spades), *Manille* (the seven of trumps), and *Basto* (the ace of clubs), are called "Matadores."

"Now move to war her sable Matadore . . .
Spadillo first, unconquerable lord,
Led off two captive trumps, and swept the board.
As many more Manillo forced to yield,
And marched a victor from the verdant field.
Him Basto followed . . ."
Pope : Rape of the Lock, canto iii.

Matamoras. Mexicans or savages.

Mat'amore (3 syl.). A poltroon, a swaggerer, a Major Bobadil (*q.v.*). A

French term composed of two Spanish words, *matar-Moros* (a slayer of Moors.)

"Your followers . . . must bandy and brawl in my court . . . like so many Matamoros."—*Sir W. Scott : Kenilworth*, chap. xvi.

Mate. *A man does not get his hands out of the tar by becoming second mate.* A second mate is expected to put his hands into the tar bucket for tarring the rigging, like the men below him. The first mate is exempt from this dirty work. The rigging is tarred by the hands, and not by brushes.

Maté (2 syl.). Paraguay tea is so called from maté, the vessel in which the herb is in Paraguay infused. These vessels are generally hollow gourds, and the herb is called *yerba de maté*.

Mate'rialism. The doctrines of a *Materialist*, who maintains that the soul and spirit are effects of matter. The orthodox doctrine is that the soul is distinct from the body, and is a portion of the Divine essence breathed into the body. A materialist, of course, does not believe in a "spiritual deity" distinct from matter. Tertullian contended that the Bible proves the soul to be "material," and he charges the "spiritual" view to the heretical doctrines of the Platonic school.

Matfellon. *Villa beatæ Mariæ de Matfellon.* Whitechapel, dedicated to Mary the Mother.

Mathew (*Father*), 1799-1856, called *The Apostle of Temperance*. His success was almost miraculous.

Math'isen. One of the three Anabaptists who induced John of Leyden to join their rebellion. (*See* JOHN OF LEYDEN.)

Math'urin (*St.*). Patron saint of idiots and fools. A pun on his name. (*See below.*)

The malady of St. Mathurin. Folly, stupidity. A French expression.

Maturins, in French argot, means *dice*, and "maturin plat," a *domino*.

"Ces deux objets doivent leur nom a leur ressemblance avec le costume des Trinitaires (vulgairement appeles *Maturins*), qui, chez nous, portaient une sontane de serge blanche sur laquelle, quand ils sortaient, ils jetaient un manteau noir."—*Francisque Michel.*

Matilda. Daughter of Lord Robert Fitzwalter. Michael Drayton has a poem of some 670 lines so called.

Matilda. Daughter of Rokeby, and niece of Mortham. She was beloved by Wilfrid, son of Oswald, but loved Redmond, her father's page, who turns out to be Mortham's son. (*Scott : Rokeby.*)

Matilda. Sister of Gessler ; in love with Arnold, a Swiss, who had saved her life when threatened by the fall of an avalanche. After the death of Gessler, who was shot by William Tell, the marriage of these lovers is consummated. (*Rossini : Guglielmo Tell, an opera.*)

Rosa Matilda. (*See* Gifford's *Baviad and Mæviad.*)

Matric'ulate means to enrol oneself in a society. The University is called our *alma mater* (propitious mother). The students are her *alumni* (foster-children), and become so by being enrolled in a register after certain forms and examinations. (Latin, *matricula* a roll.)

Matter-of-fact. Unvarnished truth, prosaic, unimaginative. Whyte Melville speaks of a " matter-of-fact swain."

Matter's afoot (*The*). Is in train, is stirring. *Il marche bien*, it goes well ; *ça ira*.

"Now let it work. Mischief, thou art afoot ;
Take thou what course thou wilt."
Shakespeare ; Julius Cæsar, iii. 2.

Matterhorn. *The matrimonial Matterhorn.* The leap in the dark. The Matterhorn is the German name for Mont Cervin, a mountain of the Pennine Alps, about 40 miles east-north-east of Mont Blanc. Above an unbroken glacier-line of 11,000 feet high, it rises in an inaccessible obelisk of rock more than 3,000 feet higher. The total elevation of the Matterhorn is 14,836 feet. Figuratively any danger, or desperate situation threatening destruction.

Matthew (*St.*) in Christian art is represented (1) as an evangelist—an old man with long beard ; an angel generally stands near him dictating his Gospel. (2) As an apostle, in which capacity he bears a purse, in reference to his calling as a publican ; sometimes he carries a spear, sometimes a carpenter's rule or square. (*See* LUKE.)

In the last of Matthew. At the last gasp, on one's last legs. This is a German expression, and arose thus : A Catholic priest said in his sermon that Protestantism was in the last of Matthew, and, being asked what he meant, replied, " The last five words of the Gospel of St. Matthew are these : ' The end of this dispensation.' " Of course he quoted the Latin version ; ours is less correctly translated " the end of the *world*."

Matthew Bramble, in Smollett's *Humphry Clinker*, is Roderick Random grown old, somewhat cynical by experience of the world, but vastly improved in taste. Chambers says, " Smollett took some of the incidents of the family tour from *Anstey's New Bath Guide*." (*English Literature*, vol. ii.)

Matthew Parker's Bible, 1572. The second edition of the " Great Bible," with corrections, etc., by Archbishop Parker.

Matthews' Bible, 1537. A version of the Bible in English, edited by John Rogers, superintendent of the English Church in Germany, and published by him under the fictitious name of Thomas Matthews.

Matthias (*St.*) in Christian art is known by the axe or halbert in his right hand, the symbol of his martyrdom. Sometimes he is bearing a stone, in allusion to the tradition of his having been stoned before he was beheaded.

Maudlin. Stupidly sentimental. *Maudlin drunk* is the drunkenness which is sentimental and inclined to tears. *Maudlin slip-slop* is sentimental chit-chat. The word is derived from Mary Magdalen, who is drawn by ancient painters with a lackadaisical face, and eyes swollen with weeping.

Maugis. The Nestor of French romance, like Hildebrand in German legend. He was one of Charlemagne's paladins, a magician and champion.

Maugis d'Aygremont. Son of Duke Bevis of Aygremont, stolen in infancy by a female slave. As she rested under a white-thorn a lion and a leopard devoured her, and then killed each other in disputing for the infant. The babe cried lustily, and Oriande la Fée, who lived at Rosefleur, hearing it, went to the white-thorn and exclaimed, " By the Powers above, this child is *mal gist* (badly lapped) ; " and ever after he was called mau-gis'. Oriande took charge of him, and was assisted by her brother Baudris, who taught him magic and necromancy. When grown a man Maugis achieved the adventure of gaining the enchanted horse Bayard, which understood like a human being all that was said, and took from Anthenor, the Saracen, the sword Flamberge or Floberge. Subsequently he gave both the horse and sword to his cousin Renaud. In the Italian romances Maugis is called " Malagi'gi " (*q.v.*). ; Renaud is called " Renaldo " (*q.v.*); Bevis is called " Buo'vo ; " the horse is called "Bayardo ; " and the sword, " Fusberta." (*Romance of Maugis d'Aygremont et de Vivian son frère.*)

Maugrab'in (*Heyraddin*). Brother of Zamet Maugrabin the Bohemian. He appears disguised as Rouge Sanglier, and pretends to be herald from Liege. (*Sir Walter Scott : Quentin Durward.*)

Mau'gys. A giant who keeps a bridge leading to a castle by a riverside, in which a beautiful lady is besieged. Sir Lybius, one of Arthur's knights, does battle with the giant ; the contest lasts a whole summer's day, but terminates with the death of the giant and liberation of the lady. (*Libeaux, a romance.*)

Maul. To beat roughly, to batter. The maul was a bludgeon with a leaden head, carried by ancient soldiery. It is generally called a " mall."

Maul (*The Giant*). A giant who used to spoil young pilgrims with sophistry. He attacked Mr. Greatheart with a club, and the combat between them lasted for the space of an hour. At length Mr. Greatheart pierced the giant under the fifth rib, and then cut off his head. (*Bunyan : Pilgrim's Progress*, pt. ii.)

Maul of Monks (*The*). Thomas Cromwell, visitor-general of English monasteries, many of which he summarily suppressed (1490-1540).

Maunciples Tale. A mediæval version of Ovid's tale about Coro'nis (*Met.* ii. 543, etc.). Phœbus had a crow which he taught to speak ; it was downy white, and as big as a swan. He had also a wife whom he dearly loved, but she was faithless to him. One day when Phœbus came home his bird 'gan sing "Cuckoo ! cuckoo ! cuckoo ! " Phœbus asked what he meant, and the crow told him of his wife's infidelity. Phœbus was very angry, and, seizing his bow, shot his wife through the heart ; but no sooner did she fall than he repented of his rashness and cursed the bird. " Nevermore shalt thou speak," said he ; " henceforth thy offspring shall be black." Moral— " Lordlings, by this ensample, take heed what you say ; be no tale-bearers, but—

> ' Wher-so thou comest amongst high or low,
> Keep wel thy tong. and think upon the crow.' "
> *Chaucer : Canterbury Tales.*

Maunds (*Royal*). Gifts distributed to the poor on Maundy Thursday (*q.v.*). The number of doles corresponds to the number of years the monarch has been regnant, and the doles used to be distributed by the Lord High Almoner. Since 1883 the doles have been money payments distributed by the Clerk of the Almonry Office. The custom began in

1368, in the reign of Edward III. James I. distributed the doles personally.

"Entries of 'al maner of things yerly yevin by my lorde of his Maundy, and my laidis, and his lordshippis children.'"—*Household Book of the Earl of Northumberland*, 1512.

Maundrel. A foolish, vapouring gossip. The Scotch say, "Haud your tongue, maundrel." As a verb it means to babble, to prate. In some parts of Scotland the talk of persons in delirium, in sleep, and in intoxication is called *maundrel*. The term is from Sir John Mandeville, the traveller, who published an account of his travels, full of idle gossip and most improbable events.

⁂ There is another verb, *maunder* (to mutter, to vapour, or wander in one's talk). This verb is from *maund* (to beg). (*See* MAUNDY THURSDAY.)

Maundy Thursday. The day before Good Friday is so called from the Latin *dies manda'ti* (the day of Christ's great mandate). After He had washed His disciples' feet, He said, "A new commandment give I unto you, that ye love one another" (St. John xiii. 34).

Spelman derives it from *maund* (a basket), because on the day before the great fast all religious houses and good Catholics brought out their broken food in maunds to distribute to the poor. This custom in many places gave birth to a fair, as the Tombland fair of Norwich, held on the plain before the Cathedral Close.

Mauri-gasima. An island near Formo'sa, said to have been sunk in the sea in consequence of the great crimes of its inhabitants. (*Kempfer*.)

Maurita'nia. Morocco and Algiers, the land of the ancient Mauri or Moors.

Mausole'um. One of the seven "wonders of the world;" so called from Mauso'lus, King of Caria, to whom Arte-mis'ia (his wife) erected at Halicarnassos a splendid sepulchral monument B.C. 353. Parts of this sepulchre are now in the British Museum.

The chief mausoleums, besides the one referred to above, are: the mausoleum of Augustus; that of Ha'drian, now called the castle of St. An'gelo, at Rome; that erected in France to Henry II. by Catherine de Medicis; that of St. Peter the Martyr in the church of St. Eusta-tius, by G. Balduccio in the fourteenth century; and that erected to the memory of Louis XVI.

Maut gets abune the Meal (*The*). malt liquor or drink gets more potent than the food eaten—that is, when men get heady or boosy.

"If the maut gets abune the meal with you, it is time for me to take myself away; and you will come to my room, gentlemen, when you want a cup of tea."—*Sir W. Scott : Redgauntlet.*

Mauthe Dog. A "spectre hound" that for many years haunted the ancient castle of Peel town, in the Isle of Man. This black spaniel used to enter the guard-room as soon as candles were lighted, and leave it at day-break. While this spectre-dog was present the soldiers forebore all oaths and profane talk. One day a drunken trooper entered the guard-house alone out of bravado, but lost his speech and died in three days. Scott refers to it in his *Lay of the Last Minstrel*, vi. stanza 26.

⁂ For the legend, see a long note at the beginning of Scott's *Peveril of the Peak*, chapter xv.

Mauvais Ton (French). Bad manners. Ill-breeding, vulgar ways.

Mauvaise Honte (French). Bad or silly shame. Bashfulness, sheepishness.

Mauvaise Plaisanterie (*A*). A rude or ill-mannered jest; a jest in bad taste.

Mavournin. Irish for darling. Erin mavournin = Ireland, my darling; Erin go bragh = Ireland for ever!

"Land of my forefathers. Erin go bragh ! . . .
Erin mavournin. Erin go bragh ! "
Campbell : Exile of Erin.

Mawther. (*See* MORTHER.)

Mawworm. A vulgar copy of Dr. Cantwell, the hypocrite, in *The Hypo-crite*, by Isaac Bickerstaff.

Max. A huntsman, and the best marksman in Germany. He was be-trothed to Ag'atha, who was to be his bride if he obtained the prize in the annual trial-shot. Having been unsuc-cessful in his practice for several days, Caspar induced him to go to the wolf's glen at midnight and obtain seven charmed balls from Sa'miel the Black Huntsman. On the day of contest, the prince bade him shoot at a dove. Max aimed at the bird, but killed Caspar, who was concealed in a tree. The prince abolished in consequence the annual fête of the trial-shot. (*Weber : Der Freis-chütz, an opera.*)

Max O'Rell. The pen name of M. Blouet, author of *John Bull and his Island*, etc.

Max'imum and **Minimum.** The *greatest* and the *least* amount; as, the maximum profits or exports, and the minimum profits or exports ; the maximum and minimum price of corn during the year. The terms are also employed in mathematics.

Max'imus or **Max'ime** (2 syl.). Officer of the prefect Alma'chius, and his cornicular. Being ordered to put Valir'ian and Tibur'cē to death because they would not worship the image of Jupiter, he took pity on his victims and led them to his own house, where Cecilia was instrumental in his conversion ; whereupon he and "all his" house were at once baptised. When Valir'ian and Tibur'cē were put to death, Maximus declared that he saw angels come and carry them to heaven, whereupon Alma'chius caused him to be beaten with whips of lead "til he his lif gan lete." (*Chaucer : Secounde Nonnes Tale.*)

May. A lovely girl who married January, an old Lombard baron, sixty years of age. She had a liaison with a young squire named Damyan, and was detected by January ; but she persuaded the old fool that his eyes were to blame and that he was labouring under a great mistake, the effect of senseless jealousy. January believed her words, and "who is glad but he?" for what is better than "a fruitful wife, and a confiding spouse?" (*Chaucer : The Marchaundes Tale.* Pope : *January and May*,)

May (the month) is not derived from Maia, the mother of Mercury, as the word existed long before either Mercury or Maia had been introduced. It is the Latin *Maius*—*i.e. Magius*, from the root *mag*, same as the Sanscrit *mah*, to grow ; and means the growing or shooting month.

May unlucky for weddings. This is a Roman superstition. Ovid says, "The common people profess it is unlucky to marry in the month of May." In this month were held the festivals of Bona Dea (the goddess of chastity), and the feasts of the dead called Lemuralia.

" Nec viduæ tædis eădem, nec virgĭnis apta
   Tempŏra ; quæ nupsit, non diuturna fuit ;
   Hæc quoque de causa, si te proverbia tangunt,
   Mente malum Maio nubĕre vulgus ait."
                       Ovid : Fasti, v. 496, etc.

Here we go gathering nuts of May. (*See* NUTS OF MAY.)

May-day. Polydore Virgil says that the Roman youths used to go into the fields and spend the calends of May in dancing and singing in honour of Flora, goddess of fruits and flowers. The early English consecrated May-day to Robin Hood and the Maid Marian, because the favourite outlaw died on that day. Stow says the villagers used to set up May-poles, and spend the day in archery, morris-dancing, and other amusements.

Evil May-day (1517), when the London apprentices rose up against the foreign residents, and did incalculable mischief. The riot lasted till May 22nd.

May-duke Cherries. Medoc, a district of France, whence the cherries first came to us.

May Meetings. A title applied to the annual gatherings, in May and June, of the religious and charitable societies, to hear the annual reports and appeals for continued or increased support. The chief meetings are the British Asylum for Deaf and Dumb Females, British and Foreign Bible Society, British and Foreign Schools, Children's Refuge, Church Home Mission, Church Missionary Society, Church Pastoral Aid Society, Clergy Orphan Society, Corporation of the Sons of the Clergy, Destitute Sailors' Asylum, Field Lane Refuge, Governesses' Benevolent Institution, Home and Colonial School Society, Irish Church Missionary Society, London City Mission, Mendicity Society, National Temperance League, Propagation of the Gospel among the Jews, Ragged School Union, Religious Tract Society, Royal Asylum of St. Anne's, Sailors' Home, Sunday School Union, Thames Church Missionary Society, United Kingdom Band of Hope, Wesleyan Missionary Society, with many others of similar character.

May Molloch, or *The Maid of the Hairy Arms.* An elf who condescends to mingle in ordinary sports, and even to direct the master of the house how to play dominoes or draughts. Like the White Lady of Avenel, May Molloch is a sort of banshee.

May-pole, May-queen, etc. Dancing round the May-pole on May-day, "going a-Maying," electing a May-queen, and lighting bonfires, are all remnants of Sun-worship, and may be traced to the most ancient times. The chimney-sweeps used to lead about a Jack-i'-the-green, and the custom is not yet quite extinct (1895).

May-pole (London). The races in the *Dunciad* take place "where the tall May-pole overlooked the Strand." On the spot now occupied by St. Mary-le-Strand, anciently stood a cross. In the place of this cross a May-pole was set up by John Clarges, a blacksmith, whose daughter Ann became the wife of Monk, Duke of Albemarle. It was taken down in 1713, and replaced by a new one erected opposite Somerset House. This second May-pole had two gilt balls and a vane on its summit. On holidays the pole was decorated with flags and garlands. It was removed in 1718, and sent by Sir Isaac Newton to Wanstead Park to support the largest telescope in Europe. (*See* UNDERSHAFT.)

"Captain Baily . . . employed four hackney coaches, with drivers in liveries, to ply at the Maypole in the Strand, fixing his own rates, about the year 1634. Bailey's coaches seem to have been the first of what are now called hackney coaches."—*Note I. The Tatler*, iv. p. 415.

May-pole. The Duchess of Kendal, mistress of George I. ; so called because she was thin and tall as a May-pole.

Mayeux. The stock name in French plays for a man deformed, vain and licentious, brave and witty.

"Mayflower" (*The*). A ship of 180 tons, which, in December, 1620, started from Plymouth, and conveyed to Massachusetts, in North America, 102 Puritans, called the "Pilgrim Fathers." They called their settlement New Plymouth.

Mayonnaise. A sauce made with pepper, salt, oil, vinegar, and the yolk of an egg beaten up together. A "may" in French is a cullender or strainer, also a "*fort plancher sur lequel on met les raisins qu' on veut fouler.*"

Mayor. The chief magistrate of a city, elected by the citizens, and holding office for twelve months.

The chief magistrate of London is The Right Hon. the Lord Mayor, one of the Privy Council. Since 1389 the chief magistrate of York has been a Lord Mayor, and in 1894 those of Liverpool and Manchester.
∴ There are two Lord Mayors of Ireland, viz. those of Dublin (1665) and of Belfast ; and four of Scotland—Glasgow, Edinburgh, Aberdeen, and Dundee.

¶ At the Conquest the sovereign appointed the chief magistrates of cities. That of London was called the Port-Reeve, but Henry II. changed the word to the Norman *maire* (our mayor). John made the office annual ; and Edward III. (in 1354) conferred the title of "The Right Hon. the Lord Mayor of London."

☛ The first Lord Mayor's Show was 1458, when Sir John Norman went by water in state, to be sworn in at Westminster ; and the cap and sword were given by Richard II. to Sir William Walworth, for killing Wat Tyler.

Mayor of Garratt. (*See* GARRATT.)

Mayor of the Bull-ring (Old Dublin). This official and his sheriffs were elected on May-day and St. Peter's Eve "to be captaine and gardian of the batchelers and the unwedded youth of the civitie." For the year the Mayor of the Bull-ring had authority to punish those who frequented brothels and houses of ill-fame. He was termed Mayor of the Bull-ring from an iron ring in the Corn Market, to which bulls for bull-baiting were tied, and if any bachelor happened to marry he was conducted by the Mayor and his followers to the market-place to kiss the bull-ring.

Mayors of the Palace (*Maire du Palais*). Superintendents of the king's household, and stewards of the royal *leudes* or companies of France before the accession of the Carlovingian dynasty.

Maz'arinades (4 syl.). Violent publications issued against Mazarin, the French minister (1650, etc.).

Mazarine Bible (*The*). The earliest book printed in movable metal type. It contains no date, but a copy in the Bibliothèque Mazarine contains the date of the illuminator Cremer (1456), so that the book must have been printed before that date. Called "Mazarine" from Cardinal Mazarin, who founded the library in 1688.

In 1873, at the Perkin's sale, Lord Ashburnham gave £3,400 for a copy in vellum, and Mr. Quaritch, bookseller, gave £2,690 for one on paper. At the Thorold sale, in 1884, Mr. Quaritch gave £3,900 for a copy. In 1887 he bought one for £2,600 ; and in 1889 he gave £2,000 for a copy slightly damaged.

Mazeppa (*Jan*), historically, was hetman of the Cossacks. Born of a noble Polish family in Podolia, he became a page in the court of Jan Casimir, King of Poland. Here he intrigued with There'sia, the young wife of a Podolian count, who had the young page lashed to a wild horse, and turned adrift. The horse dropped down dead in the Ukraine, where Mazeppa was released by a Cossack family, who nursed him in their own hut. He became secretary to the hetman, and at the death of the prince was appointed his successor. Peter I. admired him, and created him Prince of the Ukraine, but in the wars with Sweden Mazeppa deserted to Charles XII., and fought against Russia at Pulto'wa. After the loss of this battle, Mazeppa fled to Valentia, and then to Bender. Some say he died a natural death, and others that he was put to death for treason by the Czar. Lord Byron makes Mazeppa tell his tale to Charles after the battle of Pultowa. (1640-1709.)

Mazer. A cup; so called from the British *masarn* (maple); Dutch, *maeser*. Like our copus-cups in Cambridge, and the loving-cup of the London Corporation.

"A mazer wrought of the maple ware."
Spenser : Calendar (August).
"'Bring hither,' he said, 'the mazers four
My noble fathers loved of yore.'"
Sir Walter Scott : Lord of the Isles.

Maz'ikeen or *Shedeem.* A species of beings in Jewish mythology exactly resembling the Arabian Jinn or genii, and said to be the agents of magic and enchantment. When Adam fell, says the Talmud, he was excommunicated for 130 years, during which time he begat demons and spectres; for, it is written, "Adam lived 130 years and (*i.e.* before he) begat children in his own image" (Genesis v. 3). (*Rabbi Jeremiah ben Eliezar.*)

"And the Mazikeen shall not come nigh thy tents."—Psalm xci. 5 (Chaldee version).

Swells out like the Mazikeen ass. The allusion is to a Jewish tradition that a servant, whose duty it was to rouse the neighbourhood to midnight prayer, found one night an ass in the street, which he mounted. As he rode along the ass grew bigger and bigger, till at last it towered as high as the tallest edifice, where it left the man, and where next morning he was found.

Mazzi'ni-ism. The political system of Giuseppe Mazzi'ni, who filled almost every sovereign and government in Europe with a panic-terror. His plan was to establish secret societies all over Europe, and organise the several governments into federated republics. He was the founder of what is called "Young Italy," whose watchwords were "Liberty, Equality, and Humanity," whose motto was "God and the People," and whose banner was a tricolour of white, red, and green. (Born at Genoa, 1808.)

Meal or Malt (*In*). *In meal or in malt.* Directly or indirectly; some sort of subsidy. If much money passes through the hand, some profit will be sure to accrue either "in meal or in malt."

"When other interests in the country (as the cotton trade, the iron trade, and the coal trade) had been depressed, the Government had not been called upon for assistance in meal and malt."—*Sir William Harcourt : On Agricultural Depression,* 13th April, 1894.

He must pay either in meal or malt. In one way or another. A certain percentage of meal or malt is the miller's perquisite.

"If they [the Tories] wish to get the working-class vote, they have got to pay for it either in meal or in malt."—*Nineteenth Century,* August, 1892, p. 344.

Meal-tub Plot. A plot by Dangerfield against James, Duke of York, in 1679; so called because the scheme was kept in a meal-tub in the house of Mrs Cellier. Dangerfield subsequently confessed the whole affair was a forgery, and was both whipped and condemned to stand in the pillory.

Meals. In the fourteenth century breakfast hour was five; dinner, nine; supper, four. (*Chaucer's Works.*)
In the fifteenth and sixteenth centuries the breakfast hour was seven; dinner, eleven; supper, six. (*Wright : Domestic Manners.*)
Towards the close of the sixteenth century dinner advanced to noon.
In Ireland the gentry dined at between two or three in the early part of the eighteenth century. (*Swift : Country Life.*)

Mealy-mouthed is the Greek *meli-muthos* (honey-speech), and means velvet-tongued, afraid of giving offence.

Mean'der (3 syl.). To wind; so called from the Meander, a winding river of Phrygia. The "Greek pattern" in embroidery is so called.

Measure. *Out of all measure.* "*Outre mesure.*" Beyond all reasonable degree, "*Præter* (or *supra*) *modum.*"

"Thus out of measure sad."—*Shakespeare : Much Ado About Nothing,* i. 3.

To take the measure of one's foot. To ascertain how far a person will venture; to make a shrewd guess of another's character. The allusion is to "*Ex pede Herculem.*"

Measure Strength (*To*). To wrestle together; to fight, to contest.

Measure Swords (*To*). To fight a duel with swords. In such cases the seconds measure the swords to see that both are of one length.

"So we measured swords and parted."—*Shakespeare : As You Like It,* v. 4.

Measure for Measure (Shakespeare). The story is taken from a tale in G. Whetstone's *Heptam'eron*, entitled *Promos and Cassandra* (1578). Promos is called by Shakespeare, "Lord Angelo;" and Cassandra is "Isabella." Her brother, called by Shakespeare "Claudio," is named Andru'gio in the story. A similar story is given in Giovanni Giraldi Cinthio's third decade of stories.

Measure One's Length on the Ground (*To*). To fall flat on the ground; to be knocked down.

"If you will measure your lubber's length, tarry."—*Shakespeare: King Lear*, i. 4.

Measure Other People's Corn. *To measure other people's corn by one's own bushel.* To judge of others by oneself. In French, "*Mesurer les autres à son aune;*" in Latin, "*Alios suo modulo metiri.*"

Meat, Bread. These words tell a tale; both mean food in general. The Italians and Asiatics eat little animal food, and with them the word *bread* stands for food; so also with the poor, whose chief diet it is; but the English consume meat very plentifully, and this word, which simply means food, almost exclusively implies animal food. In the banquet given to Joseph's brethren, the viceroy commanded the servants "to set on bread" (Genesis xliii. 31). In Psalm civ. 27 it is said of fishes, creeping things, and crocodiles, that God giveth them their meat in due season."

To carry off meat from the graves—i.e. to be poor as a church mouse. The Greeks and Romans used to make feasts at certain seasons, when the dead were supposed to return to their graves. In these feasts the fragments were left on the tombs for the use of the ghosts.

Mec (French). Slang for king, governor, master; *méquard*, a commander; *méquer*, to command. All these are derived from the fourbesque word *maggio*, which signifies God, king, pope, doctor, seigneur, and so on, being the Latin *major*. (There are the Hebrew words *melech* and *melchi* also.)

Mecca's Three Idols. Lata, Alo'za, and Menat, all of which Mahomet overthrew.

Meche (French). "*Il y a mèche*," the same as "*Il y a moyen;*" so the negative "*Il n'y a pas mèche*" (there is no possibility). The *Dictionnaire du Bas-langage* says:

"Dans le langage typographique, lorsque des ouvriers viennent proposer leurs services dans quelque imprimerie, ils demandent *s'il y a mèche* —*i.e.* si l'on peut les occuper. Les compositeurs demandent 's'il y a mèche pour la casse,' et les pressiers demandent 's'il y a mèche pour la presse.'"—Vol. ii. p. 122.

" Soit mis dedans ceste caverne
De nul honneur il n'y a maiche."
Moralité de la Vendition de Joseph.

Medam'othi (Greek, *never in any place*). The island at which the fleet of Pantagruel landed on the fourth day of their voyage, and where they bought many choice curiosities, such as the picture of a man's voice, echo drawn to life, Plato's ideas, the atoms of Epicu'ros, a sample of Philome'la's needlework, and other objects of vertu which could be obtained in no other portion of the globe. (*Rabelais: Pantagruel*, iv. 3.)

Médard (*St.*). Master of the rain. St. Médard was the founder of the rose-prize of Salency in reward of merit. The legend says, he was one day passing over a large plain, when a sudden shower fell, which wetted everyone to the skin except himself. He remained dry as a toast, for an eagle had kindly spread his wings for an umbrella over him, and ever after he was termed *maître de la pluie*.

" S'il pleut le jour de S. Médard [8th June]
Il pleut quarante jours plus tard."

Mede'a. A sorceress, daughter of the King of Colchis. She married Jason, the leader of the Argonauts, whom she aided to obtain the golden fleece.

Mede'a's Kettle or *Caldron*, to boil the old into youth again. Medea, the sorceress, cut an old ram to pieces, and, throwing the pieces into her caldron, the old ram came forth a young lamb. The daughters of Pelias thought to restore their father to youth in the same way; but Medea refused to utter the magic words, and the old man ceased to live.

"Get thee Medea's kettle and be boiled anew."
—*Congreve. Love for Love*, iv.

Medham [*the keen*]. One of Mahomet's swords, taken from the Jews when they were exiled from Medi'na. (*See* SWORDS.)

Mediæval or **Middle Ages** begin with the Council of Chalcĕdon (451), and end with the revival of literature in the fifteenth century, according to the Rev. J. G. Dowling. According to Hallam, they begin from the downfall of the Western Empire, in 476, to the Italian expeditions of Charles VIII. of France (1494-1496).

Me'dian Apples. Pome-citrons.

Median Stone (*The*). Said to cure blindness, and, if soaked in ewe's milk, to cure the gout.

Medicine, in alchemy, was that agent which brought about the transmutation of metals, or renewed old age; the philosopher's stone, and the elixir of life.

" How much unlike art thou, Mark Antony !
Yet, coming from him, that great medicine hath
With his tinct gilded thee."
Shakespeare: Antony and Cleopatra, i. 5.

Father of Medicine. Aretæos of Cappado'cia, who lived at the close of the first and beginning of the second century, and Hippoc'ratēs of Cos (B.C. 460-357) are both so called.

Medicinal Days. The sixth, eighth, tenth, twelfth, sixteenth, eighteenth, etc., of a disease; so called because. according to Hippoc'ratēs, no " crisis " occurs on these days, and medicine may be safely administered. (*See* CRISIS.)

Medicinal Hours. Hours proper for taking medicine, viz. morning fasting, an hour before dinner, four hours after dinner, and bed-time. (*Quincy.*)

Medi'na. (*Economy*, Latin *medium*, the golden mean.) Step-sister of Elissa and Perissa, but they could never agree upon any subject. (*Spenser: Faërie Queene*, book ii.)
Medina means in Arabic " city." The city so called is " Medinat al Nabi " (city of the prophet).

Mediterranean (*Key of the*). The fortress of Gibraltar, which commands the entrance.

Me'dium (*A*), in the language of spirit-rappers, etc., is some one possessed of " odylic force," who puts the question of the interrogator to the " spirit " consulted.

Medo'ra. The betrothed of the Corsair. (*Byron: The Corsair.*)

Medo'ro (in *Orlando Furioso*). A Moorish youth of extraordinary beauty; a friend of Dardinello, King of Zuma'ra. After Dardinello was slain, Medo'ro is wounded by some unknown spear. Angelica dresses his wounds, falls in love with him, marries him, and they retire to India, where he becomes King of Cathay in right of his wife.

Medu'sa. Chief of the Gorgons. Her head was cut off by Perseus (2 syl.), and Minerva placed it in her ægis. Everyone who looked on this head was instantly changed into stone.
⁂ The tale is that Medusa, famous for her hair, presumed to set her beauty above that of Minerva : so the jealous goddess converted her rival's hair into snakes, which changed to stone anyone who looked thereon.
The most famous painting of Medusa is by Leonardo da Vinci ; it is called his *chef d'œuvre.*

Meerschaum (2 syl., German, *sea-froth.*) This mineral, from having been found on the sea-shore in rounded white

lumps, was ignorantly supposed to be sea-froth petrified ; but it is a compound of silica, magnesia, lime, water, and carbonic acid. When first dug it lathers like soap, and is used as a soap by the Tartars.

Meg. *Mons Meg.* An old-fashioned piece of artillery in the castle of Edinburgh, made at Mons, in Flanders. It was considered a palladium by the Scotch. (*See* LONG MEG.)
"Sent awa' our crown, and our sword, and our sceptre, and Mons Meg to be keepit by thae English . . . in the Tower of London [*N.B. It was restored in* 1828]."—*Scott: Rob Roy*, chap. xxvii.

A roaring Meg. A cannon given by the Fishmongers of London, and used in 1689. Burton says, " *Music is a roaring Meg against melancholy.*"

Meg Dods. An old landlady in Scott's novel called *St. Ronan's Well.*

Meg Merrilies (in Sir W. Scott's *Guy Mannering*). This character was based on that of Jean Gordon, an inhabitant of the village of Kirk Yetholm, in the Cheviot Hills, in the middle of the eighteenth century. A sketch of Jean Gordon's life will be found in *Blackwood's Magazine*, vol. i. p. 54. She is a half-crazy sibyl or gipsy.

Mega'rian School. A philosophical school, founded by Euclid, a native of Meg'ara, and disciple of Socratēs.

Mega'rians (*The*). A people of Greece proverbial for their stupidity; hence the proverb, " Wise as a Megarian "—*i.e.* not wise at all; yet *see above.*

Megathe'rium (Greek, *great-beast*). A gigantic extinct quadruped of the sloth kind.

Me'grims. A corruption of the Greek *hemi-crania* (half the skull), through the French *migraine.* A neuralgic affection generally confined to one brow, or to one side of the forehead; whims, fancies.

Meigle (in Strathmore). The place where Guinever, Arthur's queen, was buried.

Meiny (2 syl.). A company of attendants. (Norman, *meignal* and *mesnie*, a household, our *menial.*)
" With that the smiling Kriemhild forth stepped
   a little space,
And Brunhild and her meiny greeted with
   gentle grace."
     Lettsom's Nibelungen Lied, stanza 604.

Meissonier-like Exactness. Jean Louis Ernest Meissonier, R.A., a French artist, born at Lyons, 1813, exhibited in 1836 a microscopic painting called *Petit Messager*, and became proverbial for the utmost possible precision.

Meistersingers. Minstrel tradesmen of Germany, who attempted to revive the national minstrelsy of the minnesingers, which had fallen into decay. Hans Sachs, the cobbler (1494-1574), was by far the most celebrated of these poets.

Mejnoun and Leilah. A Persian love-tale, the *Romeo and Juliet* or *Pyramus and Thisbe* of Eastern romance.

Melampode (3 syl.). Black hellebore; so called from Melampus, a famous soothsayer and physician, who cured with it the daughters of Prætus of their melancholy. (*Virgil: Georgics,* iii. 550.)

" My seely sheep, like well below.
  They need not melampode :
For they been hale enough I trow,
  And liken their abode."
                    Spenser: Eclogue vii.

Mel'ancholy. Lowness of spirits, supposed at one time to arise from a redundance of black bile. (Greek, *melas cholē*.)

Mel'ancholy Jacques (1 syl.). So Jean Jacques Rousseau was called for his morbid sensibilities and unhappy spirit. (1712-1777.) The expression is from Shakespeare, *As You Like It,* ii. 1.

Melanch'thon is merely the Greek for *Schwarzerde* (black earth), the real name of this amiable reformer. (1497-1560.) Similarly, *Œcolampa'dius* is the Greek version of the German name *Hausschein*, and *Desiderius Erasmus* is one Latin and one Greek rendering of the name *Gheraerd Gheraerd*.

Melan'tius. A brave, honest soldier, who believes everyone to be true and honest till convicted of crime, and then is he a relentless punisher. (*Beaumont and Fletcher : The Maid's Tragedy.*)

Melanuros. *Abstain from the Melanurus.* This is the sixth symbol in the *Protreptics.* Melan-uros means the "black-tailed." Pythagoras told his disciples to abstain from that which has a black tail, in other words, from such pleasures and pursuits as end in sorrow, or bring grief. The Melanuros is a fish of the perch family, sacred to the terrestrial gods.

Melchior, Kaspar, and Balthazar. The three magi, according to Cologne tradition, who came from the East to make offerings to the "Babe of Bethlehem, born King of the Jews."

Melchisedec'ians. Certain heretics in the early Christian Church, who entertained strange notions about Melchis'edec. Some thought him superior to Christ, some paid him adoration, and some believed him to be Christ Himself or the Holy Ghost.

Melea'ger. Distinguished for throwing the javelin. He slew the Calydonian boar. It was declared by the fates that he would die as soon as a piece of wood then on the fire was burnt up ; whereupon his mother snatched the log from the fire and extinguished it ; but after Meleager had slain his maternal uncles, his mother threw the brand on the fire again, and Meleager died.

The death of Meleager was a favourite subject in ancient reliefs. The famous picture of Charles le Brun is in the Musée Imperiale of Paris.

Melesig'enes. So Homer is sometimes called, because one of the traditions fixes his birthplace on the banks of the Melēs, in Ionia. In a similar way we call Shakespeare the "Bard of Avon." (*See* HOMER.)

        "But higher sung
Blind Melesigenes—then Homer called."
        Milton : Paradise Regained.

Mele'tians. The followers of Mele'tius, Bishop of Lycop'olis, in Egypt, who is said to have sacrificed to idols in order to avoid the persecutions of Diocletian. A trimmer in religion.

Melia'dus (*King*). Father of Tristan ; he was drawn to a chase *par mal engin et negromance* of a fay who was in love with him, and from whose thraldom he was ultimately released by the power of the great enchanter Merlin. (*Tristan de Leonois, a romance ;* 1489.)

Melibe'us or **Melibe.** A wealthy young man, married to Prudens. One day, when Melibeus "went into the fields to play," some of his enemies got into his house, beat his wife, and wounded his daughter Sophie with five mortal wounds "in her feet, in her hands, in her ears, in her nose, and in her mouth," left her for dead, and made their escape. When Melibeus returned home he resolved upon vengeance, but his wife persuaded him to forgiveness, and Melibeus, taking his wife's counsel, called together his enemies, and told them he forgave them "to this effect and to this ende, that God of His endeles mercy wole at the tyme of oure deyinge forgive us oure giltes that we have trespased to Him in this wreeched world." (*Chaucer: Canterbury Tales.*)

N.B. This prose tale of Melibeus is a literal translation of a French story, of which there are two copies in the British Museum. (*MS. Reg.* 19, c. vii.; and *MS. Reg.* 19, c. xi.)

Meliboe'an Dye. A rich purple. Meliboea, in Thessaly, was famous for the *ostrum*, a fish used in dyeing purple.

"A military vest of purple flowed,
Lovelier than Meliboean."
Milton: Paradise Lost, xi. 242.

Melicer'tes (4 syl.). Son of Ino, a sea deity. Ath'amas imagined his wife to be a lioness, and her two sons to be lion's cubs. In his frenzy he slew one of the boys, and drove the other (named Melicertēs) with his mother into the sea. The mother became a sea-goddess, and the boy the god of harbours.

Mel'ior. A lovely fairy, who carried off Parthen'opex of Blois to her secret island in her magic bark. (*French romance* called *Parthenopex de Blois*, 12th cent.)

Melisen'dra. Charlemagne's daughter, married to his nephew Don Gwyfe'-ros. She was taken captive by the Moors, and confined seven years in a dungeon, when Gwyfe'ros rescued her. (*Don Quixote.*)

Melis'sa (in *Orlando Furioso*). The prophetess who lived in Merlin's cave. Brad'amant gave her the enchanted ring to take to Roge'ro; so, assuming the form of Atlantēs, she went to Alci'na's island, and not only delivered Roge'ro, but disenchanted all the forms metamorphosed in the island. In book xix. she assumes the form of Rodomont, and persuades Agramant to break the league which was to settle the contest by single combat. A general battle ensues.

Mell Supper. Harvest supper; so called from the French *meler* (to mix together), because the master and servants sat promiscuously at the harvest board.

Mellifluous Doctor (*The*). St. Bernard, whose writings were called a "river of Paradise." (1091-1153.)

Mel'on. The Mahometans say that the eating of a melon produces a thousand good works. So named from Melos.
Etre 'n melon. To be stupid or dull of comprehension. The melon-pumpkin or squash is soft and without heart, hence "*être un melon*" is to be as soft as a squash. So also "*avoir un cœur de melon* (or *de citrouille*)" means to have no heart at all. Tertullian says of Marcion, the heresiarch, "he has a pumpkin [*pep'onem*] in the place of a heart [*cordis loco*]." It will be remembered that Thersi'tēs, the railer, calls the Greeks "pumpkins" (*pep'onēs*).

Melons (French). Children sent to school for the first time; so called because they come from a "hot-bed," and are as delicate as exotics. At St. Cyr, the new-comers are called in school-slang "*Les melons*," and the old stagers "*Les anciens*."

Melons. There are certain stones on Mount Carmel called Stone Melons. The tradition is that Elijah saw a peasant carrying melons, and asked him for one. The man said they were not melons but stones, and Elijah instantly converted them into stones.

A like story is told of St. Elizabeth of Thuringia. She gave so bountifully to the poor as to cripple her own household. One day her husband met her with her lapful of something, and demanded of her what she was carrying. "Only flowers, my lord," said Elizabeth, and to save the lie God converted the loaves into flowers. (*The Schönberg-Cotta Family*, p. 19.)

Melpom'ene (4 syl.). The muse of tragedy. The best painting of this muse is by Le Brun, at Versailles.

Melrose Abbey (*Register of*) from 735 to 1270, published in *Fulman* (1684).

Melus'ina. The most famous of the *fées* of France. Having enclosed her father in a high mountain for offending her mother, she was condemned to become every Saturday a serpent from her waist downward. When she married Raymond, Count of Lusignan, she made her husband vow never to visit her on a Saturday; but, the jealousy of the count being excited, he hid himself on one of the forbidden days, and saw his wife's transformation. Melusina was now obliged to quit her mortal husband, and was destined to wander about as a spectre till the day of doom. Some say the count immured her in the dungeon of his castle. (*See* UNDINE.)
Cri de Mélusine. A sudden scream; in allusion to the scream of despair uttered by the fairy when she discovered the indiscreet visit of her beloved husband. (*See above.*)

Mélusines (3 syl.). Gingerbread cakes bearing the impress of a beautiful woman "*bien coiffée*," with a serpent's tail ; made by confectioners for the May fair in the neighbourhood of Lusignan, near Poitiers. The allusion is to the transformation of the fairy Melusi'na every Saturday. (*See above.*)

Melyhalt (*Lady*). A powerful subject of King Arthur, whose domains Galiot invaded. She chose Galiot as her lover.

Memento Mori (*A*). Something to put us in mind of the shortness and uncertainty of life.

"I make as good use of it [Bardolph's face] as many a man doth of a death's head or a memento mori."—*Shakespeare : Henry IV.*, iii. 3.

Memnon. Prince of the Ethiopians, who went to the assistance of his uncle Priam, and was slain by Achilles. His mother Eos was inconsolable for his death, and wept for him every morning. The Greeks used to call the statue of Am'enoph'is III., in Thebes, that of Memnon. This image, when first struck by the rays of the rising sun, is said to have produced a sound like the snapping asunder of a chord. Poetically, when Eos (morning) kisses her son at daybreak, the hero acknowledges the salutation with a musical murmur. The word is the Egyptian *mei-amun*, beloved of Ammon.

"Memnon bending o'er his broken lyre."
Darwin : Economy of Vegetation, i. 3.

Memnon. One of Voltaire's novels, designed to show the folly of aspiring to too much wisdom.

Memnon's sister. Himĕra, mentioned by Dictys Cretensis.

"Black, but such as in esteem
Prince Memnon's sister might beseem."
Milton : Il Penseroso.

The legend given by Dictys Cretensis (book vi.) is that Himera, on hearing of her brother's death, set out to secure his remains, and encountered at Paphos a troop laden with booty, and carrying Memnon's ashes in an urn. Pallas, the leader of the troop, offered to give her either the urn or the booty, and she chose the urn.

Probably all that is meant is this : Black so delicate and beautiful that it might beseem a sister of Memnon the son of Aurora or the early day-dawn.

Mem'orable. *The ever memorable.* John Hales, of Eton (1584-1656).

Mem'ory. Magliabecchi, of Florence, the book-lover, was called "the universal index and living cyclopædia." (1633-1714.) (*See* WOODFALL.)

Bard of Memory. Samuel Rogers, author of *Pleasures of Memory.* (1762-1855.)

Men in Buckram. Hypothetical men existing only in the brain of the imaginer. The allusion is to the vaunting tale of Falstaff to Prince Henry. (*Shakespeare :* 1 *Henry IV.*, ii. 4.)

Men of Kent. (*See* KENT.)

Men of Lawn. Bishops of the Anglican Church. (*See* MAN.)

Men are but Children of a Larger Growth. (*Dryden : All for Love*, iv. 1.)

Me'nah. A large stone worshipped by certain tribes of Arabia between Mecca and Medi'na. This stone, like most other Arabian idols, was demolished in the eighth year of "the flight." The "menah" is simply a rude large stone brought from Mecca, the sacred city, by certain colonists, who wished to carry with them some memento of the Holy Land.

Menal'cas. Any shepherd or rustic. The name figures in the *Eclogues* of Virgil and the *Idyls* of Theoc'ritos.

Me'nam. A river of Siam, on whose banks swarms of fire-flies are seen.

Menam'bei. A rocking-stone in the parish of Sithney (Cornwall) which a little child could move. The soldiers of Cromwell thought it fostered superstition, and rendered it immovable.

Mendicants. The four orders are the Jacobins, Franciscans, Augustinians, and Carmelites (3 syl.).

Mendo'za (*Daniel*), the Jew. A prize-fighter who held the belt at the close of the last century, and in 1791 opened the Lyceum in the Strand to teach "the noble art of boxing." (1719-1791.)

"When Humphreys stood up to the Israelite's thumps
In kerseymere breeches and touch-me-not pumps."
Mendoza the Jew.

⁂ *The Odiad* (1798) is a mock heroic on the battle between Mendoza and Humphreys. *The Art of Boxing* (1799) was written by Mendoza. *Memoirs of the Life of Daniel Mendoza* (1816). See also *Pugilistica*, vol. i. (1880).

Menech'mians. Persons exactly like each other, as the brothers Dromio. So called from the *Menechmi* of Plautus.

⁂ In the *Comedy of Errors*, not only the two Dromios are exactly like each others, but also Antiphŏlus of Ephesus is the facsimile of his brother, Antipholus of Syracuse.

Menec'rates (4 syl.). A physician of Syracuse, of such unbounded vanity that he called himself Jupiter. Philip of Macedon invited him to a banquet, but served him with incense only.

" Such was Menecrates of little worth,
Who Jove, the saviour, to be called pre-
sumed,
To whom of incense Philip made a feast."
Lord Brooke : Inquisition upon Fame, etc.

Mene'via. St. David's (Wales). Its old British name was *Henemenew.*

Meng-tse. The fourth of the sacred books of China ; so called from its author, Latinised into Mencius. It is by far the best of all, and was written in the fourth century B.C. Confucius or Kong-foo-tse wrote the other three : viz. Ta-heo (*School of Adults*), Chong-yong (*The Golden Mean*), and Lun-yu (or *Book of Maxims*).
Mother of Meng. A Chinese expression, meaning "an admirable teacher." Meng's father died soon after the birth of the sage, and he was brought up by his mother. (*Died* B.C. 317.)

Me'nie (2 syl.). A contraction of Marianne.

" And maun I still on Menie doat,
And bear the scorn that's in her e'e ?"
Burns.

Menip'pos, the cynic, called by Lucian "the greatest snarler and snapper of all the old dogs " (*cynics*).
Varro wrote in Latin *Satyræ Menippeæ.*
The Menippean Satire is a political pamphlet, partly in verse and partly in prose, designed to expose the perfidious intentions of Spain in regard to France, and the criminal ambition of the Guise family. The chief writers were Leroy (who died 1593), Pithou (1544-1596), Passerat (1534-1602), and Rapin, the poet (1540-1609).

Men'nonites (3 syl.). The followers of Simons Menno, a native of Friesland, who modified the fanatical views of the Anabaptists. (1496-1561.)

Men'struum means a *monthly dissolvent* (Latin, *mensis*), from the notion of the alchemists that it acted only at the full of the moon.

" All liquors are called menstruums which are used as dissolvents, or to extract the virtues of ingredients by infusion or decoction."—*Quincy.*

Mental Hallucinations. The mind informing the senses, instead of the senses informing the mind. There can be no doubt that the senses may be excited by the mind (from within, as well as from without). Macbeth saw the dagger of his imagination as distinctly as the dagger which he held in his hand. Malebranche declared that he heard the voice of God. Descartes thought he was followed by an invisible person, telling him to pursue his search for truth. Goethe says that, on one occasion, he met an exact counterpart of himself. Sir Walter Scott was fully persuaded that he had seen the ghost of the deceased Byron. All such hallucinations (due to mental disturbances) are of such stuff as dreams are made of.

Mentor. A guide, a wise and faithful counsellor ; so called from Mentor, a friend of Ulysses, whose form Minerva assumed when she accompanied Telemachos in his search for his father. (*Fénelon : Télémaque.*)

Me'nu. Son of Brahma, whose institutes are the great code of Indian civil and religious law.

Meo Peric'ulo (Latin). On my responsibility ; I being bond.

" ' I will vouch for Edie Ochiltree, *meo periculo,* . . .' said Oldbuck."—*Sir W. Scott : The Antiquary,* chap. xxxviii.

Mephib'osheth, in *Absalom and Achitophel,* by Dryden and Tate, is meant for Pordage, a poetaster (ii. 403).

Mephistoph'eles, Mephistoph'ilis, Mephostoph'ilus. A sneering, jeering, leering tempter. The character is that of a devil in Goethe's *Faust.* He is next in rank to Satan.

Mercador Amante—the basis of our comedy called *The Curious Impertinent* —was by Gaspar de Avila, a Spaniard.

Merca'tor's Projection is Mercator's chart or map for nautical purposes. The meridian lines are at right angles to the parallels of latitude. It is so called because it was devised by Gerhard Kauffmann, whose surname Latinised is Mercator (*Merchant*). (1512-1594.)

Merchant of Venice. A drama by Shakespeare. A similar story occurs in the *Gesta Romano'rum.* The tale of the bond is chapter xlviii., and that of the caskets is chapter xcix. Shakespeare, without doubt, is also indebted for his plot to the novelette *Il Pecorone* of Ser. Giovanni. (Fourteenth century.)
⁂ Loki made a wager with Brock and lost. He wagered his *head*, but saved it on the plea that Brock could not take his head without touching his **neck.** (*Simroch's Edda*, p. 305.)

Mer'cia. The eighth and last kingdom of the Heptarchy, between the Thames and the Humber. It was the *merc* or boundary of the Anglo-Saxons and free Britons of Wales.

Mercu'rial. Light-hearted and gay, like those born under the planet Mercury. (*Astrological notion.*)

Mercu'rial Finger (*The*). The little finger.

" The thumb, in chiromancy, we give to Venus,
The foreflnger to Jove, the midst to Saturn,
The ring to Sol, the least to Mercury."
Ben Jonson : The Alchemist, i. 1.

❣ If pointed it denotes eloquence, if square it denotes sound judgment.

Mercuriale (4 syl., French). An harangue or rebuke; so called from Mercuriale, as the first Wednesday after the great vacation of the Parliament under the old French *régime* used to be called. On this day the house discussed grievances, and reprimanded members for misconduct.

Mer'cury. Images of Mercury, or rather, shapeless posts with a marble head of Mercury on them, used to be erected by the Greeks and Romans where two or more roads met, to point out the way. (*Juvenal,* viii. 53.)

❣ There are two famous statues of this god in Paris : one in the garden of Versailles, by Lerambert, and another in the Tuileries, by Mellana.

You cannot make a Mercury of every log. Pythagoras said : " *Non ex quovis ligno Mercurius fit.*" That is, " Not every mind will answer equally well to be trained into a scholar." The proper wood for a statue of Mercury was box-wood—"*vel quod hominis pultorem præ se ferat, vel quod materies sit omnium maxime æterna.*" (*Erasmus.*)

Mercury, in astrology, " signifieth subtill men, ingenious, inconstant : rymers, poets, advocates, orators, phylosophers, arithmeticians, and busie fellowes."

Mercury Fig. (In Latin *Ficus ad Mercurium*). The first fig gathered off a fig-tree was by the Romans devoted to Mercury. The proverbial saying was applied generally to all first fruits or first works, as the " *Guide to Science* was my Mercury fig."

Mercu'tio. A kind-hearted, witty nobleman, kinsman to the Prince of Vero'na, in Shakespeare's *Romeo and Juliet.* Being mortally wounded by Tybalt, he was asked if he were hurt, and replied, " A scratch, a scratch ; marry, 'tis enough."

The Mercutio of actors. Lewis, who displayed in acting the combination of the fop and real gentleman. (1748-1811.)

Mercy. A young pilgrim who accompanied Christiana in her pilgrimage to Mount Zion. She married Matthew, Christian's son. (*Bunyan : Pilgrim's Progress,* part ii.)

Mercy. The seven corporal works of mercy are :—

(1) To tend the sick.
(2) To feed the hungry.
(3) To give drink to the thirsty.
(4) To clothe the naked.
(5) To house the homeless.
(6) To visit the fatherless and the afflicted.
(7) To bury the dead.
Matt. xxv. 35-40.

Meredith (*Owen*). The pseudonym of Edward Robert Bulwer Lytton, author of *Chronicles and Characters,* in verse (1868). He became Lord Lytton (1873-1891).

Meridian (*A*). A noonday dram of spirits.

" He received from the hand of the waiter the meridian, which was placed ready at the bar."— *Sir Walter Scott : Redgauntlet,* chap. i.

Meri'no Sheep. A Spanish breed of sheep, very valuable for their wool.

Mer'ioneth (Wales) is *maeronaeth* (a dairy farm).

Merlan (French). A whiting, or a hairdresser. Perruquiers are so called because at one time they were covered with flour like whiting prepared for the frying-pan.

" M'adressantà un merlan qui filait une perruque sur un peigne de fer."—*Chateaubriand : Mémoires à Outre-Tombe.*

Merlin. Prince of Enchanters ; also the name of a romance. He was the son of a damsel seduced by a fiend, but Blaise baptised the infant, and so rescued it from the power of Satan. He died spell-bound by his mistress Vivian in a hawthorn-bush. (*See* Spenser's *Faërie Queene,* Tennyson's *Idylls of the King,* and Ellis's *Specimens of Early English Metrical Romances.*)

The English Merlin. Lilly, the astrologer, who published two tracts under the assumed name of " Mer'linus An'glicus."

Merlin Chair (*A*). A three-wheeled invalid chair, with a double tyre to the two front wheels, the outer tyre being somewhat smaller than that on which the chair rests, so that by turning it with the hand the chair can be propelled. Named after the inventor.

Merlo or **Melo** (*Juan de*). Born at Castile in the 15th century. A dispute having arisen at Esalo'na upon the question whether Hector or Achilles was the braver warrior, the Marques de Ville'na called out in a voice of thunder, "Let us see if the advocates of Achilles can fight as well as prate." Presently there appeared in the midst of the assembly a gigantic fire-breathing monster, which repeated the same challenge. Everyone shrank back except Juan de Melo, who drew his sword and placed himself before the king (Juan II.) to protect him, for which exploit he was appointed alcayde of Alcala la Real (Granada). (*Chronica de Don Alvaro de Luna.*)

Mermaids. Sir James Emerson Tennent, speaking of the dugong, a cetacean, says, "Its head has a rude approach to the human outline, and the mother while suckling her young holds it to her breast with one flipper, as a woman holds her infant in her arm. If disturbed she suddenly dives under water, and tosses up her fish-like tail. It is this creature which has probably given rise to the tales about mermaids."
Mermaid. Mary Queen of Scots (*q.v.*).

Mermaid's Glove [*Chalina oculata*], the largest of British sponges, so called because its branches resemble fingers.

Mermaids' Purses. The empty cases of fishes' eggs, frequently cast up by the waves on the sea-beach.

Mer'opē. One of the Pleiads; dimmer than the rest, because she married a mortal.

Merops' Son or *A son of Merops.* One who thinks he can set the world to rights, but can only set it on fire. Agitators and stump orators, demagogues and Nihilists, are sons of Merops. The allusion is to Phaeton, son of Merops, who thought himself able to drive the car of Phœbus, but, in the attempt, nearly set the world on fire.

Merovin'gian Dynasty. The dynasty of Mero'vius, a Latin form of *Merwig* (great warrior). Similarly Louis is Clovis, and Clovis is *Clot-wig* (noted warrior).

Merrie England may probably mean "illustrious," from the old Teutonic *mer.* (Anglo-Saxon, *mœra,* famous.) According to R. Ferguson, the word appears in the names Marry, Merry, Merick; the French *Méra, Méreau, Merey, Mériq;* and numerous others.

(*Teutonic Name-System,* p. 368.) (*See below* MERRY.)

Merrow. A mermaid, believed by Irish fishermen to forebode a coming storm. There are male merrows, but no word to designate them. (Irish, *Muruadh* or *Murrûghach,* from *muir,* the sea, and *oigh,* a maid.)

" It was rather annoying to Jack that, though living in a place where the merrows were as plenty as lobsters, he never could get a right view of one."—*W. B. Yeates: Fairy and Folk Tales,* p. 63.

Merry. The original meaning is not *mirthful,* but active, famous ; hence gallant soldiers were called "merry men ;" favourable weather, "merry weather ;" brisk wind, "a merry gale ;" London was "merry London;" England, "merry England;" Chaucer speaks of the "merry organ at the mass ;" Jane Shore is called by Pennant the "merry concubine of Edward IV." (Anglo-Saxon, *mœra,* illustrious, great, mighty, etc.). (*See* MERRY-MEN.)
'*Tis merry in hall, when beards wag all* (2 *Henry IV.,* act v. 3). It is a sure sign of mirth when the beards of the guests shake with laughter.

Merry Andrew. So called from Andrew Borde, physician to Henry VIII., etc. To vast learning he added great eccentricity, and in order to instruct the people used to address them at fairs and other crowded places in a very *ad captandum* way. Those who imitated his wit and drollery, though they possessed not his genius, were called Merry Andrews, a term now signifying a clown or buffoon. Andrew Borde Latinised his name into *Andreas Perfora'tus.* (1500-1549.) Prior has a poem on "Merry Andrew."
⁑ The above is the usual explanation given of this phrase ; but Andrew is a common name in old plays for a varlet or manservant, as Abigail is for a waiting gentlewoman.

Merry Dancers. The northern lights, so called from their undulatory motion. The French also call them *chèvres dansantes* (dancing goats).

Merry Dun of Dover. A large mythical ship, which knocked down Calais steeple in passing through the Straits of Dover, and the pennant, at the same time, swept a flock of sheep off Dover cliffs into the sea. The masts were so lofty that a boy who ascended them would grow grey before he could reach deck again. (*Scandinavian mythology.*)

Merry Men (*My*). A chief calls his followers his merry men. (*See above.*)

Merry Men of Mey. An expanse of broken water which boils like a caldron in the southern side of the Stroma channel.

Merry Monarch. Charles II. (1630, 1660-1685).

Merry-thought. The furcula or wishing-bone in the breast of a fowl; sometimes broken by two persons, and the one who holds the larger portion has his wish, as it is said.

Merry as a Cricket, or as a Lark, or as a Grig. The French say, "*Fou* (or *Folle*) *comme le branlegai*," and more commonly "*Gai comme un pinson*" (a chaffinch). "*Branlegai*" is a dance, but the word is not in use now.

Merse. Berwickshire was so called because it was the *merc* or frontier of England and Scotland.

Mersenne (2 syl.). *The English Mersenne.* John Collins, mathematician and physicist, so called from Marin Mersenne, the French philosopher (1624-1683).

Merton (*Tommy*). One of the chief characters in the tale of *Sandford and Merton*, by Thomas Day.

Merton College. Founded by Walter de Merton, Bishop of Rochester, and Lord High Chancellor in 1264.

Meru. A fabulous mountain in the centre of the world, 80,000 leagues high, the abode of Vishnu, and a perfect paradise. It may be termed the Indian Olympos.

Merveilleuse (3 syl., *French*). The sword of Doolin of Mayence. It was so sharp that when placed edge downwards it would cut through a slab of wood without the use of force. (*See* Swords.)

⁎ Also a term applied to the 18th century French ladies' dress.

Mes'merism. So called from Friedrich Anton Mesmer, of Mersburg, in Suabia, who introduced the science into Paris in 1778. (1734-1815.)

Mesopota'mia. *The true "Mesopota'mia" ring* (*London Review*)—*i.e.* something high-sounding and pleasing, but wholly past comprehension. The allusion is to the story of an old woman who told her pastor that she "found great support in that comfortable word *Mesopotamia.*"

27

Mess = 4. Nares says because "at great dinners . . . the company was usually arranged into fours." That four made a mess is without doubt. Lyly expressly says, "Foure makes a messe, and we have a messe of masters" (*Mother Bombie*, ii. 1). Shakespeare calls the four sons of Henry his "mess of sons" (2 *Henry VI.*, act i. 4); and "Latine," English, French, and Spanish are called a "messe of tongues" (*Vocabulary*, 1617). Again, Shakespeare says (*Love's Labour's Lost*, iv. 3), "You three fools lacked me . . . to make up the mess." Though four made a mess, yet it does not follow that the "officer's mess" is so called, as Nares says, because "the company was arranged into fours," for the Anglo-Saxon *mese*, like the Latin *mensa* = table, *mes* Gothic = dish, whence Benjamin's mess, a mess of pottage, etc.

⁎ Mess, meaning confusion or litter, is the German *mischen*, to mix; our word *mash*.

Messali'na. Wife of the Emperor Claudius of Rome. Her name has become a byword for lasciviousness and incontinency. Catherine II. of Russia is called *The Modern Messali'na* (1729-1796). (*See* Marozia.)

Messali'na of Germany (*The*). Barbary of Cilley, second wife of Kaiser Sigismund (15th century).

Metalo'gicus, by John of Salisbury, the object of which is to expose the absurdity and injurious effects of "wrangling," or dialectics and metaphysics. He says, "Prattling and quibbling the masters call disputing or wrangling, but I am no wiser for such logic."

Metals. *The seven metals in alchemy.*
Gold, Apollo or the sun.
Silver, Diana or the moon.
Quicksilver, Mercury.
Copper, Venus.
Iron, Mars.
Tin, Jupiter.
Lead, Saturn.

Metamor'phic Rocks. Those rocks, including gneiss, mica-schist, clay-slate, marble, and the like, which have become more or less crystalline.

Metamorphic Words. Obsolete words slightly altered, and made current again—as "chestnut" for *castnut*, from Castana, in Thessaly; "court-cards" for *coat-cards*; "currants" for *corinths*; "frontispiece" for *frontispice* (Latin *frontispicium*) ; "Isinglass" for *hausen blase* (the sturgeon's bladder, Ger.) ; "shame-faced" for *shamefast*, as steadfast, etc. ; "sweetheart" for *sweethard*, as drunkard, dullard, dotard, niggard.

Metaphys'ics (Greek, *after-physics*). The disciples of Aristotle thought that matter or nature should be studied before mind. The Greek for matter or nature is *physis*, and the science of its causes and effects *physics*. Meta-physics is the Greek for "after-physics." Sir James Mackintosh takes a less intentional view of the case, and says the word arose from the mere accident of the compilers who sorted the treatises of Aristotle, and placed that upon mind and intelligence after that upon matter and nature. The science of metaphysics is the consideration of things in the abstract—that is, divested of their accidents, relations, and matter.

Metasta'sio. The real name of this Italian poet was Trapassi (*death*). He was brought up by Gravina, who Græcised the name. (1698-1782.)

Metathesis. A figure of speech in which letters or syllables are transposed, as "You occupew my pie [py]," instead of "You *occupy my pew ;*" *daggle-trail* for "draggle-tail," etc.

Methodical. *Most methodical doctor.* John Bassol, a disciple of Duns Scotus. (1347.)

Meth'odists. A name given (1729) by a student of Christ Church to the brothers Wesley and their friends, who used to assemble on given evenings for religious conversation.

⁂ This word was in use many centuries before the birth of Wesley and of Whitfield. Gale (1678) speaks of a religious sect called "the New Methodists" (*Court of the Gentiles*). John Spencer uses the word as one familiarly known in Cromwell's time. Even before the birth of Christ, Celsus tells us that those physicians were called "Methodists" (*methodici*) who followed medical *rules* rather than experience. Modern Methodism dates no farther back than 1729.

Primitive Methodists. Founded by Hugh Bourne (1772-1852).

Meth'uen Treaty. A commercial treaty between England and Portugal, negotiated by Paul Methuen, in 1703, whereby the Portuguese wines were received at a lower duty than those of France. This treaty was abandoned in 1836.

Meton'ic Cycle (*The*). A cycle of nineteen years, at the end of which period the new moons fall on the same days of the year, and eclipses recur. Discovered by Meton, B.C. 432.

Metra. *Qu'en dit Metra* (Louis XVI.)? Metra was a noted news-vendor of Paris before the Revolution—a notability with a cocked hat, who went about with his hands folded behind his back.

Metropol'itan (*A*). A prelate who has suffragan bishops subject to him. The two metropolitans of England are the two archbishops, and the two of Ireland the archbishops of Armagh and Dublin. In the Roman Catholic Church of Great Britain, the four archbishops of Armagh, Dublin, Cashel, and Tuam are metropolitans. The word does not mean the prelate of the metropolis in a secular sense, but the prelate of a "mother city" in an ecclesiastical sense —*i.e.* a city which is the mother or ruler of other cities. Thus, the Bishop of London is the prelate of the metropolis, but not a metropolitan. The Archbishop of Canterbury is *metropolita'nus et primus toti'us Angliæ*, and the Archbishop of York *primus et metropolita'nus Angliæ*.

Mettre de la Paille dans scs Souliers, or Mettre du Foin dans ses Bottes. To amass money, to grow rich, especially by illicit gains. The reference is to a practice, in the sixteenth century, followed by beggars to extort alms.

". . . Des quemands et belistres qui, pour abuser le monde, mettent de la paille en leurs souliers."— *Supplément du Catholicon*, ch. ix.

Me'um and Tu'um. That which belongs to me and that which is another's. *Meum* is Latin for "what is mine," and *tuum* is Latin for "what is thine." If a man is said not to know the difference between *meum* and *tuum*, it is a polite way of saying he is a thief.

"*Meum est pro'pos'itum in taberna mori.*" A famous drinking song by Walter Mapes, who died in 1210.

Mews. Stables, but properly a place for hawks on the moult. The muette was an edifice in a park where the officers of venery lodged, and which was fitted up with dog-kennels, stables, and hawkeries. They were called *muettes* from *mue*, the slough of anything ; the antlers shed by stags were collected and kept in these enclosures. (*Lacombe : Dictionnaire Portatif des Beaux-Arts.*)

Mexit'li. Tutelary god of the Aztecs, in honour of whom they named their empire Mexico. (*Southey.*)

Mezen'tius, king of the Tyrrhenians, noted for his cruelties and impiety. He was driven from his throne by his subjects, and fled to Turnus, King of the Rutuli. When Æneas arrived he fought with Mezentius, and slew both him and his son Lausus. Mezentius put his subjects to death by tying a living man to a dead one.

"He stretches out the arm of Mezentius, and fetters the dead to the living."—*C. Brontë: Shirley*, chap. xxxi.

"This is like Mezentius in Virgil. . . . . Such critics are like dead coals; they may blacken, but cannot burn."—*Broom: Preface to Poems.*

Mezzo Relie'vo. Moderate relief (*Italian*). This is applied to figures which project more than those of basso relievo (*q.v.*), but less than those of alto relievo (*q.v.*).

Mezzo Tinto (Italian, *medium tint*). So engravings in imitation of Indian-ink drawings are called.

Mezzora'mia. An earthly paradise somewhere in Africa, but accessible by only one narrow road. Gaudentio di Lucca discovered this secret road, and resided in this paradise for twenty-five years. (*Simon Berington: Gaudentio di Lucca.*)

Micah Rood's Apples. Apples with a spot of red (like blood) in the heart. Micah Rood was a prosperous farmer at Franklin. In 1693 a pedlar with jewellery called at his house, and next day was found murdered under an apple-tree in Rood's orchard. The crime was never brought home to the farmer, but next autumn all the apples of the fatal tree bore inside a red blood-spot, called "Micah Rood's Curse," and the farmer died soon afterwards.

Micawber (*Mr. Wilkins*). A great speechifier and letter-writer, projector of bubble schemes sure to lead to fortune, but always ending in grief. Notwithstanding his ill success, he never despaired, but felt certain that something would "turn up" to make his fortune. Having failed in every adventure in the old country, he emigrated to Australia, where he became a magnate. (*Dickens: David Copperfield.*)

Micawberism. Conduct similar to that of Mr. Micawber's. (*See above.*)

Mi'chael. Prince of the celestial armies, commanded by God to drive the rebel angels out of heaven. Ga'briel was next to him in command. (*See* SEVEN SPIRITS.)

Longfellow, in his *Golden Legend*, says

he is the presiding spirit of the planet Mercury, and brings to man the gift of prudence.

"The planet Mercury, whose place
Is nearest to the sun in space,
Is my allotted sphere ;
And with celestial ardour swift
I bear upon my hands the gift
Of heavenly *prudence* here."
The Miracle Play, iii.

St. Michael, in Christian art, is sometimes depicted as a beautiful young man with severe countenance, winged, and either clad in white or armour, bearing a lance and shield, with which he combats a dragon. In the final judgment he is represented with scales, in which he weighs the souls of the risen dead.

St. Michael's chair. It is said that any woman who has sat on St. Michael's chair, Cornwall, will rule the roost as long as she lives.

Michael Angelo. The celebrated painter, born 1474, died 1563. *The Michael-Angelo of battle-scenes.* Michael-Angelo Cerquozzi, a native of Rome, famous for his battle-scenes and shipwrecks. (1600-1660.)

Michel-Ange des Bamboches. Peter van Laar, the Dutch painter. (1613-1673.)

Michael-Angelo of music. Johann Christoph von Gluck, the German musical composer. (1714-1787.)

Michael-Angelo of sculptors. Pierre Puget, the French sculptor (1623-1694). Also Réné Michael Slodtz (1705-1764).

Michaelmas Day, September 29th, one of the quarter-days when rents are paid, and the day when magistrates are elected. Michael the archangel is represented in the Bible as the general of the celestial host, and as such Milton represents him. September 29th is dedicated to Michael and All Angels, and as magistrates were once considered "angels" or their representatives, they were chosen on the day of "All Angels."

"I saw another sign in heaven . . . . . seven angels [magistrates, or executors of God's judgments], having the seven last plagues . . . . filled with the wrath of God." (Rev. xv. 1.) Those ministers of religion who acted as magistrates were also called angels. "There is no power but of God. The powers that be are ordained of God."

Michal, in the satire of *Absalom and Achitophel*, by Dryden and Tate, is meant for Queen Catherine, wife of Charles II. As Charles II. is called David in the satire, and Michal was David's wife, the name is appropriate.

Michel or **Cousin Michael.** A German. Michel means a dolt; thus the French call a fool who allows himself to be taken in by thimble-rigs and card tricks *mikel.* In Old French the word *mice* occurs, meaning a fool. (*See* MICHON.)

"L'Anglais aime à être représenté comme un John Bull ; pour nous, notre type est l'Allemand Michel, qui reçoit une tape par derrière et qui demande encore ; 'Qu'y a-t-il pour votre service?'"—*Dr. Weber : De l'Allemagne,* etc.

Miching Malicho. Secret or underhand mischief ; a veiled rebuke ; a bad deed probed by disguised means. To *mich* or *meech* means to skulk or shrink from sight. *Michers* are poachers or secret pilferers. Malicho is a Spanish word meaning an "evil action ; " as a personified name it means a malefactor. (*Hamlet,* iii. 2.)

The "quarto" reads *munching mallico ;* the "folio" has *miching malicho.* Qy. The Spanish *mu'cho malhe'cho* (much mischief) ?

Michon, according to Cotgrave, is a "block, dunce, dolt, jobbernol, dullard, loggerhead." Probably *michon, Mike* (an ass), *mikel,* and *cousin Michel,* are all from the Italian *miccio,* an ass. (*See* MIKE.)

Mickleton Jury (*The*). A corruption of mickle-tourn (*magnus turnus*). The jury of court leets.ı These leets were visited Easter and Michaelmas by the county sheriffs in their *tourns.*

Microcosm. (Greek, *little world.*) So man is called by Paracelsus. The ancients considered the world as a living being ; the sun and moon being its *two eyes,* the earth its *body,* the ether its *intellect,* and the sky its *wings.* When man was looked on as the world in miniature, it was thought that the movements of the world and of man corresponded, and if one could be ascertained, the other could be easily inferred ; hence arose the system of astrology, which professed to interpret the events of a man's life by the corresponding movements, etc., of the stars. (*See* DIAPASON.)

Mid-Lent Sunday. The fourth Sunday in Lent. It is called *domin'ica refectio'nis* (refection Sunday), because the first lesson is the banquet given by Joseph to his brethren, and the gospel of the day is the miraculous feeding of the five thousand. In England it used to be called *Mothering Sunday,* from the custom of visiting the mother or cathedral church on that day to make the Easter offering.

Mi'das. *Like Midas, all he touches turns to gold.* Midas, King of Phrygia,

requested of the gods that everything he touched might be turned to gold. His request was granted, but as his food became gold the moment he touched it, he prayed the gods to take their favour back. He was then ordered to bathe in the Pacto'lus, and the river ever after rolled over golden sands.

Midas-eared. Without discrimination or judgment. Midas, King of Phrygia, was appointed to judge a musical contest between Apollo and Pan, and gave judgment in favour of the satyr ; whereupon Apollo in contempt gave the king a pair of ass's ears. Midas hid them under his Phrygian cap ; but his servant, who used to cut his hair, discovered them, and was so tickled at the "joke," which he durst not mention, that he dug a hole in the earth, and relieved his mind by whispering in it "Midas has ass's ears." Budæus gives a different version. He says that Midas kept spies to tell him everything that transpired throughout his kingdom, and the proverb "that kings have long arms" was changed in his case to "Midas has long ears." *" Ex eo in proverbium venit, quod multos otacustas*—i.e. *auricularios habebat."* (*De Asse.*) (See Pope : *Prologues to Satires.*)

✢ Domenichino (1581-1661) has a painting on the *Judgment of Midas.*

Midas has ass's ears. An exact parallel of this tale is told of Portzmach, king of a part of Brittany. It is said Portzmach had all the barbers of his kingdom put to death, lest they should announce to the public that he had the ears of a horse. An intimate friend was found willing to shave him, after swearing profound secrecy ; but not able to contain himself, he confided his secret to the sands of a river bank. The reeds of this river were used for pan-pipes and hautbois, which repeated the words "Portzmach— King Portzmach has horse's ears."

Midden. *The kitchen midden.* The dust-bin. The farmer's midden is the dunghill. The word is Scotch. (Danish, *mödding ;* Norwegian, *mudder ;* Welsh, *mwydo* (to wet), our *mud* and *mire.*)

Better marry over the midden than over the moor. Better seek a wife among your neighbours whom you know than among strangers of whom you know nothing. The midden, in Scotland, is the domestic rubbish heap.

Ilka cock craws loodest on its ain midden. In English, "Every cock crows loudest on his own dunghill." A midden is an ash-pit, a refuse-heap.

Middle Ages. A term of no definite period, but varying a little with almost every nation. In France it was from Clovis to Louis XI. (481 to 1461). In England, from the Heptarchy to the accession of Henry VII. (409 to 1485). In universal history it was from the overthrow of the Roman Empire to the revival of letters (the fifth to the fifteenth century).

Middlesex. The Middle Saxons—that is, between Essex, Sussex, and Wessex.

Midgard. The abode of the first pair, from whom sprang the human race. It was made of the eyebrows of Ymer, and was joined to Asgard by the rainbow bridge called Bifrost. (*Scandinavian mythology.*)

Asgard is the abode of the celestials. Utgard is the abode of the giants. Midgard is between the two—better than Utgard, but inferior to Asgard.

Midgard Sormen (earth's monster). The great serpent that lay in the abyss at the root of the celestial ash. (*Scandinavian mythology.*) Child of Loki.

Midi. *Chercher midi à quatorze heures.* To look for knots in a bulrush; much ado about nothing; to explain prosily what is perfectly obvious.

⁂ There is a variant of this locution: *Chercher midi où il n'est qu'onze heures,* to look for a needle in a bottle of hay; to give oneself a vast lot of trouble for nothing. At one time, hundreds of persons looked for the millennium and end of the world on fixed dates, and to them the proverb would apply.

Midlo'thian. Sir Walter Scott's *Heart of Midlothian* is a tale of the Porteous riot, in which are introduced the interesting incidents of Effie and Jeanie Deans. Effie is seduced while in the service of Mrs. Saddletree, and imprisoned for child-murder; but her sister Jeanie obtains her pardon through the intercession of the queen, and marries Reuben Butler.

Midnight Oil. Late hours.
Burning the midnight oil. Sitting up late, especially when engaged on literary work.
Smells of the midnight oil. Said of literary work, which seems very elaborate, and has not the art of concealing art. (*See* LAMP.)

Midrash'im (sing. *Midrash*). Jewish expositions of the Old Testament.

Midsummer Ale. The Midsummer banquet. Brand mentions nine ale-feasts: "Bride-ales, church-ales, clerk-ales, give-ales, lamb-ales, leet-ales, Midsummer-ales, Scot-ales, Whitsun-ales, and several more." Here "ale" does not mean the drink, but the feast in which good stout ale was supplied. The Cambridge phrase, "Will you wine with me after hall?" means, "Will you come to my rooms for dessert, when wines, fruits, and cigars will be prepared, with coffee to follow?"

Midsummer Madness. Olivia says to Malvo'lio, "Why, this is very midsummer madness" (*Twelfth Night,* iii. 4). The reference is to the rabies of dogs, which is generally brought on by Midsummer heat.

Midsummer Men. The plants called Orpine or Live-long, one of the Sedum tribe. Stonecrop is another variety of the same species of plants. Orpine is the French word for stonecrop. Live-long, so called because no plant lives longer after it is cut. It will live for months if sprinkled once a week with a little water. Sedum means the plant *sedens in rupibus* (sitting or growing on stones). It is called *midsummer men* because it used to be set in pots or shells on mid-summer eve, and hung up in the house to tell damsels whether their sweethearts were true or not. If the leaves bent to the right, it was a sign of fidelity; if to the left, the "true-love's heart was cold and faithless."

Midsummer-Moon Madness. *'Tis Midsummer-moon with you.* You are stark mad. Madness is supposed to be affected by the moon, and to be aggravated by summer heat; so it naturally follows that the full moon at mid-summer is the time when madness is most outrageous.

> "What's this midsummer moon?
> Is all the world gone a-madding?"
> *Dryden: Amphitryon,* iv. 1.

Midsummer Night's Dream. Some of the most amusing incidents of this comedy are borrowed from the *Diana* of Montemayor, a Spanish writer of pastoral romance in the sixteenth century; and probably the *Knightes Tale* in Chaucer may have furnished hints to the author.

Midsummer Night's Dream. Egēus of Athens went to Theseus, the reigning duke, to complain that his daughter Her'mia, whom he had commanded to marry Demetrius, refused to obey him, because she loved Lysander. Egeus demanded that Hermia should be put to death for this disobedience, according to the law. Hermia pleaded that Demetrius loved Hel'ena, and that his affection was reciprocated. Theseus had no power to alter the law, and gave Hermia four days' respite to consider the matter, and if then she refused the law was to take its course. Lysander proposed flight, to which Hermia agreed, and told Helena her intention; Helena told Demetrius, and Demetrius, of course, followed. The fugitives met in a wood, the favourite haunt of the fairies. Now Oberon and Tita'nia had had a quarrel about a changeling boy, and Oberon, by way of punishment, dropped on Titania's eyes during sleep some love-juice, the effect of which is to make the sleeper fall in love with the first thing seen when waking. The first thing seen by Titania was Bottom the weaver, wearing an ass's head. In the meantime King Oberon dispatched Puck to pour some of the juice on the eyes of Demetrius, that he might love Helena, who, Oberon thought refused to requite her love. Puck, by mistake, anointed the eyes of Lysander with the juice, and the first thing he saw on waking was not Hermia but Helena. Oberon, being told that Puck had done his bidding, to make all sure, dropped some of the love-juice on the eyes of Demetrius, and the first person he beheld on waking was Hermia looking for Lysander. In due time the eyes of all were disenchanted. Lysander married Hermia, Demetrius married Helena, and Titania gave the boy to her lord, King Oberon.

Midwife (Anglo-Saxon, *mid*, with ; *wíf*, woman). The nurse who is *with* the mother in her labour.

Midwife of men's thoughts. So Soc'-ratēs termed himself ; and, as Mr. Grote observes, "No other man ever struck out of others so many sparks to set light to original thought." Out of his intellectual school sprang Plato and the Dialectic system ; Euclid and the Megaric ; Aristippos and the Cyrenaic ; Antisthênês and the Cynic ; and his influence on the mind was never equalled by any teacher but One, of whom it was said, "Never man spake like this man."

Miggs (*Miss*). Mrs. Varden's maid, and the impersonation of an old shrew. (*Dickens : Barnaby Rudge.*)

Mignon. The young Italian girl who fell in love with Wilhelm Meister's apprentice, her protector. Her love not

being returned, she became insane and died. (*Goethe : Wilhelm Meister.*)

Mikado (Japan, *mi*, exalted ; *kado*, gate), is not a title of the emperor of Japan, but simply means the person who lives in the imperial palace.

Mike. To loiter. A corruption of *miche* (to skulk) ; whence, *micher* (a thief), and *michery* (theft). (Old Norse, *mak*, leisure ; Swedish, *maka ;* Saxon, *'mugan*, to creep.) (*See* MICHON.)

"Shall the blessed sun of heaven prove a micher [loiterer] ? "—*Shakespeare :* 1 *Henry IV.,* ii. 4.

Mil'an Decree (*The*). A decree made by Napoleon I., dated "Milan, Dec. 27, 1807," declaring "the whole British Empire to be in a state of blockade, and forbidding all countries either from trading with Great Britain or from even using an article of British manufacture."

This very absurd decree was killing the goose which laid the golden eggs, for England was the best customer of the very countries thus restricted from dealing with her.

Mil'an Steel. *Armed in Milan steel.* Milan was famous in the Middle Ages for its armoury. (*Froissart,* iv. 597.)

Mil'ane'se (3 syl.). A native of Milan —*i.e. mi-lano.* (Old Italian for middle-land, meaning in the middle of the Lombardian plain.)

Milden'do. The metropolis of Lilliput, the wall of which was two feet and a half in height, and at least eleven inches thick. The city was an exact square, and two main streets divided it into four quarters. The emperor's palace, called Belfab'orac, was in the centre of the city. (*Gulliver's Travels : Voyage to Lilliput,* iv.)

Mildew has nothing to do with either *mills* or *dew*. It is the Gaelic *mehl-thœw* (injurious or destructive blight).

Mile'sian Fables. The romances of Antonius Diog'enēs, described by Photius, but no longer extant. They were greedily read by the luxurious Sybarites, and appear to have been of a very coarse amatory character. They were compiled by Aristi'dēs, and translated into Latin by Sisen'na, about the time of the civil wars of Ma'rius and Sylla.

The tales of Parthe'nius Nice'nus were borrowed from them. The name is from the Milesians, a Greek colony, the first to catch from the Persians their rage for fiction. Parthenius taught Virgil Greek.

Milesian Story or *Tale* (*A*). One very wanton and ludicrous. So called from the *Milesiæ Fab'ulæ*, the immoral tendency of which was notorious. (*See above*.)

Mile'sians (*The*). The ancient Irish. The legend is that Ireland was once peopled by the Firbolgs, who were subdued by the Milesians, called the "Gaels of Ireland."

" My family, by my father's side, are all the true ould Milesians, and related to the O'Flahertys, and O'Shaughnesses, and the M'Lauchlins, the O'Donnaghans, O'Callaghans, O'Geogaghans, and all the thick blood of the nation ; and I myself am an O'Brallaghan, which is the ouldest of them all."—*Maclin : Love à la Mode.*

Milk. *To cry over spilt milk.* (*See under* CRY.)

Milk and Honey. *A land of milk and honey.* That is, abounding in all good things, or of extraordinary fertility. Joel iii. 18 speaks of " the mountains flowing with milk and honey." Figuratively used to denote all the blessings of heaven.

" Jerusalem the golden,
With milk and honey blest."

Milk and Water. Insipid, without energy or character ; baby-pap (literature, etc.).

Milk of Human Kindness (*The*). Sympathy, compassion.

Milksop (*A*). An effeminate person ; one without energy, one under petticoat government. The allusion is to very young children, who are fed on bread and milk.

Milky Way (*The*). A great circle of stars entirely surrounding the heavens. They are so crowded together that they appear to the naked eye like a " way" or stream of faint " milky " light. The Galaxy or Via Lactĕa.

A broad and ample road, whose dust is gold
And pavement stars, as stars to thee appear,
Seen in the galaxy—that Milky Way,
Thick, nightly, as a circling zone, thou seest
Powdered with stars."
Milton : Paradise Lost, vii. 577, etc.

Mill. To fight ; not from the Latin *milēs*, a soldier, but from the noun *mill*. Grinding was anciently performed by pulverising with a stone or pounding with the hand. To mill is to beat with the fist, as persons used to beat corn with a stone.

The word is Gaelic, in which there are numerous derivatives, meaning to ravage, destroy, etc.

Mills of God grind slowly (*The*). " *Dii pedes lanatos habent* " (Petronius).

Vengeance may be delayed, but it will come when least expected.

" The mills of God grind slowly, yet they grind
exceeding small ;
Though with patience He stands waiting, with
exactness He grinds all."
Longfellow : Retribution.

Millen'nium means simply a thousand years. (Latin, *mille annus*.) In Rev. xx. 2 it is said that an angel bound Satan a thousand years, and in verse 4 we are told of certain martyrs who will come to life again, and " reign with Christ a thousand years." " This," says St. John, " is the first resurrection ; " and this is what is meant by the millennium.

Miller. *To drown the miller.* (*See* DROWN, etc.)

To give one the miller is to engage a person in conversation till a sufficient number of persons have gathered together to set upon the victim with stones, dirt, garbage, and all the arms which haste supplies a mob with. (*See* MILL.)

More water glideth by the mill than wots the miller of (*Titus Andronicus*, ii. 1). Many things are done in a house which the master and mistress never dream of.

Miller. *A Joe Miller.* A stale jest. John Mottley compiled a book of facetiæ in the reign of James II., which he entitled *Joe Miller's Jests*, from a witty actor of farce during the time that Congreve's plays were in vogue. A stale jest is called a " Joe Miller," implying that it is stolen from Mottley's compilation. (Joe Miller, 1684-1738.)

Miller's Eye (*A*). Lumps of unleavened flour in bread ; so called because they are little round lumps like an eye.

To put the miller's eye out. To make broth or pudding so thin that the miller's eye would be put out or puzzled to find the flour.

Miller's Thumb (*A*). A small fish, four or five inches long, so called from its resemblance to a miller's thumb. The fish is also called *Bullhead*, from its large head.

Milliner. A corruption of *Mil'aner ;* so called from Mil'an, in Italy, which at one time gave the law to Europe in all matters of taste, dress, and elegance.

⁙ Milliner was originally applied to the male sex ; hence Ben Jonson, in *Every Man in his Humour*, i. 3, speaks of a " milliner's wife." The French have still *une modiste* and *un modiste*.

Millstone. *To look* (or *see*) *through a millstone.* To be wonderfully sharp-sighted.

"Then ... since your eies are so sharp that you can not only looke through a millstone, but cleane through the minde ..."—*Lilly: Euphues,* etc.

Millstone used for a Ferry (*A*). The saint who crossed the Irish Sea on a millstone was St. Piran, patron saint of tanners.

Millstones. *To weep millstones.* Not weep at all.

" Bid Glos'ter think on this, and he will weep—
Aye, millstones, as he lessoned us to weep."
     Shakespeare: Richard III., i. 6.

Millstones of Montisci (*The*). They produce flour of themselves, whence the proverb, "Grace comes from God, but millstones from Montisci." (*Boccaccio : Decameron,* day viii. novel 3.

Millwood (*Sarah*). The courtesan who enticed George Barnwell to robbery and murder. (*See* BARNWELL.)

Milo. An athlete of Croto'na. It is said that he carried through the stadium at Olympia a heifer four years old, and ate the whole of it afterwards. When old he attempted to tear in two an oak-tree, but the parts closed upon his hands, and while held fast he was devoured by wolves. (*See* POLYDAMUS.)

Milton borrowed from St. Avi'tus his description of Paradise (book i.), of Satan (book ii.), and many other parts of *Paradise Lost.* He also borrowed very largely from Du Bartas (1544-1591), who wrote an epic poem entitled *The Week of Creation,* which was translated into almost every European language. St. Avitus wrote in Latin hexameters *The Creation, The Fall,* and *The Expulsion from Paradise.* (460-525.)

Milton. "Milton," says Dryden, in the preface to his *Fables,* "was the poetical son of Spenser. . . . Milton has acknowledged to me that Spenser was his original."

Milton of Germany. Friedrich G. Klopstock, author of *The Messiah.* (1724-1803.) Coleridge says he is "a very German Milton indeed."

Mi'mer. The Scandinavian god of wisdom, and most celebrated of the giants. The Vanir, with whom he was left as a hostage, cut off his head. Odin embalmed it by his magic art, pronounced over it mystic runes, and ever after consulted it on critical occasions. (*Scandinavian mythology.*)

Mi'mer's Well. A well in which all wisdom lay concealed. It was at the root of the celestial ash-tree. Mimer drank thereof from the horn Gjallar. Odin gave one of his eyes to be permitted to drink of its waters, and the draught made him the wisest of the gods. (*Scandinavian mythology.*)

Mimo'sa. Niebuhr says the Mimosa " droops its branches whenever anyone approaches it, seeming to salute those who retire under its shade."

Mince (French). A bank-note. The assignats of the first republic were so called, because the paper on which they were printed was exceedingly thin. (*Dictionnaire du Bas-Langage,* ii. 139.)

Mince Pies at Christmas time are emblematical of the manger in which our Saviour was laid. The paste over the "offering" was made in form of a *cratch* or *hay-rack.* (*See* PLUM PUDDING.)

Mince pies. Slang for "the eyes." (*See* CHIVY.)

Mince the Matter. *Not to mince the matter.* To speak outright; not to palliate or gloss over the matter. Terence has "*Rem profer palam*" (*Heaut-timoroumenos,* v. 2, 41). The French say, "*Je ne le lui ai point mâche.*" About the same is the phrase "Not to put too fine a point on the matter."

Mincemeat. *To make mincemeat of.* Utterly to demolish ; to shatter to pieces. Mincemeat is meat cut up very fine.

Minch-house (*A*). A nunnery. (Anglo-Saxon, *minicem,* a nun.) Sometimes it means an ale- or road-house.

Mincing Lane (London). A corruption of Mynchen Lane; so called from the tenements held there by the mynchens or nuns of St. Helen's, in Bishopsgate Street. (*Minicen,* Anglo-Saxon for a nun ; *minchery,* a nunnery.)

Min'cio or **Min'tio.** The birthplace of Virgil. The Clitumnus, a river of Umbria, was the residence of Proper'-tius ; the Anio is where Horace had a villa ; the river Melēs, in Ionia, is the supposed birthplace of Homer. Littleton refers to all these in his *Monody on Miss Fortescue.*

Mind your Eye. Be careful or vigilant ; keep a sharp look out ; keep your eyes open to guard against mischief. School-boy wit, *Mens tuus ego.*

" ' Perhaps it may be so ' (says I) ; ' but mind your eye, and take care you don't put your foot in it.'"—*Haliburton.*

"'You must mind your eye, George ; a good many tents are robbed every week.' "—*C. Reade*

Mind your Own Business. "Seest thou a man diligent in his business, he shall stand before kings" (Prov. xxii. 29). "He who doeth his own business defileth not his fingers" (*Fielding's Proverbs*). Let every tub stand on its own bottom. Never meddle with what does not concern you.

"Bon homme, garde la vache. Chacun son métier, et les vaches son bien gardées. Chacun a ses affaires."
"Qui fa le fatti suoi, non s'embratta le mani."
"Tuâ quod nihil refert ne cures. Suum cura negotium. Tu ne quæsiveris extra."—*Horace.*

Minden Boys. The 20th Foot ; so called from their noted bravery at Minden, in Prussia, August 1, 1759. Now called "The Lancashire Fusiliers."

Minerva (in Greek, *Athe'nê*). The most famous statue of this goddess was by Phidias, the Greek sculptor. It was wood encased with ivory ; the drapery, however, was of solid gold. It represented the goddess standing, clothed with a tunic reaching to the ankles, a spear in her left hand, and an image of Victory (four cubits high — about six feet) in her right. She is girded with the ægis, has a helmet on her head, and her shield rests by her side on the ground. The entire height was nearly forty feet. This statue was anciently one of the "Seven Wonders of the World." A superb statue of the goddess was found at Velletri, but whether this was the famous statue of Phidias is not known. It is preserved in the Imperial Museum.

∴ The exquisite antique statue of *Minerva Medica* is in the Vatican of Rome.

Minerva. *Invita Minerva*, without sufficient ability ; against the grain. Thus, Charles Kean acted comedy *invita Minerva*, his *forte* lying another way. Sir Philip Sidney attempted the Horatian metres in English verse *invita Minerva*.

Minerva Press (*The*). A printing establishment in Leadenhall Street, London, famous about a century ago for its trashy, ultra-sentimental novels. These novels were remarkable for their complicated plots, and especially for the labyrinths of difficulties into which the hero and heroine got involved before they could get married to each other.

Mini'ature (3 syl.). Paintings by the Miniato'ri, a set of monks noted for painting with *minium* or red-lead. The first miniatures were the initial letters of rubrics, and as the head of the Virgin or some other saint was usually introduced into these illuminated letters, the word came to express a small likeness.

The best miniature-painters have been Holbein, Nicholas Hilliard, Isaac Oliver and his son Peter, Samuel Cooper and his brother Alexander, etc.)

Minie Rifle. (*See* GUN.)

Minims (Latin, *Fratres Min'imi*, least of the brethren). A term of self-abasement assumed by an order of monks founded by St. Francis of Paula, in 1453. The order of St. Francis of Assisi had already engrossed the "humble" title of *Fratres Mino'res* (inferior brothers). The superior of the minims is called *corrector*.

Min'ister means an inferior person, in opposition to *magister*, a superior. One is connected with the Latin *minus*, and the other with *magis*. Our Lord says, "Whosoever will be great among you, let him be your minister," where the antithesis is well preserved. The minister of a church is a man who *serves* the parish or congregation ; and the minister of the Crown is the sovereign's servant.

Minister. Florimond de Remond, speaking of Albert Babinot, one of the disciples of Calvin, says, "He was a student of the Institutes, read at the hall of the Equity school in Poitiers, and was called *la Ministerie*." Calvin, in allusion thereto, used to call him "Mr. Minister," whence not only Babinot but all the other clergy of the Calvinistic church were called *ministers*.

Minna Troil. Eldest daughter of Magnus Troil, the old Udaller of Zetland. Captain Clement Cleveland (Vaughan) the pirate loved her, and Minna reciprocated his affection, but Cleveland was killed by the Spaniards in an encounter on the Spanish main. (*Sir Walter Scott : The Pirate.*)

Minneha'ha [*Laughing-water*]. The lovely daughter of the old arrow-maker of the Daco'tahs, and wife of Hiawath'a. She died of famine. Two guests came uninvited into Hiawatha's wigwam, and the foremost said, "Behold me ! I am Famine ; " and the other said, "Behold me ! I am Fever ; " and Minnehaha shuddered to look on them, and hid her face, and lay trembling, freezing, burning. at the looks they cast upon her. "Ah ! " cried Laughing-water, "the eyes of Pauguk [death] glare upon me, I can feel his icy fingers clasping mine amidst the darkness," and she died crying, "Hiawatha ! Hiawatha ! " (*Longfellow : Hiawatha.*)

Min'ne'singers. Minstrels. The earliest lyric poets of Germany were so called, because the subject of their lyrics was *minne-sang* (love-ditty). These poets lived in the twelfth and thirteenth centuries.

Min'ories (3 syl.) (London). The cloister of the Minims or, rather, Minoresses (nuns of St. Clare). The Minims were certain reformed Franciscans, founded by St. Francis de Paula in the fifteenth century. They went barefooted, and wore a coarse, black woollen stuff, fastened with a woollen girdle, which they never put off, day or night. The word is derived from the Latin *min'imus* (the least), in allusion to the text, "I am less than *the least* of all saints" (Eph. iii. 8).

Mi'nos. A king and lawgiver of Crete, made at death supreme judge of the lower world, before whom all the dead appeared to give an account of their stewardship, and to receive the reward of their deeds.

Mi'notaur [*Minos-bull*]. The body of a man and head of a bull. Theseus slew this monster.

Minot'ti. Governor of Corinth, then under the power of the doge. In 1715 the city was stormed by the Turks, and during the siege one of the magazines in the Turkish camp blew up, killing 600 men. Byron says it was Minotti himself who fired the train, and leads us to infer that he was one of those who perished in the explosion. (*Byron: Siege of Corinth.*)

Minstrel simply means a servant or minister. Minstrels were kept in the service of kings and princes for the entertainment of guests. James Beattie has a poem in Spense'rian verse, called *The Minstrel*, divided into two books.

The last minstrel of the English stage. James Shirley, with whom the school of Shakespeare expired. (1594-1666.)

Mint. So called from the nymph Minthē, daughter of Cocy'tus, and a favourite of Pluto. This nymph was metamorphosed by Pluto's wife (Proserpine) out of jealousy, into the herb called after her name. The fable is quite obvious, and simply means that mint is a capital medicine. Minthē was a favourite of Pluto, or death, that is, was sick and on the point of death; but was changed into the herb mint, or was cured thereby.

"Could Pluto's queen, with jealous fury storm
And Minthē to a fragrant herb transform?"
Ovid.

Min'uit (2 syl.). "*Enfants de la messe de minuit*," pickpockets. Cotgrave gives "night-walking rakehells, such as haunt these nightly rites only to rob and play the knaves."

Min'ute. *Make a minute of that.* Take a note of it. A law term; a rough draft of a proceeding taken down in *minūte* or small writing, to be afterwards *engrossed*, or written larger.

Min'ute Gun. A signal of distress at sea, or a gun fired at the death of a distinguished individual; so called because a minute elapses between each discharge.

Miol'nier (3 syl.) [*the crusher*]. The magic hammer of Thor. It would never fail to hit a Troll; would never miss to hit whatever it was thrown at; would always return to the owner of its own accord; and became so small when not in use that it could be put into Thor's pocket. (*Scandinavian mythology.*)

Mir'abel. A travelled, dissipated fellow, who is proof against all the wiles of the fair sex. (*Beaumont and Fletcher: Wildgoose Chase.*)

Miracles (Latin, *miracŭlum*).

Vespasian, the Roman emperor, is said to have cured a blind man and a cripple by his touch during his stay in Alexandria.

Mahomet's miracles. He took a scroll of the Koran from the horn of a bull; a white dove came from heaven to whisper in his ear a message from God; he opened the earth and found two jars, one of honey and one of milk, as emblems of abundance; he brought the moon from heaven, made it pass through his sleeve, and return to its place in heaven; he went to heaven on his horse *Al Borak*; was taught the Koran by the angel Gabriel, etc. And yet we are told that he laid no pretensions to miracles.

The *Abbé Paris*, or more correctly François de Paris, the deacon, buried at the cemetery of St. Médard. The numberless cures performed at his tomb are said by Paley to be the best authenticated of any, except those of the Bible.

Edward the Confessor and all our sovereigns up to the time of Queen Anne are said to have cured scorbutic diseases by their touch. (*See* THAUMATURGUS.)

Miram'olin. The title of the Emperor of Morocco. A *miraman* is a temporary Turkish officer.

Mir'amont. An ignorant, testy old man, an ultra - admirer of learning. (*Fletcher : The Elder Brother.*)

Miran'da. Daughter of Prospero. (*Shakespeare : Tempest.*)

Mirror of Human Salvation. An extended "*Bib'lia Pau'perum*" (*q.v.*) with the subject of the picture explained in rhymes. Called in Latin "*Spec'ulum huma'næ salvatio'nis.*"

Mirror of King Ryence (*The*). This mirror was made by Merlin, and those who looked in it saw whatever they wished to see. (*Spenser : Faërie Queene*, bk. iii.)

Mirror of Knighthood (*The*). One of the books in Don Quixote's library, a Spanish romance at one time very popular. Butler calls *Hudibras* "the Mirror of Knighthood" (book i. 15).

"The barber, taking another book, said, 'This is the *Mirror of Knighthood.*'"—Part 1, book i. 6.]

Mirrors.

Alasnam's mirror. The "touchstone of virtue," showed if the lady beloved was chaste as well as beautiful. (*Arabian Nights : Prince Zeyn Alasnam.*)

Cambuscan's mirror. Sent to Cambuscan' by the King of Araby and Ind; it warned of the approach of ill-fortune, and told if love was returned. (*Chaucer : Canterbury Tales ; The Squire's Tale.*)

Lao's mirror reflected the mind and its thoughts, as an ordinary mirror reflects the outward seeming. (*Goldsmith : Citizen of the World*, xlv.)

Merlin's magic mirror, given by Merlin to King Ryence. It informed the king of treason, secret plots, and projected invasions. (*Spenser : Faerie Queene*, iii. 2.)

Reynard's wonderful mirror. This mirror existed only in the brain of Master Fox; he told the queen-lion that whoever looked in it could see what was done a mile off. The wood of the frame was not subject to decay, being made of the same block as King Crampart's magic horse. (*Reynard the Fox*, ch. xii.)

Vulcan's mirror showed the past, the present, and the future. Sir John Davies tells us that Cupid gave the mirror to Antin'ous, and Antinous gave it to Penelopē, who saw therein "the court of Queen Elizabeth."

Mirza. *Emir Zadah* [prince's son]. It is used in two ways by the Persians; when *prefixed* to a surname it is simply a title of honour; but when *annexed* to the surname, it means a prince of the blood royal.

Mis'creant (3 syl.) means a false believer. (French, *mis-créance.*) A term first applied to the Mahometans. The Mahometans, in return, call Christians *infidels*, and associate with the word all that we mean by "miscreants."

Mise-money. An honorarium given by the people of Wales to a new "Prince of Wales" on his entrance upon his principality. At Chester a mise-book is kept, in which every town and village is rated to this honorarium.

Littleton (*Dict.*) says the usual sum is £500. Bailey has the word in his *Dictionary.*

Misers. The most renowned are :—

(1) *Baron Aguilar* or Ephraim Lopes Pereira d'Aguilar, born at Vienna and died at Islington, worth £200,000. (1740-1802.)

(2) *Daniel Dancer.* His sister lived with him, and was a similar character, but died before him. (1716-1794.)

(3) *Colonel O'Dogherty*, though owner of large estates, lived in a windowless hut, which he entered by a ladder that he pulled up after him. His horse was mere skin and bone. He wore an old night-cap for wig, and an old brimless hat. His clothes were made up of patches, and his general appearance was that of extreme destitution.

(4) *Sir Harvey Elwes*, who died worth £250,000, but never spent more than £110 a year.

His sister-in-law inherited £100,000, but actually starved herself to death.

Her son *John*, M.P., an eminent brewer in Southwark, never bought any clothes, never suffered his shoes to be cleaned, and grudged every penny spent in food. (1714-1789.)

(5) *Foscue*, farmer-general of Languedoc, who hoarded his money in a secret cellar, where he was found dead.

(6) *Thomas Guy*, founder of Guy's Hospital. (1644-1724.)

(7) *Vulture Hopkins.*

(8) *Dick Jarrett* died worth £10,000, but his annual expenses never exceeded £6. The beer brewed at his christening was drunk at his funeral.

(9) *Messrs. Jardin*, of Cambridge.

(10) *William Jennings*, a neighbour and friend of Elwes, died worth £200,000. (1701-1797.)

(11) *The Rev. — Jonas*, of Blewbury.

(12) *John Little* left behind him £40,000, 180 wigs, 173 pairs of breeches, and an endless variety of other articles of clothing. His physician ordered him to drink a little wine for his health's sake, but he died in the act of drawing the cork of a bottle.

(13) *Ostervald*, the French banker, who died of starvation in 1790, possessed of £120,000.

(14) *John Overs*, a Southwark ferryman.

(15) *The King of Patterdale*, whose income was £800 a year, but his expenses never exceeded £30. He lived at the head of Lake Ulleswater. His last words were, "What a fortune a man might make if he lived to the age of Methuselah!" He died at the age of eighty-nine.

(16) *Guy Wilcocks*, a female miser. (*See* EUCLIO, HARPAGON, etc.)

Misere're (4 syl.). Our fifty-first psalm is so called. One of the evening services of Lent is called *misere're*, because this penitential psalm is sung, after which a sermon is delivered. The under side of a folding-seat in choir-stalls is called a *misere're;* when turned up it forms a ledge-seat sufficient to rest the aged in a kneeling position.

"Misfortune will never Leave Me till I Leave It," was the expression of Charles VII., Emperor of Germany. (1742-1745.)

Mishna. Instruction. A word applied by the Jews to the oral law. It is divided into six parts : (1) agriculture ; (2) Sabbaths, fasts, and festivals ; (3) marriage and divorce ; (4) civil and penal laws ; (5) sacrifices ; (6) holy persons and things. The commentary of the Mishna is called the Gema'ra. (Hebrew, *shanah*, to repeat.)

Misnomers.

Absalom means a *Father's Peace*, a fatal name for David's rebellious son.

Acid (sour) applied in chemistry to a class of bodies to which sourness is only accidental and by no means a universal character—thus, rock-crystal, quartz, flint, etc., are chemical acids, though no particle of acidity belongs to them.

America. So called from Amerigo Vespucci, a naval astronomer of Florence. He wrote an account of his discoveries, which were very popular in Germany, but certainly he did not discover the New World.

Ant. Go to the ant, thou sluggard. (*See* ANTS, HONEYCOMB.)

Antelope is a hopeless absurdity for the Greek *anthos-ops*, beautiful eye.

Arabic figures were not invented by the Arabs, but by the Indians.

Baffin's Bay is no bay at all.

Blacklead is a compound of carbon and iron.

Blind-worms are no more blind than *moles* are ; they have very quick and brilliant eyes, though somewhat small.

Brazilian grass does not come from Brazil, or even grow in Brazil, nor is it a grass at all. It consists of strips of a palm-leaf (*Chamærops argente'a*), and is chiefly imported from Cuba.

Bridegroom has nothing to do with groom. It is the old English *guma*, a man, *bryd-guma*.

Burgundy pitch is not pitch, nor is it manufactured or exported from Burgundy. The best is a resinous substance prepared from common frankincense, and brought from Hamburg ; but by far the larger quantity is a mixture of rosin and palm-oil.

Canopy, as if from Canopus (the star in the southern hemisphere), is the Greek *konopeion* (from *konops*, a gnat), and means a cloth to keep off gnats.

Catgut is not the gut of cats, but of sheep.

Celandine should be *chelidon*, Greek and Latin for a swallow ; so called because it was at one time supposed that swallows cured with it the blindness of their young. (*Pliny*, xxv. 50.)

China, as a name for porcelain, gives rise to the contradictory expressions British china, Sèvres china, Dresden china, Dutch china, Chelsea china, etc.; like wooden milestones, iron milestones, brass shoe-horns, iron pens, etc.

Cinerary, for a cemetery, should be "Cinery." Cinerarius is a woman's tailor.

Cuttle-bone is not bone at all, but a structure of pure chalk embedded loosely in the substance of a species of cuttlefish. It is enclosed in a membranous sac, within the body of the "fish," and drops out when the sac is opened, but it has no connection whatever with the sac or the cuttlefish.

Cleopatra's Needles were not erected by Cleopatra, or in honour of that queen, but by Thothmes III.

Crawfish for *cravis* (Latin *carabus*, a lobster, French *écrevisse*).

Cullander, a strainer, should be "colanter" (Latin *colans, colantis,* straining).

Custard, the food, is from the Welsh for curded milk ; but "custard," for a slap on the hand, should be *custid*, from the Latin *custis*, a club.

Down for *adown* (the preposition) is a strange instance of caprice, in which the omission of the negative (*a*) utterly perverts the meaning. The Saxon *dun* is an upland or hill, and *a-dun* is its opposite — *i.e.* a lowland or descent. Going *down stairs* really means "going upstairs," of ascending; and for descending we ought to say "going a-down."

Dutch clocks are not of Dutch but German (*Deutsch*) manufacture.

Elements. Fire, air, earth, and water, called the four elements, are not elements at all.

Fish, a counter, should be *fiche* (a five-sou piece), used at one time in France for card-counters. One of them, given "for the rub," was called *la fiche de consolation.*

Foxglove is not the glove of the fox, but of the fays, called *folk*—the little folk's glove; or else from *fosco*, red.

Frontispiece. A vile corruption of *frontispice* (Latin *frontispicium*, a view on the front page). The "*piece*" is *specium.* Frontispiece is an awful hybrid.

Fusiliers. These foot-soldiers now carry Enfield rifles, and not fusils.

Galvanised iron is not galvanised. It is simply iron coated with zinc, and this is done by dipping it in a zinc bath containing muriatic acid.

German silver is not silver at all, nor was the metallic mixture invented by a German, but has been in use in China time out of mind.

Gothic architecture is not the architecture of the Goths, but the ecclesiastical style employed in England and France before the Renaissance.

Guincapig. A blunder for Guiana, South America. Not a *pig* but a rodent.

Honeydew is neither *honey* nor *dew*, but an animal substance given off by certain insects, especially when hunted by ants.

Honey soap contains no honey, nor is honey in any way employed in its manufacture. It is a mixture of palm-oil soap and olive soap, each one part, with three parts of curd soap or yellow soap, scented.

Greyhound has no connection with the colour grey. It is the grayhound, or hound which hunts the *gray* or badger.

Humble pie, for *umbil pie*. The umbils of venison were served to inferior retainers and servants.

Hydrophobia (Greek, *dread of water*) applied to mad dogs is incorrect, as they will lap water and even swim in it.

Indians (*American*). A blunder of geography on the part of the early discoverers of the New World, who set their faces westward from Europe to find India, and believed they had done so

when they discovered Cat's Island, off the south coast of America.

Irish stew. A dish that is unknown in Ireland.

Iron-mask was made of velvet.

Japan lacquer contains no lac at all, but is made from the resin of a kind of nut-tree called Anacardiaceæ.

Jerusalem artichoke has no connection with Jerusalem, but with the sunflower, *girasole*, which it resembles.

Kensington Palace is not in Kensington at all, but in the parish of St. Margaret, Westminster.

Kid gloves are not kid at all, but are made of lamb-skin or sheep-skin.

Laudanum should be *ladanum*, originally made from the leaves of the *lada.* (*Pliny*, xxvi. 47.)

Longitude and latitude, the great dimension and little or broad dimension of the earth. According to the ancient notion, the world was bounded on the west by the Atlantic, but extended an indefinite length eastward. It was similarly terminated on the south by the Tropic of Cancer, whence it extended northwards, but this extent being much less than that east and west, was called the *breadth* or latitude.

Louis de Bourbon, Bishop of Liège, is made by Sir Walter Scott, in *Quentin Durward*, an "old man," whereas he was only eighteen, and a scholar at Louvain. He made his entry into his see in a scarlet jerkin and cap set jauntily on one side. (*A. Dumas: Charles the Bold.*)

Lunar caustic is not a substance from the moon, but is simply nitrate of silver, and silver is the astrological symbol of the moon.

Lunatics are not affected by the changes of the moon more than other invalids. No doubt their disorder has its periodicities, but it is not affected by the moon.

Meerschaum. (*See* MEERSCHAUM.)

Mosaic gold has no connection with Moses or the metal gold. It is an alloy of copper and zinc, used in the ancient *musivum* or tesselated work.

Mother of pearl is the inner layer of several sorts of shell. It is not the mother of pearls, as the name indicates, but in some cases the matrix of the pearl.

Natives. Oysters raised in *artificial* beds. Surely oysters in their own natural beds ought to be called the natives.

Oxygen means the generator of acids, but there are acids of which it is not the base, as hydrochloric acid. Indeed, chemists now restrict the term *acid* to compounds into which *hydrogen* enters, and oxy-acids are termed salts.

Pen means a feather. (Latin, *penna*, a wing.) A steel pen is not a very choice expression.

Philippe VI. of France was called "*Le bien fortuné*," but never was name more inappropriate. He was defeated at Sluys [*Slu-iz*], and again at Cressy; he lost Calais; and a fourth of all his subjects were carried off by the plague called the "Black Death."

Pompey's Pillar, in Alexandria, was erected neither by nor to Pompey. It was set up by the Emperor Diocletian, according to its inscription.

Prussian blue does not come from Prussia, but is the precipitate of the salt of protoxide of iron with red prussiate of potass.

Rice paper is not made from rice, but from the pith of Tung-tsau, or hollow-plant, so called because it is hollow when the pith has been pushed out.

Salt is not salt at all, and has long been wholly excluded from the class of bodies denominated salts. Table-salt is "chloride of sodium."

Salt of lemon is in reality a binoxalate of potash, with a little of the quadroxalate.

Salts. The substance of which junk bottles, French mirrors, window-panes, and opera-glasses are made is placed among the *salts*, but is no salt at all.

Sand-blind is a mere corruption of *sam* (half) blind.

Scuttle, to open a hole in a ship, means really to bolt or bar. (*See* SCUTTLE.)

Sealing-wax is not wax at all, nor does it contain a single particle of wax. It is made of shellac, Venice turpentine, and cinnabar.

Shrew-mouse is no mouse (*mus*), but belongs to the genus *sorex*.

Slave means noble, illustrious (*slavi*), but is now applied to the most ignoble and debased. (*See* BARON.)

Sovereign. The last syllable of this word is incorrect. The word should be *soverain* (Latin, *superāre ;* French, *souv-rain*). It has no connection with "reign" (Latin, *regnāre*).

Sperm oil properly means "seed oil," from the notion that it was the spawn or melt of a whale. It is chiefly taken from the *head*, not the spawn, of the "spermaceti" whale.

Titmouse (plur. *titmice*) is no mouse, but a bird. (Anglo-Saxon, *tite-máse*, little hedge-sparrow.)

Toadflax has nothing at all to do with toads. It is *tod* flax, *i.e.* flax with tods or clusters.

Tonquin beans. A geographical blunder for *tonka beans*, from Tonka, in Guinea, not Tonquin, in Asia.

Turkeys do not come from Turkey, but North America, through Spain, or India. The French call them "dindon," *i.e. d'Inde* or *coq d'Inde*, a term equally incorrect.

Turkey rhubarb neither grows in Turkey, nor is it imported from Turkey. It grows in the great mountain chain between Tartary and Siberia, and is a Russian monopoly.

Turkish baths are not of Turkish origin, nor are they baths, but hot-air rooms or thermæ.

Vallombro'sa. Milton says :—

"Thick as autumnal leaves that strew the brooks In Vallombrosa." *Paradise Lost*, i. 302.

But the trees of Vallombrosa, being pines, do not shed thickly in autumn, and the brooks are not strewed with their leaves.

Ventriloquism is not voice from the stomach at all, but from the mouth.

Well-beloved. Louis XIII. A most inappropriate title for this most detestable and detested of all kings.

Whalebone is no bone at all, nor does it possess any properties of bone. It is a substance attached to the upper jaw of the whale, and serves to strain the water which the creature takes up in large mouthfuls.

Wolf's-bane. A strange corruption. Bane is the Teutonic word for all poisonous herbs. The Greeks, mistaking banes for beans, translated it *kuamos*, as they did hen-bane (*huos-kuamos*). Now wolf's-bane is an aconite, with a pale-yellow - flower, and therefore called *white-bane* to distinguish it from the *blue* aconite. The Greek for white is *leukos*, hence "leukos-kuamos ;" but *lukos* is the Greek for wolf, and by a blunder *leukos-kuamos* (white-bean) got muddled into *lukos-kuamos* (wolf-bean). Botanists, seeing the absurdity of calling aconite a *bean*, restored the original word "bane," but retained the corrupt word *lukos* (a wolf), and hence we get the name wolf's-bane for white aconite. (*H. Fox Talbot.*)

Wormwood has nothing to do with worms or wood ; it is the Anglo-Saxon *wer mod*, man-inspiriting, being a strong tonic.

Mispris'ion. Concealment, neglect of. (French, *mépris*.)

Misprision of clerks. Mistakes in accounts arising from neglect.

Misprision of felony. Neglecting to reveal a felony when known.

Misprision of treason. Neglecting to disclose or purposely concealing a treasonable design.

Miss, Mistress, Mrs. (masteress, lady-master.) Miss used to be written Mis, and is the first syllable of Mistress; Mrs. is the contraction of *mistress*, called Mis'ess. Even in the reign of George II. unmarried ladies used to be styled Mrs.; as, Mrs. Lepel, Mrs. Bellenden, Mrs. Blount, all unmarried ladies. (See *Pope's Letters.*)

Early in Charles II.'s reign, Evelyn tells us that " lewd women began to be styled Misse; " now Mistress is more frequently applied to them. (*See* LAD.)

Miss is as Good as a Mile (*A*). A failure is a failure be it ever so little, and is no more be it ever so great; a narrow escape is an escape, and a more easy one is no more. If I miss the train by one minute, I miss it as much as if it had run a mile from the station; and if I escape an evil by the skin of my teeth, I escape, and he who escapes it easily does no more.

Missing Link (*The*). According to Darwin, the higher animals are developed from the lower ones. The lowest form of animal life is protoplasm, which develops into amœbæ (cell life), and thence, successively, into synamœbæ, gastrula, hydra, medusa, worms, hematega, ascidians, fish, amphibians, birds and reptiles, monotremata, marsupials, placental mammals, lemuridæ, monkeys [missing link], man.

Mississip'pi Bubble. The French "South-Sea Scheme," and equally disastrous. It was projected by John Law, a Scotchman, and had for its object the payment of the National Debt of France, which amounted to 208 millions sterling, on being granted the exclusive trade of Louisia'na, on the banks of the Mississippi. (1717-1720.) (*See* SOUTH SEA.)

Mist'letoe. Shakespeare calls it " the *baleful* mistletoe " (*Titus Andronicus,* ii. 3), in allusion to the Scandinavian story that it was with an arrow made of mistletoe that Balder was slain. (*See* KISSING UNDER THE MISTLETOE.)

` The word mistletoe is a corruption of *mistel-ta,* where *mist* is the German for "dung," or rather the " droppings of a bird," from the notion that the plant was so propagated, especially by the missel-thrush. *Ta* is for *tan,* Old Norse *tein,* meaning " a plant " or " shoot."

Mistletoe Bough. The tale referred to in this song, about Lord Lovel's daughter, is related by Rogers in his *Italy,* where the lady is called " Ginevra." A similar narrative is given by Collet in his *Relics of Literature,* and another is among the *Causes Célèbres.*

Marwell Old Hall, once the residence of the Seymour, and afterwards of the Dacre family, has a similar tradition attached to it, and (according to the *Post Office Directory*) " the very chest became the property of the Rev. J Haygarth, a rector of Upham."

Mistress Roper. The Marines, or any one of them ; so called by the regular sailors, because they handle the ropes like girls, not being used to them.

Mistress of the Night (*The*). The tuberose is so called because it emits its strongest fragrance after sunset. Sometimes, on a sultry evening, when the atmosphere is highly electrified, the fading flowers of the tuberose emit sparks of lucid flame.

(In the language of flowers, the tuberose signifies " the pleasures of love.")

Mistress of the World. Ancient Rome was so called, because all the known world gave it allegiance.

Mi'ta. Sister of Aude, surnamed "the Little Knight of Pearls," in love with Sir Miton de Rennes, Roland's friend. Charlemagne greeted her after a tournament with the Saracens at Fronsac, saying, " Rise, Countess of Rennes." Mita and Sir Miton were the parents of Mitaine (*q.v.*). (*Croquemitaine,* xv.)

Mitaine. Godchild of Charlemagne; her parents were Mita and Miton, Count and Countess of Rennes. She went in search of Fear fortress, and found that it only existed in the minds of the fearful, vanishing into thin air as it was approached by a bold heart and clear conscience. Charlemagne made her for this achievement Roland's squire, and she followed him on her horse *Vaillant* to Spain, and fell in the attack at Roncesvalles. (*Croquemitaine,* pt. iii.)

Mite. *Sir Matthew Mite.* A purseproud East Indian merchant, who gives his servants the most costly exotics, and overpowers everyone with the profusion of his wealth. (*S. Foote : The Nabob.*)

Lady Oldham says: "He comes amongst us preceded by all the pomp of Asia. Profusely scattering the spoils of conquered provinces, corrupting the virtue, and alienating the affections of all the old friends of the family."

Mith'ra or **Mith'ras.** The highest of the twenty-eight second-class divinities of the ancient Persians, and the ruler of the universe. Sometimes used as a synonym for the sun. The word means *friend*, and this deity is so called because he befriends man in this life, and protects him against evil spirits after death. He is represented as a young man with a Phrygian cap, a tunic, a mantle on his left shoulder, and plunging a sword into the neck of a bull. (Sanskrit, *mitram*, a friend.) (See *Thebais*, i.)

Mith'ridate (3 syl.). A confection said to be invented by Mithrida'tēs, King of Pontus and Bithyn'ia, as an antidote to poison. It contains seventy-two ingredients.

" What brave spirit could be content to sit in his shop . . . . selling Mithridatum and dragon's water to infected houses ?"—*Knight of the Burning Pestle.* (1635.)

Mitre. The episcopal mitre symbolises the cloven tongues of fire which descended on the apostles on the day of Pentecost. (Acts ii. 1-12.) Greek and Latin, *mitra*, a turban.

Mitre . Tavern (*The*). A place of resort in the time of Shakespeare : it was in Bread Street, Cheapside.

Mitten. *The Pardoner's mitten.* Whoever put this mitten on would be sure to thrive in all things.

" He that his hondë put in this metayn,
He shal have multiplying of his grayn,
Whan he hath sowen, be it whete or otes,
So that ye offre pans [pence] or ellës grootes."
Chaucer : Prologue to The Pardoneres Tale.

To give one the mitten. To reject a sweetheart ; to jilt. (Latin, *mitto*, to send [about your business], whence dismissal ; to get your dismissal.) Some say, it is to get the *mitten* instead of the *hand*.

" There is a young lady I have set my heart on, though whether she is going to give me hern, or give me the mitten, I ain't quite satisfied."—*Sam Slick : Human Nature*, p. 90.

" I don't believe but what that Hammond girl's given him the mitten, else he wouldn't a come. I wouldn't play second fiddle for any fellow."—*M. E. Wilkins : A Tardy Thanksgiving* (American).

Mit'timus (Latin). A command in writing to a gaoler, to keep the person named in safe custody. Also a writ for removing a record from one court to another. So called from the first word of the writ, " Mittimus " (*i.e.* We send . « .).

Mitton. *The Chapter of Mitton.* So the battle of Mitton was called, because so many priests took part therein. Hailes says that " three hundred ecclesiastics

fell in this battle, which was fought September 20th, 1319."

" So many priests took part in the fight that the Scots called it the Chapter of Mitton—a meeting of the clergymen belonging to a cathedral being called a chapter."—*Sir Walter Scott : Tales of a Grandfather*, x.

Mixon. *Better wed over the Mixon than over the Moor.* (*See* MIDDEN.)

Mizentop, maintop, foretop. Service in these masts has nothing whatever to do with age or merit. A " top " is a platform fixed over the head of a lower mast, resting on the trestle-trees, to spread the rigging of the topmast.

⁂ The mizenmast is the aftermost mast of a ship ; the foremast is in the forward part of a ship ; the mainmast is between these two.

" He was put into the mizentop, and served three years in the West Indies ; then he was transferred to the maintop, and served five years in the Mediterranean ; and then he was made captain of the foretop, and served six years in the East Indies ; and at last he was rated captain's coxswain in the *Druid* frigate."—*Capt. Marryat : Poor Jack*, chap. i.

Mjölnir (pron. *youl-ner*). Thor's hammer. (*See* MIOLNER.)

Mnemos'ynē (4 syl.). Goddess of memory and mother of the nine Muses. (*Classical mythology*.) The best representation of this goddess is by A. R. Mengs, the " Raphael of Germany " (1720-1779).

Moabite Stone (*The*). Presented to the British Museum by the museum of the Louvre. It was discovered by the Rev. F. Klein at Dibhan in August, 1868, and is 3 feet 10 inches high, 2 feet broad, and 14½ inches thick. The Arabs resented its removal, and splintered it into fragments, but it has been restored. The inscription, consisting of forty-four lines, gives an account of the war of Mesha, King of Moab, against Omri, Ahab, and other kings of Israel. Mesha sacrificed his eldest son on the city wall in view of the invading Israelites. He set up this stone at Kermost B.C. 900.

Moakkibat. A class of angels, according to the Mahometan mythology. Two angels of this class attend every child of Adam from the cradle to the grave. At sunset they fly up with the record of the deeds done since sunrise. Every good deed is entered ten times by the recording angel on the credit or right side of his ledger, but when an evil deed is reported the angel waits seven hours, " if haply in that time the evil-doer may repent." (*The Koran*.)

Moat. (*See under* BATTLE.)

Mob. A contraction of the Latin *mo'bile vulgus* (the fickle crowd). The term was first applied to the people by the members of the Green-ribbon Club, in the reign of Charles II. (*Northern Examiner*, p. 574.)

Mob-cap (*A*). Is a plain cap, from Dutch *mob* = a cap. Probably *mop* is another form of the same word, and all come from the Latin *mappa* (a clout), whence our word *map* (a drawing on cloth), in contradistinction to a *cartoon* (a drawing on paper).

Mo'bilise. To render soldiers liable to be moved on service out of the town where they live; to call into active service men enrolled but not on the war establishment. (Latin, *mobilis*.)

Mock-beggar Hall or **Manor.** A grand, ostentatious house, where no hospitality is afforded, neither is any charity given.

"No times observed, nor charitable lawes,
The poore receive their answer from the dawes,
Who, in their cawing language, call it plaine
Mock-begger Manour, for they come in vaine."
           Taylor: Workes.

Mockery. "*It will be a delusion, a mockery, and a snare.*" Thomas, Lord Denman, in his judgment on the case of O'Connell *v.* The Queen.

Modal'ity, in scholastic philosophy, means the *mode* in which anything exists. Kant divides our judgment into three modalities: (1) *Problematic,* touching possible events; (2) *Assertoric,* touching real events; (3) *Apodictic,* touching necessary events.

Modish (*Lady Betty*), in *The Careless Husband,* by Cibber. The name explains the character. This was Mrs. Oldfield's favourite character, and *The Tatler* (No. 10) accordingly calls this charming actress "Lady Betty Modish." (*See* NARCISSA.)

Mo'do. The fiend that urges to murder, and one of the five that possessed "Poor Tom." (*See* MAHU.) (*Shakespeare: King Lear,* iv. 1.)

Mo'dred, in the romance of *The Round Table,* is represented as the treacherous knight. He revolted from his Uncle Arthur, whose wife he seduced, was mortally wounded in the battle of Camlan, in Cornwall, and was buried in the island of Avalon.

Sir Modred. The nephew of King Arthur. He hated Sir Lancelot, sowed discord amongst the Knights of the Round Table, and tampered with the "lords of the White Horse," the brood that Hengist left. When the king went to chastise Sir Lancelot for tampering with the queen, he left Sir Modred in charge of the kingdom. Modred raised a revolt, and the king was slain in his attempt to quash it. (*Tennyson: Idylls of the King; Guinevere.*)

Mods. In Oxford a contracted form of moderations. The three necessary examinations in Oxford are the Smalls, the Mods, and the Greats. No one can take a class till he has passed the Mods. There are no Mods at Cambridge.

"While I was reading for Mods I was not so unsettled in my mind."—*Grant Allen: The Backslider,* part iii.

Mo'dus Operandi (Latin). The mode of operation; the way in which a thing is done or should be done.

Modus Vivendi (*A*). A mutual arrangement whereby persons not at the time being on friendly terms can be induced to live together in harmony. The term may be applied to individuals, to societies, or to peoples. It signifies literally a manner of living.

Mofus'sil (East Indies). The subordinate divisions of a district; the seat of government being called *sudder.* Provincial.

"To tell a man that fatal charges have been laid against him, and refuse him an opportunity for explanation, this is not even Mofussil justice."—*The Times.*

Mogul Cards. The best playing-cards were so called because the wrapper, or "duty card" (when cards were subject to excise duty) contained the portrait of the Great Mogul. Those cards which contained some mark, speck, or other imperfection, were called "Harrys."

Moha'di [*Mohammed*]. The twelfth Imaun, who is said to be living in concealment till Antichrist appears, when he will come again and overthrow the great enemy.

Mohair. (Probably the Arabic *mukhayyar,* goat's-hair cloth.) It is the hair of the Ango'ra goat, introduced into Spain by the Moors, and thence brought into Germany.

Mohak'abad' (*Al*). Abu-Rihan, the geographer and astronomer in the eleventh century.

Mohocks. A class of ruffians who in the 18th century infested the streets of London. So called from the Indian Mohawks. One of their "new inventions" was to roll persons down Snow Hill in a tub; another was to overturn coaches on rubbish-heaps. (See *Gay : Trivia*, iii.)

A vivid picture of the misdoings in the streets of London by these and other brawlers is given in *The Spectator*, No. 324.

" You sent your Mohocks next abroad,
    With razors armed, and knives ;
Who on night-walkers made inroad,
    And scared our maids and wives ;
They scared the watch, and windows broke . . ."
        Plot upon Plot (about 1713).

Mohun. Captain Hill and Lord Mohun made a dastardly attack on an actor named Mountford, on his way to Mrs. Bracegirdle's house in Howard Street. Hill was jealous of the actor, and induced the "noble lord" to join him in this "valiant quarrel." Mountford died next day. Hill fled, and was never heard of more ; Mohun was tried for his life, but acquitted. (*See* ISSACHAR.) (*Howell : State Trials*, vol. xii. p. 947.)

Mohyronus (*Edricius*). Said to cure wounds by sympathy. He did not apply his powder to the wounds, but to a cloth dipped in the blood.

Moiré Antique (French) is silk, etc., *moiré* (watered) in the *antique* style, or to resemble the material worn in olden times. The figuring of tin like frostwork or scales is called *moiré métallique*.

Mokan'na. [*See* KHORASSAN.]

Molière. *The Italian Molière.* Carlo Goldoni[i] (1707-1793).

The Spanish Molière. Leandro Fernandez Moratin (1760-1828).

Mo'linism. The system of grace and election taught by Louis Mo'lina, the Spanish Jesuit (1535-1600).

" Those Jansenists, re-nicknamed Molinists."
        Browning : The Ring and the Book.

Moll (*Kentish*). Mary Carlson, commonly known as the German Princess. She was sentenced to transportation, but, being found at large, was hanged at Tyburn in 1672.

Moll Cutpurse. Mary Frith, a woman of masculine vigour, who not unfrequently assumed man's attire. She was a notorious thief and cutpurse, who once attacked General Fairfax on Hounslow Heath, for which she was sent to Newgate. She escaped by bribery, and died at last of dropsy in the seventy-fifth year of her age. (Time of Charles I.)

Moll Flanders. A woman of extraordinary beauty, born in the Old Bailey. She was twelve years a courtesan, five times a wife, twelve years a thief, eight years a transport in Virginia ; but ultimately grew rich, lived honestly, and died a penitent. (Charles II.'s reign.) (*See* Daniel Defoe's *Moll Flanders.*)

Moll Thomson's Mark. As "Take away this bottle, it has Moll Thomson's mark on it." Moll Thomson is M. T. (*empty*).

Molly. *He's a regular Molly.* Said of a man or big boy who betties or interferes with women's work, such as kitchen business, dressmaking, personal decoration, and so on.

Molly Coddle (*A*). A pampered creature, afraid that the winds of heaven should visit him too roughly ; though a male, a Molly ; not a valetudinarian, but ever fearing lest he should be so.

Molly Maguires. An Irish secret society organised in 1843. Stout, active young Irishmen, dressed up in women's clothes, blackened faces, and otherwise disguised, to surprise those employed to enforce the payment of rents. Their victims were ducked in bog-holes, and many were beaten most unmercifully.

" The judge who tried the murderer was elected by the Molly Maguires ; the jurors who assisted him were themselves Molly Maguires. A score of Molly Maguires came forward to swear that the assassin was sixty miles from the spot on which he had been seen to fire at William Dunn, . . . and the jurors returned a verdict of Not Guilty."—W. *Hepworth Dixon: New America*, ii. 28.

Molly Mog. This celebrated beauty was an innkeeper's daughter, at Oakingham, Berks. She was the toast of all the gay sparks, in the former half of the eighteenth century, and died in 1766, at an advanced age. Gay has a ballad on this *Fair Maid of the Inn*.

Molly Mog died at the age of sixty-seven, a spinster ; Mr. Standen, of Arborfield, the enamoured swain alluded to in the ballad, died 1730. It is said that Molly's sister Sally was the greater beauty. A portrait of Gay still hangs in the inn.

Molmu'tius. A mythical king of Britain, who promulgated the laws called the Molmutine, and established the privilege of sanctuary. He is alluded to in *Cymbeline*, iii. 1 (*Shakespeare*).

Moloch. Any influence which demands from us the sacrifice of what we hold most dear. Thus, *war* is a Moloch, *king mob* is a Moloch, the *guillotine* was the Moloch of the French Revolution, etc. The allusion is to the god of the Ammonites, to whom children were "made to pass through the fire" in sacrifice. Milton says he was "worshipped in Rabba, in Argob, and Basan, to the stream of utmost Arnon." (*Paradise Lost*, book i. 392-398.)

Mo'ly. Wild garlic, called sorcerer's garlic. There are many sorts, all of which flower in May, except "the sweet moly of Montpelier," which blossoms in September. The most noted are "the great moly of Homer," the Indian moly, the moly of Hungary, serpent's moly, the yellow moly, Spanish purple moly, Spanish silver-capped moly, and Dioscor'ides's moly. Pope describes it and its effects in one of his odes, and Milton refers to it in his *Comus*. (Greek, *molu*.)

> "That moly
> That Hermēs once to wise Ulysses gave."
> *Milton: Comus*, 655-6.

Mome (*French*), says Cotgrave, is a Momus, find-fault, carping fellow. So called from Momus, the god of raillery.

> "Or cessent donques les momes,
> De mordre les escrits miens."
> *J. du Bellay : A. P. de Ronsard.*

Mo'miers (French, *men of mummery*). An Evangelical party of Switzerland, somewhat resembling our Methodists. They arose in 1818, and made way both in Germany and France.

Mommur. The realm of O'beron. (*Middle Age romance.*)

Mo'mus. One who carps at everything. Momus, the sleepy god, was always railing and carping.

Momus, being asked to pass judgment on the relative merits of Neptune, Vulcan, and Minerva, railed at them all. He said the horns of a bull ought to have been placed in the shoulders, where they would have been of much greater force ; as for man, he said Jupiter ought to have made him with a window in his breast, whereby his real thoughts might be revealed. Hence Dr. Gray says that every unreasonable carper is called a "Momus."

Momus's Lattice or Window. Momus blamed Vulcan because he did not set a window or lattice in the human breast for discerning secret thoughts.

> "Were Momus' lattice in our breasts . . ."
> *Byron: Werner*, iii. 1.

Mo'naciel'lo [*little monk*]. A sort of incubus in the mythology of Naples. It is described as a thick little man, dressed in a monk's garment and broadbrimmed hat. Those who will follow when he beckons will be led to a spot where treasure is concealed. Sometimes, however, it is his pleasure to pull the bed-clothes off, and sometimes to sit perched on a sleeper.

Monarchi'ans. A theological party of the third century, who maintained that God is one, immutable and primary. Their opponents turned upon them, and nicknamed them *Patripassians* (*q.v.*), saying that according to such a doctrine God the Father must have suffered on the cross.

Mon'archy. *Fifth-monarchy men.* Those who believed that the second coming of Christ was at hand, and that at His second coming He would establish the fifth universal monarchy. The five are these : the Assyrian, the Persian, the Macedonian, the Roman, and the Millennium.

Monday Pops. A contraction of "Monday Populars," meaning popular concerts for classical music, introduced at St. James's Hall by Mr. Arthur Chappell in 1858. There are Saturday Pops also.

Money. Shortly after the Gallic invasion, Lucius Furius built a temple to Juno Mone'ta (the *Monitress*) on the spot where the house of Manlius Capitolinus stood. This spot of the Capitol was selected because Manlius was the first man alarmed by the cackling of the sacred geese. This temple was subsequently converted into a mint, and the "ases" there coined were called *moneta*.

⁂ Juno is represented on medals with instruments of coinage, as the hammer, anvil, pincers, and die. (See *Livy*, vii. 28, and Cicero, *De Divinitate*, i. 15.)

The oldest coin of Greece bore the impress of an ox. Hence a bribe for silence was said to be an "ox on the tongue." Subsequently each province had its own impress :

Athens, an owl (the bird of wisdom).
Bœotia, Bacchus (the vineyard of Greece).
Delphos, a dolphin.
Macedonia, a buckler (from its love of war).
Rhodes, the disc of the sun (the Colossus was an image to the sun).

Rome had a different impress for each coin :

For the *As*, the head of Janus on one side, and the prow of a ship on the reverse.
The *Semi-as*, the head of Jupiter and the letter S.
The *Triens*, the head of a woman (? Rome or Minerva) and four points to denote four ounces.
The *Quadrans*, the head of Hercules and three points to denote three ounces.
The *Sextans*, the head of Mercury, and two points to denote two ounces.

Bowed money. Bent coin, given as a pledge of love.

> "Taking forth a bowed groat and an old penny bowed he gave it [*sic*] her." — *Coney-catching.* (Time, Elizabeth.)

Money makes the Mare to go. (*See* MARE.)

Monim'ia, in Otway's tragedy of *The Orphan.* Sir Walter Scott says, "More tears have been shed for the sorrows of Monimia, than for those of Juliet and Desdemona."

Monism. The doctrine of the oneness of mind and matter, God and the universe. It ignores all that is supernatural, and the dualism of mind and matter, God and creation; and, as this is the case, of course, there can be no opposition between God and the world, as unity cannot be in opposition to itself. Monism teaches that "all are but parts of one stupendous whole, whose body nature is, and God the soul;" hence, whatever is, only conforms to the cosmical laws of the universal ALL.

Haeckel, of Jena, in 1866, revived this theory, and explains it thus: "Monism (the correlative of Dualism) denotes a unitary conception, in opposition to a supernatural one. Mind can never exist without matter, nor matter without mind." As God is the same "yesterday, to-day, and for ever," creation must be the same, or God would not be unchangeable.

Monitor. So the Romans called the nursery teacher. The *Military Monitor* was an officer to tell young soldiers of the faults committed against the service. The *House Monitor* was a slave to call the family of a morning, etc.

Monitor. An ironclad with a flat deck, sharp stern, and one or more movable turrets.

Monk, in printing, is a black smear or blotch made by leaving too much ink on the part. Caxton set up his printing-press in the *scripto'rium* of Westminster Abbey; and the associations of this place gave rise to the slang expressions *monk* and *friar* for black and white defects. (*See* FRIAR, CHAPEL.)

Give a man a monk (French, "*Luy bailler le moyne*)." To do one a mischief. Rabelais says that Grangousier (after the battle of Picrocho'le) asked "what was become of Friar John;" to which Gargantua replied, "No doubt the enemy has the monk," alluding to the pugnacious feats of this wonderful churchman, who knocked men down like ninepins. (*Rabelais: Gargantua and Pantagruel,* book i. 45.)

Monk Lewis. Matthew Gregory Lewis is so called from his novel entitled *The Monk.* (1773-1818.)

Monk listening to a Bird. (*See* FELIX, HILDESHEIM.)

Monk of Westminster. Richard of Cirencester, the historian. (Fourteenth century.)

Monkey (*A*). £500. (*See* MARYGOLD.)

Monkey = the Devil; an imp of mischief. Hence, a meddlesome child is spoken to as "you little monkey;" and is called "a regular imp," or "imp of mischief." The allusion is to the old drawings of devils, with long tails and monkey ugliness.

To get (or *have*) *one's monkey up.* To be riled. Here the allusion is also to the devil or evil spirit in man; he will be "in a devil of a temper." Even taken literally, monkeys are extremely irritable and easily provoked.

Monkey, in sailor language, is the vessel which contains the full allowance of grog. Halliwell (*Archaic Dictionary*) has—

"Moncorn, 'Beere corne, barley bygge, or moncorne.'"—(1552.)

To suck the monkey. Sailors call the vessel which contains their full allowance of grog "a monkey." Hence, to "suck the monkey" is surreptitiously to suck liquor from a cask through a straw. Again, when the milk has been taken from a cocoanut, and rum has been substituted, "sucking the monkey" means drinking this rum. Probably "monkey" in all such cases is a corruption of *moncorn* (ale or beer). (See *Marryat's Peter Simple.*) (*See* MONKEY SPOONS.)

Monkey Board. The step behind an omnibus on which the conductor stands, or rather skips about like a monkey.

Monkey Boat. A long, narrow boat.

Monkey Jacket. A coat with no more tail than a monkey, or, more strictly speaking, an ape.

Monkey-puzzle. The name given to a Chilian pine, whose twisted and prickly branches puzzle even a monkey to climb.

Monkey Spoons. Spoons at one time given in Holland at marriages, christenings, and funerals. They may still be picked up occasionally at curiosity shops. The spoon at weddings was given to some immediate relative of the bride, and just below the monkey on the handle was a heart. At funerals the spoon was given to the officiating clergyman. Among the Dutch, drinking is called "sucking the monkey" (*zuiging de monky*), and one fond of drink was called "a monkey sucker." The Dutchman began the day with an appetiser—*i.e.* rum, with a pinch of salt, served in a monkey spoon (*monky lépel*); and these appetisers were freely used at weddings, christenings, and funerals.

Monkey with a Long Tail (*A*). A mortgage. A monkey (*q.v.*) is slang for £500.

Monkey's Allowance. More kicks than halfpence. The allusion is to the monkeys carried about for show; they pick up the halfpence, but carry them to the master, who keeps kicking or ill-treating the poor creatures to urge them to incessant tricks.

Monkey's Money. *I will pay you in monkey's money* ("*en monnaie de singe*") —in goods, in personal work, in mumbling and grimace. The French had a law that when a monkey passed the Petit Pont, of Paris, if it was for sale it was to pay four deniers (two-thirds of a penny) for toll; but if it belonged to a showman and was not for sale, it should suffice if the monkey went through his tricks.

"It was an original by Master Charles Charmois, principal painter to King Megistus [of France], paid for in court fashion with monkey's money."—*Rabelais: Gargantua and Pantagruel*, iv. 3.

Mon'kir and **Na'kir**, according to Mahometan mythology, are two angels who interrogate the dead immediately they are buried. The first two questions they ask are, "Who is your Lord?" and "Who is your prophet?" Their voices are like thunder, their aspects hideous, and those not approved of they lash into perdition with whips *half-iron and half-flame*. (*See* MUNKAR.)

"Do you not see those spectres that are stirring the burning coals? They are Monkir and Nakir."—*Beckford: Vathek.*

Monmouth. The town at the mouth of the Monnow.

Monmouth. The surname of Henry V. of England, who was born there.

Monmouth Cap. A soldier's cap.

"The soldiers that the Monmouth wear, On castles' tops their ensigns rear."

"The best caps were formerly made at Monmouth, where the cappers' chapel doth still remain."—*Fuller: Worthies of Wales*, p. 50.

Monmouth Street (London) takes its name from the unfortunate son of Charles II., executed for rebellion in 1685. Now Dudley Street.

Monnaie de Basoche. Worthless coin; coin not current; counters. "Brummagem halfpennies." Coins were at one time made and circulated by the lawyers of France, which had no currency beyond their own community. (*See* BASOCHIANS.)

Mono'nia (3 syl.). Munster.

"Remember the glories of Brien the brav Though the days of the hero are o'er, Though lost to Mononia, and cold in the grave, He returns to Kinko'ra [his palace] no more."
T. Moore: Irish Melodies, No. 1.

Monoph'agous. The eater of one sort of food only. (Greek, *monos phagein*.)

Monoph'ysites (4 syl.). A religious sect in the Levant, who maintained that Jesus Christ had only one nature, and that divine and human were combined in much the same way as the body and soul in man. (Greek, *monos phusis*, one nature.)

Monoth'elism consisted in the doctrine that, although Christ has two distinct natures, He never had but *one will*, His human will being merged in the divine. (Greek, *monos-thelema*, one single will.)

Monroe Doctrine. The American States are never to entangle themselves in the broils of Europe, nor to suffer the powers of the Old World to interfere in the affairs of the New; and they are to account any attempt on the part of the Old World to plant their systems of government in any part of North America dangerous to American peace and safety. James Monroe was twice president of the United States. (1816 and 1820.)

Monsieur. Philippe, Duc d'Orléans, brother to Louis XIV., was called *Monsieur;* other gentlemen were only Monsieur This or That. (1674-1723.)

Monsieur le Coadjuteur. Paul de Gondi, afterwards Cardinal de Retz (Ress). (1614-1679.)

Monsieur le Duc. Henri-Jules de Bourbon, eldest son of the Prince de Condé. (1692-1740.)

Monsieur le Grand. The Great Equerry of France.

Monsieur le Prince. Prince de Conde (1621-1686). (*See* MADAME.)

Monsieur de Paris. The public executioner or Jack Ketch of France.

"Riccardo de Albertes was a personal friend of all the 'Messieurs de Paris,' who served the Republic. He attended all capital executions, and possesses a curious library."—*Newspaper Paragraph*, January 25th, 1893.

Monsoon is a corruption of the Malay word *mooseem* (year or season). For six months it is a north-east trade-wind, and for six months a south-west.

Monster (*The*). Renwick Williams, a wretch who used to prowl about London, wounding respectable women with a double-edged knife. He was convicted of several offences in July, 1790.

The green-eyed monster. Jealousy; so called by Shakespeare in *Othello*.

> "Beware of Jealousy!
> It is a green-eyed monster that doth mock
> The meat it feeds on."   Act iii. 3.

Monsters. See each under its name, as COCKATRICE, CHICHIVACHE, CHIMÆRA, etc.

Mont, in chiromancy, is the technical word for the eminences at the roots of the fingers.

> That at the root of the
> *thumb* is the Mont de Mars.
> *index finger* is the Mont de Jupiter.
> *long finger* is the Mont de Saturne.
> *ring finger* is the Mont de Soleil.
> *little finger* is the Mont de Venus.

∵ There are two others: one between the thumb and index finger, called the Mont de Mercure, and one opposite called the Mont de Lune. (*See* FINGER.)

Mont de Piété. A pawn *depôt*. These *depôts*, called "*monti di pietà*" (charity loans), were first instituted under Leo X., at Rome, by charitable persons who wished to rescue the poor and needy from usurious money-lenders. They advanced small sums of money on the security of pledges, at a rate of interest barely sufficient to cover the working expenses of the institution. Both the name and system were introduced into France and Spain. The model Loan Fund of Ireland is formed on the same system. Public granaries for the sale of corn are called in Italian *Monti frumentarii*. "Monte" means a public or State loan; hence also a "bank."

Mont St. Michel, in Normandy, formerly called Belen. Here nine Druidesses sold to sailors the arrows to charm away storms. The arrows had to be discharged by a young man twenty-one years old.

Montagnards [the *mountain party*]. The extreme democratic politicians in the French Revolution; so called because they occupied the highest tier of benches in the hall of the National Convention. The opposite party sat on the level of the floor, called the "plain."

Mon'tague (3 syl.). The head of a faction in Vero'na (*Shakespeare: Romeo and Juliet*). The device of the family

is a *mountain* with *sharply-peaked* crest (*mont-agu* or *acu*).

Monta'nists. Heretics of the second century; so called from Monta'nus, a Phrygian, who asserted that he had received from the Holy Ghost special knowledge that had not been vouchsafed to the apostles.

Montan'to. *Signior Montanto.* A master of fence rather than a soldier; a tongue-doughty knight. It is a word of fence, and hence Ben Jonson says, "Your *punto*, your *reverso*, your *stoccata*, your *imbrocata*, your *passada*, your *montanto*." (*Every Man in his Humour*.)

Monteer Cap. So called from *monteros d'Espinoza* (mountaineers), who once formed the interior guard of the palace of the Spanish king. The way they came to be appointed is thus accounted for:—Sanchica, wife of Don Sancho Garcia, Count of Castile, entered into a plot to poison her husband, but one of the mountaineers of Espinoza revealed the plot and saved the count's life. Ever after the sovereigns of Castile recruited their body-guards from men of this estate.

Monteith'. A scalloped basin to cool and wash glasses in; a sort of punch-bowl, made of silver or pewter, with a movable rim scalloped at the top; so called from its inventor.

> "New things produce new names, and thus Monteith
> Has by one vessel saved his name from death."
>   *King.*

Montem. A custom formerly observed every three years by the boys of Eton school, who proceeded on Whit Tuesday *ad montem* (to a mound called Salt Hill), near the Bath Road, and exacted a gratuity called *salt* from all who passed by. Sometimes as much as £1,000 was thus collected. The custom was abolished in 1847.

Monte'ro-cap (*A*) properly means a huntsman's cap; but Sir Walter Scott tells us that Sir Jeffrey Hudson wore "a large Montero hat," meaning a Spanish hat with a feather. (*Peveril of the Peak*, chap. xxxv.)

Montesi'nos (*The Cave of*). Close to the castle of Rochafrida, to which a knight of the same name, who had received some cause of offence at the French court, retired. Tradition ascribes the river Guadia'na to this cave as its source, whence the river is sometimes called Montesinos.

Montezu'ma's Realm. Mexico. Montezuma, the last emperor, was seized by Cortes, and compelled to acknowledge himself a vassal of Spain (1519).

Montezu'ma's Watch. A curious stone, weighing twenty-four tons, of basaltic porphyry, in Mexico. This immense stone is cut into figures denoting the Mexican division of time, and may be termed their calendar.

Montfaucon Watch (*A*). "*Le guet de Montfaucon.*" A man hanged. Montfaucon is an eminence near Paris, once used as the Tyburn or place of execution. At one time it was crowded with gibbets, but at the Revolution they were destroyed, and it became the dustbin of the city, "*Une voirie pour les immondices de Paris et l'éscarrissage des chevaux.*" In 1841 this sink of corruption and infection was moved to "*La plaine des Vertus,*" surely a strange satire on the word.

Montgomery, in North Wales; so called from Roger de Montgomery, Earl of Shrewsbury, who won the castle of Baldwyn, lieutenant of the marchès to William the Conqueror. Before this time it was called "Tre Faldwyn."

Montgomery's division, all on one side. This is a French proverb, and refers to the Free Companies of the sixteenth century, of which Montgomery was a noted chief. The booty he took was all given to his banditti, and nothing was left to the victims. (*See* LION'S SHARE.)

Month of Sundays (*A*). An indefinite long time; never. (*See* NEVER.)

"Such another chance might never turn up in a month of Sundays."—*Boldrewood: Robbery Under Arms,* chap. xl.

Month's Mind (*A*). An irresistible longing (for something); a great desire.

"I see you have a month's mind for them."—*Shakespeare: Two Gentlemen of Verona,* i. 2.

Months.

January. So called from "Janus," the Roman deity that kept the gates of heaven. The image of Janus is represented with two faces looking opposite ways. One face is *old,* and is emblematical of time past; the other *young,* as the emblem of time future. The Dutch used to call this month *Lauw-maand* (frosty-month); the Saxons, *Wulf-monath,* because wolves were very troublesome then from the great scarcity of food. After the introduction of Christianity, the name was changed to *Se æftera geóla* (the after-yule); it was also

called *Forma-monath* (first month). In the French Republican calendar it was called *Nivôse* (snow-month, December 20th to 20th January).

February. So called from "Februa," a name of Juno, from the Sabine word *februo* (to purify). Juno was so called because she presided over the purification of women, which took place in this month. The Dutch used to term the month *Spokkel-maand* (vegetation-month); the ancient Saxons, *Sprote-cál* (from the sprouting of pot-wort or kele); they changed it subsequently to *Sol-monath* (from the returning sun). In the French Republican calendar it was called *Pluviôse* (rain-month, 20th January to 20th February).

March. So called from "Mars," the Roman war-god and patron deity. The old Dutch name for it was *Lent-maand* (lengthening-month), because the days sensibly lengthen; the old Saxon name was *Hrêth-monath* (rough month, from its boisterous winds); the name was subsequently changed to *Length-monath* (lengthening month); it was also called *Hlýd-monath* (boisterous-month). In the French Republican calendar it was called *Ventôse* (windy-month, February 20th to March 20th).

April. So called from the Latin *aperio* (to open), in allusion to the unfolding of the leaves. The old Dutch name was *Gras-maand* (grass-month); the old Saxon, *Easter-monath* (orient or paschal-month). In the French Republican calendar it was called *Germinal* (the time of budding, March 21st to the 19th of April).

May is the old Latin *magius,* softened into *maius,* similar to the Sanskrit *mah* (to grow), that is, the growing-month. The old Dutch name was *Blou-maand* (blossoming month); the Old Saxon, *Tri-milchi* (three milch), because cows were milked thrice a day in this month. In the French Republican calendar the month was called *Floréal* (the time of flowers, April 20th to May 20th).

June. So called from the "junio'res" or soldiers of the state, not from Juno, the queen-goddess. The old Dutch name was *Zomer-maand* (summer-month); the old Saxon, *Sere-monath* (dry-month), and *Lida-ærra* (joy-time). In the French Republican calendar the month was called *Prairial* (meadow-month, May 20th to June 18th).

July. Mark Antony gave this month the name of Julius, from Julius Cæsar, who was born in it. It had been previously called *Quinti'lis* (fifth-month).

The old Dutch name for it was *Hooy-maand* (hay-month) ; the old Saxon, *Mæd-monath* (because the cattle were turned into the meadows to feed), and *Lida æftevr* (the second mild or genial month). In the French Republican calendar it was called *Messidor* (harvest-month, June 19th to July 18th).

August. So called in honour of Augustus Cæsar : not because it was his birth-month, but because it was the month in which he entered upon his first consulship, celebrated three triumphs, received the oath of allegiance from the legions which occupied the Janic'ulum, reduced Egypt, and put an end to the civil wars. He was born in September. The old Dutch name for August was *Oost-vaand* (harvest-month) ; the old Saxon, *Weod-monath* (weed-month, where weed signifies vegetation in general. In the French Republican calendar it was called *Ther-midor* (hot-month, July 19th to August 17th).

September. The seventh month from March, where the year used to commence. The old Dutch name was *Herst-maand* (autumn-month) ; the old Saxon, *Gerst-monath* (barley-month), or *Hærfest-monath ;* and after the introduction of Christianity *Halig - monath* (holy-month, the nativity of the Virgin Mary being on the 8th, the exaltation of the Cross on the 14th, Holy-Rood Day on the 26th, and St. Michael's Day on the 29th). In the French Republican calendar it was called *Fructidor* (fruit-month, August 18th to September 21st).

October. The eighth month of the Alban calendar. The old Dutch name was *Wyn-maand ;* the Old Saxon, *Win-monath* (wine-month, or the time of vintage) ; it was also called *Teo-monath* (tenth - month), and *Winter - fylleth* (winter full-moon). In the French Republican calendar it was called *Vendémiaire* (time of vintage, September 22nd to October 21st).

November. The ninth Alban month. The old Dutch name was *Slaght-maand* (slaughter-month, the time when the beasts were slain and salted down for winter use) ; the old Saxon, *Wind-monath* (wind-month, when the fishermen drew their boats ashore, and gave over fishing till the next spring) ; it was also called *Blot-monath*—the same as *Slaght-maand*. In the French Republican calendar it was called *Brumaire* (fog-month, October 22nd to November 21st).

December. The tenth month of the old Alban calendar. The old Dutch name was *Winter-maand* (winter-month) ; the old Saxon, *Mid-winter-monath* (mid-winter-month) ; whereas June was *Mid-sumor-monath*. Christian Saxons called December *Se ura geóla* (the anti-yule). In the French Republican calendar it was called *Frimaire* (hoar-frost month, from November 22nd to December 20th).

Monthawi *(Al),* [*the destroyer*]. One of Mahomet's lances, confiscated from the Jews when they were exiled from Medi'na.

Montjoie St. Denis. The war-cry of the French. *Montjoie* is a corruption of *Mons Jovis,* as the little mounds were called which served as direction-posts in ancient times ; hence it was applied to whatever showed or indicated the way, as the banner of St. Denis, called the Oriflamme. The Burgundians had for their war-cry, "Montjoie St. André ; " the dukes of Bourbon, " Montjoie Notre Dame ; " and the kings of England used to have "Montjoie St. George." There seems no sufficient reason to suppose that Montjoie St. Denis is a corruption of "St. Denis mon joie"— *i.e.* "St. Denis is my hope."

Montjoie. The cry of the French heralds in the ancient tournaments ; and the title of the French king-of-arms.

Montrognon *(Baron of),* Lord of Bourglastie, Tortebesse, and elsewhere. A huge mass of muscle, who existed only to eat and drink. He was a descendant of Esau on his father's side, and of Gargantua on his mother's. He once performed a gigantic feat—he killed six hundred Saracens who happened to get in his way as he was going to dinner. He was bandy-legged, could lift immense weights, had an elastic stomach, and four rows of teeth. In *Croquemitaine* he is made one of the paladins of Charlemagne, and was one of the four knights sent in search of Croquemitaine and Fear-fortress.

Montserrat. The Catalonians aver that this mountain was riven and shattered at the Crucifixion. Every rift is filled with evergreens. Similar legends exist with regard to many other mountains. (Latin, *mons serra'tus,* the mountain jagged like a saw.)

Monumental City. Baltimore, U.S., is so called because it abounds in monuments : witness the obelisk, the 104 churches, etc.

Monumental Effigies. In the age of chivalry the woman in monumental brasses and effigies is placed on the man's right hand; but when chivalry declined she was placed on his left hand.

Monumental Figures. No. 1.

(1) Those in stone, with plain sloping roofs, and without inscriptions, are the oldest.

(2) In 1160 these plain prismatic roofs began to be ornamented.

(3) In the same century the sloping roofs gave place to armorial bearings.

(4) In the thirteenth century we see flat roofs, and figures carved on the lids.

(5) The next stage was an arch, built over the monument to protect it.

(6) The sixth stage was a chapel annexed to the church.

(7) The last stage was the head bound and feet tied, with children at the base, or cherubims at the feet.

Monumental Figures. No. 2.

Figures with their hands on their breasts, and chalices, represent *priests*.

Figures with crozier, mitre, and pontificals, represent *prelates*.

Figures with armour represent *knights*.

Figures with legs crossed represent either *crusaders* or *married men*.

Female figures with a mantle and large ring represent *nuns*.

Monumental Figures. No. 3.

Those in *scale* armour are the most ancient (time, Henry II.).

Those in *chain* armour or ring-mail come next (time, Richard I. to Henry III.).

Those with children or cherubims, between the fourteenth and seventeenth centuries.

Brasses are for the most part subsequent to the thirteenth century.

Monumental Figures. No. 4.

Saints lie to the east of the altar, and are elevated above the ground; the higher the elevation, the greater the sanctity. Martyrs are much elevated.

Holy men not canonised lie on a level with the pavement.

Founders of chapels, etc., lie with their monument built into the wall.

Monumental Inscriptions.

Capital letters and Latin inscriptions are of the first twelve centuries.

Lombardic capitals and French inscriptions, of the thirteenth century,

German text, of the fourteenth century.

English and Roman print, subsequent to the fourteenth century.

Tablets against the wall came in with the Reformation.

Moohel. A Jew whose office it is to circumcise the young Jewish boys.

Moon means "measurer" of time (Anglo-Saxon, *móna*, masc. gen.). It is masculine in all the Teutonic languages; in the Edda the *son* of Mundilfori is Mâni (moon), and *daughter* Sôl (*sun*); so it is still with the Lithuanians and Arabians, and so was it with the ancient Mexicans, Slavi, Hindus, etc. ; so that it was a most unlucky dictum of Harris, in his *Hermes*, that all nations ascribe to the Sun a masculine, and to the Moon a feminine gender. (Gothic, *mena*, masc. ; Sanskrit, *mâs*, masc., from *mâ*, to measure.) The Sanskrit *mâtram* is an instrument for measuring; hence Greek *metron*; French, *metre;* English, *meter*. The Germans have *Frau Sonne* (Mrs. Sun) and *Herr Mond* (Mr. Moon).

Moon, represented in five different phases: (1) new; (2) full; (3) crescent or decrescent; (4) half; and (5) gibbous, or more than half.

Moon, in pictures of the Assumption of the Virgin, is represented as a crescent under her feet; in the Crucifixion it is eclipsed, and placed on one side of the cross, the sun being on the other; in the Creation and Last Judgment it is also introduced by artists.

Hecate. The moon before she has risen and after she has set.

Astarte. The crescent moon, "the moon with crescent horns."

Diana. The moon in the open vault of heaven, who "hunts the clouds."

Cynthia. Same as Diana.

Selenē or *Luna.* The moon personified, properly the full moon, who loved the sleeping Endymion.

Endymion. Moonlight on a bank, field, or garden.

"How sweet the moonlight sleeps upon this bank!" *Shakespeare: Merchant of Venice,* v. 1.

Phœbe. The moon as the sister of the sun. (*See* ASTARTE, ASHTAROTH, etc.).

Moon. Astolpho found treasured in the moon everything wasted on this earth, such as misspent time and wealth, broken vows, unanswered prayers, fruitless tears, abortive attempts, unfulfilled desires and intentions, etc. All bribes were hung on gold and silver hooks; prince's favours were kept in bellows; wasted talent was kept in vases, each marked with the proper name; etc. *Orlando Furioso,* bk. xviii. (See *Rape of the Lock,* c. v.)

Moon. (*See under* MAHOMET.)

The moon is called "*triform,*" because it presents itself to us either round, or waxing with horns towards the east, or waning with horns towards the west.

Island of the moon. Madagascar is so named by the natives.

Minions of the moon. Thieves who rob by night. (See 1 *Henry IV.*, i. 2.)

Mountains of the Moon means simply White Mountains. The Arabs call a white horse "moon-coloured." (*Jackson.*)

He cries for the moon. He craves to have what is wholly beyond his reach. The allusion is to foolish children who want the moon for a plaything. The French say "He wants to take the moon between his teeth" ("*Il veut prendre la lune avec le dents*"), alluding to the old proverb about "the moon," and a "green cheese."

To cast beyond the moon. To make extravagant conjectures; to cast your thoughts or guesses beyond all reason.

To level at the moon. To be very ambitious; to aim in shooting at the moon.

You have found an elephant in the moon —found a mare's nest. Sir Paul Neal, a conceited virtuoso of the seventeenth century, gave out that he had discovered "an elephant in the moon." It turned out that a mouse had crept into his telescope, which had been mistaken for an elephant in the moon. Samuel Butler has a satirical poem on the subject called *The Elephant in the Moon.*

You would have me believe, I suppose, that the moon is a green cheese—i.e. the most absurd thing possible. A green cheese is a cream cheese which is eaten green or fresh, and is not kept to mature like other cheeses.

Man in the moon. (*See* MAN.)

Hares sacred to the moon, not because Diana was a great huntress, but because the Hindus affirm that the outline of a hare is distinctly visible on the moon.

Once in a blue moon. (*See* BLUE.)

Moon-calf is an inanimate, shapeless mass (*Pliny: Natural History*, x. 64). This abortion was supposed to be produced by the influence of the moon. The primary meaning of calf is not the young of a cow, but the issue arising "from throwing out," as a push, a protuberance; hence the calves of the legs.

"A false conception, called *mola, i.e.* moon-calf . . . a lump of flesh without shape or life."—*Holland: Pliny*, vii. 15.

Moon-drop. In Latin, *virus lunāre*, a vaporous drop supposed to be shed by the moon on certain herbs and other objects, when influenced by incantations.

"Upon the corner of the moon,
There hangs a vaporous drop profound;
I'll catch it ere it come to ground."
Shakespeare: Macbeth, iii. 5.

Moon-maker [*Sagendë Nah*], a surname given to the Veiled Prophet (*q.v.*), who caused a moon to issue from a deep well, so brilliant that the real moon was eclipsed by it.

Moon-rakers. The people of Wiltshire are so called. In the "good old times" they were noted smugglers, and one day, seeing the coastguard on the watch, they sunk in the sea some smuggled whisky. When they supposed the coast was clear they employed rakes to get their goods in hand again, when lo! the coastguard reappeared and demanded of them what they were doing. Pointing to the reflection of the moon in the water, they replied, "We are trying to rake out that cream-cheese yonder."

Moon's Men. Thieves and highwaymen who ply their trade by night.

"The fortune of us that are but Moon's-men doth ebb and flow like the sea."—*Shakespeare:* 1 *Henry IV.*, i. 2.

Moonlight Flitting (*A*). A clandestine removal of one's furniture during the night, to avoid paying one's rent or having the furniture seized in payment thereof.

Moonstone. A mineral so called on account of the play of light which it exhibits. Wilkie Collins has a novel called *The Moonstone.*

"The moonstone contains bluish-white spots, which, when held to the light, present a . . . . silvery play of colour not unlike that of the moon."—*Ure: Chemical Dictionary.*

Moor-slayer or **Mata-moros.** A name given to St. James, the patron-saint of Spain, because in almost all encounters with the Moors he came on his white horse to the aid of the Christians. So, at least, it is said.

Moors. In the Middle Ages, the Europeans called all Mahometans *Moors*, in the same manner as the Eastern nations called all inhabitants of Europe *Franks*. Camoens, in the *Lusiad*, terms the Indians "Moors." (Bk. viii.)

Moore (*Thomas*), called "Anacreon Moore," because the character of his poetry resembles that of Anacreon, the Greek poet of love and wine. He also translated Anacreon's *Odes*. (1779-1852.)

Moot Point (*A*). A doubtful or unsettled question. The Anglo-Saxon *motian* is "to debate," and a moot point is one *sub judice*, or under debate.

Moots were debates which formerly took place in the halls and libraries of Inns of Court. The benchers and the barristers, as well as the students, took an active part in these moots. Sir Simonds D'Ewes, in his *Diary* (1625-1629), says :

"I had lived mooted in law French before I was called to the bar."—*Nineteenth Century*, November, 1892, p. 775.

Mop. In many places statute fairs are held, where servants seek to be hired. Carters fasten to their hats a piece of whipcord ; shepherds, a lock of wool ; grooms, a piece of sponge, etc. When hired they mount a cockade with streamers. Some few days after the statute fair, a second, called a Mop, is held for the benefit of those not already hired. This fair mops or wipes up the refuse of the statute fair, carrying away the dregs of the servants left.

Mop. One of Queen Mab's attendants. *All mops and brooms.* Intoxicated.

Mora-stone, near Upsa'la, where the Swedes used anciently to elect their kings.

Moral. *The moral Gower.* John Gower, the poet, is so called by Chaucer. (1320-1402.)

Father of moral philosophy. Thomas Aqui'nas (1227-1274).

Moralist. *The great moralist of Fleet Street.* Dr. Johnson (1709-1784).

Moran's Collar which strangled the wearer if he deviated from the strict rules of equity. Moran was the wise councillor of Feredach the Just, an early king of Ireland, before the Christian era. Of course, the collar is an allegory of obvious meaning.

Morasteen [*great stone*]. The ancient Danes selected their king from the sacred line of royalty. The man chosen was taken to the Landsthing, or local court, and placed on the morasteen, while the magnates ranged themselves around on stones of inferior size. This was the Danish mode of installation.

Morat. *Morat and Marathon twin names shall stand* (*Childe Harold*, iii. 64). Morat, in Switzerland, is famous for the battle fought in 1476, in which the Swiss defeated Charles le Téméraire of Burgundy.

Moratorium. A legal permission to defer for a stated time the payment of a bond, debt, cheque, or other obligation. This is done to enable the creditor to pull himself round by borrowing money, selling effects, or otherwise raising funds to satisfy obligations. The device was adopted in 1891 in the Argentine Republics during the money panic caused by

the Baring Brothers' "difficulty," a default of some twenty millions sterling.

Mora'vians or *Bohemian Brethren.* A religious community tracing its origin from John Huss, expelled by persecution from Bohemia and Moravia in the eighteenth century. They are often called *The United Brethren.*

Morbleu ! (French). A corruption of *Mort de Dieu.* (*See* VENTRE ST. GRIS.)

More. *To be no more.* To exist no longer ; to be dead.

"Cassius is no more."
Shakespeare : Julius Cæsar.

More Kicks than Ha'pence. Like the monkey which plays tricks for his master. The monkey gets the kicks and the master the ha'pence.

More Last Words. When Richard Baxter lost his wife, he published a broadsheet, headed *Last Words of Mrs. Baxter,* which had an immense sale. The printer, for his own profit, brought out a spurious broadsheet, headed *More Last Words ;* but Baxter issued a small handbill with this concise sentence : "Mrs. Baxter did not say anything else."

More of More Hall. A logondary hero who armed himself with an armour of spikes ; and, concealing himself in the cave where the dragon of Wantley dwelt, slew the monster by kicking it on the mouth, where alone it was mortal.

More the Merrier (*The*). The author of this phrase was Henry Parrot.

More one has, the More he Desires (*The*). In French, *Plus il en a, plus il en veut.* In Latin, *Quo plus habent, eo plus cupiunt.*

"My more having would be a source
To make me hunger more."
Shakespeare : Macbeth, iv. 3.

More'no (3 syl.). Don Antonio Mo-rēno, a gentleman of Barcelo'na, who entertained Don Quixote with mock-heroic hospitality.

Morestone. *Would you remove More-stone ?* (*See* MORTSTONE.)

Morgan le Fay. (*See below.*) W. Morris, in his *Earthly Paradise* (August), makes Morgan the bride of Ogier the Dane, after his earthly career was ended.

Morgan le Fay, Morgaine la Fée, or **Morgana the Fairy.** Daughter of Queen Igrayne, and half-sister of King Arthur, who revealed to him the intrigues of Sir Lancelot and Guinever.

She gave him a cup containing a magic draught, and Arthur had no sooner drunk it than his eyes were opened to the perfidy of his wife and friend.

Morganat'ic Marriage (*A*). A marriage in which the wife does not take the husband's rank, because legally, or according to court bye-laws, the marriage is not recognised. This sort of marriage is effected when a man of high rank marries a woman of inferior position. The children in this case do not inherit the title or entails of the father. The word is based on the Gothic *morgjan*, "to curtail" or "limit;" and the marriage settlement was called *morgengabe* or *morgengnade*, whence the Low Latin *matrimonium ad legem morganaticam*, in which the dowry is to be considered all the portion the wife will receive, as the estates cannot pass to her or to her children.

A morganatic marriage is called "left-handed," because a man pledges his troth with his left hand instead of his right. The "hand-fasted" marriages of Scotland and Ireland were morganatic, and the "hand-fasted" bride could be put away for a fresh union.

Morgane (2 syl.). A fay to whose charge Zephyr committed young Passelyon and his cousin Bennucq. Passelyon fell in love with Morgane's daughter, and the adventures of these young lovers are related in the romance of *Perceforest*, vol. iii. (*See* MORGAN.)

Morgans. A Stock Exchange term, signifying the French 6 per cents., which were floated by the Morgans.

Morgan'te. A ferocious giant, converted by Orlando to Christianity. After performing the most wonderful feats, he died at last from the bite of a crab. (*See below*.)

Morgante Maggio're. A serio-comic romance in verse, by Pulci, of Florence (1494). He was the inventor of this species of poetry, called by the French *bernesque*, from Berni, who greatly excelled in it. Translated by Byron.

Morgia'na. The clever, faithful, female slave of Ali Baba, who pries into the forty jars, and discovers that every jar, but one, contains a man. She takes oil from the only one containing it, and, having made it boiling hot, pours enough into each jar to kill the thief concealed there. At last she kills the captain of the gang, and marries her master's son. (*Arabian Nights: Ali Baba and the Forty Thieves.*)

Morglay. A sword (*glave de la mort*, the sword of Sir Bevis of Southampton), a generic name for a sword. (*See* SWORD.)

"Had I been accompanied with my Toledo or Morglay."—*Every Woman in her Humour.*
"Carrying their morglays in their hands."—*Beaumont and Fletcher: Honest Man.*

Morgue, a dead-house, is generally associated with *mors* (death); but this is a blunder, as the word means *visage*, and was first applied to prison vestibules, where new criminals were placed to be scrutinised, that the prison officials might become familiar with their faces and general appearance.

"On me conduit donc au petit chastelet, où du guichet estant passé dans la morgue, un homme gros, court, et carré, vint à moy."—*Assoucy: La Prison de M. Dassouch* (1674), p. 35.
"Morgue. Endroit où l'on tient quelque temps ceux que l'on ecroue, afin que les guichetiers puissent les reconnaître ensuit."—*Fleming and Tibbins*, vol. ii. p. 688.

Morgue la Faye, who watched over the birth of Ogier the Dane, and after he had finished his earthly career, restored him to perpetual youth, and took him to live with her in everlasting love in the isle and castle of Av'alon.

Moribund. Declining; in a dying state; on its last legs. Turkey is called a moribund state. Institutions on the decline are called moribund. Applied to institutions, commercial companies, states, etc. (Latin, *moribundus*, ready to die.)

Moriso'nianism. The religious system of James Morison, the chief peculiarities being the doctrines of universal atonement, and the ability of man unaided to receive or reject the Gospel. James Morison, in 1841, separated from the "United Secession," now merged into the "United Presbyterian." The Morisonians call themselves the "Evangelical Union."

Morley (*Mrs.*). The name under which Queen Anne corresponded with Mrs. Freeman (the Duchess of Marlborough).

Morma, in Pepys's *Diary*, is Elizabeth, daughter of John Dickens, who died October 22nd, 1662.

Mormon. The last of a pretended line of Hebrew prophets, and the pretended author of *The Book of Mormon*, or *Golden Bible*, written on golden plates. This work was in reality written by the Rev. Solomon Spalding, but was claimed by Joseph Smith as a direct revelation to him by the angel Mormon. Spalding died in 1816; Smith, 1844.

Mormon Creed. (1) God is a person with the form and flesh of man. (2) Man is a part of the substance of God, and will himself become a god. (3) Man was not created by God, but existed from all eternity, and will never cease to exist. (4) There is no such thing as original or birth sin. (5) The earth is only one of many inhabited spheres. (6) God is president of men made gods, angels, good men, and spirits waiting to receive a tabernacle of flesh. (7) Man's household of wives is his kingdom not for earth only, but also in his future state. (8) Mormonism is the kingdom of God on earth. (*W. Hepworth Dixon : New America*, i. 24.)

Mormonism. The religious and social system of the Latter-day Saints; so called from their gospel, termed *The Book of Mormon.* Joe Smith, the founder of the system, was born in Sharon, Windsor county, Vermont; his partner was Rigdon. The manuscript, which he declared to be written on gold plates, was a novel written by Spalding. He was cited thirty-nine times into courts of law, and was at last assassinated by a gang of ruffians, who broke into his prison at Carthage, and shot him like a dog. His wife's name was Emma; he lived at Nauvoo, in Illinois; his successor was Brigham Young, a carpenter by trade, who led the "Saints" (as the Mormons are called), driven from home by force, to the valley of the Salt Lake, 1,500 miles distant, generally called Utah, but by the Mormons themselves *Deseret* (Bee-country), the New Jerusalem. Abraham is their model man, and Sarai their model woman, and English their language. Young's house was called the Bee-hive. Every man, woman, and child capable of work has work to do in the community.

Morning. The first glass of whisky drunk by Scotch fishermen in salutation to the dawn. Thus one fisherman will say to another, "Hae ye had your morning, Tam?" or "I haena had my morning, yet, Jock."

"Having declined Mrs. Flockhart's compliment of a 'morning,' . . . he made his adieus."—*Sir W. Scott : Waverley*, chap. xliv.

Morning Star of the Reformation. John Wycliffe (1324-1384).

Morocco. The name of Banks's bay horse. (*See* BANKS *and* HORSE.)

Morocco. Strong ale made from burnt malt, used in the annual feast at Sevenhalls, Westmoreland (the seat of the Hon. Mary Howard), on the opening of Milnthorpe Fair. This liquor is put into a large glass of unique form, and the person whose turn it is to drink is called the "colt." He is required to stand on one leg, and say "Luck to Sevens as long as Kent flows," then drain the glass to the bottom, or forfeit one shilling. The act is termed "drinking the constable." The feast consists of radishes, oaten cake, and butter.

Morocco Men (*The*). Public-house and perambulating touts for lottery insurances. Their rendezvous was a tavern in Oxford Market, on the Portland estate, at the close of the eighteenth century. In 1796 the great State lottery employed 7,500 Morocco men to dispose of their tickets.

Moros. The fool in the play entitled *The Longer Thou Livest the More Fool Thou Art*, by William Wager.

Morpheus (2 syl., *the Sleeper*). Son of Sleep, and god of dreams : so called because he gives these airy nothings their form and fashion.

Morrel. One of the shepherds in the *Shepherd's Calendar*, by Spenser.

Morrice (*Gil* or *Child*). The natural son of an earl and the wife of Lord Barnard or John Stewart, "brought forth in her father's house wi' mickle sin and shame," and brought up "in the gude grene wode." One day he sent Willie to the baron's hall, requesting his mother to come without delay to Greenwood, and by way of token sent with him a "gay mantel" made by herself. Willie went into the dinner-hall, and blurted out his message before all who were present, adding, "and there is the silken sarke your ain hand sewd the sleive." Lord Barnard, thinking the Child to be a paramour of his wife, forbade her to leave the hall, and, riding himself to Greenwood, slew Morrice with a broadsword, and setting his head on a spear, gave it to "the meanest man in a' his train" to carry it to the lady. When the baron returned Lady Barnard said to him, "Wi' that same spear, O pierce my heart, and put me out o' pain;" but the baron replied, "Enouch of blood by me's bin spilt. sair, sair I rew the deid," adding—

"I'll ay lament for Gil Morice,
As gin he were mine ain ;
I'll neir forget the dreiry day
On which the youth was slain."
Reliques of Ancient English Poetry, ser. iii. 1.

Dr. Percy says this pathetic tale suggested to Home the plot of *Douglas* (a tragedy).

Morris Dance, brought to England in the reign of Edward III., when John of Gaunt returned from Spain. In the dance, bells were jingled, and staves or swords clashed. It was a military dance of the Moors or Moriscos, in which five men and a boy engaged; the boy wore a *morione'* or head-piece, and was called Mad Morion. (*See* MAID MARIAN.)

Morse Alphabet (*The*). An alphabet used in telegraphic messages, invented by Professor Samuel F. B. Morse, of Massachusetts. The right-hand deflection of the electric needle corresponds to a dash, and the left-hand to a dot; and by means of dashes and dots every word may be spelt at length. Military signalling is performed in England by short and long flashes of a flag or some other instrument; the short flash corresponds with the dot, and the long with the dash. The following ten varieties will show how these two symbols are capable of endless combinations, · | · · | ·· · | · · · · | · · · · · | — | · — | — · | · · — | — · · | etc.

Mort-safe. A wrought-iron frame to prevent dead bodies from being exhumed by resurrectionists. (See *Notes and Queries,* March 14th, 1891, p. 210.)

Mortal. *I saw a mortal lot of people* —*i.e.* a vast number. Mortal is the French *à mort,* as in the sentence, "*Il y avait du monde à mort.*" Legonidec says, "*Ce mot* [mort] *ne s'emploie jamais au propre, mais seulement au figuré, avec la signification de multitude, grand nombre, foule.*"

Mortar-board. A college cap. A corruption of the French *mortier,* the cap worn by the ancient kings of France, and still used officially by the chief justice or president of the court of justice. As a college cap has a square board on the top, the mortier-board was soon transformed into mortar-board.

Mortars differ from guns, in having their trunnions placed behind the vent. They are short pieces, intended to project shells at high angles (45°), and the shells thus projected fall almost vertically on the object struck, forcing in the strongest buildings, and (bursting at the same time) firing everything around. Their splinters are very destructive.

Morte d'Arthur, compiled by Sir Thomas Malory, from French originals; edited by Southey, the poet-laureate. The compilation contains—
The Prophecies of Merlin,

The Quest of the St. Graal.
The Romance of Sir Lancelot of the Lake.
The History of Sir Tristram; etc. etc.
Tennyson has a *Morte d'Arthur* among his poems.

Mortgage. (*See* WELSH MORTGAGE.)

Morther. *Well, Mor, where have you been this long while?* (Norfolk). *I'sy, Mor, come hither!* (Norfolk). Mor or Morther means a lass, a wench. It is the Dutch *moer* (a woman). In Norfolk they call a lad a *bor,* from the Dutch *boer* (a farmer), English *boor.* "Well, bor!" and "Well, mor!" are to be heard daily in every part of the county.

> "When once a giggling morther you,
>   And I a red-faced chubby boy,
> Sly tricks you played me not a few,
>   For mischief was your greatest joy."
>   *Bloomfield: Richard and Kate.*

Mor'timer. So called from an ancestor in crusading times, noted for his exploits on the shores of the Dead Sea. (*De Mortuo Mari.*)

Mortlake Tapestry. The best English tapestry made at Mortlake (Middlesex), in the reign of James I.

> "Why, lady, do you think me
> Wrought in a loom, some Dutch-piece weaved at Mortlake?"   *City Match.*

Mortstone. *He may remove Mortstone.* A Devonshire proverb, said incredulously of husbands who pretend to be masters of their wives. It also means, "If you have done what you say, you can accomplish anything."

Morven. Fingal's realm; probably Argyllshire and its neighbourhood.

Mosa'ic Work is not connected with the proper name Moses, but with the Muses (Latin, *opus muse'um, musium,* or *musivum;* Greek, *mouseion;* French, *mosaïque;* Italian, *mosaïco*). Pliny says it was so called because these tesselated floors were first used in the grottoes consecrated to the Muses (xxxv. 21, s. 42). The most famous workman in mosaic work was Sosus of Per'gamos, who wrought the rich pavement in the common-hall, called Asaroton œcon. (*Pliny: Natural History,* xxxvi. 4, 64.)

Moscow. So called from the river Moscowa, on which it is built.
The monarch of Moscow. A large bell weighing 193 tons, 21 feet high, and 21 feet in diameter.
[*So-and-So*] *was my Moscow.* The turning-point of my good fortune, leading to future shoals and misery. The

reference is to Napoleon's disastrous expedition, when his star hastened to its setting.

"Juan was my Moscow [the ruin of my reputation]." *Byron: Don Juan,* xi. 56.

Mosen (Spanish). A corruption of Mio Señor, corresponding to the Castilian *Don.*

Moses' Horns. Exodus xxxiv. 30, "All the children of Israel saw Moses, and the skin of his face *shone,*" translated in the Vulgate, "*Cornūta esset facies sua.*" Rays of light were called horns. Hence in Habakkuk (iii. 4) we read of God, "His brightness was as the light, and He had horns [*rays of light*] coming out of His hand." Michel Angelo depicted Moses with horns, following the Vulgate.

The French translation of Habacuc, iii. 4 is:— "*Sa splendeur etait comme la lumière meme, et des rayons sortaient de sa main.*"

Moses' Rod. So the divining-rod was usually [called. The divining-rod was employed to discover water or mineral treasure. In *Blackwood's Magazine* (May, 1850) we are told that nobody sinks a well in North Somersetshire without consulting the *jowser* (as the rod-diviner is called). The Abbé Richard is stated in the *Monde* to be an extremely expert diviner of water, and amongst others discovered the "Christmas Fountain" on M. de Metternich's estate, in 1863. In the *Quarterly Review* (No. 44) we have an account of Lady Noel's divining skill. (See *World of Wonders,* pt. ix. p. 283.)

Moses Slow of Speech. The account given in the *Talmud* (vi.) is as follows:—Pharaoh was one day sitting on his throne with Moses on his lap, when the child took off the king's crown and put it on his own head. The "wise men" tried to persuade the king that this was treason, for which the child ought to be put to death; but Jethro, priest of Midian, replied, "It is the act of a child who knows no better. Let two plates" (he continued) "be set before him, one containing gold and the other red-hot coals, and you will readily see he will prefer the latter to the former." The experiment being tried, the little boy snatched up the live coal, put it into his mouth, and burnt his tongue so severely that he was ever after "heavy or slow of speech."

Moses Primrose. Son of the Rev. Dr. Primrose, very green, and with a good opinion of himself. He is chiefly known for his wonderful bargain with a

Jew at the neighbouring fair, when he gave a good horse in exchange for a gross of worthless green spectacles, with copper rims and shagreen cases. (*Goldsmith : Vicar of Wakefield.*)

Mos'lem or **Moslemin.** Plural of Mussulman, sometimes written Mussulmans. The word is Turkish, and means *true believer.*

Mosse. *Napping, as Mosse took his mare.* Wilbraham says Mosse took his mare napping, because he could not catch her when awake.

"Till day come, catch him as Mosse his grey mare, napping."—*Christmas Prince.*

Mosstrooper. A robber, a bandit. The marauders who infested the borders of England and Scotland were so called because they encamped on the *mosses.*

Mote and Beam (Matt. vii. 3-5). *In alio pedicŭlum video, in te rĭcinum non vides* (Petronius). Here *pediculum* means a louse, and *ricinum* a tyke.

Moth. Page to Don Adriano de Arma'do, all jest and playfulness, cunning and versatile. (*Shakespeare : Love's Labour's Lost.*)

Mother. *Mother and Head of all Churches.* So is St. John Lateran of Rome called. It occupies the site of the splendid palace of Plantius Latera'nus, which escheated to the Crown from treason, and was given to the Church by the Emperor Constantine. From the balcony of this church the Pope blesses the people of the whole world.

Mother Ann. Ann Lee, the "spiritual mother" of the Shakers. (1735-1784.)

Mother Bunch. (1) Mother Bunch whose fairy tales are notorious. These tales are in *Pasquil's Jests,* with the *Merriments of Mother Bunch.* (1653.)

(2) The other Mother Bunch is called *Mother Bunch's Closet newly Broke Open,* containing rare secrets of art and nature, tried and experienced by learned philosophers, and recommended to all ingenious young men and maids, teaching them how to get good wives and husbands. (1760.)

Mother Carey's Chickens. Stormy petrels. Mother Carey is *Mater Cara.* The French call these birds *oiseaux de Notre Dame* or *aves Sanctæ Mariæ.* Chickens are the young of any fowl, or any small bird.

"They are called the 'sailor's' friends, come to warn them of an approaching storm; and it is most unlucky to kill them. The legend is that each bird contains the soul of a dead seaman."

(See *Captain Marryat : Poor Jack,* where the superstition is fully related.)

Mother Carey's Goose. The great Black Petrel or Fulmar of the Pacific Ocean.

Mother Carey is plucking her goose. It is snowing. (*See* HULDA.)

Mother Country. One's native country, but the term applies specially to England, in relation to America and the Colonies. The inhabitants of North America, Australia, etc., are for the most part descendants of English parents, and therefore England may be termed the mother country. The Germans call their native country *Fatherland*.

Mother Douglas. A noted procuress, introduced in *The Minor* by Foote. She also figures in Hogarth's *March to Finchley.* Mother Douglas resided at the north-east corner of Covent Garden; her house was superbly furnished and decorated. She grew very fat, and with pious up-turned eyes used to pray for the safe return of her "babes" from battle. She died 1761.

Mother Earth. When Junius Brutus (after the death of Lucretia) formed one of the deputation to Delphi to ask the Oracle which of the three would succeed Tarquin, the response was, "He who should first kiss his mother." Junius instantly threw himself on the ground, exclaiming, "Thus, then, I kiss thee, Mother Earth," and he was elected Consul.

Mother Goose. A name associated with nursery rhymes. She was born in Boston, and her eldest daughter Elizabeth married Thomas Fleet, the printer. Mrs. Goose used to sing the rhymes to her grandson, and Thomas Fleet printed the first edition in 1719.

Mother Hubbard. The old lady whose whole time seems to have been devoted to her dog, who always kept her on the trot, and always made game of her. Her temper was proof against this wilfulness on the part of her dog, and her politeness never forsook her, for when she saw Master Doggie dressed in his fine clothes—

"The dame made a curtsey, the dog made a bow ;
The dame said, 'Your servant,' the dog said,
'Bow-wow.'"

Mother Huddle's Oven. Where folk are dried up so that they live for ever. (*Howard Pyle : Robin Hood*, 211.)

Mother Shipton lived in the reign of Henry VIII., and was famous for her prophecies, in which she foretold the death of Wolsey, Lord Percy, etc.,

and many wonderful events of future times. All her "prophecies" are still extant.

Mother-sick. Hysterical.

Mother-wit. Native wit, a ready reply ; the wit which " our mother gave us." In ancient authors the term is used to express a ready reply, courteous but not profound. Thus, when Louis XIV. expressed some anxiety lest Polignac should be inconvenienced by a shower of falling rain, the mother-wit of the cardinal replied, "It is nothing, I assure your Majesty ; the rain of Marly never makes us wet."

Mother of Believers. Ay-e'-shah, the second and favourite wife of Mahomet ; so called because Mahomet being the "Father of Believers," his wife of wives was Mother of Believers.

Mother of Books. Alexandria was so called from its library, which was the largest ever collected before the invention of printing.

Mother of Cities [*Amu-al-Bulud*]. Balkh is so called.

Mother of Pearl. The inner iridescent layers of the shells of many bivalve molluscs, especially that of the pearl oyster.

Mother of the Gracchi. A hard, strong-minded, rigid woman, without one soft point or effeminate weakness. Always in the right, and maintaining her right with the fortitude of a martyr.

Mother's Apron Strings. (*See* TIED . . .)

Mothering Sunday is Sunday in Mid-Lent, a great holiday, when the Pope blesses the golden rose, and children go home to their mothers to feast on "mothering cakes." It is said that the day received its appellation from the ancient custom of visiting their "mother church," and making offerings on the altar on that day. Used by school-children it means a holiday, when they went home to spend the day with their mother or parents.

Motion. *The laws of motion,* according to Galileo and Newton.

(1) If no force acts on a body in motion, it will continue to move uniformly in a straight line.

(2) If force acts on a body, it will produce a change of motion proportionate to the force, and in the same direction (as that in which the force acts).

(3) When one body exerts force on another, that *other* body reacts on it with equal force.

Motley. *Men of motley.* Licensed fools; so called because of their dress.

"Motley is the only wear."
Shakespeare : As You Like It, ii. 7.

Motu Pro'prio. A law brought in by Consal'vi, to abolish monopolies in the Papal States.(1757).

Mouch (*To*). To live as a vagrant.

Mouchard (French). A spy, "*qui fait comme les mouches, qui voient si bien sans en avoir l'air.*" At the close of the seventeenth century, those *petits-maitres* who frequented the Tuileries to see and be seen were called *mouchards* (fly-men). (*Dictionnaire Étymologique de Ménage.*)

Moulds. *In the moulds.* In the grave.

"After Sir John and her [the minister's wife] were . . . baith in the moulds."—*Sir W. Scott : Redgauntlet* (Letter xi.).

Mound. The largest artificial mound in Europe is Silbury Hill, near Avebury (Wiltshire). It covers 5 acres, 34 perches, and measures at the base 2,027 feet ; its diameter at top is 120 feet ; its slope is 316 feet ; perpendicular height, 107 feet ; and it is altogether one of the most stupendous monuments of human labour in the world.

Alyattes, in Asia Minor, described by Herodotus, is somewhat larger than Silbury Hill.

Mount Zion. The Celestial City or Heaven. (*Bunyan : Pilgrim's Progress.*)

"I am come from the City of Destruction, and am going to Mount Zion." (Part i.)

Mountain (*The*) or **Montagnards**. The extreme democratical party in the first French Revolution ; so called because they seated themselves on the highest benches of the hall in which the National Convention met. Their leaders were Danton and Robespierre, but under them were Marat, Couthon, Thuriot, St. André, Legendre, Camille-Desmoulins, Carnot, St. Just, and Collot d'Herbois, the men who introduced the "Reign of Terror." Extreme Radicals are still called in France the " Mountain Party," or *Montagnards*.

Old Man of the Mountain. Imaum Hassan ben Sabbah el Homairi. The Sheik Al Jebal was so called, because his residence was in the mountain fastnesses of Syria. He was the prince of a Mahometan sect called Assassins (*q.v.*), and founder of a dynasty in Syria, put an end to by the Moguls in the twelfth century. In Rymer's *Fœdera* (vol. **i.**) two letters of this sheik are inserted. It is not the province of this *Book of Fables* to dispute their genuineness.

If the mountain will not come to Mahomet, Mahomet must go to the mountain. If what I seek will not come to me without my stir, I must exert myself to obtain it ; if we cannot do as we wish, we must do as we can. When Mahomet first announced his system, the Arabs demanded supernatural proofs of his commission. " Moses and Jesus," said they, " wrought miracles in testimony of their divine authority ; and if thou art indeed the prophet of God, do so likewise." To this Mahomet replied, " It would be tempting God to do so, and bring down His anger, as in the case of Pharaoh." Not satisfied with this answer, he commanded Mount Safa to come to him, and when it stirred not at his bidding, exclaimed, " God is merciful. Had it obeyed my words, it would have fallen on us to our destruction. I will therefore go to the mountain, and thank God that He has had mercy on a stiff-necked generation."

The mountain in labour. A mighty effort made for a small effect. The allusion is to the celebrated line of Horace, " *Parturiunt montes, nasce'tur ridiculus mus,*" which Creech translates, " The travailing mountain yields a silly mouse ;" and Boileau, " *La montagne en travail enfante une souris.*"

Mountain Ash (*The*), or " Rowan-tree," botanically called *Pyrus aucuparia*, which does not belong to the same family of plants as the *fraxinus*, or Common Ash. The Mountain Ash is *icosandria*, but the Common Ash is *diandria*. The Mountain Ash is *pentagynia*, but the Common Ash is *monogynia*. The Mountain Ash is of the Natural Order *rosacœ*, but the common Ash is of the Natural Order *sepiariœ ;* yet the two trees resemble each other in many respects. The Rowan or Rown-tree is called in Westmoreland the " Wiggen-tree." It was greatly venerated by the Druids, and was called the " Witchen " by the early Britons, because it was supposed to ward off witches.

"Their spells were vain. The hags returned
To their queen in sorrowful mood,
Crying that witches have no power
Where thrives the Rowan-tree wood."
Laidley Worm of Spindleston Heughs (a ballad).

Mountain-dew. Whisky.

Mountains of Mole-hills. *To make mountains of mole-hills.* To make a

28

great fuss about trifles. "*Ex cloāca arcem facĕre*" (*Cicero*).

Mountebank. The bank or bench was the counter on which shopkeepers of yore displayed their goods. Street-vendors used to *mount* on their *bank* to patter to the public. The French word is "*saltim banque;*" and the Italian word "*Cantambanco*" (i.e. *canta in banco*, one who patters from his bank).

☙ In Italian, *montambanco* (a quack-doctor) is also in use.

"... Se disant estre quelque trabe, ou quelque Juif convert, il se feignoit medecin du roi de Perse, et comme tel il montoit la banque. C'estoit là que, pour débiter ses drogues, il étourdissoit de son babil toute l'assemblée."—*Histoire Generale des Larrons*, book i. chap. xxix.

There were temporary mountebanks as well as more regular merchants. In Attica, the names of Dolon and Susarion of Icaria are distinguished. In France, Tabaria, Tabarin, Turlupin, Gauthier-Garguille, Gros-Guillaume, Guillot-Gorju, Bo-bêche, Galimaufré, and Gringalet (a marvellous number of G's). In England, Andrew Borde, and some few others of inferior note.

Mourning.

Black. To express the privation of light and joy, the midnight gloom of sorrow for the loss sustained. The colour of mourning in Europe. It was also the colour of mourning in ancient Greece and in the Roman Empire.

Black and white striped. To express sorrow and hope. The mourning of the South-Sea Islanders.

Greyish brown. The colour of the earth, to which the dead return. The colour of mourning in Ethiopia.

Pale brown. The colour of withered leaves. The mourning of Persia.

Sky-blue. To express the assured hope that the deceased has gone to heaven. The colour of mourning in Syria, Cappadocia, and Armenia.

Deep blue, in Bokha'ra, is the colour of mourning (Hanway). The Romans in the Republic wore dark blue for mourning.

Purple and violet. To express royalty, "kings and priests to God." The colour of mourning for cardinals and the kings of France. The colour of mourning in Turkey is violet.

White. Emblem of "white-handed hope." The colour of mourning in China. Henry VIII. wore *white* for Anne Boleyn. The ladies of ancient Rome and Sparta wore white for mourning. It was the colour of mourning in Spain till 1498. In England it is still customary in some of the provinces to wear white silk hat-bands and white gloves for the unmarried.

Yellow. The sear and yellow leaf. The colour of mourning in Egypt and in

Burmah, where also it is the colour of the monastic order. In Brittany, widows' caps among the *paysannes* are yellow. Anne Boleyn wore yellow mourning for Catherine of Aragon. Some say yellow is in token of exaltation.

Mournival. Four cards all alike, as four aces, four kings, etc., in a game of cards called *Gleek*. Gleek is three cards alike.

"A mournival of aces, gleek of knaves, Just nine a-piece." *Albumazar*, iii. 5.

Poole in his *English Parnassus* called the four elements *Nature's first mournival.*

Mouse. The soul or spirit was often supposed in olden times to assume a zoömorphic form, and to make its way at death through the mouth of man in a visible form, sometimes as a pigeon, sometimes as a mouse or rat. A red mouse indicated a pure soul; a black mouse, a soul blackened by pollution; a pigeon or dove, a saintly soul.

Exorcists used to drive out evil spirits from the human body, and Harsnet gives several instances of such expulsions in his *Popular Impositions* (1604).

☙ No doubt pigeons were at one time trained to represent the departing soul, and also to represent the Holy Ghost.

Mouse, Mousie, terms of endearment. Other terms of endearment from animals are, *bird* or *birdie* (as "My bonnie bird"); *puss, pussy; lamb, lambkin;* "You little monkey" is an endearing reproof to a child. Dog and pig are used in a bad sense, as "You dirty dog;" "You filthy pig." Brave as a lion, surly as a bear, crafty as a fox, proud as a peacock, fleet as a hare, and several phrases of a like character are in common use.

"'God bless you, mouse,' the bridegroom said, And smakt her on the lips." *Warner: Alb. Eng.*, p. 17.

Mouse Tower (*The*), on the Rhine, said to be so called because Bishop Hatto (*q.v.*) was there devoured by mice. The tower, however, was built by Bishop Siegfried, two hundred years after the death of Bishop Hatto, as a toll-house for collecting the duties upon all goods which passed by. The word *maus* or *mauth* means "toll," and the toll collected on corn being very unpopular, gave rise to the tradition referred to. The catastrophe was fixed on Bishop Hatto, a noted statesman and councillor of Otho the Great, proverbial for his cunning perfidy. (*See* HATTO.)

Moussa. Moses.

Moussali. A Persian musician. Haroun al Raschid was going to divorce his late favourite Mari'dah or Marinda, but the poet Moussali sang some verses to him which so touched his heart, that he went in search of the lady and made peace with her. (*'Herbelot.*)

Mouth. *Down in the mouth.* (*See under* DOWN.)

His mouth was made, he was trained or reduced to obedience, like a horse trained to the bit.

"At first, of course, the fireworker showed fight.... but in the end 'his mouth was made,' his paces formed, and he became a very serviceable and willing animal."—*Le Fanu: House in the Churchyard,* ch. xcix.

Mouth Waters. *That makes my mouth water.* "*Cela fait venir l'eau à la bouche.*" The fragrance of appetising food excites the salivary glands. The phrase means—that makes me long for or desire it.

Moutons. *Revenons à nos moutons.* Return we to our subject. The phrase is taken from an old French play, called *L'Avocat,* by Patelin, in which a woollen-draper charges a shepherd with stealing sheep. In telling his grievance he kept for ever running away from his subject; and to throw discredit on the defendant's attorney, accused him of stealing a piece of cloth. The judge had to pull him up every moment with, "*Mais, mon ami, revenons à nos moutons*" (What about the sheep, tell me about the sheep, now return to the story of the sheep).

Movable. *The first movable.* Sir Thomas Browne (*Religio Medici*, p. 56, 27) uses the phrase, "Beyond the first movable," meaning outside the material creation. According to Ptolemy the "*primum mobile*" (the first movable and first mover of all things) was the boundary of creation, above which came the empyrean heaven, or seat of God.

Moving the Adjournment of the House. This is the only method which the rules of the house leave to a member for bringing up suddenly, and without notice, any business which is not on the order paper.

Moving the Previous Question. A parliamentary dodge for burking an obnoxious bill. The method is as follows:—A "question," or bill, is before the house, an objector does not wish to commit himself by moving its rejection, so he moves "the previous question," and the Speaker moves, from the chair, "that the question be *not* put"—that

is, that the house be not asked to come to any decision on the main question, but be invited to pass to the "orders of the day." In other words, that the subject be shelved or burked.

N.B. A motion for "the previous question" cannot be made on an amendment, nor in a select committee, nor yet in a committee of the whole house. The phrase is simply a method of avoiding a decision on the question before the House.

Moving the World. *Give me where to stand, and I will move the world.* So said Archime'des of Syracuse; and the instrument he would have used is the lever.

Mow, a heap, and **Mow,** to cut down, are quite different words. Mow, a heap, is the Anglo-Saxon *mowe;* but mow, to cut down, is the Anglo-Saxon *máw-an.*

✢ There is a third *Mow* (a wry face), which is the French *moue,* as "*Faire la moue à* [*quel qu'un*]," to make faces at someone, and "*Faire la moue,*" to pout or sulk. (Dutch, *mowe.*)

Mowis. The bridegroom of snow, who (according to American Indian tradition) wooed and won a beautiful bride; but when morning dawned, Mowis left the wigwam, and melted into the sunshine. The bride hunted for him night and day in the forests, but never saw him more.

Mozaide (2 syl.) or **Monzaida.** The "Moor," settled in Calicut, who befriended Vasco da Gama when he first landed on the Indian continent.

"The Moor attends, Mozaide, whose zealous care, To Gama's eyes revealed each treacherous snare." *Camoens: Lusiad,* bk. ix.

Much or **Mudge.** The miller's son, in Robin Hood dances, whose great feat was to bang with a bladder of peas the heads of the gaping spectators. Represents the Fool.

Much Ado about Nothing. The plot is from a novel of Belleforest, copied from one by Bandello (18th vol., vi.). There is a story resembling it in Ariosto's *Orlando Furioso,* bk. v., another in the *Geneura* of G. Turberville, and Spenser has a similar one in the *Faërie Queene,* book ii. canto iv.

Much Ado about Nothing. After a war in Messina, Claudio, Benedick, and some other soldiers went to visit Leonato the governor, when the former fell in love with Hero, the governor's daughter; but Benedick and Beatrice, being great rattle-pates, fell to jesting, and each positively disliked the other. By a slight artifice their hatred was converted into love, and Beatrice was betrothed to the Paduan lord. In regard to Hero, the day of her nuptials was fixed; but Don John, who hated Claudio and Leonato, induced Margaret, the lady's maid, to dress up like her mistress, and to talk familiarly with one Borachio, a servant of Don John's; and while this chit-chat was going on, the Don led Claudio and Leonato to overhear it. Each thought it to be Hero, and when she appeared as a bride next morning at church, they both denounced her as a light woman. The friar, being persuaded that there was some mistake, induced Hero to retire, and gave out that she was dead. Leonato now challenged Claudio for being the cause of Hero's death, and Benedick, urged on by Beatrice, did the same. At this crisis Borachio was arrested, and confessed the trick; Don John fled, the mystery was duly cleared up, and the two lords married the two ladies.

Mucia'na Cau'tio. A law-quirk, so called from Mu'cius Scæ'vola, a Roman pontifex, and the most learned of jurists.

Muc'klebackit. *Elspeth Mucklebackit,* mother of Saunders.
Little Jennie Mucklebackit. Child of Saunders.
Maggie Mucklebackit. Wife of Saunders.
Saunders Mucklebackit. The old fisherman at Musslecrag.
Steenie Mucklebackit. Eldest son of Saunders (drowned). (*Sir Walter Scott: The Antiquary.*)

Muc'klewrath. *Habakkuk Mucklewrath.* A fanatic preacher. (*Sir Walter Scott: Old Mortality.*)
John Mucklewrath. Smith at Cairnvreckan village. Dame Mucklewrath, his wife, is a perfect virago. (*Sir Walter Scott: Waverley.*)

Mud-honey. So Tennyson calls the dirty pleasures of men-about-town. (*Maud.*)

Mudar'ra. Son of a Moorish princess and Gouçalo Bustos de Salas de Lara, who murdered his uncle Rodri'go, while hunting, to avenge the death of his seven half-brothers. (*See* LARA, *The seven infants of Lara.*)

Muff (*A*). A dull, stupid person. Sir Henry Muff, one of the candidates in Dudley's interlude, called *The Rival Candidates* (1774), is a stupid, blundering

dolt. He is not only unsuccessful in his election, but he finds that his daughter has engaged herself during his absence.

Muffins and Crumpets. Muffins is *pain-moufflet.* Du Cange describes the *panis mofletus* as bread of a more delicate nature than ordinary, for the use of prebends, etc.; and says it was made fresh every day. Crumpets is *crumple-ettes,* cakes with little crumples.

Muffled Cats catch no Mice. (In Italian, "*Catta guantata non piglia sorice.*") Said of those who work in gloves for fear of soiling their fingers.

Mufti. *We went in mufti*—out of uniform, *incog.*
The French say *en pékin,* and French soldiers call civilians *pékins.* An officer who had kept Talleyrand waiting, said he had been detained by some pékins. "What are they?" asked Talleyrand. "Oh," said the officer, "we call everybody who is not *military* a pékin." "And we," said Tallyrand, "call everybody military that is not *civil.*" Mufti is an Eastern word, signifying a judge.

Mug-house. An ale-house was so called in the eighteenth century. Some hundred persons assembled in a large tap-room to drink, sing, and spout. One of the number was made chairman. Ale was served to the guests in their own mugs, and the place where the mug was to stand was chalked on the table.

Mugello. The giant slain by Averardo de Medici, a commander under Charlemagne. The tale is interesting, for it is said that the Medici took the three balls of this giant's mace for their device. Everyone knows that pawnbrokers have adopted the three balls as a symbol of their trade. (*See under* BALLS for another account.)

Muggins. A small borough magnate, a village leader. To *mug* is to drink, and Mr. Muggins is Mr. Drinker.

Muggleto'nian. A follower of one Lodovic Muggleton, a journeyman tailor, who, about 1651, set up for a prophet. He was sentenced to stand in the pillory, and was fined £500.

Mugwump (*A*). A word borrowed from the Algonquin, meaning one who acts and thinks independently. In Eliot's Indian Bible the word "centurion" in the Acts is rendered *mugwump.* Those who refuse to follow the dictum of a caucus are called in the United States *mugwumps.* The chief of the Indians of Esopus is entitled the *Mugwump*. Turncoats are mugwumps, and all political Pharisees whose party vote cannot be relied on.

"'I suppose I am a political mugwump,' said the Englishman. 'Not yet,' replied Mr. Reed. 'You will be when you have returned to your allegiance.'"—*The Liverpool Echo*, July 19th, 1886.

Mugwump Press (*The*). Those newspapers which are not organs of any special political party, but being "neither hot nor cold," are disliked by all party men."

"The Mugwump Press, whose function it is to enlighten the feeble-minded. . . ."—*The New York Tribune*, 1892.

Mulat'to (Spanish). A mule, a mongrel; applied to the male offspring of a negress by a white man. A female offspring is called a "Mulatta." (*See* CREOLE.)

Mulberry. The fruit was originally white, and became blood-red from the blood of Pyramus and Thisbē. The tale is, that Thisbē was to meet her lover at the white mulberry-tree near the tomb of Ninus, in a suburb of Babylon. Being scared by a lion, Thisbē fled, and, dropping her veil, it was besmeared with blood. Pyramus, thinking his lady-love had been devoured by a lion, slew himself, and Thisbē, coming up soon afterwards, stabbed herself also. The blood of the lovers stained the white fruit of the mulberry-tree into its present colour.

The botanical name is Morus, from the Greek *moros* (a fool); so called, we are told in the *Hortus Anglicus*, because "it is reputed the wisest of all flowers, as it never buds till the cold weather is past and gone."
In the *Seven Champions* (pt. i. chap. iv.) we are told that Eglantine, daughter of the King of Thessaly, was transformed into a mulberry-tree

Mulciber—*i.e.* Vulcan. It is said that he took the part of Juno against Jupiter, and Jupiter hurled him out of heaven. He was three days in falling, and at last was picked up, half-dead and with one leg broken, by the fishermen of the island of Lemnos. (See *Milton : Paradise Lost*, book i., 740, etc.)

Mule. Mahomet's favourite white mule was Daldah. (*See* FADDA.)

To shoe one's mule. To appropriate part of the money committed to one's trust. This is a French locution—

"*Ferrer la mule—i.e.* l'action d'un domestique qui trompe son maître sur le prix réel des choses qu'il a achetées en son nom. Elle doit son origine au pretexte, facile à employer, de la depense faite pour *ferrer la mule*."—*Encyclopedie des Proverbes Français*.

"He had the keeping and disposall of the moneys, and yet shod not his own mule."—*History of Francion* (1655).

Mull. *To make a mull of a job* is to fail to do it properly. The failure of a peg-top to spin is called a mull, hence also any blunder or failure. (Scotch, *mull*, dust, or a contraction of *muddle*.) The people of Madras are called "Mulls," because they are in a less advanced state of civilisation than the other two presidencies, in consequence of which they are held by them in low estimation. (Anglo-Saxon, *myl*, dust.)

Mulla. Awbeg, a tributary of the Blackwater, in Ireland, which flowed close by Spenser's home. Spenser is called by Shenstone "the bard of Mulla's silver stream."

Mul'mutine Laws. The code of Dunvallo Mulmutius, sixteenth King of the Britons (about B.C. 400). This code was translated by Gildas from British into Latin, and by Alfred into Anglo-Saxon. These laws obtained in England till the Conquest. (*Holinshed : History of England*, iii. 1.)

"Mulmutius made our laws,
Who was the first of Britain which did put
His brows within a golden crown, and called
Himself a king."
Shakespeare : Cymbeline, iii. 1.

∴ Mulmutius was the son of Cloten, King of Cornwall. (*See* Geoffrey of Monmouth, *British History*, ii. 17.)

Mulread'y Envelope (*The*, 1840), is an envelope resembling a half-sheet of letter-paper, when folded. The space left for the address formed the centre of an ornamental design by Mulready, the artist. When the penny postage envelopes were first introduced, these were the stamped envelopes of the day, which, however, remained in circulation only one year, and were more fit for a comic annual than anything else.

" A set of those odd-looking envelope-things,'
Where Britannia (who seems to be crucified)
flings
To her right and her left, funny people with
wings
Amongst elephants, Quakers, and Catabaw
kings,—
And a taper and wax, and small Queen's-heads
in packs,
Which, when notes are too big you must stick
on their backs."
Ingoldsby : Legends.

Multipliers. Alchemists, who pretended to multiply gold and silver. An act was passed (2 Henry IV., c. iv.) making the "art of multiplication" felony. In the *Canterbury Tales*, the Chanoun Yeman says he was reduced to poverty by alchemy, adding: " Lo, such advantage is't to multiply." (*Prologue to Chanounes Tale*.)

Multitudes. Dame Juliana Berners, in her *Booke of St. Albans*, says, in designating companies we must not use the names of multitudes promiscuously, and examples her remark thus :—

"'We say a *congregacyon* of people, a *hoost* of men, a *felyshyppynge* of jomen, and a *bevy* of ladyes ; we must speak of a *herde* of dere, swannys, cranys, or wrenys, a *sege* of herons or bytourys, a *muster* of pecockes, a *watche* of nyghtyngales, a *flyghte* of doves, a *claterynge* of choughes, a *pryde* of lyons, a *slewthe* of beeres, a *gagle* of geys, a *skulke* of foxes, a *sculle* of frerys, a *pontificalitye* of prestys, and a *superfluyte* of nonnes.'"—*Booke of St. Albans* (1486).

She adds, that a strict regard to these niceties better distinguishes "gentylmen from ungentylmen," than regard to the rules of grammar, or even to the moral law. (*See* NUMBERS.)

Multum in Parvo (Latin). Much [information] condensed into few words or into a small compass.

Mum. A strong beer made in Brunswick ; so called from Christian Mummer, by whom it was first brewed. *Mum* (a mask), hence mummer. *Mum's the word.* Keep what is told you a profound secret. (*See* MUMCHANCE.)

"Seal up your lips, and give no words but—mum."
          Shakespeare : 2 *Henry VI.*, i. 2.

Mumbo Jumbo. A bogie or bugbear in the Mandingo towns of Africa. As the Kaffirs have many wives, it not unfrequently happens that the house becomes quite unbearable. In such a case, either the husband or an agent dresses himself in disguise, and at dusk approaches the unruly house with a following, and makes the most hideous noises possible. When the women have been sufficiently scared, "Mumbo" seizes the chief offender, ties her to a tree, and scourges her with Mumbo's rod, amidst the derision of all present. Mumbo is not an idol, any more than the American Lynch, but one disguised to punish unruly wives. (See *Mungo Park : Travels in the Interior of Africa.*)

Mumchance. Silence. Mumchance was a game of chance with dice, in which silence was indispensable. (Mum is connected with mumble : German, *mumme*, a muffle ; Danish, *mumle*, to mumble.)

" And for 'mumchance,' howe'er the *cehane* may fall,
You must be *mum* for fear of spoiling all."
          Machiavell's Dogg.

Mummy is the Egyptian word *mum*, wax ; from the custom of anointing the body with wax and wrapping it in cerecloth. (Persian, *momia*, wax ; Italian, *mummia ;* French, *momie*.) (*See* BEATEN.)

Mummy Wheat. Wheat said to have been taken from some of the Egyp-tian mummies, and sown in British soil. It is, however, a delusion to suppose that seed would preserve its vitality for some hundreds of years. No seed will do so, and what is called mummy wheat is a species of corn commonly grown on the southern shores of the Mediterranean.

Mumpers. Beggars. Leland calls it a gipsy word. In Norwich, Christmas waits used to be called "Mumpers." In Lincolnshire, "Boxing-day" is called *Mumping-day* (*q.v.*). To mump is to beg. Beggars are called the "Mumping Society."

"A parcel of wretches hopping about by the assistance of their crutches, like so many Lin-coln's Inn Fields mumpers, drawing into a body to attack [infest or beset] the coach of some charitable lord."—*Ned Ward : The London Spy,* part v.

Mumping Day. St. Thomas's Day, December 21. A day on which the poor used to go about begging, or, as it was called, "going a-gooding," that is, getting gifts to procure *good things* for Christmas (*mump*, to beg).

✢ In Warwickshire the term used was "going a-corning," *i.e.* getting gifts of corn. In Staffordshire the custom is spoken of simply as "a-gooding." (*See* MUMPERS.)

Munchau'sen (*Baron*). The hero of a volume of travels, who meets with the most marvellous adventures. The incidents have been compiled from various sources, and the name is said to have pointed to Hieronymus Karl Friedrich von Münchhausen, a German officer in the Russian army, noted for his marvellous stories (1720-1797). It is a satire either on Baron de Tott, or on Bruce, whose *Travels in Abyssinia* were looked upon as mythical when they first appeared. The author is Rudolf Erich Raspe, and the sources from which the adventures were compiled, are Bebel's *Facetiæ*, Castiglione's *Cortegiano*, Bildermann's *Utopia*, and some of the baron's own stories.

Mundane Egg (*The*). In the Phœnician, Egyptian, Hindu, and Japanese systems, it is represented that the world was hatched from an egg. In some mythologies a bird is represented as laying the mundane egg on the primordial waters.

Mundilfo'ri. One of the giant race, who had a son and daughter of such surpassing beauty that their father called them Mani and Sol (*moon* and *sun*). (*Scandinavian mythology.*)

Mundun'gus. Bad tobacco.

∴ Mundungus, in Sterne's *Sentimental Journey* (1768), is meant for Samuel Sharp, a surgeon, who published *Letters from Italy*. Tobias Smollett, who published *Travels through France and Italy* (1766), "one con inual snarl," was called "Smelfungus."

Mu'nera. The daughter of Pollente, the Saracen, to whom he gave all the spoils he unjustly took from those who fell into his power. Talus, the iron page of Sir Ar'tegal, chopped off her golden hands and silver feet, and tossed her over the castle wall into the moat. (*Spenser: Faërie Queene*, bk. v. 2.)

Munkar and **Nakir.** Two black angels of appalling aspect, the inquisitors of the dead. The Koran says that during the inquisition the soul is united to the body. If the scrutiny is satisfactory, the soul is gently drawn forth from the lips of the deceased, and the body is left to repose in peace'; if not, the body is beaten about the head with iron clubs, and the soul is wrenched forth by racking torments.

Munnin. Memory; one of the two ravens that sit perched on the shoulders of Odin; the other is Hugin (thought). (*Scandinavian mythology*.)

Munta'bur [*Mount Tabor*]. The royal residence of the soldan whose daughter married Otnit, King of Lombardy.

Mu'rad. Son of Hadra'ma and Marsillus, King of Portugal, Castile, Aragon, Leon, and Valence, when those countries were held by the Moors. He was called "Lord of the Lion," because he always led about a lion in silken fetters. When he carried defiance to Charlemagne at Fronsac, the lion fell in love with Aude the Fair; Murad chastised it, and the lion tore him to pieces. (*Croquemitaine*, vii.)

Mus'cadins of Paris. French dudes or exquisites, who aped the London mashers in the first French Revolution. Their dress was top-boots with thick soles, knee-breeches, a dress-coat with long tails, and a high stiff collar, and a thick cudgel called a *constitution*. It was thought to be John Bullish to assume a huskiness of voice, a discourtesy of manners, and a swaggering vulgarity of speech and behaviour. Probably so called from being "perfumed like a popinjay."

"Cockneys of London, Muscadins of Paris."
Byron: Don Juan, viii. 124.

Muscular Christianity. Healthy or strong-minded religion, which braces a man to fight the battle of life bravely and manfully. This expression has been erroneously attributed to Charles Kingsley. (*See* his *Life*, ii. 74, 75.)

Muses. Nine daughters of Jupiter and Mnemosÿne, goddesses of poetry, history, and other arts and sciences. The paintings of Herculaneum show all nine in their respective attributes. In the National-Museum of Paris is the famous collection with which Pius VI. enriched the Vatican. Lesueur left a celebrated picture of the same subject.

Muse'um. The most celebrated are the British Museum in London; the Louvre at Paris; the Vatican at Rome; the Museum of Florence; that of St. Petersburg; and those of Dresden, Vienna, Munich, and Berlin.

A walking museum. So Longi'nus, author of a work on *The Sublime*, was called. (A.D. 213-273.)

Mushroom (an archaic form is *mushrump*). (French, *mousseron*, a white mushroom; Latin, *muscus*, moss.)

"Vocatur fungus muscārum, eo quod in lacte pulverizatus interficit muscas."—*Albertus Magnus*, vii. 345.

Music. *Father of music.* Giovanni Battista Pietro Aloisio da Palestrina. Giovanni Pierluigi da Palestrina was "the prince of musicians." (1529-1594.)

Father of Greek music. Terpander. (*Flourished* B.C. 676.)

The prince of music. G. Pietro A. da Palestrina (1529-1594).

Music hath charms, etc. ; from Congreve's *Mourning Bride*, i. 1.

Music. *Men of genius averse to music.* The following men of genius were actually averse to music: Edmund Burke; Byron had no ear for music, and neither vocal nor instrumental music afforded him the slightest pleasure. Charles Fox, Hume, Dr. Johnson, Daniel O'Connell, Robert Peel, William Pitt; Pope preferred a street organ to Handel's oratorios; the poet Rogers felt actual discomfort at the sounds of music; Sir Walter Scott, the poet Southey, and Tennyson. Seven of these twelve were actually poets, and five were orators. The Princess Mathilde (Demidoff), an excellent artist, with a veritable passion for art, may be added to those who have had a real antipathy to music.

Music of the Spheres. Pythag'oras was the first who suggested the notion so beautifully expressed by Shakespeare—

"There's not the smallest orb which thou behold'st
But in his motion like an angel sings,
Still quiring to the young-eyed cherubims."
Merchant of Venice, v. 1.

Plato says that a siren sits on each planet, who carols a most sweet song, agreeing to the motion of her own particular planet, but harmonising with all the others. Hence Milton speaks of the " celestial syrens' harmony, that sit upon the nine enfolded spheres." (*Arcades.*) (*See* NINE SPHERES.)

Maximus Tyrius says that the mere proper motion of the planets must create sounds, and as the planets move at regular intervals the sounds must harmonise.

Musical Notation. (*See* Do.)

Musical Small - coal Man (*The*). Thomas Britton (1654-1714).

Musicians. *Father of musicians.* Jubal, " the father of all such as handle the harp and organ " (Gen. iv. 21).

Musido'ra. (*See* DAMON.)

Mu'sits or **Musets.** Gaps in a hedge; places through which a hare makes his way to escape the hounds.

" The many musits through the which he goes
Are like a labyrinth to amaze his foes."
    Shakespeare: Venus and Adonis.

The passing of the hare through these gaps is termed *musing*. The word is from *musse* (old French), a little hole.

Musket is the Spanish *mosquéte*, a musket.

Muslin. So called from Mosul, in Asia, where it was first manufactured. (French, *mousseline;* Italian, *mussolino.*)

Musnud. Cushioned seats, reserved in Persia for persons of distinction.

Muspel. A region of fire, whence Surtur will collect flames to set fire to the universe. (*Scandinavian mythology.*)

Muspelheim (3 syl.). The abode of fire which at the beginning of time existed in the south. It was light, warm, and radiant; but was guarded by Surt with a flaming sword. Sparks were collected therefrom to make the stars. (*Scandinavian mythology.*) (*See* MANHEIM.)

" The Muspelheim is a noted Scandinavian poem of the 4th century. Muspelheim is the Scandinavian hell, and the subject of the poem is the Last Judgment. The great Surt or Surtur is Antichrist, who at the end of the world will set fire to all creation. The poem is in alternate verse, and shows both imagination and poetic talent."

Mustard. Connected with *must.* In 1382 Philip the Bold, Duke of Burgundy, granted to the town of Dijon, noted for its mustard, armorial bearings with the motto MOULT ME TARDE (*Multum ardeo,* I ardently desire). The arms and motto, engraved

on the principal gate, were adopted as a trade-mark by the mustard merchants, and got shortened into Moult-tarde (to burn much).

The nasturtium is of the mustard family, in Spanish *masturcio;* and the Italian *mustarda* is mustard.

Mustard. *After meat, mustard.* I have now no longer need of it. " *C'est de la moutarde après dîner.*"

Musulman (plural, *Musulmans* or *Moslems*)—that is, *Moslemin,* plural of *Moslem.* A Mahometan ; so called from the Arabic *muslim,* a believer.

Mutantur. " *Omnia mutantur, nos et mutamur in illis,*" is by Nicholas Borbonius, a Latin poet of the sixteenth century. Dr. Sandys says that the Emperor Lothair, of the Holy Roman Empire, had already said, " *Tempora mutantur, nos et muta'mur in illis.*"

Mute as a Fish. Quite silent. Some fish make noises, but these are mechanical, not organic.

Mutes at Funerals. This was a Roman custom. The undertaker, attended with lictors dressed in black, marched with the corpse; and the undertaker, as master of the ceremonies, assigned to each follower his proper place in the procession.

Mutton (French, *mouton*). A gold coin impressed with the image of a lamb.

Mutton-eating King (*The*). Charles II. of England. The witty Earl of Rochester wrote this mock epitaph on his patron :—

" Here lies our mutton-eating king,
   Whose word no man relies on :
He never *said* a foolish thing,
   And never *did* a wise one."

Come and eat your mutton with me. Come and dine with me.

Mutton-fist. A large, coarse, red fist.

Muttóns. A Stock Exchange term for the Turkish '65 loan, partly secured by the sheep-tax.

Revenons à nos moutons. (*See* MOUTONS.)

Mutual Friends. Can two persons be called *mutual* friends? Does not the word of necessity imply three or more than three? (*See* the controversy in *Notes and Queries,* June 9, 1894, p. 451.)

" A mutual flame was quickly caught,
   Was quickly, too, revealed ;
For neither bosom lodged a thought
   Which virtue keeps concealed."
     Edwin and Emma.

(Mutual = reciprocal.)

Muzzle. *To muzzle the ox that treadeth out the corn.* Not to pay for work done; to expect other persons will work for nothing. The labourer is worthy of his hire, and to withhold that hire is to muzzle the ox that treadeth out your corn.

My Eye (*All*). (*See under* ALL.)

Mynheer Closh. A Dutchman. *Closh* or *Claus* is an abbreviation of Nicholaus, a common name in Holland. Sandy, a contraction of Alexander, is a similar nickname for a Scotchman.

My'nian Sails. The ship Argo; so called because its crew were natives of Mynia.

" When his black whirlwinds o'er the ocean rolled
And rent the Mynian sails."
Camoens: Lusiad, bk. vi.

Myr'midons of the Law. Bailiffs, sheriffs' officers, and other law menials. Any rough fellow employed to annoy another is the employer's myrmidon.

The Myrmidons were a people of Thessaly who followed Achilles to the siege of Troy, and were distinguished for their savage brutality, rude behaviour, and thirst for rapine.

Myron. A Greek statuary and sculptor, born in Bœotia, B.C. 480. A fellow-disciple of Polyclētus, and a younger contemporary of Phidias. His great works are in bronze. By far the most celebrated of his statues were his Discobolus and his Cow. The cow is represented lowing. (Discobolus is a quoit or discus player.) It is said that the cow was so true to nature that a bull mistook it for a living animal.

∴ There are several similar legends. Thus it is said that Apelles painted Alexander's horse so realistically that a living horse mistook it and began to neigh. Velasquez painted a Spanish admiral so true to life, that Felipe IV. mistook the painting for the man and reproved it severely for not being with the fleet. Zeuxis painted some grapes so well that birds flew at them to peck them. Quentin Matsys painted a fly on a man's leg so inimitably that Mandyn, the artist, tried to brush it off with his handkerchief. Parrhasios, of Ephesus, painted a curtain so well that Zeuxis was deceived by it, and told him to draw it aside that he might see the picture behind it.

Myrra. An Ionian slave, the beloved concubine of Sardanapa'lus, the Assyrian king. She roused him from his indolence to oppose Arba'cēs the Mede, who aspired to his throne, and when she found that his cause was hopeless induced him to place himself on a funeral pile, which she fired with her own hand, and springing into the flames, perished with her beloved lord and master. (*Byron : Sardanapalus.*)

28*

Myr'rophores (3 syl. ; the *myrrh bearers*). The three Marys who went to see the sepulchre, bearing myrrh and spices. In Christian art they are represented as carrying vases of myrrh in their hands.

Myrtle (*The*). If you look at a leaf of myrtle in a strong light, you will see that it is pierced with innumerable little punctures. According to fable, Phædra, wife of Theseus, fell in love with Hippolotus, her step-son ; and when Hippolotus went to the arena to exercise his horses, Phædra repaired to a myrtle-tree in Trœzen to await his return, and beguiled the time by piercing the leaves with a hair-pin. The punctures referred to are an abiding memento of this tradition.

In the *Orlando Furioso* Astolpho is changed into a myrtle-tree by Acrisia.

Myrtle. The ancient Jews believed that the eating of myrtle leaves conferred the power of detecting witches; and it was a superstition that if the leaves crackled in the hands the person beloved would prove faithful.

The myrtle which dropped blood. Æneas (book iii.) is represented as tearing up the Myrtle which dropped blood. Polydorus tells us that the barbarous inhabitants of the country pierced the Myrtle (then a living being) with spears and arrows. The body of the Myrtle took root and grew into the bleeding tree.

Mysteries of Woods and Rivers. The art of hunting and fishing.

Mystery. A kind of mediæval drama, the characters and events of which were drawn from sacred history.

Mystery or **Mysterium.** Said to make up the number 666 referred to in Rev. xvii. 5. This would not be worthy notice, except for the fact that the word "mystery" was, till the time of the Reformation, inscribed on the Pope's mitre.

∴ Almost any phrase or long name can be twisted into this number. (*See* NUMBER OF THE BEAST.)

Mysteries. *The three greater mysteries* (in Christianity). The Trinity, Original Sin, and the Incarnation.

∴ Surely the resurrection of the body should be added.

Mysterious Three (*The*) of Scandinavian mythology were "Har" (the Mighty), the "Like-Mighty," and the "Third Person," who sat on three thrones above the rainbow. Then came the " Æsir," of which Odin was chief, who lived in Asgard (between the rainbow and earth) ; next come the " Vanir," or gods of the ocean, air, and clouds, of which deities Niörd was chief.

N

N. This letter represents a wriggling eel, and is called in Hebrew *nun* (a fish).

N, in Spanish, has sometimes a mark over it, thus—ñ. This mark is called a *tilde,* and alters the sense and pronunciation of a word. Thus, "pena" means *punishment,* but "peña," a *rock.* (*See* MARKS IN GRAMMAR.)

N. (One whose name is not given.) (*See* M or N.)

N, a numeral. Greek $\nu = 50$, but $,\nu =$ 50,000. Ñ (Rom.) = 900, but Ñ = 900,000.

N added to Greek words ending in a short vowel to lengthen it " by position," and "l" added to French words beginning with a vowel, when they follow a word ending with a vowel (as *si l'on* for *si on*), is called N or L " ephelcys'tic" (tagged-on) ; Greek, *epi helko*. (*See* MARKS IN GRAMMAR.)

N. H. Bugs. The letters are the initials of Norfolk Howard, in allusion to a Mr. Bugg who, in 1863, changed his name to Norfolk Howard.

nth, or **nth plus One,** in University slang, means to the utmost degree. Thus, *Cut to the nth* means wholly unnoticed by a friend. The expression is taken from the index of a mathematical formula, where *n* stands for any number, and $n + 1$, one more than any number.

Nab. The fairy which offers Orpheus for food in the infernal regions a roasted ant, a flea's thigh, butterflies' brains, some sucking mites, a rainbow-tart, and other delicacies of like nature, to be washed down with dewdrops, beer made from seven barleycorns, and the supernaculum of earth-born topers. (*King : Orpheus and Eurydice.*)

Nab. To seize without warning. A contraction of *apprehend.* (Norwegian, *nappe,* to catch at, *nap,* snatch ; Swedish, *nappa.*) Our nap (to filch or steal) is a variety of the same word.

The keeper or catch of a latch or bolt is called **the nab.**

Nab-man. A sheriff's officer. (*See* NAB.)

"Old Dornton has sent the nabman after him at last."—*Sir W. Scott : Guy Mannering* (dramatised by Terry, ii. 3).

Nabo or **Nebo.** One of the divinities of the Assyrians, supposed to be the moon. (*See* Isa. xlvi. 1.) Many of the kings of Babylon assumed the name.

Nabonassar is Nabo-n-assar, Nabo-of-Asshur or Assyria.
Nabochadanasor is Nabo-chadon (or adon)-[n]-assur, *i.e.* Nabo-king-of-Asshur or Assyria.
Nabopolassar is Nabo-[son of] pul-Assyrian.
Nebochadnezzar is Nebo-chad (or adon)-n-assur, *i.e.* Nebo or Nebo-king-of-Asshur.

.: Belchazzar is Baal-ch'-azzar, *i.e.* Baal-chadon-n-assar, or Baal-king-of-Asshur.

Nabob' (generally called Na'bob). Corruption of the Hindu word *nawab,* the plural of *naib.* An administrator of a province and commander of the Indian army under the Mogul Empire. These men acquired great wealth and lived in Eastern splendour, so that they gave rise to the phrase, "Rich as the nawâb," corrupted into "*Rich as a nabob.*" In England we apply the phrase to a merchant who has attained great wealth in the Indies, and has returned to live in his native country.

Nabonassar or **Nebo-adon-Assur.** (Nebo, Prince of Assyria.) Founder of the Babylonian and Chaldæan kingdom, and first of the dynasty of Nabonassar.

Era of Nabonassar began Wednesday, February 26th, 747 B.C., the day of Nabonassar's accession. It was used by Ptolemy, and by the Babylonians, in all their astronomical calculations.

Naboth's Vineyard. The possession of another coveted by one able to possess himself of it. (1 Kings xxi. 1-10.)

"The little Manor House property had always been a Naboth's vineyard to his father."—*Good Words,* 1887.

Nadab, in Dryden's satire of *Absalom and Achitophel,* is meant for Lord Howard, of Esrick or Escriek, a profligate who laid claim to great piety. Nadab offered incense with strange fire, and was slain by the Lord (Lev. x. 2) ; and Lord Howard, while imprisoned in the Tower, is said to have mixed the consecrated wafer with a compound of roasted apples and sugar, called lamb's-wool.

" And canting Nadab let oblivion damn,
Who made new porridge of the paschal lamb."
Absalom and Achitophel, part i. 538-9.

Na'dir. An Arabic word, signifying that point in the heavens which is directly opposite to the zenith.

From zenith down to nadir. From the

highest point of elevation to the lowest depth.

Na'dir. A representation of the planetary system.

"We then lost (1091) a most beautiful table, fabricated of different metals. . . . Saturn was of copper, Jupiter of gold, Mars of iron, the Sun of latten, Mercury of amber, Venus of tin, and the Moon of silver. . . . It was the most celebrated nadir in all England."—*Ingulphus.*

Nadir Shah. Kouli Khan, a Persian warrior. (1687-1747.)

Nag. A horse. This is an example of *n* of the article joined to the following noun, as in the word newt = an ewt. (Danish and Norwegian, *og ;* Anglo-Saxon, *eoh* or *eh ;* Latin, *eq*[*uus*] ; Dutch, *negge.*) Taylor (1630) has *naggon,* as—

"Wert thou George with thy naggon,
That foughtest with the draggon."

∵ Shakespeare's *naunt* and *nuncle* are mine-aunt and mine-uncle.

Nag, Nagging. Constant fault-finding. (Anglo - Saxon, *gnag-an,* to gnaw, bite.) We call a slight but constant pain, like a tooth-ache, a *nagging pain.*

Nag's Head Consecration. On the passing of the first Act of Uniformity in Queen Elizabeth's reign, fourteen bishops vacated their sees, and all the other sees, except Llandaff, were at the time vacant. The question was how to obtain consecration so as to preserve the succession called "apostolic" unbroken, as Llandaff refused to officiate at Parker's consecration. In this dilemma (the story runs) Scory, a deposed bishop, was sent for, and officiated at the *Nag's Head* tavern, in Cheapside, thus transmitting the succession.

∵ Such is the tale. Strype refutes the story, and so does Dr. Hook. We are told that it was not the *consecration* which took place at the *Nag's Head,* but only that those who took part in it dined there subsequently. We are furthermore told that the Bishops Barlow, Scory, Coverdale, and Hodgkins, all officiated at the consecration.

Naga. Serpents ; the king of them is Sesha, the sacred serpent of Vishnu. (*Hindu mythology.*)

Na'glfar. The giants' ship, in which they will embark on "the last day" to give battle to the gods. It is made of the nails of the dead. (Old Norse, *nagl,* a human nail, and *fara,* to make.) (*Scandinavian mythology.*) Piloted by Hrymer.

Nahushtan. Trumpery bits of brass. (2 Kings xviii. 4.)

Naiads. Nymphs of lakes, fountains, rivers, and streams. (*Classical mythology.*) (*See* FAIRY.)

Nail.

Down on the nail, Pay down on the nail. In ready money. In Latin: "*Super unguem ;*" in French: "*Sur l'ongle ;* " as, "*Boire la goutte sur l'ongle*" (*see* SUPERNACULUM), "*Payer rubis sur l'ongle,*" where *rubis* means red wine. The Latin *ungulus* (from *unguis*) means a "shot" or reckoning, hence *ungulum dare,* to pay one's reckoning.

"Quo quibus prisis, et cariagiis pleana fiat solucio super unguem."—*An Indenture dated July 15th, 1326 (Scot's Act).*

∵ O'Keefe says: "In the centre of Limerick Exchange is a pillar with a circular plate of copper about three feet in diameter, called *The Nail,* on which the earnest of all stock-exchange bargains has to be paid." (*Recollections.*)

A similar custom prevailed at Bristol, where were four pillars, called *nails,* in front of the Exchange for a similar purpose. In Liverpool Exchange there is a plate of copper called *The Nail,* on which bargains are settled.

Hung on the nail. Up the spout, put in pawn. The custom referred to is that of hanging each pawn on a nail, with a number attached, and giving the customer a duplicate thereof. Very similar to the custom of guarding hats, cloaks, walking-sticks, and umbrellas, in public exhibitions and assemblies.

To hit the nail on the head. To come to a right conclusion. In Latin, "*Rem tenes.*" The Germans have the exact phrase, "*Den Nagel auf den kopf treffen.*"

Nail (*For want of a*). "For want of a nail, the shoe is lost; for want of a shoe, the horse is lost ; and for want of a horse, the rider is lost." (*Herbert : Jacula Prudentum.*)

Nail-money. Six crowns given to the "roy des harnoys" for affixing the arms of a knight to the pavilion.

Nail fixed in the Temple (*of Jupiter*). On September 13th a nail was annually driven into the wall of the temple of Jupiter. This was originally done to tally the year, but subsequently it lapsed into a religious ceremony for warding off calamities from the city. Originally the nail was driven in the wall by the prætor maximus, subsequently by one of the consuls, and lastly by the dictator. (See *Livy,* vii. 3.)

Nail in One's Coffin. *To drive a nail into one's coffin.* To shorten life by anxiety, drink, etc. Topers call a dram "a nail in their coffin," in jocular allusion to the teetotal axiom.

" Care to our coffin adds a nail, no doubt ;
But every grin so merry draws one out."
Peter Pindar (John Wolcot): *Expostulatory Odes*, Ode xv.

Nail One's Colours to the Mast (*To*). To refuse to surrender. When the colours are nailed to the mast they cannot be lowered in proof of submission.

Nailed. Caught and secured in jail. (*See* CLOU.)
I nailed him (or *it*.) I hooked him, I pinned him, meaning I secured him. Isaiah (xxii. 23) says, "I will fasten him as a nail in a sure place." However, the idea may still be, I secured him by making him pay down the earnest on *The Nail*. (See *Pay on the Nail*, second clause.)

Nails driven into Cottage Walls. This was a Roman practice, under the notion that it kept off the plague. L. Manlius was named dictator (A.U.C. 390) " to drive the nail."
Our cottagers still *nail horseshoes* to thresholds to ward off evil spirits. Mr. Coutts, the banker, had two rusty horseshoes fastened on the highest step outside Holly Lodge.

Nails of the Cross. *The nails with which our Lord was fastened to the cross* were, in the Middle Ages, objects of great reverence. Sir John Maundeville says, "He had two in his hondes, and two in his feet ; and of on of theise the emperour of Canstantynoble made a brydille to his hors, to bere him in bataylle ; and throghe vertue thereof he overcam his enemyes " (c. vii.). Fifteen are shown as relics. (*See* IRON CROWN.)

Nain Rouge. A Lutin or goblin of Normandy, kind to fishermen. There is another called *Le petit homme rouge*.

Naivete (pron. *nah'-eve-ty*). Ingenuous simplicity ; the artless innocence of one ignorant of the conventions of society. The term is also applied to poetry, painting, and sculpture. The word is formed from the Latin *natus, natura*, etc., meaning nature without art.

Naked Lady. Meadow saffron (*Colchicum Autumnale*). Called naked because, like the almond, peach, etc., the flowers come out before the leaves. It is poetically called "the leafless orphan of the year," the flowers being orphaned or destitute of foliage. Some call it

"Naked Boy," and the "Naked Boy Courts" of London were places where meadow saffron was sold.

Naked Truth. The fable says that Truth and Falsehood went bathing ; Falsehood came first out of the water, and dressed herself in Truth's garments. Truth, unwilling to take those of Falsehood, went naked.

Nakeer. (*See* MUNKAR.)

Nala, a legendary king of India, whose love for Damayanti and subsequent misfortunes have supplied subjects for numerous poems. Dean Milman has translated into English the episode from the *Mahábhárata*, and W. Yates the famous Sanskrit poem called *Nalodaya*.

Na'ma. A daughter of the race of man, who was beloved by the angel Zaraph. Her one wish was to love purely, intensely, and holily ; but she fixed her love on a seraph, a creature, more than on her Creator ; therefore, in punishment, she was condemned to abide on earth, "unchanged in heart and frame," so long as the earth endureth ; but when time is no more, both she and her angel lover will be admitted into those courts " where love never dies." (*Moore : Loves of the Angels*, story iii.)

Namby Pamby Philips. Ambrose Philips (1671-1749). His nickname was bestowed upon him by Harry Carey, the dramatist, for his verses addressed to Lord Carteret's children, and was adopted by Pope. This was not John Philips, author of the *Splendid Shilling*. " Namby" is a baby way of pronouncing Ambrose, and "Pamby" is a jingling reduplication.
Macaulay says: "This sort of verse has been called [Namby Pamby] after the name of its author."

Name.
" What's in a name? That which we call a rose,
By any other name would smell as sweet."
Shakespeare : Romeo and Juliet, ii. 2.

To take God's name in vain. To use it profanely, thoughtlessly, or irreverently.
" Thou shalt not take the name of the Lord thy God in vain."—Exod. xx. 7.

Name. Fairies are extremely averse to having their names known, indeed there seems to be a strange identity between personality and name. Thus we are forbidden to take God's "name in vain," and when Jacob wrestled with the angel, he was anxious to know his opponent's name. (Compare the Greek *onoma* and the Latin *anima*.)

Name-son. Name-sake; also name-child, etc.

"God for ever bless your honour, I am your name-son, sure enough."—*Smollett: Adventures of Sir Launcelot Greaves.*

Name the Day. Fix the day of marriage.

Names.

To call a person names. To blackguard a person by calling him nicknames.

Names *of the Puritans.*

Praise-God Barebones. A leather-seller in Fleet Street.

If-Jesus-Christ-had-not-died-for-thee-thou-hadst-been-damned Barebones. His son; usually called Damned Dr. Barebones.

Nancy. The sailor's choice in Dibdin's exquisite song beginning, "'Twas post meridian half-past four." At half-past four he parted by signal from his Nancy; at eight he bade her a long adieu; next morn a storm arose, and four sailors were washed overboard, "but love forbade the waves to snatch our tar from Nancy"; when the storm ceased an enemy appeared, but when the battle was hottest our gallant friend "put up a prayer and thought on Nancy."

Miss Nancy. Mrs. Anna Oldfield, a celebrated actress, buried in Westminster Abbey. She died in 1730, and her remains lay in state, attended by two noblemen. She was buried in a very fine Brussels lace head-dress, a holland shift, with a tucker and double-ruffles of the same lace, new kid gloves, etc.

" 'Odious ! In woollen ? 'Twould a saint provoke !'
Were the last words that poor Narcissa spoke."
Pope: Moral Essays.

Miss Nancy. An effeminate young man.

Nancy of the Vale. A village maiden who preferred Strephon to the gay lordlings who sought her. (*Shenstone.*)

Nankeen. So called from Nankin, in China. It is the natural colour of Nankin cotton.

Nanna. Wife of Balder. When the blind-god slew her husband, she threw herself upon his funeral pile and was burnt to death.

Nannie, to whom Burns has addressed several of his songs, was Miss Fleming, daughter of a farmer in the parish of Tarbolton, Ayrshire.

Nantes (1 syl.). *Edict of Nantes.* The decree of Henri IV. of France, published from Nantes in 1598, securing

freedom of religion to all Protestants. Louis XIV. repealed this edict in 1685.

Nap. *To go nap.* To stake all the winnings on the cards in hand; hence, to risk all on one venture. Nap is a game of cards; so called from Napoleon III.

Nap (*A*), a doze or short sleep, as " To take a nap," is the Anglo-Saxon *hnæppian* or *hnapp-ian* (to take a nap; the nap of cloth is the Anglo-Saxon *hnoppa*.)

Naph'tha. The drug used by Mede'a for anointing the wedding robe of Glaucē, daughter of King Cre'on, whereby she was burnt to death on the morning of her marriage with Jason.

Na'pier's Bones. A method invented by Baron Napier, of Merchiston, for shortening the labour of trigonometrical calculations. Certain figures are arranged on little slips of paper or ivory, and simply by shifting these slips the result required is obtained. They are called *bones* because the baron used bone or ivory rods instead of cardboard.

Napoleon III. Few men have had so many nicknames.

MAN OF DECEMBER, so called because his *coup d'état* was December 2nd, and he was made emperor December 2nd, 1852.

MAN OF SEDAN, and, by a pun, *M. Sedantaire.* It was at Sedan he surrendered his sword to William I., King of Prussia (1870).

MAN OF SILENCE, from his great taciturnity.

COMTE D'ARENENBERG, the name and title he assumed when he escaped from the fortress of Ham.

BADINGUET, the name of the mason who changed clothes with him when he escaped from Ham. The emperor's partisans were called *Badingueux*, those of the empress were *Montijoyeaux*.

BOUSTRAPA is a compound of Bou[logne], Stra[sbourg], and Pa[ris], the places of his noted escapade.

RANTIPOLE = barum scarum, half-fool and half-madman.

VERHUEL. A patronymic, which cannot be here explained.

⁂ There are some very curious numerical coincidences connected with Napoleon III. and Eugénie. The last complete year of their reign was 1869. (In 1870 Napoleon was dethroned and exiled.)

Now, if to the year of coronation (1852), you add either the birth of Napoleon, or the birth of Eugénie, or the capitulation of Paris, or the date of marriage, the sum will always be 1869. For example :

1852 { Coronation.}	1852	1852	1852
1) Birth 8 of 0 Napo- 9) leon.	1) Birth 8 of 2 Eugé- 6) nie.	1) Da'e 8 of 5 mar- 3) riage.	1) Capit- 8 ulat'n 6 of 7) Paris.
1869	1869	1869	1869

And if to the year of *marriage* (1853) these dates are added, they will give 1870, the fatal year.

Napping. *To catch one napping.* To find a person unprepared or off his guard. (Anglo-Saxon, *hnappung*, slumbering.)

Nappy Ale. Strong ale is so called because it makes one nappy, or because it contains a nap or frothy head.

Naŗ'aka. The hell of the Hindus. It has twenty-eight divisions, in some of which the victims are mangled by ravens and owls; in others they will be doomed to swallow cakes boiling hot, or walk over burning sands. Each division has its name: *Rurava* (fearful) is for liars and false witnesses; *Rodha* (obstruction) for those who plunder a town, kill a cow, or strangle a man; *Sûkara* (swine) for drunkards and stealers of gold; etc.

Narcissa, in the *Night Thoughts,* was Elizabeth Lee, Dr. Young's step-daughter. In Night iii. the poet says she was clandestinely buried at Montpelier, because, being a Protestant, she was "denied the charity that dogs enjoy." (For Pope's Narcissa *see* NANCY.)

Narcissus (*The*). This charming flower is named from the son of Cephisus. This beautiful youth saw his reflection in a fountain, and thought it the presiding nymph of the place. He tried to reach it, and jumped into the fountain, where he died. The nymphs came to take up the body that they might pay it funeral honours, but found only a flower, which they called Narcissus, after the name of the son of Cephisus. (*Ovid's Metamorphoses,* iii. 346, etc.)

Plutarch says the plant is called Narcissus from the Greek *narkē* (numbness), and that it is properly *narcosis,* meaning the plant which produces numbness or palsy.

"Sweet Echo, sweetest nymph that liv'st unseen . . .
Canst thou not tell me of a gentle pair,
That likest thy Narcissus are?"
       Milton: Comus, 235, etc.

✱ Echo fell in love with Narcissus.

Nardac. The highest title of honour in the realm of Lilliput. Gulliver received this distinction for carrying off the whole fleet of the Blefuscu'dians. (*Swift: Gulliver's Travels; Voyage to Lilliput,* v.)

Narrow House *or* **Home.** A coffin; the grave. Gray calls the grave a "narrow cell."

"Each in his narrow cell for ever laid,
The rude forefathers of the hamlet sleep."
       Elegy.

Narrowdale Noon (*Till*). To defer a matter till Narrowdale noon is to defer

it indefinitely. "Christmas is coming." *Ans.,* "So is Narrowdale Noon." Your . . . was deferred or delayed, like Narrowdale Noon. Narrowdale is in Derbyshire. The Dovedale is a valley about three miles long, and nowhere more than a quarter of a mile broad. It is approached from the north by a "narrow dale," in which dwell a few cotters, who never see the sun all the winter, and when its beams first pierce the dale in the spring it is only for a few minutes in the afternoon.

Narses (2 syl.). A Roman general against the Goths; the terror of children. (473-568.) (*See* BOGIE.)

"The name of Narses was the formidable sound with which the Assyrian mothers were accustomed to terrify their infants."—*Gibbon: Decline and Fall,* etc., viii. 219.

Narwhal. Drinking-cups made of the bone of the narwhal used to be greatly valued, from the supposition that they counteracted the fatal effects of poison.

Naseby (Northamptonshire) is the Saxon *nafela* (the navel). It is so called because it was considered the navel or centre of England. Similarly, Delphi was called the "navel of the earth," and in this temple was a white stone kept bound with a red ribbon, to represent the navel and umbilical cord.

Nasi. The president of the Jewish Sanhedrim.

Na'so. The "surname" of Ovid, the Roman poet, author of *Metamorphoses.* Naso means "nose," hence Holofernes' pun: "And why Naso, but for smelling out the odoriferous flowers of fancy." (*Shakespeare: Love's Labour's Lost,* iv. 2.)

Nasser. The Arabian merchant whose fables are the delight of the Arabs. D'Herbelot tells us that when Mahomet read to them the history of the Old Testament, they cried out with one voice that Nasser's tales were the best: upon which Mahomet gave his malediction on Nasser, and all who read him.

Na'strond [*dead-man's region*]. The worst marsh in the infernal regions, where serpents pour forth venom incessantly from the high walls. Here the murderer and the perjured will be doomed to live for ever. (Old Norse, *nâ,* a dead body, and *strond,* a strand.) (*Scandinavian mythology.*) (*See* LIK-STROND.)

Nathan'iel (*Sir*). A grotesque curate in Shakespeare's *Love's Labour's Lost.*

Nation of Gentlemen. So George IV. called the Scotch when, in 1822, he visited that country.

Nation of Shopkeepers. Napoleon was not the first to call the English " a nation of shopkeepers " in contempt.

National Anthem. Both the music and words were composed by Dr. Henry Carey in 1740. However, in Antwerp cathedral is a MS. copy of it which affirms that the words and music were by Dr. John Bull ; adding that it was composed on the occasion of the discovery of Gunpowder Plot, to which the words " frustrate their knavish tricks " especially allude.

National Anthems.
Of AUSTRIA. Haydn's *Hymn to the Emperor.*
BELGIAN. The *Brabançonne.*
DENMARK. *Song of Danebrog* [a flag with a white cross, which fell from heaven in the 13th century at the prayer of Waldemar II.].
ENGLAND. *Rule Britannia,* words by Thomson, music by Handel, and *God Save the King.* (*See above.*)
FRANCE. Ancient, the *Chanson de Roland.* Since the Revolution, the *Marseillaise* and the *Chant du Départ.*
GERMANY. Arndt's *Des Deutschen Vaterland :* "Heil Dir im Siegeskranz."
HUNGARY. The *Rakoczy March.*
ITALY. *Daghela Avanti un Pa°so* [*i.e.* Move a step onward], 1821. Garibaldi's warlike *Hymn,* and Godfreoo Mameli's *Italian Brethren, Italy has Awaked,* composed by Mercantini.
RUSSIA. *God Protect the Czar.*
SCOTLAND. Several Jacobite songs, the most popular being *The King shall Enjoy his own Again, When the King Comes o'er the Water,* and *Lilliburlero* of 1688.

National Colours. (*See* COLOURS.)

National Convention. The assembly of deputies which assumed the government of France on the overthrow of the throne in 1792. It succeeded the National Assembly.

National Debt. Money borrowed by the Government, on the security of the taxes, which are pledged to the lenders for the payment of interest.
The *National Debt* in William III.'s reign was £15,730,439.
At the commencement of the American war, £128,583,635.
At the close thereof, £249,851,628.
At the close of the French war, £819,850,421.

Cancelled between 1817 and 1854, £85,538,790.
Created by Crimean war, £68,623,199.
In 1866, £802,842,949.
In 1872 it was £792,740,000.
In 1875 it was £714,797,715.
In 1879 it was £702,430,594.
In 1892 it was £677,679,571.
In 1893 it was £671,042,842.

National Exhibition. So Douglas Jerrold called a public execution at the Old Bailey. These scandals were abolished in 1868. Executions now take place in the prison yard.

National Workshops.—The English name of "Ateliers nationaux," established by the French provisional government in February, 1848, and which were abolished in three months, after a sanguinary contest.

Native. In feudal times, one born a serf. After the Conquest, the natives were the serfs of the Normans. Wat Tyler said to Richard II. :

"The firste peticion was that he scholde make alle men fre thro Ynglonde and quiete, so that there scholdo not be eny native man after that time."—*Higden : Polychronicon,* viii. 457.

Nativity (*The*) means Christmas Day, the anniversary of the birth of Jesus.
The Cave of the Nativity is under the chancel of the "church of the Nativity." In the recess, a few feet above the ground is a stone slab with a star cut in it, to mark the spot where the Saviour was born. Near it is a hollow scraped out of the rock, said to be the place where the infant Jesus was laid.
To cast a man's nativity is to construct a plan or map out of the position, etc., of the twelve houses which belong to him, and to explain the scheme.

Natty. Tidy, methodical, and neat. (Italian *netto,* French *net,* Welsh *nith.*)

Natty Bumppo, called "Leather Stocking." He appears in five of Fenimore Cooper's novels : as the Deerslayer ; the Pathfinder ; the Hawk-eye (*La Longue Carabine*), in the *Last of the Mohicans*; Natty Bumppo, in the *Pioneers ;* and the Trapper in the *Prairie,* in which he dies.

Natural (*A*). A born idiot ; one on whom education can make no impression. As nature made him, so he remains.
A natural child. One not born in lawful wedlock. The Romans called the children of concubines *natura'les,*

children according to nature, and not according to law.

"Cui pater est populus, pater est sibi nullus
   omnes;
Cui pater est populus not habet ille patrem."
                                        Ovid.

Nature. *In a state of nature.* Nude or naked.

Naught (*not "nought"*). Naught is *Ne* (negative), *aught* (anything). Saxon *nâht*, which is *ne âht* (not anything).

" A headless man had a letter [o] to write,
He who read it [*naught*] had lost his sight.
The dumb repeated it [*naught*] word for word,
And great was the man who listened and heard
   [*naught*]."   *Dr. Whewell.*

Naught, meaning bad.

"The water is naught."—2 Kings, ii. 19.

Naughty Figs (Jeremiah xxiv. 2). Worthless, vile (Anglo-Saxon *nâht*, i.e. *n* negative, *aht* aught). We still say a "naughty boy," a "naughty girl," and a "naughty child."

" One basket had very good figs, even like the figs that are first ripe. . . . The other basket had ve y naughty figs, which could not be eaten."

Navigation. *Father of navigation.* Don Henrique, Duke of Viseo, the greatest man that Portugal ever produced. (1394-1460.)

Father of British inland navigation. Francis Egerton, Duke of Bridgewater (1736-1803).

Navvy. A contraction of navigator. One employed to make railways.

" Canals were thought of as lines of inland navigation, and a tavern built by the side of a canal wa called a 'Navigation Inn.' Hence it happened that the men employed in excavating canals were called 'navigators,' shortened into navvies."— *Spencer: Principles of Sociology,* vol. i. appendix C, p. 834.

Nay-word. Pass-word. Slender, in *The Merry Wives of Windsor,* says—

" We have a nay-word how to know each other. I come to her in white and cry *Mum,* she cries *Budget,* and by that we know one another."— *Shakespeare.*

Nayres (1 syl.). The aristocratic class of India. (*See* POLEAS.)

Nazaræans or **Nazarenes** (3 syl.). A sect of Jewish Christians, who believed Christ to be the Messiah, that He was born of the Holy Ghost, and that He possessed a Divine nature; but they nevertheless conformed to the Mosaic rites and ceremonies. (*See below.*)

Nazarene (3 syl.). A native of Nazareth; hence our Lord is so called (John xviii. 5, 7; Acts xxiv. 5).

Nazareth. *Can any good thing come out of Nazareth?* (John i. 46). A general insinuation against any family or place of ill repute. Can any great man come from such an insignificant village as Nazareth?

Nazarite (3 syl.). One separated or set apart to the Lord by a vow. These Nazarites were to refrain from strong drinks, and to suffer their hair to grow. (Hebrew, *nazar,* to separate. Numb. vi. 1-21.)

Ne plus Ultra (Latin). The perfection or most perfect state to which a thing can be brought. We have Ne-plus-ultra corkscrews, and a multitude of other things.

Ne Sutor, etc. (*See* COBBLER.)

Neæra. Any sweetheart or lady-love. She is mentioned by Horace, Virgil, and Tibullus.

" To sport with Amaryllis in the shade,
Or with the tangles of Neæra's hair."
                            Milton: Lycidas.

Neapol'itan. A native of Naples; pertaining to Naples.

Near, meaning *mean,* is rather a curious play on the word *close* (close-fisted). What is " close by " is near.

Near Side and **Off Side.** Left side and right side. "Near wheel" means that to the coachman's left hand; and "near horse" (in a pair) means that to the left hand of the driver. In a four-in-hand the two horses on the left side of the coachman are the near wheeler and the near leader. Those on the right hand side of the coachman are "off horses." This, which seems an anomaly, arose when the driver *walked* beside his team. The teamster always walks with his right arm nearest the horse, and therefore, in a pair of horses, the horse on the left side is nearer than the one on his right.

Thus, 2 is the near wheeler and 1 the near leader, 4 is the off wheeler and 3 is the off leader.

1 | 3
2 | 4
Coachman.

Neat as a Bandbox. A band-box is a slight box for caps, hats, and other similar articles.

Neat as a Pin, or **Neat as a New Pin.** Very prim and tidy.

Neat as Wax. Certainly the waxen cells of bees are the perfection of neatness and good order.

Nebo, the god of science and literature, is said to have invented cuneiform writing. His temple was at Borsippa, but his worship was carried wherever Babylonian letters penetrated. Thus we had Mount Nebo in Moab, and the city of Nebo in Judea.

Nebraska, U.S. A word of Indian origin, meaning the "shallow river."

Nebuchadnezzar. A correspondent of *Notes and Queries* (July 21, 1877) says that the compound Russian word *Ne-boch-ad-ne-tzar* means, "There is no god but the czar." Of course this is not the meaning of the Babylonian proper name, but the coincidence is curious. The *-ezzar* of Nebuchadnezzar means Assyria, and appears in such words as Nabon-assar, Bel-ch-azzar, Nebo-pol-assar, Tiglath-Pil-eser, Esar-haden, and so on. Nabonassar is *Nebo-adan-Assur* (Nebo prince of Assyria); Nebuchadnezzar is *Nebo-chah-adun-Assar* (Nebo, royal prince-of Assyria). Nebo was probably an Assyrian god, but it was no unusual thing for kings to assume the names of gods, as Bel-ch-azzar, where Bel = Baal (Baal king-of Assyria.) (*See* NABO.)

Neb'uchadnez'zar. The prophet Daniel says that Nebuchadnezzar walked in the palace of the kingdom of Babylon and said, "Is not this great Babylon that I have built . . . by the might of my power, and for the honour of my majesty?" And "the same hour . . . he was driven from men, and did eat grass as oxen, and his body was wet with the dew of heaven, till his hairs were grown like eagles' feathers, and his nails like birds' claws" (iv. 29-33).

Necessity. *Make a virtue of necessity.* (*Shakespeare*: *Two Gentlemen of Verona*, iv. 1.)

"Quintilian has *laudem virtutis necessitati damus;* St. Jerome (epistle 54 section 6), *Fac de necessitate virtutem.* In the *Roman de la Rose*, line 14058, we find *S'il ne fait de necessite virtu,* and Boccaccio has 81 *come savia fatta della necessita.*

Necessity the tyrant's plea. (*Milton: Paradise Lost,* book iv. verse 393.)

Neck. "Oh that the Roman people had but one neck, that I might cut it off at a blow!" The words of Calig'ula, the Roman emperor.

To break the neck of an enterprise. To begin it successfully, and overcome the first difficulties. Well begun is half done. The allusion is to killing fowls by breaking their necks.

Neck-verse (Psalm li. 1). "Have mercy upon me, O God, according to Thy lovingkindness: according unto the multitude of Thy tender mercies blot out my transgressions." This verse was so called because it was the trial-verse of those who claimed benefit of clergy;

and if they could read it, the ordinary of Newgate said, "*Legit ut clericus,*" and the convict *saved his neck,* being only burnt in the hand and set at liberty.

"If a clerk had been taken
For stealing of bacon,
For burglary, murder, or rape.
If he could but rehearse
(Well prompt) his neck-verse,
He never could fail to escape."
British Apollo (1710).

Neck-weed. A slang term for hemp, of which the hangman's rope is made.

Neck and Crop. Entirely. The crop is the gorge of a bird.

Neck and Heels. *I bundled him out neck and heels.* There was a certain punishment formerly in vogue which consisted in bringing the chin and knees of the culprit forcibly together, and then thrusting the victim into a cage.

Neck and Neck. Very near together in merit; very close competitors. A phrase used in horse races, when two or more horses run each other very closely.

Neck or Nothing. Desperate. A racing phrase; to win by a neck or to be nowhere *i.e.* not counted at all because unworthy of notice.

Necked. *A stiff-necked people.* Obstinate and self-willed. In the Psalms we read, "Speak not with a stiff neck" (lxxv. 5); and in Jeremiah xvii. 23, "They obeyed not, but made their necks stiff;" and Isaiah (xlviii. 4) says, "Thy neck is an iron sinew." The allusion is to a wilful horse, ox, or ass, which will not answer to the reins.

Necklace. A necklace of coral or white bryony beads used to be worn round the necks of children to aid their teething. Necklaces of hyoscyamus or henbane-root have been recommended for the same purpose. In Italy coral beloques are worn as a charm against the "evil eye."

The diamond necklace (1785). (*See* DIAMOND NECKLACE.)

The fatal necklace. Cadmos received on his wedding-day the present of a necklace, which proved fatal to everyone who possessed it. Some say that Vulcan, and others that Euro'pa, gave the necklace to Cadmos. Harmonia's necklace (*q.v.*) was a similar fatal gift. (*See* FATAL GIFTS.)

Nec'romancy means prophesying by calling up the dead, as the witch of Endor called up Samuel. (Greek, *nekros,* the dead; *manteia,* prophecy.)

Nec'tar. Wine conferring immortality, and drunk by the gods. The Koran tells us "the righteous shall be given to drink pure wine sealed with musk." The food of the gods is *Ambro'sia.* (Greek *nektar.*)

Neddy (a man's name). A contraction and diminutive of Mine Edward— Mine Eddy, My N'Eddy. *Teddy* is the French *tu, toi,* form ; and *Neddy* the nunation form. (Ed', Ted, Ned.)

Neddy. A donkey ; a low cart used in Dublin; so called because its jolting keeps the riders eternally nodding.

"The 'Set-down' was succeeded by the Noddy, so called from its oscillating motion backwards and forwards."—*Sketches of Ireland* (1847).

Neddy. A dunce ; a euphemism for " an ass."

Need Makes the old Wife Trot. In German, " *Die noth macht ein alte weib traben ;* " in Italian, " *Bisogna fà trotter la vecchia ;* " in French, " *Besoin fait trotter la vieille ;* " the Scotch say, " *Need gars naked men run.*"

Needs must when the Devil Drives. The French say : " *Il faut marcher quand le diable est aux trousses ;* " and the Italians say : " *Bisogna andare, quando il diavolo è nella coda.*" If I must, I must.

" He must needs go that the Devil drives." *Shakespeare: All's Well That Ends Well,* i. 3.

Needfire. Fire obtained by friction. It has been supposed to defeat sorcery, and cure diseases assigned to witchcraft. (Danish, *gnide,* to rub.)

Needful (*The*). Ready money, cash. The one thing needful for this life.

Needham. *You are on the high-road to Needham*—to ruin or poverty. The pun is on the word need. Needham is in Suffolk. (*See* LAND OF NOD.)

Needle. *To hit the needle.* Hit the right nail on the head, to make a perfect hit. A term in archery, equal to hitting the bull's-eye.

Eye of a needle. (*See* EYE.)

Negative Pregnant (*A*). A denial which implies an affirmative, and is so interpreted. A law term.

Ne'gro. Fuller says a negro is " God's image cut in ebony."

Negro Offspring.

White father and negro mother. Offspring, mulatto, mulatta.

White father and mulatta mother. Offspring, cuarteron, -rona.

White father and cuarterona mother. Offspring, quintero, quintera.

White father and quintera mother. Offspring, white.

Negro'ni. A princess, a friend of Lucrezia di Bor'gia, Duchess of Ferra'ra. She invited to a banquet the nobles who had insulted her friend, and killed them with poisoned wine. (*Donizetti : Lucrezia di Borgia, an opera.*)

Ne'gus. So called from Colonel Francis Negus, who first concocted it, in the time of George I.

Nehalle'nia. The Flemish deity who presided over commerce and navigation.

Nehushtan (2 Kings xviii. 4). Bits of brass, worthless fragments. When Hezekiah broke in pieces the brazen serpent, he called the broken pieces Nehushtan.

" Such matters to the agitators are Nehushtan." —*Nineteenth Century,* December. 1892, p. 998.

Neiges d'Antan (*The*). A thing of the past. Literally, ")ast year's snows."

" Where are the snows of yester-year ? "
Rossetti.

" The whole has melted away like the *nei es d'antan.*"—*Nineteenth Century,* June, 1891, p. 8.3.

Neken. (*See* NEC.)

Neksheb. The city of Transoxia'na.

Nell's Point, in Barry Island. Famous for a well to which women resort on Holy Thursday, and having washed their eyes with the water of the well, each woman drops into it a pin.

Nem. Con. Unanimously. A contraction of the Latin *nem'ine contradicen'te* (no one opposing).

Nem. Diss. Without a dissentient voice. (Latin, *nem'ine dissent'iente.*)

Nem'ean Games (*The*). One of the four great national festivals of Greece, celebrated at Nem'ea, in Ar'golis, every alternate year, the first and third of each Olympiad The victor's reward was at first a crown of olive-leaves, but subsequently a garland of ivy. Pindar has eleven odes in honour of victors at these games.

Nem'ean Lion (*The*). The first of the labours of Herculês was to kill the Nemean lion (of Ar'golis), which kept the people in constant alarm. Its skin was so tough that his club made no impression on the beast, so Hercules caught it in his arms and squeezed it to death. He ever after wore the skin as a mantle.

" Ere Nemea's boast resigned his shaggy spoils.'
S' it nc. l,

Nem'esis. Retribution, or rather the righteous anger of God. A female Greek deity, whose mother was Night.

- Nemo Me Impune Lacessit. No one injures me with impunity. The motto of the Order of the Thistle. It was first used on the coins of James VI. of Scotland (James I. of England). A strange motto for Puritans to adopt (Matt. xviii. 21, 22).

Neol'ogy. The Rationalistic interpretation of Scripture. The word is Greek, and means new-(theo)-logy. Those who accept this system are called *Neolo'gians.*

Ne'optol'emos or *Pyrrhos.* Son of Achilles; called *Pyrrhos* from his yellow hair, and *Ne'optol'emos* because he was a new soldier, or one that came late to the siege of Troy. According to Virgil, it was this young man that slew the aged Priam. On his return home he was murdered by Orestes, at Delphi.

Nepen'the (3 syl.) or *Nepen'thês*, a drug to drive away care and superinduce love. Polydamna, wife of Tho'nis (or Thone, 1 syl.), King of Egypt, gave nepenthe to Helen (daughter of Jove and Leda). Homer speaks of a magic potion called *nepenthē*, which made persons forget their woes. (*Odyssey*, iv. 228.)

> " That nepenthes which the wife of Thone
> In Egypt gave the Jove-born Helena."
> *Milton : Comus*, 695, 696.

⁂ The water of Ardenne had the opposite effect.

Neper's Bones. (*See* NAPIER.)

Neph'elo-coccyg'ia. A town in the clouds built by the cuckoos. It was built to cut off from the gods the incense offered by man, so as to compel them to come to terms. (*Aristophanes : The Birds.*)

> "Without flying to Nephelo-coccygia we can meet with sharpers and bullies."—*Macaulay.*

Nephew (French *neveu*, Latin *nepos*). Both in Latin and in archaic English the word means a grandchild, or descendant. Hence, in 1 Tim. v. 4, we read—" If a woman have children or nephews [grandchildren]." Propertius has it, " *Me inter seros laudābit Roma nepotes* [posterity].''

⁂ Niece (Latin *neptis*) also means a granddaughter or female descendant. (*See* NEPOTISM.)

Nep'omuk. St. John Nepomuk, a native of Bohemia, was the almoner of Wenceslas IV., and refused to reveal to the emperor the confession of the empress. After having heroically endured torture, he was taken from the rack and cast into the Moldau. Nepomuk is the French *né*, born, and Pomuk, the village of his birth. A stone image of this saint stands on the Carl Brücke over the Moldau, in Prague. (1330-1383.)

Nep'otism. An unjust elevation of our own kinsmen to places of wealth and trust at our disposal. (Latin, *nepos*, a nephew or kinsman.)

Nep'tune (2 syl.). The sea. In Roman mythology, the divine monarch of the ocean. (*See* BEN.)

A son of Neptune. A seaman or sailor.

Neptune's Horse. Hippocampos; it had but two legs, the hinder part of the body being that of a fish. (*See* HORSE.)

Neptu'nian or **Nep'tunist.** One who follows the opinion of Werner, in the belief that all the great rocks of the earth were once held in solution in water, and have been deposited as sediment. The *Vulcanists* or *Plutonians* ascribe them to the agency of fire.

Ne'reids (2 syl.). Sea-nymphs, daughter of Nereus (2 syl.), fifty in number.

Nereids or *Nere'idēs* (4 syl.). Sea-nymphs. Camoens, in his *Lusiad*, gives the names of three— Doto, Nyse, and Neri'ne; but he has spiritualised their office, and makes them the sea-guardians of the virtuous. They went before the fleet of Ga'ma, and when the treacherous pilot supplied by Zacoc'ia, King of Mozam'bique, steered the ship of Vasco da Gama towards a sunken rock, these guardian nymphs pressed against the prow, lifting it from the water and turning it round. The pilot, looking to see the cause of this strange occurrence, beheld the ruin of the rock which had nearly proved the ruin of the whole fleet (bk. ii.)

Ne'reus (2 syl.) A sea-god, represented as a very old man, whose special dominion was the Æge'an Sea.

Neri'ne (3 syl.). One of the Nereids. (*See* NYSE.)

Neris'sa. Portia's waiting-maid; clever, self-confident, and coquettish. (*Shakespeare : Merchant of Venice.*)

Ne'ro. Emperor of Rome. Some say he set fire to Rome to see "how Troy would look when it was in flames:" others say he forbade the flames to be put out, and went to a high tower, where he sang verses to his lute "Upon the Burning of Old Troy."

A Nero. Any bloody-minded man, relentless tyrant, or evil-doer of extraordinary savagery.

Nero of the North. Christian II. of Denmark (1480, 1534-1558, 1559).

Nero's Friend. After Nero's fall, when his statues and monuments were torn down by order of the Senate, and every mark of dishonour was accorded to his memory, some unknown hand during the night went to his grave and strewed it with violets.

Nesr. An idol of the ancient Arabs. It was in the form of a vulture, and was worshipped by the tribe of Hemyer.

Nesrem. A statue some fifty cubits high, in the form of an old woman. It was hollow within for the sake of giving secret oracles. (*Arabian mythology.*)

Nessus. *Shirt of Nessus.* A source of misfortune from which there is no escape; a fatal present; anything that wounds the susceptibilities. Thus Renan has "the Nessus-shirt of ridicule." Hercules ordered Nessus (the centaur) to carry his wife Dejani'ra across a river. The centaur ill-treated the woman, and Hercules shot him with a poisoned arrow. Nessus, in revenge, gave Dejani'ra his tunic, saying to whomsoever she gave it would love her exclusively. Dejani'ra gave it to her husband, who was devoured by poison as soon as he put it on; but, after enduring agony, the hero threw himself on a funeral pile, and was consumed. (*See* HARMONIA'S ROBE.)

" While to my limbs th' envenomed mantle clings,
  Drenched in the centaur's black, malignant
    gore."
        West: Triumphs of the Gout (*Lucian*).

Nest. *To feather one's nest.* (*See* FEATHER.)

Nest-egg (*A*). Some money laid by. The allusion is to the custom of placing an egg in a hen's nest to induce her to lay her eggs there. If a person has saved a little money, it serves as an inducement to him to increase his store.

Nestor. King of Pylos, in Greece; the oldest and most experienced of the chieftains who went to the siege of Troy. A "Nestor" means the oldest and wisest man of a class or company. (*Homer: Iliad.*)

Nestor of the chemical revolution. A term applied by Lavoisier to Dr. Black. (1728-1799.)

Nestor of Europe. Leopold, King of Belgium (1790, 1831-1865).

Nesto'rians. Followers of Nesto'-rius, Patriarch of Constantinople in the fifth century. He maintained that Christ had two distinct natures, and that Mary was the mother of His human nature, which was the mere shell or husk of the divine.

Neth'inim. The hewers of wood and drawers of water for the house of God, an office which the Gibeonites were condemned to by Joshua (Joshua ix. 27). The word means *given* to God.

Nettle. Camden says the Romans brought over the seed of this plant, that they might have nettles to chafe their limbs with when they encountered the cold of Britain.

Nettles. *It is ill work plucking nettles with bare hands,* or belling the cat. It is ill work to interefere in matters which cannot but prove disagreeable or even worse. In French, *"Attacher le grelot."*

Nettoyer (French). *"Nettoyer une personne, c'est à dire luy gagner tout son argent."* (*Oudin: Curiositez Françoises.*) Our English phrase, "I cleaned him out," is precisely tantamount to it.

Never. There are numerous locutions to express this idea; as—
  At the coming of the Coquelicgrues (*Rabelais: Pantagruel*).
  At the Latter Lammas. (*See* LAMMAS.)
  On the Greek Calends (*q.v.*).
  In the reign of Queen Dick. (*See* DICK.)
  On St. Tib's Eve. (*See* TIB'S EVE.)
  In a month of five Sundays.
  (In) la semaine des trois jeudis.
  When two Fridays come together.
  When three Sundays come together.
  When Dover and Calais meet. (*See* DOVER.)
  When Dudman and Ramehead meet. (*See* DUDMAN.)
  When the world grows honest.
  When the Yellow River runs clear.

Never Say Die. Never despair; never give up.

Nevers. Il Conte di Nevers, the husband of Valentina. Being asked by the Governor of the Louvre to join in the massacre of the Protestants, he replied that his family contained a long list of warriors, but not one assassin. He was one of the Catholics who fell in the dreadful slaughter. (*Meyerbeer: Gli Ugonotti, an opera.*)

New Brooms sweep Clean. New servants work hard; new masters keep a sharp look out. (In French, "*Il n'est rien tel que balai neuf.*")

New Christians. Certain Jews of Portugal, who yielded to compulsion and suffered themselves to be baptised, but in secret observed the Mosaic ceremonies. (Fifteenth century.)

New Jerusalem. The paradise of Christians, in allusion to Rev. xxi.

New Man. The regenerated man. In Scripture phrase the unregenerated state is called the old man (*q.v.*).

New Style. The reformed or Gregorian calendar, adopted in England in September, 1752.

New Testament. The oldest MSS. extant are :—(1) The Codex Sinait'icus (𝕏), published at the expense of Alexander II. of Russia since the Crimean war. This codex contains nearly the whole of the Old and New Testaments, and was discovered in the convent of St. Catherine on Mount Sinai, by Constantius Tischendorf. It is ascribed to the fourth century. (2) The Codex Vatica'nus (B), in the Vatican Library. Written on vellum in Egypt about the fourth century. (3) The Codex Alexandri'nus (A), belonging to the fifth century. It was presented to Charles I. in 1628 by Cyrillus Lucaris, Patriarch of Alexandria, and is preserved in the British Museum. It consists of four folio volumes on parchment, and contains the Old and New Testaments (except the first twenty-four chapters of St. Matthew) and the Epistle of Clement to the Corinthians.

New World. America ; the Eastern Hemisphere is called the Old World.

New Year's Day. January 1st. The ancient Romans began their year in March ; hence such words as September, October, November, December, meaning the 7th, 8th, 9th, 10th month, had a rational meaning. Since the introduction of the Christian era, Christmas Day, Lady Day, Easter Day, and March 1st have in turns been considered as New Year's Day ; but since the reform of the calendar in the sixteenth century, January 1st has been accepted as New Year's Day, because it was the eighth day after the Nativity, when Jesus was circumcised (Luke ii. 21). (*See* NEW STYLE.)

⁂ The civil and legal year began March 25th till after the alteration of the style, in 1752, when it was fixed, like the historic year, to January 1st. In Scotland the legal year was changed to January 1st as far back as 1600 ; the proclamation was made Nov. 27, 1599.

New Year's Gifts. The Greeks transmitted the custom to the Romans,

and the Romans to the early Britons. The Roman presents were called *strenæ*, whence the French term *étrenne* (a New Year's gift). Our forefathers used to bribe the magistrates with gifts on New Year's Day—a custom abolished by law in 1290, but even down to the reign of James II. the monarchs received their *tokens*.

N.B. Nonius Marcellus says that Tatius, King of the Sabines, was presented with some branches of trees cut from the forest sacred to the goddess Strenia (*strength*), on New Year's Day, and from this happy omen established the custom.

News. The letters $\begin{smallmatrix} & N & \\ E & & W \\ & S & \end{smallmatrix}$ used to be prefixed to newspapers to show that they obtained information from the four quarters of the world, and the supposition that our word news is thence derived is at least ingenious ; but the old-fashioned way of spelling the word, *newes*, is fatal to the conceit. The French *nouvelles* seems to be the real source. (*See* NOTARICA.)

"News is conveyed by letter, word, or mouth,
And comes to us from North, East, West, and
South."   *Witt's Recreations.*

Newcastle (Northumberland) was once called Moncaster, from the monks who settled there in Anglo-Saxon times ; it was called Newcastle from the castle built there by Robert, son of the Conqueror, in 1080, to defend the neighbourhood from the Scots.

Newcastle (Staffordshire) is so called from the new castle built to supply the place of an older one which stood at Chesterton-under-Line, about two miles distant.

Carry coals to Newcastle. A work of supererogation, Newcastle being the great seat of coals. The Latins have "*Aquam mari infundĕre*" ("To pour water into the sea ") ; "*Si'dera cœlo addĕre*" ("To add stars to the sky ") ; "*Noctŭas Athe'nas*" ("To carry owls to Athens," which abounds in them).

Newcastle Programme. (*See* PEOPLE'S CHARTER.)

Newcome (*Colonel*). A character in Thackeray's novel called *The Newcomes.*

Newcomes. Strangers newly arrived.

Newgate. Before this was set up, London had but three gates : Aldgate, Aldersgate, and Ludgate. The new one was added in the reign of Henry I.

Newgate. Nash, in his *Pierce Penilesse,*

says that Newgate is "a common name for all prisons, as *homo* is a common name for a man or woman."

Newgate Fashion. Two by two. Prisoners used to be conveyed to Newgate coupled together in twos.

> "Must we all march?
> Yes, two and two, Newgate fashion."
> *Shakespeare: 1 Henry IV.*, iii. 3.

Newgate Fringe. The hair worn under the chin, or between the chin and the neck. So called because it occupies the position of the rope when men are about to be hanged.

Newgate Knocker (*A*). A lock of hair twisted into a curl, usually worn by costermongers and other persons of similar stations in life. So called because it resembles a knocker, and the wearers of it are too often inmates of Newgate. Newgate as a prison is abolished, but many phrases referring to the prison still remain.

Newland. *An Abraham Newland.* A bank-note, so called from Abraham Newland, one of the governors of the Bank of England in the early part of the nineteenth century, to whom the notes were made payable.

> "I've often heard say
> Sham Abr'am you may,
> But must not sham Abraham Newland."
> *The Eaglet.*

"Trees are notes issued from the bank of Nature, and as current as those payable to Abraham Newland."—*G. Colman : The Poor Gentleman*, i. 2.

Newton (*Sir Isaac*) discovered the prismatic colours of light. (1642-1727.)

> "Nature and Nature's laws lay hid in night,
> God said, 'Let Newton be,' and all was light."
> *Pope.*

The Newton of Harmony. Jean Philippe Rameau was so called from his work entitled a *Dissertation on the Principles of Harmony.* (1683-1764.)

Newton'ian Philosophy. The astronomical system at present received, together with that of universal gravitation. So called after Sir Isaac Newton, who established the former and discovered the latter. (*See* APPLE.)

Next Door to. . . . . Very nearly ; as "next door to a fool."

Next to Nothing. A very little. As, "It will cost next to nothing," "He eats next to nothing."

Ni'belung. A mythical king of Norway, whose subjects are called Nibelungers and territory the Nibelungenland. There were two contemporary kings in this realm, against whom Siegfried,

Prince of the Netherlands, fought. He slew the twelve giants who formed their paladins with 700 of their chiefs, and made their country tributary (Lay iii.). The word is from *nebel* (darkness), and means the children of mist or darkness. (*See* NIBELUNGEN-LIED.)

Nibelung Hoard. A mythical mass of gold and precious stones, which Siegfried obtained from the Nibelungs, and gave to his wife Kriemhild as her marriage portion. It was guarded by Albric the dwarf. After the murder of Siegfried, his widow removed the hoard to Worms ; here Hagan seized it, and buried it secretly beneath "the Rhine at Lochham," intending at a future time to enjoy it, "but that was ne'er to be." Kriemhild married Etzel with the view of avenging her wrongs. In time Günther, with Hagan and a host of Burgundians, went to visit King Etzel, and Kriemhild stirred up a great broil, at the end of which a most terrible slaughter ensued. (*See* KRIEMHILD.)

> "'Twas much as twelve huge waggons in four
> whole nights and days
> Could carry from the mountain down to the
> salt sea bay ;
> Though to and fro each waggon thrice journeyed
> every day.
>
> "It was made up of nothing but precious stones
> and gold ;
> Were all the world bought from it, and down
> the value told,
> Not a mark the less would there be left than
> erst there was I ween."
> *Nibelungen-Lied*, xix.

Nibelungen-Lied. A famous German epic of the thirteenth century, probably a compilation of different lays. It is divided into two parts, one ending with the death of Siegfried, and the other with the death of Kriemhild, his widow. The first part contains the marriage of Günther, King of Burgundy, with Queen Brunhild ; the marriage of Siegfried with Kriemhild, his death by Hagan, the removal of the "Nibelungen hoard" to Burgundy, and its seizure by Hagan, who buried it somewhere under the Rhine. This part contains nineteen lays, divided into 1,188 four-line stanzas. The second part contains the marriage of the widow Kriemhild with King Etzel, the visit of the Burgundians to the court of the Hunnish king, and the death of all the principal characters, including Hagan and Kriemhild. This part, sometimes called *The Nibelungen-Nöt*, from the last three words, contains twenty lays, divided into 1,271 four-line stanzas. The two parts contain thirty-nine lays, 2,459 stanzas, or 9,836 lines. The tale is based on a legend in the Völsunga Saga.

Nibelungen-Nôt. The second part of the famous German epic called the *Nibelungen-Lied* (*q.v.*).

Nibelungers. Whoever possessed the "Nibelungen hoard" (*q.v.*). Thus at one time certain people of Norway were so called, but when Siegfried possessed himself of the hoard he was called King of the Nibelungers; and at the death of Siegfried, when the hoard was removed to Burgundy, the Burgundians were so called. (*See* NIBELUNG.)

∵ In all these Teutonic names *ie* = *e*, and *ei* = *i*.

Nic Frog. (*See* FROG.)

Nice. *The Council of Nice.* The first œcumenical council of the Christian Church, held under Constantine the Great at Nice, or Nicæa, in Asia Minor, to condemn the Arian heresy (325). The seventh œcumenical council was also held at Nice (787).

Nice as Ninepence. A corruption of "Nice as nine-pins." In the game of nine-pins, the "men" are set in three rows with the utmost exactitude or nicety. Nine-pence is an Irish shilling of 1561. (*See* NINEPENCE.)

Nice'an Barks or **Nycean Barks.** Edgar Poe, in his lyric *To Helen*, says—

> "Helen, thy beauty is to me
> Like those Nicean barks of yore,
> That gently o'er a perfumed sea
> The weary, way-worn wanderer bore
> To his own native shore."

The way-worn wanderer was Dionysos or Bacchus, after his renowned conquests. His native shore was the Western Horn, called the Amalthēan Horn. And the Nicean barks were vessels sent from the island Nysa, to which in infancy Dionysos was convoyed to screen him from Rhea. The perfumed sea was the sea surrounding Nysa, a paradisal island.

Nicene Creed. (*See* NICE, COUNCIL OF.)

Niche. *A niche in the Temple of Fame.* The Temple of Fame was the Panthe'on, converted (1791) into a receptacle for illustrious Frenchmen. A niche in the temple is a place for a monument recording your name and deeds.

Nicholas (*St.*). The patron saint of boys, as St. Catherine is of girls. In Germany, a person assembles the children of a family or school on the 6th December (the eve of St. Nicholas), and distributes gilt nuts and sweetmeats; but if any naughty child is present, he receives the redoubtable punishment of the *klaubauf*. The same as *Santa Claus* and the Dutch *Kriss Kringle* (*q.v.*). (*See* SANTA KLAUS.)

St. Nicholas. Patron saint of parish clerks. This is because he was the patron of scholars, who used to be called *clerks*.

St. Nicholas. Patron saint of sailors, because he allayed a storm on a voyage to the Holy Land.

St. Nicholas. The patron saint of Russia.

St. Nicholas. The patron saint of Aberdeen.

St. Nicholas, in Christian art, is represented in episcopal robes, and has either three purses or golden balls, or three children, as his distinctive symbols. The three purses are in allusion to the three purses given by him to three sisters to enable them to marry. The three children allude to the legend that an Asiatic gentleman sent his three boys to school at Athens, but told them to call on St. Nicholas for his benediction; they stopped at Myra for the night, and the innkeeper, to secure their baggage, murdered them in bed, and put their mangled bodies into a pickling-tub with some pork, intending to sell the whole as such. St. Nicholas had a vision of the whole affair, and went to the inn, when the man confessed the crime, and St. Nicholas raised the murdered boys to life again. (*See* Hone's *Everyday Book*, vol. i. col. 1556; Maitre Wace, *Metrical Life of St. Nicholas*.)

Clerks or *Knights of St. Nicholas.* Thieves; so called because St. Nicholas was their patron saint; not that he aided them in their wrong-doing, but because on one occasion he induced some thieves to restore their plunder. Probably St. Nicholas is simply a pun for Nick, and thieves may be called the devil's clerks or knights with much propriety.

"I think yonder come prancing down the hills from Kingston a couple of St. Nicholas's clerks."
—*Rowley: Match at Midnight* (1633).

Nick, in Scandinavian mythology, is a water-wraith or kelpie. There are nicks in sea, lake, river, and waterfall. Both Catholic and Protestant clergy have laboured to stir up an aversion to these beings. They are sometimes represented as half-child, half-horse, the hoofs being reversed, and sometimes as old men sitting on rocks wringing the water from their hair. This kelpie must not be confounded with the *nix* (*q.v.*).

Old Nick is the Scandinavian wraith under the form and fashion of an old man. Butler says the word is derived from Nicholas Machiavel, but this can be only a poetical satire, as the term existed many years before the birth of that Florentine.

> " Nick Machiavel had ne'er a trick
> (Though he gives name to our old Nick)
> But was below the least of these."
> *Hudibras,* iii. 1.

Old Nick. Grimm says the word Nick is Neken or Nikken, the evil spirit of the North. In Scandinavia there is scarcely a river without its Nikr or wraith. (*See* NICKAR and NICOR. Anglo-Saxon *nicor,* a monster.)

He nicked it. Won, hit, accomplished it. A nick is a winning throw of dice. Hence Florio (p. 280) says: " To tye or nicke a caste of dice."

To nick the nick. To hit the exact moment. Tallies used to be called " nicksticks." Hence, to make a record of anything is " to nick it down," as publicans nick a score on a tally.

In the nick of time. Just at the right moment. The allusion is to tallies marked with nicks or notches. Shakespeare has, " 'Tis now the prick of noon " (*Romeo and Juliet,* ii. 4), in allusion to the custom of pricking tallies with a pin, as they do at Cambridge University still. If a man enters chapel just before the doors close, he would be just in time to get nicked or pricked, and would be at the nick or prick of time.

Nicka-Nan Night. The night preceding Shrove Tuesday is so called in Cornwall, because boys play tricks and practical jokes on that night.

Nickar or *Hnickar.* The name assumed by Odin when he impersonates the destroying principle. (*Grimm: Deutsche Mythologie.*)

Nickel Silver. A mixed metal of copper, zinc, and nickel, containing more nickel than what is called " German silver." From its hardness it is well adapted for electroplating. (German, *nickel,* which also means a strumpet.)

Nicker. One who nicks or hits a mark exactly. Certain night-larkers, whose game was to break windows with halfpence, assumed this name in the early part of the eighteenth century.

> " His scattered pence the flying Nicker flings,
> And with the copper shower the casement rings."
> *Gay: Trivia,* iii.

Nick'leby (*Mrs.*). An endless talker, always introducing something quite foreign to the matter in hand, and pluming herself on her penetration. (*Dickens: Nicholas Nickleby.*)

Nickname. " An eke name," written *A neke name.* An additional name, an ag-nomen. The " eke " of a beehive is the piece added to the bottom to enlarge the hive. (*See* NOW-A-DAYS.)

Nicknames. *National Nicknames :*

For an *American* of the United States, " Brother Jonathan " (*q.v.*).

For a *Dutchman,* " Nic Frog " (*q.v.*), and " Mynheer Closh " (*q.v.*).

For an *Englishman,* " John Bull." (*See* BULL.)

For a *Frenchman,* " Crapaud " (*q.v.*), Johnny or Jean, Robert Macaire.

For *French Canadians,* " Jean Baptiste."

For *French reformers,* " Brissotins."

For *French peasantry,* " Jacques Bonhomme."

For a *Glaswegian,* " Glasgow Keelie."

For a *German,* " Cousin Michael " or " Michel " (*q.v.*).

For an *Irishman,* " Paddy."

For a *Liverpudlian,* " Dicky Sam."

For a *Londoner,* " A Cockney " (*q.v.*).

For a *Russian,* " A bear."

For a *Scot,* " Sawney " (*q.v.*).

For a *Swiss,* " Colin Tampon " (*q.v.*).

For a *Turk,* " Infidel."

Nick'nev'en. A gigantic malignant hag of Scotch superstition. Dunbar has well described this spirit in his *Flyting of Dunbar and Kennedy.*

Nicodemused into Nothing, that is, the prospects of one's life ruined by a silly name ; according to the proverb, " Give a dog a bad name and hang him." It is from Sterne's *Tristram Shandy* (vol. i. 19), on the evil influence of a silly name on the mind of the bearer of it.

> " How many Cæsars and Pompeys ... by mere inspiration of the names have been rendered worthy of them ; and how many ... might have done ... well in the world ..., had they not been Nicodemused into nothing."
> (This is, to call a man Nicodemus would be enough to sink a navy.)

Nicola'itans. The followers of Nicoläus (second century). They were Gnostics in doctrine and Epicureans in practice.

Nic'olas. (*See* NICHOLAS.)

Nicor (*A*). A sea-devil, in Scandinavian mythology, who eats sailors.

> " My brother saw a nicor in the Northern sea. It was three fathoms long, with the body of a bison-bull, and the head of a cat, the beard of a man, and tusks an ell long, lying down on its breast. It was watching for the fishermen."— *Kingsley : Hypatia,* chap. xii.

Nic'otine (3 syl.) is so named from Jean Nicot, Lord of Villemain, who purchased some tobacco at Lisbon in 1560, introduced it into France, and had the honour of fixing his name on the plant. Our word tobacco is from the Indian *tabaco* (the tube used by the Indians for inhaling the smoke).

Nidhögg. The monster serpent, hid in the pit Hvergelmer, which for ever gnaws at the roots of the mundane ash-tree Yggdrasil'. (*Scandinavian mythology*.)

Niece. (*See* NEPHEW.)

Niflheim (2 syl., *mist-home*). The region of endless cold and everlasting night, ruled over by Hela. It consists of nine worlds, to which are consigned those who die of disease or old age. This region existed "from the beginning" in the North, and in the middle thereof was the well Hvergelmeer, from which flowed twelve rivers. (Old Norse, *nifl*, mist; and *heim*, home.) In the South was the world called Muspelheim (*q.v.*). (*Scandinavian mythology*.) (*See* HVERGELMER MANHEIM.)

Night. The celebrated statue of *Night*, in Florence, is the *chef d'œuvre* of Michael Angelo. In the gallery of the Luxembourg, Paris, is the famous picture of *Night* by Rubens; and at Versailles is the painting of Mignard.

Nightcap (*A*). A glass of grog before going to bed. Supposed to promote sleep.

"The nightcap is generally a little whisky left in the decanter. To do it honour it is taken neat. Then all get up and wish 'good-night.' "—*Max O'Rell : Friend MacDonald*, iii.

Nightingale. Tereus, King of Thrace, fetched Philome'la to visit his wife; but when he reached the "solitudes of Heleas" he dishonoured her, and cut out her tongue that she might not reveal his conduct. Tereus told his wife that Philomela was dead, but Philomela made her story known by weaving it into a peplus, which she sent to her sister, the wife of Tereus, whose name was Procnē. Procnē, out of revenge, cut up her own son and served it to Tereus; but as soon as the king discovered it he pursued his wife, who fled to Philomela, her sister. To put an end to the sad tale, the gods changed all three into birds; Tereus (2 syl.) became the *hawk*, his wife the *swallow*, and Philomela the *nightingale*.

Arcadian nightingales. Asses.

Cambridgeshire nightingales. Edible frogs. Liège and Dutch "nightingales" are edible.

Nightmare (*A*). A sensation in sleep as if something heavy were sitting on our breast. (Anglo-Saxon, *mara*, an incubus.) This sensation is called in French *cauchemar*. Anciently it was not unfrequently called the *night-hag*, or the *riding of the witch*. Fu'seli used to eat raw beef and pork chops for supper to produce nightmare, that he might draw his horrible creations. (*See* MARE'S NEST.)

"I do believe that the witch we call Mara has been dealing with you."—*Sir Walter Scott : The Betrothed*, chap. xv.

Nightmare of Europe. Napoleon Bonaparte (1769, 1804-1814, 1821).

Nihilists. A radical society of the maddest proclivities, which started into existence in 1848, under the leadership of Herzen and Bakunin. Their professed object was to annihilate all laws of social community, and reform the world *de novo*. The following is their code :—

(1) Annihilate the idea of a God, or there can be no freedom.
(2) Annihilate the idea of right, which is only might.
(3) Annihilate civilisation, property, marriage, morality, and justice.
(4) Let your own happiness be your only law.

Ni'hilo. *Ex nihilo nihil fit.* From nothing comes nothing—*i.e.* every effect must have a cause. It was the dictum of Xenophanēs, founder of the Eleatic school (sixth century), to prove the eternity of matter. We now apply the phrase as equivalent to "You cannot get blood from a stone." You cannot expect clever work from one who has no brains.

When all is said, "deity" is an exception.

Nil Admira'ri. To be stolidly indifferent. Neither to wonder at anything, nor yet to admire anything.

Nil Desperandum. Never say die; never give up in despair.

Nile. The Egyptians used to say that the swelling of the Nile was caused by the tears of Isis. The feast of Isis was celebrated at the anniversary of the death of Osi'ris, when Isis was supposed to mourn for her husband.

The hero of the Nile. Horatio, Lord Nelson (1758-1805).

Nil'ica or *Sephal'ica.* A plant in the blossoms of which the bees sleep.

Nimble as a Cat on a hot Bakestone. In a great hurry to get away. The bake-stone in the north is a large stone on which bread and oat-cakes are baked.

Nimble as Ninepence. (*See* NINE-PENCE.)

Nimbus characterises *authority* and *power*, not sanctity. The colour indicates the character of the person so invested:—The nimbus of the Trinity is *gold;* of angels, apostles, and the Virgin Mary, either *red* or *white;* of ordinary saints, *violet;* of Judas, *black;* of Satan, some very dark colour. The form is generally a circle or half-circle, but that of Deity is often triangular.

The nimbus was used by heathen nations long before painters introduced it into sacred pictures of saints, the Trinity, and the Virgin Mary. Proserpine was represented with a nimbus; the Roman emperors were also decorated in the same manner, because they were *divi.*

Nim′ini Pim′ini. Affected simplicity. Lady Emily, in the *Heiress*, tells Miss Alscrip the way to acquire the paphian Mimp is to stand before a glass and keep pronouncing nimini pimini. "The lips cannot fail to take the right plie." (*General Burgoyne*, iii. 2.)

This conceit has been borrowed by Charles Dickens in his *Little Dorrit*, where Mrs. General tells Amy Dorrit—

"*Papa* gives a pretty form to the lips. *Papa, potatoes, poultry, prunes,* and *prism.* You will find it serviceable if you say to yourself on entering a room, *Papa, potatoes, poultry, prunes,* and *prism, prunes* and *prism.*"

Nimrod. "A mighty hunter before the Lord" (Gen. x. 9), which the Targum says means a "sinful hunting of the sons of men." Pope says of him, he was "a mighty hunter, and his prey was man;" so also Milton interprets the phrase. (*Paradise Lost*, xii. 24, etc.)

The legend is that the tomb of Nimrod still exists in Damascus, and that no dew ever "falls" upon it, even though all its surroundings are saturated with it.

Nimrod. Any tyrant or devastating warrior.

Nimrod, in the *Quarterly Review*, is the *nom-de-plume* of Charles James Apperley, of Denbighshire, who was passionately fond of hunting. Mr. Pittman, the proprietor, kept for him a stud of hunters. His best productions are *The Chase, the Turf, and the Road.* (1777-1843.)

Nincompoop. A poor thing of a man. Said to be a corruption of the Latin *non compos* [*mentis*], but of this there is no evidence.

Nine. Nine, five, and three are mystical numbers—the diapa′son, diapente, and diatri′on of the Greeks. Nine consists of a trinity of trinities. According to the Pythagorean numbers, man is a full chord, or eight notes, and deity comes next. Three, being the trinity, represents a perfect *unity;* twice three is the perfect *dual;* and thrice three is the perfect *plural.* This explains the use of nine as a mystical number, and also as an exhaustive plural, and consequently no definite number, but a simple representative of plural perfection. (*See* DIAPASON.)

(1) *Nine indicating perfection* or *completion :—*

Deucalion's ark, made by the advice of Prome′theus, was tossed about for nine days, when it stranded on the top of Mount Parnassus.

Rigged to the nines or *Dressed up to the nines.* To perfection from head to foot.

There are nine earths. Hela is goddess of the ninth. Milton speaks of "nine-enfolded spheres." (*Arcades.*)

There are *nine worlds in Niftheim.*

There are *nine heavens.* (*See* HEAVENS.)

Gods. Macaulay makes Porsĕna swear by the nine gods. (*See* NINE GODS.)

There are *nine orders of angels.* (*See* ANGELS.)

There are the *nine korrigan* or fays of Armorica.

There were *nine muses.*

There were *nine Gallicenæ* or virgin priestesses of the ancient Gallic oracle. The serpents or Nagas of Southern Indian worship are nine in number.

There are *nine worthies* (*q.v.*); and nine worthies of *London.* (*See* WORTHIES.)

There were *nine rivers of hell*, according to classic mythology. Milton says the gates of hell are "thrice three-fold; three folds are brass, three iron, three of adamantine rock. They had nine folds, nine plates, and nine linings." (*Paradise Lost*, ii. 645.)

Fallen angels. Milton says, when they were cast out of heaven, "Nine days they fell." (*Paradise Lost*, vi. 871.)

Vulcan, when kicked out of heaven, was nine days falling, and then lighted on the island Lemnos.

Nice as ninepence. (*See* NICE.)

(2) Examples of the use of nine *as an exhaustive plural :—*

Nine tailors make a man does not mean the number nine in the ordinary acceptation, but simply the plural of tailor without relation to number. As a tailor is not so robust and powerful as the ordinary run of men, it requires more than one to match a man. (*See* TAILORS.)

A nine days' wonder is a wonder that lasts more than a day; here nine equals "several."

A cat has nine lives—i.e. a cat is popularly supposed to be more tenacious of life than animals in general.

Possession is nine points of the law—i.e. several points, or every advantage a person can have short of right.

There are *nine crowns* recognised in heraldry. (*See* CROWNS.)

A *fee* asked a Norman peasant to change babes with her, but the peasant replied, "No, not if your child were nine times fairer than my own." (*Fairy Mythology,* p. 473.)

(3) *Nine as a mystic number.* Examples of its superstitious use:—

The Abracadabra was worn nine days, and then flung into a river.

Cadency. There are nine marks of cadency.

Cat. The whip for punishing evildoers was a *cat-o'-nine-tails,* from the superstitious notion that a flogging by a " trinity of trinities " would be both more sacred and more efficacious.

Diamonds. (*See* " Diamond Jousts," *under the word* DIAMOND.)

Fairies. In order to see the fairies, a person is directed to put "nine grains of wheat on a four-leaved clover."

Hel has dominion over nine worlds.

Hydra. The hydra had nine heads. (*See* HYDRA.)

Leases used to be granted for 999 years, that is *three* times *three-three-three.* Even now they run for ninety-nine years, the dual of a trinity of trinities. Some leases run to 9,999 years.

At the *Lemu'ria,* held by the Romans on the 9th, 11th, and 13th of May, persons haunted threw black beans over their heads, pronouncing nine times the words: " Avaunt, ye spectres from this house ! " and the exorcism was complete. (See *Ovid's Fasti.*)

Magpies. To see nine magpies is most unlucky. (*See* MAGPIE.)

Odin's ring dropped eight other rings every *ninth night.*

Ordeals. In the ordeal by fire, nine hot ploughshares were laid lengthwise at unequal distances.

Peas. If a servant finds nine green peas in a peascod, she lays it on the lintel of the kitchen door, and the first man that enters in is to be her cavalier.

Seal. The people of Feroes say that the seal casts off its skin every ninth month, and assumes a human form to sport about the land. (*Thiele,* iii. 51.)

Styx encompassed the infernal regions in nine circles.

Toast. We drink a *Three-times-three* to those most highly honoured.

Witches. The weird sisters in *Macbeth* sang, as they danced round the cauldron, " Thrice to thine, and thrice to mine, and thrice again to make up nine ; " and then declared " the charm wound up."

Wresting thread. Nine knots are made on black wool as a charm for a sprained ankle.

(4) *Promiscuous examples :—*

Niobe's children lay nine days in their blood before they were buried.

Nine buttons of official rank in China.

Nine of Diamonds (*q.v.*). The curse of Scotland.

There are nine mandarins (*q.v.*).

Planets. The nine are: (1) Mercury, (2) Venus, (3) Earth, (4) Mars, (5) the Planetoids, (6) Jupiter, (7) Saturn, (8) Uranus, (9) Neptune.

According to the Ptolemaic system, there were seven planets, the Firmament or the Fixt, and the Crystalline. Above these nine came the Primum Mobile or First Moved, and the Empyrean or abode of Deity.

The followers of Jai'na, a heterodox sect of the Hindus, believe all objects are classed under nine categories. (*See* JAINAS.)

Shakespeare speaks of the "ninth part of a hair."

" I'll cavil on the ninth part of a hair."
                                   1 Hen. IV., iii 1.

Nine. *To look nine ways.* To squint.

Nine. The superlative of superlatives in Eastern estimation. It is by nines that Eastern presents are given when the donor wishes to extend his bounty to the highest pitch of munificence.

" He [Dakianos] caused himself to be preceded by nine superb camels. The *first* was loaded with 9 suits of gold adorned with jewels ; the *second* bore 9 sashes, the hilts and scabbards of which were adorned with diamonds ; upon the *third* camel were 9 suits of armour ; the *fourth* had 9 suits of horse furniture ; the *fifth* had 9 cases full of sapphires ; the *sixth* had 9 cases full of rubies ; the *seventh,* 9 cases full of emeralds ; the *eighth* had 9 cases full of amethysts ; and the *ninth* had 9 cases full of diamonds."—*Comte de Caylus: Oriental Tales ; Dakianos and the Seven Sleepers.*

Nine Crosses. Altar crosses, processional crosses, roods on lofts, reliquary crosses, consecration crosses, marking crosses, pectoral crosses, spire crosses, and crosses pendent over altars. (*Pugin : Glossary of Ecclesiastical Ornaments.*)

Nine Crowns. (*See* CROWNS.)

Nine Days' Wonder (*A*). Something that causes a great sensation for a few days, and then passes into the limbo of things forgotten. In Bohn's *Handbook of Proverbs* we have " A wonder lasts nine days, and then the puppy's eyes are open," alluding to cats and dogs, which are born blind. As much as to say, the eyes of the public are blind in astonishment for nine days, but then their eyes are open, and they see too much to wonder any longer.

"*King :* You'd think it strange if I should marry her.
Gloster : That would be ten days' wonder, at the least.
King : That's a day longer than a wonder lasts."
       Shakespeare : 3 *Henry VI.,* iii. 2.

Nine Gods (*The*). (1) Of the Etruscans : Juno, Minerva, and Tin'ia (*the three chief*) ; the other six were Vulcan, Mars, and Saturn, Herculēs, Summānus, and Vedius.

"Lars Porsēna of Clusium
By the nine gods he swore
That the great house of Tarquin
Should suffer wrong no more."
Macaulay : Lays of Ancient Rome (*Horatius*, i.).

(2) Of the Sabines (2 syl.). Herculēs, Romulus, Esculapius, Bacchus, Ænēas, Vesta, Santa, Fortuna, and Fidēs.

Nine Points of the Law. Success in a law-suit requires (1) a good deal of money ; (2) a good deal of patience ; (3) a good cause ; (4) a good lawyer ; (5) a good counsel ; (6) good witnesses ; (7) a good jury ; (8) a good judge ; and (9) good luck.

Nine Spheres (*The*). Milton, in his *Arcades,* speaks of the "celestial syrens' harmony that sit upon the nine enfolded spheres." The nine spheres are those of the Moon, of Mercury, of Venus, of the Sun, of Mars, of Jupiter, of Saturn, of the Firmament, and of the Crystalline. Above these nine heavens or spheres come the Primum Mobile, and then the Heaven of the heavens, or abode of Deity and His angels.

The earth was supposed to be in the centre of this system.

Nine Worthies. Joshua, David, and Judas Maccabæus ; Hector, Alexander, and Julius Cæsar ; Arthur, Charlemagne, and Godfrey of Bouillon.

"Nine worthies were they called, of different rites—
Three Jews, three pagans, and three Christian knights."
       Dryden : The Flower and the Leaf.

Nine worthies (privy councillors to William III.) :—
Whigs : Devonshire, Dorset, Monmouth, and Edward Russell.
Tories : Caërmarthen, Pembroke, Nottingham, Marlborough, and Lowther.
Nine worthies of London. (*See* WORTHIES.)

Ninepence. *Nimble as ninepence.* Silver ninepences were common till the year 1696, when all unmilled coin was called in. These ninepences were very *pliable* or nimble, and, being bent, were given as love tokens, the usual formula of presentation being *To my love, from my love.* (*See* NICE AS NINEPENCE.)

Nin'ian (*St.*). The apostle of the Picts (fourth and fifth centuries).

Ninon de l'Enclos, noted for her beauty, wit, and gaiety. She had two natural sons, one of whom fell in love with her, and blew out his brains when he discovered the relationship. (1615-1706.)

Ni'nus. Son of Belus, husband of Semir'amis, and the reputed builder of Nineveh.

Niobe (3 syl.). The personification of female sorrow. According to Grecian fable, Niobe was the mother of twelve children, and taunted Lato'na because she had only two—namely, Apollo and Diana. Lato'na commanded her children to avenge the insult, and they caused all the sons and daughters of Niobe to die. Niobe was inconsolable, wept herself to death, and was changed into a stone, from which ran water. "Like Niobe, all tears" (*Hamlet.*)

The group of Niobe and her children, in Florence, was discovered at Rome in 1583, and was the work either of Scopas or Praxit'eles.

The Niobe of nations. So Lord Byron styles Rome, the "lone mother of dead empires," with "broken thrones and temples ;" a "chaos of ruins ;" a "desert where we steer stumbling o'er recollections." (*Childe Harold,* canto iv. stanza 79.)

Niord. The Scandinavian sea-god. He was not one of the Æsīr. Niörd's son was Frey (the fairy of the clouds), and his daughter was Freyja. His home was Noatun. Niörd was not a sea-god, like Neptune, but the Spirit of water and air. The Scandinavian Neptune was Ægīr, whose wife was Skadi.

Nip (*A*). As a "nip of whisky," a "nip of brandy," "just a nip." A nipperkin was a small measure. (Dutch, *nippen,* a sip.)

Nip in the Bud. Destroy before it has developed. "Nip sin in the bud," Latin, "*Obsta principiis,*" "*Venienti occurite morbo.*" "Resist beginnings."

Nip-cheese or **Nip-farthing.** A miser, who nips or pinches closely his cheese and farthings. (Dutch, *nippen.*)

Nipperkin (*A*). A small wine and beer measure. Now called a "nip."

"His hawk-economy won't thank him for't
Which stops his petty nipperkin of port."
Peter Pindar : Hair Powder.

Nirva'na. Annihilation, or rather the final deliverance of the soul from transmigration (in Buddhism). Sanskrit, *nir*, out ; *vâna*, blow. (*See* GAUTAMA.)

Nishapoor and **Tous.** Mountains in Khorassan where turquoises are found.

Nisi Prius. *A Nisi Case*, a cause to be tried in the assize courts. *Sittings at Nisi Prius*, sessions of Nisi Prius Courts, which never try criminal cases. *Trial at Nisi*, a trial before judges of assize. An action at one time could be tried only in the court where it was brought, but Magna Charta provided that certain cases, instead of being tried at Westminster in the superior courts, should be tried in their proper counties before judges of assize. The words "Nisi Prius" are two words on which the following clause attached to the writs entirely hinges :—"We command you to come before our justices at Westminster on the morrow of All Souls", NISI PRIUS justiciarii domini regis ad assisas capiendas venerint—*i.e.* unless previously the justices of our lord the king come to hold their assizes at (the court of your own assize town)."

Nis'roch. An idol of the Ninevites represented in their sculptures with a hawk's head. The word means *Great Eagle*.

Nit. One of the attendants of Queen Mab.

Nitouche (*St.*) or *Mie Touche* (Touch-me-not). A hypocrite, a demure-looking pharisee. The French say, *Faire la Sainte Nitouche*, to pretend to great sanctity, or look as if butter would not melt in your mouth.

"It is certainly difficult to believe hard things of a woman who looks like Ste. Nitouche in profile."—*J. O. Hobbes : Some Emotions and a Moral*, chap. iii.

Nix (mas.), **Nixie** (fem.). Kind busybody. Little creatures not unlike the Scotch *brownie* and German *kobold*. They wear a red cap, and are ever ready to lend a helping hand to the industrious and thrifty. (*See* NICK.)

"Another tribe of water-fairies are the Nixes, who frequently assume the appearance of beautiful maidens."—*T. F. T. Dyer : Folk-lore of Plants*, chap. vii. p. 90.

Nixon. Red-faced.

"Like a red-faced Nixon."—*Pickwick.*

Nizam'. A title of sovereignty in Hyderabad (India), derived from *Nizam-ul-mulk* (regulator of the state), who obtained possession of the Deccan at the beginning of the 18th century. The name *Cæsar* was by the Romans used precisely in the same manner, and has descended to the present hour in the form of *Kaiser* (of the German Empire).

Njörd. God of the winds and waves. (*Edda.*)

No Man is a Hero to his own Valet. Montaigne (1533-1592) said : "*Peu d'hommes ont esté admirés par leurs domestiques.*" Mad. Cornuel (who died 1694) wrote to the same effect : "*Il n'y a pas de grand homme pour son valet de chambre.*"

"A prophet is not without honour save in . . . . his own house."—*Matt.* xiii. 56.

No More Poles. Give over work. The cry in hop-gardens when the pickers are to cease working.

"When the sun set, the cry of 'No more poles' resounded, and the work of the day was done."—*The Ludgate Monthly : Hops and Hop-pickers*, November, 1891.

No-Popery Riots. Those of Edinburgh and Glasgow, February 5th, 1779. Those of London, occasioned by Lord George Gordon, in 1780.

Noah's Ark (Genesis vi. 15) was about as big as a medium-sized church, that is, from 450 to 500 feet long, from 75 to 85 feet broad, and from 45 to 50 feet high, with one window in the roof. Toy arks represent it with rows of windows on each side, which is incorrect.

Noah's Ark. A white band spanning the sky like a rainbow ; if east and west expect dry weather, if north and south expect wet.

Noah's Wife [Noraida], according to legend, was unwilling to go into the ark, and the quarrel between the patriarch and his wife forms a very prominent feature of *Noah's Flood*, in the Chester and Townley Mysteries.

"Hastow nought herd, quod Nicholas, also
The sorwe of Noë with his felaschippe
That he had or he gat his wyf to schipe ?"
Chaucer : Canterbury Tales, 3,534.

Noakes (*John*) or **John o' Noakes.** A fictitious name, formerly made use of by lawyers in actions of ejectment. His name was generally coupled with that of *Tom Styles*. Similarly, *John Doe* and *Richard Roe* were used. The Roman names were *Titius* and *Seius* (*Juv. Sat.* iv. 13). All these worthies are the hopeful sons of Mrs. Harris.

Nob (*The*). The head. For *knob*.

Nob of the First Water (*A*). A mighty boss; a grand panjandrum (*q.v.*). First water refers to diamonds. (*See* DIAMONDS.)

Nobs and Snobs. Nobles and pseudo-nobles. (*See* MOB, SNOB.)

Noble. An ancient coin, so called on account of the superior excellency of its gold. Nobles were originally disposed of as a reward for good news, or important service done. Edward III. was the first who coined rose nobles (*q.v.*), and gave 100 of them to Gobin Agace of Picardy, for showing him a ford across the river Somme, when he wanted to join his army.

The Noble. Charles III. of Navarre (1361-1425). Soliman *Tchelibi*, Turkish prince at Adrianople (died 1410).

Noble Soul. The surname given to Khosrû I., the greatest monarch of the Sassanian dynasty. (* , 531-579.)

Noblesse Oblige (French). Noble birth imposes the obligation of high-minded principles and noble actions.

Noctes Ambrosia'næ. While Lockhart was writing *Vale'rius*, he was in the habit of taking walks with Professor Wilson every morning, and of supping with Blackwood at Ambrose's, a small tavern in Edinburgh. One night Lockhart said, "What a pity there has not been a short-hand writer here to take down all the good things that have been said!" and next day he produced a paper from memory, and called it *Noctes Ambrosiana.* That was the first of the series. The part ascribed to Hogg, the Ettrick Shepherd, is purely supposititious.

Noc'tuas Athe'nas Ferre. To carry coals to Newcastle. Athens abounded with owls, and Minerva was therefore symbolised by an owl. To send owls to Athens would be wasteful and extravagant excess.

Nod. *A nod is as good as a wink to a blind horse.* Whether you nod or whether you wink, if a horse is blind he knows it not; and a person who *will* not see takes no notice of hints and signs. The common use of the phrase, however, is the contrary meaning, viz. "I twig your meaning, though you speak darkly of what you purpose; but mum's the word."

"A nod is as good as a wink to a blind horse; and there are certain understandings, in public as well as in private life, which it is better for all parties not to put into writing."—*The Nineteenth Century* (July, 1893, p. 6).

Nod (*The Land of*). (*See* LAND OF NOD.)

Noddy. A *Tom Noddy* is a very foolish or half-witted person, "a noodle." The marine birds called Noddies are so silly that anyone can go up to them and knock them down with a stick. A donkey is called a Neddy Noddy.

✢ Minshew has a capital guess derivation, well fitted for a Dictionary of Fable. He says, "Noddy, a fool, so called because he *nods* his head when he ought to speak." Just as well derive wise-man from why, because he wants to know the *why* of everything.

Nodel. The lion in the beast-epic called *Reynard the Fox.* Nodel represents the regal element of Germany; Isengrim, the wolf, represents the baronial element; and Reynard represents the church element.

Noël. Christmas day, or a Christmas carol. A contraction of *nouvelles* (tidings), written in old English, *nowells.*

> " A child this day is born,
> A child of high renown,
> Most worthy of a sceptre,
> A sceptre and a crown.
> Nowells, nowells, nowells !
> Sing all we may,
> Because that Christ, the King,
> Was born this blessed day."
> *Old Carol.*

Noko'mis. Daughter of the Moon. Sporting one day with her maidens on a swing made of vine canes, a rival cut the swing, and Nokomis fell to earth, where she gave birth to a daughter named Weno'nah.

No'lens Vo'lens. Whether willing or not. Two Latin participles meaning "being unwilling (or) willing."

Noli me Tan'gere. Touch me not. The words Christ used to Mary Magdalene after His resurrection. It is the motto of the Order of the Thistle. A plant of the genus *impatiens.* The seed-vessels consist of one cell in five divisions, and when the seed is ripe each of these, on being touched, suddenly folds itself into a spiral form and leaps from the stalk. (*See Darwin : Loves of the Plants,* ii. 3.)

Noll. *Old Noll.* Oliver Cromwell was so called by the Royalists. Noll is a familiar contraction of Oliver—*i.e.* Ol' with an initial liquid.

Nolle Pros'equi [*Don't prosecute*]. A petition from a plaintiff to stay a suit. (*See* NON PROS.)

No'lo Episcopa'ri. [*I am unwilling to accept the office of bishop.*] A very general notion prevails that every bishop at consecration uses these words. Mr. Christian, in his notes to Blackstone, says, "The origin of these words and of this vulgar notion I have not been able to discover; the bishops certainly give no such refusal at present, and I am inclined to think they never did at any time in this country." When the see of Bath and Wells was offered to Beveridge, he certainly exclaimed, "*Nolo episcopari;*" but it was the private expression of his own heart, and not a form of words, in his case. Chamberlayne says in former times the person about to be elected bishop modestly refused the office twice, and if he did so a third time his refusal was accepted. (*Present State of England.*)

Nom. "*Nom de guerre*" is French for a "war name," but really means an assumed name. It was customary at one time for everyone who entered the French army to assume a name; this was especially the case in the times of chivalry, when knights went by the device of their shields or some other distinctive character in their armour, as the "Red-cross Knight."

"*Nom de plume.*" English-French for the "pen name," and meaning the name assumed by a writer who does not choose to give his own name to the public; as *Peter Pindar*, the *nom de plume* of Dr. John Wolcot; *Peter Parley*, of Mr. Goodrich; *Currer Bell*, of Charlotte Brontë; *Cuthbert Bede*, of the Rev. Edward Bradley, etc.

Nom'ads. Wanderers who live in tents; pastoral tribes without fixed residence. (Greek, *nomădĕs*: from *nŏmŏs*, a pasture.)

Nom'inalists. A sect founded by Roscelin, Canon of Compiègne (1040–1120). He maintained that if the Father, Son, and Holy Ghost are *one God*, they cannot be three distinct *persons*, but must be simply three *names* of the same being; just as father, son, and husband are three distinct names of one and the same man under different conditions. Abélard, William Occam, Buridan, Hobbes, Locke, Bishop Berkeley, Condillac, and Dugald Stewart are the most celebrated disciples of Roscelin. (*See* REALISTS.)

Non Angli sed Angeli, si forent Christiani. Words attributed to Gregory (the Great) in 573 when some British children reduced to slavery were shown him at Rome. Gregory was at the time about thirty-five years of age, and was both abbot and cardinal-deacon.

Non Bis in Idem (Latin). Not twice for the same thing—*i.e.* no man can be tried a second time on the same charge.

Non-Com. (*A*). A non-commissioned officer in the army.

Non Compos Mentis or **Non Com.** Not of sound mind; a lunatic, idiot, drunkard, or one who has lost memory and understanding by accident or disease.

Non Con. (*See* NONCONFORMIST.)

Non Est. A contraction of *Non est inventus* (not to be found). They are the words which the sheriff writes on a writ when the defendant is not to be found in his bailiwick.

Non mi Recordo, a shuffling way of saying "I don't choose to answer that question." It was the usual answer of the Italian courier and other Italian witnesses when on examination at the trial of Queen Caroline, wife of George IV., in 1820.

"The Italian witnesses often created amusement, when under examination, by the frequent answer, '*Non mi recordo.*'"—*Cassell's History of England*, vol. vii. iv. 16.

Non Plus ("no more" can be said on the subject). When a man is *come to a non-plus* in an argument, it means that he is unable to deny or controvert what is advanced against him. "To non-plus" a person is to put him into such a fix.

Non Pros. for *Non pros'oqui* (not to prosecute). The judgment of *Non pros.* is one for costs, when the plaintiff stays a suit.

Non Sequitur (*A*). A conclusion which does not follow from the premises stated.

"The name began with *B* and ended with *G*. Perhaps it was *Waters.*" — *Dickens: Nicholas Nickleby*, p. 198.

Nonce. *For the nonce.* A corruption of *for then anes* (for then once), meaning for this once. "An apron" for *a naperon* is an example of *n* transferred the other way. We have some half-dozen similar examples in the language, as "tother day"—*i.e. the other* or *that other* = the other. Nuncle used in *King Lear*, which was originally *mine-uncle*. An arrant knave is a narrant knave. (*See* NAG.)

Nonconformists. The 2,000 clergymen who, in 1662, left the Church of England, rather than conform or submit to the conditions of the Act of Uniformity—*i.e.* "unfeigned assent to all and everything contained in the Book of Common Prayer." The word is loosely used for Dissenters generally.

Nones (1 syl.), in the Roman calendar.

On March the 7th, June, July,
October too, the NONES you spy ;
Except in these, those Nones appear
On the 5th day of all the year.
If to the Nones you add an 8
Of every IDE you'll find the date.
E. C. B.

Nonjurors. Those clergymen who refused to take the oath of allegiance to the new government after the Revolution. They were Archbishop Sancroft with eight other bishops, and four hundred clergymen, all of whom were ejected from their livings. (1691.)

Nonne Prestes Tale. A thrifty widow had a cock, "hight Chaunt'e-clere," who had his harem ; but "damysel Per'tilote" was his favourite, who perched beside him at night. Chaunteclere once dreamt that he saw a fox who "tried to make arrest on his body," but Pertilote chided him for placing faith in dreams. Next day a fox came into the poultry-yard, but told Chaunteclere he merely came to hear him sing, for his voice was so ravishing he could not deny himself that pleasure. The cock, pleased with this flattery, shut his eyes and began to crow most lustily, when Dan Russell seized him by the throat and ran off with him. When they got to the wood, the cock said to the fox, "I should advise you to eat me, and that anon." "It shall be done," said the fox, but as he loosed the cock's neck to speak the word, Chaunteclere flew from his back into a tree. Presently came a hue and cry after the fox, who escaped with difficulty, and Chaunteclere returned to the poultry-yard wiser and discreeter for his adventure. (*Chaucer : Canterbury Tales.*)

This tale is taken from the old French "*Roman de Renart.*" The same story forms also one of the fables of Marie of France, "*Don Coc et Don Werpil.*"

Nor. The giant, father of Night. He dwelt in Utgard. (*Scandinavian mythology.*)

Norfolk. The folk north of Kent, Essex, and Suffolk.

Norfolk-Howards. Bugs. A man named Bugg, in 1863, changed his name into Norfolk-Howard.

Norfolk Street (Strand), with Arundel, Surrey, and Howard Streets, were the site of the house and grounds of the Bishop of Bath and Wells, then of the Lord High Admiral Seymour, and afterwards of the Howards, Earls of Arundel and Surrey, from whom it came into the possession of the Earl of Norfolk.

Norma. A vestal priestess who has been seduced. She discovers her paramour in an attempt to seduce her friend, also a vestal priestess, and in despair contemplates the murder of her base-born children. The libretto is a melodrama by Romani, music by Belli'ni (1831.) (*Norma, an opera.*)

Normandy. *The Poles are the vintagers in Normandy.* The Norman vintage consists of apples beaten down by poles. The French say, "*En Normandie l'on vendange avec la gaule,*" where gaule is a play on the word Gaul, but really means a pole.

The Gem of Normandy. Emma, daughter of Richard I. (*-1052.)

Norna. The well of Urda, where the gods sit in judgment, and near which is that "fair building" whence proceed the three maidens called Urda, Verdandi, and Skulda (*Past, Present, and Future*). (*Scandinavian mythology.*)

Norna of the Fitful Head. A character in Sir Walter Scott's *Pirate*, to illustrate that singular kind of insanity which is ingenious in self-imposition, as those who fancy a lunatic asylum their own palace, the employés thereof their retinue, and the porridge provided a banquet fit for the gods. Norna's real name was Ulla Troil, but after her amour with Basil Mertoun (Vaughan), and the birth of a son, named Clement Cleveland, she changed her name out of shame. Towards the end of the novel she gradually recovered her right mind.

Nornir or **Norns.** The three fates of Scandinavian mythology, Past, Present, and Future. They spin the events of human life sitting under the ash-tree Yggdrasil (*Igg'-dra-sil'*).

⁂ Besides these three Norns, every human creature has a personal Norn or Fate. The home of the Norns is called in Scandinavian mythology "Doomstead."

Norris'ian Professor. A Professor of Divinity in Cambridge University

This professorship was founded in 1760 by John Norris, Esq., of Whitton in Norfolk. The four divinity professors are Lady Margaret's Professor of Divinity, Regius Professor of Divinity, Norrisian Professor, and Hulsean Professor.

Norroy. North-roy or king. The third king-of-arms is so called, because his office is on the north side of the river Trent; that of the south side is called Clarencieux (*q.v.*).

Norte. Violent northern gales, which visit the Gulf of Mexico from September to March. In March they attain their maximum force, and then immediately cease. (Spanish, *nórte*, the north.)

North (*Christopher*). A *nom-de-plume* of Professor Wilson, of Gloucester Place, Edinburgh, one of the chief contributors to *Blackwood's Magazine*.

North. *He's too far north for me.* Too canny, too cunning to be taken in; very hard in making a bargain. The inhabitants of Yorkshire are supposed to be very canny, especially in driving a bargain.

North-east Passage (*The*). A way to India from Europe round the north extremity of Asia. It had been often attempted even in the 16th century. Hence Beaumont and Fletcher:

" That everlasting cassock, that has worn
As many servants out as the North-east Passage
Has consumed sailors."
The Tamer Tamed, ii. 2.

North Side of the Altar (*The*). The side on which the Gospel is read. The north is the dark part of the earth, and the Gospel is the light of the world which shineth in darkness—" *illuminare his qui in tenebris et in umbrâ mortis sedent.*" Facing the altar from the body of the church, the north side is on your left.

North Side of a Churchyard. The poor have a great objection to be buried on the north side of a churchyard. They seem to think only evil-doers should be there interred. Probably the chief reason is the want of sun. On the north side of Glasgow cathedral is shown the hangman's burial place.

There is, however, an ecclesiastical reason:—The east is *God's* side, where His throne is set; the west, *man's* side, the Galilee of the Gentiles; the south, the side of the " *spirits made just*" *and angels*, where the sun shines in his strength; the north, the *devil's* side, where Satan and his legion lurk to catch the unwary. Some churches have still 29

a " devil's door" in the north wall, which is opened at baptisms and communions to let the devil out.

" As men die, so shall they arise; if in faith in the Lord, towards the south . . . and shall arise in glory; if in unbelief . . . towards the north, then are they past all hope."—*Coverdale: Praying for the Dead.*

Northamptonshire Poet. John Clare, son of a farmer at Helpstone. (1793-1864.)

Northern Bear. Russia.

Northern Gate of the Sun. The sign of Cancer, or summer solstice; so called because it marks the northern tropic.

Northern Lights. The Auro'ra Boreä'lis, ascribed by the northern savages to the merriment of the ghosts. (*See* AURORA.)

Northern Wagoner (*The*). Ursa Major, called " Charles's wain," or wagon. The constellation contains seven large stars. " King Charles's Wain " is absurd. " Charles' Wain " is a blunder for the " Churls' or Peasants' Wain."

" By this the northern wagoner has set
His sevenfold team behind the stedfast star [*the polo-star*]." *Spenser: Faërie Queene*, i. 2.

Norval. An aged peasant and his son in Home's tragedy of *Douglas*.

Norway (*Maid of*). Margaret, infant queen of Scotland. She was the daughter of Eric II., King of Norway, and Margaret, daughter of Alexander III. of Scotland. She never actually reigned, as she died on her passage to Scotland in 1290.

Nose. *Bleeding of the nose.* Sign of love.

"' Did my nose ever bleed when I was in your company?' and, poor wretch, just as she spake this, to show her true heart, her nose fell a-bleeding."—*Boulster: Lectures*, p. 130.

Bleeding of the nose. Grose says if it bleeds one drop only it forebodes sickness, if three drops the omen is still worse; but Melton, in his *Astrologaster*, says, " If a man's nose bleeds one drop at the *left* nostril it is a sign of good luck, and *vice versâ*."

Led by the nose. Isaiah xxxvii. 29 says, " Because thy rage against Me . . . is come up into Mine ears, therefore will I put My hook in thy nose . . . and will turn thee back. . . ." Horses, asses, etc., led by bit and bridle, are led by the nose. Hence Iago says of Othello, he was " led by the nose as asses are " (i. 3). But buffaloes, camels, and bears are actually led by a ring inserted into their nostrils.

Golden nose. Tycho Brahe, the Danish astronomer. Having lost his nose in a duel with Passberg, he adopted a golden one, which he attached to his face by a cement which he carried about with him.

" That eminent man who had a golden nose, Tycho Brahe."—*Marryat : Jutland and the Danish Isles,* p. 305.

⁂ General Zelislaus, having lost his right hand in battle, had a golden one given him by Boleslaus III.

To count noses. To count the numbers of a division. It is a horse-dealer's term, who counts horses by the nose, for the sake of convenience. Thus the *Times,* comparing the House of Commons to Tattersall's, says, " Such is the counting of noses upon a question which lies at the basis of our constitution."

To cut off your nose to spite your face, or . . . *to be revenged on your face.* To act out of pique in such a way as to injure yourself: as to run away from home, to marry out of pique, to throw up a good situation in a fit of ill temper, etc., or any similar folly.

To keep one's nose to the grin'-stone. To keep one hard at work. Tools, such as scythes, chisels, etc., are constantly sharpened on a stone or with a grin'-stone. The nose of a stair is the edge, and " nose " in numerous phrases stands for the person's self. In French *nez* is so used in some phrases.

' " From this . . . he kept Bill's nose to the grinding-stone."—*W. B. Yeats: Fairy Tales of the Irish Peasantry,* p. 237.

Paying through the nose. Grimm says that Odin had a poll-tax which was called in Sweden a nose-tax ; it was a penny per nose or poll. (*Deutsche Rechts Alterthümer.*) (*See* NOSE TAX, RHINO.)

To snap one's nose off. To speak snappishly. " Ready to snap one's nose off."

To " pull (or wring) the nose," *tirer* or *arracher le nez* is to affront by an act of indignity ; to snap one's nose is to affront by speech. Fighting dogs snap at each other's noses.

To wipe [one's] nose. To affront a person ; to give one a blow on the nose. Similarly, *to wipe a person's eye ; to fetch one a wipe over the knuckles,* etc., connected with the Anglo-Saxon verb *hweop-an,* to whip, to strike (our whip).

" She was so nose-wipt, slighted, and disdained."—*Nares' Glossary,* p. 619.

⁂ " To wipe off a score," " to wipe a person down," meaning to cajole or pacify ; from the Anglo-Saxon *wipian,* to wipe, cleanse. Hence to fleece one out of his money. Quite another verb to that given above.

To take pepper in the nose. To take offence.

" A man is testy, and anger wrinkles his nose ; such a man takes pepper in the nose."—*Optick Glasse of Humors* (1639).

To turn up one's nose. To express contempt. When a person sneers he turns up the nose by curling the upper lip.

Under your [very] nose. This is French also : " *Au nez et à la barbe de quelqu'un* " (" Just before your face "). Nose = face in numerous locutions, both in French and English ; as, " *Montrer son nez ;*" " *Régarder quelqu'un sous le nez ;*" " *Mettre le nez à la fenêtre,*" etc.

Nose-bag (*A*). A visitor to a house of refreshment who brings his own victuals and calls for a glass of water or lemonade. The reference is to carrying the feed of a horse in a nose-bag to save expense.

Nose Literature.

" Knows he, that never took a pinch,
  Nosey, the pleasure thence that flows ?
Knows he the titillating joy
  Which my nose knows ?
O nose, I am as proud of thee
  As any mountain of its snows ;
I gaze on thee, and feel that pride
  A Roman knows."
    F. C. H[usenbeth], translated from the
      French of *O. Basselin.*

Chapter on Noses, in *Tristram Shandy,* by L. Sterne.
On the Dignity, Gravity, and Authority of Noses, by Taglicozzi or Tagliacozzo (1597).
De Virginitate (sec. 77). A chapter in Kornmann.
The Noses of Adam and Eve, by Mlle. Bourignon.
Pious Meditations on the Nose of the Virgin Mary, by J. Petit.
Review of Noses (Louis Brevitatis), by Théophile Raynaud.
Sermon on Noses (*La Diceria de' Nasi*), by Annibal Caro (1584).

Nose Tax (*The*). In the ninth century the Danes imposed on Irish houses a poll tax, historically called the " Nose Tax," because those who neglected to pay the ounce of gold were punished by having their nose slit.

Nose of Wax (*A*). Mutable and accommodating (faith). A waxen nose may be twisted any way.

" Sed addunt etiam simile quoddam non aptissimum ; Eas esse quoddammodo nasum cereum, posse fingi, flectique in omnes modos, et omnium institutio inservire."—*Juelli Apologia, Ecc. Angl.,* sec. 6.

Nose Out of Joint. *To put one's nose out of joint* is to supplant a person in another's good graces. To put another person's nose where yours is now. There is a good French locution, "*Lui couper l'herbe sous le pied.*" (In Latin, "*Aliquem de jure suo dejicere.*") Sometimes it means to humiliate a conceited person.

"Fearing now least this wench which is brought over hither should put your nose out the joynt, comming betweene home and you."— *Terence in English* (1614).

Nosey. The Duke of Wellington was lovingly so called by the soldiery. His "commander's nose" was a very distinguishing feature of the Iron Duke.

Nos'not-Bo'cai [*Bo'-ky*]. Prince of Purgatory. Purgatory is the "realm of Nosnot-Bocai."

"Sir, I last night received command
To see you out of Fairy land,
Into the realm of Nosnot-Bocai ;
But let not fear or sulphur choak-ye,
For he's a fiend of sense and wit."
King : Orpheus and Eurydice.

Nostrada'mus (*Michael*). An astrologer who published an annual "Almanack," very similar in character to that of "Francis Moore," and a *Recueil of Prophecies*, in four-line stanzas, extending over seven centuries. (1503-1566.)

The Nostradamus of Portugal. Gonçalo Annës Bandarra, a poet-cobbler, whose lucubrations were stopped by the Inquisition. (Died 1556.)

As good a prophet as Nostradamus—i.e. so obscure that none can make out your meaning. Nostrada'mus was a provincial astrologer of the sixteenth century, who has left a number of prophecies in verse, but what they mean no one has yet been able to discover. (*French proverb.*)

Nostrum means *Our own.* It is applied to a quack medicine, the ingredients of which are supposed to be a secret of the compounders. (Latin.)

Not, in riding and driving.

"Up a hill hurry not,
Down a hill flurry not,
On level ground spare him not."
On a Milestone in Yorkshire (near Richmond).

Not at Home. Scipio Nasica was intimate with the poet Ennius. One day, calling on the poet, the servant said, "Ennius is not at home," but Nasica could see him plainly in the house. Well, he simply walked away without a word. A few days later Ennius returned the visit, and Nasica called out, "Not at home." Ennius instantly recognised the voice, and remonstrated. "You are a nice fellow" (said Nasica) ; "why, I believed your slave, and you won't believe me."

This tale is often attributed to Dean Swift, but, if authentic, it was a borrowed *mot.*

Not Worth a Rap. (*See* RAP.)

Not Worth a Rush. (*See* RUSH.)

Not Worth a Straw. (*See* STRAW.)

Not Worth Your Salt. Not worth your wages. The Romans served out rations of salt and other necessaries to their soldiers and civil servants. These rations were called by the general name of salt (*sal*), and when money was substituted for these rations, the stipend went by the name of *sal-arium.*

Not'ables (in French history). An assembly of nobles or notable men, selected by the king, of the House of Valois, to form a parliament. They were convened in 1626 by Richelieu, and not again till 1787 (a hundred and sixty years afterwards), when Louis XVI. called them together with the view of relieving the nation of some of its pecuniary embarrassments. The last time they ever assembled was November 6th, 1788.

Notarica.

A. E. I. O. U. Austria's Empire Is Over all Universal. (*See* A. E. I. O. U.)

Æra. A. ER. A—i.e. Anno ERat Augusti. (*See* ÆRA.)

Cabal. Clifford, Ashley, Buckingham, Arlington, Lauderdale. (*See* CABAL.)

Clio. Chelsea, London, Islington, Office. (*See* CLIO.)

Hempe. "When hempe is spun, England is done." *Henry, Edward, Mary, Philip, Elizabeth.* (*See* HEMPE.)

Hip ! hip ! hurrah ! Hierosolyma Est Perdita. (*See* HIP.)

Ichthus. Ie'sous CHristos THeou Uios Soter. (*See* ICHTHUS.)

I. T. N. O. T. G. A. O. T. U. (*It-notga-otu*)—*i.e. In The Name Of The Great Architect Of The Universe.* A Freemason's notarica.

Koli. King's Own Light Infantry (the 51st Foot).

Limp. Louis, Iames, Mary, Prince. (*See* LIMP.)

Maccabees. Mi Camokah, Baelim Jehovah. (*See* MACCABÆUS.)

News. North, East, West, South. (*See* NEWS.)

Smectym'nuus. Stephen Marshall, Edmund Calamy, Thomas Young, Matthew Newcomen, Uwilliam Spurstow. (*See* SMEC.)

Tory. True Old Royal Yeoman.

The following palindrome may be added : E.T.L.N.L.T.E. *Eat to live, Never live to eat.* In Latin thus : E.U.V.N.V.U.E. *Edas ut vivas, ne vivas ut edas.*

Whig. We Hope In God.
Wise. Wales, Ireland, Scotland, England—i.e. Wales, Ireland, and Scotland added to England.

Notary Public. A law officer whose duty it is to attest deeds, to make authentic copies of documents, to make protests of bills, and to act as a legal witness of any formal act of public concern.

Notation or **Notes.** (*See* Do.)

Notch. *Out of all notch.* Out of all bounds. The allusion is to the practice of fitting timber : the piece which is to receive the other is *notched upon ;* the one to fit into the notch is said to be *notched down.*

Note of Hand (*A*). A promise to pay made in writing and duly signed.

Nothing. "A tune played by the picture of nobody." (*Shakespeare : Tempest*, iii. 2.)

Notori'ety. *Depraved taste for notoriety :—*
Cleom'brotos, who leaped into the sea. (*See* CLEOMBROTOS.)
Emped'ocles, who leaped into Etna. (*See* EMPEDOCLES.)
Heros'tratos, who set fire to the temple of Diana. (*See* DIANA.)
William Lloyd, who broke in pieces the Portland vase. (1845.)
Jonathan Martin, who set fire to York Minster. (1829.)

Nottingham (Saxon, *Snotingaham*, place of caves). So called from the caverns in the soft sandstone rock. Montecute took King Edward III. through these subterranean passages to the hill castle, where he found the "gentle Mortimer" and Isabella, the dowager-queen. The former was slain, and the latter imprisoned. The passage is still called "Mortimer's Hole."
Nottingham poet. Philip James Bailey, author of *Festus.* Born at Bashford-in-the-Burgh, Nottingham. (1816.)

Nottingham Lambs. The roughs of Nottingham.

Nourmahal'. Sultana. The word means *Light of the Harem.* She was afterwards called Nourjehan (*Light of the World*). In *Lalla Rookh*, the tale called *The Light of the Harem* is this: Nourmahal was estranged for a time from the love of Selim, son of Acbar'. By the advice of Namou'na, she prepares a love-spell, and appears as a

lute-player at a banquet given by "the imperial Selim." At the close of the feast she tries the power of song, and the young sultan exclaims, "If Nourmahal had sung those strains I could forgive her all ;" whereupon the sultana threw off her mask, Selim "caught her to his heart," and, as Nourmahal rested her head on Selim's arm, "she whispers him, with laughing eyes, 'Remember, love, the Feast of Roses.'" (*Thomas Moore.*)

Nous (1 syl.). Genius, natural acumen, quick perception, ready wit. The Platonists used the word for *mind*, or the *first cause.* (Greek, *nous*, contraction of *noos·* Pronounce *nouce.*)

Nous Avons Changé Tout Cela. A facetious reproof to a dogmatic prig who wants to lay down the law upon everything, and talks contemptuously of old customs, old authors, old artists, and old everything. The phrase is taken from Molière's *Médecin Malgré Lui,* act ii. sc. vi. (1666.)

"*Géronte.* Il n'y a qu' seule chose qui m'a choqué ; c'est l'endroit du foie et du cœur. Il n'e semble que vous les placez autrement qu'ils ne sont ; que le cœur est du côté gauche, et le foie du côté droit.
Sganarelle. Oui ; cela étoit autrefois ainsi ; mais nous avons changé tout cela, et nous faisons maintenant la médecine d'une méthode toute nouvelle.
Géronte. C'est ce que je ne savois pas, et je vous demande pardon de mon ignorance."

Nova'tians. Followers of Novatia'nus, a presbyter of Rome in the third century, who would never allow anyone who had lapsed to be readmitted into the church.

November 17. (*See* QUEEN'S DAY.)

Novum Or'ganum. The great work of Lord Bacon.

Now-a-days. A corruption of In-our-days, *I' nour days.* (*See* APRON, NAG, NICKNAME, NUGGET, etc.)

Now-now. *Old Anthony Now-now.* An itinerant fiddler, meant for Anthony Munday, the dramatist who wrote *City Pageants.* (*Chettle : Kindhart's Dream*, 1592.)

No'wheres (2 syl.). (*See* MEDAMOTHI.)

Noyades (2 syl.). A means of execution adopted by Carrier at Nantes, in the first French Revolution, and called *Carrier's Vertical Deportation.* Some 150 persons being stowed in the hold of a vessel in the Loire, the vessel was scuttled, and the victims drowned. Nero, at the suggestion of Anice'tus, drowned his mother in this same manner. (French, *noyer*, to drown.)

Nucta, or miraculous drop which falls in Egypt on St. John's day (June), is supposed to have the effect of stopping the plague. Thomas Moore refers to it in his *Paradise and the Peri*.

Nude. Rabelais wittily says that a person without clothing is dressed in " grey and cold " of a comical cut, being "nothing before, nothing behind, and sleeves of the same." King Shrovetide, monarch of Sneak Island, was so arrayed. (*Rabelais : Gargantua*, iv. 29.) The nude statues of Paris are said to be draped in " cerulean blue."

Nugget of. Gold. Nugget, a diminutive of *nug* or *nog*, as logget is of *log*. " A nog of sugar " (Scotch) is a lump, and a " nugget of gold " is a small lump. So a " log of wood " is a billet (Latin, *lignum*), and " loggets " (Norfolk) are sticks of toffy cut up into small lumps.

A correspondent in *Notes and Queries* says *nog* is a wooden ball used in the game of shinney. *Nig*, in Essex, means a " piece ; " and a *noggin* of bread means a hunch.

Nulla Linea. (*See* LINE.)

Nulli Secun'dus Club. The Coldstream Guards.

Nu'ma. The second king of Rome, who reduced the infant state to order by wise laws.

Numan'cia. A tragedy by Cervantes, author of *Don Quixote*, but never published in his lifetime.

Number Nip. The gnome king of the Giant Mountains. (*Musæus : Popular Tales*.)

" She was like one of those portly dowagers in Number Nip's society of metamorphose and turnips."—*Le Fanu : The House in the Churchyard*, p. 132.

Number One. Oneself.

To take care of number one, is to look after oneself, to seek one's own interest ; to be selfish.

Number of the Beast. " It is the number of a man, and his number is Six hundred threescore and six " (Rev. xiii. 18). This number has been applied to divers persons previously assumed to be Antichrist ; as Apostătes, Benedictos, Diocletian, Evanthas, Julian (the Apostate), Lampetis, Lateinos, Luther, Mahomet, Mysterium, Napoleon I., Nikĕtēs, Paul V., Silvester II., Trajan,

and several others. Also to certain phrases supposed to be descriptive of the Man of Sin, as Vicar - General of God, Arnoume (*I renounce*), Kakos Ode'gos (*bad guide*), Abinu Kadescha Papa (*our holy father the pope*), e.g. :—

M	a	o	m	e	t	i	s	
40,	1,	70,	40,	5,	300,	10,	200	= 666

L	a	t	e	i	n	o	s	
50,	1,	300,	5,	10,	50,	70,	200	= 666

L	u	th	r	a	n	o	s	
30,	400,	9,	100,	1,	50,	70,	6	= 666

The Nile is emblematic of the year.

N	e	i	l	o	s	
50,	5,	10,	30,	7,	200	= 365

Numbers (from 1 to 13), theological symbols :—

(1) The Unity of God.
(2) The hypostatic union of Christ, both God and man.
(3) The Trinity.
(4) The number of the Evangelists.
(5) The wounds of the Redeemer : two in the hands, two in the feet, one in the side.
(6) The creative week.
(7) The gifts of the Holy Ghost (Rev. i. 12). Seven times Christ spoke on the cross.
(8) The number of the beatitudes (Matt. v. 3-11).
(9) The nine orders of angels (*q.v.*).
(10) The number of the Commandments.
(11) The number of the apostles who remained faithful.
(12) The original college.
(13) The final number after the conversion of Paul.

Numbers.

Army of soldiers. *Regiment*, etc.
Assembly of people.
Batch or *Caste* of bread.
Bench of bishops, magistrates, etc.
Bevy of roes, quails, larks, pheasants, ladies, etc.
Board of directors.
Brood of chickens, etc.
Catch of fish taken in nets, etc.
Clump of trees.
Cluster of grapes, nuts, stars, etc.
Collection of pictures, curiosities, etc.
Company of soldiers.
Congregation of people at church, etc.
Covey of game birds.
Crew of sailors.
Crowd of people.
Drove of horses, ponies, beasts, etc.
Drum, a crush of company.
Federation. A trade union.
Fell of hair.
Fleet of ships.
Flight of bees, birds, stairs, etc.
Flock of birds, sheep, geese, etc.
Forest of trees.
Galaxy of beauties.
Gang of slaves, prisoners, thieves, etc.
Haul of fish caught in a net.
Head of cattle.
Herd of bucks, deer, harts, seals, swine, etc.
Hive of bees.

Host of men.
House of senators.
Legion of "foul fiends."
Library of books.
Litter of pigs, whelps, etc.
Menagerie of wild beasts.
Mob of roughs, wild cattle, etc.
Multitude of men. In law, more than ten.
Muster of peacocks.
Mute of hounds.
Nest of rabbits, ants, etc.; shelves, etc.
Nursery of trees, shrubs, etc.
Pack of hounds, playing cards, grouse, etc.
Panel of jurymen.
Pencil of rays, etc.
Pile of books, wood stacked, etc.
Posse (a sheriff's). Posse (2 syl.).
Pride of lions.
Rabble of men ill-bred and ill-clad.
Regiment (*A*) of soldiers.
Rookery of rooks and seals, also of unhealthy houses.
Roulcau of money.
School of whales, etc.
Set of china, or articles assorted.
Shoal of mackerel.
Shock of hair, corn, etc.
Skein of ducks, thread, worsted.
Skulk of foxes.
Society (*A*). Persons associated for some mutual object.
Stack of corn, hay, wood (piled together).
String of horses.
Stud of mares.
Suit of clothes.
Suite of rooms.
Swarm of bees, locusts, etc.
Take of fish.
Team of oxen, horses, etc.
Tribe of goats.

Numbers. *Odd Numbers.* "*Numero Deus impare gaudet*" (*Virgil : Eclogues*, viii. 75). Three indicates the "beginning, middle, and end." The Godhead has three persons; so in classic mythology Hecate had threefold power; Jove's symbol was a triple thunderbolt, Neptune's a sea-trident, Pluto's a three-headed dog; the Fates were three, the Furies three, the Graces three, the Horæ three; the Muses three-times-three. There are seven notes, nine planets, nine orders of angels, seven days a week, thirteen lunar months, or 365 days a year, etc.; five senses, five fingers on the hand and toes on the foot, five vowels, five continents, etc. etc. A volume might be filled with illustrations

of the saying that "the gods delight in odd numbers." (*See* ODD, NINE.)

Numbers. *To consult the Book of Numbers* is to call for a division of the House, or to put a question to the vote. (*Parliamentary wit.*)

Numbers. Pythagoras looked on numbers as influential principles.

1 is Unity, and represents Deity, which has no parts.

2 is Diversity, and therefore disorder. The principle of strife and all evil.

3 is Perfect Harmony, or the union of unity and diversity.

4 is Perfection. It is the first square ($2 \times 2 = 4$).

5 is the prevailing number in Nature and Art.

6 is Justice (Perfect Harmony being 3, which multiplied by Trinity = 6).

7 is the climacteric number in all diseases. Called the Medical Number (2 syl.).

2. The Romans dedicated the second month to Pluto, and the second day of the month to the Manes. They believed it to be the most fatal number of all.

∴ 4 and 6 are omitted, not being prime numbers ; 4 is the multiple of 2, and 6 is the multiple of 3.

Numerals. All our numerals and ordinals up to a million (with one exception) are Anglo-Saxon. The one exception is the word Second, which is French. The Anglo-Saxon word was *other*, as First, Other, Third, etc. Million is the Latin *millio* (*-onis*).

∴ There are some other odd exceptions in the language : Spring, summer, and winter are native words, but autumn is Latin. The days of the week are native words, but the names of the months are Latin. We have *dæg*, *monath*, *gear ;* but minute is Latin, and hour is Latin through the French.

Numerals (Greek). (*See* EPISEMON.)

Numero. *Homme de numero*—that is "*un homme fin en affaires.*" M. Walckenaer says it is a shop phrase, meaning that he knows all the numbers of the different goods, or all the private marks indicative of price and quality.

"Il n'étoit lors, de Paris jusqu'à Rome,
Galant qui sût si bien le nun ero."
La Fontaine : Richard Minutolo.

Numid'icus. Quintus Cæcilius Metellus, commander against Jugurtha, of Numidia, about 100 B.C.

Nunation. Adding *N* to an initial vowel, as *Nol* for Ol[iver], *Nell* for Ell[en], *Ned* for Ed[ward].

Nunc Dimittis. The canticle of Simeon is so called, from the first two words in the Latin version (Luke ii. 29-32).

Nunc Stans. The everlasting Now.

"It exists in the *nunc stans* of the schoolmen—the eternal Now that represented the consciousness of the Supreme Being in mediæval thought." —*Nineteenth Century*, December, 1892, p. 953.

Nuncu'pative Will. A will or testament made by word of mouth. As a general rule, no will is valid unless reduced to writing and signed; but soldiers and sailors may simply declare their wish by word of mouth. (Latin, *nuncupo*, to declare.)

Nunky pays for all. (*See* SAM.)

Nuremberg Eggs. Watches. Watches were invented at Nuremberg about 1500, and were egg-shaped.

Nurr and Spell or *Knor* and *Spill*. A game resembling trapball, and played with a wooden ball called a *nurr* or *knor*. The ball is released by means of a spring from a little brass cup at the end of a tongue of steel called a *spell* or *spill*. After the player has touched the spring, the ball flies into the air, and is struck with a bat. In *scoring*, the distances are reckoned by the score feet, previously marked off by a Gunter's chain. The game is played frequently in the West Riding of Yorkshire.

Nurse an Omnibus (*To*) is to try and run it off the road. This is done by sending a rival omnibus close at its heels, or, if necessary, one before and one behind it, to pick up the passengers. As a nurse follows a child about regardless of its caprices, so these four-wheel nurses follow their rival.

Nurseries. In the language of horse-racing, handicaps for two-year-old horses. These horses can be run only with horses of their own age, after the 1st September; and before the 1st July must not run more than six furlongs in length.

Nursery Tales. Well-known ones :—

ARABIAN NIGHTS: *Aladdin's Lamp, The Forty Thieves, Sinbad the Sailor,* and hundreds more.
CARROLL (*Lewis*): *Alice in Wonderland, Hunting the Snark,* etc.
D'AULNOY (*Mme.*): *King of the Peacocks, The Blue Bird,* and many others.
FOUQUE. De la Motte: *Undine.*
GOLDSMITH (*Oliver*): *Goody Twoshoes.* 1765.
GRIMM: *Goblin Tales.*
JOHNSON (*Richard*): *The Seven Champions of Christendom.*
KNATCHBULL-HUGESSEN (Lord Brabourne): *Stories for Children,* etc.
LE SAGE: *The Devil on Two Sticks.*
PERRAULT, Charles (A Frenchman): *Blue Beard, Little Red Riding Hood, Puss in Boots, Riquet with the Tuft, Sleeping Beauty,* etc.
RIDLEY (*James*): *Tales of the Genii.*
SCANDINAVIAN: *Jack and the Beanstalk, Jack the Giant-killer,* and some others.

SOUTHEY: *The Three Bears.*
STRAPAROLA (an Italian): *Fortunatus.*
SWIFT (*Dean*): *Gulliver's Travels.*
VILLENEUVE (*Mme.*): *Beauty and the Beast.*

⁂ It is said that the old nursery rhyme about an old woman tossed in a blanket was written as a satire against the French expedition of Henry V., and the cobwebs to be swept from the sky were the points of contention between the King of England and the King of France.

Nut. *A hard nut to crack.* A difficult question to answer; a hard problem to solve. (Anglo-Saxon, *hnut,* a nut.)

He who would eat the nut must first crack the shell. The gods give nothing to man without great labour, or "*Nil sine magno vita labōre dedit mortalibus.*" "*Qui nucleum esse vult, frangit nucem*" (Plautus). In French, "*Il faut casser le noyau pour en avoir l'amande.*" It was Heraclīdes who said, "Expect nothing without toil."

If you would reap, you also must plough ;
For bread must be earned by the sweat of the brow.   E. C. B.

Nuts of May. *Here we go gathering nuts of May.* A corruption of knots or sprigs of May. We still speak of "love-knots," and a bunch of flowers is called a "knot."

Nuts. Heads; so called from their resemblance to nuts. Probably "crack," applied to heads, is part of the same figure of speech.

" To go off their nuts about ladies,
As dies for young fellars as fights."
          Sims: *Dagonet Ballads (Polly).*

It is time to lay our nuts aside (Latin, *Relin'quere nuces*). To leave off our follies, to relinquish boyish pursuits. The allusion is to an old Roman marriage ceremony, in which the bridegroom, as he led his bride home, scattered nuts to the crowd, as if to symbolise to them that he gave up his boyish sports.

That's nuts to him. A great pleasure, a fine treat. Nuts, among the Romans, made a standing dish at dessert ; they were also common toys for children; hence, to put away childish things is, in Latin, to put your nuts away.

Nut-brown Maid. Henry, Lord Clifford, first Earl of Cumberland, and Lady Margaret Percy, his wife, are the originals of this ballad. Lord Clifford had a miserly father and ill-natured stepmother, so he left home and became the head of a band of robbers. The ballad was written in 1502, and says that the "Not-browne Mayd" was wooed and won by a knight who gave out that he was a banished man. After describing the hardships she would have to undergo if she married him, and finding her love true to the test, he revealed himself to be an earl's son, with large hereditary estates in Westmoreland. (*Percy : Reliques*, series ii.)

Nutcrack Night. All Hallows' Eve, when it is customary in some places to crack nuts in large quantities.

Nutcrackers. The 3rd Foot ; so called because at Albue'ra they cracked the heads of the Polish Lancers, then opened and retreated, but in a few minutes came again into the field and did most excellent service. Now called " The East Kent."

Nutshell. *The Iliad in a nutshell.* Pliny tells us that Cicero asserts that the whole Iliad was written on a piece of parchment which might be put into a nutshell. Lalanne describes, in his *Curiosités Bibliographiques*, an edition of Rochefoucault's *Maxims*, published by Didot in 1829, on pages one inch square, each page containing 26 lines, and each line 44 letters. Charles Toppan, of New York, engraved on a plate one-eighth of an inch square 12,000 letters. The Iliad contains 501,930 letters, and would therefore occupy 42 such plates engraved on both sides. Huet has proved by experiment that a parchment 27 by 21 centimètres would contain the entire Iliad, and such a parchment would go into a common-sized nut ; but Mr. Toppan's engraving would get the whole Iliad into half that size. George P. Marsh says, in his *Lectures*, he has seen the entire Arabic Koran in a parchment roll four inches wide and half an inch in diameter. (*See* ILIAD.)

To lie in a nutshell. To be explained in a few words; to be capable of easy solution.

Nym (*Corporal*). One of Falstaff's followers, and an arrant rogue. Nim is to steal. (*Merry Wives of Windsor.*)

Ny'se (2 syl.). One of the Nereids (*q.v.*).

" The lovely Nysë and Neri'në spring,
  With all the vehemence and speed of wing."
            Camoens: Lusiad, bk. ii.

O

O. This letter represents an eye, and is called in Hebrew *ain* (an eye).

O. *The fifteen O's* are fifteen prayers beginning with the letter O. (See *Horæ Beatissimæ Virginis Mariæ.*)

The Christmas O's. For nine days before Christmas (at 7 o'clock p.m.) are seven antiphones (3 syl.), each beginning with O, as *O Sapientia, O Radix*, etc.

O'. An Irish patronymic. (Gaelic *ogha*; Irish, *oa*, a descendant.)

O', in Scotch, means " of," as " Tam-o'-Shanter."

O.H.M.S. On His [or Her] Majesty's Service.

O.K. A telegraphic symbol for " All right" (*orl korrect*, a Sir William Curtis's or Ar'temus Ward's way of spelling " all correct").

O. P. Riot (*Old Price Riot*). When the new Covent Garden theatre was opened in 1809, the charges of admission were increased ; but night after night for three months a throng crowded the pit, shouting " O. P." (*old prices*) ; much damage was done, and the manager was obliged at last to give way.

O tem'pora ! O mores ! Alas ! how the times have changed for the worse ! Alas ! how the morals of the people are degenerate !

O Yes ! O Yes ! O Yes ! French, *oyez* (hear ye).

    " Fame with her loud'st O yes !
      Cries, ' This is he.' "
        Shakespeare : Troilus and Cressida, iv. 5.

Oaf. A corruption of *ouph* (elf). A foolish child or dolt is so called from the notion that all idiots are changelings, left by the fairies in the place of the stolen ones.

    " This guiltless oaf his vacancy of sense
      Supplied, and amply too, by innocence."
        Byron : Verses found in a Summer-house.

Oak. *Worn on May 29th.* May 29th was the birthday of Charles II. It was in the month of September that he concealed himself in an oak at Boscobel. The battle of Worcester was fought on Wednesday, September 3rd, 1651, and Charles arrived at Whiteladies, about three-quarters of a mile from Boscobel House, early the next morning. He returned to England on his birthday, when the Royalists displayed a branch of oak in allusion to his hiding in an oak-tree.

To sport one's oak. To be "not at home" to visitors. At the Universities the " chambers" have two doors, the usual room-door and another made of oak, outside it ; when the oak is shut or " sported " it indicates either that the occupant of the room is out, or that he does not wish to be disturbed by visitors.

Oak and Ash. The tradition is, if the oak gets into leaf before the ash we may expect a fine and productive year; if the ash precedes the oak in foliage, we may anticipate a cold summer and unproductive autumn. In the years 1816, 1817, 1821, 1823, 1828, 1829, 1830, 1838, 1840, 1845, 1850, and 1859, the ash was in leaf a full month before the oak, and the autumns were unfavourable. In 1831, 1833, 1839, 1853, 1860, the two species of trees came into leaf about the same time, and the years were not remarkable either for plenty or the reverse; whereas in 1818, 1819, 1820, 1822, 1824, 1825, 1826, 1827, 1833, 1834, 1835, 1836, 1837, 1842, 1846, 1854, 1868, and 1869, the oak displayed its foliage several weeks before the ash, and the summers of those years were dry and warm, and the harvests abundant.

Oak-tree. (*See* PHILRMON.)
The oak-tree was consecrated to the god of thunder because oaks are said to be more likely to be struck by lightning than other trees.

Oaks (*The*). One of the three great classic races of England. The Derby and Oaks are run at Epsom, and the St. Leger at Doncaster. The Oaks, in the parish of Woodmanstone, received its name from Lambert's Oaks, and an inn, called the "Hunter's Club," was rented of the Lambert family. It afterwards became the residence of General Burgoyne, from whom it passed to the 11th Earl of Derby. It was Edward Smith Stanley, 12th Earl of Derby, who originated the Oak Stakes, May 14, 1779. On his death, in 1834, the estate was sold to Sir Charles Guy, and was then held by Joseph Smith. The Oaks Stakes are for fillies three years old. (*See* DERBY.)

Oaks Famous in Story.

(1) *Owen Glendower's Oak*, at Shelton, near Shrewsbury, was in full growth in 1403, for in this tree Owen Glendower witnessed the great battle between Henry IV. and Henry Percy. Six or eight persons can stand in the hollow of its trunk. Its girth is 40¼ feet.

(2) *Cowthorpe Oak*, near Wetherby, in Yorkshire, will hold seventy persons in its hollow. Professor Burnet states its age to be 1,600 years.

(3) *Fairlop Oak*, in Hainault Forest, was 36 feet in circumference a yard from the ground. It was blown down in 1820.

(4) The *Oak of the Partisans,* in Parcy

29*

Forest, St. Ouen, in the department of the Vosges, is 107 feet in height. It is 700 years old. (1895.)

(5) The *Bull Oak*, Wedgenock Park, was growing at the time of the Conquest.

(6) The *Winfarthing Oak* was 700 years old at the time of the Conquest.

(7) *William the Conqueror's Oak*, in Windsor Great Park, is 38 feet in girth.

(8) *Queen's Oak*, Huntingfield, Suffolk, is so named because near this tree Queen Elizabeth shot a buck.

(9) *Sir Philip Sidney's Oak*, near Penshurst, was planted at his birth in 1554, and has been memorialised by Ben Jonson and Waller.

(10) The *Ellerslie Oak*, near Paisley, is reported to have sheltered Sir William Wallace and 300 of his men.

(11) The *Swilcar Oak*, in Needwood Forest, Staffordshire, is between 600 and 700 years old.

(12) The *Abbot's Oak*, near Woburn Abbey, is so called because the Woburn abbot was hanged on one of its branches in 1537, by order of Henry VIII.

(13) The *Major Oak*, Sherwood Forest, Edwinstowe, according to tradition, was a full-grown tree in the reign of King John. The hollow of the trunk will hold 15 persons, but of late years a new bark has considerably diminished the opening. Its girth is 37 or 38 feet, and the head covers a circumference of 240 feet.

(14) The *Parliament Oak*, Clipston, in Sherwood Forest, Notts, is the tree under which Edward I., in 1282, held his parliament. He was hunting in the forest, when a messenger came to tell him of the revolt of the Welsh. He hastily convened his nobles under the oak, and it was resolved to march at once against Llewellyn, who was slain. The oak is still standing (1895), but is supported by props.

(15) *Robin Hood's Larder* is an oak in that part of Sherwood Forest which belongs to the Duke of Portland. The tradition is that Robin Hood, the great outlaw, used this oak, then hollow, as his larder, to put the deer he had slain out of sight. Not long ago some schoolgirls boiled their kettle in the hollow of the oak, and burnt down a large part; but every effort has been made to preserve what remains from destruction.

(16) The *Reformation Oak*, on Mousehold Heath, near Norwich, is where the the rebel Ket held his court in 1549, and when the Rebellion was stamped out, nine of the ringleaders were hanged on this tree.

Oakum. Untwisted rope; used for caulking the seams (*i.e.* spaces between the planks) of a ship. It is forced in by chisel and mallet.

To pick oakum. To make oakum by untwisting old ropes. A common employment in prisons and workhouses.

Oan'nes. The Chaldean sea-god. It had a fish's head and body, and also a human head; a fish's tail, and also feet under the tail and fish's head. In the day-time he lived with men to instruct them in the arts and sciences, but at night retired to the ocean. Anedotēs or Idotion was a similar deity, so was the Dagon [*dag-On*, fish On] of the Philistines.

Oar. *To put your oar into my boat.* To interfere with my affairs. "Paddle your own canoe, and don't put your oar into my boat." "*Bon homme, garde ta vache.*" "Never scald your lips with another man's porridge" (*Scotch*). "*Croyez moi chacun son metier, et les vaches sont bien gardées.*"

"I put my oar in no man's boat."—*Thackeray.*

Oars. *To rest on one's oars.* To take an interval of rest after hard work. A boating phrase.

To toss the oars. To raise them vertically, resting on the handles. It is a form of salute.

O'asis. *A perfect o'asis.* A fertile spot in the midst of a desert country, a little charmed plot of land. The reference is to those spots in the desert of Africa where wells of water or small lakes are to be found, and vegetation is pretty abundant. (Coptic word, called by Herodotos *auasis.*)

Oath. The sacred oath of the Persians is *By the Holy Grave—i.e.* the Tomb of Shah Besa'de, who is buried in Casbin. (*Strut.*)

Oaths. Rhadamanthus imposed on the Cretans the law that men should not swear by the gods, but by the dog, ram, goose, and plane-tree. Hence Socrates would not swear by the gods, but by the dog and goose.

Oats. *He has sown his wild oats.* He has left off his gay habits and is become steady. The thick vapours which rise on the earth's surface just before the lands in the north burst into vegetation, are called in Denmark *Lok kens havre* (Loki's wild oats). When the fine weather succeeds, the Danes say, "*Loki has sown his wild oats.*"

Ob. and **Sol.** Objection and solution. Contractions formerly used by students in academical disputations.

Obadi'ah. A slang name for a Quaker.

Obadiah. One of the servants of Mr. Shandy. (*Sterne: Tristram Shandy.*)

Obam'bou. The devil of the Camma tribes of Africa. It is exorcised by noise like bees in flight.

Ob'elisk. (*See* DAGGER.)

Ob'elus. A small brass coin (nearly 1d. in value) placed by the Greeks in the mouth of the dead to pay Charon for ferrying the body over the river Styx. Same as *obŏlos,* an obol.

O'bermann. The impersonation of high moral worth without talent, and the tortures endured by the consciousness of this defect. (*Étienne Pivert de Sénancour: Obermann.*)

O'beron. King of the Fairies, whose wife was Titan'ia. Shakespeare introduces both O'beron and Titan'ia, in his *Midsummer Night's Dream.* (*Auberon,* anciently *Alberon,* German *Alberich,* king of the elves.)

O'beron the Fay. A humpty dwarf only three feet high, but of angelic face, lord and king of Mommur. He told Sir Huon his pedigree, which certainly is very romantic. The lady of the Hidden Isle (Cephalo'nia) married Neptane'bus, King of Egypt, by whom she had a son called Alexander the Great. Seven hundred years later Julius Cæsar, on his way to Thessaly, stopped in Cephalonia, and the same lady, falling in love with him, had in time another son, and that son was Oberon. At his birth the fairies bestowed their gifts—one was insight into men's thoughts, and another was the power of transporting himself to any place instantaneously. He became a friend to Huon (*q.v.*), whom he made his successor in the kingdom of Mommur. In the fulness of time, falling asleep in death, legions of angels conveyed his soul to Paradise. (*Huon de Bordeaux, a romance.*)

Oberthal (*Count*). Lord of Dordrecht, near the Meuse. When Bertha, one of his vassals, asked permission to marry John of Leyden, the count refused, resolving to make her his mistress. This drove John into rebellion, and he joined the Anabaptists. The count was taken prisoner by Gio'na, a discarded servant, but liberated by John. When John was crowned Prophet-king, the count entered his banquet-hall to arrest him, and perished with John in the flames of the burning palace. (*Meyerbeer : Le Prophète, a romance.*)

Obi'dah. An allegory in the *Rambler*, designed to be a picture of human life. It is the adventures and misfortunes which a young man named Obi'dah met with in a day's journey.

Obid'icut. The fiend of lust, and one of the five that possessed "poor Tom." (*Shakespeare : King Lear*, iv. 1.)

O'biism. Serpent-worship. From Egyptian *Ob* (the sacred serpent). The African sorceress is still called *Obi*. The Greek *ophis* is of the same family. Moses forbade the Israelites to inquire of Ob, which we translate wizard.

Ob'iter dictum (Latin). An incidental remark, an opinion expressed by a judge, but not judicially. An *obiter dictum* has no authority beyond that of deference to the wisdom, experience, and honesty of the person who utters it; but a judicial sentence is the verdict of a judge bound under oath to pronounce judgment only according to law and evidence.

Object means forecast, or that on which you employ forecast. (Latin, *ob jacio.*)

Ob'olus. *Give an ob'olus to old Belisa'rius.* Tzetzes, a writer of the twelfth century, says that Belisarius, stripped of all his wealth and honours, was reduced to beggary in his grey old age; that he lived in a mud hut, from the window of which he hung an alms-bag, and that he used to cry to the passers-by, "Give an ob'olus to poor old Belisa'rius, who rose by his merits and was cast down by envy."

Obsequies are the funeral honours, or those which follow a person deceased. (Latin, *ob-sequor.*)

Obstacle Race (*An*). A race over obstacles such as gates, nets, sails laid on the ground, through hoops or tubs, etc.

Obstinate. The name of an inhabitant of the City of Destruction, who advised Christian to return to his family, and not run on fools' errands. (*Bunyan : Pilgrim's Progress*, pt. i.)

Obverse (*The*). Of a coin or medal. That side which contains the principal device. Thus, the obverse of our money coin is the side which contains the sovereign's head. The other side is called the " reverse."

O'by. A river in Russia. The word means *Great River*. Thomson the poet says it is the *ultima thule* of the habitable globe.

Occam (*William of*), surnamed *Doctor Singula'ris et Invincib'ilis*. He was the great advocate of Nominalism. (1270-1347.)

Occam's Razor. *Entia non sunt multiplicanda* (entities are not to be multiplied). With this axiom Occam dissected every question as with a razor.

Occasion. A famous old hag, quite bald behind. Sir Guyon seized her by the forelock and threw her to the ground. Still she railed and reviled, till Sir Guyon gagged her with an iron lock; she then began to use her hands, but Sir Guyon bound them behind her. (*Spenser : Faërie Queene*, book ii.)

Occult Sciences. Magic, alchemy, and astrology; so called because they were occult or mysteries (secrets).

Oce'ana. An ideal republic by James Harrington, on the plan of Plato's *Atlantis*. Also the title of one of James Anthony Froude's books.

Oc'hiltree (*Edie*). A gaberlunzie man or blue-coat beggar, in Sir Walter Scott's *Antiquary*. The original of this bedesman was Andrew Gemmelles.

Octa'vian. Chief character of *The Mountaineers*, a drama by George Colman. He goes mad out of love for Donna Floranthe, whom he suspects of loving another; but Roque, a blunt old *attaché*, seeks him, tells him Floranthe is faithful, and induces him to return.

Octa'vo. A book where each sheet of paper is folded into eight leaves; contracted thus—8vo. (Italian, *un' ottavo ;* French, *in octavo ;* Latin, *octo*, eight.)

Oc'ypus, son of Podalir'ius and Asta'sia, was eminent for his strength, agility, and beauty; but used to deride those afflicted with the gout. This provoked the anger of the goddess who presided over that distemper, and she sent it to plague the scoffer. (*Lucian.*)

Od. (*See* ODYLE.)

Odd Numbers. *Luck in odd numbers.* A major chord consists of a fundamental or tonic, its major third, and its just fifth. According to the Pythagore'an system, "all nature is a harmony," man is a full chord; and all beyond is Deity, so that *nine* represents deity. As the odd numbers are the fundamental notes of nature, the last being deity, it will be easy to see how they came to be considered the great or lucky numbers. In China, odd numbers belong to heaven, and v.v. (*See* DIAPASON, NUMBER.)

"Good luck lies in odd numbers... They say, there is divinity in odd numbers, either in nativity, chance, or death."—*Shakespeare: Merry Wives of Windsor*, v. 1.

✢ No doubt the odd numbers 1, 3, 5, 7, 9, play a far more important part than the even numbers. *One* is Deity, *three* the Trinity, *five* the chief division (*see* FIVE), *seven* is the sacred number, and *nine* is three times three, the great climacteric.

Odd and Even. According to Pythagoras, by the number of syllables in a man's name, the side of his infirmity may be predicted ; *odd* being left, *even* being right.

Thus, to give only one or two examples : *Nelson* (even) lost his right arm and right eye. Raglan (even) lost his right arm at Waterloo. The fancy is quite worthless, but might afford amusement on a winter's night.

Odd's or **Od's**, used in oaths ; as—
Odd's bodikins ! or *Odsbody !* means "God's body," of course referring to incarnate Deity.
Od's heart ! God's heart.
Od's pittikins ! God's pity.
Od's plessed will ! (*Merry Wives of Windsor*, i. 1.)
Od rot 'em ! (*See* DRAT.)
Od-zounds ! God's wounds.

Odds. *By long odds.* By a great difference ; as, "He is the best man by long odds." A phrase used by betting men. In horse-racing, *odds* are offered in bets on favourite horses ; so, in the Cambridge and Oxford races, long odds are laid on the boat which is expected to win.
That makes no odds. No difference ; never mind ; that is no excuse. An application of the betting phrase.

Ode. *Prince of The Ode.* Pierre de Ronsard, a French lyrist. (1524-1585.)

Odhærir. The mead or nectar made of Kvasir's blood, kept in three jars. The second of these jars is called *Sohn*, and the *Bohn*. Probably the nectar is the "spirit of poetry." (*Scandinavian mythology.*)

Odin. Chief god of the Scandinavians.
His *real name* was Siggë, son of Fridulph, but he assumed the name of Odin when he left the Tanaïs, because he had

been priest of Odin, supreme god of the Scythians. He became the All-wise by drinking from Mimer's fountain, but purchased the distinction at the cost of one eye. His one eye is the Sun.
The *father* of Odin was Bör.
His *brothers* are Vilë and Ve.
His *wife* is Frigga.
His *sons*, Thor and Balder.
His *mansion* is Gladsheim.
His *seat*, Valaskjalf.
His *court* as war-god, Valhalla.
His *hall*, Einherian.
His *two black ravens* are Hugin (thought) and Munin (memory).
His *steed*, Sleipnir (*q.v.*).
His *ships*, Skidbladnir and Naglfar.
His *spear*, Gungner, which never fails to hit the mark aimed at.
His *ring*, Draupner, which every ninth night drops eight other rings of equal value.
His *throne* is Hlidskjalf.
His *wolves*, Geri and Freki.
He will be ultimately swallowed up by the wolf Fenris or Fenrir. (*Scandinavian mythology.*)
The vow of Odin. A matrimonial or other vow made before the "Stone of Odin," in the Orkneys. This is an oval stone, with a hole in it large enough to admit a man's hand. Anyone who violated a vow made before this stone was held infamous.

O'dium Theolog'icum. The bitter hatred of rival religionists. No wars so sanguinary as holy wars ; no persecutions so relentless as religious persecutions ; no hatred so bitter as theological hatred.

O'Doherty (*Sir Morgan*). Papers contributed to *Blackwood's Magazine* by William Maginn', LL.D., full of wit, fun, irony, and eloquence. (1819-1842.)

Odor Lucri (Latin). The sweets of gain ; the delights of money-making.
"Every act of such a person is seasoned with the *odor lucri*." —*Sir Walter Scott: The Betrothed* (Introduction).

Odori'co (in *Orlando Furio'so*). A Biscayan, to whom Zerbi'no commits Isabella. He proves a traitor and tries to ravish her, but, being interrupted by a pirate crew, flies for safety to Alphonzo's court. Here Almo'nio defies him, and overcomes him in single combat. King Alphonzo gives the traitor to the conqueror, and he is delivered bound to Zerbino, who awards him as a punishment to attend Gabri'na for one year as her champion, and to defend her against every foe. He accepts the charge, but hangs Gabrina to an elm.

Almonio in turn hangs Odorico to an elm.

Odour. *In good odour ; in bad odour.* In favour, out of favour ; in good repute, in bad repute. The phrases refer to the "odour of sanctity" (*q.v.*).

Odour of Sanctity (*In the*). The Catholics tell us that good persons die in the "odour of sanctity ; " and there is a certain truth in the phrase, for, when one honoured by the Church dies, it is not unusual to perfume the room with incense, and sometimes to embalm the body. Homer tells us (*Iliad*, xxiii.) that Hector's body was washed with rose - water. In Egypt the dead are washed with rose-water and perfumed with incense (*Maillet : Letters*, x. p. 88). Herodŏtos says the same thing (*History*, ii. 86-90). When the wicked and those hated die, no such care is taken of them.

"In both the Greek and Western Church incense is used, and the aroma of these consecrated oils follows the believer from birth to death."— *Nineteenth Century,* April, 1894, p. 584.

✶ The Catholic notion that priests bear about with them an odour of sanctity may be explained in a similar manner : they are so constantly present when the censers diffuse sweet odour, that their clothes and skin smell of the incense.

✶ Shakespeare has a strong passage on the disodour of impiety. Antiŏchus and his daughter, whose wickedness abounded, were killed by lightning, and the poet says :—

" A fire from heaven came and shrivelled up
 Their bodies, e'en to loathing ; for they so
  stunk
 That all those eyes adored them ere their fall
 Scorned now their hand should give them
  burial." *Pericles, Prince of Tyre,* ii. 4.

Odrys'ium Carmen. The poetry of Orpheus, a native of Thrace, called Odrysia tellus, because the Od'rys's were its chief inhabitants.

O'dur. Husband of Freyja, whom he deserted. (*Scandinavian mythology.*)

Od'yle (2 syl.). That which emanates from a medium to produce the several phenomena connected with mesmerism, spirit-rapping, table-turning, and so on. The productions of these "manifestations" is sometimes called *od'ylism.* Baron Reichenbach called it Od force, a force which becomes manifest wherever chemical action is going on.

Od'yssey. The poem of Homer which records the adventures of *Odysseus* (Ulysses) in his home-voyage from Troy. The word is an adjective formed out of

the hero's name, and means the *things* or *adventures* of Ulysses.

Œ'dipus. *I am no Œdipus.* I cannot guess what you mean. Œdipus guessed the riddle of the Sphinx, and saved Thebes from her ravages. (*See* SPHINX.)

Œil. *A l'œil.* On credit, for nothing. Corruption of the Italian *a uffo* (gratis). In the French translation of *Don Quixote* is this passage :—

"Ma femme, disait Sancho Pança, ne m'a jamais dit oui que quand il fallait dire non. Or elles sont toutes de même . . . Elles sont toutes bonnes à pendre . . . passé cela, elles ne valent pas ce que j'ai dans l'œil."

Œil de Bœuf (*L'*). A large reception-room (*salle*) in the palace of Versailles, lighted by round windows so called. The ceiling, decorated by Van der Meulen, contained likenesses of the children of Louis XIV. (seventeenth and eighteenth centuries).

Les Fastes de l' Œil de Bœuf. The annals of the courtiers of the Grand Monarque ; anecdotes of courtiers generally. The *œil de bœuf* is the round window seen in entresols, etc. The ante-room where courtiers waited at the royal chamber of Versailles had these ox-eye windows, and hence they were called by this name.

Off (Saxon, *of ;* Latin, *ab,* from, away). The house is a *mile* off—*i.e.* is "away" or "from" us a mile. The word preceding off defines its scope. To be " *well* off " is to be away or on the way towards well-being ; to be *badly* off is to be away or on the way to the bad. In many cases "off" is part of a compound verb, as to cut-off (away), to peel-off, to march-off, to tear-off, to take-off, to get-off, etc. The off-side of horses when in pairs is that to the *right* hand of the coachman, the horses on his *left*-hand side are called the " near " horses. This, which seems rather anomalous, arises from the fact that all teamsters walk beside their teams on the left side, so that the horses on the left side are near him, and those on the right side are farther off.

He is well off ; he is badly off. He is in good circumstances ; he is straitened in circumstances, *être bien* [or *mal*] *dans ses affaires.* In these phrases "off" means *fares,* "he fares well [or ill] ; his affairs go-off well [or ill]. (Anglo-Saxon, *of-faran.*)

Off-hand. Without preparation ; impromptu. The phrase, "in hand," as, "It was long in hand," means that it was long in operation, or long a-doing ;

so that "off-hand" must mean it was not "in hand."

Off his Head. Delirious, deranged, not able to use his head ; so "off his feed," not able to eat or enjoy his food. The latter phrase is applied to horses which refuse to eat their food.

Off the Hooks. Indisposed and unable to work. A door or gate off the hooks is unhinged, and does not work properly. Also, dead.

Off with his Head! So much for Buckingham! (*Colley Cibber : The Tragical History of Richard III.*, altered from Shakespeare.)

Offa's Dyke, which runs from Beachley to Flintshire, was not the work of Offa, King of Mercia, but was repaired by him. It existed when the Romans were in England, for five Roman roads cross it. Offa availed himself of it as a line of demarcation that was sufficiently serviceable, though by no means tallying with his territory either in extent or position.

Og, King of Bashan, according to Rabbinical mythology, was an antediluvian giant,· saved from the flood by climbing on the roof of the ark. After the passage of the Red Sea, Moses first conquered Sihon, and then advanced against the giant Og (whose bedstead, made of iron, was above 15 feet long and nearly 7 feet broad, *Deut. iii. 11*). The Rabbins say that Og plucked up a mountain to hurl at the Israelites, but he got so entangled with his burden, that Moses was able to kill him without much difficulty.

Og, in the satire of *Absalom and Achitophel*, by Dryden and Tate, is Thomas Shadwell, who succeeded Dryden as poet-laureate. Dryden called him MacFlecknoe, and says "he never deviates into sense." He is called Og because he was a very large and fat man. (*Part ii.*)

Og'hams. The alphabet in use among the ancient Irish and some other Celtic nations prior to the ninth century.

"The oghams seem to have been merely tree-runes. The Irish regarded the oghams as a forest, the individual characters being trees (feada), while each cross-stroke is called a twig (fleasg)." —*Isaac Taylor : The Alphabet*, vol. ii. chap. viii. p. 226.

Oghris. The lion that followed Prince Murad like a dog. (*Croquemitaine.*)

O'gier the Dane (2 syl.). One of the paladins of King Charlemagne.

Various fairies attended at his birth, and bestowed upon him divers gifts. Among them was Morgue, who when the knight was a hundred years old embarked him for the isle and castle of Av'alon, "hard by the terrestrial paradise." The vessel in which he sailed was wrecked, and Ogier was in despair, till he heard a voice that bade him "fear nothing, but enter the castle which I will show thee." So he got to the island and entered the castle, where he found a horse sitting at a banquet-table. The horse, whose name was Papillon, and who had once been a mighty prince, conducted him to Morgue the Fay, who gave him (1) a ring which removed all infirmities and restored him to ripe manhood ; (2) a Lethean crown which made him forget his country and past life ; and (3) introduced him to King Arthur. Two hundred years rolled on, and France was invaded by the Paynims. Morgue now removed the crown from Ogier's head and sent him to defend "*le bon pays de France.*" Having routed the invaders, Morgue took him back to Avalon, and he has never reappeared on this earth of ours. (*Ogier le Danois ; a romance.*)

O'gier the Dane. Represented as the Knave of Spades in the French pack. He is introduced by Ariosto in his *Orlando Furioso.*

The swords of Ogier the Dane. Curta'na (*the cutter*), and Sauvagine. (See *Morris : Earthly Paradise*, August.)

Ogleby (*Lord*). A superannuated nobleman who affects the gaiety and graces of a young man. (*Clandestine Marriage*, by Garrick and Colman the Elder.)

O'gres of nursery mythology are giants of very malignant dispositions, who live on human flesh. It is an Eastern invention, and the word is derived from the Ogurs, a desperately savage horde of Asia, who overran part of Europe in the fifth century. Others derived it from Orcus, the ugly, cruel man-eating monster so familiar to readers of Bojardo and Ariosto. The female is *Ogress.*

O'Groat. (*See* JOHN O' GROAT.)

Ogyg'ian Deluge. A flood which overran a part of Greece while Og'ygēs was king of Attica. There were two floods so called—one in Bœotia, when the lake Copa'is overflowed its banks ; and another in Attica, when the whole territory was laid waste for two hundred years (B.C. 1764).

Varro tells us that the planet Venus underwent a great change in the reign of Ogyges (3 syl.). It changed its diameter, its colour, its figure, and its course.

✵ Ogyges Deluge occurred more than 200 years before Deucalion's Flood.

Oi Polloi, properly *Hoi Polloi.* (Greek.) The commonalty, the many. In University slang the "poll men," or those who take degrees without "honours."

Oignement de Bretaigne (French). A sound drubbing. Oignement is a noun corruptly formed from *hogner.* In Lyons boys called the little cuffs which they gave each other *hognes.*

> "Frère Eleuthere a trenchoisons,
> Et j'ay orgement de Bretaigne ;
> Qui garist de roigne et de taigne."
> *Le Martyre de S. Denis,* etc., p. 129.

Oignons d'Egypte. The flesh-pots of Egypt. Hence "*regretter les oignons d'Egypte,*" to sigh for the flesh-pots of Egypt, to long for luxuries lost and gone.

Je plume oignons. I scold or grumble. Also *peler des oignons* in the same sense. A corruption of *hogner,* to scold or grumble.

> "*Grifon.* Que fais-tu là?
> *Braymault.* Je plume ongnons."
> *La Quarte Journée du Mistere de la Passion.*
> "Pas ne savoit ongnons peler."
> *Villon: Ballade* ii.

Oil. *To strike oil.* To make a happy hit or valuable discovery. The phrase refers to hitting upon or discovering a bed of petroleum or mineral oil.

Oil of Palms. Money. *Huile* is French slang for "money," as will appear from the following quotation :—
"*Il faudra que vostre bourse fusse les frais de vostre curiosité ; il faut de la pecune, il faut de l'huile.*" (*La Fausse Coquette,* ii. 7 ; 1694.)

Oil on Troubled Waters. *To pour oil on troubled waters,* as a figure of speech, means to soothe the troubled spirit. "A soft answer turneth away wrath."

As a physical fact, Professor Horsford, by emptying a vial of oil upon the sea in a stiff breeze, did actually still the ruffled surface. Commodore Wilkes, of the United States, saw the same effect produced in a violent storm off the Cape of Good Hope, by oil leaking from a whale-ship.

Origin of the phrase : The phrase is mentioned by the Venerable Bede in his *Ecclesiastical History,* written in Latin,

and completed in 735. Stapleton translated the book in 1565. St. Aidan, it appears, gave his blessing to a young priest who was to set out by land, but return by water, to convoy a young maiden destined for the bride of King Oswin or Oswy. St. Aidan gave the young man a cruse of oil to pour on the sea if the waves became stormy. A storm did arise, and the young priest, pouring oil on the waves, did actually reduce them to a calm. Bede says he had the story from "a most creditable man in Holy Orders."

✵ St. Aidan died in 694, and Bede died in 735. There is no question in archæology so often asked to be explained as this.

Oil the Knocker (*To*). To fee the porter. The expression is from Racine, "*On n'entre point chez lui sans graisser le marteau*" ("No one enters *his* house without oiling the knocker"). (*Les Plaideurs.*)

Ointment. Money. From the fable *De la Vieille qui Oint la Palme au Chevalier* (thirteenth century).

> "Vole'bant autem præfa'ti clerici al'iquem ha'berê lega'tum natio'nê Roma'num, que unguentis Anglicis, auro scilicet et argento solent ad qualibet inclina'ri."—*Gervais de Canterbury : Chronicle; Scriptores decem* ii., 1533.

Olaf or **Olave** (*St.*). The first Christian king of Norway, slain in battle by his pagan subjects in 1030. He is usually represented in royal attire, bearing the sword or halbert of his martyrdom, and sometimes carrying a loaf of bread, as a rebus on his name, which in Latin is *Holofius* or *Whole-loaf.* (Born 995.)

Old Bags. John Scott, Lord Eldon ; so called from his carrying home with him in different bags the cases still pending his judgment. (1751-1838.)

Old Blade (*An*). "*Un vieux routier*" (an old stager), meaning one up to snuff. (*See* SNUFF.)

Old Bonâ Fide. Louis XIV. (1638, 1643-1715).

Old Boots. *Like old boots.* Famously. "Cheeky as old boots," very saucy. "He ran like old boots," *i.e.* very fast. The reference is to the nursery story of the *Seven-leagued Boots, old* being simply a word of fondness, as "Well, old boy," etc. The allusion, suitable enough in many phrases, becomes, when used in slang, very remotely applicable.

Old Dominion. Virginia. Every Act of Parliament to the Declaration of

Independence designated Virginia " the Colony and Dominion of Virginia." Captain John Smith, in his *History of Virginia* (1629), calls this " colony and dominion" *Ould Virginia*, in contradistinction to *New England*, and other British settlements.

Old England. This term was first used in 1641, twenty-one years after our American colony of New Virginia received the name of New England.

Old Faith Men. (See PHILIPPINS.)

Old Fogs. The 87th Foot; so called from the war-cry " *Fag-an-Bealach* " (Clear the way), pronounced *Faug-a-bollagh*. The 87th Foot is now called "The Royal Irish Fusiliers."

Old Fox. Marshal Soult; so called by the soldiers because of his strategic abilities and never-failing resources. (1769-1851.) (See FOX.)

Old Gentleman (*The*). The devil; a cheating card.

Old Glory. The United States' Flag. Sir Francis Burdett (1770-1844).

Old Gooseberry. *To play* [*or play up*] *old gooseberry.* To be a third person; to be *de trop*. *Old Gooseberry* is the name given to a person accompanying an engaged couple.

Old Grog. Admiral Edward Vernon; so called by British sailors from his wearing a grogram cloak in foul weather. (1684-1757.)

Old Hands, supernumeraries who have been used to the work. "New hands" are those new to the work.

Old Harry. The devil. (See HARRY.)

Old Humphrey. The *nom-de-plume* of George Mogridge, of London, author of several interesting books for children. (Died 1854.)

Old Mortality. The itinerant antiquary in Sir Walter Scott's novel of that name. It is said to be a picture of Robert Paterson, a Scotchman, who busied himself in clearing the moss from the tombstones of the Covenanters.

Old News. Stale news. Hawker's (or piper's) news. " *Le secret de polichinelle*."

A pinch for old news. A schoolboy's punishment to one of his mates for telling as news what is well known.

Old Noll. (*See* NOLL.)

Old Noll's Fiddler. (*See* FIDDLER.)

Old Port School. Old-fashioned clergymen, who stick to Church and State, old port and " orthodoxy."

Old Reeky. (*See* AULD REEKIE.)

Old Rowley. Charles II. was so called from his favourite racehorse. A portion of the Newmarket racecourse is still called Rowley Mile, from the same horse.

Old Salt (*An*). An experienced sailor.

Old Scratch. The devil; so called from *Schratz* or *Skratti*, a demon of Scandinavian mythology. (*See* NICK.)

Old Song. *Went for an old song.* Was sold for a mere trifle, for a nominal sum or price.

Old Style—New Style. Old Style means computed according to the unreformed calendar. New Style means computed according to the calendar reformed and corrected by Gregory XIII. in 1582. The New Style was introduced into England, in 1752, during the reign of George II., when Wednesday, September 2nd, was followed by Thursday, September 14th. This has given rise to a double computation, as Lady Day, March 25th, Old Lady Day, April 6th ; Midsummer Day, June 24th, Old Midsummer Day, July 6th ; Michaelmas Day, September 29th, Old Michaelmas Day, October 11th ; Christmas Day, December 25th, Old Christmas Day, January 6th.

Old Tom. Cordial gin. Thomas Norris, one of the men employed in Messrs. Hodges' distillery, opened a gin palace in Great Russell Street, Covent Garden, and called the gin concocted by Thomas Chamberlain, one of the firm of Hodges, " Old Tom," in compliment to his former master.

Old Women, in theatrical parlance, means actresses who take the part of " old women." In full companies there are first and second " old women." The term *Old Men* is similarly used.

Old World. So Europe, Asia, and Africa are called when compared with North and South America (the New World).

Old as Adam. Generally used as a reproof for stating as news something well known. " That's as old as Adam," or was known as far back as the days of Adam. (*See* OLD AS METHUSELAH.)

Old as Methuselah. Of great age. Methuselah was the oldest man that ever lived. (*See above.*)

Old as the Hills. "Old as Panton Gates." (*See* PANTON GATES.)

Old Age Restored to Youth. "*La fontaine de Jouvence fit rejovenir la gent.*" The broth of Medea did the same. Grinding old men young. Ogier's Ring (*q.v.*) restored the aged to youth again. The Dancing Water restores the aged woman to youth and beauty. (*See* WATER.)

Old Dogs will not Learn New Tricks. In Latin, "*Senex psittacus negligit ferulam*" (An old parrot does not mind the stick). When persons are old they do not readily fall into new ways.

Old Lady of Threadneedle Street. The Bank of England, situated in Threadneedle Street. So called from a caricature by Gilray, dated 22nd May, 1797, and entitled *The Old Lady in Threadneedle Street in Danger*. It referred to the temporary stopping of cash payments 26th February, 1797, and one pound bank-notes were issued 4th March the same year.

Old Man Eloquent. ISOCRA'TES ; so called by Milton. When he heard of the result of the battle of Chæronæ'a, which was fatal to Grecian liberty, he died of grief.

> " That dishonest victory
> At Chæronæ'a, fatal to liberty,
> Killed with report that Old Man Eloquent."
> *Milton : Sonnets.*

Old Man of the Moon (*The*). The Chinese deity who links in wedlock predestined couples. (*See* MAN IN THE MOON.)

> " The Chinese have a firm belief in marriages being made in heaven. A certain deity, whom they call the 'Old Man of the Moon,' links with a silken cord all predestined couples."—*J. N. Jordan : Modern China (Nineteenth Century,* July, 1886, p. 45).

Old Man of the Mountain. Hassanben-Sabah, the sheik Al Jebal, and founder of the sect called Assassins (*q.v.*).

Old Man of the Sea. In the story of *Sinbad the Sailor,* the Old Man of the Sea, hoisted on the shoulders of Sinbad, clung there and refused to dismount. Sinbad released himself from his burden by making the Old Man drunk. (*Arabian Nights.*)

Oldbuck. An antiquary : from the character of Jonathan Oldbuck, a whimsical virtuoso in Sir Walter Scott's *Antiquary.*

Oldcastle (*Sir John*), called *the Good Lord Cobham,* the first Christian martyr among the English nobility (December 14th, 1417).

Old'enburg Horn. A horn long in the possession of the reigning princes of the House of Oldenburg, but now in the collection of the King of Denmark. According to tradition, Count Otto of Oldenburg, in 967, was offered drink in this silver-gilt horn by a "wild woman," at the Osenborg. As he did not like the look of the liquor, he threw it away, and rode off with the horn.

Oldest Nation and most ancient of all languages. Psammetichus of Egypt, wishing to penetrate these secrets, commanded that two infants should be brought up in such seclusion that they should never hear a single word uttered. When they had been thus secluded for two years, the boys both cried out to the keeper, "*Becos ! Becos !*" a Phrygian word for *Bread,* so Psammetichus declared the Phrygian language to be man's primitive speech. (*See* LANGUAGE.)

O'leum Adde Camino. To pour oil on fire ; to aggravate a wound under pretence of healing it. (*Horace : Satires,* ii. 3, 321.)

Olib'rius (*An*). The wrong man in the wrong place. Olib'rius was a Roman senator, proclaimed emperor by surprise in 472, but he was wholly unsuited for the office.

Ol'ifaunt. *Lord Nigel Olifaunt of Glenvarloch,* on going to court to present a petition to King James I., aroused the dislike of the Duke of Buckingham ; Lord Dalgarno gave him the cut direct, when Nigel struck him, and was obliged to seek refuge in Alsatia. After various adventures he married Margaret Ramsay, the watchmaker's daughter. (*Sir Walter Scott : Fortunes of Nigel.*)

Oligar'chy [*olly-gar'-ky*]. A government in which the supreme power is vested in a class. (Greek, *oligos,* the few ; *archē,* rule.)

Olin'do. The Mahometan king of Jerusalem, at the advice of his magician, stole an image of the Virgin, and set it up as a palladium in the chief mosque. The image was stolen during the night, and the king, unable to discover the perpetrator, ordered all his Christian subjects to be put to the sword. Sofronia, to prevent this wholesale massacre, accused herself of the deed, and was condemned to be burnt alive. Olindo, her lover, hearing of this, went to the king and took on himself the blame; whereupon both were condemned to death, but were saved by the intercession of Clorinda. (*Jerusalem Delivered*.)

O'lio or **Oglio**. A mixture or medley of any sort. (Spanish, *olla*, a pot for boiling similar to what the French call their *pot au feu*. The olio is the mixture of bread, vegetables, spices, meat, etc., boiled in this pot.)

Ol'ive (2 syl.). Sacred to Pallas Athe'nē. (*See* OLIVE-TREE.)

EMBLEM of (1) *Chastity*. In Greece the newly-married bride wore an olive-garland; with us the orange-blossom is more usual.

(2) *Fecundity*. The fruit of the olive is produced in vast profusion; so that olive-trees are valuable to their owners. (*See* ORANGE-BLOSSOMS.)

(3) *Merit*. In ancient Greece a crown of olive-twigs was the highest distinction of a citizen who had deserved well of his country.

(4) *Peace*. An olive-branch was anciently a symbol of peace. The vanquished who sued for peace carried olive-branches in their hands. And an olive-twig in the hands of a king (on medals), as in the case of Numa, indicated a reign of peace.

To hold out the olive branch. To make overtures of peace.

(5) *Prosperity*. David says, "I am like a green olive-tree in the house of God" (Psalm lii. 8).

(6) *Victory*. The highest prize in the Olympic games was a crown of olive-leaves.

ORIGIN *of the olive-tree*. The tale is, that Athēnē (Minerva) and Poseidon (Neptune) disputed the honour of giving a name to a certain city of Greece, and agreed to settle the question by a trial of which could produce the best gift for the new city. Athēnē commanded the earth to bring forth the olive-tree, Poseidon commanded the sea to bring forth the war-horse. Athēnē's gift was adjudged the better, and the city was called Athens.

Ol'ive Branches. Children of a parent. It is a Scripture term: "Thy wife shall be as a fruitful vine . . . thy children like olive plants round about thy table" (Psalm cxxviii. 3).

Oliver. Son and heir of Sir Rowland de Boys, who hated his youngest brother Orlando, and persuaded him to try a wrestling match with a professed wrestler, hoping thus to kill his brother; but when Orlando proved victorious, Oliver swore to set fire to his chamber when he was asleep. Orlando fled to the forest of Arden, and Oliver pursued him; but one day, as he slept in the forest, a snake and a lioness lurked near to make him their prey; Orlando happened to be passing, and slew the two monsters. When Oliver discovered this heroic deed he repented of his ill-conduct, and his sorrow so interested the Princess Celia that she fell in love with him, and they were married. (*Shakespeare: As You Like It.*)

Ol'iver or **Oliv'ier**. Charlemagne's favourite paladin, who, with Roland, rode by his side. He was Count of Genes, and brother of the beautiful Aude. His sword was called *Haute-claire*, and his horse *Ferrant d' Espagne*.

A Rowland for an Oliver. Tit for tat, *quid. pro quo*. Dr. J. N. Scott says that this proverb is modern, and owes its rise to the Cavaliers in the time of the Civil wars in England. These Cavaliers, by way of rebuff, gave the anti-monarchical party a General Monk for their Oliver Cromwell. As Monk's Christian name was *George*, it is hard to believe that the doctor is correct. (*See* ROLAND.)

Oliv'etans. Brethren of "Our Lady of Mount Ol'ivet," an offshoot of the Benedictine order.

Oliv'ia. Niece of Sir Toby Belch. Malvo'lio is her steward, Maria her woman, Fabian and a clown her male servants. (*Shakespeare: Twelfth Night.*)

Olivia. A female Tartuffe (*q.v.*) in Wycherley's *Plain Dealer*. A consummate hypocrite, of most unblushing effrontery.

Olla Podri'da. Odds and ends, a mixture of scraps. In Spain it takes the place of the French *pot au feu*, into which every sort of eatable is thrown and stewed. (*See* OLIO.) Used figuratively, the term means an incongruous mixture, a miscellaneous collection of any kind, a medley.

Ol'lapod. An apothecary, always trying to say a witty thing, and looking for wit in the conversation of others. When he finds anything which he can construe into "point" he says, "Thank you good sir; I owe you one." He had a military taste, and was appointed "cornet in the volunteer association of cavalry" of his own town. (*G. Colman : The Poor Gentleman.*)

Olym'pia (in *Orlando Furioso*). Countess of Holland, and wife of Bire'no. Cymosco of Friza wanted to force her to marry his son Arbantēs, but Arbantēs was slain. This aroused the fury of Cymosco, who seized Bireno, and would have put him to death if Orlando had not slain Cymosco. Bireno having deserted Olympia, she was bound naked to a rock by pirates; but Orlando delivered her and took her to Ireland. Here King Oberto espoused her cause, slew Bireno, and married the young widow. (Bks. iv., v.)

Olym'piad, among the ancient Greeks, was a period of four years, being the interval between the celebrations of their *Olympic Games*.

Olympian Jove, or rather *Zeus* (1 syl.) A statue by Phidias, and reckoned one of the "Seven Wonders of the World." Pausanias (vii. 2) says when the sculptor placed it in the temple at Elis, he prayed the god to indicate whether he was satisfied with it, and immediately a thunderbolt fell on the floor of the temple without doing the slightest harm.

⁂ The statue was made of ivory and gold, and though seated on a throne, was 60 feet in height. The left hand rested on a sceptre, and the right palm held a statue of Victory in solid gold. The robes were of gold, and so were the four lions which supported the footstool. The throne was of cedar, embellished with ebony, ivory, gold, and precious stones. (*See* MINERVA.)

It was placed in the temple at Elis B.C. 433, was removed to Constantinople, and perished in the great fire of A.D. 475. It was completed in 4 years, and of course the materials were supplied by the Government of Elis.

The "Homer of Sculptors" died in prison, having been incarcerated on the trumpery charge of having introduced on a shield of one of his statues a portrait of himself.

Olympic Games. Games held by the Greeks at Olym'pia, in Elis, every fourth year, in the month of July.

Olympus. On the confines of Macedonia and Thessaly, where the fabulous court of Jupiter was supposed to be held. It is used for any pantheon, as "Odin, Thor, Balder, and the rest of the Northern Olympus." The word means

all bright or *clear.* In Greek the word is *Olumpos.*

O'Lynn (*Brian*). Slang for gin. (*See* CHIVY.)

Om. A Sanscrit word, somewhat similar to *Amen.* When the gods are asked to rejoice in a sacrifice, the god Savitri cries out *Om* (Be it so). When Pravâhan is asked if his father has instructed him, he answers *Om* (Verily). Brahmans begin and end their lessons on the Veda with the word *Om,* for "unless *Om* precedes his lecture, it will be like water on a rock, which cannot be gathered up; and unless it concludes the lecture, it will bring forth no fruit."

Om mani padein hum. These are the first six syllables taught the children of Tibet and Mongolia, and the last words uttered by the dying in those lands. It is met with everywhere as a charm.

O'man's Sea. The Persian Gulf.

Ombre. A Spanish game of cards called *the royal game of ombre.* Prior has an epigram on the subject. He says he was playing ombre with two ladies, and though he wished to lose, won everything, for Fortune gave him "success in every suit but hearts." Pope has immortalised the game in his *Rape of the Lock.*

O'mega. *The alpha and omega.* The first and the last, the beginning and the end. Alpha is the *first* and omega the *last* letter of the Greek alphabet.

Omens. (*See* ILL OMENS.)

Omeyinger Saga. An historical tradition of Scandinavia.

Om'nibus. The French have a good slang term for these conveyances. They call an omnibus a "Four Banal" (parish oven).

∴ Of course, omnibus (for all) is the oblique case of omnes (2.ll). Yet Howitt, in his *Visits to Remarkable Places* (1840), says "Cabs and cars and omnibi and stages" (p. 200). The plural of omnibus is "omnibuses."

Om'nium (Latin, *of all*). The particulars *of all* the items, or the assignment *of all* the securities, of a government loan.

Om'nium Gath'erum. Dog Latin for a *gathering* or collection *of all* sorts of persons and things; a miscellaneous gathering together without regard to suitability or order.

Omorca. The goddess who was sovereign of the universe when it was first created. It was covered with water and darkness, but contained some few animals of monster forms, representations of which may be seen in the Temple of Bel. (*Berosius*.)

Om'phale (3 syl.). The masculine but attractive Queen of Lydia, to whom Herculēs was bound a slave for three years. He fell in love with her, and led an effeminate life spinning wool, while Om'phale wore the lion's skin and was lady paramount.

∵ The celebrated picture of Hercules spinning in the presence of Omphale, by Annibal Carracci, is in the Farnese Gallery.

On dit (French). A rumour, a report; as, "There is an *on dit* on Exchange that Spain will pay up its back dividends."

On the Loose. Dissolute (which is *dis-solutus*). "Living on the loose" is leading a dissolute life, or out on the spree.

On the Shelf. *Passé*, no longer popular, one of the "has-beens." The reference is not to pawns laid on the shelf, but to books no longer read, and clothes no longer worn, laid by on the shelf.

One-horse System (*A*). A one-sided view; looking at all things from one standpoint; bigotry.

One - horse Universities. Petty local universities.

"The provincial University of Toronto was thrown open to Nonconformists, unluckily not before the practice of chartering sectarian institutions had been introduced, and Canada had been saddled with 'one-horse universities.'"—*Prof. Goldwin Smith: Nineteenth Century*, July, 1886, p. 21.

One Step from the Sublime to the Ridiculous. Tom Paine said, "The sublime and the ridiculous are often so nearly related that it is difficult to class them separately. One step above the sublime makes the ridiculous, and one step above the ridiculous makes the sublime again."

One too Many for Him (*I was*). I outwitted him; or "One too much for you."

"You have lost, old fellow; I was one too much for you."—*Gaboriau: The Mystery of Orcival*, chap. x.

One Touch of Nature Makes the whole World Kin. (*Shakespeare: Troilus and Cressida*, iii. 3.)

Onion Pennies. Roman coins dug up at Silchester; so called from one Onion, a giant, who, the country people say, inhabited the buried city. Silchester used to be called by the British

Ard-Oneon—i.e. Ardal Onion (the region of Einion or Onion).

Only (*The*). Jean Paul Friedrich Richter (1763-1825). Carlyle says, "In the whole circle of literature we look in vain for his parallel." (German, *Der Einzigë*.)

On'slow, invoked by Thomson in his *Autumn*, was Arthur Onslow, the Speaker of the House of Commons, termed *clarum ac venera'bile nomen*. It was said of him that "his knowledge of the Constitution was only equalled by his attachment to it."

O'nus (Latin). The burden, the blame, the responsibility; as, "The whole *onus* must rest on your own shoulders."

O'nus Proban'di. The obligation of proof; as, "The *onus probandi* rests with the accuser."

Onyx is Greek for a finger-nail; so called because the colour of an onyx resembles that of the finger-nail.

O'pal. From the Greek *ops* (the eye). Considered unlucky for the same reason that peacocks' feathers in a house are said to be unlucky. A peacock's feather, being full of eyes, act as spies in a house, prying into one's privacy. Similarly, it is unlucky to introduce the eye-stone or opal into a house, because it will interfere with the sanctity of domestic privacy. (*See* CERAUNIUM).

"Not an opal
Wrapped in a bay-leaf in my left fist,
To charm their eyes with."
Ben Jonson: New Inn, i. 6.

Opal of Alphonso XII. (of Spain) seemed to be fatal. The king, on his wedding day, presented an opal ring to his wife (Mercedes, daughter of the Duke of Montpensier), but her death occurred soon afterwards. Before the funeral the king gave the ring to his sister (Maria del Pilar), who died a few days afterwards. The king then presented the ring to his sister-in-law (the Princess Christina, youngest daughter of the Duke of Montpensier), who died within three months. Alphonso, astounded at these fatalities, resolved to wear the ring himself, but died also within a very short time. The Queen Regent then attached the ring to a gold chain, which she suspended on the neck of the Virgin of Almudena of Madrid. (*See* FATAL GIFTS.)

Open Air Mission. A mission founded in 1853. Its agents preach in the open air, especially at races, fairs, and on occasions when large numbers of people congregate.

Open Question (*An*). A statement, proposal, doctrine, or supposed fact, respecting which each individual is allowed to entertain his own private opinion. In the House of Commons every member may vote as he likes, regardless of party politics, on an open question. In the Anglican Church it is an open question whether the Lord's Supper should be taken fasting (before breakfast), or whether it may be taken at noon, or in the evening. Indubitably the institution was founded by Christ "after supper;" but Catholics and the High Ritualistic party insist on its being taken fasting.

Open Secret (*An*). A piece of information generally known, but not yet formally announced.

" "It was an open secret that almost every one [of Lord Palmerston's ecclesiastical appointments] was virtually made by Lord Shaftesbury." —*Leisure Hour*, 1887.

Open, Ses′amë. The charm by which the door of the robber's dungeon flew open. The reference is to the tale of *The Forty Thieves*, in the *Arabian Nights*.

"These words were the only 'open sesame' to their feelings and sympathies."—*E. Shelton*.

"The spell loses its power, and he who should hope to conjure with it would find himself as much mistaken as Cassim when he stood crying, 'Open, Wheat,' 'Open, Barley,' to the door which obeyed no sound but 'Open, Sesame.' "

Open the Ball (*To*). To lead off the first dance; to begin anything which others will assist in carrying out.

Ophe′lia. Daughter of Polo′nius the chamberlain. Hamlet fell in love with her, but after his interview with the Ghost, found it incompatible with his plans to marry her. Ophelia, thinking his "strange conduct" the effect of madness, becomes herself demented, and in her attempt to gather flowers is drowned. (*Shakespeare : Hamlet.*)

Opin′icus. A fabulous monster, composed of dragon, camel, and lion, used in heraldry. It forms the crest of the Barber Surgeons of London.

O′pium-eater (*The English*) was Thomas de Quincey, author of *Confessions*. (1785-1850.)

Oppidan of Eton. A student not on the foundation, but who boards in the town. (Latin, *oppidum*.)

Optimë (plural, *op-ti-mēs*), in Cambridge phraseology, is a graduate in honours below a wrangler. Of course, the Latin *optimus* (a best man) is the *fons et origo* of the term. Optimës are of two grades : a man of the higher group is termed a *senior* optimë, while one of the inferior class is called a *junior* optimë.

Op′timism, in moral philosophy, is the doctrine that "whatever is, is right," that everything which happens is for the best.

O′pus Ma′jus. The great work of Roger Bacon.

Opus Op′eran′tis, in theology, means that the personal piety of the person who does the act, and not the act itself, causes it to be an instrument of grace. Thus, in the Eucharist, it is the faith of the recipient which makes it efficient for grace.

Opus Opera′tum, in theology, means that the act conveys grace irrespectively of the receiver. Thus baptism is said by many to convey regeneration to an infant in arms.

Or Ever. Ere ever. (Saxon, *ær*, before.)

" Or ever I had seen that day, Horatio."
Shakespeare : Hamlet, i. 2.
" Dying or ere they sicken."
Macbeth, iv. 3.

Oracle. The answer of a god or inspired priest to an inquiry respecting the future ; the deity giving responses ; the place where the deity could be consulted, etc.

Oracle. The following are famous responses :—
(1) When Crœsus consulted the Delphic oracle respecting a projected war, he received for answer, " *Crœsus Halyn penetrans magnum, pervertet opum vim*" (When Crœsus passes over the river Halys, he will overthrow the strength of an empire). Crœsus supposed the oracle meant he would overthrow the enemy's empire, but it was his own that he destroyed.
(2) Pyrrhus, being about to make war against Rome, was told by the oracle : "*Aio te, Æacide, Roma′nos vin′cere posse*" (I say, Pyrrhus, that you the Romans can conquer), which may mean either *You, Pyrrhus, can overthrow the Romans*, or *Pyrrhus, the Romans can overthrow you*.
(3) Another prince, consulting the oracle concerning a projected war, received for answer, " *Ibis redi′bis nunquam per bella peribis*" (You shall go shall return never you shall perish by the war). It will be seen that the whole

gist of this response depends on the place of the omitted comma; it may be *You shall return, you shall never perish in the war*, or *You shall return never, you shall perish in the war*, which latter was the fact.

(4) Philip of Macedon sent to ask the oracle of Delphi if his Persian expedition would prove successful, and received for answer—

"The ready victim crowned for death
Before the altar stands."

Philip took it for granted that the "ready victim" was the King of Persia, but it was Philip himself.

(5) When the Greeks sent to Delphi to know if they would succeed against the Persians, they were told—

"Seed-time and harvest, weeping sires shall tell
How thousands fought at Salamis and fell."

But whether the Greeks or the Persians were to be "the weeping sires," deponent stateth not, nor whether the thousands "about to fall" were to be Greeks or Persians. (*See* PUNCTUATION.)

(6) When Maxentius was about to encounter Constantine, he consulted the guardians of the Sibylline Books as to the fate of the battle, and the prophetess told him, "*Illo die hostem Romanōrum esse periturum*," but whether Maxentius or Constantine was "the enemy of the Roman people" the oracle left undecided.

(7) In the Bible we have a similar equivoke: When Ahab, King of Israel, was about to wage war on the king of Syria, and asked Micaiah if Ramoth-Gilead would fall into his hands, the prophet replied, "Go, for the Lord will deliver the city into the hands of the king" (1 Kings xxii. 15, 35). Ahab thought that he himself was *the king* referred to, but the city fell into the hands of *the king* of Syria.

There are scores of punning prophecies equally equivocal.

Oracle (*Sir*). A dogmatical person, one not to be gainsaid. The ancient oracles professed to be the responses of the gods, from which there could be no appeal.

"I am Sir Oracle,
And when I ope my lips let no dog bark."
Shakespeare: Merchant of Venice, i. 1.

To work the oracle. To induce another to favour some plan or join in some project.

"They fetched a rattling price through Starlight's working the oracle with those swells."—
Boldrewood: Robbery under Arms, chap. xii.

Oracle of the Church (*The*). St. Bernard. (1091-1153.)

Oracle of the Holy Bottle, Bacbuc, near Cathay, in Upper Egypt. Books iv. and v. of Rabelais are occupied by the search for this oracle. The ostensible object was to obtain an answer to a question which had been put to sibyl and poet, monk and fool, philosopher and witch, judge and "sort," viz. "whether Panurge should marry or not?" The whole affair is a disguised satire on the Church. The celibacy of the clergy was for a long time a moot point of great difficulty, and the "Holy Bottle" or cup to the laity was one of the moving causes of the "great schisms" from the Roman Catholic Church. The crew setting sail for the Bottle refers to Anthony, Duke of Vendôme, afterwards king of Navarre, setting out in search of religious truth. Bacbuc is the Hebrew for a bottle. The anthem sung before the fleet set sail was *When Israel went out of bondage*, and all the emblems of the ships bore upon the proverb "*In vino veritas.*" Bacbuc is both the Bottle and the priestess of the Bottle.

Oracle of Sieve and Shears (*The*). This method of divination is mentioned by Theoc'ritos. The *modus operandi* was as follows:—The points of the shears were stuck in the rim of a sieve, and two persons supported them with their finger-tips. Then a verse of the Bible was read aloud, and St. Peter and St. Paul were asked if it was A, B, or C (naming the persons suspected). When the right person was named, the sieve would suddenly turn round.

"Searching for things lost with a sieve and shears."—*Ben Jonson: Alchemist*, i. 1.

Oracles were extremely numerous, and very expensive to those who consulted them. The most famous were Dodona, Ammon (in Libya), Delphos, Delos, that of Trophonius (in Bœotia), and that of Venus in Paphos.

Oracle of APOLLO, at Delphi, the priestess of which was called the Pythoness ; at Delos, and at Claros.
Oracle of Diana, at Colchis ; of ESCULAPIUS, at Epidaurus, and another in Rome.
Oracle of HERCULES, at Athens, and another at Gades.
Oracle of JUPITER, at Dodona (the most noted) ; another at Ammon, in Libya ; another at Crete.
Oracle of MARS, in Thrace : MINERVA, in Mycenæ ; PAN, in Arcadia.
Oracle of TRIPHO'NIUS, in Bœotia, where only men made the responses.
Oracle of VENUS, at Paphos, another at Aphaca, and many others.

In most of the temples women, sitting on a tripod, made the responses.

Orange Lilies (*The*). The 35th Foot. Called "orange" because their facings were *orange* till 1832; and "lilies" because they were given white plumes in recognition of their gallantry in the battle of Quebec in 1759, when they routed the Royal Roussillon French Grenadiers. The white plume was discontinued in 1800. The 35th Foot is now called the "The Royal Sussex."

William of Orange. William III. of England (1650, 1689-1702). "Orange" is a corruption of Arausio, in the department of Vaucluse, some sixteen miles from Avignon. The town was the capital of a principality from the eleventh to the sixteenth century. The last sovereign was Philibert de Châlons, whose sister married William, Count of Nassau. William's grandson (William) married Mary, eldest daughter of Charles I., and their eldest son was our William III., referred to in the text.

Orange Lodges or *Clubs* are referred to in *Hibernia Curiosa*, published in 1769. Thirty years later the Orangemen were a very powerful society, having a "grand lodge" extending over the entire province of Ulster, and ramifying through all the centres of Protestantism in Ireland." (*See next article, and* ORANGEMAN.)

Orange Peel. A nickname given to Sir Robert Peel when Chief Secretary for Ireland (1812-1818), on account of his strong anti - Catholic proclivities. (*See above, and* ORANGEMAN.)

Orange-tawny. The ancient colour appropriated to clerks and persons of inferior condition. It was also the colour worn by the Jews. Hence Lord Bacon says, "Usurers should have orange-tawny bonnets, because they do Judaise" (Essay xli.). Bottom the weaver asked Quince what coloured beard he was to wear for the character of Pyr'amus: "I will discharge it in either your straw-coloured beard, your orange-tawny beard, your purple-ingrain beard, or your French crown-colour, which is a perfect yellow." (*Midsummer Night's Dream*, i. 2.)

Orange Blossoms Worn at Weddings. The Saracen brides used to wear orange blossoms as an emblem of fecundity; and occasionally the same emblem may have been worn by European brides ever since the time of the Crusades; but the general adoption of wreaths of orange blossoms for brides is comparatively a modern practice, due especially to the recent taste for flower-language. The subject of bridal decorations being made a study, and the orange flower being found suitable, from the use made of it by the ancient Saracens, it was introduced by modistes as a fit ornament for brides. The notion once planted, soon became a custom, now very generally adopted by those who study the conventions of society, and follow the accepted fashions. (*See* OLIVE.)

To gather orange blossoms. To look for a wife. A bride wears orange blossoms to indicate the hope of fruitfulness, no tree being more prolific. An orange tree of moderate size will yield three or four thousand oranges in a year; and the blossom being white, is a symbol of innocence and chastity. The orange was also used by Cardinal Wolsey as a pomander. It is said that some sweet oranges turn bitter by neglect.

Orangeman. A name given by Roman Catholics to the Protestants of Ireland, on account of their adhesion to William III. of the House of Orange; they had been previously called "Peep-of-Day Boys." The Roman party were Jac'obites. (*See* ORANGE LODGES.)

Oran'ia. The lady-love of Am'adis of Gaul.

Orator Henley. The Rev. John Henley, who for about thirty years delivered lectures on theological, political, and literary subjects. (1692-1756.)

Orbil'ian Stick (*The*). A cane or birch-rod.

Orbilius was the schoolmaster who taught Horace, and Horace calls him *Plago'sus* (the flogger). (Ep. ii. 71.)

Orc (in *Orlando Furioso*). A sea-monster that devoured men and women. He haunted the seas near Ireland. Orlando threw an anchor into his open jaws, and then dragged the monster to the Irish coast, where he died.

Or'ca. The Orkney Islands, or Orcades.

Or'chard properly means a kitchen garden, a yard for herbs. (Saxon, *ort-geard—i.e.* wort-yard.) Wort enters into the names of numerous herbs, as mug-wort, liver-wort, spleen-wort, etc.

" The hortyard entering [he] admires the fair
  And pleasant fruits."   *Sandys.*

Or'cus. The abode of the dead; death. (*Roman mythology.*)

Or'deal (Saxon, *great judgment*), instituted long before the Conquest, and not abolished till the reign of Henry III.

Ordeals were of several kinds, but the most usual were by *wager of battle*, by *hot* or *cold water*, and by *fire*. This method of "trial" was introduced from the notion that God would defend the right, even by miracle if needful.

(1) *Wager of battle*, was when the accused person was obliged to fight any-one who charged him with guilt. This ordeal was allowed only to persons of rank.

(2) *Of fire*, was another ordeal for persons of rank only. The accused had to hold in his hand a piece of red-hot iron, or had to walk blindfold and bare-foot among nine red-hot plough-shares laid at unequal distances. If he escaped uninjured he was accounted innocent, *aliter non*. This might be performed by deputy.

(3) *Of hot water*, was an ordeal for the common people. The accused was required to plunge his arm up to the elbow in scalding hot water, and was pronounced guilty if the skin was in-jured in the experiment.

(4) *Of cold water*, was also for the common people. The accused, being bound, was tossed into a river; if he *sank* he was acquitted, but if he *floated* he was accounted guilty.

(5) *Of the bier*, when a person suspected of murder was required to touch the corpse; if guilty the "blood of the dead body would start forth afresh."

(6) *Of the cross*. Plaintiff and de-fendant had to stand with their arms crossed over their breasts, and he who could endure the longest won the suit.

(7) *Of the Eucharist*. This was for clergymen suspected of crime. It was supposed that the elements would choke him, if taken by a guilty man.

(8) *Of the corsned*, or consecrated bread and cheese. Godwin, Earl of Kent, is said to have been choked when he submitted to this ordeal, being accused of the murder of the king's brother.

"This sort of ordeal was by no means unusual. Thus in Ceylon, a man suspected of theft is re-quired to bring what he holds dearest before a judge, and placing a heavy stone on the head of his substitute, says "May this stone crush thee to death if I am guilty of this offence."

In Tartary, an ostiack sets a wild bear and an hatchet before the tribunal, saying, as he swallows a piece of bread, "May the bear devour me, and the hatchet chop off my head, if I am guilty of the crime laid to my charge."

(9) *Of lot*, two dice, one marked by a cross, being thrown.

Ordeal. *It was a fiery ordeal.* A severe test. (*See above*, No. 2.)

Order! When members of the House of Commons and other debaters call out *Order*, they mean that the per-son speaking is transgressing the rules of the House.

Order of the Cockle. Created by St. Louis in 1269, in memory of a dis-astrous expedition made by sea for the succour of Christians. Perrot says it scarcely survived its foundation.

Order of the Day (*The*), in parlia-mentary parlance, is applied to the prearranged agenda of "Private Mem-bers' Bills." On Tuesdays these bills always stand after "notices of motions." (*See* PREVIOUS QUESTION.)

To move for the Order of the Day is a proposal to set aside a government measure on a private members' day (Tuesday), and proceed to the pre-arranged agenda. If the motion is carried, the agenda must be proceeded with, unless a motion "to adjourn" is carried.

Orders. *In Orders* or *In Holy Orders*. Belonging to the clerical order or rank.

To take Orders. To become a clergy-man.

❧ The word "order" means not only a mandate, but also an official rank, and in the Catholic Church, a "rule" of life, as *Ordo albus* (white friars or Au-gustines), *Ordo niger* (black friars or Dominicans). In "Holy Orders" is in the plural number, because in the Pro-testant Church there are three ranks of clergymen — deacons, priests, and bishops. In the Catholic Church there are four major orders and four minor ones. According to Du Cange, the *Ordinēs majōrēs* are Subdeaconātus, Deaconātus, Presbyterātus, and Episco-pālis (Subdeacon, Deacon, Priest, and Bishop).

Orders of Architecture. These five are the classic orders: Tuscan, Doric, Ionic, Corinthian, and Composite.

The following was the *usual* practice:
CORINTHIAN, for temples of Venus, Flora, Pro-serpine, and the Water Nymphs.
DORIC, for temples of Minerva, Mars, and Her-cules.
IONIC, for temples of Juno, Diana, and Bacchus.
TUSCAN, for grottoes and all rural deities.

Ordigale. The otter in the tale of *Reynard the Fox* (part iii.).

Or'dinary (*An*). One who has an "ordinary or regular jurisdiction" in his own right, and not by deputation. Thus a judge who has authority to take cog-nisance of causes in his own right is an ordinary. A bishop is an ordinary in his own diocese, because he has authority to take cognisance of ecclesiastical matters therein ; but an archbishop is the ordinary of his province, having authority in his own right to receive appeals therein from inferior jurisdictions. The chaplain of Newgate was also called the ordinary thereof.

Ordinary (*An*). A public dinner where each guest pays his quota ; a table d'hôte.

"'Tis almost dinner; I know they stay for you at the ordinary."—*Beaumont and Fletcher : Scornful Lady,* iv. 1.

Orcad (plural, *Orèads* [3 syl.] or *Oreädes* [4 syl.]). Nymphs of the mountains. (Greek, ὄρος, a mountain.)

Oreilles. Sir W. Scott (*Waverley,* x.) speaks of *vinum primæ notæ* thus :— "*C'est des deux oreilles,*" that is, it is strong and induces sleep. It makes one "*Dormir sur les deux oreilles.*" Littré, however, says, "Though wine *d'une oreille* is excellent, that of *deux oreilles* is execrable."

"Vin d'une oreille, le bon vin ; vin de deux oreilles le mauvais. On appelle, ainsi le bon vin, parce que le bon vin fait pencher la tête de celui qui le goûte d'un côté seulement : et le mauvais vin, parce qu'on secoue la tête, et par consequent le deux oreilles."

Ore'lio. The steed of Don Roderick, the last of the Goths, noted for its speed and symmetry. (*See* HORSE.)

Orella'na. The river Amazon in America ; so called from Orellana, lieutenant of Pizarro.

Orfeo and Heuro'dis. The tale of Orpheus and Euryd'icē, with the Gothic machinery of elves or fairies.

Or'gies (2 syl.). Drunken revels, riotous feasts ; so called from the nocturnal festivals in honour of Bacchus. (Greek, *orgē,* violent emotion.)

Orgoglio (pron. *Or-golé'-yo*). The word is Italian, and means "Arrogant Pride," or *The Man of Sin.* A hideous giant as tall as three men ; he was son of Earth and Wind. Finding the Red Cross Knight at the fountain of Idleness, he beats him with a club and makes him his slave. Una, hearing of these mischances, tells King Arthur, and Arthur liberates the knight and slays the giant. *Moral :* The Man of Sin had power given him to "make war with the saints and to overcome them" for "forty and two months" (Rev. xiii. 5, 7), then the "Ancient of Days came," and overcame him (Dan. vii. 21, 22). (*Spenser : Faërie Queene,* book i.)

⁂ Arthur first cut off Orgoglio's *left*

arm—*i.e.* Bohemia was first cut off from the Church of Rome. He then cut off the giant's *right leg—i.e.* England ; and, this being cut off, the giant fell to the earth, and was afterwards dispatched.

Or'gon. Brother-in-law of Tartuffe. His credulity is proverbial : he almost disbelieved his senses, and saw everyone and everything through the *couleur de rose* of his own honest heart. (*Molière : Tartuffe.*)

Oria'na. The beloved of Am'adis of Gaul, who called himself Beltene'bros when he retired to the Poor Rock. (*Am'adis de Gaul,* ii. 6.)

Queen Elizabeth is sometimes called the "peerless Oriana," especially in the madrigals entitled the *Triumphs of Oria'na* (1601).

Oria'na. The nurseling of a lioness, with whom Esplandian, son of Oria'na and Am'adis of Gaul, fell in love, and for whom he underwent all his perils and exploits. She is represented as the fairest, gentlest, and most faithful of womankind.

O'riande [*O'-re-ond*]. A fay who lived at Rosefleur, and brought up Maugis d'Aygremont (*q.v.*). When her *protégé* grew up she loved him "*d'un si grand amour, qu'elle doute fort qu'il ne se départe d'avecques elle.*" (*Romance de Maugis d'Aygremont et de Vivian son Frère.*)

O'riel. A fairy whose empire lay along the banks of the Thames, when King Oberon held his court in Kensington Gardens. (*Tickell : Kensington Gardens.*)

Orientation. The placing of the east window of a church due east, that is, so that the rising sun may at noon shine on the altar. Anciently, churches were built with their axes pointing to the rising sun on the saint's day ; so that a church dedicated to St. John was not parallel to one dedicated to St. Peter. The same practice prevailed both in Egypt and ancient Greece.

Modern churches are built as nearly due east and west as circumstances will allow, quite regardless of the saint's day.

Oriflamme (3 syl.). First used in France as a national banner in 1119. It consisted of a crimson flag mounted on a gilt staff (*un glaive tout doré où est attaché une bannière vermeille*). The flag was cut into three "vandykes" to represent "tongues of fire," and between each was a silken tassel. This celebrated standard was the banner of St. Denis;

but when the Counts of Vexin became possessed of the abbey the banner passed into their hands. In 1082 Philippe I. united Vexin to the crown, and the sacred Oriflamme belonged to the king. It was carried to the field after the battle of Agincourt, in 1415. The romance writers say that "mescreans" (infidels) were blinded by merely looking on it. In the *Roman de Garin* the Saracens are represented as saying, "If we only set eyes on it we are all dead men" ("*Se's attendons tuit sommes mors et pris*"). Froissart says it was no sooner unfurled at Rosbecq than the fog cleared off, leaving the French in light, while their enemies remained in misty darkness still. (*Or*, gold, referring to the staff ; *flamme*, flame, referring to the tongues of fire.)

Or'igenists. An early Christian sect who drew their opinions from the writings of Origen. They maintained Christ to be the Son of God only by adoption, and denied the eternity of future punishments.

Original Sin. That corruption which is born with us, and is the inheritance of all the offspring of Adam. As Adam was the federal head of his race, when Adam fell the taint and penalty of his disobedience passed to all his posterity.

Oril'o or **Orillo** (in *Orlando Furioso*, book viii.). A magician and robber who lived at the mouth of the Nile. He was the son of an imp and fairy. When any limb was lopped off he restored it by his magic power, and when his head was cut off he put it on his neck again. Astolpho encountered him, cut off his head, and fled with it. Orillo mounted his horse and gave chase. Meanwhile Astolpho with his sword cut the hair from the head. Life was in one particular hair, and as soon as that was severed the head died, and the magician's body fell lifeless.

Orin'da, called the "Incomparable," was Mrs. Katherine Philipps, who lived in the reign of Charles II., and died of small-pox. Her praises were sung by Cowley, Dryden, and others. (See *Dryden's Ode To the Memory of Mrs. Anne Killigrew.*)

Ori'on. A giant hunter, noted for his beauty. He was blinded by Œnop'ion, but Vulcan sent Cedalion to be his guide, and his sight was restored by exposing his eyeballs to the sun. Being slain by Diana, he was made one of the

constellations, and is supposed to be attended with stormy weather. "*Assurgens fluctu nimbo'sus Orion.*" (*Virgil : Æneid*, i. 539.)

"As beautiful as Orion." *Homer : Iliad*, xviii.

Wife of Orion. Sidē.
Dogs of Orion. Arctoph'onos and Ptoöph'agos.

Orkborne (*Dr.*). A learned student, very dry and uncompanionable ; very particular over his books, and the tutor of Eugenia, the niece of Sir Hugh. He is a character in *Camilla*, the third novel of Mme. D'Arblay. Eugenia was deformed owing to an accident partly caused by her uncle ; and Sir Hugh, to make the best compensation in his power, appointed Dr. Orkborne to educate her, and also left her heiress to his estates.

"Mr. Oldbuck hated putting to rights as much as Dr. Orkborne, or any other professed student." —*Scott: Antiquary.*

Orkneys. Either the Teutonic *Orkn-eys* (the water or islands of the whirlpool), in allusion to the two famous whirlpools near the Isle of Swinna ; or else the Norwegian *Orkeyjar* (northern islands), the Hebrides being the *Sudreyjar*, or southern islands.

Orlando. The youngest son of Sir Rowland de Boys. At a wrestling match the banished duke's daughter, Rosalind, who took a lively interest in Orlando, gave him a chain, saying, " Gentleman, wear this for me." Orlando, flying because of his brother's hatred, met Rosalind in the forest of Arden, disguised as a country lad, seeking to join her father. In time they become acquainted with each other, and the duke assented to their union. (*Shakespeare : As You Like It.*) (*See* OLIVER.)

Orlando, called Rotolando or Roland, and Rutlandus in the Latin chronicles of the Middle Ages, the paladin, was lord of Anglant, knight of Brava, son of Milo d'Anglesis and Bertha, sister of Charlemagne. Though married to Aldabella, he fell in love with Angel'ica, daughter of the infidel king of Cathay ; but Angelica married Medo'ro, a Moor, with whom she fled to India. When Orlando heard thereof he turned mad, or rather his wits were taken from him for three months by way of punishment, and deposited in the moon. Astolpho went to the moon in Elijah's chariot, and St. John gave him an urn containing the lost wits of Orlando. On reaching earth again, Astolpho first bound the madman, then holding the urn to his nose, the errant wits returned, and Orlando, cured of his madness and love, recovered from his temporary derangement. (*Orlando Furioso*.) (*See* ANGELICA.)

Orlando or Roland was buried at Blayes, in the church of St. Raymond; but his body was removed afterwards to Roncesvalles, in Spain.

Orlando's horn or *Roland's horn*. An ivory horn called Olivant, mentioned frequently by Boiardo and Ariosto.

" Per acto bello, Rolandus ascendit in montem, et rediit retro ad vism Runciavallis. Tunc insonuit tuba sua eburnea ; et tantâ virtute insonuit, quod flatu omnis ejus tuba per medium scissa, et venæ colli ejus et nervi rupti fuisse feruntur."

Orlando's sword. Durinda'na, which once belonged to Hector.

Orlando Furioso. An epic poem in forty-six cantos, by Ariosto (digested by Hoole into twenty-four books, but retained by Rose in the original form). The subject is the siege of Paris by Agramant the Moor, when the Saracens were overthrown. In the pagan army were two heroes—Rodo'mont, called the Mars of Africa, and Roge'ro. The latter became a Christian convert. The poem ends with a combat between these two, and the overthrow of Rodomont.

The anachronisms of this poem are most marvellous. We have Charlemagne and his paladins joined by King Edward of England, Richard Earl of Warwick, Henry Duke of Clarence, and the Dukes of York and Gloucester (bk. vi.). We have cannons employed by Cymosco, King of Friza (bk. iv.), and also in the siege of Paris (bk. vi.). We have the Moors established in Spain, whereas they were not invited over by the Saracens for nearly 300 years after Charlemagne's death. In book xvii. we have Prester John, who died 1202; in the last three Constantine the Great, who died 337.

Orlando Innamora'to (Roland the paladin in love). A romantic epic in three books, by the Count Boiardo of Scandiano, in Italy (1495).

There is a burlesque in verse of the same title by Berni of Tuscany (1538), author of *Burlesque Rhymes*.

Orleans. *Your explanation is like an Orleans comment*—*i.e.* Your comment or explanation makes the matter more obscure. The Orleans College was noted for its wordy commentaries, which darkened the text by overloading it with words. (*A French proverb*.)

Or'mandine (3 syl.). The necromancer who by his magic arts threw St. David for seven years into an enchanted

sleep, from which he was redeemed by St. George. (*The Seven Champions of Christendom*, i. 9.)

Or'mulum. A paraphrase of Scripture in Anglo-Saxon verse; so called from the name of the author, Orm or Ormin (13th cent.).

Ormusd or **Ormuzd.** The principle or angel of light and good, and creator of all things, according to the Magian system. (*See* AHRIMAN.)

Oromas'des (4 syl.). The first of the Zoroastrian trinity. The divine goodness of Plato; the deviser of creation (the father). The second person is Mithras, the eternal intellect, architect of the world; the third, Ahrim'anës (Psychē), the mundane soul.

O'roönda'tês. Only son of a Scythian king, whose love for Stati'ra (widow of Alexander the Great, and daughter of Dari'us) leads him into numerous dangers and difficulties, which he surmounts. (*La Calprenède : Cassandra, a romance*.)

Oro'sius (*General History of*), from Creation to A.D. 417, in Latin by a Spanish presbyter of the 5th century, was translated into Anglo-Saxon by Alfred the Great.

Orotalt, according to the Greek writers, was the Bacchus of the ancient Arabs. This, however, is a mistake, for the word is a corruption of *Allah Taala* (God the Most High).

Orpheus (2 syl.). A Thracian poet who could move even inanimate things by his music. When his wife Eurydicē died he went into the infernal regions, and so charmed King Pluto that Eurydice was released from death on the condition that Orpheus would not look back till he reached the earth. He was just about to place his foot on the earth when he turned round, and Eurydice vanished from him in an instant. Pope introduces this tale in his *St. Cecilia's Ode*.

The tale of Orpheus is thus explained: Aëdoneus, King of Thespro'tia, was for his cruelty called Pluto, and having seized Eurydicē as she fled from Aristæos, detained her captive. Orpheus obtained her release on certain conditions, which he violated, and lost her a second time.

There is rather a striking resemblance between the fate of Eurydicē and that of Lot's wife. The former was emerging from hell, the latter from Sodom. Orpheus looked back and Eurydice was snatched away, Lot's wife looked back and was converted into a pillar of salt.

A Scandinavian Orpheus. "Odin was so eminently skilled in music, and could sing airs so tender and melodious, that the rocks would expand with delight, while the spirits of the infernal regions would stand motionless around him, attracted by the sweetness of his strains." (*Scandinavia*, by Crichton and Wheaton, vol. i. p. 81.)

Orpheus of Highwaymen. So Gay has been called on account of his *Beggar's Opera*. (1688-1732.)

Orrery. An astronomical toy to show the relative movements of the planets, etc., invented by George Graham, who sent his model to Rowley, an instrument maker, to make one for Prince Eugène. Rowley made a copy of it for Charles Boyle, third Earl of Orrery, and Sir Richard Steele named it an orrery out of compliment to the earl. One of the best is Fulton's, in Kelvin Grove Museum, West End Park, Glasgow.

Orsin. One of the leaders of the rabble that attacked Hudibras at a bear-baiting. He was "famous for wise conduct and success in war." Joshua Gosling, who kept the bears at "Paris Garden," in Southwark, was the academy figure of this character.

Orsi'ni (*Maffio*). A young Italian nobleman, whose life was saved by Genna'ro at the battle of Rim'ini. Orsi'ni became the staunch friend of Genna'ro, but both were poisoned at a banquet given by the Princess Neg'roni. (*Donizetti : Lucrezia di Borgia, an opera.*) This was the name of the conspirator who attempted the life of Napoleon III.

Orson. Twin brother of Valentine, and son of Bellisant, sister of King Pepin and wife of Alexander, Emperor of Constantinople. The twin brothers were born in a wood near Orleans, and Orson was carried off by a bear, which suckled him with her cubs. When he grew up he was the terror of France, and was called the *Wild Man of the Forest*. He was reclaimed by Valentine, overthrew the Green Knight, and married Fezon, the daughter of Duke Savary of Aquitaine. (French, *ourson*, a little bear.) (*Valentine and Orson.*)

Orthodox Sunday, in the Eastern Church, is the First Sunday in Lent, to commemorate the restoration of images in 843.

⁎⁎ In the Church of England, on the first day in Lent, usually called "Ash Wednesday," the clergy are directed to read "the . . . sentences of God's cursing against impenitent sinners."

Orts. Crumbs; refuse. (Low German, *ort—i.e.* what is left after eating.)

I shall not eat your orts—i.e. your leavings.

"Let him have time a beggar's orts to crave."
    Shakespeare : Rape of Lucrece.

Ortus. "*Ortus a quercu, non a sal'ice.*" Latin for "sprung from an oak, and not from a willow"—*i.e.* stubborn stuff; one that cannot bend to circumstances.

Ortwine (2 syl.). Knight of Metz, sister's son of Sir Hagan of Trony, a Burgundian in the *Nibelungen Lied*.

Orvie'tan (3 syl.) or *Venice treacle*, once believed to be a sovereign remedy against poison. From Orvieto, a city of Italy, where it is said to have been first used.

"With these drugs will I, this very day, compound the true orvietan."—*Sir Walter Scott : Kenilworth*, chap. xiii.

Os Sacrum. (*See* LUZ.) A triangular bone situate at the lower part of the vertebral column, of which it is a continuation. Some say that this bone was so called because it was in the part used in sacrifice, or the sacred part ; Dr. Nash says it is so called "because it is much bigger than any of the vertebræ ;" but the Jewish rabbins say the bone is called sacred because it resists decay, and will be the germ of the "new body" at the resurrection. (*Hudibras*, part iii. canto 2.)

Osbaldistone. Nine of the characters in Sir Walter Scott's *Rob Roy* bear this name. There are (1) the London merchant and Sir Hildebrand, the heads of two families ; (2) the son of the merchant is Francis, the *pretendu* of Diana Vernon ; (3) the "distinguished" offspring of the brother are Percival *the sot*, Thorncliffe *the bully*, John *the gamekeeper*, Richard *the horse-jockey*, Wilfred *the fool*, and Rashleigh *the scholar*, by far the worst of all. This last worthy is slain by Rob Roy, and dies cursing his cousin Frank, whom he had injured in every way he could contrive.

Oseway (*Dame*). The ewe in the tale of *Reynard the Fox*.

Osi'ris (in Egyptian mythology). Judge of the dead, and potentate of the kingdom of the ghosts. This brother and husband of Isis was worshipped under the form of an ox. The word means *Many-eyed*.

Osīris is the moon, husband of Isis.

"We see Osiris represented by the moon, and by an eye at the top of fourteen steps. These steps symbolise the fourteen days of the waxing moon."—*J. N. Lockyer*, in the *Nineteenth Century*, July, 1892, p. 31.

Osiris is used to designate any waning luminary, as the setting sun, as well as the waning moon or setting planet.

∵ Osiris is the *setting* sun, but the *rising* sun is Horus, and the *noonday* sun Ra.

Osmand. A necromancer, who by his enchantments raised up an army to resist the Christians. Six of the Champions of Christendom were enchanted by Osmand, but St. George restored them. Osmand tore off his hair in which lay his spirit of enchantment, bit his tongue in two, disembowelled himself, cut off his arms, and then died. (*The Seven Champions of Christendom*, i. 19.)

Osnaburg. *The Duke of York was Bishop of Osnaburg.* Not prelate, but sovereign-bishop. By the treaty of Westphalia, in 1648, it was decreed that the ancient bishopric should be vested alternately in a Catholic bishop and a Protestant prince of the House of Luneburg. Frederick, Duke of York, was the last sovereign-bishop of Osnaburg. In 1803 the district was attached to Hanover, and it now forms part of the kingdom of Prussia.

Osnaburg. A kind of coarse linen made of flax and tow, originally imported from Osnaburg.

Osprey or **Os'pray** (a corruption of Latin *ossifragus*, the bone-breaker). The fish-eagle, or fishing hawk (*Pandion haliaëtus*).

Ossa. *Heaping Pe'lion upon Ossa.* Adding difficulty to difficulty; fruitless efforts. The allusion is to the attempt of the giants to scale heaven by piling Mount Ossa upon Mount Pelion.

"Ter sunt conāti imponĕre Pelio Ossam."
Virgil: Georgics, i. 281.

Osse'o. Son of the Evening Star. When "old and ugly, broken with age, and weak with coughing," he married Oweenee, youngest of the ten daughters of a North hunter. She loved him in spite of his ugliness and decrepitude, because "all was beautiful within him." One day, as he was walking with his nine sisters-in-law and their husbands, he leaped into the hollow of an oak-tree, and came out "tall and straight and strong and handsome;" but Oweenee at the same moment was changed into a weak old woman, "wasted, wrinkled, old, and ugly;" but the love of Osse'o

was not weakened. The nine brothers and sisters-in-law were all transformed into birds for mocking Osseo and Oweenee when they were ugly, and Oweenee, recovering her beauty, had a son, whose delight as he grew up was to shoot at his aunts and uncles, the birds that mocked his father and mother. (*Longfellow : Hiawatha*, xii.).

Os'sian. The son of Fingal, a Scottish warrior-bard who lived in the third century. The poems called *Ossian's Poems* were first published by James M'Pherson in 1760, and professed to be translations from Erse manuscripts collected in the Highlands. This is not true. M'Pherson no doubt based the poems on traditions, but not one of them is a translation of an Erse manuscript; and so far as they are Ossianic at all, they are Irish, and not Scotch.

Ostend' Manifesto. A declaration made in 1857 by the Ministers of the United States in England, France, and Spain, "that Cuba must belong to the United States."

Oster-Monath. The Anglo - Saxon name of April.

Ostler, jocosely said to be derived from *oat-stealer*, but actually from the French *hostelier*, an innkeeper.

Os'tracis'm. Oyster-shelling, blackballing, or expelling. Clis'thenēs gave the people of Attica the power of removing from the state, without making a definite charge, any leader of the people likely to subvert the government. Each citizen wrote his vote on an earthenware tablo (*ostracon*), whence the term.

Os'trich. When hunted the ostrich is said to run a certain distance and then thrust its head into a bush, thinking, because it cannot see, that it cannot be seen by the hunters. (*See* CROCODILE.)

Ostrich Brains. It was Heliogab'alus who had battues of ostriches for the sake of their brains. Smollett says "he had six hundred ostriches compounded in one mess." (*Peregrine Pickle.*)

Ostrich Eggs in Churches. Ostrich eggs are suspended in several Eastern churches as symbols of God's watchful care. It is said that the ostrich hatches her eggs by gazing on them, and if she suspends her gaze even for a minute or so, the eggs are addled. Furthermore, we are told that if an egg is bad the ostrich will break it; so will God deal with evil men.

> "Oh! even with such a look, as fables say
> The mother ostrich fixes on her eggs,
> Till that intense affection
> Kindle its light of life."
> *Southey: Thalaba.*

Ostrich Stomachs. Strong stomachs which will digest anything. The ostrich swallows large stones to aid its gizzard, and when confined where it cannot obtain them will swallow pieces of iron or copper, bricks, or glass.

Ostringers, Sperviters, Falconers. Ostringers are keepers of goshawks and tercelles. Sperviters are those who keep sparrowhawks or muskets. Falconers are those who keep any other kind of hawk, being long-winged. (*Markham: Gentleman's Academie, or Booke of S. Albans.*)

Oswald's Well commemorates the death of Oswald, Christian king of Northumbria, who fell in battle before Penda, pagan king of Mercia, in 642.

Othello (in Shakespeare's tragedy so called). A Moor, commander of the Venetian army, who eloped with Desdemo'na. Brabantio accused him of necromancy, but Desdemona, being sent for, refuted the charge. The Moor, being then sent to drive the Turks from Cyprus, won a signal victory. On his return, Iago played upon his jealousy, and persuaded him that Desdemona intrigued with Cassio. He therefore murdered her, and then stabbed himself.

Othello the Moor. Shakespeare borrowed this tale from the seventh of Giovanni Giraldi Cinthio's third decade of stories. Cinthio died 1573.

Othello's Occupation's Gone (Shakespeare). "*Jam quadrigæ meæ decucurrērunt*" (*Petronius*). I am laid on the shelf; I am no longer the observed of observers.

Other Day (*The*). The day before yesterday. The Old English *other* was used for second, as in Latin, *unus*, *alter*, *tertius*; or *proximus*, *alter*, *tertius*. Starting from to-day, and going backwards, yesterday was the *proximus ab illo*; the day before yesterday was the *altera ab illo*, or the other day; and the day preceding that was *tertius ab illo*, or three days ago. Used to express "a short time ago."

Oth'man, Os'man, or Oth'oman, surnamed the *Conqueror*. Founder of the Turkish power, from whom the empire is called the *Ottoman*, and the

Turks are called *Osmans, Othmans, Osmanli*, etc. Peter the Great, being hemmed in by the Turks on the banks of the Pruth, was rescued by his wife, Catherine, who negotiated a peace with the Grand Vizier.

O'tium cum Dig. [*dignita'te*]. Retirement after a person has given up business and has saved enough to live upon in comfort. The words are Latin, and mean "retirement with honour." They are more frequently used in jest, familiarity, and ridicule.

Otos. A giant, brother of Ephialtēs (*q.v.*). Both brothers grew nine inches every month. According to Pliny, Otos was forty-six cubits (sixty-six feet) in height. (*Greek fable.*) (*See* GIANTS.)

O'Trigger (*Sir Lucius*) in *The Rivals* (Sheridan).

Oui (French for "yes"). A contraction of *Hoc illud*. Thus, *hoc-ill', ho'-il, o'il, oil, oï, oui.*

Out. *Out of God's blessing into the warm sun.* One of Ray's proverbs, meaning from good to less good. "*Ab equis ad asinos.*" When the king says to Hamlet "How is it that the clouds still hang on you?" the prince answers, "No, my lord, I am too much i' the sun," meaning, "I have lost God's blessing, for too much of the sun"— *i.e.* this far inferior state.

> "Thou out of heaven's benediction comest
> To the warm sun."
> *Shakespeare: King Lear,* ii. 2.

To have it out. To contest either physically or verbally with another to the utmost of one's ability; as, "I mean to have it out with him one of these days;" "I had it out with him" —*i.e.* "I spoke my mind freely and without reserve." The idea is that of letting loose pent-up disapprobation.

Out-Herod Herod (*To*). To go beyond even Herod in violence, brutality, or extravagant language. In the old miracle plays Herod was the type of tyranny and violence, both of speech and of action.

Out and Out. Incomparably, by far, or beyond measure; as, "He was out and out the best man." "It is an out-and-outer" means nothing can exceed it. It is the word *utter*, the Anglo-Saxon *útærre*.

Out in the Fifteen—*i.e.* in the rebel army of the Pretender, in 1715

(George I.). (*Howitt : History of England*, vol. iv. p. 347.)

Out in the Forty-five—*i.e.* in the rebel army of the Young Pretender, in 1745 (George II.). (*Howitt : History of England*, vol. iv. p. 506.)

Out of Harness. Not in practice, retired. A horse out of harness is one not at work.

Out of Pocket. To be out of pocket by a transaction is to suffer loss of money thereby. More went out of the pocket than came into it.

Out of Sorts. Indisposed, in bad spirits. The French locution is rather remarkable—*Ne pas être dans son assiette.* "To sort" is to arrange in order, "a sort" is one of the orders so sorted."
Out of sorts. In printers' language, means not having sufficient of some particular letter, mark, or figure.

Out of the Wood. "You are not out of the wood yet," not yet out of danger. "Don't shout till you are out of the wood," do not think yourself safe till you are quite clear of the threatened danger. When freebooters were masters of the forests no traveller was safe till he had got clear of their hunting ground.

Ou'tis (Greek, *nobody*). A name assumed by Odysseus in the cave of Polyphēmos. When the monster roared with pain from the loss of his eye, his brother giants demanded from a distance who was hurting him : "Nobody," thundered out Polyphemos, and his companions went their way. Odysseus in Latin is Ulysses.

Outrigger. The leader of a unicorn team. The Earl of Malmesbury, in 1867, so called the representative of the minority in the three-cornered constituency.

Outrun the Constable. (*See under* CONSTABLE.)

Outworks, in fortification. All the works between the enceinte (*q.v.*) and the covered way (*q.v.*).

Ou'zel. The blackbird; sometimes the thrush is so called. (Anglo-Saxon, *ōsle,* a blackbird.) Bottom speaks of the "ousel cock, so black of hue with orange tawny bill." (*Midsummer Night's Dream.*)

Ova'tion. A triumph; a triumphal reception or entry of the second order ; so called from *ovis,* a sheep, because the Romans sacrificed a sheep to a victorious general to whom an ovation was accorded, but an ox to one who had obtained a "triumph."

Over. (Greek, *huper;* Latin, *super;* German, *über ;* Anglo-Saxon, *ofer.*)

Over, in cricket, means that the fielders are to go over to the other side. This is done when five balls have been delivered from one end. It used to be four. The bowling is taken up at the opposite wicket.

Over and Over Again. Very frequently. (In Latin, *Itĕrum iterumque.*)

Over Edom will I cast my Shoe (Psalm lx. 8; cviii. 9). Will I march. "Over Edom will I cast my shoe, over Philistia will I triumph."

"Every member of the Travellers' Club who could pretend to have cast his shoe over Edom, was constituted a lawful critic."—*Sir W. Scott: The Talisman* (Introduction).

Over the Left. (*See* LEFT.)

O'verdo (*Justice*), in Ben Jonson's *Bartholomew Fair.*

Overreach (*Sir Giles*). The counterpart of Sir Giles Mompesson, a noted usurer outlawed for his misdeeds. He is an unscrupulous, grasping, proud, hard-hearted rascal in *A New Way to Pay Old Debts,* by Massinger.

Overture. A piece of music for the opening of a concert. To "make an overture to a person" is to be the first to make an advance either towards a reconciliation or an acquaintance. (French, *ouverture,* opening.)

Overy. *St. Mary Overy* (Southwark). John Overie was a ferryman, who used to ferry passengers from Southwark to the City, and accumulated a hoard of wealth by penurious savings. His daughter Mary, at his decease, became a nun, and founded the church of St. Mary Overy on the site of her father's house.

Ovid. *The French Ovid.* Du Bellay, one of the Pleiad poets ; also called the "father of grace and elegance." (1524-1560.)

Ow'ain (*Sir*). The Irish knight who passed through St. Patrick's purgatory by way of penance. (*Henry of Saltrey: The Descent of Owain.*)

Owen Meredith. Robert Bulwer Lytton.

Owl. *I live too near a wood to be scared by an owl.* I am too old to be frightened by a bogie ; I am too old a stager to be frightened by such a person as you.

Owl, the emblem of Athens. Because owls abound there. As Athe'na (Minerva) and Athe'næ (Athens) are the same word, the owl was given to Minerva for her symbol also.

Owl-light. Dusk; the blind man's holiday. French, "*Entre chien et loup.*"

Owl in an Ivy Bush (*Like an*). Very ugly, a horrible fright [of a fellow]. Said of (or to) a person who has dressed his head unbecomingly, or that has a scared look, an untidy head of hair, or that looks inanely wise. The ivy bush was supposed to be the favourite haunt of owls, and numerous allusions to this supposition might be readily cited.

" Good ivy, say to us what birds hast thou ?
None but the owlet that cries ' How, how ! ' "
Carol (time Henry V I.).

Owl was a Baker's Daughter (*The*). According to legend, our Saviour went into a baker's shop to ask for something to eat. The mistress of the shop instantly put a cake into the oven for Him, but the daughter said it was too large, and reduced it half. The dough, however, swelled to an enormous size, and the daughter cried out, " Heugh ! heugh ! heugh ! " and was transformed into an owl. Ophelia alludes to this tradition in the line—

" Well, God 'ield you ! They say the owl was a baker's daughter."—*Shakespeare : Hamlet.* iv. 5.

Owlery. A haunt or abode of owls.

Owlglass (German, *Eulenspiegel*). Thyl, son of Klaus (Eulenspiegel) prototype of all the knavish fools of modern times. He was a native of Brunswick, and wandered about the world playing all manner of tricks on the people he encountered. (Died 1350.)

Ox. Emblematic of St. Luke. It is one of the four figures which made up Ezekiel's cherub (i. 10). The ox is the emblem of the priesthood, and has been awarded to St. Luke because he begins his gospel with the Jewish priest sacrificing in the Temple. (*See* LUKE.)

The ox is also the emblem of St. Frideswide, St. Leonard, St. Sylvester, St. Medard, St. Julietta, and St. Blandina.

He has an ox on his tongue. (Latin, *Bovem in lingua habe're*, to be bribed to silence.) The Greeks had the same expression. The Athenian coin was stamped with the figure of an ox. The French say, "*Il a un os dans la bouche,*" referring to a dog which is bribed by a bone.

The black ox hath trampled on you (*The Antiquary*). Misfortune has come

to your house. You are henpecked. A black ox was sacrificed to Pluto, the infernal god, as a white one was to Jupiter.

The black ox never trod upon his foot (common proverb). He never knew sorrow. He is not married. (*See above.*)

The dumb ox. St. Thomas Aqui'nas ; so named by his fellow students at Cologne, on account of his dulness and taciturnity. (1224-1274.)

Albertus said, " We call him the dumb ox, but he will give one day such a bellow as shall be heard from one end of the world to the other." (*Alban Butler.*)

Ox-eye. A cloudy speck which indicates the approach of a storm. When Elijah heard that a speck no bigger than a " man's hand " might be seen in the sky, he told Ahab that a torrent of rain would overtake him before he could reach home (1 Kings xvii. 44, 45). Thomson alludes to this storm signal in his *Summer*.

Ox of the Deluge. The Irish name for a great black deer, probably the *Megace'ros Hiber'nicus*, or Irish elk, now extinct.

Oxford. *The College Ribbons.*

Balliol, pink, white, blue, white, pink.
Brasenose, black, and gold edges.
Christ Church, blue, with red cardinal's hat.
Corpus, red and blue stripe.
Exeter, black, and red edges.
Jesus, green, with white edges.
Lincoln, blue, with mitre.
Magdalen, black and white.
Merton, blue, and white edges, with red cross.
New College, three pink and two white stripes.
Oriel, blue and white.
Pembroke, pink, white, pink.
Queen's, red, white, blue, white, blue, white, red.
St. John's, yellow, black, red.
Trinity, blue, with double dragon's head, yellow and green, or blue, with white edges.
University, blue, and yellow edges.
Wadham, light blue.
*Worcester,*blue,white,pink,white,blue.
HALLS.
St. Alban's, blue, with arrow-head.
St. Edmond's, red, and yellow edges.
St. Mary, white, black, white.
Magdalen, black, and blue edges.

Oxford Blues. The Royal Horse Guards were so called in 1690, because of their blue facings.

Oxford Boat Crew. Dark blue. Cambridge boat crew, light blue.

Oxford Movement. (*See* TRACTS FOR THE TIMES.)

Oxford Stroke (in rowing). A long, deep, high-feathered stroke, excellent in very heavy water. The Cambridge stroke is a clear, fine, deep sweep, with a very low feather, excellent in smooth water. The Cambridge pull is the best for smooth water and a short reach, but the Oxford for a "lumpy" river and a four-mile course.

Oxgang, as a land measure, was no certain quantity, but as much as an ox could gang over or cultivate. Also called a *bovate*. The Latin *jugum* was a similar term, which Varro defines "*Quod juncti boves uno die exarāre : possunt.*"

Eight oxgangs made a carucate. If an oxgang was as much as one ox could cultivate, its average would be about fifteen acres.

O'yer and Te:'miner (*Courts of*) are general gaol deliveries, held twice a year in every county. *Oyer* is French for *to hear*—*i.e.* hear in court or try ; and *terminer* is French for *to conclude*. The words mean that the commissioners appointed are to hear and bring to an end all the cases in the county.

Oyster. *Fast as a Kentish oyster, i.e.* hermetically sealed. Kentish oysters are proverbially good, and all good oysters are fast closed.

Oyster. *No more sense than an oyster.* This is French : "*Il raisonne comme une huitre.*" Oysters have a mouth, but no head.

Oyster Part (*An*). An actor who appears, speaks, or acts only once. Like an oyster, he opens but once.

Oyster and Huitre (French) are variants of the same Latin word, *ostrĕa*. Old French *uistre*, *uître*, *huitre*.

Oysters. *Who eats oysters on St. James's Day will never want.* St. James's Day is the first day of the oyster season (August 5th), when oysters are an expensive luxury eaten only by the rich. By 6, 7 Vict., c. 79, the oyster season begins September 1, and closes April 30.

Oz. (for ounce). z made with a tail (ʒ) resembles the old terminal mark ʒ, indicating a contraction—as viʒ. a contraction of *vi*[*delicet*] ; quibʒ, a contraction of *quibus ;* sʒ, a contraction of *sed* (but), and so on.

30

P. This letter is a rude outline of a man's mouth, the upright being the neck. In Hebrew it is called *pe* (the mouth).

P. *The five P's.* William Oxberry was so called, because he was Printer, Poet, Publisher, Publican, and Player. (1784-1824.)

P [alliterative]. In 1548, Placentius, a Dominican monk, wrote a poem of 253 hexameter verses (called *Pugna Porcōrum*), every word of which begins with the letter *p*. It opens thus :—

"Praise Paul's prize pig's prolific progeny."

∴ In English heroics the letter *A* or *T* would be far more easy, as they would give us articles.

P.C. (*patres conscripti*). The Roman senate. The hundred senators appointed by Romulus were called simply *patres ;* a second hundred added by Tatius, upon the union of the Sabines with the Romans, were called *patres mino'run: gentium ;* a third hundred subsequently added by Tarquin'ius Priscus were termed *patres conscripti,* an expression applied to a fourth and fifth hundred *conscribed* to the original patres or senators. Latterly the term was applied to the whole body.

P., P.P., P.P.P. (in music). P = piano, pp = pianissimo, and ppp = pianississimo. Sometimes pp means *più piano* (more softly).

∵ So f = forte, ff = fortissimo, and fff = fortississimo.

P.P.C. (*pour prendre congé*). For leave-taking ; sometimes written on the address cards of persons about to leave a locality when they pay their farewell visits. In English, *paid parting call.*

P.S. (*post-scriptum*). Written afterwards—*i.e.* after the letter or book was finished. (Latin.)

P's and Q's. *Mind your P's ...d Q's.* Be very circumspect in your behaviour.

Several explanations have been suggested, but none seems to be wholly satisfactory. The following comes nearest to the point of the caution :—In the reign of Louis XIV., when wigs of unwieldy size were worn, and bows were made with very great formality, two things were specially required, a "step" with the feet, and a low bend of the body. In the latter the wig would be very apt to get deranged, and even to fall off. The caution, therefore, of the French dancing-master to his pupils was, "Mind your P's [*i.e. pieds*, feet] and Q's [*i.e. queues*, wigs]."

Paba'na (*The*) or **Peacock Dance.** A grave and stately Spanish dance, so called from the manner in which the lady held up her skirt during the performance.

Pacific Ocean (*The*). So called by Magellan, because he enjoyed calm weather and a placid sea when he sailed across it. All the more striking after the stormy and tempestuous passage of the adjoining straits.

The Pacific.
Amadeus VIII., Count of Savoy. (1383, 1391-1439; died 1451.)
Frederick III., Emperor of Germany. (1415, 1440-1493.)
Olaus III. of Norway. (*, 1030-1093.)

Packing a Jury. Selecting persons on a jury whose verdict may be relied on from proclivity, far more than on evidence.

Pac'olet. A dwarf in the service of Lady Clerimond. He had a winged horse, which carried off Valentine, Orson, and Clerimond from the dungeon of Ferragus to the palace of King Pepin, and afterwards carried Valentine to the palace of Alexander, Emperor of Constantinople, his father. (*Valentine and Orson.*)
It is a horse of Pacolet. (French.) A very swift one, that will carry the rider anywhere; in allusion to the enchanted flying horse of wood, belonging to the dwarf Pac'olet. (*See above*.)

"I fear neither shot nor arrow, nor any horse how swift soever he may be, not though he could outstrip the Pegasus of Perseus or of Pacolet, being assured that I can make good my escape." —*Rabelais: Gargantua*, bk. ii. 24.

Pacto'lus. *The golden sands of the Pactolus.* The gold found in the Pacto'lian sands was from the mines of Mount Tmo'lus; but the supply ceased at the commencement of the Christian era. (*See* MIDAS.) Now called Bagouly.

Padding. The filling-up stuff of serials. The padding of coats and gowns is the wool, etc., put in to make the figure of the wearer more shapely. Figuratively, stuff in books or speeches to spin them out.

Paddington Fair. A public execution. Tyburn, where executions formerly took place, is in the parish of Paddington. Public executions were abolished in 1868.

Paddle Your Own Canoe. Mind your own business. The caution was given by President Lincoln, of North America.

Paddock. *Cold as a paddock.* A paddock is a toad or frog; and we have the corresponding phrases "cold as a toad," and "cold as a frog." Both are cold-blooded. "Paddock calls." (*Macbeth*, i. 1.)

Paddi-whack means an Irish wag, wag being from the Saxon *wåg-ian.*

Paddy. An Irishman. A corruption of St. Patrick, Irish *Padhrig.*

Pad'ua was long supposed by the Scotch to be the chief school of necromancy; hence Sir Walter Scott says of the Earl of Gowrie—
"He learned the art that none may name
  In Padua, far beyond the sea."
    Lay of the Last Minstrel.

Paduasoy or **Padësoy.** A silk stuff originally made at Padua.

Pæan. The physician of the celestial gods; the deliverer from any evil or calamity. (Greek, *pauo*, to make to cease.)

Pæan. A hymn to Apollo, and applied to the god himself. We are told in Dr. Smith's *Classical Dictionary*, that this word is from Pæan, the physician of the Olympian gods; but surely it could be no honour to the Sun-god to be called by the name of his own vassal. Hermsterhuis suggests *pauo*, to make to cease, meaning to make diseases to cease; but why supply *diseases* rather than any other noun? The more likely derivation, *me judice*, is the Greek verb *paio*, to dart; Apollo being called the "fardarter." The hymn began with "*Io Pæan.*" Homer applies it to a triumphal song in general.

Pagan properly means "belonging to a village" (Latin, *pagus*). The Christian Church fixed itself first in cities, the centres of intelligence. Long after it had been established in towns, idolatrous practices continued to be observed in rural districts and villages, so pagan and villager came to mean the same thing. (*See* HEATHEN.)

Pagan Works of Art. In Rome there are numerous works of art intended for Pagan deities and Roman emperors perverted into Christian notabilities.
ANGELS, in St. Peter's of Rome, are old Pagan statues of Cupids and winged genii.
GABRIEL, in St. Peter's of Rome, is an old Pagan statue of the god Mercury.

JOHN THE BAPTIST, in St. Peter's of Rome, is made out of a statue of Hercules.

ST. CATHERINE, in St. Peter's of Rome, is made out of a statue of the goddess Fortūna.

ST. GILES (or EGIDIUS), in St. Peter's of Rome, is a statue of Vulcan.

ST. PAUL. Sixtus V. perverted the original statue of Marcus Aurēlius Antonīnus into that of St. Paul. This beautiful marble column, 170 feet in height, contains a spiral of bas-reliefs of the wars of the Roman emperor, wholly out of character with the statue which surmounts it.

ST. PETER. The same Pope (Sixtus V.) converted the original statue of Trajan, on Trajan's column, into a statue of St. Peter. This exquisite column, like that of Antoninus, contains a spiral of bas-reliefs, representing the wars of Trajan. Surmounted by St. Peter, the perversion is absolutely ludicrous. In St. Peter's of Rome the statue of St. Peter was meant for the old Roman god Jupiter.

VIRGIN MARY. This statue, in St. Peter's of Rome, is in reality a statue of Isis, standing on the crescent Moon.

See *Twentieth Century*, 1892 : ROME.

Page. A boy attendant. (Russian, *paj*, a boy ; Greek, *pais* ; Italian, *paggio ;* Spanish, *page ;* Welsh, *bachgen*. But page, the leaf of a book, is the Latin *pagina*.)

Page (*Mr. and Mrs.*). Inhabitants of Windsor. The lady joins with Mrs. Ford to trick Sir John Falstaff.

Anne Page. Daughter of the above, in love with Fenton. Slender, the son of a country squire, shy, awkward, and a booby, greatly admires the lady, but has too faint a heart to urge his suit further than to sigh in audible whispers, "Sweet Anne Page ! "

William Page. A school-boy, the brother of Anne. (*Shakespeare : The Merry Wives of Windsor*.)

Pago'da. A temple in China, Hindustan, etc. (Hindustanee, *boot-khuda*, abode of God ; Persian, *put-gada*, idolhouse ; Spanish, *pagoda*.)

Paint. The North American Indians paint their faces only when they go to war ; hostilities over, they wash it off.

Paint the Lion (*To*), on board ship, means to strip a person naked and then smear the body all over with tar. (*See Notes and Queries*, 6th August, 1892.)

Painter. The rope which binds a ship's boat to the ship. (Latin, *panthĕra ;* French, *pantiere*, a drag-net ; *panteur*, a stretcher.)

I'll cut your painter for you. I'll send you to the right about in double quick time. If the painter is cut, of course the boat drifts away.

Painter of the Graces. Andrea Appia'ni is so called. (1754-1817.)

Painter of Nature. Remi Belleau, author of *Loves and Transformations of the Precious Stones.* One of the Pleiad

poets is so called, and well deserves the compliment. The *Shepherd's Calendar* of Spenser is largely borrowed from Belleau's *Song on April.* (1528-1577.)

Painters and Artists. *Characteristics of great artists.* The brilliant truth of a Watteau, the dead reality of a Poussin, the touching grace of a Reynolds.

"The colouring of Titian, the expression of Rubens, the grace of Raphael, the purity of Domenichino, the correggioscity of Correggio, the learning of Poussin, the airs of Guido, the taste of the Caracci, the grand contour of Angelo."— *Sterne.*

"The April freshness of Giotto, the piety of Fra Angelo, the virginal purity of the young Raphael, the sweet gravity of John Bellini, the philosophic depth of Da Vinci, the sublime elevation of Michael Angelo, the suavity of Fra Bartolommeo, the delicacy of the Della Robbia, the restrained powers of Roscellini."

Defects of great artists.

In MICHAEL ANGELO the ankles are too narrow.

In TITIAN the palm of the thumb is too prominent.

In RAPHAEL the ears are badly drawn.

In PINTURICCHIO both ears and hands are badly drawn.

Prince of painters. Parrhas'ios, the Greek painter, so called himself. (Fifth century B.C.)

Apelles of Cos. (Fourth century B.C.)

Painting. It is said that Apelles, being at a loss to delineate the foam of Alexander's horse, dashed his brush at the picture in despair, and did by accident what he could not accomplish by art.

Pair Off. When two members of Parliament, or two opposing electors, agree to absent themselves, and not to vote, so that one neutralises the vote of the other. The Whips generally find the pairs for members.

Paishdad'ian Dynasty. The Kai-Omurs dynasty of Persia was so called from the third of the line (Houshung), who was surnamed *Paishdad*, or the just lawgiver (B.C. 910-870). (*See* KAI OMURS.)

Paix. *La Paix des Dames.* The treaty concluded at Cambray, in 1529, between François I. and Charles V. of Germany ; so called because it was brought about by Louise of Savoy (mother of the French king) and Margaret, the emperor's aunt.

Pal (*A*). A gipsy-word, meaning a brother, or companion.

Palace originally meant a dwelling on the Pal'atine Hill of Rome. This hill was so called from Pa'lēs, a pastoral deity, whose festival was celebrated on April 21st, the "birthday of Rome," to commemorate the day when Rom'ulus, the wolf-child, drew the first furrow at the foot of the hill, and thus laid the foundation of the "Roma Quadra'ta," the most ancient part of the city. On this hill Augustus built his mansion, and his example was followed by Tibe'rius and Nero. Under the last-named emperor, all private houses on the hill had to be pulled down to make room for "The Golden House," called the Pala'tium, the palace of palaces. It continued to be the residence of the Roman emperors to the time of Alexander Seve'rus. (*See* PALLACE.)

Pal'adin. An officer of the Pala'tium or Byzantine palace, a high dignitary.

Paladins. The knights of King Charlemagne. The most noted are Allory de l'Estoc; Astolfo; Basin de Genevois; Fierambras or Ferumbras; Florismart; Ganelon, the traitor; Geoffroy, Seigneur de Bordelois, and Geoffroy de Frises; Guerin, Duc de Lorraine; Guillaume de l'Estoc, brother of Allory; Guy de Bourgogne; Hoël, Comte de Nantes; Lambert, Prince de Bruxelles; Malagi'gi; Nami or Nayme de Bavière; Ogier or Oger the Dane; Olivier, son of Regnier, Comte de Gennes; Orlando (*see* Roland); Otuël; Richard, Duc de Normandie; Rinaldo; Riol du Mans; Roland, Comte de Cenouta, son of Milon and Dame Berthe, Charlemagne's sister; Samson, Duc de Bourgogne; and Thiry or Thiery d'Ardaine. Of these, twelve at a time seemed to have formed the coterie of the king. (Latin, *palatīnus*, one of the palace.)

" Who bear the bows were knights in Arthur's reign,
Twelve they, and twelve the peers of Charlemain." *Dryden: The Flower and the Leaf.*

Palæ'mon, originally called Melicertēs. Son of Ino; called Palæmon after he was made a sea-god. The Roman Portu'nus, the protecting god of harbours, is the same. (*See* PALEMON.)

Palais des Thermes. Once the abode of the Roman government of Gaul, as well as of the kings of the first and second dynasties. Here Julius fixed his residence when he was Cæsar of Gaul. It is in Paris, but the only part now extant is a vast hall, formerly the chamber of cold baths (*frigida'rium*), restored by Napoleon III.

Palame'dēs of Lombardy joined the squadron of adventurers with his two brothers, Achilles and Sforza, in the allied Christian army. He was shot by Clorinda with an arrow. (*Tasso: Jerusa'em Delivered,* book iii. c. ii. 4.)

He is a Palamedes. A clever, ingenious person. The allusion is to the son of Nauplios, who invented measures, scales, dice, etc. He also detected that the madness of Ulysses was only assumed.

Sir Palame'dēs. A Saracen knight overcome in single combat by Sir Tristram. Both loved Isolde, the wife of King Mark; and after the lady was given up by the Saracen, Sir Tristram converted him to the Christian faith, and stood his godfather at the font. (*Thomas the Rhymer.*)

Pal'amon and Arcite (2 syl.). Two young Theban knights who fell into the hands of "Duke Theseus," and were shut up in a donjon at Athens. Both fell in love with Emily, the duke's sister-in-law. In time they obtained their liberty, and the duke appointed a tournament, promising Emily to the victor. Arcite prayed to Mars to grant him victory, Pal'amon prayed to Venus to grant him Emily, and both obtained their petition. Arcite won the victory, but, being thrown from his horse, died; Pal'amon, therefore, though not the winner, won the prize for which he fought. The story is borrowed from *Le Teseide* of Boccaccio. *The Black Horse,* a drama by John Fletcher, is the same tale; so called because it was a black horse from which Arcite was thrown. (*Chaucer: The Knight's Tale.*)

Palat'inate (4 syl.). The province of a palatine, as the Palatinate of the Rhine, in Germany. A palatine is an officer whose court is held in the royal palace, also called a palace-greave or pfalzgraf. There were three palatine counties in England — viz. Chester, Durham, and Lancaster, in which the count exercised a royal authority, just as supreme as though he had been the regal tenant of the palace itself.

Pala'ver comes from the Portuguese *palavra* (talk), which is *palaver,* a council of African chiefs.

"Comparisons are odorous: palabras [words], neighbour Verges." — *Shakespeare: Much Ado about Nothing,* iii. 4.

Pale. *Within the pale of my observation—i.e.* the scope thereof. The dominion of King John and his successors in Ireland was marked off, and the part belonging to the English crown was called the *pale,* or the part paled off.

Pale Faces. So Indians call the European settlers.

Pale'mon. "The pride of swains" in Thomson's *Autumn*; a poetical representation of *Boaz*, while the "lovely young Lavin'ia" is *Ruth*.

Palemon, in love with the captain's daughter, in Falconer's *Shipwreck*.

Palermo Razors. Razors of supreme excellence, made in Palermo.

" It is a rayser, and that's a very good one,
It came lately from Palermo."
Damon and Pithias, i. 227.

Pa'lēs. The god of shepherds and their flocks. (*Roman mythology.*)

Palestine Soup. Soup made of Jerusalem artichokes. This is a good example of blunder begetting blunder. Jerusalem artichoke is a corruption of the Italian *Girasole articiocco*—*i.e.* the "sunflower artichoke." From *girasole* we make Jerusalem, and from *Jerusalem* artichokes we make Palestine soup.

Pales'tra (3 syl.). Either the act of wrestling, etc., or the place in which the Grecian youths practised athletic exercises. (Greek, *palē*, wrestling.)

Palestri'na or **Pelestri'na.** An island nearly south of Venice, noted for its glass-houses.

Giovanni Pierluigi da Palestrina, called "The Prince of Music." (1529-1594.)

Paletot [*pal'-e-to*]. A corruption of *palla-toque*, a cloak with a hood. Called by Piers Plowman a *paltock*. The hood or toque has disappeared, but the word remains the same.

Pa'limpsest. A parchment on which the original writing has been effaced, and something else has been written. (Greek, *palin*, again; *psao*, I rub or efface.) When parchment was not supplied in sufficient quantities, the monks and others used to wash or rub out the writing in a parchment and use it again. As they did not wash or rub it out entirely, many works have been recovered by modern ingenuity. Thus Cicero's *De Republica* has been restored; it was partially erased to make room for a commentary of St. Augustine on the Psalms. Of course St. Augustine's commentary was first copied, then erased from the parchment, and the original MS. of Cicero made its appearance.

"Central Asia is a palimpsest; everywhere actual barbarism overlays a bygone civilisation."
—*The Times.*

Pal'indrome (3 syl.). A word or line which reads backwards and forwards alike, as *Madam*, also *Roma tibi subito motibus ibit amor*. (Greek, *palin dromo*, to run back again.) (*See* SOTADIC.)

✣ The following Greek palindrome is very celebrated :—

ΝΙΨΟΝΑΝΟΜΗΜΑΤΑΜΗΜΟΝΑΝΟΨΙΝ

(Wash my transgressions, not only my face). The legend round the font at St. Mary's, Nottingham. Also on the font in the basilica of St. Sophia, Constantinople ; also on the font of St. Stephen d'Egres, Paris ; at St. Menin's Abbey, Orléans ; at Dulwich College ; and at the following churches: Worlingsworth (Suffolk), Harlow (Essex), Knapton (Norfolk), Melton Mowbray (it has been removed to a neighbouring hamlet), St. Martin's, Ludgate (London), and Hadleigh (Suffolk). (See *Ingram: Churches of London*. vol. ii. ; *Malcolm: Londinum Redivivum*, vol. iv. p. 356 ; *Allen: London*, vol. iii. p. 530.)

∴ It is said that when Napoleon was asked whether he could have invaded England, he answered "Able was I ere I saw Elba."

Pal'inode (3 syl.). A song or discourse recanting a previous one. A good specimen of the palinode is *Horace*, book i. ode 16, translated by Swift. Watts has a palinode in which he retracts the praise bestowed upon Queen Anne. In the first part of her reign he wrote a laudatory poem to the queen, but he says that the latter part deluded his hopes and proved him a false prophet. Samuel Butler has also a palinode to recant what he said in a previous poem to the Hon. Edward Howard, who wrote a poem called *The British Princes*. (Greek, *palin odē*, a song again.)

Pal'inu'rus (in English, *Palinure*). Any pilot; so called from Palinurus, the steersman of Æne'as.

" Oh I think how to his [*Pitt's*] latest day,
When death, just hovering, claimed his prey,
With Palinure's unaltered mood,
Firm at his dangerous post he stood ;
Each call for needful rest repelled,
With dying hand the rudder held,
Till in his fall with fateful sway
The steerage of the realm gave way."

Palissy Ware. Dishes and other similar articles covered with models from nature of fish, reptiles, shells, flowers, and leaves, most carefully coloured and in high relief, like the wares of Della Robbia. Bernard Palissy was born at Saintes. (1510-1590.)

Pall, the covering thrown over a coffin, is the Latin *pallium*, a square piece of cloth used by the Romans to throw over their shoulders, or to cover them in bed ; hence a coverlet.

Pall, the long sweeping robe, is the Roman *palla*, worn only by princes and women of honest fame. This differed greatly from the *pallium*, which was worn by freemen and slaves, soldiers, and philosophers.

" Sometimes let gorgeous Tragedy
In sceptred pall come sweeping by."
          Milton : Il Penseroso.

Pall-bearers. The custom of appointing men of mark for pall-bearers, ʌas come to us from the Romans. Julius Cæsar had magistrates for his pall-bearers ; Augustus Cæsar had senators ; Germanicus had tribunes and centurions ; Æmil'is L. Paulus had the chief men of Macedonia who happened to be at Rome at the time ; but the poor were carried on a plain bier on men's shoulders. ᴏ₃⁻ᐟ,

Pall Mall. A game in which a palle or iron ball is struck through an iron ring with a mall or mallet.

Pallace is by Phillips derived from *pallicia*, pales or paled fences. In Devonshire, a *palace* means a " storehouse ;" in Totness, "a landing-place enclosed but not roofed in." (*See* PALACE.)

" All that cellar and the chambers over the same, and the little pallace and landing-place adjoining the River Dart."—*Lease granted by the Corporation of Totness in 1703.*

"Out of the ivory palaces" (Psalm xlv. 8)— *i.e.* store-places or cabinets made of ivory. For " palaces " read *pallaces.*

Palla'dium. Something that affords effectual protection and safety. The Palla'dium was a colossal wooden statue of Pallas in the city of Troy, said to have fallen from heaven. It was believed that so long as this statue remained within the city, Troy would be safe, but if removed, the city would fall into the hands of the enemy. The statue was carried away by the Greeks, and the city burnt by them to the ground.

The Scotch had a similar tradition attached to the great stone of Scone, near Perth. Edward I. removed it to Westminster,—and it is still framed in the Coronation Chair of England. (*See* CORONATION, SCONE.)

Palladium of Rome. Anci'le (*q.v.*).

Palladium of Meg'ara. A golden hair of King Nisus. (*See* SCYLLA, ÉDEN HALL.)

Pallas. A name of Minerva, sometimes called Pallas Minerva. According to fable, Pallas was one of the Titans, of giant size, killed by Minerva, who flayed him, and used his skin for armour ; whence she was called Pallas Minerva. More likely the word Pallas is from *pallo,* to brandish ; and the compound

means Minerva who brandishes the spear.

Pallet. The painter in Smollett's *Peregrine Pickle.* A man without one jot of reverence for ancient customs or modern etiquette.

Pal'liate (3 syl.) means simply to cloak. (Latin, *pallium,* a cloak.)

" That we should not dissemble nor cloke them [our sins] . . . . but confess them with a humble, lowly, and obedient heart."—*Common Prayer Book.*

Palm. *An itching palm.* A hand ready to receive bribes. The old superstition is that if your palm itches you are going to receive money.

" Let me tell you, Cassius, you yourself
Are much condemned to have an itching palm."
          Shakespeare : Julius Cæsar, iv. 3.

To bear the palm. To be the best. The allusion is to the Roman custom of giving the victorious gladiator a branch of the palm-tree.

Palm Off (*To*) *wares, tricks, etc., upon the unwary.* The allusion is to jugglers, who conceal in the palm of their hand what they pretend to dispose of in some other way. These jugglers were sometimes called *palmers.*

" You may palm upon us new for old."
          Dryden.

Palm Oil. Bribes, or rather money for bribes, fees, etc.

"In Ireland the machinery of a political movement will not work unless there is plenty of palm-oil to prevent friction."—*Irish Seditions from 1792 to 1880,* p. 39.

"The rich may escape with whole skins, but those without 'palm-oil' have scant mercy."— *Nineteenth Century,* Aug., 1892, p. 312.

Palm Sunday. The Sunday next before Easter. So called in memory of Christ's triumphant entry into Jerusalem, when the multitude strewed the way with palm branches and leaves. (John xii.)

Sad Palm Sunday. March 29, 1463, the day of the battle of Towton, the most fatal of all the battles in the domestic war between the White and Red Roses. Above 37,000 Englishmen were slain.

" Whose banks received the blood of many thousand men,
On 'Sad Palm Sunday' slain, that Towton field we call . . .
The bloodiest field betwixt the White Rose and the Red."
          Drayton : Polyolbion, xxviii.

Palm Tree is said to grow faster for being weighed down. Hence it is the symbol of resolution overcoming calamity. It is believed by Orientals to have sprung from the residue of the clay of which Adam was formed.

Palmer. A pilgrim privileged to carry a palm-staff. In Fosbroke's *British Monachism* we read that "certain prayers and psalms being said over the pilgrims, as they lay prostrate before the altar, they were sprinkled with holy water, and received a consecrated palm-staff. Palmers differed from pilgrims in this respect: a pilgrim made his pilgrimage and returned to public or private life; but a palmer spent all his days in visiting holy shrines, and lived on charity.

"His sandals were with travel tore,
 Staff, budget, bottle, scrip he wore;
 The faded palm-branch in his hand
 Showed pilgrim from the Holy Land."
        Sir Walter Scott: Marmion, i. 27.

Pal'merin of England. A romance of chivalry, in which Palmerin is the hero. There is another romance called *Palmerin de Oliva.* (See *Southey's Palmerin.*)

Palmy Days. Prosperous or happy days, as those were to a victorious gladiator when he went to receive the palm branch as the reward of his prowess.

Palsy. *The gentlemen's palsy*, ruin from gambling. (*Elizabeth's reign.*)

Paludamentum. A distinctive mantle worn by a Roman general in the time of war. This was the "scarlet robe" in which Christ was invested. (Matt. xxvii. 28.)

"They flung on him an old scarlet paludamentum—some cast-off war-cloak with its purple laticlave from the Prætorian wardrobe."—*Farrar: Life of Christ*, chap. lx. p. 429.

Pam. The knave of clubs, short for *Pamphile*, the French word for the knave of clubs.

"Dr. Johnson's derivation of Pam from palm, because 'Pam' triumphs over other cards, is extremely comic. Of course, Pam is short for *Pamphile*, the French name for the knave of clubs."
—*Notes and Queries* (W. W. Skeat, 1 May, 1886), p. 358.

Pam'ela. The title of the finest of Richardson's novels, which once enjoyed a popularity almost equal to that of the romances of Sir Walter Scott.

Pamela. Lady Edward Fitzgerald (died 1831).

Pampas. Treeless plains, some 2,000 miles long and from 300 to 500 broad, in South America. They cover an area of 750,000 square miles. It is an Indian word meaning *flats* or *plains*.

Pamper, according to Junius, is from the Latin *pam'pinus*, French *pampre* (vine-tendril). Hence Milton—

"Where any row
 Of fruit-trees, over-woody, reached too far
 Their pampered boughs, and needed hands to check
 Fruitless embraces." *Paradise Lost*, v. 214.

The Italian *pambera'to* (well-fed) is a compound of *pane* (bread) and *bere* (drink).

Pamphlet, said to be from Pamphila, a Greek lady, whose chief work is a commonplace book of anecdotes, epitomes, notes, etc. Dr. Johnson suggests *par-un-filet* (held "by a thread")—*i.e.* stitched, but not bound; another derivation is *pag'inæ fila'tæ* (pages tacked together). It was anciently written *panfletus, pamfle'te*, and by Caxton *vaux, flet.*

Pamphyle (3 syl.). A sorceress who converted herself into an owl (*Apuleius*). There was another Pamphylē, the daughter of Apollo, who first taught women to embroider with silk.

"In one very remote village lives the sorceress Pamphylē, who turns her neighbours into various animals. ... Lucius, peeping ... thro' a chink in the door, [saw] the old witch transform herself into an owl."—*Pater: Marius the Epicurean*, chap. v.

Pan. The personification of deity displayed in creation and pervading all things. As flocks and herds were the chief property of the pastoral age, Pan was called the god of flocks and herds. He is also called the god of *hylē*, not the "woods" only, but "all material substances." The lower part was that of a goat, because of the asperity of the earth; the upper part was that of a man, because ether is the "hegemonic of the world;" the lustful nature of the god symbolised the spermatic principle of the world; the libbard's skin was to indicate the immense variety of created things; and the character of "blameless Pan" symbolised that wisdom which governs the world. (Greek, *pan*, everything.) (*Phornutus: De Natura Deorum*, xxvii. 203.)

"Universal Pan,
 Knit with the Graces and the Hours in dance,
 Led on the eternal spring."
        Milton: Paradise Lost, iv. 266.

⁂ In the National Museum of Naples is the celebrated marble of "Pan teaching Apollo to play on the panpipe."

The Great Pan. François Marie Arouet de Voltaire, also called the *Dictator of Letters.* (1694-1778.)

Panace'a. A universal cure. Panacea was the daughter of Escula'pios (god of medicine). The name is evidently composed of two Greek words *pan-akeomai* (all I cure). Of course the medicine that cures is the daughter or child of the healing art.

Panace'a. An Orkney proverb says the well of Kildinguie and the dulse (*sea-weed*) of Guiodin will cure every malady save Black Death. (*Sir Walter Scott: The Pirate*, chap. xxix.) (*See* AZOTH.)

Other famous panaceas.

Prince Ahmed's apple, or apple of Samarcand, cured all disorders. (*See under* APPLE.)

The balsam of Fierabras (*q.v.*).

The Prome'thean unguent rendered the body invulnerable.

Aladdin's ring (*q.v.*) was a preservative against all the ills which flesh is heir to.

Sir Gilbert's sword. Sir T. Malory, in his *History of Prince Arthur* (i. 116), says:—

"Sir Launcelot touched the wounds of Sir Meliot with Sir Gilbert's sword, and wiped them with the cerecloth, and anon a wholler man was he never in all his life."

(*See also* ACHILLES' SPEAR, MEDEA'S KETTLE, REYNARD'S RING [*see* RING], PAN'THERA, etc.)

Panama'. A word which, in 1892, became synonymous with government corruptions. M. de Lesseps undertook to cut a sea passage through the Isthmus of Panama, and in order to raise money from the general public, bribed French senators, deputies, and editors of journals to an enormous extent. An investigation was made into the matter in 1892, and the results were most damaging. In the beginning of 1893 Germany was charged with a similar misappropriation of money connected with the Guelph Fund, in which Prince Ludwig of Bavaria was involved.

"On the other side of the Vosges people will exult that Germany has also her Panama."— *Reuter's Telegram*, Berlin, January 2nd, 1893.

Pancake (2 syl.) is a pudding or "cake" made in a frying-pan. It was originally to be eaten after dinner, to stay the stomachs of those who went to be shriven. The Shrove-bell was called the Pancake Bell, and the day of shriving "Pancake Tuesday."

Pancaste (3 syl.). An Athenian hetæra, and her companion in sin, Phrynē, were the models of *Venus Rising from the Sea*, by Apellēs. (*See* PHRYNE.)

Pancras (*St.*). Patron saint of children. He was a noble Roman youth, martyred by Diocle'tian at the age of fourteen (A.D. 304). (*See* NICHOLAS.)

St. *Pancras*, in Christian art, is represented as treading on a Saracen and bearing either a stone and sword, or a book and palm-branch. The allusions are to his hatred of infidelity, and the implements of his martyrdom.

Pan'darus. Leader of the Lycians in the Trojan war, but represented as a pimp in mediæval romances. (*See* PANDER.)

Pandects of Justin'ian (*The*), found at Amalfi (1137), gave a spur to the study of civil law which changed the whole literary and legal aspect of Europe. The word means much the same as "cyclopædia." (Greek, *pan*, everything; *dech'-omai*, I receive.)

Pandemo'nium (*A*). *A perfect pandemonium.* A bear-garden for disorder and licentiousness. In allusion to the parliament of hell in Milton's *Paradise Lost*, book i. (Greek, *pan daimon*, every demon.) (*See* CORDELIERS.)

Pander. *To pander to one's vices* is to act as an agent to them, and such an agent is termed a pander, from Pan'dărus, who procures for Tro'ilus the love and graces of Cressida. In *Much Ado about Nothing* it is said that Troilus was "the first employer of pandars" (v. 2). (*Shakespeare: Troilus and Cressida; Chaucer: Troilus and Cresseide.*)

"Let all pitiful goers-between be called to the world's end after my name, call them all 'Pandars.' Let all constant men be 'Troiluses,' all false women be 'Cressids,' and all brokers-between, 'Pandars.' Say, Amen."—*Troilus and Cressida*, iii. 2.

Pando'ra's Box (*A*). A present which seems valuable, but which is in reality a curse; as when Midas was permitted, according to his request, to turn whatever he touched into gold, and found his very food became gold, and therefore uneatable. Prometheus made an image and stole fire from heaven to endow it with life. In revenge, Jupiter told Vulcan to make a female statue, and gave her a box which she was to present to the man who married her. Prometheus distrusted Jove and his gifts, but Epime'theus, his brother, married the beautiful Pando'ra, and received the box. Immediately the bridegroom opened the box all the evils that flesh is heir to flew forth, and have ever since continued to afflict the world. The last thing that flew from the box was Hope.

Panel (*A*), means simply a piece of rag or skin. (Latin, *pannus;* Greek, *pe'nos.*) In law it means a piece of parchment containing the names of jurors. *To empanel a jury* is to enter their names on the panel or roll. The panels of a room are the framed wainscot which supplies the place of tapestry, and the panels of doors are the thin boards like wainscot.

Pangloss (*Dr.*). A learned pedant, very poor and very conceited, pluming himself on the titles of LL.D. and A.SS. (Greek, "All-tongue.") (*Colman : Heir-at-Law.*)

Pan'ic. On one occasion Bacchus, in his Indian expeditions, was encompassed with an army far superior to his own ; one of his chief captains, named Pan, advised him to command all his men at the dead of night to raise a simultaneous shout. The shout was rolled from mountain to mountain by innumerable echoes, and the Indians, thinking they were surrounded on all sides, took to sudden flight. From this incident, all sudden fits of great terror have been termed *panics*. (*See* Judges vii. 18-21.)

Theon gives another derivation, and says that the god Pan struck terror into the hearts of the giants, when they warred against heaven, by blowing into a sea-shell.

Panjan'drum. *The Grand Panjandrum.* A village boss, who imagines himself the "Magnus Apollo" of his neighbours. The word occurs in Foote's farrago of nonsense which he composed to test the memory of old Macklin, who said he had brought his memory to such perfection that he could remember anything by reading it over once.

⁂ I myself knew a man at college who could do the same. He would repeat accurately one hundred lines of Greek by reading them twice over, although he could not accurately translate them. His memory was marvellous, but its uselessness was still more so.

Pan'tables. *To stand upon one's pantables.* To stand upon one's dignity. Pantables are slippers, and the idea is *se tenir sur le haut bout—i.e.* to remit nothing.

"Hee standeth upon his pantables, and regardeth greatly his reputation."—Saker : Narbonus (1590).

Pantag'ruel'. So called because he was born during the drought which lasted thirty and six months, three weeks, four days, thirteen hours, and a little more, in that year of grace noted for having "three Thursdays in one week." His father was Gargantua, the giant, who was four hundred fourscore and forty-four years old at the time ; his mother, Badebec, died in giving him birth ; his grandfather was Grangousier (*q.v.*). He was so strong that he was chained in his cradle with four great iron chains, like those used in ships of the largest size ; being angry at this, he stamped out the bottom of his bassanet, which was made of weavers'

30*

beams, and, when loosed by the servants, broke his bonds into five hundred thousand pieces with one blow of his infant fist. When he grew to manhood he knew all languages, all sciences, and all knowledge of every sort, out-Solomoning Solomon in wisdom. Having defeated Anarchus, King of the Dipsodes, all submitted except the Almirods. Marching against these people, a heavy rain fell, and Pantagruel covered his whole army with his tongue. While so doing, Alcofri'bas crawled into his mouth, where he lived six months, taking toll of every morsel that his lord ate. His immortal achievement was his voyage from Uto'pia in quest of the "oracle of the Holy Bottle" (*q.v.*).

> "Wouldst thou not issue forth . . .
> To see the third part in this earthy cell
> Of the brave acts of good Pantag'ruel'."
> *Rabelais : To the Spirit of the Queen of Navarre.*

⁂ Pantagruel was the last of the race of giants.

"My thirst with Pantagruel's own would rank."
—Punch, June 15th, 1893, p. 17.

Pantag'ruel' (meant for Henri II., son of François I.), in the satirical romance of Rabelais, entitled *History of Gargantua and Pantagruel.*

Pantagruelion. *The great Pantag'ruelion law case* (Lord Busqueue *v.* Lord Suckfist). This case, having nonplussed all the judges in Paris, was referred to Lord Pantagruel for decision. The writs, etc., were as much as four asses could carry, but the arbiter determined to hear the plaintiff and defendant state their own cases. Lord Busqueue spoke first, and pleaded such a rigmarole that no one on earth could unravel its meaning ; Lord Suckfist replied, and the bench declared "We have not understood one single circumstance of the defence." Then Pantagruel gave sentence, but his judgment was as obscure and unintelligible as the case itself. So, as no one understood a single sentence of the whole affair, all were perfectly satisfied, a "thing unparalleled in the annals of the law." (*Rabelais : Pantagruel,* book ii.)

Pantag'ruel'ion Herb (*The*). Hemp ; so called "because Pantagruel was the inventor of a certain use which it serves for, exceeding hateful to felons, unto whom it is more hurtful than strangle-weed to flax."

"The figure and shape of the leaves are not much different from those of the ash-tree or the agrimony, the herb itself being so like the Eupato'rio that many herbalists have called it the 'Domestic Eupatorio,' and the Eupatorio the 'Wild Pantagruelion.'"—Rabelais : Pantagruel, iii. 49.

Pantaloon. A feeble-minded old man, the foil of the clown, whom he aids and abets in all his knavery. The word is derived from the dress he used to wear, a loose suit down to the heels.

"That Licentio that comes a-wooing is my man Tranio bearing my port, that we might beguile the old pantaloon."—*Shakespeare: Taming of the Shrew,* iii. 1.

Pantaloon. Lord Byron says the Venetians were called the *Planters of the Lion—i.e.* the Lion of St. Mark, the standard of the republic; and further tells us that the character of "pantaloon," being Venetian, was called *Piantaleone* (Planter of the Lion). (*Childe Harold,* bk. iv. stanza 14, note 9.)

Playing Pantaloon. Playing second fiddle; being the cat's-paw of another; servilely imitating.

Pantechnicon. A place where all sorts of manufactured articles are exposed for sale; a storehouse for furniture.

Panthe´a, wife of Abradatus, King of Susa. Abradatus joined the Assyrians against Cyrus, and his wife was taken captive. Cyrus refused to visit her, that he might not be tempted by her beauty to outstep the bounds of modesty. Abradatus was so charmed by this continence that he joined the party of Cyrus, and, being slain in battle, his wife put an end to her life, and fell on the body of her husband.

"Here stands Lady Rachel Russell—there the arch-virago old Bess of Hardwicke. The one is our English version of Panthea of Arria; the other of Xantippe in a coif and peaked stomacher."—*Mrs. Lynn Linton: Nineteenth Century,* Oct., 1891, p. 605.

Panthe´a (Greek). Statues carrying symbols of several deities, as in the medal of Antoni´nus Pius, where Sera´pis is represented by a *modius,* Apollo by *rays,* Jupiter Ammon by *ram's horns,* Pluto by a *large beard,* and Æscula´pius by a *wand,* around which a serpent is twined.

Panthe´on. The finest is that erected in Rome by Agrippa (son-in-law of Augustus). It is circular, 150 feet in diameter, and the same in height. It is now a church, with statues of heathen gods, and is called the Rotunda. In Paris the Pantheon was the church of St. Geneviève, built by Louis XV., finished 1790. Next year the Convention called it the Pantheon, and set it apart as the shrine of those Frenchmen whom their country wished to honour ("*aux grands hommes la patrie reconnaissante*"). (Greek. *pantes theoi,* all the gods.)

Panther. *The Spotted Panther* in Dryden's *Hind and Panther* means the Church of England full of the spots of error; whereas the Church of Rome is faultless as the milk-white hind.

" The panther, sure the noblest next the hind, And fairest creature of the spotted kind; Oh, could her inborn stains be washed away, She were too good to be a beast of prey."
Part i.

Pan´thera. A hypothetical beast which lived in the East. Reynard affirmed that he had sent her majesty the queen a comb made of panthera bone, " more lustrous than the rainbow, more odoriferous than any perfume, a charm against every ill, and a universal panacea." (*H. von Alkmar: Reynard the Fox.*) (1498.)
She wears a comb made of panthera bone.
She is all perfection. (*See above.*)

Pantile Shop. A meeting-house, from the fact that dissenting chapels were often roofed with pantiles. Hence pantile was used in the sense of dissenting. Mrs. Centlivre, in the *Gotham Election,* contrasts the pantile crew with a good churchman.

Pan´tomime (3 syl.), according to etymology, should be *all* dumb show, but in modern practice it is partly dumb show and partly grotesque speaking. Harlequin and Columbine never speak, but Clown and Pantaloon keep up a constant fire of fun. Dr. Clarke says that Harlequin is the god *Mercury,* with his short sword called " herpē; " he is supposed to be invisible, and to be able to transport himself to the ends of the earth as quick as thought. Columbine, he says, is *Psyche* (the soul); the old man is *Charon;* and the Clown *Momus* (the buffoon of heaven), whose large gaping mouth is an imitation of the ancient masks. (*Travels,* iv. 459.)
The best Roman pantomimists were Bathylus (a freedman of Mæcēnas), Pylădēs, and Hylas.

Panton Gates. *Old as Panton Gates.* A corruption of Pandon Gates at Newcastle-on-Tyne.

Pantry. (French, *paneterie* (2 syl.); Latin, *panarium,* from *panis,* bread.) An archaic form is " panary." The keeper of a pantry was at one time called a " panterer." (French, *panterer.*)

Panurge (2 syl.). A companion of Pantag'ruel's, not unlike our Rochester and Buckingham in the reign of the mutton-eating king. Panurge was a desperate rake, was always in debt, had a dodge for every scheme, knew everything and something more, was a boon companion of the mirthfullest temper and most licentious ōias ; but was timid of danger, and a desperate coward. He enters upon ten thousand adventures for the solution of this knotty point. " Whether or not he ought to marry ? " and although every response is in the negative, disputes the ostensible meaning, and stoutly maintains that no means yes. (Greek for *factotum*.) (*Rabelais*.)

. *Panurge*, probably meant for Calvin, though some think it is Cardinal Lorraine. He is a licentious, intemperate libertine. a coward and knave. Of course, the satire points to the celibacy of the clergy.

"Sam Slick is the thoroughbred Yankee, bold, cunning, and, above all, a merchant. In short, he is a sort of Republican Panurge."—*Globe*.

As Panurge asked if he should marry. Asking advice merely to contradict the giver of it. Panurge asked Pantag'ruel' whether he advised him to marry, "Yes," said Pantagruel. When Panurge urged some strong objection, "Then don't marry," said Pantagruel ; to which the favourite replied, "His whole heart was bent on so doing." "Marry then, by all means," said the prince, but Panurge again found some insuperable barrier. And so they went on ; every time Pantagruel said "Yea," new reasons were found against this advice ; and every time he said "Nay," reasons no less cogent were discovered for the affirmative. (*Rabelais : Gargantua and Pantagruel*, bk. iii. 9.)

❦ Besides Pantag'ruel', Panurge consulted lots, dreams, a sibyl, a deaf and dumb man, the old poet Rominagrobis, the chiromancer Herr Trippa, the theologian Hippothadée, the physician Rondib'ilis, the philosopher Trouillogan, the court fool Triboulet, and, lastly, the Oracle of the Holy Bottle.

Panyer Stone (*The*). A stone let into the wall of a house in Panyer Alley. It is a rude representation of a boy sitting on a pannier. (French, *panier ;* Latin, *panarium*, a bread-basket.) The stone has the following inscription :—

"When you have sought the city round, Yet still this is the highest ground. August 27th, 1688."

❦ This is not correct, for there are higher spots both in Cornhill, and in Cannon Street.

Pap. *He gives pap with a hatchet.* He does or says a kind thing in a very brusque and ungracious manner. The Spartan children were fed by the point of a sword, and the Teuton children with hatchets, or instruments so called—probably of the doll type. "Ursus," in Victor Hugo's novel of "*L'Homme qui Rit*," gives "pap with a hatchet."

Papa, Father. The former is Greek *pappas* (father) ; Chaldee, *abba*. For many centuries after the Conquest, the "gentry" taught their children to use the word "papa," but this custom is now almost gone out.

Papal Slippers (*The*) are wrought with a cross of rubies over each instep.

Paper. So called from the papy'rus or Egyptian reed used at one time for the manufacture of a writing material. Bryan Donkin, in 1803, perfected a machine for making a sheet of paper to any required length.

Paper a House (*To*), in theatrical phraseology, means to fill a house with "deadheads," or non-paying spectators, admitted by paper orders. The women admitted thus, not being dressed so smartly as the paying ones, used to cover their shoulders with a "scarlet opera cloak," often lent or hired for the occasion.

Paper King. John Law, the projector of the Mississippi Scheme. (1671-1729.)

Paper Marriages. Weddings of dons, who pay their fees in bank-notes.

Paper-stainer (*A*). An author of small repute.

Paph'ian. Relating to Venus, or rather to Paphos, a city of Cyprus, where Venus was worshipped ; a Cyprian ; a prostitute.

Papimany. The country of the Papimans ; the country subject to the Pope, or any priest-ridden country, as Spain. (*Rabelais : Gargantua and Pantag'ruel*, iv. 45.)

Papy'ra. The goddess of printing ; so called from papy'rus, the Nile-reed, from which at one time paper was made, and from which it borrows its name.

" Till to astonished realms Papyra taught To paint in mystic colours sound and thought, With Wisdom's voice to print the page sublime, And mark in adamant the steps of Time."
Darwin: Loves of the Plants, canto ii.

Papy'ri. Written scrolls made of the Papy'rus, found in Egypt and Hercula'neum.

Par. (*A*). A newspaper paragraph. (*Press slang.*)

Par (*At*). Stock at par means that it is to be bought at the price it represents. Thus, £100 stock in the 2½ per cent. quoted at par would mean that it would require £100 to invest in this stock; if quoted at £105, it would be £5 above par; if at £95, it would be £5 below par. (Latin, *par*, equal.)

Paracel'sists. Disciples of Paracelsus in medicine, physics, and mystic sciences. A Swiss physician. (1493-1541.)

Paraclete. The advocate; one *called to* aid or support another. (The word paraclete is from the Greek *para-kaleo*, to call to; and advocate is from the Latin *ad-voco*, the same thing.)

Paradise. The Greeks used this word to denote the extensive parks and pleasure-grounds of the Persian kings. (Persian, *pardēs;* Greek, *paradeisos*.) (*See* CALAYA.)

"An old word, 'paradise,' which the Hebrews had borrowed from the Persians, and which at first designated the 'parks of the Achemenidæ,' summed up the general dream."—*Renan: Life of Jesus,* xi.

Upper and Lower Paradise. The rabbins say there is an earthly or lower paradise under the equator, divided into seven dwellings, and twelve times ten thousand miles square. A column reaches from this paradise to the upper or heavenly one, by which the souls mount upwards after a short sojourn on the earthly one.

The ten dumb animals admitted to the Moslem's paradise are :—

(1) The dog Kratim, which accompanied the Seven Sleepers.

(2) Balaam's ass, which spoke with the voice of a man to reprove the disobedient prophet.

(3) Solomon's ant, of which he said, "Go to the ant, thou sluggard . . ."

(4) Jonah's whale.

(5) The ram caught in the thicket, and offered in sacrifice in lieu of Isaac.

(6) The calf of Abraham.

(7) The camel of Saleh.

(8) The cuckoo of Belkis.

(9) The ox of Moses.

.10) Mahomet's mare, called Borak.

Paradise Lost. Satan rouses the panic-stricken host of fallen angels to tell them about a rumour current in Heaven of a new world about to be created. He calls a council to deliberate what should be done, and they agree to send Satan to search out for the new world. Satan, passing the gulf between Hell and Heaven and the limbo of Vanity, enters the orb of the Sun (in the guise of an angel) to make inquiries as to the new planet's whereabouts; and, having obtained the necessary information, alights on Mount Nipha'tēs, and goes to Paradise in the form of a cormorant. Seating himself on the Tree of Life, he overhears Adam and Eve talking about the prohibition made by God, and at once resolves upon the nature of his attack. Gabriel sends two angels to watch over the bower of Paradise, and Satan flees. Raphael is sent to warn Adam of his danger, and tells him the story of Satan's revolt and expulsion out of Heaven, and why and how this world was made. After a time Satan returns to Paradise in the form of a mist, and, entering the serpent, induces Eve to eat of the forbidden fruit. Adam eats "that he may perish with the woman whom he loved." Satan returns to Hell to tell his triumph, and Michael is sent to lead the guilty pair out of the garden. (*Milton*.)

Paradise Regained (in four books). The subject is the Temptation. Eve, being tempted, fell, and lost Paradise; Jesus, being tempted, resisted, and regained Paradise. (*Milton*.)

Paradise Shoots. The lign aloe; said to be the only plant descended to us from the Garden of Eden. When Adam left Paradise, it is said, he took with him a shoot of this tree, which he planted in the land where he settled, and from which all other lign aloes have been propagated.

Paradise of Fools. The Hindus, Mahometans, Scandinavians, and Roman Catholics have devised a place between Paradise and "Purgatory" to get rid of a theological difficulty. If there is no sin without intention, then infants and idiots cannot commit sin, and if they die cannot be consigned to the purgatory of evil-doers; but, not being believers or good-doers, they cannot be placed with the saints. The Roman Catholics place them in the Paradise of Infants and the Paradise of Fools.

Paradise and the Pe'ri. The second tale in Moore's poetical romance of *Lalla Rookh*. The Peri laments her expulsion from Heaven, and is told she will be readmitted if she will bring to the Gate of Heaven the "gift most dear to the Almighty." *First* she went to a battle-field, where the tyrant Mahmoud, having won a victory, promised life to a young warrior, but the warrior struck the tyrant with a dart. The wound, however, was not mortal, so "The tyrant lived, the hero fell." The Peri took to Heaven's Gate the last drop of the patriot's blood as her offering, but the gates would not open to her. *Next* she flew to Egypt, where the plague was raging, and saw a young man dying; presently his betrothed bride sought him out, caught the disease, and both died. The Peri took to Heaven's Gate the last sigh of that self-sacrificed damsel, but the offering was not good enough to open the gates to her. *Lastly*, she flew to Syria, and there saw an innocent child and guilty old man. The vesper call sounded, and the child knelt down to prayer. The old man wept with repentance, and knelt to pray beside the child. The Peri offered the *Repentant Tear*, and the gates flew open to receive the gift.

Parallel. *None but himself can be his parallel.* Wholly without a peer; "*Quæris Alcīdæ parem;*" "*nemo proximus nec secundus.*" There are many similar sentences; for example :—

"Nemo est, nisi ipse."—*Seneca: Hercules Furens*, i. 84. (Seneca lived B.C. 58-32.)

" And but herself admits no parallel."
   Massinger : Duke of Millaine, iii. 4.   (1662.)
"None but himself himself can parallel."
   Anagram on John Lilburn.   (1658.)
" Is there a treachery like this in baseness . . .
   None but itself can be its parallel."
   Theobald : Double Falsehood, iii. 1.   (1721.)

Paramatta. A fabric of wool and cotton. So called from a town in New South Wales, where the wool was originally bought.

Parapet. Fortification, the shot-proof covering of a mass of earth on the exterior edge of the ramparts. The openings out through the parapets to permit guns to fire in the required direction are called *embrasures :* about 18 feet is allowed from one embrasure to another, and the solid intervening part is called the *merlon.* An indented parapet is a battlement. (Italian, *parapetto*, breastwork.)

Paraphernalia means all that a woman can claim at the death of her husband beyond her jointure. In the Roman law her paraphernalia included the furniture of her chamber, her wearing apparel, her jewels, etc. Hence personal attire, fittings generally, anything for show or decoration. (Greek, *parapherne*, beyond dower.)

Parasite (Greek, *para sitos*, eating at another's cost). A plant or animal that lives on another; hence a hanger-on,

who fawns and flatters for the sake of his food.

Parc aux Cerfs [*deer parks*]. A mansion fitted up in a remote corner of Versailles, whither girls were inveigled for the licentious pleasure of Louis XV. The rank of the person who visited them was scrupulously kept concealed; but one girl, more bold than the rest, rifled the pockets of M. le Comte, and found that he was no other than the king. Madame de Pompadour did not shrink from superintending the labours of the royal valets to procure victims for this infamous establishment. The term is now used for an Alsatia, or haven of shipwrecked characters.

"Boulogne may be proud of being '*parc aux cerfs*' to those whom remorseless greed drives from their island home."—*Saturday Review.*

Parcæ. The Fates. The three were Clotho, Lach'esis, and At'ropos. (*Latin mythology.*) Parcæ is from *pars*, a lot; and the corresponding Moiræ is from *meros*, a lot. The Fates were so called because they decided the lot of every man.

Parchment. So called from Per'gamon in Lesser Asia, where it was used for purposes of writing when Ptol'emy prohibited the exportation of paper from Egypt.

Pardon Bell. The Angĕlus bell. So called because of the indulgence once given for reciting certain prayers forming the *angelus.*

Par'douneres Tale, in Chaucer, is *Death and the Rioters.* Three rioters in a tavern agreed to hunt down Death and kill him. As they went their way they met an old man, who told them that he had just left him sitting under a tree in the lane close by. Off posted the three rioters, but when they came to the tree they found a great treasure, which they agreed to divide equally. They cast lots which was to carry it home, and the lot fell to the youngest, who was sent to the village to buy food and wine. While he was gone the two who were left agreed to kill him, and so increase their share; but the third bought poison to put into the wine, in order to kill his two *confrères.* On his return with his stores, the two set upon him and slew him, then sat down to drink and be merry together; but, the wine being poisoned, all the three rioters found Death under the tree as the old man had said.

Pari Passu. At the same time; in equal degrees; two or more schemes carried on at once and driven forward with equal energy, are said to be carried on *pari passu*, which is Latin for *equal strides* or the equally measured pace of persons marching together.

"The cooling effects of surrounding matter go on nearly *pari passu* with the heating."—*Grove: Correlation of Physical Forces*, p. 64.

Pa'rian Chronicle. A chronological register of the chief events in the mythology and history of ancient Greece during a series of 1,318 years, beginning with the reign of Cecrops, and ending with the archonship of Diogne'tos. It is engraved on Parian marble, and was found in the island of Paros. It is one of the Arunde'lian Marbles (*q.v.*).

Pa'rian Verse. Ill-natured satire; so called from Archil'ochos, a native of Paros.

Pa'rias or **Par'iahs.** The lowest class of the Hindu population, below the four castes. Literally drummers, from *parai*, a large drum.

"The lodgers overhead may perhaps be able to take a more comprehensive view of public questions ; but they are political Helots, they are the Pariahs of our constitutional Brahminism."—*The Times*, March 20, 1867.

Par'idel. A young gentleman that travels about and seeks adventure, because he is young, rich, and at leisure. (*See below.*)

"Thee, too, my Paridel, she marked thee there,
Stretched on the rack of a too-easy chair,
And heard thy everlasting yawn confess
The pains and penalties of idleness."
            Pope: Dunciad, iv. 341.

Sir Paridel. A male coquette, whose delight was to win women's hearts, and then desert them. The model was the Earl of Westmoreland. (*Spenser: Faërie Queene*, bk. iii. cant. 10 ; bk. iv. c. 1.)

Paris or *Alexander.* Son of Priam, and cause of the siege of Troy. He was hospitably entertained by Menela'os, King of Sparta ; and eloped with Helen, his host's wife. This brought about the siege. Post-Homeric tradition says that Paris slew Achilles, and was himself slain either by Pyrrhos or Philocte'tēs. (*Homer: Iliad.*)

Paris. Kinsman to the Prince of Ve-ro'na, the unsuccessful suitor of Juliet. (*Shakespeare: Romeo and Juliet.*)

Paris. Rabelais says that Gargantua played on the Parisians who came to stare at him a practical joke, and the men said it was a sport "par ris" (to be laughed at) ; wherefore the city was called Par-'is. It was called before Leuco'tia, from the "white skin of the ladies." (Greek, *leukŏtes*, whiteness.) (*Gargantua and Pantagruel*, bk. i. 17.)

Paris, called by the Romans "Lute'tia Parisio'rum" (the mud-city of the Parisii). The Parisii were the Gallic tribe which dwelt in the "Ile du Palais" when the Romans invaded Gaul. (*See* ISIS.)

Mons. de Paris. The public executioner of Paris.

Little Paris. The "Galleria Vittorio Emanuele" of Milan is so called on account of its brilliant shops, its numerous cafés, and its general gay appearance.

Brussels, the capital of Belgium, situate on the Senne, is also called "Little Paris."

Paris-Garden. A bear-garden; a noisy, disorderly place. In allusion to the bear-garden so called on the Thames bank-side, kept by Robert de Paris in the reign of Richard II.

"Do you take the court for a Paris-garden ?"—*Shakespeare: Henry VIII.*, v. 3.

Parish Registers. Bills of mortality. George Crabbe, author of *The Borough*, has a poem in three parts, in ten-syllable verse with rhymes, entitled *The Parish Register*.

Paris'ian. Made at Paris; after the mode of Paris ; a native of Paris ; like a native of Paris.

Paris'ian Wedding (*The*). The massacre of St. Bartholomew, part of the wedding festivity at the marriage of Henri of Navarre and Margaret of France.

"Charles IX., although it was not possible for him to recall to life the countless victims of the Parisian Wedding, was ready to explain those murders to every unprejudiced mind."—*Motley: Dutch Republic*, iii. 9.

Parisienne (*La*). A celebrated song by Casimir Delavigne, called the *Marseillaise* of 1830.

"Paris n'a plus qu'un cri de gloire :
        En avant marchons,
        Contre leurs canons.
A travers le feu des battaillons,
        Courons à la victoire ! "

Parisi'na, the beautiful young wife of Azo. She falls in love with Hugo, her stepson, and betrays herself to her husband in a dream. Azo condemns his son to be executed, but the fate of Parisina, says Byron, is unknown. (*Parisina.*)

Frizzi, in his *History of Ferrara*, tells us that Parisi'na Malatesta was the second wife of Niccolo, Marquis of Este ; that she fell in love with Ogo, her stepson, and that the infidelity of Parisina was revealed by a servant named Zoe'sē.

He says that both Ogo and Parisina were beheaded, and that the marquis commanded all the faithless wives he knew to be beheaded to the Moloch of his passion.

Pariza'de (4 syl.). A lady whose adventures in search of the Talking Bird, Singing Tree, and Yellow Water, are related in the *Story of the Sisters who Envied their Younger Sister*, in the *Arabian Nights*. This tale has been closely imitated in *Chery and Fairstar* (*q.v.*).

Parkership. The office of pound-keeper; from *parcus* (a pound).

Parks. There are in England 334 parks stocked with deer; red deer are kept in 31 of them. The oldest is Eridge Park, in Sussex, called in Domesday Book *Reredfelle* (Rotherfield). The largest private deer park is Lord Egerton's, Tatton, in Cheshire, which contains 2,500 acres. Blenheim Park contains 2,800 acres, but only 1,150 acres of it are open to deer. Almost as extensive as Tatton Park are Richmond Park, in Surrey; Eastwell Park, in Kent; Grimsthorpe Park, in Lincolnshire; Thoresby Park, in Notts; and Knowesley Park, in Lancashire. (*E. P. Shirley: English Deer Parks*.) Woburn Park is 3,500 acres.

Parlance. *In common parlance.* In the usual or vulgar phraseology. An English-French word; the French have *parler, parlant, parlage*, etc.—to speak, speaking, talk—but not parlance.

Parlement (French). A crown court, where, in the old *régime*, councillors were allowed to plead, and where justice was administered in the king's name. The Paris Parlement received appeals from all inferior tribunals, but its own judgments were final. It took cognisance of all offences against the crown, the peers, the bishops, the corporations, and all high officers of state; and, though it had no legislative power, had to *register* the royal edicts before they could become law. Abolished by the Constituent Assembly in 1790.

Parliament.

" My Lord Coke tells us *Parliament* is derived from ' parler le ment ' (to speak one's mind). He might as honestly have taught us that *firmament* is ' firma mentis ' (a farm for the mind), or ' fundament ' the bottom of the mind."—*Rymer: On Parliaments.*

The Addled Parliament (between April 5th, 1614, and June 7th, 1615); so called because it remonstrated with the king on his levying "benevolences," but passed no acts.

The Barebone Parliament. The Parliament convened July 4th, 1653; over-ridden by Praise-God Barebone.

The Black Parliament. Held by Henry VIII. in Bridewell.

The Club Parliament. (*See* PARLIAMENT OF BATS.)

The Convention Parliament. Two Parliaments were so called: one in 1660, because it was not held by the order of the king, but was convened by General Monk; the second was convened January 22nd, 1689, to confer the crown on William and Mary.

The Devil's Parliament. The Parliament convened at Coventry by Henry VI., in 1459, which passed attainders on the Duke of York and his supporters.

The Drunken Parliament. The Parliament assembled at Edinburgh, January 1st, 1661, of which Burnet says the members "were almost perpetually drunk."

The Good Parliament (1376, in the reign of Edward III., while the Black Prince was still alive). So called from the severity with which it pursued the unpopular party of the Duke of Lancaster.

Grattan's Parliament (1782-1801). In 1782 Grattan moved the "Declaration of Rights," repudiating the right of the British Parliament to interfere in the government of Ireland. Pitt pronounced the Parliament unworkable.

The Illiterate or *Lack-learning Parliament.* (*See* UNLEARNED PARLIAMENT.)

The Little Parliament. Same as "the Barebone Parliament" (*q.v.*).

The Long Parliament sat 12 years and 5 months, from November 2nd, 1640, to April 20th, 1653, when it was dissolved by Cromwell; but a fragment of it, called "The Rump," continued till the Restoration, in 1660.

Historian of the Long Parliament. Thomas May, buried in Westminster Abbey. (1595-1650.)

The Mad Parliament, in the reign of Henry III. (1258), was so called from its opposition to the king. It insisted on his confirming the Magna Charta, and even appointed twenty-four of its own members, with Simon de Montfort as president, to administer the government.

The Merciless (or *Unmerciful*) *Parliament* (from February 3rd to June 3rd, 1388). A junto of fourteen tools of Thomas, Duke of Gloucester, which assumed royal prerogatives, and attempted to depose Richard II.

The Mongrel Parliament (1681), held at Oxford, consisting of Whigs and Tories, by whom the Exclusion Bill was passed.

The Pacific Parliament. A triennial Parliament, dissolved August 8th, 1713. It signed the treaty of peace at Utrecht, after a war of eleven years.

The Pensioner (or *Pensionary*) *Parliament* (from May 8th, 1661, to January 24th, 1678 [*i.e.* 16 years and 260 days]). It was convened by Charles II., and was called "Pensionary" from the many pensions it granted to the adherents of the king.

The Rump Parliament, in the Protectorate; so called because it contained the rump or fag-end of the Long Parliament (1659). It was this Parliament that voted the trial of Charles I.

The Running Parliament. A Scotch Parliament; so called from its constantly being shifted from place to place.

The Unlearned or *Lawless Parliament* (*Parliamentum Indoctum*) (1404). So called by Sir E. Coke, because it contained no lawyer.

The Unmerciful Parliament, in the reign of Richard II.; so called by the people from its tyrannical proceedings.

The Useless Parliament. The Parliament convened by Charles I., on June 18th, 1625; adjourned to Oxford, August 1st; and dissolved August 12th; having done nothing but offend the king.

The Wondermaking Parliament. The same as "The Unmerciful Parliament;" convened February 3rd, 1388. By playing into the hands of the Duke of Gloucester it checkmated the king.

Parliament Soldiers. The soldiers of General Monk, who restored Charles II. to the throne.

" Ring a ding-ding; ring a ding-ding!
The Parliament soldiers are gone for the king.
Some they did laugh, and some they did cry
To see the Parliament soldiers go by.
[To fetch back the king.]"

Parliament of Bats (*The*), 1426, during the regency in the reign of Henry VI. So called because the members, being forbidden by the Duke of Gloucester to wear swords, armed themselves with clubs or bats.

Parliament of Dunces. Convened by Henry IV. at Coventry, in 1404, and so called because all lawyers were excluded from it.

Parliamenta'rian (*A*). One who favoured the Parliament in opposition to Charles I.

Parlour (*A*). The reception room in a religious house where the religious see their friends   (French, *parlour*.)

Par'lous. A corrupt form of *perilous*, in slang = our modern use of "awful," amazing, wondrous.

" Oh! 'tis a parlous lad."
  Shakespeare: As You Like It, iii. 2.

Parme'nianists. A name given to the Don'atists; so called from Parmenia'nus, Bishop of Carthage, the great antagonist of Augustine.

Par'mesan'. A cheese made at Parma, in Italy.

Parnassos (Greek), **Parnassus** (Latin). A mountain near Delphi, in Greece. It has two summits, one of which was consecrated to Apollo and the Muses, the other to Bacchus. It was anciently called Larnassos, from *larnax*, an ark, because Deucalion's ark stranded there after the flood. After the oracle of Delphi was built at its foot it received the name of Parnassos, which Peucerus says is a corruption of *Har Nahas* (hill of divination). The Turks call it *Liakura*.

Parnassus. The region of poetry. Properly a mountain of Phocis, in Greece, sacred to Apollo and the Muses. "Where lies your vein? Are you inclined to soar to the higher regions of Parnassus or to flutter round the base of the hill?" (*The Antiquary*)—*i.e.* Are you going to attempt the higher walks of poetry, such as epic and dramatic, or some more modest kind, as simple song?

To climb Parnassus. To write poetry.

Parochial. Relating to a parish. Hence, petty, narrow. (*See* LITTLE ENGLANDERS.)

Parody. *Father of Parody.* Hippo'nax of Ephesus. The word parody means an ode which perverts the meaning of another ode. (Greek, *para ōdē*.)

Parole (French). A verbal promise given by a soldier or prisoner of war, that he will not abuse his leave of absence; the watchword of the day.

Parol'les (3 syl.). A man of vain words, who dubs himself "captain," pretends to knowledge which he has not, and to sentiments he never feels. (French, *paroles*, a creature of empty words.) (*Shakespeare: All's Well that Ends Well*.)

" I know him a notorious liar,
Think him a great way fool, solely a coward;
Yet these fixed evils sit so fit on him
That they take place . . . ."   Act i. 1.

He was a mere Parolles in a pedagogue's wig. A pretender, a man of words, and a pedant. The allusion is to the bragging, faithless, slandering villain mentioned above.

" Rust, sword ; cool, blushes ; and. Parolles, live
Safest in shame ; being fooled, by fooling
thrive ;
There's place and means for every man alive."
Shakespeare: All's Well that Ends Well, iv. 3.

Parr. *Old Parr.* Thomas Parr lived in the reigns of ten sovereigns ; married a second wife when he was 120 years old, and had a child by her. He was a husbandman, born at Salop in 1483, and died 1635, aged 152 years. Mr. Thoms, in his *Records of Longevity,* denies the truth of Parr's great age.

Par'ricide (3 syl.). *La Belle Parricide.* Beatrice Cenci (*-1599.)

Parrot-coal. A name given to anthracite because of the crackling or chattering noise it makes when burnt.

Parsees or *Ghebers.* Fire-worshippers. We use the word for Persian refugees driven out of their country by the persecutions of the Mussulmans. They now inhabit various parts of India. (The word means *People of Pars* or *Fars —i.e.* Persia.)

Parsley. *He has need now of nothing but a little parsley—i.e.* he is dead. The Greeks decked tombs with parsley, because it keeps green a long time.

δεῖσθαι σελίνου, he needs parsley ; that is, he is dead, and should be strewed with parsley.

Parson, says Blackstone, is " *perso'na ecclesiæ,* one that hath full rights of the parochial church." (*See* CLERICAL TITLES.)

" Among wyves and wodewes ich am ywoned sute
    [wont to set],
Yparroked [impaled] in puwes. The person hit
    knoweth."
    Robert Langland : Piers Plowmes Vision.

"God give you good morrow, master person "
(*i.e.* Sir Nathaniel, a parson).—*Shakespeare: Love's Labour's Lost,* iv. 2.

Parson Adams. A simple-minded country clergyman of the eighteenth century, in Fielding's *Joseph Andrews.*

Fielding says that Parson Adams at the age of fifty was provided with a handsome income of £23 a year (1740). Timothy Burrell, Esq., in 1715, bequeathed to his nephew Timothy the sum of £20 a year, to be paid during his residence at the University, and to be continued to him until he obtained some preferment worth at least £30 a year. (*Sussex Archæological Collections,* vol. iii. p. 172.) (*See* PASSING RICH.)

Parson Bate. A stalwart, choleric, sporting parson, editor of the *Morning Post* in the latter half of the eighteenth century. He was afterwards Sir Henry Bate Dudley, Bart.

" When Sir Henry Bate Dudley was appointed an Irish dean, a young lady of Dublin said, " Oh, how I long to see our dane. They say he is a very handsome man, and that he fights like an angel."
—*Cassell's Magazine: London Legends,* iii.

Parson Trulliber, in Fielding's *Joseph Andrews.* A slothful, ignorant, and self-willed bigot.

∵ Other parsons famous in story are the Rev. Micah Balwidder, the vicar of Bray, Brocklehurst, Dr. Primrose, the parson in Goldsmith's *Deserted Village,* the parson in Chaucer's *Canterbury Tales,* and some others.

Parsons (*Walter*), the giant porter of King James, died in 1622. (*Fuller's Worthies.*)

Part. The character assigned to an actor in a play.

Part. A portion, piece, or fragment.
For my part. As far as concerns me.
For the most part. Generally, as a rule.
In good part. Favourably.
Part and parcel. An essential part, portion, or element.

Partant pour la Syrie. The national air of the French Empire. The words were composed by M. de Laborde in 1809 ; the music by Queen Hortense, mother of Napoleon III. It is a ballad, the subject of which is as follows :—Young Dunois followed the count, his lord, to Syria, and prayed the Virgin "that he might prove the bravest warrior, and love the fairest maiden." After the battle, the count said to Dunois, " To thee we owe the victory, and my daughter I give to thee." Moral : " *Amour à la plus belle ; honneur au plus vaillant.*"

Parthe'nia. Mistress of Ar'galus, in the *Arcadia,* of Sir Philip Sydney.

Parthen'opē (4 syl.). Naples ; so called from Parthenopē, the siren, who threw herself into the sea out of love for Ulysses, and was cast up on the bay of Naples.

Parthenope'an Republic. That of Naples, from January 22, 1799, to the June following.

Parti (*A*). An eligible person for a big marriage.

" Prince Frederick Leopold is a *parti,* as he has inherited the bulk of his father's immense fortune [twenty-four millions sterling]."—*Newspaper Paragraph,* 1885.

Particular Baptists. That branch of the Baptist Dissenters who limit the Sacrament of the Lord's Supper to those who have been recipients of adult baptism. Open Baptists admit any baptised person to receive it.

Particularists. Those who hold the doctrine of particular election and reprobation.

Parting.

" Parting is such sweet sorrow,
That I shall say ' Good Night' till it be morrow."
Shakespeare : Romeo and Juliet, ii. 2.

Parting Cup (*A*), was, by the ancient Romans, drunk in honour of Mercury to insure sound sleep. (*See* Ovid, *Fasti,* ii. 635.) (*See* STIRRUP CUP.)

Partington. A Mrs. Malaprop, or Tabitha Bramble, famous for her misuse of hard words. (*B. P. Shillaber ;* an American author.)

Dame Partington and her mop. A taunt against those who try to withstand progress. The newspapers say that a Mrs. Partington had a cottage at Sidmouth, in Devonshire. In November, 1824, a heavy gale drove the seawaves into her house, and the old lady laboured with a mop to sop the wet up, till she was obliged to take refuge in the upper part of the house. The Rev. Sydney Smith, speaking on the Lords rejection of the Reform Bill, October, 1831, compares them to Dame Partington with her mop, trying to push back the Atlantic. "She was excellent," he says, "at a slop or puddle, but should never have meddled with a tempest."

Part'let. The hen in Chaucer's *Nun's Priest's Tale,* and in the tale of *Reynard the Fox* (fourteenth century). So called from the partlet or loose collar of "the doublet," referring to the frill-like feathers round the neck of certain hens. (A partlet was a ruff worn in the 16th century by women.)

" In the barn the tenant cock
Close to partlet perched on high."
Cuningham.

Sister Partlet with her hooded head, allegorises the cloistered community of nuns in Dryden's *Hind and Panther,* where the Roman Catholic clergy are likened to barnyard fowls.

Partridge. The attendant of Jones, half - barber and half - schoolmaster ; shrewd, but simple as a child. His simplicity, and his strong excitement at the play-house, when he went to see Garrick in *Hamlet,* are admirably portrayed. (*Fielding : Tom Jones.*)

Partridge's Day (*St.*), September 1, the first day of partridge shooting.

Par'tula, according to Tertullian, was the goddess of pregnancy, who determined the time of gestation. (*Aulus Gellius,* iii. c. 16.)

Parturiunt Montes. "*Parturient montes, nascētur ridiculus mus.*" The Egyptian king Tachos sustained a long war against Artaxerxes Ochus, and sent to the Lacedemonians for aid. King Agesilaos went with a contingent, but when the Egyptians saw a little, ill-dressed lame man, they said: "*Parturiebat mons ; formidabat Jupiter ; ille vero murem peperit.*" ("The mountain laboured, Jupiter stood aghast, and a mouse ran out.") Agesilaos replied, "You call me a mouse, but I will soon show you I am a lion."

Party. Person or persons under consideration. "This is the next party, your worship"—*i.e.* the next case to be examined. "This is the party that stole the things"—the person or persons accused. (French, *partie,* a person.)

" If an evil spirit trouble any, one must make a
smoke . . . and the party shall be no more vexed."
—Tobit vi. 7.

Party Spirit. The animus or feeling of a party man.

Par'venu' (French). An upstart ; one who has risen from the ranks.

Parvis (London). The "place" or court before the main entrance of a cathedral. In the parvis of St. Paul's lawyers used to meet for consultation, as brokers do in exchange. The word is now applied to the room above the church porch. (*Paravīsus,* a Low Latin corruption of *paradisus,* a church close.)

" A sergeant of lawe, war and wys,
That often hadde ben atté parvys."
Chaucer : Canterbury Tales (Introduction).

Parviz' [*Victorious*]. Surname of Khosru or Chosroes II., the grandson of Khosru *the Magnificent.* The reigns of Khosru I. and II. were the golden period of Persian history. Parviz' kept 15,000 female musicians, 6,000 household officers, 20,500 saddle-mules, 960 elephants, 200 slaves to scatter perfumes when he went abroad, 1,000 sekabers to water the roads before him, and sat on a pillared throne of almost inconceivable splendour.

The horse of Chosroes Parviz. Shibdiz, the Persian Bucephalos. (*See* HORSE.)

Parys'atis. Wife of Darius Nothos. (A corruption of *Peri 'Zadchēr* [fairy bird - of - Paradise], sometimes called *Azad'chĕr* [bird-of-Paradise].)

Pascal's Thoughts. *Pensées sur la Religion* (1670). Fugitive reflections and short sentences chiefly of a religious character, by Blaise Pascal (1623-1662).

Pasch Eggs (pron. *Pask*). Easter eggs, given as an emblem of the resurrection. They are generally coloured. Not unfrequently a name written with grease, which does not absorb the colouring matter, causes a pasch egg to appear with a name on it.

The day before Easter Sunday is called *Egg Saturday.*

Donner un œuf, pour avoir un bœuf. Giving a sprat to catch a mackerel. To give an egg at Easter under the expectation of receiving a more substantial present later on.

Pasha of Three Tails (*A*). There are three grades of pashas distinguished by the number of horse-tails on their standard. In war the horse-tail standard is carried before the pasha, and planted in front of his tent. The highest rank of pashas are those of three tails; the grand vizier is always *ex officio* such a pasha. Pashas of two tails are governors of provinces; it is one of these officers that we mean when we speak of a pasha in a general way. A pasha of one tail is a sanjak or lowest of provincial governors. (The word pasha is the Persian *pa*, support of *Shah*, the ruler.)

Pasque Eggs. (*See* PASCH EGGS.)

Pasquina'de (3 syl.). A lampoon or political squib, having ridicule for its object; so called from Pasqui'no, an Italian tailor of the fifteenth century, noted for his caustic wit. Some time after his death a mutilated statue was dug up, representing either Ajax supporting Menela'os, or Menela'os carrying the dead body of Patroc'los, or else a gladiator, and was placed at the end of the Braschi Palace near the Piazza Navo'ni. As it was not clear what the statue represented, and as it stood opposite Pasquin's house, the Italians called it "Pasquin." The Romans made this torso the depository of their political, religious, and personal satires, which were therefore called *Pasquin-songs* or Pasquinades. In the Capitol is a rival statue called Marforio, to which are affixed replies to the Pasquinades.

Pass. *A pass* or *A common pass.* An ordinary degree, without honours.

Where a person is allowed to pass up the senate-house to his degree without being "plucked." (*See* PLUCK.)

Well to pass. Well to do. Here "pass" is the synonym of *fare* (Saxon, *faran*, to go or pass). Shakespeare has the expression, "How *goes* it?"—*i.e.* How fares it, how passes it?

Passe Brewell. Sir Tristram's horse. Sir Tristram was one of the round-table knights. (*History of Prince Arthur*, ii. 68.)

Passe-partout. A sort of picture-frame. The middle is cut out to the size of the picture, and the border or edge is embossed, so as to present a raised margin. The *passe-partout* and picture, being backed and faced with a glass, are held together by an edging of paper which shows on the glass face. The word means something to "pass over all."

A master-key is also called a *passe-partout* (a pass through all the rooms).

Passelourdin (3 syl.). A great rock near Poitiers, where there is a very narrow hole on the edge of a precipice, through which the university freshmen are made to pass, to "matriculate" them. The same is done at Mantua, where the freshmen are made to pass under the arch of St. Longi'nus. Passe-lourdan means "lubber-pass."

Pass'elyon. A young foundling brought up by Morgane la Fée. He was detected in an intrigue with Morgane's daughter, and the adventures of this amorous youth are related in the romance called *Perceforest*, vol. iii.

Passing Bell (*The*). It now means the bell tolled to announce the death of one who has died in the parish; but originally it meant the bell which announced that the person was *in extrēmis*, or passing from time into eternity.

"When a person lies in agony, the bells of the parish he belongs to are touched with the clappers until either he dies or recovers again. As soon as this sign is given, everybody in the street, as well as in the houses, falls on his knees, offering prayer for the sick person." (*See* lxvii. of the Canon Law.)—*Diary of the Duke of Stettin's Journey.*

Passing Fair. Admirably fair. (Dutch, *passen*, to admire.)

Passing Rich. Goldsmith tells us in his *Deserted Village*, that the clergyman was "passing rich with £40 a year." This is no covert satire, but a sober fact. Equal to about £350.

"A man he was to all the country dear,
And passing rich with forty pounds a year."
Goldsmith : Deserted Village.

In Norway and Sweden the clergy are paid from £20 to £40 a year, and in France £40 a year is the usual stipend of the working clergy. Of St. Yves it was said (1251-1303) :—

"Il distribuait, avec une sainte profusion aux pauvres, les revenus de son bénéfice et ceux de son patrimoine, qui étaient de £60 de rente, alors une somme très notable, particulièrement en Basse Bretagne."—*Dom Lobineau: Lives of the Saints of Great Britain.*

Passion Flower.

The *leaf* symbolises the spear.
The five *anthers*, the five wounds.
The *tendrils*, the cords or whips.
The column of the *ovary*, the pillar of the cross.
The *stamens*, the hammers.
The three *styles*, the three nails.
The *fleshy threads* within the flowers, the crown of thorns.
The *calyx*, the glory or nimbus.
The *white* tint, purity.
The *blue* tint, heaven.
It keeps open three days ; symbolising the three years' ministry. (Matt. xii. 40.)

(*See* PIKE'S HEAD.)

Passionists. Certain priests of the Roman Catholic Church, who mutually agreed to preach "Jesus Christ, and Him crucified." The founder of this "congregation" was Paul Francis, surnamed *Paul of the Cross.* (1694-1775.)

Pass'over. A Jewish festival to commemorate the deliverance of the Israelites, when the angel of death (that slew the first-born of the Egyptians) *passed over* their houses, and spared all who did as Moses commanded them.

Passy-measure or **Passing-measure.** A slow, stately dance ; a corruption of the Italian *passamezzo* (a middle pace or step). It is called a cinque measure, because it consists of five measures — "two singles and a double forward, with two singles side." (*Collier.*)

Passy-measure Pavin. A pavin is a stately dance (*see* PAVAN) ; a passy-measure pavin is a reeling dance or motion, like that of a drunken man, from side to side. Sir Toby Belch says of Dick Surgeon—

"He's a rogue and a passy-measure pavin. I hate a drunken rogue." — *Shakespeare : Twelfth Night*, v. 1.

Pasteboard. A visiting card ; so called from the material of which it is made.

Paston Letters. The first two volumes appeared in 1787, entitled *Original Letters written during the Reigns of Henry VI., Edward IV., and Richard III. by various Persons of Rank ;* edited by Mr. (afterwards Sir John) Fenn. They are called Paston because chiefly written by or to members of the Paston family in Norfolk. They passed from the Earl of Yarmouth to Peter le Neve, antiquary ; then to Mr. Martin, of Palgrave, Suffolk ; were then bought by Mr. Worth, of Diss ; then passed to the editor. Charles Knight calls them "an invaluable record of the social customs of the fifteenth century" (the time of the Wars of the Roses), but of late some doubt has been raised respecting their authenticity. Three extra volumes were subsequently added.

Pastorale of Pope Gregory, by Alfred the Great.

Patavin'ity. A provincial idiom in speech or writing ; so called from Patavium (*Padua*), the birthplace of Livy. (*See* PATOIS.)

Patch. A fool ; so called from the motley or patched dress worn by licensed fools.

"What a pied ninny's this ! thou scurvy patch !"
Shakespeare : The Tempest, iii. 2.

Cross-patch. An ill-tempered person. (*See above.*)

Not a patch upon. Not to be compared with ; as, "His horse is not a patch upon mine," "My patch is better than his garment."

Patch (*To*). To express certain political views. The allusion is to the custom, in Queen Anne's reign, of wearing on the face little black patches. If the patch was on the right cheek, it indicated that the wearer was a Whig ; if on the left cheek, that she was a Tory ; if on the forehead between the eyes, or on both cheeks, that she was of no political bias. (*See* COURT PLASTER.)

"Whatever might be her husband's politics, she was at liberty to patch as she pleased."— *Nineteenth Century,* February, 1890, p. 58.

Patelin. The artful dodger. The French say, *Savoir son Patelin* (to know how to bamboozle you). Patelin is the name of an artful cheat in a farce of the fifteenth century so called. On one occasion he wanted William Josseaume to sell him cloth on credit, and artfully fell on praising the father of the merchant, winding up his laudation with this *ne plus ultra :* "He did sell on credit, or even lend to those who wished to borrow." This farce was reproduced in 1706 by Brueys, under the name of *L'Avocat Patelin.*

"Consider, sir, I pray you, how the noble Patelin, having a mind to extol to the third heaven the father of William Josseaume, said no more than this : 'And he did lend to those who were desirous to borrow of him.'"—*Rabelais: Pantagruel,* iii. 4.

Patelinage. Foolery, buffoonery; acting like Patelin in the French farce.

"I never in my life laughed so much as at the acting of that Patelinage."—*Rabelais: Pantagruel,* iii. 34.

Patent Rolls. Letters patent collected together on parchment rolls. Each roll is a year, though in some cases the roll is subdivided into two or more parts. Each sheet of parchment is numbered, and called a membrane: for example, the 8th or any other sheet, say of the 10th year of Henry III., is cited thus: "Pat. 10, Hen. III., m. 8." If the document is on the back of the roll it is called dorso, and "d" is added to the citation.

Pat'er Nos'ter. The Lord's Prayer; so called from the first two words in the Latin version. Every tenth bead of a rosary is so called, because at that bead the Lord's Prayer is repeated. Formerly applied to the Rosary beads.

Pater Patrum. St. Gregory of Nyssa was so entitled by the Nicæan Council. (332-395.)

Paternoster Row (London) was so named from the rosary or paternoster makers. We read of "one Robert Nikke, a paternoster maker and citizen, in the reign of Henry IV." Some say it was so called because funeral processions on their way to St. Paul's began their *pater noster* at the beginning of the Row, and went on repeating it till they reached the church-gate.

Pathfinder. Major-General John Charles Fremont, who conducted four expeditions across the Rocky Mountains. (1842.)

Pathfinder, in Fenimore Cooper's five novels, is Natty Bumppo, called the Pathfinder, the Deerslayer, the Hawkeye, and the Trapper. (*See* NATTY BUMPPO.)

Patience cry the Lepers. A punning proverbial phrase. Lepers seek diligently the herb patience (*lapathum*) to relieve them from their suffering.

Patient (*The*). Albert IV., Duke of Austria. (1377-1404.) (*See* HELENA.)

Patient Gris'el, *Grisil'des, Grisild, Grisilde,* or *Grisildis,* according to Chaucer, was the wife of Wautier, Marquis of Sal'uces (*Clerkes Tale*). According to Boccaccio, Griselda, a poor country lass, became the wife of Gualtie're, Marquis of Saluzzo (*Tenth Day,* novel x.). She is put upon by her husband in the most wanton and gratuitous

manner, but bears it all, not only without a murmur, but even without loss of temper. She is the model of patience under injuries. The allegory means that God takes away our children and goods, afflicts us in sundry ways, and tries us "so as with fire;" but we should always say, "The Lord gave, and the Lord hath taken away; blessed be the name of the Lord."

Patin. Brother of the Emperor of Rome, who fought with Am'adis of Gaul, and had his horse killed under him.

Pat'ina. A beautiful surface deposit or fine rust, with which, in time, buried coins and bronzes become covered. It is at once preservative and ornamental, and may be seen to advantage in the ancient bronzes of Pompeii. (Greek, *patanē,* a paten.)

Patmos (*My*). My solitude, my place of banishment from society, my out-of-the-way home. As "Good-b'ye, I must go to my Patmos." The allusion, of course, is to the banishment of St. John to the island of Patmos, in the reign of Domitian.

Patois (2 syl.). Dialectic peculiarity, provincialism. Asinius Pollio noticed something of the kind in Livy, which he called *patavinitas,* from Patavium, Livy's birth-town.

Patri-Passians. One of the most ancient sectaries of the Christian Church, who maintained the oneness of the Godhead. The founder was Praxeas, of Phrygia, in the second century. The appellation was given to them by their opponents, who affirmed that, according to their theory, the Father must have suffered on the cross.

Patrician, properly speaking, is one of the *patres* or fathers of Rome. These patres were the senators, and their descendants were the patricians. As they held for many years all the honours of the state, the word came to signify the magnates or nobility of a nation.

N.B. In Rome the patrician class was twice augmented: first by Tatius, after the Sabine war, who added a whole "century;" and again by Tarquinius Priscus, who added another. The Sabine century went by the name of patricians of the senior races (*majo'rum gentium*), and the Tarquinian patricians were termed of the junior creation (*mino'rum gentium*).

Patrick. Chambers says, "We can trace the footsteps of St. Patrick almost from his cradle to his grave by the names of places called after him." Thus, assuming the Scottish origin, he was born at *Kil-patrick* (the cell of Patrick), in Dumbartonshire; he resided for some time at *Dal-patrick* (the district of Patrick), in Lanarkshire; and visited *Cragphadrig* (the rock of Patrick), near Inverness. He founded two churches, *Kirk-patrick* in Kirkcudbright, and *Kirk-patrick* in Dumfries; and ultimately sailed from *Port-patrick*, leaving behind him such an odour of sanctity that among the most distinguished families of the Scottish aristocracy Patrick has been a favourite name down to the present day.

Arriving in England, he preached at *Patter-dale* (Patrick's valley), in Westmoreland; and founded the church of *Kirk-patrick*, in Durham. Visiting Wales, he walked over *Sarn-badrig* (causeway of Patrick), which now forms a dangerous shoal in Carnarvon Bay; and, departing for the Continent, sailed from *Llan-badrig* (church of Patrick), in the isle of Anglesea. Undertaking his mission to convert the Irish, he first landed at *Innis-patrick* (island of Patrick), and next at *Holm-patrick*, on the opposite shore of the mainland, in the county of Dublin. Sailing northwards, he touched at the Isle of Man, called *Innis-patrick*, where he founded another church of *Kirk-patrick*, near the town of Peel. Again landing on the coast of Ireland, in the county of Down, he converted and baptised the chieftain Dichu on his own threshing-floor, an event perpetuated in the word *Saul—i.e. Sabbal-patrick* (barn of Patrick). He then proceeded to *Temple-patrick*, in Antrim; and from thence to a lofty mountain in Mayo, ever since called *Croagh-patrick*. In East Meath he founded the abbey of *Domnach-Padraig* (house of Patrick), and built a church in Dublin on the spot where *St. Patrick's Cathedral* now stands. In an island of Lough Derg, in Donegal, there is *St. Patrick's Purgatory;* in Leinster, *St. Patrick's Wood;* at Cashel, *St. Patrick's Rock.* There are scores of *St. Patrick's Wells* from which he drank; and he died at *Saul,* March 17th, 493. (*Book of Days.*)

∵ St. Patrick's real name was Succat, changed first into Cothraige, then to Magonus, and afterwards (on his ordination) to Patricius. (*See* Dr. Todd, in the *Proceedings of the Royal Irish Academy*, vol. vi.)

Patrick's Cave (*St.*), through which was a descent to purgatory, for the behoof of the living who wished to expiate their evil deeds before death.

Patrick's Cross (*St.*). The same shape as St. Andrew's Cross (X), only different in colour, viz. red on a white field. (*See* ANDREW.)

Patrick's Grave (*St.*), in the yard of Downpatrick cathedral. The visitor is shown a spot where some of the mould has been removed, and is told that pilgrims take away a few grains as a charm, under the belief that the relic will insure good health, and help to atone for sin.

Patrick's Monument (*St.*), in the cemetery of Downpatrick cathedral. Visitors are shown the spot where the "saint" was buried, but, on asking why there is no memorial, is informed that both Protestants and Catholics agreed to erect a suitable one, but could not agree upon the inscription. Whatever the Protestants erected in the day the Catholics pulled down at night, and *vice versâ*. Tired of this toil of Penelopē, the idea was abandoned, and the grave was left unmarked by monumental stone.

Patrick's Purgatory (*St.*), Ireland, described in the Italian romance called *Guerino Meschino*. Here gourmands are tantalised with delicious banquets which elude their grasp, and are at the same time troubled with colic. (*See* TANTALUS.)

Patrick and the Serpent (*St.*). According to tradition, St. Patrick cleared Ireland of its vermin; one old serpent resisted him; but St. Patrick overcame it by cunning. He made a box, and invited the serpent to enter it. The serpent objected, saying it was too small; but St. Patrick insisted it was quite large enough to be comfortable. After a long contention, the serpent got in to prove it was too small, when St. Patrick slammed down the lid, and threw the box into the sea. To complete this wonderful tale, the legend says the waves of the sea are made by the writhings of this serpent, and the noise of the sea is that of the serpent imploring the saint to release it.

Pat'rico or **Pater-cove.** Hedge priests who for a fee married people under a hedge, as Abraham-men (*q.v.*).

Patroc'los. The gentle and amiable friend of Achilles, in Homer's *Iliad*. When Achilles refused to fight in order to annoy Agamem'non, he sent his friend Patroc'los to battle, and he was slain by Euphorbos.

Patten. Martha or Patty, says Gay, was the daughter of a Lincolnshire farmer, with whom the village blacksmith fell in love. To save her from wet feet when she went to milk the cows, the village Mulciber invented a clog, mounted on iron, which he called *patty*, after his mistress. This pretty fable is of no literary value, as the word is the French *patin* (a high-heeled shoe or skate), from the Greek *pa'ein* (to walk).

' The patten now supports each frugal dame,
    Which from the blue-eyed Patty takes its
    name."   *Gay: Trivia,* i.

Pattens - Money (*Chapins de la Reina*). A subsidy levied in Spain on all crown tenants at the time of a royal marriage.

Patter. To chatter, to clack. Dr. Pusey thinks it is derived from *Paternoster* (the Lord's Prayer). The priest recited it in a low, mumbling voice till he came to the words, " and lead us not into temptation," which he spoke aloud, and the choir responded, " but deliver us from evil." In our reformed Prayer Book, the priest is directed to say the whole prayer " with a *loud* voice." Probably the "pattering of rain"—*i.e.* the rain coming with its pit-pat, is after all the better derivation.

∴ Gipsy talk is so called from the French *patois*. (*See* PATAVINITY.)

Pattern. A corruption of patron. As a patron is a guide, and ought to be an example, so the word has come to signify an artistic model. (French, *patron* Latin, *patrōnus*.)

Pattieson (*Mr. Peter*). Introduced by Sir Walter Scott in the Introductions of the *Heart of Midlothian* and *Bride of Lammermoor*. He is represented as "assistant" at Gandercleugh, and author of the *Tales of My Landlord*, published posthumously by Jedidiah Cleishbotham.

Paul (*St.*). Patron saint of preachers and tentmakers. Originally called Saul. The name was changed in honour of Sergius Paulus, whom he converted.

His symbols are a sword and open book, the former the instrument of his martyrdom, and the latter indicative of the new law propagated by him as the apostle of the Gentiles. He is represented of short stature, with bald head and grey, bushy beard.

Born at Giscalis, a town of Judæa, from which he r·moved, with his parents, to Tarsus, of Cilicia.

Tribe, that of Benjamin.
Taught by Gamaliel.
Beheaded by a sword in the fourteenth year of Nero. On the same day as Peter was crucified.
Buried in the Ostian Way.
(See *Eusebius : Hieronymus.*)

Paul Pry. An idle, meddlesome fellow, who has no occupation of his own, and is always interfering with other folk's business. (*John Poole : Paul Pry, a comedy.*) The original was Thomas Hill.

Paul and Virginia. A tale by Bernardin de St. Pierre. At one time this little romance was as popular as *Uncle Tom's Cabin.*

Paul the Hermit (*St.*) is represented as an old man, clothed with palm-leaves, and seated under a palm-tree, near which are a river and loaf of bread.

Paul of the Cross. Paul Francis, founder of the Passionists. (1694-1775.)

Paul's Man (*A*). A braggart; a captain out of service, with a long rapier ; so called because St. Paul's Walk was at one time the haunt of stale knights. Jonson called Bobadil (*q.v.*) a Paul's man.

Paul's Pigeons. The boys of St. Paul's School, London.

Paul's Walkers. Loungers who frequented the middle of St. Paul's, which was the Bond Street of London up to the time of the Commonwealth. (*See* Ben Jonson's *Every Man out of his Humour*, where are a variety of scenes given in the interior of St. Paul's. Harrison Ainsworth describes these " walkers " in his novel entitled *Old St. Paul's*.)

" The young gallants . . . used to meet at the central point, St. Paul's : and from this circumstance obtained the appellation of *Paul's Walkers*, as we now say *Bond Street Loungers*."—*Moser : European Magazine,* July, 1807.

Paul'ianists. A sect of heretics so called from Paulia'nus Samosa'tanus (Paul of Samosa'ta), elected Bishop of Antioch in 262. He may be considered the father of the Socinians.

Paulicians. A religious sect of the Eastern Empire, an offshoot of the Manichæ'ans. It originated in an Armenian named Paul, who lived under Justinian II. Neander says they were the followers of Constantine of Mananalis, and were called Paulicians because the apostle Paul was their guide. He says they rejected the worship of the Virgin and of saints, denied the doctrine of transubstantiation, and maintained the right of everyone to read the Scriptures freely.

Pauli'na, wife of Antig'onus, a Sicilian nobleman, takes charge of Queen Hermi'one, when unjustly sent to prison by her jealous husband, and after a time presents her again to Leontes as a statue "by that rare Italian master, Julio Romano." (*Shakespeare : Winter's Tale.*)

Paulo. The cardinal, brother of Count Guido Franceschi'ni, who advised his scapegrace bankrupt brother to marry an heiress, in order to repair his fortune. (*Robert Browning : The Ring and the Book.*)

Pa'van or **Pavin.** *Every pavan has its galliard* (Spanish). Every sage has his moments of folly. Every white must have its black, and every sweet its sour. The pavan was a stately Spanish dance, in which the ladies and gentlemen stalked like peacocks (Latin, *pavo'nes*), the gentlemen with their long robes of office, and the ladies with trains like peacocks' tails. The pavan, like the minuet, ended with a quick movement called the *galliard*, a sort of gavot'te.

Pavilion of Prince Ahmed (*The*). This pavilion was so small it could be covered with the hand, and yet would expand so largely as to encamp a whole army. (*Arabian Nights : Ahmed and Pari-Banon.*) (*See* SOLOMON'S CARPET.)

Pawnbroker. *The three golden balls.* The Lombards were the first moneylenders in England, and those who borrowed money of them deposited some security or pawn. The Medici family, whose arms were *three gilded pills,* in allusion to their profession of medicine, were the richest merchants of Florence, and greatest money-lenders. (*See* BALLS.)

❖ Roscoe, in his *Life of Lorenzo de Medici*, gives a different solution. He says that Averardo de' Medici, a commander under Charlemagne, slew the giant Mugello, whose club he bore as a trophy. This club or mace had three iron balls, which the family adopted as their device.

Pawn is the Latin *pign*[us] (a pawn or pledge).

Pawnee. *Brandy pawnee.* Brandy grog. (Hindu, *pa'ni*, water.)

Pax. The "kiss of peace." Also a sacred utensil used when mass is celebrated by a high dignitary. It is sometimes a crucifix, sometimes a tablet, and sometimes a reliquary. The pax is omitted on Maundy Thursday, from horror at the kiss of Judas.

Pay (sea term). To cover with pitch. (Latin, *picare*, to cover with pitch.)
Here's the devil to pay, and no pitch hot. (*See under* DEVIL.)

Pay (*To*). To discharge a debt. (French, *payer.*)
Who's to pay the piper ? Who is to stand Sam ? who is to pay the score? The phrase comes from the tradition about the Pied Piper of Hameln, who agreed to cure the town of rats and mice ; when he had done so, the people of Hameln refused to pay him, whereupon he piped again, and led all the children to Koppelberg Hill, which closed over them.

❖ From the corresponding French phrase, "*payer les violons,*" it would seem to mean who is to pay the fiddler or piper if we have a dance [on the green] ; who is going to stand Sam ?

Pay (*To*). To slacken a cable ; as, "Pay away" [more cable] ; that is, "discharge" more cable. (French, *payer.*)

Pay (*To*). To requite, to punish.
I'll pay him out. I'll be a match for him, I'll punish him.

"They with a foxe-tale him soundly did paye."
          The King and Northerne Man (1640).

Pay off old Scores (*To*). To pay off a debt, whether of money or revenge.

Pay with the Roll of the Drum (*To*). Not to pay at all. No soldier can be arrested for debt when on the march.

"How happy the soldier who lives on his pay,
And spends half-a-crown out of sixpence a day ;
He cares not for justices, beadles, or bum,
But pays all his debts with the roll of the drum."   *O'Keefe.*

Payn'ising. A process of preserving and hardening wood invented by Mr. Payne. (*See* KYANISE.)

Pea-jacket (*A*). Dutch, *pig* or *pije*, a coarse thick cloth or felt. A "pije jacket."

Peace. *The Perpetual Peace.* The peace concluded January 24th, 1502, between England and Scotland. But a few years afterwards the battle of Flodden Field was fought.

Peace-makers (*The*). The nickname of the Bedfordshire regiment. So called from having no battles on the colours.

Peace of Antal'cidas (*The*), between Artaxerxes and the states of Greece. It was brought about by Antal'cidas, the Spartan (B.C. 387).

Peace of God. In 1035 the clergy interfered to prevent the constant feuds between baron and baron; they commanded all men to lay down their arms on pain of excommunication. The command and malediction were read daily from the pulpits by the officiating priests after the proper gospel:—"May they who refuse to obey be accursed, and have their portion with Cain, the first murderer; with Judas, the arch-traitor; and with Dathan and Abi'ram, who went down alive into the pit. May they be accursed in the life that now is; and in that which is to come may their light be put out as a candle." So saying, all the candles were instantly extinguished, and the congregation had to make its way in the dark out of church as it best could.

Peace with Honour. The rallying cry of the late Lord Beaconsfield; it originated with his speech after the Berlin Conference (1878), when he stated that he had brought back Peace with Honour.

Peaceful (*The*). Kang-wâng, third of the Thow dynasty of China, in whose reign no one was either put to death or imprisoned. (1098-1152.)

Peach. To inform, to "split;" a contraction of *impeach*.

Peacock. *Let him keep peacock to himself.* Let him keep to himself his eccentricities. When George III. had partly recovered from one of his attacks, his Ministers got him to read the King's Speech, but he ended every sentence with the word "peacock." The Minister who drilled him said that peacock was an excellent word for ending a sentence, only kings should not let subjects hear it, but should whisper it softly. The result was a perfect success: the pause at the close of each sentence had an excellent effect.

By the peacock! A common oath which at one time was thought sacred. The fabled incorruptibility of the peacock's flesh caused the bird to be adopted as a type of the resurrection.

Peacock's Feather Unlucky (*A*). The peacock's tail is emblem of an Evil Eye, or an ever-vigilant traitor. The tale is this: Argus was the chief Minister of Osiris, King of Egypt. When the king started on his Indian expedition, he left his queen, Isis, regent, and Argus was to be her chief adviser. Argus, with one hundred spies (called eyes), soon made himself so powerful and formidable that he shut up the queen-regent in a strong castle, and proclaimed himself king. Mercury marched against him, took him prisoner, and cut off his head; whereupon Juno metamorphosed Argus into a peacock, and set his eyes in its tale.

Peak (*The*), Derbyshire. "The Queen of Scots' Pillar" is a column in the cave of the peak as clear as alabaster, and so called because Mary Queen of Scots proceeded thus far, and then returned.

Peal. *To ring a peal* is to ring 5,040 changes; any number of changes less than that is technically called a *touch* or *flourish*. Bells are first *raised*, and then *pealed*. (Qy. Latin *pello*, to strike?)

"This society rung . . . . a true and complete peal of 5,040 grandsire triples in three hours and fourteen minutes."—*Inscription in Windsor Curfew Tower.*

Pearl (*The*). Diosco'idēs and Pliny mention the belief that pearls are formed by drops of rain falling into the oyster-shells while open; the rain-drops thus received being hardened into pearls by some secretions of the animal.

According to Richardson, the Persians say when drops of spring-rain fall into the pearl-oyster they produce pearls.

"Precious the tear as that rain from the sky
Which turns into pearls as it falls on the sea."
                    Thomas Moore.

"Pearls . . . are believed to be the result of an abnormal secretory process caused by an irritation of the mollusk consequent on the intrusion into the shell of some foreign body, as a grain of sand, an egg of the mollusk itself, or perhaps some cercarian parasite."—*G. F. King: Gems, etc.,* chap. xii. p. 211.

✲ Cardan says that pearls are polished by being pecked and played with by doves. (*De Rerum Varietate,* vii. 34.)

Pearl. For Cleopatra melting her pearl in honour of Antony, *see* CLEOPATRA.

A similar act of vanity and folly is told by Horace (2 *Satire,* iii. verse 239). Clodius, son of Æsop the tragedian, drew a pearl from his ear of great value, melted it in a strong acid, and drank to the health of Cecilia Metella. This story is referred to by Valerius Maximus, Macrobius, and Pliny. Horace says,

"Qui sanior, ac si
Illud idem in rapidum flumen jaceretve cloacam?'

Sir Thomas Gresham, it is said, when Queen Elizabeth dined with him at the

City banquet, melted a pearl worth £15,000, and drank to her health.

"Here fifteen thousand pounds alone clap goes
Instead of sugar, Gresham drinks the pearl
Unto his queen and mistress."
Thomas Heywood.

Pearl of the East. Zenobia, Queen of Palmyra (reigned 266-272).

Peasant Bard. Robert Burns, the lyric poet of Scotland. (1759-1796.)

Peasant-boy Philosopher (*The*). James Ferguson. (1710-1776.)

Peasants' War (*The*), between 1500 and 1525. It was a frequent rising of the peasantry of Swabia, Franconia, Saxony, and other German states, in consequence of the tyranny and oppression of the nobles. In 1502 was the rebellion called the *Laced Shoe*, from its cognisance; in 1514, the *League of Poor Conrad;* in 1523, the *Latin War*. The insurgents were put down, and whereas they had been whipped before with scourges, they were now chastised with scorpions.

Peascod. Father of Peasblossom, if Bottom's pedigree may be accepted.

"I pray you commend me to Mistress Squash your mother, and to Master Peascod your father, good Master Peasblossom."—*Shakespeare: Midsummer Night's Dream,* iii. 1.

Winter for shoeing, peascod for wooing. The allusion in the latter clause is to the custom of placing a peascod with nine peas in it on the door-lintel, under the notion that the first man who entered through the door would be the husband of the person who did so. Another custom is alluded to by Browne—

"The peascod greene oft with no little toyle
Hee'd seeke for in the fattest, fertil'st soile,
And rend it from the stalke to bring it to her,
And in her bosome for acceptance woo her."
Britannia's Pastorals.

Pec. Eton slang for money. A contraction of the Latin *pecu'nia*.

Pecca'vi. *To cry pecca'vi.* To acknowledge oneself in the wrong. It is said that Sir Charles Napier, after the battle of Hyderabad, in 1843, used this word as a pun upon his victory — "*Peccāvi*" (I have sinned, *i.e.* Sinde).

Peck (*A*). Some food. "To have a peck," is to have something to eat. *Peckish.* Hungry, or desirous of something to eat. Of course "peck" refers to fowls, etc., which peck their food.

"When shall I feel peckish again."—*Disraeli: Sybil,* book vi. chap. iii.

Pecker. *Keep your pecker up.* As the mouth is in the head, *pecker* (the mouth) means the head; and to "keep your pecker up," means to keep your head up, or, more familiarly, "keep your tail up;" "never say die."

Peckham. *All holiday at Peckham.* —*i.e.* no appetite, not peckish; a pun on the word peck, as going to Bedfordshire is a pun on the word bed.
Going to Peckham. Going to dinner.

Peck'sniff. A canting hypocrite, who speaks homilies of morality, does the most heartless things "as a duty to society," and forgives wrong-doing in nobody but himself. (*Dickens: Martin Chuzzlewit.*)

Peculiar. A parish or church exempt from episcopal jurisdiction, as a royal chapel, etc.

Peculiars (*The Court of*). A branch of the Court of Arches having jurisdiction over the "peculiars" of the archbishop of Canterbury. (*See above.*)

Pecu'lium. *My own peculium.* Private and individual property or possession. The Roman slaves were allowed to acquire property, over which their masters had no right or control; this was called their pecu'lium.

Pecuniary. From *pecus*, cattle, especially sheep. Varo says that sheep were the ancient medium of barter and standard of value. Ancient coin was marked with the image of an ox or sheep. We have the Gold Sheep (*mouton d'or*) and Gold Lamb (*agneau d'or*) of ancient France, so called from the figure struck on them, and worth about a shilling. (Latin, *pecuniarius, pecunia*.)

Ped'agogue (3 syl.) means a boy-leader. It was a slave whose duty it was to attend the boy whenever he left home. A schoolmaster "leads" his boys, morally and otherwise. (Greek, *pais agō'geus*.)

Pedlar is not a tramp who goes on his feet, as if from the Latin *pedes* (feet), but a man who carries a *ped* or hamper without a lid, in which are stored fish or other articles to hawk about the streets. In Norwich there is a place called the Ped-market, where women expose eggs, butter, cheese, etc., in open hampers.

Pedlar's Acre (Lambeth). According to tradition, a pedlar of this parish left a sum of money, on condition that his picture, with a dog, should be preserved for ever in glass in one of the church-windows. In the south window of the middle aisle, sure enough, such a picture exists; but probably it is a rebus on *Chapman*, the name of some benefactor. In Swaffham church there is a portrait of one John Chapman, a great benefactor, who is represented as a pedlar with his pack; and in that town a similar tradition exists.

Pedlars' French. The slang of the Romany folk. Even Bracton uses the word Frenchman as a synonym of foreigner, and it is not long since that everyone who could not speak English was called a Frenchman. The Jews, with a similar width, used the word Greek.

" Instead of Pedlars' French, gives him plain language." — *Beaumont and Fletcher: Faithful Friends*, i. 2.

Peebles. *Poor Peter Peebles.* The pauper litigant in *Redgauntlet*, by Sir Walter Scott.

Peel. *A Peel district.* - A clerical district (not a parish) devised by Sir Robert Peel.

Peeler (*A*). Slang for a policeman; so called from Sir Robert Peel, who reconstructed the police system. *Bobby*, being the nickname of Robert, is applied to the same force. (*See* BOBBY.)

Peeler. It is an extraordinary circumstance that this word, now applied to a policeman or thief-catcher, was in the sixteenth century applied to robbers. Holinshed, in his *Scottish Chronicle* (1570), refers to Patrick Dunbar, who " delivered the countrie of these peelers." Thomas Mortimer, in his *British Plutarch ;* Milton, in his *Paradise Regained* (book iv.); and Dryden, all use the word " peeler " as a plunderer or robber. The old Border towers were called " peels." The two words are, of course, quite distinct.

Peep. To look at. As a specimen of the ingenuity of certain etymologists in tracing our language to Latin and Greek sources, may be mentioned Mr. Casaubon's derivation of *peep* from the Greek *opipteuo* (to stare at). (*Pe-pe-pe bo !*)

Playing bo-peep or *peep-bo*. Hiding or skulking from creditors ; in allusion to the infant nursery game.

Peep-o'-Day Boys. The Irish insurgents of 1784 ; so called because they used to visit the houses of their opponents (called *defenders*) at peep of day searching for arms or plunder.

Peeping Tom of Coventry. Leofric, Earl of Mercia and Lord of Coventry, imposed some very severe imposts on the people of Coventry, which his countess, Godi'va, tried to get mitigated. The earl, thinking to silence her importunity, said he would comply when she had ridden naked from one end of the town to the other. Godi'va took him at his word, actually rode through the town naked, and Leofric remitted the imposts. Before Godi'va started, all the inhabitants voluntarily confined themselves to their houses, and resolved that anyone who stirred abroad should be put to death. A tailor thought to have a peep, but was rewarded with the loss of his eyes, and has ever since been called Peeping Tom of Coventry. There is still a figure in a house at Coventry said to represent Peeping Tom.

⁂ Matthew of Westminster (1307) is the first to record the story of Lady Godi'va : the addition of Peeping Tom dates from the reign of Charles II. In Smithfield Wall is a grotesque figure of the inquisitive tailor in " flowing wig and Stuart cravat."

In regard to the terms made by Leofric, it may be mentioned that Rudder, in his *History of Gloucester*, tells us that " the privilege of cutting wood in the Herduoles was granted to the parishioners of St. Briavel's Castle, in Gloucestershire, on precisely similar terms by the Earl of Hereford, who was at the time lord of Dean Forest.

Tennyson, in his *Godiva*, has reproduced the story.

Peerage of the Apostles. In the preamble of the statutes instituting the Order of St. Michael, founded in 1469 by Louis XI., the archangel is styled " my lord," and is created a knight. The apostles had been already ennobled and knighted. We read of " the Earl Peter," " Count Paul," " the Baron Stephen," and so on. Thus, in the introduction of a sermon upon St. Stephen's Day, we have these lines :—

" Contes vous vueille la patron
De St. Estieul le baron."

" The Apostles were gentlemen of bloude . . . and Christ . . . might, if He had esteemed of the vayne glorye of this world, have borne coat armour."—*The Blazon of Gentrie*.

I myself was intimate with a rector who always laid especial stress on the word Lord, applied to Jesus Christ.

Peers of the Realm. The five orders of duke, marquis, earl, viscount, and baron. The word peer is the Latin *parēs* (equals), and in feudal times all great vassals were held equal in rank,

The following is well fitted to a dictionary of Phrase and Fable :—

"It is well known that, although the English aristocracy recruits itself from the sons of *barbers*, as Lord Tenterden ; merchant *tailors*, as Count Craven ; *mercers*, as the Counts of Coventry, etc., it will never tolerate poverty within its ranks. The male representative of Simon de Montfort is now a saddler in Tooley Street ; the great-grandson of Oliver Cromwell, a porter in Cork market ; and Stephen James Penny, Verger of St. George's, Hanover Square, is a direct descendant of the fifth son of Edward III."—*The Gaulois.*

Peg or **Peggy**, for Margaret, corrupted into Meg or Meggy. Thus, *Pat* or *Patty* for Martha ; *Poll* or *Polly*, for Mary, corrupted into Moll or Molly ; etc.

Peg too Low (*A*). Low-spirited, moody. Our Saxon ancestors were accustomed to use peg-tankards, or tankards with a peg inserted at equal intervals, that when two or more drank from the same bowl, no one might exceed his fair proportion. We are told that St. Dunstan introduced the fashion to prevent brawling.

I am a peg too low means, I want another draught to cheer me up.

"Come, old fellow, drink down to your peg !
But do not drink any farther, I beg."
    Longfellow : Golden Legend, iv.

To take one down a peg. To take the conceit out of a braggart or pretentious person. The allusion here is not to peg-tankards, but to a ship's colours, which used to be raised and lowered by pegs ; the higher the colours are raised the greater the honour, and to take them down a peg would be to award less honour.

"Trepanned your party with intrigue,
And took your grandees down a peg."
    Butler : Hudibras, ii. 2.

There are always more round pegs than round holes. Always more candidates for office than places to dispose of.

Peg'asos (Greek ; *Pegasus*, Latin). The inspiration of poetry, or, according to Boiardo (*Orlando Inamorato*), the horse of the Muses. A poet speaks of his Peg'asus, as "My Pegasus will not go this morning," meaning his brain will not work. "I am mounting Pegasus" —*i.e.* going to write poetry. "I am on my Pegasus," *i.e.* engaged in writing verses.

Peg'asus or Peg'asos, according to classic mythology, was the winged horse on which Beller'ophon rode against the Chimæra. When the Muses contended with the daughters of Pi'eros, Hel'icon rose heavenward with delight ; but Peg'asos gave it a kick, stopped its ascent, and brought out of the mountain the soul-inspiring waters of Hippocrene [*Hip'-po-creen*],

Pegg (*Katharine*). One of the mistresses of Charles II., daughter of Thomas Pegg, of Yeldersey, in Derbyshire, Esquire.

Pegging Away (*Keep*). Keep on attacking, and you will assuredly prevail. "But screw your courage to the sticking-place, and we'll not fail" (*Macbeth*). Patience and perseverance will overcome mountains. It was President Lincoln who gave this advice to the Federals in the American civil war.

Peine Forte et Dure. A species of torture applied to contumacious felons. In the reign of Henri IV. the accused was pressed to death by weights ; in later reigns the practice prevailed of tying the thumbs tightly together with whipcord, to induce the accused to plead. The following persons were pressed to death by weights :—Juliana Quick, in 1442 ; Anthony Arrowsmith, in 1598 ; Walter Calverly, in 1605 ; Major Strangways, in 1657 ; and even in 1741 a person was pressed to death at the Cambridge assizes. Abolished 1772.

Pela'gianism. The system or doctrines taught by Pela'gius (*q.v.*). He denied what is termed birth-sin or the taint of Adam, and he maintained that we have power of ourselves to receive or reject the Gospel.

Pela'gius. A Latinised Greek form of the name Morgan—the Welsh *môr*, like the Greek *pel'agos*, meaning the sea.

Pelf. *Filthy pelf.* Money. The word was anciently used for refuse or rubbish. "Who steals my purse steals *trash*." Filthy means ungodly ; the Scripture expression is "unrighteous mammon." It is certainly not connected with *pilfer*, as it is usually given ; but it may possibly be with the Anglo-Saxon *pila*, a pile or heap.

⁂ The old French word *pelfre* means spoil.

Pel'ias. The huge spear of Achilles, which none but the hero could wield ; so called because it was cut from an ash growing on Mount Pel'ion, in Thessaly.

Pel'ican, in Christian art, is a symbol of charity. It is also an emblem of Jesus Christ, by "whose blood we are healed" (Eucherius and Jerome). (*See below.*)

Pelican. A mystic emblem of Christ, called by Dante *nostro Pelicano*, St.

Hieronymus gives the story of the pelican restoring its young ones destroyed by serpents, and his salvation by the blood of Christ. The *Bestia'rium* says that Physiol'ogus tells us that the pelican is very fond of its brood, but when the young ones begin to grow they rebel against the male bird and provoke his anger, so that he kills them; the mother returns to the nest in three days, sits on the dead birds, pours her blood over them, revives them, and they feed on the blood. (*Bibl. Nat. Belg.*, No. 10,074.)

> "Than sayd the Pellycane,
>   When my byrdts be slayne
> With my bloude I them reuyue [revive].
>   Scrypture doth record,
> The same dyd our Lord,
> And rose from deth to lyue."
>   *Skelton: Armoury of Birdts.*

Pelicans. The notion that pelicans feed their young with their blood arose from the following habit:—They have a large bag attached to their under bill. When the parent bird is about to feed its brood, it macerates small fish in this bag or pouch, then pressing the bag against its breast, transfers the macerated food to the mouths of the young.

A pelican in her piety is the representation of a pelican feeding her young with her blood. The Romans called filial love piety, hence Virgil's hero is called *pius* Æne'as, because he rescued his father from the flames of Troy.

Peli'des. Son of Peleus (2 syl.)—that is, Achilles, the hero of Homer's *Iliad*, and chief of the Greek warriors that besieged Troy.

> "When, like Peli'des, bold beyond control,
> Homer raised high to heaven the loud impetuous
>   song."   *Beattie: Minstrel.*

Pel'ion. *Heaping Ossa upon Pelion.* Adding difficulty to difficulty, embarrassment to embarrassment, etc. When the giants tried to scale heaven, they placed Mount Ossa upon Mount Pelion for a scaling ladder.

> "Ter sunt conāti impōnĕre Pēlio Ossam."
>   *Virgil: Georgics,* i. 281.

⁂ A noteworthy hexameter verse. The *i* of "conati" does not elide, nor yet the *o* of "Pelio."

Pell-mell. Headlong; in reckless confusion. From the players of pall-mall, who rush heedlessly to strike the ball. The "pall" is the ball (Italian, *palla*), and the "mall" is the mallet or bat (Italian, *maglia*; Latin, *malleus*). Sometimes the game is called "pall mall;" and sometimes the ground set apart for the game, as Pall Mall, London.

⁂ It is not quite certain that *pell-mell* is the same compound word as pall-mall.

Pelle'an Conqueror. Alexander the Great, born at Pella, in Macedo'nia.

> "Remember that Pellean conqueror."
>   *Milton: Paradise Regained,* ii.

Pel'leas (*Sir*). One of the knights of the Round Table. In the *Faërie Queene* he goes after the "blatant beast" when it breaks the chain with which it had been bound by Sir Calidore.

Pells. *Clerk of the Pells.* An officer of the Exchequer, whose duty it was to make entries on the *pells* or parchment rolls. Abolished in 1834.

Pel'ops. Son of Tan'talos, cut to pieces and served as food to the gods. The More'a was called Peloponne'sos or the "island of Pelops," from this mythical king.

The ivory shoulder of the sons of Pelops. The distinguishing or distinctive mark of anyone. The tale is that Deme'ter ate the shoulder of Pelops when it was served up by Tan'talos, and when the gods put the body back into the cauldron to restore it to life, he came forth lacking a shoulder. Demeter supplied an ivory shoulder, and all his descendants carried this mark in their bodies. (*See* Pythagoras.)

Pelo'rus. Cape di Faro, a promontory of Sicily. (*Virgil: Æneid,* iii. 6, 7.)

> "As when the force
> Of subterranean wind transports a hill
> Torn from Pelorus."
>   *Milton: Paradise Lost,* bk. i. 232.

Pelos [*mud*]. Father of Physigna'thos, king of the frogs. (*Battle of the Frogs and Mice.*)

Pelt, in printing. Untanned sheepskins used for printing-balls. (French, *pelte;* Latin, *pellis,* a skin.)

Pen Name, sometimes written *nom-de-plume.* A fictitious name assumed by an author who does not wish to reveal his real name. (*See* Nom de Guerre.)

Pen and Feather are varieties of the same word, the root being the Sanskrit *pat,* to fly. (We have the Sanskrit *pattra,* a wing or instrument for flying; Latin, *petna* or *penna,* pen; Greek, *pteron;* Teutonic, *phathra;* Anglo-Saxon, *fether;* our "feather.")

⁂ Analogous examples are Tear and Larme, Nag and Equus, Wig and Peruke, Heart and Cœur, etc.

Penang Lawyers. Clubs. Penang sticks come from Penang, or the Prince of Wales Island, in the Malaccas.

Pena'tes (3 syl.). The household gods of the Romans.

Pencil of Rays. All the rays that issue from one point, or that can be focussed at one point (Latin, *penicillus*, little tail, whence *penicillum*, a painter's brush made of the hair of a cow's tail) ; so called because they are like the hairs of a paint-brush, except at the point where they aggregate.

Pendennis (*Arthur*). The hero of Thackeray's novel, entitled *The History of Pendennis*, etc.
Major Pendennis. A tuft - hunter, similar in character to Macklin's celebrated Sir Pertinax M'Sycophant.

Penden'te Li'te (Latin). Pending the suit; while the suit is going on.

Pendrag'on. A title conferred on several British chiefs in times of great danger, when they were invested with dictatorial power : thus Uter and Arthur were each appointed to the office to repel the Saxon invaders. Cassibelaun was pendragon when Julius Cæsar invaded the island ; and so on. The word *pen* is British for head, and *dragon* for leader, ruler, or chief. The word therefore means *summus rex* (chief of the kings).
So much for fact, and now for the fable : Geoffrey of Monmouth says, when Aure'lius, the British king, was poisoned by Ambron, during the invasion of Pascentius, son of Vortigern, there "appeared a star at Winchester of wonderful magnitude and brightness, darting forth a ray, at the end of which was a globe of fire in form of a dragon, out of whose mouth issued forth two rays, one of which extended to Gaul and the other to Ireland." Uter ordered two golden dragons to be made, one of which he presented to Winchester, and the other he carried with him as his royal standard, whence he received the name of Uter Pendragon. (Books viii. xiv. xvii.)

Penel'ope (4 syl.). *The Web* or *Shroud of Penelope.* A work "never ending, still beginning ; " never done, but ever in hand. Penelopë, according to Homer, was pestered by suitors while her husband, Ulysses, was absent at the siege of Troy. To relieve herself of their importunities, she promised to make a choice of one as soon as she had finished weaving a shroud for her father-in-law. Every night she unravelled what she had done in the day, and so deferred making any choice till Ulysses returned, when the suitors were sent to the right-about without ceremony.

Penel'ophon. The beggar loved by King Cophetua. (*See* COPHETUA.)

Penel'va. A knight whose adventures and exploits form a supplemental part of the Spanish romance entitled *Am'adis of Gaul.* The first four books of the romance, and the part above referred to, were by Portuguese authors— the former by Vasco de Lobeira, of Oporto, who died 1403 ; the latter by an unknown author.

Penetra'lia. The private rooms of a house ; the secrets of a family. That part of a Roman temple into which the priest alone had access ; here were the sacred images, here the responses of the oracles were made, and here the sacred mysteries were performed. The Holy of Holies was the penetralia of the Jewish Temple. (Latin plural of *penetrālis.*)

Penfeather (*Lady Penelope*). The lady patroness of the Spa. (*Sir Walter Scott : St. Ronan's Well.*)

Peninsular War. The war carried on, under the Duke of Wellington, against the French in Portugal and Spain, between 1808 and 1812.

Penitential Psalms. The seven psalms expressive of contrition—viz. the vi., xxxii., xxxviii., li., cii., cxxx., cxliii., of the Authorised Version, or vi., xxxi., xxxvii., l., ci., cxxix., cxliii., of the Vulgate.

Penmanship.
The "Good King Réné," titular king of Naples in the middle of the fifteenth century, was noted for his initial letters.
St. Thecla, of Isauria, wrote the entire Scriptures out without a blot or mistake.
St. Theodosius wrote the Gospels in letters of gold without a single mistake or blur. (*See* Longfellow's *Golden Legend,* iv.) (*See* ANGEL.)

Penmanship. Dickens says of John Bell, of the Chancery, that he wrote three hands : one which only *he himself* could read, one which only his clerk could read, and one which nobody could read. Dean Stanley wrote about as bad a hand as man could write.

Pennals [*pen-cases*]. So the Freshmen of the Protestant universities of Germany were called, from the *pennale* or inkhorn which they carried with them when they attended lectures.

Pen'nalism. Fagging, bullying, petty persecution. The pennals or freshmen of the Protestant universities were the fags of the elder students, called *schorists.* Abolished at the close of the seventeenth century. (*See above.*)

Pennant. The common legend is, that when Tromp, the Dutch admiral, appeared on our coast, he hoisted a broom on his ship, to signify his intention of sweeping the ships of England from the sea; and that the English admiral hoisted a horsewhip to indicate his intention of drubbing the Dutch. According to this legend, the pennant symbolises a horsewhip, and it is not unfrequently called "the whip."

Penniless (*The*). The Italians called Maximilian I. of Germany *Pochi Danari.* (1459, 1493-1519.)

Penny (in the sense of pound). Sixpenny, eightpenny, and tenpenny nails are nails of three sizes. A thousand of the first will weigh six pounds; of the second, eight pounds; of the third, ten pounds.

Penny sometimes expresses the duodecimal part, as tenpenny and elevenpenny silver—meaning silver 10-12ths and 11-12ths fine.

"One was to be tenpenny, another eleven, another sterling silver."—*Weidenfeld: Secrets of the Adepts.*

Penny (*A*) (Anglo-Saxon, *pening* or *penig*). For many hundred years the unit of money currency, hence *pening-monegre* (a money-changer). There were two coins so named, one called the greater = the fifth part of a shilling, and the other called the less = the 12th part of a shilling.

My penny of observation (*Love's Labour's Lost,* iii. 1). My pennyworth of wit; my natural observation or mother-wit. Probably there is some pun or confusion between *penetration* and "penny of observation" or "penn'orth of wit."

A penny for your thoughts. See Heywood's *Dialogue,* pt. ii. 4. (*See* PENNYWORTH.)

Penny-a-liner (*A*). A contributor to the local newspapers, but not on the staff. At one time these collectors of news used to be paid a penny a line, and it was to their interest to spin out their report as much as possible. The word remains, but is now a misnomer.

Penny Dreadfuls. Penny sensational papers, which delight in horrors.

Penny-father (*A*). A miser, a penurious person, who "husbands" his pence.

"Good old penny-father was glad of his liquor."
*Pasquil: Jests (*1629).

Penny Gaff (*A*). A theatre the admission to which is one penny. Properly a gaff is a ring for cockfighting, a sensational amusement which has been made to yield to sensational dramas of the Richardson type. (Irish, *gaf,* a hook.)

Penny Hop (*A*). A rustic dancing club, in which each person pays a penny to the fiddler. In towns, private dancing parties were at one time not uncommon, the admission money at the doors being one penny.

Penny Lattice-house (*A*). A low pothouse. Lattice shutters are a public-house sign, being the arms of Fitz-warren, which family, in the days of the Henrys, had the monopoly of licensing vintners and publicans.

Penny Pots. Pimples and spots on the tippler's face, from the too great indulgence in penny pots of beer.

Penny Readings. Parochial entertainments, consisting of readings, music, etc., for which one penny admission is charged.

Penny Saved (*A*). *A penny saved is twopence gained.* In French, "*Un centime épargné en vaut deux.*"

Well, suppose a man asks twopence apiece for his oranges, and a haggler obtains hundred at a penny apiece, would he save 200 pence by his bargain? If so, let him go on spending, and he will soon become a millionaire. Or suppose, instead of paying £1,000 for a bad bet, I had not wagered any money at all, would this have been worth £2,000 to me?

Penny Weddings. Wedding banquets in Scotland, to which a number of persons were invited, each of whom paid a small sum of money not exceeding a shilling. After defraying the expenses of the feast, the residue went to the newly-married pair, to aid in furnishing their house. Abolished in 1645.

"Vera true, vera true. We'll have a' to pay . . . a sort of penny-wedding it will prove, where all men contribute to the young folks' maintenance."—*Sir Walter Scott: Fortunes of Nigel,* chap. xxvii.

Penny Wise. Unwise thrift. The whole proverb is *Penny wise and pound foolish,* like the man who lost his horse from his penny wisdom in saving the expense of shoeing it afresh when one of its shoes was loose.

Pennyroyal. Flea-bane, the odour being, as it is supposed, hateful to fleas.

This is a real curiosity of blundering derivation. The Latin word is *pulēcium*, the flea destroyer, from *pulex*, a flea, softened into pulēgium, and corrupted into the English - Latin *pule'-regium*. "Pule," changed first into *puny*, then into *penny*, gives us "penny-regium," whence "penny-royal." The French call the herb *pouliot*, from *pou* (a louse or flea).

Pennyweight. So called from being the weight of an Anglo-Norman penny. Dwt. is d = penny wt.

Pennyworth or **Pen'oth.** A small quantity, as much as can be bought for a penny. Butler says, " This was the pen'oth of his thought" (*Hudibras*, ii. 3), meaning that its scope or amount was extremely small.

He has got his pennyworth. He has got due value for his money.

To turn an honest penny. To earn a little money by working for it.

Pen'sion is something *weighed out.* Originally money was weighed, hence our *pound.* When the Gauls were bribed to leave Rome the ransom money was weighed in scales, and then Brennus threw his sword into the weight-pan. (Latin, *pendo*, to weigh money.)

Pen'sioners at the Universities and Inns of Court. So called from the French *pension* (board), *pensionnaire* (a boarder, one who pays a sum of money to dine and lodge with someone else).

Pen'tacle. A five-sided head-dress of fine linen, meant to represent the five senses, and worn as a defence against demons in the act of conjuration. It is also called Solomon's Seal (*signum Salamo'nis*). A pentacle was extended by the magician towards the spirits when they proved contumacious.

" And on her head, lest spirits should invade,
A pentacle, for more assurance, laid."
        Rose: Orlando Furioso, iii. 21.

The Holy Pentacles numbered forty-four, of which seven were consecrated to each of the planets Saturn, Jupiter, Mars, and the Sun ; five to both Venus and Mercury : and six to the Moon. The divers figures were enclosed in a double circle, containing the name of God in Hebrew, and other mystical words.

Pentap'olin. An imaginary chieftain, but in reality the drover of a flock of sheep. Don Quixote conceived him to be the Christian King of the Garamantians, surnamed the *Naked Arm*, because he always entered the field with his right arm bare. The driver of a flock from the opposite direction was dubbed by the Don the Emperor Alifanfaron of the isle of Taproba'na, a pagan. (*Cervantes : Don Quixote*, pt. i. bk. iii. 4.)

Pentap'olis. (Greek, *pente polis*.)
(1) The five cities of the plain : Sodom, Gomorrah, Admah, Zebo'im, and Zoar ; four of which were consumed with fire, and their site covered with the Lake Asphalti tēs, or the Dead Sea.
(2) The five cities of Cyrena'ica, in Egypt : Bereni'cē, Arsin'oe, Ptolema'is, Cyre'nĕ, and Apollo'nia.
(3) The five cities of the Philistines : Gaza, Gath, As'calon, Ash'dod, and Ekron.
(4) The five cities of Italy in the exarchate of Ravenna : Rim'ini, Pesaro, Fano, Sinigaglia, and Anco'na. These were given by Pepin to the Pope.
(5) The Dorian pentapolis : Cni'dos, Cos, Lindos, Ial'ysos, and Cami'ros.

Pentateuch. The first five books of the Old Testament, supposed to be written by Moses. (Greek, *pente*, five ; *teuchos*, a book.)

The Chinese Pentateuch. The five books of Confucius : - (1) The *Shoo-King*, or *Book of History ;* (2) The *Lee-King*, or *Book of Rites ;* (3) The *Book of Odes*, or *Chinese Homer ;* (4) The *Yih-King*, or *Book of Changes ;* and (5) The *Chun-Ts'eu*, or *Spring and Autumn Annals.*

The Samaritan Pentateuch. A version of the Pentateuch in the Samaritan character. It varies in some measure from the Jewish version. Not earlier than the fourth, nor later than the seventh, century. (See *Apocrypha : 2 Esdras* xiv. 21-48.)

Pen'tecost (Greek, *pentecostê*, fiftieth). The festival held by the Jews on the fiftieth day after the Passover ; our Whit-Sunday.

Penthesile'a. Queen of the Amazons, slain by Achilles. Sir Toby Belch says to Maria, in the service of Olivia —

"Good-night, Penthesilea [my fine woman]."—
Shakespeare : Twelfth Night, ii. 2.

Pent'house (2 syl.). A hat with a broad brim. The allusion is to the hood of a door, or coping of a roof. (Welsh, *penty ;* Spanish, *pentice ;* French, *appentice,* also *pente,* a slope.)

Pentreath (*Dolly*). The last person who spoke Cornish. Daines Barrington went from London to the Land's End to visit her. She lived at Mousehole.

" Hail, Mousehole ! birthplace of old Doll Pentreath,
The last who jabbered Cornish, so says Daines . . . "
        Peter Pindar (Ode xxi., To Myself).

Peony (*The*). So called, according to fable, from Pæon, the physician who cured the wounds received by the gods in the Trojan war. The seeds were, at one time, worn round the neck as a charm against the powers of darkness. Virgil and Ovid speak of its sanative virtues. Others tell us Pæon was a chieftain who discovered the plant.

"Vetustissima inventu pæonia est, nomenque auctoris retinet, quam quidam pentorobon appellant, alii glycysiden."—*Pliny*, xxv. 10.

People. *The people's friend.* Dr. William Gordon, the philanthropist. (1801-1849.)

People's Charter (*The*). The six points of the People's Charter, formulated in 1848, are:—

Manhood Suffrage (now practically established).

Annual Parliaments.

Vote by Ballot (established).

Abolition of Property.

Qualification for Members of Parliament (the Qualification Test is abolished).

Equal Electoral Districts.

Pepper. *To pepper one well.* To give one a good basting or thrashing.

To take pepper i' the nose. To take offence. The French have a similar locution, "*La moutarde lui monte au nez.*"

"Take you pepper in your nose, you mar our sport."—*The Spanish Gipsy*, iv. 190.

Pepper Gate. *When your daughter is stolen close Pepper Gate.* Pepper Gate used to be on the east side of the city of Chester. It is said that the daughter of the mayor eloped, and the mayor ordered the gate to be closed up. "Lock the stable-door when the steed is stolen." (*Albert Smith : Christopher Tadpole*, chap. i.)

Pepper-and-Salt. A light grey colour, especially applied to cloth for dresses.

Peppercorn Rent (*A*). A nominal rent. A pepper-berry is of no appreciable value, and given as rent is a simple acknowledgment that the tenement virtually belongs to the person to whom the peppercorn is given.

Peppy Bap. A large erratic boulder, east of Leith.

Per Saltum (Latin). *By a leap.* A promotion or degree given without going over the ground usually prescribed. Thus, a clergyman on being made a bishop has the degree of D.D. given him *per saltum—i.e.* without taking the

B.D. degree, and waiting the usual five years.

"They dare not attempt to examine for the superior degree but elect *per saltum.*"—*Nineteenth Century*, January, 1893, p. 66.

Perce'forest (*King*). A prose romance, printed at Paris in 1528, and said to have been discovered in a cabinet hid in the massive wall of an ancient tower on the banks of the Humber, named Burtimer, from a king of that name who built it. The MS. was said to be in Greek, and was translated through the Latin into French.

It is also used for *Perceval*, an Arthurian knight, in many of the ancient romances.

Perceval (*Sir*), of Wales. A knight of the Round Table, son of Sir Pellinore, and brother of Sir Lamerock. He went in quest of the St. Graal (*q.v.*). Chrétien de Troyes wrote the *Roman de Perceval.* (1541-1596.) Menessier wrote the same in verse.

Per'cinet. A fairy prince, who thwarts the malicious designs of Grognon, the cruel stepmother of Gracio'sa. (*Fairy Tales.*)

Percy [*pierce-eye*]. When Malcolm III. of Scotland invaded England, and reduced the castle of Alnwick, Robert de Mowbray brought to him the keys of the castle suspended on his lance; and, handing them from the wall, thrust his lance into the king's eye; from which circumstance, the tradition says, he received the name of "Pierce-eye," which has ever since been borne by the Dukes of Northumberland.

"This is all a fable. The Percies are descended from a great Norman baron, who came over with William, and who took his name from his castle and estate in Normandy."—*Sir Walter Scott : Tales of a Grandfather*, iv.

Per'dita. Daughter of Leontēs and Hermi'onē of Sicily. She was born when her mother was imprisoned by Leontes out of causeless jealousy. Paulina, a noble lady, hoping to soften the king's heart, took the infant and laid it at its father's feet; but Leontes ordered it to be put to sea, under the expectation that it would drift to some desert island. The vessel drifted to Bohemia, where the infant was discovered by a shepherd, who brought it up as his own daughter. In time Florizel, the son and heir of the Bohemian king Polixenes, fell in love with the supposed shepherdess. The match was forbidden by Polixenes, and the young lovers fled, under the charge of Camillo, to Sicily. Here the story is cleared up, Polixenes and Leontes are

31

reconciled, and the young lovers married. (*Shakespeare : Winter'sTale.*) Polixĕnes (4 syl.), Leontes (3 syl.)

Perdrix, toujours Perdrix. Too much of the same thing. Walpole tells us that the confessor of one of the French kings reproved him for conjugal infidelity, and was asked by the king what he liked best. "Partridge," replied the priest, and the king ordered him to be served with partridge every day, till he quite loathed the sight of his favourite dish. After a time, the king visited him, and hoped he had been well served, when the confessor replied, " *Mais oui, perdrix, toujours perdrix.*" "Ah! ah!" replied the amorous monarch, "and one mistress is all very well, but not ' *perdrix, toujours perdrix.*' "

"Soup for dinner, soup for supper, and soup for breakfast again." — *Farquhar : The Inconstant,* iv. 2.

Père Duchêne. Jacques Réné Hébert, one of the most profligate characters of the French Revolution. He was editor of a vile newspaper so called, containing the grossest insinuations against Marie Antoinette. (1755-1794.)

Père la Chaise, the Parisian cemetery, is the site of a great monastery founded by Louis XIV., of which his confessor, Père la Chaise, was made the superior. After the Revolution, the grounds were laid out for a public cemetery ; first used in May, 1804.

Peregrine (3 syl.) ran away from home, and obtained a loan of £10 from Job Thornbury, with which he went abroad and traded ; he returned a wealthy man, and arrived in London on the very day Job Thornbury was made a bankrupt. Having paid the creditors out of the proceeds made from the hardwareman's loan, he married his daughter. (*George Colman the Younger : John Bull.*)

Peregrine Falcon (*A*). The female is larger than the male, as is the case with most birds of prey. The female is the *falcon* of falconers, and the male the *tercel.* It is called peregrine from its wandering habits.

Per'egrine Pic'kle. The hero of Smollett's novel so called. A savage, ungrateful spendthrift ; fond of practical jokes to the annoyance of others, and suffering with evil temper the misfortunes brought on by his own wilfulness.

Perfec'tionists. A society founded by Father Noyes in Oneida Creek. They take St. Paul for their law-giver, but read his epistles in a new light. They reject all law, saying the guidance of the Spirit is superior to all human codes. If they would know how to act in matters affecting others, they consult "public opinion," expressed by a committee ; and the "law of sympathy" so expressed is their law of action. In material prosperity, this society is unmatched by all the societies of North America. (*W. Hepworth Dixon : New America,* vii. 20, 21.)

Perfide Albion ! (French). The words of Napoleon I.

Per'fume (2 syl.) means simply "from smoke" (Latin, *per fumum*), the first perfumes having been obtained by the combustion of aromatic woods and gums. Their original use was in sacrifices, to counteract the offensive odours of the burning flesh.

Perfumed Terms of the Time. So Ben Jonson calls euphemisms.

Pe'ri (plur. PERIS). Peris are delicate, gentle, fairy-like beings of Eastern mythology, begotten by fallen spirits. They direct with a wand the pure in mind the way to heaven. These lovely creatures, according to the Koran, are under the sovereignty of Eblis ; and Mahomet was sent for their conversion, as well as for that of man.

" Like peris' wands, when pointing out the road For some pure spirit to the blest abode."
Thomas Moore : Lalla Rookh, pt. i.

Per'icles, Prince of Tyre (*Shakespeare*). The story is from the '*Gesta Romano'rum,* where Periclĕs is called "Apollo'nius, *King* of Tyre." The story is also related by Gower in his *Confessio Amantis* (bk. viii.).

Pericles' Boast. When Pericles, Tyrant of Athens, was on his death-bed, he overheard his friends recounting his various merits, and told them they had omitted the greatest of all, that no Athenian through his whole administration had put on mourning through his severity—*i.e.* he had caused no Athenian to be put to death arbitrarily.

Peril'lo Swords. *Perillo* is a "little stone," a mark by which Julian del Rey, a famous armourer of Tole'do and Zaragoza, authenticated the swords of his manufacture. All perillo swords were made of the steel produced from the mines of Mondragon. The swords given by Katharine of Aragon to Henry VIII. on his wedding-day were all *Perillo* blades.

The most common inscription was, "*Draw me not without reason, sheathe me not without honour.*"

Perillos and the Brazen Bull. Perillos of Athens made a brazen bull for Phal'aris, Tyrant of Agrigentum, intended for the execution of criminals. They were shut up in the bull, and, fires being lighted below the belly, the metal was made "red hot." The cries of the victims, reverberating, sounded like the lowing of the bull. Phalaris admired the invention, but tested it on Perillos himself. (*See* INVENTORS.)

Perilous Castle. The castle of Lord Douglas was so called in the reign of Edward I., because good Lord Douglas destroyed several English garrisons stationed there, and vowed to be revenged on anyone who should dare to take possession of it. Sir Walter Scott calls it "Castle Dangerous." (*See* Introduction of *Castle Dangerous*.)

Per'ion. A fabulous king of Gaul, father of "Amadis of Gaul." His encounter with the lion is one of his best exploits. It is said that he was hunting, when his horse reared and snorted at seeing a lion in the path. Perion leaped to the ground and attacked the lion, but the lion overthrew him ; whereupon the king drove his sword into the belly of the beast and killed him. (*Amadis de Gaul*, chap. i.)

Peripatet'ics. *Founder of the Peripatetics*—Aristotle, who used to teach his disciples in the covered walk of the Lycēum. This colonnade was called the *perip'atos*, because it was a place for walking about (*peri pateo*).

Peris. (*See* PERI.)

Peris'sa (excess or prodigality ; Greek, *Perissos*). Step-sister of Elissa and Medi'na. These ladies could never agree on any subject. (*Spenser : Faërie Queene*, bk. ii.)

Per'iwig. (*See* PERUKE.)

Periwink'le. The bind-around plant. (Anglo-Saxon, *pinewincle ;* French, *pervenche ;* Latin, *pervincio,* to bind thoroughly.) In Italy it used *to be wreathed round* dead infants, and hence its Italian name, *fior di morto.*

Perk. *To perk oneself.* To plume oneself on anything. (Welsh, *percu,* to smarten or plume feathers, *perc,* neat.) *You begin to perk up a bit—i.e.* to get a little fatter and more plump after an illness. (*See above.*)

Perku'nos. God of the elements. The Sclavonic Trinity was Perku'nos, Rikollos, and Potrimpos. (*Grimm : Deutsche Mythologie.*)

Perm'ian Strata. So called from Perm, in Russia, where they are most distinctly developed.

Pernelle (*Madame*). A scolding old woman in Molière's *Tartuffe.*

Perpendiculars. Parties called crushes, in which persons have to stand almost stationary from the time of entering the suite of rooms to the time of leaving them.

"The night before I duly attended my mother to three fashionable crowds, 'perpendiculars' is the best name for them, for there is seldom more than standing room."—*Edna Lyall: Donovan,* chap. ix.

Perpet'ual Motion. Restlessness ; fidgety or nervous disquiet ; also a chimerical scheme wholly impracticable. Many have tried to invent a machine that shall move of itself, and never stop ; but, as all materials must suffer from wear and tear, it is evident that such an invention is impossible.

"It were better to be eaten to death with rust, than to be scoured to nothing with perpetual motion."—*Shakespeare : 2 Henry IV.,* i. 2.

Pers. Persia ; called Fars. (French, *Perse.*)

Persecutions (*The ten great*). (1) Under Nero, A.D. 64 ; (2) Domitian, 95 ; (3) Trajan, 98 ; (4) Hadrian, 118 ; (5) Pertinax, 202, chiefly in Egypt ; (6) Maximin, 236 ; (7) Decius, 249 ; (8) Valerian, 257 ; (9) Aurelian, 272 ; (10) Diocletian, 302.

"It would be well if these were the only religious persecutions ; but, alas ! those on the other side prove the truth of the Founder : 'I came not to send peace [on earth], but a sword' (Matt. x. 34). Witness the long and relentless persecutions of the Waldenses and Albigenses, the six or seven crusades, the wars of Charlemagne against the Saxons, and the thirty years' war of Germany. Witness, again, the persecution of the Guises, the Bartholomew slaughter, the wars of Louis XIV. on the revocation of the Edict of Nantes, the Dragonnades, and the wars against Holland. Witness the bitter persecutions stirred up by Luther, which spread to England and Scotland. No wars so lasting, so relentless, so bloody as religious wars. It has been no thin red line."

Persep'olis, called by the Persians "The Throne of Jam-sheid," by whom it was founded. Jam-sheid removed the seat of government from Balk to Istakhar.

Per'seus (2 syl.). A bronze statue in the Loggia dei Lanzi, at Florence. The best work of Benvenuto Cellini (1500-1562).

Perseus' flying horse. A ship.
"Perseus conquered the head of Medu'sa, and did make Peg'ase, the most swift ship, which he always calls Perseus' flying horse."—*Destruction of Troy.*

" The strong-ribbed bark through liquid mountains cut . . .
Like Perseus' horse."
    Shakespeare: Troilus and Cressida, i. 3.

Perseve're (3 syl.). This word comes from an obsolete Latin verb, *sevēro* (to stick rigidly) ; hence *sevērus* (severe or rigid). Asseverate is to stick rigidly to what you say ; persevere is to stick rigidly to what you undertake till you have accomplished it. (*Per-sevēro.*)

Persian Alexander (*The*). Sandjar (1117-1158). (*See* ALEXANDER.)

Persian Bucepha'los (*The*). Shebdiz, the charger of Chosroes Parviz. (*See* BUCEPHALOS.)

Person (Latin, *persona,* a mask ; *persona'tus,* one who wears a mask, an actor). A " person " is one who impersonates a character. Shakespeare says, " All the world's a stage, and all the men and women merely players " or persons. When we speak of the " person of the Deity " we mean the same thing, the *character* represented, as that of the Father, or that of the Son, or that of the Holy Ghost. There is no more notion of corporeality connected with the word than there is any assumption of the body of Hamlet when an actor impersonates that character.

Persona Grata (Latin). An acceptable person ; one liked.
" The Count [Münster] is not a *persona grata* at court, as the royal family did not relish the course he took in Hanoverian affairs in 1866."—*Truth,* October 22nd, 1885.

Perth is Celtic for a bush. The county of Perth is the county of bushes.
Fair Maid of Perth. Catherine Glover, daughter of Simon Glover, glover, of Perth. Her lover is Henry Gow, *alias* Henry Smith, *alias* Gow Chrom, *alias* Hal of the Wynd, *the* armourer, fosterson of Dame Shoulbred. (*Sir Walter Scott : Fair Maid of Perth.*)
The Five Articles of Perth were those passed in 1618 by order of James VI., enjoining the attitude of kneeling to receive the elements ; the observance of Christmas, Good Friday, Easter, and Pentecost ; the right of confirmation, etc. They were ratified August 4, 1621, called *Black Saturday,* and condemned in the General Assembly of Glasgow in 1638.

Peru. *That's not Peru.* Said of something utterly worthless. A French

expression, founded on the notion that Peru is the El Dorado of the world.

Peru'vian Bark, called also *Jesuit's Bark,* because it was introduced into Spain by the Jesuits. "Quinine," from the same tree, is called by the Indians *quinquina.* (*See* CINCHONA.)

Peruke or **Periwig.** Menage ingeniously derives these words from the Latin *pilus* (" hair "). Thus, *pilus, pelus, pelu'tus, pelu'ticus, pelu'tica, peru'a, perruque.* The wigs are first mentioned in the 16th century ; in the next century they became very large. The fashion began to wane in the reign of George III. Periwig is a corrupt form of the French word *perruque.*

Pescec'ola. The famous swimmer drowned in the pool of Charybdis. The tale says he dived once into the pool, and was quite satisfied with its horrors and wonders ; but the King Frederick then tossed in a golden cup, which Pescecola dived for, and was never seen again. (*See Schiller's Diver.*)

Pess'imist. One who fancies everything is as bad as possible. (Latin, *pess'imus,* the worst.)

Petard'. *Hoist on his own petard.* Caught in his own trap, involved in the danger he meant for others. The petard was a conical instrument of war employed at one time for blowing open gates with gunpowder. The engineers used to carry the petard to the place they intended to blow up, and fire it at the small end by a fusee. Shakespeare spells the word *petar :* " 'Tis the sport to have the engineer hoist with his own petar." (*Hamlet,* ii. 4.)
"Turning the muzzles of the guns Magdalawards, and getting a piece of lighted rope [the party] blazed away as vigorously as possible . . . and tried to hoist Theodore on his own petard."—*Daily paper.*

Petaud. *'Tis the court of King Petaud, where everyone is master.* There is no order or discipline at all. This is a French proverb. Petaud is a corruption of *peto* (I beg), and King Petaud means king of the beggars, in whose court all are equal. (*See* ALSATIA.)

Peter. (*See* BLUE PETER.)
Great Peter. A bell in York Minster, weighing 10¾ tons, and hung in 1845.
Lord Peter. The Pope in Swift's *Tale of a Tub.*
Rob Peter to pay Paul. (*See* ROBBING.)
St. Peter. Patron saint of fishers and fishmongers, being himself a fisherman.

St. *Peter, in Christian art, is represented as an old man, bald, but with a flowing beard; he is usually dressed in a white mantle and blue tunic, and holds in his hand a book or scroll. His peculiar symbols are the keys, and a sword, the instrument of his martyrdom.

He has got St. Peter's fingers—i.e. the fingers of a thief. The allusion is to the fish caught by St. Peter with a piece of money in its mouth. They say that a thief has a fish-hook on every finger.

Peter Botte Mountain, in the island of Mauritius; so called from a Dutchman who scaled its summit, but lost his life in coming down. It is a rugged cone, more than 2,800 feet in height.

Peter Parley. The *nom de plume* of Samuel G. Goodrich, an American (1793-1860).

Peter Peebles. *Peter Peebles' Lawsuit.* In Sir Walter Scott's novel of *Redgauntlet,* Peter is a litigious hard-hearted drunkard, poor as a church-mouse, and a liar to the backbone. His "ganging plea" is Hogarthian comic, as Carlyle says.

Peter-pence. An annual tribute of one penny, paid at the feast of St. Peter to the see of Rome. At one time it was collected from every family, but afterwards it was restricted to those "who had the value of thirty pence in quick or live stock." This tax was collected in England from 740 till it was abolished by Henry VIII.

Peter Pindar. The *nom de plume* of Dr. John Wolcot (*Wool-cut*), of Dodbrooke, Devonshire. (1738-1819.)

Peter Por'cupine. William Cobbett, when he was a Tory. We have *Peter Porcupine's Gazette* and the *Porcupine Papers,* in twelve volumes. (1762-1835.)

Peter Wilkins was written by Robert Pultock, of Clifford's Inn, and sold to Dodsley, the publisher, for £20.

Peter of Provence came into possession of Merlin's wooden horse. There is a French romance called *Peter of Provence and the Fair Magalo'na,* the chief incidents of which are connected with this flying charger.

Peter the Great of Russia built St. Petersburg, and gave Russia a place among the nations of Europe. He laid aside his crown and sceptre, came to England, and worked as a common labourer in our dockyards, that he might teach his subjects how to build ships.

Peter the Hermit (in Tasso), "the holy author of the crusade" (bk. i.). It is said that six millions of persons assumed the cross at his preaching.

Peter the Wild Boy, found 1725 in a wood near Hameln, in Hanover, at the supposed age of thirteen. (Died 1785.)

Peterboat. A boat made to go either way, the stem and stern being both alike.

Pe'terborough (Northamptonshire). So called from the monastery of St. Peter, founded in 655. Tracts relating to this monastery are published in Sparke's collection.

Pe'terloo. The dispersal of a large meeting in St. Peter's Field, Manchester, by an armed force, August 16th, 1819. The assemblage consisted of operatives, and the question was parliamentary reform. The word, suggested by Hunt, is a parody upon what he absurdly called "the bloody butchers of Waterloo."

It is a most exaggerated phrase. The massacre consisted of six persons accidentally killed by the rush of the crowd, when the military and some 400 special constables appeared on the field.

Petit-Maître. A fop; a lad who assumes the manners, dress, and affectations of a man. The term arose before the Revolution, when a great dignitary was styled a *grand-maître,* and a pretentious one a *petit-maître.*

Petit Serjeantry. Holding lands of the Crown by the service of rendering annually some small implement of war, as a bow, a sword, a lance, a flag, an arrow, and the like. Thus the Duke of Wellington holds his country seat at Strathfieldsaye and Apsley House, London, by presenting a flag annually to the Crown on the anniversary of the battle of Waterloo. The flag is hung in the guard-room of the state apartments of Windsor Castle till the next anniversary, when it becomes the perquisite of the officer of the guard. The Duke of Marlborough presents also a flag on the anniversary of the battle of Blenheim. for his estate at Blenheim. This also is placed in the guard-room of Windsor Castle.

Petitio Princip'ii (*A*). A begging of the question, or assuming in the premises the question you undertake to prove. Thus, if a person undertook to prove the infallibility of the pope, and were to take for his premises—(1) Jesus Christ promised to keep the apostles and their successors in all the truth ; (2) the popes are the regular successors of the apostles, and therefore the popes are infallible—it would be a vicious syllogism from a *petitio principii.*

Petitioners and Abhorrers. Two political parties in the reign of Charles II. When that monarch was first restored he used to grant everything he was asked for ; but after a time this became a great evil, and Charles enjoined his loving subjects to discontinue their practice of "petitioning." Those who agreed with the king, and disapproved of petitioning, were called *Abhorrers;* those who were favourable to the objectionable practice were nicknamed *Petitioners.*

Petrarch. *The English Petrarch.* Sir Philip Sidney ; so called by Sir Walter Raleigh. Cowper styles him "the warbler of poetic prose." (1554-1586.)

Pet'rel. *The stormy petrel.* So named, according to tradition, from the Italian *Petrello* (little Peter), in allusion to St. Peter, who walked on the sea. Our sailors call them "Mother Carey's chickens." They are called *stormy* because in a gale they surround a ship to catch small animals which rise to the surface of the rough sea ; when the gale ceases they are no longer seen.

Pet'rified (3 syl.). *The petrified city.* Ishmonie, in Upper Egypt, is so called from the number of petrified bodies of men, women, and children to be seen there. (Latin, *petra-fio,* to become rock.)

Petrobrus'sians or **Petrobrus'ians.** A religious sect, founded in 1110, and so called from Peter Bruys, a Provençal. He declaimed against churches, asserting that a stable was as good as a cathedral for worship, and a manger equal to an altar. He also declaimed against the use of crucifixes.

Pet'ronel. *Sir Petronel Flash.* A braggadocio, a tongue-doughty warrior.

"Give your scholler degrees and your lawyer his fees,
And some dice for Sir Petronell Flash."
Brit. Bibl.

Petru'chio. A gentleman of Verona who undertakes to tame the haughty Katharine, called *the Shrew.* He marries her, and without the least personal chastisement brings her to lamb-like

submission. (*Shakespeare: Taming of the Shrew.*)

Petticoat. A woman.
"There's a petticoat will prove to be the cause of this."—*Hawley Smart: Struck Down,* chap. xi,

Petticoat Government. Female rule.

Petticoat and Gown. The dress. When the gown was looped up, the petticoat was an important item of dress.

The poppy is said to have a red petticoat and a green gown ; the daffodil, a yellow petticoat and green gown ; a candle, a white petticoat; and so on in our common nursery rhymes—

1 " The king's daughter is coming to town,
    With a red petticoat and a green gown."
2 " Daffadown dilly is now come to town,
    In a yellow petticoat and a green gown."

Petto. *In petto.* In secrecy, in reserve (Italian, *in the breast*). The pope creates cardinals *in petto—i.e.* in his own mind—and keeps the appointment to himself till he thinks proper to announce it.
"Belgium, a department of France *in petto—i.e.* in the intention of the people."—*The Herald,* 1837.

Petty Cu'ry (Cambridge) means "The Street of Cooks." It is called *Parva Coke'ria* in a deed dated 13 Edward III. Probably at one time it was part of the Market Hall. It is a mistake to derive Cury from *Écurie.* Dr. Pegge derives it from *cura're,* to cure or dress food.

Peutinge'rian Map. A map of the roads of the ancient Roman world, constructed in the time of Alexander Seve'rus (A.D. 226), made known to us by Conrad Peutinger, of Augsburg.

Pev'eril of the Peak. Sir Geoffrey the Cavalier, and Lady Margaret his wife ; Julian Peveril, their son, in love with Alice Bridgenorth, daughter of Major Bridgenorth, a Roundhead ; and William Peveril, natural son of William the Conqueror, ancestor of Sir Geoffrey. (*Sir Walter Scott: Peveril of the Peak.*)

Pewter. *To scour the pewter.* To do one's work.
" But if she neatly scour her pewter,
  Give her the money that is due t' her."
King: Orpheus and Eurydice.

Phædria [*wantonness*]. Handmaid of Acrasia the enchantress. She sails about Idle Lake in a gondola. Seeing Sir Guyon she ferries him across the lake to the floating island, where Cymoch'les attacks him. Phædria interposes, the combatants desist, and the little wanton ferries the knight Temperance over the lake again. (*Spenser: Faërie Queene,* ii.)

Pha'eton. The son of Phœbus, who undertook to drive the chariot of the sun, was upset, and caused great mischief; Libya was parched into barren sands, and all Africa was more or less injured, the inhabitants blackened, and vegetation nearly destroyed.

" Gallop apace, you fiery-footed steeds,
Towards Phœbus' mansion ; such a waggoner
As Phaeton would whip you to the west,
And bring in cloudy night immediately."
    Shakespeare: Romeo and Juliet, iii. 2.

Pha'eton. A sort of carriage ; so called from the sun-car driven by Phaeton. (*See above.*)

Phaeton's bird. The swan. Cyenus was the friend of Phaeton, and lamented his fate so grievously that Apollo changed her into a swan, and placed her among the constellations.

Phalanx. The close order of battle in which the heavy-armed troops of a Grecian army were usually drawn up. Hence, any number of people distinguished for firmness and solidity of union.

Phal'aris. *The brazen bull of Phal'aris.* Perillos, a brass-founder of Athens, proposed to Phal'aris, Tyrant of Agrigentum, to invent for him a new species of punishment ; accordingly, he cast a brazen bull, with a door in the side. The victim was shut up in the bull and roasted to death, but the throat of the engine was so contrived that the groans of the sufferer resembled the bellowings of a mad bull. Phal'aris commended the invention, and ordered its merits to be tested by Perillos himself.

The epistles of Phal'aris. Certain letters said to have been written by Phal'aris, Tyrant of Agrigen'tum, in Sicily. Boyle maintained them to be genuine, Bentley affirmed that they were forgeries. No doubt Bentley is right.

Phalog, in the satire of *Absalom and Achitophel*, by Dryden and Tate, is Mr. Forbes, a Scotchman.

Phantom Ship. (*See* CARMILHAN.)

" Or of that phantom ship, whose form
Shoots like a meteor through the storm ;
When the dark scud comes driving hard,
And lowered is every topsail yard . . .
And well the doomed spectators know
'Tis harbinger of wreck and woe."
    Sir Walter Scott : Rokeby, ii. 11.

Pha'on. A young man greatly illtreated by Furor, and rescued by Sir Guyon. He loved Claribel, but Phile'mon, his friend, persuaded him that Claribel was unfaithful, and, to prove his words, told him to watch in a given place. He saw what he thought was Claribel holding an assignation with what seemed to be a groom, and, rushing forth, met the true Claribel, whom he slew on the spot. Being tried for the

murder, it came out that the groom was Philemon, and the supposed Claribel only her lady's maid. He poisoned Phil'emon, and would have murdered the handmaid, but she escaped, and while he pursued her he was attacked by Furor. This tale is to expose the intemperance of revenge. (*Spenser : Faërie Queene*, ii. 4, 28.)

Phar'amond. King of the Franks and a knight of the Round Table. He is said to have been the *first* king of France. This reputed son of Marcomir and father of Clo'dion, is the hero of one of Calprenède's novels.

Pha'raoh (2 syl.). The king. It is the Coptic article P and the word *ouro* (king). There are eleven of this title mentioned in Holy Scripture : —

i. *Before Solomon's time.*

(1) The Pharaoh contemporary with Abraham (Gen. xii. 25).

(2) The good Pharaoh who advanced Joseph (Gen. xli.).

(3) The Pharaoh who "knew not Joseph " (Exod. i. 8).

(4) The Pharaoh who was drowned in the Red Sea (Exod. xiv. 28) ; said to be Menephthes or Meneptah, son of Ram'eses II.

(5) The Pharaoh that protected Hadad (1 Kings xi. 19).

(6) The Pharaoh whose daughter Solomon married (1 Kings iii. 1 ; ix. 16).

ii. *After Solomon's time.*

(7) Pharaoh Shishak, who warred against Rehobo'am (1 Kings xiv. 25, 26).

(8) Pharaoh Shabakok, or " So," with whom Hoshea made an alliance (2 Kings xvii. 4).

(9) The Pharaoh that made a league with Hezeki'ah against Sennacherib, called Tirhākah (2 Kings xviii. 21 ; xix. 9).

(10) Pharaoh Necho, who warred against Josi'ah (2 Kings xxiii. 29, etc.).

(11) Pharaoh Hophra, the ally of Zedeki'ah (Jer. xliv. 30) ; said to be Apries, who was strangled B.C. 570. (*See* KING.)

⁂ After Solomon's time the titular word *Pharaoh* is joined to a proper name.

iii. *Other Pharaohs of historic note.*

(1) Cheops or Suphis I. (Dynasty IV.), who built the great pyramid.

(2) Cephrenes or Suphis II., his brother, who built the second pyramid.

(3) Mencheres, his successor, who built the most beautiful pyramid of the three.

(4) Memnon or A-menophis III. (Dynasty XVIII.), whose musical statue is so celebrated.

(5) Sethos I., the Great (Dynasty XIX.), whose tomb was discovered by Belzoni.

(6) Sethos II., called Proteus (Dynasty XIX.), who detained Helen and Paris in Egypt.

(7) Phuōris or Thuōris, who sent aid to Priam in the siege of Troy.

(8) Rampsinītus or Rameses Nĕter, the miser (Dynasty XX.), mentioned by Herodŏtos.

(9) Osorthon IV. or Osorkon (Dynasty XXIII.), the Egyptian Hercules.

Pharaoh, in Dryden's satire of *Absalom and Achitophel,* means Louis XIV. of France.

" If Pharaoh's doubtful succour he [Charles II.]
should use,
A foreign aid would more incense the Jews
[English nation]."

Pharaoh who Knew not Joseph. Supposed to be Menephtah, son of Rameses the Great. Rider Haggard adopts this hypothesis. After Rameses the Great came a period of confusion in Egypt, and it is supposed the Pharaoh who succeeded was a usurper. No trace of the destruction of Pharaoh and his host has been discovered by Egyptologists.

His wife was Asia, daughter of Mozahem. Pharaoh cruelly maltreated her for believing in Moses. He fastened her hands and feet to four stakes, and laid a millstone on her as she lay exposed to the scorching sun ; but God took her, without dying, into Paradise. (*Sale : Al Koran,* lxvi. *note.*)

Among women, four have been perfect : Asia, wife of Pharaoh ; Mary, daughter of Imran ; Khadījah, daughter of Khowailed (Mahomet's first wife); and Fatima, Mahomet's daughter. Attributed to Mahomet.

Pharaoh who made Joseph his Viceroy. Supposed to be Osertesen II. There is a tablet in the sixth year of his reign which is thought to represent Jacob and his household.

Pharaoh's Chicken. The Egyptian vulture, so called from its frequent representation in Egyptian hieroglyphics.

Pharaoh's Daughter, who brought up Moses, Bathia.

" Bathia, the daughter of Pharaoh, came, attended by her maidens, and entering the water she chanced to see the box of bulrushes, and, pitying the infant, she rescued him from death."
—*The Talmud.*

Pharian Fields, Egypt. So called from Pharos, an island on the coast, noted for its lighthouse.

"And passed from Pharian fields to Canaan land." *Milton : Psalm* cxiv.

Pharisees means "separatists" (Heb. *parash,* to separate), men who looked upon themselves as holier than other men, and therefore refused to hold social intercourse with them. The Talmud mentions the following classes : —

(1) The "Dashers," or "Bandy-legged" (*Nikfi*), who scarcely lifted their feet from the ground in walking, but "dashed them against the stones," that people might think them absorbed in holy thought (Matt. xxi. 44).

(2) The "Mortars," who wore a "mortier," or cap, which would not allow them to see the passers-by, that their meditations might not be disturbed. "Having eyes, they saw not" (Mark viii. 18).

(3) The "Bleeders," who inserted thorns in the borders of their gaberdines to prick their legs in walking.

(4) The "Cryers," or "Inquirers;" who went about crying out, "Let me know my duty, and I will do it" (Matt. xix. 16-22).

(5) The "Almsgivers," who had a trumpet sounded before them to summon the poor together (Matt. vi. 2).

(6) The "Stumblers," or "Bloody-browed" (*Kizai*), who shut their eyes when they went abroad that they might see no women, being "blind leaders of the blind" (Matt. xv. 14). Our Lord calls them "blind Pharisees," "fools and blind."

(7) The "Immovables," who stood like statues for hours together, "praying in the market places" (Matt. vi. 5).

(8) The "Pestle Pharisees" (*Medinkia*), who kept themselves bent double like the handle of a pestle.

(9) The "Strong-shouldered" (*Shikmi*), who walked with their back bent as if carrying on their shoulders the whole burden of the law.

(10) The "Dyed Pharisees," called by our Lord "Whited Sepulchres," whose externals of devotion cloaked hypocrisy and moral uncleanness. (*Talmud of Jerusalem, Berakoth,* ix : *Sota,* v. 7 ; *Talmud of Babylon, Sota,* 22 b.)

Pha'ros. A lighthouse ; so called from the lighthouse built by Sostratus Cnidius in the island of Pharos, near the port of Alexandria, in Egypt. It was 450 feet high, and could be seen at the distance of 100 miles. Part was blown down in 793. This Pharos was one of the Seven Wonders of the World.

Pharsa'lia. An epic in Latin hexameters by Lucan. The battle of Pharsalia was between Pompey and Cæsar. Pompey had 45,000 legionaries, 7,000 cavalry, and a large number of auxiliaries; Cæsar had 22,000 legionaries and 1,000 cavalry. Pompey's battle-cry was "*Hercules invictus*;" that of Cæsar was "*Venus victrix.*" On this occasion Cæsar won the battle.

Pheasant. So called from Phasis, a stream of the Black Sea.

· "There was formerly at the fort of Poti a preserve of pheasants, which birds derive their European name from the river Phasis (the present Rion)."—*Lieut.-General Monteith.*

Phe'be (2 syl.). A shepherdess. (*Shakespeare: As You Like It.*)

Phelis, called *the Fair.* The wife of Sir Guy, Earl of Warwick. (*See* GUY.)

Phenom'enon (plural, *phenom'ena*) means simply what has appeared (Greek, *phainomai*, to appear). It is used in science to express the visible result of an experiment. In popular language it means a prodigy. (Greek, *phainomĕnon*.)

Phid'ias. *The French Phidias.* Jean Goujon (1510-1572); also called the *Correggio of sculptors.* (2) J. B. Pigalle (1714-1785).

Phiga'lian Marbles. A series of twenty-three sculptures in alto-relievo, discovered in 1812 at Phiga'lia, in Arca'dia, and in 1814 purchased for the British Museum. They represent the combat of the Centaurs and Lapithæ, and that of the Greeks and Am'azons. They are part of the "Elgin Marbles" (*q.v.*).

Philadelph'ia Stones, called *Christian Bones.* It is said that the walls of Philadelphia, in Turkey, were built of the bones of Christians killed in the Holy Wars. This idle tale has gained credit from the nature of the stones, full of pores and very light, not unlike petrified bones. Similar incrustations are found at Knaresborough and elsewhere.

Philan'der (in *Orlando Furioso*). A sort of Joseph. (*See* GABRINA.)

Philan'dering. Coquetting with a woman; paying court, and leading her to think you love her, but never declaring your preference. The word is coined from Philander, the Dutch knight who coquetted with Gabri'na (*q.v.*).

Philanthropist (*The*). John Howard, who spent much of his life in visiting the prisons and hospitals of Europe. (1726-1790.) (Greek, *phil-anthrōpos.*)

31*

Phile'mon and Baucis entertained Jupiter and Mercury when everyone else refused them hospitality. Being asked to make a request, they begged that they might both die at the same time. When they were very old, Philemon was changed into an oak, and Baucis into a linden tree. (*Ovid: Metamorphoses,* iii. 631, etc.)

Philip. *Philip, remember thou art mortal.* A sentence repeated to the Macedonian king every time he gave an audience.

Philip sober. When a woman who asked Philip of Macedon to do her justice was snubbed by the petulant monarch, she exclaimed, "Philip, I shall appeal against this judgment." "Appeal!" thundered the enraged king, "and to whom will you appeal?" "To Philip sober," was her reply.

St. Philip is usually represented bearing a large cross, or a basket containing loaves, in allusion to St. John vi. 5-7.

Philip Nye (in *Hudibras*). One of the assembly of Dissenting ministers, noted for his ugly beard.

Philip Quarl. A castaway sailor, solaced on a desert island by a monkey. Imitation of Robinson Crusoe. (1727.)

Philippe Égalité. Louis Philippe Joseph, Duc d'Orléans (1747-1793).

Philip'pic. A severe scolding; an invective. So called from the orations of Demos'thenes against Philip of Macedon, to rouse the Athenians to resist his encroachments. The orations of Cicero against Anthony are called "Philippics."

Philip'pins. A Russian sect; so called from the founder, Philip Pustoswiät. They are called *Old Faith Men,* because they cling with tenacity to the old service books, old version of the Bible, old hymn-book, old prayer-book, and all customs previous to the reforms of Nekon, in the 17th century.

Philips (*John*), author of *The Splendid Shilling,* wrote a georgic on *Cider* in blank verse—a serious poem modelled upon Milton's epics.

" Philips, Pomona's bard, the second thou
 Who nobly durst, in rhyme-unfettered verse,
 With British freedom sing the British song."
     Thomson: Autumn.

Philis'ides (4 syl.). Philip Sidney (*Phili' Sid*). Spenser uses the word in the *Pastoral Æglogue on the Death of Sir Philip.*

· "Philisides is dead."

Philistines, meaning the ill-behaved and ignorant. The word so applied arose in Germany from the Charlies or Philisters, who were in everlasting collision with the students; and in these "town and gown rows" identified themselves with the town, called in our universities "the snobs." Matthew Arnold, in the *Cornhill Magazine*, applied the term Philistine to the middle class, which he says is "ignorant, narrow-minded, and deficient in great ideas," insomuch that the middle-class English are objects of contempt in the eyes of foreigners.

Philis'tines (3 syl.). Earwigs and other insect tormentors are so called in Norfolk. Bailiffs, constables, etc. "The Philistines are upon thee, Samson" (Judges xvi.).

Philis'tinism. A cynical indifference and supercilious sneering at religion. The allusion is to the Philistines of Palestine.

Phillis. A play written in Spanish by Lupercio Leonardo of Argensola. (See *Don Quixote*, vol. iii. p. 70.)

Philoc'lea, in Sidney's *Arcadia*, is Lady Penelope Devereux, with whom he was in love; but the lady married another, and Sir Philip transferred his affections to Frances, eldest daughter of Sir Francis Walsingham.

Philocte'tēs. The most famous archer in the Trojan war, to whom Hercules, at death, gave his arrows. He joined the allied Greeks, with seven ships, but in the island of Lemnos, his foot being bitten by a serpent, ulcerated, and became so offensive that the Greeks left him behind. In the tenth year of the siege Ulysses commanded that he should be sent for, as an oracle had declared that Troy could not be taken without the arrows of Herculēs. Philoctetēs accordingly went to Troy, slew Paris, and Troy fell.

⁂ The *Philoctetēs* of Sophoclēs is one of the most famous Greek tragedies. Laharpe wrote a French tragedy, and Warren, in 1871, a metrical drama on the same subject.

Phil'omel or **Philome'la.** (*See* NIGHTINGALE.)

Philome'lus. The Druid bard that accompanied Sir Industry to the *Castle of Indolence.* (*Thomson*, canto ii. 34.)

Philopœ'men, general of the Achæan league, made Epaminondas his model. He slew Mechan'idas, tyrant of Sparta, and was himself killed by poison.

Philos'opher. The sages of Greece used to be called *sophoi* (wise men), but Pythag'oras thought the word too arrogant, and adopted the compound *philosoph'oi* (lover of wisdom), whence "philosopher," one who courts or loves wisdom.

Philosopher. "There was never yet philosopher who could endure the toothache patiently, however they have writ the style of gods, and made a push at chance and sufferance." (*Shakespeare: Much Ado About Nothing*, v. 1.)

The Philosopher. Marcus Aure'lius Antoni'nus is so called by Justin Martyr. (121, 161-180.)

Leo VI., Emperor of the East. (866, 886-911.)

Porphyry, the Antichristian. (233-305.)

The Philosopher of China. Confucius. His mother called him *Little Hillock*, from a knob on the top of his head. (B.C. 551-479.)

The Philosopher of Ferney. Voltaire; so called from his château of Ferney, near Gene'va. (1694-1778.)

The Philsopher of Malmesbury. Thomas Hobbes, author of *Leviathan.* (1588-1679.)

The Philosopher of Persia. Abou Ebn Sina, of Shiraz. (Died 1037.)

The Philosopher of Samosa'ta. Lucan.

"Just such another feast as was that of the Lapithæ, described by the philosopher of Samosata."—*Rabelais: Pantagruel,* book iv. 15.

The Philosopher of Sans-Souci'. Frederick the Great (1712, 1740-1786).

The Philosopher of Wimbledon. John Horne Took, author of *Diversions of Purley.* (1736-1812.)

Philosopher with the Golden Thigh. Pythagoras. General Zelislaus had a golden hand, which was given him by Bolislaus III. when he lost his right hand in battle. Nuad had an artificial hand made of silver by Cred.

"Quite discard the symbol of the old philosopher with the golden thigh."—*Rabelais: Pantagruel* (Prologue to book v.).

Philosopher's Egg (*The*). A preservative against poison, and a cure for the plague; a panacea. The shell of a new egg being pricked, the white is blown out, and the place filled with saffron or a yolk of an egg mixed with saffron.

Philosopher's Stone. The way to wealth. The ancient alchemists thought there was a substance which would convert all baser metals into gold. This substance they called the philosopher's stone. Here the word stone is about equal to the word substratum, which is compounded of the Latin *sub* and *stratus* (spread-under), the latter being related to the verb *stand, stood,* and meaning something on which the experiment stands. It was, in fact, a red powder or amalgam to drive off the impurities of baser metals. (Stone, Saxon, *stán*.)

Philosopher's stone. According to legend, Noah was commanded to hang up the true and genuine philosopher's stone in the ark, to give light to every living creature therein.

Inventions discovered in searching for the philosopher's stone. It was in searching for this treasure that Bötticher stumbled on the invention of Dresden porcelain manufacture ; Roger Bacon on the composition of gunpowder ; Geber on the properties of acids ; Van Helmont on the nature of gas ; and Dr. Glauber on the "salts" which bear his name.

Philosopher's Tree (*The*), or *Diana's tree.* An amalgam of crystallised silver, obtained from mercury in a solution of silver ; so called by the alchemists, with whom Diana stood for silver.

Philosophers.

The Seven Sages or *Wise Men of Greece.* Thalēs, Solon, Chilon, Pit'tacos, Bias, Cleobu'los, Periander ; to which add Sosi'adēs, Anacharsis the Scythian, Myson the Spartan, Epimen'idēs the Cretan, and Pherecy'dēs of Syros.

Philosophers of the Acade'mic sect. Plato, Speusippos, Xenoc'ratēs, Pol'emon, Cratēs, Crantor, Arcesila'os, Care'adēs, Clitom'achos, Philo, and Anti'ochos.

Philosophers of the Cynic sect. Antis'thenēs, Diog'enēs of Sino'pē, Mon'imos, Onesic'ritos, Cratēs, Metroc'lēs, Hippar'chia, Menippos, and Menede'mos of Lamps'acos.

Philosophers of the Cyrena'ic sect. Aristippos, Hege'sias, Annic'eris, Theodo'ros, and Bion.

Philosophers of the Eleac or *Eret'riac sect.* Phædo, Plis'thenēs, and Menede'mos of Eret'ria.

Philosophers of the Eleat'ic sect. Xenoph'anes, Parmen'idēs, Melissos, Zeno of Tarsos, Leucippos, Democ'ritos, Protag'oras, and Anaxarchos.

Philosophers of the Epicure'an sect. Epicu'ros, and a host of disciples.

Philosophers of the Heracli'tan sect. Heracli'tos ; the names of his disciples are unknown.

Philosophers of the Ionic sect. Anaximander, Anaxim'enēs, Anaxag'oras, and Archela'os.

Philosophers of the Italic sect. Pythag'oras, Emped'oclēs, Epicharmos, Archy'tas, Alcmæon, Hip'pasos, Philola'os, and Eudoxos.

Philosophers of the Megar'ic sect. Euclid, Eubu'lidēs, Alex'inos, Euphantos, Apollo'nios, Chron'os, Diodo'ros, Ich'thyas, Clinom'achos, and Stilpo.

Philosophers of the Peripatet'ic sect. Aristotle, Theophrastos, Straton, Lyco, Aristo, Critola'os, and Diodo'ros.

Philosophers of the Sceptic sect. Pyrrho and Timon.

Philosophers of the Socratic sect. Soc'ratēs, Xen'ophon, Æs'chinēs, Crito, Simon, Glauco, Simmias, and Ce'bēs.

Philosophers of the Stoic sect. Zeno, Cleanthēs, Chrysippos, Zeno the Less, Diog'enes of Babylon, Antip'ater, Panætios, and Posido'nios.

Philosophy. *Father of Philosophy.* Albrecht von Haller, of Berne. (1708-1777.)

Philot'imē. The word means *lover of honour.* The presiding Queen of Hell, and daughter of Mammon. (*Spenser : Faërie Queene,* ii.)

" And fair Philotimē, the rightly hight,
The fairest wight that wonneth under sky."
                          Book ii. canto vii.

Philox'enos of Cythēra. A most distinguished dithyrambic poet. He was invited to the court of Dionysius of Syracuse, who placed some poems in his hand to correct. Philoxenos said the only thing to do was to run a line through them and put them in the fire. For this frankness he was cast into prison, but, being released, he retired to Ephesus. The case of Voltaire and Frederick II. the Great of Prussia is an exact parallel.

" Bolder than Philoxenus,
Down the veil of truth I tear."
Amand Charlemagne : Les Grandes Vérités.

Philox'enos of Leucadia. A great epicure, who wished he had the neck of a crane, that he might enjoy the taste of his food the longer. (*Aristotle : Ethics,* iii. 10.)

Philt'er (*A*). A draught or charm to incite in another the passion of love. The Thessalian philters were the most renowned, but both the Greeks and Romans used these dangerous potions, which sometimes produced insanity. Lucre'tius is said to have been driven mad by a love-potion, and Calig'ula's death is attributed to some philters administered to him by his wife, Cæ-so'nia. Brabantio says to Othello—

"Thou hast practised on her [Desdemona] with foul charms,
Abused her delicate youth with drugs or min-erals
That weaken motion."
Shakespeare: Othello, i. 1.

..** ("Philter," Greek, *philtron, philos,* loving.)

Phi'neus (2 syl.). A blind king of Thrace, who had the gift of prophecy. Whenever he wanted to eat, the Harpies came and took away or defiled his food.

"Blind Tham'yris, and blind Mœonidēs,
And Tire'sias, and Phi'neus, prophets old."
Milton: Paradise Lost, iii. 34.

Phiz, the face, is a contraction of physiognomy.

Phiz. Hablot K. Browne, who illus-trated the *Pickwick Papers,* etc.

Phleg'ethon. A river of liquid fire in Hadēs. (Greek, *phlego,* to burn.)

"Fierce Phlegethon,
Whose waves of torrent fire inflame with rage."
Milton: Paradise Lost, ii.

Phleg'ra, in Macedonia, was where the giants attacked the gods. Encel'ados was the chief of the giants.

Phlogiston. The principle or ele-ment of heat, according to Stahl. When latent the effect is imperceptible, but when operative it produces all the effects of heat from warmth to com-bustion. Of course, this theory has long been exploded. (Greek, *phlogis'ton,* in-flammable.)

Phocensian Despair. Desperation which terminates in victory. In the days of Philip, King of Macedon, the men of Phocis had to defend themselves single-handed against the united forces of all their neighbours, because they presumed to plough a sacred field belonging to Delphi. The Phocensians suggested that they should make a huge pile, and that all the women and children should join the men in one vast human sacrifice. The pile was made, and everything was ready, but the men of Phocis, before mounting the pile, rushed in desperation on the foe, and obtained a signal victory.

Pho'cion, surnamed *The Good,* who resisted all the bribes of Alexander and his successor. It was this real patriot who told Alexander to turn his arms against Persia, their common enemy, rather than against the states of Greece, his natural allies.

"Phocion the Good, in public life severe,
To virtue still inexorably firm."
Thomson · Winter.

Phœbē. The moon, sister of Phœbus.

Phœbus. The sun or sun-god. In Greek mythology Apollo is called Phœbos (the sun-god), from the Greek verb *phao* (to shine).

"The rays divine of vernal Phœbus shine."
Thomson: Spring.

Phœnix. Said to live a certain number of years, when it makes in Arabia a nest of spices, sings a melo-dious dirge, flaps his wings to set fire to the pile, burns itself to ashes, and comes forth with new life, to repeat the former one. (*See* PHŒNIX PERIOD.)

"The enchanted pile of that lonely bird,
Who sings at the last his own death-lay,
And in music and perfume dies away."
Thomas Moore: Paradise and the Peri.

Phœnix, as a sign over chemists' shops, was adopted from the association of this fabulous bird with alchemy. Paracelsus wrote about it, and several of the al-chemists employed it to symbolise their vocation.

A phœnix among women. A phœnix of his kind. A paragon, unique; because there was but one phœnix at a time.

"If she be furnished with a mind so rare,
She is alone the Arabian bird."
Shakespeare: Cymbeline, i. 7.

The Spanish Phœnix. Lope de Vega is so called by G. H. Lewes.

"Insigne poeta, a cuyo verso o prosa
Ninguno le aventaja ni aun Mega."

Phœnix Alley (London). The alley leading to the Phœnix theatre, now called Drury Lane.

Phœnix Park (Dublin). A corrup-tion of the Gaelic *Fion-uisc* (fair water), so called from a spring at one time re-sorted to as a chalybeate spa.

Phœnix Period or *Cycle,* generally supposed to be 500 years; Tacitus tells us it was 250 years; R. Stuart Poole that it was 1,460 Julian years, like the Sothic Cycle; and Lipsius that it was 1,500 years. Now, the phœnix is said to have appeared in Egypt five times: (1) in the reign of Sesostris; (2) in the reign of Am-asis; (3) in the reign of Ptolemy Philadelphos; (4) a year or two prior to the death of Tiberius; and (5) in A.D. 334, during the reign of Constantine. These dates being accepted, a Phœnix Cycle consists of 300 years: thus, Sesostris, B.C. 866; Am-asis, B.C. 566; Ptolemy, B.C. 266; Tiberius, A.D. 34; Constantine, A.D. 334. In corroboration of this suggestion it must be borne in mind that Jesus Christ, who died A.D. 34, is termed *the Phœnix* by monastic writers. Tacitus mentions the first three of these appearances. (*Annales,* vi. 28.)

Phœnix Theatre. (*See* PHŒNIX ALLEY.)

Phœnix Tree. The palm. In Greek, *phoinix* means both phœnix and palm-tree.

"Now I will believe . . . that in Arabia
There is one tree, the phœnix' throne—one phœnix
At this hour reigneth there."
Shakespeare : The Tempest, iii. 3.

Phoo'ka or **Pooka.** A spirit of most malignant disposition, who hurries people to their destruction. He sometimes comes in the form of an eagle, and sometimes in that of a horse, like the Scotch kelpie (*q.v.*). (*Irish superstition.*)

Phor'cos. "The old man of the sea." He was the father of the three Graiæ, who were grey from their birth, and had but one eye and one tooth common to the three. (*Greek mythology.*)

Phor'mio. A parasite who accommodates himself to the humour of everyone. (*Terence : Phormio.*)

Phryg'ians. An early Christian sect, so called from Phrygia, where they abounded. They regarded Monta'nus as their prophet, and laid claim to the spirit of prophecy.

Phry'ne (2 syl.). A courtesan or Athenian hetæra. She acquired so much wealth by her beauty that she offered to rebuild the walls of Thebes if she might put on them this inscription : "Alexander destroyed them, but Phryne the hetæra rebuilt them." The Cnidian Venus of Praxit'elēs was taken from this courtesan. Apelles' picture of *Venus Rising from the Sea* was partly from his wife Campaspe, and partly from Phryne, who entered the sea with dishevelled hair as a model.

Phylac'tery. A charm or amulet. The Jews wore on their wrist or forehead a slip of parchment bearing a text of Scripture. Strictly speaking, a phylactery consisted of four pieces of parchment, enclosed in two black leather cases, and fastened to the forehead or wrist of the left hand. One case contained Ex. xiii. 1-10, 11-16 ; and the other case, Deut. vi. 4-9, xi. 13-21. The idea arose from the command of Moses, "Therefore shall ye lay up these my words in your heart . . . and bind them for a sign upon your hand . . . as frontlets between your eyes" (Deut. xi. 18). (Greek, *phylactērion,* from the verb *phylasso,* to watch.)

Phyl'lis. A country girl. (*Virgil : Eclogues,* iii. and v.)

" Country messes,
Which the neat-handed Phyllis dresses."
Milton : L'Allegro.

Phyllis and Brunetta. Rival beauties who for a long time vied with each other on equal terms. For a certain festival Phyllis procured some marvellous fabric of gold brocade to outshine her rival ; but Brunetta dressed the slave who bore her train in the same material, clothing herself in simple black. Upon this crushing mortification Phyllis went home and died. (*Spectator.*)

Phyl'lising the Fair. Philandering —making soft speeches and winning faces at them. Garth says of Dr. Atterbury—

" He passed his easy hours, instead of prayer,
In madrigals and phyllising the fair."
The Dispensary, i.

Phynnod'deree [*the Hairy-one*]. A Manx spirit, similar to the Scotch "brownie," and German "kobold." He is said to be an outlawed fairy, and the offence was this : He absented himself without leave from Fairy-court on the great levée-day of the Harvest-moon, being in the glen of Rushen, dancing with a pretty Manx maid whom he was courting.

Physician. *The Beloved Physician.* Lucius, supposed to be St. Luke, the evangelist (Col. iv. 14).
The Prince of Physicians. Avicenna, the Arabian (980-1037).

Physician or Fool. Plutarch, in his treatise *On the Preservation of Health,* tells us that Tiberius was wont to say, "A man of thirty is his own physician or a fool."

Physician, heal Thyself. "First cast out the beam from thine own eye, and then shalt thou see clearly to cast out the mote which is in thy brother's eye."

Physigna'thos [*one who swells the cheeks*]. King of the Frogs, and son of Pelus [mud], slain by Troxartas, the Mouse-king.

" Great Physignathos I, from Peleus' race,
Begot in fair Hydromede's embrace,
Where, by the nuptial bank that paints his side,
The swift Erid'anus delights to glide."
Parnell : Battle of the Frogs, bk. i.

Pi'arists, or *Brethren of the Pious School.* A religious congregation founded in the 16th century by Joseph of Calasanza, for the better instruction and education of the middle and higher classes.

Pic-nic. Dr. John Anthony derives it from the Italian *piccola nicchia* (a small task), each person being set a small task towards the general entertainment. (French, *pique-nique*.)

∴ The modern custom dates from 1802, but pic-nics, called *êrănoi*, where each person contributed something, and one was appointed "master of the feast," are mentioned by Homer, in his *Odyssey*, i. 226.

Pic'ador (Spanish). A horseman; one who in bull fights is armed with a gilt spear (*pica-dorada*), with which he pricks the bull to madden him for the combat.

Picards. An immoral sect of fanatics in the 15th century; so called from Picard of Flanders, their founder, who called himself the New Adam, and tried to introduce the custom of living nude, like Adam in Paradise.

You are as hot-headed as a Picard. This is a French expression, and is tantamount to our "Peppery as a Welshman."

Picaroon. A pirate; one who plunders wrecks. (French, *picoreur, picorer*, to plunder; Scotch, *pikary*, rapine; Spanish, *picaron*, a villain.)

Pic'atrix. The pseudonym of a Spanish monk, author of a book on demonology, collected from the writings of 224 Arabic magicians. It was dedicated to King Alfonso.

"At the time when I was a student in the University of Toulouse, that same reverend Picatrix, rector of the Diabolical Faculty, was wont to tell us that devils did naturally fear the bright glancing of swords, as much as the splendour and light of the sun."—*Rabelais: Pantagruel,* iii. 23.

Piccadil'ly (London). So called from Piccadilla Hall, the chief depôt of a certain sort of lace, much in vogue during the reign of Queen Elizabeth. The lace was called *piccadilly lace*, from its little spear-points (a diminutive of *pica*, a pike or spear). In the reign of James I. the high ruff was called a *piccadilly*, though divested of its lace edging. Barnaby Rice, speaking of the piccadillies, says— "He that some forty years sithen should have asked after a piccadilly, I wonder who would have understood him, and would have told him whether it was fish or flesh" (1614). Another derivation is given in the *Glossographia* (1681). Piccadilly, we are there told, was named from Higgins' famous ordinary near St. James's, called Higgins's *Picka-dilly*, "because he made his money by selling piccadillies" (p. 495). (See also *Hone: Everyday Book*, vol. ii. p. 381.)

"Where Sackville Street now stands was Piccadilla Hall, where piccadillies or turnovers were sold, which gave name to Piccadilly."—*Pennant.*

Picci'nists (1774-1780). A French musico-political faction, who contended that pure Italian music is higher art than the mixed German school. In other words, that music is the Alpha and Omega of opera, and the dramatic part is of very minor importance.

Niccolo Piccino, of Naples (1728-1801), was the rival of Christopher Glück, of Bohemia, and these two musicians gave birth to a long paper war. Those who sided with the Italian were called Piccinists, those who sided with the German were called Glückists.

Pick. To throw; same as *pitch*. The instrument that throws the shuttle is called the *picker*. (Anglo-Saxon, *pyc-an*, to throw, pull, or pick.)

"I'll pick you o'er the pales."
Shakespeare: Henry VIII., v. 3.

Pick Straws (*To*). To show fatigue or weariness, as birds pick up straws to make their nests (or bed).

"Their eyelids did not once pick straws,
And wink, and sink away;
No, no; they were as brisk as bees,
And loving things did say."
Peter Pindar: Orson and Ellen, canto v.

Pick a Hole in his Coat (*To*). To find fault with one; to fix on some small offence as censurable.

"And shall such mob as thou, not worth a groat,
Dare pick a hole in such a great man's coat?"
Peter Pindar: Epistle to John Nichols.

Pickanin'ny. A young child. A West Indian negro word. (Spanish, *pequēno*, little; *nino*, child.)

Pick'elher'ringe (5 syl.). A buffoon is so called by the Dutch.

Pickers and Stealers. The hands. In French *argot* hands are called *harpes*, which is a contracted form of *harpions*; and harpion is the Italian *arpione*, a hook used by thieves to pick linen, etc., from hedges. A *harpe d'un chien* means a dog's paw, and "*Il mania très bien ses harpes*" means he used his fingers very dexterously.

"*Rosencrantz.* My lord, you once did love me.
Hamlet. And do still, by these pickers and stealers."—*Shakespeare: Hamlet,* iii. 3.

Pickle. *A rod in pickle.* One ready to chastise with at any moment. Pickled means preserved for use. (Danish, *pekel*.)

I'm in a pretty pickle. In a sorry plight, or state of disorder.

"How cam'st thou in this pickle?"
Shakespeare: Tempest, v. 1.

Pickwick (*Mr. Samuel*). The hero of the *Pickwick Papers*, by Charles Dickens. He is a simple-minded, benevolent old gentleman, who wears spectacles, breeches, and short black gaiters, has a bald head, and "good round belly." He founds a club, and travels with its members over England, each member being under his guardianship.

Pickwickian. *In a Pickwickian sense.* An insult whitewashed. Mr. Pickwick accused Mr. Blotton of acting in " a vile and calumnious manner," whereupon Mr. Blotton retorted by calling Mr. Pickwick "a humbug." It finally was made to appear that both had used the offensive words only in a Pickwickian sense, and that each had, in fact, the highest regard and esteem for the other. So the affront was adjusted, and both were satisfied.

" Lawyers and politicians daily abuse each other in a Pickwickian sense."—*Bowditch.*

Pic'rochole, King of Lernē. A Greek compound, meaning " bitter-bile," or choleric. The rustics of Utopia one day asked the cake-bakers of Lernē to sell them some cakes, but received only abuse ; whereupon a quarrel ensued. When Picrochole was informed thereof, he marched with all his men against Utopia. King Grangousier tried to appease the choleric king, but all his efforts were in vain. At length Gargantua arrived, defeated Picrochole, and put his army to the rout. (*Rabelais : Gargantua,* bk. i.)

King Picrochole's statesman. One who without his host reckons of mighty achievements to be accomplished. The Duke of Smalltrash, Earl of Swashbuckler, and Captain Durtaille advised King Picrochole to divide his army into two parts : one was to be left to carry on the war in hand, and the other to be sent forth to make conquests. They were to take England, France and Spain, Asia Minor, the Greek Islands, and Turkey, Germany, Norway, Sweden, Russia, etc., and to divide the lands thus taken among the conquerors. Echeph'ron, an old soldier, replied—"A shoemaker bought a ha'poth of milk ; with this he was going to make butter, the butter was to buy a cow, the cow was to have a calf, the calf was to be changed for a colt, and the man was to become a nabob; only he cracked his jug, spilt his milk, and went supperless to bed." (*Rabelais : Gargantua,* bk. i. 33.)

⁕ In 1870 the French emperor (Napoleon III.) was induced to declare war against Germany. He was to make a demonstration and march in triumph to Berlin. Having taken Berlin, he was to march to Italy to restore the Pope to his dominions, and then to restore the Queen of Spain to her throne ; but he failed in the first, lost his throne, and Paris fell

into the hands of the allied Prussian army.

His uncle's " Berlin Decree," for the subjection of Great Britain, was a similar miscalculation. This decree ordained that no European state was to deal with England ; and, the trade of England being thus ruined, the kingdom must perforce submit to Napoleon. But as England was the best customer of the European states, the states of Europe were so impoverished that they revolted against the dictator, and. the battle of Waterloo was his utter downfall.

Picts. The inhabitants of Albin, north-east of Scotland. The name is usually said to be the Latin *picti* (painted [or tattooed] with woad), but in the Irish chronicles the Picts are called *Pictones, Pietores, Piccardaig,* etc.

Picts' Houses. Those underground buildings more accurately termed "earth houses," as the Pict's House at Kettleburn, in Caithness.

Picture. A model, or beau-ideal, as, *He is the picture of health ; A perfect picture of a house.* (Latin, *pictūra.*)

The Picture. Massinger has borrowed the plot of this play from Bandello of Piedmont, who wrote *novelles* or tales in the fifteenth century.

Picture Bible. (*See* BIBLIA.)

Picture Galleries.

London is famous for its Constables, Turners, Landseers, Gainsboroughs, etc.

Madrid for its Murillos, Van Dycks, Da Vincis, Rubenses, etc.

Dresden for its Raphael, Titian, and Correggio.

Amsterdam for its Dutch masters.

Rome for its Italian masters.

Pictures. (*See* CABINET, CARTOONS, etc.)

Pie. *Looking for a pie's nest* (French). Looking for something you are not likely to find. (*See below.*)

He is in the pie's nest (French). In a fix, in great doubt, in a quandary. The pie places her nest out of reach, and fortifies it with thorny sticks, leaving only a small aperture just large enough to admit her body. She generally sits with her head towards the hole, watching against intruders.

" Je m'en vay chercher un grand peut-estre. Il est au nid de la pie."—*Rabelais.*

Pie Corner (London). So named from an eating-house—the [*Mag*]*pie.*

Pie Poudre. A court formerly held at a fair on St. Giles's Hill, near Winchester. It was originally authorised by the Bishop of Winton from a grant of Edward IV. Similar courts were held elsewhere at wakes and fairs for the rough-and-ready treatment of pedlars and hawkers, to compel them and those with whom they dealt to fulfil their contracts. (French, *pied poudreux*, dusty foot. A vagabond is called in French *pied poudreux*.)

" Have its proceedings disallowed or
Allowed, at fancy of pie-powder."
Butler: Hudibras, pt. ii. 2.

Piebald. Party-coloured. A corruption of *pie-bailed,* speckled like a pie. The words Ball, Dun, and Favel are frequently given as names to cows. "Ball" means the cow with a mark on its face; "Dun" means the cow of a dun or brownish-yellow colour; and "Favel" means the bay cow. (*Ball,* in Gaelic, means a mark; *ballach,* speckled.)

Pied de la Lettre (*Au*). Quite literally.

" Of course, you will not take everything I have said quite *au pied de la lettre.*"—*Fra. Ollæ: A Philosophical Trilogy.*

Pied Piper of Ham'elin. The Pied Piper was promised a reward if he would drive the rats and mice out of Hameln (Westphalia). This he did, for he gathered them together by his pipe, and then drowned them in the Weser. As the people refused to pay him, he next led the children to Koppelberg Hill, where 130 of them perished (July 22nd, 1376). (*See* HATTO.)

" To blow the pipe his lips he wrinkled,
And green and blue his sharp eyes twinkled ...
And ere three notes his pipe had uttered ...
Out of the houses rats came tumbling—
Great rats, small rats, lean rats, brawny rats,
Brown rats, black rats, grey rats, tawny rats,
And step by step they followed him dancing,
Till they came to the river Weser."
Robert Browning.

⁑ Hameln, on the river Hamel, is where the Rattenfänger played this prank. It is said that the children did not perish in the mountain, but were led over it to Transylvania, where they formed a German colony.

Pierre. A conspirator in Otway's *Venice Preserved.* He is described as a patriot of the bluntest manners, and a stoical heart.

Uglier than Pierre du Coignet (French). Coignères was an advocate-general in the reign of Philippe de Valois, who stoutly opposed the encroachments of the Church. The monks, in revenge, called, by way of pun, those grotesque monkey-like figures carved in stone, used in church architecture, *pierres du Coignet* or *pierres du Coignères.* At Notre Dame de Paris they used to extinguish their torches in the mouths and nostrils of these figures, which thus acquired a superadded ugliness. (See *Recherches de Pasquier,* iii. chap. xxvii.)

" You may associate them with Master Peter du Coignet ... in the middle of the porch ... to perform the office of extinguishers, and with their noses put out the lighted candles, torches, tapers, and flambeaux."—*Rabelais.*

Pierrot [*pe'er-ro'*]. A character in French pantomime representing a man in growth and a child in mind and manners. He is generally the tallest and thinnest man that can be got, has his face and hair covered with white powder or flour, and wears a white gown with very long sleeves, and a row of big buttons down the front. The word means Little Peter.

Piers. The shepherd who relates the fable of the *Kid and her Dam,* to show the danger of bad company. (*Spenser: Shepherd's Calendar.*)

Piers Plowman. The hero of a satirical poem of the fourteenth century. He falls asleep, like John Bunyan, on the Malvern Hills, and has different visions, which he describes, and in which he exposes the corruptions of society, the dissoluteness of the clergy, and the allurements to sin, with considerable bitterness. The author is supposed to be Robert or William Langland.

Pieta'. A representation of the Virgin Mary embracing the dead body of her Son. Filial or parental love was called *piety* by the Romans. (*See* PIOUS.)

Pi'etists. A sect of Lutherans in the seventeenth century, who sought to introduce a more moral life and a more "evangelical" spirit of doctrine into the reformed church. In Germany the word *Pietist* is about equal to our vulgar use of Methodist.

Pie'tro (2 syl.). The putative father of Pompil'ia, criminally assumed as his child to prevent certain property from passing to an heir not his own. (*Robert Browning: The Ring and the Book,* ii. 580.) (*See* RING.)

Pig (*The*) was held sacred by the ancient Cretans, because Jupiter was suckled by a sow; it was immolated in the mysteries of Eleusis; was sacrificed to Hercules, to Venus, the Lares (2 syl.), and all those who sought relief from bodily ailments. The sow was sacrificed to Ceres (2 syl.), "because it taught men to turn up the earth ; " and in Egypt it was slain on grand weddings on account of its fecundity.

Pig. In the forefeet of pigs is a very small hole, which may be seen when the hair has been carefully removed. The tradition is that the legion of devils entered by these apertures. There are also round it some six rings, the whole together not larger than a small spangle ; they look as if burnt or branded into the skin, and the tradition is that they are the marks of the devil's claws when he entered the swine (Mark v. 11-15). (*See* CHRISTIAN TRADITIONS.)

Riding on a pig. It was Jane, afterwards Duchess of Gordon, who, in 1770, undertook for a wager to ride down the High Street of Edinburgh, in broad daylight, on the back of a pig, and she won her bet.

Some men there are love not a gaping pig (*Merchant of Venice*, iv. 1). Marshal d'Albert always fainted at the sight of a roast sucking pig. (*See* ANTIPATHY, CAT.)

The same is said of Vaugheim, the renowned Hanoverian huntsman. Keller used to faint at the sight of smoked bacon.

Pig-back, Picka-back, or *a-Piggerback*, does not mean as a pig is carried by a butcher, but as a *piga* or *child* is carried. It should be written *apiggaback.* A butcher carries a pig *head downwards*, with its legs over his shoulders ; but a child is carried with its arms round your neck, and legs under your arms.

"She carries the other a pickapack upon her shoulders."—*L'Estrange.*

Pig-eyes. Very small black eyes, like those of a pig. Southey says, " Those eyes have taught the lover flattery." The ace of diamonds is called " a pig's eye."

Pig Hunt (*A*). A village sport, in which a certain number of persons blindfolded hunt a small pig confined by hurdles within a limited space. The winner, having caught the pig, tucks it under his arm, and keeps it as his prize.

Pig-iron. This is a mere play upon the word sow. When iron is melted it runs off into a channel called a sow, the lat'eral branches of which are called the pigs ; here the iron cools, and is called pig-iron.

Pig and Tinderbox. The Elephant and Castle.

Pig and Whistle. The bowl and

wassail, or the wassail-cup and wassail. A *piggen* is a pail, especially a milk-pail ; and a *pig* is a small bowl, cup, or mug, making " milk and wassail ; " similar to the modern sign of *Jug and Glass*— *i.e.* beer and wine. Thus a crockery-dealer is called a *pig-wife.*

Pig in a Poke (*A*). A blind bargain. The French say *Acheter chat en poche.* The reference is to a common trick in days gone by of substituting a cat for a sucking-pig, and trying to palm it off on greenhorns. If anyone heedlessly bought the article without examination he bought a " cat " for a " pig ; " but if he opened the sack he " let the cat out of the bag," and the trick was disclosed. The French *chat en poche* refers to the fact, while our proverb regards the trick. Pocket is diminutive of poke.

Pigs. (*See* BARTHOLOMEW PIGS.)

He has brought his pigs to a pretty market. He has made a very bad bargain ; he has managed his business in a very bad way. Pigs were the chief articles of sale with our Saxon herdsmen, and till recently the village cottager looked to pay his rent by the sale of his pigs.

He follows me about like an Anthony pig, or such and such a one is a *Tantony pig ;* meaning a beggar, a hanger-on. Stow says that the officers of the market used to slit the ears of pigs unfit for food. One day one of the proctors of St. Anthony's Hospital tied a bell about a pig whose ear was slit, and no one would ever hurt it. The pig would follow like a dog anyone who fed it.

Please the pigs. If the Virgin permits. (Saxon, *piga*, a virgin.) In the Danish New Testament "maiden" is generally rendered *pigen.* " Pig Cross," dedicated to the Virgin Mary, is *Virgin Cross*, or the *Lady Cross.* So also " Pig's Hill," " Pig's Ditch," in some instances at least, are the field and diggin' attached to the Lady's Chapel, though in others they are simply the hill and ditch where pigs were offered for sale. Another etymology is *Please the pixies* (fairies), a saying still common in Devonshire.

It is somewhat remarkable that *pige* should be Norse for maiden, and *hog* or *og* Gaelic for young generally. Thus *ogan* (a young man), and *goie* (a young woman).

Pigskin (*A*). A gentleman's saddle, made of pigskin. " To throw a leg across a pigskin " is to mount a horse.

Pigtails (*The*). The Chinese; so called because the Tartar tonsure and braided queue are very general.

"We laid away telling one another of the pigtails till we both dropped off to sleep."—*Tales about the Chinese.*

Pigeon (*To*). To cheat, to gull one of his money by almost self-evident hoaxes. Pigeons are very easily gulled, caught by snares, or scared by malkins. One easily gulled is called a *pigeon*. The French *pigeon* means a dupe.

"Je me deffieroy tantost que tu serois un de ceux qui ne se laissent si facilement pigeonner à telles gens."—*Les Dialogues de Jacques Tahureau,* (1585).

Flying the pigeons. Stealing coals from a cart or sack between the coal-dealer's yard and the house of the customer.

Flying the blue pigeon. Stealing the lead from off the roofs of churches or buildings of any kind.

To pigeon a person is to cheat him clandestinely. A gullible person is called a pigeon, and in the sporting world sharps and flats are called "rooks and pigeons." The brigands of Spain used to be called *palomos* (pigeons); and in French argot a dupe is called *pechon*, or *peschon de ruby ;* where *pechon* or *peschon* is the Italian *piccione* (a pigeon), and *de ruby* is a pun on *dérobé*, bamboozled.

To pluck a pigeon. To cheat a gullible person of his money. To fleece a green-horn. (*See* GREENHORN.)

" 'Here comes a nice pigeon to pluck.' said one of the thieves."—*C. Reade.*

Pigeon, Pigeons. Pitt says in Mecca no one will kill the blue pigeons, because they are held sacred.

The black pigeons of Dodo'na. Two black pigeons, we are told, took their flight from Thebes, in Egypt; one flew to Libya, and the other to Dodo'na, in Greece. On the spot where the former alighted, the temple of Jupiter Ammon was erected ; in the place where the other settled, the oracle of Jupiter was established, and there the responses were made by the black pigeons that inhabited the surrounding groves. This fable is probably based on a pun upon the word *peleiai*, which usually means "old women," but in the dialect of the Epi'rots signifies pigeons or doves.

Mahomet's pigeon. (*See* MAHOMET.)

In Russia pigeons are not served for human food, because the Holy Ghost assumed the likeness of a dove at the baptism of Jesus; and part of the marriage service consists in letting loose two pigeons. (See *The Sporting Magazine,* January, 1825, p. 307.)

Pigeon lays only two eggs. Hence the Queen says of Hamlet, after his fit he will be—

" As patient as the female dove
When that her golden couplets are disclosed [*i.e* hatched]." *Hamlet,* v. 1.

He who is sprinkled with pigeon's blood will never die a natural death. A sculptor carrying home a bust of Charles I. stopped to rest on the way; at the moment a pigeon overhead was struck by a hawk, and the blood of the bird fell on the neck of the bust. The sculptor thought it ominous, and after the king was beheaded the saying became current.

Flocks of wild pigeons presage the pestilence, at least in Louisia'na. Longfellow says they come with "naught in their craws but an acorn." (*Evangeline.*)

Pigeon-English or **Pigeon-talk.** A corruption of *business-talk.* Thus : business, bidginess, bidgin, pidgin, pigeon. A mixture of English, Portuguese, and Chinese, used in business transactions in "The Flowery Empire."

" The traders care nothing for the Chinese language, and are content to carry on their business transactions in a hideous jargon called " pigeon English."—*The Times.*

Pigeon-hole (*A*). A small compartment for filing papers. In pigeon-lockers a small hole is left for the pigeons to walk in and out.

Pigeon-livered. Timid, easily frightened, like a pigeon. The bile rules the temper, and the liver the bile.

Pigeon Pair. A boy and girl, twins. It was once supposed that pigeons always sit on two eggs which produce a male and a female, and these twin birds live together in love the rest of their lives.

Pigg. (*See under the word* BREWER.)

Piggy-wiggy or **Piggy-whidden.** A word of endearment ; a pet pig, which, being the smallest of the litter, is called by the diminutive *Piggy*, the *wiggy* being merely alliterative.

Pightel or **Pigh'tle.** A small parcel of land enclosed with a hedge. In the eastern counties called a *pi'kle.*

" Never had that novelty in manure wr itened the . . . pightels of Court Farm."—*Miss Mitford: Our Village,* p. 68.

Pigmy. A dwarf. In fabulous history the pigmies were a nation of dwarfs devoured by cranes. (*See* PYGMIES.)

Pigsney or **Pigsnie.** A word of

endearment to a girl. (Diminutive of the Anglo-Saxon *piga*, a little girl.)

Pigwiggin. An elf in love with Queen Mab. He combats the jealous O'beron with great fury. (*Drayton: Nymphidia.*)

Pike's Head (*A*). A pike's head has all the parts of the crucifixion of Christ. There are the cross, three nails, and a sword distinctly recognisable. The German tradition is that when Christ was crucified all fishes dived under the waters in terror, except the pike, which, out of curiosity, lifted up its head and beheld the whole scene. (*See* PASSION FLOWER.)

Pikestaff. *Plain as a pikestaff.* Quite obvious and unmistakable. The pikestaff was the staff carried by pilgrims, which plainly and somewhat ostentatiously announced their "devotion." It has been suggested that "pikestaff" is a corruption of "packstaff," meaning the staff on which a pedlar carries his pack, but there is no need for the change.

Pilate Voice. A loud ranting voice. In the old mysteries all tyrants were made to speak in a rough ranting manner. Thus Bottom the Weaver, after a rant "to show his quality," exclaims, "That's 'Ercles' vein, a tyrant's vein;" and Hamlet describes a ranting actor as "out-heroding Herod."

"In Pilate voys he gan to cry,
And swor by armés, and by blood and bones."
  Chaucer: Canterbury Tales, 3126.

Pilate's Wife, who warned Pilate to have nothing to do with Jesus, is called Procla. (*E. Johnson: The Rise of Christendom*, p. 416.) Others call her Justitia, evidently an assumed name.

Pila'tus (*Mount*) in Switzerland. The similarity of the word with the name of Pontius Pilate has given rise to the tradition that the Roman Governor, being banished to Gaul by Tiberius, wandered to this mount and threw himself into a black lake on its summit. But Mont Pileatus means the "hatted mountain," because it is frequently capped with clouds.

※ The story goes, that once a year Pilate appears in his robes of office, and whoever sees the ghost will die before the year is out. In the sixteenth century a law was passed forbidding anyone to throw stones in the lake, for fear of bringing a tempest on the country.

There is a town called Pilate in the island of Hispaniola, and a Mont Pilate in France.

Pilch. The flannel napkin of an infant; a buff or leather jerkin. (Anglo-Saxon *pylce*, a pilch.)

Pilcher. A scabbard. (Anglo-Saxon, *pylce;* Latin, *pellis*, skin.)

"Will you pluck your sword out of his pilcher?"
  —*Shakespeare: Romeo and Juliet*, iii. 1.

Pilgarlic or **Pill'd Garlic** (*A*). One whose hair has fallen off from dissipation. Stow sáys of one getting bald: "He will soon be a peeled garlic like myself." Generally a poor wretch avoided and forsaken by his fellows. The editor of *Notes and Queries* says that garlic was a prime specific for leprosy, so that garlic and leprosy became inseparably associated. As lepers had to pill their own garlic, they were nicknamed *Pil-garlics*, and anyone shunned like a leper was so called likewise. (To pill = to peel; *see* Gen. xxx. 37.)

※ It must be borne in mind that at one time garlic was much more commonly used in England than it is now.

"After this [feast] we jogged off to bed for the night; but never a bit could poor pilgarlic s.eep one wink, for the everlasting jingle of bells."—*Rabelais: Pantagruel*, v. 7.

Pilgrim Fathers (*The*). The 102 English, Scotch, and Dutch Puritans who, in December, 1620, went to North America in the ship called the *Mayflower*, and colonised Maine, New Hampshire, Vermont, Massachusetts, and Connecticut.

Pil'grimage (3 syl.). The chief places in the West were (1) Walsingham and Canterbury (England); (2) Fourvières, Puy, and St. Denis (France); (3) Rome, Loretto, Genetsano, and Assisi (Italy); (4) Compostella, Guadalupe, and Montserrat (Spain); (5) Oetting, Zell, Cologne, Trier, and Einsiedeln (Germany). Chaucer has an admirable account, chiefly in verse, of a pilgrimage to Becket's tomb in Canterbury Cathedral. The pilgrims beguile the weariness of the way by telling tales. These *Canterbury Tales* were never completed.

Pillar Saints or *Styli'tēs*. A class of ascetics, chiefly of Syria, who took up their abode on the top of a pillar, from which they never descended. (*See* STYLITES.)

Pillar to Post. *Running from pillar to post*—from one thing to another without any definite purpose. This is an allusion to the *manége*. The pillar is the centre of the riding ground, and the posts are the columns at equal distances, placed two and two round the circumference of the ring.

Pillars of Heaven (*The*). The Atlas Mountains are so called by the natives.

Pillars of Hercules (*The*). The opposite rocks at the entrance of the Mediterranean Sea, one in Spain and the other on the African continent. The tale is that they were bound together till Hercules tore them asunder in order to get to Gadēs (Cadiz). The ancients called them Calpē and Ab′yla; we call them Gibraltar Rock and Mount Hacho, on which stands the fortress of Ceu′ta (Ku′tah).

Pil′lory. The following eminent men have been put in the pillory for literary offences:—Leighton, for tracts against Charles I.; Lilburn, for circulating the tracts of Dr. Bastwick; Bastwick, for attacking the Church of England; Warton the publisher; Prynne, for a satire on the wife of Charles I.; Daniel Defoe, for a pamphlet entitled *The Shortest Way with Dissenters*, etc.

Pilot, according to Scaliger, is from an old French word, *pile* (a ship).

Pilot Balloon (*A*). A political feeler; a hint thrown out to ascertain public opinion on some moot point.

"As this gentleman is in the confidence of ministers, it is fair to assume that he was deputed to start this statement as a pilot balloon."—*News-paper leader*, 1885.

Pilot Fish. So called because it is supposed to pilot the shark to its prey.

Pilot that weathered the Storm (*The*). William Pitt, son of the first Earl of Chatham. George Canning, in 1802, wrote a song so called in compliment to William Pitt, who steered us safely through the European storm stirred up by Napoleon.

Pilpay′ or *Bidpay*. The Indian Æsop. His compilation was in Sanskrit, and entitled *Pantcha-Tantra*. Khosru (Chosroes) the Great, of Persia, ordered them to be translated into Pehlvi, an idiom of Medish, at that time the language of Persia. This was in the middle of the sixth century.

Pim′lico (London). At one time a district of public gardens much frequented on holidays. According to tradition, it received its name from Ben Pimlico, famous for his nut-brown ale. His tea-gardens, however, were near Hoxton, and the road to them was termed Pimlico Path, so that what is

now called Pimlico was so named from the popularity of the Hoxton resort.

"Have at thee, then, my merrie boyes, and beg for old Ben Pimlico's nut-brown ale."—*Newes from Hogsdon* (1598).

Pimlico. *To walk in Pimlico.* To promenade, handsomely dressed, along Pimlico Path.

"Not far from this place were the Asparagus Gardens and Pimlico Path, where were fine walks, cool arbours, etc., much used by the citizens of London and their families."—*Nat. Hist. Surrey*, v. 221.

Pin (*A*). A cask holding 4½ gallons of ale or beer. This is the smallest of the casks. Two pins = a firkin or 9 gallons, and 2 firkins = a kilderkin or 18 gallons.

Pin. *Not worth a pin.* Wholly worthless.

I don't care a pin, or *a pin's point*. In the least.

The pin. The centre; as, "the pin of the heart" (*Shakespeare: Romeo and Juliet*, ii. 4). The allusion is to the pin which fastened the clout or white mark on a target in archery.

Weak on his pins. Weak in his legs, the legs being a man's pegs or supporters.

A merry pin. A roysterer.

We are told that St. Dunstan introduced the plan of pegging tankards, to check the intemperate habits of the English in his time. Called "pin-tankards."

In merry pin. In merry mood, in good spirits. Pegge, in his *Anonymiana*, says that the old tankards were divided into eight equal parts, and each part was marked with a silver pin. The cups held two quarts, consequently the quantity from pin to pin was half a Winchester pint. By the rules of "good fellowship" a drinker was supposed to stop drinking *only at a pin*, and if he drank beyond it, was to drink to the next one. As it was very hard to stop exactly at the pin, the vain efforts gave rise to much mirth, and the drinker had generally to drain the tankard. (*See* PEG.)

"No song, no laugh, no jovial din
Of drinking wassail to the pin."
    Longfellow: Golden Legend.

I do not pin my faith upon your sleeve. I am not going to take your *ipse dixit* for gospel. In feudal times badges were worn, and the partisans of a leader used to wear his badge, which was pinned on the sleeve. Sometimes these badges were changed for specific purposes, and persons learned to doubt. Hence the phrase, "You wear the badge, but I do not intend to pin my faith on your sleeve."

He tirled at the pin. Rattled at the latch to give notice that he was about to enter. The pin was not only the latch of chamber-doors and cottages, but the "rasp" of castles used instead of the modern knocker. It was attached to a ring, which produced a grating sound to give notice to the warder.

> " Sae licht he jumped up the stair,
> And tirled at the pin ;
> And wha sae ready as hersel'
> To let the laddie in."
> *Charlie is my Darling.*

Pin Money. A lady's allowance of money for her own personal expenditure. Long after the invention of pins, in the fourteenth century, the maker was allowed to sell them in open shop only on January 1st and 2nd. It was then that the court ladies and city dames flocked to the depôts to buy them, having been first provided with money by their husbands. When pins became cheap and common, the ladies spent their allowances on other fancies, but the term pin money remained in vogue.

It is quite an error to suppose that pins were invented in the reign of François I., and introduced into England by Catherine Howard, the fifth wife of Henry VIII. In 1347 just 200 years before the death of François, 12,000 pins were delivered from the royal wardrobe for the use of the Princess Joan. So that pins were not only manufactured in England, but were of *high repute* even in the reign of Henry IV. (1399-1413).

Policy of Pin Pricks. A policy of petty annoyances. The term came into prominence during the strained relations between England and France in 1898, and probably took its rise from a passage in the Paris *Matin* of November 8th, 1898.

Pinabel'lo or **Pin'abel** (in *Orlando Furioso*). Son of Anselmo, King of Maganza. Marphi'sa, having overthrown him, and taken the steed of his dame, Pinabello, at her instigation, decreed that nothing would wipe out the disgrace except a thousand dames and a thousand warriors unhorsed, and spoiled of their arms, steed, and vest. He was slain by Brad'amant.

Pinch'beck. So called from Christopher Pinchbeck, a musical-clock maker, of Fleet Street. (Died 1732.) The word is used for Brummagem gold ; and the metal is a compound of copper, zinc, and tin.

> "Where, in these pinchbeck days, can we hope to find the old agricultural virtue in all its purity ? "—*Anthony Trollope: Framley Parsonage.*

Pindar. *The French Pindar.* Jean Dorat (1507-1588). Also Ponce Denis Lebrun (1729-1807).

The Italian Pindar. Gabriello Chiabrera ; whence *Chiabreresco* is in Italian tantamount to " Pindaric. " (1552-1637.)

Peter Pindar. Dr. John Wolcott (1738-1812).

Pindar of England. George, Duke of Buckingham, most extravagantly declared Cowley to be the Pindar, Horace, and Virgil of England.

In Westminster Abbey, the last line of Gray's tablet claims the honour of British Pindar for the author of *The Bard.*

> " She [Britain] felt a Homer's fire in Milton's strains,
> A Pindar's rapture in the lyre of Gray."

Pindar and the Bees. (*See* PLATO.)

Pindar of Wakefield (*George-a-Green*) has given his name to a celebrated house on the west side of the Gray's Inn Road ; and a house with that name still exists in St. Chad's Row, on the other side of the street. (*The Times.*) (*See* PINDER.)

Pinda'ric Verse. Irregular verse ; a poem of various metres, but of lofty style, in imitation of the odes of Pindar. *Alexander's Feast,* by Dryden, is the best specimen in English.

Pinder. One who impounds cattle, or takes care of the cattle impounded ; thus George-a-Green was the " Pinder of Wakefield," and his encounter with Robin Hood, Scarlet, and Little John forms the subject of one of the Robin Hood ballads. (Anglo-Saxon *pund,* a fold.)

Pindo'rus (in *Jerusalem Delivered*). One of the two heralds ; the other is Arideus.

Pine-bender (*The*). Sinis, the Corinthian robber ; so called because he used to fasten his victims to two pine-trees bent towards the earth, and then leave them to be rent asunder by the rebound.

Pink (*A*). The flower is so called because the edges of the petals are pinked or notched. (*See below.*)

Pink of Perfection (*The*). The acmē ; the beau-ideal. Shakespeare has "the pink of courtsey" (*Romeo and Juliet,* ii. 4) ; the pink of politeness. (Welsh, *pwnc,* a point, an acmē ; our *pink,* to stab ; *pinking,* cutting into points.)

Pi'ony or **Peony.** A flower; so called from the chieftain Paion, who discovered it. (*Saxon Leechdoms*, i.)

Piou-piou. An infantry soldier. This is probably a corruption of *pion*, a pawn or foot-soldier. Cotgrave, however, thinks the French foot-soldiers are so called from their habit of pilfering chickens, whose cry is *piou piou*.

Pi'ous (2 syl.). The Romans called a man who revered his father *pius;* hence Antoni'nus was called *pius*, because he requested that his adopted father (Hadrian) might be ranked among the gods. Æne'as was called *pius* because he rescued his father from the burning city of Troy. The Italian word *pietà* (*q.v.*) has a similar meaning.

The Pious. Ernst I., founder of the House of Gotha. (1601-1674.)

Robert, son of Hugues Capet. (971, 996-1031.)

Eric IX. of Sweden. (*, 1155-1161.)

Pip. The hero of Dickens's *Great Expectations.* He is first a poor boy, and then a man of wealth.

Pipe. Anglo-Saxon *pip*, a pipe or flute.

Put that into your pipe and smoke it. Digest that, if you can. An expression used by one who has given an adversary a severe rebuke. The allusion is to the pipes of peace and war smoked by the American Indians.

Put your pipe out. Spoil your piping or singing; make you sing another tune, or in another key. "Take your shine out" has a similar force.

As you pipe, I must dance. I must accommodate myself to your wishes.

To pipe your eye. To snivel; to cry.

Pipe Rolls or *Great Rolls of the Pipe.* The series of Great Rolls of the Exchequer, beginning 2 Henry II., and continued to 1834, when the Pipe Office was abolished. These rolls are now in the Public Record Office, Chancery Lane.

"Take, for instance the Pipe Rolls, that magnificent series of documents on which, from the middle of the 12th century until well on in the 19th, we have a perfect account of the Crown revenue, rendered by the sheriffs of the different counties."—*Notes and Queries*, June 3, 1893, p. 421.

Office of the Clerk of the Pipe. A very ancient office in the Court of Exchequer, where leases of Crown lands, sheriffs' accounts, etc., were made out. It existed in the reign of Henry II., and was abolished in the reign of William IV. Lord Bacon says, "The office is so called because the whole receipt of the court is finally conveyed into it by means of divers small pipes or quills, as water into a cistern.

Pipe of Peace. The North American Indians present a pipe to anyone they wish to be on good terms with. To receive the pipe and smoke together is to promote friendship and goodwill, but to refuse the offer is virtually a declaration of hostility.

Pipeclay. Routine; fossilised military dogmas of no real worth. In government offices the term *red-tape* is used to express the same idea. Pipeclay was at one time largely used by soldiers for making their gloves, accoutrements, and clothes look clean and smart.

Pipelet. A *concierge* or French door-porter; so called from a character in Eugène Sue's *Mysteries of Paris.*

Piper. *The Pied Piper.* (*See* PIED.)

Who's to pay the piper? (*See* PAY.)

Tom Piper. So the piper is called in the morris dance.

⁂ There is apparently another Tom Piper, referred to by Drayton and others, of whom nothing is now known. He seems to have been a sort of Mother Goose, or *raconteur* of short tales.

"Tom Piper is gone out, and mirth bewailes,
He never will come in to tell us tales."

Piper that Played before Moses (*By the*). *Per tibicinem qui coram Mose modulatus est.* This oath is from *Tales in Blackwood* [*Magazine*, May, 1838]: *Father Tom and the Pope* (name of the tale). (*Notes and Queries*, April 2, 1887, p. 276.)

Piper's News or *Hawker's News, Fiddler's News.* News known to all the world. "*Le secret de polichinelle.*"

Piping Hot. Hot as water which pipes or sings.

Pippa Passes. A little leaven leaveneth the whole lump. Some casual influence has dropped good seed, which has taken root and beareth fruit to perfection. The words are the title of a dramatic poem by Robert Browning. Pippa is a chaste-minded, light-hearted peasant maiden, who resolves to enjoy New Year's Day, her only holiday. Various groups of persons overhear her as she passes-by singing her innocent ditties, and some of her stray words, falling into their hearts, act with secret but sure influence for good. (1842.)

Piræus. Now called the port Leo'në.

Pirie's Chair. "The lowest seat o' hell." "If you do not mend your ways, you will be sent to Pirie's chair, the lowest seat of hell."

" In Pirie's chair you'll sit, I say,
    The lowest seat o' hell ;
If ye do not amend your ways,
    It's there that ye must dwell."
        Child's English and Scottish Ballads:
            The Courteous Knight.

⁂ Pirie or pyrrie means a sudden storm at sea (Scotch *pirr*). "They were driven back by storme of winde and pyrries of the sea." (*North : Plutarch*, p. 355.)

Pirith'oös. King of the Lapithæ, proverbial for his love of Theseus (2 syl.), King of Athens.

Pis-aller (French). As a shift ; for want of a better ; a *dernier ressort ;* better than nothing.

"She contented herself with a *pis-aller*, and gave her hand . . . in six months to the son of the baronet's steward."—*Sir W. Scott: Waverley,* chap. v.

Pisa'nio. A servant noted for his attachment to Im'ogen. (*Shakespeare : Cymbeline.*)

Piso's Justice. *That is Piso's justice.* Verbally right, but morally wrong. Seneca tells us that Piso condemned a man on circumstantial evidence for murder ; but when the suspect was at the place of execution, the man supposed to have been murdered exclaimed, "Hold, hold ! I am the man supposed to have been killed." The centurion sent back the prisoner to Piso, and explained the case to him ; whereupon Piso condemned all three to death, saying, "*Fiat justitia.*" The man condemned is to be executed because sentence of death has been passed upon him, and *fiat justitia ;* the centurion is to be executed because he has disobeyed orders, and *fiat justitia ;* the man supposed to have been murdered is to be executed because he has been the cause of death to two innocent men, and *fiat justitia etsi cœlum ruat.*

Pistol. Falstaff's lieutenant or ancient ; a bully, but a coward, a rogue, and always poor. (*Shakespeare : 1 and 2 Henry IV. ; Merry Wives of Windsor.*)

Pis'tols. So called from Pistoja, in Tuscany, where they were invented in 1545. (Latin, *pistorium.*)
To discharge one's pistol in the air. To fight a man of straw ; to fight harmlessly in order to make up a foolish quarrel.

"Dr. Réville has discharged his pistol in the air [that is, he pretends to fight against me, but discharges his shot against objections which I never made]."—*W. E. Gladstone: Nineteenth Century,* November, 1885.

Pistris, Pistrix, Pristis, or **Pristrix.** The sea-monster sent to devour Androm'eda. In ancient art it is represented with a dragon's head, the neck and head of a beast, fins for the forelegs, and the body and tail of a fish. In Christian art the pistris was usually employed to represent the whale which swallowed Jonah. (*Aratus : Commentaries.*) Aratus died A.D. 213.

Pit-a-pat. *My heart goes pit-a-pat.* Throbs, palpitates. "Pat" is a gentle blow (Welsh, *ffat*), and "pit" is a mere ricochet expletive. We have a vast number of such ricochet words, as "fiddle - faddle," "harum - scarum," "ding-dong," etc.

" Anything like the sound of a rat
    Makes my heart go pit-a-pat."
        Browning : Pied Piper of Hamelin.

Pitch. *Touch pitch, and you will be defiled.* "The finger that touches rouge will be red." "Evil communications corrupt good manners." "A rotten apple injures its companions."

Pitch and Pay. Pitch down your money and pay at once. There is a suppressed pun in the phrase : "to pay a ship " is to pitch it.

" The word is pitch and pay—trust none."
        Shakespeare : Henry V., ii. 3.

Pitch into Him. Thrust or dart your fists into him.

Pitcher. *The pitcher went once too often to the well.* The dodge was tried once too often, and utterly failed. The same sentiment is proverbial in most European languages.

Pitch'ers. *Little pitchers have long ears.* Little folk or children hear what is said when you little think it. The ear of a pitcher is the handle, made in the shape of a man's ear. The handle of a cream-ewer and of other small jugs is quite out of proportion to the size of the vessel, compared with the handles of large jars.

Pithos. A large jar to keep wine or oil in. Winckelmann has engraved a copy of a curious bas-relief representing Diogēnēs occupying a pithos and holding conversation with Alexander the Great. (Greek *pithos*, a large wine jar.)

Pi'tri (plur. PITARAS). An order of divine beings in Hindu mythology inhabiting celestial regions of their own, and receiving into their society the spirits of those mortals whose funeral rites have been duly performed.

Pitt Diamond or *The Regent*. Called *Pitt* diamond because it once belonged to Mr. Pitt, grandfather of the famous Earl of Chatham. Called the *Regent* diamond from the Duke of Orleans, Regent of France, who purchased it. This famous diamond was worn in the sword-hilt of Napoleon, and now belongs to the King of Prussia.

Pitt's Mark. The printer's name and place of business affixed to printed books, according to William Pitt's Act, 39 Geo. III., c. 79.

Pitt's Pictures or *Billy Pitt's Pictures*. Blind windows; so called because many windows were blocked up when William Pitt augmented the Window Tax in 1784, and again in 1797.

Pit'tacus (Greek, *Pittakos*). One of the "Seven Sages" of Greece. His great sayings were: (1) "Know the right time" ("*Gno'thi kairon*"), and (2) "'Tis a sore thing to be eminent" ("*Chalepon esthlon emmenai*").

Pit'tance. An allowance of victuals over and above bread and wine. Anthony du Pinet, in his translation of Pliny, applies the term over and over again to figs and beans. The word originally comes from the people's piety in giving to poor mendicants food for their subsistence. (Probably connected with *pietas*. Monkish Latin, *pietancia*; Spanish, *pitar*, to distribute a dole of food; *pitancero*, one who distributes the dole, or a begging friar who subsists by charity.)

Pix'ies (2 syl.). The Devonshire Robin Goodfellows; said to be the spirits of infants who have died before baptism. The Pixy monarch holds his court like Titania, and sends his subjects on their several tasks. The word is a diminutive of Pix, probably the same as Puck. (Swedish, *pyke;* old English, *pouk, bug, bogie;* Danish, *pog* and *pokker*.)

"Ne let the pouke nor other evil sprites . . .
Fray us with things that be not."
Spenser: Epithalamion.

Pixy-led (Devonshire), **Poake-ledden** (Worcestershire). Misled into bogs and ditches.

Place aux Dames. Make way for the ladies; give place to the ladies; the ladies first, if you please. Indirectly it means women beat the men hollow in every contest.

Place'bo. One of the brothers of January, an old baron of Lombardy. When January held a family council to know whether he should marry, Placebo very wisely told him to do as he liked, for says he—

"A ful gret fool is eny counselour,'
That servith any lord of high honour,'
That dar presume, or oönës [once] thenken it,
That his counseil' schuld pass his lordës wit."
Chaucer: The Marchaundes Tale, line 9,121, etc.

To sing Placebo. To seek to please; to trim in order not to offend. The word Placebo is often used to denote vespers for the dead, from the fact that it is the first word of the first Antiphon of that Office.

Pla'giarist means strictly one who kidnaps a slave. Martial applies the word to the kidnappers of other men's brains. Literary theft unacknowledged is called *plagiarism*. (Latin, *plagia'rius*.)

Plain (*The*). The Girondists were so called in the National Convention, because they sat on the level floor or plain of the hall. After the overthrow of the Girondists this part of the House was called the marsh or swamp (*marais*), and included such members as were under the control of the Mountain (*q.v.*).

Plain Dealer (*The*). Wycherly was so called, from his celebrated comedy of the same title. (1640-1715.)

"The Countess of Drogheda inquired for the *Plain Dealer*. 'Madame,' says Mr. Fairbeard, 'since you are for the "Plain Dealer," there he is for you,' pushing Mr. Wycherly towards her."—*Cibber: Lives of the Poets*, p. 252.

Plan of Campaign (*The*). Often cited shortly as "The Plan," promulgated by John Dillon in October, 1886. It provided that Irish tenants on an estate should band together, and determine what abatement of rent they considered to be called for. If the landlord accepted the abatement, well and good; if not, the tenants were to pay into a campaign fund the amount offered to the landlord, and the money thus funded should be used in fighting the landlord if he went to law to recover his rents.

"The Plan of Campaign proposed to reduce rents by an average of some 30 per cent."—*Nineteenth Century*, April, 1894, p. 566.

.˙. In 1885 the Land Commission reduced all the rents from 10 to 14 per cent.; so that 30 per cent. more would equal from 40 to 45 per cent.

Planets.

i. In *astrology* there are seven planets:—

APOLLO, the sun, represents gold.
DIANA, the moon, represents silver.
MERCURY represents quicksilver.
VENUS represents copper.
MARS represents iron.
JUPITER represents tin.
SATURN represents lead.

ii. In *heraldry* the arms of royal personages used to be blazoned by the names of planets, and those of noblemen by precious stones,instead of the corresponding colours.

SOL—topaz—or (*gold*)—bezants.
LUNA—pearl—argent (*silver*)—plates.
SATURN—diamond—sable (*black*)—pellets.
MARS—ruby—gules (*red*)—torteaux.
JUPITER—sapphire—azure (*blue*)—hurts.
VENUS—emerald—vert (*green*)—pommes.
MERCURY—amethyst—purpure (*violet*)—golpes.

Inferior planets. Mercury and Venus; so called because their orbits are within the orbit of the earth.

Superior planets. Mars, the Planetoids, Jupiter, Saturn, U'ranus, and Neptune; so called because their orbits are outside the earth's orbit—*i.e.* farther from the sun.

iii. Planets represented by symbols.

MERCURY, ☿; VENUS, ♀; EARTH, ⊕; MARS, ♂; the PLANETOIDS, in the order of discovery—①, ②, ③, etc.; JUPITER, ♃; SATURN, ♄; URANUS, ♅; NEPTUNE, ♆; the SUN, ☉; the MOON, ☽.

iv. The planets in Greece were symbolised by seven letters:

JUPITER, υ (*u-psilon*); MARS, o (*o-micron*); MERCURY, ε (*e-psilon*); THE MOON, α (*alpha*); SATURN, ω (*o-mega*); THE SUN, ι (*iota*): VENUS, η (*eta*).

To be born under a lucky [or *unlucky*] *planet.* According to astrology, some planet, at the birth of every individual, presides over his destiny. Some of the planets, like Jupiter, are lucky; and others, like Saturn, are unlucky. In casting a horoscope the heavens must be divided into twelve parts or houses, called (1) the House of Life; (2) the House of Fortune; (3) the House of Brethren; (4) the House of Relations; (5) the House of Children; (6) the House of Health; (7) the House of Marriage; (8) the House of Death; (9) the House of Religion; (10) the House of Dignities; (11) the House of Friends and Benefactors; (12) the House of Enemies. Each house had one of the heavenly bodies as its *lord*. (*See* STAR IN THE ASCENDANT.)

Planet-struck. A blighted tree is said to be planet-struck. Epilepsy, paralysis, lunacy, etc., are attributed to the malignant aspects of the planets. Horses are said to be planet-struck when they seem stupefied, whether from want of food, colic, or stoppage. The Latin word is *siderātus*.

"Evidentissimum id fuit,quod quacunque equo invectus est, ibi haud secus quam pestifero sidere icti pavebant."—*Livy*, viii. 9.

Plank (*A*). Any one principle of a political platform. (*See* PLATFORM.)

Plank. *To walk the plank.* To be about to die. Walking the plank was a mode of disposing of prisoners at sea, much in vogue among the South Sea pirates in the 17th century.

Plantagenet, from *planta genistæ* (broom-plant), the family cognisance first assumed by the Earl of Anjou, the first of his race, during a pilgrimage to the Holy Land, as a symbol of humility. (*Sir George Buck : Richard III.*) Died 1622.

Plaster of Paris. Gypsum, found in large quantities in the quarries of Montmartre, near Paris.

Plate (*A*). A race in which a prize is given out of the race fund, or from some other source, without any *stakes* being made by the owners of the horses engaged. Usually entrance money is required. (*See* SWEEPSTAKES, HANDICAP, PLATE, SELLING RACE, WEIGHT-FOR-AGE RACE.)

∵ Plate, meaning silver, is the Spanish *plata*.

Plat'en, among printers, is the power or weight which presses on the tympan (*q.v.*), to cause the impression of the letters to be given off and transferred to the sheet. (French, *plat*, flat.)

∵ In type-writing machines, the platen is the feeding roller on which the paper rests to receive the proper impressions.

Plates or **Plates of Meat.** Slang for feet. One of the chief sources of slang is rhyme. Thus *meat* rhymes with feet, and " warming my plates " is slang for warming my feet. Similarly, " Rory O'More " is slang for door, and " there came a knock at the Rory O'More " means there was a knock at the door. A prescott is slang for waistcoat. (*See* CHIVY.)

Platform, in the United States, is the policy of a political or religious party. Of course the meaning is the policy on which the party stands. An American revival. Each separate principle is a *plank* of the platform.

Queen Elizabeth, in answer to the *Supplication* of the Puritans (offered to the Parliament in 1586), said she "had examined the platform, and account it most prejudicial to the religion established, to her crown, her government, and her subjects."

Again, the Rev. John Norris writes, in 1687, that Plato said, "God created τῶν ὄντων μέτρα, implying that all things were formed according to His special platforms, meaning the ideas formed in the divine mind."

The word has been resuscitated in North America. Lily, in 1581, says he "discovered the whole platform of the conspiracie." (*Discovery of the New World*, p. 115.)

"Their declaration of principles—their 'platform,' to use the appropriate term—was settled and published to the world. Its distinctive elements, or 'planks,' are financial."—*The Times*.

Plato. His original name was Aris'-toclēs, but he was called *Platōn* from the great breadth of his shoulders.

The German Plato. Friedrich Heinrich Jacobi (1743-1819).

The Jewish Plato. Philo Judæus, an Alexandrine philosopher. (Flourished 20-40.)

The Puritan Plato. John Howe, the Nonconformist (1630-1706).

Plato and the Bees. When Plato was an infant, some bees settled on his lips when he was asleep, indicating that he would become famous for his honeyed words. The same is said of Sophŏclēs, Pindar, St. Ambrose, St. Chrysostom, and others.

" And as when Plato did i' the cradle thrive,
Bees to his lips brought honey from their hive."
     W. Browne: Britannia's Pastorals, ii.

Plato's Year. A revolution of 25,000 years, in which period the stars and constellations return to their former places in respect to the equinoxes.

" Cut out more work than can be done
In Plato's year, but finish none."
     Butler : Hudibras, pt. iii. 1.

Platonic Bodies. The five regular geometric solids described by Plato—viz. the tetrahedron, hexahedron, octahedron, dodecahedron, and icosahedron, all of which are bounded by like, equal, and regular planes.

Platonic Love. Spiritual love between persons of opposite sexes. It is the friendship of man and woman, without mixture of what is usually called love. Plato strongly advocated this pure affection, and hence its distinctive name.

Platonic Puritan (*The*). John Howe, the Nonconformist divine. (1630-1706.)

Platonism. The philosophical system of Plato ; *dialectics*. Locke maintains that the mind is by nature a sheet of white paper, the five senses being the doors of knowledge. Plato maintained the opposite theory, drawing a strong line of demarcation between the province of thought and that of sensations in the production of ideas. (*See* DIALECTICS.)

It is characterised by the doctrine of pre-existing eternal ideas, and teaches the immortality and pre-existence of the soul, the dependence of virtue upon discipline, and the trustworthiness of cognition.

In *theology*, he taught that there are two eternal, primary, independent, and incorruptible causes of material things —*God* the maker, and *matter* the substance.

In *psychology*, he maintained the ultimate unity and mutual dependence of all knowledge.

In *physics*, he said that God is the measure of all things, and that from God, in whom reason and being are one, proceed human reason and those "ideas" or laws which constitute all that can be called *real* in nature.

Platter with Two Eyes (*A*). Emblematical of St. Lucy, in allusion to her sending her two eyes to a nobleman who wanted to marry her for the exceeding beauty of her eyes. (*See* LUCY.)

Play. "This may be play to you, 'tis death to us." The allusion is to the fable of the boys throwing stones at some frogs. (*Roger L'Estrange*.)

As good as a play. So said King Charles when he attended the discussion of Lord Ross's " Divorce Bill."

Play the Deuce. The Irish say, *Play the pooka.* Pooka or Pouke is an evil spirit in the form of a wild colt, who does great hurt to benighted travellers.

Played Out. Out of date ; no longer in vogue ; exhausted.

"Valentines, I suppose, are played out, said Milton."—*Truth: Queer Story*, Feb. 18, 1886.

Playing to the Gods. Degrading one's vocation *ad captandum vulgus*. The gods, in theatrical phrase, are the spectators in the uppermost gallery, the *ignobile vulgus*. The ceiling of Drury Lane theatre was at one time painted in imitation of the sky, with Cupids and other deities here and there represented. As the gallery referred to was near the ceiling, the occupants were called the gods. In French this gallery is nick-named *paradis*.

Please the Pigs. (*See under* PIGS.)

Pleased as Punch. Greatly delighted. Our old friend Punch is always singing with self-satisfaction in all his naughty ways, and his evident "pleasure" is contagious to the beholders.

"You could skip over to Europe whenever you liked ; mamma would be pleased as Punch."—*R. Grant*.

Pleasure. It was Xerxes who offered a reward to anyone who could invent a new pleasure.

Plebe'ians. Common people: properly it means the free citizens of Rome, who were neither patricians nor clients. They were, however, free landowners, and had their own "gentēs." (Latin, *plebes,* 2 syl.)

Pleb'iscite (3 syl.). A decree of the people. In Roman history, a law enacted by the "comitia" or assembly of tribes. In France, the resolutions adopted in the Revolution by the voice of the people, and the general votes given during the Second Empire—such as the general vote to elect Napoleon III. emperor of the French.

Pledge. *I pledge you in this wine— i.e.* I drink to your health or success.

> "Drink to me only with thine eyes,
> And I will pledge with mine."
> *Ben Jonson (translated from Philostratus)*
> second century.

To pledge. To guarantee. Pledging a drinker's security arose in the tenth century, when it was thought necessary for one person to watch over the safety of a companion while in the act of drinking. It was by no means unusual with the fierce Danes to stab a person under such circumstances.

> "If I
> Were a huge man, I should fear to drink at meals,
> Lest they should spy my windpipe's dangerous notes.
> Great men should drink with harness on their throats." *Timon of Athens,* i. 2.

Plei'ades (3 syl.) means the "sailing stars" (Greek, *pleo,* to sail), because the Greeks considered navigation safe at the return of the Pleiades, and never attempted it after those stars disappeared.

The PLEIADES were the seven daughters of Atlas and Plēionē (Πληιόνη). They were transformed into stars, one of which (Merōpē) is invisible out of shame, because she alone married a human being. Some call the invisible star "Electra," and say she hides herself from grief for the destruction of the city and royal race of Troy.

i. *The Pleiad of Alexandria.* A group of seven contemporary poets in the reign of Ptolemy Philadelphos; so called in reference to the cluster of stars in the back of Taurus. Their names are—Callim'achos, Apollo'nios of Rhodes, Ara'tos, Philiscos (called *Homer the Younger*), Ly'cophron, Nicander, and Theoc'ritos.

✢ There are in reality eleven stars in the Pleiades.

ii. *The literary Pleiad of Charlemagne.* Alcuin (*Albi'nus*), Angilbert (*Homer*), Adelard (*Augustine*), Riculfe (*Damœtas*), Charlemagne (*David*), Varnefrid, and Eginhard.

iii. *The first French Pleiad.* Seven contemporary poets in the sixteenth century, in the reign of Henri III., who wrote French poetry in the metres, style, and verbiage of the ancient Greek and Latin poetry. Of these, Ronsard was by far the most talented; but much that would be otherwise excellent is spoilt by pedantry and Frenchified Latin. The seven names are Ronsard, Dorat, Du Bellay, Remi-Belleau, Jodelle, Baïf, and Thiard.

The second French Pleiad. Seven contemporary poets in the reign of Louis XIII., very inferior to the "first Pleiad." Their names are Rapin, Commire, Larue, Santeuil, Ménage, Dupérier, and Petit.

iv. *The lost Pleiad.* Electra, one of the Pleiades, wife of Dardanus, disappeared a little before the Trojan war (B.C. 1193), that she might be saved the mortification of seeing the ruin of her beloved city. She showed herself occasionally to mortal eye, but always in the guise of a comet. Mons. Fréret says this tradition arose from the fact that a comet does sometimes appear in the vicinity of the Pleiades, rushes in a northerly direction, and passes out of sight. (See *Odyss.* v. and *Iliad,* xviii.)

Letitia Elizabeth Landon published, in 1829, a poem entitled *The Lost Pleiad.*

(*See above,* PLEIADES.)

Plét is a lash like a knout, but not made of raw hides. (Russian, *pletu,* a whip.)

Pleydell (*Mr. Paulus*). An advocate in Edinburgh, formerly sheriff of Ellangowan.

> "Mr. Counsellor Pleydell was a lively, sharp-looking gentleman, with a professional shrewdness in his eye, and, generally speaking, a professional formality in his manner; but this he could slip off on a Saturday evening, when .. he joined in the ancient pastime of High Jinks."— *Sir W. Scott: Guy Mannering,* xxxix.

Pli'able. One of Christian's neighbours, who went with him as far as the Slough of Despond, and then turned back again. (*Bunyan: Pilgrim's Progress,* pt. i.)

Pliny. *The German Pliny.* Konrad von Gesner, of Zürich (1516-1565).

Pliny of the East. (*See* ZAKARIJA.)

Pliny's Doves. In one of the rooms on the upper floor of the museum of the Capitol at Rome are the celebrated Doves of Pliny, one of the finest and most perfectly preserved specimens of ancient mosaic. It represents four doves drinking, with a beautiful border surrounding the composition. The mosaic is formed of natural stones, so small that 160 pieces cover only a square inch. It is supposed to be the work of Sosus, and is described by Pliny as a proof of the perfection to which that art had arrived. He says:—

"At Pergamos is a wonderful specimen of a dove drinking, and darkening the water with the shadow of her head ; on the lip of the vessel are other doves pluming themselves."

This exquisite specimen of art was found in Villa Adria'na, in 1737, by Cardinal Furietti, from whom it was purchased by Clement XIII.

Plith. A piece of iron made hot and put into an iron box, to be held for punishment by a criminal. (*See* PLET.)

Plon-plon. The sobriquet of Prince Napoleon Joseph Charles Bonaparte, son of Jerome Bonaparte. He was nicknamed *Craint-plon* (Fear-bullet) in the Crimean war (1854-1856), a nickname afterwards perverted into *Plon-plon*. (1822-1891.)

Plot, in a theatrical sense, does not only mean the incidents which lead to the development of a play, but half a dozen other things ; thus, the " scene plot " is a list of the various scenes to be used; the "flyman's plot " is a list of the articles required by the flyman in the "flies ; " there is also the " gasman's plot ; " the " property plot " is a list of all the properties required in the play, for which the manager is responsible.

Plotcock. The old Scotch form of the Roman Pluto, by which Satan is meant. Chaucer calls Plato the " king of Faërie," and Dunbar names him " Pluto the elrich incubus."

Plough. *Fond, Fool, or White Plough.* The plough dragged about a village on Plough Monday. Called *white*, because the mummers who drag it about are dressed in white, gaudily trimmed with flowers and ribbons. Called *fond* or *fool*, because the procession is fond or foolish—not serious, or of a business character.

Plough Monday. The first Monday after Twelfth Day is so called because it is the end of the Christmas holidays, and the day when men return to their plough or daily work. It was customary on this day for farm labourers to draw a plough from door to door of the parish, and solicit " plough-money" to spend in a frolic. The queen of the banquet was called Bessy. (*See* DISTAFF.)

Plover. *To live like a plover, i.e.* to live on nothing, to live on air. Plovers do not, however, live on air, but feed largely on small insects. They also eat worms, which they hunt for in newly-ploughed fields.

Plowden. " *The case is altered,*" *quoth Plowden.* Plowden was a priest, very unpopular, and in order to bring him into trouble some men inveigled him into attending mass performed by a layman, and then impeached the layman for so doing. Being brought before the tribunal, the cunning priest asked the layman if it was he who officiated. " Yes," said the man. " And are you a priest ? " said Plowden. " No," said the man. " Then," said Plowden, turning to the tribunal, " that alters the case, for it is an axiom with the church, ' No priest, no mass.' "

Plowman. *The Vision of Piers Plowman* is a satirical poem by W. [or R.] Langland, completed in 1362. The poet supposes himself falling asleep on the Malvern Hills, and in his dream sees various visions of an allegorical character, bearing on the vices of the times. In one of the allegories, the Lady An'ima (*the soul*) is placed in Castle Caro (*flesh*) under the charge of Sir Constable In-wit, and his sons See-well, Hear-well, Work-well, and Go-well. The whole poem consists of nearly 15,000 verses, and is divided into twenty parts, each part being called a *passus*, or separate vision.

Pluck. To reject a candidate for literary honours because he is not up to the required mark. The rejected candidate is said to be *plucked*.

When degrees are conferred the name of each person is read out before he is presented to the Vice-Chancellor. The proctor used at one time to walk once up and down the room, and anyone who objected to the degree being conferred might signify his dissent by *plucking or twitching the proctor's gown. This was occasionally done by tradesmen to whom the candidate was in debt ; but now all persons likely to be objected to, either by tradesmen or examiners, know it beforehand, and keep away. They are virtually plucked, but not really so.

A case of pluck. An instance of one who has been plucked : as " Tom Jones is a case of pluck," *i.e.* is a plucked man.

A man of pluck. Of courage or spirit. The pluck is the heart, liver, and whatever else is " plucked " away from the chest of a sheep or hog. We also use the expressions bold *heart*, lily-*livered*, a man of another *kidney*, *bowels* of mercy, a *vein* of fun, it raised his *bile*, etc. (*See* LIVER.)

Pluck his Goose. *I'll pluck his goose for him.* That is: I'll cut his crest, I'll lower his pride, I'll make him eat umble pie. Comparing the person to a goose, the threat is to pluck off his feathers in which he prides himself.

Plucked Pigeon (*A*). One fleeced out of his money; one plucked by a rook or sharper.

"There were no smart fellows whom fortune had troubled, . . . no plucked pigeons or winged rooks, no disappointed speculators, no ruined miners."—*Sir W. Scott : Peveril of the Peak*, c. xi.

Plugson of Undershot. Carlyle's typical commercial Radical in the middle of the 19th century, who found that no decent Tory would shake hands with him; but at the close of the century found free-competition company with latter-day Tories.

"There are two motive forces which may impel the Plugsons of Toryism . . . the pressure is not great enough to . . . overcome the *vis inertia* of Plugson and Co."—*Nineteenth Century*, Dec., 1892, p. 878.

Plum. *A plum bed* (Devonshire). A soft bed, in which the down lies light.

The dough plums well (Devonshire). Rises well, and will not be heavy.

The cake is nice and plum (Devonshire). Light. (*Plump*, swelled out.)

He is worth a plum. The Spanish *pluma* means both plumage and wealth. Hence *tiene pluma* (he has feathered his nest). We arbitrarily place this desideratum at £100,000, and the man who has realised only £50,000 has got only half a plum. "Either a plum or a plum-stone"—i.e. "*Aut Cæsar aut nullus.*"

Plume Oneself (*To*). To be conceited of . . . ; to boast of . . . A plume is a feather, and to plume oneself is to feather one's own conceit.

"Mrs. Bute Crawley . . . plumed herself upon her resolute manner of performing [what she thought right]."—*Thackeray : Vanity Fair.*

Plumes. *In borrowed plumes.* Assumed merit; airs and graces not merited. The allusion is to the fable of the jackdaw who dressed up in peacock's feathers.

Plumper (*A*). Every elector represented in Parliament by two members has the power of voting for both candidates at an election. To give a plumper is to vote for only one of the candidates, and not to use the second vote. If he votes for two candidates of opposite politics, his vote is termed a *split* vote.

Plunger. One who *plunges*, or spends money recklessly in bets, etc. The Marquis of Hastings was the first person so called by the turf. One night he played three games of draughts for £1,000 a game, and lost all three. He then cut a pack of cards for £500 a cut; and lost £5,000 in an hour and a half. He paid both debts at once before he left the room.

Plus Ultra. The motto in the royal arms of Spain. It was once *Ne plus ultra*, in allusion to the pillars of Hercules, the *ne plus ultra* of the world; but after the discovery of America, and when Charles V. inherited the crown of Aragon and Castile, with all the vast American possessions, he struck out *ne*, and assumed the words *plus ultra* for the national motto, as much as to say Spain and the *plus ultra* country.

Plush (*John*). A gorgeous footman, conspicuous for his plush breeches.

To take plush. To take a subordinate place in the ministry, where one can only act as a government flunkey.

" Lord Rosebery perhaps remembers that, years ago, a young politician who had just finished his education, was warned by an old and affectionate teacher 'not to take plush . . .' The reply was, 'I have been offered plush tied with red tape, and have refused it.'"—*Nineteenth Century*, Jan., 1892, p. 137.

Plu'to. The grave, or the god of that region where the dead go to before they are admitted into Elysium or sent to Tar'taros.

" Brothers, be of good cheer, this night we shall sup with Pluto."—*Leonidas to the three hundred Spartans before the battle of Thermopylæ.*

" Give the untasted portion you have won . . .
To those who mock you, gone to Pluto's reign."
Thomson : Castle of Indolence, canto 1.

Pluto. Many artists of great repute have painted this god, the three most famous being that by Jule-Romain (1492 1516), a pupil of Raphael, in Mantua; one by Augustin Carrache (1558-1601), in Modēna, generally called *Il Famoso*; and the third by Luc Giordano (1632-1701), in the gallery of the Palace Riccardi. Raphael has introduced Pluto in his *Assembly of the Gods.*

⁂ In the Villa Albani of Rome is the famous antique statue of Pluto and Cerberus.

Pluton'ic Rocks. Granites, and certain porphyries, supposed to be of igneous, but not of volcanic, origin. So called by Lyell from Pluto, the principle of elemental fire.

Plutus. *Rich as Plutus.* In Greek mythology Plutos is the god of riches. Plutus and Pluto are widely different.

Plymouth Brethren. A sect that protests against all sectarianism, and advocates the unity of the church; some even go so far as to advocate a community of goods. So called from Plymouth, where they sprang into existence in 1830.

Plymouth Cloak (*A*). A good stout cudgel. In the time of the Crusades many men of good family used to land at Plymouth utterly destitute. They went to a neighbouring wood, cut themselves a good stout club, and, stopping the first passenger that passed by, provided themselves with money and clothing. (*Fuller: Worthies.*)

Pocahontas. Daughter of Powhatan, an Indian chief of Virginia, who rescued Captain John Smith when her father's hand was on the point of killing him. She subsequently married John Rolfe, and was baptised under the name of Rebecca. (1595-1617.) (See *Old and New London*, ii. 481.)

Pocket (diminutive of *poche*, a pouch). *To put one's hand in one's pocket.* To give money (generally to some charity). *Put your pride in your pocket.* Lay your pride aside for the nonce. *To be in pocket.* To be a gainer by some transaction. *To be out of pocket.* To be a loser by some transaction.

Pocket an Insult (*To*). To submit to an insult without apparent displeasure.

Pocket Borough (*A*). A borough where the influence of the magnate is so powerful as to be able to control the election of any candidate he may choose to support. Well nigh a thing of the past since the introduction of voting by ballot.

Pocket Judgment (*A*). A bond under the hand of a debtor, countersigned by the sovereign. This bond can be enforced without legal process, but has quite fallen into disuse.

Pocket Pistol (*A*). A dram-flask for the pocket, in "self-defence," because we may be unable to get a dram on the road.

Pocket Pistol (*Queen Bess's*). A formidable piece of ordnance given to Queen Elizabeth by the Low Countries in recognition of her efforts to protect them in their reformed religion. It used to overlook the Channel from Dover Cliffs, but in 1894 was removed to make room for a battery of modern guns. It is said that it contains in

Flemish the equivalent of the following words:—

   " Load me well and keep me clean,
   And I'll carry a ball to Calais Green."

But this translation is only fanciful.

Poco, rather, as a *poco forte, poco animato.*

Pococurante (5 syl.). Insouciant, devil-may-care, easy-go-lucky. As the " Pococurante Guardsman " (the imperturbable and impassive . . .). Also used for one who in argument leaves the main gist and rides off on some minor and indifferent point.

Pococurantism. Insouciance, imperturbability. Also indifference to important matters, but concern about trifles.

Podgers. Toadies, venerators (real or pretended) of everything and everyone with a name. (*John Hollingshead: The Birthplace of Podgers, a farce.*)

Podsnap. A type of the heavy gentry, lumbering and straight-backed as Elizabethan furniture. (*Dickens: Our Mutual Friend.*)

Podsnap'pery. The etiquette of the fossil gentry, stiff-starched and extremely proper.

   " It may not be so in the Gospel according to Podsnappery .. but it has been the truth since the foundations of the universe were laid."—*Our Mutual Friend.*

Poe (*Edgar Allan*). The alias of Arthur Gordon Pym, the American poet. (1811-1849.)

Poet Squab. So Rochester calls Dryden, who was very corpulent. (1631 1701.)

Poets (Greek, *poieo*, to make). Skalds of Scandinavia (etym., *scalla*, to sing, Swedish, etc.) Minnesingers of the Holy Empire (Germany), love-singers. Troubadours of Provence in France (*troubar*, to invent, in the Provençal dialect). Trouvères of Normandy (*trouver*, to invent, in the Walloon dialect). Bards of Wales (*bardgan*, a song, Celtic).

Poet of Haslemere (*The*). Alfred Tennyson (Lord Tennyson), poet laureate (1809-1893). (*See* BARD.)

Poet of the poor. Rev. George Crabbe (1754-1832).

Prince of poets. Edmund Spenser is so called on his monument in Westminster Abbey. (1553-1598.)

Prince of Spanish poets. Garcila'so de la Vega, frequently so called by Cervantes. (1503-1536.)

Quaker poet (The). Bernard Barton (1784-1849).

Poets' Corner *(The).* In Westminster Abbey. The popular name given to the south corner, because some sort of recognition is made of several British poets of very varied merits. As a national Valhalla, it is a national disgrace. It is but scant honour to be ranked with Davenant, Mason, and Shadwell. Some recognition is taken of five of our first-class poets — viz. Chaucer, Dryden, Milton, Shakespeare, and Spenser. Wordsworth and Tennyson are recognised, but not Byron, Pope, Scott, and Southey. Gray is very properly acknowledged, but not Cowper. Room is found for Longfellow, an American, but none for Burns and Hogg, both Scotchmen.

Poets Laureate, appointed by letters patent.

	Appointed.	Buried.
BEN JONSON	1615-6	Westminster Abbey.
SIR WM. DAVENANT (!)	1638	Westminster Abbey.
JOHN DRYDEN	1670	Westminster Abbey.
THOMAS SHADWELL (!) ..	1688	
NAHUM TATE (!) ..	1692	..
NICHOLAS ROWE* ..	1715	Westminster Abbey.
LAWRENCE EUSDEN (!) ..	1718	
COLLEY CIBBER* ..	1730	
WILLIAM WHITEHEAD (!)	1757	
THOMAS WARTON* ..	1785	
HENRY JAMES PYE (!)	1790	
ROBERT SOUTHEY ..	1813	
WM. WORDSWORTH ..	1843	
ALFRED TENNYSON (Lord)	1850	Westminster Abbey.
ALFRED AUSTIN	1896	

The following are sometimes included, though not appointed by letters patent :—Chaucer, Gower, John Key, Bernard, Skelton, Rob. Whittington, Richard Edwards, Spenser, and Sam. Daniel.

(!) Six of the fifteen known only by their names. * Three others quite third-rate poets. The remaining six were distinguished men.

⁂ A poet laureate is one who has received a laurel crown. There were at one time "doctors laureate," "bachelors laureate," etc.

Poetaster. A very inferior poet. The suffix *-aster* is depreciative (compare "oleaster,"). At one time we had also "grammatic - aster," "politic - aster," "critic-aster," and some others. (Italian, *poetastro,* a paltry poet.)

Poetical. *(See* AONIAN.)

Poetical Justice. That ideal justice which poets exercise in making the good happy, and the bad unsuccessful in their evil schemes.

Poetry on the Greek Model. *(See* CHIABRERESCO.)

Father of English poetry. Geoffrey Chaucer (1328 - 1400); so called by Dryden. Spenser calls him "the pure well of English undefiled." He was not the first English poet, but was so superior to his predecessors that he laid the foundation of a new era. He is sometimes termed "the day-starre," and Spenser the "sun-rise" of English poetry.

Po'gram. A "creak-shoes," a Puritanical starch mawworm.

Poille. An Apu'lian horse. The horses of Apulia were very greatly valued at one time. Richard, Archbishop of Armagh in the fourteenth century, says of St. Thomas, "Neither the mule of Spain, the courser of Apulia, the repe'do of Ethiopia, the elephant of Asia, the camel of Syria, nor the English ass, is bolder or more combative than he."

> "Therto so horsly, and so quyk of ye,
> As if a gentil Poille hys courser were ;
> For certès, fro his tayl unto his cere
> Nature ne art ne couthe him nought amend."
> *Chaucer : Canterbury Tales,* line 10,536.

Poins. One of the companions of Sir John Falstaff. *(Shakespeare : 1 and 2 Henry IV.)*

Point. Defined by Euclid as "that which hath no parts." Playfair defines it as "that which has position but not magnitude," and Legendre says it "is a limit terminating a line ;" but none of these definitions can be called either philosophical or exact. A point is not necessarily a "limit terminating a line," for if so a point could not exist, even in imagination, without a line. Besides, Legendre's definition presupposes that we know what a *line* is ; but assuredly a "point" precedes a "line," as a line precedes a "superficies." To arrive at Legendre's idea we must begin with a solid, and say a superficies is the "limit terminating each face of a solid," lines are the "limits terminating a superficies," and points are the "limits terminating a line." In regard to Euclid's definition, we say : *Ex nihilo nihil fit.*

In good point (French, *embonpoint,* plump.) (See *Stretch a point.*)

To carry one's point. To gain the object sought for. The allusion is to archery.

To dine on potatoes and point. To have potatoes without salt, a very meagre dinner indeed. When salt was very dear, and the cellar was empty, parents used to tell their children to point their potato to the salt cellar, and eat it. This was potato and point. In the tale of *Ralph Richards the Miser,* we are told that he gave his boy dry bread, and whipped him for pointing it towards the cupboard where a bit of cheese was kept in a bottle.

To make a point of [*doing something*]. To consider the matter as a point of duty. The reference is to the old Roman way of voting by ballot. The ballot tablets were thrown by the voters into a chest, and were afterwards counted by *points marked on a tablet*, and to obtain every vote was to " carry every point " (" *Omne talit punctum*" [*Horace*]). Hence a point of duty or point of conscience is a plank on the platform of duty or conscience.

To stretch a point. To exceed what is strictly right. Points were the tagged laces used in ancient dress: hence, to " truss a point," to truss or tie the laces which held the breeches ; to " stretch a point " is to stretch these laces, so as to adjust the dress to extra growth, or the temporary fulness of good feeding. At Whitsuntide these points or tags were given away by the churchwardens.

"Their points being broken, down fell their hose."—*Shakespeare : 1 Henry IV.*, ii. 4.

Point-blank. Direct. A term in gunnery ; when a cannon is so placed that the line of sight is parallel to the axis and horizontal, the discharge is point-blank, and is supposed to go direct to the object without a curve. In French *point blanc* is the white mark or bull's eye of a target, to hit which the ball or arrow must not deviate in the least from the exact path.

" Now art thou within point-blank of our juris-diction regal."—*Shakespeare:* 2 *Henry VI.*, iv. 7.

Point d'Appui (French). A standpoint ; a fulcrum ; a position from which you can operate ; a pretext to conceal the real intention. Literally the point of support.

" The material which gives name to the dish is but the *point d'appui* for the literary cayenne and curry-powder, by which it is recommended to the palate of the reader."—*The Athenæum.*

Point de Judas (French). The number 13. The twelve apostles and our Lord made thirteen at the Last Supper.

Point-devise. Punctilious : minutely exact. Holofernes says, " I abhor such insociable and *point de vise* companions, such rackers of orthography." (French, *point de vise.*)

" You are rather *point de vise* in your accoutre-ments."—*Shakespeare: As You Like It*, iii. 2.

Points. *Armed at all points.* " *Armé de toutes pièces*," or " *Armé jusqu' aux dents*." " Armed at all points exactly *cap-à-pie*,"

To stand on points. On punctilios ; delicacy of behaviour.

" This fellow doth not stand upon points."— *Shakespeare : Midsummer Night's Dream*, v. 1.

Points of the Escutcheon. There are nine points distinguished in heraldry by the first nine letters of the alphabet —three at top, A, B, C ; three down the middle, D, E, F ; and three at the bottom, G, H, I. The first three are *chiefs ;* the middle three are the *collar point, fess point*, and *nombril* or *navel point ;* the bottom three are the *base* points.

Poison. It is said that poisons had no effect on Mithrida'tes, King of Pontus. This was Mithridates VI., called the Great, who succeeded his father at the age of eleven, and fortified his constitution by drinking antidotes to poisons which might at any moment be administered to him by persons about the court. (*See* AQUA TOFANA.)

Poison Detectors.

Aladdin's ring was a preservative against every evil.

Gundoforus. No one could pass with poison the gate of Gundofŏrus.

Nourgehan's bracelet. When poison was present the stones of this bracelet seemed agitated.

Opals turn pale at the approach of poison.

Peacocks ruffle their feathers at the sight of poison.

Rhinoceros. If poison is put into a cup made of rhinoceros' horn, the liquid will effervesce.

Sign of the Cross was supposed in the Middle Ages to be a poison detector.

Venetian glass will shiver at the approach of poison. (*See also* PHILO-SOPHER'S EGG.)

Poison of Khaïbar refers to the poisoned leg of mutton of which Mahomet partook while in the citadel of Khaïbar. It was poisoned by Zaïnab, a Jewess, and Mahomet felt the effects of the poison to the end of his life.

Poisoners (*Secret*).

(1) Locusta, a woman of ancient Rome, who was employed by the Empress Agrippi'na to poison her husband Claudius.' Nero employed the same woman to poison Britannicus and others.

(2) The Borgias (Pope Alexander VI. and his children, Cæsar and Lucrezia) were noted poisoners.

(3) Hieronyma Spara and Toffania, of Italy. (*See* AQUA TOFANA.)

(4) Marquise de Brinvilliers, a young profligate Frenchwoman, taught the art

by an officer named Sainte Croix, who learnt it in Italy. (See *World of Wonders*, part vii. p. 203.)

(5) Lavoisin and Lavigoreux, French midwives and fortune-tellers.

(6) Anna Maria Zweinziger, sentenced to death in 1811.

In English history we have a few instances : *e.g.* Sir Thomas Overbury was so murdered by the Countess of Somerset. King James, it has been said, was a victim to similar poisoning, by Villiers, Duke of Buckingham.

Pois'son d'Avril. An April fool. The *poisson d'Avril* is the mackerel, and we have the expression " You silly mackerel," and silly indeed are those who allow themselves to be caught by the palpable jokes engendered on the 1st of April. The Scotch say "hunting the gowk" (cuckoo). It is said that the best explanation is a reference to Matt. xxix. 2.

∴ The mackerel, says Oudin, is called the *poisson d'Avril*, "*parce que les macquereaux se prennent et se mangent environ ce mois-la.*"

A correspondent of *Notes and Queries* (June 20, 1891, p. 494) says that the April fish is the *aurata*, sacred to Venus.

Poke. A bag, pouch, or sack.

Poke. A lazy person, a loafer, a dawdler.

Poke. To thrust or push against ; to thrust or butt with the horns. Also to busy oneself without any definite object.

" Poking about where we had no business."— *Kingsley: Two Years Ago.*

To poke fun at one is to make one a laughing-stock.

" At table he was hospitable and jocose, always poking good-natured fun at Luke."—*E. Lynn Lynton: Lizzie Lorton of Greyrigg*, chap. xii.

Poke Bonnet: A long, straight, projecting bonnet, formerly commonly worn by women.

Poker. *A poker set leaning against the upper bars of a fire to draw it up.* This is to make a cross to keep off Lob, the house spirit, who loves to lie before the fire, and, like Puck and Robin Goodfellow, dearly loves mischief and practical jokes.

Poker Pictures. Drawings executed by the point of a hot poker or " heater " of an Italian iron. By charring different parts more or less, various tints are obtained.

Poker Talk. Gossip, fireside chitchat.

" Gaston rattled forth this specimen of poker talk lightly."—*Mrs. Edwardes: A Girton Girl,* ch. ii.

32

Pokers. The 'squire Bedels who carry a silver mace or poker before the Vice-Chancellor are so called at Cambridge.

Poky. Cramped, narrow, confined ; as, a poky corner. Also poor and shabby.

" The ladies were in their pokiest old headgear."—*Thackeray : The Newcomes,* chap. lvii.

Po'lack. An inhabitant of Poland. (French, *Polaque.*)

" So frowned he once, when, in angry parle,
He smote the sledded Polacks on the ice."
Shakespeare : Hamlet, i. 1.

Polarisation of Light is the absorption of those rays which are at right angles to the rays preserved : Thus A B

  A   G   is one ray in which A is re-
  ① C⊝D E⊕F   flected to B and B to A ;
  B   H   C D is a ray, in which C is reflected to D and D to C. In E G F H, if the light is polarised, either E F or G H is absorbed. A B and C D are the poles of light, or the directions in which the rays are reflected.

Po'leas (2 syl.). The labouring class of India.

" Poleas the labouring lower clans are named,
By the proud Nayres the noble rank is claimed."

Poles. *Under bare poles.* Said of a ship when all her sails are furled.

Polichinelle. *Le secret de . . .* (*See* SECRET.)

Polinesso (in *Orlando Furioso*). Duke of Albany, who falsely accused Gencu'ra of incontinency, and was slain in single combat by Ariodantes.

Polish off. To finish out of hand. In allusion to articles polished.

I'll polish him off in no time means I'll set him down, I'll give him a drubbing.

To polish off a meal is to eat it quickly, and not keep anyone waiting.

Political Economy. This term was invented by François Quesnay, the French physician. (1694-1774.)

Polixene (3 syl.). The name assumed by Madelon in Molière's *Précieuses Ridicules.*

Polix'enes (4 syl.), King of Bohemia, being invited to Sicily by King Leontes, excites unwittingly the jealousy of his friend, because he prolongs his stay at the entreaty of Queen Hermi'one. Leontes orders Camillo to poison the royal guest, but, instead of doing so, Camillo flees with him to Bohemia. In time Florizel, the son and heir of Polixenes, falls in love with Perdita, the lost daughter of

Leontes. Polixenes forbids the match, and the young lovers, under the charge of Camillo, flee to Sicily. Polixenes follows the fugitives, the mystery of Perdita is cleared up, the lovers are married, and the two kings resume their friendship. (*Shakespeare : Winter's Tale.*)

Poll. *To go out in the poll.* To take an ordinary degree—a degree without university "honours." (Greek, *hoi polloi*, the many.)

Poll Degree. (*See above.*)

Poll Men. Those of the "hoi polloi," *the many*, not the honour-men.

Pollentē. The puissant Saracen, father of Mu'néra. He took his station on "Bridge Perilous," and attacked everyone who crossed it, bestowing the spoil upon his daughter. Sir Artegal slew the monster. Pollente is meant for Charles IX. of France, sadly notorious for the slaughter of Protestants on St. Bartholomew's Eve. (*Spenser : Fërie Queene*, book v. 2.)

Pollio, to whom Virgil addresses his Fourth Eclogue, and to whom he ascribes the remarkable advent of the "golden age," was the founder of the first public library of Rome. (B.C. 76-A.D. 4.)

Pollux. *The horses of Castor and Pollux.* Cyll'aros and Har'pagos. Seneca and Claudian give Cyllaros to Castor, but Virgil (*Georgic* iii.) to Pollux. The two brothers mount it alternately on their return from the infernal regions. Har'pagos, the horse from Harpa'gium in Phrygia, was common to both brothers.

Polly. Mary. The change of M for P in pet names is by no means rare ; *e.g.*—

Margaret. Maggie or Meggy, becomes Peggie, and Pegg or Peg.

Martha. Matty becomes Patty.

Mary. Molly becomes Polly or Poll. Here we see another change by no means unusual—that of *r* into *l* or *ll*. Similarly, *Sarah* becomes Sally ; *Dorothea*, Dora, becomes Dolly ; *Harry*, Hal.

Polo'nius. An old courtier, garrulous, conceited, and politic. He was father of Ophe'lia, and lord chamberlain to the king of Denmark. (*Shakespeare : Hamlet.*)

Polo'ny. A vulgar corruption of *Bolo'gna sausage.*

Polt-foot. A club-foot. Ben Jonson calls Vulcan, who was lame, the "polt-footed philosopher." (Swedish, *bult*, a club ; *bulta*, to beat ; our *bolt*.)

Poltron. A bird of prey, with the talons of the hind toes cut off to prevent its flying at game. (Latin, *pollicetruncato*, deprived of its toe or thumb.)

Poltroon'. A coward. Menage derives it from the Italian *poltro*, a bed, because cowards feign themselves sick a-bed in times of war. Saumaise says it means "maimed of the thumb," because in times of conscription those who had no stomach for the field disqualified themselves by cutting off their right thumb. More probably a poltroon is a hawk that will not or cannot fly at game. (*See above.*)

Polybo'tes (4 syl.). One of the giants who fought against the gods. The sea-god pursued him to the island of Cos, and, tearing away part of the island, threw it on him and buried him beneath the mass. (*Greek fable.*) (*See* GIANTS.)

Polycle'tus. A statuary of Sic'yon, who deduced a canon of the proportions of the several parts of the human body, and made a statue of a Persian bodyguard, which was admitted by all to be a model of the human form, and was called "The Rule" (the standard).

Polyc'rates (4 syl.), Tyrant of Samos, was so fortunate in all things that Amasis, King of Egypt, advised him to chequer his pleasures by relinquishing something he greatly prized. Whereupon Polycrătēs threw into the sea a beautiful seal, the most valuable of his jewels. A few days afterwards a fine fish was sent him as a present, and in its belly was found the jewel. Amasis, alarmed at this good fortune, broke off his alliance, declaring that sooner or later this good fortune would fail ; and not long afterwards Polycrates was shamefully put to death by Orœtēs, who had invited him to his court.

"Richard [Mutimer], in surveying his guests, . . . had feelings not unlike those which lulled King Polycrates of old."—*G. Gissing : Demos*, chap. xii.

Polycrates' Ring. (*See above.*)

Polycrat'icon, in eight books, by John of Salisbury. This is his chief work, and is an *exposé* of the frivolities of courtiers and philosophers. It is learned, judicious, and very satirical. (He died 1182.)

Polyd'amas. A Grecian athlete of immense size and strength. He killed a fierce lion without any weapon, stopped a chariot in full career, lifted a mad bull, and died at last in attempting to stop a falling rock. (*See* MILO.)

Pol'ydore (3 syl.). The name assumed by Guide'rius, in Shakespeare's *Cymbeline.*

Polyphe'me (3 syl.). One of the Cyclops, who lived in Sicily. He was an enormous giant, with only one eye, and that in the middle of his forehead. When Ulysses landed on the island, this monster made him and twelve of his crew captives ; six of them he ate, and then Ulysses contrived to blind him, and make good his escape with the rest of the crew. Polypheme was most passionately in love with Galate'a, a sea-nymph, but Galate'a had set her heart on the shepherd Acis, whom Polypheme, in a fit of jealousy, crushed beneath a rock.

In the gallery of the Farnēse palace is a superb painting of Polyphēmus, in three parts ; (1) playing a flute to Galatea ; (2) hurling a rock at Acis ; and (3) pursuing the ships of Ulysses. Poussin has also introduced, in one of his landscapes, Polyphemus sitting on a rock and playing a flute.

Po'ma Alcinoo Dare (2 syl.). (*See* ALCINOO.)

Poma'tum. So called because it was originally made by macerating over-ripe apples in grease. (*Dr. John Quincy : Lexicon Physico-Medicum*, 1723.)

Pommard (French). Beer. This is a pun on the word *pomme.* The Normans called cider *pommé ;* whence *pomat*, a sort of beer.

"Ils tiennent leure chaloupes . . . bien pourvues ou garnies de pain, de vin, de pomat, cidre, outre d'autre boisson. . . ."—*Cleirac : Les Us et Coutumes de la Mer*, p. 127.

Pommel. The pommel of a saddle is the apple of it, called by the French *pommeau.* The Spaniards use the expression *pomo de espada* (the pommel of a sword). To "pommel a person" is to beat him with the pommel of your sword. The ball used as an ornament on pointed roofs is termed a *pomel.* (Latin, *pomum*, an apple.)

Pomo'na. Fruit; goddess of fruits and fruit-trees—one of the Roman divinities. (Latin, *pomum.*)

" Bade the wide fabric unimpaired sustain
Pomo'na's store, and cheese, and golden grain."
Bloomfield : Farmer's Boy.

Pom'padour, as a colour, is claret purple. The 56th Foot is called the Pompadours, from the claret facings of their regimental uniforms. There is an old song supposed to be an elegy on John Broadwood, a Quaker, which introduces the word :—

" Sometimes he wore an old brown coat,
Sometimes a pompadore ,
Sometimes 'twas buttoned up behin l.
And sometimes down before."

Pompey. A generic name for a black footman, as Abigail used to be of a lady's maid. Moll or Molly is a cook ; Betty, a housemaid ; Sambo, a black " buttons ;" etc. One of Hood's jokes for a list of library books was, *Pompeii ; or, Memoirs of a Black Footman, by Sir W. Gill.* (Sir W. Gell wrote a book on Pompeii.) Pompey is also a common name for a dog.

Pompey's Pillar, in Alexandria. A pillar erected by Publius, Prefect of Egypt, in honour of the Emperor Diocletian, to record the conquest of Alexandria in 296. It has about as much right to be called *Pompey's* pillar as the obelisk of Heliop'olis, re-erected by Ram'eses II. at Alexandria, has to be called *Cleopatra's Needle*, or Gibraltar Rock to be called a Pillar of Her'culēs.

Pompey's pillar is a Corinthian column nearly 100 feet high, the shaft being of red granite.

Pompilia. The bride of Count Guido Franceschi'ni, who is brutally treated by him, but makes her escape under the protection of a young priest, named Caponsacchi. She subsequently gives birth to a son, but is stabbed to death by her husband. (*Robert Browning : The Ring and the Book.*) (*See* RING.)

Pongo. The terrible monster of Sicily. A cross between a " land-tiger and sea-shark." He devoured five hundred Sicilians, and left the island for twenty miles round without inhabitant. This amphibious monster was slain by the three sons of St. George. (*The Seven Champions of Christendom*, iii. 2.) A loose name for African anthropoid apes.

Ponoc'ratēs (4 syl.). Gargantua's tutor, in the romance of *Pantag'ruel and Gargantua*, by Rabelais.

Pons Asino'rum. The fifth proposition, book i., of Euclid—the first difficult theorem, which dunces rarely get over for the first time without stumbling. It is anything but a "bridge ;" it is really *pedica asinorum*, the "dolt's stumbling-block."

Pontefract Cakes. Liquorice lozenges impressed with a castle ; so called from being made at Pontefract.

" Pont'efract pronounce " Pomfret."

Pontiff means one who has charge of the bridges. According to Varro, the highest class of the Roman priesthood had to superintend the construction of the bridges (*pontes*). (See *Ramsay : Roman Antiquities*, p. 51.)

"Well has the name of Pontifex been given
  Unto the church's head, as the chief builder
  And architect of the invisible bridge
  That leads from earth to heaven."
      Longfellow : Golden Legend, v.

❦ Here Longfellow follows the general notion that "pontiff" is from *pons-facio*, and refers to the tradition that a Roman priest threw over the Tiber, in the time of Numa, a *sublician*, or wooden bridge.

Sublicius means made of timber or piles. There were subsequently eight stone bridges, and Æmilius converted the sublician bridge into a stone one. There were fifteen pontiffs in the time of Sylla.

Pontius Pilate's Body-Guard. The 1st Foot Regiment, now called the Royal Scots, the oldest regiment in the service. When called *Le Regiment de Douglas*, and in the French service, they had a dispute with the Picardy regiment about the antiquity of their respective corps. The Picardy officers declared they were on duty on the night of the Crucifixion, when the colonel of the 1st Foot replied, "If we had been on guard, we should not have slept at our posts."

Pony (*A*). Twenty-five pounds. A sporting term ; a translation crib = to carry one over a difficulty.
Pony in vingt-et-un. The person on the right-hand of the dealer, whose duty it is to collect the cards for the dealer ; so called from the Latin *ponc*, "behind," being behind the dealer.

Poona. A sovereign. *Lingua Franca* for pound.

Poor. *Poor as Job.* The allusion is to Job, who was by Satan deprived of everything he possessed.
Poor as Lazarus. This is the beggar Lazarus, full of sores, who was laid at the rich man's gate, and desired to be fed from the crumbs that fell from Dives' table (Luke xvi. 13-31).
Poor as a church mouse. In a church there is no cupboard or pantry, where mice most do congregate.
There are none poor but those whom God hates. This does not mean that poverty is a punishment, but that the only poverty worthy of the name is poverty of God's grace. In this sense Dives may be the poor man, and Lazarus the beggar abounding in that "blessing of the Lord which maketh rich."

Poor Jack or **John** (*A*). Dried hake. We have "john-dory," a "jack" (pike), a "jack shark," and a "jack of Dover." Probably the word Jack is

a mere play on the word "Hake," and John a substitute for Jack.

"'Tis well thou art not fish ; if thou hadst, thou
  hadst been poor-john."—*Shakespeare : Romeo and Juliet*, i. 1.

∴ We have a similar perversion in the school-boy proof that a pigeon-pie is a fish-pie. A pigeon-pie is a pie-john, and a pie-john is a jack-pie, and a jack-pie is a fish-pie.

Poor Man. The blade-bone of a shoulder of mutton, so called in Scotland. In some parts of England it is termed a "poor knight of Windsor," because it holds the same relation to Sir Loin as a Windsor knight does to a baronet. Sir Walter Scott tells of a Scotch laird who, being asked by an English landlord what he would have for dinner, produced the utmost consternation by saying, "I think I could relish a morsel of a poor man." (See *Bride of Lammermoor*, chap. xix.)

Poor Richard. The assumed name of Benjamin Franklin in a series of almanacks from 1732 to 1757. These almanacks contain maxims and precepts on temperance, economy, cleanliness, chastity, and other homely virtues ; and to several of the maxims are added the words, "as poor Richard says." Nearly a century before Robert Herrick had brought out a series of almanacks under the name of *Poor Robin's Almanack*.

Poor Tassel (*A*). A poor hand, a bad workman, no great shakes. The tassel or tiercel was a male goshawk, restricted to princes, and called a "tassel gentle."

"Venturing this opinion to the brick-maker, he laughingly replied, 'Come, then, and try your hand at a brick.' The trial, however, proved me a 'poor tassel,' amidst the jeers and laughter of the men."—*C. Thomson : Autobiography*, p. 52.

Poorer than Irus (*"Iro pauperior"*). Irus was the beggar employed by the suitors of Penelope to carry to her their tokens of love. When Ulysses returned home, Irus attempted to prevent his entering the gates, but Ulysses felled him to the ground, and threw the dead body into the road.

Pop the Question (*To*). To propose or make an offer of marriage. As this important demand is supposed to be unexpected, the question is said to be popped.

Pope lived at Twickenham. (1688-1744.)

"For though not sweeter his own Homer sings,
  Yet is his life the more endearing song."
      Thomson : Winter.

Pope (1 syl.), in Latin *popa* (plur. *popæ*). A priest who knocked on the head the ox offered in sacrifice, and cut it up, a very small part being burnt, and all the rest distributed to those concerned in the sacrifice. Wine was poured between the horns, but the priest first sipped it, and all those who assisted him. After the beast had been stunned it was stabbed, and the blood was caught in a vessel used for the purpose, for the shedding of blood was indispensable in every sacrifice. It was the duty of the pope to see that the victim to be sacrificed was without spot or blemish, and to ascertain that it had never been yoked to the plough. The head was crowned with a fillet, and the horns gilt. Apparently the Roman soldiers of Pontius Pilate made a mockery imitation of these Roman and Greek sacrifices.

Pope. *The Pope changing his name.* According to Plati'na, Sergius II. was the first pope who changed his name on ascending the papal chair. His proper name was Hogsmouth. Chambers says his name was "Peter di Porca," and it was the name Peter he changed, out of deference to St. Peter, thinking it arrogant to style himself Peter II. (844-847).

I know no more about it than the Pope of Rome—than a man living as far off as the Cham of Tartary or Pope of Rome.

Drunk like a pope. Benedict XII. was an enormous eater and such a wine-drinker that he gave rise to the bacchanalian expression, *bibāmus papaliter.* (*See* DRUNK.)

Pope. *Titles assumed by the popes.*
Universal Bishop. Prior to Gregory the Great.
Servus Servōrum. Assumed by Gregory the Great in 591.
The Lamb of God which taketh away the Sins of the World. Martin IV. in 1281.
Divine Majesty ; Husband of the Church ; Prince of the Apostles ; Key of the whole Universe ; the Pastor and Physician possessed of all Power both in Heaven and Earth. Leo X. in 1513.
Monarch of Christendom ; Vice-God ; Lord God the Pope. Paul V. in 1635.
Master of the World ; the Universal Father ; Viceregent of the Most High. Subsequent to Paul V.
(See *Brady : Clavis Calendaria*, 247.)

Pope Joan. Said to have succeeded Leo IV. Gibbon says, "Two Protestants, Blondel and Bayle, annihilated her ; " but Mosheim seems half-inclined to believe there was such a person. The vulgar tale is that Joan conceived a violent passion for the monk Folda, and in order to get admission to him assumed the monastic habit. Being clever and popular, she got to be elected pope.

Pope's Sermon (*A*). Only once has a pope been known to preach a sermon in three hundred years. In 1847 a great crowd had assembled to hear the famous Padre Ventura preach in Santa Andrea della Valle, at Rome, but the preacher failed to appear ; whereupon Pius IX. ascended the pulpit, and gave a sermon. (*De Liancourt : History of Pius IX.*)

The Pope's slave. So Cardinal Cajetan calls the Church. (Sixteenth century.)

Pope's Tiara (*The*). He calls himself (1) Head of the Catholic or Universal Church ; (2) Sole Arbiter of its Rights ; and (3) Sovereign Father of all the kings of the earth. From these assumptions he wears a triple crown—one as High Priest, one as Emperor, and one as King. (See *Brady*, 250, 251.)

‥ For the first five centuries the Bishops of Rome wore a bonnet, like other ecclesiastics.

Pope Hormasdas (514-523) placed on his bonnet the crown sent him by Clovis.

Boniface VIII. (1224-1303) added a second crown during his struggles with Philip the Fair.

John XXII. (1410-1415) assumed the third crown.

Popefigland. An island inhabited by the Gaillardets (French, *gaillard*, gay people), rich and free, till, being shown one day the pope's image, they exclaimed, "A fig for the pope ! " whereupon the whole island was put to the sword. Its name was then changed to Popefigland, and the people were called Popefigs.

Pop'injay. A butterfly man, a fop ; so called from the popinjay or figure of a bird shot at for practice. The jay was decked with parti-coloured feathers so as to resemble a parrot, and, being suspended on a pole, served as a target. He whose ball or arrow brought down the bird by cutting the string by which it was hung, received the proud title of "Captain Popinjay," or "Captain of the Popinjay," for the rest of the day, and was escorted home in triumph. (See *Old Mortality*, ch. ii.)

" I then, all smarting with my wounds being cold,
To be so pestered with a popinjay,
Answered neglectingly I know not what,
He should or he should not."
    Shakespeare: 1 *Henry IV.*, 1. 3.

The Festival of the Popinjay. The first Sunday in May. (*See above.*)

Popish Plot. A plot in the reign of Charles II. to massacre the Protestants, burn London, and assassinate the king. Titus Oates invented this "wise" scheme, and obtained great wealth by revealing it; but ultimately he was pilloried, whipped, and imprisoned. (*See* GUN-POWDER PLOT.)

Poplar (*The*). (Latin, *popŭlus*, from *populus*, the people.) Being symbolical of the people, both because its leaves are dark on one side and white on the other, and also because they are never still, but blown about by the least gust of wind. In France, to the present day, the poplar is an emblem of democracy. There are black and white poplars, and the aspen-tree is one of the species.

The white poplar was consecrated to Her'cŭlēs, because he destroyed Ka'kos in a cavern of Mount Aventine, which was covered with poplars. In the moment of triumph the hero plucked a branch from one of the trees and bound it round his head. When he descended to the infernal regions, the heat caused a profuse perspiration which blanched the under surface of the leaves, while the smoke of the eternal flames blackened the upper surface. Hence the Hercu'lean poplar has its leaves black on one side and white on the other.

Porcelain (3 syl.), from *porcelana*, "a little pig." So called by the Portuguese traders, from its resemblance to cowrie-shells, the shape of which is not unlike a pig's back. The Chinese earthenware being white and glossy, like the inside of the shells, suggested the application of the name. (*See* Marryatt's *History of Pottery and Porcelain*.)

Porch (*The*). A philosophic sect, generally called Stoics (Greek, *stoa*, a porch), because Zeno, the founder, gave his lectures in the Athenian picture gallery, called the porch Pœ'cilē.

"The successors of Socratēs formed societies which lasted several centuries; the Academy, the Porch, the Garden."—*Professor Seeley: Ecce Homo.*

Porcupine. (*See* PETER.)

Porcus. *The Latins call me "porcus."* A sly reproof to anyone boasting, showing off, or trying to make himself appear greater than he is. The fable says that a wolf was going to devour a pig, when the pig observed that it was Friday, and no good Catholic would eat meat on a Friday. Going on together, the wolf said to the pig, "They seem to call you by many names." "Yes," said the pig,

"I am called swine, grunter, hog, and I know not what besides. The Latins call me *porcus*." "Porpus, do they?" said the wolf, making an intentional blunder. "Well, porpoise is a fish, and we may eat fish on a Friday." So saying, he devoured him without another word.

Porcus Litera'rum. A literary glutton, one who devours books without regard to quality.

Pork! Pork! Sylvester, in his translation of Du Bartas, gives this instead of *caw, caw*, as the cry of the raven.

Pork. Sir Thomas Browne says that the Jews abstain from pork not from fear of leprosy, as Tacitus alleges, but because the swine is an emblem of impurity. (*Vulgar Errors*.)

Pork, Pig. The former is Norman-French, the latter Saxon.

"Pork, I think, is good Norman-French; and so, when the brute lives, and is in charge of a Saxon slave, she goes by her Saxon name; but becomes a Norman, and is called *pork*, when she is carried to the castle-hall."—*Sir Walter Scott: Ivanhoe.*

Porphyr'ion. One of the giants who made war with the gods. He hurled the island of Delos against Zeus (Jupiter); but Zeus, with the aid of Hercŭlēs, overcame him. (*Greek fable.*) (*See* GIANTS.)

Porridge. *Everything tastes of porridge.* However we may deceive ourselves, whatever castles in the air we may construct, the fact of home life will always intrude. Sir Walter Scott tells us of an insane man who thought the asylum his castle, the servants his own menials, the inmates his guests. "Although," said he, "I am provided with a first-rate cook and proper assistants, and although my table is regularly furnished with every delicacy of the season, yet so depraved is my palate that everything I eat tastes of porridge." His palate was less vitiated than his imagination.

Port, meaning larboard or left side, is an abbreviation of *porta il timone* (carry the helm). Porting arms is carrying them on the left hand.

"To heel to port" is to lean on the left side (Saxon, *hyldan*, to incline). "To lurch to port" is to leap or roll over on the left side (Welsh, *llercian*).

" She gave a heel, and then a lurch to port,
And, going down head-foremost, sunk in short,"
Byron: Don Juan.

Port. An air of music; martial music. Hence Tytler says, "I have never been able to meet with any of the ports here referred to" (*Dissertation on Scotch Music*). The word is Gaelic.

Port Royal Society. In 1637, Le Maître, a celebrated advocate, resigned the honour of being *Counseiller d' État*, and with his brother De Sericourt consecrated himself to the service of religion. The two brothers retired to a small house near the Port Royal of Paris, where in time they were joined by their three other brothers—De Sacy, De St. Elme, and De Valmont. Afterwards, being obliged to remove, they fixed their residence a short distance from the city, and called it Port Royal des Champs. These illustrious recluses were subsequently joined by other distinguished persons, and the community was called the Society of Port Royal.

Port Wine. *Lord Pembroke's port wine.* This renowned wine is thus made—

27 gallons of rough cider,
13 gallons of Bone Carlo wine, } To make a hogs-
3 gallons of brandy.   } head of port.

Porte (*The*) or *The Sublime Porte.* The Ottoman Empire. In the Byzantine Empire, the gates of the palace were the place of assembly for judicial and legal administration. The word *sublime* is French for "lofty," and the term was adopted naturally, as French has long been the language of diplomacy. The whole building contains four Turkish departments of state—viz. (1) the Grand Vizierat ; (2) the Foreign Office ; (3) the Interior ; and (4) the State Council.

"The government is to blame for not having done all in its power, like the Porte."—*The Times.*

Porteous Riot. This notorious tumult took place at Edinburgh in September, 1736. Porteous was captain of the city guard. At the examination of a criminal named Wilson, Captain Porteous, fearing a rescue, ordered the guards to fire on the mob, which had become tumultuous ; in this discharge six persons were killed, and eleven wounded. Porteous was tried for this attack and condemned to death, but reprieved. The mob, at his reprieve, burst into the jail where he was confined, and, dragging him to the Grassmarket (the usual place of execution), hanged him by torchlight on a dyer's pole.

Por'tia. A rich heiress in *The Merchant of Venice*, in love with Bassa'nio. Her father had ordained that three caskets should be offered to all who sought her hand—one of gold, one of silver, and one of lead—with this proviso : he only who selected the casket which contained the portrait of the lady should possess her hand and fortune. (*Shakespeare.*)

Portland Stone. So called from the island of Portland, where it is quarried. It hardens by exposure to the atmosphere. St. Paul's Cathedral and Somerset House (London) are built of this stone.

Portland Vase. A cinerary urn of transparent dark-blue glass, long in possession of the Barberi'ni family. In 1770 it was purchased by Sir William Hamilton, for 1,000 guineas, and came afterwards into the possession of the Duchess of Portland. In 1810, the Duke of Portland, one of the trustees of the British Museum, allowed it to be placed in that institution for exhibition. William Lloyd, in 1845, dashed it to pieces ; it has since been carefully repaired, but is not now shown to the public. It is ten inches high, and six in diameter at the broadest part.

Portmanteau Word (*A*). A word, like post, which contains several meanings packed together ; as, post (a stake), post for letters, post paper, slow as a post, fast as a post, post-horses, and so on.

Portobello Arms. A public-house sign. The *Mirror* says : "In 1739, after the capture of Portobello, Admiral Vernon's portrait dangled from every sign-post, and he may figuratively be said to have sold the ale, beer, porter, and purl of England for six years." The *Portobello Arms* is a mere substitution for the admiral.

Portso'ken Ward (London). The *soken* or franchise at the *port* or gate. It was formerly a guild called the "English Knighten Guild," because it was given by King Edgar to thirteen knights for services done by them. (*See* KNIGHTEN-GUILD.)

Portugue'se (3 syl.). A native of Portugal, the language of Portugal, pertaining to Portugal, etc. ; as Camoëns was a Portuguese, and wrote in Portuguese.

Po'ser. The bishop's examining chaplain ; the examiner at Eton for the King's College fellowship. (Welsh, *posiaw*, to examine ; French, *poser ;* Latin, *pono*.) Hence, a puzzling question.

Posse. *A whole posse of men.* A large number ; a crowd. (*See next article.*)

Posse Comita′tus (Latin). Power of the county. The whole force of the county—that is, all the male members of a county over fifteen, who may be summoned by a sheriff to assist in preventing a riot, the rescue of prisoners, or other unlawful disorders. Clergymen, peers, and the infirm are exempt.

Posset properly means a drink taken before going to bed ; it was milk curdled with wine.

"In his morning's draught ... his concerves or cates ... and when he goeth to bedde his posset smoaking hot."—*Man in the Moone* (1609).

Post means *placed*. (Latin, *positus*.)

Post. A piece of timber placed in the ground.

A military post. A station where a man is placed, with instructions not to quit it without orders.

An official post is where a man is placed in office.

To post accounts is to place them under certain heads in methodical order. (*Trench.*)

Post haste. Travelling by relays of horses, or where horses are placed on the road to expedite the journey.

Post office. An office where letters are placed.

Post paper. So called from its watermark, a post-horn, or a post-boy blowing his horn.

"The old original post [paper] with the stamp in the corner representing a post-boy riding for life, and twanging his horn."—*Mrs. Gaskell: Cranford*, chap. v.

Stiff as a post. That is, stiff [in the ground] like a gate-post.

To run your head against a post. To go to work heedlessly and stupidly, or as if you had no eyes.

Post Factum (Latin). After the act has been committed.

Post Meridian (Latin). After noon.

" 'Twas post meridian half-past four, By signal I from Nancy parted."
Dibdin : Sea Songs.

Post-mortem (Latin). After death ; as a post-mortem examination for the purpose of ascertaining the cause of death.

Post-mortem Degree (*A*). A degree after having failed at the poll.

" He had not even the merit of being a plodding man, and he finally took what used to be called a *post-mortem* degree."—*My Rectors*, p. 63.

Post Obit. An agreement to pay for a loan a larger sum of money, together with interest at death. (Latin *post ob′itum*, after the death of the person named in the bond.)

Poste Restante (French). To remain at the post till called for. In the British post-office letters so addressed are kept one month, and then returned to the writer.

Posted. *Well posted up in the subject.* Thoroughly informed. The metaphor is from posting up accounts, where one can see everything at a glance.

Posterio′ri. An argument *a posterio′ri* is one from effects to cause. Thus, to prove the existence of God *a posterio′ri*, we take the works of creation and show how they manifest power, wisdom, goodness, and so on ; and then we claim the inference that the maker of these things is powerful, wise, and good. Robinson Crusoe found the footprints of a man on the sand, and inferred that there must be a man on the island besides himself. (*See* PRIORI.)

Post′humus (*Le′ona′tus*). Husband of Imo′gen. Under the erroneous persuasion of his wife's infidelity, he plots her death, but his plot miscarries. (*Shakespeare : Cymbeline.*)

Posting-Bills. Before the Great Fire the space for foot-passengers in London was defended by rails and posts ; the latter served for theatrical placards and general announcements, which were therefore called *posters* or posting-bills.

Posy properly means a copy of verses presented with a bouquet. It now means the verses without the flowers, as the " posy of a ring," or the flowers without the verses, as a " pretty posy."

" He could make anything in poetry, from the posy of a ring to the chronicle of its most heroic wearer."—*Stedman : Victorian Poets* (Landor), p. 47.

Pot. This word, like "father," " mother," " daughter," etc., is common to the whole A′ryan family. Greek, *potēr*, a drinking-vessel ; Latin, *poc-ulum* —*i.e.* potaculum ; Irish and Swedish, *pota* ; Spanish, *pote* ; German, *pott* ; Danish, *potte* ; French, Welsh, Anglo-Saxon, *pott*, etc.

Gone to pot. Ruined, gone to the bad. The allusion is to the pot into which refuse metal is cast to be remelted, or to be discarded as waste.

"Now and then a farm went to pot."—*Dr. Arbuthnot.*

The pot calls the kettle black. This is said of a person who accuses another of faults committed by himself. The French say, " The shovel mocks the poker " (*La pelle se moque du fourgon*).

To betray the pot to the roses. To betray the rose pot—that is, the pot which contains the rose-nobles. To "let the cat out of the bag." (French, *Decouvrir le pot aux roses.*)

Brazen and earthen pots. Gentlemen and artisans, rich and poor, men of mark and those unstamped. From the fable of the *Brazen and Earthen Pots.*

" Brazen and earthen pots float together in juxtaposition down the stream of life."—*Pall Mall Gazette.*

Pot-boilers. Articles written for periodicals or publishers, and pictures of small merit drawn or painted for the sake of earning daily bread, or making the pot supply needful food.

Pot-luck. *Come and take pot-luck with me.* Come and take a family dinner at my house. The French *pot au feu* is the ordinary dinner of those who dine at home.

Pot Paper. A Dutch paper ; so called from its bearing a pot as its watermark.

Pot-Pourri (French). A mixture of dried sweet-smelling flower-petals and herbs preserved in a vase. Also a hotchpotch or olla podri'da. In music, a medley of favourite tunes strung together. (*See* PASTICCIO.)

Pourri means dead [flowers], and pot-pourri, strictly speaking, is the vase containing the sweet mixture.

Pot Valiant. Made courageous by liquor.

Pot-de-Bière. French slang for an Englishman.

Pot of Hospitality (*The*). The *pot au feu* which in Ireland used to be shared with anyone who dropped in at mealtimes, or required refreshment.

" And the 'pot of hospitality' was set to boil upon the fire, and there was much mirth and heartiness and entertainment."—*Nineteenth Century,* Oct., 1891, p. 643.

Potage (*Jean*). The Jack Pudding of the French stage ; very like the German " Hanswurst," the Dutch "Pickel herringe," and the Italian " Macaro'ni."

Potato-bogle. So the Scotch call a scarecrow. The head of these bird-bogies being a big potato or a turnip.

Potato-bury (*A*). A pit or trench for preserving potatoes for winter use. A turnip-bury is a similar pit for turnips.

Pota'to-talk. (German, *Kartoffel gesprach.*) That chit-chat common in Germany at the five o'clock tea-drinkings, when neighbours of the "gentler sex" take their work to the house of muster

32*

and talk chiefly of the dainties of the table, their ingredients, admixture, and the methods of cooking them.

Poteen (pron. *pu-teen*). Whisky that has not paid duty. (Irish *poitin*, diminutive of *poite*, a pot.)

" Come and taste some good poteen That has not paid a rap to the Queen."

Pother or *Bother*. Mr. Garnett states this to be a Celtic word, and says it often occurs in the Irish translations of the Bible, in the sense of *to be grieved or troubled in mind.* (Greek, *pŏtheo*, to regret.)

" Friends, cried the umpire, cease your pother, The creature's neither one nor t'other." *The Chameleon.*

Pothooks. The 77th Foot ; so called because the two sevens resemble two pothooks. Now called the Second Battalion of the Middlesex Regiment. The first battalion is the old 57th.

Pot'iphar's Wife. According to the Koran her name was Zuleika, but some Arabian writers call her Rail.

Pots. A Stock Exchange term, signifying the " North Staffordshire Railway stock." Of course, the word means " the potteries." (*See* STOCK EXCHANGE SLANG.)

Potter. To go poking about, meddling and making, in a listless, purposeless manner. *Pudder, podder, pother, bother,* and *puddle* are varieties of the same word. To pudder is to stir with a puddering pole ; hence, to confuse. Lear says of the tempest—" May the great gods that keep this dreadful pudder o'er our head," meaning confusion. To puddle iron is to stir it about with a puddering-pole.

Potwallopers, before the passing of the Reform Bill (1832), were those who claimed a vote because they had boiled their own pot in the parish for six months. (Saxon, *weallan* to boil ; Dutch, *opwallen ;* our *wallop.*)

Strictly speaking, a pot-walloper is one who wallops or boils his own pot-au-feu.

Poult, a young turkey. **Pullet,** a young chicken. (Latin, *pullus,* the young of any animal ; whence *poultry,* young domestic fowls ; *filly,* a young horse ; *foal ;* French, *poule ;* Italian, *pollo,* etc.)

Pound. The unit of weight (Latin, *pondus,* weight) ; also cash to the value of twenty shillings sterling, because in the Carlovingian period the Roman pound (twelve ounces) of pure silver was coined into 240 silver pennies. The symbols £ and *lb.* are for *libra,* the Latin for a pound. (*See* PENNY for POUND.)

Pound of Flesh. The whole bargain, the exact terms of the agreement, the bond *literatim et verbatim.* The allusion is to Shylock, in *The Merchant of Venice,* who bargained with Antonio for a " pound of flesh," but was foiled in his suit by Portia, who said the bond was expressly a pound of flesh, and therefore (1) the Jew must cut the exact quantity, neither more nor less than a just pound ; and (2) in so doing he must not shed a drop of blood.

Poundtext (*Peter*). An "indulged pastor " with the Covenanters' army. (*Sir Walter Scott : Old Mortality.*)

Pourceaugnac (*Monsieur de*) (pron. *Poor-sone-yak*). A pompous country gentleman who comes to Paris to marry Julie, but the lady has a lover of her own choice, and Monsieur is so mystified and played upon by Julie and her *ami du cœur* that he relinquishes his suit in despair. (*Molière : Pourceaugnac.*)

Poussin. *The British Poussin.* Richard Cooper, painter and engraver, well known for his *Views of Windsor.* (*-1806.)
Gaspar Poussin. So Gaspar Dughet, the French painter, is called. (1613-1675.)

Pouting Place of Princes (*The*). Leicester Square is so called by Pennant, because George II., when Prince of Wales, having quarrelled with his father, retired to Leicester House ; and his son Frederick, Prince of Wales, did the same, for the very same reason.

Poverty ... Love. " When poverty comes in at the door, love flies out at the window." " *Sine Cerere et Baccho friget Venus.*"

Powder. *I'll powder your jacket for you.* A corruption of *poudrer* (to dust). (*See* DUST.)

" Lo ! in powdur [dust] ye schall slepe,
For out of powdur fyrst ye came."
Quoted by Halliwell under "Poudre."

Not worth powder and shot. " *Le jeu ne vaut pas la chandelle.*" The thing shot won't pay the cost of powder and shot.

Poyning's Law or *Statute of Drogheda* (pron. *Dro'he-dah*). An Act of Parliament made in Ireland in 1495 (10 Henry VII., chap. 22), declaring all general statutes hitherto made in England to be in force in Ireland also. It received its name from Sir Edward

Poyning, Lieutenant of Ireland at the time.

P.P., Clerk of this Parish. The name given to a volume of memoirs, written by Dr. Arbuthnot, as a satire on Bishop Burnet's *Own Times.*

Præmonstraten'sian Monks. (*See* PREMONSTRATENSIAN.)

Præmuni're. A barbarous word from the Latin *præmone'ri* (to be forewarned). The words of the writ begin " *Præmunire facias A.B.*"—*i.e.* " Cause A. B. to be forewarned," to appear before us to answer the contempt wherewith he stands charged. If A. B. refuses to do so, he loses all civil rights, and before the reign of Elizabeth might have been slain by anyone with impunity.

Pragmat'ic Sanction. *Sanctio* in Latin means a "decree or ordinance with a penalty attached," or, in other words, a "penal statute." *Pragmat'icus* means "relating to state affairs," so that Pragmatic Sanction is a penal statute bearing on some important question of state. The term was first applied by the Romans to those statutes which related to their provinces. The French applied the phrase to certain statutes which limited the jurisdiction of the Pope ; but generally it is applied to] an ordinance fixing the succession in a certain line.
Pragmatic Sanction of Charles VII. (*of France*), 1438, defining and limiting the power of the Pope in France. By this ordinance the authority of a general council was declared superior to the dictum of the Pope : the clergy were forbidden to appeal to Rome on any point affecting the secular condition of the nation ; and the Roman pontiff was forbidden to appropriate a vacant benefice, or to appoint either bishop or parish priest.
Pragmatic Sanction of St. Louis, 1268, forbade the court of Rome to levy taxes or collect subscriptions in France without the express sanction of the king. It also gave plaintiffs in the ecclesiastical courts the right to appeal to the civil courts. The " Constitutions of Clarendon " were to England what the " Pragmatic Sanction " was to France.
Pragmatic Sanction of Germany, 1713. Whereby the succession of the empire was made hereditary in the female line, in order to transmit the crown to Maria Theresa, the daughter of Charles VI.
This is emphatically the Pragmatic Sanction. unless some qualifying word or date is added, to restrict it to some other instrument.

Pragmatic Sanction of Naples, 1759, whereby Carlos II. of Spain ceded the succession to his third son in perpetuity.

Prairie Fever (*The*). An enthusiastic love of prairie life, which seems to be part of our being, to strengthen our strength, invigorate our spirit, and endow us with new life.

"What with gallops by day and the wild tales by the night watch-fires, I became intoxicated with the romance of my new life ; I had caught the prairie fever."—*Mayne Reid: The Scalp Hunters, ch. iii.*

Prating Sophists. The doctors of the Sorbonne were so called by Budæus of Paris. (1467-1540.)

Prayer-book Parade. The promenade in fashionable watering-places and other places of resort, after morning service on Sundays till luncheon or early dinner-time.

Praying-wheels. It is said that the Buddhists pray by machinery ; that they put prayers into a wheel, and unroll them by the length. This notion arises from a misconception. Saky'a-muni, the Buddha, is said to have "turned the wheel of the law"—*i.e.* to have preached Buddhism incessantly—we should say as a horse in a mill.

Pre-Ad'amites. Before Adam was created. Isaac de la Peyreri maintained that only the Jews are descended from Adam, and that the Gentiles are descended from a race of men existing before Adam ; as the book of Genesis is the history of the Jews only, it does not concern itself with other races. (1655.)

Pre-Raphaelites. A term introduced by Hunt and his friends, who wished to intimate that they preferred the simplicity and truthfulness of the painters who preceded Raphael. The term now signifies a very minute imitation of nature, brilliant colouring, and not much shadow.

Preacher (*The*). Solomon, the author of Ecclesiastes (*the Preacher*).
The glorious preacher. Saint John Chrysostom. (347-407.)
The king of preachers. Louis Bourdaloue. (1632-1704.)
The little preacher. Samuel de Marets, Protestant controversialist. (1599-1663.)

Prebend, meaning a "clergyman attached to a prebendal stall," is a vulgarism. The prebend is the stipend given out of the revenues of the college or cathedral ; he who enjoys the prebend

is the prebendary. (Latin, *præbeo*, to give.)

Preca'rious is what depends on our prayers or requests. A *precarious tenure* is one that depends solely on the will of the owner to concede to our prayer ; hence uncertain, not to be depended on. (Latin, *precor*.)

Precep'tor. The superior of a precep'tory was called by the Templars a *Knight Preceptor;* a "Grand Preceptor" was the head of all the preceptories, or houses of the Knights Templars, in an entire province, the three of highest rank being the Grand Preceptors of Jerusalem, Tripolis, and Antioch. Houses of these knights which were not preceptories were called *commanderies.*

Précieuses Ridicules (in Molière's comedy so called). Aminte and Polixène, who assume the airs of the Hôtel de Rambouillet, a coterie of savants of both sexes in the seventeenth century. The members of this society were termed *précieuses—i.e.* "persons of distinguished merit"—and the *précieuses ridicules* means a ridiculous apeing of their ways and manners.

Precio'sa. The heroine of Longfellow's *Spanish Student*, threatened with the vengeance of the Inquisition.

Precious Stones. (1) *Each month*, according to the Poles, is under the influence of a precious stone :—

January	.. Garnet	.. *Constancy.*
February	.. Amethyst	.. *Sincerity.*
March	.. Bloodstone..	*Courage.*
April..	.. Diamond	.. *Innocence.*
May ..	.. Emerald	.. *Success in love.*
June ..	.. Agate	.. *Health and long life.*
July ..	.. Cornelian	.. *Content.*
August.	.. Sardonyx	.. *Conjugal felicity.*
September..	Chrysolite	.. *Antidote to madness.*
October	.. Opal ..	.. *Hope.*
November ..	Topaz	.. *Fidelity.*
December ..	Turquoise	.. *Prosperity.*

(2) *In relation to the signs of the Zodiac :—*

Aries	.. Ruby.	Libra ..	.. Jacinth.
Taurus	.. Topaz.	Scorpio	.. Agate.
Gemini	.. Carbuncle.	Sagittarius	.. Amethyst.
Cancer	.. Emerald.	Capricornus	Beryl.
Leo	.. Sapphire.	Aquarius	.. Onyx.
Virgo	.. Diamond.	Pisces..	.. Jasper.

(3) *In relation to the planets :—*

Saturn	.. Turquoise	.. *Lead.*
Jupiter	.. Cornelian	.. *Tin.*
Mars ..	.. Emerald	.. *Iron.*
Sun ..	.. Diamond	.. *Gold.*
Venus	.. Amethyst	.. *Copper.*
Mercury	.. Loadstone	.. *Quicksilver.*
Moon	.. Crystal	.. *Silver.*

✵ The ancients divided precious stones into male and female. The darker stones were called the male, and the light ones were called the females. Male sapph'res approach indigo in colour, but the female ones are sky-blue. Theophartos mentions the distinction.

Preco'cious means ripened by the sun before it has attained its full growth ; premature ; a development of mind or body beyond one's age. (Latin, *præ coquo*.)

"Many precocious trees, and such as have their spring in winter, may be found."—*Brown.*

Prel'ate means simply a man preferred, a man promoted to an ecclesiastical office which gives him jurisdiction over other clergymen. Cardinals, bishops, abbots, and archdeacons were at one time so called, but the term is restricted in the Protestant Church to bishops. (Latin, *præfero, prælatus.*)

Preliminary Canter (*A*). Metaphorically, means something which precedes the real business in hand. The reference is to the preliminary canter of horses before the race itself begins.

"The real business of the sessions commenced last night. . . . Everything that has preceded the introduction of this measure has been a preliminary canter."—*Newspaper paragraph,* April 14th, 1894.

Premier Pas. *Ce n'est que le premier pas qui coûte.* Pythagoras used to say, "The beginning is half the whole."

"Incipe Dimidium facti est cœpisse."—*Ausonius.*
"Dimidium facti, qui cœpit, habet."—*Horace.*
"Well begun is half done."

✢ The reverse of these proverbs is : "*C'est le plus difficile que d'écorcher la queue.*"

Premonstraten'sian or *Norbertine Order.* Founded in the twelfth century by St. Norbert, who obtained permission, in 1120, to found a cloister in the diocese of Laon, in France. A spot was pointed out to him in a vision, and he termed the spot *Pré Montré* or *Pratum Monstra'tum* (the meadow pointed out). The order might be called the reformed Augustine, or the White canons of the rule of St. Augustine.

Prendre un Rat par la Queue. To pick a pocket. This proverb is very old —it was popular in the reign of Louis XIII.

Prepense (2 syl.). *Malice prepense* is malice designed or before deliberated. (Latin, *præ pensus.*)

Prepos'terous means "the cart before the horse." (Latin, *præ posterus,* the first last and the last first.)

Presbyterian. (*See* BLUE.)

Prescott. A waistcoat. Rhyming slang. (*See* CHIVY.)

Pres'ents. *Know all men by these presents—i.e.* by the writings or documents now present. (Latin, *per presentes,* by the [writings] present.)

Preserver [*Sotēr*]. Ptolemy I. of Egypt was called *Soter* by the Rhodians, because he compelled Deme'trios to raise the siege of Rhodes. (B.C. 367, 323-285.)

Press-money and **Press-men** do not mean money given to *impress* men into the service and men so impressed ; but ready money, and men ready for service. When a recruit has received the money, he binds himself to be ready for service whenever his attendance is required. Similarly, a *press-gang* is a gang to get ready men. (Old French *prest,* now *prêt ;* Italian *presto.*)

Prester John, according to Mandeville, a lineal descendant of Ogier the Dane. This Ogier penetrated into the north of India, with fifteen barons of his own country, among whom he divided the land. John was made sovereign of Teneduc, and was called *Prester* because he converted the natives. Another tradition says he had seventy kings for his vassals, and swept by his subjects only three times in a year. In *Much Ado about Nothing,* Benedick says:—

"I will fetch you a tooth-picker from the farthest inch of Asia ; bring you the length of Prester John's foot : fetch you a hair off the great Cham's beard . . rather than hold three words' conference with this harpy."—Act ii. 1.

Prester John (in *Orlando Furioso,* bk. xvii.), called by his subjects Sena'pus, King of Ethiopia. He was blind. Though the richest monarch of the world, he pined "in plenty's lap with endless famine," for whenever his table was spread hell-born harpies flew away with the food. This was in punishment of his great pride and impiety in wishing to add Paradise to his dominion. The plague was to cease "when a stranger came to his kingdom on a winged horse." Astolpho came on his flying griffin, and with his magic horn chased the harpies into Cocy'tus. The king sent 100,000 Nubians to the aid of Charlemagne ; they were provided with horses by Astolpho, who threw stones into the air, which became steeds fully equipped (bk. xviii.) and were transported to France by Astolpho, who filled his hands with leaves, which he cast into the sea, and they instantly became ships (bk. xix.). When Agramant was dead, the Nubians were sent back to their country, and the ships turned to leaves and the horses to stones again.

Prestige. This word has a strangely metamorphosed meaning. The Latin *præstig'iæ* means juggling tricks, hence *prestidig'itateur* (French), one who juggles with his fingers. We use the word for that favourable impression which results from good antecedents. The history of the change is this: Juggling tricks were once considered a sort of enchantment; to enchant is to charm, and to charm is to win the heart.

Presto. Quick. A name given to Swift by the Duchess of Shrewsbury, a foreigner. Of course, the pun is obvious: *presto* means swift (or quick).

Preston and his Mastiffs. *To oppose Preston and his mastiffs* is to be foolhardy, to resist what is irresistible. Christopher Preston established the Bear Garden at Hockley-in-the-Hole in the time of Charles II. The Bible says he that employs the sword "shall perish by the sword," and Preston was killed in 1709 by one of his own bears.

"... I'd as good oppose
Myself to Preston and his mastiffs loose."
Oldham: III. Satyr of Juvenal.

Pretender. *The Old Pretender.* James F. E. Stuart, son of James II. (1688-1766.)

The Young Pretender. Charles Edward Stuart, son of the "Old Pretender." (1720-1788.)

"God bless the king, I mean the faith's defender;
God bless—no harm in blessing—the Pretender.
Who that Pretender is, and who is king—
God bless us all!—that's quite another thing."
John Byrom.

Pretenders. Tanyoxarkēs, in the time of Camby'ses, King of Persia, pretended to be Smerdis; but one of his wives felt his head while he was asleep, and discovered that he had no ears.

Lambert Simnel and Perkin Warbeck, in the reign of Henry VIII.

Otrefief, a monk, pretended to be Demetrius, younger son of Czar Ivan Basilowitz II., murdered by Boris in 1598. In 1605 Demetrius "the False" became Czar, but was killed at Moscow the year following, in an insurrection.

Pre'text. A pretence. From the Latin *prætexta*, a dress embroidered in the front worn by the Roman magistrates, priests, and children of the aristocracy between the age of thirteen and seventeen. The *prætexta'tæ* were dramas in which actors personated those who wore the prætexta; hence persons who pretend to be what they are not.

Prettyman (*Prince*), who figures sometimes as a fisherman's son, and sometimes as a prince, to gain the heart of Cloris. (*Buckingham: The Rehearsal.*)

Prevarica'tion. The Latin word *varico* is to straddle, and *prævaricor*, to go zigzag or crooked. The verb, says Pliny, was first applied to men who ploughed crooked ridges, and afterwards to men who gave crooked answers in the law courts, or deviated from the straight line of truth. (*See* DELIRIUM.)

Prevent. Precede, anticipate. (Latin *præ-venio*, to go before.) And as what goes before us may hinder us, so prevent means to hinder or keep back.

"My eyes prevent the night watches."—Psalm cxix. 148.
"Prevent us, O Lord, in all our doings."—*Common Prayer Book.*

Previous Question. (*See* QUESTION.)

Pri'am. King of Troy when that city was sacked by the allied Greeks. His wife's name was Hec'uba; she was the mother of nineteen children, the eldest of whom was Hector. When the gates of Troy were thrown open by the Greeks concealed in the Wooden Horse, Pyrrhos, the son of Achilles, slew the aged Priam. (See *Homer's Iliad* and *Virgil's Æne'id.*)

Pri'amond. Son of Ag'apē, a fairy. He was very daring, and fought on foot with battle-axe and spear. He was slain by Cam'balo. (*Spenser: Faërie Queene*, bk. iv.) (*See* DIAMOND.)

Pria'pus, in classical mythology, is a hideous, sensual, disgusting deity, the impersonation of the principle of fertility. (*See* BAAL PEOR, etc.)

Prick-eared. So the Roundheads were called, because they covered their heads with a black skull-cap drawn down tight, leaving the ears exposed.

Prick the Garter. (*See* FAST AND LOOSE.)

Pride, meaning ostentation, finery, or that which persons are proud of. Spenser talks of "lofty trees yclad in summer's pride" (verdure). Pope, of a "sword whose ivory sheath [was] inwrought with envious pride" (ornamentation); and in this sense the word is used by Jacques in that celebrated passage—

"Why, who cries out on pride [dress]
That can therein tax any private party?
What woman in the city do I name
When that I say 'the city woman bears
The cost of princes on unworthy shoulders'?
... What is he of baser function
That says his bravery [finery] is not of my
cost?" *Shakespeare: As You Like It*, ii. 7.

Fly pride, says the peacock, proverbial for pride. (*Shakespeare: Comedy of Errors,* iv. 3.) The pot calling the kettle "black face."

Sir Pride. First a drayman, then a colonel in the Parliamentary army. (*Butler: Hudibras.*)

Pride of the Morning. That early mist or shower which promises a fine day. The Morning is too proud to come out in her glory all at once—or the proud beauty being thwarted weeps and pouts awhile. Keble uses the phrase in a different sense when he says:—

" Pride of the dewy Morning,
The swain's experienced eye
From thee takes timely warning,
Nor trusts the gorgeous sky."
Keble: 25th Sunday after Trinity.

Pride's Purge. The Long Parliament, not proving itself willing to condemn Charles I., was *purged* of its unruly members by Colonel Pride, who entered the House with two regiments of soldiers, imprisoned sixty members, drove one hundred and sixty out into the streets, and left only sixty of the most complaisant.

Pridwen. The name of Prince Arthur's shield.

" He henge an his sweore [neck] acne sceld deore,
His nome on Brutise [in British] Pridwen ihaten
[called]."
Layamon: Brut (twelfth century).

Prid'win. Same as *pridwen.* This shield had represented on it a picture of the Virgin.

" The temper of his sword, the tried 'Excaliber,'
The bigness and the length of ' Rone,' his noble
spear,
With ' Pridwin,' his great shield, and what the
proof could bear." *Drayton.*

Priest . . . Knight. *I would rather walk with Sir Priest than Sir Knight.* I prefer peace to strife.

Priest of the Blue-bag. A barrister. A blue-bag is a cant name for a barrister. (*See* BARRISTER'S BAG.)

" He [O'Flynn] had twice pleaded his own cause, without help of attorney, and showed himself as practised in every law quibble . . . as if he had been a regularly ordained priest of the blue bag.".
—*C. Kingsley: Alton Locke,* chap. xx.

Prig. A knavish beggar in the *Beggar's Bush,* by Beaumont and Fletcher.

Prig. A coxcomb, a conceited person. Probably the Anglo-Saxon *pryt* or *pryd.*

Prig. To filch or steal. Also a pickpocket or thief. The clown calls Autol'ycus a " prig that haunts wakes, fairs, and bear - baitings." (*Shakespeare: Winter's Tale,* iv. 3.)

In Scotch, *to prig* means to cheapen, or haggle over the price asked ; *priggin* means cheapening.

Prima Donna (Italian). A first-class lady ; applied to public singers.

Prima Facie (Latin). At first sight. A *prima facie* case is a case or statement which, without minute examination into its merits, seems plausible and correct.

It would be easy to make out a strong *prima facie* case, but I should advise the more cautious policy of *audi alteram partem.*

Primary Colours. (*See* COLOURS.)

Prime (1 syl.). In the Catholic Church the first canonical hour after lauds. Milton terms sunrise " that sweet hour of prime." (*Paradise Lost,* bk. v. 170.)

" All night long . . . came the sound of chanting . . . as the monks sang the service of matins, lauds, and prime."—*Shorthouse: John Inglesant,* chap. i. p. 10.

Primed. Full and ready to deliver a speech. We say of a man whose head is full of his subject, " He is primed to the muzzle." Of course, the allusion is to firearms.

Primero. A game at cards.

" I left him at primero with the Duke of Suffolk."—*Shakespeare: Henry VIII.,* i. 2.

** " Four cards were dealt to each player, the principal groups being flush, prime, and point. Flush was the same as in ' poker,' *prime* was one card of each suit, and *point* was reckoned as in ' piquet.' "—*Cyclopœdia of Games,* p. 270.

Primitive Fathers (*The*). The five Christian fathers supposed to be contemporary with the Apostles : viz. Clement of Rome (30-102) ; Barnabas, cousin of Mark the Evangelist, and schoolfellow of Paul the Apostle ; Hermas, author of *The Shepherd* ; Ignatius, martyred A.D. 115 ; and Polycarp (85-169).

The first two *Epistles to the Corinthians* are probably by Clement Romãnus, but everything else ascribed to him is undoubtedly spurious.

The epistle ascribed to Barnabas is of very doubtful authenticity.

Hermas.—It is very doubtful whether this is a proper name at all ; and, if a proper name, many think it is a Hermas in the second century, brother of Pius I.

Polycarp, some say, was a pupil of John the Evangelist, by whom he was made Bishop of Smyrna, addressed in the Revelation ; but if the Revelation was written in 96, Polycarp was not eleven years old at the time, and could not possibly have been a bishop. It is extremely doubtful whether he knew the Evangelist at all, and certainly he did not know either the "ourth Gospel or the Book of the Revelation.

Primrose (*George*). Son of the worthy Vicar of Wakefield. He went to Amsterdam to teach the people English, but forgot that he could not do so till he knew something of Dutch himself. (*Goldsmith: Vicar of Wakefield.*)

Moses Primrose. Brother of the above, noted for giving in barter a good horse for a gross of worthless green spectacles with copper rims and shagreen cases. (*Goldsmith: Vicar of Wakefield.*)

Mrs. Deborah Primrose. Mother of the

above; noted for her motherly vanity, her skill in housewifery, and her desire to be genteel. Her *wedding gown* is a standing simile for things that "wear well." Her daughters' names are Olivia and Sophia. (*Goldsmith: Vicar of Wakefield*.)

The Rev. Dr. Primrose. Husband of Mrs. Deborah, and Vicar of Wakefield. As simple-minded and unskilled in the world as Goldsmith himself, unaffectedly pious, and beloved by all who knew him. (*Goldsmith: Vicar of Wakefield*.)

Primrose. A curious corruption of the French *primeverole*, Italian *primeverola*, compounds of the Latin *prima vera* (first spring *flower*). Chaucer calls the word *primirole*, which is a contraction of the Italian *prime'rola*. The flower is no *rose* at all.

Pri'mum Mo'bile, in the Ptolema'ic system of astronomy, was the tenth (not ninth) sphere, supposed to revolve from east to west in twenty-four hours, carrying with it all the other spheres. The eleven spheres are: (1) Diana or the Moon, (2) Mercury, (3) Venus, (4) Apollo or the Sun, (5) Mars, (6) Jupiter, (7) Saturn, (8) the starry sphere or that of the fixed stars, (9) the crystalline, (10) the primum mo'bile, and (11) the empyre'an. Ptolemy himself acknowledged only the first nine; the two latter were devised by his disciples. The motion of the crystalline, according to this system, causes the precession of the equinoxes, its axis being that of the ecliptic. The motion of the primum mobile produces the alternation of day and night; its axis is that of the equator, and its extremities the poles of the heavens.

"They pass the planets seven, and pass the
    'fixed' [starry sphere],
And that crystal'lin sphere . . . and that 'First-
    Moved.'"   *Milton: Paradise Lost,* iii. 482.

Primum Mobile is figuratively applied to that machine which communicates motion to several others; and also to persons and ideas suggestive of complicated systems. Socratēs was the primum mobile of the Dialectic, Megaric, Cyrena'ic, and Cynic systems of philosophy.

Pri'mus. The archbishop, or rather "presiding bishop," of the Episcopal Church of Scotland. He is elected by the other six bishops, and presides in Convocation, or meetings relative to church matters.

Prince. The Latin prin'cipēs formed one of the great divisions of the Roman infantry; so called because they were originally the *first* to begin the fight. After the Hasta'ti were instituted, this privilege was transferred to the new division.

Prince. (*See* BLACK.)

Prince of alchemy. Rudolph II., Emperor of Germany, also called The German Hermes Trismegistus.

Prince of gossips. Samuel Pepys, noted for his gossiping *Diary,* commencing January 1st, 1659, and continued for nine years. (1632-1703)

Prince of grammarians. (*See* GRAMMARIANS.)

Prince of Peace. The Messiah (Isaiah ix. 6).

Prince of the Power of the Air. Satan (Eph. ii. 2).

Prince of the vegetable kingdom. So Linnæus calls the palm-tree.

Prince of Wales (*The*). This title arose thus: When Edward I. subdued Wales, he promised the Welsh, if they would lay down their arms, that he would give them a native prince. His queen having given birth to a son in Wales, the new-born child was entitled Edward, Prince of Wales; and ever since then the eldest son of the British sovereign has retained the title.

Prince of Wales Dragoon Guards. The 3rd Dragoon Guards.

Prince Rupert's Drops. Drops of molten glass, consolidated by falling into water. Their form is that of a tadpole. The thick end may be hammered pretty smartly without its breaking, but if the smallest portion of the thin end is nipped off, the whole flies into fine dust with explosive violence. These toys, if not invented by Prince Rupert, were introduced by him into England.

Prince's Peers. A term of contempt applied to peers of low birth. The son of Charles VII. of France (afterwards Louis XI.), in order to weaken the influence of the aristocracy, created a host of riff-raff peers, such as tradesmen, farmers, and mechanics, who were tools in his hands.

Princox or **Princocks.** (Probably from *prime* and *cock*.) Capulet calls Tybalt a *princox,* or wilful spoilt boy. (*Shakespeare: Romeo and Juliet*.)

Prink. *She was prinked in all her finery.* Adorned. Prink and prank. Dutch *pronken,* to make a show; German *prangen,* Danish *prange,* Swedish *prunka.*

Printer's Devil. The newest apprentice lad in the press-room, whose duty it is to run errands, and to help the pressmen.

Printing used to be called the *Black Art*, and the boys who assisted the pressmen were called *imps*. (*See under* DEVIL.)

Printers' Marks.
? is ℈—that is, the first and last letters of *quæstio* (question).

! is ⁱₒ. *Io* in Latin is the interjection of joy.

§ is a Greek p (π), the initial letter of *paragraph*.

* is used by the Greek grammarians to arrest attention to something striking (*asterisk* or star).

† is used by the Greek grammarians to indicate something objectionable (*obelisk* or dagger).

(*See* MARKS IN GRAMMAR.)

Printing. (*See* EM.)
Father of English printing. William Caxton (1412-1491).

✲ It is a mistake to suppose that Caxton (1471) was the first printer in England. A book has been accidentally discovered with the date 1478 (Oxford). The Rev. T. Wilson says, "The press at Oxford existed ten years before there was any press in Europe, except those at Haarlem and Mentz. The person who set up the Oxford press was Corsellis."

Prio'ri. An argument *a priori* is one from cause to effect. To prove the existence of God *a priori*, you must show that every other hypoth'esis is more unlikely, and therefore this hypothesis is the most likely. All mathematical proofs are of this kind. (*See* POSTERIORI.)

Priscian's Head. *To break Priscian's head* (in Latin, "*Diminuĕre Priscia'ni cap'ut*"). To violate the rules of grammar. Priscian was a great grammarian of the fifth century, whose name is almost synonymous with grammar.

"Priscian's head is often bruised without remorse."—*P. Thompson.*

"And held no sin so deeply red
As that of breaking Priscian's head."
          Butler: Hudibras, pt. ii. 2.

Priscill'ianists. Followers of Priscillian, a Spaniard; an heretical sect which sprang up in Spain in the fourth century. They were a branch of the Manichæans.

Prisoner at the Bar. The prisoner in the dock, who is on his trial; so called because anciently he stood at the bar which separated the barristers from the common pleaders.

Prisoner of Chillon'. François de Bonnivard, a Frenchman confined for six years in the dungeon of the Chateau de Chillon, by Charles III. of Savoy. Lord Byron, in his poem so called, has welded together this incident with Dante's *Count Ugoli'no.* (*See* CHILLON.)

Pri'thu. The favourite hero of the Indian Purânas. Vena having been slain for his wickedness, and leaving no offspring, the saints rubbed his right arm, and the friction brought forth Prithu. Being told that the earth had suspended for a time its fertility, Prithu went forth to punish it, and the Earth, under the form of a cow, fled at his approach; but being unable to escape, promised that in future "seed-time and harvest should never fail."

Priu'li. Senator of Venice, noted for his unbending pride, and his unnatural harshness to his daughter Belvide'ra. (*Otway : Venice Preserved.*)

Privolvans'. The antagonists of the Subvolvans, in S. Butler's satirical poem called *The Elephant in the Moon.*

"These silly ranting Privolvans
Have every summer their campaigns,
And muster like the warlike sons
Of Rawhead and of Bloodybones."
          v. 85. etc.

Privy Council. The council chosen by the sovereign to administer public affairs. It consists of the Royal Family, the two Primates, the Bishop of London, the great officers of State, the Lord Chancellor and Judges of the Courts of Equity, the Chief Justices of the Courts of Common Law, the Judge Advocate, some of the Puisne Judges, the Speaker of the House of Commons, the Ambassadors, Governors of Colonies, Commander-in-Chief, Master-General of the Ordnance, First Lord of the Admiralty, Vice-President of the Board of Trade, Paymaster of the Forces, President of the Poor-law Board, etc. etc.; a committee of which forms the Cabinet or Ministry. The number of neither the Privy Council nor Cabinet is fixed, but the latter generally includes about fifteen or sixteen gentlemen specially qualified to advise on different departments of state business. Much of the business of the Privy Council is performed by Boards or subdivisions, as the *Board of Trade*, the *Board of Quarantine*, the *Committee of Council on Education*, etc.

Privy Seal. The seal which the sovereign uses in proof of assent to a document. In matters of minor importance it is sufficient to pass the privy seal, but instruments of greater moment must have the great seal also.

Pro and Con. (Latin). For and against. "Con." is a contraction of *contra*.

Pro Tanto. As an instalment, good enough as far as it goes, but not final; for what it is worth.

"I heard Mr. Parnell accept the Bill of 1886 as a measure that would close the differences between the two countries; but since then he stated that he had accepted it as a *pro tanto* measure. ... It was a parliamentary bet, and he hoped to make future amendments on it."—*Mr. Chamberlain's speech*, April 10th, 1893.

Pro Tem'pore (3 syl.). Temporarily; for the time being, till something is permanently settled. Contracted into *pro tem.*

Probate of a Will. A certified copy of a will by an officer whose duty it is to attest it. The original is retained in the court registry, and executors act on the proved copy. Anyone may see an official copy of any will at the registry office on payment of a shilling.

Probe. *I must probe that matter to the bottom*—must narrowly examine into it. The allusion is to a surgeon probing a wound, or searching for some extraneous substance in the body.

Prob'ole (3 syl.), as applied to Jesus Christ, is this: that He was divine only because He was divinely begotten; in fact, He was a shoot of the divine stem. This heterodox notion was combated by Irenæus, but was subsequently revived by Monta'nus and Tertullian. The word is properly applied to the process of a bone—that is, a bone growing out of a normal bone. (Greek, *pro-ballo*.)

Procès-Verbal. A minute and official statement of some fact.

"We (says the procès-verbal) asked him what use he had made of the pistol [i.e. We, says the official report, etc.]."—*The Times (Law Report).*

Procession of the Black Breeches. This is the heading of a chapter in vol. ii. of Carlyle's *French Revolution.* The chapter contains a description of the mob procession, headed by Santerre carrying a pair of black satin breeches on a pole. The mob forced its way into the Tuileries on June 20th, 1792, and presented the king (Louis XVI.) with the bonnet rouge and a tricolour cockade.

Proclaim on the Housetop. To proclaim or make known to everyone; to blab in public. Dr. Jahn says that the ancient Jews "ascended their roofs to announce anything to the multitude, to pray to God, and to perform sacrifices" (Matt. x. 27).

"No secret can escape being proclaimed from the housetop."—*London Review.*

Proclivity. *His proclivities are all evil.* His tendencies or propensities have a wrong bias. The word means downhill tendency. (Latin, *proclivis.*)

Procris. *Unerring as the dart of Procris.* When Procris fled from Ceph'alus out of shame, Diana gave her a dog that never failed to secure its prey, and a dart which not only never missed aim, but which always returned of its own accord to the shooter. (*See* CEPHALUS.)

Procrustes' Bed. Procrustes was a robber of Attica, who placed all who fell into his hands upon an iron bed. If they were longer than the bed, he cut off the redundant part; if shorter, he stretched them till they fitted it. Any attempt to reduce men to one standard, one way of thinking, or one way of acting, is called placing them on Procrustes' bed, and the person who makes the attempt is called Procrustes. (*See* GIRDLE.)

"Tyrant more cruel than Procrustes old,
Who to his iron-bed by torture fits
Their nobler parts, the souls of suffering wits."
Mallet: Verbal Criticism.

Procrus'tean. Pertaining to Procrustes, and his mode of procedure. (*See above.*)

Prodigal. Festus says the Romans called victims wholly consumed by fire *prod'igæ hostiæ* (victims prodigalised), and adds that those who waste their substance are therefore called prodigals. This derivation can hardly be considered correct. Prodigal is *pro-ago* or *prod-igo* (to drive forth), and persons who had spent all their patrimony were "driven forth" to be sold as slaves to their creditors.

Prodigul (The). Albert VI., Duke of Austria. (1418-1463.)

Prodigy. *The prodigy of France.* Guillaume Budé; so called by Erasmus. (1467-1540.)

The prodigy of learning. Samuel Hahnemann, the German, was so called by J. Paul Richter. (1755-1843.)

Profane means literally before the temple (Latin, *pro fanum*). Those persons who came to the temple and were not initiated were called profane by the Romans.

Pro'file (2 syl.) means shown by a thread. (Italian, *profilo; * Latin, *filum*, a thread.) A profile is an outline. In sculpture or painting it means to give the contour or side-face.

Profound (*The*). Richard Middleton, theologian. (* -1304.)

The Profound Doctor. Thomas Bradwarden, a schoolman. (Fourteenth century.)

Most Profound Doctor. Ægidius de Columna, a Sicilian schoolman. (Died 1316.)

Prog. Food (connected with *prod*, and perhaps *prov*[*ender*]). Burke says, "You are the lion, and I have been endeavouring to prog [procure food] for you."

" So saying, with a smile she left the rogue
  To weave more lines of death, and plan for
    prog." *Dr. Wolcot : Spider and Fly.*

Progn'e or **Prok'ne.** The swallow. (*See* NIGHTINGALE.)

" As Progne or as Philome'la mourns . .
That finds the nest by cruel hands dispoiled ; . .
So Bradamant laments her absent knight."
        Orlando Furioso, book xxiii.

Progress. *To report progress,* in parliamentary language, is to conclude for the night the business of a bill, and defer the consideration of all subsequent items thereof -till the day nominated by the chief Minister of the Crown.

Projec'tion. *Powder of projection,* or the " Philosopher's Stone." A powder supposed to have the virtue of changing baser metals into gold or silver. A little of this powder, being cast into molten metal of the baser sort, was to *project* from it pure gold or silver. Education may be called the true " powder of projection."

Proletaire (3 syl.). One of the rabble. *Prolétaires* in French means the lowest and poorest class in the community. *Proleta'rian,* mean or vulgar. The sixth class of Servius Tullius consisted of *proletarii* and the *capite censi—i.e.* breeders and human *heads.* The *proletaries* could not enter the army, but were useful as breeders of the race (*proles*). The *capite censi* were not enrolled in the census by the value of their estates, but simply by their polls.

Proleta'riat. Commonalty. (*See* PROLETAIRE.)

" Italy has a clerical aristocracy, rich, idle, and corrupt ; and a clerical proletariat, needy and grossly ignorant."—*The Times.*

Prome'theus (3 syl.) made men of clay, and stole fire from heaven to animate them. For this he was chained by Zeus to Mount Cau'casus, where an eagle preyed on his liver daily. The word means Forethought, and one of his brothers was Epime'theus or Afterthought.

" Faster bound to Aaron's charming eyes
Than is Prometheus tied to Caucasus."
    Shakespeare : Titus Andronicus, ii. 1.

Prome'thean. Capable of producing fire ; pertaining to Prome'theus (*q.v.*).

Prome'thean Fire. The vital principle ; the fire with which Prometheus quickened into life his clay images. (*See* PROMETHEUS.)

" I know not where is that Promethean heat
That can thy life relume."
    Shakespeare : Othello, v. 2.

Prome'thean Unguent (*The*). Made from a herb on which some of the blood of Prometheus (3 syl.) had fallen. Medea gave Jason some of this unguent, which rendered his body proof against fire and warlike instruments.

Prome'theans. The first invention which developed into Bryant and May's " safety matches." They were originally made in 1805 by Chancel, a French chemist, who tipped cedar splints with paste of chlorate of potash and sugar. On dipping one of these matches into a little bottle containing asbestos wetted with sulphuric acid, it burst into flame on drawing it out. It was not introduced into England till after the battle of Waterloo. (*See* HUGH PERRY.)

Promise of Odin (*The*). The most binding of all promises to a Scandinavian. In making this promise the person passed his hand through a massive silver ring kept for the purpose ; or through a sacrificial stone, like that called the " Circle of Stennis."

" I will bind myself to you . . . by the promise of Odin, the most sacred of our northern rites."—*Sir W. Scott : The Pirate,* chap. xxii.

Promised Land or *Land of Promise.* Canaan ; so called because God promised Abraham, Isaac, and Jacob that their offspring should possess it.

Prone'sia (in *Orlando Furioso*). One of Logistilla's handmaids, famous for her wisdom.

Proof. A printed sheet to be examined and approved before it is finally printed. The *first* proof is that which contains all the workman's errors ; when these are corrected the impression next taken is called a *clean* proof and is submitted to the author ; the final impression, which is corrected by the reader *ad unguem,* is termed the *press* proof.

Proof Prints. The first impressions of an engraving. *India-proofs* are those taken off on India-paper. *Proofs before lettering* are those taken off before the plate is sent to the writing engraver. After the proofs the orders of merit are

—(1) the prints which have the letters only in outline; (2) those in which the letters are shaded with a black line; (3) those in which some slight ornament is introduced into the letters; (4) those in which the letters are filled up quite black.

Proof Spirit. A mixture of equal parts (by weight) of alcohol and water. The *proof* of spirit consists in little bubbles or beads which appear on the top of the liquor after agitation. When any mixture has more alcohol than water it is called *over* proof, and when less it is termed *under* proof.

Prooshan Blue (*My*). A term of great endearment. After the battle of Waterloo the Prussians were immensely popular in England, and in connection with the Loyal True Blue Club gave rise to the toasts, "The True Blue" and the "Prussian Blue." Sam Weller addresses his father as "Vell, my Prooshan Blue."

Propagan'da. The name given to the "congregation" *de propaganda fide*, established at Rome by Gregory XV., in 1622, for propagating throughout the world the Roman Catholic religion. Any institution for making religious or political proselytes.

Proper Names used as Common Nouns.

Crebillon = terrible.
Dumas = imaginative
Fénelon = fabulous.
Le Sage = humorous.
Molière = comic.
Montaigne = thoughtful.
Rabelais = unclean.
Rousseau = amorous.
Victor Hugo = incendiary.
Zola = licentious : *Zolaesque*, in the manner or style of Zola, the French novelist.

Property Plot (*The*), in theatrical language, means a list of all the "properties" or articles which will be required in the play produced. Such as the bell, when Macbeth says, "The bell invites me;" the knock, when it is said, "Heard you that knocking?" tables, chairs, banquets, tankards, etc., etc.

Prophesy upon Velvet (*To*). To prophesy what is already a known fact. Thus, the issue of á battle flashed to an individual may, by some chance, get to the knowledge of a "sibyl," who may securely prophesy the issue to others; but such a prediction would be a "prophecy on velvet;" it goes on velvet slippers without fear of stumbling.

"If one of those three had spoken the news over again . . . the old lady [or sibyl] prophesies upon velvet."—*Sir W. Scott; The Pirate, ch. xxi.*

Prophet (*The*). Mahomet is so called. (570-632.)

The Koran says there have been 200,000 prophets, only six of whom have brought new laws or dispensations; Adam, Noah, Abraham, Moses, Jesus, and Mahomet.

The Prophet. Jo'achim, Abbot of Fio're. (1130-1202.)

Prophet of the Syrians. Ephraem Syrus (4th century).

The Great Prophets. Isaiah, Jeremiah, Ezekiel, and Daniel; so called because their writings are more extensive than the prophecies of the other twelve.

The Minor or Lesser Prophets. Hose'a, Joel, Amos, Obadiah, Micah, Jonah, Nahum, Habak'kuk, Zephani'ah, Haggai, Zechari'ah, and Mal'achi; so called because their writings are less extensive than those of the four Great Prophets.

Prophetess (*Tho*). Ay-e'shah, the second wife of Mahomet; so called, not because she had any gift of prophecy, but simply because she was the favourite wife of the "prophet:" she was, therefore, emphatically "Mrs. Prophet."

Propositions, in logic, are of four kinds, called A, E, I, O. "A" is a universal affirmative, and "E" a universal negative; "I" a particular affirmative, and "O" a particular negative.

"Asserit A, negat E, verum generaliter ambo!
Asserit I, negat O, sed particulariter ambo."

A asserts and E denies some *universal* proposition;
I asserts and O denies, but with *particular* precision.

Props, in theatrical slang, means properties, of which it is a contraction. Everything stored in a theatre for general use on the stage is a "prop," but these stores are the manager's props. An actor's "props" are the clothing and other articles which he provides for his own use on the stage. In many good theatres the manager provides everything but tights and a few minor articles; but in minor theatres each actor must provide a wardrobe and properties.

Proro'gue (2 syl.). *The Parliament was prorogued.* Dismissed for the holidays, or suspended for a time. (Latin, *pro-rogo,* to prolong.) If dismissed entirely it is said to be "dissolved."

Pro.'s. Professionals—that is, actors by profession.

"A big crowd slowly gathers,
And stretches across the street;
The pit door opens sharply,
And I hear the trampling feet;
And the quiet pro.'s pass onward
To the stage-door up the court."
Sims; Ballads of Babylon; Forgotten, etc.

Prosce′nium. The front part of the stage, between the drop-curtain and orchestra. (Greek, *proskēnion ;* Latin, *proscēnium.*)

Proscrip′tion. A sort of hue and cry ; so called because among the Romans the names of the persons proscribed were written out, and the tablets bearing their names were fixed up in the public forum, sometimes with the offer of a reward for those who should aid in bringing them before the court. If the proscribed did not answer the summons, their goods were confiscated and their persons outlawed. In this case the name was engraved on brass or marble, the offence stated, and the tablet placed conspicuously in the market-place.

Prose means straightforward speaking or writing (Latin, *ora′tio pro′sa—i.e. proversa*), in opposition to foot-bound speaking or writing, *oratio vincta* (fettered speech—*i.e.* poetry).

Prose. *Il y a plus de vingt ans que je dis de la prose, sans que j'en susse rien.* I have known this these twenty years without being conscious of it. (*Molière : Le Bourgeois Gentilhomme.*)

"'Really,' exclaimed Lady Ambrose, brightening, '*Il y a plus de vingt ans que je dis de la prose, sans que j'en susse rien.*' And so it seems that I have known history without suspecting it, just as Mons. Jourdain talked prose."—*Mallock: The New Republic,* bk. iii. chap. 2.

Father of Greek prose. Herod′otos (B.C. 484-405).
Father of English prose. Wycliffe (1324-1384) ; and Roger Ascham (1515-1568).
Father of French prose. Villehardouin (pron. *Veal-hard-whah′n.*) (1167-1213.)

Proselytes (3 syl.) among Jewish writers were of two kinds—viz. "The proselyte of righteousness" and the "stranger of the gate." The former submitted to circumcision and conformed to the laws of Moses. The latter abstained from offering sacrifice to heathen gods, and from working on the Sabbath. "The stranger that is within thy gate" = the stranger of the gate.

"I must confess that his society was at first irksome ; but . . . I now have hope that he may become a stranger of the gate."—*Eldad the Pilgrim,* ch. iii.

Proser′pina or **Pros′erpine** (3 syl.). One day, as she was amusing herself in the meadows of Sicily, Pluto seized her and carried her off in his chariot to the infernal regions for his bride. In her terror she dropped some of the lilies she had been gathering, and they turned to daffodils.

"O Proserpina,
For the flowers now, that frighted thou let'st fall
From Dis's waggon ! daffodils,
That come before the swallow dares, and take
The winds of March with beauty."
Shakespeare : Winter's Tale, iv. 4.

Proserpine's Divine Calidore. Sleep. In the beautiful legend of *Cupid and Psyche,* by Apuleius, after Psyche had long wandered about searching for her lost Cupid, she is sent to Proserpine for "the casket of divine beauty," which she was not to open till she came into the light of day. Psyche received the casket, but just as she was about to step on earth, she thought how much more Cupid would love her if she was divinely beautiful ; so she opened the casket and found the calidore it contained was sleep, which instantly filled all her limbs with drowsiness, and she slept as it were the sleep of death.

This is the very perfection of allegory. Of course, sleep is the only beautifier of the weary and heart-sick ; and this calidore Psyche found before Cupid again came to her.

Prosper′ity Rob′inson. Viscount Goderich, Earl of Ripon, Chancellor of the Exchequer in 1823. In 1825 he boasted in the House of the prosperity of the nation, and his boast was not yet cold when the great financial crisis occurred. It was Cobbett who gave him the name of "Prosperity Robinson."

Pros′pero. Rightful Duke of Milan, deposed by his brother. Drifted on a desert island, he practised magic, and raised a tempest in which his brother was shipwrecked. Ultimately Prospero *broke his wand,* and his daughter married the son of the King of Naples. (*Shakespeare : Tempest.*)

Protag′oras of Abde′ra was the first who took the name of "Sophist." (B.C. 480-411.)

Prote′an. Having the aptitude to change its form : ready to assume different shapes. (*See* PROTEUS.)

Protec′tionist. One who advocates the imposition of import duties, to "protect" home produce or manufactures.

Protector. The Earl of Pembroke (1216).
Humphrey, Duke of Gloucester (1422-1447).
Richard, Duke of Gloucester (1483).
The Duke of Somerset (1548).
The Lord Protector of the Commonwealth. Oliver Cromwell (1653-1658).

Protesila'os, in Fénelon's *Télémaque*, is meant to represent Louvois, the French Minister of State.

Prot'estant. One of the party who adhered to Luther at the Reformation. These Lutherans, in 1529, "protested" against the decree of Charles V. of Germany, and appealed from the Diet of Spires to a general council. A Protestant now means one of the Reformed Church.

Protestant Pope. Clement XIV.

Proteus (pron. *Pro'-tuce*). *As many shapes as Proteus—i.e.* full of shifts, aliases, disguises, etc. Proteus was Neptune's herdsman, an old man and a prophet. He lived in a vast cave, and his custom was to tell over his herds of sea-calves at noon, and then to sleep. There was no way of catching him but by stealing upon him during sleep and binding him ; if not so captured, he would elude anyone who came to consult him by changing his shape, for he had the power of changing it in an instant into any form he chose.

The changeful Proteus, whose prophetic mind,
The secret cause of Bacchus' rage divined,
Attending, left the flocks, his scaly charge,
To graze the bitter weedy foam at large."
          Camoens : Lusiad, vi.

Pro'teus. One of the two gentlemen of Verona ; his serving-man is Launce. Valentine is the other gentleman, whose serving-man is Speed. (*Shakespeare : Two Gentlemen of Verona.*)

Prothala'mion. Marriage song by Edmund Spenser, peculiarly exquisite—probably the noblest ever sung.

Proto-martyr. The first martyr. Stephen the deacon is so called (Acts v. vii.).

Pro'tocol. The first rough draft or original copy of a despatch, which is to form the basis of a treaty. (Greek, *proto-kōleon,* a sheet glued to the front of a manuscript, and bearing an abstract of the contents and purport. (*Harmolaus Barbarus.*)

Protoplasm, Sarcode. The material or cells of which all living things are built up. Each is a jelly-like substance, the former being the nucleus of plants and the latter of animals. Max Schultz proved the identity of these substances.

∵ Protoplasm is not a simple but a complicated structure, sometimes called a "colony of plasts," or nuclear granules. (Greek, *proto-plasma,* the first model ; *proto-sarkodes,* the first flesh-like entity.)

Protozo'a. The lowest class of animal life (Greek, *protos zoön*). In a figurative sense, a young aspirant for literary honours: "They were young intellectual protozoa."

Proud (*The*). Otho IV., Emperor of Germany. (1175, 1209-1218.)

Tarquin II. of Rome. *Superbus.* (Reigned B.C. 535-510, died 496.)

The proud Duke. Charles Seymour, Duke of Somerset. He would never suffer his children to sit in his presence, and would never speak to his servants except by signs. (Died 1748.)

Proud as Lucifer ; proud as a peacock.

Proud'fute (*Oliver*). A boasting bonnet-maker of Perth. His widow is Magdalen or Maudie. (*Sir Walter Scott : Fair Maid of Perth.*)

Prout. (*See under* FATHER.)

Prov'ince means a country previously conquered. (Latin, *pro vinco.*)

Provin'cial. Like or in the manner of those who live in the provinces.

Provincial of an Order. The superior of all the monastic houses of a province.

Prudent Tree (*The*). Pliny calls the mulberry the most prudent of all trees, because it waits till winter is well over before it puts forth its leaves. Ludovico Sforza, who prided himself on his prudence, chose a mulberry-tree for his device, and was called "*Il Moro.*"

Prud'homme. *A Mons. Prud'homme.* A man of experience and great prudence, of estimable character and practical good sense. Your Mons. Prud'homme is never a man of genius and originality, but what we in England should term a "Quaker of the old school."

The council of prud'hommes. A council of arbiters to settle disputes between masters and workmen.

Prunello. Stuff. Prunello really means that woollen stuff of which common ecclesiastical gowns used to be made ; it was also employed for the uppers of women's boots and shoes ; everlasting. A corruption of Brignoles.

" Worth makes the man, and want of it the fellow ;
The rest is all but leather or prunello."
          Pope: Essay on Man, iv.

Prussia means *near Russia,* the country bordering on Russia. In Neo-Latin, *Borussia ;* in Slavonic, *Porussia ; po* in Slavonic signifying "near."

Prussian Blue. So called because it was discovered by a Prussian, viz.

Diesbach, a colourman of Berlin, in 1710. It is sometimes called *Berlin* blue.

Prus'sic Acid means the acid of Prussian blue. It is now termed in science hydrocyan'ic acid, because it is made from a cyanide of iron.

Psalm cv. 28. The Prayer Book version is : "They were not obedient unto his word."
The Bible version and the new version is : "They rebelled not against his word."

Psalms. Seventy-three psalms are inscribed with David's name, twelve with that of Asaph the singer ; eleven go under the name of the Sons of Korah, a family of singers ; one (*i.e.* Ps. xc.) is attributed to Moses. The whole compilation is divided into five books : bk. 1, from i. to xli. ; bk. 2, from xlii. to lxxii. ; bk. 3, from lxxiii. to lxxxix. ; bk. 4, from xc. to cvi. ; bk. 5, from cvii. to cl.

Psalmist. *The sweet psalmist of Israel.* King David, who composed many of the Bible Psalms. (*See* Psalm lxxii. 20.)

Psalter of Tara (*The*). It contains a narrative of the early kings of Ireland from Ollam Fodlah to B.C. 900.

" Their tribe, they said, their high degree,
Was sung in Tara's Psaltery."
Campbell : O'Connor's Child.

Psaphon's Birds (*Psaph'onis aves*). Puffers, flatterers. Psaphon, in order to attract the attention of the world, reared a multitude of birds, and having taught them to pronounce his name, let them fly.

" To what far region have his songs not flown,
Like Psaphon's birds, speaking their master's name." *Moore : Rhymes on the Road,* iii.

Psycar'pax [*granary thief*]. Son of Troxartas, King of the Mice. The Frog-king offered to carry the young prince over a lake, but scarcely had he got mid-way when a water-hydra appeared, and King Frog, to save himself, dived under water. The mouse, being thus left on the surface, was drowned, and this catastrophe brought about the battle of the Frogs and Mice.

" The soul of great Psycarpax lives in me,
Of great Troxartas' line."
Parnell : Battle of the Frogs and Mice, i.

Psyche [*Sy'ke*]. A beautiful maiden beloved by Cupid, who visited her every night, but left her at sunrise. Cupid bade her never seek to know who he was, but one night curiosity overcame her prudence, and she went to look at him.

A drop of hot oil fell on his shoulder, awoke him, and he fled. Psyche next became the slave of Venus, who treated her most cruelly ; but ultimately she was married to Cupid, and became immortal. Mrs. Henry Tighe has embodied in six cantos this exquisite allegory from Apuléios.

This subject was represented by Raphael in a suite of thirty-two pictures, and numerous artists have taken the loves of Cupid and Psyche for their subject ; as, for example, Canova, Gerard, Chaudet, etc. The cameo of the Duke of Marlborough is said to have been the work of Tryphon of Athens.

∴ Raphael's illustrations of the adventures of Psyche were engraved for a superb edition in 4to (*De la Fable de Psyche*), published by Henri Didot.

" Fair Psyche, kneeling at the ethereal throne,
Warmed the fond bosom of unconquered love."
Darwin : Economy of Vegetation, iv.

Psychography. Spirit - writing ; writing said by spiritualists to be done by spirits.

Ptolema'ic System. The system of Claudius Ptolemæus, a celebrated astronomer of Palu'sium, in Egypt, of the eleventh century. He taught that the earth is fixed in the centre of the universe, and the heavens revolve round it from east to west, carrying with them the sun, planets, and fixed stars, in their respective spheres. He said that the Moon was next above the earth, then Mercury, then Venus ; the Sun he placed between Venus and Mars, and after Mars, Jupiter and Saturn, beyond which came the two crystalline spheres.

∴ This system was accepted, till it was replaced in the sixteenth century by the Copernican system.

Public. The people generally and collectively ; the members generally of a state, nation, or community.

Public-house Signs. Much of a nation's history, and more of its manners and feelings, may be gleaned from its public-house signs. A very large number of them are selected out of compliment to the lord of the manor, either because he is the " great man " of the neighbourhood, or because the proprietor is some servant whom " it delighted the lord to honour ; " thus we have the *Earl of March*, in compliment to the Duke of Richmond : the *Green Man* or gamekeeper, married and promoted " to a public." When the name and titles of the lord have been exhausted, we get his cognisance or his favourite pursuit, as the *Bear and Ragged Staff*, the *Fox and Hounds*. As the object of the sign is to speak to the feelings and attract, another fruitful source is either some national hero or great battle ; thus we get the *Marquis of Granby* and the *Duke of Wellington*, the *Waterloo* and the *Alma*. The proverbial loyalty of our nation has naturally shown itself in our tavern signs, giving us the *Victoria*, *Prince of Wales*, the *Albert*, the *Crown*, and so on. Some signs indicate a speciality of the house, as the *Bowling Green*, the *Skittles ;* some a political bias, as the *Royal Oak ;* some are an attempt at wit, as the *Five Alls ;* and some are purely fanciful. The following list will serve to exemplify the subject :—

The Angel. In allusion to the angel that saluted the Virgin Mary.

The Bag o' Nails. A corruption of " Bacchanals."

The Bear. From the popular sport of bear-baiting.

The Bear and Bacchus, in High Street, Warwick. A corruption of *Bear and Baculus—i.e.* Bear and Ragged Staff, the badge of the Earl of Warwick.

The Bear and Ragged Staff. The cognisance of the Earl of Warwick, the Earl of Leicester, etc.

The Bell. In allusion to races, a silver bell having been the winner's prize up to the reign of Charles II.

La Belle Sauvage. (*See* BELL SAVAGE.)

The Blue Boar. The cognisance of Richard III.

The Blue Pig (Bevis Marks). A corruption of the *Blue Boar.* (*See above.*)

The Boar's Head. The cognisance of the Gordons, etc.

The Bolt-in-Tun. The punning heraldic badge of Prior Bolton, last of the clerical rulers of Bartholomew's, previous to the Reformation.

Bosom's Inn. A public-house sign in St. Lawrence Lane, London ; a corruption of *Blossom's Inn,* as it is now called, in allusion to the hawthorn blossoms surrounding the effigy of St. Lawrence on the sign.

The Bowling Green. Signifying that there are arrangements on the premises for playing bowls.

The Bull. The cognisance of Richard, Duke of York. The *Black Bull* is the cognisance of the house of Clare.

The Bull's Head. The cognisance of Henry VIII.

The Bully Ruffian. A corruption of the *Bellerophon* (a ship).

The Castle. This, being the arms of Spain, symbolises that Spanish wines are to be obtained within. In some cases, without doubt, it is a complimentary sign of the manor castle.

The Cat and Fiddle. A corruption of *Caton Fidèle—i.e.* Caton, the faithful governor of Calais. In Farringdon (Devon) is the sign of *La Chatte Fidèle,* in commemoration of a faithful cat. Without scanning the phrase so nicely, it may simply indicate that the game of *cat* (trap-ball) and a *fiddle* for dancing are provided for customers.

The Cat and Mutton, Hackney, which gives name to the Cat and Mutton Fields.

The Cat and Wheel. A corruption of " St. Catherine's Wheel ; " or an announcement that *cat* and balance-*wheels* are provided for the amusement of customers.

The Chequers. (1) In honour of the Stuarts, whose shield was " checky," like a Scotch plaid. (2) In commemoration of the licence granted by the Earls of Arundel or Lords Warrenne. (3) An intimation that a room is set apart for merchants and accountants, where they can be private and make up their accounts, or use their " chequers " undisturbed. (*See* LATTICE.)

The Coach and Horses. This sign signifies that it is a posting-house, a stage-coach house, or both.

The Cock and Bottle. By some said to be a corruption of the " Cork and Bottle," meaning that wine is sold there in bottles. (*See* suggested explanation on p. 267.)

The Cow and Skittles. The cow is the real sign, and alludes to the dairy of the hostess, or some noted dairy in the neighbourhood. Skittles is added to indicate that there is a *skittle ground* on the premises.

The Cross Keys. Common in the mediæval ages, and in allusion to St. Peter, or one of the bishops whose cognisance it is—probably the lord of the manor or the patron saint of the parish church. The cross keys are emblems of the papacy, St. Peter, the Bishop of Gloucester, St. Servatus, St. Hippol'ytus, St. Geneviève, St. Petronilla, St. Osyth, St. Martha, and St. Germa'nus.

The Devil. A public-house sign two doors from Temple Bar, Fleet Street. The sign represents St. Dunstan seizing the devil by the nose. (*See under* DEVIL, *Proverbial Phrases.*)

The Dog and Duck. Tea gardens at Lambeth (suppressed) ; to signify that the sport so called could be seen there. A duck was put into water, and a dog set to hunt it ; the fun was to see the duck diving and the dog following it under water.

The Red Dragon. The cognisance of Henry VII. or the principality of Wales.

The Spread Eagle. The arms of Germany; to indicate that German wines may be obtained within.

The Fox and Goose. To signify that there are arrangements within for playing the royal game of Fox and Goose.

St. George and the Dragon. In compliment to the patron saint of England, and his combat with the dragon. The legend is still stamped upon our gold coin.

The George and Cannon. A corruption of "George Canning."

The Globe. The cognisance of Alfonso, King of Portugal; and intimating that Portuguese wines may be obtained within.

The Goat in Golden Boots. A corruption of the Dutch *Goed in der Gouden Boots* (the god Mercury in his golden sandals).

The Goat and Compasses. A Puritan sign, a corrupt hieroglyphic reading of "God encompasses us."

The Black Goats. A public-house sign, High Bridge, Lincoln, formerly *The Three Goats*—i.e. *three gowts* (gutters or drains), by which the water from the Swan Pool (a large lake that formerly existed to the west of the city) was conducted into the bed of the Witham.

The Golden Cross. This refers to the ensigns carried by the Crusaders.

The Grecian Stairs. A corruption of "The Greesen or Stairs" (Greesen is *gree,* a step, our *de-gree*). The allusion is to a flight of steps from the New Road to the Minster Yard. In Wickliffe's Bible, Acts xxi. 40 is rendered—"Poul stood on the greezen."

" Let me speak like yourself, and lay a sentence
  Which, like a grize or step, may help these
    lovers
  Into your favour."
Shakespeare : Othello, i. 3.

The Green Man. The late gamekeeper of the lord of the manor turned publican. At one time these servants were dressed in green.

The Green Man and Still—i.e. the herbalist bringing his herbs to be distilled.

The Hare and Hounds. In compliment to the sporting squire or lord of the manor.

The Hole-in-the-Wall (London). So called because it was approached by a passage or "hole" in the wall of the house standing in front of the tavern.

The Iron Devil. A corruption of "Hirondelle" (the swallow). There are numerous public-house signs referring

to birds; as, the *Blackbird,* the *Thrush,* the *Peacock,* the *Martin,* the *Bird-in-the-Hand,* etc. etc.

The Three Kings. A public-house sign of the mediæval ages, in allusion to the three kings of Cologne, the Magi who presented offerings to the infant Jesus. Very many public-house signs of the mediæval period had a reference to ecclesiastical matters, either because their landlords were ecclesiastics, or else from a superstitious reverence for "saints" and "holy things."

The Man Laden with Mischief. A public-house sign, Oxford Street, nearly opposite to Hanway Yard. The sign is said to have been painted by Hogarth, and represents a man carrying a woman and a good many other creatures on his back.

The Marquis of Granby (London, etc.). In compliment to John Manners, eldest son of John, third Duke of Rutland —a bluff, brave soldier, generous, and greatly beloved by his men.

" What conquest now will Britain boast,
  Or where display her banners ?
Alas ! in Granby she has lost
  True courage and good Manners."

The Packhorse. To signify that packhorses could be hired there.

The Palgrave's Head. A public-house sign near Temple Bar, in honour of Frederick, Palgrave of the Rhine.

The Pig and Tinder Box. A corrupt rendering of *The Elephant and Castle;* the " pig " is really an elephant, and the " tinder-box " the castle on its back.

The Pig and Whistle. Wassail is made of apples, sugar, and ale.

The Plum and Feathers. A public-house sign near Stoken Church Hill, Oxford. A corruption of the "Plume of Feathers," meaning that of the Prince of Wales.

The Queen of Bohemia. In honour of Lady Elizabeth Stuart. (*See* BOHEMIA.)

The Queer Door. A corruption of *Cœur Doré* (Golden Heart).

The Rose. A symbol of England, as the *Thistle* is of Scotland, and the *Shamrock* of Ireland.

The Red Rose. The badge of the Lancastrians in the Civil War of the Roses.

The White Rose. The badge of the Yorkists in the Civil War of the Roses.

The Rose of the Quarter Sessions. A corruption of *La Rose des Quatre Saisons.*

The Salutation and Cat. The " Salutation" (which refers to the angel saluting the Virgin Mary) is the sign of the house, and the " Cat " is added to signify that arrangements are made for playing *cat* or tipcat.

The Saracen's Head. In allusion to what are preposterously termed "The Holy Wars;" adopted probably by some Crusader after his return home, or at any rate to flatter the natural sympathy for these Quixotic expeditions.

The Ship, near Temple Bar, and opposite *The Palgrave's Head ;* in honour of Sir Francis Drake, the circumnavigator.

The Ship and Shovel. Referring to Sir Cloudesley Shovel, a favourite admiral in Queen Anne's reign.

The Seven Stars. An astrological sign of the mediæval ages.

The Three Suns. The cognisance of Edward IV.

The Sun and the Rose. The cognisance of the House of York.

The Swan with Three Necks. A public-house sign in Lad Lane, etc. ; a corruption of "three nicks" (on the bill).

The Swan and Antelope. The cognisance of Henry V.

The Talbot [*a hound*]. The arms of the Talbot family.

The Turk's Head. Alluding to the Holy Wars, when the Crusaders fought against the Turks.

The Unicorn. The Scottish supporter in the royal arms of Great Britain.

The White Hart. The cognisance of Richard II. ; the *White Lion*, of Edward IV., as Earl of March ; the *White Swan*, of Henry IV. and Edward III.

Publicans of the New Testament were the provincial underlings of the Magister or master collector who resided at Rome. The taxes were farmed by a contractor called the Manceps ; this Manceps divided his contract into different societies ; each society had a Magister, under whom were a number of underlings called *Publica'ni* or servants of the state.

Pucelle (*La*). The Maid of Orle'ans, Jeanne d'Arc (1410-1431). (See *Shakespeare's* 1 *Henry VI.*, v. 4.)

Puck or *Robin Goodfellow.* A fairy and merry wanderer of the night, "rough, knurly-limbed, faun-faced, and shock-pated, a very Shetlander among the gossamer-winged" fairies around him. (See *Shakespeare's Midsummer Night's Dream*, ii. 1 ; iii. 1.)

Pucka, an Indian word in very common use, means real, *bona fide ;* as, "He is a commander, but not a pucka one" (*i.e.* not officially appointed, but only

acting as such, *pro tempore*). "The queen reigns, but her ministers are the pucka rulers." A suffragan bishop, an honorary canon, a Lynch-judge, a lieutenant-colonel, the temporary editor of a journal, are not "pucka," or *bona fide* so.

Pudding. (*See* JACK.)

Pudding-time properly means just as dinner is about to begin, for our forefathers took their pudding before their meat. It also means in the nick of time.

> " But Mars . . .
> In pudding-time came to his aid."
> *Butler: Hudibras*, i. 2.

Pudens. A soldier in the Roman army, mentioned in 2 Tim. iv. 21, in connection with Linus and Claudia. According to tradition, Claudia, the wife of Pudens, was a British lady ; Linus, otherwise called Cyllen, was her brother ; and Lucius, "the British king," the grandson of Linus. Tradition further adds that Lucius wrote to Eleutherus, Bishop of Rome, to send missionaries to Britain to convert the people.

Puff. Exaggerated praise. The most popular etymology of this word is *pouff*, a coiffure employed by the ladies of France in the reign of the Grand Monarque to announce events of interest, or render persons patronised by them popular. Thus, Madame d'Egmont, Duke of Richelieu's daughter, wore on her head a little diamond fortress, with moving sentinels, after her father had taken Port Mahon; and the Duchess of Orleans wore a little nursery, with cradle, baby, and toys complete, after the birth of her son and heir. These, no doubt, were pouffs and puffs, but Lord Bacon uses the word puff a century before the head-gear was brought into fashion. Two other etymons present themselves : the old pictures of Fame puffing forth the praises of some hero with her trumpet ; and the puffing out of slain beasts and birds in order to make them look plumper and better for food—a plan universally adopted in the abattoirs of Paris. (German, *puffen*, to brag or make a noise; and French, *pouf*, our puff.)

Puff, in *The Critic*, by Sheridan. An impudent literary quack.

Puff-ball. A sort of fungus. The word is a corruption of Puck or Pouk ball, anciently called Puck-fist. The Irish name is Pooka-foot. (Saxon, *Pulkerfist*, a toadstool.) Shakespeare alludes to this superstition when Pros'pero summons amongst his elves—

"You whose pastime
Is to make midnight mushrooms."
Shakespeare: Tempest, v. 1.

Puffed Up. Conceited ; elated with conceit or praise ; filled with wind. A *puff* is a tartlet with a very light or puffy crust.

"That no one of you be puffed up one against another."—1 Cor. iv. 6.

Pug, a variant of *puck*, is used to a child, monkey, dog, etc., as a pet term.
You mischievous little pug. A playful reproof to a favourite.

Pug. A mischievous little goblin in Ben Jonson's drama of *The Devil is an Ass*.

Pugna Porco'rum (*Battle of the Pigs*). The most celebrated poem of alliterative verse, extending to 253 Latin hexameters, in which every word begins with *p*.

Puisne Judges means the younger-born judges, at one time called *puny* judges. They are the four inferior judges of the Court of Queen's Bench, and the four inferior judges of the Court of Common Pleas. (French, *puisné*, subsequently born ; Latin, *post natus*.)

Pukwa'na (North American Indian). The curling smoke of the Peace-pipe ; a signal or beacon.

Pull. *A long pull, a strong pull, and a pull all together*—*i.e.* a steady, energetic, and systematic co-operation. The reference may be either to a boat, where all the oarsmen pull together with a long and strong pull at the oars ; or it may be to the act of hauling with a rope, when a simultaneous strong pull is indispensable.

Pull Bacon (*To*). To spread the fingers out after having placed one's thumb on the nose.

"The officers spoke to him, when the man put his fingers to his nose and pulled bacon."—*Leeds Police Report*, Oct. 6, 1887.

Pull Devil, Pull Baker. Let each one do the best for himself in his own line of business, but let not one man interfere in that of another.

"It's all fair pulling, 'pull devil, pull baker ;' someone has to get the worst of it. Now it's us [bushrangers], now it's them [the police] that gets . . . rubbed out."—*Boldrewood : Robbery under Arms*, chap. xxxvii.

Pulling. A jockey trick, which used to be called "playing booty"—*i.e.* appearing to use every effort to come in first, but really determined to lose the race.

"Mr. Kemble [in the *Iron Chest*] gave a slight touch of the jockey, and 'played booty.' He seemed to do justice to the play, but really ruined its success."—*George Colman the Younger*.

Pumblechook (*Uncle*). He bullied Pip when only a poor boy, but when the boy became wealthy was his lick-spittle, fawning on him most servilely with his "May I, Mr. Pip" [have the honour of shaking hands with you] ; "Might I, Mr. Pip" [take the liberty of saluting you]. (*Dickens : Great Expectations*.)

Pummel or **Pommel.** To beat black and blue. (French; *pommeler*, to dapple.)

Pump. To sift, to extract information by indirect questions. In allusion to pumping up water.

" But pump not me for politics."
Otway.

Pumpernickel. Brown George or rye-bread used by Westphalian peasants. *His Transparency of Pumpernickel*. So the *Times* satirised the minor German princes, "whose ninety men and ten drummers constituted their whole embattled host on the parade-ground before their palace ; and whose revenue was supplied by a percentage on the tax levied on strangers at the Pumpernickel Kursaal." (July 18, 1866.)
Thackeray was author of the phrase.

Pun is the Welsh *pun*, equivalent ; it means a word equally applicable to two things. The application should be remote and odd in order to give piquancy to the play. (*See* CALEMBOURG.)

Pun and Pickpocket. *He who would make a pun would pick a pocket*. Dr. Johnson is generally credited with this silly dictum (1709-1784), but Dennis had said before to Purcell, "Any man who would make such an execrable pun would not scruple to pick my pocket" (1657-1734). (*Sir W. H. Pyne : Wine and Walnuts*, vol. ii. p. 277.)

The "execrable pun" was this : Purcell rang the bell for the *drawer* or waiter, but no one answered it. Purcell, tapping the table, asked Dennis "why the table was like the tavern ?" Ans. "Because there is no drawer in it."

Punch, from the Indian word *puny* (five) ; so called from its five ingredients —viz. spirit, water, lemon, sugar, and spice. It was introduced into England from Spain, where it is called *ponche*. It is called "Contradiction," because it is composed of *spirits* to make it strong, and *water* to make it weak ; of *lemon-juice* to make it sour, and *sugar* to make it sweet.

Mr. Punch. A Roman mime called Maccus was the original of Punch. A statuette of this buffoon was discovered in 1727, containing all the well-known features of our friend—the long nose and goggle eyes, the hunch back and protruding breast.

The most popular derivation of Punch and Judy is *Pontius cum Judæis* (Matt. xxvii. 19), an old mystery play of *Pontius Pilate and the Jews;* but the Italian *policinello* seems to be from *pollicē,* a thumb (Tom-thumb figures), and our Punch is from *paunch.*

The drama or story of our Punch and Judy is attributed to Silvio Fiorillo, an Italian comedian of the seventeenth century. The tale is this : Punch, in a fit of jealousy, strangles his infant child, when Judy flies to her revenge. She fetches a bludgeon, with which she be- labours her husband, till Punch, exaspe- rated, seizes another bludgeon and beats her to death, then flings into the street the two dead bodies. The bodies attract the notice of a police officer, who enters the house. Punch flees for his life ; being arrested by an officer of the In- quisition, he is shut up in prison, from which he escapes by means of a golden key. The rest is an allegory, showing how Punch triumphs over all the ills that flesh is heir to. (1) En'nui, in the shape of a dog, is overcome ; (2) Disease, in the disguise of a doctor, is kicked out ; (3) Death is beaten to death ; and (4) the Devil himself is outwitted.

Pleased as Punch. (*See* PLEASED.)

Punch. *A Suffolk punch.* A short, thick-set cart-horse.

" I did hear them call their child Punch, which pleas'd me mightily, that word having become a word of common use for everything that is thick and short."—*Pepys's Diary.*

Punc'tual. No bigger than a point, exact to a point or moment. (Latin, *ad punctum.*) Hence the angel, describing this earth to Adam, calls it " This spa- cious earth, this punctual spot "—*i.e.* a spot no bigger than a point. (*Milton : Paradise Lost,* viii. 23.)

Punctuality. *Punctuality is the politeness of kings.* Attributed to Louis XVIII.

Punctuation. The following advice of Bishop Orleton to Gourney and Mal- travers in 1327 is an excellent example of the importance of punctuation :— *Edwardum occidere nolite timere bonum est*—" Refrain not to kill King Edward is right." If the point is placed after the first word, the sentence reads, " Not

to kill the king is right ; " but if after the second word, the direction becomes, " Refrain not ; to kill the king is right." (*See* ORACLE.)

Pundit. An East Indian scholar, skilled in Sanskrit, and learned in law, divinity, and science. We use the word for a *porcus litera'rum,* one more stocked with book lore than deep erudition.

Pu'nic Apple. A pomegranate ; so called because it is the pomum or "apple" belonging to the genus *Pu'nica.*

Pu'nic Faith. Treachery, violation of faith. " Punic faith " is about equal to "Spanish honesty." The Puni (a corruption of Pœni) were accused by the Romans of breaking faith with them, a most extraordinary instance of the "pot calling the kettle black ; " for whatever infidelity the Carthaginians were guilty of, it could scarcely equal that of their accusers.

The Roman *Pœni* is the word *Phœni* (Phœnicians), the Carthaginians being of Phœnician descent.

" Our Punic faith
Is infamous, and branded to a proverb."
Addison : Cato, ii.

Punish a Bottle (*To*). To drink a bottle of wine or spirits. When the contents have been punished, the empty bottles are " dead men."

" After we'd punished a couple of bottles of old Crow whisky . . . he caved in all of a sudden [he got completely powerless]."—*The Barton Experi- ment,* chap. xiv.

Punjab [*five rivers*]. They are the Jelum, Chenab, Ravee, Be'as, and Sutlej ; called by the Greeks *pente-potamia.*

Pup properly means a little boy or girl. A little dog is so called because it is a pet. An insect in the third stage of existence. (Latin, *pupus,* fem. *pupa ;* French, *poupée,* a doll ; German, *puppe.*)

Purbeck (Dorsetshire). Noted for a marble used in ecclesiastical ornaments. Chichester cathedral has a row of columns of this limestone. The columns of the Temple church, London ; the tomb of Queen Eleanor, in Westminster Abbey ; and the throne of the archbishop in Canterbury cathedral, are other speci- mens.

Purgatory. The Jewish Rabbi be- lieved that the soul of the deceased was consigned to a sort of purgatory for twelve months after death, during which time it was allowed to visit its dead body and the places or persons it es- pecially loved. This intermediate state they called by various names, as "the bosom of Abraham," "the garden of Eden," "upper Gehenna." The Sabbath was always a free day, and prayer was supposed to benefit those in this intermediate state.

Purita'ni (*I*). *The Puritans.* Elvi'ra, daughter of Lord Walton, a Puritan, is affianced to Lord Arthur Talbot, a Cavalier. On the day of espousals, Lord Arthur aids Henrietta, the widow of Charles I., to escape ; and Elvira, thinking him faithless, loses her reason. On his return to England, Lord Arthur explains the circumstances, and the two lovers vow that nothing on earth shall part them more. The vow is scarcely uttered, when Cromwell's soldiers enter and arrest Lord Talbot for treason ; but as they lead him forth to execution a herald announces the defeat of the Stuarts, and free pardon to all political prisoners, whereupon Lord Arthur is liberated, and marries Elvira. (*Bellini : I Puritani ; libretto by C. Pepoli*.)

Pu'ritans. Seceders from the Reformed Church ; so called because they rejected all human traditions and interference in religion, acknowledging the sole authority of the "pure Word of God," without "note or comment." Their motto was : "The Bible, the whole Bible, and nothing but the Bible." The English Puritans were sometimes by the Reformers called *Precisionists*, from their preciseness in matters called "indifferent." Andrew Fuller named them *Non-conformists*, because they refused to subscribe to the Act of Uniformity.

Purkinge's Figures. In optics, figures produced on a wall of uniform colour when a person entering a dark room with a candle moves it up and down approximately on a level with the eyes. From the eye near the candle an image of the retinal vessels will appear projected on the wall.

Purler (*A*). A cropper, or heavy fall from one's horse in a steeplechase or in the hunting-field (probably allied to *hurl* and *whirl*).

"Seraph's white horse . . . cleared it, but falling with a mighty crash, gave him a purler on the opposite side."—*Ouida: Under Two Flags,* chap. vi.

Pur'lieu (2 syl.). French *pouralle lieu* (a place free from the forest laws). Henry II., Richard I., and John made certain lands forest lands ; Henry III. allowed certain portions all round to be severed. These "rues," or forest borders were freed from that servitude which was laid on the royal forests. The

"perambulation" by which this was effected was technically called *pourallée.*

" In the purlieus of this forest stands
A sheepcote fenced about with olive-trees."
Shakespeare: As You Like It, iv. 3.

Purple (blue and red) indicates the *love of truth even unto martyrdom.* (*See under* Colour, for its symbolisms, etc.)

Purple (*Promotion to the*). Promotion to the rank of cardinal in the Roman Catholic Church.

" Dr. Moran's promotion to the purple is certain."—*Newspaper paragraph.*

Purpure [purple]. One of the colours of an heraldic escutcheon. It is expressed by vertical lines running down towards the left hand (as you look at the shield lying before you) ; "Vert" runs the contrary way.

PURPLE. VERT.

English heralds vary escutcheons by seven colours ; foreign heralds by nine. (*See* Heralds.)

Pursy, Pursiness. Broken-winded, or in a bloated state in which the wind is short and difficult. (French, *poussi-f,* same meaning.)

A fat and pursy man. Shakespeare has " pursy Insolence," the insolence of Jesurun, "who waxed fat and kicked." In *Hamlet* we have " the fatness of these pursy times "—*i.e.* wanton or self-indulgent times.

Purura'vas and Urva'si. An Indian myth similar to that of "Apollo and Daphne." Purûravas is a legendary king who fell in love with Urva'si, a heavenly nymph, who consented to become his wife on certain conditions. These conditions being violated, Urvasi disappeared, and Pururavas, inconsolable, wandered everywhere to find her. Ultimately he succeeded, and they were indissolubly united. (*See* Psyche.)

Pu'seyite (3 syl.). A High Churchman ; so called from Dr. Pusey, of Oxford, a chief contributor to the *Tracts for the Times.* (*See* Tractarians.)

Puss. A cat, hare, or rabbit. (Irish, *pus,* a cat.) It is said that the word, applied to a hare or rabbit, is from the Latin *lepus,* Frenchified into *le pus.* True or not, the pun may pass muster.

" Oh, puss, it bodes thee dire disgrace,
When I defy thee to the race.
Come, 'tis a bet ; nay, no denial,
I'll lay my shell upon the trial."
The Hare and the Tortoise.

Puss in Boots [*Le Chat Botté*], from the *Eleventh Night* of Straparola's

Italian fairy tales, where Constantine's cat procures his master a fine castle and the king's heiress. First translated into French in 1585. Our version is taken from that of Charles Perrault. There is a similar one in the Scandinavian nursery tales. This clever cat secures a fortune and a royal partner for his master, who passes off as the Marquis of Car'abas, but is in reality a young miller without a penny in the world.

Put. A clown, a silly shallow-pate, a butt, one easily "put upon."

" Queer country puts extol Queen Bess's reign."
Bramson.

Put the Cart before the Horse. (*See* CART.)

Put up the Shutters (*To*). To announce oneself a bankrupt.

Do you think I am going to put up the shutters if we can manage to keep going ?

Putney and Mortlake Race. The annual eight-oared boat-race between the two universities of Cambridge and Oxford.

Putting on Frills (American). Giving oneself airs.

Putting on Side. Giving oneself airs. Side is an archaic word for a train or trailing gown ; also long, as " his beard was side." A side-coat means a long trailing coat. (Anglo-Saxon *sid*, great, wide, long — as *sid-feax*, long hair.)

" I do not like side frocks for little girls."—
Skinner.

Pygma'lion. A statuary of Cyprus, who hated women and resolved never to marry, but fell in love with his own statue of the goddess Venus. At his earnest prayer the statue was vivified, and he married it. (*Ovid : Metamorphoses*, x. ; *Earthly Paradise*, August.)

" Few, like Pygmalion, doat on lifeless charms,
 Or care to clasp a statue in their arms."
S. Jenyns : Art of Dancing, canto i.

✶ In Gilbert's comedy of *Pygmalion and Galatēa*, the sculptor is a married man, whose wife (Cynisca) was jealous of the animated statue (Galatēa), which, after enduring great misery, voluntarily returned to its original state. This, of course, is mixing up two Pygmalions, wide as the poles apart.

John Marston wrote certain satires called *The Metamorphoses of Pygmalion's Image*. These satires were suppressed, and are now very rare.

Pyg'mies (2 syl.). A nation of dwarfs on the banks of the Upper Nile. Every spring the cranes made war upon them and devoured them. They cut down every corn-ear with an axe.

When Hercules went to the country they climbed up his goblet by ladders to drink from it ; and while he was asleep two whole armies of them fell upon his right hand, and two upon his left ; but Hercules rolled them all in his lion's skin. It is easy to see how Swift has availed himself of this Grecian legend in his *Gulliver's Travels*. Stanley met with a race of Pygmies in his search for Emin Pasha.

Pyl'ades and Orestes. Two model friends, whose names have become proverbial for friendship, like those of Damon and Pythias, David and Jonathan.

Pyramid. The largest is that of Cholula, in Mexico, which covers fifty acres of ground. The largest in Egypt is that of Cheops, near Cairo, which covers thirteen acres. Sir William Tite tells us it contains ninety million cubic feet of stone, and could not be now built for less than thirty millions of money (sterling).

Pyr'amus. The lover of Thisbë. Supposing Thisbe to be torn to pieces by a lion, he stabbed himself, and Thisbe, finding the dead body, stabbed herself also. Both fell dead under a mulberry-tree, which has ever since borne blood-red fruit. Shakespeare has a travesty of this tale in his *Midsummer Night's Dream*. (*Ovid : Metamorphoses*, bk. iv.)

Pyroc'les and Musido'rus. Heroes whose exploits, previous to their arrival in Arcadia, are detailed in the *Arca'dia* of Sir Philip Sidney.

Pyrodes (3 syl.), son of Clias was so called, according to Pliny (vii. 56), because he was the first to strike fire from flint. (Greek, *pur*, fire ; = *ignitus*.)

Pyrrha. *Sæculum Pyrrhæ.* The Flood. Pyrrha was the wife of Deucalion (*Horace :* 1 *Odes*, ii. 6). So much rain has fallen, it looks as if the days of Pyrrha were about to return.

Pyr'rhic Dance, the most famous war-dance of antiquity, received its name from Pyrrichos, a Dorian. It was danced to the flute, and its time was very quick. Julius Cæsar introduced it into Rome. The *Romaika*, still danced in Greece, is a relic of the ancient Pyrrhic dance.

" Ye have the Pyrrhic dance as often,
 Where is the Pyrrhic phalanx gone ?"
Byron.

Pyrrhic Victory (*A*). A ruinous victory. Pyrrhus, after his victory over the Romans, near the river Siris, said to those sent to congratulate him, "One more such victory and Pyrrhus is undone."

"The railway companies see that in fighting their customers they gain but a very Pyrrhic sort of victory."—*Newspaper article*, Feb. 13th, 1893.

Pyrrho. A sceptic. Pyrrho was the founder of the sceptical school of philosophy. He was a native of Elis, in Peloponne'sos.

" Blessed be the day I 'scaped the wrangling crew
From Pyrrho's maze and Epicurus' sty."
Beattie: Minstrel.

Pyrrho'nian School (*The*). The sceptical platform founded by Pyrrho. (*See above.*)

Pyr'rhonism. Infidelity. (*See above.*)

Pythag'oras, son of Mnesarchos, was called son of Apollo or Pythios, from the first two syllables of his name; but he was called Pytha-goras because the Pythian oracle predicted his birth.

Pythagoras, generally called *The Long-haired Sa'mian.* A native of Sa'mos, noted for his manly beauty and long hair. The Greeks applied the phrase to any venerable man or philosopher.

Pythagoras maintained that he distinctly recollected having occupied other human forms before his birth at Samos: (1) He was Æthal'ides, son of Mercury; (2) Euphorbos the Phrygian, son of Pan'-thoos, in which form he ran Patroclos through with a lance, leaving Hector to dispatch the hateful friend of Achilles; (3) Hermoti'mos, the prophet of Clazome'næ; and (4) a fisherman. To prove his Phrygian existence he was taken to the temple of Hera, in Argos, and asked to point out the shield of the son of Pan-thoos, which he did without hesitation. (*See* RAT.)

The golden thigh of Pythagoras. This thigh he showed to Ab'aris, the Hyperborean priest, and exhibited it in the Olympic games.

Abaris, priest of the Hyperbo'reans, gave him a dart, by which he was carried through the air, over inaccessible rivers, lakes and mountains; expelled pestilence; lulled storms; and performed other wonderful exploits.

Pythagoras maintained that the soul has three vehicles: (1) the *ethereal*, which is luminous and celestial, in which the soul resides in a state of bliss in the stars; (2) the *luminous*, which suffers the punishment of sin after death; and (3) the *terrestrial*, which is the vehicle it occupies on this earth.

Pythagoras asserted he could write on the moon. His plan of operation was to write on a looking-glass in blood, and place it opposite the moon, when the inscription would appear photographed or reflected on the moon's disc.

Pythagoras. Mesmerism was practised by Pythagoras, if we may credit Iamblichus, who tells us that he tamed a savage Daunian bear by "stroking it gently with his hand;" subdued an eagle by the same means; and held absolute dominion over beasts and birds by "the power of his voice," or "influence of his touch."

Pythagore'an System. Pytha'goras taught that the sun is a movable sphere in the centre of the universe, and that all the planets revolve round it. This is substantially the same as the Copernican and Newtonian systems.

Pyth'ian Games. The games held by the Greeks at Pytho, in Phocis, subsequently called Delphi. They took place every fourth year, the second of each Olympiad.

Pythias. (*See* DAMON.)

Py'thon. The monster serpent hatched from the mud of Deucalion's deluge, and slain near Delphi by Apollo.

Q

Q. *Q in a corner.* Something not seen at first, but subsequently brought to notice. The thong to which seals are attached in legal documents is in French called the *queue*; thus we have *lettres scellées sur simple queue* or *sur double queue*, according to whether they bear one or two seals. In documents where the seal is attached to the deed itself, the corner where the seal is placed is called the *queue*, and when the document is sworn to the finger is laid on the *queue*.

In a merry Q (cue). Humour, temper; thus Shakespeare says, "My cue is villanous melancholy" (*King Lear*, i. 2).

Old Q. The fifth Earl of March, afterwards Duke of Queensberry.

Q.E.D. *Quod erat demonstrandum.* Three letters appended to the theorems of Euclid, meaning: Thus have we proved the proposition stated above, as we were required to do.

Q.E.F. *Quod erat facien'dum.* Three letters appended to the problems of Euclid, meaning: Thus have we done or drawn the figure required by the proposition.

Q.P. *Quantum placet.* Two letters used in prescriptions, meaning the quantity may be as little or much as you like. Thus, in a cup of tea we might say "Milk and sugar *q.p.*"

Q.S. *Quantum sufficit.* Two letters appended to prescriptions, and meaning as much as is required to make the pills up. Thus, after giving the drugs in minute proportions, the apothecary is told to "mix these articles in liquorice *q.s.*"

Q.V. (Latin, *quantum vis*). As much as you like, or *quantum valeat*, as much as is proper.

q.v. (Latin, *quod vide*). Which see.

Quack or **Quack Doctor**; once called *quack-salver*. A puffer of salves. (Swedish, *qvak-salfvare*; Norwegian, *qvak-salver*; German, *quacksalber*.)

" "Saltimbancoes, quacksalvers, and charlatans deceive the vulgar."—*Sir Thomas Browne*.

Quacks. Queen Anne's quack oculists were William Read (tailor), who was knighted, and Dr. Grant (tinker).

Quad. *To be in quad.* To be confined to your college-grounds or quadrangle; to be in prison.

Quadra. The border round a bas-relief.

In the Santa Croce of Florence is a quadra round a bas relief representing the Madonna, in white terra-cotta. Several other figures are introduced.

Quadrages'ima Sunday. The first Sunday in Lent; so called because it is, in round numbers, the fortieth day before Easter.

Quadrages'imals. The farthings or payments made in commutation of a personal visit to the mother-church on Mid-Lent Sunday; also called Whitsun farthings.

Quadrilat'eral. The four fortresses of Peschie'ra and Mantua on the Mincio, with Vero'na and Legna'go on the Ad'igë. Now demolished.

The Prussian Quadrilateral. The fortresses of Luxemburg, Coblentz, Sarre-louis, and Mayence.

Quadril'le (2 syl., French) means a small square: a dance in which the persons place themselves in a square. Introduced into England in 1813 by the Duke of Devonshire. (Latin, *quadrum*, a square.)

Le Pantalon. So called from the tune to which it used to be danced.

L'Été. From a country-dance called

pas d'été, very fashionable in 1800; which it resembles.

La poule. Derived from a country-dance produced by Julien in 1802, the second part of which began with the imitation of a cock-crow.

Trenise. The name of a dancing-master who, in 1800, invented the figure.

La pastourelle. So named from its melody and accompaniment, which are similar to the *vilanelles* or peasants' dances.

Quad'riloge (3 syl.). Anything written in four parts or books, as *Childe Harold*. Anything compiled from four authors, as the *Life of Thomas à Becket*. Any history resting on the testimony of four independent authorities, as *The Gospel History*.

"The very authors of the Quadriloge itselfe or song of foure parts . . . doe all with one pen and mouth acknowledge the same."—*Lambarde: Perambulation*, p. 55.

Quadriv'ium. The four higher subjects of scholastic philosophy up to the twelfth century. It embraced music, arithmetic, geometry, and astronomy. The *quadrivium* was the "fourfold way" to knowledge; the *tri'vium* (*q.v.*) the "threefold way" to eloquence; both together comprehended the seven arts or sciences. The seven arts are enumerated in the following hexameter :—

" Lingua, Tropus, Ratio, Numerus, Tonus, Angulus, Astra."

And in the two following :—

" *Gram.* loquitur, *Dia.* vera docet, *Rhet.* verba colorat.
Mus. cadit, *Ar.* numerat, *Geo.* ponderat, *Ast.* colit astra."

Quadroon'. A person with one-fourth of black blood; the offspring of a mulatto woman by a white man. The mulatto is half-blooded, one parent being white and the other black. (Latin, *quatuor*, four.) (*See* LAMB.)

Quad'ruple Alliance of 1674. Germany, Spain, Denmark, and Holland formed an alliance against France to resist the encroachments of Louis XIV., who had declared war against Holland. It terminated with the treaty of Nimeguen in 1678.

Quadruple Alliance of 1718-1719. An alliance between England, France, Germany, and Holland, to guarantee the succession in England to the House of Hanover ; to secure the succession in France to the House of Bourbon ; and to prohibit Spain and France from uniting under one crown. Signed at Paris.

Quadruple Alliance of 1834. **The**

alliance of England, France, Spain, and Portugal for the purpose of restoring peace to the Peninsula, by putting down the Carlists or partisans of Don Carlos.

Quæstio Vexa'ta. An open question.

Quail. A bird, said to be very salacious, hence a prostitute or courtesan.

" Here's Agamemnon, an honest fellow enough, and one that loves quails."—*Shakespeare: Troilus and Cressida,* v. 1.

The *Iliad* of Homer is based on the story that Agamemnon, being obliged to give up his mistress, took the mistress of Achilles to supply her place. This brought about a quarrel between Agamemnon and Achilles, and Achilles refused to have anything more to do with the siege of Troy.

Quaint means odd, peculiar. A *quaint phrase* means a fanciful phrase, one not expressed in the ordinary way.

" His garment was very quaint and odd ; . . . a long, long way behind the time."—*Dickens: Christmas Stories ; Cricket on the Hearth,* chap. i.

Quaker. It appears from the *Journal* of George Fox, who was imprisoned for nearly twelve months in Derby, that the Quakers first obtained the appellation (1650) by which they are now known from the following circumstance :— " Justice Bennet, of Derby," says Fox, " was the first to call us Quakers, because I bade him quake and tremble at the word of the Lord." The system of the Quakers is laid down by Robert Barclay in fifteen theses, called *Barclay's Apology,* addressed to Charles II.

" Quakers (that, like lanterns, bear
Their light within them) will not swear."
       Butler: Hudibras, ii. 2.

Qualm. A sudden fit of illness, or sickly languor. Hence, a qualm of conscience = a twinge or uneasiness of conscience.

Quanda'ry. A perplexity; a state of hesitation.

Quanquam or *Cancan.* A slang manner of dancing quadrilles permitted in the public gardens of Paris, etc. The word cancan is a corruption of the Latin *quamquam,* a term applied to the exercises delivered by young theological students before the divinity professors. Hence it came to signify " babble," " jargon," anything crude, *jejune,* etc.

Quaranti'ne (3 syl.). The forty days that a ship suspected of being infected with some contagious disorder is obliged to lie off port. (Italian, *quarantina,* forty ; French, *quarantaine*.)

To perform quarantine is to ride off port during the time of quarantine. (*See* FORTY.)

Quarll (*Philip*). A sort of Robinson Crusoe, who had a chimpanzee for his " man Friday." The story relates the adventures and sufferings of an English hermit named Philip Quarll.

Quarrel. A short, stout arrow used in the crossbow. (A corruption of *carrial ;* Welsh, *chwarel ;* French, *carreau.* So called because the head was originally *carré* or four-sided. Hence also a *quarrel* or *quarry of glass,* meaning a square or diamond-shaped pane ; *quarier,* a square wax-candle, etc.)

" Quarelles qwayntly swappez thorowe knyghtez
With iryne so wekyrly, that wynche they
never."
       Morte d'Arthure.

Quarrel. *To quarrel over the bishop's cope*—over something which cannot possibly do you any good ; over goat's wool. This is a French expression. The newly-appointed Bishop of Bruges entered the town in his cope, which he gave to the people ; and the people, to part it among themselves, tore it to shreds, each taking a piece.

Quarrel with your Bread and Butter (*To*). To act contrary to your best interest ; to snarl at that which procures your living, like a spoilt child, who shows its ill-temper by throwing its bread and butter to the ground. To cut off your nose to be avenged on your face.

Quarry (*A*). The place where stone, marble, etc., are dug out and squared. (French, *quarré,* formed into square blocks.) (*Tomlinson.*)

Quarry. Prey. This is a term in falconry. When a hawk *struck* the object of pursuit and clung to it, she was said to " bind ; " but when she *flew off* with it, she was said to " carry." The " carry " or " quarry," therefore, means the prey carried off by the hawk. It is an error to derive this word from the Latin *quæro* (to seek).

" To tell the manner of it,
Were on the quarry of these murdered deer
To add the death of you."
       Shakespeare: Macbeth, iv. 3.

Quart d'Heure (*Mauvais*). A time of annoyance. The time between the arrival of the guests and the announcement of dinner is emphatically called the *mauvais quart d'heure ;* but the phrase has a much larger application : thus we say the Cabinet Ministers must have had a *mauvais quart d'heure* when opening a number of telegrams of a troublesome character.

Quarter. *To grant quarter.* To spare the life of an enemy in your power. Dr. Tusler says :—" It originated from an agreement anciently made between the Dutch and the Spaniards, that the ransom of a soldier should be the quarter of his pay." (French, *donner* and *demander quartier*.)

Quarter-days in England and Ireland:—

(1) *New Style:* Lady Day (March 25th), Midsummer Day (June 24th), Michaelmas Day (September 29th), and Christmas Day (December 25th).

(2) *Old Style:* Old Lady Day (April 6th), Old Midsummer Day (July 6th), Old Michaelmas Day (October 11th), and Old Christmas Day (January 6th).

Quarter-days in Scotland:—

Candlemas Day (February 2nd), Whit-Sunday (May 15th), Lammas Day (August 1st), and Martinmas Day (Nov. 11).

Quarter Waggoner. A book of sea-charts. Waggoner, or rather *Baron von Waggonaer*, is a folio volume of sea-charts, pointing out the coasts, rocks, routes, etc. Dalrymple's *Charts* are called *The English Waggoner*. "Quarter" is a corruption of quarto

Quarters. Residence or place of abode ; as, *winter quarters*, the place where an army lodges during the winter months. We say "this quarter of the town," meaning this district or part ; the French speak of the *Latin Quartier* —*i.e.* the district or part of Paris where the medical schools, etc., are located ; the Belgians speak of *quartiers à louer*, lodgings to let ; and bachelors in England often say, "Come to my quarters"—*i.e.* apartments. All these are from the French verb *écarter* (to set apart).

"There shall be no leavened bread be seen with thee, neither shall there be leaven seen . . . in all thy quarters [any of thy houses]."—Exodus xiii. 7.

Quarterdeck. The upper deck of a ship from the main-mast to the poop ; if no poop, then from the main-mast to the stern. In men-of-war it is used as a promenade by officers only.

Quartermaster. The officer whose duty it is to attend to the *quarters* of the soldiers. He superintends the issue of stores, food, and clothing. (*See* QUARTERS.)

As a nautical term, a quartermaster is a petty officer who, besides other duties, attends to the steering of the ship.

Quartered. (*See* DRAWN.)

Quarto. A book half the size of folio —*i.e.* where each sheet is folded into quarters or four leaves. 4to is the contraction. (The Italian, *libro in quarto ;* French, *in quarto ·* from Latin *quartus*.)

Quarto-De'cimans, who, after the decision of the Nicene Council, maintained that Easter ought to be held on the fourteenth day of the first lunar month near the vernal equinox, whether that day fell on a Sunday or not.

Quashee. A cant generic name of a negro ; so called from a negro named Quassi. (*See* QUASSIA.)

Quasi (Latin). Something which is not the real thing, but may be accepted in its place ; thus a

Quasi contract is not a real contract, but something which may be accepted as a contract, and has the force of one.

Quasi tenant. The tenant of a house sub-let.

Quasimo'do. A foundling, hideously deformed, but of amazing strength, in Victor Hugo's *Notre Dame de Paris.*

Quasimodo Sunday. The first Sunday after Easter ; so called because the "Introit" of the day begins with these words :—" *Quasi modo gen'iti infantes*" (1 Pet. ii. 2). Also called "Low Sunday," being the first Sunday after the grand ceremonies of Easter.

Quas'sia. An American plant, or rather genus of plants, named after Quassi, a negro.

"Linnæus applied this name to a tree of Surinam in honour of a negro, Quassi, . . . who employed its bark as a remedy for fever ; and enjoyed such a reputation among the natives as to be almost worshipped by some,"—*Lindley and Moore : Treatise of Botany,* part ii. p. 947.)

Quatorziennes (fourteeners). Persons of recognised position in society who hold themselves in readiness to accept an invitation to dinner when otherwise the number of guests would be thirteen. (*See* THIRTEEN.)

Queen. Greek, *gyne* (a woman) ; Sanskrit, *goni ;* Swedish, *qvenna ;* Gothic, *queins ;* Anglo-Saxon, *cwen.* (*See* SIR.)

Queen, "woman," is equivalent to "mother." In the translation of the Bible by Ulfilas (fourth century), we meet with *gens* and *gino* ("wife" and "woman") ; and in the Scandinavian languages *karl* and *kone* still mean "man" and "wife." (*See* KING.)

"He [Jesus] saith unto His mother, Woman, behold thy son."—St. John xix. 26.

Queen (*The White*). Mary Queen of Scots ; so called because she dressed in *white* mourning for her French husband.

Queen Anne is Dead. The reply made to the teller of stale news.

Queen Anne's Bounty. A fund created out of the firstfruits and tenths, which were part of the papal exactions before the Reformation. The *firstfruits* are the whole first year's profits of a clerical living, and the *tenths* are the tenth part annually of the profits of a living. Henry VIII. annexed both these to the Crown, but Queen Anne formed them into a perpetual fund for the augmentation of poor livings and the building of parsonages. The sum equals about £14,000 a year.

Queen Anne's Style (of architecture). Noted for many angles, gables, quaint features, and irregularity of windows.

Queen Consort. Wife of a reigning king.

Queen Dick. Richard Cromwell is sometimes so called. (*See* DICK, GREEK CALENDS.)

Queen Dowager. The widow of a deceased king.

Queen Passion (*The Great*). Love.

" The gallant Jew
Of mortal hearts the great queen passion knew."
Peter Pindar : Portfolio ; Dinah.

Queen Quintessence. Sovereign of Etéléchie (*q.v.*), in the romance of *Gargantua and Pantag'ruel*, by Rabelais.

Queen Regnant. A queen who holds the crown in her own right, in contradistinction to a *Queen Consort*, who is queen only because her husband is king.

Queen-Square Hermit. Jeremy Bentham, who lived at No. 1, Queen Square, London. He was the father of the political economists called Utilitarians, whose maxim is, " The greatest happiness of the greatest number." (1748-1832.)

Queen of Hearts. Elizabeth, daughter of James I. This unfortunate Queen of Bohemia was so called in the Low Countries, from her amiable character and engaging manners, even in her lowest estate. (1596-1662.)

Queen of Heaven, with the ancient Phœnicians, was Astartē ; Greeks, Hera ; Romans, Juno ; Trivia, Hecate, Diana, the Egyptian Isis, etc., were all so called ; but with the Roman Catholics it is the Virgin Mary.

In Jeremiah vii. 18 : " The children gather wood, . . . and the women knead dough to make cakes to the queen of heaven," *i.e.* probably to the Moon, to which the Jews, at the time, made drink-offerings and presented cakes. (Compare chapter xliv. 16-18.)

Queen of the Dripping-pan. A cook.

Queen of the Eastern Archipel'-ago. The island of Java.

Queen of the May. A village lass chosen to preside over the parish sports on May Day. Tennyson has a poem on the subject.

Queen of the North. Edinburgh. (*See* the proper name for other queens.)

Queen of the Northern Seas. Elizabeth, who greatly increased the English navy, and was successful against the Spanish Armada, etc.

Queen's Bench or *King's Bench*. One of the courts of law, in which the monarch used to preside in person.

Queen's College (Oxford), founded in 1340 by Robert de Eglesfield, and so called in compliment to Queen Philippa, whose confessor he was.

Queen's College (Cambridge), founded in 1448 by Margaret of Anjou, consort of Henry VI. Refounded by Elizabeth Woodville.

Queen's Day. November 17th, the day of the accession of Queen Elizabeth, first publicly celebrated in 1570, and still kept as a holiday at the Exchequer, as it was at Westminster school.

Nov. 17 at Merchant Taylors' school is a holiday also, now called Sir Thomas White's Founder's Day.

" A rumour is spread in the court, and hath come to the eares of some of the most honourable counsell, how that I on the Queen's day last past did forbid in our college an oration to bee made in praise of Her Majesty's government, etc."—*Dr. Whittaker to Lord Burghley* (May 14th, 1590).

Queen's English (*The*). Dean Alford wrote a small book on this subject, whence has arisen three or four phrases, such as " clipping the Queen's English," " murdering the Queen's English," etc. Queen's English means grammatical English.

Queen's Heads. A name given to postage stamps in Queen Victoria's reign, from their bearing a likeness of her head.

Queen's Pipe (*The*). A name given in Queen Victoria's reign to an oven at the Victoria Docks for destroying (by the Inland Revenue authorities) refuse and worthless tobacco, contraband goods, etc. In 1892 the oven was replaced by a furnace.

Queen's Ware. Glazed earthenware of a creamy colour,

Queen's Weather. A fine day for a fête ; so called because Queen Victoria was, for the most part, fortunate in having fine weather when she appeared in public.

Queenhithe (London). The hithe or strand for lading and unlading barges and lighters in the city. Called "queen" from being part of the dowry of Eleanor, Queen of Henry II.

Queenstown (Ireland), formerly called the Cove of Cork. The name was changed in 1850, out of compliment to Queen Victoria, when she visited Ireland with her husband, and created her eldest son Earl of Dublin.

Queer. Counterfeit money.
To shove the queer. To pass counterfeit money.

Queer Card (*A*). A strange or eccentric person. In whist, etc., when a wrong card is played, the partner says to himself, "That is a queer card," which, being transferred to the player, means he is a queer card to play in such a manner. Hence any eccentric person, who does not act in accordance with social rules, is a "queer card."

Queer Chap is the German *querkopf*, a cross-grained fellow.

Queer Street. *To live in Queer Street.* To be of doubtful solvency. To be one marked in a tradesman's ledger with a *quære* (inquire), meaning, make inquiries about this customer.
That has put me in Queer Street. That has posed or puzzled me queerly. In this phrase *queer* means to puzzle ; and Queer Street = puzzledom.

Quonoy. A corruption of *quintefeuil* (five-leaved), the armorial device of the family.

Querelle d'Allemand. A contention about trifles, soon provoked and soon appeased. (*See* QUEUE.)

Quern-Biter. The sword of Haco I. of Norway. (*See* SWORD.)

> " Quern-biter of Hacon the Good,
> Wherewith at a stroke he hewed
> The millstone through and through."
> *Longfellow.*

Quer'no. Camillo Querno, of Apulia, hearing that Leo X. was a great patron of poets, went to Rome with a harp in his hand, and sang his *Alexias*, a poem containing 20,000 verses. He was introduced to the Pope as a buffoon, but was promoted to the laurel.

> " Rome in her Capitol saw Querno sit,
> Throned on seven hills, the Antichrist of wit."
> *Dunciad,* ii.

Querpo (2 syl.). *Shrill Querpo* in Garth's *Dispensary*, was Dr. Howe.
In querpo. In one's shirt-sleeves ; in undress. (Spanish, *en cuerpo*, without a cloak.)

> " Boy, my cloak and rapier ; it fits not a gentleman of my rank to walk the streets in querpo."—*Beaumont and Fletcher: Love's Cure,* ii. 1.

Questa Cortesissima (Italian). Most courteous one ; a love term used by Dante to Beatrice.

> " I set myself to think of that most courteous one (*questa cortesissima*), and thinking of her there fell upon me a sweet sleep."—*Mrs. Oliphant: Makers of Florence* (Dante's description).

Questa Gentilissima (Italian). Most gentle one ; a love term used by Dante to Beatrice.

> " Common mortals stand and gaze with bated breath while that most gentle one (*questa gentilissima*) goes on her way."—*Mrs. Oliphant: Makers of Florence,* p. 25.

Question. *To move the previous question.* No one seems able to give any clear and satisfactory explanation of this phrase. Erskine May, in his *Parliamentary Practice,* p. 303 (9th edition), says : "It is an ingenious method of avoiding a vote upon any question that has been proposed, but the technical phrase does little to elucidate its operation. When there is no debate, or after a debate is closed, the Speaker ordinarily puts the question as a matter of course, . . . but by a motion for the previous question, this act may be intercepted and forbidden. The custom [used to be] 'that the question be now put,' but Arthur Wellesley Peel, while Speaker, changed the words 'be now put' into '*be not put.*'" The former process was obviously absurd. To continue the quotation from Erskine May : "Those who wish to avoid the putting of the main question, vote against the previous (or latter question) ; and if it be resolved in the negative, the Speaker is prevented from putting the main question, as the House has refused to allow it to be put. It may, however, be brought forward again another day."
Of course this is correct, but what it means is quite another matter ; and why " the main question " is called the " previous question " is past understanding.

Question. When members of the House of Commons or other debaters call out *Question*, they mean that the person speaking is wandering away from the subject under consideration.

Questionists. In the examinations for degrees in the University of Cambridge it was customary, at the beginning of the January term, to hold "Acts," and the candidates for the

Bachelor's degree were called "Questionists." They were examined by a moderator, and afterwards the fathers of other colleges "questioned" them for three hours—*i.e.* one whole hour and parts of two others. (I began my Act about a quarter to eleven and finished about half-past one.) It was held altogether in Latin, and the words of dismissal uttered by the Regius Professor indicated what class you would be placed in, or whether the respondent was plucked, in which case the words were simply "*Descendas domine.*"

Questions and Commands. A Christmas game, in which the commander bids his subjects to answer a question which is asked. If the subject refuses, or fails to satisfy the commander, he must pay a forfeit or have his face smutted.

"While other young ladies in the house are dancing, or playing at questions and commands, she [the devotee] reads aloud in her closet."—*The Spectator*, No. 354 (Hotspur's Letter), April 16, 1712.

Queu'bus. *The equinoctial of Queu-bus.* This line has Utopia on one side and Medam'othi on the other. It was discovered on the Greek Kalends by Outis after his escape from the giant's cave, and is ninety-one degrees from the poles.

"Thou wast in very gracious fooling last night, when thou spokest of Pigrogrom'itus, the Vapians passing the equinoctial of Queu'bus. 'Twas very good, i' faith."—*Shakespeare: Twelfth Night*, ii. 3.

Queue. *Gare la queue des Allemands.* Before you quarrel, count the consequences. (*See* QUERELLE.)

Queux. The seneschal of King Arthur.

Quey Calves are dear Veal. Quey calves are female calves, which should be kept and reared for cows. Calves for the butcher are generally bull calves. The proverb is somewhat analogous to killing the goose which lays the golden egg. (Danish *quie*, a heifer.)

Qui. *To give a man the qui.* When a man in the printing business has had notice to quit, his fellow-workmen say they "have given him the qui." Here qui is the contraction of *quie'tus* (discharge). (*See* QUIETUS.)

Qui s'Excuse, s'Accuse. He who apologises condemns himself.

Qui-Tam. A lawyer; so called from the first two words in an action on a penal statute. *Qui tam pro dom'inâ Regi'nâ, quam pro se-ipso, sequitur* (Who sues on the Queen's account as much as on his own).

Qui Vive? (French). Who goes there? The challenge of a sentinel.
To be on the qui vive. On the alert; to be quick and sharp; to be on the tip-toe of expectation, like a sentinel. (*See above.*)

Quia Emptores. A statute passed in the reign of Edward I., and directed against the formation of new manors, whereby feudal lords were deprived of their dues. It is so called from its first two words.

Quibble. An evasion; a juggling with words, is the Welsh *chwibiol* (a trill), and not the Latin *quid libet* (what you please), as is generally given.

Quick. Living; hence animated, lively; hence fast, active, brisk (Anglo-Saxon, *cwic*, living, alive). Our expression, "Look alive," means *Be brisk.*
Quick at meat, quick at work. In French, "*Bonne bête s'échauffe en mangeant,*" or "*Hardi gagneur, hardi mangeur.*" The opposite would certainly be true: *A dawdle in one thing is a dawdle in all.*
The quick and dead. The living and the dead.

Quick Sticks (*In*). Without more ado; quickly. To cut one's stick (*q.v.*) is to start off, and to cut one's stick quickly is to start off immediately.

Quickly (*Dame*). Hostess of a tavern in Eastcheap. (*Shakespeare: Henry IV.*, parts 1 and 2.)
Mistress Quickly. Servant of all-work to Dr. Caius. She says: "I wash, wring, brew, bake, scour, dress meat and drink, make the beds, and do all myself." She is the go-between of three suitors to Anne Page, and to prove her disinterestedness she says: "I would my master had Mistress Anne, or I would Master Slender had her, or in sooth I would Master Fenton had her. I will do what I can for them all three, for so I have promised; and I'll be as good as my word; but speciously for Master Fenton." (*Shakespeare: Merry Wives of Windsor.*)

Quicksand is sand which shifts its place as if it were alive. (*See* QUICK.)

Quickset is living hawthorn set in a hedge, instead of dead wood, hurdles, and palings. (*See* QUICK.)

Quicksilver is *argen'tum vivum* (living silver), silver that moves about like a living thing. (Anglo-Saxon, *cwicseolfor*.)

> "Swift as quicksilver
> It courses through the natural gates
> And alleys of the body."
> *Shakespeare: Hamlet*, i. 5.

Quid, a sovereign ; **Half a Quid,** half a sovereign ; **Quids,** cash or money generally. A suggested derivation may be mentioned. Quo = anything, and *Quid pro quo* means an equivalent generally. If now a person is offered anything on sale he might say, I have not a *quid* for your *quo*, an equivalent 'n cash.

> "Then, looking at the gold piece, she added, ' I guess you don't often get one of these quids.'"— *Liberty Review*, June 9, 1894, p. 437.

Quid Libet. *Quid-libets and quod-libets.* Nice and knotty points, very subtile, but of no value. Quips and quirks. (Latin.)

Quid of Tobacco. A corruption of *cud* (a morsel). We still say " chew the cud."

Quid pro Quo. Tit for tat ; a return given as good as that received ; a Roland for an Oliver ; an equivalent.

Quid Rides. It is said that Lundy Foot, a Dublin tobacconist, set up his carriage, and asked Emmett to furnish him with a motto. The words of the motto chosen were *Quid rides.* The witticism is, however, attributed to H. Callender also, who, we are assured, supplied it to one Brandon, a London tobacconist.

> "Rides," in English, one syllable. In Latin (why do you laugh?) it is a word of two syllables.

Quiddity. The essence of a thing, or that which differentiates it from other things. Schoolmen say *Quid est* (what is it?) and the reply is, the *Quid* is so and so, the *What* or the nature of the thing is as follows. The latter *quid* being formed into a barbarous Latin noun becomes *Quidditas.* Hence *Quid est* (what is it)? Answer: *Talis est quidditas* (its essence is as follows).

> "He knew . . .
> Where entity and quiddity
> (The ghosts of defunct bodies) fly."
> *Butler: Hudibras*, i. 1.

Quiddity. A crotchet ; a trifling distinction. (*See above.*)

Quidnunc. A political Paul Pry ; a pragmatical village politician ; a political botcher or jobber. Quidnunc is the chief character in Murphy's farce of *The Upholsterer, or What News ?* The words are Latin, and mean "What now ?" "What has turned up?" The original of this political busybody was the father

of Dr. Arne and his sister, Mrs. Cibber, who lived in King Street, Covent Garden. (See *The Tatler*, 155, etc.)

> "Familiar to a few quidnuncs."—*The Times.*

> "The Florentine quidnuncs seem to lose sight of the fact that none of these gentlemen now hold office."—*The Times.*

Quidnunkis. Monkey politicians. Gay has a fable called *The Quidnunkis,* to show that the death not even of the duke regent will cause any real gap in nature. A monkey who had ventured higher than his neighbours fell from his estate into the river below. For a few seconds the whole tribe stood panic-struck, but as soon as the stream carried off Master Pug, the monkeys went on with their gambols as if nothing had occurred.

> "Ah, sir ! you never saw the Ganges;
> There dwell the nation of Quidnunkis
> (So Monomotapa calls monkeys)."
> *Gay: Tales.*

Qui'etist (*A*). One who believes that the most perfect state of man is when the spirit ceases to exercise any of its functions, and is wholly passive. This sect has cropped up at sundry times ; but the last who revived it was Michael Moli'nos, a Spanish priest, in the seventeenth century.

Quie'tus. The writ of discharge formerly granted to those barons and knights who personally attended the king on a foreign expedition. At their discharge they were exempt from the claim of scutage or knight's fee. Subsequently the term was applied to the acquittance which a sheriff receives on settling his account at the Exchequer ; and, later still, to any discharge of an account : thus Webster says—

> "You had the trick in audit-time to be sick till I had signed your quietus."—*Duchess of Malfy* (1623).

Quietus. A severe blow ; a settler ; death, or discharge from life.

> "Who would fardels bear . . .
> When he himself might his quietus make
> With a bare bodkin ?"
> *Shakespeare: Hamlet*, iii. 1.

Quill-drivers. Writing clerks.

Quillet. An evasion. In French " pleadings" each separate allegation in the plaintiff's charge, and every distinct plea in the defendant's answer used to begin with *qu'il est ;* whence our *quillet,* to signify a false charge, or an evasive answer.

> "Oh, some authority how to proceed ;
> Some tricks, some quillets, how to cheat the devil."
> *Shakespeare: Love's Labour's Lost*, iv. 3.

Quilp. A hideous dwarf, both fierce

and cunning, in *The Old Curiosity Shop*, by Dickens.

Quinap'alus. The Mrs. Harris of "authorities in citations." If anyone wishes to clench an argument by some quotation, let him cite this ponderous collection.

" What says Quinapalus: 'Better a witty fool, than a foolish wit."—*Shakespeare : Twelfth Night*, i. 5.

Quinbus Flestrin. The man-mountain. So the Lilliputians called Gulliver (chap. ii.). Gay has an ode to this giant.

" Bards of old of him told,
When they said Atlas' head
Propped the skies."
Gay : Lilliputian Ode.

Quince (*Peter*). A carpenter, and manager of the play in *Midsummer Night's Dream*. He is noted for some strange compounds, such as laughable tragedy, lamentable comedy, tragical mirth, etc.

Quino'nes (*Suero de*), in the reign of Juan II., with nine other cavaliers, held the bridge of Orbigo against all comers for thirty-six days, overthrowing in that time seventy-eight knights of Spain and France. Quinones had challenged the world, and such was the result.

Quinquages'ima Sunday (Latin, *fiftieth*). Shrove Sunday, or the first day of the week which contains Ash-Wednesday. It is so called because in round numbers it is the fiftieth day before Easter.

Quinsy. This is a curious abbreviation. The Latin word is *cynanchia*, and the Greek word *kunanché*, from *kuon anche*, dog strangulation, because persons suffering from quinsy throw open the mouth like dogs, especially mad dogs. From *kunanche* comes ku'anchy, kuansy, quinsy.

Quintessence. The fifth essence. The ancient Greeks said there are four elements or forms in which matter can exist—fire, or the imponderable form ; air, or the gaseous form ; water, or the liquid form ; and earth, or the solid form. The Pythagore'ans added a fifth, which they called *ether*, more subtile and pure than fire, and possessed of an orbicular motion. This element, which flew upwards at creation, and out of which the stars were made, was called the *fifth essence ;* quintessence therefore means the most subtile extract of a body that can be procured. It is quite an error to suppose that the word means an essence five times distilled, and that the term came from the alchemists. Horace speaks of " kisses which Venus has

imbued with the quintessence of her own nectar."

" Swift to their several quarters hasted then
The cumbrous elements—earth, flood, air, fire ;
But this ethereal quint'essence of heaven
Flew upward . . . and turned to stars
Numberless as thou seest."
Milton : Paradise Lost, iii. 716.

Quintil'ians. Disciples of Quintil'ia, held to be a prophetess. These heretical Christians made the Eucharist of bread and cheese, and allowed women to become priests and bishops.

Quip Modest (*The*). Sir, it was done to please myself. Touchstone says : " If I sent a person word that his beard was not well cut, and he replied he cut it to please himself," he would answer with the quip modest, which is six removes from the lie direct ; or, rather, the lie direct in the sixth degree.

Quis custodiet Custo'des ? [The shepherds keep watch over the sheep], but who is there to keep watch over the shepherds ?

Quisquil'iæ. Light, dry fragments of things : the small twigs and leaves which fall from trees ; hence rubbish, refuse.

Quit. Discharged from an obligation, " acquitted."

" To John I owed great obligation ;
But John unhappily thought fit
To publish it to all the nation—
Now I and John are fairly quit."
Prior.

Cry quits. When two boys quarrel, and one has had enough, he says, " Cry quits," meaning, " Let us leave off, and call it a drawn game." So in an unequal distribution, he who has the largest share restores a portion and " cries quits," meaning that he has made the distribution equal. Here quit means "acquittal" or discharge.

Double or quits. In gambling, especially in a small way, one of the players says to the other, " Double or quits ? " —that is, the next stake shall be double the present one, or the winnings shall be returned to the loser, in which case both players would leave off as they began.

Quit Rent. A rent formerly paid by a tenant whereby he was releaved from feudal service.

Quixa'da (*Gutierre*). Lord of Villagarcia. He discharged a javelin at Sire de Haburdin with such force as to pierce the left shoulder, overthrow the knight, and pin him to the ground. Don Quixote calls himself a descendant of this brave knight.

Quixote (*Don*) is intended for the Duke of Lerma. (*Rawdon Brown.*)

Don Quixote. The romance so called is a merciless satire by Cervantes on the chivalric romances of the Middle Ages, and had the excellent effect of putting an end to knight-errantry.

Don Quixote's horse. Ros'inante (Spanish, *rocin-ante*, a jade previously). (*See* HORSE.)

The wooden-pin wing-horse on which he and Sancho Panza mounted to achieve the liberation of Dolori'da and her companions was called *Algie'ro Clavile'no* (*wooden-pin wing-bearer*).

Quixote of the North. Charles XII. of Sweden, sometimes called the *Madman.* (1682, 1697-1718.)

Quixot'ic. Having foolish and unpractical ideas of honour, or schemes for the general good, like Don Quixote, a half-crazy reformer or knight of the supposed distressed.

Quiz. One who banters or chaffs another. Daly, manager of the Dublin theatre, laid a wager that he would introduce into the language within twenty-four hours a new word of no meaning. Accordingly, on every wall, or all places accessible, were chalked up the four mystic letters, and all Dublin was inquiring what they meant. The wager was won, and the word remains current in our language.

Quo Warranto. A writ against a defendant (whether an individual or a corporation) who lays claim to something he has no right to; so named because the offender is called upon to show *quo warranto* [rem] *usurpa'vit* (by what right or authority he lays claim to the matter of dispute).

Quod. *To be in quod*—in prison. A corruption of *quad*, which is a contraction of quadrangle. The quadrangle is the prison enclosure in which the prisoners are allowed to walk, and where whippings used to be inflicted.

"Flogged and whipped in quod."
    Hughes: Tom Brown's Schooldays.

Quodling (*The Rev. Mr.*). Chaplain to the Duke of Buckingham. (*Sir Walter Scott: Peveril of the Peak.*)

" Why,' said the duke, 'I had caused my little Quodling to go through his oration thus : That whatever evil reports had passed current during the lifetime of the worthy matron whom they had restored to dust that day, Malice herself could not deny that she was *born* well, *married* well, *lived* well, and *died* well ; since she was born in Shadwell, married to Cresswell, lived in Camberwell and did in Bridewell."—*Peveril of the Peak*, chap. xliv

Quondam (Latin). Former. We say, *He is a quondam schoolfellow*—my former schoolfellow; *my quondam friend, the quondam candidate*, etc.; also *the quondam chancellor*, etc.

" My quondam barber, but ' his lordship' now."
                                        Dryden.

Quo'rum. Such a number of persons as are necessary to make up a committee or board; or certain justices without the presence of whom the rest cannot act. Thus, suppose the commission to be named A, B, C, D, E, etc., it would run—" Of these I wish [A, B, C, D, or E] to be one " (*quorum unum esse volumus*). These honoured names are called "Justices of the Quorum." Slender calls Justice Shallow justice of the peace and quorum. (*Shakespeare: Merry Wives of Windsor*, i. 1.)

Quos Ego. A threat of punishment for disobedience. The words are from Virgil's *Æneid* (i. 135), and were uttered by Neptune to the disobedient and rebellious winds.

"Neptune had but to appear and utter a *quos ego* for these wind-bags to collapse, and become the most subservient of salaried public servants."— *Truth*, January, 1886.

Quot. *Quot linguas calles, tot homines vales.* As many languages as you know, so many separate individuals you are worth. Attributed to Charles V.

Quota (Latin). The allotted portion or share; the rate assigned to each. Thus we say, " Every man is to pay his quota towards the feast."

Quotem (*Caleb*). A parish clerk and Jack-of-all-trades, in *The Wags of Windsor*, by Colman.

R

R in prescriptions. The ornamental part of this letter is the symbol of Jupiter (♃), under whose special protection all medicines were placed. The letter itself (*Recipe*, take) and its flourish may be thus paraphrased : " Under the good auspices of Jove, the patron of medicines, take the following drugs in the proportions set down." It has been suggested that the symbol is for *Responsum Raphae'lis*, from the assertion of Dr. Napier and other physicians of the seventeenth century, that the angel Raphael imparted them.

R is called the dog-letter, because a dog in snarling utters the letter r-r-r-r, r-r, r-r-r-r-r, etc.—sometimes preceded by a g.

"Irritata canis quod RR quam plurima dicat."
                             Lucillus.
"[R] tnat's the dog's name. R is for the dog."
—*Shakespeare: Romeo and Juliet,* ii. 4.

The three R's. Sir William Curtis being asked to give a toast, said, "I will give you the three R's—writing, reading, and arithmetic."

"The House is aware that no payment is made except on the 'three R's.'"—*Mr. Cory, M.P.: Address to the House of Commons,* February 28th, 1867.

R. A. P. Rupees, annas, and pies, in India; corresponding to our £ s. d.

R. I. P. *Requiescat in pace.*

R. M. T. In the reign of William III. all child-stealers (*comprachios*) apprehended were branded with red-hot iron : R (rogue) on the shoulders ; M (man-slayer) on the right-hand ; and T (thief) on the left.

Rab'agas. A demagogue in the kingdom of the king of Monaco. He was won over to the court party by being invited to dine at the palace. (*M. Sardou : Rabagas,* 1872.)

Rabbi Abron of Trent. A fictitious sage and wonderful linguist, "who knew the nature of all manner of herbs, beasts, and minerals." (*Reynard the Fox,* xii.)

Rabbi Bar-Coch'ba, in the reign of the Emperor Hadrian, made the Jews believe that he was the Messiah, because he had the art of breathing fire. (*Beckmann : History of Inventions.*)

Rabbit. *A Welsh rabbit.* Toasted cheese, or rather bread and cheese toasted together. (Qy. "rare-bit.")

Rab'elais. *The English Rabelais.* Swift, Sterne, and Thomas Amory have been so called. Voltaire so calls Swift.
The modern Rabelais. William Maginn (1794-1842).

Rabelais' Dodge. Rabelais one day was at a country inn, and finding he had no money to pay his score, got himself arrested as a traitor who was forming a project to poison the princes. He was immediately sent to Paris and brought before the magistrates, but, as no tittle of evidence was found against him, was liberated forthwith. By this artifice he not only got out of his difficulty at the inn, but he also got back to Paris free of expense. Fathered on Tarleton also.

Rabelais'ian Licence. The wild grotesque of Rabelais, whether in words or artistic illustrations.

Rabica'no or **Rabican.** The name of Astolpho's horse. Its sire was Wind, and its dam Fire. It fed on unearthly food. (*Orlando Furioso.*)
Argalia's steed in *Orlando Innamorato* is called by the same name. (*See* HORSE.)

Raboin or **Rabuino** (French). The devil ; so called from the Spanish *rubo* (a tail). In the mediæval ages it was vulgarly asserted that the Jews were born with tails ; this arose from a confusion of the word rabbi or rabbins with raboin or rabuino.

Rab'sheka, in the satire of *Absalom and Achitophel,* by Dryden and Tate, is meant for Sir Thomas Player. Rabshakeh was the officer sent by Sennacherib to summon the Jews to surrender, and he told them insolently that resistance was in vain. (2 Kings xviii.)

"Next him, let railing Rabsheka have place—
So full of zeal, he has no need of grace."
                          (Pt. ii.)

Raby (*Aurora*). The model of this exquisite sketch was Miss Millbank, as she appeared to Lord Byron when he first knew her. Miss Millpond (a little farther on in the same canto) is the same lady after marriage. In canto i., Donna Inez is an enlarged portrait of the same person. Lord Byron describes himself in the first instance under the character of Don Juan, and in the last as Don José.

Races. *Goodwood Races.* So called from Goodwood Park, in which they are held. They begin the last Tuesday of July, and continue four days, of which Thursday (the "cup-day") is the principal. These races are very select, and admirably conducted. Goodwood Park was purchased by Charles, first Duke of Richmond, of the Compton family, then resident in East Lav'ant, a village two miles north of Chichester.
The Newmarket Races. There are seven annual race meetings at Newmarket : (1) The Craven ; (2) first spring ; (3) second spring ; (4) July ; (5) first October ; (6) second October ; (7) the Houghton.
The Epsom. So called from Epsom Downs, where they are held. They last four days.
The Derby. The second day (Wednesday) of the great May meeting at Epsom, in Surrey ; so called from the Earl of Derby, who instituted the stakes in 1780. This is the great "Classic Race" for colts and fillies three years old.
The Oaks. The fourth day (Friday)

of the great Epsom races; so called from "Lambert's Oaks," erected on lease by the "Hunter's Club." The Oaks estate passed to the Derby family, and the twelfth earl established the stakes so called. This is the great "classic race" for fillies three years old.

The St. Leger. The great Doncaster race; so called from Colonel St. Leger, who founded the stakes in 1776. This is the great "classic race" for both colts and fillies of three years old. Horses that have competed in the Derby and Oaks may take part in the St. Leger.

Ascot Races, held on Ascot Heath, in Berks.

Races (Lengths run).

(i) *Under a mile and a half:*—
The Newmarket Stakes, 1 mile 2 furlongs.

The Prince of Wales's Stakes (at Leicester), rather less.

The Eclipse Stakes, 1¼ mile.

The Kempton Park Stakes, 1½ mile.

The Lancashire Plate (at the September Manchester meeting) is only 7 furlongs.

In 1890 the Duke of Portland won all these five races; *Ayrshire* won two of them, and *Donovan* the other three.

(ii) *Long distances (between 1¾ and 3 miles):*—
The Great Northampton Stakes, 1¾ mile.

Ascot (Gold Vase), 2 miles.
Ascot (Gold Cup), 2½ miles.
Ascot (Alexander Plate), 3 miles.
The Chester Cup, 2½ miles.
The Great Metropolitan Stakes (in the Epsom Spring Meeting), 2¼ miles.
The Hardwicke Stakes, the Goodwood Cup, 2½ miles (in July), and the Doncaster Cup, 2·634 miles (in September), are long races.

Rach'aders. The second tribe of giants or evil genii, who had frequently made the earth subject to their kings, but were ultimately punished by Shiva and Vishnoo. (*Indian mythology.*)

Rache. A "setter," or rather a dog said to hunt wild beasts, birds, and even fishes by scent. The female was called a *brache*—*i.e.* bitch-rache. (Saxon, *ræcc*; French, *braque.*)

"A leyshe of ratches to renne an hare."—
Skelton: Magnificence.

Rack. A flying scud, drifting clouds. (Icelandic, *rek,* drift; verb, *recka,* to drive.)

"The cloud-capped towers, the gorgeous palaces,
The solemn temples, the great globe itself,
Yea, all which it inherit, shall dissolve
And . . . leave not a rack behind."
Shakespeare: Tempest, iv. 1.

33*

Rack. The instrument of torture so called was a frame in which a man was fastened, and his arms and legs were *stretched* till the body was lifted by the tension several inches from the floor. Not unfrequently the limbs were forced thereby out of their sockets. Coke says that the rack was first introduced into the Tower by the Duke of Exeter, constable of the Tower, in 1447, whence it was called the "Duke of Exeter's daughter." (Dutch, *rak*; verb, *rakken,* to stretch; Danish, *rag*; Anglo-Saxon, *reac.*)

Rack-rent. The actual value or rent of a tenement, and not that modified form on which the rates and taxes are usually levied. (Saxon, *ræcan,* to stretch; Dutch, *racken.*)

"A rent which is equivalent, or nearly equivalent in amount, to the full annual value of the land, is a rack-rent."—*Encyclopædia Britannica,* vol. xx. p. 403.

Rack and Manger. Housekeeping. *To lie at rack and manger.* To live at reckless expense.

"When Virtue was a country maide,
And had no skill to set up trade,
She came up with a carrier's jade,
And lay at rack and manger."
Life of Robin Goodfellow. (1628.)

Rack and Ruin. Utter destitution. Here "rack" is a variety of *wrack* and wreck.

"The worst of all University snobs are those unfortunates who go to rack and ruin from their desire to ape their betters."—*Thackeray: Book of Snobs,* chap. xv. p. 87.

Racket. Noise or confusion, like that of persons playing racket or tennis.

Racy. Having distinctive piquancy, as *racy wine.* It was first applied to wine, and, according to Cowley, comes to us from the Spanish and Portuguese *raiz* (root), meaning having a radical or distinct flavour; but probably it is a corruption of "relishy" (French, *reléché,* flavorous).

"Rich, racy verse, in which we see
The soil from which they come, taste, smell, and see."
Cowley.

Racy Style. Piquant composition, the very opposite of mawkish.

Radcliffe Library (Oxford). Founded by Dr. John Radcliffe, of Wakefield, Yorkshire. (1650-1714.)

"When King William [III.] consulted [Radcliffe] on his swollen ankles and thin body, Radcliffe said, 'I would not have your Majesty's two legs for your three kingdoms.'"—*Leigh Hunt: The Town,* chap. vi.

Radegaste. A tutelary god of the Slavi. The head was that of a cow, the breast was covered with an ægis, the left hand held a spear, and a cock surmounted its helmet. (*Slavonic mythology.*)

Rad'egund. Queen of the Am'azons, "half like a man." Getting the better of Sir Art'egal in a single combat, she compelled him to dress in "woman's weeds," with a white apron before him, and to spin flax. Brit'omart, being informed by Talus of his captivity, went to the rescue, cut off the Amazon's head, and liberated her knight. (*Spenser: Faërie Queene*, book v. 4-7.)

St. Radegonde or *Radegund*, wife of Clothaire, King of France.

St. Radegonde's lifted stone. A stone sixty feet in circumference, placed on five supporting stones, said by the historians of Poitou to have been so arranged in 1478, to commemorate a great fair held on the spot in the October of that year. The country people insist that Queen Radegonde brought the impost stone on her head, and the five uprights in her apron, and arranged them all as they appear to this day.

Radevore (3 syl.). Tapestry.

" This woful lady ylern'd had in youthe
So that she worken and embrowden kouthe,
And weven in stole [the loom] the radevore,
As hyt of wommen had be woved yore."
                              Chaucer.

Rad'ical. An ultra-Liberal, verging on republican opinions. The term was first applied as a party name in 1818 to Henry Hunt, Major Cartwright, and others of the same clique, who wished to introduce *radical reform* in the representative system, and not merely to disfranchise and enfranchise a borough or two. Lord Bolingbroke, in his *Discourses on Parties*, says, "Such a remedy might have wrought a *radical cure* of the evil that threatens our constitution."

Radiometer. The name of an instrument invented by Crookes for measuring the mechanical effect of radiant energy. It is like a miniature anemometer, and is made to revolve by the action of light, the cups of the anemometer being replaced by discs coloured white on one side and black on the other, and the instrument is enclosed in a glass globe from which the air has been exhausted, so that no heat is transmitted.

Radit Usque ad Cutem. He fleeced him to the skin; he sucked him dry. He shaved off all his hair (instead of only trimming it).

Rag. A tatter, hence a remnant, hence a vagabond or ragamuffin.

" Lash hence these overweening rags of France."
        Shakespeare: Richard III., v. 3.

Rag. A cant term for a farthing. Paper money not easily convertible is called "rag-money."

" Money by me ? Heart and good-will you might,
But surely, master, not a rag of money."
        Shakespeare: Comedy of Errors, iv. 4.

Rag (*The*). The Army and Navy Club. "The rag," of course, is the flag.

" By the way, come and dine to-night at the Rag,' said the major."—*Truth, Queer Story*, April 1, 1886.

Rag-water. Whisky. (*Thieves' jargon.*)

Rags of Antisthenes. *Rank pride may be seen peering through the rags of Antis'thenes' doublet.* (*See* ANTISTHENES.)

Rags and Jags. Rags and tatters. A jagged edge is one that is toothed.

" Hark, hark ! the dogs do bark,
    The beggars are coming to town ;
Some in rags and some in jags,
    And some in silken gown."
                    Nursery Rhyme.

Ragamuffin (French, *maroufle*). A *muff* or muffin is a poor thing of a creature, a "regular muff;" so that a ragamuffin is a sorry creature in rags.

" I have led my ragamuffins where they are peppered."—*Shakespeare:* 1 *Henry IV.*, v. 3.

Ragged Robin. A wild-flower. The word is used by Tennyson to mean a pretty damsel in ragged clothes.

" The prince
Hath picked a ragged robin from the hedge."
    Tennyson: Idylls of the King ; Enid.

Raghu. A legendary king of Oude, belonging to the dynasty of the Sun. The poem called the *Raghu-vansa*, in nineteen cantos, gives the history of these mythic kings.

Ragman Roll originally meant the "Statute of Rageman" (*De Ragemannis*), a legate of Scotland, who compelled all the clergy to give a true account of their benefices, that they might be taxed at Rome accordingly. Subsequently it was applied to the four great rolls of parchment recording the acts of fealty and homage done by the Scotch nobility to Edward I. in 1296 ; these four rolls consisted of thirty-five pieces sewn together. The originals perished, but a record of them is preserved in the Rolls House, Chancery Lane.

Ragnarok [*twilight of the gods*]. The day of doom, when the present world and all its inhabitants will be annihilated. Vidar of Vali will survive the conflagration, and reconstruct the universe on an imperishable basis. (*Scandinavian mythology*.)

> " And, Frithiof, mayst thou sleep away
> Till Ragnarok, if such thy will."
>   *Frithiof-Saga: Frithiof's Joy.*

Ragout is something "more-ish," something you will be served twice to. (Latin, *re-gustus*, tasted again ; French, *re-goûte*.)

Ra'hu. The demon that causes eclipses. One day Rahu stole into Valhalla to quaff some of the nectar of immortality. He was discovered by the Sun and Moon, who informed against him, and Vishnu cut off his head. As he had already taken some of the nectar into his mouth, the head was immortal, and he ever afterwards hunted the Sun and Moon, which he caught occasionally, causing eclipses. (*Hindu mythology*.)

Rail. *To sit on the rail.* To shuffle off a direct answer ; to hedge or to fence ; to reserve the decision of one's vote. Here rail means the fence, and "to sit on the rail" to sit on one side. A common American phrase.

> " If he said ' Yes,' there was an end to any church support at once ; if ' No,' he might as well go home at once. So he tried to sit on the rail again."—*T. Terrell: Lady Delmar*, chap. i.

Railway Abbreviations.

C. & D. Collected and delivered—*i.e.* the rate quoted includes the entire charge from sender to consignee. Such goods are collected by the railway company and delivered according to the address at the price stated.

S. to S. From station to station. This does not include collecting and delivering.

O. R. Owner's risk.

C. R. Company's risk.

O. C. S. On company's service ; such parcels go free.

C. by B. Collection from the sender to the barge, both included.

O/C. Overcharged.

O/S. Outstanding.

Railway King. George Hudson, of Yorkshire, chairman of the North Midland Company, and for a time the Dictator of the railway speculations. In one day he cleared the large sum of £100,000. It was the Rev. Sydney Smith who gave him this designation. (1800-1871.)

Railway Signals. (*See* FLAG SIGNALS.)

Railways.

A. & B. R. Aylesbury and Buckingham Railway.

B. & L. J. R. Bourn and Lynn Joint Railway.

B. & M. R. Brecon and Merthyr Railway.

B. & N. C. R. Belfast and Northern Counties Railway.

Cal. R. Caledonian Railway.

Cam. R. Cambrian Railway.

C. K. & P. R. Cockermouth, Keswick, and Penrith Railway.

C. L. C. Cheshire Lines Committee, embracing the G. N., M. S. & L., and Mid. Coys.

C. V. R. Colne Valley and Halstead Railway.

C. W. & C. R. Central Wales and Carmarthen Railway.

C. & C. R. Carmarthen and Cardigan Railway.

D. R. & C. R. Denbigh, Ruthin, and Corwen Railway.

E. L. R. East London Railway.

E. & W. J. R. East and West Junction Railway.

Fur. R. Furness Railway.

G. & K. R. Garstang and Knotend Railway.

G. & S. W. R. Glasgow and South-Western Railway.

G. E. R. Great Eastern Railway.

G. N. S. R. Great Northern of Scotland Railway.

G. N. R. Great Northern Railway.

G. N. I. R. Great Northern of Ireland Railway.

G. S. & W. R. Great Southern and Western Railway.

G. W. R. Great Western Railway.

H. R. Highland Railway.

I. of M. R. Isle of Man Railway.

I. of W. R. Isle of Wight Railway.

L. & Y. R. Lancashire and Yorkshire Railway.

L. B. & S. C. R. London, Brighton, and South Coast Railway.

L. C. & D. R. London, Chatham, and Dover Railway.

L. D. & E. C. R. Lancashire, Derby, and East Coast Railway.

L. & N. W. R. London and North-Western Railway.

L. & S. W. R. London and South-Western Railway.

L. T. & S. R. London, Tilbury, and Southend Railway.

M. & M. R. Manchester and Milford Railway.

M. S. & L. R. Manchester, Sheffield, and Lincolnshire Railway.

M. S. J. & A. R. Manchester, South Junction, and Altrincham Railway.

M. & C. R. Maryport and Carlisle Railway.

Met. R. Metropolitan Railway.

Met. D. R. Metropolitan District Railway.

M. R. Midland Railway.

M. W. R. Mid-Wales Railway.

M. G. W. I. R. Midland Great-Western of Ireland Railway.

N. & B. R. Neath and Brecon Railway.

N. & B. J. R. Northampton and Banbury Junction Railway.

N. B. R. North British Railway.

N. E. R. North-Eastern Railway.

N. L. R. North London Railway.

N. S. R. North Staffordshire Railway.

P. & T. R. Pembroke and Tenby Railway.

R. R. Rhymney Railway.

S. & W. & S. B. R. Severn and Wye and Severn Bridge Railway.

S. & D. J. R. Somerset and Dorset Joint Railway.

S. E. R. South-Eastern Railway.

S. M. & A. R. Swindon, Marlborough, and Andover Railway.

T. V. R. Taff Vale Railway.

W. & L. R. Waterford and Limerick Railway.

W. & P. R. R. Watlington and Princes Risboro' Railway.

W. R. Wigtownshire Railway.

W. M. & C. Q. R. Wrexham, Mold, and Connah's Quay Railway.

Rain. *To rain cats and dogs.* In northern mythology the cat is supposed to have great influence on the weather, and English sailors still say, "The cat has a gale of wind in her tail," when she is unusually frisky. Witches that rode upon the storms were said to assume the form of cats; and the stormy north-west wind is called the *cat's-nose* in the Harz even at the present day.

The dog is a signal of *wind*, like the wolf, both which animals were attendants of Odin, the storm-god. In old German pictures the wind is figured as the "head of a dog or wolf," from which blasts issue.

The *cat* therefore symbolises the downpouring rain, and the *dog* the strong gusts of wind which accompany a rainstorm; and a "rain of cats and dogs" is a heavy rain with wind. (*See* CAT AND DOG.)

❧ The French *catadoupe* or *catadupe* means a waterfall.

Rain Gauge. An instrument or contrivance for measuring the amount of rain which falls on a given surface.

Rainbow. (*See* CIRCLE OF ULLOA.)

Rainbow Chasers. Problematical politicians and reformers, who chase rainbows, which cannot possibly be caught, to "find the pot of gold at the foot thereof." This alludes to an old joke, that a pot of gold can be dug up where the rainbow touches the earth.

Raining Tree (*The*). The Til, a linden-tree of the Canaries, mentioned by a host of persons. Mandelolo describes it minutely, and tells us that the water which falls from this tree suffices for a plentiful supply for men and beasts of the whole island of Fierro, which contains no river. Glas assures us that "the existence of such a tree is firmly believed in the Canaries" (*History of the Canary Islands*). Cordeyro (*Historia Insulana*, book ii. chap. v.) says it is an emblem of the Trinity, and that the rain is called *Agua Santa*. Without doubt a rain falls from some trees (as the lime) in hot weather.

Rainy Day (*A*). Evil times.

Lay by something for a rainy day. Save something against evil times.

Raise the Wind. To obtain ready money by hook or crook. A sea phrase. What wind is to a ship, money is to commerce.

> "I've tried queer ways
> The wind to raise,
> But ne'er had such a blow."
> *Judy* (My Lost Dog), Mar. 27, 1889.

Rajah. (Sanskrit for king, cognate with the Latin *reg* or *rex*.) Maha-rajah means the "great rajah."

Rake. A libertine. A contraction of rakehell, used by Milton and others.

> "And far away amid their rakehell bands
> They speed a lady left all succourless."
> *Francis Quarles.*

Rak'shas. Evil spirits who guard the treasures of Kuvera, the god of riches. They haunt cemeteries and devour human beings; assume any shape at will, and their strength increases as the day declines. Some are hideously ugly, but others, especially the female spirits, allure by their beauty. (*Hindu mythology*.)

Rakush. Rustem's horse in the *Shah Nameh* of Firdusi, the Homer of Korassan. (*See* HORSE.)

Ra'leigh. Sir Walter Scott introduces in *Kenilworth* the tradition of his laying down his cloak on a miry spot for the queen to step on.

> "Hark ye, Master Raleigh, see thou fail not to wear thy muddy cloak, in token of penitence, till our pleasure be further known."—*Sir Walter Scott: Kenilworth*, chap. xv.

Rally is *re-alligo*, to bind together again. (French *rallier*.) In Spenser it is spelt re-allie—

> " Before they could new consels re-allie."
> *Faërie Queene.*

> " Yes, we'll rally round the flag, boys,
> We'll rally once again."
> *G. F. Root · Battle-cry of Freedom*, stanza i.

Ralph or **Ralpho.** The squire of Hudibras. The model was Isaac Robinson, a zealous butcher in Moorfields, always contriving some queer art of church government. He represents the Independent party, and Hudibras the Presbyterian. Ralph rhymes with *half* and *safe.*

> " He was himself under the tyranny of scruples as unreasonable as those of . . . Ralpho."—*Macaulay.*

Ralph Roister Doister. The title of the earliest English comedy ; so called from the chief character. Written by Nicholas Udall. (16th century.)

Ram. The usual prize at wrestling matches. Thus Chaucer says of his Mellere, " At wrastlynge he wolde bere away the ram." (*Canterbury Tales : Prologue* 550.)

Ram Feast (*The*). May morning is so called at Holne, near Dartmoor, because on that day a ram is run down in the " Ploy Field." It is roasted whole, with its skin and fur, close by a granite pillar. At mid-day a scramble takes place for a slice, which is supposed to bring luck to those who get it. Said to be a relic of Baal worship in England.

Ram and Teazle (*The*). A public-house sign, is in compliment to the Clothiers' Company. The *ram* with the golden fleece is emblematical of wool, and the *teazle* is used for raising the nap of wool spun and woven into cloth.

Ram of the Zodiac (*The*). This is the famous Chrysomallon, whose golden fleece was stolen by Jason in his Argonautic expedition. It was transposed to the stars, and made the first sign of the Zodiac.

> The Vernal signs the Ram begins ;
> Then comes the Bull ; in May the Twins :
> The Crab in June ; next Leo shines ;
> And Virgo ends the northern signs.   *E. C. B.*

Ram's Horn (*A*). A loud, vulgar, unpolished speaker. A smooth-tongued orator is called a " silver trumpet."

Rama. The seventh incarnation of Vishnu.

The first was the *fish* ; the second, the *tortoise ;* the third, the *boar ;* the fourth, the *man-lion ;* the fifth, the *dwarf ;* the sixth, *Parus'u-Rama*, son of Jamadagni :

the seventh, RAMA, son of Das'aratha, King of Ayodhyâ ; the eighth, *Krishna* or *Crishna ;* the ninth, *Buddha ;* and the last (tenth) will be *Kalki*, and the consummation of all things—a kind of millennium.

Rama performed many wonderful exploits, such as killing giants, demons, and monsters. He won Sita to wife because he was able to bend the bow of Siva.

Rama-Yana. The history of Rama, the best great epic poem of ancient India, and worthy to be ranked with the *Iliad* of Homer.

Ram'adan. The ninth month of the Mahometan year, and the Mussulman's Lent or Holy Month.

> " November is the financial Ramadan of the Sublime Porte."—*The Times.*

That is, when the Turkish Government promises all kinds of financial reforms and curtailments of national expenses.

Rambouillet. *Hôtel de Rambouillet.* The *réunion* of rank and literary genius on terms of equality ; a *coterie* where sparkling wit with polished manners prevails. The Marquise de Rambouillet, in the seventeenth century, reformed the French *soirées*, and purged them of the gross morals and licentious conversation which at that time prevailed. The present good taste, freedom without licentiousness, wit without *double entendre*, equality without familiarity, was due to this illustrious Italian. The *Précieuses Ridicules* of Molière was a satire on those her imitators who had not her talent and good taste. Catherine, Marquise de Rambouillet (1588-1665).

Rameo Samoo. The conjurer who swallowed swords, and could twist himself into a knot as if he had neither bones nor joints.

Ram'eses (3 syl.). The title of an ancient Egyptian dynasty ; it means *Offspring of the Sun.* This title was first assumed towards the close of the Eighteenth Dynasty, and ran through the Nineteenth. Rameses III. is called Rhampsini'tos by Herod'otos. Sesostris is supposed to be identical with Rameses the Great. (Eses, *i.e.* Isis.)

Ram'iel (2 syl.). One of the fallen angels cast out of heaven. The word means *one that exalts himself against God.*

Raminago'bris. A cat ; a vile poet. La Fontaine in several of his fables gives this name to the cat. Rabelais under this name satirises Guillaume Crétin, an old French poet in the reigns of Charles VIII., Louis XII., and François I. (*Rabelais : Pantagruel*, iii. 21.)

Rampal'lian. A term of contempt ; probably it means a rampant or wanton woman ; hence in *A New Trick to Cheat the Devil* (1639) we have this line : "And bold rampallian-like, swear and drink drunk."

"Away, you scullion ! you rampallian ! you fustilarian ! I'll tickle your catastrophe."—*Shakespeare : 2 Henry IV.*, ii. 1.

Ramsay the Rich. Ramsay used to be called the Crœsus of our English abbeys. It had only sixty monks of the Benedictine order to maintain, and its revenues allowed £1,000 a year to the abbot, and £100 a year for each of its monks.

David Ramsay. The old watchmaker near Temple Bar.

Margaret Ramsay. His daughter, who became the bride of Lord Nigel. (*Sir Walter Scott : Fortunes of Nigel.*)

Ramsbottom (*Mrs.*). A vile speller of the Queen's English. It was the signature of Theodore Hook in his letters published in the *John Bull* newspaper, 1829.

Ra'na. Goddess of the sea, and wife of the sea-god Aeger. (*Scandinavian mythology.*)

" 'May Rana keep them in the deep,
   As is her wont,
And no one save them from the grave,'
   Cried Helgehont."
         Frithiof-Saga ; The Banishment.

Randem-Tandem. A tandem of three horses. (*University term.*)

Random (*Roderick*). A young Scotch scapegrace in quest of fortune ; at one time basking in prosperity, at another in utter destitution. He is led into different countries, whose peculiarities are described ; and into all sorts of society, as that of wits, sharpers, courtiers, courtesans, and so on. Though occasionally lavish, he is inherently mean ; and though possessing a dash of humour, is contemptibly revengeful. His treatment of Strap is revolting to a generous mind. Strap lends him money in his necessity, but the heartless Roderick wastes the loan, treats Strap as a mere servant, fleeces him at dice, and cuffs him when the game is adverse. (*Smollett : Roderick Random.*)

Rank and File. Soldiers of any grade below that of lance-sergeant are so called, collectively, in military phraseology, and any two soldiers of such

grade are spoken of as "a file ;" thus, 100 rank and file would equal 50 file, that is, 50 men standing behind each other in a row. No soldier ever talks of *files* in the plural, or about "a file of fours." As there are two in a "rank," there is a *left* file and a *right* file ; and men may move in "single file" or in "double file." A line of soldiers drawn up side by side or abreast is a rank.

Rank distinguished by Colour. In China the emperor, empress, and prince imperial wear yellow ; the other wives of the emperor wear violet ; high state officers wear blue ; officials of lower rank wear red ; and the general public wear black or some dark shade.

Ranks. *Risen from the ranks.* From mean origin ; a self-made man. A military term applied to an officer who once served as a private soldier. Such an officer is now often called a "ranker."

Ran'tipole (3 syl.). A harum-scarum fellow, a madcap (Dutch, *randten*, to be in a state of idiotcy or insanity, and *pole*, a head or person). The late Emperor Napoleon III. was called *Rantipole*, for his escapades at Strasbourg and Boulogne. In 1852 I myself saw a man commanded by the police to leave Paris within twenty-four hours for calling his dog Rantipole.

"Dick, be a little rantipolish."—*Colman : Hein. at-Law.*

Ranz des Vaches. Simple melodies played by the Swiss mountaineers on their Alp-horn when they drive their herds to pasture, or call them home (*pour. ranger des vaches*, to bring the cows to their place).

Rap. *Not worth a rap.* The rap was a base halfpenny, intrinsically worth about half a farthing, issued for the nonce in Ireland in 1721, because small coin was so very scarce. There was also a coin in Switzerland called a *rappe*, worth the seventh of a penny.

"Many counterfeits passed about under the name of raps."—*Swift : Drapier's Letters.*

Rape (1 syl.). The division of a county. Sussex is divided into six rapes, each of which has its river, forest, and castle. *Herepp* is Norwegian for a parish district, and rape in Doomsday Book is used for a district under military jurisdiction. (Icelandic *hreppr*, a district.)

Rape of the Lock. Lord Petre, in a thoughtless moment of frolic gallantry, cut off a lock of Arabella Fermor's hair ; and this liberty gave rise to a bitter feud between the two families, which Alexander Pope has worked up into the best heroi-comic poem of the language. The first sketch was published in 1712 in two cantos. The machinery of sylphs and gnomes is most happily conceived. Pope, under the name of Esdras Barnevelt, apothecary, says the poem is a covert satire on Queen Anne and the Barrier Treaty. In the poem the lady is called Belinda, and the poet says she wore on her neck two curls, one of which the baron cut off with a pair of scissors borrowed from Clarissa. Belinda, in anger, demanded back the ringlet, but it had flown to the skies and become a meteor there. (*See* COMA BERENI'CES.)

'Say, what strange motive, goddess, could compel
A well-bred lord to assault a gentle belle ;
O say, what stranger cause, yet unexplored,
Could make a gentle belle reject a lord."
            Introduction to the Poem.

Raph'ael. The sociable archangel who travelled with Tobi'as into Me'dia and back again, instructing him on the way how to marry Sara and to drive away the wicked spirit. Milton introduces him as sent by God to advertise Adam of his danger. (*See* SEVEN SPIRITS.)

" Raphael, the sociable spirit, hath deigned
To travel with Tobias, and secured
His marriage with the seven-times-wedded
maid."   *Paradise Lost,* v. 221-3.

Raphael, according to Longfellow, is the angel of the Sun, who brings to man the " gift of faith."

" I am the angel of the Sun,
Whose flaming wheels began to run
  When God Almighty's breath
Said to the darkness and the night,
'Let there be light,' and there was light,—
  I bring the gift of faith."
      Golden Legend : The Miracle Play, iii.

St. Raphael, the archangel, is usually distinguished in Christian art by a pilgrim's staff, or carrying a fish, in allusion to his aiding Tobias to capture the fish which performed the miraculous cure of his father's eyesight.

The French Raphael. Eustace Lesueur (1617-1655).

Raphael of Cats (*The*). Godefroi Mind, a Swiss painter, noted for his cats. (1768-1814.)

Rapparee'. A wild Irish plunderer ; so called from his being armed with a raparv or half-pike. (Irish *rappire,* a robber.)

Rappee. A coarse species of snuff, manufactured from dried tobacco by an instrument called in French a *râpe,* " instrument en metal percé de plusieurs trous. dont on se sert pour réduire les corps en pulpe ou en fragments. On se

sert surtout de la râpe dans les ménages, pour le sucre, le chocolat, le poivre ; et dans les usines, pour le tabac, les betteraves, les pommes de terre qu'on réduit en fécule, etc." (*Bouillet : Dictionnaire des Sciences.*)

Ra'ra A'vis (Latin, *a rare bird*). A phenomenon ; a prodigy ; a something quite out of the common course. Black swans are now familiar to us ; they are natives of Australia, and have given its name to the " Swan river." At one time a black swan was emphatically a *rara avis.*

" Rara avis in terris nigroque simillima cygne."
                    Juvenal.

Rare Ben. So Shakespeare called Ben Jonson, the dramatist. (1574-1637.) Aubrey says that this inscription on his tablet in the " Poets' Corner," Westminster Abbey, " was done at the charge of Jack Young (afterwards knighted), who, walking there when the grave was covering, gave the fellow eighteenpence to cut it." At the late relaying of the pavement, this stone was unhappily removed. When Sir William Davenant was interred in Westminster Abbey, the inscription on his covering-stone was, " O rare Sir William Davenant " —showing how nearly the sublime and the ridiculous often meet.

Raree Show. A peep-show ; a show carried about in a box.

Rascal. Originally applied in the chase to a lean, worthless deer, then a collective term for the commonalty, the mob ; and popularly to a base fellow. Shakespeare says, " Horns ! the noblest deer hath them as huge as the rascal " [deer]. Palsgrave calls a starving animal, like the lean kine of Pharaoh, " a rascall refus beest " (1530). The French have *racaille* (riff-raff).

" Come, you thin thing ; come, you rascal."—
Shakespeare : 2 Henry IV., v. 4.

Rascal Counters. Pitiful or paltry £ s. d. Brutus calls money paltry compared with friendship, etc.

" When Marcus Brutus grows so covetous,
To lock such rascal counters from his friends,
Be ready, gods, with all your thunderbolts,
Dash him to pieces."
      Shakespeare : Julius Cæsar, iv. 5.

Rasher. A slice, as a rasher of bacon.

Rash'leigh Osbaldistone. An accomplished but deceitful villain, called " the scholar." He is the youngest of the six hopeful sons of Sir Hildebrand Osbaldistone. The six brothers were nicknamed " the sot," " the bully," " the gamekeeper," " the horse-jockey," "the fool," and the crafty "scholar." (*Sir Walter Scott: Rob Roy.*)

Ra'siel. The angel who was the tutor of Adam. (*Talmud.*)

Raspberry. Rhyming slang for "heart," as "it made my raspberry beat." (*See* CHIVY.)

Ras'selas. Prince of Abyssinia, in Dr. Johnson's romance so called.

"'Rasselas' is a mass of sense, and its moral precepts are certainly conveyed in striking and happy language. The mad astronomer who imagined that he possessed the regulation of the weather and the distribution of the seasons, is an original character in romance ; and the happy valley in which Rasselas resides is sketched with poetical feeling."—*Young.*

Rat. The Egyptians and Phrygians deified rats. The people of Basso'ra and Cambay to the present time forbid their destruction. In Egypt the rat symbolised "utter destruction ;" it also symbolised "judgment," because rats always choose the best bread for their repast.

Rat. Pliny tells us (bk. viii. ch. lvii.) that the Romans drew presages from these animals, and to see a *white* rat foreboded good fortune. The bucklers at Lanu'vium being gnawed by rats presaged ill-fortune, and the battle of the Marses, fought soon after, confirmed this superstition. Proserpine's veil was embroidered with rats.

Irish rats rhymed to death. It was once a prevalent opinion that rats in pasturages could be extirpated by anathematising them in rhyming verse or by metrical charms. This notion is frequently alluded to by ancient authors. Thus, Ben Jonson says: "Rhyme them to death, as they do Irish rats" (*Poetaster*) ; Sir Philip Sidney says: "Though I will not wish unto you . . . to be rimed to death, as is said to be done in Ireland" (*Defence of Poesie*) ; and Shakespeare makes Rosalind say: "I was never so berhymed since . . . I was an Irish rat," alluding to the Pythagore'an doctrine of the transmigration of souls (*As You Like It*, iii. 2). (*See* CHARM.)

I smell a rat. I perceive there is something concealed which is mischievous. The allusion is to a cat smelling a rat.

Rat (*To*). To forsake a losing side for the stronger party. It is said that rats forsake ships not weatherproof. A rat is one who rats or deserts his party. Hence workmen who work during a strike are called "rats."

" Averting . . .
    The cup of sorrow from their lips,
    And fly like rats from sinking ships."
            Swift: Epistle to Mr. Nugent.

Rat (*Un*). A purse. Hence, a young boy thief is called a *Raton*. A sort of pun on the word *rapt* from the Latin *rapto*, to carry off forcibly. *Courir le rat*, to rob or break into a house at night-time.

To take a rat by the tail, or *Prendre un rat par la queue*, is to cut a purse. A phrase dating back to the age of Louis XIII., and inserted in Cotgrave's *Dictionary.* Of course, a cutpurse would cut the purse at the string or else he would spill the contents.

Rat, Cat, and Dog.

" The Rat, the Cat, and Lovell the Dog,
    Rule all England under the hog."

❧ The *Rat*, i.e. Rat-cliff ; the *Cat*, i.e. Cat-esby ; and *Lovel the dog*, is Francis, Viscount Lovel, the king's "spaniel." The *hog* or boar was the crest of Richard III. William Collingham, the author of this rhyme (1413), was put to death for his pregnant wit.

Rat-killer. Apollo received this aristocratic soubriquet from the following incident :—Crinis, one of his priests, having neglected his official duties, Apollo sent against him a swarm of rats : but the priest, seeing the invaders coming, repented and obtained forgiveness of the god, who annihilated the swarms which he had sent with his far-darting arrows. For this redoubtable exploit the sun-god received the appellation of Apollo the Rat-killer. (*Classic mythology.*)

Rat'atosk. The squirrel that runs up and down the mythological tree Yggdrasil'. (*Scandinavian mythology.*)

Ratten (*To*). To annoy for refusing to join a trade union, or for not submitting to its demands. This is done by destroying or taking away a workman's tools, or otherwise incapacitating him from doing work. "To rat" is to desert one's party ; to work for less than the price fixed by a trade union ; and "ratten" is to act the part of a rat. (*See* RAT.)

Rattlin (*Jack*). A famous naval character in Smollett's *Roderick Random.* Tom Bowling is another naval character in the same novel.

Raul. *Sir Raul di Nangis*, the Huguenot, in love with Valenti'na, daughter of the Comte de St. Bris, governor of the Louvre. Being sent for by Marguerite, he is offered the hand of Valentina in marriage, but rejects it, because he fancies she is betrothed to the Comte de Nevers. Nevers is slain in the

Bartholomew massacre, and Valentina confesses her love for Raul. They are united by Marcello, an old Puritan servant, but scarcely is the ceremony ended when both are shot by the musketeers under the command of St. Bris. (*Meyerbeer : Gli Ugonotti, an opera.*)

Rava'na, according to Indian mythology, was fastened down between heaven and earth for 10,000 years by Siva's leg, for attempting to move the hill of heaven to Ceylon. He is described as a demon giant with ten faces. (*Hindu mythology.*)

Ravelin (*The*) or *demi-lune*, in fortification. A work with two faces, forming a salient angle, placed beyond the main ditch, opposite the curtain (*q.v.*), and separated from the covered way (*q.v.*) by a ditch which runs into the main ditch.

Raven. A bird of ill omen. They are said to forebode death and bring infection. The former notion arises from their following an army under the expectation of finding dead bodies to raven on ; the latter notion is a mere offshoot of the former, seeing pestilence kills as fast as the sword.

" The boding raven on her cottage sat,
And with hoarse croakings warned us of our
fate."   *Gay : Pastorals ; The Dirge.*

" Like the sad-presaging raven that tolls
The sick man's passport in her hollow beak,
And, in the shadow of the silent night,
Does shake contagion from her sable wing."
    Marlowe : Jew of Malta (1633).

Raven. Jovianus Ponta'nus relates two skirmishes between ravens and kites near Beneventum, which prognosticated a great battle. Nice'tas speaks of a skirmish between crows and ravens as presaging the irruption of the Scythians into Thrace. He also tells us that his friend Mr. Draper, in the flower of his age and robust health, knew he was at the point of death because two ravens flew into his chamber. Cicero was forewarned of his death by the fluttering of ravens, and Macaulay relates the legend that a raven entered the chamber of the great orator the very day of his murder, and pulled the clothes off his bed. Like many other birds, ravens indicate by their cries the approach of foul weather, but "it is ful unleful to beleve that God sheweth His prevy counsayle to crowes, as Isidore sayth."

He has the foresight of a raven. A raven was accounted at one time a prophetic bird. (*See above.*)

" Of inspired birds ravens are accounted the most prophetical. Accordingly, in the language of that district, ' to have the foresight of a raven' is to this day a proverbial expression."—*Macaulay : History of St. Kilda, p. 174.*

Ravens bode famine. When a flock of ravens forsake the woods we may look for famine and mortality, because " ravens bear the characters of Saturn, the author of these calamities, and have a very early perception of the bad disposition of that planet." (See *Athenian Oracle,* Supplement, p. 476.)

" As if the great god Jupiter had nothing else to doe but to dryve about jacke-dawes and ravens."—*Carneades.*

Ravens were once as white as swans, and not inferior in size ; but one day a raven told Apollo that Coro'nis, a Thessalian nymph whom he passionately loved, was faithless. The god shot the nymph with his dart ; but, hating the tell-tale bird—

" He blacked the raven o'er,
And bid him prate in his white plumes no more."
    Addison : Translation of Ovid, bk. ii.

Ravens in Christian art. Emblems of God's Providence, in allusion to the ravens which fed Elijah. St. Oswald holds in his hand a raven with a ring in its mouth ; St. Benedict has a raven at his feet ; St. Paul the Hermit is drawn with a raven bringing him a loaf of bread, etc.

The fatal raven, consecrated to Odin, the Danish war-god, was the emblem on the Danish standard. This raven was said to be possessed of necromantic power. The standard was termed *Landeyda* (the desolation of the country), and miraculous powers were attributed to it. The fatal raven was the device of Odin, god of war, and was said to have been woven and embroidered in one noontide by the daughters of Regner Lodbrok, son of Sigurd, that dauntless warrior who chanted his death-song (the *Krakamal*) while being stung to death in a horrible pit filled with deadly serpents. If the Danish arms were destined to defeat, the raven hung his wings ; if victory was to attend them, he stood erect and soaring, as if inviting the warriors to follow.

" The Danish raven, lured by annual prey,
Hung o'er the land incessant."
    Thomson : Liberty, pt. iv.

The two ravens that sit on the shoulders of Odin are called Hugin and Munnin (*Mind and Memory*).

One raven will not pluck another's eyes out (German, " *Keine krähe hackt der anderen die augen aus*"). Friends will not " peach" friends ; you are not to take for granted all that a friend says of a friend.

Ravenglass (Cumberland). A corruption of *Afon-glass* (Blue river).

Ra'venstone. The stone gibbet of Germany; so called from the ravens which are wont to perch on it. (German *rabenstein*.)

"Do you think
I'll honour you so much as save your throat
From the Ravenstone, by choking you myself?"
Byron: Werner, ii. 2.

Ra'venswood (*Allan, Lord of*). A decayed Scotch nobleman of the Royalist party.

Master Edgar Ravenswood. His son, who falls in love with Lucy Ashton, daughter of Sir William Ashton, Lord-Keeper of Scotland. The lovers plight their troth at the Mermaid's Fountain, but Lucy is compelled to marry Frank Hayston, laird of Bucklaw. The bride, in a fit of insanity, attempts to murder the bridegroom and dies in convulsions. Bucklaw recovers, and goes abroad. Colonel Ashton, seeing Edgar at the funeral of Lucy, appoints a hostile meeting; and Edgar, on his way to the place appointed, is lost in the quicksands of Kelpies-flow. (*Sir Walter Scott: Bride of Lammermoor*.)

In Donizetti's opera of *Lucia di Lammermoor*, Bucklaw dies of the wound inflicted by the bride, and Edgar, heartbroken, comes on the stage and kills himself, that "his marriage with Lucy, forbidden on earth, may be consummated in heaven."

Raw. *To touch one on the raw.* To mention something that makes a person wince, like touching a horse on a raw place in cleaning him.

Raw Lobster (*A*). A policeman. Lobsters before they are boiled are a dark blue. A soldier dressed in scarlet is a lobster; a policeman, or sort of soldier, dressed in dark blue is a raw lobster. The name was given to the new force by the *Weekly Dispatch* newspaper, which tried to write it down.

Rawhead and Bloody-Bones. A bogie at one time the terror of children.

"Servants awe children and keep them in subjection by telling them of Rawhead and Bloody-bones."—*Locke.*

Ray'mond (in *Jerusalem Delivered*). Master of 4,000 infantry, Count of Toulouse, equal to Godfrey in the "wisdom of cool debate" (bk. iii.). This Nestor of the Crusaders slew Aladine, the king of Jerusalem, and planted the Christian standard upon the tower of David (bk. xx.).

Rayne or **Raine** (Essex). *Go and say your prayers at Raine.* The old church

of Raine, built in the time of Henry II., famous for its altar to the Virgin, and much frequented at one time by pregnant women, who went to implore the Virgin to give them safe deliverance.

Razed Shoes, referred to in *Hamlet*, are slashed shoes.

"Would not this, sir ... with two Provençal roses on my razed shoes, get me a fellowship in a cry of players, sir?"—Act iii. 2.

Razee (*raz-za*). A ship of war cut down to a smaller size, as a seventy-four reduced to a frigate. (French, *raser*.)

Razor. *Hewing blocks with a razor.* Livy relates how Tarquinius Priscus, defying the power of Attus Navius, the augur, said to him, "Tell me, if you are so wise, whether I can do what I am now thinking about." "Yes," said Navius. "Ha! ha!" cried the king; "I was thinking whether I could cut in twain that whetstone with a razor." "Cut boldly!" answered the augur, and the king cleft it in twain at one blow.

Raz'zia. An incursion made by the military into an enemy's country, for the purpose of carrying off cattle or slaves, or for enforcing tribute. It is an Arabic word much employed in connection with Algerine affairs.

"War is a razzia rather than an art to the ... merciless Pelissier."—*The Standard.*

Re (Latin). . Respecting; in reference to; as, "*re* Brown," in reference to the case of Brown.

Reach of a river. The part which lies between two points or bends; so called because it *reaches* from point to point.

"When he drew near them he would turn from each,
And loudly whistle till he passed the Reach."
Crabbe: Borough.

Read between the Lines. (*See under* LINES.)

Reade or **Read** (*Simon*), alluded to by Ben Jonson in the *Alchemist*, i. 2, was Simon Read, of St. George's, Southwark, professor of physic. Rymer, in his *Fœdêra*, vol. xvi., says, "he was indicted for invoking evil spirits in order to find out the name of a person who, in 1608, stole £37 10s. from Tobias Mathews, of St. Mary Steynings, London.

Reader. In the University of Oxford, one who reads lectures on scientific subjects. In the Inns of Court, one who reads lectures in law. In printing, one who reads and corrects the proof-sheets of any work before publication; a corrector of the press.

Ready (*The*). An elliptical expression for ready-money. Goldsmith says, "*Æs in presenti perfectum format*" ("Ready-money makes a man perfect"). (*Eton Latin Grammar.*)

"Lord Strut was not very flush in the 'ready.'"
—*Dr. Arbuthnot.*

Ready - to - Halt. A pilgrim that journeyed to the Celestial city on crutches. He joined the party under the charge of Mr. Greatheart, but "when he was sent for" he threw away his crutches, and, lo! a chariot bore him into Paradise. (*Bunyan : Pilgrim's Progress*, part ii.)

Real Jam. Prime stuff, a real treat, something delightful. Of course, the allusion is to jam given to children for a treat.

"There must have been a charming climate in Paradise, and [the] connubial bliss [there] . . . was real jam."—*Sam Slick : Human Nature.*

Real Presence. The doctrine that Christ Himself is really and substantially present in the bread and wine of the Eucharist after consecration.

Rear-mouse or **Rere-mouse.** The bat. (Anglo-Saxon *hrere-mus*, the fluttering-mouse ; verb, *hrere-an*, to flutter.) Of course, the "bat" is not a winged mouse.

Reason. *The Goddess of Reason*, November 10th, 1793. Mlle. Candeille, of the Opéra, was one of the earliest of these goddesses, but Mme. Momoro, wife of the printer, the Goddess of Liberty, was the most celebrated. On November 10th a festival was held in Notre Dame de Paris in honour of Reason and Liberty, when women represented these "goddesses." Mlle. Candeille wore a red Phrygian cap, a white frock, a blue mantle, and tricolour ribbons. Her head was filleted with oak-leaves, and in her hand she carried the pike of Jupiter-Peuple. In the cathedral a sort of temple was erected on a mound, and in this "Temple of Philosophy" Mlle. Candeille was installed. Young girls crowned with oak-leaves were her attendants, and sang hymns in her honour. Similar installations were repeated at Lyons and other places. (*See* LIBERTY, *Goddess of.*)

Mlle. Maillard, the actress, is mentioned by Lamartine as one of these goddesses, but played the part much against her will.
Mlle. Aubray was another Goddess of Reason.

Rebec'ca. Daughter of Isaac the Jew, in love with Ivanhoe. Rebecca, with her father and Ivanhoe, being taken prisoners, are confined in Front de Bœuf's castle. Rebecca is taken to the turret chamber and left with the old sibyl there ; but when Brian de Bois Guilbert comes and offers her insult she spurns him with heroic disdain, and, rushing to the verge of the battlements, threatens to throw herself over if he touches her. Ivanhoe, who was suffering from wounds received in a tournament, is nursed by Rebecca. Being again taken prisoner, the Grand Master commands the Jewish maiden to be tried for sorcery, and she demands a trial by combat. The demand is granted, when Brian de Bois Guilbert is appointed as the champion against her ; and Ivanhoe undertakes her defence, slays Brian, and Rebecca is set free. To the general disappointment of novel-readers, after all this excitement Ivanhoe tamely marries the lady Rowen'a, a "vapid piece of still life." Rebecca pays the newly-married pair a wedding visit, and then goes abroad with her father to get out of the way. (*Sir Walter Scott : Ivanhoe.*)

Rebec'caites (4 syl.). Certain Welsh rioters in 1843, whose object was to demolish turnpike gates. The name was taken from Rebekah, the bride of Isaac. When she left her father's house, Laban and his family "blessed her," and said, "Let thy seed possess the gate of those that hate them" (Gen. xxiv. 60).

Rebellion (*The*). The revolts in behalf of the House of Stuart in 1715 and 1745 ; the former in behalf of the Chevalier de St. George, son of James II., called the Old Pretender, and the latter in favour of Charles Edward, usually termed the Young Pretender.

The Great Rebellion. The revolt of the Long Parliament against Charles I. (1612-1616.)

The Great Irish Rebellion, 1789. It was caused by the creation of numerous Irish societies hostile to England, especially that called "The United Irishmen." There have been eight or nine other rebellions. In 1365 the Irish applied to France for soldiers ; in 1597 they offered the crown of Ireland to Spain ; in 1796 they concluded a treaty with the French Directory.

Rebus (Latin, *with things*). A hieroglyphic riddle, "*non verbis sed rebus.*" The origin of the word and custom is this: The basochiens of Paris, during the carnival, used to satirise the current follies of the day in squibs called *De rebus quæ geruntur* (on the current events). That these squibs might not be accounted libellous, they employed hieroglyphics either wholly or in part

Reception (*To get a*), in theatrical language means to be welcomed with applause from the front, when you make your first appearance for the night. This signifies that the audience recognises your established reputation.

Re'chabites (3 syl.). A religious sect founded by Jonadab, son of Rechab, who enjoined his family to abstain from wine and to dwell in tents. (Jer. xxxv. 6, 7.)

Receipt is a direction for compounding or mixing together certain ingredients to make something required. It also means a written discharge to a debtor for the payment of a debt.

Recipe (3 syl.), **Receipt.** Recĭpe is Latin for *take*, and contracted into ℞ is used in doctor's prescriptions. The dash through the R is an abbreviated form of ♃, the symbol of Jupiter, and ℞ means *Recĭpe, deo volente.*

Reck his own Rede (*To*). Give heed to his own counsel. (Old English, *Rec*[*an*], to heed; *Ræd*, counsel, advice.)

Reckon (*I*). A peculiar phraseology common in the Southern States of America. Those in New England say, "I guess." (*See* Calculate.)

Reckoning without your Host. To guess what your expenses at an hotel will be before the bill has been delivered; to enter upon an enterprise without knowing the cost.

"We thought that now our troubles were over ; . . . but we reckoned without our host."—*Macmillan's Magazine*, 1887.

Recla'im (2 syl.). To turn from evil ways. This is a term in falconry, and means to *call back* the hawk to the wrist. This was done when it was unruly, that it might be smoothed and tamed. (Latin, *re-clamo.*)

Recorded. *Death recorded* means that the sentence of death is *recorded* or written by the recorder against the criminal, but not verbally pronounced by the judge. This is done when capital punishment is likely to be remitted. It is the verbal sentence of the judge that is the only sufficient warrant of an execution. The sovereign is now not consulted about any capital punishment.

Rec'reant is one who cries out (French, *récrier*); alluding to the judicial combats, when the person who wished to give in cried for mercy, and was held a coward and infamous. (*See* Craven.)

Rector. (*See* Clerical Titles.)

Reculer pour Mieux Sauter. To run back in order to give a better jump forwards; to give way a little in order to take up a stronger position.

"Where the empire sets its foot, it cannot withdraw without much loss of credit, whereas *reculer pour mieux sauter* must often be the most effective action in that tide of European civilisation, which is slowly, but surely, advancing into the heart of the Dark Continent."—*Nineteenth Century*, December, 1892, p. 990.

Recul'ver. The antiquities of this place are fully described in *Antiquitates Rutupinæ*, by Dr. Battley (1711). It was a Roman fort in the time of Claudius.

Red. The colour of magic.

"Red is the colour of magic in every country, and has been so from the very earliest times. The caps of fairies and musicians are well-nigh always red."—*Yeates: Fairy and Folk Tales of the Irish Peasantry*, p. 61.

Red applied to gold. Hence a gold watch is a "red kettle."

' Thou shew'st an honest nature ; weep'st for thy
                    master ;
There's a red rogue to buy the handkerchief."
          Beaumont and Fletcher: Mad Lover, v. 4.

Red Basque Cap. The cognisance of Don Carlos, pretender to the Spanish throne.

Red Book. The book which gave account of the court expenditure in France before the Revolution was so called because its covers were red. We have also a "Red Book" in manuscript, containing the names of all those who held lands *per baro'niam* in the reign of Henry II., with other matters pertaining to the nation before the Conquest. (*Ryley*, 667.)

Red Book of the Exchequer (*The*). *Liber Rubens Scaccarii* in the Record Office. It was compiled in the reign of Henry III. (1246), and contains the returns of the tenants *in capite* in 1166, who certify how many knights' fees they hold, and the names of those who hold or held them, also much other matter from the Pipe Rolls and other sources. It has not yet (1895) been printed, but is described in Sims' *Manual* (p. 41), Thomas's *Handbook* (p. 255), and in the *Record Report* of 1837 (pp. 166-177). A separate account of it was printed by Hunter in 1837. It contains the only known fragment of the Pipe Roll of Henry II., and copies of the important Inquisition returned into the exchequer in 13 John. It is *not* written in *red ink*. (*Communicated by A. Oldham.*)

Red Boots. *A pair of red boots.* A Tartar phrase, referring to a custom of cutting the skin of a victim round the upper part of the ankles, and then stripping it off at the feet. A Tartar will say, "When you come my way again, I will give you a pair of red boots to go home in."

Red-breasts. Bow Street runners, who wore a scarlet waistcoat.

"The Bow Street runners ceased out of the land soon after the introduction of the new police. I remember them very well as standing about the door of the office in Bow Street. They had no other uniform than a blue dress-coat, brass buttons ... and a bright red cloth waistcoat. ... The slang name for them was 'Red-breasts.'"—*Dickens: Letters*, vol. ii. p. 178.

Red Button (*A*). A mandarin of the first class, whose badge of honour is a red button in his cap.

"An interview was granted to the admiral [Elliot] by Kishen, the imperial commissioner, the third man in the empire, a mandarin of first class and red button."—*Howitt: History of England*, 1841, p. 471.

Red Cap (*Mother*). An old nurse "at the Hungerford Stairs." Dame Ursley or Ursula, another nurse, says of her rival—

"She may do very well for skipper's wives, chandlers' daughters, and such like, but nobody shall wait on pretty Mistress Margaret ... excepting and saving myself."—*Sir Walter Scott: Fortunes of Nigel.*

Red Coats in fox-hunting (or scarlet) is a badge of royal livery, fox-hunting being ordained by Henry II. a royal sport.

Red Cock. *The red cock will crow in his house.* His house will be set on fire.

"'We'll see if the red cock craw not in his bonnie barn-yard ae morning.' 'What does she mean?' said Mannering. ... 'Fire-raising,' answered the ... dominie."—*Sir Walter Scott: Guy Mannering*, chap. iii.

Red Com'yn. Sir John Comyn of Badenoch, son of Marjory, sister of King John Balhol; so called from his ruddy complexion and red hair, to distinguish him from his kinsman "Black Comyn," whose complexion was swarthy and hair black. He was stabbed by Sir Robert Bruce in the church of the Minorites at Dumfries, and afterwards dispatched by Lindesay and Kirkpatrick.

Red Cross (*The*). The badge of the royal banner of England till those of St. Patrick and St. Andrew were added.

"The fall of Rouen (1419) was the fall of the whole province ... and the red cross of England waved on all the towers of Normandy."—*Howitt: History of England*, vol. i. p. 545.

Red Cross Knight, in Spenser's *Faërie Queene*, is the impersonation of holiness, or rather the spirit of Christianity. Politically he typifies the Church of England. The knight is sent forth by the queen to slay a dragon which ravaged the kingdom of Una's father. Having achieved this feat, he marries Una (*q.v.*). (Book i.)

Red Feathers (*The*). The Duke of Cornwall's Light Infantry. They cut to pieces General Wayne's brigade in the American War, and the Americans vowed to give them no quarter. So they mounted red feathers that no others might be subjected to this threat. They still wear red puggarees on Indian service. (*See* LACEDÆMONIANS.)

Red Flag (*A*). (i) In the *Roman* empire it signified war and a call to arms.

(ii) Hoisted by *British* seamen, it indicates that no concession will be made.

As a railway signal, it intimates danger, and warns the engine-driver to stop.

(iii) In *France*, since 1791, it has been the symbol of insurrection and terrorism.

(iv) It is a synonym of Radicalism and Anarchy.

"Mr. Chamberlain sticks to the red flag, and apparently believes in its ultimate success."—*Newspaper paragraph*, January, 1886.

Red Hand of Ulster. In an ancient expedition to Ireland, it was given out that whoever first touched the shore should possess the territory which he touched; O'Neill, seeing another boat likely to outstrip his own, cut off his left hand and threw it on the coast. From this O'Neill the princes of Ulster were descended, and the motto of the O'Neills is to this day "*Lamh dearg Eirin*" (red hand of Erin). (*See* HAND.)

Red-handed. In the very act; with red blood still on his hand.

"I had some trouble to save him from the fury of those who had caught him red-handed."—*The Times (a correspondent).*

Red Hat (*The*). The cardinalate.

"David Beatoun was born of good family .... and was raised to a red hat by Pope Paul III."—*Prince: Parallel History*, vol. ii. p. 81.

Red Heads. (*See* SCHIITES.)

Red Herring (*The*) of a novel is a hint or statement in the early part of the story to put the reader on the wrong scent. In all detective stories a red herring is trailed across the scent. The allusion is to trailing a red herring on the ground to destroy the scent and set the dogs at fault. A "red herring" is a herring dried and smoked.

Red Herring. *Drawing a red herring across the path.* Trying to divert attention from the main question by some side-issue. A red herring drawn across a fox's path destroys the scent and sets the dogs at fault.

Neither fish, flesh, nor good red herring.
Something insipid and not good eating.
Neither one thing nor another.

Red Indians (of Newfoundland).
So called because they daub their skin,
garments, canoes, weapons, and almost
everything with red ochre.

"Whether it is merely a custom, or whether
they daub their skin with red ochre to protect it
from the attacks of mosquitos and black-flies,
which swarm by myriads in the woods and wilds
during the summer, it is not possible to say."—
Lady Blake: Nineteenth Century, Dec. 1888, p. 905.

Red Kettle (*A*). Properly a gold
watch, but applied, in thieves' slang, to
any watch.

Gold is often called red, hence "red
ruddocks" (gold coin).

Red-laced Jacket. *Giving a man a
red-laced jacket.* Military slang for giving a soldier a flogging.

Red Land (*The*). The jurisdiction
over which the Vehmgericht of Westphalia extended.

Red-lattice Phrases. Pot-house
talk. Red-lattice at the doors and windows was formerly the sign that an ale-
house was duly licensed ; hence our
chequers. In some cases "lattice" has
been converted into *lettuce,* and the
colour of the alternate checks changed to
green : such a sign used to be in Brownlow Street, Holborn. Sometimes, without doubt, the sign had another meaning,
and announced that "tables" were
played within ; hence Gayton, in his
Notes on Don Quixote (p. 340), in
speaking of our public-house signs, refers to our notices of "billiards, kettle-
noddy-boards, tables, truncks, shovelboards, fox-and-geese, and the like."
It is quite certain that shops with the
sign of the chequers were not uncommon
among the Romans. (*See* a view of the
left-hand street of Pompeii, presented by
Sir William Hamilton to the Society of
Antiquaries.) (*See* LATTICE.)

"I, I, I myself sometimes, leaving the fear of
heaven on the left hand, . . . am fain to shuffle, to
hedge and to lurch ; and yet you, rogue, will ensconce your rags . . . your red-lattice phrases . . .
under the shelter of your honour."—*Shakespeare:
Merry Wives of Windsor,* ii. 2.

Red Laws (*The*). The civil code of
ancient Rome. Juvenal says, "*Per lege
rubras majoram leges*" (*Satires,* xiv. 193).
The civil laws, being written in vermil-
lion, were called *rubrica,* and *rubrica
vetāvit* means, It is forbidden by the
civil laws.

The prætor's laws were inscribed in *white* letters
as Quintilian informs us (xii. 3 "*prætores edicta
sua in albo proponebant*"), and imperial rescripts
were written in purple.

Red-letter Day. A lucky day ; a
day to be recalled with delight. In
almanacks, saints' days and holidays are
printed in red ink, other days in black.

"That day, . . . writes the doctor, was truly a red-
letter day to me."—*Wauters: Stanley's Er[ ]n Expedition,* chap. vi. p. 111.

Red Man. The French say that a
red man commands the elements, and
wrecks off the coast of Brittany those
whom he dooms to death. The legend
affirms that he appeared to Napoleon
and foretold his downfall.

Red Men. W. Hepworth Dixon tells
us that the Mormons regard the Red
Indians as a branch of the Hebrew race,
who lost their priesthood, and with it
their colour, intelligence, and physiognomy, through disobedience. In time the
wild-olive branch will be restored, become white in colour, and will act as a
nation of priests. (*New America,* i. 15.)

Red Rag (*The*). The tongue. In
French, *Le chiffon rouge ;* and *balancer
le chiffon rouge* means to prate.

"Discovering in his mouth a tongue,
He must not his palaver balk ;
So keeps it running all day long,
And fancies his red rag can talk."
Peter Pindar : Lord B. and his Motions.

Red Republicans. Those extreme
republicans of France who scruple not
to dye their hands in blood in order to
accomplish their political object. They
used to wear a red cap. (*See* CARMAG-
NOLE.)

Red Rose Knight (*The*). Tom
Thumb or Tom-a-lin. Richard Johnson, in 1597, published a "history of
this ever-renowned soldier, the Red Rose
Knight, surnamed the Boast of England. . . . "

Red Rot (*The*). The Sun-dew (*q.v.*);
so called because it occasions the rot in
sheep.

Red Sea. The sea of the Red Man—
i.e. Edom. Also called the "sedgy sea,"
because of the sea-weed which collects
there.

Red-shanks. A Highlander ; so
called from a buskin formerly worn by
them ; it was made of undressed deer's
hide, with the red hair outside.

Red Snow and *Gory Dew.* The
latter is a slimy damp-like blood which
appears on walls. Both are due to the
presence of the algæ called by botanists
Palmella cruenta and *Hœmatococcus san-
guineus,* which are of the lowest forms
of vegetable life.

Red Tape. Official formality; so called because lawyers and government officials tie their papers together with red tape. Charles Dickens introduced the phrase.

"There is a good deal of red tape at Scotland Yard, as anyone may find to his cost who has any business to transact there."—*W. Terrell: Lady Delmar*, bk. iii. 2.

Red Tape. Dressing Edward VI.

" First a shirt was taken up by the Chief Equerry-in-Waiting,
who passed it to the First Lord of the Buck-hounds,
who passed it to the Second Gentleman of the Bedchamber,
who passed it to the Head Ranger of Windsor Forest,
who passed it to the Third Groom of the Stole,
who passed it to the Chancellor Royal of the Duchy of Lancashire,
who passed it to the Master of the Wardrobe,
who passed it to Norroy King-of-Arms,
who passed it to the Constable of the Tower,
who passed it to the Chief Steward of the Household,
who passed it to the Hereditary Grand Diaperer,
who passed it to the Lord High Admiral of England,
who passed it to the Archbishop of Canterbury,
who passed it to the First Lord of the Bedchamber,
who put it on the young king."
Mark Twain: The Prince and the Pauper, p. 143.

Red Tapism. The following is from *Truth*, Feb. 10th, 1887, p. 207:—There was an escape of gas at Cambridge Barracks, and this is the way of proceeding: The escape was discovered by a private, who reported it to his corporal; the corporal reported it to the colour-sergeant, and the colour-sergeant to the quartermaster-sergeant. The quartermaster-sergeant had to report it to the quartermaster, and the quartermaster to the colonel commanding the regiment. The colonel had to report it to the commissariat officer in charge of the barracks, and the commissariat officer to the barrack-sergeant, who had to report it to the divisional officer of engineers. This officer had to report it to the district officer of engineers, and he to the clerk of works, Royal Engineers, who sends for a gasman to see if there is an escape, and report back again. While the reporting is going on the barracks are burnt down.

Red Tincture. That preparation which the alchemists thought would convert any baser metal into gold. It is sometimes called the Philosopher's Stone, the Great Elixir, and the Great Magisterium. (*See* WHITE TINCTURE.)

Redan'. The simplest of fieldworks, and very quickly constructed. It consists simply of two faces and an angle formed thus Λ, the angle being towards the object of attack. A corruption of *redens.* (Latin.)

Redder (*The*). The adviser, the person who redes or interferes. Thus the proverb, "The redder gets aye the warst lick of the fray."

" Those that in quarrels interpose
Must wipe themselves a bloody nose."

Redding-straik (*A*). A blow received by a peacemaker, who interferes between two combatants to *red* or separate them; proverbially, the severest blow a man can receive.

"Said I not to ye,'Make not, meddle not ;' beware of the redding-straik ?"—*Sir W. Scott: Guy Mannering*, chap. xxvii.

Redgaunt'let. The sobriquet of Fitz-Aldin, given him from the great slaughter which he made of the Southron, and his reluctance to admit them to quarter. The sobriquet was adopted by him as a surname, and transmitted to his posterity. A novel by Sir W. Scott. (*See* chap. viii.)

Redgaunt'let. A novel told in a series of letters by Sir Walter Scott. Sir Edward Hugh Redgauntlet, a Jacobite conspirator in favour of the Young Pretender, Charles Edward, is the hero. When George III. was crowned he persuaded his niece, Lilias Redgauntlet, to pick up the glove thrown down by the king's champion. The plot ripened, but when the prince positively refused to dismiss his mistress, Miss Walkinshaw—a *sine quâ non* with the conspirators—the whole enterprise was given up. General Campbell arrived with the military, the prince left Scotland, Redgauntlet, who embarked with him, became a prior abroad, and Lilias, his niece, married her brother's friend, Allan Fairford, a young advocate.

Redgaunt'let (*Sir Aberick*). An ancestor of the family so called.

Sir Edward. Son of Sir Aberick, killed by his father's horse.

Sir Robert. An old Tory in *Wandering Willie's Tale.* He has a favourite monkey called "Major Weir." *Sir John,* son and successor of Sir Robert. *Sir Redwald,* son of Sir John.

Sir Henry Darsie. Son of Sir Redwald. *Lady Henry Darsie,* wife of Sir Henry Darsie. *Sir Arthur Darsie* alias *Darsie Latimer,* son of Sir Henry and the above lady. *Miss Lilias* alias *Greenmantle,* sister of Sir Arthur ; she marries Allan Fairford.

Sir Edward Hugh. A political enthusiast and Jacobite conspirator, uncle of

Sir Arthur Darsie. He appears as
"Laird of the Lochs," "Mr. Herries, of
Birrenswork," and "Mr. Ingoldsby."
"When he frowned, the puckers of his
brow formed a horseshoe, the special
mark of his race." (*Sir Walter Scott :
Redgauntlet.*)

Redlaw (*Mr.*). The haunted man,
professor of chemistry in an ancient
college. Being haunted, he bargained
with his spectre to leave him, and the
condition imposed was that Redlaw (go
where he would) should give again "the
gift of forgetfulness" bestowed by the
spectre. From this moment the chemist
carried in his touch the infection of
sullenness, selfishness, discontent, and
ingratitude. On Christmas Day the
infection ceased, and all those who had
suffered by it were restored to love and
gratitude. (*Dickens : The Haunted Man.*)

Redmain. Magnus, Earl of Northumberland, was so called not from his
red or bloody hand, but on account of
his long red beard or mane. He was
slain in the battle of Sark (1449).

"He was remarkable for his long red beard, and
was therefore called by the English Magnus Red-
beard ; but the Scotch in derision called him
'Magnus with the Red Mane.'"—*Godscroft*, fol.
178.

Redmond O'Neale. Rokeby's page,
who is beloved by Rokeby's daughter
Matilda. Redmond turns out to be
Mortham's son and heir, and marries
Matilda. (*Sir Walter Scott : Rokeby.*)

Reductio ad Absurdum. A proof
of inference arising from the demonstration that every other hypothesis involves
an absurdity. Thus, suppose I want to
prove that the direct road from two given
places is the shortest, I should say, "It
must either be the shortest or not the
shortest. If *not* the shortest, then some
other road is the direct road ; but there
cannot be two shortest roads, therefore
the direct road must be the shortest."

Reduplicated or **Ricochet Words**,
of intensifying force. Chit-chat, click-
clack, clitter-clatter, dilly-dally, ding-
dong, drip-drop, fal-lal, flim-flam, fiddle-
faddle, flip-flop, fluffy-fluffy, flippity-
floppity, handy-pandy, harum-scarum,
helter-skelter, heyve-keyve (*Halliwell*),
hibbledy-hobbledy, higgledy-piggledy,
hob-nob, hodge-podge, hoity-toity,
hurly-burly, mish-mash, mixy-maxy
(*Brockett*), namby-pamby, niddy-noddy,
niminy-piminy, nosy-posy, pell-mell,
pit-pat, pitter-patter, random-tandem,
randy-dandy, ribble-rabble, riff-raff,
roly-poly, rusty-fusty-crusty, see-saw,

shilly-shally, slip-slop, slish-slosh, snick-
snack, spitter-spatter, splitter-splutter,
squish-squash, teeny-tiny, tick-tack,
tilly-valley, tiny-totty, tip-top, tittle-
tattle, toe-toes, wee-wee, wiggle-waggle,
widdy-waddy (*Halliwell*), widdle-
waddle, wibble-wobble, wish-wash,
wishy-washy ; besides a host of rhyming
synonyms, as bawling-squawling, mew-
ling-pewling, whisky-frisky, musty-
fusty, gawky-pawky, slippy-sloppy,
rosy-posy, right and tight, wear and
tear, *high* and *mighty*, etc. ; and many
more with the Anglo-Saxon letter-
rhyme, as *safe* and *sound*, jog-trot, etc.

Ree. Right. Thus teamers say to a
leading horse, "Ree ! " when they want
it to turn to the right, and "Hey ! " for
the contrary direction. (Saxon, *reht ;*
German, *recht ;* Latin, *rectus ;* various
English dialects, *reet*, whence *reetle*, "to
put to rights.")

"Who with a hey and ree the beasts command."
Micro-Cynicon (1599).

Riddle me, riddle me ree. Expound
my riddle rightly.

Reed. *A broken reed.* Something
not to be trusted for support. Egypt is
called a broken reed, to which Hezekiah
could not trust if the Assyrians made
war on Jerusalem, "which broken reed
if a man leans on, it will go into his
hand and pierce it." Reed walking
sticks are referred to.

A bruised reed, in Bible language,
means a believer weak in grace. A
bruised reed [God] will not break.

Reed Shaken by the Wind (*A*),
in Bible language, means a person blown
about by every wind of doctrine. John
the Baptist (said Christ) was not a "reed
shaken by the wind," but from the very
first had a firm belief in the Messiahship
of the Son of Mary, and this conviction
was not shaken by fear or favour.

Reef. *He must take in a reef or so.*
He must reduce his expenses ; he must
retrench. A reef is that part of a sail
which is between two rows of eyelet-
holes. The object of these eyelet-holes
is to reduce the sail reef by reef as it is
required.

Reekie (*Auld*). Chambers says :
"An old patriarchal laird (Durham of
Largo) was in the habit of regulating
the time of evening worship by the appearance of the smoke of Edinburgh.
. . . When it increased in density, in
consequence of the good folk preparing
supper, he would . . . say, 'It is time
noo, bairns, to tak the buiks and gang

to our beds, for yonder's auld Reekie, I see, putting on her night-cap.'"

"Yonder is auld Reekie. You may see the smoke hover over her at twenty miles' distance."
—*Sir W. Scott : The Abbot*, xvii.

Reel. *Right off the reel.* Without intermission. A reel is a device for winding rope. A reel of cotton is a certain quantity wound on a bobbin. (Anglo-Saxon *reōl*.)

"We've been travelling best part of twenty-four hours right off the reel."—*Boldrewood : Robbery under Arms*, chap. xxxi.

Reel. A Scotch dance. (Gaelic, *righil*.)

Reeves Tale. Thomas Wright says that this tale occurs frequently in the jest- and story-books of the sixteenth and seventeenth centuries. Boccaccio has given it in the *Decameron*, evidently from a fabliau, which has been printed in Barbazan under the title of *De Gombert et des Deux Clers*. Chaucer took the story from another fabliau, which Wright has given in his *Anecdota Literaria*, p. 15.

Refresh'er. A fee paid to a barrister daily in addition to his retaining fee, to remind him of the case intrusted to his charge.

Refreshments of public men, etc.

BRAHAM'S favourite refreshment was bottled porter.

BYRON almost lived on uncanny foods, such as garlic pottage, raw artichokes and vinegar, broths of bitter herbs, saffron biscuits, eggs and lemons.

CATALANI'S favourite refreshment was sweetbreads.

CONTRALTO SINGERS can indulge even in pork and pease-pudding.

COOK (*G. F.*) indulged in everything drinkable.

DISRAELI (Lord Beaconsfield), champagne.

EMERY, cold brandy and water.

GLADSTONE, an egg beaten up in sherry.

HENDERSON, gum arabic and sherry.

INCLEDON (*Mrs.*), Madeira.

JORDAN (*Mrs.*), Calves'-foot jelly dissolved in warm sherry.

KEAN (*Edmund*), beef-tea for breakfast ; brandy neat.

KEMBLE (*both John and Charles*), rump-steaks and kidneys. John indulged in opium.

LEWIS, oysters and mulled wine.

MALIBRAN, a dozen native oysters and a pint of half-and-half.

SIDDONS (*Mrs.*), mutton-chops, either neck or chump, and porter.

SMITH (*William*), coffee.

SOPRANOS eschew much butcher's meat, which baritones may indulge in.

TENORS rarely indulge in beef-steaks and sirloins.

WOOD (*Mrs.*), draught porter.

Rega'le (2 syl.). To entertain like a king. (Latin, *rega'lis*, like a king, kingly.)

Re'gan and Gon'eril. Two of the daughters of King Lear, and types of unfilial daughters. (*Shakespeare : King Lear.*)

Regatta (*Italian*). Originally applied to the contests of the gondoliers at Venice.

Regent (*The*). (*See* SHIPS.)

Regent's Park (London). This park was originally attached to a palace of Queen Elizabeth, but at the beginning of the seventeenth century much of the land was let on long leases, which fell in early in the nineteenth century. The present park was formed under the direction of Mr Nash, and received its name in compliment to George IV., then Prince Regent.

Regime de la Calotte. Administration of government by ecclesiastics. The *calotte* is the small skull-cap worn over the tonsure.

Regiment de la Calotte. A society of witty and satirical men in the reign of Louis XIV. When any public character made himself ridiculous, a calotte was sent to him to " cover the bald or brainless part of his noddle." (*See above.*)

Regi'na (*St.*), the virgin martyr, is depicted with lighted torches held to her sides, as she stands fast bound to the cross on which she suffered martyrdom.

Regiomonta'nus. The Latin equivalent of *Königsberger*. The name adopted by Johann Müller, the mathematician. (1436-1476.)

Re'gium Do'num (Latin). An annual grant of public money to the Presbyterian, Independent, and Baptist ministers of Ireland. It began in 1672, and was commuted in 1869.

Re'gius Professor. One who holds in an English university a professorship founded by Henry VIII. Each of the five Regius Professors of Cambridge receives a royally-endowed stipend of about £40. In the universities of Scotland they are appointed by the Crown. The present stipend is about £400 or £500.

Reg'ulars (*The*). All the British troops except the militia, the yeomanry, and the volunteers. There are no ir-regulars in the British army, but such a force exists among the black troops.

Rehobo'am (*A*). A clerical hat.

"He [Mr. Helstone] was short of stature [and wore] a rehoboam, or shovel hat, which he did not ... remove."—"*Currer Bell*": *Shirley*, chap. i.

Rehoboam. *A rehoboam of claret or rum* is a double jeroboam. (2 Chr. xiii. 3.)

1 rehoboam = 2 jeroboams or 32 pints.
1 jeroboam = 2 tappet-hens or 16 pints.
1 tappet-hen = 2 magnums or 8 pints.
1 magnum = 2 quarts or 4 pints.

Reign of Terror. The period in the French Revolution between the fall of the Girondists and overthrow of Robes-pierre. It lasted 420 days, from May 31st, 1793, to July 27th, 1794.

Reimkennar (*A*). A sorceress, a pythoness; one skilled in numbers. Sorcery and Chaldean numbers are sy-nonymous terms. The Anglo-Saxon *rim-stafas* means charms or conjuration, and the Norse *reim-kennar* means one skilled in numbers or charms. Norna of the Fitful Head was a Reimkennar, "a con-troller of the elements."

Reins. *To give the reins.* To let go unrestrained; to give licence.
To take the reins. To assume the guidance or direction.

Reins (*The*). The kidneys, supposed by the Hebrews and others to be the seat of knowledge, pleasure, and pain. The Psalmist says (xvi. 7), "My reins instruct me in the night season," *i.e.* my kidneys, the seat of knowledge, instruct me how to trust in God. Solomon says (Prov. xxiii. 16), "My reins shall rejoice when [men] speak right things," *i.e.* truth ex-cites joy from my kidneys; and Jeremiah says (Lam. iii. 13), God "caused His arrows to enter into my reins," *i.e.* sent pain into my kidneys. (Latin, *ren*, a kidney.)

Rel'dresal. Principal secretary for private affairs in the court of Lilliput, and great friend of Gulliver. When it was proposed to put the Man-Mountain to death for high treason, Reldresal moved as an amendment, that the "traitor should have both his eyes put out, and be suffered to live that he might serve the nation." (*Swift: Gulliver's Travels; Voyage to Lilliput*.)

Relics. A writer in the *Twentieth Century* (1892, article ROME) says: "Some of the most astounding relics are officially shown in Rome, and publicly adored by the highest dignitaries of the Christian Church, with all the magnifi-cence of ecclesiastical pomp and ritual." The following are mentioned :—

A BOTTLE OF THE VIRGIN'S MILK.
THE CRADLE AND SWADDLING CLOTHES of the infant Jesus.
THE CROSS OF THE PENITENT THIEF
THE CROWN OF THORNS.
THE FINGER OF THOMAS, with which he touched the wound in the side of Jesus.
HAIR OF THE VIRGIN MARY.
THE HANDKERCHIEF OF ST. VERON'ICA, on which the face of Jesus was miraculously pictured.
HAY OF THE MANGER in which the infant Jesus was laid.
HEADS OF PETER, PAUL, AND MATTHEW.
THE INSCRIPTION set over the cross by the order of Pilate.
NAILS used at the crucifixion.
PIECE OF THE CHEMISE of the Virgin Mary.
THE SILVER MONEY given to Judas by the Jewish priests, which he flung into the Temple and was expended in buying the potters' field as a cemetery for strangers.
THE TABLE on which the soldiers cast lots for the coat of Jesus.

⁂ Brady mentions many others, some of which are actually impossibilities, as, for example, a rib of the *Verbum caro factum*, a vial of the sweat of St. Michael when he contended with Satan, some of the rays of the star which guided the wise men. (See *Clavis Calendaria*, p. 240.)

Relief (*The*). In fortification, the general height to which the defensive masses of earth are raised. The direc-tions in which the masses are laid out are called the *tracings*.

Rem Acu. You have hit the mark; you have hit the nail on the head. *Rem acu tetigisti* (Plautus). A phrase in archery, meaning, You have hit the white, or the bull's-eye.

"'*Rem acu* once again,' said Sir Piercie."—*The Monastery*, chap. xvi.

Remember. The last injunction of Charles I., on the scaffold, to Bishop Juxon. A probable solution of this mysterious word is given in *Notes and Queries* (February 24th, 1894, p. 144). The substance is this: Charles, who was really at heart a Catholic, felt persuaded that his misfortunes were a divine visita-tion on him for retaining the church property confiscated by Henry VIII., and made a vow that if God would re-store him to the throne, he would restore this property to the Church. This vow may be seen in the British Museum. His injunction to the bishop was to re-member this vow, and enjoin his son Charles to carry it out. Charles II., however, wanted all the money he could get, and therefore the church lands were never restored.

Remig'ius (*St.*). Rémy, bishop and confessor, is represented as carrying a vessel of holy oil, or in the act of anointing therewith Clovis, who kneels before him. When Clovis presented himself for baptism, Rémy said to him, " Sigambrian, henceforward burn what thou hast worshipped, and worship what thou hast burned." (438-533.)

Remis atque Velis (Latin). With oars and sails. Tooth and nail ; with all despatch.

"We were going *remis atque velis* into the interests of the Pretender, since a Scot had presented a Jacobite at court."—*Sir W. Scott: Redgauntlet* (conclusion).

Renaissance (French). A term applied in the arts to that peculiar style of decoration revived by Raphael, and which resulted from ancient paintings exhumed in the pontificate of Leo X. (16th century). The French Renaissance is a Gothic skeleton with classic details.

Renaissance Period (*The*). That period in French history which began with the Italian wars in the reign of Charles VIII. and closed with the reign of Henri II. It was the intercourse with Italy, brought about by the Italian war (1494-1557), which "regenerated" the arts and sciences in France ; but as everything was Italianised—the language, dress, architecture, poetry, prose, food, manners, etc.—it was a period of great false taste and national deformity.

Renard. *Une queue de renard.* A mockery. At one time a common practical joke was to fasten a fox's tail behind a person against whom a laugh was designed. "Panurge never refrained from attaching a fox's tail or the ears of a leveret, behind a Master of Arts or Doctor of Divinity, whenever he encountered them."—*Rabelais: Gargantua,* ii. 16. (*See* REYNARD.)

"C'est une petite vipère
Qui n'epargneroit pas son père,
Et qui par nature ou par art
Scait couper la queuë au renard."
Beaucaire: L'Embarras de la Foire.

Renarder (French). To vomit, especially after too freely indulging in intoxicating drinks. Our word *fox* means also to be tipsy.

"Il luy visite la machoire,
Quand l'autre luy renarde aux yeux.
Le baume qu'ils venoient de'boire
Pour se le rendre a qui mieux mieux."
Sieur de St. Amant: Chambre de Desbauché.

Rena'ta. Renée, daughter of Louis XII. and Anne of Bretagne, married Hercules, second son of Lucretia Borgia and Alphonso.

Renaud. French form of Rinaldo (*q.v.*).

Renault of Montauban. In the last chapter of the romance of *Aymon's Four Sons,* Renault, as an act of penance, carries the hods of mortar for the building of St. Peter's, at Cologne.

"Since I cannot improve our architecture, ... I am resolved to do like Renault of Montauban, and I will wait on the masons. . . . As it was not in my good luck to be cut out for one of them, I will live and die the admirer of their divine writings."—*Rabelais: Prologue to Book V. of Pantagruel.*

Rendezvous. The place to which you are to repair, a meeting, a place of muster or call. Also used as a verb. (French, *rendez,* betake ; *vous,* yourself.)

His house is a grand rendezvous of the *élite* of Paris.
The Imperial Guard was ordered to rendezvous in the Champs de Mars.

René (2 syl.). *Le bon Roi René.* Son of Louis II., Duc d'Anjou, Comte de Provence, father of Margaret of Anjou. The last minstrel monarch, just, joyous, and debonair ; a friend to chase and tilt, but still more so to poetry and music. He gave in largesses to knights-errant and minstrels (so says Thiebault) more than he received in revenue. (1408-1480.)

"Studying to promote, as far as possible, the immediate mirth and good humour of his subjects . . . he was never mentioned by them excepting as *Le bon Roi René,* a distinction . . . due to him certainly by the qualities of his heart, if not by those of his head."—*Sir Walter Scott: Anne of Geierstein,* chap. xxix.

René Leblanc. Notary-public of Grand Pré (Nova Scotia), the father of twenty children and 159 grandchildren. (*Longfellow: Evangeline.*)

Rep'artee' properly means a smart return blow in fencing. (French, *repartir,* to return a blow.)

Repenter Curls. The long ringlets of a lady's hair. *Repentir* is the French for a penitentiary, and *les repentirs* are the girls sent there for reformation. *Repentir,* therefore, is a Lock Hospital or Magdalen. Now, Mary Magdalen is represented to have had such long hair that she wiped off her tears therewith from the feet of Jesus. Hence, Magdalen curls would mean the long hair of a Mary Magdalen made into ringlets.

Reply Churlish (*The*). Sir, you are no judge ; your opinion has no weight with me. Or, to use Touchstone's illustration: "If a courtier tell me my beard is not well cut, and I disable his judgment, I give him the reply churlish, which is the fifth remove from the lie direct, or, rather, the lie direct in the fifth degree."

Reproof Valiant (*The*). Sir, allow me to tell you that is not the truth. To use Touchstone's illustration: "If a courtier tells me my beard is not well cut, and I answer, 'That is not true,' I give him the reply valiant, which is the fourth remove from the lie direct, or rather, the lie direct in the fourth degree."

The reproof valiant, the countercheck quarrelsome, the lie circumstantial, and the lie direct, are not clearly defined by Touchstone. The following, perhaps, will give the distinction required: *That* is not true ; How *dare* you utter such a falsehood ; *If* you said so, you are a liar ; You are a liar, or you lie.

Republican Queen. Sophie Charlotte, wife of Frederick I. of Prussia.

Republicans. (*See* BLACK.)

Resolute (*The*). John Florio, the philologist, tutor to Prince Henry ; the Holofernes of Shakespeare. (1545-1625.)
The resolute doctor. John Baconthorp (*-1346).
The most resolute doctor. Guillaume Durandus de St. Pourçain (*-1332).

Rest (*The*). A contraction of *resid'ue* —thus, *resid', resit, res't.*

Rest on One's Oars. (*See* OARS.)

Res'tive (2 syl.) means inclined to resist, resist-ive, obstinate or self-willed. It has nothing to do with *rest* (quiet).

Restora'tionists. The followers of Origen's opinion that all persons, after a purgation proportioned to their demerits, will be restored to Divine favour and taken to Paradise. Mr. Ballow, of America, has introduced an extension of the term, and maintains that all retribution is limited to this life, and at the resurrection all will be restored to life, joy, and immortality.

Resurrection Men. Grave robbers. First applied to Burke and Hare, in 1829, who rifled graves to sell the bodies for dissection, and sometimes even murdered people for the same purpose.

Resurrection Pie is made of broken cooked meat. Meat *réchauffé* is sometimes called "resurrection meat."

Retia'rius. A gladiator who made use of a net, which he threw over his adversary.

" As in thronged amphitheatre of old,
The wary Retiarius trapped his foe."
Thomson: Castle of Indolence, canto ii.

Retort Courteous (*The*). Sir, I am not of your opinion ; I beg to differ from you ; or, to use Touchstone's illustration, "If I said his beard was not cut well, he was in the mind it was." The

lie seven times removed ; or rather, the lie direct in the seventh degree.

Reuben Dixon. A village schoolmaster " of ragged lads."

" Mid noise, and dirt, and stench, and play, and prate,
He calmly cuts the pen or views the slate."
Crabbe: Borough, letter xxiv.

Reveillé [*re-vay'-ya*]. The beat of drum at daybreak to warn the sentries that they may forbear from challenging, as the troops are awake. (French, *réveiller,* to awake.)

Revenons à nos Moutons. (*See* MOUTONS.)

Reverend. An archbishop is *the Most Reverend* [Father in God] ; a bishop, *the Right Reverend ;* a dean, *the Very Reverend ;* an archdeacon, *the Venerable ;* all the rest of the clergy, *the Reverend.*

Revetments, in fortifications. In " permanent fortification " the sides of ditches supported by walls of masonry are so called. (*See* COUNTERFORTS.)

Review. The *British Review* was nicknamed " My Grandmother." In *Don Juan,* Lord Byron says, he bribed " *My Grandmother's Review,* the British." The editor took this in dudgeon and gave Byron the lie, but the poet turned the laugh against the reviewer.

" Am I flat, I tip ' My Grandmother ' a bit of prose."—*Noctes Ambrosianæ.*

Revi'se (2 syl.). The second proofsheet submitted to an author or " reader."

" I at length reached a vaulted room, . . . and beheld, seated by a lamp and employed in reading a blotted revise . . . the author of Waverley."—*Sir Walter Scott: Fortunes of Nigel* (Introduction).

Revival of Letters in England dates from the commencement of the eleventh century.

Revival of Painting and Sculpture began with Niccola Pisano, Giunta, Cimabue, and Giotto (2 syl.).

Revo'ke (2 syl.). When a player at cards can follow suit, but plays some other card, he makes a revoke, and by the laws of whist the adversaries are entitled to score three points.

" Good heaven ! Revoke ? Remember, if the set
Be lost, in honour you should pay the debt."
Crabbe: Borough.

Revulsion (in philosophy). Part of a substance set off and formed into a distinct existence ; as when a slip is cut from a tree and planted to form a distinct plant of itself. Tertullian the Montanist taught that the second person of the Trinity was a revulsion of the Father.) (Latin, *revulsio, re-vello*, to pull back.)

Rewe. A roll or slip ; as Ragman's Rewe. (*See* RAGMAN.)

"There is a whole world of curious history contained in the phrase 'ragman's rewe,' meaning a list, roll, catalogue, . . . charter, scroll of any kind. In *Piers Plowman's Vision* it is used for the pope's bull."—*Edinburgh Review.* July, 1870.
"In Fescenium was first invented the joylitee of mynstrelsie and syngyng merrie songs for makyng laughter, hence called 'Fescennina Carmina,' which I translate a 'Ragman's Rewe' or Bible."—*Udall.*

Reyn'ard the Fox. The hero in the beast-epic of the fourteenth century. This prose poem is a satire on the state of Germany in the Middle Ages. Reynard typifies the church ; his uncle, Isengrin the wolf, typifies the baronial element ; and Nodel the lion, the regal. The word means deep counsel or wit. (Gothic, *raginohart*, cunning in counsel ; Old Norse, *hreinn* and *ard ;* German, *reineke*.) Reynard is commonly used as a synonym of fox. (*Heinrich von Alkmaar.*)

"Where prowling Reynard trod his nightly round." *Bloomfield: Farmer's Boy.*

Reynard the Fox. Professedly by Hinreck van Alckmer, tutor of the Duke of Lorraine. This name is generally supposed to be a pseudonym of Hermann Barkhusen, town clerk and book printer in Rostock. (1498.)

False Reynard. So Dryden describes the Unitarians in his *Hind and Panther.* (*See* RENARD.)

"With greater guile
False Reynard fed on consecrated spoil ;
The graceless beast by Athana'sius first
Was chased from Nice, then by Socinus nursed."
Part i. 51-54.

Reynar'dine (3 syl.). The eldest son of Reynard the Fox, who assumed the names of Dr. Pedanto and Crabron. (*Reynard the Fox.*)

Reynold of Montalbon. One of Charlemagne's knights and paladins.

Rezio. (*See* DOCTOR REZIO.)

Rhadaman'thos. One of the three judges of hell ; Minos and Æacos being the other two. (*Greek mythology.*)

Rhampsini'tos. The Greek form of Ram'eses III., the richest of the Egyptian kings, who amassed seventy-seven millions sterling, which he secured in a treasury of stone, but by an artifice of the builder he was robbed every night.

Herodotos (bk. ii. chap. 121) tells us that two brothers were the architects of the treasury, and that they placed in the wall a removable stone, through which they crept every night to purloin

the store. The king, after a time, noticed the diminution, and set a trap to catch the thieves. One of the brothers was caught in the trap, but the other brother, to prevent detection, cut off his head and made good his escape.

∴ This tale is almost identical with that of Trophonios, told by Pausanias. Hyrieus (3 syl.) a Bœotian king employed Trophonios and his brother to build him a treasury. In so doing they also contrived to place in the wall a removable stone, through which they crept nightly to purloin the king's stores. Hyrieus also set a trap to catch the thief, and one of the brothers was caught ; but Trophonios cut off his head to prevent detection, and made good his escape. There cannot be a doubt that the two tales are in reality one and the same.

Rhapsody means songs strung together. The term was originally applied to the books of the *Iliad* and *Odyssey,* which at one time were in fragments. Certain bards collected together a number of the fragments, enough to make a connected "ballad," and sang them as our minstrels sang the deeds of famous heroes. Those bards who sang the *Iliad* wore a *red* robe, and those who sang the *Odyssey* a *blue* one. Pisis'tratos of Athens had all these fragments carefully compiled into their present form (Greek *rapto*, to sew or string together ; *odē,* a song.)

Rhene (1 syl.). The Rhine. (Latin, *Rhenus.*)

"To pass
Rhene or the Danaw [Danube]."
Milton: Paradise Lost, bk. i. 353.

Rhine or **Rhineland.** The country of Gunther, King of Burgundy, is so called in the *Nibelungen-Lied.*

"Not a lord of Rhineland could follow where he flew." *Lettsom's Nibelungen-Lied,* st. 210.

Rhi'no. Ready money. (*See* NOSE.) May not this explain the phrase "paying through the nose" (*par le nez*), that is, paying ready rhino. Rhino = money is very old.

"Some, as I know,
Have parted with their ready rhino."
The Seaman's Adieu (1670).

Rhod'alind. A princess famous for her "knightly" deeds ; she would have been the wife of Gon'dibert, but he wisely preferred Birtha, a country girl, the daughter of the sage As'tragon.

Rhodian Bully (*The*). The colossus of Rhodes.

"Yet fain wouldst thou the crouching world bestride.
Just like the Rhodian bully o'er the tide."
Peter Pindar: The Lusiad, canto 2.

Rho'dian Law. The earliest system of marine law known to history ; compiled by the Rhodians about 900 B.C.

Rhone. *The Rhone of Christian eloquence.* St. Hil'ary ; so called from the vehemence of his style. (300-368.)

Rhopal'ic Verse (*wedge-verse*). A line in which each successive word has more syllables than the one preceding it (Greek, *rhopalon*, a club, which from the handle to the top grows bigger.)

Rem tibi confeci, doctissime, dulcisonorum.
Spes deus æternæ-est stationis conciliator.
Hope ever solaces   miserable individuals.
 1   2   3   4   5

Rhyme. *Neither rhyme nor reason.* Fit neither for amusement nor instruction. An author took his book to Sir Thomas More, chancellor in the reign of Henry VIII., and asked his opinion. Sir Thomas told the author to turn it into rhyme. He did so, and submitted it again to the lord chancellor. " Ay ! ay ! " said the witty satirist, " that will do, that will do. 'Tis rhyme now, but before it was neither rhyme nor reason."

Rhymer. *Thomas the Rhymer.* Thomas Learmount, of Ercildoune, who lived in the thirteenth century. This was quite a different person to Thomas Rymer, the historiographer royal to William III. (who flourished 1283). (*See* TRUE THOMAS.)

Rhyming to Death. The Irish at one time believed that their children and cattle could be " eybitten," that is, be-witched by an evil eye, and that the " eybitter," or witch could "rime" them to death. (*R. Scott: Discovery of Witch-craft*.) (*See* RATS.)

Rib'aldry is the language of a ribald. (French, *ribaud ;* Old French, *ribaudie ;* Italian, *ribalderia*, the language of a vagabond or rogue.)

Ribbon Dodge (*The*). Plying a person secretly with threatening letters in order to drive him out of the neigh-bourhood, or to compel him to do some-thing he objects to. The Irish Ribbon men sent threatening letters or letters containing coffins, cross-bones, or dag-gers, to obnoxious neighbours.

Ribbonism. A Catholic association organised in Ireland about 1808. Its two main objects were (1) to secure " fixity of tenure," called the tenant-right ; and (2) to deter anyone from taking land from which a tenant has been ejected. The name arises from a ribbon worn as a badge in the button-hole.

Ribston Pippin. So called from Ribston, in Yorkshire, where Sir Henry Goodricke planted three pips, sent to him from Rouen, in Normandy. Two pips died, but from the third came all the Ribston apple-trees in England.

Ricardo, in the opera of *I Purita'ni,* is Sir Richard Forth, a Puritan, com-mander of Plymouth fortress. Lord Walton promised to give him his daugh-ter Elvi'ra in marriage, but Elvira had engaged her affections to Lord Arthur Talbot, a Cavalier, to whom ultimately she was married.

Ricciardet'to. Son of Agmon and brother of Bradamante. (*Ariosto : Or-lando Furioso*.)

Rice Christians. Converts to Chris-tianity for worldly benefits, such as a supply of rice to Indians. Profession of Christianity born of lucre, not faith.

Rice thrown after a Bride. It was an Indian custom, rice being, with the Hindûs, an emblem of fecun-dity. The bridegroom throws three handfuls over the bride, and the bride does the same over the bridegroom. With us the rice is thrown by neighbours and friends. (*See* MARRIAGE KNOT.)

Rich as Crœsus. (*See* CRŒSUS.)

Rich as a Jew. This expression arose in the Middle Ages, when Jews were almost the only merchants, and were certainly the most wealthy of the people. There are still the Rothschilds among them, and others of great wealth.

Richard Cœur de Lion. (*See* BOGIE.)

" His tremendous name was employed by the Syrian mothers to silence their infants ; and if a horse suddenly started from the way, his rider was wont to exclaim, ' Dost thou think King Richard is in the bush ? ' "—*Gibbon: Decline and Fall*, etc., xi. 146.

Richard II.'s Horse. Roan Barbary. (*See* HORSE.)

" Oh, how it yearned my heart when I beheld
  In London streets, that coronation day,
  When Bolingbroke rode on roan Barbary,
  That horse that thou so often hast bestrid,
  That horse that I so carefully have dressed."
        Shakespeare : Richard II., v. 5.

Richard III.'s Horse. White Surrey. (*See* HORSE.)

" Saddle White Surrey for the field to-morrow."
        Shakespeare : Richard III., v. 8.

Richard Roe. (*See* DOE.)

Richard is Himself again. These words are not in Shakespeare's *Richard III.*, but were interpolated from Colley Cibber by John Kemble.

Richard of Cirencester. Some-times called " The Monk of West-minster," an early English chronicler. His chronicle *On the Ancient State of Britain* was first brought to light by Dr. Charles Julius Bertram, professor of English at Copenhagen in 1747; **but**

the original (like the original of Macpherson's *Ossian* and of Joe Smith's *Book of Mormon*) does not exist, and grave suspicion prevails that all three are alike forgeries. (*See* SANCHONIATHO.)

Richar'da, wife of Nicholas d'Este. A widow who, with her son Hercules, was dispossessed of her inheritance by Lionello and Borso. Both were obliged to go into exile, but finally Hercules recovered his lordship.

Richborough, Richeboro', or Ratesburgh (a Roman fort in the time of Claudius), called by Alfred of Beverley, Richberge; by the Saxons (according to Bede) Reptacester, and by others Ruptimuth; by Orosius, the port and city of Rhutubus; by Ammianus, Rhutupiæ Statio; by Antoninus, Rhitupis Portus; by Tacitus, Portus Trutulensis for Rhutupensis; by Ptolemy, Rhutupiæ. (*Camden.*)

Rick Mould. This is an April fool joke transferred to hay-harvest. The joke is this: some greenhorn is sent a good long distance to borrow a rickmould, with strict injunction not to drop it. The lender places something very heavy in a sack or bag, which he hoists on the greenhorn's back. He carries it carefully in the hot sun to the hayfield, and gets well laughed at for his pains.

Rickety Stock. Stock bought or sold for a man of straw. If the client cannot pay, the broker must.

Ricochet [*rikko-shay*]. Anything repeated over and over again. The fabulous bird that had only one note was called the ricochet; and the rebound on water termed *ducks and drakes* has the same name. Marshal Vauban (1633-1707) invented a battery of rebound called the *ricochet battery,* the application of which was ricochet firing.

Riddle. Josephus relates how Hiram, King of Tyre, and Solomon had once a contest in riddles, when Solomon won a large sum of money; but he subsequently lost it to Abde'mon, one of Hiram's subjects.

Riddle. Plutarch states that Homer died of chagrin because he could not solve a certain riddle. (*See* SPHINX.)

Father of riddles. So the Abbé Cotin dubbed himself, but posterity has not confirmed his right to the title. (1604-1682.) (*See* REE.)

Riddle of Claret (*A*). Thirteen bottles, a magnum and twelve quarts.

So called because in golf matches the magistrates invited to the celebration dinner presented to the club a "riddle of claret," sending it in a riddle or sieve.

Ride. *To ride abroad with St. George, but at home with St. Michael;* said of a hen-pecked braggart. St. George is represented as riding on a war charger whither he listed; St. Michael, on a dragon. Abroad a man rides, like St. George, on a horse which he can control and govern; but at home he has "a dragon" to manage, like St. Michael. (French.)

Ride for a Fall (*To*). To ride a race and lose it intentionally.

"There were not wanting people who said that government had 'ridden for a fall,' in their despair of carrying out their policy."—*Newspaper paragraph,* November, 1885.

Ride up Holborn Hill (*To*). To go to the gallows.

"I shall live to see you ride up Holborn Hill."—*Congreve: Love for Love.*

Rider. An addition to a manuscript, like a codicil to a will; an additional clause tacked to a bill in parliament; so called because it *over-rides* the preceding matter when the two come into collision.

"Perhaps Mr. Kenneth will allow me to add the following as a rider to his suggestion."—*Notes and Queries,* "M.N."

Riderhood (*Rogue*). The villain in Dickens's *Our Mutual Friend.*

Ridicule (*Father of*). François Rabelais (1495-1553).

Riding [*of Yorkshire*]. Same as *trithing* in Lincolnshire; the jurisdiction of a third part of a county, under the government of a reeve (*sheriff*). The word *ding* or *thing* is Scandinavian, and means a legislative assembly; hence the great national diet of Norway is still called a *stor-thing* (great legislative assembly), and its two chambers are the *lag-thing* (law assembly) and the *odels-thing* (freeholders' assembly). Kent was divided into *laths,* Sussex into *rapes,* Lincoln into *parts.* The person who presided over a trithing was called the *trithing-man;* he who presided in the lath was called a *lath-grieve.*

Ridol'phus (in *Jerusalem Delivered*). One of the band of adventurers that joined the Crusaders. He was slain by Argantes (bk. vii.).

Ridot'to (Italian). An assembly where the company is first entertained to music, and then joins in dancing. The word originally meant music reduced to a full score. (Latin, *reductus.*)

Rien'zi (*Nicolò Gabri'ni*). The Reformer at Rome (1313-1354). Bulwer Lytton (Lord Lytton) has a novel called *Rienzi*, and Wagner an opera.

Rif or **Rifle** (French). *Avoir rifle et rafle.* To have everything. Also, the negative, *N'avoir ni rif ni raf* (to have nothing).

> " Hélas ! j'ai goute miseraigne,
> J'ai rifle et rafle, et roigne et taigne."
> *Les Miracles de Ste. Geneviève.*

Riff-raff. The offscouring of society, or rather, "refuse and sweepings." *Rief* is Anglo-Saxon, and means a rag ; *Raff* is also Anglo-Saxon, and means sweepings. (Danish, *rips-raps*.) The French have the expression *"Avoir rifle et rafle,"* meaning to have everything ; whence *radoux* (one who has everything), and the phrase " *Il n'a laissé ni rif ni raf*" (he has left nothing behind him).

> " I have neither ryff nor ruff [rag to cover me nor roof over my head]."—*Sharp : Coventry Myst.,* p. 224.
> " Ilka man agayne his gud he gaffe
> That he had tane with ryfe and raffe."
> *Quoted by Halliwell in his Archaic Dictionary.*

Rifle is from the German *reifeln* (to hollow into tubes). In 1851 the French *minié* rifle was partially supplied to the British army. In 1853 it was superseded by the *Enfield* rifle, which has three grooves. Sir William Armstrong's gun, which has numerous small sharp grooves, was adopted by the government in 1859. The Whitworth gun has a polygonal bore, with a twist towards the muzzle. ("Rifle" is Norwegian for a groove or flute.)

∴ Rifles are either "breech-loaders" or "magazine rifles." Breech-loading rifles load at the breech instead of at the muzzle ; magazine rifles are those which contain a chamber with extra cartridges.

The chief breech-loading rifles are the Ballard, the Berdan, the Chaffee, the Chassepot (a French needle-gun, 1870-1871), the Flobert-Gras (an improved Chassepot, 1874-1880), the Greene, the Hall, the Minie-Henry (Great Britain, 1890), the Maxim, the Magnard, the Minie, the Morgensten, the Peabody, the Peabody-Martini (Turkey), the Scott, the Sharp, the Springfield (United States, 1893), the Werder (Bavaria), the Werndi, the Whittemore, the Westley-Richards, and the Winchester.

∴ The *magazine* or *repeating-rifles* are also very numerous. The best known to the general public are Colt's revolver and the Winchester repeating-rifle of 1892. They are of three classes : (1) those in which the magazine is *in the stock* ; (2) those in which the magazine is a tube parallel with the barrel (as in Colt's revolver) : and (3) those in which the magazine is either a fixed or detachable box near the lock. The once famous Enfield rifle was loaded at the muzzle. In Spencer's rifle the magazine was in the stock.

Rift in the Lute (*A*). A small defect which mars the general result.

> " Unfaith in aught is want of faith in all.
> It is the little rift within the lute
> That by-and-by will make the music mute,
> And, ever widening, slowly, silence all."
> *Tennyson : Merlin and Vivien ; Vivien's Song,* verses 1, 2.

Rig. A piece of fun, a practical joke. The Scotch say of a man who indulges in intoxication, "He goes the *rig*." The same word is applied in Scotland to a certain portion or division of a field. A wanton used to be called a *rig*. (French, *se rigoler*, to make merry.)

> " He little thought when he set out
> Of running such a rig."
> *Cowper : John Gilpin.*

Rig. To dress ; whence *rigged out*, to *rig oneself*, to *rig a ship*, *well-rigged*, etc. (Anglo-Saxon, *wrigan*, to dress ; *hrægl*, a garment.)

> "Jack was rigged out in his gold and silver lace, with a feather in his cap."—*L'Estrange.*

Rig-Marie. Base coin. The word originated from one of the billon coins struck in the reign of Queen Mary, which bore the words *Reg. Maria* as part of the legend.

∴ Billon is mixed metal for coinage, especially silver largely alloyed with copper.

Rigadoon. A French figure-dance invented by Isaac Rig'adon.

> " And Isaac's Rigadoon shall live as long
> As Raphael's painting, or as Virgil's song."
> *Jenyns : Art of Dancing,* canto ii.

Rig'dum Fun'nidos, in Carey's burlesque of *Chrononhotonthologos.*

Rigdum Funnidos. A sobriquet given by Sir Walter Scott to John Ballantyne, his publisher. So called because he was full of fun. (1776-1821.)

> " A quick, active, intrepid little fellow, . . . full of fun and merriment, . . . all over quaintness and humorous mimicry, . . . a keen and skilful devotee of all manner of field-sports, from fox-hunting to badger-baiting inclusive."—*Lockhart.*

Right Foot. *Put the shoe on the right foot first.* The twelfth symbol of the *Protreptics* of Iamblichus. This audition is preserved in our word "awkward," which means "left-handed" (*awke*, the left hand), seen also in the French *gauche*. Pythagoras meant to teach that his disciples should walk discreetly and wisely, not basely and feebly or gauchely.

Right Foot Foremost. In Rome a boy was stationed at the door of a mansion to caution visitors not to cross the threshold with their left foot, which would have been an ill omen.

Right Hand. The right-hand side of the Speaker, meaning the Ministerial benches. In the French Legislative Assembly *the right* meant the Monarchy men. In the National Convention the Girondists were called the *right hand*, because they occupied the Ministerial benches.

Right as a Trivet. The trivet is a

metallic plate-stand with three legs. Some fasten to the fender and are designed to hold the plate of hot toast, etc. (Anglo-Saxon, *thryfot*, three-foot, tripod.)

Right of Way (*The*). The legal right to make use of a certain passage whether high-road, by-road, or private road. Watercourses, ferries, rivers, etc., are included in the word "ways." Private right of way may be claimed by immemorial usage, special permission, or necessity; but a funeral *cortège* or bridal party having passed over a certain field does not give to the public the right of way, as many suppose.

Rights. *Declaration of Rights.* An instrument submitted to William and Mary, on their being called to the throne, setting forth the fundamental principles of the constitution. The chief items are these: The Crown cannot levy taxes, nor keep a standing army in times of peace; the Members of Parliament are free to utter their thoughts, and a Parliament is to be convened every year; elections are to be free, trial by jury is to be inviolate, and the right of petition is not to be interfered with.

Riglet. A thin piece of wood used for stretching the canvas of pictures; and in printing to regulate the margin, etc. (French, *reglet*, a rule or regulator; Latin, *reg'ula*, a rule.)

Rig'ol. A circle or diadem. (Italian, *rigolo*, a little wheel.)

"[Sleep] That from this golden rigol hath divorced
So many English kings."
Shakespeare: 2 Henry IV., iv. 4.

Rigolette (3 syl.). A grisette, a courtesan; so called from Rigolette, in Eugène Sue's *Mysteries of Paris.*

Rigoletto. An opera describing the agony of a father obliged to witness the prostitution of his own child. The libretto is borrowed from the drama called *Le Roi s'Amuse*, by Victor Hugo; the music is by Guiseppe Verdi.

Rigwoodie. Unyielding; stubborn. A rigwiddie is the chain which crosses the back of a horse to hold up the shafts of a cart (*rig* = back, *withy* = twig.)

"Withered beldams, auld and droll,
Rigwoodie hags."
Burns: Tam O'Shanter.

Rile. *Don't rile the water.* Do not stir up the water and make it muddy. *The water is riled*—muddy and unfit to drink. Common Norfolk expressions; also, a boy is *riled* (out of temper). *I'sy*, together, *Joe Smith was regularly riled*, is

34

quite Norfolk. The American *roil* has the same meaning. A corruption of [*em*]*broil*. (French, *brouiller;* our *broil.*) The adjective *rily*, turbid, angry, is more common.

Ri'mer. Chief god of Damascus; so called from the word *rimë*, a "pomegranate," because he held a pomegranate in his right hand. The people bore a pomegranate in their coat armour. The Romans called this god Jupiter Cassius, from Mount Cassius, near Damascus.

Rimfaxi [*Frost-mane*]. The horse of Night, the foam of whose bit causes dew. (*Scandinavian mythology.*)

Rimmon. A Syrian god, whose seat was Damascus.

" Him followed Rimmon, whose delightful seat
Was fair Damascus, on the fertile bank
Of Ab'bana and Pharphar, lucid streams."
Milton: Paradise Lost, bk. i. 467.

Rimthur'sar. Brother of Y'mer. They were called the "Evil Ones." (*Scandinavian mythology.*)

Rinaldo (in *Jerusalem Delivered*). The Achilles of the Christian army. "He despises gold and power, but craves renown" (bk. i.). He was the son of Bertoldo and Sophia, and nephew of Guelpho, but was brought up by Matilda. At the age of fifteen he ran away and joined the Crusaders, where he was enrolled in the adventurers' squadron. Having slain Gernando, he was summoned by Godfrey to public trial, but went into voluntary exile. The pedigree of Rinaldo, of the noble house of Este, is traced from Actius on the male side and Augustus on the female to Actius VI. (bk. xvii.).

Rinaldo (in *Orlando Furioso*). Son of the fourth Marquis d'Este, cousin of Orlando, Lord of Mount Auban or Albano, eldest son of Amon or Aymon, nephew of Charlemagne, and Bradamant's brother. (*See* ALBA'NO.) He was the rival of his cousin Orlando, but Angelica detested him. He was called "Clarmont's leader," and brought an auxiliary force of English and Scotch to Charlemagne, which "Silence" conducted into Paris.

Rinaldo or *Renaud*, one of the paladins of Charlemagne, is always painted with the characteristics of a borderer—valiant, ingenious, rapacious, and unscrupulous.

Ring. If a lady or gentleman is willing to marry, but not engaged, a ring should be worn on the index finger of the left hand; if engaged, on the second finger; if married, on the third finger; but if either has no desire to marry, on the little finger. (*Mme. C. de la Tour.*)

A ring worn on the forefinger indicates a haughty, bold, and overbearing spirit; on the long finger, prudence, dignity, and discretion; on the marriage finger, love and affection; on the little finger, a masterful spirit.

Ring given in marriage, because it was anciently used as a *seal*, by which orders were signed (Gen. xxxviii. 18; Esther iii. 10-12); and the delivery of a ring was a sign that the giver endowed the person who received it with all the power he himself possessed (Gen. xli. 42). The woman who had the ring could issue commands as her husband, and was in every respect his representative.

"In the Roman espousals, the man gave the woman a ring by way of pledge, and the woman put it on the third finger of her left hand, because it was believed that a nerve ran from that finger to the heart."—*Macrobius: Sat.* vii. 15.

Ring. *The Ring and the Book.* An idyllic epic by Robert Browning, founded on a *cause célèbre* of Italian history (1698). Guido Franceschi'ni, a Florentine nobleman of shattered fortune, by the advice of his brother, Cardinal Paulo, marries Pompilia, an heiress, to repair his state. Now Pompilia was only a supposititious child of Pietro, supplied by Violante for the sake of preventing certain property from going to an heir not his own. When the bride discovered the motive of the bridegroom, she revealed to him this fact, and the first trial occurs to settle the said property. The count treats his bride so brutally that she quits his roof under the protection of Caponsacchi, a young priest, and takes refuge in Rome. Guido follows the fugitives and arrests them at an inn; a trial ensues, and a separation is permitted. Pompilia pleads for a divorce, but, pending the suit, gives birth to a son at the house of her putative parents. The count, hearing thereof, murders Pietro, Violante, and Pompilia; but, being taken red-handed, is executed.

Ring (*The*). The space set apart for prize-fighters, horse-racing, etc. So called because the spectators stand round in a ring.

Ring. *To make a ring.* To combine in order to control the price of a given article. Thus, if the chief merchants of any article (say salt, flour, or sugar) combine, they can fix the selling price, and thus secure enormous profits.

Ring. *It has the true ring*—has intrinsic merit; bears the mark of real talent. A metaphor taken from the custom of judging genuine money by its "ring" or sound. Ring, a circlet, is the Anglo-Saxon *hring*; ring, to sound a bell, etc., is the verb *hring-an*.

Ring Down. Conclude, end at once. A theatrical phrase, alluding to the custom of ringing a bell to give notice for the fall of the curtain. Charles Dickens says, "It is time to ring down on these remarks." (*Speech at the Dramatic Fête.*)

Ring Finger. Priests used to wear their ring on the fore-finger (which represents the Holy Ghost) in token of their spiritual office. (*See* WEDDING FINGER.)

The *ring* finger represents the *humanity* of Christ, and is used in matrimony, which has only to do with humanity. (*See* FINGER BENEDICTION.)

Ring finger. Aulus Gellius tells us that Appia'nus asserts in his Egyptian books that a very delicate nerve runs from the fourth finger of the left hand to the heart, on which account this finger is used for the marriage ring. (*Noctes,* x. 10.)

The *fact* has nothing to do with the question; that the ancients *believed* it is all we require to know. In the Roman Catholic Church, the thumb and first two fingers represent the Trinity: thus the bridegroom says, "In the name of the Father," and touches the thumb; "in the name of the Son," and touches the first finger; and "in the name of the Holy Ghost" he touches the long or second finger. The next finger is the husband's, to whom the woman owes allegiance next to God. The *left* hand is chosen to show that the woman is to be subject to the man. In the Hereford, York, and Salisbury missals, the ring is directed to be put first on the thumb, then on the first finger, then on the long finger, and lastly on the ring-finger, *quia in illo dig'ito est quædam vena pro-ce'dens usque ad cor.*

The ring finger. Mr. Henry Swinburne, in his *Treatise of Spousals*, printed 1680 (p. 208), says: "The finger on which this ring [the wedding-ring] is to be worn is the fourth finger of the left hand, next unto the little finger; because by the received opinion of the learned . . . in ripping up and anatomising men's bodies, there is a vein of blood, called *vena amoris*, which passeth from that finger to the heart."

Ring Posies or *mottoes.*

(1) A E I (Greek for "*Always*").
(2) For ever and for aye.
(3) In thee, my choice, I do rejoice.
(4) Let love increase.

(5) May God above Increase our love.
(6) Not two but one, Till life is gone.
(7) My heart and I, Until I die.
(8) When this you see, Then think of me.
(9) Love is heaven, and heaven is love.
(10) Wedlock, 'tis said, In heaven is made.

Right to wear a gold ring. Amongst the Romans, only senators, chief magistrates, and in later times knights, enjoyed the *jus annuli aurei.* The emperors conferred the right upon whom they pleased, and Justinian extended the privilege to all Roman citizens.

Ring a Ding-ding.

" Ring a ding-ding, ring a ding-ding !
The Parliament soldiers are gone to the king ;
Some they did laugh, and some they did cry,
To see the Parliament soldiers go by."

The reference is to the several removals of Charles I. from one place of captivity to another, till finally he was brought to the block. The Parliament party laughed at their success, the Royalists wept to see the king thus treated.

Ring in the Ear. A sign of slavery or life-long servitude.

"Then Eldad took an awl, and, piercing his [Jetur's] ears against the doorpost, made him his servant for ever. The elders pronounced a blessing, and Eldad put a ring through the ears of Jetur, as a sign that he was become his property."
—*Eldad the Pilgrim*, chap. i.

Ring of Invisibility (*The*), which belonged to Otnit, King of Lombardy, given to him by the queen-mother when he went to gain in marriage the soldan's daughter. The stone of the ring had the virtue of directing the wearer the right road to take in travelling. (*The Heldenbuch.*) (*See* GYGES' RING.)

Ring One's Own Bell (*To*). To be one's own trumpeter. Bells are rung to announce any joyous event, or the advent of some celebrity.

Rings Noted in Fable.

Agramant's ring. This enchanted ring was given by Agramant to the dwarf Brunello, from whom it was stolen by Brad'amant and given to Melissa. It passed successively into the hands of Roge'ro and Angelica (who carried it in her mouth). (*Orlando Furioso*, bk. v.)

The ring of Amasis. The same as the ring of Polycratēs (*q.v.*).

The Doge's ring. The doge of Venice, on Ascension Day, used to throw a ring into the sea from the ship *Bucentaur*, to denote that the Adriatic was subject to the republic of Venice as a wife is subject to her husband.

The ring of Edward the Confessor. It is said that Edward the Confessor was once asked for alms by an old man,

and gave him his ring. In time some English pilgrims went to the Holy Land, and happened to meet the same old man, who told them he was John the Evangelist, and gave them the identical ring to take to "Saint" Edward. It was preserved in Westminster Abbey.

The ring of Gyges (2 syl.) rendered the wearer invisible when its stone was turned inwards.

The ring of Ogier, given him by the Morgue de Fay. It removed all infirmities, and restored the aged to youth again. (*See* OGIER.)

Polyc'ratēs' ring was flung into the sea to propitiate Nem'esis, and was found again by the owner inside a fish. (*See* GLASGOW ARMS.)

The ring of Pope Innocent. On May 29th, 1205, Pope Innocent III. sent John, King of England, four gold rings set with precious stones, and in his letter says the gift is emblematical. He thus explains the matter : The rotundity signifies *eternity*—remember we are passing through time into eternity. The number signifies the four virtues which make up constancy of mind—viz. "justice, fortitude, prudence, and temperance." The material signifies "wisdom from on high," which is as gold purified in the fire. The green emerald is emblem of "faith," the blue sapphire of "hope," the red garnet of "charity," and the bright topaz of "good works." (*Rymer: Fœdera*, vol. i. 139.)

Reynard's wonderful ring. This ring, which existed only in the brain of Reynard, had a stone of three colours—red, white, and green. The *red* made the night as clear as the day ; the *white* cured all manner of diseases, and the *green* rendered the wearer of the ring invincible. (*Reynard the Fox*, chap. xii.)

He must have got possession of Reynard's ring. He bore a charmed life ; he was one of Nature's favourites ; all he did prospered. Reynard affirmed that he had sent King Lion a ring with three gems—one *red*, which gave light in darkness ; one *white*, which cured all pains and wounds, even those arising from indigestion and fever ; and one *green*, which guarded the wearer from every ill both in peace and war. (*Alkmar : Reynard the Fox*, 1498.)

Solomon's ring, among other wonderful things, sealed up the refractory Jins in jars, and cast them into the Red Sea.

Ringing Changes. Bantering each other ; turning the tables on a jester. The allusion is to bells. (*See* PEAL.)

Ringing the Changes. A method of swindling by changing gold and silver in payment of goods. For example : A man goes to a tavern and asks for two-pennyworth of whisky. He lays on the counter half a sovereign, and receives nine shillings and tenpence in change. "Oh!" (says the man) "give me the half-sovereign back, I have such a lot of change." He then takes up ten shillings in silver and receives back the half-sovereign. The barmaid is about to take up the silver when the man says, "Give me a sovereign in lieu of this half-sovereign and ten shillingsworth of silver." This is done, and, of course, the barmaid loses ten shillings by the trans-action.

Ringing Island. The Church of Rome. It is an *island* because it is isolated or cut off from the world. It is a *ringing* island because bells are inces-santly ringing : at matin and vespers, at mass and at sermon-time, at noon, vigils, eves, and so on. It is entered only after four days' fasting, without which none in the Romish Church enter holy orders.

Ringleader. The person who opens a ball or leads off a dance (see *Holly-band's Dictionary*, 1593). The dance referred to was commenced by the party taking hands round in a ring, instead of in two lines as in the country dance. The leader in both cases has to set the figures. One who organises and leads a party.

Riot. *To run riot.* To act in a very disorderly way. Riot means debauchery or wild merriment.

" See, Riot her luxurious bowl prepares."
Tableau of Cebes.

Rip (*A*). *He's a regular rip. A rip of a fellow. A precious rip.* Applied to children, means one who rips or tears his clothes by boisterous play, careless-ness, or indifference. Anglo-Saxon *ryp*[*an*], to spoil, to tear, to break in pieces.

He is a sad rip. A sad rake or de-bauchee ; seems to be a perversion of rep, as in demirep, meaning rep, *i.e.* rep-robate.

" Some forlorn, worn-out old rips, broken-kneed and broken-winded."— *Du Maurier : Peter Ibbet-son*, part vi. p. 376.

Rip. *To rip up old grievances* or *sores.* To bring them again to recollection, to recall them. The allusion is to breaking up a place in search of something hidden and out of sight. (*Anglo-Saxon.*)

" They ripped up all that had been done from the beginning of the Rebellion."— *Clarendon.*

Rip Van Winkle slept twenty years in the Kaatskill mountains. (*See* WINKLE.)

Ripaille. *I am living at Ripaille*—in idleness and pleasure. (French, *faire Ripaille.*) Amadeus VIII., Duke of Savoy, retired to Ripaille, near Geneva, where he threw off all the cares of state, and lived among boon companions in the indulgence of unrestrained pleasure. (*See* SYBARITE.)

Riph'ean or **Rhiphæ'an Rocks.** Any cold mountains in a north country. The fabled Rhiphæan mountains were in Scythia.

" Cold Riphean rocks, which the wild Russ
Believes the stony girdle of the world."
Thomson : Autumn.

The poet here speaks of the Weliki Camenypoys (*great stone girdle*) supposed by the early Russians to have girded the whole earth.

Rip'on. *True as Ripon steel.* Ripon used to be famous for its steel spurs, which were the best in the world. The spikes of a Ripon spur would strike through a shilling-piece without turning the point.

Riquet with a Tuft, from the French *Riquet à la Houppe*, by Charles Per-rault, borrowed from *The Nights of Straparola*, and imitated by Madame Villeneuve in her *Beauty and the Beast*. Riquet is the beau-ideal of ugliness, but had the power of endowing the person he loved best with wit and intelligence. He falls in love with a beautiful woman as stupid as Riquet is ugly, but possess-ing the power of endowing the person she loves best with beauty. The two marry and exchange gifts.

Rise. *To take a rise out of one.* Hot-ten says this is a metaphor from fly-fish-ing ; the fish *rise* to the fly, and are caught.

Rising in the Air. In the Middle Ages, persons believed that saints were sometimes elevated from the ground by religious ecstasy. St. Philip of Neri was sometimes raised to the height of several yards, occasionally to the ceiling of the room. Ignatius Loyola was some-times raised up two or three feet, and his body became luminous. St. Robert de Palentin was elevated in his ecstasies eighteen or twenty inches. St. Dunstan, a little before his death, was observed to rise from the ground. And Girolamo Savonarola, just prior to execution, knelt in prayer, and was lifted from the floor of his cell into mid-air, where he remained suspended for a considerable time. (*Acta Sanctorum.*)

Rivals. "Persons dwelling on opposite sides of a river." Forsyth derives these words from the Latin *riva'lis,* a riverman. Cælius says there was no more fruitful source of contention than river-right, both with beasts and men, not only for the benefit of its waters, but also because rivers are natural boundaries. Hence Ariosto compares Orlando and Ag'rican to "two hinds quarrelling for the river-right" (xxiii. 83).

River Demon or **River Horse** was the Kelpie of the Lowlands of Scotland.

River of Paradise. St. Bernard, Abbot of Clairvaux, "the Last of the Fathers," was so called. (1091-1153.)

River Flowing from the Ocean Inland. The stream from the Bay of Tadjoura, on the north-east coast of Africa. It empties itself into Lake Assal.

Rivers. *Miles in length.*
2,578, the Nile, the longest river in Africa.
2,762, the Volga, the longest river in Europe.
3,314, the Yang-tze-Kiang, the longest river in Asia.
3,716, the Mississippi, the longest river in America.

Roach. *Sound as a roach* (French, *Sain comme une roche*). Sound as a rock.

Road. *Gentlemen of the road* or *Knights of the road.* Highwaymen. In the latter a double pun is implied. A first-class highwayman, like Robin Hood, is a "Colossus of Roads."
King of Roads [Rhodes]. John Loudon Macadam (1756-1836).
The law of the road—
" The law of the road is a paradox quite,
　In riding or driving along ;
If you go to the left you are sure to go right,
　If you go to the right you go wrong."

Road or **Roadstead,** as " Yarmouth Roads," a place where ships can ride at anchor. (French, *rader,* to anchor in a *rade ;* Anglo-Saxon, *rad,* a road or place for riding.)

Road-agent. A highwayman in the mountain districts of North America.
" Road-agent is the name applied in the mountains to a ruffian who has given up honest work in the store, in the mine, in the ranch. for the perils and profits of the highway."—*W. Hepworth Dixon: New America,* i. 14.

Roads. *All roads lead to Rome.* All efforts of thought converge in a common centre.

Roan. A reddish-brown. **This is** the Greek *eruthron* or *eruthræon ;* whence the Latin *rufum.* (The Welsh have *rhudd ;* German, *roth ;* Anglo-Saxon, *rud ;* our *ruddy.*)

Roan Barbary. The famous charger of Richard II., which ate from his royal hand. (*See* RICHARD II.)

Roarer. A broken-winded horse is so called from the noise it makes in breathing.

Roaring Boys or **Roarers.** The riotous blades of Ben Jonson's time, whose delight it was to annoy quiet folk. At one time their pranks in London were carried to an alarming extent.
" And bid them think on Jones amidst this glee,
In hope to get such roaring boys as he."
　　　　Legend of Captain Jones (1659).

Roaring Forties (*The*). What seamen understand by this term is a zone of strong winds about lat. 40° S., where a strong wind prevails throughout the year, from W.N.W. to E.S.E. There is a similar zone in the northern hemisphere, but the current of the wind is interrupted by the prevalence of land. The tendency, however, is from W.S.W. to E.N.E.

Roaring Game (*The*). So the Scotch call the game of curling.

Roaring Trade. *He drives a roaring trade.* He does a great business ; his employees are driven till all their wind is gone. Hence *fast, quick.* (*See above.*)

Roast. *To rule the roast.* To have the chief direction ; to be paramount.
⁂ It is usually thought that "roast" in this phrase means *roost,* and that the reference is to a cock, who decides which hen is to roost nearest to him ; but the subjoined quotation favours the idea of " council."
" John, Duke of Burgoyne, ruled the rost, and governed both King Charles . . . and his whole realme."—*Hall : Union* (1548).

Roasting One. *To give one a roasting.* To banter him, to expose him to sharp words. Shakespeare, in *Hamlet,* speaks of roasting " in wrath and fire."

Rob. A sort of jam. It is a Spanish word, taken from the Arabic *roob* (the juice of fruit).
Faire un rob (in whist). To win the rubber ; that is, either two successive games, or two out of three. Borrowed from the game of bowls.

Rob Roy [*Robert the Red*]. A nickname given to Robert M'Gregor, who assumed the name of Campbell when the clan M'Gregor was outlawed by the Scotch Parliament in 1662. He may be termed the Robin Hood of Scotland.

"Rather beneath the middle size than above it, his limbs were formed upon the very strongest model that is consistent with agility.... Two points in his person interfered with the rules of symmetry: his shoulders were so broad ... as to give him the air of being too square in respect to his stature; and his arms, though round, sinewy, and strong, were so very long as to be rather a deformity."—*Sir Walter Scott: Rob Roy McGregor*, xxiii.

Robber. The highwayman who told Alexander that he was the greater robber of the two was named Dion'idēs. The tale is given in *Evenings at Home* under the title of *Alexander and the Robber*.

Robber. Edward IV. of England was called by the Scotch *Edward the Robber*.

Robbing Peter to pay Paul. On December 17th, 1550, the abbey church of St. Peter, Westminster, was advanced to the dignity of a cathedral by letters patent; but ten years later it was joined to the diocese of London again, and many of its estates appropriated to the repairs of St. Paul's Cathedral. (*Winkle: Cathedrals.*)

"Tanquam siquis crucifigeret Paulum ut redimeret Petrum." (Twelfth century.)
"It was not desirable to rob St. Peter's altar in order to build one to St. Paul."—*Viglius: Com. Dec. Denarii*, i. 9 (1569).

Robert. *King Robert of Sicily.* A metrical romance of the Trouveur, taken from the *Story of the Emperor Jovinian* in the *Gesta Romano'rum*, and borrowed from the *Talmud*. It finds a place in the *Arabian Nights*, the Turkish *Tutinameh*, the Sanskrit *Pantschatantra*, and has been *réchauffé* by Longfellow under the same name.

Robert, Robin. A highwayman.

Robert François Damiens, who attempted to assassinate Louis XV., is called "Robert the Devil." (1714-1757.)

Robert Macaire. *He's a Robert Macaire.* A bluff, free-living, unblushing libertine, who commits the most horrible crimes without stint or compunction. It is a character in M. Daumier's drama of *L'Auberge des Adrets*. His accomplice is Bertrand, a simpleton and villain. (*See* MACAIRE.)

Robert Street (Adelphi, London). So called from Robert Adams, the builder.

Robert le Diable. The son of Bertha and Bertramo. The former was daughter of Robert, Duke of Normandy, and the latter was a fiend in the guise of a knight. The opera shows the struggle in Robert between the virtue inherited from his mother, and the vice imparted by his father. He is introduced as a libertine; but Alice, his foster-sister, places in his hand the will of his mother, "which he is not to read till he is worthy." Bertramo induces him to gamble till he loses everything, and finally claims his soul; but Alice counterplots the fiend, and finally triumphs by reading to Robert the will of his mother. (*Meyerbeer: Roberto il Diavolo, an opera.*)

Robert the Devil. Robert, first Duke of Normandy; so called for his daring and cruelty. The Norman tradition is that his wandering ghost will not be allowed to rest till the Day of Judgment. He is also called *Robert the Magnificent.* (1028-1035.)

Robert of Brunne, that is, of Bourne, in Lincolnshire. His name was Robert Manning, author of an old English *Chronicle*, written in the reign of Edward III. It consists of two parts, the first of which is in octosyllabic rhymes, and is a translation of Wace's *Brut;* the second part is in Alexandrine verse, and is a translation of the French chronicle of Piers de Langtoft, of Yorkshire.

" Of Brunne I am, if any me blame,
    Robert Mannyng is my name ...
    In the thrid Edwardes tyme was I
    When I wrote alle this story."
            Preface to Chronicle.

Robert's Men. Bandits, marauders, etc. So called from Robin Hood, the outlaw.

Robespierre's Weavers. The fishwomen and other female rowdies who joined the Parisian Guard, and helped to line the avenues to the National Assembly in 1793, and clamour "Down with the Girondists!"

Robin Goodfellow. A "drudging fiend," and merry domestic fairy, famous for mischievous pranks and practical jokes. At night-time he will sometimes do little services for the family over which he presides. The Scotch call this domestic spirit a *brownie;* the Germans, *kobold* or *Knecht Ruprecht.* The Scandinavians called it *Nissë God-dreng.* Puck, the jester of Fairy-court, is the same.

" Either I mistake your shape and making quite,
    Or else you are that shrewd and knavish sprite
    Called Robin Goodfellow. ...
    Those that Hob-goblin call you, and sweet Puck,
    You do their work, and they shall have good
        luck."
Shakespeare: Midsummer Night's Dream, ii. 1.

(*See* FAIRY.)

Robin Gray (*Auld*). Words by Lady Anne Lindsay, daughter of the Earl of Balcarres, and afterwards Lady Barnard, in 1772, written to an old Scotch tune called "The bridegroom grat when the sun gaed down." Auld Robin Gray was the herdsman of her father. When Lady Anne had written a part, she called her younger sister for advice. She said, "I am writing a ballad of virtuous distress in humble life. I have oppressed my heroine with sundry troubles: 'for example, I have sent her Jamie to sea, broken her father's arm, made her mother sick, given her Auld Robin Gray for a lover, and want a fifth sorrow; can you help me to one?" "Steal the cow, sister Anne," said the little Elizabeth; so the cow was stolen awa', and the song completed.

Robin Hood is first mentioned by the Scottish historian Fordun, who died in 1386. According to Stow, he was an outlaw in the reign of Richard I. (twelfth century). He entertained one hundred tall men, all good archers, with the spoil he took, but "he suffered no woman to be oppressed, violated, or otherwise molested; poore men's goods he spared, abundantlie relieving them with that which by theft he got from abbeys and houses of rich carles." He was an immense favourite with the common people, who have dubbed him an earl. Stukeley says he was Robert Fitzooth, Earl of Huntingdon. (*See* ROBERT.)

According to one tradition, Robin Hood and Little John were two heroes defeated with Simon de Montfort at the battle of Evesham, in 1265. Fuller, in his *Worthies*, considers him an historical character, but Thierry says he simply represents a class—viz. the remnant of the old Saxon race, which lived in perpetual defiance of the Norman oppressors from the time of Hereward.

Other examples of similar combinations are the Cumberland bandits, headed by Adam Bell, Clym of the Clough, and William of Cloudesley.

An old sporting magazine of December, 1808, says the true name of Robin Hood was Fitzooth, and Fitz being omitted leaves Ooth, and converting *th* into *d* it became "Ood." He was grandson of Ralph Fitzooth, Earl of Kyme, a Norman, who came to England in the reign of William Rufus. His maternal grandfather was Gilbert de Gaunt, Earl of Lincoln, and his grandmother was Lady Roisia de Bere, sister to the Earl of Oxford. His father was under the guardianship of Robert, Earl of Oxford, who, by the king's order, gave him in marriage the third daughter of Lady Roisia. (*Notes and Queries*, May 21st, 1887.)

✱ The traditions about Fulk Fitz-Warine, great-grandson of Warine of Metz, so greatly resemble those connected with "Robin Hood," that some suppose them to be both one. Fitz-Warine quarrelled with John, and when John was king he banished Fulk, who became a bold forester. (See *Notes and Queries*, November 27th, 1886, pp. 421-424.)

Bow and arrow of Robin Hood. The traditional bow and arrow of Robin Hood are religiously preserved at Kirklees Hall, Yorkshire, the seat of Sir George Armytage; and the site of his grave is pointed out in the park.

Death of Robin Hood. He was bled to death treacherously by a nun, instigated to the foul deed by his kinsman, the prior of Kirklees, Yorkshire, near Halifax. Introduced by Sir Walter Scott in *Ivanhoe*.

Epitaph of Robin Hood.

> " Hear, underneath this latil stean,
> Laiz Robert earl of Huntington ;
> Nea arcir ver az hie sae geud,
> An pipl kauld him Robin Heud.
> Sich utlaz az he an hiz men
> Vll England nivr si agen."
> ｜Obit. 24, Kalend Dikembris, 1247.

✱ Notwithstanding this epitaph, it is generally thought that Robin Hood died in 1325, which would bring him into the reign of Edward II., not Richard I., according to Sir Walter Scott.

In the accounts of King Edward II.'s household is an item which states that "Robin Hood received his wages as king's valet, and a gratuity on leaving the service." One of the ballads relates how Robin Hood took service under this king.

Many talk of Robin Hood who never shot with his bow. Many brag of deeds in which they took no part. Many talk of Robin Hood, and wish their hearers to suppose they took part in his adventures, but they never put a shaft to one of his bows; nor could they have bent it even if they had tried.

To sell Robin Hood's pennyworth is to sell things at half their value. As Robin Hood stole his wares, he sold them, under their intrinsic value, for just what he could get on the nonce.

Robin Hood and Guy of Gisborne. Robin Hood and Little John, having had a tiff, part company; when Little John falls into the hands of the sheriff of Nottingham, who binds him to a tree.

Meanwhile, Robin Hood meets with Guy of Gisborne, sworn to slay the "bold forrester." The two bowmen struggle together, but Guy is slain, and Robin Hood rides till he comes to the tree where Little John is bound. The sheriff mistakes him for Guy of Gisborne, and gives him charge of the prisoner. Robin cuts the cord, hands Guy's bow to Little John, and the two soon put to flight the sheriff and his men. (*Percy: Reliques*, etc., series i.)

Robin Hood Wind (*A*). A cold thaw-wind. Tradition runs that Robin Hood used to say he could bear any cold except that which a thaw-wind brought with it.

Robin Mutton (*A*). A simpleton.

"Do you see this ram? His name is Robin. Here, Robin, Robin, Robin. . . . We will get a pair of scales, and then you, Robin Mutton [Panurge], shall be weighed against Tup Robin, . . . etc."—*Rabelais: Pantagruel*, iv. 7.

Robin Redbreast. The tradition is that when our Lord was on His way to Calvary, a robin picked a thorn out of His crown, and the blood which issued from the wound falling on the bird dyed its breast with red. (*See* CHRISTIAN TRADITIONS.)

Robin Redbreasts. Bow Street runners were so called from their red waistcoats.

Robin and Makyne (2 syl.). An ancient Scottish pastoral. Robin is a shepherd for whom Makyne sighs. She goes to him and tells her love, but Robin turns a deaf ear, and the damsel goes home to weep. After a time the tables are turned, and Robin goes to Makyne to plead for her heart and hand; but the damsel replies—

"The man that will not when he may
   Sall have nocht when he wald."
         Percy: Reliques, etc., series ii.

Robin of Bagshot. Noted for the number of his aliases (*see* ALIAS); but Deeming had nine : viz. Williams, Ward, Swanston, Levey, Lord Dunn, Lawson, Mollatt, Drewe, and Baron Swanston.

"You have as many aliases as Robin of Bagshot."

Robinson Crusoe. Alexander Selkirk was found in the desert island of Juan Fernandez, where he had been left by Captain Stradling. He remained on the island four years and four months, when he was rescued by Captain Rogers, and brought to England. The embryo of De Foe's novel may be seen in Captain Burney's interesting narrative.

Robinsonians. They were followers of John Robinson, of Leyden. The Brownists were followers of Robert Brown. The Brownists were most rigid separatists ; the Robinsonians were only semi-separatists.

Roc. A fabulous white bird of enormous size, and such strength that it can "truss elephants in its talons," and carry them to its mountain nest, where it devours them. (*Arabian Nights ; The Third Calender, and Sinbad the Sailor*.)

Roch (*St.*). Patron of those afflicted with the plague, because he devoted his life to their service, and is said to intercede for them in his exaltation. He is depicted in a pilgrim's habit, lifting his dress to display a plague-spot on his thigh, which an angel is touching that he may cure it. Sometimes he is accompanied by a dog bringing bread in his mouth, in allusion to the legend that a hound brought him bread daily while he was perishing in a forest of pestilence.

St. Roch's Day (August 16th), formerly celebrated in England as a general harvest-home, and styled "the great August festival." The Anglo - Saxon name of it was *harfest* (herb-feast), the word *herb* meaning autumn (German *herbst*), and having no relation to what we call herbs.

St. Roch et son chien. Inseparables. Darby and Joan.

Roche. *Men of la vieille roche.* Old-fashioned men ; men of fossilised ideas ; non-progressive men. A geological expression.

"Perhaps it may be justly attributed to a class of producers, men of *la vieille roche*, that they have been so slow to apprehend the changes which are daily presenting themselves in the requirements of trade."—*The Times.*

Sir Boyle Roche's bird. Sir Boyle Roche, quoting from Jevon's play (*The Devil of a Wife*), said on one occasion in the House, "Mr. Speaker, it is impossible I could have been in two places at once, unless I were a bird."

"Presuming that the duplicate card is the knave of hearts, you may make a remark on the ubiquitous nature of certain cards, which, like Sir Boyle Roche's bird, are in two places at once."—*Drawing-room Magic.*

Rochelle Salt. So called because it was discovered by an apothecary of Rochelle, named Seignette, in 1672.

Roches (*Catharine des*) had a collection of poems written on her, termed *La Puce de Grands-jours de Poitiers*.

Rochester, according to Bede, derives its name from "Hrof," a Saxon chieftain. (*Hrofs-ceaster*, Hrof's castle.)

Rock. A quack; so called from one Rock, who was the "Holloway" of Queen Anne's reign.

"Oh, when his nerves had once received a shock, Sir Isaac Newton might have gone to Rock."
          Crabbe: Borough.

The Ladies' Rock. A crag in Scotland under the castle rock of Stirling, where ladies used to witness tournaments.

"In the castle hill is a hollow called *The Valley* about a square acre in extent, used for justings and tournaments. On the south side of the valley is a small rocky pyramidical mount, called *The Ladies' Hill* or *Rock,* where the ladies sat to witness the spectacle."—*Nimmo: History of Stirlingshire,* p. 282.

People of the Rock. The inhabitants of Hejaz or Arabia Petræa.

Captain Rock. A fictitious name assumed by the leader of the Irish insurgents in 1822.

Rock ahead (*A*). A sea-phrase, meaning that a rock is in the path of the ship, which the helmsman must steer clear of; a danger threatens; an opponent; an obstruction.

"That yonker . . . has been a rock ahead to me all my life."—*Sir W. Scott: Guy Mannering,* chap. liv.

Rock Cork. A variety of asbestos, resembling cork. It is soft, easily cut, and very light.

Rock Crystal. The specimens which enclose hair-like substances are called *Thetis's hair-stone, Venus's hair-stone, Venus's pencils, Cupid's net, Cupid's arrows,* etc.

Rock Day. The day after Twelfth-day, when, the Christmas holidays being over, women returned to their rock or distaff.

Rococo. *C'est du rococo.* It is mere twaddle; Brummagem finery; make-believe. (Italian *roco,* uncouth.)

Roco'co Architecture. A debased style, which succeeded the revival of Italian architecture, and very prevalent in Germany. The ornamentation is without principle or taste, and may be designated ornamental design run mad. The Rock-temple of Ellora, in India, is most lavishly decorated.

"The sacristy of St. Lorenzo . . . was the beginning of that wonderful mixture of antique regularity with the capricious bizarrerie of modern times, the last barren fruit of which was the rococo."—*H. Grimm: Michel Angelo,* vol. ii. chap. xi. p. 173.

Roco'co Jewellery, strictly speaking, means showy jewellery made up of several different stones. Moorish decoration and Watteau's paintings are rococo. The term is now generally used depreciatingly for flashy, gaudy. Louis XIV.

34*

furniture, with gilding and ormolu, is sometimes termed rococo.

Rod. *To kiss the rod.* (*See* KISS THE ROD.)

Rod-men. Anglers, who use line and fishing-rod.

"You will be nearly sure to meet one or two old rod-men sipping their toddy there."—*J. K. Jerome. Three Men in a Boat,* chap. xvii.

Rod in Pickle (*A*). A scolding in store. The rod is laid in pickle to keep it ready for use.

Rod'erick, the thirty-fourth and last of the Visigothic kings, was the son of Theod'ofred, and grandson of King Chindasuin'tho. Witi'za, the usurper, put out the eyes of Theod'ofred, and murdered Favil'a, a younger brother of Roderick; but Roderick, having recovered his father's throne, put out the eyes of the usurper. The sons of Witi'za, joining with Count Julian, invited the aid of Muza ibn Nozeir, the Arab chief, who sent Tarik into Spain with a large army. Roderick was routed at the battle of Guadale'te, near Xeres de la Fronte'ra (July 17th, 711). Southey has taken this story for an epic poem in twenty-five books—blank verse. (*See* RODRIGO.)

Rod'erick Random. (*See* RANDOM.)

Roderigo. A Venetian gentleman in Shakespeare's *Othello.* He was in love with Desdemona, and when the lady eloped with Othello, hated the "noble Moor." Iago took advantage of this temper for his own ends, told his dupe the Moor will change, therefore "put money in thy purse." The burden of his advice was always the same—"Put money in thy purse."

This word is sometimes pronounced Rod'r-igo: *e.g.* "It is as sure as you are Roderigo;" and sometimes Rode-ri'go: *e.g.* "On, good Roderigo; I'll deserve your pains." (Act i. scene 1.)

Rodhaver. The lady-love of Zal, a Persian hero. Zal wanted to scale her bower, and Rodhaver let down her long tresses to assist him; but the lover managed to climb to his mistress by fixing his crook into a projecting beam. (*Champion: Ferdosi.*)

Rodilar'dus. A huge cat which scared Panurge, and which he declared to be a puny devil. The word means "gnaw-bacon" (Latin, *rodo-lardum*). (*Rabelais: Gargantua and Pantagruel,* iv. 67.)

Rodol'pho (*Count*). The count, returning from his travels, puts up for the night at an inn near his castle. While in bed, a lady enters his chamber, and speaks to him of her devoted love. It is Ami'na, the somnambulist, who has wandered thither in her sleep. Rodolpho perceives the state of the case, and quits the apartment. The villagers, next morning, come to congratulate their lord on his return, and find his bed occupied by a lady. The tongue of scandal is loud against her, but the count explains to them the mystery, and his tale is confirmed by their own eyes, which see Ami'na at the moment getting out of the window of a mill, and walking in her sleep along the edge of a roof under which the wheel of the mill is rolling with velocity. She crosses the crazy bridge securely; and everyone is convinced of her innocence. (*Bellini : La Sonnambula.*) (*See* AMINA, ELVINO.)

Rod'omont (in *Orlando Inamorato* and *Orlando Furioso*). King of Sarza or Algiers, Ulien's son, and called the "Mars of Africa." He was commander both of horse and foot in the Saracen army sent against Charlemagne, and may be termed the Achilles of the host. His lady-love was Dor'alis, Princess of Grana'da, who ran off with Mandricardo, King of Tartary. At Roge'ro's wedding-feast Rodomont rode up to the king of France in full armour, and accused Roge'ro, who had turned Christian, of being a traitor to King Agramant, his master and a renegade; whereupon Roge'ro met him in single combat, and slew him. (*See* ROGERO.)

"Who more brave than Rodomont?"—*Cervantes : Don Quixote.*

Rod'omonta'de (4 syl.). From Rodomont, a brave but braggart knight in Bojardo's *Orlando Inamorato.* He is introduced into the continuation of the story by Ariosto (*Orlando Furioso*), but the braggart part of his character is greatly toned down. Neither Rodomont nor Hector deserves the opprobium which has been attached to their names. (*See* RODOMONT.)

Rodrigo [*Rod-ree'-go*] or **Roderick**, King of Spain, conquered by the Arabs. He saved his life by flight, and wandered to Guadalet'e, where he saw a shepherd, and asked food. In return he gave the shepherd his royal chain and ring. He passed the night in the cell of a hermit, who told him that by way of penance he must pass certain days in a tomb full of snakes, toads, and lizards. After three days the hermit went to see him, and he was unhurt, "because the Lord kept His

anger against him." The hermit went home, passed the night in prayer, and went again to the tomb, when Rodrigo said, "They eat me now, they eat me now, I feel the adder's bite." So his sin was atoned for, and he died.

Rogation Days. The Monday, Tuesday, and Wednesday before Ascension Day. Rogation is the Latin equivalent of the Greek word "Litany," and on the three Rogation days "the Litany of the Saints" is appointed to be sung by the clergy and people in public procession. ("Litany," Greek *litaneia,* supplication. "Rogation," Latin *rogatio,* same meaning.)

Rogation Week used to be called *Gang Week,* from the custom of ganging round the country parishes to mark their bounds. Similarly, the weed Milkwort is still called Rogation or Gangflower, from the custom of decorating the pole (carried on such occasions by the charity children) with these flowers.

Rogel of Greece. A knight, whose exploits and adventures form a supplemental part of the Spanish romance entitled *Am'adis of Gaul.* This part was added by Feliciano de Silva.

Roger. The cook in Chaucer's *Canterbury Tales.* " He cowde roste, sethe, broille, and frie. Make mortreux, and wel bake a pye; " but Herry Bailif, the host, said to him—

" Now telle on, Roger, and loke it be good ;
For many a Jakk of Dover hastow sold.
That hath be twyes hoot and twyes cold."
Verse 4343.

Roger Bontemps. (*See* BONTEMPS.)
The Jolly Roger. The black flag, the favourite ensign of pirates.

"Set all sail, clear the deck, stand to quarters, up w'th the Jolly Roger !"—*Sir Walter Scott: The Pirate,* chap. xxxi.

Roger of Bruges. Roger van der Weyde, painter. (1455-1529.)
Roger de Coverley. A dance invented by the great-grandfather of Roger de Coverley, or Roger of Cowley, near Oxford. Named after the squire described in Addison's *Spectator.*
Roger of Hoveden or Howden, in Yorkshire, continued Bede's *History* from 732 to 1202. The reigns of Henry II. and Richard I. are very fully given. The most matter-of-fact of all our old chroniclers; he indulges in no epithets or reflections.

Roge'ro, Ruggiero, or **Rizieri** of Risa (in *Orlando Furioso*), was brother of Marphi'sa, and son of Rogero and Galacella. He married Brad'amant,

Charlemagne's niece, but had no issue. Galacella being slain by Ag'olant and his sons, Rogero was nursed by a lioness. Rogero deserted from the Moorish army to the Christian Charles, and was baptised. His marriage with Bradamant and election to the crown of Bulgaria conclude the poem.

Rogero was brought up by Atlantes, a magician, who gave him a shield of such dazzling splendour that everyone quailed who set eyes on it. Rogero, thinking it unknightly to carry a charmed shield, threw it into a well.

"Who more courteous than Rogero?"—*Cervantes: Don Quixote.*

Rogero (in *Jerusalem Delivered*), brother of Bœmond, and son of Roberto Guiscardo, of the Norman race, was one of the band of adventurers in the crusading army. Slain by Tisaphernes. (Bk. xx.)

Rogue Ingrain (*A*). Ingrain colours are what we call "fast colours," colours which will not fly or wash out. A rogue ingrain means one rotten to the core, one whose villainy is deep-seated.

"'Tis ingrain, sir; 'twill endure wind and weather."—*Shakespeare: Twelfth Night,* i. 5.

Roi Panade [*King of Slops*]. Louis XVIII. was so nicknamed. (1755, 1814-1824.)

Roland, Count of Mans and Knight of Blaives, was son of Duke Milo of Aiglant, his mother being Bertha, the sister of Charlemagne. His sword was called Durandal, and his horse Veillantiff. He was eight feet high, and had an open countenance, which invited confidence, but inspired respect. In Italian romance he is called *Orlando*, his sword *Duranda'na*, and his horse *Veyliantl'no*. (See *Song of Roland*.)

"I knew of n one to compare him to but the Archangel Michael."—*Croquemitaine,* iii.

Roland. Called the Christian Theseus (2 syl.), or the Achilles of the West.

Roland or *Rolando* (*Orlando* in Italian). One of Charlemagne's paladins and nephews. He is represented as brave, loyal, and simple-minded. On the return of Charlemagne from Spain, Roland, who commanded the rear-guard, fell into an ambuscade at Roncesvalles, in the Pyrenees, and perished with all the flower of French chivalry (778). He is the hero of Theroulde's *Chanson de Roland;* the romance called *Chroniq de Turpin;* Boiardo's epic *Orlando in Love* (Italian); and Ariosto's epic of *Orlando Mad* (Italian).

Roland, after slaying Angoulaffre, the Saracen giant, in single combat at Fronsac, asked as his reward the hand of Aude, daughter of Sir Gerard and Lady Guibourg; but they never married, as Roland fell at Roncesvalles, and Aude died of a broken heart. (*Croquemitaine,* xi.)

A Roland for an Oliver. A blow for a blow, tit for tat. Roland and Oliver were two of the paladins of Charlemagne, whose exploits are so similar that it is very difficult to keep them distinct. What Roland did Oliver did, and what Oliver did Roland did. At length the two met in single combat, and fought for five consecutive days on an island in the Rhine, but neither gained the least advantage. (*See* in *La Légende des Siècles,* by Victor Hugo, the poem entitled *Le Mariage de Roland.*)

The etymologies connecting the proverb with Charles II., General Monk, and Oliver Cromwell, are wholly unworthy of credit, for even Shakespeare alludes to it: "England all Olivers and Rolands bred" (1 *Henry VI.,* i. 2); and Edward Hall, the historian, almost a century before Shakespeare, writes—

"But to have a Roland to resist an Oliver, he sent solempne ambassadors to the Kyng of Englande, offeryng hym hys doughter in mariage."—*Henry VI.*

(*See* OLIVER, BRECHE.)

∵ In French, *à bon chat bon rat.*

To die like Roland. To die of starvation or thirst. It is said that Roland, the great paladin, set upon in the defile of Roncesvalles, escaped the general slaughter, and died of hunger and thirst in seeking to cross the Pyrenees.

"Post ingentem Hispano'rum cædem prope Pyrenæi saltus juga ... siti miserrime extinctum. Inde nostri intolera'bili siti et immi'ti volentes significa're se torquê, face're aiunt, Rolandi morte se erire."—*John de la Bruiere Champia: Re Gi bus'lu xvi,* 5.

Faire le Roland. To swagger.

Like the blast of Roland's horn. When Roland was set upon by the Gascons at Roncesvalles, he sounded his horn to give Charlemagne notice of his danger. At the third blast it cracked in two, but so loud was the blast that birds fell dead and the whole Saracen army was panic-struck. Charlemagne heard the sound at St. Jean Pied de Port, and rushed to the rescue, but arrived too late.

"Oh, for one blast of that dread horn
On Fontarabian echoes borne,
That to King Charles did come."
    Sir Walter Scott: Marmion, vi. 33.

Song of Roland. Part of the *Chansons de Geste,* which treat of the achievements of Charlemagne and his paladins. William of Normandy had it sung at the head of his troops when he came to invade England.

Song of Roland. When Charlemagne had been six years in Spain, by the advice of Roland, his nephew, he sent Ganelon on an embassy to Marsillus, the pagan king of Saragossa. Ganelon, out of jealousy, betrayed to Marsillus the route which the Christian army designed to take on its way home, and the pagan king arrived at Roncesvalles just as Roland was conducting through the pass a rearguard of 20,000 men. Roland fought till 100,000 Saracens lay slain, and only 50 of his own men survived. At this juncture another army, consisting of 50,000 men, poured from the mountains. Roland now blew his enchanted horn, and blew so loudly that the veins of his neck started. Charlemagne heard the blast, but Ganelon persuaded him that it was only his nephew hunting the deer. Roland died of his wounds, but in dying threw his trusty sword Durandal into a poisoned stream, where it remained.

Roland de Vaux (*Sir*). Baron of Triermain, who woke Gyneth from her long sleep of five hundred years and married her. (*Sir Walter Scott : Bridal of Triermain.*)

Rolandseck Tower, opposite the Drachenfels. The legend is that when Roland went to the wars, a false report of his death was brought to his betrothed, who retired to a convent in the isle of Nonnewerth. When Roland returned home flushed with glory, and found that his lady-love had taken the veil, he built the castle which bears his name, and overlooks the nunnery, that he might at least see his heart-treasure, lost to him for ever.

Roll. *The flying roll of Zechariah* (v. 1-5). "Predictions of evils to come on a nation are like the Flying Roll of Zechariah." This roll (twenty cubits long and ten wide) was full of maledictions, threats, and calamities about to befall the Jews. The parchment being unrolled fluttered in the air.

Rolls [*Chancery Lane, London*]. So called from the records kept there in rolls of parchment. The house was originally built by Henry III. for converted Jews, and was called "Domus Converso'rum." It was Edward III. who appropriated the place to the conservation of records. "Conversi" means laymonks. (*Ducange*, vol. ii. p. 703.)

Glover's Roll. A copy of the lost *Roll of Arms*, made by Glover, Somerset herald. It is a roll of the arms borne by Henry III., his princes of the

blood, barons, and knights, between 1216 and 1272.

The Roll of Caerlaverock. An heraldic poem in Norman-French, reciting the names and arms of the knights present at the siege of Caerlaverock, in 1300.

Rolling Stone. *A rolling stone gathers no moss.*

Greek :   Λιθος κυλινδομενος το φυκος ου ποιει. (*Erasmus : Proverbs ; Assiduitas.*)

Latin :   Saxum volutum non obducitur musco (*or* Saxum volubile, etc.)

Planta quæ sæpius transfertur non coalescit. (*Fabius.*)

Sæpius plantata arbor fructum profert exiguum.

French : Pierre qui roule n'amasse jamais mousse.

La pierre souvent remuée n'amasse pas volontiers mousse.

Pierre souvent remuée n'attire pas mousse.

Italian : Pietra mossa non fa muschio.

"*Three removes are as bad as a fire.*"

" I never saw an oft-removed tree,
Nor yet an oft-removed family,
That throve so well as those that settled be."

Rollrich or **Rowldrich Stones**, near Chipping Norton (Oxfordshire). A number of large stones in a circle, which tradition says are *men* turned to stone. The highest of them is called *the King*, who "would have been king of England if he could have caught sight of Long Compton," which may be seen a few steps farther on ; five other large stones are called the knights, and the rest common soldiers.

Roly-poly (pron. *rowl-y powl-y*). A crust with jam rolled up into a pudding ; a little fat child. Roly is a thing rolled with the diminutive added. In some parts of Scotland the game of nine-pins is called *rouly-pouly.*

Roma'ic. Modern or Romanised Greek.

Roman (*The*).

Jean Dumont, the French painter, *le Romain* (1700-1781).

Stephen Picart, the French engraver, *le Romain* (1631-1721).

Giulio Pippi, *Giulio Romano* (1492-1546).

Adrian van Roomen, the mathematician, *Adria'nus Roma'nus* (1561-1615).

Most learned of the Romans. Marcus Terentius Varro (B.C. 116-28).

Last of the Romans. Rienzi (1310-1354).

Last of the Romans. Charles James Fox (1749-1806.) (*See* SIDNEY.)

Ultimus Romanorum. Horace Walpole (1717-1797). (*See* LAST.)

Roman Birds. Eagles ; so called because the ensign of the Roman legion was an eagle.

" Roma'nas aves propria legio'num nu'mina."— *Tacitus.*

Roman Remains in England. The most remarkable are the following :—

The pharos, church, and trenches in Dover.

Chilham Castle, Richborough, and Reculver forts.

Silchester (Berkshire), Dorchester, Nisconium (Salop), and Caerleon, amphitheatres.

Hadrian's wall, from Tyne to Boulness.

The wall, baths, and Newport Gate of Lincoln.

Verulam, near St. Albans.

York (Eboracum), where Sevērus and Constantius Chlorus died, and Constantine the Great was born.

Bath, etc.

Roman de Chevalier de Lyon, by Maitre Wace, Canon of Caen in Normandy, and author of *Le Brut.* The romance referred to is the same as that entitled *Ywain and Gawain.*

Roman de la Rose. (*See* ILIAD, *The French.*)

Roman des Romans. A French version of *Am'adis of Gaul,* greatly extended, by Gilbert Saunier and Sieur de Duverdier.

Romance. A tale in prose or verse the incidents of which are hung upon what is marvellous and fictitious.

These tales were originally written in the Romance language (*q.v.*), and the expression, "In Romance we read," came in time to refer to the tale, and not to the language in which it was told.

Romance of chivalry may be divided into three groups :—(1) that relating to Arthur and his Round Table ; (2) that relating to Charlemagne and his paladins ; (3) that relating to Am'adis and Pal'merin. In the first are but few fairies ; in the second they are shown in all their glory ; in the third (which belongs to Spanish literature) we have no fairies, but the enchantress Urganda la Desconeci'da.

⁂ It is misleading to call such poetical tales as the *Bride of Abydos, Lalla Rookh,* and the *Chansons of the Mouvères,* etc., *Romances.*

Romanes'que (3 syl.).

In painting. Fanciful and romantic rather than true to nature.

In architecture. Byzantine, Lombard, Saxon, and, indeed, all the debased Roman styles, between the time of Constantine (350) and Charlemagne (800).

In literature. The dialect of Languedoc, which smacks of the Romance.

Roman'ic or Romance Languages. Those modern languages which are the immediate offspring of Latin, as the Italian, Spanish, Portuguese, and French. Early French is emphatically so called ; hence Bouillett says, " *Le roman était universellement parlé en Gaule au dixième siècle.*"

" Frankis speech is called Romance, So say clerks and men of France." *Robert Le Brunn.*

Ro'manism. Popery, or what resembles Popery, the religion of modern Rome. (A word of implied reproach.)

Roman'tic School. The name assumed, at the beginning of the nineteenth century, by a number of young poets and critics in Germany, who wished to limit poetry and art to romance. Some twenty-five years later Victor Hugo, Lamartine, and Dumas introduced it into France.

Roma'nus (*St.*), a Norman bishop of the seventh century, is depicted fighting with a dragon, in allusion to the tale that he miraculously conquered a dragon which infested Normandy.

Roma'ny. Gipsy language, the speech of the Roma or Zinca'li. This has nothing to do with Rome.

" A learned Sclavonian . . . said of Rommany, that he found it interesting to be able to study a Hindu dialect in the heart of Europe."—*Leland : English Gipsies,* chap. viii. p. 109.

Rome. Virgil says of Romulus, " *Mavortia condet mœnia. Romanosque suo de nomine dicet* " (*Æneid,* i. 276). The words of the Sibyl, quoted by Servius, are " Ρωμαιοι Ρωμον παιδες." Romulus is a diminutive or word of endearment for Romus.

The etymology of Rome from *Roma* (mother of Romulus and Remus), or from *Romulus,* the legendary founder of the city, or from *ruma* (a dug), in allusion to the fable of a wolf suckling the outcast children, is not tenable. Niebuhr derives it from the Greek word *rhoma* (strength), a suggestion confirmed by its other name Valentia, from *valens* (strong). Michelet prefers *Rumo,* the ancient name of the river Tiber.

Rome. *Founders of Rome.* (1)Romulus, the legendary founder, B.C. 752; (2) Camillus was termed the *Second Romulus,* for saving Rome from the Gauls, B.C. 365; (3) Caius Ma′rius was called the *Third Romulus,* for saving Rome from the Teuto′nes and Cimbri, B.C. 101.

From Rome to May. A bantering expression, equivalent to the following:—
"From April to the foot of Westminster Bridge;" "*Inter pascha Rennesque feror*" (*Reinardus,* ii. 690); "*Inter Cluniacum et Sancti festa Johannis obit*" (*Reinardus,* iv. 972); "*Cela s'est passé entre Maubeuge et la Pentecôte.*"

'Tis ill sitting at Rome and striving with the Pope. Never tread on a man's corns. "Never wear a brown hat in Friesland" (*q.v.*).

"Mr. Harrison the steward, and Gudyell the butler, are no very fond o' us, and it's ill sitting at Rome and striving with the pope, sae I thought it best to flit before ill came."—*Sir W. Scott: Old Mortality,* chap. viii.

Oh, that all Rome had but one head, that I might strike it off at a blow! Caligula, the Roman emperor, is said to have uttered this amiable sentiment.

When you go to Rome, do as Rome does—i.e. conform to the manners and customs of those amongst whom you live, and don't wear a brown hat in Friesland. St. Mon′ica and her son St. Augustine, said to St. Ambrose: At Rome they fast on Saturday, but not so at Milan; which practice ought to be observed? To which St. Ambrose replied, "When I am at Milan, I do as they do at Milan; but when I go to Rome, I do as Rome does." (*Epistle* xxxvi.) Compare 2 Kings v. 18, 19.

Rome of the West. Aachen, or Aix la Chapelle, the favourite city of Charlemagne, where, when he died, he was seated, embalmed, on a throne, with the Bible on his lap, his sword (La Joyeuse) by his side, the imperial crown on his head, and his sceptre and shield at his feet. So well had the Egyptians embalmed him, that he seemed only to be asleep.

Rome was not Built in a Day. Achievements of great pith and moment are not accomplished without patient perseverance and a considerable interval of time. The French say, "*Grand bien ne vient pas en peu d'heures,*" but the English proverb is to be found in the French also: "*Rome n'a pas été faite en un jour.*" (1615.)

Rome was not built in a day, like Anchiale, of Cilicia, where Sardanapalus was buried. It is said that Anchiale was actually built in a day.

Rome's best Wealth is Patriotism. So said Mettius Curtius, when he jumped into the chasm which the soothsayers gave out would never close till Rome threw therein "its best wealth."

Romeo (*A*). A devoted lover; a lady's man; from Romeo in Shakespeare's tragedy. (See *Romeo and Juliet.*)

" James in an evil hour went forth to woo
  Young Juliet Hart, and was her Romeo."
         Crabbe: Borough.

Romeo and Juliet (*Shakespeare*). The story is taken from a poetical version by Arthur Brooke of ·Boisteau's novel, called *Rhomeo and Julietta.* Boisteau borrowed the main incidents from a story by Luigi da Porto, of Vicenza (1535), entitled *La Giulietta.* In many respects it resembles the *Ephesi′aca* (in ten books) of Ephe′sius Xenophon, whose novel recounts the loves of Habroc′omas and Anthia.

Rom′ulus. *We need no Romulus to account for Rome.* We require no hypothetical person to account for a plain fact.

☸ Romulus and Remus were suckled by a wolf; Atalanta by a she-bear.

Ron or **Rone.** The name of Prince Arthur's spear, made of ebony.

" His spere he nom [took] an honde, tha Ron was
   thaten [called]."
      Layamon: Brut (twelfth century).

Ronald. Lord Ronald gave Lady Clare a lily-white doe as a love-token, and the cousins were to be married on the following day. Lady Clare opened her heart to Alice the nurse, and was then informed that she was not Lady Clare at all, but the nurse's child, and that Lord Ronald was rightful heir to the estate. "Lady" Clare dressed herself as a peasant, and went to reveal the mystery to her lord. Ronald replied, "If you are not the heiress born, we will be married to-morrow, and you shall still be Lady Clare." (*Tennyson.*)

Roncesvalles (4 syl.). A defile in the Pyrenees, famous for the disaster which here befell the rear of Charlemagne's army, on the return march from Saragossa. Ganelon betrayed Roland, out of jealousy, to Marsillus, King of the Saracens, and an ambuscade attacking the Franks, killed every man of them. Amongst the slain were Roland, Oliver, Turpin, and Mitaine, the emperor's godchild. An account of this attack is given in the epilogue of *Croquemitaine;* but the historical narrative is derived from Eginhard.

Rondo. *Father of the rondo.* Jean Baptiste Davaux ; but Gluck was the first to introduce the musical rondo into France, in the opera of *Orpheus.*

Rone (1 syl.). (*See* RON.)

Ron'yon or **Ronion.** A term of contempt to a woman. It is the French *rogneux* (scabby, mangy).

"You hag, you baggage, you polecat, you ronyon ! out, out !"—*Shakespeare : Merry Wives of Windsor,* iv. 2.

" 'Aroint thee, witch !' the rump-fed ronyon cries." *Shakespeare : Macbeth,* i. 3.

Rood Lane (London). So called from a rood or " Jesus on the Cross " placed there, and in Roman Catholic times held in great veneration.

Rood-loft (*The*). The screen between the nave and chancel, where the rood or crucifix was elevated. In some cases, on each side of the crucifix were either some of the evangelists or apostles, and especially the saint to whom the church was dedicated.

" And then to zee the rood-loft,
Zo bravely zet with zaints."
Percy : Ballad of Plain Truth, ii. 292.

Roodselken. Vervain, or " the herb of the cross."

" Hallowed be thou, vervain, as thou growest in the ground,
For in the Mount of Calvary thou wast found.
Thou healedst Christ our Saviour, and staunchedst His bleeding wound.
In the name of Father, Son and Holy Ghost, I take thee from the ground."
Folkard : Plant Lore, p. 47.

Rook (*A*). A cheat. " To rook," to cheat ; " to rook a pigeon," to fleece a greenhorn. Sometimes it simply means, to win from another at a game of chance or skill. (*See* ROOKERY.)

" 'My Lord Marquis,' said the king, 'you rooked me at piquet last night, for which disloyal deed thou shalt now atone, by giving a couple of pieces to this honest youth, and five to the girl.' "—*Sir Walter Scott : Peveril of the Peak,* chap. xxx.

Rook's Hill (Lavant, Chichester), celebrated for the local tradition that the golden calf of Aaron is buried there.

Rook'ery (3 syl.). Any low neighbourhood frequented by thieves and vagabonds. A person fleeced or liable to be fleeced is a pigeon, but those who prey upon these " gulls " are called rooks.

" The demolition of rookeries has not proved an efficient remedy for overcrowding."—*A. Egmont Hake : Free Trade in Capital,* chap. xv.

Rooky Wood (*The*). Not the wood where rooks do congregate, but the *misty* or dark wood. The verb *reek* (to emit vapour) had the preterite *roke,*

rook, or *roak ;* hence Hamilton, in his *Wallace,* speaks of the " rooky mist."

" Light thickens, and the crow
Makes wing to the roaky wood."
Shakespeare : Macbeth, iii. 2.

Room. *Your room is better than your company,* occurs in Green's *Quip for an Upstart Courtier.*

Roost. A strong current or furious tide betwixt island groups.

" This lofty promontory is constantly exposed to the current of a strong and furious tide, which setting in betwixt the Orkney and Zetland islands, and running with force only inferior to that of the Pentland Frith, . . . is called the Roost of Sumburgh [from the headland]."—*Sir Walter Scott : The Pirate,* chap. i.

Roost. *Gone to roost.* Gone to bed. (Anglo-Saxon, *hrost.*)

" The chough and crow to roost are gone."
Glee (words by Joanna Baillie, music by Bishop).

Rope. The Brahmin teaches that " whoever hangs himself will wander eternally with a rope round his neck." (*Asiatic Researches.*)

Rope. *To fight with a rope round one's neck.* To fight with a certainty of being hanged unless you conquer.

" You must send in a large force ; . . . for, as he fights with a rope round his neck, he will struggle to the last."—*Kingston : The Three Admirals,* viii.

To give one rope enough. To permit a person to continue in wrong-doing, till he reaps the consequences.

Rope. *You carry a rope in your pocket* (French). Said of a person very lucky at cards, from the superstition that a bit of rope with which a man has been hanged, carried in the pocket, secures luck at cards.

" ' You have no occupation ?' said the Bench, inquiringly, to a vagabond at the bar. ' Beg your worship's pardon, was the rejoinder : ' I deal in bits of halter for the use of gentlemen as plays.' "—*The Times (French correspondent).*

Rope-dancer (*The*). Yvo de Grentmesnil, the crusader, one of the leaders of Robert, Duke of Normandy's party against Henry I. of England.

" Ivo was one of those who escaped from Antioch when it was besieged. He was let down by a rope over the wall, and hence called 'The Rope-dancer.' "—*Gentleman's Magazine.*

Rope-dancers. Jacob Hall, in the reign of Charles II., greatly admired by the Duchess of Cleveland.

Richer, the celebrated rope-dancer at Sadler's Wells (1658).

Signora Violante, in the reign of Queen Anne.

The Turk who astonished everyone who saw him, in the reign of George II.

Froissart (vol. iv. chap. xxxviii. fol. 47) tells us of " a mayster from Geane," who either slid or walked down a rope suspended to the highest house on St. Michael's bridge and the tower of Our Lady's church, when Isabel of Bavaria made her public entry into Paris. Some say he descended dancing, placed a crown on Isabel's head, and then reascended.

A similar performance was exhibited in London, February 19th, 1546, before Edward VI. The rope was slung from the battlements of St. Paul's steeple. The performer of this feat was a man from Aragon.

The same trick was repeated when Felipe of Spain came to marry Queen Mary. (See *Holinshed : Chronicle*, iii. p. 1121.)

Rope-walk [*barristers' slang*]. Old Bailey practice. Thus, " Gone into the rope-walk " means, he has taken up practice in the Old Bailey. (*See* ROPES.)

The ways of London low life are called "ropes," and to *know the ropes* means to be *au fait* with the minutiæ of all sorts of dodges. (*See* ROPES.)

Ropes. *Fought back to the ropes.* Fought to the bitter end. A pugilistic phrase.

" It is a battle that must be fought game, and right back to the ropes."—*Boldrewood : Robbery Under Arms*, chap. xxxiii.

Ropes. Tricks, artifices. A term in horse-racing. To rope a horse is to pull it in or restrain its speed, to prevent its winning a race. When a boxer or any other athlete loses for the purpose, he is accused of roping. " To know the ropes " is to be up to all the dodges of the sporting world. Of course, the *ropes* mean the reins.

" I am no longer the verdant country squire, the natural prey of swindlers, blacklegs, and sharks. No, sir, I 'know the ropes,' and these gentry would find me but sorry sport."—*Truth : Queer Story*, September 3rd, 1885.

Ropes. *She is on her high ropes.* In a distant and haughty temper. The allusion is to a rope-dancer, who looks down on the spectators. The French say, *Etre monté sur ses grands chevaux* (to be on your high horse).

Roper. Margaret Roper was buried with the head of her father, Sir Thomas More, in her arms.

" Her, who clasped in her last trance
Her murdered father's head." *Tennyson.*

Mistress Roper. A cant name given to the *marines* by British sailors. The wit, of course, lies in the awkward way that marines handle the ship's ropes.

To marry Mistress Roper is to enlist in the marines.

Roque (1 syl.). A blunt, feeling old man in the service of Donna Floranthe. (*George Colman : The Mountaineers.*)

Saint Roque. Patron saint of those who suffer from plague or pestilence; this is because " he worked miracles on the plague-stricken, while he was himself smitten with the same judgment."

Roque Guinart. A famous robber, whose true name was Pédro Rocha Guinarda, leader of *los Nicerros*, which, with the *los Cadelles*, levied heavy contributions on all the mountain districts of Catalo'nia in the seventeenth century. He was a Spanish Rob Roy, and was executed in 1616. (*Pellicer.*)

Roquelaure. A cloak; so called from the Duke de Roquelaure. (George II.)

" 'Your honour's roquelaure,' replied the corporal, 'has not once been had on since the night before your honour received your wound.'"—*Sterne : Tristram Shandy ; Story of Le Fevre.*

Rory O'More. Slang for *a door*. (Explained under the word CHIVY.)

Ros-crana. Daughter of Cormac, King of Moi-lena, wife of Fingal. (*Ossian : Tamora*, iv.)

Ro'sa (*Salva'tor*). An Italian painter, noted for his scenes of savage nature, gloomy grandeur, and awe-creating magnificence. (1615-1673.)

" Whate'er Lorrain light touched with softened hue,
Or savage Rosa dashed, or learnèd Poussin drew."
Thomson : Castle of Indolence, canto i.

Rosabelle. The favourite palfrey of Mary Queen of Scots. (*See* HORSE.)

" I could almost swear I am at this moment mounted on my own favourite Rosabelle, who was never matched in Scotland for swiftness, for ease of motion, and for sureness of foot."—*Sir W. Scott : The Abbot*, chap. xxxvi.

Rosa'lia or **St. Rosalie.** A native of Palermo, who was carried by angels to an inaccessible mountain, where she lived for many years in the cleft of a rock, a part of which she wore away with her knees in her devotions. If anyone doubts it, let him know that a rock with a hole in it may still be seen, and folks less sceptical have built a chapel there, with a marble statue, to commemorate the event.

" That grot where olives nod,
Where, darling of each heart and eye,
From all the youths of Sicily,
St. Rosalie retired to God."
Sir Walter Scott : Marmion, i. 23.

St. Rosalia, in Christian art, is depicted in a cave with a cross and skull, or else in the act of receiving a rosary or chaplet of roses from the Virgin.

Ros'alind. Daughter of the banished duke, but brought up with Celia in the court of Frederick, the duke's brother, and usurper of his dominions. When Rosalind fell in love with Orlando, Duke Frederick said she must leave his house and join her father in the forest of Arden. Celia resolved to go with her, and the two ladies started on their journey. For better security, they changed their names and assumed disguises ; Celia dressed herself as a peasant-girl, and took for the nonce the name of Aliena : Rosalind dressed as her brother, and called herself Gan'ymede. They took up their quarters in a peasant's cottage, where they soon encountered Orlando, and (to make a long tale short) Celia fell in love with Oliver, the brother of Orlando, and Rosalind obtained her father's consent to marry Orlando. (*Shakespeare : As You Like It.*)

Ros'alind, in the *Shepherds' Calendar,* is the maiden vainly beloved by Colin Clout, as her choice was fixed on a shepherd named Menalcas. (*See below.*)

Ros'alinde (3 syl.). The anagram of "Rose Danil" or "Rose Daniel," with whom Spenser was in love, but the young lady married John Florio, lexicographer. In the *Shepherds' Calendar* Rose is called "Rosalinde," and Spenser calls himself "Colin Clout." Shakespeare introduces John Florio in *Love's Labour's Lost,* under the imperfect anagram Holofernes ('*Hnes Floreo*).

Ros'aline (3 syl.). A negress of sparkling wit and great beauty, attending on the Princess of France, and loved by Lord Biron', a nobleman in the suite of Ferdinand, King of Navarre. (*Shakespeare : Love's Labour's Lost.*)

Ros'amond (*Fair*). Higden, monk of Chester, says : "She was the fayre daughter of Walter, Lord Clifford, concubine of Henry II., and poisoned by Queen Elianor, A.D. 1177. Henry made for her a house of wonderfull working, so that no man or woman might come to her. This house was named Labyrinthus, and was wrought like unto a knot in a garden called a maze. But the queen came to her by a clue of thredde, and so dealt with her that she lived not long after. She was buried at Godstow, in an house of nunnes, with these verses upon her tombe :—

"Hic jacet in tumba Rosa mundi, non Rosa
   munda ;
Non redolet, sed olet, quæ redole're solet."
Here Rose the graced, not Rose the chaste, re-
   poses ;
The smell that rises is no smell of roses. *E. C. B.*

. Rosamond Clifford is introduced by Sir Walter Scott in two of his novels— *The Talisman* and *Woodstock.*

"Jane Clifford was her name, as books aver ;
Fair Rosamond was but her *nom de guerre.*"
   Dryden ; Epilogue to Henry II.

Rosa'na. Daughter of the Queen of Armenia. She aided the three sons of St. George to quench the seven lamps of the Knight of the Black Castle. (*The Seven Champions of Christendom,* ii. 8-9.) (*See* LAMPS.)

Ro'sary [*the rose article*]. A name given to the bead-roll employed by Roman Catholics for keeping count of their repetitions of certain prayers. It consists of three parts, each of which contains five mysteries connected with Christ or His virgin mother. The entire roll consists of 150 *Ave Marias,* 15 *Pater Nosters,* and 15 doxologies. The word is said by some to be derived from the chaplet of beads, perfumed with roses, given by the Virgin to St. Dominic. (This cannot be correct, as it was in use A.D. 1100.) Others say the first chaplet of the kind was made of rosewood ; others, again, maintain that it takes its name from the "Mystical Rose," one of the titles of the Virgin. The set is sometimes called "fifteens," from its containing 15 "doxologies," 15 "Our Fathers," and 10 times 15 or 150 "Hail Marys." (Latin, *rosarium.*)

. The "Devotion of the Rosary" takes different forms :—(1) *the Greater Rosary,* or recitation of the whole fifteen mysteries ; (2) *the Lesser Rosary,* or recitation of one of the mysteries ; and (3) *the Living Rosary,* or the recitation of the fifteen mysteries by fifteen different persons in combination.
In regard to the "rosewood," this etymology is extremely doubtful. The beads are now made of berries, wood, stone, ivory, metal, etc., sometimes of considerable value.

Ros'ciad. A satire published by Charles Churchill in 1761 ; it canvasses the faults and merits of the metropolitan actors.

Ros'cius. A first-rate actor ; so called from the Roman Roscius, unrivalled for his grace of action, melody of voice, conception of character, and delivery. He was paid thirty pounds a day for acting ; Pliny says four thousand a year, and Cicero says five thousand.

"What scene of death hath Roscius now to act ?"
   Shakespeare : 3 *Henry VI.,* v. 6.

Another Roscius. So Camden terms Richard Burbage (1566-1619).

The British Roscius. Thomas Betterton, of whom Cibber says, "He alone was born to speak what only Shakespeare knew to write." (1635-1710.)

David Garrick (1716-1779).

The Roscius of France. Michel Boyron, generally called Baron. (1653-1729.)

The Young Roscius. William Henry West Betty, who in fifty-six nights realised £34,000. (Died 1874, aged 84.)

Rose. Sir John Mandeville says— A Jewish maid of Bethlehem (whom Southey names Zillah) was beloved by one Ham'uel, a brutish sot. Zillah rejected his suit, and Hamuel vowed vengeance. He gave out that Zillah was a demoniac, and she was condemned to be burnt; but God averted the flames, the stake budded, and the maid stood unharmed under a rose-tree full of white and red roses, then "first seen on earth since Paradise was lost."

Rose. An emblem of England. It is also the cognisance of the Richmonds, hence the rose in the mouth of one of the foxes which support the shield in the public-house called the *Holland Arms,* Kensington. The daughter of the Duke of Richmond (Lady Caroline Lennox) ran away with Mr. Henry Fox, afterwards Baron Holland of Foxley. So the Fox stole the *Rose* and ran off with it.

Rose. In the language of flowers, different roses have a different signification. For example :—

The Burgundy Rose signifies simplicity and beauty.

The China Rose, grace or beauty ever fresh.

The Daily Rose, a smile.

The Dog Rose, pleasure mixed with pain.

A Faded Rose, beauty is fleeting.

The Japan Rose, beauty your sole attraction.

The Moss Rose, voluptuous love.

The Musk Rose, capricious beauty.

The Provence Rose, my heart is in flames.

The White Rose Bud, too young to love.

The White Rose full of buds, secrecy.

A wreath of Roses, beauty and virtue rewarded.

The Yellow Rose, infidelity.

Rose. *The red rose,* says Sir John Mandeville, sprang from the extinguished brands heaped around a virgin martyr at Bethlehem, named Zillah. (*See* ROSE.)

The Red Rose [of Lancaster]. (*See* ROSES, *The Wars of the Roses.*)

The Red Rose (as a public-house sign). Camden says the red rose was the accepted badge of Edmund Plantagenet, who was the second son of Henry III., and of the first Duke of Lancaster, surnamed Crouchbacke. It was also the cognisance of John of Gaunt, second Duke of Lancaster, in virtue of his wife, who was godchild of Edmund Crouchbacke, and his sole heir. (*See above.*)

The white rose, says Sir John Mandeville, sprang from the unkindled brands heaped around the virgin martyr at Bethlehem. (*See* ROSE.)

The White Rose (as a public-house sign) was *not* first adopted by the Yorkists during the contest for the crown, as Shakespeare says. It was an hereditary cognisance of the House of York, and had been borne by them ever since the title was first created. It was adopted by the Jacobins as an emblem of the Pretender, because his adherents were obliged to abet him *sub rosa* (in secret).

No rose without a thorn. "There is a crook in every lot" (*Boston*); "No joy without alloy;" "There is a poisondrop in man's purest cup;" "Every path hath its puddle" (*Scotch*).

French : "Il n'y a point de roses sans épines," or "Point de rose sans épine ;" "Il n'est si gentil mois d'Avril qui n'ait son chapeau de grésil."

Italian : "Non v'è rosa senza spina ;" "Ogni medaglia ha il suo reverso."

Latin : "Nihil est ab omni parte beatum" (*Horace :* 2 *Odes,* x. 27); "Curtæ nescio quid semper abest rei."

Under the rose (*sub rosa*). In strict confidence. Cupid gave Harpoc'rates (the god of silence) a rose, to bribe him not to betray the amours of Venus. Hence the flower became the emblem of silence. It was for this reason sculptured on the ceilings of banquet-rooms, to remind the guests that what was spoken *sub vino* was not to be uttered *sub divo.* In 1526 it was placed over confessionals. The banquet-room ceiling at Haddon Hall is decorated with roses. (French, *parler sous la rose.*)

Rose (in Christian art). The attribute of St. Dorothe'a, who carries roses in a basket; of St. Casilda, St. Elizabeth of Portugal, and St. Rose of Viterbo, who carry roses either in their hands or caps. St. Rosa'lia, St. An'gelus, St. Rose of Lima, St. Ascylus, St. Victoria, etc., wear crowns of roses.

> "Rose, elle a vecu ce que vivent les roses
>   L'espace d'un matin."
> *Malherbe: A Mme. du Perrier, sur la Morte*
>   *de sa Fille.*

> Like other roses, thy sweet rose survived
>   While shone the morning sun, then drooped
>   and died.   *E. C. B.*

Rose for **Rose-noble.** A gold coin worth 6s. 8d. struck in 1344, under Edward III.; so called because it had a rose, the badge of the Lancastrians and Yorkists.

" De la pistole,
De la guinée, et de l'obole,
Du louis d'or, du ducaton,
De la rose, et du patagon."
Jacques Moreau, in Virgils Travesti.

Rose Sunday. The fourth Sunday in Lent, when the Pope blesses the "Golden Rose." He dips it in balsam, sprinkles it with holy water, and incenses it. Strange as it may seem, Pope Julius II., in 1510, and Leo X. both sent the sacred rose to Henry VIII. In 1856 Isabella II. of Spain received the "Rose;" and both Charlotte, Empress of Mexico, and Eugénie, Empress of France, were honoured by it likewise.

The Rose Alley ambuscade. The attack on Dryden by hired ruffians in the employ of Rochester and the Duchess of Portsmouth, December 18th, 1679. This scandalous outrage was in revenge of a satire by Mulgrave, erroneously attributed to Dryden.

Attacks of this kind were not uncommon in "the age of chivalry;" witness the case of Sir John Coventry, who was waylaid and had his nose slit by some young men of rank for a reflection on the king's theatrical amours. This attack gave rise to the "Coventry Act" against maiming and wounding. Of a similar nature was the cowardly assassination of Mr. Mountford, in Norfolk Street, Strand, by Lord Mohun and Captain Hill, for the hypothetical offence of his admiration for Mrs. Bracegirdle.

The Rose coffee-house, formerly called "The Red Cow," and subsequently "Will's," at the western corner of Bow Street, where John Dryden presided over the literature of the town. "Here," says Malcolm, "appeal was made to him upon every literary dispute." (*Spence : Anecdotes*, p. 263.)

This coffee-house is referred to as "Russell Street Coffee House," and "The Wits' Coffee-house."

" Will's continued to be the resort of the wits at least till 1710. Probably Addison established his servant [Button] in a new house about 1712."— *Spence : Anecdotes*, p. 263.

This Button had been a servant of the Countess of Warwick, whom Addison married; and Button's became the headquarters of the Whig *literati*, as Will's had been of the Tory.

Rose of Jericho. Also called *Rosa Mariæ* or *Rose of the Virgin*.

Rose of Raby (*The*). Cicely, the twelfth and youngest daughter of Ralph Neville, Earl of Westmoreland. (1415-1495.)

Roses. *The Wars of the Roses.* A civil contest that lasted thirty years, in which eighty princes of the blood, a larger portion of the English nobility, and some 100,000 common soldiers were slain. It was a contest between the Lancastrians and Yorkists, whose supporters wore in their caps as badges a red or white rose. the *Red* rose (*gules*) being the cognisance of the House of Lancaster, and the *White* rose (*argent*) being the badge of the House of York. (1455-1485.)

Ro'semary is *Ros-mari'nus* (sea-dew), and is said to be "useful in love-making." The reason is this : Both Venus, the love-goddess, and Rosemary or sea-dew, were offspring of the sea ; and as Love is Beauty's son, Rosemary is his nearest relative.

" The sea his mother Venus came on ;
And hence some reverend men approve
Of rosemary in making love."
Butler : Hudibras, pt. ii. c. 1.

Rosemary, an emblem of remembrance. Thus Ophelia says, "There's rosemary, that's for remembrance." According to ancient tradition, this herb strengthens the memory. As Hungary water, it was once very extensively taken to quiet the nerves. It was much used in weddings, and to wear rosemary in ancient times was as significant of a wedding as to wear a white favour. When the Nurse in *Romeo and Juliet* asks, "Doth not rosemary and Romeo begin both with a [*i.e.* one] letter?" she refers to these emblematical characteristics of the herb. In the language of flowers it means "Fidelity in love."

Rosemary Lane (London), now called *Royal Mint Street.*

Rosewood. So called because when cut it yields a perfume like that of roses.

Ro'sencrantz and Guild'enstern. Time-serving courtiers, willing to betray anyone, and do any "genteel" dirty work to please a king. (*Shakespeare : Hamlet.*)

Roset'ta (Africa). The orchards of Rosetta are filled with turtle-doves.

" Now hangs listening to the doves
In warm Rosetta."
T. Moore : Paradise and the Peri.

Rosetta Stone (*The*). A stone found in 1799 by M. Boussard, a French officer of engineers, in an excavation made at Fort St. Julien, near Rosetta. It has an inscription in three different languages —the hieroglyphic, the demotic, and the Greek. It was erected B.C. 195, in honour of Ptolemy Epiph'anes, because he remitted the dues of the sacerdotal body. The great value of this stone is that it furnished the key whereby the Egyptian hieroglyphics have been deciphered.

Rosicru'cians. Not *rosa crux*, rose cross, but *ros crux*, dew cross. Dew was considered by the ancient chemists as the most powerful solvent of gold; and *cross* in alchemy is the synonym of light, because any figure of a cross contains the three letters L V X (light). "Lux" is the menstruum of the red dragon (*i.e.* corporeal light), and this gross light properly digested produces gold, and dew is the digester. Hence the Rosicrucians are those who used dew for digesting lux or light, with the object of finding the philosopher's stone.

> " As for the Rosycross philosophers,
> Whom you will have to be but sorcerers,
> What they pretend to is no more
> Than Trismegistus did before,
> Pythagoras, old Zoroaster,
> And Apollonius their master."
> *Butler : Hudibras,* pt. ii. 5.

Ross (Celtic). A headland ; as Roslin, Culross, Rossberg, Montrose, Roxburg, Ardrossan, etc.

Ross, from the Welsh *rhos* ("a moor"); found in Welsh and Cornish names, as Rossal, Rusholme, etc.

The Man of Ross. A name given to John Kyrle, a native of Whitehouse, in Gloucestershire. He resided the greater part of his life in the village of Ross, Herefordshire, and died 1724.

> " Who taught that heaven-directed spire to rise ?
> ' The Man of Ross,' each lisping babe replies."
> *Pope : Moral Essays.*

Rosse (2 syl.). A famous sword which the dwarf Elberich gave to Otwit, King of Lombardy. It struck so fine a cut that it left no " gap." It shone like glass, and was adorned with gold. (*See* Sword and Balmung.)

> " This sword to thee I give : it is all bright of hue ;
> Whatever it may cleave, no gap will there ensue,
> From Al'mari I brought it, and Rossë is its name ;
> Wherever swords are drawn, 'twill put them all to shame." *The Heldenbuch.*

Ross'el. One of Reynard's sons. The word means " reddish." (*Reynard the Fox.*)

Rossignol (French). *Rossignol d'Arcadie.* A donkey ; so called because its *bray* is quite as remarkable as the nightingale's song, and Arcadia is called the land of asses and fools. (*See* Fen Nightingale.)

Ros'trum. A pulpit ; properly the beak of a ship. In Rome, the pulpit from which orators addressed the public was ornamented with the rostra or ship-prows taken from the Carthaginians.

Ro'ta or **Rota Men.** A political club formed in 1651 by Harrington, author of *Ocēana.* Its objects were to introduce rotation in office, and voting by ballot. It met at the *Turk's Head,* in New Palace Yard, Westminster, where the members drew up a popular form of commonwealth, which will be found in Harrington's *Oce'ana.* It was called Rota because a third part of the members were *roted out* by ballot every year, and were not eligible for re-election for three years.

Rota Aristote'lica (Aristotle's wheel). A problem in mechanics founded on the motion of a wheel about its axis. First noticed by Aristotle.

Rota Romana. An ecclesiastical court composed of twelve Catholic prelates, to adjudicate when a conflict of rights occurs.

Rote. *To learn by rote* is to learn by turning words round and round in the memory as a wheel. To "learn by heart" is to learn thoroughly (French, *apprendre par cœur*). Shakespeare speaks of the "heart of loss," meaning *entire loss,* and to love with "all our heart" is to love thoroughly. (Latin, *rota,* a wheel.)

> " Take hackney'd jokes from Miller got by rote."
> *Byron : English Bards, etc.*

Rothschild [*Red Shield*]. Mayer Amschel, in 1763, made his appearance in Hanover barefoot, with a sack on his shoulders and a bundle of rags on his back. Successful in trade, he returned to Frankfort and set up a small shop, over which hung the signboard of a *red shield.* As a dealer in old coins he became known to William I., Elector of Hesse-Cassel, who appointed him confidential agent. The serene elector being compelled to fly his country, Mayer Amschel took charge of his cash, amounting to £250,000. When Napoleon was banished to Elba, and the elector returned, Amschel was dead, but his son Anselm restored the money, an act of noble honesty which the elector mentioned at the Congress of Vienna. Hence arose the greatness of the house, which assumed the name of the Red Shield. In 1863 Charles received six millions sterling as his personal share and retiring pension from the firm of the five brothers

Rotten Row. Muster row. Camden derives the word from *rotteran* (to muster) ; hence *rot*, a file of six soldiers. Another derivation is the Norman *Ratten Row* (roundabout way), being the way corpses were carried to avoid the public thoroughfares. Others suggest *Route du roi;* and others the Anglo-Saxon *rot*, pleasant, cheerful ; or *rotten*, referring to the soft material with which the road is covered.

Rotundity of the Belt (Washington Irving). Obesity ; a large projecting paunch ; what Shakespeare calls a "fair round belly with good capon lined." (*As You Like It*, ii. 7.)

Roué. The profligate Duke of Orleans, Regent of France, first used this word in its modern sense. It was his ambition to collect round him companions as worthless as himself, and he used facetiously to boast that there was not one of them who did not deserve to be broken on the *wheel*—that being the most ordinary punishment for malefactors at the time ; hence these profligates went by the name of Orleans' roués or wheels. The most notorious roués were the Dukes of Richelieu, Broglie, Biron, and Brancas, together with Canillac and Nocé ; in England, the Dukes of Rochester and Buckingham.

A notorious roué. A libertine.

Rouen. *Aller à Rouen.* To go to ruin. The French are full of these puns, and our merry forefathers indulged in them also.

(1) *Il a fait son cours à Asnières.* He knows nothing ; he graduated at Dunse [Dunce] College.

(2) *Aller à Cachan.* To give leg-bail, or "*se cacher*" [*de ses créanciers*] ; to go to Hyde [Hide] Park.

(3) *Aller à Dourdan.* To go to be whipped (*douder, être battu*) ; to be on the road to Flogny.

(4) *Vous êtes de Lagny, vous n'avez pas hâte.* I see you are a man of Laggon. Don't hurry yourself, Mr. Slowcoach.

(5) *Il est de Lunel, Il a une chambre à Lunel, Il est des Luniers d'Orléans*, or *Il est Logé à la Lune.* He is a lunatic.

(6) *Envoyer à Mortaigne.* To be slain, or sent to Deadham.

(7) *Aller à Patras.* To die ; to be gathered to one's fathers (*ad patres*).

(8) *Aller à Versailles.* To be going to the bad. Here the pun is between *Versa-illes* and *renverser.* This wretched pun is about equal to such a phrase as "Going to Downham."

The Bloody Feast of Rouen (1356). Charles the Dauphin gave a banquet to his private friends at Rouen, to which his brother-in-law Charles the Bad was invited. While the guests were at table King Jean entered the room with a numerous escort, exclaiming, "Traitor, thou art not worthy to sit at table with my son !" Then, turning to his guards, he added, "Take him hence ! By holy Paul, I will neither eat nor drink till his head be brought me !" Then, seizing an iron mace from one of the men-at-arms, he struck another of the guests between the shoulders, exclaiming, "Out, proud traitor ! by the soul of my father, thou shalt not live !" Four of the guests were beheaded on the spot.

Rouge (*A*), *i.e.* a red cap, a red republican, a democrat.

"She had all the furious prejudices and all the instinctive virtues in her of an uncompromising Rouge."—*Ouida: Under Two Flags*, chap. xxxiv.

Rouge Croix. One of the pursuivants of the heraldic establishment. So called from the red cross of St. George, the patron saint of England.

Rouge Dragon. The pursuivant founded by Henry VII. ; it was the ensign of Cadwaladyr, the last king of the Britons, an ancestor of Henry Tudor.

Rouge et Noir (French, *red and black*). A game of chance ; so called because of the red and black diamonds marked on the board. The dealer deals out to noir first till the sum of the pips exceeds thirty, then to rouge in the same manner. That packet which comes nearest to thirty-one is the winner of the stakes.

Rough-hewn. Shaped in the rough, not finished, unpolished, ill-mannered, raw ; as a "rough-hewn seaman" (Bacon) ; a "rough-hewn discourse" (Howel).

Rough Music, called in Somersetshire *skimmity-riding*, and by the Basques *toberac.* A ceremony which takes place after sunset, when the performers, to show their indignation against some man or woman who has outraged propriety, assemble before the house, and make an appalling din with bells, horns, tin pans, and other noisy instruments.

Rough-shod. *Riding rough-shod over one.* Treating one without the least consideration. The allusion is to riding a horse rough-shod.

Rough and Ready. Said to be derived from Colonel Rough, who was in the battle of Waterloo. The story says that the Duke of Wellington used to say "Rough and ready, colonel," and the family adopted the words as their motto.

Rough and Ready. So General Zachary Taylor, twelfth president of the United States, was called. (1786-1853.)

Roughs (*The*). The coarse, ill-behaved rabble, without any of the polish of good breeding.

Roun'cival. Large; of gigantic size. Certain large bones of antediluvian animals were at one time said to be the bones of the heroes who fell with Roland in Roncesvalles. "Rounceval peas" are those large peas called "marrowfats," and a very large woman is called a *rouncival*.

"Hereof, I take it, it comes that seeing a great woman, we say she is a *rouncival*."—*Mandeville.*

Round. A watchman's beat. He starts from one point, and comes round again to the same place.

To walk the Round. The lawyers used frequently to give interviews to their clients in the Round church; and "walking the Round" meant loitering about the Round church, under the hope of being hired for a witness.

Round (*To*). To whisper. (Anglo-Saxon, *runian*; German, *raunen*, to whisper.) (*See* ROUNDED.)

That lesson which I will round you in the ear—which I will whisper in your ear. (*Bunyan: Pilgrim's Progress.*)

"France .... rounded in the ear with [by] ... commodity [self-interest] hath resolved to [on] a most base ... peace."—*Shakespeare : King John,* ii. 1.

"And ner the feend he drough as nought ne were, Ful prively, and rouned in his'eere, 'Herkë, my brother, herkë, by thi faith ...'"   *Chaucer: Canterbury Tales,* 7132.

Round Dealing. Honest, straightforward dealing, without branching off into underhand tricks, or deviating from the straight path into the by-ways of finesse.

"Round dealing is the honour of man's nature."—*Bacon.*

Round Numbers (*In*). In whole numbers, without regarding the fractions. Thus we say the population of the British Isles is forty millions in round numbers, and that of London four millions (1895). The idea is that what is round is whole or perfect, and, of course, fractions, being broken numbers, cannot belong thereto

Round Peg. *Round peg in the square hole,* and *square peg in the round hole.* The wrong man in the wrong place; especially applied to government officials. The expression was used in 1855, by Mr. Layard, speaking of the "Administration Reform Association." The allusion is to such games as cribbage, German tactics, etc.

In 1804, Sydney Smith, in his *Moral Philosophy,* said : "You choose to represent the various parts in life by holes upon a table. ... We shall generally find that the triangular person has got into the square hole, the oblong into the triangular hole, and the round person has squeezed himself into the square hole."

Round Robin. A petition or protest signed in such a way that no name heads the list. Of course, the signatures are placed in a circular form. The device is French, and the term is a corruption of *rond* (round) *ruban* (a ribbon). It was first adopted by the officers of government as a means of making known their grievances.

Round Sum. *A good round sum.* A large sum of money. Shakespeare says the Justice has a "big round belly, with good capon lined ; " and the notion of puffed out or bloated is evidently the idea of Shylock when he says to Bassa'nio, "'Tis a good round sum."

Round Table. Made by Merlin at Carduel for Uter Pendragon. Uter gave it to King Leodegraunce, of Camelyard, and King Leodegraunce gave it to Arthur when the latter married Guinever, his daughter. It seated 150 knights, and a place was left in it for the San Graal.

What is usually meant by Arthur's Round Table is a smaller one for the accommodation of twelve favourite knights. Henry VIII. showed François I. the table at Winchester, which he said was the one used by the British king.

The Round Table, says Dr. Percy, was not peculiar to the reign of King Arthur, but was common in all the ages of chivalry. Thus the King of Ireland, father of the fair Christabelle, says in the ballad—

"Is there never a knighte of my round table This matter will undergo ?"   *Sir Cauline.*

Round Table. In the eighth year of Edward I., Roger de Mortimer established a Round Table at Kenilworth for "the encouragement of military pastimes." At this foundation 100 knights and as many ladies were entertained at the founder's expense. About seventy years later, Edward III. erected a splendid table at Windsor. It was 200 feet in diameter, and the expense of entertaining the knights thereof amounted to £100 a week.

A round table. A tournament. "So called by reason that the place wherein they practised those feats was environed with a strong wall made in a round form" (*Dugdale*). We still talk of *table-land.*

Holding a round table. Proclaiming or holding a grand tournament. Matthew of Paris frequently calls justs and tournaments *Hastilu'dia Mensæ Rotundæ* (lance games of the Round Table).

Knights of the Round Table. There were 150 knights who had "sieges" at the table. King Leodegraunce brought over 100 when, at the wedding of his daughter Guinever, he gave the table to King Arthur; Merlin filled up twenty-eight of the vacant seats, and the king elected Gawaine and Tor; the remaining twenty were left for those who might prove worthy. (*History of Prince Arthur,* 45, 46.)

Knights of the Round Table. The most celebrated are *Sirs* Acolon,* Ag'-ravain, Am'oral of Wales, Ball'amore,* Banier, Beaumans,* Beleo'bus,* Bevidere, Belvour,* Bersunt,* Bliom'beris, Borro *or* Bors * (Arthur's natural son), Brandiles, Brunor, Caradoc the Chaste (the only knight who could quaff the golden cup), Col'grevance, Din'adam, Driam, Dodynas the Savage, Eric, Floll,* Galahad *or* Galaad the Modest,* Gareth,* Gaheris,* Galohalt,* Gawain *or* Gauwin the Gentle * (Arthur's nephew), Grislet,* Hector of Mares (1 syl.) *or* Ector of Marys,* Iwein *or* Ewaine * (also written Yvain), Kay,* Ladynas, Lamereck *or* Lamerock,* Lancelot *or* Launcelot du Lac * (the seducer of Arthur's wife), Lanval of the Fairy Lance, Lavain, Lionell,* Lucan, Marhaus,* Melia'dus, Mordred the Traitor (Arthur's nephew), Morolt *or* Morhault of the Iron Mace, Pag'inet,* Palamede *or* Palame'dès,* Phar'amond, Pell'eas,* Pell'inore, Persuant of Inde (meaning of the *indigo* or blue armour), Per'civall,* Peredur, Ryence, Sag'ra-mour le Desirus, Sa'gris,* Super'bilis,* Tor *or* Torres * (reputed son of Aries the cowherd), Tristram *or* Tristran the Love-lòrn,* Tur'quine,* Wig'alois, Wig'amor, Ywain (*see* Iwein).

∴ The thirty marked with a star (*) are seated with Prince Arthur at the Round Table, in the frontispiece of the *Famous History of the Renowned Prince Arthur.*

" There Galaad sat with manly grace,
    Yet maiden meekness in his face ;
There Morolt of the iron mace,
    And love-lorn Tristrem there;
And Dinadam with lively glance,
And Lanval with the fairy lance,
And Mordred with his looks askance,
    Brunor and Bevidere.
Why should I tell of numbers more ?
Sir Cay, Sir Banier, and Sir Bore,
    Sir Caradoc the keen,
The gentle Gawa'in's courteous lore,
Hector de Mares, and Pellinore,
And Lancelot, that evermore
    Looked stol'n-wise on the queen."
Sir Walter Scott: Bridal of Triermain, ii. 15.

Knights of the Round Table. Their chief exploits occurred in quest of the San Graal or Holy Cup, brought to Britain by Joseph of Arimathe'a.

Harcourt's Round Table. (*See* HARCOURT'S . . .)

Round as a Ball; . . . as an apple, as an orange, etc.

Roundabout (*A*). A Pict's camp.

" His desire of his companion a Pict's camp, or Roundabout."—*Sir W. Scott: The Antiquary,* chap. i.

Roundheads. Puritans; so called because they wore their hair short, while the Royalists wore long hair covering their shoulders.

" And ere their butter 'gan to coddle,
A bullet churnd i' th' Roundhead's noddle."
Men Miracles, p. 43 (1656).

Roundle, in heraldry, is a charge of a round or circular form. They are of eight sorts, distinguished by their tinctures: (1) a *Bezant,* tincture " or ; " (2) a *Plate,* tincture " argent ; " (3) a *Torteau,* tincture " gules ; " (4) a *Hurt,* tincture " azure ; " (5) an *Ogress or Pellet,* tincture " sable ; " (6) a *Golpe,* tincture " purpure ; " (7) a *Guze,* tincture " sanguine ; " (8) an *Orange,* tincture " tenney."

Rounfl. So the Britons called ogres, and the servants or attendants of the ogres they called *Grewnds.*

Rouse (*A*). A contraction of ca-rousal, a drinking bout. (Swedish, *rus ;* Norwegian, *ruus,* drunkenness ; Dutch, *roes,* a bumper.) Rouse (1 syl.).

" The king doth wake to-night, and takes his rouse."   Shakespeare : Hamlet. i. 4.

Rou'sing. *A rousing good fire.* Rousing means large, great; hence a *rousing falsehood (mendacium magnif'i-cum).*

Rout (*A*). A large evening party. (Welsh, *rhawter,* a crowd.) (*See* DRUM, HURRICANE, etc.)

Rou'tiers. Adventurers who made war a trade and let themselves out to anyone who would pay them. So called because they were always on the *route* or moving from place to place. (Twelfth century.)

Rove (1 syl.). To shoot with roving arrows—*i.e.* arrows shot at a roving mark, either in height or distance.

To shoot at rovers. To shoot at certain marks of the target so called; to shoot at random without any distinct aim.

"Unbelievers are said by Clobery to 'shoot at rovers.'"—*Divine Glimpses*, p. 4 (1659).

Running at rovers. Running wild; being without restraint.

Row (rhyme with *now*). A tumult. It used to be written *roue*, and referred to the night encounters of the roués or profligate bon-vivants whose glory it was to attack the "Charleys" and disturb the peace. (See ROUE.)

Row (rhyme with *low*). *The Row* means "Paternoster Row," famous for publishing firms and wholesale booksellers, or Rotten Row (*q.v.*). (Anglo-Saxon, *rāw*, a line.)

Row'dy (rhyme with *cloudy*). A ruffian brawler, a "rough," a riotous or turbulent fellow, whose delight is to make a row or disturbance.

Rowe'na. A Saxon princess, and bride of Ivanhoe. (*Sir Walter Scott: Ivanhoe.*)

Rowland. (See ROLAND.)
Childe Rowland. Youngest brother of the "fair burd Helen." Guided by Merlin, he undertook to bring back his sister from Elf-land, whither the fairies had carried her, and succeeded in his perilous exploit. (*Ancient Scotch ballad.*)

"Childe Rowland to the dark tower came;
His word was still 'Fie, foh, and fum,
I smell the blood of a Britishman.'"
Shakespeare: King Lear, iii. 4.

Rowley (*Thomas*). The fictitious priest of Bristol, said by Chatterton to have been the author of certain poems which he (Chatterton) published.

Rowned in the Ear. Whispered in the ear. The old word *rown*, *rowned* (to whisper, to talk in private). Polonius says to the king in *Hamlet*—"Let his queen-mother all alone entreat him to show his grief—let her be rowned with him;" not blunt and loud, but in *private converse.* (See ROUND, To.)

Roxburghe Club for printing rare works or MSS., the copies being rigidly confined to members of the club. It was called after John, Duke of Roxburghe, a celebrated collector of ancient literature, who died 1812. Since the establishment of this club, others of a similar character have sprung up, as (1) the Camden, Cheetham, Percy, Shakespeare, Surtees, and Wharton, in England; (2) the Abbotsford, Bannatyne, Maitland, and Spalding, in Scotland: and (3) the Celtic Society of Ireland.

Roy (*Le*) [or **la Reine**] **s'avisera.** This is the royal veto, last put in force March 11, 1707, when Queen Anne refused her assent to a Scotch Militia Bill.

During the agitation for Catholic emancipation, George III. threatened a veto, but the matter was not brought to the test.

Royal Arms worn by a subject. (See LANE.)

Royal Goats (*The*). The Royal Welsh Fusiliers, noted for their nanny-goat. This gallant regiment was at Blenheim, Oudenarde, Malplaquet, Dettingen, Vittoria, Alma, Inkermann, and many another field.

Royal Merchant. In the thirteenth century the Venetians were masters of the sea, and some of their wealthy merchants—as the Sanu dos, the Justinia'ni, the Grimal'di, and others—erected principalities in divers places of the Archipelago, which their descendants enjoyed for many centuries. These self-created princes were called "royal merchants." (*Warburton.*)

"Glancing an eye of pity on his losses,
That have of late so huddled on his back,
Enough to press a royal merchant down."
Shakespeare: Merchant of Venice, iv. 1.

⁂ Sir Thomas Gresham was called a "royal merchant."

Royal Road to Learning. Euclid, having opened a school of mathematics at Alexandria, was asked by King Ptolemy whether he could not explain his art to him in a more compendious manner. "Sire," said the geometrician, "there is no royal road to learning."

Royal Titles. (1) Of England— Henry IV. was styled *His Grace;* Henry VI., *His Excellent Grace;* Edward IV., *High and Mighty Prince;* Henry VII., *His Grace* and *His Majesty;* Henry VIII., *His Highness*, then *His Majesty*. Subsequently kings were styled *His Sacred Majesty*. Our present style is *Her Most Gracious Majesty.*

(2) *Royal titles*, their meaning: Abimelech (*Father King*). Autocrat (*self-potentate*, i.e. *absolute*). Cæsar (*in compliment*

to Julius Cæsar). Calif (*successor*). Cham (*chieftain*). Czar (*autocrat*, a contraction of *Samodersheta*). Darius (*holder of the empire*). Duke (*leader*). Emperor (*commander*). Hospodar (*Slavonic, master of the house*). Kaiser (*Cæsar*). Khan (*provincial chief*). Khedive (*suzerain*). King (*father*). Landgrave (*land reeve*). Maharajah (*great sovereign*). Margrave (*border reeve*). Nejus (*lord protector*). Nizam (*ruler*). Pharaoh (*light of the world*). Queen (*mother*). Rajah (*prince or sovereign*). Shah or Padishah (*protector, sceptred protector*). Sheik (*elder*). Sultan (*ruler*).

Royston (Herts) means king's town ; so called in honour of King Stephen, who erected a cross there. (French, *roy*.)
A Royston horse and Cambridge Master of Arts will give way to no one. A Cambridgeshire proverb. Royston was a village famous for malt, which was sent to London on horseback. These heavy-laden beasts never moved out of the way. The Masters of Arts, being the great dons of Cambridge, had the wall conceded to them by the inhabitants out of courtesy.

Rozinante (4 syl.). A wretched jade of a riding-horse. Don Quixote's horse was so called. (Spanish, *rocin-ante*, a hack before.)
   " It is the only time he will sit behind the wretched Rosinante, and it would be Quixotic of him to expect speed."—*London Review.*

(*See* HORSE.)

Ruach. The Isle of Winds, visited by Pantag'ruel and his fleet on their way to the Oracle of the Holy Bottle, is the isle of windy hopes and unmeaning flattery. The people of this island live on nothing but wind, eat nothing but wind, and drink nothing but wind. They have no other houses but weathercocks, seeing everyone is obliged to shift his way of life to the ever-changing caprice of court fashion ; and they sow no other seeds but the wind-flowers of promise and flattery. The common people get only a fan-puff of food very occasionally, but the richer sort banquet daily on huge mill-draughts of the same unsubstantial stuff. (*Rabelais : Pantag'ruel*, iv. 43.)

Rub. An impediment. The expression is taken from bowls, where "rub" means that something hinders the free movement of your bowl.
   " Without rub or interruption."—*Swift.*
   " Like a bowle that runneth in a smooth allie, without anie rub."—*Stanihurst,* p. 10.

Rubber of Whist (*A*). A game of cards called "whist." "Rubber" is

transferred from bowls, in which the collision of two balls is a rubber, because they rub against each other.

Rubens' Women. The portrait of Helena Forman or Fourment, his second wife, married at the age of 16, introduced in several of his historical paintings ; but the woman in *Rubens and His Wife*, in the Munich gallery, is meant for Isabella Brandt, of Antwerp, his first wife.

Ru'bi. One of the Cherubim or "Spirits of Knowledge," who was present when Eve walked in Paradise. He felt the most intense interest in her, and longed, as the race increased, to find one of her daughters whom he could love. He fixed upon Lir'is, young and proud, who thirsted for knowledge, and cared not what price she paid to obtain it. After some months had elapsed, Liris asked her angel lover to let her see him in his full glory ; so Rubi showed himself to her in all his splendour, and she embraced him. Instantly Liris was burnt to ashes by the radiant light, and the kiss she gave on the angel's forehead became a brand, which shot agony into his brain. That brand was " left for ever on his brow," and that agony knew no abatement. (*Thomas Moore : Loves of the Angels,* story ii.)

Ru'bicon. *To pass the Rubicon.* To adopt some measure from which it is not possible to recede. Thus, when the Austrians, in 1859, passed the Tici'no, the act was a declaration of war against Sardinia ; and in 1866, when the Italians passed the Adige, it was a declaration of war against Austria. The Rubicon was a small river separating ancient Italy from Cisalpine Gaul (the province allotted to Julius Cæsar). When Cæsar crossed this stream he passed beyond the limits of his own province and became an invader of Italy.

Rubo'nax. Sir Philip Sidney says, Rubonax " was driven by a poet's verses to hang himself." (*Defence of Poesie.*)

Rubric (from the Latin *rubrica*, "red ochre," or "vermilion"). An ordinance or law was by the Romans called a rubric, because it was written with vermilion, in contradistinction to prætorian edicts or rules of the court, which were posted on a *white* ground. (*Juvenal,* xiv. 192.)
   "*Rubrica vetavit*" = the law has forbidden it. (*Persius,* v. 99.)
   " Prætores edicta sua in albo proponebant, ac rubricas [*i.e.* jus civile] translaterunt."—*Quintilian,* xii. 3, 11.

"Rules and orders directing how, when, and where all things in divine service are to be performed were formerly printed in red characters (now generally in italics), and called rubrics."—*Hook: Church Dictionary.*

Ru'by. The King of Ceylon has the finest ruby ever seen. "It is a span long, as thick as a man's arm, and without a flaw." Kublai-Khan offered the value of a city for it, but the king answered that he would not part with it if all the treasures of the world were laid at his feet. (*Marco Polo.*)

Ruby (*The*). The ancients considered the ruby to be an antidote of poison, to preserve persons from plague, to banish grief, to repress the ill effects of luxuries, and to divert the mind from evil thoughts.

Ruby (*The Perfect*). The philosopher's stone. (*See* FLOWER OF THE SUN.)

Ruch'iel. God of the air. (Hebrew, *ruch*, air; *el*, god.) (*Jewish mythology.*)

Rudder. *Who won't be ruled by the rudder must be ruled by the rock.* Who won't listen to reason must bear the consequences, like a ship that runs upon a rock if it will not answer the helm.

Ruddock. The redbreast, "sacred to the household gods." The legend says if a redbreast finds a dead body in the woods it will "cover it with moss." Drayton alludes to this tradition—

" Covering with moss the dead's unclosed eye,
The little redbreast teacheth charitie."
                                        The Owl.

Shakespeare makes Arvir'agus say over Imogen—

"Thou shalt not lack
The flower that's like thy face, pale primrose ; nor
The azured harebell . . . the ruddock would
With charitable bill . . . bring thee all these."
                                        Cymbeline, iv. 2.

So also in the folk tale of *The Babes in the Wood*—

"The Robins so red
Fresh strawberry-leaves did over them spread."

Ruddy-mane [*Bloody-hand*]. The infant son of Sir Mordant: so called because his hand was red with his mother's blood. She had stabbed herself because her husband had been paralysed by a draught from an enchanted stream. (*Spenser: Faërie Queene*, bk. ii. 1, 3.)

Rudge (*Barnaby*). A half-witted lad, who had for his companion a raven. (*Dickens : Barnaby Rudge.*)

Ru'diger (3 syl.). Margrave of Bechelar'en, a wealthy Hun, liegeman of King Etzel. In the *Nibelungen-Lied* he is represented as a most noble character. He was sent to Burgundy by King Etzel, to conduct Kriemhild to Hungary if she would consent to marry the Hunnish king. When Gunther and his suite went to pay a visit to Kriemhild, he entertained them all most hospitably, and gave his daughter in marriage to Kriemhild's youngest brother, Gis'elher ; and when the broil broke out in the dining-hall of King Etzel, and Rudiger was compelled to take part against the Burgundians, he fought with Kriemhild's second brother, Gernot. Rudiger struck Gernot "through his helmet," and the prince struck the margrave "through shield and morion," and "down dead dropped both together, each by the other slain." —*Nibelungen-Lied.*

Rudol'phine Tables (*The*). *Tabulæ Rudolphinæ*, 1627. Astronomical calculations begun by Tycho Brahé, and continued by Kepler, under the immediate patronage of Kaiser Rudolph II., after whom Kepler named the work.

Rudolph gave Tycho Brahé an annuity of £1,500 sterling. George III. gave Herschel an annuity of £200.

Rudolstadt (*La Comtesse de*), or "Consuelo," who marries the Count of Rudolstadt. (*Romance by George Sand : Madame Dudevant.*) (*See* CONSUELO.)

Rudra. Father of the tempest-gods. The word means "run about crying," and the legend says that the boy ran about weeping because he had no name, whereupon Brahma said, "Let thy name be Rud-dra." (Sanskrit, *rud*, weep ; *dra*, run.) (*Vedic mythology.*)

Rue, to grieve for something done, to repent, is the Anglo-Saxon *reow*, contrition; German, *reue*. Rue (1 syl.).

Rue, called "herb of grace," because it was employed for sprinkling holy water. Without doubt it was so used symbolically, because *to rue* means to be sorry, and penitence brings the water of grace with it. (Latin, *ruta*, from the Greek *rhuo*, so called because it sets persons free from disease and death.) (*See* DIFFERENCE.) Ophelia says—

"There's rue for you, and here's some for me !
we may call it 'herb of grace' o' Sundays."—
Shakespeare: Hamlet, iv. 5.

Rue. A slip of land (free of all manorial charges and claims) encompassing or bounding manorial land. It certainly is not derived from the French *rue*, a street, nor is it a corruption of *row*. (*See* REWE.)

Rewe is a roll or slip, hence Ragman's rewe or roll (*q.v.*).

"There is a whole world of curious history contained in the phrase Ragman's rewe, meaning a roll. In *Piers Plowman's Vision*, the pope's bull is called a rewe."—*Edinburgh Review*, July, 1870.

Ruffe (1 syl.). A game at cards, now called *slamm ;* also playing a trump, when one cannot follow suit.

"A swaggerer is one that plays at ruffre, from whence he took the denomination of ruffyn."—*J. H. (Gent.) Satirical Epigrams,* 1619.

Ruffian Hall. That part of West Smithfield which is now the horse-market, where "tryals of skill were plaid by ordinary ruffianly people with sword and buckler." (*Blount,* p. 562.)

Rufus (*The Red*). William II. of England. (1056, 1087–1100.)
Otho II. of Germany ; also called *The Bloody.* (955, 973–983.)
Gilbert de Clare, Earl of Gloucester, son-in-law of Edward I. (Slain 1313.)

Ruggie'ro. (*See* ROGERO.)

Rukenaw (*Dame*). The ape's wife in the tale of *Reynard the Fox.* The word means noisy insolence.

Rule (*St.*) or **St. Reg'ulus,** a monk of Patræ in Achaia, is the real saint of Scotland. He was the first to colonise its metropolitan see, and to convert the inhabitants (370). The name Killrule (*Cella Reg'uli*) perpetuates this fact. St. Andrew superseded the Achæan.

"But I have solemn vows to pay . . .
To far St. Andrew's bound,
Within the ocean-cave to pray,
Where good St. Rule his holy lay
Sung to the billow's sound."
Sir Walter Scott : Marmion, i. 20.

Rule, Britannia. Words by Thomson, author of *The Seasons ;* music by Dr. Arne. It first appeared in a masque entitled *Alfred,* in which the name of David Mallett is associated with that of James Thomson, and some think he was the real author of this "political hymn." (August 1, 1740.)

Rule Nisi. A "rule" is an order from one of the superior courts, and a "rule nisi" is such an order "to show cause." That is, the rule is to be held absolute *unless* the party to whom it applies can "show cause" why it should not be so.

Rule of Thumb (*The*). A rough guess-work measure. Measuring lengths by the thumb. In some places the heat required in brewing is determined by dipping the thumb into the vat.

Rule of thumb. In the legend of *Knockmany Fin,* Mr. Coul says :—

" 'That baste Cucullin [is coming], . . . for my thumb tells me so.' To which his wife replies : 'Well, my Cully, don't be cast down. . . . Maybe I'll bring you better out of this scrape than ever you could bring yourself by your rule of thumb [referring to the pricking of the thumb].' "—*W. B. Yeats : Fairy Tales of the Irish Pea-antry,* p. 270.
Again, p. 274, Fin knew by the "pricking of his thumb" that the giant Cucullin would arrive at two o'clock. In these cases the "rule of thumb" refers to the prognostics of the thumb, referred to by the witches of Macbeth. "By the pricking of my thumbs, something evil this way comes."

Rule of the Road (*The*).

"The rule of the road's an anomaly quite,
In riding or driving along :
If you go to the left you are sure to go right.
If you go to the right you go wrong."

It is not so in France.

Rule the Roost (*To*). The cock rules which of the hens is to have the honour of roosting nearest him. (*See* under ROAST.)

"Geate you nowe up into your pulpittes like bragginge cocks on the rowst, flappe your winges and crowe out aloude."—*Jewell.*

Rum. Queer, quaint, old-fashioned. This word was first applied to Roman Catholic priests, and subsequently to other clergymen. Thus Swift speaks of "a rabble of tenants and rusty dull rums" (country parsons). As these "rusty dull rums" were old-fashioned and quaint, a "rum fellow" came to signify one as odd as a "rusty dull rum."

✢ Professor De Morgan thought that the most probable derivation was from booksellers trading with the West Indies. It is said that in the eighteenth century they bartered books for rum, but set aside chiefly such books as would not sell in England.

Ru'minate (3 syl.). To think, to meditate upon some subject ; properly, "to chew the cud" (Latin, *ru'mino*).

"To chew the cud of sweet and bitter fancy."—*Milton.*
"On a flowery bank he chews the cud."—*Dryden.*

Rumolt. Gunther's chief cook.

"Sore toiled the chief cook, Rumolt; ah ! how h's orders ran
Among his understrappers ! how many a pot and pan,
How many a mighty cauldron rattled and rang again !
They dressed a world of dishes for the expected train."
Lettsom's Nibelungen-Lied, stanza 8½.

Rump-fed, that is, fed on scraps, such as liver, kidneys, chitlings, and other kitchen perquisites.

"Aroint thee, witch ! the rump-fed ronyon cries." *Shakespeare : Macbeth,* i. 3.

✢ A ronyon or ronian is a kitchen

wench fed on scraps (French, *rognon*, a kidney).

Rump Parliament. Oliver Cromwell (1648) sent two regiments to the House of Commons to coerce the members to condemn Charles I. Forty-one were seized and imprisoned in a lower room of the House, 160 were ordered to go home, and the sixty favourable to Cromwell were allowed to remain. These sixty were merely the fag-end or *rump* of the whole House. (*See* PRIDE'S PURGE.)

The name was revived again in the protectorate of Richard Cromwell. Subsequently the former was called *The Bloody Rump*, and the latter *The Rump of a Rump.*

"The few,
Because they're wasted to the stumps,
Are represented best by rumps."
Butler: Hudibras, pt. iii. 2.

Rumpelstilzchen[*Rumple-stilts-skin*]. A passionate little deformed dwarf. A miller's daughter was enjoined by a king to spin straw into gold, and the dwarf did it for her, on condition that she would give him her first child. The maiden married the king, and grieved so bitterly when her first child was born that the dwarf promised to relent if within three days she could find out his name. Two days were spent in vain guesses, but the third day one of the queen's servants heard a strange voice singing—

"Little dreams my dainty dame
Rumpelstilzchen is my name."

The queen, being told thereof, saved her child, and the dwarf killed himself with rage. (*German Popular Stories.*)

Rumping Dozen. A corruption of *Rump and Dozen*, meaning a rump of beef and a dozen of claret; or a rump steak and dozen oysters.

Run. *A long run, a short run.* We say of a drama, "It had a long run," meaning it attracted the people to the house, and was represented over and over again for many nights. The allusion is to a runner who continues his race for a long way. The drama ran on night after night without change.

In the long run. In the final result. This allusion is to race-running: one may get the start for a time, but in the long run, or entire race, the result may be different. The hare got the start, but in the long run the patient perseverance of the tortoise won the race.

To go with a run. A seaman's phrase. A rope goes with a run when it is let

go entirely, instead of being slackened gradually.

Run Amuck. (*See* AMUCK.)
"It was like a Malay running amuck, only with a more deadly weapon."—*The Times.*
"Frontless and satire-proof he scours the streets.
And runs an Indian-muck at all he meets."
Dryden: The Hind and the Panther.

Run a Rig (*To*). To play a trick, to suffer a sportive trick. Thus, John Gilpin, when he set out, "little thought of running such a rig" as he suffered. Florio gives as a meaning of rig, "the tricks of a wanton;" hence frolicsome and deceptive tricks. The rig of a ship means the way it is rigged, hence its appearance; and, as pirates deceive by changing the rig of their vessel, so rig came to mean a trick to deceive, a trick, a frolicsome deception.

Run Riot (*To*). To run wild. A hunting term, meaning to run at a whole herd.

Run Thin (*To*). To start from a bargain. When liquor runs thin it indicates that the cask is nearly empty.

Run a Man Down (*To*). To abuse, depreciate. A hunting term.

Run of the House (*The*). *He has the run of the house.* Free access to it, and free liberty to partake of whatever comes to table. A "run of events" means a series of good, bad, and indifferent, as they may chance to succeed each other. And the "run of the house" means the food and domestic arrangements as they ordinarily occur.

Runs. *The tub runs*—leaks, or lets out water. In this and all similar phrases the verb run means to "be in a running state." Thus we have "the ulcer runs," "the cup runs over," "the rivers run blood," "the field runs with blood."

Runs may Read (*He that*). The Bible quotation in Habakkuk ii. 2 is, "Write the vision, and make it plain, that he may run that readeth it." Cowper says—
"But truths, on which depends our main concern . . .
Shine by the side of every path we tread
With such a lustre, he that runs may read."
Tirocinium.

Running. *Quite out of the running.* Quite out of court, not worthy of consideration. A horse which has been "scratched" is quite out of the running. (*See* SCRATCHED.)

Running Footman. The last of these menials died out with the infamous Duke of Queensberry. In the early part of the eighteenth century no great house was complete without some half-dozen of them. Their duty was to run before and alongside the fat Flemish mares of the period, and advise the innkeeper of the coming guests. The pole which they carried was to help the cumbrous coach of their master out of the numerous sloughs on the northern and western high-roads. (*See* BOW STREET RUNNERS, ESTAFETTE.)

Running Leather. *His shoes are made of running leather.* He is given to roving. Probably the pun is between *roan* and *run.*

Running Thursday. In the beginning of the reign of William III. a rumour ran that the French and Irish Papists had landed; a terrible panic ensued, and the people betook themselves to the country, running for their lives. Joseph Perry says: "I was dismally affrighted the day called Running Thursday. It was that day the report reached our town, and I expected to be killed" (his *Life*). The day in question was Thursday, Dec. 13, 1688.

Running Water. No enchantment can subsist in a living stream; if, therefore, a person can interpose a brook betwixt himself and the witches, spritos, or goblins chasing him, he is in perfect safety. Burns' tale of *Tam o' Shanter* turns upon this superstition.

Running the Hood. It is said that an old lady was passing over Haxey Hill, when the wind blew away her hood. Some boys began tossing it from one to the other, and the old lady so enjoyed the fun that she bequeathed thirteen acres of land, that thirteen candidates might be induced to renew the sport on the 6th of every January.

Runcible Spoon (*A*). A horn spoon with a bowl at each end, one the size of a table-spoon and the other the size of a tea-spoon. There is a joint midway between the two bowls by which the bowls can be folded over.

Runes. The earliest alphabet in use among the Gothic tribes of Northern Europe. The characters were employed either for purposes of secrecy or for divination. *Run* is Gaelic for "secret," and *helrún* means "divination."

There were several sorts of runes in Celtic mythology: as (1) the *Evil Rune*, employed when evil was invoked; (2) the *Securable Rune*, to secure from misadventure; (3) the *Victorious Rune*, to procure victory over enemies; (4) *Medicinal Rune*, for restoring to health the indisposed, or for averting danger; and (5) the *Maledictory Rune*, to bring down curses on enemies. (Compare Balaam and Balak.)

Runic Rhymes. Rhymes in imitation of the *Edda* or *Book of Runic Mythology*; rude, old-fashioned poetry of a Runic stamp.

Runic Wands. Willow wands with mystic characters inscribed on them, used by the Scandinavians for magic ceremonies.

Runnymede. The *nom de guerre* of Disraeli in the *Times.* (1805-1881.)

Rupee. A silver coin = 2s. English (a florin). A lac of rupees = £10,000 sterling. Since the depreciation of silver the value of a rupee is considerably less.

∵ In 1870 an ounce of silver was worth 60½d.; in 1876 it fell to 49d.; to-day (May, 1895) it is quoted between 58d. and 59d.; and at New York at 67¾d. per ounce.

Rupert of Debate. Edward Geoffrey, fourteenth Earl of Derby. It was when he was Mr. Stanley, and the opponent of the great O (*i.e.* O'Connell), that Lord Lytton so describes him. (1799-1869.)

"The brilliant chief, irregularly great,
Frank, haughty, bold—the Rupert of Debate."
New Timon.

Rupert's Balls, or *Prince Rupert's Drops.* Glass bubbles first brought to England by Prince Rupert. Each bubble has a tail, and if the smallest part of the tail is broken off the bubble explodes. The French term is *larme Batavique*, because these toys were invented in Holland.

"The first production of an author . . . is usually esteemed as a sort of Prince Rupert's drop, which is destroyed entirely if a person make on it but a single scratch."—*Household Words.*

Rupert's Head (*Sir*), Devonshire. The legend is that the young wife of Sir Rupert Leigh eloped with a paramour, and the guilty pair, being pursued, were overtaken on the Red Cliff. The woman fell over the cliff, and the paramour sneaked off; but Sir Rupert let himself down some thirty feet, took up the fallen woman, and contrived to save her. She was terribly mutilated, and remained a sad disfigured cripple till death, but Sir Rupert nursed her with unwearied zeal. From this story the cliff received its name.

Rush. *Not worth a rush.* Worthless. The allusion is to the practice of strewing floors with rushes before carpets were invented. Distinguished guests had clean fresh rushes, but those of inferior grade had either the rushes which had been already used by their superiors, or none at all. The more modern expression is "Not worth a straw."

"Strangers have green rushes, when daily guests are not worth a rush."—*Lilly: Sappho and Phaon.*

Friar Rush. Will-o'-the-Wisp; a strolling demon, who once on a time got admittance into a monastery as a scullion, and played the monks divers pranks. (*See* FRIAR'S LANTHORN.)

Rush-bearing Sunday. A Sunday, generally near the time of the festival of the saint to whom the church is dedicated, when anciently it was customary to renew the rushes with which the church floor was strewed. The festival is still observed at Ambleside, Westmoreland, on the last Sunday in July, the church being dedicated to St. Anne, whose day is July 26. The present custom is to make the festival a flower Sunday, with rushes and flowers formed into fanciful devices. The preceding Saturday is a holiday, being the day when the old rushes were removed.

Rush'van. The angel who opens and shuts the gates of Paradise or Al Janat. (*The Koran.*)

Ruskine'se (3 syl.). Words and phrases introduced by Ruskin, or coined *à la* Ruskin. The word is used in *The Times* :—

" Such writers as Ruskin and Carlyle have made for themselves technical terms, words, and phrases ; some of which will be incorporated into the language . . . while others may remain emblems of Ruskinese and Carlylism."— June 11, 1869.

Russ. The Russian language; a Russian.

Rus'sel. A common name given to a fox, from its russet colour.

" Dann Russel, the fox, stert up at oones,
And by the garget hente Chaunteclere
And on his bak toward the wood him bere."
Chaucer: The Nonne Prestes Tale.

Russia. "Great Russia" is Muscovy. "White *or* Little Russia" is that part acquired in 1654 by Alexei Mikalowitch, including Smolensk. The emperor is called the "Czar of All the Russias." (*See* BLACK RUSSIA.)

Rus'sian. The nickname of a Russian is "a Bear," or the "Northern Bear."

Rustam. The Deev-bend and Persian Her'cules, famous for his victory over the white dragon named Asdeev'. He was the son of Zàl, prince of Sedjistan. The exploits attributed to him must have been the aggregate of exploits performed by numerous persons of the same name. His combat for two days with Prince Isfendiar is a favourite subject with the Persian poets. The name of his horse was Reksh. Matthew Arnold's poem, *Sohrab and Rustam*, gives an account of

Rustam fighting with and killing his son Sohrab.

Rusty. *He turns rusty.* Like a rusty bolt, he sticks and will not move.

Rusty-Fusty. That odour and filth which accumulates on things and in places not used.

" Then from the butchers we bought lamb and sheepe,
Beer from the alehouse, and a broome to sweepe
Our cottage, that for want of use was musty,
And most extremely rusty-fusty dusty."
Taylor: Workes, ii. 24.

Ruyde'ra. The duenna of Belerma. She had seven daughters, who wept so bitterly at the death of Durandarte, that Merlin, out of pity, turned them into lakes or estuaries. (*Don Quixote,* pt. ii. bk. ii. ch. 6.)

Ry. A Stock Exchange expression for any sharp or dishonest practice. It originated in an old stock-jobber, who had practised upon a young man, and, being compelled to refund, wrote on the cheque, "Please to pay to R. Y." etc., in order to avoid direct evidence of the transaction.

Rye-house Plot. A conspiracy to assassinate Charles II. and his brother James on their way from Newmarket. As the house in which the king was lodging accidentally caught fire, the royal party left eight days sooner than they had intended, and the plot miscarried. It was called the Rye House Plot because the conspirators met at the Rye House Farm, in Hertfordshire. (1683.)

Rykell (*John*). A celebrated tregetour in the reign of Henry V. (*See* TREGETOUR.)

" Maister John Rykell sometime tregitour
Of noble Henry, kinge of Englande,
And of France the mighty conquerour."
John Lidgate: Dance of Macabre.

Rykelot. A magpie (?) ; a little rook. The German *roche*, Anglo-Saxon *hroc*, seem to be cognate words. The last syllable is a diminutive.

Rymar (*Mr. Robert*). Poet at the Spa. (*Sir Walter Scott: St. Ronan's Well.*)

Ryme. The Frost giant, the enemy of the elves and fairies. At the end of the world this giant is to be the pilot of the ship *Naglefarë.* (*Scandinavian mythology.*)

Ryot. A tenant in India who pays a usufruct for his occupation. The Scripture parable of the husbandmen refers to such a tenure ; the lord sent for his rent, which was not money but fruits, and the husbandmen stoned those who were sent, refusing to pay their "lord." Ryots have an hereditary and perpetual right of occupancy so long as they pay the usufruct, but if they refuse or neglect payment may be turned away.

Ryparog'rapher (Greek). So Pliny calls Pyri'cus the painter, because he confined himself to the drawing of ridiculous and gross pictures, in which he greatly excelled. Rabelais was the ryparographer of wits. (Greek, *ruparos*, foul, nasty.)

Rython. A giant of Bretagne, slain by King Arthur.

"Rython, the mighty giant slain
By his good brand, relieved Bretagne."
Sir Walter Scott: Bridal of Triermain, ii. 11.

S.

S. *You have crossed your S* (French). You have cheated me in your account ; you have charged me pounds where you ought to have charged shillings, or shillings where you ought to have charged pence. In the old French accounts, *f* (= *s*) stood for sous or pence, and *f* for francs. To cross your *f* meant therefore to turn it fraudulently into *f*.

S.P.Q.R. Senātus Populus Que Romānus (the Roman Senate and People). Letters inscribed on the standards of ancient Rome.

S.S. Collar. The collar consists of a series of the letter S in gold, either linked together or set in close order, on a blue and white ribbon. (*See* COLLAR OF S.S.)

"On the Wednesday preceding Easter, 1465, as Sir Anthony was speaking to his royal sister, on his knees, all the ladies of the court gathered round him, and bound to his left knee a band of gold, adorned with stones fashioned into the letters S.S. (*souvenance*, or remembrance) and to this band was suspended an enamelled Forget-me-not."—*Lord Lytton : Last of the Barons*, bk. iv. 5.

S.S.S. (Latin *stra'tum super stra'tum*). Layer over layer.

S.T.P. stands for *Sanctæ Theologiæ Professor. Professor* is the Latin for Doctor. D.D.—*i.e. Divinity Doctor* or Doctor of Divinity—is the English equivalent of the Latin S.T.P.

Saadia (*Al*). A cuirass of silver which belonged to King Saul, and was lent to David when he was armed for the encounter with Goliath. This cuirass fell into the hands of Mahomet, being part of the property confiscated from the Jews on their expulsion from Medi'na.

Sabbath Day's Journey (Exodus xvi. 29 ; Acts i. 12), with the Jews was not to exceed the distance between the ark and the extreme end of the camp. This was 2,000 cubits, somewhat short of an English mile. (Exodus xvi. 29 ; Acts i. 12.)

" Up to the hill by Hebron, seat of giants old,
No journey of a Sabbath Day, and loaded so."
Milton : Samson Agonistes.

Sabbath of Sound (*The*). Silence.

Sabbath'ians. The disciples of Sabbathais Zwi, the most remarkable "Messiah" of modern times. At the age of fifteen he had mastered the Talmud, and at eighteen the Cabbala. (1641-1677.)

Sabbat'ical Year. One year in seven, when all land with the ancient Jews was to lie fallow for twelve months. This law was founded on Exodus xxiii. 10, etc. ; Leviticus xxv. 2-7 ; Deuteronomy xv. 1-11.

Sabe'ans. An ancient religious sect ; so called from Sabi, son of Seth, who, with his father and brother Enoch, lies buried in the Pyramids. The Sabeans worshipped one God, but approached Him indirectly through some created representative, such as the sun, moon, stars, etc. Their system is called *Sabeanism* or the *Sabean faith.* The Arabs were chiefly Sabeans before their conversion.

Sabe'anism. The worship of the sun, moon, and host of heaven. (Chaldee, *tzaba*, a host.)

Sa'beism means *baptism*—that is, the " religion of many baptisms ; " founded by Boudasp or Bodhisattva, a wise Chaldean. This sect was the root of the party called " Christians of St. John," and by the Arabs *El Mogtasila.*

Sabel'lians. A religious sect ; so called from Sabellius, a Libyan priest of the third century. They believed in the unity of God, and said that the Trinity merely expressed three relations or states of one and the same God.

Sa'biens is the Aramean equivalent of the word " Baptists." (*See below.*)

" The sects of Hemerobaptists, Baptists, and Sabiens (the Mogtasila of the Arabian writers) in the second century filled Syria, Palestine, and Babylonia."—*Renan : Life of Jesus*, chap. xii.

Sable denotes—of the *ages* of man, the last ; of *attributes*, wisdom, prudence, integrity, singleness of mind ; of *birds*, the raven or crow ; of *elements*, the earth ; of *metals*, iron or lead ; of *planets*, Saturn; of *precious stones*, the diamond; of *trees*, the olive; of *animals*, a sort of weasel.

Sable black. Expressed in heraldry by horizontal lines crossing perpendicular ones.

In English heraldry escutcheons are varied by seven colours; foreign heralds add two more.

A suit of sables. A rich courtly dress. By the statute of apparel (24 Henry VIII. c. 13) it is ordained that none under the degree of an earl shall use sables. Bishop tells us that a thousand ducats were sometimes given for a "face of sables" (*Blossoms*, 1577). Ben Jonson says, "Would you not laugh to meet a great councillor of state in a flat cap, with trunk-hose . . . and yond haber-dasher in a velvet gown trimmed with sables?" (*Discoveries.*)

"So long? Nay, then, let the devil wear black, for I'll have a suit of sables."—*Shakespeare: Hamlet*, iii. 2.

Sablonnière (*La*). The sand-pits. So the Tuileries were called to the four-teenth century. Towards the end of that century *tiles* were made there, but the sand-pits were first called the Tile-works or Tuileries in 1416. At the beginning of the sixteenth century, Nicolas de Neuville built a house in the vicinity, which he called the "Hôtel des Tuileries." This property was purchased in 1518 by François I. for his mother.

Sabra. Daughter of Ptolemy, King of Egypt, rescued by St. George from the fangs of the giant, and ultimately married to her deliverer. She is repre-sented as pure in mind, saintly in char-acter, a perfect citizen, daughter, and wife. Her three sons, born at a birth, were named Guy, Alexander, and David. Sabra died from the "pricks of a thorny brake."

Sabreur. *Le beau sabreur* [the hand-some or famous swordsman]. Joachim Murat (1767-1815).

Sabri'na (Latin). The Severn. In Milton's *Comus* we are told she is the daughter of Locrine "that had the sceptre from his father, Brute," and was living in concubinage with Estrildis. His queen, Guendolen, vowed vengeance against Estrildis and her daughter, gathered an army together, and over-threw Locrine by the river Sture. Sabrina fled and jumped into the river. Nereus took pity on her, and made her "goddess of the Severn," which is poetically called Sabri'na.

Saccharine Principle in Things (*The*). Mr. Emerson means by this phrase, the adaptation of living beings to their conditions—the becoming callous to pains that have to be borne, and the acquirement of liking for labours that are necessary.

Saccharis'sa. A name bestowed by Waller on Lady Dorothea Sidney, eldest daughter of the Earl of Leicester, for whose hand he was an unsuccessful suitor, for she married the Earl of Sun-derland.

"The Earl of Leicester, father of Algernon Sidney, the patriot, and of Waller's *Saccharissa*, built for himself a stately house at the north corner of a square plot of 'Lammas land' be-longing to the parish of St. Martin's, which plot henceforth became known to Londoners as 'Leicester Fields.'"—*Cassell's Magazine: London Legends*, ii.

Saccharissa turns to Joan (*Fenton : The Platonic Spell*). The gloss of novelty being gone, that which was once thought unparalleled proves only ordinary. Fen-ton says before marriage many a woman seems a Saccharissa, faultless in make and wit, but scarcely is "half Hymen's taper wasted" when the "spell is dissolved," and "Saccharissa turns to Joan."

Sacco Benedetto or **Saco Bendi'to** [the blessed sack or cloak]. A yellow garment with two crosses on it, and painted over with flames and devils. In this linen robe persons condemned by the Spanish Inquisition were arrayed when they went to the stake. The word sack was used for any loose upper garment hanging down the back from the shoulders; hence "sac-friars" or *fratrēs sacc'ati*.

Sachem. A chief among some of the North American Indian tribes.

Sachentege (3 syl.). An instrument of torture used in Stephen's reign, and thus described in the Anglo-Saxon Chronicle: "It was fastened to a beam, having a sharp iron to go round the throat and neck, so that the person tortured could in no wise sit, lie, nor sleep, but that he must at all times bear all the iron."

Sack. Any dry wine, as sherry sack, Madeira sack, Canary sack, and Palm sack. (A corruption of the French *sec*, dry.)

Sack. A bag. According to tradition, it was the last word uttered before the tongues were confounded at Babel. (Saxon, *sæc;* German, *sack;* Welsh, *sach;* Irish, *sac;* French, *sac;* Latin, *saccus;* Italian, *sacco;* Spanish, *sáco;* Greek, *sakkos ;* Hebrew, *sak ;* Swedish, *sâck ;* etc., etc.)

To get the sack or *To give one the sack*. To get discharged by one's employer. Mechanics travelling in quest of work carried their implements in a bag or sack ; when discharged, they received back the bag that they might replace in it their tools, and seek a job elsewhere. Workmen still often carry a bag of tools, but so much is done by machines that bags of tools are decreasing.

The Sultan puts into a sack, and throws into the Bosphorus, any one of his harem he wishes out of the way.

There are many cognate phrases, as *To give one the bag*, and *Get the bag*, which is merely substitutional. *To receive the canvas* is a very old expression, referring to the substance of which the sack or bag was made. The French *Trousser vos quilles* (pack up your ninepins or toys) is another idea, similar to "Pack up your tatters and follow the drum." (*See* CASHIER.)

Sack Race (*A*). A village sport in which each runner is tied up to the neck in a sack. In some cases the candidates have to make short leaps, in other cases they are at liberty to run as well as the limits of the sack will allow them.

Sackbut. A corruption of *sambuca*. (Spanish, *sacabuche ;* Portuguese, *saquebuxo ;* French, *saquebute ;* Latin, *sacra buccina*, sacred trumpet.)

Sack'erson. The famous bear kept at "Paris Garden" in Shakespeare's time. (*See* PARIS GARDEN.)

Sacrament. Literally, "a military oath" taken by the Roman soldiers not to desert their standard, turn their back on the enemy, or abandon their general. We also, in the sacrament of baptism, take a military oath "to fight manfully under the banner of Christ." The early Christians used the word to signify "a sacred mystery," and hence its application to the Baptism and Eucharist, and in the Roman Catholic Church to marriage, confirmation, etc.

The five sacraments are Confirmation, Penance, Orders, Matrimony, and Extreme Unction. (See *Thirty-nine Articles*, Article xxxv.)

The seven sacraments are Baptism, Confirmation, the Eucharist, Penance, Orders, Matrimony, and Extreme Unction.

The two sacraments of the Protestant Church are Baptism and the Lord's Supper.

Sacramenta'rians. Those who believe that no change takes place in the eucharistic elements after consecration, but that the bread and wine are simply emblems of the body and blood of Christ. They were a party among the Reformers who separated from Luther.

Sacred Anchors, in Greek vessels, were never let go till the ship was in the extremity of danger.

Sacred City. (*See* HOLY CITY.)

Sacred Heart. The "Feast of the Sacred Heart of Jesus" owes its origin to a French nun, named Mary Margaret Alacoque, of Burgundy, who practised devotion to the Saviour's heart in consequence of a vision. The devotion was sanctioned by Pope Clement XII. in 1732.

Sacred Isle, or *Holy Island*. Ireland was so called because of its many saints, and Guernsey for its many monks. The island referred to by Thomas Moore in his *Irish Melodies* (No. II.) is Scattery, to which St. Sena'nus retired, and vowed that no woman should set foot thereon.

"Oh, haste and leave this sacred isle,
Unholy bark, ere morning smile."
St. Senanus and the Lady.

Enhallow (from the Norse *Eyinhalga*, Holy Isle) is the name of a small island in the Orkney group, where cells of the Irish anchorite fathers are said still to exist.

Sacred War.

(1) A war undertaken by the Amphictyon'ic League against the Cirrhæans, in defence of Delphi. (B.C. 594-587.)

(2) A war waged by the Athenians for the restoration of Delphi to the Pho'cians, from whom it had been taken. (B.C. 448-447.)

(3) A war in which the Phocians, who had seized Delphi, were conquered by Philip of Macedon. (B.C. 346.)

Sacred Way (*The*) in ancient Rome, was the street where Romulus and Tatius (the Sabine) swore mutual alliance. It does not mean the "holy street," but the "street of the oath."

Sacred Weed (*The*). Vervain. (*See* HERBA SACRA.)

Sacrifice. *Never sacrifice a white cock*, was one of the doctrines of Pythagoras, because it was sacred to the moon. The Greeks went further, and said, "Nourish a cock, but sacrifice it not," for all cockerels were sacred either to the sun or moon, as they announced the hours. The

35

cock was sacred also to the goddess of wisdom, and to Escula'pios, the god of health; it therefore represented *time*, *wisdom*, and *health*, none of which are ever to be sacrificed. (See *Iamblichus : Protreptics*, symbol xviii.)

Sacrifice to the Graces is to render oneself agreeable by courteous conduct, suavity of manners, and fastidiousness of dress. The allusion is to the three Graces of classic mythology.

Sa'cring Bell. The little bell rung to give notice that the "Host" is approaching. Now called sanctus bell, from the words "*Sanctus, sanctus, sanctus, dominus, Deus Sabaoth*," pronounced by the priest. (French, *sacrer ;* Latin, *sacer*.)

" He heard a little sacring bell ring to the elevation of a to-morrow mass."—*Reginald Scott : Discovery of Witchcraft* (1584).

"The sacring of the kings of France."—*Temple.*

Sa'cripant. A braggart, a noisy hectorer. He is introduced by Alexander Passoni, in a mock-heroic poem called *The Rape of the Bucket.*

Sa'cripant (in *Orlando Furioso*). King of Circassia, and a Saracen.

Sad Bread (Latin, *panis gravis*). Heavy bread, ill-made bread. Shakespeare calls it " distressful bread "—not the bread of distress, but the *panis gravis* or ill-made bread eaten by the poor.

Sad Dog (*He's a*). *Un triste sujet.* A playful way of saying a man is a debauchee.

Sadah. The sixteenth night of the month Bayaman. (*Persian mythology.*)

Sadda. One of the sacred books of the Guebres or Parsis containing a summary of the Zend-Avesta.

Sadder and a Wiser Man (*A*).

" A sadder and a wiser man
He rose the morrow morn."
Coleridge : The Ancient Mariner.

Saddle. *Set the saddle on the right horse.* Lay the blame on those who deserve it.

Lose the horse and win the saddle. (See LOSE.)

Saddletree (*Mr. Bartoline*). The learned saddler. (*Sir Walter Scott : The Heart of Midlothian.*)

Sad'ducees. A Jewish party which denied the existence of spirits and angels, and, of course, disbelieved in the resurrection of the dead; so called from Sadoc (*righteous man*), thought to be the name of a priest or rabbi some three centuries before the birth of Christ. As they did

not believe in future punishments, they punished offences with the utmost severity.

Sadi or **Saadi.** A Persian poet styled the "nightingale of thousand songs," and " one of the four monarchs of eloquence." His poems are the *Gulistan* or *Garden of Roses*, the *Bostan* or *Garden of Fruits*, and the *Pend-Nameh*, a moral poem. He is admired for his sententious march. (1184-1263.)

Sadler's Wells (London). There was a well at this place called *Holy Well*, once noted for "its extraordinary cures." The priests of Clerkenwell Priory used to boast of its virtues. At the Reformation it was stopped up, and was wholly forgotten till 1683, when a Mr. Sadler, in digging gravel for his garden, accidentally discovered it again. Hence the name. In 1765 Mr. Rosoman converted Sadler's garden into a theatre.

Sadle'rian Lectures. Lectures on Algebra delivered in the University of Cambridge, and founded in 1710 by Lady Sadler.

Sæhrimnir [*Sza-rim'-ner*]. The boar served to the gods in Valhalla every evening ; by next morning the part eaten was miraculously restored. (*Scandinavian mythology.*)

Safa, in Arabia, according to Arabian legend, is the hill on which Adam and Eve came together, after having been parted for two hundred years, during which time they wandered homeless over the face of the earth.

Safety Matches. In 1847 Schrötter, an Austrian chemist, discovered that red phosphorus gives off no fumes, and is virtually inert ; but being mixed with chlorate of potash under slight pressure it explodes with violence. In 1855 Herr Böttger, of Sweden, put the red phosphorus on the *box* and the phosphorus on the *match*, so that the match must be rubbed on the box to bring the two together. (*See* PROMETHEANS, LUCIFERS.)

Saffron. *He hath slept in a bed of saffron.* In Latin *dormivit in sacco croci*, meaning he has a very light heart, in reference to the exhilarating effects of saffron.

" With genial joy to warm his soul,
Helen mixed saffron in the bowl."

Saffron Veil. The Greek and Latin brides wore a *flammeum* or yellow veil, which wholly enveloped them. (*See* SAOPHRON.)

Saga (plural **Sagas**). The northern mythological and historical traditions, chiefly compiled in the twelfth and three following centuries. The most remarkable are those of *Lodbrok, Hervara, Vilkina, Volsunga, Blomsturvalla, Ynglinga, Olaf Tryggva-Sonar*, with those of *Jomsvikingia* and of *Knytlinga* (which contain the legendary history of Norway and Denmark), those of *Sturlinga* and *Eryrbiggia* (which contain the legendary history of Iceland), the *Heims-Kringla* and *New Edda*, due to Snorro-Sturleson.

All these legends are short, abrupt, concise, full of bold metaphor and graphic descriptions.

Sa'gan of Jerusalem, in Dryden's *Absalom and Achitophel*, is designed for Dr. Compton, Bishop of London; he was son of the Earl of Northampton, who fell in the royal cause at the battle of Hopton Heath. The Jewish sagan was the vicar of the sovereign pontiff. According to tradition, Moses was Aaron's sagan.

∵ The Sagan was the vicar of the Jewish pontiff. Thus they called Moses " Aaron's Sagan."

Sages (*The Seven*). (*See* WISE MEN.)

Sag'itta'rius, the archer, represents the Centaur Chiron, who at death was converted into the constellation so called. (*See next article.*)

Sag'ittary. A terrible archer, half beast and half man, whose eyes sparkled like fire, and struck dead like lightning. He is introduced into the Trojan armies by Guido da Colonna.

"The dreadful Sagittary
Appals our numbers."
Shakespeare : Troilus and Cressida, v. 5.

Sag'ramour le De'sirus. A knight of the Round Table, introduced in the *Morte d'Arthur, Lancelot du Lac*, etc.

Sahib (in Bengalee, *Saheb*). Equal to our Mr., or rather to such gentlemen as we term "Esquires." *Sahiba* is the lady. (Arabic for *lord, master*.)

Sail. *You may hoist sail.* Cut your stick, be off. Maria saucily says to Viola, dressed in man's apparel—

"Will you hoist sail, sir ? Here lies your way."
—*Shakespeare : Twelfth Night*, i. 5.

To set sail. To start on a voyage.
To strike sail. (*See* STRIKE.)

Sail before the Wind (*To*). To prosper, to go on swimmingly, to meet with great success, to go as smoothly and rapidly as a ship before the wind.

Sailing under False Colours. Pretending to be what you are not. The allusion is to pirate vessels, which hoist any colours to elude detection.

Sailing within the Wind or **Sailing close to the Wind.** Going to the very verge of propriety, or acting so as just to escape the letter of the law. The phrase, of course, is nautical.

" The jokes [of our predecessors] might have been broader than modern manners allow, . . . but . . . the masher sails nearer the wind than did his ruder forefathers."—*Nineteenth Century*, November, 1892, p. 795.

" Ea defended himself by declaring that he did not tell Hasisadra anything ; he only sent her a dream. This was undoubtedly sailing very near the wind."—*Nineteenth Century*, June, 1891, p. 911.

Sailor King. William IV. of England, who entered the navy as midshipman in 1779, and was made Lord High Admiral in 1827. (1765, 1830-1837.)

Saint. Kings and princes so called :—
Edward the Martyr (961, 975-978).
Edward the Confessor (1004, 1042-1066).
Eric IX. of Sweden (*, 1155-1161).
Ethelred I., King of Wessex (*, 866-871).
Eugenius I., pope (*, 654-657).
Felix I., pope (*, 269-274).
Ferdinand III. of Castile and Leon (1200, 1217-1252).
Julius I., pope (*, 337-352).
Kâng-he, second of the Manchoo dynasty of China, who assumed the name of Chin-tsou-jin (1661-1722).
Lawrence Justini'ni, Patriarch of Venice (1380, 1451-1465).
Leo IX., pope (1002, 1049-1054).
Louis IX. of France (1215, 1226-1270).
Olaus II. of Norway, brother of Harald III., called " St. Olaf the Double Beard " (984, 1026-1030).
Stephen I. of Hungary (979, 997-1038).
Dom Fernando, son of King John of Portugal, was, with his brother Henry, taken prisoner by the Moors at the siege of Tangier. The Portuguese general promised to give Ceuta for their ransom, and left Fernando in prison as their surety. The Portuguese government refused to ratify the condition, and Fernando was left in the hands of the Moors till he died. For this patriotic act he is regarded as a *saint*, and his day is June 5th. His brother Edward was king at the time. (1402-1443.)

St. Bees' College (Cumberland), situated on the bay formed by *St. Bees' Head*, founded by Dr. Law, Bishop of Chester, in 1816. St. Bees' was so called from a nunnery founded here in 650, and dedicated to the Irish saint named Bega. A "man of wax" is a "Bees' man."

St. Cecil'ia, born of noble Roman parents, and fostered from her cradle in the Christian faith, married Valirian. One day she told him that an angel, "whether she was awake or asleep, was ever beside her." Valirian requested to see this angel, and she said he must be baptised first. Valirian was baptised and suffered martyrdom. When Cecilia was brought before the Prefect Alma'chius, and refused to worship the Roman deities, she was "shut fast in a bath kept hot both night and day with great fires," but "felt of it no woe." Almachius then sent an executioner to cut off her head, "but for no manner of chance could he smite her fair neck in two." Three days she lingered with her neck bleeding, preaching Christ and Him crucified all the while ; then she died, and Pope Urban buried the body. "Her house the church of St. Cecily is hight" unto this day. (*Chaucer: Secounde Nonnes Tale.*) (*See* CECILIA.)

⁂ Towards the close of the seventeenth century an annual musical festival was held in Stationers' Hall in honour of St. Cecilia.

St. Cuthbert's Duck. The eider duck.

St. Distaff. (*See* DISTAFF.)

St. Elmo, called by the French *St. Elme.* The electric light seen playing about the masts of ships in stormy weather. (*See* CASTOR AND POLLUX.)

" And sudden breaking on their raptured sight,
Appeared the splendour of St. Elmo's light."
Hoole's Furioso, book ix.

St. Francis. (*See* FRANCIS.)

St. George's Cross, in heraldry, is a Greek cross gules upon a field argent. The field is represented in the Union Jack by a narrow fimbriation. It is the distinguishing badge of the British navy.

St. George's flag is a smaller flag, without the Union Jack.

St. John Long. An illiterate quack, who professed to have discovered a liniment which had the power of distinguishing between disease and health. The body was rubbed with it, and if irritation appeared it announced secret disease, which the quack undertook to cure. He was twice tried for manslaughter : once in 1830, when he was fined for his treatment of Miss Cashan, who died ; and next in 1831, for the death of Mrs. Lloyd. Being acquitted, he was driven in triumph from the Old Bailey in a nobleman's carriage, amid the congratulations of the aristocracy.

⁂ St. John is pronounced *Sin'jin,* as in that verse of Pope's—

" Awake, my St. John ! leave all meaner things
To low ambition and the pride of kings."
Essay on Man.

St. John's Eve, St. Mark's Eve, and **Allhallow Even,** are times when poets say the forms of all such persons as are about to die in the ensuing twelve months make their solemn entry into the churches of their respective parishes. On these eves all sorts of goblins are about. Brand says, "On the Eve of John the Baptist's nativity bonfires are made to purify the air (vol. i. p. 305).

St. Johnstone's Tippet. A halter ; so called from Johnstone the hangman.

"Sent to heaven wi' a St. Johnstone's tippit about my hause."—*Sir Walter Scott: Old Mortality,* chap. viii.

St. Leger Sweepstakes. The St. Leger race was instituted in 1776, by Colonel St. Leger, of Park Hill, near Doncaster, but was not called the "St. Leger" till two years afterwards, when the Marquis of Rockingham's horse *Allabaculia* won the race. (*See* DERBY, LEGER.)

St. Leon became possessed of the elixir of life, and the power of transmuting the baser metals into gold, but these acquisitions only brought him increased misery. (*William Goodwin: St. Leon.*)

St. Lundi (*La*). St. Monday. Monday spent by workmen in idleness. One of the rules enjoined by the Sheffield unionists was that no work should be permitted to be done on a Monday by any of their members.

St. Michael's Chair. The projecting stone lantern of a tower erected on St. Michael's Mount, Cornwall. It is said that the rock received its name from a religious house built to commemorate the apparition of St. Michael on one of its craggy heights. (*See* MICHAEL.)

St. Monday. A holiday observed by journeyman shoemakers and other inferior mechanics, and well-to-do merchants.

In the *Journal of the Folk-lore Society,* vol. i. p. 245, we read that, "While Cromwell's army lay encamped at Perth, one of his zealous partisans, named Monday, died, and Cromwell offered a reward for the best lines on his death. A shoemaker of Perth brought the following, which so pleased Cromwell that he not only gave the promised reward, but made also a decree that shoemakers should be allowed to make Monday a standing holiday.

> " Blessed be the Sabbath Day,
> And cursed be worldly pelf ;
> Tuesday will begin the week,
> Since Monday's hanged himself."

St. Si'monism. The social and political system of St. Simon. He proposed the institution of a European parliament, to arbitrate in all matters affecting Europe, and the establishment of a social hierarchy based on capacity and labour. He was led to his " social system" by the apparition of Charlemagne, which appeared to him one night in the Luxembourg, where he was suffering a temporary imprisonment. (1760-1825.)

⁜ For other saints, *see* the names.

St. Stephen's. The Houses of Parliament are so called, because, at one time, the Commons used to sit in St. Stephen's Chapel.

St. Stephen's Loaves. Stones.

> "Having said this, he took up one of St. Stephen's loaves, and was going to hit him with it."—*Rabelais: Pantagruel,* v. 8.

St. Thomas's Castle. The penitentiary in St. Thomas's parish, Oxford, where women of frail morals are kept under surveillance.

St. Wilfrid's Needle, often called " St. Winifred's Needle." In the crypt of Ripon Minster is a passage regarded as a test of chastity.

Saints. *City of Saints.* (*See under* CITY *and* HOLY CITY.)

Sai'vas (2 syl.). Worshippers of Siva, one of the three great Indian sects ; they are at present divided into —

(1) *Dandins* or staff-bearers, the Hindu mendicants ; so called because they carry a *danda* or small staff, with a piece of red cloth fixed on it. In this piece of cloth the Brahmanical cord is enshrined.

(2) *Yogins.* Followers of Yoga, who practise the most difficult austerities.

(3) *Lingavats,* who wear the Linga emblem on some part of their dress.

(4) *Paramahansas,* ascetics who go naked, and never express any want or wish.

(5) *Aghorins,* who eat and drink whatever is given them, even ordure and carrion.

(6) *Urdhaba'hus,* who extend one or both arms over their head till they become rigidly fixed in this position.

(7) *Akas'mukhins,* who hold up their faces to the sky till the muscles of the neck become contracted.

Sa'ker. A piece of light artillery. The word is borrowed from the saker hawk. (*See* FALCON.)

> " The cannon, blunderbuss, and saker,
> He was the inventor of and maker."
>   *Butler: Hudibras,* i. 2.

Sakhrat [*Sak-rah'*]. A sacred stone, one grain of which endows the possessor with miraculous powers. It is of an emerald colour ; its reflection makes the sky blue. (*Mahometan mythology.*)

Sak'ta. A worshipper of a Sakti, or female deity, in Hindu mythology. The Saktas are divided into two branches, the Dakshin'acha'rins and the Vam'acha'-rins (the followers of the right-hand and left-hand ritual). The latter practise the grossest impurities. (Sanskrit, *sakti,* power, energy.)

Sa-kun'tala. Daughter of St. Vis'-wa'mita, and Menakâ a water-nymph. Abandoned by her parents, she was brought up by a hermit. One day King Dushyanta came to the hermitage during a hunt, and persuaded Sakuntala to marry him, and in due time a son was born. When the boy was six years old, she took it to its father, and the king recognised his wife by a ring which he had given her. She was now publicly proclaimed his queen, and Bhârata, his son and heir, became the founder of the glorious race of the Bhâratas. This story forms the plot of the celebrated drama of Kâlida'sa, called *Sakuntala,* made known to us by Sir W. Jones.

Sak'ya-Mu'ni. Sakya, the hermit, founder of Buddhism.

Sal Prunella. A mixture of refined nitre and soda for sore throats. Prunella is a corruption of Brunelle, in French *sel de brunelle,* from the German *breune* (a sore throat), *braune* (the quinsy).

Salacaca'bia or **Salacac'aby of Apicius.** An uneatable soup of great pretensions. King, in his *Art of Cookery,* gives the recipe of this soup: " Bruise in a mortar parsley-seed, dried peneryal, dried mint, ginger, green coriander, stoned raisins, honey, vinegar, oil, and wine. Put them into a *cacab'ulum,* with three crusts of Pycentine bread, the flesh of a pullet, vestine cheese, pine-kernels, cucumbers, and dried onions, minced small ; pour soup over all, garnish with snow, and serve up in the cacab'ulum."

> " At each end there are dishes of the salacacabia of the Romans : one is made of parsley, pennyroyal, cheese, pinetops, honey, vinegar, brine, eggs, cucumbers, onions, and hen-livers ; the other is much the same as soup maigre."—*Smollett: Peregrine Pickle.*

Sal'ace (3 syl.). The sea, or rather the *salt* or *briny* deep; the wife of Neptune.

"Triton, who boasts his high Neptunian race,
Sprung from the god by Salace's embrace."
Camoens: Lusiad, book vi.

Salad Days. Days of inexperience, when persons are very green.

"My salad days.
When I was green in judgment."
Shakespeare: Antony and Cleopatra, i. 5.

A pen'orth of salad oil. A strapping; a castigation. It is a joke on All Fools' Day to send one to the saddler's for a "pen'orth of salad oil." The pun is between "salad oil," as above, and the French *avoir de la salade,* "to be flogged." The French *salader* and *salade* are derived from the *salle* or saddle on which schoolboys were at one time birched. A block for the purpose used to be kept in some of our public schools. Oudin translates the phrase "*Donner la salle à un escolier*" by "*Scopar un scolari innanzi à tutti gli altri.*" (*Recherches Italiennes et Françoises,* part ii. 508.)

Salamander, in Egyptian hieroglyphics, is a human form pinched to death with the cold. (*See* UNDINES.)

Salamander. A sort of lizard, fabled to live in fire, which, however, it quenched by the chill of its body. Pliny tells us he tried the experiment once, but the creature was soon burnt to a powder. (*Natural History,* x. 67; xxix. 4.) Salamanders are not uncommon, especially the spotted European kind (Greek, *salamandria*).

Salamander. François I. of France adopted as his badge "a lizard in the midst of flames," with the legend "*Nutrisco et extinguo*" ("I nourish and extinguish"). The Italian motto from which this legend was borrowed was, "*Nudrisco il buono e spengo il reo*" ("I nourish the good and extinguish the bad"). Fire purifies good metal, but consumes rubbish. (*See ante.*)

Salamander. Anything of a fiery-red colour. Falstaff calls Bardolph's nose "a burning lamp," "a salamander," and the drink that made such "a fiery meteor" he calls "fire."

"I have maintained that salamander of yours with fire any time this two-and-thirty years."
—*Shakespeare:* 1 *Henry IV.,* iv. 3.

Salamander's Wool. Asbestos, a fibrous mineral, affirmed by the Tartars to be made "of the root of a tree." It is sometimes called "mountain flax," and is not combustible.

Sal'ary. The salt rations. The Romans served out rations of salt and

other necessaries to their soldiers and civil servants. The rations altogether were called by the general name of salt, and when money was substituted for the rations the stipend went by the same name. (Latin, *sala'rium,* from *sal, salt.*)

Salchichon. A huge Italian sausage. Thomas, Duke of Genoa, a boy of Harrow school, was so called, when he was thrust forward by General Prim as an "inflated candidate" for the Spanish throne.

Sale by the Candle. A species of auction. An inch of candle being lighted, he who made the bid as the candle gave its expiring wink was declared the buyer; sometimes a pin is stuck in a candle, and the last bidder before the pin falls out is the buyer.

Sa'lem is Jireh-Salem, or Jerusalem.

"Melchisedec, King of Salem . . . being by interpretation . . . King of peace."—Hebrews vii. 1, 2.

Salic Law. The law so called is one chapter of the Salian code regarding succession to salic lands, which was limited to heirs male to the exclusion of females, chiefly because certain military duties were connected with the holding of those lands. In the fourteenth century females were excluded from the throne of France by the application of the Salic law to the succession of the crown.

"Which Salique, as I said, 'twixt Elbe and Sala,
Is at this day in Germany called Meisen,'
Shakespeare: Henry V., i. 2.

⁂ Philippe VI. of France, in order to raise money, exacted a tax on salt, called *Gabelle,* which was most unpopular and most unjustly levied. Edward III. called this iniquitous tax "Philippe's *Salic* law." (Latin, *sal, salt.*)

Saliens (*The*). A college of twelve priests of Mars instituted by Numa. The tale is that a shield fell from heaven, and the nymph Egēria predicted that wherever that shield was preserved the people would be the dominant people of the earth. To prevent the shield from being surreptitiously taken away, Numa had eleven others made exactly like it, and appointed twelve priests for guardians. Every year these young patricians promenaded the city, singing and dancing, and they finished the day with a most sumptuous banquet, insomuch that *saliares cœna* became proverbial for a most sumptuous feast. The word "saliens" means dancing.

> " Nunc est bibendum . . .
> . . . nunc Saliaribus
> Ornăre pulvinar Deorum
> Tempus erat dapibus."
> *Horace : 1 Odes,* xxxvii. 2-4.

Salient Angles, in fortification, are those angles in a rampart which point outwards towards the country; those which point inwards towards the place fortified are called " re-entering 'angles."

Salisbury Cathedral. Begun in 1220, and finished in 1258; noted for having the loftiest spire in the United Kingdom. It is 400 feet high, or thirty feet higher than the dome of St. Paul's.

Salisbury Craigs. Rocks near Edinburgh; so called from the Earl of Salisbury, who accompanied Edward III. on an expedition against the Scots.

Sallee. A seaport on the west coast of Morocco. The inhabitants were formerly notorious for their piracy.

Sallust of France. César Vichard, Abbé de St. Réal; so called by Voltaire. (1639-1692.)

Sally. Saddle. (Latin, *sella;* French, *selle.*)

> " The horse . . . stopped his course by degrees,
> and went with his rider . . . into a pond to drink;
> and there sat his lordship upon the sally."—*Lives of the Norths.*
> " Vaulting ambition . . . o'erleaps its *sell,*
> And falls o' the other . . ."
> *Shakespeare : Macbeth,* i. 7.

Sally Lunn. A tea-cake; so called from Sally Lunn, the pastrycook of Bath, who used to cry them about in a basket at the close of the eighteenth century. Dalmer, the baker, bought her recipe, and made a song about the buns.

Sallyport. The postern in fortifications. It is a small door or *port* whence troops may issue unseen to make *sallies,* etc. (Latin, *salio,* to leap.)

Sal'macis. A fountain of Caria, which rendered effeminate all those who bathed therein. It was in this fountain that Hermaphrodĭtus changed his sex. (*Ovid : Metamorphoses,* iv. 285, and xvi. 319.)

> " Thy moist limbs melted into Salmacis."
> *Swinburne : Hermaphroditus.*

Sal'magun'di. A mixture of minced veal, chicken, or turkey, anchovies or pickled herrings, and onions, all chopped together, and served with lemon-juice and oil; said to be so called from Salmagondi, one of the ladies attached to the suite of Mary de Medicis, wife of Henri IV. of France. She either invented the dish or was so fond of it that it went by her name.

Salmon (Latin, *salmo,* to leap). The leaping fish.

Salmon, *as food for servants.* At one time apprentices and servants stipulated that they should not be obliged to feed on salmon more than five days in a week. Salmon was one penny a pound.

> " A large boiled salmon would now-a-days have indicated most liberal housekeeping ; but at that period salmon was caught in such plenty (1679) . . . that, instead of being accounted a delicacy, it was generally applied to feed the servants, who are said sometimes to have stipulated that they should not be required to eat food so luscious and surfeiting . . . above five times a week."—*Sir W. Scott: Old Mortality,* chap. vii.

Salmo'neus (3 syl.). A king of Elis, noted for his arrogance and impiety. He wished to be called a god, and to receive divine honour from his subjects. To imitate Jove's thunder he used to drive his chariot over a brazen bridge, and darted burning torches on every side to imitate lightning, for which impiety the king of gods and men hurled a thunderbolt at him, and sent him to the infernal regions.

Sal'sabil. A fountain in Paradise. (*Al Koran,* xxvi.)

> " Mahomet was taking his afternoon nap in his Paradise. A houri had rolled a cloud under his head, and he was snoring serenely near the fountain of Salsabil."—*Croquemitaine,* ii. 8.

Salt. Flavour, smack. The salt of youth is that vigour and strong passion which then predominates. Shakespeare uses the term on several occasions for strong amorous passion. Thus Iago refers to it as "hot as monkeys, salt as wolves in pride" (*Othello,* iii. 3). The Duke calls Angelo's base passion his "salt imagination," because he supposed his victim to be Isabella, and not his betrothed wife whom the Duke forced him to marry. (*Measure for Measure,* v. 1.)

> " Though we are justices, and doctors, and churchmen, Master Page, we have some salt of our youth in us."—*Merry Wives of Windsor,* ii. 3.

Spilling salt was held to be an unlucky omen by the Romans, and the superstition has descended to ourselves. In Leonardo da Vinci's famous picture of the Lord's Supper, Jùdas Iscariot is known by the salt-cellar knocked over accidentally by his arm. Salt was used in sacrifice by the Jews, as well as by the Greeks and Romans; and it is still used in baptism by the Roman Catholic clergy. It was an emblem of purity and the sanctifying influence of a holy life on others. Hence our Lord tells His disciples they are " the salt of the earth." Spilling the salt after it was placed on the head of the victim was a bad omen, hence the superstition.

A covenant of salt (Numbers xviii. 19). A covenant which could not be broken. As salt was a symbol of incorruption, it, of course, symbolised perpetuity.

"The Lord God of Israel gave the kingdom . . . to David . . . by a covenant of salt."—2 Chronicles xiii. 5.

Cum grano sa'lis. With great limitation; with its grain of salt, or truth. As salt is sparingly used in condiments, so is truth in the remark just made.

He won't earn salt for his porridge. He will never earn a penny.

Not worth one's salt. Not worth the expense of the food he eats.

To eat a man's salt. To partake of his hospitality. Among the Arabs to eat a man's salt was a sacred bond between the host and guest. No one who has eaten of another's salt should speak ill of him or do him an ill turn.

"One does not eat a man's salt . . . at these dinners. There is nothing sacred in . . . London hospitality."—*Thackeray.*

To sit above the salt—in a place of distinction. Formerly the family *saler* (salt cellar) was of massive silver, and placed in the middle of the table. Persons of distinction sat *above* the "saler"—*i.e.* between it and the head of the table; dependents and inferior guests sat below.

"We took him up above the salt and made much of him."—*Kingsley: Westward Ho!* chap. xv.

True to his salt. Faithful to his employers. Here salt means salary or interests. (See above, *To eat a man's salt.*)

"M. Waddington owes his fortune and his consideration to his father's adopted country[France], and he is true to his salt."—*Newspaper paragraph,* March 6, 1893.

Salt. A sailor, especially an old sailor; *e.g.* an old salt.

Salt Bread or *Bitter Bread.* The bread of affliction or humiliation. Bread too salt is both disagreeable to the taste and indigestible.

"Learning how hard it is to get back when once exiled, and how salt is the bread of others."—*Mrs. Oliphant: Makers of Florence,* p. 85.

Salt-cellar (*A*). A table salt-stand. (French, *salière*; Latin, *salarium.*)

Salt Hill (Eton). The mound at Eton where the Eton scholars used to collect money from the visitors on Montem day. The mound is still called *Salt Hill,* and the money given was called *salt.* The word salt is similar to the Latin *sala'rium* (salary), the pay given to Roman soldiers and civil officers. (*See* MONTEM, SALARY.)

∴ Cakes of salt are still used for money in Abyssinia and Thibet.

Salt Junk. (*See* JUNK.)

Salt Lake. It has been stated that three buckets of this water will yield one of solid salt. This cannot be true, as water will not hold in solution more than twenty-five per cent. of saline matter. The Mormons engaged in procuring it state that they obtain one bucket of salt for every five buckets of water. (*Quebec Morning Chronicle.*)

Salt Ring. An attempt to monopolise the sale of salt by a ring or company which bought up some of the largest of our salt-mines.

Salt River. *To row up Salt River.* A defeated political party is said to be rowed up Salt River, and those who attempt to uphold the party have the task of rowing up this ungracious stream. J. Inman says the allusion is to a small stream in Kentucky, the passage of which is rendered both difficult and dangerous by shallows, bars, and an extremely tortuous channel.

Salt an Invoice (*To*) is to put the extreme value upon each article, and even something more, to give it piquancy and raise its market value, according to the maxim, *sal sapit omnia.* The French have the same expression: as "*Vendre bien salé*" (to sell very dear); "*Il me l'a bien salé*" (He charged me an exorbitant price); and generally *saler* is to pigeon one.

Salt in Beer. In Scotland it was customary to throw a handful of salt on the top of the mash to keep the witches from it. Salt really has the effect of moderating the fermentation and fining the liquor.

Salt in a Coffin. It is still not uncommon to put salt into a coffin, and Moresin tells us the reason; Satan hates salt, because it is the symbol of incorruption and immortality. (*Papatus,* p. 154.)

Salt Losing its Savour. "If salt has lost its savour, wherewith shall it be salted?" If men fall from grace, how shall they be restored? The reference is to rock-salt, which loses its saltness if exposed to the hot sun.

"Along one side of the Valley of Salt (that towards Gibul) there is a small precipice about two men's lengths, occasioned by taking away of the salt. I broke a piece off that was exposed to the sun, rain, and air; though it had the sparks and particles of salt, yet it had perfectly lost its savour. The inner part, however, retained its saltness."—*Maundrel, quoted by Dr. Adam Clarke.*

Salt on His Tail (*Lay*). Catch or apprehend him. The phrase is based on the direction given to small children to lay salt on a bird's tail if they want to catch it.

"His intelligence is so good, that were you to come near him with soldiers or constables, . . . I shall answer for it you will never lay salt on his tail."—*Sir W. Scott: Redgauntlet*, chap. xi.

Saltarello, "*le fils de la Folie et de Pulcinello.*" A supposititious Italian dancer, sent to amuse Bettina in the court of the Grand Duke Laurent. Bettina was a servant on a farm, in love with the shepherd Pippo. But when she was taken to court and made a countess, Pippo was forbidden to approach her. Bettina languished, and to amuse her a troop of Italian dancers was sent for, of which Saltarello was the leader. He soon made himself known to Bettina, and married her. Bettina was a "mascotte" (*q.v.*), but, as the children of mascottes are mascottes also, the prince became reconciled with the promise that he should be allowed to adopt her first child. (*La Mascotte.*)

⁂ Hence a Saltarello is an assumed covert to bring about a forbidden marriage and hoodwink those who forbade it.

Saltpetre (French, *saltpetre*), *sel de pierre, parcequ'il forme des efflorescences salines sur les murs*. (*Bouillet: Dict. des Sciences.*)

Salu'te (2 syl.). According to tradition, on the triumphant return of Maximilian to Germany, after his second campaign, the town of Augsburg ordered 100 rounds of cannon to be discharged. The officer on service, fearing to have fallen short of the number, caused an extra round to be added. The town of Nuremberg ordered a like salute, and the custom became established.

Salute, in the British navy, between two ships of equal rank, is made by firing an equal number of guns. If the vessels are of unequal rank, the superior fires the fewer rounds.

Royal salute, in the British navy, consists (1) in firing twenty-one great guns, (2) in the officers lowering their swordpoints, and (3) in dipping the colours.

Salutations.

Shaking hands. A relic of the ancient custom of adversaries, in treating of a truce, taking hold of the weapon-hand to ensure against treachery.

Lady's curtsey. A relic of the ancient custom of women going on the knee to men of rank and power, originally to beg mercy, afterwards to acknowledge superiority.

Taking off the hat. A relic of the

35*

ancient custom of taking off the helmet when no danger is nigh. A man takes off his hat to show that he dares stand unarmed in your presence.

Discharging guns as a salute. To show that no fear exists, and therefore no guns will be required. This is like "burying the hatchet" (*q.v.*).

Presenting arms—*i.e.* offering to give them up, from the full persuasion of the peaceful and friendly disposition of the person so honoured.

Lowering swords. To express a willingness to put yourself unarmed in the power of the person saluted, from a full persuasion of his friendly feeling.

Salve (1 syl.) is the Latin *sal'via* (sage), one of the most efficient of mediæval remedies.

" To other woundes, and to broken armes, Some hadde salve, and some hadde charmes."
Chaucer: Canterbury Tales, line 2,715.

Salve. To flatter, to wheedle. The allusion is to salving a wound.

Salve (2 syl.). Latin " hail," " welcome." The word is often woven on door-mats.

Sam. *Uncle Sam.* The United States Government. Mr. Frost tells us that the inspectors of Elbert Anderson's store on the Hudson were Ebenezer Wilson and his uncle Samuel Wilson, the latter of whom superintended in person the workmen, and went by the name of "Uncle Sam." The stores were marked E.A.—U.S. (*Elbert Anderson, United States*). and one of the employers, being asked the meaning, said U.S. stood for "Uncle Sam." The joke took, and in the War of Independence the men carried it with them, and it became stereotyped.

To stand Sam. To be made to pay the reckoning. This is an Americanism, and arose from the letters U.S. on the knapsacks of the soldiers. The government of Uncle Sam has to pay, or " stand Sam " for all. (*See above.*)

Sam Weller. Servant of Mr. Pickwick, famous for his metaphors. He is meant to impersonate the wit, shrewdness, quaint humour, and best qualities of London low life. (*Charles Dickens: Pickwick Papers.*)

Sa'mael. The prince of demons, who, in the guise of a serpent, tempted Eve; also called the angel of death. (*Jewish demonology.*)

Sam'anides (3 syl.). A dynasty of ten kings in Western Persia (902-1004), founded by Ismail al Sam'ani.

Sama'ria, according to 1 Kings xvi. 24, means the hill of Shemer. Omri "bought the hill Samaria of Shemer for two talents of silver, and built on the hill, and called the name of [his] city . . . after the name of Shemer . . . *Samaria*." (B.C. 925.)

Samaritan. *A good Samaritan.* A philanthropist, one who attends upon the poor to aid them and give them relief. (Luke x. 30-37.)

Sambo. A pet name given to anyone of the negro race. The term is properly applied to the male offspring of a negro and mulatto, the female offspring being called Zamba. (Spanish, *zambo*, bow-legged ; Latin, *scambus*.)

Samedi (French). Saturday. A contraction of *Saturni-dies*. In French, *m* and *n* are interchangeable, whence *Saturne* is changed to *Saturne*, and contracted into *Sa'me*. M. Masson, in his French etymologies, says it is *Sabbati dies*, but this cannot be correct. MARDI is *Martis-dies*, VENDREDI is *Veneris dies*, JEUDI is *Jovis-dies*, etc. (The day of Saturn, Mars, Venus, Jove, etc.)

Sa'mian. *The Samian poet.* Simon'-idēs the satirist, born at Samos.

Samian Letter (*The*). The letter Y, used by Pythag'oras as an emblem of the straight narrow path of virtue, which is one, but, if once deviated from, the farther the lines are extended the wider becomes the breach.

" When reason doubtful, like the Samian letter,
Points him two ways, the narrower the better."
                                        Dunciad, iv.

Samian Sage (*The*). Pythag'oras born at Samos ; sometimes called " the Samian." (Sixth century B.C.)

                        " 'Tis enough,
In this late age, adventurous to have touched
Light on the numbers of the Samian sage."
                                        Thomson.

Samia'sa. A seraph, who fell in love with Aholiba'mah, a granddaughter of Cain, and when the flood came, carried her under his wing to some other planet. (*Byron : Heaven and Earth.*)

Samiel, the Black Huntsman of the Wolf's Glen. A satanic spirit, who gave to a marksman who entered into compact with him seven balls, six of which were to hit infallibly whatever was aimed at, but the seventh was to deceive. The person who made this compact was termed *Der Frei'schutz*. (*Weber : Der Freischutz, libretto by Kind.*)

Sa'miel Wind, or Simoom'. A hot suffocating wind that blows occasionally in Africa and Arabia. (Arabic, *samma*, suffocatingly hot.)

" Burning and headlong as the Samiel wind."
                Thomas Moore: Lalla Rookh, pt. i.

Sammael. The chief of evil spirits, who is for ever gnashing his teeth over the damned. Next to him is Ashmedai (Asmodeus). (*Cabalists.*)

Samoor. The south wind of Persia, which so softens the strings of lutes, that they can never be tuned while it lasts. (*Stephen : Persia.*)

" Like the wind of the south o'er a summer lute
Hushed all its music, and withered its frame."
                Thomas Moore: The Fire Worshippers.

Samosa'tian Philosopher. Lucian of Samos'ata. (Properly *Samos'a-tan*.)

Sampford Ghost (*The*). A kind of exaggerated " Cock Lane ghost " (*q.v.*), which " haunted " Sampford Peverell for about three years in the first decade of the 19th century. The house selected was occupied by a man named Chave, and besides the usual knockings, the inmates were beaten ; in one instance a powerful " unattached arm " flung a folio Greek Testament from a bed into the middle of a room. The Rev. Charles Caled Colton (credited as the author of these freaks) offered £100 to anyone who could explain the matter except on supernatural grounds. No one, however, claimed the reward. Colton died 1832.

Sampi. A Greek numeral. (*See* EPISEMON.)

Sampler. A pattern, A piece of fancy-sewed or embroidered work done by girls for practice.

Samp'son. *A dominie Sampson.* A humble pedantic scholar, awkward, irascible, and very old-fashioned. The character occurs in Sir Walter Scott's *Guy Mannering*.

Samson. Any man of unusual strength ; so called from the Judge of Israel.

The British Samson. Thomas Topham, son of a London carpenter. He lifted three hogsheads of water, weighing 1,836 pounds, in the presence of thousands of spectators assembled in Bath Street, Coldbath Fields, May 28th, 1741. Being plagued by a faithless woman, he put an end to his life in the flower of his age. (1710-1753.)

The Kentish Samson. Richard Joy, who died 1742, at the age of 67. His tombstone is in St. Peter's churchyard, Isle of Thanet.

Samson Carrasco. (See *Don Quixote*, pt. ii. bk. i. chap. iv.)

San Benito (*The*). The vest of penitence. It was a coarse yellow tunic worn by persons condemned to death by the Inquisition on their way to the *auto da fé;* it was painted over with flames, demons, etc. In the case of those who expressed repentance for their errors, the flames were directed downwards. Penitents who had been taken before the Inquisition had to wear this badge for a stated period. Those worn by Jews, sorcerers, and renegades bore a St. Andrew's cross in red on back and front.

San Chris'tobal. A mountain in Grana'da, seen by ships arriving from the African coast ; so called because colossal images of St. Christopher were erected in places of danger, from the superstitious notion that whoever cast his eye on the gigantic saint would be free from peril for the whole day.

San Suen'a. Zaragoza.

Sance-bell. Same as " Sanctus-bell." (*See* SACRING-BELL.)

San'cha. Daughter of Garcias, King of Navarre, and wife of Fernan Gonsa'lez of Castile. She twice saved the life of the count her husband ; once on his road to Navarre, being waylaid by personal enemies and cast into a dungeon, she liberated him by bribing the gaoler. The next time was when Fernan was waylaid and held prisoner at Leon. On this occasion she effected his escape by changing clothes with him.

꙾ The tale resembles that of the Countess of Nithsdale, who effected the escape of her husband from the Tower on February 23rd, 1715 ; and that of the Countess de Lavalette, who, in 1815, liberated the count her husband from prison by changing clothes with him.

Sancho Panza, the squire of Don Quixote, was governor of Barata'ria, according to Cervantes. He is described as a short, pot-bellied rustic, full of common sense, but without a grain of "spirituality." He rode upon an ass, *Dapple*, and was famous for his proverbs. Panza, in Spanish, means *paunch*.

A Sancho Panza. A justice of the peace. In allusion to Sancho, as judge in the isle of Barata'ria.

Sancho Panza's wife, called Terēsa, pt. ñ. i. 5 ; Maria, pt. ii. iv. 7 ; Juāna, pt. i. 7 ; and Joan, pt. i. 21.

Sancho. The model painting of this squire is Leslie's *Sancho and the Duchess.*

Sanchoni'atho. A forgery of the nine books of this "author" was printed at Bremen in 1837. The "original" was said to have been discovered in the convent of St. Maria de Merinhâo by Colonel Pereira, a Portuguese; but it was soon discovered (1) that no such convent existed, (2) that there was no colonel in the Portuguese service of the name, and (3) that the paper of the MS. displayed the water-mark of an Osnabrück paper-mill. (*See* RICHARD OF CIRENCESTER.)

Sanctum Sancto'rum. A private room into which no one uninvited enters. The reference is to the Holy of Holies in the Jewish Temple, a small chamber into which none but the high priest might enter, and that only on the Great Day of Atonement. A man's private house is his sanctuary ; his own special private room in that house is the sanctuary of the sanctuary, or the *sanctum sancto'rum.*

Sancy' Diamond. So called from Nicholas de Harlay, Sieur de Sancy, who bought it for 70,000 francs (£2,800) of Don Antonio, Prince of Crato and King of Portugal *in partibus*. It belonged at one time to Charles the Bold of Burgundy, who wore it with other diamonds at the battle of Granson, in 1476 ; and after his defeat it was picked up by a Swiss soldier, who sold it for a gulden to a clergyman. The clergyman sold it sixteen years afterwards (1492) to a merchant of Lucerne for 5,000 ducats (£1,125). It was next purchased (1495) by Emanuel the Fortunate of Portugal, and remained in the house of Aviz till the kingdom was annexed to Spain (1580), when Don Antonio sold it to Sieur de Sancy, in whose family it remained more than a century. On one occasion the sieur, being desirous of aiding Henri I. in his struggle for the crown, pledged the diamond to the Jews at Metz. The servant entrusted with it, being attacked by robbers, swallowed the diamond, and was murdered, but Nicholas de Harlay subsequently recovered the diamond out of the dead body of his unfortunate messenger. We next find it in the possession of James II., who purchased it for the crown of England. James carried it with him in his flight to France in 1688, when it was sold to Louis XIV. for £25,000. Louis XV. wore it at his coronation, but during the Revolution it was again sold. Napoleon in his high and palmy days bought it, but it was sold in 1835 to

Prince Paul Demidoff for £80,000. The prince sold it in 1830 to M. Levrat, administrator of the Mining Society, who was to pay for it in four instalments; but his failing to fulfil his engagement became, in 1832, the subject of a lawsuit, which was given in favour of the prince. We next hear of it in Bombay; and in 1867 it was transmitted to England by the firm of Forbes & Co. It now belongs to the Czar.

Sand (*George*). The *nom de plume* of Madame Dudevant, a French authoress, assumed out of attachment to Jules Sand or Sandeau, a young student, in conjunction with whom she published her first novel, *Rose et Blanche*, under the name of "Jules Sand." (1804-1876.)

Sand. *A rope of sand.* Something nominally effective and strong, but in reality worthless and untrustworthy.

My sand of life is almost run. The allusion is to the hour-glass.

"Alas! dread lord, you see the case wherein I stand, and how little sand is left to run in my poor glass."—*Reynard the Fox*, iv.

Sand-blind. Virtually blind, but not wholly so; what the French call *ber-lue*; our *par-blind*. (Old English suffix *sam*, half; or Old High German *sand*, virtually.) It is only fit for a Launcelot Gobbo to derive it from *sand*, a sort of earth.

"This is my true-begotten father, who, being more than sand-blind, high-gravel blind, knows me not."—*Shakespeare: Merchant of Venice*, ii. 2.

Sand-man is about (*The*). (*See* DUSTMAN.)

Sands. *Footprints on the sands of Time* (*Longfellow: Psalm of Life*). This beautiful expression was probably suggested by a letter of the First Napoleon to his Minister of the Interior respecting the poor-laws:—"It is melancholy [he says] to see time passing away without being put to its full value. Surely in a matter of this kind we should endeavour to do something, that we may say that we have not lived in vain, that we may leave some impress of our lives on the sands of Time."

To number sands. To undertake an endless or impossible task.

"Alas! poor duke, the task he undertakes Is numbering sands and drinking oceans dry." *Shakespeare: Richard II.*, ii. 2.

San'dabar. An Arabian writer, celebrated for his *Parables*. He lived about a century before the Christian era.

Sandal. *A man without sandals.* A prodigal; so called by the ancient Jews, because the seller gave his sandals to the buyer as a ratification of his bargain. (Ruth iv. 7.)

Sandals of Theram'enes (4 syl.), which would fit any foot. Theramenes, one of the Athenian oligarchy, was nicknamed "the trimmer" (*cothurnus*, a sandal or boot which might be worn on either foot), because no dependence could be placed on him. He blew hot and cold with the same breath. The proverb is applied to a trimmer.

Sandal'phon. One of the three angels who receive the prayers of the Israelites, and weave crowns for them. (*Longfellow*.)

Sandalwood. A corruption of Santalwood, a plant of the genus *San'-talum* and natural order *Santala'ceæ*.

Sandbanks. Wynants, a Dutch artist, is famous for his homely pictures, where sandbanks form a most striking feature.

Sandema'nians or *Glassites*. A religious party expelled from the Church of Scotland for maintaining that national churches, being "kingdoms of this world," are unlawful. Called Glassites from John Glass, the founder (1728), and called Sandemanians from Robert Sandĕman, who published a series of letters on the subject in 1755.

Sand'en [*sandy-den*]. The great palace of King Lion, in the tale of *Reynard the Fox.*

Sandford and Merton. Thomas Day's tale so called.

Sandjar. One of the Seljuke Sultans of Persia; so called from the place of his birth. Generally considered the *Persian Alexander.* (1117-1158.)

Sandschaki or **Sandschaki-sherif** [*the standard of green silk*]. The sacred banner of the Mussulmans. It is now enveloped in four coverings of green taffeta, enclosed in a case of green cloth. The standard is twelve feet high, and the golden ornament (a closed hand) which surmounts it holds a copy of the Koran written by the Calif Osman III. In times of peace this banner is guarded in the hall of the "noble vestment," as the dress worn by "the prophet" is styled. In the same hall are preserved the sacred teeth, the holy beard, the sacred stirrup, the sabre, and the bow of Mahomet.

Sandwich. A piece of meat between two slices of bread; so called from the Earl of Sandwich (the noted "Jemmy Twitcher"), who passed whole days in gambling, bidding the waiter bring him for refreshment a piece of meat between two pieces of bread, which he ate without stopping from play. This contrivance was not first hit upon by the earl in the reign of George III., as the Romans were very fond of "sandwiches," called by them *offula.*

Sandwichman (*A*). A perambulating advertisement displayer, with an advertisement board before and behind.

" The Earl of Shaftesbury desired to say a word on behalf of a very respectable body of men, ordinarily called ' sandwiches.' " — *The Times,* March 16th, 1867.

Sang Bleu. Of high aristocratic descent. The words are French, and mean *blue blood,* but the notion is Spanish. The old families of Spain who trace their pedigree beyond the time of the Moorish conquest say that their venous blood is blue, but that of common people is black.

Sang Froid (French, "cool blood"), meaning indifference ; without temper or irritation.

Sangaree'. A West Indian drink, consisting of Madeira wine, syrup, water, and nutmeg.

San'glamore (3 syl.). Braggadochio's sword. (*Spenser : Faërie Queene.*)

San'glier (*Sir*). Meant for Shan O'Neil, leader of the Irish insurgents in 1567. (*Spenser : Faërie Queene*, v.)
Sanglier des Ardennes. Guillaume de la Marck, driven from Liège, for the murder of the Bishop of Liège, and beheaded by the Archduke Maximilian. (1446-1485.)

Sangra'do (*Dr.*), in the romance of *Gil Blas,* prescribes warm water and bleeding for every ailment. The character is a satire on Helvetius. (Book ii. 2.)

" If the Sangra'dos were ignorant, there was at any rate more to spare in the veins then than there is now."—*Daily Telegraph.*

Sangreal. The vessel from which our Saviour drank at the Last Supper, and which (as it is said) was afterwards filled by Joseph of Arimathe'a with the blood that flowed from His wounds. This blood was reported to have the power of prolonging life and preserving chastity. The quest of this cup forms the most fertile source of adventures to the knights of the Round Table. The story of the Sangreal or Sangraal was first written in verse by Chrestien de Troyes (end of the tenth century), thence Latinised (thirteenth century), and finally turned into French prose by Gautier Map, by "order of Lord Henry" (Henry III.). It commences with the genealogy of our Saviour, and details the whole Gospel history; but the prose romance begins with Joseph of Arimathe'a. Its quest is continued in *Percival,* a romance of the fifteenth century, which gives the adventures of a young Welshman, raw and inexperienced, but admitted to knighthood. At his death the sangreal, the sacred lance, and the silver trencher were carried up to heaven in the presence of attendants, and have never since been seen on earth.

Tennyson has a poem entitled *The Holy Grail.*

Sanguine [*murrey*]. One of the nine colours used by foreign heralds in escutcheons. It is expressed by lines of vert and purpure crossed, that is, diagonals from right to left crossing diagonals from left to right. (*See* TENNE.)

Tenné and Sanguine are not used by English heralds. (*See* HERALDS.)

Sanguinary James (*A*). A sheep's head not singed. A jemmy is a sheep's head ; so called from James I., who introduced into England the national Scotch dish of "singed sheep's head and trotters." No real Scotch dinner is complete without a haggis, a sheep's head and trotters, and a hotch-potch (in summer), or cocky leekie (in winter).
A cocky leekie is a fowl boiled or stewed with leeks or kale—*i.e.* salt beef and curly greens.

Gimmer (a sheep) cannot be the origin of Jemmy, as the G is *always* soft.

San'hedrim. The Jewish Sanhedrim probably took its form from the seventy elders appointed to assist Moses in the government. After the captivity it seems to have been a permanent consistory court. The president was called "Ha-Nasi" (the prince), and the vice-president "Abba" (father). The seventy sat in a semicircle, thirty-five on each side of the president ; the "father" being on his right hand, and the "hacan," or sub-deputy, on his left. All questions of the "Law" were dogmatically settled by the Sanhedrim, and those who refused obedience were excommunicated. (Greek, *sunedrion,* a sitting together.)
Sanhedrim, in Dryden's satire of *Absalom and Achitophel,* stands for the British Parliament.

" The Sanhedrim long time as chief he ruled,
Their reason guided, and their passion cooled."

Sanjaksherif. The flag of the prophet. (Turkish, *sanjak*, a standard.)

Sans Culottes (French, *without trousers*). A name given by the aristocratic section during the French Revolution to the popular party, the favourite leader of which was Henriot. (1793.)

Sans Culottides. The five complementary days added to the twelve months of the Revolutionary Calendar. Each month being made to consist of thirty days, the riff-raff days which would not conform to the law were named in honour of the *sans culottes*, and made idle days or holidays.

Sans-culottism. Red republicanism.

Sans Peur et Sans Reproche. Pierre du Terrail, Chevalier de Bayard, was called *Le chevalier sans peur et sans reproche.* (1476-1524.)

Sans Souci (French). Free and easy, void of care. There is a place so called near Potsdam, where Frederick II. (the Great) built a royal palace.

Enfans Sans Souci. The Tradesmen's company of actors, as opposed to the Lawyers', called "Basochians" (*q.v.*). This company was organised in France in the reign of Charles VIII., for the performance of short comedies, in which public characters and the manners of the day were turned into ridicule. The manager of the "Care-for-Nothings" (*sans souci*) was called "The Prince of Fools." One of their dramatic pieces, entitled *Master Pierre Pathelin*, was an immense favourite with the Parisians.

Sansca'ra. The ten essential rites of Hindus of the first three castes : (1) at the conception of a child ; (2) at the quickening ; (3) at birth ; (4) at naming ; (5) carrying the child out to see the moon ; (6) giving him food to eat ; (7) the ceremony of tonsure ; (8) investiture with the string ; (9) the close of his studies ; (10) the ceremony of "marriage," when he is qualified to perform the sacrifices ordained.

Sansfoy [*Infidelity*]. A Saracen "who cared for neither God nor man," encountered by St. George and slain. (*Spenser : Faërie Queene*, book i. 2.)

Sansjoy [*Without the peace of God*]. Brother of Sansfoy (*Infidelity*) and Sansloy (*Without the law of God*). He is a paynim knight, who fights with St. George in the palace grounds of Pride, and would have been slain if Duessa had not rescued him. He is carried in the car of Night to the infernal regions,

where he is healed of his wounds by Escula'pius. (*Spenser : Faërie Queene*, book i. 4, 5.)

Sansloy [*Irreligion*], brother of Sansfoy (*q.v.*). Having torn off the disguise of Archima'go and wounded the lion, he carries off Una into the wilderness. Her shrieks arouse the fauns and satyrs, who come to her rescue, and Sansloy flees. Una is Truth, and, being without Holiness (the Red-Cross Knight), is deceived by Hypocrisy. As soon as Truth joins Hypocrisy, instead of Holiness, Irreligion breaks in and carries her away. The reference is to the reign of Queen Mary, when the Reformation was carried captive, and the lion was wounded by the "False-law of God." (*Spenser : Faërie Queene*, book i. 2.)

In book ii. Sansloy appears again as the cavalier of Perissa or Prodigality.

Sansonetto (in *Orlando Furioso*). A Christian regent of Mecca, vicegerent of Charlemagne.

Santa Casa (Italian, the holy house). The reputed house in which the Virgin Mary lived at Nazareth, miraculously translated to Fiume, in Dalmatia, in 1291, thence to Recana'ti in 1294, and finally to Macera'ta, in Italy, to a piece of land belonging to the Lady Loretto.

Santa Claus or **Santa Klaus.** A corrupt contraction of Sankt Nikolaus (*Sank'ni kolaus—i.e.* St. Nicolas), the patron saint of children. The vigil of his feast is still held in some places, but for the most part his name is now associated with Christmas-tide. The old custom used to be for someone, on December 5th, to assume the costume of a bishop and distribute small gifts to "good children." The present custom is to put toys and other little presents into a stocking or pillow-case late on Christmas Eve, when the children are asleep, and when they wake on Christmas morn each child finds in the stocking or bag hung at the bedside the gift sent by Santa Claus. St. Nicholas' day is December 6. The Dutch *Kriss Kringle*.

Saophron. The girdle worn by Grecian women, whether married or not. The bridegroom loosed the bride's girdle, whence "to loose the girdle" came to mean to deflower a woman, and a prostitute was called "a woman whose girdle is unloosed" (Γυνὴ λυσίζωνος).

Sapphics. A Greek and Latin metre, so named from Sappho, the inventor. Horace always writes this metre in four-line stanzas, the last being an Adon'ic. There must be a cæsura at the fifth foot of each of the first three lines, which runs thus:—

—◡|——|—‖◡◡|—◡|—◡

The Adonic is—

—◡◡|—◡ *or* ——

The first and third stanzas of the famous *Ode* of Horace (i. 22) may be translated thus, preserving the metre:—

He of sound life, who ne'er with sinners
    wendeth,
Needs no Maurish bow, such as malice bendeth,
Nor with poisoned darts life from harm de-
    fendeth,
        Fuscus believe me.

Once I, unarmed, was in a forest roaming,
Singing love lays, when i' the secret gloaming
Rushed a huge wolf, which, though in fury
    foaming,
        Did not aggrieve me.   *E. C. B.*

Sappho of Toulouse. Clémence Isaure (2 syl.), a wealthy lady of Toulouse, who instituted in 1490 the "Jeux Floraux," and left funds to defray their annual expenses. She composed a beautiful *Ode to Spring.* (1463-1513.)

Sar'acen Wheat (French, *Blé-sarrasin*). Buck-wheat; so called because it was brought into Spain by the Moors or Saracens. (*See* BUCKWHEAT.)

Sar'acens. Ducange derives this word from *Sarah* (Abraham's wife); Hottinger from the Arabic *saraca* (to steal); Forster from *sahra* (a desert); but probably it is the Arabic *sharakyoun* or *sharkeyn* (the eastern people), as opposed to Mag'haribë (the western people —*i.e.* of Morocco). Any unbaptised person was called a Saracen in mediæval romance. (Greek, *Surakēnos.*)

"So the Arabs, or Saracens, as they are called
. . . gave men the choice of three things."—*E. A. Freeman: General Sketch*, chap. vi. p. 117.

Saragoz'a. *The Maid of Saragoza.* Augustina, who was only twenty-two when, her lover being shot, she mounted the battery in his place. The French, after besieging the town for two months, had to retreat, August 15th, 1808.

Sar'aswa'ti. Wife of Brahma, and goddess of fine arts. (*Hindu mythology*).

Sar'casm. A flaying or plucking off of the skin; a cutting taunt. (Greek, *sarkazo*, to flay, etc.)

Sarce'net (2 syl.). A corruption of *Saracennet*, from its Saracenic or Oriental origin.

Sarcenet Chidings. Loving rebukes, as those of a mother to a young child— "You little rogue," etc.

"The child reddened . . . and hesitated, while the mother, with many a fye . . . and such sarcenet chidings as tender mothers give to spoiled children . . ."—*Sir W. Scott: The Monastery*, ii.

Sarcoph'agus. A stone, according to Pliny, which consumed the flesh, and was therefore chosen by the ancients for coffins. It is called sometimes *lapis Assius*, because it was found at Assos of Lycia. (Greek, *sarx*, flesh; *phagein*, to eat or consume.)

Sardanapa'lus. King of Nineveh and Assyria, noted for his luxury and voluptuousness. His effeminacy induced Arba'ces, the Mede, to conspire against him. Myrra, an Ionian slave, and his favourite concubine, roused him from his lethargy, and induced him to appear at the head of his armies. He won three successive battles, but being then defeated, was induced by Myrra to place himself on a funeral pile, which she herself set fire to, and then jumping into the flames, perished with her beloved master. (Died B.C. 817.) (*Byron: Sardanapalus.*)

A Sardanapalus. Any luxurious, extravagant, self-willed tyrant. (*See above*.)

Sardanapalus of China. Cheo-tsin, who shut himself and his queen in his palace, and set fire to the building, that he might not fall into the hands of Woo-wong, who founded the dynasty of Tchow (B.C. 1154-1122). It was Cheo-tsin who invented the chopsticks.

Sardin'ian Laugh. Laughing on the wrong side of one's mouth. The *Edinburgh Review* says: "The ancient Sardinians used to get rid of their old relations by throwing them into deep pits, and the sufferers were expected to feel delighted at this attention to their well-being." (July, 1849.)

Sardon'ic Smile, Grin, or Laughter. A smile of contempt: so used by Homer.

"The Sardonic or Sardinian laugh. A laugh caused, it was supposed, by a plant growing in Sardinia, of which they who ate died laughing." —*Trench: Words*, lecture iv. p. 176.

The *Herba Sardon'ia* (so called from Sardis, in Asia Minor) is so acrid that it produces a convulsive movement of the nerves of the face, resembling a painful grin. Byron says of the Corsair, *There was a laughing devil in his sneer.*

"'Tis envy's safest, surest rule
To hide her rage in ridicule;
The vulgar eye the best beguiles
When all her snakes are decked with smiles,
Sardonic smiles by rancour raised."
        Swift: Pheasant and Lark.

Sar'donyx. An orange-brown cornelian. Pliny says it is called *sard* from Sardis, in Asia Minor, where it is found, and *onyx*, the nail, because its colour resembles that of the skin under the nail (xxxvii. 6).

Sarnia. Guernsey. Adjective, *Sarnian.*

"Sometimes ... mistakes occur in our little bits of Sarnian intelligence."—*Mrs. Edwardes : A Girton Girl,* chap. iii.

Sarpe'don. A favourite of the gods, who assisted Priam when Troy was besieged by the allied Greeks. When Achilles refused to fight, Sarpe'don made great havoc in battle, but was slain by Patroc'los. (*Homer : Iliad.*)

Sars'en Stones. The "Druidical" sandstones of Wiltshire and Berkshire are so called. The early Christian Saxons used the word Saresyn as a synonym of pagan or heathen, and as these stones were popularly associated with Druid worship, they were called Saresyn or heathen stones. Robert Ricart says of Duke Rollo, "He was a Saresyn come out of Denmark into France." Another derivation is the Phœnician *sarsen* (a rock), applied to any huge mass of stone that has been drawn from the quarry in its rude state.

✴ These boulders are no more connected with the Druids than Stonehenge is (*q.v.*).

Sartor Resartus. (*The Tailor Patched.*) By Thomas Carlyle.

Diogenes Teufelsdröckh is Carlyle himself, and *Entepfuhl* is his native village of Ecclefechan.

The Rose Goddess, according to Froude, is Margaret Gordon, but Strachey is *Blumine, i.e.* Kitty Kirkpatrick, daughter of Colonel Achilles Kirkpatrick, and *Rose Garden* is Strachey's garden at Shooter's Hill. The duenna is Mrs. Strachey.

The Zahdarms are Mr. and Mrs. Buller, and *Toughgut* is Charles Buller.

Philistine is the Rev. Edward Irving.

Sash Window is a window that moves up and down in a groove. (French, *chassis,* a sash or groove.)

Sassan'ides (4 syl.). The first Persian dynasty of the historic period ; so named because Ard'eshir, the founder, was son of Sassan, a lineal descendant of Xerxes.

Sassenach (ch = k). A Keltic word for a Saxon, or for the English language.

Sa'tan, in Hebrew, means *enemy.*

"To whom the Arch-enemy
(And hence in heaven called Satan)."
    Milton : Paradise Lost, bk. i. 81, 82.

Satan's Journey to Earth (*Milton : Paradise Lost,* iii. 418 to the end). He starts from Hell, and wanders a long time about the confines of the Universe, where he sees Chaos and Limbo. The Universe is a vast extended plain, fortified by part of the ethereal quintessence out of which the stars were created. There is a gap in the fortification, through which angels pass when they visit our earth. Being weary, Satan rests awhile at this gap, and contemplates the vast Universe. He then transforms himself into an angel of light and visits Uriel, whom he finds in the Sun. He asks Uriel the way to Paradise, and Uriel points out to him our earth. Then plunging through the starry vault, the waters above the firmament, and the firmament itself, he alights safely on Mount Niphātes, in Armenia.

Satan'ic. *The Satanic School.* So Southey called Lord Byron and his imitators, who set at defiance the generally received notions of religion. Of English writers, Byron, Shelley, Moore, and Bulwer are the most prominent ; of French writers Rousseau, Victor Hugo, Paul de Kock, and George Sand.

Sat'ire (2 syl.). Scaliger's derivation of this word from *satyr* is untenable. It is from *sat'ura* (full of variety), *sat'ura lanx,* a hotchpotch or olla podrida. As *max'umus, optu'mus,* etc., became *maximus, optimus,* so "satura" became *sat'ira.* (*See* Dryden's Dedication prefixed to his *Satires.*)

Father of satire. Archil'ochos of Paros (B.C. seventh century).

Father of French satire. Mathurin Regnier (1573-1613).

Father of Roman satire. Lucilius (B.C. 148-103).

"Lucilius was the man who, bravely bold,
To Roman vices did the mirror hold ;
Protected humble goodness from reproach,
Showed worth on foot, and rascals in a coach."
    Dryden : Art of Poetry, c. ii.

Saturday. (*See* BLACK SATURDAY.)

Saturn or *Kronos* [*Time*] devoured all his children except Jupiter, Neptune, and Pluto. Jupiter means *air,* Neptune *water,* and Pluto *the grave.* These Time cannot consume.

Saturn is a very evil planet to be born under. "The children of the sayd Saturne shall be great jangeleres and chyders ... and they will never forgyve tyll they be revenged of theyr quarell." (*Compost of Ptholomeus.*)

Saturn, with the ancient alchemists, designated lead.

Saturn's Tree, in alchemy, is a deposit of crystallised lead, massed together in the form of a "tree." It is produced by a shaving of zinc in a solution of the acetate of lead. In alchemy Saturn = lead. (*See* DIANA'S TREE.)

Saturna'lia. A time of licensed disorder and misrule. With the Romans it was the festival of Saturn, and was celebrated the 17th, 18th, and 19th of December. During its continuance no public business could be transacted, the law courts were closed, the schools kept holiday, no war could be commenced, and no malefactor punished. Under the empire the festival was extended to seven days.

Saturnian Days. Days of dulness, when everything is venal.

> " Then rose the seed of Chaos and of Night
> To blot out order and extinguish light,
> Of dull and venal a new world to mould,
> And bring Saturnian days of lead and gold."
> *Dunciad,* iv.

⁂ They are *lead* to indicate dulness, and *gold* to indicate venality.

Satur'nian Verses. Old-fashioned. A rude composition employed in satire among the ancient Romans. Also a peculiar metre, consisting of three iambics and a syllable over, joined to three trochees, according to the following nursery metre :—

> " The queen was in the par-lour . . . ."
> The maids were in the garden . . ."

" The Fescennine and Saturnian were the same, for as they were called Saturnian from their ancientness, when Saturn reigned in Italy, they were called Fescennine from Fescennina [*sic*], where they were first practised."—*Dryden: Dedication of Juvenal.*

Sat'urnine (3 syl.). A grave, phlegmatic disposition, dull and heavy. Astrologers affirm that such is the disposition of those who are born under the influence of the leaden planet Saturn.

Sat'yr. The most famous representation of these goat-men is that of Praxit'eles, a sculptor of Athens in the fourth century B.C.

Sat'yrane (3 syl.). A blunt but noble knight who delivered Una from the fauns and satyrs. The meaning is this : Truth, being driven from the towns and cities, took refuge in caves and dens, where for a time it lay concealed. At length Sir Satyrane (Luther) rescues Una from bondage ; but no sooner is this the case than she falls in with Archima'go, to show how very difficult it was at the Reformation to separate Truth from Error. (*Spenser : Faërie Queene,* bk. i.)

Sauce means " salted food," for giving a relish to meat, as pickled roots, herbs, and so on. (Latin, *salsus.*)

The sauce was better than the fish. The accessories were better than the main part. This may be said of a book in which the plates and getting up are better than the matter it contains.

To serve the same sauce. To retaliate ; to give as good as you take ; to serve in the same manner.

" After him another came unto her, and served her with the same sauce ; then a third . . ."—*The Man in the Moon,* etc. (1609).

Sauce (*To*). To intermix.

" Then she fell to sauce her desires with threatenings."—*Sidney.*

" Folly sauced with discretion."—*Shakespeare : Troilus and Cressida,* i. 2.

Sauce to the Goose is Sauce to the Gander. (*See* GANDER.)

Saucer Eyes. Big, round, glaring eyes.

> " Yet when a child (bless me !) I thought
> That thou a pair of horns had'st got,
> With eyes like saucers staring."
> *Peter Pindar : Ode to the Devil.*

Saucer Oath. When a Chinese is put in the witness-box, he says : " If I do not speak the truth may my soul be cracked and broken like this saucer." So saying, he dashes the saucer on the ground. The Roman Catholic imprecation, known as " Bell, Book, and Candle " (*q.v.*), and the Jewish marriage custom of breaking a wine-glass, are of a similar character.

Saucy. Rakish, irresistible ; or rather that care-for-nobody, jaunty, daring behaviour which has won for many of our regiments the term as a compliment. It is also applied metaphorically to some inanimate things, as " saucy waves," which dare attack the very moon ; the " saucy world," which dares defy the very gods ; the " saucy mountains," " winds," " wit," and so on.

"But still the little petrel was saucy as the waves."
Eliza Cook : The Young Mariners, stanza 7.

Saul, in Dryden's satire of *Absalom and Achitophel,* is meant for Oliver Cromwell. As Saul persecuted David and drove him from Jerusalem, so Cromwell persecuted Charles II. and drove him from England.

> " They who, when Saul was dead, without a blow
> Made foolish Ishbosheth [Richard Cromwell]
> the crown forego." Part i. lines 57, 58.

Saul among the prophets ? The Jews said of our Lord, " How knoweth this man letters, having never learned ? " (John vii. 15.) Similarly at the conversion of Saul, afterwards called Paul, the Jews said in substance, " Is it possible that Saul can be a convert ? " (Acts ix. 21.) The proverb applies to a person who unexpectedly bears tribute to a party or doctrine that he has hitherto vigorously assailed. (1 Sam. x. 12.)

Saut Lairds o' Dunscore (*The*). Lords or gentlefolk who have only a name but no money. The tale is that the "puir wee lairds of Dunscore" clubbed together to buy a stone of salt, which was doled out to the subscribers in small spoonfuls, that no one should get more than his due quota.

Sav'age (2 syl.). One who lives in a wood (Greek, *hulē*, a forest; Latin, *silva;* Spanish, *salvage;* Italian, *selvaggio;* French, *sauvage*).

Save. *To save appearances.* To do something to obviate or prevent exposure or embarrassment.

Save the Mark. In archery when an archer shot well it was customary to cry out "God save the mark!"—*i.e.* prevent anyone coming after to hit the same mark and displace my arrow. Ironically it is said to a novice whose arrow is nowhere.

God save the mark! (1 *Henry IV.*, i. 3). Hotspur, apologising to the king for not sending the prisoners according to command, says the messenger was a "popinjay," who made him mad with his unmanly ways, and who talked "like a waiting gentlewoman of guns, drums, and wounds (God save the mark!)"—meaning that he himself had been in the brunt of battle, and it would be sad indeed if "his mark" was displaced by this court butterfly. It was an ejaculation of derision and contempt.

✷ So (in *Othello*, i. 1) Iago says he was "his Moorship's ancient; bless the mark!" expressive of derision and contempt.

In like manner (in *The Merchant of Venice*, ii. 2), Launcelot Gobbo says his master [Shylock] is a kind of devil, "God bless the mark!"

So (in *The Ring and the Book*) Browning says:

" Deny myself [to] pleasure you,
The sacred and superior. Save the mark !"

The *Observer* (Oct. 26, 1894) speaks of "the comic operas (save the mark!) that have lately been before us." An ejaculation of derision and contempt.

And Mr. Chamberlain (in his speech, September 5th, 1894) says:

"The policy of this government, which cal's itself (God save the mark!) an English government . . ."

✷ Sometimes it refers simply to the perverted natural order of things, as

"travelling by *night* and resting (save the mark!) by day." (*U. S. Magazine,* October, 1894.)

✷ And sometimes it is an ejaculated prayer to avert the ill omen of an observation, as (in *Romeo and Juliet*) where the nurse says:

" I saw the wound, I saw it with mine eyes (God save the mark!) upon his manly breast."

Savoir Faire (French). Ready wit; skill in getting out of a scrape; hence "*Vivre de son savoir-faire,*" to live by one's wits; "*Avoir du savoir-faire,*" to be up to snuff, to know a thing or two.

" He had great confidence in his *savoir-faire.*"— *Sir W. Scott: Guy Mannering,* chap. xxxiv.

Savoy (*The*). A precinct of the Strand, London, noted for the palace of Savoy, originally the seat of Peter, Earl of Savoy, who came to England to visit his niece Eleanor, wife of Henry III. At the death of the earl the house became the property of the queen, who gave it to her second son, Edmund (Earl of Lancaster), and from this period it was attached to the Duchy of Lancaster. When the Black Prince brought Jean *le Bon*, King of France, captive to London (1356), he lodged him in the Savoy Palace, where he remained till 1359, when he was removed to Somerton Castle, in Lincolnshire. In 1360 he was lodged in the Tower; but, two months afterwards, was allowed to return to France on certain conditions. These conditions being violated by the royal hostages, Jean voluntarily returned to London, and had his old quarters again assigned to him, and died in 1364. The rebels under Wat Tyler burnt down the old palace in 1381; but it was rebuilt in 1505 by Henry VII., and converted into a hospital for the poor, under the name of St. John's Hospital. Charles II. used it for wounded soldiers and sailors. St. Mary-le-Savoy or the Chapel of St. John still stands in the precinct, and has recently been restored.

N.B. Here, in 1552, was established the first flint-glass manufactory.

Saw. In Christian art an attribute of St. Simon and St. James the Less, in allusion to the tradition of their being sawn to death in martyrdom.

Sawdust Parlance (*In*). Circus parlance. Of course, the allusion is to the custom of sifting sawdust over the arena to prevent the horses from slipping.

Sawny or **Sandy.** A Scotchman ; a contraction of "Alexander."

Saxifrage. So called because its tender rootlets will penetrate the hardest rock, and break it up.

Saxon Castles.

Alnwick Castle, given to Ivo de Vesey by the Conqueror.

Bamborough Castle (Northumberland), the palace of the kings of Northumberland, and built by King Ida, who began to reign 559 ; now converted into charity schools and signal-stations.

Carisbrook Castle, enlarged by Fitz-Osborne, five centuries later.

Conisborough Castle (York).

Goodrich Castle (Herefordshire).

Kenilworth Castle, built by Kenelm, King of Mercia. Kenil-worth means Kenhelm's dwelling.

Richmond Castle (York), belonging to the Saxon earl Edwin, given by the Conqueror to his nephew Alan, Earl of Bretagne ; a ruin for three centuries. The keep remains.

Rochester Castle, given to Odo, natural brother of the Conqueror.

Saxon Characteristics (architectural).

(1) The quoining consists of a long stone set at the corner, and a short one lying on it and bonding into the wall.

(2) The use of large heavy blocks of stone in some parts, while the rest is built of Roman bricks.

(3) An arch with straight sides to the upper part instead of curves.

(4) The absence of buttresses.

(5) The use in windows of rude balusters.

(6) A rude round staircase west of the tower, for the purpose of access to the upper floors.

(7) Rude carvings in imitation of Roman work. (*Rickman.*)

Saxon Duke (in *Hudibras*). John Frederick, Duke of Saxony, a very corpulent man. When taken prisoner, Charles V. said, "I have gone hunting many a time, but never saw I such a swine before."

Saxon English. The "Lord's Prayer" is almost all of it Anglo-Saxon. The words *trespasses, trespass,* and *temptation* are of Latin origin. The substitution of "debts" and "debtors" (as "forgive us our debts as we forgive our debtors") is objectionable. Perhaps "Forgive us our wrongdoings, as we forgive them who do wrong to us"

would be less objectionable. The latter clause, "lead us not into temptation," is far more difficult to convert into Anglo-Saxon. The best suggestion I can think of is "lead us not in the ways of sinners," but the real meaning is "put us not to the test." We have the word assay (Assay us not), which would be an excellent translation, but the word is not a familiar one.

Saxon Relics.

The church of Earl's Barton (Northamptonshire). The tower and west doorway.

The church of St. Michael's (St. Albans), erected by the Abbot of St. Albans in 948.

The tower of Bosham church (Sussex)

The east side of the dark and principal cloisters of Westminster Abbey, from the college dormitory on the south to the chapter-house on the north. Edward the Confessor's chapel in Westminster Abbey, now used as the Pix office.

The church of Darenth (Kent) contains some windows of manifest Saxon architecture.

With many others, some of which are rather doubtful.

Saxon Shore. The coast of Norfolk, Suffolk, Essex, Kent, Sussex, and Hampshire, where were castles and garrisons, under the charge of a count or military officer, called *Comes Littoris Saxonici per Britanniam.*

Fort Branodunum (Brancaster) was on the Norfolk coast.

Gariannonum (Burgh) was on the Suffolk coast.

Othona (Ithanchester) was on the Essex coast.

Regulbium (Reculver), Rutupiæ (Richborough), Dubris (Dover), P. Lemanis (Lyme), were on the Kentish coast.

Anderida (Hastings or Pevensey), Portus Adurni (Worthing), were on the Sussex coast.

Say. *To take the say.* To taste meat or wine before it is presented, in order to prove that it is not poisoned. The phrase was common in the reign of Queen Elizabeth.

" Nor deem it meet that you to him convey
The proffered bowl, unless you taste the say."
Rose : Orlando Furioso, xxi. 61.

Sbirri (Italian). A police-force which existed in the pope's dominions. They were domiciled in private houses.

" He points them out to his sbirri and armed ruffians."—*The Daily Telegraph.*

Scævola [*left-handed*]. So Caius Mucius was called, because, when he entered the camp of Porsenna as a spy, and was taken before the king, he deliberately held his hand over a lamp till it was burnt off, to show the Etruscan that he would not shrink from torture.

Scaffold, Scaffolding. A temporary gallery for workmen. In its secondary sense it means the postulates and rough scheme of a system or sustained story. (French, *échafaud*, *échafaudage*.) (*See* CINTER.)

Scaglio'la. Imitation marble, like the pillars of the Pantheon, London. The word is from the Italian *scáglia* (the dust and chips of marble); it is so called because the substance (which is gypsum and Flanders glue) is studded with chips and dust of marble.

Scales. The Koran says, at the judgment day everyone will be weighed in the scales of the archangel Gabriel. His good deeds will be put in the scale called "Light," and his evil ones in the scale called "Darkness;" after which they will have to cross the bridge Al Serát, not wider than the edge of a scimitar. The faithful will pass over in safety, but the rest will fall into the dreary realms of Jehennam.

Scallop Shell. Emblem of St. James of Compostella, adopted, says Erasmus, because the shore of the adjacent sea abounds in them. Pilgrims used them for cup, spoon, and dish; hence the punning crest of the Disington family is a scallop shell. On returning home, the pilgrim placed his scallop shell in his hat to command admiration, and adopted it in his coat-armour. (Danish, *schelp*, a shell; French, *escalope*.)

" I will give thee a palmer's staff of ivory and a scallop-shell of beaten gold."—*The Old Wives' Tale.* (1595.)

Scalloped [*scollopt*]. Having an edge like that of a scallop shell.

Scammoz'zi's Rule. The jointed two-foot rule used by builders, and invented by Vincent Scammozzi, the famous Italian architect. (1540-1609.)

Scamp [*qui exit ex campo*]. A deserter from the field; one who *decamps* without paying his debts. *S* privative and *camp*. (*See* SNOB.)

Scandal means properly a pitfall or snare laid for an enemy; hence a stumbling-block, and morally an aspersion. (Greek, *skan'dalon*.)

" We preach Christ crucified, unto the Jews a [scandal]."—1 Cor. i. 23.

The Hill of Scandal. So Milton calls the Mount of Olives, because King Solomon built thereon "an high place for Chemosh, the abomination of Moab; and for Moloch, the abomination of the children of Ammon " (1 Kings xi. 7).

Scandal-broth. Tea. The reference is to the gossip held by some of the womenkind over their " cups which cheer but not inebriate." Also called " Chatter-broth."

"'I proposed to my venerated visitor . . . to summon my . . . housekeeper . . . with the tea-equipage; but he rejected my proposal with disdain. . . .' 'No scandal-broth,' he exclaimed, 'No unidea'd woman's chatter for me.'"—*Sir W. Scott: Peveril of the Peak* (Prefatory letter).

Scan'dalum Magna'tum [*scandal of the magnates*]. Words in derogation of peers, judges, and other great officers of the realm. What St. Paul calls " speaking evil of dignities."

Scanderbeg. A name given by the Turks to George Castriota, the patriot chief of Epi'rus. The word is a corruption of *Iskander-beg*, Prince Alexander (1414-1467).

Scanderbeg's Sword must have Scanderbeg's Arm—*i.e.* None but Ulysses can draw Ulysses' bow. Scanderbeg is a corruption of Iskander-beg (Alexander the Great), not the Macedonian, but George Castriota, Prince of Albania, so called by the Turks. Mahomet wanted to see his scimitar, but when presented no one could draw it; whereupon the Turkish emperor sent it back as an imposition; but Iskander-beg replied, he had only sent his majesty the sword without sending the arm that drew it. (*See* ROBIN HOOD.)

Scandinavia. Norway, Sweden, Denmark, and Iceland. Pliny speaks of Scandia as an island.

Scant-of-grace (*A*). A madcap; a wild, disorderly, graceless fellow.

" You, a gentleman of birth and breeding, . . . associate yourself with a sort of scant-of-grace, as men call me."—*Sir W. Scott: Kenilworth*, iii.

Scant'ling, a small quantity, is the French *échantillon*, a specimen or pattern.

" A scantling of wit."—*Dryden.*

Scapegoat. The Biajùs or aborigenes of Borneo observe a custom bearing a considerable resemblance to that of the scapegoat. They annually launch a small bark laden with all the sins and misfortunes of the nation, which, says Dr. Leyden, "they imagine will fall on the unhappy crew that first meets with it."

The scapegoat of the family. One made to bear the blame of the rest of the family; one always chidden and found fault with, let who may be in the wrong. The allusion is to a Jewish custom: Two goats being brought to the altar of the tabernacle on the Day of Atonement, the high priest cast lots; one was *for the Lord,* and the other *for Azaz'el.* The goat on which the first lot fell was sacrificed, the other was the scapegoat; and the high priest having, by confession, transferred his own sins and the sins of the people to it, the goat was taken to the wilderness and suffered to escape.

Scaph'ism. Locking up a criminal in the trunk of a tree, bored through so as just to admit the body. Five holes were made—one for the head, and the others for the hands and legs. These parts were anointed with honey to invite the wasps. In this situation the criminal would linger in the burning sun for several days. (Greek, *skaphē,* anything scooped out.)

Scapin. A "barber of Seville;" a knavish valet who makes his master his tool. (*Molière: Les Fourberies de Scapin.*)

Scar'amouch. A braggart and fool, very valiant in words, but a poltroon. According to Dyche, the Italian posture-master, Tiberio Fiurelli, was surnamed Scaramouch Fiurelli. He came to England in 1673, and astonished John Bull with feats of agility.

" Stout Scaramoucha with rush-lance rode in,
And ran a tilt with centaure Arlequin."
Dryden: The Silent Woman (Epilogue).

Scaramouch Dress (*A*), in Molière's time, was black from top to toe; hence he says, "Night has put on her 'scaramouch dress.'"

Scarborough Warning. No warning at all; blow first, then warning. In Scarborough robbers used to be dealt with in a very summary manner by a sort of Halifax gibbet-law, lynch-law, or an *à la lanterne.* Another origin is given of this phrase: It is said that Thomas Stafford, in the reign of Queen Mary, seized the castle of Scarborough, not only without warning, but even before the townsfolk knew he was afoot (1557). (*See* GONE UP.)

" This term *Scarborow warning* grew, some say,
By hasty hanging for rank robbery there.
Who that was met, but sus'pect in that way,
Straight he was trust up, whatever he were."
J. Heywood.

Scarlet. *Though your sins be as scarlet, they shall be as white as snow* (Isa. i. 18). The allusion is to the scarlet fillet tied round the head of the scapegoat.

Though your sins be as scarlet as the fillet on the head of the goat to which the high priest has transferred the sins of the whole nation, yet shall they be forgiven and wiped out.

Scarlet (*Will*). One of the companions of Robin Hood.

Scarlet Coat. Worn by fox-hunters. (*See* RED COAT.)

Scarlet Woman. Some controversial Protestants apply the words to the Church of Rome, and some Romanists, with equal "good taste," apply them to London. The Book of Revelation says, "It is that great city which reigneth over the kings of the earth," and terms the city "Babylon" (chap. xvii.).

Scavenger's Daughter. An instrument of torture invented by Sir William Skevington, lieutenant of the Tower in the reign of Henry VIII. As Skevington was the father of the instrument, the instrument was his daughter.

Sceatta. Anglo-Saxon for "money," or a little silver coin. A *sceat* was an Anglo-Saxon coin.

Scene Painters. The most celebrated are—

Inigo Jones, who introduced the first appropriate decorations for masques.

D'Avenant, who produced perspective scenes in 1656, for *The Siege of Rhodes.*

Betterton was the first to improve the scenic effects in "Dorset Gardens;" his artist was Streater.

John Rich may be called the great reformer of stage scenery in "Covent Garden."

Richards, secretary of the Royal Academy; especially successful in *The Maid of the Mill.* His son was one of the most celebrated of our scene-painters.

Philip James de Loutherbourg was the greatest scene-artist up to Garrick's time. He produced the scenes for *The Winter's Tale,* at the request of that great actor.

John Kemble engaged William Capon, a pupil of Novosielski, to furnish him with scenery for Shakespeare's historic plays.

Patrick Nasmyth, in the North, produced several unrivalled scenes.

Stanfield is well known for his scene of *Acis and Galatē'a.*

William Beverley is the greatest scene-painter of modern times.

Frank Hayman, Thomas Dall, John

Laguerre. William Hogarth, Robert Dighton, Charles Dibdin, David Roberts, Grieve, and Phillips have all aided in improving scene-painting.

Scene Plot. (*See* PLOT.)

Scent. *We are not yet on the right scent.* We have not yet got the right clue. The allusion is to dogs following game by their scent.

Sceptic (Greek) means one who thinks for himself, and does not receive on another's testimony. Pyrrho founded the philosophic sect called "Sceptics," and Epicte'tus combated their dogmas. In theology we apply the word to those who will not accept Revelation.

Sceptre. That of Agamemnon is the most noted. Homer says it was made by Vulcan, who gave it to the son of Saturn. It then passed successively to Jupiter, to Mercury, to Pelops, to Atreus (2 syl.), to Thyestes (3 syl.), and then to Agamemnon. It was found at Phocis, whither it had been taken by Electra. It was looked on with great reverence, and several miracles are attributed to it. It was preserved for many years after the time of Homer, but ultimately disappeared.

Scheherazade [*She-he'-ra-zay'-de*]. Daughter of the Grand Vizier of the Indies. The Sultan Schahriah, having discovered the infidelity of his sultana, resolved to marry a fresh wife every night and have her strangled at daybreak. Scheherazade entreated to become his wife, and so amused him with tales for a thousand and one nights that he revoked his cruel decree, bestowed his affection on his amiable and talented wife, and called her "the liberator of the sex." (*Arabian Nights.*)

Schel'trum. An army drawn up in a circle instead of in a square.

Scheme is something entertained. Scheme is a Greek word meaning what is had or held (*sche'o*); and entertain is the Latin *teneo*, to have or hold, also.

Schiedam. Hollands gin, so called from Schiedam, a town where it is principally manufactured.

Schiites. (*See* SHIITES.)

Schlem'ihl (*Peter*). The name of a man who sold his shadow to the devil, in Chamisso's tale so called. It is a synonym for any person who makes a desperate and silly bargain.

Scholas'tic. Anselm of Laon, *Doctor Scholasticus.* (1050-1117.)

Epipha'nius *the Scholastic.* An Italian scholar. (Sixth century.)

Scholastic Divinity. Divinity subjected to the test of reason and argument, or at least "darkened by the counsel of words." The Athanasian creed is a favourable specimen of this attempt to reduce the mysteries of religion to "right reason;" and the attempts to reconcile the Mosaic cosmogony with modern geology smack of the same school.

Schools.

The six old schools : Eton, Harrow, Winchester, Charterhouse, Westminster, and Rugby.

⁂ Some add St. Paul's, Merchant Taylors', and Shrewsbury.

The six modern schools : Marlborough, Wellington, Clifton, Cheltenham, Repton, and Haileybury.

⁂ Charterhouse has been removed to the hills of Surrey.

St. Paul's has migrated to the West End.

Schoolmaster Abroad (*The*). Lord Brougham said, in a speech (Jan. 29, 1828) on the general diffusion of education, and of intelligence arising therefrom, "Let the soldier be abroad, if he will; he can do nothing in this age. There is another personage abroad . . . the schoolmaster is abroad; and I trust to him, armed with his primer, against the soldier in full military array."

Schoolmen. Certain theologians of the Middle Ages; so called because they lectured in the cloisters or cathedral schools founded by Charlemagne and his immediate successors. They followed the fathers, from whom they differed in reducing every subject to a system, and may be grouped under three periods—

First Period. PLATONISTS (from ninth to twelfth century).

(1) Pierre Abélard (1079-1142).
(2) Flacius Albinus Alcuin (735-804).
(3) John Scotus Erigĕna.
(4) Anselm. *Doctor Scholasticus.* (1050-1117.)
(5) Berenga'rius of Tours (1000-1088).
(6) Gerbert of Aurillac, afterwards Pope Sylvester II. (930-1003).
(7) John of Salisbury (1110-1180).
(8) Lanfranc, Archbishop of Canterbury. (1005-1089.)
(9) Pierre Lombard. *Master of the Sentences,* sometimes called the founder of school divinity. (1100-1164.)
(10) John Roscelinus (eleventh century).

Second Period, or *Golden Age of Scholasticism*. ARISTOTELIANS (thirteenth and fourteenth centuries).

(1) Alain de Lille. *Universal Doctor.* (1114-1203.)

(2) Albertus *Magnus*, of Padua. (1193-1280.)

(3) Thomas Aquinas. *The Angelic Doctor.* (1224-1274.)

(4) Augustine *Triumphans*, Archbishop of Aix. *The Eloquent Doctor.*

(5) John Fidanza Bonaventure. *The Seraphic Doctor.* (1221-1274.)

(6) Alexander of Hales. *Irrefrangible Doctor.* (Died 1245.)

(7) John Duns Scotus. *The Subtle Doctor.* (1265-1308.)

Third Period. NOMINALISM REVIVED. (To the seventeenth century.)

(1) Thomas de Bradwardine. *The Profound Doctor.* (1290-1348.)

(2) John Buridan (1295-1360).

(3) William Durandus de Pourçain. *The Most Resolving* or *Resolute Doctor.* (Died 1332.)

(4) Giles, Archbishop of Bourges. *The Doctor with Good Foundation.*

(5) Gregory of Rim'ini. *The Authentic Doctor.* (Died 1357.)

(6) Robert Holkot. An English divine.

(7) Raymond Lully. *The Illuminated Doctor.* (1234-1315.)

(8) Francis Mairon, of Digne, in Provence.

(9) William Occam. *The Singular* or *Invincible Doctor.* (Died 1347.)

(10) François Suarez, the last of the schoolmen. (1548-1617.)

Schoolmistress (*The*), by Shenstone, is designed for a "portrait of Sarah Lloyd," the dame who first taught the poet himself. She lived in a thatched house before which grew a birch tree.

Scian. (*See* CEAN.)

Science. *The Gay Science* or "*Gay Saber.*" The poetry of the Troubadours, and in its extended meaning poetry generally.

Science Persecuted.

(1) Anaxagoras of Clazom'enæ held opinions in natural science so far in advance of his age that he was accused of impiety, thrown into prison, and condemned to death. Pericles, with great difficulty, got his sentence commuted to fine and banishment.

(2) Virgilius, Bishop of Salzburg, denounced as a heretic by St. Boniface for asserting the existence of antipodes. (Died 784.)

(3) Galileo was imprisoned by the Inquisition for maintaining that the earth moved. In order to get his liberty he "abjured the heresy," but as he went his way whispered half-audibly, "*E pur si muove*" ("but nevertheless it does move"). (1564-1642.)

(4) Gebert, who introduced algebra into Christendom, was accused of dealing in the black arts, and shunned as a magician.

(5) Friar Bacon was excommunicated and imprisoned for diabolical knowledge, chiefly on account of his chemical researches. (1214-1294.)

(6) Dr. Faust, the German philosopher, suffered in a similar way in the sixteenth century.

(7) John Dee. (*See* DEE.)

(8) Robert Grosseteste. (*See* GROSTED.)

(9) Averroes, the Arabian philosopher, who flourished in the twelfth century, was denounced as a heretic and degraded solely on account of his great eminence in natural philosophy and medicine. (He died 1226.)

(10) Andrew Crosse, electrician, who asserted that he had seen certain animals of the genus *Acarus*, which had been developed by him out of inorganic elements. Crosse was accused of impiety, and was shunned as a "profane man," who wanted to arrogate to himself the creative power of God. (1784-1855.)

Scien'ter Nes'ciens et Sapien'te Indoctus was how Gregory the Great described St. Benedict.

Scio's Blind Old Bard. Homer. Scio is the modern name of Chios, in the Æge'an Sea.

" Smyrna, Chios, Colophon', Salamis', Rhodos,
    Argos, Athe'næ,
Your just right to call Homer your son you
    must settle between ye."

Scipio dismissed the Iberian Maid (*Paradise Regained*, ii.). Referring to the tale that the conqueror of Spain not only refused to see a beautiful princess who had fallen into his power after the capture of New Carthage, but that he restored her to her parents, and actually gave her great presents that she might marry the man to whom she had been betrothed. (*See* CONTINENCE.)

The Lusian Scipio. Nunio.

" The Lusian Scipio well may speak his fame,
  But nobler Nunio shines a greater name ;
  On earth's green bosom, or on ocean grey,
  A greater never shall the sun survey."
           Camoens : Lusiad, bk. viii.

Scissors to Grind. Work to do; purpose to serve.

"That the Emperor of Austria [in the Servian and Bulgarian war, 1885] has his own scissors to grind goes without saying ; but for the present it is Russia who keeps the ball rolling."—*Newspaper paragraph*, November, 1885.

Sclavon'ic. The language spoken by the Russians, Servians, Poles, Bohemians, etc. ; anything belonging to the Sclavi.

Scobel'lum. A very fruitful land, but the inhabitants "exceeded the cannibals for cruelty, the Persians for pride, the Egyptians for luxury, the Cretans for lying, the Germans for drunkenness, and all nations together for a generality of vices." In vengeance the gods changed all the people into beasts : drunkards into swine, the lecherous into goats, the proud into peacocks, scolds into magpies, gamblers into asses, musicians into song-birds, the envious into dogs, idle women into milch-cows, jesters into monkeys, dancers into squirrels, and misers into moles. Four of the Champions of Christendom restored them to their normal forms by quenching the fire of the Golden Cave." (*The Seven Champions of Christendom*, iii. 10.)

Scone (pron. *Skoon*). Edward I. removed to London, and placed in Westminster Abbey, the great stone upon which the kings of Scotland were wont to be crowned. This stone is still preserved, and forms the support of Edward the Confessor's chair, which the British monarchs occupy at their coronation. It is said to have been brought from Ireland by Fergus, son of Eric, who led the Dalriads to the shores of Argyllshire. (*See* TANIST-STONE.)

" Ni fallat fatum, Scoti, quocunque locatum
Invenient lapidem, regnare tenentur ibidem."
Lardner, i. p. 67.

Unless the fates are faithless found
And prophets' voice be vain,
Where'er is placed this stone, e'en there
The Scottish race shall reign.

Score. A reckoning ; to make a reckoning ; so called from the custom of marking off "runs" or "lengths," in games by the score feet. (*See* NURR, SPELL, TALLY.)

Scornful Dogs will eat dirty Puddings. In emergency men will do many things they would scorn to do in easy circumstances. Darius and Alexander will drink dirty water and think it nectar when distressed with thirst. Kings and queens, to make good their escape in times of danger, will put on the most menial disguise. And hungry

men will not be over particular as to the food they eat.

"'All nonsense and pride,' said the laird. . . . 'Scornful dogs will eat dirty puddings.'"—*Sir W. Scott : Redgauntlet*, chap. xi.

Scor'pion. It is said that scorpions have an oil which is a remedy against their stings. The toad also is said to have an antidote to its "venom."

" 'Tis true. a scorpion's oil is said
To cure the wounds the venom made,
And weapons dressed with salves restore
And heal the hurts they gave before."
Butler : Hudibras, iii. 2.

Scor'pions. Whips armed with metal or knotted cords.

"My father chastised you with whips, but I will chastise you with scorpions."—1 Kings xii. 11.

Scot. The same as Scythian in etymology ; the root of both is Sct. The Greeks had no *c*, and would change *t* into *th*, making the root *skth*, and by adding a phonetic vowel we get *Skuth-ai* (Scythians), and *Skoth-ai* (Scoths). The Welsh disliked *s* at the beginning of a word, and would change it to *ys ;* they would also changed *c* or *k* to *g*, and *th* to *d ;* whence the Welsh root would be Ysgd, and Skuth or Skoth would become *ysgod*. Once more, the Saxons would cut off the Welsh *y*, and change the *g* back again to *c*, and the *d* to *t*, converting the Ysgod to Scot.

N.B. Before the third century Scotland was called Caledonia or Alban.

Scot-free. Tax-free, without payment. (*See below*.)

Scot and Lot. A levy on all subjects according to their ability to pay. Scot means tribute or tax, and lot means allotment or portion allotted. To pay scot and lot, therefore, is to pay the ordinary tributes and also the personal tax allotted to you.

Scots Greys. The 2nd Dragoons, the colour of whose horses is grey. (Heavy-armed.)

Scots wha hae. Words by Robert Burns, to the music of an old Scotch tune called *Hey Tuttie Taittie. The Land o' the Leal* is to the same tune.

Scotch. The people or language of Scotland.
Highland Scotch. Scottish Gaelic.
Lowland Scotch. The English dialect spoken in the lowlands of Scotland.
∴ *Broad Scotch.* The official language of Scotland in the fifteenth and sixteenth centuries. Sometimes used in novels and in verse.

Scotch Breakfast (*A*). A substantial breakfast of sundry sorts of good things to eat and drink. The Scotch are famous for their breakfast-tables and tea-fights. No people in the world are more hospitable.

Scotch Mist. A thick fog with drizzling rain, common in Scotland.

"A Scotch fog will wet an Englishman through."
—*Common saying.*

Scotch Pint (*A*). A Scotch pint = 2 English quarts.

Scotch Pound (*A*) was originally of the same value as an English pound, but after 1355 it gradually depreciated, until in 1600 it was but one-twelfth of the value of an English pound, that is about 1s. 8d.

Scotch Shilling = a penny sterling. The Scotch pound in 1600 was worth 20d., and as it was divided into twenty shillings, it follows that a Scotch shilling was worth one penny English.

Sco'tia. Now applied poetically to Scotland, but at one time Ireland was so called. Hence Claudius says—

" When Scots came thundering from the Irish
    shores,
And ocean trembled, struck with hostile oars."

Scotists. Followers of Duns Scotus, who maintained the doctrine of the Immaculate Conception in opposition to Thomas Aqul'nas.

"Scotists and Thomists now in peace remain."
Pope: Essay on Criticism.

Scotland. St. Andrew is the patron saint of this country, and tradition says that the remains of the apostle were brought by Reg'ulus, a Greek monk, to the eastern coast of Fife in 368. (*See* RULE, *St.*)

Scotland a fief of England. Edward I. founded his claim to the lordship of Scotland on these four grounds :—(1) the ancient chroniclers, who state that Scotch kings had occasionally paid homage to the English sovereigns from time immemorial. Extracts are given from St. Alban, Marianus Scotus, Ralph of Diceto, Roger of Hoveden, and William of Malmesbury. (2) From charters of Scotch kings: as those of Edgar, son of Malcolm, William, and his son Alexander II. (3) From papal rescripts : as those of Honorius III., Gregory IX., and Clement IV. (4) By an extract from *The Life and Miracles of St. John of Beverley.* The tenor of this extract is quite suited to this *Dictionary of Fable :* In the reign of Adelstan the Scots invaded England and committed great devastation. Adelstan went to drive them back, and, on reaching the Tyne,

found that the Scotch had retreated. At midnight St. John of Beverley appeared to him, and bade him cross the river at daybreak, for he "should discomfit the foe." Adelstan obeyed the vision, and reduced the whole kingdom to subjection. On reaching Dunbar on his return march, he prayed that some sign might be vouchsafed to him to satisfy all ages that "God, by the intercession of St. John, had given him the kingdom of Scotland." Then struck he with his sword the basaltic rocks near the coast, and the blade sank into the solid flint "as if it had been butter," cleaving it asunder for "an ell or more," and the cleft remains even to the present hour. Without doubt there is a fissure in the basalt, and how could it have come there except in the way recorded above ? And how could a sword cut three feet deep into a hard rock without miraculous aid ? And what could such a miracle have been vouchsafed for, except to show that Adelstan was rightful lord of Scotland ? And if Adelstan was lord, of course Edward should be so likewise. Q. E. D. (*Rymer : Fœdera,* vol. i. pt. ii. p. 771.)

Scotland Yard (London). So called from a palace built there for the reception of the kings of Scotland when they visited England. Pennant tells us it was originally given by King Edgar to Kenneth of Scotland when he came to London to pay homage.

Scotland Yard. The headquarters of the Metropolitan Police, whence all public orders to the force proceed.

" Mr. Walpole has only to speak the word in Scotland Yard, and the parks will be cleared."—*Pall Mall Gazette.*

Scott. *The Walter Scott of Belgium.* Hendrick Conscience. (Born 1812.)

The Southern Scott. Lord Byron calls Ariosto the Sir Walter Scott of Italy. (*Childe Harold,* iv. 40.)

Scotus (*Duns*). Died 1309. His epitaph at Cologne is—

"Scotia me genuit, Anglia me suscepit,
    Gallia me docuit, Colonia me tenet."

Scourge of Christians. Noureddin-Mahmûd of Damascus. (1116-1174.)

Scourge of God. (1) Attila, king of the Huns. A. P. Stanley says the term was first applied to Attila in the Hungarian Chronicles. In Isidore's Chronicle the Huns are called *Virga Dei.* (*,* 434-453.)

(2) Gen'seric, king of the Vandals, who went about like a destroying angel "against all those who had, in his opinion, incurred the wrath of God."

(Probably the word Godegesal (*Goth-gesal*, God-given) was purposely twisted into *God-gesil* (God's scourge) by those who hated him, because he was an Arian. God-gesal (or *Deoda'tus*) was the common title of the contemporary kings, like our *Dei Gratiâ*. (*, 429-477.)

Scourge of Princes. Pietro Areti'no was so called for his satires. (1492-1556.)

Scouring. *I 'scaped a scouring*—a disease. Scouring is a sort of flux in horses and cattle. (Latin, *Malum præ-tervehi* ; French, *L'échapper belle*.)

Scowerers. A set of rakes in the eighteenth century, who, with the Nic'-kers and Mohocks, committed great annoyances in London and other large towns.

" Who, has not heard the Scowerers' midnight
        fame ?
Who has not trembled at the Mohocks' name ?
Was there a watchman took his hourly rounds,
Safe from their blows and new-invented
        wounds ?"   *Gay : Trivia*, iii.

Scrape. *I've got into a sad scrape* —a great difficulty. We use rub, squeeze, pinch, and scrape to express the same idea. Thus Shakespeare says, " Ay; there's the rub" (difficulty) ; " I have got into tribulation " (a squeeze, from the Latin *trib'ulo*, to squeeze) ; " I am come to a pinch " (a difficulty). Some think the word a corrupt contraction of *escapade*, but Robert Chambers thinks it is borrowed from a term in golf. A rabbit's burrow in Scotland, he says, is called a " scrape," and if the ball gets into such a hole it can hardly be played. The rules of the game allow something to the player who " gets into a scrape." (*Book of Days*.)

Scrape an Acquaintance (*To*). The *Gentleman's Magazine* says that Hadrian went one day to the public baths, and saw an old soldier, well known to him, scraping himself with a potsherd for want of a flesh-brush. The emperor sent him a sum of money. Next day Hadrian found the bath crowded with soldiers scraping themselves with potsherds, and said, " Scrape on, gentlemen, but you'll not scrape acquaintance with me." (*N. S.*, xxxix. 230.)

Scratch. *Old Scratch.* Scrat, the house-demon of the North. (Icelandic, *scratti*, an imp.) (*See* DEUCE, NICK, etc.)

Scratch (*A*). One who in a race starts from the scratch, other runners in the same race being a yard or so in advance. The scratch runner generally is one who has already won a similar race.

Coming up to the scratch—up to the mark ; about to do what we want him to do. In prize-fighting a line is scratched on the ground, and the toe of the fighter must come up to the scratch.

Scratch Cradle. A game played with a piece of string stretched across the two hands. The art is so to cross the thread as to produce a resemblance to something, and for another so to transfer it to his own hands as to change the former figure into some other resemblance. A corruption of " cratch cradle " (the manger cradle), because the first figure represents a cradle, supposed to be the cradle of the infant-Jesus.

Scratch Crew (*A*), in a boat-race, means a random crew ; not a regular crew.

Scratch Eleven (*A*), or " scratch team," in cricket, means eleven men picked up anyhow ; not a regular team.

Scratch Race (*A*). A race of horses, men, boys, etc., without restrictions as to age, weight, previous winnings, etc.

Scratched. A horse is said to be scratched when its name is scratched out of the list of runners. " Tomboy was scratched for the Derby at ten a.m. on Wednesday," and no bet on that horse made subsequently would be valid.

Screw (*A*), meaning a small quantity, is in allusion to the habit of putting a small quantity of small articles into a " screw of paper."

An old screw. One who keeps his money tight, and doles it out in screws or small quantities.

To put on the screw. To press for payment, as a screw presses by gradually-increasing pressure.

Raised your screw. Raised your wages.

"' Has Tom got his screw raised ?' said Milton."
—*Truth : Queer Story*, 18th February, 1886.

Screw Loose (*A*). Something amiss. The allusion is to joinery kept together by screws.

Screw Plot (*The*). 1708, when Queen Anne went to St. Paul's to offer thanksgivings for the victory of Oudenarde. The tale is that the plotters took out certain screw-bolts from the beams of the cathedral, that the roof might fall on the queen and her suite and kill them.

" Some of your Machiavelian crew
    From heavy roof of Paul
Most traitorously stole every screw,
    To make that fabric fall ;
And so to catch Her Majesty,
    And all her friends beguile."
            Plot upon Plot (about 1713).

Screwed. Intoxicated. A playful synonym of *tight*, which again is a playful synonym of *blown out*.

Screwed on Right. *His head was screwed on right.* He was clear-headed and right-thinking.

" His heart was in the right place . . . and his head was screwed on right, too."—*Boldrewood: Robbery under Arms*, xv.

Screwed on the wrong way. Crotchety, ungainly, not right.

Scribe (1 syl.), in the New Testament, means a doctor of the law. Thus, in Matthew xxii. 35, we read, " Then one of them, which was a *lawyer*, asked Him, Which is the great commandment of the law ? " Mark (xii. 28) says, " One of the *scribes* came and asked Him, Which is the first commandment of all ? "

In the Old Testament the word is used more widely. Thus Seraiah is called the scribe (secretary) of David (2 Sam. viii. 17) ; in the Book of Chronicles " Jael the scribe " was an officer in the king's army, who reviewed the troops and called over the muster-roll. Jonathan, Baruch, Gemariah, etc., who were princes, were called scribes. Ezra, however, called " a ready scribe in the law of Moses," accords with the New Testament usage of the word.

Scrible'rus (*Marti'nus*). A merciless satire on the false taste in literature current in the time of Pope. Cornelius Scrible'rus, the father of Martin, was a pedant, who entertained all sorts of absurdities about the education of his son. Martin grew up a man of capacity ; but though he had read everything, his judgment was vile and taste atrocious.

Scrim'mage. A tussle ; a slight battle. From the obsolete *scrimer*, a fencer ; French, *escrimeur ;* same root as *escarmouch*, our *skirmish*.

" Prince Ouffur at this skrymage, for all his pryde,
Fled full fast and sought no guide."
MS. Lansdowne, 200, f. 10.

Scripto'res Decem. A collection of ten ancient chronicles on English history, edited by Roger Twysden and John Selden. The ten chroniclers are Simeon of Durham, John of Hexham, Richard of Hexham, Ailred of Rieval, Ralph de Diceto (Archdeacon of London), John Brompton of Jorval, Gervase of Canterbury, Thomas Stubbs, William Thorn of Canterbury, and Henry Knighton of Leicester.

Scripto'res Quinque. A collection of five chronicles on the early history of England, edited by Thomas Gale.

Scripto'res Tres [*the three writers*]. Meaning Richard of Cirencester, Gildas Badon'icus, and Nennius of Bangor. Julius Bertram, professor of English at Copenhagen, professed to have discovered the first of these treatises in 1747, in the royal library of that city. Its subject is *De Situ Britanniæ*, and in 1757 he published it along with the two other treatises, calling the whole *The Three Writers on the Ancient History of the British Nations.* Bertram's forgery was completely exposed by J. E. Mayor, in his preface to *Ricardi de Cirencestria Speculum Historiale.* (*See* SANCHONI-ATHO.)

Scripto'rium. An apartment in every abbey where writers transcribed service-books for the choir and books for the library. (*Warton.*)

Scriptures. (*See* SEVEN BIBLES.)

Scu'damore (*Sir*). The lover of Am'oret, whom he finally marries. (*Spenser : Faërie Queene*, book iii. iv.)

Scudding under Bare Poles. In seaman's language to *scud* means to drive before a gale with no sails, or only just enough to keep the vessel ahead of the sea ; " scudding under bare poles " is being driven by the wind so violently that no sail at all is set. Figuratively it means to cut and run so precipitately as to leave no trace behind.

Scullabogue Massacre. In the Irish rebellion of 1798 Scullabogue House, Wexford, was seized by the rebels and used for a prison. Some thirty or forty prisoners confined in it were brought out and shot in cold blood, when the news of a repulse of the rebels at New Ross arrived (5th June, '98). The barn at the back of the house was filled with prisoners and set on fire, and Taylor, in his history, written at the time and almost on the spot, puts the number of victims at 184, and he gives the names of several of them.

Sculls. (*See* DIAMOND . . .)

Sculpture. *Fathers of French sculpture.*

Jean Goujon (1510-1572).
Germain Pilon (1515-1590).

Scutch. The scrapings of hides ; also refuse of flax. (English, *scotch*, to cut ; Saxon, *sceadan*.) We have the word in the expression, " You have scotched the snake, not killed it."

" About half a mile from the southern outfall are two manufactories, where the refuse from the London tanneries, known as scutch, is operated upon."—*The Times*.

Scuttle. *To scuttle a ship* is to bore a hole in it in order to make it sink. Rather strangely, this word is from the same root as our word *shut* or bolt (Saxon *scyttel*, a lock, bolt, or bar). It was first applied then to a roof with a door or lid, then to a hatchway in the deck of a ship with a lid, then to a hole in the bottom of a ship plugged up ; then comes the verb to pull out the plug, and leave the hole for the admission of water.

Scuttle (of coals, etc.) is the Anglo-Saxon, *scutel*, a basket.

" The Bergen [Norway] fishwomen . . . in every direction are coming . . . with their scuttles swinging on their arms. In Bergen fish is never carried in any other way." — *H. H. Jackson: Glimpses of Three Coasts*, pt. iii. p. 235.

Scuttle Out (*To*). To sneak off quickly, to skedaddle, to cut and run. Anglo-Saxon *sceotan*, to flee precipitately ; *scitel*, an arrow ; *sceota*, a darting fish, like the trout ; *scot*, an arrow, etc.

Scylla, daughter of Nisus, promised to deliver Meg'ara into the hands of Minos. To redeem this promise she had to cut off a golden hair on her father's head, which she effected while he was asleep. Minos, her lover, despised her for this treachery, and Scylla threw herself from a rock into the sea. At death she was changed into a lark, and Nisus into a hawk. Scylla turned into a rock by Circe " has no connection " with the daughter of Nisus.

" Think of Scylla's fate.
Changed to a bird, and sent to fly in air,
She dearly pays for Nisus' injured hair."
Pope: Rape of the Lock, iii.

Scylla. Glaucus, a fisherman, was in love with Scylla ; but Circē, out of jealousy, changed her into a hideous monster, and set dogs and wolves to bark round her incessantly. On this Scylla threw herself into the sea and became a rock. It is said that the rock Scylla somewhat resembles a woman at a distance, and the noise of the waves dashing against it is not unlike the barking of dogs and wolves.

" Glaucus, lost to joy,
Curst in his love by vengeful Circe's hate,
Attending wept his Scylla's hapless fate."
Camoens : Lusiad, bk. vi.

Avoiding Scylla, he fell into Charybdis. Trying to avoid one error, he fell into another ; or, trying to avoid one danger, he fell into another equally fatal. Scylla and Charybdis are two rocks between Italy and Sicily. In one was a cave where " Scylla dwelt," and on the other Charybdis dwelt under a fig-tree. Ships which tried to avoid one were often wrecked on the other rock. It was Circe

who changed Scylla into a frightful sea-monster, and Jupiter who changed Charybdis into a whirlpool.

" When I shun Scylla your father, I fall into Charybdis your mother "—*Shakespeare : Merchant of Venice,* iii. 5.

Between Scylla and Charybdis. Between two difficulties or fatal works.

To fall from Scylla into Charybdis—out of the frying-pan into the fire.

Scythian or **Tartarian Lamb** (*The*). Agnus Scythicus, a kind of fern, called the borametz, or polypodium of Cayenne. It is said to resemble a lamb, and even in some cases to be mistaken for one.

Scythian Defiance. When Darius approached Scythia, an ambassador was sent to his tent with a bird, a frog, a mouse, and five arrows, then left without uttering a word. Darius, wondering what was meant, was told by Gobrias it meant this : Either fly away like a bird, and hide your head in a hole like a mouse, or swim across the river, or in five days you will be laid prostrate by the Scythian arrows.

Sea. Any large collection of water, more or less enclosed ; hence the expression " molten sea," meaning the great brazen vessel which stood in Solomon's temple (2 Chronicles iv. 5, and 1 Kings vii. 26). We have also the Mediterranean Sea, the Black Sea, the White Sea, the Red Sea, the Sea of Galilee, the Dead Sea, etc. ; and even the Nile, the Euphrates, and the Tigris are sometimes called seas by the prophets. The world of water is the ocean. (Anglo-Saxon, *sae*.)

The Old Man of the sea (*Arabian Nights*). A creature encountered by Sinbad the Sailor in his fifth voyage. This terrible Old Man contrived to get on the back of Sinbad, and would neither dismount again nor could he be shaken off. At last Sinbad gave him some wine to drink, which so intoxicated him that he relaxed his grip, and Sinbad made his escape.

At sea. Quite at sea. Wide of the mark ; quite wrong ; like a person in the open ocean without compass or chart.

Sea-blue Bird of March (*The*). The wheatear, not the kingfisher.

Sea Deities.

Amphitrite (4 syl.). Wife of Poseidon (3 syl.), queen goddess of the sea.

N.B. Neptune had no wife.

Doto, a sea-nymph, mentioned by Virgil.

Galatēa, a daughter of Nereus.

Glaucus, a fisherman of Bœotia, afterwards a marine deity.

Ino, who threw herself from a rock into the sea, and was made a seagoddess.

Neptune (2 syl.), king of the ocean.

The Nereids (3 syl.) or Nereïdes (4 syl.), fifty in number.

Nereus (2 syl.) and his wife Doris. Their palace was at the bottom of the Mediterranean Sea. His hair was seaweeds.

Oceănos and his wife Tethys. Oceănos was not god of the sea, but of the *ocean*, supposed to form a boundary round the world.

Oceanïdes (5 syl.). Daughters of Oceănos.

Palēmon, the Greek Portumnus.

Portumnus, the protector of harbours.

Poseidon (3 syl.), the Greek Neptune.

Proteus (2 syl.), who assumed every variety of shape.

Sirens (*The*). Sea nymphs who charmed by song.

Tethys, wife of Oceanos, and daughter of Uranus and Terra.

Thetis, a daughter of Nereus and mother of Achillēs.

Triton, son of Poseidon (3 syl.).

✵ The Naiads or Naiădes (3 syl.) were *river* nymphs.

Sea-girt Isle. England. So called because, as Shakespeare has it, it is "hedged in with the main, that water-walled bulwark" (*King John*, ii. 1).

"Th's precious stone set in the silver sea,
Which serves it in the office of a wall,
Or as a moat defensive to a house,
Against the envy of less happier lands."
  Shakespeare: King Richard II., ii. 1.

Sea-green Incorruptible (*The*). So Carlyle called Robespierre in his *French Revolution*.

"The song is a short one, and may perhaps serve to qualify our judgment of the 'sea-green incorruptible.'"—*Notes and Queries*, September 19th, 1891, p. 226.

Sea Legs. *He has got his sea legs.* Is able to walk on deck when the ship is rolling; able to bear the motion of the ship without sea-sickness.

Sea Serpent. Pontoppidan, in his *Natural History of Norway*, speaks of sea serpents 600 feet long. The great sea serpent was said to have been seen off the coast of Norway in 1819, 1822, 1837. Hans Egede affirms that it was seen on the coast of Greenland in 1734. In 1815, 1817, 1819, 1833, and in 1869, it made its appearance near Boston. In 1841 it was "seen" by the crew of Her Majesty's frigate *Dædalus*, in the South Atlantic Ocean. In 1875 it was seen by the crew of the barque *Pauline*. Girth, nine feet.

Seaboard. That part of a country which *borders* on the *sea;* the coast-line. It should be *seabord*. (French, *bord*, the edge.)

Seal. The sire is called a bull, its females are cows, the offspring are called pups; the breeding-place is called a rookery, a group of young seals is called a pod. The male seal till it is full grown is called a bachelor. A colony of seals is called a herd. A *sealer* is a seal-hunter, seal-hunting is called *sealing*, and the seal trade *sealery*.

Seamy Side (*The*). The "wrong" or worst side; as, the "seamy side of Australia," "the seamy side of life." Thus, in velvet, in Brussels carpets, in tapestry, etc., the "wrong" side shows the seams or threads of the pattern exhibited on the right side.

"You see the seamy side of human nature in its most seamy attire."—*Review of R. Buchanan's play Alone in London*, November, 1885.
"My present purpose is to call attention to the seamy side of the Australian colonies. There is, as we know, such a thing as cotton-backed satin; but the colonists take care to show us only the face of the goods."—*Nineteenth Century*, April, 1891, p. 524.

Seasons (*The*). In art. The four seasons have often been sculptured or painted by artists:

POUSSIN drew his symbolic characters from the Old Testament. Thus, Adam and Eve in Paradise represent Spring; Ruth in the cornfields represents Summer; Joshua and Caleb bringing grapes from the Land of Promise represent Autumn; and the Deluge represents Winter.

The Ancient Greeks characterised Spring by Mercury, Summer by Apollo, Autumn by Bacchus, and Winter by Hercules.

M. Girondet painted for the King of Spain four pictures, with allegoric character, from the Herculaneum.

Seba'ra'im (4 syl.). Rabbis who lived after the Talmud was finished, and gave their judgment on traditionary difficulties (*Al derek sebaroth*, "by way of opinion"). (*Buxtorf.*)

Sebastian (*St.*). Patron saint of archers, because he was bound to a tree and shot at with arrows. As the arrows stuck in his body, thick as pins in a pin-cushion, he was also made patron saint of pin-makers. And as he was a centurion, he is patron saint of soldiers.

The English St. Sebastian. St. Edmund, the martyr-king of East Anglia.

He gave himself up to his enemies under the hope of saving his people by this sacrifice. The Danes first scourged him with rods, and then, binding him to a tree, shot arrows at him, and finally cut off his head. A legend tells how a wolf guarded the head till it was duly interred. The monastery and cathedral of St. Edmundsbury were erected on the place of his burial.

Sebas'tianistes. Persons who believe that Dom Sebastian, who fell in the battle of Alcazarquebir in 1578, will return to earth, when Brazil will become the chief kingdom of the earth.

⁂ A similar tradition is attached to several other names.

Second. (*See* Two.)

Second-hand. Not new or original; what has already been the property of another; as, "second-hand books," "second-hand clothes," etc.

Second Sight. The power of seeing things invisible to others; the power of foreseeing future events by means of shadows thrown before them. Many Highlanders claim this power, which the ancient Gaels called shadow-sight (*taischitaraugh*).

" Nor less availed his optic sleight,
And Scottish gift of second sight."
Trumbull.

Second Wind (*The*), in running. All animals soon after the start get out of breath, but, as the body becomes heated, breathing becomes more easy, and endures till fatigue produces exhaustion; this is called the *second wind*.

"That mysterious physical readjustment, known in animals as 'second breath,' came to the rescue of his fainting frame."—*The Barton Experiment*, chap. x.

Second of Time (*A*). The sixtieth part of an hour was called by the Romans *scrupŭlum*, and the sixtieth part of a minute was *scrupŭlum secundum*.

Sec'ondary Colours. (*See under* Colours.)

Secret de Polichinelle (*Le*). No secret at all. A secret known to all the world; old news. We have also "Hawker's News," "Piper's News." The secrets of Polichinelle are "stage whispers" told to all the audience.

" Entre nous, c'est qu'on appelle
Le secret de polichinelle."
La Mascotte, ii. 12.

Secular Clergy (*The*). The parish clergy who live in the world, in contradistinction to monks, who live in monasteries, etc., out of the world. (Latin, *secularis*.)

Sec'ular Games. Those held by the Romans only once in a century. While the kings reigned they were held in the Campus Martius, in honour of Pluto and Proserpine, and were instituted in obedience to the Sibylline verses, with the promise that "the empire should remain in safety so long as this admonition was observed."

" Datē, quæ precāmur
Temp'ore sacro
Quo Sibyllini monuēre versus."
Horace: Carmen Seculare, A.U.C., 737.'

Sedan Chairs. So called from *sedes* (Latin, "a seat"). Their introduction into England is by Hume (vol. iv. 505) erroneously attributed to the Duke of Buckingham, who, it is said, gave great offence by employing men as beasts of burden. Sir S. Duncombe used one in 1634, when Buckingham was a boy, and we find it spoken of as far back as 1581. It was introduced into France (in 1617) by the Marquis de Montbrun, and called *chaise à porteurs*.

⁂ It is generally said that these chairs were first made at Sedan, on the Meuse; but this is not at all probable, as, without doubt, the invention was introduced into France from England.

Sedrat. The lotus-tree which stands on the right-hand side of the invisible throne of Allah. Its branches extend wider than the distance between heaven and earth. Its leaves resemble the ears of an elephant. Each seed of its fruit encloses a houri; and two rivers issue from its roots. Numberless birds sing among its branches, and numberless angels rest beneath its shade.

See'dy. Weary, worn out, out of sorts; run to seed. A hat or coat is termed seedy when it has become shabby. A man is seedy after a debauch, when he looks and feels out of sorts.

Seel. To close the eyelids of a hawk by running a thread through them; to hoodwink. (French, *ciller*, *cil*, the eyelash.)

" She that so young could give out such a seeming,
To seel her father's eyes up, close as oak."
Shakespeare: Othello, iii. 3.

See'murgh. The wonderful bird that could speak all the languages of the world, and whose knowledge embraced past, present, and future events. (*Persian mythology*.)

Seian Horse (*The*). A possession which invariably brought ill luck with it. Hence the Latin proverb "*Ille homo habet equum Seianum.*" Cneius Seius had an Argive horse, of the breed of

Diomed, of a bay colour and surpassing beauty, but it was fatal to its possessor. Seius was put to death by Mark Antony. Its next owner, Cornelius Dolabella, who bought it for 100,000 sesterces, was killed in Syria during the civil wars. Caius Cassius, who next took possession of it, perished after the battle of Philippi by the very sword which stabbed Cæsar. Antony had the horse next, and after the battle of Actium slew himself.

Like the gold of Tolosa and Hermione's necklace, the Seian or Sejan horse was a fatal possession.

Seidlitz Water. Natural mineral water from a spring in the village of Seidlitz, in Bohemia. (*See* SELTZER.)

Seiks (pron. *Seeks*). A religious sect in Hindustan, founded in 1500. They profess the purest Deism, and are distinguished from the Hindus by worshipping one invisible god. The word means *lion*, and was applied to them on account of their heroic resistance to the Moslem. Ultimately they subdued Lahore, and established a military commonwealth in the Punjab, etc.

✢ In 1849 the Punjab was annexed to the British empire.

Selah. in the Psalms. Matthœon, the musical critic, says the word is equivalent to *da capo*, and is a direction to the choir to repeat the psalm down to the part thus indicated.

Sela'ma or **Sele'meh.** The headland of the Persian Gulf, commonly called Cape Musseldom. The Indians throw cocoanuts, fruits, and flowers into the sea when they pass this cape, to secure a propitious voyage. (*Morier.*)

"Breezes from the Indian sea
Blow round Selama's sainted cape."
Moore : Fire Worshippers.

Sele'nē. The moon-goddess; sometimes, but improperly, called Diana, as Diana is always called the chaste huntress; but Selene had fifty daughters by Endymion, and several by Zeus, one of whom was called "The Dew" (*Erse*). Diana is represented with bow and arrow running after the stag; but Selene is represented in a chariot drawn by two white horses; she has wings on her shoulders and a sceptre in her hand.

Seleu'cidæ. The dynasty of Seleucus. Seleucus succeeded to a part of Alexander's vast empire. The monarchy consisted of Syria, a part of Asia Minor, and all the eastern provinces.

Se'lim. Son of Abdallah and cousin of Zuleika (3 syl.). When Giaffir (2 syl.) murdered Abdallah, he took Selim and brought him up as his own son. The young man fell in love with Zuleika, who thought he was her brother; but when she discovered he was Abdallah's son, she promised to be his bride, and eloped with him. As soon as Giaffir discovered this he went after the fugitives, and shot Selim. Zuleika killed herself, and the old pacha was left childless. The character of Selim is bold, enterprising, and truthful. (*Byron: Bride of Abydos.*)

Se'lim (son of Akbar). The name of Jehanguire, before his accession to the throne. He married Nourmahal' (the Light of the Harem). (*See* NOURMAHAL).

Sel'juks. A Perso-Turkish dynasty which gave eleven kings and lasted 138 years (1056-1194). It was founded by Togrul Beg, a descendant of Seljuk, chief of a small tribe which gained possession of Boka'ra.

Sell. A saddle. "Vaulting ambition . . . o'erleaps its sell" (*Macbeth*, i. 7). (Latin, *sella;* French, *selle*.) Window *sill* is the Anglo-Saxon *syl* (a basement).

"He left his loftie steed with golden sell."
Spenser : Faërie Queene, II. 2.

Sell, sold. Made a captive, as a purchased slave. St. Paul says he was "sold under sin" (Rom. vii. 14). (Anglo-Saxon, *sell-an*, to give.)

A sell. A "do," a deception, a "take-in." Street vendors who take in the unwary with catchpennies, chuckle like hens when they have laid an egg, "Sold again, and got the money! "

Selling Race (*A*), in which horses to be sold are run. These horses must have the sale price ticketed. The winner is generally sold by auction, and the owner gets both the selling price and the stakes. If at the auction a price is obtained above the ticketed price it is divided between the second-best horse and the race-fund. (*See* HANDICAP, SWEEPSTAKES, PLATE, WEIGHT-FOR-AGE RACE.)

The owner of any of the horses may claim any horse in a selling race at the price ticketed.

Selling the Pass. This is a phrase, very general in all Ireland, applied to those who turn queen's or king's evidence, or who impeach their comrades for money. The tradition is that a regiment of soldiers was sent by Crotha, "lord of Atha," to hold a pass against the invading army of Trathal, "King of Cael." The pass was betrayed for money. The Fir-bolgs being subdued, Trathal assumed the title of " King of Ireland."

Selt'zer Water. A corruption of *Selters Water ;* so called from the Lower Selters, near Limburg (Nassau).

Semir'amis of the North. Margaret of Denmark, Sweden, and Norway. (1353-1412.)

Catherine II. of Russia (1729-1796).

Sena'nus *(St.)* fled to the island of Scattery, and resolved that no female form should ever step upon it. An angel led St. Can'ara to the island, but the recluse refused to admit her. Tom Moore has a poem on this legend, *St. Senanus and the Lady.* (*Irish Melodies,* No. 1. (*See* KEVIN.)

Sen'eca. *The Christian Sen'eca.* Bishop Hall of Norwich. (1574-1656.)

Senior Op'time (3 syl.) A Cambridge University expression meaning one of the second-class in the mathematical tripos. The first class consists of Wranglers.

∵ In the University of Cambridge every branch is divided into three classes, and the three classes are called a tripos. In the mathematical tripos, those of the *first* class are called *wranglers,* those of the second class are *senior optimes* (3 syl.), and those of the third class *junior optimes.* Law, classical, and other triposes have no distinctive names, but are called Class I., II., or III. of the respective tripos.

Sennac'herib, whose army was destroyed by the Angel of Death, is by the Orientals called King Moussal. (*D'Herbelot, notes to the Koran.*)

Se'nnight. A week ; seven nights. *Fort'night,* fourteen nights. These words are relics of the ancient Celtic custom of beginning the day at sunset, a custom observed by the ancient Greeks, Babylonians, Persians, Syrians, and Jews, and by the modern representatives of these people. In Gen. i. we always find the evening precedes the morning ; as, " The evening and the morning were the first day," etc.

Sen'tences (3 syl.). The four books of Sentences, by Pierre Lombard, the foundation of scholastic theology of the middle period. (*See* SCHOOLMEN.)

Master of the Sentences. Pierre Lombard, schoolman. (Died 1164.)

Sen'tinel. Archd. Smith says, " It is one set to watch the *sentina* (Lat.) or hold of a ship," but the Fr. *sentier,* a path or " beat," is far more probable. (French, *sentinelle ;* Italian, *sentinella ;* the French *sentier* is from the Latin *semita.*)

Sepoy. The Indian soldier is so called, says Bishop Heber, from *sip,* a bow, their principal weapon in olden times. (*Sipahi,* a soldier.)

Sept. A clan (Latin, *septum,* a fold), all the cattle, or all the voters, in a given enclosure.

September Massacres. An indiscriminate slaughter of Loyalists confined at the time in the Abbaye and other French prisons. Danton gave order for this onslaught after the capture of Verdun by the allied Prussian army. It lasted the 2nd, 3rd, and 4th of September, 1792. As many as 8,000 persons fell in this massacre, among whom was the Princess de Lamballe.

Septuages'ima Sunday. In round numbers, seventy days before Easter. The third Sunday before Lent. Really only sixty-eight days before Easter.

Sep'tuagint. A Greek version of the Old Testament, so called because it was made, in round numbers, by seventy Jews ; more correctly speaking, by seventy-two. Dr. Campbell disapproves of this derivation, and says it was so called because it was sanctioned and authorised by the Jewish San'hedrim or great council, which consisted of seventy members besides the high priest. This derivation falls in better with the modern notion that the version was made at different times by different translators between B.C. 270 and 130. (Latin, *septuaginta,* seventy.)

∵ The Septuagint contains the Apocrypha. According to legend, the Septuagint was made at Alexandria by seventy-two Jews in seventy-two days.

Serag'lio. The palace of the Turkish sultan, situated in the Golden Horn, and enclosed by walls seven miles and a half in circuit. The chief entrance is *the Sublime Gate ;* and the chief of the large edifices is the *Harem,* or " sacred spot," which contains numerous houses, one for each of the sultan's wives, and others for his concubines. The black eunuchs form the inner guard, and the white eunuchs the second guard. The Seraglio may be visited by strangers ; not so the Harem.

Ser'aphim. An order of angels distinguished for fervent zeal and religious ardour. The word means " to burn." (*See* Isaiah vi. 2.)

" Thousand celestial ardours [seraphs] where he stood
Veiled with his gorgeous wings, up springing light,
Flew through the midst of heaven."
Milton : Paradise Lost, v. 249,

Sera'pis. The Ptolemaic form of the Egyptian *Osi'ris.* The word is a corruption of *osor'apis* (dead apis, or rather "osirified apis"), a deity which had so many things in common with Osi'ris that it is not at all easy to distinguish them.

Serapis. Symbol of the Nile and of fertility.

Serat (*Al*). The ordeal bridge over which everyone will have to pass at the resurrection. It is not wider than the edge of a scimitar, and is thrown across the gulf of hell. The faithful, says the Koran, will pass over in safety, but sinners will fall headlong into the dreary realm beneath.

Serbo'nian Bog or **Serbo'nis.** A mess from which there is no way of extricating oneself. The Serbonian bog was between Egypt and Palestine. Strabo calls it a lake, and says it was 200 stadia long, and 50 broad; Pliny makes it 150 miles in length. Hume says that whole armies have been lost therein. Typhon lay at the bottom of this bog, which was therefore called *Typhon's Breathing Hole.* It received its name from Sebaket-Bardoil, a king of Jerusalem, who died there on his return from an expedition into Egypt.

"Now, sir, I must say I know of no Serbonian bog deeper than a £5 rating would prove to be."—*B. Disraeli (Chanc. of the Exch.), Times,* March 19, 1867.

"A gulf profound as that Serbonian bog,
Betwixt Damiata and Mount Cassius old,
Where armies whole have sunk."
　　　　Milton: Paradise Lost, ii. 592.

Sereme'nes (4 syl.). Brother-in-law of King Sardanapa'lus, to whom he entrusts his signet-ring to put down a rebellion headed by Arba'ces the Mede and Bel'esis, the Chaldean soothsayer. He is slain in a battle with the insurgents. (*Byron: Sardanapalus.*)

Serena'de (3 syl.). Music performed in the *serene—i.e.* in the open air at eventide (Latin, *sere'num,* whence the French *sérénade* and Italian *serenata*).

"Or serenate which the starved lover sings
To his proud fair."
　　　　Milton: Paradise Lost, iii. 769.

Sere'ne (2 syl.). A title given to certain German princes. Those princes who used to hold under the empire were entitled *Serene* or *Most Serene Highnesses.*

It's all serene. All right (Spanish, *sere'no,* "all right"—the sentinel's countersign). *Sereno,* the night-watch.

"'Let us clearly understand each other.' 'All serene,' responded Foster."—*Watson: The Web of the Spider.* chap. vii.

36

Serif and **Sanserif.** The former is a letter in typography with the "wings" or finishing-strokes (as T); the latter is without the finishing-strokes (as T).

Serjeants-at-Law. French, *frères-serjens,* a corruption of *fratres-servientes* of the Templars.

Sermon Lane (Doctors Commons, London). A corruption of *Shere-moniers Lane* (the lane of the money-shearers or clippers, whose office it was to cut and round the metal to be stamped into money). The Mint was in the street now called Old Change. (*Maitland: London,* ii. 880.)

Serpent. An attribute of St. Cecilia, St. Euphe'mia, and many other saints, either because they trampled on Satan, or because they miraculously cleared some country of such reptiles. (*See* DAGON.)

Serpent, in Christian art, figures in Paradise as the tempter.

The brazen serpent gave newness of life to those who were bitten by the fiery dragons and raised their eyes to this symbol. (Numb. xxi. 8.)

It is generally placed under the feet of the Virgin, in allusion to the promise made to Eve after the fall. (Gen. iii. 15.)

Satan is called the great serpent because under the form of a serpent he tempted Eve. (Rev. xii. 9.)

⁂ It is rather strange that, in Hindu mythology, hell is called Narac (the region of serpents). (*Sir W. Jones.*)

Serpent metamorphoses. Cadmos and his wife Harmo'nia were by Zeus converted into serpents and removed to Elysium. Escula'pius, god of Epidau'ros, assumed the form of a serpent when he appeared at Rome during a pestilence. Therefore is it that the goddess of Health bears in her hand a serpent.

"O wave, Hygeia, o'er Britannia's throne
Thy serpent-wand, and mark it for thine own."
　　　　Darwin: Economy of Vegetation, iv.

Jupiter Ammon appeared to Olym'pia in the form of a serpent, and became the father of Alexander the Great.

'When glides a silver serpent, treacherous guest!
And fair Olympia folds him to her breast."
　　　　Darwin: Economy of Vegetation, i. 2.

Jupiter Capitoli'nus, in a similar form, became the father of Scipio Africanus.

The serpent is emblematical—

(1) Of wisdom. "Be ye therefore wise as serpents, and harmless as doves" (Matt. x. 16).

(2) Of subtilty. "Now the serpent was more subtil than any beast of the field" (Gen. iii. 1).

It is said that the ceras'tēs hides in sand that it may bite the horse's foot and get the rider thrown. In allusion to this belief, Jacob says, "Dan shall be . . . an adder in the path, that biteth the horse's heels, so that his rider shall fall backward" (Gen. xlix. 17).

It is said that serpents, when attacked, swallow their young, and eject them again on reaching a place of safety.

Thomas Lodge says that people called Sauveurs have St. Catherine's wheel in the palate of their mouths, and therefore can heal the sting of serpents.

The Bible also tells us that it stops up its ears that it may not be charmed by the charmer. (Ps. lviii. 4.)

The serpent is symbolical—

(1) Of deity, because, says Plutarch, "it feeds upon its own body ; even so all things spring from God, and will be resolved into deity again." (*De Iside et Osiride,* i. 2, p. 5 ; and *Philo Byblius.*)

(2) Of eternity, as a corollary of the former. It is represented as forming a circle and holding its tail in its mouth.

(3) Of renovation. It is said that the serpent, when it is old, has the power of growing young again "like the eagle," by casting its slough, which is done by squeezing itself between two rocks.

(4) Of guardian spirits. It was thus employed by the ancient Greeks and Romans, and not unfrequently the figure of a serpent was depicted on their altars. In the temple of Athen'a at Athens, a serpent was kept in a cage, and called "the Guardian Spirit of the Temple." This serpent was supposed to be animated by the soul of Erictho'nius.

To cherish a serpent in your bosom. To show kindness to one who proves ungrateful. The Greeks say that a husbandman found a serpent's egg, which he put into his bosom. The egg was hatched by the warmth, and the young serpent stung its benefactor.

" Therefore think him as a serpent's egg
    Which, hatched, would (as his kind) grow dangerous." *Shakespeare: Julius Cæsar,* ii. 1.

Their ears have been serpent-licked. They have the gift of foreseeing events, the power of seeing into futurity. This is a Greek superstition. It is said that Cassandra and Hel'enus were gifted with the power of prophecy, because serpents licked their ears while sleeping in the temple of Apollo.

The seed of the woman shall bruise the serpent's head (Gen. iii. 15). The serpent bruised the *heel* of man ; but Christ, the "seed of the woman," bruised the serpent's *head.*

Serpent's food. Fennel is said to be the favourite food of serpents, with the juice of which it restores its sight when dim.

Serpents. Brazilian wood is a panacea against the bite of serpents. The Countess of Salisbury, in the reign of James I., had a bedstead made of this wood, and on it is the legend of "*Honi soit qui mal y pense.*"

Serpentine Verses. Such as end with the same word as they begin with. The following are examples :—

"Crescit amor nummi, quantum ipsa pecunia crescit."
(Greater grows the love of pelf, as pelf itself grows greater.)
" Ambo florentes ætatibus, Arcades ambo."
(Both in the spring of life, Arcadians both.)

Serrapur'da. High screens of rep cloth, stiffened with cane, used to enclose a considerable space round the royal tent of the Persian army.

Servant (*Faithful*). (*See* ADAM.)

Serve. *I'll serve him out*—give him a *quid pro quo.* This is the French *desserver,* to do an ill turn to one.

To serve a rope. To roll something upon it to prevent it from being fretted. The "service" or material employed is spun yarn, small lines, sennit, ropes, old leather, or canvas.

Servus Servo'rum (*Latin*). The slave of slaves, the drudge of a servant. The style adopted by the Roman pontiffs ever since the time of Gregory the Great is *Servus Servorum Dei.*

" Alexander episcopus, servus servorum Dei, Karissimo filio Willielmo salutem."—*Rymer : Fœdera,* i. p. 1.

Ses'ame (3 syl.). Oily grain of the natural order Pedalia'ceæ, originally from India. In Egypt they eat sesame cakes, and the Jews frequently add the seed to their bread. The cakes made of sesame oil, mixed with honey and preserved citron, are considered an Oriental luxury ; sesame is excellent also for puddings. (*See* OPEN SESAME.)

" Among the numerous objects . . . was a black horse. . . . On one side of its manger there was clean barley and sesame, and the other was filled with rose-water."—*Arabian Nights (Third Calender).*

Se'sha. King of the serpent race, on which Vishnu reclines on the primeval waters. It has a thousand heads, on one of which the world rests. The coiled-up sesha is the emblem of eternity. (*Hindu mythology.*)

Set Off (*A*). A commercial expression. The credits are set off against the debits, and the balance struck.

Set off to advantage. A term used by jewellers, who set off precious stones by appropriate " settings."

Set Scene. In theatrical parlance, a scene built up by the stage carpenters, or a furnished interior, as a drawing-room, as distinguished from an ordinary or shifting scene.

Set-to (*A*). A boxing match, a pugilistic fight, a scolding. In pugilism the combatants are by their seconds " set to the scratch " or line marked on the ground.

Set'ebos. A deity of the Patagonians, introduced by Shakespeare into his *Tempest.*

" His art is of such power,
It would control my dam's god, Setebos,
And make a vassal of him." *Tempest,* i. 2.

Seth'ites (2 syl.). A sect of the second century, who maintained that the Messiah was Seth, son of Adam.

Setting a Hen. Giving her a certain number of eggs to hatch. The whole number for incubation is called a *setting.*

Setting a Saw. Bending the teeth alternately to the right or left in order to make it work more easily.

Setting of a Jewel. The frame of gold or silver surrounding a jewel in a ring, brooch, etc.

" This precious stone set in the silver sea."
Shakespeare : Richard II., ii. 1.

Setting of Plaster or **Paint.** Its hardening.

Setting of Sun, Moon, and Stars. Their sinking below the horizon.

Setting the Thames on Fire. (*See* THAMES.)

Settle your Hash (*Tb*). " To cook his goose;" or " make mince-meat of him." Our slang is full of similar phrases.

" About earls as goes mad in their castles,
And females what settles their hash."
Sims : Dagonet Ballads (*Polly*).

Seven (Greek, *hepta ;* Latin, *septem ;* German, *sieben ;* Anglo-Saxon, *seofan ;* etc.). A holy number. There are seven days in creation, seven spirits before the throne of God, seven days in the week, seven graces, seven divisions in the Lord's Prayer, seven ages in the life of man, and the just fall " seven times a day." There are seven phases of the moon, every seventh year was sabbatical, and seven times seven years was the jubilee. The three great Jewish feasts lasted seven days, and between the first and second of these feasts were seven

weeks. Levitical purifications lasted seven days. We have seven churches of Asia, seven candlesticks, seven stars, seven trumpets, seven spirits before the throne of God, seven horns, the Lamb has seven eyes, ten times seven Israelites go to Egypt, the exile lasts the same number of years, and there were ten times seven elders. Pharaoh in his dream saw seven kine and seven ears of corn, etc.

It is frequently used indefinitely to signify a long time, or a great many ; thus in the *Interlude of the Four Elements,* the dance of Apetyte is called the best " that I have seen this seven yere." Shakespeare talks of a man being " a vile thief this seven year."

Seven Bibles (*The*) or *Sacred Books.*
(1) The *Bible* of Christians. (Canon completed A.D. 494 ; Old Testament as we have it, B.C. 130.)
(2) The *Eddas* of the Scandinavians.
(3) The *Five Kings* of the Chinese. " King " here means web-of-cloth on which they were originally written.
(4) The *Koran* of the Mohammedans. (Seventh century, A.D.)
(5) The *Tri Pitikes* of the Buddhists. (Sixth century B.C.)
(6) The *Three Vedas* of the Hindûs. (Twelfth century B.C.)
(7) *Zendavesta* of the Persians. (Twelfth century B.C.)

Seven Bodies in Alchemy. Sun is gold, moon silver, Mars iron, Mercury quicksilver, Saturn lead, Jupiter tin, and Venus copper.

" The bodies seven, eek, lo hem heer anoon ;
Sol gold is, and Luna silver we threpe,
Mars yren, Mercurie quyksilver we clepe ;
Saturnus leed, and Jubitur is tyn ;
And Venus coper, by my fader kyn."
Chaucer : Prol. of the Chanounes Yemanes Tal.

Seven Champions of Christendom is by Richard Johnson, who lived in the reigns of Elizabeth and James I.
(1) St. George of England was seven years imprisoned by the Almi'dor, the black King of Morocco.
(2) St. Denys of France lived seven years in the form of a hart.
(3) St. James of Spain was seven years dumb out of love to a fair Jewess.
(4) St. Anthony of Italy, with the other champions, was enchanted into a deep sleep in the Black Castle, and was released by St. George's three sons, who quenched the seven lamps by water from the enchanted fountain.
(5) St. Andrew of Scotland, who delivered six ladies who had lived seven years under the form of white swans.

(6) St. Patrick of Ireland was immured in a cell where he scratched his grave with his own nails.

(7) St. David of Wales slept seven years in the enchanted garden of Ormandine, but was redeemed by St. George.

Seven Churches of Asia.

(1) Ephesos, founded by St. Paul, 57, in a ruinous state in the time of Justinian.

(2) Smyrna, still an important seaport. Polycarp was its first bishop.

(3) Per'gamos, renowned for its library.

(4) Thyati'ra, now called Ak-hissar (the *White Castle*).

(5) Sardis, now a small village called Sart.

(6) Philadelph'ia, now called Allah Shehr (*City of God*), a miserable town.

(7) Laodice'a, now a deserted place called Eski-hissar (the *Old Castle*).

⁂ It is strange that all these churches, planted by the apostles themselves, are now Mahometan. Read what Gamaliel said, Acts v. 38, 39.

Seven Deadly Sins (*The*). Pride, Wrath, Envy, Lust, Gluttony, Avarice, and Sloth.

Seven Dials (London). A column with seven dials formerly stood in St. Giles, facing the seven streets which radiated therefrom.

" Where famed St. Giles's ancient limits spread
An in-railed column rears its lofty head.
Here to seven streets seven dials count the day,
And from each other catch the circling ray."
Gay: Trivia, ii.

Seven Joys of the Virgin. (*See* MARY.)

Seven Sages of Greece.

(1) Solon of Athens, whose motto was, "Know thyself."

(2) Chilo of Sparta—"Consider the end."

(3) Thalēs of Mile'tos—"Who hateth suretyship is sure."

(4) Bias of Prie'nē—"Most men are bad."

(5) Cleobu'los of Lindos—"The golden mean," or "Avoid extremes."

(6) Pittacos of Mityle'nē—"Seize Time by the forelock."

(7) Periander of Corinth—"Nothing is impossible to industry."

First, *Solon*, who made the Athenian laws:
While *Chilo*, in Sparta, was famed for his saws :
In Mile'tos did *Thales* astronomy teach ;
Bias used in Prie'ne his morals to preach ;
Cleobulos, of Lindos, was handsome and wise ;
Mityle'ne 'gainst thraldom saw *Pittacos* rise ;
Periander is said to have gained through his court
The title thr*v Myson*. the Chenian, ought.
E. C. B.

Seven Senses. *Scared out of my seven senses.* According to very ancient teaching, the soul of man, or his "inward holy body," is compounded of the seven properties which are under the influence of the seven planets. Fire animates, earth gives the sense of feeling, water gives speech, air gives taste, mist gives sight, flowers give hearing, the south wind gives smelling. Hence the seven senses are animation, feeling, speech, taste, sight, hearing, and smelling. (*See* COMMON SENSE.) (*See* Ecclesiastes xvii. 5.)

Seven Sisters. Seven culverins so called, cast by one Borthwick.

" And these were Borthwick's 'Sisters Seven,'
And culverins which France had given ;
Ill-omened gift ! The guns remain
The conqueror's spoil on Flodden plain."
Sir Walter Scott : Marmion, IV.

Seven Sleepers. Seven noble youths of Ephesos, who fled in the Decian persecution to a cave in Mount Celion. After 230 years they awoke, but soon died, and their bodies were taken to Marseilles in a large stone coffin, still shown in Victor's church. Their names are Constantine, Dionysius, John, Maxim'ian, Malchus, Martin'ian, and Serap'ion. This fable took its rise from a misapprehension of the words, "They fell asleep in the Lord"—*i.e.* died. (*Gregory of Tours: De Gloria Martyrum*, i. 9.) (See *Koran*, xviii. ; *Golden Legend*, etc.)

Seven Sorrows of the Virgin. (*See* MARY.)

Seven Spirits stand before the Throne of God: Michael, Gabriel, Lamael, Raphael, Zachariel, Anael, and Oriphel. (*Gustavini*.)

Seven Spirits of God (*The*). (1) the Spirit of Wisdom, (2) the Spirit of Understanding, (3) the Spirit of Counsel, (4) the Spirit of Power, (5) the Spirit of Knowledge, (6) the Spirit of Righteousness, and (7) the Spirit of Divine Awfulness.

Seven Virtues (*The*). Faith, Hope, Charity, Prudence, Justice, Fortitude, and Temperance. The first three are called "the holy virtues." (*See* SEVEN DEADLY SINS.)

Seven Weeks' War (*The*). From June 8th to July 26th, 1866, between Prussia and Austria, for German supremacy. Italy was allied to Prussia. Hostilities broke out between Austria and Italy July 25th, but the Bavarians were defeated the following day (July 26th).

The Treaty of Prague was signed August 23rd, 1866, and that of Vienna October 3rd. By these treaties, Austria was wholly excluded from Germany, and Prussia was placed at the head of the German States.

Seven Wise Masters. Lucien, son of Dolopăthus, received improper advances from his stepmother, and, being repelled, she accused him to the king of offering her violence. By consulting the stars the prince found out that his life was in danger, but that the crisis would be passed without injury if he remained silent for seven days. The wise masters now take up the matter; each one in turn tells the king a tale to illustrate the evils of inconsiderate punishments, and as the tale ends the king resolves to relent; but the queen at night persuades him to carry out his sentence. The seven days being passed, the prince also tells a tale which embodies the whole truth, whereupon the king sentences the queen to lose her life. This collection of tales, called *Sandabar's Parables*, is very ancient, and has been translated from the Arabic into almost all the languages of the civilised world. John Rolland, of Dalkeith, turned it into Scotch metre.

Seven Wonders of the World.

(i) *Of Antiquity.*

The *Pyramids* first, which in Egypt were laid;
Then *Babylon's Gardens* for Amy'tis made:
Third, *Mauso'lus's Tomb* of affection and guilt;
Fourth, the *Temple of Dian*, in Ephesus built;
Fifth, *Colossos of Rhodes*, cast in brass, to the sun;
Sixth, *Jupiter's Statue*, by Phidias done;
The *Pharos of Egypt*, last wonder of old,
Or the *Palace of Cyrus*, cemented with gold.
E. C. B.

(ii) *Of the Middle Ages.*
(1) The Colise'um of Rome.
(2) The Catacombs of Alexandria.
(3) The Great Wall of China.
(4) Stonehenge.
(5) The Leaning Tower of Pisa.
(6) The Porcelain Tower of Nankin.
(7) The Mosque of St. Sophia at Constantinople.

Seven Years' Lease. Leases run by seven years and its multiples, from the ancient notion of what was termed "climacteric years," in which life was supposed to be in special peril. (*Levinus Lemnius.*) (*See* CLIMACTERIC YEARS.)

Seven Years' War (*The*). The third period of the War of the "Austrian Succession," between Maria Theresa of Austria and Friedrich II. of Prussia. It began 1756, and terminated in 1763. At the close, Silesia was handed over to Prussia.

Seven Years' War between Sweden and Denmark (1563-1570). Erik XIV. of Sweden was poisoned, and his successor put an end to the war.

Several = separate; that which is severed or separate; each, as "all and several."

Azariah was a leper, and "dwelt in a several house" (2 *Kings* xv. 5).

Severn. (*See* SABRINA.)

Seve'rus (*St.*). Patron saint of fullers, being himself of the same craft.

The Wall of Severus. A stone rampart, built in 208 by the Emperor Seve'rus, between the Tyne and the Solway. It is to the north of Hadrian's wall, which was constructed in 120.

Sèvres Ware. Porcelain of fine quality, made at the French government works at Sèvres. Chiefly of a delicate kind, for ornament rather than use.

Sew the Button on. Jot down at once what you wish to remember, otherwise it may be lost or forgotten.

Sex. (*See* GENDER WORDS.)

Sexages'ima Sunday. The second Sunday before Lent; so called because in round numbers it is sixty days before Easter.

Sex'tile (2 syl.). The aspect of two planets when distant from each other sixty degrees or two signs. This position is marked thus *. As there are twelve signs, two signs are a *sixth*.

" In sextile, square, and trine, and opposite
Of noxious efficacy."
Milton: Paradise Lost, x. 659.

Sex'ton. A corruption of sa'cristan, an official who has charge of the *sacra*, or things attached to a specific church, such as vestments, cushions, books, boxes, tools, vessels, and so on.

Seyd [*Seed*]. Pacha of the More'a, assassinated by Gulnare, his favourite concubine. (*Byron : The Corsair*.)

Sforza. The founder of the illustrious house which was so conspicuous in the fifteenth and sixteenth centuries, was the son of a day-labourer. His name was Giacomuzzo Attendolo, changed to Sforza from the following incident:—Being desirous of going to the wars, he consulted his hatchet thus: he flung it against a tree, saying, "If it sticks fast, I will go." It did stick fast, and he enlisted. It was because he threw it with such amazing force that he was called Sforza, the Italian for force.

Sforza (in *Jerusalem Delivered*) of Lombardy. He, with his two brothers, Achilles and Palame'des, were in the squadron of adventurers in the allied Christian army.

Shack. A scamp. To shack or shackle is to tie a log to a horse, and send it out to feed on the stubble after harvest. A shack is either a beast so shackled, the right of sending a beast to the stubble, or the stubble itself. Applied to men, a shack is a jade, a stubble-feeder, one bearing the same ratio to a well-to-do man as a jade sent to graze on a common bears to a well-stalled horse. (Anglo-Saxon, *sceacul*; Arabic, *shakal*, to tie the feet of a beast.)

Shaddock. A large kind of orange, so called from Captain Shaddock, who first transplanted one in the West Indies. It is a native of China and Japan.

Shades. Wine vaults. The Brighton Old Bank, in 1819, was turned by Mr. Savage into a smoking-room and gin-shop. There was an entrance to it by the Pavilion Shades, and Savage took down the word *bank*, and inserted instead the word *shades*. This term was not inappropriate, as the room was in reality shaded by the opposite house, occupied by Mrs. Fitzherbert.

Shadoff or **Shadoof.** A contrivance in Egypt for watering lands for the summer crops. It consists of a long rod weighted at one end, so as to raise the bucket attached by a rope to the other end.

Shadow. A ghost. Macbeth says to the ghost of Banquo—

> "Hence, horrible shadow! unreal mockery,
>   hence!"   *Shakespeare : Macbeth*, iii. 4.

He would quarrel with his own shadow. He is so irritable that he would lose his temper on the merest trifle. (*See* SCHLE-MIHL.)

Gone to the bad for the shadow of an ass. Demosthenes says a young Athenian once hired an ass to Meg'ara. The heat was so great and the road so exposed, that he alighted at midday to take shelter from the sun under the shadow of the poor beast. Scarcely was he seated when the owner passed by, and laid claim to the shadow, saying he let the ass to the traveller, but not the ass's shadow. After fighting for a time, they agreed to settle the matter in the law courts, and the suit lasted so long that both were ruined. "If you must quarrel, let it be for something better than the shadow of an ass."

May your shadow never be less. When students have made certain progress in the black arts, they are compelled to run through a subterranean hall with the devil after them. If they run so fast that the devil can only catch their shadow, or part of it, they become first-rate magicians, but lose either all or part of their shadow. Therefore, the expression referred to above means, May you escape wholly and entirely from the clutches of the foul fiend.

A servant earnestly desireth the shadow (Job vii. 2)—the time of leaving off work. The people of the East measure time by the length of their shadow, and if you ask a man what o'clock it is, he will go into the sun, stand erect, and fixing his eye where his shadow terminates, will measure its length with his feet; having done so, he will tell you the hour correctly. A workman earnestly desires his shadow, which indicates the time of leaving off work.

Shadow (*To*). To follow about like a shadow. This is done by some person or persons appointed to watch the movements and keep *au fait* with the doings of suspicious characters.

> "He [Jesus] was shadowed by spies, who were stirring up the crowd against Him."—*Longman's Magazine*, 1891, p. 238.

Shady. *On the shady side of forty*—the wrong side, meaning more than forty. As evening approaches the shadows lengthen, and as man advances towards the evening of life he approaches the shady side thereof. As the beauty of the day is gone when the sun declines, the word shady means inferior, bad, etc.; as, a shady character, one that will not bear the light; a shady transaction, etc.

Shaf'alus. So Bottom the weaver and Francis Flute the bellows-mender, call Ceph'alus, the husband of Procris.

> "*Pyramus :* Not Shafalus to Procrus was so true.
> *Thisbe :* As Shafalus to Procrus, I to you."
>   *Shakespeare : Midsummer Night's Dream*, v. 1.

Sha'fites (2 syl.). One of the four sects of the Sunnites or orthodox Moslems ; so called from Al-Shafei, a descendant of Mahomet. (*See* SHIITES.)

Shaft. *I will make either a shaft or bolt of it.* I will apply it to one use or another. The bolt was the crossbow arrow, the shaft was the arrow of the long-bow.

Shatton (*Sir Piercie*). In this character Sir Walter Scott has made familiar to us the euphuisms of Queen Elizabeth's age. The fashionable cavalier or pedantic fop, who assumes the high-flown style rendered fashionable by Lyly, was grandson of old Overstitch the tailor. (*Sir Walter Scott : Monastery.*)

Shah. *Have you seen the Shah ?* A query implying a hoax, popular with street arabs when the Shah of Persia visited England. (1873.)

Shah-pour, *the Great* (Sapor II.). Surnamed *Zu-lectaf* (shoulder-breaker), because he dislocated the shoulders of all the Arabs taken in war. The Romans called him *Post'humus,* because he was born after the death of his father Hormuz II. He was crowned in the womb by the Magi placing the royal insignia on the body of his mother.

Shahzada. A prince, the son of a king. (*Anglo-Indian.*)

Shakedown. *Come and take a shakedown at my house*—a bed. The allusion is to the time when men slept upon litter or clean straw. (*See below,* SHAKES.)

Shakers. Certain agamists founded in North America by Ann Lee, called "Mother Ann," daughter of a poor blacksmith born in Toad Lane (Todd Street), Manchester. She married a smith named Stanley, and had four children, who died in infancy, after which she joined the sect of Jane Wardlaw, a tailoress, but was thrown into prison as a brawler. While there she said that Jesus Christ stood before her, and became one with her in form and spirit. When she came out and told her story six or seven persons joined her, and called her "the Lamb's bride." Soon after this she went to America and settled at Water Vliet, in New York. Other settlements were established in Hancock and Mount Lebanon.

"The Shakers never marry, form no earthly ties, believe in no future resurrection."—*W. Hepworth Dixon : New America,* vii. 12.

Shakes. *No great shakes.* Nothing extraordinary ; no such mighty bargain. The reference is to shingle for the roof of shanties, or to stubble left after harvest for the poor.

"The cabin itself is quite like that of the modern settlers, but the shingles, called shakes, . . . make the wood roof unique." — *Harper's Weekly,* July 18th, 1891, p. 534.

I'll do it in a brace of shakes—instantly, as soon as you can shake twice the dice-box.

Shakespeare, usually called "Gentle Will."

His wife was Anne Hathaway, of Shottery, about eight years older than himself.

He had one son, named Hamnet, who died in his twelfth year, and two daughters.

Ben Jonson said of him—"And though thou hadst small Latin and less Greek . . ."

Milton calls him "Sweetest Shakespeare, fancy's child," and says he will go to the well-trod stage to hear him "warble his native wood-notes wild." (*L'Allegro,* 133.)

Akenside says he is "Alike the master of our smiles and tears." (*Ode* i.)

Dryden says of him—"He was a man who of all modern and perhaps ancient poets, had the largest and most comprehensive soul."

Young says—"He wrote the play the Almighty made." (*Epistle to Lord Lansdowne.*)

Mallett says—"Great above rule. . . . Nature was his own." (*Verbal Criticism.*)

Collins says he "joined Tuscan fancy to Athenian force." (*Epistle to Sir Thomas Hanmer.*)

Pope says—

"Shakespeare (whom you and every play-house bill
Style "the divine." "the matchless," what you will)
For gain, not glory, winged his roving flight,
And grew immortal in his own despite."
        Imitations of Horace, Ep. i.

The dedication of Shakespeare's Sonnets has provoked much controversy. It is as follows :—

TO THE ONLIE BEGETTER OF
THESE INSUING SONNETS
MR. W. H. ALL HAPPINESSE
AND THAT ETERNITIE
PROMISED
BY
OUR EVER-LIVING POET
WISHETH

—that is, Mr. William Herbert [afterwards Lord Pembroke] wisheth to [the Earl of Southampton] the only begetter or instigator of these sonnets, that happiness and eternal life which [Shakespeare] the ever-living poet speaks of. The rider is—

THE WELL-WISHING
ADVENTURER IN
SETTING
FORTH.   T. T.

That is, Thomas Thorpe is the adventurer who speculates in their publication. (See *Athenæum,* Jan. 25, 1862.)

Shakspeare. There are six accredited signatures of this poet, five of which are attached to business documents, and one is entered in a book called *Florio,* a translation of Montaigne, published in

1603. A passage in act ii. s. 2 of *The Tempest* is traced directly to this translation, proving that the *Florio* was possessed by Shakespeare before he wrote that play.

The Shakespeare of divines. Jeremy Taylor (1613-1667).

The Shakespeare of eloquence. So Barnave happily characterised the Comte de Mirabeau (1749-1791).

The Spanish Shakespeare. Calderon (1601-1687).

Shaking Hands. Horace, strolling along the Via Sacra, shook hands with an acquaintance. *Arreptâque manu, " Quid agis dulcissimĕ rerum ? "*

Æneas, in the temple of Dido, sees his lost companions enter, and *" avidi conjungere dextras ardebant "* (*Æn.*, i. 514.)

Nestor shook hands with Ulysses on his return to the Grecian camp with the stolen horses of Rhesus.

And in the Old Testament, when Jehu asked Jehonadab if his "heart was right" with him, he said, "If it be, give me thine hand," and Jehonadab gave him his hand.

Shaky. Not steady; not in good health; not strictly upright; not well prepared for examination; doubtfully solvent. The allusion is to a table or chair out of order and shaky.

Shallow. A weak-minded country justice, intended as a caricature of Sir Thomas Lucy, of Charlecote. He is described as one who had been a madcap in his youth, and still dotes on his wild tricks; he is withal a liar, a blockhead, and a rogue. (*Shakespeare: Merry Wives of Windsor*, and 2 *Henry IV.*)

Shalott (*Lady of*). A poem by Tennyson, the tale of which is similar to that of Elaine the "fair maid of Astolat" (*q.v.*). Part I. describes the island of Shalott, and tells us that the lady passed her life so secluded there that only the farm-labourers knew her. Part II. tells us that the lady passed her time in weaving a magic web, and that a curse would light on her if she looked down the river towards Camelot. Part III. describes how Sir Lancelot, in all his bravery, rode to Camelot, and the lady looked at him as he rode along. Part IV. says that the lady entered a boat, having first written her name on the prow, and floated down the river to Camelot, but died on the way. When the boat reached Camelot, Sir Lancelot, with all the inmates of the palace, came to look at it. They read the name on

the prow, and Sir Lancelot exclaimed, "She has a lovely face, and may God have mercy on the lady of Shalott ! "

Shambles means *benches* (Anglo-Saxon, *scamel; * Latin, *scamnum*, and the diminutive *scamellum*, a little bench). The benches or banks on which meat is exposed for sale. (*See* BANK.)

" Whatsoever is sold in the shambles, that eat, asking no question."—1 Cor. x. 25.

Sham'rock, the symbol of Ireland, because it was selected by St. Patrick to prove to the Irish the doctrine of the Trinity. (Irish and Gaelic, *seam-rog*.)

Shamrock. According to the elder Pliny, no serpent will touch this plant.

Shan Van Voght. This excellent song (composed 1798) may be called the Irish *Marseillaise.* The title of it is a corruption of *An t-sean bean bochd* (the poor old woman—*i.e.* Ireland). (*Halliday-Spurling: Irish Minstrelsy*, p. 13.) The last verse is—

" Will Ireland then be free ?
　　Said the Shan Van Voght ? (repeat)
Yes, Ireland shall be free
From the centre to the sea,
Hurrah for liberty !
　　Said the Shan Van Voght."

Shande'an Exactness. Sir Walter Scott says, "The author proceeds with the most unfeeling prolixity to give a minute detail of civil and common law, of the feudal institutions, of the architecture of churches and castles, of sculpture and painting, of minstrels, players, and parish clerks. . . Tristram can hardly be said to be fairly born, though his life has already attained the size of half a volume." (*See below.*)

" With a Shandean exactness . . . Lady Anne begins her memoirs of herself nine months before her nativity, for the sake of introducing a beautiful quotation from the Psalms."—*Bioj. Borealis*, p. 260.

Shandy. Captain Shandy is called *Uncle Toby.* He was wounded at the siege of Namur, and had retired from the service. He is benevolent and generous, simple as a child, brave as a lion, and gallant as a courtier. His modesty with Widow Wadman and his military tastes are admirable. He is said to be drawn for Sterne's father. (*Tristram Shandy.*)

Mrs. Elizabeth Shandy, mother of Tristram. The *beau-ideal* of nonentity. Sir Walter Scott describes her as a "good lady of the poco-curante school." (*Sterne : Tristram Shandy.*)

Tristram Shandy. The hero of Sterne's novel so called.

Walter Shandy, Tristram's father. He is a metaphysical Don Quixote in his way, full of superstitious and idle conceits. He believes in long noses and propitious names, but his son's nose is crushed, and his name is Tristram instead of Trismegistus. (*Sterne : Tristram Shandy.*)

Shandygaff is a mixture of beer and ginger-beer. (*See* SMILER.)

Shanks' Nag. *To ride Shanks' nag* is to go on foot, the shanks being the legs. A similar phrase is "Going by the marrow-bone stage" or by Walker's 'bus. (Anglo-Saxon, *scanca*, shanks.)

Shannon. *Dipped in the Shannon.* One who has been dipped in the Shannon loses all bashfulness. At least, *sic aiunt.*

Shanty. A log-hut. (Irish, *sean*, old ; *tig*, house.)

Shanty Songs. Songs sung by sailors at work, to ensure united action. They are in sets, each of which has a different cadence adapted to the work in hand. Thus, in sheeting topsails, weighing anchor, etc., one of the most popular of the shanty songs runs thus :—

> " I'm bound away, this very day,
> I'm bound for the Rio Grande.
> Ho, you, Rio !
> Then fare you well, my bonny blue bell,
> I'm bound for the Rio Grande."

(French, *chanter*, to sing ; a sing-song.)

Shark. A swindler, a pilferer, one who snaps up things like a shark, which eats almost anything, and seems to care little whether its food is alive or dead, fish, flesh, or human bodies.

> " These thieves doe rob us with our owne good will,
> And have Dame Nature's warrant for it still ;
> Sometimes these sharks doe worke each other's wrack,
> The ravening belly often robs the backe."
> *Taylor's Workes,* ii. 117.

The shark flies the feather. This is a sailor's proverb founded on observation. Though a shark is so voracious that it will swallow without distinction everything that drops from a ship into the sea, such as cordage, cloth, pitch, wood, and even knives, yet it will never touch a pilot-fish (*q.v.*) or a fowl, either alive or dead. It avoids sea-gulls, sea-mews, petrels, and every feathered thing. (*St. Pierre : Studies,* i.)

Sharp (*Becky*). The impersonation of intellect without virtue in Thackeray's *Vanity Fair.* (*See* SEDLEY.)

> " Becky Sharp, with a baronet for a brother-in-law and an earl's daughter for a friend, felt the hollowness of human grandeur, and thought she was happier with the Bohemian artists in Soho."
> —*The Express.*

Sharp. *Sharp's the word.* Look out, keep your eyes open and your wits about you. When a shopman suspects a

36*

customer, he will ask aloud of a brother-shopman if "Mr. Sharp is come in ;" and if his suspicion is confirmed, will receive for answer, "No, but he is expected back immediately." (*Hotten.*)

Sharp-beak. The Crow's wife in the tale of *Reynard the Fox.*

Sharp-set. Hungry. A term in falconry. (*See* HAWK.)

> " If anie were so sharpe-set as to eat fried flies, buttered bees, stued snails, either on Fridaie or Sundaie, he could not be therefore indicted of haulte treason."—*Stanihurst : Ireland,* p. 19 (1580).

Shave. *To shave a customer.* Hotten says, when a master-draper sees anyone capable of being imposed upon enter his shop, he strokes his chin, to signify to his assistant that the customer may be shaved.

I shaved through ; he was within a shave of a pluck. I just got through [my examination] ; he was nearly rejected as not up to the mark. The allusion is to carpentry.

Shaveling. A lad ; a young man. In the year 1348 the clergy died so fast of the Black Death that youths were admitted to holy orders by being shaven. " William Bateman, Bishop of Norwich, dispensed with sixty shavelings to hold rectories and other livings, that divine service might not cease in the parishes over which they were appointed. (*Blomfield : History of Norfolk,* vol. iii.)

Shaving. Bondmen were commanded by the ancient Gauls to shave, in token of servitude.

In the Turkish seraglio the slaves are obliged to shave their chins, in token of their servitude.

She Stoops to Conquer. This comedy owes its existence to an incident which actually occurred to its author. When Goldsmith was sixteen years of age, a wag residing at Ardagh directed him, when passing through that village, to Squire Fetherstone's house as the village inn. The mistake was not discovered for some time, and then no one enjoyed it more heartily than Oliver himself.

Shear Steel. Steel which has been sheared. When the bars have been converted into steel, they are *sheared into short pieces,* and forged again from a pile built up with layers crossed, so as to produce a web-like texture in the metal by the crossing of the fibres. Great toughness results from this mode of manipulation, and the steel thus produced is used for shears and other instruments where a hard sharp edge is required.

Sheb-seze. The great fire festival of the Persians, when they used to set fire to large bunches of dry combustibles, fastened round wild beasts and birds, which, being then let loose, the air and earth appeared one great illumination. The terrified creatures naturally fled to the woods for shelter, and it is easy to conceive the conflagration they produced. (*Richardson : Dissertation.*)

She'ba (*Queen of*). The Assyrians say her name was Macqueda, but Arabs call her Belkis.

Shebeen. A small Irish store for the sale of whisky and something else, as bacon, eggs, general provisions, and groceries.

" Drinking your health wid Shamus
O'Shea at Katty's shebeen."
Tennyson : To-morrow, stanza 2.

Sheep. *Ram* or *tup,* the sire ; *ewe,* the dam ; *lamb,* the new-born sheep till it is weaned, when it is called a *hogget ;* the tup-lamb being a " tup-hogget," and the ewe-lamb a " ewe-hogget ; " if the tup is castrated it is called a wether-hogget.

After the removal of the *first* fleece, the tup-hogget becomes a *shearling,* the ewe-hogget a *grimmer,* and the wether-hogget a dinmont (hence the name " Dandy Dinmont ").

After the removal of the *second* fleece, the shearling becomes a *two-shear tup,* the grimmer a *ewe,* and the dinmont a *wether.*

After the removal of the *third* fleece, the ewe is called a *twinter-ewe ;* and when it ceases to breed, a *draft-ewe.*

The Black Sheep (Kârà-koin-loo). A tribe which established a principality in Armenia, that lasted 108 years (1360-1468) ; so called from the device of their standard.

The White Sheep (Ak-koin-loo). A tribe which established a principality in Armenia, etc., on the ruin of the Black Sheep (1468-1508) ; so called from the device of their standard.

To cast a sheep's eye at one is to look askance, like a sheep, at a person to whom you feel lovingly inclined.

" But he, the beast, was casting sheep's eyes at her."—*Colman : Broad Grins.*

Sheet Anchor. *That is my sheet anchor* —my chief stay, my chief dependence. The sheet anchor is the largest and heaviest of all. The word is a corruption of Shote-anchor, the anchor shot or thrown out in stress of weather. Many

ships carry more than one sheet-anchor outside the ship's waist.

"The surgeon no longer bleeds. If *y*ou ask him 'why this neglect of what was once considered the *sheet anchor* of practice in certain diseases?' he will . . ."—*The Times.*

Sheik (Arabic, *elder*). A title of respect equal to the Italian *signo're,* the French *sieur,* Spanish *senor,* etc. There are seven sheiks in the East, all said to be direct descendants of Mahomet, and they all reside at Mecca.

Sheki'nah (*shachan,* to reside). The glory of the Divine Presence in the shape of a cloud of fire, which rested on the mercy-seat between the Cherubim.

Shekinah or Shechinah is not a biblical word. It was first mentioned in the Jerusalem Targum. The Sheckinah was not supposed to dwell in the Second Temple. Its responses were given either by the Urim and Thummim of the high priest, by prophets, or orally. (*See* Deut. iii. 24 ; and Luke xvi. 2.)

Sheldo'nian Theatre. The " Senate House " of Oxford ; so called from Gilbert Sheldon, Archbishop of Canterbury, who built it. (1598-1669.)

Shelf. *Laid on the shelf,* or *shelved.* A government officer no longer actively employed ; an actor no longer assigned a part ; a young lady past the ordinary age of marriage ; a pawn at the broker's ; a question started and set aside. All mean laid up and put away.

Shell (*A*) is a hollow iron ball, with a fuze-hole in it to receive a fuze, which is a plug of wood containing gunpowder. It is constructed to burn slowly, and, on firing, the piece ignites, and continues to burn during its flight till it falls on the object. at which it is directed, when it bursts, scattering its fragments in all directions.

Shell Jacket (*A*). An undress military jacket.

Shell of an Egg. After an egg in the shell has been eaten, many persons break or crush the empty shell. Sir Thomas Brown says this was done originally " to prevent house-spirits from using the shell for their mischievous pranks." (Book v., chap. xxiii.)

Shells on churches, tombstones, and used by pilgrims :

(1) If dedicated to James the Greater, the scallop-shell is his recognised emblem. (*See* JAMES.) If *not,* the allusion is to the vocation of the apostles generally, who were fishermen, and Christ said He would make them "fishers of men."

(2) On tombstones, the allusion is to

the earthly body left behind, which is the mere *shell* of the immortal soul.

(3) Carried by pilgrims, the allusion may possibly be to James the Greater, the patron saint of pilgrims, but more likely it originally arose as a convenient drinking-cup, and hence the pilgrims of Japan carry scallop shells.

Shemit'ic. Pertaining to Shem, descendant of Shem, derived from Shem.

The Shemitic languages are Chaldee, Syriac, Arabic, Hebrew, Samaritan, Ethiopic, and old Phœnician. The great characteristic of this family of languages is that the roots of words consist of three consonants.

Shemitic nations or *Shemites* (2 syl.). (*See above.*)

Shepherd. *The shepherd.* Moses who fed the flocks of Jethro, his father-in-law.

" Sing, heavenly muse, that on the secret top
    Of Oreb or of Sinai didst inspire
That shepherd, who first taught the chosen seed
In the beginning how the heavens and earth
Rose out of chaos."
         Milton : Paradise Lost, bk. i. 8.

N.B. Oreb, or Horeb and Sinai, are two heights of one mountain.

Shepherd Kings or *Hyksos.* Some 2,000 years B.C. a tribe of Arabian shepherds established themselves in Lower Egypt, and were governed by their own chiefs. Man'etho says " they reigned 511 years;" Eratos'thenēs says 470 years; Africa'nus, 284 years ; Eusebius, 103 years. Some say they extended over five dynasties, some over three, some limit their sway to one ; some give the name of only one monarch, some of four, and others of six. Bunsen places them B.C. 1639 ; Lepsius, B.C. 1842 ; others, 1900 or 2000. If there ever were such kings, they were driven into Syria by the rulers of Upper Egypt. (*Hyk*, ruler ; *shos*, shepherd.)

Shepherd Lord (*The*). Henry, the tenth Lord Clifford, sent by his mother to be brought up by a shepherd, in order to save him from the fury of the Yorkists. At the accession of Henry VII. he was restored to all his rights and seigniories. (Died 1523.)

⁂ The story is told by Wordsworth in *The Song for the Feast of Brougham Castle.*

Shepherd of Banbury (*The*). The ostensible author of a Weather Guide. He styles himself John Claridge, Shepherd : but the real author is said to have been Dr. John Campbell. (First published in 1744.)

Shepherd of Salisbury Plain (*The*). Said to be David Saunders, noted for his homely wisdom and practical piety. Mrs. Hannah More wrote the religious tract so entitled, and makes the hero a Christian Arcadian.

Shepherd of the Ocean (*The*). So Sir Walter Raleigh is called by Spenser, in his poem entitled *Colin Clout's Come Home Again.* (1552-1618.)

Shepherd's Sundial (*The*). The scarlet pimpernel, which opens at a little past seven in the morning, and closes at a little past two. When rain is at hand, or the weather is unfavourable, it does not open at all.

Shepherded. Watched and followed as suspicious of mischief, as a shepherd watches a wolf.

" Russian vessels of war are everywhere being carefully ' shepherded' by British ships, and it is easy to see that such a state of extreme tension cannot be continued much longer without an actual outbreak."—*Newspaper leader,* April 27th, 1885.

Sheppard (*Jack*). Son of a carpenter in Smithfield, noted for his two escapes from Newgate in 1724. He was hanged at Tyburn the same year. (1701-1724.)

Shepster Time. The time of sheep-shearing.

Sheriffmuir. *There was mair lost at the Shirramuir.* Don't grieve for your losses, for worse have befallen others before now. The battle of Sheriffmuir, in 1715, between the Jacobites and Hanoverians was very bloody ; both sides sustained heavy losses, and both sides claimed the victory.

She'va, in the satire of *Absalom and Achitophel*, by Dryden and Tate, is designed for Sir Roger Lestrange. (Part ii.)

Shewbread. Food for show only, and not intended to be eaten except by certain privileged persons. The term is Jewish, and refers to the twelve loaves which the priest " showed " or exhibited to Jehovah, by placing them week by week on the sanctuary table. At the end of the week, the priest who had been in office was allowed to take them home for his own eating ; but no one else was allowed to partake of them.

Shewri-while. A spirit-woman that haunts Mynydd Llanhilleth mountain, in Monmouthshire, to mislead those who attempt to cross it.

Shiahs. (*See* SHIITES.)

Shib'boleth. The password of a secret society : the secret by which those of a party know each other. The

Ephraimites quarrelled with Jephthah, and Jephthah gathered together the men of Gilead and fought with Ephraim. There were many fugitives, and when they tried to pass the Jordan the guard told them to say Shibboleth, which the Ephraimites pronounced Sibboleth, and by this test it was ascertained whether the person wishing to cross the river was a friend or foe. (Judges xii. 1-16.)

> "Their foes a deadly shibboleth devise."
> *Dryden: Hind and Panther*, pt. iii.

Shield.

The Gold and Silver Shield. Two knights coming from different directions stopped in sight of a trophy shield, one side of which was gold and the other silver. Like the disputants about the colour of the chameleon, the knights disputed about the metal of the shield, and from words they proceeded to blows. Luckily a third knight came up at this juncture, to whom the point of dispute was referred, and the disputants were informed that the shield was silver on one side and gold on the other. This story is from Beaumont's *Moralities.* It was reprinted in a collection of *Useful and Entertaining Passages in Prose*, 1826.

The other side of the shield. The other side of the question. The reference is to the "Gold and Silver Shield." (*See above.*)

That depends on which side of the shield you look at. That depends on the standpoint of the speaker. (*See above.*)

Shield-of-Arms. Same as *Coat of Arms ;* so called because persons in the Middle Ages bore their heraldic devices on their shields.

Shield of Expectation (*The*). The naked shield given to a young warrior in his virgin campaign. As he achieved glory, his deeds were recorded or symbolised on his shield.

Shields. The most famous in story are the *Shield of Achilles* described by Homer, of *Hercules*, described by Hesiod, and of Æneas described by Virgil.

Other famous bucklers described in classic story are the following :—That of

Agamemnon, a gorgon.
Amýcos (son of Poseidon or Neptune), a crayfish, symbol of prudence.
Cadmos and his descendants, a dragon, to indicate their descent from the dragon's teeth.
Eteôcles (4 syl.), one of the seven heroes against Thebes, a man scaling a wall.
Hector, a lion.
Idoméneus (4 syl.), a cock.
Menelãos, a serpent at his heart ; alluding to the elopement of his wife with Paris.

Parthenopœos, one of the seven heroes, a sphinx holding a man in its claws.
Ulysses, a dolphin. Whence he is sometimes called Delphinosemos.

⁎ Servius says that the *Greeks* in the siege of Troy had, as a rule, Neptune on their bucklers, and the *Trojans* Minerva.

It was a common custom, after a great victory, for the victorious general to hang his buckler on the walls of some temple.

The clang of shields. When a chief doomed a man to death, he struck his shield with the blunt end of his spear, by way of notice to the royal bard to begin the death-song. (*See* Æ'GIS.)

> "Cairbar rises in his arms,
> The clang of shields is heard."
> *Ossian: Temora*, i.

Shi-ites (2 syl.). Those Mahometans who do not consider the Sunna, or oral law, of any authority, but look upon it as apocryphal. They wear *red* turbans, and are sometimes called "Red Heads." The Persians are Shiites. (Arabic, *shiah*, a sect.) (*See* SUNNITES.)

Shillelagh (pronounce *she-lay-lah*). An oaken sapling or cudgel (Irish).

Shilling. Said to be derived from *St. Kilian*, whose image was stamped on the "shillings" of Würzburg. Of course this etymology is of no value. (Anglo-Saxon, *scylling* or *scilling*, a shilling).

⁎ According to Skeat, from the verb *scylan* (to divide). The coin was originally made with a deeply-indented cross, and could easily be divided into halves or quarters.

Shilly Shally. A corruption of "Will I, shall I," or "Shall I, shall I."

> "There's no delay, they ne'er stand shall I,
> shall I,
> Hermog'enes with Dal'lila doth dally."
> *Taylor's Workes*, iii. 3 (1630).

Shim'ci (2 syl.), in Dryden's satire of *Absalom and Achitophel*, is designed for Slingsby Bethel, the lord mayor.

> "Shimei, whose youth did early promise bring,
> Of zeal to God and hatred to his king ;
> Did wisely from expensive sins refrain,
> And never broke the Sabbath but for gain."
> Part 1, lines 548—551.

Shi'nar. The land of the Chaldees.

Shindy. A row, a disturbance. To kick up a shindy, to make a row. (Gipsy, *chinda*, a quarrel.)

Shin'gebis, in North American Indian mythology, is a diver who dared the North Wind to single combat. The Indian Boreas rated him for staying in his dominions after he had routed away the flowers, and driven off the sea-gulls and herons. Shin'gebis laughed at him, and the North Wind went at night and tried to blow down his hut and put out his fire. As he could not do this, he defied the diver to come forth and wrestle with him. Shin'gebis obeyed the summons, and sent the blusterer howling to his home. (*Longfellow : Hiawatha.*) (*See* KABIBONOKKA.)

Ship (the device of Paris). Sauval says, " *L'île de la cité est faite comme un grand navire enfoncé dans la vase, et échoué au fil de l'eau vers le milieu de la Seine.*" This form of a ship struck the heraldic scribes, who, in the latter half of the Middle Ages, emblazoned it in the shield of the city. (*See* VENGEUR.)

When my ship comes home. When my fortune is made. The allusion is to the argosies returning from foreign parts laden with rich freights.

Ship Letters. These are to indicate when a ship is fully laden, and this depends on its destination.

F.W. (Fresh Water line), *i.e.* it may be laden till this mark touches the water when loading in a fresh-water dock or river.

I.S. (Indian Summer line). It was to be loaded to this point in the Indian seas in summer time.

S. The summer draught in the Mediterranean.

W. The winter draught in the Mediterranean.

W.N.A. (Winter North Atlantic line).

Ship-shape. As methodically arranged as things in a ship; in good order. When a vessel is sent out temporarily rigged, it is termed "jury-rigged" (*i.e. jour-y,* meaning *pro tem.,* for the day or time being). Her rigging is completed while at sea, and when the jury-rigging has been duly changed for ship-rigging, the vessel is in "ship-shape," *i.e.* due or regular order.

Ship of the Desert. The camel.

" Three thousand camels his rank pastures fed,
Arabia's wandering ships, for traffic bred."
G. Sandys: Paraphrase from Job (1610).

Ships. There are three ships often confounded, viz. the *Great Harry,* the *Regent,* and the *Henry Grâce de Dieu.*

The GREAT HARRY was built in the third year of Henry VII. (1488). It was a two-decker with three masts, and was accidentally burnt at Woolwich in 1553.

The REGENT was burnt in 1512 in an engagement with the French.

The HENRY GRÂCE DE DIEU was built at Erith in 1515. It had three decks and four masts. It was named

Edward, after the death of Henry VIII. in 1547. There is no record of its destruction.

"Though we are not acquainted with all the particular ships that formed the navy of Henry VIII., we know that among them were two very large ones, viz. the *Regent,* and the *Henry Grace de Dieu.* The former being burnt in 1512, in an engagement with the French, occasioned Henry to build the latter."—*Willet : Naval Architecture,* xi. 158.

Ships of the Line. Men-of-war large enough to have a place in a line of battle. They must not have less than two decks or two complete tiers of guns.

Shipton. (*See* MOTHER.)

Shire and **County.** When the Saxon kings created an earl, they gave him a shire or division of land to govern. At the Norman conquest the word count superseded the title of earl, and the earldom was called a county. Even to the present hour we call the wife of an earl a countess. (Anglo-Saxon, *scire,* from *sciran,* to divide.)

He comes from the shires; has a seat in the shires, etc.—in those English counties which terminate in "shire:" a belt running from Devonshire and Hampshire in a north-east direction. In a general way it means the midland counties.

✲ Anglesey in Wales, and twelve counties of England, do not terminate in "shire."

Shire Horses originally meant horses bred in the midland and eastern shires of England, but now mean any draught-horses of a certain character which can show a registered pedigree. The sire and dam, with a minute description of the horse itself, its age, marks, and so on, must be shown in order to prove the claim of a "shire horse." Shire horses are noted for their great size, muscular power, and beauty of form; stallions to serve cart mares.

Clydesdale horses are Scotch draught-horses, not equal to shire horses in size, but of great endurance.

A hackney is not a thoroughbred, but nearly so, and makes the best roadster, hunter, and carriage-horse. Its action is showy, and its pace good. A first-class roadster will trot a mile in two and a half minutes. American trotters sometimes exceed this record. The best hackneys are produced from thorough sires mated with half-bred mares.

Shirt. (*See* NESSUS.)

Shirt for ensign. When Sultan Saladin died, he commanded that no ceremony should be used but this: A priest was to carry his shirt on a lance, and say: "Saladin, the conqueror of the East, carries nothing with him of all his wealth and greatness, save a shirt for his shroud and ensign." (*Knolles: Turkish History.*)

Close sits my shirt, but closer my skin— i.e. My property is dear to me, but dearer my life ; my belongings sit close to my heart, but "*Ego proximus mihi.*"

Shittim Wood. The acacia.

"The scented acacia of Palestine furnished the shittim wood so much esteemed by the ancient Jews."—*Bible Flowers*, p. 142.

Shivering Mountain. Mam Tor, a hill on the Peak of Derbyshire ; so called from the waste of its mass by "shivering"—that is, breaking away in "shivers" or small pieces. This shivering has been going on for ages, as the hill consists of alternate layers of shale and gritstone. The former, being soft, is easily reduced to powder, and, as it crumbles away, small "shivers" of the gritstone break away from want of support.

Shoddy properly means the flue and fluff thrown off from cloth in the process of weaving. This flue, being mixed with new wool, is woven into a cloth called shoddy - *i.e.* cloth made of the flue "shod" or thrown off. Shoddy is also made of old garments torn up and re-spun. The term is used for any loose, sleazy cloth, and metaphorically for literature of an inferior character compiled from other works. (*Shed*, provincial pret. "shod ;" *shoot*, obsolete pret. *shotten.*)

Shoddy characters. Persons of tarnished reputation, like cloth made of shoddy or refuse wool.

Shoe. (*See* CHOPINE.)

Shoe. It was at one time thought unlucky to put on the left shoe before the right, or to put either shoe on the wrong foot. It is said that Augustus Cæsar was nearly assassinated by a mutiny one day when he put on his left shoe first.

"Auguste, cet empereur qui gouverna avec tant de sagesse, et dont le règne fut si florissant, restoit immobile et consterné lorsqu'il lui arrivoit par mégarde de mettre le soulier droit au pied gauche, et le soulier gauche au pied droit."—*St. Foix.*

A shoe too large trips one up. A Latin proverb, "*Calceus major subvertit.*" An empire too large falls to pieces ; a business too large comes to grief ; an ambition too large fails altogether.

Loose thy shoe from off thy foot, for the place whereon thou standest is holy (Josh.

v. 15). Loosing the shoe is a mark of respect in the East, among Moslems and Hindus, to the present hour. The Mussulman leaves his slippers at the door of the mosque. The Mahometan moonshee comes barefooted into the presence of his superiors. The governor of a town, in making a visit of ceremony to a European visitor, leaves his slippers at the tent entrance, as a mark of respect. There are two reasons for this custom : (1) It is a mark of humility, the shoe being a sign of dignity, and the shoeless foot a mark of servitude. (2) Leather, being held to be an unclean thing, would contaminate the sacred floor and offend the insulted idol. (*See* SANDAL.)

Plucking off the shoe among the Jews, smoking a pipe together among the Indians, breaking a straw together among the Teutons, and shaking hands among the English, are all ceremonies to confirm a bargain, now done by "earnest money."

Put on the right shoe first. One of the auditions of Pythagoras was this: "When stretching forth your feet to have your sandals put on, first extend your right foot, but when about to step into a bath, let your left foot enter first." Iamblichus says the hidden meaning is that worthy actions should be done heartily, but base ones should be avoided. (*Protreptics*, symbol xii.).

Throwing the wedding-shoe. It has long been a custom in England, Scotland, and elsewhere, to throw an old shoe, or several shoes, at the bride and bridegroom when they quit the bride's home, after the wedding breakfast, or when they go to church to get married. Some think this represents an assault and refers to the ancient notion that the bridegroom carried off the bride with force and violence. Others look upon it as a relic of the ancient law of exchange, implying that the parents of the bride give up henceforth all right of dominion to their daughter. This was a Jewish custom. Thus, in Deut. xxv. 5-10 we read that the widow refused by the surviving brother, asserted her independence by "loosing his shoe ;" and in the story of Ruth we are told "that it was the custom" in exchange to deliver a shoe in token of renunciation. When Boaz, therefore, became possessed of his lot, the kinsman's kinsman indicated his assent by giving Boaz his shoe. When the Emperor Wladimir proposed marriage to the daughter of Reginald, she rejected him, saying, "I will not take off my shoe to the son of a slave,"

Luther being at a wedding, told the bridegroom that he had placed the husband's shoe on the head of the bed, "*afin qu'il prit ainsi la domination et le gouvernement.*" (*Michel: Life of Luther.*)

In *Anglo-Saxon marriages* the father delivered the bride's shoe to the bridegroom, who touched her with it on the head to show his authority.

In *Turkey* the bridegroom, after marriage, is chased by the guests, who either administer blows by way of adieux, or pelt him with slippers. (*Thirty Years in the Harem*, p. 330.)

Another man's shoes. "To stand in another man's shoes." To occupy the place or lay claim to the honours of another. Among the ancient Northmen, when a man adopted a son, the person adopted put on the shoes of the adopter. (*Brayley: Graphic Illustrator ; 1834.*)

In the tale of *Reynard the Fox* (fourteenth century), Master Reynard, having turned the tables on Sir Bruin the Bear, asked the queen to let him have the shoes of the disgraced minister ; so Bruin's shoes were torn off and put upon Reynard, the new favourite.

Another pair of shoes. Another matter.

"But how a world that notes his [the Prince of Wales's] daily doings—the everlasting round of weary fashion, the health-returnings, speeches, interviewings—can grudge him some relief, without compunction, them's quite another pair of shoes."—*Punch,* 17th June, 1891.

Dead men's shoes. Waiting or looking for dead men's shoes. Counting on some advantage to which you will succeed when the present possessor is dead.

⁂ "A man without sandals" was a proverbial expression among the Jews for a prodigal, from the custom of giving one's sandals in confirmation of a bargain. (*See* Deut. xxv. 9, Ruth iv. 7.)

Over shoes, over boots. In for a penny, in for a pound.

"Where true courage roots,
The proverb says, 'once over shoes, o'er boots.'"
Taylor's Workes, ii. 145 (1690).

To die in one's shoes. To die on the scaffold.

"And there's Mr. Fuse, and Lieutenant Tregooze,
And there is Sir Carnaby Jenks, of the Blues,
All come to see a man die in his shoes."
Barham.

To shake in one's shoes. To be in a state of nervous terror.

To step into another man's shoes. To take the office or position previously held by another.

"'That will do, sir,' he thundered, 'that will do. It is very evident now what would happen if you stepped into my shoes."—*Good Words,* 1887.

Waiting for my shoes. Hoping for my death. Amongst the ancient Jews the transfer of an inheritance was made by the new party pulling off the shoe of the possessor. (*See* Ruth iv. 7.)

Whose shoes I am not worthy to bear (Matt. iii. 11). This means, "I am not worthy to be his humblest slave." It was the business of a slave recently purchased to loose and carry his master's sandals. (*Jahn: Archæologica Biblica.*)

Shoe-loosed. A man without shoes ; an unnatural kinsman, a selfish prodigal (Hebrew). If a man refused to marry his brother's widow, the woman pulled off his shoe in the presence of the elders, spat in his face, and called him "shoe-loosed." (Deut. xxv. 9.)

Shoe Pinches. *No one knows where the shoe pinches like the wearer.* This was said by a Roman sage who was blamed for divorcing his wife, with whom he seemed to live happily.

"For, God it wot, he sat ful still and song,
When that his scho ful bitterly him wrong."
Chaucer: Canterbury Tales, 6,014.

Shoe a Goose (*To*). To engage in a silly and fruitless task.

Shoe the Anchor (*To*). To cover the flukes of an anchor with a broad triangular piece of plank, in order that the anchor may have a stronger hold in soft ground. The French have the same phrase : *ensoler l'ancre.*

Shoe the Cobbler (*To*). To give a quick peculiar movement with the front foot in sliding.

Shoe the Horse (*To*). (French, *Ferrer la mule.*) Means to cheat one's employer out of a small sum of money. The expression is derived from the ancient practice of grooms, who charged their masters for "shoeing," but pocketed the money themselves.

Shoe the Wild Colt (*To*). To exact a fine called "footing" from a newcomer, who is called the "colt." Colt is a common synonym for a greenhorn, or a youth not broken in. Thus Shakespeare says—"Ay, that's a colt indeed, for he doth nothing but talk of his horse." (*Merchant of Venice,* i. 2.)

Shoes. *Scarpa's shoes* for curing club feet, etc. Devised by Antonio Scarpa, an Italian anatomist.

Shoemakers. The patron saints of shoemakers are St. Crispin and his brother Crispian, who supported themselves by making shoes while they preached to the people of Gaul and Britain. In compliment to these saints the trade of shoemaking is called "the gentle craft."

Shoot the Moon (*To*). To remove house furniture by night to avoid distraint.

Shoot the Sun (*To*). To take a nautical observation.

"Unless a man understood how to handle his vessel, it would be very little use his being able to 'shoot the sun,' as sailors call it."—*Notes and Queries*, November 19th, 1892, p. 403.

Shooting-iron (*A*). A gun.

"Catch old Stripes [a tiger] coming near my bullock, if he thought a 'shooting-iron' anywhere about."—*Cornhill*, July, 1883 (*My Tiger Watch*).

Shooting Stars, called in ancient legends the "fiery tears of St. Lawrence," because one of the periodic swarms of these meteors is between the 9th and 14th of August, about the time of St. Lawrence's festival, which is on the 10th.

Shooting stars are said by the Arabs to be firebrands hurled by the angels against the inquisitive Jinns or Genii, who are for ever clambering up on the constellations to peep into heaven.

Shop. *To talk shop.* To talk about one's affairs or business, to illustrate by one's business, as when Ollipod the apothecary talks of a uniform with rhubarb-coloured facings.

Shop-lifting is secretly purloining goods from a shop. Dekker speaks of the lifting-law—*i.e.* the law against theft. (Gothic, *hlifan*, to steal; *hliftus*, a thief; Latin, *levo*, to disburden.)

Shore (*Jane*). Sir Thomas More says, "She was well-born, honestly brought up, and married somewhat too soon to a wealthy yeoman." The tragedy of *Jane Shore* is by Nicholas Rowe.

Shoreditch, according to tradition, is so called from Jane Shore, who, it is said, died there in a ditch. This tale comes from a ballad in Pepys' collection; but the truth is, it receives its name from Sir John de Soerdich, lord of the manor in the reign of Edward III.

" I could not get one bit of bread
    Whereby my hunger might be fed. . . .
So, weary of my life, at length .
    I yielded up my vital strength
Within a ditch . . . which since that day
    Is Shoreditch called, as writers say."

Duke of Shoreditch. The most successful of the London archers received this playful title.

"Good king, make not good Lord of Lincoln Duke of Shoreditch!"—*The Poore Man's Peticion to the Kinge.* (1603.)

Shorne (*Sir John*) or **Master John Shorne,** well known for his feat of conjuring the devil into a boot. He was one of the uncanonised saints, and was prayed to in cases of ague. It seems that he was a devout man, and rector of North Marston, in Buckinghamshire, at the close of the thirteenth century. He blessed a well, which became the resort of multitudes and brought in a yearly revenue of some £500.

"To Maister John Shorne, that blessed man borne,
    For the ague to him we apply.
Which juggleth with a bote ; I beschrewe his herte rote
    That will trust him, and it be I."
                    Fantassic of Idolatrie.

Short. *My name is Short.* I'm in a hurry and cannot wait.

",Well, but let us hear the wishes (said the old man) ; my name is short, and I cannot stay much longer."—*W. Yeats: Fairy Tales of the Irish Peasantry*, p. 240.

Short Stature (*Noted Men of*). Aetius, commander of the Roman army in the days of Valentinian ; Agesilāus (5 syl.) "*Statura fuit humili, et corpore exiguo, et claudius altero pede*" (*Nepos*); Alexander the Great, scarcely middle height ; Attila, "the scourge of God," broad-shouldered, thick-set, sinewy, and short ; Byron, Cervantes, Claverhouse, Condé the Great, Cowper, Cromwell, Sir Francis Drake, Admiral Kepple (called "Little Kepple "), Louis XIV., barely 5 feet 5 inches; Marshal Luxembourg, nicknamed "the Little"; Mehemet Ali, Angelo ; Napoleon I., le petit caporal, was, according to his school certificate, 5½ feet: Lord Nelson, St. Paul, Pepin le Bref, Philip of Macedon (scarcely middle height), Richard Savage, Shakespeare ; Socratēs was stumpy ; Theodore II., King of the Goths, stout, short of stature, very strong (so says *Cassiodorus*) ; Timon the Tartar, self-described as lame, decrepit, and of little weight ; Dr. Isaac Watts, etc.

Shot. *Hand out your shot* or *Down with your shot*—your reckoning or quota, your money. (Saxon, *sceat;* Dutch, *schot.*) (*See* SCOT AND LOT.)

" As the fund of our pleasure, let us each pay his shot."
                    Ben Jonson.

He shot wide of the mark. He was altogether in error. The allusion is to shooting at the mark or bull's-eye in archery, but will now apply to our modern rifle practice.

Shot in the Locker. *I haven't a shot in the locker*—a penny in my pocket or in my purse. If a sailor says there is not a shot in the locker, he means the ship is wholly without ammunition, powder and shot have all been expended.

Shot Window (*A*)—*i.e.* shot-out or projecting window, and not, as Ritson explains the word, a "window which opens and shuts." Similarly, a projecting part of a building is called an *out-shot*. The aperture to give light to a dark staircase is called a "shot window."

"My sie flew to the shot window. . . . 'St. Mary!
sweet lady, here come two well-mounted gallants.'"—*Sir W. Scott: The Monastery*, chaps. xiv. and xxviii.

Shotten Herring. A lean spiritless creature, a Jack-o'-Lent, like a herring that has shot or ejected its spawn. Herrings gutted and dried are so called also.

"Though they like shotten-herrings are to see,
Yet such tall souldiers of their teeth they be,
That two of them, like greedy cormorants,
Devour more then six honest Protestants."
Taylor's Workes iii. 5.

Shoulder. *Showing the cold shoulder*. Receiving without cordiality some one who was once on better terms with you. (*See* COLD.)

The government shall be upon his shoulders (Isaiah ix. 6). The allusion is to the key slung on the shoulder of Jewish stewards on public occasions, and as a key is emblematic of government and power, the metaphor is very striking.

Straight from the shoulder. With full force. A boxing term.

"He was letting them have it straight from the shoulder."—*T. Tyrell: Lady Delmar*, chap. v.

Shovel-board. A game in which three counters were shoved or slid over a smooth board; a game very popular in the sixteenth and seventeenth centuries; the table itself, and sometimes even the counters were so called. Slender speaks of "two Edward shovelboards." (*Shakespeare: Merry Wives of Windsor*, i. 1.)

Show. *Show him an egg, and instantly the whole air is full of feathers*. Said of a very sanguine man.

Shrew-mouse. A small insectivorous mammal, resembling a mouse in form. It was supposed to have the power of injuring cattle by running over them; and to provide a remedy our forefathers used to plug the creature into a hole made in an ash-tree, any branch of which would cure the mischief done by the mouse. (Anglo-Saxon, *screawa*, a shrew-mouse; mouse is expletive.)

Shrieking Sisterhood (*The*). Women who clamour about "women's rights."

"By Jove, I suppose my life wouldn't be worth a moment's purchase if I made public these sentiments of mine at a meeting of the Shrieking Sisterhood."—*The World*, 24th February, 1892, p. 25.

Shrimp. A child, a puny little fellow, in the same ratio to a man as a shrimp to a lobster. *Fry* is also used for children. (Anglo-Saxon, *scrine-an*, to shrink; Danish, *skrumpe*; Dutch, *krimpen*.)

"It cannot be this weak and writhled shrimp
Would strike such terror to his enemies."
Shakespeare: 1 Henry VI., ii. 3.

Shropshire. A contraction of Shrewsbury-shire, the Saxon *Scrobbesburh* (shrub-borough), corrupted by the Normans into *Sloppes-burie*, whence our *Salop*.

Shrovetide Cocks. Shrove Tuesday used to be the great "Derby Day" of cock-fighting in England.

"Or martyr beat, like Shrovetide cocks, with bats."
Peter Pindar: Subjects for Painters.

Shunamite's House (*The*). An inn kept for the entertainment of the preachers at Paul's Cross. These preachers were invited by the bishop, and were entertained by the Corporation of London from Thursday before the day of preaching, to the following Thursday morning. (*Maitland: London*, ii. 949.)

Shunt. A railway term. (Anglo-Saxon, *scun-ran*, to shun.)

Shut up. Hold your tongue. Shut up your mouth.

Shy. *To have a shy at anything*. To fling at it, to try and shoot it.

Shylock. The grasping Jew, who "would kill the thing he hates." (*Shakespeare: Merchant of Venice*.)

Shylock (*A*). A grasping money-lender. (*See above*.)

"Respectable people withdrew from the trade, and the money-lending business was entirely in the hands of the Shylocks. . . . Those who had to borrow coin were obliged to submit to the expensive subterfuges of the Shylocks, from whose net once caught, there was little chance of escape."—*A. Egmont-Hake: Free Trade in Capital*, chap. vii.

Si, the seventh note in music, was not introduced till the seventeenth century. The original scale introduced by Guido d'Arezzo consisted of only six notes. (*See* ARETINIAN SYLLABLES.)

Si Quis. A notice to all whom it may concern, given in the parish church before ordination, that a resident means to offer himself as a candidate for holy orders; and SI QUIS — *i.e. if anyone* knows any just cause or impediment thereto, he is to declare the same to the bishop.

Si'amese Twins. Yoke-fellows, inseparables; so called from two youths (Eng and Chang), born of Chinese parents at Bang Mecklong. Their bodies were united by a band of flesh, stretching from breast-bone to breast-bone. They married two sisters, and had offspring. (1825-1872.)

Siamese Twins. The Biddenden Maids, born 1100, had distinct bodies, but were joined by the hips and shoulders. They lived to be thirty-four years of age.

Sib'beridge (3 syl.). Banns of marriage. (Anglo-Saxon *sibbe*, alliance; whence the old English word *sibrede*, relationship, kindred.) (*See* GOSSIP.)

"For every man it schuldë drede
And Nameliche in his sibrede."
Gower : Confessio Amantis.

Sibyl. (*See* AMALTHÆA.)

Sibyls. Plato speaks of only *one* (the Erythræan); Martian Capella says there were *two*, the *Erythræan* and the *Phrygian;* the former being the famous "Cumæan Sibyl;" Solinus and Jackson, in his *Chronologic Antiquities*, maintains, on the authority of Ælian, that there were *four*—the *Erythræan*, the *Samian*, the *Egyptian*, and the *Sardian;* Varro tells us there were *ten*, viz. the Cumæan (who sold the books to Tarquin), the Delphic, Egyptian, Erythræan, Hellespontine, Libyan, Persian, Phrygian, Samian, and Tiburtine.

⁂ The name of the Cumæan sibyl was Amalthæa.

"How know we but that she may be an eleventh Sibyl or a second Cassandra?"—*Rabelais : Gargantua and Pantagruel,* iii. 16.

Sibyls. The mediæval monks reckoned twelve Sibyls, and gave to each a separate prophecy and distinct emblem :—

(1) The *Lib'yan* Sibyl : "The day shall come when men shall see the King of all living things." *Emblem*, a lighted taper.

(2) The *Sa'mian* Sibyl : "The Rich One shall be born of a pure virgin." *Emblem*, a rose.

(3) The *Cuman* Sibyl : "Jesus Christ shall come from heaven, and live and reign in poverty on earth." *Emblem*, a crown.

(4) The *Cumæan* Sibyl : "God shall be born of a pure virgin, and hold converse with sinners." *Emblem*, a cradle.

(5) The *Erythræan* Sibyl : "Jesus Christ, Son of God, the Saviour." *Emblem*, a horn.

(6) The *Persian* Sibyl : "Satan shall

be overcome by a true prophet." *Emblem*, a dragon under the Sibyl's feet, and a lantern.

(7) The *Tiburtine* Sibyl : "The Highest shall descend from heaven, and a virgin be shown in the valleys of the deserts." *Emblem*, a dove.

(8) The *Delphic* Sibyl : "The Prophet born of the virgin shall be crowned with thorns." *Emblem*, a crown of thorns.

(9) The *Phrygian* Sibyl : "Our Lord shall rise again." *Emblem*, a banner and a cross.

(10) The *European* Sibyl : "A virgin and her Son shall flee into Egypt." *Emblem*, a sword.

(11) The *Agrippi'ne* Sibyl : "Jesus Christ shall be outraged and scourged." *Emblem*, a whip.

(12) The *Hellespontic* Sibyl : "Jesus Christ shall suffer shame upon the cross." *Emblem*, a T cross.

This list of prophecies is of the sixteenth century, and is manifestly a clumsy forgery or mere monkish legend. (*See below*, SIBYLLINE VERSES.)

The most famous of the ten sibyls was Amalthæa, of Cumæ in Æo'lia, who offered her nine books to Tarquin the Proud. The offer being rejected, she burnt three of them; and after the lapse of twelve months, offered the remaining six at the same price. Again being refused, she burnt three more, and after a similar interval asked the same price for the remaining three. The sum demanded was now given, and Amalthæa never appeared again. (*Livy.*)

Sibyl. The Cumæan sibyl was the conductor of Virgil to the infernal regions. (*Æneid*, vi.)

Sibyl. A fortune-teller.

"How they will fare it needs a sibyl to say." —*The Times.*

Sibylline Books. The three surviving books of the Sibyl Amalthæa were preserved in a stone chest underground in the temple of Jupiter Capitoli'nus, and committed to the charge of custodians chosen in the same manner as the high priests. The number of custodians was at first two, then ten, and ultimately fifteen. The books were destroyed by fire when the Capitol was burnt (A.D. 670).

Sibylline Books. A collection of poetical utterances in Greek, compiled in the second century (138-167). The collection is in eight books, relates to Jesus Christ, and is entitled *Ora'cula Sibyli'na.*

Sibylline Leaves. The Sibylline prophecies were written in Greek, upon palm-leaves. (*Varro.*)

Sibylline Verses. When the Sibylline books were destroyed (*see above*), all the floating verses of the several Sibyls were carefully collected and deposited in the new temple of Jupiter. Augustus had some 2,000 of these verses destroyed as spurious, and placed the rest in two gilt cases, under the base of the statue of Apollo, in the temple on the Palatine Hill; but the whole perished when the city was burnt in the reign of Nero. (See *Sibyls* [of the mediæval monks].)

Siccis pedibus [*with dry feet*]. Metaphorically, without notice.

"It may be worth noticing that both Mrs. Shelley and Mr. Rossetti pass over the line *siccis pedibus*."—*Notes and Queries* (26th May, 1893, p. 417).

Sice (1 syl.). A sizing, an allowance of bread and butter. "He'll print for a sice." In the University of Cambridge the men call the pound loaf, two inches of butter, and pot of milk allowed for breakfast, their "sizings;" and when one student breakfasts with another in the same college, the bed-maker carries his sizings to the rooms of the entertainer. (*See* SIZINGS.)

Sicil'ian Dishes (*Sicŭlæ dapēs*) were choice foods. The best Roman cooks were Sicilians. Horace (3 *Odes*, i. 18) tells us that when a sword hangs over our head, as in the case of Damoclês, not even "*Siculæ dapēs dulcem elaborabunt saporem.*"

Sicil'ian Vespers. The massacre of the French in Sicily, which began at the hour of vespers on Easter Monday in 1282.

Sick Man (*The*). So Nicholas of Russia (in 1844) called the Ottoman Empire, which had been declining ever since 1586.

"I repeat to you that the sick man is dying; and we must never allow such an event to take us by surprise."—*Annual Register*, 1853.

N.B. Don John, Governor-General of the Netherlands, writing in 1579 to Philip II. of Spain, calls the Prince of Orange "the sick man," because he was in the way, and he wanted him "finished."

"'Money' (he says in his letter) 'is the gruel with which we must cure this sick man [for spies and assassins are expensive drugs]'."—*Motley: Dutch Republic*, bk. v. 2.

Sick as a Cat. (*See* SIMILES.)

Sick as a Dog. (*See* SIMILES.)

Sick as a Horse. Nausea unrelieved by vomiting. A horse is unable to vomit, because its diaphragm is not a complete partition in the abdomen,

perforated only by the gullet, and against which the stomach can be compressed by the abdominal muscles, as is the case in man. Hence the nausea of a horse is more lasting and more violent. (See *Notes and Queries*, C. S. xii., August 15th, 1885, p. 134.)

Siddons (*Mrs.*). Sidney Smith says it was never without awe that he saw this tragedy queen *stab the potatoes;* and Sir Walter Scott tells us, while she was dining at Ashestiel, he heard her declaim to the footman, "You've brought me water, boy! I asked for beer."

Side of the Angels. *Punch*, Dec. 10, 1864, contains a cartoon of Disraeli, dressing for an Oxford *bal masqué*, as an angel, and underneath the cartoon are these words—

"The question is, is man an ape or an angel? I am on the side of the angels."—*Disraeli's Oxford Speech, Friday, Nov. 25* (1864).

Sidney (*Algernon*), called by Thomson, in his *Summer*, "The British Cassius," because of his republican principles. Both disliked kings, not from their misrule, but from a dislike to monarchy. Cassius was one of the conspirators against the life of Cæsar, and Sidney was one of the judges that condemned Charles I. to the block (1617-1683).

Sidney (*Sir Philip*). The academy figure of Prince Arthur, in Spenser's *Faërie Queene*, and the poet's type of magnanimity.

Sir Philip Sidney, called by Sir Walter Raleigh "the English Petrarch," was the author of *Arcadia*. Queen Elizabeth called him "the jewel of her dominions;" and Thomson, in his *Summer*, "the plume of war." The poet refers to the battle of Zutphen, where Sir Philip received his death-wound. Being thirsty, a soldier brought him some water; but as he was about to drink he observed a wounded man eye the bottle with longing looks. Sir Philip gave the water to the wounded man, saying, "Poor fellow, thy necessity is greater than mine." Spenser laments him in the poem called *Astrophel* (*q.v.*).

Sidney's sister, Pembroke's mother. Mary Herbert (*née* Sidney), Countess of Pembroke, poetess, etc. (Died 1621.) The line is by William Browne (1645).

Sidney-Sussex College, Cambridge, founded by Lady Frances Sidney, Countess of Sussex, in 1598.

Sieg'fried (2 syl.). Hero of the first part of the *Nibelungen-Lied*. He was the youngest son of Siegmund and Sieglind, king and queen of the Netherlands, and was born in Rhinecastle called Xanton. He married Kriemhild, Princess of Burgundy, and sister of Günther. Günther craved his assistance in carrying off Brunhild from Issland, and Siegfried succeeded by taking away her talisman by main force. This excited the jealousy of Günther, who induced Hagan, the Dane, to murder Sieg'fried. Hagan struck him with a sword in the only vulnerable part (between the shoulder-blades), while he stooped to quench his thirst at a fountain. (*Nibelungen-Lied.*)

Horny Siegfried. So called because when he slew the dragon he bathed in its blood, and became covered all over with a horny hide which was invulnerable, except in one spot between the shoulders, where a linden-leaf stuck. (*Nibelungen-Lied*, st. 100.)

Siegfried's cloak of invisibility, called "tarnkappe" (*tarnen*, to conceal; *kappe*, a cloak). It not only made the wearer invisible, but also gave him the strength of twelve men. (Tarnkappe, 2 syl.)

> " The mighty dwarf successless strove with the
>   mightier man ;
> Like to wild mountain lions to the hollow hill
>   ·   they ran ;
> He ravished there the tarnkappe from strug-
>   gling Albric's hold,
> And then became the master of the hoarded
>   gems and gold."
>   *Lettsom: Fall of the Nibelungers*, Lied iii.

Sieg'lind (2 syl.). Mother of Siegfried, and Queen of the Netherlanders. (*The Nibelungen-Lied.*)

Sien'na (3 syl.). The paint so called is made of terra di Siena, in Italy.

Sier'ra (3 syl., Spanish, *a saw*). A mountain whose top is indented like a saw ; a range of mountains whose tops form a saw-like appearance ; a line of craggy rocks ; as Sierra More'na (where many of the incidents in *Don Quixote* are laid), Sierra Neva'da (the snowy range), Sierra Leo'ne (in West Africa, where lions abound), etc.

Sies'ta (3 syl.) means "the sixth hour"—*i.e.* noon. (Latin, *sexta hora*). It is applied to the short sleep taken in Spain during the mid-day heat. (Spanish, *sesta*, sixth hour ; *sestéar*, to take a mid-day nap.)

Sieve and Shears. The device of discovering a guilty person by sieve and shears is to stick a pair of shears in a sieve, and give the sieve into the hands

of two virgins, then say : "By St. Peter and St. Paul, if you [or you] have stolen the article, turn shears to the thief." Sometimes a Bible and key are employed instead, in which case the key is placed in a Bible.

Sif. Wife of Thor, famous for the beauty of her hair. Loki having cut it off while she was asleep, she obtained from the dwarfs a new fell of golden hair equal to that which he had taken.

Sight for "multitude" is not an Americanism, but good Old English. Thus, in *Morte d'Arthur*, the word is not unfrequently so employed ; and the high-born dame, Juliana Berners, lady prioress in the fifteenth century of Sopwell nunnery, speaks of a *bomynable syght of monkes* (a large number of friars).

" Where is so huge a syght of mony."—*Palsgrave: Acolastus* (1540).

Sight (*Far*). Zarga, the Arabian heroine of the tribe Jadis, could see at the distance of three days' journey. Being asked by Hassân the secret of her long sight, she said it was due to the ore of antimony, which she reduced to powder, and applied to her eyes as a collyrium every night.

Sign your Name. It is not correct to say that the expression "signing one's name" points to the time when persons could not write. No doubt persons who could not write made their mark in olden times as they do now, but we find over and over again in ancient documents these words : "This [grant] is signed with the sign of the cross for its greater assurance (or) greater inviolability," and after the sign follows the name of the donor. (See *Rymer's Fœdera*, vol. i. pt. i.)

Signs instead of words. A symbolic language made by gestures. Members of religious orders bound to silence, communicate with each other in this way. John, a monk, gives, in his *Life of St. Odo*, a number of signs for bread, tart, beans, eggs, fish, cheese, honey, milk, cherries, onions, etc. (See *Sussex Archæological Collection*, vol. iii. p. 190.)

Significa'vit. A writ of Chancery given by the ordinary to keep an excommunicate in prison till he submitted to the authority of the Church. The writ, which is now obsolete, used to begin with "*Significavit nobis venerabilis pater*," etc. Chaucer says of his Sompnour—

" And also ware him of a ' significavit.'"
Canterbury Tales (*Prologue*), 664.

Sigun'a. Wife of Loki. She nurses him in his cavern, but sometimes, as she carries off the poison which the serpents gorge, a portion drops on the god, and his writhings cause earthquakes. (*Scandinavian mythology.*)

Si'gurd. The Norse Siegfried (*q.v.*). He falls in love with Brynhild, but, under the influence of a love-potion, marries Gudrun, a union which brings about a volume of mischief.

Si'gurd the Horny. A German romance based on a legend in the Sagas. An analysis of this legend is published by Weber in his *Illustrations of Northern Antiquities.* (*See* SIEGFRIED, *Horny.*)

Sikes (*Bill*). A ruffian housebreaker of the lowest grade in *Oliver Twist*, by Charles Dickens.

Sikh. (Hindu *sikh*, disciple.) The Sikhs were originally a religious body like the Mahometans, but in 1764 they formally assumed national independence. Since 1849 the Sikhs have been ruled by the English.

Silbury, near Marlborough. An artificial mound, 130 feet high, and covering seven acres of ground. Some say it is where "King Sel" was buried; others, that it is a corruption of *Solis-bury* (mound of the sun); others, that it is Sel-barrow (great tumulus), in honour of some ancient prince of Britain. The Rev. A. C. Smith is of opinion that it was erected by the Celts about B.C. 1600. There is a natural hill in the same vicinity, called St. Martin's Sell or Sill, in which case sill or sell means seat or throne. These etymologies of Silbury must rest on the authority of those who have suggested them.

Sil'chester (Berks) is Silicis castrum (flint camp), a Saxon-Latin form of the Roman Calleva or Galleva. Galleva is the Roman form of the British *Gwal Vawr* (great wall), so called from its wall, the ruins of which are still striking. Leland says, "On that wall grow some oaks of ten cart-load the piece." According to tradition King Arthur was crowned here; and Ninnius asserts that the city was built by Constantius, father of Constantine the Great.

Silence gives Consent, Latin, "*Qui tacet consenti're vide'tur;*" Greek, "*Auto de to sigan homologountos esti sou*" (Euripidês); French, "*Assez consent qui ne dit mot;*" Italian, "*Chi tace confessa.*"

[a] But that you shall not say I yield, being silent,
  I would not speak."
    Shakespeare: Cymbeline, ii. 3.

Silent (*The*). William I., Prince of Orange (1533-1584).

Sile'nus. The foster-father of Bacchus, fond of music, and a prophet, but indomitably lazy, wanton, and given to debauch. He is described as a jovial old man, with bald head, pug nose, and face like Bardolph's.

Sil'houet'te (3 syl.). A black profile, so called from Etienne de Silhouctte, Contrôleur des Finances, 1757, who made great savings in the public expenditure of France. Some say the black portraits were called Silhouettes in ridicule; others assert that Silhouette devised this way of taking likenesses to save expense.

Silk. *Received silk,* applied to a barrister, means that he has obtained licence to wear a silk gown in the law courts, having obtained the degree or title of sergeant.

Silk Gown. A queen's counsel. So called because his canonical robe is a black silk gown. That of an ordinary barrister is made of stuff or prunello.

Silk Purse. *You cannot make a silk purse of a sow's ear.* "You cannot make a horn of a pig's tail." A sow's ear may somewhat resemble a purse, and a curled pig's tail may somewhat resemble a twisted horn, but a sow's ear cannot be made into a silk purse, nor a pig's tail into a cow's horn.

"You cannot make, my lord, I fear,
A velvet purse of a sow's ear."
   Peter Pindar: Lord B. and His Motions.

Silken Thread. In the kingdom of Lilliput, the three great prizes of honour are "fine silk threads six inches long, one blue, another red, and a third green." The emperor holds a stick in his hands, and the candidates "jump over it or creep under it, backwards or forwards, as the stick indicates," and he who does so with the greatest agility is rewarded with the blue ribbon, the second best with the red cordon, and the third with the green. The thread is girt about their loins, and no ribbon of the Legion of Honour, or Knight of the Garter, is won more worthily or worn more proudly. (*Gulliver's Travels.*)

Silly is the German *selig* (blessed), whence the infant Jesus is termed "the harmless silly babe," and sheep are called "silly," meaning harmless or innocent. As the "holy" are easily taken in by worldly cunning, the word came to signify "gullible," "foolish." (*See* SIMPLICITY.)

Silly Season (*The*), for daily news-papers, is when Parliament is not in session, and all sorts of "silly" stuff are vamped-up for padding. Also called the "Big Gooseberry Season," because para-graphs are often inserted on this subject.

Silu'ria—that is, Hereford, Mon-mouth, Radnor, Brecon, and Glamorgan. The "sparkling wines of the Silurian vats" are cider and perry.

" From Silurian vats, high-sparkling wines
Foam in transparent floods."
Thomson : Autumn.

Silu'rian Rocks. A name given by Sir R. Murchison to what miners call *gray-wacke*, and Werner termed *transi-tion rocks*. Sir Roderick called them Silurian because it was in the region of the ancient Silurēs that he investigated them.

Silva'na. A maga or fata in Tasso's *Amadi'gi*, where she is made the guar-dian spirit of Alido'ro.

Silvanella. A beautiful maga or fata in Bojardo, who raised a tomb over Narcissus, and then dissolved into a fountain. (Lib. ii. xvii. 56, etc.)

Silver was, by the ancient alchemists, called Diana or the Moon.

Silver. The Frenchman employs the word *silver* to designate money, the wealthy Englishman uses the word *gold*, and the poorer old Roman *brass* (æs).

Silver and gold articles are marked with five marks : the maker's private mark, the standard or assay mark, the hall mark, the duty mark, and the date mark. The standard mark states the proportion of silver, to which figure is added a lion passant for England, a harp crowned for Ireland, a thistle for Edin-burgh, and a lion rampant for Glasgow. (For the other marks, *see* MARK.)

Silver Cooper (*The*). A kidnapper. "To play the silver cooper," to kidnap. A cooper is one who *coops up* another.

"You rob and you murder, and you want me to . . . play the silver cooper."—*Sir W. Scott: Guy Mannering*, chap. xxxiv.

Silver Fork School. Those novelists who are sticklers for etiquette and the graces of society, such as Theodore Hook, Lady Blessington, Mrs. Trollope, and Sir Edward Bulwer Lytton (Lord Lytton).

Silver-hand. Nuad, the chieftain who led back the tribe of the Danaans from Scotland to Ireland, whence they had migrated. Nuad of the Silver-hand had an artificial hand of silver made by Cred, the goldsmith, to supply the loss

sustained from a wound in the battle of Moytura. Miach, son of Dian Kect, set it on the wrist. (*O'Flaherty : Ogygia*, part iii. chap. x.) (*See* IRON HAND.)

Silver Lining. The prospect of better days, the promise of happier times. The allusion is to Milton's *Comus*, where the lady lost in the wood resolves to hope on, and sees a "sable cloud turn forth its silver lining to the night."

Silver Pheasant (*A*). A beautiful young lady of the high aristocracy.

" One would think you were a silver pheasant, you give yourself such airs."—*Ouida : Under Two Flags.*

Silver Spoon. *Born with a silver spoon in one's mouth.* Born to luck and wealth. The allusion is to silver spoons given as prizes and at christenings. The lucky man is born with it in his mouth, and needs not stop to earn it.

" One can see, young fellow, that you were born with a silver spoon in your mouth."—*Longman's Magazine,* 1886.

Silver Star of Love (*The*). When Gama was tempest-tossed through the machinations of Bacchus, the "Silver Star of Love" appeared to him, calmed the sea, and restored the elements to harmony again.

" The sky and ocean blending, each on fire,
Seemed as all Nature struggled to expire ;
When now the Silver Star of Love appeared,
Bright in the East her radiant front she reared."
Camoëns : Lusiad, bk. vi.

Silver Streak (*The*). The British Channel.

" Steam power has much lessened the value of the silver streak as a defensive agent."—*News-paper paragraph*, November, 1885.

Silver-Tongued. William Bates, the Puritan divine. (1625-1699.)

Anthony Hammond, the poet, called *Silver-tongue*. (1668-1738.)

Henry Smith, preacher. (1550-1600.)

Joshua Sylvester, translator of Du Bartas. (1563-1618.)

Silver Trumpet (*A*). A smooth-tongued orator. A rough, unpolished speaker is called a ram's horn.

Silver Weapon. *With silver wea-pons you may conquer the world*, is what the Delphic oracle said to Philip of Macedon, when he went to consult it. Philip, acting on this advice, sat down before a fortress which his staff pro-nounced to be impregnable. "You shall see," said the king, "how an ass laden with gold will find an entrance."

Silver Wedding. The twenty-fifth anniversary, when, in Germany, the woman has a silver wreath presented her.

On the fiftieth anniversary, or GOLDEN WEDDING, the wreath is of gold.

Silver of Guthrum, or *Guthram's Lane.* Fine silver; so called because in the thirteenth and fourteenth centuries the principal gold- and silver-smiths resided there.

Silverside of Beef (*The*). The upper side of a round, which not only shows the shining tissue uppermost, but, when carved cold has a silvery appearance. Generally boiled.

Sim'eon (*St.*) is usually depicted as bearing in his arms the infant Jesus, or receiving Him in the Temple.

Similes in common use:—

BALD as a coot.
BITTER as gall, as soot.
BLACK as ink, as a coal, as a crow.
BLIND as a bat, a beetle, a mole.
BLUNT as a hedge-hook.
BRAVE as Alexander.
BRIGHT as silver.
BRITTLE as glass.
BROWN as a berry.
BUSY as a bee.
CHATTER like a jay.
CLEAR as crystal.
COLD as ice, as a frog, as charity.
COOL as a cucumber.
CROSS as the tongs, as two sticks.
DARK as pitch [pitch-dark].
DEAD as a door-nail.
DEAF as a post.
DRY as a bone.
FAIR as a lily.
FALSE as hell.
FAT as a pig, as a porpoise.
FLAT as a flounder, as a pancake.
FLEET as the wind, as a racehorse.
FREE as air.
GAY as a lark.
GOOD as gold.
GREEN as grass.
HARD as iron, as a flint.
HARMLESS as a dove.
HEAVY as lead.
HOARSE as a hog, as a raven.
HELPLESS as a babe.
HOLLOW as a drum.
HOT as fire, as an oven, as a coal.
HUNGRY as a hunter.
LIGHT as a feather, as day.
LIMP as a glove.
LOUD as thunder.
MERRY as a grig, as a cricket.
MILD as Moses, as milk.
NEAT as wax, as a new pin.
OBSTINATE as a pig (pig-headed.)
OLD as the hills, as Methuselah.
PALE as a ghost.
PATIENT as Job.
PLAIN as a pikestaff.
PLAYFUL as a kitten.
PLUMP as a partridge.
POOR as a rat, as a church mouse, as Job.
PROUD as Lucifer.
RED as blood, as a fox, a rose, a brick.
ROUGH as a nutmeg-grater.
ROUND as an orange, a ball.
RUDE as a bear.
SAFE as the bank [of England], or the stocks.
SAVAGE as a bear, as a tiger, as a bear with a sore head.
SICK as a cat, a dog, a horse, a toad.
SHARP as a needle.
SLEEP like a top.
SLOW as a snail, as a tortoise.
SLY as a fox, as old boots.
SOFT as silk, as velvet, as soap.
SOUND as a roach, as a bell.
SOUR as vinegar, as verjuice.

STARE like a stuck pig.
STEADY as Old Time.
STIFF as a poker.
STRAIGHT as an arrow.
STRONG as iron, as a horse, as brandy.
SURE as a gun, as fate, as death and taxes.
SURLY as a bear.
SWEET as sugar.
SWIFT as lightning, as the wind, as an arrow.
THICK as hops.
THIN as a lath, as a whipping-post.
TIGHT as a drum.
TOUGH as leather.
TRUE as the Gospel.
VAIN as a peacock.
WARM as a toast.
WEAK as water.
WET as a fish.
WHITE as driven snow, as milk, as a swan, as a sheet, as chalk.
WISE as a serpent, as Solomon.
YELLOW as a guinea, as gold, as saffron.

Similia Similibus Curantur. Like cures like. (*See under* HAIR : *Take a hair of the dog that bit you.*)

Simmes' Hole. The cavity which Captain John C. Simmes maintained existed at the North and South Poles.

Simnel Cakes. Rich cakes eaten in Lancashire in Mid-Lent. Simnel is the German *semmel*, a manchet or roll; Danish and Norwegian *simle ;* Swedish, *simla.* In Somersetshire a teacake is called a *simlin.* A simnel cake is a *cake* manchet, or rich semmel. The eating of these cakes in Mid-Lent is in commemoration of the banquet given by Joseph to his brethren, which forms the first lesson of Mid-Lent Sunday, and the feeding of five thousand, which forms the gospel of the day. (*See* MID-LENT.)

Simon (*St.*) is represented with a saw in his hand, in allusion to the instrument of his martyrdom. He sometimes bears fish in the other hand, in allusion to his occupation as a fishmonger.

Simon Magus. Isidore tells us that Simon Magus died in the reign of Nero, and adds that he (Simon) had proposed a dispute with Peter and Paul, and had promised to fly up to heaven. He succeeded in rising high into the air, but at the prayers of the two apostles he was cast down to earth by the evil spirits who had enabled him to rise into the air.

Milman, in his *History of Christianity*, vol. ii. p. 51, tells another story. He says that Simon offered to be buried alive, and declared that he would reappear on the third day. He was actually buried in a deep trench, "but to this day," says Hippolytus, "his disciples have failed to witness his resurrection."

Simon Pure. The real man. In Mrs. Centlivre's *Bold Stroke for a Wife*, a Colonel Feignwell passes himself off for Simon Pure, and wins the heart of Miss

Lovely. No sooner does he get the assent of her guardian, than the veritable Quaker shows himself, and proves, beyond a doubt, he is the real Simon Pure.

Simony. Buying and selling church livings; any unlawful traffic in holy things. So called from Simon Magus, who wanted to purchase the "gift of the Holy Ghost," that he might have the power of working miracles. (Acts viii. 9-23.)

Simony. The friar in the tale of *Reynard the Fox;* so called from Simon Magus.

Simple (*The*). Charles III. of France. (879, 893-929.)

Simples cut. (*See* BATTERSEA.)

Simple Simon. A simpleton. The character is introduced in the wellknown nursery tale, the author of which is unknown.

Simplicity is *sine plica*, without a fold; as duplicity is *duplex plica*, a double fold. *Conduct* "without a fold" is *straightforward*, but *thought* without a fold is mere childishness. It is "tortuity of thought" that constitutes philosophic wisdom, and "simplicity of thought" that prepares the mind for faith.

"The flat simplicity of that reply was admirable."—*Vanbrugh and Cibber : The Provoked Husband*, i.

Simplon Road. Commenced in 1800 by Napoleon, and finished in 1806. It leads over a shoulder of what is called *the Pass of the Simplon* (Switzerland).

Sin, according to Milton, is twinkeeper with Death of the gates of Hell. She sprang full-grown from the head of Satan.

"... Woman to the waist, and fair,
But ending foul in many a scaly fold
Voluminous and vast, a serpent armed
With mortal sting." *Paradise Lost*, ii. 650-653.

Original sin. (*See* ADAM.)

Sin-eaters. Persons hired at funerals in ancient times, to take upon themselves the sins of the deceased, that the soul might be delivered from purgatory.

"Notice was given to an old sire before the door of the house, when some of the family came out and furnished him with a cricket [low stool], on which he sat down facing the door ; then they gave him a groat which he put in his pocket, a crust of bread which he ate, and a bowl of ale which he drank off at a draught. After this he got up from the cricket and pronounced *the ease and rest of the soul departed, for which he would pawn his own soul.*"—*Bagford's letter on Leland's Collectanea*, i. 76.

Since're (2 syl.) properly means without wax (*sine cera*). The allusion is to the Roman practice of concealing flaws in pottery with wax, or to honey from which all the wax has been extracted. (See *Trench : On the Study of Words*, lect. vii. p. 322.)

Sin'dhu'. The ancient name of the river Indus. (Sanskrit, *syand*, to flow.)

Sin'don. A thin manufacture of the Middle Ages used for dresses and hangings ; also a little round piece of linen or lint for dressing the wound left by trepanning. (Du Cange gives its etymology *Cyssus tenuis ;* but the Greek *sindon* means "fine Indian cloth." India is *Sind*, and China *Sina*.)

Sine Die (Latin). No time being fixed ; indefinitely in regard to time. When a proposal is deferred *sine die*, it is deferred without fixing a day for its reconsideration, which is virtually "for ever."

Sine quā Non. An indispensable condition. Latin, *Sine qua non potest es'se* or *fieri* (that without which [the thing] cannot be, *or* be done).

Si'necure [*si'-ne-kure*]. An enjoyment of the money attached to a benefice without having the trouble of the "cure" ; also applied to any office to which a salary is attached without any duties to perform. (Latin, *sine cura*, without cure, or care.)

Sinews of War. Money, which buys the sinews, and makes them act vigorously. Men will not fight without wages, and the materials of war must be paid for.

Sing a Song o' Sixpence. (*See* MACARONIC VERSE.)

Sing my Music, and not Yours, said Guglielmi to those who introduced their own ornaments into his operas, so eminently distinguished for their simplicity and purity. (1727-1804.)

Sing Old Rose. *Sing Old Rose and burn the bellows.* "Old Rose" was the title of a song now unknown ; thus, Izaak Walton (1590-1683) says, "Let's sing *Old Rose.*" *Burn the bellows* is said to be a schoolboy's perversion of *burn libellos.* At breaking-up time the boys might say, "Let's sing *Old Rose* [a popular song], and burn our schoolbooks" (*libellos*). This does not accord with the words of the wellknown catch, which evidently means "throw aside all implements of work."

"Now we're met like jovial fellows,
Let us do as wise men tell us,
Sing *Old Rose* and burn the bellows."

Sing Out. To cry or squall from chastisement.

To sing small. To cease boasting and assume a lower tone.

Sing-su-hay. A lake of Thibet, famous for its gold sands.

" Bright are the waters of Sing-su-hay
And the golden floods that thitherward stray."
          Thomas Moore: Paradise and the Peri.

Singapores (3 syl.), in Stock-Exchange phraseology, means, " British Indian Extension Telegraph Stock." (*See* STOCK-EXCHANGE SLANG.)

Singing Apple was a ruby apple on a stem of amber. It had the power of persuading anyone to anything merely by its odour, and enabled the possessor to write verses, make people laugh or cry, and itself sang so as to ravish the ear. The apple was in the desert of Libya, and was guarded by a dragon with three heads and twelve feet. Prince Chery put on an armour of glass, and the dragon, when it saw its thousand reflections in the armour and thought a thousand dragons were about to attack it, became so alarmed that it ran into its cave, and the prince closed up the mouth of the cave. (*Countess d'Aunoy: Cherry and Fairstar.*) (*See* SINGING-TREE.)

Singing-Bread, consecrated by the priest *singing.* (French, *pain à chanter.*) The reformers directed that the sacramental bread should be similar in fineness and fashion to the round bread-and-water singing-cakes used in private Masses.

Singing Chambermaids, in theatrical parlance, mean those smart young light comedy actresses who perform chambermaids and are good singers.

Singing Tree. A tree whose leaves were so musical that every leaf sang in concert. (*Arabian Nights: Story of the Sisters who Envied their Younger Sister.*) (*See* SINGING APPLE.)

Singing in Tribulation. Confessing when put to the torture. Such a person is termed in gaol slang a " canary bird."

" ' This man, sir, is condemned to the galleys for being a canary-bird.' ' A canary-bird !' exclaimed the knight. ' Yes, sir,' added the arch-thief; ' I mean that he is very famous for his singing.' ' What !' said Don Quixote : ' are people to be sent to the galleys for singing ?' ' Marry, that they are,' answered the slave ; ' for there is nothing more dangerous than singing in tribulation.' "—*Cervantes: Don Quixote,* iii. 8.

Single-Speech Hamilton. The Right Hon. W. G. Hamilton, Chancellor of the Exchequer in Ireland, spoke one speech, but that was a masterly torrent of eloquence which astounded everyone. (November 13th, 1755.)

" No one likes a reputation analogous to that of 'single-speech Hamilton.' "—*The Times.*
" Or is it he, the wordy youth,
    So early trained for statesman's part,
Who talks of honour, faith, and truth,
    As themes that he has got by heart,
Whose ethics Chesterfield can teach,
    Whose logic is from Single-speech ?"
    Sir Walter Scott: Bridal of Triermain, ii. 4.

Sin'ister (Latin, *on the left hand*). According to augury, birds, etc., appearing on the left-hand side forbode ill-luck ; but, on the right-hand side, good luck. Thus, *corva sinistra* (a crow on the left-hand) is a sign of ill-luck which belongs to English superstitions as much as to the ancient Roman or Etruscan. (*Virgil: Eclogues,* i. 18.)

" That raven on yon left-hand oak
    (Curse on his ill-betiding croak)
Bodes me no good." *Gay: Fable* xxxvii.

Sinister. (*See* BAR SINISTER.)

Sinning One's Mercies. Being ungrateful for the gifts of Providence.

" I know your good father would term this 'sinning my mercies.' "—*Sir W. Scott: Redgauntlet.*

Si'non. A Greek who induced the Trojans to receive the wooden horse. (*Virgil: Æneid,* ii. 102, etc.) Anyone deceiving to betray is called " a Sinon."

" And now securely trusting to destroy,
As erst false Sinon snared the sons of Troy."
          Camoëns: Lusiad, bk. i.

Sintram. The Greek hero of the German romance, *Sintram and his Companions,* by Baron Lamotte Fouqué.

Sintram's famous sword was called " Welsung." The same name was given to Dietlieb's sword. (*See* SWORD.)

Sir. Latin, *senex;* Spanish, *señor;* Italian, *signor;* French, *sieur;* Norman, *sire;* English, *sir.* According to some, Greek ἀναξ is connected with *Sir;* on the analogy of ἐμ-μι (εἰμι) = Latin *sum;* ἄμπερες = Latin *semper;* ὑπος = Latin *sapa.*

Sir (a clerical address). Clergymen had at one time *Sir* prefixed to their name. This is not the *Sir* of knighthood, but merely a translation of the university word *dominus* given to graduates, as " *Dominus* Hugh Evans," etc.

Sir Oracle. (*See* ORACLE.)

Sir Roger de Coverley. An imaginary character by Addison ; type of a benevolent country gentleman of the eighteenth century. Probably the model was William Boevey, lord of the manor of Flaxley.

Si'ren. A woman of dangerous blandishments. The allusion is to the fabulous sirens said by Greek and Latin poets to entice seamen by the sweetness of their song to such a degree that the listeners forgot everything and died of hunger (Greek, *sire'nes*, entanglers). In Homeric mythology there were but two sirens; later writers name three, viz. Parthen'ope, Lig'ea, and Leucos'ia; but the number was still further augmented by those who loved "lords many and gods many."

"There were several sirens up and down the coast; one at Panormus, another at Naples, others at Surrentum, but the greatest number lived in the delightful Capreæ, whence they passed over to the rocks [Sirenu'sæ] which bear their name."—*Inquiry into the Life of Homer.*

Sirens. Plato says there are three kinds of sirens—the *celestial*, the *generative*, and the *cathartic*. The first are under the government of Jupiter, the second under the government of Neptune, and the third under the government of Pluto. When the soul is in heaven, the sirens seek, by harmonic motion, to unite it to the divine life of the celestial host; and when in Hadēs, to conform them to the infernal regimen; but on earth they produce generation, of which the sea is emblematic. (*Proclus: On the Theology of Plato*, bk. vi.)

Sirius. The Dog-star; so called by the Greeks from the adjective *seirios*, hot and scorching. The Romans called it *canic'ula*; and the Egyptians, *sothis.*

Sirloin of Beef. A corruption of Surloin. (French, *surlonge*.) *La partie du boeuf qui reste après qu'on en a coupé l'épaule et la cuisse.* In Queen Elizabeth's "Progresses," one of the items mentioned under March 31st, 1573, is a "sorloyne of byf." Fuller tells us that Henry VIII. jocularly knighted the surloin. If so, James I. could claim neither wit nor originality when, at a banquet given him at HOGTON Tower, near Blackburn, he said, "Bring hither that surloin, sirrah, for 'tis worthy of a more honourable post, being, as I may say, not *sur*loin, but *sir*loin."

"Dining with the Abbot of Reading, he [Henry VIII.] ate so heartily of a loin of beef that the abbot said he would give 1,000 marks for such a stomach. 'Done!' said the king, and kept the abbot a prisoner in the Tower, won his 1,000 marks, and knighted the beef."—See *Fuller: Church History*, vi. 2, p. 299 (1655).

Sis'yphus (Latin; *Sisuphos*, Greek). A fraudulent avaricious king of Corinth, whose task in the world of shades is to roll a huge stone to the top of a hill, and fix it there. It so falls out that the stone no sooner reaches the hill-top than it bounds down again.

Sit Bodkin (*To*). (*See* BODKIN.)

Sit Out (*To*). To remain to the end. Not to join, as "to sit out a dance."

Sit Under ... (*To*). To attend the ministry of ...

"On a Sunday the household marched away in separate groups to half-a-dozen edifices, each to sit under his or her favourite minister."—*W. M. Thackeray.*

Sit Up (for anyone) (*To*). To await the return of a person after the usual hour of bed-time.

"His own maid would sit up for him."—*George Eliot.*

Sit Upon (*To*). To snub, squash, smother, set down; the Latin *insideo.* Charlotte Brontë, in *Shirley* (xxviii.), uses a phrase which seems analagous: Miss Keeldar says she mentioned the mischance to no one—"I preferred to cushion the matter."

"Mr. Schwann and his congeners should be most energetically sat upon by colleagues and opponents alike, by everyone, in fact, who has the welfare of the empire at heart."—*The World*, April 6th, 1892, p. 19.

Sit on the Rail or **Fence** (*To*). To refuse to promise your support to a party; to reserve your vote.

"In American slang, he was always sitting on the rail between Catholics and Huguenots."—*The Times.*

Sit on Thorns (*To*) or **on Tenterhooks.** To be in a state of anxiety, fearful that something will go wrong.

Sitâ. Wife of Râma or Vishnu incarnate, carried off by the giant Ravana. She was not born, but arose from a furrow when her father Jan'aka, King of Mith'ila, was ploughing. The word means "furrow."

Sitting in Banco. The judges of the courts of law at Westminster are said to be "sitting in banco" so long as they sit together on the benches of their respective courts—that is, all term time. Banco is the Italian for "bench."

Sieve and Shears. (*See under* ORACLE.)

Si'va (Indian). The destroyer who, with Brahma and Vishnu, forms the divine trinity of the Brahmins. He has five heads, and is the emblem of fire. His wife is Parvati or Parbutta (Sanscrit, *auspicious*).

Six. *Six thrice or three dice.* Everything or nothing. "*Cæsar aut nullus.*" The Greeks and Romans used to play with three dice. The highest throw was three sixes, and the lowest three aces. The aces were left blank, and three aces were called "three dice." (*See* CÆSAR.)

Six-and-Eightpence used to be called a "noble" (*q.v.*), the third of a pound. The half-noble was often called "ten groats," and was in Shakespeare's time the usual lawyer's fee.

"As fit as ten groats is for the hand of an attorney."—*Shakespeare: All's Well that Ends Well*, ii. 2.

Six Articles (33 Henry VIII.) enjoins the belief in (1) the real presence of Christ in the Eucharist; (2) the sufficiency of communion in one kind; (3) the celibacy of the priests; (4) the obligation of vows of chastity; (5) the expediency of private masses; and (6) the necessity of auricular confession.

Six-hooped Pot. A two-quart pot. Quart pots were bound with three hoops, and when three men joined in drinking each man drank his hoop. Mine host of the *Black Bear* calls Tressalian "A six-hooped pot of a traveller," meaning a first-class guest, because he paid freely, and made no complaints. (*Kenilworth*, chap. iii.)

Six Members. The six members that Charles I. went into the House of Commons to arrest were Lord Kimbolton, Pym, Hollis, Hampden, Sir Arthur Haselrig, and Stroud. Being warned in time, they made good their escape.

Six Months' War. The Franco-Prussian (July 28th, 1870, to January 28th, 1871).

Six Nations (*The*). The Iroquois confederacy since the Tuscaroras was added.

Six Points. (*See* PEOPLE'S CHARTER.)

Six-Principle Baptists (*The*). Those whose creed is Hebrews iv. 1, 2.

Sixes and Sevens (*All*). Ill-assorted; not matched; higgledy-piggledy.

To be at sixes and sevens. Spoken of things, it means in confusion; spoken of persons, it means in disagreement or hostility. "Six, yea seven," was a Hebrew phrase meaning an indefinite number; hence we read in Job (v. 19), "He [God] shall deliver thee in six troubles, yea in seven," etc. What is indefinite is confused. Our modern phrase would be five or six things here, and five or six things there, but nothing in proper order.

"Old Odcombs odness makes not thee uneven,
Nor carelessly set all at six and seven."
Taylor: Workes, ii. 71 (1630).

Long and short sixes. Certain dip candles, common in the first half of the nineteenth century. Long sixes were those eight inches long, short sixes were thicker and about five inches long. Called sixes because six went to a pound.

Sixteen-string Jack. John Rann, a highwayman, noted for his foppery. He wore sixteen tags, eight at each knee. (Hanged in 1774.)

"Dr. Johnson said that Gray's poetry towered above the ordinary run of verse as Sixteen-string Jack above the ordinary foot-pad."—*Boswell: Life of Johnson.*

Si'zar. A poor scholar whose assize of food is given him. Sizars used to have what was left at the fellows' table, because it was their duty at one time to wait on the fellows at dinner. Each fellow had his sizar. (*Cambridge University.*)

Sizings. The quota of food allowed at breakfast, and also food "sized for" at dinner. At Cambridge, the students are allowed meat for dinner, but tart, jelly, ale, etc., are obtained only by paying extra. These articles are called sizings, and those who demand them *size* for them. The word is a contraction of assize, a statute to regulate the size or weight of articles sold. (*See* SICE.)

"A size is a portion of bread or drinke: it is a farthing which schollers in Cambridge have at the buttery. It is noted with the letter S "—*Minshen.* (See also *Ellis: Literary Letters*, p. 178.)

Skains-mate or **Skeins-mate.** A dagger-comrade; a fencing-school companion; a fellow cut-throat. Skain is an Irish knife, similar to the American bowie-knife. Swift, describing an Irish feast, says, "A cubit at least the length of their skains." Green, in his *Quip for an Upstart Courtier*, speaks of "an ill-favoured knave, who wore by his side a skane, like a brewer's bung-knife."

"Scurvy knave! . . . I am none of his skains-mates."—*Shakespeare: Romeo and Juliet*, ii. 4.

Skald. An old Norse poet, whose aim was to celebrate living warriors or their ancestors; hence they were attached to courts. Few complete Skaldic poems have survived, but a multitude of fragments exist.

Skedad'dle. To run away, to be scattered in rout. The Scotch apply the word to the milk spilt over the pail in carrying it. During the late American war, the New York papers said the Southern forces were "skedaddled" by the Federals. (Saxon, *scedan*, to pour out; Chaldee, *scheda;* Greek, *skeda'o*, to scatter.)

Skeggs. *Miss Carolina Wilhelmi'na Amelia Skeggs.* A pretender to gentility who boasts of her aristocratic connections, but is atrociously vulgar, and complains of being "all of a muck of sweat." (*Goldsmith : Vicar of Wakefield*.)

Skel'eton. *There is a skeleton in every house.* Something to annoy and to be kept out of sight.

That is my skeleton—my trouble, the "crook in my lot."

A woman had an only son who obtained an appointment in India, but his health failed, and his mother longed for his return. One day he wrote a letter to his mother, with this strange request: "Pray, mother, get someone who has no cares and troubles to make me six shirts." The widow hunted in vain for such a person, and at length called upon a lady who told her to go with her to her bedroom. Being there she opened a closet which contained a human skeleton. "Madam," said the lady, "I try to keep my trouble to myself, but every night my husband compels me to kiss that skeleton." She then explained that the skeleton was once her husband's rival, killed in a duel. "Think you I am happy?" The mother wrote to her son, and the son wrote home: "I knew when I gave the commission that everyone had his cares, and you, mother, must have yours. Know then that I am condemned to death, and can never return to England. Mother, mother! there is a skeleton in every house."

Skeleton Jackets. Jackets on which the trousers buttoned, very commonly worn by boys in the first quarter of the nineteenth century. In the illustrations of Kate Greenaway, *The Pickwick Papers, Nicholas Nickleby*, etc., are plenty of such skeleton suits. Shell-jackets are short fatigue jackets worn especially by military officers.

Skevington's Daughter, corrupted into *Scavenger's Daughter*, was an instrument of torture invented by Skevington, lieutenant of the Tower under Henry VIII. It consisted of a broad hoop of iron in two parts, fastened together by a hinge. The victim was made to kneel while the hoop was passed under his legs; he was then squeezed gradually till the hoop could be got over his back, where it was fastened.

Skibbereen and Connemara (in Ireland). Types of poverty and distress.

"You would then see the United Kingdom one vast Skibbereen or Connemara; you might convert its factories into poor-houses, and its parks into potters' fields to bury strangers in."—*C. Thomson : Autobiography*, p. 307.

Skibbereen Eagle (*The*). The chief amang ye takin' notes. It was the *Skibbereen*, or *West Cork Eagle* newspaper, that solemnly told Lord Palmerston that it had "got its eye both upon him and on the Emperor of Russia." This terrible warning has elevated the little insignificant town of Skibbereen, in the southwest coast of Ireland, quite into a Lilliputian pre-eminence. Beware, beware, ye statesmen, emperors, and thrones, for the *Skibbereen Eagle* has its eye upon you!

Skid. A drag to check the wheels of a carriage, cart, etc., when going down hill. (Anglo-Saxon, *scid*, a splinter.)

Skiddaw. *Whenever Skiddaw hath a cap, Scruffell wots full well of that.* When my neighbour's house is on fire mine is threatened; When you are in misfortune I also am a sufferer; When you mourn I have cause also to lament. Skiddaw and Scruffell are two neighbouring hills—one in Cumberland and the other in Annandale in Scotland. When Skiddaw is capped with clouds, it will be sure to rain ere long at Scruffell. (*Fuller : Worthies*.)

Skied. Pictures are said to be skied when they are hung so high as not to be easily seen.

"Bad pictures are hung on the line by dozens, and many excellent ones are rejected or skied."
—*Truth*, p. 431 (September 17, 1885).

Skillygolee. Slip-slop, wish-wash, twaddle, talk about gruel. "Skilly" is prison-gruel or, more strictly speaking, the water in which meat has been boiled thickened with oatmeal. Broth served on board the hulks to convicts is called *skilly.*

"It is the policy of Cursitor Street and skilly-golee."—*The Daily Telegraph.*

Skimble-Skamble. Rambling, worthless. "Skamble" is merely a variety of *scramble*, hence "scambling days," those days in Lent when no regular meals are provided, but each person "scrambles" or shifts for himself. "Skimble" is added to give force. (*See* REDUPLICATED WORDS.)

"And such a deal of skimble-skamble stuff
As put me from my faith."
Shakespeare : 1 *Henry IV.*, iii. 1.

"With such scamble-scemble, spitter-spatter,
As puts me cleane beside the money-matter."
Taylor's Workes, ii. 39 (1630).

Skim'mington. *To ride the skimmington*, or *Riding the stang.* To be hen-pecked. Grose tells us that the man rode behind the woman, with his face to the horse's tail. The man held a distaff, and the woman beat him about the jowls with a ladle. As the procession passed a house where the woman was paramount, each gave the threshold a sweep. The "stang" was a pole supported by two stout lads, across which the rider was made to stride. Mr. Douce derives "skimmington" from the *skimming*-ladle with which the rider was buffeted.

The custom was not peculiar to Scotland and England; it prevailed in Scandinavia; and Hoefnagel, in his *Views in Seville* (1591), shows that it existed in Spain also. The procession is described at length in *Hudibras*, pt. ii. ch. ii.

"'Hark ye, Dame Ursley Suddlechop,' said Jenkin, starting up, his eyes flashing with anger: 'remember, I am none of your husband, and if I were you would do well not to forget whose threshold was swept when they last rode the skimmington upon such another scolding jade as yourself.'"—*Scott: Fortunes of Nigel*.

Skin. *To sell the skin before you have caught the bear.* To count of your chickens before they are hatched. In the South Sea mania (1720), dealing in bear-skins was a great stock-jobbing item, and thousands of skins were sold as mere time bargains. Shakespeare alludes to a similar practice :—

" The man that once did sell the lion's skin
While the beast lived, was killed with hunting
him."   *Henry V.*, iv. 3.

Skin a Flint. To be very exacting in making a bargain. The French say, " *Tondre sur un œuf.*" The Latin, *lana capri'na* (goat's wool), means something as worthless as the skin of a flint or fleece of an eggshell. (*See* SKINFLINT.)

Skin of his Teeth. *I am escaped with the skin of my teeth* (Job xix. 20). Just escaped, and that is all—having lost everything.

Skinfaxi, in Scandinavian mythology, is the " shining horse which draws Daylight over the earth." (*See* HORSE.)

Skinflint. A pinch-farthing; a niggard. In the French, " *pince-maille.*" *Maille* is an old copper coin.

Skinners. A predatory band in the American Revolutionary War which roamed over the neutral ground robbing and fleecing those who refused to take the oath of fidelity. (*See* ECORCHEURS.)

Skirt. *To sit upon one's skirt.* To insult, or seek occasion of quarrel. Tarlton, the clown, told his audience the reason why he wore a jacket was that "no one might sit upon his skirt." Sitting on one's skirt is, like stamping

on one's coat in Ireland, a fruitful source of quarrels, often provoked.

" Crosse me not, Liza, nether be so perte,
For if thou dost, I'll sit upon thy skirte."
    The Abortive of an Idle Howre (1620).
    (Quoted by Halliwell : *Archaic Words.*)

Skogan (*Henry*). A poet in the reign of Henry IV. Justice Shallow says he saw Sir John Falstaff, when he was a boy, " break Skogan's head at the court gate, when he [Sir John] was a crack [child] not thus high." (*2 Henry IV.*, iii. 2.)

" Scogan ? What was he ?
Oh, a fine gentleman, and a master of arts
Of Henry the Fourth's times, that made disguises
For the king's sons, and writ in ballad royal
Daintily well."
    Ben Jonson: The Fortunate Isles (1626).

John Skogan. The favourite buffoon of the court of King Edward IV. *Scogin's Jests* were published by Andrew Borde, a physician, in the reign of Henry VIII.

Skopts, Skopti, or *White Doves*, A Russian religious sect who, taking Matt. xix. 12 and Luke xxiii. 29 as the bases of their creed, are all eunuchs, and the women are mutilated in a most barbarous manner, as they deem it a Christian grace not to be able to bear children. They are vegetarians and total abstainers. Origen was a Skopt in everything but name.

" Look at the Mormons, the Skopts, the Shakers, the Howling Dervishes, the Theosophists, and the Fakirs."—*With the Immortals*, vol. ii. p. 50.

Skull. *You shall quaff beer out of the skulls of your enemies.* (Scandinavian.) Skull means a cup or dish; hence a person who washes up cups and dishes is called a scullery-maid. (Scotch, *skoll*, a bowl; French, *écuelle*; Danish, *skaal*, a drinking-vessel; German, *schale;* our *shell.*)

Skurry (*A*). A scratch race, or race without restrictions.

Hurry-skurry. A confused bustle through lack of time; in a confused bustle. A reduplicated or ricochet word.

Sky, slang for pocket. Explained under the word CHIVY (*q.v.*).

Sky. To elevate, ennoble, raise. It is a term in ballooning; when the ropes are cut, the balloon mounts upwards to the skies. (*See* SKIED.)

" We found the same distinguished personage doing his best to sky some dozen or so of his best friends [referring to the peers made by Gladstone]."—*The Times*, November 16, 1869.

If the sky falls we shall catch larks. A bantering reply to those who suggest some very improbable or wild scheme,

Sky-blue. Milk and water, the colour of the skies.

" Its name derision and reproach pursue,
And strangers tell of three times skimmed sky-blue."   *Bloomfield: Farmer's Boy.*

Sky-rakers, strictly speaking, is a sail above the fore-royal, the main-royal, or the mizzen-royal, more frequently called " sky-scrapers." In general parlance any top-sail is so called.

" Dashed by the strange wind's sport, we were sunk deep in the green sea's trough ; and before we could utter an ejaculatory prayer, were upheaved upon the crown of some fantastic surge, peering our sky-rakers into the azure vault of heaven."—*C. Thomson: Autobiography,* p. 120.

Skye (*Isle of*) means the isle of gaps or indentations (Celtic, *skyb,* a gap). Hence also the Skibbereen of Cork, which is *Skyb-bohreen,* the byway gap, a pass in a mountain to the sea.

Skylark. A spree.

Skylark, among sailors, is to mount the highest yards (called sky-scrapers), and then slide down the ropes for amusement. (*See* LARK.)

Slander, Offence. Slander is a stumbling-block or something which trips a person up (Greek, *skan'dalon,* through the French *esclandre*). Offence is the striking of our foot against a stone (Latin, *ob fendo,* as *scopulum offendit navis,* the ship struck against a rock).

Slang. Slangs are the greaves with which the legs of convicts are fettered ; hence convicts themselves ; and slang is the language of convicts.

Slang. The difficulty of tracing the *fons et origo* of slang words is extremely great, as there is no law to guide one. Generally, a perversion and a pun may be looked for, as *Monseigneur* = toe (*q.v.*), *Monpensier* = ventre (*i.e. monpanse,* my paunch or belly), etc. (*See* SANDIS, SQUASH, and numerous other examples in this dictionary. For rhyming slang *see* CHIVY.)

Slap-bang, in sport, means that the gun was discharged incessantly ; it went slap here and bang there. As a term of laudation it means " very dashing," both words being playful synonyms of "dashing," the repetition being employed to give intensity. *Slap-bang, here we are again,* means, we have "popped" in again without ceremony. Pop, slap, bang, and dash are interchangeable.

❉ Dickens uses the word to signify a low eating-house.

" They lived in the same street, walked to town every morning at the same hour, dined at the same slap-bang every day."

Slap-dash. In an off-hand manner. The allusion is to the method of colouring rooms by slapping and dashing the walls, so as to imitate paper. At one time slap-dash walls were very common.

Slap-up. *Prime slap-up* or *slap-bang-up.* Very exquisite or dashing. Here *slap* is a playful synonym of *dashing,* and " up " is the Latin *super,* as in " superfine." The dress of a dandy or the equipage of an exquisite is " slap-up," " prime slap-up," or " slap-bang-up."

" [The] more slap-up still have the shields painted on the panels with the coronet over."—*Thackeray.*

Slate. *He has a slate* or *tile loose.* He is a little cracked ; his head or roof is not quite sound.

Slate Club (*A*). A sick benefit club for working-men. Originally the names of the members were entered on a folding slate ; in the universities the names of members are marked on a board, or on boards ; hence such expressions as " his name is on the boards," " I have taken my name off the boards."

Slate One (*To*). To criticise, expose in print, show up, reprove. A scholastic term. Rebellious and idle boys are slated, that is, their names are set down on a slate to expose their offence, and some punishment is generally awarded.

" The journalists there lead each other a dance.
If one man 'slates' another for what he has done,
It is pistols for two, and then coffin for one."
Punch (*The Pugnacious Penmen*), 1885.

Slating (*A*). A slashing review.

"He cut it up root and branch. . . . He gave it what he technically styled 'a slating' ; and as he threw down his pen . . . he muttered, ' I think I've pretty well settled that dunce's business.'"—*The World,* February 24th, 1892, p. 24.

Slave (1 syl.). This is an example of the strange changes which come over some words. The Slavi were a tribe which once dwelt on the banks of the Dnieper, and were so called from *slav* (noble, illustrious) ; but as, in the lower ages of the Roman empire, vast multitudes of them were spread over Europe in the condition of captive servants, the word came to signify a slave.

Similarly, *Goths* means the good or godlike men ; but since the invasion of the Goths the word has become synonymous with barbarous, bad, ungodlike.

Distraction is simply " dis-traho," as *diversion* is " di-verto." The French still employ the word for recreation or amusement, but when *we* talk of being distracted we mean anything but being amused or entertained,

Sleave. *The ravelled sleave of care* (*Shakespeare: Macbeth*). The sleave is the knotted or entangled part of thread or silk, the raw edge of woven articles. Chaucer has "sleeveless words" (words like ravellings, not knit together to any wise purpose) ; Bishop Hall has "sleaveless rhymes" (random rhymes) ; Milton speaks of "sleeveless reason" (reasoning which proves nothing) ; Taylor the water-poet has "sleeveless message" (a simple message ; it now means a *profitless* one). The weaver's *slaie* is still used. (Saxon, *slæ*, a weaver's reed ; Danish, *slöjfe*, a knot.)

"If all these faife, a beggar-woman may
A sweet love-letter to her hands convay,
Or a neat laundresse or a hearb-wife can
Carry a sleevelesse message now and than."
Taylor's Workes, ii. 111 (1630).

Sleck-stone. The ebon stone used by goldsmiths to slecken (polish) their gold with. Curriers use a similar stone for smoothing out creases of leather ; the *slecker* is also made of glass, steel, etc. (Icelandic, *slikr*, our word *sleek*.)

Sledge-hammer. *A sledge-hammer argument.* A clincher ; an argument which annihilates opposition at a blow. The sledge-hammer is the largest sort of hammer used by smiths, and is wielded by both hands. The word *sledge* is the Saxon *slecge* (a sledge).

Sleep (Anglo-Saxon *slæpen*). Crabbe's etymology of *doze* under this word is exquisite :—

"Doze, a variation from the French *dors* and the Latin *dormio* (to sleep), which was anciently *dermio*, and comes from the Greek *derma* (a skin), because people lay on *skins* when they slept"!—*Synonyms.*

To sleep away. To pass away in sleep, to consume in sleeping ; as, to sleep one's life away.

To sleep off. To get rid of by sleep.

Sleep like a Top. When peg-tops and humming-tops are at the acme of their gyration they become so steady and quiet that they do not seem to move. In this state they are said to sleep. Soon they begin to totter, and the tipsy movement increases till they fall. The French say, *Dormir comme un sabot*, and *Mon sabot dort.* (*See* SIMILES.)

Sleeper (*The*). Epimen'idēs, the Greek poet, is said to have fallen asleep in a cave when a boy, and not to have waked for fifty-seven years, when he found himself possessed of all wisdom. Rip Van Winkle, in Washington Irving's tale, is supposed to sleep for twenty years, and wake up an old man, unknowing and unknown. (*See* KLAUS.)

Sleepers. Timbers laid asleep or resting on something, as the sleepers of a railway. (Anglo-Saxon, *slæpere*.)

The Seven Sleepers. (*See* SEVEN.)

Sleeping Beauty. From the French *La Belle au Bois Dormante*, by Charles Perrault (*Contes du Temps*). She is shut up by enchantment in a castle, where she sleeps a hundred years, during which time an impenetrable wood springs up around. Ultimately she is disenchanted by a young prince, who marries her. Epimen'idēs, the Cretan poet, went to fetch a sheep, and after sleeping fifty-seven years continued his search, and was surprised to find when he got home that his younger brother was grown grey. (*See* RIP VAN WINKLE.)

Sleepless Hat (*A*). A worthless, worn-out hat, which has no *nap.*

Sleepy Hollow. The name given, in Washington Irving's *Sketch Book*, to a quiet old-world village on the Hudson.

Sleeve. *To hang on one's sleeve.* To listen devoutly to what one says ; to surrender your freedom of thought and action to the judgment of another. The allusion is to children hanging on their mother's sleeve.

To have in one's sleeve is to offer a person's name for a vacant situation. Dean Swift, when he waited on Harley, had always some name in his sleeve. The phrase arose from the custom of placing pockets in sleeves. These sleeve-pockets were chiefly used for memoranda, and other small articles.

To laugh in one's sleeve. To ridicule a person not openly but in secret ; to conceal a laugh by hiding your face in the large sleeves at one time worn by men. *Rire sous cape.*

To pin to one's sleeve, as, "I shan't pin my faith to your sleeve," meaning, "I shall not slavishly believe or follow you." The allusion is to the practice of knights, in days of chivalry, pinning to their sleeve some token given them by their ladylove. This token was a pledge that he would do or die.

Sleeve of Care. (*See* SLEAVE.)

Sleeve of Hildebrand (*The*), from which he shook thunder and lightning.

Sleeveless Errand. A fruitless errand. It should be written *sleaveless*, as it comes from *sleave*, ravelled thread, or the raw-edge of silk. In *Troilus and Cressida*, Thersi'tës the railer calls Patroclus an "idle immaterial skein of sleive silk" (v. 1).

Sleight of Hand is artifice by the hand. (Icelandic, *slædgh;* German, *schlich,* cunning or trick.)

"And still the less they understand,
The more they admire his sleight of hand."
  Butler: Hudibras, pt. ii. c. 3.

Sleip'nir (2 syl.). Odin's grey horse, which had eight legs, and could carry his master over sea as well as land. (*Scandinavian mythology.*)

Slender. A country lout, a booby in love with Anne Page, but of too faint a heart to win so fair a lady. (*Shakespeare: Merry Wives of Windsor.*)

Sleuth-Hound. A blood-hound which follows the *sleuth* or track of an animal. (*Slot,* the track of a deer, is the Anglo-Saxon *slæting;* Icelandic, *sloth,* trail; Dutch, *sloot.*)

"There is a law also among the Borderers in time of peace, that whoso denieth entrance or sute of a sleuth-hound in pursuit made after fellons and stolen goods, shall be holden as accessarie unto the theft."—*Holinshed: Description of Scotland,* p. 14.

Slewed. Intoxicated. When a vessel changes her tack, she staggers and gradually heels over. A drunken man moves like a ship changing her angle of sailing. (Probably from the Icelandic, *snua,* turn.)

"Mr. Hornby was just a bit slewed by the liquor he'd taken."—*W. C. Russell: A Strange Voyage,* chap. xii. p. 25.

Slick (*Sam*). A Yankee clock-maker and pedlar, wonderfully 'cute, a keen observer, and with plenty of "soft sawder." Judge Haliburton wrote the two series called *Sam Slick, or the Clock-maker.*

Slick Off. To finish a thing there and then without stopping; to make a clean sweep of a job in hand. Judge Haliburton's *Sam Slick* popularised the word. (German, *schlicht,* sleek, polished, hence *clean;* Icelandic, *slíke,* sleek.) We say, "To do a thing clean off" as well as "slick off."

Sliding Scale. A schedule of payment which slides up and down as the article to which it refers becomes dearer or cheaper. In government duty it varies as the amount taxed varies.

Slip. *Many a slip 'twixt the cup and the lip.* Everything is uncertain till you possess it. (*See* ANCÆOS.)

"Multa cadunt inter calicem supremaque labra."
  Horace.

To give one the slip. To steal off unperceived; to elude pursuit. A *sea-phrase.* In fastening a cable to a buoy, the home end is slipped through the hawse-pipe. To give the slip is to cut

away the cable, so as to avoid the noise of weighing anchor.

Slippers. The Turks wear *yellow* slippers; the Arme'nians, *red;* and the Jews, *blue.*

Slipshod, applied to literature, means a loose, careless style of composition; no more fit for the public eye than a man with his shoes down at heels.

Slipslop. A ricochet word meaning wishy-washy. (Anglo-Saxon, *slip-an,* to melt, which makes *slopen* in the past participle.)

Sloane MSS. 3,560 MSS. collected by Sir Hans Sloane, now in the British Museum. The museum of Sir Hans formed the basis of the British Museum. (1660-1753.)

Slogan. A war-cry, a Scotch gathering-cry. (Anglo-Saxon, *sleán,* to fight, pret. *slog;* Gaelic, *sluagh-gairm,* an army-yell.)

Slop (*Dr.*). A choleric physician in Sterne's *Tristram Shandy.*

Dr. Slop. Sir John Stoddart, M.D., a choleric physician who assailed Napoleon most virulently in *The Times,* of which he was editor. (1773-1856.)

Slops (*The*). The police; originally "ecilop."

"I dragged you in here and saved you,
  And sent out a gal for the slops ;
Ha ! they're acomin', sir ! Listen !
  The noise and the shoutin' stops."
  Sims: Ballads of Babylon (The Matron's Story).

Slo'pard (*Dame*). The wife of Grimbard, the brock (or badger), in the tale of *Reynard the Fox.*

Slope (1 syl.). To decamp; to run away.

Slough of Despond. A deep bog which Christian has to cross in order to get to the Wicket Gate. Help comes to his aid. Neighbour Pliable went with Christian as far as the Slough, and then turned back again. (*Bunyan: Pilgrim's Progress,* part i.).

Slow. Stupid, dull. A "quick boy" is one who is sharp and active. *Awfully slow,* slang for very stupid and dull.

Slow Coach. A dawdle. As a slow coach in the old coaching-days "got on" slowly, so one that "gets on" slowly is a slow coach.

Slubber-Degullion. A nasty, paltry fellow. A *slub* is a roll of wool drawn out and only slightly twisted; hence to *slubber,* to twist loosely, to do things by halves, to perform a work carelessly. *Degullion* is compounded of the word "gull," or the Cornish "gullan," a simpleton.

"Quoth she, 'Although th u hast deserved,
Base slubber-degullion, to be served
As thou didst vow to deal with me."
    Butler: Hudibras, i. 3.

Slug-abed (*A*). A late riser.
"The buttercup is no slug-abed."—*Notes and Queries* (Aug. 11, 1894, p. 1118, col. 2).

Slumland. The localities of the destitute poor who dwell in the slums.
"Not only have we the inhabitants of Slumland to deal with, but a steadily growing number of skilled and fairly educated artisans."—*Nineteenth Century*, December, 1892, p. 888.

Slums. "The back slums"—*i.e.* the purlieus of Westminster Abbey, etc., where vagrants get a night's lodging.

Sly (*Christopher*). A keeper of bears and a tinker, son of a pedlar, and a sad, drunken sot. In the Induction of Shakespeare's comedy called *Taming of the Shrew*, he is found dead drunk by a lord, who commands his servants to put him to bed, and on his waking to attend upon him like a lord, to see if they can bamboozle him into the belief that he is a great man, and not Christopher Sly at all. The "commonty" of *Taming of the Shrew* is performed for his delectation. The trick was played by the Caliph Haroun Alraschid on Abou Hassan, the rich merchant, in the tale called *The Sleeper Awakened* (*Arabian Nights*), and by Philippe *the Good*, Duke of Burgundy, on his marriage with Eleanor, as given in Burton's *Anatomy of Melancholy* (pt. ii. sec. 2, num. 4).

Sly-Boots. One who appears to be a dolt, but who is really wide awake; a cunning dull.
"The frog called the lazy one several times, but in vain ; there was no such thing as stirring him, though the sly-boots heard well enough all the while."—*Adventures of Abdalla*, p. 32 (1729).

Sly Dog. *You're a sly dog.* "*Un fin matois.*" A playful way of saying, You pretend to be disinterested, but I can read between the lines.

Sly as a Fox. (*See* SIMILES.)

Slyme (*Chevy*). In *Martin Chuzzlewit*, by Charles Dickens.

Small. *Small by degrees and beautifully less.* Prior, in his *Henry and Emma*, wrote "Fine by degrees," etc.

Small-back. Death. So called because he is usually drawn as a skeleton.
"Small-back must lead down the dance with us all in our time."—*Sir Walter Scott.*

37

Small Beer. "To suckle fools and chronicle small beer." (Iago in the play of *Othello*, ii. 1.)
He does not think small beer of himself. He has a very good opinion of number one.
"To express her self-esteem [it might be said] that she did not think small beer of herself."—*De Quincey: Historical Essays.*

Small-endians. The Big-endians of Lilliput made it a point of orthodoxy to crack their eggs at the big end; but were considered heretics for so doing by the Small-endians, who insisted that eggs ought to be broken at the small end. (*Swift: Gulliver's Travels.*)

Small Hours of the Morning (*The*). One, two, three, four, etc., before daybreak. A student who sits up all night, and goes to bed at one, two, three, etc., is said to work till the small hours of the morning, or to go to bed in the small hours of the morning.

Smalls. *In for his smalls ; Passed his smalls*—his "Little-go," or previous examination ; the examination for degree being the "Great-go," or "Greats."

Smart Money. Money paid by a person to obtain exemption from some disagreeable office or duty ; in *law* it means a heavy fine ; and in recompense it means money given to soldiers or sailors for injuries received in the service. It either makes the person "smart," *i.e.* suffer, or else the person who receives it is paid for smarting.

Smash. *Come to smash*—to ruin. *Smashed to pieces*, broken to atoms. Smash is a corruption of *mash ;* Latin, *mastico*, to bite to pieces. (*See* SLOPE.)
"I have a great mind to . . . let social position go to smash."—*Eggleston: Faith Doctor*, p. 63.

Smec (in *Hudibras*). A contraction of Smectymnuus, a word made from the initial letters of five rebels—
Stephen Marshal.
Edward Calamy.
Thomas Young.
Matthew Newcomen.
William Spurstow, who wrote a book against Episcopacy and the Common Prayer. (*See* NOTARICA.)
"The handkerchief about the neck,
Canonical cravat of Smec."
    Butler: Hudibras, pt. i. 5.

Smectym'nuans. Anti-Episcopalians.

Smectym'nuus. (*See* SMEC.)

Smell (an acute sense). James Mitchell was deaf, dumb, and blind from birth, "but he distinguished persons by their smell, and by means of the same sense formed correct judgments as to character." (*Nineteenth Century*, April, 1894, p. 579.)

Smell a Rat (*To*). To suspect something about to happen. The allusion is to a cat or dog smelling out vermin.

I smell treason. I discern treason involved ; I have some aim that would lead to treason.

Smelling Sin. Shakespeare says, " Do you smell a fault ? " (*King Lear*, i. 1) ; and Iago says to Othello, " One may smell in this a will most rank." Probably the smell of dogs may have something to do with such phrases, but St. Jerome furnishes even a better source. He says that St. Hilarion had the gift of knowing what sins or vices anyone was inclined to by simply smelling either the person or his garments ; and by the same faculty he could discern good feelings and virtuous propensities. (*Life of Hilarion*, A.D. 390.)

Smells of the Lamp. Said of a literary production manifestly laboured. Plutarch attributes the phrase to Pytheas the orator, who said, " The orations of Demos'thenēs smell of the lamp," alluding to the current tale that the great orator lived in an underground cave lighted by a lamp, that he might have no distraction to his severe study.

Smelts (Stock-Exchange term), meaning " English and Australian copper shares." (*See* STOCK-EXCHANGE SLANG.)

Smiler, the name of a drink, is a mixture of bitter beer and lemonade. In the United States, a drink of liquor is called a " smile," and the act of treating one at the bar is giving one a " smile." Of course this is metaphorical. (*See* SHANDY-GAFF.)

Smith. A proper name. (*See* BREWER.)

Smith of Nottingham. Ray, in his *Collection of Proverbs*, has the following couplet :—

" The little Smith of Nottingham,
  Who doth the work that no man can."

Applied to conceited persons who imagine that no one is able to compete with themselves.

Smith's Prize-man. One who has obtained the prize (£25), founded in the University of Cambridge by Robert Smith, D.D. (once master of Trinity), for proficiency in mathematics and natural philosophy. There are annually two

prizes, awarded to two commencing Bachelors of Arts.

Smithfield. The smooth field (Anglo-Saxon, *smethe*, smooth), called in Latin *Campus Planus*, and described by Fitz-Stephen in the twelfth century as a " plain field where every Friday there is a celebrated rendezvous of fine horses brought thither to be sold."

Smoke. To detect, or rather to get a scent, of some plot or scheme. The allusion is to the detection of robbers by the smoke seen to issue from their place of concealment.

No smoke without fire. Every slander has some foundation. The reverse proverb, " No fire without smoke," means no good without some drawback.

To end in smoke. To come to no practical result. The allusion is to kindling, which smokes, but will not light a fire.

To smoke the calumet (or *pipe*) *of peace.* (*See* CALUMET.)

Smoke Farthings. An offering given to the priest at Whitsuntide, according to the number of chimneys in his parish.

" The Bishop of Elie hath out of everie parish in Cambridgeshire a certain tribute called . . . *smoke-farthings*, which the churchwardens do levie according to the number of . . . chimneys that be in a parish."—*MSS. Baker*, xxxix. 326.

Smoke Silver. A modus of 6d. in lieu of tithe firewood.

Snack. *The snack of a door* (Norfolk). The latch. Generally called the " sneck " (*q.v.*).

To take a snack. To take a morsel.

To go snacks. To share and share alike.

Snails have no sex, " *chacun remissant les deux sexes.*" (Anglo-Saxon, *snægl*).

Snake-Stones. Small rounded stones or matters compounded by art, and supposed to cure snake-bites. Mr. Quekett discovered that two given to him for analysis were composed of vegetable matters. Little perforated stones are sometimes hung on cattle to charm away adders.

Snake in the Grass. A secret enemy ; an enemy concealed from sight. Rhyming slang, " a looking-glass."

" Latet anguis in herba."
Virgil, Eclogue iii. 93.

Snakes in his Boots (*To have*). To suffer from D.T. (*delirium tremens*). This is one of the delusions common to those so afflicted.

" He's been pretty high on whisky for two or three days, . . . and they say he's got snakes in his boots now."—*The Barton Experiment*, chap. ix.

Snap-Dragons. (*See* FLAP-DRAGON.)

Snap of the Fingers. *Not worth a snap of the fingers.* A fico. (*See* FIG.)

Snap One's Nose Off. (*See under* NOSE.)

Snarling Letter (Latin, *lit'era cani'na*). The letter *r*. (*See* R.)

Sneck Posset. To give one a sneck posset is to slam the door in his face (Cumberland and Westmoreland). The "sneck" or snick is the latch of a door, and to "sneck the door in one's face" is to shut a person out. Mrs. Browning speaks of "nicking" the door.

"The lady closed
That door, and nicked the lock."
Aurora Leigh, book vi. line 1,067.

Probably allied to *niche*, to put the latch into its niche.

Sneezed. *It is not to be sneezed at—* not to be despised. (*See* SNUFF.)

Sneezing. Some Catholics attribute to St. Gregory the use of the benediction "God bless you," after sneezing, and say that he enjoined its use during a pestilence in which sneezing was a mortal symptom, and was therefore called the death-sneeze.   Aristotle mentions a similar custom among the Greeks; and Thucyd'idēs tells us that sneezing was a crisis symptom of the great Athenian plague. The Romans followed the same custom, and their usual exclamation was "*Absit omen!*" We also find it prevalent in the New World among the native Indian tribes, in Sennaar, Monomatapa, etc. etc.

∴ It is almost incredible how ancient and how widely diffused is the notion that sneezing is an omen which requires to be averted. The notion prevailed not only in ancient Greece and Rome, but is existent in Persia, India, and even Africa. The rabbins tell us that Jacob in his flight gave a sneeze, the evil effects of which were averted by prayer.
In the conquest of Florida, when the Spaniards arrived, the Cazique, we are told, sneezed, and all the court lifted up their hands and implored the sun to avert the evil omen.
In the rebellion of Monomatapa, in Africa, the king sneezed, and a signal of the fact being given, all the faithful subjects instantly made vows and offerings for his safety. The same is said respecting Sennaar, in Nubia, in Sweden, etc.
The *Sadder* (one of the sacred books of the Parsees) enjoins that all people should have recourse to prayer if a person sneezes, because sneezing is a proof that the "Evil Spirit is abroad."
Foote, in his farce of *Dr. Last in His Chariot*, makes one of the consulting doctors ask why, when a person sneezes, all the company bows? and the answer given was that "sneezing is a mortal symptom which once depopulated Athens."
"In Sweden . . . . you sneeze, and they cry God bless you."—*Longfellow*.

Snickersnee. A large clasp-knife, or combat with clasp-knives. ("Snick," [Icelandic *snikka*, to clip ; verb, *smitte*,

to cut. "Snee" is the Dutch *snee*, an edge ; *snijden*, to cut.) Thackeray, in his *Little Billee*, uses the term "snickersnee."

"One man being busy in lighting his pipe, and another in sharpening his snickersnee."—*Irvin"*: *Bracebridge Hall*, p. 462.

Snider Rifle. (*See* GUN.)

Snob. Not a gentleman ; one who arrogates to himself merits which he does not deserve. Thackeray calls George IV. a snob, because he assumed to be "the greatest gentleman in Europe," but had not the genuine stamp of a gentleman's mind. (*S* privative and *nob*.)

Snood. *The lassie lost her silken snood.* The snood was a riband with which a Scotch lass braided her hair, and was the emblem of her maiden character. When she married she changed the snood for the curch or coif ; but if she lost the name of virgin before she obtained that of wife, she "lost her silken snood," and was not privileged to assume the curch. (Anglo-Saxon, *snōd*.)

Snooks. An exclamation of incredulity ; a Mrs. Harris. A person tells an incredible story, and the listener cries *Snooks*—gammon ; or he replies, *It was Snooks*—the host of the Château d'Espagne. This word "snook" may be a corruption of Noakes or Nokes, the mythical party at one time employed by lawyers to help them in actions of ejectment. (*See* STYLES.)

Snore. *You snore like an owl.* It is very generally believed that owls snore, and it is quite certain that a noise like snoring proceeds from their nests ; but this is most likely the "purring" of the young birds, nestling in comfort and warmth under the parent wing.

Snow King. Gustavus Adolphus, of Sweden. (1594, 1611-1632.)

"At Vienna he was called in derision the Snow King, who was kept together by the cold, but would melt and disappear as he approached a warmer soil."—*Dr. Crichton : Scandinavia*, vol. ii. p. 61.

Snowdo'nia. The district which contains the mountain range of Snowdon.

The King of Snowdonia. Moel-y-Wyddfa (*the conspicuous peak*), the highest in South Britain. (3,571 feet above the sea-level.)

Snowdrop (*The*). Tickell's fable is that King Albion's son fell in love with Kenna, daughter of Oberon, but Oberon in anger drove the lover out of fairyland. Albion's son brought an army to avenge the indignity, and was slain. Kenna

applied the herb moly to the wounds,
hoping to restore life; but the moment
the juice of the herb touched the dead
body it was converted into a snowdrop.
Called the Fair Maid of February.

Snuff. *Up to snuff.* Wide awake,
knowing, sharp; not easily taken in or
imposed upon; alive to scent (Dutch,
snuffen, to scent, *snuf;* Danish, *snöfte*).
Took it in snuff—in anger, in huff.

"You'll mar the light by taking it in snuff."
    Shakespeare: Love's Labour's Lost, v. 2.
"Who, . . . when it next came there, took it
in snuff."—*Shakespeare :* 1 *Henry IV.,* i. 3.

Snuff Out. *He was snuffed out*—put
down, eclipsed. The allusion is to a
candle snuffed with snuffers.

Soane Museum, formed by Sir John
Soane, and preserved in its original
locality, No. 13, Lincoln's Inn Fields,
the private residence of the founder. Sir
John Soane died in 1837.

Soap. An English form of *savon,* the
French for soap.
How are you off for soap ? (for money
or any other necessity). The insurgent
women of Paris, in February, 1793, went
about crying, " *Du pain et du savon !* "
(bread and soap).

" A deputation of washwomen petitioned the
Convention for soap, and their plaintive cry was
heard round the Salle de Manège, ' *Du pain et du
savon !* '"—*Carlyle : French Revolution,* pt. iii. bk.
iii. 1.

Soap (*Castile*). A hard white soap
made of olive oil, sometimes mottled
with ferruginous matter.

There are also Marseilles soap, Spanish soap,
Venetian soap, and marine soap (usually made of
cocoanut oil and used with sea-water).

Soaped-pig Fashion (*In*). Vague;
a method of speaking or writing which
always leaves a way of escape. The
allusion is to the custom at fairs, etc., of
soaping the tail of a pig before turning
it out to be caught by the tail.

" He is vague as may be ; writing in what is
called the 'soaped-pig' fashion."—*Carlyle : The
Diamond Necklace,* chap. iv.

Soapy Sam. Samuel Wilberforce,
Bishop of Oxford, and afterwards of
Winchester. (1805-1873.) It is somewhat remarkable that the floral decorations above the stall of the bishop and
of the principal of Cuddesdon, were
S. O. A. P. (the initials of **S**am **O**xon
and **A**lfred **P**ott. When Samuel Wilberforce went to inspect the building he
was dismayed at seeing his sobriquet
thus perpetuated.

Someone asking the bishop why he was so
called, the bishop replied, " Because I am often in
hot water, and always come out with clean
hands."

Sober or **Sobrius** is the Latin *s* privative, and *ebrius,* drunk. (*S* privative is for *seorsum.*)

Sober as a Judge—*i.e.* grave and
sedate. (*See* SIMILES.)

Sobri'no (in *Orlando Furioso*). One
of the most valiant of the Saracen army.
He is called the Sage. He was aged,
and counselled Ag'ramant to give up the
war and return home, or, if he rejected
that advice, to entrust the fight to single
combat, on condition that the nation of
the champion overthrown should pay
tribute to the other. Roge'ro was chosen
for the pagan champion, and Rinaldo for
the Christian, but Agramant broke the
league. Sobri'no soon after this received
the rite of baptism.
Don Quixote asks—

" Who more prudent than Sobrino ?"

So'briquet (French). A nickname.
Ménage thinks the etymology is the
Latin *subridic'ulum* (somewhat ridiculous); Count de Gebelin suggests the
Romance words *sopra-quest* (a name acquired over and above your proper
names) ; while Leglay is in favour of
soubriquet, a word common in the fourteenth century to express a sound of
contempt, half whistle and half jeer,
made by raising quickly the chin. Probably *sous-brechet,* where *brechet* means
the breast, seen in our word " brisket."

So'cialism (3 syl.). The political
and social scheme of Robert Owen, of
Montgomeryshire, who in 1816 published
a work to show that society was in a
wretched condition, and all its institutions and religious systems were based
on wrong principles. The prevailing
system is competition, but Owen maintained that the proper principle is co-
operation ; he therefore advocated a
community of property and the abolition of degrees of rank. (1771-1858.)
The Socialists are called also Owenites
(3 syl.). In France the Fourierists and
St. Simonians are similar sorts of communists, who receive their designations
from Fourier and St. Simon (*q.v.*).

Société de Momus. One of the
minor clubs of Paris for the reunion of
song-writers and singers. The most
noted of these clubs was the *Caveau,* or
in full *Les Diners du Caveau,* founded in
1733 by Piron, Crébillon, jun., and Collet. This club lasted the Revolution.
In the Consulate was formed *Les Diners
du Vaudeville,* for the *habitués* of the
drama ; these *diners* were held in the
house of Julliet, an actor. In 1806 the

old *Caveau* was revived under the name of the *Caveau Moderne*, and the muster was once a month at a restaurant entitled *La Rocher de Cancale*, famous for fish dinners, and Laujon (the French Anacreon) was president. Béranger belonged to this club, which lasted ten years. In 1824 was founded the *Gymnase Lyrique*, which, like the *Caveau*, published an annual volume of songs; this society was dissolved in 1841. In 1834 was founded *La Lice Chansonnière*, for those who could not afford to join the *Caveau* or the *Gymnase*, to which we owe some of the best French songs.

Society. The upper ten thousand, or "the upper ten." When persons are in "society," they are on the visiting lists of the fashionable social leaders. The "society" of a district are the great panjandrums thereof.

"All the society of the district were present at the prince's ball."—*Newspaper paragraph*, December, 1885.

Sock [*comedy*]. The Greek comic actors used to wear a sandal and sock. The difference between the sock and the tragic buskin was this—the sock went only to the ankle, but the buskin extended to the knee. (*See* BUSKIN.)

"Then to the well-trod stage anon,
If Jonson's learned sock be on."
Milton: L'Allegro.

Sock a Corpse (*To*). To shroud it. (French, *sac*, a cerement or shroud.)

"1591. Item paid for a sheet to sock a poor man that died at Byneons, 1s. 6d."—*Parish Register.*

Soc'rates. The greatest of the ancient philosophers, whose chief aim was to amend the morals of his countrymen, the Athe'nians. Cicero said of him that "he brought down philosophy from the heavens to earth;" and he was certainly the first to teach that "the proper study of mankind is man." Socrates resisted the unjust sentence of the senate, which condemned to death the Athenian generals for not burying the dead at the battle of Arginu'sæ.

"Socra'tes—
Who, firmly good in a corrupted state,
Against the rage of tyrants single stood
Invincible."   *Thomson: Winter.*

Socrates used to call himself "the midwife of men's thoughts." Out of his intellectual school sprang those of Plato and the Dialectic system; Euclid and the Megaric; Aristippos and the Cyrena'ic; Antis'thenes and the Cynic.

Sodom. *Apples of Sodom* or *mad apples*. Strabo, Tacitus, and Josephus describe them as beautiful externally and filled with ashes. These "apples"

are in reality gall-nuts produced by the insect called *Cynips insa'na.*

Sof'farides (3 syl.). A dynasty of four kings, which lasted thirty-four years and had dominion over Khorassan, Seïstan, Fars, etc. (873-907); founded by Yacoub ebn Laïth, surnamed *al Soffar* (the brazier), because his father followed that trade in Seïstan.

Soft. *He's a soft*—half a fool. The word originally meant effeminate, unmanly; hence soft in brains, silly, etc., "soft in courage." (3 *Henry VI.*, ii. 2.)

Soft Sawder. Flattery, adulation. A play is intended between solder (pronounced *sawder*) and sawder, a compound of *saw* (a saying). Soft solder, a composition of tin and lead, is used for soldering zinc, lead, and tin; hard solder for brass, etc. (French, *soudure*, Latin, *solïdus*.)

Soft Soap. Flattery, complimentary words. (*See* SOAPY SAM.)

Soft as Soap—as "silk," as "velvet." (*See* SIMILES.)

Soft Fire makes Sweet Malt (*A*). Too fierce a fire would burn malt and destroy its sweetness, and too much hurry or precipitation spoils work. "Soft and fair goes far;" "Love me little, love me long;" "Slow and steady wins the race;" "He who is in haste fishes in an empty pond;" "The more haste the worse speed;" "He who walks too hastily will stumble in a plain way;" "Hastily and well never met;" "It is good to have a hatch before the door;" "Hasty climbers have sudden falls."

Soft Words Butter no Parsnips, or "Fair words," etc. Saying "Be thou fed" will not feed a hungry man. "Good words will not fill a sack." To "butter parsnips" means also "*dorer la pilule*" ("soft words will not gild the pill of distress").

Softly. *To walk softly.* To be out of spirits. In Greece, mourners for the dead used to cut off their hair, go about muffled, and walk softly to express want of spirit and strength. When Elijah denounced the judgments of heaven against Ahab, that wicked king "fasted, and lay in sackcloth, and went softly" to show that his strength was exhausted with sorrow (1 Kings xxi. 27). Isaiah says, "I shall go softly all my years in the bitterness of my soul" (xxxviii. 15). The Psalmist says, "My clothing was sackcloth . . . I walked as [for] a friend or brother." The French *Je vais douce-ment* means precisely the same thing: "I go softly," because I am indisposed, out of sorts, or in low spirits.

Softy. A soft, simple person.

"She were but a softy after all."—*Mrs. Gaskell: Sylvia's Lovers*, chap. xv.

Soho! The cry made by huntsmen when they uncouple the dogs in hunting the hare. Also to pointers and setters when they make a point. Tally-ho! (*q.v.*) is the cry when a fox breaks cover. *So!* or *see!* is to call attention, and *ho!* is virtually "hie after him."

" Now is the fox drevin to hole. Hoo to hym!
    Hoo! Hoo!
For and he acpe out he will you alle undo."
        Excerpta Historica, p. 279.

" If ye hounte at the hare, ye shall say, atte un-coupling, *hors de couple, avaunt!* And after, three times, *Sohow! Sohow! Sohow!*"—*A fifteenth-century translation of Reliquæ Antiquæ.*

" When a stag breaks covert the cry is 'tayho!' ... when a hare ... 'soho!'"—*Herbert: Field Sports*, vol. iii. appendix B, p. 313.

⁂ Of course "Ho!" is often used merely to call attention. Thus we say to one in advance, "Ho! stop!" and " Ho! every one that thirsteth, come ye to the waters" (Isaiah lv. 1). This use of the word is a contracted form of *haloo!* In the hunting-field " So-ho " is doubt-less a cry to encourage the dogs to follow up the quarry.

Soi-disant (French). Self-styled, would-be.

Soil. *To take soil.* A hunting term, signifying that the deer has taken to the water. Soil, in French, is the mire in which a wild boar wallows. (Danish, *söl*, mire; Swedish, *söla*, to wallow.)

" Fida went downe the dale to seeke the hinde,
And founde her taking soyle within a flood."
        Browne: Britannia's Pastorals, i. 84.

Soil the Milk before Using It. Yorkshire for " Sile the milk, etc."—*i.e.* strain it, or skim it. A sile is a sieve or strainer.

" Take a handeful of sauge, and stampe it, and temper it with hate ale, and sythene syle it thorowe a hate clothe."—*MS. Lincoln*, A i. 17 f 281.

" Drink the licoure siled thorgh a clothe."—*MS. in Mr. Pettigrew's possession* (fifteenth century).

So'journ (2 syl.) is the Italian *sog-giorno—i.e.* sub-giorno; Latin, *sub-diur-nus* (for a day, temporally).

Sol (Latin). The sun.

" And when Dan Sol to slope his wheels began."
        Thomson: Castle of Indolence, canto i.

Sol. The term given by the ancient alchemists to gold. Silver was *luna*.

Sol in the Edda was the daughter of Mundilfori, and sister of Ma'ni. She was so beautiful that at death she was placed in heaven to drive the sun-chariot. Two horses were yoked to it, named Arvakur and Alsvith (*watchful* and *rapid*). (*Scandinavian mythology.*) (*See* MANI.)

Sol-fa. (*See* DO, RE, etc.)

Solan Goose. The gannet. (French, *Oie de Soland* (*ou*) *d'Écosse;* Icelandic, *sula*.)

Sola'no. *Ask no favour during the Solano* (Spanish). Ask no favour during a time of trouble, panic, or adversity. The Solano of Spain is a south-east wind, extremely hot, and loaded with fine dust. It produces giddiness and irritation. Called the Sirocco in Italy.

Solatium (*A*). A recompense; a sop; a solace. (Latin, *solātium*.)

" It may be that Mr. Elden will be persuaded to take one, by way of solatium for his defeat in Somersetshire."—*Newspaper paragraph*, December, 1885.

Soldan or **Sowdan.** A corruption of sultan, meaning in mediæval romance the Saracen king; but, with the usual inaccuracy of these writers, we have the Soldan of Egypt, the Soudan of Persia, the Sowdan of Babylon, etc., all repre-sented as accompanied by grim Saracens to torment Christians.

The Soldan, meant for Felipe of Spain, who used all his power to bribe and seduce the subjects of Elizabeth. Queen Mercilla sent to negotiate a peace, but the ambassador sent was treated like a dog, referring to Felipe's detention of the deputies sent by the States of Hol-land. Sir Artegal demands of the sol-dan the release of the damsel " held as wrongful prisoner," and the soldan " swearing and banning most blasphe-mously," mounts his " high chariot," and prepares to maintain his cause. Prince Arthur encounters him " on the green," and after a severe combat uncovers his shield, at sight of which the soldan and all his followers take to flight. The " swearing and banning" refer to the excommunications thundered out against Elizabeth; the " high chariot" is the Spanish Arma'da; the " green" is the sea; the " uncovering of the shield" in-dicates that the Arma'da was put to flight, not by man's might, but by the power of God. *Flavit Jehovah et dis-sipa'ti sunt* (God blew, and they were scattered). (*Spenser: Faërie Queene*, v. 8.)

Soldats (*Des*). Money. Shakespeare, in *The Merry Wives of Windsor*, ii. 2, has " Money is a good soldier, sir, and will on." Doubtless the French use of the word is derived from the proverbial truth that "Money is the sinews of war," combined with a pun on the word *solidus* (the pay of a soldier). The Norman *sould* (i.e. *sould*) means "wages;" Swedish, *besolda*, to pay; Danish, *besolde*, to pay wages; the French *soldat*, our *soldier*, a hireling or mercenary, and the French *sol* or *sou*.

Soldier originally meant a hireling or mercenary; one paid a *solidus* for military service; but hireling and soldier convey now very different ideas. (*See above.*)

To come the old soldier over one. To dictate peremptorily and profess superiority of knowledge and experience.

Soldier's Heart. A complaint common in the English army, indicated by a weak voice and great feebleness of the chest, for which soldiers are discharged. It is said to be the result of the present system of drill, which enforces expansion of the chest by restraining free breathing.

Soldiers' Battles (*The*). Malplaquet, 1709, and Inkermann, 1854, were both "soldiers' battles."

Soldiers of Fortune. Chevaliers de l'industrie; men who live by their wits. Referring to those men in mediæval times who let themselves for hire into any army.

"His father was a soldier of fortune, as I am a sailor."—*Sir W. Scott : The Antiquary*, chap. xx.

Soldiering. A barrack term for furbishing up of accoutrements.

"I got the screws last night, but I was busy soldiering till too late."—*J. H. Ewing : Story of a Short Life*, p. 35.

Solecism (3 syl.). Misapplication of words; an expression opposed to the laws of syntax; so called from the city of Soli, in Cilicia, where an Athenian colony settled, and forgot the purity of their native language. (*Suidas.*)

Sol'emn. Habitual, customary. (Latin, *sollemnis*, strictly speaking means "once a year," "annual," *solus-annus*.)

"Silent night with this her solemn bird" [*i.e.* the nightingale, the bird familiar to night].— *Milton : Paradise Lost*, v.

✸ Of course the usual meaning of "solemn" is devout; but an annual festival, like Good Friday, etc., may be both devout and serious. The Latin for "it is usual," is *solemne est*, and to "solemnise" is to celebrate an annual custom.

The Solemn Doctor. Henry Goethals

was so called by the Sorbonne. (1227-1293.)

Solemn League and Covenant, for the suppression of Popery and Prelacy, adopted by the Scotch Parliament in 1638, and accepted by the English in 1643. Charles II. swore to the Scotch that he would abide by it and therefore they crowned him in 1651 at Dunbar; but at the Restoration he not only rejected the covenant, but had it burnt by the common hangman.

Soler. An upper room, a loft, a garret. (Latin, *solarium*.)

"Hastily than went thai all,
And soght him in the maydens hall,
In chambers high, es noght at hide,
And in solers on ilka side."
Ywaine and Gawin, 807.

Solid Doctor. Richard Middleton, a cordelier; also called the *Profound Doctor*. (*-1304.)

Solingen. The Sheffield of Germany, famous for swords and fencing-foils.

Solomon. *The English Solomon.* James I., called by Sully "the wisest fool in Christendom." (1566, 1603-1625.)

Henry VII. was so called for his wise policy in uniting the York and Lancaster factions. (1457, 1485-1509.)

Solomon of France. Charles V., *le Sage.* (1337, 1364-1380.)

St. Louis or Louis IX. (1215, 1226-1270.)

Solomon's Carpet. (*See* CARPET.)

Solomon's Ring. The rabbins say Solomon wore a ring with a gem that told him all he desired to know.

Solon of Parnassus. So Voltaire called Boileau, in allusion to his *Art of Poetry.* (1636-1711.)

So long. Good-bye, till we meet again.

Sol'stice (2 syl.). The summer solstice is June 21st; the winter solstice is December 22nd; so called because, on arriving at the corresponding points of the ecliptic, the sun is stopped and made to approach the equator again. (Latin, *sol sistit* or *stat*, the sun stops.)

Sol'yman, king of the Turks (in *Jerusalem Delivered*), whose capital was Nice. Being driven from his kingdom, he fled to Egypt, and was there appointed leader of the Arabs (bk. ix.). He and Argantes were by far the most doughty of the pagan knights. Solyman was slain by Rinaldo (bk. xx.), and Argantes by Tancred.

Soma. The moon, born from the eyes of Atri, son of Brahma; made the sovereign of plants and planets. Soma ran away with Tara (*Star*), wife of Vrihaspata, preceptor of the gods, and Buddha was their offspring. (*Hindu mythology.*)

To drink the Soma. To become immortal. In the Vedic hymns the Soma is the moon-plant, the juice of which confers immortality, and exhilarates even the gods. It is said to be brought down from heaven by a falcon. (*Scandinavian mythology.*)

Somag'ia (singular *somagium*). Horse-loads. Italian, *soma*, a burden; *soma'ro*, a beast of burden, an ass. (*See* SUMPTER.)

Sombre'ro. A Spanish hat with a very wide brim.

Somerset. Anciently *Sumorsæte* or *Sumorsæt—i.e.* *Suth-mor-sæt* (south moor camp).

Som'erset or **Somersault.** A leap in which a person turns head over heels in the air and lights on his feet. (Latin, *super saltus;* French, *soubresaut.*) Sometimes a person will turn twice or thrice in the air before he touches the ground.

" First that could make love faces, or could do
  The valter's sombersalts."
            Donne: Poems, p. 300.

Somerset House occupies the site of a princely mansion built by Somerset the Protector, brother of Lady Jane Seymour, and uncle of Edward VI. At the death of Somerset on the scaffold it became the property of the Crown, and in the reign of James I. was called Denmark House in honour of Anne of Denmark, his queen. Old Somerset House was pulled down in the eighteenth century, and the present structure was erected by Sir William Chambers in 1776.

Somoreen. (*See* ZAMORIN.)

Son (or *descendant of*). Norman, *Fitz- ;* Gaelic, *Mac;* Welsh, *Ap-* (sometimes contracted into P, as P-richard); Irish, *O';* Hebrew and Arabic, *Ben-*, all prefixes: English, *-son;* Russian, *-vitch* or *-witch*, postfixes.

Son of Be'lial. One of a wicked disposition ; a companion of the wicked. (*See* Judges xix. 22.)

"Now the sons of Eli were sons of Belial, they knew not the Lord."—1 *Samuel* ii. 12.

Son of Dripping (*A*). A man cook, a turnspit.

"Yet, son of dripping . . . let us halt ;
Soft fires, the proverb tells us, make sweet malt."
       Peter Pindar: The Lousiad, canto ii.

Son of One Year. A child one year old ; similarly a " son of sixty years," etc. (Exodus xii. 5.)

Son of Perdition. Judas Iscariot. (John xvii. 12.)

Son of perdition. Antichrist, who not only draws others to perdition, but is himself devoted to destruction. (2 Thessalonians ii. 3.)

Son of the Morning. A traveller. An Oriental phrase, alluding to the custom of rising early in the morning to avoid the mid-day heat, when on one's travels.

Son of the Star [*Bar Cochab*]. A name assumed by Simon the Jew, in the reign of Hadrian, who gave himself out to be the " Star out of Jacob " mentioned in Numbers xxiv. 17.

Sons of God. Angels, genuine Christians, or believers who are the sons of God by adoption.

"As many as are led by the Spirit of God, they are the sons of God."—Romans viii. 14.

Sons of God. When Judæa was a theocracy the representative of God on earth was by the Jews called *god;* hence angels, rulers, prophets, and priests were called gods. Moses as the messenger of Jehovah was "a god to Pharaoh" (Exodus vii. 1) ; magistrates generally were called *gods;* thus it is said, "Thou shalt not revile the gods, nor curse the ruler of thy people" (Exodus xxii. 28). By a still further extension, anyone who gave a message to another was his god, because he " inspired him," as Moses was a god to Aaron his spokesman (Exodus iv. 16). Our Lord refers to this use of the word in John x. 34. (*See also* Genesis vi. 2, 4 ; Job i. 6 ; ii. 1 ; Psalm lxxxii. 6 ; Exodus iv. 22, 23 ; Hosea xi. 1.)

Sons of the Band. Soldiers rank and file. (2 Chronicles xxv. 13.)

Sons of the Mighty. Heroes. (Psalm xxix. 1.)

Sons of the Prophets. Disciples or scholars belonging to the " college of the prophets," or under instruction for the ministry. In this sense we call the University where we were educated our " Alma ma'ter." (*See* 1 Kings xx. 35.)

Sons of the Sorceress. Those who study and practise magic. (Isaiah lvii. 3.)

Song. *Father of modern French song.* Panard ; also called the " La Fontaine of the Vaudeville." (1691-1765.)

Song of Degrees. The fifteen Psalms, cxx. to cxxxiv. ; so called because they are prophetic of the return or "going up" from captivity. Some think there is a connection between these Psalms and the fifteen steps of the Temple porch. (Ezekiel xl. 22-26.) In the Revised Version called "Song of Ascents."

Song of Roland, the renowned nephew of Charlemagne, slain in the pass of Roncesvalles. At the battle of Hastings, Taillefer advanced on horseback before the invading army, and gave the signal for onset by singing this famous song.

" Taillefer, who sung well and loud,
  Came mounted on a charger proud ;
  Before the duke the minstrel sprang,
  And the *Song of Roland* sang."
  Brut of Wace (translated).

Song of Songs. The Canticles, or "Solomon's Song."

Sonna or **Sunna.** The Mishna or oral law of the Mahometans. Reland (*De Relig. Mahom.*, p. 54) says these traditions were orally delivered by Mahomet, and subsequently committed to writing. Albulpharn'gius asserts that Ali, the son-in-law and cousin of Mahomet, was set aside because he refused to regard the oral traditions of the prophet of the same authority as the Koran. (*Hist. Dynast.*, 182.) (Arabic, *sunna*, tradition.) (*See* SUNNITES.)

Sonnam'bula (*La*). (*See* AMINA, ELVINO.)

Sonnet. *Prince of the sonnet.* Joachim du Bellay, a French sonneteer (1524-1560) ; but Petrarch better deserves the title. (1334-1374.)

Sop. *A sop in the pan.* A *bonne-bouche*, tit-bit, dainty morsel ; a piece of bread soaked in the dripping of meat caught in a dripping-pan ; also a bribe. (*See below.*)
To give a sop to Cer'berus. To give a bribe, to quiet a troublesome customer. Cerberus is Pluto's three-headed dog, stationed at the gates of the infernal regions. When persons died the Greeks and Romans used to put a cake in their hands as a sop to Cerberus, to allow them to pass without molestation.

Soph. A student at Cambridge is a Freshman for the first term, a Junior Soph for the second year, and a Senior Soph for the third year. The word Soph is a contraction of "sophister," which is the Greek and Latin *sophistēs* (a sophist). At one time these students

had to maintain a given question in the schools by opposing the orthodox view of it. These opponencies are now limited to Law and Divinity degrees.

Sophi or **Safi** [*mystic*], applied in Persia to ascetics generally, was given to Sheik Juneyd u Dien, grandfather of Shah Ismail, a Mahometan sectary or Shiite, who claimed descent, through Ali, from the twelve saints.

So'phis. The twelfth dynasty of Persia, founded by Shah Ismail I., grandson of Sheik Juneyd (1509). (*See above.*)

Soph'ia (*St.*), at Constantinople, is not dedicated to a saint named Sophi'a, but to the "Logos," or Second Person of the Trinity, called *Hagia Sophia* (Sacred Wisdom).

Sophist, Sophistry, Sophism, Sophisticator, etc. These words have quite run from their legitimate meaning. Before the time of Pythagoras (B.C. 586-506) the sages of Greece were called *sophists* (wise men). Pythagoras out of modesty called himself a *philosopher* (a wisdom-lover). A century later Protag'oras of Abde'ra resumed the title, and a set of quibblers appeared in Athens who professed to answer any question on any subject, and took up the title discarded by the Wise Samian. From this moment sophos and all its family of words were applied to "wisdom falsely so called," and philo-sophos to the "modest search after truth."

Sorbon'ica. The public disputations sustained by candidates for membership of the Sorbonne. They began at 5 a.m. and lasted till 7 p.m.

Sorbonne. The institution of theology, science, and literature in Paris founded by Robert de Sorbon, Canon of Cambrai, in 1252. In 1808 the buildings were given to the University, and since 1821 have been the *Académie universitaire de Paris.*

Sorceress. (*See* CANIDIA, CIRCE, etc. etc.)

Sordello. A poem by Robert Browning, showing the conflict of a minstrel about the best way of making his influence felt, whether personally or by the power of song.

Sori'tes (Greek). A heaped-up or cumulative syllogism. The following will serve as an example :—
All men who believe shall be saved.

All who are saved must be free from sin.

All who are free from sin are innocent in the sight of God.

All who are innocent in the sight of God are meet for heaven.

All who are meet for heaven will be admitted into heaven.

Therefore all who believe will be admitted into heaven.

The famous Sorites of Themistocles was: That his infant son commanded the whole world, proved thus:—

My infant son rules his mother.
His mother rules me.
I rule the Athenians.
The Athenians rule the Greeks.
The Greeks rule Europe.
And Europe rules the world.

Sorrows of Werther. A novel by Goethe. The heroine is Charlotte.

Sortēs Bib'licæ. Same as the Sortēs Virgilia'næ (*q.v.*), only the Bible was substituted for the works of the poet.

Sortes Virgilia'næ. Telling one's fortune by consulting the Æne'id of Virgil. You take up the book, open it at random, and the passage you touch at random with your finger is the oracular response. Seve'rus consulted the book, and read these words : " Forget not thou, O Roman, to rule the people with royal sway." Gordia'nus, who reigned only a few days, hit upon this verse: " Fate only showed him on the earth, but suffered him not to tarry." But, certainly, the most curious instance is that given by Dr. Wellwood respecting King Charles I. and Lord Falkland while they were both at Oxford. Falkland, to amuse the king, proposed to try this kind of augury, and the king hit upon bk. iv. ver. 615-620, the gist of which passage is that " evil wars would break out, and the king lose his life." Falkland, to laugh the matter off, said he would show his Majesty how ridiculously the " lot " would foretell the next fate, and he lighted on book xi. ver. 152-181, the lament of Evander for the untimely death of his son Pallas. King Charles, in 1643, mourned over his noble friend, who was shot through the body in the battle of Newbury.

Sorts. *Out of sorts.* Not in good health and spirits. The French *être dérangé* explains the metaphor. If cards are out of sorts they are deranged, and if a person is out of sorts the health or spirits are out of order.

In printers' language it means out of

some particular letter, in which case they substitute for a time another letter.

To run upon sorts. In printing, said of work which requires an unusual number of certain letters, etc. ; as an index, which requires a disproportionate number of capitals.

Sos'ia. The living double of another, as the brothers Antiph'olus and brothers Dromio in the *Comedy of Errors*, and the Corsican brothers in the drama so called. Sosia is a servant of Amphit'-ryon, in Plautus's comedy so called. It is Mercury who assumes the double of Sosia, till Sosia doubts his own identity. Both Dryden and Molière have adapted this play to the modern stage, but the *Comedy of Errors* is based on another drama of the same author, called the *Menæchmi*. (*See* AMPHITRYON.)

Sotadics or **Sotad'ic Verse.** One that reads backwards and forwards the same, as " llewd did I live, and evil I did dwell." So called from Sot'ades, the inventor. These verses are also called palindromic. (*See* PALINDROME.)

N.B. ll is the old way of writing a capital L.

Sothic Year. The Persian year consists of 365 days, so that a day is lost in four years, and the lost bits in the course of 1,460 years amount to a year. This period of 1,460 years is called a *sothic period*, and the reclaimed year made up of the bits is called a *sothic year*. (Greek, *sothis*, the dog-star, at whose rising it commences.)

Soul. The Moslems fancy that it is necessary, when a man is bow-strung, to relax the rope a little before death occurs to let the soul escape. The Greeks and Romans seemed to think that the soul made its escape with life out of the death-wound.

Soul. The Moslems say that the souls of the faithful assume the forms of snow-white birds, and nestle under the throne of Allah until the resurrection.

Soul. Heracli'tus held the soul to be a spark of the stellar essence : " *scintilla stellaris essentiæ.*" (*Macrobius : Somnium Scipioris,* lib. i. cap. 14.)

> " Vital spark of heavenly flame,
> Quit, oh ! quit this mortal frame."
> *Pope : The Dying Christian to his Soul.*

Soul, in Egyptian hieroglyphics, is represented by several emblems, as a basket of fire, a heron, a hawk with a human face, and a ram.

Soul Cakes. Cakes given in Staffordshire and Cheshire on All Souls' Day, to the poor who go *a-souling*, *i.e.* begging for soul-cakes. The words used are—

" Soul, soul, for soul-cake
Pray you, good mistress, a soul cake."

Soul and Spirit. ἡ ψυχὴ (the soul) contains the passions and desires, which animals have in common with man. τὸ πνεῦμα (the spirit) is the highest and distinctive part of man. In 1 Thess. Paul says, " I pray God your whole spirit, soul, and body be preserved blameless unto the coming of our Lord Jesus Christ." (*See also* Heb. iv. 12 ; 1 Cor. ii. 14 and 15 ; xv. 45, 46.)

Soul of a Goose or **Capon.** The liver, called by the French *ame*. The renowned Strasbourg "*patés de foie gras*" are made of these souls.

" Draw out all the entrails . . . but leave the soul."—*Brigg: English Dictionary of Cookery.*

Sound, a narrow sea, is the Anglo-Saxon *sund;* hence such words as Bo-marsund, etc.

Sound Dues. A toll or tribute which was levied by the king of Denmark on all merchant vessels passing through the *Sound.* (Abolished 1857.)

Sound as a Bell. Quite sound. A cracked bell is useless as a bell.

" Blinde Fortune did so happily contrive,
That we, as sound as bells, did safe arive
At Dover." *Taylor's Workes.* ii. 22 (1630).

Sound as a Roach. Quite sound. A pun upon *roach* or *roche* the fish, and the French *roche*, a rock.

Soundings. In nautical language, the depths of water in rivers, harbours, along shores, etc.

Sour Grapes. Things despised because they are beyond our reach. Many men of low degree call titles and dignities " sour grapes ; " and men of no parts turn up their noses at literary honours. The phrase is from Æsop's fable called *The Fox and the Grapes.*

Sour Grapeism. An assumed contempt or indifference to the unattainable. (*See above.*)

" There, economy was always ' elegant,' and money-spending always ' vulgar' and ostentation —a sort of sour grapeism. which made us very peaceful and satisfied."—*Mrs. Gaskell: Cranford,* chap. i.

South-Sea Scheme or **Bubble.** A stock-jobbing scheme devised by Sir John Blunt, a lawyer. The object of the company was to buy up the National Debt, and to be allowed the sole privilege of trading in the South Seas. The £100 shares soon realised ten times that sum, but the whole bubble burst in 1720

and ruined thousands. (1710-1720.) The term is applied to any hollow scheme which has a splendid promise, but whose collapse will be sudden and ruinous. (*See* MISSISSIPPI BUBBLE.)

Southampton Street (London). So called in compliment to the noble family of that title, allied to the Bedford family, the proprietors.

Southampton's Wise Sons. In the early part of the present century, the people of Southampton cut a ditch for barges between Southampton and Red-bridge ; but as barges could go without paying dues through the "Southampton Water," the ditch or canal was never used. This wise scheme was compared to that of the man who cut two holes through the wall—one for the great cat and the other for its kitten.

Southern Gate of the Sun. The sign Capricornus or winter solstice. So called because it is the most southern limit of the sun's course in the ecliptic.

Soutras. The discourses of Buddha. (*See* TRIPITAKA.)

Sovereign: A strangely misspelled word, the last syllable being mistaken for the word *reign*. It is the Latin *supern* (supreme over all), with the *p* changed to *v*. The French *souverain* is nearer the Latin word ; Italian, *sovrano;* Spanish, *soberano.*

Sovereign, a gold coin of the value of twenty shillings, was first issued by Henry VIII., and so called because he was represented on it in royal robes.

Sow (to rhyme with "now"). *You have got the wrong sow by the ear*. Sow is a large tub with two ears or handles ; it is used for pickling or *sowsing*. The expression means, therefore, You have got hold of the wrong vessel, or, as the Latin phrase has it, " *Pro am'phorâ ur'ceus* " (You have brought me the little jug instead of the great gotch). French, *seau* (a bucket).

You have got the right sow by the ear. You have hit upon the very thing.

Sow. (*See* PIG IRON.)

Spa or **Spa Water.** A general name for medical springs. So called from Spa, in Belgium, in the seventeenth century the most fashionable watering-place in Europe.

Spade. *Why not call a spade a spade ?* Do not palliate his sins by euphemisms.

" We call a nettle but a nettle, and the faults of fools but folly."—*Shakespeare : Coriolanus*, ii. 1.
" I have learned to call wickedness by its own terms : a fig a fig, and a spade a spade."—*John Knox,*

Spades in cards. A corruption of the Spanish *spados*, pikes or swords, called by the French *piques* (pikes).

Spadish Language (*In*). In plain English without euphuism; calling a spade a "spade."

"Had I attempted to express my opinions in full 'Spadish' language, I should have had to say many harder things."—*Fra Olla.*

Spa'fiel'ds (London). So called from "the London Spa," the name of certain tea-gardens once celebrated for their "spa-water."

Spag'iric Art. Alchemy.

Spag'iric Food. Cagliostro's "elixir of immortal youth" was so called from the Latin word *spagir'icus* (chemical). Hence, chemistry is termed the "spag'-iric art," and a chemist is a spag'irist.

Spagnaletto [*the little Spaniard*]. José Ribera, the painter. Salva'tor Rosa and Guerci'no were two of his pupils. (1588-1656.)

Spaie. A red deer of the third year.

"The young male is called in the first yeere a *calfe*, in the second a *broket*, the third a *spaie*, the fourth a *stagon* or *stag*, the fifth a *great stag*, the sixth an *hart*, and so foorth unto his death."—*Harrison.*

Spain. *Château d'Espagne.* (*See* CASTLE.)

Patron saint of Spain. St. James the Greater, who is said to have preached the Gospel in Spain, where what are called his "relics" are preserved.

Span New. (*See* SPICK.)

Spaniel. The Spanish dog, from *español*, through the French.

Spanish Blades. A sword is called a tole'do, from the great excellence of the Toletan steel.

Spanish Brutus (*The*). Alfonzo Perez de Guzman (1258-1309). Lope de Vega has celebrated this hero. When besieged, he was threatened with the death of his son, who had been taken prisoner, unless he surrendered. Perez replied by throwing a dagger over the walls, and his son was put to death in his sight.

Spanish Main. The circular bank of islands forming the northern and eastern boundaries of the Caribbe'an Sea, beginning from Mosquito, near the isthmus, and including Jamaica, St. Domingo, the Leeward Islands, and the Windward Islands, to the coast of Vene-zue'la in South America.

"We turned conquerors, and invaded the main of Spain."—*Bacon.*

Spanish Money. Fair words and compliments. The Spanish government is a model of dishonest dealings, the byword of the commercial world, yet no man is more irate than a Spaniard if any imputation is laid to his charge as inconsistent with the character of a man of honour.

Spanish Worm. A nail concealed in a piece of wood, against which a carpenter jars his saw or chisel. So called from Spanish woods used in cabinet-work.

Spank (*A*). A slap to urge one to greater energy. (*See below.*)

Spanker (*A*). A fore-and-aft sail set upon the mizen-mast of a three-masted vessel, and the jigger-mast of a four-masted vessel. There is no spanker in a one- or two-masted vessel of any rig. A "spanker" used to be called a "driver." (*Supplied by an old sailor of long service.*)

Spanking. Large, rapid, strong; as a "spanking big fellow," a "spanking speed," a "spanking breeze." A nautical term. (*See above.*)

Spare the Rod and Spoil the Child. Solomon (Prov. xiii. 24) says: "He that spareth the rod hateth his son;" but Samuel Butler, in his *Hudibras* (pt. ii. canto 1, line 843), says:

" Love is a boy, by poets styled,
Then spare the rod, and spoil the child."

Sparkling Heat. Heat greater than *white* heat.

"There be several degrees of heat in a smith's forge, according to the purpose of their work : (1) a bloud-red heat ; (2) a white flame heat ; (3) a sparkling or welding heat, used to weld barrs or pieces of iron."—*Kennett : MS. Lansd.*, 1033, f. 388.

Spartan Dog. A blood-hound ; a blood-thirsty man.

" O Spartan dog,
More fell than anguish, hunger, or the sea."
Shakespeare : Othello, v. ii.

Spasmod'ic School. A name applied by Professor Aytoun to certain authors of the nineteenth century, whose writings are distinguished by spasmodic or forced conceits. Of this school the most noted are Carlyle, Bailey (author of *Festus*), Alexander Smith, Sydney Dobell, etc.

Speaker's Eye. *To catch the Speaker's eye.* The rule in the House of Commons is that the member whose rising to address the House is first observed by the Speaker is allowed precedence.

Speaking. *They are on speaking terms.* They just know each other.

They are not on speaking terms. Though they know each other, they do not even salute each other in the street, or say "How d'ye do?"

Speaking Heads and **Sounding Stones.**

(1) Jabel Nagus [*mountain of the bell*], in Arabia Petræa, gives out sounds of varying strength whenever the sand slides down its sloping flanks.

(2) The white dry sand of the beach in the isle of Eigg, of the Hebrides, produces, according to Hugh Miller, a musical sound when walked upon.

(3) The statue of Memnon, in Egypt, utters musical sounds when the morning sun darts on it.

(4) The speaking head of Orpheus, at Lesbos, is said to have predicted the bloody death which terminated the expedition of Cyrus the Great into Scythia.

(5) The head of Minos, brought by Odin to Scandinavia, is said to have uttered responses.

(6) Gerbert, afterwards Pope Sylvester II., constructed a speaking head of brass (tenth century).

(7) Albertus Magnus constructed an earthen head in the thirteenth century, which both spoke and moved. Thomas Aqui'nas broke it, whereupon the mechanist exclaimed, "There goes the labour of thirty years!"

(8) Alexander made a statue of Escula'pios which spoke, but Lucian says the sounds were uttered by a man concealed, and conveyed by tubes to the statue.

(9) The "ear of Dionysius" communicated to Dionysius, Tyrant of Syracuse, whatever was uttered by suspected subjects shut up in a state prison. This "ear" was a large black opening in a rock, about fifty feet high, and the sound was communicated by a series of channels not unlike those of the human ear.

Spear. Cairbar asks if Fingal comes in peace, to which Mor-annal replies: "In peace he comes not, king of Erin, I have seen his forward spear." If a stranger kept the point of his spear forward when he entered a strange land, it was a declaration of war; if he carried the spear on his shoulder with the point behind him, it was a token of friendship. (*Ossian: Temora*, i.)

Achilles' spear. Te'lephus, King of Mys'ia, in attempting to hinder the Greeks from marching through his country against Troy, was wounded by Achilles' spear, and was told by an oracle that the wound could be cured

only by the weapon that gave it; at the same time the Greeks were told that they would never reach Troy except by the aid of Te'lephus. So, when the Mys'ian king repaired to Achilles' tent, some of the rust of the spear was applied to the wound, and, in return for the cure which followed, Telephus directed the Greeks on their way to Troy.

" Telephus æterna consumptus tabe perisset
Si non quæ noc'uit dextra tulisset opem." *Ovid.*

The spear of Te'lephus could both kill and cure. (*Plutarch.*) (See *Achilles' spear.*)

The heavy spear of Valence was of great repute in the days of chivalry.

Arthur's spear. Rone or Ron.

To break a spear. To fight in a tournament.

Spear-half. The male line. The female line was called by the Anglo-Saxons the Spindle-half (*q.v.*).

Spear of Ithuriel (*The*), the slightest touch of which exposed deceit. Thus when Ithuriel touched with his spear Satan squatting like a toad close to the ear of Eve, the "toad" instantly resumed the form of Satan. (*Milton: Paradise Lost*, bk. iv. 810-814.)

"The acute pen of Lord Halles, which, like Ithuriel's spear, conjured so many shadows from Scottish history, dismissed among the rest those of Banquo and Fleance."—*Sir W. Scott.*

Special Pleading. Quibbling; making your own argument good by forcing certain words or phrases from their obvious and ordinary meaning. A pleading in law means a written statement of a cause *pro* and *con.*, and "special pleaders" are persons who have been called to the bar, but do not speak as advocates. They advise on evidence, draw up affidavits, state the merits and demerits of a cause, and so on. After a time most special pleaders go to the bar, and many get advanced to the bench.

Specie, Species, means simply what is visible. As things are distinguished by their visible forms, it has come to mean *kind* or *class.* As drugs and condiments at one time formed the most important articles of merchandise, they were called *species*—still retained in the French *épices*, and English *spices.* Again, as bank-notes represent money, money itself is called *specie*, the thing represented.

Spectacles, the device of Thackeray in drawings made by him. In *Punch*, vol. xx. No. 495, p. 8, is a butcher's boy chalking up "No Popery," and the tray forms a pair of spectacles, showing it was designed by Thackeray.

Spectre of the Brocken. The Brocken is the highest summit of the Hartz mountains in Hanover. This summit is at times enveloped in a thick mist, which reflects in a greatly magnified degree any form opposite at sunset. In one of De Quincey's opium-dreams there is a powerful description of the Brocken spectre.

Spectrum, Spectra, Spectre (Latin, *specto*, to behold). In optics a spectrum is the image of a sunbeam beheld on a screen, after refraction by one or more prisms. Spectra are the images of objects left on the eye after the objects themselves are removed from sight. A *spectre* is the apparition of a person no longer living or not bodily present.

Specu'late means to look out of a watch-tower, to spy about (Latin). Metaphorically, to look at a subject with the mind's eye, to spy into it; in *commerce*, to purchase articles which your mind has speculated on, and has led you to expect will prove profitable. (*Specula'ris lapis* is what we should now call window-glass.)

Speech. *Speech was given to conceal or disguise men's thoughts.* Voltaire. But erroneously fathered on Talleyrand.

Speed. A great punster, the serving-man of Valentine, one of the Two Gentlemen of Vero'na. Launce is the serving-man of Proteus, the other gentleman. (*Shakespeare : Two Gentlemen of Verona.*)

Spell (*A*), in workman's language, means a portion of time allotted to some particular work, and from which the men are relieved when the limited time expires.
To spell is to relieve another at his work.
Spell ho ! An exclamation to signify that the allotted time has expired, and men are to be relieved by another set.
A pretty good spell. A long bout or pull, as a "spell at the capstan," etc. (The German *spiel* means a performance as well as a play, game, or sport.)

Spellbinders. Orators who hold their audience spellbound. The word came into use in America in the presidential election of 1888.

"The Hon. Daniel Dougherty says : 'The proudest day of his life was when he beheld his name among the "spell-binders" who held the audience in rapture with their eloquence.' —*Liberty Review*, July 7th, 1894, p. 13.

Spelter. A commercial name for zinc. Also an abbreviation of spelter-solder.

Spence. A *salle à manger*, the room in which meals are taken, a dining-room; also a store-room or pantry. (*Dispensorium*, Old French *dispense*, a buttery.)

"The rest of the family held counsel in the spence."—*Sir W. Scott: The Monastery*, chap. xxx.

Spencer. An outer coat without skirts ; so named from the Earl Spencer, who wore this dress. (George III.)

Spendthrift. The Danish *thrift* is the noun of the word *thrive* (to increase or prosper). Shakespeare says, "I have a mind presages me such thrift" (increase, profit). As our frugal ancestors found *saving* the best way to grow rich, they applied the word to frugality and careful management. A spendthrift is one who spends the thrift or saving of his father, or, as Old Adam says, the "thrifty hire I saved." (*As You Like It.*)

Spenser (*Edmund*), called by Milton "the sage and serious Spenser." Ben Jonson, in a letter to Drummond, states that the poet "died for lake of bread." (1553-1599.)

Spenserian Metre (*The*). The metre in which Spenser's *Faërie Queene* is written. It is a stanza of nine iambic lines, all of ten syllables except the last, which is an Alexandrine. Only three different rhymes are admitted into a stanza, and these rhymes are thus disposed : Lines 1 and 3 rhyme ; lines 2, 4, 5, 7 rhyme ; lines 6, 8, 9 rhyme ; thus :—

```
1 - - - - - - - - - - ride
2 - - - - - - - - - - low
3 - - - - - - - - - - side
4 - - - - - - - - - - throw
5 - - - - - - - - - - snow
6 - - - - - - - - - - had
7 - - - - - - - - - - blow
8 - - - - - - - - - - lad
9 - - - - - - - - - - - - sad (an alex-
                              andrine).
```

Spent. Weary. A hunting term. A deer is said to be spent when it stretches out its neck, and is at the point of death. In sea language, a broken mast is said to be "spent."

Spheres. *The music or harmony of the spheres.* Pythag'oras, having ascertained that the pitch of notes depends on the rapidity of vibrations, and also that the planets move at different rates of motion, concluded that the sounds made by their motion must vary according to their different rates of motion. As all things in nature are harmoniously made, the different sounds must harmonise, and the combination he called the "harmony of the spheres." Kepler has a treatise on the subject.

Sphinx (*The Egyptian*). Half a woman and half a lion, said to symbolise the "rising of the Nile while the sun is in Leo and Virgo." This "saying" must be taken for what it is worth.

Sphinx. Lord Bacon's ingenious resolution of this fable is a fair specimen of what some persons call "spiritualising" incidents and parables. He says that the whole represents "science," which is regarded by the ignorant as "a monster." As the figure of the sphinx is heterogeneous, so the subjects of science "are very various." The female face "denotes volubility of speech;" her wings show that "knowledge like light is rapidly diffused;" her hooked talons remind us of "the arguments of science which enter the mind and lay hold of it." She is placed on a crag overlooking the city, for "all science is placed on an eminence which is hard to climb." If the riddles of the sphinx brought disaster, so the riddles of science "perplex and harass the mind."

You are a perfect sphinx—You speak in riddles. *You are nothing better than a sphinx*—You speak so obscurely that I cannot understand you. The sphinx was a sea-monster that proposed a riddle to the Thebans, and murdered all who could not guess it. Œdipus solved it, and the sphinx put herself to death. The riddle was this—

" What goes on four feet, on two feet, and three,
But the more feet it goes on the weaker it be?"

Spice. A small admixture, a flavouring; as, "He is all very well, but there's a spice of conceit about him." Probably the French *espèce*.

"God's bountè is all pure, without ony espece of evyll."—*Caxton: Mirrour of the World*, i.

Spick and Span New. Quite and entirely new. A *spic* is a spike or nail, and a *span* is a chip. So that a spick and span new ship is one in which every nail and chip is new. Halliwell mentions "span new." According to Dr. Johnson, the phrase was first applied to cloth just taken off the *spannans* or stretchers. (Dutch, *spikspelderniew*.)

Spider.
Bruce and the spider. In the spring of 1305, Robert Bruce was crowned at Scone king of Scotland, but, being attacked by the English, retreated first to the wilds of Athole, and then to the little island of Rathlin, off the north coast of Ireland, and all supposed him to be dead. While lying perdu in this island, he one day noticed a spider near his bed try six times to fix its web on a beam in the ceiling. "Now shall this spider (said Bruce) teach me what I am to do, for I also have failed six times." The spider made a seventh effort and succeeded; whereupon Bruce left the island (in the spring of 1307), collecting together 300 followers, landed at Carrick, and at midnight surprised the English garrison in Turnberry Castle; he next overthrew the Earl of Gloucester, and in two years made himself master of well nigh all Scotland, which Edward III. declared in 1328 to be an independent kingdom. Sir Walter Scott tells us, in his *Tales of a Grandfather* (p. 26, col. 2), that in remembrance of this incident, it has always been deemed a foul crime in Scotland for any of the name of Bruce to injure a spider.

" I will grant you, my father, that this valiant burgess of Perth is one of the best-hearted men that draws breath . . . He would be as loth, in wantonness, to kill a spider, as if he were a kinsman to King Robert of happy memory."—*Sir Walter Scott: Fair Maid of Perth*, ch. ii.

Frederick the Great and the spider. While Frederick II. was at Sans Souci, he one day went into his ante-room, as usual, to drink a cup of chocolate, but set his cup down to fetch his handkerchief from his bedroom. On his return he found a great spider had fallen from the ceiling into his cup. He called for fresh chocolate, and next moment heard the report of a pistol. The cook had been suborned to poison the chocolate, and, supposing his treachery had been found out, shot himself. On the ceiling of the room in Sans Souci a spider has been painted (according to tradition) in remembrance of this story.

Spider. When Mahomet fled from Mecca he hid in a certain cave, and the Koreishites were close upon him. Suddenly an acacia in full leaf sprung up at the mouth of the cave, a wood-pigeon had its nest in the branches, and a spider had woven its net between the tree and the cave. When the Koreishites saw this, they felt persuaded that no one could have recently passed that way, and went on.

Spider anciently supposed to envenom everything it touched. In the examination into the murder of Sir Thomas Overbury, one of the witnesses deposed "that the countess wished him to get the strongest poison that he could . . ." Accordingly he brought seven great spiders.

" There may be in the cup
A spider steeped, and one may drink, depart,
And yet partake no venom."
Shakespeare: Winter's Tale, ii, 1.

Spider. According to old wives' fable, fever may be cured by wearing a spider in a nutshell round the neck.

"Cured by wearing a spider hung round one's neck in a nutshell."   *Longfellow: Evangeline.*

Spiders will never set their webs on a cedar roof. (*Caughey : Letters*, 1845.)

Spiders spin only on dark days.

" The subtle spider never spins,
But on dark days, his slimy gins."
  S. *Butler : On a Nonconformist*, iv.

Spider. The shoal called the Shambles at the entrance of Portland Roads was very dangerous before the breakwater was constructed. According to legend, at the bottom of the gigantic shaft are the wrecks of ships seized and sunk by the huge spider *Kraken*, called also the *fish-mountain.*

Spid'ireen or **Spidereen.** The anonyma of ships. If a sailor is asked what ship he belongs to, and does not choose to tell, he will say, "The spidireen frigate with nine decks." Officers who will not tell their quarters, give B.K.S. as their address. (*See* B.K.S.)

Spigot. *Spare at the spigot and spill at the bung.* To be parsimonious in trifles and wasteful in great matters, like a man who stops his beer-tub at the vent-hole and leaves it running at the bung-hole.

Spilt Milk. (*See* CRY.)

Spindle-half. The female line. A Saxon term. The spindle was the pin on which the thread was wound from the spinning-wheel. (*See* SPEAR-HALF.)

Spinning Jenny. Jennie is a diminutive and corruption of engine ('ginie). A little engine invented by James Hargreaves, a Lancashire weaver, in 1767. It is usually said that he so called it after his wife and daughter; but the name of his wife was Elizabeth, and he never had a daughter.

Spino'za's System. The "system of Spinoza" is that matter is eternal, and that the universe is God.

Spinster. An unmarried woman. The fleece which was brought home by the Anglo-Saxons in summer, was spun into clothing by the female part of each family during the winter. King Edward *the Elder* commanded his daughters to be instructed in the use of the distaff. Alfred the Great, in his will, calls the female part of his family the *spindle side ;* and it was a regularly received axiom with our frugal forefathers, that no young woman was fit to

be a wife till she had spun for herself a set of body, table, and bed linen. Hence the maiden was termed a spinner or spinster, and the married woman a wife or "one who has been a spinner." (Anglo-Saxon, *wif*, from the verb *wyfan* or *wefan*, to weave.)

⁂ The armorial bearings of women are not painted on a *shield*, like those of men, but on a *spindle* (called a "lozenge"). Among the Romans the bride carried a distaff, and Homer tells us that Kryseis was to spin and share the king's bed.

Spirit. *To give up the spirit.* To die. At death the "spirit is given back to Him who gave it."

Spirit-writing. Pneumatology. Alleged visible writing by spirits.

Spirits. Inflammable liquors obtained by distillation. This is connected with the ancient notion of bottle-imps (*q.v.*), whence these liquors were largely used in the black arts.

Spirits. There are four spirits and seven bodies in alchemy. The spirits are quicksilver, orpiment, sal-ammoniac, and brimstone. (*See* SEVEN BODIES.)

" The first sp'rit quyksilver called is:
  The second orpiment : the thrid I wis
Sal armoni'ac ; and the ferth bremstoon."
Chaucer : Prol. of the Chanounes Yemanes Tale.

Spirits. There were formerly said to be three in animal bodies :—

(1) The animal spirits, seated in the brain ; they perform through the nerves all the actions of sense and motion.

(2) The vital spirits, seated in the heart, on which depend the motion of the blood and animal heat.

(3) The natural spirits, seated in the liver, on which depend the temper and "spirit of mind."

Spirits (*Elemental*). There are four sorts of elemental spirits, which rule respectively over the four elements. The *fire* spirits are SALAMANDERS ; the *water* spirits UNDINES (2 syl.) ; the *air* spirits SYLPHS ; and the *earth* spirits GNOMES (1 syl.).

Spirited Away. Kidnapped ; allured. Kidnappers who beguiled orphans, apprentices, and others on board ship in order to sell them to planters in Barbadoes and Virginia, were called "spirits." Mr. Doyle (*English in America*, p. 512) finds the word used in this sense in official papers as early as 1657. (*Notes and Queries*, 17th December, 1892.)

Spiritual Mother. So Joanna Southcott is addressed by her disciples. (1750-1814.)

Spiritualism or **Spiritism.** A system which started up in America in 1848. It professes that certain living persons have the power of holding communion with the " spirits of the dead." Nineteenth century spiritualism probably owes its origin to Andrew Jackson Davis, "the seer of Poughkeepsie."

Spirt or **Spurt.** A sudden convulsive effort (Swedish, *spruta ;* Danish, *sprude ;* Icelandic, *spretta,* to start ; our *spout,* to throw up water in a jet).

Spitalfields (London). A spital is a charitable foundation for the care of the poor, and these were the fields of the almshouse founded in 1197 by Walter Brune and his wife Rosia.

Spite of His Teeth (*In*). In spite of opposition ; though you snarl and show your teeth like an angry dog.

Spitfire. An irascible person, whose angry words are like fire spit from the mouth of a fire-eater.

Spitting for Luck. Boys often spit on a piece of money given to them for luck. Boxers spit upon their hands for luck. Fishwomen not unfrequently spit upon their hansel (*i.e.* the first money they take) for luck. Spitting was a charm against fascination among the ancient Greeks and Romans. Pliny says it averted witchcraft, and availed in giving to an enemy a shrewder blow.

" Thrice on my breast I spit to guard me safe
  From fascinating charms." *Theocritus.*

Spittle or **Spital.** An hospital.

" A spittle or hospitall for poore folks diseased ; a spittle, hospitall, or lazarhouse for lepers."— *Baret : Alveaire* (1580).

Spittle Sermons. Sermons preached formerly at the Spittle in a pulpit erected expressly for the purpose. Subsequently they were preached at Christchurch, City, on Easter Monday and Tuesday. Ben Jonson alludes to them in his *Underwoods,* ap. Gifford, viii. 414.

Splay is a contraction of display (to unfold ; Latin, *dis-plico*). A *splay window* is one in a V-shape, the external opening being very wide, to admit as much light as possible, but the inner opening being very small. A *splay-foot* is a foot displayed or turned outward. A *splay-mouth* is a wide mouth, like that of a clown.

Spleen was once believed to be the seat of ill-humour and melancholy. The herb spleenwort was supposed to remove these splenic disorders.

Splendid Shilling. A mock-heroic poem by John Philips. (1676-1708.)

Splice. To marry. Very strangely, " splice " means to *split* or *divide.* The way it came to signify *unite* is this : Ropes' ends are first untwisted before the strands are interwoven. Joining two ropes together by interweaving their strands is "splicing" them. Splicing wood is joining two boards together, the term being borrowed from the sailor. (German, *spleissen,* to split.)

Splice the Main Brace. (*See* MAIN BRACE.)

To get spliced is to get married or tied together as one.

Spoke (verb). When members of the House of Commons and other debaters call out *Spoke,* they mean that the person who gets up to address the assembly has spoken already, and cannot speak again except in explanation of something imperfectly understood.

Spoke (noun). *I have put my spoke into his wheel.* I have shut him up. The allusion is to the pin or spoke used to lock wheels in machinery.

Don't put your spoke into my wheel. Don't interfere with my business ; Let my wheel turn, and don't you put a pin in to stop it or interrupt its movement. The Dutch have " *Een spaak in t'wiel steeken,*" to thwart a purpose.

When solid wheels were used, the driver was provided with a pin or spoke, which he thrust into one of the three holes made to receive it, to skid the cart when it went down-hill. The carts used by railway navvies, and tram-waggons used in collieries, still have a wheel " spoked " in order to skid it.

Sponge. *Throw up the sponge.* Give up ; confess oneself beaten. The metaphor is from boxing matches.

" We must stand up to our fight now, or throw up the sponge. There's no two ways about the matter."—*Boldrewood : Robbery under Arms,* chap. xxxi.

" We hear that the followers of the Arab chief have thrown up the sponge."—*Newspaper paragraph,* April 2nd, 1888.

Spontaneous Combustion. Taking fire without the intervention of applied heat. Greasy rags heaped together, hay stacked in a damp state, coal-dust in coal mines, cinders and ashes in dust bins, are said to be liable to spontaneous combustion.

Spoon. (*See* APOSTLE-SPOONS.)
He hath need of a long spoon that

eateth with the devil. Shakespeare alludes to this proverb in the *Comedy of Errors,* iv. 3; and again in the *Tempest,* ii. 2, where Stephano says: "Mercy! mercy! this is a devil . . . I will leave him, I have no long spoon."

> "Therefor behoveth him a ful long spoon
> That schal ete with a feend."
> *Chaucer: The Squieres Tale,* 10,916.

Spoon (*A*). One who is spoony, or sillily love-sick on a girl.

"He was awful spoons at the time."—*Truth (Queer Story),* March 25th, 1886.

Spooning, in rowing, is dipping the oars so little into the water as merely to skim the surface. The resistance being very small, much water is thrown up and more disturbed.

Spoony. Lovingly soft. A seaphrase. When a ship under sail in a sea-storm cannot bear it, but is obliged to put right before the wind, she is said to "spoon;" so a young man under sail in the sea of courtship "spoons" when he cannot bear it, but is obliged to put right before the gale of his lady's "eyebrow."

Sporran (Gaelic). The heavy pouch worn in front of the philibeg of a Highlander's kilt.

Sport a Door or **Oak.** To keep an outer door shut. In the Universities the College rooms have two doors, an outer and an inner one. The outer door is called the *sporting door,* and is opened with a key. When shut it is to give notice to visitors that the person who occupies the rooms is not at home, or is not to be disturbed. The word *sport* means to exhibit to the public, as, "to sport a new equipage," "to sport a new tile [hat]," etc.; whence to have a new thing, as "to sport an ægro'tat [sick-leave];" or merely to show to the public, as "sport a door or oak." The word is a contraction of *support.* (French, *supporter,* to sustain, carry; Latin, *supporto.*)

Sporting Seasons in England.

Those marked thus (*) are fixed by Act of Parliament.

*Black Game,** from August 20th to December 10th; but in Somerset, Devon, and New Forest, from September 1st to December 10th.
Blackcock, August 20th to December 10th.
Buck hunting, August 20th to September 17th.
*Bustard,** September 1st to March 1st.
Red Deer hunted, August 20th to September 30th.
Male Deer (Ireland),** October 20th to June 10th.
Fallow Deer (Ireland), June 20th to Michaelmas.
Eels, (about) April 20th to October 28th.
Fox hunting, (about) October to Lady Day.
Fox Cubs, August 1st to the first Monday in November.
Grouse shooting,** August 12th to December 10th.
Hares, March 12th to August 12th.
Hind, hunted in October and again between April 10th and May 20th.

Moor Game (Ireland),** August 20th to December 10th.
Oyster season, August 5th to May.
Partridge shooting,** September 1st to February 1st.
Pheasant shooting,** October 1st to February 1st.
Ptarmigan, August 12th to December 10th.
Quail, August 12th to January 10th.
Rabbits, between October and March. Rabbits, as vermin, are shot at any time.
*Salmon,** February 1st to September 1st.
Salmon, rod fishing,** November 1st to September 1st.
Trout fishing, May 1st to September 10th.
Trout, in the Thames, April 1st to September 10th.
Woodcocks, (about) November to January.

For Ireland and Scotland there are special game-laws. (*See* TIME OF GRACE.)

N.B. Game in *England:* hare, pheasant, partridge, grouse, and moor-fowl; in *Scotland,* same as England, with the addition of ptarmigan; in *Ireland,* same as England, with the addition of deer, black-game, landrail, quail, and bustard.

Spouse (*Spouze,* 1 syl.) means one whom sponsors have answered for. In Rome, before marriage, the friends of the parties about to be married met at the house of the woman's father to settle the marriage contract. This contract was called *sponsa'lia* (espousals): the man and woman were *spouses.* The contracting parties were each asked, "*An spondes*" (Do you agree?), and replied "*Spondeo*" (I agree).

Spouse of Jesus. "Our seraphic mother, the holy Tere'sa," born at Av'ila in 1515, is so called in the Roman Catholic Church.

Spout. *Up the spout.* At the pawnbroker's. In allusion to the "spout" up which brokers send the articles ticketed. When redeemed they return down the spout—*i.e.* from the store-room to the shop.

"As for spoons, forks, and jewellery, they are not taken so readily to the smelting-pot, but to wellknown places where there is a pipe [spout] which your lordships may have seen in a pawnbroker's shop. The thief taps the pipe, it is lifted up, and in the course of a minute a hand comes out, covered with a glove, takes up the article, and gives out the money for it."—*Lord Shaftesbury: The Times,* March 1st, 1869.

Sprat. *To bait with a sprat to catch a mackerel.* To give a small thing under the hope of getting something much more valuable. The French say, "A pea for a bean." (*See* GARVIES.)

Spread-eagle (*To*). To fly away like a spread-eagle; to beat. (*Sporting term.*)

"You'll spread-eagle all the [other] cattle in a brace of shakes."—*Ouida: Under Two Flags,* chap. ix.

Spread-eagle Oratory. "A compound of exaggeration, effrontery, bombast, and extravagance, mixed with metaphors, platitudes, threats, and irreverent appeals flung at the Almighty."

(*North American Review*, November, 1858.)

Spring Gardens (London). So called from a playfully contrived waterwork, which, on being unguardedly pressed by the foot, sprinkled the bystanders with water. (James I., etc.)

Spring Tide. The tide that springs or leaps or swells up. These full tides occur at the new and full moon, when the attraction of both sun and moon act in a direct line, as thus—

☾ ◯ ✳ or ✳ ⊕ ●

Sprout-kele. The Saxon name for February. Kele is colewort, the great pot-wort of the ancient Saxons ; the broth made thereof was also called *kele*. This important pottage herb begins to sprout in February. (*Verstegan*.)

Spruce. Smart, dandified. Hall tells us it is a contraction of Prussian-like, *à la Prusse*, and gives the subjoined quotation :—

"After them came Sir Edward Hayward, and with him Sir Thomas Parre, in doublets of crimson velvet, faced on the breast with chains of silver, and over that short cloaks of crimson satin, and on their heads hats after dancers' fashion, with feathers in them. They were apparelled after the fashion of Prussia or Spruce."

∵ In confirmation of this it may be mentioned that "Spruce leather" is certainly a corruption of Prussian leather ; Spruce-beer is beer made from the Spruce or Prussian fir, and Danzig, in Prussia, is famous for the beverage.

Spun (*To be*). Exhausted, undone, ruined.

"I shall be spun. There is a voice within
    Which tells me plainly I am all undone ;
For though I toil not, neither do I spin,
    I shall be spun."   *Robert Murray* (1863).

Spun Out. As "the tale was spun out" that is, prolonged to a disproportionate length. It is a Latin phrase, and the allusion is to the operation of spinning and weaving. Cicero says, "*Tenu'o deducta poemata filo*"—that is, poems spun out to a fine thread.

Spunging House. A victualling house where persons arrested for debt are kept for twenty-four hours, before lodging them in prison. The houses so used are generally kept by a bailiff, and the person lodged is spunged of all his money before he leaves.

Spur Money. Money given to redeem a pair of spurs. Gifford says, in the time of Ben Jonson, in consequence of the interruptions to divine service occasioned by the ringing of the spurs worn, a small fine was imposed on those who entered church in spurs. The enforcement of this fine was committed to the beadles and chorister-boys.

Spurs. *Ripon spurs.* The best spurs were made at Ripon, in Yorkshire.

"If my spurs be not right Rippon."
        Ben Jonson: Staple of News.

The Battle of Spurs. The battle of Guinnegate, fought in 1513, between Henry VIII. and the Duc de Longueville. So called because the French used their spurs in flight more than their swords in fight.

The Battle of the Spurs. The battle of Courtrai, in 1302. So called because the victorious Flemings gathered from the field more than 700 gilt spurs, worn by French nobles slain in the fight.

To dish up the spurs. In Scotland, during the times of the Border feuds, when any of the great families had come to the end of their provisions the lady of the house sent up a pair of spurs for the last course, to intimate that it was time to put spurs to the horses and make a raid upon England for more cattle.

"He dishes up the spurs in his helpless address, like one of the old Border chiefs with an empty larder."—*The Daily Telegraph.*

To win his spurs. To gain the rank of knighthood. When a man was knighted, the person who dubbed him presented him with a pair of gilt spurs.

Spy. Vidocq, the spy in the French Revolution, was a short man, vivacious, vain, and talkative. He spoke of his feats with real enthusiasm and gusto.

Spy (of *Vanity Fair*). Leslie Ward, successor of "Ape" (Pellegrini, the caricaturist).

Spy Wednesday. The Wednesday before Good Friday, when Judas bargained to become the spy of the Jewish Sanhedrim. (Matt. xxvi. 3-5, 14-16.)

Squab Pie. Pie made of squabs— *i.e.* young pigeons ; also a pie made of mutton, apples, and onions.

"Cornwall squab-pie, and Devon white-pot brings,
And Leicester beans and bacon, fit for kings."
        King : Art of Cookery.

Squad. *The awkward squad* consists of recruits not yet fitted to take their places in the regimental line. Squad is a mere contraction of squadron.

Squalls. *Look out for squalls.* Expect to meet with difficulties. A nautical term.

"If this is the case, let the ministry look out for squalls."—*Newspaper paragraph*, July 6th, 1894

Square. To put oneself in the attitude of boxing, to quarrel. (Welsh, *cwer'*—i.e. *cweryl, cwerylu*, to quarrel.)

> " Are you such fools
> To square for this ? "
> *Shakespeare: Titus Andronicus*, ii. 1.

Square the Circle. To attempt an impossibility. The allusion is to the mathematical question whether a circle can be made which contains precisely the same area as a square. The difficulty is to find the precise ratio between the diameter and the circumference. Popularly it is 3·14159 . . . . the next decimals would be 26537, but the numbers would go on *ad infinitum*.

Squash. A sort of pumpkin, called by the American Indians *ascutaquash*.

Squib (*A*). A political joke, printed and circulated at election times against a candidate, with intent of bringing him into ridicule, and influencing votes.

> " Parodies, lampoons, rightly named squibs, fire and brimstone, ending in smoke, with a villainous smell of saltpetre."—*Dean Hole: Rose-garden and Pulpit.*

Squint-eyed [*Guerci'no*]. Gian Francesco Barbie'ri, the great painter. (1590-1666.)

Squintife'go. Squinting.

> " The squintifego maid
> Of Isis awe thee, lest the gods for sin
> Should with a swelling dropsy stuff thy skin."
> *Dryden: Fifth Satire of Juvenal.*

Squire of Dames. Any cavalier who is devoted to ladies. Spenser, in his *Faërie Queene* (bk. iii. chap. vii.) introduces the "squire," and records his adventure.

Sta'bat Ma'ter. The celebrated Latin hymn on the Crucifixion, which forms a part of the service during Passion week, in the Roman Catholic Church. It was composed by Jacopone, a Franciscan of the thirteenth century, and has been set to music by Pergole'se, also by Rossi'ni.

In the catalogue of the Library of Burgundy, No.13,993, is the following:—

> " Item. fol. 77. Benedictus Papa XII. composuit hanc orationem : ' Stabat Mater dolorosa iuxta crucem,' etc., concessitque cuilibet confesso pœnitenti dicenti eam pro qualibet vice 30 dies indulgentium." (Sixteenth century.)

Stable-door. *Locking the stable-door after the horse* [or *steed*] *is stolen.* Taking precautions after the mischief is done.

Stable Keys, as those of cow-houses, have frequently a perforated flint or horn appended to them. This is a charm to guard the creatures from nightmare. The flint is to propitiate the gnomes, and the horn to obtain the good graces of Pan, the protector of cattle.

Staff. *I keep the staff in my own hand.* I keep possession ; I retain the right. The staff was the ancient sceptre, and therefore, figuratively, it means, power, authority, dignity, etc.

To part with the staff. To lose or give up office or possession. (*See above.*)

> "Give up your staff, sir, and the king his realm."
> *Shakespeare : 2 Henry VI.*, ii. 3.

To put down one's staff in a place. To take up one's residence. The allusion is to the tent-staff : where the staff is placed, there the tent is stretched, and the nomad resides.

To strike my staff. To lodge for the time being.

> "Thou mayst see me at thy pleasure, for I intend to strike my staff at yonder hostelry."— *Cæsar Borgia*, xv.

Staff of Life (*The*). Bread, which is the *support* of life. Shakespeare says, "The boy was the very staff of my age." The allusion is to a staff which supports the feeble in walking.

Stafford. *He has had a treat in Stafford Court.* He has been thoroughly cudgelled. Of course the pun is on the word staff, a stick. The French have a similar phrase—"*Il a esté au festin de Martin Baston*" (He has been to Jack Drum's entertainment).

Stafford Law. Club law. A beating. The pun is on the word *staff*, a stick. (Italian, *Braccésca licenza*.) (*Florio*, p. 66.) (*See above.*)

Stag. The reason why a stag symbolises Christ is from the superstition that it draws serpents by its breath from their holes, and then tramples them to death. (See *Pliny : Nat. Hist.*, viii. 50.)

Stag in Christian art. The attribute of St. Julian Hospitaller, St. Felix of Valois, and St. Aidan. When it has a crucifix between its horns it alludes to the legendary tale of St. Hubert. When luminous it belongs to St. Eustachius.

Stags, in Stock Exchange phraseology, are persons who apply for the allotment of shares in a joint-stock company, not because they wish to hold the shares, but because they hope to sell the allotment at a premium. If they fail in this they forbear to pay the deposit and the allotment is forfeited. (*See* BEAR, BULL.)

Stagi'rite or **Stagyrite** (3 syl.). (Greek, *στάγειρος*.) Aristotle, who was

born at Stagi'ra, in Macedon. Generally called Stag'irite in English verse.

"In one rich soul
Plato the Stagyrite, and Tully joined."
Thomson: Summer.
" And rules as strict his laboured work confine
As if the Stagirite o'erlooked each line."
Pope: Essay on Criticism.
" And all the wisdom of the Stagirite.
Enriched and beautified his studious mind."
Wordsworth.

Stain. A contraction of *distain.*
(Latin, *dis-tingere,* to discolour.)

Stalking-horse. A mask to conceal
some design; a person put forward to
mislead; a sham. Fowlers used to conceal themselves behind horses, and went
on stalking step by step till they got
within shot of the game.

N.B. To *stalk* is to walk with strides,
from the Anglo-Saxon *stælcan.*

"He uses his folly like a stalking-horse, and
under the presentation of that he shoots his wit."
—*Shakespeare: As You Like It,* v. 4.

Stammerer (*The*).
Louis II. of France, *le Bégue.* (846,
877-879.)
Michael II., Emperor of the East, *le
Bégue.* (*, 820, 829.)
Notker or Notger of St. Gall. (830-
912.)

Stamp. '*Tis of the right stamp*—has
the stamp of genuine merit. A metaphor taken from current coin, which is
stamped with a recognised stamp and
superscription.

Stampede. A sudden panic in a
herd of buffaloes, causing them to rush
away pell-mell. The panic-flight of the
Federals at Bull Run, near the Poto'mac,
U.S., in 1861, was a stampede.

Stand. *To stand for a child.* To be
sponsor for it; to stand in its place and
answer for it.

Stand Nunky (*To*). (*See* NUNKY.)

Stand Off (*To*). To keep at a distance.

Stand Out (*To*). *I'll stand it out*—
persist in what I say. A mere translation of "persist" (Latin, *per-sisto* or
per-sto).

Stand Sam (*To*). (*See* SAM.)

Stand Treat (*To*). To pay the expenses of a treat.

Stand Upon (*To*). As *To stand upon
one's privilege* or *on punctilios;* this is
the Latin *insisto.* In French, " *Insister
sur son privilege* or *sur des vétilles.*"

Stand to a Bargain (*To*), to abide
by it, is simply the Latin *stare conventis,
conditionibus stare, pactis stare,* etc.

Stand to his Guns (*To*). To persist in a statement; not to give way. A
military phrase.

"The Speaker said he hoped the gallant gentle-
man would try to modify his phrase; but Colonel
Saunderson still stood to his guns."—*Daily
Graphic,* 3rd February, 1893. '

Stand to Reason (*To*), or *It stands
to reason,* is the Latin *constāre, constat.*

Standing Dish (*A*). An article of
food which usually appears at table.
Cibus quotidiānus.

Standing Orders. Rules or instructions constantly in force.
Standing orders. Those bye-laws of
the Houses of Parliament for the conduct of their proceedings which stand in
force till they are either rescinded or
suspended. Their suspension is generally caused by a desire to hurry through
a Bill with unusual expedition.

Standing Stones. (*See* STONES.)

Standard. *American standard of* 1776.
A snake with thirteen rattles, about to
strike, with the motto " DON'T TREAD ON
ME."

Standards.
Standard of Augustus. A globe, to
indicate his conquest of the whole
world.
Standard of Edward I. The arms of
England, St. George, St. Edmond, and
St. Edward.
Standard of Mahomet. (*See* SANDS-
CHAKI.)
Standard of the Anglo-Saxons. A
white horse.
Royal Standard of Great Britain. A
banner with the national arms covering
the entire field.
The Celestial Standard. So the Turks
call their great green banner, which they
say was given to Mahomet by the angel
Gabriel. (*See* SANDSCHAKI.)
Constantinople (*Standard of*), called
Lab'arum. It consisted of a silver-
plated spear with a cross-beam, from
which hung a small silk banner, bearing
the portrait of the reigning family and
the famous monogram.
Danish Standard. A raven.
Egypt (*ancient*). An eagle stripped of
its feathers, an emblem of the Nile; the
head of an ox.
Franks (*ancient*). A tiger or wolf;
but subsequently the Roman eagle.
Gauls (*ancient*). A lion, bull, or bear.
Greco-Egyptian Standard. A round-
headed table-knife or a semicircular fan.
Greece (*ancient*). A purple coat on the
top of a spear.

(1) *Athens*, Minerva, an olive, an owl.
(2) *Corinth*, a pegasus or flying horse.
(3) *Lacedæmon*, the initial letter L, in Greek (Λ).
(4) *Messi'na*, the initial letter M.
(5) *Thebes*, a sphinx.

Heliop'olis. On the top of a staff, the head of a white eagle, with the breast stripped of feathers and without wings. This was the symbol of Jupiter and of the Lagïdes.

Jews (ancient), ("degel") belonged to the four tribes of Judah, Reuben, Ephraim, and Dan. The Rabbins say the standard of Judah bore a *lion*, that of Reuben a *man*, that of Ephraim a *bull*, and that of Dan the *cherubim* (Gen. xlix. 3-22). They were ornamented with white, purple, crimson, and blue, and were embroidered.

Persia (ancient). The one adopted by Cyrus, and perpetuated, was a golden eagle with outstretched wings; the colour white.

Persian Standard. A blacksmith's apron. Kaivah, sometimes called Gao, a blacksmith, headed a rebellion against Biver, surnamed *Deh-ak* (ten vices), a merciless tyrant, and displayed his apron as a banner. The apron was adopted by the next king, and continued for centuries to be the national standard. (B.C. 800.)

Roman Standards. In the rude ages a wisp of straw. This was succeeded by bronze or silver devices attached to a staff. Pliny enumerates five—viz. the eagle, wolf, minotaur, horse, and boar. In later ages the image of the emperor, a hand outstretched, a dragon with a silver head and body of taffety. Ma'rius confined all promiscuous devices to the cohorts, and reserved the eagle for the exclusive use of the legion. This eagle, made of gold and silver, was borne on the top of a spear, and was represented with its wings displayed, and bearing in one of its talons a thunderbolt.

Turkish Standards.
(1) Sanjak Cherif (Standard of the Prophet), green silk. This is preserved with great care in the Seraglio, and is never brought forth except in time of war.
(2) The Sanjak, red.
(3) The Tug, consisting of one, two, or three horse-tails, according to the rank of the person who bears it. Pachas with three tails are of the highest dignity, and are entitled *beglerbeg* (prince of princes). Beys have only one horse-tail. The tails are fastened to the end of a gilt lance, and carried before the pacha or bey.
(4) The Alem, a broad standard which, instead of a spear-head, has in the middle a silver plate of a crescent shape.

Standards of Individuals.

AUGUSTUS (*Of*). A globe, to indicate his "empire of the world."

EDWARD I. (*Of*). The arms of England, St. George, St. Edmund, and St. Edward.

MAHOMET (*Of*). See under *Turkish Standards*.

Standards (*Size of*) varied according to the rank of the person who bore them. The standard of an *emperor* was eleven yards in length; of a *king*, nine yards; of a *prince*, seven yards; of a *marquis*, six and a half yards; of an *earl*, six yards; of a *viscount* or *baron*, five yards; of a *knight-banneret*, four and a half yards; of a *baronet*, four yards. They generally contained the arms of the bearer, his cognisance and crest, his motto or war-cry, and were fringed with his livery.

The Battle of the Standard, between the English and the Scotch, at Cuton Moor, near Northallerton, in 1138. Here David I., fighting on behalf of Matilda, was defeated by King Stephen's general Robert de Moubray. It received its name from a ship's mast erected on a waggon, and placed in the centre of the English army; the mast displayed the standards of St. Peter of York, St. John of Beverley, and St. Wilfred of Ripon. On the top of the mast was a little casket containing a consecrated host. (*Hailes : Annals of Scotland*, i. p. 85.)

Stang. *To ride the stang*. To be under petticoat government. At one time a man who ill-treated his wife was made to sit on a "stang" or pole hoisted on men's shoulders. On this uneasy conveyance the "stanger" was carried in procession amidst the hootings and jeerings of his neighbours. (Saxon, *stæng*, a pole.) (*See* SKIMMINGTON.)

Stanhope (*A*). A light open one-seated carriage, with two or four wheels. Invented by a Mr. Stanhope.

Stanhope Lens. A cylindrical lens with spherical ends of different radii. The covering of the tube into which the lens is fitted is called the "cap."

Stank Hen (*A*). A moor-hen. (*Stagnum* [Latin], a pool, pond, or stank [tank still common]; *sto*, to stand.)

Stannary Courts. Courts of record in Cornwall and Devon for the administration of justice among the tinners. (Latin, *stannum*, tin.)

Star (*A*), in theatrical language, means a popular actor.

Star (in Christian art). St. Bruno bears one on his breast; St. Dominic, St. Humbert, St. Peter of Alcan'tare, one over their head, or on their forehead, etc.

Star. The ensign of knightly rank. A star of some form constitutes part of the insignia of every order of knighthood.

His star is in the ascendant. He is in luck's way; said of a person to whom some good fortune has fallen and who is very prosperous. According to astrology, those leading stars which are above the horizon at a person's birth influence his life and fortune; when those stars are in the ascendant, he is strong, healthy, and lucky; but when they are depressed below the horizon, his stars do not shine on him, he is in the shade and subject to ill-fortune.

"The star of Richelieu was still in the ascendant."—*St. Simon.*

Star Chamber. A court of civil and criminal jurisdiction at Westminster, abolished in the reign of Charles I. So called because the ceiling or roof was decorated with gilt stars. Its jurisdiction was to punish such offences as the law had made no provision for.

∵ The chamber where the "starrs" or Jewish documents were kept was a separate room. The Star Chamber was the *Caměra Stellāta*, not *Caměra Starrāta*.

"It is well known that, before the banishment of the Jews by Edward I., their contracts and obligations were denominated . . . starra, or stars. . . . The room in the exchequer where the chests . . . were kept was . . . the starr-chamber."—*Blackstone: Commentaries,* vol. ii. book iv. p. 266, *a note.*

Star-crossed. Not favoured by the stars; unfortunate.

Star of Bethlehem (*The*), botanically called *ornithogalum.* The French peasants call it "*La dame d'onze heures,*" because it opens at eleven o'clock. Called "star" because the flower is star-shaped; and "Bethlehem" because it is one of the most common wild flowers of Bethlehem and the Holy Land generally.

Star of the South. A splendid diamond found in Brazil in 1853.

Stars and Garters! (*My*). An expletive, or mild kind of oath. The stars and garters of knighthood. Shakespeare makes Richard III. swear "By my George, my garter, and my crown!" (*Richard III.*, iv. 4.)

Stars and Stripes (*The*) or the **Star-spangled Banner,** the flag of the United States of North America.

The first flag of the United States, raised by Washington June 2, 1776, consisted of thirteen stripes, alternately red and white, with a blue canton emblazoned with the crosses of St. George and St. Andrew.
In 1777 Congress ordered that the canton should have thirteen white stripes in a blue field.
In 1794 (after the admission of Vermont and Kentucky) the stripes and stars were each increased to fifteen.
In 1818 S. R. Reid suggested that the original thirteen stripes should be restored, and a star be added to signify the States in the union.
∵ The flag preceding 1776 represented a coiled rattlesnake with thirteen rattles, and the motto *Don't tread on me.* This was an imitation of the Scotch thistle and the motto *Nemo me impune lacessit.*

"Oh! say, does that star-spangled banner yet wave
O'er the land of the free and the home of the brave?"

Starboard and Larboard, Star- is the Anglo-Saxon *steor,* rudder, *bord,* side; meaning the right side of a ship (looking forwards). Larboard is now obsolete, and "port" is used instead. *To port the helm* is to put the helm to the larboard. Byron, in his shipwreck (*Don Juan*), says of the ship—

"She gave a heel [*i.e.* turned on one side], and then a lurch to port,
And going down head foremost, sunk, in short."

Starch. Mrs. Anne Turner, half-milliner, half-procuress, introduced into England the French custom of using yellow starch in getting up bands and cuffs. She trafficked in poison, and being concerned in the murder of Sir Thomas Overbury, appeared on the scaffold with a huge ruff. This was done by Lord Coke's order, and was the means of putting an end to this absurd fashion.

"I shall never forget poor Mistress Turner, my honoured patroness, peace be with her! She had the ill-luck to meddle in the matter of Somerset and Overbury, and so the great earl and his lady slipt their necks out of the collar, and left her and some half-dozen others to suffer in their stead."—*Sir Walter Scott: Fortunes of Nigel,* viii.

Starry Sphere. The eighth heaven of the Peripatetic system; also called the "Firmament."

"The Crystal Heaven is this, whose rigour guides And binds the starry sphere."
Camoens : Lusiad, bk. x.

Starvation Dundas. Henry Dundas, first Lord Melville, who was the first to introduce the word *starvation* into the language, on an American debate in 1775. (Anglo-Saxon, *steorfcn*, to perish of hunger; German, *sterben ;* Dutch, *sterven.*)

Starved with Cold. Half-dead with cold. (Anglo-Saxon, *steorfan*, to die.)

Stations. *The fourteen stations of the Catholic Church.* These are generally called "Stations of the Cross," and the whole series is known as the *via Calvaria* or *via Crucis.* Each station represents some item in the passage of Jesus from the Judgment Hall to Calvary, and at each station the faithful are expected to kneel and offer up a prayer in memory of the event represented by the fresco, picture, or otherwise. They are as follows:—

(1) Jesus is condemned to death.
(2) Jesus is made to bear His cross.
(3) Jesus falls the first time under His cross.
(4) Jesus meets His afflicted mother.
(5) Simon the Cyrenean helps Jesus to carry His cross.
(6) Veronica wipes the face of Jesus.
(7) Jesus falls the second time.
(8) Jesus speaks to the daughters of Jerusalem.
(9) Jesus falls the third time.
(10) Jesus is stripped of His garments.
(11) Jesus is nailed to the cross.
(12) Jesus dies on the cross.
(13) Jesus is taken down from the cross.
(14) Jesus is placed in the sepulchre.

Stati'ra. A stock name of those historical romances which represented the fate of empires as turning on the effects produced on a crack-brained lover by some charming Manda'na or Statira. In La Calprenède's *Cassandra*, Statira is represented as the perfection of female beauty, and is ultimately married to Oroonda'tes.

Sta'tor [*the stopper or arrestor*]. When the Romans fled from the Sabines, they stopped at a certain place and made terms with the victors. On this spot they afterwards built a temple to Jupiter, and called it the temple of Jupiter Stator or Jupiter who caused them to stop in their flight.

" Here, Stator Jove and Phœbus, god of verse
    The votive tablet I suspend."   *Prior.*

Statue. The largest ever made was the Colossos of Rhodes ; the next largest is the statue of Bavaria, erected by Louis I., King of Bavaria. The Bartholdi statue of Liberty is also worthy of mention. (*See* LIGHTHOUSES.)

Statue. It was Pygmalion who fell in love with a statue he had himself made.

Statue. Of all the projects of Alexander, none was more hare-brained than his proposal to have Mount Athos hewed into a statue of himself. It is said he even arranged with a sculptor to undertake the job.

Status of Great Men. (*See* GREAT MEN.)

Statute Fairs. (*See* MOP.)

Steak. Beef-steak is a slice of beef fried or broiled. In the north of Scotland a slice of salmon *fried* is called a "salmon-steak." Also cod and hake split and fried. (Icelandic, *steik, steikja*, roast.)

Steal. A handle. *Stealing*—putting handles on (Yorkshire). This is the Anglo-Saxon *stela* (a stalk or handle).

"Steale or handell of a staffe, manche, hantel." *Palsgrave.*

Steal a Horse. *One man may steal a horse, but another must not look over the hedge.* Some men are chartered libertines, while others are always eyed with suspicion. (Latin : " *Dat veniam corvis, vexat censura columbas.*")

Steal a March on One (*To*). To come on one unexpectedly, as when an army steals a march or appears unexpectedly before an enemy.

Steam-kettles. Contemptuous name applied to vessels propelled by steam-power, whether steamers, men-of-war, or any other craft.

"These steam-kettles of ours can never be depended upon. I wish we could go back to the good old sailing ships. When we had them we knew what we were about. . . . Now we trust to machinery, and it fails us in time of need."— *Kingston : The Three Admirals*, chap. xvi.

Steelyard (London, adjoining Dowgate) ; so called from being the place where the king's steelyard or beam was set up, for weighing goods imported into London.

Steenie (2 syl.). A nickname given by James I. to George Villiers, Duke of Buckingham. The half-profane allusion is to Acts vi. 15, where those who looked on Stephen the martyr " saw his face as it had been the face of an angel."

Steeple-engine. A form of marine engine common on American river-boats.

Steeple-Jack (*A*). A man who ascends a church spire to repair it. This is done by a series of short ladders, tied one to another as the man ascends, the topmost one being securely tied to the point of the spire. Not many men have nerve enough for the dangerous work of a steeple-Jack.

Steeplechase. A horse-race across fields, hedges, ditches, and obstacles of every sort that happen to lie in the way. The term arose from a party of foxhunters on their return from an unsuccessful chase, who agreed to race to the village church, the steeple of which was in sight ; he who first touched the church with his whip was to be the

winner. The entire distance was two miles.

¨ The Grand National Steeplechase is run on the Aintree course, Liverpool.

Stel'vio. *The pass of the Stelvio.* The highest carriage-road in Europe (9,176 feet above the sea-level). It leads from Bor'mio to Glurns.

Sten'tor. *The voice of a Stentor.* A very loud voice. Stentor was a Greek herald in the Trojan war. According to Homer, his voice was as loud as that of fifty men combined.

Stento'rian Lungs. Lungs like those of Stentor.

Sten'toropho'nic Voice. A voice proceeding from a speaking-trumpet or stentorophonic tube, such as Sir Samuel Moreland invented to be used at sea.

" I heard a formidable noise
　Loud as the stentrophonic voice,
That roared far off, ' Dispatch ! and strip ! ' "
　　　　Butler : Hudibras, iii. 1.

Stepfather and **Father-in-law.** The stepfather is the father of one bereaved of his natural father by death. A *stepmother* is the mother of one bereaved of his mother by death. A stepfather must be married to a widow, and thus become the stepfather of her children by a previous husband; and a stepmother must be married to a widower, and thus become the stepmother of his children by a former wife. Similarly, stepson and stepdaughter must be the son and daughter by the father or mother deceased, the relict marrying again. FATHER-IN-LAW and MOTHER-IN-LAW are the father and mother of the wife to her husband, and of the husband to the wife. Similarly, sons-in-law and daughters-in-law are the sons and daughters of the parents of the wife to the husband and of the husband to the wife. (Anglo-Saxon, *steop,* bereaved.)

Stephen. *Crown of St. Stephen.* The crown of Hungary.

" If Hungarian independence should be secured through the help of Prince Napoleon, the Prince himself should receive the crown of St. Stephen."
—*Kossuth : Memoirs of my Exile* (1880).

Stephen's Bread (*St.*). Stones. *Fed with St. Stephen's bread.* Stoned. In French, " *Miches de St. Etienne.*" In Italian, " *Pan di St. Stefano.*" Of course the allusion is to the stoning of Stephen.

Stephens (*Joanna*) professed to have made a very wonderful discovery, and Drummond, the banker, set on foot a subscription to purchase her secret. The sum she asked was £5,000. When £1,500 had been raised by private subscription, government voted £3,500. The secret was a decoction of soap, swine's cresses, honey, egg-shells, and snails, made into pills, and a powder to match. Joanna Stephens got the money and forthwith disappeared.

Stepney Papers. A voluminous collection of political letters between Mr. Stepney, the British minister, and our ambassadors at various European courts, the Duke of Marlborough, and other public characters of the time. Part of the correspondence is in the British Museum, and part in the Public Record Office. It is very valuable, as this was the period called the Seven Years' War. The original letters are preserved in bound volumes, but the whole correspondence is in print also. (Between 1692 and 1706.)

Sterling Money. Spelman derives the word from *esterlings,* merchants of the Hanse Towns, who came over and reformed our coin in the reign of John. Others say it is *starling* (little star), in allusion to a star impressed on the coin. Others refer it to Stirling Castle in Scotland, where money was coined in the reign of Edward I. (*Sir Matthew Hale.*)

" In the time of King Richard I., monie coined in the east parts of Germany began to be of especiall request in England for the puritie thereof, and was called Easterling monie, as all the inhabitants of those parts were called Easterlings ; and shortly after some of that countrie, skillfull in mint matters and allaies, were sent for into this realm to bring the coine to perfection, which since that time was called of them sterling for Easterling."—*Camden.*

Stern. *To sit at the stern; At the stern of public affairs.* Having the management of public affairs. The stern is the *steer-ern*—*i.e.* steer-place; and to sit at the stern is " to sit at the helm."

" Sit at chiefest stern of public weal."
　　　　Shakespeare: 1 *Henry VI.,* i. 1.

Sternhold (*Thomas*) versified fifty-one of the Psalms. The remainder were the productions of Hopkins and some others. Sternhold and Hopkins' Psalms used to be attached to the Common Prayer Book.

" Mistaken choirs refuse the solemn strain
Of ancient Sternhold." *Crabbe: Borough.*

Sterry (in *Hudibras*). A fanatical preacher, admired by Hugh Peters.

Stewing in their own Gravy. Especially applied to a besieged city. The besiegers may leave the hostile city to suffer from want of food, loss of commerce, confinement, and so on. The phrase is very old, borrowed perhaps from the Bible, "Thou shalt not seethe a kid in its mother's milk." Chaucer says—

"In his own gress I made him frie,. For anger and for verry jalousie." Prologue to the *Wife of Bathes Tale*.

∴ We are told that the Russian ambassador, when Louis Philippe fortified Paris, remarked, if ever again Paris is in insurrection, it "can be made to stew in its own gravy (jus)"; and Bismarck, at the siege of Paris, in 1871, said, the Germans intend to leave the city "to seethe in its own milk."—See *Snell: Chronicles of Twyford*, p. 295.

"He relieved us out of our purgatory . . . after we had been stewing in our own gravy."—*The London Spy*, 1716.

Stick. *A composing stick* is a hand instrument into which a compositor places the letters to be set up. Each row or line of letters is pushed home and held in place by a movable "setting rule," against which the thumb presses. When a stick is full, the matter set up is transferred to a "galley" (*q.v.*), and from the galley it is transferred to the "chase" (*q.v.*). Called a *stick* because the compositor *sticks* the letters into it.

Stickler. One who obstinately maintains some custom or opinion; as a stickler for Church government. (*See below.*)

A stickler about trifles. One particular about things of no moment. Sticklers were the seconds in ancient single combats, very punctilious about the minutest points of etiquette. They were so called from the white stick which they carried in emblem of their office.

"I am willing . . . to give thee precedence, and content myself with the humbler office of stickler."—*Sir Walter Scott: Fair Maid of Perth*, chap. xvi.

Stiff. An I.O.U.; a bill of acceptance. "Hard," means hard cash. "Did you get it stiff or hard?" means by an I.O.U. or in cash. Of course "stiff" refers to the stiff interest exacted by money lenders.

"His 'stiff' was floating about in too many directions, at too many high figures."—*Ouida: Under Two Flags*, chap. vii.

Stig'mata. Impressions on certain persons of marks corresponding to some or all of the wounds received by our Saviour in His trial and crucifixion. The following claim to have been so stigmatised:

(1) MEN. Angelo del Paz (all the marks); Benedict of Reggio (the crown of thorns), 1602; Carlo di Saeta (the lance-wound); Dodo, a Premonstratensian monk (all the marks); Francis of Assisi (all the marks, which were impressed on him by a seraph with six

wings), September 15th, 1224; Nicholas of Ravenna, etc.

(2) WOMEN. Bianca de Gazeran; St. Catharine of Sienna; Catharine di Raconisco (the crown of thorns), 1583; Cecilia di Nobili of Nocera, 1655; Clara di Pugny (mark of the spear), 1514; "Estatica" of Caldaro (all the marks), 1842; Gabriella da Piezolo of Aquila (the spear-mark), 1472; Hieronyma Carvaglio (the spear-mark, which bled every Friday); Joanna Maria of the Cross; Maria Razzi of Chio (marks of the thorny crown); Maria Villani (ditto); Mary Magdalen di Pazzi; Mechtildis von Stanz; Ursula of Valencia; Veronica Guliani (all the marks), 1694; Vincenza Ferreri of Valencia, etc.

Stigmatise. To puncture, to brand (Greek, *stigma*, a puncture). Slaves used to be branded, sometimes for the sake of recognising them, and sometimes by way of punishment. The branding was effected by applying a red-hot iron marked with certain letters to their forehead, and then rubbing some colouring matter into the wound. A slave that had been branded was by the Romans called a *stigmat'ic*, and the brand was called the *stigma*.

Stigmites, or **St. Stephen's Stones,** are chalced'onies with brown and red spots.

Stiletto of the Storm (*The*). Lightning.

Still. Cornelius Tacitus is called *Cornelius the Still* in the *Fardle of Facions*, "still" being a translation of the Latin word *tacitus*.

"Cornelius the Stylle in his firste book of his yerely exploietes called in Latine Ansales . . ."—Ch. iii. s. 3 (1555).

Still Sow. A man cunning and selfish; one wise in his own interest; one who avoids talking at meals that he may enjoy his food the better. So called from the old proverb, "The still sow eats the wash" or "draff."

"We do not act that often jest and langh; 'Tis old but true, 'Still swine eat all the draugh.'" *Shakespeare: Merry Wives of Windsor*, iv. 2.

Still Waters Run Deep. Silent and quiet conspirators or traitors are most dangerous; barking dogs never bite; the fox barks not when he would steal the lamb.

"Smooth runs the water where the brook is deep; And in his simple show he harbours treason. The fox barks not when he would steal the lamb; No, no, my sovereign, Gloucester is a man Unsounded yet, and full of deep deceit." *Shakespeare: 2 Henry VI.*, iii. 1.

Stilling (*John Henry*), surnamed *Jung*, the mystic or pietist; called by Carlyle the German *Dominie Sampson;* "awkward, honest, irascible, in old-fashioned clothes and bag-wig." A real character. (1740-1817.)

Sti'lo No'vo. New-fangled notions. When the calendar was reformed by Pope Gregory XIII. (1582), letters used to be dated *stilo novo*, which grew in time to be a cant phrase for any innovation.

"And so I leave you to your *stilo novo*."
Beaumont and Fletcher.

Stimulants of Great Men.

BONAPARTE took snuff when he wished to stimulate his intellect, or when he was greatly annoyed.
BRAHAM (the singer) drank bottled porter.
The REV. WILLIAM BULL, the Nonconformist, was an inveterate smoker.
LORD BYRON took gin and water.
G. F. COOKE took all sorts of stimulants.
LORD ERSKINE took large doses of opium.
GLADSTONE'S restorative is an egg beaten up in sherry.
HOBBES drank cold water.
ED. KEAN drank raw brandy.
J. KEMBLE was an opium eater.
NEWTON smoked.
POPE drank strong coffee.
WEDDERBURNE (the first Lord Ashburton) placed a blister on his chest when he was about to make a great speech. (*Dr. Paris: Pharmacologia.*)

Stink'omalee'. So Theodore Hook called University College, London. The fun of the sobriquet is this: the buildings stand on the site of a large rubbish store or sort of refuse field, into which were cast potsherds and all sorts of sweepings. About the same time the question respecting Trincomalee in Ceylon was in agitation, so the wit spun the two ideas together, and produced the word in question, which was the more readily accepted as the non-religious education of the new college, and its rivalry with Oxford and Cambridge, gave for a time very great offence to the High Church and State party.

Stip'ulate (3 syl.). The word is generally given from the Latin *stipula* (a straw), and it is said that a straw was given to the purchaser in sign of a real delivery. Isidore (v. 24) asserts that the two contracting parties broke a straw between them, each taking a moiety, that, by rejoining the parts, they might prove their right to the bargain. With all deference to the Bishop of Seville, his "fact" seems to belong to limbo-lore. All bargains among the Romans were made by asking a question and replying to it. One said, *An stipem vis?* the other replied, *Stipem volo* ("Do you require money?" "I do"); the next question and answer were, *An dabis? Dabo* ("Will you give it?" "I will"); the third question to the surety, *An spondes?* to which he replied, *Spondeo* ("Will you be security?" "I will"), and the bargain was made. So that stipulate is compounded of *stips-volo* (*stip'ulo*), and the tale about breaking the straws seems to be concocted to bolster up a wrong etymology.

"Stir Up" Sunday. The last Sunday in Trinity. So called from the first two words of the collect. It announces to schoolboys the near approach of the Christmas holidays.

Stirrup (*A*). A rope to climb by. (Anglo-Saxon, *sti'g-ra'p*, a climbing rope. The verb *sti'g-an* is to climb, to mount.)

Stirrup Cup. A "parting cup," given in the Highlands to guests on leaving when their feet are in the stirrups. In the north of the Highlands called "cup at the door." (*See* COFFEE.)

"Lord Marmion's bugles blew to horse;
Then came the stirrup-cup in course;
Between the baron and his host
No point of courtesy was lost."
Sir Walter Scott: Marmion, i. 21.

Stirrup Oil. A beating; a variety of "strap oil" (*q.v.*). The French *De l'huile de cotret* (faggot or stick oil).

Stiver. *Not a stiver.* Not a penny. The stiver was a Dutch coin, equal to about a penny. (Dutch, *stuiver*.)

Stock. From the verb to *stick* (to fasten, make firm, fix).
Live stock. The fixed capital of a farm.
Stock in trade. The fixed capital.
The village stocks, in which the feet are stuck or fastened.
A gun stock, in which the gun is stuck or made fast.
It is on the stocks. It is in hand, but not yet finished. The stocks is the frame in which a ship is placed while building, and so long as it is in hand it is said to be or to lie on the stocks.

Stock Exchange Slang. *See each article:*

Backwardation.	Floaters.
Bears.	Fourteen Hundred.
Berthas.	Kite.
Berwicks.	Lame Duck.
Brums.	Leeds.
Bulls.	Morgans.
Caleys.	Muttons.
Claras.	Pots.
Cohens.	Singapores.
Contango.	Smelts.
Dogs.	Stag.
Dovers.	Yorks.

Stock, Lock, and Barrel. Every part, everything. Gun-maker's phrase.

"Everything is to be sold off—stock, lock, and barrel."

Stockdove. The wild pigeon; so called because it breeds in the stocks of hollow trees, or rabbit burrows.

Stockfish. *I will beat thee like a stockfish.* Moffet and Bennet, in their *Health's Improvement* (p. 262), inform us that dried cod, till it is beaten, is called buckhorn, because it is so tough; but after it has been beaten on the stock, it is termed stockfish. (In French, *etriller quelqu'un*, a double carillon, "to a pretty tune.")

"Peace! thou wilt be beaten like a stockfish else."—*Jonson: Every Man in his Humour*, iii. 2.

Stocking. (*See* BLUE STOCKING.)

Stockwell Ghost. A supposed ghost that haunted the village of Stockwell, near London, in 1772. The real author of the strange noises was Anne Robinson, a servant. (*See* COCK LANE GHOST.)

Sto'ics. *Founder of the Stoic school.* Zeno of Athens. These philosophers were so called because Zeno used to give his lectures in the *Stoa Pœcilé* of Athens. (Greek, *stoa*, a porch.)
Epicte'tus was the founder of the New Stoic school.

" The ancient Stoics in their porch
  With fierce dispute maintained their church,
  Beat out their brains in fight and study
  To prove that virtue is a body,
  That bonum is an animal,
  Made good with stout polemic bawl."
      Butler : Hudibras, ii. 2.

Stole (Latin, *stola*). An ecclesiastical vestment, also called the Orarium. "*Deinde circumdat collum suum stola, quæ et Orarium dicitur.*" It indicates "*Obedientiam fiilii Dei et jugum servitutis, quod pro salute hominum portävit.*" Deacons wear the stole over the left shoulder, and loop the two parts together, that they may both hang on the right side. Priests wear it over both shoulders. (See *Ducange : Stola*.)

Stolen Things are Sweet. A sop filched from the dripping-pan, fruit procured by stealth, and game illicitly taken, have the charm of dexterity to make them the more palatable. Solomon says, "Stolen waters are sweet, and bread eaten in secret [*i.e.* by stealth] is pleasant."

" From busie cooks we love to steal a bit
  Behind their backs, and that in corners eat ;
  Nor need we here the reason why entreat ;
  All know the proverb, 'Stolen bread is sweet.'"
      History of Joseph, n. d.

Stomach. Appetite: "He who hath no stomach for this fight." (*Shakespeare: Henry V.*, iv. 3.)

Appetite for honours, etc., or ambition: "Wolsey was a man of an unbounded stomach." (*Henry VIII.*, iv. 2.)
Appetite or inclination : "Let me praise you while I have the stomach." (*Merchant of Venice*, iii. 5.)
Stomach. To swallow, to accept with appetite, to digest.
To stomach an insult. To swallow it and not resent it.

" If you must believe, stomach not all."—*Shakespeare: Antony and Cleopatra*, iii. 4.

Stomach, meaning "wrath," and the verb "to be angry," is the Latin *stom'-achus, stomacha'ri*.

" Peli'dæ stomachum cedere nescii." *Horace*.
  ("The stomach [wrath] of relentless Achilles.")
" Stomachabatur si quid asperius dixerim."—*Cicero*. (" His stomach rose if I spoke sharper than usual.")

The fourth stomach of ruminating animals is called the *aboma'sus* or *aboma'sum* (from *ab-oma'sum*).

Stone (1 syl.). The sacred stone of the Caa'ba (*q.v.*) is, according to Arab tradition, the guardian angel of Paradise turned into stone. When first built by Abraham into the wall of the shrine it was clear as crystal, but it has become black from being kissed by sinful man.
A hag-stone. A flint with a natural perforation through it. Sometimes hung on the key of an outside door to ward off the hags. Sometimes such a stone used to be hung round the neck "for luck" ; sometimes on the bedstead to prevent nightmare ; and sometimes on a horse-collar to ward off disease.
Leave no stone unturned. Omit no minutiæ if you would succeed. After the defeat of Mardonius at Platæa (B.C. 477), a report was current that the Persian General had left great treasures in his tent. Polycrätes (4 syl.) the Theban sought long but found them not. The Oracle of Delphi, being consulted, told him " to leave no stone unturned," and the treasures were discovered.

Stone Age (*The*). The period when stone implements were used. It preceded the bronze age.

Stone Blind. Wholly blind.

Stone Cold. Cold as a stone.

Stone Dead. Dead as a stone.

Stone Jug. Either a stone jar or a prison. The Greek word κέραμος (*kerä'mos*) means either an earthen jar or a prison, as in χαλκέῳ εν κεράμῳ (*chalkĕo en keramŏ*), in a brazen prison. When Venus complained to the immortals that Diomed had wounded her, Dïōnē bade her cheer up, for other immortals had suffered also, but had borne up under their affliction ; as Mars, for example, when Otos and Ephialtēs bound him . . . and kept him for thirteen months χωλκέω εν κεράμω (in a brazen prison, or brazen jug). (*Homer: Iliad*, v. 381, etc. ; *see also* ix. 469.) Ewing says *keramos*, potter's earth or pottery, was also a prison, because prisoners were made to work up potters' earth into jugs and other vessels. Thus we say, "He was sent to the treadmill, meaning, to prison to work in the treadmill.

Stone Soup or St. Bernard's Soup. A beggar asked alms at a lordly mansion, but was told by the servants they had nothing to give him. "Sorry for it," said the man, "but will you let me boil a little water to make some soup of this stone?" This was so novel a proceeding, that the curiosity of the servants was aroused, and the man was readily furnished with saucepan, water, and a spoon. In he popped the stone, and begged for a little salt and pepper for flavouring. Stirring the water and tasting it, he said it would be the better for any fragments of meat and vegetables they might happen to have. These were supplied, and ultimately he asked for a little catsup or other sauce. When fully boiled and fit, each of the servants tasted it, and declared that stone soup was excellent. (*La soupe au caillou.*)

Stone Still. Perfectly still ; with no more motion than a stone.

"I will not struggle ; I will stand stone still."
     Shakespeare: King John, iv. 1.

Stone of the Broken Treaty. Limerick. About a century and a half ago England made a solemn compact with Ireland. Ireland promised fealty, and England promised to guarantee to the Irish people civil and religious equality. When the crisis was over England handed Ireland over to a faction that has ever since bred strife and disunion. (*Address of the Corporation of Limerick to Mr. Bright*, 1868.)

"The 'stone of the broken treaty' is there, and from early in the morning till late at night groups gather round it, and foster the tradition of their national wrongs."—*The Times*.

Stone of Stumbling. This was much more significant among the Jews than it is with ourselves. One of the Pharisaic sects, called *Nikfi* or "Dashers," used to walk abroad without lifting their feet from the ground. They were for ever "dashing their feet against the

stones," and "stumbling" on their way.

Stone of Tongues. This was a stone given to Otnit, King of Lombardy, by his father dwarf Elberich, and had the virtue, when put into a person's mouth, of enabling him to speak perfectly any foreign language. (*The Heldenbuch.*)

Stones.

Aerolites, or stones which have fallen from heaven. J. Norman Lockyer says the number of meteors which fall daily to the earth "exceeds 21 millions." (*Nineteenth Century*, Nov., 1830, p. 787.) The largest aerolith on record is one that fell in Brazil. It is estimated to weigh 14,000 lbs. In 1806 a shower of stones fell near L'Aigle, and M. Biot was deputed by the French Government to report on the phenomenon. He found between two and three thousand stones, the largest being about 17 lbs. in weight.

Eagle stones. (*See* EAGLE-STONES.)

Health stones. Purites (2 syl.) found in Geneva and Savoy. So called from the notion that it loses its steel-blue colour if the person in possession of one is in ill health.

Square stones. The most ancient idols were square stones. The head and limbs were subsequent additions.

Touchstones. (*q.v.*)

Stones. After the Moslem pilgrim has made his seven processions round the Caaba, he repairs to Mount Arafat, and before sunrise enters the valley of Mena, where he throws seven stones at each of three pillars, in imitation of Abraham and Adam, who thus drove away the devil when he disturbed their devotions.

Standing stones. The most celebrated groups are those of Stonehenge, Avebury, in Wiltshire, Stennis in the Orkneys, and Carnac in Brittany. .

The Standing Stones of Stennis, in the Orkneys, resemble Stonehenge, and, says Sir W. Scott, furnish an irresistible refutation of the opinion that these circles are Druidical. There is every reason to believe that the custom was prevalent in Scandinavia as well as in Gaul and Britain, and as common to the mythology of Odin as to Druidism. They were places of public assembly, and in the Eyrbiggia Saga is described the manner of setting apart the Helga Feli (Holy Rocks) by the pontiff Thorolf for solemn meetings.

¶ *Stones fallen down from Jupiter.* Anaxag'oras mentions a stone that fell from Jupiter in Thrace, a description of which is given by Pliny. The Ephesians asserted that their image of Diana came from Jupiter. The stone at Emessa, in Syria, worshipped as a symbol of the sun, was a similar meteorite. At Aby'-dos and Potidæ'a similar stones were preserved. At Corinth was one venerated as Zeus. At Cyprus was one dedicated to Venus, a description of which is given by Tacitus and Maximus Tyr'ius. Hero'-dian describes a similar stone in Syria. The famous Caa'ba stone at Mecca is a similar meteor. Livy recounts three falls of stones. On November 27th, 1492, just as Maximilian was on the point of en-gaging the French army near Ensisheim, a mass weighing 270 lbs. fell between the combatants; part of this mass is now in the British Museum. In June, 1866, at Knyahinya, a village of Hungary, a shower of stones fell, the largest of which weighs above 5 cwt.; it was broken in the fall into two pieces, both of which are now in the Imperial Collection at Vienna. On December 13th, 1795, in the village of Thwing, Yorkshire, an aërolite fell weighing 56 lbs., now in the British Museum. On September 10th, 1813, at Adare, in Limerick, fell a similar stone, weighing 17 lbs., now in the Oxford Museum. On May 1st, 1860, in Guernsey county, Ohio, more than thirty stones were picked up within a space of ten miles by three; the largest weighed 103 lbs. (*Kesselmeyer and Dr. Otto Buchner: The Times,* November 14th, 1866.)

¶ *You have stones in your mouth.* Said to a person who stutters or speaks very indistinctly The allusion is to Demos'-thenēs, who cured himself of stuttering by putting pebbles in his mouth and declaiming on the sea-shore.

> "The orator who once
> Did fill his mouth with pebble stones
> When he harangued,"
> *Butler: Hudibras,* i. 1.

Precious stones. Said to be dew-drops condensed and hardened by the sun.

Stonebrash. A name given in Wilt-shire to the subsoil of the north-western border, consisting of a reddish calcareous loam, mingled with flat stones; a soil made of small stones or broken rock.

Stonehenge, says Geoffrey of Mon-mouth, was erected by Merlin (the magi-cian) to perpetuate the treachery of Hengist, who desired a friendly meeting with Vortigern, but fell upon him and his 400 attendants, putting them all to the sword. Aurelius Ambrosius asked Merlin to recommend a sensible memento of this event, and Merlin told the king

to transplant the "Giants' Dance" from the mountain of Killaraus, in Ireland. These stones had been brought by the giants from Africa as baths, and all pos-sessed medicinal qualities. Merlin trans-planted them by magic. This tale owes its birth to the word "stan-hengist," which means *uplifted stones,* but "hen-gist" suggested the name of the tradi-tional hero.

Stonewall Jackson. Thomas J. Jackson, one of the Confederate generals in the American war. The name arose thus: General Bee, of South Caroli'na, observing his men waver, exclaimed, "Look at Jackson's men; they stand like a stone wall!" (1826-1863.)

Stonewall (*To*). To adopt purely defensive measures; to play against time (used of the batsman, who, for this reason, is often called a *stonewaller.*)

Stony Arabia. A mistranslation of *Arabia Petræa,* where Petræa is sup-posed to be an adjective formed from the Greek *petros* (a stone), and not, as it really is, from the city of Petra, the capital of the Nabathæans. This city was called *Thamud* (rock-built). (*See* YEMEN.)

Stool of Repentance. A low stool placed in front of the pulpit in Scotland, on which persons who had incurred an ecclesiastical censure were placed during divine service. When the service was over the "penitent" had to stand on the stool and receive the minister's rebuke. Even in the present century this method of rebuke has been repeated.

"Colonel Knox . . . tried to take advantage of a merely formal proceeding to set Mr. Gladstone on the stool of repentance."—*The Times.*

Stops. Organs have no fixed number of stops; some have sixty or more, and others much fewer. A stop is a collec-tion of pipes similar in tone and quality, running through the whole or part of an organ. They may be divided into mouth-pipes and reed-pipes, according to structure, or into (1) metallic, (2) reed, (3) wood, (4) mixture or compound stops, according to material. The fol-lowing are the chief:—

(1) *Metallic.* Principal (so called be-cause it is the first stop tuned, and is the standard by which the whole organ is regulated), the open diapason, dulci-ana, the 12th, 15th, tierce or 17th, lari-got or 19th, 22nd, 26th, 29th, 33rd, etc. (being respectively 12, 15, 17, etc., notes above the open diapason).

(2) *Reed* (metal reed pipes). Bassoon,

cremona, hautboy or oboe, trumpet, vox-humana (all in unison with the open diapason), clarion (an octave above the diapason and in unison with principal).

(3) *Wood.* Stopt diapason, double diapason, and most of the flutes.

(4) *Compound or mixture.* Flute (in unison with the principal), cornet, mixture or furniture, sesquialtera, cymbel, and cornet.

⁂ Grand organs have, in addition to the above, from two to two and a half octaves of pedals.

Stops, strictly speaking, are three-fold, called the *foundation* stop, the *mutation* stop. and the *mixture* stop.

The *foundation* stop is one whose tone agrees with the normal pitch of the digital struck, or some octave of it.

The *mutation* stops produce a tone that is neither the normal pitch nor yet an octave of the digital struck.

The *mixture* stop needs no explanation.

Among varieties of organ-stops may be mentioned the *complete* stop, which has one pipe or reed to a note. The *compound* stop, which has more than one pipe or reed to a note. The *flue* stop, composed of flue-pipes. The *incomplete* (or imperfect) stop, which has less than the full number of pipes. The *manual* stop, corresponding to the manual keyboard. The *open* stop, which has the pipes open at the upper end. The *pedal* stop, as distinguished from the "manual" stop. The *solo* stop, the *string* stop, etc.

Store (1 syl.). *Store is no sore.* Things stored up for future use are no evil. Sore means grief as well as wound, our *sorrow.*

Stork, a sacred bird, according to the Swedish legend received its name from flying round the cross of the crucified Redeemer, crying *Styrka! styrka!* (Strengthen! strengthen!). (See *Christ,* in CHRISTIAN TRADITIONS.)

Storks are the sworn foes of snakes. Hence the veneration in which they are held. They are also excellent scavengers. (Stork, Anglo-Saxon, *storc.*)

" 'Twill profit when the stork, sworn foe of snakes,
Returns, to show compassion to thy plants."
Philips: Cyder, bk. i.

Storks' Law or *Lex Ciconaria.* A Roman law which obliged children to maintain their necessitous parents in old age, " in imitation of the stork." Also called " Antipelargia."

Storm in a Teapot. A mighty to-do about a trifle. "A storm in a puddle."

Storms. The inhabitants of Comacchio, a town in Central Italy, between the two branches of the Po, rejoice in storms because then the fish are driven into their marshes.

" Whose townsmen loathe the lazy calm's repose,
And pray that stormy waves may lash the beach." *Rose's Orlando Furioso,* ii. 41.

Cape of Storms. So Bartholomew Diaz named the south cape of Africa in 1486,

but King John II. changed it into the *Cape of Good Hope.*

Stormy Petrel (*A*). An ill omen ; a bad augury.

" Dr. von Esmarch is regarded at court as a stormy petrel, and every effort was made to conceal his visit to the German emperor."—*The World,* 6th April, 1892, p. 15.

Stornello Verses are those in which certain words are harped on and turned about and about. They are common among the Tuscan peasants. The word is from *torna're* (to return).

" I'll tell him the *white,* and the *green,* and the *red,*
Mean our country has flung the vile yoke from her head ;
I'll tell him the *green,* and the *red,* and the *white*
Would look well by his side as a sword-knot so bright ;
I'll tell him the *red,* and the *white,* and the *green*
Is the prize that we play for, a prize we will win." *Notes and Queries.*

Stor'thing (pron. *stor-ting*). The Norwegian Parliament, elected every three years (Norse, *stor,* great ; *thing,* court.)

Stovepipe Hat (*A*). A chimney-pot hat (*q.v.*).

" High collars, tight coats, and tight sleeves were worn at home and abroad, and, as though that were not enough, a stovepipe hat was worn."—*Illustrated Sporting and Dramatic News,* September, 1891.

Stowe (1 syl.). *The fair majestic paradise of Stowe* (*Thomson : Autumn*). The principal seat of the Duke of Buckingham.

Stowe Nine Churches. A hamlet of Stowe, Northamptonshire. The tradition is that the people of this hamlet wished to build a church, and made nine ineffectual efforts to do so, for every time the church was finished the devil came by night and knocked it down again.

Stra'bo (*Walafridus*). A German monk. (807-849.)

Stradiva'rius (*Antonio*). A famous violin-maker, born at Cremo'na. Some of his instruments have fetched £400. (1670-1728.) (*See* CREMONAS.)

Straight as an Arrow. (*See* SIMILES.)

Strain (1 syl.). *To strain courtesy.* To stand upon ceremony. Here, strain is to stretch, as parchment is strained on a drum-head. When strain means to filter, the idea is pressing or squeezing through a canvas or woollen bag.

Strain at a gnat and swallow a camel. To make much fuss about little peccadillos, but commit offences of real magnitude. " Strain at " is *strain out* or *off* (Greek, *di-ulizo*). The allusion is to the practice of filtering wine for fear of swallowing an insect, which was "unclean." Tyndale has "strain out" in his version. Our expression "strain at" is a corruption of *strain-ut*, "ut" being the Saxon form of out, retained in the words *ut-most*, *utter*, *uttermost*, etc.

The quality of mercy is not strained (*Merchant of Venice*, iv. 1)—constrained or forced, but cometh down freely as the rain, which is God's gift.

Stral'enheim (*Count of*). A feudal baron who hunted Werner like a partridge in order to obtain his inheritance. Ulric, Werner's son, saved him from the Oder, but subsequently murdered him. (*Byron: Werner*.)

Strand (London). The bank of the Thames (Saxon for a beach or shore); whence *stranded*, run ashore or grounded.

Strange (1 syl.). Latin, *extra* (without); whence *extra'neus* (one without); old French, *estrange*; Italian, *strano*, etc. Stranger, therefore, is *extra'neus*, one without.

Stranger of the Gate (*The*). (*See under* PROSELYTE.)

Strangers Sacrificed. It is said that Busi'ris, King of Egypt, sacrificed to his gods all strangers that set foot on his territories. Diomed, King of Thrace, gave strangers to his horses for food. (*See* DIOMEDES.)

" Oh fly, or here with strangers' blood imbrued
Busiris' altars thou shalt find renewed:
Amidst his slaughtered guests his altars stood
Obscene with gore, and baked with human
blood."   *Camoens: Lusiad*, book ii.

Strap Oil. A beating. A corruption of strap 'eil, *i.e.* German *theil* (a dole). The play is palpable. The "April fool" asks for a pennyworth of strap 'eil, that is dole of the strap, in French *l'huile de cotret*. (Latin, *stroppus*.)

Strappa'do. A military punishment formerly practised; it consisted of pulling an offender to a beam and then letting him down suddenly; by this means a limb was not unfrequently dislocated. (Italian, *strappa're*, to pull.)

" Were I at the strappado or the rack, I'd give
no man a reason on compulsion."—*Shakespeare:*
1 *Henry IV.*, ii. 4.

Strasburg Goose (*A*). A goose fattened, crammed, and confined in order to enlarge its liver. Metaphorically, one crammed with instruction and kept from healthy exercise in order to pass examinations.

"The anæmic, myopic, worn-out creature who
comes to [the army]—a new kind of Strasburg
goose."—*Nineteenth Century*, January, 1893, p. 26.

Strat'agem means generalship. (Greek, *strate'gos*, a general; *stratos-ago*, to lead an army.)

Straw. Servants wishing to be hired used to go into the market-place of Carlisle (Carel) with a straw in their mouth. (*See* MOP.)

" At Carel I stuid wi' a strae i' my mouth,
The weyves com roun' me in custers;
' What weage dus te ax, canny lad?' says yen."
          Anderson: Cumberland Ballads.

Straw, chopped or otherwise, at a wedding, signifies that the bride is no virgin. Flowers indicate purity or virginity, but straw is only the refuse from which corn has been already taken.

A little straw shows which way the wind blows. Mere trifles often indicate the coming on of momentous events. They are shadows cast before coming events.

A man of straw. A man without means; a Mrs. Harris; a sham. In French, " *Un homme de paille*," like a malkin. (*See* MAN OF STRAW.)

I have a straw to break with you. I am displeased with you; I have a reproof to give you. In feudal times possession of a fief was conveyed by giving a straw to the new tenant. If the tenant misconducted himself, the lord dispossessed him by going to the threshold of his door and breaking a straw, saying as he did so, " As I break this straw, so break I the contract made between us." In allusion to this custom, it is said in *Reynard the Fox*—" The kinge toke up a straw fro' the ground, and pardoned and forguf the Foxe," on condition that the Fox showed King Lion where the treasures were hid (ch. v.).

In the straw. " *Être en couche* " (in bed). The phrase is applied to women in childbirth. The allusion is to the straw with which beds were at one time usually stuffed, and not to the litter laid before a house to break the noise of wheels passing by. The Dutch of Haarlem and Enckhuysen, when a woman is confined, expose a pin-cushion at the street-door. If the babe is a boy, the pin-cushion has a red fringe, if a girl a white one.

Not to care a straw for one. In Latin, " [*Aliquem*] *nihili, flocci, nauci, pili, teruncii facĕre*." To hold one in no esteem; to defy one as not worth your steel.

Not worth a straw. Worthless. In French, " *Je n'en donnerais pas un fêtu* (or *un zeste*)." Not worth a rap; not worth a pin's point; not worth a fig (*q.v.*); not worth a twopenny dam, etc.

She wears a straw in her ear. She is looking out for another husband. This is a French expression, and refers to the ancient custom of placing a straw between the ears of horses for sale.

The last straw. The only hope left; the last penny.

'Tis the last straw that breaks the horse's (or *camel's*) *back*. In weighing articles, as salt, tea, sugar, etc., it is the last pinch which turns the scale; and there is an ultimate point of endurance beyond which calamity breaks a man down.

To carry off the straw (*"Enlever la paille"*). To bear off the belle. The pun is between "pal," a slang word for a favourite, and "paille," straw. The French *palot* means a "pal." Thus Gervais says—

> "Mais, oncore un coup, man palot."
> *Le Coup d'Œil Purin*, p. 64.

To catch at a straw. To hope a forlorn hope. A drowning man will catch at a straw.

To make bricks without straw. To attempt to do something without the proper and necessary materials. The allusion is to the exaction of the Egyptian taskmasters mentioned in Exodus v. 6-14. Even to the present, "bricks" in India, etc., are made of mud and straw dried in the sun. To make plum-puddings without plums.

To stumble at a straw. "*Nodos in scirpo quærĕre*." To look for knots in a bulrush (which has none). To stumble in a plain way.

To throw straws against the wind. To contend uselessly and feebly against what is irresistible; to sweep back the Atlantic with a besom.

Strawberry means the straying plant that bears berries (Anglo-Saxon, *streow berie*). So called from its runners, which stray from the parent plant in all directions.

Strawberry Preachers. So Latimer called the non-resident country clergy, because they *strayed* from their parishes, to which they returned only once a year. (Anglo-Saxon, *streowan*, to stray.)

Streak of Silver (*The*). The British Channel. So called in the *Edinburgh Review*, October, 1870.

Street and Walker (*Messrs.*). "In the employ of Messrs. Street and Walker." Said of a person out of employment. A gentleman without means,

whose employment is walking about the streets.

Stretch'er. An exaggeration; a statement stretched out beyond the strict truth. Also a frame on which the sick or wounded are carried; a frame on which painters' canvas is stretched; etc.

Strike (*A*). A federation of workmen to quit work unless the masters will submit to certain stated conditions. *To strike* is to leave off work, as stated above. (Anglo-Saxon, *strïc-an*, to go.)

> "Co-operation .... prevents strikes by .... identifying the interests of labour and capital."—
> R. T. Ely: *Political Economy*, part iv. chap. iv. 262.

Strike (1 syl.). *Strike, but hear me!* So said Themis'tocles with wonderful self-possession to Eurybi'ades, the Spartan general. The tale told by Plutarch is this: Themistocles strongly opposed the proposal of Eurybiades to quit the bay of Sal'amis. The hot-headed Spartan insultingly remarked that "those who in the public games rise up before the proper signal are scourged." "True," said Themistocles, "but those who lag behind win no laurels." On this, Eurybiades lifted up his staff to strike him, when Themistocles earnestly but proudly exclaimed, "Strike, but hear me!"

To strike hands upon a bargain or *strike a bargain*. To confirm it by shaking or striking hands.

Strike Amain. Yield or suffer the consequences. The defiance of a man-of-war to a hostile ship. To strike amain is to lower the topsail in token of submission. To wave a naked sword amain is a symbolical command to a hostile ship to lower her topsail.

Strike a Bargain (*To*). In Latin, *fœdus ferīre*; in Greek, *horkia temein*. The allusion is to the Greek and Roman custom of making sacrifice in concluding an agreement or bargain. After calling the gods to witness, they struck—*i.e.* slew—the victim which was offered in sacrifice. The modern English custom is simply to strike or shake hands.

Strike Sail. To acknowledge oneself beaten; to eat umble pie. A maritime expression. When a ship in fight or on meeting another ship, lets down her topsails at least half-mast high, she is said to *strike*, meaning that she submits or pays respect to the other.

> "Now Margaret
> Must strike her sail, and learn awhile to serve
> When kings command."
> *Shakespeare*: 3 *Henry VI.*, iii. 3.

Strike while the Iron is Hot. In French, "*Il faut battre le fer pendant qu'il est chaud.*" Either act while the impulse is still fervent, or do what you do at the right time. The metaphor is taken from a blacksmith working a piece of iron, say a horse-shoe, into shape. It must be struck while the iron is red-hot or it cannot be moulded into shape. Similar proverbs are: "Make hay while the sun shines," "Take time by the forelock."

String. *Always harping on one string.* Always talking on one subject; always repeating the same thing. The allusion is to the ancient harpers; some, like Paganini, played on one string to show their skill, but more would have endorsed the Apothecary's apology—"My poverty, and not my will, consents."

Stripes. A tiger. In India a tiger is called Master Stripes.

"Catch old Stripes come near my bullock, if he thought a 'shooting-iron' was anywhere about. Even if there were another Stripes, he would not show himself that night. — *Cornhill Magazine* (*My Tiger Watch*), July, 1883.

Strode. *The babes of Strode are born with tails.*

" As Becket, that good saint, sublimely rode,
Thoughtless of insult, through the town of Strode,
What did the mob? Attacked his horse's rump
And cut the tail, so flowing, to the stump.
What does the saint? Quoth he, ' For this vile trick
The town of Strode shall heartily be sick.'
And lo ! by power divine, a curse prevails—
The babes of Strode are born with horse's tails."
Peter Pindar: Epistle to the Pope.

Stroke. The oarsman who sits on the bench next the coxswain, and sets the stroke of the oars.

Stromkarl. A Norwegian musical spirit. Arndt informs us that the Strömkarl has eleven different musical measures, to ten of which people may dance, but the eleventh belongs to the night-spirit, his host. If anyone plays it, tables and benches, cups and cans, old men and women, blind and lame, babies in their cradles, and the sick in their beds, begin to dance. (*See* FAIRY.)

Strong—as iron, as a horse, as brandy. (*See* SIMILES.)

Strong-back. One of Fortunio's servants. He was so strong he could carry any weight upon his back without difficulty. (*Grimm's Goblins ; Fortunio.*)

Strong-bow. Richard de Clare, Earl of Strigul. Justice of Ireland. (*-1176.)

Stron'tian. This mineral receives its name from Strontian, in Argyleshire, where it was discovered by Dr. Hope, in 1792.

Struldbrugs. Wretched inhabitants of Luggnagg, an imaginary island a hundred leagues south-east of Japan. These human beings have the privilege of eternal life without those of immortal vigour, strength, and intellect. (*Swift · Gulliver's Travels.*)

"Many persons think that the picture of the Stulbrugs (*sic*) was intended to wean us from a love of life . . . but I am certain that the dean never had any such thing in view."—*Paley's Natural Theology* (Lord Brougham's note, bk. i. p. 140).

Stub'ble Geese, called in Devonshire *Arish Geese.* The geese turned into the stubble-fields or arrishers, to pick up the corn left after harvest. (*See* EARING.)

Stuck Pig. *To stare like a stuck pig.* A simile founded on actual observation. Of course, the *stuck* pig is the pig in the act of being killed. (*See* SIMILES.)

Stuck Up. An Australian phrase for robbed on the highway. (*See* GONE UP.)

Stuck-up People. Pretentious people ; parvenus ; nobodies who assume to be somebodies. The allusion is to birds, as the peacock, which sticks up its train to add to its "importance" and "awe down" antagonists.

Stuck his Spoon in the Wall. Took up his residence. Sometimes it means took up his long home, or died. In primitive times a leather strap was very often nailed to the wall, somewhere near the fireplace, and in this strap were stuck such things as scissors, spoons for daily use, pen-case, and so on. In Barclay's *Ship of Fools* is a picture of a man stirring a pot on the fire, and on the wall is a strap with two spoons stuck into it.

Stuff Gown. An outer barrister, or one without the bar. (*See* BARRISTER.)

Stumers, in the language of the turf, are fictitious bets recorded in the books of bookmakers, and published in the papers, to deceive the public by running up the odds on a horse which is not meant to win.

Stump. *To take to the stump.* To roam about the country speechifying.

To stump the country. To go from town to town making [political] speeches.

"The Irish members have already taken to the stump."—*A Daily Journal.*

Stump Orator (in America). A person who harangues the people from the stump of a tree or other chance elevation; a mob orator.

Stump Up. Pay your reckoning; pay what is due. Ready money is called stumpy or stumps. An Americanism, meaning money paid down on the spot—*i.e.* on the stump of a tree. (*See* Nail.)

Stumps. *To stir one's stumps.* To get on faster; to set upon something expeditiously. The stumps properly are wooden legs fastened to stumps or mutilated limbs. (Icelandic, *stumpr*.)

" This makes him stirre his stumps."
        The Two Lancashire Lovers (1640).

Stumped Out. Outwitted; put down. A term borrowed from the game of cricket.

Stupid Boy. St. Thomas Aqui'nas, nicknamed the Dumb Ox by his schoolfellows. (1224-1274.)

Sty or **Stye.** *Christ styed up to heaven.* Halliwell gives *sty* = a ladder, and the verb would be to go to heaven, as it were, by Jacob's ladder. The Anglo-Saxon verb *stigan* means to ascend.

" The beast . . .
Thought with his winges to stye above the
ground."
        Spenser : Faërie Queene, bk. i. canto xi. 25.

Styg'ian (3 syl.). Infernal; pertaining to Styx, the fabled river of hell.

" At that so sudden blaze the Stygian throng
Bent their aspect."
        Milton : Paradise Lost, x. 453.

Style (1 syl.) is from the Latin *stylus* (an iron pencil for writing on waxen tablets, etc.). The characteristic of a person's writing is called his style. Metaphorically it is applied to composition and speech. Good writing is *stylish,* and, metaphorically, smartness of dress and deportment is so called.

" Style is the dress of thought, and a well-dressed thought, like a well-dressed man, appears to great advantage."—*Chesterfield : Letter* ccxl. p. 361.

Styles. *Tom Styles* or *John a Styles,* connected with *John o' Noakes* in actions of ejectment. These mythical gentlemen, like John Doe and Richard Roe, are no longer employed.

" And, like blind Fortune, with a sleight
Convey men's interest and right
From Stiles's pocket into Nokes's."
        Butler : Hudibras, iii. 3.

Styli'tes or *Pillar Saints.* By far the most celebrated are Simeon the Stylite of Syria, and Daniel the Stylite of Constantinople. Simeon spent thirty-seven years on different pillars, each loftier and narrower than the preceding. The last was sixty-six feet high. He died in 460, aged seventy-two. Daniel lived thirty-three years on a pillar, and was not unfrequently nearly blown from it by the storms from Thrace. He died in 494. Tennyson has a poem on Simeon Stylites.

" I, Simeon of the Pillar by surname,
Stylites among men—I, Simeon,
The watcher on the column till the end."
        Tennyson.

Styx. The river of Hate, called by Milton "abhorrèd Styx, the flood of burning hate" (*Paradise Lost,* ii. 577). It was said to flow nine times round the infernal regions. (Greek, *stug'eo,* to hate.)

⁂ The Styx is a river of Egypt, and the tale is that Isis collected the various parts of Osiris (murdered by Typhon) and buried them in secrecy on the banks of the Styx. The classic fables about the Styx are obviously of Egyptian origin. Charon, as Diodōrus informs us, is an Egyptian word for a "ferryman," and styx means "hate."

" The Thames reminded him of Styx."—*M. Taine.*

        Styx, the dread oath of gods.

" For by the black infernal Styx I swear
(That dreadful oath which binds the Thunderer)
'Tis fixed !"   *Pope : Thebais of Statius,* i.

Suav'iter in Modo (Latin). An inoffensive manner of doing what is to be done. *Suaviter in modo, fortiter in re,* doing what is to be done with unflinching firmness, but in the most inoffensive manner possible.

Sub Cultro Liquit. He left me in the lurch, like a toad under the harrow, or an ox under the knife.

Sub Hasta. By auction. When an auction took place among the Romans, it was customary to stick a spear in the ground to give notice of it to the public. In London we hang from the first-floor window a strip of bed-room carpet.

Sub Jo've (Latin). Under Jove; in the open air. Jupiter is the deified personification of the upper regions of the air, Juno of the lower regions, Neptune of the waters of the sea, Vesta of the earth, Ceres of the surface soil, Hades of the invisible or under-world.

Sub-Lapsa'rian, Supra-Lapsarian. The *sub*-lapsarian maintains that God devised His scheme of redemption *after* the "lapse" or fall of Adam, when He elected some to salvation and left others to run their course. The *supra*-lapsarian maintains that all this was ordained by God from the foundation of the world, and therefore *before* the "lapse" or fall of Adam.

Sub Rosa. (*See* ROSE.)

Sublime Port. Wine merchants say the port of 1820 is the true. "Sublime Port." Of course, the play is on the Porta Sublima or Ottoman empire.

Sublime Porte (*The*). The Ottoman empire. It is the French for Porta Sublima, the "lofty gate." Constantinople has twelve gates, and near one of these gates is a building with a lofty gateway called "Bab-i-humajun." In this building resides the vizier, in the same are the offices of all the chief ministers of state, and thence all the imperial edicts are issued. The French phrase has been adopted, because at one time French was the language of European diplomacy.

Submerged (*The*) or **The Submerged Tenth.** The proletariat, sunk or submerged in poverty; the gutter-class; the waifs and strays of society.

"All but the 'submerged' were bent upon merrymaking."—*Society,* November 12th, 1892, p. 1273.

"If Mr. Booth has not inaugurated remedial work among the submerged tenth, he has certainly set the fashion of writing and talking about them."—*Newspaper paragraph,* October 13th, 1891.

Submit means simply "to lower," and the idea usually associated with the word is derived from a custom in gladiatorial sports: When a gladiator acknowledged himself vanquished he lowered (*submitted*) his arms as a sign that he gave in; it then rested with the spectators to let him go or put him to death. If they wished him to live they held their thumbs *down,* if to be put to death they held their thumbs *upwards.*

Subpœ'na is a writ given to a man commanding him to appear in court, to bear witness or give evidence on a certain trial named in the writ. It is so called because the party summoned is bound to appear *sub pœna centum libro'rum* (under a penalty of £100). We have the verb to *subpœna.*

Sub'sidy means literally a sediment; that which is on the ground. It is a military term. In battle the Romans drew up their army in three divisions: first, the light-armed troops made the attack, and, if repulsed, the pike-men came up to their aid; if these two were beaten back, the swordsmen (*prin'cipes*) advanced; and if they too were defeated, the reserve went forward. These last were called subsidies because they remained *resting on their left knee* till their time of action. Metaphorically, money

aid is called a subsidy. (Latin, *subsideo,* to subside.)

Substitution of Service (*The*), in Ireland. Instead of serving a process personally, the name of the defaulter was posted on the walls of a Catholic chapel in the parish or barony, or in some other public place.

Subtle Doctor. John Duns Scotus, one of the schoolmen. (1265-1308.)

Subvol'vans or **Subvolva'ni.** The antagonists of the Privolvans in Samuel Butler's satirical poem called *The Elephant in the Moon.*

"The gallant Subvolvani rally,
And from their trenches make a sally."
Verse 83, etc.

Succes'sion Powder. The poison used by the Marquise de Brinvilliers in her poisonings, for the benefit of successors. (*See* POISONERS.)

Succinct means undergirded; hence concise, terse. (Latin, *sub-cinctus.*)

Succoth. The Jewish feast of tabernacles or tents, which began on the 15th Tisri (September), and lasted eight days. It was kept in remembrance of the sojourn in the wilderness, and was a time of grand rejoicing. Those who kept it held in their hands sprigs of myrtle, palm-branches, and willow-twigs. The Pentateuch was read on the last eight days.

Suck the Monkey. (*See* MONKEY.)

Sucking Young Patricians. The younger sons of the aristocracy, who sponge on those in power to get places of profit and employment.

Suckle. *To suckle fools and chronicle small beer.* Iago says women are of no use but to nurse children and keep the accounts of the household. (*Shakespeare: Othello,* ii. 1.)

Sucre. *Manger du sucre.* Applause given by claqueurs to actors is called *sucre* (sugar). French actors and actresses make a regular agreement with the manager for these hired applauders. While inferior artists are obliged to accept a mere murmur of approval, others receive a "salvo of bravos," while those of the highest rôle demand a "furore" or *éclat de rire,* according to their line of acting, whether tragedy or comedy. Sometimes the manager is bound to give actors "sugar to eat" in the public journals, and the agreement is that the announcement of their name shall be preceded with the words "celebrated," "admirable," and so on. The following is part of the agreement of a French actor on renewing his engagement (1869) :—" Que cinquante claqueurs au moins feraient manger du sucre dès l'entrée en scène, et que l'actrice rivale serait privée de cet agrément." (*See* CLAQUE.)

Suds (*Mrs.*). A facetious name for a washwoman or laundress. Of course, the allusion is to soap-suds.

To be in the suds—in ill-temper. According to the song, "Ne'er a bit of comfort is upon a washing day," all are put out of gear, and therefore out of temper.

Suffolk. The folk south of Norfolk.

Suf'frage means primarily the hough or pastern of a horse ; so called because it bends *under*, and not over, like the knee-joint. When a horse is lying down and wants to rise on his legs, it is this joint which is brought into action ; and when the horse stands on his legs it is these "ankle-joints" which support him. Metaphorically, voters are the pastern joints of a candidate, whereby he is supported.

A *suffragan* is a titular bishop who is appointed to assist a prelate ; and in relation to an archbishop all bishops are suffragans. The archbishop is the horse, and the bishops are his pasterns.

Sugar-candy. Rhyming slang for "brandy."

Sugar-lip. Hâfiz, the great Persian lyrist. (*-1389.)

Sugar and Honey. Rhyming slang for "money." (*See* CHIVY.)

Sugared Words. Sweet, flattering words. When sugar was first imported into Europe it was a very great dainty. The coarse, vulgar idea now associated with it is from its being cheap and common.

Sui Gen'eris (Latin). Having a distinct character of its own ; unlike anything else.

Sui Juris. Of one's own right ; the state of being able to exercise one's legal rights—*i.e.* freedom from legal disability.

Suicides were formerly buried ignominiously on the high-road, with a stake thrust through their body, and without Christian rites. (*Chambers : Encyclopædia*, lx. p. 184, col. 1.)

" They buried Ben at four cross roads,
With a stake in his inside."
Hood : Faithless Nelly Gray.

Suisse. *Tu fais suisse.* You live alone ; you are a misanthrope. Suisse means porter or door-keeper, hence "*Parler au Suisse*" ("Ask the porter," or "Enquire at the porter's lodge"). The door-keeper lives in a lodge near the main entrance, and the solitariness of his position, cut off from the house and servants, gave rise to the phrase. At one time these porters were for the most part Swiss.

Suit (1 syl.). *To follow suit.* To follow the leader ; to do as those do who are taken as your exemplars. The term is from games of cards.

Suit of Dittos (*A*). A suit of clothes in which coat, waistcoat, and trousers are all of one cloth.

Sullt [*starvation*]. The knife which the goddess Hel (*q.v.*) is accustomed to use when she sits down to eat from her dish Hunger.

Sultan of Persia. Mahmoud Gazni, founder of the Gaznivide dynasty, was the first to assume in Persia the title of Sultan (A.D. 999).

Sultan's Horse, Deadly (*The*).

" Byzantians boast that on the clod
Where once the Sultan's horse hath trod
Grows neither grass, nor shrub, nor tree."
Swift : Pethox the Great.

Sulta'na. A beautiful bird, allied to the moorhen, with blue feathers, showing beautiful metallic gloss, generally with red beak and legs.

" Some purple-winged sultana."
Moore : Paradise and the Peri.

Summa Diligentia. On the top of a diligence. "Cæsar crossed the Alps 'summa diligentia.'" This is a famous schoolboy joke, and one of the best of the kind.

Summer. The second or autumnal summer, said to last thirty days, begins about the time that the sun enters Scorpio (October 23rd). It is variously called—

(1) St. Martin's summer (*L'été de St. Martin*). St. Martin's Day is the 11th November.

"Expect St. Martin's summer, halcyon days."
Shakespeare : 1 Henry VI., i. 2.

(2) All Saints' summer (All Saints' is the 1st November), or All Hallowen summer.

" Then followed that beautiful season,
Called by the pious Arcadian peasants the summer of All Saints."
Longfellow : Evangeline.

" Farewell, All Hallowen summer." — *Shakespeare : 1 Henry IV., i. 2.*

(3) St. Luke's little summer (St. Luke's day is 18th October).

Summer King (*The*). Amadeus of Spain.

Summons. Peter and John de Carvajal, being condemned to death on circumstantial evidence, appealed without success to Ferdinand IV. of Spain. On their way to execution they declared their innocence, and summoned the king to appear before God within thirty days. Ferdinand was quite well on the thirtieth day, but was found dead in his bed next morning. (*See* WISHART.)

Summum Bonum. The chief excellence ; the highest attainable good.

SOCRATES said knowledge is virtue, and ignorance is vice.

ARISTOTLE said that happiness is the greatest good.

BERNARD DE MANDEVILLE and HELVETIUS contended that self-interest is the perfection of the ethical end.

BENTHAM and MILL were for the greatest happiness of the greatest number.

HERBERT SPENCER places it in those actions which best tend to the survival of the individual and the race.

LETOURNEAU places it in utilitarianism.

Sumpter Horse or **Mule.** One that carries baggage. (Italian, *soma*, a burden.) (*See* SOMAGIA.)

Sumptuary Laws. Laws to limit the expenses of food and dress, or any luxury. The Romans had their sumptuary laws (*leges sumptuārii*). Such laws have been enacted in many states at various times. Those of England were all repealed by 1 James I., c. 25.

Sun. Hebrew, *Elohim* (God) ; Greek, *helios* (the sun) ; Breton, *heol ;* Latin, *sol ;* German, *sonne ;* Anglo-Saxon, *sunne.* As a deity, called Ado'nis by the Phœnicians, and Apollo by the Greeks and Romans.

Sun. Harris, in his *Hermēs,* asserts that all nations ascribe to the sun a masculine and the moon a feminine gender. For confutation *see* MOON.

City of the Sun. Rhodes was so called because the sun was its tutelar deity. The Colossos of Rhodes was consecrated to the sun. On or Heliopolis, Egypt.

Sun (*The*), called in Celtic mythology Sunna (*fem.*), lives in constant dread of being devoured by the wolf Fenris. It is this contest with the wolf to which eclipses are due. According to this

mythology, the sun has a beautiful daughter who will one day reign in place of her mother, and the world will be wholly renovated.

Horses of the Sun.

Arva'kur, Aslo, and Alsvidur. (*Scandinavian mythology.*)

Brontē (*thunder*), Eo'os (*day-break*), Ethiops (*flashing*), Ethon (*fiery*), Erythre'os (*red-producers*), Philoge'a (*earth-loving*), Pyr'ois (*fiery*). All of them " breathe fire from their nostrils." (*Greek and Latin mythology.*)

The horses of Aurora are Abrax and Pha'eton. (*See* HORSE.)

¶ *More worship the rising than the setting sun,* said Pompey ; meaning that more persons pay honour to ascendant than to fallen greatness. The allusion is, of course, to the Persian fire-worshippers.

Heaven cannot support two suns, nor earth two masters. So said Alexander the Great when Darius (before the battle of Arbe'la) sent to offer terms of peace. Beautifully imitated by Shakespeare :—

" Two stars keep not their motion in one sphere ;
Nor can one England brook a double reign,
Of Harry Percy and the Prince of Wales."
         1 Henry IV., v. 4.

Here lies a she-sun, and a he-moon there (Donne). Epithalamium on the marriage of Lady Elizabeth, daughter of James I., with Frederick, elector palatine. It was through this unfortunate princess, called " Queen of Bohemia " and " Queen of Hearts," that the family of Brunswick succeeded to the British throne. Some say that Lord Craven married (secretly) the " fair widow."

Sun-burst. The fanciful name given by the ancient Irish to their national banner.

" At once, like a sun-burst, her banner unfurled."
         Thomas Moore : Irish Melodies, No. 6.

Sun Inn. In compliment to the ill-omened House of York. The *Sun Inn,* Westminster, is the badge of Richard II.

Sun and Moon Falling. By the old heralds the arms of royal houses were not emblazoned by colours, but by sun, moon, and stars. Thus, instead of or (*gold*), a royal coat has the *sun ;* instead of argent (*silver*), the *moon ;* instead of the other five heraldic colours, one of the other five ancient planets. In connection with this idea, read Matt. xxiv. 29 : " Immediately after the tribulation of those days shall the *sun* be darkened, and the *moon* shall not give her light, and the *stars* shall fall from heaven, and the powers of the heavens shall be shaken." (*See* PLANETS.)

Sun in one's Eyes (*To have the*). To be tipsy.

Sun of Righteousness. Jesus Christ. (Mal. iv. 3.)

Sunday. *Impor'ant battles fought on Sunday.* Barnet, Bull Run, Carberry Hill, Friedland, Fuentes d'Onoro, Jarnac, THE GLORIOUS FIRST OF JUNE (Lord Howe's great victory), Killiecrankie, Kunersdorf, Leipsig, Lepanto, Lincoln, Newbury, RAMILLIES, Ravenna, Saarbruck (the "baptism of fire"), SEDAN, Seringapatam, Stony Creek, of the Thirty, Toulouse, Towton, Vienna, Vimiera, WATERLOO, WORCESTER.

Sunday Saint. One who observes the ordinances of religion, and goes to church on a Sunday, but is worldly, grasping, indifferently honest, and not "too moral" the following six days.

Sundays. *When three Sundays come together.* (*See* NEVER.)

Sundew, the *Drosĕra*, which is from the Greek *drosos*, dew. So called from the dew-like drops which rest on the hairy fringes of the leaves.

> " By the lone fountain's secret bed,
> Where human footsteps rarely tread ;
> Mid the wild moor or silent glen,
> The sundew blooms unseen by men,
> And, ere the summer's sun can rise,
> Drinks the pure water of the skies."
> *The Wild Garland.*

Sunflower (*The*). Clytie, a waternymph, was in love with Apollo, but meeting no return, she died and was changed into a sunflower, which still turns to the sun through its daily course.

> " The sunflower turns on the god, when he sets,
> The same look which she turned when he rose."
> *T. Moore*: (*Believe me if all those endearing young charms*).

> " I will not have the mad Clytie,
> Whose head is turned by the sun."
> *Hood.*

⁂ What we call a sunflower is the *Helianthus,* so called, not because it follows the sun, but because it resembles a picture sun. A bed of these flowers will turn in every direction, regardless of the sun. The Turnsole is the *Heliotrōpium,* quite another order of plants.

Sunna or **Sonna.** The Oral Law, or the precepts of Mahomet not contained in the Koran, collected into a volume. Similar to the Jewish Mishna, which is the supplement of the Pentateuch. (Arabic, *sunna,* custom, rule of conduct.)

Sunnites (2 syl.). Orthodox Mahometans, who consider the Sunna or Oral Law as binding as the Koran. They wear *white* turbans. The heterodox Moslems are called Shiites or Shiahs (*q.v.*).

Suo Jure (Latin). In one's own right.

Suo Marte (Latin). By one's own strength or personal exertions.

Super, Supers. In theatrical parlance, " supers " means supernumeraries, or persons employed to make up crowds, processions, dancing or singing choirs, messengers, etc., where little or no speaking is needed.

Supercil'ious (5 syl.). Having an elevated eyebrow ; hence contemptuous, haughty. (Latin, *super-cilium.*)

Supernac'ulum. The very best wine. The word is Low Latin for " upon the nail," meaning that the wine is so good the drinker leaves only enough in his glass to make a bead on his nail. The French say of first-class wine, "It is fit to make a ruby on the nail " (*faire rubis sur l'ongle*), referring to the residue left which is only sufficient to make a single drop on the nail. Tom Nash says, " After a man has drunk his glass, it is usual, in the North, to turn the bottom of the cup upside down, and let a drop fall upon the thumb-nail. If the drop rolls off, the drinker is obliged to fill and drink again." Bishop Hall alludes to the same custom: "The Duke Tenterbelly . . . exclaims . . . ' Let never this goodly-formed goblet of wine go jovially through me ; ' and then he set it to his mouth, stole it off every drop, save a little remainder, which he was by custom to set upon his thumb-nail and lick off."

> " 'Tis here ! the supernaculum : twenty years
> Of age, if 'tis a day." *Byron: Werner,* i. 1.

Supernaculum. Entirely. To drink supernaculum is to leave no heel-taps ; to drink so as to leave just enough not to roll off one's thumb-nail if poured upon it, but only to remain there as a wine-bead.

> " This is after the fashion of Switzerland. Clear off neat, supernaculum."—*Rabelais: Gargantua and Pantagruel,* bk. i. 5.

> " Their jests were supernaculum,
> I snatched the rubies from each thumb,
> And in th's crystal have them here.
> Perhaps you'll like it more than beer."
> *King: Orpheus and Eurydice.*

Superstition. That which survives when its companions are dead. (Latin, *supersto.*) Those who escaped in battle were called *superstĭtēs.* Superstition is religious credulity, or that religion which remains when real religion is dead.

Paul said to the Athenians that he perceived they were " too superstitious."—Acts XV. 22.

Supped all his Porridge (*He has*). Eaten his last meal ; he is dead.

Supper of Trimalchio (*A*). A supper for gourmands of the upper classes in the reign of Nero. It forms a section of *Petronii Arbitri Satyricon.*

Supplica'tion. This word has greatly changed its original meaning. The Romans used it for a thanksgiving after a signal victory (*Livy*, iii. 63). ("*His rebus gestis, supplicatio a senatu decreta est*" [*Cæsar : Bell. Gall.*, ii.].) The word means the act of folding the knees (*sub-plico*). We now use the word for begging or entreating something.

Sure as Demoivre. Abraham Demoivre, author of *The Doctrine of Chances, or Method of Calculating the Probabilities of Events at Play*, was proverbially accurate in his calculations. It was Pope who said, "Sure as Demoivre, without rule or line."
Sure as a gun, as fate, as death and taxes, etc. (*See* SIMILES.)

"Surest Way to Peace is a constant Preparation for War." Fox, afterwards Bishop of Hereford, to Henry VIII. (In Latin, "*Si vis pacem, para bellum.*")

Surety. One who takes the place of another, a substitute, a hostage.

Surfeit Water. Cordial water to cure surfeits.

"Water that cures surfeits. A little cold distilled poppywater is the true surfeit water."—*Locke.*

Surgeon is the Greek form of the Latin word *manufacturer.* The former is *cheir-ergein* (to work with the hand), and the latter *manu-facere* (to do or make with the hand).

Surloin of Beef. (*See* SIRLOIN.)

Surlyboy. Yellow hair. (Irish, *surley buie.*)

Sur'name (2 syl.). The over-name ; either the name written over the Christian name, or given over and above it ; an additional name. For a long time persons had no family name, but only one, and that a personal name. Surnames are not traced farther back than the latter part of the tenth century.
Surnames of places.

In *ford*, in *ham*, and *ley*, and *ton*, The most of English surnames run.

Sur'plice (2 syl.). Over the fur robe. (Latin, *super-pellicium.*) The clerical robe worn over the bachelor's ordinary dress, which was anciently made of sheepskin. The ancient Celts and Germans also wore a garment occasionally over their fur skins.

Durandus says : "The garments of the Jewish priesthood were girt tight about them, to signify the *bondage of the law ;* but the surplice of the Christian priest is loose, to signify the *freedom of the gospel.*"

Surrey. Anglo-Saxon, *Suth-rea* (south of the river—*i.e.* the Thames), or *Suth-ric* (south kingdom).
Saddle White Surrey for the field to-morrow (Shakespeare : *Richard III.*). Surrey is the Syrian horse, as Roan Barbary in *Richard II.* is the Barbary horse or barb. (*See* HORSE.)

Surt or **Surtur.** The guardian of Muspelheim, who keeps watch day and night with a flaming sword. At the end of the world he will hurl fire from his hand and burn up both heaven and earth. (*Scandinavian mythology.*)

Susan (*St.*). The patron saint who saves from infamy and reproach. This is from her fiery trial recorded in the tale of Susannah and the Elders.
⁂ This wife of Joiachim, being accused of adultery, was condemned to death by the Jewish elders ; but Daniel proved her innocence, and turned the tables on her accusers, who were put to death instead. (*The Apocrypha.*)

Sussex. The territory of the South Saxons (*Suth-Seaxe*).

Sutor. *Ne sutor*, etc. (*See* COBBLER.)
Stick to the cow. Boswell, one night sitting in the pit of Covent Garden theatre with his friend Dr. Blair, gave an extempore imitation of a cow, which the house applauded. He then ventured another imitation, but failed, whereupon the doctor advised him in future to "stick to the cow."

Suttee (Indian). A pure and model wife (Sanskrit, *sati*, chaste, pure) ; a widow who immolates herself on the funeral pile of her deceased husband. Abolished by law in British India.

Sval'in. The dashboard placed by the gods before the sun-car to prevent the earth from being burnt up. The word means "cooling." (*Scandinavian mythology.*)

Swaddler. A contemptuous synonym for Protestant used by the Roman Catholics. Cardinal Cullen, in 1869, gave notice that he would deprive of the sacrament all parents who sent their children to be taught in mixed Model schools, where they were associated with "Presbyterians, Socinians, Arians, and Swaddlers." (See *Times*, September 4, 1869.)

The origin of the term is as follows:—
"It happened that Cennick, preaching on Christmas Day, took for his text these words from St. Luke's Gospel: 'And this shall be a sign unto you; ye shall find the babe wrapped in swaddling clothes lying in a manger.' A Catholic who was present, and to whom the language of Scripture was a novelty, thought this so ridiculous that he called the preacher a swaddler in derision, and this unmeaning word became a nickname for 'Protestant,' and had all the effect of the most opprobrious appellation." (*Southey: Life of Wesley*, ii. 153.)

Swag. Luggage, knapsack, a bundle; also food carried about one. *Swag-shop*, a store of minor, or cheap-priced goods. (Scotch, *sweg*.)

"[Palliser] began to retrace the way by which he had fled, and, descending carefully to the spot where he had thrown off his swag, found it as he had left it."—*Watsons The Web of the Spider*, chap. v.

Swag. Plenty. Rhyming slang: A bag-full means plenty, and by omitting full, "bag" remains to rhyme with swag. (*See* CHIVY.)

Swagger. Bluster; noisy boasting.

Swainmote. (*See* SWANIMOTE.)

Swal'low. According to Scandinavian tradition, this bird hovered over the cross of our Lord, crying "*Svala! svala!*" (Console! console!) whence it was called *svalow* (the bird of consolation). (*See* CHRISTIAN TRADITIONS.)

The *swallow* is said to bring home from the sea-shore a stone which gives sight to her fledglings.

"Seeking with eager eyes that wondrous stone
which the swallow
Brings from the shore of the sea to restore the
sight of its fledglings."
Longfellow: Evangeline, part i.

It is lucky for a swallow to build about one's house. This is a Roman superstition. Ælian says that the swallow was sacred to the Pena'tēs or household gods, and therefore to injure one would be to bring wrath upon your own house.

It is unlucky to kill a swallow.

"Perhaps you failed in your foreseeing skill,
For swallows are unlucky birds to kill."
Dryden: Hind and Panther, part iii.

One swallow does not make spring. You are not to suppose winter is past because you have seen a swallow; nor that the troubles of life are over because you have surmounted one difficulty.

Swan. Fionnua'la, daughter of Lir, was transformed into a swan, and condemned to wander for many hundred years over the lakes and rivers of Ireland till the introduction of Christianity into that island. T. Moore has a poem entitled *The Song of Fionnuala*. (*Irish Melodies*, No. 11.)

The male swan is called a *cob*, the female a *pen;* a young swan is called a *cygnet*.

Swan. Erman says of the *Cygnus olor*, "This bird, when wounded, pours forth its last breath in notes most beautifully clear and loud." (*Travels in Siberia*, translated by Cooley, vol. ii.)

Emilia says, "I will play the swan, and die in music." (*Othello*, v. 2.)

"'What is that, mother?' 'The swan, my love.
He is floating down to his native grove . . .
Death darkens his eyes and unplumes his wings,
Yet the sweetest song is the last he sings.
Live so, my son, that when death shall come,
Swan-like and sweet, it may waft thee home.'"
Dr. G. Doane.

Swan. Mr. Nicol says of the *Cygnus mu'sicus* that its note resembles the tones of a violin, though somewhat higher. Each note occurs after a long interval. The music presages a thaw in Iceland, and hence one of its great charms.

Swan. A nickname for a blackamoor. (*See* LUCUS A NON LUCENDO.)

"Ethiopem voca'mus cygnum."
Juvenal, viii. 32.

A black swan. A curiosity, a *rara avis*. The expression is borrowed from the well known verse "*Rara avis in terris, nigroque simillima cycno*."

"'What! is it my *rara avis*, my black swan?'"—
Sir Walter Scott: The Antiquary.

Swan. *Swan, a public-house sign,* like the peacock and pheasant, was an emblem of the parade of chivalry. Every knight chose one of these birds, which was associated in his oath with God, the Virgin, or his lady-love. Hence their use as public-house signs.

The White Swan, a public-house sign, is in compliment to Anne of Cleves, descended from the Knight of the Swan.

Swan with Two Necks. A corruption of "Swan with Two Nicks." The Vintners' Company mark their swans with two nicks in the beak.

N.B. Royal swans are marked with five nicks—two lengthwise, and three across the bill.

Swan-hopping. A corruption of Swan Upping—that is, taking the swans up the River Thames for the purpose of marking them. (*See above.*)

Swan of Avon (*The*), or **Sweet Swan of Avon.** Shakespeare is so called by Ben Jonson because his home was on the Avon. (1564-1616.)

Swan of Cambray (*The*). Fénelon, Archbishop of Cambray, and author of *Telemachus*. (1651-1715.)

Swan of Mantua (*The*), or **The Mantuan Swan**. Virgil, who was born at Mantua. (B.C. 70-29.)

Swan of Meander (*The*). Homer, who lived on the banks of the Meander, in Asia Minor. (Fl. B.C. 950.)

Swan of Padua (*The*). Count Francesco Algarotti. (1712-1764.)

Swans . . . Geese. *All your swans are geese.* All your fine promises or expectations have proved fallacious. "Hope told a flattering tale." The converse, *All your geese are swans*, means all your children are paragons, and whatever you do is in your own eyes superlative work.

Swan'imote. A court held thrice a year before forest verderers by the steward of the court. So called because the swans or swains were the jurymen. (*Swans, swains*, or *sweins*, freeholders; Anglo-Saxon, *swan* or *swein*, a herdsman, shepherd, youth; our *swain*.)

⁘ This court was incident to a forest, as the court of pie-powder or piepoudre to a fair.

Swarga. The paradise of Indra, and also of certain deified mortals, who rest there under the shade of the five wonderful trees, drink the nectar of immortality called Am'rita, and dance with the heavenly nymphs.

Swashbuckler. A ruffian; a swaggerer. "From swashing," says Fuller, "and making a noise on the buckler." The sword-players used to "swash" or tap their shield, as fencers tap their foot upon the ground when they attack. (*Worthies of England.*) (A.D. 1662.) (*See* SWINGE-BUCKLER.)

"A bravo, a swashbuckler, one that for money and good cheere will follow any man to defend him ; but if any danger come, he runs away the first, and leaves him in the lurch."—*Florio.*

Swear now means to take an oath, but the primitive sense is merely to *aver* or *affirm;* when to affirm on oath was meant, the word *oath* was appended, as "I swear by oath." Shakespeare uses the word frequently in its primitive sense ; thus Othello says of Desdemona—

"She swore, in faith 'twas strange, 'twas passing strange."   *Othello,* i. 3.

Swear Black is White (*To*). To swear to any falsehood.

Swear by my Sword (*Hamlet*, i. 5) —that is, "by the cross on the hilt of my sword." Again in *Winter's Tale,* "Swear by this sword thou wilt perform my bidding" (ii. 3). Holinshed says, "Warwick kisses the cross of King Edward's sword, as it were a vow to his promise ; " and Decker says, "He has sworn to me on the cross of his pure Tole'do" (*Old Fortunatus*).

Sweat. *To sweat a client.* To make him bleed; to fleece him.

To sweat coin. To subtract part of the silver or gold by friction, but not to such an amount as to render the coin useless as a legal tender. The French use *suer* in the same sense, as " *Suer son argent*," to sweat his money by usury. "*Vous faites suer le bonhomme—tel est votre dire quand vous le pillez.*" (*Harangue du Capitaine la Carbonnade.*) (1615.)

Sweating Sickness appeared in England about a century and a half after the *Black Death.* (1485.) It broke out amongst the soldiers of Richmond's army, after the battle of Bosworth Field, and lasted five weeks. It was a violent inflammatory fever, without boils or ulcers. Between 1485 and 1529 there were five outbreaks of this pest in England, the first four being confined to England and France; but the fifth spread over Germany, Turkey, and Austria.

Swedenbor'gians, called by themselves "the New Jerusalem Church " (Rev. xxi. 2). Believers in the doctrines taught by Emanuel Swedenborg (1688-1772). Their views of salvation, inspiration of Scripture, and a future state, differ widely from those of other Christians ; and as to the Trinity, they believe it to be centred in the person of Jesus Christ (Col. ii. 9). (*Supplied by the Auxiliary New Church Missionary Society.*)

Swedish Nightingale. Jenny Lind (Madame Goldschmidt), a native of Stockholm, and previous to her marriage a public singer. (1821-1886.)

Sweep. *To sweep the threshold.* To announce to all the world that the woman of the house is paramount. When the procession called "Skimmington" passed any house where the woman was dominant, each one gave the threshold a sweep with a broom or bunch of twigs. (*See* SKIMMINGTON.)

Sweepstakes (*A*). A race in which stakes are made by the owners of horses engaged, to be awarded to the winner or other horse in the race. In all sweepstakes entrance money has to be paid to the race fund. (*See* PLATE, SELLING-RACE, HANDICAP, WEIGHT-FOR-AGE RACE.)

If the horse runs, the full stake must be paid ; but if it is withdrawn, a forfeit only is imposed.

✤ Also a gambling arrangement by which the successful bettor sweeps up or carries off all the other stakes. It is sometimes applied to a game of cards in which one of the players may win all the tricks or all the stakes.

Sweet as sugar. (*See* SIMILES.)

Sweet Singer of Israel. King David (B.C. 1074-1001).

Sweet Singers. A puritanical sect in the reign of Charles II., etc., common in Edinburgh. They burnt all storybooks, ballads, romances, etc., denounced all unchaste words and actions, and even the printed Bible.

Sweet Voices. Backers, votes. Coriolanus speaks with contempt of the sweet voices of the Roman mob voters.

Sweetheart. A lover, male or female.

Swell Mob. The better-dressed thieves and pickpockets. A " swell " is a person showily dressed ; one who puffs himself out beyond his proper dimensions, like the frog in the fable.

Swi Dynasty. The twelfth Imperial dynasty of China, founded by Yang-kien, Prince of Swi, A.D. 587. He assumed the name of Wen-tee (King Wen).

Swift as lightning, as the wind, as an arrow, etc. (*See* SIMILES.)

Swim (*In the*). In society. The upper crust of society. An angler's phrase. A lot of fish gathered together is called a *swim*, and when an angler can pitch his hook in such a place he is said to be " in a good swim." To know persons in the swim is to know society folk, who always congregate together.

" Cottontree, who knows nearly everybody in the swim of European society . . . informs him that Lucy Annerley is the daughter of Sir Jonas Stevens."—A. C. Gunter : Mr. Potter of Texas, book iii. chap. xiv.

Swindle. To cheat ; from the German *schwindeln*, to totter. It originally meant those artifices employed by a tradesman to prop up his credit when it began to totter, in order to prevent or defer bankruptcy.

Swine. *Boar* or *brawn*, the sire ; *sow*, the dam ; *sucklings*, the new-born pigs. A castrated boar-pig is called **a** *hog* or *shot*. Young pigs for the butcher are called *porkers*.

A sow-pig after her first litter becomes a *brood-sow*, and her whole stock of pigs cast at a birth is called a *litter* or *farrow of pigs*.

Swing (*Captain*). The name assumed by certain persons who sent threatening letters to those who used threshing machines: (1830-1833.) The tenor of these letters was as follows :—" Sir, if you do not lay by your threshing machine, you will hear from Swing."

" Excesses of the Luddites and Swing."—*The Times*.

Swinge-buckler. A roisterer, a rake. The continuation of *Stow's Annals* tells us that the " blades " of London used to assemble in West Smithfield with sword and buckler, in the reign of Queen Elizabeth, on high days and holidays, for mock fights called " bragging " fights. They swashed and swinged their bucklers with much show of fury, " but seldome was any man hurt." (*See* SWASHBUCKLER.)

" There was I, and little John Doit of Staffordshire, and black George Barnes, and Francis Pickbone, and Will Squele, a Cotswold man ; you had not four such swinge-bucklers in all the Inns-ofcourt ; and, I may say to you, we knew where the bona-robas were."—*Shakespeare: 2 Henry IV.*, iii. 2.

Swiss. The nickname of a Swiss is " Colin Tampon " (*q.v.*).

No money, no Swiss—*i.e.* no servant. The Swiss have ever been the mercenaries of Europe—willing to serve anyone for pay. The same was said of the ancient Ca'rians. In the hotels of Paris this notice is common : " *Demandez* [or *Parlez*] *au Suisse* " (Speak to the porter).

Swiss Boy (*The*). Music by Moscheles.

Swiss Family Robinson. An abridged translation of a German tale by Joachim Heinrich Kampe, tutor to Baron Humboldt.

Swithin (*St.*). *If it rains on St. Swithin's day* (15th July), *there will be rain for forty days*. (*See* GERVAIS.)

" St. Swithin's day, gif ye do rain, for forty days it will remain ;
St. Swithin's day, an ye be fair, for forty days 'twill rain nae mair."

The French have two similar proverbs—" *S'il pleut le jour de St. Médan* " (8th June), " *il pleut quarante jours plus tard ;* " and " *S'il pleut le jour de St. Gervais* " (19th June), " *il pleut quarante jours après*."

The legend is that St. Swithin, Bishop of Winchester, who died 862, desired t̶ be buried in the church-*yard* of the minster, that the "sweet rain of heaven might fall upon his grave." At canonisation the monks thought to honour the saint by removing his body into the choir, and fixed July 15th for the ceremony; but it rained day after day for forty days, so that the monks saw the saints were averse to their project, and wisely abandoned it.

The St. Swithin of Scotland is St. Martin of Bouillons. The rainy saint in Flanders is St. Godeliève; in Germany, the Seven Sleepers.

Switzers. Swiss mercenaries. "Where are my Switzers? Let them guard the door" (*Hamlet*, iv. 5).

Swollen Head. Excessive conceit. One who has a greatly exaggerated opinion of himself is said to suffer from swollen head.

Sword. *Owners' names for their swords.*

(1) AGRICANE'S was called *Tranch'era.* Afterwards BRANDEMART'S.

(2) ALI'S sword was *Zulfagar.*

(3) ANTONY'S was Philippan, so named from the battle of Philippi. (*Shakespeare: Antony and Cleopatra*, ii. 4.)

(4) ARTEGAL'S was called *Chrysa'or.* (*Spenser: Faërie Queene.*)

(5) ARTHUR'S was called *Escalibar, Excalibar,* or *Caliburn;* given to him by the Lady of the Lake.

(6) SIR BEVIS'S OF HAMPTOUN was called *Morglay.*

(7) BITEROLF'S was called *Schrit.*

(8) BRAGGADOCHIO'S was called *Sanglamore.* (*Faërie Queene.*)

(9) CÆSAR'S was called *Crocea Mors* (yellow death). (See *Commentaries*, bk. iv. 4.)

(10) CHARLEMAGNE'S were *Joyeuse* or *Fusberta Joyo'sa,* and *Flamberge;* both made by Galas.

(11) THE CID'S was called *Cola'da;* the sword *Tizo'na* was taken by him from King Bucar.

(12) CLOSAMONT'S was called *Haute-claire,* made by Galas.

(13) DIETRICH'S was *Nagelring.*

(14) DOOLIN'S OF MAYENCE was called *Merveilleuse* (wonderful).

(15) ECK'S was called *Sacho.*

(16) EDWARD THE CONFESSOR'S was called *Curta'na* (the cutter), a blunt sword of state carried before the sovereigns of England at their coronation, emblematical of mercy.

(17) ENGLISH KINGS' (the ancient) was called *Curta'na.*

(18) FRITHIOF'S was called *Angurva-del* (stream of anguish).

(19) HACO I.'S OF NORWAY was called *Quern-biter* (foot-breadth).

(20) HIEME'S was called *Blutgang.*

(21) HILDEBRAND'S was *Brinnig.*

(22) IRING'S was called *Waskë.*

(23) KOLL, THE THRALLS, *Greysteel.*

(24) LAUNCELOT OF THE LAKE'S, *Ar'oundight.*

(25) MAHOMET'S were called *Dhu' l Fakar* (the trenchant), a scimitar; *Al Battar* (the beater); *Medham* (the keen); *Halef* (the deadly).

(26) MAUGIS'S or MALAGIGI'S was called *Flamberge* or *Floberge.* He gave it to his cousin Rinaldo. It was made by Wieland.

(27) OGIER THE DANE'S, *Courtain* and *Sauvagine,* both made by Munifican.

"He [Ogier] drew Courtain, his sword, out of its sheath."—*Morris: Earthly Paradise*, 634.

(28) OLIVER'S was *Haute-Claire.*

(29) ORLANDO'S was called *Durinda'na* or *Durindan,* which once belonged to Hector, and is said to be still preserved at Rocamadour, in France.

(30) OTUEL'S was *Corrouque* (2 syl.).

(31) RINALDO'S was called *Fusberta* or *Flamberge* (2 syl.). (*See above,* MAUGIS.)

(32) ROGERO'S was called *Balisarda.* It was made by a sorceress.

(33) ROLAND'S was called *Durandal,* made by Munifican. This is the French version of *Orlando and Durandana.*

(34) SIEGFRIED'S was called *Balmung,* in the *Nibelungen-Lied.* It was made by Wieland. Also *Gram. Mimung* was lent to him by Wittich.

(35) SINTRAM'S was called *Welsung.*

(36) STRONG-I'-THE-ARM'S, *Baptism, Florence,* and *Graban,* by Ansias.

(37) THORALF SKOLINSON'S—*i.e.* Thoralf the Strong, of Norway—was called *Quern-biter* (foot-breadth).

(38) WIELAND. The swords made by the divine blacksmith were *Flamberge* and *Balmung.*

Sword-makers.

ANSIAS, GALAS, and MUNIFICAN made three swords each, and each sword took three years a-making.

ANSIAS. The three swords made by this cutler were *Baptism, Florence,* and *Graban,* all made for Strong-i'-the-Arm.

GALAS. The three swords made by this cutler were *Flamberge* (2 syl.) and *Joyeuse* for Charlemagne; and *Haute-claire* for Closamont.

MUNIFICAN. The three swords made by this cutler were *Durandal,* for Roland;

Sauvagine and *Courtain* for Ogier the Dane.

WIELAND ("the divine blacksmith") also made two famous swords—viz. *Flamberge*, for Maugis; and *Balmung*, for Siegfried.

N.B. Oliver's sword, called *Glorious*, hacked all the nine swords of Ansias, Galas, and Munifican "a foot from the pommel." (*Croquemitaine*.)

An alphabetical list of the famous swords:—

Al Battar (the beater), one of Mahomet's swords.

Angurva (stream of anguish), Frithiof's sword.

Ar'oundight(? *Æron-diht*), the sword of Launcelot of the Lake.

Balisarda, Rogero's sword, made by a sorceress.

Balmung, one of the swords of Siegfried, made by Wieland, "the divine blacksmith."

Baptism, one of the swords of Strong-i'-the-Arm, which took Ansias three years to make.

Blutgang (blood-fetcher), Hieme's sword.

Brinnig (flaming), Hildebrand's sword.

Culiburn, Arthur's sword.

Chrysaor (sword of gold, *i.e.* as good as gold). Artegal's sword.

Colada, the Cid's sword.

Corrougue, Otuel's sword.

Courtain (the short sword), one of the swords of Ogier the Dane, which took Munifican three years to make.

Crocea Mors (yellow death), Cæsar's sword.

Curtana (? the short sword). (See *Edward the Confessor* and *English kings*.)

Dhu' l Fakâr (the trenchant), Mahomet's scimitar.

Durandal, same as *Durandan*, Roland's sword, which took Munifican three years to make.

Durandan or *Durandana* (the inflexible), Orlando's sword.

Escalibar or *Excalibar*, the sword of King Arthur. (*Ex cal[ce]liber[are]*, to liberate from the stone.) (See below, SWORD EXCALIBAR.)

Flamberge or *Floberge* (? syl., the flame-cutter), one of Charlemagne's swords, and also the sword of Rinaldo, which took Gallas three years to make.

Flamborge, the sword of Maugis or Malagigi, made by Wieland, "the divine blacksmith."

Florence, one of the swords of Strong-i'-the-Arm, which took Ansias three years to make.

Fusberta Joyosa, another name for *Joyeuse* (*q.v.*).

Glorious, Oliver's sword, which hacked to pieces the nine swords made by Ausias, Galas, and Munifican.

Graban (the grave-digger), one of the swords of Strong-i'-the-Arm, which took Ansias three years to make,

Gram (grief), one of the swords of Siegfried.

Greysteel, the sword of Koll the Thrall.

Haute-claire (2 syl., very bright), both Closamont's and Oliver's swords were so called. Closamont's sword took Gallas three years to make.

Halef (the deadly), one of Mahomet's swords.

Joyeuse (2 syl., joyous), one of Charlemagne's swords, which took Gallas three years to make.

Mandousian swords (*q.v.*).

Medham (the keen), one of Mahomet's swords.

Merveilleuse (the marvellous), Doolin's sword.

Minung, the sword that Wittich lent Siegfried.

Morglay, i.e. mor-glaif (big glaive), Sir Bevis's sword.

Nagelring (nail-ring), Dietrich's sword.

Philippan. The sword of Antony, one of the triumvirs.

Quern-biter (a foot-breadth), both Haco I. and Thoralf Skolinson had a sword so called.

Sacho, Eck's sword.

Samsamha Haroun-al-Raschid's sword.

Sanglamore (the big bloody glaive), Braggadochio's sword.

Sauvagine (3 syl., the relentless), one of the swords of Ogier the Dane, which took Munifican three years to make.

Schrit or *Schritt* (? the lopper), Biterolf's sword.

Tizóna (the poker), King Bucar's sword. (See CID.)

Tranchéra (the trenchant), Agricane's sword.

Waske (2 syl.), Iring's sword.

Welsung, both Dietlieb and Sintram had a sword so called.

Zuflagar, Ali's sword.

Sword Excalibar (*The*). At the death of Uter Pendragon there were many claimants to the crown; they were all ordered to assemble in "the great church of London," on Christmas Eve, and found a sword stuck in a stone and anvil with this inscription: "He who can draw forth this sword, the same is to be king." The knights tried to pull it out, but were unable. One day, when a tournament was held, young Arthur wanted a sword and took this one, not knowing it was a charmed instrument, whereupon he was universally acknowledged to be the God-elected king. This was the sword of Excalibar. (*History of Prince Arthur*, i. 3.)

The enchanted sword (in *Amadis of Gaul*). Whoever drew this sword from a rock was to gain access to a subterranean treasure. (Cap. cxxx. *See also* caps. lxxii. and xcix.)

Sword of God (*The*), Khaled Ibn al Waled was so called for his prowess at the battle of Muta.

Sword of Rome (*The*). Marcellus, who opposed Hannibal, (B.C. 216-214.)

Sword of the Spirit (*The*). The Word of God (Eph. vi. 17).

¶ **Sword** (phrases and proverbs).

At swords' point. In deadly hostility, ready to fight each other with swords.

Poke not fire with a sword. This was a precept of Pythagoras, meaning add not fuel to fire, or do not irritate an angry man by sharp words which will only increase his rage. (See *Iamblichus: Protreptics*, symbol ix.)

To put to the sword. To slay.

Your tongue is a double-edged sword. You first say one thing and then the contrary; your argument cuts both ways. The allusion is to the double-edged sword out of the mouth of the Son of Man—one edge to condemn, and the other to save. (Rev. i. 16.)

Yours is a Delphic sword—it cuts both ways. Erasmus says a Delphic sword is that which accommodates itself to the *pro* or *con.* of a subject. The reference is to the double meanings of the Delphic oracles, called in Greek *Delphikē machaira.*

Sword and Cloak Plays. So Calderon called topical or modern comedies, because the actors wore cloaks and swords (worn by gentlemen of the period) instead of heraldic, antique, or dramatico-historic dresses, worn in tragedy.

Swords Prohibited. Gaming ran high at Bath, and frequently led to disputes and resort to the sword, then generally carried by well-dressed men. Swords were therefore prohibited by Nash in the public rooms; still they were worn in the streets, when Nash, in consequence of a duel fought by torchlight by two notorious gamesters, made the rule absolute—"That no swords should on any account be worn in Bath."

Sworn Brothers, "in the Old English law, were persons who by mutual oath covenanted to share each other's fortune." (*Burrill*.)

Sworn at Highgate. (*See* HIGHGATE.)

Syb'arite (3 syl.). A self-indulgent person; a wanton. The inhabitants of Syb'aris, in South Italy, were proverbial for their luxurious living and self-indulgence. A tale is told by Seneca of a Sybarite who complained that he could not rest comfortably at night, and being asked why, replied, "He found a rose-leaf doubled under him, and it hurt him." (*See* RIPAILLE.)

"All is calm as would delight the heart
Of Sybarite of old."
        Thomson: Castle of Indolence, canto i.

Sybarite. The Sybarites taught their horses to dance to the sound of a pipe. When the Crotonians marched against Sybaris they began to play on their pipes, whereupon all the Sybarite horses drawn out in array before the town began to dance; disorder soon prevailed in the ranks, and the victory was quick and easy.

Sycamore and **Sycomore.** Sycamore is the plane-tree of the maple family (*Acer pseudo-platănus*, or greater maple). The sycomore is the Egyptian fig-tree (Greek, *sukomoros, sukos,* a fig). The tree into which Zacchæus climbed (Luke xix. 4) to see Christ pass is wrongly called a sycamore or maple, as it was the sycomore or wild fig. The French have translated the word correctly—"*Il montait sur un sycomore pour le voir.*"

Syc'ophant, from the Greek *sukophantēs,* "fig-blabbers." The men of Athens passed a law forbidding the

exportation of figs; the law was little more than a dead letter, but there were always found mean fellows who, for their own private ends, impeached those who violated it; hence sycophant came to signify first a government toady, and then a toady generally.

"I here use 'sycophant' in its original sense, as a wretch who flatters the prevailing party by informing against his neighbours, under pretence that they are exporters of prohibited figs."—*Coleridge: Biography,* vol. iii. chap. x. p. 286.

Syc'orax. A witch, whose son was Cal'iban. (*Shakespeare : The Tempest.*)

Sye'nite. A granite so called from Syene, in Egypt, its great quarry.

Syl'logism. The five hexameter verses which contain the symbolic names of all the different syllogistic figures are as follow :—

"Barbara, Celārent, Darii, Feriōque, *priōris.*
Cesāre, Camestres, Festinō, Barōkō, *secundœ.*
Tertia, Darapti, Disāmis, Datīsi, Felapton,
Bokardō, Ferisōn, *habet. Quarta insuper addit*
Bramantip,Camēnes, Dimāris, Fesāpo, Fresison.

N.B. The vowel

A universal affirmative.
E universal negative.
I particular affirmative.
O particular negative.

Taking the first line as the standard, the initial letters of all the words below it show to which standard the syllogism is to be reduced; thus, Barōkō is to be reduced to "Barbara," Cesāre to "Celārent," and so on.

Sylphs, according to Middle Age belief, are the elemental spirits of air; so named by the Rosicrucians and Cabalists, from the Greek *silphē* (a butterfly or moth). (*See* GNOMES.)

Sylphs. Any mortal who has preserved inviolate chastity may enjoy intimate familiarity with these gentle spirits. All coquettes at death become sylphs, "and sport and flutter in the fields of air."

"Whoever, fair and chaste,
Rejects mankind, is by some sylph embraced."
        Pope: Rape of the Lock, i.

Sylvam Lignum Ferre (*In*). To carry coals to Newcastle. The French say, "*Porter de l'eau à la rivière.*" To do a work of supererogation; to paint the lily, or add another perfume to the violet, or perform any other superfluous or ridiculous excess.

Sylvester (*St.*). The pope who converted Constantine the Great and his mother by "the miracle of restoring to life a dead ox." The ox was killed by a magician for a trial of skill, and he who restored it to life was to be accounted the servant of the true God. This tale is manifestly an imitation of the Bible story of Elijah and the prophets of Baal. (1 Kings xviii.)

Syl'vius Bo'nus. Supposed to be Coil the Good, a contemporary of Auso'nius, who often mentions him; but not even the titles of his works are known. He was a British writer.

Symbol originally meant the corresponding part of a tally, ticket, or coin cut in twain. The person who presented the piece which fitted showed a "symbol" of his right to what he claimed. (Greek, *sun ballo*, to put or cast together.)

Symbols of Saints.

SAINTS.	SYMBOLS.
Agatha	Carrying her breasts in a dish.
Agathon	A book and crozier.
Agnes	A lamb at her side.
Anasta'sia	A palm branch.
Andrew	A saltire cross.
Anne	A book in her hand.
Anthony	A tau cross, with a bell at the end, and a pig by his side.
Apollo'nia	A tooth and palm branch. She is applied to by those who suffer from toothache.
Asaph and Aydan	A crozier.
Barbara	A book and palm branch.
Barnabas	A staff in one hand and an open book in the other; or a rake.
Bartholomew	A knife; or a processional cross.
Blaise	Iron combs, with which his body was torn to pieces.
Bridget	A crozier and book.
Catherine	An inverted sword, or large wheel.
Cecilia	Playing on a harp or organ.
Christopher	A gigantic figure carrying Christ over a river.
Clare	A palm branch.
Clement	A papal crown, or an anchor. He was drowned with an anchor tied round his neck; also a pot.
Crispin and Crispian }	Two shoemakers at work.
Cuthbert	St. Osbald's head in his hand.
David	A leek, in commemoration of his victory over the Saxons.
Denys	Holding his mitred head in his hand.
Dorothy	Carrying a basket of fruit.
Edward the Confessor }	Crowned with a nimbus, and holding a sceptre.
Elizabeth	St. John and the lamb at her feet.
Faith	A gridiron.
Felix	An anchor.
Flower	Her head in her hand, and a flower sprouting out of her neck.
Francis	A seraph inflicting the five wounds of Christ; or a lily on a trampled globe.
Fyacre	Arrayed in a long robe, praying and holding his beads in one hand.
Gabriel	A flower-pot full of lilies between him and the Virgin.
George	Mounted on horseback, and transfixing a dragon.
Giles	A hind, with its head in the saint's lap.
Ignatius	The monogram I.H.S. on the breast or in the sky, circled with a glory. Fairhold says the mystery of the Trinity was thus revealed to him.
James the Greater }	A pilgrim's staff; or a scallop shell.

SAINTS.	SYMBOLS.
James the Less	A fuller's pole. He was killed by Simon the fuller.
John Baptist	A camel-hair garment, small rude cross, and a lamb at his feet.
John Evangelist	A chalice, out of which a dragon or serpent is issuing, and an open book; or a young man with an eagle in the background. (Ezekiel vii. 1-10.)
Jerome	A blue hat, and studying a large folio volume,
Jude	With a club or lance.
Julian	Ferrying travellers across a stream.
Lawrence	A book and gridiron.
Louis	A king kneeling, with the arms of France at his feet; a bishop blessing him, and a dove descending on his head.
Loy	A crozier and hammer. He is the patron saint of smiths.
Lucy	With a short staff in her hand, and the devil behind her; or with eyes in a dish. (See LUCY.)
Luke	Sitting at a reading-desk, beneath which appears an ox's head; or pictorially engaged upon a Bambino. (Ezekiel vii. 1-10.)
Margaret	Treading on a dragon, or piercing it with the cross.
Mark	A man seated writing, with a lion couchant at his feet.
Martin	On horseback, dividing his cloak with a beggar behind him on foot.
Mary the Virgin	Carrying the child Jesus, and a lily is somewhere displayed.
Mary Magdalen	A box of ointment.
Matthew	With a halberd, with which Nadabar killed him. As an evangelist, he holds a pen, with which he is writing on a scroll. The most ancient symbol is a man's face. (Ezekiel vii. 1-10.)
Michael	In armour, with a cross, or else holding scales, in which he is weighing souls.
Nicholas	A tub with naked infants in it. He is patron saint of children.
Paul	A sword and a book. Dressed as a Roman.
Peter	Keys and a triple cross; or a fish; or a cock.
Philip	A pastoral staff, surmounted with a cross. He was hung on a tall pillar.
Roche	A wallet, and a dog with a loaf in its mouth sitting by. He shows a boil in his thigh.
Sebastian	Bound to a tree, his arms tied behind him, and his body transfixed with arrows. Two archers stand by his side; sometimes presenting a sheaf of arrows to the Lord.
Simon	A saw, because he was sawn asunder.
Stephen	A book and a stone in his hand.
Theodora	The devil holding her hand, and tempting her.
Theodore	Armed with a halberd in his hand, and with a sabre by his side.
Thomas	With a builder's rule, or a stone in his hand, or holding the lance with which he was slain at Meliapour.
Thomas of Canterbury }	Kneeling, and a man behind him striking at him with a sword.
Ursula	A book and arrows, She was shot through with arrows by the Prince of the Huns.

(See APOSTLES, EVANGELISTS, etc.)

Symbols of other sacred characters.

Abraham ..	..	An old man grasping a knife, ready to strike his son Isaac, who is bound on an altar. An angel arrests his hand, and a ram is caught in the thicket.
David ..	..	Kneeling, above is an angel with a sword. Sometimes he is represented playing a harp.
Esau ..	..	With bow and arrows, going to meet Jacob.
Job	..	Sitting naked on the ground, with three friends talking to him.
Joseph ..	..	Conversing with his brothers. Benjamin is represented as a mere boy.
Judas Iscariot ..		With a money bag. In the last supper he has knocked over the salt with his right elbow.
Judith ..	..	With Holofernes' head in one hand, and a sabre in the other.
Noah		Is represented as looking out of the ark window at a dove, which is flying to the ark, olive branch in its beak.
King Saul ..		Is represented as arrayed in a rich tunic and crowned. A harp is placed behind him.
Solomon ..	..	Is represented in royal robes, standing under an arch.

Symbolism of Colours, whether displayed in dresses, the background of pictures, or otherwise:

Black typifies grief, death.

Blue, hope, love of divine works; (in dresses) divine contemplation, piety, sincerity.

Pale blue, peace, Christian prudence, love of good works, a serene conscience.

Gold, glory and power.

Green, faith, gladness, immortality, the resurrection of the just; (in dresses) the gladness of the faithful.

Pale green, baptism.

Grey, tribulation.

Purple, justice, royalty.

Red, martyrdom for faith, charity; (in dresses) divine love.

Rose-colour, martyrdom. Innocent III. says of martyrs and apostles, " *Hi et illi sunt flores rosarum et lilia convallium.*" (*De Sacr. alto Myst.*, i. 64.)

Saffron, confessors.

Scarlet, the fervour and glory of witnesses to the Church.

Silver, chastity and purity.

Violet, penitence.

White, purity, temperance, innocence, chastity, faith; (in dresses) innocence and purity.

Symbolism of Metals and Gems.

Amethyst typifies humility.

Diamond, invulnerable faith.

Gold, glory, power.

Sardonyx, sincerity.

Sapphire, hope.

Silver, chastity, purity.

Syrens of the Ditch. Frogs. So called by Tasso.

Syr'ia, says Richardson, derives its name from *Suri* (a delicate rose) ; hence *Suristan* (the land of roses). The Jews called Syria *Aram*.

Syrtis. A quicksand. Applied especially to a part of the African coast. (Greek *syrtis*.)

T

T, in music, stands for *Tutti* (all), meaning all the instruments or voices are to join. It is the opposite of S for *Solo*.

-t- inserted with a double hyphen between a verb ending with a vowel and the pronouns *elle, il,* or *on,* is called " t ephelcystic," as, *aime-t-il, dire-t-on.* (*See* N, MARKS IN GRAMMAR.)

Marked with a T. Criminals convicted of felony, and admitted to the benefit of clergy, were branded on the brawn of the thumb with the letter T (*thief*). The law was abolished by 7 and 8 George IV., c. 27.

It fits to a T. Exactly. The allusion is to work that mechanics square with a T-rule, especially useful in making right angles, and in obtaining perpendiculars on paper or wood.

The saintly T*'s.* Sin Tander, Sin Tantony, Sin Tawdry, Sin Tausin, Sin Tedmund, and Sin Telders ; otherwise St. Andrew, St. Anthony, St. Audry, St. Austin [Augustine], St. Edmund, and St. Ethelred. Tooley is St. Olaf.

T.Y.C., in the language of horseracing, means the Two-Year-Old Course scurries. Under six furlongs.

T-Rule (*A*). A ruler shaped like a Greek T. (*See above.*)

Tab. *An old Tab.* An old maid; an old tabby or cat. So called because old maids usually make a cat their companion.

Tab'ard. The *Tabard*, in Southwark, is where Chaucer supposes his pilgrims to have assembled. The tabard was a jacket without sleeves, whole before, open on both sides, with a square collar, winged at the shoulder like a cape, and worn by military nobles over their armour. It was generally emblazoned with heraldic devices. Heralds still wear a tabard.

" Item . . . à chascun ung grand tabart
De cordelier, jusques aux pieds."
Le Petit Testament de Maistre François Villon.

Tab'ardar. A sizar of Queen's College, Oxford. So called because his gown has tabard sleeves—that is, loose sleeves, terminating a little below the elbow in a point.

Tab'arin. *He's a Tabarin*—a merry Andrew. Tabarin was the fellow of Mondor, a famous vendor of quack medicines in the reign of Charles IX. By his antics and coarse wit he collected great crowds, and both he and his master grew rich. Tabarin bought a handsome château in Dauphiné, but the aristocracy out of jealousy murdered him.

Tabby, a cat, so called because the brindlings of the tabby were thought to resemble the waterings of the silk of the name. (French, *tabis;* Italian, etc., *tabi;* Persian, *retabi,* a rich figured silk.)

" Demurest of the tabby kind,
The pensive Selima reclined." *Gay.*

Tabula Rasa (Latin). A clean slate on which anything can be written.

" When a girl has been taught to keep her
mind a *tabula rasa* till she comes to years of
discretion, she will be more free to act on her
own natural impulses."—*W. S. R.*

Table. *Apellēs' table.* A pictured table, representing the excellency of sobriety on one side, and the deformity of intemperance on the other.

Tables of Celēs. Cebes was a Theban philosopher, a disciple of Socrates, and one of the interlocutors of Plato's *Phædo.* His *Tables* or *Tableau* supposes him to be placed before a tableau or panorama representing the life of man, which the philosopher describes with great accuracy of judgment and splendour of sentiment. This tableau is sometimes appended to *Epictĕtus.*

Table of Pythag'oras. The common multiplication table, carried up to ten. The table is parcelled off into a hundred little squares or cells. (*See* TABULÆ.)

Knights of the Round Table. A military order instituted by Arthur, the "first king of the Britons," A.D. 516. Some say they were twenty-four in number, some make the number as high as 150, and others reduce the number to twelve. They were all seated at a round table, that no one might claim a post of honour.

The Twelve Tables. The tables of the Roman laws engraved on brass, brought from Athens to Rome by the decemvirs.

Turning the tables. Rebutting a charge by bringing forth a counter-charge. Thus, if a husband accuses his wife of extravagance in dress, she "turns the tables upon him " by accusing him of extravagance in his club. The Romans prided themselves on their tables made of citron wood from Maurita'nia, inlaid with ivory, and sold at a most extravagant price—some equal to a senator's income. When the gentlemen accused the ladies of extravagance, the ladies retorted by reminding the gentlemen of what they spent in tables. Pliny calls this taste of the Romans *mensa'rum insania.*

It is also used for *" audi alteram partem,"* and the allusion is then slightly modified—" We have considered the wife's extravagance ; let us now look to the husband's."

" We will now turn the tables, and show the
hexameters in all their vigour."—*The Times.*

Table d'Hôte [*the host's table*]. An ordinary. In the Middle Ages, and even down to the reign of Louis XIV., the landlord's table was the only public dining-place known in Germany and France. The first restaurant was opened in Paris during the reign of the *Grand Monarque,* and was a great success.

Table Money. Money appropriated to the purposes of hospitality.

Table-Turning. The presumed art of turning tables without the application of mechanical force. Said by some to be the work of departed spirits, and by others to be due to a force akin to mesmerism. Jackson Davis (the Seer of Poughkeepsie), a cobbler, professed, in 1848, to hear " spirit voices in the air." (*See* SPIRITUALISM.)

Tableaux Vivants (French, *living pictures*). Representations of statuary groups by living persons, invented by Madame Genlis while she had charge of the children of the Duc d'Orléans.

Tabooed. Devoted. Forbidden. This is a Polynesian term, and means consecrated or set apart. Like the Greek *anathema,* the Latin *sacer,* the French *sacre,* etc., the word has a double meaning—one to consecrate, and one to incur the penalty of violating the consecration. (*See* TAPU.)

Tab'orites (3 syl.). A sect of Hussites in Bohemia. So called from the fortress Tabor, about fifty miles from Prague, from which Nicholas von Hussineez, one of the founders, expelled the Imperial army. They are now incorporated with the Bohemian Brethren.

Tabouret. The right of sitting in the presence of the queen. In the ancient French court certain ladies had the *droit de tabouret* (right of sitting on a tabouret in the presence of the queen). At first it was limited to princesses; but subsequently it was extended to all the chief ladies of the queen's household; and later still the wives of ambassadors, dukes, lord chancellor, and keeper of the seals, enjoyed the privilege. Gentlemen similarly privileged had the *droit de fauteuil.*

" Qui me résisterait
   La marquise a le tabouret."
    Beranger : Le Marquis de Carabas.

Tab'ulæ Toleta'næ. The astronomical tables composed by order of Alphonso X. of Castile, in the middle of the thirteenth century, were so called because they were adapted to the city of Tole'do.

"'His Tables Tolletanes forth he brought,
Ful wel corrected, ne ther lakked nought."
    Chaucer : Canterbury Tales, 11,585.

Ta'ce (2 syl.). *Latin for candle.* Silence is most discreet. *Tace* is Latin for "be silent," and candle is symbolical of *light.* The phrase means "keep it dark," do not throw light upon it. Fielding, in his *Amelia* (chap. x.), says, " *Tace,* madam, is Latin for candle." There is an historical allusion worth remembering. It was customary at one time to express disapprobation of a play or actor by throwing a candle on the stage, and when this was done the curtain was immediately drawn down. Oultor (vol. i. p. 6), in his *History of the Theatres of London,* gives us an instance of this which occurred January 25th, 1772, at Covent Garden theatre, when the piece before the public was *An Hour Before Marriage.* Someone threw a candle on the stage, and the curtain was dropped at once.

"There are some auld stories that cannot be ripped up again with entire safety to all concerned. *Tace* is Latin for candle."—*Sir W. Scott : Redgauntlet,* chap. xi. (Sir Walter is rather fond of the phrase.)

"Mum, William, mum. *Tace* is Latin for candle."—*W. B. Yeats: Fairy Tales of the Irish Peasantry,* p. 250.

N.B. We have several of these old phrases; one of the best is, " Brandy is Latin for goose " (*q.v.*).

Tache'brune (2 syl.). The horse of Ogier le Dane. The word means "brown-spot." (*See* HORSE.)

Tænia Rationis. Show of argument. Argument which seems *prima facie* plausible and specious, but has no real depth or value.

"Mr. Spencer is again afflicted with his old complaint *tænia rationis,* and takes big words for real things."—*Fra Olla ; Mr. Spencer's First Principles.*

Taë'-pings. Chinese rebels. The word means *Universal Peace,* and arose thus: Hung-sew-tseuen, a man of humble birth, and an unsuccessful candidate for a government office, was induced by some missionary tracts to renounce idolatry, and found the society of Taë-ping, which came into collision with the imperial authorities in 1850. Hung now gave out that he was the chosen instrument in God's hands to uproot idolatry and establish the dynasty of Universal Peace; he assumed the title of Taë-ping-wang (*Prince of Universal Peace*), and called his five chief officers princes. Nankin was made their capital in 1860, but Colonel Gordon (called Chinese Gordon) in 1864 quelled the insurrection, and overthrew the armies of Hung.

Taf'fata or **Taffety.** A fabric made of silk: at one time it was watered; hence Taylor says, "No taffaty more changeable than they." " *Notre mot* taffeta *est formé, par onomatopée, du bruit que fait cette étoffe.*" (Francisque-Michel.)

∵ The fabric has often changed its character. At one time it was silk and linen, at another silk and wool. In the eighteenth century it was lustrous silk, sometimes striped with gold.

Taffata phrases. Smooth sleek phrases, euphemisms. We also use the words fustian, stuff, silken, shoddy, buckram, velvet, satin, lutestring, etc., etc., to qualify phrases and literary compositions spoken or written.

" Taffata phrases, silken terms precise,
Three-piled hyperboles."
    Shakespeare : Love's Labour's Lost, v. 2.

Taffy. A Welshman. So called from David, a very common Welsh name. David, familiarly Davy, becomes in Welsh Taffid, Taffy.

Tag Rag, and Bobtail. The *vulgus ignobile.* A "tag" is a doe in the second year of her age; a "rag," a herd of deer at rutting time; "bobtail," a fawn just weaned.

∵ According to Halliwell, a sheep of the first year is called a *tag.* Tag is sometimes written *shag.*

" It will swallow us all up, ships and men, shag, rag, and bobtail."—*Rabelais : Pantagruel,* iv. 33.

Tag'hairm (2 syl.). A means employed by the Scotch in inquiring into futurity. A person wrapped up in the hide of a fresh-slain bullock was placed beside a waterfall, or at the foot of a precipice, and there left to meditate on the question propounded. Whatever his fancy suggested to him in this wild situation passed for the inspiration of his disembodied spirit.

> " Last evening-tide
> Brian an augury hath tried,
> Of that kind which must not be
> Unless in dread extremity,
> The Taghairm called."
> *Sir Walter Scott: Lady of the Lake,* iv. 4.

Ta'herites (3 syl.). A dynasty of five kings who reigned in Khorassan for fifty-two years (820-872). So called from the founder, Taher, general of the Calif's army.

Tail. *Lion's tail.* Lions, according to legend, wipe out their footsteps with their tail, that they may not be tracked. *Twisting the lion's tail.* (*See* TWIST-ING.)

He has no more tail than a Manx cat. There is a breed of cats in the Isle of Man without tails.

Tails. The men of Kent are born with tails, as a punishment for the murder of Thomas à Becket. (*Lambert: Peramb.*) (*See* the *Spectator*, 173.)

" For Becket's sake, Kent always shall have tails."
Andrew Marvel.

Tails. It is said that the Ghilane race, which number between 30,000 and 40,000, and dwell " far beyond the Sennaar," have tails three or four inches long. Colonel du Corret tells us he carefully examined one of this race named Bellal, the slave of an emir in Mecca, whose house he frequented. (*World of Wonders,* p. 206.)
The Niam-niams of Africa are tailed, so we are told.

Tails. The Chinese men were made to shave their heads and wear a queue or tail by the Manchu Tartars, who, in the seventeenth century, subdued the country, and compelled the men to adopt the Manchu dress. The women were allowed to compress their feet as before, although the custom is not adopted by the Tartars.

** *"Anglicus a tergo caudam gerit"* probably refers to the pigtails once worn.

Tailors. *The three tailors of Tooley Street.* Canning says that three tailors of Tooley Street, Southwark, addressed a petition of grievances to the House of Commons, beginning—" We, the people of England." (*See* VAUGHAN.)

Nine tailors make a man. The present scope of this expression is that a tailor is so much more feeble than another man that it would take nine of them to make a man of average stature and strength. There is a tradition that an

orphan lad, in 1742, applied to a fashionable London tailor for alms. There were nine journeymen in the establishment, each of whom contributed something to set the little orphan up with a fruit barrow. The little merchant in time became rich, and adopted for his motto, " Nine tailors made me a man," or " Nine tailors make a man." This certainly is not the origin of the expression, inasmuch as we find a similar one used by Taylor a century before that date, and referred to as of old standing, even then.

" Some foolish knave, I thinke, at first began
The slander that three taylers are one man."
Taylor: Workes, iii. 73*(1630).

** Another suggestion is this: At the death of a man the tolling bell is rung thrice three tolls ; at the death of a woman it is rung only three-two tolls. Hence nine tolls indicate the death of a man. Halliwell gives *telled* = told, and a tolling-bell is a teller. In regard to " make," it is the French *faire,* as *On le faisait mort, i.e.* some one gave out or made it known that he was dead.

"The fourme of the Trinitie was founded in manne.... Adam our forefather, ... and Eve of Adam the secundo personne, and of them both was the third persone. At the death of a manne three bells schulde be ronge as his knyll, in worscheppe of the Trinitie—for a womanne, who is the secunde personne of the Trinitie, two belles schulde be rungen."—*An old English Homily for Trinity Sunday.* (See Strutt: *Manners and Customs,* vol. iii. p. 176.)

Tailor's Sword (*A*), or **A Tailor's Dagger.** A needle.

" The tailors cross-legged on their boards,
Needle-armed, hand-extended, prepared
To stab the black cloth with their swords [to
make up mourning]
The instant that death is declared."
Peter Pindar: Great Cry and Little Wool, Epist. i.

Take a Back Seat (*To*). To be set aside ; to be deferred for the present. A parliamentary phrase.

" When there seemed to be a tendency ... to make the Irish question, in the cant of the day, ' take a back seat,' Unionist indignation knew no bounds."—*The Daily Graphic,* February 9th, 1893.

Take a Hair of the Dog that Bit You. After a debauch, take a little wine the next day. Take a cool draught of ale in the morning, after a night's excess. The advice was given literally in ancient times, " If a dog bites you, put a hair of the dog into the wound," on the homœopathic principle of "*Similia similibus curantur*" (like cures like).

Take in Tow (*To*). Take under guidance. A man who takes a lad in tow acts as his guide and director. To tow a ship or barge is to guide and draw it along by tow-lines.

"Too proud for bards to take in tow my name."
Peter Pindar ; Future Laureate, Part ii,

Take Mourning (*To*). Attending church the Sunday after a funeral. It is the custom, especially in the northern counties, for all the mourners, and sometimes the bearers also, to sit in a specific pew all together the Sunday after a funeral. It matters not what place of worship they usually attend—all unite in the "taking mourning."

Take Tea with Him (*I*), *i.e.* I floor my adversary by winning every rubber. If he beats me in billiards, he "has me on toast." (*Indian slang*.)

Takin' the Beuk. A Scotch phrase for family worship.

Taking On. Said of a woman in hysterics; to fret; to grieve passionately, as, "Come, don't take on so!"

" Lance, who . . . took upon himself the whole burden of Dame Debbitch's . . . 'taking on,' as such fits of *passio hysterica* are usually termed."
—*Sir W. Scott : Peveril of the Peak*, chap. XXVI.

Taking a Sight. Putting the right thumb to the nose and spreading the fingers out. This is done as much as to say, "Do you see any green in my eye?" "Tell that to the marines;" "*Credat Judæus, non ego.*" Captain Marryat tells us that some "of the old coins of Denmark represent Thor with his thumb to his nose, and his four fingers extended in the air;" and Panurge (says Rabelais, *Pantagruel*, book ii. 19) "suddenly lifted his right hand, put his thumb to his nose, and spread his fingers straight out" to express incredulity.

" The sacristan he says no word that indicates a doubt,
But puts his thumb unto his nose, and spreads his fingers out."   *Ingoldsby : Nell Cook.*

Taking Time by the Forelock. Seize the present moment; "*Carpe diem.*" Time personified is represented with a lock of hair on his forehead but none on the rest of his head, to signify that time past cannot be used, but time present may be seized by the forelock.

Tal'botype (3 syl.). A photographic process invented in 1839 by Fox Talbot, who called it "the Calotype Process." (*See* DAGUERREOTYPE.)

Tale (1 syl.). A tally; a reckoning. In Exod. v. we have *tale of bricks.* A measure by number, not by weight.

An old wife's tale. Any marvellous legendary story.

To tell tales out of school. To utter abroad affairs not meant for the public ear.

Tale of a Tub (*The*). A ridiculous narrative or tale of fiction. The reference is to Dean Swift's tale so called.

Talent, meaning cleverness or "gift" of intelligence, is a word borrowed from Matt. xxv. 14-30.

Ta'les (2 syl.). Persons in the court from whom the sheriff or his clerk makes selections to supply the place of jurors who have been empanelled, but are not in attendance. It is the first word of the Latin sentence which provides for this contingency. (*Tales de circumstant'ibus.*)

" To serve for jurymen or tales.
    Butler : Hudibras, part iii. 8.

To pray a talēs. To pray that the number of jurymen may be completed. It sometimes happens that jurymen are challenged, or that less than twelve are in the court. When this is the case the jury can request that their complement be made up from persons in the court. Those who supplement the jury are called *talesmen*, and their names are set down in a book called a *talesbook.*

Tal'gol (in *Hudibras*), famous for killing flies, was Jackson, butcher of Newgate Street, who got his captain's commission at Naseby.

Tal'isman. A figure cut or engraved on metal or stone, under the influence of certain planets. In order to free any place of vermin, the figure of the obnoxious animal is made in wax or consecrated metal, in a planetary hour, and this is called the talisman. (*Warburton*.)

" He swore that you had robbed his house,
And stole his talismanic louse."
    S. Butler : Hudibras, part iii. 1.

Talisman. The Abraxas Stone is a most noted talisman. (*See* ABRAXAS.) In Arabia a talisman is still used, consisting of a piece of paper, on which are written the names of the Seven Sleepers and their dog, to protect a house from ghosts and demons. The talisman is supposed to be sympathetic, and to receive an influence from the planets, which it communicates to the wearer.

Talk. *To talk over.* To discuss, to debate; also to gain over by argument.

Talk Shop. (*See* SHOP.)

Talkee Talkee. (A reduplication of *talk* with termination *ee*, borrowed in ridicule from some attempt of dark races to speak English.) A copius effusion of talk with no valuable result.

Talking Bird. A bird that spoke with a human voice, and could call all other birds to sing in concert. (*The Sisters who Envied their Younger Sister ; Arabian Nights.*) (*See* GREEN BIRD.)

Tall Men. Champions (a Welsh phrase) ; brave men.

"You were good soldiers, and tall fellows."—
Shakespeare: Merry Wives of Windsor, ii. 2.

"The undaunted resolution and stubborn ferocity of Gwenwyn . . . had long made him beloved among the 'Tall Men,' or champions of Wales."—
Sir W. Scott: The Betrothed, chap. i.

Talleyrand, anciently written *Tailleran*, is the sobriquet derived from the words "*tailler les rangs*," "cut through the ranks."

Tally (*A*). The price paid for picking a bushel of hops. It varies (1891) from 1½d. to 2½d.

Tally. To correspond. The tally used in the Exchequer was a rod of wood, marked on one face with notches corresponding to the sum for which it was an acknowledgment. Two other sides contained the date, the name of the payer, and so on. The rod was then cleft in such a manner that each half contained one written side and half of every notch. One part was kept in the Exchequer, and the other was circulated. When payment was required the two parts were compared, and if they "tallied," or made a tally, all was right ; if not, there was some fraud, and payment was refused. Tallies were not finally abandoned in the Exchequer till 1834. (French, *tailler*, to cut.)

⁕ In 1834 orders were issued to destroy the tallies. There were two cartloads of them, which were set fire to at six o'clock in the morning, and the conflagration set on fire the Houses of Parliament, with their offices, and part of the Palace of Westminster.

To break one's tally (in Latin, "*Confringere tesseram*"). When public houses were unknown, a guest entertained for a night at a private house had a tally given him, the corresponding part being kept by the host. It was expected that the guest would return the favour if required to do so, and if he refused he "violated the rites of hospitality," or *confregisse tesseram*. The "white stone" spoken of in the Book of the Revelation is a tessera which Christ gives to His disciples.

To live tally is to live unwed as man and wife. A tally-woman is a concubine, and a tally-man is the man who keeps a mistress. These expressions are quite common in Cheshire, Yorkshire, and Lancashire. In mines a tin label is attached to each tub of coals, bearing the name of the man who sent it to the bank, that the weighman may credit it to the right person. As the tallies of the miner and weighman agree, so the persons who agree to live together tally with each other's taste.

Tally-ho! is the Norman hunting cry *Taillis au !* (To the coppice). The tally-ho was used when the stag was viewed in full career making for the coppice. We now cry "Tally-ho!" when the fox breaks cover. The French cry is "*Taïaut !*"

Tallyman (*A*). A travelling draper who calls at private houses to sell wares on the tally system—that is, part payment on account, and other parts when the man calls again.

Talmud (*The*). About 120 years after the destruction of the Temple, the rabbi Judah began to take down in writing the Jewish traditions ; his book, called the *Mishna*, contains six parts : (1) Agriculture and seed-sowing ; (2) Festivals ; (3) Marriage ; (4) Civil affairs ; (5) Sacrifices ; and (6) what is clean and what unclean. The book caused immense disputation, and two Babylonish rabbis replied to it, and wrote a commentary in sixty parts, called the *Babylonian Talmud*. *Gemara* (imperfect). This compilation has been greatly abridged by the omission of Nos. 5 and 6.

Talpot or **Talipot Tree.** A gigantic palm. When the sheath of the flower bursts it makes a report like that of a cannon.

" They burst, like Zeilan's giant palm,
  Whose buds fly open with a sound
  That shakes the pigmy forest round."
        Moore: Fire Worshippers.

Zeilan is Portuguese for Ceylon.

Talus. *Sir Artegal's iron man.* Spenser, in his *Faërie Queene*, makes Talus run continually round the island of Crete to chastise offenders with an iron flail. He represents executive power—"swift as a swallow, and as lion strong." In Greek mythology, Talos was a man of brass, the work of Hephæstos (Vulcan), who went round the island of Crete thrice a day. Whenever he saw a stranger draw near the island he made himself red-hot, and embraced the stranger to death.

Tam-o'-Shanter's Mare. *Remember Tam-o'-Shanter's mare.* You may pay too dear for your whistle, as Meg lost her tail, pulled off by Nannie of the "Cutty-sark."

" Think, ye may buy the joys owre dear—
  Remember Tam-o'-Shanter's mare."
        Burns.

Tamarisk, from a Hebrew word meaning to cleanse, so called from its absterstve qualities. The Romans wreathed the brows of criminals with tamarisk. The Arabs make cakes called *manna* of the hardened juice extracted from this tree.

Tame Cat (*A*). A harmless dangler after a married woman ; a cavalier servant ; a cicisbeo.

" He soon installed himself as a tame cat in the MacMungo mansion."—*Truth (Queer Story)*, October, 1885.

Tam'erlane (3 syl.). A corruption of Timour *Lengh* (Timour the Lame), one of the greatest warrior-kings that ever lived. Under him Persia became a province of Tartary. He modestly called himself *Ameer* (chief), instead of sultan or shah. (1380-1405.)

Taming of the Shrew. The plot was borrowed from a drama of the same title, published by S. Leacroft, of Charing Cross, under the title of *Six Old Plays on which Shakespeare Founded his Comedies*. The induction was borrowed from Heuterus' *Rerum Burgumdarum* (lib. iv.), a translation of which was published in 1607 by E. Grimstone, and called *Admirable and Memorable Histories*. Dr. Percy thinks that the ballad of *The Frolicksome Duke, or the Tinker's Good Fortune*, published in the Pepys Collection, may have suggested the induction. (*See* SLY.)

Tammany (*St.*). Tammany was of the Delaware nation in the seventeenth century, and became a chief, whose rule was wise and pacific. He was chosen by the American democrats as their tutelary saint. His day is May 1st. Cooper calls him Tammenund, but the correct word is *Tamanend.*

Tammany Ring. A cabal or powerful organisation of unprincipled officials, who enriched themselves by plundering the people. So called from Tammany Hall, the head-quarters of the high officials of the U.S., whose nefarious practices were exposed in 1871.

Tammuz. (*See* THAMMUZ.)

Tan'cred (in *Jerusalem Delivered*) shows a generous contempt of danger. Son of Eudes and Emma (sister of Robert Guiscard), Bœmoud or Bohemond was his cousin. Tancred was the greatest of all the Christian warriors except Rinaldo. His one fault was " woman's love," and that woman Clorinda, a Pagan (bk. i.). He brought

800 horse from Tuscany and Campania to the allied Christian army. He slew Clorinda (not knowing her) in a night combat, and lamented her death with great lamentation (bk. xii.). Being wounded, he was nursed by Ermin'ia, who was in love with him (bk. xix.).

Tan'dem. At length. A pun applied to two horses driven one before the other. This Latin is of a similar character to *plenum sed* (full butt).

Tandem D.O.M. *Tandem Deo optimo maximo* (Now at the end ascribe we praise to God, the best and greatest).

Tangie. The water sprite of the Orkneys ; from Danish *tang* (sea-weed), with which it is covered. The tangie sometimes appears in a human form, and sometimes as a little apple-green horse.

Tanist (*A*). One who held lands in Ireland under the Celtic law of tanistry. The chief of a sept. (Irish, *tanaiste,* heir apparent to a chief.)

" Whoever stood highest in the estimation of the class was nominated ' Tanist,' or successor."— *E. Lawless : Story of Ireland*, chap. iii. p. 27.

Tanist Stone. A monolith erected by the Celts at a coronation. We read in the Book of Judges (ix. 6) of Abimelech, that a "pillar was erected in Shechem" when he was made king ; and (2 Kings xi. 14) it is said that a pillar was raised when Joash was made king, " as the manner was." The *Lia Fail* of Ireland was erected in Icolmkil for the coronation of Fergus Eric. This stone was removed to Scone, and became the coronation chair of Scotland. It was taken to Westminster by Edward I., and is the coronation chair of our sovereigns. (Celtic, *Tanist,* the heir-apparent.)

Tankard of October (*A*). A tankard of the best and strongest ale, brewed in October.

" He was in high favour with Sir Geoffrey, not merely on account of his sound orthodoxy and deep learning, but [also for] his excellent skill in playing at bowls, and his facetious conversation over a pipe and tankard of October."—*Sir W. Scott : Peveril of the Peak*, chap. iv.

Tanner. Sixpence. (The Italian *danaro,* small change ; Gipsy, *tawno,* little one. Similarly a *thaler* is called a *dollar.*)

Tanner. A proper name. (*See* BREWER.)

Tanner of Tamworth. Edward IV. was hunting in Drayton Basset when a tanner met him. The king asked him several questions, and the tanner, taking him for a highway robber, was very chary. At last they swopped horses; the tanner gave the king his gentle mare Brocke, which cost 4s., and the king gave the tanner his hunter, which soon threw him. Upon this the tanner paid dearly for changing back again. Edward now blew his horn, and when his courtiers came up in obedience to the summons, the tanner, in great alarm, cried out, " I *hope* I shall be hanged tomorrow " (*i.e.* I expect); but the king gave him the manor of Plumpton Park, with 300 marks a year. (*Percy: Reliques, etc.*)

Tann'häu'ser (3 syl.). A legendary hero of Germany, who wins the affections of Lisaura; but Lisaura, hearing that Sir Tannhäuser has set out for Venusberg to kiss the queen of love and beauty, destroys herself. After living some time in the cave-palace, Sir Tannhäuser obtains leave to visit the upper world, and goes to Pope Urban for absolution. " No," said his holiness, " you can no more hope for mercy than this dry staff can be expected to bud again." On this the knight returned to Venusberg. In a few days the papal staff actually did bud, and Urban sent for Sir Tannhäuser, but the knight was nowhere to be found.

Tansy. A corruption of the Greek word *athanasia,* immortality, as *thansa, tansy.* So called because it is "a sort of everlasting flower." (*Hortus Anglicus,* vol. ii. p. 366.)

Tan'talise. To excite a hope and disappoint it. (*See next article.*)

Tan'talos (Latin, *Tantalus*), according to fable, is punished in the infernal regions by intolerable thirst. To make his punishment the more severe, he is plunged up to his chin in a river, but whenever he bends forward to slake his thirst the water flows from him.

" So bends tormented Tantalus to drink,
While from his lips the refluent waters shrink;
Again the rising stream his bosom laves,
And thirst consumes him 'mid circumfluent waves."
Darwin: Loves of the Plants, ii. 419.

Tantalus. Emblematical of a covetous man, who the more he has the more he craves. (*See* COVETOUS.)

Tantalus. A parallel story exists among the Chipouyans, who inhabit the deserts which divide Canada from the United States. At death, they say, the soul is placed in a stone ferry-boat, till judgment has been passed on it. If the judgment is averse, the boat sinks in the stream, leaving the victim chin-deep in water, where he suffers endless thirst,

and makes fruitless attempts to escape to the Islands of the Blessed. (*Alexander Mackenzie: Voyages in the Interior of America.*) (1789, 1792, 1793.)

Tanthony (*St. Anthony*). In Norwich are the churches called Sin Telder's (*St. Ethelred's*), Sin Tedmund's (*St. Edmund's*), Sin Tander's (*St. Andrew's*), and Sin Tausin's (*St. Austin's*). (*See* TAWDRY.)

Tantum Ergo. The most popular of the Eucharistic hymns sung in the Roman Catholic churches at Benediction with the Holy Sacrament. So called from the first two words of the last stanza but one of the hymn *Pange Lingua.*

Taou. The sect of Reason, founded in China by Laou-Tsze, a contemporary of Confu'cius. He was taken to heaven on a black buffalo. (B.C. 523.)

Tap the Admiral. To suck liquor from a cask by a straw. Hotten says it was first done with the rum-cask in which the body of Admiral Lord Nelson was brought to England, and when the cask arrived the admiral was found " high and dry."

Tap the Till (*To*). To pilfer from a till.

Tap-up Sunday. The Sunday preceding the fair held on the 2nd October, on St. Catherine's Hill, near Guildford, and so called because any person, with or without a licence, may open a "tap," or sell beer on the hill for that one day.

Tapis. *On the tapis.* On the carpet; under consideration; now being ventilated. An English-French phrase, referring to the tapis or cloth with which the table of the council-chamber is covered, and on which are laid the motions before the House.

" My business comes now upon the tapis."—
Farquhar: The Beaux Stratagem, iii. 3.

Tapisserie. *Faire tapisserie.* To play gooseberry-picker; to be mere chaperon for the sake of "propriety." " *Se dit des personnes qui assertent à un bal ou à quelque autre grande réunion sans y prendre part.*"

"You accepted out of pure kindness *faire tapisserie;* Mrs. Arbuthnot, you are too amiable."—
Mrs. Edwardes: A Girton Girl, chap. xxvi.

Tappit-hen (*A*). A huge pewter measuring-pot, containing at least three English quarts. Readers of *Waverley* will remember (in chap. xi.) the Baron Bradwardine's tappit-hen of claret from Bordeaux. To have a tappit-hen under the belt is to have swallowed three quarts of claret. *A hen and chickens* means large and small drinking mugs or pewter pots. A tappit was served from the tap. (*See* JEROBOAM.)

" Weel she lo'ed a Hawick gill,
And leugh to see a tappit-hen."

Tapster, says E. Adams (*English Language*), properly means a bar-*maid;* " -ster " is the Anglo-Saxon feminine suffix -*estre*, which remains in *spin-ster* (a female spinner).

∴ This is only a half-truth. After the thirteenth century, the suffix -*ster* was used for an agent of either sex. We have *barrister, gamester, punster,* etc., and Wickliffe uses *songster* for a male singer. (See *Dr. Morris : Historic Outlines,* p. 89.)

Tapu, among the South Sea Islanders, means " devoted " in a religious sense. Thus, a temple is *tapu*, and he who violates a temple is tapu. Not only so, but everyone and everything connected with what is tapu becomes tapu also. Thus, Captain Cook was tapu because some of his sailors took rails from a " temple " of the Hawaiians to supply themselves with fuel, and, being devoted, he was slain. Our *taboo* is the same word.

Tarabolus or **Tantrabolus.** *We shall live till we die, like Tarabolus* [or *Tantrabolus*]. Tarabolus, Ali Pacha, was grand vizier in 1693, and was strangled in 1695 by order of Mustapha II.

We shall live till we die, like Tantrabolus, is said to be a Cornish proverb. There is a cognate saying, " Like Tantrabolus, who lived till he died."

•• Tantarabobs means the devil. Noisily playful children are called Tantrabols.

Tarakee, the Brahmin, was the model of austere devotion. He lived 1,100 years, and spent each century in some astounding mortification.

1st century. He held up his arms and one foot towards heaven, fixing his eyes on the sun the whole time.

2nd century. He stood on tiptoe the whole time.

8th century. He stood on his head, with his feet towards the sky.

9th century. He rested wholly on the palm of one hand.

11th century. He hung from a tree with his head downwards.

" One century he lived wholly on water, another wholly on air, another steeped to the neck in earth, and for another century he was always enveloped in fire. I don't know that the world has been benefited by such devotion."—*Maurice: History of Hindostan.*

Tarant'ism. The dancing mania, extremely contagious. It broke out in Germany in 1374, and in France in the Great Revolution, when it was called the *Carmagnole.* Clergymen, judges, men and women, even the aged, joined the mad dance in the open streets till they fell from exhaustion.

Taran'tula. This word is derived from Taranto the city, or from Thara the river in Apulia, in the vicinity of which the venomous hairy spiders abound. (*Kircher: De Arte Mag.*)

Tarentella or **Tarantella.** Tunes and dances in triplets, supposed to cure the dancing mania.

Tariff. A list in alphabetical order of the duties, drawbacks, bounties, etc., charged or allowed on exports and imports. The word is derived from Tari'fa, a seaport of Spain about twenty miles from Gibraltar, where the Moors, during the supremacy in Spain, levied contributions according to a certain scale on vessels entering the Mediterranean Sea. (French, *tarif;* Spanish, *tarifa.*)

Tarpaulins or **Tars.** Sailors; more frequently called *Jack Tars.* Tarpaulins are tarred cloths used commonly on board ship to keep articles from the sea-spray, etc.

The more correct spelling is tar-palling, from *pall,* Latin *pallium,* a cloak or cloth.

Tarpe'ian Rock. So called from Tarpeia, a vestal virgin, the daughter of Spurius Tarpeius, governor of the citadel on the Capit'oline Hill. Tarpeia agreed to open the gates to the Sabines if they would give her " what they wore on their arms " (meaning their bracelets). The Sabines, " keeping their promise to the ear," crushed her to death with their shields, and she was buried in that part of the hill called the Tarpeian Rock. Subsequently, traitors were cast down this rock and so killed.

" Bear him to the rock Tarpeian, and from thence
Into destruction cast him."
Shakespeare : Coriolanus, iii. 1.

Tarred. *All tarred with the same brush.* All alike to blame ; all sheep of the same flock. The allusion is to the custom of distinguishing the sheep of any given flock by a common mark with a brush dipped in tar.

Tarring and Feathering. The first record of this punishment is in 1189 (1 Rich. I.). A statute was made that any robber voyaging with the crusaders " shall be first shaved, then boiling pitch shall be poured upon his head, and a cushion of feathers shook over it." The wretch was then to be put on shore at the very first place the ship came to. (*Rymer: Foedera,* i. 65.)

Tarrinzeau Field. The bowling-green of Southwark. So called because it belonged to the Barons Hastings, who were Barons Tarrinzeau and Mauchline.

Tartan Plaid. A plaid is a long shawl or scarf—some twelve yards of narrow cloth wrapped round the waist, or over the chest and one shoulder, and reaching to the knees. It may be chequered or not; but the English use of the word in such a compound as Scotch-plaids, meaning chequered cloth, is a blunder for Scotch tartans. The tartan is the chequered pattern, every clan having its own tartan. A tartan-plaid is a Scotch scarf of a tartan or checked pattern.

Tartar, the deposit of wine, means "infernal stuff," being derived from the word Tar'taros (*q.v.*). Paracelsus says, "It is so called because it produces oil, water, tincture, and salt, which burn the patient as the fires of Tartarus burn."

Tar'taros (Greek), **Tartarus** (Latin). That part of the infernal regions where the wicked are punished. (*Classic mythology.*)

❣ The word "Hell" occurs seventeen times in the English version of the New Testament. In seven of these the original Greek is "Gehenna," in nine "Hades," and in one instance it is "Tartaros" (2 Peter ii. 4) σειραῖς ζόφου ταρταρώσας, παρέδωκεν. It is a very great pity that the three words are translated alike, especially as Gehenna and Hades are not synonymous, nor should either be confounded with Tartarus. The Anglo-Saxon verb *hél-an* means to cover, hence *hell* = the grave or Hades.

Tartuffe (2 syl.). The principal character of Molière's comedy so called. The original was the Abbé de Roquette, a parasite of the Prince de Condé. It is said that the name is from the Italian *tartuffoli* (truffles), and was suggested to Molière on seeing the sudden animation which lighted up the faces of certain monks when they heard that a seller of truffles awaited their orders. Bickerstaff's play, *The Hypocrite*, is an English version of *Tartuffe*.

Tassel-Gentle. The *tiercel* is the male of the goshawk. So called because it is a *tierce* or third less than the female. This is true of all birds of prey. The tiercel-gentle was the class of hawk appropriate to princes. (*See* HAWK.)

"O for a falconer's voice
To lure this tassel-gentle back again!"
Shakespeare: Romeo and Juliet, ii. 2.

Tasselled Gentleman. A fop; a man dressed in fine clothes. A corruption of *Tercel-gentle* by a double blunder: (1) Tercel, erroneously supposed to be *tassel,* and to refer to the tags and tassels worn by men on their dress; and (2) gentle corrupted into gentlemen, according to the Irish exposition of the verse, "The gentle shall inherit the earth."

Ta'tianists. The disciples of Tatian, who, after the death of Justin Martyr, "formed a new scheme of religion; for he advanced the notion of certain invisible æons, branded marriage with the name of fornication, and denied the salvation of Adam." (*Irenæus: Adv. Hereses* (ed. Grabe), pp. 105, 106, 262.)

❣ Two Tatians are almost always confounded as one person in Church history, although there was at least a century between them. The older Tatian was a Platonic philosopher, born in Syria, and converted to Christianity by Justin the Martyr. He was the author of a *Discourse to the Greeks*, became a Gnostic, and founded the sect of the Tatianists. The other Tatian was a native of Mesopotamia, lived in the fourth century, and wrote in very bad Greek a book called *Diatessaron*, supposed to be based on four Gospels, but what four is quite conjectural.

Tatterdemal'ion. A ragamuffin.

Tattoo. A beat on the drum at night to recall the soldiers to their barracks. It sounded at nine in summer and eight in winter. (French, *tapoter* or *tapotez tous.*)

The devil's tattoo. Drumming with one's finger on the furniture, or with one's toe on the ground—a monotonous sound, which gives the listener the "blue devils."

Tattoo (*To*). To mark the skin, especially the face, with indelible pigments rubbed into small punctures. (Tahitan, *tatu ;* from *ta,* mark.)

Tau. *Marked with a tau, i.e.* with a cross. Tertullian says, "*Hæc est litera Græcorum* τ, *nostra autem* T, *species crucis.*" And Cyprian tells us that the sign of the cross on the forehead is the mark of salvation.

"This reward (Ezek. ix. 4) is for those whose foreheads are marked with Tau."—*Bp. Andrews : Sermons* (Luke xvii. 32).

Taurus [*the Bull*] indicates to the Egyptians the time for ploughing the earth, which is done with oxen.

Mount Taurus, in Asia. In Judges xv. 3-19 we have an account of Samson and the jawbone, but probably Chamor (translated an *ass*) was the name of a hill or series of hills like Taurus, and should not have been translated. Similarly, Lehi (translated a *jawbone*) is probably a proper name also, and refers to a part of Chamor. If so, the meaning is, When he (Samson) came to Lehi, the summit of Mount Chamor, seeing a moist boulder, he broke it off and rolled it on his foes. Down it bounded, crushing "heaps upon heaps" of the Philistines. Where the boulder was broken off a spring of water jetted out, and with this water Samson quenched his thirst.

⁂ What is now called the Mountain of St. Patrick was previously called "Mount Eagle"—in Irish, *Cruachan Aichle*.

Tawdry. Showy, worthless finery; a corruption of St. Audrey. At the annual fair of St. Audrey, in the isle of Ely, showy lace called St. Audrey's lace was sold, and gave foundation to our word tawdry, which means anything gaudy, in bad taste, and of little value. (*See* TANTHONY.)

"*Tawdry*. 'Astrigmenta, timbriæ, seu fasciolæ, emptæ nundinis S. Ethelredæ.'"—*Henshawe*.
"Come, you promised me a tawdry lace and a pair of sweet gloves."—*Winter's Tale*, iv. 4.

Tawny (*The*). Alexandre Bonvici'no the historian, called *Il Moretto*. (1514-1564.)

Taylor, called *The Water-Poet*, who confesses he never learnt so much as the accidence. He wrote fourscore books, and afterwards opened an ale-house in Long Acre. (1580-1654.)

"Taylor, their better Charon, lends an oar,
Once swan of Thames, though now he sings no more."   *Dunciad*, iii.

Taylor's Institute. The Fitzwilliam Museum of Oxford. So called from Sir Robert Taylor, who made large bequests towards its erection. (1714-1788.)

Tchin. The military system adopted in the municipal and momestic regimen of Russia.

"Peter the Great established what is here [in Russia] the 'tchin,' that is to say, he applied the military system to the general administration of the empire."—*De Custine: Russia*, chap. vii.

Tchow Dynasty. The third imperial dynasty of China. which gave thirty-four kings, and lasted 866 years (B.C. 1122-256). It was so called from the seat of government.

Te Deum, etc., is usually ascribed to St. Ambrose. but is probably of a much later date. It is said that St. Ambrose

improvised this hymn while baptising St. Augustine. In allusion to this tradition, it is sometimes called "the Ambrosian Hymn."

Te Deum (of ecclesiastical architecture) is a "theological series" of carved figures in niches: (1) of angels, (2) of patriarchs and prophets, (3) of apostles and evangelists, (4) of saints and martyrs, (5) of founders. In the restored west front of Salisbury cathedral there is a "Te Deum," but the whole 123 original figures have been reduced in number.

Te Ig'itur. One of the service-books of the Roman Catholic Church, used by bishops and other dignitaries. So called from the first words of the canon, " *Te igitur, clementissime Pater*." *Oaths upon the Te Igitur.* Oaths sworn on the *Te Igitur* service-book, regarded as especially solemn.

Teague (*A*). An Irishman, about equal to Pat or Paddy. Sometimes we find the word Teague-lander. Teague is an Irish servant in Farquhar's *Twin Rivals ;* in act iii. 2 we find the phrase "a downright Teague," meaning a regular Irish character — blundering, witty, fond of whisky, and lazy. The name is also introduced in Shadwell's play, *The Lancashire Witches*, and *Teague O' Divelly, the Irish Priest* (1688).

"Was't Carwell, brother James, or Teague, That made thee break the Triple League?" *Rochester : History of Insipids*.

Teakettle Broth consists of hot water, bread, and a small lump of butter, with pepper and salt. The French *soup maigre*.

Tean or **Teian Poet.** Anacreon, who was born at Teos, in Io'nia. (B.C. 563-478.)

Teanlay Night. The vigil of ᐧAll Souls, or last evening of October, when bonfires were lighted and revels held for succouring souls in purgatory.

Tear (to rhyme with " snare "). *To tear Christ's body.* To use imprecations. The common oaths of mediæval times were by different parts of the Lord's body : hence the preachers used to talk of " tearing God's body by imprecations."

"Her othes been so greet and so dampnable. That 't is grisly for to hiere hëm swere. Our blisful Lordës body thay to-tere." *Chaucer: Canterbury Tales*, 13,889.

Tear (to rhyme with " fear "). *Tear and larme.* (Anglo - Saxon, *tæher ;* Gothic, *tagr ;* Greek, *dakru ;* Latin, *lacrim-a ;* French, *lar'm*.)

Tears of Eos. The dew-drops of the morning were so called by the Greeks. Eos was the mother of Memnon (*q.v.*), and wept for him every morning.

St. Lawrence's tears. Falling stars. St. Lawrence was roasted to death on a gridiron, and wept that others had not the same spirit to suffer for truth's sake as he had. (*See* LAWRENCE.)

Tear Handkerchief (*The*). A handkerchief blessed by the priest and given, in the Tyrol, to a bride, to dry her tears. At death, this handkerchief is laid in her coffin over the face of the deceased.

Teaspoon (*A*). £5,000. (*See* SPOON.)

Tea'zle (*Lady*). A lively, innocent country maiden, married to Sir Peter, who is old enough to be her father. Planted in the hotbed of London gaiety, she formed a *liaison* with Joseph Surface, but, being saved from disgrace, repented and reformed. (*Sheridan : School for Scandal.*) (*See* TOWNLY.)

Teazle (*Sir Peter*). A man who had remained a bachelor till he had become old, when he married a girl from the country, who proved extravagant, fond of pleasure, selfish, and vain. Sir Peter was always gibing his wife for her inferior rank, teasing her about her manner of life, and yet secretly liking what she did, and feeling proud of her. (*Sheridan : School for Scandal.*)

Teck (*A*). A detective. Every suspicious man is a "teck" in the eyes of a thief. Of course, the word is a contraction of [de]tec[tive].

Teeth.

From the teeth outwards. Merely talk ; without real significance.

"Much of the . . . talk about General Gordon lately was only from the teeth outwards."—*The Daily News*, 1886.

To set one's teeth on edge. (*See* EDGE.) *He has cut his eye-teeth.* He is "up to snuff ; " he has "his weather-eye open." The eye-teeth are cut late—

Months.
First set—5 to 8, the four centr'l incisors
7 „ 10 „ lateral incisors.
12 „ 16 „ anterior molars.
14 „ 20 „ the eye-teeth.
Years.
Second set—5 to 6, the anterior molars.
7 „ 8 „ incisors.
9 „ 10 „ bicuspids.
11 „ 12 „ eye-teeth.

In spite of his teeth. In opposition to his settled purpose or resolution. Holinshed tells us of a Bristol Jew, who suffered a tooth to be drawn daily for seven days before he would submit to the extortion of King John. (*See* JEW'S EYE.)

"In despite of the teeth of all the rhyme and reason."—*Shakespeare: Merry Wives of Windsor*, v. 4.

To cast into one's teeth. To utter reproaches.

"All his faults observed,
Set in a note-book, learned, and conned by rote,
To cast into my teeth."
Shakespeare: Julius Cæsar, iv. 3.

The skin of his teeth. (*See* SKIN.)

Teeth. The people of Ceylon and Malabar used to worship the teeth of elephants and monkeys. The Siamese once offered to a Portuguese 700,000 ducats to redeem a monkey's tooth.

Wolf's tooth. An amulet worn by children to charm away fear.

Teeth are Drawn (*His*). His power of doing mischief is taken from him. The phrase comes from the fable of *The Lion in Love*, who consented to have his teeth drawn and claws cut, in order that a fair damsel might marry him. When the teeth were drawn and claws cut off, the father of the maid fell on the lion and slew him.

Teeth of the Wind (*In the*). With the wind dead against us, with the wind blowing in or against our teeth.

"To strive with all the tempest in my teeth."
Pope.

Teetotal. Those who sign the abstinence pledge are entered with O. P. (*old pledge*) after their name. Those who pledge themselves to abstain wholly from alcoholic drinks have a T (*total*) after their name. Hence, T = total abstainer.

⁂ The tale about Dick Turner, a plasterer or fish-hawker at Preston, in Lancashire, who stammered forth, " I'll have nowt to do with the moderation botheration pledge ; I'll be reet down t—total, that or nowt," is not to be relied on.

It is said that Turner's tombstone contains this inscription : " Beneath this stone are deposited the remains of Richard Turner, author of the word *Teetotal* as applied to abstinence from all intoxicating liquors, who departed this life on the 27th day of October, 1846, aged 56 years."

Teetotum (*A*). A working-man's club in which all intoxicants are prohibited.

" You can generally depend upon getting your money's worth if you go to a teetotum."—*Stephen Remarx*, chap. v.

Teian Muse (*The*). Anacreon, a native of Teion, in Paphlagonia. (B.C. 563-478.)

Teinds. Tithes.

"Taking down from the window-seat that amusing folio (*The Scottish Coke upon Littleton*), he opened it, as if instinctively, at the tenth title of Book Second, 'of Teinds or Tythes.'"—*Sir W. Scott: The Antiquary*, chap. xxxv.

N.B. Those entitled to tithes were called in Scotland "teind-masters."

Telamo'nēs. Supporters. (Greek, *telamŏn*.) Generally applied to figures of men used for supporters in architure. (*See* ATLANTES.)

Telegram. *Milking a telegram.* A telegram is said to be "milked" when the message sent to a specific party is surreptitiously made use of by others.

"They receive their telegrams in cipher to avoid the risk of their being 'milked' by rival journals."—*The Times*, August 14th, 1869.

Telem'achos. The only son of Ulysses and Penel'ope. After the fall of Troy he went, under the guidance of Mentor, in quest of his father. He is the hero of Fénelon's prose epic called *Télémaque*.

Tell (*William*). The boldest of the Swiss mountaineers. The daughter of Leu'thold having been insulted by an emissary of Albrecht Gessler, the enraged father killed the ruffian and fled. William Tell carried the assassin across the lake, and greatly incensed the tyrannical governor. The people rising in rebellion, Gessler put to death Melch'tal, the patriarch of the district, and, placing the ducal cap of Austria on a pole, commanded the people to bow down before it in reverence. Tell refused to do so, whereupon Gessler imposed on him the task of shooting an apple from his little boy's head. Tell succeeded in this perilous trial of skill, but, letting fall a concealed arrow, was asked with what object he had secreted it. "To kill thee, O tyrant," he replied, "if I had failed in the task imposed on me." Gessler now ordered the bold mountaineer to be put in chains and carried across the lake to Küssnacht Castle "to be devoured alive by reptiles," but, being rescued by the peasantry, he shot Gessler and liberated his country. (*Rossini : Guglielmo Tell, an opera.*)

⁎⁎ Kissling's monument at Altorf (1892) has four reliefs on the pedestal: (1) Tell shooting the apple ; (2) Tell's leap from the boat ; (3) Gessler's death ; and (4) Tell's death at Schachenbach.

William Tell. The story of William Tell is told of several other persons :

(1) Egil, the brother of Wayland Smith. One day King Nidung commanded him to shoot an apple off the

head of his son. Egil took two arrows from his quiver, the straightest and sharpest he could find. When asked by the king why he took *two* arrows, the god-archer replied, as the Swiss peasant to Gessler, "To shoot thee, tyrant, with the second if the first one fails."

(2) Saxo Grammaticus tells nearly the same story respecting Toki, who killed Harald.

(3) Reginald Scot says, "Puncher shot a pennie on his son's head, and made ready another arrow to have slain the Duke Remgrave, who commanded it." (1584.)

(4) Similar tales are told of Adam Bell, Clym of the Clough, William of Cloudeslie and Henry IV., Olaf and Eindridi, etc.

Tellers of the Exchequer. A corruption of *talliers*—*i.e.* tally-men, whose duty it was to compare the tallies, receive money payable into the Exchequer, give receipts, and pay what was due according to the tallies. Abolished in the reign of William IV. The functionary of a bank who receives and pays bills, orders, and so on, is still called a "teller."

Tem'ora. One of the principal poems of Ossian, in eight books, so called from the royal residence of the kings of Connaught. Cairbar had usurped the throne, having killed Cormac, a distant relative of Fingal ; and Fingal raised an army to dethrone the usurper. The poem begins from this point with an invitation from Cairbar to Oscar, son of Ossian, to a banquet. Oscar accepted the invitation, but during the feast a quarrel was vamped up, in which Cairbar and Oscar fell by each other's spears. When Fingal arrived a battle ensued, in which Fillan, son of Fingal, the Achilles of the Caledonian army, and Cathmor, brother of Cairbar, the bravest of the Irish army, were both slain. Victory crowned the army of Fingal, and Ferad-Artho, the rightful heir, was restored to the throne of Connaught.

Temper. To make trim. The Italians say, *tempera're la lira*, to tune the lyre ; *temperare una penna*, to mend a pen ; *temperáre l'oriuólo*, to wind up the clock. In Latin, *temperare calamum* is "to mend a pen." Metal well tempered is metal made trim or meet for its use, and if not so it is called *ill-tempered*. When Otway says, "Woman, nature made thee to temper man," he means to make him trim, to soften his nature, to mend him.

Templars or **Knights Templars.** Nine French knights bound themselves, at the beginning of the twelfth century, to protect pilgrims on their way to the Holy Land, and received the name of Templars, because their arms were kept in a building given to them for the purpose by the abbot of the convent called the Temple of Jerusalem. They used to call themselves the "Poor Soldiers of the Holy City." Their habit was a long white mantle, to which subsequently was added a red cross on the left shoulder. Their famous war-cry was "Bauseant," from their banner, which was striped black and white, and charged with a red cross; the word *Bauseant* is old French for a black and white horse.

Seal of the Knights Templars (two knights riding on one horse). The first Master of the Order and his friend were so poor that they had but one horse between them, a circumstance commemorated by the seal of the order. The order afterwards became wealthy and powerful.

Temple (*London*) was once the seat of the Knights Templars. (*See above.*)

Temple. The place under inspection, from the Latin verb *tueor*, to behold, to look at. It was the space marked out by the Roman augurs as the field of observation. When augurs made their observations they marked out a space within which the sign was to occur. Rather remarkable is it that the Greek *theos* and Latin *deus* are nouns from the verbs *theaomai* and *tueor*, meaning the "presence" in this space marked out by the augurs.

Temple (*A*). A kind of stretcher, used by weavers for keeping Scotch carpeting at its proper breadth during weaving. The weaver's temple is a sort of wooden rule with teeth of a pothook form.

Temple Bar, called "the City Golgotha," because the heads of traitors, etc., were exposed there. (Removed 1878.)

Temple of Solomon. Timbs, in his *Notabilia*, p. 192, tells us that the treasure provided by David for this building exceeded 900 millions sterling (!). The building was only about 150 feet long and 105 wide. Taking the whole revenue of the British empire at 100 millions sterling annually, the sum stated by Timbs would exhaust nine years of the whole British revenue. The kingdom of David was not larger than Wales, and by no means populous.

Temples (*Pagan*) in many respects resembled Roman Catholic churches. There was first the vestibule, in which were the piscina with lustral water to sprinkle those who entered the edifice; then the nave (or *naos*), common to all comers; then the chancel (or *adytum*) from which the general public was excluded. In some of the temples there was also an *apsis*, like our apse; and in some others there was a portico, which not unfrequently was entered by steps or "degrees"; and, like churches, the Greek and Roman temples were consecrated by the pontiff.

∴ The most noted temples were that of Vulcan, in Egypt; of Jupiter Olympus, and of Apollo, in Delphos; of Diana, in Ephesus; the Capitol and the Pantheon of Rome; the Jewish temple, built by Solomon, and that of Herod the Great.

Tempora Mutantur. (*See* MUTANTUR.)

Ten. Gothic, *tai-hun* (two hands); Old German, *ze-hen*, whence *zehn, zen*.

Ten Commandments (*The*). The following rhyme was written under the two tables of the commandments:—

"PRSVR Y PRFCT MN
VR KP THS PRCPTS TN.

The vowel E
Supplies the key."

Ten Commandments (*The*). Scratching the face with the ten fingers of an angry woman; or a blow with the two fists of an angry man, in which the "ten commandments are summarised into two."

" Could I come near your beauty with my nails,
  I'd set my ten commandments in your face."
      Shakespeare: 2 *Henry VI.,* i. 3.

"' I daur you to touch him,' spreading abroad her long and muscular fingers, garnished with claws, which a vulture might have envied. ' I'll set my ten commandments on the face of the first loon that lays a finger on him.'—*Sir W. Scott: Waverley,* chap. xxx.

Tench is from the Latin *tinc-a*, so called, says Aulus Gellius, because it is *tincta* (tinted).

Tend in the Eyes. Dutch, "*Iemand naar de oogen te zien.*" The English equivalent is, "to wait on his nod" or beck.

" Her gentlewomen, like the Nereides,
  So many mermaids, tended her i' the eyes."
      Shakespeare: Antony and Cleopatra, ii. 2.

Tendon. (*See* ACHILLES.)

Ten'glio. A river in Lapland on whose banks roses grow.

" I was surprised to see upon the banks of this river roses of as lovely a red as any that are in our own gardens."—*M. de Maupertuis.*

Ten'iers. Malplaquet, in France, famous for the victory of the Duke of Marlborough and Prince Eugene over the French under Marshal Villars on September 11, 1709.

"Her courage tried
On Teniers' dreadful field."
Thomson: Autumn.

The Scottish Teniers. Sir David Wilkie (1785-1841).

Tenner (*A*). A ten-pound note. A "fiver" is a five-pound note.

Tennis Ball of Fortune. Pertinax, the Roman emperor, was so called. He was first a seller of charcoal, then a schoolmaster, then a soldier, and lastly an emperor, but in three months he was dethroned and murdered.

Tennyson (*Alfred*). *Bard of Arthurian Romance.* His poems on the legends of King Arthur are—(1) *The Coming of Arthur;* (2) *Geraint and Enid;* (3) *Merlin and Vivien;* (4) *Lancelot and Elaine;* (5) *The Holy Grail;* (6) *Pelleas and Ettare;* (7) *Guinevere;* (8) *The Passing of Arthur.* Also *The Morte d'Arthur, Sir Galahad, The Lady of Shallott.* (1810-1892.)

Tenpenny Nails. Very large nails, 1,000 of which would weigh 10 lbs. Four-penny nails are those which are much smaller, as 1,000 of them would weigh only 4 lbs.; two-penny nails, being half the size, 1,000 of them would weigh only 2 lbs. Then we come to the ounce nails, 1,000 weighing only 8, 12, or 16 ounces, the standard unit being always 1,000 nails. Penny is a corruption of pounder, *poun'er, pun'er, penny,* as two-penny nails, four-penny nails, ten-penny nails, etc., according to the weight of 1,000 of them.

Tenson. A subdivision of the *chanzos* or poems of love and gallantry by the Troubadours. When the public jousts were over, the lady of the castle opened her "court of love," in which the combatants *contended* with harp and song.

Tent. *Father of such as dwell in tents.* Jabal. (Genesis iv. 20.)

Tent (*Skidbladnir's*) would cover a whole army, and yet fold up into a parcel not too big for the pocket. (*Arabian Nights.*)

Ten'terden. *Tenterden steeple was the cause of Goodwin Sands.* The reason alleged is not obvious; an apparent *non-sequitur.* Mr. More, being sent with a commission into Kent to ascertain the cause of the Goodwin Sands, called together the oldest inhabitants to ask their opinion. A very old man said, " I

believe Tenterden steeple is the cause." This reason seemed ridiculous enough, but the fact is, the Bishop of Rochester applied the revenues for keeping clear the Sandwich haven to the building of Tenterden steeple. (*See* GOODWIN SANDS.)

∴ Some say the stone collected for strengthening the wall was used for building the church tower.

Tenterhooks. *I am on tenterhooks,* or *on tenterhooks of great expectation.* My curiosity is on the full stretch, I am most curious or anxious to hear the issue. Cloth, after being woven, is stretched or "tentered" on hooks passed through the selvages. (Latin, *tentus,* stretched, hence "tent," canvas stretched.)

" He was not kept an instant on the tenterhooks of impatience longer than the appointed moment."—*Sir W. Scott: Redgauntlet,* chap. xvi.

Tenth Legion (*The*), or the *Submerged Tenth.* The lowest of the proletariat class. A phrase much popularised in the last quarter of the nineteenth century by "General" Booth's book, *In Darkest England.* (*See* SUBMERGED.)

Tenth Wave. It is said that every tenth wave is the biggest. (*See* WAVE.)

" At length, tumbling from the Gallic coast, the victorious tenth wave shall ride, like the boar, over all the rest."—*Burke.*

Tercel. The male hawk. So called because it is one-third smaller than the female. (French, *tiers.*)

Terence. *The Terence of England, the mender of hearts,* is the exquisite compliment which Goldsmith, in his *Retaliation,* pays to Richard Cumberland, author of *The Jew, The West Indian, The Wheel of Fortune,* etc. (1732-1811.)

Tere'sa (*St.*). The reformer of the Carmelites, canonised by Gregory XV. in 1621. (1515-1582.) (*See* SANCHO PANZA.)

Term Time, called, since 1873, LAW SESSIONS.

Michaelmas Sessions begin November 2nd, and end December 21st.
Hilary Sessions begin January 11th, and end the Wednesday before Easter.
Easter Sessions begin the Tuesday after Easter-week, and end the Friday before Whit-Sunday.
Trinity Sessions begin the Tuesday after Whit-sun-week, and end August 8th.

Term Time of our Universities. There are three terms at Cambridge in a year, and four at Oxford, but the two middle Oxford terms are two only in name, as they run on without a break. The three Cambridge terms are Lent, Easter, and Michaelmas. The four

Oxford terms are Lent, Easter + Trinity, and Michaelmas.

LENT—
  Cambridge, begins January 13th, and ends on the Friday before Palm Sunday.
  Oxford, begins January 14th, and ends on the Saturday before Palm Sunday.

EASTER—
  Cambridge, begins on the Friday of Easter-week, and ends Friday nearest June 20th.
  Oxford, begins on the Wednesday of Easter-week, and ends Friday before Whit-Sunday. The continuation, called "Trinity term," runs on till the second Saturday of July.

MICHAELMAS—
  Cambridge, begins October 1st, and ends December 16th.
  Oxford, begins October 10th, and ends December 17th.

Ter'magant. The author of *Junius* says this was a Saxon idol, and derives the word from *tyr magan* (very mighty); but perhaps it is the Persian *tir-magian* (Magian lord or deity). The early Crusaders, not very nice in their distinctions, called all Pagans *Saracens*, and muddled together Magianism and Mahometanism in wonderful confusion, so that Termagant was called the god of the Saracens, or the co-partner of Mahound. Hence Ariosto makes Ferrau "blaspheme his Mahound and Termagant" (*Orlando Furioso*, xii. 59); and in the legend of *Syr Guy* the Soudan or Sultan is made to say—

  " So help͛ me, Mahoune, of might,
  And Termagaunt, my God so bright."

Termagant was at one time applied to men. Thus Massinger, in *The Picture*, says, "A hundred thousand Turks assailed him, every one a Termagant [Pagan]." At present the word is applied to a boisterous, brawling woman. Thus Arbuthnot says, "The eldest daughter was a termagant, an imperious profligate wretch." The change of sex arose from the custom of representing Termagant on the stage in Eastern robes, like those worn in Europe by females.

  "'Twas time to counterfeit, or that hot termagant Scot [Douglas] had paid me scot and lot too."—*Shakespeare: 1 Henry IV.*, v. 4.

Outdoing Termagant (*Hamlet*, iii. 2). In the old play the degree of rant was the measure of villainy. Termagant and Herod, being considered the *beau-ideal* of all that is bad, were represented as settling everything with club law, and bawling so as to split the ears of the groundlings. Bully Bottom, having ranted to his heart's content, says, "That is Ercles' vein, a tyrant's vein." (*See* HEROD.)

Terpsichore (properly *Terp-sik'-o-re*, but often pronounced *Terp'-si-core*). The goddess of dancing. *Terpsichore'an*,

relating to dancing. Dancers are called "the votaries of Terpsichore."

Terra Firma. Dry land, in opposition to water; the continents as distinguished from islands. The Venetians so called the mainland of Italy under their sway; as, the Duchy of Venice, Venetian Lombardy, the March of Treviso, the Duchy of Friu'li, and Istria. The continental parts of America belonging to Spain were also called by the same term.

Terrestrial Sun (*That*). Gold, which in alchemy was the metal corresponding to the sun, as silver did to the moon. (*Sir Thomas Browne: Religio Medici*, p. 149, 3.)

Terrible (*The*). Ivan IV. [or II.] of Russia. (1529, 1533-1584.)

Ter'rier is a dog that "takes the earth," or unearths his prey. Dog Tray is merely an abbreviation of the same word. Terrier is also applied to the hole which foxes, badgers, rabbits, and so on, dig under ground to save themselves from the hunters. The dog called a *terrier* creeps into these holes like a ferret to rout out the victim. (Latin, *terra*, the earth.) Also a land-roll or description of estates.

  ∴ There are short- and long-haired terriers.
  (1) *Short-haired*: the black-and-tan, the schipperke, the bull-terrier, and the fox-terrier.
  (2) *Long-haired*: the Bedlington, the Dandy Dinmont, and the Irish, Scotch, and Yorkshire terrier.

Terry Alts. Insurgents of Clare, who appeared after the Union, and committed numerous outrages. These rebels were similar to "the Thrashers" of Connaught, "the Carders," the followers of "Captain Rock" in 1822, and the Fenians (1869).

Ter'tium Quid. A third party which shall be nameless. The expression originated with Pythago'ras, who, defining bipeds, said—

  " Sunt *bipes* homo, et avis, et tertium quid."
  " A man is a biped, so is a bird, and a third thing (which shall be nameless)."

Iamblichus says this third thing was Pythagoras himself. (*Vita Pyth.*, cxxvii.)

In chemistry, when two substances chemically unite, the new substance is called a *tertium quid*, as a neutral salt produced by the mixture of an acid and alkali.

Terza Rima. A poem in triplets, in which the second or middle line rhymes with the first and third lines of the succeeding triplets. In the beginning of the poem lines 1 and 3 rhyme independently, and the poem must end with the first line of a new triplet. Dante's *Divine Comedy* is in this metre, and Byron has adopted it in *The Prophecy of Dante.* The scheme is as follows:—

```
−1a -
x2a - feel - - - - - - - (a new rhyme for 1b and 2b).
−3a -
  1b- heal
x2b - - - - cries - - - - (a new rhyme for 1c and 4c).
  3b- steal
  1c - - - - skies
x2c - - - - - - - place - (a new rhyme for 1d and 3d).
  3c - - - - arise
  1d - - - - - race
x2d - - - - - - - - - - - (a new rhyme for 1e and 2e).
  3d - - - - - space
  etc.  etc.
```

Tessera'rian Art. The art of gambling. (Latin, *tessera*, a die.)

Tester. A sixpence. Called *testone* (*teste*, a head) because it was stamped on one side with the *head* of the reigning sovereign. Similarly, the head canopy of a bed is called its tester (Italian, *testa ;* French, *teste, tête*). Copstick in Dutch means the same thing. Worth 12d. in the reign of Henry VIII., but 6d. in the reign of Elizabeth.

" Hold, there's a tester for thee."—*Shakespeare :* 2 *Henry IV.,* iii. 2.

Testers are gone to Oxford, to study at Brazenose. When Henry VIII. debased the silver testers, the alloy broke out in red pimples through the silver, giving the royal likeness in the coin a blotchy appearance ; hence the punning proverb.

Tête-à-tête. A confidential conversation.

Tête Bottée [*Booted Head*]. The nickname of Philippe des Comines.

"You, Sir Philip des Comines, were at a hunting-match with the duke your master ; and when he alighted after the chase, he required your services in drawing off his boots. Reading in your looks some natural resentment, he ordered you to sit down in turn, and rendered you the same office. . . . but . . . no sooner had he plucked one of your boots off than he brutally beat it about your head. . . . and his privileged fool Le Glorieux gave you the name of *Tête Bottée.*"—*Sir W. Scott : Quentin Durward*, chap. xxx.

Tete du Pont. The barbican or watch-tower placed on the head of a drawbridge.

Tether. *He has come to the end of his tether.* He has outrun his fortune ; he has exhausted all his resources. The reference is to a cable run out to the bitter end (*see* BITTER END), or to the lines upon lines in whale fishing. If the whale runs out all the lines it gets away and is lost.

Horace calls the end of life "*ultima linea rerum,*" the end of the goal, referring to the white chalk mark at the end of a racecourse.

Teth'ys. The sea, properly the wife of Oce'anos.

" The golden sun above the watery bed
Of hoary Tethys raised his beamy head."
Hoole's Ariosto, bk. viii.

Tetragram'maton. The four letters, meaning the four which compose the name of Deity. The ancient Jews never pronounced the word Jehovah composed of the four sacred letters JHVH. The word means " I am," or " I exist " (Exod. iii. 14) ; but Rabbi Bechai says the letters include the three times—past, present, and future. Pythagoras called Deity a Tetrad or Tetractys, meaning the " four sacred letters."

The words in different languages :—

Arabic, ALLA.
Assyrian, ADAD.
Brahmins, JOSS.
Danish, GODH.
Dutch, GODT.
East Indian, ZEUL and ESAI.
Egyptian, ZEUT, AUMN, AMON.
French, DIEU.
German, GOTT.
Greek, ZEUS.
Hebrew, JHVH, ADON.
Irish, DICH.
Italian, IDIO.
Japanese, ZAIN.
Latin, DEUS.
Malayan, EESF.
Persian, SORU, SYRA.
Peruvian, LLAN.
Scandinavian, ODIN.
Spanish, DIOS.
Swedish, GODD, GOTH.
Syriac, ADAD.
Tahitan, ATUA.
Tartarian, TYAN.
Turkish, ADDI.
Vaudois, DIOU.
Wallachian, SEUE.

" Such was the sacred Tetragrammaton.
Things worthy silence must not be revealed."
Dryden : Britannia Rediviva.

[We have the Egyptian Θωνθ, like the Greek Θεος.]

Tetrap'la. The Bible, disposed by Origen under four columns, each of which contained a different Greek version. The versions were those of Aquila, Symmachus, Theodosian, and the Septuagint.

Teucer. Brother of Ajax *the Greater*, who went with the allied Greeks to the siege of Troy. On his return home, his father banished him the kingdom for not avenging on Ulysses the death of his brother. (*Homer : Iliad.*)

Teutons. Thuath-duiné (north men). Our word *Dutch* and the German *Deutsch* are variations of the same word, originally written *Theodisk.*

Teuton'ic Knights. An order which the Crusades gave birth to. Originally only Germans of noble birth were admissible to the order. (Abolished by Napoleon in 1800.)

Th (Θ, *theta*). The sign given in the verdict of the Areopăgus of condemnation to death (θάνατος).

"Et potis es vitio nigrum præfigere theta."—
Persius.

∵ T (τελέωσις) meant absolution, and A = *non liquet*. In the Roman courts C meant condemnation, A absolution, and N L (*non liquet*) remanded.

Tha'is (2 syl.). An Athenian courtesan who induced Alexander, when excited with wine, to set fire to the palace of the Persian kings at Persep'olis.

" The king seized a flambeau with zeal to destroy ;
Thaïs led the way to light him to his prey,
And, like another Helen, fired another Troy."
        Dryden : Alexander's Feast.

Thal'aba. The Destroyer, son of Hodei'rah and Zei'nab (*Zeno'bia*) ; hero of a poem by Southey, in twelve books.

Thales. (*See* SEVEN SAGES.)

Thales'tris. Queen of the Am'azons, who went with 300 women to meet Alexander the Great, under the hope of raising a race of Alexanders.

"This was no Thalestris from the fields, but a quiet domestic character from the fireside."—*C. Brontë's Shirley,* chap. xxviii.

Thali'a. One of the muses, generally regarded as the patroness of comedy. She was supposed by some, also, to preside over husbandry and planting, and is represented leaning on a column holding a mask in her right hand, etc.

Thames (1 syl.). The Latin *Thamesis* (the broad Isis, where *isis* is a mere variation of *esk, ouse, uisg,* etc., meaning water). The river Churn unites with the Thames at Cricklade, in Wiltshire, where it was at one time indifferently called the Thames, Isis, or Thamesis. Thus, in the Saxon Chronicle we are told the East Anglians " overran all the land of Mercia till they came to Cricklade, where they forded the Thames." In Camden's *Britannia* mention is made of Summerford, in Wiltshire, on the east bank of the " Isis " (*cujus vocabulum Temis juxta vadum, qui appellātur Summerford*). Canute also forded the Thames in 1016 in Wiltshire. Hence Thames is not a compound of the two rivers Thame and Isis at their junction, but of Thamesis. Tham is a variety of the Latin *amnis,* seen in such words as North-ampton, South-ampton, Tam-worth, etc. Pope perpetuates the notion that Thames = Thame and Isis in the lines—

" Around his throne the sea-born brothers stood ;
Who swell with tributary urns his flood :—
First the famed authors of his ancient name,
The winding Isis and the fruitful Thame !
The Kennet swift, for silver eels renowned ;
The Loddon slow, with verdant alders crowned ;

Cole, whose dark streams his flowery islands lave ;
And chalky Wey that rolls a milky wave ;
The blue transparent Vandalis appears ;
The gulphy Lee his sedgy tresses rears ;
And sullen Mole that hides his diving flood ;
And silent Darent stained with Danish blood."
        Pope : Windsor Forest.

He'll never set the Thames on fire. He'll never make any figure in the world ; never plant his footsteps on the sands of time. The popular explanation is that the word *Thames* is a pun on the word *temse,* a corn-sieve ; and that the parallel French locution *He will never set the Seine on fire* is a pun ón *seine,* a drag-net ; but these solutions are not tenable. There is a Latin saw, "*Tiberim accendĕre nequaquam potest,*" which is probably the *fons et origo* of other parallel sayings. Then, long before our proverb, we had " To set the Rhine on fire " (*Den Rhein anzünden*), 1630, and *Er hat den Rhein und das Meer angezündet,* 1580.

∵ There are numerous similar phrases : as " He will never set the Liffey on fire ; " to " set the Trent on fire ; " to " set the Humber on fire ; " etc. Of course it is possible to set water on fire, but the scope of the proverb lies the other way, and it may take its place beside such sayings as " If the sky falls we may catch larks."

Tham'muz. The Syrian and Phœnician name of Ado'nis. His death happened on the banks of the river Adonis, and in summer-time the waters always become reddened with the hunter's blood. (*See* Ezekiel viii. 14.)

"Thammuz came next behind,
Whose annual wound on Lebanon allured
The Syrian damsels to lament his fate
In amorous ditties all a summer's day,
While smooth Adonis from his native rock
Ran purple to the sea, supposed with blood
Of Thammuz yearly wounded."
    Milton : Paradise Lost, bk. iii. 446-452.

Tham'yris. A Thracian bard mentioned by Homer (*Iliad,* ii. 595). He challenged the Muses to a trial of skill, and, being overcome in the contest, was deprived by them of his sight and power of song. He is represented with a broken lyre in his hand.

" Blind Thamyris and blind Mæon'idēs [Homer],
And Tiresias and Phineus, prophets old."
    Milton : Paradise Lost, iii. 35-36.

∵ " Tiresias " pronounce *Ti'-re-sas;* " Phineus " pronounce *Fi'nuce.*

That. Seven "thats" may follow each other, and make sense.

" For be it known that we may safely write
Or say that ' that *that*' that that man wrote was right ;
Nay, e'en that that *that,* that ' that THAT' has followed,
Through six repeats, the grammar's rule has hallowed ;
And that that *that* that *that* ' that THAT' began
Repeated seven times is right, deny't who can."

" My lords, with humble submission *that* that I say is this : That that that ' that that' that that gentleman has advanced is not *that* that he should have proved to your lordships."—*Spectator,* No. 86.

That's the Ticket. That's the right thing to do; generally supposed to be a corruption of " That's the etiquette," or proper mode of procedure, according to the programme ; but the expanded phrase " That's the ticket for soup" seems to allude to the custom of showing a ticket in order to obtain a basin of soup given in charity.

Thatch. A straw hat. A hat being called a tile, and the word being mistaken for a roof-tile, gave rise to several synonyms, such as roof, roofing, thatch, etc.

Thau′matur′gus. A miracle-worker; applied to saints and others who are reputed to have performed miracles. (Greek, *thauma ergon*.)

Prince Alexander of Hohenlohe, whose power was looked upon as miraculous.

Apollo′nius of Tya′na, Cappadocia (A.D. 3-98). (*See* his *Life*, by Philos′tratus.)

St. Bernard of Clairvaux, called " the Thaumaturgus of the West." (1091-1153.)

St. Francis d'Assisi, founder of the Franciscan order. (1182-1226.)

J. Joseph Gassner, of Bratz, in the Tyrol, who, looking on disease as a possession, exorcised the sick, and his cures were considered miraculous. (1727-1779.)

Gregory, Bishop of Neo-Cæsare′a, in Cappado′cia, called emphatically " the Thaumaturgus," from the numerous miracles he is reported to have performed. (212-270.)

St. Isidorus. (*See* his *Life*, by Damascius.)

Jannes and *Jambres*, the magicians of Pharaoh who withstood Moses.

Blaise Pascal. (1623-1662.)

Ploti′nus, and several other Alexandrine philosophers. (205-270.) (*See* the *Life of Plotinus*, by Porphyry.)

Proclus. (412-415.) (*See* his *Life*, by Marinus.)

Simon Magus, of Samaria, called " the Great Power of God." (Acts viii. 10.)

Several of the *Sophists*. (See *Lives of the Philosophers*, by Eunapius.)

Sospitra possessed the omniscient ρower of seeing all that was done in every part of the globe. (*Eunapius: Œdeseus.*)

Vincent de Paul, founder of the " Sisters of Charity." (1576-1660.)

⁂ Peter Schott has published a treatise on natural magic called *Thaumaturgus Physicus.* (*See below.*)

Thaumaturgus. Filumĕna is called

Thaumaturga, a saint unknown till 1802, when a grave was discovered with this inscription on tiles : " LUMENA PAXTE CYMFI, which, being rearranged, makes *Pax tecum Filumena*. Filumena was at once accepted as a saint, and so many wonders were worked by " her " that she has been called *La Thaumaturge du Dixneuvième Siècle*.

Theag′enes and Charicle′a. The hero and heroine of an erotic romance in Greek by Heliodo′rus, Bishop of Trikka (fourth century).

Theban Bard or **Eagle.** Pindar, born at Thebes. (B.C. 518-439.)

Theban Legion. The legion raised in the Thebaïs of Egypt, and composed of Christian soldiers, led by St. Maurice. This legion is sometimes called " the Thundering Legion " (*q.v.*).

Thebes (1 syl.), called *The Hundred-Gated*, was not Thebes of Bœotia, but of Thebaïs of Egypt, which extended over twenty-three miles of land. Homer says out of each gate the Thebans could send forth 200 war - chariots. (Egyptian, *Taape* or *Taouab*, city of the sun.)

> " The world's great empress on the Egyptian plain,
> That spreads her conquests o'er a thousand states,
> And pours her heroes through a hundred gates,
> Two hundred horsemen and two hundred cars
> From each wide portal issuing to the wars."
> *Pope: Iliad*, i.

Thec′la (*St.*), styled in Greek martyrologies the *proto-martyress*, as St. Stephen is the *proto-martyr*. All that is known of her is from a book called the *Periods*, or *Acts of Paul and Thecla*, pronounced apocryphal by Pope Gela′sius, and unhappily lost. According to the legend, Thecla was born of a noble family in Ico′nium, and was converted by the preaching of St. Paul.

Theist, Deist, Atheist, Agnostic. A *theist* believes there is a God who made and governs all creation ; but does not believe in the doctrine of the Trinity, nor in a divine revelation.

A *deist* believes there is a God who created all things, but does not believe in His superintendence and government. He thinks the Creator implanted in all things certain immutable laws, called the *Laws of Nature*, which act *per se*, as a watch acts without the supervision of its maker. Like the theist, he does not believe in the doctrine of the Trinity, nor in a divine revelation.

The *atheist* disbelieves even the existence of a God. He thinks matter is eternal, and what we call "creation" is the result of natural laws.

The *agnostic* believes only what is knowable. He rejects revelation and the doctrine of the Trinity as "past human understanding." He is neither theist, deist, nor atheist, as all these are past understanding.

Thelusson Act. The 39th and 4th George III., cap. 98. An Act to prevent testators from leaving their property to accumulate for more than twenty-one years. So called because it was passed in reference to the last will and testament of the late Mr. Thelusson, in which he desired his property to be invested till it had accumulated to some nineteen millions sterling.

The'not. An old shepherd who relates to Cuddy the fable of *The Oak and the Briar*, with the view of curing him of his vanity. (*Spenser: Shepherd's Calendar.*)

Theoc'ritus. *The Scottish Theocritus.* Allan Ramsay, author of *The Gentle Shepherd*. (1685-1758.)

Theod'omas. A famous trumpeter at the siege of Thebes.

" At every court ther cam loud menstralcye
That never trompèd Joab for to heere.
Ne ne Theodomas yit half so cleere
At Thebes, when the citè was in doute."
Chaucer: Canterbury Tales, 9,592.

Theodo'ra (in *Orlando Furioso*), sister of Constantine, the Greek Emperor. Greatly enraged against Roge'ro, who slew her son, she vowed vengeance. Rogero, captured during sleep, being committed to her hands, she cast him into a foul dungeon, and fed him on the bread of affliction till Prince Leon released him.

Theod'orick. One of the heroes of the *Nibelung*, a legend of the Sagas. This king of the Goths was also selected as the centre of a set of champions by the German minnesängers (*minstrels*), but he is called by these romancers Diderick of Bern (*Vero'na*).

Theon's Tooth. The bite of an ill-natured or carping critic. " *Dente Theonino circumrodi,*" to be nastily aspersed. (*Horace: Epistles*, i. 18, 82.) Theon was a carping grammarian of Rome.

Theosophy (the society was founded in November, 1875). It means divine wisdom, the "wisdom religion," the "hidden wisdom." It is borrowed from Ammonius Saccas of the third century A.D. Theosophists tell us there has ever been a body of knowledge, touching the universe, known to certain sages, and communicated by them in doles, as the world was able to bear the secrets. Certainly Esdras supports this hypothesis. Of the two hundred books Jehovah said :—

"The first that thou hast written publish openly, that the worthy [esoterics] and the unworthy [exoterics] may read it ; but keep the seventy last that thou mayst deliver them *only* to such as be wise among the people, for in them is wisdom and the stream of knowledge."—2 Esdras xiv. 45-47.

"At my first approach to the 'Wisdom Religion,' I rather resented the necessity of having to master the profusion of technical terms which Madame Blavatsky very freely s rinkles about her *Key to Theosophy*, such as DAVACHAN BUDDI, ATMA, MANAS, SAMADHI, etc."—*F. J. Gould.*

Therapeu'tæ. The Therapeutæ of Philo were a branch of the Essenes. The word Essenes is Greek, and means "doctors" (*essaioi*), and Therapeutæ is merely a synonym of the same word.

There'sa. Daughter of the Count Palatine of Pado'lia, beloved by Mazeppa. The count, her father, was very indignant that a mere page should presume to fall in love with his daughter, and had Mazeppa bound to a wild horse and set adrift. As for Theresa, Mazeppa never knew her future history. Theresa was historically not the daughter, but the young wife, of the fiery count. (*Byron: Mazeppa.*)

Thermido'rians. Those who took part in the *coup d'état* which effected the fall of Robespierre, with the desire of restoring the legitimate monarchy. So called because the Reign of Terror was brought to an end on the ninth Thermidor of the second Republican year (July 27th, 1794). Ther'midor or "Hot Month" was from July 19th to August 18th. (*Duval: Souvenirs Thermidoriens.*)

Thersi'tes. A deformed, scurrilous officer in the Greek army which went to the siege of Troy. He was always railing at the chiefs, and one day Achilles felled him to the earth with his fist and killed him. (*Homer : Iliad.*)

" He squinted, halted, gibbous was behind,
And pinched before, and on his tapering head
Grew patches only of the flimsiest down.
. . . . Him Greece had sent to Troy,
The miscreant, who shamed his country most."
Cowper's Translation, book ii.

A Thersitēs. A dastardly, malevolent, impudent railer against the powers that be. (*See above.*)

Theseus (2 syl.). Lord and governor of Athens, called by Chaucer Duke Theseus. He married Hippol'ita, and as he returned home with his bride, and Emily her sister, was accosted by a crowd of

female suppliants, who complained of Creon, King of Thebes. The Duke forthwith set out for Thebes, slew Creon, and took the city by assault. Many captives fell into his hands, amongst whom were the two knights named Pal'amon and Arcite (*q.v.*). (*Chaucer : The Knight's Tale.*)
The Christian Theseus. Roland the Paladin.

Thes'pians. Actors. (*See below.*)

Thes'pis, Thes'pian. Dramatic. Thespis was the father of Greek tragedy.

> "The race of learned men,
> .... oft they snatch the pen,
> As if inspired, and in a Thespian rage ;
> Then write."
> *Thomson : Castle of Indolence,* c. i. 52.

> " Thespis, the first professor of our art,
> At country wakes sang ballads from a cart."
> *Dryden : Prologue to Sophonisba.*

Thessalian. Deceitful, fraudulent ; hence Θεσσαλῶν νόμισμα = fraud or deceit. Θεσσαλῶν σόφισμα = double dealing, referring to the double-dealing of the Thessalians with their confederates, a notable instance of which occurred in the Peloponnesian War where, in the very midst of the battle, they turned sides, deserting the Athenians and going over to the Lacedæmonians. The Locrians had a similar bad repute, whence Λοκρῶν σύνθημα ; but of all people, the Spartans were most noted for treachery.

Thes'tylis. Any rustic maiden. In the *Idylls* of Theoc'ritos, Thestylis is a young female slave.

> " And then in haste her bower she leaves,
> With Thestylis to bind the sheaves."
> *Milton : L'Allegro.*

Thick. *Through thick and thin* (Dryden). Through evil and through good report ; through stoggy mud and stones only thinly covered with dust.

> " Through perils both of wind and limb
> She followed him through thick and thin."
> *Butler : Hudibras.*

⁂ "Thick and thin blocks" are pulley-blocks with two sheaves of different thickness, to accommodate different sizes of ropes.

Thick-skinned. Not sensitive ; not irritated by rebukes and slanders. **Thin-skinned**, on the contrary, means impatient of reproof or censure ; their skin is so thin it annoys them to be touched.

Thief. (*See* AUTOLYCUS, CACUS, etc.)

Thieves' Latin. Slang ; dog, or dog's Latin ; gibberish.

> " What did actually reach his ears was disguised so completely by the use of cant words and the thieves' Latin, called slang, that he . . . could make no sense of the conversation."—*Sir W. Scott : Redgauntlet,* chap. xiii.

> " He can vent Greek and Hebrew as fast as I can thieves' Latin."—*Sir W. Scott : Kenilworth,* chap. xxix,

Thieves on the Cross, called Gesmas (the impenitent) and Desmas (afterwards "St. Desmas," the penitent thief) in the ancient mysteries. Hence the following charm to scare away thieves :

> " Impartibus meritis pendent tria corpora ramis
> Desmas et Gesmas, media est divina potestas ;
> Alta petit Desmas, infelix, infima, Gesmas :
> Nos et res nostras conservet summa potestas,
> Hos versus dicas, ne tu furto tua perdas."

Thimble. Scotch, *Thummle*, originally "Thumb-bell," because it was worn on the thumb, as sailors still wear their thimbles. It is a Dutch invention, introduced into England in 1695 by John Lofting, who opened a thimble manufactory at Islington.

Thimble-rig. A cheat. The cheating game so called is played thus : A pea is put on a table, and the conjurer places three or four thimbles over it in succession, and then sets the thimbles on the table. You are asked to say under which thimble the pea is, but are sure to guess wrong, as the pea has been concealed under the man's nail.

Thin-skinned. (*See above,* THICK-SKINNED.)

Thin Red Line (*The*). The old 93rd Highlanders were so described at the battle of Balaclava by Dr. W. H. Russell, because they did not take the trouble to form into square. "Balaclava" is one of the honour-names on their colours, and their regimental magazine is named *The Thin Red Line.*

Thin as a Whipping-post. As a lath ; as a wafer. (*See* SIMILES.)

> " I assure you that, for many weeks afterwards, I was as thin as a whipping-post."—*Kingston : The Three Admirals,* chap. vi.

> " ' I wish we had something to eat,' said Tom. ' I shall grow as thin as a whipping-post . . . I suspect.' "—*Kingston : The Three Admirals,* chap. xi.

Think about It (*I'll*). A courteous refusal. When the sovereign declines to accept a bill, the words employed are *Le roi* (or *la reine*) *s'avisera.*

Thirteen Unlucky. The Turks so dislike the number that the word is almost expunged from their vocabulary. The Italians never use it in making up the numbers of their lotteries. In Paris no house bears the number, and persons, called Quartorziennes (*q.v.*), are reserved to make a fourteenth at dinner parties.

> " Jamais on ne devrait
> Se mettre a table treize,
> Mais douze c'est parfait."
> *La Mascotte (an opera),* i. 5.

Sitting down thirteen at dinner, in old Norse mythology, was deemed unlucky, because at a banquet in the Valhalla,

Loki once intruded, making thirteen guests, and Baldur was slain.

In Christian countries the superstition was confirmed by the Last Supper of Christ and His twelve apostles, but the superstition itself is much anterior to Christianity.

Twelve at a dinner table, supposing one sits at the head of the table and one at the bottom, gives a party to these two, provided a couple is divided; but thirteen, like any other odd number, is a unicorn.

Thirteens. *Throwing the thirteens about.* A thirteen is an Irish shilling, which, prior to 1825, was worth 13 pence, and many years after that date, although reduced to the English standard, went by the name of "thirteens." When Members of Parliament were chaired after their election, it was by no means unusual to carry a bag or two of "thirteens," and scatter the money amongst the crowd.

Thirteenpence-halfpenny. A hangman. So called because thirteen-pence-halfpenny was at one time his wages for hanging a man. (*See* HANG-MAN.)

Thirty. A man at thirty must be either a fool or a physician. (*Tiberius.*)

Thirty Tyrants. The thirty magistrates appointed by Sparta over Athens, at the termination of the Peloponnesian war. This "reign of terror," after one year's continuance, was overthrown by Thrasybu'los (B.C. 403).

The Thirty Tyrants of the Roman empire. So those military usurpers are called who endeavoured, in the reigns of Vale'rian and Gallie'nus (253-268), to make themselves independent princes. The number thirty must be taken with great latitude, as only nineteen are given, and their resemblance to the thirty tyrants of Athens is extremely fanciful. They were—

In the East.	Illyricum.
(1) Cyri'adês.	(11) Ingen'uus.
(2) Macria'nus.	(12) Regillianus.
(3) Balista.	(13) Aure'olus.
(4) Odena'thus.	
(5) Zeno'bia.	*Promiscuous.*
	(14) Saturni'nus in Pontus.
In the West.	(15) Trebellia'nus in Isauria.
(6) Post'humus.	
(7) Lollia'nus.	(16) Piso in Thessaly.
(8) Victori'nus and his mother Victoria.	(17) Va'lens in Achaia.
	(18) Æmilia'nus in Egypt.
(9) Ma'rius.	(19) Celsus in Africa.
(10) Tet'ricus.	

Thirty Years' War. A series of wars between the Catholics and Protestants of Germany in the seventeenth century. It began in Bohemia in 1618, and ended in 1648 with the "peace of Westphalia."

Thisbe. A Babylonish maiden beloved by Piramus. They lived in contiguous houses, and as their parents would not let them marry, they contrived to converse together through a hole in the garden wall. On one occasion they agreed to meet at Ninus' tomb, and Thisbe, who was first at the spot, hearing a lion roar, ran away in a fright, dropping her garment on the way. The lion seized the garment and tore it. When Piramus arrived and saw the garment, he concluded that a lion had eaten Thisbe, and he stabbed himself. Thisbe returning to the tomb, saw Piramus dead, and killed herself also. This story is travestied in the *Midsummer Night's Dream,* by Shakespeare.

Thistle (*The*). The species called *Silybum Mariānum,* we are told, owes the white markings on its leaves to the milk of the Virgin Mary, some of which fell thereon and left a white mark behind. (*See* CHRISTIAN TRADITIONS.)

Thistles are said to be a cure for stitch in the side, especially the species called "Our Lady's Thistle." According to the *Doctrine of Signatures,* Nature has labelled every plant, and the prickles of the thistle tell us the plant is efficacious for *prickles* or stitches in the side. (*See* TURMERIC.)

Thistle Beds. Withoos, a Dutch artist, is famous for his homely pictures where thistle-beds abound.

Thistle of Scotland. The Danes thought it cowardly to attack an enemy by night, but on one occasion deviated from their rule. On they crept, barefooted, noiselessly, and unobserved, when one of the men set his foot on a thistle, which made him cry out. The alarm was given, the Scotch fell upon the night-party, and defeated them with terrible slaughter. Ever since the thistle has been adopted as the insignia of Scotland, with the motto "*Nemo me impune lacessit.*" This tradition reminds us of Brennus and the geese. (*See also* STARS AND STRIPES.)

Thistle. The device of the Scotch monarchs was adopted by Queen Anne; hence the riddle in Pope's pastoral proposed by Daphnis to Strephon :

"Tell me ... in what more happy fields
The thistle springs, to which the lily yields ?"
Pope: Spring.

In the reign of Anne the Duke of Marlborough made the "lily" of France yield to the thistle of Queen Anne. The lines are a parody of Virgil's *Eclogue,* iii. 104-108.

Thomas (*St.*). Patron saint of architects. The tradition is that Gondof'orus, king of the Indies, gave him a large sum of money to build a palace. St. Thomas spent it on the poor, "thus erecting a superb palace in heaven."

The symbol of St. Thomas is a builder's square, because he was the patron of masons and architects.

Christians of St. Thomas. In the southern parts of Mal'abar there were some 200,000 persons who called themselves "Christians of St. Thomas" when Gama discovered India. They had been 1,300 years under the jurisdiction of the patriarch of Babylon, who appointed their materene (archbishop). When Gama arrived the head of the Malabar Christians was Jacob, who styled himself "Metropolitan of India and China." In 1625 a stone was found near Siganfu with a cross on it, and containing a list of the materenes of India and China.

Sir Thomas. The dogmatical prating squire in Crabbe's *Borough* (letter x.).

Thomas-a-Kempis. Thomas Hammerlein of Kempen, an Augustinian, in the diocese of Cologne. (1380-1471.)

Thomas the Rhymer. Thomas Learmont, of Ercildoune, a Scotchman, in the reign of Alexander III., and contemporary with Wallace. He is also called Thomas of Ercildoune. Sir Walter Scott calls him the "Merlin of Scotland." He was magician, prophet, and poet, and is to return again to earth at some future time when Shrove Tuesday and Good Friday change places.

❃ Care must be taken not to confound "Thomas the Rhymer" with Thomas Rymer, the historiographer and compiler of the *Fœdera*.

Thomasing. In some rural districts the custom still prevails of "Thomasing"—that is, of collecting small sums of money or obtaining drink from the employers of labour on the 21st of December—"St. Thomas's Day." December 21st is still noted in London as that day when every one of the Common Council has to be either elected or re-elected, and the electors are wholly without restriction except as to age and sex. The aldermen and their officers are not elected on St. Thomas's Day.

Thom'ists. Followers of Thomas Aqui'nas, who denied the doctrine of the immaculate conception maintained by Duns Scotus.

" Scotists and Thomists now in peace remain."
Pove: Essay on Criticism. 444.

Thomson (*James*), author of *The Seasons* and *Castle of Indolence*, in 1729 brought out the tragedy of *Sophonisba*, in which occurs the silly line: " O Sophonisba, Sophonisba, O ! " which a wag in the pit parodied into " O Jemmy Thomson, Jemmy Thomson, O ! " (1700-1748.)

Thone (1 syl.) or **Thonis.** Governor of a province of Egypt. His wife was Polydamnia. It is said by post-Homeric poets that Paris took Helen to this province, and that Polydamnia gave her a drug named nepenthes to make her forget her sorrows, and fill her with joy.

" Not that nepenthes which the wife of Thone
In Egypt gave to love-lorn Helena,
Is of such power to stir up joy as this."
Milton: Comus, 695-697.

Tho'pas (*Sir*). Native of Poperyng in Flanders ; a capital sportsman, archer, wrestler, and runner. He resolved to marry no one but an "elf queen," and set out for fairy-land. On his way he met the three-headed giant Olifaunt, who challenged him to single combat. Sir Thopas got permission to go back for his armour, and promised to meet him next day. Here mine host interrupts the narrative as "intolerable nonsense," and the "rime " is left unfinished.

" An elf queen wol I have, I wis,
For in this world no woman is
Worthy to be my mate."
Chaucer : Rime of Sir Thopas.

Thor. Son of Odin, and god of war.

His *attendant* was THIALFI, the swift runner.
His *belt* was MEGINGJARDIR or MEGINJARD, which doubled his strength whenever he put it on.
His *goats* were CRACK, GRIND, CRASH, and CHASE.
His *hammer* or *mace* was MJOLNIR.
His *palace* was BILSKIRNIR (Bright Space), where he received the warriors who had fallen in battle.
His *realm* was TRUDVANG.
His *wife* was SIF (Love).

❃ He is addressed as *Asa Thor* or *Ring Thor* (Winged Thor, *i.e.* Lightning). (*Scandinavian mythology.*)

The word enters into many names of places, etc., as Thorsby in Cumberland, Thunderhill in Surrey, Thurso in Caithness, Torthorwald (*i.e.* "Hill of Thor-in-the-wood") in Dumfriesshire, Thursday, etc.

Thorn. *The Conference of Thorn* met October, 1645, at Thorn, in Prussia, to remove the difficulties which separate Christians into sects. It was convoked by Lad'islaus IV. of Poland, but no good result followed the conference.

Thorn in the Flesh (*A*). Something to mortify ; a skeleton in the cupboard. The allusion is to a custom common amongst the ancient Pharisees, one class of which used to insert thorns in the borders of their gaberdines to prick their legs in walking and make them bleed. (*See* PHARISEES.)

Thorns. Calvin (*Admonitio de Reliquiis*) gives a long list of places claiming to possess one or more of the thorns which composed the Saviour's crown. To his list may be added Glastonbury Abbey, where was also the spear of Longius or Longinus, and some of the Virgin's milk.

The thorns of Dauphiné will never prick unless they prick the first day. This proverb is applied to natural talent. If talent does not show itself early, it will never do so—the truth of which application is very doubtful indeed.

" Si l'espine non picque quand nai,
  A pene que picque jamai."
                Proverb in Dauphine.

Thorps-men. Villagers. This very pretty Anglo-Saxon word is worth restoring. (*Thorpe*, Anglo-Saxon, a village.)

Thoth. The Hermes of Egyptian mythology. He is represented with the head of an ibis on a human body. He is the inventor of the arts and sciences, music and astronomy, speech and letters. The name means "Logos" or "the Word."

Though Lost to Sight, to Memory Dear. A writer in *Harper's Magazine* tells us that the author of this line was Ruthven Jenkyns, and that the poem, which consists of two stanzas each of eight lines, begins each stanza with " Sweetheart, good-bye," and ends with the line, " Though lost to sight, to memory dear." The poem was published in the *Greenwich Magazine for Marines* in 1701 or 1702.

Thousand. Everyone knows that a *dozen* may be either twelve or thirteen, a *score* either twenty or twenty-one, a *hundred* either one hundred or one hundred and twenty, and a thousand either one thousand or one thousand two hundred. The higher numbers are the old Teutonic computations. Hickes tells us that the Norwegians and Icelandic people have two sorts of decad, the lesser and the greater called "Tolfræd." The lesser thousand $= 10 \times 100$, but the greater thousand $= 12 \times 100$. The word *tolf*, equal to *tolv*, is our *twelve*. (*Institutiones Grammaticæ*, p. 43.)

" Five score of men, money, or pins,
  Six score of all other things." *Old Saw.*

Thousand Years as One Day (*A*). (1 Peter iii. 8.) Precisely the same is said of Brahma. " A day of Brahma is as a thousand revolutions of the Yoogs, and his might extendeth also to a thousand more." (*Kreeshna : Bhagavat Geeta.*)

Thrall. A slave ; bondage ; wittily derived from *drill*, in allusion to the custom of drilling the ear of a slave in token of servitude, a custom common to the Jews. (Deut. xv. 17.) Our Saxon forefathers used to pierce at the churchdoor the ears of their bond-slaves. (Anglo-Saxon, *thrael*, slave or bondman.)

Thread. *The thread of destiny—i.e.* that on which destiny depends. The Greeks and Romans imagined that a grave maiden called Clotho spun from her distaff the destiny of man, and as she spun one of her sisters worked out the events which were in store, and At'ropos cut the thread at the point when death was to occur.

A St. Thomas's thread. The tale is that St. Thomas planted Christianity in China, and then returned to Mal'abar. Here he saw a huge beam of timber floating on the sea near the coast, and the king endeavouring, by the force of men and elephants, to haul it ashore, but it would not stir. St. Thomas desired leave to build a church with it, and, his request being granted, he dragged it easily ashore with a piece of packthread. (*Faria y Sousa.*)

Chief of the Triple Thread. Chief Brahmin. Oso'rius tells us that the Brahmins wore a symbolical Tessera of three threads, reaching from the right shoulder to the left. Faria says that the religion of the Brahmins proceeded from fishermen, who left the charge of the temples to their successors on the condition of their wearing some threads of their nets in remembrance of their vocation ; but Oso'rius maintains that the triple thread symbolises the Trinity.

" Terna fila ab hu'mero dex'tero in latus sinis'-
  trum gerunt, ut designent trinam in natu'ra
  divi'na ratio'nem."

Threadneedle Street. A corruption of *Thryddanen* or *Thryddenal Street*, meaning third street from " Chepesyde" to the great thoroughfare from London Bridge to " Bushop Gate " (consisting of New Fyshe Streate, Gracious Streate, and Bushop Gate Streate). (Anglo-Saxon, *thrydda* or *thrydde*, third.)

Another etymology is *Thrig-needle* (three-needle street), from the three needles which the Needlemaker's Company bore in their arms. It begins from the Mansion House, and therefore the Bank stands in it.

The Old Lady in Threadneedle Street. The directors of the Bank of England were so called by William Cobbett, because, like Mrs. Partington, they tried with their broom to sweep back the Atlantic waves of national progress.

"A silver curl-paper that I myself took off the shining locks of the ever-beautiful old lady of Threadneedle Street [a bank-note]."—*Dickens: Dr. Marigold.*

Three. Pythagoras calls three the perfect number, expressive of "beginning, middle, and end," wherefore he makes it a symbol of Deity. The world was supposed to be under the rule of three gods, viz. Jupiter (heaven), Neptune (sea), and Pluto (Hades). Jove is represented with three-forked lightning, Neptune with a trident, and Pluto with a three-headed dog. The Fates are three, the Furies three, the Graces three, the Harpies three, the Sibylline books three ; the fountain from which Hylas drew water was presided over by three nymphs, and the Muses were three times three ; the pythoness sat on a tripod. Man is three-fold (body, soul, and spirit) ; the world is three-fold (earth, sea, and air) ; the enemies of man are three-fold (the world, the flesh, and the devil) ; the Christian graces are threefold (Faith, Hope, and Charity) ; the kingdoms of Nature are threefold (mineral, vegetable, and animal) ; the cardinal colours are three in number (red, yellow, and blue), etc. (*See* NINE, which is three times three.)

∴ Even the Bible consists of the Old Testament, the New Testament, and the Apocrypha. Our laws have to pass the Commons, Lords, and Crown.

Three Bishoprics (*The*). So the French call the three cities of Lorraine, Metz, and Verdun, each of which was at one time under the lordship of a bishop. They were united to the kingdom of France by Henri II. in 1552. Since the Franco-German war they have been attached to Germany.

Three-Decker (*A*). The pulpit, reading-desk, and clerk's desk arranged in a church, towering one above the other. Now an obsolete arrangement.

"In the midst of the church stands . . . the offensive structure of pulpit, reading-desk, and clerk's desk ; in fact, a regular old three-decker in full sail westward."—*The Christian Remembrancer,* July, 1852, p. 92.

Three Chapters (*The*). Three books, or parts of three books—one by Theodore of Mopsuestia, one by Theodoret of Cyprus, and the third by Ibas, Bishop of Edessa. These books were of a Nestorian bias on the subject of the incarnation and two natures of Christ. The Church took up the controversy warmly, and the dispute continued during the reign of Justinian and the popedom of Vigilius. In 553 the *Three Chapters* were condemned at the general council of Constantinople.

Three Estates of the Realm are the nobility, the clergy, and the commonalty. In the collect for *Gunpowder Treason* we thank God for "preserving (1st) the king, and (2nd) the three estates of the realm ; " from which it is quite evident that the sovereign is not one of the three estates, as nine persons out of ten suppose. These three estates are represented in the two Houses of Parliament. (*See* FOURTH ESTATE.)

Three Holes in the Wall (*The*), to which Macaulay alluded in his speech, September 20th, 1831, are three holes or niches in a ruined mound in the borough of Old Sarum, which before the Reform sent two members to Parliament. Lord John Russell (March, 1831) referred to the same anomaly. (See *Notes and Queries,* March 14th, 1885, p. 213.)

Three Kings' Day. Epiphany or Twelfth Day, designed to commemorate the visit of the "three kings" or Wise Men of the East to the infant Jesus. (*See under* KINGS.)

Three-pair Back (*Living up a*). Living in a garret, which is got at by mounting to the third storey by a back staircase.

Three-quarters or $\frac{3}{4}$. Rhyming slang for the neck. This certainly is a most ingenious perversion. "Threequarters of a *peck*" rhymes with *neck*, so, in writing, an expert simply sets down $\frac{3}{4}$. (*See* CHIVY.)

Three R's (*The*). (*See under* R.)

Three Sheets in the Wind. Unsteady from over-drinking, as a ship when its sheets are in the wind. The sail of a ship is fastened at one of the bottom corners by a rope called a "tack ; " the other corner is left more or less free as the rope called a "sheet" is disposed ; if quite free, the sheet is said to be "in the wind," and the sail flaps and flutters without restraint. If all the three sails were so loosened, the ship would "reel and stagger like a drunken man."

"Captain Cuttle looking, candle in hand, at Bunsby more attentively, perceived that he was three sheets in the wind, or, in plain words, drunk."—*Dickens: Dombey and Son.*

Three-tailed Bashaw. (*See* BA-SHAW.)

Three Tuns. A fish ordinary in Billingsgate, famous as far back as the reign of Queen Anne.

Threshers. Members of the Catholic organisation instituted in 1806. One object was to resist the payment of tithes. Their threats and warnings were signed "Captain Thresher."

Threshold. Properly the door-sill, but figuratively applied to the beginning of anything; as, the threshold of life (*infancy*), the threshold of an argument (*the commencement*), the threshold of the inquiry (*the first part of the investigation*). (Saxon, *thœrscwald*, door-wood; German, *thürschwelle;* Icelandic, *throsulldur.* From *thür* comes our *door.*)

Thrift-box. A money-box, in which thrifts or savings are put. (*See* SPEND-THRIFT.)

Throgmorton Street (London). So named from Sir Nicholas Throckmorton, head of the ancient Warwickshire family, and chief banker of England in the reign of Queen Elizabeth.

Through-stone (*A*). A flat gravestone, a stone coffin or sarcophagus, also a bond stone which extends over the entire thickness of a wall. In architecture, called "Perpent" or "Perpend Stones" or "Throughs." (French, *Pierre parpainge.*)

"Od! he is not stirring yet, mair than he were a through-stane."—*Sir W. Scott: The Monastery* (Introduction).

Throw. *To throw the helve after the hatchet.* (*See* HELVE.)

Throw. *Throw lots of dirt, and some will stick.* Find plenty of fault, and some of it will be believed. In Latin, *Fortiter calumniāri, aliquid adhærēbit.*

Throw Up the Sponge (*To*). (*See* SPONGE.)

Throw your Eye on. Give a glance at. In Latin, *oculos* [*in aliquem*] *conjicĕre.*

"Hubert, Hubert, throw thine eye
On yon young boy."
      Shakespeare: King John, iii. 3.

Throwing an Old Shoe for Luck. (*See under* SHOE.)

"Now, for goode luck caste an old shoe after me."—*Haywood* (1693-1756).

"Ay, with all my heart, there's an old shoe after you."—*The Parson's Wedding* (*Dodsley,* vol. ix. p. 499).

Thrums. Weaver's ends and fagends of carpet, used for common rugs. (The word is common to many languages, as Icelandic, *thraum;* German, *trumm;*

Dutch, *drom;* Greek, *thrumma;* all meaning "fag-ends" or "fragments.")

"Come, sisters, come. cut thread and thrum;
   Quail, crush, conclude, and quell!"
      Shakespeare: Midsummer Night's Dream, v. 1.

Thread and thrum. Everything, good and bad together.

Thrummy Cap. A sprite described in Northumberland fairy tales as a "queer-looking little auld man," whose exploits are generally laid in the cellars of old castles.

Thug [*a cheat*]. So a religious fraternity in India was called. Their patron goddess was Devî or Kâli, wife of Si'va. The Thugs lived by plunder, to obtain which they never halted at violence or even murder. In some provinces they were called "stranglers" (*phansigars*), in the Tamil tongue "noosers" (*ari tulukar*), in the Canarese "catgut thieves" (*tanti kalleru*). They banded together in gangs mounted on horseback, assuming the appearance of merchants; some two or more of these gangs concerted to meet as if by accident at a given town. They then ascertained what rich merchants were about to journey, and either joined the party or lay in wait for it. This being arranged, the victim was duly caught with a lasso, plundered, and strangled. (Hindu, *thaga*, deceive.)

Thuggee (2 syl.). The system of secret assassination preached by Thugs; the practice of Thugs.

Thuig or **Tuig** (Norse). The mounds raised by the old Scandinavians where their courts were held. The word is met with in Iceland, in the Shetlands, and elsewhere in Scotland.

Thule (2 syl.). Called by Drayton *Thuly.* Pliny, Solīnus, and Mela take it for Iceland. Pliny says, "It is an island in the Northern Ocean discovered by Pyth'eas, after sailing six days from the Orcadēs." Others, like Camden, consider it to be Shetland, still called Thylens-el (isle of Thylē) by seamen, in which opinion they agree with Mari'nus, and the descriptions of Ptolemy and Tacitus. Bochart says it is a Syrian word, and that the Phœnician merchants who traded to the group called it *Gezirat Thulē* (isles of darkness). Its certain etymology is unknown; it may possibly be the Gothic *Tiule*, meaning the "most remote land," and connected with the Greek *telos* (the end).

"Where the Northern Ocean, in vast whirls,
Boils round the naked melancholy isles
Of farthest Thule."   *Thomson: Autumn.*

39*

Ultima Thulē. The end of the world ; the last extremity. Thule was the most northern point known to the ancient Romans.

"Tibi serviat Ultima Thule."
Virgil : Georgics, i. 30.

"Peshawar cantonment is the Ultima Thule of British India."—*Nineteenth Century,* Oct., 1893, p. 533.

Thumb. When a gladiator was vanquished it rested with the spectators to decide whether he should be slain or not. If they wished him to live, they *shut up* their thumbs in their fists (*police compresso favor judicabatur*) ; if to be slain, they *turned out* their thumbs. Adam, in his *Roman Antiquities* (p. 287), says, "If they wished him to be saved, they *pressed down* their thumbs ; if to be slain, they *turned up* [held out] their thumbs." (*Pliny,* xxviii. 2 ; *Juvenal,* iii. 36 ; *Horace :* 1 *Epist.,* xviii. 66.)

⁂ It is not correct to say, if they wished the man to live they held their thumbs *downwards ;* if to be slain, they held their thumbs upwards. "*Police compressio*" means to hold their thumbs *close.*

"Where, influenced by the rabble's bloody will,
With thumbs bent back, they popularly kill."
Dryden : Third Satire.

By the pricking of my thumbs, something wicked this way comes. Another proverb says, "*My little finger told me that.*" When your *ears turn hot and red,* it is to indicate that someone is speaking about you. When a *sudden fit of "shivering"* occurs, it is because someone is treading on the place which is to form your grave. When the *eye itches,* it indicates the visit of a friend. When the *palm itches,* it shows that a present will shortly be received. When the *bones ache,* it prognosticates a coming storm. Plautus says, "*Timeo quod rerum gesserim hic ita dorsus totus prurit.*" (*Miles Gloriosus.*) All these and many similar superstitions rest on the notion that "coming events cast their shadows before," because our "angel," ever watchful, forewarns us that we may be prepared. Sudden pains and prickings are the warnings of evil on the road ; sudden glows and pleasurable sensations are the couriers to tell us of joy close at hand. These superstitions are relics of demonology and witchcraft.

⁂ In ancient Rome the augurs took special notice of the palpitation of the heart, the flickering of the eye, and the pricking of the thumb. In regard to the last, if the pricking was on the left hand it was considered a very bad sign, indicating mischief at hand.

Do you bite your thumb at me ? Do you mean to insult me ? The way of expressing defiance and contempt was by snapping the finger or putting the thumb in the mouth. Both these acts are termed a *fico,* whence our expressions "Not worth a fig," "I don't care a fig for you." Decker, describing St. Paul's Walk, speaks of the biting of thumbs to beget quarrels. (*See* GLOVE.)

"I see Contempt marching forth, giving mee the fico with his thombe in his mouth."—*Wits Miserie* (1596).

"I will bite my thumb at them ; which is a disgrace to them, if they bear it."—*Shakespeare : Romeo and Juliet,* i. 1.

Every honest miller has a thumb of gold. Even an honest miller grows rich with what he prigs. Thus Chaucer says of his miller—

"Wel cowde he stelē and tollen thries,
And yet he had a thomb of gold parde [was what is called an 'honest miller']."
Canterbury Tales (Prologue, 565).

Rule of thumb. Rough measure. Ladies often measure yard lengths by their thumb. Indeed the expression "sixteen nails make a yard" seems to point to the thumb-nail as a standard. Countrymen always measure by their thumb.

Tom Thumb. (*See* TOM.)
Under one's thumb. Under the influence or power of the person named.

Thumb-nail Legacies. Legacies so small that they could be written on one's thumb-nail.

"'Tis said, some men may make their wills
On their thumb-nails, for aught they can bestow."
Peter Pindar : Lord B. and his Motions.

Thum'bikins or **Thumbscrew.** An instrument of torture largely used by the Inquisition. The torture was compressing the thumb between two bars of iron, made to approach each other by means of a screw. Principal Carstairs was the last person put to this torture in Britain ; he suffered for half an hour at Holyrood, by order of the Scotch Privy Council, to wring from him a confession of the secrets of the Argyll and Monmouth parties.

Thunder. The giant who fell into the river and was killed, because Jack cut the ropes that suspended the draw-bridge, and when the giant ventured to cross it the bridge fell in. (*Jack the Giant Killer.*)

Thunder (*Sons of*) [*Boaner'gēs*]. James and John, the sons of Zebedee (Mark iii. 17). So called because they asked to be allowed to consume with lightning those who rejected the mission of Christ. (Luke ix. 54 ; Mark iii. 17.)

Thunder and Lightning or **Tonnant.** Stephen II. of Hungary (1100, 1114-1131).

Thunders of the Vatican. The anathemas and denunciations of the Pope, whose palace is the Vatican of Rome.

Properly speaking, the Vatican consists of the Papal palace, the court and garden of Belvedere, the library, and the museum, all on the right bank of the Tiber.

Thunderbolt of Italy. Gaston de Foix, nephew of Louis XII. (1489-1512.)

Thunderbolts. Jupiter was depicted by the ancients as a man seated on a throne, holding a sceptre in his left hand and thunderbolts in his right. Modern science has proved there are no such things as thunderstones, though many tons of bolides (2 syl.), aërolites (3 syl.), meteors, or shooting stars (of stony or metallic substance) fall annually to our earth. These "air-stones," however, have no connection with thunder and lightning.

" Be ready, gods, with all your thunderbolts ;
    Dash him to pieces ! "
            Shakespeare: Julius Cæsar, iv. 3.

Thunderer (*The*). A name applied to *The Times* newspaper, in allusion to an article by Captain Ed. Sterling, beginning thus :—

" We thundered forth the other day an article on the subject of social and political reform."— *The Times.*

Thundering Legion. Under cover of a thunderstorm which broke over them they successfully attacked the Marcomanni. (*See* LEGION, THEBAN LEGION.)

∵ This is a mere legend of no historic value. The legion was so called at least a century before the reign of Aurelius ; probably because it bore on its shields or ensigns a representation of Jupiter Tonans.

Thun'stone. The successor of King Arthur. (*Nursery Tale : Tom Thumb.*)

Thursday. That is, Thor's day. In French, *Jeudi—i.e.* Jove's day.

Thursday. (*See* BLACK.)
When three Thursdays meet. Never (*q.v.*). In French, "*Cela arrivera la semaine des trois jeudis.*"
    Maundy Thursday. (*See* MAUNDY THURSDAY.)

Tiara. A composite emblem. Its primary meaning is purity and chastity —the foundation being of fine linen. The gold band denotes supremacy. The first cap of dignity was adopted by Pope Damasus II. in 1048. The cap was surmounted with a high coronet in 1295 by Boniface VIII. The second coronet was added in 1335 by Benedict XII., to indicate the prerogatives of spiritual and temporal power combined in the Papacy. The third coronet is indicative of the Trinity, but it is not known who first adopted it ; some say Urban V., others John XXII., John XXIII., or Benedict XII.

"The symbol of my threefold dignity, in heaven, upon earth, and in purgatory."—*Pope Pius IX.* (1871.)

∵ The triple crown most likely was in imitation of that of the Jewish high priest.

"On his head was a white turban, and over this a second striped with dark blue. On his forehead he wore a plate of gold, on which the name of Jehovah was inscribed. And, being at once high priest and prince, this was connected with a triple crown on the temples and back of the head."—*Eldad the Pilgrim,* chap. x.

Tib. *St. Tib's Eve.* Never. A corruption of St. Ubes. There is no such saint in the calendar as St. Ubes, and therefore her eve falls on the "Greek Kalends" (*q.v.*), neither before Christmas Day nor after it.

Tib and Tom. Tib is the ace of trumps, and Tom is the knave of trumps in the game of Gleek.

"That gamester needs must overcome,
    That can play both Tib and Tom."
            Randolph: Hermaphrodite, p. 640.

Tiber, called *The Yellow Tiber,* because it is discoloured with yellow mud.
"Verticibus rapidis, et multa flavus are'na."
            Virgil: Æneid, vii. 31.

Tibul'lus. *The French Tibullus.* Evariste Désiré Desforges, Chevalier de Parny (1753-1814).

Tibur'ce (3 syl.) or **Tiburce** (2 syl.). Brother of Valirian, converted by the teaching of St. Cecilia, his sister-in-law, and baptised by Pope Urban. Being brought before Almachius the prefect, and commanded to worship the image of Jupiter, both the brothers refused, and were decapitated. (*Chaucer: Secounde Nonnes Tale.*)

" Al this thing sche unto Tiburce told (3 syl.),
    And after this Tiburce, in good entente (2 syl.),
    With Valiri'an to Pope Urban wente."
            Chaucer: Canterbury Tales, 12,276.

Tiburtius's Day (*St.*). April 14th. The cuckoo sings from St. Tiburtius's Day (April 14th) to St. John's Day (June 24th).

This most certainly is not correct, as I have heard the cuckoo even in August ; but without doubt July is the month of its migration generally.

The proverb says :

" July, prepares to fly ; August, go he must."

∵ It is said that he migrates to Egypt.

Tick. *To go on tick*—on ticket. In the seventeenth century, *ticket* was the ordinary term for the written acknowledgment of a debt, and one living on credit was said to be *living on tick*. Betting was then, and still is to a great extent, a matter of tick—*i.e.* entry of particulars in a betting-book. We have an Act of Parliament prohibiting the use of betting tickets : " Be it enacted, that if any person shall play at any of the said games . . . (otherwise than with and for ready money), or shall bet on the sides of such as shall play . . . a sum of money exceeding £100 at any one time . . . upon ticket or credit . . . he shall," etc. (16 Car. II. cap. 16.)

" If a servant usually buy for the master upon tick, and the servant buy some things without the master's order . . . the master is liable."—*Chief Justice Holt (Blackstone,* chap. xv. p. 468).

Ticket. *That's the ticket* or *That's the ticket for soup.* That's the right thing. The ticket to be shown in order to obtain something. Some think that the word "ticket" in this phrase is a corruption of *etiquette.*

What's the ticket ? What is the arrangement ?

" 'Well,' said Bob Cross, 'what's the ticket, youngster ? Are you to go aboard with us ? "—*Captain Marryat.*

Ticket of Leave (*A*). A warrant given to convicts to have their liberty on condition of good behaviour.

Tickle the Public (*To*). When an actor introduces some gag to make the audience laugh, "*il chatouille le public.*" One of the most noted chatouilleurs was Odry, a French actor.

Tide-rode, in seaman phrase, means that the vessel at anchor is swung about by the force of the tide. Metaphorically, a person is tide-rode when circumstances over which he has no control are against him, especially a sudden glut in the market. Tide-rode, ridden at anchor with the head to the tide ; *wind-rode,* with the head to the wind.

Tide-waiters. Those who vote against their opinions. S. G. O. (the Rev. Lord Osborne), of the *Times,* calls the clergy in Convocation whose votes do not agree with their convictions " ecclesiastical tide-waiters."

Tidy means in *tide,* in season, in time. We retain the word in even-tide, spring-tide, and so on. Tusser has the phrase, " If the weather be fair and tidy," meaning seasonable. Things done punctually and in their proper season are sure to be done orderly, and what is

orderly done is neat and well arranged. Hence we get the notion of methodical, neat, well-arranged, associated with tidy. (Danish, *tidig,* seasonable, favourable.)

How are you getting on ? Oh ! pretty *tidily*—favourably. (*See above.*)

A tidy fortune. A nice little bit of money. Tidy means neat, and neat means comfortable.

Tied. *Tied to your mother's apron-strings.* Not yet out of nursery government ; not free to act on your own responsibility. The allusion is to tying naughty young children to the mother's or nurse's apron.

Tied House (*A*). A retail shop, stocked by a wholesale dealer, and managed by some other person not the owner of the stock. The wholesale dealer appoints the manager.

" There are tied houses in the drapery, grocery, dairy, boot and shoe, hardware, liquor, and book trades. Whiteley's, if rumour is to be trusted, is a tied house ; and the majority of Italian restaurants in London begin by being tied to the Gattis."
—*Liberty Review,* 14th April, 1894, p. 310, col. 1.

Tied-up. Married ; tied up in the marriage-knot.

" When first the marriage-knot was tied
Between my wife and me."
Walkingame's Arithmetic.

Tiffin (Indian). Luncheon ; refreshment. (*Tiff,* a draught of liquor.)

Ti'ger (*A*) properly means "a gentleman's attendant, and *page* a lady's attendant ; but the distinction is quite obsolete, and any servant in livery who rides out with his master or mistress is so called ; also a boy in buttons attendant on a lady, like a page ; a parasite.

" ' Yes,' she cried gaily over the banisters, " my fiacre and my tiger are waiting."—*A Fellow of Trinity,* chap. xv.

Tiger-kill (*A*). An animal tied up by hunters in a jungle to be killed by a tiger. This is a lure to attract the tiger preparatory to a tiger-hunt.

Tigers. The car of Bacchus was drawn by tigers, and tigers are generally drawn by artists crouching at the feet of Bacchus. Solomon (Prov. xx. 1) says " Strong drink is raging " (like a tiger). In British India a tiger is called "Brother Stripes."

Tigernach. Oldest of the Irish annalists. His annals were published in Dr. O'Connor's *Rerum Hibernicarum Scriptores Veteres,* at the expense of the Duke of Buckingham (1814-1826).

Tight. Intoxicated.

Tigris [*the Arrow*]. So called from the rapidity of its current. Hiddekel is

"The Dekel," or Diglath, a Semitic corruption of *Tigra*, Medo-Persic for arrow. (Gen. ii. 14.)

"Flu'mini, a celerita'te qua defluit Tigri nomen est ; quia Persica lingua, tigrim *sagittam* appellant."—*Quintus Curtius.*

Tike. *A Yorkshire tike.* A clownish rustic. In Scotland a dog is called a tyke (Icelandic, *tik*) ; hence, a snarling, obstinate fellow.

Tilbert (*Sir*). The cat in the tale of *Reynard the Fox.* (*See* TYBALT.)

Tile. A hat. (Anglo-Saxon, *tigel ;* Latin, *tego*, to cover.)

Tile Loose. *He has a tile loose.* He is not quite *compos mentis ;* he is not all there.

Tile a Lodge, in Freemasonry, means to close the door, to prevent anyone uninitiated from entering. Of course, to tile a house means to finish building it, and to tile a lodge is to complete it.

Timber-toe (*A*). A wooden leg ; one with a wooden leg.

Time. *Time and tide wait for no man.*

" For the next inn he spurs amain,
In haste alights, and scuds away—
But time and tide for no man stay."
    Somerville: The Sweet-scented Miser.

Take [or *Seize*] *Time by the forelock* (*Tha'les of Mile'tus.*). Time is represented as an old man, quite bald, with the exception of a single lock of hair on the forehead. Shakespeare calls him " that bald sexton, Time." (*King John*, iii. 1.)

Time is, Time was, Time's past. Friar Bacon made a brazen head, and it was said if he heard his head speak he would succeed in his work in hand, if not he would fail. A man named Miles was set to watch the head, and while Bacon was sleeping the head uttered these words : " TIME IS ; " and half an hour afterwards it said " TIME WAS ; " after the expiration of another half-hour it said " TIME'S PAST," fell down, and was broken to pieces.

" Like Friar Bacon's brazen head, I've spoken ;
Time is, time was, time's past."
    Byron: Don Juan, i. 217-8.

Time-bargain (*A*), in Stock, is a speculation, not an investment. A time-bargain is made to buy or sell again as soon as possible and receive the difference realised. An investment is made for the sake of the interest given.

Time of Grace. The lawful season for venery, which began at Midsummer and lasted to Holyrood Day. The fox

and wolf might be hunted from the Nativity to the Annunciation ; the roebuck from Easter to Michaelmas ; the roe from Michaelmas to Candlemas ; the hare from Michaelmas to Midsummer ; and the boar from the Nativity to the Purification. (*See* SPORTING SEASONS.)

Time-honoured Lancaster. Old John of Gaunt. His father was Edward III., his son Henry IV., his nephew Richard II. of England ; his second wife was Constance, daughter of Peter the Cruel of Castile and Leon ; his only daughter married John of Castile and Leon ; his sister Johanna married Alphonso, King of Castile. Shakespeare calls him " time-honoured " and " old ; " honoured he certainly was, but was only fifty-nine at his death. Hesiod is called *Old*, meaning " long ago."

Times (*The*). A newspaper, founded by John Walter. In 1785 he established *The Daily Universal Register*, but in 1788 changed the name into *The Times, or Daily Universal Register.* (*See* THUNDERER.)

Timo'leon. The Corinthian who so hated tyranny that he murdered his own brother Timoph'anes when he attempted to make himself absolute in Corinth

" The fair Corinthian boast
Timoleon, happy temper, mild and firm,
Who wept the brother while the tyrant bled.
    Thomson: Winter.

Timon of Athens. The misanthrope. Shakespeare's play so called. Lord Macaulay uses the expression to "out-Timon Timon "—*i.e.* to be more misanthropical than even Timon.

Tin. Money. A depreciating synonym for silver, called by alchemists " Jupiter."

Tine-man (*The*). The Earl of Douglas, who died 1424. (See *Sir W. Scott : Tales of a Grandfather*, chap. xviii.)

Ting. The general assembly of the Northmen, which all capable of bearing arms were bound to attend on occasions requiring deliberation and action. The words Volksthing and Storthing are still in use.

" A shout filled all the Ting, a thousand swords
Clashed loud approval."
    Frithiof-Saga (The Parting).

Tinker. The man who *tinks*, or beats on a kettle to announce his trade. John Bunyan (1628-1688) was called *The inspired Tinker.*)

Tintag'el or **Tintag'il.** A strong castle on the coast of Cornwall, the reputed birth-place of King Arthur.

" When Uthur in Tintagil passed away."
    Tennyson: The Coming of Arthur.

Tin'tern Abbey. Wordsworth has a poem called *Lines Composed a few Miles above Tintern Abbey*, but these lines have nothing whatever to do with the famous ruin, not even once alluding to it.

Tintoretto, the historical painter. So called because his father was a dyer (*tintore*). His real name was Jacopo Robusti. He was nicknamed *Il Furioso*, from the rapidity of his productions. (1512-1594.)

Tip. Private information, secret warning. In horse-racing, it means such secret information as may guide the person tipped to make bets advantageously. A "straight tip" comes straight or direct from the owner or trainer of the horse in question. A man will sometimes give the police the "tip," or hint where a gang of confederates lie concealed, or where law-breakers may be found. Thus, houses of ill-fame and keepers of clandestine gaming houses in league with the police, receive the "tip" when spies are on them or legal danger is abroad.

"If he told the police, he felt assured that the 'tip' would be given to the parties concerned, and his efforts would be frustrated."—*Mr. Stead's defence*, November 2nd, 1885.

He gave me a tip—a present of money, a bribe. (*See* DIBS.)

Tip of my Tongue. *To have a thing on the tip of my tongue* means to have it so pat that it comes without thought; also, to have a thing on the verge of one's memory, but not quite perfectly remembered. (In Latin, *in labris natat.*)

Tip One the Wink (*To*). To make a signal to another by a wink. Here tip means "to give," as tip in the previous example means "a gift."

Tiph'any, according to the calendar of saints, was the mother of the Three Kings of Cologne. (*See* COLOGNE.)

Ti'phys. A pilot. He was the pilot of the Argonauts.

" Many a Tiphys ocean's depths explore,
To open wondrous ways untried before."
Hoole's Ariosto, bk. viii.

Tipperary Rifle (*A*). A shillelagh or stick made of blackthorn. At Ballybrophy station an itinerant vendor of walking-sticks pushed up close to their Royal Highnesses [the Prince and Princess of Wales] . . . The Prince asked him what he wanted, and the man replied, "Nothing, your honour, but to ask your honour to accept a present of a Tipperary rifle," and so saying he handed his Royal Highness a stout

hawthorn. The Prince sent the man a sovereign, for which a gentleman offered him 25s. "No," said the man, "I would not part with it for twenty-five gold guineas." In a few minutes the man had sold *all* his sticks for princely prices. (April 25th, 1885.)

Tippling Act (*The*), 24 Geo. II., chap. 40, which restricted the sale of spirituous liquors retailed on credit for less than 20s. at one time. In part repealed. A "tippler" originally meant a tavern-keeper or tapster, and the tavern was called a "tippling-house." At Boston, Lincolnshire, in 1577, five persons were appointed "tipplers of Lincoln beer," and no "other tippler [might] draw or sell beer " . . . under penalties.

Tippling House. A contemptuous name for a tavern or public-house.

Tipstaff. A constable so called because he carried a staff tipped with a bull's horn. In the documents of Edward III. allusion is often made to his staff. (See *Rymer's Fœdera.*)

Tiptoe of Expectation (*On the*). All agog with curiosity. I am like one standing on tiptoe to see over the shoulders of a crowd.

Tirer une Dent. To draw a man's tooth, or extort money from him. The allusion is to the tale told by Holinshed of King John, who extorted 10,000 marks from a Jew living at Bristol by extracting a tooth daily till he consented to provide the money. For seven successive days a tooth was taken, and then the Jew gave in.

Tire'sias. *Blind as Tire'sias.* Tiresias the Theban by accident saw Athe'na bathing, and the goddess struck him with blindness by splashing water in his face. She afterwards repented doing so, and, as she could not restore his sight, conferred on him the power of soothsaying, and gave him a staff with which he could walk as safely as if he had his sight. He found death at last by drinking from the well of Tilpho'sa.

" Juno the truth of what was said denied,
Tiresias, therefore, must the cause decide."
Addison: Transformation of Tiresias.

Tiring Irons. Iron rings to be put on or taken off a ring as a puzzle. Lightfoot calls them "tiring irons never to be untied."

Tirled. *He tirlĕd at the pin.* He twiddled or rattled with the latch before opening the door. Guillaume di Lorris, in his *Romance of the Rose* (thirteenth century), says, "When persons visit a friend they ought not to bounce all at once into the room, but should announce their approach by a slight cough, or few words spoken in the hall, or a slight shuffling of their feet, so as not to take their friends unawares." The pin is the door-latch, and before a visitor entered a room it was, in Scotland, thought good manners to fumble at the latch to give notice of your intention to enter. (Tirl is the Anglo-Saxon *thwer-an*, to turn ; Dutch *dwarlen*, our twirl, etc. ; or Danish *trille*, German *triller*, Welsh *treillio ;* our *trill*, to rattle or roll.)

> " Right quick he mounted up the stair,
> And tirlèd at the pin."
> > *Charlie is my Darling.*

Tiro'nian Sign (*The*). The symbol (&) for "and" or the Latin *et*. Said to have been invented by Tullius Tiro, Cicero's freed-man. (*See* MARKS IN GRAMMAR.)

Tiryns. An ancient city of Ar'golis in Greece, famous for its Cyclopean architecture. The "Gallery of Tiryns" is the oldest and noblest structure of the heroic ages. It is mentioned by Homer, and still exists.

Tiryn'thian Swain. Hercules is so called by Spenser, but he is more frequently styled the *Tirynthian Hero*, because he generally resided at Tiryns, a town of Ar'golis.

Tit. A horse.

> " They scorned the coach, they scorned the rails,
> Two spanking tits with streaming tails."
> > *The End of All Things.*

> " What spurres need now for an untamed titt."
> > *Barnefield : Affectionate Shepherd* (1594).

Tit for Tat. J. Bellenden Ker says this is the Dutch "*Dit vor dat*" (this for.that) ; "*Quid pro quo*." Heywood uses the phrase "tat for tat," perhaps the French phrase, "*tant pour tant*."

Ti'tan. The sun, so called by Ovid and Virgil.

> ' And fleckèd Darkness like a drunkard reels
> From forth Day's path and Titan's fiery wheels."
> > *Shakespeare : Romeo and Juliet*, ii. 3.

The Titans. The children of Heaven and Earth, who, instigated by their mother, deposed their father, and liberated from Tar'taros their brothers the Hundred-handed giants, and the Cyclopes. (*Classic mythology.*)

Titan's War with Jove (*The*). The Titans set their brother Cronos on the throne of heaven ; and Zeus [*Zuce*] tried to dethrone him. The contest lasted ten years, when Zeus became the conqueror and hurled the Titans into hell.

✣ This must not be confounded with the war of the giants, which was a revolt against Zeus, and was soon put down by the help of the other gods and the aid of Herculës. (*See* GIANTS.)

Titan'ia. Wife of O'beron, king of the fairies. According to the belief in Shakespeare's age, fairies were the same as the classic nymphs, the attendants of Diana. The queen of the fairies was therefore Diana herself, called Titania by Ovid (*Metamorphoses*, iii. 173). (*Keightley : Fairy Mythology.*)

Titho'nus. A beautiful Trojan beloved by Auro'ra. He begged the goddess to grant him immortality, which request the goddess granted ; but as he had forgotten to ask for youth and vigour he soon grew old, infirm, and ugly. When life became insupportable he prayed Aurora to remove him from the world ; this, however, she could not do, but she changed him into a grasshopper. Synonym for "an old man."

> " An idle scene Tithonus acted
> When to a grasshopper contracted."
> > *Prior : The Turtle and Sparrows.*

> " Thinner than Tithonus was
> Before he faded into air."
> > *Tales of Miletus*, ii.

Titi (*Prince*). Frederick, Prince of Wales, eldest son of George II. Seward, a contemporary, tells us that Prince Frederick was a great reader of French memoirs, and that he himself wrote memoirs of his contemporaries under the pseudonym of "Prince Titi."

> There was a political fairy tale by St. Hyacinthe (1684-1740) called the *History of Prince Titi*. Ralph also wrote a *History of Prince Titi*. These histories are manifestly covert reflections on George II. and his belongings.

Titian [*Tiziano Vecellio*]. An Italian landscape painter, celebrated for the fine effects of his clouds. (1477-1576.)

> " Not Titian's pencil e'er could so array,
> So fleece with clouds the pure ethereal space."
> > *Thomson : Castle of Indolence*, canto i.

The French Titian. Jacques Blanchard, the painter (1600-1638).

The Titian of Portugal. Alonzo Sanchez Coello (1515-1590).

Tit'ivate (3 syl.). To tidy up ; to dress up ; to set in order. "Titi" is a variant of *tidy ;* and "vate" is an affix, from the Latin *vado* (to go), meaning "to go and do something."

Tittle Tattle. Tattle is prate. (Dutch *tateren*, Italian, *tatta-mella*.) Tittle is little, same as tit in titmouse, little tit, tit-bit.

"Pish! Why do I spend my time in tittle-tattle?"
Otway: Cheats of Scapin, i. 1.

Titular Bishops. The name now given to the Roman Catholic dignitaries formerly known as Bishops *in partibus.* (*See* IN PARTIBUS).

Titus. The penitent thief, called Desmas in the ancient mysteries. (*See* DUMACHUS.)

Titus the Roman Emperor was called "the delight of men." (40, 79-81.) *The Arch of Titus* commemorates the capture of Jerusalem, A.D. 70.

Tit'yos. A giant whose body covered nine acres of land. He tried to defile Latōna, but Apollo cast him into Tartarus, where a vulture fed on his liver, which grew again as fast as it was devoured. (*Greek fable.*) (*See* GIANTS.)

⁂ Promētheus (3 syl.) was chained to Mount Caucasus, and had his liver gnawed by a vulture or eagle. (*See also* ST. GEORGE, who delivered Sabra, chained to a rock.)

Tit'yre Tus. Dissolute young scapegraces, whose delight was to worry the watchmen, upset sedans, wrench knockers off doors, and be rude to pretty women, at the close of the seventeenth century. The name comes from the first line of Virgil's first Eclogue, "*Tityre tu patulæ recubans sub tegmine fagi*" (Tityre Tus loved to lurk in the dark night looking for mischief). "Tus" = *tuze*.

Tit'yrus. Any shepherd. So called in allusion to the name familiar from its use in Greek idyls and Virgil's first Eclogue. In the *Shepherd's Calendar* Spenser calls Chaucer by this name:

"Heroes and their feats
Fatigue me, never weary of the pipe
Of Tityrus, assembling as he sang
The rustic throng beneath his favourite beech."
Cowper.

Tizo'ne. One of the favourite swords of the Cid, taken by him from King Bucar. His other favourite sword was Cola'da. Tizona was buried with him. (*See* SWORD.)

Tizzy (*A*). A sixpence. A variant of *tester*. In the reign of Henry VIII. a "testone" was a shilling, but only sixpence in the reign of Elizabeth. (French, *teste, tête*, the [monarch's] head.)

To (1) (to rhyme with *do*). To be compared to; comparable to. Thus, Sir Thomas Browne (*Religio Medici*) says: "There is no torture *to* the rack of a disease" (p. 69, 20); and again, "No reproach *to* the scandal of a story." And Shakespeare says:—

"There is no woe *to* his correction,
Nor *to* his service no such joy on earth.'
Two Gentlemen of Verona, ii. 4.

To. Altogether; wholly. .

"If the podech be burned to . . . we save the byshope hath put his fote in the potte."—*Tyndale.*

To-do. *Here's a pretty to-do.* Disturbance. The French *affaire*—i.e. *à faire* (to do).

To Rights. In apple-pie order. *To put things to rights.* To put every article in its proper place. In the United States of America the phrase is used to signify directly. (Latin, '*rectus,* right.)

"I said I had never heard it, so she began to rights and told me the whole thing."—*Story of the Sleigh-ride.*

To Wit. For example. (Anglo-Saxon, *wit-an*, to know.)

To (2) (to rhyme with *so, foe*, etc.).

To En (*The*). The One—that is, the Unity. This should be *To hen* properly.

To On (*The*). The reality.

To Pan (*The*). The totality.

"So then he falls back upon force as the "ultimate of ultimates," as the TO EN, the TO ON, and the TO PAN of creation."—*Fra. Olla.*

Toads. The device of Clovis was three toads (or botes, as they were called in Old French), but after his baptism the Arians greatly hated him, and assembled a large army under King Candat to put down the Christian king. While on his way to meet the heretics, he saw in the heavens his device miraculously changed into three lilies *or* on a banner *azure.* He had such a banner instantly made, and called it his *liflambe.* Even before his army came in sight of King Candat, the host of the heretic lay dead, slain, like the army of Sennacherib, by a blast from the god of battles. (*Raoul de Prèsles: Grans Croniques de France.*)

"It is wytnessyd of Maister Robert Gagwyne that before thyse dayes all French kynges used to here in their armes iii Todys, but after this Clodoveus had recognised Cristes relygyon iii Floure de lys were sent to hym by diuyne power, sette in a shylde of azure, the whiche syns that been borne of all French kynges."—*Fabian's Chronicle.*

The toad, ugly and venomous, wears yet a precious jewel in its head. Fenton says: "There is to be found in the heads of old and great toads a stone they call borax or stelon, which, being used as rings, give forewarning against venom" (1569). These stones always bear a figure resembling a toad on their surface.

Lupton says: "A toad-stone, called *crepaudia*, touching any part envenomed by the bite of a rat, wasp, spider, or other venomous beast, ceases the pain and swelling thereof." In the Londesborough Collection is a silver ring of the fifteenth century, in which one of these toad-stones is set. The stone was supposed to sweat and change colour when poison was in its proximity. Technically called the Batrachyte or Batrachos, an antidote of all sorts of poison.

Toads unknown in Ireland. It is said that St. Patrick cleared the island of all "varmint" by his malediction.

Toad-eater. At the final overthrow of the Moors, the Castilians made them their servants, and their active habits and officious manners greatly pleased the proud and lazy Spaniards, who called them *mi todita* (my factotum). Hence a cringing officious dependent, who will do all sorts of dirty work for you, is called a *todita* or *toad-eater*.

Pulteney's toad-eater. Henry Vane. So called by Walpole (1742).

Toady. (*See* TOAD-EATER.)

Toast. A name given, to which guests are invited to drink in compliment. The name at one time was that of a lady. The word is taken from the toast which used at one time to be put into the tankard, and which still floats in the loving-cup, and also the cups called copus, bishop, and cardinal, at the Universities. Hence the lady named was the toast or savour of the wine—that which gave the draught piquancy and merit. The story goes that a certain beau, in the reign of Charles II., being at Bath, pledged a noted beauty in a glass of water taken from her bath; whereupon another roysterer cried out he would have nothing to do with the liquor, but would have the toast—*i.e.* the lady herself. (*Rambler*, No. 24.)

"Let the toast pass, drink to the lass."—*Sheridan: School for Scandal.*

"Say, why are beauties praised and honoured most,
The wise man's passion and the vain man's toast."   *Pope: Rape of the Lock*, canto i.

Tobit, sleeping one night outside the wall of his courtyard, was blinded by sparrows "muting warm dung into his eyes." His son Tobias was attacked on the Tigris by a fish, which leapt out of the water to assail him. Tobias married Sara, seven of whose betrothed lovers had been successively carried off by the evil spirit Asmodeus. Asmodeus was driven off by the angel Azarias, and,

fleeing to the extremity of Egypt, was bound. Old Tobit was cured of his blindness by applying to his eyes the gall of the fish which had tried to devour his son. (*Apocrypha: Book of Tobit.*)

Tobo'so. *Dulcin'ea del Toboso.* Don Quixote's lady. Sancho Panza says she was "a stout-built sturdy wench, who could pitch the bar as well as any young fellow in the parish." The knight had been in love with her when he was simply a gentleman of the name of Quix'ada. She was then called Aldonza Lorenzo (daughter of Lorenzo Corchuelo and Aldonza Nogales); but when the gentleman became a don, he changed the style of address of the village damsel into one more befitting his new rank. (*Cervantes: Don Quixote*, bk. i. chap. i.)

"'Sir,' said Don Quixote, 'she is not a descendant of the ancient Caii, Curtii, and Scipios of Rome; nor of the modern Colonas and Orsini; nor of the Rebillas and Villanovas of Valencia; neither is she a descendant of the Palafoxes, Newcas, Rocabertis, Corellas, Lunas, Alagones, Ureas, Fozes, and Gurreas of Aragon: neither does the Lady Dulcinea descend from the Cerdas, Manriquez, Mendozas, and Guzmans of Castile; nor from the Aloncastros, Pallas, and Menezes of Portugal; but she derives her origin from a family of Toboso, near Mancha'" (bk. ii. chap. v.).

⁂ In English the accent of Dulcinea is often on the second syllable, but in Spanish it is on the third.

"Ask you for whom my tears do flow so?
Why, for Dulcinea del Toboso."
    Don Quixote's Love-song.

Tobo'sian. *The rampant Man'chegan lion shall be united to the white Tobosian dove.* Literally, Don Quixote de la Mancha shall marry Dulcin'ea del Toboso. Metaphorically, "None but the brave deserve the fair."

Toby (*the dog*), in Punchinello, wears a frill garnished with bells, to frighten away the devil from his master. This is a very old superstition. (*See* PASSING BELL.)

The Chinese and other nations make a great noise at death to scare away evil spirits. "Keening" is probably based on the same superstition.

Toby. *The high toby*, the high-road; *the low toby*, the by-road. A highwayman is a "high tobyman;" a mere footpad is a "low tobyman."

"So we can do a touch now . . . as well as you grand gentlemen on the high toby."—*Boldrewood: Robbery under Arms*, chap. xxvi.

Toddy. A favourite Scotch beverage compounded of spirits, hot water, and sugar. The word is a corruption of *taudi*, the Indian name for the saccharine juice of palm spathes. The Sanskrit is *toldi* or *taldi*, from *tal* (palm-juice). (*Rhind: Vegetable Kingdom.*)

Toes. The most dexterous man in the use of his toes in lieu of fingers was William Kingston, born without hands or arms. (See *World of Wonders*, pt. x.; *Correspondence*, p. 65.)

Tofana. An old woman of Naples immortalised by her invention of a tasteless and colourless poison, called by her the *Manna of St. Nicola of Bari*, but better known as *Aqua Tofa'na*. Above 600 persons fell victims to this insidious drug. Tofana died 1730.

Hieronyma Spara, generally called *La Spara*, a reputed witch, about a century previously, sold a similar elixir. The secret was revealed by the father confessors, after many years of concealment and a frightful number of deaths.

Tog. *Togs*, dress. (Latin, *toga*.) "Togged out in his best" is dressed in his best clothes. *Toggery* is finery.

Toga. The Romans were called *to-ga'ti* or *gens toga'ta*, because their chief outer dress was a toga.

Toga'd or **Togated Nation** (*The*). *Gens togāta*, the Romans, who wore togas. The Greeks wore "palls," and were called the *gens pallia'ta ;* the Gauls wore breeches, and were called *gens braccata*. (*Toga*, *pallium*, and *braccæ*.)

Tole'do. Famous for its swords. "The temper of Tole'dan blades is such that they are sometimes packed in boxes, curled up like the mainsprings of watches"!! Both Livy and Polyb'ius refer to them.

Tolmen (in French, *Dolmen*). An immense mass of stone placed on two or more vertical ones, so as to admit a passage between them. (Celtic, *tol* or *dol*, table; *men*, stone.)

The Constantine Tolmen, Cornwall, consists of a vast stone 33 feet long, 14½ deep, and 18½ across. This stone is calculated to weigh 750 tons, and is poised on the points of two natural rocks.

Tolo'sa. *He has got the gold of Tolosa.* (Latin proverb meaning "His ill-gotten wealth will do him no good.") Cæpio, in his march to Gallia Narbonensis, stole from Toulouse (*Tolosa*) the gold and silver consecrated by the Cimbrian Druids to their gods. In the battle which ensued both Cæpio and his brother consul were defeated by the Cimbrians and Teutons, and 112,000 Romans were left dead on the field. (B.C. 106.)

Tom. Between "Tom" and "Jack" there is a vast difference. "Jack" is the sharp, shrewd, active fellow, but Tom the honest dullard. Counterfeits are "Jack," but Toms are simply bulky examples of the ordinary sort, as Tom-toes. No one would think of calling the thick-headed, ponderous male cat a Jack, nor the pert, dexterous, thieving daw a "Tom." The former is instinctively called a Tom-cat, and the latter a Jack-daw. The subject of "Jack" has been already set forth. (*See* Jack.) Let us now see how Tom is used :—

Tom o' Bedlam (*q.v.*). A mendicant who levies charity on the plea of insanity.

Tom-cat. The male cat.

Tom Drum's entertainment. A very clumsy sort of horse-play.

Tom Farthing. A born fool.

Tom Fool. A clumsy, witless fool, fond of stupid practical jokes, but very different from a "Jack Pudding," who is a wit and bit of a conjurer.

Tom Long. A lazy, dilatory sluggard.

Tom Lony. A simpleton.

Tom Noddy. A puffing, fuming, stupid creature, no more like a "Jack-a-dandy" than Bill Sikes to Sam Weller.

Tom Noodle. A mere nincompoop.

Tom the Piper's son. A poor stupid thief who got well basted, and blubbered like a booby.

Tom Thumb. A man cut short or stinted of his fair proportions. (For the Tom Thumb of nursery delight, *see next page*.)

Tom Tidler. An occupant who finds it no easy matter to keep his own against sharper rivals. (*See* Tom Tidler's Ground.)

Tom Tiller. A hen-pecked husband.

Tom Tinker. The brawny, heavy blacksmith, with none of the wit and fun of a "Jack Tar," who can tell a yarn to astonish all his native village.

Tom Tit. The "Tom Thumb" of birds.

Tom-Toe. The clumsy, bulky toe, "bulk without spirit vast." Why the great toe? "For that being one o' the lowest, basest, poorest of this most wise rebellion, thou goest foremost." (*Shakespeare : Coriolanus*, i. 1.)

Tom Tug. A waterman, who bears the same relation to a Jack Tar as a cart-horse to an Arab. (*See* Tom Tug.)

Great Tom of Lincoln. A bell weighing 5 tons 8 cwt.

Mighty Tom of Oxford. A bell weighing 7 tons 12 cwt.

Old Tom. A heavy, strong, intoxicating sort of gin.

Long Tom. A huge water-jug.

Tom Folio. Thomas Rawlinson, the bibliomaniac. (1681-1725.)

Tom Fool's Colours. Red and yellow, or scarlet and yellow, the colours of the ancient motley.

Tom Foolery. The coarse, witless jokes of a Tom Fool. (*See above.*)

Tom Long. *Waiting for Tom Long—i.e.* a wearisome long time. The pun, of course, is on the word *long*.

Tom Raw. The griffin; applied at one time to a subaltern in India for a year and a day after his joining the army.

Tom Tailor. A tailor.

" ' We rend our hearts, and not our garments.'— ' The better for yourselves, and the worse for Tom Taylor,' said the baron."—*Sir W. Scott : The Monastery*, chap. xxv.

Tom Thumb, the nursery tale, is from the French *Le Petit Poucet*, by Charles Perrault (1630), but it is probably of Anglo-Saxon origin. There is in the Bodleian Library a ballad about Tom Thumb, " printed for John Wright in 1630."

Tom Thumb. The son of a common ploughman and his wife, who was knighted by King Arthur, and was killed by the poisonous breath of a spider, in the reign of King Thunstone, the successor of Arthur. (*Nursery tale.*)

Tom Tidler's Ground. The ground or tenement of a sluggard. The expression occurs in Dickens's Christmas story, 1861. Tidler is a contraction of " the idler " or *t'idler*. The game so called consists in this: Tom Tidler stands on a heap of stones, gravel, etc.; other boys rush on the heap crying, " Here I am on Tom Tidler's ground," and Tom bestirs himself to keep the invaders off.

Tom Tug. A waterman. In allusion to the tug or boat so called, or to tugging at the oars.

Tom and Jerry — *i.e.* Corinthian Tom and Jerry Hawthorn, the two chief characters in Pierce Egan's *Life in London*, illustrated by Cruikshank.

Tom, Dick, and Harry. A set of nobodies; persons of no note; persons unworthy notice. Jones, Brown, and Robinson are far other men: they are the vulgar rich, especially abroad, who give themselves airs, and look with scorn on all foreign ways which differ from their own.

Tom o' Bedlams. A race of mendicants. The Bethlem Hospital was made to accommodate six lunatics, but in 1644 the number admitted was forty-four, and applications were so numerous that many inmates were dismissed half-cured. These " ticket-of-leave men " used to wander about as vagrants, chanting mad songs, and dressed in fantastic dresses, to excite pity. Under cover of these harmless " innocents," a set of sturdy rogues appeared, called Abram men, who shammed lunacy, and committed great depredations.

" With a sigh like Tom o' Bedlam."
                Shakespeare: King Lear, i. 2.

Tomboy. A romping girl, formerly used for a harlot. (Saxon, *-tumbere*, a dancer or romper; Danish, *tumle*, " to tumble about ;" French, *tomber ;* Spanish, *tumbar ;* our tumble.) The word may either be tumbe-boy (one who romps like a boy), or a *tumber* (one who romps), the word *boy* being a corruption.

                    " A lady
So fair . . . to be partner'd
With tomboys."
          Shakespeare: Cymbeline, i. 6.

Halliwell gives the following quotation :—

" Herodias dougter that was a tumb-estre, and tumblede before [the king] and other grete lordes of the contré, he granted to geve hure whatevere she would bydde."

Tomahawk. A war-hatchet. The word has slight variations in different Indian tribes, as *tomehagen, tumnahagen, tamoihecan,* etc. When peace was made between tribes in hostility, the tomahawks were buried with certain ceremonies; hence, to " bury the hatchet " means to make peace.

Tomb of Our Lord. This spot is now covered by " The Church of the Holy Sepulchre." A long marble slab is shown on the pavement as the tombstone. Where the Lord was anointed for His burial three large candlesticks stand covered with red velvet. The identity of the spot is doubtful.

Tommy Atkins (*A*). A British soldier, as a Jack Tar is a British sailor. The term arose from the little pocket ledgers served out, at one time, to all British soldiers. In these manuals were to be entered the name, the age, the date of enlistment, the length of service, the wounds, the medals, and so on of each individual. The War Office sent with each little book a form for filling it in, and the hypothetical name selected, instead of John Doe and Richard Roe (selected by lawyers), or M. N. (selected by the Church), was " Tommy Atkins."

The books were instantly so called, and it did not require many days to transfer the name from the book to the soldier.

Tommy Dodd. The "odd" man who, in tossing up, either wins or loses according to agreement with his confederate. There is a music-hall song so called, in which Tommy Dodd is the "knowing one."

Tommy Shop. Where wages are paid to workmen who are expected to lay out a part of the money for the good of the shop. Tommy means bread or a penny roll, or the food taken by a workman in his handkerchief ; it also means goods in lieu of money. A Tom and Jerry shop is a low drinking-room.

To morrow never Comes. A reproof to those who defer till to-morrow what should be done to-day.

"' I shall acquaint your mother, Miss May, with your pretty behaviour to-morrow.'—' I suppose you mean to-morrow come never,' answered Magnolia."—*Le Fanu : The House in the Churchyard*, p. 118.

Tonans. *Delirium tonans.* Loud talk, exaggeration, gasconade. *Blackwood's Magazine* (1869) introduced the expression in the following clause :—

"Irishmen are the victims of that terrible malady that is characterised by a sort of subacute raving, and may, for want of a better name, be called 'delirium tonans.'"

Tongue of the Trump (*The*). The spokesman or leader of a party. The trump means a Jew's harp, which is vocalised by the tongue.

"The tongue of the trump to them a'."
                                        Burns.

Tongues.
The Italian is pleasant, but without sinews, as still fleeting water.

The French—delicate, but like an overnice woman, scarce daring to open her lips for fear of marring her countenance.

Spanish—majestical, but fulsome, running too much on the letter *o ;* and terrible, like the devil in a play.

Dutch—manlike, but withal very harsh, as one ready at every word to pick a quarrel.

We (the English), in borrowing from them, give the strength of consonants to the Italian ; the full sound of words to the French ; the variety of terminations to the Spanish ; and the mollifying of more vowels to the Dutch. Thus, like bees, we gather the honey of their good properties and leave the dregs to themselves. (*Camden.*)

Tonna (*Mrs.*), Charlotte Elizabeth,

the author of *Personal Recollections.* (1792-1846.)

Ton'sure (2 syl.). *The tonsure of St. Peter* consists in shaving the crown and back of the head, so as to leave a ring or "crown" of hair.

The tonsure of James consists in shaving the entire front of the head. This is sometimes called "the tonsure of Simon the Magician," and sometimes "the Scottish tonsure," from its use in North Britain.

Tonsures vary in size according to rank.

For *clerics* the tonsure should be 1 inch in diameter. (*Gastaldus*, ii. sect. i. chap. viii.)

For those in *minor orders* it should be 1½ inch. (Council of Palencia under Urban VI.)

For *sub-deacon* 1¾ inch. (*Gastaldus*, xi. sect. i. chap. viii.)

For a *deacon* 2 inches. (*Gastaldus*, xi. sect. i. chap. ix.)

For a *priest* 2½ inches. (Council of Palencia.)

Tontine (2 syl.). A legacy left among several persons in such a way that as anyone dies his share goes to the survivors, till the last survivor inherits all. So named from Lorenzo Tonti, a Neapolitan, who introduced the system into France in 1653.

Tony Lumpkin. A young clownish bumpkin in *She Stoops to Conquer*, by Oliver Goldsmith.

Too Many for [**Me**] or *One too many for* [*me*]. More than a match. "*Il est trop fort pour moi.*"

"The Irishman is cunning enough ; but we shall be too many for him."—*Mrs. Edgeworth.*

Tooba or **Touba** [*eternal happiness*]. The tree Touba, in Paradise, stands in the palace of Mahomet. (*Sale : Preliminary Discourse to the Koran.*)

Tool. *To tool a coach.* To drive one; generally applied to a gentleman Jehu, who undertakes for his own amusement to drive a stage-coach. To tool is to use the tool as a workman ; a coachman's tools are the reins and whip with which he tools his coach or makes his coach go.

Tooley Street. A corruption of St. Olaf—*i.e.* 'T-olaf, Tolay, Tooly. Similarly, Sise Lane is St. Osyth's Lane.

Toom Tabard [*empty jacket*]. A nickname given to John Baliol, because of his poor spirit, and sleeveless appointment to the throne of Scotland. The honour was an "empty jacket," which he enjoyed a short time and then lost. He died discrowned in Normandy.

Tooth. Greek, *odont'*; Latin, *dent'*; Sanskrit, *dant'*; Gothic, *tunth'*; Anglo-Saxon, *tóth*, plural, *téth*.

Golden tooth. (*See* GOLDEN.)
Wolf's tooth. (*See* TEETH.)
In spite of his teeth. (*See* TEETH.)

Tooth and Egg. A corruption of *Tutanag*, a Chinese word for spelter, the metal of which canisters are made, and tea-chests lined. It is a mixture of English lead and tin from Quintang.

Tooth and Nail. In right good earnest, like a rat or mouse biting and scratching to get at something.

Top. (*See* SLEEP.)

Top-heavy. Liable to tip over because the centre of gravity is too high. Intoxicated.

Top Ropes. *A display of the top-ropes.* A show of gushing friendliness; great promise of help. The top-rope is the rope used in hauling the top-mast up or down.

"This display of the top-ropes was rather new to me, for time had blurred from my memory the 'General's' rhapsodies."—*C. Thomson : Autobiography*, p. 189.

Top-sawyer. A first-rate fellow. The sawyer that takes the upper stand is always the superior man, and gets higher wages.

Topham. *Take him, Topham.* Catch him if you can ; lay hold of him, tip-staff. Topham was the Black Rod of the House of Commons in the reign of Charles II., very active in apprehending "suspects" during the supposed conspiracy revealed by Titus Oates. "Take him, Topham," became a proverbial saying of the time, much the same as "Who stole the donkey?" "How are your poor feet?" and so on.

"Till 'Take him, Topham' became a proverb, and a formidable one, in the mouth of the people."
—*Sir Walter Scott : Peveril of the Peak*, chap. xx.

To'phet. A valley near Jerusalem, where children were made to "pass through the fire to Moloch." Josi'ah threw dead bodies, ordure, and other unclean things there, to prevent all further application of the place to religious use. (2 Kings xxiii. 10, 11.) Here Sennacherib's army was destroyed. (Isaiah xxx. 31-33.) The valley was also called "Gehinnom" (valley of Hinnom), corrupted into Gehenna ; and Rabbi Kimchi tells us that a perpetual fire was kept burning in it to consume the dead bodies, bones, filth, and ordure deposited there. (Hebrew, *toph*, a drum. When children were offered to Moloch, their shrieks were drowned by beat of drum.)

Top'ic. This word has wholly changed its original meaning. It now signifies a subject for talk, a theme for discussion or to be written about ; but originally "topics" were what we call *commonplace books ;* the "sentences" of Peter Lombard were theological topics. (Greek, *topikos*, from *topos*, a place.)

Topsy. A slave-girl, who impersonates the low moral development but real capacity for education of the negro race. Her reply to Aunt Ophelia, who questioned her as to her father and mother, is worthy Dickens. After maintaining that she had neither father nor mother, her solution of her existence was "I 'spects I growed." (*Mrs. Beecher Stowe : Uncle Tom's Cabin.*)

Topsy-turvy. Upside down. (Anglo-Saxon, *top side turn-aweg.*) As Shakespeare says, "Turn it topsy-turvy down." (1 *Henry IV.*, iv. 1.) (*See* HALF-SEAS OVER.)

Toralva. The licentiate who was conveyed on a cane through the air, with his eyes shut. In the space of twelve hours he arrived at Rome, and lighted on the tower of Nona, whence, looking down, he witnessed the death of the constable de Bourbon. The next morning he arrived at Madrid, and related the whole affair. During his flight through the air the devil bade him open his eyes, and he found himself so near the moon that he could have touched it with his finger. (*Cervantes : Don Quixote*, pt. ii. bk. iii. chap. v.)

Torne'a. A lake, or rather a river of Sweden, which rises from a lake in Lapland, and runs into the Gulf of Bothnia, at the town called Torne'a or Torne.

"Still pressing on beyond Tornea's lake."
Thomson : Winter.

Torqua'to—*i.e.* Torquato Tasso, the poet. (1544-1595.) (*See* ALFONSO.)

"And see how dearly earned Torquato's fame."
Lord Byron : Childe Harold, iv. 36.

Torquema'da (Inquisitor-general of Spain, 1420-1498). A Dominican of excessive zeal, who multiplied confiscations, condemnations, and punishments to a frightful extent ; and his hatred of the Jews and Moors was diabolical.

"General Strelnikoff was the greatest scoundrel who defiled the earth since Torquemada."—*Stepniak : The Explosion of the Winter Palace*, February, 1880.

Torr's MSS., in the library of the dean and chapter of York Minster. These voluminous records contain the clergy list of every parish in the diocese of York, and state not only the date of each vacancy, but the cause of each removal, whether by death, promotion, or otherwise.

Torralba (*Doctor*), who resided some time in the court of Charles V. of Spain. He was tried by the Inquisition for sorcery, and confessed that the spirit Cequiel took him from Vall'adolid' to Rome and back again in an hour and a half. (*Pelicer.*)

Torre (*Sir*) (1 syl.). Brother of Elaine, and son of the lord of As'tolat. A kind blunt heart, brusque in manners, and but little of a knight. (*Tennyson : Idyls of the King ; Elaine.*)

Torricelli, an Italian mathematician (1608-47), noted for his explanation of the rise of water in a common barometer. Galileo explained the phenomenon by the *ipse dixit* of " Nature abhors a vacuum."

Torso. A statue which has lost its head and members, as the famous "torso of Hercules." (Italian, *torso*.)

∴ The *Torso Belvedere*, the famous torso of Hercules, in the Vatican, was discovered in the fifteenth century. It is said that Michael Angelo greatly admired it.

Tortoise which Supports the Earth (*The*) is Chukwa ; the elephant (between the tortoise and the world) is Maha-pudma.

Torture (2 syl.). The most celebrated instruments of torture were the *rack*, called by the English "the Duke of Exeter's daughter ; " the *thumbikins*, or thumbscrews, the *boots*, the *pincers*, the *manacles*, and the *scavenger's daughter* (*q.v.*).

To'ry. This word, says Defoe, is the Irish *toruigh*, used in the reign of Queen Elizabeth to signify a band of Catholic outlaws who haunted the bogs of Ireland. It is formed from the verb *toruig-him* (to make sudden raids). Golius says—"Tory, *silvestris, montana, avis, homo, et utrumque ullus haud ibi est*" (Whatever inhabits mountains and forests is a Tory). Lord Macaulay says—" The name was first given to those who refused to concur in excluding James from the throne." He further says—" The bogs of Ireland afforded a refuge to Popish outlaws, called *tories*." Tory-hunting was a pastime which has even found place in our nursery rhymes—"I went to the wood and I killed a tory."

F. Crossley gives as the derivation, *Taobh-righ* (Celtic), " king's party."

H. T. Hore, in *Notes and Queries*, gives *Tuath-righ*, " partisans of the king."

G. Borrow gives *Tar-a-ri*, " Come, O king."

∴ In 1832, after the Reform Act, the Tory party began to call themselves " Conservatives," and after Gladstone's Bill of Home Rule for Ireland, in 1886, the Whigs and Radicals who objected to the bill joined the Conservatives, and the two combined called themselves " Unionists." In 1895 the Queen sent for Lord Salisbury, who formed a Unionist government.

Totem Pole (*A*). A pole, elaborately carved, erected before the dwelling of certain American Indians. It is a sort of symbol, like a public-house sign or flagstaff.

" Imagine a huge log, forty or fifty feet high, set up flagstaff fashion in front or at the side of a low one-storied wooden house, and carved in its whole height into immense but grotesque representations of man, beast, and bird. . . . [It is emblematic of] family pride, veneration of ancestors . . . and legendary religion. Sometimes [the totem] is only a massive pole, with a bird or some weird animal at the top, . . . the crest of the chief by whose house it stands. . . . Sometimes it was so broad at the base as to allow a doorway to be cut through it. Usually the whole pole was carved into grotesque figures one above the other, and the effect heightened . . . by dabs of paint—blue, red, and green."—*Nineteenth Century*, December, 1892, p. 993.

Totemism. Totem is the representation of a symbol by an animal, and totemism is the system or science of such symbolism. Thus, in Egyptian mythology, what is represented as a pig or hippopotamus by one tribe, is (for some totemic reason) represented as a crocodile by another.

" The apparent wealth of [Egyptian] mythology depends on the totemism of the inhabitants of the Nile Valley. . . . Each district had its own special animal as the emblem of the tribe dwelling in that locality."—*Lockyer : Nineteenth Century*, July 1892, p. 51.

Toto Cœlo. Entirely. The allusion is to augurs who divided the heavens into four parts. Among the Greeks the left hand was unlucky, and the right lucky. When all four parts concurred a prediction was certified *toto cœlo*. The Romans called the east *Antica*, the west *Postica*, the south *Dextra*, and the north *Sinistra*.

" Even when they are relaxing those general requirements . . . the education differs *toto cœlo* from instruction induced by the tests of an examining body."—*Nineteenth Century*, January, 1893, p. 23.

Totus Teres atque Rotundus. Finished and completely rounded off.

Touch. *In touch with him. En rapport ;* in sympathy. The allusion is to the touchstone, which shows by its colour what metal has touched it.

Touch. *To keep touch*—faith, fidelity. The allusion is to " touching " gold and other metals on a touchstone to prove them. Shakespeare speaks of "friends of noble touch" (proof).

> " And trust me on my truth,
> If thou keep touch with me,
> My dearest friend, as my own heart,
> Thou shalt right welcome be."
> *George Barnwell* (1730).

Touch At (*To*). To go to a place without stopping at it.

> "The next day we touched at Sidon." — *Acts* xxvii. 3.

Touch Bottom (*To*). To know the worst. A sea-phrase.

> "It is much better for the ministry to touch bottom at once and know the whole truth, than to remain any longer in suspense."—*Newspaper paragraph*, January, 1886.

Touch Up (*To*). To touch a horse with a whip for greater speed. To touch up a picture, etc., is to give it a few touches to improve it.

Touch and Go (*A*). A very narrow escape ; a very brief encounter. A metaphor derived from driving when the wheel of one vehicle touches that of another passing vehicle without doing mischief. It was a touch, but neither vehicle was stopped, each went on its way.

Tou'chet. When Charles IX. introduced Henri of Navarre to Marie Touchet, he requested him to make an anagram on her name, and Henri thereupon wrote the following :—*Je charme tout.*

Touchstone. A dark, flinty schist, called by the ancients *Lapis Lydius ;* called touchstone because gold is tried by it, thus : A series of needles are formed (1) of pure gold ; (2) of 23 gold and 1 copper ; (3) of 22 gold and 2 copper, and so on. The assayer selects one of these and rubs it on the touchstone, when it leaves a reddish mark in proportion to the quantity of copper alloy. Dr. Ure. says : "In such small work as cannot be assayed . . . the assayers . . . ascertain its quality by 'touch.' They then compare the colour left behind, and form their judgment accordingly."

⁂ The fable is, that Battus saw Mercury steal Apollo's oxen, and Mercury gave him a cow to secure his silence on the theft. Mercury, distrustful of the man, changed himself into a peasant, and offered Battus a cow and an ox if he would tell him the secret. Battus, caught in the trap, told the secret, and Mercury changed him into a touchstone. (*Ovid : Metamorphoses,* ii.)

> "Gold is tried by the touchstone, and men by gold."—*Bacon.*

Touchstone. A clown whose mouth is filled with quips and cranks and witty repartees. (*Shakespeare : As You Like It.*) The original one was Tarlton.

Touchy. Apt to take offence on slight provocation. *Ne touchez pas, "Noli me tangere,"* one not to be touched.

Tour. *The Grand Tour.* Through France, Switzerland, Italy, and home by Germany. Before railways were laid down, this tour was made by most of the young aristocratic families as the finish of their education. Those who merely went to France or Germany were simply tourists.

Tour de Force. A feat of strength.

Tourlourou. Young unfledged soldiers of the line, who used to be called "Jean-Jean."

> "Les Tourlourous sont les nouveaux enrolés, ceux qui n'ont pas encore de vieilles moustaches, et qui flanent sur les boulevards en regardant les images, les paillasses, et en cherchant des payses." —*Paul de Kock : Un Tourlourou,* chap. xiii.

Tournament or **Tournay.** A tilt of knights ; the chief art of the game being so to manœuvre or *turn* your horse as to avoid the adversary's blow. (French, *tournoiement,* verb, *tournoyer.*)

Tournament of the Drum. A comic romance in verse by Sir David Lindsay ; a ludicrous mock tournament.

Tournament of Tottenham. A comic romance, printed in Percy's *Reliques.* A number of clowns are introduced, practising warlike games, and making vows like knights of high degree. They ride tilt on cart-horses, fight with plough-shares and flails, and wear for armour wooden bowls and saucepan lids. It may be termed the "high life below stairs" of chivalry.

Tour'nemine (3 syl.). *That's Tournemine.* Your wish was father to the thought. Tournemine was a Jesuit of the eighteenth century, of a very sanguine and dreamy temperament.

Tours. Geoffrey of Monmouth says : "In the party of Brutus was one Turo'nes, his nephew, inferior to none in courage and strength, from whom Tours derived its name, being the place of his sepulture. Of course, this fable is wholly worthless historically. Tours is the city of the Tu'ronēs, a people of Gallia Lugdunensis.

Tout (pronounce *towt*). To ply or seek for customers. "A touter" is one who touts. (From Tooting, where persons on their way to the court held at Epsom were pestered by "touts."

"A century or two ago, when the court took up its quarters at Epsom ... [many of] the inhabitants used to station themselves at the point where the roads fork off to Epsom by Tooting and Merton, and 'tout' the travellers to pass through Tooting. It become a common expression for carriage-folk to say, 'The Toots are on us again.'"—*Walford: Greater London*, vol. ii. p. 530.

Tout Ensemble (French). The whole massed together; the general effect.

Tout est Perdu Hormis L'Honneur, is what François I. wrote to his mother after the battle of Pa'via.

Tout le Monde. Everyone who is anyone.

Tower of Hunger. Gualandi. (*See* UGOLI'NO.)

Tower of London. The architect of this remarkable building was Gundulphus, Bishop of Rochester, who also built or restored Rochester keep, in the time of William I. In the Tower lie buried Anne Boleyn and her brother; the guilty Catherine Howard, and Lady Rochford her associate; the venerable Lady Salisbury, and Cromwell the minister of Henry VIII.; the two Seymours, the admiral and protector of Edward VI.; the Duke of Norfolk and Earl of Sussex (Queen Elizabeth's reign); the Duke of Monmouth, son of Charles II.; the Earls of Balmerino and Kilmarnock, and Lord Lovat; Bishop Fisher and his illustrious friend More.

Towers of Silence. Towers in Persia and India, some sixty feet in height, on the top of which Parsees place the dead to be eaten by vultures. The bones are picked clean in the course of a day, and are then thrown into a receptacle and covered with charcoal.

"A procession is then formed, the friends of the dead following the priests to the Towers of Silence on Malabar Hill."—*Col. Floyd-Jones.*

∴ The Parsees will not burn or bury their dead, because they consider a dead body impure, and they will not suffer themselves to defile any of the elements. They carry their dead on a bier to the Tower of Silence. At the entrance they look their last on the dead, and the corpse-bearers carry the dead body within the precincts and lay it down to be devoured by vultures which crowd the tower. (*Nineteenth Century*, Oct., 1893, p. 611.)

Town (*A*) is the Anglo-Saxon *tún*, a plot of ground fenced round or enclosed by a hedge; a single dwelling; a number of dwelling-houses enclosed together forming a village or burgh.

"Our ancestors in time of war ... would cast a ditch, or make a strong hedge about their houses, and houses so environed ... got the name *tunes* annexed unto them (as Cote-tun, now Cotton, the cote or house fenced in or *tuned* about; North-tun, now Norton ... South-tun, now Sutton). In troublous times whole 'thorpes' were fenced in,

and took the name of *tunes* (towns), and then 'stedes' (now *cities*), and 'thorpes' (villages), and *burghs* (burrows) ... got the name of townes."—*Restitution*, p. 232.

Town and Gown Row (*A*). A collision, often leading to a fight, in the English universities between the students or gownsmen, and non-gownsmen—principally bargees and roughs. (*See* PHILISTINES.)

Toyshop of Europe (*The*). So Burke called Birmingham. Here "toy" does not refer to playthings for children, but small articles made of steel. "Light toys" in Birmingham mean mounts, small steel rings, sword hilts, and so on; while "heavy steel toys" mean champagne-nippers, sugar-cutters, nut-crackers, and all similar articles.

∵ A whim or fancy is a toy. Halliwell quotes (*MS. Harl.* 4888), "For these causes ... she ran at random ... as the toy took her."

It also means an anecdote or trifling story. Hence Latimer (1550) says, "And here I will tell you a merry toy."

Tracing of a Fortress (*The*). The outline of the fortification, that is, the directions in which the masses are laid out.

Tracts for the Times. Published at Oxford during the years 1833-1841, and hence called the *Oxford Tracts*.

A. *i.e.* Rev. John Keble, M.A., author of the *Christian Year*, fellow of Oriel, and formerly Professor of Poetry at Oxford.

B. Rev. Isaac Williams, Fellow of Trinity; author of *The Cathedral, and other Poems*.

C. Rev. E. B. Pusey, D.D., Regius Professor of Hebrew, and Canon of Christ Church.

D. Rev. John Henry Newman, D.D., Fellow of Oriel, writer of the celebrated Tract No. 90, which was the last.

E. Rev. Thomas Keble.

F. Sir John Provost, Bart.

G. Rev. R. F. Wilson, of Oriel.

Tracta'rians. Those who concur in the religious views advocated by the *Oxford Tracts*.

Tracy. *All the Tracys have the wind in their faces.* Those who do wrong will always meet with punishment. William de Traci was the most active of the four knights who slew Thomas à Becket, and for this misdeed all who bore the name were saddled by the Church with this ban: "Wherever by sea or land they go, the wind in their face shall ever blow." Fuller, with his usual *naïveté*, says, "So much the better in hot weather, as it will save the need of a fan."

Trade. (*See* BALANCE.)

Trade Mark. A mark adopted by a manufacturer to distinguish his productions from those made by other persons.

Trade Winds. Winds that trade or tread in one uniform track. In the northern hemisphere they blow from the *north-east*, and in the southern hemisphere from the *south-east*, about thirty degrees each side of the equator. In some places they blow six months in one direction, and six in the opposite. It is a mistake to derive the word from *trade* (commerce), under the notion that they are "good for trade." (Anglo-Saxon, *tredde-wind*, a treading wind—*i.e.* wind of a specific "beat" or tread; *tredan*, to tread.)

Trade follows the Flag. Colonies promote the trade of the mother country. The reference is to the custom of planting the flag of the mother country in every colony.

Tradesmen's Signs, removed by Act of Parliament, 1764. The London Paving Act, 6 Geo. III. 26, 17.

Traditions. (*See* CHRISTIAN TRADITIONS.)

Trafa Meat. Meat prohibited as food by Jews from some ritual defect. It was sold cheap to general butchers, but at one time the law forbade the sale. In 1285 Roger de Lakenham, of Norwich, was fined for selling "Trafa meat."

Tragedy. The goat-song (Greek, *tragos-odē*). The song that wins the goat as a prize. This is the explanation given by Horace (*De Arte Poetica*, 220). (*See* COMEDY.)

Tragedy. The first English tragedy of any merit was *Gorboduc*, written by Thomas Norton and Thomas Sackville. (See *Ralph Roister Doister*.)

The Father of Tragedy. Æschylos the Athenian. (B.C. 525-426.) Thespis, the Richardson of Athens, who went about in a waggon with his strolling players, was the first to introduce dialogue in the choral odes, and is therefore not unfrequently called the "Father of Tragedy or the Drama."

" Thespis was first who, all besmeared with lee,
Began this pleasure for posterity."
Dryden : Art of Poetry (*Tragedy*), c. iii.

Father of French Tragedy. Garnier (1534-1590).

Trail. *The trail of the serpent is over them all.* Sin has set his mark on all. (*Thomas Moore : Paradise and the Peri.*)

Traitors' Bridge. *A loyal heart may be landed under Traitors' Bridge.* Traitor's Bridge, in the Tower, was the way by which persons charged with high treason entered that State prison.

Traitors' Gate opens from the Tower of London to the Thames, and was the gate by which persons accused of treason entered their prison.

Trajan's Column commemorates his victories over the Dacians. It was the work of Apollodorus. The column of the *Place Vendôme*, Paris, is a model of it.

Trajan's Wall. A line of fortifications stretching across the Dobrudscha from Czernavoda to the Black Sea.

Tram (*A*). A car which runs on a tramway (*q.v.*). Trams in collieries were in use in the seventeenth century, but were not introduced into our streets till 1868.

Tramway or **Tram Rails.** A railway for tram-carts or waggons, originally made of wooden rails. Iron rails were first laid down in 1738, but apparently were called "dram-roads" (Greek, *dram-ein*, to run). We are told there were waggons called drams (or trams). Benjamin Outram, in 1800, used *stone* rails at Little Eaton, Derbyshire; but the similarity between *tram* and *Outram* is a mere coincidence. Perhaps he was the cause of the word *dram* being changed to *tram*, but even this is doubtful. (See *Rees' Cyclopædia*.)

"Trams are a kind of sledge on which coals are brought from the place where they are hewn to the shaft. A tram has four wheels, but a sledge is without wheels."—*Brand: History of Newcastle-upon-Tyne*, vol. ii. p. 681, n. (1789).

Tramecksan and Slamecksan. The high heels and low heels, the two great political factions of Lilliput. The high heels are the Tories, and the low heels the Radicals of the kingdom. "The animosity of these two factions runs so high that they will neither eat, nor drink, nor speak to each other." The king was a low heel in politics, but the heir-apparent a high heel. (*Swift: Gulliver's Travels; Voyage to Lilliput*, chap. iv.)

Trammel means to catch in a net. (French, *tramail, trame*, a woof; verb, *tramer*, to weave.)

Tra′mon′tane (3 syl.). The north wind; so called by the Italians because to them it comes over the mountains. The Italians also apply the term to German, French, and other artists born north of the Alps. French lawyers, on the other hand, apply the word to *Italian* canonists, whom they consider too Romanistic. We in England generally call overstrained Roman Catholic notions " Ultramontane."

Translator (*A*). A cobbler, who translates or transmogrifies two pairs of worn-out shoes into one pair capable of being worn; a reformer, who tries to cobble the laws.

"The dull *à la mode* reformers or translators have pulled the church all to pieces and know not how to patch it up again."—*Mercurius Pragmaticus* (March, 1647, No. 27).

Translator-General. So Fuller, in his *Worthies*, calls Philemon Holland, who translated a large number of the Greek and Latin classics. (1551-1636.)

Trap. A carriage, especially such as a phäeton, dog-cart, commercial sulky, and such like. It is not applied to a gentleman's close carriage. Contraction of *trappings* (whatever is "put on," furniture for horses, decorations, etc.).

"The trap in question was a carriage which the Major had bought for six pounds sterling."—*Thackeray: Vanity Fair*, chap. lxvii.

Traps. Luggage, as "Leave your traps at the station," "I must look after my traps," etc. (*See above.*)

"The traps were packed up as quickly as possible, and the party drove away."—*DailyTelegraph.*

Trapa′ni. The Count de Trapani was the ninth child of Mary Isabel and Ferdinand II. of the two Sicilies. He married the Archduchess Mary, daughter of Leopold II., Grand Duke of Tuscany. N.B. Francis de Paul, usually called Louis-Emmanuel, Count of Trapani, was born in 1827.

Trapa′ni. The Spaniards, in pitiless raillery of the Spanish marriages, called the *trapos* or dishclouts used by waiters in the *cafés* to wipe down the dirty tables *trapani*.

Trapper, in America, is one whose vocation is to set traps for wild animals for the sake of their furs.

The Trapper. (*See* NATTY BUMPPO.)

Trappists. A religious order, so called from La Trappe, an abbey of the Cistercian order, founded in the middle of the twelfth century.

Tras′go. Same as Duende (*q.v.*).

Travels in the Blue. A brown study; in cloudland.

"Finding him gone for 'travels in the blue,' I respected his mood, and did not resent his long mutism."—*Remington Annual*, 1889, p. 61.

Traveller's Licence. The long bow; exaggeration.

"If the captain has not taken 'traveller's licence,' we have in Norway a most successful development of peasant proprietorship."—*W. Bowerman.*

Travia′ta. An opera representing the progress of a courtesan. The libretto is borrowed from a French novel, called *La Dame aux Camélias*, by Alexandre Dumas, jun. It was dramatised for the French stage. The music of the opera is by Giuseppe Verdi.

Tre, Pol, Pen.

" By their Tre, their Pol, and Pen,
Ye shall know the Cornish men."

The extreme east of Cornwall is noted for *Tre*, the extreme west for *Pol*, the centre for *Pen*.

On December 19th, 1891, the following residents are mentioned by the *Launceston Weekly News* as attending the funeral of a gentleman who lived at Tre-hummer House, Tresmere :—Residents from Trevell, Tresmarrow, Treglith, Trebarrow, Treludick, etc., with Treleaven the Mayor of Launceston.

Treacle [*tree-k′l*] properly means an antidote against the bite of wild beasts (Greek, *thē′riaka* [pharmăka], from *thēr* a wild beast). The ancients gave the name to several sorts of antidotes, but ultimately it was applied chiefly to Venice treacle (*thē′riaca androchi*), a compound of some sixty-four drugs in honey.

⁂ Sir Thomas More speaks of "a most strong treacle (*i.e.* antidote) against these venomous heresies." And in an old version of Jeremiah viii. 22, " balm" is translated treacle—"Is there no treacle at Gilead? Is there no phisitian there?"

Treading on One's Corns. (*See* CORNS.)

Treasures. *These are my treasures;* meaning the sick and poor. So said St. Lawrence when the Roman prætor commanded him to deliver up his treasures. He was then condemned to be roasted alive on a gridiron (258).

One day a lady from Campa′nia called upon Corne′lia, the mother of the Gracchi, and after showing her jewels, requested in return to see those belonging to the famous mother-in-law of Africanus.

Cornelia sent for her two sons, and said to the lady, "These are my jewels, in which alone I delight."

Treas'ury of Sciences. Bokhara (Asia), the centre of learning. It has 103 colleges, with 10,000 students, besides a host of schools and 360 mosques.

Tree. The oldest in the world—

(1) De Candolle considers the deciduous *cypress of Chapultepec*, in Mexico, one of the oldest trees in the world.

(2) The *chestnut-trees on Mount Etna*, and the Oriental *plane-tree* in the valley of Bujukdere, near Constantinople, are supposed to be of about the same age.

(3) The Rev. W. Tuckwell says the "oldest tree in the world is the *Soma cypress* of Lombardy. It was forty years old when Christ was born."

Trees of a patriarchal age.

I. OAKS.

(1) *Damorey's Oak*, Dorsetshire, 2,000 years old. Blown down in 1703.

(2) The great *Oak of Saintes*, in the department of Charente Inférieure, is from 1,800 to 2,000 years old.

(3) The *Winfarthing Oak*, Norfolk, and the *Bentley Oak* were 700 years old at the time of the Conquest.

(4) *Cowthorpe Oak*, near Wetherby, Yorkshire, according to Professor Burnet, is 1,600 years old.

(5) *William the Conqueror's Oak*, Windsor Great Park, is at least 1,200 years old.

(6) The *Bull Oak*, Wedgenock Park, and the *Plestor Oak*, Colborne, were in existence at the time of the Conquest.

(7) The *Oak of the Partisans*, in the forest of Parey, St. Ouen, is above 650 years old. *Wallace's Oak*, at Ellersley, near Paisley, was probably fifty years older. Blown down in 1859.

(8) *Owen Glendower's Oak*, Shelton, near Shrewsbury, is so called because that chieftain witnessed from its branches the battle between Henry IV. and Harry Percy, in 1403. Other famous oaks are those called *The Twelve Apostles* and *The Four Evangelists*.

(9) In the Dukeries, Nottinghamshire, are some oaks of memorable age and renown : (*a*) In the Duke of Portland's Park is an oak called *Robin Hood's Larder*. It is only a shell, held together with strong iron braces.

The *Parliament Oak*, Clipston, Notts, is said to be above 1,000 years old. We are told that Edward I., hunting in Sherwood Forest, was informed of the Welsh revolt, and summoned a "parliament" of his barons under this oak, and it was agreed to make war of extermination on Wales. Others say it was under this tree that King John assembled his barons and decreed the execution of Prince Arthur. The Parliament Oak is split into two distinct trees, and though both the trunks are hollow, they are both covered with foliage and acorns atop during the season.

The *Major Oak*, in the park of Lord Manvers, is a veritable giant. In the hollow trunk fifteen persons of ordinary size may find standing room. At its base it measures 90 feet, and at 5 feet from the ground about 35 feet. Its head covers a circumference of 270 yards.

Another venerable oak (some say 1,500 years old) is *Greendale Oak*, about half a mile from Welbeck Abbey. It is a mere ruin supported by props and chains. It has a passage through the bole large enough to admit three horsemen abreast, and a coach-and-four has been driven through it.

The *Seven Sisters Oak*, in the same vicinity, is so called because the trunk was composed of seven stems. It still stands, but in a very dilapidated state.

II. YEWS.

(1) Of *Braburn*, in Kent, according to De Candolle, is 3,000 years old.

(2) The *Scotch yew at Fortingal*, in Perthshire, is between 2,500 and 3,000 years.

(3) Of *Darley churchyard*, Derbyshire, about 2,050 years.

(4) Of *Crowhurst*, Surrey, about 1,400.

(5) The three at *Fountains Abbey*, in Yorkshire, at least 1,200 years. Beneath these trees the founders of the abbey held their council in 1132.

(6) The yew grove of *Norbury Park*, Surrey, was standing in the time of the Druids.

(7) The yew-trees at *Kingsley Bottom*, near Chichester, were standing when the sea-kings landed on the Sussex coast.

(8) The yew-tree of *Harlington churchyard*, Middlesex, is above 850 years old.

(9) That at *Ankerwyke House*, near Staines, was noted when Magna Charta was signed in 1215, and it was the trysting tree for Henry VIII. and Anne Boleyn.

III. MISCELLANEOUS.

(1) The *eight olive-trees on the Mount of Olives* were flourishing 800 years ago, when the Turks took Jerusalem.

(2) The *lime-tree in the Grisons* is upwards of 590 years old.

⁑ The *spruce* will reach to the age of 1,200 years.

¶ *The poet's tree.* A tree grows over the tomb of Tan-Sein, a musician of incomparable skill at the court of Akbar, and it is said that whoever chews a leaf of this tree will have extraordinary melody of voice. (*W. Hunter.*)

" His voice was as sweet as if he had chewed the leaves of that enchanted tree which grows over the tomb of the musician Tan-Sein."—*Moore: Lalla Rookh.*

¶ *The singing tree.* Each leaf was a mouth, and every leaf joined in concert. (*Arabian Nights.*)

He is altogether up the tree. Quite out of the swim, nowhere in the competition list.

Up a tree. In a difficulty, in a mess. It is said that Spurgeon used to practise his students in extempore preaching, and that one of his young men, on reaching the desk and opening the note containing his text, read the single word "Zacchæus" as his text. He thought a minute or two, and then delivered himself thus:— " Zacchæus was a little man, so am I; Zacchæus was up a tree, so am I; Zacchæus made haste and came down, and so do I."

Tree of Buddha (*The*). The bo-tree.

Tree of Knowledge (*The*). Genesis ii. 9.

Tree of Liberty. A tree set up by the people, hung with flags and devices, and crowned with a cap of liberty. The Americans of the United States planted poplars and other trees during the war of independence, "as symbols of growing freedom." The Jacobins in Paris planted their first tree of liberty in 1790. The symbols used in France to decorate their trees of liberty were tricoloured ribbons, circles to indicate unity, triangles to signify equality, and a cap of liberty. Trees of liberty were planted by the Italians in the revolution of 1848.

Tree of Life. Genesis ii. 9.

Trees. *Trees burst into leaf—*

		earliest		latest
Ash		May 13th,		June 14th.
Beech	,,	April 19th,	,,	May 7th.
Damson	,,	March 28th,	,,	May 13th.
Horse-chestnut	,,	March 17th,	,,	April 19th.
Larch	,,	March 21st,	,,	April 14th.
Lime	,,	April 6th,	,,	May 2nd.
Mulberry	,,	May 12th,	,,	June 23rd.
Oak	,,	April 10th,	,,	May 26th.
Poplar	,,	March 6th,	,,	April 19th.
Spanish chestnut	,,	April 20th,	,,	May 20th.
Sycamore	,,	March 28th,	,,	April 23rd.

¶ *Trees of the Sun and Moon.* Oracular trees growing " at the extremity of India," mentioned in the Italian romance of Guerino Meschino.

Tregea'gle. *To roar like Tregeagle—* very loudly. Tregeagle is the giant of Dosmary Pool, on Bodmin Downs (Cornwall), whose allotted task is to bale out the water with a limpet-shell. When the wintry blast howls over the downs, the people say it is the giant roaring. (*See* GIANTS.)

Tregetour. A conjurer or juggler. (From Old French, *tresgiat* = a juggling trick.) The performance of a conjurer was anciently termed his "minstrelsy; " thus we read of Janio the juggler—" Janio ie tregettor, facienti ministralsiam suam coram rege . . . 20s." (*Lib. Comput. Garderobæ, an.* (4 Edw. II. fol. 86), *MS. Cott. Nero,* chap. viii.)

Tremont. Boston in Massachusetts was once so called, from the three hills on which the city stands.

Trench-the-Mer. The galley of Richard *Cœur de Lion ;* so called from its "fleetness." Those who sailed in it were called by the same name.

Trencher. *A good trencher-man.* A good eater. The trencher is the platter on which food is cut (French, *trancher,* to cut), by a figure of speech applied to food itself.

He that waits for another's trencher, eats many a late dinner. He who is dependent on others must wait, and wait, and wait, happy if after waiting he gets anything at all.

" Oh, how wretched
Is that poor man that hangs on princes' favours !
There is, betwixt that smile he would aspire to,
That sweet aspect of princes, and their ruin,
More pangs and fears than wars or women have."
Shakespeare : Henry VIII., iii. 2.

Trencher Cap. The mortar-board cap worn at college; so called from the trenchered or split boards which form the top. Mortar-board is a perversion of the French *mortier*.

Trencher Friends. Persons who cultivate the friendship of others for the sake of sitting at their board, and the good things they can get.

Trencher Knight. A table knight, a suitor from cupboard love.

Trenchmore. A popular dance in the sixteenth and seventeenth centuries.

" Nimble-heeled mariners . . . capering . . sometimes a Morisco, or Trenchmore of forty miles long."—*Taylor the Water-Poet.*

Tres'sure (2 syl.). A border round a shield in heraldry. The origin of the tressure in the royal arms of Scotland is traced by heralds to the ninth century. They assert that Charlemagne granted it to King Achaius of Scotland in token of alliance, and as an assurance that "the lilies of France should be a defence to the lion of Scotland." Chalmers insinuates that these two monarchs did not even know of each other's existence.

Trèves (1 syl.). *The Holy Coat of Trèves.* A relic preserved in the cathedral of Trèves. It is said to be the seamless coat of our Saviour, which the soldiers would not rend, and therefore cast lots for. (John xix. 23, 25.) The Empress Hele'na, it is said, discovered this coat in the fourth century.

Trevéthy Stone. St. Clear, Cornwall. A cromlech. Trevédi, in British, means a *place of graves.*

Tria Juncta in Uno. The motto of the Order of the Bath.

Triads. Three subjects more or less connected formed into one continuous poem or subject : thus the *Creation, Redemption,* and *Resurrection* would form a triad. The conquest of England by the *Romans, Saxons,* and *Normans* would form a triad. *Alexander the Great, Julius Cæsar,* and *Napoleon Bonaparte* would form a triad. So would *Law, Physic,* and *Divinity.* The Welsh triads are collections of historic facts, mythological traditions, moral maxims, or rules of poetry disposed in groups of three.

Trials at Bar. Trials which occupy the attention of the four judges in the superior court, instead of at *Nisi Prius.* These trials are for very difficult causes, and before special juries. (See *Wharton : Law Lexicon,* article " Bar.")

Tri'amond. Son of Ag'apē, a fairy; very daring and very strong. He fought on horseback, and employed both sword and shield. He married Can'acē. (*Spenser : Faërie Queene,* bk. iv.) (*See* PRIAMOND.)

Triangles. *Tied up at the triangles.* A machine to which a soldier was at one time fastened when flogged.

" He was tied up at the triangles, and branded 'D.'"—*Ouida: Under Two Flags,* chap. vii.

Triangular Part of Man (*The*). The body. Spenser says, "The divine part of man is *circular,* but the mortal part is triangular." (*Faërie Queene,* book ii. 9.)

Tribune. *Last of the Tribunes.* Cola di Rienzi, who assumed the title of "Tribune of liberty, peace, and justice." Rienzi is the hero of one of Lord Lytton's most vigorous works of fiction. (1313-1354.)

Tribune of the People (*A*). A democratic leader.

"Delmar had often spoken of Alman, and of his power in the East End, and she had come to the conclusion that he was no ordinary man, this tribune of the people."—*T. Terrell : Lady Delmar,* bk. ii. chap. viii.

Trice. *I'll do it in a trice.* The hour is divided into minutes, seconds, and trices or thirds. I'll do it in a minute, I'll do it in a second, I'll do it in a trice.

Trick. *An old dog learns no tricks.* When persons are old they do not readily conform to new ways. The Latin proverb is " *Senex psittacus negligit ferulam ;* " the Greeks said, " *Nekron iat'reuein kai geronta nou'thetein tauton esti ;* " the Germans say, " *Ein alter hund ist nicht gut kundigen.*"

Tricolour. Flags or ribbons with three colours, assumed by nations or insurgents as symbols of political liberty. The present European tricolour ensigns are, for—

Belgium, black, yellow, red, divided vertically.

France, blue, white, red, divided vertically. (*See below.*)

Holland, red, white, blue, divided horizontally.

Italy, green, white, red, divided vertically.

Tricolour of France. The insurgents in the French Revolution chose the three colours of the city of Paris for their symbol. The three colours were first devised by Mary Stuart, wife of François II. The *white* represented the royal house of France ; the *blue,* Scotland ; and the *red,* Switzerland, in compliment to the Swiss guards, whose livery it was. The heralds afterwards tinctured the shield of Paris with the three colours, thus expressed in heraldic language: " *Paris portait de gueules, sur vaisseau d'argent, flottant sur des ondes de même, le chef cousu de France* " (a ship with *white* sails, on a *red* ground, with a *blue* chef). The usual tale is that the insurgents in 1789 had adopted for their flag the two colours, *red and blue,* but that Lafayette persuaded them to add the Bourbon *white,* to show that they bore no hostility to the king. The first flag of the Republicans was *green.* The tricolour was adopted July 11th, when the people were disgusted with the king for dismissing Necker.

" If you will wear a livery, let it at least be that of the city of Paris—blue and red."—*Dumas: Six Years Afterwards,* chap. xv.

Triest'e (2 syl.). Since 1816 it has

borne the title of "the most loyal of towns."

Tri'gon. The junction of three signs. The zodiac is partitioned into four trigons, named respectively after the four elements: the *watery* trigon includes Cancer, Scorpio, and Pisces; the *fiery,* Aries, Leo, and Sagittarius; the *earthy,* Taurus, Virgo, and Capricornus; and t'ie *airy,* Gemini, Libra, and Aquarius.

Tril'ogy. A group of three tragedies. Everyone in Greece who took part in the poetic contest had to produce a trilogy and a satyric drama. We have only one specimen, and that is by Æschylos, embracing the *Agamemnon,* the *Choëphorœ,* and the *Eumen'idēs.*

Trimilki. The Anglo-Saxon name for the month of May, because in that month they began to milk their kine three times a day.

Trimmer. One who runs with the hare and holds with the hounds. George Savile, Marquis of Halifax, adopted the term in the reign of Charles II. to signify that he was neither an extreme Whig nor an extreme Tory. Dryden was called a *trimmer,* because he professed attachment to the king, but was the avowed enemy of the Duke of York.

Trin'culo. A jester in Shakespeare's *Tempest.*

Trine. In astrology, a planet distant from another one-third of the circle is said to be in trine; one-fourth, it is in square; one-sixth or two signs, it is in sextile; but when one-half distant, it is said to be "opposite."

" In sextile, square, and trine, and opposite
Of noxious efficacy."
Milton: Paradise Lost, x. 659.

N.B. Planets distant from each other six signs or half a circle have opposite influences, and are therefore opposed to each other.

Trin'ity. Tertullian (160-240) introduced this word into Christian theology. The word triad is much older. Almost every mythology has a threefold deity. (*See* THREE.)

American Indians. Otkon, Messou, and Atahuata.

Brahmins. Their "tri-murti" is a three-headed deity, representing Brahma (as creator), Vishnu (as preserver), and Siva (as destroyer).
Celts. Hu, Ceridwen, and Craiwy.
Cherusci. A three-headed god called Triglat.
Chinese have the triple goddess Pussa.
Druids. Taulac, Fan, and Mollac.
Egyptians. Osiris, Isis, and Horus.
Eleusinian Mysteries. Bacchus, Persephone (4 syl.), and Demeter.
Goths. Woden, Frigga, and Thor.
Greece (*ancient*). Zeus (1 syl.), Aphrodite, and Apollo.

Iesini of Britain. Got, Ertha, and Issus.
Mexicans. Vitzputzli, Tlaloc, and Tezcatlipoca.
Peruvians. Aponti, Chureonti, and Intequuequi.
Persians (*ancient*). Their "Triplasian deity" was Oromasdes, Mithras, and Arim'anes.
Phœnicians. Astaroth, Mileom, and Chemoth.
Romans (*ancient*). Jupiter (divine power), Minerva (divine Logos or wisdom), and Juno (called "amor et delicium Jovis").—*Vossius: De Theologia Gentil,* viii. 12. Their three chief deities were Jupiter, Neptune, and Pluto.
Scandinavians. Odin (who gave the breath of life), Hænir (who gave sense and motion), and Lodur (who gave blood, colour, speech, sight, and hearing).
Tyrians. Belus, Venus, and Tamuz, etc.
∴ Orpheus (2 syl.). His triad was Phanēs, Uranos, and Kronos.
Plato. His triad was To Ag'athon (Goodness), Nous or Eternal Wisdom (architect of the World) (*see* Proverbs iii. 19), and Psychē (the mundane soul).
Pythag'oras. His triad was the Monad or Unity, Nous or Wisdom, and Psychē.

Trinoban'tës (4 syl.). Inhabitants of Middlesex and Essex, referred to in Cæsar's *Gallic Wars.* This word, converted into Trinovantes, gave rise to the myth that the people referred to came from Troy.

Trino'da Necessitas. The three contributions to which all lands were subject in Anglo-Saxon times, viz.— (1) *Bryge-bot,* for keeping bridges and high roads in repair; (2) *Burg-bot,* for *Fyrd,* for maintaining the military and keeping fortresses in repair; and (3) naval force of the kingdom.

Tripit'aka means the "triple basket," a term applied to the three classes into which the canonical writings of the Buddha are divided—viz. the Soutras, the Vina'ya, and the Abidharma. (*See these words.*)

Triple Alliance.

A treaty entered into by England, Sweden, and Holland against Louis XIV. in 1668. It ended in the treaty of Aix-la-Chapelle. (*See next page.*)

A treaty between England, France, and Holland against Charles XII. This league was called the Quadruple after Germany joined it. (1717.)

A third (1789) between Great Britain, Holland, and Russia, against Catherine of Russia in defence of Turkey.

A fourth in 1883, between Germany, Italy, and Austria, against France and Russia.

Tripos. A Cambridge term, meaning the *three honour classes* into which the best men are disposed at the final examination, whether of Mathematics, Law, Theology, or Natural Science, etc. The word is often emphatically applied to the voluntary classical examination,

Trismegis'tus [*thrice greatest*]. Hermēs, the Egyptian philosopher, or Thoth, councillor of Osi'ris, King of Egypt, to whom is attributed a host of inventions —amongst others the art of writing in hieroglyphics, the first code of Egyptian laws, harmony, astrology, the lute and lyre, magic, and all mysterious sciences.

Tristram (*Sir*), *Tristrem, Tristan,* or *Tristam.* Son of Rouland Rise, Lord of Ermonie, and Blanche Fleur, sister of Marke, King of Cornwall. Having lost both his parents, he was brought up by his uncle. Tristram, being wounded in a duel, was cured by Ysolde, daughter of the Queen of Ireland, and on his return to Cornwall told his uncle of the beautiful princess. Marke sent to solicit her hand in marriage, and was accepted. Ysolde married the king, but was in love with the nephew, with whom she had guilty connection. Tristram being banished from Cornwall, went to Brittany, and married Ysolt *of the White Hand,* daughter of the Duke of Brittany. Tristram then went on his adventures, and, being wounded, was informed that he could be cured only by Ysolde. A messenger is dispatched to Cornwall, and is ordered to hoist a white sail if Ysolde accompanies him back. The vessel came in sight with a white sail displayed; but Ysolt *of the White Hand,* out of jealousy, told her husband that the vessel had a *black* sail flying, and Tristram instantly expired. Sir Tristram was one of the knights of the Round Table. Gotfrit of Strasbourg, a German *minnesänger* (minstrel) at the close of the twelfth century, composed a romance in verse, entitled *Tristan et Isolde.* It was continued by Ulrich of Turheim, by Honry of Freyberg, and others, to the extent of many thousand verses. The best edition is that of Breslau, two vols. 8vo, 1823. (*See* YSOLT, HERMITE.)

Sir Tristram's horse. Passet'reul.

Triton. Son of Neptune, represented as a fish with a human head. It is this sea-god that makes the roaring of the ocean by blowing through his shell.

" Hear old Triton blow his wreathëd horn [hear
    the sea roar]." *Wordsworth.*

A Triton among the minnows. The sun among inferior lights. *Luna inter minores ignes.*

Triumph. A word formed from thriambos, the Dionysiac hymn.

"Some . . . have assigned the origin of . . . triumphal processions to the mythic pomps of Dionysus, after his conquests in the East, the very word *triumph* being . . . the Dionysiac hymn."—*Pater; Marius the Epicurean,* chap. xii.

Trivet. *Right as a trivet.* (*See* RIGHT.)

Tri'via. Goddess of streets and ways. Gay has a poem in three books so entitled.

    " Thou, Trivia, aid my song.
Through spacious streets conduct thy bard
    along . . .
To pave thy realm, and smooth the broken ways,
Earth from her womb a flinty tribute pays."
                    Gay: Trivia, bk. i.

Trivial, strictly speaking, means " belonging to the beaten road." (Latin, *trivium,* which is not *tres viæ* [three roads], but from the Greek *tribo* [to rub], meaning the worn or beaten path.) As what comes out of the road is common, so trivial means of little value. Trench connects this word with *trivium* (*tres viæ* or cross ways), and says the gossip carried on at these places gave rise to the present meaning of the word.

Trivium. The three elementary subjects of literary education up to the twelfth century—Grammar, Rhetoric, and Logic. (*See* QUADRIVIUM.)

N.B. Theology was introduced in the twelfth century.

Troc'hilus (*The*), says Barrow, " enters with impunity into the mouth of the crocodile. This is to pick from the teeth a leech which greatly torments the creature.

        " Not half so bold
The puny bird that dares, with teasing hum,
Within the crocodile's stretched jaws to come."
            Thomas Moore; Lalla Rookh, pt. i.

Trog'lodytes (3 syl.). A people of Ethiopia, south-east of Egypt. Remains of their cave dwellings are still to be seen along the banks of the Nile. There were Troglodytes of Syria and Arabia also, according to Strabo. Pliny (v. 8) asserts that they fed on serpents. (Greek, *trog'lē,* a cave ; *duo,* to get into.)

"King François, of eternal memory . . . abhorred these hypocritical snake-eaters."—*Rabelais: Gargantua and Pantagruel (Ep. Ded.* iv.).

Trog'lodyte. A person who lives so secluded as not to know the current events of the day, is so self-opinionated as to condemn everyone who sees not eye to eye with himself, and scorns everything that comes not within the scope of his own approval ; a detractor ; a critic. The *Saturday Review* introduced this use of the word. (*See above.*)

‥ Miners are sometimes facetiously called Troglodytes.

Tro'ilus (3 syl.). The prince of chivalry, one of the sons of Priam, killed by Achilles in the siege of Troy (*Homer's Iliad*). The loves of Troilus and Cressida, celebrated by Shakespeare and Chaucer, form no part of the old classic tale.

As true as Troilus. Troilus is meant by Shakespeare to be the type of constancy, and Cressid the type of female inconstancy. (*See* CRESSIDA.)

> " After all comparisons of truth . . .
> ' As true as Troilus' shall crown up the verse,
> And sanctify the numbers."
> *Troilus and Cressida,* iii. 2.

Tro'ilus and Cres'sida (*Shakespeare*). The story was originally written by Lollius, an old Lombard author, and since by Chaucer (*Pope*). Chaucer's poem is from Boccaccio's *Filostrato*.

Trois pour Cent. A cheap hat.

> " Running with bare head about,
>   While the town is tempest-tost,
> 'Prentice lads unheeded shout
> That their three-per-cents. are lost."
> *Désaugiers : Le Pilier du Café.*

Trojan. *He is a regular Trojan.* A fine fellow, with good courage and plenty of spirit; what the French call a *brave homme*. The Trojans in Homer's *Iliad* and Virgil's *Æneid* are described as truthful, brave, patriotic, and confiding.

> " There they say right, and like true Trojans."
> *Butler : Hudibras,* i. 1.

Trojan War (*The*). The siege of Troy by the Greeks. After a siege of ten years the city was taken and burnt to the ground. The last year of the siege is the subject of Homer's *Iliad ;* the burning of Troy and the flight of Ænēas is a continuation by Virgil in his *Æneid*.

The Trojan War, by Henry of Veldig, (Waldeck), a minnesinger (twelfth century) is no translation of either Homer or Virgil, but a German adaptation of the old tale. By far the best part of this poetical romance is where Lavinia tells her tale of love to her mother.

Trolls. Dwarfs of Northern mythology, living in hills or mounds ; they are represented as stumpy, misshapen, and humpbacked, inclined to thieving, and fond of carrying off children or substituting one of their own offspring for that of a human mother. They are called hill-people, and are especially averse to noise, from a recollection of the time when Thor used to be for ever flinging his hammer after them. (Icelandic, *troll*.) (*See* FAIRY.)

> " Out then spake the tiny Troll,
> No bigger than an emmet he."
> *Danish ballad, Eline of Villenskov.*

Trolly. A cart used in mines and on railways. A railway trolly is worked by the hand, which moves a treadle ; a coal-mine trolly used to be pushed by trolly-boys ; ponies are now generally

employed instead of boys. (Welsh, *trol*, a cart ; *trolio*, to roll or trundle, whence " to troll a catch "—*i.e.* to sing a catch or round.)

Trompée. *Votre religion a été trompée.* You have been greatly imposed upon. Similarly, " *Suprendre la religion de quelqu'un* " is to deceive or impose upon one. Cardinal de Bonnechose used the former phrase in his letter to *The Times* respecting the Report of the Œcumenical Council, and it puzzled the English journals, but was explained by M. Notterelle. (See *The Times*, January 1st, 1870.)

⁂ We use the word *faith* both for " credulity " and " religion " — *e.g.* " Your faith (credulity) has been imposed upon." The " Catholic faith," " Mahometan faith," " Brahminical faith," etc., virtually mean " religion."

Troness, Tronis, or **Trophy Money,** or **Trophy Tax.** " A duty of fourpence [in the pound] paid annually by housekeepers or their landlords, for the drums, colours [trophies], etc., of the companies or regiments of militia." (*Dr. Scott's Bailey's Dictionary.*)

Troopers mean troopships, as " Indian troopers," ships for the conveyance of troops to India, especially between February and October, when the annual reliefs of British forces in India are made. Similarly, whaler is a ship for whaling.

Troops of the Line. All numbered infantry or marching regiments, except the foot-guards.

Tropho'nios (Greek), Latin, *Tropho'nius*. *He has visited the cave of Trophonius* (Greek). Said of a melancholy man. The cave of Trophonius was one of the most celebrated oracles of Greece. The entrance was so narrow that he who went to consult the oracle had to lie on his back with his feet towards the cave, whereupon he was caught by some unseen force and violently pulled inside the cave. After remaining there a time, he was driven out in similar fashion, and looked most ghastly pale and terrified ; hence the proverb.

Trou'badours (3 syl.). Minstrels of the south of France in the eleventh, twelfth, and thirteenth centuries ; so called from the Provençal verb *troubar* (to invent). Our word *poet* signifies exactly the same thing, being the Greek for " create." (*See* TROUVÈRES.)

Trouble means a moral whirlwind. (Latin, *turbo*, a whirlwind; Italian, *turbare ;* French, *troubler.*) Disturb is from the same root. The idea pervades all such words as *agitation, commotion, vexation,* a tossing up and down, etc.

Trouil'logan's Advice. Do and do not; yes and no. When Pantag'-ruel asked the philosopher Trouillogan whether Panurge should marry or not, the philosopher replied "Yes." "What say you?" asked the prince. "What you have heard," answered Trouillogan. "What have I heard," said Pantagruel. "What I have spoken," rejoined the sage. "'Good,'' said the prince; "but tell me plainly, shall Panurge marry or let it alone?" "Neither," answered the oracle. "How?" said the prince; "that cannot be." "Then both," said Trouillogan. (*Rabelais : Gargantua and Pantagruel,* iii. 35.)

Trout is the Latin *troct-a*, from the Greek *troktēs*, the greedy fish (*trogo,* to eat). The trout is very voracious, and will devour any kind of animal food.

"[Roland] was ... engaged in a keen and animated discussion about Lochleven trout and sea trout, and river trout, and bull trout, and char which never rise to the fly, and par which some suppose [to be] infant salmon, and herlings which frequent the Nith, and vendisses which are only found in the castle loch of Lochmaben."—*Sir W. Scott : The Abbot,* chap. xxii.

Trouveres (2 syl.) were the troubadours of the *north* of France, in the twelfth, thirteenth, and fourteenth centuries. So called from *trouver*, the Walloon verb meaning "to invent." (*See* TROUBADOURS.)

Trovato're (*Il*) (4 syl.). Manri'co, the son of Garzia, brother of the Comte di Luna. Verdi's opera so called is taken from the drama of Gargia Guttierez, which is laid in the fifteenth century. Trovatore means a troubadour.

Trows. Dwarfs of Orkney and Shetland mythology, similar to the Scandinavian Trolls. There are land-trows and sea-trows. "Trow tak' thee" is a phrase still used by the island women when angry with their children.

Troxar'tas [*bread-eater*]. King of the mice and father of Psycar'pax, who was drowned.

"Fix their council ...
Where great Troxartas crowned in glory
reigns ...
Psycar'pax' father, father now no more !"
Parnell : Battle of the Frogs and Mice, bk. i.

Troy-Novant (London). This name gave rise to the tradition that Brute, a Trojan refugee, founded London and called it New Troy; but the word is British, and compounded of *Tri-nou-hant* (inhabitants of the new town). Civitas Trinobantum, the city of the Trinobantes, which we might render "New-townsmen."

"For noble Britons sprong from Trojans bold,
And Troy-novant was built of old Troyes ashes
cold."   *Spenser : Faerie Queene,* iii. 9.

Troy-town has no connection with the Homeric "Troy," but means a maze, labyrinth, or bower. (Welsh *troi,* to turn ; *troedle,* a trodden place [? street], whence the archaic *trode,* a path or track ; Anglo-Saxon *thraw-an,* to twist or turn.) There are numerous Troys and Troy-towns in Great Britain and North America. The upper garden of Kensington Palace was called "the siege of Troy."

⁂ A Troy-town is about equivalent to "Julian's Bower," mentioned in Halliwell's *Archaic Dictionary.*

Troy Weight means "London weight." London used to be called *Troy-novant.* (*See above.*) The general notion that the word is from *Troyes,* a town of France, and that the weight was brought to Europe from Grand Cairo by crusaders, is wholly untenable, as the term Troy Weight was used in England in the reign of Edward the Confessor. Troy weight is old London weight, and Avoirdupois the weight brought over by the Normans. (*See* AVOIRDUPOIS.)

Truce of God. In 1040 the Church forbade the barons to make any attack on each other between sunset on Wednesday and sunrise on the following Monday, or upon any ecclesiastical fast or feast day. It also provided that no man was to molest a labourer working in the fields, or to lay hands on any implement of husbandry, on pain of excommunication. (*See* PEACE OF GOD.)

Truces. *Faithless and fatal truces.*

The Emperor Antonius Caracalla destroyed the citizens of Alexandria, at one time, and at another cut off the attendants of Artabanus, King of Persia, under colour of marrying his daughter.

Jacob's children destroyed the Shechemites to avenge the rape of Dinah.

Gallienus, the Roman Emperor, put to death the military men in Constantinople.

Antonius, under colour of friendship, enticed Artavasdes of Armenia ; then, binding him in heavy chains, put him to death.

Truchue'la. A very small trout with which Don Quixote was regaled at the road-side inn where he was dubbed knight. (*Cervantes : Don Quixote*, bk. i. chap. ii.)

True Blue—that is, "Coventry blue," noted for its fast dye. An epithet applied to a person of inflexible honesty and fidelity.

True-lovers' Knot is the Danish *trolovelses knort*, "a betrothment bond," not a compound of *true* and *lover*. Thus in the Icelandic Gospel the phrase, "a virgin espoused to a man," is, *er trulofad var einum mannë*.

" Three times a true-love's knot I tie secure ;
Firm be the knot, firm may his love endure."
Gay's Pastorals : The Spell.

True as Touch. The reference is to gold tested by the touchstone (*q.v.*).

" If thou lovest me too much
It will not prove as true as touch."
Love me Little, Love me Long (1570).

True Thomas and the Queen of Elfland. An old romance in verse by Thomas the Rhymer.

True Thomas. Thomas the Rhymer was so called from his prophecies, the most noted of which was the prediction of the death of Alexander III. of Scotland, made to the Earl of March in the Castle of Dunbar the day before it occurred. It is recorded in the *Scotichron'icon* of Fordun. (1430.) (*See* RHYMER.)

Truepenny. Hamlet says to the Ghost, "Art thou there, Truepenny?" Then to his comrades, "You hear this fellow in the cellarage?" (i. 5). And again, "Well said, old mole; canst work?" Truepenny means *earth-borer* or *mole* (Greek, *trupanon*, *trupao*, to bore or perforate), an excellent word to apply to a ghost "boring through the cellarage" to get to the place of purgatory before cock-crow. Miners use the word for a run of metal or metallic earth, which indicates the presence and direction of a lode.

Trulli. Female spirits noted for their kindness to men. (*Randle Holms : Academy of Armory.*)

Trump. *To trump up.* To devise or make up falsely; to concoct.

Trump Card. The French *carte de triomphe* (card of triumph).

Trumpet. *To trumpet one's good deeds.* The allusion is to the Pharisaic sect called the *Almsgivers*, who had a trumpet sounded before them, ostensibly to summon the poor together, but in reality to publish abroad their abnegation and benevolence.

You sound your own trumpet. The allusion is to heralds, who used to announce with a flourish of trumpets the knights who entered a list.

Trumpeter. *Your trumpeter is dead* —*i.e* you are obliged to sound your own praises because no one will do it for you.

Trumpets (*Feast of*). A Jewish festival, held on the first two days of Tisri, the beginning of the ecclesiastical year.

Trundle. A military earthwork above Goodwood. The area is about two furlongs. It has a double vallum. The situations of the portæ are still to be traced in the east, west, and north. The fortifications of the ancient Britons being circular, it is probable that the Trundle is British. The fortified encampments of the Romans were square; examples may be seen at the Broyle, near Chichester, and on Ditching Hill.

Truss his Points (*To*). To tie the points of hose. The points were the cords pointed with metal, like shoe-laces, attached to doublets and hose; being very numerous, some second person was required to "truss" them or fasten them properly.

"'I hear the gull [Sir Piercie] clamorous for someone to truss his points. He will find himself fortunate if he lights on anyone here who can do him the office of groom of the chamber."—*Sir W. Scott : The Monastery*, chap. xvi.

Trusts. The combinations called rings or corners in the commercial world. The chief merchants of an article (say sugar, salt, or flour) combine to fix the selling price of a given article and thus secure enormous profits. These enterprises are technically called "trusts," because each of the merchants is on trust not to undersell the others, but to remain faithful to the terms agreed on.

Truth. *Pilate said, "What is truth?"* This was the great question of the Platonists. Plato said we could know truth if we could sublimate our minds to their original purity. Arcesila'os said that man's understanding is not capable of knowing what truth is. Car'neadēs maintained that not only our understanding could not comprehend it, but even our senses are wholly inadequate to help us in the investigation. Gorgias the Sophist said, "What is right but what we prove to be right? and what is truth but what we believe to be truth?"

Truth in a Well. This expression is attributed both to Clean'thēs and to Democ'ritos the derider.

"Naturam accusa, quæ in profundo veritatem (ut ait Democritus) penitus abstruserit."—*Cicero: Academics*, i. 10.

Try'anon. Daughter of the fairy king who lived on the island of Oléron. "She was as white as lily in May," and married Sir Launfal, King Arthur's steward, whom she carried off to "Oliroun her jolif isle," and, as the romance says—

"Since saw him in this land no man,
Ne no more of him tell I n'can
For soothe without lie."
Thomas Chestre: Sir Launfal (15th century).

Try'gon. A poisonous fish. It is said that Tele'gonos, son of Ulysses by Circē, coming to Ith'aca to see his father was denied admission by the servants; whereupon a quarrel ensued, and his father, coming out to see what was the matter, was accidentally struck with his son's arrow, pointed with the bone of a trygon, and died.

"The lord of Ithaca,
Struck by the poisonous trygon's bone, expired."
West: Triumphs of the Gout (Lucian).

Tsin Dynasty. The fourth Imperial Dynasty of China, founded by Tchaosiang-wáng, prince of Tsin, who conquered the "fighting kings" (*q.v.*). He built the Wall of China (B.C. 211).

Tsong Dynasty. The nineteenth Imperial Dynasty of China, founded by Tchao-quang-yn, the guardian and chief minister of Yông-lee. He was a descendant of Tchuang-tsong, the Tartar general, and on taking the yellow robe assumed the name of Taë-tsou (great ancestor). This dynasty, which lasted 300 years, was one of the most famous in Chinese annals. (960-1276.)

Tu Autem. Come to the last clause. In the long Latin grace at St. John's College, Cambridge, the last clause used to be "*Tu autem misere're mei, Domine. Amen.*" It was not unusual, when a scholar read slowly, for the senior Fellow to whisper "*Tu autem*"—*i.e.* Skip all the rest and give us only the last sentence.

Tu l'as Voulu, George Dandin ('*Tis your own fault, George Dandin*). You brought this upon yourself; as you have made your bed so you must lie on it. (*See* DANDIN.)

Tu Quoque. *The tu quoque style of argument.* Personal invectives; argument of personal application; *argumentum ad hominem.*

"We miss in this work his usual *tu quoque* style."—*Public Opinion.*

Tu-ral-lu, the refrain of comic songs, is a corruption of the Italian *turluru,* and the French *turlureau* or *turelure.* "Loure" is an old French word for a bagpipe, and "toure loure" means a refrain on the bagpipe. The refrain of a French song published in 1697 is—

"Toure loure, lourirette,
Lironfa, toure lourira."
Suite du Théâtre Italien, iii. p. 453.

Tub. *A tale of a tub.* A cock-and-bull story: a rigmarole, nonsensical romance. The *Tale of a Tub* is a religious satire by Dean Swift.

Throw a tub to the whale. To create a diversion in order to avoid a real danger; to bamboozle or mislead an enemy. In whaling, when a ship is threatened by a whole school of whales, it is usual to throw a tub into the sea to divert their attention, and to make off as fast as possible.

A tub of naked children. Emblematical of St. Nicholas, in allusion to two boys murdered and placed in a pickling tub by a landlord, but raised to life again by this saint. (*See* NICHOLAS.)

Tub, Tubbing. Tubs, in rowing slang, are gig pairs of college boat clubs, who practice for the term's races. They are pulled on one side when a pair-oar boat in uniform makes its appearance. Tubbing is taking out pairs under the supervision of a coach to train men for taking part in the races.

Tub-woman (*A*). A drawer of beer at a country public-house.

"The common people had always a tradition that the queen's [Anne] grandmother . . . had been a washerwoman, or, as Cardinal York asserted, a tub-woman—that is, a drawer of beer at a country publichouse."—*Howell: History of England; Anne,* p. 171.

Tuba [*happiness*]. A tree of Paradise, of gigantic proportions, whose branches stretch out to those who wish to gather their produce; not only all luscious fruits, but even the flesh of birds already cooked, green garments, and even horses ready saddled and bridled. From the root of this tree spring the rivers of Paradise, flowing with milk and honey, wine and water, and from the banks of which may be picked up inestimable gems.

Tuck. A long narrow sword. (Gaelic, *tuca,* Welsh *twca,* Italian *stocco,* German *stock,* French *estoc.*) In *Hamlet* the word is erroneously printed "stuck," in Malone's edition.

"If he by chance escape your venomous tuck,
Our purpose may hold there." Act iv. 7.

A good tuck in or *tuck out*. A good feed. To *tuck* is to full, a *tucker* is a fuller. Hence, to cram. The fold of a dress to allow for growth is called a *tuck*, and a little frill on the top thereof is called a *tucker*. (Anglo-Saxon, *tuc-ian*.)

I'll tuck him up. Stab him, do for him. Tuck is a small dirk used by artillerymen. (*See above*.)

Tucker. Food. "A tuck in," a cram of food. (*See above*.)

"'No,' said Palliser, 'we've no food.' 'By Jove!' said the other, 'I'll search creation for tucker to-night. Give me your gun.'"—*Watson: The Web of the Spider*, chap. xii.

Tuffet (*A*). A small tuft or clump. Strange that this word, so universally known, has never been introduced into our dictionaries, to the best of my knowledge.

"Little Miss Muffet
Sat on a tuffet
Eating her curds and whey . . ."
Nursery Rhymes.

Tuft. A nobleman or fellow commoner. So called at Oxford because he wears a gold tuft or tassel on his college cap.

Tuft-hunter. A nobleman's toady; one who tries to curry favour with the wealthy and great for the sake of feeding on the crumbs which fall from the rich man's table. A University term. (*See above*.)

Tug. A name by which collegers are known at Eton. Either from *tog* (the gown worn in distinction to Oppidans), or from "*tough mutton*."

"A name in college handed down
From mutton tough or ancient gown."
The World, February 17, 1883 (p. 31).

Tug of War (*The*), a rural sport, in which a number of men or boys, divided into two bands, lay hold of a strong rope and pull against each other till one side has tugged the other over the dividing line.

Tuileries (*Paris*) [*tile-kilns*]. The palace was on the site of some old tile-kilns. (*See* SABLONNIÈRE.)

Tulcan Bishops. Certain Scotch bishops appointed by James I., with the distinct understanding that they were to hand over a fixed portion of the revenue to the patron. A *tulcan* is a stuffed calf-skin, placed under a cow that withholds her milk. The cow, thinking the "tul-can" to be her calf, readily yields her milk to the milk-pail.

Tulip. The *turban plant;* Persian, *thoulyb'* (*thoulyban*, a turban), by which name the flower is called in Persia.

My tulip. A term of endearment to animals, as "Gee up, my tulip!" or "Kim up, my tulip!" Perhaps a pun suggested by the word *tool*. A donkey is a costermonger's tool.

Tulip Mania. A reckless mania for the purchase of tulip-bulbs in the seventeenth century. Beckmann says it rose to its greatest height in the years 1634-1637. A root of the species called Viceroy sold for £250; Semper Augustus, more than double that sum. The tulips were grown in Holland, but the mania which spread over Europe was a mere stock-jobbing speculation.

Tumbledown Dick. Anything that will not stand firmly. Dick is Richard, the Protector's son, who was but a tottering wall at best.

Tun. Any vessel, even a goblet or cup. (Anglo-Saxon *tunne*.)

"Tun, such a cup as jugglers use to show divers tricks by."—*Minsheu: Spanish Dictionary.*

Tunding. A thrashing with ashen sticks given to a school-fellow by one of the monitors or "præfects" of Winchester school, for breach of discipline. (Latin *tundo*, to beat or bruise.)

Tune the Old Cow Died of (*The*). Advice instead of relief; remonstrance instead of help. As St. James says (ii. 15, 16), "If a brother or sister be naked, and destitute of daily food, and one of you say to them, Depart in peace, be ye warmed and filled; not-withstanding ye give them not those things which are needful to the body; what doth it profit?" Your words are the tune the old cow died of. The reference is to the well-known song—

"There was an old man, and he had an old cow,
But he had no fodder to give her,
So he took up his fiddle and played her the tune—
'Consider, good cow, consider,
This isn't the time for the grass to grow.
Consider, good cow, consider.'"

Tuneful Nine. The nine Muses: Calli'opē (*epic poetry*), Clio (*history*), Era'tō (*elegy* and *lyric poetry*), Euterpē (*music*), Melpom'enē (*tragedy*), Poly-hym'nia (*sacred song*), Terpsic'horē (*dancing*), Thali'a (*comedy*), Ura'nia (*astronomy*).

Tuning Goose. The entertainment given in Yorkshire when the corn at harvest was all safely stacked.

Tunis'ian. The adjective form of Tunis.

Tun'kers. A politico-religious sect of Ohio. They came from a small

German village on the Eder. They believe all will be saved; are Quakers in plainness of dress and speech ; and will neither fight, nor go to law. Both sexes are equally eligible for any office. Celibacy is the highest honour, but not imperative. They are also called Tumblers, and incorrectly Dunkers. Tunker means "to dip a morsel into gravy," "a sop into wine," and as they are Baptists this term has been given them ; but they call themselves "the harmless people." (*W. Hepworth Dixon : New America,* ii. 18.)

Tur'caret. One who has become rich by hook or by crook, and, having nothing else to display, makes a great display of his wealth. A chevalier in Le Sage's comedy of the same name.

Tureen'. A deep pan for holding soup. (French, *terrine,* a pan made of *terre,* earth.)

Turf (*The*). The racecourse ; the profession of horse-racing, which is done on turf or grass. One who lives by the turf, or whose means of living is derived from running horses or betting on races.

" All men are equal on the turf and under it."— *Lord George Bentinck.*

Turk. Slave, villain. A term of reproach used by the Greeks of Constantinople.
You young Turk, a playful reprimand to a young mischievous child.

Turk Gregory. Gregory VII., called Hildebrand, a furious Churchman, who surmounted every obstacle to deprive the emperor of his right of investiture of bishops. He was exceedingly disliked by the early reformers.

"Turk Gregory never did such deeds in arms as I have done this day."—1 *Henry IV.,* v. 3.

Turkey. The bird with a red wattle. A native of America, at one time supposed to have come from Turkey.

Turkish Spy was written by John Paul Mara'na, an Italian, who had been imprisoned for conspiracy. After his release he retired to Mon'aco, where he wrote the *History of the Plot.* Subsequently he removed to Paris, and produced his *Turkish Spy,* in which he gives the history of the last age.

Turlupin, a punster or farceur, with *turlupinade,* and the verb *turlupiner.* It was usual in the 17th century for play-writers in Italy and France to change their names. Thus Le Grand called himself Belleville in tragedy, and Turlupin in farce ; Hugues Guéret took

the name of Fléchelles ; and Jean Baptiste Poquelin called himself Molière, but there was a Molière before him who wrote plays.

Turmeric, like berberry, being yellow, was supposed to cure the yellow jaundice. According to the *doctrine of signatures,* Nature labels every plant with a mark to show what it is good for. Red plants are good for fever, white ones for rigor. Hence the red rose is supposed to cure hæmorrhage. (*See* THISTLES.)

Turncoat. As the dominions of the duke of Saxony were bounded in part by France, one of the early dukes hit upon the device of a coat *blue* one side, and *white* the other. When he wished to be thought in the *French* interest he wore the white outside ; otherwise the outside colour was blue. Whence a Saxon was nicknamed Emmanuel Turncoat. (*Scots' Magazine,* October, 1747.) Without going to history, we have a very palpable etymon in the French *tourne-côte* (turn-side). (*See* COAT.)

Turning the Tables. (*See under* TABLES.)

Turnip-Garden (*The*) So called by the Jacobites. George II. was called the "Turnip-hougher" [hoer], and his hiring of troops was spoken of as "selling the turnips," or "trying to sell his roots." Hanover at the time was eminently a pastoral country.

Turnip Townsend. The brother-in-law of Sir Robert Walpole, who, after his retirement from office in 1731, devoted himself to the improvement of agriculture.

Turnspit Dog. One who has all the work but none of the profit; he turns the spit but eats not of the roast. The allusion is to the dog used formerly to turn the spit in roasting. Topsel says, "They go into a wheel, which they turn round about with the weight of their bodies, so dilligently . . . . that no drudge . . . . can do the feate more cunningly." (1697.)

Turpin, *Archbishop of Rheims.* A mythological contemporary of Charlemagne. His chronicle is supposed to be written at Vienne, in Dauphiny, whence it is addressed to Leoprandus, Dean of Aquisgranensis(Aix-la-Chapelle). It was not really written till the end of the eleventh century, and the probable author was a canon of Barcelo'na.

The romance turns on the expedition of Charlemagne to Spain in 777, to defend one of his allies from the aggressions of some neighbouring prince. Having conquered Navarre and Aragon, he returned to France. The chronicle says he invested Pampelu'na for three months without being able to take it; he then tried what prayer could do, and the walls fell down of their own accord, like those of Jericho. Those Saracens who consented to become Christians were spared; the rest were put to the sword. Charlemagne then visited the sarcophagus of James, and Turpin baptised most of the neighbourhood. The king crossed the Pyrenees, but the rear commanded by Roland was attacked by 50,000 Saracens, and none escaped.

Turtle Doves. Rhyming slang for a pair of gloves. (*See* CHIVY.)

Tussle. A struggle, a skirmish. A corruption of *tousle* (German, *zausen*, to pull); hence a dog is named *Towser* (pull 'em down). In the *Winter's Tale* (iv. 4.), Autol'ycus says to the Shepherd, "I *toze* from thee thy business" (*pump or draw out of thee*). In *Measure for Measure*, Escalus says to the Duke, "We'll *touze* thee joint by joint" (v. 1.).

Tut. A word used in Lincolnshire for a phantom, as the *Spittal Hili Tut. Tom Tut will get you* is a threat to frighten children. *Tut-gotten* is panic-struck. Our *tush* is derived from the word *tut*.

Tutivil'lus. The demon who collects all the words skipped over or mutilated by priests in the performance of the services. These literary scraps or shreds he deposits in that pit which is said to be paved with "good intentions" never brought to effect. (*Piers Plowman*, p. 547; *Townley Mysteries*, pp. 310, 319; etc.).

Twa Dogs of Robert Burns, perhaps suggested by the Spanish *Colloquio de Dos Perros*, by Cervantes.

Twangdillo, the fiddler, lost one leg and one eye by a stroke of lightning on the banks of the Ister.

" Yet still the merry bard without regret
Bears his own ills, and with his sounding shell
And comic phiz relieves his drooping friends.
He tickles every string, to every note
He bends his pliant neck, his single eye
Twinkles with joy, his active stump beats time."
                    Somerville: Hobbinol.

Tweeds. Checked cloths for trousers, etc. The origin of this name is supposed to have been a blunder for "tweels," somewhat blotted and badly written in 1829. The Scotch manufacturer sent a consignment of these goods to James Locke, of London, who misread the word, and as they were made on the banks of the Tweed, the name was appropriated and accordingly adopted.

∴ However, the Anglo-Saxon *twaed* (duplex), which gave rise to *tweddlin* (cloth that is tweeled), and *twedden sheets*, is more likely to have given rise to the word. In fact, *tweels* and *tweddles* both mean cloth in which the woof crosses the warp vertically.

Tweedledum and Tweedledee.

" Some say compared to Bononcini
That mynheer Handel's but a ninny;
Others aver that he to Handel
Is scarcely fit to hold a candle.
Strange all this difference should be
'Twixt Tweedledum and Tweedledee."
                    J. Byrom.

This refers to the feud between the Bononcinists and Handelists. The Duke of Marlborough and most of the nobility took Bononcini by the hand; but the Prince of Wales, with Pope and Arbuthnot, was for Handel. (*See* GLUCKISTS.)

Twelfth (*The*), the 12th of August. The first day of grouse-shooting.

Twelfth Cake. The drawing for king and queen is a relic of the Roman Saturna'lia. At the close of this festival the Roman children drew lots with beans to see who would be king. Twelfth Day is twelve days after Christmas, or the Epiphany.

Twelfth Night (*Shakespeare*). The serious plot is taken from Belleforest's *Histoires Tragiques*. The comic parts are of Shakespeare's own invention. (*See* BEFANA.)

Twelve. *Each English archer carries twelve Scotchmen under his girdle.* This was a common saying at one time, because the English were unerring archers, and each archer carried in his belt twelve arrows (*Sir Walter Scott: Tales of a Grandfather*. vii.).
The Twelve. All the prelates of the Roman Catholic Church. Of course the Twelve Apostles.

" The Pope identifies himself with the ' Master,' and addresses those 700 pre'ates as the ' Twelve.' "
—*The Times*, December 11, 1869.

Twelve Tables. The earliest code of Roman law, compiled by the Decemviri, and cut on twelve bronze tables or tablets (*Livy*, iii. 57; *Diodorus*, xii. 56.)

Twickenham. *The Bard of Twickenham.* Alexander Pope, who lived there for thirty years. (1688-1744.)

Twig. *I twig you ; do you twig my meaning ?* I catch your meaning ; I understand. (Irish, *twigim*, I notice.)

Twinkling. (*See* BED-POST.)

Twins. A constellation and sign of the zodiac (May 21st to June 21st).

" When now no more the alternate twins are fired,
Short is the doubtful empire of the night."
          Thomson: Summer.

Twist (*Oliver*). A boy born in a workhouse, starved and ill-treated ; but always gentle, amiable, and pureminded. Dickens's novel so called.

Twisting the Lion's Tail. Seeing how far the "Britishers" will bear provocation. "To give the lion's tail another twist" is to tax the British forbearance a little further. No doubt the kingdom is averse to war with civilised nations, and will put up with a deal rather than apply to the arbitration of arms. Even victory may be bought too dearly. Such provocation may provoke a growl, but there will the matter end.

Twitcher. *Jemmy Twitcher.* A name given to John, Lord Sandwich (1718-1792), noted for his *liaison* with Miss Ray, who was shot by the Rev. "Captain" Hackman out of jealousy. His lordship's shambling gait is memorialised in the *Heroic Epistle.*

" See Jemmy Twitcher shambles—stop, stop thief ! "

Twitten. A narrow alley.

Two. The evil principle of Pythagoras. Accordingly the second day of the second month of the year was sacred to Pluto, and was esteemed unlucky.

Two an unlucky number in our dynasties. Witness Ethelred II. *the Unready*, forced to abdicate ; Harold II., slain at Hastings ; William II., shot in New Forest ; Henry II., who had to fight for his crown, etc. ; Edward II., murdered at Berkeley Castle ; Richard II., deposed ; Charles II., driven into exile ; James II., forced to abdicate ; George II. was worsted at Fontenoy and Lawfeld, his reign was troubled by civil war, and disgraced by General Braddock and Admiral Byng.

It does not seem much more lucky abroad : Charles II. of France, after a most unhappy reign, died of poison ; Charles II. of Navarre was called *The Bad ;* Charles II. of Spain ended his dynasty, and left his kingdom a wreck ; Charles II. of Anjou (*le Boiteux*) passed almost the whole of his life in captivity ; Charles II. of Savoy reigned only nine months, and died at the age of eight.

François II. of France was peculiarly unhappy, and after reigning less than two years, sickened and died ; Napoleon II. never reigned at all, and Napoleon III., really the second emperor, was a most disastrous prince ; Franz II. of Germany lost all his Rhine possessions, and in 1806 had to renounce his title of emperor.

Friedrich II., Emperor of Germany, was first anathematised, then excommunicated, then dethroned, and lastly poisoned.

Jean II. of France, being conquered at Poitiers, was brought captive to England by the Black Prince ; Juan II. of Aragon had to contend for his crown with his own son Carlos.

It was Felipe II. of Spain who sent against England the "Invincible Armada"; it was Francesco II. of the Two Sicilies who was driven from his throne by Garibaldi ; it was Romulus II. in whom terminated the empire of the West ; Peter II. of Russia died at the age of fifteen, and he was a disgrace to the name of Menschikoff ; Pietro II. de Medicis was forced to abdicate, and died of shipwreck ; James II. of Scotland was shot by a cannon at the siege of Roxburgh ; James II. of Majorca, after losing his dominions, was murdered. Alexander II. of Scotland had his kingdom laid under an interdict ; Alexander II., the Pope, had to contend against Honorius II., the anti-pope ; Alexis II., Emperor of the East, was placed under the ward of his father and mother, who so disgusted the nation by their cruelty that the boy was first dethroned and then strangled ; Andronicus II., Emperor of Greece, was dethroned ; Henri II. of France made the disastrous peace called *La Paix Malheureuse,* and was killed by Montgomery in a tournament ; etc. etc. (*See* JANE *and* JOHN.)

Two Eyes of Greece. Athens and Sparta.

Two Fridays. *When two Fridays come together.* Never (*q.v.*).

Two Gentlemen of Vero'na. The story of Proteus and Julia was borrowed from the pastoral romance of *Diana,* by George of Montemayor, a Spaniard, translated into English by Bartholomew Younge in 1598. The love adventure of Julia resembles that of Viola, in *Twelfth Night.*

Two Strings to his Bow (*He has*). He is provided against contingencies ; if one business or adventure should fail, he has another in reserve; two sweet-hearts; two devices, etc.

Latin : " Duabus anchoris nititur " (*i.e.* " He is doubly moored "), or " Duabus anchoris sis fultus."

Greek : " Επι δυοιν οσμειν."

French : " Il a deux cordes à son arc."

Italian : " Navigar per piu venti."

Two of a Trade never agree. The French say, *Fin contre fin n'est bon à faire doublure—i.e.* Two materials of the same nature never unite well together.

" E'en a beggar sees with woe
A beggar to the house-door go."

Greek : " Kai ptōchos ptōcho phth-onei." (*Hesiod.*)

Latin : " Etiam mendīcus mendico invidit." " Figŭlus figulo invidet, faber fabro " (" Potter envies potter, and smith smith ").

Twopenny Damn. A vague im-precation, said to have been commonly used by the great Duke of Wellington. Some have derived it from the Hindu *dám, dawm* = an ancient copper coin, of which 1,600 went to the rupee. Concerning this derivation Dr. Murray says that it is ingenious, but has no foundation in fact. Goldsmith, in the *Citizen of the World,* uses the expression, "Not that I care three damns."

Tyb'alt. A Capulet; a "fiery" young noble. (*Shakespeare : Romeo and Juliet.*)

It is the name given to the *cat* in the story of *Reynard the Fox.* Hence Mer-cutio says, "Tybalt, you rat-catcher, will you walk?" (iii. 1); and again, when Tybalt asks, "What wouldst thou have with me?" Mercutio answers, "Good king of cats! nothing but one of your nine lives" (iii. 1).

Tyburn is *Twa-burne,* the "two rivulets;" so called because two small rivers met in this locality.

Tyburn's triple tree. A gallows, which consists of two uprights and a beam resting on them. ˉ Previous to 1783 Tyburn was the chief place of execu-tion in London, and a gallows was permanently erected there. In the reign of Henry VIII. the average number of persons executed annually in England was 2,000. The present number is under twelve.

Kings of Tyburn. Public executioners. (*See* HANGMEN.)

Tyburn Ticket. Under a statute of William III. prosecutors who had

secured a capital conviction against a criminal were exempted from all parish and ward offices within the parish in which the felony had been committed. Such persons obtained a Tyburn Ticket, which was duly enrolled and might be sold. The *Stamford Mercury* (March 27th, 1818) announces the sale of one of these tickets for £280. The Act was repealed by 58 Geo. III., c. 70. ˌ

Tybur'nia (London). Portman and Grosvenor Squares district, described by Thackeray as "the elegant, the pros-perous, the polite Tyburnia, the most re-spectable district of the habitable globe.'

T'Year—*i.e.* to-year; as, *to-day, to-night, to-morrow.* (Anglo-Saxon, *to-dæge, to-geare.*)

Tyke. (*See* TIKE.)

Tyler Insurrection. *Wat Tyler's insurrection.* An insurrection headed by Wat Tyler and Jack Straw, in con-sequence of a poll-tax of three groats to defray the expenses of a war with France. (1381.)

Tyl'wyth Teg [*the Fair Family*], A sort of Kobold family, but not of diminutive size. They lived in the lake near Brecknock. (*Davies : Mythology, etc., of the British Druids.*)

Type. Pica (*large type*), *litera picá ta,* the great black letter at the beginning of some new order in the liturgy.

Brevier' (*small type*), used in printing the breviary.

Primer, now called "long primer," (*small type*), used in printing small prayer-books called *primers.*

A fount of types. In an ordinary fount the proportion of the various letters is usually as follows :—

a 8,500	h 6,400	o 8,000	v 1,200
b 1,600	i 8,000	p 1,700	w 2,000
c 3,000	j 400	q 500	x 4 0
d 4,400	k 800	r 6,200	y 2,000
e 12,000	l 4,000	s 8,000	z 200
f 2,500	m 3,000	t 9,000	, 4,500 ; 800
g 1,700	n 8,000	u 3,400	: 2,000 : 600

Typhœ'us. A giant with a hundred heads, fearful eyes, and a most terrible voice. He was the father of the Harpies. Zeus [*Zuce*] killed him with a thunder-bolt, and he lies buried under Mount Etna. (*Hesiod : Theogony.*) (*See* GIANTS.)

Ty'phon. Son of Typhœ'us, the giant with a hundred heads. He was so tall that he touched the skies with his head. His offspring were Gorgon, Geryon, Cerbĕrus, and the hydra of Lernē. Like his father, he lies buried under Etna. (*Homer : Hymns.*) (*See* GIANTS.)

Typhoon'. The evil genius of Egyptian mythology; also a furious whirling wind in the Chinese seas. (Typhoon or typhon, the whirling wind, is really the Chinese *t'ai-fun* [the great wind].)

" Beneath the radiant line that girts the globe,
The circling Ty'phon, whirled from point to
    point,
Exhausting all the rage of all the sky,
And dire Ecneph'ia, reign."
Thomson: Summer.

Tyr. Son of Odin, and younger brother of Thor. The wolf Fenrir bit off his hand. (*Scandinavian mythology.*)

Tyrant did not originally mean a despot, but an absolute prince, and especially one who made himself absolute in a free state. Napoleon III. would have been so called by the ancient Greeks. Many of the Greek tyrants were pattern rulers, as Pisis'tratos and Pericles, of Athens ; Per'iander, of Corinth ; Dionysios the Younger, Gelon, and his brother Hi'ero, of Syracuse ; Polyc'ratēs, of Samos ; Phi'dion, of Argos, etc. etc. (Greek, *turannos*, an absolute king, like the Czar of Russia.)

Tyrant of the Chersonese. Milti'adēs was so called, and yet was he, as Byron says, " Freedom's best and bravest friend." (*See* THIRTY TYRANTS.)

A tyrant's rein. A ranting, bullying manner. In the old moralities the tyrants were made to rant, and the loudness of their rant was proportionate to the villainy of their dispositions. Hence to out-Herod Herod is to rant more loudly than Herod ; to o'erdo Termagant is to rant more loudly than Termagant. (*See* PILATE, VOICE.)

Tyre, in Dryden's satire of *Absalom and Achitophel,* means Holland ; Egypt means France.

" I mourn, my countrymen, your lost estate . . .
Now all your liberties a spoil are made,
Egypt and Tyrus intercept your trade."
Part i. 700-707.

Tyrtæus. *The Spanish Tyrtæus.* Manuel José Quinta'na, whose odes stimulated the Spaniards to vindicate their liberty at the outbreak of the War of Independence. (1772-1857.)

U

U.S. The United States of North America.

Ube'da. Orbaneia, painter of Ubeda, sometimes painted a cock so preposterously designed that he was obliged to write under it, " This is a cock." (*Cervantes : Don Quixote,* pt. ii. bk. i. 3.)

Udal Tenure. The same as "allodial tenure," the opposite of "feudal tenure." Feudal tenure is the holding of a tenement of land under a feudal lord. Udal tenure is a sort of freehold, held by the right of long possession. (Icelandic, *othal,* allodial.)

Ugly means hag-like. Mr. Dyer derives it from *ouph-lic,* like an ough or goblin. The Welsh *hagr,* ugly, would rather point to *hag-lic,* like a hag ; but we need only go to the Old English verb *ugge,* to feel an abhorrence of, to stand in fear of. (Icelandic, *uggligr, uggr,* horror.)

" For tha paynes are so felle and harde . . . .
That ilk man may ugge bothe yhowng and
    awlde."
Hampole, MS. Bowes, p. 189.

Ugly. (*See* PIERRE *du Coignet.*)

Ugly as Sin.

" Sin is a creature of such hideous mien
That to be hated needs but to be seen."
Pope.

Ugoli'no, Count of Pisa, deserted his party the Ghibellines, and with the hope of usurping supreme power in Pisa formed an alliance with Giovanni Visconti, the head of the Guelphic party, who promised to supply him secretly with soldiers from Sardinia. The plot was found out, and both were banished. Giovanni died, but the latter joined the Florentines, and forced the Pisans to restore his territories. In 1284 Genoa made war against Pisa, and Count Ugoli'no treacherously deserted the Pisans, causing their total overthrow. At length a conspiracy was formed against him, and in 1288 he was cast with his two sons and two grandsons into the tower of Gualandi, where they were all starved to death. Dante, in his *Inferno,* has given the sad tale an undying interest.

N.B. Count Ugolino was one of the noble family of Gheradesca, and should be styled Ugolino Count of Gheradesca.

Uhlan (German). A horse-soldier chiefly employed in reconnoitering, skirmishing, and outpost duty.

Uka'se (2 syl.). A Russian term for an edict either proceeding from the senate or direct from the emperor. (Russian, *ukaza,* an edict.)

Ul-Erin. "The Guide of Ireland." A star supposed to be the guardian of that island. (*Ossian : Temora,* iv.)

Ula'nia, Queen of Perdu'ta or Islanda, sent a golden shield to Charlemagne, which he was to give to his bravest paladin. Whoever could win the shield from this paladin was to claim the hand of Ulania in marriage. (*Orlando Furioso*, bk. xv.)

Ule'ma. In Turkey, either a member of the college or the college itself. The Ulema consists of the imaums, muftis, and cadis (ministers of religion, doctors of law, and administrators of justice). "Ulema" is the plural of *ulim*, a wise man.

"The Ulema is not an ecclesiastical body, except so far as law in Mahometan countries is based on the Koran."—*Creasy: Ottoman Turks*, vi. 105.

Ul'ler. The god of archery and the chase. No one could outstrip him in his snow-shoes. (*Scandinavian mythology*.)

Ullin. Fingal's aged bard. (*Ossian*.) *Lord Ullin's Daughter.* A ballad by Campbell. She eloped with the chief of Ulva's Isle, and, being pursued, induced a boatman to row them over Lochgyle during a storm. The boat was overwhelmed just as Lord Ullin and his retinue reached the lake. In an agony of distress, he now promised to forgive the fugitives, but it was too late: "the waters wild rolled o'er his child, and he was left lamenting."

Ul'ric. Son of Count Siegendorf. He rescues Stral'enheim from the Oder, but, being informed by his father that the man he had saved is the enemy of their house, he murders him. (*Byron: Werner.*) *St. Ulric.* Much honoured by fishermen. He died 973 on ashes strewed in the form of a cross upon the floor.

Ulster. A long loose overcoat, worn by males and females, and originally made of frieze cloth in Ulster.

Ulster. *The Red Hand of Ulster.* (*See under* HAND, *The open red hand.*)

Ulster Badge. A sinister hand, erect, open, and couped at the wrist (*gules*), sometimes borne in a canton, and sometimes on the escutcheon. (*See under* HAND *as above.*)

Ulster King of Arms. Chief heraldic officer of Ireland. Created by Edward VI. in 1552.

Ultima Thule. (*See* THULE.)

Ultima'tum (Latin). A final proposal, which, if not accepted, will be followed by hostile proceedings.

Ul'timum Vale (Latin). A finishing stroke, a final coup.

" Atropos, cutting off the thread of his life, gave an *ultimum vale* to my good fortune."—*The Seven Champions of Christendom*, iii. 4.

Ul'timus Romano'rum. So Horace Walpole was preposterously called. (1717-1797.) (*See* LAST OF THE ROMANS.)

⁘ Carlyle so called Dr. Johnson, but he might, with greater propriety, be termed "the last of the Catos." (1709-1784.)

Pope called Congreve "Ultimus Romanōrum." (1670-1729.) (*See* LAST OF THE ROMANS.)

Ultra Vires. Beyond their legitimate powers. Said of a company when exceeding the licence given to it by Act of Parliament. Thus if a company, which had obtained an Act of Parliament to construct a railway from London to Nottingham were to carry its rails to York, it would be acting *ultra vires*. If the Bank of England were to set up a mint on their premises, it would be acting *ultra vires*.

Ultramontane Party. The ultra-Popish party in the Church of Rome. Ultramontane opinions or tendencies are those which favour the high "Catholic" party. Ultramontane ("beyond the Alps") means Italy or the Papal States. The term was first used by the French, to distinguish those who look upon the Pope as the fountain of all power in the Church, in contradistinction to the Gallican school, which maintains the right of self-government by national churches. (*See* TRAMONTANE.)

Ulys'ses (3 syl.), King of Ith'aca, a small rocky island of Greece. He is represented in Homer's *Iliad* as full of artifices, and, according to Virgil, hit upon the device of the wooden horse, by which Troy was ultimately taken. (The word means *The Angry* or *Wrathful*.)

After the fall of Troy, Ulysses was driven about by tempests for ten years before he reached home, and his adventures form the subject of Homer's other epic, called the *Odyssey*.

Ulysses. When Palame'des summoned Ulysses to the Trojan war, he found him in a field ploughing with a team of strange animals, and sowing salt instead of barley. This he did to feign insanity, that he might be excused from the expedition. The incident is employed to show what meagre shifts are sometimes resorted to to shuffle out of plain duties.

Ulysses (*The*). Albert III., Margrave of Brandenburg. He was also called "*The Achilles*" (*q.v.*). (1414-1486.)

The Ulysses of the Highlands. Sir

Evan Cameron, lord of Lochiel, surnamed "The Black." (Died 1719.) His son Donald was called "The Gentle Lochiel."

Ulysses' Bow. Only Ulysses could draw his own bow, and he could shoot an arrow through twelve rings. By this sign Penel'ope recognised her husband after an absence of twenty years.

Ulysses' bow was prophetic. It belonged at one time to Eu'rytus of Œchal'ia.

"This bow of mine sang to me of present war
. . . 'I have heard but once of such a weapon . . .
the bow of Odysseus,' said the queen."—*H. Rider Haggard: The World's Desire,* bk. ii. chap. i.

Uma, consort of Siva, famous for her defeat of the army of Chanda and Munda, two demons. She is represented as holding the head of Chanda in one of her four hands, and trampling on Munda. The heads of the army, strung into a necklace, adorn her body, and a girdle of the same surrounds her waist.

Umber. The paint so called was first made in Umbr.a, Italy.

Umble-pie. A pie made of umbles—*i.e.* the liver, kidneys, etc., of a deer. These "refuse" were the perquisites of the keeper, and umble-pie was a dish for servants and inferiors.

"The keeper hath the skin, head, umbles, chine, and shoulders."—*Holinshed: Chronicle,* i. 204.

Umbra. *Obsequious Umbra,* in Garth's *Dispensary,* is Dr. Gould.

Umbrage. *To take umbrage.* To take offence. Umbrage means shade (Latin, *umbra*), a gloomy view.

Umbrella. Common in *London* in 1710. First used in *Edinburgh* by Dr. Spens. First used in Glasgow in 1780. Mentioned by Drayton in his *Muses Elizium* (1630); but Drayton evidently refers to a sort of fan. Quarles's *Emblems* (1635) also uses the word to signify the Deity hidden in the manhood of Christ. "Nature is made th' umbrella of the Deity" (bk. iv. emblem 14). Drayton's lines are:

" And like umbrellas, with their feathers,
    Shield you in all sorts of weathers."

The *Graphic* tells us, "An umbrella is now being made in London for an African potentate which, when unfurled, will cover a space sufficient for twelve persons. The stick is . . . fifteen feet long."—March 18th, 1894, p. 270.

The Tatler, in No. 238 (October 17th, 1710), says:

" The young gentlemen belonging to the Custom House . . . borrowed the umbrella from Wilk's coffee-house."

So that umbrellas were kept on hire at that date.

✶ Jonas Hanway (born 1712) used an umbrella in London to keep off the rain, and created a disturbance among the sedan porters and public coachmen. So that probably umbrellas were not commonly used in the streets at the time.

" The tucked-up semstress walks with hasty strides,
While streams ran down her oiled umbrella's sides."   *Swift: A City Shower* (1710).
" Or underneath th' umbrella's oily shed
Safe thro' the wet on clinking pattens tread."
       Gay: Trivia, bk. i. (1711).

Umbrella, as, *under Gladstone's umbrella,* means dominion, regimen, influence. The allusion is to the umbrella which, as an emblem of sovereignty, is carried over the Sultan of Morocco. In *Travels of Ali Bey* (*Penny Magazine,* December, 1835, vol. iv. 480), we are told, "The retinue of the sultan was composed of a troop of from fifteen to twenty men on horseback. About 100 steps behind them came the sultan, mounted on a mule, with an officer bearing his umbrella, who rode beside him on a mule. . . . Nobody but the sultan himself [not even] his sons and brothers, dares to make use of it."

" As a direct competitor for the throne—or, strictly speaking, for the shereefian umbrella—he [Muley Abbas] could scarcely hope to escape."— *Nineteenth Century,* August, 1892, p. 314.

✶ In 1874 the sacred umbrella of King Koffee Kalcalli, of the Ashantees, was captured. It was placed in the South Kensington Museum.

U'na (*Truth,* so called because truth is *one*). She starts with St. George on his adventure, and being driven by a storm into "Wandering Wood," retires for the night to Hypocrisy's cell. St. George quits the cell, leaving Una behind. In her search for him she is caressed by a lion, who afterwards attends her. She next sleeps in the hut of Superstition, and next morning meets Hypocrisy dressed as St. George. As they journey together Sansloy meets them, exposes Hypocrisy, kills the lion, and carries off Una on his steed to a wild forest. Una fills the air with her shrieks, and is rescued by the fauns and satyrs, who attempt to worship her, but, being restrained, pay adoration to her ass. She is delivered from the satyrs and fauns by Sir Satyrane, and is told by Archi'mago that St. George is dead, but subsequently hears that he is the captive of Orgoglio. She goes to King Arthur for aid, and the king both slays Orgoglio and rescues the knight. Una now takes St. George to the house of Holiness, where he is carefully nursed, and then leads him to Eden, where their union is consummated. (*Spenser : Faërie Queene*, bk. i.) (*See* LION.)

Una Serranilla [*a little mountain song*], by Mendo'za, Marquis of Santillana, godfather of Diego Hurtado de Mendoza. This song, of European celebrity, was composed on a little girl found by the marquis tending her father's flocks on the hills, and is called *The Charming Milk-maiden of Sweet Fin'ojo'sa.*

Un'anel'ed (3 syl.). Unanointed ; without extreme unction. (Saxon *œll* means "oil," and *an-œll* to "anoint with oil.")

" Unhouseled [without the last sacrament], disappointed, unaneled."
    Shakespeare : Hamlet, i. 5.

Uncas, the son of Chingachcook ; called in French *Le Cerf Agile* (Deerfoot) ; introduced into three of Fenimore Cooper's novels—viz. *The Last of the Mohicans, The Pathfinder, and The Pioneer.*

Un'cial Letters. Letters an inch in size. From the fifth to the ninth century. (Latin *uncia,* an inch.)

Uncircumcised in Heart and Ears (Acts vii. 51). Obstinately deaf and wilfully obdurate to the preaching of the apostle. Heathenish, and perversely so.

Uncle. *Don't come the uncle over me.* In Latin, " *Ne sis patruus mihi* " (*Horace : 2 Sat.*, iii. 88)—*i.e.* do not overdo your privilege of reproving or castigating me. The Latin notion of a *patruus* or uncle left guardian was that of a severe castigator and reprover. Similarly, their idea of a step-mother was a woman of stern, unsympathetic nature, who was unjust to her step-children, and was generally disliked.

" Metuentes patruæ verbera linguæ."—*Horace :*
3 *Odes*, xii. 3.

Uncle. *Gone to my uncle's.* Uncle's is a pun on the Latin word *uncus,* a hook. Pawnbrokers employed a hook to lift articles pawned before spouts were adopted. " Gone to the *uncus* " is exactly tantamount to the more modern phrase " Up the spout." The pronoun was inserted to carry out the pun. In French, " *C'est chez ma tante.*" At the pawnbroker's.

Uncle Sam. (*See* SAM.)

Uncle Tom. A negro slave, noted for his fidelity, piety, and the faithful discharge of all his duties. Being sold, he has to submit to the most revolting cruelties. (*Mrs. Beecher Stowe : Uncle Tom's Cabin.*)

⁂ This tale was founded on the story of *Josiah Henson* (1787), told to Mrs. Stowe by Henson himself.

Unco has two meanings : As an *adjective* it means unknown, strange, unusual ; but as an *adverb* it means very— as unco good, unco glad, etc. The "unco guid" are the pinchbeck saints, too good by half.

"The race of the 'unco guid' is not yet quite extinct in Scotland."—*A Daily Journal.*

Uncumber (*St.*), formerly called St Wylgeforte. " Women changed her name " (says Sir Thomas More) " because they reken that for a pecke of otys she will not faile to *uncumber* them of their husbondys." The tradition says that the saint was very beautiful, but, wishing to lead a single life, prayed that she might have a beard, after which she was no more cumbered with lovers. " For a peck of oats," says Sir Thomas More, " she would provide a horse for an evil housebonde to ride to the Devill upon."

" If a wife were weary of a husband, she offered oats at Poules . . . to St. Uncumber."—*Michael Woode* (1554).

Un'der-cur'rent metaphorically means something at work which has an opposite tendency to what is visible or apparent. Thus in the Puritan supremacy there was a strong under-current of loyalty to the banished prince. Both in air and water there are frequently two currents, the upper one running in one direction, and the under one in another.

Under-spur-leather. An understrapper ; a subordinate ; the leather strap which goes under the heel of the boot to assist in keeping the spur in the right place.

" Everett and Dangerfield . . . were subordinate informers—a sort of under-spur-leathers, as the cant term went."—*Sir W. Scott : Peveril of the Peak,* chap. xli.

Under the Rose [*sub ro'sa*]. (*See* article ROSE.)

Under Weigh. The undertaking is already begun. A ship is said to be under weigh when it has drawn its anchors from their moorings, and started on its voyage.

Under which King, Bezonian ? Which horn of the dilemma is to be taken ? (*See* BEZONIAN.)

Underwriter. *An underwriter at Lloyds.* One who insures a ship or its merchandise to a stated amount. So called because he writes his name under the policy.

Undine' (2 syl.). The water-nymph, who was created without a soul, like all others of her species. By marrying a mortal she obtained a soul, and with it all the pains and penalties of the human race. (*La Motte Fouqué: Undine.*)

⁂ Founded on a tale told by Paracelsus in his *Treatise on Elemental Sprites.* (*See* FAIRY, SYLPHS.)

Ungrateful Guest (*The*). (*See* GUEST.)

Unguem. *Ad unguem.* To the minutest point. To finish a statue *ad unguem* is to finish it so smoothly and perfectly that when the nail is run over the surface it can detect no imperfection.

Unhinged. *I am quite unhinged.* My nerves are shaken, my equilibrium of mind is disturbed : I am like a door which has lost one of its hinges.

Unhou'selled (3 syl.). Without having had the Eucharist in the hour of death. To *housel* is to administer the "sacrament" to the sick in danger of death. Housel is the Saxon *husel* (the Eucharist). Lye derives it from the Gothic *hunsa* (a victim).

U'nicorn. According to the legends of the Middle Ages, the unicorn could be caught only by placing a virgin in his haunts ; upon seeing the virgin, the creature would lose its fierceness and lie quiet at her feet. This is said to be an allegory of Jesus Christ, who willingly became man and entered the Virgin's womb, when He was taken by the hunters of blood. The one horn symbolises the great Gospel doctrine that Christ is one with God. (*Guillaume, Clerc de Normandie Trouvère.*)

⁂ The unicorn has the legs of a buck, the tail of a lion, the head and body of a horse, and a single horn in the middle of its forehead. The horn is white at the base, black in the middle, and red at the tip. The body of the unicorn is white, the head red, and eyes blue. The oldest author that describes it is Cte'sias (B.C. 400) ; Aristotle calls it the Wild Ass ; Pliny, the Indian Ass ; Lobo also describes it in his *History of Abyssinia.*

Unicorn. James I. substituted a unicorn, one of the supporters of the royal arms of Scotland, for the red dragon of Wales, introduced by Henry VII. Ariosto refers to the arms of Scotland thus :

"Yon lion placed two unicorns between
That rampant with a silver sword is seen.
Is for the king of Scotland's banner known."
Hoole, iii.

Unicorn. According to a belief once popular, the unicorn by dipping its horn into a liquid could detect whether or not it contained poison. In the designs for gold and silver plate made for the Emperor Rudolph II. by Ottavio Strada is a cup on which a unicorn stands as if to essay the liquid.

Driving unicorn. Two wheelers and one leader. The leader is the *one horn.* (Latin, *unum cornu,* one horn.)

Unicorns. So whale-fishers call narwhals, from the long twisted tusks, often eight feet long.

Unigen'itus (Latin, *The Only-Begotten*). A Papal bull, so called from its opening sentence, "*Unigen'itus Dei Filius.*" It was issued in condemnation of Quesnel's *Réflexions Morales*, which favoured Jansenism ; the bull was issued in 1713 by Clement XI., and was a *damnatio in globo — i.e.* a condemnation of the whole book without exception. Cardinal de Noailles, Archbishop of Paris, took the side of Quesnel, and those who supported the archbishop against the pope were termed "Appelants." In 1730 the bull was condemned by the civil authorities of Paris, and the controversy died out.

Union Jack. The national banner of Great Britain and Ireland. It consists of three united crosses—that of St. George for England, the saltire of St. Andrew for Scotland, and the cross of St. Patrick for Ireland.

In the Union Jack the white edging of St. George's cross shows the white field. In the saltire the cross is reversed on each side, showing that the other half of the cross is covered over. The broad white band is the St. Andrew's cross ; the narrow white edge is the white field of St. Patrick's cross.

In regard to the word "Jack," some say it is *Jacque* (James), the name of the king who united the flags, but this is not correct. *Jacque* is a surcoat emblazoned with St. George's cross. James I. added St. Andrew's cross, and St. Patrick's cross was added in 1801. (*Jaque,* our "jacket.")

Technically described thus :

"The Union Flag shall be azure, the Crosses saltire of St. Andrew and St. Patrick quarterly per saltire, counterchanged, argent and gules, the latter fimbriated of the second, surmounted by the Cross of St. George of the third, fimbriated as the saltire."—*By order of the Council*.

"Jaque, de l'allemand *jacke*, espèce de petite casaque militaire qu' on portait au moyen âge sur les armes et sur la cuirasse."—*Bouillet: Dictionnaire Universel*.

Union Rose (*The*). The York and Lancaster, the petals of which are white and red; the white representing the white rose of the House of York, and the red representing the red rose of the House of Lancaster.

Unionists. A Whig and Radical party opposed to Home Rule in Ireland. It began in 1886, and in 1895 joined the Conservative government.

Unita'rians, in England, ascribe their foundation to John Biddle (1615-1662). Milton (?), Locke, Newton, Lardner, and many other men of historic note were Unitarians.

United Kingdom. The name adopted on January 1st, 1801, when Great Britain and Ireland were united.

United States. The thirty-six states of North America composing the Federal Republic. Each state is represented in the Federal Congress by two senators, and a number of representatives proportionate to the number of inhabitants. The nickname of a United States man is "a Brother Jonathan," and of the people in the aggregate "Brother Jonathan" (*q.v.*). Declared their independence July 4th, 1776.

U'nities. (*See* ARISTOTELIAN.)

Universal Doctor. Alain de Lille (1114-1203).

U'niverse (3 syl.). According to the Peripatetics, the universe consists of eleven spheres enclosed within each other like Chinese balls. The eleventh sphere is called the empyre'an or heaven of the blessed. (*See* HEAVEN.)

U'niver'sity. First applied to collegiate societies of learning in the twelfth century, because the *universitas litera'rum* (entire range of literature) was taught in them — *i.e.* arts, theology, law, and physic, still called the "learned" sciences. Greek, Latin, grammar, rhetoric, and poetry are called *humanity studies*, or *humaniorēs literæ*, meaning "lay" studies in contradistinction to divinity, which is the study of *divine* things. (*See* CAD.)

Unknown. *The Great Unknown.* Sir Walter Scott. So called because the *Waverley Novels* were at first published anonymously. It was James Ballantyne who first applied the term to the unknown novelist.

Unlicked or **Unlicked Cub.** A loutish, unmannerly youth. According to tradition, the bear cub is misshapen and imperfect till its dam has licked it into form.

Unlucky Gifts. (*See* FATAL GIFTS.)

Unmanned (2 syl.). A man reduced to tears. It is a term in falconry applied to a hawk not yet subservient to man; metaphorically, having lost the spirit, etc., of a man.

Unmarried Men of Note. (*See* WIVES.)

Unmentionables. Breeches.

"Corinthians and exquisites from Bond Street, sporting an eye-glass, . . . waiting-men in laced coats and plush unmentionables of yellow, green, blue, red, and all the primary colours."—*Rev. N. S. Wheaton: Journal* (1830).

Unready (*The*). Ethelred II.—*i.e.* lacking *rede* (counsel). (*, 978-1016.)

Unrighteous [*Adok'imos*]. St. Christopher's name before baptism. It was changed to Christ-bearer because he carried over a stream a little child, who (according to tradition) proved to be Jesus Christ.

Unwashed (2 syl.). It was Burke who first called the mob "the great unwashed," but the term "unwashed" had been applied to them before, for Gay uses it.

"The king of late drew forth his sword
(Thank God, 'twas not in wrath),
And made, of many a squire and lord,
An unwashed knight of Bath."
A Ballad on Quadrille.

Up. *The House is up.* The business of the day is ended, and the members may rise up from their seats and go home.

A.B. is up. A.B. is on his legs, in for a speech.

"*Up, Guards, and at them!*" Creasy, in his *Fifteen Decisive Battles*, states that the Duke of Wellington gave this order in the final charge at the battle of Waterloo. It has been utterly denied by recent writers, but it is the fashion to deny or discredit all cherished traditions. I, for one, wish the tradition were true, because, like Nelson's mot at Trafalgar, it gives a memorable interest to the charge; but alas! we are informed that it was not the Guards, but the 52nd light infantry which broke the column of the French Imperial Guard in the final charge, and "honour to whom honour is due."

Up a Tree. Shelved; nowhere; done for. A 'possum up a gum-tree. (*See under* TREE.)

Up the Spout. In pawn. (*See* SPOUT.)

Up to Snuff. (*See* SNUFF.)

Up to the Hub. Hub is an archaic word for the nave of a wheel, the hilt of a weapon, or the mark aimed at in quoits. If a cart sinks in the mud up to the hub, it can sink no lower; if a man is thrust through with a sword up to the hub, the entire sword has passed through him; and if a quoit strikes the hub, it is not possible to do better. Hence the phrase means fully, entirely, as far as possible. It is not American, but archaic English. (*See* HUB.)

" I shouldn't commune with nobody that didn't believe in election up to the hub."—*Mrs. Stowe: Dred*, vol. i. p. 311.

Up to the Mark. In good condition of health; well skilled in proposed work. "Not up to the mark" means a cup too low, or not sufficiently skilled.

Up-turning of his Glass. *He felt that the hour for the up-turning of his glass was at hand.* He knew that the sand of life was nearly run out, and that death was about to turn his hour-glass upside down.

Upas-tree or *Poison-tree of Macassar.* Applied to anything baneful or of evil influence. The tradition is that a putrid stream rises from the tree which grows in the island of Java, and that whatever the vapour touches dies. This fable is chiefly due to Foersch, a Dutch physician, who published his narrative in 1783. "Not a tree," he says, "nor blade of grass is to be found in the valley or surrounding mountains. Not a beast or bird, reptile or living thing, lives in the vicinity." He adds that on "one occasion 1,600 refugees encamped within fourteen miles of it, and all but 300 died within two months." This fable Darwin has perpetuated in his *Loves of the Plants.* Bennett has shown that the Dutchman's account is a mere traveller's tale, for the tree while growing is quite innocuous, though the juice may be used for poison; the whole neighbourhood is most richly covered with vegetation; men can fearlessly walk under the tree, and birds roost on its branches. A upas tree grows in Kew Gardens, and flourishes amidst other hot-house plants.

" On the blasted heath
Fell Upas sits, the hydra-tree of death."
. *Darwin: Loves of the Plants*, iii. 233.

Upper Crust. The lions or crack men of the day. The phrase was first used in *Sam Slick*. The upper crust was at one time the part of the loaf placed before the most honoured guests. Thus, in Wynkyn de Worde's *Boke of Kervinge* (carving) we have these directions: "Then take a lofe in your lyfte hande, and pare ye lofe rounde about; then cut the ouer-cruste to your souerayne . . ." Furnwall, in *Manners and Meales*, etc., says the same thing—" Kutt the vpper cruste for your souerayne."

" I want you to see Peel, Stanley, Graham, Shiel, Russell, Macaulay, old Joe, and so on. They are all upper crust here."

Upper Storey. The head. "Ill-furnished in the upper storey;" a head without brains.

Upper Ten Thousand or **The Upper Ten.** The aristocracy. The term was first used by N. P. Willis, in speaking of the fashionables of New York, who at that time were not more than ten thousand in number.

Uproar is not compounded of *up* and *roar*, but is the German *auf-ruhren* (to stir up).

Upsee-Dutch. A heavy Dutch beer; *Upsee-Freese* a Friesland strong ale; *Upsee English*, a strong English ale. *Upsee Dutch* also means tipsy, stupid with drink.

" I do not like the dulness of your eye,
It hath a heavy cast; 'tis upsee-Dutch,
And says you are a lumpish whoremaster."
Ben Jonson: The Alchemist, iv. 4.

" Yet whoop, Barnaby! off with thy liquor,
Drink upsees out, and a fig for the vicar."
Sir Walter Scott: Lady of the Lake, vi. 5.

"Teach me how to take the German upsy freeze, the Danish rouser, the Switzer's stoop of Rhenish."
—*Dekker: Gull's Hornbook* (1600).

Up'set Price. The price at which goods sold by auction are first offered for competition. If no advance is made they fall to the person who made the upset price. Our "reserved bid" is virtually the same thing.

Urbi et Orbi [*To Rome and the rest of the world*]: A form used in the publication of Papal bulls.

Urd [*The Past*]. Guardian of the sacred fount called Urda, where the gods sit in judgment. (*Scandinavian mythology*.)

Urda or **Urdan Fount** (*The*). The sacred fount of light and heat, situated over the Rainbow Bridge, Bifrost. (*Scandinavian mythology*.)

Urda, Verdandi, and Skulda. The three Nornir (*Past, Present,* and *Future*) who dwell in a beautiful hall below the ash-tree Yggdrasil'. Their employment is to engrave on a shield the destiny of man. (*Scandinavian mythology*.)

❧ Urd (*Past*) takes the threads from Verdandi (*Present*), and Verdandi takes them from Skuld (*Future*).

¶ "What is that which was *to-morrow* and will be *yesterday*?" Verdandi stands between Skuld (*to-morrow*) and Urd (*yesterday*).

Urgan. A mortal born and christened, but stolen by the king of the fairies and brought up in elf-land. He was sent to Lord Richard, the husband of Alice Brand, to lay on him the "curse of the sleepless eye" for killing his wife's brother Ethert. When Lord Richard saw the hideous dwarf he crossed himself, but the elf said, "I fear not sign made with a bloody hand." Then forward stepped Alice and made the sign, and the dwarf said if any woman would sign his brow thrice with a cross he should recover his mortal form. Alice signed him thrice, and the elf became "the fairest knight in all Scotland, in whom she recognised her brother Ethert." (*Sir Walter Scott: Alice Brand; Lady of the Lake*, iv. 12.)

Urganda la Desconeci'da. An enchantress or sort of Mede'a in the romances belonging to the Am'adis and Pal'merin series, in the Spanish school of romance.

Ur'gel. One of Charlemagne's paladins, famous for his "giant strength."

Uriah. *Letter of Uriah.* (2 Sam. xi. 15.) (*See* LETTER . . .)

U'riel. "Regent of the Sun," and "sharpest-sighted spirit of all in heaven." (*Milton: Paradise Lost*, iii. 690.) Longfellow, in the *Golden Legend*, makes Raphael the angel of the Sun, and Uriel the minister of Mars. (*See* RAPHAEL.)

" I am the minister of Mars,
The strongest star among the stars.
  My songs of power prelude
The march and battle of man's life,
And for the suffering and the strife
  I give him fortitude."
              The Miracle Play, iii.

U'rim, in Garth's *Dispensary*, is Dr. Atterbury.

" Uri m was civil, and not void of sense,
Had humour and courteous confidence. . . .
Constant at feasts, and each decorum knew,
And soon as the dessert appeared, withdrew."
                        Canto i.

Urim and Thummim consisted of three stones, which were deposited in the double lining of the high priest's breastplate. One stone represented *Yes*, one *No*, and one *No answer is to be given*. When any question was brought to the high priest to be decided by " Urim," the priest put his hand into the " pouch" and drew out one of the stones, and according to the stone drawn out the question was decided. (Lev. viii. 8; I Sam. xxviii. 6.)

Ursa Major. Calisto, daughter of Lyca'on, was violated by Jupiter, and Juno changed her into a bear. Jupiter placed her among the stars that she might be more under his protection. Homer calls it *Arktos* the bear, and *Hamaxa* the waggon. The Romans called it *Ursa* the bear, and *Septemtrio'nes* the seven ploughing oxen; whence "Septentriona'lis" came to signify the north. The common names in Europe for the seven bright stars are " the plough," " the waggon," " Charles's wain," " the Great Bear," etc.

· Boswell's father used to call Dr. Johnson *Ursa Major*. (*See* BEAR.)

Ursa Minor. Also called *Cynosu'ra*, or " Dog's tail," from its circular sweep. The pole star is *a* in the tail. (*See* CYNOSURE.)

St. Ursula and the eleven thousand virgin martyrs. Ursula was a British princess, and, as the legend says, was going to France with her virgin train, but was driven by adverse winds to Cologne, where she and her 11,000 companions were martyred by the Huns. This extravagant legend is said to have originated in the discovery of an inscription to *Ursula et Undecimilla Virgines*, " the virgins Ursula and Undecimilla;" but by translating the latter name, the inscription reads " Ursula and her 11,000 virgins." Visitors to Cologne are shown piles of skulls and human bones heaped in the wall, faced with glass, which the verger asserts are the relics of the 11,000 martyred virgins. (*See* VIRGINS.)

Used Up. *Worn out, tired out, utterly fatigued,* or *exhausted*. Used up alludes to articles used up. Worn out alludes to dresses and articles worn out by use. Exhausted alludes to wells, water, etc., dried up. Tired out means tired utterly.

" Being out night after night, she got kinder used up."—*Sam Slick: Human Nature*, p. 192.

Ush'er means a porter. (Old French, *huisher*, a door; whence *huissier*, an usher; Latin, *ostiarius*.) One who stands at the door to usher visitors into the presence. (Scotch, *Wishart*.)

Us'quebau'gh (3 syl.). Whisky (Irish, *uisge-beatha*, water of life). Similar to the Latin *aqua vitæ*, and the French *eau de vie*.

Ut. Saxon *out*, as Utoxeter, in Staffordshire; Utrecht, in Holland; "outer camp town"; the "out passage," so called by Clotaire because it was the grand passage over or out of the Rhine before that river changed its bed. *Utmost* is out or outer-most. (*See* UTGARD.)

"Strain at [*ut,* "out"] a gnat, and swallow a camel."—Matt. xxiii. 24.

Ut Quean Laxis, etc. This hymn was composed in 770. Dr. Busby, in his *Musical Dictionary*, says it is ascribed to John the Baptist, but has omitted to inform us by whom. (*See* Do.)

U'ta. Queen of Burgundy, mother of Kriemhild and Gunther. (*The Nibelungen-Lied.*)

U'ter. Pendragon (chief) of the Britons; by an adulterous amour with Igerna (wife of Gorlois, Duke of Cornwall) he became the father of Arthur, who succeeded him as king of the Silures.

U'terine (3 syl.). *A uterine brother* or *sister*. One born of the same mother but not of the same father. (Latin, *uterus*, the womb.)

Ut'gard (Old Norse, *outer ward*). The circle of rocks that hemmed in the ocean which was supposed to encompass the world. The giants dwelt among the rocks. (*Scandinavian mythology.*)

Utgard-Lok. The demon of the infernal regions. (*Scandinavian mythology.*)

U'ti Posside'tis (*Latin*, as you at present possess them). The belligerents are to retain possession of all the places taken by them before the treaty commenced.

U'ticen'sis. Cato the Younger was so called from U'tica, the place of his death.

Utilita'rians. A word first used by John Stuart Mill; but Jeremy Bentham employed the word "Utility" to signify the doctrine which makes "the happiness of man" the one and only measure of right and wrong.

"Oh, happiness, our being's end and aim....
For which we bear to live, or dare to die."
Pope: Essay on Man, Epistle iv.

Uto'pia properly means *nowhere* (Greek, *ou topos*). It is the imaginary island of Sir Thomas More, where everything is perfect—the laws, the morals, the politics, etc. In this romance the evils of existing laws, etc., are shown by contrast. (1516.) (*See* WEISSNICHTWO.)

Uto'pia, the kingdom of Grangousier. When Pantagruel' sailed thither from France and had got into the main ocean, he doubled the Cape of Good Hope and made for the shores of Melinda. "Parting from Me'damoth, he sailed with a northerly wind, passed Me'dam, Gelasem, and the Fairy Isles; and keeping Uti to the left and Uden to the right, ran into the port of Utopia, distant about three and a half leagues from the city of the Amaurots." (*Medamoth*, from no place; *Me'dam*, nowhere; *Gelasem*, hidden land; *Uti*, nothing at all; *Uden*, nothing; *Utopia*, no place, distant three and a half leagues from *Amauros*, the vanishing point — all Greek.) (*See* QUEUBUS.)

Uto'pian. An impracticable scheme for the improvement of society. Any scheme of profit or pleasure which is not practicable. (*See* UTOPIA.)

U'traquists [*Both - kinders*]. The followers of Huss were so called, because they insisted that both the elements should be administered to all communicants in the Eucharist. (Latin, *utraque specie*, in both kinds.)

Utter and Inner Barristers. An utter or outer barrister means (in some cases at least) a full-fledged barrister, one licensed to practise. An inner barrister means a student. (*See Nineteenth Century*, No. 1892, p. 775, *note*.)

Uz'ziel. The angel next in command to Gabriel. The word means "Strength of God." Uzziel is commanded by Gabriel to "coast the south with strictest watch." (*Milton: Paradise Lost*, iv. 782.)

V

V represents a hook, and is called in Hebrew *vav* (a hook).

V. D. M. on monuments is *Vir Dei Minis'ter*, or *Verbi Dei Minister*.

V. D. M. I. Æ. (*Verbum Dei manet in æternum*). The word of God endureth for ever. The inscription on the livery of the servants of the Duke of Saxony and Landgrave of Hesse, the Lutheran princes, at the Diet of Spires in 1526.

V. V. V., the letters found on the coin of the 20th Roman legion, stand for " Valeria, Vicesima, Victrix."

Vacuum now means a space from which air has been expelled. Descartes says, "If a vacuum could be effected in a vessel, the sides would be pressed into contact." Galileo said, "Nature abhors a vacuum," to account for the rise of water in pumps. (*See* POINT.)

Vac′uum Boylea′num. Such a vacuum as can be produced by Boyle's improved air-pump, the nearest approach to a vacuum practicable with human instruments.

The *Guerickian* vacuum is that produced by ordinary air-pumps, so called from Otto von Guericke, who devised the air-pump.
The *Torricellian* vacuum is the vacuum produced by a mercury-pump.

Va′de Mecum [*a go-with-me*]. A pocket-book, memorandum-book, pocket cyclopædia, lady's pocket companion, or anything else which contains many things of daily use in a small compass.

Væ Victis! Woe to the vanquished.

Vail (*To*). To lower; to cast down. Brutus complained that he had not lately seen in Cassius that courtesy and show of love which he used to notice; to which Cassius replies, "If I have vailed [lowered] my looks, I turn the trouble of my countenance merely on myself. Vexed I am of late . . . [and this may] give some soil to my behaviour."

" His hat, which never vailed to human pride,
Walker with reverence took and laid aside."
Dunciad, iv.

Vails. Blackmail in the shape of fees to servants. (From the Latin verb *valeo*, to be worth, to be of value; French, *valoir*.) The older form was *avails*.

" Vails to servants being much in fashion."
Russell: Representative Actors.

Vain as a Peacock. (*See* SIMILES.)

Valdar′no. The valley of the Arno, in Tuscany.

" — the Tuscan artist [Galileo] views
At evening from the top of Fesole,
Or in Valdarno?"
Milton: Paradise Lost, bk. i. 207-209.

Vale of Avo′ca in Wicklow, Ireland.

" Sweet Vale of Avoca, how calm could I rest
In thy bosom of shade, with the friends I love best."
T. Moore: Irish Melodies, No. 1 (*The Meeting of the Waters.*)

Vale of Tears. This world. (*See* BACA.)

Vale the Bonnet (*To*). To cap to a superior; hence to strike sail, to lower (French, *avaler*, to take off.)

" My wealthy Andrew docked in sand,
Vailing her high-top lower than her ribs."
Shakespeare: Merchant of Venice, i. 1.

Valens or **Vala′nus.** Mercury was the son of Valens and Phoro′nis. This Mercury is called Tropho′nius in the regions under the earth. (*Cicero: De Nat. Deorum*, iii. 22.)

" Ciclin′ius [Mercury] riding in his hirachee
Fro Venus V′lanus might this palais see."
Chaucer: Compl. of Mars and Venus.

Valentia. The southern part of Scotland was so called from the Emperor Valens.

Valentine. A corruption of *galantin* (a lover, a dangler), a gallant. St. Valentine was selected for the sweethearts' saint because of his name. Similar changes are seen in gallant and valiant.

Valentine. One of the Two Gentlemen of Vero′na; his serving-man is Speed. The other gentleman is Proteus, whose serving-man is Launce. (*Shakespeare: Two Gentlemen of Verona.*)

Valentine, in Congreve's *Love for Love.* Betterton's great character.

Valentine (*The Brave*). Brother of Orson and the son of Bellisant, sister of King Pepin and wife of Alexander, Emperor of Constantinople. The twin brothers were born in a wood, near Orleans, and while their mother went in search of Orson, who had been carried off by a bear, Pepin happened to see Valentine and took him under his charge. He married Clerimond, niece of the Green Knight. (*Valentine and Orson.*)

Valentin′ians. An ancient sect of Gnostics. So called from Valentinus, their leader.

Vale′rian or **Valirian.** Husband of St. Cecilia. Cecilia told him she was beloved by an angel who frequently visited her, and Valerian requested he might be allowed to see this constant visitant. Cecilia told him he should do so provided he went to Pope Urban and got baptised. On returning home, he saw the angel in his wife's chamber, who gave to Cecilia a crown of roses, and to himself a crown of lilies, both of which he brought from Paradise. The angel then asked Valerian what would please him best, and he answered that his brother might be brought " to saving faith " by God's grace. The angel approved of the petition, and said both should be holy martyrs. Valerian being brought before Alma′chius, the prefect, was commanded to worship the image of Jupiter, and, refusing to do so, was led forth to execution. (*Chaucer: Secounde Nonnes Tale.*) (*See* CECILIA.)

Vale'rian (the herb). An irresistible attraction to cats. (The word is from the Latin *valēre*, to be well, and hence to make well and keep well.) It is an excitant, antispasmodic, tonic, and emmenagogue. The "Father of Botany" says:

"Valerian hath been had in such veneration, that no brothes, pottage, or physical meates are worth anything, if this be not at one end."

Valhalla, in Scandinavian mythology, is the great hall or refectory of Gladsheim, the palace of the Æsir or Asgard. The *Times*, speaking of Westminster Abbey, says "The Abbey is our Valhalla."

"We both must pass from earth away,
Valhalla's joys to see ;
And if I wander there to-day,
To-morrow may fetch thee."
Frithiof-Saga, lay xi.

Valiant (*The*). Jean IV. of Brittany. (1389-1442.)

Valis'e (2 syl.). A small leather portmanteau. (French, *valise*.)

Valkyriur or **Valkyries.** The twelve nymphs of Valhalla. They were mounted on swift horses, and held drawn swords in their hands. In the *mêlée* of battle they selected those destined to death, and conducted them to Valhalla, where they waited upon them, and served them with mead and ale in cups of horn called skulls. The chief were Mista, San'grida, and Hilda. Valkyriur means "chooser of the slain."

"Mista black, terrific maid,
Sangrida and Hilda see."
Gray: Fatal Sisters.

Valla (*Laurentius*). One of the first scholars of the Renaissance, noted for his Latin sermons, and his admirable Latin translations of Herodotus and Thucydides.

Val'lary Crown. A crown bestowed by the ancient Romans on the soldier who first surmounted the vallum of an enemy's camp.

Valley of Humiliation. The place where Christian encountered Apollyon, just before he came to the "Valley of the Shadow of Death." (*Bunyan: Pilgrim's Progress*, pt. i.)

Valley of the Shadow of Death, through which Christian had to pass in order to get to the Celestial City. The prophet Jeremiah describes it as a "wilderness, a land of deserts and of pits, a land of drought and of the shadow of death" (ii. 6); and the Psalmist says, "Though I walk through the valley of the shadow of death, I will fear no evil,

for Thou art with me ; Thy rod and Thy staff they comfort me" (xxiii. 4).

"The light there is darkness, and the way full of traps and gins to catch the unwary."—*Bunyan: Pilgrim's Progress*, pt. i.

Vallombro'sa. Milton says, "Thick as autumnal leaves that strew the brooks in Vallombrosa" (*Paradise Lost*, i. 302) ; but as the trees of Vallombrosa are chiefly pines, they do not strew the brooks with autumnal leaves. The beech and chestnut trees are by no means numerous.

Valorem. *Ad valōrem.* A sliding scale of duty on excisable articles, regulated according to their market value.

Thus, tea at 4s. per pound would pay more duty than tea at 2s. per pound.

Vamp. *To vamp up an old story.* To vamp is to put new uppers to old boots. Vampes were short hose covering the feet and ankles. (Perhaps the French *avant-pied*, the fore-part of the foot.)

Vampire. An extortioner. According to Dom Calmet, the vampire is a dead man who returns in body and soul from the other world, and wanders about the earth doing mischief to the living. He sucks the blood of persons asleep, and these persons become vampires in turn.

The *vampire* lies as a corpse during the day, but by night, especially at full moon, wanders about. Sir W. Scott, in his *Rokeby* (part iii. chap. ii. s. 3) alludes to the superstition, and Lord Byron in his *Giaour* says,

"But first on earth, as vampire sent,
Thy corse shall from the tomb be rent,
Then ghastly haunt thy native place
And suck the blood of all thy race."

Van of an army is the French *avant ;* but van, a winnowing machine, is the Latin *vannus*, our *fan*.

The Spirit of the Van. A sort of fairy which haunts the Van Pools in the mountains of Carmarthen on New Year's Eve. She is dressed in white, girded with a golden girdle ; her golden hair is very long, and she sits in a golden boat, which she urges along with a golden oar. A young farmer fell in love with her and married her, but she told him if he struck her thrice she would quit him for ever. After a time they were invited to a christening, and in the midst of the ceremony she burst into tears. Her husband struck her, and asked why she made such a fool of herself. "I weep," she said, "to see the poor babe brought into a vale of misery and tears." They were next invited to the funeral of the same child, and she could not resist laughing. Her husband struck her again, and asked the same question. "I laugh," she said, "to think how joyous a thing it is that the child has left a world of sin for a world of joy and innocence." They were next invited to a wedding, where the bride was young and the man advanced in years. Again she wept, and said aloud, "It is the devil's compact. The bride has sold herself for gold." Her husband bade her hold her peace, struck her, and she vanished for ever from his sight. (*Welsh mythology.*)

Van (pl. **Vanir**), in Scandinavian mythology. Gods of the ocean, air, fountains, and streams.

Vandal. One who destroys beautiful objects to make way for what he terms "improvements," or to indulge his own caprice. When Gen'seric with his Vandals captured Rome in A.D. 455, he mutilated the public monuments regardless of their worth or beauty.

"The word 'vandalism' was invented by the Abbé Grégoire, *à propos* of the destruction of works of art by revolutionary fanatics."—*Nineteenth Century* (Aug., 1893, p. 272).

Vandy'ck. *The Vandyck of sculpture.* Antoine Coysevox (1640-1720).
The English Vandyck. William Dobson, painter (1610-1647).

Vandy'ke (2 syl.). To scollop an edge after the fashion of the collars painted by Vandyck in the reign of Charles I. The scolloped edges are said to be vandyked.

Vanessa is Miss Esther Vanhomrigh, and Cade'nus is Dean Swift. While he was still married to Stella [Miss Hester Johnson, whose tutor he had been] Miss Vanhomrigh fell in love with him, and requested him to marry her, but the dean refused. The proposal became known to his wife (?), and both the ladies died soon afterwards. Hester Johnson was called Stella by a pun upon the Greek *aster*, which resembles Hester in sound, and means a "star." Miss Vanhomrigh was called Van-essa by compounding *Van*, the first syllable of her name, with *Essa*, the pet form of Esther. Cade'nus is simply *deca'nus* (dean) slightly transposed.

Vanity Fair. A fair established by Beelzebub, Apollyon, and Legion, for the sale of all sorts of vanities. It was held in the town of Vanity, and lasted all the year round. Here were sold houses, lands, trades, places, honours, preferments, titles, countries, kingdoms,

lusts, pleasures, and delights of all sorts. (*Bunyan: Pilgrim's Progress*, pt. i.)

Va'noc. Son of Merlin, one of Arthur's Round-Table Knights.

" Young Vanoc of the beardless face
(Fame spoke the youth of Merlin's race),
O'erpowered at Gyneth's footstool, bled,
His heart's blood dyed her sandals red."
Sir Walter Scott: Bridal of Triermain, ii. 25.

Vantage Loaf. The thirteenth loaf of a baker's dozen.

Vari'na. Swift, in his early life, professed to have an attachment to Miss Jane Waryng, and Latinised her name into Varina. (*See* VANESSA.)

Varnish, from the French *vernis;* Italian, *ver'nice*. Sir G. C. Lewis says the word is a corruption of Bereni'ce, famous for her amber hair, which was dedicated in the temple of Arsin'oë, and became a constellation. (*See* BERENICE.)

Varro, called "the most learned of the Romans." (B.C. 116-28.)

Varun'a. The Hindu Neptune. He is represented as an old man riding on a sea-monster, with a club in one hand and a rope in the other. In the Vedic hymns he is the night-sky, and *Mitra* the day-sky. Varuna is said to set free the "waters of the clouds."

Vassal. A youth. In feudal times it meant a feudatory, or one who held lands under a " lord." In law it means a bondservant or political slave, as "England shall never be the vassal of a foreign prince." Christian says, in his *Notes on Blackstone*, that the corruption of the meaning of vassal into slave "is an incontrovertible proof of the horror of feudalism in England." (Welsh, *gwas*, a boy or servant; *gwasan*, a page; like the French *garçon*, and Latin *puer;* Italian, *vassallo*, a servant.)

Vath'ek. The hero of Beckford's fairy romance. He is a haughty, effeminate monarch, induced by a malignant genius to commit all sorts of crimes. He abjures his faith, and offers allegiance to Eblis, under the hope of obtaining the throne of the pre-Adamite sultans.

Vat'ican. The palace of the Pope; so called because it stands on the Vati'can Hill. Strictly speaking, the Vatican consists of the Papal palace, the court and garden of Belvidere, the library, and the museum.

"The sun of the Vatican sheds glory over the Catholic world."—*The Times.*

The thunders of the Vati'can. The anathemas of the Pope, which are issued from the Vatican.

The Council of the Vatican. The twenty-first General or Œcumenical Council. It commenced in 1869, Pius IX. being Pope. (*See* COUNCILS.)

Vaude'ville (2 syl.). A corruption of *Val de Vire*, or in Old French, *Vau de Vire*, the native valley of Oliver Basselin, a Norman poet, the founder of a certain class of convivial songs, which he called after the name of his own valley. These songs are the basis of modern *vaudeville*.

Father of the Vaudeville. Oliver Basselin, a Norman poet. (Fifteenth century.)

Vau'girard. *The deputies of Vaugirard.* Only one individual. This applies to all the false companies in which the promoter represents the directors, chairman, committee, and entire staff. The expression is founded on an incident in the reign of Charles VIII. of France: The usher announced to the king "The deputies of Vaugirard." "How many are there?" asked the king. "Only one, and please your majesty," was the answer. (*See* TAILORS.)

Vaux'hall or *Fauxhall* (2 syl.). Called after Jane Vaux, who held the copyhold tenement in 1615, and was the widow of John Vaux, the vintner. Chambers says it was the manor of Fulke de Breauté, the mercenary follower of King John, and that the word should be Fulke's Hall. Pepys calls it Fox Hall, and says the entertainments there are "mighty divertising." (*Book of Days.*)

Thackeray, in *Vanity Fair* (chap. vi.), sketches the loose character of these "divertising" amusements.

Ve. Brother of Odin and Vili. He was one of the three deities who took part in the creation of the world. (*Scandinavian mythology.*)

Veal, Calf. The former is Norman, and the latter Saxon. (*See* BEEF, PORK.)

"Mynheer Calf becomes Monsieur de Veau in the like manner. He is Saxon when he requires tendance, but takes a Norman name when he becomes matter of enjoyment."—*Sir Walter Scott : Ivanhoe.*

Ve'das or **Ve'dams.** The generic name of the four sacred books of the Hindus. It comprises (1) the *Rig* or *Rish Veda;* (2) *Yajar* or *Yajush Veda;* (3) the *Sama* or *Saman Veda ;* and (4) the *Atharva'na* or *Ezour Veda.* (Sanskrit, *vid,* know; Chaldee, *yed-a;* Hebrew, *id-o ;* Greek, *eid-o ;* Latin, *video*, etc.)

Vehm'gerichte or *Holy Vehme Tribunal.* A secret tribunal of Westphalia, said to have been founded by Charlemagne. (*See* FEHM-GERICHT.)

Veil. At one time men wore veils, as St. Ambrose testifies. He speaks of the "silken garments and the veils interwoven with gold, with which the bodies of rich men are encompassed." (St. Ambrose lived 340-397.)

Veiled Prophet of Khorassan. The first poetical tale in Thomas Moore's *Lalla Rookh.*

The Veiled Prophet of Khorassan was Hakim ben Allah, surnamed the Veiled (*Mokanna*), founder of an Arabic sect in the eighth century. Having lost an eye, and being otherwise disfigured in battle, he wore a veil to conceal his face, but his followers said it was done to screen his dazzling brightness. He assumed to be a god, and maintained that he had been Adam, Noah, and other representative men. When encompassed by Sultan Mahadi, he first poisoned all his followers at a banquet, and then threw himself into a burning acid, which wholly destroyed his body.

Vendémiaire (4 syl.), in the French Republican calendar, was from September 22 to October 21. The word means "Vintage."

Vendetta. The blood-feud, or duty of the nearest kin of a murdered man to kill the murderer. It prevails in Corsica, and exists in Sicily, Sardinia, and Calabria. It is preserved among the Druses, Circassians, Arabs, etc. (Latin, *vindicta.*)

Vendredi (French), Friday. (Latin, *Veněris dies.* Here *Vener* is metamorphosed into *Vendre.* The Italian is *Venerdi.*)

Venerable. *The Venerable.* Bede, the ecclesiastical historian. (672-735.)

The Venerable Doctor. William de Champeaux, founder of realism. (Twelfth century.)

Peter, Abbot of Clugny. (1093-1156.)

Vengeur (*Le*). A man-of-war commanded by Cambrone. The tale is this : June 1, 1794, Lord Howe encountered the French fleet off Ushant. Six ships were taken by the English admiral, and the victory was decisive : but *Le Vengeur*, although reduced to a mere hulk, refused to surrender, and, discharging a last broadside, sank in the waves, while the crew shouted "*Vive la République !*" The Convention ordered a medal to be struck with this legend—*Le Triomphe* *du Vengeur.* It is almost a pity that this thoroughly French romance should lack one important item — a grain of truth. The day of this victory is often called "The Glorious First of June." The historic fact is, the ship sank, with the crew crying for help, which was readily given by the British foe.

> "We'll show the haughty British race
> The Frenchman can such honour boast—
> That when one *Vengeur* we have lost,
> Another hastes to take her place.
> *Translated by J. Oxenford.*

Veni, Crea′tor Spiritus. A hymn of the Roman Breviary used on the Feast of Pentecost. It has been ascribed to Charlemagne, but Mone thinks that Pope Gregory I. was the author.

Veni, Sancte Spiritus. A Latin hymn in rhyme, ascribed to Robert, King of France, also to Archbishop Langton.

Veni, Vidi, Vici. It was thus that Julius Cæsar announced to his friend Amintius his victory at Zela, in Asia Minor, over Pharna′cēs, son of Mithrida′tēs, who had rendered aid to Pompey. (*Plutarch.*)

Ve′nial Sin. One that may be pardoned ; one that does not forfeit grace. In the Catholic Church sins are of two sorts, mortal and venial ; in the Protestant Church there is no such distinction ; but see Matt. xii. 31.

Venice Glass. The drinking glasses of the Middle Ages, made at Venice, were said to break into shivers if poison were put into them.

> *Doge.* "'Tis said that our Venetian crystal has
> Such pure antipathy to poison, as
> To burst, if aught of venom touches it."
> *Byron : The Two Foscari,* v. 1.

Venice glass, from its excellency, became a synonym for *perfection.*

Venice of the West. Glasgow.

"Another element in the blazon of the 'Venice of the West' is a fish laid across the stem of the tree, 'in base,' as the heralds say."—*J. H. Burton.*

Ven′ison. Anything taken in hunting or by the chase. Hence Jacob bids Esau to go and get venison such as he loved (Gen. xxvii. 3), meaning the wild kid. The word is simply the Latin *vena′tio* (hunting), but is now restricted to the flesh of deer.

Ven′om. *The venom is in the tail.* The real difficulty is the conclusion. The allusion is to the scorpion, which has a sting in its tail.

The French say, "It is always most difficult to flay the tail" (*Il n'y a rien de plus difficile à écorcher que la queue*).

Venomous Preacher (*The*). Robert Traill (1642-1716).

Ventilate a Subject (*To*). To moot it, to throw it out for discussion that it may be winnowed or sifted. To ventilate a room is to let air and light into it, to drive away bad gases, etc. So in ventilating a subject, light is thrown on it, and all that is false, extraneous, or doubtful is blown away.

Ventre-saint-Gris ! The usual oath of Henri IV. About equal to "*Corpus Christi.*" A similar juron is "*Par le ventre de Dieu*" (*Ventre-dieu !* or *Ventrebleu !*). Cris for Christ is familiarised by our common phrase "the criss-cross or cris-cross row" ; and if *saint* refers to Christ we have a similar phrase in St. Saviour's. Rabelais has "*Par sainct Gris*" ; and William Price, "the Arch-Druid," who died in 1893, describes himself in the *Medical Directory* as "Decipherer of the Pedigree of Jessu Grist." Chaucer writes the word "Crist."

⁂ Mr. F. Adams has sent me two quotations from the *Romance of Huon de Bordeau,* from a MS. dated 1250—

> "Abes, dist Karles, tort avés, par saint Crist."
> (Line 1,473.)
> "Sire, dist Hues, tort aves, par saint Crist."
> (Line 2,218.)

But a correspondent of *Notes and Queries* sends this quotation—

> "Ce prince [Henri IV.] avoit pris l'habitude d'employer cette expression, 'Ventre-saint-Gris,' comme une espèce de jurement, lorsqu'il étoit encore infant, ses gouverneurs craignant qu'il ne s' habitual à jurer . . . lui avoient permis de dire 'Ventre-saint-Gris,' qui étoit un terme derision qu'ils appliquoent aux Franciscans . . . de la couleur de leur habillements."—Feb. 10th, 1894, p. 113.

Ventril′oquism, "speaking from the belly." From the erroneous notion that the voice of the ventriloquist proceeded from his stomach. The best that ever lived was Brabant, the "engastrimist" of François I. (Latin, *venter-loquor.*)

Venus. Love : the goddess of love ; courtship. Copper was called Venus by the alchemists. (*See* APHRODITE.)

> "Venus smiles not in a house of tears."
> *Shakespeare : Romeo and Juliet,* iv. 1.

Venus is the name of the second planet from the sun, and the nearest heavenly body to the earth except the moon.

Statues of Venus. The most celebrated statues of this goddess are the Venus de Medici, the Aphrodite of Praxit′elēs, the Venus of Milo, the Venus Victorious of Cano′va, and the Venus of Gibson.

Capitoline Venus (*The*). In the Capitoline Museum of Rome.

Canova's Venus is the most noted of modern sculpture. (1757-1822.)

Ura'nian Venus of the *Lusiad* is the impersonation of heavenly love. She pleads to Destiny for the Lusians, and appears to them in the form of "the silver star of love." Plato says she was the daughter of Heaven (*U'ranos*), and Xenophon adds that "she presided over the love of wisdom and virtue, the pleasures of the *soul*." 'Nigidius says that this "heavenly Venus" was not born from the sea-foam, but from an egg which two fishes conveyed to the sea-shore. This egg was hatched by two pigeons whiter than snow, and gave birth to the Assyrian Venus, who instructed mankind in religion, virtue, and equity. (*See* APHRODITE.)

Venus in astrology "signifiethe white men or browne . . . . joyfull, laughter, liberall, pleasers, dauncers, entertayners of women, players, perfumers, musitions, messengers of love."

> " Venus loveth ryot and dispense."
> *Chaucer : Canterbury Tales*, 6,282.

My Venus turns out a whelp (Latin). All my swans are changed to geese ; my cake is dough. In dice the best cast (three sixes) was called "Venus," and the worst (three aces) was called "Canis." My win-all turns out to be a lose-all.

The Island of Venus in the *Lusiad* is a paradisa'ical island raised by "Divine Love," as a reward for the heroes of the poem. Here Venus, the ocean-goddess, gave her hand to Gama, and committed to him the empire of the sea. It was situate "near where the bowers of Paradise are placed," not far from the mountains of Ima'us, whence the Ganges and Indus derive their source. This paradise of Love is described in the ninth book.

⁂ We have several parallel Edens, as the "gardens of Alcin'ous," in the *Odyssey*, bk. vii. ; the "island of Circē," *Odyssey*, x. ; the "Elysium" of Virgil, *Æneid*, vi. ; the "island and palace of Alci'na" or Vice, in *Orlando Furioso*, vi. vii. ; the "country of Logistilla" or Virtue, in the same epic, bk. x. ; the description of "Paradise," visited by Astolpho, the English duke, in bk. xxxiv. ; the "island of Armi'da," in Tasso's *Jerusalem Delivered*; the "bower of Acras'ia," in Spenser's *Faërie Queene*; the "palace with its forty doors," the keys of which were entrusted to prince Agib, whose adventures form the tale of the "Third Calendar," in *The Arabian Nights' Entertainments*. etc. E. A. Poe

calls Eden "Aiden," which he rhymes with "laden." (*The Raven*, 16.) (*See* VENUSBERG.)

Venus Anadyom'ene (6 syl.). Venus rising from the sea, accompanied by dolphins.

Venus Genetrix. Worshipped at Rome, especially on April day, as the mother of Æneas, and patroness of the Julian race.

Venus Victrix. Venus, as goddess of victory, represented on numerous Roman coins.

Venus de Medicis, supposed to be the production of Cleom'enēs of Athens, who lived in the second century before the Christian era. In the seventeenth century it was dug up in the villa of Hadrian, near Tivoli, in eleven pieces ; but it is all ancient except the right arm. It was removed in 1680, by Cosmo III., to the Imperial Gallery at Florence, from the Medici Palace at Rome.

> " So stands the statue that enchants the world,
> So bending tries to veil the matchless boast,
> The mingled beauties of exulting Greece."
> *Thomson : Summer.*

Venus of Cnidus. The *undraped* statue of Praxit'eles (4 syl.) purchased by the ancient Cnidians, who refused to part with it, although Nicome'dēs, King of Bithyn'ia, offered to pay off their national debt as a price for it. The statue was subsequently removed to Constantinople, and perished in the great fire during the reign of Justinian. (A.D. 80.)

Praxiteles made also a *draped* statue of the same goddess, called the "Venus of Cos."

Venus of Milo or **Melos.** The statue, with three of Hermēs, was discovered in 1820 by Admiral Dumont in Milo or Melos, one of the Greek islands, whence its name. It now stands in the Louvre.

Ve'nusberg'. The mountain of delight and love, where Lady Venus holds her court. Human beings occasionally are permitted to visit her, as Heinrich von Limburg did, and the noble Tannhäuser (*q.v.*) ; but as such persons run the risk of eternal perdition, Eckhardt the Faithful, who sat before the gate, failed not to warn them against entering. (*German Legend : Children of Limburg, a poem.* (1337.) (See *The Island of Venus.*)

Vera Causa. A cause in harmony with other causes already known. A fairy godmother may be assigned in story as the cause of certain marvellous effects, but is not a *vera causa.* The revolution of the earth round the sun may be assigned as the cause of the four seasons, and is a *vera causa.*

Verba'tim et Litera'tim. Accurately rendered, word for word and letter for letter.

Verbum Sap. [*A word to the wise.*] A hint is sufficient to any wise man ; a threat implying if the hint is not taken I will expose you. (Latin, *Verbum sapienti.*)

Verbum Sat. [*A word is enough.*] Similar to the above. (Latin, *Verbum sat* [*satienti*]. A word to the wise is enough.)

Ve're Adep'tus. One admitted to the fraternity of the Rosicrucians.

" In Rosycrucian lore as learned
As he the Vere-adeptus earned."
Butler : Hudibras.

Verger. The officer in a church who carries the rod or mace. (Latin, *verga,* a wand.)

Vernon, mentioned by Thomson in his *Summer,* was Admiral Edward Vernon, who attacked Carthage'na in 1741 ; but the malaria reached the crew, and, as the poet says—

" To infant weakness sunk the warrior's arms."

Diana Vernon. An enthusiastic Royalist of great beauty and talent. (*Sir Walter Scott : Rob Roy.*)

Verone'se (3 syl.). A native of Vero'na, pertaining to Verona, etc. ; a Paul Veronese, Paul a native of Verona ; a Veronese fashion, and so on.

Veron'ica. It is said that a maiden handed her handkerchief to our Lord on His way to Calvary. He wiped the sweat from His brow, returned the handkerchief to the owner, and went on. The handkerchief was found to bear a perfect likeness of the Saviour, and was called *Vera-Icon'ica* (true likeness), and the maiden was ever after cailed St. Veronica. One of these handkerchiefs is preserved at St. Peter's church in Rome, and another in Milan cathedral.

Versailles of Poland. The palace of the Counts of Braniski, which now belongs to the municipality of Bialystok.

Versaillese (*The*). The government troops, in the presidency of M. Thiers. The Communist troops were called the Federals, short for the " Federated National Guards."

Versi Bernes'chi. Jocose poetry.

So called from Francesco Berni, the Italian poet. (1490-1536.)

Vert [*green*], in heraldry, signifies love, joy, and abundance. It is represented on the shields of noblemen by the emerald, and on those of kings by the planet Venus.

⁂ In heraldry vert is symbolically expressed by diagonal lines running from right to left of the shield. Lines running the reverse way—*i.e.* from left to right—mean purpure.

N.B. English heralds vary escutcheons by only seven colours, but foreign heralds employ nine colours. (*See* HERALDS.)

Vertum'nus. The god of the seasons, who married Pomo'na. August 12th was his festival. (*Roman mythology.*)

Ver'ulam Buildings (London). So named in compliment to Lord Bacon, who was Baron Verulam and Viscount St. Albans.

Vervain. Called " holy herb," from its use in ancient sacred rites. Also called " pigeons' grass," " Juno's tears," and " simpler's joy." Supposed to cure scrofula, the bite of rabid animals, to arrest the diffusion of poison, to avert antipathies, to conciliate friendships, and to be a pledge of mutual good faith ; hence it was anciently worn by heralds and ambassadors. (*See* ROODSELKEN.) Verbena is the botanical name.

"The term Verbena (quasi *herbena*) originally denoted all those herbs that were held sacred on account of their being employed in the rites of sacrifice."—*Mill : Logic,* book iv. chap. v. p. 485.

Vesi'ca Piscis (Latin, *fish-bladder*). The ovoidal frame or glory which, in the twelfth century, was much used, especially in painted windows, to surround pictures of the Virgin Mary and of our Lord. It is meant to represent a fish, from the anagram ICHTHUS. (*See* NOTARICA.)

Vesper Hour is said to be *between the dog and the wolf;* " betwixt and between," neither day nor night ; a breed between the dog and wolf ; too much day to be night, and too much night to be day. Probably the phrase was suggested by the terms "dog watch" (which begins at four), and " dark as a wolf's mouth."

Sicilian Vespers. Easter Monday, March 30, 1282. So called because John of Pro'cida on that day led a band of conspirators against Charles d'Anjou and his French countrymen in Sicily. These

Frenchmen greatly oppressed the Sicilians, and the conspirators, at the sound of the vesper bell, put them all to the sword without regard to age or sex.
The Fatal Vespers. October 26th, 1623. A congregation of some 300 persons had assembled in a small gallery over the gateway of the French ambassador, in Blackfriars, to hear Father Drury, a Jesuit, preach. The gallery gave way, and about 100 of the congregation were precipitated into the street and killed. Drury and a priest named Redman were also killed. This accident was, according to the bigotry of the times, attributed to God's judgment against the Jesuits. (*Stow: Chronicles.*) (*See* St. Luke xiii. 4.)

Vesta, in Roman mythology, was the Home-goddess, called by the Greeks "Hestia." She was custodian of the sacred fire brought by Æneas from Troy. This fire was lighted afresh annually on March day, and to let it go out would have been regarded as a national calamity.

Vestal Virgin. A nun, a religieuse; properly a maiden dedicated to the service of the goddess Vesta. The duty of these virgins was to keep the fire of the temple always burning, both day and night. They were required to be of spotless chastity. (*See* IMMURING.)

Veto (*Monsieur and Madame*). Louis XVI. and Marie Antoinette. So called by the Republicans, because the Constituent Assembly allowed the king to have the power of putting his veto upon any decree submitted to him. (1791.)

Monsieur Veto swore he'd bide
To the constitution true;
But he cast his oath aside,
Teaching us the like to do.
Madame Veto swore one day
All the Paris rout to slay;
But we snapped the tyrant's yoke,
Turning all her threats to smoke.
E. C. B.

Vetturino [*Vettu-ree'no*], in Italy, is one who for hire conveys persons about in a *vet'tura* or four-wheeled carriage; the owner of a livery stable; a guide for travellers. The two latter are, of course, subsidiary meanings.

"We were accosted in the steamer by a well-dressed man, who represented himself to be a *vetturino*."—*The Times (One of the Alpine Club).*

Vi'a Doloro'sa. The way our Lord went to the Hall of Judgment, from the Mount of Olives to Golgotha, about a mile in length.

Vial. *Vials of wrath.* Vengeance, the execution of wrath on the wicked.

The allusion is to the seven angels who pour out upon the earth their vials full of wrath. (Rev. xvi.)

Viat'icum (Latin). The Eucharist administered to the dying. The word means "money allowed for a journey," and the notion is that this sacrament will be the spirit's passport to Paradise.

Vic'ar. *Rector,* one who receives both great and small tithes. *Vicar* receives only the small tithes. At the Reformation many livings which belonged to monasteries passed into the hands of noblemen, who, not being in holy orders, had to perform the sacred offices *vica-riously.* The clergyman who offi iated for them was ca'led their *vicar* or representative, and the law enjoined that the lord should allow him to receive the use of the glebe and all tithes except those accruing from grain (such as corn, barley, oats, rye, etc.), hay, and wood.

The term Vicar is now applied to the minister of a district church, though he receives neither great nor small tithes; his stipend arising partly from endowment, partly from pew-rents, and in part from fees, voluntary contributions, offerings, and so on. The vicar of a pope is a Vicar-apostolic, and the vicar of a bishop is a curate or vicar in charge.

A lay vicar is a cathedral officer who sings certain portions of the service. The Pope is called the "Vicar of Christ."

Vicar of Bray (*The*). *Let who will be king, I will be vicar of Bray still.* Brome says of Simon Alleyn that he "lived in the reigns of Henry VIII., Edward VI., Mary, and Elizabeth. In the first two reigns he was Protestant, in Mary's reign he turned Papist, and in the next reign recanted—being resolved, whoever was king, to die Vicar of Bray." (1540-1588.) Others say it is Pendleton.

Ray refers to Simon Symonds, a vicar who was Independent in the Protectorate, Churchman in the reign of Charles II., Papist under James II., and Moderate Protestant under William and Mary.

The well-known song, "I will be Vicar of Bray," was written by an officer in Colonel Fuller's regiment. This vicar lived in the reigns of Charles II., James II., William III., Anne, and George I.

Vicar of Wakefield (*The*). Dr. Primrose.

Vice (1 syl.), in Old English moralities, was a buffoon who wore a cap with ass's ears.

Vi'ce Versa (Latin). The reverse; the terms of the case being reversed.

Victor Emmanuel of Italy, called *King Honest-Man,* for his honest concessions to the people of constitutional freedom promised by his father and by himself in less prosperous circumstances.

Vierge (2 syl.). A curious conversion in playing-cards occurs in reference to this word. The invention is Indian, and the game is called "The Four Rajahs." The pieces are the king, his general or *fierche,* the elephant or *phil,* the horsemen, the camel or *ruch,* and the infantry. The French corrupted *fierche* (general) into "vierge," and then converted "virgin" into *dame.* Similarly they corrupted *phil* into "fol" or "fou" (knave); *ruch* is our "rook." At one time playing-cards were called "the Books of the Four Kings," and chess "the Game of the Four Kings." It was for chess, and not cards, that Walter Sturton, in 1278, was paid 8s. 5d., according to the wardrobe rolls of Edward I., "*ad opus regis ad ludendum adquatuor reges.*" Malkin said it was no great proof of our wisdom that we delighted in cards, seeing they were "invented for a fool." Malkin referred to the vulgar tradition that cards were invented for the amusement of Charles VI., the idiot king of France; but it was no proof that Jacquemin Gringonneur *invented* cards because "he painted and gilded three packs for the king in 1392."

View-holloa. The shout of huntsmen when a fox breaks cover = "Gone away!" (*See* SOHO, TALLY-HO.)

Vignette (2 syl.) means properly a likeness having a border of vine-leaves round it. (French, "little vine, tendril.")

Vi'king. A pirate. So called from the *vik* or creek in which he lurked. The word is wholly unconnected with the word "king." There were *sea-kings,* sometimes, but erroneously, called "vikings," connected with royal blood, and having small dominions on the coast. These sea-kings were often vikingr or vikings, but the reverse is not true that every viking or pirate was a sea-king. (Icelandic *vikingr,* a pirate.)

Village Blacksmith (*The*), in Longfellow's poem, we are told in an American newspaper, was Henry Francis Moore, of Medford, Massachusetts, born 1830. But as the *Village Blacksmith* was published in 1842, this is impossible, as Moore was not then twelve years of

age, and could not have had a grown-up daughter who sang in the village choir.

Vil'lain means simply one attached to a villa or farm. In feudal times the lord was the great landowner, and under him were a host of tenants called villains. The highest class of villains were called *regardant,* and were annexed to the manor; then came the *Coliberti* or *Burēs,* who were privileged vassals; then the *Bord'arii* or cottagers (Saxon, *bord,* a cottage), who rendered certain menial offices to their lord for rent; then the *Coscets, Cottarii,* and *Cotmanni,* who paid partly in produce and partly in menial service; and, lastly, the villains in *gross,* who were annexed to the person of the lord, and might be sold or transferred as chattels. The notion of wickedness and worthlessness associated with the word is simply the effect of aristocratic pride and exclusiveness—not, as Christian says in his *Notes on Blackstone,* "a proof of the horror in which our forefathers held all service to feudal lords." The French *vilain* seems to connect the word with *vile,* but it is probable that vile is the Latin *vilis vile* (of no value), and that the noun *vilain* is independent of *villein,* except by way of pun. (*See* CHEATER.)

"I am no villain [base-born]; I am the youngest son of Sir Rowland de Boys; he was my father, and he is thrice a villain [rascal] that says such a rather begot villains [bastards]."—*Shakespeare: As You Like It,* i. 1.

Villiers. Second Duke of Buckingham. (1627-1688.)

Villoner. (French.) To cheat. Villon was a poet in the reign of Louis XI., but more famous for his cheats and villainies than for his verses. Hence the word *villoner,* "to cheat, to play a rogue's trick." (*Rabelais: Pantagruel,* iv. 17; note *by Molleux.*)

Vincent (*St.*). Patron saint of drunkards. This is from the proverb—

"If on St. Vincent's Day [Jan. 22] the sky is clear, More wine than water will crown the year."

Vincent de la Rosa. The son of a poor labourer who had served as a soldier. According to his own account, "he had slain more Moors than ever Tunis or Morocco produced; and as for duels, he had fought a greater number than ever Gantë had, or Luna either, or Diego Garcia de Paredez, always coming off victorious, and without losing a drop of blood." He dressed "superbly," and though he had but three suits, the villagers thought he had ten or a dozen, and more than twenty plumes of feathers. This gay young spark soon caught the affections of Leandra, only child of an opulent farmer. The giddy girl eloped with him ; but he robbed her of all her money and jewels, and left her in a cave to make the best of her way home again. (*Cervantes : Don Quixote*, pt. i. iv. 20.)

Vin'dicate (3 syl.), to justify, to ayenge, has a remarkable etymon. Vindicius was a slave of the Vitelli, who informed the Senate of the conspiracy of the sons of Junius Brutus to restore Tarquin, for which service he was rewarded with liberty (*Livy*, ii. 5) ; hence the rod with which a slave was struck in manumission was called *vindicta*, a Vindicius rod (*see* MANUMIT) ; and to set free was in Latin *vindica're in libertatem*. One way of settling disputes was to give the litigants two rods, which they crossed as if in fight, and the person whom the prætor *vindicated* broke the rod of his opponent. These rods were called *vindiciæ*, and hence vindicate, meaning to "justify." To avenge is simply to justify oneself by punishing the wrongdoer.

Vi'ne (1 syl.). The Rabbins say that the fiend buried a lion, a lamb, and a hog at the foot of the first vine planted by Noah ; and that hence men receive from wine ferocity, mildness, or wallowing in the mire. (*See* MIDRASH.)

Vinegar (*Hannibal's*). Livy tells us that when Hannibal led his army over the Alps to enter Rome he used vinegar to dissolve the snow, and make the march less slippery. Of course this tradition is fabulous. Where did the vinegar come from ? Nepos has left a short memoir of Hannibal, but says nothing about the vinegar. (Livy, B.C. 59 to A.D. 17 ; Nepos about the same time ; Hannibal, B.C. 247-183.)

Vin'egar Bi'ble. Printed at the Clarendon Press, Oxford, 1717. So called because it has the word vinegar instead of vineyard in the running head-line of Luke xxii.

Vineyard Controversy. A paper war provoked by the Hon. Daines Barrington, who entered the lists to overthrow all chroniclers and antiquaries from William of Malmesbury to Samuel Pegge, respecting the vineyards of Domesday Book. He maintained that the vines were currants, and the vineyards currant-gardens.

Vi'no. *In vino veritas.* In wine is truth, meaning when persons are more or less intoxicated they utter many things they would at other times conceal or disguise. (Latin.)

Vin'try Ward (London). So called from the Vintry, or part occupied by the Vintners or wine-merchants from Bordeaux, who anciently settled on this part of the Thames' bank. They landed their wines here, and, till the 28th Edw. I., were obliged to sell what they landed within forty days.

Vi'num Theolog'icum. The best wine in the nation. Holinshed says it was so called because religious men would be sure "neither to drinke nor be served of the worst, or such as was anie waies vined by the vintner ; naie, the merchant would have thought that his soule would have gone streightwaie to the devil if he would have served them with other than the best." (i. 282.)

Violet, said to have sprung from the blood of Ajax ; but how the blood of the mad boaster could produce this modest flower is past understanding. (Latin, *viola ;* Greek, *ιον.*)

" As when stern Ajax poured a purple flood,
The violet rose, fair daughter of his blood."
Dr. Young : The Instalment.

Chemical test paper is steeped in syrup of violets ; used to detect acids and alkalis. If an acid is present, it will change the violet paper into red, an alkali will turn the paper green. Slips of white paper stained with the juice of violets (kept from the air) will serve the same purpose. Litmus and turmeric are also used for similar purposes. The paper should be unsized.

Vi'olet. The colour indicates the *love of truth* and the *truth of love.* Pugin says it is used for black in mourning and fasting.

The violet on the tyrant's grave. (*Tennyson : Aylmer's Field.*) The reference is to Nero's grave. It is said that some unknown hand went by night and strewed violets over his grave. Even Nero had one who loved him. Lemprière states that the statues of Nero, at death, "were crowned with garlands of flowers."

"*I would give you some violets, but they withered all when my father died.*" So says Ophelia to the Queen. The violet in flower-language is emblematical of *innocence*, and Ophelia says the King, the Queen, and even Hamlet himself now he has killed Polonius, are unworthy of this symbol. Now my father is dead *all* the violets are withered, all the court family are stained with blood-guiltiness.

This entire posy may be thus paraphrased : Both you and I are under a spell, and there is "herb of grace" to disenchant us ; there's a " daisy" to caution you against expecting that such wanton love as yours will endure long; I would have given you a "violet" if I could, but now that my father is killed all of you are blood-guilty. (*Shakespeare: Hamlet*, iv. 5.)

Violet (*Corporal*). Napoleon Bonaparte. When Bonaparte was banished to Elba he told his friends he would return with the violets, and "Corporal Violet" was the favourite toast of his partisans. When he broke his *parole* and reached Frejus, a gang of women assembled with violets, which were freely sold. The shibboleth was, "Do you like violets?" If the answer given was "*Oui*," the person was known not to be a confederate; but if the answer was "*Eh bien*," the respondent was recognised as an adherent.

Violet-crowned City. Aristophănēs calls Athens ἰοστέφ-νος (*Equitēs*, 1323 and 1329), and again in the *Acharnians*, 637. Macaulay uses the phrase, "city of the violet crown." Ion (*a violet*) was a representative king of Athens, whose four sons gave names to the four Athenian classes; and Greece in Asia Minor was called "Ion-ia." Athens was the city of Ion, crowned king, and hence the "Ion crowned" or violet-crowned.

Similarly Paris is called the "City of Lilies," by a pun on the word Louis (*lys*, a lily).

Violin. The following musicians are very celebrated: Arcangelo Corelli, noted for the melodious tones he produced (1653 - 1713); Pierre Gaviniés, native of Bordeaux, founder of the French school of violinists, noted for the sweetness of his tones (1722-1800); Nicolo Pagani'ni, whose mastery over the instrument has never been equalled, especially known for his musical feats on one string (1784 - 1840); Gaetan Pugnani, of Turin, founder of the Italian school of violinists; his playing was "wild, noble, and sublime" (1727-1803); Giuseppe Tartini, of Padua, whose performance was plaintive but full of grace (1698-1770); G. B. Viotti, of Piedmont, whose playing was noted for grandeur and audacity, fire and excitement (1753-1824). (*See* CREMONAS.)

The best makers of violins. Gaspar di Salo (1560-1610); Nicholas Amati, of Cremona (1596-1684); Antonio Stradivari, his pupil (1670-1728); Joseph A. Guarneri (1683 - 1745). *Almost equal.* Joseph Steiner (1620 - 1667); Matthias Klotz (1650-1696). (*See* FIDDLE.)

Vi'olon'. A temporary prison. Galignani says: "In the time of Louis XI. the Salle-de-Perdus was so full of turbulent clerks and students that the bailiff of the palace shut many up in the lower room of the *conciergerie* (prison) while the courts were sitting; but as they were guilty of no punishable offence, he allowed them a *violin* to wile away the tedium of their temporary captivity."

M. Génin says the seven penitential psalms were called in the Middle Ages the psalte'rion, and to put one to penance was in French expressed by *mettre au psalterion*. As the psaltery was an instrument of music, some witty Frenchman changed psalte'rion to *violon*, and in lieu of *mettre au psalte'rion* wrote *mettre au violon*.

"A ┌risonnier et lui furent mis au salterion."
    Antiquités Nationales de Millin, iv. p. 6.

Vi'per and File. The biter bit. Æsop says a viper found a file, and tried to bite it, under the supposition that it was good food; but the file said that its province was to bite others, and not to be bitten. (*See* SERPENT.) The viper of real life does not bite or masticate its food, but swallows it whole.

"I fawned and smiled to plunder and betray,
Myself betrayed and plundered all the while;
So gnawed the viper the corroding file."
    Beattie: Minstrel.

"Thus he realised the moral of the fable: the viper sought to bite the file, but broke his own teeth."—*The Times.*

Vir'gil. In the *Gesta Romanorum* Virgil is represented as a mighty but benevolent enchanter. This is the character that Italian tradition always gives him, and it is this traditional character that furnishes Dante with his conception of making Virgil his guide through the infernal regions. From the *Æne'id* grammarians illustrated their rules, rhetoricians selected the subjects of their declamations, and Christians looked on the poet as half-inspired; hence the use of his poems in divination. (*See* SORTES VIRGILIANÆ.)

∴ Dante makes Virgil the personification of *human* wisdom, Beatrice of that wisdom which comes of *faith*, and St. Bernard of *spiritual* wisdom. Virgil conducts Dante through the Inferno, Beatrice through Purgatory, and St. Bernard through Paradise.

¶ Virgil was wise, and as craft was considered a part of wisdom, especially over-reaching the spirits of evil, so he is represented by mediæval writers as outwitting the demon. On one occasion, it is said, he saw an imp in a hole of a mountain, and the imp promised to teach the poet the black art if he released him. Virgil did so, and after learning all the imp could teach him, expressed amazement that one of such imposing stature could be squeezed into so small a rift. The imp said, " Oh, that is not wonderful," and crept into the hole to show Virgil how it was done, whereupon Virgil closed up the hole and kept the imp there. (*Een Schone Historie Van Virgilius*, 1552.)

This tale is almost identical with that of the *Fisherman and the Genius* in the *Arabian Nights*. The fisherman trapped in his net a small copper vessel, from which, when opened, an evil genius came out, who told the fisherman he had vowed to kill the person who released him. The fisherman began to mock the genius, and declared it was quite impossible for such a monster to squeeze himself into so small a vessel. The genius, to convince the fisherman, metamorphosed himself into smoke and got into the vessel, whereupon the fisherman clapped down the lid and flung the vessel back into the sea.

The Swiss tale of *Theophrastus and the Devil* is another analogous story. Theophrastus liberates the devil from a hollow tree, and the sequel is like those given above. (*Gorres: Folksbücher*, p. 226.)

☙ There are numerous tales of the devil outwitted.

The Christian Virgil. Marco Girolamo Vida, author of *Christias* in six books, an imitation of the *Æneid.* (1490-1566.)

The Virgil and Horace of the Christians. So Bentley calls Aurelius Clemens Prudentius, a native of Spain, who wrote Latin hymns and religious poems. (348-*.)

Le Virgile au Rabot. (*Au rabot* is difficult to render into English. " Virgil with a Plane " is far from conveying the idea. " The Virgil of Planers," or " The Virgil of the Plane," is somewhat nearer the meaning.) Adam Billaut, the poetical carpenter and joiner, was so called by M. Tissot, both because he used the plane and because one of his chief *recueils* is entitled *Le Rabot.* He is generally called *Maître Adam.* His roaring Bacchanalian songs seem very unlike the Eclogues of Virgil, and the only reason for the title seems to be that Virgil was a husbandman and wrote on husbandry, while Billaut was a carpenter and wrote on carpentry. (*-1662.)

Virgil′ius, *Bishop of Salzburg,* an Irishman, whose native name was Feargil or Feargal. He was denounced as a heretic for asserting the existence of antipodes. (Died 784.) (*See* SCIENCE.)

Virgin. One of the constellations. (August 23rd to September 23rd.) Astræa, goddess of justice, was the last of the deities to quit our earth, and when she returned to heaven became the constellation *Virgo.*

" When the bright Virgin gives the beauteous days." *Thomson: Autumn.*

Virgin Mary's Guard (*The*). The Scotch guard of France, organised in 1448 by Charles VII. Louis XI. made the Virgin Mary their colonel. Disbanded in 1830.

Virgin Mary's Peas (*The*). Near Bethlehem are certain crystallisations in limestone so called.

Virgin Queen (*The*). Queen Elizabeth (1533, 1558-1603).

Virgins. *The eleven thousand virgins of Cologne,* according to the legend, were born at Bao'za in Spain, which contained only 12,000 families. The bones exhibited were taken from an old Roman cemetery, across which the wall of Cologne ran, and which were exposed to view after the siege in 1106. (*See* URSULA.)

Virginal. An instrument used in convents to lead the virginals or hymns to the Virgin. It was a quilled keyboard instrument of two or three octaves, common in the reign of Elizabeth.

Virtuo′so. A man fond of virtu or skilled therein ; a *dilettante.*

Vis Iner′tiæ. That property of matter which makes it resist any change. Thus it is hard to set in motion what is still, or to stop what is in motion. Figuratively, it applies to that unwillingness of change which makes men " rather bear the ills they have than fly to others they know not of."

Vish′nu [*Indian*]. The Preserver, who forms with Brahma and Siva the divine triad of the system of Hinduism.

☙ Vishnu rides on an eagle ; Brahma on a goose.

Vi′tal Spark of Heavenly Flame. (*Pope.*) Heracli′tus held the soul to be a spark of the stellar essence. (*Macrobius : In Somnium Scipionis*, i. 14.)

Vitel′lius. A glutton. So named from Vitellius the Roman emperor, who took emetics after a meal that he might have power to swallow another.

Vitex. Called Abraham's balm, Agnus Castus, and the chaste-tree. In the language of flowers it means "insensibility to love." Dioscorĭdēs, Pliny, and Galen mention the plant, and say that the Athenian ladies, at the feast of Ceres, used to strew their couches with vitex leaves as a palladium of chastity. In France a beverage is made of the leaves by distillation, and is (or was at one time) given to novitiates to wean their hearts from earthly affections. *Vitex*, from *vieo*, to bind with twigs; so called from the flexible nature of the twigs.

Vitru'vius. There were two Roman architects of this name. The one best known was Marcus Vitruvius Pollio, who wrote a book on architecture. *The English Vitruvius.* Inigo Jones (1572-1652).

Vit'ulos. The scourgings which the monks inflicted on themselves during the chanting of the psalms.

Vitus (*St.*). *St. Vitus's dance*, once widely prevalent in Germany and the Low Countries, was a "dancing mania." So called from the supposed power of St. Vitus over nervous and hysterical affections.

> " At Strasbourg hundreds of folk began
> To dance and leap, both maid and man ;
> In open market, lane, or street,
> They skipped along, nor cared to eat,
> Until their plague had ceased to fright us.
> 'Twas called the dance of holy Vitus."
> *Jan of Konigshaven (an old German chronicler).*

St. Vitus's Dance. A description of the jumping procession on Whit-Tuesday to a chapel in Ulm dedicated to St. Vitus, is given in *Notes and Queries*, September, 1856. (*See* TARANTISM.)

Vi'va Vo'ce. Orally ; by word of mouth. A *viva voce* examination is one in which the respondent answers by word of mouth. (Latin, " with the living voice.")

Viv'ien. A wily wanton in Arthur's court " who hated all the knights." She tried to seduce " the blameless king," and succeeded in seducing Merlin, who, "overtalked and overworn, told her his secret charm "—

> " The which if any wrought on anyone
> With woven paces and with waving arms,
> The man so wrought on ever seemed to lie
> Closed in the four walls of a hollow tower,
> From which was no escape for evermore."

Having obtained this secret, the wanton "put forth the charm," and in the hollow oak lay Merlin as one dead,

" lost to life, and use, and name, and fame." (*Tennyson : Idyls of the King ; Vivien.*)

Vixen. A female fox. Metaphorically, a woman of villainous and ungovernable temper. (Anglo-Saxon, *fixen.*)

Vixe're. "*Vixere fortes ante Agamemnona*" (Horace). You are not the first great man that ever lived, though you boast so mightily. Our own age does not monopolise the right of merit.

Viz. A contraction of *videlicet*. The *z* is a corruption of ȝ, a common mark of contraction in the Middle Ages ; as habȝ—*i.e. habet ;* omnibȝ—*i.e. omnibus ;* viȝ—*i.e. videlicet.*

Vogue (1 syl.). A French word. "In vogue" means in repute, in the fashion. The verb *voguer* means to sail or move forwards. Hence the idea of sailing with the tide.

Vogue la Galère. Let the world go how it will ; "*arrive qui pourra.*"

Vole. *He has gone the vole—i.e.* been everything by turns. Vole is a deal at cards that draws the whole tricks. The verb *vole* means to win all the tricks. Vole is a French word *Faire la vole—i.e.* "*Faire seul toutes les levées,*" *de voler—i.e.* enlever.

> "Who is he [Edie Ochiltree]? Why, he has gone the vole—has been sold'er, ballad-singer, travelling tinker, and now a beggar."—*Sir W. Scott: The Antiquary*, chap. iv.

Volta'ic Battery. An apparatus for accumulating electricity. So called from Volta, the Italian, who first contrived it.

Voltaire. His proper name was François Marie Arouet. The word Voltaire is simply an anagram of Arouet L. I. (*le jeune*). Thus have we Stella, Astrophel (*q.v.*), Vanessa and Cadenus (*q.v.*), and a host of other names in anagrams.

Voltaire, the infidel, built the church at Ferney, which has this inscription : "*Deo erexit Voltaire.*" Cowper alludes to this anomaly in the following lines :

> " Nor he who, for the bane of thousands born,
> Built God a church, and laughed His Word to scorn."

Voltaire. Dr. Young said of him—
> " Thou art so witty, profligate and thin,
> Thou seem'st a Milton, with his Death and Sin."

An excellent comparison between *Voltaire* and *Gibbon* is given by Byron in *Childe Harold*, canto iii. 106, 107. *The German Voltaire.* Johann Wolfgang von Goethe (1749-1838).

Christoph Martin Wieland (1733-1813).

The Polish Voltaire. Ignatius Krasicki (1774-1801).

Vol'ume (2 syl.). A roll. Anciently books were written on sheets fastened together lengthwise and rolled; some were rolled on a pin or roller. The rolls were placed erect on shelves. Each one was labelled in red letters or *rubrics.* Rolls of great value were packed in cases or boxes. (Latin, *volvo,* to roll up.)

Vox et Præterea Nihil. Echo; a threat not followed out. When the Lacedemonian plucked the nightingale, on seeing so little substance he exclaimed, "*Vox tu es, et nihil præterea.*" (φωνά τυ τις ἐσσὶ, καὶ οὐδὲν ἄλλο. *Plut. Opp. Mor. Apophthegmata Laconica.*)

Vox Populi Vox Dei. This does not mean that the voice of the many is wise and good, but only that it is irresistible. You might as well try to stop the tide of the Atlantic as to resist the *vox populi.* As God's laws cannot be withstood, neither can the popular will. After Edward II. had been dethroned by the people in favour of his son (Edward III.), Simon Mepham, Archbishop of Canterbury, preached from these words as his text.

Vul'can. The divine blacksmith, whose workshop was on Mount Etna, where the Cyclops assisted him in forging thunderbolts for Jove. He was also called Mulciber.

Vulcan's Badge. That of cuckoldom. Venus was Vulcan's wife, but her amour with Mars gave Vulcan the badge referred to.

Vul'canised Indiarubber. Indiarubber combined with sulphur by vulcanic agency or heat, by which means the caoutchouc absorbs the sulphur and becomes carbonised.

Vul'canist. One who supports the Vulcanian or Plutonian theory, which ascribes the changes on the earth's surface to the agency of fire. These theorists say the earth was once in a state of igneous fusion, and that the crust has gradually cooled down to its present temperature.

Vulgar Errors.

Aristotle taught that women have more teeth than men.

From an account given in Genesis ii. 21 it was once generally believed that a woman has one rib more than a man.

It is a vulgar error to suppose that beetles and moles are blind.

It is a vulgar error to suppose that lowly-organised animals are as sensible of pain as the highly-organised are.

To exhaust the subject of vulgar errors would require many pages of this Dictionary. Every reader will be able to add to the few examples given above. (*See* UPAS TREE.)

VXL, a monogram on lockets, etc., stands for U XL (*you excel*).

W

Wa'bun. Son of Mudjekee'wis (North-American Indian), East-Wind, the Indian Apollo. Young and beautiful, he chases Darkness with his arrows over hill and valley, wakes the villager, calls the Thunder, and brings the Morning. He married Wabun-Annung (*q.v.*), and transplanted her to heaven, where she became the Morning Star. (*Longfellow: Hiawatha.*)

Wa'bung An'nung, in North American Indian mythology, is the Morning Star. She was a country maiden wooed and won by Wabun, the Indian Apollo, who transplanted her to the skies. (*Longfellow: Hiawatha.*)

Wade (1 syl.), to go through watery places, is the Anglo-Saxon *wad* (a ford), *wadan* (to ford or go [through a meadow]). (*See* WEYD-MONAT.)

General Wade, famous for his military highways in the Highlands, which proceed in a straight line up and down hill like a Roman road, and were made with a crown, instead of being lowest in the middle.

" Had you seen but these roads before they were made,
You would hold up your hands and bless General Wade."

Wade's Boat, named Guin'gelot. Wade was a hero of mediæval romance, whose adventures were a favourite theme in the sixteenth century. Mons. F. Michel has brought together all he could find about this story, but nevertheless, the tale is very imperfectly known.

" They can so moché craft of Wadës boot,
So moché broken harm whan that hem list,
That with hem schuld I never lyv in rest."
Chaucer: Canterbury Tales, 9,298.

Wadham College (Oxford) was founded by Nicholas Wadham in 1613.

Wad'man (*Widow*). A comely widow who tries to secure Uncle Toby for her second husband. Amongst other wiles she pretends that she has something in her eye, and gets Uncle Toby to look for it; as the kind-hearted hero of Namur does so, the widow gradually places her face nearer and nearer the captain's mouth, under the hope that he will kiss her and propose. (*Sterne : Tristram Shandy.*)

Wag Beards (*To*). "'Tis merry in hall when beards wag all"—*i.e.* when feasting goes on.

" Then was the minstrel's harp with rapture
  heard ;
    The song of ancient days gave huge delight ;
  With pleasure too did wag the minstrel's beard,
    For Plenty courted him to drink and bite."
        Peter Pindar : Elegy to Scotland.

Wages. Giles Moore, in 1659, paid his mowers sixteenpence an acre. In 1711 Timothy Burrell, Esq., paid twentypence an acre ; in 1686 he paid Mary his cook fifty shillings a year ; in 1715 he had raised the sum to fifty-five shillings. (*Sussex Archæological Collections*, iii. pp. 163, 170.)

✢ For wages in the reign of Henry VIII., *see* preface of vol. i. *Letters and Papers of the Reign of Henry VIII.*, edited by J. S. Brewer, pp. 108-119.

Wages of Sin (*The*). *To earn the wages of sin.* To be hanged, or condemned to death.

"I believe some of you will be hanged unless you change a good deal. It's cold blood and bad blood that runs in your veins, and you'll come to earn the wages of sin."—*Boldrewood : Robbery under Arms*, ii.

" The wages of sin is death."—Rom. vi. 23.

Wagoner. (*See* BOOTES.)

Waha'bites (3 syl.). A Mahometan sect, whose object is to bring back the doctrines and observances of Islam to the literal precepts of the *Koran ;* so called from the founder, Ibn-abd-ul-Wahab.

Waifs and Strays. "Waifs" are stolen goods, which have been waived or abandoned by the thief. "Strays" are domestic animals which have wandered from their owners and are lost temporarily or permanently.

Waifs and strays of London streets. The homeless poor.

Waistcoat. *The M. B. waistcoat.* The clerical waistcoat. (*See* M.B.)

Waiters upon Providence. Those who cling to the prosperous, but fall away from decaying fortunes.

"The side of the Puritans was deserted at this period by a numerous class of ... prudential persons, who never forsook them till they became unfortunate. These sagacious personages were called ... waiters upon Providence, and deemed it a high delinquency towards heaven to afford countenance to any cause longer than it was favoured by fortune."—*Sir W. Scott : Peveril of the Peak*, chap. iv.

Waits. Street musicians, who serenade the principal inhabitants at Christmas-time, especially on Christmas Eve. From Rymer's *Fœdera* we learn it was the duty of musical watchmen " to pipe the watch" nightly in the king's court four times from Michaelmas to Shrove-Thursday, and three times in the summer ; and they had also to make "the bon gate" at every door, to secure them against "pyckeres and pillers." They form a distinct class from both the watch and the minstrels. Oboes were at one time called " waits."

" Dr. Busby says the word is a corruption of *wayghtes*, hautbo s, transferred from the instruments to the performers."—*Dictionary of Music.*

Wake (1 syl.). To keep vigils. (Anglo-Saxon, *wæccan.*) A vigil celebrated with junketing and dancing.

"It may, therefore, be permitted them [the Irish] on the dedication day, or other solemn days of martyrs, to make them bowers about the churches, and refresh themselves, feasting together after a good religious sort ; killing their oxen now to the praise of God and increase of charity, which they were wont before to sacrifice to the devil."—*Gregory the Great to Melitus* [Melitus was an abbot who came over with St. Augustine].

"Waking a Witch." If a "witch" was obdurate, the most effectual way of obtaining a confession was by what was termed " waking her." For this purpose an iron bridle or hoop was bound across her face with four prongs thrust into her mouth. The " bridle" was fastened behind to the wall by a chain in such a manner that the victim was unable to lie down ; and in this position she was kept sometimes for several days, while men were constantly by to keep her awake. In Scotland some of these bridles are still preserved.

Walbrook Ward (London) is so called from a brook which once ran along the west wall of Walbrook Street.

Walcheren Expedition. A well-devised scheme, ruined by the stupidity of the agent chosen to carry it out. Lord Castlereagh's instructions were " to advance instantly in full force against Antwerp," but Lord Chatham wasted his time and strength in reducing Flushing. Ultimately, the red-tape "Incapable " got possession of the island of Walcheren, but 7,000 men died of malaria, and as many more were permanently disabled.

Wal'demar's Way. So the Milky Way is called in Denmark. This was Waldemar or Valdemar the Victorious, who substituted the Danebrog for the national banner of Denmark.

Walden'ses. So called from Peter Waldo, a citizen of Lyons, who founded a preaching society in 1176.

Waldo, a copse between Lav'ant and Goodwood (Sussex). Same as *weald*. *wold, wald, walt,* "a wood." (Anglo-Saxon.) The final *o* is about equivalent to "the," as *hælo*, the whole, *i.e.* health ; *mænegeo,* the many—*i.e.* multitude, etc.

Wales. The older form is *Wealhas* (plural of *Wealh*), an Anglo-Saxon word denoting foreigners, and applied by them to the ancient Britons; hence, also, *Corn-wall*, the horn occupied by the same "refugees." *Wälschland* is a German name for Italy ; *Valais* are the non-German districts of Switzerland ; the parts about Liège constitute the *Walloon* country. The Welsh proper are Cimbri, and those driven thither by the Teutonic invaders were refugees or strangers. (*See* WALNUT.)

Walk (in *Hudibras*) is Colonel Hewson, so called from Gayton's tract.
To walk. This is a remarkable word. It comes from the Anglo-Saxon *wealcan* (to roll); whence *wealcere*, a fuller of cloth. In Percy's *Reliques* we read—

" She cursed the weaver and the walker,
The cloth that they had wrought."

To walk, therefore, is to roll along, as the machine in felting hats or fulling cloth.

Walk Chalks. An ordeal used on board ship as a test of drunkenness. Two parallel lines being chalked on the deck, the supposed delinquent must walk between them without stepping on either.

Walk Spanish. *To make a man walk Spanish* is to give him the sack ; to give him his discharge. In 1885 one of the retired captains in the Trinity House Establishment said, "If I had to deal with the fellow, I would soon make him walk Spanish, I warrant you."

Walk not in the Public Ways. The fifth symbol of the *Protreptics* of Iamblichus, meaning follow not the multitude in their evil ways; or, wide is the path of sin and narrow the path of virtue, few being those who find it. The "public way" is the way of the public or multitude, but the way of virtue is *personal* and separate. The arcana of Pythagoras were not for the common people, but only for his chosen or elect disciples.

" Broad is the way that leadeth to destruction, but narrow is the path of truth and holiness."

41

Walk the Plank (*To*). (*See* PLANK.)

Walk through One's Part (*To*). A theatrical phrase, meaning to repeat one's part at rehearsal verbally, but without dressing for it or acting it. To do anything appointed you in a listless indifferent manner.

" A fit of dulness, such as will at times creep over all the professors of the fine arts, arising either from fatigue or contempt of the present audience, or that caprice which tempts painters, musicians, and great actors . . . to walk through their parts, instead of exerting themselves with the energy which acquired their fame."—*Sir W. Scott : Redgauntlet,* chap. xix.

Walker, a proper name, is generally supposed to be *wealcere*, a fuller, but the derivation of ancient names from trades is to be received with great caution. It is far more probable that Walker is derived from the old High German *walah*, Anglo-Saxon *wealh*, a foreigner or borderer; whence Wallack, Walk, Walkey, Walliker, and many others. (*See* BREWER.)
Helen Walker. The prototype of Jeanie Deans. Sir Walter Scott caused a tombstone to be erected over her grave in the churchyard of Irongray, stewartry of Kirkcudbright. In 1869 Messrs. A. and C. Black caused a headstone of red freestone to be erected in Carlaverock churchyard to the memory of Robert Paterson, the Old Mortality of the same novelist, buried there in 1801.
Hookey Walker. John Walker was an outdoor clerk at Longman, Clementi, and Co.'s, Cheapside, and was noted for his eagle nose, which gained him the nickname of *Old Hookey.* Walker's office was to keep the workmen to their work, or report them to the principals. Of course it was the interest of the employées to throw discredit on Walker's reports, and the poor old man was so badgered and ridiculed that the firm found it politic to abolish the office ; but *Hookey Walker* still means a tale not to be trusted. (*John Bee.*)

Walker's 'Bus. *To go by Walker's 'bus,* to walk. Similarly, "To go by the Marrowbone stage," "To ride Shank's pony."

Walking Gentleman (*A*), in theatrical parlance, means one who has little or nothing to say, but is expected to deport himself as a gentleman when before the lights.

Walking Sword (*A*). A short, light sword, when long swords wielded by two hands were in use. (*See* Sir W. Scott's *Abbot,* chap. xx.)

Walkyries (*The*). (*See* VALKYRIES.)

Wall (*The*), from the Tyne to Boulness, on the Solway Firth, a distance of eighty miles. Called—

The Roman Wall, because it was the work of the Romans.

Agricola's Wall, because Agricola made the south bank and ditch.

Hadrian's Wall, because Hadrian added another vallum and mound parallel to Agricola's.

The Wall of Severus, because Severus followed in the same line with a stone wall, having castles and turrets.

The Picts' Wall, because its object was to prevent the incursions of the Picts.

The wall of Antoni'nus, now called *Graeme's Dyke*, from Dunglass Castle on the Clyde to Blackness Castle on the Forth, was made by Lollius Urbicus, legate of Antoninus Pius, A.D. 140. It was a turf wall.

Wall. *To give the wall.* Nathaniel Bailey's explanation of this phrase is worth perpetuating. He says it is "a compliment paid to the female sex, or those to whom one would show respect, by letting them go nearest the wall or houses, upon a supposition of its being the cleanest. This custom," he adds, "is chiefly peculiar to England, for in most parts abroad they will give them the right hand, though at the same time they thrust them into the kennel."

To take the wall. To take the place of honour, the same as to choose "the uppermost rooms at feasts." (Matt. xxiii. 6.) At one time pedestrians gave the wall to persons of a higher grade in society than themselves.

"I will take the wall of any man or maid of Montague's."—*Shakespeare: Romeo and Juliet*, i. 1.

To go to the wall. To be put on one side; to be shelved. This is in allusion to another phrase, "Laid by the wall" —*i.e.* dead but not buried; put out of the way.

To hang by the wall. To hang up neglected; hence, not to be made use of. (*Shakespeare : Cymbeline*, iii. 4.)

Wall-eyed properly means "withered-eyed." Persons are wall-eyed when the white is unusually large, and the sight defective ; hence Shakespeare has *wall-eyed wrath*, wall-eyed slave, etc. When King John says, "My rage was *blind*," he virtually says his "wrath was wall-eyed." (Saxon, *hwelan*, to wither. The word is often written *whall-eyed*, or *whallied*, from the verb *whally*.)

Walls have Ears. The Louvre was so constructed in the time of Catherine de Medicis, that what was said in one room could be distinctly heard in another. It was by this contrivance that the suspicious queen became acquainted with state secrets and plots. The tubes of communication were called the auriculaires, and were constructed on the same principle as those of the confessionals. The "Ear of Dionysius" communicated to him every word uttered in the state prison. (*See* SPEAKING HEADS, 9.)

Wallace's Larder. (*See* LARDER.)

Wallflower. So called because it grows on old walls and ruined buildings. It is a native plant. Similarly, *wall-cress, wall-creeper*, etc., are plants which grow on dry, stony places, or on walls. *Wall-fruit* is fruit trained against a wall. (*See* WALNUT.)

Herrick has a pretty fancy on the origin of this flower. A fair damsel was long kept in durance vile from her lover ; but at last

" Up she got upon a wall,
Tempting down to slide withal ;
But the silken twist untied,
So she fell, and, bruised, she died.

"Love, in pity of the deed,
And her loving luckless speed,
Turned her to this plant we call
Now the 'Flower of the wall.'"

Young ladies who sit out against the wall, not having partners during a dance, are called " wallflowers."

Walloons. Part of the great Romaic stock. They occupied the low track along the frontiers of the German-speaking territory, as Artois, Hainault, Namur, Liège, Luxemburg, with parts of Flanders and Brabant. (*See* WALES.)

"The Wallons . . . are the Romanised Gauls, lineal representatives of the ancient Belgæ."—*Encyclopædia Britannica*, vol. xxi. p. 332.

Wal'lop. To thrash. Sir John Wallop, in the reign of Henry VIII., was sent to Normandy to make reprisals, because the French fleet had burnt Brighton. Sir John burnt twenty-one towns and villages, demolished several harbours, and "walloped" the foe to his heart's content.

Wallsend Coals. Originally from Wallsend, on the Tyne, but now from any part of a large district about Newcastle.

Wal'nut [*foreign nut*]. It comes from Persia, and is so called to distinguish it from those native to Europe, as hazel, filbert, chestnut. (Anglo-Saxon, *walh*, foreign; *hnutu*, nut.)

"Some difficulty there is in cracking the name thereof. Why wallnuts, having no affinity to a wall, should be so called. The truth is, *gual* or *wall* in the old Dutch signifieth 'strange' or 'exotic' (whence *Welsh*, foreigners); these nuts being no natives of England or Europe, but probably first fetched from Persia, and called by the French *nux persique*."—*Fuller: Worthies of England.*

Walnut Tree. It is said that the walnut tree thrives best if the nuts are beaten off with sticks, and not gathered. Hence Fuller says, "Who, like a nut tree, must be manured by beating, or else would not bear fruit" (bk. ii. ch. 11). The saying is well known that—

"A woman, a spaniel, and a walnut tree,
The more you beat them the better they be."
Taylor, the Water-Poet.

Walpurgis Night. The eve of May Day, when the old pagan witch-world was supposed to hold high revelry under its chief on certain high places. The Brocken of Germany was a favourite spot for these revelries.

Walpurgis was a female saint concerned in the introduction of Christianity into Germany. She died February 25th, 779.

"He changed hands, and whisked and rioted like a dance of Walpurgis in his lonely brain."—*J. S. Le Fanu: The House in the Churchyard*, p. 109.

Walston (*St.*). A Briton who gave up all his wealth, and supported himself by manual husbandry. Patron saint of husbandmen; usually depicted with a scythe in his hand, and cattle in the background. Died mowing, 1016.

Walter Multon, Abbot of Thornton-upon-Humber, in Lincolnshire, was immured in 1443. In 1722, an old wall being taken down, his remains were found with a candlestick, table, and book. Stukeley mentions the fact. In 1845 another instance of the same kind was discovered at Temple Bruer, in Lincolnshire.

Wal'tham Blacks. (*See* BLACK ACT.)

Walton. *An Izaak Walton.* One devoted to "the gentle craft" of angling. Izaak Walton wrote a book called *The Complete Angler, or Contemplative Man's Recreation.* (1655.)

❖ "Gentle" is a pun. Gentles are the larvæ of flesh-flies used as bait in angling.

Walton Bridle (*The*). The "gossip's or scold's bridle." One of these bridles is preserved in the vestry of the church of Walton-on-Thames. Iron bars pass round the head, and are fastened by a padlock. In front, a flat piece of iron projects, and, this piece of iron being thrust into the mouth, effectually prevents the utterance of words. The relic at Walton is dated 1633, and the donor was a person named Chester, as appears from the inscription:

"Chester presents Walton with a bridle
To curb women's tongues that talk too idle."

❖ It is also called a "brank." (Teutonic, *pranque*, "a bridle.")

Wam'ba. Son of Witless, and jester of Cedric "the Saxon," of Rotherwood. (*Sir Walter Scott: Ivanhoe.*)

Wan means thin. (Anglo-Saxon, *wan*, "deficient"; our *wane*, as the "waning moon.") As wasting of the flesh is generally accompanied with a grey pallor, the idea of leanness has yielded to that of the sickly hue which attends it. (Verb *wan-ian*, to wane.)

Wand. *The footman's wand.* (*See* under RUNNING FOOTMEN.)

Wandering Jew.
(1) *Of Greek tradition.* Aris'teas, a poet who continued to appear and disappear alternately for above 400 years, and who visited all the mythical nations of the earth.

(2) *Of Jewish story.* Tradition says that Kartaph'ilos, the door-keeper of the Judgment Hall, in the service of Pontius Pilate, struck our Lord as he led Him forth, saying, "Go on faster, Jesus"; whereupon the Man of Sorrows replied, "I am going, but thou shalt tarry till I come again." (*Chronicle of St. Alban's Abbey*; 1228.)

∴ The same *Chronicle*, continued by Matthew Paris, tells us that Kartaphilos was baptized by Ananias, and received the name of Joseph. At the end of every hundred years he falls into a trance, and wakes up a young man about thirty.

Another legend is that Jesus, pressed down with the weight of His cross, stopped to rest at the door of one Ahasue'rus, a cobbler. The craftsman pushed him away, saying, "Get off! Away with you, away!" Our Lord replied, "Truly I go away, and that quickly, but tarry thou till I come." Schubert has a poem entitled *Ahasuer* (the Wandering Jew). (*Paul von Eitzen*; 1547.)

A third legend says that it was Ananias, the cobbler, who haled Jesus before the judgment seat of Pilate, saying to Him, "Faster, Jesus, faster!"

(3) In *Germany* the Wandering Jew is associated with John Buttadæus, seen at Antwerp in the thirteenth century,

again in the fifteenth, and a third time in the sixteenth. His last appearance was in 1774 at Brussels. Signor Gualdi about the same time made his appearance at Venice, and had a portrait of himself by Titian, who had been dead at the time 130 years. One day he disappeared as mysteriously as he had come. (*Turkish Spy*, vol. ii.)

(4) The *French* call the Wandering Jew Isaac Laquedem, a corruption of Lake'-dion. (*Mitternacht Diss. in Jno.* xxi. 19; 1640.)

Wandering Jew. Salathiel ben Sadi, who appeared and disappeared towards the close of the sixteenth century, at Venice, in so sudden a manner as to attract the notice of all Europe. Croly in his novel called *Salathiel*, and Southey in his *Curse of Kehama*, trace the course of the Wandering Jew, but in utter violation of the general legends. In Eugène Sue's *Le Juif Errant*, the Jew makes no figure of the slightest importance to the tale.

The Wandering Jew. Alexandre Dumas wrote a novel called *Isaac Laquedem*. Sieur Emmerch relates the legend.

Ed. Grenier has a poem on the subject, *La Mort du Juif Errant*, in five cantos.

Halévy has an opera on the same subject, words by Scribe.

Doré has illustrated the legend.

Wandering Willie or **Willie Steenson.** The blind fiddler who tells the tale of Redgauntlet. (*Sir Walter Scott: Redgauntlet.*)

Wandering Wood, in book i. of Spenser's *Faërie Queene*, is where St. George and Una encounter Error, who is slain by the knight. Una tries to persuade the Red Cross knight to leave the wood, but he is self-willed. Error, in the form of a serpent, attacks him, but the knight severs her head from her body. The idea is that when Piety will not listen to Una or Truth, it is sure to get into "Wandering Wood," where Error will attack it; but if it listens then to Truth it will slay Error.

Wans Dyke, Sir Richard Colt Hoare tells us, was a barrier erected by the Belgæ against the Celts, and served as a boundary between these tribes. Dr. Stukeley says the original mound was added to by the Anglo-Saxons when they made it the boundary-line of the two kingdoms of Mercia and Wessex. It was also used by the Britons as a defence against the Romans, who attacked them

from the side of Gloucestershire and Oxfordshire.

In its most perfect state it began at Andover, in Hampshire, ran through the counties of Berkshire, Wiltshire, and Somersetshire, and terminated in the "Severn Sea" or Bristol Channel. It was called Wodenes Dyke by the Saxons, contracted into Wondes-dyke, and corrupted to Wans-dyke, as Wodenes-dæg is into Wed'nes-day. (*See* WAT'S DYKE.)

Want or **Went.** A road. Thus "the four-want way," the spot where four roads meet. Chaucer uses the expression "a privie went" (private road), etc.

Wants, meaning "gloves." According to the best Dutch authorities, the word is a corruption of the French *gant*, Italian *quanto*, our "gauntlets."

"Wanten are worn by peasants and working people when the weather is cold. They are in shape somewhat like boxing-gloves, having only a thumb and no fingers. They are made of a coarse woollen stuff."—*Teding von Berkhout: Letter from Breda.*

Wantley. (*See* DRAGON.)

Wa'pentake. A division of Yorkshire, similar to that better known as a *hundred.* The word means "touch-arms," it being the custom of each vassal, when he attended the assemblies of the district, "to touch the spear of his overlord in token of homage." Victor Hugo, in his novel of *L'Homme qui Rit*, calls a tipstaff a "wapentake." (Anglo-Saxon, *wapen*, arms; *tacan*, to touch.)

Wapping Great means astonishingly great. (Anglo-Saxon, *wafian*, to be astonished; *wafung*, amazement.) A "wapper" is a great falsehood.

War of the Meal-sacks. After the battle of Beder, Abu Sofian summoned two hundred fleet horsemen, each with a sack of meal at his saddle-bow (the scanty provision of an Arab for a foray), and sallied forth to Medi'na. Mahomet went forth at the head of a superior force to meet him, and Abu Sofian with his horsemen, throwing off their meal-sacks, fled with precipitation.

War of the Roses. (*See* ROSES.)

Ward. A district under the charge of a warden. The word is applied to the subdivisions of Cumberland, Westmoreland, and Durham, which, being contiguous to Scotland, were placed under the charge of lord wardens of the marches, whose duty it was to protect these counties from inroads. (*See* HUNDRED.)

Ward (*Artemus*). (*See* ARTEMUS WARD.)

Ward Money, Ward-penny, or **Wardage.** Money paid for watch and ward. (*Domesday*.)

Warden-pie. Pie made of the Warden pear. Warden pears are so called from Warden Abbey, Berks, where they are grown in great profusion.

" Myself with denial I mortify
With a dainty bit of a Warden-pie."
The Friar of Orders Grey.

Ware. (*See* BED.)

War'lock. A wandering evil spirit; a wizard. (Anglo-Saxon, *wær-loga*, a deceiver, one who breaks his word. Satan is called in Scripture "the father of lies," the arch-warlock.)

Warm Reception (*A*). A hot opposition. Also, a hearty welcome.

" The Home Rule members are prepared to give the Coercion Bill a warm reception ; Mr. Parnell's followers will oppose it tooth and nail."—*Newspaper paragraph*, May 19th, 1885.

Warm as a Bat. Hot as burning coal. In South Staffordshire that slaty coal which will not burn, but which lies in the fire till it becomes red-hot, is called " bat."

Warming-pan (*A*). One who keeps a place warm for another, *i.e.* holds it temporarily for another. The allusion is to the custom in public schools of making a fag warm his "superior's" bed by lying in it till the proper occupant was ready to turn him out.

" If Mr. Mellor took a judgeship, Grantham might object to become a warming-pan for ambitious lawyers."—*Newspaper paragraph*, March 5th, 1886.

Warming-pan. (*See* JACOBITES.)

Warning Stone. Anything that gives notice of danger. Bakers in Wiltshire and some other counties used to put a " certain pebble " in their ovens, and when the stone turned white it gave the baker warning that the oven was hot enough for his bakings.

Warp (*To*). A sea term, meaning to shift the position of a vessel. This is done by means of a rope called a *warp*. *Kedging* is when the warp is bent to a kedge, which is let go, and the vessel is hove ahead by the capstan.

" The potent rod
Of Amram's son [Moses], in Egypt's evil day,
Waved round the coast, up-called a pitchy cloud
Of locusts, warping [shifting about] in the eastern wind." *Milton: Paradise Lost*, i. 338.

⁂ In Lancashire, warping means laying eggs; and boys, on finding a bird's nest, will ask—"And how many eggs has she warped ? "

Warp and Weft, or **Woof.** The " warp " of a fabric are the longitudinal threads; the " weft " or " woof " are threads which run from selvage to selvage.

" Weave the warp and weave the woof,
The winding-sheet of Edward's race ;
Give ample room and verge enough
The characters of hell to trace."
Gray : The Bard.

Warrior Queen (*The*). Boadicea, Queen of the Iceni.

" When the British warrior queen,
Bleeding from the Roman rods,
Sought, with an indignant mien,
Counsel of her country's gods. ..."
Cowper : Boadicea.

The Iceni were the faithful allies of Rome ; but, on the death of Prasutagus, king of that tribe, the Roman procurator took possession of the kingdom of Prasutagus ; and when the widow Boadicea complained thereof, the procurator had her beaten with rods like a slave.

Warwick. (Anglo-Saxon, *wær-wic*, contracted from *wæring-wic* (the fortified or garrisoned town). A translation of the ancient British name *Caer Leon*.

Warwick Lane (City). The site of a magnificent house belonging to the famed Beauchamps, Earls of Warwick.

Warwolf. (*See* WERWOLF.)

Washed Out (*I am thoroughly*). I am thoroughly exhausted or done up ; I have no strength or spirit left in me.

Washing. *Wash your dirty linen at home* (French). The French say the English do not follow the advice of washing their dirty linen *en famille*—meaning that they talk openly and freely of the faults committed by ministers, corporations, and individuals. All may see their dirty linen ; and as for its washing, let it be but washed, and the English care not who has the doing of it. Horace (2 *Ep.*, i. 220) says, " *Vine'ta egomet cædam mea* " (I do my own washing at home). Though the French assert that we disregard this advice, we have the familiar proverb, "It is an ill bird that fouls its own nest."

Washington of Columbia. Simon Bolivar (1785-1831).

Was'sail (2 syl.). A salutation used on New Year's Eve and New Year's Day over the spiced-ale cup, hence called the "wassail bowl." (Anglo-Saxon, *Wæs hæl*, be whole, be well.)

Wassailers. Those who join a wassail ; revellers, drunkards.

" I should be loath
To meet the rudeness and swilled insolence
Of such late wassailers."
Milton : Comus (The Lady).

Wastlers. Wandering musicians; from *wastle*, to wander. The carol-singers in Sussex are called wastlers.

Wat. A familiar name for a hare.

" By this, poor Wat, far off upon a hill,
Stands on his hinder legs, with listening ear."
            Shakespeare : Venus and Adonis.

Wat's Dyke (Flintshire). A corruption of Wato's Dyke. Wato was the father of Weland, the Vulcan of Northern mythology, and the son of King Vilkinr by a mermaid. This dyke extends from the vicinity of Basingwerk Abbey, in a south - easterly direction, into Denbighshire. The space between it and Offa's Dyke, which in some parts is three miles, and in others not above 500 yards, is neutral ground, " where Britons, Danes, and Saxons met for commercial purposes." (*See* WAN'S DYKE.)

" There is a famous thing
Called Offa's Dyke, that reacheth far in length.
All kinds of ware the Danes might thither bring ;
It was free ground, and called the Briton's
            strength.
Wat's Dyke, likewise, about the same was set,
Between which two both Danes and Britons met,
And traffic still.
        Churchyard : Worthiness of Wales (1587).

Watch Night. December 31st, to see the Old Year out and the New Year in by a religious service. John Wesley grafted it on the religious system, but it has been followed by most Christian communities.

"Southey in his biography of the evangelist (Wesley) denounces watch-night as another of Wesley's objectionable institutions."—*Nottingham Guardian*, January 1, 1895, p. 5.

Watch on Board Ship. There are two sorts of watch—the *long* watch of four hours, and the *dog* watch of two, from 4 to 6; but strictly speaking a watch means four hours. The dog watches are introduced to prevent one party always keeping watch at the same time. (*See* WOLF, *Between dog and wolf*, DOG-WATCH.)

12 to 4 p.m.	Afternoon watch.
4 to 6	„	First dog-watch.
6 to 8	„	Second dog-watch.
8 to 12	„	First night watch.
12 to 4 a.m.	Middle watch.
4 to 8	„	Morning watch.
8 to 12	„	Forenoon watch.

There are two divisions which perform duty alternately—the starboard watch and the port watch. The former is called the captain's watch in the merchant service, often under the command of the second mate ; the port watch is under the command of the first mate.

The Black Watch. The gallant 42nd, linked with the 73rd, now called the Royal Highlanders. The 42nd was the first corps raised for the royal service in the Highlands. Their tart'an (1729) consisted of dark blue and dark green, and was called black from the contrast which their dark tartans furnished to the scarlet and white of the other regiments.

Watch'et. Sky-blue. (Anglo-Saxon, *waadchet*, probably dye of the woad plant.)

Water. (*See* DANCING WATER.)
The Father of Waters. The Mississippi (Indian, *Miche Sepe*), the chief river of North America. The Missouri is its child. The Irrawaddy is so called also.

Water. *Blood thicker than water.* (*See under* BLOOD.)
Court holy water. Fair but empty words. In French, "*Eau bénite de cour.*"
In deep water. In difficulties ; in great perplexity.
It makes my mouth water. It is very alluring ; it makes me long for it. Saliva is excited in the mouth by strong desire. The French have the same phrase : " *Cela fait venir l'eau à la bouche.*"
More water glideth by the mill than wots the miller of (*Titus Andronicus,* ii. 1). The Scotch say, " Mickle water goes by the miller when he sleeps." (*See under* MILLER.)
O'er muckle water drowned the miller. (*See* DROWN THE MILLER.) The weaver, in fact, is hanged in his own yarn. The French say, " *Un embarras de richesse.*"
Of the first water. Of the highest type ; very excellent. (*See under* DIAMOND.)
Smooth water runs deep. Deep thinkers are persons of few words ; barking dogs do not bite. There are two or three French proverbs of somewhat similar meaning. For example : " *En eau endormie point ne se fe ;*" again, " *L'eau qui dort est pire que celle qui court.*" A calm exterior is far more to be feared than a tongue-doughty Bobadil.
The modest water saw its God and blushed. The allusion is to Christ's turning water into wine at the marriage feast. Richard Crashaw (1670) wrote the Latin epigram in pentameter verse.

"Nympha pudica Deum vidit et erubuit."

To back water. To row backwards in order to reverse the forward motion of a boat in rowing.
To carry water to the river. To carry coals to Newcastle. In French, " *Porter de l'eau à la rivière.*"
To fish in troubled water. The French saying is, " *Pêcher en eau troublé,*" i.e. " *Profiter des époques de trouble et de révolution pour faire ses affaires et sa fortune.* (*Hilaire Le Gai.*)

To hold water. That won't hold water.
That is not correct; it is not tenable.
It is a vessel which leaks.

To keep one's head above water. To
remain out of debt. When immersed in
water, while the head is out of water,
one is not drowned.

To throw cold water on a scheme. To
discourage the proposal; to speak of it
slightingly.

Water. *The coldest water known.*
Colder than the water of Nonacris
(*Pliny*, xiii. 2).

Colder than the water of Dircē. "*Dircē
et Nemῠ fontes sunt frigidissimi æstate,
inter Bilbilim et Segobregam, in ripa fere
Salonis amnis.*" (*Martial.*)

Colder than the water of Dircenna.
(*Martial*, i. 51.)

Colder than the Conthoporian Spring
of Corinth, that froze up the gastric
juices of those that sipped it.

Water-gall. The dark rim round
the eyes after much weeping. A peculiar appearance in a rainbow which indicates more rain at hand. "Gall" is the
Anglo-Saxon *gealew* (yellow).

" And round about her tear-distainèd eye
  Blue circles streamed, like rainbows in the sky ;
  These watergalls ... foretell new storms."
        Shakespeare : Rape of Lucrece.

Water-hole. *The big water-hole.*
The bed of the sea ; the ocean.

" We've got to the big water-hole at last ...
'Tis a long way across."—*Boldrewood : Robbery
under Arms*, chap. xii.

Water-logged. Rendered immovable by too much water in the hold.
When a ship leaks and is water-logged,
it will not make any progress, but is
like a log on the sea, tossed and stationary.

Water-Poet. John Taylor, the
Thames waterman. (1580-1654.)

" I must confess I do want eloquence,
And never scarce did learn my accidence,
For having got from ' possum' to ' posset,'
I there was gravelled, nor could farther get."
        Taylor the Water-Poet.

Water-sky (*A*), in Arctic navigation, is a dark or brown sky, indicating
an open sea. An *ice-sky* is a white one,
or a sky tinted with orange or rose-
colour, indicative of a frozen sea. (*See*
ICE-BLINK.)

Water Stock (*To*). To add extra
shares. Suppose a "trust" (*q.v.*) consists
of 1,000 shares of £50 each, and the profit
available for dividend is 40 per cent.,
the managers "water the stock," that
is, add another 1,000 fully paid-up shares
to the original 1,000. There are now
2,000 shares, and the dividend, instead

of £40 per cent., is reduced to £20 ; but
the shares are more easily sold, and the
shareholders are increased in number.

Water of Jealousy (*The*). If a
woman was known to commit adultery
she was to be stoned to death, according
to the Mosaic law. (Deut. xxii. 22.) If,
however, the husband had no proof, but
only suspected his wife of infidelity, he
might take her before the Sanhedrim to
be examined, and if she denied it, she
was given the "water of jealousy"
to drink (Numb. v. 11-29). In this
water some of the dust of the sanctuary
was mixed, and the priest said to the
woman, "If thou hast gone aside may
Jehovah make this water bitter to thee,
and bring on thee all the curses written
in this law." The priest then wrote on
a roll the curses, blotted the writing
with the water, gave it to the woman,
and then handed to her the "water
of jealousy" to drink.

Water Tasting like Wine. Pliny
(ii. 103) tells us of a fountain in the Isle
of Andros, in the temple of Bacchus,
which every year, on January 5th, tasted
like wine.

Baccius de Thermis (vi. 22) gives
numerous examples of similar vinous
springs.

In Lanternland there was a fountain
in the middle of the temple, the water of
which had the flavour of the wine which
the drinker most liked. (*Rabelais : Pantagruel*, v. 42.)

Waters (*Sanitary*).

For anæmia, Schwalbach, St. Moritz.
  „ articular rheumatism, Aix les Bains.
  „ asthma, Mont Dore.
  „ atonic gout, Royat.
  „ biliary obstructions, Carlsbad.
  „ calculous disorders, Vichy and Contrexéville.
  „ diabetes, Neuenahr and Carlsbad.
  „ gout, Aix les Bains.
  „ gouty and catarrhal dyspepsia, Homburg and
      Kissingen.
  „ obesity, Marienbad.
  „ plethoric gout, Carlsbad.
  „ scrofulous glandular affections, Kreuznacn.
  „ skin diseases, Aix la Chapelle and Constadt.
  „ throat affections, La Bourbonne, Aix-les-
      Bains, Uriage, Auterets, Eaux Bonnes.

Waterloo Cup (*The*). A dog prize.
Waterloo is on the banks of the Mersey,
about three miles north of Liverpool.

Waterworks (*The*). The shedding
of tears. Many other meanings also.

" ' Oh, miss, I never thought to have seen this
day,' and the waterworks began to play."—
Thackeray.

Watling Street. A road extending
east and west across South Britain. Beginning at Dover, it ran through Canterbury to London, and thence to Cardigan. The word is a corruption of

Vitellina strata, the paved road of Vitellius, called by the Britons *Guet'alin*. Poetically the "Milky Way" has been called the Watling Street of the sky.

"Secunda via principalis dicitur Watelingstreate, tendens ab euro-austro in zephyrum septentrionalem. Incipit . . . a Dovaria . . . usque Cardigan."—*Leland.*

Watteau. "*Peintre de fêtes galantes du roi.*" (1684-1721.)

Wave. *The ninth wave.* A notion prevails that the waves keep increasing in regular series till the maximum arrives, and then the series begins again. No doubt when two waves coalesce they form a large one, but this does not occur at fixed intervals. The most common theory is that the tenth wave is the largest, but Tennyson says the ninth.

" And then the two
Dropt to the cove, and watch'd the great sea fall,
Wave after wave, each mightier than the last,
Till last, a ninth one, gathering half the deep
And full of voices, slowly rose and plunged
Roaring, and all the wave was in a flame."
    Tennyson: The Holy Grail.

Wax-bond End (*A*). A thread waxed with cobbler's wax and used for binding whips, fishing-rods, ropes, etc., for sewing boots and shoes, etc. It is *waxed* and used for a *bond*.

Way-bit. *A Yorkshire way-bit.* A large overplus. Ask a Yorkshireman the distance of any place, and he will reply so many miles and a way-bit (*wee-bit*); but the way-bit will prove a frightful length to the traveller who imagines it means only a *little* bit over. The Highlanders say, "A mile and a *bittock*," which means about two miles.

Ways and Means. A parliamentary term, meaning the method of raising the supply of money for the current requirements of the state.

Wayfaring Tree (*The*). The Guelder rose (*q.v.*).

" Wayfaring Tree ! What ancient claim
Hast thou to that right pleasant name ?
Was it that some faint pilgrim came
   Unhopedly to thee,
In the brown desert's weary way,
'Midst thirst and toil's consuming sway,
And there, as 'neath thy shade he lay,
   Blessed the Wayfaring Tree ?"   *W. H.*

Wayland, the Scandinavian Vulcan, was son of the sea-giant Wate, and the sea-nymph Wac-hilt. He was bound apprentice to Mimi the smith. King Nidung cut the sinews of his feet, and cast him into prison, but he escaped in a feather-boat. (Anglo-Saxon *weallan*, to fabricate.)

Wayland Smith's Cave. A cromlech near Lambourn, Berkshire. Scott, in his *Kenilworth* (chap. xiii.), says, "Here lived a supernatural smith, who would shoe a traveller's horse for a ' consideration.' His fee was sixpence, and if more was offered he was offended."

Wayland Wood (near Watton, Norfolk), said to be the scene of the *Babes in the Wood*, and a corruption of "Wailing Wood."

Wayleaves. Right of way through private property for the laying of water-pipes and making of sewers, etc., provided that only the surface-soil is utilised by the proprietor.

"Mr. Woods made an attempt to get the House of Commons to commit itself to the proposition : That the present system of royalty rents and wayleaves is injurious to the great industries."—*Liberty Review,* April 14th, 1894, p. 307.

Wayzgoose. An entertainment given to journeymen, or provided by the journeymen themselves. It is mainly a printers' affair, which literary men and commercial staffs may attend by invitation or sufferance. The word *wayz* means a " bundle of straw," and *wayz-goose* a " stubble goose," properly the crowning dish of the entertainment. The Dutch *wassen* means " to wax fat." The Latin *anser sigatum*. (*See* BEANFEAST, HARVEST GOOSE.)

" In the midlands and north of England, every newspaper has its wayzgoose."—*The Pall Mall Gazette,* June 26th, 1894.

We. Coke, in the *Institutes*, says the first king that wrote *we* in his grants was King John. All the kings before him wrote *ego* (I). This is not correct, as Richard *Lion-heart* adopted the royal we. (*See Rymer's Fœdera.*)

We Three. *Did you never see the picture of "We Three"?* asks Sir Andrew Aguecheek—not meaning himself, Sir Toby Belch, and the clown, but referring to a public-house sign of *Two Loggerheads*, with the inscription, " We three loggerheads be," the third being the spectator.

We Left Our Country for Our Country's Good. We are transported convicts. The line occurs in a prologue written by George Barrington (a notorious pickpocket) for the opening of the first playhouse at Sydney, in Australia, 16th January, 1796.

" True patriots we, for be it understood,
  We left our country for our country's good."

Weak as Water. (*See* SIMILES.)

Weak-kneed Christian or **Politician** (*A*). Irresolute; not thorough; a Laodicean, neither hot nor cold.

"If any weak-kneed Churchman, now hesitating between his [political] party and his Church, is trying to persuade himself that no mischief is in the air, let him take warning."—*Newspaper paragraph*, October 16th, 1883.

Weap'on Salve. A salve said to cure wounds by sympathy. The salve is not applied to the wound, but to the instrument which gave the wound. The direction "Bind the wound and grease the nail" is still common when a wound has been given by a rusty nail. Sir Kenelm Digby says the salve is sympathetic, and quotes several instances to prove that "as the sword is treated the wound inflicted by it feels. Thus, if the instrument is kept wet, the wound will feel cool; if held to the fire, it will feel hot;" etc.

" But she has ta'en the broken lance,
And washed it from the clotted gore,
And salved the splinter o'er and o'er."
Sir Walter Scott: Lay of the Last Minstrel, iii. 23.

∴ If grease must be used to satisfy the ignorant, it can do no harm on the rusty nail, but would certainly be harmful on the wound itself.

Wear. *Never wear the image of Deity in a ring.* So Pythagoras taught his disciples, and Moses directed that the Jews should make no image of God. Both meant to teach their disciples that God is incorporeal, and not to be likened to any created form. (See *Iamblichus: Protreptics*, symbol xxiv.)

Never wear a brown hat in Friesland. (*See* HAT.)

To wear the wooden sword. (*See* WOODEN.)

To wear the willow. (*See* WILLOW.)

To wear one's heart upon one's sleeve. (*See under* HEART.)

Weasel. *Weasels suck eggs.* Hence Shakespeare—

"The weazel Scot
Comes sneaking, and so sucks the princely egg."
Henry V., i. 2.

"I can suck melancholy out of a song, as a weazel sucks eggs."—*As You Like It*, ii. 5.

To catch a weasel asleep. To expect to find a very vigilant person nodding, off his guard; to suppose that one who has his weather-eye open cannot see what is passing before him. The French say, *Croir avoir trouvé la pie au nid* (To expect to find the pie on its nest). The vigilant habits of these animals explain the allusions.

Weather Breeder (*A*). A day of unusual fineness coming suddenly after a series of damp dull ones, especially at the time of the year when such a genial

day is not looked for. Such a day is generally followed by foul weather.

Weather-cock. By a Papal enactment made in the middle of the ninth century, the figure of a cock was set up on every church-steeple as the emblem of St. Peter. The emblem is in allusion to his denial of our Lord thrice before the cock crew twice. On the second crowing of the cock the warning of his Master flashed across his memory, and the repentant apostle "went out and wept bitterly."

Weather-eye. *I have my weather-eye open.* I have my wits about me; I know what I am after. The weather-eye is towards the wind to forecast the weather.

Weather-gage. *To get the weather-gage of a person.* To get the advantage over him. A ship is said to have the weather-gage of another when it has got to the windward thereof.

" Were the line
Of Rokeby once combined with mine,
I gain the weather-gage of fate."
Sir Walter Scott: Rokeby.

Weather-glass (*The Peasant's*) or "Poor man's warning." The scarlet pimpernel, which closes its petals at the approach of rain.

" Closed is the pink-eyed pimpernel:
'Twill surely rain; I see with sorrow,
Our jaunt must be put off to-morrow."
Dr. Jenner.

Web of Life. The destiny of an individual from the cradle to the grave. The allusion is to the three Fates who, according to Roman mythology, spin the thread of life, the pattern being the events which are to occur.

Wed is Anglo Saxon, and means a *pledge*. The ring is the pledge given by the man to avouch that he will perform his part of the contract.

Wedding Anniversaries.

The 5th anniversary is called the *Wooden* wedding,

The 10th anniversary is called the *Tin* wedding,

The 15th anniversary is called the *Crystal* wedding,

The 20th anniversary is called the *China* wedding,

The 25th anniversary is called the *Silver* wedding,

The 50th anniversary is called the *Golden* wedding,

The 60th anniversary is called the *Diamond* wedding. From the nature of the gifts suitable for each respective anniversary.

Wedding Finger. Macrobius says the thumb is too busy to be set apart, the forefinger and little finger are only half protected, the middle finger is called *med'icus*, and is too opprobrious for the purpose of honour, so the only finger left is the *pronubus* or wedding finger. (*See* RING, FINGERS.)

Wedding Knives. Undoubtedly, one knife or more than one was in Chaucer's time part of a bride's paraphernalia. Allusions to this custom are very numerous.

" See, at my girdle hang my wedding knives."
            Dekker: Match Me in London (1631).

Wednesday. Woden-es or Odin-es Day, called by the French " Mercredi " (Mercury's Day). The Persians regard it as a " red-letter day," because the moon was created on the fourth day. (Genesis iv. 14-19.)

·: But the last Wednesday of November is called " Black Wednesday."

Weed of Worcester (*The*). The elm, which is very common indeed in the county.

Weeds. *Widow's weeds.* (Anglo-Saxon, *wæd*, a garment.) There are the compounds *wæd-brēc* (breeches or garment for the breech), *wædless* (naked or without clothing), and so on. Spenser speaks of

" A goodly lady clad in hunter's weed."

Weeping Brides. A notion long prevailed in this country that it augured ill for a matrimonial alliance if the bride did not weep profusely at the wedding. As no witch could shed more than three tears, and those from her left eye only, a copious flow of tears gave assurance to the husband that the lady had not " plighted her troth " to Satan, and was no witch.

Weeping Cross. *To go by Weeping Cross.* To repent, to grieve. In ancient times weeping crosses were crosses where penitents offered their devotions. In Stafford there is a weeping cross.

"Few men have wedded . . . their paramours . . . but have come home by Weeping Cross."—
Florio: Montaigne.

Weeping Philosopher. Heracli'tos. So called because he grieved at the folly of man. (Flourished B.C. 500.)

Weeping Saint (*The*). St. Swithin. So called from the tradition of forty days' rain, if it rains on July 15th.

Weigh Anchor. Be off, get you gone. To weigh anchor is to lift it from its moorings, so that the ship may start

on her voyage. As soon as this is done the ship is *under-weigh—i.e.* in movement. (Saxon, *wægan*, to lift up, carry.)

"Get off with you ; come, come ! weigh anchor.''
  —*Sir W. Scott: The Antiquary.*

Weighed in the Balance, and found Wanting. The custom of weighing the Maharajah of Travancore in a scale against gold coin is still in use, and is called *Talabbaram.* The gold is heaped up till the Maharajah rises well in the air. The priests chant their Vedic hymns, the Maharajah is adored, and the gold is distributed among some 15,000 Brahmins, more or less.

Weight. *A dead weight.* (*See* DEAD.)

Weight-for-age Race (*A*). A sort of handicap (*q.v.*), but the weights are apportioned according to certain conditions, and not according to the dictum of a " capper." Horses of the same age carry similar weights *cæteris paribus.* (*See* SELLING - RACE, PLATE, SWEEPSTAKES.)

Weissnichtwo (*vice-neccht-vo*). I know not where; Utopia; Kennaquhair; an imaginary place in Carlyle's *Sartor Resartus.* (*See* UTOPIA.)

Welcher. (*See* WELSHER.)

Weld or **Wold.** The dyer's-weed (*resēda luteōla*), which yields a beautiful yellow dye. (Anglo-Saxon, *geld* or *gold*, our yellow, etc.)

Well Begun is Half Done. " The beginning is half the whole." (*Pythagoras.*)
French: " Heureux commencement est la moitié de l'œuvre." " Ce n'est que le premier pas qui coûte."
Latin: " Incipe dimidium facti est cœpisse." (*Ausonius.*)
" Dimidium facti, qui cœpit, habet."
                        Horace.
" Facilius est incitare currentem, quam commovere languentem." (*Cicero.*)

Well-beloved. Charles VI. of France, *le Bien-aimé.* (1368, 1380-1422.)

Well-founded Doctor. Ægid'ius de Columna. (*-1316.)

Well of English Undefiled. So Geoffrey Chaucer is spoken of by Spenser in the *Faërie Queene*, iv. 2. (1328-1400.)

Well of St. Keyne [*Cornwall*]. The reputed virtue of this well is that whichever of a married pair first drinks its waters will be the paramount power of the house. Southey has a ballad on the subject. The gentleman left the bride at the church door, but the lady took a bottle of the water to church.

Well of Samaria, now called *Nablûs*, is seventy-five feet deep.

Well of Wisdom. This was the well under the protection of the god Mimir (*q.v.*). Odin, by drinking thereof, became the wisest of all beings. (*Scandinavian mythology.*)

Wells (Somersetshire). So called from St. Andrew's Well.

Weller (*Sam*). Pickwick's factotum. His wit, fidelity, archness, and wide-awakedness are inimitable. (*Dickens: Pickwick Papers.*)

Tony Weller. Father of Sam. Type of the old stage-coachman; portly in size, and dressed in a broad-brimmed hat, great-coat of many capes, and top-boots. His stage-coach was his castle, and elsewhere he was as green as a sailor on *terra firma*. (*Dickens: Pickwick Papers.*)

Wellington. *Arthur Wellesley, Duke of Wellington,* called "The Iron Duke," from his iron constitution and iron will. (1769-1852.)

Wellington's horse, Copenhagen. (Died at the age of twenty-seven.) (*See* HORSE.)

Le Wellington des Joueurs. Lord Rivers was so called in Paris.

"Le Wellington des Joueurs lost £23,000 at a sitting, beginning at twelve at night, and ending at seven the following morning."—*Edinburgh Review,* July, 1844.

Welsh Ambassador (*The*). The cuckoo. Logan, in his poem *To the Cuckoo* calls it the "messenger of Spring"; but the Welsh ambassador means that the bird announces the migration of Welsh labourers into England for summer employment.

"Why, thou rogue of universality, do I not know thee? This sound is like the cuckoo, the Welsh ambassador."—*Dampet: A Trick to Catch the Old One,* iv. 5.

Welsh Main. Same as a "battle royal." (*See* BATTLE.)

Welsh Mortgage (*A*). A pledge of land in which no day is fixed for redemption.

Welsh Rabbit. Cheese melted and spread over buttered toast. The word rabbit is a corruption of rare-bit.

"The Welshman he loved toasted cheese,
Which made his mouth like a mouse-trap."
When Good King Arthur Ruled the Land.

Welsh'er. One who lays a bet, but absconds if he loses. It means a Welshman, and is based upon the nursery rhyme, "Taffy was a Welshman, Taffy was a thief."

Wench (*A*) is the Anglo-Saxon word *wencle*, a child. It is now chiefly used derogatorily, and the word *wenching* is quite offensive. In the Midland counties, when a peasant addresses his wife as "my wench," he expresses endearment.

Wench, like *girl*, was at one time applied to either sex. Chaucer has "yonge-girls" for youngsters of both sexes. We find the phrase "knave-girl" used for boys; and Isaac, in the *Ormulum,* is called a wench or wenchel. Similarly, "maid" is applied to both sexes, hence the compound *mæden-fœmne,* a female child or maiden.

Wer'ner, alias *Kruitzner,* alias *Count Siegendorf.* Being driven from the dominion of his father, he wandered about as a beggar for twelve years. Count Stral'enheim, being the next heir, hunted him from place to place. At length Stral'enheim, travelling through Silesia, was rescued from the Oder by Ulric, and lodged in an old palace where Werner had been lodging for some few days. Werner robbed Stral'enheim of a rouleau of gold, but scarcely had he done so when he recognised in Ulric his lost son, and chid him for saving the count. Ulric murdered Stral'enheim, and provided for his father's escape to Siegendorf castle, near Prague. Werner recovered his dominion, but found that his son was a murderer, and imagination is left to fill up the future fate of both father and son. (*Byron: Werner.*)

Wer'ther. The sentimental hero of Goethe's romance called *The Sorrows of Werther.*

Werwolf (French, *loup-garou*). A bogie who roams about devouring infants, sometimes under the form of a man, sometimes as a wolf followed by dogs, sometimes as a white dog, sometimes as a black goat, and occasionally invisible. Its skin is bullet-proof, unless the bullet has been blessed in a chapel dedicated to St. Hubert. This superstition was once common to almost all Europe, and still lingers in Brittany, Limousin, Auvergne, Servia, Wallachia, and White Russia. In the fifteenth century a council of theologians, convoked by the Emperor Sigismund, gravely decided that the *loup-garou* was a reality. It is somewhat curious that we say a "bug-bear," and the French a "bug-wolf." ("Wer-wolf" is Anglo-Saxon *wer,* a man, and wolf—a man in the semblance of a wolf. "Gar" of *gar-ou* is *wer* or *war*, a man; and "ou," a corruption of *ore*, an ogre.)

⁕ Ovid tells the story of Lycāon, King of Arcadia, turned into a wolf because he tested the divinity of Jupiter by serving up to him a "hash of human flesh."

Herodotus describes the Neuri as sorcerers, who had the power of assuming once a year the shape of wolves.

Pliny relates that one of the family of Antæus was chosen annually, by lot, to be transformed into a wolf, in which shape he continued for nine years.

St. Patrick, we are told, converted Vereticus, King of Wales, into a wolf.

Wesleyan. A follower of John Wesley (1703-1791), founder of the Wesleyan Methodists.

Wessex, or **West Saxon Kingdom,** included Hants, Dorset, Wilts, Somerset, Surrey, Gloucestershire, and Bucks.

Westmoreland [*Land of the West Moors*]. Geoffrey of Monmouth says (iv. 17) that Mar or Ma'rius, son of Arvir'-agus, one of the descendants of Brutus the Trojan wanderer, killed Rodric, a Pict, and set up a monument of his victory in a place which he called "Westmar-land," and the chronicler adds that the "inscription of this stone remains to this day." (Saxon, *West-moring-land*.)

Wet. *To have a wet.* To have a drink.

Wet-bob and **Dry-bob.** At Eton a wet-bob is a boy who goes in for boating, but a dry-bob is one who goes in for cricket.

Wet Finger (*With a*), easily, directly. "*D'un tour de main*." The allusion is to the old custom of spinning, in which the spinner constantly wetted the forefinger with the mouth.

" I can bring myself round with a wet finger."—
Sir W. Scott: Redgauntlet, chap. xxiii. (and in many other places).

" The spirit being grieved and provoked. . . .
will not return again with a wet finger."—*Gouge :
Whole Armour of God*, p. 458 (1616).

" I can find
One with a wet finger that is stark blind."
Trial of Love and Fortune (1598).

Flores. " Canst thou bring me thither ?
Peasant.   With a wet finger."
Wisdom of Dr. Dodypoll (1600).

Wetherell (*Elizabeth*). A pseudonym adopted by Miss Susan Warner, an American writer, author of *The Wide Wide World,* and other works.

Wexford Bridge Massacre. In the great Irish Rebellion of 1798, May 25th, some 14,000 Irish insurgents attacked Wexford, defeated the garrison, put to death all those taken prisoners,

and on the 30th frightened the town into a surrender. They treated the Protestants with the utmost barbarity, and, after taking Enniscorthy, encamped on Vinegar Hill (*q.v.*). When informed that Wexford was retaken by the English, the insurgents massacred about a thousand Protestant prisoners in cold blood.

Weyd-monat. The Anglo-Saxon name for June, "because the beasts did then *weyd* in the meadow, that is to say, go and feed there." (*Verstegan.*)

Whale. Not a fish, but a cetaceous mammal.

A *group* of whales is called a school.
The *fat* is called blubber.
The *female* is called a cow.
The *fore-limbs* are called paddles.
The *male* is called a bull-whale.
The *spear* used in whale-fishing is called a harpoon.
The *young* of whales is a cub or calf.

TOOTHED - WHALES include sperm-whales and dolphins.

WHALE-BONE WHALES include rorquals and humpbacks.

Whale. *Very like a whale.* Very much like a cock-and-bull story; a fudge. Hamlet chaffs Polo'nius by comparing a cloud to a camel, and then to a weasel, and when the courtier assents Hamlet adds, "Or like a whale"; to which Polonius answers, "Very like a whale." (Act iii. 2.)

Whalebone (2 syl.). *White as whalebone.* Our forefathers seemed to confuse the walrus with the whale; ivory was made from the teeth of the walrus, and "white as whalebone" is really a blunder for "white as walrus-ivory."

Wharncliffe (2 syl.). *A Wharncliffe meeting* is a meeting of the shareholders of a railway company, called for the purpose of obtaining their assent to a bill in Parliament bearing on the company's railway. So called from Lord Wharncliffe, its originator.

Wharton. *Philip Wharton, Duke of Northumberland,* described by Pope in the *Moral Essays* in the lines beginning—

" Wharton, the scorn and wonder of our days."

A most brilliant orator, but so licentious that he wasted his patrimony in drunkenness and self-indulgence. He was outlawed for treason, and died in a wretched condition at a Bernardine convent in Catalonia. (1698-1731.)

What we Gave we Have, What we Spent we Had, What we Had we Lost. Epitaph of the Good Earl of Courtenay. (*Gibbon : History of the Courtenay Family.*)

The epitaph in St. George's church, Doncaster, runs thus :

> "How now, who is here ?
> I, Robin of Doncastere
> And Margaret, my feere.
> That I spent, that I had ;
> That I gave, that I have ;
> That I left, that I lost."

This is a free translation of Martial's distich—

> "Extra fortunam est quidquid donatur amicis
> Quas dederis, solas semper habebis opes."

What's What. *He knows what's what.* He is a shrewd fellow not to be imposed on. One of the senseless questions of logic was "*Quid est quid ?*"

> " He knew what's what, and that's as high
> As metaphysic wit can fly."
> *Butler : Hudibras,* part i. canto 1.

Whately, Archbishop of Dublin, nicknamed at Oxford "the White Bear" (White from his white overcoat, and Bear from the rude, unceremonious way in which he would trample upon an adversary in argument). (1787-1863.)

Wheal or *Huel* means a tin-mine. (*Cornwall.*)

Wheatear (the bird) has no connection with either *wheat* or *ear*, but it is the Anglo-Saxon *hwit* (white), *ears* (rump). Sometimes called the White-rump, and in French *blanculet* (the little blanc-cul). So called from its white rump.

Wheel. Emblematical of St. Catharine, who was put to death on a wheel somewhat resembling a chaff-cutter.

St. Dona'tus bears a wheel set round with lights.

St. Euphe'mia and St. Willigis both carry wheels.

St. Quintin is sometimes represented with a broken wheel at his feet.

To put one's spoke into another man's wheel. (*See under* SPOKE.)

Wheel of Fortune (*The*). Fortuna, the goddess, is represented on ancient monuments with a wheel in her hand, emblematical of her inconstancy.

> " Though Fortune's malice overthrow my state,
> My mind exceeds the compass of her wheel."
> *Shakespeare : 3 Henry VI.,* iv. 3.

Whelps. Fifth-rate men of war. Thus, in Howell's letters we read, "At the return of this fleet two of the *whelps* were cast away " ; and in the *Travels of Sir W. Brereton* we read, " I went aboard one of the king's ships, called the ninth *whelp*, which is . . . . 215 ton and

tonnage in king's books." In Queen Elizabeth's navy was a ship called *Lion's Whelp,* and her navy was distinguished as first, second . . . tenth *whelp.*

Whetstone. (*See* ACCIUS NAVIUS.)

Whetstone of Witte (*The*) (1556), by Robert Recorde, a treatise on algebra. The old name for algebra was the " Cossic Art," and *Cos Ingenii* rendered into English is " the Whetstone of Wit." It will be remembered that the maid told the belated traveller in the *Fortunes of Nigel* that her master had " no other books but her young mistress's Bible . . . . and her master's *Whetstone of Witte,* by Robert Recorde."

Whig is from *Whiggam-more,* a corruption of *Ugham-more* (pack-saddle thieves), from the Celtic *ugham* (a pack-saddle). The Scotch insurgent Covenanters were called pack-saddle thieves, from the pack-saddles which they used to employ for the stowage of plunder. The Marquis of Argyle collected a band of these vagabonds, and instigated them to aid him in opposing certain government measures in the reign of James I., and in the reign of Charles II. all who opposed government were called the *Argyle whiggamors,* contracted into whigs. (*See* TORY.)

> " The south-west counties of Scotland have seldom corn enough to serve them all the year round, and, the northern parts producing more than they used, those in the west went in summer to buy at Leith the stores that came from the north. From the word *whiggam,* used in driving their horses, all that drove were called the *whiggamors,* contracted into *whigs.* Now, in the year before the news came down of Duke Hamilton's defeat, the ministers animated their people to rise and march to Edinburgh ; and they came up, marching on the head of their parishes, with an unheard-of fury, praying and preaching all the way as they came. The Marquis of Argyle and his party came and headed them, they being about 6,000. This was called the " Whiggamors' Inroad " ; and ever after that, all who opposed the court came in contempt to be called *whigs.* From Scotland the word was brought into England, where it is now one of our unhappy terms of disunion."—*Bishop Burnet : Own Times.*

Whig'gism. The political tenets of the Whigs, which may be broadly stated to be political and religious liberty. Certainly Bishop Burnet's assertion that they are " opposed to the court " may or may not be true. In the reigns of Charles II. and his brother James, no doubt they were opposed to the court, but it was far otherwise in the reign of William III., George I., etc., when the Tories were the anti-court party.

Whip (*A*), in the Legislative Assemblies, is a person employed to whip up members on either side. The Whips give notice to members that a motion is expected when their individual vote may be desirable. The circular runs: "A motion is expected when your vote is 'earnestly' required." If the word "earnestly" has only one red-ink dash under it the receiver is *expected* to come, if it has two dashes it means that he *ought* to come, if it has three dashes it means that he *must* come, if four dashes it means "stay away at your peril." These notices are technically called "RED WHIPS." (*Annual Register*, 1877, p. 86.)

A whip. A notice sent to a member of Parliament by a "whip" (*see above*) to be in his place at the time stated when a "division" is expected.

Whip. *He whipped round the corner* —ran round it quickly. (Dutch, *wippen;* Welsh, *chwipwio*, to whip; *chwip*, a flick or flirt.)

He whipped it up in a minute. The allusion is to the hoisting machine called a whip. A *single* whip is a rope passing over one pulley; a *double* whip is a rope passed over two single pulleys attached to a yard-arm.

Whip-dog Day. October 18 (St. Luke's Day). Brand tells us that a priest about to celebrate mass on St. Luke's Day, happened to drop the pyx, which was snatched up by a dog, and this was the origin of Whip-dog Day. (*Popular Antiquities*, ii. 273.)

Whip with Six Strings (*The*). Called "the Bloody Statute." The religious code of six articles enacted by Convocation and Parliament in the reign of Henry VIII. (1539).

Whipping Boy. A boy kept to be whipped when a prince deserved chastisement. Mungo Murray stood for Charles I., Barnaby Fitzpatrick for Edward VI. (*Fuller: Church History*, ii. 342.) D'Ossat and Du Perron, afterwards cardinals, were whipped by Clement VIII. for Henri IV. of France. Also called a whip-boy.

Whis'kers. A security for money. John de Castro of Portugal, having captured the castle of Diu, in India, borrowed of the inhabitants of Goa 1,000 pistoles for the maintenance of his fleet, and gave one of his whiskers as security of payment, saying, "All the gold in the world cannot equal the value of this natural ornament, which I deposit in your hands."

Whis'ky. Contracted from the Gaelic *ooshk-'a-pai* (water of health).

Usquebaugh, Irish *uisge-'a-bagh* (water of life); *eau de vie*, French (water of life).

L.L. whisky. (*See* L.L. WHISKY.)

Whisky, drink divine (the song) was by O'Leary, not by John Sheehan.

⁂ As a pretty general rule the Scotch word is whiskey, and the Irish word whisky, without the *e*.

Whisky-drinker. *The Irish whisky-drinker.* John [Jack] Sheehan, author of *The Irish Whisky-drinker's Papers* in *Bentley's Miscellany.*

Whist. Cotton says that "the game is so called from the silence that is to be observed in the play." Dr. Johnson has adopted this derivation; but Taylor the Water-poet (1650), Swift (1728), and Barrington (1787) called the game *Whisk*, to the great discomfiture of this etymology. Pope (1715) called it whist.

⁂ The first known mention of whist in print was in a book called *The Motto*, published in 1621, where it is called *whisk*. The earliest known use of the present spelling is in Butler's *Hudibras* (1663).

" Let nice Piquette the boast of France remain,
And studious Ombre be the pride of Spain ;
Invention's praise shall England yield to none,
While she can call delightful Whist her own."
Alexander Thomson: A poem in eight cantos on Whist. (Second edition, 1792.)

Whistle (noun). *Champion of the whistle.* The person who can hold out longest in a drinking bout. A Dane, in the train of Anne of Denmark, had an ebony whistle placed on the table, and whoever of his guests was able to blow it when the rest of the company were too far gone for the purpose was called the champion. Sir Robert Laurie of Maxwelton, after a rouse lasting three nights and three days, left the Dane under the table and blew his requiem on the whistle.

To wet one's whistle. To take a drink. Whistle means a pipe (Latin, *fistula ;* Saxon, *hwistle*), hence the wind-pipe.

"So was hir joly whistal well y-wet."
Chaucer : Canterbury Tales.

You paid too dearly for your whistle. You paid dearly for something you fancied, but found that it did not answer your expectation. The allusion is to a story told by Dr. Franklin of his nephew, who set his mind on a common whistle, which he bought of a boy for four times its value. Franklin says the ambitious who dance attendance on court, the miser who gives this world and the next for gold, the libertine who ruins his health for pleasure, the girl who marries a brute for money, all pay "too much for their whistle."

Worth the whistle. Worth calling; worth inviting; worth notice. The dog is worth the pains of whistling for. Thus Heywood, in one of his dialogues consisting entirely of proverbs, says, "It is a poor dog that is not worth the whistling." Goneril says to Albany—

> "I have been worth the whistle."
> *Shakespeare : King Lear,* iv. 2.

Whistle (verb). *You may whistle for that.* You must not expect it. The reference is to sailors whistling for the wind. "They call the winds, but will they come when they do call them ? "

> " Only a little hour ago
> I was whistling to St. Antonio
> For a capful of wind to fill our sail,
> And instead of a breeze he has sent a gale."
> *Longfellow : Golden Legend,* v.

You must whistle for more. In the old whistle-tankards, the whistle comes into play when the tankard is empty, to announce to the drawer that more liquor is wanted. Hence the expression, If a man wants liquor, *he must whistle for it.*

Whistle Down the Wind (*To*). To defame a person. The cognate phrase "blown upon" is more familiar. The idea is to whistle down the wind that the reputation of the person may be blown upon.

Whistle for the Wind. (*See* CAPFULL.)

> " What gales are sold on Lapland's shore !
> How whistle rash bids tempests roar ! "
> *Sir Walter Scott : Rokeby,* ii. 11.

White denotes purity, simplicity, and candour; innocence, truth, and hope.

The ancient Druids, and indeed the priests generally of antiquity, used to wear white vestments, as do the clergy of the Established Church of England when they officiate in any sacred service. The magi also wore white robes.

The head of Osiris, in Egypt, was adorned with a white tiara; all her ornaments were white; and her priests were clad in white.

The priests of Jupiter, and the Flamen Diālis of Rome, were clothed in white, and wore white hats. The victims offered to Jupiter were white. The Roman festivals were marked with white chalk, and at the death of a Cæsar the national mourning was white; white horses were sacrificed to the sun, white oxen were selected for sacrifice by the Druids, and white elephants are held sacred in Siam.

The Persians affirm that the divinities are habited in white.

White Bird (*The*). Conscience, or the soul of man. The Mahometans have preserved the old Roman idea in the doctrine that the souls of the just lie under the throne of God, like white birds, till the resurrection morn.

> " A white bird, she told him once . . . he must carry on his bosom across a crowded public place —his own soul was like that."—*Pater : Marius the Epicurean,* chap. ii.

White Brethren or **White-clad Brethren.** A sect in the beginning of the fifteenth century. Mosheim says (bk. ii. p. 2, chap. v.) a certain priest came from the Alps, clad in white, with an immense concourse of followers all dressed in white linen also. They marched through several provinces, following a cross borne by their leader. Boniface X. ordered their leader to be burnt, and the multitude dispersed.

White Caps. A rebellious party of zealous Mahometans, put down by Kienlŏng the Chinese emperor, in 1758. So called from their head-dress.

White Caps. An influential family in Kerry (Ireland), who acted a similar part as Judge Lynch in America. When neighbours became unruly, the white caps visited them during the night and beat them soundly. Their example was followed about a hundred years ago in other parts of Ireland.

White Caps (1891). A party in North America opposed to the strict Sabbatarian observance. So called because they wear high white caps. First heard of at Okawaville, Illinois.

White-coat (*A*). An Austrian soldier. So called because he wears a white coat. Similarly, an English soldier is called a red-coat. In old Rome, *ad saga ire* meant to " become a soldier," and *tunere sagum* to enlist, from the *sagum* or military cloak worn by the soldier, in contradistinction to the *toga* worn by the citizen in times of peace.

White Cockade. The badge worn by the followers of Charles Edward, the Pretender.

White Company (*The*). " *Le Blanche Compagnie.*" A band of French cutthroats organised by Bertrand du Guesclin and led against Pedro the Cruel.

> " Se faisoient appeller ' La Blanche Compagnie,' parce qu'ils portoient tous une croix blanche sur l'épaule, comme voulant témoigner qu'ils n'avoient pris les armes que pour abolir le Judaïsme en Espagne, et combattre le Prince qui le protégesit."—*Mémoires Historiques.*

White Czar (*The*). Strictly speaking means the Czar of Muscovy; the

King of Muscovy was called the White King from the white robes which he wore. The King of Poland was called the Black King.

"Sunt qui principem Moscoviæ *Album Regem* nuncupant. . Ego quidem causam diligenter quierēbam, cur regis albi nomine appellaretur, cum nemo principum Moscoviæ eo titulo antea [Ivan III.] esset usus . . . Credo autem ut Persam nunc propter *rubea* tegumenta capitis 'Kissil-passa' (*i. e.* rubeum caput) vocant; ita reges Moscoviæ propter *alba* tegumenta 'Albos Reges' appellari."—*Sigismund.*

"The marriage of the Czarevitch with the Princess Alex of Hesse (2 syl.) will impress the Oriental mind with the expectation that the Empress of India and the White Czar will henceforth . . . labour to avoid the . . mischief of disagreement."—*The Standard,* April 21st, 1894.

White Elephant. *King of the White Elephant.* The proudest title borne by the kings of Ava and Siam. In Ava the white elephant bears the title of "lord," and has a minister of high rank to superintend his household.

The land of the White Elephant. Siam.

To have a white elephant to keep. To have an expensive and unprofitable dignity to support, or a pet article to take care of. For example, a person moving is determined to keep a pet carpet, and therefore hires his house to fit his carpet. The King of Siam makes a present of a white elephant to such of his courtiers as he wishes to ruin.

White Feather. *To show the white feather.* To show cowardice. No game-cock has a white feather. A white feather indicates a cross-breed in birds.

Showing the white feather. Some years ago a bloody war was raging between the Indians and settlers of the back-woods of North America. A Quaker, who refused to fly, saw one day a horde of savages rushing down towards his house. He set food before them, and when they had eaten the chief fastened a white feather over the door as a badge of friendship and peace. Though many bands passed that house, none ever violated the covenant by injuring its inmates or property.

White Friars. The Carmelites. So called because they dressed in white.

Whitefriars, London. So called from a monastery of White Friars which formerly stood in Water Lane.

Whitefriars. A novel, by Emma Robinson.

White Harvest (*A*). A late harvest, when the ground is white of a morning with hoarfrost. The harvest of 1891 was a white harvest.

White Hat. (*See under* HAT.)

White Horse of Wantage (Berkshire), cut in the chalk hills. This horse commemorates a great victory gained by Alfred over the Danes, in the reign of his brother Ethelred I. The battle is called the battle of Æscesdun (Ashtree-hill). The horse is 374 feet long, and may be seen at the distance of fifteen miles. (*Dr. Wise.*)

An annual ceremony was once held, called "Scouring the White Horse."

White Horses. Foam-crested waves.

"The resemblance . . . has commonly been drawn between the horse [and the waves], in regard to his mane, and the foam-tipped waves, which are still called white horses."—*W. E. Gladstone: Nineteenth Century,* November, 1885.

White House. The presidential mansion in the United States. It is a building of freestone, painted white, at Washington. Figuratively, it means the Presidency; as, "He has his eye on the White House." (*See* WHITEHALL.)

White Ladies [*Les Dames Blanches*]. A species of fée in Normandy. They lurk in ravines, fords, bridges, and other narrow passes, and ask the passenger to dance. If they receive a courteous answer, well; but if a refusal, they seize the churl and fling him into a ditch, where thorns and briars may serve to teach him gentleness of manners.

⁂ The most famous of these ladies is La Dame d'Aprigny, who used to occupy the site of the present Rue St. Quentin, at Bayeux, and La Dame Abonde. "Vocant dom'inam *Abundiam* pro eo quod dom'ibus, quas frequentant, abundan'tiam bono'rum tempora'lium præsta're putantur non al'iter tibi sentiendum est neque al'iter quam quemad'modum de illis audivisti." (*William of Auverane,* 1248.) (*See* BEERCHTA.)

"One kind of these the Italians *Fata* name;
The French call *Fée;* we *Sybils;* and the same
Others *White Dames,* and those that them have seen,
Night Ladies some, of which Habundia's queen."
Hierarchie, viii. p. 597.

The White Lady. The legend says that Bertha promised the workmen of Neuhaus a sweet soup and carp on the completion of the castle. In remembrance thereof, these dainties were given to the poor of Bohemia on Maundy Thursday, but have been discontinued.

The most celebrated in Britain is the *White Lady of Avenel,* the creation of Sir Walter Scott.

White Lady of German legend. A being dressed in white, who appears at the castle of German princes to forebode a death. She last appeared, it is said, in

1879, just prior to the death of Prince Waldemar. She carries a bunch of keys at her side, and is always dressed in white. The first instance of this apparition occurred in the sixteenth century and the name given to the lady is Bertha von Rosenberg (in Bohemia).

∴ Twice, we are told, she has been heard to speak, once in December, 1628, when she said, " I wait for judgment ! " and once at the castle of Neuhaus, in Bohemia, when she said to the princes, " 'Tis ten o'clock."

The White Lady of Ireland. The Banshee.

White Lies. A conventional lie, such as telling a caller that Mrs. A. or Mrs. B. is not at home, meaning not " at home " to that particular caller.

It is said that Dean Swift called on a " friend," and was told by Jeames that " master is not at home." After a time this very " friend " called on the dean, and Swift, opening the window, shouted, " Not at home." When the friend expostulated, Swift said, " I believed your footman when he said his master was not at home ; surely you can believe the master himself when he tells you he is not at home."

White Moments of Life (*The*). The red-letter days or happy moments of life. The Romans used to mark unlucky days, in their calendars, with *black chalk*, and lucky ones with *white* chalk ; hence *Notare diem lactea gemma* or *alba* means to mark a day as a lucky one.

" These, my young friend, these are the white moments of one's life."—*Sir W. Scott: The Antiquary*, chap. iii.

White Moon (*Knight of the*). Sampson Carrasco assumed this character and device, in order to induce Don Quixote to abandon knight errantry, and return home. The Don, being worsted, returned home, lingered a little while, and died. (*Cervantes: Don Quixote*, pt. ii. bk. iv. chap. 12, etc.)

White Night (*A*). A sleepless night; hence the French phrase " *Passer une nuit blanche.*"

White Poplar. This tree was originally the nymph Leuce, beloved by Pluto, and at death the infernal Zeus metamorphosed her into a white poplar, which was ultimately removed into Elysium.

White Rose. The House of York, whose emblem it was.

The White Rose. Cardinal de la Pole. (1500-1558.)

White Rose of England. So Perkin Warbeck or Osbeck was always addressed by Margaret of Burgundy, the sister of Edward IV. (*-1449.) Lady Catherine Gordon, given by James IV. as wife to Perkin Warbeck, was called " The White Rose." She married three times more after the death of Warbeck.

The White Rose of Raby. Cecily, wife of Richard, Duke of York, and mother of Edward IV. and Richard III. She was the youngest of twenty-one children.

White Sheep [*Ak-koin-loo*]. A tribe of Turkomans, so called from their standards. The Sophive'an dynasty of Persia was founded by one of this tribe.

White Squall. One which produces no diminution of light, in contradistinction to a *black* squall, in which the clouds are black and heavy.

White Stone. *Days marked with a white stone.* Days of pleasure ; days to be remembered with gratification. The Romans used a white stone or piece of chalk to mark their lucky days with on the calendar. Those that were unlucky they marked with black charcoal. (*See* RED-LETTER DAY.)

White Stone (Rev. ii. 17). *To him that overcometh will I give . . . a white stone ; and in the stone a new name* [*is*] *written which no man knoweth saving he that receiveth it* [*i.e.* the stone]. In primitive times, when travelling was difficult for want of places of public accommodation, hospitality was exercised by private individuals to a great extent. When the guest left, the host gave him a small white stone cut in two ; on one half the host wrote his name, and on the other the guest ; the host gave the guest the half containing his [host's] name, and *vice versâ*. This was done that the guest at some future time might return the favour, if needed. Our text says, " I will give him to eat of the hidden manna "—*i.e.* I will feed or entertain him well, and I will keep my friendship, sacred, inviolable, and known only to himself.

White Surrey. The horse of Richard III. (*See* HORSE.)

" Saddle White Surrey for the field."
Shakespeare : Richard III., v. 3.

White Tincture. That preparation which the alchemists believed would convert any baser metal into silver. It is also called the Stone of the Second Order, the Little Elixir, and the Little Magisterium. (*See* RED TINCTURE.)

White Water-lotus [*Pe-lien-kaou*]. A secret society which greatly disturbed the empire of China in the reign of Kea-King. (1796-1820.)

White Widow. The Duchess of Tyrconnel, wife of Richard Talbot, Lord-deputy of Ireland under James II., created Duke of Tyrconnel a little before the king's abdication. After the death of Talbot, a female, supposed to be his duchess, supported herself for a few days by her needle. She wore a white mask, and dressed in white. (*Pennant : London,* p. 147.)

White Witch (*A*). A cunning fellow ; one knowing in white art in contradistinction to black art.

"Two or three years past there came to these parts one . . . what the vulgar call a white witch, a cunning man, and such like."—*Sir W. Scott: Kenilworth,* chap. ix.

White as Driven Snow. (*See* SIMILES.)

White in the Eye. It is said that the devil has no white in his eyes, and hence the French locution, "*Celui qui n'a point de blanc en l'œil.*" "Do you see any white in my eye ? " is asked by one who means to insinuate he is no fool or no knave—that is, he is not like the devil with no white in the eye.

Whitebait Dinner. The ministerial dinner that announces the near close of the parliamentary session. Sir Robert Preston, M.P. for Dover, first invited his friend George Rose (Secretary of the Treasury) and an elder brother of the Trinity House to dine with him at his fishing cottage on the banks of Dagenham Lake. This was at the close of the session. Rose on one occasion proposed that Mr. Pitt, their mutual friend, should be asked to join them ; this was done, and Pitt promised to repeat his visit the year following, when other members swelled the party. This went on for several years, when Pitt suggested that the muster should be in future nearer town, and Greenwich was selected. Lord Camden next advised that each man should pay his quota. The dinner became an annual feast, and was until lately (1892) a matter of course. The time of meeting was Trinity Monday, or as near Trinity Monday as circumstances would allow, and therefore was near the close of the session.

Whiteboys. A secret agrarian association organised in Ireland about the year 1759. So called because they wore white shirts in their nightly expeditions. In 1787 a new association appeared, the members of which called themselves "Right-boys." The Whiteboys were originally called "Levellers," from their throwing down fences and levelling enclosures. (*See* LEVELLERS.)

Whitehall (London) obtained its name from the white and fresh appearance of the front, compared with the ancient buildings in York Place. (*Brayley : Londoniana.*) (*See* WHITE HOUSE.)

Whitewashed. Said of a person who has taken the benefit of the Insolvent Act. He went to prison covered with debts and soiled with "dirty ways : " he comes out with a clean bill to begin the contest of life afresh.

Whit-leather. The skin of a horse cured and whitened for whip-thongs, hedging-gloves, and so on.

"Thy gerdill made of whitlether whange . . .
Is turned now to velvet."
MS. Lansd., 241.

Whitsunday. White Sunday. The seventh Sunday after Easter, to commemorate the "Descent of the Holy Ghost" on the day of Pentecost. In the Primitive Church the newly-baptised wore white from Easter to Pentecost, and were called *alba'ii* (white-robed). The last of the Sundays, which was also the chief festival, was called emphatically *Domin'ica in Albis* (Sunday in White).

Another etymology is *Wit* or *Wisdom* Sunday, the day when the Apostles were filled with wisdom by the Holy Ghost.

"This day Wit-sonday is cald.
For wisdom and wit serene fald,
Was zonen to the Apostles as this day."
Cambr. Univer. MSS., Dd. i. 1, p. 234.

(Compare *Witten-agemote.*)

"We ought to kepe this our Witsonday bicause the law of God was then of the Holy Wyght or Ghost deliured gostly ynto vs."—*Taverner* (1540).
"This day is called Wytsonday because the Holy Ghost brought wytte and wysdom into Christis disciples . . . and filled them full of ghostly wytte."—*In die Pentecostis* (printed by Wynken de Worde).

Whittington. (*See under* CAT ; also WITTINGTON.)

Riley in his *Munimenta Gildhallæ Londenensis* (p. xviii.) says *achat* was used at the time for "trading" (*i.e.* buying and selling), and that Whittington made his money by *achat*, called *acat.* We have the word in *cater, caterer.*

.·. As much error exists respecting Dick Whittington, the following account will be useful. He was born in Gloucestershire, in the middle of the fourteenth century, and was the son of a knight of good property. He went to London to learn how to become a merchant. His master was a relative, and took a great interest in the boy, who subsequently married Alice, his master's daughter. He became very rich, and was four times Mayor of London, but the first time was before the office was created Lord Mayor by Richard II. He died in 1423, during his year of office, about sixty-three years of age.

Whittle (*A*). A knife. (Anglo-Saxon *hwytel*, a knife; *hwæt*, sharp or keen.)

"Walter de Aldeham holds land of the king in the More, in the county of Salop, by the service of paying to the king yearly at his exchequer two knives [whittles], whereof one ought to be of that value or goodness that at the first stroke it would cut asunder in the middle a hasle-rod of a year's growth, and of the length of a cubit, which service ought to be . . . on the morrow of St. Michael. . . The said knives [whittles] to be delivered to the chamberlain to keep for the king's use."—*Blount: Ancient Tenures.*

Whittle Down. To cut away with a knife or whittle; to reduce; to encroach. In Cumberland, underpaid schoolmasters used to be allowed *Whittle-gait*—*i.e.* the privilege of knife and fork at the table of those who employ them.

The Americans "whittled down the royal throne;" "whittled out a commonwealth;" "whittle down the forest trees;" "whittle out a railroad;" "whittle down to the thin end of nothing." (Saxon, *hwytel,* 'a large knife.)

"We have whittled down our loss extremely, and will not allow a man more than 350 English slain out of 4,000."—*Walpole.*

Whitworth Gun. (*See* GUN.)

Whole Duty of Man. Tenison, Bishop of Lincoln, says the author was Dr. Chaplin, of University College, Oxford. (*Evelyn: Diary.*)

Thomas Hearne ascribes the authorship to Archbishop Sancroft.

Some think Dr. Hawkins, who wrote the introduction, was the author.

The following names have also been suggested.—Lady Packington (assisted by Dr. Fell), Archbishop Sterne, Archbishop Woodhead, William Fulham, Archbishop Frewen (President of Magdalen College, Oxford), and others.

Whole Gale (*A*). A very heavy wind. The three degrees are a *fresh* gale, a *strong* gale, and a *heavy* or *whole* gale.

Whom the Gods Love Die Young [*Herodotos*]. Cited in *Don Juan,* canto iv. 12 (death of Haidee).

Wick, Wicked, and in French *Méche, Méchant.* That the two English words and the two French words should have similar resemblances and similar meanings is a remarkable coincidence, especially as the two adjectives are quite independent of the nouns in their etymology. "Wick" is the Anglo-Saxon *weoce,* a rush or reed, but "wicked" is the Anglo-Saxon *wæc* or *wac,* vile. So "méche" is the Latin *myxa,* a wick, but "méchant" is the old French *mes-chéant,* unlucky.

Wicked Bible. (*See* BIBLE.)

Wicked Prayer Book (*The*). Printed 1686, octavo. The Fourteenth Sunday after Trinity reads :—

"Now the works of the flesh are manifest, which are these: adultery, fornication, uncleanness, idolatry . . . they who do these things shall inherit the kingdom of God."

(Of course, "shall inherit" should be *shall not inherit.*)

Wicked Weed (*The*). Hops.

"After the introduction into England of the wicked weed called hops."—*Return to Edward VI.'s Parliament,* 1524.

Wicket-gate. The entrance to the road that leadeth to the Celestial City. Over the portal is the inscription— "KNOCK, AND IT SHALL BE OPENED UNTO YOU." (*Bunyan: Pilgrim's Progress.*)

Wicliffe (*John*), called "The Morning Star of the Reformation." (1324-1384.)

Wide-awake. Felt hats are so called by a pun, because they never have a *nap* at any time; they are always wide awake.

Wide'nostrils (3 syl.). (French, *Bringuenarilles.*) A huge giant, who subsisted on windmills, and lived in the island of Tohu. When Pantagruel and his fleet reached this island no food could be cooked because Widenostrils had swallowed "every individual pan, skillet, kettle, frying-pan, dripping-pan, boiler, and saucepan in the land," and died from eating a lump of butter. Tohu and Bohu, two contiguous islands (in Hebrew, *toil* and *confusion*), mean lands laid waste by war. The giant had eaten everything, so that there was "nothing to fry with," as the French say—*i.e.* nothing left to live upon.

Widow. (*See* GRASS WIDOW.)

Widow (in *Hudibras*). The relict of Aminadab Wilmer or Willmot, an Independent, slain at Edgehill. She had £200 left her. Sir Hudibras fell in love with her.

Widow Bird. A corruption of Whydaw bird. So called from the country of Whydaw, in Western Africa. The blunder is perpetuated in the scientific name given to the genus, which is the Latin *Vid'ua,* a widow.

Widow's Cap. This was a Roman custom. Widows were obliged to wear "weeds" for ten months. (*Seneca: Epistles,* lxv.)

Widow's Piano. Inferior instruments sold as bargains; so called from the ordinary advertisement announcing that a *widow lady* is compelled to sell her piano, for which she will take half-price.

Widow's Port. A wine sold for port, but of quite a different family. As a widow retains her husband's name after her husband is taken away, so this mixture of potato spirit and some inferior wine retains the name of port, though every drop of port is taken from it.

"We have all heard of widow's port, and of the instinctive dread all persons who have any respect for their health have for it."—*The Times.*

Wie'land (2 syl.). The famous smith of Scandinavian fable. He and Amilias had a contest of skill in their handicraft. Wieland's sword cleft his rival down to the thighs ; but so sharp was the sword, that Amilias was not aware of the cut till he attempted to stir, when he divided into two pieces. This sword was named Balmung.

Wife is from the verb to weave. (Saxon *wefan*, Danish *væve*, German *weben*, whence *weib*, a woman, one who works at the distaff.) Woman is called the *distaff*. Hence Dryden calls Anne "a distaff on the throne." While a girl was spinning her wedding clothes she was simply a spinster ; but when this task was done, and she was married, she became a wife, or one who had already woven her allotted task.

Alfred, in his will, speaks of his male and female descendants as those of the *spear-side* and those of the *spindle-side*, a distinction still observed by the Germans ; and hence the effigies on graves of spears and spindles.

Wig. A variation of the French *perruque*, Latin *pilucca*, our *periwig* cut short. In the middle of the eighteenth century we meet with thirty or forty different names for wigs : as the artichoke, bag, barrister's, bishop's, brush, bush [buzz], buckle, busby, chain, chancellor's, corded wolf's paw, Count Saxe's mode, the crutch, the cut bob, the detached buckle, the Dalmahoy (a bobwig worn by tradesmen), the drop, the Dutch, the full, the half-natural, the Jansenist bob, the judge's, the ladder, the long bob, the Louis, the periwig, the pigeon's wing, the rhinoceros, the rose, the scratch, the she-dragon, the small back, the spinach seed, the staircase, the Welsh, and the wild boar's back.

A bigwig. A magnate. Louis XIV. had long flowing hair, and the courtiers, out of compliment to the young king, wore perukes. When Louis grew older he adopted the wig, which very soon encumbered the head and shoulders of the aristocracy of England and France. Lord Chancellors, judges, and barristers still wear big wigs. Bishops used to wear them in the House of Lords till 1880.

" An ye fa' over the cleugh, there will be but ae wig left in the parish, and that's the minister's."
—*Sir Walter Scott : The Antiquary.*

Make wigs. A perruquier, who fancied himself "married to immortal verse," sent his epic to Voltaire, asking him to examine it and give his "candid opinion" of its merits. The witty patriarch of Ferney simply wrote on the MS. "Make wigs, make wigs, make wigs," and returned it to the barber-poet. (*See* SUTOR, *Stick to the cow.*)

Wig (*A*). A head. Similarly, the French call a head a *binette*. As "*Quelle binette !*" or "*Il a une drôle de binette !*" M. Binet was the court wig-maker in the reign of Louis XIV. "*M. Binet, qui foit les perruques du roy, demeure Rue des Petits-Champs.*" (*Almanack des addresses sous Louis XIV.*)

" Fleas are not lobsters, dash my wig."
S. Butler: Hudibras.

Wig. War (Anglo-Saxon). The word enters into many names of places, as Wigan in Lancashire, where Arthur is said to have routed the Saxons.

Wight (*Isle of*) means probably channel island. (Celtic *gwy*, water ; *gwyth*, the channel.) The inhabitants used to be called Uuhtii or Gwythii, the inhabitants of the channel isle.

❖ According to the famous *Anglo-Saxon Chronicle*, the island is so called from Wihtgar, great grandson of King Cerdic, who conquered it. All eponymic names—that is, names of *persons*, like the names of *places*, are more fit for fable than history : as *Cissa*, to account for Cissanceaster (Chichester) ; *Horsa* to account for Horsted ; *Hengist* to account for Hengistbury ; *Brutus* to account for Britain ; and so on.

Wig'wam'. An Indian hut (America). The Knisteneaux word is *wigwaum*, and the Algonquin *wêkou-om-ut*, contracted into *wekouom* (ou = w, as in French), whence *wêkwom*.

Wild (*Jonathan*), the detective, born at Wolverhampton, in Staffordshire. He brought to the gallows thirty-five highwaymen, twenty-two housebreakers, and ten returned convicts. He was himself hanged at Tyburn for housebreaking "amidst the execrations of an enraged populace, who pelted him with stones to the last moment of his existence." (1682-1725.) Fielding has a novel entitled *Jonathan Wild*.

Wild Boar. An emblem of warlike fury and merciless brutality.

Wild Boy of Hamelin or *Man of Nature*, found in the forest of Hertswold, Hanover. He walked on all fours, climbed trees like a monkey, fed on grass and leaves, and could never be taught to articulate a single word. Dr. Arbuthnot and Lord Monboddo sanctioned the notion that this poor boy was really an unsophisticated specimen of the *genus homo;* but Blumenbach showed most conclusively that he was born dumb, of weak intellect, and was driven from his home by a stepmother. He was discovered in 1725, was called Peter the Wild Boy, and died at Broadway Farm, near Berkhampstead, in 1785, at the supposed age of seventy-three.

Wild Children.
(1) *Peter the Wild Boy.* (*See above.*)
(2) Mlle. Lablanc, found by the villagers of Soigny, near Châlons, in 1731 : she died at Paris in 1785, at the supposed age of sixty-two.
(3) A child captured by three sportsmen in the woods of Cannes (France) in 1798. (See *World of Wonders*, p. 61, Correspondence.)

Wild-goose Chase. A hunt after a mare's nest. This chase has two defects : First, it is very hard to catch the goose ; and, secondly, it is of very little worth when it is caught.
To lead one a wild-goose chase. To beguile one with false hopes, or put one on the pursuit of something not practicable, or at any rate not worth the chase.

Wild Huntsman.
The German tradition is that a spectral hunter with dogs frequents the Black Forest to chase the wild animals. (*Sir Walter Scott : Wild Huntsman.*)
The French story of *Le Grand Veneur* is laid in Fontainebleau Forest, and is considered to be "St. Hubert." (*Father Matthieu.*)
The English name is "Herne the Hunter," who was once a keeper in Windsor Forest. In winter time, at midnight, he walks about Herne's Oak, and blasts trees and cattle. He wears horns, and rattles a chain in a "most hideous manner." (*Merry Wives of Windsor*, iv. 4.)
Another legend is that a certain Jew would not suffer Jesus to drink out of a horse-trough, but pointed to some water in a hoof-print as good enough for "such

an enemy of Moses," and that this man is the "Wild Huntsman." (*Kuhn von Schwarz : Nordd. Sagen*, p. 499.)

Wild Oats. *He is sowing his wild oats*—indulging the buoyant folly of youth ; living in youthful dissipation. The idea is that the mind is a field of good oats, but these pranks are wild oats or weeds sown amongst the good seed, choking it for a time, and about to die out and give place to genuine corn. The corresponding French phrase is "*Jeter ses premiers faux*," which reminds us of Cicero's expression, "*Nondum illi deferbuit adolescentia*." (*See* OATS.)

Wild Women [*Wildë Frauën*] of Germany resemble the Ellë-maids of Scandinavia. Like them, they are very beautiful, have long flowing hair, and live in hills. (*See* WUNDERBURG.)

Wild Women. A term at one time applied to the advocates of women's rights. The movement in favour of female suffrage speedily outgrew vulgar prejudices, motions in favour of it passed the House of Commons, and the term very soon became obsolete.

"Let anyone commend to these female runagates quietness, duty, home-staying, and the whole cohort of wild women is like an angry beehive, which a rough hand has disturbed."—*Nineteenth Century*, March, 1892, p. 463.

Wild as a March Hare. The hare in spring, after one or two rings, will often run straight on end for several miles. This is especially the case with the buck, which therefore affords the best sport.

Wilde. *A John* or *Johnny Wilde* is one who wears himself to skin and bone to add house to house and barn to barn. The tale is that John Wilde, of Rodenkerchen, in the isle of Rügen, found one day a glass slipper belonging to one of the hill-folks. Next day the little brownie, in the character of a merchant, came to redeem it, and John asked as the price "that he should find a gold ducat in every furrow he ploughed." The bargain was concluded, and the avaricious hunks never ceased ploughing morning, noon, nor night, but died within twelve months from over-work. (*Rügen tradition.*)

Wile away Time (not *While*). It is the same word as "guile," to "beguile the time " (*fall'ere tempus*).

"To wile each moment with a fresh delight."
Lowell : Legend of Brittany, part i. stanza 6.

Wilfrid (*St.*). Patron saint of bakers, being himself of the craft. (634-709.)
St. Wilfrid's Needle is a narrow

passage in the crypt of Ripon cathedral, built by Odo, Archbishop of Canterbury, and used to try whether virgins deserve the name or not. It is said that none but virgins can pass this ordeal.

Wil'helm Mei'ster (2 syl.). The first true German novel. It was by Goethe, who died 1832, aged eighty-three.

Will not when They may. *Those who will not when they may, when they will they shall have nay.*

"Qui ne prend le bien quand il peut, il ne l'a pas quand il veut."
"Quand le bien vient, on le doit prendre."
"Saisir en tout l'occasion et l'à-propos est un grand élément de bonheur et de succès."

Wil'liam (2 syl.; in *Jerusalem De-livered*), Archbishop of Orange. An ecclesiastical warrior, who besought Pope Urban on his knees that he might be sent in the crusade. He took 400 armed men in his train from his own diocese.

William, youngest son of William Rufus. He wore a casque of gold, and was the leader of a large army of British bow-men and Irish volunteers in the crusading army. (*Tasso: Jerusalem Delivered*, bk. iii.)

✥ English history teaches that William Rufus was never married. (*See* ORLANDO FURIOSO.)

Belted Will. William, Lord Howard, warden of the Western Marches. (1563-1640.)

"His Bilboa blade, by Marchmen felt,
Hung in a broad and studded belt :
Hence, in rude phrase, the borderers still
Called noble Howard ' Belted Will.' "
Sir Walter Scott: Lay of the Last Minstrel, v. 16.

St. William of Aquitaine was one of the soldiers of Charlemagne, and helped to chase the Saracens from Languedoc. In 808 he renounced the world, and died 812. He is usually represented as a mailed soldier.

St. William of Mallavalle or *Maleval.* A French nobleman of very abandoned life ; but, being converted, he went as pilgrim to Jerusalem, and on his return retired to the desert of Malavalle. He is depicted in a Benedictine's habit, with armour lying beside him. (Died 1157.)

St. William of Montpelier is represented with a lily growing from his mouth, with the words *Ave Maria* in gold letters on it.

St. William of Monte Virgine is drawn with a wolf by his side. (Died 1142.)

St. William of Norwich was the celebrated child said to have been crucified by the Jews in 1137. He is represented as a child crowned with thorns, or crucified, or holding a hammer and nails in his hands, or wounded in his side with a knife. (See *Polyolbion*, song xxiv.)

✥ In Percy's *Reliques* (bk. i. 3) there is a tale of a lad named Hew, son of Lady Helen, of Merryland town (Milan), who was allured by a Jew's daughter with an apple. She stuck him with a penknife, rolled him in lead, and cast him into a well. Lady Helen went in search of her boy, and the child's ghost cried out from the bottom of the well—

"The lead is wondrous heavy, mither,
   The well is wondrous deip ;
A keen penknife sticks in my heirt, mither ;
   A word I dounae speik." (*See* HUGH).

St. William of Roeschild is represented with a torch flaming on his grave. (Died 1203.)

St. William of York is depicted in pontificals, and bearing his archiepiscopal cross. (Died 1154.)

William II. The body of this king was picked up by Purkess, a charcoal-burner of Minestead, and conveyed in a cart to Winchester. The name of Purkess is still to be seen in the same village.

" A Minestead churl, whose wonted trade
   Was burning charcoal in the glade,
   Outstretched amid the gorse
The monarch found ; and in his wain
He raised, and to St. Swithin's fane
   Conveyed the bleeding corse." *W. S. Rose.*

William III. It was not known till the discovery of the correspondence of Cardonnel, secretary of Marlborough, by the Historical MS. Commission in 1869, that our Dutch king was a great eater. Cardonnel, writing from The Hague, October, 1701, to Under-Secretary Ellis, says—"It is a pity his majesty will not be more temperate in his diet. Should I eat so much, and of the same kinds, I dare say I should scarce have survived it so long, and yet I reckon myself none of the weakest constitutions."

William of Cloudes'lie (2 syl.). A noted outlaw and famous archer of the "north countrie." (*See* CLYM OF THE CLOUGH.)

William of Newburgh (Gulielmus Neu-brigensis), monk of Newburgh in York-shire, surnamed Little, and sometimes called *Gulielmus Parvus*, wrote a history in five books, from the Conquest to 1197, edited by Thomas Hearne, in three volumes, octavo, Oxford, 1719. The Latin is good, and the work ranks with that of Malmesbury. William of New-burgh is the first writer who rejects Geoffrey of Monmouth's Trojan descent of the old Britons, which he calls a "figment made more absurd by Geoffrey's impudent and impertinent lies." He is, however, quite as fabulous an historian as the "impudent" Geoffrey. (1136-1208.)

William I., King of Prussia and Emperor of Germany, was called by his detractors *Kaiser Tartuffe.*

Willie-Wastle (the child's game). Willie Wastle was governor of Hume Castle, Haddington. When Cromwell sent a summons to him to surrender, he replied—

"Here I, Willie Wastle,
Stand firm in my castle,
And all the dogs in the town
Shan't pull Willie Wastle down."

Willow. *To handle the willow—i.e.* the cricket bat.

To wear the willow. To go into mourning, especially for a sweetheart or bride. Fuller says, "The willow is a sad tree, whereof such as have lost their love make their mourning garlands." The psalmist tells us that the Jews in captivity "hanged their harps upon the willows" in sign of mourning. (cxxxvii.)

Willow Garland. An emblem of being forsaken. "All round my hat I wear a green willow." So Shakespeare: "I offered him my company to a willow-tree . . . . to make him a garland, as being forsaken." (*Much Ado About Nothing*, ii. 1.) The very term *weeping* willow will suffice to account for its emblematical character.

Willow Pattern. To the right is a lordly mandarin's country seat. It is two storeys high to show the rank and wealth of the possessor; in the foreground is a pavilion, in the background an orange-tree, and to the right of the pavilion a peach-tree in full bearing. The estate is enclosed by an elegant wooden fence. At one end of the bridge is the famous willow-tree, and at the other the gardener's cottage, one storey high, and so humble that the grounds are wholly uncultivated, the only green thing being a small fir-tree at the back. At the top of the pattern (left-hand side) is an island, with a cottage; the grounds are highly cultivated, and much has been reclaimed from the water. The two birds are turtle-doves. The three figures on the bridge are the mandarin's daughter with a distaff nearest the cottage, the lovers with a boat in the middle, and nearest the willow-tree the mandarin with a whip.

The tradition. The mandarin had an only daughter named Li-chi, who fell in love with Chang, a young man who lived in the island home represented at the top of the pattern, and who had been her father's secretary. The father overheard them one day making vows of love under the orange-tree, and sternly forbade the unequal match; but the lovers contrived to elope, lay concealed for a while in the gardener's cottage, and thence made their escape in a boat to the island home of the young lover. The enraged mandarin pursued them with a whip, and would have beaten them to death had not the gods rewarded their fidelity by changing them both into turtle-doves. The picture is called the willow pattern not only because it is a tale of disastrous love, but because the elopement occurred "when the willow begins to shed its leaves."

Willy-nilly. *Nolens volens;* willing or not. *Will-he, nill-he,* where nill is *n'* negative, and *will,* just as *nolens* is *n'-volens.*

Wil'mington, invoked by Thomson in his *Winter,* is Sir Spencer Compton, Earl of Wilmington, the first patron of our poet, and Speaker of the House of Commons.

Wil't or **Welk,** to wither. This is the Dutch and German *welken* (to fade). Spenser says, "When ruddy Phœbus 'gins to welk in west"—*i.e.* fade in the west.

"A wilted debauchee is not a fruit of the tree of life."—*J. Cook: The Orient,* p. 149.

Wilt'shire (2 syl.) is Wilton-shire, Wilton being a contraction of Wily-town (the town on the river Wily).

Win'chester. According to the authority given below, Winchester was the Camelot of Arthurian romance. Hanmer, referring to *King Lear,* ii. 2, says Camelot is Queen Camel, Somersetshire, in the vicinity of which "are many large moors where are bred great quantities of geese, so that many other places are from hence supplied with quills and feathers." Kent says to the Duke of Cornwall—

"Goose, if I had you upon Sarum Plain,
I'd drive ye cackling home to Camelot."

With all due respect to Hanmer, it seems far more probable that Kent refers to Camelford, in Cornwall, where the Duke of Cornwall resided, in his castle of Tintag'el. He says, "If I had you on Salisbury Plain [where geese abound], I would drive you home to Tintagel, on the river Camel." Though the Camelot of Shakespeare is Tintagel or Camelford, yet the Camelot of King Arthur may be Queen Camel; and indeed visitors are still pointed to certain large entrenchments at South Cadbury (Cadbury Castle) called by the inhabitants "King Arthur's Palace."

"Sir Balin's sword was put into marble stone, standing as upright as a great millstone, and it swam down the stream to the city of Camelot—that is, in English, Winchester."—*History of Prince Arthur*, 44.

Wind Egg. An egg without a shell. Dr. Johnson's notion that the wind egg does not contain the principle of life is no more correct than the superstition that the hen that lays it was impregnated, like the "Thracian mares," by the wind. The usual cause of such eggs is that the hen is too fat.

Winds. *Poetical names of the winds.* The *North* wind, Aquilo or Bo'reas; *South*, Notus or Auster; *East*, Eu'rus; *West*, Zephyr or Favonius; *North-east*, Arges'tës; *North-west*, Corus; *South-east*, Volturnus; *South-west*, Afer ventus, Af'ricus, Africā'nus, or Libs. The Thra'scias is a north wind, but not due north.

"Boreas and Cæcias, and Argestes loud,
And Thrascias rend the woods, and seas upturn ;
Notus and Afer, black with thunderous clouds,
From Serralio'na. Thwart of these, as fierce,
Forth rush . . . . Eurus and zephyr . . . .
Sirocco and Libecchio [Libycus]."
Milton : Paradise Lost, x. 699-706.

Special winds.

(1) The ETESIAN WINDS are refreshing breezes which blow annually for forty days in the Mediterranean Sea. (Greek, *et'os*, a year.)

(2) The HARMATTAN. A wind which blows periodically from the interior parts of Africa towards the Atlantic. It prevails in December, January, and February, and is generally accompanied with fog, but is so dry as to wither vegetation and cause human skin to peel off.

(3) The KHAMSIN. A fifty days' wind in Egypt, from the end of April to the inundation of the Nile. (Arabic for fifty.)

(4) The MISTRAL. A violent northwest wind blowing down the Gulf of Lyons; felt particularly at Marseilles and the south-east of France.

(5) The PAMPERO blows in the summer season, from the Andes across the pampas to the sea-coast. It is a dry, north-west wind.

(6) The PUNA WINDS prevail for four months in the Puna (table-lands of Peru). The most dry and parching winds of any.

When they prevail it is necessary to protect the face with a mask, from the heat by day and the intense cold of the night.

(7) SAM'IEL or SIMOOM'. A hot, suffocating wind that blows occasionally in Africa and Arabia. Its approach is indicated by a redness in the air. (Arabic, *samoon*, from *samma*, destructive.)

(8) The SIR'CCO. A wind from Northern Africa that blows over Italy, Sicily, etc., producing extreme languor and mental debility.

(9) The SOLA'NO of Spain, a south-east wind, extremely hot, and loaded with fine dust. It produces great uneasiness ; hence the proverb, "Ask no favour during the Solano." (*See* TRADE WINDS.)

To take or *have the wind.* To get or keep the upper hand. Lord Bacon uses the phrase. "To have the wind of a ship" is to be to the windward of it.

Windfall. Unexpected legacy ; money which has come *de cælo*. Some of the English nobility were forbidden by the tenure of their estates to fell timber, all the trees being reserved for the use of the Royal Navy. Those trees, however, which were *blown* down were excepted, and hence a good wind was often a great godsend.

Windmills. Don Quixote de la Mancha, riding through the plains of Montiel, approached thirty or forty windmills, which he declared to Sancho Panza "were giants, two leagues in length or more." Striking his spurs into Rosinante, with his lance in rest, he drove at one of the "monsters dreadful as Typhœus." The lance lodged in the sail, and the latter, striking both man and beast, lifted them into the air, shivering the lance to pieces. When the valiant knight and his steed fell to the ground they were both much injured, and Don Quixote declared that the enchanter Freston, "who carried off his library with all the books therein," had changed the giants into windmills " out of malice." (*Cervantes : Don Quixote*, bk. i. ch. viii.)

To fight with windmills. To combat chimeras. The French have the same proverb, " *Se battre contre des moulins à vent.*" The allusion is, of course, to the adventure of Don Quixote referred to above.

To have windmills in your head. Fancies, chimeras. Similar to " bees in your bonnet" (*q.v.*). Sancho Panza says—

"Did I not tell your worship they were windmills? and who would have thought otherwise, except such as had windmills in their head?"— *Cervantes: Don Quixote*, bk. i. ch. viii.

Windmill Street. When Charnel chapel, St. Paul's, was taken down by the Protector Somerset, in 1549, more than 1,000 cart-loads of bones were removed to Finsbury Fields, where they formed a large mound, on which three windmills were erected. It was from these mills that the street obtained its name. (*Leigh Hunt.*)

Window. (Norwegian, *vindue*.) A *French* window opens like folding doors; a *sash* window is in two parts, called sashes, one or both of which are made to slide up and down about half way.

Wine. A *magnum* of wine is two quarts; a *tappit-hen* of wine or rum is a double magnum; a *jeroboam* of wine or rum is a double "tappit-hen"; and a *rehoboam* (*q.v.*) is a double jeroboam.

Wine. The French say of wine that makes you stupid, it is *vin d'âne;* if it makes you maudlin, it is *vin de cerf* (from the notion that deer weep); if quarrelsome, it is *vin de lion;* if talkative, it is *vin de pie;* if sick, it is *vin de porc;* if crafty, it is *vin de renard;* if rude, it is *vin de singe*. (*See below.*)

Win of ape (Chaucer). "I trow that ye have drunken win of ape"—*i.e.* wine to make you drunk; in French, *vin de singe*. There is a Talmud parable which says that Satan came one day to drink with Noah, and slew a lamb, a lion, a pig, and an ape, to teach Noah that man before wine is in him is a *lamb*, when he drinks moderately he is a *lion*, when like a sot he is a *swine*, but after that any further excess makes him an *ape* that senselessly chatters and jabbers.

Wine-month. (Anglo-Saxon, *Win-monath*.) The month of October, the time of vintage.

Wine Mingled with Myrrh (Mark xv. 23). Called by the Romans *Murrhina* (vinum myrrha conditum), given to malefactors to intoxicate them, that their sufferings from crucifixion might be somewhat deadened.

"'Falernum' (that *divina potio*) was flavoured with myrrh."

Win'trith. The same as St. Boniface, the apostle of Germany, an Anglo-Saxon, killed by a band of heathens in 755.

Wing, Wings. Wing of a house, wing of an army, wing of a battalion or squadron, etc., are the side-pieces which start from the main body, as the wings of birds.

Don't try to fly without wings. Attempt nothing you are not fit for. A French proverb.

On the wing. Au vol, about to leave.

To clip one's wings. To take down one's conceit; to hamper one's action. In French, *Rogner les ailes* [*à quelqu'un*].

To lend wings. To spur one's speed.

"This sound of danger lent me wings."
R. L. Stevenson.

To take one under your wing. To patronise and protect. The allusion is to a hen gathering her chicks under her wing.

To take wing. To fly away; to depart without warning. (French, *s'envoler*.)

Wings of Azrael (*The*). (*See* Azrael.)

Winged Rooks. Outwitted sharpers. A rook is a sharper, and a rookery the place of resort for sharpers. A rook is the opposite of a pigeon; a rook cheats, a pigeon is the one cheated.

"This light, young, gay in appearance, the thoughtless youth of wit and pleasure—the pigeon rather than the rook—but the heart the same sly, shrewd, cold-blooded calculator."—*Sir W. Scott: Peveril of the Peak*, chap. xxviii.

Win'ifred (*St.*). Patron saint of virgins, because she was beheaded by Prince Caradoc for refusing to marry him. She was Welsh by birth, and the legend says that her head falling on the ground originated the famous healing well of St. Winifred in Flintshire. She is usually drawn like St. Denis, carrying her head in her hand. Holywell, in Wales, is St. Winifred's Well, celebrated for its "miraculous" virtues.

Winkle (*Rip van*). A Dutch colonist of New York. He met with a strange man in a ravine in the Kaatskill Mountains. Rip helps him to carry a keg, and when they reach the destination Rip sees a number of odd creatures playing nine-pins, but no one utters a word. Master Winkle seizes the first opportunity to take a sip at the keg, falls into a stupor, and sleeps for twenty years. On waking, his wife is dead and buried, his daughter is married, his native village has been remodelled, and America has become independent. (*Washington Irving*.)

Wint-monath [*Wind-month*]. The Anglo-Saxon name for November.

Winter, Summer. We say of an old man, "His life has extended to a hundred winters;" but of a blooming girl, "She has seen sixteen summers."

Winter's Tale (*Shakespeare*). Taken from the *Pleasant History of Dorastus and Fawnia* by Robert Green. Dorastus is called by Shakespeare Florizel and Doricles, and Fawnia is Perdita. Leontes of the *Winter's Tale* is Egistus in the novel, Polixenes is Pandosto, and Hermi'one is Bellaria.

Wipple-tree or **Whipultre.** Mentioned in Chaucer's *Knight's Tale*, is the cornel-tree or dogwood (*Cornus sanguinea*) (= whiffle-tree, from whiffle = to turn).

Wisdom-tooth. The popular name for the third molar in each jaw. Wisdom-teeth appear between 17 and 25.

Wisdom of Many and the Wit of One (*The*). This is Lord John Russell's definition of a proverb.

Wise (*The*).
ALBERT II., Duke of Austria, called *The Lame and Wise.* (1289, 1330-1358.)
ALFONSO X. (or IX.) of Leon, and IV. of Castile, called *The Wise* and *The Astronomer.* (1203, 1252-1285.)
ABEN-ESRA, a Spanish rabbi, born at Toledo. (1119-1174.)
CHARLES V. of France, called *Le Sage.* (1337, regent 1358-1360, king 1364-1380.)
CHE-TSOU, founder of the fourteenth dynasty of China, called *Hou-pe-lae* (the model ruler), and his sovereignty *The Wise Government.* (1278-1295.)
COMTE DE LAS CASES, called *Le Sage.* (1766-1842.)
FREDERICK, Elector of Saxony. (1463, 1544-1554.)
JOHN V. of Brittany, called *The Good and Wise.* (1389, 1399-1442.)
¶ *Nathan the Wise.* A drama by Lessing, based on a story in the *Decameron.* (Day x., Novel 3.)

Wise as a Serpent. This refers to the serpent which tempted Eve, or more probably to the old notion that serpents were extremely wise.

Wise as Solomon. (*See* SIMILES.)

Wise as the Mayor of Banbury. A blundering Sir William Curtis. The mayor referred to insisted that Henry III. reigned in England before Henry II.

The following is a fact which happened to myself in 1880. I was on a visit to a country mayor of great wealth, whose house was full of most exquisite works of art. I was particularly struck with a choice china figure, when the mayor told me how many guineas he had given for it, and added, "Of course you know 'who' it is meant for. It is John Knox signing Magna Charta."

Wise as the Women of Mungret. At Mungret, near Limerick, was a famous monastery, and one day a deputation was sent to it from Cashel to try the skill of the Mungret scholars. The head of the monastery had no desire to be put to this proof, so they habited several of their scholars as women, and sent them forth to waylay the deputation. The Cashel professors met one and another of these "women," and asked the way, or distance, or hour of the day, to all which questions they received replies in Greek. Thunderstruck with this strange occurrence, they resolved to return, saying, "What must the scholars be if even the towns-women talk in Greek?"

Wise Men or **Wise Women.** Fortune-tellers.

Wise Men of Greece. (*See* SEVEN SAGES.)

Wise Men of the East. The three Magi who followed the guiding star to Bethlehem. They are the patron saints of travellers. (*See* MAGI, SEVEN SAGES.)

Wise Men of Gotham (*The*). (*See* GOTHAM.)

Wiseacre. A corruption of the German *weissager* (a soothsayer or prophet). This, like the Greek *sophism*, has quite lost its original meaning, and is applied to dunces, wise only "in their own conceit."
There is a story told that Ben Jonson, at the *Devil's Tavern*, in Fleet Street, said to a country gentleman who boasted of his landed estates, "What care we for your dirt and clods? Where you have an acre of land, I have ten acres of wit." The landed gentleman retorted by calling Ben "Good Mr. Wiseacre." The story may pass for what it is worth.

Wisest Man of Greece. So the Delphic oracle pronounced Soc'rates to be, and Socrates modestly made answer, "'Tis because I alone of all the Greeks know that I know nothing."

Wish-wash. A reduplication of wash. Any thin liquor for drinking.

Wishy-washy. A reduplication of washy. Very thin, weak, and poor; wanting in substance or body.

Wishart (*George*). One of the early reformers of Scotland, condemned to the stake by Cardinal Beaton. While the fire was blazing about him he said: "He who from yon high place beholdeth me with such pride shall be brought low, even to the ground, before the trees which supplied these faggots have shed their leaves." It was March when Wishart uttered these words, and the cardinal died in June. (*See* SUMMONS.)

Wishing-bone. (*See* MERRY-THOUGHT.)

Wishing-cap. Fortuna'tus had an inexhaustible purse and a wishing-cap, but these gifts proved the ruin of himself and his sons. The object of the tale is to show the vanity of human prosperity.

Wishing - coat. *Willie Wynkin's wishing-coat.* An Irish locution.

"I wish I had here Willie Wynkin's wishing-coat."—*Howard Pyle : Robin Hood,* p. 200.

Wishing-rod (*The*) of the Nibelungs was of pure gold. Whoever had it could keep the whole world in subjection. It belonged to Siegfried, but when the "Nibelung hoard" was removed to Worms this rod went also.

" And there-among was lying the wishing-rod of gold,
  Which whoso could discover might in subjection hold
All this wide world as master, with all that dwell therein."
         Lettsom's Nibelungen-Lied, st. 1160.

Wisp. *Will o' the Wisp.* (*See* IGNIS FATUUS.)

Wisp of Straw (*A*). Sign of danger. Often hung under the arch of a bridge undergoing repairs, to warn watermen; sometimes in streets to warn passengers that the roof of a house is under repair. The Romans used to twist straw round the horns of a tossing ox or bull, to warn passers-by to beware, hence the phrase *fœnum habet in cornu,* the man is crotchety or dangerous. The reason why straw (or hay) is used is because it is readily come-at-able, cheap, and easily wisped into a bundle visible some long way off.

Wit. *To wit, viz.* that is to say. A translation of the French *savoir.* Wit is the Anglo-Saxon *witan* (to know). I divide my property into four parts, *to wit,* or *savoir,* or *namely,* or *that is to say* . . . .

Wits. Five wits. (*See under* FIVE.)

Witch. By drawing the blood of a witch you deprive her of her power of sorcery. Glanvil says that when Jane Brooks, the demon of Tedworth, bewitched a boy, his father scratched her face and drew blood, whereupon the boy instantly exclaimed that he was well.

"Blood will I draw on thee ; thou art a witch."
    Shakespeare: 1 Henry VI., i. 5.

Hammer for Witches (*Malleus Maleficarum*). A treatise drawn up by Heinrich Institor and Jacob Sprenger, systematising the whole doctrine of witchcraft, laying down a regular form of trial, and a course of examination. Innocent VIII. issued the celebrated bull *Summis Desiderantes* in 1484, directing inquisitors and others to put to death all practisers of witchcraft and other diabolical arts.

✷ Dr. Sprenger computes that as many as nine millions of persons have suffered death for witchcraft since the bull of Innocent. (*Life of Mohammed.*) As late as 1705 two women were executed at Northampton for witchcraft.

Witch-finder. Matthew Hopkins, who, in the middle of the seventeenth century, travelled through the eastern counties to find out witches. At last Hopkins himself was tested by his own rule. Being cast into a river, he floated, was declared to be a wizard, and was put to death. (See above, *Hammer for Witches.*)

Witch Hazel. A shrub supposed to be efficacious in discovering witches. A forked twig of the hazel was made into a divining-rod for the purpose.

Witch of Endor. A divining woman consulted by Saul when Samuel was dead. She called up the ghost of the prophet, and Saul was told that his death was at hand. (1 Sam. xxviii.)

Witch's Bridle. An instrument of torture to make obstinate witches confess. (*Pitcairn,* vol. i. part ii. p. 50.) (*See* WAKING A WITCH.)

Witches' Sabbath. The muster at night-time of witches and demons to concoct mischief. The witch first anointed her feet and shoulders with the fat of a murdered babe, then mounting a broomstick, distaff, or rake, made her exit by the chimney, and rode through the air to the place of rendezvous. The assembled witches feasted together, and concluded with a dance, in which they all turned their backs to each other.

Witchcraft. The epidemic demonopathy which raged in the fifteenth, sixteenth, and seventeenth centuries.

Witenagemot. The Anglo-Saxon parliament.

" The famous assembly of our forefathers was called by various names [as] *Mycel Gemot*,(or great meeting) ; the Witenagemot (or meeting of the wise) ; and sometimes the Mycel Getheaht (or great thought).—*Freeman: The Norman Conquest,* i. 3.

Wit'ham. *You were born, I suppose, at Little Witham.* A reproof to a noodle. The pun, of course, is on little wit. Witham is in Lincolnshire.

"I will be sworn she was not born at Wittham, for Gaffer Gibbs . . . says she could not turn up a single lesson like a Christian."—*Sir Walter Scott: Heart of Mid-Lothian,* chap. xxxii.

Puns of this sort are very common. (*See* BEDFORDSHIRE, NOD, DUNCE, CRIPPLEGATE, SHANKS' NAG, etc.)

Withe (1 syl.). When Delilah asked Samson what would effectually bind him he told her "green withes," but when she called in the Philistines he snapped his bonds like tow. Also spelt *with*. A boy, being asked what part of speech is *with*, replied a noun, and being reproved for ignorance made answer: "Please, sir, Samson was bound with seven withs."

"It seems impossible that Samson can be held by such green withes [*i.e.* that a great measure can be carried by such petty shifts]."—*The Times.*

Withers of a Horse (*The*) are the muscles which unite the neck and shoulders. The skin of this part of a horse is often galled by the pommel of an ill-fitting saddle, and then the irritation of the saddle makes the horse wince. In 1 *Henry IV.,* ii. 1, one of the carriers gives direction to the ostler to ease the saddle of his horse, *Cut.* "I prythee, Tom, beat Cut's saddle . . . the poor jade is wrung on the withers," that is, the muscles are wrung, and the skin galled by the saddle. And Hamlet says (iii. 2):

"Let the galled jade wince, our withers are un-
    wrung."

That is, let those wince who are galled; as for myself, my withers are not wrung, and I am not affected by the "bob."

Within the Pale. (*See under* PALE.)

Witney (Oxfordshire) is the Anglo-Saxon *Witen-ey,* the island of Wisemen—*i.e.* of the Witenagemot or national parliament.

Wit'tington. (*See* WHIT INGTON.)

"Beneath this stone lies Wit ington,
    Sir Richard rightly named,
Who three times Lord Mayor served in London,
    In which he ne'er was blamed.
He rose from indigence to wealth
    By industry and that,
For lo ! he scorned to gain by stealth
    What he got by a cat."
Epitaph (destroyed by the fire of London).

Witwold. *A Sir Jerry Witwold.* A pert, talkative coxcomb, vain of a little learning ; one who swims with the stream of popular opinion, and gives his judgment on men and books as if he were Sir Oracle. A great pretender to virtue and

modesty, like Mr. Pecksniff, but always nosing out smut and obscenity, which he retails with virtuous indignation.

Wives of Literary Men. The following literary men, among many others, made unhappy marriages :

ADDISON.	LYTTON.
ARISTOTLE.	MILTON (first wife).
BACON (LORD).	MOLIÈRE.
BOCCACCIO.	MORE.
BYRON.	PITTACUS.
DANTE.	RACINE.
DICKENS.	ROUSSEAU (J. J.).
DURER (ALBERT).	SCALIGER (both
EURIPIDES.	wives).
GARRICK.	SHAKESPEARE.
HAYDN.	SHELLEY (first wife).
HOOKER.	SOCRATES.
JOHNSON (DR.).	STEELE.
JONSON (BEN).	STERNE.
KNOX.	WYCHERLEY (first
LILLY (second wife).	wife).

Wo! Stop! (addressed to horses). "Ho !" or "Hoa !" was formerly an exclamation commanding the knights at tournaments to cease from all further action. (*See* WOO'SH.)

"Scollers, as they read nuch of love, so when they once fall in love, there is no ho with them till they have their love."—*Cobler of Canterburie* (1608).

Woo' or **Woo'e.** Stop, addressed to a horse. The Latin word *ohè* has the same meaning. Thus Horace (1 *Sat.* v. 12)', "*Ohe, jam satis est.*"

Woo'sh, when addressed to horses, means "Bear to the left." In the West of England they say *Woag*—*i.e.* wag off (Anglo-Saxon, *woh,* a bend or turn). Woo'sh is "Move off a little."

Woo-tee Dynasty. The eighth Imperial dynasty of China, established in the south Liou-yu. A cobbler, having assassinated the two preceding monarchs, usurped the crown, and took the name of Woo-tee (*King Woo*), a name assumed by many of his followers.

Woden. Another form of Odin (*q.v.*). The word is incorporated in Wodensbury (Kent), Wednesbury (Suffolk), Wansdyke (Wiltshire), Wednesday, etc.

Woe to Thee, O Land, *when thy king is a child.* This famous sentence is from Ecclesiastes x. 6. Often quoted in Latin, *Væ terris ubi rex est puer.*

Woful. *Knight of the Woful Countenance.* The title given by Sancho Panza to Don Quixote. (Bk. iii. chap. v.) After his challenge of the two royal lions (pt. ii. bk. i. chap. xvii.), the adventurer called himself *Knight of the Lions.*

Wokey. *Wicked as the Witch of Wokey.* Wookey-hole is a noted cavern in Somersetshire, which has given birth to as many weird stories as the Sibyls'

Cave in Italy. The Witch of Wokey was metamorphosed into stone by a "lerned wight" from Gaston, but left her curse behind, so that the fair damsels of Wokey rarely find "a gallant." (*Percy: Reliques*, iii. 14.)

Wolf (in music). In almost all stringed instruments (as the violin, organ, piano, harp, etc.) there is one note that is not true, generally in the bass string. This false note is by musicians called a "wolf."

❖ The squeak made in *reed* instruments by unskilful players is termed a "goose."

" Nature hath implanted so inveterate a hatred atweene the wolfe and the sheepe, that, being dead, yet in the operation of Nature appeareth there a sufficient trial of their discording nature ; so that the enmity betweene them seemeth not to dye with their bodies ; for if there be put upon a harpe . . . strings made of the intralles of a sheepe, and amongst them . . . one made of the intralles of a wolfe . . . the musician . . . cannot reconcile them to a unity and concord of sounds, so discording is that string of the wolf-."—*Ferne : Blazon of Gentrie* (1586).

❖ Here Mr. Ferne attributes the musical "wolf" to a wolf-gut string ; but the real cause is a faulty interval. Thus, the interval between the fourth and fifth of the major scale contains nine commas, but that between the fifth and the sixth only eight. Tuners generally distribute the defects, but some musicians prefer to throw the whole onus on the "wolf" keys.

Wolf. (Anglo-Saxon, *wulf*.)

Fenris. The wolf that scatters venom through air and water, and will swallow Odin when time shall be no more.

Sköll. The wolf that follows the sun and moon, and will swallow them ultimately. (*Scandinavian mythology*.)

The Wolf. So Dryden calls the Presbytery in his *Hind and Panther*.

"Unkennelled range in thy Polonian plains,
A fiercer foe the insatiate Wolf remains."

She-wolf of France. Isabella *le Bel*, wife of Edward II. According to a tradition, she murdered the king by burning his bowels with a hot iron, or by tearing them from his body with her own hands.

" She-wolf of France, with unrelenting fangs,
That tear'st the bowels of thy mangled mate."
Gray : The Bard.

Between dog and wolf. In Latin, "*Inter canem et lupum*"; in French, "*Entre chien et loup.*" That is, neither daylight nor dark, the blind man's holiday. Generally applied to the evening dusk.

Dark as a wolf's mouth. Pitch dark.

He has seen a wolf. Said of a person who has lost his voice. Our forefathers used to say that if a man saw a wolf before the wolf saw him he became dumb, at least for a time.

" Vox quoque Mœrin
Jam fugit ipsa ; lupi Mœrin vide're prio'res."
Virgil : Bucolica, eclogue ix.

"'Our young companion has seen a wolf,' said Lady Hameline, 'and has lost his tongue in consequence.'"—*Scott : Quentin Durward*, ch. xviii.

To see a wolf is also a good sign, inasmuch as the wolf was dedicated to Odin, the giver of victory.

He put his head into the wolf's mouth. He exposed himself to needless danger. The allusion is to the fable of the crane that put its head into a wolf's mouth in order to extract a bone. The fable is usually related of a fox instead of a wolf. (*French.*)

Holding a wolf by the ears. So Augustus said of his situation in Rome, meaning it was equally dangerous to keep hold or to let go. Similarly, the British hold of Ireland is like that of Augustus. The French use the same locution : *Tenir le loup par les oreilles.*

To cry "Wolf!" To give a false alarm. The allusion is to the well-known fable of the shepherd lad who used to cry "Wolf!" merely to make fun of the neighbours, but when at last the wolf came no one would believe him.

In Chinese history it is said that Yëuwàng, of the third Imperial dynasty, was attached to a courtesan named Pao-tse, whom he tried by various expedients to make laugh. At length he hit upon the following : He caused the tocsins to be rung as if an enemy were at the gates, and Pao-tse laughed immoderately to see the people pouring into the city in alarm. The emperor, seeing the success of his trick, repeated it over and over again ; but at last an enemy really did come, and when the alarm was given no one paid attention to it, and the emperor was slain. (B.C. 770.) (*See* AMYCLÆAN SILENCE.)

To keep the wolf from the door. To keep out hunger. We say of a ravenous person " He has a wolf in his stomach," an expression common to the French and Germans. Thus *manger comme un loup* is to eat voraciously, and *wolfsmagen* is the German for a keen appetite.

Wolf, *Duke of Gascony.* One of Charlemagne's knights, and the most treacherous of all, except Ganelon. He sold his guest and his family. He wore browned steel armour, damasked with silver ; but his favourite weapon was the gallows. He was never in a rage, but cruel in cold blood.

> "It was Wolf, Duke of Gascony, who was the originator of the plan of tying wetted ropes round the temples of his prisoners, to make their eye-balls start from their sockets. It was he who had them sewed up in freshly-stripped bulls' hides, and exposed to the sun till the hides in shrinking broke their bones."—*Croquemitaine*, iii.

Wolf Men. Giraldus Cambrensis tells us (*Opera*, vol. v. p. 119) that Irishmen can be "changed into wolves." Nennius asserts that the "descendants of wolves are still in Ossory," and "they retransform themselves into wolves when they bite." (*Wonders of Eri*, xiv.)

⁜ These Ossory men-wolves are of the race of Laighne Fxlaidh.

Wolf-month or **Wolf-monath.** The Saxon name for January, because "people are wont always in that month to be in more danger of being devoured by wolves than in any other." (*Verstegan*.)

Wolf's-bane. The Germans call all poisonous herbs "banes," and the Greeks, mistaking the word for "beans," translated it by *kŭ'amoi*, as they did "hen-bane" (*huos ku'amos*). Wolf's-bane is an aconite with a pale yellow flower, called therefore the *white*-bane to distinguish it from the *blue* aconite. White-bean would be in Greek *leukos kuamos*, which was corrupted into *lukos kuamos* (wolf-bean); but botanists, seeing the absurdity of calling aconite a "bean," restored the original German word "bane," but retained the corrupt word *lukos* (wolf), and hence the ridiculous term "wolf's-bane." (*H. Fox Talbot*.)

⁜ This cannot be correct: (1) *bane* is not German; (2) *huos kuamos* would be hog-bean, not hen-bane; (3) How could Greeks mistranslate German? The truth is, wolf-bane is so called because meat saturated with its juice was supposed to be a wolf-poison.

Wolves. It is not true that wolves were extirpated from the island in the reign of Edgar. The tradition is based upon the words of William of Malmesbury (bk. ii. ch. viii.), who says that the tribute paid by the King of Wales, consisting of 300 wolves, ceased after the third year, because "*nullum se ulterius posse inveni're professus*" (because he could find no more—*i.e.* in Wales); but in the tenth year of William I. we find that Robert de Umfraville, knight, held his lordship of Ríddlesdale in Northumberland by service of defending that part of the kingdom from "wolves." In the forty-third year of Edward III.

Thomas Engarne held lands in Pitchley, Northamptonshire, by service of finding dogs at his own cost for the destruction of "wolves" and foxes. Even in the eleventh year of Henry VI. Sir Robert Plumpton held one bovate of land in the county of Notts by service of "frighting the wolves" in Shirewood Forest.

Wonder. *A nine days' wonder.* Something that causes a sensational astonishment for a few days, and is then placed in the limbo of "things forgot." Three days' amazement, three days' discussion of details, and three days of subsidence. (*See* NINE, *and* SEVEN.)

¶ *The eighth wonder.* The palace of the Escurial in Toledo, built by Felipe II. to commemorate his victory over the French at St. Quentin. It was dedicated to San Lorenzo, and Juan Baptista de Toledo, the architect, took a gridiron for his model—the bars being represented by rows or files of buildings, and the handle by a church. It has 1,860 rooms, 6,200 windows and doors, 80 staircases, 73 fountains, 48 wine cellars, 51 bells, and 8 organs. Its circumference is 4,800 feet (nearly a mile). Escurial is *scoria ferri*, iron dross, because its site is that of old iron works. (*See* TUILERIES.)

An eighth wonder. A work of extraordinary mechanical ingenuity, such as the Great Wall of China, the dome of Chosroes in Madain, St. Peter's of Rome, the Menai suspension bridge, the Thames tunnel, the bridge over the Niagara, Eddystone lighthouse, the Suez Canal, the railroad over Mont Cenis, the Atlantic cable, etc.

¶ *The Three Wonders of Babylon.*
The Palace, eight miles in circumference.
The Hanging Gardens.
The Tower of Babel, said by some Jewish writers to be twelve miles in height! Jerome quotes contemporary authority for its being four miles high. Strabo says its height was 660 feet.

Wonder-worker. St. Gregory, of Neo-Cæsare'a, in Pontus. So called because he "recalled devils at his will, stayed a river, killed a Jew by the mere effort of his will, changed a lake into solid earth, and did many other wonderful things." (*See* THAUMATURGUS.)

Wood. *Knight of the Wood* or *Knight of the Mirrors.* So called because his coat was overspread with numerous small mirrors. It was Sampson Carrasco, a bachelor of letters, who adopted the disguise of a knight under the hope of overthrowing Don Quixote, when he would have imposed upon him the penalty of returning to his home for two years; but it so happened that Don Quixote was the victor, and Carrasco's scheme was abortive. As *Knight of the White Moon* Carrasco again challenged the Man'chegan lunatic, and overthrew him; whereupon the vanquished knight was obliged to return home, and quit the profession of knight-errantry for twelve months. Before the term expired he died. (*Cervantes : Don Quixote,* pt. ii. bk. i. 11, etc. ; bk. iv. 12.)

Wood. *Don't cry* [or *halloo*] *till you are out of the wood.* Do not rejoice for having escaped danger till the danger has passed away.

Wood's Halfpence. A penny coined by William Wood, to whom George I. granted letters patent for the purpose. (*See* DRAPIER'S LETTERS.)

" Sir Walter's [Scott] real belief in Scotch one-pound notes may be advantageously contrasted with Swift's forced frenzy about Wood's half-pence, more especially as Swift really did understand the defects of Wood's scheme, and Sir Walter was absolutely ignorant of the currency controversy in which he engaged."—*The Times.*

Woodbind. The bindweed or wild convolvulus. This is quite a different plant to the woodbine. It is a most troublesome weed in orchards, as its roots run to a great depth, and its long, climbing stalks bind round anything near it with persistent tenacity. It is one of the most difficult weeds to extirpate, as every broken fragment is apt to take root.

Woodbine. The honeysuckle or bee-wort; or perhaps the convolvulus.

" Where the bee
Strays diligent, and with extracted balm
Of fragrant woodbine loads his little thigh."
Phillips.

Shakespeare says—

"So doth the woodbine the sweet honeysuckle
Gently entwist."
Midsummer Night's Dream, iv. 1.

Gone where the woodbine twineth. To the pawnbroker's, up the spout, where, in Quebec, "on cottage walls the woodbine may be seen twining." (*A correspondent of Quebec supplied this.*)

Woodcock (*A*). A fool is so called from the supposition that woodcocks are without brains. Polonius tells his daughter that protestations of love are "springes to catch woodcocks." (*Shakespeare : Hamlet,* i. 3.)

Wooden Horse (*The*). Babiĕca,

Peter of Provence had a wooden horse named Babiĕca. (*See* CLAVILEN'O.)

"This very day may be seen in the king's armoury the identical peg with which Peter of Provence turned his Wooden Horse, which carried him through the air. It is rather bigger than the pole of a coach, and stands near Babieca's saddle."—*Don Quixote,* pt. i. bk. iv. 19.

Wooden Horse (*To ride the*). To sail aboard a ship, brig, or boat, etc.

" He felt a little out of the way for riding the wooden horse."—*Sir Walter Scott : Redgauntlet,* chap. xv.

Wooden Horse of Troy. Virgil tells us that Ulysses had a monster wooden horse made after the death of Hector, and gave out that it was an offering to the gods to secure a prosperous voyage back to Greece. The Trojans dragged the horse within their city, but it was full of Grecian soldiers, who at night stole out of their place of concealment, slew the Trojan guards, opened the city gates, and set fire to Troy. Menelãos was one of the Greeks shut up in it. It was made by Epeios (Latin, *Epẽus*).

Cambuscan's wooden horse. The *Arabian Nights* tells us of Cambuscan's horse of brass, which had a pin in the neck, and on turning this pin the horse rose into the air, and transported the rider to the place he wanted to go to. (*See* CLAVILENO.)

Wooden Mare (*The*). "The mare foaled of an acorn." An instrument of torture to enforce military discipline, used in the reign of Charles II. and long after. The horse was made of oak, the back was a sharp ridge, and the four legs were like a high stool. The victim was seated on the ridge, with a firelock fastened to each foot.

" Here, Andrews, wrap a cloak round the prisoner, and do not mention his name . . . unless you would have a trot on the wooden horse."— *Sir Walter Scott : Old Mortality,* chap. ix.

Wooden Spoon. The last of the honour men—*i.e.* of the Junior Optimes, in the Cambridge University. Sometimes two or more "last" men are bracketed together, in which case the group is termed the spoon bracket. It is said that these men are so called because in days of yore they were presented with a wooden spoon, while the other honour men had a silver or golden one, a spoon being the usual *prix de mérite* instead of a medal. (*See* WOODEN WEDGE.)

Wooden Sword. *To wear the wooden sword.* To keep back sales by asking too high a price. Fools used to wear wooden swords or " daggers of lath."

Wooden Wall. When the Greeks sent to Delphi to ask how they were to defend themselves against Xerxes, who had invaded their country, the evasive answer given was to this effect—

Pallas hath urged, and Zeus, the sire of all,
Hath safety prom ised in a wooden wall ;
Seed-time and harvest, weeping sires shall tell
How thousands fought at Salamis and fell.

Wooden walls of Old England. The ships of war. We must now say, " The iron walls of Old England."

Wooden Wedge. Last in the classical tripos. When, in 1824, the classical tripos was instituted at Cambridge, it was debated by what name to call the last on the list. It so happened that the last on the list was Wedgewood, and the name was accepted and moulded into Wooden-wedge. (*See* WOODEN SPOON.)

Woodfall, brother of the Woodfall of Junius, and editor of the *Morning Chronicle.* Woodfall would attend a debate, and, without notes, report it accurately next morning. He was called *Memory Woodfall.* (1745-1803.) W. Radcliffe could do the same.

Woodwar'dian Professor. The professor of geology in the University of Cambridge. This professorship was founded in 1727 by Dr. Woodward.

Wool. *Dyed in the wool.* A hearty good fellow. Cloth which is wool-dyed (not piece-dyed), is true throughout "and will wash."

No wool is so white that a dyer cannot blacken it. No one is so free from faults that slander can find nothing to say against him ; no book is so perfect as to be free from adverse criticism.

" Maister Mainwaring's much abuzed,
Most grievously for things accused,
    And all the dowlish [devilish] pack ;
E'en let mun all their poison spit,
My lord, there is no wooll zo whit
    That dyers can't make black."
    Peter Pindar: Middlesex Election, letter iii.

Wool-gathering. *Your wits are gone wool-gathering.* As children sent to gather wool from hedges are absent for a trivial purpose, so persons in a " brown study " are absent-minded to no good purpose.

" But, my dear, if my wits are somewhat wool-gathering and unsettled, my heart is as true as a star."—*Harriet B. Stowe.*

Woollen. In 1666 an Act of Parliament was'passed for "burying in woollen only," which was intended for " the encouragement of the woollen manufactures of the kingdom, and prevention of the exportation of money for the buying

and importing of linen." Repealed in 1814.

" 'Odious ! in woollen ! 'twould a saint provoke !'
    (Were the last words that poor Narcissa spoke).
'No : let a charming chintz and Brussels lace
Wrap my cold limbs, and shade my lifeless face.
One would not, sure, be frightful when one's
    dead ;
And—Betty—give the cheeks a little red.'"
        Pope: Moral Essays, Ep. i.

This was the ruling passion strong in death. At the time this was written it was compulsory to bury in woollen. Narcissa did not dread death half 'so much as being obliged to wear flannel instead of her fine mantles. Narcissa was Mrs. Oldfield, the actress, who died 1731.

Woollen goods. (*See* LINEN GOODS.)

Woolsack. *To sit on the woolsack.* To be Lord Chancellor of England, whose seat in the House of Lords is called the woolsack. It is a large square bag of wool, without back or arms, and covered with red cloth. In the reign of Queen Elizabeth an Act of Parliament was passed to prevent the exportation of wool ; and that this source of our national wealth might be kept constantly in mind woolsacks were placed in the House of Peers, whereon the judges sat. Hence the Lord Chancellor, who presides in the House of Lords, is said to " sit on the woolsack," or to be " appointed to the woolsack."

Woolwich Infant (*The*). (*See* GUN.)

Worcester (*Woost'-er*). A contraction of *Wicii-ware-ceaster* (the camp-town of the Wicii people). *Ware* means people, and *Wicii* was a tribe name.

Worcester College (Oxford), founded by Sir Thomas Cookes, of Bentley, Worcestershire. Created a baronet by Charles II.

Word. *A man of his word.* One whose word may be depended on ; trustworthy.

As good as his word. In French, " *Un homme de parole.*" One who keeps his word.

By word of mouth. Orally. As "he took it down by word of mouth " (as it was spoken by the speaker).

I take you at your word. In French, " *Je vous prend au mot.*" I will act in reliance of what you tell me.

Pray, make no words about it. In French, " *N'en dites mot.*" Don't mention it ; make no fuss about it.

Speak a good word for me. In French, " *Dites un mot en ma faveur.*"

To pass one's word. In French,

" Donner sa parole." To promise to do something required.

Upon my word. Assuredly; by my troth.

"Upon my word, you answer . . . discreetly."
—*Jane Austen.*

Upon my word and honour ! A strong affirmation of the speaker as to the truth of what he has asserted.

Word (*The*). The second person of the Christian Trinity. (John i. 1.)

Word to the Wise (*A*). *" Verbum sap."*

Words. *Soft words butter no parsnips.* In Scotland an excellent dish is made of parsnips and potatoes beaten up with butter. (*See* BUTTER.)

Many words will not fill a bushel. Mere promises will not help the needy. If we say to a beggar, " Be thou filled," is he filled ?

The object of words is to conceal thoughts. (*See* LANGUAGE.)

To have words with one. To quarrel; to have an angry discussion. Other phrases to the same effect are — *They exchanged words together ; There passed some words between them* (in French, *" Ils ont en quelques paroles "*).

Working on the Dead Horse, doing work which has been already paid for. Such work is a dead horse, because you can get no more out of it.

World. *A man of the world.* One acquainted with the ways of public and social life.

A woman of the world. A married woman. (*See above.*)

"*Touchstone.* To-morrow will we be married.
Audrey. I do desire it with all my heart ; and I
hope it is no dishonest desire to be a woman of
the world."—*Shakespeare : As You Like It,* v. 3.

All the world and his wife. Everyone without exception.

To go to the world. To get married. The Catholics at one time exalted celibacy into " a crown of glory," and divided mankind into celibates and worldlings (or laity). The former were monks and nuns, and the latter were the *monde* (or people of the world). Similarly they divided literature into sacred and profane.

"Everyone goes to the world but I, and I may
sit in a corner and cry heigho ! for a husband."—
Shakespeare : Much Ado About Nothing, ii. 1.

"If I may have your ladyship's good will to go
to the world, Isabel and I will do as we may."—
All's Well that Ends Well, i. 3.

World (*The*). *The world, the flesh, and the devil.* " The world," *i.e.* the things of this world, in contradistinction

42

to religious matters; " the flesh," *i.e.* love of pleasure and sensual enjoyments ; " the devil," *i.e.* all temptations to evil of every kind, as theft, murder, lying, blasphemy, and so on.

Worm. *To have a worm in one's tongue.* To be cantankerous; to snarl and bite like a mad dog.

"There is one easy artifice
That seldom has been known to miss—
To snarl at all things right or wrong,
Like a mad dog that has a worm in's tongue.'
Samuel Butler : Upon Modern Critics.

To worm out information. To elicit information indirectly and piecemeal.

To worm oneself into another's favour. To insinuate oneself in an underhand manner into the good graces of another person.

‡ A worm is a spiral instrument resembling a double corkscrew, used for drawing wads and cartridges from cannon, etc.

Worms, in Germany, according to tradition, is so called from the Lindwurm or dragon slain by Siegfried under the linden tree.

"Yet more I know of Siegfried that well your
ear may hold.
Beneath the linden tree he slew the dragon
bold ;
Then in its blood he bathed him, which turned
to horn his skin,
So now no weapon harms him, as oft hath
proven been." *Nibelungen,* st. 104.

Wormwood. The tradition is that this plant sprang up in the track of the serpent as it writhed along the ground when driven out of Paradise.

Worse than a Crime. *It was worse than a crime, it was a blunder.* Said by Talleyrand of the murder of the Duc d'Enghien by Napoleon I.

Wor'ship means state or condition of worth, hence the term " his worship," meaning his *worthyship.* " Thou shalt have *worship* in the presence of them that sit at meat with thee " (Luke xiv. 10) means " Thou shalt have *worth-ship* [value or appreciation]." In the marriage service the man says to the woman, " With my body I thee worship, and with all my worldly goods I thee endow " —that is, I confer on you my rank and dignities, and endow you with my wealth ; the worthship attached to my person I share with you, and the wealth which is mine is thine also.

Never worship the gods unshod. So taught Pythagoras, and he meant in a careless and slovenly manner. (See *Iamblichus : Protreptics,* symbol 3.) The Jews took off their shoes when they entered holy ground (Exodus iii. 5).

This custom was observed by the ancient Egyptians. Mahometans and Brahmins enter holy places bare-footed; indeed, in British India, inferiors take off their shoes when they enter the room of a British officer, or the wife of an officer. The idea is that shoes get covered with dust, and holy ground must not be defiled by dirt. (*Justin Martyr: Apology*, i. 62.)

The command given to the disciples by Christ was to shake off the dust of their feet when they left a city which would not receive them.

Worsted. Yarn or thread made of wool; so called from Worsted in Norfolk, now a village, but once a large market-town with at least as many thousand inhabitants as it now contains hundreds. (*Camden.*)

Worth = betide.

"Thus saith the Lord God: Howl ye, wo worth the day!"—*Ezekiel* xxx. 2.
  "Wo worth the chase! wo worth the day
  That costs thy life, my gallant grey."
             Sir Walter Scott.

Worthies (*The Nine*). (*See* NINE.)

¶ *The Nine Worthies of London.*

(1) *Sir William Walworth*, fishmonger, who stabbed Wat Tyler, the rebel. Sir William was twice Lord Mayor. (1374, 1380.)

(2) *Sir Henry Pritchard*, who (in 1356) feasted Edward III., with 5,000 followers; Edward the Black Prince; John, King of Austria; the King of Cyprus; and David, King of Scotland.

(3) *Sir William Sevenoke*, who fought with the Dauphin of France, built twenty almshouses and a free school. (1418.)

(4) *Sir Thomas White*, merchant tailor, son of a poor clothier. In 1553 he kept the citizens loyal to Queen Mary during Wyatt's rebellion. Sir John White founded St. John's College, Oxford, on the spot where "two elms grew from one root."

(5) *Sir John Bonham*, entrusted with a valuable cargo for the Danish market, and made commander of the army raised to stop the progress of the great Solyman.

(6) *Christopher Croker.* Famous at the siege of Bordeaux, and companion of the Black Prince when he helped Don Pedro to the throne of Castile.

(7) *Sir John Hawkwood.* One of the Black Prince's knights, and immortalised in Italian history as Giovanni Acuti Cavaliero.

(8) *Sir Hugh Caverley.* Famous for ridding Poland of a monstrous bear.

(9) *Sir Henry Malererer*, generally called Henry of Cornhill, who lived in the reign of Henry IV. He was a crusader, and became the guardian of "Jacob's well."

The chronicle of these worthies is told in a mixture of prose and verse by Richard Johnson, author of *The Seven Champions of Christendom.* (1592.)

❖ Among these nine worthies we miss the names of Whittington, Gresham, and Sir John Lawrence (Lord Mayor in 1664), second to none.

Wound. *Bind the wound, and grease the weapon.* This is a Rosicrucian maxim. These early physicians applied salve to the weapon instead of to the wound, under the notion of a magical reflex action. Sir Kenelm Digby quotes several anecdotes to prove this sympathetic action.

Wra'ith. The spectral appearance of a person shortly about to die. It appears to persons at a distance, and forewarns them of the event." (*Highland superstition.*) (*See* FAIRY.)

Wrang'ler, in Cambridge phrase, is one who has obtained a place in the highest mathematical tripos. The first man of this class is termed the *senior* wrangler, the rest are arranged according to respective merit, and are called *second, third, fourth,* etc., wrangler, as it may be. In the Middle Ages, when letters were first elevated to respectability in modern Europe, college exercises were called *disputations,* and those who performed them *disputants,* because the main part consisted in pitting two men together, one to argue *pro* and the other *con.* In the law and theological "schools" this is still done for the bachelor's and doctor's degrees. The exercise of an opponent is called an *opponency.* Wrangling is a word-battle carried on by *twisting* words and trying to obfuscate an opponent—a most excellent term for the disputations of schoolmen. The opponency begins with an essay on the subject of dispute.

Wrath's Hole (Cornwall). The legend is that Bolster, a gigantic wrath or evil spirit, paid embarrassing attention to St. Agnes, who told him she would listen to his suit when he filled with his blood a small hole which she pointed out to him. The wrath joyfully accepted the terms, but the hole opened into the sea, and the wrath, being utterly exhausted, St. Agnes pushed him over the cliff.

Wrax'en. Overstretched, strained, rank. *They go to school all the week, and get wraxen. The wind are quite*

*wraxen. The child fell and wraxed his
ankle.* (Anglo-Saxon, *wræc*, miserable,
wretched.)

Wright of Norwich. *Do you know
Dr. Wright of Norwich?* A reproof
given to a person who stops the decanter
at dinner. Dr. Wright, of Norwich, was
a great diner-out and excellent talker.
When a person stops the bottle and is
asked this question, it is as much as to
say, Dr. Wright had the privilege of
doing so because he entertained the
table with his conversation, but you
are no Dr. Wright, except in stopping
the circulation of the wine.

A similar reproof is given in the
combination room of our Universities
in this way : The bottle-stopper is
asked if he knows A or B (*any name*),
and after several queries as to who A
or B is, the questioner says, "He was
hanged," and being asked what for, replies, "For stopping the bottle."

Write. *To write up.* To bring into
public notice or estimation by favourable criticisms or accounts of, as to write
up a play or an author.

Write Like an Angel (*To*). (*See
under* ANGEL.)

Wrong. *The king* (or *queen*) *can do no
wrong.*

"It seems incredible that we should have to
remind Lord Redesdale that the sovereign 'can
do no wrong,' simply because the sovereign can
do nothing except by and with the advice and
consent of the ministers of the Crown."—*The
Times.*

Wrong End of the Stick (*You have
got hold of the*). You have quite misapprehended the matter ; you have got the
wrong sow by the ear. There is another
form of this phrase which determines the
allusion. The toe of the stick is apt to
be fouled with dirt, and when laid hold
of defiles the hand instead of supporting
the feet.

Wrong Side of the Blanket (*The*).
(*See* BLANKET.)

Wrong Side of the Cloth (*That is
the*). The inferior aspect. In French,
l'envers du drap.

Wrong Sow by the Ear (*You have
the*). You have made a mistake in
choice ; come to the wrong shop or box ;
or misapprehended the subject. Pigs are
caught by the ear. (*See* SOW.)

Wrong 'un (*A*). A horse which has
run at any flat-race meeting not recognised by the Jockey Club is technically
so called, and is boycotted by the club.

Wroth Money or **Wroth Silver.**
Money paid to the lord in lieu of castle
guard for military service ; a tribute
paid for killing accidentally some person
of note ; a tribute paid in acknowledgment of the tenancy of unenclosed land.
Dugdale, in his *History of Warwickshire,* says :—

"There is a certain rent due unto the lord of
this Hundred (*i.e.* of Knightlow, the property of
the Duke of Buccleuch), called wroth-money, or
wrath-money, or swarff-penny. . . *Denarii vice-
comiti vel aliis castellanis persoluti ob castrorum
præsidium vel excubias agendas* (*Sir Henry Spelman : Glossary*). The rent must be paid on Martinmas Day, in the morning at Knightlow Cross,
before sun-rise. The party paying it must go
thrice about the cross and say, 'The wrath-
money,' and then lay it [varying from 1d. to
2s. 3d.] in a hole in the said cross before good
witnesses, or forfeit a white bull with red nose
and ears. The amount thus collected reached in
1892 to about 9s., and all who complied with the
custom were entertained at a substantial breakfast at the Duke's expense, and were toasted in
a glass of rum and milk."

Wulstan (*St.*). A Saxon Bishop of
Worcester, who received his see from
Edward the Confessor. Being accused
of certain offences, and ordered to resign
his see, he planted his crozier in the
shrine of the Confessor, declaring if any
of his accusers could draw it out he
would submit to resign ; as no one
could do so but St. Wulstan himself, his
innocence was admitted. This sort of
"miracle" is the commonest of legendary wonders. Arthur proved himself
king by a similar "miracle."

Wunderberg or *Underberg,* on the
great moor near Salzberg, the chief
haunt of the Wild-women. It is said to
be quite hollow, and contains churches,
gardens, and cities. Here is Charles V.
with crown and sceptre, lords and
knights. His grey beard has twice encompassed the table at which he sits,
and when it has grown long enough to
go a third time round it Antichrist will
appear. (*German superstition.*) (*See
BARBAROSSA.*)

Wyn-monath [*Wine - month*]. The
Anglo - Saxon name for October, the
month for treading the wine-vats. In
Domesday Book the vineyards are perpetually mentioned.

Wynd. *Every man for his own hand,
as Henry Wynd fought.* Every man for
himself ; every man seeks his own advantage. When the feud between Clan
Chattan and Clan Kay was decided by
deadly combat on the North Inch of
Perth, one of the men of Clan Chattan
deserted, and Henry Wynd, a bandy-
legged smith, volunteered for half-a-
crown to supply his place. After killing

one man he relaxed in his efforts, and on being asked why, replied, "I have done enough for half-a-crown." He was promised wages according to his deserts, and fought bravely. After the battle he was asked what he fought for, and gave for answer that he fought "for his own hand ;" whence the proverb. (*Sir Walter Scott : Tales of a Grand-father*, xvii.)

Wyo'ming (3 syl.). In 1778 a force of British provincials and Indians, led by Colonel Butler, drove the settlers out of the valley, and Queen Esther toma-hawked fourteen of the fugitives with her own hand, in revenge for her son's death. Campbell has founded his *Ger-trude of Wyoming* on this di-aster, but erroneously makes Brandt leader of the expedition, and calls the place Wy'-oming.

"Susquehanna's side, fair Wyoming."

X

X on beer-casks indicates beer which paid ten shillings duty, and hence it came to mean beer of a given quality. Two or three crosses are mere trade-marks, intended to convey the notion of twice or thrice as strong as that which pays ten shillings duty.

Xan'thos [*reddish yellow*]. Achilles' wonderful horse. Being chid by his master for leaving Patroclos on the field of battle, the horse turned his head re-proachfully, and told Achilles that he also would soon be numbered with the dead, not from any fault of his horse, but by the decree of inexorable destiny. (*Iliad*, xix.) (*Compare* Numbers xxii. 28-30.)

⁂ Xanthos and Balios (swift as the wind) were the offspring of Podargē the harpy and Zephyros. (*See* HORSE.)

Xanthos, the river of Troas. Elian and Pliny say that Homer called the Scamander "Xanthos" or the "Gold-red river," because it coloured with such a tinge the fleeces of sheep washed in its waters. Others maintain that it was so called because a hero named Xanthos defeated a body of Trojans on its banks, and pushed half of them into the stream, as in the battle of Blenheim the Duke of Marlborough drove the French into the Danube.

Xanthus. A large shell like those as-cribed to the Tritons. The volutes generally run from right to left ; and if the Indians find a shell with the volutes running in the contrary direction, they persist that one of their gods has got into the shell for concealment.

Xantip'pe or **Xanthip'pe** (3 syl.). Wife of the philosopher Socratēs. Her bad temper has rendered her name proverbial for a conjugal scold.

" Be she as foul as was Florentius' love,
   As old as Sibyl, and as curst and shrewd
   As Socrates' Xanthippe, or a worse,
   She moves me not."
            Shakespeare : Taming of the Shrew, i. 2.

Xenoc'ratēs. A disciple of Plato, noted for his continence and contempt of wealth. (B.C. 396-314.)

" Warmed by such youthful beauty, the severe
   Xenocrates would not have more been chaste."
            Orlando Furioso, xi. 8.

Xerx'es (2 syl.). A Greek way of writing the Persian Ksathra or Kshatra, a royal title assumed by Isfundear, son of Gushtasp, *darawesh.* (*See* DARIUS.)

When Xerxes invaded Greece he con-structed a pontoon bridge across the Dardanelles, which, being swept away by the force of the waves, so enraged the Persian despot that he "inflicted three hundred lashes on the rebellious sea, and cast chains of iron across it." This story is probably a Greek myth, founded on the peculiar construction of Xerxes' second bridge, which consisted of three hundred boats, lashed by iron chains to two ships serving as supporters. As for the scourging, without doubt it was given to the engineers and not to the waves.

Xerxes' Tears. It is said that when Xerxes, King of Persia, reviewed his magnificent and enormous army before starting for Greece, he wept at the thought of slaughter about to take place. " Of all this multitude, who shall say how many will return ? " Em-erson, in his *English Traits*, chap. iv., speaks of the Emperor Charlemagne viewing the fleet of the Norsemen in the Mediterranean Sea with tears in his eyes, and adds, "There was reason for these Xerxes' tears."

Xerxes wept at the prospective loss he expected to suffer in the invasion prepared, but Charlemagne wept at the prospective disruption of his kingdom by the hardy Norsemen.

Xime'na. The Cid's bride.

Xit. Royal dwarf to Edward VI.

Xu'ry. A Moresco boy, servant to Robinson Crusoe. (*De Foe : Robinson Crusoe.*)

Y

Y. A letter resembling "y" was the Anglo-Saxon character for th (hard); hence y*, y‘, y‘, etc., are sometimes made to stand for *the, that, this.*

Y. *See* SAMIAN LETTER.

Ya'coub ebn La'ith, surnamed *al Soffar* (the brazier), because his father followed that trade in Seistan, was captain of a bandit troop, raised himself to the sovereignty of Persia, and was the first independent monarch of that country of the Mahometan faith. (873-875.)

Yacu-mama [*mother of waters*]. A fabulous sea-snake, fifty paces long and twelve yards in girth, said to lurk in the lagunes of South America, and in the river Amazon. This monster draws into its mouth whatever passes within a hundred yards of it, and for this reason an Indian will never venture to enter an unknown lagune till he has blown his horn, which the yacu-mama never fails to answer if it is within hearing.. By this means the danger apprehended is avoided. (*Waterton.*)

Ya'hoo. A savage; a very ill-mannered person. In *Gulliver's Travels* the Yahoos are described as brutes with human forms and vicious propensities. They are subject to the Houyhnhnms, or horses with human reason.

Ya'ma. Judge of departed souls, the Minos of the Hindus. He is represented as of a green colour, and sits on a buffalo.

Yamuna. A sacred river of the Hindus, supposed by them to have the efficacy of removing sin.

Yankee. A corruption of "English." The word got into general use thus: In 1713 one Jonathan Hastings, a farmer at Cambridge, in Massachusetts, used th? word as a puffing epithet, meaning genuine, American-made, wh.t .anuot be surpassed, etc.; as, a "Yankee horse," "Yankee cider," and so on. The students in Harvard College, catching up the term, called Hastings, "Yankee Jonathan."' It soon spread, and became the jocose pet name of the New Englander. Since then the term has been extended to any American of the Northern States. (Indian corruption of Anglais or English, thus: *Yengees, Yenghis, Yanghis, Yankees.*)

Yankee Doodle is Nankee Doodle (Oliver Cromwell), who went to Oxford "with a single feather fastened in a macaroni knot," whence the rhyme—

"Nankee Doodle came to town upon his little pony,
Stuck a feather in his hat, and called it macaroni."

The brigade under Lord Percy marched out of Boston playing this air "by way of contempt," but were told they should dance to it soon in another spirit.

Yar'mouth Bloater. A red herring, for which .Yarmouth is very famous. (*Lex Balatronicum.*)

Yarmouth Capons. Red herrings.

Yawn. Greek, *chaino;* German, *gahnen;* Anglo-Saxon, *gān-ian.*

Yea, Yes. *Yea* and *nay* are in answer to questions framed in the affirmative; as, "Art thou a prophet?" Yea or nay. *Yes* and *no* to questions framed in the negative; as, "Art thou not a prophet?" Yes or no. (*George P. Marsh :. Lectures on the English Language.*) (*See* his note on the celebrated passage of Sir Thomas More, who rebukes Tyndale for using *no* instead of *nay,* p. 422.)

Year. *Annus magnus.* The Chaldaic astronomers observed that the fixed stars shift their places at about the rate of a degree in seventy-two years, according to which calculation they will perform one revolution in 25,920 years at the end of which time they will return to their "as you were." This revolution of the fixed stars is the *annus magnus.* The Egyptians made it 30,000 years, and the Arabians 49,000. (See *Abulhasan's Meadows of Gold.*)

¶ *For a year and a day.* In law many acts are determined by this period of time—*e.g.* if a person wounded does not die within a year and a day, the offender is not guilty of murder; if an owner does not claim an estray within the same length of time, it belongs to the lord of the manor; a year and a day is given to prosecute appeals, etc.

Yellow. Anglo-Saxon, *geolu,* yellow; Italian, *giallo;* Danish, *gnul;* Icelandic, *gull,* our *gold,* yellow metal.

Yellow indicates jealousy, inconstancy, and adultery. In France the doors of traitors used to be daubed with yellow. In some countries the law ordains that Jews be clothed in yellow, because they betrayed our Lord. Judas in mediæval pictures is arrayed in yellow. In Spain the vestments of the executioner are either red or yellow—the former to indicate blood-shedding, and the latter treason.

Yellow, in blazonry, is gold, the symbol of love, constancy, and wisdom.

Yellow, in Christian symbolism, also gold, is emblematical of faith. St. Peter is represented in a robe of a golden yellow colour. In China yellow is the imperial colour.

Yellow-bellies. Frogs, fenmen. The Mexicans are so called.

"When the Queen's Prize was won at Wimbledon, July 21st, 1885, by Sergeant Bulmer, 2nd Lincoln, his victory was hailed with 'Well done, yellow-belly!' in allusion to his being a Lincolnshire man."—*Notes and Queries*, August 22nd, 1885, p. 146.

"Ah, then, agin, it kin scarce be Mexikins neyther. It ur too fur no'th for any o' them yellow-bellies."—*Captain Mayne Reid: The War Trail*, chap. lxxi.

Yellow Book of France. A report drawn up by government every year since 1861, designed to furnish historians with reliable information of the state, external and internal, of the French nation. It is called Yellow from the colour of its cover. It corresponds to our "Blue Book" and the "White Books" of Germany and Portugal.

Yellow-boy (*A*). A gold sovereign.

"John did not starve the cause: there wanted not yellow-boys to fee counsel."—*Arbuthnot: John Bull.*

Yellow-boy (*A*). A bankrupt. The French call a bankrupt *Safranier*, and *Aller au safran* means to be made a bankrupt. The allusion is to the ancient custom of painting the house of a traitor yellow. It will be remembered that the house of the Petit Bourbon was long so stigmatised on account of the treason of the Constable Bourbon.

Yellow Caps. A notable insurrection in China, in the reign of Hân-ling-tee (168-189), headed by Tchang-keo, and so called from the caps worn by the rebels, which were all of the imperial colour.

Yellow Dwarf. A certain queen had a daughter named ALL-FAIR, of incomparable beauty. One day the queen went to consult the Desert-Fairy, but, being weary, lay down to rest, and fell asleep. On waking she saw two lions approaching, and was greatly terrified. At this juncture the Yellow Dwarf arrested her attention, and promised to save her from the lions if she would consent to give him ALL-FAIR for his bride. The queen made the promise, and an orange-tree opened, into which the queen entered, and escaped the lions.

The queen now sickened, and ALL-FAIR went to consult the Desert-Fairy, but, like her mother, was threatened by the lions, and promised to be the dwarf's bride if he would contrive her escape. Next morning she awoke in her own room, and found on her finger a ring made of a single red hair, which could not be got off. The princess now sickened, and the States resolved to give her in marriage to the powerful king of the Gold Mines. On the day of espousals the Yellow Dwarf came to claim his bride, carried her off on his Spanish cat, and confined her in Steel Castle. In the meantime the Desert-Fairy made the king of the Gold Mines her captive. One day a mermaid appeared to the captive king, carried him to Steel Castle, and gave him a sword made of one entire diamond. Thus armed, the king went in, and was first encountered by four sphinxes, then by six dragons, then by twenty-four nymphs. All these he slew with the syren sword, and then came to the princess. Here he dropped his sword, which the Yellow Dwarf took possession of. The Yellow Dwarf now made the king his captive, and asked if he would give up the princess. "No," said the king; whereupon the dwarf stabbed him to the heart; and the princess, seeing him fall, threw herself upon the dead body and died also. (*Countess D'Aulnoy: Fairy Tales.*)

Yellow Jack. The flag displayed from lazarettos, naval hospitals, and vessels in quarantine. (*See* UNION JACK.)

Yellow Jack (*The*). The yellow fever.

"Raymond and all his family died of yellow fever, and Fernando ... had passed a few weeks recovering from a touch of yellow Jack."—*A. C. Gunter: Baron Montez*, book iv. chap. x.

Yellowhammer (*The*). The eggs of this bird are spotted with red. The tradition is that the bird fluttered about the Cross, and got stained with the blood in its plumage, and by way of punishment its eggs were doomed ever after to bear marks of blood. 'Tis a very lame story, but helps to show how in former times every possible thing was made to bear some allusion to the Redeemer. Because the bird was "cursed," boys who abstain from plundering the eggs of small birds, were taught that it is as right and proper to destroy the eggs of the bunting as to persecute a Jew. (*See* CHRISTIAN TRADITIONS.)

.⁎. Hammer is a corruption of the German *ammer*, a bunting.

Ye'men. Arabia Felix. Felix is a mistranslation by Ptolemy of Yemen, which means to the "right"—*i.e.* of Mecca. (*See* STONY ARABIA.)

" Beautiful are the maids that glide
On summer-eves through Yemen's dales."
Thomas Moore: Fire-Worshippers.

Yeoman (*A*) was anciently a forty-shilling freeholder, and as such qualified to vote, and serve on juries. In more modern times it meant a farmer who cultivated his own freehold. Later still, an upper farmer, tenant or otherwise, is often called a yeoman.

" His family were yeomen of the richer class, who for some generations had held property."—
R. C. Jebb : Richard Bentley, chap. i. p. 2.

Yeoman's Service. Regular hard work; effectual service; excellent service whether in a good or bad cause. The reference is to the yeomen of the Free Companies.

" The whole training of Port Royal did him yeoman's service."—*Shorthouse: Sir Percival*, p. 56.

" We found a long knife, and a knotted handkerchief stained with blood, with which Claude had no doubt recently done yeoman's service."
—*Miss Robinson: Whitefriars*, chap. viii.

Yeomen of the Guard. The beefeaters (*q.v.*).

Yeth-Hounds. Dogs without heads, said to be the spirits of unbaptised children, which ramble among the woods at night, making wailing noises. (*Devonshire.*)

Yezd (1 syl.). Chief residence of the Fire-worshippers. Stephen says they have kept the sacred fire alight above 3,000 years, without suffering it to go out for a second. The sacred fire is on the mountain Ater Quedah (*Mansion of the Fire*), and he is deemed unfortunate who dies away from the mountain. (*Persia.*)

" From Yezd's eternal ' Mansion of the Fire,'
Where aged saints in dreams of heaven expire."
Thomas Moore: Lalla Rookh, pt. i.

Ygg'drasil'. The ash-tree, whose roots run in three directions: one to the Asa-gods in heaven, one to the Frostgiants, and the third to the under-world. Under each root is a fountain of wonderful virtues. In the tree, which drops honey, sit an eagle, a squirrel, and four stags. At the root lies the serpent Nithhöggr gnawing it, while the squirrel Ratatöskr runs up and down to sow strife between the eagle at the top and the serpent. (*Scandinavian mythology.*)

" The Nornas besprinkle
The ash Yggdrassil."
Lord Lytton: Harold, bk. viii.

Y'mir. The personification of Chaos, or the first created being, produced by the antagonism of heat and cold. He is called a giant, and was nourished by the four milky streams which flowed from the cow Audhum'la. While he slept, a man and woman grew out of his left arm, and sons from his feet. Thus was generated the race of the frost-giants. (*Hrimthursar.*)

Odin and his two brothers slew Ymir, and threw his carcase into the Ginnun'gagap (abyss of abysses), when his blood formed the water of the earth, his gore the ocean, his bones the mountains, his teeth the rocks, his skull the heavens, his brains the clouds, his hair plants of every kind, and his eyebrows the wall of defence against the giants. (*Scandinavian mythology.*)

Yn'iol. An earl of decayed fortune, father of Enid, ousted from his earldom by his nephew Ed'yrn, son of Nudd, called the "Sparrow-hawk." When Edyrn was overthrown in single combat by Prince Geraint', he was compelled to restore the earldom to Yn'iol. (*Tennyson: Idyls of the King; Enid.*)

Yo'ke (1 syl.). Greek *zugon*, Latin *jugum*, French *joug*, Dutch *juk*, German *joch*, Anglo-Saxon *geoc* (pron. *yoc*).

To pass under the yoke. To suffer the disgrace of a vanquished army. The Romans made a yoke of three spears—two upright and one resting on them. When an army was vanquished, the soldiers had to lay down their arms, and pass under this archway of spears.

Yor'ick. The King of Denmark's jester, " a fellow of infinite jest and most excellent fancy." (*Hamlet*, v. 1.) In *Tristram Shandy* Sterne introduces a clergyman of that name, meant for himself.

York, when it was Saxon, was called Eorwic, and the legend is that a Duke of Effroc being drowned at the foot of the wall caused this name to be given to the city. Southwark Wall was also called the Effroc Wall or Stone. (*Victor Hugo: L'Homme qui Rit*, pt. ii. bk. iii. 1.)

York is *Eure-wic* (pron. *Yorric*), and means the town on the Eure, now called the Ouse. The Romans Latinised the word *Eure* or *Evre* into "Evora" or "Ebora," and *wic* into "vicum;" whence Ebora-vicum, contracted into *Ebor'acum*.

York Stairs (London), by Inigo Jones. The only remains left of the splendid mansion of the Buckinghams. The site is part of the precincts of a palace belonging to the bishops of Norwich. It then passed to Charles Brandon, Duke of Suffolk, then to the archbishops of York, then to the Crown, then to the Duke of Buckingham, who rebuilt it. The second Duke of Buckingham pulled it down, and converted it into the five streets, etc., called respectively, "George," "Villiers," "Duke," "Of," "Buckingham." The gate leading to the Thames is the only part of this mansion which remains.

Yorks (a Stock-Exchange term), the Great Northern Railway Ordinary Stock, the York line. Similarly, there are the Berwicks, the Brums, the Dovers, the Leeds, the Pots or Potteries, the Singapores, and so on. (*See* STOCK-EXCHANGE SLANG.)

Yorkshire. *I'se Yorkshire, too.* I am as deep as you are, and am not to be bamboozled. The North-countrymen are proverbially "long-headed and cannie." A tale is told of a Yorkshire rustic under cross-examination. The counsel tried to make fun of him, and said to him, " Well, farmer, how go calves at York?" "Well, sir," said the farmer, " on four legs, and not on two." "Silence in the court!" cried the baffled bigwig, and tried again. "Now, farmer —remember you are on your oath—are there as many fools as ever in the West Riding?" " Well, no, sir, no; we've got our share, no doubt; but there are not so many as when *you* were there."

Young Chevalier. Charles Edward Stuart, the second Pretender. (1720-1788.)

Young England. A set of young noblemen and aristocratic gentlemen who tried to revive the formality and court manners of the Chesterfield school. They wore white waistcoats, patronised the pet poor, looked down upon shopkeepers, and were altogether Red-Tape Knights. Disraeli has immortalised their ways and manners, but scarcely a *caput mortuum* of their folly now remains.

Young Germany. A literary school headed by Heinrich Heine, whose aim was to liberate politics, religion, and manners from the old conventional trammels.

Young Italy. A league of Italian refugees, who associated themselves with the French republican party, called the *Charbonnerie Démocratique (q.v.).* It was organised at Marseilles by Mazzini, and its chief object was to diffuse republican principles.

Your Petitioners shall ever Pray, etc. The part omitted is, if a petition to the Crown, "for your Majesty's most prosperous reign"; but if to Parliament, the suppressed words are, "for the prosperous success of this high and honourable court of Parliament."

Youth Restored. Iola'us was restored to youth, as Euripĭdēs says.

Phaon, the beloved of Sappho, was restored to youth on the behalf of Venus.

Æson was restored to youth by Medæa, and so was Jason.

The muses of Bacchus and their husbands were restored to youth, according to Æschўlos.

Ysolde, Ysonde, or *Iseult.* Daughter of the Queen of Ireland. Sir Tristram, being wounded, was cured by Ysolde, and on his return to Cornwall gave his uncle such a glowing description of the young princess that he sent to ask her hand in marriage. Ysolde married King Mark of Cornwall, but entertained a criminal passion for the nephew. This attachment being discovered by the king, he banished Tristram from Cornwall. Sir Tristram went to Wales, where he performed prodigies of valour, and his uncle invited him back again. The guilty intercourse being repeated, Sir Tristram was banished a second time, and went to Spain, Ermonie, and Brittany. In this last place he met with Ysolt *of the White Hand,* daughter of the Duke of Brittany, whom he married. After many marvellous exploits he was severely wounded, and, being told that no one could cure him but Ysolde, he sent a messenger to Cornwall, and told him if the queen consented to accompany him he was to hoist a white flag. The queen hastened to succour her lover, but Ysolt told her husband that the vessel was coming with a *black* sail displayed. Sir Tristram, in an agony of despair, fell on his bed and instantly expired. Soon as Ysolde heard thereof, she flung herself on the corpse and died also. King Mark buried the two in one grave, and planted over it a rose-bush and vine, which so intermingled their branches as they grew up that no man could separate them.

Ysolt of the White Hand. Daughter of the Duke of Brittany and wife of Sir Tristram. (*See above.*)

Yue-Laou, in Chinese mythology, is the old man of the moon, who unites with a silken cord all predestined couples, after which nothing can prevent their union.

Yuga. A mundane period of years, four of which have already passed, making up an aggregate of four million solar years. In the first period men were innocent and free from disease, in the second their life was shortened by one quarter. In the first period *devotion* was man's object, in the second *spiritual knowledge*, in the third *sacrifice*. Compare the Hindu legend with the account given in Genesis.

Yule (1 syl.). Christmas time.

Yule Log. A great log of wood laid in ancient times across the hearth-fire on Christmas Eve. This was done with certain ceremonies and much merry-making. (Norwegian, *juul*, Christmas.)

" Ever at Yuletide, when the great log flamed
  In chimney corner, laugh and jest went round."
      Aldrich: Wyndham Towers, stanza 5.

Yule Swain (*The*). A kind of Santa Klaus among the Lapps. He is eleven feet high, and rides on a goat. He appears on St. Thomas's Day, and continues his visits till Christmas Eve ; but where he comes from and whither he goes nobody has the least idea.

Yuletide has been held as a sacred festival by numberless nations.

Christians hold December 25th as the anniversary of the birth of Jesus.
 China on the same day celebrates the birth of Buddha, s n of Mâya. (*Bunsen.*)
Druids held during the winter solstice the festival of Nolagh. (*Higgins.*)
Egypt held that Horus, son of Isis, was born towards the close of December. (*Le Clerk de Septchenes.*)
Greece celebrated in the winter solstice the birth of Dewēter (*Ceres*), Dionÿsos (*Bacchus*), and Heraklēs (*Hercules*).
India. Numerous Indian tribes keep Yuletide as a religious festival. (*Monier Williams.*)
Mexico holds in the winter solstice the festival of Capacrame. (*History of the Indies*, vol. ii. p. 354.)
Persia at the same period honours the birth of Mithras. (*Gross.*)
Rome celebrated on December 25th the festival " Nu alis Solis Invicta."
Scandinavia held at Yuletide the festival called Jul, in honour of Freya, son of Odin.

Yum'boes (2 syl.). Fairies of African mythology, about two feet high, of a white colour, and dressed like the people of Jaloff. Their favourite haunt is the range of hills called The Paps.

" When evening's shades o'er Goree's isle extend,
The nimble Yumboes from The Paps descend,
Slily approach the natives' huts, and steal
With secret hand the pounded coos coos meal."
      Keightley: Fairy Mythology.

Y'ves (*St.*) (1 syl.). Patron saint of lawyers, being himself a lawyer. As he used his knowledge of the law in defending the oppressed, he is called in Brittany " the poor man's advocate."

" Advocātus, sed non latro,
  Res miranda populo."
      Hymn to St. Yves.

Y'veto't (pron. *Eve-tó*). *The King of Yvetot.* Yvetot is a town in Normandy, and the king referred to is the lord of the town, called *roi d'Yvetot* in old chronicles. The tradition is that Clotaire, son of Clovis, having slain Gaulthier, lord of Yvetot, before the high altar of Soissons, made atonement by conferring the title of *king* on the heirs of the murdered man.

" Il était un roi d'Yvetot
  Peu connu dans l'histoire ;
Se levant tard, se couchant tôt,
  Dormant fort bien sans gloire,
Et couronné par Jeanneton
D'un simple bonnet de coton,
    Dit-on.
Oh ! oh ! oh ! oh ! ah ! ah ! ah ! ah !
Quel bon petit roi c'était, là ! là ! là !"
     Beranjer: Roi d'Yvetot (1813).

A king there was, " roi d'Yvetot" clept,
  But little known in story ;
Went soon to bed, till daylight slept,
  And soundly without glory.
His royal brow in cotton cap
Would Janet, when he took his nap,
    Enwrap.
Ah ! ah ! ah ! ah ! ho ! ho ! ho ! ho !
A famous king this " roi d'Yvetot."
     E. C. B.

Z

Za'bian. *The Zabian world of fashion.* The world of fashion that worships the stars, or men and women of notoriety. A Zabian is a worshipper of the sun, moon, and stars. The Chaldees and ancient Persians were Zabians.

" This is the new meteor, admired with so much devotion by the Zabian world of fashion."—*Belgravia*, No. 1.

Zacoc'ia. King of Mozam'bec. Camoens, in his *Lusiad*, says that he received Vasco da Gama and his men with great hospitality, believing them to be Mahometans, but the moment he discovered that they were Christians all his kindness turned to the most rancorous hate. He tried to allure them into ambush, but, failing in this, sent to Gama a pilot to conduct the fleet to Momba'ze (2 syl.), where the whole party would have been killed or reduced to slavery. This treachery failed also, because Venus drove the fleet in a contrary direction by a storm. The faithless pilot lastly attempted to run the ships upon hidden rocks, but the Nereids came to the rescue, and the pilot threw himself into the sea to escape the anger of the Portuguese adventurer. (*Camoens: Lusiad*, bks. i. ii.)

42*

Zad'kiel (3 syl.). Angel of the planet Jupiter. (*Jewish mythology.*)

Zadkiel. The pen-name of Lieutenant Morrison, author of the *Prophetic Almanac.*

Za'doc, in Dryden's satire of *Absalom and Achitophel,* is designed for Sancroft, Archbishop of Canterbury.

"Zadoc the priest, whom (shunning power and place),
His lowly mind advanced to David's [Charles II.] grace."
        Part i. lines 801-2.

Zakari'ja ibn Muhammed, surnamed *Kazwini,* from Kaswîn, the place of his birth. De Sacy calls him "the Pliny of the East." (1200-1283.)

Zakkum. A tree growing in the Muhammadan hell, from which a food is prepared for the damned of inexpressible bitterness.

"How will it be for him whose food is Zakkûm?"—*The Koran.*

Zal. Son of Sâm Nerimân, exposed on Mount Elburz, because he was born with white hair, and therefore supposed to be the offspring of a deer. He was brought up by the wonderful bird Seemurgh (*q.v.*), and when claimed by his father, received from the foster-bird a feather to give him insight into futurity. (*Persian mythology.*)

Za'nēs. The statues dispersed about the grounds on which the public games of Greece were celebrated. They were the produce of fines imposed on those who infringed the regulations.

Zano'ni. Hero of a novel so called by Lord Lytton. Zanoni is supposed to possess the power of communicating with spirits, prolonging life, and producing gold, silver, and precious stones.

Zan'y. More correctly, **Zanny** (Italian *zanni,* a buffoon; Latin *sannio,* "sanna" means a grimace, and "sanneo" one who makes grimaces).

"For indeed,
He's like the 'zani' to a tumbler
That tries thereafter him to make men laugh."
B. *Jonson: Every Man out of his Humour,* iv. 2.

"He belonged to one of those dramatic companies called zanni, who went about the country reciting and acting."—*John Inglesant,* chap. xxvii.

Zel. A Moorish cymbal.

"Where, some hours since, was heard the swell
• Of trumpet, and the clash of zel."
        Thomas Moore: Fire-Worshippers.

Zel'ica was in love with Azim. Azim left his native Bokhara to join the Persian army, and was taken captive by the Greeks. Report said "he was dead;" Zel'ica lost her reason, joined the harem of the Veiled Prophet as "one of the elect of Paradise," and became "priestess of the faith." When Azim joined the prophet's band, Zelica was appointed to lure him to his destruction, both of body and soul. They meet—Azim tells her to fly with him, but she tells him she is the prophet's bride, and flees from his embrace. After the death of the prophet Zelica puts on his veil, and Azim, thinking he sees the prophet, rushes on her and kills her. (*Thomas Moore: Veiled Prophet of Khorassan; Lalla Rookh.*)

Zelo'tes (3 syl.) or *Sicarii* were pious assassins among the Jews, who imposed on themselves the task of killing all who broke the Mosaic law. (*Mishnah: Sanhedrim,* ix. 6.)

"Simon Zelotes was probably a disciple of Judas the Gaulonite, leader of a party of the Kenaim (Sicarii)."—*Renan: Life of Jesus,* ix.

Zem. The sacred well of Mecca. According to Arab tradition, this is the very well that was shown to Hagar when Ishmael was perishing of thirst. Mecca is built round it.

Zen'chis Khan [*great chief*]. A title assumed in 1206 by Temoudin, a Persian rebel, in the presence of 100 tribes. His progress was like that of a destroying angel, and by his sword Persia became part of the vast Mogul empire.

Zend-Aves'ta. The great work of Zoroaster, or rather Zarathustra, the Mede, who reformed the Magian religion. It is the Avesta or "Living Word," written in the Zend language (B.C. 490). It now contains the Yacna, the Vispered, the Vendidad, and the Khordah-Avesta.

"The sacred writings of the Parsees have usually been called *Zend-Avesta* by Europeans ; but this is, without doubt, an inversion of the proper order of the words, as the Pahlavi books always style them 'Avistâk-va-Zand' (text and commentary)."—*Hong: Essays on the Parsis,* Essay iii. p. 19.

Zenel'ophon. A corruption of *Penelophon.* The beggar-maid loved by King Cophe'tua.

"The magnanimous and most illustrate king Cophetua set eye upon the pernicious and indubitate beggar Zenelophon."—*Shakespeare: Love's Labour's Lost,* iv. 1.

Ze'nith, Na'dir. Zenith is the point of the heavens immediately over the head of the spectator. Na'dir is the opposite point, immediately beneath the spectator's feet. (French, *zénith, nadir.*)

Zephon [*searcher of secrets*]. The cherub despatched by Gabriel to find Satan, after his flight from hell. Ithu'riel goes with him. (*Milton: Paradise Lost,* iv. 788-796.)

Zeph'yr. The west wind, the son of Æ'olus and Auro'ra, and the lover of Flora. (*Roman mythology.*)

Pas de zephyr. Standing on one foot and balancing the other backwards and forwards.

Zeus (1 syl.). The Grecian Jupiter. The word means the "living one." (Sanskrit, *Djaus*, heaven.) (*See* JU-PITER.)

Zeux'is (2 syl.), a Grecian painter, is said to have painted some grapes so well that the birds came and pecked at them.

" E'en as poor birds, deceived with painted grapes,
Do surfeit by the eye, and pine the maw."
    Shakespeare: Venus and Adonis.

Zif. Hypothetical stock, entered in "salted accounts," to give a colourable balance " to the good." (Hebrew *ziphr*, a book.) (*Vidocq : Les Voleurs,* vol. ii. pp. 81, 87.)

Zig. A prodigious cock, which stands with its feet on the earth and touches heaven with its head When its wings are spread it darkens the sun, and causes a total eclipse. This cock crows before the Lord, and delighteth Him. (*Babylonish Talmud.*)

Zig. A chum, a comrade. (Italian *zigno*, a newt or little lizard.) It generally means *un mauvais camarade*, unless otherwise qualified. (*French argot.*)

"Only the bon zig Rac."—*Ouida: Under Two Flags,* chap xxv.

Zim and Jim. "His house was made a habitation for Zim and Jim, and every unclean thing " (*Godly Man's Portion,* 1663). The marginal reading of Isa. xii. 21, 22, explains *Zim* to be wild beasts, and *Jim* jackals.

Zimri, in Dryden's *Absalom and Achitophel,* is the second Duke of Buckingham. Like the captain who conspired against Asa, King of Judah, he "formed parties and joined factions," but pending the issue " he was drinking himself drunk in the house of Arza, steward of his house." (1 Kings xvi. 9.)

" Some of the chiefs were princes in the land ;
In the first rank of these did Zimri stand ;
A man so various that he seemed to be
Not one, but all mankind's epitome.
Stiff in opinions, always in the wrong,
Was everything by starts, and nothing long."
    Part i. 543-548.

Zin'cali. Gipsies ; so called in Spain from *Sinte* or *Sind* (India) and *calo* (black), the supposition being that they came from Hindustan, which no doubt is true. The Persian *Zangi* means an Ethiopian or Egyptian.

Zin'dikites (3 syl.). An heretical Mahometan sect, who disbelieve in God, the resurrection, and a future life. They think that the world is the production of four eternal elements, and that man is a microcosm of the world.

Zineu'ra, in the *Decameron* of Boccaccio (day ii. novel 9), is the Imogen of Shakespeare's *Cymbeline.* In male attire Zineura assumed the name of Sicura'no da Finale, and Imogen of Fide'le. Zineura's husband was Bernard Lomellin, and the villain was Ambrose. Imogen's husband was Posthumus Leonatus, and the villain Iachimo. In Shakespeare, the British king Cymbeline takes the place assigned by Boccaccio to the sultan.

Zion. *Daughter of Zion.* Jerusalem or its inhabitants. The city of David stood on Mount Zion. Zion and Jerusalem were pretty much in the same relation to each other as Old and New Edinburgh. (Hebrew, *Tsiyon*, a hill.)

Zist. " *Se trouver entre le zist et le zest.*" To be in a quandary ; in a state of perfect bewilderment. Also, to shilly shally. " Zest " is anything of no value, as " *Cela ne vaut pas un zest* " (It is not worth a fig). " Zist " is the same word slightly varied.

Zobeide (2 syl.). A lady of Bagdad, whose history is related in the *Three Calenders.* The Kalif Haroun-al-Raschid married her. (*Arabian Nights.*)

Zo'diac. An imaginary belt or zone in the heavens, extending about eight degrees each side of the ecliptic.

Signs of the Zodiac. The zodiac is divided into twelve equal parts, proceeding from west to east ; each part is thirty degrees, and is distinguished by a sign. Beginning with "Aries," we have first six *northern* and then six *southern* signs—*i.e.* six on the north side and six on the south side of the equator ; beginning with "Capricornus," we have six *ascending* and then six *descending* signs—*i.e.* six which ascend higher and higher towards the north, and six which descend lower and lower towards the south. The six northern signs are: *Aries* (the ram), *Taurus* (the bull), *Gemini* (the twins), spring signs ; *Cancer* (the crab), *Leo* (the lion), *Virgo* (the virgin), summer signs. The six southern are : *Libra* (the balance), *Scorpio* (the scorpion), *Sagitta'rius* (the archer), autumn signs ; *Capricor'nus* (the goat), *Aqua'rius* (the water-bearer), and *Pisces* (the fishes), winter signs. (Greek, *zo-on*, living creatures.)

> Our vernal signs the RAM begins,
> Then comes the BULL, in May the TWINS ; –
> The CRAB in June, next LEO shines,
> And VIRGO ends the northern signs.
>
> The BALANCE brings autumnal-fruits,
> The SCORPION stings, the ARCHER shoots ;—
> December's GOAT brings wintry blast,
> AQUARIUS rain, the FISH come last.   *E. C. B.*

Zohar. The name of a Jewish book containing cabalistic expositions of the "books of Moses." Traditionally ascribed to Rabbi Simon ben Yochi, first century ; but probably belonging to the thirteenth century.

> "The renowned Zohar is written in Aramaic, and is a commentary on the Pentateuch, according to its divisions into fifty-two hebdomadal lessons."—*Encyclopædia Britannica*, vol. xii. p. 813.

Zoilism. Harsh, ill-tempered criticism ; so called from Zoilos (*q.v.*).

Zoilos (Latin, *Zoilus*). *The sword of Zoilos.* The pen of a critic. Zoilos was a literary Thersi'tēs, shrewd, witty, and spiteful. He was nicknamed *Home'ro-mastix* (Homer's scourge), because he mercilessly assailed the epics of Homer, and called the companions of Ulysses in the island of Circē "weeping porkers" (" *choirid'ia klaionta* "). He also flew at Plato, Isoc'rates, and other high game.

> "Pendentem volo Zoilum videre." *Martial.*

Zola-ise. To write like Zola, the French novelist, the last quarter of the nineteenth century. Zola was noted for his realistic novels. His speciality was the exposition of the licentious habits of the French. His historic novel, called the *Débâcle*, exposed the breakdown of Napoleon III. and his army in the Franco-German war (1870-1871). Zola died in 1903. He took an active part in the celebrated Dreyfus agitation.

Other parts of speech from Zola are Zolaesque, Zolaisation, Zolaiser, etc.

❧ The most complimentary meaning of Zolaesque is *the terrible descriptive* style of writing. The more general meaning is licentious and coarsely erotic.

Zollverein, meaning customs union, a commercial union of German states for the purpose of establishing a uniform tariff of duties. (Begun 1819.)

Zo'phiel. An angelic scout of " swiftest wing." The word means " God's spy." (*Milton : Paradise Lost*, vi. 355.)

Zoraida (3 syl.). Daughter of Agimora'to of Algiers, who becomes a Christian and elopes with Ruy Perez de Viedma, an officer of Leon. The story is told in an episode of *Don Quixote*, called *The Captive's Life and Adventures.* (Bk. iv. chap. ix.-xi.)

Zoraide (3 syl.) or **Zoraida.** The name of a yacht belonging to the squadron at Cowes. This name is taken from Rossini's *Zoraidi et Coradin.*

Zounds ! An oath, meaning God's wounds.

Zulal. That stream of Paradise, clear as crystal and delicious as nectar, which " the spirits of the just made perfect" drink of.

Zulei'ka. Daughter of Giaffir, Pacha of Aby'dos. She is all purity and loveliness. Her intelligence, joyousness, undeviating love, and strict regard to duty are beautifully portrayed. She promises to flee with Selim and become his bride ; but her father, Giaffir, shoots her lover, and Zuleika dies of a broken heart. (*Byron : Bride of Abydos.*)

Zuleika. The wife of Joseph.

> " It is less costly than the others, and it is remarkable that, although his wife's name, Zuleika (according to tradition), is inserted in the certificates given to pilgrims, no grave having that name is shown."—*The Times* (*Report of the visit of the Prince of Wales to the mosque of Hebron*).

Zulfa'gar. Ali's sword. (*See* SWORD.)